From, Holly. 2004

Congratulations...

on your purchase of the most complete interstate services guide **ever printed!**

Developed over many years and updated annually, ***the Next EXIT®*** will save time, money and frustration. This travel tool will help you find services along the USA Interstate Highway System like nothing you have ever used.

PO Box 888
Garden City, UT 84028
theNextEXIT.com

How to use *the Next EXIT®*

(1)

TENNESSEE

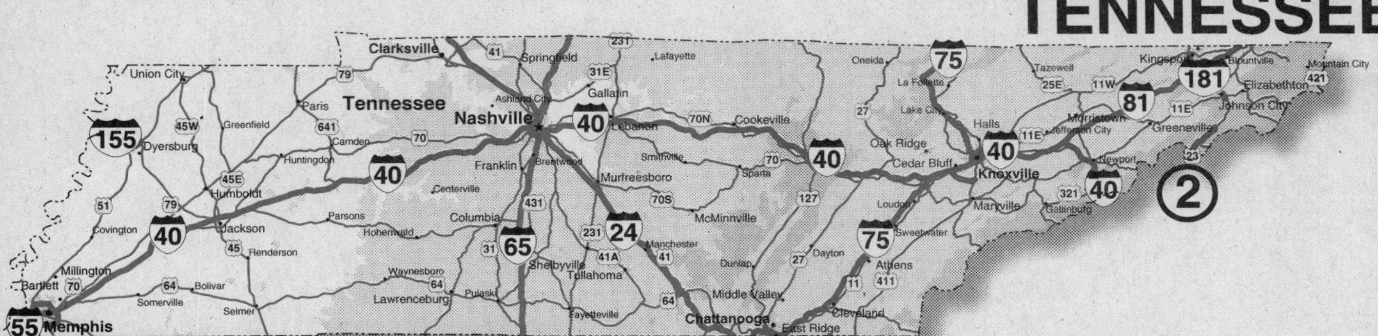

(2)

(4) **Interstate 40**

(3) E ↕ W

Knoxville

Exit #	Services
369	Watt Rd, **N...gas:** Flying J/Conoco/diesel/LP/24hr/@, Speedco, **S...gas:** Exxon, Petro/Mobil/diesel/24hr/@, TA/BP/Burger King/Perkins/Pizza Hut/diesel/24hr/@, **other:** Blue Beacon
I-40 E and I-75 N run together 17 mi (6)	
368	I-75 and I-40, no facilities
364	US 321, TN 95, Lenoir City, Oak Ridge, **N...gas:** Shell, **other:** Crosseyed Cricket Camping(2mi), **S...food:** Ruby Tuesday(4mi)
360	Buttermilk Rd, **N...**Soaring Eagle RV Park
356	TN 58 N, Gallaher Rd, to Oak Ridge, **N...gas:** BP/diesel, **food:** Huddle House, Simply Subs, **lodging:** Day's Inn, Family Inn/rest., Kings Inn, **other:** 4 Seasons Camping, **S...gas:** Citgo/diesel

(5) **Harriman**

352	TN 58 S, Kingston, **N...lodging:** Knight's Inn, **other:** NAPA, **S...gas:** Exxon/diesel, RaceWay, Shell, **food:** DQ, Hardee's, McDonald's, Pizza Hut, Sonic, Subway, Taco Bell, **lodging:** Comfort Inn
347	US 27, Harriman, **N...gas:** Phillips 66/Subway/diesel, **food:** Cancun Mexican, Hardee's, KFC, LJ Silver, McDonald's, Pizza Hut, Ruby Tuesday, Taco Bell, Wendy's, **lodging:** Best Western, to Frozen Head SP, Big S Fork NRA, **S...gas:** BP, Exxon, Shell/Krystal/diesel/24hr, **food:** Cracker Barrel, Reno's Grill, Shoney's, **lodging:** Holiday Inn Express, Super 8, **2-3 mi S...food:** Capt D's, Domino's, Subway, **other:** HOSPITAL, Advance Parts, Goody's, Kroger, Radio Shack, Wal-Mart SuperCtr/gas/24hr

(1).....state name
(2).....map with interstate highways
(3).....directional arrow
(4).....interstate highway #
(5).....city locator strip
(6).....services accessed from the exit

Exit

Most states number exits by the nearest mile marker(mm). Some use consecutive numbers, in which case mile markers are given. Mile markers are the little green vertical signs beside the interstate at one mile intervals which indicate distance from the southern or western border of a state. Odd numbered interstates run north/south, even numbers run east/west.

Services

Services are listed alphabetically by name in the order...**gas, food, lodging, other** services(including camping). "HOSPITAL" indicates an exit from which a hospital may be accessed, but it may not be close to the exit. Services located away from the exit may be referred to by "access to," or "to...," and a distance may be given. A directional notation is also given, such as "**N...**".

Directional Arrows

Read services from the page according to your direction of travel; i.e., if traveling from North to South or East to West, read services DOWN the page. If traveling S to N or W to E, then read services UP the page.

N ↕ S   E ↕ W

the Next EXIT, inc. makes no warranty regarding the accuracy of the information contained in this publication. This information is subject to change without notice.

Table of Contents

Abbreviations used in *the Next EXIT®*:

AFB	Air Force Base	NP	National Park
B&B	Bed&Breakfast	NRA	Nat Rec Area
Bfd	Battlefield	pk	park
bldg	building	pkwy	parkway
Ctr	Center	rest.	restaurant
Coll	College	nb	northbound
$	Dollar	sb	southbound
Mem	Memorial	eb	eastbound
Mkt	Market	wb	westbound
Mtn	Mountain	SP	state park
mm	mile marker	SF	state forest
N...	north side of exit	Sprs	springs
S...	south side of exit	st	street, state
E...	east side of exit	sta	station
W...	west side of exit	TPK	Turnpike
NM	National Monument	USPO	Post Office
NHS	Nat Hist Site	whse	warehouse
NWR	Nat Wildlife Reserve	@	truckstop
NF	National Forest	red print	RV accessible

For Trans Canada Highway(TCH) information, please visit our website at ***www.thenextexit.com***

Fireflies and Funerals

by

Mark Watson

Winter, 2004

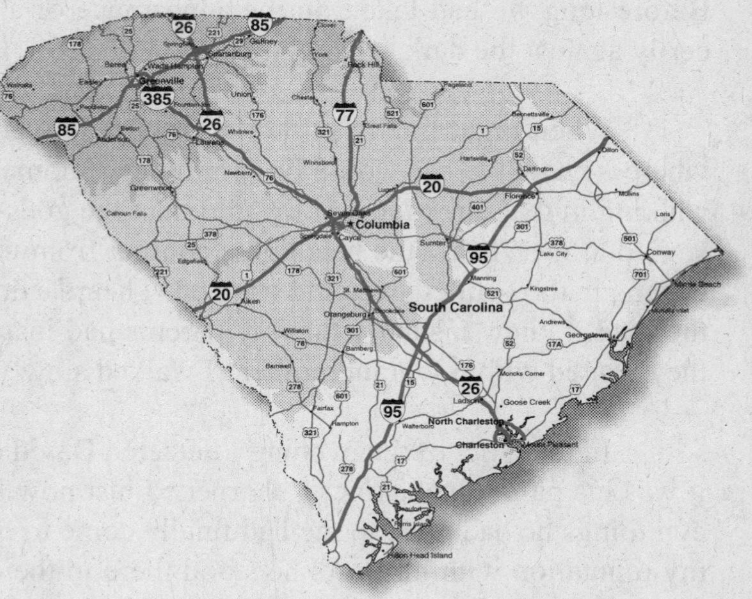

Serious Firefly Country

As children we loved playing outside in the summer evening. After the work was done on our South Carolina farm, frolicking barefoot on the centipede grass of our yard in the cool of the day was reward for whatever we had accomplished. With no school for a couple of months, we were satisfied even though we knew the next morning would bring back the chores. We did lots of things. When our cousins came from up north, we played hide and seek, red light-green light and red rover. We rode bikes and played with our dogs. Sometimes I would take off running down a row in one of Daddy's fields, racing to the end only to turn around and race home again, enjoying the soft, freshly plowed soil underneath my feet. And there were the fireflies.

Someone in the Design Department was either testing a new idea or giving southern children something to do at night when they created these. Production must have forgotten to turn the machine off, because we had these glowing insects by the zillions. I never heard them called "fireflies" until years later when a scientist advertised that he would buy them for a penny apiece for cancer research. They were "lightning bugs" to us. Because of the flashing nature of their hindquarters, on a dark night you had to be looking directly at them in order to catch one at the moment it "lightens." Then, if you didn't think too much about the feelings of the bug, you could pull him apart mid-flash and use the lit end for all kinds of things. No matter what they were called it would be difficult to catch enough of them by hand to turn any kind of profit, but on the evening they buried my uncle, I came out pretty well.

One June morning the phone rang with the news that my uncle had died. My father's emotion was noticeable as he left home to help with the arrangements, and there was a cloud of gloom everywhere. I felt it all right, but at the age of nine I did not comprehend the depth of that event. It would take time and maturity to understand its effects, but in the aftermath of those few days arose an opportunity for which I shall thank my uncle when I see him.

Everybody went to the funeral service several afternoons later except me, including my older brother, David. Someone must have rounded his age upward, because, once again, he got to go somewhere and I did not. A neighborhood friend came over before dark and we busied ourselves playing in the yard while I waited for my family to return. As dusk converted to dark the cotton fields surrounding our house came alive with lightning bugs, each tiny flash being replicated by countless others. When we ran out of things to do we started snatching at the twinkling lights, improving our capture skills with each catch. Then somebody came up with the notion of pasting the fluorescent end of the insects to our faces. This gave meaning to an empty pursuit, so we began to focus all our efforts, gathering them in by the dozens, relieving them of their hind parts and sticking them on. Before long we had taken on the appearance of alien creatures whose light emitting faces glowed eerily against the dark.

When night finally settled in my friend went home and I began looking down the driveway where I knew the car would be turning any moment. Straining my ears for their coming, I started walking in that direction. At this moment the gods-of-get-even looked down from the big board and smiled at me. I saw the headlights coming from town and heard the engine slowing, but instead of turning in they pulled over and stopped. I heard a door open and shut and then the car continued down the road. I knew instantly that my parents had instructed my brother to stay at home with me while they visited with my grandmother. I walked slowly toward the road.

In the quiet of the evening I detected David coming toward me, then heard him stop. Perhaps it was his natural spookiness, sharpened just now by attending a funeral or maybe he feared all the evil things he had done to me had finally come to light, but the next few moments firmly established my reputation with him. As he stood there in the driveway peering into the night I moved steadily toward him. I sensed him swallowing when he asked, "Mark?" No power on earth could have made me speak when I discovered his dilemma. Moving closer, I heard him breathe, "Mark??" this time with real concern. I thought, "if only I had lit up my hands too!" The distance between us narrowed to a few feet, and his flight mechanism activated as he turned to escape the glowing terror. I knew it was his final plea when, in an elevated, cracking voice he fairly begged, "Maarrk??" I also knew he would retaliate, so I paused just another second and answered, finally, "David! Did I scare you?"

He let out with a blood chilling, "yaaaaagh," and I knew it was time to leave. It was a good thing I had a head start as he chased me back to the yard, around the house and then out through the cotton fields. His adrenalin rush, ignited by pure horror was matched only by my own, fueled by my desire to avoid his wrath. He stood at the edge of the field where I hid shouting and shaking his fists until his threats finally subsided. I kept my distance until our parents returned from grandmother's house, not really fearing for my life, but not altogether willing to take the chance.

To this day, any encounter with these remarkable insects evokes for me an image of retribution and justice. While plowing along interstate highways into firefly country, it is comforting to remember a time when events conspired in my behalf. There were many opportunities to even the score as time went by, but none so divinely appointed and so satisfying as the Night of the Lightning Bugs.

Interstate 10

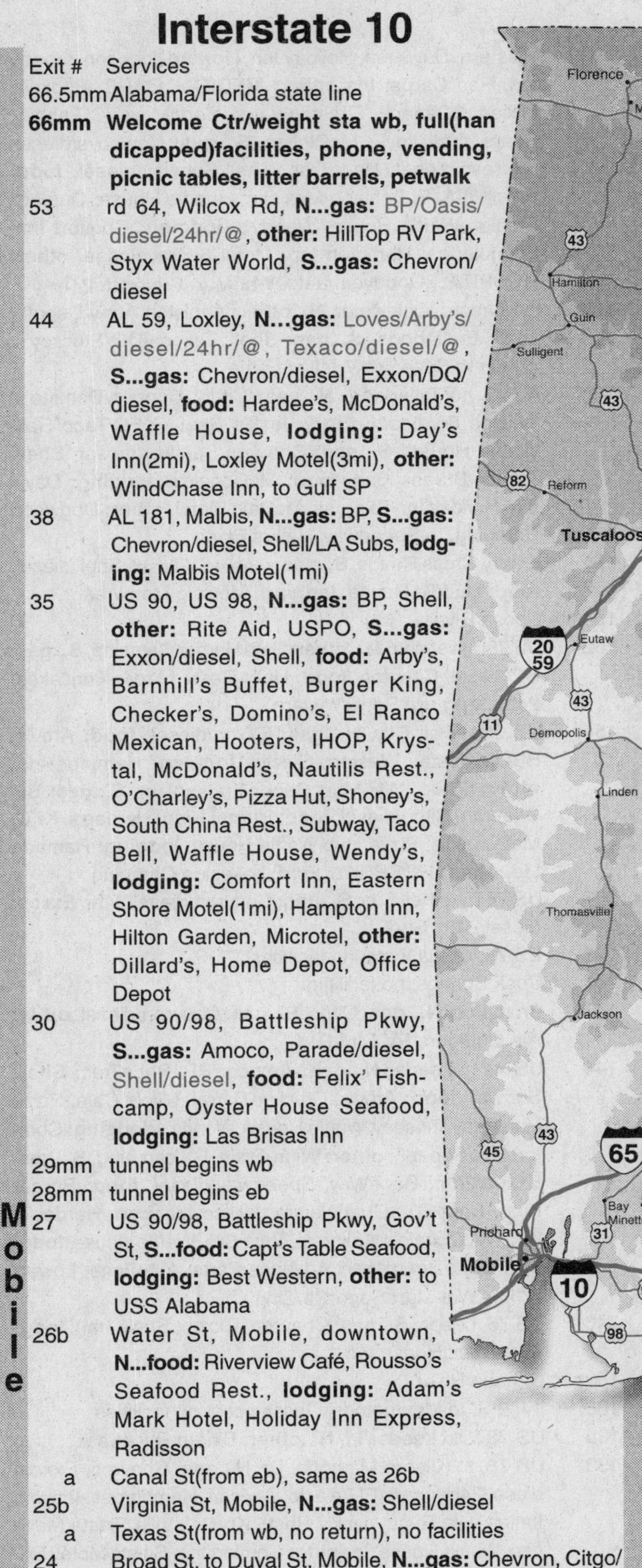

E ↕ W

Exit # Services

66.5mm Alabama/Florida state line

66mm Welcome Ctr/weight sta wb, full(handicapped)facilities, phone, vending, picnic tables, litter barrels, petwalk

53 rd 64, Wilcox Rd, **N...gas:** BP/Oasis/diesel/24hr/@, **other:** HillTop RV Park, Styx Water World, **S...gas:** Chevron/diesel

44 AL 59, Loxley, **N...gas:** Loves/Arby's/diesel/24hr/@, Texaco/diesel/@, **S...gas:** Chevron/diesel, Exxon/DQ/diesel, **food:** Hardee's, McDonald's, Waffle House, **lodging:** Day's Inn(2mi), Loxley Motel(3mi), **other:** WindChase Inn, to Gulf SP

38 AL 181, Malbis, **N...gas:** BP, **S...gas:** Chevron/diesel, Shell/LA Subs, **lodging:** Malbis Motel(1mi)

35 US 90, US 98, **N...gas:** BP, Shell, **other:** Rite Aid, USPO, **S...gas:** Exxon/diesel, Shell, **food:** Arby's, Barnhill's Buffet, Burger King, Checker's, Domino's, El Ranco Mexican, Hooters, IHOP, Krystal, McDonald's, Nautilis Rest., O'Charley's, Pizza Hut, Shoney's, South China Rest., Subway, Taco Bell, Waffle House, Wendy's, **lodging:** Comfort Inn, Eastern Shore Motel(1mi), Hampton Inn, Hilton Garden, Microtel, **other:** Dillard's, Home Depot, Office Depot

30 US 90/98, Battleship Pkwy, **S...gas:** Amoco, Parade/diesel, Shell/diesel, **food:** Felix' Fishcamp, Oyster House Seafood, **lodging:** Las Brisas Inn

29mm tunnel begins wb

28mm tunnel begins eb

Mobile

27 US 90/98, Battleship Pkwy, Gov't St, **S...food:** Capt's Table Seafood, **lodging:** Best Western, **other:** to USS Alabama

26b Water St, Mobile, downtown, **N...food:** Riverview Café, Rousso's Seafood Rest., **lodging:** Adam's Mark Hotel, Holiday Inn Express, Radisson

a Canal St(from eb), same as 26b

25b Virginia St, Mobile, **N...gas:** Shell/diesel

a Texas St(from wb, no return), no facilities

24 Broad St, to Duval St, Mobile, **N...gas:** Chevron, Citgo/diesel

23 Michigan Ave, **N...gas:** Exxon, **other:** $General

22b a AL 163, Dauphin Island Pkwy, **N...gas:** Amoco, **lodging:** Villager Lodge, **S...gas:** Citgo, Exxon/Subway/24hr, Shell/diesel, Texaco/café, **food:** Checker's, Gone Fishin Café, Hoboy's Seafood, Waffle House, **other:** $General

20 I-65 N, to Montgomery

17 AL 193, Tillmans Corner, to Dauphin Island, **N...gas:** Chevron/Blimpie/24hr, Citgo, **food:** BBQ, Burger King, Golden Corral, IHOP, McDonald's, Ruby Tuesday, **other:** HOSPITAL, Big 10 Tire, Lowe's Whse, PawPaw's RV Ctr, Wal-Mart SuperCtr/24hr

ALABAMA

Interstate 10

E ↔ W

Theodore

15b a US 90, Tillmans Corner, to Mobile, **N...gas:** BP, Chevron/24hr, Conoco/diesel, RaceTrac, Shell, **food:** Arby's, Azteca Mexican, Burger King, Canton Buffet, Checker's, CiCi's, Godfather's, KFC, McDonald's, Papa John's, Pizza Hut, Pizza Inn, Popeye's, Shoney's, Subway, Taco Bell, Thai Cuisine, Waffle House, **lodging:** Best Western, Comfort Inn, Day's Inn, Econolodge, Guesthouse Inn, Hampton Inn, Holiday Inn, Motel 6, Red Roof Inn, Suite 1, Super 8, Travelodge, **other:** AutoZone, CarQuest, Family$, Firestone/auto, FoodWorld/24hr, Goodyear, K-Mart, O'Reilly Parts, Radio Shack, Rite Aid, Walgreen, Winn-Dixie, **S...gas:** Chevron/24hr, Conoco/diesel, Shell/diesel, **food:** Hardee's, Waffle House, **other:** Johnny's RV Ctr, auto repair, transmissions

13 to Theodore, **N...gas:** Amoco/McDonald's/diesel/24hr, Conoco, Pilot/Citgo/Wendy's/diesel/24hr/@, Shell/Subway, **food:** Waffle House, **other:** Greyhound Prk, **S...gas:** Chevron/diesel, **other:** I-10 Kamping, Bellingraf Gardens

11 new exit

4 AL 188 E, to Grand Bay, **N...gas:** Shell/DQ/Stuckey's, TA/BP/diesel/rest./24hr/@, **food:** Waffle House, **S...gas:** Chevron/24hr, **food:** Hardee's, **other:** Trav-L-Kamp

1mm Welcome Ctr eb, full(handicapped)facilities, info, phone, picnic tables, litter barrels, petwalk, RV dump

0mm Alabama/Mississippi state line

Interstate 20

E ↔ W

Exit # Services

215mm Alabama/Georgia state line,Central/Eastern time zone

213mm Welcome Ctr wb, full(handicapped)facilities, info, phone, vending, picnic tables, litter barrels, petwalk, RV dump, 24hr security

210 AL 49, Abernathy, **N...**fireworks, **S...**fireworks

209mm Tallapoosa River

208mm weigh sta wb

205 AL 46, to Heflin, **N...gas:** BP/diesel, Shell/diesel

199 AL 9, Heflin, **N...gas:** Shell/Subway/Taco Bell/diesel/24hr, **food:** Hardee's, Pop's Charburgers, **lodging:** Howard Johnson, **other:** Ford, **S...gas:** BP/diesel, Chevron, **food:** Huddle House

198mm Talladega Nat Forest eastern boundary

191 US 431, to US 78, **S...**Talladega Scenic Drive, Cheaha SP

Anniston

188 to US 78, to Anniston, **N...gas:** Shell, SuperMart, **food:** BBQ, Cracker Barrel, DQ, IHOP, KFC, LoneStar Steaks, Subway, Waffle House, Wendy's, Zaxby's, **lodging:** Holiday Inn Express, Jameson Inn, Sleep Inn, Wingate Inn, **other:** Harley-Davidson, Honda, Lowe's Whse

185 AL 21, to Anniston, **N...gas:** BP/diesel, Chevron/24hr, Shell, **food:** Applebee's, Arby's, Burger King, Capt D's, Domino's, Hardee's, Krystal, McDonald's, O'Charley's, Piccadilly's, Pizza Hut, Quincy's, Red Lobster, Shoney's, Taco Bell, Waffle House, Western Sizzlin, **lodging:** Best Western, Day's Inn, Holiday Inn, Howard Johnson, Liberty Inn, Red Carpet Inn, **other:** MEDICAL CARE, BooksA-Million, $General, Firestone/auto, FoodMax, JC Penney, Sears, mall, to Ft McClellan, **S...gas:** Cowboys/diesel, Express/diesel, RaceTrac, Shell/Subway/diesel, **food:** Chick-fil-A, El Poblano Mexican, Huddle House, Outback Steaks, Waffle House, Wendy's, **lodging:** Comfort Inn, Econolodge, Hampton Inn, Motel 6, Travelodge, **other:** HOSPITAL, Goodyear/auto, Wal-Mart SuperCtr/24hr

179 to Munford, Coldwater, **N...other:** Anniston Army Depot

173 AL 5, Eastaboga, **S...gas:** Shell, Texaco/DQ/Stuckey's, **other:** to Speedway/Hall of Fame

168 AL 77, to Talladega, **N...gas:** Citgo, Conoco/Domino's, Phillips 66/diesel, **food:** Jack's Rest., KFC/Taco Bell, Waffle House, **S...gas:** Chevron/Subway/diesel, Shell, Texaco/Burger King, **food:** McDonald's, **lodging:** Day's Inn, Holiday Inn Express, McCaig Motel, **other:** Dogwood Camping, to Speedway, Hall of Fame

165 Embry Cross Roads, **S...gas:** Chevron/diesel, Shell/diesel, **food:** Huddle House, **lodging:** McCaig Motel/rest.

164mm Coosa River

Pell City

162 US 78, Riverside, **N...other:** Safe Harbor Camping, **S...gas:** BP/diesel, Chevron, **food:** Hal's Rest., Mary's Pancakes/24hr, **lodging:** Best Western

158 US 231, Pell City, **N...gas:** Exxon/diesel, **food:** Arby's, BBQ, Krystal, Western Sizzlin, **lodging:** Hampton Inn, **other:** $Tree, Wal-Mart SuperCtr/gas/24hr, **S...gas:** BP, Chevron, Citgo/diesel, **food:** Burger King, Hardee's, KFC, McDonald's, Pizza Hut, Waffle House, **lodging:** Ramada Ltd, **other:** HOSPITAL, Ford, Lakeside Camping

156 US 78 E, to Pell City, **S...gas:** Chevron/diesel/24hr, Exxon/diesel/24hr, Shell

153 US 78, Chula Vista, no facilities

152 Cook Springs, no facilities

147 Brompton, **N...gas:** Citgo, **S...gas:** Chevron/diesel, **other:** Ala Outdoors RV Ctr/LP

Leeds

144 US 411, Leeds, **N...gas:** Amoco, BP, RaceTrac, Shell/Subway, **food:** Arby's, Cracker Barrel, Milo's Café, Pizza Hut, Ruby Tuesday, Waffle House, Wendy's, **lodging:** Comfort Inn, Super 8, **other:** Winn-Dixie, RV camping, **S...gas:** Exxon/24hr, RaceWay, Speedway/diesel, **food:** Burger King, Capt D's, Guadalajara Jalisco Mexican, Hardee's, KFC, McDonald's, Quincy's, Taco Bell, Waffle House, **lodging:** Day's Inn, **other:** Advance Parts, AutoZone, Lowe's Whse, Wal-Mart SuperCtr/24hr

140 US 78, Leeds, **S...gas:** Chevron, Exxon, Shell(1mi), **lodging:** GuestHouse Inn

139mm Cahaba River

136 I-459 S, to Montgomery, Tuscaloosa, no facilities

135 US 78, Old Leeds Rd, **N...other:** B'ham Racetrack

133 US 78, to Kilgore Memorial Dr, **N...gas:** Chevron, Exxon/diesel/24hr, **food:** El Palacio Mexican, Hamburger Heaven, Italian Villa Rest., Jack's Rest., Krystal, Villa Fiesta Mexican, Waffle House, **lodging:** Comfort Inn, Siesta Motel, Super 8, **other:** MEDICAL CARE, **S...gas:** BP, **food:** Arby's, BBQ, China Buffet, Gus' Hotdogs, McDonald's, Subway, **lodging:** Best Western, Hampton Inn, Holiday Inn Express,

Interstate 20

E ↕ W

other: $Tree, Ford, Graham Tire, Sam's Club, Wal-Mart, same as 132

132b a US 78, Crestwood Blvd, **N...gas:** Exxon, **food:** Barnhill's Buffet, Krystal, Waffle House, **other:** Chevrolet, **S...gas:** BP, Crown/24hr, Shell/24hr, **food:** Arby's, Capt D's, China Garden, Denny's, Hooters, IHOP, KFC, Logan's Roadhouse, McDonald's, O'Charley's, Omelet Shop, Olive Garden, Pizza Hut, Red Lobster, Ruby Tuesday, Shoney's, Taco Bell, Wendy's, **lodging:** Delux Inn, USA Lodge, **other:** HOSPITAL, Circuit City, Home Depot, JC Penney, K-Mart, OfficeMax, Sears/auto, Waldenbooks, mall

130b US 11, 1st Ave, **N...gas:** BP, Chevron/24hr, Citgo, **lodging:** Bama Motel, **other:** Advance Parts, AutoZone, Colonial RV Ctr, Food Fair, **S...food:** Capt D's, McDonald's, **lodging:** Interstate Inn, Relax Inn

a I-59 N, to Gadsden

I-59 S and I-20 W run together from B'ham to Meridian, MS

129 Airport Blvd, **N...lodging:** Ramada Inn, **other:** airport, **S...gas:** Conoco, Shell, **food:** Hardee's, **lodging:** Day's Inn, Holiday Inn, **other:** transmissions

128 AL 79, Tallapoosa St, **N...gas:** Cowboys/Blimpie/diesel, Shell

126b 31st St, downtown, to Sloss Furnaces, **N...gas:** Conoco, Shell, **food:** McDonald's

a US 31, US 280, 26th St, Carraway Blvd, downtown, to UAB

125b 22nd St, to downtown, **N...lodging:** Sheraton

a 17th St, to downtown, Civic Ctr

124b a I-65, S to Montgomery, N to Nashville

123 US 78, Arkadelphia Rd, **N...gas:** BP, Chevron/24hr, Pilot/Wendy's/diesel/24hr, **food:** Popeye's, **lodging:** La Quinta, **S...other:** HOSPITAL, to Legion Field

121 Bush Blvd(from wb, no return), Ensley, **N...gas:** BP, Exxon, **food:** Bob's Burger

120 AL 269, 20th St, Ensley Ave, **N...food:** KFC, **other:** GMC/Pontiac, Breeze RV, **S...gas:** BP, Chevrolet, **other:** HOSPITAL, Chrysler/Plymouth/Jeep, Hyundai, Toyota

119b Ave I(from wb), no facilities

a Scrushy Pkwy, Gary Ave, **N...gas:** BP, Chevron/diesel, **food:** Burger King, McDonald's, Seafood Delite, Subway, Taco Bell, **other:** Food Fair, Family$, **S...gas:** Exxon, Mobil, **food:** Omelet Shoppe, **other:** HOSPITAL

118 AL 56, Valley Rd, Fairfield, **S...food:** Papa John's, **lodging:** Fairfield Inn, Villager Lodge, **other:** Home Depot, NTB, Sears, Winn-Dixie

115 Allison-Bonnett Memorial Dr, **N...gas:** Citgo/diesel, Phillips 66, RaceTrac, Shell/diesel, **food:** Church's, Guadalajara Grill, Subway

113 18th Ave, to Hueytown, **S...gas:** Chevron/diesel, **food:** McDonald's

112 18th St, 19th St, Bessemer, **N...gas:** Conoco, RaceTrac, **food:** Church's, Jack's Rest., **other:** OK Tire, **S...gas:** Chevron, **food:** Arby's, Burger King, Krystal, McDonald's, **other:** Lowe's Whse

Bessemer

109 new exit

108 US 11, AL 5 N, Academy Dr, **N...gas:** Exxon, **food:** Applebee's, BBQ, Cracker Barrel, Santa Fe Steaks, Waffle House, **lodging:** Best Western, Comfort Inn, Holiday Inn Express, Jameson Inn, **S...gas:** BP, Citgo/Church's/diesel, **food:** Burger King, Jade Garden, Chinese, McDonald's, Milo's Burgers, Sonic, **lodging:** Day's Inn, Hampton Inn, **other:** HOSPITAL, Big 10 Tire, $Tree, Ford, Radio Shack, Wal-Mart SuperCtr/24hr, Winn-Dixie, to civic ctr

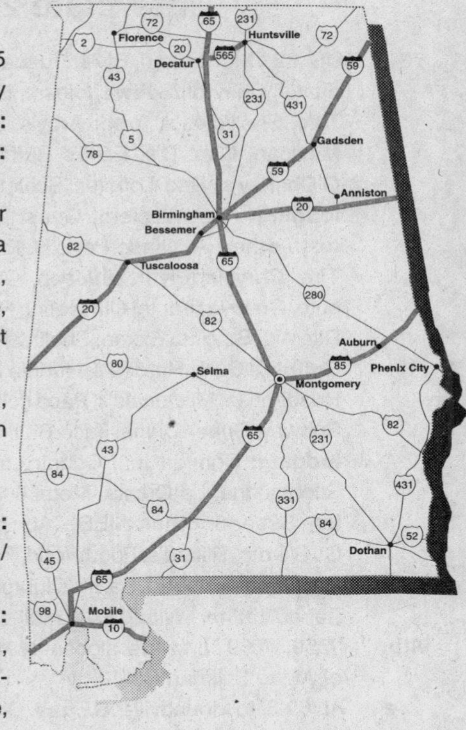

106 I-459 N, to Montgomery

104 Rock Mt Lake, **S...gas:** Flying J/Conoco/diesel/LP/rest./24hr/@

100 to Abernant, **N...gas:** Citgo, **other:** McCalla Camping, **S...gas:** BP, Exxon, Petro/Chevron/diesel/rest./24hr/@, **other:** Tannehill SP(3mi)

97 US 11 S, AL 5 S, to W Blocton, **S...gas:** BP/KFC/diesel, Exxon/Subway/diesel, Shell/diesel, **food:** Dot's Farmhouse Rest., Jack's Rest.

89 Mercedes Dr, **N...lodging:** Wellesley Inn, **S...other:** Mercedes Auto Plant

86 Vance, to Brookwood, **N...gas:** Shell/diesel/rest./24hr/@

85mm rest area both lanes, full(handicapped)facilities, phone, vending, picnic tables, litter barrels, petwalk, RV dump

Tuscaloosa

79 US 11, University Blvd, Coaling, **S...gas:** Chevron/diesel

77 Cottondale, **N...gas:** Amoco/McDonald's, TA/BP/Subway/Taco Bell/diesel/@, Wilco/Wendy's/diesel/24hr, **food:** Pizza Hut, Ruby Tuesday, **lodging:** Hampton Inn, Microtel, **other:** SpeedCo, USPO, truckwash

76 US 11, E Tuscaloosa, Cottondale, **N...gas:** Citgo, Exxon, Shell/diesel, **food:** Burger King, Cracker Barrel, Waffle House, **lodging:** Comfort Inn, Scottish Inn, **other:** transmissions, **S...gas:** Pilot/Subway/diesel/24hr/@, Shell/diesel, **lodging:** Sleep Inn

ALABAMA

Interstate 20

E ↔ W — Tuscaloosa

73 US 82, McFarland Blvd, Tuscaloosa, **N...gas:** BP/diesel, Chevron/Subway/diesel, Exxon, Parade, RaceTrac, Shell/diesel, **food:** Arby's, Burger King, Cancun Mexican, Capt D's, Ezell's Buffet, Krystal, LJ Silver, O'Charley's, Red Lobster, Schlotsky's, Waffle House, **lodging:** Best Western, Guest Lodge, Shoney's Inn/rest., **other:** Advance Parts, AllTransmissions, Big 10 Tire, Chrysler/Plymouth/Jeep, Circuit City, Firestone/auto, Goodyear/auto, OfficeMax, Pontiac/Cadillac/GMC, Rite Aid, **S...gas:** Exxon, Shell/diesel, **food:** Chili's, DQ, Guthrie's Café, Hardee's, Huddle House, KFC, Logan's Roadhouse, McDonald's, Papa John's, Pizza Hut, Sonic, Subway, Super China, Taco Bell, Taco Casa, Wendy's, **lodging:** Comfort Inn, Country Inn Suites, Day's Inn, Econolodge, La Quinta, Motel 6, Quality Inn, Ramada Inn, Super 8, **other:** MEDICAL CARE, BooksAMillion, CVS Drug, Dillard's, FoodWorld, Ford, Isuzu, NAPA, Office Depot, Rite Aid, Sam's Club/gas, U-Haul, Wal-Mart SuperCtr/24hr, Winn-Dixie, mall

71b I-359, Al 69 N, to Tuscaloosa, **N...other:** HOSPITAL, U of AL, to Stillman Coll

a AL 69 S, to Moundville, **S...gas:** Chevron, Exxon/diesel, Shell/diesel, **food:** Arby's, BBQ, Hooters, IHOP, LoneStar Steaks, OutBack Steaks, Pizza Hut, Ryan's, Waffle House, Wendy's, **lodging:** Courtyard, Fairfield Inn, Jameson Inn, **other:** Advance Parts, K-Mart, Lowe's Whse, Mazda/VW, to Mound SM

68 Northfort-Tuscaloosa Western Bypass, no facilities

64mm Black Warrior River

62 Fosters, **N...gas:** BP

52 US 11, US 43, Knoxville, **N...gas:** Exxon/diesel, **other:** Knoxville Camping

45 AL 37, Union, **N...food:** Cotton Patch Rest., **S...gas:** BP/diesel/rest./24hr, **food:** Hardee's, Southfork Rest./24hr, **lodging:** Western Inn/rest., **other:** Greene Co Greyhound Park

40 AL 14, Eutaw, **N...other:** to Tom Bevill Lock/Dam, **S...gas:** BP, HOSPITAL

39mm rest area wb, full(handicapped)facilities, phone, vending, picnic tables, litter barrels, petwalk, RV dump

38mm rest area eb, full(handicapped)facilities, phone, vending, picnic tables, litter barrels, petwalk, RV dump

32 Boligee, **N...gas:** BP/diesel/rest./24hr, **S...gas:** Chevron/Subway/24hr

27mm Tombigbee River, Tenn-Tom Waterway

23 Epes, to Gainesville, no facilities

17 AL 28, Livingston, **S...gas:** BP/diesel/24hr, Chevron/Subway/24hr, Noble/Citgo/Janet's/Waffle King/diesel/24hr/@, Shell/diesel, **food:** Burger King, Pizza Hut, **lodging:** Comfort Inn, Western Inn(1mi), **other:** repair/24hr

8 AL 17, York, **S...gas:** BP/diesel/rest., **lodging:** Day's Inn/Briar Patch Rest., **other:** HOSPITAL

1 to US 80 E, Cuba, **N...gas:** Phillips 66/diesel/rest., **S...gas:** Chevron, Dixie

.5mm **Welcome Ctr eb, full(handicapped)facilities, phone, vending, picnic tables, litter barrels, petwalk, RV dump**

I-20 E and I-59 N run together from Meridian, MS to B'ham

0mm Alabama/Mississippi state line

Interstate 59

N ↔ S — Ft Payne, Gadsden

Exit #	Services

241.5mm Alabama/Georgia state line, Central/Eastern time zone

241mm Welcome Ctr sb, full(handicapped)facilities, phone, vending, picnic tables, litter barrels, petwalk, RV dump

239 to US 11, Sulphur Springs Rd, **E...other:** Sequoyah Caverns Camping(4mi)

231 AL 40, AL 117, Hammondville, Valley Head, **E...other:** Sequoyah Caverns Camping(5mi), **W...gas:** Shell

222 US 11, to Ft Payne, **E...gas:** Shell, **1-2 mi E...food:** Arby's, Bojangles, Jack's Rest., KFC, Krystal, Subway, **lodging:** Ft Payne Inn, **W...gas:** Shell/diesel, **food:** Waffle King

218 AL 35, Ft Payne, **E...gas:** Conoco/diesel, **food:** Capt D's, Durango's Mexican, McDonald's, New China, Papa John's, Pizza Hut, Shoney's, Taco Bell, Wendy's, **lodging:** Mtn View Motel(2mi), **other:** Advance Parts, AutoZone, Buick/Pontiac, Chrysler/Dodge, Goodyear/auto, **W...gas:** Chevron, Cowboys/diesel, Exxon, **food:** Burger King, Cracker Barrel, Hardee's, Ryan's, Ruby Tuesday, Subway, Waffle House, **lodging:** Day's Inn, Econolodge, Holiday Inn Express, **other:** HOSPITAL, Ford/Lincoln/Mercury, Kia, K-Mart, Radio Shack, Wal-Mart SuperCtr/gas/24hr

205 AL 68, Collinsville, **E...gas:** Chevron, **food:** Jack's Rest., **lodging:** Howard Johnson, **other:** to Little River Canyon, Weiss Lake, **W... gas:** Conoco/diesel, Shell, **other:** MEDICAL CARE

188 AL 211, to US 11, Reece City, Gadsden, **E...gas:** Chevron/24hr, **food:** Maw'nPaw's Rest., **W...gas:** BP/diesel

183 US 431, US 278, Gadsden, **E...gas:** BP/diesel, Shell, **food:** Waffle House, Wendy's, **lodging:** Holiday Inn Express, Ramada Ltd, Rodeway Inn, **other:** st police, **W...gas:** Chevron/24hr, Exxon, Texaco, **food:** KFC/Taco Bell, Krystal, McDonald's, Pizza Hut, Quincy's, Subway, **lodging:** Econolodge

182 I-759, to Gadsden, no facilities

181 AL 77, Rainbow City, to Gadsden, **E...gas:** BP/diesel/24hr@, **food:** Austin's Steaks, **lodging:** Day's Inn, **W...gas:** Cowboys/diesel, **food:** Cracker Barrel, DQ, Hardee's, Ruby Tuesday, Subway, Waffle House, **lodging:** Best Western, Comfort Inn

174 to Steele, **E...other:** truck tire service, **W...gas:** Chevron/diesel, JetPep/diesel/@

168mm rest area sb, full(handicapped)facilities, phone, vending, picnic tables, litter barrels, petwalk, RV dump

Interstate 59

N ↑ S

166 US 231, Whitney, to Ashville, **E...gas:** Chevron, Discount/gas, **W...gas:** Shell/Taco Bell/diesel/24hr, **food:** Jack's Rest., Subway

165mm rest area nb, full(handicapped)facilities, phone, vending, picnic tables, litter barrels, petwalk, RV dump

156 to US 11, AL 23, Springville, to St Clair Springs, no facilities

154 AL 174, Springville, to Odenville, **W...gas:** BP/ Subway, Chevron, Exxon, Shell/diesel, **food:** Gulf Seafood, Jack's Rest., McDonald's

148 to US 11, Argo, **E...gas:** BP

143 Mt Olive Church Rd, Deerfoot Pkwy, no facilities

141 to Trussville, Pinson, **E...gas:** Amoco/diesel, BP/diesel, Shell/diesel, **food:** Applebee's, Arby's, Cracker Barrel, LoneStar Steaks, McDonald's, Papa Johns, Pizza Hut, Subway, Taco Bell, Waffle House, Wendy's, **lodging:** Comfort Inn, Holiday Inn Express, Jameson Inn, **W...gas:** Chevron/24hr, Exxon, Shell, **food:** Arby's, Chick-fil-A, Bennigan's, Backyard Burger, Burger King, Krystal, Milo's Burgers, Monterrey Mexican, Ruby Tuesday, **other:** CVS Drug, Kohl's, Radio Shack, Sam's Club, Wal-Mart SuperCtr/24hr, Western Foods

137 I-459 S, to Montgomery, Tuscaloosa

134 to AL 75, Roebuck Pkwy, **W...gas:** BP/diesel, Chevron, Mobil, **food:** Barnhill's Buffet, Burger King, Capt D's, Chick-fil-A, ChuckeCheese, Church's, McDonald's, Milo's Burgers, Monterrey Mexican, O'Charley's, Papa John's, Pasquale's Pizza, Rally's, Steak'n Shake, Subway, Taco Bell, Wendy's, **lodging:** Best Inn, **other:** HOSPITAL, Chevrolet, CVS Drug, Dodge, $Tree, Firestone/auto, FoodGiant, Ford, Goodyear/auto, Honda, Hyundai, Jo-Ann Fabrics, Lincoln/Mercury, Mazda/Kia, Mr Transmissions, NTB, Rite Aid, USPO, VW, Wal-Mart SuperCtr/24hr, Winn-Dixie

133 4th St, to US 11(from nb), **W...gas:** Exxon, **food:** Arby's, Catfish Cabin Rest., Checker's, Krystal, Shoney's, Waffle House, **other:** Chrysler/Plymouth, Mazda, mall, accesses same as 134

132 US 11 N, 1st Ave, **W...gas:** Exxon, Chevron/24hr, **food:** Pizza Hut, accesses same as 131

131 77th Ave(from nb), **E...gas:** Chevron, Exxon, **food:** Burger King, Church's, Rally's, Subway, Taco Bell, **other:** CVS Drug, NAPA, U-Haul, accesses same as 132

130 I-20, E to Atlanta, W to Tuscaloosa

I-59 S and I-20 W run together from B'ham to Mississippi. **See Alabama Interstate 20.**

Interstate 65

N ↑ S

Exit # Services

366mm Alabama/Tennessee state line

365 AL 53, to Ardmore, **E...lodging:** Budget Inn

364mm Welcome Ctr sb, full(handicapped)facilities, info, phone, vending, picnic tables, litter barrels, petwalk, RV dump

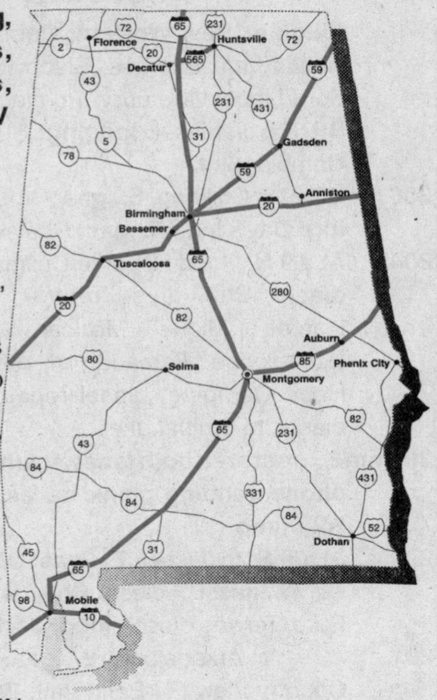

361 Elkmont, **W...gas:** Citgo/diesel/ rest./repair/@, Exxon/diesel, **other:** antiques

354 US 31 S, to Athens, **W...gas:** Chevron/ Subway, Conoco, **food:** Dairy Queen, **lodging:** Athens Hotel/rest., Budget Inn, Mark Hotel, **other:** HOSPITAL

351 US 72, to Athens, Huntsville, **E...gas:** BP/diesel, Exxon, RaceTrac, Shell/Subway, **food:** Burger King, Cracker Barrel, McDonald's, Waffle House, Wendy's, **lodging:** Comfort Inn, Country Hearth Inn, Hampton Inn, **other:** R Stover Candy, **W...gas:** Chevron/24hr, Texaco/diesel, **food:** Applebee's, Arby's, Hardee's, Hungry Fisherman, Krystal, Shoney's, Sonic, **lodging:** Best Western, Day's Inn, Sleep Inn, Super 8, **other:** HOSPITAL, Chevrolet, Chrysler/Plymouth/Jeep, $Tree, Big 10 Tire, Ford/ Lincoln/Mercury, Goodyear/auto, Staples, Wal-Mart SuperCtr/gas/24hr, to Joe Wheeler SP

340b I-565, to Huntsville, to Ala Space & Rocket Ctr

a AL 20, to Decatur, **W...gas:** Conoco/diesel, RaceTrac, **2 mi W...lodging:** Courtyard, Hampton Inn

337mm Tennessee River

334 AL 67, Priceville, to Decatur, **E...gas:** Amoco/diesel, RaceTrac/diesel/24hr, **lodging:** Day's Inn, Super 8, **W...gas:** BP/diesel, Chevron, Pilot/Subway/diesel/ 24hr/@, Texaco, **food:** BBQ, DQ, Hardee's, Krystal, McDonald's, Waffle House, **lodging:** Comfort Inn, Hampton Inn, **other:** HOSPITAL

328 AL 36, Hartselle, **W...gas:** BP, Chevron/diesel, Cowboys/ diesel, Shell, **food:** BBQ, Huddle House, **lodging:** Express Inn

325 Thompson Rd, to Hartselle, **W...lodging:** Express Inn

322 AL 55, to US 31, to Falkville, Eva, **E...gas:** BP/diesel/ rest., **W...gas:** Chevron

318 US 31, to Lacon, **E...gas:** Texaco/DQ/Stuckey's, **lodging:** Lacon Motel

310 AL 157, Cullman, West Point, **E...gas:** BP, Chevron, Conoco/Subway/diesel, Shell/diesel/24hr, Texaco/ Wendy's/diesel, **food:** Arby's, Baxter's Steaks, Burger King, Cracker Barrel, Dairy Queen, Denny's, KFC, McDonald's, Ruby Tuesday, Taco Bell, Waffle House,

ALABAMA

Interstate 65

N ↕ S

lodging: Best Western, Comfort Inn, Hampton Inn, Holiday Inn Express, Sleep Inn, **other:** HOSPITAL, Ford/Lincoln/Mercury, Pontiac/Buick/GMC, **W...gas:** BP, Exxon/diesel, **lodging:** Super 8, **other:** Cullman Camping(2mi)

308 US 278, Cullman, **E...gas:** Omelet Shoppe/24hr, **lodging:** Day's Inn, **W...gas:** Chevron/24hr

304 AL 69 N, Good Hope, to Cullman, **E...gas:** BP, Exxon/diesel, Shell/diesel/rest/@, Texaco/diesel, **food:** Hardee's, Miguel's Mexican, Waffle House, **lodging:** Econolodge, Ramada Inn, **other:** HOSPITAL, Good Hope Camping, diesel repair, laundry, **W...**JetPep/diesel, to Smith Lake

301mm E...rest area both lanes, full(handicapped)facilities, phone, vending, picnic tables, litter barrels, petwalk, RV dump

299 AL 69 S, to Jasper, **E...gas:** Citgo, **other:** Millican RV Ctr, **W...gas:** BP/diesel, Chevron/diesel, Conoco/diesel, Pure, Texaco/diesel, **food:** Jack's Rest.

291 AL 91, to Arkadelphia, **E...gas:** Chevron/diesel, **other:** Country View RV Park(1mi), **W...gas:** Shell/diesel/@, **food:** GoodDays Rest.

291mm Warrior River

289 to Blount Springs, **W...gas:** Texaco/DQ/Stuckey's, **other:** to Rickwood Caverns SP

287 US 31 N, to Blount Springs, **E...gas:** Chevron/diesel, Citgo/diesel

284 US 31 S, AL 160 E, Hayden, **E...gas:** Conoco/diesel, Phillips 66, Shell/diesel

282 AL 140, Warrior, **E...gas:** Chevron/24hr, Exxon/McDonald's, FuelZ/diesel, **food:** Hardee's, Jack's Rest., Pizza Hut, **W...gas:** BP

281 US 31, to Warrior, **E...other:** Chevrolet

280 to US 31, to Warrior, **E...other:** Chevrolet

279mm Warrior River

275 to US 31, Morris, no facilities

272 Mt Olive Rd, **E...other:** Gardendale Kamp(1mi), **W...gas:** Chevron/24hr, Shell, Texaco/diesel

271 Fieldstown Rd, **E...gas:** BP, Chevron/24hr, Exxon, RaceTrac, Shell, **food:** Arby's, Dairy Queen, Guthrie's Diner, KFC, McDonald's, Milo's Burgers, Pizza Hut, Ruby Tuesday, Shoney's, Subway, Taco Bell, Waffle House, Wendy's, **other:** MEDICAL CARE, AutoZone, Chevrolet, Kia/Subaru, Walgreen, Wal-Mart SuperCtr/gas/24hr, **W...food:** Cracker Barrel, **lodging:** Best Western

Birmingham

267 Walkers Chapel Rd, to Fultondale, **E...gas:** Shell/diesel, **food:** Burger King, O'Charley's, Outback Steaks, Waffle House, **lodging:** Hampton Inn, Holiday Inn Express, **other:** Lowe's Whse, **1 mi E...gas:** BP, **food:** Hardee's, Jack's Rest., Taco Bell, **other:** CVS Drug, $General, Rite Aid, USPO, Winn-Dixie, **W...gas:** Chevron/diesel

266 US 31, Fultondale, **E...gas:** Chevron/24hr, **lodging:** Day's Inn, Super 8

264 41st Ave, **W...gas:** Flying J/CountryMktdiesel/24hr/@

263 33rd Ave, **E...gas:** Chevron/diesel, **lodging:** Apex Motel, **W...gas:** Crown, Exxon

262b a 16th St, Finley Ave, **E...gas:** Bama/diesel, BP, Texaco/diesel/@, **W...gas:** Chevron/24hr, Citgo/diesel/24hr, Conoco/diesel/@, **food:** Capt D's, McDonald's, Popeye's

Birmingham

261b a I-20/59, E to Gadsden, W to Tuscaloosa, no facilities

260b a 6th Ave, **E...gas:** BP, Shell, **food:** Nicki's Rest., Mrs Winner's, Popeye's, **lodging:** Tourway Inn, **other:** Buick, Nissan, **W...gas:** Chevron, **food:** Church's, **lodging:** Adams Inn, **other:** to Legion Field

259b a University Blvd, 4th Ave, 5th Ave, **E...food:** Waffle House, **lodging:** Best Western, **other:** HOSPITAL, Food Fair, **W...gas:** Chevron, **other:** Goodyear

258 Green Springs Ave, **E...gas:** Chevron, Citgo, **food:** Exotic Wings

256b a Oxmoor Rd, **E...gas:** Exxon/diesel, Mobil, Shell, **food:** Burger King, Cuco's Mexican, KFC, Krystal, Lovoy's Italian, McDonald's, **lodging:** Howard Johnson, **other:** Firestone/auto, Food World, Goodyear/auto, Jo-Ann Fabrics, K-Mart, Office Depot, **W...gas:** BP, Chevron/24hr, **food:** BBQ, Hardee's, Shoney's, **lodging:** Comfort Inn, Fairfield Inn, Guesthouse Inn, Holiday Inn/rest., Microtel, Red Roof Inn, Super 8, **other:** Batteries+

255 Lakeshore Dr, **E...gas:** BP, **other:** HOSPITAL, to Samford U, **W...gas:** Chevron, Citgo, **food:** Arby's, Capt D's, Chili's, Chick-fil-A, Dragon Chinese, Hooters, IHOP, Landry's Seafood, LoneStar Steaks, O'Charley's, Outback Steaks, Schlotsky's, Taco Bell, Tony Roma, Wendy's, **lodging:** Best Suites, La Quinta, Residence Inn, TownePlace Suites, **other:** BooksAMillion, Bruno's Foods, $Tree, Goody's, Lowe's Whse, OfficeMax, Old Navy, Sam's Club, Wal-Mart SuperCtr/24hr, mall

Birmingham

254 Alford Ave, Shades Crest Rd, **E...gas:** Chevron, **W...gas:** BP, Citgo

252 US 31, Montgomery Hwy, **E...gas:** BP, Chevron, Shell, **food:** Arby's, Capt D's, ChuckeCheese, Milo's Burgers, Piccadilly's, Pizza Hut, Taco Bell, Waffle House, **lodging:** Comfort Inn, Hampton Inn, The Motor Lodge/rest., **other:** HOSPITAL, GMC/Saturn/Isuzu, Lincoln/Mercury, Aamco, **W...gas:** BP, Chevron, Exxon, Shell, **food:** BBQ, Burger King, Chick-fil-A, Damon's, Krystal, LoneStar Steaks, McDonald's, Mexicao Lindo, Outback Steaks, Schlotsky's, Subway, Waffle House, **lodging:** Day's Inn, Quality Inn, **other:** BooksAMillion, Bruno's Food, Buick, Chevrolet, Chrysler/Plymouth/Jeep, Circuit City, Eckerd, Goodyear/auto, Hancock Fabrics, Honda, Kia, Nissan, Pontiac, Rite Aid, Toyota, transmissions

250 I-459, US 280, no facilities

247 AL 17, Valleydale Rd, **E...gas:** BP, **food:** BBQ, **W...gas:** Mobil, RaceTrac, Shell, **food:** Arby's, Backyard Burger, IHOP, Milo's Burgers, Papa John's, RagTime Café, Waffle House, **lodging:** Hampton Inn, InTown Motel, La Quinta, Suburban Lodge, **other:** $General, Rite Aid, Walgreen

ALABAMA

Interstate 65

N ↕ S

246 AL 119, Cahaba Valley Rd, **E...other:** to Oak Mtn SP, **W...gas:** BP/diesel, Cowboys/Subway, RaceTrac, Shell, **food:** Applebee's, Arby's, BBQ, Blimpie, Buffalo's Café, Capt D's, Chick-fil-A, Cracker Barrel, Dairy Queen, Golden Corral, Hardee's, KFC, Krystal, McDonald's, O'Charley's, Pier Rest., Pizza Hut, Schlotsky's, Shoney's, Sonic, Taco Bell, Two Pesos Mexican, Waffle House, Wendy's, **lodging:** Best Western, Comfort Inn, Hampton Inn, Holiday Inn Express, Ramada Ltd, Sleep Inn, Travelodge, HOSPITAL, CVS Drug, Firestone/auto, Harley-Davidson, Winn-Dixie

242 Pelham, **E...gas:** Chevron/diesel/24hr, Exxon/diesel, Shell, **W...lodging:** Shelby Motel(2mi), **other:** KOA(1mi)

238 US 31, Alabaster, Saginaw, **E...gas:** BP/diesel, **W...gas:** Chevron/diesel, Cannon/gas, Shell, **food:** Waffle House, **2 mi W...food:** Arby's, **lodging:** Shelby Motel, **other:** HOSPITAL

234 Shelby Co Airport, **E...gas:** BP/Subway/diesel, **W...gas:** Chevron/diesel/24hr, Shell/diesel

231 US 31, Saginaw, **E...gas:** BP/diesel, Shell, **food:** BBQ, Capt D's, Golden China, Los Potrillos Mexican, McDonald's, **lodging:** Holiday Inn Express, **other:** Burton RV Ctr, $Tree, Radio Shack, Wal-Mart SuperCtr/gas/24hr, **W...food:** Donna's Café

228 AL 25, to Calera, **E...gas:** Citgo/diesel, Shell/diesel, **lodging:** Best Western, Day's Inn, **W...food:** Hardee's(1mi), **lodging:** Parkside Motel, **other:** to Brierfield Works SP

227mm Buxahatchie Creek

219 Union Grove, Thorsby, **E...gas:** Chevron/diesel/24hr, Exxon/Subway/diesel, **food:** Peach Queen Camping, **W...gas:** Shell, **food:** Smokey Hollow Rest.

213mm rest area both lanes, full(handicapped)facilities, phone, vending, picnic tables, litter barrels, petwalk, RV dump

Clanton

212 AL 145, Clanton, **E...gas:** Chevron/diesel, **W...gas:** BP/Subway, Headco/diesel, **other:** HOSPITAL, One Big Peach

208 Clanton, to Lake Mitchell, **W...gas:** Exxon/diesel/24hr, **food:** Shoney's, **lodging:** Guesthouse Inn, **other:** Heaton Pecans, Dandy RV Ctr

205 US 31, AL 22, to Clanton, **E...gas:** Amoco, Shell/diesel, **food:** McDonald's, Waffle House, **lodging:** Best Western, Day's Inn, Scottish Inn, **other:** Peach Park, to Confed Mem Park, **W...gas:** BP/diesel/The Store, Chevron/diesel/24hr, **food:** Burger King, Capt D's, Hardee's, Heaton Pecans, KFC, Subway, Taco Bell, **lodging:** Key West Inn, **other:** Durbin Farms Mkt, Wal-Mart SuperCtr/gas/24hr(2mi)

200 to Verbena, **E...gas:** BP/diesel, **W...gas:** Shell/DQ/Stuckey's/diesel, **other:** RV camping

186 US 31, Pine Level, **E...other:** Confederate Mem Park(13mi), **W...gas:** BP/diesel, Chevron/24hr, Citgo/diesel, Conoco/diesel, **food:** Vivian's Café, **lodging:** motel, **other:** HOSPITAL

181 AL 14, to Prattville, **E...gas:** Chevron/diesel/24hr, Entec/diesel, **W...gas:** Amoco, Citgo, Conoco/diesel, Exxon, Shell/DQ/diesel, **food:** Cracker Barrel, Ruby Tuesday, Waffle House, **lodging:** Best Western, Comfort Inn, Super 8, **other:** HOSPITAL

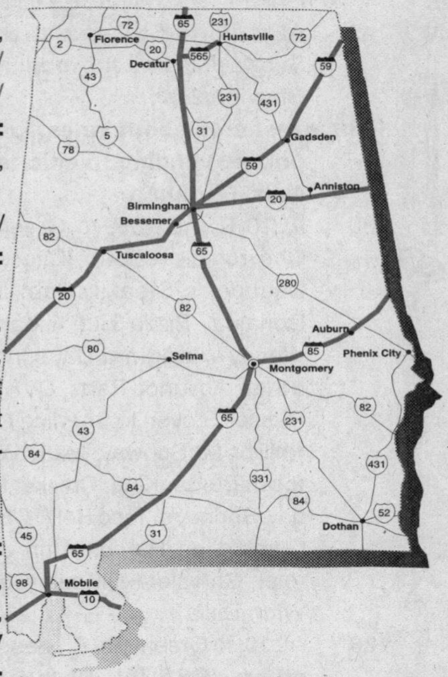

179 US 82 W, Millbrook, **E...gas:** Chevron/diesel, **food:** Asian Grill, **other:** K&K RV Park, **W...gas:** Amoco/diesel, BP/diesel, Citgo, Exxon/Subway/24hr, Shell, **food:** Burger King, Hardee's, Longhorn Steaks, McDonald's, O'Charley's, Steak'n Shake, Waffle House, **lodging:** Econolodge, Hampton Inn, Holiday Inn, Jameson Inn, **other:** Lowe's Whse

176 AL 143 N(from nb, no return), Millbrook, Coosada, no facilities

Montgomery

173 AL 152, North Blvd, to US 231, no facilities

172mm Alabama River

172 Clay St, Herron St, downtown, **E...lodging:** Embassy Suites, **W...gas:** Chevron

171 I-85 N, Day St, no facilities

170 Fairview Ave, **E...gas:** Citgo/Subway, **food:** China King, Church's, Krystal, McDonald's, **other:** Advance Parts, AutoZone, CVS Drug, Rite Aid, **W...gas:** Exxon, **food:** Hardee's, **other:** Calhoun Foods, Family$

169 Edgemont Ave(from sb), **E...gas:** Amoco, **other:** carwash

168 US 80 E, US 82, South Blvd, **E...gas:** BP/diesel, Cowboy's, Entec/diesel, TA/Citgo/diesel/rest./24hr/@, **food:** Arby's, Capt D's, KFC, McDonald's, Pizza Hut, Shoney's, Taco Bell, Waffle House, **lodging:** Best Inn, Knight's Inn, Travel Inn, **other:** HOSPITAL, **W...gas:** Amoco, Race-Way, Shell/Subway/diesel, Speedy/diesel, **food:** Dairy Queen, Hardee's, Wendy's, **lodging:** Comfort Inn, Day's Inn, Econolodge, Inn South, Ramada Inn, Valu Inn

167 US 80 W, to Selma, **1 mi W...gas:** Citgo, PaceCar, **food:** Church's, Subway, **other:** CVS Drug

164 US 31, Hope Hull, **E...gas:** Amoco/24hr, Saveway/diesel/24hr, Texaco, **lodging:** Lakeside Motel, **other:** KOA, **W...gas:** BP/Burger King, Chevron/24hr, Liberty/Subway, **food:** Waffle House, **lodging:** Best Western

158 to US 31, **E...gas:** Shell/DQ/Stuckey's

151 AL 97, to Letohatchee, **W...gas:** Amoco/diesel, BP

ALABAMA

Interstate 65

N ↕ S

Greenville

142 AL 185, to Ft Deposit, **E...gas:** BP/diesel, Shell/Subway/diesel/24hr, **food:** Priester's Pecans, **W...gas:** Chevron/24hr

133mm rest areas both lanes, full(handicapped)facilities, phone, vending, picnic tables, litter barrels, petwalk, RV dump

130 AL10 E, AL 185, to Greenville, **E...gas:** BP/diesel, Chevron/diesel/24hr, Citgo, Shell/24hr, **food:** Arby's, Beaugez's Steaks, Capt D's, Hardee's, KFC, McDonald's, Pizza Hut, Steak'n Shake, Waffle House, Wendy's, **lodging:** Day's Inn, Econolodge, Thrifty Inn, **other:** Advance Parts, CVS Drug, $General, Goody's, Russell Stover, to Sherling Lake Park, **W...gas:** Exxon, Phillips 66/Subway, Texaco/diesel, Bates Turkey Rest., **food:** Burger King, Cracker Barrel, Krystal, Ruby Tuesday, Shoney's, Taco Bell/TCBY, **lodging:** Best Western, Comfort Inn, Hampton Inn, Jameson Inn, **other:** Chevrolet, Chrysler/Plymouth/Dodge/Jeep, Wal-Mart/auto, Winn-Dixie

128 AL 10, to Greenville, **E...gas:** Shell/Smokehouse/diesel, **other:** HOSPITAL, **W...gas:** Amoco

114 AL 106, to Georgiana, **W...gas:** Amoco, Chevron/24hr, **other:** auto repair

107 AL 8, to Garland, no facilities

101 AL 29, to Owassa, **E...gas:** BP/diesel, **W...gas:** Exxon/diesel

96 AL 83, to Evergreen, **E...gas:** Chevron/24hr, Shell, **food:** Burger King, Hardee's, KFC/Taco Bell, McDonald's, **other:** HOSPITAL, **W...gas:** BP, Citgo/Subway/diesel, **food:** Pizza Hut, Waffle House, **lodging:** Comfort Inn, Day's Inn, Evergreen Inn

93 US 84, to Evergreen, **E...gas:** Exxon, Shell/diesel, **other:** PineCrest RV Park, **W...gas:** BP/diesel

89mm rest area sb, full(handicapped)facilities, phone, vending, picnic tables, litter barrels, petwalk, RV dump

85mm rest area nb, full(handicapped)facilities, phone, vending, picnic tables, litter barrels, petwalk, RV dump

83 AL 6, to Lenox, **E...gas:** Exxon/diesel/LP, Shell, **food:** Louise's Rest., **other:** Sunshine RV Park(4mi)

77 AL 41, to Range, **E...gas:** BP, **W...gas:** Amoco, Shell/Stuckey's/diesel, Texaco/diesel, **food:** Ranch House Rest.

69 AL 113, to Flomaton, **E...gas:** Chevron/Subway, Shell/diesel/24hr, **food:** Angel Ridge Rest., **W...gas:** Conoco/diesel/24hr, **food:** Huddle House

Atmore

57 AL 21, to Atmore, **E...gas:** Exxon/BBQ/diesel, Shell/diesel, **food:** Creek Family Rest., **lodging:** Best Western, **other:** Indian Bingo, **W...gas:** BP/diesel, **other:** to Kelley SP

54 Escambia Cty Rd 1, **E...gas:** BP/Subway/diesel, Citgo/diesel, **other:** to Creek Indian Res

45 to Perdido, **W...gas:** Amoco/diesel

37 AL 287, to Bay Minette, **E...gas:** BP

34 to AL 59, to Bay Minette, Stockton, **E...**HOSPITAL

31 AL 225, to Stockton, **E...other:** to Blakeley SP, Confederate Mem Bfd, **W...gas:** Conoco/diesel

29mm Tensaw River

28mm Middle River

25mm Mobile River

22 Creola, **E...**marine ctr, **W...other:** I-65 RV Park(3mi)

19 US 43, to Satsuma, **E...gas:** Chevron/diesel/24hr, Pilot/Arby's/diesel/24hr, **food:** McDonald's, Waffle House, **W...gas:** BP, **other:** I-65 RV Park(5mi)

15 AL 41, **E...gas:** Chevron, **lodging:** Plantation Motel, **W...gas:** Citgo/diesel

13 AL 158, AL 213, to Saraland, **E...gas:** BP/diesel, Shell/Krystal/diesel/24hr, **food:** Ruby Tuesday, Shoney's, Waffle House, **lodging:** Comfort Inn, Day's Inn, Holiday Inn Express, **other:** Plantation Motel(1mi), Wal-Mart SuperCtr/24hr, **W...gas:** Exxon, **food:** Blimpie, Pizza Inn, **lodging:** Hampton Inn

10 W Lee St, **E...gas:** Citgo, Conoco, Shell/Subway, **lodging:** Howard Johnson Express

9 I-165 S, to Mobile, to I-10 E

8b a US 45, to Prichard, **E...gas:** Chevron/24hr, Shell/diesel, **food:** Church's, My Seafood Café, **lodging:** Star Motel, **other:** Family$, Tiger Foods, **W...gas:** Amoco/24hr, Conoco/diesel, Exxon, Pride Trkstp/diesel, RaceWay, **food:** Burger King, Domino's, Golden Egg Café, McDonald's

5b US 98, Moffett Rd, **E...gas:** Exxon/diesel, **food:** Burger King, Church's, Sub King, **other:** Advance Parts, Big 10 Tire, **W...gas:** MinuteStop/diesel, **lodging:** Super 8

a Spring Hill Ave, **E...gas:** Amoco, Chevron, Shell/diesel, **food:** BBQ, Dairy Queen, KFC, McDonald's, **other:** HOSPITAL, AutoZone, Big 10 Tire, CarQuest, Family$, Tiger Foods, **W...gas:** Chevron/diesel/24hr, Exxon, Shell/diesel, **food:** Waffle House, **lodging:** Extended Stay America

4 Dauphin St, **E...gas:** Amoco/diesel, Shell, **food:** Checker's, Chick-fil-A, Cracker Barrel, Godfather's, Hong Kong Island, Krystal, McDonald's, Popeye's, Subway, Taco Bell, TCBY, Waffle House, Wendy's, **lodging:** Comfort Suites, Executive Inn, Red Roof Inn, **other:** Cadillac/Pontiac/GMC, $General, FoodWorld, Hyundai, Lowe's Whse, Mercedes, Mr Transmission, Rite Aid, Subaru, Wal-Mart SuperCtr/24hr, same as 3 & 5a, **W...**HOSPITAL

Mobile

3 Airport Blvd, to Airport, **E...gas:** BP, **food:** Burger King, Hooters, Piccadilly's, Schlotsky's, Wendy's, **lodging:** Marriott, **other:** HOSPITAL, Acura/Jaguar/Infiniti, Barnes&Noble, Best Buy, BooksAMillion, Daewoo, Dillard's, Firestone/auto, Ford, Goodyear/auto, Harley-Davidson, Mitsubishi, Nissan, Old Navy, Saab,

Interstate 65

Saturn, Sears/auto, Staples, Target, mall, **W...gas:** Exxon/Subway, Shell, Spur/diesel, **food:** American Café, Arby's, Bumpers Grill, Burger King, Carrabba's, Chen Chinese, Chili's, ChuckeCheese, Denny's, El Chico, El Monterey Mexican, Fatzo's Café, IHOP, JR's Smokehouse, LoneStar Steaks, Los Rancheros Mexican, O'Charley's, Olive Garden, Outback Steaks, Pizza Hut, Popeye's, Quizno's, Red Lobster, S China Seafood, Shoney's, Tony Roma, Waffle House, Wanfu Mongolian, **lodging:** Airport Plaza Hotel, Best Inn, Best Value Inn, Best Western, Courtyard, Day's Inn, Drury Inn, Fairfield Inn, Hampton Inn, InTowne Suites, La Quinta, Motel 6, Ramada Inn, Residence Inn, **other:** BooksAMillion, Bruno's Food, Circuit City, $Tree, Home Depot, Jo-Ann Fabrics, Michael's, OfficeMax, Office Depot, PepBoys, Radio Shack, Sam's Club, SteinMart, U-Haul, to USAL

1b a — US 90, Government Blvd, **E...gas:** Chevron, **food:** Burger King, McAlister's Deli, Steak'n Shake, **lodging:** Guesthouse Inn, **other:** Aamco, Audi/VW, BMW, Buick/Isuzu/Volvo, Chevrolet, Chrysler/Jeep, Dodge, Family$, Honda, Kia, Lexus, Lincoln/Mercury, Mazda, Toyota, **W...gas:** Shell/diesel, **food:** Waffle House, **lodging:** Rest Inn

0mm — I-10, E to Pensacola, W to New Orleans. I-65 begins/ends on I-10, exit 20.

Interstate 85

Exit #	Services
80mm	Alabama/Georgia state line, Chattahoochee River
79	US 29, to Lanett, **E...gas:** Amoco/diesel, Lo-Bucks/24hr, **food:** Arby's, Burger King, BBQ, Capt D's, Hardee's, KFC, Krystal, Magic Wok Chinese, McDonald's, San Marcos Mexican, Subway, Taco Bell, Waffle House/24hr, Wendy's, **other:** Advance Parts, $General, Radio Shack, Wal-Mart SuperCtr/gas/24hr, transmissions, to West Point Lake, **W...gas:** Conoco, Phillips 66/diesel, **food:** Domino's, Shoney's, Sonic, **lodging:** Day's Inn, Econolodge, Super 8, **other:** AutoZone, CVS Drug, Kroger, Parts+
78.5mm	**Welcome Ctr sb, full(handicapped)facilities, phone, vending, picnic tables, litter barrels, petwalk**
77	AL 208, to Huguley, **E...gas:** Amoco/diesel/24hr, Chevron/WaffleKing/diesel/24hr, **food:** Waffle House, **lodging:** Holiday Inn Express, **other:** Chevrolet, Chrysler/Dodge, Ford/Lincoln/Mercury
76mm	Eastern/Central time zone
70	AL 388, to Cusseta, **E...gas:** Perlis/Subway/diesel/rest./24hr/@
66	to Andrews Rd, no facilities
64	US 29, to Opelika, **E...gas:** Amoco, **lodging:** IGuesthouse Inn
62	US 280/431, to Opelika, **E...gas:** Amoco, BP/diesel, Chevron, Shell/Church's/diesel/24hr, **food:** Burger King, Denny's, McDonald's, Shoney's, Subway, **lodging:** Budget Inn, Day's Inn, Econolodge, Holiday Inn, Knight's Inn, Motel 6, **other: Lakeside RV Park(4.5mi)**, **W...gas:** Conoco, Shell, **food:** Cracker Barrel, Waffle House, Western Sizzlin, **lodging:** Comfort Inn, Travelodge, **other:** Chevrolet, Chrysler/Plymouth/Dodge, Ford, GNC, Hyundai, Jeep, Toyota, USA Stores/famous brands
60	AL 51, AL 169, to Opelika, **E...gas:** Amoco/diesel, RaceTrac, **food:** Hardee's, **W...gas:** Shell/Krystal/diesel, **food:** Wendy's, **lodging:** Econolodge, **other:** HOSPITAL
58	US 280 W, to Opelika, **E...other:** golf, museum, **W...gas:** BP, Chevron/Subway, **food:** Dairy Queen, Golden Corral, Outback Steaks, Taco Bell, **lodging:** Ramada Ltd, **other:** HOSPITAL, Lowe's Whse
57	Glenn Ave, **W...gas:** Exxon, Conoco/diesel, **lodging:** Hilton Garden, Plaza Motel, Super 8
51	US 29, to Auburn, **E...gas:** Amoco/diesel/24hr, **lodging:** Hampton Inn, **other:** to Chewacla SP, **W...gas:** Exxon/diesel, Raceway, **food:** McDonald's, Philly Connection, Waffle House, **lodging:** Auburn U Hotel/Conf Ctr, Comfort Inn, Econolodge, Heart of Auburn Motel, **other:** Ford/Lincoln/Mercury/Mitsubishi, to Auburn U
44mm	**rest area both lanes, full(handicapped)facilitie s, phone, vending, picnic tables, litter barrels, petwalk, RV dump, 24hr security**
42	US 80, AL 186 E, Wire Rd, **E...other:** to Tuskegee NF, diesel repair/tires, **W...gas:** Amoco/diesel
38	AL 81, to Tuskegee, **E...**to Tuskegee NHS
32	AL 49 N, to Tuskegee, **E...gas:** Amoco/diesel
26	AL 229 N, to Tallassee, **E...gas:** Texaco/diesel, **W...**HOSPITAL

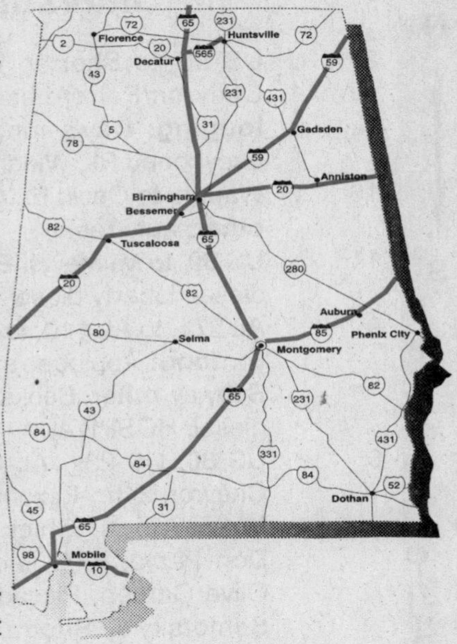

Interstate 85

N ↕ S — Montgomery

22 US 80, to Shorter, **E...gas:** Amoco/diesel, Chevron/Petro/diesel/rest., Exxon/diesel, **lodging:** Day's Inn, **other:** to Macon Co Greyhound Pk, Windrift RV Park

16 Waugh, to Cecil, **E...gas:** BP/Subway/diesel, **other:** auto repair

11 US 80, to Mt Meigs, **E...gas:** Exxon/Subway/diesel, Liberty/diesel, **W...gas:** Chevron/24hr

9 AL 271, to AL 110, to Auburn U/Montgomery, **E...food:** Applebee's, Arby's, Atlanta Bread, Subway, **other:** BooksAMillion, **W...gas:** Citgo/diesel, HOSPITAL

6 US 80, US 231, AL 21, East Blvd, **E...gas:** Chevron/24hr, Exxon/diesel/24hr, RaceTrac, **food:** Arby's, Chick-fil-A, Cracker Barrel, Don Pablo, KFC, McAlister's, O'Charley's, Olive Garden, Piccadilly's, Roadhouse Grill, Schlotsky's, Shogun Japanese, Smokey Bones BBQ, SteakOut, Subway, Taco Bell, Up The Creek Grill, Waffle House, Wendy's, Wings Grill, Zaxby's, **lodging:** Baymont Inn, Best Inn, Comfort Inn, Courtyard, Extended Stay America, Fairfield Inn, Hampton Inn, La Quinta, Quality Inn, Ramada Inn, Residence Inn, SpringHill Suites, Studio+, Wingate Inn, **other:** Home Depot, Lowe's Whse, Pontiac/Cadillac, Radio Shack, USPO, **1 mi E...food:** Copeland's, TGIFriday, Tony Roma, Wal-Mart SuperCtr/24hr, **W...gas:** Amoco, Citgo, Shell, **food:** Burger King, Church's, KFC, LoneStar Steaks, McDonald's, OutBack Steaks, Ruby Tuesday, Waffle House, **lodging:** Best Western, Comfort Suites, Motel 6, Holiday Inn, **other:** BMW, Buick, Chevrolet, Chrysler/Jeep, Ford, Hyundai, Isuzu, Kia, Lexus, Mazda, Mitsubishi, Nissan, Sam's Club/gas, Toyota, VW, to Gunter AFB, **1 mi W...food:** IHOP, **other:** Circuit City, Sears/auto, mall

4 Perry Hill Rd, **E...other:** DENTIST, Bruno's Foods, Rite Aid, **W...gas:** Chevron/24hr

3 Ann St, **E...gas:** BP/diesel, Chevron, **food:** Arby's, BBQ, Capt D's, Domino's, Great Wall Chinese, Hardee's, KFC, Krystal, McDonald's, Pizza Hut, Taco Bell, Waffle House, Wendy's, **lodging:** Day's Inn, **other:** Big 10 Tire, **W...gas:** Amoco, Entec, Exxon, **lodging:** Stay Lodge

2 Forest Ave, **E...other:** CVS Drug, **W...**HOSPITAL

1 Court St, Union St, downtown, **E...gas:** Amoco/diesel, Exxon, **W...**to Ala St U

0mm I-85 begins/ends on I-65, exit 171 in Montgomery.

Interstate 459(Birmingham)

N ↕ S — Birmingham

Exit # Services

33b a I-59, N to Gadsden, S to Birmingham. I-459 begins/ends on I-59, exit 137.

32 US 11, Trussville, **E...gas:** Chevron/diesel/24hr, Citgo, RaceTrac/24hr, Shell, Texaco/Wendy's/diesel, **food:** A&W/KFC, Arby's, BBQ, Chili's, Jack's Rest., McDonald's, Waffle House, **lodging:** Hampton Inn, **other:** BooksAMillion, Harley-Davidson, Home Depot, Lowe's Whse, Mazda, Michael's, Pontiac/GMC/Buick, Staples, Target, **W...gas:** BP/24hr, **lodging:** Best Inn(3mi)

31 Derby Parkway, **W...other:** B'ham Race Course

29 I-20, E to Atlanta, W to Birmingham

27 Grants Mill Rd, **S...gas:** Exxon/diesel

23 Liberty Parkway, no facilities

19 US 280, Mt Brook, Childersburg, **N...gas:** Chevron, **other:** Barnes&Noble, **1-2 mi S...gas:** Exxon, **food:** Arby's, Burger King, Chick-fil-A, McDonald's, Piccadilly's, Ruby Tuesday, **lodging:** Courtyard, Drury Inn, Fairfield Inn, Hampton Inn, Hilton, Holiday Inn Express, Homestead Suites, Marriott, Sheraton, Studio Inn

17 Acton Rd, **N...gas:** Shell/diesel/24hr, **food:** BBQ, Krystal, McDonald's

15b a I-65, N to Birmingham, S to Montgomery

13 US 31, Hoover, Pelham, **N...gas:** Chevron, Shell, **food:** BBQ, Chick-fil-A, DQ, LongHorn Steaks, McDonald's, Quizno's, Schlotsky's, Shoney's, SteakOut, Subway, **lodging:** Comfort Inn, Day's Inn, Hampton Inn, Holiday Inn, RiverChase Inn, **other:** MEDICAL CARE, Acura, BooksAMillion, Bruno's Foods, Buick, Cadillac, Chevrolet, Chrysler/Plymouth/Jeep, Circuit City, Eckerd, Firestone, Goodyear, Honda, Kia, Mitsubishi, Mr Transmissions, Toyota, **S...gas:** Crown Gas, Shell/diesel/24hr, Circle K, **food:** BBQ, Burger King, CiCi's, Grady's Grill, McDonald's, Olive Garden, Omelet Shoppe, Piccadilly's, Sun's Chinese, Taco Bell, Wendy's, **lodging:** AmeriSuites, Courtyard, Winfrey Hotel, **other:** Barnes&Noble, Bruno's Foods, CVS Drug, GNC, Infiniti, JC Penney, K-Mart, Mercedes, Michael's, Wal-Mart(1mi), mall

10 AL 150, Waverly, **N...gas:** Chevron, Shell, **S...gas:** BP/diesel/24hr, Exxon, **food:** Mei China, AmeriSuites(1mi), GNC, Walgreen, Winn-Dixie

6 AL 52, to Bessemer, **N...gas:** BP, **S...gas:** Crown, Exxon/24hr, Shell, **food:** Arby's, McDonald's, Pizza Hut, Taco Bell, Waffle House, Wendy's, **lodging:** Sleep Inn, **other:** MEDICAL CARE, CVS Drug, Winn-Dixie

1 AL 18, Bessemer, **N...gas:** Shell/diesel, **S...gas:** BP/diesel, **food:** China King, McDonald's, Subway, **other:** FoodWorld, to Tannehill SP

0mm I-459 begins/ends on I-20/59, exit 106.

Interstate 8

E
W

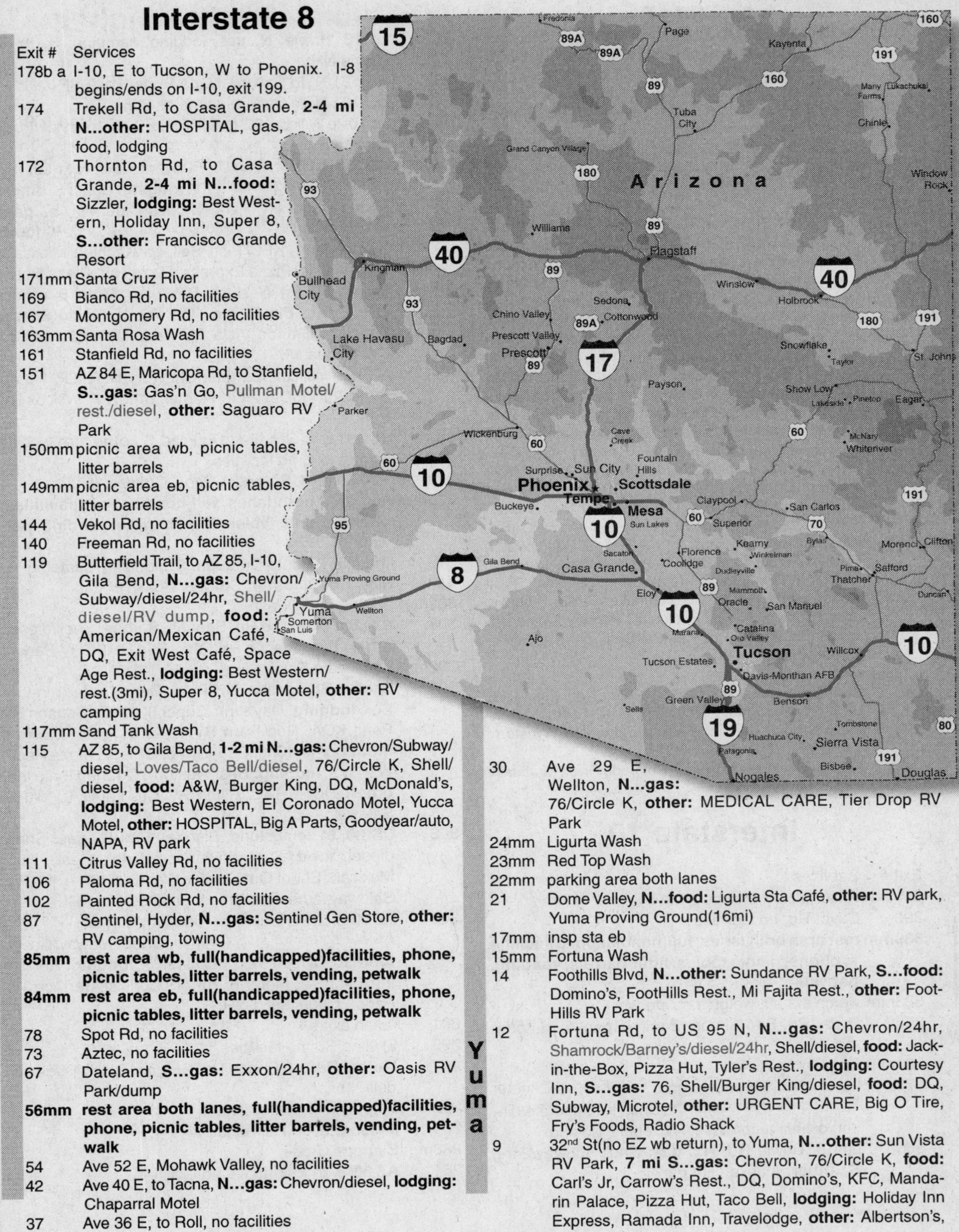

Exit # Services

178b a I-10, E to Tucson, W to Phoenix. I-8 begins/ends on I-10, exit 199.

174 Trekell Rd, to Casa Grande, **2-4 mi N...other:** HOSPITAL, gas, food, lodging

172 Thornton Rd, to Casa Grande, **2-4 mi N...food:** Sizzler, **lodging:** Best Western, Holiday Inn, Super 8, **S...other:** Francisco Grande Resort

171mm Santa Cruz River

169 Bianco Rd, no facilities

167 Montgomery Rd, no facilities

163mm Santa Rosa Wash

161 Stanfield Rd, no facilities

151 AZ 84 E, Maricopa Rd, to Stanfield, **S...gas:** Gas'n Go, Pullman Motel/rest./diesel, **other:** Saguaro RV Park

150mm picnic area wb, picnic tables, litter barrels

149mm picnic area eb, picnic tables, litter barrels

144 Vekol Rd, no facilities

140 Freeman Rd, no facilities

119 Butterfield Trail, to AZ 85, I-10, Gila Bend, **N...gas:** Chevron/Subway/diesel/24hr, Shell/diesel/RV dump, **food:** American/Mexican Café, DQ, Exit West Café, Space Age Rest., **lodging:** Best Western/rest.(3mi), Super 8, Yucca Motel, **other:** RV camping

117mm Sand Tank Wash

115 AZ 85, to Gila Bend, **1-2 mi N...gas:** Chevron/Subway/diesel, Loves/Taco Bell/diesel, 76/Circle K, Shell/diesel, **food:** A&W, Burger King, DQ, McDonald's, **lodging:** Best Western, El Coronado Motel, Yucca Motel, **other:** HOSPITAL, Big A Parts, Goodyear/auto, NAPA, RV park

111 Citrus Valley Rd, no facilities

106 Paloma Rd, no facilities

102 Painted Rock Rd, no facilities

87 Sentinel, Hyder, **N...gas:** Sentinel Gen Store, **other:** RV camping, towing

85mm rest area wb, full(handicapped)facilities, phone, picnic tables, litter barrels, vending, petwalk

84mm rest area eb, full(handicapped)facilities, phone, picnic tables, litter barrels, vending, petwalk

78 Spot Rd, no facilities

73 Aztec, no facilities

67 Dateland, **S...gas:** Exxon/24hr, **other:** Oasis RV Park/dump

56mm rest area both lanes, full(handicapped)facilities, phone, picnic tables, litter barrels, vending, petwalk

54 Ave 52 E, Mohawk Valley, no facilities

42 Ave 40 E, to Tacna, **N...gas:** Chevron/diesel, **lodging:** Chaparral Motel

37 Ave 36 E, to Roll, no facilities

Yuma

30 Ave 29 E, Wellton, **N...gas:** 76/Circle K, **other:** MEDICAL CARE, Tier Drop RV Park

24mm Ligurta Wash

23mm Red Top Wash

22mm parking area both lanes

21 Dome Valley, **N...food:** Ligurta Sta Café, **other:** RV park, Yuma Proving Ground(16mi)

17mm insp sta eb

15mm Fortuna Wash

14 Foothills Blvd, **N...other:** Sundance RV Park, **S...food:** Domino's, FootHills Rest., Mi Fajita Rest., **other:** FootHills RV Park

12 Fortuna Rd, to US 95 N, **N...gas:** Chevron/24hr, Shamrock/Barney's/diesel/24hr, Shell/diesel, **food:** Jack-in-the-Box, Pizza Hut, Tyler's Rest., **lodging:** Courtesy Inn, **S...gas:** 76, Shell/Burger King/diesel, **food:** DQ, Subway, Microtel, **other:** URGENT CARE, Big O Tire, Fry's Foods, Radio Shack

9 32nd St(no EZ wb return), to Yuma, **N...other:** Sun Vista RV Park, **7 mi S...gas:** Chevron, 76/Circle K, **food:** Carl's Jr, Carrow's Rest., DQ, Domino's, KFC, Mandarin Palace, Pizza Hut, Taco Bell, **lodging:** Holiday Inn Express, Ramada Inn, Travelodge, **other:** Albertson's,

ARIZONA

Interstate 8

E ↕ W

Buick/Cadillac/GMC, Chevrolet, Dillard's, Ford/Lincoln/Mercury, Honda, Lowe's Whse, Mazda, Mervyn's, Michael's, PepBoys, Plymouth/Jeep/Dodge, Sears/auto, Toyota, Walgreen, **access to services on 4th Ave**

7 Araby Rd, **S...gas:** 76/Circle K/diesel, **other:** La Mesa Ctr, Windhaven RV Park, to AZWU

3 AZ 280 S, Ave 3E, **N...gas:** Yuma 3E/diesel, **food:** Burger King, **S...other:** Big A Parts, **3 mi S...food:** KFC, Pizza Hut, Wendy's(6mi), **other:** to Marine Corp Air Sta

2 US 95, 16th St, Yuma, **N...gas:** Barneys/diesel/café, 76/Circle K, **food:** Cracker Barrel, Denny's, Musick's Rest., Penny's Diner/24hr, **lodging:** Best Western, Day's Inn, Fairfield Inn, La Fuente Inn, Motel 6, OakTree Inn, Shilo Inn/rest., **other:** auto/tire repair, **Services on Pacific Ave S...food:** Peter Piper Pizza, Sonic, Subway, Wienerschnitzel, **other:** Big O Tire, NAPA, Kia, Sam's Club, Wal-Mart SuperCtr/24hr, **S...gas:** Arco/diesel/24hr, Chevron/Blimpie/diesel, Mobil/Wendy's/diesel, Shamrock, Shell, **food:** Applebee's, Burger King, Carl's Jr, IHOP, Jack-in-the-Box, Wendy's, Village Inn Pizza, **lodging:** Comfort Inn, Interstate 8 Inn, Motel 6, Super 8, **other:** HOSPITAL, Home Depot, Staples, U-Haul, **services on 4th Ave S...gas:** Chevron, 76/Circle K, Shell, **food:** Arby's, Burger King, China Boy, Church's, Del Taco, HomeTown Buffet, HongKong Buffet, Jack-in-the-Box, JB's, KFC, McDonald's, Papa John's, Rally's, Red Lobster, Rocky's Pizza, Taco Bell, Wienerschnitzel, **lodging:** Holiday Inn Express, Interstate 8 Inn, Radisson, Travelodge, **other:** AutoZone, Checker Parts, Dillard's, Fry's Foods, Hastings Books, JC Penney, Office Depot, Radio Shack, Rite Aid, SavOn Drug, SW Foods, Target, U-Haul, mall

1.5mm weigh sta both lanes

1 Giss Pkwy, Yuma, **N...other:** to Yuma Terr Prison SP, **S on 4th Ave...gas:** 76/Circle K, Shell, **food:** Jack-in-the-Box, Yuma Landing Rest., **lodging:** Best Western, Yuma Inn

0mm Arizona/California state line, Colorado River, Mountain/Pacific time zone

Interstate 10

E ↕ W

Exit # Services

391mm Arizona/New Mexico state line

390 Cavot Rd, no facilities

389mm rest area both lanes, full(handicapped)facilities, phone, picnic tables, litter barrels, vending, petwalk

383mm weigh sta eb, weigh/insp sta wb

382 Portal Rd, San Simon, **2 mi N...**gas, food, lodging

381mm San Simon River

378 Lp 10, San Simon, **N...gas:** 4K/Chevron/Chester Fried Chicken/diesel/24hr, Shell/Kactus Kafe/diesel, **other:** auto/diesel/RV repair, lodging

366 Lp 10, Bowie Rd, **N... gas:** Shell/Subway/24hr, **S...other:** Alaskan RV park

362 Lp 10, Bowie, **N...**gas, lodging, camping, **S...**to Ft Bowie NHS

355 US 191 N, to Safford, **N...**to Roper Lake SP

352 US 191 N, to Safford, same as 355

Willcox

344 Lp 10, to Willcox, **S...gas:** Willcox Diesel Service/truck repair

340 AZ 186, to Rex Allen Dr, Ft Grant Field, **N...gas:** Rip Griffin/Subway/diesel/24hr, **lodging:** Super 8, **other:** Magic Circle RV Park, Stout's CiderMill, **S...gas:** Chevron/diesel/24hr, Mobil/diesel, 76/Circle K, **food:** Burger King, KFC/Taco Bell, La Kachina Mexican, McDonald's, Pizza Express, Pizza Hut, Plaza Rest., **lodging:** Best Western, Day's Inn, Motel 6, **other:** HOSPITAL, Big O Tire, IGA Foods, Radio Shack, Safeway, Grande Vista RV Park, Dick's Repair, to Chiricahua NM

336 AZ 186, Willcox, **S...gas:** Chevron/diesel/LP, **1-3 mi S...lodging:** Desert Inn Motel, **other:** Ft Willcox RV Park

331 US 191 S, to Sunsites, Douglas, **S...other:** to Cochise Stronghold, no facilities

322 Johnson Rd, **S...gas:** Citgo/DQ/diesel/gifts

320mm rest area both lanes, full(handicapped)facilities, phone, picnic tables, litter barrels, vending, petwalk

318 Triangle T Rd, to Dragoon, **S...**lodging, camping

312 Sibyl Rd, **S...other:** Stuckey's/gas/RV park

309mm Adams Peak Wash

306 AZ 80, Pomerene Rd, Benson, **S...gas:** Shell/diesel, **other:** Pato Blanco RV Park, San Pedro RV Park

305mm San Pedro River

Benson

304 Ocotillo St, Benson, **N...food:** Denny's, Jack-in-the-Box, **lodging:** Day's Inn, Super 8, **other:** Benson RV Park, KOA, Red Barn RV Park, **S...gas:** Chevron, **food:** Burger King, Country Folks Rest., Plaza Rest., Wendy's, **lodging:** Best Western, QuarterHorse Inn, **other:** HOSPITAL, Dillon RV Ctr, Family$, NAPA, Safeway

303 US 80, to Tombstone, Bisbee, **1 mi S...gas:** Shell/diesel, **food:** Beijing Chinese, Reb's Rest., Ruiz Mexican, Shoot Out Steaks, Wendy's, **other:** NAPA, Safeway, auto/diesel/repair, to Douglas NHL

302 AZ 90 S, to Ft Huachuca, Benson, **S...gas:** Gas City/A&W/Pizza Hut/TCBY/diesel, Shell/Subway/diesel, **food:** KFC/Taco Bell, McDonald's, **lodging:** Holiday Inn Express, Motel 6, **other:** Cochise Terrace RV Park, Ft Huachuca NHS

301 ranch exit eb

299 Skyline Rd, no facilities

297 Mescal Rd, J-6 Ranch Rd, **N...gas:** QuickPic/diesel/deli/24hr

292 Empirita Rd, no facilities

289 Marsh Station Rd, no facilities

288mm Cienega Creek

281 AZ 83 S, to Patagonia, no facilities

Interstate 10

E
W

279 Vail/Wentworth Rd, **N...food:** Vail Steakhouse, **other:** to Colossal Caves

275 Houghton Rd, **N...other:** to Saguaro NM, camping, **S...**to fairgrounds

273 Rita Rd, **S...**fairgrounds

270 Kolb Rd, **N...gas:** Chevron/diesel, **S...other:** Voyager RV Resort

269 Wilmot Rd, **N...gas:** Chevron/A&W/diesel, **lodging:** Travel Inn, **other:** RV park, **S...**RV park

268 Craycroft Rd, **N...gas:** Conoco/diesel, TTT/diesel/rest./24hr, 76/Circle K, **S...**diesel repair

267 Valencia Rd, **N...gas:** Arco/Jack-in-the-Box, **other:** Pima Air Museum, **S...**airport

265 Alvernon Way, Davis-Monthan AFB, no facilities

264b a Palo Verde Rd, **N...gas:** Chevron/Wendy's/diesel, **food:** Carl's Jr, Denny's, Waffle House, **lodging:** Crossland Suites, Day's Inn, Fairfield Inn, Holiday Inn, Red Roof Inn, **other:** Hannon RV Ctr, **S...gas:** QuikMart/gas, **food:** Arby's, McDonald's, Motel 6, **lodging:** Ramada Inn, Studio 6 Suites, **other:** Beaudry RV Ctr, Camping World RV Resort, La Mesa RV Ctr, Factory Outlet/famous brands

263b Kino Pkwy N, no facilities

a Kino Pkwy S, **S...gas:** Shamrock, **food:** Fry's Foods, **other:** to Tucson Intn'l Airport

262 Benson Hwy, Park Ave, **S...gas:** Arco/24hr, Chevron, Shell, JB's, **food:** McDonald's, Navaronne Rest., Waffle House, **lodging:** Howard Johnson, Jct Inn, Motel 6, Quality Inn, Rodeway Inn

Tucson

261 6th/4th Ave, **N...gas:** Chevron, **lodging:** Budget Inn, Econolodge, **S...food:** Burger King, Carrow's Rest., Silver Saddle Steaks, **lodging:** Rodeway Inn, Sandman Inn, Lazy 8 Motel, **other:** Spanish Trail

260 I-19 S, to Nogales

259 22nd St, Starr Pass Blvd, **N...gas:** 76/Circle K/diesel, **S...gas:** 76, Kettle, **food:** Waffle House, Comfort Inn, Holiday Inn Express, Howard Johnson, Knight's Inn, Motel 6, Super 8, Travel Inn

258 Congress St, Broadway St, **N...gas:** Circle K/76, **food:** Garcia's Rest., **lodging:** Holiday Inn, InnSuites Motel, Motel 6, Quality Hotel Suites, Ramada Inn, Travelodge, **S...food:** Bennigan's, Carl's Jr, Whataburger, **lodging:** Days Inn, Pueblo Inn

257a St Mary's Rd, **N...gas:** 76/diesel, **other:** HOSPITAL, **S...gas:** Shell/24hr, **food:** Burger King, Denny's, Furr's Cafeteria, Jack-in-the-Box, **lodging:** La Quinta, **other:** Pim Comm Coll

257 Speedway Blvd, **N...gas:** 7-11/24hr, **lodging:** Best Western, **other:** HOSPITAL, Old Town Tucson, museum, U of AZ, **S...gas:** Arco/diesel/24hr

256 Grant Rd, **N...food:** Sonic, diesel/transmission repair, **S...gas:** Exxon, 76/Circle K, Shell, **food:** Del Taco, IHOP, Subway, Waffle House, **lodging:** Baymont Inn, Hampton Inn, Motel 6, Rodeway Inn, Shoney's Inn, **1 mi S...gas:** Circle K, **food:** McDonald's, **other:** Walgreen

255 AZ 77 N, to Miracle Mile

254 Prince Rd, **N...gas:** Circle K, **other:** U-Haul, tires, **S...other:** Prince of Tucson RV Park, golf

252 El Camino del Cerro, Ruthrauff Rd, **N...gas:** Arco/24hr

251 Sunset Rd, **N...other:** auto parts

250 Orange Grove Rd, **N...gas:** Arco/24hr, Circle K, **food:** Wendy's, **other:** Mitsubishi, **N on Thornydale...gas:** Costco/gas, **food:** Casa Molina Mexican, Little Caesar's, **other:** Big O Tire, Home Depot

248 Ina Rd, **N...gas:** Chevron/diesel, Conoco/diesel, Exxon/Circle K, **food:** Arby's, Burger King, Carl's Jr, China House, DQ, Hooters, Jack-in-the-Box, LJ Silver, McDonald's, Perkins, Pizza Hut, Rubio's Grill, Taco Bell, Waffle House, **lodging:** InTown Suites, Motel 6, **other:** CarQuest, Discount Tire, Fry's Foods, Hancock Fabrics, Office Depot, OfficeMax, Osco Drug, PepBoys, Target, **S...gas:** Exxon/Circle K, **food:** Denny's, **lodging:** Comfort Inn, Park Inn, Red Roof Inn

246 Cortaro Rd, **N...gas:** Chevron/Arby's/diesel, **food:** IHOP, Wendy's, **S...gas:** Shell/diesel, **food:** Burger King, Cracker Barrel, KFC, McDonald's, **lodging:** Best Western, Day's Inn, Holiday Inn Express, Ramada Ltd, Super 8, **other:** USPO, Wal-Mart SuperCtr/24hr, access to RV camping

243 Avra Valley Rd, **S...other:** Saguaro NM(13mi), RV camping, airport

240 Tangerine Rd, to Rillito, **S...**USPO

236 Marana, **S...gas:** Chevron/diesel/LP, 76/Circle K, **other:** Sun RV Park, auto repair

232 Pinal Air Park Rd, **S...**Pinal Air Park

228mm wb pulloff, to frontage rd

226 Red Rock, **S...**USPO

219 Picacho Peak Rd, **N...gas:** Citgo/DQ, **S...other:** Pichaco Peak RV Park, to Picacho Peak SP

212 Picacho(from wb), **N...gas:** Premium Gas, **lodging:** Picacho Motel/RV Park, **other:** USPO

211b AZ 87 N, AZ 84 W, to Coolidge

a Picacho(from eb), **S...other:** Picacho RV Park, state prison

208 Sunshine Blvd, to Eloy, **S...gas:** Flying J/Conoco/diesel/LP/rest./24hr/@, Pilot/diesel/24hr/@

ARIZONA

Interstate 10

E ↕ W

203 Toltec Rd, to Eloy, **N...gas:** Chevron/McDonald's/24hr, Circle K/diesel, **food:** Carl's Jr, El Zarape Rojo Mexican, Waffle House, **lodging:** Super 8, Toltec Inn, **other:** Blue Beacon, Golden Corridor RV Park, diesel/tire repair, **S...gas:** Exxon/diesel, TA/A&W/Taco Bell/diesel/24hr/@, **food:** Pizza Hut

200 Sunland Gin Rd, Arizona City, **N...gas:** Petro/Mobil/diesel/rest./24hr/@, Pilot/Subway/diesel/24hr, **food:** Burger King, **lodging:** Day's Inn, Sunland Inn/rest., **other:** Blue Beacon, Las Colinas RV Park, **S...gas:** Loves/Arby's/Baskin-Robbins/diesel/24hr, **food:** Golden 9 Rest., **lodging:** Motel 6, Quail Run RV Resort

199 I-8 W, to Yuma, San Diego

198 AZ 84, to Eloy, Casa Grande, **N...lodging:** Sunland Inn, **S...food:** Wendy's, **other:** Tanger Outlet Ctr/famous brands, Buena Tierra RV Pk

Casa Grande

194 AZ 287, to Casa Grande, **N...other:** Sunscape RV Park(7mi), **S...gas:** Arco/diesel/24hr, Chevron/DQ, **food:** Burger King, Cracker Barrel, Del Taco, Denny's, **lodging:** Best Western, Comfort Inn, Holiday Inn, Super 8, **other:** HOSPITAL, Factory Stores/famous brands, Palm Creek RV/golf Resort, **2 mi S...gas:** Chevron, 76/Circle K, **food:** Arby's, China King, Church's, Filiberto's Mexican, Golden Corral, Jack-in-the-Box, JB's, Little Caesar's, McDonald's, Peter Piper Pizza, Sizzler, Sonic, Subway, Wendy's, **other:** Albertson's, American CarCare, Basha's Foods, Fry's Foods, Goodyear/auto, GreenBax, JC Penney, OfficeMax, PepBoys, Radio Shack, Walgreen, Wal-Mart SuperCtr/24hr, to Casa Grande Ruins NM

190 McCartney Rd, **N...other:** to Central AZ Coll

185 AZ 387, to Casa Grande, Casa Grande Ruins NM, **S...other:** hwy patrol, RV camping

183mm rest area wb, full(handicapped)facilities, phone, picnic tables, litter barrels, vending, petwalk

181mm rest area eb, full(handicapped)facilities, phone, picnic tables, litter barrels, vending, petwalk

175 AZ 587 N, Casa Blanca Rd, **S...gas:** Shell/diesel, **other:** Casa Blanca RV Camping

173mm Gila River

167 Riggs Rd, to Sun Lake, **N...gas:** Chevron

Chandler

164 AZ 347 S, Queen Creek Rd, to Maricopa, **N...other:** to Chandler Airport

162b a Maricopa Rd N, **S...other:** Firebird Sports Park, Gila River Casino

160 Chandler Blvd, to Chandler, **N...gas:** Exxon/Circle K, Mobil, **food:** Burger King, Damon's, Denny's, Marie Callender's, Perkins, Sizzler, Whataburger/24hr, **lodging:** Fairfield Inn, Hampton Inn, Homewood Suites, Red Roof Inn, Southgate Motel, Super 8, Wyndham Garden, **other:** Firestone/auto, to Compadre Stadium, to Williams AFB, **S...gas:** Chevron, Citgo/7-11, Phillips 66/diesel, **food:** Cracker Barrel, Del Taco, Hooters, Holiday Inn Express, InTown Suites, La Quinta, **lodging:** Wellesley Inn, **other:** HOSPITAL, Brakes+, Discount Tire

159 Ray Rd, **N...gas:** 76/Circle K, Shell/diesel, **food:** Buca Italian, Carrabba's, Charleston's Rest., In-n-Out, Luby's, McDonald's, Outback Steaks, Red Lobster, **lodging:** Courtyard, **other:** Borders Books, CompUSA, Ford, Home Depot, Lowe's Whse, Sam's Club, **S...gas:** Exxon/Circle K/diesel, **food:** BBQ, Boston Mkt, IHOP/24hr, Jack-in-the-Box, Macaroni Grill, Mimi's Café, On-the-Border, Peter Piper Pizza, Pizza Hut, Ruby Tuesday, Subway, Sweet Tomato, Wendy's, **lodging:** Extended Stay America, **other:** Albertson's/24hr, Barnes&Noble, Best Buy, FootHills Carwash, Jo-Ann Fabrics, Mervyn's, Michael's, OfficeMax, Old Navy, Osco, Ross, Smith's Food/drug/24hr, SteinMart, SunDevil AutoCare, Target

158 Warner Rd, **N...gas:** 76/Circle K, **S...gas:** Arco/24hr, 76/Circle K, **food:** Burger King, ChuckeCheese, DQ, Malaya Mexican, McDonald's, Quizno's, Ruffino's Italian, Taco Bell, **other:** Basha's Foods, Big O Tire, Goodyear/auto, Osco Drug, Wild Oats Foods

157 Elliot Rd, **N...gas:** Chevron, Circle K, **food:** Applebee's, Arby's, Blackeyed Pea, Burger King, Chili's, Coco's, Country Harvest Buffet, Eastside Mario's, Fuddrucker's, Kyoto Japanese, Mi Amigos Mexican, Olive Garden, Red Robin Rest., Schlotsky's, Sooper Salad, Subway, Taco Bell, Village Inn Rest., Wendy's, **lodging:** Country Suites, **other:** Cadillac/GMC, Circuit City, Costco, Discount Tire, Dodge, Fiddlesticks Funpark, Ford/Lincoln/Mercury, GNC, Honda, Nissan, OfficeMax, PetsMart, Saturn, SportsAuthority, Staples, Toyota, U-Haul, Wal-Mart, **S...gas:** Mobil/diesel, 76/Circle K, **food:** Burrito Co, China Star, KFC, McDonald's, Peter Piper Pizza, Pizza Hut, Sub Factory, Taco John's, **lodging:** Best Western, Quality Inn, **other:** MEDICAL CARE, Checker Parts, Radio Shack, Walgreen

Phoenix

155 Baseline Rd, Guadalupe, **N...gas:** Mobil, 76/Circle K, Shell/diesel, **food:** Carl's Jr, Jack-in-the-Box, Rusty Pelican Seafood, Shoney's, Waffle House, **lodging:** AmeriSuites, Candlewood Studios, Holiday Inn Express, InnSuites, Ramada Ltd, Residence Inn, **other:** AZ Mills Factory Shops, JC Penney Outlet, Marshall's, Pro Auto Parts, Savco Drugs, **S...food:** Aunt Chilada's Mexican, Denny's, **lodging:** Homestead Village, Motel 6, **other:** Fry's Electronics

154 US 60 E, AZ 360, Superstition Frwy, to Mesa, **N...other:** to Camping World(off Mesa Dr)

Interstate 10

E ↕ W

Phoenix

153b a AZ 143 N, Broadway Rd E, to Sky Harbor Airport, **N...food:** Denny's, **lodging:** Comfort Suites, Courtyard, Fairfield Inn, Hilton, La Quinta, MainStay Suites, Red Roof Inn, Sheraton, Sleep Inn, **other:** to Diablo Stadium, **S...gas:** Shell/A&W/Taco Bell/24hr, **food:** Del Taco, **lodging:** Hampton Inn

152 40th St, **N...gas:** Cardlock/diesel, Shell/diesel, **other:** U Phoenix, **S...gas:** 76/Circle K, **food:** Burger King

151mm Salt River

151b a 28th St, 32nd St, University Ave, **N...lodging:** Extended Stay America, La Quinta, Radisson, **other:** AZSU, U Phoenix, **S...gas:** 76/Circle K

150b 24th St E(from wb), **N...**Air Nat Guard, **gas:** Exxon, **food:** Durado's Rest., **lodging:** Golden 9 Motel/rest., Knight's Inn, Motel 6, Rodeway Inn, **S...lodging:** Best Western/rest.

a I-17 N, to Flagstaff

149 Buckeye Rd, **N...other:** Sky Harbor Airport

148 Washington St, Jefferson St, **N...gas:** Chevron, Exxon, Tiemco/diesel, **food:** Carl's Jr, McDonald's, Rally's, **lodging:** Motel 6, Rodeway Inn, **other:** to Sky Harbor Airport, **S...gas:** 76/Circle K, **other:** HOSPITAL

147b a AZ 51 N, AZ 202 E, to Squaw Peak Pkwy, no facilities

146 16th St, **N...gas:** 76/Circle K, **food:** KFC, **S...gas:** 76/Circle K, **food:** Church's, Jack-in-the-Box, Ramiro's Mexican, **other:** K-Mart

145 7th St, **N...food:** McDonald's, **other:** Walgreen, **S...gas:** Chevron, 76/Circle K, Shell, **other:** HOSPITAL, to America West Arena

144 7th Ave, Amtrak, central bus dist

143c 19th Ave, US 60, no facilities

b a I-17, N to Flagstaff, S to Phoenix

142 27th Ave(from eb, no return), **N...gas:** Circle K, 7-11, **lodging:** Comfort Inn, **S...gas:** Pacific Pride/diesel

141 35th Ave, **N...gas:** 76/Circle K, **food:** Jack-in-the-Box, Rita's Mexican, **S...gas:** Shell

140 43rd Ave, **N...gas:** Citgo/7-11, Exxon/CircleK/diesel, Mobil, **food:** KFC, Little Caesar's, Mixteca Mexican, Smitty's Foods, Subway, Wendy's, **other:** Big O Tire, Food City, Fry's Foods, Radio Shack, Walgreen

139 51st Ave, **N...gas:** Chevron/diesel, 76/Circle K, Citgo/7-11, **food:** Burger King, Domino's, El Pollo Loco, Little China, McDonald's, Sonic, Waffle House, **lodging:** CrossLand Suites, InTown Suites, Motel 6, Red Roof Inn, Travelodge, **other:** Discount Tire, Goodyear/auto, **S...gas:** DiscountZone/diesel, **food:** Carl's Jr, IHOP, Taco Bell, **lodging:** Fairfield Inn, Hampton Inn, Super 8, Travelers Inn

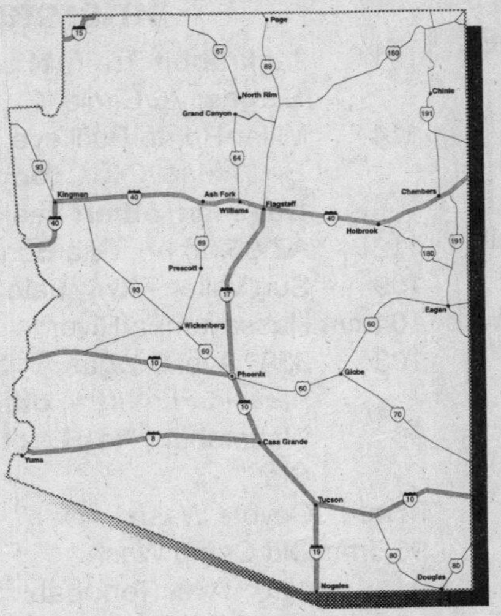

138 59th Ave, **N...gas:** 76/Circle K, Shamrock, 7-11, **food:** Armando's Mexican/24hr, **other:** AutoZone, Checker Parts, Walgreen, **S...gas:** Pilot/Wendy's/diesel/24hr, **food:** Waffle House, Whataburger/24hr

137 67th Ave, **N...gas:** QT, 76/Circle K, Texaco, **food:** Church's, **S...gas:** Flying J/Conoco/CountryMkt/diesel/LP/24hr/@

136 75th Ave, **N...gas:** Chevron, 76/Circle K, **food:** Denny's, Taco Bell, Whataburger, **other:** Ford, Home Depot, Lowe's Whse, Staples, Wal-Mart SuperCtr/24hr, **S...gas:** Arco/24hr

135 83rd Ave, **N...gas:** 76/Circle K, **food:** Arby's, Burger King, Jack-in-the-Box, Waffle House, **lodging:** Comfort Suites, Econolodge, **other:** Sam's Club

134 91st Ave, Tolleson, no facilities

133b Lp 101 N, no facilities

a 99th Ave, **S...food:** Pilot/diesel/24hr/@

132 107th Ave(from eb), no facilities

131 115th Ave, to Cashion, **N...gas:** Mobil, **S...other:** to Phoenix International Raceway

Phoenix

129 Dysart Rd, to Avondale, **N...gas:** Chevron, Shell/diesel, **food:** In-n-Out, Jack-in-the-Box/24hr, Palermo's Pizza, **other:** Fry's Foods, OfficeMax, Wal-Mart SuperCtr/24hr, **S...food:** KFC, McDonald's, Subway, Towns Square Café, Waffle House, Whataburger, **lodging:** Comfort Inn, Super 8, **other:** Chevrolet, Chrysler/Plymouth/Dodge/Jeep, Home Depot, Walgreen

128 Litchfield Rd, **N...gas:** Mobil/Blimpie/diesel, **food:** Applebee's, Bennett's BBQ, Chili's, Cracker Barrel, Denny's, Fazoli's, McDonald's, On the Border, Pizza Factory, Taco Cabana, TGIFriday, Wendy's, **lodging:** Hampton Inn, Holiday Inn Express, **other:** Michael's, Target, Wigwam Outlet Stores/famous brands, Wigwam Resort(3mi), to Luke AFB, **S...gas:** Chevron, Mobil/Blimpie, **food:** Arby's, Bamboo Inn Rest., Burger King, JB's, Peter Piper Pizza, Schlotsky's, Taco Bell, **lodging:** Best Western, **other:** MEDICAL CARE, Albertson's, Checker Parts, Goodyear/auto, Pontiac/GMC, Radio Shack

126 PebbleCreek Pkwy, to Estrella Park, no facilities

125mm Roosevelt Canal

124 Cotton Lane, to AZ 303, **N...**st prison, **S...other:** Scenic Destiny RV Park

ARIZONA

Interstate 10

E ↕ W

121	Jackrabbit Trail, **N...gas:** Phillips 66/diesel, **S...gas:** 76/Circle K
114	Miller Rd, to Buckeye, **S...gas:** Loves/A&W/Taco Bell/diesel/24hr, **food:** Burger King, **lodging:** Day's Inn, **other:** Leaf Verde RV Park
112	AZ 85, to I-8, Gila Bend, no facilities
109	Sun Valley Pkwy, Palo Verde Rd, no facilities
104mm	Hassayampa River
103	339th Ave, **S...gas:** Rip Griffin/Subway/Pizza Hut/diesel/LP/24hr/@, **other:** truckwash
98	Wintersburg Rd, **S...other:** to Palo Verde Nuclear Sta
97mm	Coyote Wash
95.5mm	Old Camp Wash
94	411th Ave, Tonopah, **S...gas:** Chevron/diesel, Shell/Subway/diesel/LP/24hr, **food:** Joe&Alice's Café/24hr, **lodging:** Mineral Wells Motel, **other:** USPO, tires/repair, Saddle Mtn RV Park
86mm	**rest area both lanes, full(handicapped)facilities, phone, picnic tables, litter barrels, petwalk, vending**
81	Salome Rd, Harquahala Valley Rd, no facilities
69	Ave 75E, no facilities
53	Hovatter Rd, no facilities
52mm	**rest area both lanes, full(handicapped)facilities, phone, vending, picnic tables, litter barrels, petwalk**
45	Vicksburg Rd, **S...gas:** Shamrock/diesel/rest./24hr, Jobski's Diesel Repair/towing
31	US 60 E, to Wickenburg, **12 mi N...other:** food, camping
26	Gold Nugget Rd, no facilities
19	Quartzsite, to US 95, Yuma, **N...gas:** Chevron, Shell/diesel, **food:** Taco Mio, **other:** CarQuest, **other:** Roadrunner Foods, RV camping
18mm	Tyson Wash
17	to US 95, Quartzsite, **N...gas:** Mobil/Burger King/LP, Pilot/Subway/DQ/diesel/24hr, **food:** Best Chinese, McDonald's, Ponderosa Grill, Ted's Bullpen Rest., **other:** RV camping, **S...gas:** Loves/A&W/Taco Bell/diesel/24hr, **lodging:** Best Western, **other:** Desert Gardens RV Park
11	Dome Rock Rd, no facilities
5	Tom Wells Rd, **N...gas:** Beacon/diesel/24hr
4.5mm	**rest area both lanes, full(handicapped)facilities, phone, vending, picnic tables, litter barrels, petwalk**
3.5mm	**eb...**AZ Port of Entry, **wb...**weigh sta
1	Ehrenberg, to Parker, **N...other:** KOA, **S...gas:** Flying J/Wendy's/Cookery/diesel/LP/24hr/@, **lodging:** Best Western
0mm	Colorado River, Arizona/California state line, Mountain/Pacific time zone

Interstate 15

N ↕ S

Exit #	Services
29.5mm	Arizona/Utah state line
27	Black Rock Rd, no facilities
21mm	turnout sb
18	Cedar Pocket, **S...other:** Virgin River Canyon RA, parking area
16mm	truck parking both lanes
15mm	truck parking nb
14mm	truck parking nb
10mm	truck parking nb
9	Farm Rd, no facilities
8.5mm	Virgin River
8	Littlefield, Beaver Dam, **E...other:** RV park, **1 mi W**...gas/diesel, food, lodging, camping
0mm	Arizona/Nevada state line, Pacific/Mountain time zone

Interstate 17

Flagstaff

N ↕ S

Exit #	Services
341	McConnell Dr, I-17 begins/ends. **See Arizona Interstate 40, exit 195b.**
340b a	I-40, E to Gallup, W to Kingman
339	Lake Mary Rd(from nb), Mormon Lake, access to same as 341. **E...gas:** 76/diesel
337	AZ 89A S, Oak Creek Canyon, to Sedona, Ft Tuthill RA
333	Kachina Blvd, Mountainaire Rd, **E...lodging:** Sled Dog B&B, **W...gas:** 76/Subway
331	Kelly Canyon Rd, no facilities
328	Newman Park Rd, no facilities
326	Willard Springs Rd, no facilities
322	Pinewood Rd, to Munds Park, **E...gas:** Chevron/diesel, Woody's/diesel, **food:** Lone Pine Rest., **other:** Motel in the Pines/RV camp, USPO, **W...gas:** Exxon, **other:** Munds RV Park, RV repair
322mm	Munds Canyon
320	Schnebly Hill Rd, no facilities
317	Fox Ranch Rd, no facilities
316mm	Woods Canyon
315	Rocky Park Rd, no facilities
313mm	scenic view sb, litter barrels
306	Stoneman Lake Rd, no facilities
300mm	runaway truck ramp sb
298	AZ 179, to Sedona, Oak Creek Canyon, **7-15 mi W...food:** Burger King, Poco Café, **lodging:** Best Western, Hilton Garden, Holiday Inn Express, Quality Inn, Radisson, Wildflower Inn
297mm	**rest area both lanes, full(handicapped)facilities, phone, picnic tables, litter barrels, vending, petwalk**

Interstate 17

N ↕ S

293mm Dry Beaver Creek

293 Cornville Rd, McGuireville Rd, to Rimrock, **E...gas:** XpressFuel, **food:** McGuireville Café, **lodging:** Beaver Creek Golf Resort(3mi), **W...gas:** 76/diesel

289 Middle Verde Rd, Camp Verde, **E...gas:** Mobil/diesel, Shell/diesel, **food:** Rockets Café, Sonic, **lodging:** Cliff Castle Lodge/casino, **other:** to Montezuma Castle NM, **W...other:** Distant Drums RV Park

288mm Verde River

287 AZ 260, to AZ 89A, Cottonwood, Payson, **E...gas:** Arco, Chevron, Shell/Subway/diesel/RVdump/LP/24hr, **food:** A&W/KFC, Burger King, DQ, Denny's, McDonald's, Pizza Hut/Taco Bell, **lodging:** Comfort Inn, Day's Inn, Super 8, **other:** Basha's Foods, Trails End RV Park, **W...gas:** Chevron/diesel/24hr, **other:** to Jerome SP, RV camping, **12-14 mi W...food:** Jack-in-the-Box, **lodging:** Best Western, Quality Inn, **other:** HOSPITAL, to DeadHorse SP

285 Camp Verde, Gen Crook Tr, **E...other:** to Ft Verde SP

281mm brake check area nb

278 AZ 169, Cherry Rd, to Prescott, no facilities

268 Dugas Rd, Orme Rd, no facilities

269mm Ash Creek

265.5mm Agua Fria River

262b a AZ 69 N, Cordes Jct Rd, to Prescott, **E...gas:** Chevron/24hr, Shell/Subway/diesel/24hr, **food:** McDonald's, **other:** Lights On Motel/RV Park, **W...food:** Papa's Place Steaks

262mm Big Bug Creek

259 Bloody Basin Rd, to Crown King, Horse Thief Basin RA, no facilities

256 Badger Springs Rd, no facilities

252 Sunset Point, W...scenic view/rest area both lanes, full(handicapped)facilities, phone, picnic tables, litter barrels, vending

248 Bumble Bee, **W...other:** HorseThief Basin RA

244 Squaw Valley Rd, Black Canyon City, **E...gas:** Chevron/diesel/24hr, Shell/diesel, **food:** Medicine Horse Café, Smokin Joe's Cantina, Squaw Peak Steaks, **other:** KOA

243.5mm Agua Fria River

242 Rock Springs, Black Canyon City, **E...**KOA, **W...gas:** Chevron/diesel/24hr, Shell, **food:** Lazy JB Rest., Rock Springs Café, **lodging:** Bradshaw Mtn RV Resort

239.5mm Little Squaw Creek

239mm Moore's Gulch

236 Table Mesa Rd, no facilities

232 New River, no facilities

231.5mm New River

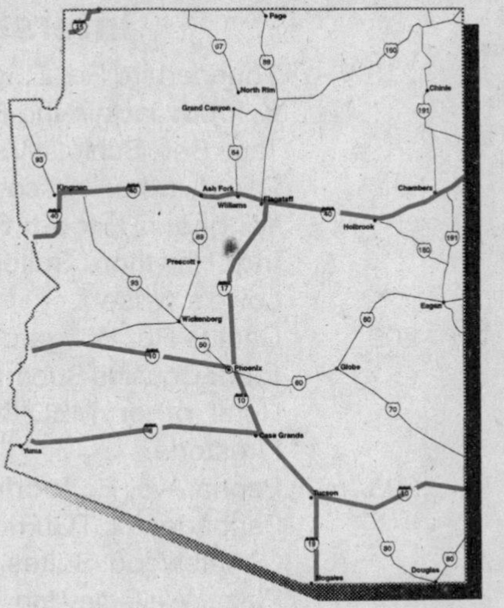

229 Anthem Way, Desert Hills Rd, **E...gas:** Mobil/diesel, **food:** McDonald's, Subway, **other:** Osco Drug, Safeway, **W...gas:** Chevron/Burger King, Mobil/Blimpie, **lodging:** Comfort Suites, **other:** Prime Outlets/famous brands/food court

227mm Dead Man Wash

225 Pioneer Rd, **W...other:** Pioneer RV Park, museum

223 AZ 74, Carefree Hwy, to Wickenburg, **E...gas:** Chevron, **food:** McDonald's, **other:** Albertson's, **W...other:** Lake Pleasant Park, camping

219mm Skunk Creek

218 Happy Valley Rd, no facilities

217 Pinnacle Peak Rd, no facilities

217b Deer Valley Rd, Rose Garden Ln, **E...gas:** Exxon, Shell/diesel, **food:** Burger King, Jack-in-the-Box, McDonald's, Sonic, Taco Bell, Wendy's, **W...gas:** 76/Circle K, Shell/diesel, **food:** Cracker Barrel, Denny's, Schlotsky's, Waffle House, Wendy's, **lodging:** Budgetel, Day's Inn, Extended Stay America, **other:** N Phoenix RV Park

215 AZ 101 W, **W...lodging:** Country Inn Suites, **other:** HOSPITAL, Target

214b a Yorkshire Dr, Union Hills Dr, **E...gas:** Shamrock, 76/Circle K, **W...gas:** Arco, **food:** ClaimJumper Rest., Jack-in-the-Box, Macaroni Grill, Souper Salad, Subway, Tony Roma, **lodging:** Motel 6, Sleep Inn, Wyndham Garden, **other:** HOSPITAL, Costco/gas, OfficeMax, Radio Shack, Ross, Target

Scottsdale

212b a Bell Rd, Scottsdale, to Sun City, **E...gas:** Chevron/diesel, Exxon, Mobil, **food:** Coco's, IHOP/24hr, Jack-in-the-Box, LJ Silver, McDonald's, Quizno's, Sonic, Waffle House, Wendy's, **lodging:** Best Western, Comfort Inn, Fairfield Inn, Motel 6, **other:** Checker Parts, Chevrolet, Dodge, Drug Emporium, Ford/Lexus/Isuzu, Lincoln/Mercury, Nissan/Infiniti, Pontiac/Buick/GMC, Smith's Foods, Toyota, U-Haul, **W...gas:** Mobil, **food:** Applebee's, Denny's, Good Egg Rest., HomeTown Buffet, Hooters, Sizzler, Village Inn Rest., **lodging:** Fairfield Inn, Red Roof Inn, **other:** Fry's Foods, Sam's Club

211 Greenway Rd, **E...gas:** 7-11, **lodging:** Embassy Suites, La Quinta, **other:** MEDICAL CARE

ARIZONA

Interstate 17

N ↕ S

210 Thunderbird Rd, **E...gas:** Arco, Exxon, 76/Circle K, **food:** Jack-in-the-Box, McDonald's, Pizza Hut/Taco Bell, Schlotsky's, Wendy's, **lodging:** Home Depot, **other:** Osco Drug, Safeway, Walgreen, **W...gas:** QT, **food:** Fazoli's, McDonald's, **lodging:** Hawthorn Suites, **other:** Fry's Electronics, Lowe's Whse

209 Cactus Rd, **W...gas:** Chevron/24hr, Citgo/7-11, **food:** Cousins Subs, Denny's, **lodging:** Red Lion Hotel, **other:** MEDICAL CARE, Basha's Foods, Firestone

Phoenix

208 Peoria Ave, **E...food:** Fajita's, LoneStar Steaks, Pappadeaux, TGIFriday, **lodging:** AmeriSuites, Candlewood Suites, Comfort Suites, Crowne Plaza, Wellesley Inn, **W...gas:** 76/Circle K, **food:** Bennigan's, Black Angus, Burger King, China Gate, Coco's, El Torito, FlashBacks Café, Italian Oven, Mamma Mia's, Olive Garden, Red Lobster, Sizzler, Souper Salad, Wendy's, **lodging:** Premier Inn, Sheraton, **other:** Barnes&Noble, Circuit City, Firestone/auto, Macy's, Michael's, Sears/auto, Staples, mall

208.5mm Arizona Canal

207 Dunlap Ave, **E...gas:** 76, **food:** Blimpie, Fuddrucker's, Outback Steaks, Sweet Tomato, **lodging:** Courtyard, Parkway Inn, Sierra Suites, SpringHill Suites, TownPlace Suites, **other:** Aamco, Firestone, mall, **W...gas:** Exxon/LP, Circle K, **food:** Bobby McGee's, Denny's, Schlotsky's, Subway, **other:** Circuit City, OfficeMax, U-Haul

206 Northern Ave, **E...gas:** Mobil, 76/Circle K, Shell/diesel, **food:** Boston Mkt, Burger King, Denny's/24hr, El Pollo Loco, Marie Callender's, McDonald's, Papa John's, Pizza Hut, South China Buffet, Starbucks, Subway, **lodging:** Hampton Inn, **other:** Albertson's, Checker Parts, USPO, Walgreen, **W...gas:** Arco, **food:** DQ, Furr's Dining, Village Inn Rest., Winchell's, **lodging:** Motel 6, Residence Inn, Super 8, **other:** K-Mart, NAPA AutoCare

205 Glendale Ave, **E...gas:** Circle K/24hr, **food:** BBQ, **other:** VETERINARIAN, **W...gas:** Exxon/diesel, Circle K, **food:** Jack-in-the-Box, **other:** to Luke AFB

204 Bethany Home Rd, **E...gas:** Arco/24hr, 76/Circle K, Shell/Church's, **food:** Isberto's Mexican/24hr, McDonald's, Subway, Teriyaki Grill, Whataburger, **other:** Desert Mkt Foods, **W...gas:** Chevron/diesel, Exxon, **other:** Food City, transmissions/24hr

203 Camelback Rd, **E...gas:** Arco/24hr, Circle K, **food:** Blimpie, Burger King, Church's, Country Boy's Rest./24hr, Denny's/24hr, Pizza Hut, Taco Villa, **other:** Buick, Chrysler/Plymouth/Jeep/Dodge, Volvo, Discount Tire, Firestone/auto, Checker Parts, NAPA, Walgreen, **W...gas:** Mobil, QT, **food:** DQ, Denny's, Jack-in-the-Box, McDonald's, Taco Bell, Tacos Mexico, Treulich's Rest., **lodging:** Comfort Inn, **other:** AutoZone, Chevrolet, Firestone/auto, to Grand Canyon U

202 Indian School Rd, **E...gas:** Arco/24hr, **food:** Alberto's Mexican, Filiberto's Mexican/24hr, Jimmy's Rest., Pizza Hut, Pizza Mia, Subway, **other:** Albertson's Foods, **W...gas:** Exxon, Circle K, Shell, **food:** Hunter Steaks, JB's, Wendy's, **lodging:** Motel 6, Super 8, **other:** MEDICAL CARE, auto repair

201 Thomas Rd, **E...gas:** Circle K, **food:** Arby's, Denny's, Jack-in-the-Box, McDonald's, Roman's Pizza, Taco Bell/24hr, **lodging:** Day's Inn, EZ Inn, La Quinta, **W...food:** Burger King, **other:** Ford, NAPA

Phoenix

200b McDowell Rd, Van Buren, **E...food:** Wendy's, **other:** Goodyear, **W...lodging:** Travelodge

a I-10, W to LA, E to Phoenix

199b Jefferson St(from sb), Adams St(from nb), Van Buren St(from nb), **E...gas:** Circle K/76/24hr, **food:** Jack-in-the-Box, McDonald's, **lodging:** Sandman Motel, **other:** to st capitol, **W...gas:** Circle K/76, KFC, **food:** La Canasta Mexican, Pete's Fish'n Chips, **other:** Penny Pincher Parts, PepBoys, SW Foods

a Grant St, no facilities

198 Buckeye Rd(from nb), **W...**RV Ctr

197 US 60, 19th Ave, Durango St, to st capitol, **E...food:** Whataburger/24hr

196 7th St, Central Ave, **E...food:** Burger King, **other:** HOSPITAL, Amtrak Sta

195b 7th St, Central Ave, **E...gas:** Exxon/24hr, Circle K, Trailside Gas/diesel/24hr, **food:** McDonald's, Taco Bell, **lodging:** EZ 8 Motel/rest., **other:** HOSPITAL

a 16th St(no EZ return from sb), **E...other:** Checker Parts, Food City, Smitty's Foods, Walgreen, to Sky Harbor Airport

194 I-10 W, to AZ 51, Squaw Peak Pkwy, to Sky Harbor Airport

I-17 begins/ends on I-10, exit 150a.

Interstate 19

Exit # Services

I-19 uses kilometers (km)

N ↕ S

Tucson

101b a I-10, E to El Paso, W to Phoenix. I-19 begins/ends on I-10, exit 260.

99 AZ 86, Ajo Way, **E...gas:** Conoco, 76/Circle K, **food:** DQ, Hamburger Stand, Peter Piper Pizza, Pizza Hut, Subway, Taco Bell, **other:** Fry's Foods, GNC, Jo-Ann Fabrics, Mervyn's, Osco Drug, Radio Shack, U-Haul, Walgreen, **W...gas:** Chevron/

Interstate 19

N S

diesel/24hr, Conoco/diesel, 76/Circle K, **food:** Bamboo Chinese, Burger King, **other:** HOSPITAL, IGA Foods, to Old Tucson, museum

98 Irvington Rd, **E...gas:** Arco/24hr, **other:** Fry's Foods, **W...gas:** Chevron, **food:** China Olive Buffet, McDonald's, **other:** Food4Less, Home Depot, OfficeMax, Target

95b a Valencia Rd, **E...food:** Church's, Donut Wheel, Eegee's Café, Jack-in-the-Box, KFC, McDonald's, Sonic, Taco Loco, Yokohama RiceBowl, **other:** AutoZone, Checker Parts, IGA Foods, Radio Shack, USPO, **W...gas:** Chevron, 76/Circle K, **food:** Applebee's, Arby's, Burger King, Carl's Jr, Denny's, Golden Corral, IHOP, Papa John's, Pizza Hut, Taco Bell, Wendy's, **other:** MEDICAL CARE, Big O Tire, CarQuest, Osco Drug, Walgreen, Wal-Mart SuperCtr/24hr, repair, transmissions

92 San Xavier Rd, **W...other:** to San Xavier Mission

91.5km Santa Cruz River

87 Papago Rd, no facilities, emergency phones sb

80 Pima Mine Rd(no sb return), **E...food:** Agave Rest., Diamond Casino

75 Helmut Peak Rd, to Sahuarita, no facilities

69 US 89 N, Green Valley, **E...food:** Denny's, Pizza Hut, Schlotsky's, Subway, **other:** Basha's Food, Radio Shack, Wal-Mart, **W...gas:** 76/diesel, **food:** Burger King, DQ, Rigoberto's Mexican, Taco Bell/TCBY, **lodging:** Holiday Inn Express, **other:** Big O Tire, Ford/Lincoln/Mercury, Green Valley RV Resort, Safeway, Titan Missile Museum

65 Esperanza Blvd, to Green Valley, **E...gas:** Shell/repair, **W...gas:** Exxon/diesel, **food:** AZ Family Rest., La Placita Mexican, Oasis Rest., **lodging:** Baymont Inn, Best Western, **other:** Walgreen

63 Continental Rd, Green Valley, **E...food:** KFC, Quail Valley Rest., **other:** USPO, **2 mi E...other:** San Ignacio Golf Club/rest., **W... gas:** Exxon, **food:** McDonald's, Taco Bell, **other:** MEDICAL CARE, Goodyear/auto, HealthFoods, NAPA, Osco Drug, Safeway, Walgreen, to Madera Cyn RA

56 Canoa Rd, **W...lodging:** San Ignacio Inn

54km rest area both lanes, full(handicapped)facilities, phone, picnic tables, litter barrels, vending, petwalk

48 Arivaca Rd, Amado, **2 mi E...other:** Mtn View RV Park, **W...gas:** Amado Plaza

42 Agua Linda Rd, to Amado, **E...other:** Mtn View RV Park

Nogales

40 Chavez Siding Rd, Tubac, **3-5 mi E...gas:** Tubac Mkt/diesel/deli, **other:** Tubac Golf Resort

34 Tubac, **E...gas:** Tubac Mkt/diesel, **food:** Montura Rest., **other:** Tubac Golf Resort, USPO, to Tubac Presidio SP

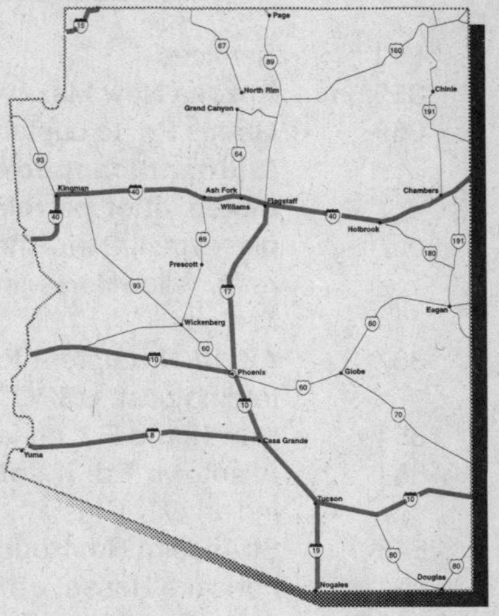

29 Carmen, Tumacacori, **E...**gas, food, lodging, **other:** to Tumacacori Nat Hist Park

25 Palo Parado Rd, no facilities

22 Peck Canyon Rd, insp sta nb

17 Rio Rico Dr, Calabasas Rd, **E...food:** Sunset Grill, **W...gas:** Chevron, Gas4Less, **food:** Cayatano Grill, La Placita Mexican, **other:** IGA Foods, Rio Rico Resort, USPO, RV camping

12 AZ 289, to Ruby Rd, **E...gas:** Pilot/Wendy's/diesel/24hr, **other:** to Pena Blanca Lake RA

8 US 89, AZ 82(exits left from sb), Nogales, **1-3 mi E...gas:** 76/Circle K, Shell/diesel, **food:** Denny's, Medici's Rest., **lodging:** Americana Motel, Best Western, Day's Inn, **other:** HOSPITAL, Goodyear/auto, U-Haul, Mi Casa RV Park

4 AZ 189 S, Mariposa Rd, Nogales, **E...gas:** Chevron/DQ, FasTrip, 76, **food:** Arby's, ChinaStar, Denny's, Exquisito Mexican, KFC, McDonald's, Rooster's Grill, Shakey's, Taco Bell, Yokohama Rest., **lodging:** Americana Motel, Best Western, Motel 6, Super 8, **other:** Chevrolet, Ford/Lincoln/Mercury, JC Penney, K-Mart, Pontiac/Buick/GMC, Radio Shack, Safeway, Veterans Foods, Walgreen, Wal-Mart SuperCtr/24hr(N Grand Ave), **W...gas:** Phillips 66/diesel, **food:** Carl's Jr, IHOP, **lodging:** Holiday Inn Express, Chrysler/Plymouth/Dodge/Jeep

1 Western Ave, Nogales, **W...**HOSPITAL

0km I-19 begins/ends in Nogales, Arizona/Mexico Border, **1/2 mi...gas:** 76/Circle K, Shell/repair, **food:** Burger King, Domino's, Jack-in-the-Box, McDonald's, Peter Piper Pizza, **other:** AutoZone, Basha's Mercado, CarQuest, Checker Parts, Family$, NAPA, PepBoys, Walgreen, bank, museum

ARIZONA

Interstate 40

E ↕ W

Exit #	Services
359.5mm	Arizona/New Mexico state line
359	Grants Rd, to Lupton, **N...rest area both lanes, full(handicapped)facilities, phone, picnic tables, litter barrels, petwalk, gas:** Speedy's/diesel/rest./24hr, **other:** Tee Pee Trading Post/rest., YellowHorse Indian Gifts, **S...other:** Indian Mkt/gas
357	AZ 12 N, Lupton, to Window Rock, **N...other:** trading post, USPO
354	Hawthorne Rd, no facilities
351	Allentown Rd, **N...other:** Cheese Indian Store, Indian City Gifts
348	St Anselm Rd, Houck, **N...gas:** Chevron, **food:** Pancake House, **other:** Ft Courage Food/gifts
347.5mm	Black Creek
346	Pine Springs Rd, no facilities
345mm	Box Canyon
344mm	Querino Wash
343	Querino Rd, no facilities
341	Ortega Rd, Cedar Point, **N...gas:** Armco/gas/gifts
340.5mm	insp/weigh sta both lanes
339	US 191 S, to St Johns, **S...gas:** Conoco/diesel/24hr, **other:** USPO
333	US 191 N, Chambers, **N...gas:** Chevron/diesel, **other:** to Hubbell Trading Post NHS, RV camping, **S...gas:** Mobil, Best Western/rest., **other:** USPO
330	McCarrell Rd, no facilities
325	Navajo, **S...gas:** Shell/Subway/Navajo Trading Post/diesel/24hr
323mm	Crazy Creek
320	Pinta Rd, no facilities
316mm	Dead River, picnic area both lanes, litter barrels
311	Painted Desert, **N...other:** Petrified Forest NP, Painted Desert
303	Adamana Rd, **N...**Stewarts/gifts, **S...gas:** Painted Desert Indian Ctr/gas
302.5mm	Big Lithodendron Wash
301mm	Little Lithodendron Wash
300	Goodwater, no facilities
299mm	Twin Wash
294	Sun Valley Rd, **N...**RV camping, **S...gas:** AZ StageStop/gifts
292	AZ 77 N, to Keams Canyon, **N...gas:** Conoco/Burger King/diesel/24hr/@, **food:** Red Baron
289	Lp 40, Holbrook, **N...gas:** Chevron/diesel, Hatch's/diesel, **food:** Denny's, Jerry's Rest., Mesa Rest., **lodging:** Best Inn, Best Western, Comfort Inn, Day's Inn, Econolodge, Motel 6, Ramada Ltd, Relax Inn, Sahara Inn, **other:** KOA
286	Lp 40, Holbrook, **N...gas:** 76/Circle K, Shamrock/diesel, **food:** KFC, McDonald's, Pizza Hut, Roadrunner Café, Taco Bell, Holiday Inn Express, Super 8, **other:** Checker Parts, KOA, OK RV Park, **S...gas:** Chevron/diesel/repair, MiniMart/gas, 76/repair, Super Fuels, Woody's/diesel, **food:** DQ, **lodging:** Budget Inn, El Rancho Motel, Western Holiday Motel/rest., **other:** HOSPITAL, Ford/Lincoln/Mercury, Plymouth/Jeep/Dodge, museum, rockshops, transmissions
285	US 180 E, AZ 77 S, Holbrook, **1 mi S...gas:** Pacific Pride/diesel, **food:** Butterfield Steaks, Pizza Hut, Wayside Mexican, **lodging:** Best Western, Wigwam Motel, **other:** Safeway, RV repair, to Petrified Forest NP
284mm	Leroux Wash
283	Perkins Valley Rd, Golf Course Rd, **S...gas:** Shell/Country Host Rest./diesel/24hr/@
280	Hunt Rd, Geronimo Rd, **N...other:** Geronimo Trading Post
277	Lp 40, Joseph City, **N...gas:** Love's/A&W/Subway/diesel/24hr/@, **S...other:** to Cholla Lake CP, RV camping
274	Lp 40, Joseph City, **N...**gas, food, lodging, RV camping
269	Jackrabbit Rd, **S...gas:** Jackrabbit Trading Post/gas/diesel
264	Hibbard Rd, no facilities
257	AZ 87 N, to Second Mesa, **N...other:** to Homolovi Ruins SP, camping, **S...other:** SW Indian Ctr
256.5mm	Little Colorado River
255	Lp 40, Winslow, **N...gas:** Shell/rest./RV park, **food:** China Inn Rest., **lodging:** Holiday Inn Express, **S...gas:** Flying J/CountryMkt/diesel/LP/24hr/@, **food:** Sonic, **lodging:** Best Western(2mi)
253	N Park Dr, Winslow, **N...gas:** Chevron, Pilot/SenorD's/diesel/RV dump/24hr/@, **food:** Arby's, Capt Tony's Pizza, Denny's, Pizza Hut, **other:** Big O Tire, Checker Parts, Wal-Mart, **S...gas:** Gas Depot, **food:** Alfonso's Mexican, KFC, McDonald's, Subway, Taco Bell, **lodging:** Best Western, Econolodge, Motel 6, **other:** HOSPITAL, Basha's Foods, Family$, NAPA, Safeway
252	AZ 87 S, Winslow, **S...gas:** Shell/diesel, **food:** Entre Chinese, **lodging:** Day's Inn, Rest Inn, Super 8, Travelodge, **other:** NAPACare
245	AZ 99, Leupp Corner, no facilities
239	Meteor City Rd, Red Gap Ranch Rd, **S...other:** Meteor City Trading Post, to Meteor Crater
235mm	**rest area both lanes, full(handicapped)facilities, info, phone, picnic tables, litter barrels, petwalk**
233	Meteor Crater Rd, **S...gas:** Mobil/Subway/Meteor Crater RV Park, **other:** to Meteor Crater NL
230	Two Guns, no facilities

Holbrook

Holbrook

Winslow

Interstate 40

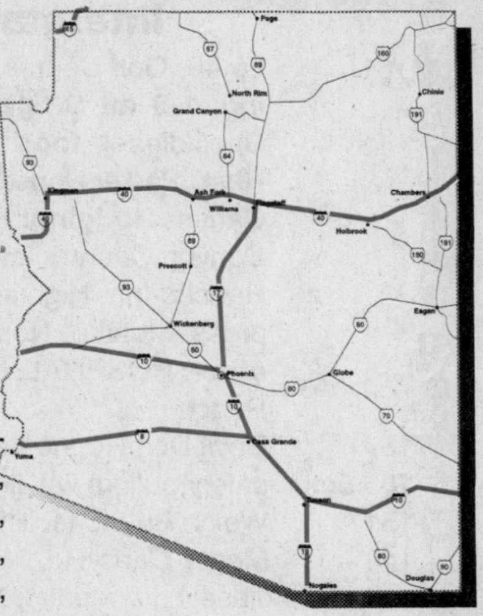

229.5mm Canyon Diablo
225 Buffalo Range Rd, no facilities
219 Twin Arrows, no facilities
218.5mm Padre Canyon
211 Winona, **N...gas:** Shell/diesel/repair, **other:** Winona Trading Post
207 Cosnino Rd, no facilities
204 to Walnut Canyon NM, no facilities
201 US 89, to Flagstaff, **N...gas:** Conoco/diesel, 76/repair, Xpress/diesel, **food:** Arby's, Burger King, Del Taco, Jack-in-the-Box, McDonald's, Pizza Hut, Quizno's, Ruby Tuesday, Sizzler, Taco Bell, Wendy's, Village Inn Rest., **lodging:** Best Western, Day's Inn, Hampton Inn, Howard Johnson, Super 8, Travelodge, **other:** HOSPITAL, Aamco, Checker's Parts, Dillard's, Discount Tire, Flagstaff RV Ctr, Goodyear/auto, JC Penney, KOA, OfficeMax, Safeway, Savers/gas, Sears/auto, Toyota, mall, **S...gas:** Mobil/diesel, **lodging:** Fairfield Resort, Residence Inn
198 Butler Ave, Flagstaff, **N...gas:** Chevron, Conoco/diesel, Shell, **food:** Burger King, Country Host Rest., Cracker Barrel, Denny's, McDonald's, Sonic, Taco Bell, **lodging:** Econolodge, Holiday Inn, Inn Suites, Howard Johnson, Motel 6, Ramada Ltd, Super 8, Travelodge, **other:** NAPA, Sam's Club, **1 mi N on US 89...gas:** 76/diesel, **food:** China House, Denny's, Kachina Mexican, KFC, Yippee-ei-o Steaks, **lodging:** Best Western, Frontier Motel, Red Roof Motel, Relax Inn, Rodeway Inn, Royal Inn, 66 Motel, Travelodge, Timberline Motel, Wonderland Motel, **other:** Albertson's, AutoZone, Big A Parts, Buick/Pontiac/GMC, Firestone, Fry's Foods, High Country Tire/auto, Kia, Nissan/Subaru, Plymouth/Dodge, Smith's Foods, U-Haul, Wienerschnitzel, **S...gas:** Mobil, Sinclair/Little America/diesel/motel/@, **food:** Black Bart's Steaks/RV Park
197.5mm Rio de Flag
195b US 89A N, McConnell Dr, Flagstaff, **N...gas:** Chevron, Conoco/diesel, Exxon/Wendy's/diesel, Gasser/diesel, Giant/diesel, Mobil, 76/diesel, Shell/diesel, Circle K, **food:** Arby's, Blimpie, Burger King, Buster's Rest., Carl's Jr, Cilantro's Mexican, Chili's, China Garden, Coco's, DQ, Del Taco, Denny's, Domino's, Fazoli's, IHOP, Jack-in-the-Box, Fuddrucker's, Furr's Café, KFC, McDonald's, Olive Garden, Perkins, Pizza Hut, Quizno's, Red Lobster, Roma Pizza, Sizzler, Souper Salad, Strombolli's, Subway, Taco Bell, TCBY, Village Inn Rest., **lodging:** AZ Motel, AmeriSuites, AutoLodge, Comfort Inn, Crystal Inn, Day's Inn, Econolodge, Embassy Suites, Fairfield Inn, Hampton Inn, Hilton, La Quinta, Motel 6, Quality Inn, Ramada Ltd, Rodeway Inn, Sleep Inn, **other:** Barnes&Noble, Basha's Foods, CarQuest, Checker Parts, Discount Tire, Hastings Books, Jo-Ann Crafts, K-Mart, Michael's, Osco Drug, Safeway, Staples, Target, Walgreen, Wal-Mart
a I-17 S, AZ 89A S, to Phoenix
192 Flagstaff Ranch Rd, no facilities
191 Lp 40, Flagstaff, to Grand Canyon, **5 mi N...food:** DQ, **lodging:** Best Western, Budget Host, Comfort Inn, Day's Inn, Econolodge, Embassy Suites, Radisson, Super 8, Travelodge
190 A-1 Mountain Rd, no facilities
189.5mm Arizona Divide, elevation 7335
185 Transwestern Rd, Bellemont, **N...gas:** Conoco/Subway/diesel/24hr, **lodging:** Microtel, **S...food:** 66 Roadhouse Grill, **other:** Harley-Davidson
183mm rest area wb, full(handicapped)facilities, phone, picnic tables, litter barrels, vending, weather info, petwalk
182mm rest area eb, full(handicapped)facilities, phone, picnic tables, litter barrels, vending, weather info, petwalk
178 Parks Rd, **N...food:** Rack&Bull Café, **other:** Ponderosa Forest RV Park, gas
171 Pittman Valley Rd, Deer Farm Rd, **S...lodging:** Quality Inn/rest.
167 Garland Prairie Rd, Circle Pines Rd, **N...other:** KOA
165 AZ 64, to Williams, to Grand Canyon, **4 mi N...gas:** Shell/diesel, **other:** KOA, Red Lake Camping(9mi), **2-4 mi S...food:** Red's Steaks, **lodging:** Econolodge, Motel 6, Super 8, Travelodge, **other:** RV Ctr
163 Williams, **N...gas:** Chevron/Subway/diesel, **lodging:** Fairfield Inn, **other:** Cyn Gateway RV Park, to Grand Canyon, **S...gas:** Mobil/diesel, Shell/diesel, Circle K, **food:** Buckle's Rest., Jack-in-the-Box, McDonald's, Pizza Hut, **lodging:** Budget Host, Downtowner Motel, Econolodge, Gateway Motel, Holiday Inn, Howard Johnson Express, Rodeway Inn, Rte 66 Inn, Super 8, **other:** USPO, same as 161

ARIZONA

Interstate 40

E Williams Wm

161 Lp 40, Golf Course Dr, Williams, **N...**RV camping, **1-3 mi S...gas:** Chevron/diesel, Mobil, Shell/diesel, **food:** DQ, Denny's, Old Smoky Rest., Parker House Rest., Red's Steaks, Rosa's Cantina, **lodging:** Best Western, Budget Host, Canyon Country Inn, Comfort Inn, Day's Inn, El Rancho Inn, Highlander Motel, Holiday Inn Express, Motel 6, Norris Motel, Westerner Motel, **other:** HOSPITAL, NAPA, Safeway, Railside RV Ranch

157 Devil Dog Rd, no facilities

155.5mm safety pullout wb, litter barrels

151 Welch Rd, no facilities

149 Monte Carlo Rd, **N...gas:** Monte Carlo Trkstp/diesel/café/repair/24hr

148 County Line Rd, no facilities

146 AZ 89, Ash Fork, to Prescott, **N...gas:** Mobil, **lodging:** Ash Fork Inn/rest., **other:** KOA

144 Ash Fork, **N...lodging:** Ash Fork Inn/rest., **other:** KOA, **S...gas:** Chevron, **other:** Exxon/diesel/RV park

139 Crookton Rd, to Rte 66, no facilities

132mm weigh sta both lanes

123 Lp 40, to Rte 66, Seligman, **N... gas:** Shell/diesel, **other:** to Grand Canyon Caverns, **S...gas:** Chevron/Subway/diesel/24hr

121 Lp 40, to Rte 66, Seligman, **N...gas:** Chevron/A&W

109 Anvil Rock Rd, no facilities

108mm Markham Wash

103 Jolly Rd, no facilities

96 Cross Mountain Rd, no facilities

91 Fort Rock Rd, no facilities

87 Willows Ranch Rd, no facilities

83mm Willow Creek

79 Silver Springs Rd, no facilities

75.5mm Big Sandy Wash

73.5mm Peacock Wash

71 US 93 S, to Wickenburg, Phoenix, no facilities

66 Blake Ranch Rd, **N...gas:** Petro/Mobil/diesel/rest./24hr/@, **food:** Pizza Hut, **other:** Blake Ranch RV Park, Blue Beacon, **S...gas:** Beacon/diesel/café

60mm Frees Wash

59 DW Ranch Rd, **N...gas:** Love's/Subway/diesel/24hr

57mm Rattlesnake Wash

Kingman

53 AZ 66, Andy Devine Ave, to Kingman, **N...gas:** Chevron, Flying J/Conoco/diesel/LP/24hr/@, Mobil/diesel, Terrible's/diesel, **food:** Arby's, Burger King, Denny's, Jack-in-the-Box, McDonald's, Pizza Hut, Taco Bell, **lodging:** Day's Inn, Motel 6, Silver Queen Motel, Super 8, Travel Inn, Travelodge, **other:** Basha's Foods, Blue beacon, Goodyear/auto, K-Mart, KOA(1mi), TireWorld, diesel repair, **S...gas:** Exxon/repair, 76/diesel, Shell/repair, **food:** ABC Rest., JB's, Lo's Chinese, Sonic, **lodging:** Best Value Inn, Best Western, Comfort Inn, Day's Inn, High Desert Inn, Lido Motel, Mojave Inn, **other:** MEDICAL CARE, Chrysler/Jeep/Dodge, NAPA, Uptown Drug

51 Stockton Hill Rd, Kingman, **N...gas:** Arco/24hr, Chevron, 76/Circle K, **food:** Cracker Barrel, Del Taco, KFC, Papa John's, Sonic, Taco Bell/24hr, Uncle's Chinese, Whataburger, **other:** HOSPITAL, Albertson's, AutoZone, Checker Parts, Chevrolet/Buick/Pontiac/Cadillac, Ford/Lincoln/Mercury, Honda, Hyundai, Nissan, Smith's Foods, Toyota, Walgreen, Wal-Mart/auto, KOA(2mi), **S...gas:** 76/Circle K, Shell/diesel, **food:** Alfonso's Mexican, A-O Steaks, Pizza Hut, **other:** MEDICAL CARE, CarQuest, Family$, Hastings Books, JC Penney, Radio Shack, Safeway

48 US 93 N, Beale St, Kingman, **N...gas:** Chevron, Exxon/diesel, Mobil/diesel/RV dump, Pilot/Subway/diesel/24hr, Shell/diesel/24hr, TA/76/Popeye's/diesel/24hr, Woody's, **food:** Chan Chinese, Wendy's, **lodging:** Budget Inn, Economy Inn, Frontier Motel, **S...gas:** Chevron/diesel/24hr, Circle K, **food:** Calico's Rest., Carl's Jr, **lodging:** AZ Inn, Motel 6, Quality Inn, **other:** CarQuest, Ft Beale RV Park, museum

46.5mm Holy Moses Wash

44 AZ 66, Oatman Hwy, McConnico, to Rte 66, **S...gas:** Crazy Fred's Fuel/diesel/café, **other:** truckwash, Canyon West RV Park(3mi)

40.5mm Griffith Wash

37 Griffith Rd, no facilities

35mm Black Rock Wash

32mm Walnut Creek

28 Old Trails Rd, no facilities

26 Proving Ground Rd, **S...other:** Ford Proving Grounds

25 Alamo Rd, to Yucca, **N...gas:** Micromart/diesel/diner

23mm rest area both lanes, full(handicapped)facilities, phone, picnic tables, litter barrels, vending, petwalk

21mm Flat Top Wash

20 Gem Acres Rd, no facilities

18.5mm Illavar Wash

15mm Buck Mtn Wash

13.5mm Franconia Wash

13 Franconia Rd, no facilities

9 AZ 95 S, to Lake Havasu City, Parker, London Br, **S...gas:** Pilot/Wendy's/diesel/24hr/@

4mm weigh sta both lanes

2 Needle Mtn Rd, no facilities

1 Topock Rd, to Bullhead City, Oatman, Havasu NWR, **N...**gas, food, camping

0mm Arizona/California state line, Colorado River, Mountain/Pacific time zone

Interstate 30

E

W

Little Rock

Exit # Services

143b a I-40, E to Memphis, W to Ft Smith. I-30 begins/ends on I-40, exit 153b.

142 15th St, **S...gas:** Phillips 66

141b US 70, Broadway St, downtown, **N...gas:** Exxon, US Fuel, **food:** Burger King, **other:** AllTel Arena, Kroger, U-Haul, **S...gas:** Citgo, SuperStop, **food:** Arby's, KFC, McDonald's, Popeye's, Taco Bell, Wendy's

a AR 10, Cantrell Rd, Markham St, downtown

141mm Arkansas River

140 9th St, 6th St, downtown, **N...gas:** Exxon, Shell, Texaco, **food:** Pizza Hut, **lodging:** Best Western, **S...gas:** Phillips 66, **food:** Waffle House, **lodging:** Masters Inn

139b I-630, downtown

a AR 365, Roosevelt Rd, **N...gas:** Exxon, **S...gas:** Texaco, **other:** Family$, Kroger, NAPA

138b I-530 S, US 167 S, US 65 S, to Pine Bluff, no facilities

a I-440 E, to Memphis, airport

135 W 65th St, **N...gas:** Exxon/diesel, Shell/diesel, **lodging:** Day's Inn, **S...lodging:** Ramada Ltd

134 Scott Hamilton Dr, **S...gas:** Exxon/diesel, **food:** Waffle House, **lodging:** Motel 6, Red Roof Inn

Little Rock

133 Geyer Springs Rd, **N...gas:** Exxon, **food:** Church's, Sim's BBQ, Subway, Whataburger, **other:** transmissions, **S...gas:** Conoco, Phillips 66, Shell, Total, **food:** Arby's, Backyard Burgers, Blimpie, Burger King, Dixie Café, El Chico, KFC, Mazzio's, McDonald's, Pizza Inn, Taco Bell, TCBY, Waffle House, Wendy's, Western Sizzlin, **lodging:** Comfort Inn, Hampton Inn, Rest Inn, Super 8, **other:** Goodyear/auto, Harvest Foods

132 US 70, University Ave, **N...gas:** Fina, **food:** Pizza Hut, **other:** Chevrolet, Ford/Lincoln/Mercury

131 Chicot Rd, **S...gas:** Shell/Popeye's, **food:** Dixie Café, McDonald's, Ryan's, Santa Fe Café, Waffle House, **lodging:** Knight's Inn, Motel 6, Plantation Inn, Ramada Ltd, Super 7 Inn, **other:** Capps RV Ctr, Firestone, Wal-Mart SuperCtr/24hr

130 AR 338, Baseline Rd, Mabelvale, **N...gas:** Express/diesel, **lodging:** Cimarron Inn, King Motel, **other:** Harley-Davidson, **S...gas:** Phillips 66, Shell, **food:** McDonald's, Pizza Hut, Popey's, Sonic, Wendy's, same as 131

129 I-430 N, no facilities

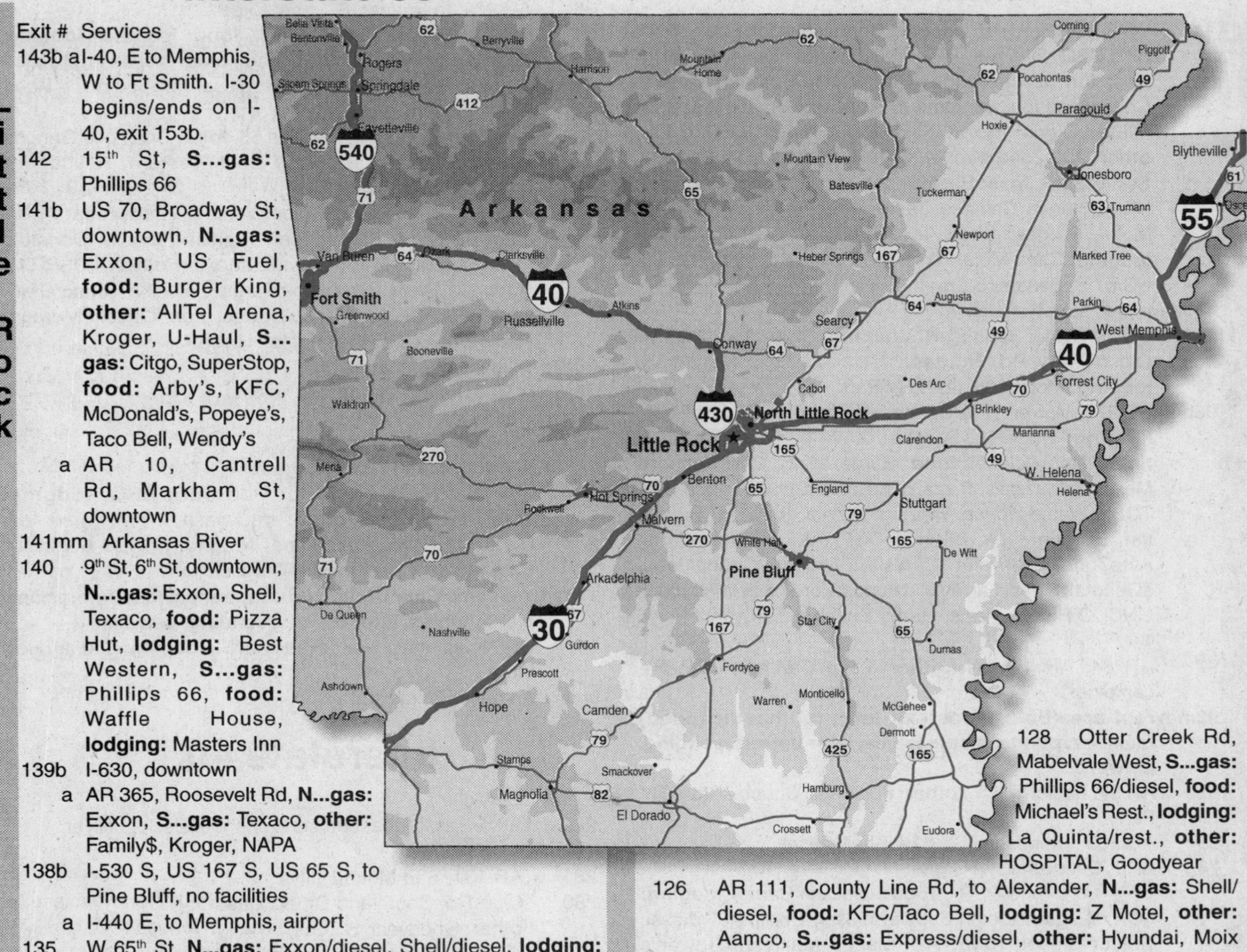

128 Otter Creek Rd, Mabelvale West, **S...gas:** Phillips 66/diesel, **food:** Michael's Rest., **lodging:** La Quinta/rest., **other:** HOSPITAL, Goodyear

126 AR 111, County Line Rd, to Alexander, **N...gas:** Shell/diesel, **food:** KFC/Taco Bell, **lodging:** Z Motel, **other:** Aamco, **S...gas:** Express/diesel, **other:** Hyundai, Moix RV Ctr

123 AR 183, Reynolds Rd, to Bryant, Bauxite, **N...gas:** Phillips 66, Shell/Blimpie, **food:** Arby's, Backyard Burgers, Burger King, Catfish Barn, Cracker Barrel, De-Light China, KFC, Pizza Hut, Ruby Tuesday, TaMolly's Mexican, Waffle House, **lodging:** Comfort Inn, Holiday Inn Express, **other:** Harvest Foods, Radio Shack, Wal-Mart SuperCtr/gas/24hr, **S...gas:** Exxon/diesel, Phillips 66, Total/diesel, **food:** Little Caesar's, McDonald's, Sonic, Subway, Taco Bell, Wendy's, **lodging:** Super 8, **other:** Foster's Foods, Isuzu

121 Alcoa Rd, **N...gas:** Pilot/Subway/diesel/24hr/@ Texaco, **other:** Buick/Pontiac/GMC, Chrysler/Plymouth/Dodge/Jeep, **S...gas:** Texaco/diesel, **lodging:** Branch Hollow RV Park, **other:** Chevrolet, Ford/Lincoln/Mercury, Mayflower RV Ctr

118 Congo Rd, **N...gas:** Texaco/diesel, **food:** CiCi's, Dixie Café, Mi Familia Mexican, Santa Fe Grill, Weng's Chinese, **lodging:** Relax Inn, **other:** Brown's Store, Home Depot, **S...gas:** Citgo, Exxon, Fina, Shell, **food:** Arby's, Backyard Burger, Burger King, Colton's Steaks, DQ, La Hacienda Mexican, Sonic, Taco Bell, TCBY, Waffle House, Wendy's, Western Sizzlin, **lodging:** Best Western, Day's Inn, Econolodge, Ramada Inn, **other:** Advance Parts, Family$, GMC, GNC, Hastings Books, JC Penney, Kroger, RV City, USPO, Wal-Mart SuperCtr/gas/24hr

ARKANSAS

Interstate 30

E ↕ W

117 US 64, AR 5, AR 35, **N...gas:** Conoco/diesel, Shell, **food:** Bo's BBQ, Denny's, Pizza Hut, Waffle House, **lodging:** Best Inn, Econolodge, Ramada Inn, Sleep Cheap, Cedarwood Inn, Benton Inn, **S...other:** HOSPITAL, **S on Military...gas:** Exxon, Fina, **food:** Arby's, McDonald's, **other:** AutoZone, Kroger, O'Reilly Parts, Radio Shack

116 Sevier St, **N...gas:** Shell/diesel, Texaco, **food:** Ed&Kay's Rest., Hunan Chinese, Tastee Freeze, **lodging:** Troutt Motel, **S...gas:** Shell, Texaco/diesel, US Fuel/diesel, **lodging:** Capri Motel

Malvern

114 US 67 S, Benton, **S...gas:** Shell(1mi)

113mm insp sta eb, st police

111 US 70 W, Hot Springs, **N...lodging:** Cloud 9 RV Park

106 Old Military Rd, **N...gas:** Fina/JJ's Rest./diesel/@, **lodging:** Motel 106, JB'S RV Park

98b a US 270, Malvern, Hot Springs, **N...food:** Fish Nest Rest., **lodging:** Super 8, **S...gas:** Fina/diesel, Phillips 66, Shell/Blimpie/diesel, **food:** Burger King, Chili Pepper's Mexican, Mazzio's, Pizza Hut, Sonic, Subway, Taco Bell, TCBY, Waffle House, Western Sizzlin, **lodging:** Budget Inn, Economy Inn, **other:** HOSPITAL, Advance Parts, AutoZone, Chevrolet, Chrysler/Plymouth/Dodge/Jeep, $General, $Tree, Family Mkt Foods, Ford/Lincoln/Mercury, GNC, O'Reilly's Parts, Radio Shack, USPO, Wal-Mart/auto

97 AR 84, AR 171, **N...other:** Lake Catherine SP, RV camping

93mm rest area(both lanes exit left), full(handicapped) facilities, phone, picnic tables, litter barrels, vending, petwalk

91 AR 84, Social Hill, **S...other:** Social Hill Country Store/RV Park

83 AR 283, Friendship, **S...gas:** Shell/diesel

78 AR 7, Caddo Valley, **N...gas:** Fina/diesel/24hr, Shell/diesel, Total/A&W/diesel/24hr, **food:** Cracker Barrel, **lodging:** KOA, **S...gas:** Exxon/Subway/diesel, Phillips 66/diesel, Texaco/diesel, **food:** Art&Mary's Mexican, Bowen's Rest., McDonald's, Pizza Hut, Taco Bell, Waffle House, Wendy's, **lodging:** Best Western, Comfort Inn, Day's Inn, Econolodge, Holiday Inn Express, Quality Inn, Super 8, **other:** to Hot Springs NP, De Gray SP

Arkadelphia

73 AR 8, AR 26, AR 51, Arkadelphia, **N...gas:** Citgo/diesel, Shell, **food:** McDonald's, Western Sizzlin, **other:** Plymouth/Jeep, Wal-Mart SuperCtr/24hr, **S...gas:** Exxon/diesel, Shell, **food:** Andy's Rest., Burger King, Mazzio's, Subway, Taco Tico, TCBY, **other:** HOSPITAL, AutoZone, Brookshire Foods, Fred's Drug, JC Penney, O'Reilly's Parts, Pontiac/Buick/GMC, USPO

69 AR 26 E, Gum Springs, no facilities

63 AR 53, Gurdon, **N...gas:** Citgo/diesel/rest., **lodging:** Best Value Inn, **S...gas:** Shell/diesel/rest.

56mm rest area both lanes, full(handicapped)facilities,vend ing, picnic tables, litter barrels, vending, petwalk

54 AR 51, Gurdon, Okolona, no facilities

46 AR 19, Prescott, **N...gas:** Citgo/diesel/24hr, Fina/diesel, **S...gas:** Love's/Hardee's/diesel/24hr/@, **food:** Pizza Hut, **other:** Crater of Diamonds SP

44 AR 24, Prescott, **N...gas:** Rip Griffin/Phillips 66/Subway/diesel/24hr/@, **S...gas:** Norman's 44 Trkstp/diesel/rest./@, **food:** Sonic, **lodging:** Econolodge, **other:** HOSPITAL, to S Ark U

36 AR 299, to Emmet, **S...gas:** Citgo

31 AR 29, Hope, **N...gas:** Shell, **food:** Pitt Grill, **lodging:** Econolodge, Village Inn/RV park, **other:** carwash, st police, **S...gas:** Exxon, Texaco, Total/diesel, **food:** Andy's Rest., KFC, **lodging:** Economy Inn

Hope

30 AR 4, Hope, **N...gas:** Phillips 66, **food:** Dos Loco Gringos, Western Sizzlin, **lodging:** Best Western, Holiday Inn Express, Super 8, **other:** Wal-Mart SuperCtr/gas/24hr, Millwood SP, **S...gas:** Exxon/Wendy's, Shell, **food:** Amigo Juan Mexican, Burger King, Catfish King, McDonald's, Pizza Hut, Taco Bell, **lodging:** Day's Inn, **other:** HOSPITAL, Advance Parts, Brookshire's/gas, Buick/Pontiac/GMC/Chevrolet, Chrysler/Jeep/Dodge, Ford/Lincoln/Mercury, Radio Shack, Old Washington Hist SP

26mm weigh sta both lanes

18 rd 355, Fulton, **N...gas:** BP/diesel

17mm Red River

12 US 67, Fulton, no facilities

7 AR 108, Mandeville, **N...gas:** Flying J/Conoco/Cookery/diesel/LP/24hr/@, **food:** Red Barn BBQ, **lodging:** Texarkana RV Park, **other:** truckwash

2 US 67, AR 245, Texarkana, **N...gas:** Phillips 66/diesel, **S...gas:** BP/diesel, **food:** T-Town Diner

1.5mm Welcome Ctr eb, full(handicapped)facilities, info, phone, picnic tables, litter barrels, vending, petwalk

1 US 71, Jefferson Ave, Texarkana, **S...lodging:** Country Host Inn

0mm Arkansas/Texas state line

Interstate 40

W E ↕ W

Exit # Services

285mm Arkansas/Tennessee state line, Mississippi River

282mm weigh sta wb

Memphis

281 AR 131, S to Mound City

280 Club Rd, Southland Dr, **N...gas:** Pilot/Wendy's/diesel/@, **other:** Goodyear, **S...gas:** Flying J/Conoco/LP/diesel/rest./@, Petro/diesel/rest./24hr/@, Pilot/Subway/DQ/diesel/@, **food:** KFC/Taco Bell, McDonald's, Waffle House, **lodging:** Best Western, Express Inn, Sunset Inn, Super 8, **other:** Blue Beacon, SpeedCo Lube

279b I-55 S(from eb)

a Ingram Blvd, **N...lodging:** Classic Inn, Comfort Inn, Day's Inn, Red Roof Inn, **other:** Ford, Greyhound Park, U-Haul, **S...gas:** Citgo/diesel, Exxon, Shell, **food:** Waffle House, Western Sizzlin, **lodging:** Econolodge, Hampshire Inn, Hampton Inn, Holiday Inn, Howard Johnson, Motel 6, Relax Inn, **other:** Chrysler/Plymouth/Dodge/Jeep, same as 280

278 AR 77, 7th St, Missouri St, **N...gas:** Citgo/Blimpie/24hr, **S...gas:** Citgo/diesel, Express, Exxon, Love's/diesel/24hr, RaceTrac, Shell/diesel/rest./24hr, **food:** Backyard Burger, BBQ, Bonanza, Burger King, Cracker Barrel, Domino's, KFC, Krystal, Little Caesar's, Mrs Winner's, McDonald's, Pizza Hut, Pizza Inn, Shoney's, Subway, Taco Bell, TCBY, Wendy's, **lodging:** Quality Inn, Ramada Ltd, **other:** HOSPITAL, Chief Parts, Goodyear/auto, Hancock Fabrics, Kroger, Radio Shack, Sawyers RV Park, Sears, Walgreen, Wal-Mart SuperCtr/24hr

277 I-55 N, to Jonesboro, no facilities

Interstate 40

E ↕ W

276 AR 77, Rich Rd, to Missouri St(from eb), **S...gas:** Exxon, Phillips 66, Shell, **food:** Bonanza, Burger King, McDonald's, **lodging:** Ramada Ltd, **other:** Wal-Mart SuperCtr/24hr, same as 278

275 AR 118, Airport Rd, **S...other:** Hog Pen Funpark

274mm Welcome Ctr wb, full(handicapped)facilities, info, phone, picnic tables, litter barrels, petwalk

273mm weigh sta both lanes

271 AR 147, to Blue Lake, **S...gas:** Exxon, Phillips 66/PJ's Store/diesel/24hr, Shell, **other:** to Horseshoe Lake, RV camping

265 US 79, AR 218, to Hughes, **S...food:** Bole's Foods

260 AR 149, to Earle, **N...gas:** Citgo/Subway, TA/BP/Burger King/Taco Bell/diesel/24hr/@, Super 8, **lodging:** KOA, **S...gas:** Shell, **other:** diesel repair

256 AR 75, to Parkin, **N...gas:** Express/diesel/rest., **other:** to Parkin SP(12mi)

247 AR 38 E, to Widener, no facilities

245mm St Francis River

Forrest City

243mm rest area wb, full(handicapped)facilities, phone, vending, picnic tables, litter barrels, petwalk

242 AR 284, Crowley's Ridge Rd, **N...other:** to Village Creek SP, camping, HOSPITAL

241b a AR 1, Forrest City, **N...gas:** BP/diesel, Phillips 66/Krystal/diesel, **food:** Denny's, HoHo Chinese, Wendy's, **lodging:** Comfort Inn, Day's Inn, Econolodge, Hampton Inn, Holiday Inn, Super 8, **other:** Chevrolet/Pontiac/Buick, Ford/Lincoln/Mercury, Plymouth/Dodge, st police, **S...gas:** Citgo, Exxon, Shell, **food:** Bonanza, Burger King, Dragon China, KFC, McDonald's, Mrs Winners, Old South Pancakes, Pizza Hut, Subway, Taco Bell, Waffle House, **lodging:** Best Western, **other:** Advance Parts, $General, $Tree, Food Giant, SavALot, Wal-Mart SuperCtr/gas/24hr

239 new exit

235mm rest area eb, full(handicapped)facilities, phone, vending, picnic tables, litter barrels, petwalk

234mm L'Anguille River

233 AR 261, Palestine, **N...gas:** Love's/A&W/Subway/diesel/24hr/@, **lodging:** Rest Inn, **S...gas:** BP/diesel/24hr

221 AR 78, Wheatley, **N...gas:** Exxon, Phillips 66/diesel, **lodging:** motel, **other:** Goodyear/repair, Wheatley RV Park, **S...gas:** Express/Subway/diesel, FuelMart/KFC/diesel/@

Brinkley

216 US 49, AR 17, Brinkley, **N...gas:** Citgo/diesel, Exxon/diesel, Shell/KFC/diesel, **food:** Western Sizzlin, **lodging:** Amerihost, Best Inn, Day's Inn, Super 8/RV/rest., **S...gas:** Express/diesel/24hr, Exxon/diesel, Phillips 66, **food:** BBQ, KFC, Laura's Diner, McDonald's, Pizza Hut, Sonic, Subway, Taco Bell, Waffle House, **lodging:** Best Western, Brinkley Inn(2mi), Heritage Inn/RV Park, **other:** $General, Firestone, Kroger, NAPA, Radio Shack, Wal-Mart

205mm Cache River

202 AR 33, to Biscoe, no facilities

200mm White River

199mm rest areas both lanes, full(handicapped)facilities, vending, picnic tables, litter barrels, no phones

193 AR 11, to Hazen, **N...gas:** Exxon, **S...gas:** Citgo/diesel, Shell/diesel/24hr, **food:** Outdoor Café, Subway, **lodging:** Super 8, Travel Inn

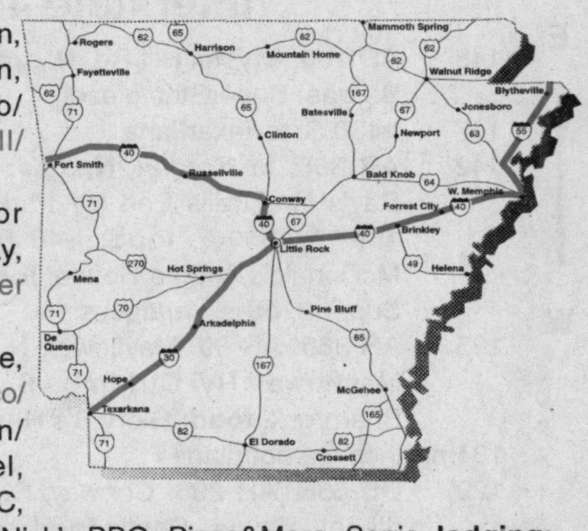

183 AR 13, Carlisle, **S...gas:** Conoco/diesel, Exxon/Subway/diesel, Phillips 66/KFC, Texaco, **food:** Nick's BBQ, Pizza&More, Sonic, **lodging:** Best Western, Carlisle Motel

175 AR 31, Lonoke, **N...gas:** Fina/diesel, Exxon/diesel, **food:** McDonald's, **lodging:** Day's Inn, Economy Inn/rest., Super 8, **S...gas:** Shell/Subway, **food:** KFC/Taco Bell, Pizza Hut, Sonic, **lodging:** Perry's Motel/rest., **other:** Chevrolet

169.5 insp sta both lanes

169 AR 15, Remington Rd, no facilities

165 Kerr Rd, no facilities

161 AR 391, Galloway, **N...gas:** Love's/A&W/diesel/24hr/@, **S...gas:** Petro/Mobil/diesel/24hr/@, Pilot/Subway/DQ/diesel/24hr/@, TruckOMat/diesel, **lodging:** Galloway Inn, **other:** Blue Beacon, CB Shop

159 I-440 W, to airport

157 AR 161, to US 70, **N...gas:** Exxon/diesel, **S...gas:** Citgo/diesel, Phillips 66/diesel, Super S Stop, Shell/diesel, **food:** Burger King, KFC/Taco Bell, McDonald's, Sonic, Subway, Waffle House, **lodging:** Comfort Inn, Day's Inn, Masters Inn, Red Roof Inn, Rest Inn, Super 8

Little Rock

156 Springhill Dr, **N...gas:** Phillips 66, **food:** Cracker Barrel, **lodging:** Fairfield Inn, Holiday Inn Express, Residence Inn

155 US 67 N, US 167, to Jacksonville, Little Rock AFB, **1 mi N on US 167...gas:** Phillips 66, Shell, **food:** Applebee's, Carino's Italian, Chili's, ChuckeCheese, Denny's, Furr's Café, KFC, McDonald's, Outback Steaks, Pizza Hut, Wendy's, **lodging:** Comfort Inn, Hampton Inn, Holiday Inn Express, La Quinta, **other:** Firestone, Best Buy, Chrysler/Plymouth/Dodge, Circuit City, Dillard's, Home Depot, JC Penney, Lowe's Whse, Office Depot, PepBoys, Target, mall

154 to Lakewood(from eb)

153b I-30 W, US 65 S, to Little Rock, no facilities

a AR 107 N, JFK Blvd, **N...gas:** Exxon, Express, Shell, **food:** Schlotsky's, **lodging:** Travelodge, **S...gas:** Exxon, **food:** Waffle House, **lodging:** Country Inn Suites, Hampton Inn, Holiday Inn, Howard Johnson, Motel 6, **other:** HOSPITAL

152 AR 365, AR 176, Camp Pike Rd, Levy, **N...gas:** Shell, US Fuel, **food:** Burger King, EggRoll Express, KFC/Taco Bell, Little Caesar's, McDonald's, Pizza Hut, Rally's, Sim's BBQ, Sonic, Subway, US Pizza, Wendy's, **other:** AutoZone, Fred's Drug, Kroger, Wal-Mart/24hr, **S...gas:** Phillips 66, Shell, **food:** Church's, **other:** HOSPITAL, Chevrolet, Family$, Kroger, Radio Shack, Sav-A-Lot

150 AR 176, Burns Park, Camp Robinson, **S...other:** info, camping

ARKANSAS

Interstate 40

148 AR 100, Crystal Hill Rd, **N...gas:** Shell, **other:** repair, **S...gas:** SuperStop/diesel

147 I-430 S, to Texarkana

142 AR 365, to Morgan, **N...gas:** Total/diesel, **lodging:** Day's Inn, Trails End RV Park, **S...gas:** Shell/A&W/Subway/diesel, **food:** I-40 Rest., KFC/Taco Bell, McDonald's, Waffle House, **lodging:** Comfort Suites, Super 8, **other:** antiques

135 AR 365, AR 89, Mayflower, **N...gas:** Hess, **lodging:** Mayflower RV Ctr(1mi), **S...gas:** Exxon/diesel, Shamrock, **food:** Glory B's Rest.

134mm insp sta both lanes

129 US 65B, AR 286, Conway, **S...gas:** Citgo, Express/diesel, Exxon, Shell, **food:** Amazon Grill, Arby's, Subway, **lodging:** Budget Inn, Clements Motel, Continental Motel, **other:** HOSPITAL,Chrysler/Plymouth/Dodge/Jeep, st police

127 US 64, Conway, **N...gas:** BP, Exxon, **food:** Denny's, Waffle House, **lodging:** Best Western, Day's Inn, Economy Inn, Hampton Inn, Ramada Inn, **other:** Chevrolet, Ford/Mercury, GMC/Buick/Pontiac, Goodyear/auto, Honda, Moix RV Ctr, Nissan, Superior Tire, Toyota, repair/transmissions, to Lester Flatt Park, **S...gas:** RaceWay, Shell/Subway/diesel, Total, **food:** Burger King, Church's, Colton's Steaks, Hardee's, KFC/Taco Bell, LJ Silver, Mazzio's, McDonald's, Pizza Inn, Quizno's, Rally's, TCBY, Wendy's, Western Sizzlin, **lodging:** Kings Inn, **other:** AutoZone, Family$, Hancock Fabrics, Kroger, Radio Shack, Walgreen

125 US 65, Conway, **N...gas:** Conoco/diesel, Exxon, Shell/Subway/diesel/24hr, **food:** Acapulco Mexican, Cracker Barrel, El Chico, Hardee's, MktPlace Grill, McDonald's, Ole South Rest., **lodging:** Comfort Inn, **other:** JC Penney, Office Depot, **S...gas:** Citgo, Exxon/diesel, Fina, **food:** Backyard Burger, Burger King, CiCi's, Evergreen Chinese, Fazoli's, IHOP, McAlister's Deli, Outback Steaks, Ryan's, Shakey's Custard, Sonic, Subway, Village Inn Rest., Waffle House, Wendy's, **lodging:** Holiday Inn Express, Howard Johnson, Motel 6, Stacy Motel, Super 8, **other:** HOSPITAL, $General, $Tree, Hastings Books, Kelly Tire, Lowe's Whse, Wal-Mart SuperCtr/gas/24hr

124 AR 25 N(from eb), to Conway, **S...gas:** Shell, **food:** DQ, Mazzio's, **other:** U-Haul

120mm Cadron River

117 to Menifee, no facilities

112 AR 92, Plumerville, **S...other:** USPO

108 AR 9, Morrilton, **S...gas:** Phillips 66/24hr, Shell/diesel/24hr, **food:** Bonanza, KFC, Mkt Place Café, McDonald's, Pizza Hut, Subway, TCBY, Waffle House, Wendy's, **lodging:** Super 8, **other:** HOSPITAL, Chevrolet/Buick/Pontiac, $General, Ford/Lincoln/Mercury, Goodyear, GMC, Kroger, Radio Shack, Wal-Mart SuperCtr/gas/24hr, to Petit Jean SP(21mi), RV camping

107 AR 95, Morrilton, **N...gas:** Shell/diesel, **food:** Morrilton Rest., **lodging:** Scottish Inn, KOA, **S...gas:** Love's/A&W/Wendy's/diesel/24hr/@, Shell, **lodging:** Day's Inn, **other:** CarQuest

101 Blackwell, **N...other:** Utility Trailer Sales

94 AR 105, Atkins, **N...gas:** BP/McDonald's/diesel, **gas:** Citgo/Subway/diesel/24hr, **food:** I-40 Grill, KFC/Taco Bell, Sonic, **other:** $General, repair

88 Pottsville, **S...other:** truck repair

84 US 64, AR 331, Russellville, **N...gas:** FlyingJ/Conoco/Country Mkt/diesel/LP/24hr/@, Exxon/diesel, **S...gas:** Phillips 66, Pilot/Subway/Wendy's/diesel/24hr/@, **food:** CiCi's, Hardee's, Hunan Chinese, McDonald's, Ryan's, Sonic, Waffle House, Western Sizzlin, **lodging:** Comfort Inn, Ramada Inn, **other:** AutoZone, Chevrolet, Chrysler/Jeep, Hastings Books, JC Penney, K-Mart, Lowe's Whse, Nissan, PriceCutter Foods/24hr, Staples, USPO, Wal-Mart/auto, **2 mi S...lodging:** Classic Inn, Merrick Motel

81 AR 7, Russellville, **N...gas:** SuperStop/diesel, **lodging:** Econolodge, Knight's Inn, Motel 6, **other:** Outdoor RV Ctr, **S...gas:** Exxon/diesel/24hr, Phillips 66/diesel/24hr, Shell/24hr, **food:** Arby's, Burger King, Colton's Steaks, Cracker Barrel, Dixie Café, New China, Pizza Inn, Ruby Tuesday, Santa Fe Café, Subway, Waffle House, **lodging:** Best Western, Day's Inn, Economy Inn, Fairfield Inn, Hampton Inn, Holiday Inn, Super 8, **other:** antiques, **2 mi S...gas:** Fina, **food:** El Acapulco Mexican, LJ Silver, Mazzio's, McDonald's, Pizza Hut, Taco Bell, Taco John's, Wataburger, Wendy's, **other:** HOSPITAL, Goodyear/auto, to Lake Dardanelle SP, RV camping

80mm Dardanelle Reservoir

78 US 64, Russellville, **S...other:** to Lake Dardanelle SP, RV camping

74 AR 333, London, no facilities

72mm rest area wb, full(handicapped)facilities, phone, picnic tables, litter barrels, vending, petwalk

70mm overlook wb lane

68mm rest area eb, full(handicapped)facilities, phone, picnic tables, litter barrels, vending, petwalk

67 AR 315, Knoxville, no facilities

64 US 64, Clarksville, Lamar, **S...gas:** Shell/diesel/24hr, **food:** Pizza Pro, **lodging:** Dad's Dream RV Park

58 AR 21, AR 103, Clarksville, **N...gas:** Phillips 66/24hr, Shell/diesel, **food:** BBQ, KFC, Mazzio's, McDonald's, Old South Pancakes, Pizza Hut, Pizza Pro, Sonic, Taco Bell, Waffle House, Wendy's, Woodard's Rest., **lodging:** Best Western, Budget Inn, Comfort Inn, Economy Inn, Super 8, **other:** HOSPITAL, Chevrolet, **S...gas:** Shell/diesel/rest./24hr, **other:** Chrysler/Dodge/Jeep, Ford/Lincoln/Mercury, Wal-Mart SuperCtr/gas/24hr

57 AR 109, Clarksville, **N...gas:** Citgo, Conoco, **food:** Subway, **S...gas:** Shell/A&W/diesel

55 US 64, AR 109, Clarksville, **N...gas:** Citgo/diesel, **food:** Hardee's, Lotus Chinese, Pizza Hut, Waffle Inn, **lodging:** Day's Inn, Hampton Inn, **other:** st police, **S...gas:** Exxon, **food:** Western Sizzlin

47 AR 164, Coal Hill, no facilities

41 AR 186, Altus, **S...lodging:** Pine Ridge RV Park, **other:** winery

37 AR 219, Ozark, **S...gas:** Exxon, Love's/A&W/Subway/diesel/24hr/@, Shell/McDonald's, **food:** KFC/Taco Bell, **lodging:** Day's Inn, McNutt RV Park, **other:** HOSPITAL

36mm rest area both lanes, full(handicapped)facilities, phone, picnic tables, litter barrels, petwalk

ARKANSAS

Interstate 40

E ↔ W

Ft Smith

35 AR 23, Ozark, **3 mi S...gas:** Total/diesel, **food:** Hardee's, **lodging:** Oxford Inn, **other:** HOSPITAL

24 AR 215, Mulberry, **2 mi S...gas:** Total, **other:** camping

20 Dyer, **N...gas:** Conoco/diesel, **S...gas:** Shell/diesel, **lodging:** Mill Creek Inn

13 US 71 N, to Fayetteville, **N...gas:** Exxon, Phillips 66/diesel, Shell, **food:** Burger King, Cracker Barrel, Dairy Queen, KFC, La Fiesta Mexican, Mazzio's, Subway, Taco Bell, **lodging:** Alma RV Park, Howard Johnson, Meadors Inn, **other:** $General, KOA(2mi), O'Reilly Parts, to U of AR, Lake Ft Smith SP, **S...gas:** Citgo/Piccadilly's/diesel, **food:** Braum's, McDonald's, Sonic, **lodging:** Day's Inn, **other:** Coleman Drug, CV's Foods, NAPA/lube/repair, Wal-Mart

12 I-540 N, to Fayetteville, **N...other:** to Lake Ft Smith SP

9mm weigh sta both lanes

7 I-540 S, US 71 S, to Ft Smith, Van Buren, **S...** HOSPITAL

5 AR 59, Van Buren, **N...gas:** Citgo, Fina/diesel, Phillips 66, **food:** Arby's, Burger King, McDonald's, Santa Fe Café, Schlotsky's, **lodging:** Holiday Inn Express, **other:** Radio Shack, Wal-Mart SuperCtr/gas/24hr, **S...gas:** Citgo, Shell/diesel/24hr, **food:** Braum's, Big Jake's Steaks, Geno's Pizza, Gringo's TexMex, KFC/Taco Bell, Little Caesar's, Mazzio's, Rick's Ribs, Sonic, Subway, Waffle House, Wendy's, **lodging:** Best Western, Motel 6, Super 8, **other:** CV's Foods, $General, Ford, Overland RV Park, Walgreen, diesel repair

3 Lee Creek Rd, **lodging:** Park Ridge Camping

2.5mm Welcome Ctr eb, full(handicapped)facilities, info, phone, picnic tables, litter barrels, vending, petwalk

1 Dora, to Ft Smith(from wb), no facilities

0mm Arkansas/Oklahoma state line

Interstate 55

N ↔ S

Blytheville

Exit # Services

72mm Arkansas/Missouri state line

72 State Line Rd, weigh sta sb

71 AR 150, Yarbro, **W...gas:** Citgo/diesel

68mm Welcome Ctr sb, full(handicapped)facilities, phone, picnic tables, litter barrels, petwalk

67 AR 18, Blytheville, **E...food:** Burger King, Chinese Buffet, Day's Inn, **other:** $Tree, Wal-Mart SuperCtr/24hr, **W...gas:** BP/Blimpie/diesel, Citgo/diesel, Texaco, **food:** Bonanza, Casa Mexican, Grecian Steaks, Hardee's, KFC, Mazzio's, McDonald's, Perkins, Pizza Inn, River Rd Buffet, Sonic, Subway, Taco Bell, Wendy's, **lodging:** Comfort Inn, Drury Inn, Hampton Inn, Holiday Inn, **other:** HOSPITAL, JC Penney

63 US 61, to Blytheville, **E...gas:** BP/diesel, **W...gas:** Citgo/diesel/24hr, Dodge's Store/diesel, Shell/McDonald's/diesel/24hr, Texaco/diesel, **lodging:** Best Western, Delta K Motel, Royal Inn(2mi), **other:** Chevrolet, Nissan, RV Park

57 AR 148, Burdette, **E...other:** Cotton Bowl Tech

53 AR 158, Victoria, Luxora, no facilities

48 AR 140, to Osceola, **E...gas:** BP/diesel, Shell/diesel, **lodging:** Best Western/rest., Deerfield Inn, Holiday Inn Express, **3 mi E...food:** McDonald's, Pizza Inn, Sonic, Subway, **other:** HOSPITAL

45mm rest area nb, full(handicapped)facilities, picnic tables, litter barrels, petwalk

44 AR 181, Keiser, no facilities

41 AR 14, Marie, **E... other:** to Hampson SP/museum

36 AR 181, to Wilson, Bassett, no facilities

35mm rest area sb, full(handicapped)facilities, picnic tables, litter barrels, phones, petwalk

34 AR 118, Joiner, no facilities

23b a US 63, AR 77, to Marked Tree, Jonesboro, ASU, **W...gas:** Citgo, **lodging:** Travel Air Motel

21 AR 42, Turrell, **W...gas:** FuelMart/Subway/diesel/24hr/@

17 AR 50, to Jericho, no facilities

14 rd 4, to Jericho, **E...gas:** Citgo/diesel/24hr, **W...gas:** Citgo/Stuckey's, **lodging:** Best Holiday RV Park

10 US 64 W, Marion, **E...gas:** BP, Citgo/Subway, Express/diesel, Shell/McDonald's/diesel, **food:** KFC/Taco Bell, Marion Diner, Sonic, Tops BBQ, **lodging:** Hallmarc Inn, **other:** Family$, Winn-Dixie, **W...gas:** BP, Shell, **lodging:** Best Western, Journey Inn, **other:** to Parkin SP(23mi)

9mm weigh sta both lanes

W Memphis

8 I-40 W, to Little Rock, no facilities

278 AR 77, Missouri St, 7th St, **E...gas:** Citgo/Blimpie/24hr, **W... gas:** Citgo/diesel, Express, Exxon, Love's/diesel/24hr, Shell/diesel/24hr, Texaco, **food:** Backyard Burger, Bojangles, Bonanza, Burger King, Cracker Barrel, Domino's, Krystal, Mrs Winner's, McDonald's, Pizza Hut, Pizza Inn, Shoney's, Subway, Taco Bell, Wendy's, **lodging:** Ramada Ltd, **other:** Blue Beacon, Chief Parts, Goodyear/auto, Kroger, Sears, USPO, Walgreen, Wal-Mart SuperCtr/24hr

279b I-40 E, to Memphis

a Ingram Blvd, **E...lodging:** Comfort Inn, Red Roof Inn, **other:** Ford, Greyhound Track, U-Haul, **W...gas:** Citgo/diesel, Shell, **food:** Earl's Rest., Grandy's, Waffle House, Western Sizzlin, **lodging:** American Inn, Best Western, Econolodge, Hampton Inn, Holiday Inn, Howard Johnson, Motel 6, Relax Inn, **other:** Chevrolet, Chrysler/Plymouth/Dodge/Jeep

ARKANSAS

Interstate 55

Exit #	Services
4	King Dr, Southland Dr, **E...gas:** Flying J/Conoco/diesel/LP/rest./24hr/@, Petro/diesel/rest./24hr/@, Pilot/DQ/Subway/diesel/@, **food:** KFC/Taco Bell, McDonald's, Waffle House, **lodging:** Best Western, Deluxe Inn, Express Inn, Super 8, **other:** Blue Beacon, SpeedCo, **1/2 mi E...gas:** Pilot/Wendy's/diesel/24hr/@, **other:** Goodyear, **W...food:** Pancho's Mexican, **lodging:** Sunset Inn
3b a	US 70, Broadway Blvd, AR 131, Mound City Rd(exits left from nb), **W...lodging:** Budget Inn
2mm	weigh sta nb
1	Bridgeport Rd, no facilities
0mm	Arkansas/Tennessee state line, Mississippi River

Interstate 430 (Little Rock)

Exit #	Services
13b a	I-40. I-430 begins/ends on I-40, exit 147.
12	AR 100, Maumelle, **W...gas:** Citgo, **other:** NAPA
10mm	Arkansas River
9	AR 10, Cantrell Rd, **W...**Pinnacle Mtn SP
8	Rodney Parham Rd, **E...gas:** Conoco, Shell, **food:** El Chico, McDonald's, Mt Fuji Japanese, **lodging:** Baymont Inn, **other:** Kroger, USA Drug, **W...gas:** Exxon, **food:** Black Angus Steaks, Burger King, ChuckeCheese, CiCi's, Dixie Café, El Acapulco Mexican, Frank's Café, LoneStar Steaks, Olive Garden, Small's Burgers, Wendy's, **lodging:** Best Western, **other:** Cadillac, Firestone, Harvest Foods, K-Mart, Waldenbooks
6	I-630, Kanis Rd, Markham St, to downtown, **E...lodging:** Comfort Inn, Motel 6, SpringHill Suites, **W...gas:** Exxon, Texaco, **food:** Denny's, Rega's Grill, Waffle House, Wendy's, **lodging:** AmeriSuites, Courtyard, Embassy Suites, Extended Stay America, Holiday Inn, La Quinta, Ramada Ltd
5	Shackleford Rd, **W...**HOSPITAL
4	AR 300, Col Glenn Rd, **W...**Nissan
1	AR 5, Stagecoach Rd, no facilities
0mm	I-30. I-430 begins/ends on I-30, exit 129.

Interstate 440 (Little Rock)

Exit #	Services
11	I-40.
10	US 70, no facilities
8	Faulkner Lake Rd, **W...gas:** BP/mart
7	US 165, to England, **S...**museum
6mm	Arkansas River
5	Fourche Dam Pike, LR Riverport, **N...gas:** Exxon, Shell, **food:** McDonald's, **lodging:** Travelodge, **S...gas:** Fina/diesel/@, Total/diesel
4	Lindsey Rd, no facilities
3	Bankhead Dr, **N...lodging:** Comfort Inn, **other:** LR Airport, **S...gas:** Conoco, **food:** Waffle House, **lodging:** Day's Inn, Holiday Inn, Holiday Inn Express
1	AR 365, Confederate Blvd, no facilities
0mm	I-440 begins/ends on I-30, exit 138.

Interstate 540 (Fayetteville)

Exit #	Services
93	US 71B, Bentonville, I-540 begins/ends on US 71 N.
88	AR 72, Bentonville, Pea Ridge, **E...gas:** Conoco, **food:** A&W, Dowd's Catfish, River Grille, **lodging:** Courtyard
86	US 62, AR 102, Bentonville, Rogers, **E...gas:** Exxon, **other:** Wal-Mart SuperCtr/diesel/24hr, Pea Ridge NMP, **W...gas:** EZ Mart, Phillips 66/diesel, **food:** Hardee's, McDonald's, Sonic, Subway, **lodging:** Hartland Motel, Quality Inn, **other:** GMC/Pontiac/Buick, Wal-Mart Visitor Ctr
85	US 71B, AR 12, Bentonville, Rogers, **E...gas:** Citgo/diesel, **food:** Applebee's, Atlanta Bread, Carino's Italian, Chili's, CiCi's, Colton's Steaks, Dixie Café, IHOP, KFC, King Buffet, McDonald's, On-the-Border, Quizno's, Small's Rest., Sonic, **lodging:** AmeriSuites, Candlewood Suites, Fairfield Inn, Hampton Inn, Hartland Lodge, Regency Inn, **other:** Barnes&Noble, Belk, Honda, Kohl's, Lowe's Whse, Office Depot, Old Navy, Beaver Lake SP, Prairie Creek SP, **W...gas:** Exxon, **food:** Braum's, Denny's, Waffle House, **lodging:** Comfort Inn, Hilton Garden, Holiday Inn Express, SpringHill Suites, Super 8, **other:** HOSPITAL
83	AR 94 E, Pinnacle Hills Pkway, **E...food:** Hillbilly Smokehouse, Rib House, **other:** Horse Shoe Bend Park, **W...food:** Plaza Rest., **lodging:** Embassy Suites
81	Pleasant Grove Rd, **W...**Green Country RV Park
78	AR 264, Lowell, Cave Sprgs, Rogers, **E...gas:** EZ Mart, Phillips 66, **food:** DQ, McDonald's, Sonic, Subway, Taco Bell, Super 8, **other:** New Hope RV Ctr
76	Wagon Wheel Rd, no facilities
73	Elm Springs Rd, **E...gas:** Total, **food:** AQ Chicken House, **other:** Goodyear
72mm	weigh sta nb
72	US 412, Springdale, Siloam Springs, **E...gas:** Citgo, EZ Mart, Exxon, Phillips 66/Subway, **food:** Armadillo Grill, Braum's, Denny's, McDonald's, Sonic, Taco Bell, Waffle House, Wendy's, **lodging:** Baymont Inn, Best Western, Comfort Inn, Day's Inn, Executive Inn, Extended Stay America, Hampton Inn, Hartland Inn, Holiday Inn, Residence Inn, Springdale Motel, **W...gas:** Pilot/Burger King/diesel/24hr/@, Total, Cracker Barrel, KFC, Santa Fe Café, **other:** Fred's Drug, Hancock Fabrics
69	Johnson, **1-2 mi E...gas:** EZ Mart, **food:** Hooter's, Ryan's, Shogun Japanese, **lodging:** Mill Inn
67	US 71B, Fayetteville, **E...**HOSPITAL
66	AR 112, **E...gas:** Citgo, **lodging:** Day's Inn, **W...**ROTC Grill, Acura/Chevrolet/Honda/Toyota
65	Porter Rd, no facilities
64	AR 16 W, AR 112 E, Wedington Dr, **E...food:** AQ Chicken House, **lodging:** Radisson, **W...gas:** Citgo/McDonald's, Exxon, EZ Mart, Phillips 66, **food:** Sonic, Subway, **lodging:** Country Inn Suites, Holiday Inn Express, Quality Inn
62	US 62, AR 180, Farmington, **E...gas:** Citgo, EZ Mart, Shell, **food:** Arby's, Burger King, Charlie's Chicken, Hardee's, JO China, McDonald's, Mexico Viejo, Sonic, Taco Bell, Taiwan Chinese, Waffle House, Wendy's, **lodging:** Best Western, Red Roof Inn, **other:** USA Drug, **W...gas:** EZ Mart, **food:** Braum's, Denny's, **lodging:** Clarion, Hampton Inn, Regency 7 Motel, Super 8, **other:** Wal-Mart SuperCtr/gas/24hr
60	AR 112, AR 265, Razorback Rd, **E...**to U of AR
58	Greenland, **W...gas:** Phillips 66/diesel, **food:** Lib's Rest.
53	AR 170, West Fork, **E...gas:** EZ Mart, **other:** Winn Creek RV Resort(4mi), **W...**to Devils Den SP
45	AR 74, Winslow, **W...**to Devils Den SP
34	AR 292, to US 71, Chester, **E...**Ozark Mtn Smokehouse
29	AR 282, to US 71, Mountainburg, **E...gas:** Conoco, **food:** Silver Bridge Rest., **other:** to Lake Ft Smith SP
24	AR 282, to US 71, Rudy, **E...**KOA, Boston Mtns Scenic Lp
20	to US 71, **E...food:** KFC, Taco Bell, **lodging:** Day's Inn

I-540 N begins/ends on I-40, exit 12.

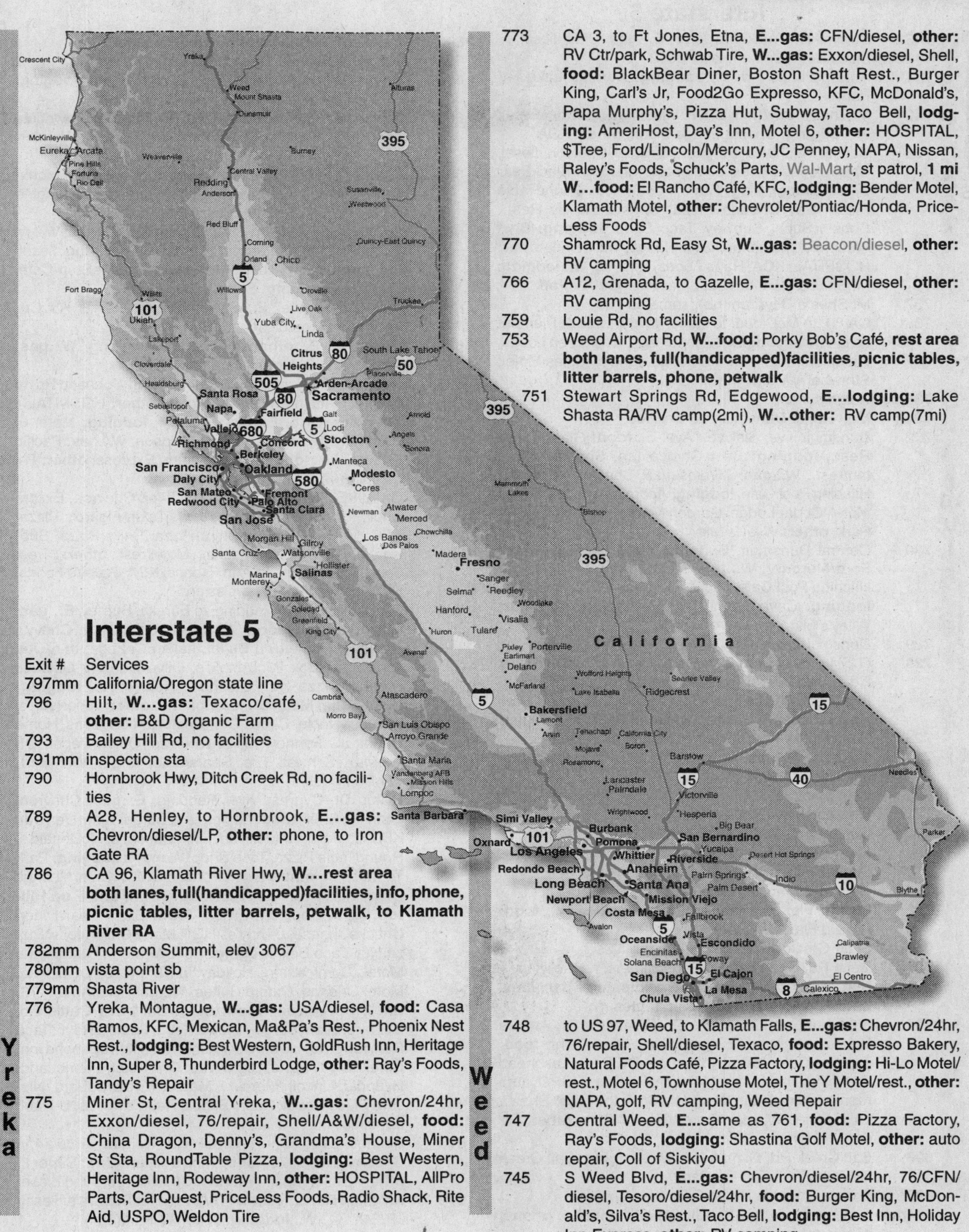

Interstate 5

N
S

Exit # Services

797mm California/Oregon state line

796 Hilt, **W...gas:** Texaco/café, **other:** B&D Organic Farm

793 Bailey Hill Rd, no facilities

791mm inspection sta

790 Hornbrook Hwy, Ditch Creek Rd, no facilities

789 A28, Henley, to Hornbrook, **E...gas:** Chevron/diesel/LP, **other:** phone, to Iron Gate RA

786 CA 96, Klamath River Hwy, **W...rest area both lanes, full(handicapped)facilities, info, phone, picnic tables, litter barrels, petwalk, to Klamath River RA**

782mm Anderson Summit, elev 3067

780mm vista point sb

779mm Shasta River

776 Yreka, Montague, **W...gas:** USA/diesel, **food:** Casa Ramos, KFC, Mexican, Ma&Pa's Rest., Phoenix Nest Rest., **lodging:** Best Western, GoldRush Inn, Heritage Inn, Super 8, Thunderbird Lodge, **other:** Ray's Foods, Tandy's Repair

Yreka

775 Miner St, Central Yreka, **W...gas:** Chevron/24hr, Exxon/diesel, 76/repair, Shell/A&W/diesel, **food:** China Dragon, Denny's, Grandma's House, Miner St Sta, RoundTable Pizza, **lodging:** Best Western, Heritage Inn, Rodeway Inn, **other:** HOSPITAL, AllPro Parts, CarQuest, PriceLess Foods, Radio Shack, Rite Aid, USPO, Weldon Tire

773 CA 3, to Ft Jones, Etna, **E...gas:** CFN/diesel, **other:** RV Ctr/park, Schwab Tire, **W...gas:** Exxon/diesel, Shell, **food:** BlackBear Diner, Boston Shaft Rest., Burger King, Carl's Jr, Food2Go Expresso, KFC, McDonald's, Papa Murphy's, Pizza Hut, Subway, Taco Bell, **lodging:** AmeriHost, Day's Inn, Motel 6, **other:** HOSPITAL, $Tree, Ford/Lincoln/Mercury, JC Penney, NAPA, Nissan, Raley's Foods, Schuck's Parts, Wal-Mart, st patrol, **1 mi W...food:** El Rancho Café, KFC, **lodging:** Bender Motel, Klamath Motel, **other:** Chevrolet/Pontiac/Honda, Price-Less Foods

770 Shamrock Rd, Easy St, **W...gas:** Beacon/diesel, **other:** RV camping

766 A12, Grenada, to Gazelle, **E...gas:** CFN/diesel, **other:** RV camping

759 Louie Rd, no facilities

753 Weed Airport Rd, **W...food:** Porky Bob's Café, **rest area both lanes, full(handicapped)facilities, picnic tables, litter barrels, phone, petwalk**

751 Stewart Springs Rd, Edgewood, **E...lodging:** Lake Shasta RA/RV camp(2mi), **W...other:** RV camp(7mi)

Weed

748 to US 97, Weed, to Klamath Falls, **E...gas:** Chevron/24hr, 76/repair, Shell/diesel, Texaco, **food:** Expresso Bakery, Natural Foods Café, Pizza Factory, **lodging:** Hi-Lo Motel/rest., Motel 6, Townhouse Motel, The Y Motel/rest., **other:** NAPA, golf, RV camping, Weed Repair

747 Central Weed, **E...**same as 761, **food:** Pizza Factory, Ray's Foods, **lodging:** Shastina Golf Motel, **other:** auto repair, Coll of Siskiyou

745 S Weed Blvd, **E...gas:** Chevron/diesel/24hr, 76/CFN/diesel, Tesoro/diesel/24hr, **food:** Burger King, McDonald's, Silva's Rest., Taco Bell, **lodging:** Best Inn, Holiday Inn Express, **other:** RV camping

CALIFORNIA

Interstate 5

N ↕ S

Mt Shasta

743 Summit Dr, Truck Village Dr, **E...gas:** CFN/diesel

742mm Black Butte Summit, elev 3912

741 Abrams Lake Rd, **W...lodging:** Abrams Lake RV Park

740 Mt Shasta City(from sb), **E...gas:** Pacific Pride/diesel/LP, **lodging:** Shasta Lodge Motel, **other:** KOA

738 Central Mt Shasta, **E...gas:** 76/diesel, Chevron/diesel, Shell/diesel/LP, Texaco/diesel/24hr, **food:** BlackBear Diner, Burger King, Ray's FoodPlace, RoundTable Pizza, Say Cheese Pizza, Shasta Family Rest., Subs'n Such, Subway, Taco Shop, **lodging:** Best Western, Choice Inn, Econolodge, Travel Inn, **other:** HOSPITAL, KOA, Ray's Foods, Rite Aid, **W...lodging:** Mt Shasta Resort/rest., Lake Siskiyou RV Park

737 Mt Shasta City(from nb), same as 738

736 CA 89, to McCloud, to Reno, **1 mi E...food:** Piemont Italian Diner, **lodging:** Econolodge, Evergreen Lodge, Finlandia Motel, Mt Aire Lodge, Pine Needles Motel, Strawberry Valley Inn

Dunsmuir

735mm weigh sta sb

734 Mott Rd, to Dunsmuir, no facilities

732 Dunsmuir Ave, Siskiyou Ave, **E...food:** GlassHouse Rest., **lodging:** Best Choice Inn, Shasta Alpine Inn/rest., **W...gas:** 76/diesel/LP, Shell/diesel, **food:** Hitching Post Café, **lodging:** Acorn Inn, Cave Springs Motel, Cedar Lodge, Garden Motel, Hedge Creek RV Park, **other:** Wiley's Mkt

730 Central Dunsmuir, **E...food:** Pizza Factory, **other:** Ford/Mercury, **W...gas:** Texaco/diesel/LP, **food:** Hitching Post Café, Micki's Burgers, Shelby's Dining, **lodging:** Cave Springs Motel, Travelodge, **other:** Wiley's Mkt

729 Dunsmuir(from nb)

728 (727 from nb)Crag View Dr, Dunsmuir, Railroad Park Rd, **E...gas:** Tesoro/diesel, **food:** Burger Barn, **lodging:** Best Choice Inn, Oak Tree Inn, Railroad Park Resort/motel, **W...other:** Railroad Park RV camping

726 Soda Creek Rd, to Pacific Crest Trail, no facilities

724 Castella, **W...gas:** Chevron/diesel, **other:** RV camping, Castle Crags SP

723mm vista point nb

723 Sweetbrier Ave, no facilities

721 Conant Rd, no facilities

720 Flume Creek Rd, no facilities

718 Sims Rd, **W...other:** RV camping, phone

714 Gibson Rd, no facilities

712 Pollard Flat, **E...gas:** Exxon/diesel/LP/24hr, **food:** Pollard Flat USA Rest.

710 Slate Creek Rd, La Moine, no facilities

707 Delta Rd, Dog Creek Rd, to Vollmers, no facilities

705mm rest area both lanes, full(handicapped)facilities, phone, litter barrels, picnic tables

704 (702 from nb)Lakeshore Dr, Riverview Dr, Antlers Rd, to Lakehead, **E...gas:** Shell/diesel/24hr, **food:** Top Hat Café, **lodging:** Antlers RV Park, Lakehead Camping, Neu Lodge Motel/café, **other:** USPO, auto repair, towing/24hr, **W...gas:** 76/LP, **lodging:** Shasta Lake Motel/RV, Lakeshore Villa RV Park, **other:** RV service/dump

698 Salt Creek Rd, Gilman Rd, **W...lodging:** Salt Creek RV Park, Trail End RV Park

695 Shasta Caverns Rd, to O'Brien, camping

694mm rest area nb, full(handicapped)facilities, phone, picnic tables, litter barrels, petwalk

693 (from sb)Packers Bay Rd, **other:** boating

692 Turntable Bay Rd, no facilities

690 Bridge Bay Rd, **W...food:** Tail of a Whale Rest., **lodging:** Bridge Bay Motel

689 Fawndale Rd, Wonderland Blvd, **E...lodging:** Fawndale Lodge, Fawndale Oaks RV Park, **W...lodging:** Wonderland RV Park

687 Wonderland Blvd, Mountain Gate, **E...other:** Bear Mountain RV Resort, Mountain Gate RV Park, Marine/engine repair, Ranger Sta, **W...gas:** 76/LP/diesel

685 CA 151, Shasta Dam Blvd, Project City, Central Valley, **W...gas:** Chevron/diesel/LP, Shell/Burger King/diesel/LP, **food:** Bakery&Grill, McDonald's, StageStop Café, Taco Den, **lodging:** Shasta Dam Motel

684 Pine Grove Ave, **E...other:** Cousin Gary's RV Ctr, **W...gas:** Exxon/diesel

682 Oasis Rd, **E...other:** CA RV Ctr/camping, **W...gas:** Arco/24hr, LP, **other:** st patrol

681b (from sb, no re-entry)CA 273, Market St, Johnson Rd, to Central Redding, **W...gas:** Exxon, **other:** HOSPITAL

681 Twin View Blvd, **E...gas:** 76/24hr, **lodging:** Motel 6, Ramada Ltd, **other:** Harley-Davidson, **W...gas:** Pacific Pride/diesel, **lodging:** Holiday Inn Express, **other:** RV camping

Redding

680 CA 299E, **1/2 mi W...gas:** Arco/24hr, Chevron, Exxon, Shell, **food:** BBQ Pit, Arby's, Carl's Jr, Figaro's Pizza, KFC, McDonald's, Murphy's Pizza, Phil's Pizza, Subway, TCBY, **lodging:** River Inn Motel/rest., **other:** $Tree, Food Connection, Jo-Ann Fabrics, KOA, Raley's Foods, RV Ctr, ShopKO, transmissions

678 CA 299 W, CA 44, Redding, to Eureka, Burney, **E...gas:** Chevron, Shell, **food:** Applebee's, Carl's Jr, Chevy's Mexican, Hometown Buffet, Italian Cottage, In-n-Out, Jack-in-the-Box, McDonald's, Olive Garden, Outback Steaks, Pizza Hut, Quizno's, Red Robin, **lodging:** Holiday Inn, Motel 6, Red Lion Inn, **other:** Albertson's, Barnes&Noble, Circuit City, Costco, Food4Less, Home Depot, JC Penney, Kragen's Parts, Office Depot, OfficeMax, Schwab Tire, Sears/auto, Target, Wal-Mart, WinCo Foods

677 Hilltop Dr, Cypress Ave, Redding, **E...gas:** Chevron/24hr, 76, Shell, **food:** Applebee's, Burger King, Carl's Jr, KFC, La Palomar Mexican, Little Caesar's, McDonald's, RoundTable Pizza, Taco Shop, Wendy's, **lodging:** Park Terrace Inn, **other:** Buick/Pontiac/GMC, K-Mart, Longs Drug, Mervyn's, Rite Aid, Ross, mall, **1/4 mi E on Hilltop...gas:** Chevron, Exxon, **food:** Black Bear Diner, ChuckeCheese, Denny's, IHOP, Marie Callender's, Pizza Hut, Taco Bell, **lodging:** Best Western, Cattlemens Motel, Comfort Inn, Holiday Inn Express, La Quinta, Motel Orleans, Oxford Suites, **W...gas:** GasAmart, 76, Shell, USA/diesel, **food:** BBQ, California Cattle Co, Denny's, Giant Burger, Lyon's Rest., Perko's Rest., Taco Den, **lodging:** Howard Johnson, Motel 6, Vagabond Inn, **other:** Big A Parts, Big O Tire, Chevrolet, FabricLand, Hyundai, Lincoln/Mercury, Mazda/Toyota/Subaru, Nissan, Office Depot, Radio Shack, Raley's Foods, U-Haul, transmissions

675 Bechelli Lane, Churn Creek Rd, **E...gas:** Arco/24hr, Chevron/diesel, 76, **food:** Taco Bell, **lodging:** Super 8, **other:** diesel repair, **W...gas:** Shell/Burger King/diesel

673 Knighton Rd, **E...gas:** TA/76/Pizza Hut/Popeye's/diesel/LP/24hr/@, **W...lodging:** JGW RV Park(3mi)

CALIFORNIA

Interstate 5

670 Riverside Ave, **1 mi W...lodging:** JGW RV Park

668 Balls Ferry Rd, Anderson, **E...gas:** Beacon, 76/diesel, **food:** Burger King, Denny's, El Mariachi Mexican, McDonald's, Papa Murphy's, Perko's Rest., RoundTable Pizza, Subway, Taco Bell, Walkabout Creek Deli/gifts, **lodging:** Best Western/rest., Valley Inn, **other:** MEDICAL CARE, $Tree, NAPA, Rite Aid, Safeway, Schwab Tires, **W...gas:** Beacon/diesel, Chevron, Exxon/diesel, Shell, **food:** City Grill, Giant Burger, Goodtimes Pizza, KFC, Koffee Korner Rest., **other:** Holiday Food/drugs, Kragen Parts, Owen's Drugs, RV Ctr

667 CA 273, Factory Outlet Blvd, **W...gas:** Shell/diesel, TowneMart/diesel, **food:** Arby's, LJ Silver, **lodging:** AmeriHost, **other:** GNC, Prime Outlets/famous brands, farmers mkt

665 (from sb)Cottonwood, **E...food:** Branding Iron Rest., **lodging:** Travelers Motel

664 Gas Point Rd, to Balls Ferry, **E...gas:** CFN/diesel, Chevron/MeanGene's/diesel/LP, Exxon/diesel/LP, **lodging:** Travelers Motel, **other:** Jim's Auto Repair, **W...gas:** Beacon/diesel/LP, 76/diesel, **other:** Sentry Foods

662 Bowman Rd, to Cottonwood, **E...gas:** Pacific Pride/diesel, Shell/A&W/diesel

660mm weigh sta both lanes

659 Snively Rd, Auction Yard Rd, no facilities

657 Hooker Creek Rd, Auction Yard Rd, **E...other:** trailer sales

656mm rest area both, full(handicapped)facilities, phone, picnic tables, litter barrels, petwalk

653 Jellys Ferry Rd, **E...lodging:** Bend RV Park

652 Wilcox Golf Rd, no facilities

650 CA 36W(from sb), Red Bluff, **3/4 mi W...other:** Hwy Patrol

649 CA 36, CA 99, Red Bluff, **E...gas:** Exxon/diesel, 76, Shell/diesel, **food:** Burger King, Perko's Rest., KFC, McDonald's, RoundTable Pizza, Subway, **lodging:** Best Inn, Motel 6, Super 8, **W...gas:** Gas4Less, USA/diesel, **food:** Carl's Jr, Denny's, Egg Roll King, Marie's Rest., Riverside Dining, Shari's/24hr, Subway, Wild Bill's Steaks, Winchell's, **lodging:** Cinderella Motel, Idle Wheels RV Park, Red Bluff Inn, Travelodge, Value Lodge, **other:** AutoZone, Food4Less, Sears

647 Diamond Ave, Red Bluff, **E...gas:** Exxon, **food:** Red Rock Café, **lodging:** Day's Inn, Motel Orleans/rest., **other:** HOSPITAL,**W...gas:** Arco/diesel/24hr, Beacon/diesel, Chevron, **food:** Arby's, Country Waffles, Crystal Oven Rest., Feedbag Rest., Italian Cottage, Jack-in-the-Box, Pepe's Pizza, Taco Bell/24hr, Yogurt Alley, **lodging:** Crystal Motel, Flamingo Motel, Sky Terrace Motel, Triangle Motel, **other:** Chevrolet/Cadillac, $Tree, Ford/Mercury, K-Mart, Kragen Parts, Radio Shack, Raley's Food/drug, Staples, Wal-Mart/auto

642 Flores Ave, to Proberta, Gerber, **2 mi E...other:** Wal-Mart Dist Ctr

636 CA 811, Gyle Rd, to Tehama, **E...other:** RV camping(7mi)

633 Finnel Rd, to Richfield, no facilities

633mm rest area both lanes, full(handicapped)facilities, phone, picnic tables, litter barrels, petwalk

631 A9, Corning Ave, Corning, **E...gas:** Chevron/24hr, Citgo/7-11, Exxon, Shell/diesel/LP, 76/diesel, **food:** Burger King, Casa Ramos Mexican, Marcos Pizza, Olive Pit Rest., Papa Murphy's, Rancho Grande Mexican, RoundTable Pizza, Taco Bell, **lodging:** AmeriHost, Best Western, Budget Inn, Economy Inn, Heritage RV Park, Olive City Inn, 7 Inn Motel/RV Park, **other:** Clark Drug, Ford/Mercury/Kia, Holiday Mkt/deli, Kragen Parts, NAPA, Pontiac/Chevrolet/Buick, Rite Aid, Safeway/24hr, Tires+, **W...food:** Giant Burger, **lodging:** Corning RV Park

630 South Ave, Corning, **E...gas:** Petro/Exxon/diesel/rest./@, TA/Arco/Arby's/Subway/diesel/24hr/@, **food:** Jack-in-the-Box, McDonald's, **lodging:** Day's Inn, Shilo Inn/rest./24hr, **other:** Blue Beacon, Goodyear, RV Ctr, RV camping(1-6mi), Woodson Br SRA

628 CA 99W, Liberal Ave, no facilities

621 CA 7, no facilities

619 CA 32, Orland, **E... gas:** Gas4Less, 76, **food:** Burger King, Berry Patch Rest., Subway, **lodging:** Amberlight Motel, Orlanda Inn, **W...gas:** Sportsmans/diesel, USA, **food:** Taco Bell, **lodging:** Green Acres RV Park, Old Orchard RV Park

618 CA 16, **E...gas:** Beacon/diesel/24hr, CFN/diesel, **food:** Pizza Factory, **lodging:** Orland Inn, **other:** Longs Drug, Schwab Tires, laundry

614 CA 27, no facilities

610 Artois, no facilities

608mm rest area both lanes, full(handicapped)facilities, phone, picnic tables, litter barrels, petwalk, RV dump

607 CA 39, Blue Gum Rd, Bayliss, **2-3 mi E...lodging:** Blue Gum Motel/rest.

603 CA 162, Willows, to Oroville, **E...gas:** Arco/24hr, Chevron/24hr, Shell/diesel, **food:** BlackBear Diner, Burger King, Denny's/24hr, Java Jim's Café, KFC, McDonald's, RoundTable Pizza, Subway/TCBY, Taco Bell/24hr, **lodging:** Best Western/rest., CrossRoads West Inn, Day's Inn, Super 8/RV Park, **other:** HOSPITAL, CHP, **W...food:** Nancy's Café/24hr, **other:** Wal-Mart, RV Park(8mi), airport

601 CA 57, **E...gas:** CFN/diesel

595 Norman Rd, to Princeton, **E...**to Sacramento NWR

591 Delevan Rd, no facilities

588 Maxwell(from sb), access to camping

586 Maxwell Rd, **E...other:** Delavan NWR, **W...gas:** CFN/diesel, Chevron, **lodging:** Maxwell Inn/rest., **other:** Maxwell Parts, NAPA

583 rest area both lanes, full(handicapped)facilities, phone, picnic tables, litter barrels, petwalk

578 CA 20 W, Colusa, **W...gas:** Beacon/diesel, **food:** Orv's Rest., **other:** HOSPITAL, hwy patrol

CALIFORNIA

Interstate 5

577 CA 20 E, Williams, **E...gas:** Shell/Togo's/diesel/24hr, **food:** Carl's Jr, Taco Bell, **lodging:** Holiday Inn Express, **W...gas:** Arco/24hr, CFN/diesel, Chevron/diesel/24hr, 76, Shell/diesel, **food:** A&W, Burger King, Cairo's Italian, Caliente Café, DQ, Denny's, Granzella's Deli, McDonald's/RV parking, Wendy's, Williams Chinese Rest., **lodging:** Capri Motel, Comfort Inn, El Rancho Motel, Granzella's Inn, Motel 6, StageStop Motel, Travelers Motel, **other:** HOSPITAL, NAPA, U-Haul, USPO, ValuRite Drug, camping, hwy patrol

575 Husted Rd, to Williams, no facilities

569 Hahn Rd, to Grimes, no facilities

567 frontage rd(from nb), to Arbuckle, **E...gas:** Beacon/diesel, **food:** El Jaliscience Mexican, **W...gas:** CFN/diesel

566 Arbuckle, to College City, **E...gas:** Pacific Pride/diesel, 76, **food:** Boyd's GasHouse Grill, **W... gas:** Beacon/diesel

559 Yolo/Colusa County Line Rd, no facilities

557mm rest area both lanes, full(handicapped)facilities, phone, picnic tables, litter barrels, petwalk

556 E4, Dunnigan, **E...gas:** Chevron/24hr, Shell/diesel, **food:** Bill&Kathy's Rest., Jack-in-the-Box, **lodging:** Best Value Inn, Best Western, **other:** USPO, **W...gas:** 76, **lodging:** Camper's RV Park

554 rd 8, **E...gas:** Pilot/Wendy's/diesel/24hr/@, **lodging:** Budget 8 Motel, HappyTime RV Park, **W...gas:** Beacon/diesel

562 I-505(from sb), to San Francisco, callboxes begin sb

548 Zamora, **E...gas:** Pacific Pride/diesel, Shell, **other:** Zamora Minimart, camping, **W...other:** USPO

542 Yolo, **1 mi E...**gas

541 CA 16W, Woodland, **3 mi W...other:** HOSPITAL

540 West St, **W...food:** Denny's

538 CA 113 N, E St, Woodland, **E...lodging:** Valley Oaks Inn, **W...gas:** CFN/diesel, Shell, **food:** Denny's, **lodging:** Best Western, **other:** Woodland Opera House(1mi)

537 CA 113 S, Main St, Woodland, to Davis, **E...other:** Cadillac/Pontiac, Chrysler/Jeep, Nissan, tires, **W...gas:** Exxon/diesel, 76/diesel, **food:** Burger King, Denny's, McDonald's, Primo's Rest., Subway, Taco Bell, Teriyaki Rest., Wendy's, **lodging:** Comfort Inn, Motel 6, **other:** Food4Less

536 rd 102, **E...gas:** Exxon, Shell, **food:** Jack-in-the-Box, **other:** Target, museum, **W...gas:** Chevron, **other:** CHP

531 rd 22, W Sacramento, no facilities

530mm Sacramento River

529mm rest area sb, full(handicapped)facilities, phone, picnic tables, litter barrels, petwalk

528 Airport Rd, **E...other:** airport

525b CA 99, 70, to Marysville, Yuba City, no facilities

525a Del Paso Rd, **E...other:** Arco Arena, no facilities

522 I-80, E to Reno, W to San Francisco

521b a Garden Hwy, West El Camino, **W...food:** Carl's Jr, **lodging:** Courtyard, Hilton Garden, Homestead Village, Residence Inn

520 Richards Blvd, **E...gas:** Chevron/24hr, **food:** Hungry Hunter Rest., Lyon's Rest./24hr, McDonald's, Monterey Rest., **lodging:** Day's Inn, Governor's Inn, Hawthorn Suites, Super 8, **W...gas:** Rivermart Gas, Shell, **food:** El Rey Rest., **lodging:** Best Western/rest., Capitol Inn, Comfort Suites, La Quinta, Motel 6, Super 8

519b J St, Old Sacramento, Hist SP, **E...lodging:** Holiday Inn, Vagabond Inn, **W...lodging:** Embassy Suites, **other:** Railroad Museum

519a Q St, Sacramento, downtown

518 US 50, CA 99, Broadway, **E...**multiple facilities downtown

516 Sutterville Rd, **E...gas:** 76/diesel/repair, Shell/repair, **other:** Land Park, zoo

515 Fruitridge Rd, Seamas Rd, no facilities

514 43rd Ave, Riverside Blvd(from sb), **E...gas:** 76/repair, 7-11

513 Florin Rd, **E...gas:** Arco/24hr, Chevron/24hr, Shell/repair/24hr, **food:** Rosalinda's Mexican, RoundTable Pizza, Subway, **other:** Bel Air Foods, Kragen Parts, Longs Drug, **W...food:** Burger King, JimBoy's Tacos, RoundTable Pizza, Shari's, Starbucks, Wendy's, **other:** Marshall's, Radio Shack, Rite Aid

512 CA 160, Pocket Rd, Meadowview Rd, to Freeport, **E...gas:** Shell/24hr, United/diesel, **food:** IHOP, McDonald's, Togo's, **other:** Home Depot, Staples, **W...food:** Pizza Hut

508 Laguna Blvd, **E...gas:** Chevron, Shell, 76/diesel/LP

506 Elk Grove Blvd, no facilities

504 Hood-Franklin Rd, no facilities

498 Twin Cities Rd, to Walnut Grove, no facilities

493 Walnut Grove Rd, Thornton, no facilities

490 Peltier Rd, no facilities

487 Turner Rd, no facilities

485 CA 12, Lodi, **E...gas:** Arco/diesel/24hr, Chevron/Subway/diesel/LP/@, Flying J/diesel/24hr/@, NW/diesel, 76/diesel, **food:** Burger King, McDonald's, Rocky's Rest./24hr, Taco Bell, Wendy's, **lodging:** Microtel, **other:** Blue Beacon, **W... other:** Tower Park Marina Camping(5mi)

481 Eight Mile Rd, **3 mi E...lodging:** KOA

478 Hammer Lane, Stockton, **E...gas:** Arco/24hr, 76/Circle K, **food:** Adalberto's Mexican, Carl's Jr, KFC, Little Caesar's, Shirason Japanese, **other:** Raley's Foods, Smart Foods, **W...gas:** Exxon/diesel/24hr, QuikStop, **food:** Arby's, Burger King, Jack-in-the-Box, JimBoy's Tacos, Subway, Taco Bell, **lodging:** InnCal

477 Benjamin Holt Dr, Stockton, **E...gas:** Arco, Chevron/24hr, QuikStop, **food:** Pizza Guys, **lodging:** Motel 6, **W...gas:** Shell, 7-11, Lyon's/24hr, **food:** McDonald's, RoundTable Pizza, Subway/TCBY, Wong's Chinese, **other:** Marina Foods

476 March Lane, Stockton, **E...gas:** Citgo/7-11, **food:** Applebee's, Arroyo's Mexican, Black Angus, Carl's Jr, Denny's, El Torito, Jack-in-the-Box, Kowloon Chinese, Marie Callender, Red Lobster, StrawHat Pizza, Taco Bell, Tony Roma, Wendy's, **lodging:** Ramada(2mi), Red Roof Inn, **other:** MEDICAL CARE, Longs Drug, Marshall's, OfficeMax, Smart Foods, **W...gas:** 76/diesel/24hr, 7-11, **food:** Carrow's Rest., In-n-Out, Old Spaghetti Factory, **lodging:** Extended Stay America, La Quinta, Super 8, Travelodge, **other:** Home Depot

475 Alpine Ave, Country Club Blvd, **E...gas:** Shell/repair, **W...gas:** Citgo/7-11, USA/Baskin-Robbins/Subway/diesel, Safeway/gas

474b Country Club Blvd(from nb)

474a Monte Diablo Ave, **W...other:** Aamco

473 Pershing Ave(from nb), **W...gas:** Arco, **lodging:** Travelodge

472 CA 4 E, to CA 99, Fresno Ave, downtown

471 CA 4 W, Charter Way, **E...gas:** Chevron/24hr, Shell/24hr, United/diesel, **food:** Burger King, Delta Foods, Denny's,

Interstate 5

N
S

McDonald's, **lodging:** Best Western, Motel 6, **other:** Kragen Parts, transmissions, **W...gas:** Beacon/Country MktPlace/TCBY/diesel/@, 76/diesel/rest./24hr, **food:** Carrow's Rest., Taco Bell, **lodging:** Motel 6

470 8th St, Stockton, **W...gas:** CAStop/diesel, **lodging:** Econolodge, **other:** Triad Drug

469 Downing Ave, **W...food:** Cirelli's Pizzaria, **other:** Food4Less/gas, Weston Ranch Drug

468 French Camp, Stockton Airport, **E...gas:** Exxon/Togo's/diesel, **lodging:** Pan Pacific RV, **W...other:** HOSPITAL

467b Mathews Rd, **E...gas:** CFN/diesel, **other:** RV Ctr, tires/repair, **W...other:** HOSPITAL

467a El Dorado St(from nb)

465 Sharpe Depot, Roth Rd, **E...other:** Kenworth, Western Star Trucks, truck repair

463 Lathrop Rd, **E...gas:** Chevron/24hr, Exxon/diesel, Joe's/Subway/TCBY/diesel/@, TowerMart/diesel, **food:** Country Kitchen, **lodging:** Country Inn Suites, Day's Inn, **W...other:** Dos Reis CP, RV camping

Tracy

462 Louise Ave, **E...gas:** Arco/24hr, 76, **food:** A&W/KFC, Carl's Jr, Denny's, Jack-in-the-Box, McDonald's, Taco Bell, **lodging:** Holiday Inn Express

461 CA 120, Manteca, to Sonora, **E...other:** Oakwood Lake Resort Camping

460 Manthey Rd, **E...gas:** Exxon/diesel, **W...food:** fruitstand/deli

458b I-205, to Oakland(from sb, no return), no facilities

458a 11th St, Defense Depot, to Tracy, **2 mi W...gas:** gas/diesel/food

457 Kasson Rd, to Tracy, **W... gas:** CFN/diesel

452 CA 33 S, Vernalis, no facilities

449b a CA 132, to Modesto, **W...other:** The Orchard Campground

446 I-580(from nb, exits left, no return), no facilities

445mm Westley Rest Area both lanes, full(handicapped)facilities, picnic tables, litter barrels, phone, RV dump, petwalk

441 Ingram Creek, Howard Rd, Westley, **E...gas:** Beacon/diesel, Bobby Ray's/diesel/rest./24hr/@, Chevron/diesel/24hr, 76/diesel/24hr, **food:** Carl's Jr, McDonald's, **lodging:** Day's Inn, Econolodge, Holiday Inn Express, Super 8, **W...gas:** Shell/diesel/24hr, **food:** Ingram Creek Rest., fruits

434 Sperry Ave, Del Puerto, Patterson, **E...gas:** Arco/24hr, 76/Subway/diesel, **food:** Denny's, Del Lago Steaks, Jack-in-the-Box, Wendy's, **lodging:** Best Western

430mm vista point nb

428 Fink Rd, Crow's Landing, no facilities

423 Stuhr Rd, Newman, **5 mi E...**food, lodging, **other:** HOSPITAL, RV camping

422mm vista point sb

418 CA 140E, Gustine, **E...gas:** 76/diesel, Shell/diesel

409 weigh sta both lanes

407 CA 33, Santa Nella, **E... gas:** Arco, Pilot/Del Taco/diesel/24hr/@, Shell/diesel, TA/76/diesel/rest./24hr/@, **food:** Andersen's Rest., Burger King, Carl's Jr, **lodging:** Best Western, Holiday Inn Express, **W...gas:** Beacon/diesel, Chevron/24hr, Rotten Robbie/diesel, Shell, **food:** Denny's, McDonald's, Taco Bell, **lodging:** Motel 6, Ramada Inn

403b a CA 152, Los Banos, **6 mi E...other:** HOSPITAL, **W...lodging:** Super 8, **other:** San Luis RV Park

391 CA 165N, Mercy Springs Rd, **W...gas:** Shell

386 rest area both lanes, full(handicapped)facilities, phone, picnic tables, litter barrels, petwalk

385 Nees Ave, to Firebaugh, **W...gas:** Exxon/CFN/Subway/TCBY/diesel

379 Shields Ave, to Mendota, no facilities

372 Russell Ave, no facilities

368 Panoche Rd, **W...gas:** Chevron, 76, Shell/Foster's Freeze/diesel/burgers/@, **lodging:** Apricot Tree Motel/rest., Shilo Inn, **other:** Palms Mkt

365 Manning Ave, to San Joaquin, no facilities

357 Kamm Ave, no facilities

349 CA 33 N, Derrick Ave, no facilities

337 CA 33 S, CA 145 N, to Coalinga

334 CA 198, Huron, to Lemoore, **E...gas:** Shell/Subway/diesel/24hr/@, **lodging:** Harris Ranch Inn/rest., **W...gas:** Chevron, CFN/diesel, Mobil/diesel, 76/Circle K, **food:** Burger King, Carl's Jr, Cazuela's Mexican, Denny's, McDonald's, Oriental Express Chinese, Red Robin Rest., Taco Bell, Windmill Mkt/deli, **lodging:** Best Western, Big County Inn, Motel 6, Pleasant Valley Inn, **other:** HOSPITAL

325 Jayne Ave, to Coalinga, **W...gas:** Arco/24hr, **lodging:** Almond Tree RV Park, **other:** HOSPITAL

320mm rest area both lanes, full(handicapped)facilities, phone, picnic tables, litter barrels, petwalk

319 CA 269, Lassen Ave, to Avenal, **W...**gas/diesel, food, lodging, st prison

309 CA 41, Kettleman City, **E...gas:** Beacon/diesel, CFN/diesel, Chevron, Exxon/Subway/TCBY/diesel, Mobil/diesel/24hr, 76, Shell, **food:** Carl's Jr, In-n-Out, Jack-in-the-Box, McDonald's, Mike's Roadhouse Café, Pizza Hut/Taco Bell, TCBY, **lodging:** Best Western, Super 8, **other:** Travelers RV Park

305 Utica Ave, no facilities

288 Twisselman Rd, no facilities

278 CA 46, Lost Hills, **E...gas:** Shell/diesel, **other:** to Kern NWR, **W...gas:** Arco/24hr, Beacon/diesel, Chevron/diesel/24hr, Pilot/Wendy's/diesel/24hr/@, 76/24hr, Shell, **food:** Carl's Jr, Denny's, Jack-in-the-Box, **lodging:** Day's Inn, Motel 6, **other:** KOA

268 Lerdo Hwy, to Shafter, **3 mi E...gas:** Minimart/gas

262 7th Standard Rd, Rowlee Rd, to Buttonwillow, no facilities

259mm Buttonwillow Rest Area both lanes, full(handicapped) facilities, phone, picnic tables, litter barrels, petwalk

CALIFORNIA

Interstate 5

N ↕ S Buttonwillow

257 CA 58, Buttonwillow, to Bakersfield, **E...gas:** Arco/24hr, Bruce's/A&W/diesel/@, Chevron/diesel/24hr, Mobil/Subway/TCBY/diesel/@, TA/76/Taco Bell/diesel/24hr/@, Shell/diesel, **food:** Carl's Jr, Denny's, McDonald's, Zippy Freeze, **lodging:** FirstValue Inn, Motel 6, Super 8, Willow Inn, **other:** Roger's Produce/gifts, **W...gas:** Exxon/diesel

253 Stockdale Hwy, **E...gas:** Exxon/IHOP/diesel/24hr, 76/24hr, **food:** Jack-in-the-Box, **lodging:** Best Inn, Best Western, **W...other:** Tule Elk St Reserve

246 CA 43, to Taft, Maricopa, **other:** to Buena Vista RA

244 CA 119, to Pumpkin Center, no facilities

239 CA 223, Bear Mtn Blvd, to Arvin, **W...other:** RV camping

234 Old River Rd, no facilities

228 Copus Rd, no facilities

225 CA 166, to Mettler, **2-3 mi E...**gas/diesel, food

221 I-5 and CA 99(from nb, exits left, no return), no facilities

219b a Laval Rd, Wheeler Ridge, **E...gas:** Chevron, TA/diesel/rest./@, **food:** Burger King, Pizza Hut, Subway, Taco Bell, TCBY, **other:** Blue Beacon, repair, **W...gas:** Petro/Mobil/diesel/24hr/@, **food:** McDonald's, Starbucks, Wendy's, **lodging:** Best Western

218 truck weigh sta sb

215 Grapevine, **E...gas:** Mobil, **food:** Denny's, Jack-in-the-Box, RanchHouse Rest., **W...gas:** 76/diesel, Shell/Taco Bell/diesel/@, **food:** Farmer's Table Rest., **lodging:** Countryside Inn

210 Ft Tejon Rd, **W...other:** to Ft Tejon Hist SP, towing/repair

209mm brake check area nb

207 Lebec Rd, **W...other:** USPO, CHP, antiques, towing

206mm rest areas both lanes, full(handicapped)facilities, phone, vending, picnic tables litter barrels, petwalk

205 Frazier Mtn Park Rd, **W...gas:** Arco, Chevron/Subway/diesel/24hr, Flying J/diesel/LP/rest./motel/24hr/@, Shell/Quizno's/diesel, **food:** Jack-in-the-Box, Los Pinos Mexican, **lodging:** BestRest Inn, **other:** Auto Parts+, towing/repair/radiators/transmissions, to Mt Pinos RA

204 Tejon Pass, elev 4144

202 Gorman Rd, to Hungry Valley, **E...gas:** Chevron/diesel/LP, **food:** Carl's Jr, Gorman Plaza Café, Sizzler, **lodging:** Econolodge, **W...gas:** Mobil, **food:** McDonald's, **other:** auto repair

199 CA 138 E(from sb), Lancaster Rd, to Palmdale, no facilities

198b a Quail Lake Rd, CA 138 E(from nb), no facilities

195 Smokey Bear Rd, Pyramid Lake, **W...other:** Pyramid Lake RV Park

191 Vista del Lago Rd, **W...other:** visitors ctr

186mm brake inspection area sb, motorist callboxes begin sb

183 Templin Hwy, **W...other:** Ranger Sta, RV camping

176b a Lake Hughes Rd, Parker Rd, Castaic, **E...gas:** Arco, Citgo/7-11, Castaic Trkstp/diesel/rest./24hr/@, Giant/Chevron/Popeye's/diesel/24hr/@, Shell, **food:** Burger King, Café Mike, Carl's Jr, Del Taco, Domino's, Foster Freeze, McDonald's, Subway, Zorba's Rest., **lodging:** Castaic Inn, Comfort Inn, Day's Inn, **other:** Ralph's Food, Rite Aid, to Castaic Lake, **W...gas:** Mobil, 76/Circle K/Pizza Hut/Taco Bell/repair, **food:** Jack-in-the-Box, **lodging:** Comfort Suites, **other:** auto repair

Santa Clarita

173 Hasley Canyon Rd, **W...food:** Ameci Pizza/pasta

172 CA 126 W, to Ventura, no facilities

171mm weigh sta sb

171 Rye Canyon Rd(from sb), **W...gas:** Shell, **food:** Del Taco, Jack-in-the-Box, Tommy's Burgers, **other:** funpark

170 CA 126 E, Magic Mtn Pkwy, Saugus, **E...lodging:** Best Western/rest., **W... gas:** Chevron, **food:** El Torito, Hamburger Hamlet, Marie Callender's, Red Lobster, Wendy's, **lodging:** Hilton Garden, **other:** Six Flags of CA

169 Valencia Blvd, no facilities

168 McBean Pkwy, **E...other:** HOSPITAL, **W...food:** Baskin-Robbins, Chili's, ChuckeCheese, ClaimJumper Rest., Indian Cuisine, JambaJuice, Macaroni Grill, Starbucks, Subway, Wood Ranch BBQ, **other:** Circuit City, Marshall's, Michael's, Old Navy, Staples, Vons Foods, WorldMkt

167 Lyons Ave, Pico Canyon Rd, **E...gas:** Chevron/24hr, 76/Circle K, Shell/diesel, **food:** Burger King, **other:** Chevrolet, **W...gas:** Arco/24hr, Mobil/Blimpie, Shell, **food:** Carl's Jr, Chuy's Chinese, Coco's, Del Taco, Denny's, Foster's Freeze, El Pollo Loco, Fortune Express Chinese, Floridinos Italian, IHOP, In-n-Out, Jack-in-the-Box, McDonald's, Outback Steaks, Taco Bell, Yamato Japanese, **lodging:** Comfort Inn, Extended Stay America, Fairfield Inn, Hampton Inn, Residence Inn, **other:** Camping World RV Service, GNC, Ralph's Foods, SteinMart, Wal-Mart/auto

166 Calgrove Blvd, **E...food:** Carrows Rest.

162 CA 14 N, to Palmdale, no facilities

161b Balboa Blvd, no facilities

160a I-210, to San Fernando, Pasadena

159 Roxford St, Sylmar, **E...gas:** Chevron/diesel, Mobil/diesel, **food:** Denny's/24hr, McDonald's, **lodging:** Good Nite Inn, Motel 6

158 I-405 S(from sb, no return), no facilities

157b a SF Mission Blvd, Brand Blvd, **E...gas:** Mobil, 76/24hr, **food:** Carl's Jr, In-n-Out, Pollo Gordo, Popeye's, **other:** HOSPITAL, AutoZone, Rite Aid

Los Angeles Area

156b CA 118, no facilities

156a Paxton St, Brand Ave(from nb), **E...gas:** Arco, Chevron, Shell/24hr, **food:** Carnita's Mexican, Taco Bell, Winchell's

155b Van Nuys Blvd(no EZ nb return), **E...gas:** Mobil, 76, **food:** Jack-in-the-Box, KFC, McDonald's, Pizza Hut, Popeye's, **other:** AutoZone, **W...food:** Domino's

155a Terra Bella St(from nb), **E...gas:** Arco, Citgo

154 Osborne St, to Arleta, **E...gas:** Arco/24hr, 76, **food:** Papa's Tacos, Peter Piper Pizza, **other:** Food4Less, Target, **W...gas:** Mobil/Burger King, 7-11, **food:** Mi Taco

153b CA 170(from sb), to Hollywood, no facilities

152a Sheldon St, **E...food:** Big Jim's Rest., **other:** HOSPITAL, auto repair

152 Lankershim Blvd, Tuxford, **E...gas:** Shell/diesel, **W...other:** radiators

151 Penrose St, no facilities

150b Sunland Blvd, Sun Valley, **E...gas:** Mobil, 76, 7-11, **food:** Acapulco Rest., Carl's Jr, El Pollo Loco, Good Fortune Chinese, Town Café, **lodging:** Scottish Inn, **W...gas:** Exxon, Shell, **food:** Dimion's Rest., El Mexicano's, McDonald's

150a GlenOaks Blvd(from nb), **E...gas:** Arco, **lodging:** Willows Motel

149 Hollywood Way, **E...food:** Carrow's, **W...gas:** Shell/diesel, **other:** U-Haul, airport

Interstate 5

N S

Los Angeles Area

148 Buena Vista St, **W...gas:** Exxon/diesel, **food:** Jack-in-the-Box, **lodging:** Buena Vista Motel, Quality Inn, Ramada Inn

147 Scott Rd, to Burbank, **E...gas:** Sevan/diesel, **W...food:** Krispy Kreme, Outback Steaks, Panda Express, Starbucks, Wendy's, **other:** Best Buy, Lowe's Whse, Marshall's, Michael's, Staples, Target

146b Burbank Blvd, **E...gas:** 76/repair, **food:** CA Pizza, Carl's Jr, Chevy's Mexican, ChuckeCheese, Crabby Bob's, El Pollo Loco, Great Wall Buffet, Harry's Rest., IHOP, In-n-Out, KooRooRoo Kitchen, Marie Callender, McDonald's, Popeye's, Shakey's Pizza, Subway, Taco Bell, Tommy's Burgers, Wienerschnitzel, Yoshinoya, **lodging:** Holiday Inn, **other:** Barnes&Noble, Circuit City, CompUSA, K-Mart, Macy's, Mervyn's, Office Depot, Ralph's Foods, Ross, SavOn Drug, Sears, Von's Foods, **W...gas:** Chevron, **food:** Subway

146a Olive Ave, Verdugo, **E...food:** Black Angus, Brewhouse Rest., Fuddrucker's, **lodging:** Holiday Inn, **other:** Radio Shack, Sears, **W...other:** HOSPITAL, Chevrolet

145b Alameda Ave, **E...gas:** Chevron, **food:** Starbucks, **other:** Ralph's Foods, SavOn Drug, **W...gas:** Arco, Mobil/diesel, Shell, **lodging:** Burbank Inn, **other:** U-Haul

145a Western Ave, **W...other:** Gene Autrey Museum

144b a CA 134, Ventura Fwy, Glendale, Pasadena, no facilities

142 Colorado St, no facilities

141a Los Feliz Blvd, **E...other:** HOSPITAL, **W...other:** Griffith Park, zoo

140b Glendale Blvd, **E...gas:** 76, Shell, **other:** auto repair

140a Fletcher Dr(from sb), **E...other:** U-Haul, **W...gas:** Arco/24hr, Chevron, 76, **food:** Charburger, Rick's Drive-In, **other:** Ralph's Foods

139b a CA 2, Glendale Fwy, no facilities

138 Stadium Way, Figueroa St, **E...other:** Home Depot, **W...other:** to Dodger Stadium

137b a CA 110, Pasadena Fwy, no facilities

136b Broadway St(from sb), industrial area

136a Main St, **E...gas:** Chevron/24hr, 76, **food:** Burgers+, Chinatown Express, McDonald's, Mr Pizza, **other:** HOSPITAL, Parts+

135c I-10 W(from nb), Mission Rd(from sb), **E...gas:** Chevron, 76, **food:** Jack-in-the-Box, McDonald's, **lodging:** Howard Johnson, **other:** HOSPITAL

135b Ceasar Chavez Ave, **W...other:** HOSPITAL

135a 4th St, Soto St, no facilities

134b Ca 60 E(from sb), Soto St(from nb)

134a CA 60 W, Santa Monica Fwy, no facilities

133 Euclid Ave(from sb), Grand Vista(from nb), **E...gas:** Arco, USA/diesel, **W...gas:** Mobil, Shell, **other:** HOSPITAL

132 Calzona St, Indiana St, **E...gas:** Arco/diesel

131b Indiana St(from nb)

131a Olympic Blvd, **E...food:** McDonald's, **W...food:** Jack-in-the-Box, King Taco, **other:** HOSPITAL

130c b I-710, to Long Beach, Eastern Ave, **E...food:** McDonald's

130a Triggs St(from sb), **E...food:** Winchell's, **other:** outlet mall, **W... gas:** 76/diesel, **food:** Denny's/24hr, **lodging:** Destiny Inn, **other:** Ford

129 Atlantic Blvd N, Eastern Ave(from sb), **E...food:** Carl's Jr, **other:** outlet mall/famous brands, **W...food:** Denny's, Steven's Steaks

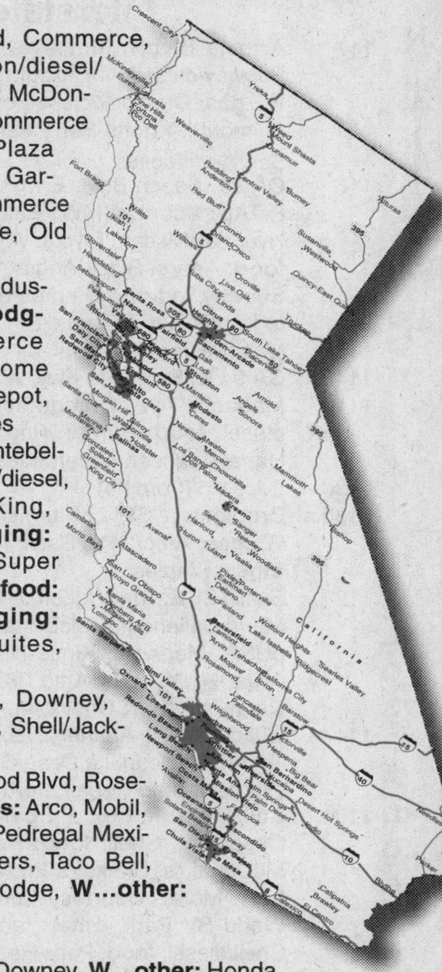

128b Washington Blvd, Commerce, **E...gas:** Chevron/diesel/repair/24hr, **food:** McDonald's, **lodging:** Commerce Hotel, Crowne Plaza Hotel, Wyndham Garden, **other:** Commerce Casino, Firestone, Old Navy, mall

128a Garfield Blvd, industrial area, **E...lodging:** Commerce Hotel, **other:** Home Depot, Office Depot, **W...other:** Staples

126b Slauson Ave, Montebello, **E...gas:** Shell/diesel, **food:** Burger King, Subworks, **lodging:** Best Western, Super 8, **W...gas:** Arco, **food:** Denny's, **lodging:** Guesthouse Suites, Ramada Inn

126a Paramount Blvd, Downey, **E...gas:** Circle K, Shell/Jack-in-the-Box

125 CA 19 S, Lakewood Blvd, Rosemead Blvd, **E...gas:** Arco, Mobil, Thrifty, **food:** El Pedregal Mexican, Sam's Burgers, Taco Bell, **lodging:** Econolodge, **W...other:** Ford

124 I-605, no facilities

123 Florence Ave, to Downey, **W...other:** Honda

122 Imperial Hwy, Pioneer Blvd, **E...gas:** Chevron, **food:** IHOP, Jack-in-the-Box, McDonald's, Red Lobster, Subway, Wendy's, **lodging:** Best Western, **other:** Audi/Porsche, BMW, Firestone/auto, Payless Foods, Rite Aid, Target, **W...gas:** Shell, **food:** Denny's, HongKong Express, Pizza Hut, Rally's, Sizzler, Tacos Mexico, **lodging:** Anchor Inn, Comfort Inn, Vistaland Motel, **other:** Ford

121 San Antonio Dr, to Norwalk Blvd, **E...food:** IHOP, McDonald's, Outback Steaks, **lodging:** Marriott, **W...gas:** 76, **other:** Hall's Automotive

120b Firestone Blvd(exits left from nb)

120a Rosecrans Ave, **E...gas:** Arco/24hr, Mobil/diesel, Shell/diesel, **food:** Burger King, Casa Adelita Mexican, Jim's Burgers, KFC, Pizza Hut/Taco Bell, Taco Joe, **other:** HOSPITAL, BigSaver Foods, **W...gas:** Arco/24hr, **food:** El Pollo Loco, **other:** El Monte RV Ctr, Nissan

119 Carmenita Rd, Buena Park, **E...gas:** Arco, 76/diesel, **food:** Burger King, Carrows, Jack-in-the-Box, Pizza Hut/Taco Bell, **lodging:** Motel 6, **other:** Ford Trucks, Lowe's Whse, **W...gas:** Arco/24hr, Mobil, **food:** Carl's Jr, China Express, Galaxy Burger, **lodging:** Best Western, Dynasty Suites, Super 8

118 Valley View Blvd, **E...gas:** Arco/24hr, **food:** Carl's Jr, In-n-Out, Red Robin, **lodging:** Holiday Inn, **other:** Staples, **W...gas:** Chevron, Shell/diesel, **food:** Blimpie, Denny's, El Pollo Loco, Taco Tio, Winchell's, **lodging:** Residence Inn, **other:** Thompson RV Ctr, to Camping World

CALIFORNIA

Interstate 5

N ↕ S

Los Angeles Area

117 Artesia Blvd, Knott Ave, **E...gas:** 76/24hr, Shell/ Subway/diesel/24hr, **lodging:** Extended Stay America, **W...gas:** Cardlock/diesel, **other:** Chevrolet, Chrysler/ Plymouth, Knotts Berry Farm, to Camping World RV Service/supplies

116 CA 39, Beach Blvd, **E...gas:** Chevron, **other:** HOSPITAL, Acura, BMW, Buick/Pontiac/GMC, Honda, Hyundai, Nissan, Toyota, VW, **W...gas:** Chevron, Mobil, **food:** Arby's, Black Angus, Denny's, KFC, Pizza Hut, Subway, **lodging:** Hampton Inn, Red Roof Inn, **other:** to Knotts Berry Farm

115 Manchester(from nb)

114b CA 91 E, Riverside Fwy, **W...**to airport

114a Magnolia Ave, Orangethorpe Ave, **E...gas:** Mobil/ diesel, **food:** Burger King, Taco Bell, **other:** BMW, Harley-Davidson, Mercedes, Nissan

113c CA 91 W(from nb)

113b a Brookhurst St, LaPalma, **E...gas:** Chevron/24hr, **W...gas:** Arco/24hr, Shell, **food:** La Estrella Mexican, **other:** Staples

112 Euclid St, **E...gas:** Mobil, 7-11, **food:** Chris&Pitt's BBQ, Marie Callender's, McDonald's, Subway, **other:** CompUSA, Mervyn's, Kings Drug, OfficeMax, Old Navy, Wal-Mart, **W...gas:** Arco, 76, **food:** Arby's, Burger King, Denny's, **other:** Chevrolet, SavOn Drug

111 Lincoln Ave, to Anaheim, **E...gas:** Shell/diesel, **food:** El Triunfo Mexican, La Casa Garcia Mexican, **W...other:** Discount Auto Repair, Ford

110b Ball Rd(from sb), **E...gas:** Arco, Chevron/diesel, Citgo/7-11, Shell, **food:** Burger King, El Pollo Loco, McDonald's, Shakey's Pizza, Subway, **lodging:** Anaheim Motel, Courtesy Lodge, Day's Inn, Traveler's World RV Park, **other:** laundry, **W...gas:** Arco/24hr, Shell/diesel, **food:** Paris Rest., Spaghetti Sta, **lodging:** Best Western, Budget Inn, Day's Inn, Sheraton, **other:** Camping World RV Service/supplies

110a Harbor Blvd, **E...gas:** Shell, **lodging:** Day's Inn, Holiday Inn, **W...**to Disneyland, **food:** Acapulco Mexican, IHOP, McDonald's, Millie's Rest., Tony Roma, **lodging:** Anaheim Resort, Best Inn, Best Western, Carousel Inn, Castle Inn Suites, Desert Inn, Fairfield Inn, Howard Johnson, ParkVue Inn, Ramada Inn, Saga Inn, Tropicana Inn, same as 111

109 Katella Ave, Disney Way, **E...gas:** Arco, 76/repair, **food:** CA Country Café, Denny's, El Torito, McDonald's, Ming Delight, Mr Stox Dining, **lodging:** Angel Inn, Ramada Inn, Travelodge, **W...gas:** 7-11, **food:** Del Taco, Flakey Jake's, Thai&Thai, **lodging:** Arena Inn, Comfort Inn, Desert Palms Suites, Extended Stay America, Hilton, Holiday Inn Express, Marriott, Peacock Suites, Portofino Inn, Radisson, Red Roof Inn, Residence Inn, Super 8, to Disneyland

107c St Coll Blvd, City Drive, **E...lodging:** Hilton Suites, **W...lodging:** Doubletree Hotel

107b a CA 57 N, Chapman Ave, **E...gas:** Mobil, **food:** Burger King, Del Taco, Denny's, **lodging:** Hilton Suites, Motel 6, Ramada Inn, **other:** HOSPITAL, to Edison Field, **W...food:** Krispy Kreme, **lodging:** Country Inn/café, DoubleTree, **other:** HOSPITAL

106 CA 22 W(from nb), Garden Grove Fwy, Bristol St, no facilities

105b N Broadway, Main St, **E...gas:** 76, **food:** Carl's Jr, FoodCourt, Jamba Juice, Polly's Café, Rubio's Grill, Starbucks, **lodging:** Red Roof Inn, **other:** Barnes&Noble, BMW, Macy's, Nordstrom's, OfficeMax, Robinsons-May, SavOn Drug, Bowers Museum, mall, **W...lodging:** Golden West Motel, Travel Inn

105a 17th St, **E...gas:** 76/diesel/24hr, **food:** IHOP, McDonald's, **lodging:** Grand Courtyard Inn, **other:** Chevrolet, **W...gas:** Chevron, 7-11, **food:** Marisco's Seafood, Norm's Rest.

104b Santa Ana Blvd, Grand Ave, **E on Grand...food:** Chabela's Mexican, Denny's, Marie Callender, Popeye's, RoundTable Pizza, Taco Bell, Wienerschnitzel, **other:** Factory2U, Food4Less, Goodyear, Kragen Parts, SavOn Drug, Target

Mission Viejo

104a (103c from nb), 4th St, 1st St, to CA 55 N, **E...gas:** Chevron, Shell, **food:** Del Taco

103b CA 55 S, to Newport Beach, no facilities

103a CA 55 N(from nb), to Riverside

102 Newport Ave(from sb), **W...gas:** Arco

101b Red Hill Ave, **E...gas:** Arco/repair, Mobil/diesel, Shell/ repair, **food:** Del Taco, Wendy's, **lodging:** Key Inn, **other:** Drug Emporium/24hr, 1$World, U-Haul, **W...gas:** Arco/24hr, Chevron/24hr, 76/Circle K, **food:** R&R Pizza, Taco Bell, **other:** Stater Bros Foods

101a Tustin Ranch Rd, **E...food:** McDonald's, **other:** Acura, Buick, Cadillac, Chevrolet, Costco, Dodge, Ford/Lincoln/ Mercury, Infiniti, K-Mart, Lexus, Mazda, Nissan, Pontiac, Toyota

100 Jamboree Rd, **E...gas:** Shell, **food:** Black Angus, Buca Italian, Burger King, CA Pizza, El Pollo Loco, In-n-Out, KooRooRoo Kitchen, Macaroni Grill, On the Border, Red Robin, **other:** AAA, Barnes&Noble, Circuit City, Costco, Loehmann's, Lowe's Whse, OfficeMax, Old Navy, Ralph's Foods, Rite Aid, Ross, Target

99 Culver Dr, **E...gas:** Shell/24hr, **food:** Bullwinkle's Rest., Denny's, Starbucks

97 Jeffrey Rd, no facilities

96 Sand Canyon Ave, Old Towne, **W...gas:** 76/Circle K, Denny's, **food:** Jack-in-the-Box, Knollwood Burgers, **lodging:** La Quinta, **other:** Traveland USA RV Park, Irvine RV Ctr

95 CA 133, Laguna Fwy, S Laguna Beach, N to Riverside, toll

94b Alton Pkwy, **E...gas:** Shell, **food:** Carl's Jr, Taco Bell, **other:** Costco, OfficeMax, **W...food:** Chang's Bistro, Dave&Buster's, **lodging:** DoubleTree

94a I-405 N(from nb)

92b Bake Pkwy, same as 92a

92a Lake Forest Dr, Laguna Hills, **E...gas:** Chevron/24hr, Shell/diesel, **food:** Aldo's Italian, Black Angus, Burger King, Diedrich Coffee, Del Taco, Hunter Steaks, IHOP, Jack-in-the-Box, JuiceStop, McDonald's, Mimi's Café, Pizza Hut, Subway, Taco Bell, Teriyaki Japanese, **lodging:** Best Western, Irvine Suites, Travelodge, **other:** MEDICAL CARE, Audi/Jeep, Chevrolet, Ford/Lincoln/Mercury, GMC/ Kia, Honda, Isuzu, Jaguar, Mazda, Mercedes/Suzuki, Pep-Boys, Staples, Subaru, Toyota, VW, **W...gas:** Chevron/ 24hr, Shell, **food:** Café Italia, Carl's Jr, Coco's, Del Taco, McDonald's, Subway, **lodging:** Comfort Inn, Courtyard, Quality Suites, Travelodge, **other:** AZ Leather, BMW, Books Etc, JC Penney

91 El Toro Rd, **E...gas:** Arco/24hr, Chevron/diesel, Mobil, Shell/diesel, USA, **food:** Arby's, Bakers Square, Baskin-Robbins, Denny's, Fuddrucker's, Jack-in-the-Box, KFC, McDonald's, MegaBurger, Red Lobster, Scarantino's Rest., Souper Salad, Wendy's, **other:** House of Fab-

Interstate 5

N ↕ S

rics, K-Mart, Office Depot, SavOn Drug, **W...gas:** Chevron/diesel/24hr, Shell/24hr, 76, **food:** Bennigan's, Biersch Brewery Rest., CA Pizza, Carrows, Coco's, El Torito, Island Burgers, Kings FishHouse, KooRooRoo Kitchen, LoneStar Steaks, Monterey Seafood, Onami Seafood Buffet, Pizza Hut, Trader Joe's, **lodging:** Laguna Hills Lodge, **other:** HOSPITAL, Circuit City, Firestone/auto, JC Penney, Just Tires, Longs Drugs, Macy's, Marshall's, Sears/auto, Walgreen, mall

90 Alicia Pkwy, Mission Viejo, **E...gas:** Chevron/24hr, 76/diesel, **food:** Carl's Jr, Del Taco, Denny's, Little Caesar's, Subway, Wendy's, Winchell's, **other:** Albertson's, America's Tire, Buick/Pontiac/Mazda, Firestone, Mervyn's, Kragen Parts, Target, **W...food:** Togo's

89 La Paz Rd, Mission Viejo, **E...gas:** Arco/24hr, Mobil, UltrMar/repair, **food:** Diedrich's Coffee, KFC, Pizza Hut, Taco Bell, **other:** Albertson's, **W...gas:** Chevron, 76, 7-11, **food:** Claim Jumper Rest., Del Taco, Flamingo Mexican, Jack-in-the-Box, McDonald's, Outback Steaks, Quizno's, Spasso's Italian, Wienerschnitzel, **lodging:** Holiday Inn, **other:** Best Buy, Borders Books&Café, CompUSA, Goodyear/auto, Jo-Ann Fabrics, Winston Tire, to Laguna Niguel Pk

87 Oso Pkwy, Pacific Park Dr, **E...gas:** Chevron/repair, Mobil, 76/repair, **food:** Carl's Jr, **lodging:** Fairfield Inn

86 Crown Valley Pkwy, **E...gas:** Arco, Chevron, 76, **food:** Coco's, Mexican Cantina, **other:** HOSPITAL, Macy's, OfficeMax, mall, **W...gas:** Chevron/diesel, **other:** Aamco

Capistrano

85b Avery Pkwy, **E...gas:** Shell/diesel, **food:** Booster's Grill, Carrow's, Del Taco, Jack-in-the-Box, McDonald's, Sheesh Kabob, **other:** Acura/Volvo, America's Tire, Goodyear, Infiniti, Land Rover, Lexus, Parts+, Staples, **W...gas:** Arco, Shell/diesel/24hr, **food:** A's Burgers, Buffy's Rest., In-n-Out, **lodging:** Laguna Inn, **other:** Firestone/auto, GMC/Cadillac, Mercedes

85a CA 73 N toll

83 Junipero Serra Rd, to San Juan Capistrano, **W...gas:** Shell, UltraMar/diesel

82 CA 74, Ortego Hwy, **E...gas:** Chevron/diesel, Shell/repair, 76, **food:** Denny's, **lodging:** Best Western, **other:** MEDICAL CARE, **W...gas:** Arco, Chevron/24hr, **food:** Burger King, Carl's Jr, Del Taco, Jack-in-the-Box, McDonald's, Pedro's Tacos, Walnut Grove Rest., **lodging:** Mission Inn

San Clemente

81 Camino Capistrano, **E...other:** Peugeot/VW, **W...gas:** Chevron, **food:** Harry's Rest., KFC, Starbucks, **other:** Goodyear, Pic'n Sav Foods, Rite Aid, Ross, Von's Food

79 CA 1, Pacific Coast Hwy, Capistrano Bch, **1 mi W...gas:** Arco/24hr, 76, Shell, **food:** A's Burgers, Carl's Jr, Del Taco, Denny's, Jack-in-the-Box, McDonald's, Subway, **lodging:** Dana Point Inn, DoubleTree, Hilton, Ramada Inn, **other:** Chevrolet, Chrysler/Jeep, Honda, Nissan, Saturn, Toyota, USPO

78 Camino de Estrella, San Clemente, **E...gas:** 76/diesel/24hr, **food:** Bakers Square, Big City Bagel, Café Expresso, Carl's Jr, China Well, JuiceStop, Rubio's Grill, Subway, Trader Joe's, **other:** HOSPITAL, Ralph's Foods, SavOn Drug/24hr, Stater Bros Foods, **W...gas:** Arco/diesel, **other:** K-Mart, Las Golondrienas, Kragen Parts, Pic'n Sav Foods

76 Ave Pico, **E...gas:** Mobil, **food:** Carrow's, McDonald's, NY Pizza, **other:** Albertson's, GNC, **W...gas:** Chevron, Shell/diesel, **food:** BurgerStop, Del Taco, Denny's/24hr, Pizza Hut, Stuft Pizza, Subway, Waffle Lady, **lodging:** Country Side Inn, **other:** Books Etc, $Less, Ralph's Foods, SavOn Drug, Staples, USPO

75 Ave Palizada, Ave Presidio, **W...gas:** Arco, UltraMar, 7-11, **food:** Antoine's Café, Baskin-Robbins, KFC, Subway, **lodging:** Holiday Inn, **other:** Albertson's, Ford

74 El Camino Real, **E...gas:** Chevron/24hr, **food:** Pedro's Tacos, same as 75, **W...gas:** Mobil, 76, 7-11, **food:** China Taste, FatBurger, KFC, LoveBurger, Taco Bell, Tommy's Rest./24hr, **other:** Kragen Parts, Radio Shack, Ralph's Foods

73 Ave Calafia, Ave Magdalena, **E...gas:** 76, Shell, 7-11, **food:** Beef Cutter Rest., Coco's, El Marianchi Rest., Jack-in-the-Box, Pedro's Tacos, **lodging:** C-Vu Inn, El Rancho Motel, LaVista Inn, Quality Suites, San Clemente Motel, Trade Winds Motel, Travelodge, **other:** Amato Tire, **W...lodging:** San Clemente Inn, **other:** to San Clemente SP

72 Cristianitios Ave, **E...lodging:** San Mateo RV Park/dump, **W...other:** to San Clemente SP

71 Basilone Rd, **W...other:** San Onofre St Beach

67mm weigh sta both lanes

66mm viewpoint sb

62 Las Pulgas Rd, no facilities

59 Aliso Creek rest area both lanes, full(handicapped)facilities, phone, vending, picnic tables, litter barrels, petwalk, RV dump

Oceanside

54c Oceanside Harbor Dr, **W...gas:** Chevron, Mobil, **food:** Burger King(1mi), Del Taco, Denny's/24hr, **lodging:** Comfort Inn, Sandman Hotel, Travelodge, The Bridge Motel, **other:** to Camp Pendleton

54b Hill St(from sb), to Oceanside, **W...gas:** Mobil, **food:** Carrow's Rest., **lodging:** Comfort Inn

54a Ca 76 E, Coast Hwy, no facilities

53 Mission Ave, Oceanside, **E...gas:** Arco/24hr, Mobil/diesel, 76/LP, **food:** Arby's, Armando's Tacos, Burger King, China Dynasty, El Charrito Mexican, Jack-in-the-Box, KFC, McDonald's, Mission Donuts, Pizza Hut, **lodging:** Econolodge, Ramada Ltd, **other:** CarQuest, NAPA, PepBoys, Valu+ Foods, **W...food:** Carrow's, El Pollo Loco, Mandarin Chinese, Wendy's, **lodging:** GuestHouse Inn, **other:** AutoZone, Grocery Outlet, 99c Store, Office Depot, Radio Shack, Rite Aid

CALIFORNIA

Interstate 5

N ↕ S

Carlsbad

52 Oceanside Blvd, **E...gas:** Arco, **food:** Domino's, IHOP, McDonald's, Papa John's, Pizza Hut, Rosarita's Café, Subway, Taco Bell, **other:** Boney's Foods, Longs Drug, 98c Store, Ralph's Food, SavOn Drug, Von's Food, CHP, **W...gas:** Shell/24hr, **lodging:** Best Western

51c Cassidy St(from sb), **W...gas:** Citgo/7-11, Mobil, 76, **other:** HOSPITAL

51b CA 78, Vista Way, Escondido, **E...gas:** Chevron/24hr, 76, **food:** Applebee's, Golden Taipei, McDonald's, Mimi's Café, Olive Garden, Tony Roma, **other:** Best Buy, Cost+, JC Penney, Macy's, Marshall's, Mervyn's, Michael's, Robinsons-May, Saturn, Sears/auto, Staples, Starbucks, Stater Bros Foods, Target, Wal-Mart, **W...food:** Hunter Steaks

51a Las Flores Dr, no facilites

50 Elm Ave, Carlsbad Village Dr, **E...gas:** Shell/24hr, **food:** Lotus Thai Bistro, **W...gas:** Carlsbad/LP, Chevron/repair/24hr, 76, UltraMar, **food:** Carl's Jr, Denny's/24hr, Jack-in-the-Box, KFC/Taco Bell, Mikko Japanese, **lodging:** Motel 6, **other:** Albertson's

49 Tamarack Ave, **E...gas:** Chevron/24hr, Exxon/diesel, **food:** Village Kitchen, **lodging:** Carlsbad Lodge, Super 8, Travel Inn, **other:** GNC, Rite Aid, Von's Foods, **W...gas:** 76/repair/24hr, **food:** Koko Palms Rest.

48 Cannon Rd, Car Country Carlsbad, **E...other:** Acura, Buick, Chevrolet/Cadillac, Ford, Honda, Isuzu, Lexus, Lincoln/Mercury, Mazda, Mercedes, Toyota, VW

47 Carlsbad Blvd, Palomar Airport Rd, **E...gas:** Chevron, Mobil/diesel, Citgo/7-11, **food:** Carl's Jr, Denny's, Hadley Orchard's Foods, IslandsBurgers, Pat&Oscar's Rest., Subway, Strauss Brewery Rest., Taco Bell, TGIFriday, **lodging:** Holiday Inn, **other:** Costco, **W...gas:** Shell/diesel, **food:** ClaimJumper Rest., In-n-Out, Marie Callender's, McDonald's, **lodging:** Hilton, **other:** S Carlsbad St Bch

45 Poinsettia Lane, **W...gas:** Chevron, **food:** El Pollo Loco, Jack-in-the-Box, Panda Buffet, Raintree Grill, Subway, **lodging:** Inn of America, Motel 6, Quality Inn, Ramada, **other:** Ralph's Food, Rite Aid, Volvo

44 La Costa Ave, **E...**vista point, **W...gas:** Chevron/diesel

Encinitas

43 Leucadia Blvd, **E...lodging:** Holiday Inn Express, **W...gas:** Shell/autocare, Texaco/diesel

41b Encinitas Blvd, **E...gas:** Arco/diesel, Chevron, Exxon, **food:** Chin's Chinese, Coco's, Del Taco, Stuft Pizza, **other:** Albertson's, Chevrolet, Nissan, SavOn Drug, to Quail Botanical Gardens, **W...gas:** Shell, **food:** Denny's, Wendy's, **lodging:** Best Western/rest., Day's Inn

41a Santa Fe Dr, to Encinitas, **E...gas:** Shell, 7-11/24hr, **food:** Carl's Jr, Papa Tonie's Pizza, **W...gas:**76/Burger King, **food:** NY Pizza, **other:** HOSPITAL, Rite Aid, Von's Foods

40 Birmingham Dr, **E...gas:** Chevron, Shell, **food:** Taco Bell, **lodging:** Country Inn, **W...gas:** Arco/24hr

39mm viewpoint sb

39 Manchester Ave, **E...gas:** 76, **other:** to MiraCosta College

37 Lomas Santa Fe Dr, Solana Bch, **E...food:** Pizza Nova, Samurai Rest., **other:** Ross, Von's Foods, We-R-Fabrics, **W...gas:** Mobil, Shell/diesel, **food:** Carl's Jr, Starbucks, Thai Kitchen, **other:** Discount Tire, Henry's Foods, Marshall's, SavOn Drug, Staples

San Diego Area

36 Via de La Valle, Del Mar, **E...gas:** Chevron, Mobil, **food:** Burger King, Chevy's Mexican, KooRoo Kitchen, McDonald's, Milton's Deli, Pasta Pronto, Papachino's Italian, Taste of Thai, Tony Roma's, **other:** Albertson's, **W...gas:** Arco/24hr, Shell/diesel, **food:** Denny's, FishMkt Rest., Red Tracton's Rest., **lodging:** Hilton, **other:** racetrack

34 Del Mar Heights Rd, **E...gas:** Shell/diesel, **W...gas:** Citgo/7-11, **food:** Bloomberg's Rest., Jack-in-the-Box, Mexican Grill, **other:** Longs Drug, Von's Foods

33b Carmel Valley Rd, **E...gas:** Arco, Shell/repair, **food:** Taco Bell, Tio Leo's Mexican, **lodging:** DoubleTree Hotel, Hampton Inn, Marriott

33a CA 56 E, no facilities

31 I-805(from sb), no facilities

29 Genesee Ave, **E...other:** HOSPITAL, **1 mi W...**gas, food, lodging

28b La Jolla Village Dr, **E...food:** Italian Bistro, **lodging:** Embassy Suites, Hyatt, Marriott, **other:** HOSPITAL, to LDS Temple, **W...gas:** Mobil/diesel, **food:** BJ's Grill, CA Pizza, Domino's, El Torito, Islands Burgers, Pasta Bravo, RockBottom Café, Rubio's Grill, TGIFriday, Trader Joe's, **lodging:** Radisson, **other:** HOSPITAL, Marshall's, Radio Shack, Ralph's Foods, Ross, SavOn Drug, Whole Foods

28a Nobel Dr(from nb), **E...lodging:** Hyatt, **other:** LDS Temple, **W...**same as 28b

27 Gilman Dr, La Jolla Colony Dr, no facilities

26b CA 52 E, San Clemente Canyon, Ardath Rd(from nb)

26a Ardath Rd(from nb)

23b CA 274, Balboa Ave, **1 mi E...gas:** Shell, **food:** Del Taco, **other:** Albertson's, **W...gas:** Citgo/7-11, Mobil, 76/repair, **food:** Arby's, In-n-Out, Wienerschnitzel, **lodging:** Comfort Inn, SleepyTime Motel, Super 8, **other:** HOSPITAL, Ford, Nissan, Plymouth, Toyota, Winston Tire, Mission Bay Pk

23a Grand Ave, Garnet Ave, **W...other:** Cadillac

22 Clairemont Dr, Mission Bay Dr, **E...gas:** 76, Shell, **food:** Carl's Jr, HomeTown Buffet, Jack-in-the-Box, KFC, McDonald's, Subway, **lodging:** Best Western, **other:** Chevrolet/VW, Rite Aid, **W...**to Sea World Dr

21 Sea World Dr, Tecolote Dr, **E...gas:** Arco, Shell, **other:** Circle K, Firestone, **W...lodging:** Hilton, **other:** Old Town SP

20 I-8, W to Nimitz Blvd, E to El Centro, CA 209 S(from sb), to Rosecrans St

19 Old Town Ave, **E...gas:** Arco/24hr, Shell, **lodging:** Ramada Inn, Travelodge

18b Washington St, **E...lodging:** Comfort Inn

18a Pacific Hwy Viaduct, Kettner St

17b India St, Front St, Sassafras St, **E...gas:** Mobil, 76, **W...gas:** Exxon, **lodging:** Motel 6, Super 8, **other:** airport, civic ctr

17a Hawthorn St, Front St, **W...gas:** Exxon, **other:** HOSPITAL

16b 6th Ave, downtown

16a CA 163 N, 10th St, **E...other:** AeroSpace Museum, **W...gas:** Shell, **lodging:** Budget Motel, El Cortez Motel, Holiday Inn, Radisson, Marriott, **other:** HOSPITAL

15c b CA 94 E(from nb), Pershing Dr, B St, civic ctr, downtown

15a CA 94 E, J St, Imperial Ave(from sb),no facilities

14b Cesar Chavez Pkwy

14a CA 75, to Coronado, **W...**toll rd to Coronado

13b National Ave SD, 28th St, **E...other:** AutoZone, **W...gas:** Shell

13a CA 15 N, to Riverside, no facilities

CALIFORNIA

Interstate 5

N ↕ S

San Diego Area

12 Main St, National City, no facilities
11b 8th St, National City, **E...gas:** Mobil, Shell/24hr, **lodging:** Budget Inn, EZ 8 Motel, Holiday Inn, Howard Johnson, Ramada Inn, Super 8, Value Inn, **W...gas:** Chevron/diesel, **other:** MEDICAL CARE
11a Harbor Dr, Civic Center Way, no facilities
10 Bay Marina, 24th St, Mile of Cars Way, **1/2 mi E...food:** Denny's, In-n-Out
9 CA 54 E, no facilities
8b E St, Chula Vista, **E...gas:** Mobil, **lodging:** Motel 6, **W...food:** Anthony's Fish Grotto, **lodging:** GoodNite Inn
8a H St, **E...gas:** Arco/diesel, Chevron, 7-11, **other:** HOSPITAL, Dodge, Goodyear, motel
7b J St(from sb), **W...other:** Marina Pkwy
7a L St, **E...gas:** Citgo/7-11, 76, Shell/diesel, **food:** Golden Pagoda Chinese, **lodging:** Best Western, **other:** AutoZone, NAPA, Grocery Outlet, Office Depot
6 Palomar St, **E...gas:** Arco, **food:** China King, Del Taco, HomeTown Buffet, Jack-in-the-Box, KFC, McDonald's, **lodging:** Palomar Inn, **other:** Office Depot, Ralph's Foods, **E on Broadway...food:** Yoshinoya, **other:** Costco, Michael's, Ross, Target
5b Main St, to Imperial Beach, **E...gas:** Arco, **food:** AZ Chinese, Garcia's Mexican
5a CA 75(from sb), Palm Ave, to Imperial Beach, **E...gas:** Arco, 7-11, **food:** Papa John's, Tasty China, **W...gas:** Arco, Citgo/7-11, Mobil, Shell/repair/24hr, **food:** Boll Weevil Diner, Burger King, Carl's Jr, Carrow's, El Pollo Loco, Lydia's Mexican, McDonald's, Rally's, Red Hawk Steaks, Roberto's Mexican, Subway, Taco Bell, Wienerschnitzel, **lodging:** Super 8, **other:** AutoZone, CarQuest, Goodyear/auto, Home Depot, Kragen Parts, Mervyn's, 99c Store, SavOn Drug, Von's Foods
4 Coronado Ave(from sb), **E...gas:** Chevron/service, Shell/service, 7-11, **food:** Denny's, Taco Bell, **lodging:** EZ 8 Motel, San Diego Inn, **W...gas:** Arco/24hr, Shell/diesel/repair, **lodging:** Day's Inn, **other:** to Border Field SP
3 CA 905, Tocayo Ave, **W...gas:** Citgo/7-11
2 Dairy Mart Rd, **E...gas:** Arco/24hr, Circle K, **food:** Burger King, Carl's Jr, Coco's, McDonald's, Roberto's Mexican, **lodging:** Americana Inn, Ramada Ltd, Super 8, Valli-Hi Motel, **other:** CarQuest, Radio Shack, Pacifica RV Resort
1b Via de San Ysidro, **E...gas:** Chevron, Exxon, Mobil, 76, **food:** Denny's, Si Senor Mexican, **other:** Max's Foods, NAPA, **W...gas:** Chevron, **food:** Denny's, KFC, **lodging:** Economy Inn, International Inn/RV park, Motel 6
1a I-805 N(from nb), Camino de la Plaza(from sb), **E...food:** Burger King, El Pollo Loco, Jack-in-the-Box, KFC, McDonald's, Subway, **lodging:** Flamingo Motel, Gateway Inn, Holiday Motel, Travelodge, **W...other:** factory outlet, border parking
0 US/Mexico Border, California state line, customs, I-5 begins/ends.

Interstate 8

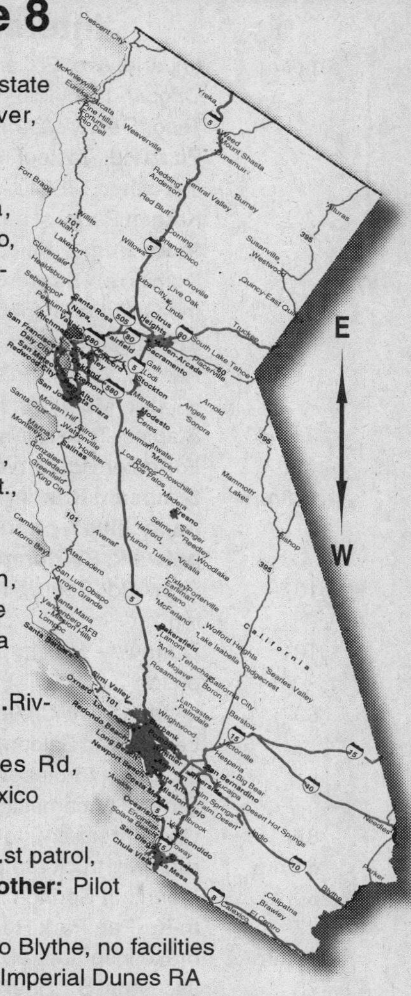

Yuma

Exit # Services
172.5mm California/Arizona state line, Colorado River, Pacific/Mountain time zone
172 4th Ave, Yuma, **N...**Ft Yuma Casino, **S...gas:** Chevron, 76/Circle K, Shell/24hr, **food:** Domino's, Jack-in-the-Box, Little Caesar's, Mi Rancho Mexican, Yuma Landing Rest., **lodging:** Best Western, Interstate 8 Inn, Yuma Inn, **other:** Rivers Edge RV Park, to Yuma SP
170 Winterhaven Dr, **S...**Rivers Edge RV Park
166 CA 186, Algodones Rd, Andrade, **S...**to Mexico
165mm CA Insp Sta
164 Sidewinder Rd, **N...**st patrol, **S...gas:** Shell/LP, **other:** Pilot Knob RV Park
159 CA 34, Ogilby Rd, to Blythe, no facilities
156 Grays Well Rd, **N...**Imperial Dunes RA
155mm rest area both lanes(exits left), full(handicapped)facilities, picnic tables, litter barrels, petwalk
151 Gordons Well, no facilities
146 Brock Research Ctr Rd, no facilities
143 CA 98, Midway Well, to Calexico, no facilities
131 CA 115, VanDerLinden Rd, to Holtville, **5 mi N...**gas, food, lodging, RV camping
128 Bonds Corner Rd, no facilities
125 Orchard Rd, Holtville, **4 mi N...**gas/diesel, food
120 Bowker Rd, no facilities
118b a CA 111, to Calexico, **1 mi N...gas:** Shell/diesel/café, **other:** RV park
116 Dogwood Rd, **N...other:** RV camping

El Centro

115 CA 86, 4th St, El Centro, **N...gas:** Arco/24hr, Chevron, Citgo/7-11/diesel, Shell/diesel, USA, **food:** Carl's Jr, Fong Chinese, Foster's Freeze, Jack-in-the-Box, McDonald's, Rally's, **lodging:** Holiday Inn Express, Motel 6, **other:** El Sol Foods, Firestone/auto, Goodyear/auto, Ford/Lincoln/Mercury, U-Haul, radiators, **S...gas:** Mobil/A&W/Subway/Pizza Hut/diesel/@, **food:** Taco Bell, **lodging:** Best Western, Casa Real Inn, EZ 8 Motel, **other:** Buick/Cadillac/Pontiac, Chevrolet, Chrysler/Plymouth/Dodge/Jeep, Honda, Max Foods, Desert Trails RV Park

E ↕ W

CALIFORNIA

Interstate 8

E ↕ W — El Centro

114 Imperial Ave, El Centro, **N...gas:** Chevron/service, Citgo/7-11/diesel, Shell, USA/diesel, **food:** Del Taco, Denny's/24hr, Domino's, KFC, McDonald's, Pizza Hut, TasteeFreez Burgers, **lodging:** Ramada Inn, **other:** MEDICAL CARE, Vacation Inn/RV Park, Kragen Parts, st patrol, **1-3 mi N...gas:** Arco/24hr, **food:** Burger King, Carl's Jr, Carrow's, Church's, Domino's, 4Seasons Buffet, Golden Corral, Jack-in-the-Box, Papa John's, Sizzler, Taco Bell, Wendy's, **lodging:** Brunners Inn, Day's Inn, Super 8, **other:** Aamco, Albertson's, Costco/gas, Goodyear/auto, K-Mart, Mervyn's, PepBoys, Rite Aid, Sears/auto, Staples, Toyota, Wal-Mart, Winston Tire

111 Forrester Rd, to Westmorland, no facilities

108mm Sunbeam Rest Area both lanes, full(handicapped)facilities, phone, picnic tables, litter barrels, petwalk, RV dump

107 Drew Rd, Seeley, **N...**RV camping, **S...**RV camping

101 Dunaway Rd, Imperial Valley, elev 0 ft, **N...**st prison

89 Imperial Hwy, CA 98, Ocotillo, **N...gas:** Shell/diesel, Lazy Lizard Saloon, Ocotillo Motel/RV Park, USPO, **S...gas:** 76/diesel/repair, **food:** Desert Kitchen, **other:** RV camping

87 CA 98(from eb), to Calexico, no facilities

81mm runaway truck ramp, eb

80 Mountain Springs Rd, no facilities

77 In-Ko-Pah Park Rd, **N...**phone, towing

75mm brake insp area eb, phone

73 Jacumba, **S...gas:** Shell/diesel/towing/24hr, **other:** NAPA, RV camping

65 CA 94, Boulevard, to Campo, **S...gas:** MtnTop/diesel, **food:** Burning Tree Rest., **lodging:** Buena Vista Motel, to McCain Valley RA

63mm Tecate Divide, elev 4140 ft

61 Crestwood Rd, Live Oak Springs, **S...food:** Country Broiler Rest., **lodging:** Live Oak Sprs Country Inn, **other:** FoodSource/diesel/24hr, Vacation Inn/RV Park, RV camping, info

62mm Crestwood Summit, elev 4190 ft

54 Kitchen Creek Rd, Cameron Station, **S...**food, RV camping

51 rd 1, Buckman Spgs Rd, to Lake Morena, **S...**gas/diesel/LP, food, lodging, RV camping, Lake Morena CP(7mi), Potrero CP(19mi), **rest area both lanes, full(handicapped)facilities, phone, picnic tables, litter barrels, petwalk, RV dump**

47 rd 1, Sunrise Hwy, Laguna Summit, elev 4055 ft, **N...**to Laguna Mtn RA

45 Pine Valley, Julian, **N...food:** Major's Diner, **other:** to Cuyamaca Rancho SP

44mm Pine Valley Creek

42mm elev 4000 ft

40 CA 79, Japatul Rd, Descanso, **N...**to Cuyamaca Rancho SP, gas, food

37mm vista point eb, elev 3000 ft

36 E Willows, **N...**Alpine Sprs RV Park, Viejas Indian Res, casino

33 W Willows Rd, to Alpine, **N...**Alpine Sprs RV Park, Viejas Res, casino, **S...**ranger sta

31mm elev 2000 ft

30 Tavern Rd, to Alpine, **N...gas:** Shell/diesel, UltrMar/diesel, **S...gas:** 76/Circle K, Shell, **food:** BBQ, Breadbasket Rest., Carl's Jr, La Carreta Mexican, LJ Silver, Mediterraneo Italian, Panda Machi, **lodging:** Countryside Inn, **other:** MEDICAL CARE, Alpine Mkt Foods, Radio Shack, Rite Aid, city park

27 Dunbar Lane, Harbison Canyon, **N...other:** RV camping

25mm elev 1000 ft

24mm map stop wb, phone

23 Lake Jennings Pk Rd, Lakeside, **N...gas:** Arco/Jack-in-the-Box/diesel/24hr, to Lake Jennings CP, **other:** RV camping, **S...gas:** Citgo/7-11, **food:** Burger King, Jilberto's Tacos, Marechiaro's Pizza, **other:** Eitsmoes RV Ctr, Flinn Sprgs CP

22 Los Coches Rd, Lakeside, **N...gas:** 76/Circle K, Citgo/7-11, Mobil/service, **food:** Laposta Mexican, Pizza Pro, **other:** PillCo Drug, RV camping, **S...gas:** Shell/diesel, **food:** Denny's, McDonald's, Subway, Taco Bell, **other:** Radio Shack, Von's Foods, Wal-Mart/auto

El Cajon

20b Greenfield Dr, to Crest, **N...gas:** Chevron/diesel, Exxon/diesel/24hr, Shell, 7-11/YumYum, **food:** Janet's Café, McDonald's, Panchos Taco, **other:** HOSPITAL, AutoZone, Ford, 99c Store, RV camping, auto repair, st patrol, **S...gas:** Mobil/LP

20a E Main St(from wb, no EZ return), **N...food:** Main St Grill, Pernicano's Italian, **lodging:** Budget Inn, Embasadora Motel, **other:** Ford, Vactioner RV Park, **S...food:** Coco's, **other:** Cadillac

19 2nd St, CA 54, El Cajon, **N...gas:** Arco/24hr, Chevron, Regent/diesel, **food:** Taco Shop, **other:** Parts+, Von's Foods, **S...gas:** 76, Shell/A&W/diesel, **food:** Arby's, Burger King, Carl's Jr, DQ, Golden Corral, IHOP, Jack-in-the-Box, KFC, McDonald's, Pizza Hut, Subway, Taco Bell, **other:** Firestone/auto, Ralph's Foods, Radio Shack, Rite Aid, Walgreen

18 Mollison Ave, El Cajon, **N...gas:** Chevron, **food:** Denny's, **lodging:** Best Western, Plaza Inn, **S...gas:** Arco/24hr, **food:** Taco Bell, **lodging:** Super 8, Valley Motel

17c Magnolia Ave, CA 67(from wb), to Santee, **N...food:** LJ Silver, **other:** Albertson's, JC Penney, K-Mart, mall, same as 19, **S...gas:** Shell/service, **food:** Mexican Rest., Perry's Café, Wienerschnitzel, **lodging:** MidTown Motel, Motel 6, Travelodge, **other:** Nudo's Drug

Interstate 8

E ↕ W

San Diego Area

17b CA 67(from eb), **N...other:** JC Penney, Sears/auto, mall, same as 19 & 21

17a Johnson Ave(from eb), **N...food:** Applebee's, Boston Mkt, Burger King, LJ Silver, Subway, **other:** Albertson's, Chevrolet, Home Depot, Honda, JC Penney, K-Mart, Marshall's, Mervyn's, Rite Aid, Robinson-May, Sears/auto, mall, **S...other:** Aamco, Isuzu, Saturn

16 Main St, **N...gas:** Arco/24hr, 7-11, **food:** Denny's/24hr, Sombrero Mexican, **lodging:** ThriftLodge, **other:** Lexus, **S...gas:** 76, Chevron, **other:** Nissan, brakes/transmissions

15 El Cajon Blvd(from eb), **N...lodging:** Day's Inn, **S...gas:** Mobil/diesel, Shell, **food:** BBQ, **other:** Chrysler/Plymouth

14c Severin Dr, Fuerte Dr(from wb), **N...gas:** Arco/24hr, Mobil, 7-11, **food:** Anthony's Fish Rest., Charcoal House Rest., **lodging:** Econo Inn, Holiday Inn Express, **S...food:** Brigantine Seafood Rest.

14b a CA 125, to CA 94, no facilities

13b Jackson Dr, Grossmont Blvd, **N...gas:** Arco/24hr, Chevron, Mobil, Shell, 7-11/24hr, **food:** Arby's, Burger King, Chili's, ChuckeCheese, Fuddrucker's, KFC, Olive Garden, Red Lobster, Taco Bell, **other:** Barnes&Noble, Cost+, Dodge, Kragen Parts, Macy's, Staples, Target, USPO, mall, **S...food:** Chile Bandido, Jack-in-the-Box, **other:** Circuit City, Discount Tire, Firestone/auto, Hyundai, Isuzu, Ralph's Foods, VW

13a Spring St(from eb), El Cajon Blvd(from wb), **N... other:** Dodge/Kia, Jeep, **S...lodging:** Travelodge

12 Fletcher Pkwy, to La Mesa, **N...gas:** Shell, 7-11, **food:** Bakers Square, Boston Mkt, Chili's, McDonald's, **lodging:** EZ 8 Motel, **other:** MEDICAL CARE, Albertson's, Costco, **S...food:** La Salsa Mexican, **lodging:** Motel 6, **other:** Chevrolet, RV Park

11 70th St, Lake Murray Blvd, **N...gas:** Shell, **food:** Pepper's Mexican, Subway, **other:** MEDICAL CARE, **S...gas:** Mobil, Shell/diesel/repair, 7-11, **food:** Aiken's Deli, Denny's, La Casa Maria Mexican, **other:** HOSPITAL, Marie Callender's, **1/4 mi S...**multiple services on El Cajon Blvd

10 College Ave, **N...gas:** Chevron, **other:** Katz's Mkt, USPO, **S...other:** MEDICAL CARE, to San Diego St U

9 Waring Rd, **N...food:** Nicolosi's Italian, **lodging:** Best Inn, Good Nite Inn, Madrid Suites

8 Fairmont Ave(7 from eb), to Mission Gorge Rd, **N...gas:** Arco/24hr, Citgo/7-11, Mobil/diesel, Shell, UltraMar/diesel, **food:** Arby's, Boll Weevil Diner, Boston Mkt, Burger King, Carl's Jr, Chili's, Coco's, Happy Chef, Jack-in-the-Box, El Pollo Loco, KFC, Krazy Pete's Diner, McDonald's, Rally's, Subway, Taco Bell, Tio Leo's Mexican, **lodging:** Super 8, **other:** HOSPITAL, Discount Tire, Home Depot, Longs Drugs, NAPA, Radio Shack, Rite Aid, Toyota, Von's Foods

San Diego Area

7b a I-15 N, CA 15 S, to 40th St

6b I-805, N to LA, S to Chula Vista

6a Texas St, Qualcomm Way, **N...gas:** Chevron, same as 5

5 Mission Ctr Rd, **N...gas:** Chevron, **food:** Bennigan's, Chevy's Mexican, Dave&Buster's, Hogi Yogi, Hooters, In-n-Out, Mandarin Cuisine, Outback Steaks, Quizno's, Taco Bell, Togo's, **lodging:** Marriott, **other:** Best Buy, Borders Books&Café, Chevrolet, Crown Books, Ford, Lincoln/Mercury, Loehmann's, Macy's, Michael's, Nordstrom Rack, Old Navy, Robinson-May, Sak's Off 5th, Staples, mall, **S...gas:** Arco/24hr, **food:** Benihana, Denny's, Todai Rest., Wendy's, **lodging:** Comfort Inn, Hilton, Radisson, Ramada Ltd, Red Lion Inn, **other:** Chrysler/Plymouth, Dodge, GMC/Pontiac, Mazda, Subaru

4c b CA 163, Cabrillo Frwy, **S...**to downtown, zoo

4a Hotel Circle Dr(from eb), CA 163 (from wb)

3a Hotel Circle, Taylor St, **N...gas:** Chevron, **food:** DW Ranch Rest., Hunter Steaks, **lodging:** Best Western Hanalei, Comfort Suites, Handlery Hotel, Motel 6, Red Lion Hotel, Town&Country Motel, **other:** cinema, golf, **S...gas:** Chevron, **food:** Albie's Rest., Valley Kitchen, **lodging:** Best Western, Econolodge, Extended Stay America, Hawthorn Suties, Holiday Inn, Hotel Circle Inn, Howard Johnson, King's Inn/rest., Quality Resort, Ramada Inn, Regency Plaza, Travelodge, Vagabond Inn

2c Morena Blvd(from wb)

2b I-5, N to LA, S to San Diego

CALIFORNIA

Interstate 8

San Diego Area (E ↕ W)

2a Rosecrans St(from wb), CA 209, **S...gas:** Chevron, **food:** Burger King, Del Taco, Denny's, In-n-Out, Jack-in-the-Box, McDonald's, Perry's Café, Rally's, **lodging:** Arena Inn, Best Western, Day's Inn, Holiday Inn, Howard Johnson, Quality Inn, Rio Motel, Super 8, **other:** Chrysler/Jeep, Circuit City, Goodyear/auto, House of Fabrics, Pic'n Save, Staples, SaveOn Drug

1 W Mission Bay Blvd, Sports Arena Blvd(from wb), **N...**to SeaWorld, **S...food:** Arby's, Coco's, Embers Café, McDonald's, **lodging:** EZ 8 Motel, Holiday Inn Express, **other:** Home Depot

0mm I-8 begins/ends on Sunset Cliffs Blvd, **N...**Mission Bay Park, **1/4 mi W...gas:** Mobil/service, Shell, **food:** Anthony's Rest., Jack-in-the-Box, Kaiserhof Deli

Interstate 10

Blythe (E ↕ W)

Exit # Services

245mm California/Arizona state line, Colorado River, Pacific/Mountain time zone

244mm inspection sta wb

243 Riviera Dr, **S...other:** Riviera RV Camp

241 US 95, Intake Blvd, Blythe, **N...gas:** Shell, UltraMar, **food:** Steaks'n Cakes Rest., **lodging:** Best Western, Desert Winds Motel, Travelers Inn Express, **other:** diesel repair/24hr, to Needles, **S...**McIntyre Park

240 7th St, **N...gas:** Chevron/service, EZ, **food:** Blimpie, Foster's Freeze, **lodging:** Astro Motel, Blue Line Motel, Blythe Inn, Budget Inn, Comfort Suites, Dunes Motel, **other:** MEDICAL CARE, Albertson's, AutoZone, Chrysler/Dodge/Jeep, Ford, Rite Aid, RV repair/LP

239 Lovekin Blvd, Blythe, **N...gas:** Mobil/Subway/diesel, Shell, **food:** Carl's Jr, Del Taco, Jack-in-the-Box, La Casita Dos Mexican, McDonald's, Pizza Hut, Popeye's, Sizzler, **lodging:** Best Value Inn, Best Western, Comfort Inn, EZ 8 Motel, Hampton Inn, Legacy Inn, Royal Pacific Inn, **other:** MEDICAL CARE, Goodyear, K-Mart, Radio Shack, **S...gas:** Arco/diesel/24hr, Chevron/diesel/24hr/@, 76/diesel, Shell/DQ, UltraMar, **food:** Burger King, Denny's, KFC, Townes Square Café/24hr, Taco Bell, **lodging:** Holiday Inn Express, Motel 6, Super 8, **other:** Chevrolet/Pontiac/Buick/Cadillac, city park/RV dump

236 CA 78, Neighbours Blvd, to Ripley, **N...gas:** Shell/service, **S...**to Cibola NWR

232 Mesa Dr, **N...gas:** Chevron, 76/diesel/rest./24hr, **S...gas:** Mesa Verde/diesel

231 weigh sta wb

222 Wileys Well Rd, **N...rest area both lanes, full(handicapped)facilities, phone, picnic tables, litter barrels, petwalk, S...**to st prison

217 Ford Dry Lake Rd, no facilities

201 Corn Springs Rd, no facilities

192 CA 177, Rice Rd, Desert Center, to Lake Tamarisk, **N...gas:** Stanco/diesel/repair/24hr, **food:** Family Café, **other:** USPO, camping

189 Eagle Mtn Rd, no facilities

182 Red Cloud Rd, no facilities

177 Hayfield Rd, no facilities

173 Chiriaco Summit, **N...gas:** Chevron/diesel/café/24hr, **other:** Patton Museum, truck/tire repair

168 to Twentynine Palms, to Mecca, Joshua Tree NM, **N...**wildlife viewing

162 frontage rd, no facilities

159mm Cactus City Rest Area both lanes, full(handicapped)facilities, picnic tables, litter barrels, petwalk

156mm 0 ft elevation

Indio

146 Dillon Rd, to CA 86, to CA 111 S, Coachella, **N...gas:** Chevron/24hr, Loves/Carl's Jr/diesel/24hr/@, Shell/24hr, **S...gas:** TA/Arco/Taco Bell/TCBY/diesel/24hr/@, Shell/Jack-in-the-Box, **other:** casino

145 (from eb), CA 86 S

144 CA 111 N, CA 86 S, Indio, **N...lodging:** Holiday Inn Express, **other:** Classic RV Park, Fantasy Sprgs Casino, **1 mi S...other:** Audi/VW, Chevrolet, Ford/Lincoln/Mercury, Isuzu, Mazda, Nissan

143 Jackson St, Indio, **S...gas:** Circle K, **other:** Big A Parts, NAPA, auto repair

142 Monroe St, Central Indio, **N...other:** RV camping, **S...gas:** Circle K, 76, Shell/diesel/LP, **food:** Alicia's Mexican, Carrow's, Denny's, In-n-Out(1mi), **lodging:** Best Western, Comfort Inn, Holiday Motel, Motel 6, Quality Inn, Super 8, **other:** HOSPITAL, Target, auto/transmissions

139 Jefferson St, Indio Blvd, **N...other:** RV camping, hwy patrol, **2 mi S...lodging:** Best Western, Motel 6

137 Washington St, Country Club Dr, to Indian Wells, **N...gas:** Arco/24hr, **food:** Burger King, Coco's, Del Taco, **lodging:** Comfort Suites, Motel 6, **other:** Buick/Pontiac/GMC, Ford/Lincoln/Mercury, Honda, Toyota, U-Haul, 10k Trails RV Park, **S...gas:** Mobil/diesel, 76/Circle K, **food:** Carl's Jr, Lili's Chinese, Subway, **other:** MEDICAL CARE, Goodyear/auto

Palm Sprgs

134 Cook St, to Indian Wells, **S...lodging:** Courtyard, Residence Inn, **other:** Emerald Desert RV Resort

131 Monterey Ave, Thousand Palms, **N...gas:** Arco/24hr, **food:** Jack-in-the-Box, **S...food:** IHOP, Taco Bell, **other:** Costco/gas, Home Depot

130 Ramon Rd, Bob Hope Dr, **N...gas:** Chevron/24hr, Flying J/diesel/LP/rest./24hr/@, Mobil/diesel, UltraMar, **food:** Carl's Jr, Del Taco, Denny's, In-n-Out, McDonald's, **lodging:** Red Roof Inn, **other:** truckwash, **S...other:** HOSPITAL, Agua Caliente Casino/rest.

126 Date Palm Dr, Rancho Mirage, **S...gas:** Arco/24hr, UltraMar

Interstate 10

E ↕ W

Palm Sprgs

123 Gene Autry Tr, Palm Dr, to Desert Hot Sprgs, **N...gas:** Arco, **other:** camping, **3 mi S...**to Gene Autry Trail

120 Indian Ave, to N Palm Sprgs, **N...gas:** 76/Circle K, Denny's, **food:** Le Chiquita Tacos, **lodging:** Motel 6, **S...gas:** Chevron, Pilot/DQ/Wendy's/diesel/24hr/@, **food:** Jack-in-the-Box, **other:** HOSPITAL

117 CA 62, to Yucca Valley, Twentynine Palms, to Joshua Tree NM

114 Whitewater, many windmills

113mm rest area both lanes, full(handicapped)facilities, phone, picnic tables, litter barrels

112 CA 111(from eb), to Palm Springs, **S...food:** Outback Steaks(9mi)

11 Verbenia Ave, no facilities

106 Main St, to Cabazon, **N...gas:** Shell/diesel, **food:** Burger King, Denny's, **S...gas:** Arco/diesel/24hr

104 Cabazon, **N...gas:** Shell/A&W/diesel/24hr, **food:** Coco's, **other:** Premium Outlets/famous brands, Hadley Orchard Fruits, Morongo Casino/rest.

103 Fields Rd, **N...gas:** Chevron, **food:** McDonald's, **other:** Premium Outlets/famous brands, Morongo Reservation/casino

102.5mmBanning weigh sta both lanes

102 Ramsey St(from wb), no facilities

101 Hargrave St, Banning, **N...gas:** Shell/diesel/LP, **other:** Parts+, transmissions

100 CA 243, 8th St, Banning, **N...gas:** Chevron, **food:** Ahloo Chinese, Banning Burger, Carolina Seafood, Wing Chinese Garden, **other:** MEDICAL CARE, My Oriental Mkt, Star Parts, **S...other:** RV camping

Banning

99 22nd St, to Ramsey St, **N...gas:** Arco/24hr, Mobil, **food:** Carl's Jr, Carrow's, Chelo's Tacos, Del Taco, KFC, McDonald's, Pizza Hut, Sizzler, Starbucks, Taco Bell, Wendy's, **lodging:** Day's Inn, Hacienda Inn, Super 8, Travelodge, **other:** Banning RV Ctr, Ford, Plymouth/Jeep/Dodge, Winston Tire

98 Sunset Ave, Banning, **N...gas:** Chevron/diesel, UltraMar/24hr, **food:** Domino's/Donut Factory, Gus Jr #7 Burger, Subway, **other:** AutoZone, Chevrolet, Radio Shack, Rite Aid, Save-U Foods

96 Highland Springs Ave, **N...gas:** Arco/24hr, Chevron, UltraMar/diesel, **food:** Burger King, Denny's, Guy's Italian, Jack-in-the-Box, Little Caesar's, Subway, **other:** Food4Less, Kragen Parts, Radio Shack, Stater Bros Foods, Walgreen, **S...gas:** Arco/24hr, **food:** Baskin-Robbins, Carl's Jr, **other:** Albertson's, K-Mart, Rite Aid, hwy patrol

Beaumont

95 Pennsylvania Ave, Beaumont, **N...gas:** Circle K, **food:** ABC Rest., Rusty Lantern Rest., **lodging:** Windsor Motel, **other:** Miller's RV Ctr, Tom's RV Ctr

94 CA 79, Beaumont, **N...gas:** Arco, 76, **food:** Baker's DriveThru, Gus Burgers, McDonald's, El Rancho Steaks, YumYum Donuts/24hr, **lodging:** Best Western, Budget Host, **S...food:** Denny's, **other:** RV camping

93 CA 60 W, to Riverside, no facilities

92 San Timoteo Canyon Rd, Oak Valley Pkwy, **N...**golf, **S...**golf

91mm rest area wb, full(handicapped)facilities, phone, picnic tables, litter barrels, petwalk

90 Cherry Valley Blvd, no facilities

89 Singleton Rd(from wb), to Calimesa, no facilities

88 Calimesa Blvd, **N...gas:** Arco/24hr, Chevron/Burger King/diesel, Shell, **food:** McDonald's, Subway, Taco Bell, **lodging:** Calimesa Inn, **other:** Stater Bros Foods, bank, **S...food:** Big Boy, Jack-in-the-Box

87 County Line Rd, to Yucaipa, **N...gas:** FasTrip/gas, Shell/diesel, **food:** Del Taco, **lodging:** Calimesa Inn, **other:** auto repair/tires

86mm Wildwood Rest Area eb, full(handicapped)facilities, phone, picnic tables, litter barrels, petwalk

85 Live Oak Canyon Rd, Oak Glen, **N...food:** Cedar Mill Rest.

83 Yucaipa Blvd, **N...gas:** Arco/24hr, Chevron, **food:** Baker's DriveThru

82 Wabash Ave(from wb), no facilities

81 Redlands Blvd, Ford St, **S...gas:** 76, **food:** Griswold's Smorgasbord

80 Cypress Ave, University St, **N...**HOSPITAL, to U of Redlands

79b a CA 38, 6th St, Orange St, Redlands, **N...gas:** Arco, Chevron, **food:** Redland Rest., Ricky's Mexican, **lodging:** Budget Inn, Stardust Motel, **other:** Goodyear, Stater Bros Foods, Viking Tire, **S...gas:** 76, Shell, **food:** Boston Mkt, **other:** Albertson's, Kragen Parts, Lincoln/Mercury, NAPA, Office Depot, Von's Foods

77c (77b from wb)Tennessee St, **N...other:** Home Depot, **S...gas:** Shell, **food:** Arby's, Bakers DriveThru, Burger King, Carl's Jr, Coco's, El Pollo Loco, Foster's Donuts, Papa John's, Shakey's Pizza, Subway, Taco Bell, Vince's Spaghetti, **lodging:** Best Western, Dynasty Suites, **other:** Ford, Tri-City Mall, USPO

CALIFORNIA

Interstate 10

E ↕ W

San Bernardino

77b (77c from wb)CA 30, to Highlands, **S...**to Tri-City Mall

77a Alabama St, **N...gas:** Chevron, **food:** Denny's, Tom's Chiliburgers, **lodging:** Motel 6, 7 West Motel, Super 8, **other:** Ford, VW, U-Haul, **S...gas:** Chevron, Shell/diesel, **food:** Del Taco, IHOP, McDonald's, Nick's Burgers, Zabella's Mexican, **lodging:** Best Western, GoodNite Inn, **other:** Aamco, Chief Parts, Chevrolet, Goodyear/auto, Hyundai, K-Mart, Longs Drug, Mervyn's, Nissan, PepBoys, Pic'n Sav Foods, Ross, Toyota, Tri-City Mall

76 California St, **N...other:** museum, **S...gas:** Arco/24hr, 76, Shell/LP/24hr, **food:** Applebee's, Jack-in-the-Box, Jose's Mexican, **other:** Food4Less, Wal-Mart/auto, Winston Tire, RV camping

75 Mountain View Ave, Loma Linda, **N...gas:** Mobil/diesel, **S...food:** FarmerBoys Burgers, Lupe's Mexican, Subway

74 Tippecanoe Ave, Anderson St, **N...gas:** Arco, **food:** Denny's, In-n-Out, **other:** Costco/gas, Staples, **S...gas:** 76/diesel, **food:** Baker's DriveThru, Blimpie, Del Taco, HomeTown Buffet, KFC, Kool Kactus Café, Napoli Italian, Taco Bell, Wienerschnitzel, **other:** Audi, Harley-Davidson, Honda, Jaguar, Saab, Saturn, transmissions, to Loma Linda U

73b a Waterman Ave, **N...gas:** 76, Shell/diesel/24hr, **food:** Black Angus, Bobby McGee's, Beef Bowl Chinese, Chili's, Coco's, El Torito, IHOP/24hr, Lotus Garden Chinese, Mimi's Café, Olive Garden, Outback Steaks, Red Lobster, Sizzler, Souplantation, Starbucks, TGIFriday, Thai Garden, Tony Roma, Yamazato Japanese, **lodging:** Comfort Inn, EZ 8 Motel, Hilton, La Quinta, Super 8, Travelodge, **other:** Best Buy, Circuit City, CompUSA, Home Depot, Office Depot, OfficeMax, Sam's Club, **S...gas:** Arco/24hr, Beacon/diesel/rest., **food:** Burger King, Carl's Jr, Gus Jr Burger #8, McDonald's, Popeye's, Taco Bell, **lodging:** Motel 6, **other:** Staples, Camping World RV Service/supplies

72 I-215, CA 91, no facilities

71 Mt Vernon Ave, Sperry Ave, **N...gas:** Arco/24hr, Colton Trkstp/diesel/LP/rest./@, **food:** Peppersteak Rest., **lodging:** Colony Inn, **other:** brake/muffler, repair

70b 9th St, **N...gas:** Mobil, **food:** Baskin-Robbins, Burger King, Carrow's Rest./24hr, Denny's, Jeremiah's Steaks, KFC, LaVilla Mexican, McDonald's, P&G's Burgers, Piccadilly's, Taco Bell, **lodging:** ThriftLodge, **other:** Parts+, Stater Bros Foods

70a Rancho Ave, **N...gas:** Arco/diesel, **food:** Antonio's Pizza, Del Taco, Diane's Coffee, Wienerschnitzel

69 Pepper Dr, **N...gas:** Shell, **food:** Baker's DriveThru, **other:** Acacia RV, Ford

68 Riverside Ave, to Rialto, **N...gas:** Arco/24hr, Chevron, 10 Trkstp/diesel, **food:** Burger King, China Palace, Coco's, HomeTown Buffet, Izumi Japanese, Jack-in-the-Box, McDonald's, Taco Joe's, **lodging:** Best Western, Rialto Motel, Ross, **other:** Wal-Mart, diesel repair, **S...gas:** Cardlock Fuels/diesel

66 Cedar Ave, to Bloomington, **N...gas:** Arco/24hr, Chevron, Mobil, **food:** Baker's DriveThru, Burger King, FarmerBoys Burgers, **other:** USPO, **S...gas:** Citgo/7-11

64 Sierra Ave, to Fontana, **N...gas:** Arco/24hr, Mobil, Shell, **food:** Applebee's, Arby's, Burger King, China Cook, ChuckeyCheese, DQ, Denny's, Del Taco, In-n-Out, Jack-in-the-Box, KFC, La Buffa Mexican, McDonald's, Millie's Kitchen, Papa John's, Pizza Hut/Taco Bell, Popeye's, Spires Rest., Subway, Wienerschnitzel, **lodging:** Comfort Inn, Econolodge, Motel 6, **other:** Aamco, **other:** HOSPITAL, Albertson's, Chevrolet, $Tree, Food4Less, Goodyear/auto, Honda/GMC, Kia, KidsRUs, K-Mart, Kragen Parts, Mazda, Nissan, PepBoys, Pic'n Sav Foods, Radio Shack, Rite Aid, SavOn Drug, Stater Bros Foods, Winston Tire, **S...gas:** Circle K, **food:** Burger Basket, China Buffet, Mervyn's, **other:** Ross, Target

63 Citrus Ave, **N...gas:** 76, UltarMar/gas, **food:** Baker's DriveThru, Taqueria Mexican, **other:** Ford

61 Cherry Ave, **N...gas:** Arco/24hr, Chevron/Taco Bell, Mobil/diesel/24hr, **food:** Carl's Jr, Jack-in-the-Box, **lodging:** Circle Inn Motel, **other:** Ford Trucks, **S...gas:** 3 Sisters Trkstp/diesel/@, 76/Circle K, **other:** Peterbilt

59 Etiwanda Ave, Valley Blvd, no facilities

58b a I-15, N to Barstow, S to San Diego

57 Milliken Ave, **N...gas:** Arco, Chevron, Mobil/Subway/diesel, 76/Del Taco/diesel, Shell/diesel, **food:** Burger King, Carl's Jr, Coco's, CoffeeBean, Cucina Italian, Dave&Buster's, FoodCourt, In-n-Out, McDonald's, NY Grill, RainForest Café, Rubio's Rest., Tokyo Japanese, Wendy's, Wienerschnitzel, Wolfgang Puck Café, **lodging:** AmeriSuites, Country Suites, **other:** America's Tire, JC Penney, Sam's Club, mall, **S...gas:** TA/76/diesel/rest./24hr/@, **other:** RV Ctr

56 Haven Ave, Rancho Cucamonga, **N...gas:** Mobil, Benihana, **food:** Black Angus, Crabby's Seafood, El Torito, Quizno's, Tony Roma, **lodging:** Extended Stay America, Hilton, Holiday Inn, La Quinta, **S...food:** Panda Chinese, TGIFriday, **lodging:** Fairfield Inn

55b a Holt Blvd, to Archibald Ave, **N...gas:** Circle K, Mobil/diesel, **food:** Burger Town, Joey's Pizza, Subway, **other:** MEDICAL CARE

54 Vineyard Ave, **N...food:** Del Taco, Popeye's, Rocky's Foods, Sizzler, Taco Bell, **other:** Chief Parts, Rite Aid, Stater Bros Foods, **S...gas:** Arco/24hr, Circle K, Mobil,

Interstate 10

E ↕ W

Ontario

Shell, **food:** Cuisine of India, Denny's, In-n-Out, Marie Callender, Michael J's Rest., Rosa's Italian, Spires Rest., Yoshinoya Japanese, **lodging:** Best Western, Country Suites, DoubleTree Inn, Express Inn, Good-Nite Inn, Ramada Ltd, Red Roof Inn, Residence Inn, Sheraton, Super 8, **other:** Chevrolet/Cadillac

53 San Bernardino Ave, 4th St, to Ontario, **N...gas:** Arco, Chevron, Circle K, Shell, **food:** Baskin-Robbins, Burger King, Carl's Jr, Del Taco, Jack-in-the-Box, Popeye's, Sizzler, Taco Bell/24hr, **lodging:** Motel 6, Quality Inn, **other:** Chief Parts, K-Mart, Radio Shack, Ralph's Foods, Rite Aid, **S...gas:** Arco/24hr, Exxon/A&W/diesel/24hr, 76, **food:** Denny's, Gordo's Mexican, KFC, McDonald's, Pizza Hut, YumYum Donut, **lodging:** CA Inn, Travelodge, West Coast Inn

51 CA 83, Euclid Ave, to Ontario, Upland, **N...food:** Coco's Rest.

50 Mountain Ave, to Mt Baldy, **N...gas:** Arco, Chevron, Mobil, Shell/A&W/diesel, **food:** BBQ, Carrow's, Denny's, El Burrito, El Torito, Green Burrito, Happy Wok Chinese, Mimi's Café, Mi Taco, Subway, Trader Joe's, **lodging:** Super 8, **other:** Home Depot, Longs Drug, Mervyn's of CA, Staples, **S...gas:** 76/diesel, **food:** Baskin-Robbins, Carl's Jr, Tacos Mexico, **other:** Albertson's, Food4Less, Rite Aid, Target, USPO

49 Central Ave, to Montclair, **N...gas:** Chevron, Mobil, Shell/24hr, 7-11, **food:** Acapulco Mexican, Burger King, El Pollo Loco, KFC, McDonald's, Subway, Tom's Burgers, **other:** MEDICAL CARE, Borders Books, Circuit City, Firestone/auto, Goodyear/auto, Hi-Lo Auto Supply, JC Penney, Macy's, Office Depot, Ross, Sears/auto, mall, same as 48, **S...gas:** 76, **food:** Jack-in-the-Box, LJ Silver, Wienerschnitzel, **other:** Acura, Costco/gas, Honda, Infiniti, K-Mart, Nissan

48 Monte Vista, **N...gas:** Shell, **food:** Black Angus, Olive Garden, Red Lobster, Tony Roma, **other:** HOSPITAL, Nordstrom's, Robinson-May, mall, same as 49

47 Indian Hill Blvd, to Claremont, **N...gas:** Mobil, **food:** Bakers Square, Tony Roma, **lodging:** Howard Johnson, Travelodge, **S...gas:** Chevron/McDonald's, 76/diesel, Shell, 7-11, **food:** Burger King, Carl's Jr, Chili's, In-n-Out, RoundTable Pizza, Wienerschnitzel, **lodging:** Ramada Inn, **other:** MEDICAL CARE, Albertson's, America's Tire, AutoZone, Ford, Kia, Pic'n Sav, Radio Shack, Toyota

46 Towne Ave, **N...gas:** 7-11, **food:** Jack-in-the-Box

45b Garey Ave(from eb), to Pomona, **N...gas:** Delta, **other:** SavOn Drug, **S...gas:** Arco/24hr, Chevron, Shell/diesel, **other:** HOSPITAL

45a White Ave, Garey Ave, to Pomona, same as 46a

Los Angeles Area

44 (43 from eb)Dudley St, Fairplex Dr, **N...gas:** Arco, 76, **food:** Coppacabana Rest., Denny's, **lodging:** LemonTree Motel, Sheraton, **S...gas:** Chevron/24hr, Mobil, Texaco/diesel, 7-11, **food:** Jack-in-the-Box, McDonald's

42b CA 71 S(from eb), to Corona

42a I-210 N, CA 57 S, no facilities

41 Kellogg Dr(from eb), **S...**to Cal Poly Inst

40 Via Verde, no facilities

38b Holt Ave, to Covina, **N...food:** Blake's Steaks/seafood, **lodging:** Embassy Suites

38a Grand Ave

37b Barranca St, Grand Ave, **N...gas:** Arco, Shell/repair, **food:** Bailey's Rest., Charley Brown Steaks/lobster, Coco's, El Torito, Magic Recipe Rest., Marie Callender, Mariposa Mexican, Monterrey Rest., **lodging:** Best Western, Hampton Inn, Holiday Inn, **S...food:** In-n-Out, McDonald's, **lodging:** Comfort Inn

37a Citrus Ave, to Covina, **N...gas:** Chevron, Mobil, Shell, **food:** Burger King, Carl's Jr, Chili's, Del Taco, IHOP, Jack-in-the-Box, Mandarin Express, TGIFriday, Winchell's, **other:** Acura, Buick, GMC, Honda, Lincoln/Mercury, Longs Drug, Marshall's, Mazda, Mervyn's, Office Depot, Old Navy, Ralph's Foods, Ross, Target, Volvo/VW, **S...gas:** 76/autocare, **food:** Trader Joe's, **lodging:** Comfort Inn, 5 Star Inn, **other:** HOSPITAL, Cadillac

36 CA 39, Azusa Ave, to Covina, **N...gas:** Arco/24hr, Chevron, 76, **food:** Black Angus, McDonald's, Papa John's, Red Lobster, Steak Corral, Subway, **lodging:** El Dorado Motel, **other:** Chrysler/Plymouth, Circuit City, Jeep, **S...gas:** Mobil, Shell, **food:** Carrow's, **other:** Dodge, Honda, Hummer, Jaguar, Mazda, Mercedes, Mitsubishi, Nissan, Saab, Saturn, Toyota

35 Vincent Ave, Glendora Ave, **N...gas:** Arco/24hr, Chevron/24hr, Mobil, 76, **food:** KFC, Pizza Hut, Wienerschnitzel, **S...gas:** 76, **food:** Applebee's, Chevy's Mexican, Red Robin, **other:** Barnes&Noble, Best Buy, JC Penney, Macy's, Robinson-May, Sears/auto, SportMart, mall

CALIFORNIA

Interstate 10

E ↕ W

Los Angeles Area

34 Pacific Ave, **N...other:** CarQuest, **S...gas:** Mobil, **other:** HOSPITAL, K-Mart, Goodyear/auto, JC Penney, Jo-Ann Fabrics, Sears, mall, same as 35

33 La Puente Ave, **N...gas:** Chevron, **food:** China Palace, Denny's, Guadalajara Grill, McDonald's, Quizno's, Starbucks, **lodging:** Motel 6, Radisson, Home Depot, Staples, **S...gas:** Arco, **lodging:** Baldwin Motel, **other:** Harley-Davidson, Saturn, U-Haul

32b Francisquito Ave, to La Puente, **N...food:** In-n-Out, **other:** hwy patrol, **S...gas:** Chevron, **food:** Carl's Jr, In-n-Out, Wienerschnitzel, **lodging:** Grand Park Inn

31c a (31b from wb)Frazier St, Baldwin Pk Blvd, **N...gas:** Arco, Chevron, Shell, 7-11, **food:** Burger King, Jack-in-the-Box, McDonald's, Pizza Hut/Taco Bell, **other:** HOSPITAL, Food4Less, OfficeMax, Target, **S...food:** In-n-Out, **other:** Altman's RV Ctr

31b a (31a from wb)I-605 S, to Long Beach

29b Valley Blvd, Peck Rd, **N...gas:** Chevron, **food:** Denny's, **lodging:** Motel 6, **other:** Ford, Dodge, Goodyear, Honda, K-Mart, Nissan, Toyota/Lexus, **S...gas:** Mobil, Shell, **food:** Del Taco, McDonald's, Teriyaki Bowl, **other:** MEDICAL CARE, PepBoys, Pontiac/GMC

29a S Peck Rd(from eb), no facilities

28 Santa Anita Ave, to El Monte, **N...gas:** Shell/diesel, **other:** Chevrolet, Hyundai, **S...gas:** 76, 7-11

27 Baldwin Ave(from eb), **S...gas:** Arco/24hr, **food:** Denny's, Edward's Steaks, same as 27b a

26b CA 19, Rosemead Blvd, Pasadena, **N...food:** Denny's, IHOP, **lodging:** Ramada Inn, **other:** MEDICAL CARE, Goodyear/auto, Target

26a Walnut Grove Ave, no facilities

25b San Gabriel Blvd, **N...gas:** Arco, Mobil, Shell/autocare, **food:** Carl's Jr, Popeye's, Taco Bell, Teriyaki Bowl, Wienerschnitzel, **lodging:** Budget Motel, **other:** MEDICAL CARE, AutoZone, San Gabriel Foods, **S...gas:** Arco, **food:** Burger King, **other:** SavOn Drug

25a Del Mar Ave, to San Gabriel, **N...gas:** 76, **other:** auto repair, **S...gas:** Arco, Chevron

24 New Ave, to Monterey Park, **N...gas:** Mobil, to Mission San Gabriel

23b Garfield Ave, to Alhambra, **N...**HOSPITAL, **S...gas:** Shell, Texaco

23a Atlantic Blvd, Monterey Park, **N...gas:** Mobil, 76, **food:** Del Taco, Pizza Hut, Popeye's, **other:** HOSPITAL, **S...other:** Firestone/auto

22 Fremont Ave, **N...**HOSPITAL, tuneup, **S...gas:** 7-11

21 I-710, Long Beach Fwy, Eastern Ave(from wb)

20b a Eastern Ave(from eb), City Terrace Dr, **S...gas:** Chevron/service, **food:** McDonald's

19c Soto St(from wb), **N...gas:** Shell, **other:** HOSPITAL, **S...gas:** Mobil, Shell, **food:** Burger King

Los Angeles Area

19b I-5(from wb), US 101 S, N to Burbank, S to San Diego

19a State St, **N...**HOSPITAL

17 I-5 N

16b I-5 S(from eb)

16a Santa Fe Ave, San Mateo St, **S...gas:** Shell, **other:** Hertz Trucks, industrial area

15b Alameda St, **N...**downtown, **S...**industrial area

15a Central Ave, **N...gas:** Shell/repair

14b San Pedro Blvd, **S...**industrial

14a LA Blvd, **N...**conv ctr, **S...other:** Kragen Parts, Radio Shack, Rite Aid

13 I-110, Harbor Fwy, no facilities

12 Hoover St, Vermont Ave, **N...gas:** Mobil, Texaco, **food:** Burger King, King Donuts, **other:** PepBoys, Thrifty Drug, Toyota, **S...gas:** Chevron, Shell, **food:** Jack-in-the-Box, **other:** Office Depot, Staples

11 Western Ave, Normandie Ave, **N...gas:** Chevron, Mobil, **food:** McDonald's, Winchell's, **other:** AutoZone, Food4Less, Radio Shack, SavOn Drug, **S...**Chevron, Texaco, Goodyear

10 Arlington Ave, **N...gas:** Chevron, Mobil

9 Crenshaw Blvd, **S...gas:** Chevron, Thrifty, **other:** U-Haul

8 La Brea Ave, **N...gas:** Chevron, Shell/diesel/repair, **other:** Walgreen, transmissions, **S...gas:** Chevron, AutoZone, Ralph's Foods

7b Washington Blvd, Fairfax Ave, **S...gas:** Mobil, same as 8

7a La Cienega Blvd, Venice Ave(from wb), **N...gas:** Chevron/24h, **other:** Firestone/auto, **S...gas:** Arco/24hr, Mobil, **food:** Carl's Jr, McDonald's, Pizza Hut, Subway, **other:** Staples

6 Robertson Blvd, Culver City, **N...gas:** Arco, Chevron, Mobil, **other:** museum, **S...food:** Del Taco, Albertson's, **other:** OfficeMax, SavOn Drug, Ross

5 National Blvd, **N...gas:** 76, 7-11, **other:** Rite Aid, Von's Foods

4 Overland Ave, **S...gas:** Arco/24hr, Mobil, 76, Shell, **food:** Winchell's

3b a I-405, N to Sacramento, S to Long Beach, no facilities

2c b Bundy Dr, **N...gas:** 76, **food:** Eddy's Café, Taco Bell

2a Centinela Ave, to Santa Monica, **N...food:** Don Antonio's Mexican, Taco Bell, **S...food:** McDonald's, Trader Joe's, **lodging:** Santa Monica Hotel

1c 20th St(from wb), Cloverfield Blvd, 26th St(from wb), **N...gas:** Arco, Shell/repair, **other:** HOSPITAL

1b Lincoln Blvd, CA 1 S, **N...food:** Denny's, **lodging:** Holiday Inn, **other:** Jo-Ann Fabrics, Macy's, Sears, auto repair, mall, **S...gas:** Chevron/24hr, **food:** Jack-in-the-Box, **other:** Firestone/auto, U-Haul

1a 4th, 5th,(from wb) **N...other:** Macy's, Sears

0 Santa Monica Blvd, to beaches, I-10 begins/ends on CA 1.

Interstate 15

N ↕ S

Exit #	Services
298	California/Nevada state line, facilities located at state line, Nevada side.
291	Yates Well Rd, **W...**golf
286	Nipton Rd, **E...**E Mojave Nat Scenic Area, to Searchlight
281	Bailey Rd, no facilities
276mm	brake check area for trucks, nb
272	Cima Rd, no facilities
270mm	**Valley Wells Rest Area both lanes, full(handicapped)facilities, phone, picnic tables, litter barrels, petwalk**
265	Halloran Summit Rd, **E...gas:** Hilltop Gas/diesel, **other:** towing/tires/repair
259	Halloran Springs Rd, **E...gas:** Lo Gas/diesel/café
248	to Baker(from sb), access to same as 239
246	CA 127, Kel-Baker Rd, Baker, to Death Valley, **W...gas:** Arco/24hr, Chevron/Taco Bell/24hr, Mobil/Denny's/diesel, 76/diesel, Shell/Jack-in-the-Box/diesel, Texaco/A&W/Pizza Hut/TCBY, UltraMar/DQ/diesel/@, **food:** Arby's, BunBoy Rest., Burger King, Del Taco, Mad Greek Café, **lodging:** Royal Hawaiian Motel, **other:** Arnold's Mkt/repair, Baker Auto Parts, Baker Mkt Foods, Gen Store/NAPA, World's Largest Thermometer, repair
245	to Baker(from nb), access to same as 239
239	Zzyzx Rd, no facilities
233	Rasor Rd, **E...gas:** Rasor Rest Sta/diesel/24hr
230	Basin Rd, no facilities
221	Afton Rd, to Dunn, no facilities
217mm	**rest area both lanes, full(handicapped)facilities, phone, picnic tables, litter barrels, petwalk**
213	Field Rd, no facilities
206	Harvard Rd, to Newberry Springs, **W...other:** Lake Dolores Resort/WaterPark(1mi), Twin Lakes RV Park
198	Minneola Rd, **W...gas:** Mobil/diesel, **other:** to Lake Dolores Resort(5mi)
197mm	agricultural insp sta sb
196	to Yermo, no facilities
194	Calico Rd, **E...gas:** International Café/gas, **other:** repair
191	Ghost Town Rd, **E...gas:** Arco/24hr, Vegas/diesel/rest./24hr/@, **food:** Jack-in-the-Box, Peggy Sue's 50s Diner, **lodging:** OakTree Inn, **W...gas:** Clink's #2/diesel/@, Texaco, **lodging:** Jenny Rose' Rest., **other:** Calico GhostTown(3mi), KOA, to USMC Logistics
189	Ft Irwin Rd, **W...gas:** 76/diesel, RV camping
186	CA 58 W, to Bakersfield, **W...other:** RV camping
184	E Main, Barstow, to I-40, **E...gas:** Chevron, Mobil/diesel, Shell/repair, **food:** Burger King, Krissy's Café, McDonald's, Straw Hat Pizza, Tom's Burgers, **lodging:** Best Western, **other:** Pic'n Sav, mall, **S of I-40...gas:** Arco/24hr, **other:** Wal-Mart/auto, **W...gas:** Arco/24hr, Chevron, 76/Circle K/Subway/TCBY, Shell, **food:** Arby's, Burger King, Carl's Jr, Carrow's Rest., China Gourmet, Coco's, Del Taco, Denny's, Firehouse Italian, Golden Dragon, IHOP, Jack-in-the-Box, KFC, LJ Silver, Sizzler, Taco Bell, **lodging:** AstroBudget Motel, Best Motel, Budget Inn, Comfort Inn, Day's Inn, Desert Inn, Econolodge, Economy Inn, Executive Inn, Quality Inn, Ramada Inn, Super 8, **other:** AutoZone, Goodyear, Kragen Parts, Radio Shack, U-Haul/LP, Von's Foods
184a	I-40 E(from nb), I-40 begins/ends
183	CA 247, Barstow Rd, **E...gas:** 76/Circle K, UltraMar/Pizza Hut/gas, **other:** Rite Aid, Stater Bros Foods, **W...gas:** Chevron/24hr, **other:** HOSPITAL, Food4Less, Mojave River Valley Museum, st patrol,
181	L St, W Main, Barstow, **W...gas:** Arco/24hr, Chevron, TA/diesel/rest./@, **food:** BunBoy Rest., Pizza Palace, **lodging:** Holiday Inn Express, **other:** tires/towing
179	CA 58, to Bakersfield
178	Lenwood, to Barstow, **E...gas:** Chevron/diesel, Flying J/CountryMkt/diesel/24hr/@, Mobil/Blimpie, Shell/24hr, 76/Wendy's/diesel, **food:** Arby's, Burger King, Carl's Jr, Del Taco, Denny's, El Pollo Loco, FoodCourt, In-n-Out, Jack-in-the-Box, KFC, Panda Express, Starbucks, Subway, Taco Bell, Tommy's Burgers, **other:** Tanger Outlet/famous brands, **W...gas:** Arco/24hr, Pilot/DQ/diesel/24hr/@, Rip Griffin/Subway/diesel/24hr/@, **food:** McDonald's, **lodging:** GoodNite Inn, **other:** truck repair
175	Outlet Ctr Dr, Sidewinder Rd, **4 mi E...other:** factory outlets
169	Hodge Rd, no facilities
165	Wild Wash Rd, no facilities
161	Dale Evans Pkwy, to Apple Valley, **W...**airport
154	Stoddard Wells Rd, to Bell Mtn, **E...food:** Peggy Sue's 50s Diner, **other:** KOA, **W...gas:** Mobil, 76, Shell, **food:** Denny's, **lodging:** Howard Johnson, Motel 6, Queens Motel

CALIFORNIA

Interstate 15

N ↕ S

Victorville

153.5mm Mojave River
153b E St, no facilities
153a CA 18 E, D St, to Apple Valley, **E...gas:** 76, **other:** HOSPITAL, **W...gas:** Arco/24hr
151b Mojave Dr, Victorville, **E...gas:** 76/diesel/24hr, **lodging:** Budget Inn, **W...gas:** UltraMar, **lodging:** Economy Inn, Sunset Inn, **other:** transmissions
151a La Paz Dr, Roy Rogers Dr, **E...gas:** Chevron, Texaco/A&W/TCBY, USA, **food:** Carl's Jr, China Palace, Dairy Queen, HomeTown Buffet, IHOP, Jack-in-the-Box, **lodging:** New Corral Motel, **other:** Asian Mkt, Costco/gas, Daewoo, Food4Less/24hr, Goodyear/auto, Harley-Davidson, Honda, Jo-Ann Fabrics, Pic'n Sav Foods, Rite Aid, Toyota, Winston Tire, same as 144, **W...gas:** Arco/24hr
150 CA 18 W, Palmdale Rd, Victorville, **E... gas:** Arco/24hr, Chevron, Shell, Texaco/diesel/24hr, **food:** Baker's Drive-Thru, Burger King, Carl's Jr, Denny's, Don's Rest., Jack-in-the-Box, KFC, Richie's Diner, YumYum Donuts, **lodging:** Best Western, **other:** Cadillac/GMC, Dodge/Plymouth, PepBoys, **W...gas:** Arco/24hr, Chevron, Mobil, Shell, Thrifty, **food:** Andrew's Rest., Coco's, Del Taco, Los Domingos Mexican, LJ Silver, McDonald's, Pina's Mexican, Pizza Hut, Subway, Taco Bell, Tom's #21 Rest., **lodging:** Budget Inn, EZ 8 Motel, Ramada Inn, **other:** HOSPITAL, Aamco, AutoZone, Buick/Pontiac, Chevrolet/Hyundai, Chrysler/Jeep, Ford/Lincoln/Mercury, Honda/Toyota, Kamper's Korner RV, Kia, Nissan, Ralph's Foods, Target, Town&Country Tire, mall
147 Bear Valley Rd, to Lucerne Valley, **E...gas:** Arco/24hr, Chevron, Citgo/7-11, Mobil, 76/Circle K, Shell, **food:** A&W, Arby's, Baker's Drive-Thru, Burger King, Carl's Jr, Del Taco, Dragon Express, Hogi Yogi, John's Pizza, KFC, LJ Silver, Los Toritos Mexican, Marie Callender, McDonald's, Panda Express, Red Robin, Pizza Palace, Shakey's Pizza, Stein'n Steer, Straw Hat Pizza, TNT Café, Wienerschnitzel, Winchell's, **lodging:** American Inn, Day's Inn, Econolodge, Red Roof Inn, Super 8, **other:** America's Tire, AutoZone, Circuit City, Firestone/auto, Home Depot, Kragen Parts, Michael's, Range RV, Staples, Wal-Mart/auto, funpark, **W...gas:** Chevron/Church's, UtraMar, **food:** Applebee's, Archibald's Drive-Thru, Baja Fresh Grill, ChuckeCheese, El Pollo Loco, El Tio Pepe Mexican, Greenhouse Café, Jack-in-the-Box, Olive Garden, Outback Steaks, Red Lobster, RoadHouse Grill, Starbucks, Subway, Tony Roma, **other:** Barnes&Noble, Best Buy, JC Penney, Lowe's Whse, Mervyn's, OfficeMax, Sears/auto, mall
143 Main St, to Hesperia, Phelan, **E...gas:** Shell, Texaco/A&W/Popeyes/diesel, UltraMar/DQ/pizza, **food:** Burger King, Denny's, In-n-Out, Jack-in-the-Box, **W...gas:** Arco/24hr, **food:** Baker's Drive-thru, **lodging:** Holiday Inn Express, RV camping
141 US 395, to Adelanto, **W...gas:** Pilot/Wendy's/diesel/24hr/@, **food:** Newt's Outpost Café, **other:** repair
138 Oak Hill Rd, **E...gas:** Arco/24hr, **food:** Summit Inn/café, **W...other:** RV camping, LP
132 Cajon Summit, elevation 4260, brake check sb
131 CA 138, to Palmdale, Silverwood Lake, **E...gas:** Chevron/McDonald's/24hr, **other:** repair, **W...gas:** 76/Del Taco/Circle K/LP, Shell/diesel, **lodging:** Best Western
131mm weigh sta both lanes, elevation 3000
129 Cleghorn Rd, no facilities
124 Kenwood Ave, no facilities
123 I-215 S, to San Bernardino, **E...gas:** Arco/24hr, to Glen Helen Park
122 Glen Helen Parkway, no facilities
119 Sierra Ave, **W...gas:** Arco/Jack-in-the-Box/diesel/24hr, Shell/Del Taco/diesel/@, to Lytle Creek RA
116 Summit Ave, no facilities
115b a CA 210, Highland Ave, **E...**to Lake Arrowhead
113 Base Line Rd, **E...gas:** USA, **food:** Denny's, Jack-in-the-Box, Starbucks, **lodging:** AmeriHost, **W...gas:** Speedway
112 CA 66, Foothill Blvd, **E...gas:** Chevron, **food:** Arby's, ClaimJumper Rest., Coco's, Golden Spoon, In-n-Out, Subway, Taco Bell, Wienerschnitzel, **other:** Circuit City, Costco, Food4Less, Mervyn's, Michael's, Office Depot, OfficeMax, Radio Shack, Target, Wal-Mart/auto, **1-2 mi W...gas:** Arco, Mobil, **food:** Blimpie, BrewPub, Carl's Jr, China Hut, Denny's, FarmerBoys, Jack-in-the-Box, Old Spaghetti Factory, **lodging:** Best Western, **other:** MEDICAL CARE, AutoZone, Barnes&Noble, Best Buy, Discount Tire, Home Depot, Lowe's Whse, SteinMart, stadium

Ontario

110 4th St, **W...gas:** Arco/24hr, Mobil/Subway, Texaco/Burger King/diesel, **food:** Dave&Buster's, Carl's Jr, Chevy's Mexican, Coco's, CucinaCucina, Del Taco, FoodCourt, Jack-in-the-Box, KFC, Krispy Kreme, McDonald's, Mi Casa Mexican, NY Grill, Pat Oscar's Rest., Quizno's, Rubio's, Starbucks, Tokyo-Tokyo, Wienerschnitzel, **lodging:** AmeriSuites, **other:** America's Tire, Costco/gas, JC Penney, Ontario Mills Mall, Sam's Club
109b a I-10, E to San Bernardino, W to LA
108 Jurupa St, **E...other:** Affordable RV, BMW, Buick, Chrysler/Jeep/Dodge, GMC/Pontiac, Honda, Lexus, Mitsubishi, Nissan, Saturn, Toyota, Volvo, **W...gas:** Arco/24hr, Carl's Jr, Ford, Lincoln/Mercury, funpark
106 CA 60, E to Riverside, W to LA
103 Limonite Ave, no facilities
100 6th St, Norco Dr, **E...gas:** Arco/24hr, Chevron/24hr, **food:** Jack-in-the-Box, McDonald's, Old Town Norco, **W...gas:** Arco/24hr, UltraMar/diesel, **food:** Country Jct Rest.

Interstate 15

N
S

98 2nd St, **W...gas:** Shell/diesel, Texaco, 7-11, **food:** Burger King, Del Taco, Denny's, Domino's, Fazoli's, In-n-Out, KFC, Little Caesar's, Marie Callender, Miguel's Jr, Wienerschnitzel, **lodging:** Howard Johnson Express, **other:** MEDICAL CARE, America's Tire, AutoZone, Big O Tire, Chrysler/Plymouth, Dodge, Ford, Jeep, Mitsubishi, Pontiac, Norco RV, Staples, Target

97 Yuma Dr, Hidden Valley Pkwy, **W...gas:** Chevron, 76, Shell/diesel, **food:** Alberto's Arby's, Mexican, Carl's Jr, Gus Jr, Dairy Queen, McDonald's, Papa John's, Quizno's, Rubio's, Starbucks, Wendy's, **other:** Albertson's, Kragen Parts, SavOn Drug, Staples, Winston Tire

96b a CA 91, to Riverside, beaches, no facilities

95 Magnolia Ave, **E...gas:** Chevron/diesel, **W...gas:** Mobil, Shell, **food:** Burger King, Carl's Jr, Coco's, Donut Star, Little Caesar's, Lotus Garden, McDonald's, Pizza Palace, Sizzler, Subway, Zendejas Mexican, **other:** Kragen Parts, Ralph's Foods, Rite Aid, Sav-On Drug, Stater Bros Foods

93 Ontario Ave, to El Cerrito, **W...gas:** Arco/24hr, Chevron/24hr, **food:** Jack-in-the-Box, McDonald's, Porky's Pizza, Quizno's, Wienerschnitzel, **other:** Albertson's, Home Depot, Sam's Club, USPO, Wal-Mart/auto

92 El Cerrito Rd, **E...gas:** 76/Circle K

91 Cajalco Rd, no facilities

90 Weirick Rd, **E...other:** 7 Oaks Gen Store

88 Temescal Cyn Rd, Glen Ivy, **W...gas:** Arco/diesel/24hr, **food:** Carl's Jr, Tom's Farms, **other:** RV camping

85 Indian Truck Trail, no facilities

81 Lake St, no facilities

78 Nichols Rd, **W...gas:** Arco/24hr, **other:** VF Outlet/famous brands, auto repair

77 CA 74, Central Ave, Lake Elsinore, **E...gas:** Arco/24hr, Chevron, Mobil, **food:** Burger King, Douglas Burgers, Italian Deli, **W...other:** craft mall

Lake Elsinore

75 Main St, Lake Elsinore, **W...gas:** 76, Circle K, UltraMar/diesel, **lodging:** Elsinore Motel

73 Railroad Cyn Rd, to Lake Elsinore, **E...gas:** 76/Circle K, **food:** Denny's, El Pollo Loco, In-n-Out, KFC, Papa John's, Wienerschnitzel, **other:** GNC, Kragen Parts, Von's Foods, Wal-Mart/auto, **W...gas:** Arco, Chevron, Mobil/diesel, 7-11, **food:** Carl's Jr, Coco's, Del Taco, Don Jose's Mexican, Green Burrito, McDonald's, Pizza Hut, Sizzler, Subway, Taco Bell, **lodging:** Lake Elsinore Hotel/casino, Lake View Inn, Travel Inn, **other:** MEDICAL CARE, Albertson's, AutoZone, Big O Tire, Chevrolet, Firestone, Ford, Goodyear/auto, NAPA, Radio Shack, SavOn Drug, Stater Bros Foods

71 Bundy Cyn Rd, **W...gas:** Arco/24hr, **food:** Jack-in-the-Box

69 Baxter Rd, no facilities

68 Clinton Keith Rd, **E...HOSPITAL**

65 California Oaks Rd, Kalmia St, **E...gas:** Chevron, Mobil/diesel, 76/Circle K, Shell/Burger King/diesel, Texaco/diesel, **food:** Carl's Jr, DQ, KFC, McDonald's, Papa John's, Stew's Rest., **other:** Albertson's, Goodyear/auto, Kragen Parts, Rite Aid, SavOn Drug, Target, **W...gas:** Arco/24hr, **food:** Carrow's, Jack-in-the-Box, **other:** funpark

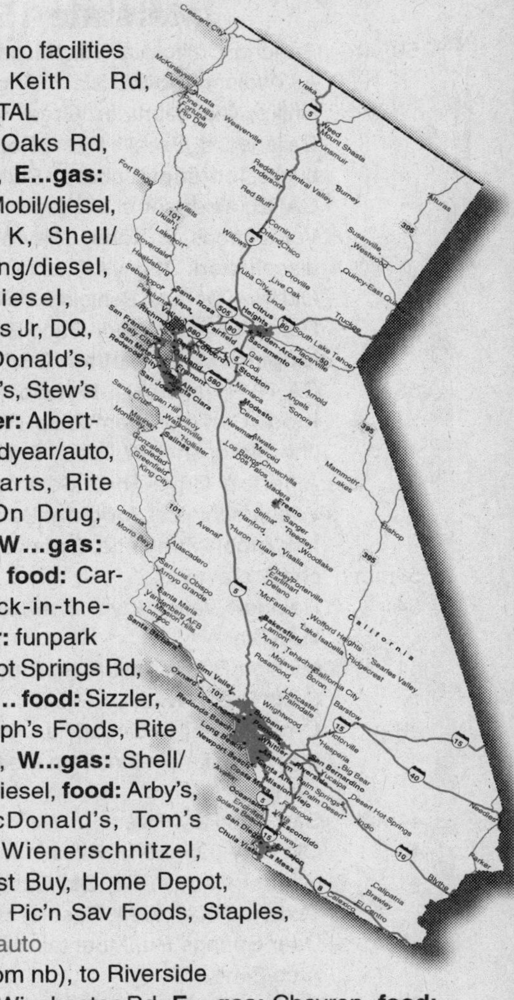

64 Murrieta Hot Springs Rd, to I-215, **E... food:** Sizzler, **other:** Ralph's Foods, Rite Aid, Ross, **W...gas:** Shell/Popeyes/diesel, **food:** Arby's, IHOP, McDonald's, Tom's Burgers, Wienerschnitzel, **other:** Best Buy, Home Depot, 99c Store, Pic'n Sav Foods, Staples, Wal-Mart/auto

63 I-215 N(from nb), to Riverside

Temecula

61 CA 79 N, Winchester Rd, **E... gas:** Chevron, **food:** Carl's Jr, Coco's, 5&Diner, Godfather's, McDonald's, Mimi's Café, On the Border, Roadhouse Grill, Souplantation, Taco Bell, TGIFriday, **other:** MEDICAL CARE, Aamco, America Tire, Big O Tire, Costco/gas, Food 4Less, Goodyear, Dodge, Ford, Honda/Acura, K-Mart, Kragen Parts, Mervyn's, PepBoys, Ralph's Food, Robinsons-May, Toyota, VW, **W...gas:** Arco/24hr, Chevron/diesel, Mobil, UltraMar, **food:** Arby's, Banzai Japanese, Billy B's Burgers, ChungKing Chinese, DQ, Del Taco, El Pollo Loco, Filippi's Café, Golden Corral, Guadalajara Mexican, Hungry Hunter, In-n-Out, Jack-in-the-Box, Richie's Diner, Sizzler, Tecate Grill, Tony Roma's, Wendy's, **lodging:** Best Western, Comfort Inn, Temecula Valley Inn, **other:** MEDICAL CARE, Big A Parts, NAPA, Rancho Richardson's RV, Stater Bros Foods, Winston Tire, st patrol

CALIFORNIA

Interstate 15

N ↕ S

59 Rancho California Rd, **E...gas:** Mobil, 76, Shell/A&W/diesel, **food:** Black Angus, Buddie's Pizza, Chili's, ClaimJumper, Great Grains Bread, Marie Callender's, Oscar's Rest., RoundTable Pizza, Starbucks, **lodging:** Embassy Suites, **other:** MEDICAL CARE, Albertson's, Michael's, SavOn Drug, Target, Von's Foods, **W...gas:** Chevron/repair, 76/Circle K/diesel, **food:** Denny's, Domino's, KFC, McDonald's, OldTown Donuts, Penfold's Mexican, Rick's Burgers, Rosa's Café, SW Grill, Taco Bell, Taco Grill, Togo's, **lodging:** Motel 6, **other:** USPO

58 CA 79 S, Temecula, to Indio, **E...gas:** Mobil, 7-11, **food:** Carl's Jr, Temecula Pizza, **lodging:** Rancho Motor Inn, **W...gas:** Shell/diesel/24hr, **food:** Alberto's Drive-Thru Mexican, Hungry Howie's, Wienerschnitzel, **lodging:** Butterfield Inn, Ramada Inn, **other:** Firestone, Goodyear/auto, RV service

55mm check sta nb

54 Rainbow Valley Blvd, **2 mi E...**gas, food, **W...**CA Insp Sta

51 Mission Rd, to Fallbrook, **2 mi E...food:** Rainbow Oaks Rest., **W...**HOSPITAL

46 CA 76, Pala, to Oceanside, **W...gas:** Mobil, **lodging:** La Estancia Inn, Pala Mesa Resort, **other:** RV camp

44mm San Luis Rey River

43 Old Hwy 395, no facilities

41 Gopher Canyon Rd, Old Castle Rd, **1 mi E...gas:** Texaco/diesel, Welk Resort, **other:** RV camping

37 Deer Springs Rd, Mountain Meadow Rd, **W...gas:** Arco/24hr

34 Centre City Pkwy(from sb)

33 El Norte Pkwy, **E...gas:** Arco/24hr, Shell/diesel, Texaco, **food:** Arby's, DQ, IHOP, Taco Bell, **lodging:** Best Western, **other:** Goodyear, SavOn Drug, Von's Foods, **W...gas:** 76, Circle K, **food:** Jack-in-the-Box, Wendy's, **other:** Von's Foods

32 CA 78, to Oceanside, **1 mi E on Mission...gas:** Mobil, **food:** Carl's Jr, ChuckeCheese, Denny's, Jack-in-the-Box, LJ Silver, Wienerschnitzel, **lodging:** Motel 6, Mt Vernon Inn, PalmTree Lodge, Super 8, **other:** AutoZone, PepBoys, K-Mart, U-Haul

31 Valley Pkwy, **E...gas:** Arco/24hr, **food:** Chili's, Coco's, McDonald's, Olive Garden, Togo's, Yoshinoya, **other:** HOSPITAL, Albertson's, Circuit City, Infiniti, mall, **W...gas:** 7-11, **food:** Burger King, Carl's Jr, Coco's, Del Taco, La Salsa, **lodging:** Comfort Inn, Holiday Inn Express, **other:** Mervyn's, Staples, Target

30 9th Ave, Auto Parkway, **W...gas:** Shell, **food:** Applebee's, Starbucks, Subway, Taco Bell, **other:** Home Depot, WorldMkt, same as 25

29 Felicita Rd, no facilities

Escondido

28 Centre City Pkwy(from nb, no return), **E...food:** Center City Café, **lodging:** Palms Inn

27 Via Rancho Pkwy, to Escondido, **E...gas:** Chevron/24hr, Shell, **food:** FoodCourt, Red Lobster, Red Robin, **other:** JC Penney, Macy's, Nordstrom's, Robinsons-May, Sears/auto, Animal Zoo, mall, **W...gas:** Shell/Subway/diesel, **food:** CA Coffee, McDonald's, Olive House Café, Tony's Steer

26 W Bernardo Dr, to Highland Valley Rd, Palmerado Rd, no facilities

24 Rancho Bernardo Rd, to Lake Poway, **E...gas:** Arco/24hr, Mobil, **other:** Baron's Foods, Von's Foods, **W...gas:** 76/Circle K, Shell/repair, Texaco/diesel/repair, **food:** Elephant Bar Rest., **lodging:** Holiday Inn, Travelodge

23 Bernardo Ctr Dr, **E...gas:** Chevron, 7-11, **food:** Burger King, Carl's Jr, Coco's, Denny's, Hunan Chinese, Jack-in-the-Box, Quizno's, Rubio's Grill, Taco Bell, **other:** Firestone/auto, Goodyear/auto, SavOn Drug

22 Camino del Norte, **E...**HOSPITAL, same as 17, **W...food:** Bernardo Pizza, Togo Eatery

21 Carmel Mtn Rd, **E...gas:** Chevron, Shell, Texaco, **food:** Baskin-Robbins, Boston Mkt, CA Pizza, Carl's Jr, Chevy's Mexican, ClaimJumper, El Pollo Loco, In-n-Out, Islands Burgers, JambaJuice, Marie Callender, McDonald's, Olive Garden, Oscar's Rest., Rubio's Grill, Schlotsky's, Subway, Taco Bell, TGIFriday, Wendy's, **lodging:** Residence Inn, **other:** Barnes&Noble, Borders Books, Circuit City, Home Depot, K-Mart, Marshall's, Mervyn's, Michael's, Ralph's Foods, Rite Aid, Ross, Staples, Trader Joes, USPO, **W... gas:** Chevron, 7-11, **food:** Jack-in-the-Box, Roberto's Mexican, **other:** Albertson's, Office Depot

19 CA 56 W, Ted Williams Pkwy, **E...food:** Tony's Pizza

18 Rancho Penasquitos Blvd, Poway Rd, **E... gas:** Arco/24hr, **food:** Manhattan Deli, **W...gas:** Exxon, Mobil, 76, 7-11, **food:** Burger King, IHOP, Little Caesar's, McDonald's, Subway, Taco Bell, **lodging:** La Quinta

17 Mercy Rd, Scripps Poway Pkwy, no facilities

16 Mira Mesa Blvd, to Lake Miramar, **E... food:** ChuckeCheese, Denny's, Filippi's Pizza, Golden Crown Chinese, **lodging:** Quality Suites, **other:** Medco Drug, USPO, **W...gas:** Arco/24hr, Mobil, 76, Shell, **food:** Applebee's, Arby's, Burger King, Café China, In-n-Out, Islands Burgers, Jack-in-the-Box, Jamba Juice, Little Caesar's, McDonald's, Mimi's Café, On the Border, Rubio's Grill, Starbucks, Subway, Wendy's, **other:** MEDICAL CARE, Albertson's, Barnes&Noble, Home Depot, Longs Drug, Old Navy, Pic'n Sav Foods, Ralph's Foods, Rite Aid, Ross, SavOn Drug, USPO

Interstate 15

N ↕ S

San Diego Area

15 Carroll Canyon Rd, to Miramar College, **E...food:** Carl's Jr
14 Pomerado Rd, Miramar Rd, **W...gas:** Arco/diesel, Chevron, Mobil, Shell/24hr, Texaco/diesel, **food:** Acapulco Mexican, Amber's Rest., Carl's Jr, Keith's Rest., Marie Callender's, Pizza Hut, Subway, **lodging:** Best Western, Budget Inn, Holiday Inn, **other:** Aamco, Audi/Porsche/VW, Kragen Parts, Land Rover, NAPA
13 Miramar Way, US Naval Air Station
12 CA 163 S(from sb), to San Diego, no facilities
11 to CA 52, no facilities
10 Clairemont Mesa Blvd, **W...food:** Carl's Jr, Giovanni's Pizza, McDonald's, Mr Chick Rest., Subway, Sunny Donuts, Taco Bell, Wendy's
9 CA 274, Balboa Ave, no facilities
8 Aero Dr, **W...gas:** Arco/24hr, Shell, **food:** Baja Fresh, D'Amato's Pizza, Fong Chinese, Jack-in-the-Box, McDonald's, Roberto's Café, Sizzler, Starbucks, Stix Chinese, Submarina, Taco Bell, **lodging:** Best Western, Holiday Inn, **other:** Fry's Electronics, Radio Shack, Von's Foods, Wal-Mart/auto
7b Friars Rd W, **W...**San Diego Stadium
7a Friars Rd E, no facilities
6b I-8, E to El Centro, W to beaches
6a Adams Ave, downtown
5b El Cajon Blvd, downtown
5a University Ave, downtown
3 I-805, N to I-5, S to San Ysidro
2b (2c from nb)CA 94 W, downtown
2a Market St, downtown
1c National Ave, Ocean View Blvd
1b (from sb)I-5 S, to Chula Vista
1a (from sb)I-5 N. I-15 begins/ends on I-5

Interstate 40

E ↕ W

California uses road names/numbers. Exit number is approximate mile marker.

Exit # Services
155 Colorado River, California/Arizona state line, Pacific/Mountain time zone
153 Park Moabi Rd, to Rte 66, **N...**boating, camping
149mm weigh sta eb, insp wb
148 5 Mile Rd, to Topock, Rte 66, no facilities

Needles

144 US 95 S, E Broadway, Needles, **N...gas:** Arco/24hr, Chevron/diesel, Shell/diesel, **food:** Burger King, Vito's Pizza, **other:** MEDICAL CARE, Basha's Foods, Rite Aid, U-Haul, **S...lodging:** Super 8
142 J St, Needles, **N...gas:** 76/24hr, **food:** Jack-in-the-Box, McDonald's, **lodging:** Travelers Inn, **other:** NAPA, **S...food:** Denny's, **lodging:** Day's Inn, Motel 6, **other:** st patrol
141 W Broadway, River Rd, Needles, **N...gas:** Chevron/diesel/24hr, **food:** Denny's, KFC, **lodging:** Best Motel, Econolodge, River Valley Motel, Stardust Motel, Travelodge, **other:** Goodyear/auto, diesel repair, **S...gas:** Arco/24hr, Chevron/diesel/24hr, Mobil/diesel, Shell/DQ/24hr, **food:** Carl's Jr, Hui's Rest., Taco Bell, **lodging:** Best Chalet Inn, Best Western, Budget Inn, Relax Inn, **other:** Chevrolet/Cadillac/Buick/GMC, RV/tire/repair
139 River Rd Cutoff(from eb), **N...**rec area, Hist Rte 66, **other:** KOA, Desert View RV Park
133 US 95 N, to Searchlight, Las Vegas, to Rte 66, no facilities
120 Water Rd, no facilities
115 Mountain Springs Rd, High Springs Summit, elev 2770
107 Goffs Rd, **N...**gas/diesel/food, Hist Rte 66
106mm rest area both lanes, full(handicapped)facilities, phone, picnic tables, litter barrels, petwalk
100 Essex Rd, Essex, **N...**to Providence Mtn SP, Mitchell Caverns
78 Kelbaker Rd, to Amboy, Kelso, to E Mojave Nat Preserve, **S...**Hist Rte 66, **other:** RV camping
50 Ludlow, **N...gas:** 76/DQ/24hr, **S...gas:** Chevron/24hr, **lodging:** Ludlow Motel
33 Hector Rd, to Hist Rte 66, no facilities
28mm rest area both lanes, full(handicapped)facilities, phone, picnic tables, litter barrels, petwalk
23 Ft Cady Rd, **N...gas:** Wesco/diesel/24hr, **S...lodging:** Newberry Mtn Motel/RV Park
18 Newberry Springs, **N...other:** UltraMar/diesel, **S...gas:** Shell/Taco Bell/LP, **other:** RV camp
12 Barstow-Daggett Airport, **N...**airport
7 Daggett, **N...gas:** Daggett Trkstp/diesel, **other:** RV camping(2mi), to Calico Ghost Town
5 Nebo St, to Hist Rte 66, no facilities
2 USMC Logistics Base, no facilities

CALIFORNIA

Interstate 40

E ↕ W Barstow

1 Montara Rd, Barstow, **N...gas:** Chevron, Mobil/diesel, Shell/repair, **food:** Burger King, Krissy's Café, McDonald's, Straw Hat Pizza, Tom's Burgers, **lodging:** Best Western, **other:** Pic'n Sav Foods, **1 mi N...gas:** Arco/24hr, Chevron, 76/Circle K/Subway/TCBY, Shell, **food:** Arby's, Burger King, Carl's Jr, Carrow's Rest., China Gourmet, Coco's, Del Taco, Denny's, FireHouse Italian, Golden Dragon, IHOP, Jack-in-the-Box, KFC, LJ Silver, Sizzler, Taco Bell, **lodging:** AstroBudget Motel, Best Motel, Budget Inn, Comfort Inn, Day's Inn, Desert Inn, Econolodge, Economy Inn, Executive Inn, Quality Inn, Ramada Inn, Super 8, **other:** AutoZone, Kragen Parts, Radio Shack, U-Haul/LP, Von's Foods, **S...gas:** Arco/24hr, **other:** Wal-Mart/auto

0mm I-40 begins/ends on I-15 in Barstow.

Interstate 80

E ↕ W Truckee

Exit #	Services
208	California/Nevada state line
201	Farad, no facilities
199	Floristan, no facilities
194	Hirschdale Rd, **N...**to Boca Dam, Stampede Dam, **S...gas:** United Trails Gen Store, **other:** RV camping, boating, camping
191	weigh sta wb
190	Prosser Village Rd, no facilities
188	CA 89 N, CA 267, Truckee, to N Shore Lake Tahoe, **N...other:** Coachland RV Park, USFS, **S...gas:** 76, Shell, **food:** El Toro Bravo Mexican, Ponderosa Deli, Taco Sta, WagonTrain Café, **lodging:** Best Western, Truckee Hotel, **other:** info, same as 184
186	Central Truckee(no eb return), **S...gas:** 76, **food:** El Toro Bravo Mexican, Ponderosa Café, Wagontrain Café, **lodging:** Star Hotel, Swedish House B&B
185	CA 89 S, to N Lake Tahoe, **N...gas:** Sierra Superstop, 7-11, **food:** Burger King, DQ, La Bamba Mexican, Little Caesar's, Pizza Jct, Pizza Shack, Port of Subs, Sizzler, **other:** MEDICAL CARE, Allied Parts, Book Shelf, CarQuest, Gateway Pets, GNC, NAPA, New Moon Natural Foods, Rite Aid, Safeway, **S...gas:** Shell, **food:** Burger King, KFC, McDonald's, Pizzaria, Subway, **lodging:** Super 8, Truckee Inn, **other:** Albertson's, Longs Drugs, auto repair, to Squaw Valley, RV camping
184	Donner Pass Rd, Truckee, **N...gas:** Shell/diesel, **lodging:** Sunset Inn, **other:** factory outlet/famous brands, **S...gas:** Chevron/diesel/24hr, 76, **food:** Beginning Rest., Donner House Rest., Donner Lake Pizza, **lodging:** Alpine Country Lodge, Holiday Inn Express, **other:** chain service, to Donner SP, RV camping
181mm	vista point both lanes
180	Donner Lake(from wb), **S...lodging:** Donner Lake Village Resort
177mm	**Donner Summit, elev 7239, rest area both lanes, full(handicapped)facilities, view area, phone, picnic tables, litter barrels, petwalk**
176	Castle Park, Boreal Ridge Rd, **S...lodging:** Boreal Inn/rest., **other:** Pacific Crest Trailhead, skiing
174	Soda Springs, Norden, **S...gas:** 76/LP/diesel, **lodging:** Donner Summit Lodge, **other:** chain services
171	Kingvale, **S...gas:** Shell
168	Rainbow Rd, to Big Bend, **S...lodging:** Rainbow Lodge/rest., **other:** RV camping
166	Big Bend(from eb), ranger sta, RV camping, same as 168
165	Cisco Grove, **N...other:** RV camping, skiing, snowmobiling, **S...gas:** Chevron/24hr, **other:** chain serv
164	Eagle Lakes Rd, **N...other:** RV camping
161	CA 20 W, to Nevada City, Grass Valley, no facilities
160	Yuba Gap, **S...other:** snowpark, phone, picnic tables, boating, camping, skiing
158	Laing Rd, **S...lodging:** Rancho Sierra Inn/café
157mm	vista point wb
158a	Emigrant Gap(from eb), **S...gas:** Shell/Burger King/diesel/24hr, **lodging:** Rancho Sierra Inn/café, phone
156	Nyack Rd, Emigrant Gap, **S...gas:** Shell/Burger King/diesel, **food:** Nyack Café
155	Blue Canyon, no facilities
150	Drum Forebay, no facilities
148b	Baxter, **N...other:** RV camping, chainup services, food, phone
148a	Crystal Springs, no facilities
146	Alta, no facilities
145	Dutch Flat, **N...food:** Monte Vista Rest., **other:** RV camping, **S...gas:** Tesoro/diesel, **other:** CHP, chainup services
143	Gold Run(from wb), **N...**gas/diesel, food, phone, chainup
143mm	**rest area both lanes, full(handicapped)facilities, phone, picnic tables, litter barrels, petwalk**
142	Gold Run, **N...**gas/diesel, food, phone, chainup services
140	Magra Rd, Rollins Lake Rd, Secret Town Rd, no facilities
139	Rollins Lake Road(from wb), RV camping
135	CA 174, Colfax, to Grass Valley, **N...gas:** Chevron, 76/diesel, **food:** McDonald's, Pizza Factory, Rosy's Café, Taco Bell, Togo's, **lodging:** Colfax Motel, **other:** Sierra Mkt Foods, NAPA, **S...gas:** Chevron/diesel, Tesoro/diesel, **food:** Dave's Tacos, Shang Garden Chinese, Subway, Sierra RV Ctr
133	Canyon Way, to Colfax, **N...food:** Dingus McGee's, **S...food:** California Cantina, Mexican Villa Rest., **other:** Chevrolet, Sierra NV Tire/repair
131	Cross Rd, to Weimar, park&ride, RV camping
130	W Paoli Lane, to Weimar, **S...gas:** Weimar Store/diesel
129	Heather Glen, elev 2000 ft, no facilities

Colfax

Interstate 80

E ↕ W

Auburn

128 Applegate, **N...gas:** Beacon/diesel, **lodging:** Firehouse Motel, **other:** chainup services

125 Clipper Gap, Meadow Vista, **S...other:** RV camping, park&ride

124 Dry Creek Rd, **N...other:** CA Conservation Corps, **S...other:** park&ride

123 Bell Rd, **N...other:** HOSPITAL, KOA(3mi), **S...food:** HQ House Rest.

121 Foresthill Rd, Ravine Rd, Auburn, **N...other:** RV camping/dump, **S...gas:** 76, **food:** Burger King, Ikeba's Burgers, Jack-in-the-Box, Sizzler, **lodging:** Best Western, Country Squire Inn/rest., same as 117

120 (from eb)Lincolnway, Auburn, **N...gas:** Flyers Gas, Sierra, Thrifty, **food:** Arby's, Denny's, JimBoy's Tacos, Pizza Hut, Taco Bell/24hr, Wienerschnitzel, Wimpy's Burgers, **lodging:** Best Inn, Foothills Motel, Motel 6, Sleep Inn, Super 8, **S...gas:** Arco/diesel/24hr, Chevron/diesel/24hr, 76, Shell/diesel, **food:** Bakers Square, Baskin-Robbins, Burger King, Burrito Shop, Carl's Jr, Country Waffle, DQ, Ikea's Burgers, Izzy's BurgerStop, Jack-in-the-Box, KFC, LaBonte's Rest., Lyon's Rest., McDonald's, Sizzler, Thai Cuisine, **lodging:** Best Western, Country Squire Inn, Travelodge, **other:** Raley's Foods

120 Russell Ave(from wb), **S...gas:** Shell/diesel, **other:** Ryder Trucks, U-Haul, same as 117

119c Elm Ave, Auburn, **N...gas:** 76, Shell, **food:** Blimpie, Foster's Freeze, Taco Bell, **lodging:** Holiday Inn, **other:** Albertson's, Grocery Outlet, Longs Drug, Staples, Thrifty Foods, U-Haul, **S...gas:** Sierra

119b CA 49, Auburn, to Grass Valley, Placerville, **N...gas:** Shell, **food:** In-n-Out, Marie Callender's, **lodging:** Holiday Inn, **other:** MEDICAL CARE, Staples, Thrifty Foods, **S...food:** Chevy's FreshMex(2mi)

119a Maple St, Nevada St, Old Town Auburn, **S...gas:** Budget, **food:** Tiopete Mexican

118 Ophir Rd, **N...food:** Pizza Lunch, Pop's Place Foods

116 CA 193, to Lincoln, **S...other:** Gamel RV Ctr

115 Newcastle, **N...other:** transmissions, **S...gas:** Arco/diesel/24hr, Exxon/diesel, **food:** Denny's, CHP

112 Penryn, **N...gas:** Beacon/diesel/LP, **food:** CattleBaron's Café, Old Ground Cow Rest.

110 Horseshoe Bar Rd, to Loomis, **N...food:** Burger King, Taco Bell, Raley's Foods, RoundTable Pizza

109 Sierra College Blvd, **N...gas:** Chevron/McDonald's/diesel, Citgo/7-11, 76/diesel, **food:** Carl's Jr, **lodging:** Day's Inn, **other:** Camping World RV Service/supplies, KOA

108 Rocklin Rd, **N...gas:** Beacon, Exxon, **food:** Arby's, Baskin-Robbins, Blimpie, Burger King, Carl's Jr, China Gourmet, Denny's, Jack-in-the-Box, Jasper's Giant Burgers, KFC, Outback Steaks, Papa Murphy's, Red Pepper Café, RoundTable Pizza, Starbucks, Subway, Swank's Dinner Theatre, Taco Bell, **lodging:** Howard Johnson, Ramada Ltd, **other:** MEDICAL CARE, Camping World RV Service, CarQuest, Fabric Shop, Gamel RV Ctr, GNC, Harley-Davidson, Kragen Parts, Land Rover, Longs Drug, Radio Shack, Safeway, **S...gas:** Arco/24hr, **food:** Susanne Rest./bakery, **lodging:** Rocklin Park Hotel

106 CA 65, to Lincoln, Marysville, **1 mi N on Stanford Ranch Rd... gas:** 76, Shell, **food:** Applebee's, Carl's Jr, Jack-in-the-Box, **lodging:** Comfort Suites, **other:** Barnes&Noble, FoodSource, Costco, JC Penney, Macy's, Marshall's, Nordstrom's, Old Navy, Wal-Mart

105b Taylor Rd, to Rocklin(from eb), **N...food:** Cattlemen's Rest., **other:** Albertson's(1mi), Complete RV Ctr, **S...gas:** 76/Burger King, **lodging:** Hilton Garden, Larkspur Landing Hotel, Residence Inn, **other:** HOSPITAL

105a Atlantic St, Eureka Rd, **S...gas:** Pacific Pride/diesel, 76, Shell, **food:** Brookfield's Rest., Black Angus, Carver's Steaks, In-n-Out, Taco Bell, Wendy's, **lodging:** Marriott, **other:** America'sTire, Buick/GMC, Chevrolet, Ford, CompUSA, Home Depot, Nissan, OfficeMax, Sam's Club, mall

103b a Douglas Blvd, **N...gas:** Arco/24hr, Beacon, Exxon, 76, **food:** BBQ, Burger King, ClaimJumper, Delicia's Mexican, Jack-in-the-Box, KFC, McDonald's, Mtn Mike's Pizza, Taco Bell, Taquiera Mexican, **lodging:** Best Western, Extended Stay America, Heritage Inn, **other:** HOSPITAL, Big O Tire, Chevrolet, $Tree, Firestone/auto, Goodyear, Kragen Parts, Michael's, Old Navy, Radio Shack, Ross, Trader Joe, **S...gas:** Arco/24hr, Chevron/24hr, Shell, Carrow's/24hr, **food:** Carl's Jr, Del Taco, Denny's, Outback Steaks, Quality Inn, Oxford Suites, **other:** Albertson's, Lincoln/Mercury, Mervyn's, Office Depot, Rite Aid

102 Riverside Ave, Auburn Blvd, to Roseville, **N...gas:** Arco/24hr, **other:** MEDICAL CARE, **S...gas:** Exxon/diesel, Shell, UltraMar, **food:** California Burgers, Jack-in-the-Box, JimBoy's Tacos, **other:** AutoZone, BMW Motorcycles, K-Mart, Riebes Parts, Schwab Tire, Village RV Ctr, Winston Tire

CALIFORNIA

Interstate 80

E ↕ W

Citrus Hts

100 Antelope Rd, to Citrus Heights, **N...gas:** 76, 7-11, **food:** Burger King, Carl's Jr, Del Taco, Giant Pizza, KFC, Little Caesar's, LJ Silver, McDonald's, RoundTable Pizza, Subway, Taco Bell, Wendy's, **other:** Albertson's, $Tree, Raley's Foods, Rite Aid, USPO

100mm weigh sta both lanes

98 Greenback Lane, Elkhorn Blvd, Orangedale, Citrus Heights, **N...gas:** 76/service, Circle K, **food:** Carl's Jr, Leyva's Mexican, McDonald's, Pizza Hut, Subway, Taco Bell, **other:** MEDICAL CARE, Longs Drug, Safeway

96 Madison Ave, **N...gas:** Beacon/24hr, Shell, **food:** Brookfield's Rest., Denny's, Foster's Freeze, **lodging:** Motel 6, Super 8, **other:** Scandia Funpark, to McClellan AFB, **S...gas:** Arco/24hr, 76, Shell/repair, 7-11, **food:** A&W, Boston Mkt, Burger King, Carl's Jr, El Pollo Loco, Eppie's Rest., Humberto's Mexican, IHOP, Jack-in-the-Box, LJ Silver, McDonald's, Subway, Taco Bell, T-Bonz Steaks, Wienerschnitzel, **lodging:** Holiday Inn, La Quinta, **other:** Acura/Porsche, America's Tire, Chevrolet, Ford/Isuzu, Goodyear, Office Depot, PepBoys, Target, U-Haul

94b Auburn Blvd, **S...food:** Burger King, **lodging:** Travelodge, to same as 94

94a Watt Ave, **N...lodging:** Day's Inn, **other:** McClellan AFB, **S... gas:** Arco/24hr, 76/diesel, Shell, 7-11, **food:** Burger King, Carl's Jr, Carrow's Rest., Church's, DQ, Denny's, Golden Egg Café, KFC, Pizza Hut, Taco Bell, Wendy's, **lodging:** Best Inn, Motel 6, Travelodge, **other:** Firestone

93 Longview Dr, no facilities

92 Winters St, no facilities

Sacramento

91 Raley Blvd, Marysville Blvd, to Rio Linda, **N...gas:** Arco/24hr, Chevron/diesel/24hr, **food:** Angelina's Pizza, **S...other:** Mkt Basket Foods, tires

90 Norwood Ave, **N...gas:** Arco/Jack-in-the-Box/24hr, Shell/diesel, **food:** McDonald's, Subway, **other:** Chief Parts, Rite Aid, SavMax Foods

89 Northgate Blvd, Sacramento, **N...other:** Fry's Electronics, **S...gas:** Circle K, Shell, Texaco/diesel, Valero/diesel, **food:** Burger King, Carl's Jr, IHOP, KFC, Lamp Post Pizza, LJ Silver, McDonald's, Taco Bell, **lodging:** Extended Stay America, Red Roof Inn, **other:** Goodyear/auto, K-Mart, PepBoys, transmissions

88 Truxel Rd, **N...gas:** Shell/diesel, **food:** Applebee's, Del Taco, In-n-Out, Jamba Juice, On the Border, Quizno's, Starbucks, Steve's Place Pizza, **other:** Arco Arena, Home Depot, Michael's, Raley's Depot, Ross, Staples, Wal-Mart, mall

86 I-5, N to Redding, S to Sacramento, to CA 99 N

85 W El Camino, **N...gas:** Chevron/diesel/24hr, Shell/diesel/rest., **food:** Burger King, Subway, **lodging:** Microtel

83 Reed Ave, **N... food:** Jack-in-the-Box, Tony's Rest., **other:** Ford Trucks, diesel repair, **S...gas:** Arco/24hr

82 US 50 E, W Sacramento, no facilities

81 Enterprise Blvd, W Sacramento, **N...gas:** Chevron/24hr, Shell/24hr, Valero/diesel, Eppie's Rest/24hr, **lodging:** Granada Inn, **S...gas:** 76/diesel, **food:** Burger King, Denny's, KOA

78 Chiles Rd, no facilities

75 Mace Blvd, **S...gas:** Chevron/24hr, DieselFuel, 76, Shell, **food:** Burger King, Cindy's Rest., Denny's, Lamp Post Pizza, McDonald's, Subway, Taco Bell/24hr, Wendy's, **lodging:** Howard Johnson, Motel 6, **other:** Chevrolet/Toyota, Chrysler/Jeep, Ford/Mercury/Nissan, Honda, La Mesa RV Ctr, Mazda/VW, Nugget Mkt Foods, Pontiac/Buick/GMC, to Mace Ranch

73 Olive St(from wb, no EZ return), **N...other:** Fair Deal RV Ctr

72b a Richards Blvd, Davis, **N...gas:** Shell/24hr, **food:** In-n-Out, **lodging:** Davis Motel/Café Italia, University Park Inn, **other:** NAPA, **S...gas:** Chevron, **food:** Del Taco, KFC, RoundTable Pizza, Wendy's, **lodging:** Hawthorn Suites, Holiday Inn Express, **other:** Kragen Parts

71 to UC Davis

70 CA 113 N, to Woodland, **N...**HOSPITAL

69 Kidwell Rd, no facilities

67 Pedrick Rd, **N...gas:** 76/LP

66b Milk Farm Rd(from wb), no facilities

66a CA 113 S, Currey Rd, to Dixon, **S...gas:** Arco, CFN/diesel, 76/Popeye's, Shell/diesel, **food:** Cattlemen's Rest., Jack-in-the-Box, **1 mi S...gas:** Beacon, Citgo/7-11, **other:** Ford

64 Pitt School Rd, to Dixon, **S... gas:** Chevron/24hr, Valero, **food:** Arby's, Burger King, Chevy's Mexican, Denny's, Domino's, IHOP/24hr, LaBella's Pizza, Mary's Pizza, McDonald's, Pizza Hut, Solano Bakery, Subway, Taco Bell, Valley Grill, **lodging:** Best Western, Microtel, **other:** MEDICAL CARE, Kragen Parts, Radio Shack, Safeway

63 Dixon Rd, Midway Rd, **N...gas:** Chevron/diesel, **S...gas:** Arco/24hr, Shell/tune, **food:** Carl's Jr, KFC, Los Altos Mexican, **lodging:** Super 8, **other:** Dixon Fruit Mkt

60 Midway Rd, Lewis Rd, **N...**RV camping

59 Meridian Rd, Weber Rd, no facilities

57 Leisure Town Rd, **S...gas:** Beacon/gas, **food:** Black Oak Rest., Jack-in-the-Box, Joe's Rest., Hick'ry Pit BBQ, SplitFire Rest., **lodging:** Fairfield Inn, Motel 6, Residence Inn, Vaca Valley Inn, **other:** Chevrolet, Chrysler/Plymouth/Dodge/Jeep, Honda, Mazda, Nissan, Toyota, VW

Vacaville

56 I-505 N, to Winters, no facilities

56 Orange Dr, same as 55 and 58

55 Monte Vista Ave, **N...gas:** Beacon/diesel, Citgo/7-11, 76, Shell, **food:** Arby's, Burger King, City Sports Grill, Denny's, Hisui Japanese, IHOP, McDonald's, Murillo's Mexican, Nations Burger, NutTree Rest., Pelayo's Mexican, RoundTable Pizza, Taco Bell, Wendy's, **lodging:** Best Western, Royal Motel, Super 8, **other:** HOSPITAL, America Tire, Firestone/auto, Goodyear/auto, U-Haul, Winston Tire, transmissions, **S...gas:** Arco/24hr,

Interstate 80

E ↕ W

Chevron/24hr, **food:** Applebee's, Carl's Jr, Chevy's FreshMex, Chili's, Chubby's Diner, CoffeeTree Rest., HomeTown Buffet, In-n-Out, Italian Café, Jack-in-the-Box, KFC, Starbucks, Tahoe Joe's Rest., Togo's, **lodging:** Courtyard, **other:** CompUSA, Goodyear, Mervyn's, Michael's, Old Navy, Ross, Safeway, Sam's Club, Staples, Target, Vacaville Stores/famous brands, Wal-Mart/auto

54b Mason St, Peabody Rd, **N...gas:** Beacon/Taco Time/diesel, Petro, **lodging:** Hawthorn Suites, **other:** AutoZone, NAPA, Schwab Tire, **S...gas:** Arco, Shell/repair, **food:** Carl's Jr, Solano's Bakery, Wok'n Roll Chinese, **other:** Aegean Tires, Costco, Ford/Mercury, Goodyear/auto, PepBoys

54a Davis St, **N...gas:** Chevron/McDonald's, **food:** Outback Steaks, **other:** CarQuest, **S...gas:** QuikStop, **other:** Cecil's Repair

53 Merchant St, Alamo Dr, **N...gas:** Chevron, Shell/diesel, **food:** Adalberto's Mexican, Bakers Square, Lyon's/24hr, **lodging:** Alamo Inn, Monte Vista Motel, **S...food:** Jack-in-the-Box, KFC, McDonald's, Pizza Hut, Port Subs, **other:** Radio Shack, SavMax Foods/24hr

52 Cherry Glen Rd(from wb), no facilities

51b Pena Adobe Rd, **S...lodging:** Ranch Hotel

51a Lagoon Valley Rd, Cherry Glen, no facilities

48 N Texas St, Fairfield, **S...gas:** Arco/24hr, Chevron, Shell, **food:** Burger King, Lou's Jct Rest., RoundTable Pizza, **lodging:** EZ 8 Motel, **other:** GNC, K-Mart, Raley's Foods

47 Waterman Blvd, **N...food:** Dynasty Chinese, Hungry Hunter Rest., RoundTable Pizza, Strings Italian, TCBY, **other:** Buick/Pontiac/GMC, Chevrolet/Cadillac, Safeway, Village RV Ctr, **S...**to Travis AFB, museum

Fairfield

45 Travis Blvd, Fairfield, **N...gas:** Arco/24hr, Chevron/24hr, Shell/diesel, **food:** Burger King, Denny's, In-n-Out, McDonald's, NY Pizza, Taco Bell, **lodging:** Holiday Inn, Motel 6, **other:** Raley's Foods, Harley-Davidson, Ford, Hyundai/Daewoo, Nissan, CHP, **S...gas:** Shell, **food:** Blue Frog Brewery/rest., Chevy's Mexican, FreshChoice Rest., Great Wall Chinese, Marie Callender's, Mimi's Café, Red Lobster, Subway, **other:** HOSPITAL, Barnes&Noble, Best Buy, Circuit City, Firestone/auto, JC Penney, Macy's, Mazda, Mervyn's, Michael's, OfficeMax, Old Navy, Ross, Sears/auto, Trader Joe's, mall

44 W Texas St, Fairfield, same as 46, **N...gas:** Shell/diesel, **food:** ChuckeCheese, Gordito's Mexican, **lodging:** Sleepy Hollow Motel, **other:** Mazda/Subaru, Suzuki, Target, **S...gas:** Exxon, **food:** DQ, Jack-in-the-Box, Johanne's Diner, McDonald's, Nations Burgers, Pelayo's Mexican, **lodging:** Travelodge, **other:** Acura/Honda, Home Depot, Isuzu, Nissan, PepBoys, PostMasters, SavMax Foods, Target, Toyota, Walgreen

43 CA 12 E, Abernathy Rd, Suisun City, **S...other:** Wal-Mart, Budweiser Plant

42mm weigh sta both lanes, phone

41 Suisan Valley Rd, **S...gas:** Arco/24hr, Chevron, 76/diesel/24hr, Shell/diesel, **food:** Arby's, Bravo's Pizza, Burger King, Carl's Jr, Denny's, Green Bamboo Chinese, McDonald's, Old SF Expresso, Subway, Taco Bell, Wendy's, **lodging:** Best Western, Hampton Inn, Holiday Inn Express, Inns of America, Overnighter Lodge, **other:** Camping World RV Service, Scandia FunCtr

40 I-680(from wb)

39b CA 12 W, to Napa, Green Valley Rd, **N...other:** Longs Drug, Safeway, **S...**Saturn

39a Red Top Rd, **N...gas:** 76/Circle K/24hr, **food:** Jack-in-the-Box

36 American Canyon Rd, no facilities

34mm rest area wb, full(handicapped)facilities, info, phone, picnic tables, litter barrels, petwalk, vista parking

33b a CA 37, to San Rafael, Columbus Pkwy, **N...lodging:** Best Western

Vallejo

32 Redwood St, to Vallejo, **N...gas:** 76, **food:** Denny's, Panda Garden, **lodging:** Day's Inn, Holiday Inn, Motel 6, **other:** HOSPITAL, **S...gas:** Arco, Shell, **food:** Applebee's, Black Angus, Cham Thai Rest., Chevy's Mexican, IHOP, Little Caesar's, Lyon's Rest., McDonald's, Mtn Mike's Pizza, Olive Garden, Red Lobster, Subway, Susie's Café, Taco Bell, Wendy's, **lodging:** Comfort Inn, Ramada Inn, **other:** AutoZone, Buick/GMC, Costco, Hancock Fabrics, Home Depot, Honda, Longs Drug, OfficeMax, PepBoys, Radio Shack, Ross, Safeway, SaveMart Foods, Target, Toyota

31b Tennessee St, to Vallejo, **N... food:** Baskin-Robbins, Lucky Garden Chinese, Scotty's Rest., **other:** Grocery Outlet, Medicine Shoppe, **S... gas:** 76, Valero, **food:** Jack-in-the-Box, Pacifica Pizza, **lodging:** Great Western Inn, Quality Inn, **other:** USPO

31a Solano Ave, Springs Rd, **N...gas:** Chevron/diesel/24hr, **food:** Burger King, Church's, Nitti Gritti Rest., Schezuan Chinese, Taco Bell, **lodging:** Best Value Inn, Deluxe Inn, **other:** Ford, Albertson's, Rite Aid, U-Haul, **S...gas:** Beacon, Chemco, Chevron, QuikStop, **food:** Bud's Burgers, DQ, McDonald's, Panino Italian, Pizza Hut, RoundTable Pizza, SmorgaBob's, Subway, **lodging:** Islander Motel, **other:** Kragen Parts, Walgreen

CALIFORNIA

Interstate 80

E ↕ W

30c Georgia St, Central Vallejo, **N...gas:** Safeway, **other:** Ford, **S...gas:** Shell/Starbucks/diesel, **food:** Mandarin Chinese, **lodging:** Crest Motel
30b Benicia Rd(from wb), **S...gas:** Shell/diesel
30a I-780, to Martinez, no facilities
29b Magazine St, Vallejo, **N...gas:** Shell, **food:** Rod's Hickory Pit/24hr, **lodging:** Economy Inn, El Curtola Motel, 7 Motel, **other:** TradeWinds RV Park, **S...gas:** 7-11, **food:** McDonald's, **lodging:** Knight's Inn
29a CA 29, Maritime Academy Dr, Vallejo, **N...gas:** Arco/diesel, Chevron/24hr, **food:** Subway, **lodging:** Motel 6, Vallejo Inn
28mm toll plaza, pay toll from eb
27 Crockett Rd, Crockett, to Rodeo, **N...food:** seafood rest.
26 Cummings Skyway, to CA 4(from wb), to Martinez, no facilities
24 Willow Ave, to Rodeo, **N...gas:** 76/diesel, **food:** Straw Hat Pizza, **other:** MEDICAL CARE, NAPA, Safeway/24hr, Rodeo Drugs, USPO, **S...gas:** 76/Circle K/diesel, **food:** Burger King, Jamalo's Pizza
23 CA 4, Hercules, to Stockton, **N...gas:** Shell, **food:** Jack-in-the-Box, **S on Sycamore...food:** Burgerama, McDonald's, RoundTable Pizza, Subway, Taco Bell, Valley Ice Cream/deli, **other:** MEDICAL CARE, Albertson's, Rite Aid, USPO
22 Pinole Valley Rd, **S... gas:** Arco/24hr, Beacon, Chevron/diesel, Shell, 76, 7-11, **food:** Jack-in-the-Box, Pizza Plenty, Red Onion Rest., Rico's Mexican, Ristorante Italiano, Subway, Waffle Shop, Zip's Rest., **other:** Albertson's
21 Appian Way, **N... gas:** Beacon, **food:** McDonald's, **other:** MEDICAL CARE, Kragen Parts, Longs Drug, Safeway, **S...gas:** Valero/diesel, **food:** Burger King, Carl's Jr, HomeTown Buffet, HotDog Sta, KFC, LJ Silver, RoundTable Pizza, Sizzler, Starbucks, Taco Bell, Wendy's, **lodging:** Day's Inn, Motel 6, **other:** Albertson's, Best Buy, Goodyear/auto, K-Mart, Radio Shack
20 Richmond Pkwy, to I-580 W, **N...gas:** Chevron, **food:** McDonald's, IHOP, **other:** Barnes&Noble, Chrysler/Plymouth/Jeep, Circuit City, Ford, OfficeMax, Ross, **S...gas:** Chevron, Shell/diesel, **food:** Applebee's, Chuck Steak, In-n-Out, Outback Steaks, RoundTable Pizza, **other:** Food4Less, GoodGuys, Kragen Parts, Old Navy, Mervyn's, Staples, Target
19b Hilltop Dr, to Richmond, **N...gas:** Chevron, **food:** Chevy's Mexican, Olive Garden, Red Lobster, Subway, Tokyo Rest., **lodging:** Courtyard, Extended Stay America, **other:** Albertson's, Buick/Pontiac, Chevrolet, Firestone, JC Penney, Jo-Ann Fabrics, Macy's, Nissan, Sears/auto, mall, **S...gas:** 7-11
19a El Portal Dr, to San Pablo, **S...gas:** Shell, 76, **food:** KFC, McDonald's, **other:** Raley's Foods

Richmond

18 San Pablo Dam Rd, **N...gas:** Arco/24hr, 76, 7-11, **food:** Burger King, Denny's, KFC, McDonald's, Nations Burgers, Taco Bell, **other:** HOSPITAL, Albertson's, K-Mart, Longs Drug, **S...other:** CamperLand RV Ctr
17 Macdonald Ave(from eb), McBryde Ave(from wb), Richmond, **N...gas:** Arco/24hr, Citgo/7-11, **food:** Burger King, Church's, KFC, Taco Bell, **S...gas:** Chevron/24hr, **food:** Bakers Square, Wendy's, **other:** Albertson's, Safeway, auto repair
16 San Pablo Ave, San Pablo, to Richmond, **S...gas:** 76, Valero, **food:** Wendy's, **other:** Aamco, Dodge/Jeep, Toyota
15 Cutting Blvd, Potrero St, to I-580 Br(from wb), to El Cerrito, **N...gas:** Arco, **S... gas:** Chevron, Shell, **food:** Carrow's Rest., Church's, IHOP, Jack-in-the-Box, McDonald's, **lodging:** Best Inn, Travelodge, **other:** FoodsCo Foods, Home Depot, Honda, PepBoys, Staples, Target, Walgreen
14b Carlson Blvd, El Cerrito, **N...gas:** 76, **food:** Carlson Foods, **lodging:** 40 Flags Motel, **S...lodging:** Super 8
14a Central Ave, El Cerrito, **S...gas:** Shell/24hr, 76, Valero, **food:** Burger King, Daimo Japanese, KFC, Nations Burgers, **other:** Branch Mkt Foods, mall
13 Albany, to I-580(from eb), no facilities
12 Gilman St, to Berkeley, **N...**Golden Gate Fields Racetrack
11 University Ave, to Berkeley, **S...gas:** 76, Beacon, **other:** to UC Berkeley
10 CA 13, to Ashby Ave, no facilities
9 Powell St, Emeryville, **N...gas:** Shell, **food:** Chevy's Mexican, **lodging:** Holiday Inn, **S...gas:** Beacon, **food:** Burger King, Denny's, Lyon's Rest., Starbucks, Trader Joe's, **lodging:** Courtyard, Day's Inn, Sheraton, Woodfin Suites, **other:** Borders Books, Circuit City, Emery Bay Mkt, Good Guys, Jo-Ann Fabrics, Old Navy, Ross
8c b Oakland, to I-880, I-580, no facilities
8a W Grand Ave, Maritime St, no facilities
7mm toll plaza wb
5mm SF Bay
4 Treasure Island(exits left)
2c b Fremont St, Harrison St, Embarcadero(exits left)
1 5th St, 7th St, downtown SF

Berkeley

I-80 begins/ends at 7th St in San Francisco.

Interstate 110(LA)

E ↕ W

Exit #	Services
21	I-110 begins/ends on I-10.
20c	Adams Blvd, **E...other:** Nissan
20b	37th St, Exposition Blvd, **E...**repair, **W...gas:** Chevron/McDonald's, **lodging:** Radisson
20a	MLK Blvd, Expo Park
19b	Vernon Ave, **E...gas:** Mobil, Shell, **W...gas:** 76/24hr, Shell, **food:** Jack-in-the-Box, **other:** Ralph's Foods, Rite Aid
18b	Slauson Ave, **E...gas:** Mobil, Shell, **W...gas:** 76
18a	Gage Blvd, **E...gas:** Arco, **food:** Church's
17	Florence Ave, **E...gas:** Mobil, **food:** Jack-in-the-Box,

Interstate 110

Los Angeles Area

Exit #	Services
	W...**gas:** Arco, Chevron, Shell/24hr, **food:** Burger King, Pizza Hut
16	Manchester Ave, **E...gas:** Arco, **food:** McDonald's, **W...gas:** 76/Circle K, **food:** Church's, Jack-in-the-Box, Pam's Burgers, Popeye's
15	Century Blvd, **E...gas:** Shell/Subway, **food:** Burger King, **W...gas:** 76
14b	Imperial Hwy, **W...gas:** Shell, **food:** McDonald's
14a	I-105
13	El Segundo Blvd, **E...gas:** Shell/diesel/24hr, **W...gas:** Arco/24hr, Shell
12	Rosecrans Ave, **E...gas:** Arco/24hr, Cardlock Fuel, Chevron, **W...gas:** Chevron/McDonald's, Mobil, 7-11, **food:** Jack-in-the-Box, KFC, Subway, **other:** Chief Parts
11	Redondo Beach Blvd, **E...food:** McDonald's, Peter Pan Pizza, **W...gas:** Mobil, **other:** HOSPITAL
10b a	CA 91, **W...food:** Carl's Jr, Jack-in-the-Box, Krispy Kreme, McDonald's, Taco Bell/Pizza Hut, **other:** Albertson's, Food4Less, Sam's Club
9	I-405, San Diego Fwy
8	Torrance Blvd, Del Amo, **E...food:** Burger King, **other:** K-mart, **W...gas:** Mobil, Shell/diesel
7b	Carson St, **E...food:** KFC, **lodging:** Cali Inn, **W...gas:** Mobil, Shell, **food:** Bakers Square, Hong Kong Garden, In-n-Out, Jack-in-the-Box, **other:** HOSPITAL, Harbor Drug, Kragen Parts, Radio Shack
5	Sepulveda Blvd, **E...other:** Target, **W...gas:** Arco/24hr, Chevron, Mobil, Shell, **food:** Carl's Jr, Golden Ox Burger, McDonald's, Popeye's, Taco Bell, **lodging:** Motel 6, **other:** Food4Less, K-Mart, Rite Aid, Von's Foods
4	CA 1, Pacific Coast Hwy, **E...gas:** Shell, **food:** Jack-in-the-Box, **W...gas:** Chevron, Mobil/diesel, **food:** Denny's, El Pollo Loco, EZ TakeOut Burger, **lodging:** Best Western, **other:** HOSPITAL, Discount Parts, Honda, PepBoys
3b	Anaheim St, **E...gas:** Shell
3a	C St, **E...gas:** Shell/diesel, **other:** radiators, **W...gas:** 76 Refinery
1b	Channel St, no facilities
1a	CA 47, Gaffey Ave, no facilities
0mm	I-110 begins/ends

Interstate 205(Tracy)

Tracy

Exit #	Services
112	I-205 begins wb, ends eb, accesses I-5 nb.
9	MacArthur Dr, Tracy, **S...other:** Prime Outlet Ctr/ famous brands
8	Tracy Blvd, Tracy, **N...gas:** Chevron, Shell/diesel, **food:** Denny's/24hr, **lodging:** Holiday inn Express, Motel 6, **S...gas:** Arco/24hr, **food:** Arby's, Burger King, ChuckeCheese, In-n-Out, LJ Silver, Lyon's Rest., McDonald's, Nations Burgers, TCBY, Wendy's, Wok King, **lodging:** Best Western, Phoenix Lodge, **other:** HOSPITAL, Albertson's, Food4Less, Jo-Ann Fabrics, Kragen Parts, Longs Drugs, Walgreen, CHP
7	Corral Hollow
6	Grant Line Rd, Antioch, **N...food:** Burger King, IHOP, Taco Bell, **lodging:** Fairfield Inn, Hampton Inn, **other:** Chevrolet, JC Penney, Ross, Sears/auto, Staples, Target, Toyota, Wal-Mart/McDonald's, mall, **S...gas:** Arco/24hr, Citgo/7-11, Dik Tracy, Shell/diesel, **food:** Carl's Jr, Orchard Rest., **other:** Cadillac/Pontiac/GMC, Tracy Marine
4	11TH St(from eb), to Tracy, Defense Depot
3	Mtn House Rd, to I-580 E
2	Patterson Pass Rd, **N...**fruitstand
0mm	I-205 begins eb/ends wb, accesses I-580 wb.

Interstate 210(Pasadena)

San Dimas

Exit #	Services
49	I-10, San Bernardino Fwy. CA 57, Orange Fwy. I-210 begins/ends on I-10.
48	CA 71, Corona Fwy, no facilities
47	Raging Waters Dr, Via Verde, **S...other:** Bonelli Park, gas/LP
46	Covina Blvd, no facilities
45	Arrow Hwy, San Dimas, **N...gas:** 76, Shell, **food:** Del Taco, Denny's, McDonald's, Red Robin, Sizzler, Zendeja's Mexican, **lodging:** Comfort Suites, Red Roof Inn, **other:** Home Depot, Lowe's Whse, **S...gas:** Mobil, **food:** IHOP, Trader Joe's, **other:** DressBarn, OfficeMax, PetCo, Ralph's Foods, Rite Aid, Ross, Target
44	CA 30 E(exits left from eb), Lone Hill Ave, **S...food:** Baja Fresh, Blimpie, Coco's, Wendy's, **other:** Chevrolet, Dodge, Ford, Home Depot, Sam's Club, Toyota, Wal-Mart/auto
43	Sunflower Ave, no facilities
42	Grand Ave, to Glendora, **N...gas:** Mobil, **food:** Denny's, **other:** HOSPITAL
41	Citrus Ave, to Covina, no facilities
40	CA 39, Azusa Ave, **N...gas:** Arco/24hr, Chevron, Texaco/ Subway/Del Taco, **lodging:** Super 8, **lodging:** Western Inn, **S...gas:** 76, **food:** In-n-Out, **lodging:** Azuza Inn
39	Vernon Ave, **N...food:** Carl's Jr, Taco Bell, **other:** Costco
38	Irwindale, **N...gas:** Arco, **food:** Carl's Jr, Denny's, Don Ramon's Grill, McDonald's, Taco Bell, **other:** MEDICAL CARE, Costco, Health Valley Foods
36b	Mt Olive Dr, no facilities
36a	I-605 S, no facilities
35b a	Mountain Ave, **N...food:** Old Spaghetti Factory, **other:** BMW,

CALIFORNIA

Interstate 210

E ↕ W — Pasadena

Buick, Chevrolet, Ford/Lincoln/Mercury, Honda, Infiniti, Isuzu, Mazda, Mitsubishi, Nissan, Saturn, Staples, Subaru, Target, **S...other:** Home Depot, Ross, Wal-Mart

34 Myrtle Ave, **S...gas:** Chevron, 76, **food:** Jack-in-the-Box

33 Huntington Dr, Monrovia, **N...gas:** Shell, **food:** Acapulco Rest., Applebee's, Black Angus, Burger King, Chili's, ChuckeCheese, Lee Roy's Rest., McDonald's, Mimi's, Orange Julius, Panda Express, Quizno's, Trader Joe's, Winchell's, **lodging:** Sheraton, **other:** CompUSA, GNC, Marshall's, Office Depot, Rite Aid, **S...food:** Baja Fresh, BJ's Grill, Capistrano's, ClaimJumper, KookooRoo, Macaroni Grill, Olive Garden, Red Lobster, Souplantation, Starbucks, Subway, Tokyo Woko, Tony Roma, **lodging:** Embassy Suites, Extended Stay America, Hampton Inn, Holiday Inn, Homestead Suites, OakTree Inn, Residence Inn

32 Santa Anita Ave, Arcadia, **S...gas:** Chevron, **food:** In-n-Out, **other:** carwash

31 Baldwin Ave, to Sierra Madre, no facilities

30b a Rosemead Blvd, **N...**Shell, **S...gas:** 76

29b a San Gabriel Blvd, Madre St, **N...gas:** Arco, 76, **lodging:** Panda Inn, Ralph's Foods, Ross, **S...gas:** Arco, 76, **food:** Jack–in-the-Box, **lodging:** Best Western, Ramada Inn, **other:** Buick/Chevrolet/Pontiac/GMC, Cadillac, Circuit City, Staples, Target, Toyota

28 Altadena Dr, Sierra Madre, no facilities

27 Hill Ave, no facilities

26 Lake Ave, **N...gas:** Mobil

25b CA 134, to Ventura

25a Del Mar Blvd, CA Blvd, CO Blvd, no facilities

24 Mountain St, no facilities

23 Lincoln Ave, **S...lodging:** Lincoln Motel

22b Arroyo Blvd, **N...food:** Jack-in-the-Box, **other:** repair, **S...**to Rose Bowl

22a Berkshire Ave, Oak Grove Dr, no facilities

21 Gould Ave, **S...gas:** Arco, **food:** McDonald's, Round-Table Pizza, Trader Joes, **other:** Firestone, Just Tires, Ralph's Foods

20 Angeles Crest Hwy, no facilities

19 CA 2, Glendale Fwy, **S...other:** HOSPITAL

18 Ocean View Blvd, to Montrose

17b a Pennsylvania Ave, La Crescenta, **N...gas:** Mobil, Shell, **food:** Wienerschnitzel, **other:** Nissan, Office Depot, Toyota, Von's Foods, **S...other:** Gardenia Mkt/deli

San Fernando

16 Lowell Ave, no facilities

14 La Tuna Cyn Rd, no facilities

11 Sunland Blvd, Tujunga, **N...food:** Sizzler, **other:** Ralph's Foods, Rite Aid

9 Wheatland Ave, **N...other:** food mkt

8 Osborne St, Lakeview Terrace, **N...gas:** 7-11

6a Paxton St, no facilities

6b CA 118, no facilities

5 Maclay St, to San Fernando, **S...gas:** Chevron, 76, **food:** El Pollo Loco, McDonald's, Taco Bell, **other:** Home Depot, **other:** Office Depot, Radio Shack, Sam's Club

4 Hubbard St, **N...gas:** Chevron, **other:** Radio Shack, Rite Aid, **S...gas:** Mobil/diesel, Shell, **food:** El Caporal Mexican, Jack-in-the-Box, Shakey's Pizza, Subway

3 Polk St, **S...gas:** Arco, Chevron/24hr, 7-11

2 Roxford St, **N...**HOSPITAL, **S...lodging:** Super 8

1c Yarnell St, no facilities

1 b a I-210 begins/ends on I-5, exit 160.

Interstate 215(Riverside)

N ↕ S — San Bernardino

Exit# Services

55 I-215 begins/ends on I-15.

54 Devore, **E...gas:** Arco/24hr, Devore Minimart, **other:** KOA, **W...food:** Joe's Country Corner

50 Palm Ave, Kendall Dr, **E...gas:** Citgo/7-11, Mobil/diesel, **food:** Burger King, DQ, Popeye's, **W...gas:** Arco/24hr, **food:** Denny's

48 University Pkwy, **E...gas:** Chevron, 76/Subway/Circle K, **food:** Carl's Jr, Del Taco, IHOP, KFC, McDonald's, **other:** Ralph's Foods, **W...gas:** Arco/24hr, Shell/diesel, **food:** Jack-in-the-Box, Pizza Hut, Taco Bell, **lodging:** Motel 6, Quality Inn

46c b 27th St, **E...**golf, **W...**golf

46a CA 30 W, Highland Ave, no facilities

45b Muscuplabe Dr, **E...gas:** Shell, **other:** Chevrolet, Home Depot, SavOn Foods, Stater Bros

45a CA 30 E, Highlands, no facilities

44b Baseline Rd no facilities

44a CA 66 W, 5th St, **E...lodging:** Econolodge

43 2nd St, Civic Ctr, **E...gas:** Arco, Chevron, **food:** China Hut, Del Taco, Denny's, In-n-Out, LJ Silver, Pizza Hut/Taco Bell, **lodging:** Radisson, **other:** Ford, Food4Less, JC Penney, Kelly Tire, Marshall's, mall

42b Mill St, SBD Airport, **E...food:** McDonald's, **other:** Suzuki/Honda, **W...gas:** Shell

42a Inland Ctr Dr, **E...food:** Carl's Jr, Del Taco, Jack-in-the-Box, Macy's, Robinsons-May, Sears/auto, mall

41 Orange Show Rd, **E...gas:** Chevron, Shell, **food:** Denny's, **lodging:** Budget Inn, Knight's Inn, **other:** Chevrolet, Dodge, Firestone, Macy's, Mazda, 99c Store, Target, **W...lodging:** Villager Lodge, **other:** Cadillac, Daewoo, Giant RV, Isuzu, Jeep, Kia, Mitsubishi, Nissan, Toyota, Volvo

40b a I-10, E to Palm Springs, W to LA

39 Washington St, Mt Vernon Ave, **E...gas:** Arco/24hr, Chevron/diesel, **food:** Arby's, Bluff's Rest., Siquios Mexican, Taco Joe's, **other:** Asiana Mkt, Goodyear, Rite Aid, **W...gas:** Mobil, **food:** Burger King, Carl's Jr, Del Taco, Denny's, Jack-in-the-Box, McDonald's, Ravi's Indian Cuisine, Sassy Steer, Spike's Teriyaki, Subway, Taco Bell, Yoshinoya, Zendejas Mexican, **lodging:** Red Tile Inn, **other:** Giant RV, 99c Store, Radio Shack, RV Expo, Wal-Mart

38 Barton Rd, **E...gas:** Arco/24hr, Shell, **other:** AutoZone, **W...food:** Dorothy's Burgers

37 La Cadena Dr, **E...gas:** Shell/diesel/24hr, **food:** YumYum Rest., **lodging:** Day's Inn

36 Center St, to Highgrove, **W...gas:** 76/diesel/LP

35 Columbia Ave, **E...gas:** Arco, **W...gas:** Circle K

34b a CA 91, CA 60, Riverside, to beach cities

Riverside

33 Blaine St, 3rd St, **E...gas:** 76, Shell, Texaco/repair, UltraMar, **other:** K-Mart, **W...gas:** Arco/24hr

32 University Ave, Riverside, **W...gas:** Arco, Mobil, Shell, **food:** Baker's Drive-Thru, Baskin-Robbins, Carl's Jr, Chan's Oriental, Coco's, Del Taco, Denny's, Domino's, Green Burrito, Gus Jr #11, IHOP, Jilberto's Tacos, Papa John's, Quizno's, Starbucks, Taco Bell, Tempo Del Sol Mexican, Wienerschnitzel, Winchell's, **lodging:** Comfort Inn, Courtyard, Dynasty Suites, Hampton Inn, Motel 6, Super 8, **other:** MEDICAL CARE, Kragen Parts, Rite Aid

CALIFORNIA

Interstate 215

N ↕ S

Perris

31 MLK Blvd, El Cerrito, no facilities
30b Central Ave, Watkins Dr, no facilities
30a Fair Isle Dr, Box Springs, **E...gas:** Shell, **other:** Margon's RV, **W...gas:** 76/Taco Bell, **other:** Ford
29 CA 60 E, to Indio, **E on Day St...gas:** Arco/24hr, Shell/Del Taco/diesel, **food:** Café Chinese, Carl's Jr, HomeTown Buffet, McDonald's, Red Robin, **other:** MEDICAL CARE, Costco/gas, Home Depot, JC Penney, Mervyn's, Ralph's Foods, Robinsons-May, Sam's Club, Sears/auto, Staples, Wal-Mart, mall
28 Eucalyptus Ave, Eastridge Ave, **E on Day St...other:** Sam's Club, Wal-Mart, same as 29
27b Alessandro Blvd, **E...gas:** Arco/24hr, Mobil/diesel, **food:** Jack-in-the-Box, Dragon House Chinese, **other:** Big O Tire, auto repair, **W...gas:** Chevron
27a Cactus Air Blvd, **E...gas:** Chevron, Shell/DelTaco/diesel, **food:** Burger King, Carl's Jr
25 Van Buren Blvd, **E...other:** March Field Museum, **W...other:** Riverside Nat Cen.
23 Oleander Ave, no facilities
22 Ramona Expswy, **1 mi E on Perris Blvd...gas:** Arco/24hr, Mobil, Shell/Subway/diesel, **food:** Jack-in-the-Box, Taco Bell, **other:** Albertson's, Wal-Mart/auto
19 Nuevo Rd, **E...gas:** Arco/24hr, Mobil, 76, **food:** Burger King, Carl's Jr, China Buffet, Del Taco, El Pollo Loco, IHOP, Jenny's Rest., McDonald's, Sizzler, **other:** AutoZone, Food4Less, Rite Aid, Stater Bros Foods
17 CA 74 W, 4th St, to Perris, Lake Elsinore, **E...gas:** Shell/24hr, **W...gas:** Chevron, **food:** Denny's, Jack-in-the-Box, La Mexicana Taquiera, Popeye's, **lodging:** Best Western, Perris Inn, **other:** Chrysler/Dodge/Plymouth/Jeep, USPO
15 CA 74 E, Hemet, **E...other:** motel, Ford/Lincoln/Mercury
14 Ethanac Rd, **E...food:** KFC/Taco Bell, **other:** Richardson's RV/Marine, **W...gas:** Exxon/diesel
12 McCall Blvd, Sun City, **E...gas:** 76, UltraMar/diesel, **food:** Wendy's, **lodging:** Sun City Motel, Travelodge, **other:** HOSPITAL, **W...gas:** Chevron/diesel, Mobil, 76, Shell, **food:** Burger King, Coco's, McDonald's, **other:** MEDICAL CARE, Rite Aid, Stater Bros Foods, Von's Foods
10 Newport Rd, Quail Valley, **E...gas:** Shell/DelTaco/diesel, **food:** Cathay Chinese, Jack-in-the-Box, Subway, Taco Bell, **other:** AutoZone, GNC, Ralph's Foods, Target, **W...gas:** Arco/24hr
7 Scott Rd, no facilities
4 Clinton Keith Rd, no facilities
2 Los Alamos, **E...gas:** Shell, **food:** CA Grill, Peony Chinese, Taco Bell, Wendy's, **W...gas:** Mobil/McDonald's, **food:** ChuckeCheese, City Deli/bakery, Green Burrito, Jack-in-the-Box, Mongolian BBQ, Subway, **other:** Radio Shack, SavOn Drug, Stater Bros Foods
1 Murrieta Hot Springs, **E...food:** Carl's Jr, Del Taco, Domino's, Sizzler, **other:** Ralph's Foods, Rite Aid, Ross, USPO, Weston's Mkt
0mm I-215 begins/ends on I-15.

Interstate 280(Bay Area)

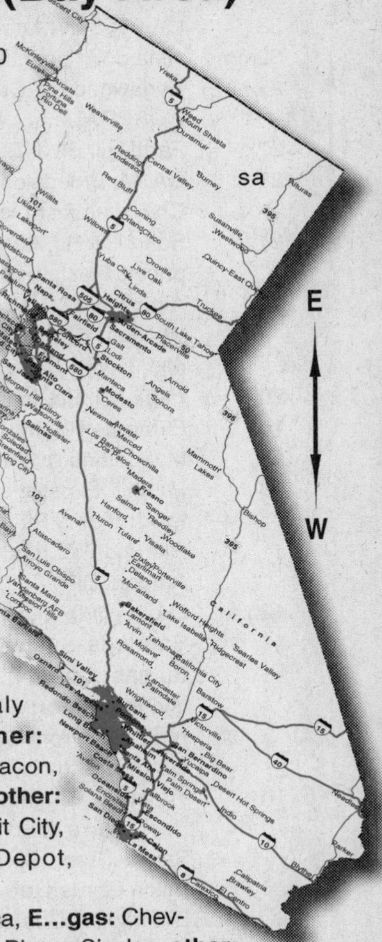

San Francisco

E ↕ W

Exit#	Services
58	4th St, downtown, I-280 begins/ends.
57	6th St, to I-80, Bay Bridge, downtown
56	Mariposa St, downtown
55	Army St, Port of SF
54	US 101 S, Alemany Blvd, Mission St, **E...gas:** Shell
52	San Jose Ave, Bosworth St(from nb, no return)
51	Geneva Ave, no facilities
50	CA 1, 19th Ave, **W...gas:** Chevron, **other:** to Bay Bridge, SFSU
49	Daly City, Westlake Dist, **E...gas:** 76/diesel/LP
48	Serramonte Blvd, Daly City(from sb), **E...other:** Chevrolet, **W...gas:** Beacon, 76, **food:** McDonald's, **other:** Macy's, Mervyn's, Circuit City, Good Guys, Office Depot, Ross
47b	CA 1, Mission St, Pacifica, **E...gas:** Chevron, **food:** RoundTable Pizza, Sizzler, **other:** HOSPITAL, Dodge, Drug Barn, Ford, Fresh Choice Foods, Home Depot, Isuzu, Jo-Ann Fabrics, Mitsubishi, Nissan, Nordstrom's, Target, mall
46	Hickey Blvd, Colma, **E...gas:** Chevron/diesel/24hr, Shell, **W...gas:** Shell/24hr, 7-11, **food:** El Torito's, Peppermill Rest., RoundTable Pizza, Sizzler, **other:** Pak'nSave Foods/24hr
45	Avalon Dr, Westborough, **W...gas:** Arco/24hr, Exxon/diesel, **food:** Denny's, McDonald's, **other:** Safeway, Walgreen/24hr, Skyline Coll
43b	I-380 E, to US 101
43a	San Bruno Ave, Sneath Lane, **E...food:** Baskin-Robbins, Petrini's Rest., **other:** Longs Drugs, **W...gas:** Beacon, 76, Chevron/24hr, 7-11, **food:** Bakers Square
42	Crystal Springs(from eb), no facilities
41	CA 35 N, Skyline Blvd(from wb, no EZ return), to Pacifica, **1 mi W...gas:** Beacon, **other:** Lunardi's Foods
40	Millbrae Ave, Millbrae, **E...gas:** Beacon, Chevron
39	Trousdale Dr, to Burlingame, E...HOSPITAL
36	Black Mtn Rd, Hayne Rd, **W...**golf, vista point
36	**Crystal Springs rest area wb, full(handicapped)facilties, phone, picnic table, litter barrels, petwalk**
35	CA 35, CA 92W(from eb), to Half Moon Bay, no facilities
34	Bunker Hill Dr, no facilities

CALIFORNIA

Interstate 280

E ↕ W

33 CA 92, San Mateo, to Half Moon Bay, no facilties
32mm vista point both lanes
29 Edgewood Rd, Canada Rd, to San Carlos, **E...other:** HOSPITAL
27 Farm Hill Blvd, **E...other:** Cañada Coll, phone
25 CA 84, Woodside Rd, Redwood City, **1 mi W...gas:** Chevron/diesel, **other:** MEDICAL CARE, USPO
24 Sand Hill Rd, Menlo Park, **E...gas:** Shell, **food:** Capriccio Rest., **other:** Longs Drug, Safeway
22 Alpine Rd, Portola Valley, **E...other:** HOSPITAL, **W...gas:** Chevron, Shell/autocare, **food:** Bianchini's Mkt, RoundTable Pizza
20 Page Mill Rd, to Palo Alto, **E...**HOSPITAL
16 El Monte Rd, Moody Rd, no facilities
15 Magdalena Ave, no facilities
13 Foothill Expswy, Grant Rd, **E...gas:** Chevron/24hr, **food:** Hick'ry Pit Rest., Pacific Steamer Pizza, **other:** Rite Aid, **W...gas:** Arco/24hr, **other:** to Rancho San Antonio CP
12b a CA 85, N to Mtn View, S to Gilroy
11 Saratoga-Sunnyvale Rd, Cupertino, Sunnyvale, **E...gas:** Chevron, **food:** Carl's Jr, **lodging:** Cupertino Inn, **other:** Goodyear, Rite Aid, repair, **W...gas:** Arco, Chevron, Shell/diesel, **food:** Croutons Rest., Outback Steaks, Togo's, **other:** Target
10 Wolfe Rd, **E...gas:** Arco/24hr, **food:** Carlos Murphy's Rest., Duke of Edinburgh Rest., Momo House Rest., Sankee Rest., Silver Wing Rest., **lodging:** Courtyard, Hilton Garden, **other:** Ranch Mkt, **W...gas:** 76, **food:** El Torito, McDonald's, Pizza, TGIFriday, **other:** FabricLand, JC Penney, Sears/auto, Vallco Fashion Park
9 Lawrence Expswy, Stevens Creek Blvd(from eb), **N...other:** Rite Aid, Safeway, Marshall's, **S...gas:** 76, 7-11, **food:** IHOP, Rock'n Tacos, **lodging:** Howard Johnson, Woodcrest Hotel
7 Saratoga Ave, **N...gas:** Arco/24hr, Chevron/24hr, 7-11, **food:** Black Angus, Burger King, Happi House, Harry's Hosbrau, McDonald's, Thai Cuisine, **other:** Albertson's, **S...gas:** 76, Exxon, Shell, **food:** Denny's, RoundTable Pizza, Tony Roma's
5c Winchester Blvd, Campbell Ave(from eb), **S...gas:** 76
5b CA 17 S, to Santa Cruz, I-880 N, to San Jose, Oakland
5a Leigh Ave, Bascom Ave, **N...gas:** Exxon, **food:** KFC
4 Meridian St(from eb), **S...gas:** Chevron/Fastpay, 76, 7-11, **food:** KFC, Taco Bell, Wienerschnitzel, **other:** Food4Less, K-Mart
3b Bird Ave, Race St, no facilities
3a CA 87, **N...lodging:** Hilton, Holiday Inn, Hotel Sainte Claire
2 7th St, to CA 82, **N...**conv ctr
1 10th St, 11th St, **N...gas:** 7-11, **other:** to San Jose St U
0mm I-280 begins/ends on US 101.

San Jose

Los Angeles Area

Interstate 405(LA)

N ↕ S

Exit # Services
73 I-5, N to Sacramento
72 Rinaldi St, Sepulveda, **E...gas:** Arco, 76, **food:** Arby's, Presidente Mexican, Subway, **other:** HOSPITAL, Toyota, **W...gas:** Shell, **lodging:** Granada Motel
71 CA 118 W, Simi Valley, no facilities
70 Devonshire St, Granada Hills, **E...gas:** Mobil, 76, Shell/diesel, **food:** Holiday Burger, Millie's Rest., Starbucks, **other:** Discount Tire, Nissan, Ralph's Foods, Rite Aid, Von's Foods
69 Nordhoff St, **E...gas:** Mobil/diesel, 7-11/24hr, **other:** MEDICAL CARE, **W...gas:** Arco
68 Roscoe Blvd, to Panorama City, **E...gas:** Exxon, 76, **food:** Burger King, Carl's Jr, Denny's, Galpin Rest., Jack-in-the-Box, McDonald's, Shakey's Pizza, **lodging:** Holiday Inn Express, **other:** AutoZone, Ford/Lincoln/Mercury/Jaguar, Saturn, **W...gas:** Shell/diesel, **food:** Coco's, Mexican Grill, Tommy's Burgers, **lodging:** Motel 6
66 Sherman Blvd, Reseda, **E...gas:** Chevron, Mobil/diesel/LP, 76, Shell, **food:** KFC, **other:** Albertson's, Rite Aid, **W...gas:** Mobil, 76/diesel/24hr, **food:** Taco Bell, **other:** HOSPITAL, USPO
65 Victory Blvd, Van Nuys, **E...gas:** 76, Mobil/diesel, **food:** El Pollo Loco, Jack-in-the-Box, **other:** Office Depot, **E on Sepulveda...food:** Wendy's, **other:** Costco, PepBoys, **W on Victory...gas:** Arco/24hr
64 Burbank Blvd, **E...gas:** Chevron, Shell, **food:** Denny's, **lodging:** Best Western
63b US 101, Ventura Fwy, no facilities
63a Ventura Blvd(from nb), **E...gas:** Mobil, **food:** Denny's, Robinsons-May, **other:** Thrifty Food, mall, **W...gas:** Chevron, 76, **food:** McDonald's, **lodging:** Radisson
63a Valley Vista Blvd(from sb), no facilities
61 Mulholland Dr, no facilities
59 Sepulveda Blvd, **W...**to Getty Ctr
57 Sunset Blvd, **E...gas:** Chevron/24hr, Shell, **other:** to UCLA, **W...lodging:** Holiday Inn, Luse Hotel
56 Waterford St, Montana Ave(from nb)
55c b Wilshire Blvd, **E...**downtown, **W...gas:** Mobil, 7-11, **other:** HOSPITAL
55a CA 2, Santa Monica Blvd, **E...gas:** Exxon, Mobil, 7-11, **food:** Chinese Cuisine, Jack-in-the-Box, Jamba Juice, NY Pizza, Starbucks, Winchell's, Yoshinoya, **W...gas:** 76/24hr, Shell/repair, 7-11, **lodging:** Best Western
54 Olympic Blvd, Peco Blvd(from sb), **E...gas:** 7-11, **food:** Pazzo Pizzaria, Subway, **W...food:** Panda Express, Starbucks, **other:** Marshall's
53 I-10, Santa Monica Fwy
52 Venice Blvd, **E...gas:** Chevron/service, Mobil, 76, Shell/diesel, 7-11, **food:** Carl's Jr, **other:** Winston Tire, **W...gas:** SP, **food:** FatBurger, **other:** services on Sepulveda
51 Culver Blvd, Washington Blvd, **E...food:** Dear John's Café, Domino's, **other: W...gas:** 76/repair
50b CA 90, Slauson Ave, to Marina del Rey, **E...gas:** Arco/24hr, **food:** Del Taco, Shakey's Pizza, **other:** Circuit City, CompUSA, Firestone/auto, Goodyear/auto, Office Depot, Pic'n Sav Foods, transmissions, **W...gas:** 76, **food:** Denny's, **other:** Albertson's

Interstate 405

N
S

Hawthorne

50a Jefferson Blvd(from sb), **E...food:** Coco's, Jack-in-the-Box, **other:** Rite Aid, **W...**to LA Airport

49 Howard Hughes Pkwy, to Centinela Ave, **E...gas:** Mobil/diesel, **food:** Sizzler, **lodging:** Ramada Inn, Sheraton, **other:** JC Penney, Macy's, Robinsons-May, mall, **W...gas:** Chevron, **food:** Dinah's Rest., Islands Burgers, On the Border, **lodging:** Extended Stay America, **other:** Radisson, Ford, Saturn, SavOn Drug, Howard Hughes Ctr, mall

48 La Tijera Blvd, **E...food:** El Pollo Loco, FatBurger, KFC, McDonald's, TGIFriday, **lodging:** Best Western, **other:** EZ Lube, 99c Store, Von's Foods, **W...gas:** Arco/24hr, Chevron/diesel/24hr, 76/Circle K, **food:** Buggy Whip Rest., **other:** Marie Callender's, USPO

47 CA 42, Manchester Ave, to Inglewood, **E...gas:** Chevron, 76/diesel/24hr, **food:** Carl's Jr, Steppin Up Rest., **lodging:** Best Western, Econolodge, **W...gas:** Arco, Shell, 76, **food:** Arby's, Burger King, Jack-in-the-Box, Randy's Donuts, **lodging:** Day's Inn, **other:** Chrysler/Jeep/Dodge, K-Mart

46 Century Blvd, **E...gas:** 76, **food:** Burger King, Casa Gamino Mexican, Flower Drum Chinese, Rally's, Subway, **lodging:** Best Western, Comfort Inn, Motel 6, Tiboli Hotel, **other:** AutoZone, **W...gas:** Arco/24hr, Chevron/diesel, 76/Circle K, Shell, **food:** Carl's Jr, Denny's, McDonald's, Taco Bell, **lodging:** Hampton Inn, Hilton, Holiday Inn, Marriott, Quality Hotel, Travelodge, Westin Hotel

45 I-105, Imperial Hwy, **E...gas:** Arco, Mobil/diesel, Shell, **food:** BBQ, El Pollo Loco, El Tarasco Mexican, Jack-in-the-Box, McDonald's, **other:** J&S Trasmissions, **W...food:** Proud Bird Rest.(1mi)

44 El Segundo Blvd, to El Segundo, **E...gas:** Arco, Chevron/24hr, **food:** Burger King, Christy's Donuts, HongKong Express, Jack-in-the-Box, Los Chorros Mexican, Pizza Hut, Rally's, Subway, Taco Bell, **other:** Albertson's, SavOn Drug, **W...food:** Denny's, **lodging:** Ramada Inn, **other:** Office Depot

43b a Rosecrans Ave, to Manhattan Beach, **E...gas:** 76, Mobil/diesel, Shell, **food:** El Pollo Loco, Pizza Hut, Starbucks, Subway, **other:** Albertson's, Best Buy, Food4Less, Home Depot, Michael's, Ross, SavOn Drug, **W...gas:** Arco, **food:** Carl's Jr, China Chef, Luigi's Rest., McDonald's, **other:** Costco/gas, Staples

42b Inglewood Ave, **E...gas:** Arco, **food:** Del Taco, Denny's, In-n-Out, Yoshinoya, **other:** Von's Foods, **W...gas:** Arco, Mobil, Shell/diesel/24hr, **other:** Drug Emporium, Goodyear/auto

42a CA 107, Hawthorne Blvd, **E...food:** Jack-in-the-Box, LA Wok, McDonald's, Papa John's, **lodging:** Best Western, Day's Inn, **other:** Freeway Drug, 99c Store, Radio Shack, **W...gas:** Arco/24hr, Mobil/diesel, Thrifty, Blimpie, Subway, Taco Bell, Yoshinoya, **other:** Goodyear, Robinson-May

40b Redondo Beach Blvd, Hermosa Beach, **E...gas:** Arco/24hr, Thrifty, **food:** Amigo's Tacos, ChuckeCheese, **other:** golf, **W...food:** Boston Mkt, RoundTable Pizza, **other:** Ralph's Foods, SavOn Drug, U-Haul

40a CA 91 E, Artesia Blvd, to Torrance, **W...gas:** Chevron, 76/24hr, **other:** Winchell's, Parts+, XpressLube/Burger King/Taco Bell

39 Crenshaw Blvd, to Torrance, **E...gas:** Arco/24hr, Chevron/24hr, Mobil/repair, Shell, 7-11, **food:** Burger King, Denny's, Pizza Hut, **other:** MEDICAL CARE, Ralph's Foods, **W...gas:** Mobil/diesel, Shell/Subway/diesel

38b Western Ave, to Torrance, **E...gas:** Arco, Chevron, Mobil/repair, 76/diesel, **food:** Del Taco, Denny's, Wendy's, Yorgo's Burgers, **other:** Albertson's, Toyota, **W...gas:** Mobil, **food:** Mill's Rest., **lodging:** Courtyard

38a Normandie Ave, to Gardena, **E...lodging:** Comfort Inn, **W...gas:** Shell/diesel, **food:** Carl's Jr, Great Steak Café, Hong Kong Express, StarBucks, Subway, Taco Bell, **lodging:** Extended Stay America, **other:** Goodyear, Office Depot

37b Vermont Ave(from sb), **W...lodging:** Holiday Inn, **other:** hwy patrol

37a I-110, Harbor Fwy, no facilities

36 Main St(from nb), no facilities

36mm weigh sta both lanes

Carson

35 Avalon Blvd, to Carson, **E...gas:** Arco/24hr, Chevron, Mobil, Shell, **food:** ChuckeCheese, Denny's, FoodCourt, Jack-in-the-Box, McDonald's, Pizza Hut, Shakey's Pizza, Sizzler, Subway, Tony Roma, **lodging:** Quality Inn, **other:** MEDICAL CARE, America's Tire, Firestone, Goodyear/auto, Ikea, JC Penney, PepBoys, Sears/auto, mall, **W...gas:** Arco/24hr, Mobil, Shell, **food:** Carl's Jr, El Charro, IHOP, **other:** Chrysler/Dodge/Jeep, Ford/Lincoln/Mercury, Isuzu, Kia, Ralph's Foods, USPO

34 Carson St, to Carson, **E...food:** Del Taco, **lodging:** Comfort Inn, **W...gas:** Mobil, 76/diesel/24hr, **food:** Carl's Jr, El Charro, IHOP, Jack-in-th-Box, Subway, **lodging:** Hilton

33b Wilmington Ave, **E...gas:** Arco/service, Chevron/repair/24hr, **food:** Carson Burgers, **W...gas:** Shell/Subway/Taco Bell/diesel, **other:** Chevrolet/Hyundai, Toyota

CALIFORNIA

Interstate 405

N ↕ S

33a Alameda St, no facilities

32d Santa Fe Ave(from nb), **E...gas:** Arco/24hr, **W...gas:** Chevron/24hr, Shell

32c b I-710, Long Beach Fwy, no facilities

32a Pacific Ave(from sb), no facilities

30b Long Beach Blvd, **E...gas:** 76, **W...gas:** Mobil, **other:** HOSPITAL, Toyota

30a Atlantic Blvd, **E...gas:** Chevron/diesel, Shell/Subway/diesel, **food:** Arby's, Black Angus, Denny's/24hr, El Patio, El Torito, Jack-in-the-Box, **other:** Mercedes, Staples, Target, Walgreen, **W...other:** HOSPITAL, Chrysler/Jeep, Nissan

29c Orange Ave(from sb), no facilities

29b a Cherry Ave, to Signal Hill, **E...gas:** Mobil/diesel, **food:** Fantastic Burgers, **other:** Ford, auto repair, **W...food:** John's Burgers, Charley Brown's Steaks/Lobster, Rib Café, **other:** BMW, Dodge, Firestone, Nissan

27 CA 19, Lakewood Blvd, **E...lodging:** Marriott, **W...gas:** Chevron, Shell/24hr, **food:** Spires Rest., Taco Bell, **lodging:** Holiday Inn, Residence Inn, **other:** HOSPITAL, Ford, Goodyear/auto, Kia, Plymouth

26b Bellflower Blvd, **E...gas:** Chevron, 76, **food:** Burger King, Carl's Jr, KFC, **other:** Chevrolet, Ford, K-Mart, Lowe's Whse, **W...gas:** Mobil/diesel, 76, **food:** Fish-Tale Rest., Hof's Rest., McDonald's, Quizno's, Wendy's, **other:** HOSPITAL, Borders Books, Circuit City, CompUSA, Goodyear/auto, Rite Aid/24hr, SavOn Drug, Sears, Target

26a Woodruff Ave(from nb), no facilities

25 Palo Verde Ave, **W...gas:** 76, **food:** Del Taco, Dr Wi Donuts, Pizza Hut/Taco Bell, Subway

24b Studebaker Rd

24a I-605 N, no facilities

23 CA 22 W, 7th St, to Long Beach, no facilities

22 Seal Beach Blvd, Los Alamitos Blvd, **E...gas:** Chevron/repair/24hr, Mobil, 76, **food:** Carl's Jr, KFC, Panda Chinese, Spagatini Grill, Winchell's, **other:** Albertson's, Goodyear/auto, Ralph's Foods, Rite Aid, Target, Winston Tire

21 CA 22 E, Garden Grove Fwy, Valley View St, **E...gas:** Mobil, Shell/diesel, **food:** Coco's, DQ, Maxwell's Seafood Rest., Sizzler, **other:** Chevrolet, Ford, Rite Aid, Von's Foods

19 Westminster Ave, to Springdale St, **E...gas:** Arco/24hr, Chevron/diesel, 76/Circle K, Thrifty, 7-11/24hr, **food:** Café Westminster, Carl's Jr, In-n-Out, KFC, La Casa Brita, McDonald's, Taco Bell, Yoshinoya, **lodging:** Motel 6, Travelodge, **other:** Albertson's, America's Tire, Home Depot, Kragen Parts, Radio Shack, Rite Aid, **W...gas:** Chevron/diesel/24hr, Shell/diesel/24hr, **food:** Pizza Hut, Subway, **lodging:** Best Western, Day's Inn

18 Bolsa Ave, Golden West St, **E...food:** Pizza Hut, Popeye's, **W...gas:** Chevron, Mobil, 76, Shell, **food:** Bennigan's, Coco's, El Torito, IHOP, Jack-in-the-Box, **other:** Best Buy, JC Penney, Jo-Ann Fabrics, Jon's Foods, Robinson-May, Sears/auto, mall

16 CA 39, Beach Blvd, to Huntington Bch, **E...gas:** Shell, **food:** Hof's Rest., Jack-in-the-Box, Mei's Chinese, **lodging:** BeachWest Inn, Princess Inn, Super 8, Westminster Inn, **other:** HOSPITAL, Buick/Pontiac/GMC, K-Mart, PepBoys, Toyota, **W...gas:** Arco, Mobil/service, 76, **food:** Arby's, Burger King, Diedrich's Coffee, El Torito, Jack-in-the-Box, Macaroni Grill, Marie Callender's, Popeye's, Starbucks, **lodging:** Holiday Inn, **other:** Barnes&Noble, Chevrolet, Chrysler/Jeep, Circuit City, Dodge, Ford/Lincoln/Mercury, Just Tires, Marshall's, Mitsubishi, OfficeMax, Plymouth, Subaru, Target, VW

Costa Mesa

15b a Magnolia St, Warner Ave, **E...gas:** Shell, **food:** Del Taco, Sizzler, **other:** CompUSA, **W...gas:** Chevron, Mobil, **food:** Bullwinkle's Rest., Carrow's, Magnolia Café, Tommy's Burgers, **lodging:** Ramada Inn, **other:** IGA Foods, SavOn Drug

14 Brookhurst Ave, Fountain Valley, **E...gas:** Arco/24hr, Chevron, Thrifty, **food:** Alberto's Mexican, Coco's, Del Taco, **lodging:** Courtyard, Residence Inn, **other:** Thompson's RV Ctr, **W...gas:** Chevron/service/24hr, Shell/diesel, **food:** Black Angus, Stix Chinese, Wendy's, **other:** MEDICAL CARE, Albertson's, Office Depot

12 Euclid Ave, **E...food:** Carl's Jr, George's Burgers, Souplantation, Taco Bell, **other:** HOSPITAL, Costco, Fry's Electronics, Office Depot, Staples, Tire Whse

11b Harbor Blvd, to Costa Mesa, **E...lodging:** La Quinta, **W...gas:** Arco, Chevron, Mobil, Shell/diesel, 7-11, **food:** Burger King, Denny's, Domino's, El Pollo Loco, IHOP, Jack-in-the-Box, KFC, LJ Silver, McDonald's, Subway, **lodging:** Costa Mesa Inn, Motel 6, Super 8, Vagabond Inn, **other:** MEDICAL CARE, Albertson's, Big O Tire, Cadillac, Chevrolet, Dodge/Acura, Ford/Lincoln/Mercury, Honda, Infiniti, JustTires, Mazda, Pontiac/Buick, Radio Shack, Rite Aid, Target, Von's Foods, Winchell's

11a Fairview Rd, **E...gas:** Shell, **other:** Barnes&Noble, Best Buy, Nordstrom's, Old Navy, **W...gas:** Chevron, Mobil, Shell, **food:** Del Taco, Jack-in-the-Box

10 CA 73, to CA 55 S(from sb), Corona del Mar, Newport Beach

9b Bristol St, **E...gas:** Chevron, Shell/24hr, **food:** Bombay Bicycle Club, Carrow's, Coco's, In-n-Out, Jack-in-the-Box, Maggiano's Rest., McDonald's, New Panda Chinese, Pizza Hut, Red Robin, Sizzler, **lodging:** Holiday Inn, Marriott Suites, Red Lion, Westin Hotel, **other:** MEDICAL CARE, Firestone/auto, Goodyear/auto, Office Depot, Michael's, Radio Shack, Rite Aid, Ross, Robinson-May, SavOn Drug, Sears/auto, Staples, Target, Von's Foods, mall, **W...gas:** Chevron, 76/diesel, Shell, 7-11, **food:** Del Taco/24hr, El Pollo Loco, Garf's Grill, McDonald's, Subway, **lodging:** DoubleTree Hotel, Hilton, Holiday Inn, **other:** PepBoys

9a CA 55, Costa Mesa Fwy, to Newport Bch, Riverside

8 MacArthur Blvd, **E...food:** Carl's Jr, Chicago Joe's, Food Court, Kokomo's Rest., McDonald's, Oasis Diner, **lodging:** Crowne Plaza Hotel, Holiday Inn, Embassy Suites, **other:** MEDICAL CARE, **W...gas:** Chevron, **food:** El Torito, Gulliver's Ribs, IHOP, **lodging:** Hilton, Marriott

Interstate 405

7 Jamboree Rd, Irvine, **E...lodging:** Courtyard, Hyatt, Residence Inn, **E on Main St...gas:** Texaco, **food:** Burger King, China West, JambaJuice, **W...food:** Asiana Rest., Daily Grill, Inka Grill, **lodging:** Marriott

5 Culver Dr, **W...gas:** Chevron, Shell, **food:** Carl's Jr, Subway, **other:** MEDICAL CARE, Ralph's Foods, Rite Aid, Wild Oats Mkt

4 Jeffrey Rd, University Dr, **E...gas:** Chevron, **food:** El Cholo Cantina, El Pollo Loco, McDonald's, Stix Chinese, Taco Bell, Togo's, **other:** Office Depot, Ralph's Foods, SavOn Drug, **W...gas:** Mobil/diesel, **food:** IHOP, Rubino's Pizza, **other:** Parkview Drug, Ralph's Foods

3 Sand Canyon Ave, **E...**HOSPITAL

2 CA 133, to Laguna Beach, no facilities

1c Irvine Center Dr, **E...food:** Dave & Buster's, Chang's Chinese Bistro, **other:** Barnes&Noble, **W...food:** Burger King

1b Bake Pkwy, **W...**Toyota

1a Lake Forest

0mm I-405 begins/ends on I-5, exit 132.

Interstate 505(Winters)

Exit #	Services
33	I-5. I-505 begins/ends on I-5.
31	CA 12A, no facilities
28	CA 14, Zamora, no facilities
24	CA 19, no facilities
21	CA 16, Woodland, to Esparto, **W...gas:** Guy's Food/fuel
17	CA 27, no facilities
15	CA 29A, no facilities
11	CA 128 W, Russell Blvd, **W...gas:** Chevron/24hr, **food:** Mexican Rest., RoundTable Pizza, **other:** MEDICAL CARE, Eagle Drug, IGA Foods
10	Putah Creek Rd, same as 11
6	Allendale Rd, no facilities
3	Midway Rd, **E...other:** RV camping
1c	Vaca Valley Pkwy, no facilities
1b	I-80 E. I-505 begins/ends on I-80.

Interstate 580(Bay Area)

Exit #	Services
79	I-580 begins/ends, accesses I-5 sb.
76b a	CA 132, Chrisman Rd, to Modesto, **E...gas:** 76/diesel, **other:** RV camping(5mi)
72	Corral Hollow Rd, no facilities
67	Patterson Pass Rd, **W...gas:** Arco/diesel/24hr
65	I-205(from eb), to Tracy
63	Grant Line Rd, to Byron, no facilities
59	N Flynn Rd, Altamont Pass, elev 1009, no facilities
57	N Greenville Rd, Laughlin Rd, Altamont Pass Rd, to Livermore Lab
56	weigh sta both lanes
55	Vasco Rd, to Brentwood, **N...gas:** Shell/diesel/deli, **S...gas:** 76, **food:** Jack-in-the-Box
54	CA 84, 1st St, Springtown Blvd, Livermore, **N...lodging:** Holiday Inn, Motel 6, Springtown Motel, **S...gas:** Chevron, Shell, 76/24hr, **food:** Applebee's, Arby's, Burger King, Happi House, Italian Express, McDonald's, StarBucks, Taco Bell, Togo's, **other:** American Tires, Longs Drug, Mervyn's, Office Depot, Ross, Safeway, Target
52	N Livermore Ave, **S...gas:** Chevron/Jack-in-the-Box, Citgo/7-11, **other:** Wal-Mart/auto
51	Portola Ave, Livermore(no EZ eb return), **S...gas:** Chevron, Shell, **other:** HOSPITAL, JC's RV Ctr
50	Airway Blvd, Collier Canyon Rd, Livermore, **N...gas:** Shell/diesel, **food:** Wendy's, **lodging:** Comfort Inn, Courtyard, Hampton Inn, Hilton Garden, Residence Inn, **other:** Costco Whse/gas, **S...food:** Cattlemen's Rest., McDonald's, **lodging:** Extended Stay America, **other:** Chrysler/Plymouth/Jeep, Lincoln/Mercury, Mazda
48	El Charro Rd, Croak Rd, no facilities
47	Santa Rita Rd, Tassajara Rd, **S...gas:** Shell, **food:** Bakers Square, Baskin-Robbins, Boston Mkt, California Burger, Ole's Mexican, McDonald's, Subway, Taco Bell, **other:** Longs Drug, Acura, BMW, Cadillac, GMC, Infiniti, Lexus, Mitsubishi, Rose Pavilion, Saab, Saturn, Volvo
46	Hacienda Dr, Pleasanton, **N...food:** Black Angus, **lodging:** AmeriSuites, **other:** Barnes&Noble, Best Buy, Mimi's, Old Navy, **S...other:** HOSPITAL, Borders Books, Staples, Wal-Mart
45	Hopyard Rd, Pleasanton, **N...gas:** 76, Minimart, **lodging:** Holiday Inn Express, **other:** Dodge, Goodyear, Nissan, Office Depot, Pak'n Sav, RV Ctr, Toyota, **S...gas:** Chevron, Shell/diesel, **food:** Burger King, Buttercup Pantry/24hr, Chevy's Mexican, Chili's, Denny's, Hungry Hunter, Lyon's Rest., Maestro's Italian, Nations Burgers, Pedro's Mexican, Taco Bell, **lodging:** Candlewood Suites, Courtyard, Hilton, Marriott, Motel 6, Sheraton, Super 8, **other:** CompUSA, Home Depot, Mercedes
44b	I-680, N to San Ramon, S to San Jose

CALIFORNIA

Interstate 580

E ↕ W

44a Foothills Rd, San Ramon Rd, **N...gas:** Chevron, Exxon, Shell, 76, **food:** Burger King, Carl's Jr, Carrow's, Coco's, Foster's Freeze, Frankie&Johnny&Luigi's, India Prince Rest., KFC, McDonald's, Outback Steaks, RoundTable Pizza, Subway, Wendy's, **lodging:** Best Western, **other:** Buick, Chevrolet, Ford, Honda, Isuzu, Grand Auto Supply, Mervyn's, Michael's, Ralph's Foods, Rite Aid, Ross, Target, **S...food:** Black Angus, **lodging:** Crowne Plaza, Residence Inn, Wyndham Garden, **other:** Chrysler/Plymouth, JC Penney, Macy's, Nordstrom's, mall

39 Eden Canyon Rd, Palomares Rd, **S...other:** rodeo park

37 Center St, Crow Canyon Rd, **N...**mall, same as 38, **S...gas:** Arco/24hr, Chevron/diesel/, 76

35 Redwood Rd, Castro Valley, (no EZ eb return), **N...gas:** Chevron, Shell, **food:** KFC, McDonald's, Sizzler, Taco Bell, **lodging:** Holiday Inn Express, **other:** Longs Drug, NAPA, Rite Aid, Safeway, **S...gas:** 7-11

34 I-238 W, to I-880, CA 238, **W off I-238...food:** Jack-in-the Box, **other:** Volvo

33 164th Ave, Miramar Ave, **E...gas:** Chevron/diesel

32b 150th Ave, Fairmont, **E...**HOSPITAL, **W...gas:** Arco, Shell, 76, **food:** Denny's, **other:** Longs Drug, Macy's

32a Grand Ave(from sb), Dutton Ave, **W...gas:** Coast, **other:** Rite Aid

30 106th Ave, Foothill Blvd, MacArthur Blvd, **W...gas:** Arco/24hr

29 98th Ave, Golf Links Rd, **E...gas:** Shell, **W...gas:** 76

27b Keller Ave, Mtn Blvd, **E...**repair

27ab Edwards Ave(from sb, no EZ return), **E...**US Naval Hospital

26a CA 13, Warren Fwy, to Berkeley

26b Seminary Rd, **E...**Observatory/Planetarium, **W...gas:** Arco/24hr

Oakland Area

25b a High St, to MacArthur Blvd, **E...gas:** Shell, 76, 7-11, **food:** Subway, **other:** Kragen Parts, **W...gas:** 76, **other:** Walgreen

24 35th Ave(no EZ sb return), **E...gas:** Exxon, 76, **food:** Taco Bell, **other:** Albertson's, **W...gas:** Chevron, QuikStop

23 Fruitvale, Coolidge Ave, **E...gas:** Shell/24hr, 7-11, **food:** McDonald's, **other:** Albertson's, Longs Drug, Safeway, **W...gas:** 76

22 Park Blvd, **E...**Shell, **W...**76

21b Grand Ave, Lake Shore, **E...gas:** Chevron, 76/24hr, 7-11, **food:** Domino's, KFC, Subway, **other:** Lucky Foods, **W...gas:** Chevron/diesel/24hr

21a Harrison St, Copeland Ave, **E...gas:** 76

19d c Ca 24 E, I-980 W, to Oakland

19b West St, San Pablo Ave, downtown

19a I-80 W

18c Market St, to San Pablo Ave, downtown

18b Powell St, Emeryville, **E...gas:** 76, **food:** Burger King, Denny's, Lyon's Rest., Starbucks, Trader Joe's, **lodging:** Day's Inn, **other:** Circuit City, Jo-Ann Fabrics, **W...gas:** Shell, **food:** Chevy's FreshMex, **lodging:** Holiday Inn

18a CA 13, Ashby Ave, Bay St, no facilities

17 University Ave, Berkeley, **E...gas:** Coast/diesel, 76, **food:** Mermaid Cambodian Seafood, **lodging:** Ramada Inn

16 Gilman St, **E...gas:** Chevron, **other:** Walgreen, Golden Gate Fields

13 Buchanan St(from eb), no facilities

13 Albany Ave, **W...**Golden Gate Field Racetrack

12 Central Ave(from eb), El Cerrito, **E...gas:** Shell

11 Bayview Ave, Carlson Blvd, **E...gas:** 76

10b Regatta Blvd, **E...gas:** gas/diesel

10a S 23rd St, Marina Bay Pkwy, **E...gas:** gas/diesel

9 Harbour Way, Cutting Blvd, **E...gas:** Cutting/diesel, **food:** El Caballo Mexican, **W...**Tire Barn

8 Canal Blvd, Garrard Blvd, **W...gas:** Chevron/diesel, **lodging:** Point Marina Inn

7b Castro St, Point Richmond, to I-80 E, downtown industrial

7a Western Drive(from wb), Point Molate, no facilities

5mm Richmond-San Rafael Toll Bridge

2a Francis Drake Blvd(from wb), to US 101 S

1b Francisco Blvd, San Rafael, **E...gas:** 76, **food:** Azul Marisco's Mexican, Burger King, Café Mesa, Foodles' Café, Subway, Wendy's, **other:** Aamco, Home Depot, Dodge/Isuzu, **W...**USPO, to San Quentin

1a US 101 N to San Rafael, I-580 begins/ends on US

Interstate 605(LA)

N ↕ S

Exit # . Services

25 Huntington Dr. I-605 begins/ends.

24 I-210, no facilities

23 Live Oak Ave, Arrow Hwy, **E...**Santa Fe Dam, **W...**Irwindale Speedway

Los Angeles Area

22 Lower Azusa Rd, LA St, no facilities

21 Ramona Blvd, **E...gas:** Mobil, **food:** Del Taco/24hr

20 I-10, E to San Bernardino, W to LA

19 Valley Blvd, to Industry, **E...gas:** Chevron, 76, **food:** McDonald's, **lodging:** Valley Inn

18 CA 60, Pamona Fwy, no facilities

17 Peck Rd, **E...gas:** Shell, **W...other:** Ford Trucks, Freightliner

16 Beverly Blvd, RoseHills Rd, no facilities

15 Whittier Blvd, **E...gas:** 76, Shell, 7-11, **food:** Carl's Jr, **lodging:** GoodNite Inn, **W...gas:** Chevron, **other:** Buick, Chrysler/Dodge, Ford, GMC, Honda, Isuzu, Jeep, Kia, Plymouth, Pontiac, Saturn, Toyota, Volvo

14 Washington Blvd, to Pico Rivera, no facilities

13 Slauson Ave, **E...gas:** Arco, Mobil, **food:** Denny's, **lodging:** Motel 6, **W...**HOSPITAL

12 Telegraph Rd, to Santa Fe Springs, **E...gas:** Chevron, Shell, **other:** st patrol

11 I-5, no facilities

10 Florence Ave, to Downey, **E... other:** Chevrolet, Honda, Sam's Club, Volvo

Interstate 605

N ↕ S — Los Angeles Area

9 Firestone Blvd, **E...gas:** 76, Shell, **food:** ChuckeCheese, KFC, McDonald's, Norm's Burgers, Taco Bell, **lodging:** Best Western, **other:** BMW, Costco, Food4Less, Staples, VW/Audi, **W...gas:** Arco, Chevron/repair, 76/diesel, **food:** Starbucks, **other:** Dodge, Office Depot, Target

8 I-105, Imperial Hwy, **E...gas:** 76, **food:** KFC, Pizza Hut/Taco Bell, **other:** SavOn Drug, **W...gas:** Arco

7 Rosecrans Ave, to Norwalk, **E...gas:** Chevron, **W...food:** Carrow's Rest, **lodging:** Motel 6

6 Alondra Blvd, **E...gas:** Chevron, **lodging:** Spires Rest., **other:** Staples, **W...gas:** Shell/24hr, Texaco/Subway

5 CA 91, no facilities

4 South St, **E...other:** Macy's, Mervyn's, Nordstrom's, Robinsons-May, Sears/auto, mall, **W...gas:** 76/service, Shell/service, Texaco/diesel, UltraMar, **other:** Buick/GMC/Pontiac, Chrysler/Plymouth, Daewoo, Dodge, Ford, Honda, Hyundai, Infiniti, Isuzu, Saturn, Toyota, Volvo

3 Del Amo Blvd, to Cerritos, **E...food:** Del Taco, Duke's Burgers, **other:** Ralph's Foods, **W...gas:** Mobil

2 Carson St, **E...gas:** Arco, 76, Shell, **food:** Jack-in-the-Box, KFC, Little Caesar's, McDonald's, Mexican Rest., Popeye's, Sky Burgers, Spike's Rest., Taco Bell, Wienerschnitzel, **lodging:** Lakewood Inn, **other:** Chief Parts, Kragen Parts, **W...gas:** Chevron/diesel, Mobil, **food:** Denny's, Del Taco, El Pollo Loco, El Torito, FoodCourt, In-n-Out, Jack-in-the-Box, Roadhouse Grill, Starbucks, TGIFriday, **other:** Barnes&Noble, GNC, Lowe's Whse, Michael's, Old Navy, Radio Shack, Ross, Sam's Club, Staples, Wal-Mart SuperCtr/24hr

1 Katella Ave, Willow St, **E...food:** McDonald's, **other:** HOSPITAL

0mm I-605 begins/ends on I-405.

Interstate 680(Bay Area)

N ↕ S

Exit #	Services
71b a	I-80 E, to Sacramento, W to Oakland, I-680 begins/ends on I-80.
70	Green Valley Rd(from eb), Cordelia, **N...other:** Longs Drug, Safeway
69	Gold Hill Rd, **W...gas:** TowerMart/diesel
65	Marshview Rd, no facilities
63	Parish Rd, no facilities
61	Lake Herman Rd, **E...gas:** Arco/Jack-in-the-Box/diesel, **W... gas:** Shell/Carl's Jr/diesel/24hr, **other:** vista point
60	Bayshore Rd, industrial park
58	I-780, to Benicia, toll plaza
55mm	Martinez-Benicia Toll Br
56	Marina Vista, to Martinez, no facilities
54	Pacheco Blvd, Arthur Rd, Concord, **W...gas:** 76/24hr, Shell/diesel/24hr
53b	CA 4 W, Pittsburg, to Richmond, **E...other:** Dodge

Concord

53a	CA 4 E, Concord, Pacheco, **E...food:** Peppermill Coffeeshop, Sullivan's Rest., Taco Bell, **lodging:** Sheraton, **other:** Ford, Hyundai, Infiniti/VW, Toyota, USPO, **W...gas:** Chevron/24hr, Exxon, 76, Shell/24hr, 7-11, **food:** Burger King, Carrow's Rest., Denny's, KFC, McDonald's, **other:** Barnes&Noble, Goodyear/auto, K-Mart, Kragen Parts, Longs Drug, Marshall's, Mervyn's, Target
51	Willow Pass Rd, Taylor Blvd, **E...food:** Benihana Rest., Denny's, El Torito, Grissini Italian, JJ North's Buffet, Marie Callender's, Red Lobster, Tony Roma, **lodging:** Hilton, **other:** MEDICAL CARE, Auto Parts Club, Circuit City, CompUSA, Cost+, Office Depot, Old Navy, Trader Joe's, Willows Shopping Ctr, **W...other:** Firestone, JC Penney, Macy's, Sears/auto
50	CA 242(from nb), to Concord
49	Gregory Lane, to Pleasant Hill, **E...gas:** Chevron, **other:** Jo-Ann Fabrics, **W...food:** Confetti Rest., Lyon's Rest., **other:** Grand Auto Supply
48	Oak Park Blvd, Geary Rd, **E...gas:** Chevron, 7-11, **food:** Subway, **lodging:** Embassy Suites, Extended Stay America, **other:** Best Buy, **W...gas:** Chevron, Shell/diesel, **food:** Black Angus, Burger King, China Rest., Sweet Tomatos, Wendy's, **lodging:** Courtyard, Holiday Inn, **other:** Mazda/Subaru, Nissan, Staples, Volvo, Walgreen
47	N Main St, to Walnut Creek, **E...gas:** Chevron/Subway, Shell, **food:** Black Diamond Brewery/rest., Fuddrucker's, Jack-in-the-Box, Taco Bell, Vino Ristorante, **lodging:** Marriott, Motel 6, Walnut Cr Motel, **other:** Cadillac, Chrysler/Jeep, Harley-Davidson, Mercedes, Target, **W...gas:** 76/diesel/24hr, 7-11, **food:** Domino's, **other:** Honda, NAPA, OfficeMax
46b	Ygnacio Rd
46a	CA 24, to Lafayette, Oakland
45	S Main St, Walnut Creek, **E...**HOSPITAL

CALIFORNIA

Interstate 680

N ↕ S

Exit	Services
43	Livorna Rd, no facilities
42b a	Stone Valley Rd, Alamo, **W...gas:** Chevron, Rotten Robbie/diesel, Shell/diesel, 7-11, **food:** Cioni's Italian, Little Caesar's, **other:** Safeway
41	El Pintado Rd, Danville, no facilities
40	El Cerro Blvd, no facilities
39	Diablo Rd, Danville, **E...gas:** 76/24hr, **food:** Taco Bell, **other:** Albertson's, Mt Diablo SP(12mi), **W...gas:** Chevron, 76, Coco's, **food:** Country Waffle Rest., Foster's Freeze, Pizza Hut, Primo's Pizza, **other:** MEDICAL CARE
San Ramon	
38	Sycamore Valley Rd, **E...gas:** Shell, **food:** Denny's, **lodging:** Econolodge, **W...gas:** Arco/diesel, Exxon, 76, **food:** Pizza Machine, Tony Roma's, **other:** Albertson's, Longs Drug
36	Crow Canyon Rd, San Ramon, **E...gas:** Shell, **food:** Burger King, Carl's Jr, Chili's, **other:** HOSPITAL, Albertson's, Rite Aid, USPO, **W...gas:** Chevron/repair/24hr, Exxon, 76, Shell/autocare, **food:** Boston Mkt, In-n-Out, Maestro's Rest., McDonald's, Taco Bell, TGIFriday, **other:** Harley-Davidson, Longs Drug, Safeway
34	Bollinger Canyon Rd, **E...gas:** Exxon, **food:** Subway, Marriott, **lodging:** Residence Inn, **other:** Borders Books, Target, Whole Foods, **W...gas:** Chevron/Foodini's, **food:** Applebee's, Chevy's Mexican, Marie Callender's, **lodging:** Courtyard, Homestead Village
31	Alcosta Blvd, to Dublin, **E...gas:** 76, 7-11, **food:** Pizza Hut, TCBY, **other:** Albertson's, Longs Drugs, **W...gas:** Chevron, Shell, **food:** Chatillon Rest., Chubby's Rest., Pizza Palace, Taco Bell, **other:** Albertson's, Walgreen
30	I-580, W to Oakland, E to Tracy
29	Stoneridge, Dublin, **E...lodging:** Hilton, **W...food:** Black Angus, **lodging:** Doubletree Hotel, Holiday Inn, **other:** Chrysler/Plymouth/Jeep, Macy's, Nordstrom's, Sears, mall
26	Bernal Ave, Pleasanton, **E...food:** Lindo's Mexican, Ring's Burgers, Vic's Bakery
22	Sunol Blvd, Castlewood Dr, Pleasanton, **1 mi E...food:** Jim's Rest., Raley's Foods
Fremont	
21b a	CA 84, Calvaras Rd, Sunol, W to Dumbarton Bridge
20	Andrade Rd, Sheridan Rd(from sb), **E...**gas/diesel/24hr
19mm	weigh sta nb
19	Sheridan Rd(from nb), no facilities
18	Vargas Rd, no facilities
16	CA 238, Mission Blvd, to Hayward, **E...gas:** Shell, **food:** McDonald's, **W...**HOSPITAL
15	Washington Blvd, Irvington Dist, **E...gas:** Quik-Stop
14	Durham Rd, to Auto Mall Pkwy, **W...gas:** 76/Subway/24hr, Shell/Jack-in-the-Box, **other:** Fry's Electronics
12	Mission Blvd, Warm Springs Dist, to I-880, **W...gas:** Exxon/diesel, **food:** Burger King, Carl's Jr, Denny's, Donut House, Jack-in-the-Box, KFC, Little Caesar's, RoundTable Pizza, Taco Bell, **lodging:** Econolodge, Quality Inn, **other:** GNC, Albertson's, Lion Foods, Longs Drug
10	Scott Creek Rd, no facilities
9	Jacklin Rd, **E...food:** Bonfare Rest., **W...gas:** Shell
8	CA 237, Calaveras Blvd, Milpitas, **E...gas:** Shell/repair, 76, **food:** Flames CoffeeShop, Hungry Hunter, Pizza Hut, Sizzler, Subway, **lodging:** Day's Inn, **other:** SuperMkt, **W...gas:** Shell, **food:** Dave&Buster's, El Torito, Lyon's Rest., McDonald's, Red Lobster, TCBY, **lodging:** Embassy Suites, Extended Stay America, **other:** MEDICAL CARE, Albertson's, Longs Drug, Mervyn's
San Jose	
6	Landess Ave, Montague Expswy, **E...gas:** Arco, 76, **food:** Burger King, Jack-in-the-Box, McDonald's, Royal Taco, StrawHat Pizza, Taco Bell, Togo's, Wienerschnitzel, **other:** Albertson's, Home Depot, Rite Aid, Target, Walgreen
5	Capitol Ave, Hostetter Ave, **E...gas:** Shell, **food:** Carl's Jr, Popeye's, **other:** SaveMart Foods, **W...gas:** Exxon, 7-11, **food:** KFC, **other:** MEDICAL CARE
4	Berryessa Rd, **E...gas:** Arco/24hr, Shell, **food:** Baskin-Robbins, Denny's, McDonald's, Ristorante Italiano, Taco Bell, **other:** Albertson's, Longs Drug, Safeway
2b	McKee Rd, **E...gas:** 76, Chevron, Shell, **food:** Burger King, Country Harvest Buffet, Donut Express, Pizza Hut, Sizzler, Togo's, Wienerschnitzel, **other:** Albertson's, PaknSave Foods, Walgreen, **W...food:** Baskin-Robbins, Foster's Freeze, McDonald's, RoundTable, Winchell's, **other:** HOSPITAL, Fabric Whse, K-Mart
2a	Alum Rock Ave, **E...gas:** Shell/diesel/24hr, **W...gas:** Exxon, 76/24hr, **food:** Carl's Jr
1d	Capitol Expswy, no facilities
1c	King Rd, Jackson Ave(from nb), **E...gas:** 76, Shell, 7-11, **food:** Jack-in-the-Box, Mi Pueblo Mexican, Taco Bell, **other:** King's SuperMkt, Walgreen
1b	US 101, to LA, SF
1a	(exits left from sb)I-680 begins/ends on I-280.

Interstate 710(LA)

E ↕ W

Exit #	Services
23	I-710 begins/ends on Valley Blvd
22b a	I-10, no facilities
20c	Chavez Ave, no facilities
20b	CA 60, Pamona Fwy, **W...gas:** Shell
20a	3rd St, no facilities
19	Whittier Blvd, Olympic Blvd, **W...gas:** Shell, **food:** McDonald's
17b	Washington Blvd, Commerce, **W...gas:** Commerce Trkstp/diesel/rest.

Interstate 710

Los Angeles Area (E ↕ W)

Exit #	Services
17a	Bandini Blvd, Atlantic Blvd, industrial
15	Florence Ave, **E...food:** KFC, **other:** Ralph's Foods, **W...**truck repair
13	CA 42, Firestone Blvd, **E...gas:** Arco, **food:** Krispy Kreme, Starbucks, **other:** Ford, Target
12b a	Imperial Hwy, **W...gas:** 76, Shell
11b a	I-105, no facilities
10	Rosecrans Ave, no facilities
9b a	Alondra Ave, **E...**Home Depot
8b a	CA 91, no facilities
7b a	Long Beach Blvd, **E...gas:** Mobil/repair, 76, **food:** Taco Bell, **W...gas:** Arco/24hr, **lodging:** Day's Inn
6	Del Amo Blvd, no facilities
4	I-405, San Diego Freeway
3b a	Willow St, **E...gas:** Chevron, **food:** Chee Chinese, **W...gas:** Mobil, **food:** Popeye's, **other:** Ralph's Foods
2	CA 1, Pacific Coast Hwy, **E...gas:** Arco/mart, Shell, UltraMar, **food:** Burger Express, Via Italia Pizza, **lodging:** LaMirage Inn, **other:** auto repair, **W...gas:** 76/service, Shell/Carl's Jr/diesel, Xpress Minimart, **food:** Alberta's Mexican/24hr, Golden Star Rest., Jack-in-the-Box, McDonald's, Tom's Burgers, Wienerschnitzel, Winchell's, **lodging:** SeaBreeze Motel, SeaBrite Motel
1d	Anaheim St, **W...gas:** Shell/LP/24hr, **other:** diesel repair
1c	Ahjoreline Dr, Piers B, C, D, E, Pico Ave, Long Beach, no facilities
1b	Pico Ave, Piers F-J, Queen Mary
1a	Harbor Scenic Dr, Piers S, T, Terminal Island, **E... lodging:** Hilton
0mm	I-710 begins/ends in Long Beach

Interstate 780(Vallejo)

Benicia (E ↕ W)

Exit #	Services
7	I-780 begins/ends on I-680.
6	E 5th St, Benicia, **N...gas:** Fast&Easy, **S...gas:** Citgo/7-11, GasCity/TCBY
5	E 2nd St, Central Benicia, **N...gas:** Exxon, **lodging:** Best Western, **S...food:** McDonald's
4	Southampton Rd, Benicia, **N...food:** Asian Bistro, Burger King, Country Waffle, Papa Murphy's, Rickshaw Express, RoundTable Pizza, Starbucks, Subway, **other:** AutoZone, Radio Shack, Raley's Foods
3b	Military West, **S...**MEDICAL CARE
3a	Columbus Pkwy, **N...gas:** Shell/Burger King/mart, **food:** Napoli Pizza/pasta, Subway, **S...**to Benicia RA
1d	Glen Cove Pkwy, **S...food:** Baskin-Robbins, Taco Bell, **other:** Safeway
1c	Laurel St, no facilities
1b a	I-780 begins/ends on I-80.

Interstate 805(San Diego)

San Diego Area (N ↕ S)

Exit #	Services
28mm	I-5(from nb). I-805 begins/ends on I-5.
27	Sorrento Valley Rd, Mira Mesa Blvd, **E...gas:** Shell, **food:** Chili's, McDonald's, **lodging:** Courtyard, Holiday Inn Express, Wyndham Garden, **other:** Staples
26	Vista Sorrento Pkwy, no facilities
25b a	La Jolla Village Dr, Miramar Rd, **1 mi E...gas:** 76/diesel, **other:** Discount Tire, Firestone/auto, **W...food:** Chang's China Bistro, **lodging:** Embassy Suites, Marriott, **other:** HOSPITAL, Nordstom's, Sears, mall
24	Governor Dr, **2 mi W...gas:** Chevron, Exxon, Mobil, 76, **food:** Carl's Jr, **other:** Rite Aid
23	CA 52, no facilities
22	Clairemont Mesa Blvd, **E...gas:** Chevron, Mobil/Subway/diesel, 76, **food:** Arby's, Burger King, Carl's Jr, Coco's, McDonald's, Quizno's, Players Grill, Rubio's Grill, Souplantation, Starbucks, **other:** Food4Less, Ford, K-Mart, **W...gas:** Arco/24hr, **food:** Carrow's, Godfather's, Oriental Buffet, **lodging:** CA Suites, Day's Inn, Motel 6
21	CA 274, Balboa Ave, **E...gas:** Arco, Chevron, Exxon/diesel, 76, Shell, **food:** Applebee's, Islands Burger, Jack-in-the-Box, **other:** Albertson's, Balboa AutoCare, Chevrolet, Dodge, Saturn, SavOn Drug
20	CA 163 N, to Escondido, no facilities
20a	Mesa College Dr, Kearney Villa Rd, **W...**HOSPITAL
18	Murray Ridge Rd, to Phyllis Place, no facilities
17b	I-8, E to El Centro, W to beaches
16	El Cajon Blvd, **E...gas:** Arco/24hr, Emerald, **food:** Church's, Venice Pizza, **other:** Albertson's, **W...gas:** 76, **food:** Wendy's
15	University Ave, **E...gas:** Chevron, **food:** Subway, **other:** Radio Shack, **W...gas:** Arco/24hr, Exxon, **other:** SavOn Drug
14	CA 15 N, 40th St, to I-15, no facilities
13b	Home Ave, MLK Ave, **E...gas:** Arco/24hr
13a	CA 94, no facilities
12b	Market St, no facilities
12a	Imperial Ave, **E...gas:** UltraMar/diesel
11b	47th St, no facilities
11a	43rd St, **W...food:** Giant Pizza, **other:** Albertson's, AutoZone, SavOn Drug
10	Plaza Blvd, National City, **E...food:** DQ, Dragon Garden

CALIFORNIA

Interstate 805

Chinese, Manila Seafood, McDonald's, Popeye's, Winchell's, **other:** HOSPITAL, AutoZone, Firestone/auto, Ralph's Foods, Well's Drug, **W...food:** Jimmy's Rest., **lodging:** Day's Inn

9 Sweetwater Rd, **E...gas:** Citgo/7-11, **lodging:** Sweetwater Inn, **W...gas:** Chevron/diesel, **food:** Carl's Jr, Casa Taco, Subway, Taco Bell, **other:** Circuit City, Food4Less, Longs Drug, Staples

8 CA 54, no facilities

7c E St, Bonita Rd, **E...food:** Applebee's, **other:** Mervyn's, Robinson-May, mall, **W...gas:** Chevron, 76, Shell, **food:** Burger King, Love's Rest., **lodging:** La Quinta, Ramada Inn

7b a H St, **E...gas:** Shell, **food:** China China, Jack-in-the-Box, Subway, Taco Bell, **other:** JC Penney, Longs Drug, Marshall's, Vons Foods, mall, RV camping

6 L St, Telegraph Canyon Rd, **E... gas:** Arco/repair, 76, **food:** McDonald's, Subway, **other:** HOSPITAL, Rite Aid, Von's Foods, Olympic Training Ctr, RV camping, **W...gas:** Mobil, 7-11

4 Orange Ave, no facilities

3 Main St, Otay Valley Rd, **E...gas:** Shell, **W...lodging:** Holiday Inn Express

2 Palm Ave, **E...gas:** Arco/24hr, Chevron/24hr, **food:** Carl's Jr, Subway, Taco Bell, **other:** MEDICAL CARE, Home Depot, Radio Shack, USPO, Von's Foods, Wal-Mart, **W...gas:** 76/diesel, **food:** KFC, McDonald's

1b CA 905, **E...**Brown Field Airport, Otay Mesa Border Crossing

1a San Ysidro Blvd, **E...gas:** Arco, Shell, **lodging:** Travelodge, Factory2U, Kragen Parts, Longs Drug, 99c Store, U-Haul, **W...gas:** Chevron, Exxon, Mobil, 76, **food:** Denny's, McDonald's, Si Senor Mexican, **lodging:** Motel 6,

I-805 begins/ends on I-5.

Interstate 880(Bay Area)

Exit #	Services
46b a	I-80 W(exits left). I-80 E/580 W.
44	7th St, Grand Ave(from sb), downtown
42b a	Broadway St, downtown, **E...lodging:** Civic Ctr Lodge, **W...**to Jack London Square
41a	Oak St, Lakeside Dr, downtown, **E...lodging:** Howard Johnson, **W...gas:** Shell/diesel
40	5th Ave, Embarcadero, **W...food:** Ark Rest., Hungry Hunter Rest., Reef Rest., **lodging:** Executive Inn, Motel 6
39b a	29th Ave, 23rd Ave, to Fruitvale, **E...gas:** Shell, **food:** Boston Mkt, DonutStar, Starbucks, **other:** Albertson's, AutoZone, GNC, Office Depot, Radio Shack, **W...gas:** 7-11, **food:** Buttercup Grill
38	High St, to Alameda, **E...lodging:** $Inn, **other:** El Monte RV Ctr, **W...gas:** Shell/diesel, **food:** McDonald's, K-Mart
37	66th Ave, Zhoney Way, **E...**coliseum
36	Hegenberger Rd, **E...gas:** Arco/24hr, Shell/diesel, **food:** Burger King, Denny's, Hungry Hunter Rest., Jack-in-the-Box/24hr, McDonald's, Sam's Hofbrau, Taco Bell, **lodging:** Comfort Inn, Day's Inn/rest., Hampton Inn, Holiday Inn, Motel 6, **other:** Pak'n Save Foods, GMC/Volvo, Freightliner, AutoParts Club, **W...gas:** Chevron, Shell, **food:** Carrows Rest., Francesco's Rest., Hegen Burgers, **lodging:** Hilton, Park Plaza Motel, Ramada Inn, **other:** Goodyear, to Oakland Airport
35	98th Ave, **W...**airport
34	Davis St, **E...gas:** Arco, 7-11, **food:** Lee's Donuts, Sergio's Pizza, **W...gas:** Shell, **food:** Burger King, Starbucks, Togo's, **other:** Costco, Home Depot, Office Depot, Wal-Mart
33b a	Marina Blvd, **E...gas:** Beacon/diesel, Marina/gas, **food:** Jack-in-the-Box, La Salsa Mexican, Starbucks, **other:** HOSPITAL, Firestone/auto, Ford, Hyundai, Kia, Kinko's, Marshall's, Nissan, Nordstrom's, OfficeMax, Old Navy, **W...gas:** Flyers/diesel, **food:** DairyBelle, Denny's, Giant Burger, KFC, Mtn Mike's Pizza, **other:** USPO
32	Washington Ave(from nb), Lewellin Blvd(from sb), **W...gas:** Arco, 76, **food:** Burrito Shop, Hometown Buffet, Jack-in-the-Box, McDonald's, Subway, **lodging:** Motel Nimitz, **other:** Longs Drug, Radio Shack, Safeway/24hr, SavMax Foods, SP Parts, Walgreen/24hr
31	I-238(from sb), to I-580, Castro Valley
30	Hesperian Blvd, **E...gas:** 76, **food:** Bakers Square, KFC, Mr Pizza, Western Superburger, **other:** House of Fabrics, Kragen Parts, Target, Wheelworks Repair, **W...gas:** Arco, Chevron, 76, **food:** Black Angus, Carrow's Rest., KFC, McDonald's, Taco Bell, **lodging:** Vagabond Inn, **other:** Albertson's
29	A St, San Lorenzo, **E...gas:** 76, **food:** McDonald's, **lodging:** Best Western, **other:** AllPro Parts, Costco, **W...gas:** 76, **food:** Burger King, StrawHat Pizza, **lodging:** Heritage Inn
28	Winton Ave, **W...gas:** Chevron, Valero/diesel, **food:** Applebee's, Sizzler, **other:** Circuit City, Firestone/auto, JC Penney, Macy's, Mervyn's, Old Navy, Ross, Sears/auto, mall
27	CA 92, Jackson St, **E...gas:** Valero, 76, 7-11, **food:** Bakers Square, Rickshaw Chinese, Subway, Taco Bell, **other:** Albertson's, Longs Drug, Rite Aid, Safeway, **W...**San Mateo Br
26	Tennyson Rd, **E...gas:** All American/diesel, 76, Shell, **food:** Jack-in-the-Box, KFC, Pizza Hut, RoundTable Pizza, **other:** Chavez Foods, Grand Parts, Walgreen, **W...gas:** Chevron, 76, Valero/diesel, 7-11, **food:** Carl's Jr, McDonald's, **other:** HOSPITAL, PepBoys

Interstate 880

N ↕ S

Fremont

24 Whipple Rd, Dyer St, **E...gas:** Chevron/24hr, 76, **food:** Denny's, McDonald's, Taco Bell, **lodging:** Motel 6, Super 8, **other:** CHP, Food4Less, Home Depot, PepBoys, **W...gas:** QuikStop/24hr, 76, Shell, **food:** Chili's, IHOP, Jollibee's Café, Jamba Juice, Krispy Kreme, La Salsa Mexican, Starbucks, Texas Roadhouse, TGIFriday, Togo's, **lodging:** Extended Stay America, **other:** Albertson's/SavOn, Borders Books, Michael's, OfficeMax, RadioShack, Wal-Mart/auto

23 Alvarado-Niles Rd, **E...gas:** Shell, 7-11, **lodging:** Radisson, **W...gas:** 76, Shell, **other:** Wal-Mart/auto

22 Alvarado Blvd, Fremont Blvd, **E...food:** Luciano European Café, Phoenix Garden Chinese, Subway, **lodging:** Motel 6, **other:** Albertson's/SavOn, Ranch Mkt Foods

21 CA 84 W, Dumbarton Br, Decoto Rd, **E...gas:** Citgo/7-11, **food:** McDonald's, **other:** Rite Aid, Walgreen

19 CA 84 E, Thornton Ave, Newark, **E...other:** Chevrolet, **W...gas:** Chevron/24hr, Exxon, Shell, 7-11, **food:** Bakers Square, Carl's Jr, KFC, RoundTable Pizza, Taco Bell, **other:** K-Mart

17 Mowry Ave, Fremont, **E...gas:** Chevron/diesel, Exxon, **food:** Applebee's, Burger King, Denny's, Hungry Hunter, KFC, Mkt Broiler, Olive Garden, **lodging:** EZ 8 Motel, Studio+ Suites, **other:** HOSPITAL, Albertson's, Cost+, Jo-Ann Fabrics, **W...food:** Bombay Garden, El Burro Mexican, FreshChoice Rest., HomeTown Buffet, Jack-in-the-Box, Lyon's Rest., McDonald's, Red Robin, Subway, Taco Bell, **lodging:** Hawthorn Suites, Holiday Inn Express, Motel 6, Woodfin Suites, **other:** Circuit City, Firestone, Ford, Goodyear/auto, Hancock Fabrics, JC Penney, Macy's, Marshall's, Mervyn's, Sears/auto, Staples, Target, mall

16 Stevenson Blvd, **W...food:** Carl's Jr, Chevy's Mexican, ChuckeCheese, Nijo Castle Rest., Sizzler, **lodging:** Hilton Garden, **other:** AAA, Costco, Food4Less, Ford, Harley-Davidson, Home Depot, JC Penney, Macy's, Mervyn's, Nissan, Pontiac/GMC, PepBoys, Saturn, Sears/auto, mall

15 Auto Mall Pkwy, **E...gas:** Chevron, **W...lodging:** Crawford Suites, **other:** BMW, Dodge/Isuzu, Honda, Hyundai, Kia, Lexus, Mercedes, Nissan, Saturn, Toyota, Volvo

14mm weigh sta both lanes

13 Fremont Blvd, Irving Dist, **W...food:** McDonald's, **lodging:** Courtyard, GoodNite Inn, Homestead Village, La Quinta, Marriott

13b Warren St(from sb), **E...lodging:** Quality Inn, **W...lodging:** Courtyard, Hampton Inn

13a Gateway Blvd(from nb), **W...lodging:** Courtyard

12 Mission Blvd, **E...**to I-680, **gas:** 76, **food:** Denny's, Togo's, **lodging:** Quality Inn

10 Dixon Landing Rd, **E...gas:** 7-11, **food:** Burger King, **lodging:** Residence Inn

San Jose

8b CA 237, Alviso Rd, Calaveras Rd, Milpitas, **E...gas:** Arco, 76, 7-11, **food:** Chili's, Denny's, Marie Callender, RoundTable Pizza, **lodging:** Best Western, Economy Inn, Travelodge, **other:** Albertson's, Kragen Parts, SavMart Foods, Walgreen, **W...food:** Applebee's, Black Angus, HomeTown Buffet, In-n-Out, Macaroni Grill, McDonald's, On the Border, Taco Bell, **lodging:** Candlewood Suites, Hampton Inn, Hilton Garden, Holiday Inn, **other:** Best Buy, Borders Books, Chevrolet, OfficeMax, Ranch Mkt Foods, Ross, Wal-Mart/auto

8a Great Mall Parkway, Tasman Dr, **E...**mall

7 Montague Expswy, **E...gas:** 76, Shell, **food:** Carl's Jr, Jack-in-the-Box, **other:** MEDICAL CARE, U-Haul, auto repair, **W...gas:** Chevron, **food:** Dave&Buster's, **lodging:** Sheraton

5 Brokaw Rd, **W...other:** Ford Trucks, CHP

4d Gish Rd, **W...other:** auto/diesel repair/transmissions

4c b US 101, N to San Francisco, S to LA

4a 1st St, **E...gas:** Shell/repair, **W...gas:** Chevron, 76, **food:** Denny's/24hr, Japanese Steaks, McDonald's, **lodging:** Adlon Hotel, Comfort Inn, Day's Inn, Holiday Inn Express, Wyndham Garden

3 Coleman St, **E...gas:** Exxon, **food:** George's Rest.

2 CA 82, The Alameda, **E...lodging:** San Jose Inn/rest., **W...gas:** Shell/repair, **food:** Cozy Rest., **lodging:** Bell Motel, Comfort Inn, Co-Z Hotel, Friendship Inn, Valley Inn, **other:** Safeway, Santa Clara U

1d Bascom Ave, to Santa Clara, **E...gas:** Shell/repair, **other:** HOSPITAL, **W...gas:** Exxon, Rotten Robbie/diesel, **food:** Burger King, Japanese Rest., Normandie House Pizza

1c Stevens Creek Blvd, San Carlos St, **E...gas:** Coast, **food:** Korean Rest., **W...gas:** Exxon, **food:** Arby's, Burger King, Lyon's Rest., Teriyaki Rest., **other:** Audi/VW, Chevrolet, Firestone/auto, Goodyear/auto, Isuzu, Longs Drugs, Macy's, Mitsubishi, Nordstrom's, Safeway, Subaru

1b I-280. I-880 begins/ends on I-280.

1a Ca 17 to Santa Cruz.

COLORADO

Interstate 25

N ↕ S

Ft Collins

Exit #	Services
299	Colorado/Wyoming state line
296	point of interest both lanes
293	to Carr, Norfolk, no facilities
288	Buckeye Rd, **3 mi W...**Rawhide Energy Project, no facilities
281	Owl Canyon Rd, **5 mi E...**KOA
278	CO 1 to Wellington, **1/2 mi W...gas:** Conoco, **food:** Shell/Burger King/Taco Bell, Subway
271	Mountain Vista Dr, **W...**Anheiser-Busch Brewery, no facilities
269b a	CO 14, to US 87, Ft Collins, **E...lodging:** Mulberry Inn, **other:** RV service, **W...gas:** Conoco, Phillips 66/diesel, **food:** Burger King, Denny's, Waffle House, **lodging:** Comfort Inn, Day's Inn, Holiday Inn, Motel 6, National 9 Inn, Plaza Inn, Ramada Inn, Super 8, **other:** to CO St U, stadium
268	Prospect Rd, to Ft Collins, **W...other:** HOSPITAL, Welcome Ctr, Harley-Davidson, Sunset RV Ctr
267mm	weigh sta both lanes
266mm	**rest area both lanes, full(handicapped)facilities, info, phone, picnic tables, litter barrels, petwalk**
265	CO 68 W, Timnath, **W...gas:** Shell, **2-3 mi W...food:** Austin's Grill, Carrabba's, Golden Corral, Hunan Chinese, IHOP, Macaroni Grill, Outback Steaks, Papa John's, Quizno's, Subway, Texas Roadhouse, Village Inn Rest., **lodging:** Courtyard, Hampton Inn, Marriott, Residence Inn, Safeway/gas, Sam's Club
262	CO 392 E, to Windsor, **E...gas:** Conoco, Phillips 66/Subway/diesel, **food:** Arby's, McDonald's(3mi), **lodging:** AmericInn, Super 8
259	Airport Rd, **E...**Wal-Mart Depot, **W...**to airport
257b a	US 34, to Loveland, **E...gas:** Shamrock/diesel/RV camping, **lodging:** Country Inn Suites, **W...gas:** Shell/diesel, **food:** Arby's(2mi), Blackeyed Pea, Chili's, Cracker Barrel, IHOP, KFC/Taco Bell, LoneStar Steaks, McDonald's, Subway, Waffle House, Wendy's, **lodging:** Best Western, Comfort Inn, Fairfield Inn, Hampton Inn, Holiday Inn Express, Super 8(2mi), **other:** HOSPITAL, Prime Outlets/famous brands, Target, RV camping, museum, to Rocky Mtn NP
255	CO 402 W, to Loveland, no facilities
254	to CO 60 W, to Campion, **E...gas:**Johnson's Corner/diesel/café/24hr, **lodging:** Budget Host, **other:** RV camping/service
252	CO 60 E, to Johnstown, Milliken, no facilities
250	CO 56 W, to Berthoud, no facilities
245	to Mead, no facilities
243	CO 66, to Longmont, Platteville, **E...gas:** Conoco, Shell, **food:** Blimpie, Scott's Rest., **other:** K&C RV Ctr, Yamaha/Suzuki, **W...**to Rocky Mtn NP, to Estes Park

Thornton

Exit #	Services
241mm	St Vrain River
240	CO 119, to Longmont, **E...gas:** Phillips 66/diesel, **food:** Wendy's, **lodging:** Best Western, Kia, Stevinson RV Ctr, **W...gas:** Conoco/Subway/diesel/24hr, Shell/diesel, **food:** Arby's, Burger King, DQ, McDonald's, Piccadilly's, Pizza Hut, Taco Bell, Waffle House, **lodging:** Best Western, Comfort Inn, Day's Inn, 1st Interstate Inn, Super 8, **other:** HOSPITAL, Del Camino RV Ctr, museum, to Barbour Ponds SP
235	CO 52, Dacono, **E...**Ford, **W...gas:** Phillips 66/diesel/LP, **other:** Harley-Davidson, to Eldora Ski Area
232	to Erie, no facilities
229	CO 7, to Lafayette, Brighton, **E...**RV camping
228	E-470, tollway, to Limon
225	144th Ave
223	CO 128, 120th Ave, to Broomfield, **E...gas:** Conoco, Shell, Sinclair, **food:** Applebee's, Burger King, Café Mexico, Damon's, Fuddrucker's, Golden Gate Chinese, LoneStar Steaks, OutBack Steaks, Pizza Hut, Shari's, **lodging:** Day's Inn, Hampton Inn, Holiday Inn, Radisson, Sleep Inn, **other:** Albertson's, Checker's Parts, Discount Tire, **W...gas:** Conoco, Shamrock/diesel, **food:** Casa Loma Mexican, Chili's, Cracker Barrel, DQ, Jade City Chinese, Perkins, Starbucks, Subway, Village Inn Rest., Wendy's, **lodging:** Comfort Inn, Fairfield Inn, La Quinta, Super 8
221	104th Ave, to Northglenn, **E...gas:** Conoco, Phillips 66, Shamrock/diesel, **food:** Burger King, Denny's, IHOP, McDonald's, Subway, Taco Bell, Taco John's, Texas Roadhouse, **other:** HOSPITAL, AutoZone, Big A Parts, Bigg's Foods, Home Depot, King's Sooper's, Target, Wal-Mart, **W...gas:** Citgo/7-11, Conoco, Shell/diesel, **food:** Applebee's, Bennigan's, Blackeyed Pea, Cinzinetti's Italian, Hop's Grill, McDonald's, Taco Bell, **lodging:** La Quinta, Ramada Ltd, **other:** Albertson's, Borders Books, Dodge, Firestone/auto, Goodyear/auto, Lowe's Whse, Marshall's, Mervyn's, Office Depot, Rite Aid, mall
220	Thornton Pkwy, **E...lodging:** Crossland Suites, **other:** HOSPITAL, Sam's Club/gas, Thornton Civic Ctr, **W...gas:** Conoco, Shamrock
219	84th Ave, to Federal Way, **E... gas:** Conoco, Shamrock, **food:** Arby's, Bonanza, Dos Verdes Mexican, Goodtimes Grill, Taco Bell, Waffle House, **other:** Radio Shack Outlet, Walgreen, **W...gas:** Shamrock/diesel, **food:** Burger King, DQ, Pizza Hut, Tokyo Bowl Japanese, Village Inn Rest., **lodging:** Motel 6, **other:** HOSPITAL, CarQuest, Discount Tire
217	US 36 W(exits left from nb), to Boulder, **W...food:** Subway, **other:** Chevrolet, Toyota
216b a	I-76 E, to I-270 E; no facilities

N

S

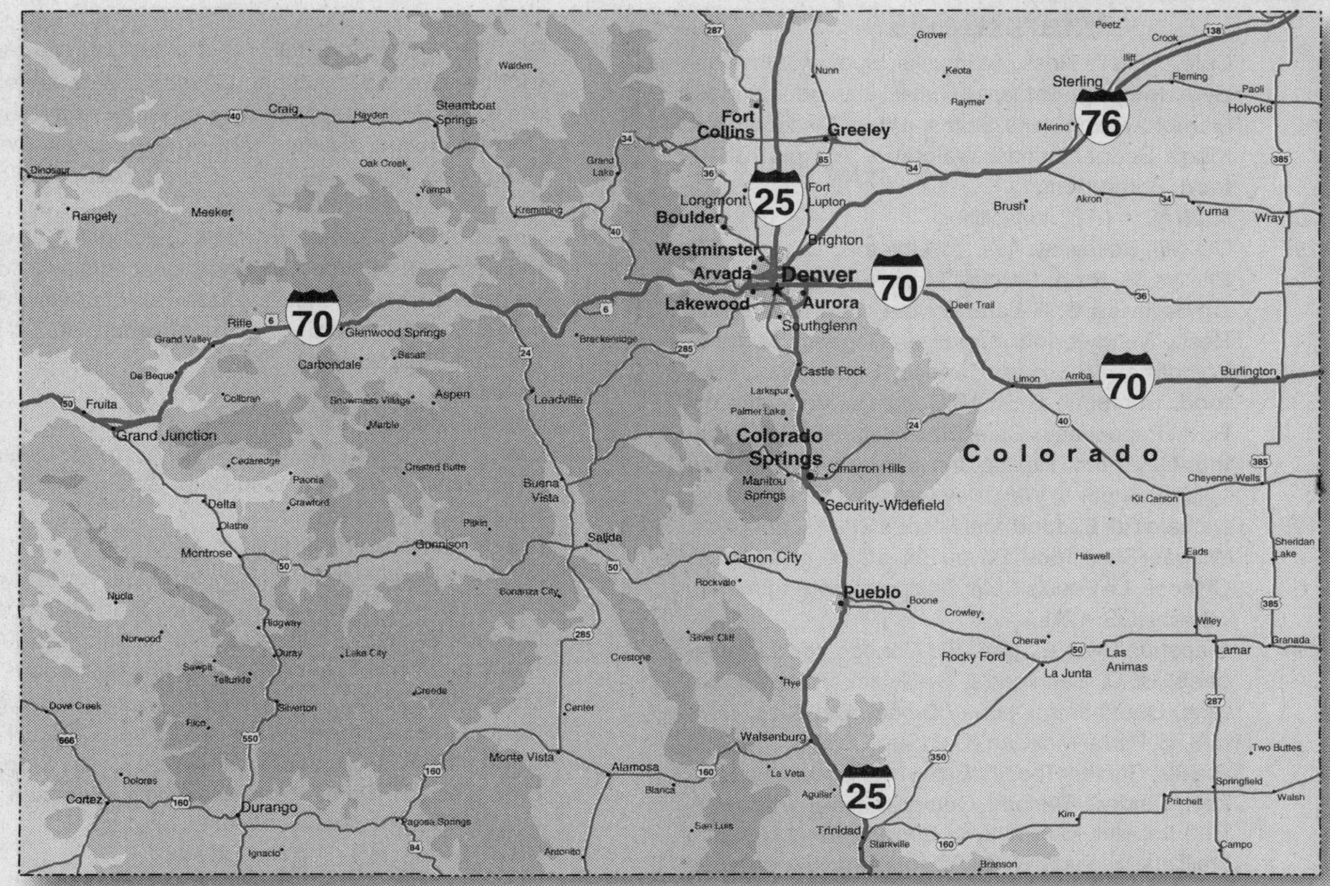

Denver Area

215 58th Ave, **E...food:** McDonald's, Taco John's, Wendy's, **lodging:** Quality Inn, **W...gas:** Conoco, Shamrock/Taco Bell/diesel/LP, **lodging**: Super 8, **other**: Malibu FunPark

214c 48th Ave, **E...**coliseum, airport, **W...food:** Village Inn Rest., **lodging:** Best Western, Holiday Inn

b a I-70, E to Limon, W to Grand Junction

213 Park Ave, W 38th Ave, 23rd St, downtown, **E...gas:** BP/McDonald's, Citgo/7-11, Shell, **food:** Burger King, Denny's, **lodging:** La Quinta, **other:** Goodyear, **W...lodging:** Regency Inn, Travelodge

212c 20th St, Denver, downtown, **W...food:** Pagliacci's Italian

b a Speer Blvd, **E...**downtown, museum, **W...gas:** Conoco, Shell, **lodging:** Ramada Inn, Residence Inn, Super 8, Travel Inn

211 23rd Ave, **E...**funpark

210c CO 33(from nb)

210b US 40 W, Colfax Ave, **W...food:** Denny's, KFC, **lodging:** Ramada Inn/rest., Red Lion Inn

a US 40 E, Colfax Ave, **E...**civic center, downtown, U-Haul

209c 8th Ave, **E...lodging:** Motel 7, **other:** Bob's Auto Parts

b 6th Ave W, US 6, **W...lodging:** Day's Inn

a 6th Ave E, Denver, downtown

208 CO 26, Alameda Ave(from sb), **E...gas:** Amoco, Shamrock/diesel, **food:** Burger King, Denny's, same as 207b

Cherry Hills

207b US 85 S, Santa Fe Dr, **E...gas:** Shamrock, **food:** Burger King, Denny's, **other:** Home Depot, **W...gas:** Shell

a Broadway, Lincoln St, **E...food:**Griff's Burgers, **other:** USPO

206b Washington St, Emerson St, **E...other:** WildOats Mkt/café, **W...other:** HOSPITAL

a Downing St(from nb), no facilities

205b a University Blvd, **W...**to U of Denver

204 CO 2, Colorado Blvd, **E...gas:** BP, Conoco, Shamrock, 7-11, **food:** Grisanti's Grill, KFC, Lazy Dog Café, Pizza Hut, Village Inn Rest., **lodging:** Day's Inn, Fairfield Inn, Ramada, **other:** Albertson's, Best Buy, CompUSA, **W...food:** Dave&Buster's, Denny's, Perkins, **lodging:** La Quinta

203 Evans Ave, **E...gas:** Shell, **food:** Denny's, KFC, **lodging:** Rockies Inn, **other:** Big O Tire, **W...lodging:** Cameron Motel, **other:** Ford

202 Yale Ave, **W...gas:** Shamrock

201 US 285, CO 30, Hampden Ave, to Englewood, Aurora, **E...gas:** BP, Conoco/LP, Phillips 66, Shamrock, Shell, **food:** Applebee's, Benihana, Blackeyed Pea, Boston Mkt, Chicago Grill, Chili's, Domino's, Houlihan's, Jason's Deli, Le Peep's Café, McDonald's, Mexican Grill, NY Deli, No Frills Grill, On-the-Border, Piccolo's

COLORADO

Interstate 25

N ↕ S

Café, Skillet's Rest., Starbucks, Subway, Uno Pizzaria, **lodging:** Embassy Suites, Hampden Lodge, Marriott, TownePlace Suites, **other:** Discount Tire, King's Sooper Foods, Walgreen, **W...gas:** Shell, **food:** Burger King

200 I-225 N, to I-70, no facilities

199 CO 88, Belleview Ave, to Littleton, **E...gas:** BP, Phillips 66, **food:** Garcia's Mexican, Harvest Rest., Off Belleview Grill, Sandwiches+, Tosh's Hacienda Rest., Wendy's, **lodging:** Hyatt Regency, Marriott, Wyndham, **W... gas:** Conoco, Shamrock/diesel, **food:** European Café, McDonald's, Mountainview Rest., Pappadeaux Café, Pizza Hut, Taco Bell, **lodging:** Day's Inn, Holiday Inn Express, HomeStead Village, Super 8, Wellesley Inn

198 Orchard Rd, **E...food:** Del Frisco's Steaks, Shepler's, **W...gas:** Shell, **food:** Bayou Bob's Café, 4Happiness Chinese, Le Peep's Café, Quizno's, **lodging:** Hilton, **other:** HOSPITAL,

197 Arapahoe Blvd, **E...gas:** BP, Conoco, **food:** Applebee's, BBQ, Bennigan's, BlackJack Pizza, Burger King, Carrabba's, Country Dinner, DeliZone, Denny's, El Parral Mexican, GoldStar Chili, GrandSlam Steaks, Gunther Toody's Rest., IHOP, Jalapeno Mexican, Landry's Seafood, Outback Steaks, Pizza Hut, Red Lobster, Schlotsky's, Subway, Taco Cabana, TrailDust Steaks, Wendy's, **lodging:** Candlewood Hotel, Courtyard, Embassy Suites, Hampton Inn, Holiday Inn, La Quinta, MainStay Suites, Motel 6, Radisson, Sheraton, Sleep Inn, Summerfield Suites, Woodfield Suites, **other:** Big A Parts, Buick/Pontiac, Chrysler/Toyota, Discount Tire, Ford, GMC/Cadillac/ Subaru, K-Mart, Lowe's Whse, Nissan, Target, USPO, **W...gas:** Phillips 66/diesel, 7-11, **food:** Arby's, Baker St Gourmet, Blackeyed Pea, Boston Mkt, Brooks Steaks, Burger King, Chevy's Mexican, DQ, GoodTimes Grill, Grady's Grill, Grisante's Grill, KFC, Lamonica's Rest., Macaroni Grill, McDonald's, Red Robin, Ruby Tuesday, Stanford's Grill, Souper Salad, Taco Bell, TCBY, Uno Pizzaria, **lodging:** Residence Inn, **other:** Albertson's, Barnes&Noble, Firestone/auto, Goodyear/auto, Office Depot, OfficeMax

196 Dry Creek Rd, **E...food:** Vasil's Rest., Landry's Seafood, **lodging:** Best Western, Bradford Suites, Country Inn Suites, Homestead Village, Quality Inn, Ramada Ltd, **other:** Studio+, **W...lodging:** Drury Inn

195 County Line Rd, **E...lodging:** Courtyard, Residence Inn, **W...food:** Alexander's Rest., Champp's Rest., Cucina Cucina, Starbucks, **lodging:** AmeriSuites, **other:** Barnes&Noble, Best Buy, Borders, CompUSA, Costco, Dillard's, Home Depot, JC Penney, Nordstrom's, OfficeMax

Castle Rock

194 CO 470 W, CO 470 E(tollway), **1 exit W on Quebec... food:** Arby's, ClaimJumper, Country Buffet, LoneStar Steaks, McDonald's, TGIFriday, **lodging:** AmeriSuites, Comfort Suites, Fairfield Inn, **other:** Barnes&Noble, Circuit City, Firestone, Home Depot, PepBoys, Sam's Club, Wal-Mart/auto/gas

193 Lincoln Ave, to Parker, **E...food:** Hacienda Colorado, **lodging:** Hilton Garden, **W...gas:** Conoco/diesel, **food:** Chipotle Grill, McDonald's, Pizza Hut/Taco Bell, Starbucks, Subway, **lodging:** Marriott, **other:** HOSPITAL, Discount Tire, Safeway

191 no facilities

190 Surrey Ridge, no facilities

188 Castle Pines Pkwy, **W...gas:** BP, Shell, **food:** La Dolce Vita, Subway, Wendy's, Wild Bean Café, **other:** King's Sooper/gas, Safeway

187 Happy Canyon Rd, no facilities

184 Founders Pkwy, Meadows Pkwy, to Castle Rock, **E...gas:** Conoco/diesel, Shell/Carl's Jr/diesel, **food:** Applebee's, Outback Steaks, Sonic, Wendy's, **other:** Starbucks, GNC, Goodyear, Home Depot, King's Sooper/24hr, Target, Walgreen, Wal-Mart SuperCtr/24hr, **W...gas:** Conoco/diesel, **food:** Blackeyed Pea, Chili's, Food Court, IHOP, McDonald's, Rockyard Café, **lodging:** Best Western, Comfort Inn, Day's Inn, Hampton Inn, Castle Rock Prime Outlet/famous brands

183 US 85 N(from nb), Sedalia, Littleton

182 CO 86, Castle Rock, Franktown, **E...gas:** Phillips 66/ diesel, Western, **food:** Little Caesar's, Mexicali Café, Nick&Willie's, **other:** st patrol, **W... gas:** Shamrock, Shell/ diesel, **food:** Burger King, KFC, McDonald's, Shari's/ 24hr, Taco Bell, Village Inn Rest., Wendy's, **lodging:** Comfort Inn, Holiday Inn Express, Quality Inn, Super 8, **other:** Chrysler/Plymouth/Dodge/Jeep, NAPA

181 CO 86, Wilcox St, Plum Creek Pkwy, Castle Rock, **E...gas:** BP, Citgo/7-11, Shamrock/diesel, **food:** DQ, Duke's Rest., Hungry Heifer Steaks, New Rock Café, Nicolo's Pizza, Pino's Café, Pizza Hut, Subway, **lodging:** Castle Rock Motel, **other:** MEDICAL CARE, Big A Parts, Ford/Lincoln/Mercury, Safeway, USPO

174 Tomah Rd, **W...**KOA(seasonal)

173 Larkspur(from sb, no return), **1 mi W...gas:** Conoco/ diesel/phone

172 South Lake Gulch Rd, Larkspur, **2 mi W...gas:** Conoco/ diesel/phone

171mm rest area both lanes, full(handicapped)facilities , phone, picnic tables, litter barrels, petwalk, RV dump

167 Greenland, no facilities

163 County Line Rd, no facilities

16.5mm Monument Hill, elev 7352

162mm weigh sta both lanes

161 CO 105, Woodmoor Dr, **E...gas:** BP, **lodging:** Falcon Inn, **W...gas:** Citgo/7-11, Conoco/diesel, **food:** Arby's, Boston Mkt, Burger King, DQ, McDonald's, Pizza Hut, Rosie's Diner, Starbucks, Subway, Taco Bell, Village Inn Rest., **other:** Big O Tire, Rite Aid, Safeway

Colorado Springs

Interstate 25

N ↕ S

Colorado Springs

158 Baptist Rd, **E...gas:** Shell/Popeye's/diesel/24hr, **food:** Jackson Creek Chinese, Subway, **other:** Ace Hardware, King's Sooper/24hr, **W...gas:** Shamrock/ diesel

156b N Entrance to USAF Academy, **W...**visitors center

a Gleneagle Dr, **E...**mining museum

153 InterQuest Pkwy

151 Briargate Pkwy, **E...lodging:** Hilton Garden, **other:** Focus on the Family Visitor Ctr, to Black Forest

150b a CO 83, Academy Blvd, **E...gas:** Shamrock/Quizno's/ diesel, Shell/diesel, **food:** Applebee's, Blimpie, Boston Mkt, Burger King, Capt D's, Chevy's Mexican, Chipotle Mexican, Country Buffet, Cracker Barrel, Denny's, Egg&I Café, Fazoli's, Grady's Grill, IHOP, Joe's Crabshack, KFC, Macaroni Grill, McDonald's, Mimi's Café, Olive Garden, On-the-Border, Panera Bread, Pizza Hut, Red Robin, Schlotsky's, Sonic, Souper Salad, Starbucks, Subway, Taco Bell, Village Inn Rest., Wendy's, **lodging:** Comfort Inn, Day's Inn, Drury Inn, Radisson, Red Roof Inn, Sleep Inn, Super 8, **other:** Advance Parts, Barnes&Noble, Best Buy, Big O Tire, Borders Books, Circuit City, CompUSA, Cub Foods, Dillard's, Firestone/auto, Home Depot, King's Soopers, NAPA, Office Depot, OfficeMax, PepBoys, Rite Aid, Sam's Club, Sears/auto, USPO, Wal-Mart SuperCtr/24hr, mall, to Peterson AFB, **W...**S Entrance to USAF Academy

149 Woodmen Rd, **E...gas:** Conoco/Subway/diesel, **food:** Carrabba's, **W...gas:** Shell, **food:** Old Chicago Pizza, Outback Steaks, TGIFriday, Zio's Italian, **lodging:** Comfort Inn, Embassy Suites, Extended Stay America, Fairfield Inn, Hampton Inn, Holiday Inn Express, Microtel

148b a Corporate Ctr Dr(exits left from sb), Nevada Ave, **E...other:** Harley-Davidson, K&C RV Ctr, **W...**New South Wales Rest.

147 Rockrimmon Blvd, **W...gas:** Shell, **lodging:** Bradford Suites, Wyndham, to Rodeo Hall of Fame

146 Garden of the Gods Rd, **E...gas:** BP, Shell/diesel, **food:** Carl's Jr, Denny's, McDonald's, Taco John's, **lodging:** Econolodge, La Quinta, Aamco, **W...gas:** Citgo/7-11, Conoco, Phillips 66, Shamrock, **food:** Applebee's, Arby's, Blackeyed Pea, Hungry Farmer Rest., Margarita's, Quizno's, Subway, Taco Bell, Village Inn Rest., Wendy's, **lodging:** AmeriSuites, Day's Inn, Holiday Inn, Quality Inn, Super 8, **other:** to Garden of Gods

145 CO 38 E, Fillmore St, **E... gas:** Citgo/7-11, Shamrock, **food:** DQ, **lodging:** Budget Host, Ramada Inn, **other:** HOSPITAL, **W... gas:** Conoco/diesel, Shell/diesel, **food:** BBQ, Waffle House, **lodging:** Best Western, Motel 6, Super 8

144 Fontanero St, no facilities

143 Uintah St, **E...gas:** Citgo/7-11, **other:** Uintah Fine Arts Ctr

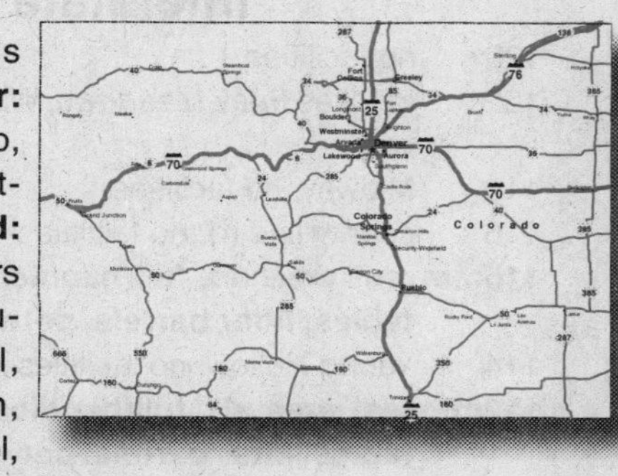

142 Bijou St, Bus Dist, **E...other:** Firestone/auto, **W...gas:** Western Gas, **food:** Denny's, Antlers **lodging:** Doubletree Hotel, Best Western, Le Baron Motel, RainTree Inn, Red Lion Hotel

141 US 24 W, Cimarron St, to Manitou Springs, **W...gas:** Conoco, Phillips 66, **food:** Burger King, Capt D's, McDonald's, Papa John's, Popeye's, Sonic, Subway, Taco John's, Texas Roadhouse, Waffle House, **lodging:** Holiday Inn Express, **other:** Acura, AutoZone, Buick/GMC/Pontiac, Chevrolet, Chrysler/Plymouth, Discount Tire, Ford, Hyundai, Infiniti, Isuzu, Lincoln/ Mercury, Mazda, Mercedes, NAPA, Nissan, Office Depot, Saturn, Subaru/Saab/VW, Suzuki, Toyota, Volvo, Wal-Mart SuperCtr/24hr, to Pikes Peak

140b US 85 S, Tejon St, **W...gas:** Conoco, Circle K, access to same as 141

a Nevada Ave, **E...lodging:** Chateau Motel, Colorado Springs Motel, Economy Inn, Howard Johnson, Chrysler/Jeep, **W...gas:** BP, Citgo/7-11, Shamrock, Shell/diesel, **food:** Burger King, Colima Mexican, KFC, Little Caesar's, McDonald's, Schlotsky's, Subway, Taco Bell, TCBY, Wienerschnitzel, Wendy's, **lodging:** American Inn, Chief Motel, Cheyenne Motel, Circle S Motel, Econolodge, Stagecoach Motel, **other:** Checker Parts, Safeway, USPO, Walgreen, access to auto dealers at 141

139 US 24 E, to Lyman, Peterson AFB

138 CO 29, Circle Dr, **E...gas:** Conoco, Shell/diesel, **lodging:** Day's Inn/Mexican Rest., Sheraton, **other:** RV repair, airport, zoo, **W...gas:** Citgo/7-11, **food:** Arby's, Burger King, Carrabba's, Carl's Jr, Chili's, Denny's, Fazoli's, Outback Steaks, Papa John's, Village Inn Rest., Subway, **lodging:** Budget Inn, DoubleTree Hotel, Fairfield Inn, Hampton Inn, La Quinta, Quality Inn, Residence Inn, **other:** Batteries+, OfficeMax, Radio Shack, Target

135 CO 83, Academy Blvd, **E...**to airport, same as 132, **W...**Ft Carson

132 CO 16, Wide Field Security, **3 mi E on US 85...gas:** Shamrock, **food:** Arby's, Burger King, KFC, McDonald's, Papa John's, Pizza Hut, Subway, Taco Bell, Wendy's, **other:** AutoZone, Checker Parts, KOA, Wal-Mart SuperCtr/24hr

128 to US 85 N, Fountain, Security, **E...gas:** Citgo/7-11, Conoco/Subway/diesel, **lodging:** Ute Motel, **other:** USPO, **W...gas:** Tomahawk/diesel/rest./24hr/@, **lodging:** 1st Interstate Inn, Super 8

125 Ray Nixon Rd, no facilities

COLORADO

Interstate 25

N ↕ S

123 no facilities
122 to Pikes Peak Meadows, **W...**Pikes Peak Intn'l Raceway
119 Midway, no facilities
116 county line rd, no facilities
115mm rest area nb, full(handicapped)facilities, picnic tables, litter barrels, petwalk
114 Young Hollow, no facilities
112mm rest area sb, full(handicapped)facilities, picnic tables, litter barrels, petwalk
110 Pinon, **W...gas:** Sinclair/Subway/diesel/repair/@, **lodging:** Pinon Tree Inn
108 Bragdon, **E...gas:** racetrack, **W...**KOA
106 Porter Draw, no facilities
104 Eden, **W...**flea market, RV Sales

Pueblo

102 Eagleridge Blvd, **E...gas:** Conoco/diesel, **food:** Burger King, Texas Roadhouse, **other:** Big O Tire, Home Depot, Sam's Club/gas, **W... gas:** Shell/Blimpie/diesel, **food:** Cactus Flower Mexican, Cracker Barrel, DJ's Steaks, IHOP, Village Inn Rest., **lodging:** Comfort Inn, Day's Inn, Econolodge, Hampton Inn, Holiday Inn, La Quinta, Motel 6, National 9 Inn, Wingate Inn, **other:** MEDICAL CARE, Harley-Davidson, frontage rds access 101
101 US 50 W, Pueblo, **E... gas:** Conoco, **food:** Denny's, Ruby Tuesday, **lodging:** Sleep Inn, **other:** Barnes&Noble, Circuit City, JC Penney, OfficeMax, Sears/auto, Wal-Mart SuperCtr/24hr, U-Haul, mall, **W...gas:** Conoco/Blimpie, Phillips 66, Shamrock/diesel, **food:** Applebee's, Arby's, Blackeyed Pea, Boston Mkt, Burger King, Carl's Jr, Country Kitchen, DQ, Domino's, Fazoli's, Gaetano's Italian, Golden Corral, King's Table Buffet, McDonald's, Pizza Hut, Red Lobster, Subway, Taco Bell, Wendy's, **lodging:** Holiday Inn, Motel 6, Quality Inn, Super 8, Villager Lodge, **other:** Advance Parts, Albertson's, Batteries+, Checker Parts, Discount Tire, Dodge, Goodyear/auto, K-Mart, Lincoln/Mercury, Lowe's Whse, Toyota, frontage rds access 102
100b 29th St, Pueblo, **E...food:** Country Buffet, KFC, **other:** King's Sooper Foods, mall, tires, **W...gas:** Amoco, Shamrock, Sinclair, **food:** Sonic, **other:** Safeway
a US 50 E, to La Junta, **E...gas:** Conoco/LP, Phillips 66, Shamrock, **food:** Little Caesar's, McDonald's, Pizza Hut, Wendy's, **lodging:** Ramada Inn/rest., Rodeway Inn, **other:** AutoZone, Furr's Foods, Goodyear
99b a Santa Fe Ave, 13th St, downtown, **W... gas:** Amoco, Wendy's, **lodging:** Best Western, Brambletree Inn, Travelers Motel, **other:** HOSPITAL, Chevrolet, Chrysler/Jeep, Ford/Subaru, Honda, Mazda, Nissan, Pontiac, VW
98b CO 96, 1st St, Union Ave Hist Dist, Pueblo, **W... gas:** Conoco, **food:** Carl's Jr, **lodging:** Jubilee Inn, Marriott
a US 50E bus, to La Junta, **E...gas:** Shamrock/diesel/24hr, **W...gas:** Shell/diesel, **food:** Sonic
97b Abriendo Ave, **W...food:** Wendy's, **lodging:** Best Western, **other:** auto repair
a Central Ave, **W...gas:** Shamrock, **food:** McDonald's, **other:** Jim's Automotive, Tire King
96 Indiana Ave, **W...gas:** Fuzzy's, **other:** HOSPITAL, Cobra Automotive
95 Illinois Ave(from sb), **W...**to dogtrack
94 CO 45 N, Pueblo Blvd, **E...other:** 5J's Auto Parts, **W...gas:** Citgo/7-11, Shamrock/diesel, **food:** Pizza Hut/Taco Bell, **lodging:** Hampton Inn, Microtel, **other:** Pueblo Greyhound Park, RV camping, fairgrounds, to Lake Pueblo SP
91 Stem Beach, no facilities
88 Burnt Mill Rd, no facilities
87 Verde Rd, no facilities
83 no facilities
77 Hatchet Ranch Rd, Cedarwood, no facilities
74 CO 165 W, Colo City, **E...gas:** Shamrock/diesel/24hr, **other:** KOA, **W...gas:** Shell/Subway/diesel, **lodging:** Greenhorn Inn/rest., **other:** Rocking B Country Store, **rest area both lanes, full(handicapped)facilities, phone, vending, picnic tables, litter barrels, petwalk**
71 Graneros Rd, access to Columbia House
67 to Apache, no facilities
64 Lascar Rd, no facilities

Walsenburg

60 Huerfano, no facilities
59 Butte Rd, no facilities
56 Red Rock Rd, no facilities
55 Airport Rd, no facilities
52 CO 69 W, Walsenburg, to Alamosa, **W...gas:** Conoco, Phillips 66/diesel/24hr, Western Gas, **food:** Alpine Rose Café(2mi), Carl's Jr(2mi), Pizza Hut, Subway(2mi), Tex' Mexican(1mi), **lodging:** Best Western, Budget Host, to Great Sand Dunes NM, San Luis Valley
50 CO 10 E, to La Junta, **W...**HOSPITAL, tourist info
49 Lp 25, to US 160 W, Walsenburg, **W...**Lathrop SP, to Cuchara Ski Valley
42 Rouse Rd, to Pryor, no facilities
41 Rugby Rd, no facilities
34 Aguilar, **E...gas:** BP/diesel/rest.
30 Aguilar Rd, no facilities
27 Ludlow, **W...**point of interest
23 Hoehne Rd, no facilities
18 El Moro Rd, **W...rest area both lanes, full(handicapped)facilities, picnic tables, litter barrels, petwalk**
15 US 350 E, Trinidad, Goddard Ave, **E...food:** Burger King, **lodging:** Super 8, **other:** Big R Foods, Family$, **W...gas:** Texaco, **food:** B Lee's Café, **lodging:** Frontier Motel/café

Interstate 25

Trinidad

14b a CO 12 W, Trinidad, **E...CO Welcome Ctr, gas:** BP, **food:** McDonald's, Pizza Hut, Subway, Taco Bell, **W...gas:** Conoco, Phillips 66, Shamrock, **food:** DQ, Domino's, El Capitan Rest., Wonderful Chinese, **lodging:** Prospect Plaza Motel, **other:** Parts+, TrueValue, RV camping, to Trinidad Lake, Monument Lake

13b Main St, Trinidad, **E...gas:** Conoco, **food:** Sonic, **lodging:** Villager Lodge, **other:** CarQuest, Safeway

a Santa Fe Trail, Trinidad, **E...lodging:** Best Western, **other:** HOSPITAL, RV camping

11 Starkville, **E...gas:** Shell/Wendy's/diesel/24hr/@, weigh/check sta, **lodging:** Budget Host/RV park, Budget Summit Inn/RV Park, to Santa Fe Trail, **W...food:** Country Kitchen, **lodging:** Holiday Inn, **other:** Big O Tire, Checker Parts, Chevrolet/Buick, Wal-Mart SuperCtr/gas/24hr

8 Springcreek, no facilities

6 Gallinas, no facilities

2 Wootten, no facilities

1mm scenic area pulloff nb

0mm Colorado/New Mexico state line, Raton Pass, elev 7834, weigh sta sb

Interstate 70

E ↕ W

Exit # Services

447mm Colorado/Kansas state line

Burlington

438 US 24, Rose Ave, Burlington, **N...gas:** Conoco, Sinclair, **food:** DQ, **lodging:** Comfort Inn, Hi-Lo Motel, Sloan's Motel, Super 8, **other:** HOSPITAL, Buick/Pontiac/GMC, CarQuest, Chevrolet, Ford, Goodyear, NAPA, **S...gas:** Amoco/diesel/24hr

437.5mm Welcome Ctr wb, full(handicapped)facilities, info, phone, picnic tables, litter barrels, petwalk, historical site

437 US 385, Burlington, **N...gas:** Conoco/diesel/rest./24hr, Phillips 66/Taco Bell/diesel/24hr, **food:** Arby's, Burger King, DQ, McDonald's, Pizza Hut, Route Steaks, Sonic, Subway/TCBY, **lodging:** Burlington Inn, Chaparral Motel, Comfort Inn, Sloan's Motel, Super 8, Western Motel, **other:** HOSPITAL, Alco, Ford/Lincoln/Mercury, Goodyear, Safeway, to Bonny St RA, RV camping

429 Bethune, no facilities

419 CO 57, Stratton, **N...gas:** Ampride/diesel/24hr, Conoco/diesel, **lodging:** Best Western Claremont/café, Marshall Ash Village Camping, Trails End Camping, **other:** auto museum

412 Vona, **1/2 mi N...**gas, phone

405 CO 59, Seibert, **N...**Shady Grove Camping, **S...gas:** Shell/A&W/diesel/24hr, **other:** SuperFoods

395 Flagler, **N...gas:** Conoco, **food:** Dairy King, Freshway Subs, **lodging:** Little England Motel, **other:** NAPA, **S...other:** Country Store/diesel/café, golf

383 Arriba, **N... gas:** Phillips 66/diesel/café, lodging, **other:** RV camping, **S...rest area both lanes full(handicapped)facilities, picnic tables, litter barrels, point of interest, petwalk**

376 Bovina, no facilities

Limon

371 Genoa, **N...**point of interest, gas, food, phone, **S...**HOSPITAL

363 US 24, US 40, US 287, to CO 71, Limon, to Hugo, **13 mi S...**HOSPITAL

361 CO 71, Limon, **N...other:** Chrysler/Dodge/Jeep, **S...gas:** Conoco/diesel, Flying J/diesel/rest./24hr, Shell/Wendy's/diesel/@, **food:** DQ, Pizza Hut, **lodging:** Midwest Inn, Silver Spur Motel(1mi), Travel Inn, **other:** KOA, st patrol

360.5mm weigh/check sta both lanes

359 to US 24, CO 71, Limon, **S...gas:** Rip Griffin/Subway/diesel/rest./24hr/@, Shell/diesel, Shamrock/diesel/24hr, **food:** Arby's, Denny's, Golden China, McDonald's, **lodging:** Best Western, Comfort Inn, Econolodge, Safari Motel, Silver Spur Motel, Super 8, Tyme Square Inn, **other:** camping

354 no facilities

352 CO 86 W, to Kiowa, no facilities

348 to Cedar Point, no facilities

340 Agate, **1/4 mi S...**gas/diesel, phone

336 to Lowland, no facilities

332mm rest area wb, full(handicapped)facilities, info, phone, picnic tables, litter barrels, vending, petwalk

328 to Deer Trail, **N...gas:** Shell/diesel, **S...gas:** Corner Gas, **food:** Deer Trail Café

325mm East Bijou Creek

323.5mm Middle Bijou Creek

Denver Area

322 to Peoria, no facilities

316 US 36 E, Byers, **N...gas:** Sinclair, **lodging:** Budget Host, **other:** SuperValu Foods, **S...gas:** Frontier/gas, **food:** Country Burger Rest., **lodging:** Lazy 8 Motel(1mi), **other:** USPO

310 Strasburg, **N...gas:** Conoco, **food:** Pizza Shop, **other:** Corner Mkt, NAPA, KOA, USPO

306mm Kiowa, Bennett, **N...rest area both lanes, full(handicapped)facilities, phone, picnic tables, litter barrels, petwalk**

305 Kiowa(from eb), no facilities

304 CO 79 N, Bennett, **N...gas:** Hank's Trkstp/diesel/24hr/@

299 CO 36, Manila Rd, **S...gas:** Shamrock/diesel/24hr, phone

COLORADO

Interstate 70

E ↕ W

295 Lp 70, Watkins, **N...gas:** Tomahawk/diesel/rest./@, **lodging:** Country Manor Motel

292 CO 36, Airpark Rd, no facilities

289 E-470 Tollway, 120th Ave, CO Springs, no facilities

288 US 287, US 40, Lp 70, Colfax Ave(exits left from wb), no facilities

286 CO 32, Tower Rd, no facilities

285 Airport Blvd, **N...**Denver Int Airport, **S...gas:** Flying J/Conoco/diesel/rest./24hr/@, **lodging:** Comfort Inn, Crystal Inn, **other:** Harley-Davidson

284 I-225 N(from eb)

283 Chambers Rd, **N...lodging:** AmeriSuites, Hilton Garden, Holiday Inn, Marriott, Sleep Inn, **S...gas:** Phillips 66, Shamrock/Taco Bell, **food:** Burger King, **lodging:** Extended Stay America, **other:** Subaru

282 I-225 S, to Colorado Springs, no facilities

281 Peoria St, **N...gas:** BP, Citgo/7-11, Conoco/Blimpie/diesel/LP/24hr, Phillips 66, **food:** Burger King, McDonald's, Village Inn Rest., **lodging:** Best Western/grill, Drury Inn, Executive Hotel, Park Inn, **S...gas:** BP, Shamrock/diesel, **food:** Airport Broker Rest., BBQ, Church's, Denny's, IHOP, KFC, Mexican Grill, Pizza Hut, Subway, Taco Bell, Waffle House, Wendy's, **lodging:** Airport Value Inn, La Quinta, Motel 6, Traveler's Inn, **other:** ARMY MED CTR, Goodyear/auto, auto/RV repair

Denver Area

280 Havana St, **N...lodging:** Embassy Suites, **other:** Office Depot

279 I-270 W, US 36 W(from wb), to Ft Collins, Boulder

278 CO 35, Quebec St, **N...gas:** Sapp Bros/Sinclair/Burger King/diesel/@, TA/diesel/rest./24hr/@, **food:** Denny's, **lodging:** Best Western, Day's Inn, Hampton Inn, Quality Inn, **S...**Stapleton Airport, **gas:** Amoco, Phillips 66, **food:** Breakfast Shop, **lodging:** Courtyard, Holiday Inn/rest., Radisson, Red Lion Hotel

277 to Dahlia St, Holly St, Monaco St, frontage rd, no facilities

276b US 6 E, US 85 N, CO 2, Colorado Blvd, **S...food:** Silver Bullet Rest.

a Vasquez Ave, **N...gas:** Pilot/Wendy's/diesel/24hr/@, **lodging:** Colonial Motel, Western Inn, **other:** Blue Beacon, Ford/Mack Trucks, **S...gas:** Citgo/7-11, **food:** Burger King, **other:** NAPA

275c York St(from eb), **N...food:** Family Kitchen Rest., **lodging:** Colonial Motel

b CO 265, Brighton Blvd, Coliseum

a Washington St, **N...gas:** Citgo/7-11, **food:** Pizza Hut, **S...gas:** Conoco, **food:** McDonald's, Muneca Mexican, Quizno's, Subway

274b a I-25, N to Cheyenne, S to Colorado Springs

273 Pecos St, **N...gas:** Safeway, **S...gas:** Conoco, Phillips 66/diesel, Circle K, **lodging:** Discount Hotel, **other:** transmissions

272 US 287, Federal Blvd, **N...gas:** Amoco, Sinclair, **food:** Burger King, Goodtimes Burgers, Hamburger Stand, Loco Pollo, McCoy's Rest., McDonald's, Pizza Hut, Subway, Taco Bell, Village Inn Rest., Wendy's, **lodging:** Motel 6, **other:** K-Mart, **S...gas:** Amoco, Conoco, 7-11, **food:** Popeye's, **lodging:** Howard Johnson/Las Palmeras Mexican

271b Lowell Blvd, Tennyson St(from wb), no facilities

a CO 95, **S...**Wild Chipmunk Amusement Park

Denver Area

270 Sheridan Blvd, **S...gas:** Shamrock, **food:** Arby's, Oriental Rest., Sunrise Café, **other:** Target, U-Haul, funpark, mall

269b I-76 E(from eb), to Ft Morgan, Ft Collins

a CO 121, Wadsworth Blvd, **N...gas:** Citgo/7-11, Conoco, LuckyMart/diesel, **food:** Applebee's, Bennigan's, Country Buffet, Fazoli's, Goodberry's Rest., Gunther Toody's Diner, Kokoro Japanese, LoneStar Steaks, McDonald's, Ruby Tuesday, Schlotsky's, Starbucks, Taco Bell, Texas Roadhouse, **other:** Advance Parts, Costco/gas, Home Depot, Lowe's Whse, OfficeMax, Office Depot, Sam's Club, Tires+, Waldenbooks, mall, **S...other:** Discount Tire

267 CO 391, Kipling St, Wheat Ridge, **N...gas:** Amoco, Shell/Carl's Jr/diesel, 7-11, **food:** Burger King, Denny's, Furr's Dining, Subway, **lodging:** American Motel, Motel 6, **other:** Chevrolet/Cadillac, Chrysler/Plymouth/Jeep, **S...gas:** Conoco, **food:** Pizza Hut/Taco Bell, Village Inn Rest., **lodging:** Comfort Inn, Holiday Inn Express, Motel 6, Super 8, **other:** RV Ctr

266 CO 72, W 44th Ave, Ward Rd, Wheat Ridge, **N...gas:** Shell, **S...gas:** Shamrock, TA/diesel/rest./24hr/@, **lodging:** Quality Inn

265 CO 58 W(from wb), to Golden, Central City, no facilities

264 Youngfield St, W 32nd Ave, **N...gas:** Conoco, **food:** GoodTimes Burgers, **lodging:** La Quinta, **S... gas:** Amoco, Conoco, Shamrock, **food:** Chili's, DQ, McDonald's, Papa John's, Pizza Hut/Taco Bell, Starbucks, Subway, **other:** Camping World RV Ctr, Casey's RV Ctr, King's Sooper/24hr, Radio Shack, Walgreen, Wal-Mart

263 Denver West Blvd, **N...lodging:** Marriott/rest., **S...other:** Barnes&Noble, Wild Oats Mkt

262 US 40 E, W Colfax, Lakewood, **N...gas:** Sinclair, **food:** Arby's, **lodging:** Hampton Inn, **other:** Home Depot, Honda, Kohl's, NAPA, U-Haul, transmissions, **S...gas:** Conoco, Shell/diesel/LP, **food:** Outback Steaks, Wendy's, **lodging:** Courtyard, Day's Inn/rest., Holiday Inn Express, Residence Inn, **other:** Chevrolet, Lexus, Target, Toyota, RV Ctr

261 US 6 E(from eb), W 6th Ave, to Denver, no facilities

260 CO 470, to Colo Springs, no facilities

Interstate 70

E ↕ W

Idaho Spgrs

259 CO 26, Golden, **N...gas:** Conoco, **lodging:** Hampton Inn(2mi), **other:** Heritage Sq Funpark, **S...**Music Hall, to Red Rock Park
257mm runaway truck ramp eb
256 Lookout Mtn, **N...**to Buffalo Bill's Grave
254 Genesee, Lookout Mtn, **N...**to Buffalo Bill's Grave, **S...gas:** Conoco/LP, **food:** Buffalo Moon Coffee, Chart House Rest., Guido's Pizza, **other:** MEDICAL CARE, USPO
253 Chief Hosa, **S...**Chief Hosa Camping, phone
252 (251 from eb), CO 74, Evergreen Pkwy, **S...gas:** BP, **food:** Burger King, El Rancho Rest., McDonald's, **lodging:** Quality Suites, **other:** Big O Tire, Home Depot, King's Sooper/deli, Wal-Mart/auto
248 (247 from eb), Beaver Brook, Floyd Hill, **S...food:** Gourmet Coffee, to Saddlerack Summit Rest., **other:** Floyd Hill Grocery/grill
244 US 6, to CO 119, Central City, to Golden, Eldora Ski Area, **N...food:** Kermit's Café Food/drink
243 Hidden Valley, no facilities
242mm tunnel
241b a rd 314, Idaho Springs West, **N...gas:** BP/McDonald's, Phillips 66, Sinclair, 7-11, Shell, **food:** A&W, BBQ, Beaujo's Pizza, Buffalo Rest., Café Expresso, JC Sweet's, King's Derby Rest., Marion's Rest., Subway, Taco Bell, **lodging:** Argo Motel, Club Hotel, Columbine Inn, Hanson Lodge, H&H Motel, Indian Springs Resort, King Henry's Motel, National 9 Motel, Peoriana Motel, 6&40 Motel/rest., The Lodge, **other:** CarQuest, NAPA, Radio Shack, Safeway, USPO
240 CO 103, **N...gas:** Texaco, **other:** 2 Bros Deli, Tommy Knockery Brewery, same as 241, **S...**to Mt Evans
239 Idaho Springs, **N... gas:** Amoco, Phillips 66, **other:** Sandwich Mine Mkt, camping
238 Fall River Rd, to St Mary's Glacier, no facilities
235 Dumont(from wb), no facilities
234 Downeyville, Dumont, weigh sta both lanes, **N...gas:** Conoco/Subway/diesel, **food:** Burger King, Starbucks, **other:** ski rentals
233 Lawson(from eb), no facilities
232 US 40 W, to Empire, Atacula/Rocky Mtn NP, **N...**to Berthoud Pass, Winterpark/Silver Creek ski areas
228 Georgetown, **S...gas:** Conoco, Phillips 66, Shamrock/diesel, **food:** Dairy King, Panda City Chinese, Red Ram rest., **lodging:** Georgetown Lodge, Super 8
226.5mm scenic overlook eb
226 Georgetown, Silver Plume Hist Dist, **N...other:** Buckley Bros Mkt, lodging, ski rentals
221 Bakerville, no facilities
220mm Arapahoe NF eastern boundary
218 no facilities

Dillon

216 US 6 W, Loveland Valley, Loveland Basin, ski areas
214mm EisenhowerTunnel, elev 11013
213mm parking area eb 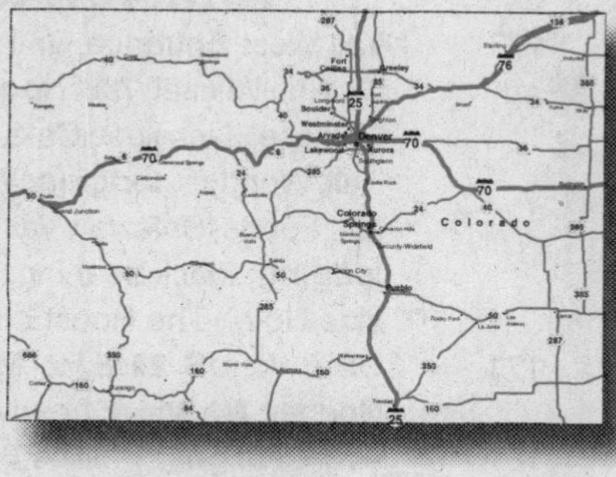
205 US 6 E, CO 9 N, Dillon, Silverthorne, **N...gas:** Citgo/7-11, Conoco, Shell/GoodTimes/diesel, **food:** Denny's, Domino's, Old Dillon Inn Mexican, Quizno's, Mtn Lyon Café, Village Inn Rest., Wendy's/24hr, **lodging:** Day's Inn, 1st Interstate Inn, Hampton Inn/rest., Luxury Suites, Sheraton, Silver Inn, **other:** CarQuest, Chevrolet, Chrysler/Plymouth/Dodge, Ford/Mercury, Prime Outlets/famous brands, **S...gas:** Phillips 66/Taco Bell, Shamrock, **food:** Arby's, BBQ, Burger King, DQ, McDonald's, Pizza Hut, Ruby Tuesday, SweetPeas, Starbucks, Subway, **lodging:** Best Western, Comfort Suites, Super 8, **other:** City Mkt Foods, Dillon Stores/famous brands, Goodyear/auto, OfficeMax
203.5mm scenic overlook both lanes, phones
203 CO 9 S, Frisco, to Breckenridge, **S...gas:** Citgo/7-11, Shamrock, Shell/24hr, **food:** A&W, Back Country Brewery/rest., BBQ, ClaimJumper Rest., Country Kitchen, KFC, Papa John's, Pizza Hut, Starbucks, Subway, Taco Bell, TCBY, Tex's Café, **lodging:** Alpine Inn, Best Western, Holiday Inn, Luxury Inn, Microtel, Ramada Ltd, Summit Inn, **other:** MEDICAL CARE, Big O Tire, NAPA, Radio Shack, Safeway, Wal-Mart/drugs, to Breckenridge Ski Area, Tiger Run RV Resort
201 Main St, Frisco, **S...gas:** Conoco, **food:** A&W, Brewery Rest., KFC, Pizza Hut, **lodging:** Bighorn Reservations, Pearl Head Lodge, Woodbridge Inn, **other:** CHIROPRACTOR, Alpine Natural Foods, to Breckenridge Ski Area
198 Officers Gulch, no facilities, emergency callbox
195 CO 91 S, to Leadville, **1 mi S...gas:** Conoco/diesel, **food:** Camp Hale Coffee, Endo's Café, **lodging:** East West Resort, Fox Pine Inn, Telemark Lodge, **other:** to Copper Mtn Ski Resort
190 S...rest area both lanes, full(handicapped)facilities, phone, picnic tables, litter barrels
189mm Vail Pass Summit, elev 10662 ft, parking area both lanes

Vail

180 Vail East Entrance, phone, services 3-4 mi S
176 Vail, **S...gas:** Amoco/diesel, **lodging:** Best Western, Vailglo, Holiday Inn, **other:** MEDICAL CARE, info, Craig's Mkt, **1 mi S...gas:** Amoco, **food:** Chicago Pizza

COLORADO

Interstate 70

E ↕ W — Vail

173 Vail West Entrance, Vail Ski Area, **N...gas:** Phillips 66, Shell/diesel, 7-11, **food:** DQ, Domino's, 1/2 Moon Chinese, Jackalope Café, McDonald's, Subway, Taco Bell, Wendy's, **lodging:** West Vail Lodge, **other:** City Mkt Foods, Safeway, Vail Drug, **S...gas:** Conoco/LP, **lodging:** Black Bear Inn, Day's Inn, Marriott Streamside Hotel, The Roost Lodge

171 US 6 W, US 24 E, to Minturn, Leadville, info, Ski Cooper, **N...food:** Leadville Café, **other:** NAPA

167 Avon, **N...gas:** Phillips 66, **food:** Pizza Hut, **other:** Goodyear, **S...food:** Burger King, China Garden, Denny's, Domino's, Quizno's, Starbucks, Subway, **lodging:** Avon Ctr Lodge, Beaver Creek Inn, Beaver Creek Condos, Christie Lodge, Comfort Inn, Seasons Hotel, **other:** City Mkt/drugs, Wal-Mart, to Beaver Creek/Arrowhead Skiing

163 Edwards, S...rest area both lanes, full(handicapped)facilities, phone, picnic tables, litter barrel, gas: Conoco, Shell/Wendy's/diesel, **food:** Canac's Kitchen, Gashaus Rest., Gore Range Brewery, Marko's Pizza, Starbucks, **lodging:** Riverwalk Inn, **other:** to Arrowhead Ski Area

162mm scenic overlook both lanes

159mm Eagle River

157 CO 131 N, Wolcott, **N...**to gas, phone, to Steamboat Ski Area

Eagle

147 Eagle, **N...gas:** Shell/Taco Bell/diesel, **food:** Burger King, McDonald's, Mi Pueblo Mexican, **lodging:** AmericInn, Comfort Inn, Holiday Inn Express, **other:** City Mkt Foods, **S...gas:** Amoco/Subway/diesel, Conoco/pizza, **food:** Eagle Diner, Wendy's, **lodging:** Best Western, Prairie Moon Motel, **other:** Suburban Lodge, FoodTown Foods, **rest area both lanes, full(handicapped)facilities, info**

140 Gypsum, **S...gas:** Phillips 66/diesel, **food:** Columbine Mkt Deli, Mexican-American Café, **other:** auto/truck repair, to camping, airport

134mm Colorado River

133 Dotsero, no facilities

129 Bair Ranch, **S...rest area both lanes, full(handicapped)facilities, picnic tables, litter barrels, petwalk**

128.5mm parking area eb

127mm tunnel wb

125mm tunnel

125 to Hanging Lake(no return eb)

123 Shoshone(no return eb), no facilities

122.5mm exit to river(no return eb)

121 Grizzly Creek, S...rest area both lanes, full(handicapped)facilities, picnic tables, litter barrels, to Hanging Lake

119 No Name, rest area both lanes, full(handicapped)facilities), RV camping, rafting

118mm tunnel

Glenwood Springs

116 CO 82 E, Glenwood Springs, to Aspen, **N...gas:** Amoco, Conoco/diesel, Shell/diesel, **food:** A&W, Fiesta Guadalajara, KFC, Mancinelli's Pizza, Pizza Hut, Smokin Willie BBQ, Tequila Rest., **lodging:** Village Inn Rest., Best Western, Glenwood Inn, Hampton Inn, Holiday Inn Express, Hotel Colorado, Hot Springs Motel, Ramada Inn, Silver Spruce Motel, Starlight Motel, **other:** Audi/VW, Land Rover, Mazda, Nissan, Saab, Suzuki, Toyota, Hot Springs Bath, **S...gas:** Conoco, Phillips 66/diesel, Sinclair, 7-11, **food:** Arby's, China Town, Domino's, Glenwood Sprs Brewpub, 19th St Diner, Quizno's, Taco Bell, Wendy's, **lodging:** Best Western, Frontier Lodge, Hotel Denver, **other:** MEDICAL CARE, City Mkt Foods, NAPA, Rite Aid, **2 mi S...**Subway, Goodyear, Honda, Wal-Mart, to Ski Sunlight

115mm rest area eb, full(handicapped)facilities, picnic tables, litter barrels

114 W Glenwood Springs, **N...gas:** Amoco/diesel, Citgo/7-11, Texaco/repair, **food:** Burger King, CharBurger, DQ, Dos Hombres Mexican, Fireside Steaks, Los Desperados Mexican, Marshall Dillon Steaks, Ocean Pearl Chinese, **lodging:** Affordable Inn, Best Value Inn, Budget Host, Colonial Inn, 1st Choice Inn, Holiday Inn, Motel 5, National 9 Inn, Ponderosa Motel, Red Mtn Inn, Super 8, Terra Vista Motel, **other:** Big O Tire, Chevrolet/Cadillac, Chrysler/Dodge/Plymouth, Ford, JC Penney, K-Mart, Lincoln/Mercury, Radio Shack, Sears, Staples, Taylor's RV Ctr, mall, **S...gas:** Conoco/diesel, **lodging:** Quality Inn

111 South Canyon, no facilities

109 Canyon Creek, no facilities

108mm parking area both lanes

105 New Castle, **N...gas:** Conoco/Subway/diesel, Kum&Go, Sinclair, **lodging:** Comfort Inn, **other:** City Mkt Foods, KOA(4mi), **S...gas:** Phillips 66

97 Silt, **N...gas:** Conoco/Blimpie/diesel/24hr, Phillips 66, **food:** Miners Claim Rest., Pizza Pro, Silt Café, **lodging:** Red River Inn(1mi), **other:** Reed's Auto Repair, Viking RV Park, to Harvey Gap SP

94 Garfield County Airport Rd, no facilities

90 CO 13 N, Rifle, **N...rest area both lanes, full(handicapped)facilities, phone, picnic tables, litter barrels, RV dump, NF Info, gas:** Amoco/24hr, Kum&Go/gas, Phillips 66/diesel, Texaco, **food:** KFC, **lodging:** Winchester Motel(1mi), **other:** HOSPITAL, USPO, **S...gas:** Conoco/diesel, Phillips 66/Subway, **food:** Burger King, McDonald's, TCBY, **lodging:** Buckskin Motel, Red River Inn/rest., Rusty Cannon Motel

87 to CO 13, West Rifle, **2 mi N...lodging:** Buckskin Motel, La Donna Motel, Shaler Motel, Winchester Motel, gas, food, phone

81 Rulison, no facilities

COLORADO

Interstate 70

75 Parachute, **N...rest area both lanes, full(handicapped)facilities, info, phone, picnic tables, litter barrels, petwalk, gas:** Sinclair/diesel, **Shell/diesel/24hr, food:** Dragon Treasure Chinese, El Rio Mexican, Outlaws Rest., **lodging:** Super 8, **other:** USPO, **S...gas:** Conoco/Wendy's/diesel, **other:** Good Sam RV Park(4mi)

63mm Colorado River

62 De Beque, **1 mi N...gas:** Conoco, **other:** food, lodging, phone, auto repair

50mm parking area eastbound, Colorado River, tunnel begins eastbound

49mm Plateau Creek

49 CO 65 S, to CO 330 E, to Grand Mesa, to Powderhorn Ski Area

47 Island Acres St RA, **N...**CO River SP, RV camping, **S...gas:** Shamrock/diesel/24hr/@, **food:** Rosie's Rest./24hr, **other:** Fawn's Gift Shop, motel, RV camping

46 Cameo, no facilities

44 Lp 70 W, to Palisade, **3 mi S...**gas, food, lodging

43.5mm Colorado River

42 Palisade, US 6, **1 mi S...**Fruitstand/store, gas, lodging, Grand River Winery

37 to US 6, to US 50 S, Clifton, Grand Jct, **1 mi S on US 6 bus...gas:** Conoco/diesel, Shamrock, Shell, **food:** Burger King, Dos Hombres Mexican, KFC, Little Caesar's, McDonald's, Papa Murphy's, Pizza Chef, Pizza Hut, Subway, Taco Bell, Texas Roadhouse, **lodging:** Best Western, **other:** MEDICAL CARE, Albertson's, Checker Parts, City Mkt Food/gas, KOA, Max Foods, Rite Aid, USPO, Walgreen, **2-3 mi S...gas:** Amoco, Phillips 66, **food:** Capt D's, Furr's Dining, **lodging:** Village Inn Rest., Wendy's, Western Sizzlin, Wienerschnitzel, Timbers Motel, **other:** AutoZone, Checker Parts, Chrysler/Plymouth/Dodge, Chevrolet, Discount Tire, Hastings Books, K-Mart, Wal-Mart SuperCtr/24hr

31 Horizon Dr, Grand Jct, **N...gas:** Shamrock, Shell/diesel, **food:** Coco's, Diorio's Pizza, Pepper's Rest., Village Inn Rest., Wendy's, **lodging:** Best Western, Comfort Inn, Grand Vista Hotel, Holiday Inn, La Quinta, Motel 6, Ramada Inn, **other:** Harley-Davidson, USPO, Zarlingo's Repair, **S...gas:** Conoco/Subway/diesel, Phillips 66, **food:** Applebee's, Burger King, Denny's, Pizza Hut, Taco Bell, **lodging:** Adams Mark Hotel, Best Western, Budget Host, Country Inn, Day's Inn/rest., Super 8, **other:** HOSPITAL, golf, to Mesa St Coll, CO NM

28 Redlands Pkwy, 24 rd, **N...**camping, **S...**recreational park/sports complex

26 US 6, US 50, Grand Jct, **N...**Mobile City RV Park, **S...gas:** Conoco/A&W/diesel/24hr/@, **food:** Otto's Rest., Westgate Inn/rest., **other:** Ford/Lincoln/Mercury, Mazda, Mercedes, Subaru, Toyota, Freightliner, radiators, **3-5 mi S...food:** BBQ, Chili's, Golden Corral, McDonald's, Outback Steaks, Red Lobster, **lodging:** Hawthorn Inn, Holiday Inn Express, **other:** Centennial RV Ctr, JC Penney, Mervyn's, Sears/auto, mall

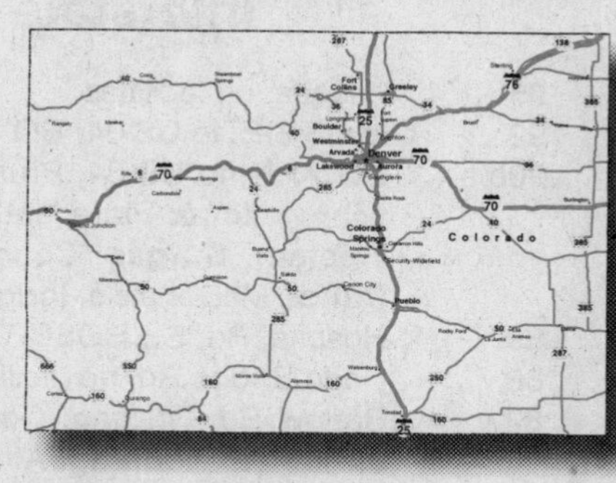

19 US 6, CO 340, Fruita, **N...gas:** Amoco, Conoco/diesel, **food:** Burger King, Pizza Pro, **lodging:** Balanced Rock Motel, **other:** HOSPITAL, CarQuest, City Mkt Foods/24hr, NAPA, USPO, **S...Welcome Ctr both lanes, full(handicapped)facilities, phone, picnic tables, litter barrels, RV dump, petwalk, gas:** Conoco/Subway/diesel/24hr, Shell/Wendy's/diesel/24hr, **food:** McDonald's, **lodging:** Comfort Inn, Super 8, **other:** CO Mon Trading Co, camping, museum, to CO NM

17mm Colorado River

15 CO 139 N, to Loma, Rangely, **N...**to Highline Lake SP, gas/diesel, phone

14.5mm weigh/check sta both lanes, phones

11 Mack, **2-3 mi N...**gas/diesel, food

2 Rabbit Valley, to Dinosaur Quarry Trail, no facilities

0mm Colorado/Utah state line

Interstate 76

Exit # Services

184mm Colorado/Nebraska state line

180 US 385, Julesburg, **N...gas:** Flying J/diesel/rest./24hr, Shell, **lodging:** Budget Host, **other:** HOSPITAL, **Welcome Ctr/rest area both lanes, full(handicapped)facilities, info, RV dump, S...gas:** Conoco/diesel

172 Ovid, **2 mi N...**gas, food

165 CO 59, Sedgewick, to Haxtun, **N...**gas/café

155 Red Lion Rd, no facilities

149 CO 55, Crook, to Fleming, **S...gas:** Sinclair/diesel/café

141 Proctor, no facilities

134 Iliff, no facilities

125 US 6, Sterling, **N...gas:** Cenex/diesel, **food:** Arby's, McDonald's, Taco Bell, Wendy's, **lodging:** Best Western, 1st Interstate Inn, **other:** HOSPITAL, N Sterling SP, museum, st patrol, **rest area both lanes(full handicapped)facilities, picnic tables, litter barrels, petwalk, vending, RV dump, S...gas:** Phillips 66/Quizno's/diesel, **food:** Country Kitchen, **lodging:** Ramada Inn, Super 8, Travelodge, Jellystone Camping

115 CO 63, Atwood, **N...gas:** Sinclair/diesel, **other:** HOSPITAL, **S...gas:** Amoco, **food:** Steakhouse

102 Merino, no facilities

COLORADO

Interstate 76

E ↕ W

Ft Morgan

95 Hillrose, no facilities
92 to US 6 E, to US 34, CO 71 S, no facilities
90b a CO 71 N, to US 34, Brush, **N...gas:** Shell/diesel/24hr/@, **food:** Pizza Hut, Wendy's, **lodging:** Best Western, **S...gas:** Conoco/diesel, **food: China Buffet,** McDonald's, **lodging:** Microtel
89 Hospital Rd, **S...**HOSPITAL, golf
86 Dodd Bridge Rd, no facilities
82 Barlow Rd, **N...gas:** Conoco/diesel, **food:** Maverick's Grill, **lodging:** Affordable Inn, Comfort Inn, **S...gas:** Phillips 66/diesel, **food:** Burger King, **other:** $Tree, Wal-Mart SuperCtr/diesel/24hr
80 CO 52, Ft Morgan, **S...gas:** Conoco/diesel/24hr, Shamrock, Shell/diesel, **food:** A&W, Arby's, DQ, KFC, McDonald's, Sonic, Subway/TCBY, Taco John's, **lodging:** Best Western/rest., Day's Inn, Super 8, **other:** HOSPITAL, AutoZone, Rite Aid
79 CO 144, to Weldona, **N...gas:** Shell/diesel
75 US 34 E, to Ft Morgan, **S...gas:** Conoco/A&W/diesel, **lodging:** motel
74.5mm weigh sta both lanes
73 Long Bridge Rd, no facilities
66b US 34 W(from wb), to Greeley
66a CO 39, CO 52, Wiggins, to Goodrich, **N...**to Jackson Lake SP, **S...gas:** Sinclair/diesel, **other: rest area both lanes, full(handicapped)facilities, picnic tables, litter barrels, petwalk, phone, vending**
64 Wiggins, no facilities
60 to CO 144 E, to Orchard, no facilities
57 rd 91, no facilities
49 Painter Rd(from wb), no facilities
48 to Roggen, **N...gas:** Shell/diesel, **lodging:** I-76 Motel
39 Keenesburg, **S...gas:** Phillips 66/diesel, **lodging:** Fine Food Rest., Keene Motel
34 Kersey Rd, no facilities
31 CO 52, Hudson, **S...gas:** Amoco/diesel, Phillips 66/diesel, **food:** El Faro Mexican, Pepper Pod Rest., **other:** auto/truck repair, RV camping
25 CO 7, Lochbuie, **N...gas:** Shell/diese
22 Bromley, **N...**HOSPITAL, **S...**Barr Lake SP
21 144th Ave, no facilities
20 136th Ave, **N...**Barr Lake RV Park
18 (from wb)E-470 tollway, to Limon
16 CO 2 W, Sable Blvd, Commerce City, **N...gas:** Shell/Blimpie/diesel/24hr/@
12 US 85 N, to Brighton, Greeley, no facilities
11 96th Ave, **N...**trailer sales, **S...**diesel repair
10 88th Ave, **N...gas:** Conoco/Blimpie/diesel, **lodging:** Holiday Inn Express, Super 8, **S...**flea mkt
9 US 6 W, US 85 S, Commerce City, **S...gas:** Shell/diesel, **other:** GMC/Freightliner, st patrol
8 CO 224, 74th Ave(no EZ eb return), **1 mi N...**NAPA, **S...gas:** Shamrock/diesel, **lodging:** Crestline Motel
6b a I-270 E, to Limon, to airport
5 I-25, N to Ft Collins, S to Colo Springs
4 Pecos St, no facilities

Denver Area

3 US 287, Federal Blvd, **N...gas:** Shamrock/diesel, **S...food:** Taco House
1b CO 95, Sheridan Blvd, no facilities
a CO 121, Wadsworth Blvd, **N...gas:** Citgo/7-11, Conoco, LuckyMart/diesel, **food:** Applebee's, Bennigan's, Country Buffet, Fazoli's, Goodberry's Rest., Gunther Toody's Diner, Kokoro Japanese, LoneStar Steaks, McDonald's, Ruby Tuesday, Schlotsky's, Starbucks, Taco Bell, Texas Roadhouse, **other:** Advance Parts, Costco/gas, Home Depot, Lowe's Whse, OfficeMax, Office Depot, Sam's Club, Tires+, Waldenbooks, mall, **S...other:** Discount Tire
0mm I-76 begins/ends on I-70, exit 169b.

Interstate 225(Denver)

Denver Area

N ↕ S

Exit # Services
12b a I-70, W to Denver, E to Limon
10 US 40, US 287, Colfax Ave, **E...gas:** Shell, **food:** KFC, McDonald's, Waffle House, **other:** RV Ctr, **W...gas:** Conoco
9 Co 30, 6th Ave, **E...gas:** Conoco, **food:** Pizza Hut, **lodging:** Super 8, **W...gas:** Phillips 66/diesel, **other:** HOSPITAL
8 Alameda Ave, **E...food:** Foley's, JC Penney, mall, **W...gas:** Conoco/mart, Shell/repair, 7-11
7 Mississippi Ave, Alameda Ave, **E...food:** Chevy's, Denny's, Jason's Deli, **lodging:** Hampton Inn, La Quinta, **other:** Best Buy, Circuit City, Sam's Club, Target, Wal-Mart
5 Iliff Ave, **E...food:** Applebee's, Carrabba's, Fuddrucker's, Hop's Rest., Joe's Crabshack, Outback Steaks, Sweet Tomato, **lodging:** Comfort Inn, Fairfield Inn, Motel 6, **W...gas:** Coastal, **food:** Dragon Boat Chinese
4 CO 83, Parker Rd, **E...lodging:** Holiday Inn, **other:** Cherry Creek SP, **W...gas:** Shell, **food:** DQ, Denny's, McDonald's, Taco Bell
2 DTC Blvd, Tamarac St, **W...gas:** Amoco, 7-11, **food:** Pizza Hut
0mm I-225 begins/ends on I-25, exit 200.

Interstate 270(Denver)

Denver Area

E ↕ W

Exit # Services
4 I-70.
3 **N...gas:** TA/Popeye's/Quizno's/Pizza Hut/diesel24hr/@, **S...** Sapp Bros/diesel/@,
2b a US 85, CO 2, Vasquez Ave, **N...gas:** Conoco, **food:** Arby's, GoodTimes Grill, KFC, McDonald's, Pizza Inn, Wendy's
1b York St, no facilities
1a I-76 E, to Ft Morgan
1c I-25 S, to Denver
0 I-25 N, to Ft Collins

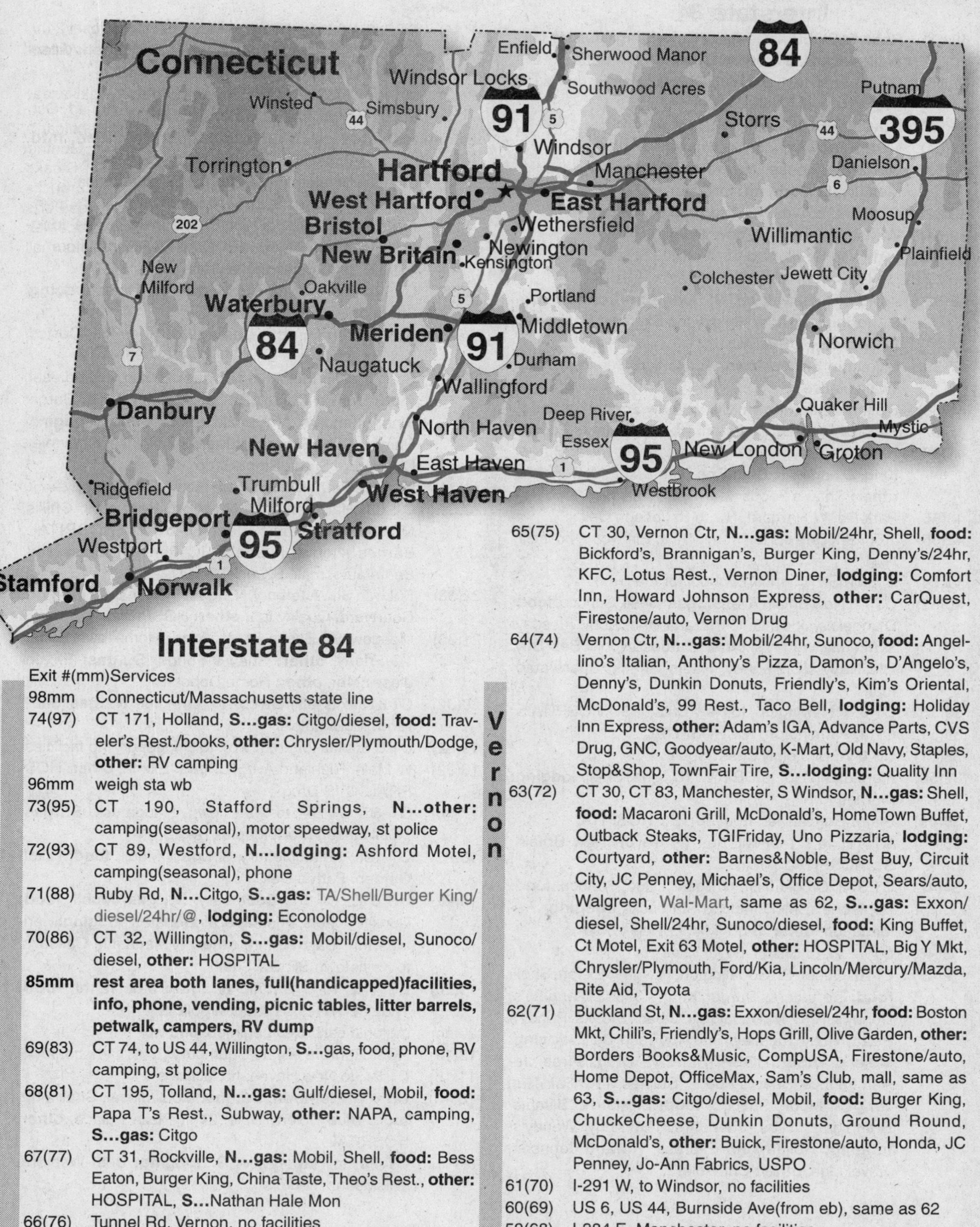

Interstate 84

Exit #(mm)Services

E ↕ W

98mm Connecticut/Massachusetts state line

74(97) CT 171, Holland, **S...gas:** Citgo/diesel, **food:** Traveler's Rest./books, **other:** Chrysler/Plymouth/Dodge, **other:** RV camping

96mm weigh sta wb

73(95) CT 190, Stafford Springs, **N...other:** camping(seasonal), motor speedway, st police

72(93) CT 89, Westford, **N...lodging:** Ashford Motel, camping(seasonal), phone

71(88) Ruby Rd, **N...**Citgo, **S...gas:** TA/Shell/Burger King/diesel/24hr/@, **lodging:** Econolodge

70(86) CT 32, Willington, **S...gas:** Mobil/diesel, Sunoco/diesel, **other:** HOSPITAL

85mm rest area both lanes, full(handicapped)facilities, info, phone, vending, picnic tables, litter barrels, petwalk, campers, RV dump

69(83) CT 74, to US 44, Willington, **S...**gas, food, phone, RV camping, st police

68(81) CT 195, Tolland, **N...gas:** Gulf/diesel, Mobil, **food:** Papa T's Rest., Subway, **other:** NAPA, camping, **S...gas:** Citgo

67(77) CT 31, Rockville, **N...gas:** Mobil, Shell, **food:** Bess Eaton, Burger King, China Taste, Theo's Rest., **other:** HOSPITAL, **S...**Nathan Hale Mon

66(76) Tunnel Rd, Vernon, no facilities

Vernon

65(75) CT 30, Vernon Ctr, **N...gas:** Mobil/24hr, Shell, **food:** Bickford's, Brannigan's, Burger King, Denny's/24hr, KFC, Lotus Rest., Vernon Diner, **lodging:** Comfort Inn, Howard Johnson Express, **other:** CarQuest, Firestone/auto, Vernon Drug

64(74) Vernon Ctr, **N...gas:** Mobil/24hr, Sunoco, **food:** Angellino's Italian, Anthony's Pizza, Damon's, D'Angelo's, Denny's, Dunkin Donuts, Friendly's, Kim's Oriental, McDonald's, 99 Rest., Taco Bell, **lodging:** Holiday Inn Express, **other:** Adam's IGA, Advance Parts, CVS Drug, GNC, Goodyear/auto, K-Mart, Old Navy, Staples, Stop&Shop, TownFair Tire, **S...lodging:** Quality Inn

63(72) CT 30, CT 83, Manchester, S Windsor, **N...gas:** Shell, **food:** Macaroni Grill, McDonald's, HomeTown Buffet, Outback Steaks, TGIFriday, Uno Pizzaria, **lodging:** Courtyard, **other:** Barnes&Noble, Best Buy, Circuit City, JC Penney, Michael's, Office Depot, Sears/auto, Walgreen, Wal-Mart, same as 62, **S...gas:** Exxon/diesel, Shell/24hr, Sunoco/diesel, **food:** King Buffet, Ct Motel, Exit 63 Motel, **other:** HOSPITAL, Big Y Mkt, Chrysler/Plymouth, Ford/Kia, Lincoln/Mercury/Mazda, Rite Aid, Toyota

62(71) Buckland St, **N...gas:** Exxon/diesel/24hr, **food:** Boston Mkt, Chili's, Friendly's, Hops Grill, Olive Garden, **other:** Borders Books&Music, CompUSA, Firestone/auto, Home Depot, OfficeMax, Sam's Club, mall, same as 63, **S...gas:** Citgo/diesel, Mobil, **food:** Burger King, ChuckeCheese, Dunkin Donuts, Ground Round, McDonald's, **other:** Buick, Firestone/auto, Honda, JC Penney, Jo-Ann Fabrics, USPO

61(70) I-291 W, to Windsor, no facilities

60(69) US 6, US 44, Burnside Ave(from eb), same as 62

59(68) I-384 E, Manchester, no facilities

CONNECTICUT

Interstate 84

E ↕ W — Hartford

58(67) Roberts St, Burnside Ave, **N...lodging:** Holiday Inn, Wellesley Inn, **S...other:** Super Stop'n Shop
57(66) CT 15 S, to I-91 S, NYC, Charter Oak Br, no facilities
56(65) Governor St, E Hartford, **S...**airport
55(64) CT 2 E, New London, downtown
54(63) Old State House, **N...other:** Ford/Isuzu, Lincoln/ Mercury, **S...lodging:** Sheraton
53(62) CT Blvd(from eb), **S...lodging:** Ramada Inn
52(61) W Main St(from eb), downtown
51(60) I-91 N, to Springfield
50(59.8) to I-91 S(from wb)
48(59.5) Asylum St, downtown, **N...lodging:** Crowne Plaza, **S...lodging:** Hilton, Holiday Inn Express, Residence Inn, **other:** HOSPITAL
47(59) Sigourney St, downtown, **N...**Hartford Seminary, Mark Twain House
46(58) Sisson St, downtown, UConn Law School
45(57) Flatbush Ave(exits left from wb), **N...**Shaw's Foods
44(56.5) Prospect Ave, **N...gas:** Exxon, Shell, **food:** Burger King, D'angelo's, Gold Roc Diner/24hr, McDonald's, **other:** Shaw's Foods
43(56) Park Rd, W Hartford, **N...**to St Joseph Coll
42(55) Trout Brk Dr(exits left from wb), to Elmwood, no facilities
41(54) S Main St, American School for the Deaf
40(53) CT 71, New Britain Ave, **S...gas:** Shell, Sunoco, **food:** D'angelo's, Joe's Grill, Pizzaria Uno, Ruby Tuesday, TGIFriday, Wendy's, **other:** Barnes&Noble, Best Buy, Old Navy, JC Penney, Radio Shack, Sears/auto, mall
39a(52) CT 9 S, Newington, to New Britain, **S...**HOSPITAL
39(51.5) CT 4, Farmington, **N...**HOSPITAL
38(51) US 6 W, Bristol, **N...gas:** Shell
37(50) Fienemann Rd, to US 6 W, **N...gas:** Shell, **lodging:** Marriott
36(49) Slater Rd(exits left from eb), **S...**HOSPITAL
35(48) CT 72, to CT 9(exits left from wb), New Britain, **S...**HOSPITAL
34(47) CT 372, Crooked St, **N...gas:** Citgo, Sunoco, **food:** Applebee's, McDonald's, Starbucks, **lodging:** Ramada Inn, **other:** Big Y Mkt, Lowe's Whse
33(46) CT 72 W, to Bristol, no facilities
32(45) Ct 10, Queen St, Southington, **N...gas:** Exxon, Shell, **food:** Bertucci's, Burger King, Chili's, D'angelo's, Denny's, KFC, McDonald's, Outback Steaks, Randy's Pizza, Ruby Tuesday, Subway, Taco Bell, **lodging:** Motel 6, **other:** HOSPITAL, CVS Drug, $Tree, Jo-Ann Fabrics, Shaw's Foods, Staples, TownFair Tire, **S...gas:** Mobil, Sunoco, **food:** Bickford's, Blimpie, Brannigan's Ribs, Friendly's, TGIFriday, Wendy's, **lodging:** Holiday Inn Express, Howard Johnson, Travelodge, **other:** Chevrolet
31(44) CT 229, West St, **N...gas:** Mobil, Sunoco/diesel/24hr, **S...gas:** Citgo, Gulf, **food:** Mack's Brick Oven, Valendino's Pizzaria, **lodging:** Residence Inn
30(43) Marion Ave, W Main, Southington, **N...**ski area, **S...gas:** Mobil/repair, **other:** HOSPITAL
42.5mm rest area eb, full(handicapped)facilities, info, phone, picnic tables, litter barrels, petwalk
29(42) CT 10, Milldale(exits left from wb), no facilities
28(41) CT 322, Marion, **S...gas:** Mobil, TA/diesel/24hr/@, **food:** Blimpie, Burger King, DQ, Dunkin Donuts, **lodging:** Day's Inn, **other:** MEDICAL CARE, radiators
27(40) I-691 E, to Meriden, no facilities
26(38) CT 70, to Cheshire, **N...food:** Silver Diner, **lodging:** Sheraton
25a(37) Austin Rd(from eb), **N...lodging:** Sheraton, Costco/ gas

Waterbury

25(36) Scott Rd, E Main St, **N...gas:** Exxon, Gulf/diesel, **food:** Dunkin Donuts, **S...gas:** Mobil, **food:** Burger King, Friendly's, McDonald's, Nino's Rest., **lodging:** Ramada Inn, Super 8, **other:** BJ's Whse, Chevrolet, CVS Drug, Super Stop&Shop
24(34) Harpers Ferry Rd, **S...gas:** Getty, Shell/24hr
23(33.5) CT 69, Hamilton Ave, **N...food:** Bertucci's, Chili's, McDonald's, Ruby Tuesday, **other:** HOSPITAL, Barnes&Noble, Filene's, JC Penney, OfficeMax, Sears/auto, mall, **S...gas:** Shell
22(33) Baldwin St, Waterbury, **N...gas:** McDonald's, **lodging:** Courtyard, Quality Inn, **other:** HOSPITAL
21(33) Meadow St, Banks St, **N...food:** HomeTown Buffet, TGIFriday, **other:** Shaw's Foods, **S...gas:** Exxon/ diesel/24hr, **other:** Home Depot
20(32) CT 8 N(exits left from eb), to Torrington, **N...gas:** Shell, **food:** McDonald's
19(32) CT 8 S(exits left from wb), to Bridgeport, no facilities
18(32) W Main, Highland Ave, **N...gas:** Exxon, **other:** HOSPITAL, CVS Drug
17(30) CT 63, CT 64, to Watertown, Naugatuck, **S...gas:** Mobil/diesel, **food:** Maples Rest.
16(25) CT 188, to Middlebury, **N...gas:** Mobil, **food:** Hilton Garden, Patty's Deli
15(22) US 6 E, CT 67, Southbury, **N...gas:** Mobil, **food:** Dunkin Donuts, Friendly's, McDonald's, **lodging:** Heritage Inn, Oaktree Inn, **other:** K-Mart/Little Caesar's, to Kettletown SP, **S...**Shell
14(20) CT 172, to S Britain, **N...gas:** Mobil/24hr, **food:** Thatcher's Rest., **other:** st police
20mm motorist callboxes begin eb, end wb
13(19) River Rd(from eb), to Southbury
11(16) CT 34, to New Haven, no facilities
10(15) US 6 W, Newtown, **S...gas:** Mobil/diesel, Shell/24hr, **food:** Blue Colony Diner/24hr, Pizza Palace, **other:** HOSPITAL
9(11) CT 25, to Hawleyville, **S...lodging:** Best Western, Hillside Inn, Microtel

Interstate 84

8(8) Newtown Rd, **N...gas:** Global, Mobil/diesel, **food:** Outback Steaks, **lodging:** Wellesley Inn, **S...gas:** BP, Shell, **food:** Bertucci's Italian, Boston Mkt, Burger King, Chili's, Denny's, Friendly's, Harold's Diner, McDonald's, Subway, Taco Bell, **lodging:** Best Western, Holiday Inn/rest., Quality Inn, **other:** Buick/Pontiac, Chrysler/Plymouth/Jeep/Kia, CVS Drug, GMC, Goodyear/auto, Radio Shack, Staples, Target, Wal-Mart

7(7) US 7N/202E, to Brookfield, New Milford, **1 exit N on Federal Rd...food:** Applebee's, **lodging:** Best Inn, **other:** Borders Books, Circuit City, Ford, Harley-Davidson, Home Depot, mall

6(6) CT 37(from wb), New Fairfield, **N...gas:** Shell, **other:** HOSPITAL, to Squantz Pond SP

5(5) CT 37, CT 39, CT 53, Danbury, **N...gas:** Exxon, **lodging:** Best Value Inn, **S...gas:** Exxon, Mobil, **food:** DeliSnack, Taco Bell, **other:** HOSPITAL, to Putnam SP

4(4) US 6 W/202 W, Lake Ave, **N...gas:** Amoco, Gulf/diesel, Shell/diesel, 7-11, **food:** McDonald's, **lodging:** Ethan Allen Inn, Super 8, Goodyear/auto, **S...**Sunoco, **lodging:** Residence Inn, to mall

3(3) US 7 S(exits left from wb), to Norwalk, **S...food:** Dave&Buster's, **other:** JC Penney, Lord&Taylor, Macy's, Sears/auto, mall

2b a(1) US 6, US 202, Mill Plain Rd, **N...gas:** Exxon, **food:** Desert Moon Café, Starbucks, **lodging:** Hilton Garden, **other:** Eckerd, Staples, **S...Welcome Ctr/weigh sta, full(handicapped)facilities, info, picnic tables, litter barrels, petwalk,** to Old Ridgebury

1(0) Sawmill Rd, **N...**Hilton Garden

0mm Connecticut/New York state line

Interstate 91

Exit #(mm)Services

58mm Connecticut/Massachusetts state line

49(57) US 5, to Longmeadow, MA, **E...gas:** Citgo, Mobil, **food:** Friendly's, Jiggy's Café, McDonald's, Rinaldi's Italian, Steve's Seafood, **lodging:** Radisson, **W...food:** Cloverleaf Café

48(56) CT 220, Elm St, **E...gas:** Mobil, **food:** Burger King, ChiChi's, Denny's, Dunkin Donuts, Friendly's, McDonald's, Ruby Tuesday, TGIFriday, Togo's, Wendy's, **other:** A&P, Filene's, Honda, Kohl's, Sear/auto, Target, same as 47

47(55) CT 190, to Hazardville, **E...gas:** Citgo, **food:** Bickford's, D'angelo's, Domino's, Dunkin Donuts, Ground Round, KFC, McDonald's, Olive Garden, Pizza Hut, Red Lobster, Taco Bell, TCBY, **lodging:** Motel 6, Red Roof Inn, **other:** HOSPITAL, Advance Parts, AutoZone, Barnes&Noble, CVS Drug, $Tree, Ford, Goodyear, Home Depot, JC Penney, Jo-Ann Fabrics, Michael's, OfficeMax, Radio Shack, Shaw's Foods, Staples, Stop&Shop Foods, Walgreen, mall, same as 48

46(53) US 5, King St, to Enfield, **E...gas:** Mobil, **food:** Astro's Rest., **W...lodging:** Super 8

45(51) CT 140, Warehouse Point, **E...gas:** Shell/Dunkin Donuts, **food:** Blimpie, Burger King, Cracker Barrel, Friendly's, Kowloon Chinese, Sofia's Pizza, **other:** Big Y Foods, Wal-Mart, to Trolley Museum, **W...gas:** Sunoco/diesel/24hr, **lodging:** Best Western

44(50) US 5 S, to E Windsor, **E...gas:** Citgo/diesel, **food:** Cavodoro's Pizza, Dunkin Donuts, E Windsor Rest., **lodging:** Holiday Inn Express

49mm Connecticut River

42(48) CT 159, Windsor Locks, **W...gas:** Gulf, same as 41

41(47) Center St(exits with 39), **W...gas:** Shell/24hr, **food:** Ad Pizzaria, **lodging:** Howard Johnson

40(46.5) CT 20, **W...**Old New-Gate Prison, airport

39(46) Kennedy Rd(exits with 41), Community Rd, **W...gas:** Shell/diesel/24hr, **other:** K-Mart, Radio Shack, Stop&Shop Foods

38(45) CT 75, to Poquonock, Windsor Area, **E...gas:** Mobil/diesel, **food:** Beanery Bistro, China Sea, Domino's, McDonald's, Subway, **other:** to Ellsworth Homestead, **W...lodging:** Courtyard, Hilton Garden, Marriott

37(44) CT 305, Bloomfield Ave, Windsor Ctr, **E...gas:** Mobil/diesel, **food:** McDonald's, **W...gas:** Citgo, **lodging:** Residence Inn

36(43) CT 178, Park Ave, to W Hartford, no facilities

35b(41) CT 218, to Bloomfield, to S Windsor, **E...**gas/diesel, food

a I-291 E, to Manchester

34(40) CT 159, Windsor Ave, **E...gas:** Texaco/diesel, **W...gas:** Citgo, **lodging:** Flamingo Inn, **other:** HOSPITAL

33(39) Jennings Rd, Weston St, **E...other:** Buick/GMC, Mazda, Saturn, repair, **W...gas:** Exxon/diesel, Mobil, **food:** Burger King, Dunkin Donuts, McDonald's, Subway, **lodging:** Red Roof Inn, Super 8, **other:** Honda, Hyundai, Jaguar, Mitsubishi, Nissan, Toyota

32b(38) Trumbull St(exits left from nb), **W...**to downtown, **food:** Crowne Plaza, **lodging:** Sheraton, **other:** HOSPITAL, Goodyear

a (exit 30 from sb), I-84 W

29b(37) Hartford, I-84 E

a(36.5) US 5 N, CT 15 N(exits left from nb), **W...**downtown, **other:** HOSPITAL, capitol, civic ctr

28(36) US 5, CT 15 S(from nb), **W...gas:** Citgo, **food:** Burger King, Wendy's

27(35) Brainerd Rd, Airport Rd, **E...gas:** Shell/diesel, **food:** McDonald's, Valle's Steaks, **lodging:** Day's Inn, **other:** Ford, to Regional Mkt

CONNECTICUT

Interstate 91

N ↕ S

26(33.5) Marsh St, **E...**Silas Deane House, Webb House, CT MVD

25(33) CT 3, Glastonbury, Wethersfield, no facilities

24(32) CT 99, Rocky Hill, Wethersfield, **E...gas:** Gulf, Mobil, 7-11, **food:** Bickford's, McDonald's, On the Border, Rasoi Grill, Subway, Susse Chalet, **lodging:** Howard Johnson, **W...gas:** Mobil, Shell/diesel, **food:** Bennigan's, China Star Buffet, Denny's, Dunkin Donuts, Giovanni's Pizza, Ground Round, HomeTown Buffet, KFC, McDonald's, D'angelo's, Red Lobster, **lodging:** Motel 6, Ramada Inn, **other:** MEDICAL CARE, A&P, AutoZone, CVS Drug, Goodyear/auto, Lowe's Whse, Marshalls, Radio Shack, TownFair Tire, Walgreen, Wal-Mart

23(29) to CT 3, West St, Rocky Hill, Vet Home, **E...lodging:** Marriott, **other:** HOSPITAL, to Dinosaur SP, **W...gas:** Citgo/diesel, Mobil, **food:** Angelo's Pizza, D'angelo's, McDonald's, Tommaso's Italian, **other:** IGA Foods

22(27) CT 9, to New Britain, Middletown, no facilities

21(26) CT 372, to Berlin, Cromwell, **E...gas:** Sunoco/diesel/repair, **food:** Krauszer's Foods, Wooster St Pizza, **lodging:** Comfort Inn, Radisson Inn/rest., **W... gas:** Citgo/diesel, Mobil/diesel, **food:** Blimpie, Burger King, Cromwell Diner/24hr, Luna Pizza, McDonald's, **lodging:** Holiday Inn, Super 8, **other:** Fabric Place, Firestone/auto, Wal-Mart

Meriden

20(23) Country Club Rd, Middle St, no facilities

22mm rest area/weigh sta nb, full(handicapped)facilities, info, phone, picnic tables, litter barrels, vending, RV dump, petwalk

19(21) Baldwin Ave(from sb), no facilities

18(20.5) I-691 W, to Marion, access to same as 16 & 17, ski area

17(20) CT 15 N(from sb), to I-691, CT 66 E, Meriden, **W...gas:** Amoco, **food:** Getty, **lodging:** Residence Inn

16(19) CT 15, E Main St, **E...gas:** Gulf/diesel, Mobil, Sunoco, **food:** American Steaks, Gianni's Rest., Huxley's Café, Olympos Diner, Subway, **lodging:** Candlewood Suites, Hampton Inn, Ramada Inn, The Inn, **other:** CVS Drug, Ford, Hancock Fabrics, Radio Shack, USPO, Volvo, **W...gas:** Amoco/24hr, Citgo/diesel, Getty/diesel, Gulf/repair, Sunoco/diesel, **food:** Bess Eaton, Boston Mkt, Burger King, Domino's, Dunkin Donuts, Friendly's, Great Wall Chinese, KFC, McDonald's, Taco Bell, Wendy's, **lodging:** East Inn, **other:** CarQuest, CVS Drug

15(16) CT 68, to Durham, **E...**golf, **W...lodging:** Courtyard, Fairfield Inn

15mm rest area sb, full(handicapped)facilities, info, phone, picnic tables, litter barrels, petwalk

14(12) CT 150(no EZ return), Woodhouse Ave, Wallingford, no facilities

13(10) US 5(exits left from nb), Wallingford, **2 mi W on US 5...gas:** Citgo/diesel, DM, **food:** Dunkin Donuts, **other:** Audi/Porche/Saab/Suzuki, Krauszners Foods, to Wharton Brook SP

12(9) US 5, Washington Ave, **E...gas:** Citgo, **food:** Boston Mkt, Burger King, China Buffet, D'angelo's, Dunkin Donuts, Friendly's, McDonald's, Rustic Oak Rest., Subway, Wendy's, **other:** CVS Drug, Stop&Shop Food, Walgreen, **W...gas:** Exxon/diesel/24hr, **food:** Athena II Diner, Danny's Pizza, Roy Rogers, **lodging:** Holiday Inn

New Haven

11(7) CT 22(from nb), North Haven, **E...gas:** Sunoco, **food:** Hunan Chinese, **other:** AutoZone, JC Penney Outlet, Radio Shack, Stop&Shop Foods, TownFair Tire, USPO, same as 12

10(6) CT 40, Hamden, to Cheshire, no facilities

9(5) Montowese Ave, **W...gas:** Sunoco, **food:** McDonald's, Sbarro's, Subway, **other:** Barnes&Noble, BJ's Whse, Circuit City, Home Depot, OfficeMax

8(4) CT 17, CT 80, Middletown Ave, **E... gas:** Amoco/Blimpie, Citgo, Exxon, Shell, Sunoco/24hr, **food:** Burger King, D'angelo's, Dunkin Donuts, Exit 8 Diner, KFC, McDonald's, Taco Bell/Pizza Hut, **lodging:** Day's Inn, **other:** Advance Parts, Lowe's Whse, K-Mart/Little Caesar's/24hr, **W...gas:** Mobil/diesel

7(3) Ferry St(from sb), Fair Haven, no facilities

6(2.5) Willow St(exits left from nb), Blatchley Ave, **W...gas:** Shell

5(2) US 5(from nb), State St, Fair Haven, **E...food:** New Star Diner

4(1.5) State St(from sb), downtown

3(1) Trumbull St, New Haven, downtown, **W...**Peabody Museum

2(.5) Hamilton St, New Haven, downtown

1(.3) CT 34W(from sb), New Haven, **W...**HOSPITAL, downtown

0mm I-91 begins/ends on I-95, exit 48.

Interstate 95

N ↕ S

Exit #(mm) Services

112mm Connecticut/Rhode Island state line

93(111) CT 216, Clarks Falls, **E...gas:** Shell/repair/24hr, to Burlingame SP, **W...gas:** Citgo/diesel, Republic/diesel/rest./@, **food:** Bess Eaton, McDonald's, **lodging:** Budget Inn, Stardust Motel

92(107) CT 2, CT 49(no EZ nb return), Pawcatuck, **E...gas:** Shell, **other:** HOSPITAL, **W...lodging:** Randall's Inn/rest.

106mm Welcome Ctr/rest area sb, full(handicapped) facilities, phone, picnic tables, litter barrels, petwalk, vending

91(103) CT 234, N Main St, to Stonington, **E...**HOSPITAL

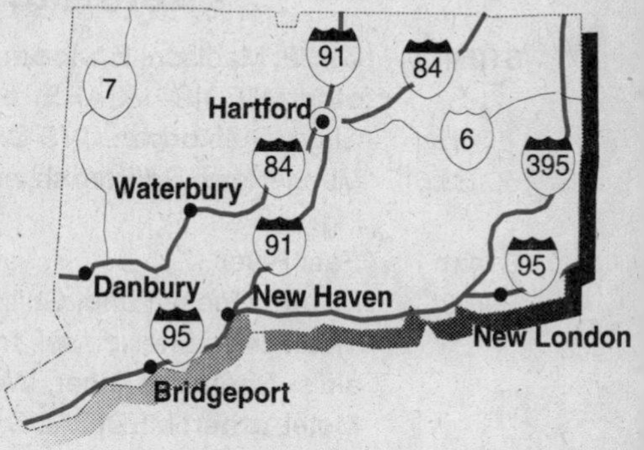

CONNECTICUT

Interstate 95

N ↕ S

Mystic

90(101) CT 27, Mystic, **E...gas:** Mobil, **food:** Bickford's, Friendly's, GoFish Rest., Jamm's Seafood, McDonald's, Newport Creamery, Steak Loft, **lodging:** AmeriSuites, Hilton, Howard Johnson, Old Mystic Motel, Seaport Lodge, **other:** Mystic Factory Outlets, aquarium, **W...gas:** Mobil, Shell/ Subway/Dunkin Donuts/diesel, **food:** Ashby's Rest., Ground Round, Pizza Grille, **lodging:** Best Western, Comfort Inn, Day's Inn, Residence Inn, **other:** Chevrolet, Chrysler/Plymouth/Dodge, Ford

100mm scneic overlook nb

89(99) CT 215, Allyn St, **W...**camping(seasonal)

88(98) CT 117, to Noank, **E...**MEDICAL CARE(7 am-11pm), airport

87(97) Sharp Hwy, Groton, **E...**Griswold SP, airport

86(96) rd 184(exits left from nb), Groton, **W...gas:** Cory's, **food:** IHOP, KFC, Rosie's Diner/24hr, Taco Bell, **lodging:** Clarion Inn/rest., Groton Suites, Morgan Suites, Super 8, **other:** Kohl's, Stop&Shop Foods, Wal-Mart, to US Sub Base

85(95) US 1 N, Groton, downtown, **E...gas:** Citgo/diesel, **food:** Norm's Diner, **other:** NAPA

94.5mm Thames River

New London

84(94) CT 32(from sb), New London, downtown

83(92) CT 32, New London, **E...**to Long Island Ferry

82a(90.5) frontage rd, New London, **E...other:** AutoZone, Brooks Drug, Goodyear, IGA Foods, TownFair Tire, same as 82, **W...food:** Chili's, ChuckeCheese, **lodging:** Fairfield Suites, Holiday Inn, SpringHill Suites, Marshall's, OfficeMax, ShopRite Foods, same as 82

82(90) CT 85, New London, **E...food:** Pizza Hut, **other:** Staples, **W...gas:** Mobil, **food:** Dairy Rest., Food-Court, Red Lobster, **lodging:** Fairfield Suites, Holiday Inn, **other:** Filene's, Home Depot, JC Penney, Macy's, Marshall's, Sears, Target, mall

81(89.5) Cross Road, **W...food:** Benoit's Rest., **other:** Bob's Store, BJ's Whse, Wal-Mart/McDonald's/drugs, Waterford Ind Park

80(89.3) Oil Mill Rd(from sb), **W...lodging:** Lamplighter Motel

76(89) I-395 N(from nb), to Norwich

75(88) US 1, to Waterford, no facilities

74(87) rd 161, to Flanders, Niantic, **E...gas:** Citgo, Exxon, Sunoco/diesel/repair, **food:** Bickford's Rest., Burger King, Dunkin Donuts, KFC, Illiano's Grill, **lodging:** Best Western, Day's Inn, Motel 6, Ramada Inn, Sleep Inn, Starlight Motel, **other:** Children's Museum, National Tire, **W...gas:** Shell, **food:** Kings Garden Chinese, McDonald's, Shack Rest., **other:** MEDICAL CARE, Brooks Drug, IGA Foods, Ford

73(86) Society Rd, no facilities

Old Lyme

72(84) to Rocky Neck SP, **2 mi E...**food, lodging, RV camping, to Rocky Neck SP

71(83) 4 Mile Rd, River Rd, to Rocky Neck SP, beaches, **1 mi E...**camping(seasonal)

70(80) US 1, CT 156, Old Lyme, **W...gas:** Shell/diesel, **food:** Bess Eaton, **lodging:** Old Lyme Inn/dining, **other:** MEDICAL CARE, A&P, Old Lyme Drug, Griswold Museum

78mm Connecticut River

69(77) US 1, CT 9 N, to Hartford, **W...food:** Saybrook Fish House, **lodging:** Comfort Inn/rest.

68(76.5) US 1 S, Old Saybrook, **E...gas:** Citgo, Mobil, Shell, **food:** Cloud 9 Deli, Pat's Country Kitchen, Sully's Seafood, **other:** Chrysler/Plymouth/Dodge/Jeep, Daewoo, Isuzu, **W... lodging:** Liberty Inn, **other:** Chevrolet/Nissan, Kia, Pontiac/GMC, Toyota

67(76) CT 154, Elm St(no EZ sb return), Old Saybrook, same as 68

66(75) to US 1, Spencer Plain Rd, **1 mi E...gas:** Citgo/ diesel/24hr, **food:** Benny's Pizzeria, CA Pizza, Cucu's Mexican, Gateway Indian Cuisine, Luigi's Italian, Paisan's Pizza, SoleMar Café, Thai Cuisine, TNT Rest., **lodging:** Day's Inn, Heritage Inn, Saybrook Motel, Super 8, **other:** ABC Hardware, transmissions, **W...**st police

Westbrook

65(73) rd 153, Westbrook, **E...gas:** Exxon/Dunkin Donuts, **food:** Denny's, **lodging:** Day's Inn, Waters Edge B&B, Westbook Inn B&B, **other:** Honda, Westbrook Factory Stores/famous brands, **W...lodging:** Super 8

64(70) rd 145, Horse Hill Rd, Clinton, **3 mi E on US 1...gas:** Shell, **food:** Dunkin Donuts, Hungry Lion Rest., **lodging:** Clinton Motel, **other:** NAPA, Radio Shack, Stop&Shop Foods

63(68) CT 81, Clinton, **E...gas:** Shell, **1 mi E on US 1... gas:** Citgo/diesel, Shell/diesel/LP, **food:** Friendly's, McDonald's, **other:** CVS Drug, **W...other:** Clinton Crossing Premium Outlets/famous brands

62(67) **E...**to Hammonasset SP, RV camping, beaches

66mm **service area both lanes, Mobil/diesel, McDonald's, atm**

CONNECTICUT

Interstate 95

61(64) CT 79, Madison, **E...food:** Panda House Chinese, **other:** MEDICAL CARE, **on US 1 E...gas:** Amoco, Citgo, Gulf, **other:** CVS Drug

60(63.5) Mungertown Rd(from sb, no return), E...food, lodging

61mm East River

59(60) rd 146, Goose Lane, Guilford, **E...gas:** Citgo/DM, Mobil/24hr, Shell/diesel, **food:** Friendly's, McDonald's, Shoreline Diner, Wendy's, **lodging:** Tower Motel, **other:** MEDICAL CARE, Chevrolet/Pontiac, Pepper's Gen Store, transmissions, **W...food:** Sachem Country Rest.

58(59) CT 77, Guilford, **on US 1 E...food:** Getty, Donut Village, Friendly's, Subway, **other:** Big Y Foods, CVS Drug, Radio Shack, to Whitfield Museum, **W...**st police

57(58) US 1, Guilford, **E...**MEDICAL CARE, **W...other:** Land Rover, Saab

56(55) rd 146, to Stony Creek, **E...lodging:** Advanced Motel, **W...gas:** Mobil, TA/Sunoco/diesel/rest./24hr/@, **food:** Dutchess Rest., Friendly's, **lodging:** MacDonald's Motel, Ramada Ltd, **other:** Stop&Shop Foods

55(54) US 1, **E...gas:** Mobil, Sunoco, Thornton, 7-11/24hr, **food:** Dunkin Donuts, McDonald's, My Dad's Rest., **lodging:** Knight's Inn, Motel 6, **other:** Dodge, Ford, Walgreen, **W...gas:** Citgo, Shell, **food:** Margarita's Mexican, Parthenon Diner/24hr, Su Casa Mexican, **lodging:** Day's Inn

54(53) Cedar St, Brushy Plain Rd, **E...gas:** Citgo/repair, Mobil, **food:** Dunkin Donuts, La Luna Ristorante, Townhouse Rest., **other:** Chevrolet, Dodge, Mitsubishi, Subaru, **W...**Krausnzer's Foods

52mm service area both lanes, Mobil/diesel/24hr, McDonald's, atm

New Haven

52(50) rd 100, North High St, **E...other:** to Trolley Museum, **W...**st police

51(49.5) US 1, Easthaven, **E...gas:** Hess, Shell, Sunoco, **food:** Boston Mkt, Chili's, Friendly's, McDonald's, **lodging:** Holiday Inn Express, **other:** Chevrolet, Lexus, **W...gas:** Mobil, Sunoco, **food:** Dunkin Donuts, King Buffet, Wendy's, **other:** A&P, AutoZone

50(49) Woodward Ave(from nb), **E...gas:** Shell, **other:** US Naval/Marine Reserve, Ft Nathan Hale

49(48.5) Stiles St(from nb), no facilities

48(48) I-91 N, to Hartford, no facilities

47(47.5) CT 34, New Haven, **E...gas:** Shell, **W... gas:** Mobil/diesel, **lodging:** Fairfield Inn, **other:** HOSPITAL

46(47) Long Wharf Dr, Sargent Dr, **E... food:** Rusty Scupper Rest., **W...gas:** Mobil/diesel, **food:** Brick Oven Pizza, **lodging:** Fairfield Inn

45(46.5) CT 10(from sb), Blvd, same as 44, **W...food:** Getty, DQ, Dunkin Donuts, McDonald's

44(46) CT 10(from nb), Kimberly Ave, **E...lodging:** Super 8, **W...food:** Getty, DQ, Dunkin Donuts, McDonald's, Wendy's, same as 45

43(45) CT 122, 1st Ave(no EZ return), West Haven, **W...gas:** Amoco, **other:** HOSPITAL, to U of New Haven

42(44) CT 162, Saw Mill Rd, **E...gas:** Mobil, **food:** Pizza Hut, **lodging:** Econolodge, **other:** Sears, **W...gas:** Shell, 7-11, **food:** American Steaks, D'angelo's, Denny's, Dunkin Donuts, Friendly's, **lodging:** Best Western, **other:** Staples

41(42) Marsh Hill Rd, to Orange

41mm service area both lanes, gas: Mobil/diesel, food: McDonald's

Milford

40(40) Old Gate Lane, Woodmont Rd, **E...gas:** Gulf/diesel/24hr, Pilot/Wendy's/diesel/24hr, Shell, **food:** Bennigan's, Cracker Barrel, D'angelo's, Duchess Rest., Dunkin Donuts, Gipper's Rest., **lodging:** Best Value Inn, Comfort Inn, Mayflower Hotel, Milford Inn

39(39) US 1, to Milford, **E...gas:** Gulf/diesel, **food:** Friendly's, Hooters, Imo's Pizza, Pizzaria Uno, **lodging:** Howard Johnson, Milford Inn, **other:** Firestone/auto, Mazda/Volvo, **W on US 1...gas:** Mobil, **food:** Baskin-Robbins, Boston Mkt, Burger King, Chili's, Dunkin Donuts, KFC, Little Caesar's, Miami Subs, Mr Sizzzl, McDonald's, Nathan's Famous, Steak&Sword Rest., Subway, Taco Bell, Wendy's, **other:** Acura, Chrysler/Jeep, Filene's, JC Penney, Michael's, Rite Aid, Sears/auto, Stop&Shop Food, TownFair Tire, USPO, Waldbaum's Foods, mall

38(38) CT 15, Merritt Pkwy, Cross Pkwy, no facilities

37(37.5) High St(from nb, no EZ return), **E...gas:** Amoco, Citgo, Gulf, Mobil, 7-11, **lodging:** ShoreLine Motel

36(37) Plains Rd, **E...gas:** Exxon/diesel, Sunoco/diesel, **lodging:** Hampton Inn, **other:** HOSPITAL

35(36) Bic Dr, School House Rd, **E...gas:** Citgo, **food:** Subway, Wendy's, **lodging:** Fairfield Inn, **other:** Buick, Chevrolet, Chrysler/Jeep, Dodge, Ford/Lincoln/Mercury, Honda, Kia, K-Mart, Pontiac/Nissan, **W...lodging:** Red Roof Inn, SpringHill Suites

Bridgeport

34(34) US 1, Milford, **E...gas:** Gulf, Shell, **food:** Denny's, Dunkin Donuts, Gourmet Buffet, McDonald's, Taco Bell, **lodging:** Devon Motel

33(33.5) US 1(from nb, no EZ return), CT 110, Ferry Blvd, **E...gas:** Citgo/diesel, Sunoco, **food:** Marina Dock Rest., **other:** Jo-Ann Fabrics, Staples, Stop&Shop Foods, Walgreen, **W...other:** Ponderosa, Home Depot, Marshalls, Wal-Mart SuperCtr/24hr

32(33) W Broad St, Stratford, **E...gas:** Amoco, **food:** Getty, **other:** Ford, repair, **W...gas:** Gulf, **food:** Dunkin Donuts

Interstate 95

N ↕ S

31(32) South Ave, Honeyspot Rd, **E...gas:** Gulf/diesel, **lodging:** Camelot Motel, **W...gas:** Citgo/diesel

30(31.5) Lordship Blvd, Surf Ave, **E...gas:** Shell/24hr, **food:** Ramada/rest., **other:** Harley-Davidson, Ryder, **W...gas:** Citgo/diesel

29(31) rd 130, Stratford Ave, Seaview Ave, **W...**HOSPITAL

28(30) CT 113, E Main St, Pembrook St

27(29.5) Lafayette Blvd, downtown, **W...lodging:** Day's Inn, **other:** HOSPITAL, Bob's Store, Sears/auto, Barnum Museum

27a(29) CT 25, CT 8, to Waterbury

26(28) Wordin Ave, downtown

25(27) CT 130(from sb, no EZ return), State St, Commerce Dr, Fairfield Ave, **E...food:** Getty, **other:** Mercedes, **W...gas:** Gulf, **food:** McDonald's

24(26.5) Black Rock Tpk, **E...food:** Fairfield Diner, **other:** Staples, **W...other:** Ford/Nissan

23(26) US 1, Kings Hwy, **E...gas:** Sunoco, **food:** McDonald's, Outback Steaks, **other:** Home Depot

22(24) Round Hill Rd(from sb), N Benson Rd, no facilities

23.5mm service area both lanes, gas: Mobil/diesel, food: FoodCourt(sb), McDonald's/24hr

21(23) Mill Plain Rd, **E...gas:** Mobil, Shell, **food:** DQ, Grotto Rest., McDonald's, Subway, **lodging:** Fairfield Inn, **other:** Brooks Drug, Stop&Shop Food

20(22) Bronson Rd(from sb), no facilities

19(21) US 1, Center St, Southport, **E...**Southport Brewing Co, **W...gas:** Shell/Dunkin Donuts/diesel, **food:** Athena Diner, **lodging:** Tequot Motel

18(20) to Westport, **E...**Sherwood Island SP, beaches, **W...gas:** Citgo, Mobil, **food:** Bertucci's Pizza, Burger King, Carver's Ice Cream, Cedar Brook Café, McDonald's, Sherwood Diner, Subway, Woodie's Roadhouse, **other:** Toyota, Radio Shack, st police

Norwalk

17(18) CT 33, rd 136, Westport, **W...gas:** FastStop Mart, **food:** Dunville's Rest., Little Nick's Pizza, Susan's Cookies

16(17) E Norwalk, **E...gas:** Mobil, Shell/diesel, **food:** Baskin-Robbins/Dunkin Donuts, Eastside Café, Penny's Diner, Subway, **other:** Rite Aid

15(16) US 7, Norwalk, to Danbury, **E...gas:** Shell

14(15) US 1, CT Ave, S Norwalk, **E...**st police, **W...gas:** Amoco, Coastal, **food:** Angela Mia's Café, Pagano's Seafood, Pizza Hut, Post Road Diner, Silver Star Diner, **other:** HOSPITAL, Barnes&Noble, Circuit City, CompUSA, Firestone, GNC, ShopRite Foods, Stop&Shop

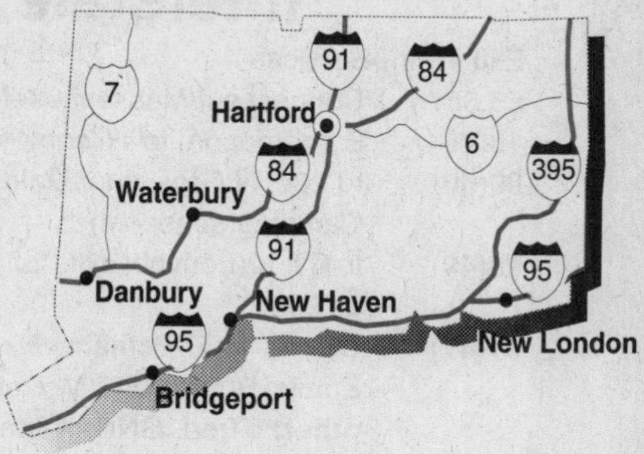

13(13) US 1(no EZ return), Post Rd, Norwalk, **W...gas:** Exxon, Mobil, Shell/24hr, **food:** American Steaks, Burger King, Driftwood Diner, Dunkin Donuts, Friendly's, IHOP, KFC, McDonald's, Pasta Fare Rest., Red Lobster, Wendy's, **lodging:** DoubleTree Hotel, **other:** Costco, Home Depot, Kohl's, LandRover, Old Navy, Radio Shack, ShopRite Foods, Staples, TownFair Tire, same as 14

12.5mm service area nb, Mobil/diesel, McDonald's

12(12) rd 136, Tokeneke Rd(from nb, no return), **W...**deli

11(11) US 1, Darien, **E...gas:** Amoco, **other:** Chevrolet, Lincoln/Mercury/Jaguar, **W...gas:** Exxon, **lodging:** Howard Johnson/rest., **other:** BMW

10(10) Noroton, **W...gas:** Citgo, Getty, Shell, **food:** Jake's Place

9.5mm service area sb, gas: Mobil/diesel, food: McDonald's

9(9) US 1, rd 106, Glenbrook, **E...food:** Indian Cuisine, **lodging:** Stamford Motor Inn, **W...gas:** Gulf, **food:** Blimpie, McDonald's, **other:** Aamco

8(8) Atlantic Ave, Elm St, **E...**U-Haul, **W... gas:** Exxon, Sunoco, **lodging:** Budget Inn, Marriott, Ramada Inn, **other:** HOSPITAL, Saturn

Stamford

7(7) CT 137, Atlantic Ave, **E...lodging:** Westin Hotel, **W...lodging:** Marriott, **other:** JC Penney, mall, same as 8

6(6) Harvard Ave, West Ave, **E...gas:** Exxon, **lodging:** Fairfield Inn, **other:** USPO, **W...gas:** Getty, Shell/24hr, **food:** Boston Mkt, Corner Deli/pizza, Subway, Taco Bell, **lodging:** Stamford Hotel, Super 8, **other:** HOSPITAL, Firestone

5(5) US 1, Riverside, Old Greenwich, **W...gas:** Mobil, Shell/24hr, **food:** Italian Ristorante, McDonald's, Taco Bell, **lodging:** Hyatt Regency, **other:** MEDICAL CARE, A&P, Caldor, Edwards Drug, Staples

4(4) Indian Field Rd, Cos Cob, **W...lodging:** Howard Johnson's, **other:** Bush-Holley House Museum

3(3) Arch St, Greenwich, **E...**Bruce Museum, **W...gas:** Shell, **other:** HOSPITAL

2mm weigh sta nb

2(1) Delavan Ave, Byram, no facilities

1mm Connecticut/New York state line

CONNECTICUT

Interstate 395

N ↕ S

Putnam

Exit #(mm)Services
55.5mm Connecticut/Massachusetts state line
100(54) E Thompson, to Wilsonville, no facilities
99(50) rd 200, N Grosvenor Dale, **E...**W Thompson Lake Camping(seasonal)
98(49) to CT 12(from nb, exits left), Grosvenor Dale, same as 99
97(47) US 44, to E Putnam, **E... food:** Dunkin Donuts, Empire Buffet, KFC, McDonald's, Subway, Wendy's, **other:** $Tree, GNC, K-Mart/Little Caesar's, Radio Shack, Stop&Shop Foods, **W...gas:** Shell/repair/24hr, Sunoco, **other:** Wal-Mart
96(46) to CT 12, Putnam, **W...food:** Heritage Rd Café, **lodging:** King's Inn, **other:** HOSPITAL
95(45) Kennedy Dr, to Putnam, **E...**Ford/Mercury, **W...** HOSPITAL
94(43) Ballouville, **E on CT 12...food:** Golden Greek Rest., **W...food:** Laurel House Rest., **lodging:** Holiday Inn Express
93(41) CT 101, to Dayville, **E...gas:** Getty, Shell/diesel, **food:** Burger King, China Garden, Dunkin Donuts, McDonald's, Subway, Zip's Diner, **other:** A&P, IGA Foods, Wibberley Tire, **W...gas:** Mobil/diesel/24hr
92(39) to S Killingly, **W...food:** Giant Pizza, **other:** st police
91(38) US 6 W, to Danielson, to Quinebaug Valley Coll
90(36) to US 6 E(from nb), to Providence, no facilities
35mm rest area both lanes, full(handicapped)facilities, gas: Mobil/diesel
89(32) CT 14, to Central Village, **E...gas:** Gulf, **other:** RV camping, **W...gas:** Citgo/7-11/diesel/24hr, Sunoco/diesel/LP/repair, **food:** Brittany Rest., Subway, **lodging:** Plainfield Motel/rest.
88(30) CT 14A to Plainfield, **E...**RV camping, **1/2 mi W...gas:** Mobil
87(28) Lathrop Rd, to Plainfield, **E...gas:** Shell/Domino's/diesel, **food:** Dunkin Donuts, HongKong Star Chinese, **lodging:** Plainfield Yankee Motel, **other:** Big Y Foods, Greyhound Park, Radio Shack, **W...gas:** Citgo, **food:** Brass Rail Rest., McDonald's, Stromboli's Pizza, **other:** MEDICAL CARE, CVS Drug
86(24) rd 201, Hopeville, **E...**Hopeville Pond SP, RV camping
85(23) CT 164, CT 138, to Pachaug, Preston, **E...other:** $Tree, RV camping
84(21) CT 12, Jewett City, **E...other:** Home Depot, Kohl's, Wal-Mart SuperCtr/24hr, **W...gas:** Citgo/7-11, Mobil/Pizza Hut/diesel, **food:** McDonald's, **other:** Val-U Foods
83a(20) CT 169(from nb), Lisbon, **E...**RV camping
83(18) rd 97, Taftville, **E...gas:** Getty/diesel, **other:** camping, repair, **W...gas:** Citgo/7-11

Norwich

82(14) to CT 2 W, CT 32 N, Norwichtown, **E...food:** Friendly's, **W...gas:** Mobil/diesel, Shell/Dunkin Donuts/diesel, **food:** McDonald's, Rena's Pizza, **lodging:** Comfort Suites, Courtyard, Rosemont Suites
81(14) CT 2 E, CT 32 S, Norwich, **E...**HOSPITAL, to Mohegan Coll
80(12) CT 82, Norwich, **E...gas:** Mobil, Shell/repair, **food:** Bess Eaton/Subway, Burger King, Dandy Donuts, Dominic's Pizza, Friendly's, KFC, McDonald's, Mr Pizza, Papa Gino's, Village Garden Chinese, Wendy's, **other:** Brooks Drug, Jo-Ann Fabrics, ShopRite Foods, Staples, TownFair Tire, **W...lodging:** Ramada Inn
79a(10) CT 2A E, to Ledyard, **E...**to Pequot Res
8.5mm nb...st police, phone
sb...Mobil, rest area, full facilities
79(6) rd 163, to Uncasville, Montville, **1 mi E...gas:** Shell/diesel, **food:** Friendly Pizza, McDonald's, Someplace Else Café
78(5) CT 32(from sb, exits left), to New London, RI Beaches
77(2) CT 85, to I-95 N, Colchester, **1/2 mi E...gas:** Shell/diesel, Dunkin Donuts, **lodging:** Oakdell Motel
0mm I-95. I-395 begins/ends on I-95, exit 76.fs

Interstate 691

E ↕ W

Meriden

Exit #(mm)Services
I-691 begins/ends on I-91, exit 18.
12(12) Preston Ave, no facilities
11(11) I-91 N, to Hartford
10(11) I-91 S, to New Haven, CT 15 S, W Cross Pkwy
8(10) US 5, Broad St, **N...gas:** Cumberland, Mobil/mart, Shell/diesel, **food:** Broad St Pizza, Chinese Gourmet, DQ
7(9) Meriden(from wb), downtown, **S...gas:** Citgo
6(8) Lewis Ave(from wb, no EZ return), to CT 71, **N... food:** Ruby Tuesday, **other:** HOSPITAL, Filene's, JC Penney, Lord&Taylor, Sears/auto, mall, **S...**Citgo
5(7) CT 71, to Chamberlain Hill(from eb, no EZ return), **N...other:** HOSPITAL, A&P, Target, mall, **S...gas:** Getty/diesel, Sunoco, **food:** McDonald's, **other:** VW
4(4) CT 322, W Main St(no re-entry from eb), **N...gas:** Citgo, **food:** Dunkin Donuts, **other:** HOSPITAL, Sal's Foods
3mm Quinnipiac River
3(1) CT 10, to Cheshire, Southington, **N...gas:** Sunoco, **food:** Tony's Pizza, Whole Donut
2(0) I-84 E, to Hartford, no facilities
1(0) I-84 W, to Waterbury, no facilities
I-691 begins/ends on I-84, exit 27.

DELAWARE

Interstate 95

N ↕ S

Exit #(mm)	Services
23mm	Delaware/Pennsylvania state line, motorist callboxes for 23 miles sb
11(22)	I-495 S, DE 92, Naamans Rd, **E...gas:** WaWa, **food:** China Star, Wendy's, **other:** K-Mart, **W...gas:** Gulf/diesel, **food:** KFC/Taco Bell, **lodging:** Howard Johnson Rest., Holiday Inn, **other:** Acme Foods, Eckerd, Home Depot, Radio Shack
10(21)	Harvey Rd(from nb, no EZ return), **1 mi E on US 13...gas:** Amoco, Exxxon/diesel, Gulf, Shell, Sunoco, 7-11, **food:** Arby's, Boston Mkt, Burger King, McDonald's, **other:** Eckerd
9(19)	DE 3, to Marsh Rd, **E...**to Bellevue SP, st police, **W...**museum
8b a(17)	US 202, Concord Pike, to Wilmington, **W...**HOSPITAL, to gas, food, lodging
7b a(16)	DE 52, Delaware Ave, **E...**HOSPITAL, to gas, food, lodging
6(15)	DE 4, MLK Blvd, **W...gas:** Gulf
5d(12)	I-495 N, to Wilmington, to DE Mem Bridge
5b a(11)	DE 141, to US 202, Newport, to New Castle, **E...lodging:** Quality Inn, Radisson
4b a(8)	DE 1, DE 7, to Christiana, **E...food:** Don Pablo, FoodCourt, Houlihan's, **other:** Circuit City, CostCo, JC Penney, Lord&Taylor, Macy's, Michael's, Sears, Strawbridge, mall, **W...food:** Applebee's, ChiChi's, Chili's, Michael's Rest., Shoney's Inn, **lodging:** Courtyard, Fairfield Inn, Hilton Garden, Red Roof Inn, **other:** HOSPITAL, Borders Books, OfficeMax
3b a(6)	DE 273, to Newark, Dover, **E...gas:** Amoco/24hr, Exxon/diesel, **food:** Bob Evans, Boston Mkt, Olive Grill Italian, Ruby Tuesday, Wendy's, **lodging:** Best Western, Comfort Suites, Hawthorn Inn, Residence Inn, **other:** Acme Foods, Jo-Ann Fabrics, **W...gas:** Getty, Shell, 7-11, **food:** Denny's, Donut Connection, Pizza Hut, **lodging:** Hampton Inn, Holiday Inn/Oliver's Rest., McIntosh Inn
5mm	**service area both lanes(exits left from both lanes), info, gas: Exxon/diesel, Mobil/diesel, food: Big Boy, Roy Rogers, Sbarro's, Taco Bell, TCBY**
1b a(3)	DE 896, to Newark, Middletown, to U of DE, **W...gas:** Exxon, Gulf/diesel, Mobil, Shell/24hr, Texaco/diesel, **food:** Boston Mkt, China Garden, Dunkin Donuts, 1st State Diner, Friendly's, Ground Round, McDonald's, TGIFriday, **lodging:** Comfort Inn, Embassy Suites, Howard Johnson, Sleep Inn
1mm	toll booth, st police
0mm	Delaware/Maryland state line, motorist callboxes for 23 miles nb

Newark

Interstate 295(Wilmington)

N ↕ S

Exit #	Services
15mm	Delaware/New Jersey state line, Delaware River, Delaware Memorial Bridge
14.5mm	toll plaza
14	DE 9, New Castle Ave, to Wilmington, **E...gas:** Amoco/24hr, Gulf, Mobil, **other:** Advance Parts, Family$, Firestone/auto, Harley-Davidson, Rite Aid, SuperFresh Foods, **W...gas:** Gulf, Shell, **food:** McDonald's, **lodging:** Day's Inn, Motel 6, Travelodge
13	US 13, US 301, US 40, to New Castle, **E...gas:** Amoco, Exxon/diesel, Sunoco/diesel, Shell, **food:** Burger King, Denny's, DogHouse, Dunkin Donuts, Golden Diner, IHOP, La Chiquita Mexican, McDonald's, Popeye's, Rascal's Seafood, Subway, Taco Bell, Wendy's, **lodging:** Quality Inn, Red Rose Inn, **other:** Cottman Transmissions, Happy Harry's Drugs, Pep-Boys, Radio Shack, Rayco Repair, Sav-A-Lot, **W... gas:** Shell, **lodging:** Ramada Inn, **other:** Kia, Nissan
12	I-495, US 202, N to Wilmington

I-295 begins/ends on I-95, exit 5.

Interstate 495

N ↕ S

Exit#	Services
11mm	I-95 N. I-495 begins/ends on I-95.
5(10)	US 13, Phila Pike, Claymont, **W...gas:** Amoco, Gulf, Sunoco, **food:** Arby's, Claymont Diner, McDonald's
4(5)	rd 3, Edgemoor Rd, **3 mi W...gas:** 7-11/gas
3(4)	12th St, **3 mi W...**HOSPITAL, gas, food
2(3)	rd 9A, Terminal Ave, Port of Wilmington, no facilities
1(1)	US 13, **E...gas:** Citgo/7-11, Shell, WaWa, **food:** Casablanca Rest., Dunkin Donuts, **lodging:** Ramada Inn, **other:** Ford, Kia
0mm	I-95 S. I-495 begins/ends on I-95.

FLORIDA
Interstate 4

E ↕ W

Exit #	Services
132	I-95, S to Miami, N to Jacksonville, FL 400. I-4 begins/ends on I-95, exit 260b.
129	to US 92(from eb, exits left)
126mm	parking area eb, litter barrels, no facilities, no security
118	FL 44, to DeLand, **N...gas:** Shell/diesel, **lodging:** Quality Inn, **other:** HOSPITAL, **S...gas:** Shell/diesel/fruit
116	Lake Helen, Orange Camp Rd, no facilities
114	FL 472, Orange City, to DeLand, **N...other:** KOA, Village RV Park, to Blue Sprgs SP
111b a	Saxon Blvd, Deltona, **N...gas:** Hess, RaceTrac, Shell, **food:** Baskin-Robbins/Dunkin Donuts, BBQ, Chili's, Denny's, Fazoli's, Perkins, Ruby Tuesday, Steak'n Shake, **other:** HOSPITAL, Lowe's Whse, Office Depot, Publix/deli, Tire Kingdom, **S...gas:** Chevron/repair, **food:** Wendy's, **other:** Albertson's
108	Dirksen Dr, DeBary, Deltona, **N...gas:** Chevron, **food:** Burger King, Shoney's, **lodging:** Hampton Inn, **S...gas:** Shell, **food:** McDonald's, Waffle House, **lodging:** Best Western/rest., **other:** Paradise Lakes Camping(3mi)
104	US 17, US 92, Sanford, **N...**Featherlite RV Ctr, **S...gas:** Citgo/Subway, **lodging:** Holiday Inn, **other:** HOSPITAL
101c	rd 46, Sanford, to FL 417 toll, to Mt Dora, **N...gas:** Amoco/Pizza Hut/diesel, **other:** Chevrolet, Ford, **S...gas:** Chevron, Citgo/diesel, Mobil, RaceTrac, Speedway/diesel, **food:** Bennigan's, Burger King, Cracker Barrel, Denny's, Don Pablo, FoodCourt, Hops Grill, Joe's Crabshack, Logan's Roadhouse, McDonald's, Olive Garden, Orlando Alehouse, OutBack Steaks, Red Lobster, Steak'n Shake, Waffle House, **lodging:** Day's Inn, Holiday Inn, SpringHill Suites, Super 8, **other:** HOSPITAL, BooksAMillion, Burdine's, Dillard's, $Tree, Eckerd, JC Penney, OfficeMax, Old Navy, Ross, Sears/auto, mall
101b a	FL 417, FL 46, FL 46a
101a	rd 46a, Sanford, Heathrow, no facilities
98	Lake Mary Blvd, Heathrow, **N...gas:** Exxon, **food:** Panera Bread, **lodging:** Courtyard, Wingate Inn, **other:** Eckerd, Walgreen, Winn-Dixie, **S...gas:** Amoco/24hr, Chevron/24hr, Citgo/7-11, **food:** Arby's, Bob Evans, Boston Mkt, Burger King, Checkers, Chevy's Mexican, Chick-fil-A, Chili's, Dunkin Donuts, Frank&Naomi's, Golden China, Japanese Steaks, KFC, Krystal, LongHorn Steaks, Macaroni Grill, McDonald's, Papa Joe's, Papa John's, Steak'n Shake, Subway, Taco Bell, TGIFriday, Uno Pizzaria, Wendy's, **lodging:** Extended Stay America, Hilton, HomeWood Suites, La Quinta, MainStay Suites, **other:** CAlbertson's, Discount Parts, Home Depot, K-Mart, Olson Tire, Publix, Staples, Starbucks, Target, USPO, Winn-Dixie, mall
95mm	**rest areas both lanes, full(handicapped)facilities, phone, vending, picnic tables, litter barrels, petwalk, 24hr security**
94	FL 434, Longwood, to Winter Springs, **N...gas:** Hess, **food:** Denny's, Imperial Dynasty, Kyoto Steaks, Miami Subs, Pizza Hut, Wendy's, **lodging:** Ramada Inn, Quality Inn, **S...gas:** Amoco, Mobil/diesel, Shell, 7-11, **food:** Boston Mkt, **lodging:** Candlewood Suites, **other:** HOSPITAL
92	FL 436, Altamonte Springs, **N...gas:** Amoco, Citgo/7-11, Exxon, Mobil, Shell/diesel, **food:** Bennigan's, Boston Mkt, Chevy's Mexican, Chick-fil-A, Cooker, Kobe Japanese, LongHorn Steaks, McDonald's, Olive Garden, Perkins, Pizza Hut, Red Lobster, Schlotsky's, Steak&Ale, Taco Bell, TGIFriday, **lodging:** Best Western, Hampton Inn, Holiday Inn, SpringHill Suites, Travelodge, **other:** Firestone/auto, **S...gas:** Amoco, Hess, Shell, **food:** Chicago Pizza, Chili's, Denny's, Fuddrucker's, **lodging:** Embassy Suites, Hilton, Homestead Village, **other:** Discount Parts, Marshall's, Michael's, Ross, Sears/auto
90b a	FL 414, Maitland Blvd, **N...gas:** 7-11/gas, **lodging:** Courtyard, Sheraton, Wellesley Inn, **S...**Maitland Art Ctr
88	FL 423, Lee Rd, **N...gas:** Marathon, 7-11/gas, Shell, **food:** Arby's, McDonald's, Waffle House, **lodging:** Comfort Inn, Holiday Inn, Motel 6, Travelers Inn, **other:** Aamco, Eckerd, Infiniti, **S...gas:** Chevron, Mobil/diesel, **food:** Denny's, Steak'n Shake, **lodging:** Fairfield Inn, Plaza Inn, **other:** BMW
87	FL 426, Fairbanks Ave(no eb re-entry), **N...gas:** Hess, **S...gas:** Amoco, **1 mi S...gas:** Shell, **food:** Burger King, Steak'n Shake, Subway, Wendy's
86	Par Ave(from eb, no re-entry), **S...gas:** Shell
85	Princeton St, **S...gas:** Chevron, Shell, **other:** HOSPITAL
84	FL 50, Colonial Dr(from wb), Ivanhoe Blvd, downtown, **N...lodging:** Holiday Inn, **S...lodging:** Radisson, Travelers Hotel
83b	US 17, US 92, FL 50, Amelia St(from eb), **N...lodging:** Holiday Inn
83a	FL 526(from eb), Robinson St, **N...lodging:** Marriott
83	South St(from wb), downtown
82c	Anderson St E, Church St Sta Hist Dist, downtown
82b	Gore Ave(from wb), **S...**HOSPITAL, downtown
82a	FL 408(toll), to FL 526, no facilities
81b c	Kaley Ave, **S...gas:** Mobil, Shell, **other:** HOSPITAL
81a	Michigan St(from wb), **N...gas:** Citgo/diesel
80b a	US 17, US 441 S, US 92 W, **S...gas:** Amoco, Exxon, Mobil, RaceTrac, **food:** Denny's/24hr, Krystal/24hr, McDonald's, Quincy's, Subway, Wendy's, **lodging:** Day's Inn

Lake Mary

Orlando

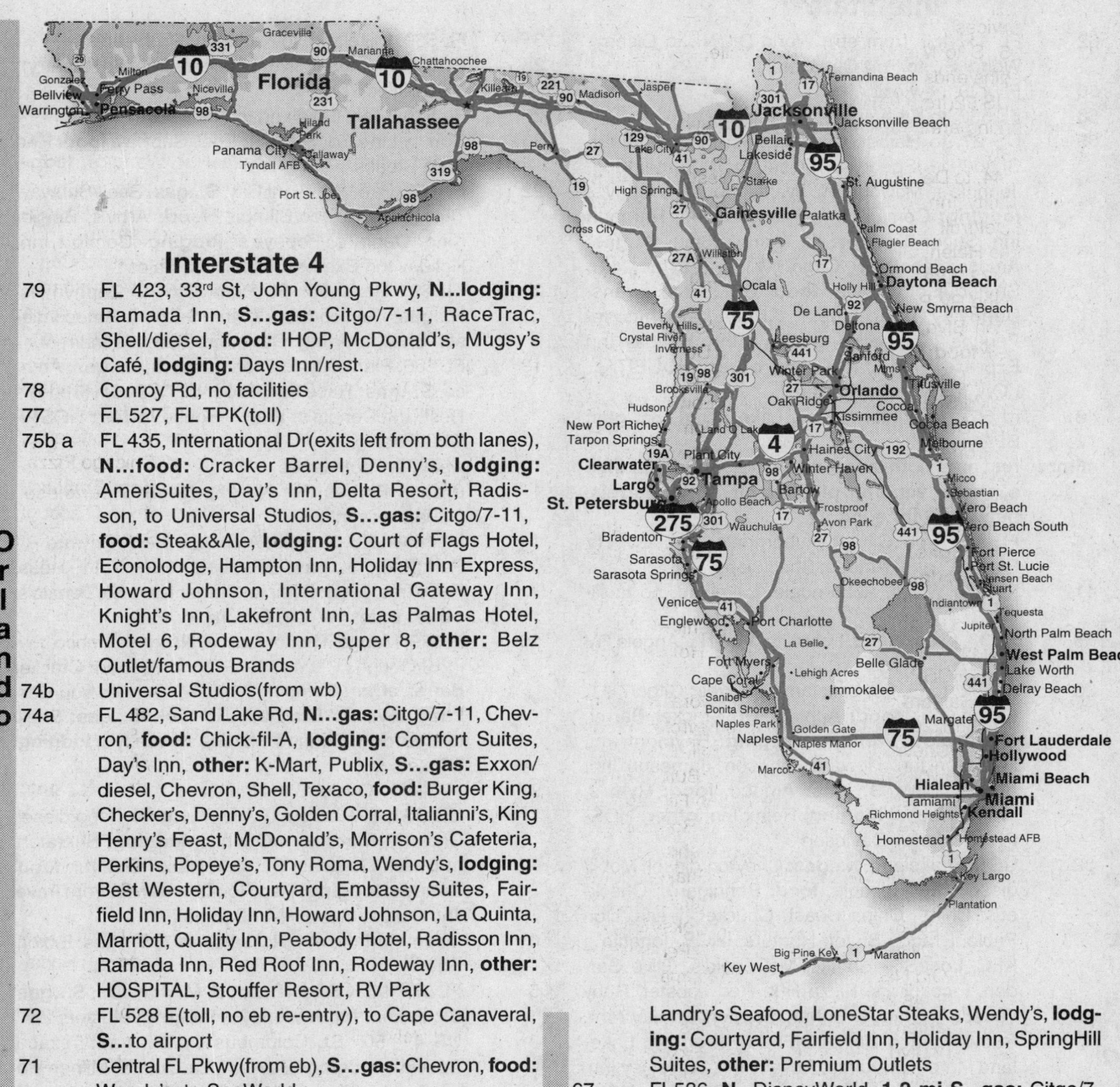

Interstate 4

Orlando

79 FL 423, 33rd St, John Young Pkwy, **N...lodging:** Ramada Inn, **S...gas:** Citgo/7-11, RaceTrac, Shell/diesel, **food:** IHOP, McDonald's, Mugsy's Café, **lodging:** Days Inn/rest.

78 Conroy Rd, no facilities

77 FL 527, FL TPK(toll)

75b a FL 435, International Dr(exits left from both lanes), **N...food:** Cracker Barrel, Denny's, **lodging:** AmeriSuites, Day's Inn, Delta Resort, Radisson, to Universal Studios, **S...gas:** Citgo/7-11, **food:** Steak&Ale, **lodging:** Court of Flags Hotel, Econolodge, Hampton Inn, Holiday Inn Express, Howard Johnson, International Gateway Inn, Knight's Inn, Lakefront Inn, Las Palmas Hotel, Motel 6, Rodeway Inn, Super 8, **other:** Belz Outlet/famous Brands

74b Universal Studios(from wb)

74a FL 482, Sand Lake Rd, **N...gas:** Citgo/7-11, Chevron, **food:** Chick-fil-A, **lodging:** Comfort Suites, Day's Inn, **other:** K-Mart, Publix, **S...gas:** Exxon/diesel, Chevron, Shell, Texaco, **food:** Burger King, Checker's, Denny's, Golden Corral, Italianni's, King Henry's Feast, McDonald's, Morrison's Cafeteria, Perkins, Popeye's, Tony Roma, Wendy's, **lodging:** Best Western, Courtyard, Embassy Suites, Fairfield Inn, Holiday Inn, Howard Johnson, La Quinta, Marriott, Quality Inn, Peabody Hotel, Radisson Inn, Ramada Inn, Red Roof Inn, Rodeway Inn, **other:** HOSPITAL, Stouffer Resort, RV Park

72 FL 528 E(toll, no eb re-entry), to Cape Canaveral, **S...**to airport

71 Central FL Pkwy(from eb), **S...gas:** Chevron, **food:** Wendy's, to SeaWorld

68 FL 535, Lake Buena Vista, **N...gas:** Chevron/24hr, Citgo/7-11, Shell, **food:** AleHouse, Burger King, Chevy's Mexican, Chili's, CrabHouse Seafood, Denny's, Dunkin Donuts, Giordano's, Hooters, IHOP, Jungle Jim's Rest., Macaroni Grill, McDonald's, Miami Subs, Olive Garden, Pebble's Dining, Perkins, Pizza Hut, Pizzaria Uno, Red Lobster, Shoney's, Sizzler, Steak'n Shake, Subway, Taco Bell, TGIFriday, Tony Roma, Waffle House, **lodging:** Comfort Inn, Day's Inn, Doubletree, Embassy Suites, Hilton, Hotel Orlando, Hyatt Hotel, Radisson, Summerfield Suites, Wyndham Hotel, **other:** Eckerd, Gooding's Foods, USPO, Walgreen, **S...gas:** Amoco, Citgo/7-11, **food:** Chick-fil-A, Landry's Seafood, LoneStar Steaks, Wendy's, **lodging:** Courtyard, Fairfield Inn, Holiday Inn, SpringHill Suites, **other:** Premium Outlets

67 Fl 536, **N...**DisneyWorld, **1-2 mi S...gas:** Citgo/7-11, **food:** Ponderosa, **lodging:** Buena Vista Suites, Caribe Royale Suites, Marriott, **other:** Eckerd, Prime Outlet, to airport

65 Osceola Pkwy, to FL 417(toll)

64b a US 192, FL 536, to FL 417(toll), to Kissimmee, **N...**to DisneyWorld, MGM, **S...gas:** 76/7-11, RaceTrac, **food:** Boston Mkt, Food Court, IHOP, Kobe Japanese, McDonald's, Shoney's, Steakhouse Foods, Waffle House, **lodging:** Hampton Inn, Homewood Suites, Howard Johnson, Hyatt Hotel, Larsen's Lodge, Radisson, **other:** Camping World RV Service/supplies(3mi), factory outlet/famous brands

FLORIDA

Interstate 4

E ↕ W

62 FL 417(toll, from eb), World Dr, **N...**to Disney-World, **S...**to Port Canaveral

60 FL 429, new exit

58 FL 532, to Kissimmee, no facilities

55 US 27, to Haines City, **N...gas:** Chevron/24hr, Citgo/7-11, Speedway/diesel, **food:** Burger King, Johnnie's, McDonald's, Waffle House, Wendy's, **lodging:** Comfort Inn, Hampton Inn, Ramada Inn, Super 8, **other:** FL CampIn(5mi), **S...gas:** Amoco/diesel, BP, Citgo/7-11, RaceTrac/24hr, Shell/diesel/service, **food:** BBQ, Bob Evans, Denny's, Grand China, GreenLeaf Chinese, Perkins/24hr, **lodging:** Day's Inn, Holiday Inn Express, Red Carpet Inn, **other:** HOSPITAL, KOA, to Cypress Gardens

48 rd 557, to Winter Haven, Lake Alfred, **S... gas:** BP/diesel

46mm rest area both lanes, full(handicapped)facilities, phone, vending, picnic tables, litter barrels, petwalk, 24hr security

44 FL 559, Polk City, to Auburndale, **N..**LeLyn RV Park, **S...gas:** Amoco, Shell/diesel

41 FL 570 W toll, Auburndale, Lakeland, no facilities

38 FL 33, to Lakeland, Polk City, **1 mi N...**Angola RV Ctr

33 rd 582, to FL 33, Lakeland, **N...gas:** Citgo/7-11, Exxon/24hr, **food:** Applebee's, Cracker Barrel, McDonald's, Wendy's, **lodging:** Baymont Inn, Hampton Inn, Howard Johnson, Jameson Inn, **other:** BMW, **S...gas:** Amoco, **food:** Ryan's, Waffle House, **lodging:** Relax Inn, **other:** HOSPITAL, Harley-Davidson

Lakeland

32 US 98, Lakeland, **N...gas:** Chevron/diesel, Mobil/diesel, Shell/Blimpie, **food:** Bennigan's, Checker's, Chili's, China Coast, ChuckeCheese, Don Pablo, Dragon Buffet, Hooters, IHOP, Johnnie's, KFC, LoneStar Steaks, McDonald's, Olive Garden, Piccadilly's, Pizza Hut, Red Lobster, Ruby Tuesday, Stacy's Buffet, Steak'n Shake/24hr, Subway, Taco Bell, TGIFriday, **lodging:** Lakeland Motel, La Quinta, Royalty Inn, Wellesley Inn, **other:** Barnes&Noble, Belk, Best Buy, Circuit City, Dillard's, $Tree, Food Lion, Goodyear/auto, Kash'n Karry, K-Mart, Olson Tire, PepBoys, Sam's Club/gas, Tire Kingdom, Walgreen, Wal-Mart SuperCtr/24hr(2mi), RV Ctr, **S...gas:** Amoco, Citgo/diesel, Coastal/diesel, RaceTrac, **food:** Bob Evans, Burger King, Denny's, LJ Silver, McDonald's, Popeye's, Roadhouse Grill, Waffle House, Wendy's, **lodging:** Best Western/rest., Day's Inn, Motel 6, Ramada Inn, Red Carpet Inn, **other:** HOSPITAL, AutoZone, Chrysler/Plymouth/Dodge, Cost+ Foods, Family$, Home Depot, Office Depot, Radio Shack, U-Haul, Winn-Dixie, transmissions

31 FL 539, Lakeland, to Kathleen, **S...**hist dist

28 FL 546, Memorial Blvd, Lakeland(from eb re-entry), no facilities

27 FL 570 E toll, Lakeland, no facilities

25 County Line Rd, **S...gas:** Shell/Subway, **food:** Red Barn Steaks

22 FL 553, Park Rd, Plant City, **S...gas:** Shell/Subway/Taco Bell, Texaco/Blimpie, **food:** Arby's, Burger King, Denny's, Popeye's, **lodging:** Comfort Inn, Holiday Inn Express, **other:** RV Sales

21 FL 39, Alexander St, Plant City, to Zephyrhills, **N...gas:** Texaco/diesel/24hr, **S...gas:** Amoco/diesel, Shell, **lodging:** Day's Inn, Ramada Inn/rest.

19 FL 566, Plant City, to Thonotosassa, **N...gas:** Amoco, **S...gas:** RaceTrac, **food:** BBQ, BuddyFreddy's Rest., McDonald's, Waffle House, **other:** HOSPITAL, Publix

19mm weigh sta both lanes

17 Branch Forbes Rd, **N...gas:** Shell, Spur/diesel, **S...**farmer's mkt

14 McIntosh Rd, **N...gas:** Amoco, **other:** Winward RV Park(2mi), **S...gas:** BP/diesel, Citgo/7-11, Hess, RaceTrac, **food:** Blimpie, Burger King, McDonald's, **other:** Bates RV Ctr, Encore RV Park

10 rd 579, Mango, Thonotosassa, **N...gas:** Amoco, Flying J/CountryMkt/diesel/LP/24hr/@, **food:** Cracker Barrel, **other:** Camping World RV Service/supplies, Lazy Day's RV Ctr, Rally RV Park, **S...gas:** Shell/diesel, **food:** Denny's, Hardee's, Wendy's, **lodging:** Masters Inn

9 I-75, N to Ocala, S to Naples

7 US 301, Hillsborough Ave, **N...gas:** Citgo/diesel, Circle K, **food:** My's Oriental, **lodging:** Sheraton, to Busch Gardens, **S...gas:** RaceTrac/24hr, **food:** Denny's, **lodging:** Red Roof Inn, **other:** ForeTravel RV, Holiday Travel RV, FL Expo Fair

6 Orient Rd(from eb), **N...**same as 7, **S...gas:** Exxon, Shell

Tampa

5 FL 574, MLK Blvd, **N...food:** McDonald's, **S...gas:** BP, Exxon, **food:** Wendy's, **lodging:** Masters Inn

3 US 41, 50th St, Columbus Dr, **N...gas:** Texaco/Subway, **lodging:** Bay Inn, La Quinta, Milner Motel, **S...gas:** Exxon/diesel, Shell, Speedway/diesel, **food:** Burger King, Checker's, Church's, KFC, McDonald's, Pizza Hut, Taco Bell, Wendy's, **lodging:** Howard Johnson, **other:** Eckerd, Family$, Kash'n Karry

2 FL 569, 40th St, **N...gas:** Citgo/diesel/24hr, Shell/diesel, **lodging:** Budget Inn, to Busch Gardens

1 FL 585, 22nd, 21st St, Hist District, Port of Tampa, **N...gas:** BP/diesel, **S...gas:** Amoco/24hr, **food:** Burger King, Hilton Garden

0mm I-4 begins/ends on I-275, exit 45b.

FLORIDA

Interstate 10

E ↕ W

Jacksonville

Exit #	Services
363mm	I-10 begins/ends on I-95, exit 351b.
362	Stockton St, to Riverside, **S...gas:** Amoco, Gate, **other:** HOSPITAL
361	US 17 S(from wb), downtown
360	FL 129, McDuff Ave, **S...gas:** Amoco, Chevron, **food:** Popeye's
359	Lenox Ave, Edgewood Ave(from wb), no facilities
358	FL 111, Cassat Ave, **N...gas:** Amoco/diesel, Chevron, Hess/Blimpie, **food:** Burger King, McDonald's, Firehouse Subs, Popeye's, **other:** AutoZone, GMC, **S...gas:** RaceTrac/24hr, **food:** Dunkin Donuts, Krispy Kreme, Taco Bell, **other:** Winn-Dixie, transmissions
357	FL 103, Lane Ave, **N...gas:** Amoco, **food:** Andy's Sandwiches, **lodging:** Day's Inn, Quality Inn, Ramada Inn, **S...gas:** Amoco, Chevron, Texaco/diesel, **food:** Burger King, Denny's, Hardee's, McDonald's, Piccadilly's, Shoney's, **lodging:** Executive Inn, Super 8, **other:** Battery Depot, Home Depot, Office Depot
356	I-295, N to Savannah, S to St Augustine
355	Marietta, **N...gas:** Gate/24hr, Texaco, **S...gas:** Amoco/diesel, **food:** Domino's
351	FL 115c, Chaffee Rd, Whitehouse, to Cecil Fields, **N...gas:** Chevron/24hr, **other:** Rivers RV Ctr, **S...gas:** Chevron, Shell/Subway/diesel/24hr, **food:** McDonald's, **other:** Winn-Dixie/gas
352mm	**rest area eb, full(handicapped)facilities, phone, vending, picnic tables, litter barrels, 24hr security**
351mm	**rest area wb, full(handicapped)facilities, phone, vending, picnic tables, litter barrels, 24hr security**
343	US 301, Baldwin, to Starke, **S...gas:** Chevron, Exxon, Pilot/diesel/24hr/@, Shell/Subway, TA/Amoco/diesel/rest./24hr/@, **food:** Burger King, McDonald's, Waffle House, **lodging:** Best Western, **other:** NAPA
336	FL 228, Macclenny, to Maxville, **N...**HOSPITAL
335	FL 121, Macclenny, to Lake Butler, **N...gas:** BP/diesel, Exxon, **food:** Connie's Kitchen, Domino's, Hardee's, KFC, McDonald's, Pizza Hut, Subway, Taco Bell/TCBY, Waffle House, Wendy's, **lodging:** Day's Inn, **other:** HOSPITAL, Discount Parts, $General, Food Lion, Radio Shack, Wal-Mart, Winn-Dixie, **S...gas:** RaceWay, Exxon/diesel, **food:** Burger King, China Garden, **lodging:** Econolodge, Travelodge
333	rd 125, Glen Saint Mary, **N...gas:** Exxon/diesel/24hr
327	rd 229, Sanderson, to Raiford, **1 mi N...**gas
324	US 90, Sanderson, to Olustee, **S...gas:** Exxon, to Olustee Bfd
318mm	**rest area both lanes, full(handicapped)facilities, phone, vending, picnic tables, litter barrels, petwalk, 24hr security**

Live Oak

Exit #	Services
303	US 441, Lake City, to Fargo, **N...gas:** BP/repair, Chevron/diesel/24hr, **other:** KOA(1mi), Oaks'n Pines RV Park, **S...gas:** SuperTest/diesel, Texaco/diesel, **lodging:** Day's Inn, **other:** HOSPITAL
301	US 41, to Lake City, **N...gas:** Amoco, **other:** Kelly's RV Park(6mi), to Stephen Foster Ctr, **S...**HOSPITAL, **S...gas:** Texaco
296b a	I-75, N to Valdosta, S to Tampa
295mm	**rest area wb, full(handicapped)facilities, phone, vending, picnic tables, litter barrels, petwalk, 24hr security**
294mm	**rest area eb, full(handicapped)facilities, phone, vending, picnic tables, litter barrels, petwalk, 24hr security**
292	rd 137, to Wellborn, no facilities
283	US 129, to Live Oak, **N...gas:** Penn/diesel, to Boys Ranch, **S...gas:** Chevron, Shell, Texaco, **food:** Huddle House, Krystal, McDonald's, Subway, Taco Bell/TCBY, Waffle House, Wendy's, **lodging:** Best Western, Econolodge, Holiday Inn Express, Royal Inn, **other:** HOSPITAL, $Tree, Wal-Mart SuperCtr/gas/24hr
275	US 90, Live Oak, **N...**to Suwannee River SP, **S...other:** HOSPITAL, United 500/diesel/repair
271mm	weigh sta both lanes
269mm	Suwannee River
265mm	**rest areas both lanes, full(handicapped)facilities, phone, vending, picnic tables, litter barrels, petwalk, 24hr security**
264mm	weigh sta both lanes
262	rd 255, Lee, **N...gas:** Exxon/diesel, **food:** Kountry Kitchen, **other:** to Suwannee River SP, **S...gas:** Citgo/diesel/@, Texaco, **food:** Red Onion Grill
258	FL 53, **N...gas:** Amoco/Burger King/diesel24hr, Citgo/diesel/24hr, **food:** Waffle House, **lodging:** Day's Inn, Holiday Inn Express, Super 8, **other:** HOSPITAL **S...lodging:** Deer Wood Inn, **other:** Jellystone Camping, Madison Camping
251	FL 14, to Madison, **N...gas:** Texaco/Arby's, **other:** HOSPITAL
241	US 221, Greenville, **N...gas:** Texaco/DQ, **S...gas:** BP/diesel
234mm	**rest area both lanes, full(handicapped)facilities, phone, picnic tables, litter barrels, petwalk, 24hr security**
233	rd 257, Aucilla, **N...gas:** Citgo, Shell/diesel

FLORIDA

Interstate 10

E ↕ W

225 US 19, to Monticello, **N...**Campers World RV Park, **S...gas:** Amoco, Chevron/McDonald's, Exxon/Wendy's, Texaco/Arby's/diesel, **food:** Huddle House, **lodging:** Day's Inn, Super 8, **other:** Alligator Lake Camping, KOA, dogtrack

217 FL 59, Lloyd, **S...gas:** BP/diesel/24hr/@, Shell/Subway/diesel/@, **lodging:** motel

209b a US 90, Tallahassee, **S...gas:** Citgo/diesel/24hr, 76, Shell, **food:** Cross Creek Rest., Subway, Waffle House, **lodging:** Best Western, **other:** Publix, Tallahassee RV Park

203 FL 61, to US 319, Tallahassee, **N...gas:** BP/diesel, Chevron, 76/Circle K, Shell, Texaco/diesel, **food:** Applebee's, Fuddrucker's, KFC, McDonald's, Pizza Hut, Popeye's, Subway, Taco Bell, TCBY, Waffle House, Wendy's, **lodging:** Motel 6, **other:** Albertson's, BooksAMillion, Discount Tire, Eckerd, Publix, Radio Shack, SteinMart, SuperLube, Wal-Mart SuperCtr/24hr(3mi), Winn-Dixie, **S...gas:** Citgo, **food:** Boston Mkt, Chick-fil-A, Don Pablo, Miami Subs, Osaka Japanese, Outback Steaks, Steak'n Shake, TGIFriday, Wings Grill, **lodging:** Cabot Lodge, Courtyard, Hilton Garden, Residence Inn, Studio+, **other:** HOSPITAL, Home Depot, Office Depot

Tallahassee

199 US 27, Tallahassee, **N...gas:** MacKenzie, **food:** Burger King, Taco Bell, Waffle House, **lodging:** Best Inn, Comfort Inn, Fairfield Inn, Hampton Inn, Holiday Inn, Microtel, Villager Lodge, **other:** Big Oak RV Park(2mi), Sam's Club, **S...gas:** Amoco/24hr, BP, Chevron/diesel, Shell, 76/Circle K, USA, **food:** BBQ, Boston Mkt, Chick-fil-A, China Buffet, China Wok, Cracker Barrel, Crystal River Seafood, DQ, Hooters, Julie's Rest., KFC, Krispy Kreme, Longhorn Steaks, McDonald's, Melting Pot Rest., Miami Subs, Papa John's, Pizza Hut, Quizno's, Red Lobster, Roadhouse Grill, Shoney's, Starbucks, Steak&Ale, Subway, TCBY, Village Inn Rest., Whataburger, Wendy's, **lodging:** Cabot Lodge, Day's Inn, Econolodge, Howard Johnson, La Quinta, Motel 6, Ramada Inn, Red Roof Inn, Super 8, **other:** Albertson's, AutoZone, Barnes&Noble, Big 10 Tire, Firestone/auto, Dillard's, Publix, Walgreen, mall

196 FL 263, Tallahassee, **S...gas:** Chevron/diesel, Shell/diesel, **food:** Steak'n Shake, Waffle House, **lodging:** Sleep Inn, **2-5 mi S...food:** Applebee's, McDonald's, Subway, **lodging:** Colony Inn, Day's Inn, Lafayette Motel, Skyline Motel, **other:** Harley-Davidson, Home Depot, Lowe's Whse, RV camping, civic ctr, museum/zoo

194mm rest area both lanes, full(handicapped)facilities, phone, vending, picnic tables, litter barrels, petwalk, 24hr security

192 US 90, to Tallahassee, Quincy, **N...gas:** Citgo, Flying J/Conoco/diesel/LP/24hr/@, **lodging:** Howard Johnson, **S...gas:** Pilot/Subway/diesel/24hr/@, **food:** Waffle House, **other:** Lakeside RV Park(4mi)

181 FL 267, Quincy, **N...gas:** Exprezit/diesel, **other:** HOSPITAL, **S...gas:** Amoco/24hr, BP/diesel, **lodging:** Holiday Inn Express, to Lake Talquin SP

174 FL 12, to Greensboro, **N...gas:** Quality, Shell/Burger King/diesel, **other:** Beaver Lake Camping

166 rd 270A, Chattahoochee, **N...**to Lake Seminole SP, **S...gas:** Shell/diesel, **other:** KOA

161mm rest area both lanes, full(handicapped)facilities, phone, vending, picnic tables, litter barrels, petwalk, 24hr security

160mm Apalachicola River, central/eastern time zone

158 rd 286, Sneads, **N...**Lake Seminole, to Three Rivers SRA

155mm weigh sta both lanes

152 FL 69, to Grand Ridge, **N...gas:** BP, Exxon, GL, **food:** Golden Lariat

142 FL 71, Oakdale, to Marianna, **N...gas:** Exprezit, Pilot/Arby's/diesel/24hr/@, **food:** BBQ, Burger King, KFC, Pizza Hut, Ruby Tuesday, Waffle House, **lodging:** Comfort Inn, Hampton Inn, Holiday Inn Express, Microtel, Super 8, **other:** HOSPITAL, Wal-Mart SuperCtr/diesel/24hr, to FL Caverns SP(8mi), **S...gas:** Chevron, Sunoco/diesel, TA/BP/diesel/rest./24hr/@, **food:** McDonald's, **lodging:** Best Western, **other:** Arrowhead Camping

136 FL 276, to Marianna, **N...gas:** Exprezit/diesel, **lodging:** Day's Inn(3mi), Executive Inn(3mi), **other:** HOSPITAL, to FL Caverns SP(8mi)

133mm rest area both lanes, full(handicapped)facilities, phone, picnic tables, litter barrels, petwalk, 24hr security

Chipley

130 US 231, Cottondale, **N...gas:** Amoco/diesel, Chevron, **food:** Hardee's, Subway

120 FL 77, Chipley, to Panama City, **N...gas:** Exprezit, Exxon/Burger King, **food:** JJ's Kitchen, KFC, McDonald's, Taco Bell, Waffle House, Wendy's, **lodging:** Day's Inn/rest., Executive Inn, Holiday Inn Express, Super 8, **other:** HOSPITAL, Wal-Mart SuperCtr/gas/24hr, **S...gas:** Exprezit, **other:** Falling Water SRA

112 FL 79, Bonifay, **N...gas:** Chevron, Exxon/diesel, **food:** Blitch's Rest., Hardee's, McDonald's, Pizza Hut, Subway, Waffle House, **lodging:** Bonifay Inn, Economy Inn, Tivoli Inn, **other:** HOSPITAL, Hidden Lakes Camping, **S...**FL Springs Camping(8mi)

104 rd 279, Caryville, no facilities

96 FL 81, Ponce de Leon, **N...**to Ponce de Leon SRA, camping, **S...gas:** Amoco/diesel/24hr, Exprezit/Subway, Exxon/diesel, **other:** Ponce de Leon Motel/RV Park, **rest area both lanes, full(handicapped)facilities, phone, picnic tables, litter barrels, petwalk, 24hr security**

FLORIDA

Interstate 10

85 US 331, De Funiak Springs, **N...gas:** Amoco, Chevron/24hr, Texaco, **food:** Arby's, Burger King, McLain's Steaks, Pizza Hut, Subway, Waffle House, **lodging:** Comfort Inn, Day's Inn, Ramada Ltd, Sundown Inn, Super 8, **other:** HOSPITAL, Family$, Wal-Mart SuperCtr/gas/24hr, Winn-Dixie, winery, **S...gas:** BP, Emerald Express/diesel, Shell, **food:** Hardee's, KFC, McDonald's, **lodging:** Best Western

70 FL 285, Eglin AFB, to Ft Walton Bch, **N...gas:** RaceWay, **S...gas:** Citgo/Subway/diesel/24hr/@, **lodging:** Ramada Ltd, **other:** repair

60mm rest area wb, full(handicapped)facilities, phone, vending, picnic tables, litter barrels, petwalk, 24hr security, weigh sta eb

58mm rest area eb, full(handicapped)facilities, phone, vending, picnic tables, litter barrels, petwalk, 24hr security

56 FL 85, Crestview, Eglin AFB, **N...gas:** Amoco/diesel, Chevron, Exxon, Mobil, Shell/diesel, **food:** Applebee's, BBQ, Burger King, Capt D's, McDonald's, Pizza Hut, Popeye's, Ryan's, Subway, Taco Bell, **lodging:** Budget Host, Econolodge, **other:** HOSPITAL, Advance Parts, AutoZone, Publix, Walgreen, Wal-Mart SuperCtr/24hr, **S...gas:** Citgo/diesel, Exxon/Subway, **food:** Arby's, Cracker Barrel, Hardee's, LaBamba Mexican, Nim's Chinese, Shoney's, Waffle House, Wendy's, Whataburger, **lodging:** Comfort Inn, Day's Inn, Hampton Inn, Holiday Inn, Jameson Inn, Super 8, **other:** Chrysler/Dodge/Plymouth/Jeep, Ford/Mercury, museum, RV camping

45 rd 189, to US 90, Holt, **N...gas:** Chevron(1mi), **other:** to Blackwater River SP, Eagle Landing RV Park, **S...gas:** Amoco/diesel, River's Edge RV Park(1mi)

31 FL 87, Milton, to Ft Walton Beach, **N...gas:** Rolling Thunder/diesel/@, Shell/Quizno's/diesel, **food:** Waffle House, **lodging:** Holiday Inn Express, **other:** Blackwater River SP, Gulf Pines Camping, **S...gas:** Amoco, Shell/diesel, **lodging:** Comfort Inn, Red Carpet Inn

31mm rest area both lanes, full(handicapped)facilities, phone, picnic tables, litter barrels, petwalk, 24hr security

28 rd 89, Milton, **N...**HOSPITAL, **S...**Cedar Lakes RV Camping(2mi)

26mm Blackwater River

26 rd 191, Bagdad, Milton, **N...gas:** Parade/Chester/diesel, **other:** HOSPITAL, **S...gas:** Chevron/DQ/Stuckey's, Petro/diesel, **other:** Pelican Palms RV Park

22 N FL 281, Avalon Blvd, **N...gas:** Amoco/24hr, Exxon, **food:** McDonald's, Oval Office Café, **S...gas:** Texaco/Subway/diesel, **food:** Waffle House, **lodging:** Red Roof Inn, **other:** By the Bay RV Park(3mi)

18mm Escambia Bay

17 US 90, Pensacola, **N...gas:** BP, **S...gas:** Exxon, **food:** DQ, **lodging:** Ramada Inn/rest.

13 FL 291, to US 90, Pensacola, **N...gas:** Amoco, Chevron, Shell/diesel, **food:** Arby's, Barnhill's Buffet, Burger King, Capt D's, Denny's, McDonald's, Peking Garden, Shoney's, Subway, Taco Bell, TCBY, Waffle House, **lodging:** La Quinta, Motel 6, Shoney's Inn, Villager Inn, **other:** AutoZone, CVS Drug, Eckerd, Food World/24hr, **S...food:** Bennigan's, ChuckeCheese, Fazoli's, Piccadilly, Pizza Hut, Popeye's, Steak&Ale, Waffle House, Wendy's, Whataburger, **lodging:** Fairfield Inn, Hampton Inn, Holiday Inn Express, Motel 6, Red Roof Inn, Residence Inn, Super 8, **other:** HOSPITAL, Big 10 Tire, Firestone/auto, Goodyear/auto, JC Penney, McRae's, Mr Transmission, Sears/auto, U-Haul, mall

12 I-110, to Pensacola, Hist Dist, Islands Nat Seashore

10b a US 29, Pensacola, **N...gas:** Exxon, Fleet/diesel, **food:** Church's, Hardee's, Waffle House, **other:** Advance Parts, Carpenter's RV Ctr, Wal-Mart SuperCtr/gas/24hr, **S...gas:** RaceTrac, Shell, **food:** BBQ, Burger King, Denny's, IHOP, McDonald's, Ruby Tuesday, Subway, Waffle House, Wendy's, **lodging:** Comfort Inn, Day's Inn, Econolodge, Executive Inn, Holiday Inn Express, Howard Johnson, Hospitality Inn, Knight's Inn, Landmark Inn, Luxury Suites, Motel 6, Palm Court, Travelodge, **other:** Buick, Ford, Hill-Kelly RV Ctr, Isuzu, Jeep, Saturn, Toyota

7b a Fl 297, Pine Forest Rd, **N...gas:** Exxon/Krystal, **lodging:** Comfort Inn, Rodeway Inn, **other:** Albertson's, Tall Oaks Camping, **S...gas:** BP, Citgo, Texaco/diesel/café, **food:** BBQ, Burger King, Cracker Barrel, Hardee's, McDonald's, Ruby Tuesday, Subway, Waffle House, **lodging:** Microtel, Ramada Ltd, Sleep Inn, **other:** Food World/24hr, Big Lagoon SRA(12mi), museum

5 US 90 A, **N...gas:** Fleet/Subway/diesel, **other:** Albertson's/gas, **S...**Leisure Lakes Camping

4mm Welcome Ctr eb, full(handicapped)facilities, info, phone, vending, picnic tables, litter barrels, petwalk, 24hr security

3mm weigh sta both lanes

0mm Florida/Alabama state line, Perdido River

FLORIDA

Interstate 75

N ↕ S

Exit # Services

472mm Florida/Georgia state line. Motorist callboxes begin sb.

470mm Welcome Ctr sb, full(handicapped)facilities, info, phone, vending, picnic tables, litter barrels, petwalk

467 FL 143, Jennings, **E...gas:** Chevron, Texaco, **other:** Budget Lodge, **W...gas:** Amoco, Exxon/Burger King/diesel, **lodging:** Jennings House, Scottish Inn, **other:** Jennings Camping

460 FL 6, Jasper, **E...gas:** Amoco/Burger King, Exxon/Huddle House/diesel, Raceway, **lodging:** Day's Inn, **other:** HOSPITAL, **W...gas:** Shell/diesel, Texaco, **food:** Sheffield's Catfish, **lodging:** Scottish Inn, **other:** Suwanee River SP

451 US 129, Jasper, Live Oak, **E...gas:** Texaco/DQ/Subway/diesel, **other:** HOSPITAL, **W...gas:** Shell, **other:** Suwanee Music Park(4mi), to FL Boys Ranch

450mm weigh sta both lanes

447mm insp sta both lanes

443mm Historic Suwanee River

439 to FL 136, White Springs, Live Oak, **E...gas:** Gate/diesel, Shell/diesel, **food:** McDonald's, **lodging:** Scottish Inn, **other:** Kelly RV Park(5mi), Lee's Camping(3mi), to S Foster Ctr, **W...gas:** Express/diesel

435 I-10, E to Jacksonville, W to Tallahassee

Lake City

427 US 90, Lake City, to Live Oak, **E...gas:** BP, B&B/diesel, Chevron/diesel/24hr, Exxon, Texaco/diesel, **food:** Applebee's, Arby's, BBQ, Blimpie, Burger King, Cracker Barrel, Domino's, Fazoli's, Hardee's, IHOP, KFC, Krystal, McDonald's, Red Lobster, Ryan's, Subway, Taco Bell, Texas Roadhouse, Waffle House, Wendy's, **lodging:** A-1 Inn, Driftwood Inn, Executive Inn, Jameson Inn, Knight's Inn, Microtel, Ramda Ltd, Rodeway Inn, Scottish Inn, **other:** AutoZone, Belk, Discount Parts, Eckerd, Food Lion, Ford/Lincoln/Mercury, Goody's, JC Penney, K-Mart, Lowe's Whse, Publix, Radio Shack, TireMart, Toyota, Wal-Mart SuperCtr/gas/24hr, In&Out RV Park, mall, **W...gas:** Amoco/LJ Silver, BP, Chevron, Marathon, Shell, Texaco/diesel, **food:** Bob Evans, Jade Fountain Chinese, Shoney's, Subway, Waffle House, **lodging:** American Inn, Best Western, Comfort Inn, Country Inn Suites, Econolodge, Gateway Inn, GuestHouse Inn, Hampton Inn, Holiday Inn, Motel 6, Travelodge, **other:** Chevrolet/Mazda, Chrysler/Plymouth/Dodge, FL Sports Hall of Fame, Travel Country RV, Wayne's RV Resort

423 FL 47, Lake City, to Ft White, **E...gas:** Texaco/diesel, **W...gas:** Amoco, BP/diesel, Chevron/Little Caesar's, Express/Subway, **food:** Anne's Kitchen, **lodging:** Motel 8, Super 8, **other:** Casey Jones Camping

414 US 41, US 441, to Lake City, High Sprs, **E...gas:** Chevron/diesel/24hr, Pitstop/gas, Texaco, **lodging:** Travelodge, **W...gas:** Amoco/diesel, BP/diesel, Pure, **food:** Huddle House, Subway, **lodging:** Diplomat Motel, Econolodge, **other:** antiques, tires, to O'Leno SP

413mm rest areas both lanes, full(handicapped)facilities, phone, vending, picnic tables, litter barrels, petwalk

409mm Santa Fe River

404 rd 236, to High Sprs, **E...gas:** Chevron/Texaco/fruits/gifts, **W...**High Sprs Camping

399 US 441, Alachua, to High Sprs, **E...gas:** Amoco, BP, **food:** BBQ, McDonald's, Pizza Hut, Subway, Waffle House, **lodging:** Comfort Inn, Travelers Inn/RV Park, **W...gas:** Amoco/Wendy's, Chevron, Citgo/Taco/Bell/diesel, Mobil, **food:** KFC, **lodging:** Day's Inn, Ramada Ltd

Gainesville

390 FL 222, to Gainesville, **E...gas:** Chevron, Exxon/McDonald's/diesel, Mobil/diesel/LP, **food:** Burger King, Schlotsky's(3mi), Wendy's, **other:** Publix, **W...gas:** Texaco/Hardee's/diesel, **food:** KeyWest Grill, **lodging:** Best Western, **other:** Buick, Chrysler/Jeep/Mercedes, Harley-Davidson, auto repair

387 FL 26, Gainesville, to Newberry, **E...gas:** Chevron, Citgo, Shell/diesel, Speedway, Texaco/diesel, **food:** BBQ, Boston Mkt, Burger King, Don Pablo's, Durango's Steaks, FoodCourt, LJ Silver, McDonald's, Perkins, Piccadilly's, Qunicy's, Red Lobster, Rigatelli's Italian, Ruby Tuesday, Semolina Grill, Subway, Wendy's, **lodging:** La Quinta, **other:** HOSPITAL, Belk, BooksAMillion, Borders Books, Eckerd, Dillard's, JC Penney, Office Depot, Sears/auto, mall, **W...gas:** BP, Chevron/diesel, Exxon/diesel, Mobil/diesel/LP, **food:** Cracker Barrel, Domino's, Godfather's, GrillMasters Seafood, Hardee's, KFC, Napolatanos Rest., Pizza Hut, Shoney's, Taco Bell, Tequila Mexican, Waffle House, **lodging:** Day's Inn, Econolodge, Fairfield Inn, Holiday Inn, **other:** Circuit City, Discount Parts, Home Depot, JiffyLube, PepBoys, Publix, Walgreen, Winn-Dixie, tires/repair

384 FL 24, Gainesville, to Archer, **E...gas:** Amoco, Chevron/diesel/24hr, Citgo, Exxon, Shell, **food:** BBQ, Bennigan's, Bob Evans, Burger King, Capt D's, Checker's, Chick-fil-A, Chili's, Guthrie's, Hops Grill, KFC, LoneStar Steaks, McDonald's, Miami Subs, Olive Garden, OutBack Steaks, Papa John's, Pizza Hut, Rafferty's, Shoney's, Steak&Ale, Steak'n Shake, Subway, Taco Bell, Texas Roadhouse, TGIFriday, Waffle House, Wendy's, **lodging:** Cabot Lodge, Courtyard, DoubleTree Hotel, Extended Stay America, Hampton Inn, Motel 6, Ramada Ltd, Red Roof Inn, Super 8, **other:** Albertson's, Barnes&Noble, Best Buy, CarQuest, $Tree, Eckerd, Firestone/auto, GNC, Goody's, Lowe's Whse, Michael's, OfficeMax, Old Navy, Publix, Radio Shack, Ross, Santa Fe Parts, Target, Wal-Mart, Winn-Dixie, **W...gas:** Mobil/diesel, **food:** Cracker Barrel, **lodging:** Wingate Inn, **other:** Sunshine RV Park, to Bear Museum

Interstate 75

382 FL 121, Gainesville, to Williston, **E...gas:** Amoco/repair, Citgo/diesel/24hr, **lodging:** Residence Inn(2mi), Travelodge, **other:** antiques, **W...gas:** BP, Chevron/diesel/24hr, Sprint/gas, **food:** Chuck-Wagon Buffet, **lodging:** Best Inn, **other:** Fred Bear Mueum

383mm rest areas both lanes, full(handiacpped)facilities, phone, vending, picnic tables, litter barrels, petwalk, 24hr security

374 rd 234, Micanopy, **E...gas:** Amoco, Chevron, **other:** antiques, fruit, to Paynes Prairie SP, **W...gas:** Amoco/repair, Citgo/diesel, Texaco, **lodging:** Knight's Inn

368 rd 318, Orange Lake, **E...gas:** Amoco, Petro/Mobil/diesel/24hr/@, **food:** Jim's BBQ/gas, Wendy's, **other:** Grand Lake RV Park(3mi), **W...gas:** BP/diesel/repair, **other:** antiques, Encore RV Park(1mi)

358 FL 326, **E...gas:** Amoco/diesel, Mobil/McDonald's/diesel, Pilot/diesel/24hr/@, Speedway/Hardee's/diesel, **other:** Liberty RV Ctr, **W... gas:** Chevron/Gator's/DQ/diesel

354 US 27, Ocala, to Silver Springs, **E...gas:** Amoco/24hr, RaceTrac, SuperTest/diesel, **food:** BBQ, Burger King, Krystal, **lodging:** Quality Inn, **other:** fruits, **W...gas:** BP/diesel, Chevron, Shell/diesel/24hr, Texaco/diesel, **food:** Damon's, Larenzo's Pizza, Waffle House, **lodging:** Budget Host, Day's Inn/café, Howard Johnson, Knight's Inn, Ramada Inn, Travelodge, **other:** Arrowhead Campsites, Oaktree Village

352 FL 40, Ocala, to Silver Springs, **E...gas:** BP/diesel, Chevron, Citgo, RaceTrac/24hr, **food:** McDonald's, Pizza Hut/Taco Bell, Wendy's, **lodging:** Day's Inn/café, Economy Inn, Holiday Inn, Motor Inn/RV park, fruits, **W...gas:** Texaco, Denny's, **food:** Golden Coast Buffet, Waffle House, **lodging:** Comfort Inn, Horne's Motel, Super 8, **other:** Holiday TravL Park

350 FL 200, Ocala, to Hernando, **E...gas:** Chevron, Citgo, RaceTrac, Shell, Texaco/diesel, **food:** Arby's, Bella Luna Italian, Bennigans, Bob Evans, Burger King, Chick-fil-A, Chili's, Fazoli's, HongKong Chinese, Hooters, Hops Grill, Krystal, Lee's Chicken, LoneStar Steaks, McDonald's, Olive Garden, Outback Steaks, Papa John's, Perkins, Pizza Hut, Quincy's, Red Lobster, Ruby Tuesday, Semolina Grill, Shell's Rest., Shoney's, Sonic, Taco Bell, TGIFriday, Tokyo Japanese, Wendy's, Western Sizzlin, **lodging:** Hampton Inn, Hilton, La Quinta, **other:** HOSPITAL, Advance Parts, Barnes&Noble, Belk, Chevrolet/Nissan/Mitsubishi, Circuit City, Discount Parts, Eckerd, $General, Goodyear/auto, Home Depot, JC Penney, Kia, K-Mart, Lowe's Whse, Pennzoil, PepBoys, Publix, Sears, Target, Walgreen, Wal-Mart SuperCtr/24hr, Winn-Dixie, fruits, mall, **W...gas:** Amoco/24hr, Chevron/24hr, **food:** Burger King, Cracker Barrel, Dunkin Donuts, KFC, Steak'n Shake/24hr, Waffle House, **lodging:** Best Western, Courtyard, Fairfield Inn, **other:** VETERINARIAN, Cadillac, Firestone/auto, KOA, Sam's Club, Camper Village RV Park

346mm rest area both lanes, full(handicapped)facilities, phone, vending, picnic tables, litter barrels, petwalk, 24hr security

341 FL 484, to Belleview, **E...gas:** Chevron/fruit/24hr, Citgo/fruit, Exxon, **food:** BBQ, museums, **W...gas:** Amoco/repair, Pilot/Arby's/DQ/diesel/24hr/@, Texaco/diesel/rest./24hr, **food:** McDonald's, Waffle House, **other:** Water-Wheel RV Park, fruit

338mm weigh sta both lanes

329 FL 44, Wildwood, to Inverness, **E...gas:** Amoco/repair, Gate/Steak'n Shake/diesel, Speedway/DQ, **food:** Burger King, Denny's, Johnnie's Rest., McDonald's, Waffle House, Wendy's, **other:** KOA, fruits, **W...gas:** Citgo/diesel/repair/24hr, Pilot/diesel/24hr/@, TA/BP/Pizza Hut/Subway/Popeye's/diesel/24hr/@, **food:** KFC, Waffle House, Day's Inn/rest., **lodging:** Super 8, Villager Inn, Wildwood Inn

328 FL TPK(from sb), to Orlando

321 rd 470, Lake Panasoffkee, to Sumterville, **E...gas:** Sunshine/diesel/rest./24hr, **other:** Coleman Correctional, **W...gas:** Amoco/Hardee's/diesel, Chevron, **other:** Countryside RV Park, flea mkt

314 FL 48, to Bushnell, **E...gas:** BP/diesel, Chevron/A&W/24hr, Citgo, Mobil/DQ/Stuckey's, **food:** KFC/Taco Bell, Shanghai Chinese, **lodging:** Best Western, **other:** Red Barn RV Camp, The Oaks Camp(1mi), to Dade Bfd HS, **W...gas:** Shell/diesel, Speedway/diesel, **food:** McDonald's, Waffle House, flea mkt

309 rd 476, to Webster, **E...**Sumter Oaks RV Park(1mi)

307mm rest areas both lanes, full(handicapped)facilities, phone, coffee, vending, picnic tables, litter barrels, petwalk

301 US 98, FL 50, to Dade City, **E...gas:** Amoco, RaceTrac, Speedway, **food:** Cracker Barrel, Denny's, McDonald's, Mexican Cantina, Waffle House, Wendy's, **lodging:** Day's Inn, **other:** HOSPITAL, Winn-Dixie, **W...gas:** Mobil/Subway/LP, **food:** Burger King, **lodging:** Hampton Inn, Holiday Inn, **other:** Florida Campland(5mi)

293 rd 41, to Dade City, **W...**Travelers Rest Resort RV Park

285 FL 52, to Dade City, New Port Richey, **E...gas:** Flying J/Country Mkt/diesel/LP/24hr/@, **other:** HOSPITAL, tires, **W... gas:** Texaco/Blimpie/diesel/24hr, **food:** Waffle House

FLORIDA

Interstate 75

N ↕ S

Tampa

279 FL 54, to Land O' Lakes, Zephyrhills, **E...gas:** Hess, RaceTrac, Shell/fruit, Texaco, **food:** ABC Pizza, Applebee's, BBQ, Blimpie, BrewMaster Steaks, Burger King, Godfather's, Subway, Waffle House, Wendy's, **lodging:** Masters Inn, **other:** Discount Parts, Ford, Publix, Walgreen, Winn-Dixie, Saddlebrook RV Resort(1mi), **W...gas:** Amoco, Circle K/ diesel, Citgo/diesel, **food:** Cracker Barrel, Denny's, KFC, McDonald's, Outback Steaks, Peacock's Grill, Remington's Steaks, Shanghai Chinese, **lodging:** Comfort Inn, Holiday Inn Express, Masters Inn, Sleep Inn, **other:** $Store, Kash'n Karry Foods, Medicine Shoppe, RV camping, USPO

278mm rest areas both lanes, full(handicapped)facilities, phone, vending, picnic tables, litter barrels, petwalk, 24hr security

275 FL 56, no facilities

274 I-275(from sb), to Tampa, St Petersburg

270 rd 581, Bruce B Downs Blvd, **E...gas:** Citgo/7-11, Hess/Blimpie/diesel, Mobil, Shell, 7-11, **food:** Burger King, Chick-fil-A, Chili's, DQ, KFC, Macaroni Grill, McDonald's, Papa John's, Quizno's, Ruby Tuesday, Steak'n Shake, Taco Bell, **lodging:** Wingate Inn, **other:** Home Depot, Kash'n Karry Food, Kauffman Tire, Publix(2mi), Walgreen, Winn-Dixie(2mi)

266 rd 582A, Fletcher Ave, **W...gas:** Shell/Subway, **food:** Wendy's, **lodging:** Courtyard, Extended Stay America, Fairfield Inn, Hampton Inn Suites, Hilton Garden, Residence Inn, Sleep Inn, **other:** HOSPITAL

265 FL 582, Fowler Ave, Temple Terrace, **E...other:** Happy Traveler RV Park(1mi), flea mkt, **W...gas:** Amoco/24hr, Chevron/diesel, **food:** Burger King, Denny's, McDonald's, **lodging:** Holiday Inn, La Quinta, Shoney's Inn/rest.(1mi), Wingate Inn, to Busch Gardens

261 I-4, W to Tampa, E to Orlando

260b a FL 574, Tampa, to Mango, **E...gas:** Chevron, Shell/Subway, **food:** McDonald's(2mi), **other:** Walgreen, **W...gas:** Amoco, Rainbow, **food:** Joe's NY Deli(2mi), **lodging:** Hilton, Radisson, Residence Inn

Brandon

257 FL 60, Brandon, **E...gas:** Amoco, Mobil, Texaco, **food:** Bennigan's, BuddyFreddy's Diner, Chili's, Domino's, Don Pablo, Grady's Grill, Macaroni Grill, Olive Garden, Outback Steaks, Red Lobster, TGIFriday, Waffle House, **lodging:** Holiday Inn Express, HomeStead Village, La Quinta, **other:** HOSPITAL, Aamco, Barnes&Noble, Best Buy, Chrysler/ Plymouth/Dodge, Dillard's, Firestone, JC Penney, Jo-Ann Fabrics, K-Mart, Marshall's, MensWhse, Michael's, PepBoys, Sam's Club, Sears/auto, Staples, mall, **W...gas:** Citgo, Shell, **food:** BBQ, Bob Evans, Burger King, Hooters, McDonald's, Subway, Sweet Tomato, Wendy's, **lodging:** Baymont Inn, Best Western, Comfort Inn, Courtyard, Day's Inn, Fairfield Inn, Red Roof Inn, **other:** Chevrolet, Circuit City, Dodge, Harley-Davidson, Home Depot, Honda, Mitsubishi/Hyundai/Suzuki/Yamaha, Nissan, Office Depot, Pontiac/GMC, funpark

256 FL 618 W(toll), to Tampa, no facilities

254 US 301, Riverview, no facilities

250 Gibsonton Dr, Riverview, **1 mi E...gas:** Amoco, Chevron, Mobil, **food:** Beef O'Brady's, Burger King, McDonald's, Subway, **other:** Alafia River RV Resort, Hidden River RV Resort(4mi), **W...gas:** Amoco(1mi)

246 FL 672, Big Bend Rd, Apollo Bch, **E...gas:** 7-11, **W...gas:** Chevron(1mi), **lodging:** Ramada Inn

240b a FL 674, Ruskin, Sun City Ctr, **E...Welcome Ctr, gas:** Chevron/24hr, **food:** BBQ, Burger King, Checker's, Denny's, Hungry Howie's, Pizza Hut, Taco Bell, Wendy's, **lodging:** Comfort Inn, Sun City Ctr Inn/rest., **other:** Kash'n Karry Foods, OilExpress, Radio Shack, Scotty's Hardware, Walgreen, Wal-Mart, SunLake RV Resort(1mi), to Little Manatee River SP, **W...gas:** Circle K/diesel, Exxon, Hess/diesel, RaceTrac, **food:** BuddyFreddy's, KFC, McDonald's, Subway, **lodging:** Holiday Inn Express, **other:** Beall's, D&K Repair, Eckerd, NAPA, Publix

238mm rest area both lanes, full(handicapped)facilities, phone, vending, picnic tables, litter barrels, petwalk, 24hr security

229 rd 683, Moccasin Wallow Rd, to Parrish, **E...**Little Manatee Sprs RV Park(10mi), **W...other:** Fiesta Grove RV Park(3mi), Frog Creek RV Park(3mi), Terra Ceia RV Village(2mi), Winterset RV Park(3mi)

Bradenton

228 I-275 N, to St Petersburg

224 US 301, Ellenton, to Bradenton, **E...gas:** Chevron/ 24hr, RaceTrac/McDonald's, Shell, **food:** Checker's, Food Court, Wendy's, **lodging:** Hampton Inn, Holiday Inn Express, **other:** Ace Hardware, Foodway, K-Mart, Publix, Walgreen, USPO, Ellenton Garden Camping(1mi), Prime Outlets/famous brands, cleaners, **W...gas:** Pilot/Subway/diesel/@, **food:** Denny's, Johnnie's Seafood, Waffle House, **lodging:** Best Western, Day's Inn(3mi), Ellenton Inn

220b a FL 64, Bradenton, to Zolfo Springs, **E...**Lake Manatee SRA, **W...gas:** Amoco/diesel, Chevron, Citgo/diesel/24hr, RaceTrac, 76/Circle K/diesel, Shell, **food:** Burger King, Cracker Barrel, Denny's, McDonald's, Subway, TCBY, Waffle House, Wendy's, **lodging:** Comfort Inn, Day's Inn, Econolodge, Holiday Inn Express, Luxury Inn, Motel 6, **other:** HOSPITAL, Encore RV Resort(1mi)

217b a FL 70, Bradenton, to Arcadia, **E...gas:** Hess/Blimpie/ Godfather's/diesel/24hr, **W...gas:** Amoco/diesel/LP, Citgo/7-11, Shell, 76/Circle K, **food:** Applebee's, Bob Evans, Chick-fil-A, Denny's, Demetrio's Rest., McDonald's, Hungry Howie's, Subway, **other:** Eckerd, K-Mart, Lowe's Whse, Olson Tire, Publix, Valvoline, HorseShoe RV Park, Pleasant Lake RV Resort

Interstate 75

N ↕ S

Sarasota

213 University Parkway, to Sarasota, **E...gas:** Mobil/Subway/TCBY/diesel, **food:** Chili's, China Coast, Monty's Pizza, Ryan's Grill, **lodging:** Holiday Inn, **other:** Publix, **W...**Sarasota Outlet Ctr/famous brands/food court, **3-6 mi W...gas:** Chevron/24hr, **food:** Applebee's, Burger King, KFC, McDonald's, Taco Bell, **lodging:** Courtyard, Residence Inn, Sleep Inn, SpringHill Suites, **other:** Ringling Museum, dog-track

210 FL 780, Fruitville Rd, Sarasota, **1 mi E...gas:** Texaco/diesel, **other:** Sun&Fun RV Park, golf, radiators, **W...gas:** Amoco/diesel/LP, BP/diesel, Chevron/24hr, Mobil/Blimpie/diesel, **food:** Applebee's, Burger King, Checker's, Chick-fil-A, Don Pablo, KFC, Longhorn Steaks, McDonald's, Perkins, Quizno's, Subway, Taco Bell, **food:** AmericInn, Hyatt(6mi), Wellesley Inn(6mi), **other:** Discount Parts, $Tree, Eckerd, GNC, Publix, Radio Shack, Target, Winn-Dixie

207 FL 758, Sarasota, **W...gas:** Mobil/Subway/diesel/repair, Speedway/diesel(2mi), Texaco/Blimpie, **food:** Arby's, BBQ, Checker's, Chili's, MadFish Grill, McDonald's, Pizza Hut, Sarasota Ale House, Steak'n Shake, Taco Bell, **lodging:** Hampton Inn, **other:** HOSPITAL, Goodyear/auto, Home Depot, Kash'n Karry, Publix, Radio Shack, Walgreen, Wal-Mart

205 FL 72, Sarasota, to Arcadia, **E...**Myakka River SP(9mi), **W...gas:** Amoco/diesel, Citgo/7-11/diesel, Mobil, **food:** Burger King, McDonald's, Subway, Waffle House, Wendy's, **lodging:** Comfort Inn, Holiday Inn Express(5mi), Ramada Ltd, **other:** Beach Club RV Resort(6mi)

200 FL 681 S(from sb), to Venice, Osprey, same as 195

195 Laurel Rd, Nokomis, **E...**Stay'n Play RV Park(1mi), **W...gas:** Hess(3mi), **other:** Encore RV Park(2mi), Scherer SP(6mi)

193 Jaracanda Blvd, Venice, **W...gas:** Chevron/Subway/diesel/24hr, Hess/Blimpie/Godfather's/diesel, Race-Trac, **food:** Cracker Barrel, McDonald's, Waffle House, **lodging:** Best Western, **other:** HOSPITAL

191 Englewood Rd, **W...other:** Ramblers Rest Resort(3mi), Venice Campground(1mi)

182 Sumter Blvd, to North Port, **W...**gas, food, lodging

179 Toledo Blade Blvd, North Port, no facilities

170 rd 769, Port Charlotte, to Arcadia, **E...gas:** Citgo/7-11/diesel, **lodging:** Hampton Inn, Holiday Inn Express, **other:** Lettuce Lake Camping(7mi), Riverside Camping(4mi), **W...gas:** Amoco/Subway/diesel, Hess/diesel, Mobil/Blimpie/diesel, 76/Circle K, **food:** Burger King, Cracker Barrel, Denny's, McDonald's, Taco Bell, Waffle House, Wendy's, **other:** HOSPITAL, Ace Hardware, Discount Parts, Eckerd, GNC, Publix, USPO, Winn-Dixie

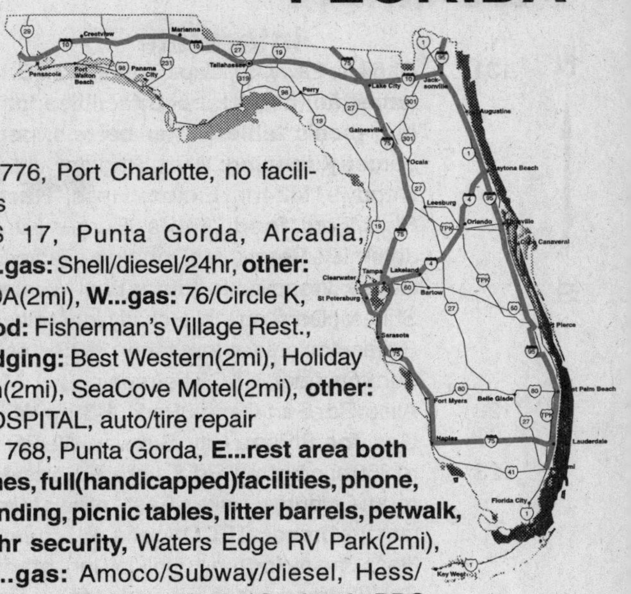

167 rd 776, Port Charlotte, no facilities

164 US 17, Punta Gorda, Arcadia, **E...gas:** Shell/diesel/24hr, **other:** KOA(2mi), **W...gas:** 76/Circle K, **food:** Fisherman's Village Rest., **lodging:** Best Western(2mi), Holiday Inn(2mi), SeaCove Motel(2mi), **other:** HOSPITAL, auto/tire repair

161 FL 768, Punta Gorda, **E...rest area both lanes, full(handicapped)facilities, phone, vending, picnic tables, litter barrels, petwalk, 24hr security,** Waters Edge RV Park(2mi), **W...gas:** Amoco/Subway/diesel, Hess/diesel, Pilot/diesel/24hr/@, **food:** BBQ, Burger King, Denny's, McDonald's, Pizza Hut, Taco Bell, Waffle House, Wendy's, **lodging:** Day's Inn, Motel 6, **other:** Alligator RV Park(2mi), Encore RV Park(2mi)

160mm weigh sta both lanes

158 rd 762, **E...**Babcock-Wells Wildlife Mgt Area, **W...gas:** Texaco/diesel, to RV camping

Ft Myers

143 FL 78, N Ft Myers, to Cape Coral, **E...gas:** Citgo/diesel, **other:** Upriver RV Park(1mi), **W...gas:** RaceTrac/diesel/24hr, **lodging:** Pioneer Village RV Resort

141 FL 80, Palm Bch Blvd, Ft Myers, **E...gas:** Chevron/diesel, Exxon/diesel, **food:** Cracker Barrel, Waffle House, **lodging:** Comfort Inn, **other:** Orange Harbor RV Park, **W...gas:** Citgo/7-11, Hess/diesel, RaceTrac, **food:** BBQ, DQ, Hardee's, Juicy Lucy's Burgers, KFC(2mi), Perkins, Pizza Hut, Subway, Taco Bell, **lodging:** Holiday Inn(6mi), Quality Inn(6mi), Ramada Inn(6mi), **other:** MEDICAL CARE, $General, Eckerd, Martin's Tire/repair, North Trail RV Ctr, Publix, Radio Shack, Scotty's Hardware

139 Luckett Rd, Ft Myers, **E...lodging:** Cypress Woods RV Resort, **W...gas:** Pilot/Subway/Grandma's Kitchen/diesel/24hr/@, **other:** Camping World RV Service/supplies, Lazy J's RV Park, RV Kountry

138 FL 82, Ft Myers, to Lehigh Acres, **W...gas:** RaceTrac/diesel, Speedway/diesel

136 FL 884, Colonial Blvd, Ft Myers, **1-3 mi W...gas:** Hess, Mobil, RaceTrac, **lodging:** Baymont Inn, Courtyard, Howard Johnson, La Quinta, Residence Inn, Wellesley Inn, **other:** HOSPITAL

FLORIDA

Interstate 75

N ↕ S

131 Daniels Pkwy, to Cape Coral, **E...rest area both lanes, full(handicapped)facilities, phone, vending, picnic tables, litter barrels, petwalk, 24hr security, lodging:** WynnStar Inn, airport, **W...gas:** Citgo/7-11/24hr, Exxon, Hess, RaceTrac/24hr, Shell/24hr, **food:** Arby's, Burger King, Denny's, Johnnie's Rest., McDonald's, Taco Bell, Waffle House, Wendy's, **lodging:** Best Western, Comfort Suites, Hampton Inn, Holiday Inn(4mi), Homewood Suites(4mi), Sleep Inn, **other:** HOSPITAL, American Van&Camper, C&C Tire/repair

128 Alico Rd, San Carlos Park, **1-3 mi W...gas:** Hess Gas, **food:** Pizza City, Subway, Wendy's

123 rd 850, Corkscrew Rd, Estero, **E...gas:** Mobil/diesel, **food:** Chiburger, Jake's Rest., **other:** Miromar Outlet/famous brands, TECO Arena, **W...gas:** Citgo/7-11, Hess/diesel, **lodging:** Holiday Inn, **other:** Koreshan St HS, Woodsmoke RV Park(4mi)

116 Bonita Bch Rd, Bonita Springs, **W...gas:** Amoco/McDonald's/24hr, Hess/diesel/24hr, **1-3 mi W...gas:** Shell/24hr, Speedway, **food:** BBQ, Burger King, KFC, Perkins, Waffle House, Wendy's, AmericInn, **lodging:** Baymont Inn, Comfort Inn, Day's Inn, Hampton Inn, Holiday Inn Express, **other:** Imperial Bonita RV Park, to gulf beaches

111 rd 846, Immokalee Rd, Naples Park, **E...gas:** Mobil, **lodging:** Hampton Inn, **W...gas:** 76/Circle K, **food:** Wendy's(2mi), **lodging:** Fairways Motel(2mi), Vanderbilt Inn(5mi), **other:** HOSPITAL, Publix, to Wiggins SP

Naples

107 rd 896, Pinebridge Rd, Naples, **E...gas:** Mobil/McDonald's/diesel/24hr, **other:** MEDICAL CARE, Publix, Walgreen, **W...gas:** Chevron/Subway/diesel24hr, RaceTrac, Shell/diesel/24hr, **food:** Applebee's, Burger King, IHOP, Perkins, Waffle House, **lodging:** Best Western, Hawthorn Suites, Hilton Garden(4mi), Knight's Inn, Ramada(3mi), **other:** Harley-Davidson

101 rd 951, to FL 84, **2 mi E...gas:** BP, Citgo/diesel, Hess, 76/Circle K/24hr, **food:** BBQ, KFC, McDonald's, Pizza Hut, **lodging:** Quality Inn, **other:** Discount Parts, Golden Gate Drug, **W...gas:** Amoco/Subway/diesel, Mobil/Subway/diesel/24hr, Shell/diesel/24hr, 76/Circle K/24hr, **food:** Burger King, Checker's, Cracker Barrel, McDonald's, Waffle House, **lodging:** Baymont Inn, Comfort Inn, Holiday Inn Express, Super 8, **other:** Mazda, Endless Summer RV Park(3mi)

100mm toll plaza both lanes

80 FL 29, to Everglade City, Immokalee, Big Cypress Nat Preserve, no facilities

71mm Big Cypress Nat Preserve, hiking, no security

63mm W...rest area both lanes, full(handicapped)facilities, phone, vending, picnic tables, litter barrels, petwalk, 24hr security

49 Gov't Rd, Snake Rd, Big Cypress Indian Reservation, **E...gas:** Shell/diesel, **other:** museum

41mm rec area eb, picnic tables, litter barrels

38mm rec area wb, picnic tables, litter barrels

35mm W...rest area both lanes, full(handicapped)facilities, phone, vending, picnic tables, litter barrels, petwalk, 24hr security

32mm rec area both lanes, picnic tables, litter barrels

25mm toll plaza wb, motorist callboxes begin/end

23 US 27, FL 25, Miami, South Bay, no facilities

22 NW 196th, Arvida Pkwy, **W...other:** Weston Tire/repair, same as 21

21 FL 84 W(from nb), Indian Trace, **W...gas:** Mobil/diesel, **food:** Antonello's Italian, Café Café, Papa John's

19 I-595 E, FL 869(toll), Sawgrass Expswy

15 Arvida Pkwy, Weston, Bonaventure, **W...gas:** Exxon, **food:** Max's Grill, Pastability Ristorante, Sporting Brew Grill, Wendy's, **other:** MEDICAL CARE, PillBox Drug, USPO

13b a Griffin Rd, **E...gas:** Shell/diesel, **food:** Burger King, DQ, Subway, Waffle House, **other:** MEDICAL CARE, Goodyear/auto, Publix, **W...gas:** Amoco/diesel, Citgo/7-11, **food:** East Coast Burrito, McDonald's, Pizza Heaven, Togo's, **other:** Home Depot, Toyota, Winn-Dixie

11b a Sheridan St, **E...gas:** Chevron, **food:** Cracker Barrel, **lodging:** Hampton Inn, **other:** HOSPITAL(3mi), Lincoln/Mercury, **W...gas:** Shell, **food:** Bilotti's Italian, DQ, Little Caesar's, McDonald's, **other:** CHIROPRACTOR, GNC, Lowe's Whse, Publix

Miami

9b a FL 820, Pine Blvd, Hollywood Blvd, **E...gas:** Amoco, **food:** Chili's, Macaroni Grill, McDonald's, Wendy's, **other:** BJ's Whse, Dodge, Home Depot, JC Penney, Walgreen, **W...gas:** Amoco, Chevron, Exxon, Mobil/diesel, **food:** IHOP, KFC, McDonald's, Miami Subs, **other:** Discount Parts, K-Mart, Pontiac/GMC/ Lexus, USPO, Walgreen, Winn-Dixie

7b a Miramar Pkwy, **E...gas:** Chevron, **food:** Dunkin Donuts/Baskin-Robbins, McDonald's, Sal's Italian, Subway, Wendy's, **lodging:** Wingate Inn, **other:** Publix, USPO, **W...**Home Depot

5 to FL 821(from sb), FL TPK(toll)

4 NW 186th, Miami Gardens Dr, **E...gas:** Amoco/24hr, Chevron/24hr, Shell/24hr, **food:** IHOP, McDonald's, Subway, **other:** Eckerd, GNC, Publix/deli

2 NW 138th, Graham Dairy Rd, **W...gas:** Mobil, **food:** DQ, DonTike Chinese, McDonald's, **other:** HOSPITAL, GNC, Publix

1b a I-75 begins/ends on FL 826, Palmetto Expswy. Multiple services on FL 826.

Interstate 95

N ↕ S

Jacksonville

Exit #	Services
382mm	Florida/Georgia state line, St Marys River, motorist callboxes begin/end.
381mm	inspection sta both lanes
380	US 17, to Yulee, Kingsland, **E...**Hance's RV Camping, **W...gas:** Amoco/24hr, Shell/24hr, **food:** Po Folks, **lodging:** Day's Inn, Holiday Inn Express
378mm	**Welcome Ctr sb, full(handicapped)facilities, phone, vending, picnic tables, litter barrels, petwalk, 24hr security**
376mm	weigh sta both lanes
373	FL 200, FL A1A, to Yulee, Callahan, Fernandina Bch, **E...gas:** Citgo/DQ/Stuckey's, Shell/repair, Texaco/Krystal, **food:** Burger King, McDonald's, Taco Bell, Wendy's, **lodging:** Comfort Inn, Hampton Inn(3mi), Nassau Holiday Motel, to Ft Clinch SP, **W...gas:** BP/diesel, Citgo/Wayfara Rest., Exxon/diesel, **food:** Waffle House
366	Pecan Park Rd, **E...gas:** BP/diesel/ice cream, Citgo/diesel, **W...**Flea&Farmer's Mkt
363b a	Duval Rd, **E...gas:** Chevron, Mobil/diesel, **W...gas:** Amoco/Subway, BP, Chevron/A&W/Taco Bell, Shell/diesel, **food:** Denny's, Waffle House, **lodging:** Admiral Benbow Inn, Clarion Hotel, Courtyard, Day's Inn, Fairfield Inn, Hampton Inn, Holiday Inn, Microtel, Quality Inn, Red Roof Inn, Valu Lodge, **other:** RV Ctr
362b a	I-295 S, Jacksonville, FL 9A, to Blount Island
360	FL 104, Dunn Ave, Busch Dr, **E...gas:** Gate/diesel, **food:** Applebee's, Hardee's, Waffle House, **lodging:** Admiral Benbow Inn, **other:** NAPA, Sam's Club, **W...gas:** Amoco, BP, Hess, Shell, Texaco, **food:** Arby's, BBQ, Burger King, Capt D's, Dunkin Donuts, KFC, Krystal, Lee's Chicken, LJ Silver, McDonald's, Pizza Hut, Popeye's, Quincy's, Rally's, Shoney's, Taco Bell, Wendy's, **lodging:** Best Western, La Quinta, Motel 6, Red Carpet Inn, Super 8, **other:** Discount Parts, Eckerd, Family$, PepBoys, Publix, Radio Shack, Winn Dixie
358b a	FL 105, Broward Rd, Heckscher Dr, **E...**zoo, **W...lodging:** Day's Inn
357mm	Trout River
357	FL 111, Edgewood Ave, **W...gas:** Amoco/repair, Citgo
356b a	FL 115, Lem Turner Rd, **E...food:** Hardee's, **W...gas:** Amoco/24hr, Hess, Shell/repair, Texaco/diesel, **food:** Burger King, Krystal, Popeye's, Rally's, Taco Bell, **other:** Discount Parts, 1 Stop Parts, Sav-A-Lot Foods, Walgreen, flea mkt
355	Golfair Blvd, **E...gas:** Shell, Texaco, **other:** carwash, flea mkt, tires, **W...gas:** Amoco/repair/24hr, Exxon, RaceTrac, **lodging:** Valu Lodge
354b a	US 1, 20th St, to Jacksonville, to AmTrak
353d	FL 114, to 8th St, **E...gas:** Amoco, McDonald's, **other:** HOSPITAL,
353c	US 23 N, Kings Rd, downtown
353b	US 90A, Union St, Sports Complex, downtown
353a	Church St, Myrtle Ave, Forsythe St, downtown
352c	Monroe St(from nb), downtown
352b a	Myrtle Ave(from nb), downtown
351d	Stockton St, HOSPITAL, downtown
351c	Margaret St, downtown
351b	I-10 W, to Tallahassee
351a	Park St, College St, HOSPITAL, to downtown, no facilities
351mm	St Johns River
350b	FL 13, San Marco Blvd
350a	Prudential Dr, Main St, Riverside Ave(from nb), to downtown
349	US 90 E(from sb), downtown, to beaches, **W... lodging:** Super 8
348	US 1 S(from sb), Philips Hwy, downtown, **W...lodging:** Scottish Inn, Super 8, **other:** Cadillac, Chevrolet, VW/Volvo
347	US 1A, FL 126, Emerson St, **E...gas:** Shell, Texaco/diesel, **food:** Subway, **W... gas:** Amoco, BP/diesel, Exxon, Gate, **food:** McDonald's, Taco Bell, **lodging:** Comfort Inn, Emerson Inn, **other:** mall
346b a	FL 109, University Blvd, **E...gas:** Amoco, Citgo, Hess/diesel, Shell, **food:** Capt D's, DQ, El Potro Mexican, Firehouse Subs, Hungry Howie's, Krystal, Pizza Hut, **other:** HOSPITAL, Rally's, Firestone/auto, Goodyear/auto, 1 Stop Parts, Tire Kingdom, Winn-Dixie, **W...gas:** BP/diesel, RaceTrac, **food:** BBQ, Buckingham Grill, Burger King, Dunkin Donuts, IHOP, OceanBay Seafood, Ryan's, Shoney's, Taco Bell, Waffle House, Wendy's, **lodging:** Comfort Lodge, Day's Inn, Ramada Inn, Red Carpet Inn, **other:** Chrysler/Plymouth, auto repair
345	FL 109, University Blvd(from nb), **E...gas:** Chevron, Gate/diesel, **W...gas:** Chevron
344	FL 202, Butler Blvd, **E...food:** Dave&Buster's, **lodging:** DoubleTree Inn, Economy Inn, Hampton Inn, Holiday Inn Express, Inns of America, Marriott, Quality Inn/café, Ramada Inn, **other:** HOSPITAL, **W...gas:** BP, Shell, Texaco/diesel, **food:** Applebee's, Cracker Barrel, Hardee's, McDonald's, Waffle House, Wendy's, **lodging:** Courtyard, Extended Stay America, Jameson Inn, La Quinta, Masters Inn, Microtel, Red Roof Inn, **other:** Studio+, Wingate Inn

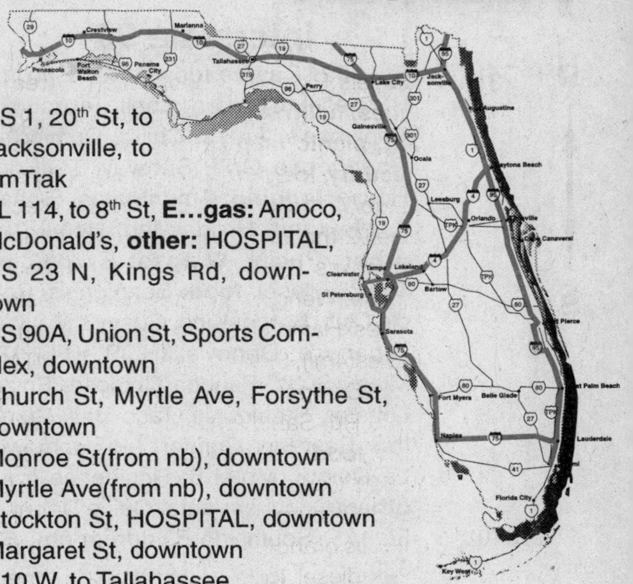

FLORIDA

Interstate 95

N ↕ S

St Augustine

341 FL 152, Baymeadows Rd, **E...gas:** Amoco, BP/diesel, Chevron, Shell, Texaco/diesel, **food:** Applebee's, Arby's, Chili's, Domino's, Hardee's, Roadhouse Grill, Subway, TGIFriday, Waffle House, **lodging:** AmeriSuites, Embassy Suites, Fairfield Inn, Holiday Inn, HomeStead Village, **other:** Publix, **W...gas:** Exxon/diesel, Shell, Texaco/diesel, **food:** Bennigan's, Bombay Bicycle Club, Burger King, Chevy's Mexican, Daruma Japanese, Denny's, IHOP, KFC, McDonald's, Miami Subs, Pagoda Chinese, Pizza Hut, Red Lobster, Steak&Ale, Taco Bell, Wendy's, **lodging:** Best Inn, Comfort Inn, Homewood Suites, La Quinta, Motel 6, Residence Inn, Studio 6, **other:** Goodyear/auto, Office Depot

340 FL 115, Southside Blvd(from nb), **E...**same as 339

339 US 1, Philips Hwy, **E...gas:** Chevron, RaceTrac, **food:** Arby's, Burger King, McDonald's, Olive Garden, Taco Bell, Waffle House, **other:** Belk, Dillard's, Ford, Gayfer's, JC Penney, Parisian, Sears/auto, Toyota, mall, **W...gas:** Amoco, Shell

337 I-295 N, to Orange Park

331mm rest area both lanes, full(handicapped)facilities, phone, vending, picnic tables, litter barrels, petwalk, 24hr security

329 rd 210, **E...gas:** Citgo/fruit, Pilot/Hardee's/diesel/24hr/@, TA/Shell/diesel/rest./@, Texaco, **food:** Waffle House, **other:** KOA, **W...gas:** Amoco, Chevron/diesel, **other:** fireworks

323 International Golf Pkwy, **E...gas:** Shell/diesel, **food:** Marvin's Steaks, Subway, **lodging:** Comfort Suites, Courtyard, Hampton Inn, Holiday Inn Express, **W...gas:** Publix, **other:** World Golf Village

318 FL 16, St Augustine, Green Cove Sprgs, **E...gas:** Chevron, Citgo/DQ, Gate/diesel/fruit, Shell, **food:** Burger King, McDonald's, Subway, Waffle House, **lodging:** GuestHouse Inn, Holiday Inn Express, Belz Outlet, **W...gas:** Exxon, Shell/diesel, **food:** BBQ, Cracker Barrel, Denny's, FoodCourt, KFC, Shoney's, Taco Bell, Wendy's, **lodging:** Best Western, Day's Inn, Hampton Inn, Ramada Ltd, Scottish Inn, Super 8, **other:** St Augustine Outlet Ctr

311 FL 207, St Augustine, **E...gas:** BP, Chevron, Hess/Subway, Indian River Fruit/gas, **other:** HOSPITAL, Indian Forest RV Park(2mi), KOA(7mi), St Johns RV Park, flea mkt, to Anastasia SP, **W...gas:** Mobil/diesel, Shell, **lodging:** Comfort Inn

305 FL 206, to Hastings, Crescent Beach, **E...gas:** Flying J/Country Mkt/diesel/24hr/@, to Ft Matanzas NM

Palm Coast

302mm rest areas both lanes, full(handicapped)facilities, phone, vending, picnic tables, litter barrels, petwalk, 24hr security

298 US 1, to St Augustine, **E...gas:** BP/diesel, Citgo/gifts/fruit, Indian River Fruit/gas, Shell/diesel, **other:** to Faver-Dykes SP, **W...gas:** Charlie T's/diesel/motel/24hr, Hess/DQ, Mobil/diesel, **food:** Waffle House

289 FL A1A(toll br), to Palm Coast, **E...gas:** BP, Exxon/diesel, **food:** Cracker Barrel, Denny's, KFC, McDonald's, Pizza Hut, Wendy's, **lodging:** Hampton Inn, Microtel, Sleep Inn, **other:** Beall's, Eckerd, Publix, **W...gas:** Chevron/diesel, Shell, Texaco, **food:** BBQ, Perkins, Steak'n Shake/24hr, Subway, Taco Bell, TCBY, **other:** Discount Parts, Ford, K-Mart, Tire Kingdom, USPO, Walgreen, Wal-Mart SuperCtr/24hr, Winn-Dixie

286mm weigh sta both lanes, phone

284 FL 100, to Bunnell, Flagler Beach, **E...gas:** Chevron/diesel/24hr, Exxon, Hess/diesel, **food:** BBQ, Burger King, Gage's Café, McDonald's, Subway, Taco Bell, **other:** $General, Winn-Dixie, **W...gas:** BP/diesel, **other:** Chrysler/Plymouth/Jeep

278 Old Dixie Hwy, **E...gas:** Citgo/7-11, **other:** Publix, Bulow RV Park(3mi), to Tomoke SP, **W...gas:** Hess/diesel, **lodging:** Day's Inn, **other:** Holiday TravL Park

273 US 1, **E...gas:** Amoco, Chevron, Citgo, Mobil/Wendy's/diesel, Shell/diesel, Denny's/24hr, **food:** McDonald's, Waffle House, Comfort Inn, **other:** RV Ctr, **W...gas:** Exxon/Burger King, **food:** DQ, **lodging:** Budget Inn, Day's Inn, Econolodge, Scottish Inn, Super 8, **other:** Encore RV Park

268 FL 40, Ormond Beach, **E... gas:** BP/Blimpie, Chevron, **food:** Applebee's, Boston Mkt, Chili's, Chick-fil-A, Denny's/24hr, Papa John's, Schlotsky's, Steak'n Shake, Subway, Taco Bell, Waffle House, Wendy's, **lodging:** Sleep Inn, **other:** Beall's, K-Mart, Lowe's Whse, Publix, USPO, Wal-Mart SuperCtr/24hr, **W...gas:** Amoco/Burger King/TCBY, Hess, Mobil/diesel, **food:** Cracker Barrel, Hampton Inn, Jameson Inn, **other:** HOSPITAL

Daytona

265 LPGA Blvd, Holly Hill, Daytona Beach, **E...gas:** Citgo/7-11, Shell/diesel, **food:** Hardee's

261b a US 92, to DeLand, Daytona Bch, **E...gas:** Amoco/diesel, Chevron/diesel, Citgo/7-11, Hess/Blimpie//diesel, Mobil, RaceTrac/24hr, Shell/diesel, **food:** Alehouse, Bob Evans, Burger King, Carrabba's, Checker's, Chick-fil-A, Cracker Barrel, Fazoli's, Friendly's, Hooters, Hops Grill, KFC, Krystal, Longhorn Steaks, Olive Garden, Pizzaria Uno,

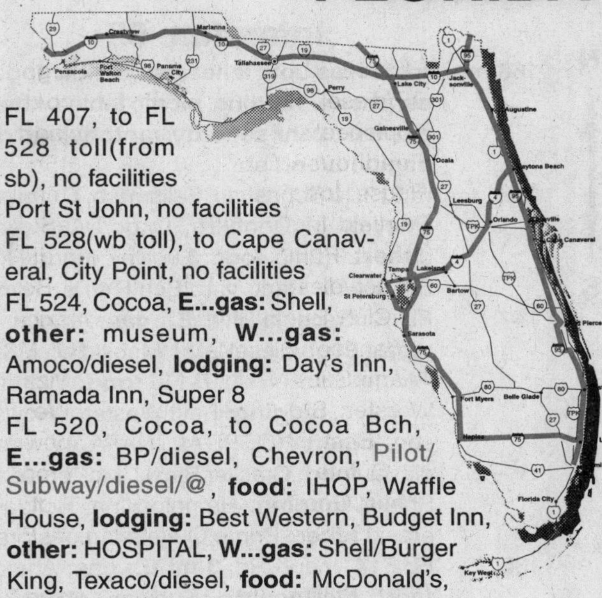

Interstate 95

N ↕ S

Daytona

Red Lobster, Roadhouse Grill, Ruby Tuesday, Shoney's, S&S Cafeteria, Subway, Taco Bell, Waffle House, **lodging:** Holiday Inn, La Quinta, Ramada Inn, Travelodge, **other:** HOSPITAL, Barnes&Noble, Best Buy, Circuit City, Dillard's, Dodge/Kia, Gayfer's, Home Depot, JC Penney, Marshall's, Michael's, OfficeMax, Old Navy, PepBoys, Ross, Sears/auto, Staples, SteinMart, Target, Walgreen, mall, to Daytona Racetrack, **W...gas:** BP/diesel, Exxon, **food:** Denny's, IHOP, McDonald's, **lodging:** Day's Inn, Super 8, **other:** RV camping, museum

260b a I-4, to Orlando, FL 400 E, to S Daytona, **E...gas:** BP/diesel, Chevron, **other:** museum

256 FL 421, to Port Orange, **E...gas:** Amoco, **food:** BBQ, Denny's/24hr, Spruce Creek Pizza, **lodging:** AmeriSuites, Hampton Inn, Holiday Inn, **other:** Lowe's Whse, **W...gas:** Amoco, Citgo/7-11, Hess, Shell/diesel, **food:** McDonald's, Subway, **other:** Publix

249b a FL 44, New Smyrna Bch, to De Land, **E...gas:** Shell/diesel/fruit, **other:** HOSPITAL, **3 mi E...gas:** Citgo, **food:** Burger King, Denny's, McDonald's, **other:** GNC, Harley-Davidson, Publix, Wal-Mart, **W...gas:** Chevron/diesel

244 FL 442, to Edgewater, **E...gas:** Chevron/diesel/24hr

231 rd 5a, Scottsmoor, **E...gas:** BP/Stuckey's/diesel, **other:** Crystal Lake RV Park

227mm rest area sb, full(handicapped)facilities, phone, vending, picnic tables, litter barrels, petwalk, 24hr security

225mm rest area nb, full(handicapped)facilities, phone, vending, picnic tables, litter barrels, petwalk, 24hr security

223 FL 46, Mims, **E...gas:** Chevron(2mi), **food:** McDonald's, **lodging:** Dickens B&B, **other:** HOSPITAL, **W...gas:** Amoco, Shell/deli, **other:** KOA/LP

220 FL 406, Titusville, **E...gas:** BP/diesel, Shell/Piccadilly's/subs, **food:** KFC, McDonald's, Subway, Wendy's, **lodging:** Day's Inn, HiWay Inn/Chinese Rest., **other:** HOSPITAL, Discount Parts, Eckerd, Fabric King, Publix, Walgreen, **W...gas:** Texaco/diesel

215 FL 50, Titusville, to Orlando, **E...gas:** BP, Circle K/gas, Coastal/diesel, Shell/DQ/diesel, Texaco/diesel, **food:** BBQ, Burger King, Denny's, Durango Steaks, McDonald's, Shoney's, Taco Bell, Waffle House, Wendy's, **lodging:** Best Western, Holiday Inn(3mi), Ramada Inn, **other:** Ford/Mercury, Lowe's Whse, Staples, Wal-Mart SuperCtr/gas/24hr, to Kennedy Space Ctr, **W...food:** Cracker Barrel, **lodging:** Day's Inn, LucksWay Inn

212 FL 407, to FL 528 toll(from sb), no facilities

208 Port St John, no facilities

205 FL 528(wb toll), to Cape Canaveral, City Point, no facilities

202 FL 524, Cocoa, **E...gas:** Shell, **other:** museum, **W...gas:** Amoco/diesel, **lodging:** Day's Inn, Ramada Inn, Super 8

201 FL 520, Cocoa, to Cocoa Bch, **E...gas:** BP/diesel, Chevron, Pilot/Subway/diesel/@, **food:** IHOP, Waffle House, **lodging:** Best Western, Budget Inn, **other:** HOSPITAL, **W...gas:** Shell/Burger King, Texaco/diesel, **food:** McDonald's, **lodging:** Ramada Inn(1mi), Super 8(1mi), **other:** Sun Coast RV Park

Melbourne

195 FL 519, Fiske Blvd, **E...gas:** Citgo/7-11, Shell/diesel(1mi), Texaco, **other:** Coast RV Park

191 rd 509, to Satellite Beach, **E...gas:** Citgo/7-11, Hess(2mi), Mobil, **food:** Denny's, McDonald's, Miami Subs, Perkins, Wendy's, **lodging:** Comfort Inn, Imperial Hotel, **other:** Eckerd, 2000 Auto Repair, to Patrick AFB, **W...gas:** Chevron/diesel, **food:** Burger King, Cracker Barrel, **lodging:** Baymont Inn

183 FL 518, Melbourne, Indian Harbour Bch, **E...gas:** Amoco, Citgo/7-11, Exxon, RaceTrac/24hr, **other:** museum, **W...**Flea Mkt

180 US 192, to Melbourne, **E...gas:** BP/diesel, Circle K, Citgo/7-11, Mobil/diesel, Speedway/diesel, **food:** Denny's, IHOP, Olive Garden, Shoney's, Steak'n Shake/24hr, Waffle House, **lodging:** Courtyard, Day's Inn, Hampton Inn, Holiday Inn Express, Howard Johnson, Travelodge, **other:** HOSPITAL, Sam's Club, Saturn, **W...gas:** Shell/diesel

176 rd 516a, to Palm Bay, **E...gas:** Chevron/diesel, Citgo/7-11, Exxon, Shell, **food:** Applebee's, Baskin-Robbins/Dunkin Donuts, Boston Mkt, Chick-fil-A, Denny's, Golden Corral, Taco Bell, Wendy's, **lodging:** Jameson Inn, Ramada Inn, **other:** Albertson's, Chevrolet, $Tree, GNC, Wal-Mart SuperCtr/gas/24hr, **W...gas:** Citgo/7-11, Sav-A-Ton/diesel, **other:** Publix, Walgreen

173 FL 514, to Palm Bay, **E...gas:** Cumberland/gas, Speedway/diesel, **other:** MEDICAL CARE, Firestone/auto, Ford, **W...gas:** Amoco/diesel, Hess, Speedway/diesel, **food:** Arby's, BBQ, Burger King, IHOP, McDonald's, Subway, Taco Bell, Waffle House, Wendy's, **lodging:** Motel 6, **other:** $General, Discount Parts, Eckerd, Goodyear/auto, Home Depot, Publix, Russell Stover, Tire Kingdom, USPO, Walgreen

FLORIDA

Interstate 95

N ↕ S

168mm **rest areas both lanes, full(handicapped)facilities, phone, vending, picnic tables, litter barrels, petwalk, 24hr security, motorist aid callboxes begin nb/end sb**

156 rd 512, to Sebastian, Fellsmere, **E...gas:** Amoco, Chevron/McDonald's, Citgo/DQ/diesel, Mobil/diesel/LP(2mi), **food:** Subway, **other:** HOSPITAL, Encore RV Park, Vero Bch RV Park(8mi)

147 FL 60, Osceola Blvd, **E...gas:** Amoco, Chevron/repair, Citgo/diesel/24hr, Mobil/diesel, Speedway, TA/diesel/24hr/@, 7-11, **food:** Waffle House, Wendy's, **lodging:** Best Western, Howard Johnson, **other:** HOSPITAL, NAPA, **W...gas:** Shell/diesel, **food:** Cracker Barrel, McDonald's, Steak'n Shake, **lodging:** Hampton Inn, Holiday Inn Express, **other:** Prime Outlets/famous brands

138 FL 614, Indrio Rd, **3 mi E...gas:** Amoco, Citgo, **food:** McDonald's, Subway, **other:** Oceanographic Institute, citrus

133mm **rest areas both lanes, full(handicapped)facilities, phone, vending, picnic tables, litter barrels, petwalk, 24hr security**

131b a FL 68, Orange Ave, **E...**to Ft Pierce SP, **W...gas:** Flying J/CountryMkt/diesel/LP/24hr/@

129 FL 70, to Okeechobee, **E...gas:** Citgo, Hess/diesel, RaceTrac, **food:** Applebee's, Golden Corral, Piccadilly's, **other:** HOSPITAL, Discount Parts, Belk, Firestone/auto, Goodyear/auto, Home Depot, Wal-Mart SuperCtr/gas/24hr, mall, **W...gas:** Amoco/diesel/24hr, Chevron, Citgo, Exxon, Mobil/Subway, Pilot/Arby's/diesel/24hr/@, Pilot/Hardee's/diesel/24hr/@, Shell, **food:** Burger King, Cracker Barrel, Denny's, KFC, McDonald's, Miami Subs, Red Lobster, Shoney's, Steak'n Shake, Taco Bell, Waffle House, Wendy's, **lodging:** CrossRoads Inn, Day's Inn, Hampton Inn, Holiday Inn Express, Motel 6, Sleep Inn, Treasure Coast Inn, to FL TPK

126 rd 712, Midway Rd, **3-5 mi E...gas:** Chevron, Mobil, Shell, **food:** Blimpie, Burger King, Subway

121 St Lucie West Blvd, **E...gas:** Chevron/24hr, Citgo/7-11, Hess/diesel, Mobil(1mi), Shell/Subway/diesel, **food:** Bob Evans, Burger King, Friendly's, Little Italy Rest.(1mi), McDonald's, Ruby Tuesday, Wendy's, **lodging:** Hampton Inn, SpringHill Suites, **other:** Publix/deli, USPO, Walgreen, **W...lodging:** MainStay Suites

118 Gatlin Blvd, to Port St Lucie, **1-2 mi E...gas:** Amoco/diesel/LP, Coastal/24hr, Mobil/Subway/diesel, **food:** Burger King, Gateway Diner, **other:** HOSPITAL,

110 FL 714, to Stuart, Palm City, no facilities

106mm **rest areas both lanes, full(handicapped)facilities, phone, vending, picnic tables. litter barrels, petwalk, 24hr security**

Ft Pierce

102 FL 713, to Stuart, Palm City, no facilities

101 FL 76, to Stuart, Indiantown, **E...gas:** Chevron/24hr, Mobil/diesel, Shell, **food:** Cracker Barrel, FlashBack Diner(5mi), McDonald's, **other:** HOSPITAL, RV camping, **W...gas:** Shell/diesel, **food:** DQ, Subway

96 rd 708, to Hobe Sound, **E...**Dickinson SP(11mi), RV camping

87b a FL 706, Jupiter, to Okeechobee, **E...gas:** Chevron, Hess, Mobil, Shell, Speedway, Texaco/diesel/24hr, **food:** Applebee's, City Grille, Dunkin Donuts, Domino's, Gator's Rest., IHOP, KFC, Little Caesar's, McDonald's, Nick's Tomato Pie, Pizza Man, Subway, Taco Bell, **lodging:** Fairfield Inn, Wellesley Inn, **other:** HOSPITAL, Discount Parts, Dodge/Mazda, Eckerd, GNC, Home Depot, PepBoys, Publix, Tire Kingdom, Walgreen, Wal-Mart, Winn-Dixie, hist sites, museum, **W...**info, RV camping, to FL TPK

83 Donald Ross Rd, **E...**HOSPITAL

79c FL 809 S(from sb), Military Trail, **W...**to FL TPK, same services as 57b(W)

79a b FL 786, PGA Blvd, **E...gas:** Mobil, Speedway, **food:** China Wok, Durango Steaks, **lodging:** Hampton Inn, Marriott, **other:** HOSPITAL, Loehmann's Foods, **W...gas:** Shell/diesel/24hr, **food:** Beacon St Café, **lodging:** DoubleTree Hotel, Embassy Suites, **other:** Publix

W Palm Beach

77 Northlake Blvd, to W Palm Bch, **E...gas:** Amoco, Citgo, Hess, Shell/diesel, **food:** Applebee's, Arby's, Burger King, Checker's, KFC, McDonald's, Taco Bell, Wendy's, **other:** HOSPITAL, Chevrolet, Chrysler/Jeep, Costco, Ford, Kia/Isuzu//Suzuki, K-Mart, Lincoln/Mercury, PepBoys, Pontiac/GMC, Staples, Suburu, VW/Mitsubishi, **W...gas:** Amoco, Chevron, Mobil/diesel, Shell, **food:** City Grille, Gator's Rest., **lodging:** Inns of America, **other:** Albertson's, OfficeMax, Publix

76 FL 708, Blue Heron Blvd, **E...gas:** Amoco, Shell, **food:** Wendy's, **W...gas:** Mobil, **food:** Burger King, Denny's, McDonald's, **lodging:** Motel 6, Super 8

Jupiter

74 FL 702, 45th St, **E...food:** Burger King, Hong Kong Café, IHOP, **lodging:** Day's Inn, Knight's Inn, **other:** HOSPITAL, Cadillac, Walgreen, **W...gas:** RaceTrac, **food:** Cracker Barrel, Taco Bell, Wendy's, **lodging:** Courtyard, Red Roof Inn, Residence Inn, **other:** Studio+, Goodyear/auto

71 Lake Blvd, Palm Beach, **E...food:** King China, **lodging:** Best Western, **other:** HOSPITAL, Best Buy, Burdine's, Dillard's, Firestone/auto, JC Penney, Lord&Taylor, Target, mall, **W...lodging:** Comfort Inn, Wellesley Inn

Interstate 95

N ↕ S

70b a FL 704, Okeechobee Blvd, **E...gas:** Exxon, **lodging:** Sheraton, **other:** Kravis Ctr, museum, **1-2 mi E...lodging:** beach motels, **W...gas:** Chevron, Goodway/diesel, Hess, Shell, Texaco, **food:** Burger King, Shell's Rest., Sub Factory, **lodging:** Holiday Inn, Omni Hotel, Radisson, **other:** Chevrolet, Circuit City, CompUSA, Dodge, Lincoln/Mercury, MensWhse, Mitsubishi

69 Belvedere Rd, **W...gas:** Shell, **food:** Burger King, Denny's, **lodging:** Courtyard, Hampton Inn, Holiday Inn/rest., Motel 6, Radisson Suites, **other:** U-Haul, to airport

68 US 98, Southern Blvd, **E...food:** Mobil, John's Subs, **other:** Publix/deli, **W...lodging:** Hilton

66 Forest Hill Blvd, **E...gas:** Mobil, **other:** golf, **W...gas:** Speedway

64 10th Ave N, **W...gas:** BP, Shell/diesel/24hr, **food:** Wendy's

63 6th Ave S, **W...**HOSPITAL

61 FL 812, Lantana Rd, **E...gas:** Shell, **food:** CrabHouse Rest., KFC, McDonald's, Subway, **lodging:** Motel 6, **other:** Beall's, Eckerd, Publix, **W...gas:** Mobil(2mi), **food:** Rosalita's Café, **other:** Costco Whse

60 Hypoluxo Rd, **E...gas:** Amoco, Mobil, Shell/diesel, Circle K, **food:** Pizza Hut, Subway, Taco Bell, Wendy's, **lodging:** Best Western, Comfort Inn, Super 8, **other:** Olson Tire, Sam's Club, Tire Kingdom, U-Haul, **W...gas:** Shell

59 Gateway Blvd, **E...**Shell/diesel, **W...food:** Blimpie, Chili's, McDonald's, Pete Rose Café, **lodging:** Hampton Inn, Holiday Inn, **other:** Target

57 FL 804, Boynton Bch Blvd, **E...gas:** Shell/repair, **food:** KFC, **lodging:** Holiday Inn Express, Relax Inn, **other:** HOSPITAL, USPO, **W...gas:** Chevron, Mobil, Shell, Texaco/diesel, 7-11, **food:** Checker's, Steak'n Shake, Subway, TGIFriday, Waffle House, Wendy's, **other:** Barnes&Noble, Office Depot, Old Navy, Publix, Radio Shack, Wal-Mart SuperCtr/24hr, Winn-Dixie

56 Woolbright Rd, **E...gas:** Shell, **other:** HOSPITAL, **W...gas:** Mobil/24hr, RaceTrac/24hr, **food:** Burger King, Cracker Barrel, McDonald's, Subway

52b a FL 806, Atlantic Ave, **W...gas:** Chevron, Mobil, Shell/diesel, **food:** Burger King, McDonald's, Miami Subs, Swiss Chalet, **lodging:** Holiday Inn, Marriott, **other:** Publix

51 rd 782, Linton Blvd, **E...gas:** Exxon, **food:** Abbey Rd Grill, DQ, McDonald's, OutBack Steaks, **other:** HOSPITAL, Circuit City, Dodge, Ford, Home Depot, Nissan, OfficeMax, Ross, Target, **W...gas:** Shell, **food:** BBQ, **other:** NAPA, Winn-Dixie, auto repair, museum

Pompano

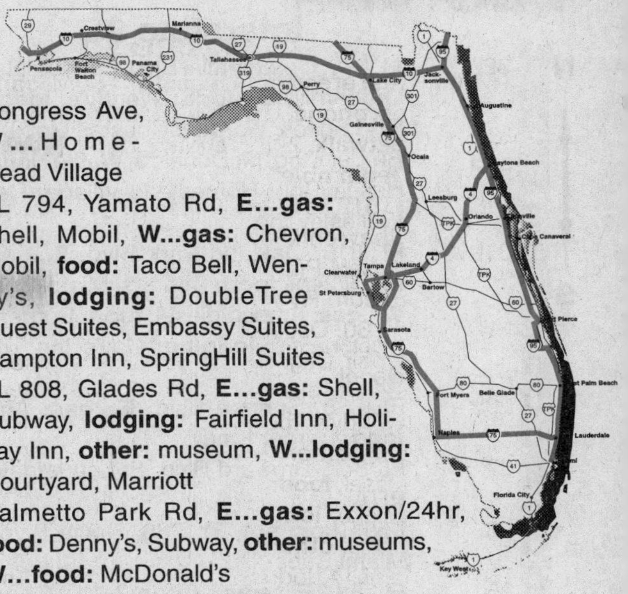

50 Congress Ave, **W...** Homestead Village

48b a FL 794, Yamato Rd, **E...gas:** Shell, Mobil, **W...gas:** Chevron, Mobil, **food:** Taco Bell, Wendy's, **lodging:** DoubleTree Guest Suites, Embassy Suites, Hampton Inn, SpringHill Suites

45 FL 808, Glades Rd, **E...gas:** Shell, Subway, **lodging:** Fairfield Inn, Holiday Inn, **other:** museum, **W...lodging:** Courtyard, Marriott

44 Palmetto Park Rd, **E...gas:** Exxon/24hr, **food:** Denny's, Subway, **other:** museums, **W...food:** McDonald's

42b a FL 810, Hillsboro Blvd, **E...gas:** Amoco, Texaco, **food:** Clock Rest., McDonald's, Popeye's, Hilton, **lodging:** La Quinta, **other:** MEDICAL CARE, Discount Parts, **W...gas:** Chevron, Mobil/diesel, **food:** Blimpie, Boston Mkt, Checker's, Denny's, Italiano Ristorante, Pizza Hut, Wolfie's Rest., **lodging:** Ramada Inn, Villager Lodge, Wellesley Inn, **other:** CompUSA, Eckerd, Home Depot

41 FL 869(toll), SW 10th, to I-75, **E...gas:** Mobil, **food:** Cracker Barrel, **lodging:** Extended Stay America, **W...lodging:** Comfort Suites, Quality Suites

39 FL 834, Sample Rd, **E...gas:** Hess, Shell/diesel, Texaco/diesel, **food:** Hops Grill(1mi), **other:** HOSPITAL, Plymouth, **W...gas:** Chevron, Mobil/diesel, Shell, Texaco/diesel, 7-11, **food:** Arby's, Blimpie, Burger King, Checker's, Cracker Barrel, Domino's, IHOP, McDonald's, Miami Subs, Subway, **other:** Costco Whse, Eckerd, Mr Grocer, Winn-Dixie

38b a Copans Rd, **E...gas:** Amoco, Mobil/7-11, **food:** McDonald's, **other:** Circuit City, Mercedes/Audi/Porsche, PepBoys, Wal-Mart, **W...gas:** Amoco/diesel, **food:** Wendy's, **other:** Home Depot, NAPA, NTB

36b a FL 814, Atlantic Blvd, to Pompano Bch, **E...food:** KFC, Miami Subs, Taco Bell, **other:** MEDICAL CARE, **1 mi W...gas:** Amoco, Mobil/diesel, Shell/repair, **other:** Chevrolet, Eckerd, Harness RaceTrack, Winn-Dixie, to FL TPK, Power Line Rd has multiple services

33b a Cypress Creek Rd, **E...gas:** Amoco, Hess, 7-11, **food:** Domino's, DownTown Pizzaria, Duffy's Diner, Jester's Grill, **lodging:** Extended Stay America, Hampton Inn, Westin Hotel, **W...gas:** Hess, Shell/repair, **food:** Arby's, Bennigan's, Burger King, Chili's, Hooters, Longhorn Steaks, McDonald's, StarLite Diner, Steak&Ale, SweetTomato, Wendy's, **lodging:** La Quinta, Marriott, Sheraton Suites, **other:** Studio+, Office Depot, OfficeMax

FLORIDA

Interstate 95

N ↕ S

Ft Lauderdale

32 FL 870, Commercial Blvd, Lauderdale by the Sea, Lauderhill, **E...food:** Wendy's, **lodging:** Crossland Suites, **W...gas:** Coastal, Mobil, Shell, **food:** Burger King, McDonald's, Waffle House, **lodging:** Holiday Inn, Homestead Village, Red Roof Inn, Wellesley Inn

31b a FL 816, Oakland Park Blvd, **E...gas:** Chevron, Mobil/24hr, **food:** Denny's, Miami Subs, Wendy's, **W...gas:** Amoco/diesel, **food:** Burger King, IHOP, McDonald's, **lodging:** Day's Inn, **other:** Home Depot

29b a FL 838, Sunrise Blvd, **E...gas:** Amoco, Shell, **food:** Burger King

27 FL 842, Broward Blvd, Ft Lauderdale, **E...**HOSPITAL

26 I-595(from sb), FL 736, Davie Blvd, **W...food:** Miami Subs

25 FL 84, **E...gas:** Citgo/7-11, Coastal/diesel, Mobil/diesel, RaceTrac/24hr, Shell, Texaco, **food:** Domino's, Dunkin Donuts, Lil Red's Rest., Little Caesar's, McDonald's, Subway, Wendy's, **lodging:** Best Western, Budget Inn, Motel 6, Sky Motel, **other:** U-Haul, Walgreen, Winn-Dixie, **W...lodging:** Ramada Inn, Red Carpet Inn, **other:** Ford Trucks

24 I-595(from nb), to I-75, **E...**to airport

23 FL 818, Griffin Rd, **E...lodging:** Hilton, Sheraton, **W...gas:** Amoco/diesel, **other:** Outdoor RV Ctr

22 FL 848, Stirling Rd, Cooper City, **E...food:** Burger King, Chevy's Mexican, Dave&Buster's, McDonald's, Taco Bell, **lodging:** Comfort Inn, Hampton Inn, SpringHill Suites, **other:** Barnes&Noble, BJ's Whse, Discount Parts, GNC, Home Depot, K-Mart/Little Caesar's, Marshall's, OfficeMax, Old Navy, Ross, to Lloyd SP, same as 21, **1/2 mi W...gas:** Circle K, **food:** Dunkin Donuts, Miami Subs, Mr M Café, Subway, **other:** MEDICAL CARE, Eckerd, PepBoys, Tire Kingdom, Walgreen

21 FL 822, Sheridan St, **E...gas:** Mobil/diesel, **food:** AleHouse Grill, Sweet Tomato, TGIFriday, **other:** Cumberland Foods, same as 22, **W...gas:** Shell, **food:** Denny's, **lodging:** Day's Inn, Holiday Inn

20 FL 820, Hollywood Blvd, **E...lodging:** Howard Johnson, **W...gas:** Mobil, **other:** HOSPITAL

19 FL 824, Pembroke Rd, **E...gas:** Shell, Texaco, **lodging:** Howard Johnson

18 FL 858, Hallandale Bch Blvd, **E...gas:** Amoco, Citgo/7-11, Exxon, Shell/Blimpie, Bakehouse Rest., **food:** BBQ, Burger King, Church's, Denny's, Dunkin Donuts, IHOP, KFC, Little Caesar's, LJ Silver, McDonald's, Miami Subs, Subway, **lodging:** Best Western, Holiday Inn Express, **other:** HOSPITAL, Goodyear/auto, Tire Kingdom, Walgreen, Winn-Dixie, laundry, **W...gas:** Amoco/Taco Bell, RaceTrac, Speedway, **other:** Discount Parts

16 Ives Dairy Rd, **E...**HOSPITAL, mall, **W...gas:** Amoco/24hr, 7-11, **food:** Subway

14 FL 860, Miami Gardens Dr, N Miami Beach, **E...**HOSPITAL, Oleta River SRA, **1/2 mi W...gas:** Amoco/24hr, Chevron, Citgo/diesel, **food:** Subway, **other:** BJ's Whse

12c US 441, FL 826, FL TPK, FL 9, **E...lodging:** Howard Johnson, Holiday Inn, **other:** HOSPITAL, **W...food:** Checker's

12b US 441(from nb), same as 12c

12a FL 868(from nb), FL TPK N, no facilities

11 NW 151st, **W...food:** McDonald's, **other:** Discount Parts, Winn-Dixie, services on US 441

10b FL 916, NW 135th, Opa-Locka Blvd, **W...gas:** Amoco, Mobil, QuikStop, **other:** motel

10a NW 125th, N Miami, Bal Harbour, **W...gas:** Shell, **food:** Burger King, Wendy's, **other:** U-Haul

9 NW 119th(from nb), **W...gas:** Amoco, **food:** BBQ, Church's, **other:** Winn-Dixie

8b FL 932, NW 103rd, **E...gas:** Exxon, Shell, 7-11, **W...gas:** Amoco, Chevron, Mobil, **food:** Dunkin Donuts

8a NW 95th, **E...gas:** Amoco, **W...gas:** Mobil, Shell, **food:** Burger King, McDonald's, **other:** HOSPITAL, Discount Parts, Ford, SavALot Foods, Walgreen

7 FL 934, NW 81st, NW 79th, **E...gas:** BP, Chevron/diesel, **W...gas:** Shell, **food:** Checker's, **lodging:** Day's Inn, **other:** Chrysler, Lincoln/Mercury, Pontiac

6b NW 69th(from sb), no facilities

6a FL 944, NW 62nd, NW 54th, **W...gas:** Shell, **food:** Burger King, McDonald's, Subway, **other:** AutoZone, U-Haul, Winn-Dixie

Miami

4b a I-195 E, Miami Beach, FL 112 W(toll), **E...**downtown, **W...**airport

3b NW 8th St(from sb)

3a FL 836 W(toll)(exits left from nb), **W...**HOSPITAL, to Orange Bowl, airport

2d I-395 E(exits left from sb), to Miami Beach

2c NW 8th, NW 14th(from sb), Miami Ave, **E...**Port of Miami, **W...**to Orange Bowl

2b NW 2nd(from nb), downtown Miami

2a US 1(exits left from sb), Biscayne Blvd, downtown Miami

1b US 41, SW 7th, SW 8th, Brickell Ave, downtown, **E...lodging:** Extended Stay America, Hampton Inn, **other:** Publix, Walgreen, **W...gas:** Shell

1a SW 25th(from sb), downtown, to Rickenbacker Causeway, Key Biscayne, **E...lodging:** Hampton Inn, **other:** museum, to Baggs SRA

0mm I-95 begins/ends on US 1. **1 mi S...gas:** Citgo

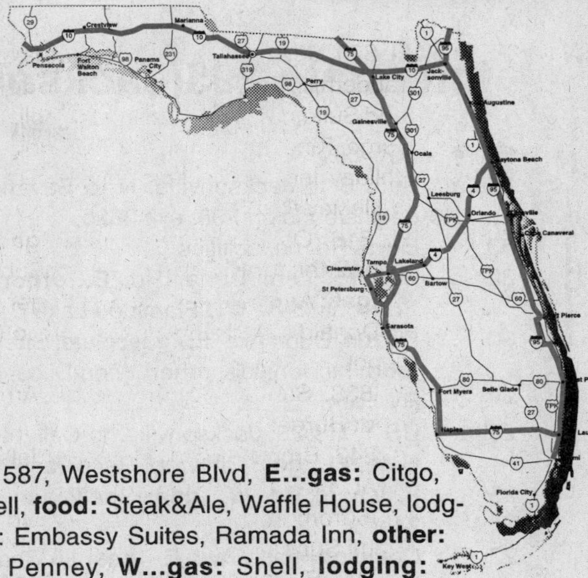

Interstate 275(Tampa)

N ↕ S

Exit #	Services
59mm	I-275 begins/ends on I-75, exit 274.
53	Bearss Ave, **E...gas:** Citgo, **W...gas:** Amoco, Chevron/diesel, Shell, food: BBQ, Burger King, McDonald's, Subway, Wendy's, lodging: Holiday Inn Express, other: Albertson's, Eckerd, GNC, Publix, Radio Shack
52	Fletcher Ave, **E...lodging:** Day's Inn, **other:** HOSPITAL, **W...gas:** BP, Citgo, **lodging:** Americana Inn
51	FL 582, Fowler Ave, **E...gas:** Shell, **food:** Burger King, McDonald's, Subway, **lodging:** Howard Johnson, Quality Inn, **W...gas:** Citgo, **lodging:** Discovery Inn, Motel 6, SleepRite Motel, **other:** **Audi**
50	FL 580, Busch Blvd, **E...gas:** Amoco, Exxon, **lodging:** Best Western, Red Roof Inn, **other:** Busch Gardens, **W...food:** KFC, **other:** flea mkt, dogtrack
49	Bird Ave(from nb), **W...gas:** Shell, Wendy's, K-Mart
48	Sligh Ave, **E...gas:** Amoco, Coastal, Spur, **W...gas:** BP, PitStop/gas, **other:** zoo
47b a	US 92, to US 41 S, Hillsborough Ave, **E...gas:** Citgo, **other:** Discount Parts, **W...gas:** Amoco
46b	FL 574, MLK Blvd, **E...gas:** Chevron, **other:** Kash&Karry, **W...other:** Cumberland Farms, McDonald's
46a	Floribraska Ave, HOSPITAL
45b	I-4 E, to Orlando, I-75
45a	Jefferson St, downtown E
44	Ashley Dr, Tampa St, downtown W
42	Howard Ave, Armenia Ave, **E...gas:** Citgo, **W...gas:** Amoco, Shell/diesel, **food:** Popeye's, **other:** HOSPITAL
41c	Himes Ave(from sb), **W...**Tampa Stadium
41b a	US 92, Dale Mabry Blvd, **E...gas:** Amoco/24hr, BP, Citgo/Hardee's, Exxon, Shell, **food:** Alexander's Rest., Carrabba's, Hops Grill, Japanese Steaks, Krystal, Lobster Louie's Crabs, Miami Subs, Pizza Hut, Rio Bravo, Ruby Tuesday, Village Inn Pancakes, **lodging:** Courtyard, **other:** MEDICAL CARE, Borders Books&Café, Office Depot, to MacDill AFB, **W...gas:** Exxon/diesel, Bennigan's, Blimpie, Burger King, Checker's, Chili's, Denny's, Dunkin Donuts, Eastside Mario's Café, LongHorn Steaks, McDonald's, Sweet Tomatos, Taco Bell, Tia's TexMex, Waffle House, Wendy's, **lodging:** Day's Inn, Howard Johnson, other: Best Buy, Circuit City, Home Depot, Wal-Mart
40b	Lois Ave, **W...gas:** Radiant/diesel, **lodging:** Westin Suites
40a	FL 587, Westshore Blvd, **E...gas:** Citgo, Shell, **food:** Steak&Ale, Waffle House, lodging: Embassy Suites, Ramada Inn, **other:** JC Penney, **W...gas:** Shell, **lodging:** Crowne Plaza, DoubleTree Hotel, Marriott
39b a	FL 60 W, **2 mi W...lodging:** Day's Inn, to airport
32	Fl 687 S, 4th St N, to US 92(no sb re-entry), no facilities
31b	FL 688 W, Ulmerton Rd, to Largo, info, airport
31a	9th St N, MLK St N(exits left from sb), no facilities
30	FL 686, Roosevelt Blvd, no facilities
28	FL 694 W, Gandy Blvd, Indian Shores, no facilities
26b a	54th Ave N, no facilities
25	38th Ave N, to beaches
24	22nd Ave N, **E...**Sunken Garden, **W...other:** Home Depot
23b	FL 595, 5th Ave N, **E...**HOSPITAL
23a	I-375, **E...**The Pier, Waterfront, downtown
22	I-175 E, Tropicana Fields, **E...**HOSPITAL
21	46th St, downtown
20	31st Ave(from nb), downtown
19	22nd Ave S, Gulfport, **W...**Citgo
18	26th Ave S(from nb)
17	FL 682 W, 54th Ave S, Pinellas Bayway, **W...food:** Bob Evans, Burger King, McDonald's, Taco Bell, **lodging:** Krystal Inn, Park Inn, to Ft DeSoto Pk, St Pete Beach
16	Pinellas Point Dr, Skyway Lane, to Maximo Park, **W...**marina
16mm	toll plaza sb
13mm	N Skyway Fishing Pier, **W...rest area both lanes, full(handicapped)facilities, phone, vending, picnic tables, litter barrels, petwalk**
10mm	Tampa Bay
7mm	S Skyway Fishing Pier, **E...rest area both lanes, full(handicapped)facilities, phone, vending, picnic tables, litter barrels, petwalk**
6mm	toll plaza nb
5	US 19, Palmetto, Bradenton, no facilities
2	US 41, Palmetto, Bradenton, no facilities
0mm	I-275 begins/ends on I-75, exit 228.

Tampa

St Petersburg

Interstate 295(Jacksonville)

Exit #	Services
35b a	I-95, S to Jacksonville, N to Savannah. I-295 begins/ends on I-95, exit 362b.
33	Duval Rd, no facilities
32	FL 115, Lem Turner Rd, **E...other:** Wal-Mart SuperCtr/24hr, **W...**Flamingo Lake Camping
30	FL 104, Dunn Ave, **E...gas:** Gate, Shell/24hr(1mi), **food:** McDonald's, **other:** Winn-Dixie, **W...**BigTree RV Park
28b a	US 1, US 23, Jacksonville, to Callahan, **E...gas:** Gate, **W...gas:** Chevron, RaceTrac/24hr
25	Pritchard Rd, **W...gas:** Shell/Taco Bell/diesel/24hr
22	Commonwealth Ave, **E...gas:** Lil Champ, Sprint, **food:** Hardee's, **lodging:** Holiday Inn, **other:** Winn-Dixie, dogtrack, **W...**Goodyear
21b a	I-10, W to Tallahassee, E to Jacksonville
19	FL 228, Normandy Blvd, **E...gas:** Amoco/24hr, Shell/diesel, **food:** Burger King, McDonald's, **other:** Food Lion, Walgreen, cleaners, st patrol, **W...gas:** Hess, RaceTrac, Shell, **food:** Hardee's, Pizza Hut, Popeye's, Subway, **other:** Discount Parts, Eckerd, Family$, K-Mart, Publix, Radio Shack, Winn-Dixie
17	FL 208, Wilson Blvd, **E...gas:** BP/diesel, Citgo/diesel/24hr, Exxon, **food:** Fazoli's, Hardee's, McDonald's(2mi), Ryan's(2mi), TCBY, **other:** Winn-Dixie(2mi)
16	FL 134, 103rd St, Cecil Field, **E...gas:** Gate/diesel, Hess, Shell/24hr, Texaco/diesel, **food:** Applebee's, Burger King, Popeye's, Wendy's, **lodging:** Hospitality Inn, **other:** Discount Parts, **W...gas:** Amoco, Chevron, Exxon/diesel, Shell, **food:** BBQ, DQ, Dragon Garden Chinese, Dunkin Donuts, IHOP, KFC, McDonald's, Miami Subs, Pizza Hut, Rally's, Subway, Taco Bell, **other:** Family$, Goodyear/auto, Publix, Walgreen, Winn-Dixie
12	FL 21, Blanding Blvd, **E...gas:** Chevron/diesel, RaceTrac, **food:** Burger King, Larry's Subs, Pizza Hut, **other:** Acura, Cadillac, Eckerd, Ford, Office Depot, Publix, Saturn, oyota, **W...gas:** Amoco, Chevron, Shell, **food:** Arby's, Bennigan's, Chili's, ChuckeCheese, Cross Creek BBQ/steaks, Denny's, Longhorn Steaks, Olive Garden, Outback Steaks, Papa John's, Red Lobster, Rio Bravo, Shoney's, Steak&Ale, Taco Bell, Tony Roma, **lodging:** Economy Motel, Hampton Inn, La Quinta, Motel 6, Red Roof Inn, **other:** HOSPITAL, Circuit City, Discount Tire, Gayfer's, Home Depot, Sam's Club, Sears/auto, Target, mall
10	US 17, FL 15, Roosevelt Blvd, Orange Park, **E... lodging:** Wilson Inn, **W...gas:** Amoco, Chevron/diesel/24hr, RaceTrac, Shell, **food:** Cracker Barrel, Damon's, Krystal, LJ Silver, McDonald's, Pizza Hut, Quincy's, Waffle House, Wendy's, **lodging:** Best Western, Comfort Inn, Day's Inn, Holiday Inn, Villager Lodge, **other:** Chrysler, Honda, Nissan, VW
7mm	St Johns River, Buckman Br
5b a	FL 13, San Jose Blvd, **E...gas:** Exxon/diesel/24hr, Shell, **food:** Applebee's, Arby's, Famous Amos, TCBY, **lodging:** Baymont Inn, Ramada Inn, **other:** Albertson's, Eckerd, Firestone/auto, Publix, **W...gas:** Shell, **food:** Baskin-Robbins, BBQ, Burger King, Chili's, Golden China, Golden Corral, Krispy Kreme, Mozzarella's Café, Pizza Hut, Renna's Pizza, Schlotsky's, **other:** Barnes&Noble, BooksAMillion, Fresh Mkt, Michael's, NAPA, Radio Shack, Sears, SteinMart, Wal-Mart
3	Old St Augustine Rd, **E...gas:** Amoco, Shell, **food:** Burger King, Denny's, McDonald's, Pizza Hut, Taco Bell, Wendy's, **other:** $General, Eckerd, Publix, Sing Food, Winn-Dixie, **W...gas:** Chevron, Lil Champ, **other:** MEDICAL CARE, Lowe's Whse, Walgreen
0mm	I-295 begins/ends on I-95, exit 337.

N ↕ S

Jacksonville

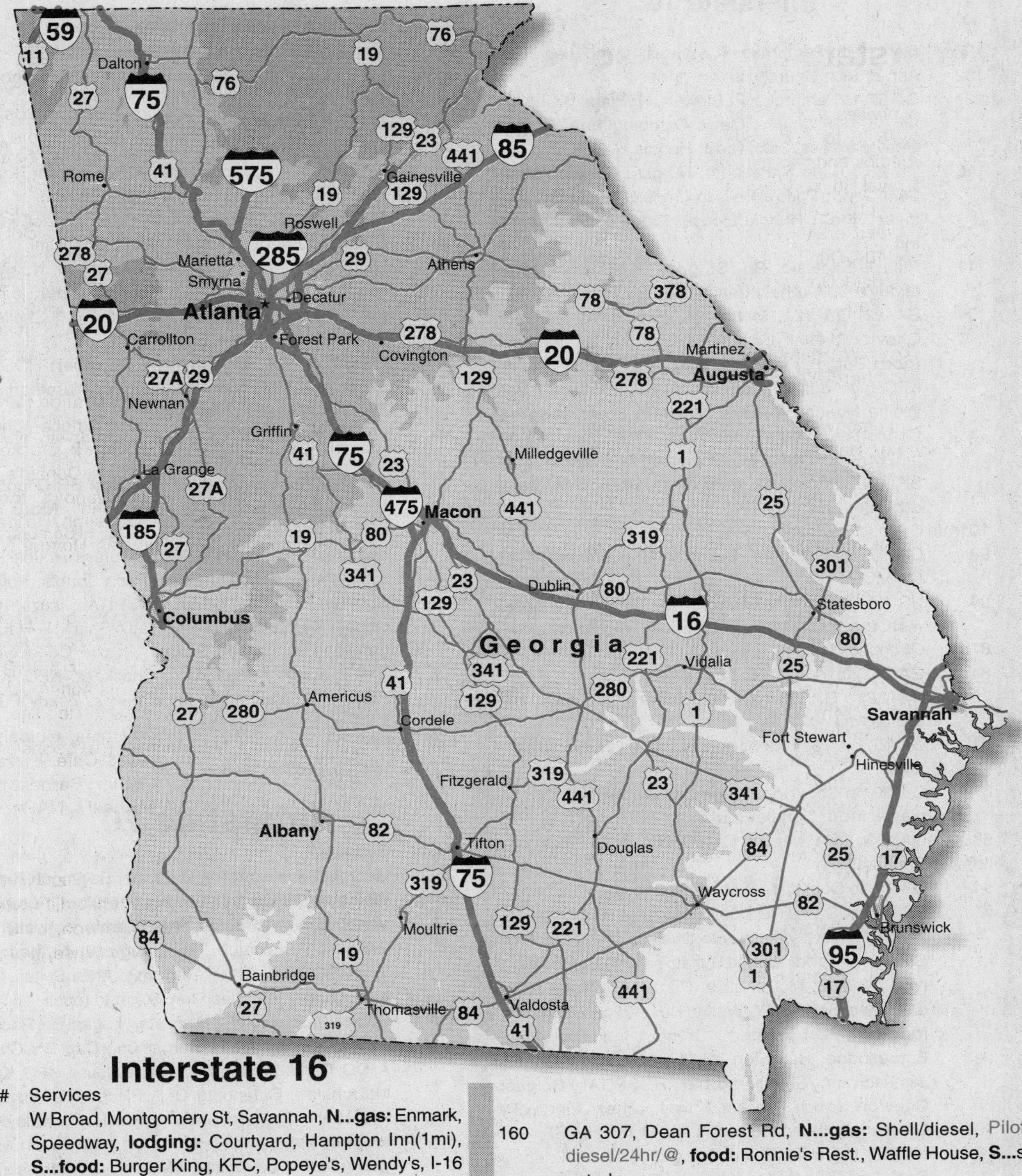

Interstate 16

E ↑ Savannah ↓ W

Exit #	Services
167	W Broad, Montgomery St, Savannah, **N...gas:** Enmark, Speedway, **lodging:** Courtyard, Hampton Inn(1mi), **S...food:** Burger King, KFC, Popeye's, Wendy's, I-16 begins/ends in Savannah.
166	US 17, Gwinnet St, Savannah, no facilities
165	GA 204, 37th St(from eb), to Ft Pulaski NM, Savannah Coll
164b a	I-516, US 80, US 17, GA 21, **1 mi S...lodging:** Budget Inn, Courtyard, Day's Inn, Holiday Inn, La Quinta
162	Chatham Pkwy, **S...gas:** Shell/Taco Maker/diesel, **other:** Lexus, Toyota
160	GA 307, Dean Forest Rd, **N...gas:** Shell/diesel, Pilot/diesel/24hr/@, **food:** Ronnie's Rest., Waffle House, **S...**st patrol
157b a	I-95, S to Jacksonville, N to Florence, no facilities
155	Pooler Pkwy, no facilities
152	GA 17, to Bloomingdale, no facilities
148	Old River Rd, to US 80, no facilities
144mm	weigh sta both lanes
143	US 280, to US 80, **N...gas:** Citgo(2mi), **S...gas:** BP, El Cheapo/diesel/café/@, **other:** Black Creek Café/golf

GEORGIA

Interstate 16

E ↕ W

(3mi)
137 GA 119, to Pembroke, Ft Stewart, no facilities
132 Ash Branch Church Rd, no facilities
127 GA 67, to Pembroke, Ft Stewart, **N...gas:** El Cheapo/diesel, Shell/diesel, Oasis Camping(1mi), **S...gas:** Chevron/diesel/24hr, **food:** Huddle House
116 US 25/301, to Statesboro, **N...gas:** Chevron/diesel/24hr, **food:** PoJo's Deli, to GA S U, **S...gas:** Shell/diesel, **food:** Huddle House, **lodging:** Red Carpet Inn
111 Pulaski-Excelsior Rd, **S...gas:** Citgo/diesel, **food:** Grady's Grill, **other:** Beaver Run RV Park
104 GA 22, GA 121, Metter, **N...gas:** BP/diesel/24hr, Chevron/diesel, Exxon, Phillips 66, Shell/diesel, **food:** Burger King, DQ, Hardee's, Huddle House, KFC/Taco Bell, McDonald's, Subway, Village Pizza, Waffle House, Wendy's, Western Steer, **lodging:** Comfort Inn, Day's Inn, Holiday Inn Express, Metter Inn, **other:** HOSPITAL, Chevrolet, Rite Aid, to Smith SP, RV camping, **S...gas:** Citgo, Phillips 66/diesel, **other:** Ford
101mm Canoochee River
98 GA 57, to Stillmore, **S...gas:** Amoco/diesel/24hr, Chevron/diesel
90 US 1, to Swainsboro, **N...gas:** BP, Citgo, Pure/diesel/rest., **food:** Oak Island Crabhouse, **other:** repair
87mm Ohoopee River
84 GA 297, to Vidalia, **N...**truck sales
78 US 221, GA 56, to Swainsboro, **N...gas:** BP/diesel(1mi)
71 GA 15, GA 78, to Soperton, **N...gas:** Chevron/diesel/24hr
67 GA 29, to Soperton, **S...gas:** Chevron/diesel, Citgo/diesel, **food:** Huddle House
58 GA 199, Old River Rd, East Dublin, no facilities

Dublin

56mm Oconee River
54 GA 19, to Dublin, **1 mi N...gas:** Chevron
51 US 441, US 319, to Dublin, **N...gas:** Amoco/diesel/24hr, BP/Subway/diesel, Exxon/diesel, Pilot/diesel/@, Shell/24hr, **food:** Arby's, Buffalo's Café, Burger King, KFC, Krystal, McDonald's, Pizza Hut, Ruby Tuesday, Taco Bell/TCBY, Waffle House/24hr, Wendy's, **lodging:** Best Western, Comfort Inn, Day's Inn, Econolodge, Hampton Inn, Holiday Inn Express, Jameson Inn, Super 8, **other:** HOSPITAL, **S...gas:** Chevron, **food:** Cracker Barrel, **other:** Pinetucky Camping(2mi), antiques, to Little Ocmulgee SP
49 GA 257, to Dublin, Dexter, **N...gas:** Chevron/Friendly Gus, **3 mi N...gas:** Shell, **food:** BBQ, Huddle House, Waffle House, Zaxby's, **other:** HOSPITAL, **S...gas:** 257 Trkstp/diesel/@
46mm rest area wb, full(handicapped)facilities, phone, picnic tables, litter barrels, vending, petwalk, RV dump
44mm rest area eb, full(handicapped)facilities, phone, picnic tables, litter barrels, vending, petwalk, RV dump
42 GA 338, to Dudley, no facilities
39 GA 26, Montrose, to Cochran, no facilities
32 GA 112, Allentown, **S...gas:** Chevron/diesel, **food:** CJ's Grill
27 GA 358, to Danville, no facilities
24 GA 96, to Jeffersonville, **N...gas:** Citgo/diesel, **S...gas:** BP/diesel/24hr, **food:** Huddle House/24hr, **lodging:** Day's Inn, **other:** to Robins AFB, museum
18 Bullard Rd, Bullard, to Jeffersonville, no facilities
12 Sgoda Rd, Huber, **N...gas:** Marathon/diesel

Macon

6 US 23, US 129A, East Blvd, Ocmulgee, **N...gas:** BP, **food:** DQ, **lodging:** Day's Inn(2mi), **other:** to airport, GA Forestry Ctr, **S...gas:** Chevron/diesel Shell/diesel, **food:** Huddle House, Subway
2 US 80, GA 87, MLK Jr Blvd, **N...other:** HOSPITAL, Ocmulgee NM, conv ctr, **S...gas:** Marathon/diesel, Saf-T-Oil/diesel, to Hist Dist
1b GA 22, to US 129, GA 49, 2nd St(from wb), **N...other:** HOSPITAL, coliseum
a US 23, Gray Hwy(from eb), **N...gas:** BP, Citgo/diesel, Exxon, Flash/diesel, Marathon, Shell, **food:** Arby's, BBQ, Burger King, Central Park, DQ, El Sombrero Mexican, Golden Corral, HongKong Express, Huddle House, Krispy Kreme, McDonald's, Papa John's, Popeye's, Subway, Taco Bell, **other:** HOSPITAL, Isuzu, Kroger, Lincoln/Mercury, Mitsubishi, Radio Shack, U-Haul, Walgreen, transmissions, **S...gas:** Amoco, Conoco/diesel, Exxon, **food:** Burger King, Checker's, KFC, Krystal, Pizza Hut, Waffle House, Wendy's, Zaxby's, **other:** Pontiac, Staples, Tires+
0mm I-75, S to Valdosta, N to Atlanta. I-16 begins/ends on I-75, exit 165 in Macon.

Interstate 20

Augusta

E ↕ W

Exit # Services
202mm Georgia/South Carolina state line, Savannah River
201mm Welcome Ctr wb, full(handicapped)facilities, phone, vending, picnic tables, litter barrels, petwalk
200 GA 104, Riverwatch Pkwy, Augusta, **N...gas:** Pilot/Wendy's/diesel/24hr/@, **lodging:** AmeriSuites, Courtyard, Quality Inn, Sleep Inn, **S...**auto repair
199 GA 28, Washington Rd, Augusta, **N...gas:** BP, RaceTrac/24hr, **food:** Applebee's, Burger King, Capt D's, Chick-fil-A, DQ, Damon's, Denny's, Huddle House, KFC, Krystal, McDonald's, Oldenburg Grill, Piccadilly's, Pizza Hut, Rhinehart's Seafood, Shogun Japanese, Waffle House, **lodging:** Day's Inn, Hampton Inn, Holiday Inn, Homewood Suites, La Quinta, Masters Inn, Radisson, Ramada Ltd, Scottish Inn, Sunset Inn, Shoney's Inn/rest., **other:** BMW/Infiniti, Hancock Fabrics, Hyundai, Lowe's Whse, Mazda, Mercedes, Toyota, **S...gas:** Amoco/24hr, Crown, 76/Circle K, Shell/diesel, **food:** Arby's, Blimpie, Bojangles, Carrabba's, China Rest., Church's, Domino's, Famous Dave's BBQ, Fazoli's, Hardee's, Hooters, Krispy Kreme, Kyoto Japanese, LoneStar Café, LJ Silver, McDonald's, Michael's Rest., Olive Garden, Outback Steaks, Red Lobster, Sonic, Subway, Taco Bell, T-Bonz

Interstate 20

E ↕ W

Steaks, TGIFriday, Thai Jong Rest., Vallarta Mexican, Waffle House, Wendy's, **lodging:** Econolodge, Fairfield Inn, Knight's Inn, Motel 6, Rodeway Inn, **other:** MEDICAL CARE, BooksAMillion, Dillard's, $General, Eckerd, FastLube, Goodyear/auto, Kroger, PepBoys, Publix, SteinMart

196b GA 232 W, **N...gas:** Amoco, Enmark, RaceTrac, 76, **food:** Applebee's, Arby's, Burger King, Checker's, China Pearl, Golden Corral, Krispy Kreme, Krystal, Ruby Tuesday, Ryan's, Salsa's Grill, Schlotsky's, Waffle House, Wendy's, **lodging:** Comfort Inn, Howard Johnson, Suburban Lodge, Travelers Inn, **other:** BiLo Foods, Home Depot, Lowe's Whse, OfficeMax, Sam's Club, Wal-Mart SuperCtr/24hr

a I-520, Bobby Jones Fwy, **S...gas:** Amoco, **other:** HOSPITAL, Best Buy, Circuit City, Target, Winn-Dixie, to airport

195 Wheeler Rd, **N...gas:** Chevron, **food:** O'Charley's, **S...gas:** BP, 76, Shell/24hr, **food:** Blimpie, **lodging:** Day's Inn, **other:** HOSPITAL, Harley-Davidson

194 GA 383, Belair Rd, to Evans, **N...gas:** Citgo/Taco Bell, Phillips 66/diesel, 76/Circle K/Blimpie/diesel, **food:** Burger King, Popeye's, Waffle House, **lodging:** Villager Lodge, **other:** Food Lion, Funsville Park, **S...gas:** Amoco/DQ/Stuckey's/diesel, Pilot/Subway/diesel/24hr/@, **food:** A&W/KFC, Cracker Barrel, Huddle House, Waffle House, **lodging:** Best Western, Econolodge, Hampton Inn, Quality Inn, Ramada Ltd, Wingate Inn

190 GA 388, to Grovetown, **N...gas:** Amoco/diesel, **food:** Waffle House, **S...gas:** Chevron/diesel, 76, KFC, **food:** McDonald's, Subway, TPS Grill

187mm weigh sta both lanes

183 US 221, Appling, to Harlem, **N...gas:** 76, **other:** Ford, **S...gas:** BP/diesel

182mm rest area both lanes, full(handicapped)facilities, phone, vending, picnic tables, litter barrels, RV dump, petwalk

175 GA 150, **N...gas:** Samuels/diesel/rest./24hr/@, **lodging:** Day's Inn, **other:** to Mistletoe SP

Thomson

172 US 78, GA 17, Thomson, **N...gas:** BP/diesel, Chevron/diesel, **food:** Waffle House, **other:** Chrysler/Dodge/Jeep, Ford/Mercury, Pontiac/GMC, **S...gas:** Amoco/DQ/diesel/24hr, Bryants, RaceTrac/diesel, 76/Blimpie/Circle K, Shell/diesel, **food:** Amigo's Mexican, Arby's, Burger King, Denny's, Domino's, Hardee's, LJ Silver, McDonald's, Pizza Hut, Taco Bell, Waffle House, Wendy's, Western Sizzlin, **lodging:** Best Western, Econolodge, Holiday Inn Express, Howard Johnson, **other:** HOSPITAL, Advance Parts, AutoZone, BiLo Foods, Buick/Chevrolet/Cadillac, CVS Drug, Family$, Food Lion, K-Mart, Lowe's Whse

165 GA 80, Camak, no facilities

160 E Cadley Rd, Norwood, no facilities

154 US 278, GA 12, Barnett, no facilities

148 GA 22, Crawfordville, **N...gas:** Amoco/diesel, **other:** to Stephens SP, **S...gas:** Pure/diesel/rest./motel/repair/@

138 GA 77, Siloam, **S...gas:** Amoco/diesel, Exxon, **other:** HOSPITAL

130 GA 44, Greensboro, weigh sta, **N...gas:** Amoco/diesel/24hr, Exxon/Subway, **food:** McDonald's, Pizza Hut, Waffle House, Wendy's, Zaxby's, **lodging:** Jameson Inn, Microtel, Thrift Court, **other:** HOSPITAL, Motel(3mi), **S...gas:** Chevron/diesel/24hr

121 Buckhead, to Lake Oconee, **S...gas:** Phillips 66

Madison

114 US 441, US 129, to Madison, **N...gas:** Chevron/Subway, Citgo, Exxon, Pilot/diesel/24hr/@, RaceTrac, **food:** Arby's, Burger King, KFC, Krystal, McDonald's, Pizza Hut, Waffle House, Wendy's, Zaxby's, **lodging:** Comfort Inn, Day's Inn, Hampton Inn, **other:** HOSPITAL, BiLo Foods, Chevrolet/Pontiac/GMC, Ingles Foods, Wal-Mart/drugs, **S...gas:** TA/BP/Popeye's/Taco Bell/diesel/@, FuelMart/diesel, Texaco, **food:** Waffle House, **lodging:** Budget Inn, Holiday Inn Express, Ramada Inn, Super 8, **other:** RV camping

113 GA 83, Madison, **N...gas:** BP, **other:** HOSPITAL, st patrol

108mm rest area wb, full(handicapped)facilities, phone, picnic tables, litter barrels, vending, RV dump, petwalk

105 Rutledge, Newborn, **N...gas:** BP/diesel, **food:** Yesterday Café, **other:** Hard Labor Creek SP

103mm rest area eb, full(handicapped)facilities, phone, picnic tables, litter barrels, vending, RV dump, petwalk

101 US 278, no facilities

98 GA 11, to Monroe, Monticello, **4 mi N...gas:** Amoco, **food:** Blue Willow Inn/rest., Log Cabin Rest., Sycamore Grill, **S...gas:** BP, Chevron/diesel

95mm Alcovy River

93 GA 142, Hazelbrand Rd, **S...gas:** Exxon/diesel, Shell/24hr, **food:** Little Philly's Hoagies, Waffle House, **lodging:** Jameson Inn, **other:** HOSPITAL

92 Alcovy Rd, **N...gas:** Chevron/diesel, Circle K/diesel, **food:** BBQ, Chick-fil-A, Krystal, McDonald's, Pizza Hut, Waffle House, Wendy's, **lodging:** Best Western/rest., Cornerstone Lodge, Day's Inn, Econolodge, Holiday Inn Express, **S...**HOSPITAL

90 US 278, GA 81, Covington, **S...gas:** BP, Citgo, RaceTrac, Shell, **food:** Arby's, Bojangles, Burger King, Capt D's, Checker's, DQ, Hardee's, KFC, Nagano Japanese, Papa John's, Shoney's, Taco Bell/Pizza Hut, Waffle House, Zaxby's, **other:** Advance Parts, Chevrolet, $General, Eckerd, Ingles Foods, K-Mart, SaveRite Foods, Tire Depot

88 Almon Rd, to Porterdale, **N...gas:** Chevron/diesel, **S...gas:** BP/Blimpie, **other:** Riverside Estates RV Camp, transmissions/repair

GEORGIA

Interstate 20

E ↕ W

Conyers

84 GA 162, Salem Rd, to Pace, **N...gas:** BJ's Whse/gas, **other:** Saturn, Super 1 RV Ctr, **S...gas:** BP/Amoco, Chevron/24hr, Phillips 66, RaceTrac, **food:** Burger King, China Kitchen, Hardee's, Los Bravos Mexican, QuikChick Express, Subway, Waffle House, **other:** Advance Parts, Eckerd, Medicine Shoppe, SaveRite Foods

83mm parking area wb

82 GA 138, GA 20, Conyers, **N...gas:** Amoco, BP/ diesel/repair, Speedway/diesel, **food:** Blimpie, ChuckeCheese, Cracker Barrel, Don Pablo, Golden Corral, IHOP, O'Charley's, On the Border, Outback Steaks, Red Lobster, Roadhouse Grill, Sonic, **lodging:** Conyers Inn, Day's Inn, Hampton Inn, Jameson Inn, La Quinta, Ramada Ltd, **other:** Chevrolet, Circuit City, Ford, Goody's, Home Depot, Kohl's, Michael's, NAPA, Office Depot, Old Navy, Staples, Tires+, U-Haul, Wal-Mart SuperCtr/24hr, **S...gas:** Chevron/24hr, QT, Shell/diesel, **food:** Arby's, Applebee's, Burger King, Capt D's, Checker's, Chili's, Chick-fil-A, Chihuahua Mexican, CiCi's, City Buffet, Donato's Pizza, Hooters, Huddle House, KFC, Krystal/24hr, LJ Silver, McDonald's, Milano Italian, Papa John's, Piccadilly's, Pizza Hut, Popeye's, Ruby Tuesday, Ryan's, Subway, Taco Bell, TCBY, Waffle House, Wendy's, **lodging:** InTown Inn, Suburban Lodge, **other:** Big 10 Tire, Cub Foods, Dodge, $General, Eckerd, Firestone/auto, GNC, Goodyear/auto, Honda, Jo-Ann Fabrics, Kroger/24hr, NTB, PepBoys, Publix, Radio Shack, Rite Aid, Target, Toyota, USPO, mall

80 West Ave, Conyers, **N...gas:** Exxon/diesel, Shell/ diesel, Speedway/diesel, **food:** Burger King, DQ, Domino's, Mrs Winner's, Subway, **lodging:** Holiday Inn, Richfield Lodge, **other:** Family$, Piggly Wiggly, **S...gas:** Exxon/diesel/24hr, **food:** Longhorn Steaks, McDonald's, Waffle House, **lodging:** Comfort Inn, **other:** Chrysler/Plymouth/Jeep, Ford, Hyundai, Just-Brakes, Kia, Mitsubishi, Nissan

79mm parking area eb

78 Sigman Rd, **N...gas:** Circle K/gas, **food:** Waffle House, **S...other:** Buick/Pontiac/GMC/Mazda, Crown RV Ctr, st police

Lithonia

75 US 278, GA 124, Turner Hill Rd, **N...gas:** BP/diesel, Citgo/diesel/24hr, **S...food:** Applebee's, Bugaboo Steaks, Chick-fil-A, KFC/Pizza Hut/Taco Bell, McDonald's, Olive Garden, **lodging:** AmeriSuites, **other:** Best Buy, Borders Books, Dillard's, JC Penney, Marshall's, Sears/auto, Staples, Tires+, mall

74 GA 124, Lithonia, **N...gas:** Chevron/24hr, Phillips 66, Shell, **food:** Capt D's, KFC/Taco Bell, McDonald's, Pizza Hut, Robert's Café, Waffle House, Wendy's, **S...gas:** Citgo/diesel/24hr, **food:** DQ, Krystal/24hr, Snuffy's Grille, Waffle House, **lodging:** Howard Johnson, **other:** CVS Drug, $General, Piggly Wiggly, Radio Shack

Atlanta Area

71 Hillandale Dr, Farrington Rd, Panola Rd, **N...gas:** Exxon/ diesel, QT/diesel, Shell/diesel, **food:** Burger King, C'est Bon Cajun, Checker's, Cracker Barrel, HotWings/pizza, KFC, McDonald's, Waffle House, Wendy's, **lodging:** Holiday Inn Express, Motel 6, Super 8, **S...gas:** BP/diesel/ 24hr, Citgo, Shell, **food:** IHOP, New China, Philly Connection, Popeye's, Wendy's, **lodging:** Sleep Inn, **other:** NAPA AutoCare, Publix, Tires+, Walgreen

68 Wesley Chapel Rd, Snapfinger Rd, **N...gas:** Exxon/diesel, Shell/diesel, **food:** Blimpie, Capt D's, Checker's, Chick-fil-A, China Café, Church's, Hardee's, KFC, LJ Silver, Popeye's, Subway, Taco Bell, 3$ Café, Waffle House, Wendy's, **lodging:** Day's Inn, Motel 6, **other:** MEDICAL CARE, Ford, GNC, Goodyear/auto, Home Depot, Ingles Foods, Wal-Mart, **S...gas:** BP, Chevron/24hr, Shell/diesel, **food:** Burger King, DQ, McDonald's, Pizza Hut, **lodging:** Super Inn

67b a I-285, S to Macon, N to Greenville

66 Columbia Dr(from eb, no return), **N...gas:** Citgo

65 GA 155, Candler Rd, to Decatur, **N...gas:** Amoco/24hr, Citgo, **food:** Blimpie, Dundee's Café, LJ Silver, Pizza Hut, Red Lobster, Supreme Fish Delight, Wendy's, **lodging:** Discover Inn, Econolodge, Howard Johnson, **other:** A-1 Foods, CVS Drug, U-Haul, **S...gas:** Chevron/24hr, Conoco, Circle K, Shell/diesel, **food:** Arby's, Burger King, Checker's, China Café, Church's, DQ, KFC, McDonald's, Rally's, Ruby Tuesday, Taco Bell, WK Wings, **lodging:** Best Western, Candler Inn, Ramada Ltd, Sunset Lodge, **other:** MEDICAL CARE, Advance Parts, Firestone/auto, JC Penney, Kroger, PepBoys, Winn-Dixie, mall

63 Gresham Rd, **S...gas:** Amoco/24hr, Citgo, Shell, **food:** Church's, **other:** auto repair

62 Flat Shoals Rd(from eb, no return), **N...gas:** Chevron, Shell

61b GA 260, Glenwood Ave, **N...gas:** BP, Chevron, **food:** KFC

a Maynard Terrace(from eb, no return), no facilities

60b a US 23, Moreland Ave, **N...gas:** Exxon, **lodging:** Atlanta Motel, **S...gas:** BP/Chinese Rest./diesel, Shell, **food:** Checker's, KFC/Taco Bell, Krystal, LJ Silver, McDonald's, Mrs Winner's, Wendy's

59b Memorial Dr, Glenwood Ave(from eb), no facilities

a Blvd, Cyclorama, **N...gas:** Chevron/Blimpie/diesel, **other:** Confederate Ave Complex, MLK Site, **S...gas:** BP

58b Hill St(from wb, no return), no facilities

a Capitol St(from wb, no return), downtown, **N...**to GA Dome, **S...**Holiday Inn

57 I-75/85, no facilities

56b Windsor St(from eb), stadium

a US 19, US 29, McDaniel St, **N...gas:** Chevron

55b Lee St(from wb), Ft McPherson, **S...gas:** BP, **food:** Church's, Popeye's, Taco Bell

a Ashby St, **S...gas:** BP, Exxon, **food:** Taco Bell, **other:** Eckerd, Sears, mall

54 Langhorn St(from wb), to Cascade Rd

53 MLK Dr, to GA 139, **N...gas:** Shell/diesel, **other:** laundry, **S...gas:** BP

Interstate 20

E ↕ W

52b a GA 280, Holmes Dr, High Tower Rd, **N...gas:** BP, **food:** Church's, McDonald's, **S...gas:** Exxon

51b a I-285, S to Montgomery, N to Chattanooga

49 GA 70, Fulton Ind Blvd, **N...gas:** Citgo/diesel/24hr, **food:** Capt D's, Hardee's, Mrs Winners, Subway, Wendy's, **lodging:** Fulton Inn, Masters Inn, Ramada Inn, Summit Inn, **S...gas:** Chevron, Citgo/diesel, Shell, **food:** Arby's, Las Cortas Mexican, McDonald's, Waffle House, **lodging:** Comfort Inn, Super 8, Travelodge

48mm Chattahoochee River

47 Six Flags Pkwy(from wb), **N...gas:** Amoco, **food:** Church's, Waffle House, **lodging:** La Quinta, Mark Inn, Sleep Inn, Wingate Inn, **other:** Arrowhead Camping, **S...lodging:** Comfort Inn, Day's Inn, **other:** Sam's Club, Six Flags Funpark

46b a Riverside Parkway, **N...gas:** Citgo, Marathon, QT, **food:** Waffle House, **lodging:** La Quinta, **other:** EZ Wash, **S...food:** Wendy's, **lodging:** Day's Inn, **other:** Sam's Club, Six Flags Funpark

44 GA 6, Thornton Rd, to Lithia Springs, **N...gas:** BP/24hr, Exxon/diesel, Phillips 66, RaceTrac, Shell, **food:** Burger King, Chick-fil-A, Courtini's Café, Hardee's, IHOP, Krystal, McDonald's, Shoney's, Subway, Taco Bell, Waffle House, Wendy's, **lodging:** Budget Inn, Hampton Inn, Knight's Inn, Shoney's Inn, Suburban Lodge, **other:** HOSPITAL, Chevrolet, CVS Drug, Ford, Kroger, Mazda, Nissan, VW, **S...lodging:** Country Inn Suites, Courtyard, Fairfield Inn, Motel 6, SpringHill Suites, **other:** Buick/GMC, Chrysler/Plymouth/Jeep, Dodge, KOA, Mitsubishi, Toyota, Wal-Mart SuperCtr/24hr, to Sweetwater Creek SP

42mm weigh sta eb

41 Lee Rd, to Lithia Springs, **N...gas:** Citgo/diesel, **food:** Hardee's, **other:** transmissions, **S...gas:** Shell, **food:** Blimpie, Waffle House

37 GA 92, to Douglasville, **N...gas:** Chevron, Citgo, RaceTrac, Shell/diesel/24hr, **food:** Arby's, BBQ, Burger King, Capt D's, Checker's, Chick-fil-A, Church's, Cracker Barrel, DQ, Hong Kong Buffet, Kenny's Rest., KFC, Krystal, McDonald's, Mrs Winner's, Papa John's, Pizza Hut, Subway, Taco Bell, Waffle House, Wendy's, **lodging:** Bilbo's Motel, Comfort Inn, Country Inn Suites, Day's Inn, Holiday Inn Express, Ramada Ltd, Super 8, **other:** HOSPITAL, Advance Parts, AutoZone, Dodge, $General, Gordy Tires, Kroger/24hr, **S...gas:** QT, RaceTrac, Shell/diesel, **food:** Pizza Hut, **other:** Aamco, Eckerd, Ingles Food, Winn-Dixie

36 Chapel Hill Rd, **N...HOSPITAL, S...gas:** BP/McDonald's/diesel/24hr, QT/24hr, Shell, **food:** Applebee's, Arby's, Blimpie, China Buffet, Hops Grill, Joe's Crabshack, Logan's Roadhouse, O'Charley's, Olive Garden, Outback Steaks, Rio Bravo, Souper Salad, TGIFriday, Waffle House, **lodging:** Hampton Inn, InTown Suites, Super 8, **other:** Borders, Circuit City, Dillard's, Eckerd, Firestone/auto, Marshall's, Michael's, OfficeMax, Old Navy, Sears/auto, Target, mall

Douglasville

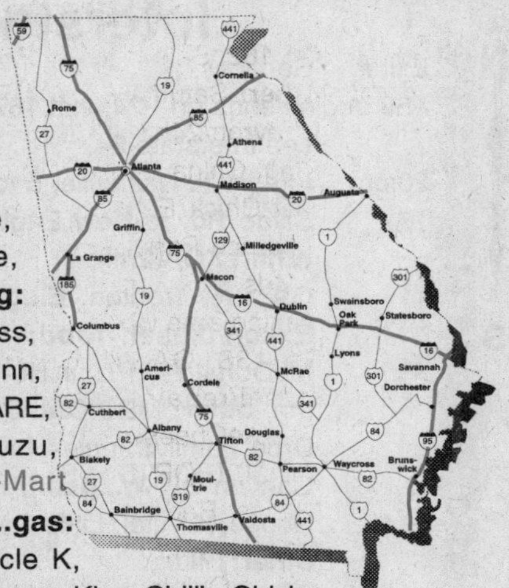

34 GA 5, to Douglasville, **N...gas:** RaceTrac, Shell, **food:** Hooters, Huddle House, Waffle House, Zaxby's, **lodging:** Holiday Inn Express, Quality Inn, Sleep Inn, **other:** MEDICAL CARE, $Tree, Honda/Isuzu, Sam's Club, Wal-Mart SuperCtr/24hr, **S...gas:** Chevron/24hr, Circle K, Shell, **food:** BBQ, Burger King, Chili's, Chick-fil-A, China Café, CiCi's, DQ, Folks Rest., Golden Corral, KFC, Krystal, LJ Silver, McDonald's, Miano's Pasta, Papa John's, Pizza Hut, Red Lobster, Ruby Tuesday, Ryan's, Subway, Taco Bell, Taco Mac, Tokyo Steaks, Waffle House, Wendy's, **lodging:** Suburban Lodge, **other:** Advance Parts, Best Buy, Cub Foods, Eckerd, Food Depot, GNC, Goodyear/auto, Home Depot, Jo-Ann Crafts, K-Mart, Kroger, Lowe's Whse, PepBoys, Publix, Radio Shack, Rite Aid, USPO

30 Post Rd, **S...gas:** Shell/diesel

26 Liberty Rd, Villa Rica, **N...gas:** Shell/diesel, **S...gas:** Wilco/Hess/diesel/24hr/@, **food:** Leather's Rest., Subway, **lodging:** American Inn

24 GA 101, GA 61, Villa Rica, **N...gas:** BP, Exxon, QT, RaceTrac, Shell/diesel, **food:** Arby's, El Tio Mexican, Hardee's, KFC/Taco Bell, Krystal, McDonald's, New China Buffet, Pizza Hut, Romero's Italian, Subway, Waffle House, Wendy's, **lodging:** Best Western, Comfort Inn, Super 8, **other:** HOSPITAL, CVS Drug, Ingles Foods, Winn-Dixie, **S...gas:** QT, Shell/diesel, **other:** Wal-Mart SuperCtr/24hr, to W GA Coll

21mm Little Tallapoosa River

19 GA 113, Temple, **N...gas:** Flying J/diesel/LP/rest./24hr/@, Pilot/Subway/Wendy's/diesel/24hr/@, **food:** BBQ, Hardee's, **S...gas:** Shell/diesel

15mm weigh sta wb

11 US 27, Bremen, Bowdon, **N...gas:** Shell/diesel, **food:** Arby's, Hardee's(2mi), McDonald's, Pizza Hut, Subway, Wendy's, **lodging:** Day's Inn, Hampton Inn, Quality Inn, **other:** HOSPITAL, $General, Ingles, Publix, Wal-Mart/grill, **S...**Shell/diesel/24hr, Waffle House, John Tanner SP

9 Waco Rd, no facilities

5 GA 100, Tallapoosa, **N...gas:** Exxon/diesel/24hr, Shell/Blimpie/diesel, **food:** Waffle House **S...gas:** Citgo/Noble/diesel/24hr/@, Big O/diesel, Pilot/KFC/Taco Bell/diesel/24hr/@, **food:** DQ, Huddle House, Waffle King, **lodging:** Comfort Inn, **other:** to John Tanner SP

1mm Welcome Ctr eb, full(handicapped)facilities, phone, vending, picnic tables, litter barrels, petwalk

0mm Georgia/Alabama state line, Eastern/Central time zone

GEORGIA

Interstate 59

N ↕ S — Trenton

Exit # Services

I-59 begins/ends on I-24, exit 167. For I-24, turn to Tennessee Interstate 24.

20mm I-24, W to Nashville, E to Chattanooga

17 Slygo Rd, to New England, **W...gas:** Citgo/diesel, **other:** KOA(2mi)

11 GA 136, Trenton, **E...gas:** Chevron/diesel, Citgo, Exxon/diesel, **food:** Asian Garden, Hardee's, McDonald's, Pizza Hut, Subway, **lodging:** Day's Inn, **other:** MEDICAL CARE, Advance Parts, CVS Drug, Family$, Ingles, Plymouth/Dodge, to Cloudland Canyon SP, **W...gas:** Amoco, Citgo, **food:** Huddle House, Krystal, Little Caesar's, Taco Bell, Wendy's, **other:** BiLo

11mm scenic area/weigh sta both lanes, litter barrels

4 Rising Fawn, **E...gas:** Citgo/diesel/24hr/@, **W...gas:** Amoco/diesel/24hr, Pilot/Subway/diesel/24hr/@, **other:** camping

0mm Georgia/Alabama state line, eastern/central time zone

Interstate 75

N ↕ S — Ringgold

Exit # Services

355mm Georgia/Tennessee state line

354mm Chickamauga Creek

353 GA 146, Rossville, **E...gas:** BP/24hr, Chevron, **lodging:** Knight's Inn, **W...gas:** Exxon/diesel/LP/24hr, Texaco, **other:** carpet outlet

352mm Welcome Ctr sb, full(handicapped)facilities, info, phone, vending, picnic tables, litter barrels, petwalk

350 GA 2, Bfd Pkwy, to Ft Oglethorpe, **E...gas:** Exxon, Sav-A-Ton/diesel, **W...gas:** Exxon/diesel, RaceTrac/24hr, Texaco, **other:** HOSPITAL, **3 mi W...gas:** Conoco/diesel/rest., **food:** BBQ Corral, Fazoli's, Taco Bell, **other:** KOA, Wal-Mart SuperCtr/24hr, to Chickamauga NP

348 GA 151, Ringgold, **E...gas:** Conoco, Golden Gallon/diesel, Texaco/diesel, **food:** Hardee's, Krystal/24hr, KFC, McDonald's, Pizza Hut, Ruby Tuesday, Subway, Taco Bell, Waffle House, **lodging:** Best Western, Day's Inn, Holiday Inn Express, Super 8, **other:** Advance Parts, CVS Drug, Chevrolet, Chrysler/Plymouth/Jeep, Family$, Ingles, RV camping, **W...gas:** Chevron/24hr, Exxon, Texaco, **food:** Wendy's, **lodging:** Comfort Inn, **other:** Ford

345 US 41, US 76, Ringgold, **E...gas:** BP, **W...gas:** Citgo/diesel/rest./24hr, Chevron, Golden Gallon, **food:** Waffle House

343mm weigh sta both lanes

341 GA 201, Tunnel Hill, to Varnell, **W...gas:** Chevron, Texaco, **other:** carpet outlets

336 US 41, US 76, Dalton, Rocky Face, **E...gas:** BP, Chevron/Blimpie, RaceTrac, Texaco, **food:** Mr Biscuit, Waffle House, **lodging:** Best Value Inn, **other:** HOSPITAL, Home Depot, **W...gas:** BP/diesel, Phillips 66, **food:** Denny's, TaGin Chinese, Tijuana Mexican, Wendy's, **lodging:** Best Western/rest., Howard Johnson, Motel 6, Royal Inn, StayLodge Inn, carpet outlets

Dalton

333 GA 52, Dalton, **E...gas:** BP/diesel, Chevron/24hr, Exxon/diesel, RaceTrac/diesel, Texaco, **food:** Applebee's, Burger King, Capt D's, Chick-fil-A, CiCi's, Cracker Barrel, Dairy Queen, Emperor Garden, Fuddrucker's, IHOP, Jimmy's Rest., JW's Rest., KFC, LJ Silver, Longhorn Steaks, Los Pablos Mexican, McDonald's, O'Charley's, Outback Steaks, Pizza Hut, Schlotsky's, Shoney's, Sonic, Steak'n Shake, Taco Bell, TCBY, Waffle House, Wendy's, **lodging:** Best Inn, Day's Inn, Hampton Inn, Travelodge, **other:** Chevrolet, Chrysler/Jeep, Ford, Isuzu, K-Mart, Kroger, Mr Transmission, Tanger Outlets/famous brands, Walgreen, **W...gas:** Texaco, **food:** Red Lobster, **lodging:** Comfort Inn, Courtyard, Country Inn Suites, Holiday Inn, Jameson Inn, Wellesley Inn, Wingate Inn, **other:** NW GA Trade/Conv Ctr

328 GA 3, to US 41, **E...gas:** BP/Blimpie, Pilot/Arby's/diesel/24hr/@, **food:** Mucho Mexico, Waffle House, Wendy's, **lodging:** Super 8, **W...**carpet outlets

326 Carbondale Rd, **E...**Chevron/diesel, **W...gas:** Citgo/diesel, Phillips 66/diesel, Pilot/diesel/@

320 GA 136, Resaca, to Lafayette, **E...gas:** Flying J/Conoco/diesel/LP/rest./24hr/@, **other:** truckwash

319mm Oostanaula River, rest area sb, full(handicapped)facilities, phone, vending, picnic tables, litter barrels, petwalk

318 US 41, Resaca, **E...gas:** Wilco/DQ/Wendy's/diesel/24hr/@, **food:** Burger King, Hardee's, **lodging:** Knight's Inn, **W...gas:** Exxon/diesel, Right Stuff Gas, **lodging:** Best Inn, Budget Inn, Duffy's Motel, Smith Motel, Super 8

317 GA 225, to Chatsworth, **E...**New Echota HS, Vann House HS

315 GA 156, Redbud Rd, to Calhoun, **E...gas:** Citgo/diesel, Exxon, **food:** Waffle House, Scottish Inn, KOA(2mi), antiques, **W...gas:** BP/Subway/diesel, Chevron, Shell, Texaco/diesel, **food:** Arby's, Shoney's, **lodging:** Best Value Inn, Howard Johnson, Ramada Ltd, **other:** HOSPITAL

Calhoun

312 GA 53, to Calhoun, **E...gas:** Texaco/diesel, **food:** Cracker Barrel, Denny's, **lodging:** Budget Host/rest., Quality Inn, Red Carpet Inn, **other:** Prime Outlets/famous brands, **W...gas:** BP/Arby's, Chevron/diesel, Citgo, Exxon, Race-Way, **food:** Bojangles, Burger King, Capt D's, Checker's, Chick-fil-A, China Cook, Dairy Queen, Domino's, Hickory House BBQ, Huddle House, IHOP, KFC, Krystal/24hr, Little Caesar's, LJ Silver, McDonald's, Pizza Hut, Ryan's, Subway, Taco Bell, Taylor's Rest., Waffle House, Wendy's, Zaxby's, **lodging:** Day's Inn, Guest Inn, Hampton Inn, Holiday Inn Express, Jameson Inn, **other:** Advance Parts, AutoZone, Chrysler/Jeep/Dodge, CVS Drug, $General, Goodyear/auto, Ingles, Kroger, Office Depot, Wal-Mart SuperCtr/gas/24hr

308mm rest area nb, full(handicapped)facilities, phone, picnic tables, litter barrels, vending, petwalk

Interstate 75

N

S

306 GA 140, Adairsville, **E...gas:** Amoco/24hr, Patty's/Texaco/diesel/24hr/@, QT/diesel, **food:** Wendy's, **lodging:** Travelodge, **W...gas:** BP/Subway, Cowboys/diesel, Exxon/diesel, **food:** Burger King, Hardee's, Taco Bell, Waffle House, **lodging:** Comfort Inn, Country Hearth Inn, Ramada Ltd, **other:** camping

296 Cassville-White Rd, **E...gas:** Amoco/diesel, Pilot/Subway/diesel/@, TA/Burger King/Popeyes/Sbarro's/diesel/24hr/@, Texaco/Blimpie/24hr, **food:** McDonald's, **W...gas:** Chevron, Citgo, Shell, Waffle House/24hr, **lodging:** Budget Host/rest., Howard Johnson, Red Carpet Inn, Super 8, Travelodge, **other:** KOA

293 US 411, to White, **E...**Shell/diesel, Texaco, Scottish Inn, **W...gas:** Chevron/diesel, Citgo/diesel/24hr, **food:** Truckline Café, Waffle House, **lodging:** Courtesy Inn, Holiday Inn, **other:** RV camping, museum, st patrol

290 GA 20, to Rome, **E...gas:** Chevron/Subway/diesel, Cowboys/diesel, Exxon/diesel, **food:** Arby's, McDonald's, Morrell's BBQ, Wendy's, **lodging:** Best Western, Comfort Inn, Country Inn Suites, Econolodge, Motel 6, Ramada Ltd, Super 8, **W...gas:** BP, Texaco, **food:** Cracker Barrel, Pruitt's BBQ, Shoney's, Waffle House, **lodging:** Day's Inn, Hampton Inn, **other:** RV camping(7mi), HOSPITAL,

288 GA 113, Cartersville, **2 mi W...gas:** Amoco/24hr, BP/diesel, **food:** Applebee's, Blimpie, Burger King, Chick-fil-A, Krystal/24hr, Mrs Winner's, Pizza Hut, Subway, Waffle House, **lodging:** Knight's Inn, Quality Inn, **other:** Kroger, to Etowah Indian Mounds(6mi)

286mm Etowah River

285 Emerson, **E...gas:** Texaco/24hr, **lodging:** Red Top Mtn Lodge, **other:** to Allatoona Dam, to Red Top Mtn SP

283 Emerson Allatoona Rd, Allatoona Landing Resort, camping

280mm Allatoona Lake

278 Glade Rd, to Acworth, **E...gas:** BP/Subway, Shell, **lodging:** Guesthouse Inn, **other:** to Glade Marina, **W...gas:** Chevron, Citgo, **food:** Burger King, Country Café, Dunkin Donuts, His&Hers Southern Buffet, Hong Kong Chinese, KFC, Krystal, Pizza Hut, Subway, Taco Bell, Waffle House, Western Sizzlin, **lodging:** Red Roof Inn, **other:** AutoZone, CVS Drug, Ingles, K-Mart, NAPA, Radio Shack

277 GA 92, **E...gas:** BP, Exxon/diesel, RaceTrac, Shell/diesel/24hr, **food:** Hardee's, Shoney's, Waffle House, **lodging:** Comfort Suites, Holiday Inn Express, Ramada Ltd, **W...gas:** Chevron/diesel, Shell/DQ/diesel, **food:** Bamboo Garden, Domino's, McDonald's, Ricardo's Mexican, Sonic, Waffle House, Wendy's, Zaxby's, **lodging:** Best Western, Day's Inn, Econolodge, Super 8, **other:** Advance Parts, CVS Drug, Publix

273 Wade Green Rd, **E...gas:** BP, Citgo/diesel, RaceTrac, **food:** Arby's, Burger King, China King, Del Taco/Mrs Winners, Dunkin Donuts, McDonald's, Papa John's, Pizza Hut/Taco Bell, Subway, Waffle House, **lodging:** Rodeway Inn, **other:** Eckerd, GNC, Goodyear/auto, Publix, **W...gas:** Amoco, Conoco, Texaco/Blimpie/diesel

Marietta

271 Chastain Rd, to I-575 N, **E...gas:** Chevron, **food:** Cracker Barrel, **lodging:** Best Western, **lodging:** Comfort Inn, Extended Stay America, Fairfield Inn, Residence Inn, Suburban Lodge, Super 8, **other:** Circuit City, Goodyear, Outlets Ltd Mall, Studio+, Wal-Mart/auto, funpark, **W...gas:** Texaco/Subway/diesel, **food:** Arby's/Mrs Winners, Del Taco, Waffle House/24hr, Wendy's, **lodging:** Country Inn Suites, SpringHill Suites, Sun Suites, **other:** museum

269 to US 41, to Marietta, **E...gas:** Chevron/24hr, Texaco/diesel, **food:** Applebee's, Atlanta Bread, Burger King, Fuddrucker's, Grady's Grill, Happy China, Itpolotis Italian, Longhorn Steaks, Manhattan Bagel, McDonald's, New China, Olive Garden, Piccadilly's, Pizza Hut, Red Lobster, Rio Bravo Cantina, Starbucks, Subway, $3 Café, Waffle House, **lodging:** Holiday Inn Express, Econolodge, Red Roof Inn, Super 8, **other:** Barnes&Noble, Big 10 Tire, Firestone/auto, Home Depot, Macy's, Publix, Sears/auto, mall, **W...gas:** BP, Exxon, **food:** Chick-fil-A, Chili's, Cooker Rest., Golden Corral, Macaroni Grill, On-the-Border, Outback Steaks, Roadhouse Grill, Steak'n Shake, TGIFriday, **lodging:** Comfort Inn, Day's Inn, Hampton Inn, Ramada Ltd, Sleep Inn, **other:** Best Buy, Buick/Pontiac/GMC, Chevrolet, Mitsubishi, NTB, Office Depot, OfficeMax, Old Navy, Kia/Toyota, Target, mall, to Kennesaw Mtn NP

268 I-575 N, GA 5 N, to Canton

267b a GA 5 N, to US 41, Marietta, **1/2 mi W...gas:** BP, Citgo, **food:** Burger King, McDonald's, Welcome Inn America, **other:** HOSPITAL,

265 GA120, N Marietta Pkwy, **W...gas:** Amoco, Shell/diesel, **lodging:** Arrival Inn, Budget Inn, Crown Inn, Sun Inn, Suburban Lodge, Travelers Motel

263 GA 120, Marietta, to Roswell, **E...gas:** Chevron/diesel/24hr, Shell/24hr, **other:** Harry's Farmers Mkt, cleaners, **W...gas:** Amoco, Exxon/diesel, **food:** Applebee's, Blackeyed Pea, Chili's, Dairy Queen, Hardee's, Longhorn Steaks, Piccadilly's, Subway, **lodging:** Best Western, Fairfield Inn, Hampton Inn, Marietta Motel, Mayflower Motel, Ramada Ltd, Regency Inn, Sheraton, Super 8, Wyndham Garden, **other:** DENTIST, U-Haul

261 GA 280, Delk Rd, to Dobbins AFB, **E...gas:** Exxon, RaceTrac, Shell/24hr, Texaco/diesel, **food:** Hardee's, KFC/Taco Bell, McDonald's, Papa John's, Spaghetti Whse, Waffle House, **lodging:** Courtyard, Drury Inn, Howard Johnson, Knight's Inn, Motel 6, Scottish Inn, Sleep Inn, Studio 6, Super 8, Travelers Inn, **W...gas:** Amoco, BP, Chevron/24hr, Shell/24hr, **food:** Cracker Barrel, D&B Rest., Waffle House, **lodging:** Best Inn, Comfort Inn, Fairfield Inn, Holiday Inn, La Quinta, Wingate Inn

GEORGIA

Interstate 75

N ↕ S

Atlanta Area

260 Windy Hill Rd, to Smyrna, **E...gas:** Amoco, BP, **food:** Applebee's, Boston Mkt, Cooker, Fuddrucker's, Houston's Rest., LePeep Rest., NY Pizza, Pappasito's Cantina, Pappadeaux Seafood, Quizno's, Schlotsky's, Subway, TGIFriday, **lodging:** Clarion Suites, Econolodge, Hawthorn Suites, Hyatt, Marriott, Ramada Inn, Travelodge, **other:** CVS Drug, **W...gas:** Chevron, Citgo, Texaco/diesel, **food:** Arby's, Chick-fil-A, Fuddrucker's, McDonald's, Popeye's, Sub Shop, $3 Café, Waffle House, Wendy's, **lodging:** Best Western, Courtyard, Day's Inn, Hilton, Masters Inn, Red Roof Inn, **other:** HOSPITAL, Target

259b a I-285, W to Birmingham, Montgomery, E to Greenville

258 Cumberland Pkwy, no facilities

257mm Chattahoochee River

256 to US 41, Northside Pkwy, no facilities

255 US 41, W Paces Ferry Rd, **W...gas:** Exxon/24hr, **E...gas:** Chevron, Shell/diesel, **food:** Caribou Coffee, Chick-fil-A, McDonald's, Dairy Queen, OK Café/24hr, Pero's Pizza, Steak'n Shake, Taco Bell, **other:** HOSPITAL, Publix

254 Moores Mill Rd, no facilities

252b Howell Mill Rd, **E...gas:** Texaco, **food:** Chick-fil-A, Domino's, Hardee's, McDonald's, **lodging:** Budget Inn, **other:** Eckerd, Goodyear, SaveRite Foods, **W...gas:** Exxon/diesel, **food:** Arby's, Green Derby Rest., KFC, Piccadilly, Sensational Subs, Taco Bell, US BBQ, Waffle House, Wendy's, **lodging:** Budget Inn, Holiday Inn, **other:** Kroger

a US 41, Northside Dr, **W...gas:** BP, Waffle House, **lodging:** Day's Inn, **other:** Firestone

251 I-85 N, to Greenville

250 Techwood Dr(from sb), 10th St, 14th St, **E...lodging:** Travelodge

249d 10th St, Spring St(from nb), **E...gas:** BP, Chevron/24hr, **food:** Checker's, Domino's, Pizza Hut, Varsity Drive-In, **lodging:** Fairfield Inn, Regency Suites, Renaissance Hotel, Residence Inn, **W...food:** McDonald's, **lodging:** Courtyard, Comfort Inn, **other:** HOSPITAL, to GA Tech

249c Williams St(from sb), downtown, to GA Dome

249b Pine St, Peachtree St(from nb), downtown, **W...lodging:** Hilton, Marriott, **other:** HOSPITAL,

249a Courtland St(from sb), downtown, **W...lodging:** Hilton, Marriott, **other:** GA St U

248d Piedmont Ave, Butler St(from sb), downtown, **W...lodging:** Courtyard, Fairfield Inn, Radisson, **other:** HOSPITAL, Ford, MLK NHS

248c GA 10 E, Intn'l Blvd, downtown, **W...lodging:** Hilton, Holiday Inn, Marriott Marquis, Radisson

248b Edgewood Ave(from nb), **W...other:** HOSPITAL, downtown, hotels

248a MLK Dr(from sb), **W...**st capitol, to Underground Atlanta

247 I-20, E to Augusta, W to Birmingham

246 Georgia Ave, Fulton St, **E...lodging:** Hampton Inn, Holiday Inn Express, **other:** stadium, **W...gas:** Amoco, **food:** KFC, **other:** to Coliseum, GSU

245 Ormond St, Abernathy Blvd, **E...lodging:** Hampton Inn, Holiday Inn Express, **other:** stadium, **W...**st capitol

244 University Ave, **E...gas:** Exxon, **W...gas:** Amoco, **food:** Mrs Winner's, **other:** Ford Trucks

243 GA 166, Lakewood Fwy, to East Point, no facilities

242 I-85 S, to airport

241 Cleveland Ave, **E...gas:** Chevron, **food:** Checker's, McDonald's, **lodging:** Palace Inn, **other:** K-Mart, **W...gas:** Shell, Texaco, **food:** Burger King, Church's, Krystal/24hr, **lodging:** American Inn, Day's Inn

239 US 19, US 41, **E...gas:** Chevron, **food:** Checker's, Waffle House, **W...gas:** Amoco, **food:** IHOP, Krystal, McDonald's, **lodging:** Best Western, **other:** USPO, to airport

238b a I-285 around Atlanta

237a GA 85 S(from sb), **W...food:** Denny's, **lodging:** Day's Inn, Day's Lodge, King's Inn

237 GA 331, Forest Parkway, **E...gas:** Chevron, Exxon, Happy Store/gas, Shell, **food:** Burger King, McDonald's, Waffle House, **lodging:** Econolodge, Motel 6, Rodeway Inn, **other:** Farmer's Mkt, Chevrolet, **W...lodging:** Day's Inn, Ramada Ltd

Jonesboro

235 US 19, US 41, GA 3, Jonesboro, **E...gas:** Phillips 66, **food:** Hardee's, Waffle House, **lodging:** Super 8, **other:** K-Mart, RV Ctr, **W...gas:** Amoco, Marathon, RaceTrac/diesel, Shell, Texaco, **food:** Checker's, Dunkin Donuts, Folks Rest., Johnny's Pizza, KFC, Krystal, McDonald's, Red Lobster, Waffle House, **lodging:** Comfort Inn, Day's Inn, Econolodge, Holiday Inn Express, Shoney's Inn/rest., **other:** HOSPITAL, Cub Foods, Dodge, Office Depot

233 GA 54, Morrow, **E...gas:** BP, Chevron, Conoco/diesel, **food:** Cracker Barrel, Krystal/24hr, Mrs Winner's, Taco Bell, Waffle House, Wendy's, **lodging:** Best Western, Drury Inn, Fairfield Inn, Red Roof Inn, **other:** MEDICAL CARE, **W...gas:** Exxon/24hr, RaceTrac, Texaco/diesel, **food:** Bennigan's, China Café, Japanese Rest., KFC, LJ Silver, McDonald's, Pizza Hut, Shoney's, Waffle House, **lodging:** Hampton Inn, Quality Inn, **other:** Acura/Cadillac, Best Buy, Chevrolet, HobbyLobby, JiffyLube, Kroger, Nissan, OfficeMax, Toyota, mall

231 Mt Zion Blvd, **E...**Honda, **W...gas:** Citgo, Conoco, Exxon, **food:** Arby's, Blimpie, Chick-fil-A, Chili's, Del Taco, Longhorn Steaks, McDonald's, Mrs Winner's, On-the-Border, Papa John's, Philly Subs, Steak'n Shake, TGIFriday, Waffle House, Wendy's, **lodging:** Country Inn Suites, Extended Stay America, Howard Johnson Express, Sleep Inn, Sun Suites, **other:** Circuit City, Goody's, Home Depot, Michael's, NTB, Old Navy, Publix, Target

228 GA 54, GA 138, Jonesboro, **E...gas:** Exxon, RaceTrac/24hr, **food:** Applebee's, Arby's, Burger King, Chick-fil-A, CiCi's, Dairy Queen, Damon's, Frontera Mexican, Golden Corral, Gregory's Grill, Hardee's, IHOP, KFC, Krystal, LJ Silver, McDonald's, Piccadilly's, Philly Connection, Shoney's, Subway, Taco Bell, Waffle House, Wendy's, **lodging:** Best Western, Day's Inn, Comfort Inn, Holiday Inn Express, Motel 6, Ramada Ltd, Shoney's Inn, **other:** HOSPITAL, Bruno's Foods, Goodyear, K-Mart, Kroger, **W...gas:** Amoco/24hr, Chevron, Citgo/diesel, **food:** Waffle House, **other:** CarMax, Chrysler/Plymouth/Jeep

Interstate 75

N

S

227 I-675 N, to I-285 E(from nb)

224 Hudson Bridge Rd, **E...gas:** BP, Citgo/24hr, Phillips 66, Texaco/Chick-fil-A/diesel, **food:** Dunkin Donuts, McDonald's, Subway, Waffle House, Wendy's, **lodging:** AmeriHost Inn, Eagle Landing Inn, **other:** HOSPITAL, CVS Drug, **W...**Teddy's Diner/24hr, Super 8

222 Jodeco Rd, **E...gas:** Amoco, Citgo/24hr, **food:** Hardee's, Waffle House, **W...gas:** BP, Chevron/diesel, **other:** KOA

221 Jonesboro Rd, **E...gas:** Flash/Chick-fil-A/diesel/24hr, **W...other:** flea market, KOA

218 GA 20, GA 81, McDonough, **E...gas:** Amoco, BP, **food:** Applebee's, Arby's, Burger King, Dairy Queen, KFC, McDonald's, Mrs Winner's, Pizza Hut, Taco Bell, Waffle House, Wendy's, **lodging:** Best Western, Budget Inn, Hampton Inn, Red Carpet Inn, **W...gas:** Shell/24hr, Speedway/diesel, **food:** Subway, Waffle House, **lodging:** Comfort Inn, Econolodge, HoJo's, Master's Inn

216 GA 155, McDonough, Blacksville, **E...gas:** Chevron/diesel, Shell, Texaco/diesel, **food:** BBQ(1mi), Blimpie, Waffle House, **lodging:** Day's Inn, Sunny Inn, Chevrolet/Pontiac, **other:** Ford/Lincoln/Mercury, **W...gas:** Amoco/diesel, BP/diesel, Citgo/diesel/24hr, Shoney's, Waffle House, **lodging:** Sleep Inn, Holiday Inn/rest.

212 to US 23, Locust Grove, **E...gas:** BP/Subway/diesel, Citgo, Exxon/diesel, Shell/diesel, **food:** Denny's, Hardee's, Huddle House, Waffle House, **lodging:** Executive Inn, Outlet Inn, Red Carpet, Scottish Inn, Travel Inn, **other:** Tanger Outlet/famous brands, **W...gas:** Chevron/diesel, **lodging:** Scottish Inn, Super 8

205 GA 16, to Griffin, Jackson, **E...gas:** BP, Citgo/diesel, **lodging:** BBQ, **W...gas:** Amoco, Chevron/diesel, Texaco/diesel

201 GA 36, to Jackson, Barnesville, **E...gas:** Sunshine/diesel/grill/24hr, TA/Subway/Taco Bell/diesel/24hr/@, Wilco/Hess/DQ/Wendy's/diesel/24hr/@, **food:** Huddle House, **other:** Blue Beacon, **W...gas:** BP, Flying J/Conoco/Hardee's/diesel/LP/24hr/@

198 Highfalls Rd, **E...gas:** Exxon(1mi), **other:** High Falls SP, **W...**High Falls RV Park

193 Johnstonville Rd, **E...**BP

190mm weigh sta both lanes

188 GA 42, **E...gas:** Shell/24hr, **lodging:** Best Value Inn, Best Western, Super 8, **other:** to Indian Spings SP, RV camping

Forsyth

187 GA 83, Forsyth, **E...food:** El Tejado Mexican, **lodging:** Econolodge, New Forsyth Inn, Regency Inn, **W...gas:** Amoco/Blimpie, Citgo/diesel, Conoco/diesel, Exxon, Texaco, **food:** Burger King, Capt D's, Hardee's, McDonald's, Pizza Hut, Subway, Taco Bell, Waffle House, Wendy's, **lodging:** Day's Inn, Tradewinds Motel, **other:** Advance Parts, CVS Drug, Family$, Piggly Wiggly/24hr, Wal-Mart

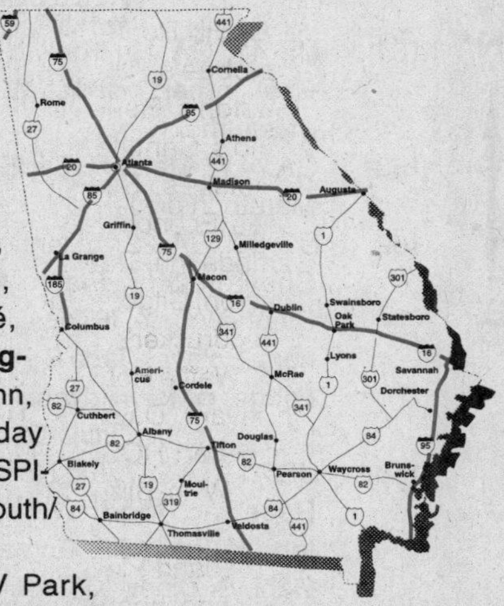

186 Tift College Dr, Juliette Rd, Forsyth, **E...**Jarrell Plantation HS, KOA, **W...gas:** BP/diesel, Chevron, Shell/24hr, **food:** Dairy Queen, Hong Kong Café, Waffle House, **lodging:** Ambassador Inn, Hampton Inn, Holiday Inn/rest., **other:** HOSPITAL, Chrysler/Plymouth/Dodge, Ingles

185 GA 18, **E...**L&D RV Park, **W...gas:** Amoco/Waffle King/24hr, Texaco/diesel, **food:** Shoney's, **lodging:** Comfort Inn, **other:** Ford, st patrol

181 Rumble Rd, to Smarr, **E...gas:** BP/Subway/diesel/24hr, Shell/diesel/24hr

179mm rest area sb, full(handicapped)facilities, phone, vending, picnic tables, litter barrels, petwalk

177 I-475 S around Macon(from sb)

175 Pate Rd, Bolingbroke(from nb, no re-entry), no facilities

172 Bass Rd, **E...**funpark, **W...**to Museum of Arts&Sciences

171 US 23, to GA 87, Riverside Dr, **E...gas:** BP, Marathon/diesel, Shell, **food:** Cracker Barrel, Huddle House/24hr, **other:** Jack&Jill's Brewery

Macon

169 to US 23, Arkwright Dr, **E...gas:** Shell/24hr, **food:** Carrabba's, Logan's Roadhouse, Outback Steaks, Waffle House, Wager's Grill, **lodging:** Courtyard, Fairfield Inn, La Quinta, Red Roof Inn, Residence Inn, Sleep Inn, Super 8, **other:** Buick/Cadillac/GMC/Saturn, **W...gas:** Amoco/diesel, Chevron/24hr, Conoco/diesel, **food:** Applebee's, Burger King, Chick-fil-A, Chili's, Cracker Barrel, Dunkin Donuts, Hooters, KFC, Krystal, Longhorn Steaks, McDonald's, Papa John's, Papoulis' Gyros, Popeye's, Rio Bravo Cantina, Ryan's, Steak'n Shake, Subway, Taco Bell, Waffle House, WhataPizza, **lodging:** Hampton Inn, Holiday Inn, Quality Inn, Ramada Ltd, Shoney's Inn/rest., Studio+, Wingate Inn, **other:** HOSPITAL, Acura, Barnes&Noble, BMW/Mitsubishi, Chrysler/Jeep/Dodge, GNC, K-Mart, Kroger, Lexus, Pontiac, Publix, Radio Shack, Rite Aid, Volvo, same as 167

167 GA 247, Pierce Ave, **E...lodging:** Budget Inn Suites, **W...gas:** Amoco/Blimpie, BP/diesel, Chevron, Exxon, Marathon/Subway/diesel, Texaco/diesel, **food:** Applebee's, Arby's, Bennigan's, Capt D's, Denny's, Pizza Hut, Red Lobster, S&S Cafeteria, Shogun Japanese, Steak-Out Rest., Texas Cattle Co, Waffle House, Wendy's, **lodging:** Ambassador Inn, Best Western/rest., Comfort Inn, Holiday Inn Express, Howard Johnson, **other:** Eckerd, Goodyear/auto

165 I-16 E, to Savannah

Interstate 75

164 US 41, GA 19, Forsyth Ave, Macon, **E...food:** Sid's Rest., **other:** hist dist, **W...gas:** BP, **other:** HOSPITAL, museum

163 GA 74 W, Mercer U Dr, **E...**to Mercer U, **W...gas:** Citgo, Marathon/diesel

162 US 80, GA 22, Eisenhower Pkwy, **W...gas:** Amoco, Chevron/24hr, Flash, **food:** Capt D's, Checker's, CityView Café, IHOP, LJ Silver, McDonald's, Mrs Winners, Subway, Taco Bell, Wendy's, **lodging:** Suburban Lodge, **other:** Advance Parts, FoodMax, Goodyear, Home Depot, Office Depot, PepBoys, Walgreen

160 US 41, GA 247, Pio Nono Ave, **E...gas:** Exxon/diesel, RaceTrac, **food:** Waffle House, **lodging:** Masters Inn, **W...gas:** BP, Enmark/diesel, **food:** Arby's, DQ, Gabby's Diner, KFC, King Buffet, McDonald's, Pizza Hut, Subway, Waffle House, **other:** Advance Parts, Eckerd, FoodMax, JiffyLube, USPO, same as 162

156 I-475 N around Macon(from nb)

155 Hartley Br Rd, **E...gas:** BP/KFC/Pizza Hut/diesel/24hr, Marathon/diesel, **food:** Wendy's, **other:** Kroger/gas, **W...gas:** Citgo, **food:** Subway, Waffle House, **lodging:** Ambassador Inn

149 GA 49, Byron, **E...gas:** Chevron/diesel, Shell/24hr, **food:** Burger King, Krystal, McDonald's, Pizza Hut, Shoney's, Waffle House, **lodging:** Best Western, Holiday Inn Express, Super 8, **other:** MidState RV Ctr, Peach Stores/famous brands, antiques, **W...gas:** BP, Citgo/diesel/24hr, Flash/diesel, Marathon, RaceTrac, **food:** Country Cupboard, DQ, Huddle House, Papa's Pizza, Popeye's, Subway, Waffle House, **lodging:** Comfort Inn, Day's Inn, Econolodge, Passport Inn, **other:** Chevrolet, Ford, NAPA

146 GA 247, to Centerville, **E...gas:** Exxon, Flash/diesel, Shell, **food:** Subway, Waffle House, **lodging:** Budget Inn, **other:** HOSPITAL, to Robins AFB, museum, **W...gas:** Pilot/Arby's/diesel/24hr/@, **lodging:** Royal Inn

145 new exit

142 GA 96, Housers Mill Rd, **E...gas:** Chevron/diesel, **other:** Ponderosa RV Park

138 Thompson Rd, **E...gas:** Phillips/Chester/diesel, **other:** HOSPITAL, **W...**airport

136 US 341, Perry, **E...gas:** Amoco, Chevron/24hr, Flash, Shell/diesel, **food:** Arby's, BBQ, Burger King, Capt D's, Chick-fil-A, Hardee's, Hong Kong Buffet, Jalisco Grill, KFC, Krystal, McDonald's, Pizza Hut, Red Lobster, Sister's Café, Subway, Taco Bell, Waffle House, Wendy's, Zaxby's, **lodging:** Best Inn, Great Inn, Hampton Inn, Jameson Inn, Ramada Ltd, Super 8, **other:** HOSPITAL, Advance Parts, $Tree, Kroger, Radio Shack, Wal-Mart SuperCtr/24hr, **W...gas:** BP, Chevron, Conoco/diesel, RaceWay/24hr, **food:** Angelina's Café, Applebee's, Green Derby Rest., **lodging:** Comfort Inn, Day's Inn, Econolodge, Holiday Inn/rest., Knight's Inn, Passport Inn, **other:** Ford, Crossroads Camping

135 US 41, GA 127, Perry, **E...gas:** BP/diesel, Exxon, Flash, Shell, Texaco, **food:** Cracker Barrel, Waffle House, **lodging:** Day's Inn, Red Carpet Inn, Relax Inn, Scottish Inn, Travelodge, **other:** Plymouth/Jeep/Dodge, GA Nat Fair, **W...food:** Mandarin Chinese, **other:** GA Patrol, Fair Harbor RV Park

134 South Perry Pkwy, **W...**Chevrolet/Buick/Pontiac/GMC, Priester's Pecans

127 GA 26, Henderson, **E...**Twin Oaks Camping, **W...gas:** Chevron, **lodging:** Henderson Lodge

122 GA 230, Unadilla, **E...gas:** Dixie, **other:** Chevrolet/Ford, **W...gas:** Phillips 66, **lodging:** Red Carpet Inn

121 US 41, Unadilla, **E...gas:** BP, Shell, Texaco/DQ/Stuckey's, **food:** Cotton Patch Rest., Subway, **lodging:** Day's Inn, Economy Inn, Scottish Inn, **other:** $General, Southern Trails RV Resort, **W...gas:** Citgo/diesel/rest./24hr/@, **lodging:** Regency Inn

118mm rest area sb, full(handicapped)facilities, phone, vending, picnic tables, litter barrels, petwalk

117 to US 41, Pinehurst, **W...gas:** BP/diesel, Danfair, **lodging:** Budget Inn

112 GA 27, Vienna, **E...gas:** Pure, **W...gas:** BP/diesel, Marathon

109 GA 215, Vienna, **E...gas:** BP/diesel, **W...gas:** Citgo/diesel, El Cheapo, Shell, **food:** Huddle House/24hr, Popeye's, **lodging:** Knight's Inn, **other:** HOSPITAL

108mm rest area nb, full(handicapped)facilities, phone, vending, picnic tables, litter barrels, petwalk

104 Farmers Mkt Rd, Cordele, **E...lodging:** Cordele Inn, **W...gas:** Phillips 66/diesel

102 GA 257, Cordele, **E...gas:** Shell, **W...food:** Pecan House, **other:** HOSPITAL

101 US 280, GA 90, Cordele, **E...gas:** Exxon/diesel, Pilot/Arby's/diesel/24hr/@, Shell, **food:** Denny's, Golden Corral, Waffle House, **lodging:** Day's Inn, Ramada Inn, **other:** Ford/Lincoln/Mercury, st patrol, **W...gas:** BP/diesel, Chevron/24hr, Liberty, RaceWay/24hr, **food:** Burger King, Capt D's, Compadres Mexican, Cracker Barrel, Cutter's Steaks, Dairy Queen, Hardee's, KFC/Pizza Hut/Taco Bell, Krystal/24hr, McDonald's, Shoney's, Subway, Wendy's, **lodging:** Best Western, Comfort Inn, Deluxe Inn, Hampton Inn, Holiday Inn Express, Premier Inn, Super 8, **other:** CVS Drug, Family$, Radio Shack, Wal-Mart SuperCtr/24hr, to Veterans Mem SP, J Carter HS

99 GA 300, GA/FL Pkwy, **W...**to Chehaw SP

97 to GA 33, Wenona, **E...lodging:** Royal Inn, **other:** RV DR RV Park, **W...gas:** TA/BP/Popeye's/Pizza Hut/diesel/24hr/@, **other:** KOA

92 Arabi, **E...gas:** Chevron/Plantation House, Phillips 66, **lodging:** Budget Inn, **W...gas:** BP, **other:** Southern Gates RV Park

85mm rest area nb, full(handicapped)facilities, phone, vending, picnic tables, litter barrels, petwalk

84 GA 159, Ashburn, **E...gas:** Shell/diesel, **W...gas:** A-1 Trkstp/diesel@, BP/Subway/diesel, **food:** Waffle King, **lodging:** motel/RV park

82 GA 107, GA 112, Ashburn, **W...gas:** BP, Chevron, Shorty's, **food:** Hardee's, Huddle House/24hr, Krystal, McDonald's, Pizza Hut, Shoney's, **lodging:** Best Western, Day's Inn, Ramada Ltd, Super 8, **other:** Chevrolet, Rite Aid, to Chehaw SP

Interstate 75

N S

Tifton

80 Bussey Rd, Sycamore, **E...gas:** Exxon/Subway, Shell, **lodging:** Budget Inn/camping, **W...gas:** Chevron/diesel

78 GA 32, Sycamore, **E...**to Jefferson Davis Memorial Park(14mi)

76mm rest area sb, full(handicapped)facilities, phone, vending, picnic tables, litter barrels, petwalk

75 Inaha Rd, **E...gas:** Chevron, **W...gas:** BP/DQ/Stuckey's

71 Willis Still Rd, Sunsweet, **W...gas:** BP/diesel

69 Chula-Brookfield Rd, **E...gas:** Phillips 66, **lodging:** Red Carpet Inn, **other:** antiques

66 Brighton Rd, no facilities

64 US 41, Tifton, **E...gas:** Chevron, **other:** HOSPITAL, $General, Food Lion, **W...gas:** Citgo/diesel

63b 8th St, Tifton, **E...gas:** Flash, Texaco, **food:** Hardee's, KFC, Krystal, McDonald's, **lodging:** Budget Inn, **other:** Belk, JC Penney, Winn-Dixie, **W... food:** Split Rail Grill, same as 63a

63a 2nd St, Tifton, **E...gas:** BP, Chevron, **food:** Arby's, Burger King, Checker's, Denny's, King Buffet, Krystal, LJ Silver, McDonald's, Pizza Hut, Red Lobster, Subway, Taco Bell, Waffle House, **lodging:** Econolodge, Super 8, **other:** Advance Parts, Buick/Pontiac/Cadillac/GMC, FoodMax, **W...gas:** Shell/diesel, **lodging:** Comfort Inn, Family Inn

62 US 82, to US 319, Tifton, **E...gas:** BP, Citgo, Exxon/diesel, **food:** Applebee's, Charles Seafood, Country Buffet, Cracker Barrel, DQ, Golden Corral, Sonic, Waffle House, Western Sizzlin, Zaxby's, **lodging:** Courtyard, Hampton Inn, Masters Inn, Microtel, **other:** Advance Parts, Ford/Lincoln/Mercury, Pecan Outlet, **W...gas:** Amoco/Subway, RaceTrac/24hr, Shell/diesel, **food:** Burger King, Capt D's, Chick-fil-A, Longhorn Steaks, Shoney's, Waffle House, Wendy's, **lodging:** Day's Inn, Holiday Inn, Ramada Ltd, Rodeway Inn, **other:** Chevrolet, Chrysler/Jeep, Honda, Lowe's Whse, Mazda, Plymouth/Dodge, Radio Shack, Toyota, Wal-Mart SuperCtr/gas/24hr

61 Omega Rd, **W...gas:** Citgo/diesel, **food:** Waffle King, **lodging:** Motel 6, **other:** Pines RV Park

60 Central Ave, Tifton, **E...gas:** Chevron, **food:** Taj Mahal Rest., **W...gas:** Pilot/Subway/Steak'n Shake/diesel/@, **other:** Amy's RV Ctr, Blue Beacon

59 Southwell Blvd, to US 41, Tifton, no facilities

55 to Eldorado, Omega, **E...gas:** Chevron/Magnolia Plantation, **W...gas:** Pure/diesel

49 Kinard Br Rd, Lenox, **E...gas:** Dixie/diesel, **lodging:** Knight's Inn, **W...gas:** BP/diesel/24hr, Phillips 66/diesel, **food:** Blimpie

47mm rest area both lanes, full(handicapped)facilities, phone, vending, picnic tables, litter barrels, petwalk

45 Barneyville Rd, **E...lodging:** Red Carpet Inn

41 Rountree Br Rd, **W...**to Reed Bingham SP

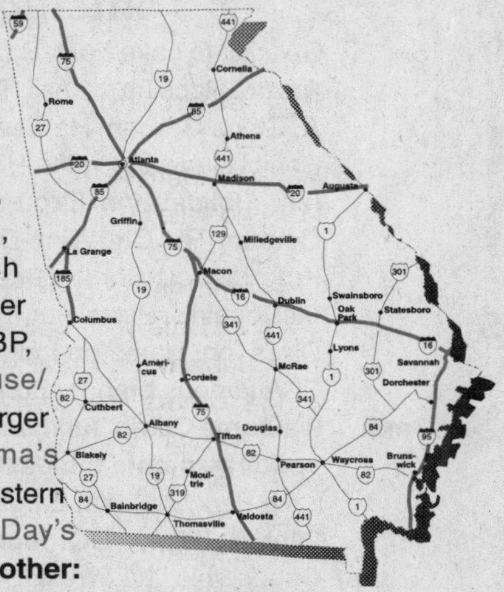

Adel

39 GA 37, Adel, Moultrie, **E...gas:** Shell/McDonald's/diesel, **food:** DQ, Hardee's, Subway, Waffle House, **lodging:** Scottish Inn, Super 8, Villager Lodge, **W...gas:** BP, Citgo/Huddle House/diesel/@, **food:** Burger King, IHOP, Mama's Table, Taco Bell, Western Sizzlin, **lodging:** Day's Inn, Hampton Inn, **other:** Factory Stores/famous brands, to Reed Bingham SP

37 Adel, no facilities

32 Old Coffee Rd, Cecil, **W...gas:** Chevron

29 US 41 N, GA 122, Hahira, Sheriff's Boys Ranch, **E...gas:** Pure, **food:** Subway, **W...gas:** BP, Citgo/Blimpie/diesel, Sav-A-Ton/Apple Valley Café/diesel/24hr, **lodging:** Super 8

23mm weigh sta both lanes

Valdosta

22 US 41 S, to Valdosta, **E...gas:** BP, Shell/Subway/diesel, **other:** HOSPITAL, Chevrolet/Mazda, Chrysler/Jeep/Toyota, Ford/Lincoln/Mercury, golf, **W...gas:** Citgo/Burger King/DQ/Stuckey's, **lodging:** Day's Inn

18 GA 133, Valdosta, **E...gas:** Amoco, Chevron, Citgo, Exxon, Shell, Texaco/diesel, **food:** Applebee's, Arby's, BBQ, Burger King, Chick-fil-A, Country Buffet, Cracker Barrel, Denny's, El Potro Mexican, Fazoli's, Hardee's, Hooters, KFC, Krystal, Little Caesar's, Longhorn Steaks, McDonald's, Outback Steaks, Red Lobster, Ruby Tuesday, Steak'n Shake, Subway, Taco Bell, Texas Roadhouse, Waffle House, Wendy's, **lodging:** Clubhouse Inn, Country Inn Suites, Courtyard, Fairfield Inn, Hampton Inn, Holiday Inn, Howard Johnson, Jolly Inn, Quality Inn, Scottish Inn, **other:** Belk, Home Depot, JC Penney, Publix, Sam's Club, Target, Wal-Mart/auto, mall, **W...gas:** BP/diesel, Shell, **lodging:** Best Western, Sleep Inn, **other:** RiverPark Camping

16 US 84, US 221, GA 94, Valdosta, **E...gas:** Amoco, BP/diesel, Chevron, Citgo/Blimpie/diesel, Phillips 66, Shell/diesel, **food:** Aligatou Japanese, Burger King, IHOP, McDonald's, Pizza Hut, Shoney's, Sonic, Waffle House, Wendy's, **lodging:** Comfort Inn, Day's Inn, Guesthouse Inn, Motel 6, New Valdosta Inn, Quality Inn, Ramada Ltd, Super 8, **other:** to Okefenokee SP, **W...** Shell/Huddle House/diesel/24hr, Austin's Steaks, Comfort Inn, Knight's Inn

13 Old Clyattville Rd, Valdosta, **W...**Wild Adventures Park

11 GA 31, Valdosta, **E...gas:** Pilot/Subway/diesel/24hr/@, Wilco/Hess/diesel/24hr/@, **food:** Waffle House, **lodging:** Travelers Inn, **W...gas:** BP, Texaco

GEORGIA

Interstate 75

N ↕ S

5 GA 376, to Lake Park, **E...gas:** Amoco, Chevron, Phillips 66, RaceTrac, Shell, Texaco, **food:** BBQ, Chick-fil-A, China Garden, Hardee's, Mama's Subs, Shoney's, Sonic, Subway, Waffle House, **lodging:** Guesthouse Inn, Holiday Inn Express, **other:** Family$, Travel Country RV Ctr, Winn-Dixie, **W...gas:** Citgo/Burger King/diesel, Shell/diesel, **food:** Cracker Barrel, McDonald's, Pizza Hut, Taco Bell, Wendy's, **lodging:** Day's Inn, Hampton Inn, Super 8, Travelodge, **other:** FSA/famous brands, SunCoast RV Ctr

3mm Welcome Ctr nb, full(handicapped)facilities, phone, vending, picnic tables, litter barrels, petwalk

2 Lake Park, Bellville, **E...gas:** Shell, TA/BP/diesel/rest./24hr/@, Texaco/DQ, **food:** Arby's, **W...gas:** Flying J/Conoco/diesel/LP/rest./24hr/@, **lodging:** Best Western

0mm Georgia/Florida state line

Interstate 85

N ↕ S

Exit # Services

179mm Georgia/South Carolina state line, Lake Hartwell, Tugaloo River

177 GA 77 S, to Hartwell, **E...gas:** BP/gifts, **food:** Dad's II Grill, **other:** to Hart SP, Tugaloo SP

176mm Welcome Ctr sb, full(handicapped)facilities, info, phone, picnic tables, litter barrels, vending, petwalk

Lavonia

173 GA 17, to Lavonia, **E...gas:** Amoco/diesel, RaceTrac/24hr, Texaco/diesel, **food:** KFC, La Cabana Mexican, McDonald's, Subway, Taco Bell, Waffle House, **lodging:** Best Western, Sleep Inn, **other:** $General, Rite Aid, **W...gas:** Exxon, Marathon, **food:** Arby's, Burger King, Hardee's, Pizza Hut, Waffle House, Wendy's, Shoney's Inn/rest., **other:** Chrysler/Plymouth, to Tugaloo SP

171mm weigh sta nb

169mm weigh sta sb

166 GA 106, to Carnesville, **E...gas:** Shell, Wilco/Hess/Wendy's/DQ/diesel/24hr/@, **W...gas:** Echo Trkstp/diesel/rest./24hr/@, **other:** repair

164 GA 320, to Carnesville, **E...gas:** Sunshine Travel/Hardee's/diesel/24hr

160mm rest area nb, full(handicapped)facilities, phone, vending, picnic tables, litter barrels, petwalk

160 GA 51, to Homer, **E...gas:** Shell/Chester's/Subway/diesel/24hr, **W...gas:** Flying J/Country Mkt/diesel/24hr/@, Petro/Pizza Hut/diesel/24hr/@, Blue Beacon

154 GA 63, Martin Br Rd, no facilities

Commerce

149 US 441, GA 15, to Commerce, **E...gas:** Citgo/diesel/rest./24hr, TA/76/diesel/rest./24hr/@, **food:** BBQ, Capt D's, Chinese Chef, Pizza Hut/Taco Bell, Shoney's, Waffle House, Zaxby's, **lodging:** Day's Inn, Guest House Inn, Hampton Inn, Holiday Inn Express, **other:** HOSPITAL, KOA, Tanger Outlet/famous brands, Wal-Mart SuperCtr/gas/24hr, **W...gas:** BP/diesel, Phillips 66, RaceTrac/diesel, Texaco, **food:** Arby's, Burger King, Checker's, Chick-fil-A, Cracker Barrel, Dairy Queen, Denny's, KFC, McDonald's, Pizza Hut, Ryan's, Subway, Waffle House, Wendy's, **lodging:** Comfort Inn, $Wise Inn, Howard Johnson, Jameson Inn, Ramada Ltd, Red Roof Inn, Super 8, **other:** Buick/Pontiac/GMC, Tanger Outlet/famous brands

147 GA 98, to Commerce, **E...gas:** FuelMart/diesel, Flash/diesel, **other:** HOSPITAL, **W...gas:** Shell

140 GA 82, Dry Pond Rd, **W...**Interstate Truck Sales

137 US 129, GA 11 to Jefferson, **E...gas:** BP, Shell, Texaco/diesel, **food:** Arby's, Hardee's, McDonald's, Waffle House, **lodging:** Comfort Inn, **other:** museum, **W...gas:** QT/diesel/24hr, **food:** Burger King, Waffle House, Wendy's, **other:** flea mkt

129 GA 53, to Braselton, **E...gas:** Shell, Texaco/diesel, **food:** Waffle House, Papa's Pizza, **lodging:** Best Western, **W...gas:** BP/Subway/diesel, Pilot/diesel/24hr/@, Pure/diesel

126 GA 211, to Chestnut Mtn, **E...gas:** Shell, **W...gas:** BP/diesel, **food:** Chateau Elan Winery/rest., **lodging:** The Lodge

120 to GA 124, Hamilton Mill Rd, **E...gas:** BP, QT/diesel, 76/Circle K, **food:** Buffalo's Café, Burger King, Dos Copas Mexican, McDonald's, Millhouse Rest., Ninja's Steaks, Subway, Wendy's, Zaxby's, **other:** Home Depot, Publix, **W...gas:** Chevron, Shell/Huddle House/diesel

115 GA 20, to Buford Dam, **W...gas:** Citgo, QT/diesel, RaceTrac, Texaco, **food:** Arby's, Bruster's, Burger King, Chang's Bistro, Chick-fil-A, Chili's, Longhorn Steaks, Macaroni Grill, McDonald's, O'Charley's, Olive Garden, Red Lobster, Subway, TGIFriday, Waffle House, **lodging:** Hampton Inn, SpringHill Suites, Wingate Inn, **other:** Best Buy, Borders Books, Circuit City, Dillard's, JC Penney, Michael's, OfficeMax, Target, mall, **1 mi W... gas:** Amoco, Chevron, Flash, Texaco, **food:** BBQ, Ryan's, Waffle House, **other:** $Tree, Honda, Lowe's Whse, Toyota, Wal-Mart SuperCtr/24hr, XpertTire, to Lake Lanier Islands

114mm rest area sb, full(handicapped)facilities, phone, vending, picnic tables, litter barrels, petwalk

113 I-985 N(from nb), to Gainesville, no facilities

112mm rest area nb, full(handicapped)facilities, phone, vending, picnic tables, litter barrels, petwalk

Suwanee

111 GA 317, to Suwanee, **E...gas:** Amoco, BP, Phillips 66/diesel, **food:** Applebee's, Arby's, Blimpie, Burger King, Cazadore's Mexican, Checker's, Chick-fil-A, Cracker Barrel, Del Taco/Mrs Winner's, Outback Steaks, Philly Connection, Pizza Hut, Subway, Taco Bell, Waffle House, Wendy's, **lodging:** Comfort Inn, Courtyard, Fairfield Inn, Holiday Inn, Howard Johnson Express, Red Roof Inn, Sun Suites, **other:** CVS Drug, Ingles, Publix, **W...gas:** Chevron/diesel/24hr, Exxon, Texaco, **food:** Denny's, McDonald's, Waffle House, **lodging:** Best Western/rest., Day's Inn, Ramada Ltd, **other:** flea mkt

109 Old Peachtree Rd, **E...gas:** QT/diesel/24hr

108 Sugarloaf Pkwy, **W...food:** Chick-fil-A, Hilton Garden, **other:** Gwinnett Civic Ctr

107 GA 120, to GA 316 E, Athens, **W...gas:** Amoco/diesel, BP, Chevron, **food:** McDonald's

106 Boggs Rd(from sb, no return), Duluth, **W...gas:** QT/diesel/24hr

Interstate 85

104 Pleasant Hill Rd, **E...gas:** Chevron/24hr, Citgo/LP, Exxon/diesel, Phillip 66, Circle K, **food:** Burger King, Chick-fil-A, Cooker, Corky's Ribs/BBQ, Grady's Grill, Dunkin Donuts, Hardee's, Krispy Kreme, O'Charley's, Popeye's, Restaurante Mexicano, Ruby Tuesday, TGIFriday, Waffle House, **lodging:** Comfort Suites, Hampton Inn Suites, Holiday Inn Express, Marriott, **other:** Best Buy, CVS Drug, Eckerd, Goodyear/auto, Home Depot, Ingles, K-Mart, Office Depot, Publix, Wal-Mart, Winn-Dixie, **W...gas:** Amoco, BP/diesel, Phillips 66/diesel, Texaco/diesel, **food:** Applebee's, Arby's, Blackeyed Pea, Burger King, Chili's, Hooters, KFC, McDonald's, Mrs Winner's, Olive Garden, Pizza Hut, Red Lobster, Ryan's, Shoney's, Steak'n Shake, Subway, Taco Bell, Waffle House, Wendy's, **lodging:** AmeriSuites, Courtyard, Day's Inn, Extended Stay America, Fairfield Inn, Ramada Ltd, Sumner Inn, Wellesley Inn, Wingate Inn, **other:** BMW, Chevrolet, Dodge, Firestone/auto, Ford/Lincoln/Mercury, Honda, Kroger, Macy's, Mazda/Hyundai, Mitsubishi, Nissan, Sears/auto, mall

103 Steve Reynolds Blvd(from nb, no return), **E...gas:** QT/diesel/24hr(1mi), **W...gas:** QT, Texaco, **food:** Dave&Buster's, Waffle House, **other:** Circuit City, Costco Whse, CompUSA, Sam's Club

102 GA 378, Beaver Ruin Rd, **E...gas:** Conoco/24hr, QT/diesel/24hr(1mi), **other:** Chevrolet, **W...gas:** Amoco/24hr, Texaco/diesel

101 Lilburn Rd, **E...gas:** QT/diesel, Texaco, **food:** Burger King, McDonald's, Shoney's Inn/rest., Studio 1, Taco Bell, **lodging:** Suburban Lodge, Super 8, **W...gas:** BP/diesel, Chevron/24hr, Citgo, Exxon, **food:** Arby's, Blimpie, Dairy Queen, Hardee's, Little Caeser's, Mexican Rest., Mrs Winner's, Papa John's, Peach's Rest., Waffle House, Wendy's, **lodging:** Red Roof Inn, Villager Lodge, **other:** Chrysler/Plymouth/Jeep, CVS Drug, Outlet Mall, Winn-Dixie

99 GA 140, Jimmy Carter Blvd, **E...gas:** Amoco/24hr, Chevron, Exxon, Phillips 66/diesel, Texaco/diesel, **food:** Bennigan's, Burger King, Chili's, Cracker Barrel, Denny's, Dunkin Donuts, KFC, Krystal, LJ Silver, McDonald's, Morrison's Cafeteria, Pizza Hut, Sizzler, Steak&Ale, Taco Bell, Waffle House, Wendy's, **lodging:** Amberley Suites, Best Western, Comfort Inn, Courtyard, Clubhouse Inn, GuestHouse Inn, La Quinta, Motel 6, Quality Inn, Rodeway Inn, **other:** MEDICAL CARE, Circuit City, Cub Foods, CVS Drug, **1 mi E...food:** Crown, Dairy Queen, ChuckeCheese, Waffle House, IHOP, Subway, Mrs Winner's, Ryan's, El Amigo's Mexican, Japanese Steaks, PoFolks, **other:** Firestone/auto, Goodyear, K-Mart, U-Haul, **W...gas:** Chevron/24hr, Phillips 66, QT/diesel/24hr, **food:** Arby's, Barnacle's Grill, Blimpie, Hooters, Pappadeaux Steak/seafood, RW GoodTimes Grill, Shoney's, Waffle House, Wendy's, **lodging:** Drury Inn, Comfort Inn, Country Inn Suites, **other:** AutoZone, Big 10 Tire, NTB, PepBoys

96 Pleasantdale Rd, Northcrest Rd, **E...food:** Burger King, **lodging:** Econolodge, **other:** West Marine, **W...gas:** BP/diesel, QT/diesel, **food:** Waffle House, **lodging:** Howard Johnson

95 I-285, no facilities

94 Chamblee-Tucker Rd, **E...gas:** Amoco, Shell, **lodging:** Masters Inn, Travel Inn, **W...gas:** QT/diesel, Texaco/diesel, **food:** Dairy Queen, Waffle House, **lodging:** Motel 6, Red Roof Inn, **other:** to Mercer U

93 Shallowford Rd, to Doraville, **E...gas:** Shell, **food:** Waffle House, Pizza 2 U, **lodging:** Global Inn, U-Haul, **W...gas:** Citgo/Circle K, Texaco/diesel, **lodging:** Quality Inn

91 US 23, GA 155, Clairmont Rd, **E...gas:** Chevron, Flash, **food:** Popeye's, IHOP, Waffle House, Mo's Pizza, **other:** CVS Drug, Firestone, Piggly Wiggly, **W...gas:** Amoco/diesel/24hr, **food:** McDonald's, Roadhouse Grill, Waffle House, Williams Seafood Rest., **lodging:** Day's Inn, Marriott, Wingate Inn, **other:** NTB, Sam's Club

89 GA 42, N Druid Hills, **E...gas:** Amoco/24hr, QT/diesel/24hr, Crown Gas, **food:** Arby's, Burger King, Chick-fil-A, Grady's Grill, McDonald's, Mexican Rest., Miami Subs, Morrison's Cafeteria, Rally's, Taco Bell, Wall St Pizza, **lodging:** Courtyard, **other:** CVS Drug, Eckerd, Firestone/auto, Target, **W...gas:** BP/diesel, Chevron, Exxon, Hess/diesel, **food:** Applebee's, BBQ, Capt D's, Denny's, Dunkin Donuts, Folks Rest, Krystal, Waffle House, **lodging:** Hampton Inn, Radisson, Red Roof Inn, Travelodge

88 Lenox Rd, GA 400 N, Cheshire Br Rd(from sb), **E...lodging:** Baymont Suites, **W...food:** Pancho's Mexican

87 GA 400 N(from nb), no facilities

86 GA 13 S, Peachtree St, **E...gas:** Amoco, BP, **food:** Denny's, Wendy's, **lodging:** La Quinta, **other:** Brake-O, **W...lodging:** Ramada Inn, Sleep Inn

85 I-75 N, to Marietta, Chattanooga

84 Techwood Dr, 14th St, **E...gas:** Amoco, BP/diesel, **food:** CheeseSteaks, La Bamba Mexican, Thai Cuisine, VVV Ristorante Italiano, **lodging:** Hampton Inn, Marriott, Sheraton, Travelodge, **other:** Woodruff Arts Ctr, **W...food:** AllStar Pizza, Blimpie, **lodging:** Courtyard, Villager Lodge, **other:** CVS Drug, Office Depot

I-85 and I-75 run together 8 miles. See Georgia Interstate 75, exits 243-249.

77 I-75 S, no facilities

76 Cleveland Ave, **E...gas:** BP, Conoco, Hess, Phillips 66/Blimpie, **food:** Arby's, Burger King, Mrs Winner's/Del Taco, WK Wings Rest., **lodging:** American Inn, Day's Inn, **other:** HOSPITAL, CVS Drug, Kroger, Radio Shack, **W...other:** Advance Parts, Chevrolet, Honda

GEORGIA

Interstate 85

N ↕ S

Atlanta Area

75 Sylvan Rd, **E...lodging:** Best Western, **W...lodging:** Mark Inn

74 Aviation Commercial Center

73b a Virginia Ave, **E...gas:** Citgo/diesel, **food:** Hardee's, IHOP, KFC, Malone's Grill, McDonald's, Morrison's Cafeteria, Pizza Hut, Schlotsky's, Waffle House, Wendy's, **lodging:** Club Hotel, Courtyard, Drury Inn, Hilton, Renaissance Hotel, Red Roof Inn, Residence Inn, **W...gas:** Chevron/24hr, Texaco, **food:** Blimpie, Happy Buddha Chinese, Hardee's, KFC, Steak&Ale, Waffle House, Crowne Plaza, **lodging:** Country Inn Suites, Econolodge, Harvey Hotel, Holiday Inn, Howard Johnson, Ramada Plaza

72 Camp Creek Pkwy

71 Riverdale Rd, Atlanta Airport, **E...food:** Ruby Tuesday, **lodging:** Comfort Suites, Courtyard, GA Conv Ctr, Microtel, Hampton Inn, Sheraton/grill, Sleep Inn, Sumner Suites, Super 8, Wingate Inn, **W...food:** Bennigan's, **lodging:** Comfort Inn, Day's Inn, Embassy Suites, Marriott, Quality Inn, Ramada, Super 8, Travelodge, Westin Hotel

69 GA 14, GA 279, **E...gas:** Chevron/24hr, **food:** Denny's, Waffle House, **lodging:** La Quinta, Radisson, **other:** CVS Drug, Goodyear/auto, **W...gas:** BP, Citgo, Conoco/diesel, Exxon/diesel, RaceTrac, Texaco, **food:** Arby's, Blimpie, Burger King, Cajun Crabhouse, Checker's, Church's, El Ranchero Mexican, KFC, Krystal, Longhorn Steaks, McDonald's, Pizza Hut, Red Lobster, ShowCase Eatery, Steak&Ale, Subway, Taco Bell, Wendy's, **lodging:** Baymont Inn, Day's Inn, Fairfield Inn, Red Roof Inn, **other:** Advance Parts, AutoZone, Cottman Transmissions, Family$, Kroger, Radio Shack, Target, U-Haul

68 I-285 Atlanta Perimeter, no facilities

66 Flat Shoals Rd, **W...gas:** BP, Chevron/diesel, Texaco/Blimpie, **food:** Supreme Fish Delight, Waffle House, **lodging:** Motel 6

64 GA 138, to Union City, **E...gas:** BP/Blimpie/diesel, **food:** Waffle House, **lodging:** Econolodge, Ramada Ltd, **other:** Buick/Pontiac/GMC, Chevrolet, Chrysler, Dodge, Ford, Honda, Kia/Nissan, Saturn, Toyota, **W...gas:** Chevron, QT, Shell, Texaco/diesel, **food:** Arby's, Burger King, Capt D's, China King, Corner Café, Cracker Barrel, IHOP, KFC, Krystal, La Fiesta Mexican, McDonald's, Papa John's, Pizza Hut, Subway, Taco Bell, Wendy's, **lodging:** Comfort Inn, Day's Inn, Holiday Inn Express, Microtel, Red Roof Inn, **other:** Aamco, Chevrolet, $Tree, Eckerd, Firestone, Goodyear/auto, Ingles, Kroger, NTB, PepBoys, Sears/auto, Wal-Mart, mall

61 GA 74, to Fairburn, **E...gas:** BP, Chevron, RaceTrac, Shell, **food:** Hickory House Rest., McDonald's, Waffle House, Wendy's, **W...gas:** Citgo/diesel, Marathon, Phillips 66/Blimpie/diesel, **lodging:** Efficiency Motel

56 Collinsworth Rd, **W...gas:** BP, Marathon/Blimpie, **food:** Frank's Rest.

51 GA 154, to Sharpsburg, **E...gas:** BP/diesel, Phillips 66/Blimpie/diesel, **food:** Hardee's, **W...gas:** Chevron/diesel, Shell/Krystal/diesel, **food:** Waffle House

Newnan

47 GA 34, to Newnan, **E...gas:** BP, Chevron/diesel, Citgo/Subway, Shell, Texaco, **food:** Applebee's, Arby's, Dunkin Donuts, Hooters, LongHorn Steaks, Red Lobster, Ruby Tuesday, Ryan's, Schlotsky's, Sprayberry's BBQ, Steak'n Shake, Texas Roadhouse, Waffle House, Wendy's, **lodging:** Hampton Inn, Jameson Inn, Springhill Suites, **other:** Circuit City, Goodyear, Goody's, Home Depot, Kohl's, Lowe's Whse, OfficeMax, Peachtree Stores/famous brands, Wal-Mart SuperCtr/24hr, **W...gas:** Exxon/diesel, HotSpot/diesel, Phillips 66, RaceTrac, **food:** Burger King, Chick-fil-A, Cracker Barrel, Golden Corral, Hardee's, IHOP, KFC, Krystal, O'Charley's, Taco Bell, Waffle House, Zaxby's, **lodging:** Best Western, Comfort Inn, Day's Inn, Holiday Inn Express, La Quinta, Motel 6, **other:** HOSPITAL, BJ's Whse, Chevrolet, Ford/Lincoln/Mercury, Hyundai, Michael's, Office Depot, Old Navy, Plymouth, Pontiac/Buick/GMC, Publix, Target, Tires+, Toyota

41 US 27/29, Newnan, **E...gas:** Pilot/diesel/24hr/@, **food:** Wendy's, **W...gas:** Amoco/diesel/24hr, BP/24hr, Flash/diesel, Phillips 66, **food:** Blimpie, McDonald's, Waffle House, **lodging:** Day's Inn, Ramada Ltd, Super 8

35 US 29, to Grantville, **W...gas:** BP/diesel, Phillips 66/diesel

28 GA 54, GA 100, to Hogansville, **E...gas:** Shell/diesel, **W...gas:** BP/diesel, Chevron/diesel, Noble's Trkstp/Janet's Rest./diesel/@, **food:** BBQ, McDonald's, Subway, Waffle House, Wendy's, **lodging:** Day's Inn, KeyWest Inn, **other:** Ingles, Flat Creek RV Park

23mm Beech Creek

22mm weigh sta both lanes

21 I-185 S, to Columbus, no facilities

18 GA 109, to Mountville, **E...gas:** Chevron/Domino's/diesel, **lodging:** Econolodge, **other:** to FDR SP, Little White House HS, **W...gas:** BP/diesel, Citgo, RaceTrac, Shell/Church's/diesel, **food:** Applebee's, Banzai Japanese, Burger King, Los Nopales Mexican, Ryan's, Subway, Waffle House, Wendy's, **lodging:** AmeriHost, Best Western, Holiday Inn Express, Jameson Inn, Super 8, **other:** Chrysler/Plymouth/Dodge/Jeep, Ford/Lincoln/Mercury, Home Depot, Honda, Hoofer's RV Park(3mi), JC Penney

LaGrange

14 US 27, to La Grange, **W...gas:** BP/24hr, Pure, Shell/Church's, **lodging:** Hampton Inn

13 GA 219, to La Grange, **E...gas:** Texaco Trkstp/diesel/24hr/@, **food:** Waffle House, **lodging:** Admiral Benbow, Day's Inn, **other:** truckwash, **W...gas:** BP/diesel, Pilot/Subway/diesel/24hr/@, **food:** McDonald's, **other:** HOSPITAL

10mm Long Cane Creek

2 GA 18, to West Point, **E...gas:** BP, Shell/Church's/diesel/24hr, **food:** KFC, **lodging:** Travelodge, **W...**to West Point Lake, camping

.5mm **Welcome Ctr nb, full(handicapped)facilities, phone, picnic tables, litter barrels, vending, petwalk**

0mm Georgia/Alabama state line, Chattahoochee River, eastern/central time zone

Interstate 95

N

S

Exit #	Services
113mm	Georgia/South Carolina state line, Savannah River
111mm	**Welcome Ctr/weigh sta sb, full(handicapped)facilities, info, phone, vending, picnic tables, litter barrels, petwalk**
109	GA 21, to Savannah, Pt Wentworth, Rincon, **E...gas:** Enmark/diesel, Pilot/diesel/24hr/@, **food:** McDonald's, Subway, Waffle House, **lodging:** Country Inn Suites, Hampton Inn, **W...gas:** 76/Circle K/diesel, **food:** Wendy's, Sea Grill Rest., **lodging:** Holiday Inn Express, Quality Inn, Ramada Ltd, Savannah Inn, Sleep Inn, Super 8
107mm	Augustine Creek
106	Jimmy DeLoach Pkwy, no facilities
104	Savannah Airport, **E...gas:** Amoco, Shell/diesel, **food:** Waffle House, **lodging:** Fairfield Inn, Hawthorn Suites, **other:** to airport, **W...gas:** Texaco/Subway, **food:** Arby's, Schlotsky's, Sonic, Zaxby's Café, **lodging:** Red Roof Inn, **other:** Home Depot, Wal-Mart SuperCtr/Radio Grill/gas/24hr
102	US 80, to Garden City, **E...gas:** Amoco, Enmark/diesel, **food:** Cracker Barrel, Huddle House, KFC, Krystal, McDonald's, Peking Chinese, Pizza Hut/Taco Bell, Waffle House, **lodging:** Best Western, Jameson Inn, Microtel, Ramada Ltd, Travelodge Suites, **other:** Food Lion, Family$, Russell Stover, to Ft Pulaski NM, museum, **W...gas:** BP, Gate/diesel, Shell, **food:** BBQ, Burger King, Domino's, El Potro Mexican, Hardee's, Italian Pizza, Subway, Wendy's, Western Sizzlin, **lodging:** Comfort Inn, Country Hearth Inn, Econolodge, **other:** CarCare
99b a	I-16, W to Macon, E to Savannah
94	GA 204, to Savannah, Pembroke, **E...gas:** Amoco/diesel, El Cheapo/24hr, Exxon, 76/Circle K, Shell/diesel, **food:** Cracker Barrel, Denny's, Hardee's, McDonald's, Perkins, **lodging:** Best Western, Clarion, Comfort Inn, Country Inn Suites, Day's Inn, Fairfield Inn, GuestHouse Inn, Hampton Inn, Holiday Inn, La Quinta, Quality Inn, Red Roof Inn, Shoney's Inn/rest., Sleep Inn, Wingate Inn, **other:** HOSPITAL, Factory Stores, **W...gas:** Chevron/diesel/24hr, Shell, **food:** Huddle House, Subway, Waffle House, **lodging:** Econolodge, Red Carpet Inn, Microtel, Super 8, **other:** Harley-Davidson, Bellaire Woods RV Park(2mi)
91mm	Ogeechee River
90	GA 144, Old Clyde Rd, to Ft Stewart, Richmond Hill SP, **E...gas:** BP(1mi), Chevron, Exxon, **food:** El Potro Mexican(1mi), Hardee's, **other:** Kroger, Waterway RV Park(3mi), **W...gas:** Shell/diesel
87	US 17, to Coastal Hwy, Richmond Hill, **E...gas:** Amoco, Chevron/diesel/24hr, Phillips 66, RaceTrac, **food:** Denny's/24hr, Huddle House, Subway, Waffle House, **lodging:** Day's Inn, Motel 6, Royal Inn, Scottish Inn, Travelodge, **W...gas:** Exxon/diesel, Speedway/diesel, 76/Circle K, TA/LJSilver/Pizza Hut/diesel/24hr/@, Texaco/diesel, **food:** Arby's, Burger King, KFC/Taco Bell, McDonald's, Waffle House, Wendy's, **lodging:** Econolodge, Hampton Inn, Holiday Inn, Ramada Inn, **other:** KOA
85mm	Elbow Swamp
80mm	Jerico River
76	US 84, GA 38, to Midway, Sunbury, **E...**hist sites, **W...gas:** Amoco, BP/diesel, **food:** Holton's Seafood, Huddle House, **other:** HOSPITAL, RV camping, museum
67	US 17, Coastal Hwy, to S Newport, **E...gas:** BP, Chevron/diesel, Shell/McDonald's, Texaco, **other:** Newport Camping(2mi), RiverFront RV Park, **W...gas:** Amoco
58	GA 99, GA 57, Townsend Rd, Eulonia, **E...gas:** Amoco/diesel, Marathon, **food:** Altman's Rest., **lodging:** Eulonia Lodge, **other:** MEDICAL CARE, **W...gas:** Amoco/diesel, Chevron/diesel/24hr, Shell/diesel, Texaco/Day's Inn/Eulonia Café, **food:** Huddle House, **lodging:** Best Inn, **other:** McIntosh Lake RV Park, Lake Harmony RV Camp
55mm	weigh sta both lanes, phone
49	GA 251, to Darien, **E...gas:** BP/diesel, Chevron/diesel/24hr, **food:** Archie's Rest.(1mi), DQ, McDonald's, Waffle House, **lodging:** Ft King George Motel, **other:** Inland Harbor RV Park, Tall Pines RV Park, **W...gas:** Amoco, Mobil/diesel, Shell/diesel, Texaco/diesel, **food:** Burger King, Huddle House, KFC/Pizza Hut/Taco Bell, TCBY, **lodging:** Comfort Inn, Hampton Inn, Holiday Inn Express, Super 8, **other:** Prime Outlets/famous brands, flea mkt
47mm	Darien River
46.5mm	Butler River
46mm	Champney River
45mm	Altamaha River
42	GA 99, **E...**to Hofwyl Plantation HS
41mm	**rest area sb, full(handicapped)facilities, info, phone, vending, picnic tables, litter barrels, petwalk**
38	GA 25, to US 17, N Golden Isles Pkwy, Brunswick, **E...gas:** Racetrac, **food:** Applebee's, Capt D's, FoodCourt, Ruby Tuesday, **lodging:** Embassy Suites, Fairfield Inn, Jameson Inn, **other:** HOSPITAL, **W...gas:** Amoco, Flash, Shell/diesel, **food:** Godfather's, Waffle House, **lodging:** Econolodge, Guest Cottage Motel, Quality Inn
36b a	US 25, US 341, Brunswick, to Jesup, **E...gas:** Amoco, Chevron/diesel/24hr, Exxon/diesel, RaceTrac, Shell/diesel, **food:** Burger King, Cracker Barrel, IHOP, KFC, Krystal/24hr, McDonald's, Pizza Hut, Shoney's, Taco Bell, Waffle House, Wendy's, **lodging:** Baymont Inn, Day's Inn, Hampton Inn, Knight's Inn, Ramada Inn, Red Roof Inn, **W...gas:** Amoco, BP/diesel, Mobil/diesel, **food:** BBQ, Capt Joe's Seafood, Denny's, Huddle House/24hr, Matteo's Italian, Minh-Shun Chinese, Subway, Waffle House, **lodging:** Best Western, Comfort Inn, Holiday Inn, Motel 6, Sleep Inn, Super 8, **other:** CVS Drug, Discount Parts, $General, Family$, Winn-Dixie

Savannah

Brunswick

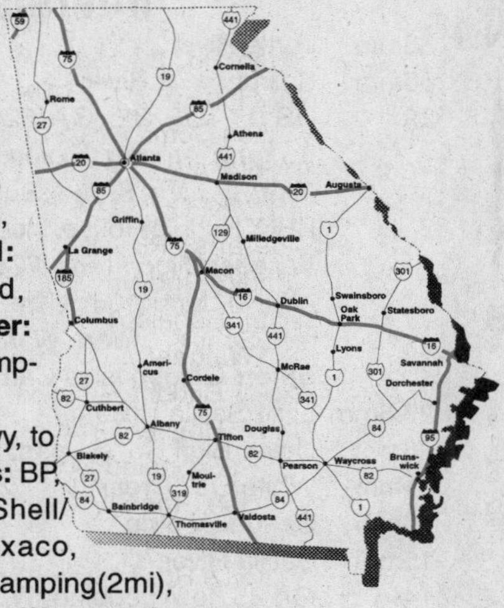

GEORGIA

Interstate 95

33mm Turtle River

30mm S Brunswick River

29 US 17, US 82, GA 520, S GA Pkwy, Brunswick, **E...gas:** Amoco, Exxon, Phillips 66/Church's/diesel, Pilot/Steak'n Shake/Subway/diesel/24hr/@ , **food:** BBQ, Huddle House, McDonald's, **other:** Blue Beacon, **W...gas:** Citgo, Flying J/Conoco/Country Mkt/diesel/LP/24hr/@ , Mobil/KrispyKreme, Shell/diesel, TA/BP/diesel/rest./24hr/@ , **food:** Waffle House, DayStop, Super 8, **other:** Golden Isles Camping

27.5mm Little Satilla River

26 Dover Bluff Rd, **E...gas:** Mobil/diesel, **food:** BBQ

21mm White Oak Creek

19mm Canoe Swamp

15mm Satilla River

14 GA 25, to Woodbine, **W...food:** BP, Sav-a-Ton/diesel/24hr, Sunshine/diesel/rest./24hr, **food:** BBQ, **lodging:** Stardust Motel(3mi)

7 Harrietts Bluff Rd, **E...gas:** Shell, Texaco/Taco Bell/diesel, **food:** Huddle House, Jack's BBQ, Wishbone Café, **W...gas:** Chevron/diesel

6.5mm Crooked River

6 Laurel Island Pkwy, **E...gas:** BP/Arby's/diesel/24hr, Cone/diesel/24hr, **other:** pecans

3 GA 40, Kingsland, to St Marys, **E...gas:** Amoco, BP, Chevron, Enmark/diesel, Mobil, Shell/Subway, Texaco/Krystal, **food:** Applebee's, BBQ, Burger King, Chick-fil-A, Cucina Italian, DQ, Dynasty Chinese, KFC, McDonald's, Pablo's Mexican, Pizza Hut, Ponderosa, Shoney's, Taco Bell, Waffle House, Wendy's, Zaxby's, **lodging:** Best Western, Comfort Inn, Country Inn Suites, Day's Inn, Hampton Inn, Holiday Inn Express, Super 8, **other:** HOSPITAL, Chevrolet/Buick, Chrysler/Plymouth/Jeep, CVS Drug, $Tree, Ford/Mercury, Kia, K-Mart, Publix, Winn-Dixie, to Submarine Base, **W...gas:** Citgo/diesel, Exxon/diesel, Pilot/diesel/@ , RaceTrac, **food:** Cracker Barrel, Waffle House, **lodging:** Econolodge, Howard Johnson, Jameson Inn, Quality Inn

1 St Marys Rd, **E...Welcome Ctr nb, full(handicapped)facilities, phone, vending, picnic tables, litter barrels, petwalk, gas:** Cisco/Blimpie/DQ/Maui Taco/Mrs Winners/diesel/@ , **food:** Pizza Hut, to Cumberland Is Nat Seashore, **W...gas:** BP/diesel, Chevron/diesel, Wilco/Hess/diesel/@ , **other:** Country Oaks RV Park, KOA

0mm Georgia/Florida state line, St Marys River

Interstate 185(Columbus)

Exit # Services

48 I-85. I-185 begins/ends on I-85.

46 Big Springs Rd, **E...**BP, **W...gas:** Shell

42 US 27, Pine Mountain, **E...gas:** BP, Shell/diesel, **food:** Waffle House, **other:** to Callaway Gardens, Little White House HS

34 GA 18, to West Point, **E...gas:** Shell/diesel/24hr

30 Hopewell Church Rd, Whitesville, **W...gas:** Amoco/diesel

25 GA 116, to Hamilton, **W...**RV camping

19 GA 315, Mulberry Grove, **W...gas:** Chevron/diesel/24hr

14 Smith Rd, no facilities

12 Williams Rd, **W...Welcome Ctr, gas:** Amoco, Shell, **food:** Church's, **lodging:** Country Inn Suites

10 US 80, GA 22, to Phenix City, **W...**Springer Opera House

8 Airport Thruway, **E...gas:** Chevron, **food:** Blimpie, China Moon, Shoney's, **other:** Advance Parts, Circuit City, Home Depot, Sam's Club, Wal-Mart, **W...gas:** Amoco, Citgo, Crown, **food:** Applebee's, Burger King, Capt D's, Hardee's, IHOP, KFC, McDonald's, Outback Steaks, Subway, Taco Bell/Pizza Hut, **lodging:** Comfort Inn, Extended Stay America, Hampton Inn, Sheraton, **other:** Cub Foods, K-Mart, Office Depot

7 45th St, Manchester Expswy, **E...gas:** Chevron, **food:** Applebee's, Burger King, Chevy's Mexican, Krystal, Ruby Tuesday, **lodging:** Baymont Inn, Courtyard, Super 8, **other:** Chevrolet/Cadillac, Dillard's, mall, **W...gas:** Amoco, BP, Chevron, Crown, **food:** Arby's, China Express, Crystal River Seafood, Dunkin Donuts, Logan's Roadhouse, McDonald's, Pizza Hut, Ryan's, Sonic, Subway, Waffle House, Wendy's, **lodging:** Fairfield Inn, Holiday Inn, Sleep Inn, **other:** HOSPITAL

6 GA 22, Macon Rd, E...food: Burger King, China Buffet, KFC, Pizza Hut, Taco Bell, Waffle House, lodging: Best Western, Comfort Inn, Day's Inn, other: Eckerd, Ford, Nissan, U-Haul, W...gas: BP, Chevron, food: Capt D's, Denny's, Longhorn Steaks, McDonald's, lodging: Efficiency Lodge, LaQuinta, other: Honda, OfficeMax, Publix

4 Buena Vista Rd, **E...gas:** BP, **food:** Arby's, Burger King, Capt D's, Chef Lee Chinese, Church's, Krystal, McDonald's, Pizza Hut, Taco Bell, Waffle House, **other:** AutoZone, Firestone/auto, Jones Foods, Super$, **W...gas:** Chevron, Crown, Spectrum

3 St Marys Rd, **W...gas:** Amoco, BP/diesel, **food:** KFC, DQ, Hardee's

1b a US 27, US 280, Victory Dr, **1-3 mi W...gas:** RaceTrac/24hr, **food:** Burger King, Denny's, KFC, McDonald's, Popeye's, **lodging:** Econolodge, Colony Inn, Day's Inn, Motel 6. I-185 begins/ends.

Interstate 285(Atlanta)

Exit # Services

62 GA 279, Roosevelt Hwy, Old Nat Hwy, **N...gas:** BP, Chevron, **lodging:** La Quinta, **S...gas:** Exxon, Shell, **food:** Burger King, Checker's, China Cafeteria, Church's, Dock's Rest., KFC, Krystal, Longhorn Steaks, McDonald's, Mrs Winner's, Popeye's, Red Lobster, Taco Bell, Waffle House, Wendy's, **lodging:** Day's Inn, Fairfield Inn, Howard Johnson, Radisson, Red Roof Inn, **other:** AutoZone, Cottman Transmissions, Family$, U-Haul

61 I-85, N to Atlanta, S to Montgomery. **Services 1 mi N...see GA I-85, exit 71.**

Interstate 285

60 GA 139, Riverdale Rd, **N...lodging:** Microtel(2mi), **S...gas:** BP, Exxon, QT/Blimpie, Shell/diesel, Speedway/diesel, **food:** Burger King, Checker's, China Café, McDonald's, Waffle House, Wendy's, **lodging:** Best Western, Day's Inn, Ramada Inn, Travelodge, **other:** Family$

59 Clark Howell Hwy, **N...**air cargo

58 I-75, N to Atlanta, S to Macon(from eb), to US 19, US 41, Forest Park, to Hapeville, **S...gas:** Amoco, Chevron/24hr, **food:** Waffle House, **lodging:** Home Lodge Motel

55 GA 54, Jonesboro Rd, **N...lodging:** Super 8, **S...gas:** Amoco, Citgo/diesel, Phillips 66, RaceTrac, Shell/diesel, **food:** Alondra's Mexican/Chinese, Arby's, DaiLai Vietnamese, McDonald's, Waffle House, **other:** Home Depot

53 US 23, Moreland Ave, to Ft Gillem, **N...gas:** Amoco, Conoco/diesel, Speedway/diesel, **S...gas:** Citgo, Shell, TA/diesel/24hr/@, **food:** Popeye's, Wendy's, **lodging:** Economy Inn

52 I-675, S to Macon

51 Bouldercrest Rd, **N...gas:** Amoco/24hr, Pilot/Wendy's/diesel/24hr, **food:** Hardee's, KFC/Pizza Hut, WK Wings, **lodging:** DeKalb Inn, **other:** Family$, Wayfield Foods, **S...gas:** Chevron/diesel

48 GA 155, Flat Shoals Rd, Candler Rd, **N...gas:** Circle K, Marathon, Shell/diesel, **food:** Arby's, Checker's, DQ, KFC/Pizza Hut, McDonald's, Taco Bell, Waffle King, WK Wings, **lodging:** Econolodge, Great American Inn, Ramada Ltd, **S...gas:** QT, Foodmart, Shell

46b a I-20, E to Augusta, W to Atlanta

44 GA 260, Glenwood Rd, **E...gas:** Marathon, Super 8, **W...gas:** Shell, **food:** Church's, Mrs Winner's, **lodging:** Glenwood Inn

43 US 278, Covington Hwy, **E...gas:** Chevron/Subway/24hr, Citgo/diesel, **other:** U-Haul, **W...gas:** Amoco/24hr, Shell/diesel, **food:** Blimpie, Checker's, KFC/Taco Bell, Mrs Winner's, Wendy's, **lodging:** Best Inn, **other:** Advance Parts, Family$, Firestone/auto

42 Marta Station

41 GA 10, Memorial Dr, Avondale Estates, **E...gas:** QT, Shell/diesel, **food:** Applebee's, Arby's, Burger King, Church's, Hardee's, McDonald's, Steak'n Shake, Waffle House, Wendy's, **lodging:** Savannah Suites, **other:** Advance Parts, AutoZone, Circuit City, Office Depot, Radio Shack, **W...gas:** Mobil, **food:** KFC, Waffle King, **lodging:** Comfort Inn

40 Church St, to Clarkston, **E...gas:** Chevron, Citgo, Shell/diesel, **food:** Waffle House, **W...gas:** Shell, **other:** HOSPITAL

39b a US 78, to Athens, Decatur, no facilities

38 US 29, Lawrenceville Hwy, **E...gas:** Phillips 66, Shell, **food:** Waffle House, **lodging:** Knight's Inn, Super 8, **other:** HOSPITAL, **W...gas:** Amoco, Shell, **food:** Waffle House, **lodging:** Masters Inn, Red Roof Inn

37 GA 236, to LaVista, Tucker, **E...gas:** Chevron, Circle K, **food:** Checker's, Chili's, Folks Rest., IHOP, O'Charley's, Olive Garden, Piccadilly's, Schlotsky's, Steak&Ale, Waffle House, **lodging:** Comfort Suites, Country Inn Suites, **other:** Firestone, Target, **W...gas:** Amoco, BP/repair, Citgo, Shell, **food:** Arby's, Blackeyed Pea, Blue Ribbon Grill, DQ, Fuddrucker's, Jason's Deli, McDonald's, Panera Bread, Philly Connection, Pizza Hut, Red Lobster, Taco Bell, Wendy's, **lodging:** Courtyard, Fairfield Inn, Holiday Inn, Radisson, **other:** Best Buy, $Tree, Goodyear/auto, JC Penney, Kroger, Macy's, Office Depot, OfficeMax, Publix, mall

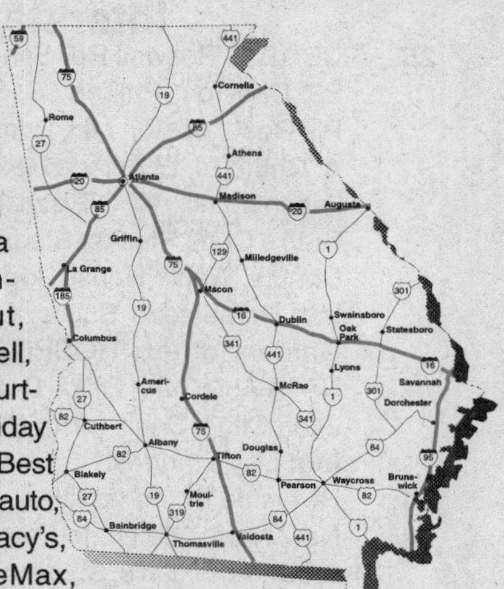

33b a I-85, N to Greenville, S to Atlanta

34 Chamblee-Tucker Rd, **E...gas:** Chevron, Citgo, Phillips 66, Shell, **food:** Arby's/Mrs Winner's, Blimpie, Galaxy Diner, Hunan Chinese, KFC/Taco Bell, S&S Cafeteria, **lodging:** Day's Inn, **other:** Advance Parts, Eckerd, Goodyear, **W...gas:** Amoco, Citgo, **food:** AllStar Grill, LoneStar Steaks, McDonald's, Waffle House

32 US 23, Buford Hwy, to Doraville, **E...gas:** Amoco/24hr, **food:** Burger King, Checker's, Chick-fil-A, El Azteca Mexican, KFC/Pizza Hut, Krystal, LJ Silver, Mrs Winners, Steak'n Shake, Wendy's, **other:** Firestone/auto, Goodyear/auto, K-Mart, OfficeMax, Target, **W...gas:** Phillips 66/diesel, **food:** Arby's, McDonald's, Szechuan Garden, Taco Bell, Waffle House, **lodging:** Comfort Inn

31b a GA 141, Peachtree Ind, to Chamblee, **W...food:** Chick-fil-A, Piccadilly, Red Lobster, Waffle House, Wendy's, **other:** Acura, Audi/VW, Buick/Pontiac, Chevrolet, CVS Drug, Dodge, Firestone, Ford, GMC, Isuzu, Kia, Lexus, Mazda, Mitsubishi, Porsche, Saab, Toyota

30 Chamblee-Dunwoody Rd, N Shallowford Rd, to N Peachtree Rd, **N...gas:** Amoco, BP, Chevron, **food:** Burger King, DQ, Del Taco, Mrs Winners, Subway, Waffle House, **other:** Kroger, **S...gas:** Exxon, Phillips 66, Shell, Texaco, **food:** Blimpie, Bombay Grill, China Express, City Café, KFC, LJ Silver, Mad Italian Rest., Malone's Grill, Papa John's, Taco Bell, Wendy's, **lodging:** Holiday Inn Select

29 Ashford-Dunwoody Rd, **N...gas:** Amoco, BP, Exxon, **food:** Applebee's, Calif Pizza, Chequer's Grill, Burger King, Denny's, Food Court, Fuddrucker's, Houlihan's, Maggiano's Italian, Mrs Winner's, Subway, **lodging:** Fairfield Inn, Holiday Inn, Marquis Hotel, Marriott, **other:** Best Buy, Firestone/auto, Goodyear/auto, Home Depot, Kroger, Marshall's, Old Navy, mall, **S...**Chevron, Conoco, Arby's, Christina's Café, Hilton Garden, Holiday Inn, Residence Inn

28 Peachtree-Dunwoody Rd(no EZ return wb), **N...food:** Burger King, Chequer's Grill, **lodging:** Comfort Suites, Concourse Hotel, Courtyard, Hampton Inn, Holiday Inn Express, Marriott, Residence Inn, Westin, Wyndham Garden, **other:** Eckerd, Goodyear/auto, OfficeMax, Publix, mall, **S...**HOSPITAL

27 US 19 N, GA 400, **2 mi N...**LDS Temple

26 Glenridge Dr(from eb), Johnson Ferry Rd

GEORGIA

Interstate 285

25 US 19 S, Roswell Rd, Sandy Springs, **N...gas:** Amoco, BP, Chevron, Phillips 66, Shell/diesel, **food:** American Pie Rest., Boston Mkt, Burger King, Checker's, Chick-fil-A, Church's, El Azteca Mexican, El Toro Mexican, IHOP, Jason's Deli, KFC/Pizza Hut, Panera Bread, Rally's, Ruth's Chris Steaks, Starbucks, 3$ Café, Togo's/Dunkin Donuts, Waffle House, **lodging:** Comfort Inn, Hampton Inn, Homestead Suites, Suburban Lodge, Wyndham Garden, **other:** HOSPITAL, Firestone/auto, K-Mart, NAPA AutoCare, Office Depot, Tires+, **S...gas:** Chevron/24hr, Citgo, Shell, **food:** Mama's Café, TGIFriday, **lodging:** Day's Inn/rest.

24 Riverside Dr, no facilities

22 New Northside Dr, to Powers Ferry Rd, **N...gas:** Shell, **food:** Bennigan's, **S...gas:** Amoco, Chevron/24hr, **food:** Blimpie, Chevy's Mexican, McDonald's, On-the-River Café, SideLines Grill, Waffle House, Wendy's, **other:** Crowne Plaza, CVS Drug

21 (from wb), **N...gas:** Shell, **food:** HillTop Café, Homestead Village, **other:** BMW

20 I-75, N to Chattanooga, S to Atlanta(from wb), to US 41 N

19 US 41, Cobb Pkwy, to Dobbins AFB, **N...gas:** BP, Amoco/24hr, Chevron/24hr, Citgo, Shell, **food:** Arby's, BBQ, Burger King, Carrabba's, Checker's, ChuckeCheese, Crabhouse Rest., Denny's, Dunkin Donuts, Folks Rest., Hardee's, Indian Cuisine, Jilly's Ribs, KFC, McDonald's, Old Hickory House Rest., Olive Garden, Pizza Hut, Red Lobster, Steak&Ale, Steak'n Shake, Sizzler, Taco Bell, Waffle House, Wendy's, **lodging:** French Quarter Hotel, Hilton, Holiday Inn, Howard Johnson, Red Roof Inn, **other:** MEDICAL CARE, Cadillac, Buick/Pontiac/Subaru, Chevrolet/Saab, Circuit City, Eckerd, Honda, Target, **S...gas:** Amoco/24hr, Chevron/24hr, **food:** Buffalo's Café, El Toro Mexican, Malone's Grill, Ruby Tuesday, Schlotsky's, **lodging:** Courtyard, Hampton Inn, Homewood Suites, Sheraton Suites, Stouffer Waverly Hotel, Sumner Suites, **other:** A&P, Barnes&Noble, JC Penney, Macy's, Sears/auto, mall

18 Paces Ferry Rd, to Vinings, **N...lodging:** Fairfield Inn, La Quinta, **S...gas:** BP, QT/24hr, Shell, **food:** Atlanta Exchange Café, Blimpie, Mrs Winner's, Subway, **lodging:** Hampton Inn, Studio+, Wyndham, **other:** Eckerd, Goodyear/auto, Home Depot, Publix

16 S Atlanta Rd, to Smyrna, **N...food:** Waffle House, **lodging:** Holiday Inn Express, **S...gas:** Exxon, Pilot/KFC/Subway/diesel/24hr/2, Texaco/diesel, RV Ctr

15 GA 280, S Cobb Dr, **E...lodging:** Microtel, **other:** U-Haul, **W...gas:** Amoco, BP/diesel, Exxon/diesel, RaceTrac, **food:** Arby's/Mrs Winners/Taco Bell, Checker's, Church's, IHOP, Krystal/24hr, McDonald's, Monterrey Mexican, Subway, Waffle House, Wendy's, **lodging:** AmeriHost, Knight's Inn, Sun Suites, **other:** HOSPITAL

14mm Chattahoochee River

13 Bolton Rd(from nb)

12 US 78, US 278, Bankhead Hwy, **E...gas:** Citgo/diesel, Petro/diesel/rest./24hr/@, **food:** McDonald's, Mrs Winner's, **other:** Blue Beacon, **W...gas:** Amoco

10b a I-20, W to Birmingham, E to Atlanta(exits left from nb), **W...**to Six Flags

9 GA 139, MLK Dr, to Adamsville, **E...gas:** Amoco, Phillips 66, **food:** KFC, McDonald's, Mrs Winner's, **other:** Family$, Winn-Dixie, **W...gas:** Chevron

7 Cascade Rd, **E...gas:** Chevron, Marathon, **other:** Kroger, **W...gas:** Amoco, Phillips 66, **food:** Applebee's, KFC, McDonald's, Mrs Winner's, Pizza Hut, Starbucks, Subway, Wendy's, **other:** HOSPITAL, Eckerd, GNC, Home Depot, Publix, Radio Shack

5b a GA 166, Lakewood Fwy, **E...gas:** Shell, **food:** Burger King, Capt D's, Checker's, DQ, Piccadilly's, Taco Bell, **other:** Circuit City, Cub Foods, CVS Drug, Goodyear, K-Mart, Kroger, mall, **W...gas:** Amoco, Conoco, Shell/diesel/24hr, Texaco, **food:** Church's, KFC, Mrs Winner's, Pizza Hut, Wendy's, **lodging:** Deluxe Inn, **other:** AutoZone, CVS Drug, Family$

2 Camp Creek Pkwy, to airport, **E...gas:** Amoco, BP, Shell/24hr, **food:** Checker's, McDonald's, Mrs Winner's, **lodging:** Clarion

1 Washington Rd, **E...gas:** BP/diesel, **W...gas:** Chevron, **lodging:** Regency Inn

Atlanta Area

Interstate 475(Macon)

N ↕ S

Exit #	Services
16mm	I-475 begins/ends on I-75, exit 177.
15	US 41, Bolingbroke, **1 mi E...gas:** Exxon/diesel/LP, Marathon/diesel
9	Zebulon Rd, **E...gas:** BP/Chin's Wok/24hr, Citgo, Shell/Pizza Hut/Taco Bell/24hr, Texaco/24hr, **food:** Buffalo's Café, Chick-fil-A, Fuddrucker's, Krystal, Margarita's Mexican, McDonald's, Papa John's, Sonic, Subway, Waffle House, Wendy's, **lodging:** Fairfield Inn, Jameson Inn, Sleep Inn, **other:** HOSPITAL, Kroger, Lowe's Whse, Radio Shack, USPO, **W...gas:** Citgo, Polly's Café
8mm	**rest area nb, full(handicapped)facilities, phone, vending, picnic tables, litter barrels, petwalk**
5	GA 74, Macon, **E...food:** Waffle House, Harley-Davidson/Suzuki, **other:** to Mercer U, **W...gas:** Exxon/Subway/Taco Bell, Marathon, Phillips 66/Church's/diesel, **food:** Fazoli's, Wok&Roll Chinese, **lodging:** Family Inn, **other:** $General, Food Lion, Tires+, to Lake Tobesofkee
3	US 80, Macon, **E...gas:** Citgo/Subway, Marathon/diesel, RaceTrac, **food:** BBQ, Cracker Barrel, Golden Corral, McDonald's, Popeye's, Waffle House, **lodging:** Best Western, Comfort Inn, Day's Inn, Discovery Inn, Economy Inn, Hampton Inn, Holiday Inn, Quality Inn, Red Carpet Inn, Regency Inn, Rodeway Inn, Super 8, Travelodge, **other:** Wal-Mart SuperCtr/gas/24hr, **1 mi E...food:** Applebee's, Chick-fil-A, KFC, Krystal, DQ, Taco Bell, **other:** Best Buy, BooksAMillion, Chrysler/Plymouth, Circuit City, CVS Drug, Dillard's, Firestone/auto, Honda, JC Penney, Jo-Ann Fabrics, Kroger, Lowe's Whse, Nissan, Sam's Club/gas, Sears/auto, Target, Toyota, mall, **W...gas:** Conoco/diesel, Shell, **food:** Burger King, **lodging:** Econolodge, Knight's Inn, Scottish Inn
0mm	I-475 begins/ends on I-75, exit 156.

Macon

Interstate 575

I-575 begins/ends on GA 5/515.

27 GA 5, Howell Br, to Ball Ground, no facilities

24 Airport Dr, no facilities

20 GA 5, to Canton, **E...gas:** Amoco, Krystal/24hr, **food:** Hardee's, McDonald's, Shoney's, **lodging:** Day's Inn, **other:** Wal-Mart/McDonald's, **W...gas:** Exxon/diesel, **food:** Waffle House

19 GA 20 E, Canton, no facilities

17 GA 140, Canton, to Roswell, no facilities

16 GA 20, GA 140, **W...gas:** Exxon

14 Holly Springs, **E...food:** Chris' Pinecrest Rest., **lodging:** Pinecrest Motel, **W...gas:** Amoco, BP, Chevron, Exxon, RaceTrac, **other:** Kroger

11 Sixes Rd, **E...gas:** Chevron, Citgo, **W...gas:** Conoco

8 Towne Lake Pkwy, to Woodstock, **E...gas:** BP, Chevron, **food:** HotRod Café, McDonald's, 1904 House Rest., Waffle House, Waffle King/24hr, **other:** Ford

7 GA 92, Woodstock, **E...gas:** Exxon, RaceTrac, Shell, **food:** Arby's, Burger King, McDonald's, Mrs Winner's, Waffle House, **lodging:** MetroLodge, **W...gas:** Amoco, **food:** IHOP, **other:** Honda, Home Depot

4 Bells Ferry Rd, **W...gas:** Chevron, QT/24hr, **food:** Arby's, Subway, Waffle House, **other:** Eckerd

3 Chastain Rd, to I-75 N, **E...gas:** BP, **W...gas:** Amoco, Shell, **food:** Arby's, Cracker Barrel, Subway, Waffle House, Wendy's, **lodging:** Comfort Inn, **other:** to Kennesaw St Coll

1 Barrett Pkwy, to I-75 N, US 41, **E...gas:** Chevron/24hr, **food:** Burger King, Hickory Ham Café, KFC, Waffle House, **other:** Barnes&Noble, Publix, **W...gas:** Chevron, Shell, **food:** McDonald's, Applebee's, Fuddrucker's, Olive Garden, Starbucks, Subway, $3 Cafe, **lodging:** Comfort Inn, Crestwood Suites, Day's Inn, Econolodge, Holiday Inn Express, Ramada Ltd, Red Roof Inn, Super 8, **other:** Home Depot, Marshall's, mall

0mm I-575 begins/ends on I-75, exit 268.

Interstate 675

Exit # Services

10mm I-285 W, to Atlanta Airport, E to Augusta. I-675 begins/ends on I-285, exit 52.

7 Ft Gillem, Anvil Block Rd, no facilities

5 Ellenwood Rd, to Ellenwood, no facilities

2 US 23, GA 42, **E...food:** El Puente Mexican, Mojoe's Café, **W...gas:** Speedway/diesel, **food:** Waffle House, **other:** Eckerd, Winn-Dixie/

1 GA 138, to I-75 N, Stockbridge, **E...gas:** Chevron/24hr, Citgo/diesel, Exxon, Marathon, Shell, **food:** Arby's, Blimpie, Buffalo's Café, Burger King, Capt D's, Checker's, DQ, Golden Corral, Hong Kong Buffet, KFC, McDonald's, Papa John's, Pizza Hut, Ryan's, Taco Bell, Waffle House, Wendy's, Zaxby's, **lodging:** Comfort Inn, Holiday Inn Express, Motel 6, Ramada Ltd, Shoney's Inn, Suburban Lodge, **other:** Advance Parts, Cub Foods, CVS Drug, Eckerd, Goodyear, Ingles Foods, Radio Shack, Wal-Mart SuperCtr/24hr, USPO, **W...gas:** RaceTrac, **food:** Applebee's, BBQ, Chick-fil-A, Damon's, Fazoli's, Frontera Mexican, IHOP, Krystal, LJ Silver, Morrison's Cafeteria, O'Charley's, Waffle House, **lodging:** Best Western, Day's Inn, Hampton Inn, **other:** HOSPITAL, Kroger, Tires+

I-675 N begins/ends on I-75, exit 227.

Interstate 985(Gainesville)

Exit # Services

I-985 begins/ends on US 23, 25mm.

24 to US 129 N, GA 369 W, Gainesville, **N...other:** HOSPITAL, GA Mtn Ctr, **S...gas:** Chevron/diesel, Citgo

22 GA 11, Gainesville, **N...gas:** BP, QT/24hr, **food:** Burger King, McDonald's, Waffle House, **lodging:** Best Western/rest., Masters Inn, Shoney's Inn/rest., **S...gas:** Citgo/diesel, Exxon, **food:** Huddle House, Waffle House

20 GA 60, GA 53, Gainesville, **N...food:** Hardee's, McDonald's, Mellow Mushroom Pizza, Mrs Winners, **lodging:** Day's Inn, Hampton Inn, Holiday Inn, Shoney's Inn/rest., **S...gas:** Citgo/diesel, **food:** Waffle House

16 GA 53, Oakwood, **N...gas:** Amoco, Citgo, **food:** Arby's, Baskin-Robbins/Dunkin Donuts, Burger King, DQ, El Sombrero Mexican, Hardee's, KFC, McDonald's, Pizza Hut, Subway, Taco Bell, Waffle House, **lodging:** Admiral Benbow Inn, Country Inn Suites, Jameson Inn, Shoney's Inn/rest., **other:** A&P, Chrysler/Jeep, Food Lion, RV Ctr, Sam's Club, **S...gas:** Amoco, Chevron, Citgo/diesel, Exxon, QT, **food:** Checker's, Mrs Winners, Waffle House, Wendy's, **lodging:** Comfort Inn, Goodyear/auto

12 Spout Springs Rd, Flowery Branch, **N...gas:** Amoco, **food:** Taco Bell, **S...gas:** BP/Subway, Chevron/diesel

8 GA 347, Friendship Rd, Lake Lanier, **N...gas:** Chevron, Phillips 66, **S...**RV Ctr

4 US 23 S, GA 20, Buford, **N...gas:** Amoco/24hr, RaceTrac/mart, Shell, **food:** Arby's, Burger King, Hardee's, Krystal, McDonald's, Shoney's, **other:** Big B Drug, Ingles Food, **S...gas:** Amoco/mart/wash, Chevron, Speedway/mart, **food:** Waffle House, **other:** $Tree, Lowe's Whse, Wal-Mart SuperCtr/24hr

0mm I-985 begins/ends on I-85.

IDAHO

Interstate 15

N ↕ S

Exit # Services

196mm Idaho/Montana state line, Monida Pass, continental divide, elev 6870

190 Humphrey, no facilities

184 Stoddard Creek Area, **E...**RV camping, **W...**Stoddard Creek Camping

180 Spencer, **E...food:** Opal Country Café, **other:** High Country Opal Store, **W...food:** Spencer Grill/RV Park

172 **E...**US Sheep Experimental Sta, no facilities

167 ID 22, Dubois, **E...gas:** Exxon/diesel/24hr, Phillips 66/diesel, **food:** Cow County Kettle, **lodging:** Crossroads Motel, **other:** Scoggins RV Park, **rest area both lanes, full(handicapped) facilities, phone, picnic table, litter barrels, petwalk, W...**to Craters NM, Nez Pearce Tr

150 Hamer, **E...other:** Goodyear, **gas**, **food**, phone

143 ID 33, ID 28, to Mud Lake, Rexburg, **W...**weigh sta both lanes

142mm roadside parking, hist site

135 ID 48, Roberts, **E...gas:** Tesoro/diesel/LP, **food:** Amy's Place, **other:** Western Wings RV Park

128 Osgood Area, **E...gas:** Sinclair/diesel

Idaho Falls

119 US 20 E, Idaho Falls, to Rexburg, **E...gas:** Sinclair/diesel, **food:** Applebee's, Brownstone Rest., Chili's, Denny's, JB's, Jaker's Steaks&Fish, Outback Steaks, Smitty's Rest., **lodging:** Best Western, Comfort Inn, Day's Inn, LeRitz Hotel, Motel 6, Quality Inn/rest., Red Lion Hotel, Shilo Inn/rest., Super 8, **other:** KOA, LDS Temple, **W...gas:** Shell

118 US 20, Broadway St, Idaho Falls, **E...gas:** Phillips 66/diesel, **food:** Arctic Circle, Domino's, JB's, Smitty's Pancakes, Wendy's, **lodging:** AmeriTel, Fairfield Inn, **other:** HOSPITAL, Buick/GMC, Ford, Harley-Davidson, Subaru, LDS Temple, **W...gas:** Chevron/diesel, Exxon, Flying J/diesel, Maverik, Phillips 66, **food:** Arby's, BBQ, Burger King, DQ, Hong Kong Chinese, Jack-in-the-Box, Little Caesar's, McDonald's, O'Brady's, Papa Murphy's, Pizza Hut, Subway, **lodging:** Comfort Inn, Motel 6, Motel West/rest., **other:** Albertson's, American RV Sales, AutoZone, RiteAid

113 US 26, to Idaho Falls, Jackson, **E...gas:** Sinclair/Dad's/diesel/24hr/@, Yellowstone/Exxon/diesel/motel/@, **other:** HOSPITAL, Targhee RV Park

108 Shelley, Firth Area, **3 mi E...gas:** Chevron, Stop'n Go/diesel, **other:** RV Park/dump

101mm rest area both lanes, full(handicapped)facilities, phone, picnic tables, litter barrels, petwalk, geological site

98 Rose-Firth Area, no facilities

94.5mm Snake River

93 US 26, ID 39, Blackfoot, **E...gas:** Chevron/24hr, Flying J/diesel/LP/24hr, Maverik, **food:** Arctic Circle, Domino's, Hogy Yogi, Homestead Rest., KFC, Little Caesar's, McDonald's, Papa Murphy's, Pizza Hut, Subway, Taco Bell, Taco Time, Wendy's, **lodging:** Best Western, Sunset Motel, Super 8, **other:** Albertson's, Checker Parts, Chrysler/Dodge/Ford/Lincoln/Mercury, Goodyear/auto, King's Discount, RiteAid, Schwab Tire, Wal-Mart SuperCtr/24hr, **W...**Phillips 66, Riverside Boot/saddleshop(4mi)

90.5mm Blackfoot River

89 US 91, S Blackfoot, **2 mi E...lodging:** Y Motel

80 Ft Hall, **W...gas:** Sinclair/diesel/rest./casino, **other:** Shoshone Bannock Tribal Museum

72 I-86 W, to Twin Falls, no facilities

Pocatello

71 Pocatello Creek Rd, Pocatello, **E...gas:** Chevron/Burger King, Phillips 66/diesel, Circle K, Shell/diesel/24hr, **food:** Applebee's, Frontier Pies, Jack-in-the Box, Perkins, Sandpiper Rest., Subway, **lodging:** AmeriTel, Best Western, Comfort Inn, Holiday Inn, Quality Inn/rest., Super 8, **other:** HOSPITAL, KOA(1mi), **W...gas:** Exxon, Sinclair, **food:** DQ, Papa Kelsey's Pizza, Senor Iguana's Mexican, SF Pizza, Sizzler, **other:** RiteAid, WinCo **Food**s, **1 mi W on Yellowstone...food:** Arby's, KFC, McDonald's, Papa Murphy's, Schlotsky's, Skipper's, Taco Bell, TCBY, Wendy's, Winger's, **other:** Albertson's, AutoZone, Ford, Fred Meyer, Radio Shack, Walgreen

69 Clark St, Pocatello, **W...other:** HOSPITAL, to ID St U, museum

67 US 30/91, 5th St, Pocatello, **E...gas:** Exxon/24hr, **1-2 mi W...gas:** Cowboys, Phillips 66/diesel, Sinclair/diesel, **food:** Elmer's Dining, McDonald's, Papa Paul's Rest., Pizza Hut, Subway, Taco Bell, Tom's Burgers, **lodging:** Best Western, Econolodge, Rainbow Motel, Sundial Inn, Thunderbird Motel, **other:** HOSPITAL, Cowboy RV Park, Del's **Food**s, Old Fort Hall, Sullivan's RV Tents, museum

63 Portneuf Area, **W...other:** to Mink Creek RA, RV camp/dump

59mm rest area/weigh sta both lanes, full(handicapped)facilities, phone, picnic table, litter barrel, vending, petwalk, hist site

58 Inkom(from sb), **1/2 mi W...gas:** Sinclair/diesel/café, **other:** Pebble Creek Ski Area

57 Inkom(from nb), same as 58

47 US 30, McCammon, to Lava Hot Springs, **E...gas:** Flying J/Conoco/diesel/LP/rest./24hr/@, Chevron/A&W/Taco Time/diesel, **food:** Subway, **other:** to Lava Hot Springs RA, McCammon RV Park

44 Lp 15, Jenson Rd, McCammon, **E...**access to **food**

40 Arimo, **E...gas:** Sinclair/diesel/deli, repair

36 US 91, Virginia, no facilities

31 ID 40, to Downey, Preston, **E...gas:** Shell/Flags West/diesel/motel/café/24hr/@, **other:** RV camping

25mm rest area sb, full(handicapped)facilities, phone, picnic tables, litter barrels, petwalk

24.5mm Malad Summit, elev 5574

22 to Devil Creek Reservoir, **E...**RV camping

17 ID 36, to Weston, to Preston, **W...food:** Deep Creek Rest.

13 ID 38, Malad City, **W...gas:** Chevron/Burger King, Phillips 66/diesel/café, **food:** Me&Lou's Rest., Papa Kelsey's Pizza/subs, **lodging:** Village Inn Motel, **other:** HOSPITAL, Chevrolet/Buick, carwash, **1 mi W...gas:** Tesoro, **food:** Chat&Chew Café, **other:** Thomas **Food**s, 3R's Tire, museum, repair

7mm Welcome Ctr nb, full(handicapped)facilities, info, phone, picnic tables, litter barrels, vending, petwalk

3 Woodruff, to Samaria, no facilities

0mm Idaho/Utah state line

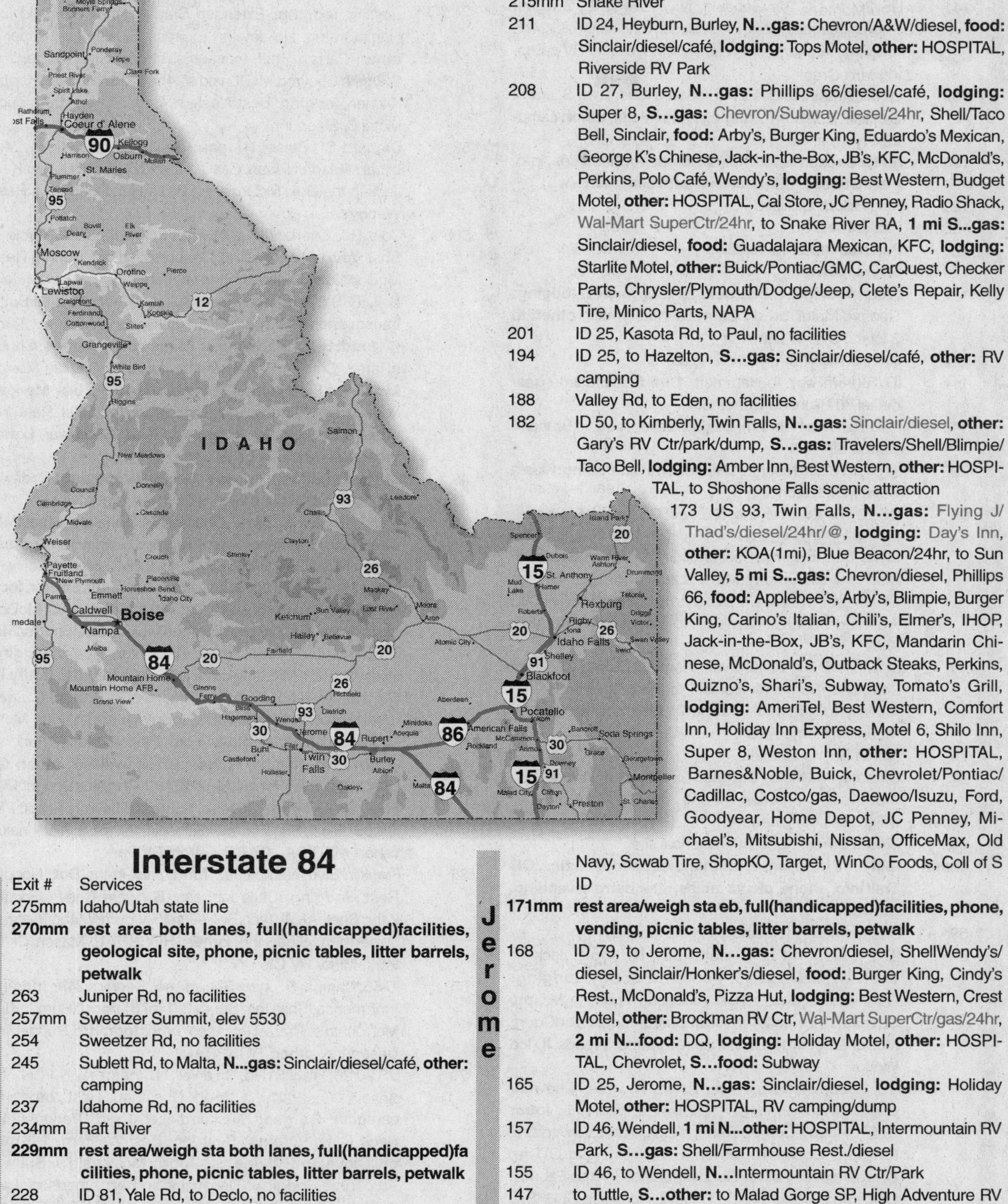

Interstate 84

E ↕ W

Exit #	Services
275mm	Idaho/Utah state line
270mm	**rest area both lanes, full(handicapped)facilities, geological site, phone, picnic tables, litter barrels, petwalk**
263	Juniper Rd, no facilities
257mm	Sweetzer Summit, elev 5530
254	Sweetzer Rd, no facilities
245	Sublett Rd, to Malta, **N...gas:** Sinclair/diesel/café, **other:** camping
237	Idahome Rd, no facilities
234mm	Raft River
229mm	**rest area/weigh sta both lanes, full(handicapped)facilities, phone, picnic tables, litter barrels, petwalk**
228	ID 81, Yale Rd, to Declo, no facilities
222	I-86, US 30 E to Pocatello, no facilities
216	ID 77, ID 25, to Declo, **N...gas:** Phillips 66/Blimpie/diesel, **other:** HOSPITAL, to Walcott SP, **S...gas:** Shell/Jake'sCafé/diesel, **other:** Frenchman's RV Park(6mi)
215mm	Snake River
211	ID 24, Heyburn, Burley, **N...gas:** Chevron/A&W/diesel, **food:** Sinclair/diesel/café, **lodging:** Tops Motel, **other:** HOSPITAL, Riverside RV Park
208	ID 27, Burley, **N...gas:** Phillips 66/diesel/café, **lodging:** Super 8, **S...gas:** Chevron/Subway/diesel/24hr, Shell/Taco Bell, Sinclair, **food:** Arby's, Burger King, Eduardo's Mexican, George K's Chinese, Jack-in-the-Box, JB's, KFC, McDonald's, Perkins, Polo Café, Wendy's, **lodging:** Best Western, Budget Motel, **other:** HOSPITAL, Cal Store, JC Penney, Radio Shack, Wal-Mart SuperCtr/24hr, to Snake River RA, **1 mi S...gas:** Sinclair/diesel, **food:** Guadalajara Mexican, KFC, **lodging:** Starlite Motel, **other:** Buick/Pontiac/GMC, CarQuest, Checker Parts, Chrysler/Plymouth/Dodge/Jeep, Clete's Repair, Kelly Tire, Minico Parts, NAPA
201	ID 25, Kasota Rd, to Paul, no facilities
194	ID 25, to Hazelton, **S...gas:** Sinclair/diesel/café, **other:** RV camping
188	Valley Rd, to Eden, no facilities
182	ID 50, to Kimberly, Twin Falls, **N...gas:** Sinclair/diesel, **other:** Gary's RV Ctr/park/dump, **S...gas:** Travelers/Shell/Blimpie/Taco Bell, **lodging:** Amber Inn, Best Western, **other:** HOSPITAL, to Shoshone Falls scenic attraction
173	US 93, Twin Falls, **N...gas:** Flying J/Thad's/diesel/24hr/@, **lodging:** Day's Inn, **other:** KOA(1mi), Blue Beacon/24hr, to Sun Valley, **5 mi S...gas:** Chevron/diesel, Phillips 66, **food:** Applebee's, Arby's, Blimpie, Burger King, Carino's Italian, Chili's, Elmer's, IHOP, Jack-in-the-Box, JB's, KFC, Mandarin Chinese, McDonald's, Outback Steaks, Perkins, Quizno's, Shari's, Subway, Tomato's Grill, **lodging:** AmeriTel, Best Western, Comfort Inn, Holiday Inn Express, Motel 6, Shilo Inn, Super 8, Weston Inn, **other:** HOSPITAL, Barnes&Noble, Buick, Chevrolet/Pontiac/Cadillac, Costco/gas, Daewoo/Isuzu, Ford, Goodyear, Home Depot, JC Penney, Michael's, Mitsubishi, Nissan, OfficeMax, Old Navy, Scwab Tire, ShopKO, Target, WinCo Foods, Coll of S ID
171mm	**rest area/weigh sta eb, full(handicapped)facilities, phone, vending, picnic tables, litter barrels, petwalk**
168	ID 79, to Jerome, **N...gas:** Chevron/diesel, ShellWendy's/diesel, Sinclair/Honker's/diesel, **food:** Burger King, Cindy's Rest., McDonald's, Pizza Hut, **lodging:** Best Western, Crest Motel, **other:** Brockman RV Ctr, Wal-Mart SuperCtr/gas/24hr, **2 mi N...food:** DQ, **lodging:** Holiday Motel, **other:** HOSPITAL, Chevrolet, **S...food:** Subway
165	ID 25, Jerome, **N...gas:** Sinclair/diesel, **lodging:** Holiday Motel, **other:** HOSPITAL, RV camping/dump
157	ID 46, Wendell, **1 mi N...other:** HOSPITAL, Intermountain RV Park, **S...gas:** Shell/Farmhouse Rest./diesel
155	ID 46, to Wendell, **N...**Intermountain RV Ctr/Park
147	to Tuttle, **S...other:** to Malad Gorge SP, High Adventure RV Park
146mm	Malad River

Jerome

IDAHO

Interstate 84

E ↕ W

141 US 26, to US 30, Gooding, **N...**HOSPITAL, **S...gas:** Phillips 66/diesel/café, Shell/diesel, Sinclair/diesel/24hr, **lodging:** Amber Inn, Hagerman Inn, **other:** RV camping

137 Lp 84, to US 30, Bliss, to Pioneer Road, **2 mi S...gas:** Sinclair/diesel/24hr, **lodging:** Y Inn Motel, **other:** camping

133mm rest area both lanes, full(handicapped)facilities, info, picnic tables, litter barrels, petwalk, phone(wb)

129 King Hill, no facilities

128mm Snake River

125 Paradise Valley, no facilities

122mm Snake River

121 Glenns Ferry, **1 mi S...gas:** Sinclair, Tesoro, **lodging:** Redford Motel, **other:** Carmela Winery/rest., **other:** to 3 Island SP, RV camping

120 Glenns Ferry(from eb), same as 121

114 ID 78(from wb), to Hammett, **1 mi S...**access to **gas**/diesel, to Bruneau Dunes SP

112 to ID 78, Hammett, **1 mi S...gas**/diesel, **food**, to Bruneau Dunes SP

99 ID 51, ID 67, to Mountain Home, **2 mi S...lodging:** Maple Cove Motel, camping

95 US 20, Mountain Home, **N...gas:** Chevron/KFC/diesel/24hr, Pilot/Arby's/diesel/24hr/@, **food:** AJ's Rest., Jack-in-the-Box, **lodging:** Best Western, Sleep Inn, **S...food:** McDonald's, Smoky Mtn Pizza, **lodging:** Hilander Motel(1mi), Towne Ctr Motel(1mi), **other:** HOSPITAL, Wal-Mart SuperCtr/gas/24hr, to Mountain Home AFB, KOA

90 to ID 51, ID 67, W Mountain Home, **S...gas:** Chevron/24hr, Shell/Burger King/diesel, **lodging:** to Hilander Motel, Maple Cove Motel, Towne Ctr Motel, **other:** KOA, to Mountain Home AFB

74 Simco Rd, no facilities

71 Orchard, Mayfield, **S...gas:** Sinclair/diesel/StageStop Motel/rest./24hr, **other:** phone

66mm weigh sta both lanes

64 Blacks Creek, Kuna Rd, historical site

62mm rest area both lanes, full(handicapped)facilities, OR Trail info, phone, picnic tables, litter barrels, vending, petwalk

59b a S Eisenman Rd, Memory Rd, no facilities

Boise

57 ID 21, Gowen Rd, to Idaho City, **N...food:** Jack-in-the-Box, McDonald's, Perkins, Subway, **lodging:** Northwest Lodge, **other:** Albertson's/**gas**, to Micron, **S...gas:** Chevron/24hr, **food:** Burger King, **Food**Court, McDonald's, **other:** Boise Stores/famous brands, ID Ice World

54 US 20/26, Broadway Ave, Boise, **N...gas:** Chevron/diesel/24hr, Flying J/Conoco/diesel/LP/24hr/@, **food:** Chili's, Hugo's Deli, Jack-in-the-Box, Subway, Wendy's, **lodging:** Courtyard, **other:** HOSPITAL, Big O Tire, Dowdie's Automotive, Goodyear/auto, Jo-Ann Fabrics, OfficeMax, Radio Shack, ShopKO, to Boise St U, **S...gas:** TA/Subway/Taco Bell/diesel/rest./24hr/@, **lodging:** Shilo Inn, **other:** Kenworth, Mtn View RV Park

53 Vista Ave, Boise, **N...gas:** Citgo/7-11, Shell/Taco Bell, Sinclair, **lodging:** Extended Stay America, Fairfield Inn, Hampton Inn, Holiday Inn Express, Quality Inn, Super 8, **other:** Parts'n Stuff, museums, st capitol, st police, zoo, **S...gas:** Chevron/McDonald's/24hr, **food:** Denny's, Kopper Kitchen, **lodging:** Best Western, Comfort Inn, InnAmerica, Motel 6, Sleep Inn

52 Orchard St, Boise, **N...gas:** Shell/Taco Bell/diesel/24hr, **other:** Mazda/Nissan, GMC, **1-2 mi N...food:** Burger King, Jack-in-the-Box, McDonald's, Pizza Hut, Raedean's Rest., Wendy's

50b a Cole Rd, Overland Rd, **N...gas:** Chevron/24hr, Circle K, Shell, **food:** Buster's Grill, Cancun Mexican, Eddie's Rest., McDonald's, Outback Steaks, Pizza Hut, Subway, Taco Bell, TCBY, **lodging:** Plaza Suites, **other:** Pontiac/Buick, transmissions, **S...gas:** Flying J/Conoco/diesel/rest./24hr/@, **food:** BBQ, Black Angus, Burger King, Carino's, Chuck-aRama, Cracker Barrel, Jamba Juice, KFC, Little Mexico, McGrath's FishHouse, On the Border, Pollo Rey Mexican, Yen Ching Chinese, **lodging:** AmeriTel, Best Rest Inn, **other:** LDS Temple, Commercial Tire, Goodyear, Lowe's Whse, Wal-Mart SuperCtr/24hr

49 I-184(exits left from eb), to W Boise, **N...lodging:** Rodeway Inn, National 9 Inn, **other:** HOSPITAL

46 ID 55, Eagle, **N...gas:** Chevron/McDonald's/diesel/24hr, Shell/Taco Bell/diesel/24hr, **lodging:** Holiday Inn Express, **other:** MEDICAL CARE, **S...**Fiesta RV Park

44 ID 69, Meridian, **N...gas:** Chevron/diesel/24hr, Sinclair, **food:** Blimpie, Bolo's Eatery, DQ, Jack-in-the-Box, KFC, McDonald's, Pizza Hut, Quizno's, RoundTable Pizza, Shari's/24hr, Taco Bell, Taco Time, Under The Onion Steaks, **lodging:** Best Western, Microtel, **other:** MEDICAL CARE, Bodily RV Ctr, Home Depot, Schwab Tire, WinCo **Foods**, **S...gas:** Shell/diesel/24hr, **food:** JB's, **lodging:** Knotty Pine Motel, Mr Sandman Motel, **other:** Ford, Playground RV Park

Nampa

38 Garrity Blvd, Nampa, **N...gas:** Chevron/diesel, **other:** Cadillac, Chevrolet/Pontiac/Buick/GMC, Chrysler/Dodge/Jeep, Ford, Swiss Village Cheese, **S...gas:** Chevron/diesel, Phillips 66/diesel, Shell/Taco Ole/diesel/24hr, **food:** McDonald's, **other:** MEDICAL CARE, Garrity RV Park

36 Franklin Blvd, Nampa, **N...food:** Jack-in-the-Box, Noodles Rest., **lodging:** Shilo Inn/rest., **S...gas:** Chevron/diesel/24hr, Shell/A&W/Taco Bell/diesel/RV dump/24hr, **lodging:** Desert Inn, Sleep Inn, **other:** HOSPITAL, Mason Cr RV Park, Minor RV Ctr

35 ID 55, Nampa, **S...gas:** Shell/diesel, Denny's/24hr, **lodging:** InnAmerica, Shilo Inn, Super 8, **1 mi S...food:** Burger King, McDonald's, Pizza Hut, Taco Time, **lodging:** Budget Inn, Desert Inn, **other:** HOSPITAL

29 US 20/26, Franklin Rd, Caldwell, **N...gas:** Flying J/Conoco/diesel/LP/rest./24hr/@, **food:** Guesthaus Rest., **other:** RV camping, **S...gas:** Sinclair/diesel, **food:** Perkins/24hr, Sage Café, **lodging:** Best Inn, Best Western, **1-2 mi S on Cleveland/Blaine St...food:** McDonald's, Subway, Taco Time, **lodging:** Desert Inn, **other:** Albertson's/**gas**, Chrysler/Plymouth/Dodge/Jeep, Honda, NAPA, Rite Aid, Wal-Mart SuperCtr/24hr, to Simplot Stadium

Interstate 84

E W

28 10th Ave, Caldwell, **N...gas:** Maverick/**gas**, **lodging:** I-84 Motel, **S...gas:** Chevron/24hr, 7-11, Tesoro, **food:** Carl's Jr, DQ, Jack-in-the-Box, Mr V's Rest., Pizza Hut, Wendy's, **lodging:** Holiday Motel/café, Sundowner Motel, **other:** HOSPITAL, Paul's Drug
27 ID 19, to Wilder, **1 mi S...gas:** Tesoro/diesel/24hr
26.5mm Boise River
26 US 20/26, to Notus, **N...other:** Camp Caldwell RV Park, **S...gas:** Chevron/diesel
25 ID 44, Middleton, **N...gas:** Shell/diesel, **food:** Bud's Burgers/shakes, **S...**weigh sta eb
17 Sand Hollow, **N...food:** Sand Hollow Café, **other:** Country Corners RV Park
13 Black Canyon Jct, **S...gas:** Sinclair/diesel/motel/rest./24hr, phone
9 US 30, to New Plymouth, no facilities
3 US 95, Fruitland, **N...gas:** Shell/A&W/diesel, Texaco/diesel/24hr(3mi), **5 mi N...other:** Neat Retreat RV Park, to Hell's Cyn RA
1mm Welcome Ctr eb, full(handicapped)facilities, info, phone, picnic tables, litter barrels, petwalk
0mm Snake River, Idaho/Oregon state line

Interstate 86

E W

Pocatello

Exit # Services
63b a I-15, N to Butte, S to SLC. I-86 begins/ends on I-15, exit 72.
61 US 91, Yellowstone Ave, Pocatello, **N...gas:** Tesoro, Exxon, Shell/diesel, **food:** Arctic Circle, Burger King, Chapala Mexican, Johnny B Goode Diner, Papa Murphy's, Pizza Hut, Subway, Super China, **lodging:** Motel 6, Ramada Inn, **other:** Checker Parts, Smith's **Food**s, **S...gas:** Flying J/Taco Bell/diesel/24hr, Phillips 66/diesel, **food:** Denny's, IHOP, Me&Lou's Rest., McDonald's, Red Lobster, Taco Bandido, **lodging:** Pine Ridge Inn, **other:** Dillard's, Ford, Grocery Outlet, Herb's RV, Home Depot, JC Penney, K-Mart, Michael's, Schwab Tire, ShopKO, Wal-Mart SuperCtr/24hr, diesel repair, mall
58.5mm Portneuf River
58 US 30, W Pocatello, **N...**RV dump, **S...gas:** Stinker/diesel
56 **N...**Pocatello Air Terminal, **S...gas:** Exxon/diesel/24hr/@
52 Arbon Valley, **S...gas:** Sinclair/Bannock Peak/diesel/@, **other:** casino
51mm Bannock Creek
49 Rainbow Rd, no facilities
44 Seagull Bay, no facilities
40 ID 39, American Falls, **N...gas:** Cenex/diesel, Sinclair, **food:** Pizza Hut, Sagebrush Rest., **lodging:** American Motel, **other:** HOSPITAL, Chevrolet/GMC, NAPA, Schwab Tire, to Am Falls RA, RV Park/dump, **S...gas:** Tesoro/diesel/café, **lodging:** Hillview Motel
36 ID 37, American Falls, to Rockland, **2 mi N...gas:** Shell/diesel/24hr, **lodging:** Falls Motel, **other:** HOSPITAL, **2 mi S...**Indian Springs RV Resort
33 Neeley Area, no facilities
31mm rest area wb, full(handicapped)facilities, phone, picnic table, litter barrel, petwalk, vending, hist site
28 **N...other:** to Massacre Rock SP, Register Rock Hist Site, RV camping/dump
21 Coldwater Area, no facilities
19mm rest area eb, full(handicapped)facilities, phone, picnic table, litter barrel, petwalk, vending, hist site
15 Raft River Area, **S...gas:** Sinclair, phone
1 I-84 E, to Ogden. I-86 begins/ends on I-84, exit 222.

Interstate 90

E W

Kellogg

Exit # Services
74mm Idaho/Montana state line, Pacific/Mountain time zone, Lookout Pass elev 4680
73mm scenic area/hist site wb
72mm scenic area/hist site eb
71mm runaway truck ramp wb
70mm runaway truck ramp wb
69 Lp 90, Mullan, **N...gas**: Exxon/diesel/24hr, Yuppie Trails/diesel, **food**: Mullan Café, **lodging**: Lookout Motel(1mi), **other**: USPO, museum
68 Lp 90(from eb), Mullan, same as 69
67 Morning District, no facilities
66 Gold Creek(from eb), no facilities
65 Compressor District, no facilities
64 Golconda District, no facilities
62 ID 4, Wallace, **S...gas**: Exxon, **food**: Pizza Factory, Sweet's Café, Wallace Café, **lodging**: Brooks Hotel, Stardust Motel, Sweet's Hotel, **other**: HOSPITAL, Depot RV Park, Excell **Food**s, Parts+, USPO, museum, repair
61 Lp 90, Wallace, **S...gas**: Exxon, **food**: Silver Lantern Drive-In, Wallace Sta Rest./gifts, **lodging**: Best Western, Brooks Hotel, Molly B-Damm Inn, **other**: info ctr, same as 62
60 Lp 90, Silverton, **N...**HOSPITAL, **S...lodging**: SilverLeaf Motel, **other**: RV camping
57 Lp 90, Osburn, **S...gas**: Shell/diesel/24hr, **other**: Blue Anchor RV Park, auto repair
54 Big Creek, **N...other**: Elk Creek Store/repair, hist site
51 Lp 90, Division St, Kellogg, **N...gas**: Conoco/diesel, **food**: Broken Wheel Rest., Trail Motel, **other**: HOSPITAL, Chevrolet/Pontiac/Buick/Cadillac, Chrysler/Dodge/Jeep, IGA **Food**, Radio Shack, Schwab Tire, Sunnyside Drug, **S...food**: Kopper Keg Café/pizza, Mansion B&B, **other**: USPO, museum
50 Hill St(from eb), Kellogg, **N...lodging**: Sunshine Inn/café, Trail Motel, **other**: IGA **Food**s, NAPA, **S...other**: Pac'n Sav **Food**s, Silver Mtn Ski/summer resort/rec area, museum
49 Bunker Ave, **N...food**: McDonald's, Sam's Drive-In, Subway, Taco John's, **lodging**: Silverhorn Motel/rest., Sunshine Inn, **other**: HOSPITAL, **S...food**: Silver Mtn/Gondola Café, Zany's Café, **lodging**: Super 8, **other**: museum, RV dump

IDAHO

Interstate 90

E W

48 Smelterville, **N...gas**: Silver Valley Car/trkstp/motel/café, **other**: RV Park, **S...lodging**: motel/café, **other**: Wayside Mkt **Foods**

45 Pinehurst, **S...gas**: Chevron, Conoco/diesel/24hr, **other**: Honda/Yamaha, Pinehurst RV, KOA, RV dump

43 Kingston, **N...gas**: Shell/diesel/24hr, **food**: Snakepit Café, **lodging**: Enaville Resort, RV camping, S...**gas**: Exxon

40 Cataldo, **N...other**: General Store, 3rd Generation Rest., RV camping

39.5mm Coeur d' Alene River

39 Cataldo Mission, **S...other**: Old Mission SP, Nat Hist Landmark

34 ID 3, Rose Lake, to St Maries, **S...gas**: Conoco/diesel, Shell/diesel, **food**: Country Chef Café, **other**: Rose Lake Gen Store, White Pines Scenic Rte

32mm chainup area/weigh sta wb

31.5mm Idaho Panhandle NF, eastern boundary, 4th of July Creek

28 4th of July Pass, elev 3069, Mullan Tree HS, ski area, snowmobile area, turnout both lanes

24mm chainup eb, removal wb

22 ID 97, Harrison, to St Maries, L Coeur d' Alene Scenic ByWay, Wolf Lodge District, **1 mi N...**Wolf Lodge Campground, **S...other**: KOA, Squaw Bay Resort(7mi)

20.5mm Lake Coeur d' Alene

17 Mullan Trail Rd, no facilities

Coeur d' Alene

15 Lp 90, Sherman Ave, Coeur d' Alene, City Ctr, **N...other**: forest info, Lake Coeur D' Alene RA/HS, **S...gas**: Cenex, Exxon/diesel/24hr, Shell, Tesoro, **food**: Michael D's Eatery, Mike's Café, Roger's Ice Cream, **lodging**: BudgetSaver Motel, El Rancho Motel, Holiday Inn Express, Holiday Motel, Red Rose Motel, Sandman Motel, Star Motel, State Motel, Sundowner Motel, **other**: Buick/Pontiac/GMC, IGA **Food**s/24hr, NAPA

14 15th St, Coeur d' Alene, **S...gas**: TAJ Mart, **other**: Jordon's Grocery

13 4th St, Coeur d' Alene, **N...gas**: Citgo/7-11, Conoco/diesel, **food**: Baskin-Robbins, Bruchi's Café, Carl's Jr, DQ, Davis Donuts, Denny's, Godfather's, IHOP, KFC, Little Caesar's, Taco John's, Wendy's, **lodging**: Comfort Inn, Fairfield Inn, **other**: Hastings Books, Kelly Tire, NAPA, Radio Shack, Schuck's Parts, Schwab Tires, same as 12, **S...gas**: Exxon/diesel, **food**: Hunter's Steaks, Subway, **other**: Chevrolet, Chrysler/Jeep, Nissan/Subaru

12 US 95, to Sandpoint, Moscow, **N...gas**: Chevron, Exxon/diesel, Holiday/diesel, Shell, **food**: Applebee's, Arby's, Burger King, Chili's, Domino's, DragonHouse Chinese, FastBurger, McDonald's, Perkins, Pizza Hut, Pizza Shoppe, Red Lobster, Taco Bell, Tomato St Italian, **lodging**: Village Inn Rest., Best Inn, Budget Host, Comfort Inn, Coeur d'Alene Inn, Holiday Inn, Motel 6, Shilo Inn, Super 8, **other**: Buick/Pontiac/GMC, Cadillac/Isuzu, Dodge, Ford/Lincoln/Mercury, Fred Meyer, Home Depot, K-Mart, Office Depot, Safeway/**gas**, Super 1 **Food**s, Tidyman's **Food**/24hr, Toyota, U-Haul, radiators, **S...gas**: Shell, **food**: Chopstix Express, Figaro's Italian, Mr Steak, Jack-in-the-Box, Schlotsky's, Shari's, TCBY, **lodging**: Ameritel, **other**: HOSPITAL, Albertson's, GNC, Rite Aid, ShopKO/drugs, Staples, same as 13

11 Northwest Blvd, **N...gas**: Shell/diesel, **S...gas**: Exxon, Qwikstop/diesel, **food**: Outback Steaks, **lodging**: Blvd Motel/RV Park, Day's Inn, Garden Motel, **other**: HOSPITAL, Honda/Kia, RiverWalk RV Park

8.5mm Welcome Ctr/weigh sta eb, rest area both lanes, full(handicapped)facilities, info, phone, picnic tables, litter barrels, petwalk

7 ID 41, to Rathdrum, Spirit Lake, **N...gas**: Exxon/diesel, **other**: Wal-Mart SuperCtr/gas/24hr, Couer d'Alene RV Park, **S...gas**: Chevron/diesel/24hr, **food**: Applebee's, Casey's Rest./brewery, DQ, KFC, **lodging**: Holiday Inn Express, U-Haul, repair

6 Seltice Way, City Ctr, **N...gas**: Citgo/7-11, Exxon/RV dump, Shell, **food**: La Cabana Mexican, Pizza Hut, **other**: MEDICAL CARE, Chevrolet, Excell **Food**s, NAPA, Nissan, Super 1 **Food**s, **S...gas**: Conoco/diesel/LP, **food**: Arby's, Big Cheese Pizza, Denny's, EasyRider Café, Godfather's, Hot Rod Café, JambaJuice, Little Caesar's, McDonald's, Papa Murphy's, Rancho Viejo Mexican, Subway, Taco Bell, Winger's Diner, **other**: Alton Tire, Shuck's Parts, Tidyman's **Food**/24hr, USPO

5 Lp 90, Spokane St, Treaty Rock HS, **N...gas**: Shell/diesel, Texaco, **food**: Andy's Rest., Bruchi's Rest., Domino's, Golden Dragon Chinese, McDuff's Rest., Rob's Sea**food**/burgers, WhiteHouse Grill, **other**: Excell **Food**s, Mazda, Schwab Tire, Seltice RV Ctr, **S...gas**: Pacific Pride/diesel, **food**: MillTown Grill, **lodging**: Best Western

2 Pleasant View Rd, **N...gas**: Flying J/Conoco/diesel/rest./LP/24hr/@, Shell, **food**: Burger King, McDonald's, Subway, Toro Viejo Mexican, **lodging**: Howard Johnson Express, **S...gas**: Exxon/24hr, **food**: Chocolate Factory/pizza/pasta, Jack-in-the-Box, **lodging**: Riverbend Inn/rest., Sleep Inn, **other**: GNC, Prime Outlets/famous brands, SunTree RV Park, dogtrack

0mm Idaho/Washington state line

Interstate 184(Boise)

E W

Boise

Exit #	Services
6mm	I-184 begins/ends on 13th St, downtown, **lodging:** Best Western, StateHouse Inn, **other:** Aamco, USPO
5	River St(from eb), **W...food:** McDonald's, **other:** Ford/Mercury
4.5mm	Boise River
3	Fairview Ave, to US 20/26 E, **W...lodging:** DoubleTree, Econolodge, Shilo Inn
2	Curtis Rd, to Garden City, **W...**HOSPITAL
1	Franklin Rd, **E...gas:** Chevron/Subway, Sinclair, **lodging:** Boise Motel, Plaza Suites, **other:** Acura/Honda, Buick/Pontiac, Dodge, **W...gas:** Sinclair, **food:** Burger King, Chili's, EatABurger, Jack-in-the-Box, Perkins, Sizzler, Starbucks, Wendy's, YenChing Chinese, **lodging:** AmeriTel, **other:** Circuit City, Costco, Dillard's, JC Penney, Mervyn's, Office Depot, Old Navy, Ross, Saturn, Target, mall
0mm	I-184 begins/ends on I-84, exit 49.

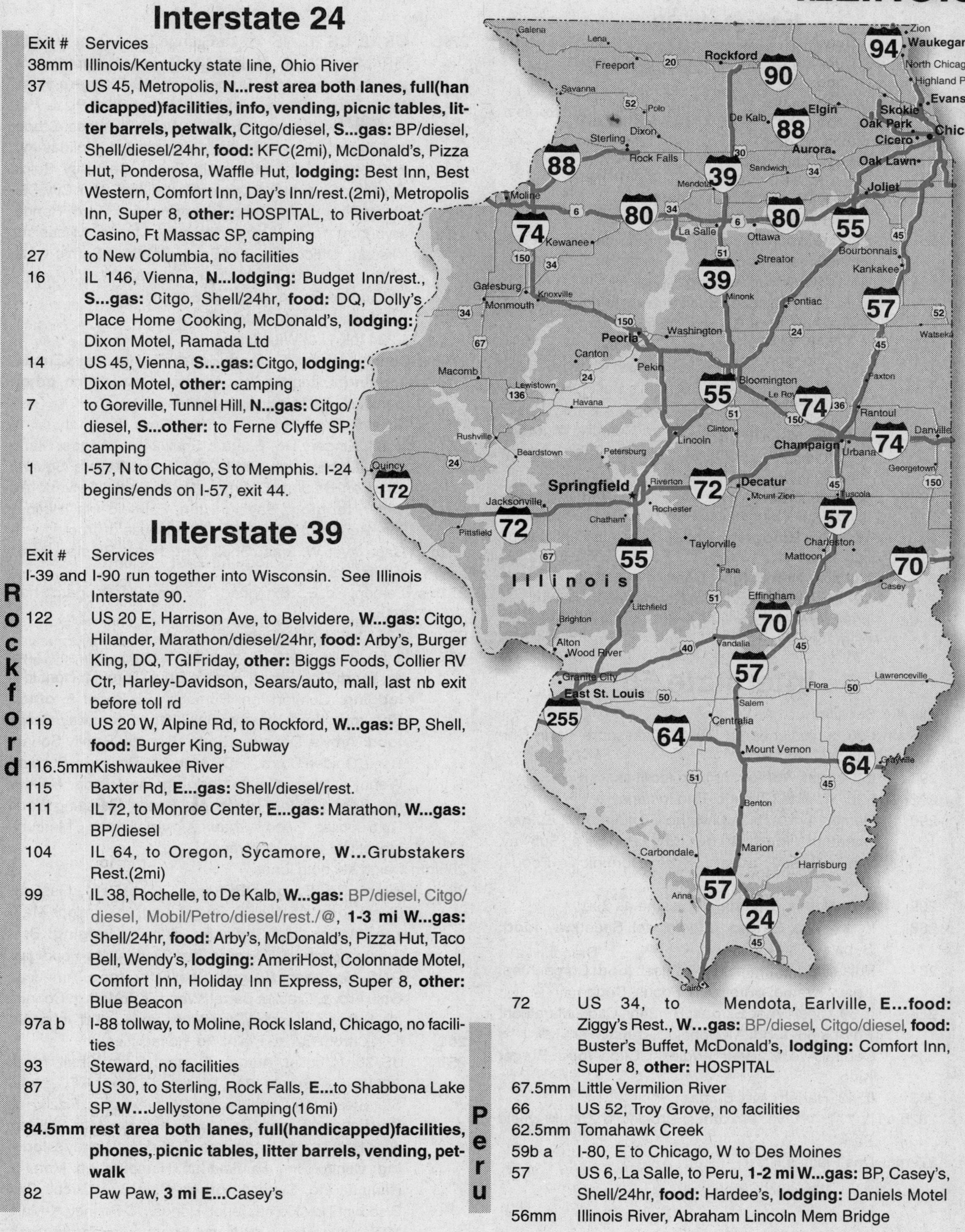

Interstate 24

E ↕ W

Exit #	Services
38mm	Illinois/Kentucky state line, Ohio River
37	US 45, Metropolis, **N...rest area both lanes, full(handicapped)facilities, info, vending, picnic tables, litter barrels, petwalk,** Citgo/diesel, **S...gas:** BP/diesel, Shell/diesel/24hr, **food:** KFC(2mi), McDonald's, Pizza Hut, Ponderosa, Waffle Hut, **lodging:** Best Inn, Best Western, Comfort Inn, Day's Inn/rest.(2mi), Metropolis Inn, Super 8, **other:** HOSPITAL, to Riverboat Casino, Ft Massac SP, camping
27	to New Columbia, no facilities
16	IL 146, Vienna, **N...lodging:** Budget Inn/rest., **S...gas:** Citgo, Shell/24hr, **food:** DQ, Dolly's Place Home Cooking, McDonald's, **lodging:** Dixon Motel, Ramada Ltd
14	US 45, Vienna, **S...gas:** Citgo, **lodging:** Dixon Motel, **other:** camping
7	to Goreville, Tunnel Hill, **N...gas:** Citgo/diesel, **S...other:** to Ferne Clyffe SP, camping
1	I-57, N to Chicago, S to Memphis. I-24 begins/ends on I-57, exit 44.

Interstate 39

N ↕ S

Rockford

Exit #	Services
	I-39 and I-90 run together into Wisconsin. See Illinois Interstate 90.
122	US 20 E, Harrison Ave, to Belvidere, **W...gas:** Citgo, Hilander, Marathon/diesel/24hr, **food:** Arby's, Burger King, DQ, TGIFriday, **other:** Biggs Foods, Collier RV Ctr, Harley-Davidson, Sears/auto, mall, last nb exit before toll rd
119	US 20 W, Alpine Rd, to Rockford, **W...gas:** BP, Shell, **food:** Burger King, Subway
116.5mm	Kishwaukee River
115	Baxter Rd, **E...gas:** Shell/diesel/rest.
111	IL 72, to Monroe Center, **E...gas:** Marathon, **W...gas:** BP/diesel
104	IL 64, to Oregon, Sycamore, **W...**Grubstakers Rest.(2mi)
99	IL 38, Rochelle, to De Kalb, **W...gas:** BP/diesel, Citgo/diesel, Mobil/Petro/diesel/rest./@, **1-3 mi W...gas:** Shell/24hr, **food:** Arby's, McDonald's, Pizza Hut, Taco Bell, Wendy's, **lodging:** AmeriHost, Colonnade Motel, Comfort Inn, Holiday Inn Express, Super 8, **other:** Blue Beacon
97a b	I-88 tollway, to Moline, Rock Island, Chicago, no facilities
93	Steward, no facilities
87	US 30, to Sterling, Rock Falls, **E...**to Shabbona Lake SP, **W...**Jellystone Camping(16mi)
84.5mm	**rest area both lanes, full(handicapped)facilities, phones, picnic tables, litter barrels, vending, petwalk**
82	Paw Paw, **3 mi E...**Casey's

Peru

Exit #	Services
72	US 34, to Mendota, Earlville, **E...food:** Ziggy's Rest., **W...gas:** BP/diesel, Citgo/diesel, **food:** Buster's Buffet, McDonald's, **lodging:** Comfort Inn, Super 8, **other:** HOSPITAL
67.5mm	Little Vermilion River
66	US 52, Troy Grove, no facilities
62.5mm	Tomahawk Creek
59b a	I-80, E to Chicago, W to Des Moines
57	US 6, La Salle, to Peru, **1-2 mi W...gas:** BP, Casey's, Shell/24hr, **food:** Hardee's, **lodging:** Daniels Motel
56mm	Illinois River, Abraham Lincoln Mem Bridge

ILLINOIS

Interstate 39

54 Oglesby, **E...gas:** BP, Casey's, Shell/24hr, **food:** Baskin-Robbins/Dunkin Donuts, Delaney's Rest., Burger King, Hardee's, McDonald's, Pizza Grill, Subway, **lodging:** Day's Inn, Holiday Inn Express, Starved Rock SP

52 IL 251, to La Salle, Peru, no facilities

51 IL 71, Oglesby, to Hennepin, no facilities

48 Tonica, **E...gas:** Casey's Store

41 IL 18, to Streator, Henry, no facilities

35 IL 17, to Wenona, Lacon, **2.5 mi E...gas:** BP/diesel/24hr, Casey's, **food:** Burger King, Buster's Family Rest., Pizza Hut, **lodging:** Super 8

27 to Minonk, **E...gas:** Shell/Subway/Woody's Rest./diesel/24hr, **1 mi E...gas:** Casey's

22 IL 116, Benson, to Peoria, no facilities

14 US 24, to El Paso, Peoria, **E...gas:** Casey's, Freedom, Shell/24hr, **food:** DQ, Elm's Buffet, Hardee's/24hr, McDonald's, Subway, Woody's Family Rest., **lodging:** Day's Inn, **other:** Ford/Mercury, **W...food:** Dabney's Rest., **lodging:** Super 8, **other:** Hickory Hill Camping

9mm Mackinaw River

Normal

8 IL 251, Lake Bloomington Rd, **E...**Lake Bloomington, **W...other:** Evergreen Lake, to Comlara Park, camping

5 Hudson, **1 mi E...gas:** Casey's

2 US 51 bus, Bloomington, Normal, no facilities

0mm I-39 begins/ends on I-55, exit 164. Facilities located N on I-55, exit 165.

Interstate 55

N ↕ S — Chicago Area

Exit # Services

295mm I-55 begins/ends on US 41, Lakeshore Dr, in Chicago.

293a to Cermak Rd(from nb), no facilities

292 I-90/94, W to Chicago, E to Indiana

290 Damen Ave, Ashland Ave(no EZ nb return), **E...gas:** Marathon, **food:** Burger King, Popeye's, Subway, White Castle, **other:** $Tree, Dominick's Foods, GNC

289 to California Ave(from nb), same as 290

288 Kedzie Ave, **E...gas:** Citgo/diesel, Speedway, **food:** Subway

287 Pulaski Rd, **E...gas:** Mobil/diesel, **food:** Burger King, Krispy Kreme, **other:** Aldi Foods, Dodge

286 IL 50, Cicero Ave, **E...gas:** BP/24hr, Citgo, Marathon, Phillips 66, **food:** McDonald's, **other:** Family$

285 Central Ave, **E...gas:** BP/diesel, Citgo, **food:** Burger King

283 IL 43, Harlem Ave, **E...gas:** Shell

282b a IL 171, 1st Ave, **W...other:** Brookfield Zoo, Mayfield Park

279mm Des Plaines River

279b US 12, US 20, US 45, La Grange Rd, **1-2 mi W...gas:** BP/24hr, Clark, Mobil, Shell, **food:** Applebee's, Arby's, Boston Mkt, Burger King, JC George's Rest., KFC, Ledo's Pizza, LJ Silver, McDonald's, Pizza Hut, Popeye's, Subway, Taco Bell, Wendy's, White Castle, **lodging:** Countryside Inn, Hampton Inn, Holiday Inn, La Grange Motel, **other:** Aldi Foods, Best Buy, Buick, Cadillac, Chevrolet, Chrysler/Plymouth, Circuit City, Discount Tire, Dodge/Jeep, Firestone/auto, Ford, Honda, Hyundai, Kohl's, Lincoln/Mercury, Mazda, Mitsubishi, Nissan, OfficeMax, PepBoys, Pontiac, Sam's Club, Saturn, Subaru, Target/drugs, Toyota, VW, Wal-Mart

a La Grange Rd, to I-294 toll, S to Indiana

277b I-294 toll(from nb), S to Indiana

a I-294 toll, N to Wisconsin

276b a County Line Rd, **E...food:** Bobak's Buffet, Max&Erma's, **lodging:** Extended Stay America, Ramada Inn, **other:** bank, **W...lodging:** AmeriSuites

c Joliet Rd(from nb)

274 IL 83, Kingery Rd, **E...gas:** Shell/24hr, **W...gas:** Marathon, Mobil/diesel, Shell/24hr, **food:** Bakers Square, Chicken Basket, Denny's, Patio Rest., Salvadore's Diner, **lodging:** Baymont Inn, Fairfield Inn, Holiday Inn, Red Roof Inn, **other:** Ford, House of Trucks

273b a Cass Ave, **W...gas:** Shell/24hr, **food:** Ripples Rest., **other:** Parts+

271b a Lemont Rd, **E...**Extended Stay America, **W...gas:** Shell/24hr

269 I-355 toll N, to W Suburbs

267 IL 53, Bolingbrook, **E...gas:** 55 Trkstp/diesel/rest./24hr/@, **food:** Bob Evans, Bono's Drive-Thru, McDonald's, **lodging:** Comfort Inn, Ramada Ltd, Super 8, **other:** Chevrolet, Ford, **W...gas:** Shell/24hr, Speedway/diesel, **food:** Arby's, Denny's, Dunkin Donuts, Family Square Rest., Golden Corral, IHOP, Mendy's, Popeye's, Subway, Wendy's, White Castle, **lodging:** AmericInn, Holiday Inn, SpringHill Inn, **other:** Aldi Foods, Camping World RV Supplies, Goodyear/auto, Jo-Ann Fabrics, Mercury/Lincoln, U-Haul, Walgreen

265mm weigh sta both lanes

263 Weber Rd, **E...gas:** BP/diesel, Citgo/7-11, GasCity/diesel, **food:** A&W/KFC, Burger King, Los Amigos Mexican, McDonald's, Starbucks, Subway, **lodging:** Best Western, **other:** Discount Tire, Dominick's Food/gas, GNC, Walgreen, **W...gas:** Shell/24hr, **food:** American Grill, Arby's, Cracker Barrel, Wendy's, **lodging:** Country Inn Suites, Extended Stay America, Howard Johnson

261 IL 126(from sb), to Plainfield, no facilities

257 US 30, to Joliet, Aurora, **E...gas:** Citgo, Shell, **food:** Applebee's, Burger King, Diamand's Rest., KFC, LoneStar Steaks, McDonald's, Old Country Buffet, Pizza Hut, Red Lobster, Samy's Grill, Steak'n Shake/24hr, Subway, Taco Bell, Texas Roadhouse, TGIFriday, Wendy's, **lodging:** Comfort Inn, Fairfield Inn, Hampton Inn, Motel 6, Ramada Ltd, Super 8, **other:** Best Buy, Circuit City, Discount Tire, Home Depot, Honda, JC Penney, K-Mart, NTB, OfficeMax, Old Navy, Sears/auto, Target, mall, **W...gas:** BP/diesel/24hr, Clark/Subway/diesel/24hr

Interstate 55

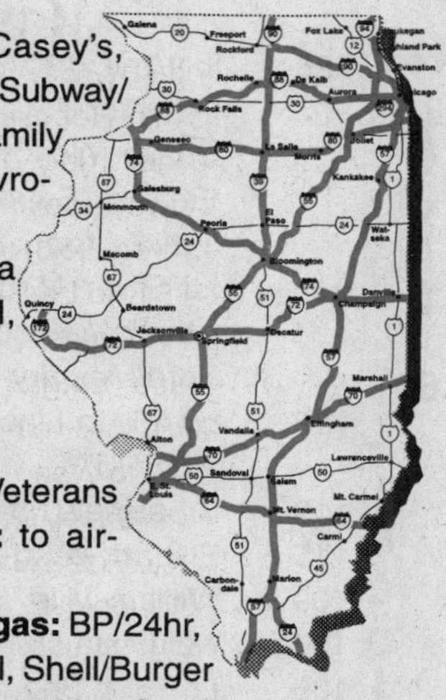

N ↕ S

Joliet

253b a US 52, Jefferson St, Joliet, **E...gas:** Phillips 66, Shell/24hr, **food:** KFC/Pizza Hut, McDonald's, Wendy's, **lodging:** Best Western, Fireside Motel, Wingate Inn, **other:** HOSPITAL, Ford/Suzuki, Rick's RV Ctr, **W...gas:** BP/diesel/24hr, **food:** Baba's Rest., Burger King, DQ, Smile of Thai Rest., Subway(1mi), **other:** HOSPITAL, Chrysler/Plymouth/Dodge/Jeep, Goodyear

251 IL 59(from nb), to Shorewood, access to same as 253 W

250b a I-80, W to Iowa, E to Toledo, no facilities

248 US 6, Joliet, **E...gas:** Speedway/diesel/24hr, **lodging:** Manor Motel, **other:** Frank's Country Store, **W...gas:** BP/McDonald's, **food:** Ivo's Grill, Lone Star Rest.(2mi), **other:** to Ill/Mich Tr

247 Bluff Rd, no facilities

245mm Des Plaines River

245 Arsenal Rd, **E...other:** Joliet Army Ammunition Plant, Exxon/Mobil Refinery

241 to Wilmington, no facilities

241mm Kankakee River

240 Lorenzo Rd, **E...gas:** Phillips 66/diesel, **W...gas:** Citgo/diesel/rest./24hr, **lodging:** Motel 55

238 IL 129 S, Braidwood, to Wilmington, no facilities

236 IL 113, Coal City, **E...food:** Good Table Rest., **other:** Chrysler/Plymouth/Dodge/Jeep, **W...gas:** Clark/diesel, **2 mi W...gas:** Citgo, Mobil/diesel/24hr, Shell, **food:** McDonald's, Subway

233 Reed Rd, **E...gas:** Marathon, **lodging:** Sun Motel, **W...other:** antiques

227 IL 53, Gardner, **E...gas:** Casey's, Gardner Haus Rest., **W...gas:** BP/diesel/24hr

220 IL 47, Dwight, **E...gas:** Amoco/Burger King/diesel/24hr, Clark/diesel/24hr, **food:** Arby's, Dwight Chinese Rest., McDonald's, Pete's Rest., Subway, Classic Motel, **lodging:** Super 8

217 IL 17, Dwight, **E...gas:** Casey's, Shell/diesel/24hr, **food:** DQ, Rte 66 Rest., **other:** Chrysler/Plymouth/Dodge/Jeep, Family$, NAPA, RadioShack

213mm Mazon River

209 Odell, **E...gas:** BP, **food:** Wishing Well Café

201 IL 23, Pontiac, **1-3 mi E...gas:** Clark/24hr, **food:** DQ, **other:** Pontiac RV Ctr, 4H RV Camp(seasonal)

198mm Vermilion River

Pontiac

197 IL 116, Pontiac, **E...gas:** BP/Subway/diesel/24hr, Shell, **food:** Arby's, Baby Bull's Rest., Burger King, Buster's Rest., KFC/Taco Bell, LJ Silver, McDonald's, Wendy's, **lodging:** Comfort Inn, Fiesta Motel(1mi), Holiday Inn Express, Super 8, **other:** HOSPITAL, Aldi Foods, AutoZone, Chevrolet/Buick, Lincoln/Mercury/Dodge, Pontiac/Cadillac, Wal-Mart/auto, st police, **W...gas:** Citgo

193mm rest area both lanes, full(handicapped)facilities, phone, picnic tables, litter barrels, vending, petwalk

187 US 24, Chenoa, **E...gas:** Casey's, Phillips 66/McDonald's, Shell/Subway/diesel/24hr, **food:** Chenoa Family Rest., Super 8, **other:** Chevrolet

178 Lexington, **E...gas:** BP/Pizza Hut/diesel, Freedom/diesel, **W...**Chevrolet

177mm Mackinaw River

171 Towanda, **E...gas:** FastStop

167 Lp 55 S(exits left from sb), Veterans Pkwy, to Normal, **S...food:** to airport

Normal

165b a US 51B, to Bloomington, **E...gas:** BP/24hr, FS/diesel, Mobil/Arby's/diesel, Shell/Burger King/24hr, **food:** Denny's, Pizza Hut, Steak'n Shake, Uncle Tom's Pancakes, **lodging:** Best Western, Holiday Inn, Motel 6, Super 8, **other:** HOSPITAL, $General, to Ill St U, **W...**NAPA

164 I-39, US 51, N to Peru, no facilities

163 I-74 W, to Peoria, no facilities

160b a US 150, IL 9, Market St, Bloomington, **E...gas:** BP, Clark, Freedom/diesel, Pilot/Wendy's/diesel/24hr/@, Shell, Speedway/diesel, TA/diesel/rest./24hr/@, **food:** Arby's, Burger King, Cracker Barrel, Culver's, KFC, McDonald's, Subway, Taco Bell, **lodging:** Best Inn, Comfort Inn, Econolodge, Hawthorn Suites, Quality Suites, **other:** HOSPITAL, Aldi Foods, Blue Beacon, Family$, NAPA, **W...gas:** Citgo/diesel, **food:** Country Kitchen, Fiesta Ranchera, Ming's Wok, Steak'n Shake/24hr, **lodging:** Country Inn Suites, Hampton Inn, Ramada Ltd, Wingate Inn, **other:** Factory Stores/famous brands, Wal-Mart SuperCtr/gas/24hr

157b Lp 55 N, Veterans Pkwy, Bloomington, **N...gas:** Clark/24hr, FS, **food:** CJ's Rest., Froggy's Pad Rest., **lodging:** Parkway Inn/rest., Sunset Inn, **other:** HOSPITAL, to airport

a I-74 E, to Indianapolis, US 51 to Decatur

154 Shirley, no facilities

149 W...rest area both lanes, full(handicapped)facilit ies, phone, picnic tables, litter barrels, vending, playground, petwalk

145 US 136, McLean, **E...**RV Ctr, **W...gas:** Citgo, Dixie/Shell/diesel/rest./24hr, **food:** McDonald's, **lodging:** Super 8

140 Atlanta, **E...**camping, **W...gas:** Phillips 66/diesel, **food:** Country-Aire Rest., **lodging:** I-55 Motel

133 Lp 55, Lincoln, **2 mi E...gas:** Citgo, **lodging:** Budget Inn, **other:** HOSPITAL, Camp-A-While Camping

127 I-155 N, to Peoria, no facilities

ILLINOIS

Interstate 55

N ↕ S

Lincoln

126 IL 10, IL 121 S, Lincoln, **E...gas:** Phillips 66/diesel/24hr, **food:** Cracker Barrel, KFC/Taco Bell, Steak'n Shake, Wendy's, **lodging:** Comfort Inn, Holiday Inn Express, Super 8, **other:** HOSPITAL, Russell Stover, **1 mi E...food:** A&W, Bonanza, Burger King, Hardee's, LJ Silver, McDonald's, **lodging:** Crossroads Motel, **other:** Aldi Foods, AutoZone, $General, Eagle Foods, Ford/Mercury, Radio Shack, Wal-Mart/auto

123 Lp 55, to Lincoln, **E...lodging:** Lincoln Inn, **other:** HOSPITAL

119 Broadwell, no facilities

115 Elkhart, **W...gas:** Shell/diesel

109 Williamsville, **E...gas:** Shell, **W...**New Salem HS

107mm weigh sta sb

105 Lp 55, to Sherman, **W...gas:** BP, Shell, **food:** Cancun Mexican, DQ, Subway, **other:** to Prairie Capitol Conv Ctr, hist sites

103mm rest area sb, full(handicapped)facilities, phone, picnic tables, litter barrels, vending, petwalk

102mm Sangamon River

102mm rest area nb, full(handicapped)facilities, phone, picnic tables, litter barrels, vending, petwalk

Springfield

100b IL 54, Sangamon Ave, Springfield, **W...gas:** BP/24hr, Shell/diesel, Speedway/diesel, **food:** Arby's, Burger King, Culver's, McDonald's, Sonic, Wendy's, **lodging:** Northfield Suites, **other:** Wal-Mart SuperCtr/gas/24hr, to Vet Mem

a **E...gas:** Citgo/diesel, **other:** Kenworth/Ryder/Volvo Trucks

98b IL 97, Springfield, **W...gas:** BP/24hr, Shell/diesel/24hr, **food:** Hardee's, McDonald's, Subway, Taco Bell, **lodging:** Best Rest Inn, Best Western, Parkview Motel, **other:** HOSPITAL, Goodyear, K-Mart, Walgreen, to Capitol Complex

a I-72, US 36 E, to Decatur, no facilities

96b a IL 29 N, S Grand Ave, Springfield, **W...gas:** BP, Citgo/diesel/24hr, **food:** Burger King, Godfather's, **lodging:** Motel 6, Red Roof Inn, Super 8, **other:** AutoZone, Buick, Cub Foods, Dodge/Jeep, Ford/Lincoln/Mercury, Hyundai, Isuzu, JC Penney, Kia, Mazda, Mitsubishi, Pontiac/GMC/Subaru, Shop'n Save, Toyota, VW, museum

94 Stevenson Dr, Springfield, **E...**KOA(7mi), **W...gas:** BP, Mobil, **food:** Arby's, Bob Evans, Cheddar's, Denny's, Hooters, Little Caesar's, LJ Silver, Maverick Steaks, McDonald's, Outback Steaks, Pizza Hut, Red Lobster, Smokey Bones BBQ, Steak'n Shake, Subway, Taco Bell, Wendy's, **lodging:** Comfort Suites, Crowne Plaza, Day's Inn/rest., Drury Inn, Hampton Inn, Holiday Inn Express, Microtel, PearTree Inn, Signature Inn, Stevenson Inn, **other:** Cadillac, Chevrolet, CVS Drug, $General, Honda, Jo-Ann Fabrics, Radio Shack, Saturn, ShopKO, USPO

92b a I-72 W, US 36 W, 6th St, Springfield, **W...gas:** Citgo/diesel/24hr, **food:** Arby's, Burger King, DQ, KFC, McDonald's, Subway, **lodging:** Super 8, Travelodge/rest., **other:** HOSPITAL, Walgreen

90 Toronto Rd, **E...gas:** BP/24hr, Qik-n-EZ/diesel, Shell, **food:** Burger King, Cracker Barrel, Hardee's, HenHouse, Hunan Chinese, McDonald's, Subway, **lodging:** Baymont Inn, Motel 6, Ramada Ltd, **other:** HOSPITAL

89mm Lake Springfield

88 E Lake Dr, Chatham, **E...other:** to Lincoln Mem Garden/Nature Ctr, st police, **W...**KOA

83 Glenarm, **W...**JJ RV Park/LP(4mi)

82 IL 104, to Pawnee, **E...**to Sangchris Lake SP, **W...gas:** Mobil/Homestead/Subway/diesel/rest./24hr/@, **other:** antiques/crafts

80 Divernon, Hist 66, **W...gas:** Clark, Phillips 66/diesel, **food:** Bearden's Rest.

72 Farmersville, **W...gas:** Mobil/diesel/24hr, Shell/24hr, Subway/TCBY, **lodging:** Art's Motel/rest.

65mm rest area both lanes, full(handicapped)facilities, phone, picnic tables, litter barrels, vending, playground, petwalk

63 IL 48, IL 127, to Raymond, no facilities

60 IL 108, to Carlinville, **E...other:** Kamper Kampanion RV Park, **W...gas:** Shell/diesel/LP/café, **lodging:** Holiday Inn/rest., **other:** to Blackburn Coll

56mm weigh sta nb

52 IL 16, Litchfield, Hist 66, **E...gas:** Amoco/24hr, Casey's, Phillips 66/diesel, Shell/24hr, **food:** Ariston Café, Burger King, China Town, DQ, Denny's, Domino's, Gardens Rest., Hardee's, Jubelt's Rest., KFC, LJ Silver/A&W, Maverick Steaks, McDonald's, Pizza Hut, Ponderosa, Subway, Taco Bell, Wendy's, **lodging:** Baymont Inn, Best Value Inn, Comfort Inn, Super 8, **other:** HOSPITAL, Aldi Foods, Dodge, $General, Ford/Mercury, Goodyear/auto, IGA Foods, Kroger, Rainmaker Camping(8mi), Wal-Mart SuperCtr/gas/24hr, **W...**st police

44 IL 138, Mt Olive, to White City, **E...gas:** Mobil/diesel, **food:** Crossroads Diner, **lodging:** Budget 10 Motel

41 to Staunton, **E...**Classic Car Museum, **W...gas:** Casey's, Phillips 66/diesel/rest./24hr, **food:** DQ, Subway, **lodging:** Super 8, **other:** HOSPITAL

37 Livingston, New Douglas, **E...**Shady-Oak Camping(4mi), **W...gas:** BP/diesel/24hr, **food:** Country Inn, Gasperoni's Café

33 IL 4, Worden, to Staunton, **W...**gas

30 IL 140, Hamel, **E...**Innkeeper Motel/rest., **W...gas:** Shell, **food:** Earnie's Café, **other:** NAPA

28mm rest area both lanes, full(handicapped)facilities, phone, picnic tables, litter barrels, vending, petwalk

Interstate 55

N ↕ S

23 IL 143, Edwardsville, **E...gas:** Mobil/dieselmart, **other:** repair, **W...**Red Barn Camping(apr-oct)
20b I-270 W, to Kansas City, no facilities
a I-70 E, to Indianapolis, no facilities
I-55 S and I-70 W run together 18 mi
18 IL 162, to Troy, **E...gas:** BP/diesel/rest./24hr/@ , Citgo/24hr,Pilot/Arby's/diesel/24hr/@ , **food:** Burger King, China King, DQ, Imo's Pizza, Jack-in-the-Box, KFC, Little Caesar's, McDonald's, Moma Mia's Café, Perkins, Pizza Hut, Subway, **lodging:** Relax Inn, **other:** HOSPITAL, Family$, SuperValu Foods, USPO, **W...gas:** Phillips 66/diesel/24hr, **food:** China Garden, Cracker Barrel, Taco Bell, **lodging:** Ramada Ltd, Red Roof Inn, Super 8, Villager Lodge
17 US 40 E, to Troy, to St Jacob
15b a IL 159, Maryville, Collinsville, **E...gas:** Citgo, Phillips 66/diesel, Shell, **food:** Sharkey's Rest., **other:** Aldi Foods, Chevrolet, $General, Family$, Ford/Lincoln/ Mercury, **W...gas:** Conoco, **lodging:** Econolodge
14mm weigh sta sb
11 IL 157, Collinsville, **E...gas:** BP/24hr, Casey's, **food:** Denny's, Hardee's, LJ Silver, McDonald's, New China, Pizza Hut, Waffle House, Wendy's, **lodging:** Best Western, Howard Johnson, Motel 6, PearTree Inn, The Inn, Travelodge, **other: W...gas:** Motomart/diesel/24hr/@ , **food:** Applebee's, Arby's, Bandana's BBQ, Bob Evans, Burger King, DQ, Ponderosa, Steak'n Shake, White Castle/24hr, **lodging:** Comfort Inn, Drury Inn, Fairfield Inn, Hampton Inn, Holiday Inn/rest., Quality Inn, Ramada Ltd, Super 8, **other:** Buick/Pontiac/GMC, Chrysler/Plymouth/ Dodge/Jeep, st police

E St Louis Area

10 I-255, S to Memphis, N to I-270
9 Black Lane(from nb, no return), **E...**Fairmount Race-Track
6 IL 111, Fairmont City, Great River Rd, **E...gas:** Phillips 66, **lodging:** Rainbo Motel, Royal Budget Inn, Cahokia Mounds SP, **W...**Horseshoe SP
5mm motorist callboxes begin at 1/2 mi intervals nb
4b a IL 203, Granite City, **E...gas:** Phillips 66/diesel/24hr, **lodging:** Western Inn, **W...gas:**Gateway/Pizza Hut/ Taco Bell/diesel/24hr/@ , **food:** Burger King, **other:** Gateway Int Raceway
3 Exchange Ave, no facilities
2 I-64 E, IL 3 N, St Clair Ave, no facilities
2b 3rd St, no facilities
2a M L King Bridge, to downtown E St Louis, no facilities
1 IL 3, to Sauget(from sb), no facilities
I-55 N and I-70 E run together 18 mi
0mm Illinois/Missouri state line, Mississippi River

Interstate 57

Chicago

N ↕ S

Exit # Services
358mm I-94 E to Indiana, I-57 begins/ends on I-94, exit 63 in Chicago.
357 IL 1, Halsted St, **E...gas:** BP, Mobil, **other:** auto repair, **W...gas:** Marathon, Phillips 66, **food:** McDonald's, **other:** Walgreen
355 111th St, Monterey Ave, **W...gas:** BP
354 119th St, no facilities
353 127th St, Burr Oak Ave, **E...gas:** Clark, Shell/Subway, Marathon, **food:** Burger King, McDonald's, Wendy's, **lodging:** Best Western, Plaza Inn, Super 8, **other:** HOSPITAL, Ace Hardware, Firestone, Ultra Foods, **W...gas:** BP/Amoco
352mm Calumet Sag Channel
350 IL 83, 147th St, Sibley Blvd, **E...gas:** Citgo, Marathon/ diesel, **food:** Denver's Rest., **W...gas:** BP, Citgo
348 US 6, 159th St, **E...gas:** Clark, Marathon, **food:** Burger King, Taco Bell, USA Rest., White Castle, **lodging:** Holiday Inn Express, **other:** Firestone/auto, U-Haul, Walgreen, **W...gas:** Citgo/diesel, Mobil/diesel
346 167th St, Cicero Ave, to IL 50, **E...gas:** BP, Citgo/diesel, **food:** Wendy's, **lodging:** Ramada Ltd, **W...gas:** Shell
345b a I-80, W to Iowa, E to Indiana, to I-294 N toll to Wisconsin
342 Vollmer Rd, **E...gas:** Shell/24hr, **other:** HOSPITAL
340b a US 30, Lincoln Hwy, Matteson, **E...gas:** BP/24hr, Citgo/diesel, Mobil, Shell, **food:** Applebee's, Benny's Steaks, Bob Evans, Boston Mkt, Burger King, ChuckeCheese, Cracker Barrel, Denny's, Empire Buffet, Fazoli's, Fuddrucker's, IHOP, JN Michael's Grill, KFC, McDonald's, Old Country Buffet, Olive Garden, Pizza Hut, Red Lobster, Starbucks, Subway, Taco Bell, Wendy's, **lodging:** Baymont Inn, Country Inn Suites, Hampton Inn, Holiday Inn/rest., Matteson Motel, **other:** Aldi Foods, Best Buy, Circuit City, $Tree, Dodge, Dominick's Foods, Goodyear/auto, Home Depot, Isuzu, JC Penney, Jo-Ann Fabrics, K-Mart, OfficeMax, Sam's Club, Sears/auto, Target, Walgreen, Wal-Mart, mall, **W...other:** Buick, Chevrolet, Daewoo, Ford, Isuzu, Kia, Mitsubishi, VW
339 Sauk Trail, to Richton Park, **E...gas:** Shell, **food:** Bob's HotDogs, McDonald's, **other:** cinema
335 Monee, **E...gas:** BP/Subway, Petro/Mobil/diesel/rest./ Blue Beacon/24hr/@ , Pilot/McDonald's/diesel/24hr/ @ , **food:** Burger King, Pizza Hut, **lodging:** Best Western, Country Host Motel, Holiday Inn Express, Super 8
332mm Prairie View Rest Area both lanes, full(handicapped)facilities, info, phone, vending, picnic tables, litter barrels, RV dump, petwalk
330mm weigh sta both lanes
327 to Peotone, **E...gas:** Casey's, Shell/Taco Bell/24hr, **food:** McDonald's
322 Manteno, **E...gas:** BP/McDonald's/24hr, Phillips 66/ Subway, **food:** Hardee's, Monical's Pizza, **lodging:** Comfort Inn, Quality Inn, **other:** Harley-Davidson, **W...gas:** GasCity/diesel

ILLINOIS

Interstate 57

N ↕ S

Kankakee

315 IL 50, Bradley, **E...gas:** Shell/Burger King/24hr, **food:** Cracker Barrel, LoneStar Steaks, Old Country Buffet, Piccolo's Rest., Pizza Hut, Red Lobster, Ruby Tuesday, TGIFriday, White Castle, **lodging:** Fairfield Inn, Hampton Inn, Holiday Inn Express, Lee's Inn, **other:** Barnes&Noble, $Tree, JC Penney, Michael's, Sears/auto, Staples, Target, mall, **W...gas:** BP/diesel, **food:** Applebee's, Arby's, Bakers Square, Boston Mkt, Coyote Canyon Steaks, Denny's, Hardee's, LJ Silver, McDonald's, Mongolian Buffet, Pizza Hut, Taco Bell, Ponderosa, Steak'n Shake, Subway, VIP's Rest., Wendy's, **lodging:** Motel 6, Northgate Motel, Quality Inn, Ramada Inn, Super 8, **other:** Aldi Foods, Buick/Nissan, Chevrolet, Honda, Hyundai, K-Mart, Lowe's Whse, Mazda, OfficeMax, RV Ctr, Wal-Mart/24hr, to Kankakee River SP

312 IL 17, Kankakee, **E...other:** Chrysler/Plymouth/Dodge, **W...gas:** BP, Clark/diesel, Shell/24hr, **food:** McDonald's, PoorBoy Rest., Subway, Uncle Johnni's Rest., Wendy's, **lodging:** Avis Motel, Day's Inn/rest., **other:** HOSPITAL, Walgreen, auto repair

310.5mm Kankakee River

308 US 45, US 52, to Kankakee, **E...**KOA(3mi), **W...gas:** Phillips 66/diesel, **lodging:** Fairview Motel, Knight's Inn, **other:** airport

302 Chebanse, **W...gas:** BP

297 Clifton, **W...gas:** Phillips 66/DQ/diesel, **food:** Char-Grilled Cheeseburgers

293 IL 116, Ashkum, **E...gas:** BP/Noble Roman/diesel, **W...food:** Loft Rest., **other:** st police

283 US 24, IL 54, Gilman, **E...gas:** BP/diesel/24hr, Citgo/diesel, Shell, **food:** Burger King, DQ, McDonald's, Monical's Pizza, Red Door Rest., **lodging:** Budget Host, Super 8, Travel Inn, **other:** Pennzoil, **W...gas:** Phillips 66/Subway/diesel, **other:** R&R RV Ctr

280 IL 54, Onarga, **E...gas:** Phillips 66, **other:** camping

272 Buckley, to Roberts, no facilities

268.5mm rest area both lanes, full(handicapped)facilities, vending, phone, picnic tables, litter barrels, petwalk

261 IL 9, Paxton, **E...gas:** Casey's, Citgo/diesel/24hr, **food:** Hardee's, Monical's Pizza, Pizza Hut, Subway, **other:** Chevrolet/Pontiac/Buick/GMC, **W...gas:** BP, Marathon, **food:** Country Garden Rest., **lodging:** Paxton Inn

250 US 136, Rantoul, **E...gas:** BP/rest./24hr, Phillips 66, **food:** Arby's, Hardee's, LJ Silver, McDonald's, Monical's Pizza, Red Wheel Rest., **lodging:** Best Western, Day's Inn/rest., Rantoul Motel, Super 8, **other:** NAPA, camping, to Chanute AFB

Champaign

240 Market St, **E...gas:** Citgo/diesel/rest., **other:** D&W Lake Camping, truck/tire repair

238 Olympian Dr, to Champaign, **W...gas:** Mobil/diesel, **food:** DQ, **lodging:** Microtel, **other:** RV/diesel repair

237b a I-74, W to Peoria, E to Urbana

235b I-72 W, to Decatur

a University Ave, to Champaign, **E...**HOSPITAL, U of Ill

229 to Savoy, Monticello, **E...gas:** Speedway/diesel, **W...lodging:** Best Western(1mi)

221.5mm rest area both lanes, full(handicapped)facilities, phones, picnic tables, litter barrels, vending, petwalk

220 US 45, Pesotum, **W...gas:** Citgo, st police

212 US 36, Tuscola, **E...gas:** FuelMart/diesel, **W...gas:** BP/24hr, Fleet/diesel/24hr, **food:** Amish Buffet, Burger King, DQ, Denny's, McDonald's, Monical's Pizza, Pizza Hut, Subway, **lodging:** AmeriHost, Holiday Inn Express, Super 8, **other:** Chevrolet/Pontiac/Buick/GMC, Firestone/auto, Ford, IGA Foods, Pamida, Tuscola Parts, Tuscola Stores/famous brands, camping

203 IL 133, Arcola, **E...gas:** Citgo/diesel, **other:** CampALot, **W...gas:** Clark, Shell/diesel, **food:** DQ, Dutch Kitchen, Hardee's, Hen House, Subway/Noble Roman, **lodging:** Arcola Inn, Comfort Inn, Knight's Inn, Country Charm Amish, **other:** $General, NAPA, Rockome Gardens, Arcola Camping

Mattoon

190b a IL 16, to Mattoon, **E...other:** HOSPITAL, Citgo, to E IL U, Fox Ridge SP, **W...gas:** BP/24hr, Clark, Phillips 66/Subway/24hr, **food:** Alamo Steaks, Arby's, Cody's Roadhouse, Cracker Barrel, DQ, El Vaquero Mexican, Fazoli's, McDonald's, Steak'n Shake/24hr, Taco Bell, Wendy's, **lodging:** Comfort Suites, Fairfield Inn, Hampton Inn, Ramada Inn/rest., Super 8, **other:** Aldi Foods, $General, Home Depot, JC Penney, Osco Drug, Sears/auto, Staples, Walgreen, Wal-Mart SuperCtr/gas/24hr, mall

184 US 45, IL 121, to Mattoon, **E...gas:** Citgo/diesel, **W...gas:** Marathon/diesel, Shell, **food:** McDonald's, **lodging:** Budget Inn, Knight's Inn, US Grant Motel, **other:** to Lake Shelbyville

177 US 45, Neoga, **E...gas:** BP/Subway/diesel, Citgo, **W...gas:** Phillips 66/diesel/24hr, Casey's(2mi)

166.5mm rest area both lanes, full(handicapped)facilities, vending, phones, picnic tables, litter barrels, petwalk, RV dump

163 I-70 E, to Indianapolis

I-57 S and I-70 W run together 6 mi

Effingham

162 US 45, Effingham, **E...gas:** Moto/24hr, **lodging:** Budget Host, **W...gas:** Phillips 66/Subway, Pilot/Harvest Grill/diesel/24hr/@, Shell/diesel, **food:** Trailways Rest., **lodging:** Effingham Motel/café, Lincoln Lodge, **other:** truck repair, Camp Lakewood(2mi)

160 IL 33, IL 32, Effingham, **E...gas:** BP, **food:** KFC, Little Caesar's, LoneStar Steaks, **lodging:** Comfort Inn, Hampton Inn, **other:** HOSPITAL, Aldi Foods, K-Mart, Kroger, Radio Shack, Walgreen, **W...food:** Flying J/diesel/24hr/@, Phillips 66, TA/Popeye's/Sbarro's/diesel/rest./@, **food:** A&W, Arby's, BBQ, Burger King/24hr, Cracker Barrel, Denny's, El Rancherito Mexican, KFC, LJ Silver, McDonald's, Ponderosa, Ryan's, Steak'n Shake/24hr, Taco Bell, TGIFriday, Wendy's, **lodging:** Best Inn, Country Inn Suites, Holiday Inn Express, Keller Hotel, Super 8, Travel Inn, Travelodge Suites, **other:** Ford/Lincoln/Mercury, Wal-Mart SuperCtr/gas/diesel/24hr

Interstate 57

N ↕ S

159 US 40, Effingham, **E...gas:** BP/24hr, Clark, Dixie/Citgo/diesel/rest./24hr/@, Phillips 66/diesel/24hr, Speedway/diesel, **food:** China Buffet, Domino's, Hardee's/24hr, Niemerg's Rest., Papa John's, Subway, **lodging:** Abe Lincoln Motel, Comfort Suites, Day's Inn, Econolodge, Howard Johnson, Paradise Motel, **other:** Family$, Firestone, SavALot Foods, **W...gas:** Petro/Mobil/diesel/rest./24hr/@, **lodging:** Best Western, **other:** Blue Beacon

I-57 N and I-70 E run together 6 mi

157 I-70 W, to St Louis, no facilities

151 Watson, **5 mi E...**Percival Springs RV Park

150mm Little Wabash River

145 Edgewood, **E...gas:** Citgo

135 IL 185, Farina, **E...gas:** Shell/diesel/rest., **other:** Ford

127 to Kinmundy, Patoka, no facilities

116 US 50, Salem, **E...gas:** Clark/diesel, Huck's, Motomart/24hr, Shell, Swifty, **food:** Austin Fried Chicken, Burger King, Hunan Garden, KFC, LJ Silver, McDonald's, Pizza Hut, Pizza Man, Subway, Taco Bell, Wendy's, **lodging:** Budget Inn, Continental Motel, Restwell Motel, **other:** AutoZone, Chrysler/Dodge/Jeep, MadPricer Foods, Radio Shack, Salem Parts, to Forbes SP, **W...gas:** Phillips 66/diesel, **food:** Applebee's, Denny's, **lodging:** Comfort Inn, Salem Inn, Super 8, **other:** Chevrolet/Buick, Ford, Salem Tires, Wal-Mart SuperCtr/24hr

Salem

114mm rest area both lanes, full(handicapped)facilities, phones, picnic tables, litter barrels, vending, petwalk, playground

109 IL 161, to Centralia, **W...gas:** Phillips 66/24hr, **other:** camping

103 Dix, **E...gas:** Phillips 66/diesel, **lodging:** Scottish Inn, **other:** camping

96 I-64 W, to St Louis, no facilities

95 IL 15, Mt Vernon, **E...gas:** BP/diesel/24hr, Marathon, Mobil, Phillips 66, **food:** Burger King, Fazoli's, Hardee's, Hunan Chinese, KFC, LJ Silver, McDonald's, Papa John's, Pasta House, Pizza Hut, Steak'n Shake/24hr, Subway, Taco Bell, Wendy's, Western Sizzlin, **lodging:** Best Inn, Best Western, Drury Inn, Econolodge, Motel 6, Super 8, Thrifty Inn, Villager Lodge, **other:** HOSPITAL, AutoZone, Chevrolet, Country Fair Foods, CVS Drug, $Tree, Ford, Harley-Davidson, JC Penney, Jo-Ann Fabrics, K-Mart, Kroger, Radio Shack, Walgreen, **W...gas:** Hucks/diesel/rest./24hr/@, Shell/7-11/24hr, TA/Popeye's/diesel/24hr/@, **food:** Applebee's, Arby's, Burger King, Chili's, Cracker Barrel, LoneStar Steaks, McDonald's, Ryan's, Sonic, **lodging:** Comfort Inn, Day's Inn, Hampton Inn, Holiday Inn, Ramada Hotel, **other:** Cadillac/Pontiac/Buick/GMC, Fannie Mae Candies, Lowe's Whse, Outlet Mall/famous brands, Quality Times RV Park, Staples, Toyota, Wal-Mart SuperCtr/24hr

Mt Vernon

92 I-64 E, to Louisville, no facilities

83 Ina, **E...gas:** BP/diesel/deli/24hr, **other:** Sherwood Camping, **W...**to Rend Lake Coll

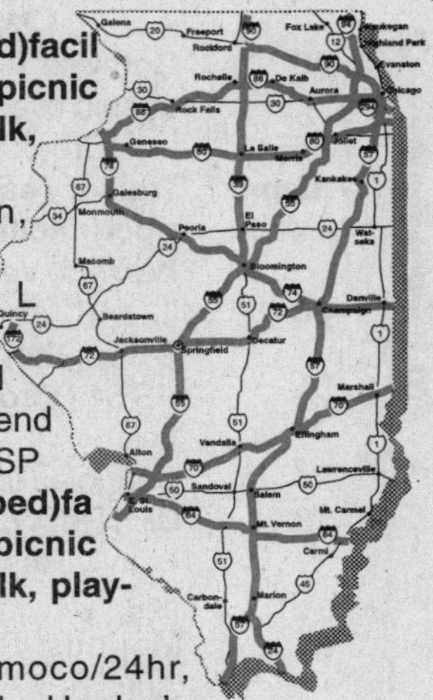

79mm rest area sb, full(handicapped)facilities, info, vending, phones, picnic tables, litter barrels, petwalk, playground

77 IL 154, to Whittington, **E...gas:** Shell/24hr, **other:** Holiday Trav-L Park, **W...lodging:** Best Western, Seasons at Rend Lake Lodge/rest., **other:** to Rend Lake, golf, Wayne Fitzgerrell SP

74mm rest area nb, full(handicapped)facilities, vending, phones, picnic tables, litter barrels, petwalk, playground

71 IL 14, Benton, **E...gas:** Amoco/24hr, BP/diesel, Citgo, **food:** Arby's, Hardee's, KFC/Taco Bell, Pizza Hut, Wendy's, **lodging:** Day's Inn/rest., Gray Plaza Motel, Motel Benton, Plaza Motel/rest., Super 8, **other:** HOSPITAL, AutoZone, KOA, Plaza Tire, **W...gas:** BP/Burger King/diesel, Shell/diesel/24hr, **food:** Bonanza, McDonald's, Subway, Taco John's, **other:** Big John Foods, CVS Drug, Wal-Mart/drugs, to Rend Lake

65 IL 149, W Frankfort, **E...gas:** BP, Citgo/diesel/24hr, GasForLess, Shell, **food:** Hardee's, KFC, LJ Silver, Mike's Drive-In, Pizza Inn, Pancakes/24hr, Sonic, **lodging:** Gray Plaza Motel, HOSPITAL, **other:** CarQuest, $General, MadPricer Foods, **W...gas:** Casey's, **food:** Burger King, Triple E+ Steaks, McDonald's, **lodging:** American Classic Inn, **other:** Chevrolet/Pontiac, CVS Drug, $Tree, K-Mart, VF Factory Stores

59 Johnston City, to Herrin, **E...gas:** Citgo, Shell/24hr, **food:** DQ, Gibby's Grill, Hardee's, McDonald's, **other:** camping(2mi), **W...other:** HOSPITAL, camping

54b a IL 13, Marion, **E...gas:** Citgo, Phillips 66/24hr, **food:** Arby's, Fazoli's, Grand Buffet, Hardee's, KFC, LJ Silver, Papa John's, Pizza Hut, Subway, Tequila's Mexican, Wendy's, Western Sizzlin, **lodging:** Day's Inn, **other:** MEDICAL CARE, Aldi Foods, AutoZone, Chevrolet/Cadillac, Family$, Ford/Lincoln/Mercury/Hyundai, Kroger/gas, Plaza Tire, Radio Shack, SavALot Foods, USPO, **W...gas:** Amoco/24hr, BP/diesel/24hr, **food:** Applebee's, Backyard Burger, Bob Evans, Burger King, McDonald's, O'Charley's, Red Lobster, Ryan's, Sonic, Steak'n Shake, Taco Bell, **lodging:** Best Inn, Drury Inn, Hampton Inn, Motel 6, Red Carpet Inn, Super 8, **other:** Buick/GMC/Pontiac/Mercedes, Chrysler/Plymouth/Dodge/Jeep, Dillard's, Harley-Davidson, Home Depot, Kia, Sam's Club/gas, Wal-Mart/auto, mall

Marion

53 Main St, Marion, **E...gas:** Shell/diesel, **food:** DQ, **lodging:** Motel Marion/camping, **other:** HOSPITAL, **W...gas:** Motomart/24hr, **food:** Cracker Barrel, Hide-Out Steaks, **lodging:** Comfort Inn, Comfort Suites, Holiday Inn Express

47mm weigh sta both lanes

45 IL 148, **1 mi E...gas:** King Tut's Food/diesel/24hr, **other:** Egyptian Hills Marina(9mi), camping, diesel repair

44 I-24 E to Nashville, no facilities

ILLINOIS

Interstate 57

N ↕ S

40 Goreville Rd, **E...other:** Ferne Clyffe SP, camping, scenic overlook, **W...gas:** Citgo/diesel/24hr
36 Lick Creek Rd, no facilities
32mm Trail of Tears Rest Area both lanes, full(handicapped)facilities, info, phones, picnic tables, litter barrels, vending, petwalk, playground
30 IL 146, Anna, Vienna, **W...gas:** Shell/diesel/rest./24hr, **other:** HOSPITAL, auto/tire repair
25 US 51 N(from nb, exits left), to Carbondale, no facilities
24 Dongola Rd, **W...gas:** Shell/diesel
18 Ullin Rd, **W...gas:** Citgo/diesel/24hr, **food:** Cheeko's Family Rest., **lodging:** Best Western, **other:** st police
8 Mounds Rd, to Mound City, **E...other:** K&K AutoTruck/diesel/repair
1 IL 3, to US 51, Cairo, **E...gas:** Amoco/diesel, BP/diesel, **lodging:** Belvedere Motel(2mi), Day's Inn, **other:** $General, Mound City Nat Cem(4mi), camping, **W...**camping
0mm Illinois/Missouri state line, Mississippi River

Interstate 64

E ↕ W

Exit # Services
131.5mm Illinois/Indiana state line, Wabash River
131mm Skeeter Mtn Welcome Ctr wb, full(handicapped)facilities, phone, vending, picnic tables, litter barrels, petwalk
130 IL 1, to Grayville, **N...gas:** Shell/24hr, **food:** Gingham House Rest., **lodging:** Best Western/rest., **other:** museum, camping, **S...gas:** Phillips 66/diesel
124mm Little Wabash River
117 Burnt Prairie, **S...gas:** Marathon/diesel, **food:** ChuckWagon Charlie's Café, **other:** antiques
110 US 45, Mill Shoals, **N...gas:** SS/diesel, **other:** Barnhill Camping
100 IL 242, to Wayne City, **N...gas:** Marathon/diesel
89 to Belle Rive, Bluford, no facilities
86mm rest area wb, full(handicapped)facilities, phone, vending, picnic tables, litter barrels, petwalk
82.5mm rest area eb, full(handicapped)facilities, phone, vending, picnic tables, litter barrels, petwalk

Mt Vernon

80 IL 37, to Mt Vernon, **2 mi N...gas:** BP/Burger King/diesel/24hr, Marathon/diesel/24hr, **lodging:** Royal Inn, **other:** camping
78 I-57, S to Memphis, N to Chicago
I-64 and I-57 run together 5 mi. See Illinois Interstate 57, exit 95.
73 I-57, N to Chicago, S to Memphis, no facilities
69 Woodlawn, no facilities
61 US 51, Richview, to Centralia, **S...**access to gas, food
50 IL 127, to Nashville, **N...**to Carlyle Lake, **S...gas:** BP/24hr, Citgo/diesel/24hr, Conoco/diesel/rest., Shell/diesel/24hr, **food:** Hardee's(3mi), McDonald's, Subway, **lodging:** Best Western, Little Nashville Inn/rest., Derrick Motel/rest.(3mi), **other:** HOSPITAL
41 IL 177, Okawville, **S...gas:** Phillips 66/Burger King/diesel/24hr/@, **food:** DQ, Hen House/24hr, Golfer's Steakhouse, **lodging:** Original Springs Motel, Super 8, **other:** Toyo Tires/truck repair
37mm Kaskaskia River
34 to Albers, **3 mi N...gas:** Casey's
27 IL 161, New Baden, **N...gas:** Shell/diesel/24hr, **food:** Good Ol' Days Rest., McDonald's, Outside Inn Rest., **other:** Chevrolet
25mm rest area both lanes, full(handicapped)facilities, info, phone, vending, picnic tables, litter barrels, petwalk
23 IL 4, to Mascoutah, **N...food:** Hardee's, McDonald's
19b a US 50, IL 158, **N...gas:** Motomart/24hr, **food:** Hero's Pizza/subs, **lodging:** Comfort Inn, **S...gas:** Citgo/diesel, **food:** Ivory Chopsticks Chinese, **other:** HOSPITAL, to Scott AFB
18mm weigh sta eb
15mm motorist callbox every 1/2 mile wb
14 O'Fallon, **N...food:** QT, Shell/24hr, Japanese Garden, Steak'n Shake/24hr, **lodging:** Baymont Inn, Extended Stay America, Holiday Inn Express, Howard Johnson, Sleep Inn, **other:** Chevrolet, CVS Drug, Ford, Nissan/Cadillac, **S...gas:** Mobil, **food:** Chevy's Mexican, DQ, Emperor's Wok, Hardee's, Jack-in-the-Box, KFC, Lion's Choice, LoneStar Steaks, McDonald's, O'Charley's, Pepper's Rest., SteakOut, Taco Bell, Western Sizzlin, **lodging:** Econolodge, Ramada Ltd, **other:** BMW, Dierberg's Foods, Home Depot, Honda, Hyundai, Kia, Mazda, Mitsubishi, Sam's Club, Subaru, Suzuki, Toyota, VW, Wal-Mart/auto/24hr
12 IL 159, to Collinsville, **N...gas:** CFM/diesel, **food:** Applebee's, Bob Evans, Carlos O'Kelly's, Carrabba's, Damon's, HideOut Steaks, Houlihan's, Joe's Crabshack, Olive Garden, Red Lobster, TGIFriday, **lodging:** Best Western Camelot, Drury Inn, Fairfield Inn, Hampton Inn, Ramada Inn/rest., Super 8, **other:** Circuit City, Michael's, 1/2Price Store, Saturn, **S...gas:** BP/24hr, Mobil, Motomart/diesel/24hr, **food:** Boston Mkt, Burger King, Capt D's, Casa Gallardo, Chili's, Denny's, Fazoli's, Hardee's, IHOP, Longhorn Steaks, LJ Silver, Mazzio's, McDonald's, Old Country Buffet, Outback Steaks, Pasta House, Ponderosa, Popeye's, Rally's, Ramon's Mexican, Ruby Tuesday, Schlotsky's, Steak'n Shake, Taco Bell, **other:** AutoTire, Best Buy, Borders, Dillard's, Famous Barr, Firestone/auto, Goodyear, JC Penney, K-Mart, Kohl's, OfficeMax, Schnuck's Foods, Target, Walgreen, mall
9 IL 157, to Caseyville, **N...gas:** BP/24hr, Phillips 66/Subway/repair, **food:** Hardee's, Wendy's, **lodging:** Western Inn, **S...gas:** BP/diesel/repair, **food:** Cracker Barrel, DQ, Domino's, McDonald's, Pizza Hut/Taco Bell, **lodging:** Best Inn, Day's Inn, Motel 6, Quality Inn
7 I-255, S to Memphis, N to Chicago, no facilities

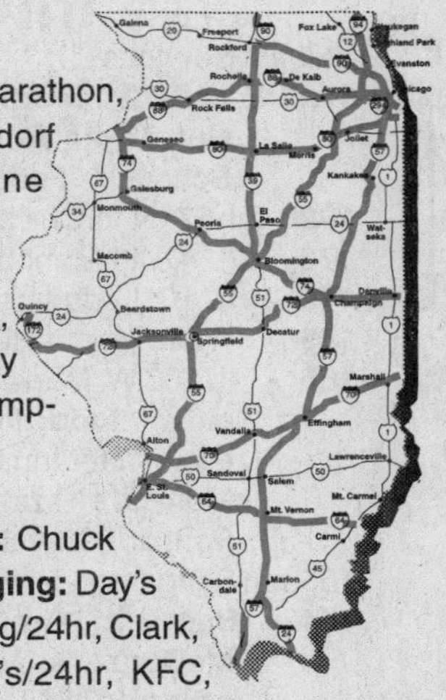

Interstate 64

E St Louis

6	IL 111, Kingshighway, **N...gas:** BP, Shell, **food:** Popeye's, **lodging:** Econo Inn
5.5mm	motorist callbox every 1/2 mi eb
5	25th St, no facilities
4	15th St, Baugh, no facilities
3	I-55 N, I-70 E, IL 3 N, to St Clair Ave, to stockyards
2b a	3rd St, MLK, **S...gas**
1	IL 3 S, 13th St, E St Louis, **N...**Casino Queen
0mm	Illinois/Missouri state line, Mississippi River

Interstate 70

Exit #	Services
156mm	Illinois/Indiana state line
155.5mm	weigh sta eb
154	US 40 W, **S...**South Fork Conv Mart
151mm	weigh sta wb
149mm	**rest area wb, full(handicapped)facilities, info, phone, picnic tables, vending, litter barrels, petwalk, camping**
147	IL 1, Marshall, **N...gas:** Jerry's Rest., **S...gas:** Casey's, Jiffy/diesel/24hr, Phillips 66/Arby's/diesel/@ , Shell/Subway, **food:** Burger King, DQ, McDonald's, Pizza Hut, Wendy's, **lodging:** Peak's Motel, Lincoln Motel(2mi), Super 8, **other:** Lincoln Trail SP, camping
136	to Martinsville, **S...gas:** BP/diesel/24hr
134.5mm	N Fork Embarras River
129	IL 49, Casey, **N...other:** RV service, KOA(seasonal), **S...gas:** Casey's, Citgo/DQ/diesel, Speedway, **food:** Hardee's, Joe's Pizza, KFC, McDonald's, Pizza Hut, **lodging:** Comfort Inn, Casey Motel(1mi)
119	IL 130, Greenup, **S...gas:** Amoco, BP/diesel, Phillips 66/Subway, **food:** DQ, Dutch Pan Rest., **lodging:** Budget Host, 5 Star Motel, **other:** MEDICAL CARE, Chevrolet, camping, hist sites
105	Montrose, **S...gas:** BP/diesel, Shell/delimart/24hr, **lodging:** Montarosa Motel/café
98	I-57, N to Chicago

Effingham

I-70 and I-57 run together 6 mi. See Illinois Interstate 57, exits 159-162.

92	I-57, S to Mt Vernon
91mm	Little Wabash River
87mm	**rest area both lanes, full(handicapped)facilities, info, phone, vending, picnic tables, litter barrels, playground, petwalk, RV dump**
82	IL 128, Altamont, **N...gas:** Casey's, Citgo/Stuckey's/Subway/24hr, Marathon, Speedway/diesel, **food:** McDonald's, **lodging:** Altamont Motel/rest., Knight's Inn, **other:** Fostoria Factory Outlet, **S...gas:** Phillips 66/diesel, **lodging:** Super 8
76	US 40, St Elmo, **N...gas:** Marathon, Phillips 66, **lodging:** Waldorf Motel, **other:** Timberline Camping(2mi)
71mm	weigh sta eb
68	US 40, Brownstown, **N...other:** Okaw Valley Kamping, Road Angel Camping, **S...**truck repair
63.5mm	Kaskaskia River
63	US 51, Vandalia, **N...food:** Chuck Wagon Café, LJ Silver, **lodging:** Day's Inn, **S...gas:** BP/Burger King/24hr, Clark, Marathon, **food:** Hardee's/24hr, KFC, McDonald's, Pizza Hut, Rancho Nuevo Mexican, Sonic, Subway, Wendy's, **lodging:** Jay's Inn, Mabry Motel, Travelodge, **other:** HOSPITAL, Aldi Foods, hist site
61	US 40, Vandalia, **S...gas:** Fastop/diesel, Phillips 66, **food:** KFC/Taco Bell, Ponderosa, **lodging:** Ramada Ltd, **other:** NAPA AutoCare, Wal-Mart

Vandalia

52	US 40, Mulberry Grove, **N...gas:** Citgo/diesel, **other:** Timber Trail Camp-In(2mi), tires/repair, antiques, **S...**Cedar Brook Camping(1mi)
45	IL 127, Greenville, **N...gas:** BP, Phillips 66/Domino's/diesel, Shell/diesel/24hr, **food:** Chang's Chinese, KFC/Taco Bell, Lu-Bob's Rest., Red Apple Rest., McDonald's, **lodging:** Best Western/rest., Budget Host, Super 8, 2 Acre Motel, **other:** HOSPITAL, Ford/Mercury, **S...**to Carlyle Lake, **food:** Circle B Steaks
41	US 40 E, to Greenville, no facilities
36	US 40 E, Pocahontas, **S... gas:** BP/diesel/24hr, Phillips 66/diesel/24hr, **lodging:** Lighthouse Lodge, Powhatan Motel/rest., Wickiup Hotel, Tahoe Motel(3mi)
30	US 40, IL 143, to Highland, **S...gas:** Shell/24hr, **food:** Blue Springs Café, **other:** Tomahawk RV Park(7mi)
26.5mm	**Silver Lake Rest Area both lanes, full(handicapped)facilities, phone, picnic tables, litter barrels, vending, petwalk**
24	IL 143, Marine, **3 mi S...food:** Ponderosa, **lodging:** Holiday Inn Express, **other:** HOSPITAL
23mm	motorist callboxes begin wb every 1/2mile
21	IL 4, Troy, **N...**gas/diesel/24hr
15b a	I-55, N to Chicago, S to St Louis, I-270 W to Kansas City

I-70 and I-55 run together 18 mi . See Illinois Interstate 55, exits 1-18.

0mm	Illinois/Missouri state line, Mississippi River

ILLINOIS

Interstate 72

E ↕ W

Exit #	Services
1 mi E of I-72...food:	McDonald's, Monical's Pizza, Pizza Hut, Texas Roadhouse, **other:** County Mkt Foods, Schnuck's Foods
182b a	I-57, N to Chicago, S to Memphis, to I-74
176	IL 47, to Mahomet, no facilities
172	IL 10, Lodge, Seymour, no facilities
169	White Heath Rd, no facilities
166	IL 105 W, Market St, **N...**Ford/Mercury, **S...gas:** Mobil/diesel, **food:** Iron Horse Rest., **lodging:** Best Western, Foster Inn, **1 mi S...food:** Hardee's, McDonald's, Monical's Pizza, Pizza Hut, **other:** Chevrolet/Buick/Pontiac, Chrysler/Plymouth/Dodge/Jeep
165mm	Sangamon River
164	Bridge St, **1 mi S...gas:** Mobil, **food:** DQ, Hardee's, McDonald's, Monical's Pizza, Pizza Hut, Subway, **other:** HOSPITAL
156	IL 48, Cisco, to Weldon, **S...**Friends Creek Camping(may-oct)(3mi)
153mm	**rest area both lanes, full(handicapped)facilities, phone, picnic tables, litter barrels, vending, petwalk**
152mm	Friends Creek
150	Argenta, no facilities
144	IL 48, Oreana, **N...gas:** Oasis Trkstp/diesel/24hr/@, **S...lodging:** Sleep Inn, **other:** HOSPITAL, Dodge, Honda
141b a	US 51 S, Decatur, **N...gas:** Shell, **food:** Applebee's, Cheddar's, Cracker Barrel, Country Kitchen, Hardee's, HomeTown Buffet, McDonald's, O'Charley's, Pizza Hut, Red Lobster, Steak'n Shake, Taco Bell, Texas Roadhouse, **lodging:** Baymont Inn, Comfort Inn, Country Inn Suites, Fairfield Inn, Hampton Inn, Ramada Ltd, Wingate Inn, **other:** Advance Parts, Bergner's, Buick/GMC, JC Penney, Lowe's Whse, Kohl's, Mitsubishi/Hyundai/Honda, Sears/auto, Staples, mall, **S...food:** Arby's, Burger King, China Buffet, Monical's Pizza, Panera Bread, Quizno's, Subway, **other:** Circuit City, Radio Shack, Sam's Club, Walgreen, Wal-Mart SuperCtr/24hr
138	IL 121, Decatur, **S...**HOSPITAL
133b a	US 36 E, US 51, Decatur, **S...gas:** Citgo, Phillips 66/diesel, **lodging:** Day's Inn, Holiday Inn Select/rest.
128	Niantic, no facilities
122	Illiopolis, to Mt Auburn, **N...gas:** Citgo
114	Buffalo, Mechanicsburg, no facilities
108	Riverton, Dawson, no facilities
107mm	Sangamon River
104	Camp Butler, **N...lodging:** Best Rest Inn, Park View Motel, **other:** golf(1mi)
103b a	I-55, N to Chicago, S to St Louis, Il 97, to Springfield

I-72 and I-55 run together 6 mi. **See IL I-55, exits 92-98.**

Exit #	Services
97b a	6th St, I-55 S, **N...gas:** Shell, **food:** Heritage House Rest., McDonald's, **lodging:** Illini Inn, Ramada Inn, Super 8, Travelodge, **other:** Mr Lincoln's Camping/LP
93	IL 4, Springfield, **N...gas:** Hucks, **food:** Applebee's, Arby's, Bakers Square, Best Buffet Chinese, Burger King, Chili's, Damon's, Denny's, Grand Buffet, Lion's Choice Rest., LoneStar Steaks, Maverick Rest., McDonald's, Ned Kelly's Steaks, Old Country Buffet, Olive Garden, Panera Bread, Pasta House, Popeye's, Sonic, Taco Bell, TGIFriday, Wendy's, **lodging:** Comfort Inn, Courtyard, Fairfield Inn, Sleep Inn, **other:** Barnes&Noble, Batteries+, Best Buy, Circuit City, Cub Foods/24hr, Gordman's, Jo-Ann Crafts, K-Mart, Kohl's, Lowe's Whse, Michael's, Office Depot, OfficeMax, Sam's Club, Sears/auto, ShopKO, Staples, Target, Walgreen, Wal-Mart/auto, **S...gas:** Meijer/diesel, **food:** Bob Evans, Burger King, O'Charley's, Steak'n Shake, **lodging:** Hampton Inn, Staybridge Suites, **other:** Cadillac, Chevrolet, Chrysler/Plymouth/Dodge/Jeep, Ford, Honda, Saturn
91	Wabash Ave, to Springfield, **N...other:** Lincoln/Mercury/Mazda, Mr Battery, **S...**RV SuperCtr
82	New Berlin, **S...gas:** Phillips 66/A&W/diesel
76	IL 123, Alexander, to Ashland, no facilities
68	to IL 104, to Jacksonville, **2 mi N...gas:** BP, Clark, **food:** Hucks Food/gas, **other:** HOSPITAL
64	US 67, to Jacksonville, **N...food:** Classic Diner, **lodging:** Comfort Inn, **other:** Hopper RV Ctr, **2 mi N...gas:** Clark/diesel, **food:** DQ, McDonald's, Subway, **lodging:** Super 8, **other:** HOSPITAL, Harpers Food/gas
60	to US 67 N, to Jacksonville, **6 mi N...**HOSPITAL, gas, food, lodging
52	to IL 106, Winchester, **N...**golf, **2 mi S...**gas, food, lodging
46	IL 100, to Bluffs, no facilities
42mm	Illinois River
35	US 54, IL 107, Griggsville, to Pittsfield, **4 mi N...**gas, food, lodging, **S...other:** HOSPITAL, camping(6mi), st police
31	New Salem, to Pittsfield, **5 mi S...**HOSPITAL, gas, food, lodging, camping
20	IL 106, Barry, **N...lodging:** Ice Market Inn, **other:** AppleBasket Farms, **S...gas:** Phillips 66/diesel/24hr, Shell/diesel/24hr, **food:** Wendy's
10	IL 96, Hull, to Payson, no facilities
4c b a	US 36 W, I-172, to Quincy
0mm	Illinois/Missouri state line, Mississippi River

Decatur
Springfield

Interstate 74

E ↕ W

Exit #	Services
221mm	Illinois/Indiana state line
220	Lynch Rd, Danville, **N...gas:** BP/diesel, **food:** Big Boy, **lodging:** Best Western, Comfort Inn, Fairfield Inn, Knight's Inn, Ramada Inn, Super 8
216	Bowman Ave, Danville, **N...gas:** Citgo/diesel, Freedom, Mobil/diesel/24hr, **food:** Godfather's, KFC
215b a	US 150, IL 1, Gilbert St, Danville, **N...gas:** Citgo/diesel, Speedway, **food:** Arby's, Hardee's, LJ Silver, McDonald's, Pizza Hut, Steak'n Shake, Subway, Taco Bell, **lodging:** Best Western, Day's Inn, **other:** HOSPITAL, Aldi Foods, Bass Tires, Ford/Lincoln/Mercury, **S...gas:** Clark, Speedway/diesel/24hr, **food:** Burger King, Monical's Pizza, **other:** AutoZone, Big R Foods, Buick/Pontiac/GMC, $General, Eagle Foods, Harley-Davidson, Forest Glen Preserve Camping(11mi)
214	G St, Tilton, no facilities
210	US 150, MLK Dr, **2 mi N...gas:** Marathon, **food:** Little Nugget Steaks, **other:** HOSPITAL, to Kickapoo SP, camping, **S...food:** PossumTrot Rest.
208mm	**Welcome Ctr wb, full(handicapped)facilities, info, phones, picnic tables, litter barrels, vending, petwalk**

Danville

Interstate 74

206 Oakwood, **N...gas:** Marathon/diesel/rest./24hr, **S...gas:** Marathon/diesel/24hr/@, Phillips 66/diesel, **food:** McDonald's, Oaks Grill, **other:** Casey's(1mi)

200 IL 49 N, to Rankin, **N...**5 Bridges RV Park

197 IL 49 S, Ogden, **S...gas:** Citgo/diesel, **food:** Billy Bud's Steaks, Lincoln House Rest.

192 St Joseph, **S...food:** DQ, **other:** antiques

185 IL 130, University Ave, no facilities

184 US 45, Cunningham Ave, Urbana, **N...lodging:** Park Inn, **S...gas:** Clark, Freedom/diesel/24hr, Speedway/Taco Bell, **food:** Cracker Barrel, Domino's, Longhorn Steaks, Ned Kelly's Steaks, Steak'nShake/24hr, **lodging:** Best Value Inn, Best Western, Eastland Suites, Motel 6, **other:** $General, Family$, Firestone/auto, NAPA, Sav-A-Lot

183 Lincoln Ave, Urbana, **S...gas:** Clark/diesel, Speedway, **food:** Urbana Garden Café, **lodging:** Holiday Inn/rest., Ramada Ltd, Sleep Inn, Super 8, **other:** HOSPITAL, to U of IL

182 Neil St, Champaign, **N...food:** Alexander's Steaks, Bob Evans, Chevy's Mexican, ChiChi's, Denny's, FoodCourt, Fortune House Chinese, Grandy's, McDonald's, Olive Garden, Subway, Taco Bell, **lodging:** Baymont Inn, Comfort Inn, Extended Stay America, La Quinta, Red Roof Inn, Super 8, **other:** Barnes&Noble, Chevrolet/Cadillac, Chrysler/Jeep, JC Penney, Kohl's, Office Depot, Osco Drug, Sears/auto, mall, same as 181, **S... gas:** Mobil, **food:** Oakley's Rest., **lodging:** Premier Motel, **other:** Jo-Ann Fabrics, NTB

181 Prospect Ave, Champaign, **N...gas:** Meijer/diesel/24hr, **food:** Applebee's, Burger King, Cheddar's, Chili's, China Town, Culver's, Damon's, Fazoli's, HomeTown Buffet, LoneStar Steaks, O'Charley's, Old Country Buffet, Outback Steaks, Red Lobster, Ryan's, Steak'n Shake/24hr, Subway, Wendy's, **lodging:** Courtyard, Drury Inn, Fairfield Inn, **other:** Aamco, Advance Parts, Best Buy, Borders Books, Circuit City, $Tree, Hyundai, Kia, Lowe's Whse, Michael's, Mitsubishi, Sam's Club/gas, Staples, Target, Tires+, Wal-Mart/auto, same as 182, **S...gas:** Clark, Freedom, Mobil, Shell, **food:** Arby's, Dos Real's Mexican, KFC, LJ Silver, **lodging:** AmeriInn, Day's Inn, Econolodge, **other:** CarX, $General, K-Mart, NAPA, Nissan, Saturn, Subaru, RV/diesel repair

179b a I-57, N to Chicago, S to Memphis

174 Lake of the Woods Rd, Prairieview Rd, **N...gas:** BP/diesel, Casey's, Mobil/diesel, **food:** PickleTree Farm Rest., Subway, **other:** R&S RV Ctr, Tin Cup Camping, Lake of the Woods SP, **S...gas:** Citgo, **food:** McDonald's

172 IL 47, Mahomet, **S...gas:** Clark, Mobil, Shell/Domino's/diesel, **food:** Arby's, DQ, HenHouse Rest., Mahomet Garden Rest., Monical's Pizza, Peking House Chinese, Subway, **lodging:** Heritage Inn, **other:** IGA Foods, NAPA, Walgreen

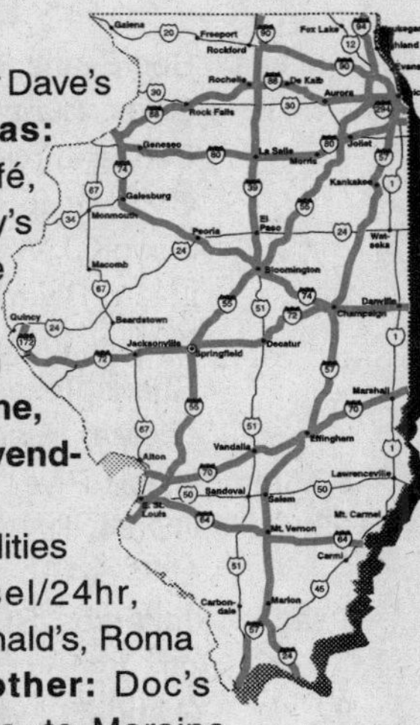

166 Mansfield, **S...gas:** BP

159 IL 54, Farmer City, **N...**Farmer Dave's Buffalo Ranch(1mi), **S...gas:** Casey's, **food:** Family Café, **lodging:** Budget Motel, Day's Inn, **other:** to Clinton Lake RA

156mm rest area both lanes, full(handicapped)facilities, phone, picnic tables, litter larrels, vending, playground, petwalk

152 US 136, to Heyworth, no facilities

149 Le Roy, **N...gas:** BP/diesel/24hr, Freedom, **food:** KFC, McDonald's, Roma Ralph's Pizza, Subway, **other:** Doc's Drug, $General, IGA Foods, to Moraine View SP, **S...gas:** Shell/Woody's Rest./diesel/24hr, **lodging:** Super 8, **other:** Clinton Lake, camping

142 Downs, **N...gas:** BP/diesel/24hr, **food:** Pizza Hut

143 135 US 51, Bloomington, **N...gas:** Clark, Mobil/diesel, **food:** McDonald's, **other:** HOSPITAL, to IL St U, **S...gas:** Shell/diesel

134b[157] Veterans Pkwy, Bloomington, **N...gas:** Clark/24hr, FS, **food:** CJ's Rest., Froggy's Rest., **lodging:** Parkway Inn/rest., Sunset Motel, **other:** airport

a I-55, N to Chicago, S to St Louis, I-74 E

I-74 and I-55 run together 6 mi. See IL 55, exit 160b a.

127[163] I-55, N to Chicago, S to St Louis, I-74 W to Peoria

125 US 150, Mitsubishi Motorway, to Bloomington

123mm weigh sta wb

122mm weigh sta eb

120 Carlock, **N...gas:** BP/diesel/repair, **food:** Countryside Rest.

114.5mm rest area both lanes, full(handicapped)facilities, vending, phone, picnic tables, litter barrels, petwalk

113.5mm Mackinaw River

112 IL 117, Goodfield, **N...gas:** Shell/Busy Corner/diesel, **other:** to Timberline RA, Jellystone Camping, Eureka Coll, Reagan Home

102b a Morton, **N...gas:** BP, Casey's, Citgo/Blimpie/diesel/24hr, Mobil/Arby's/diesel, **food:** Burger King, Country Kitchen, Cracker Barrel, Ruby Tuesday, Taco Bell, Wendy's, **lodging:** Best Western, Comfort Inn, Day's Inn, Holiday Inn Express, **other:** MEDICAL CARE, **S...gas:** Clark/24hr, Shell/Subway/diesel/24hr, **food:** China Dragon, KFC, McDonald's, Monical's Pizza, Quizno's, **other:** Chrysler/Dodge, CVS Drug, $Tree, Ford, K-Mart, Kroger

101 I-155 S, to Lincoln, no facilities

99 I-474 W, airport

98 Pinecrest Dr, no facilities

96 95c(from eb), US 150, IL 8, E Washington St, E Peoria, **N...gas:** Site, **food:** Monical's Pizza, Subway, Wendy's, **lodging:** Super 8

95b IL 116, to Metamora, **N...lodging:** Hampton Inn

a Peoria, N Main St, **S...gas:** BP/24hr, **food:** Applebee's,

ILLINOIS

Interstate 74

E ↕ W

Bob Evans, China Buffet, Godfather's, Hardee's, LJ Silver, Subway, **lodging:** Baymont Inn, Hotel East Peoria, Motel 6, **other:** Aldi Foods, Advance Parts, CVS Drug, $General, Goodyear/auto, Kroger, ShopKO, Walgreen

94 IL 40, RiverFront Dr, **S...gas:** Citgo/Burger King, Hucks/Godfather's/24hr, **food:** Papa John's, Steak'n Shake, Texas Roadhouse, **other:** Lowe's Whse, OfficeMax, Radio Shack, Wal-Mart SuperCtr/24hr

93.5mm Illinois River

93b US 24, IL 29, Peoria, **S...other:** Damon's, Sears, civic ctr

a Jefferson St, Peoria, **S...other:** Damon's, to civic ctr

92 Glendale Ave, Peoria, **S... other:** HOSPITAL, downtown

92a IL 40 N, Knoxville Ave, Peoria, **S...lodging:** Holiday Inn, **other:** HOSPITAL

91b a University St, Peoria, **1 mi N on Universtiy...gas:** BP, Phillips 66, **other:** AutoZone, Walgreen, Wal-Mart, to Expo Gardens, **S...**to Bradley U

90 Gale Ave, Peoria, **S...gas:** Speedway

89 US 150, War Memorial Dr, Peoria, **N on War Memorial...gas:** BP, Clark, Shell, **food:** Bob Evans, Burger King, Cheddar's, Denny's, Dunkin Donuts, IHOP, Ned Kelly's Steaks, Outback Steaks, Perkins/24hr, Pizza Hut, Red Lobster, Schlotsky's, Steak'n Shake, Subway, Wendy's, **lodging:** AmeriSuites, Best Western, Comfort Suites, Courtyard, Extended Stay America, Fairfield Inn, Holiday Inn, Red Roof Inn, Residence Inn, Sleep Inn, Super 8, The Inn, **other:** Chevrolet, Circuit City, Cub Foods, Famous-Barr, Firestone, JC Penney, Lowe's Whse, Pontiac/Cadillac, Sears/auto, Target, Tires+, U-Haul, Walgreen, mall

Peoria

87b a I-474 E, IL 6, N to Chillicothe, **E...**airport

82 Edwards Rd, Kickapoo, **N...gas:** Mobil/diesel/service, Shell/Subway/diesel, **food:** Jubilee Café, **other:** craft mall, to Jubilee Coll SP, **S...other:** USPO, Wildlife Prairie Park

75 Brimfield, Oak Hill, **N...gas:** Casey's, **food:** Jimall's Rest.

71 to IL 78, Elmwood, to Canton, Kewanee, no facilities

62mm rest area both lanes, full(handicapped)facilities, phone, picnic tables, litter barrels, vending, petwalk

61.5mm Spoon River

54 IL 97, Lewistown, **N...other:** TravL Park Camping(1mi), **S...gas:** Mobil/diesel(2mi)

51 Knoxville, **S...gas:** BP/diesel, Casey's, Citgo/diesel/24hr, **food:** Hardee's/24hr, McDonald's, Subway, **lodging:** Super 8

48b a E Galesburg, Galesburg, **N...lodging:** Jumer's Hotel/rest., **S...gas:** Clark, Mobil/diesel, Phillips 66, **food:** DQ, KFC, Hardee's, McDonald's, Pizza Hut, Subway, Taco Bell, Hy-Vee Foods, **lodging:** Days Inn, Economy 8, Galesburg Inn, Holiday Inn Express, Ramada Inn, Relax Inn, Super 8, Buick, **other:** Econo Foods, Firestone, Goodyear, to Sandburg Birthplace, Lincoln-Douglas Debates

Galesburg

46b a US 34, to Monmouth, **N...other:** Nichol's Diesel Service, **3 mi S...food:** Applebee's, Golden Corral, **lodging:** Country Inn Suites, **other:** HOSPITAL

32 IL 17, Woodhull, **N...gas:** BP/diesel/@, Shell, **food:** Woodhull Rest., **S...gas:** Mobil/diesel/rest./24hr/@, **food:** Homestead Rest., **other:** Shady Lakes Camping(8mi)

30mm rest area wb, full(handicapped)facilities, vending, picnic tables, litter barrels, phones, playground, petwalk, RV dump

28mm rest area eb, full(handicapped)facilities, vending, picnic tables, litter barrels, phones, playground, petwalk, RV dump

24 IL 81, Andover, **N...**Gibson's RV Park(5mi)

14mm I-80, E to Chicago, I-80/I-280 W to Des Moines

8mm weigh sta wb

6mm weigh sta eb

5b US 6, Moline, **S...gas:** Citgo, **food:** Bender's Rest., Denny's, Harold's Rest., McDonald's, Omelet Shoppe, Skyline Rest., **lodging:** Best Western, Comfort Inn, Country Inn Suites, Exel Inn, Hampton Inn, Holiday Inn, Holiday Inn Express, La Quinta, Motel 6, Skyline Inn

a I-280 W, US 6 W, to Des Moines

4b a IL 5, John Deere Rd, Moline, **N...gas:** BP, **food:** Applebee's, Carlos O'Kelly's, Old Country Buffet, Ryan's, Steak'n Shake, Wendy's, **other:** Buick, Lowe's Whse, Staples, Tires+, Wal-Mart SuperCtr/24hr, **S...gas:** Citgo, Mobil, **food:** Arby's, Burger King, Denny's, LJ Silver, ChiChi's, New Mandarin Chinese, Pizza Hut, Subway, Taco Bell, Wendy's, Winner's Circle Rest., **lodging:** Best Western, Comfort Inn, Exel Inn, Fairfield Inn, **other:** Best Buy, Chevrolet, Eagle Foods, Firestone/auto, Food Fair, Ford, Goodyear/auto, JC Penney, OfficeMax, Sears/auto, ShopKO, mall

Moline

3 23rd Ave, Moline, **N...lodging:** Super 8

2 7th Ave, Moline, **S...lodging:** Signature Inn, **other:** Goodyear/auto, to civic ctr, riverfront

1 3rd Ave(from eb), Moline, **S...gas:** PetroStop, **lodging:** Radisson, **other:** Goodyear/auto

0mm Mississippi River, Illinois/Iowa state line. **Exits 4-1 are in Iowa.**

4 US 67, Grant St, State St, Bettendorf, **N...gas:** BP, Phillips 66, Sinclair, **food:** Ross' Rest./24hr, **lodging:** Abbey Motel, Twin Bridges Motel, **other:** CarQuest, **S...food:** DQ, Village Inn Rest., **other:** $General, NAPA

3 Middle Rd, Locust St, Bettendorf, **S...gas:** BP, **food:** Bennigan's, Bishop's Cafeteria, Fortune Garden Chinese, MaidRite Café, McDonald's, Pizza Hut, Subway, Taco Bell, **lodging:** Econolodge, Holiday Inn, **other:** HOSPITAL, Goodyear/auto, ShopKO, Walgreen, mall

Bettendorf

Interstate 74

E ↕ W

2 US 6 W, Spruce Hills Dr, Bettendorf, **N...gas:** BP/diesel, Phillips 66, **food:** Old Chicago Pizza, **lodging:** Courtyard, Heartland Inn, Signature Inn, Jumer's Hotel/rest., **other:** U-Haul, **S...food:** Applebee's, Bob Evans, Burger King, Country Kitchen, Godfather's, Hardee's, KFC, Panera Bread, Red Lobster, Subway, Day's Inn, **lodging:** Fairfield Inn, Hampton Inn, **other:** Cub Foods, Buick/Pontiac, Cadillac, Isuzu, Kohl's, Gordman's, Lowe's Whse, Sam's Club, st patrol

1 53rd St, Hamilton, **N... gas:** BP, **food:** Ruby Tuesday, **other:** Borders Books, Harley-Davidson, Michael's, Old Navy, Ultimate Electronics, **S...gas:** Phillips 66, **food:** Arby's, Golden Corral, IHOP, Krispy Kreme, Quizno's, Steak'n Shake, Village Inn Rest., Wendy's, **lodging:** Sleep Inn, **other:** MEDICAL CARE, Best Buy, Staples, Target, Wal-Mart SuperCtr/24hr/gas

0mm I-74 begins/ends on I-80, exit 298. **Exits 1-4 are in Iowa.**

Interstate 80

E ↕ W

Chicago Area

Exit # Services

163mm Illinois/Indiana state line

161 US 6, IL 83, Torrence Ave, **N...gas:** BP, **food:** Arby's, Bob Evans, Chili's, Dixie Kitchen, Hooters, IHOP, Olive Garden, On-the-Border, Oriental Palace, Wendy's, **lodging:** Comfort Suites, Day's Inn, Extended Stay America, Fairfield Inn, Red Roof Inn, Sleep Inn, Super 8, **other:** Best Buy, Chrysler/Plymouth/Jeep, Dominick's Foods, Firestone/auto, Home Depot, JustTires, K-Mart, PepBoys, Radio Shack, **S...gas:** Gas City, Marathon, Mobil, **food:** Al's Diner, Brown's Chicken/pasta, Burger King, Dunkin Donuts, Golden Crown Rest., McDonald's, Pappy's Gyro's, **other:** Auto Clinic, Chevrolet, OfficeMax, Saab, Sam's Club, SunRise Foods, Walgreen

160b I-94 W, to Chicago, tollway begins wb, ends eb

a IL 394 S, to Danville, no facilities

159mm Oasis, **gas:** Mobil/diesel, **food:** Burger King, TCBY

157 IL 1, Halsted St, **N...gas:** Citgo/diesel, Clark, Marathon/diesel, **food:** Burger King, Yellow Ribbon Rest., **lodging:** Best Western, Comfort Inn, Econolodge, Hilton Garden, Holiday Inn Express, Motel 6, Park Inn, **S...gas:** Shell, Speedway, **food:** Applebee's, Arby's, Boston Mkt, Dunkin Donuts, Fannie May Candies, KFC, McDonald's, Popeye's, Shooter's Buffet, Subway, Taco Bell, Washington Square Rest., Wendy's, **lodging:** Rodeway Inn, Super 8, Villager Lodge, **other:** Chevrolet, $Tree, Firestone/auto, Goodyear/auto, Home Depot, Jewel-Osco, K-Mart, OfficeMax, PepBoys, Target

156 Dixie Hwy(from eb), **S...**golf

155 I-294 N, Tri-State Tollway, toll plaza, no facilities

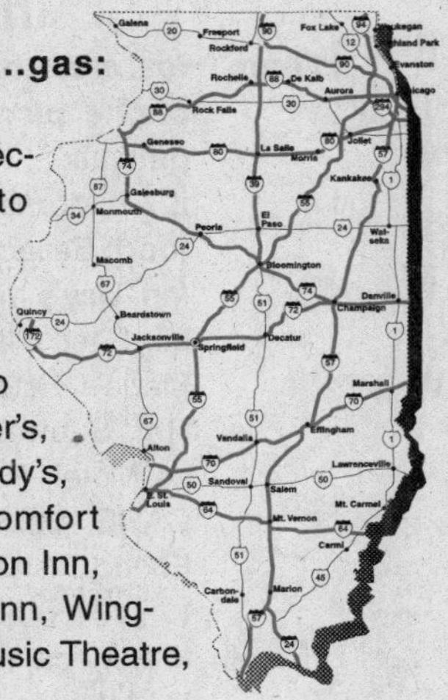

154 Kedzie Ave(from eb), **N...gas:** Speedway, **S...**HOSPITAL

151b a I-57(exits left from both directions), N to Chicago, S to Memphis

148b a IL 43, Harlem Ave, **N...gas:** Speedway/Subway/diesel, **food:** Burger King, Chicago Café, Cracker Barrel, Culver's, Papa John's, Quizno's, Wendy's, **lodging:** Baymont Inn, Comfort Suites, Fairfield Inn, Hampton Inn, Holiday Inn Select, Sleep Inn, Wingate Inn, **S...other:** World Music Theatre, Windy City Camping

147.5mm weigh sta wb

145b a US 45, 96th Ave, **N...gas:** Gas City, **S...gas:** BP, Clark, Gas City/diesel, Shell/diesel/24hr, **food:** Burger King, DQ, Denny's, McDonald's(3mi), Mindy's Ribs, Morgan's Grill, Subway, White Castle, Wendy's, **lodging:** Super 8, **other:** camping(2mi)

143mm weigh sta eb

137 US 30, New Lenox, **N...food:** Les Bros Rest., **other:** K-Mart, **S...gas:** Speedway/diesel, **food:** Burger King, KFC, McDonald's, New Lenox Rest., Pizza Hut, Taco Bell, **other:** Eagle Foods, Jewel-Osco/gas, Walgreen

Joliet

134 Briggs St, **N...gas:** Speedway, **other:** HOSPITAL, **S...gas:** BP/repair/24hr, Citgo/diesel

133 Richards St, no facilities

132b a US 52, IL 53, Chicago St, no facilities

131.5mm Des Plaines River

131 US 6, Meadow Ave, **N...**to Riverboat Casino

130b a IL 7, Larkin Ave, **N...gas:** Citgo, Clark, Marathon/24hr, Shell/24hr, Speedway, Thornton/diesel, **food:** Bellagio Pizzaria, Bob Evans, Burger King, ChuckeCheese, Dunkin Donuts, Pizza Hut, Steak'n Shake, Subway, Taco Bell, TCBY, Wendy's, White Castle, **lodging:** Comfort Inn, Holiday Inn Express, Microtel, Motel 6, Red Roof, Super 8, **other:** HOSPITAL, Aldi Foods, Chevrolet/Mitsubishi, Cub Food/drug, Ford, Goodyear/auto, K-Mart, NTB, PepBoys, Radio Shack, Sam's Club, Wal-Mart, to Coll of St Francis, **S...**auto repair

127 Houbolt Rd, to Joliet, **N...gas:** BP/deli, Citgo/7-11, **food:** Burger King, Cracker Barrel, McDonald's, **lodging:** Fairfield Inn, Hampton Inn, Ramada Ltd, **other:** Harley-Davidson

126b a I-55, N to Chicago, S to St Louis

125.5mm Du Page River

122 Minooka, **N...gas:** Citgo/diesel/24hr, **S...gas:** BP/24hr, Pilot/Arby's/diesel/24hr/@, **food:** DQ, McDonald's, Subway, Wendy's, **other:** SuperValu Foods

119mm rest area wb, full(handicapped)facilities, vending, phones, picnic tables, litter barrels, playground, petwalk

ILLINOIS

Interstate 80

E ↕ W

117mm **rest area eb, full(handicapped)facilities, vending, phone, picnic tables, litter barrels, playground, petwalk**

112 IL 47, Morris, **N...gas:** BP/diesel/24hr, Citgo/diesel, **food:** Bellacino's, **lodging:** Best Western, Comfort Inn, Day's Inn, Holiday Inn, **S...gas:** BP, Clark, Mobil, Shell/24hr, **food:** Burger King, Culver's, KFC, Maria's Ristorante, McDonald's, Morris Diner, Pizza Hut, Subway, Taco Bell, Wendy's, **lodging:** Morris Motel, Park Motel, Super 8, **other:** MEDICAL CARE, Aldi Foods, Chevrolet/Buick/Cadillac, Eagle Foods, Fisher Parts, Ford, Radio Shack, Walgreen, Wal-Mart SuperCtr/24hr, to Stratton SP

105 to Seneca, no facilities

97 to Marseilles, **S...other:** Prairie Lakes Resort/rest., to Illini SP, RV camping

93 IL 71, Ottawa, **N...gas:** Mobil/24hr, Shell/diesel/24hr, **other:** Skydive Chicago RV Park(2mi), **S...food:** Hank's Farm Rest., **other:** HOSPITAL

92.5mm Fox River

90 IL 23, Ottawa, **N...gas:** BP/Subway, **food:** Cracker Barrel, Taco Bell, **lodging:** Hampton Inn, Holiday Inn Express, **other:** HOSPITAL, Buick/Pontiac/Cadillac, Ford/Lincoln/Mercury/Kia, Chrysler/Jeep, Honda, **S...gas:** BP/diesel/LP, **food:** Shell/24hr, China Inn, Country Kitchen, Dunkin Donuts, Hardee's, McDonald's, KFC, Ponderosa, **lodging:** Comfort Inn, Sands Motel, Super 8, Surrey Motel, Travelodge, **other:** Ace RV Ctr, Harley-Davidson, K-Mart, Kroger, USPO, Wal-Mart/drugs

81 IL 178, Utica, **N...**KOA(2mi), **S...gas:** BP, Shell/diesel, **food:** Duffy's Tavern(2mi), Jimmy Johns Sandwiches, **lodging:** Starved Rock Inn, **other:** Hickory Hollow Camping, to Starved Rock SP

79b a I-39, US 51, N to Rockford, S to Bloomington

77.5mm Little Vermilion River

77 IL 351, La Salle, **S...gas:** FS/24hr, Flying J/Country Mkt/diesel/24hr/@, **food:** UpTown Grill, **lodging:** Daniels Motel, **other:** st police

Peru

75 IL 251, Peru, **N...gas:** BP, Crazy D's/diesel, Shell/diesel/rest./24hr, **food:** Arby's, Champ's Grill, McDonald's, Taco Bell, **lodging:** Comfort Inn, Econolodge, Motel 6, Super 8, Tiki Inn/RV Park/rest., **other:** antiques, **S...gas:** BP, **food:** Applebee's, Bob Evans, Culver's, DQ, Dunkin Donuts, Mi Margarita, Red Lobster, Steak'n Shake, Subway, Wendy's, **lodging:** Fairfield Inn, Ramada Ltd, **other:** HOSPITAL, AutoZone, Buick/Pontiac/GMC, Chevrolet/Mercedes, Chrysler/Jeep, EconoFoods, Goodyear/auto, Home Depot, HyVee Foods, JC Penney, Jo-Ann Fabrics, K-Mart, Mitsubishi, Nissan, Sears, Staples, Target, Toyota, Walgreen, Wal-Mart/drugs, mall

73 Plank Rd, **N...gas:** Sapp Bros/Burger King/diesel/@, **other:** camping

70 IL 89, to Ladd, **N...gas:** Casey's, **S...lodging:** Motel Riviera, **3 mi S...food:** Hardee's, Pizza Hut, **other:** HOSPITAL

61 I-180, to Hennepin, no facilities

56 IL 26, Princeton, **N...gas:** Pilot/diesel/24hr/@, **lodging:** Super 8, **S...gas:** BP/24hr, Phillips 66, Shell, **food:** Burger King, Country Kitchen, KFC, McDonald's, Red Apple Rest., Taco Bell, Wendy's, **lodging:** BirdsNest Motel, Comfort Inn, Day's Inn, Motor Lodge/rest., **other:** HOSPITAL, AutoZone, Chevrolet/Pontiac/Buick/Cadillac, $General, Eagle Foods, Pennzoil, Sullivan's Food/gas, Wal-Mart SuperCtr/gas/24hr

51.5mm **rest area both lanes, full(handicapped)facilities, phone, picnic tables, litter barrels, vending, playground, petwalk, RV dump**

45 IL 40, **N...gas:** Marathon/diesel/rest., **lodging:** Day's Inn/rest., **other:** to Ronald Reagan Birthplace(21mi), **S...other:** Hennepin Canal SP, camping

44mm Hennepin Canal

33 IL 78, Annawan, **S...gas:** Citgo/diesel, Phillips 66/diesel, **food:** Olympic Flame Rest., **lodging:** Holiday Inn Express, **other:** to Johnson-Sauk Trail SP

27 to US 6, Atkinson, **N...gas:** BP/diesel/24hr, Casey's, Mobil/diesel/rest./24hr, **other:** Ford

19 IL 82, Geneseo, **N...gas:** Citgo, Phillips 66/diesel/24hr, **food:** DQ, Hardee's, McDonald's, Pizza Hut, Subway, **lodging:** Deck Motel/diner, Oakwood Motel, Royal Motel, Super 8, **other:** HOSPITAL, $General, Ford, Hutchcraft RV Ctr, Wal-Mart/drugs, **S...food:** KFC

10 I-74, W to Moline, E to Peoria, no facilities

9 US 6, to Geneseo, no facilities

7 Colona, **N...gas:** Conoco/diesel/rest.

E Moline

5mm Rock River

4a IL 5, IL 92, W to Silvis, **S...other:** to Quad City Downs, Lundeen's Camping

b I-88, IL 92, E to Rock Falls, no facilities

2mm weigh sta both lanes

1.5mm **Welcome Ctr eb, full(handicapped)facilities, info, phone, picnic tables, litter barrels, petwalk, scenic overlook**

1 IL 84, 20th St, E Moline, Great River Rd, **N...gas:** BP, **food:** Bridgeview Burgers, Brothers Rest., **other:** camping, **3 mi S... gas:** Citgo, **other:** camping

0mm Illinois/Iowa state line, Mississippi River

Interstate 88

E ↕ W

Chicago Area

Exit #	Services
139.5mm	I-88 begins/ends on I-290.
139	I-294, S to Indiana, N to Milwaukee
138mm	toll plaza
137	IL 83 N, Cermak Rd, **N...lodging:** Rennaisance, Marriott, **other:** Nieman-Marcus
136	IL 83 S, Midwest Rd(from eb), **N...gas:** Costco/gas, **other:** Cost+, Nordstrom's, Old Navy
134	Highland Ave(no EZ wb return), **N...food:** Bennigan's, Buca Italian, Taylor Brewing Co, TGIFriday, **lodging:** Embassy Suites, Homestead Studios, Red Roof Inn, **other:** HOSPITAL, Circuit City, CompUSA, Firestone, JC Penney, mall, **S...food:** Parkers Ocean Grill
132	I-355 N(from wb)
131	I-355 S(from eb)
130	IL 53(from wb), no facilities
127	Naperville Rd, **S...food:** Bob Evans, Buona Beef, Chevy's Mexican, McDonald's, TGIFriday, Wendy's, **lodging:** Best Western, Day's Inn, Holiday Inn, Homestead Suites, **other:** Ford, Kia, Office Depot
125	Winfield Rd, **N...**HOSPITAL, **S...food:** Max&Erma's, Red Robin, Rockbottom Brewery, **lodging:** AmeriSuites
123	IL 59, **N...S...gas:** Mobil/diesel, **food:** Cracker Barrel, Steak'n Shake, Subway, Wendy's, White Hen Pantry, **lodging:** Country Inn Suites, Extended Stay America, Hawthorn Suites, Red Roof Inn, Sleep Inn
119	Farnsworth Ave, **N...gas:** BP, **food:** Jacaranda's Mexican, Papa Bear Rest., **lodging:** Best Western, Motel 6, **other:** Ford/Mercury/Lincoln/Mitsubishi, **S...gas:** Clark, Marathon, Phillips 66, Shell, **food:** Goody's Drive-Thru, McDonald's, Subway, Taco Bell, White Hen Pantry, **other:** Goodyear
118mm	toll plaza
117	IL 31, IL 56, to Aurora, Batavia, **N...gas:** Citgo, Marathon, **food:** A&W, Raimondo's Pizza, Tastee Freez, White Hen Pantry, **S...gas:** Mobil, Thornton's, **food:** Culver's, Denny's, Mayberry's Rest., McDonald's, Popeye's, Togo's/Baskin-Robbins/Dunkin Donuts, **lodging:** Baymont Inn, Howard Johnson, **other:** HOSPITAL, AutoZone, Firestone, GNC, Jewel/Osco, Radio Shack, U-Haul
115	Orchard Rd, **N...other:** Chrysler/Plymouth/Dodge/Jeep, Ford/Lincoln/Mercury, Isuzu, Nissan, Pontiac, Saturn, Subaru, **S...gas:** Citgo/7-11, **food:** Chili's, IHOP, Wendy's, **lodging:** Hampton Inn, **other:** Home Depot
114	IL 56W, to US 30(from wb, no EZ return), to Sugar Grove
109	IL 47(from eb, no EZ return), to Black Berry Hist Farm

DeKalb

Exit #	Services
94	Peace Rd, to IL 38, **N...**HOSPITAL
93mm	Dekalb Oasis/24hr both lanes, **gas:** Mobil/diesel, **food:** McDonald's
93mm	toll plaza
92	IL 38, IL 23, Annie Glidden Rd, to DeKalb, **N...lodging:** Super 8, **2-3 mi N...gas:** BP, Clark, **food:** Burger King, Happy Wok Chinese, Jct Rest., La Magaritas Mexican, McDonald's, Pagliai's Pizza, Pizza Hut, Pizza Villa, Taco Bell, Wendy's, Yen Ching Chinese, **lodging:** Baymont Inn, Best Western, Stadium Inn, Travelodge, **other:** Ford, Illini Tire, to N IL U
91mm	toll plaza
78	I-39, US 51, S to Bloomington, N to Rockford
76	IL 251, Rochelle, **N...gas:** BP/Blimpie/diesel, Casey's, Marathon, Shell, **food:** Olive Branch Rest., **other:** HOSPITAL, Dodge, Ford/Lincoln/Mercury, GMC, Goodyear
55	IL 26, Dixon, **N...gas:** BP/diesel, **food:** Pizza Hut, **lodging:** Comfort Inn, Quality Inn, Super 8, **1-2 mi N...gas:** Clark Gas, **food:** Hardee's, Hometown Pantry, **lodging:** Best Western, **other:** HOSPITAL, to Ronald Reagan Birthplace, to John Deere HS, to St Parks
54mm	toll plaza
44	US 30(last free exit eb), **N...**gas, food, lodging, camping
41	IL 40, Rock Falls, to Sterling, **1-2 mi N...gas:** Clark, Marathon, Mobil/24hr, Shell/deli, **food:** Arby's, Arthur's Deli, Bennigan's, Burger King, Culver's, First Wok Chinese, Hardee's, KFC, McDonald's, Perna's Pizza, Red Apple Rest., Subway, **lodging:** All Seasons Motel, Country Inn Suites, Holiday Inn, Super 8, **other:** HOSPITAL, AutoZone, Eagle Foods, Goodyear/auto, Harley-Davidson, Sav-A-Lot, Walgreen, Wal-Mart
36	to US 30, Rock Falls, Sterling, no facilities
26	IL 78, to Prophetstown, Morrison, **N...other:** to Morrison-Rockwood SP, camping, **S...gas:** Conoco/diesel
18	Erie, to Albany, no facilities
10	Hillsdale, to Port Byron, **S...gas:** Citgo/diesel, Phillips 66/diesel, **food:** Mama J's Rest.
6	IL 92 E, to Joslin, **1 mi S...other:** Sunset Lake Camping
2	Former IL 2, no facilities
1b a	I-80, W to Des Moines, E to Chicago
0mm	I-88 begins/ends on I-80, exit 4b. IL 5, IL 92, W to Silvis, to Quad City Downs, Lundeen's Camping

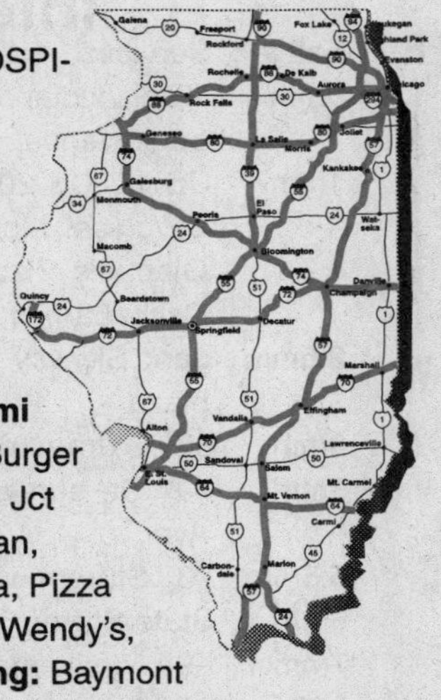

ILLINOIS

Interstate 90

E ↔ W

Chicago Area

Exit #	Services
0mm	Illinois/Indiana state line, Chicago Skyway Tool Rd begins/ends
1mm	US 12, US 20, 106th St, Indianapolis Blvd, **N...gas:** BP/diesel, Mobil, Shell/diesel, **S...food:** Burger King, Giappo's Pizza, KFC, McDonald's, **other:** Jewel-Osco, Larry's Repair
2.5mm	**gas:** Skyway Oasis, **food:** McDonald's, **other:** toll plaza
3mm	87th St(from wb), no facilities
5mm	79th St, services along 79th St and Stoney Island Ave
5.5mm	73rd St(from wb), no facilities
6mm	State St(from wb), no facilities
7mm	I-94 N(mile markers decrease to IN state line)

I-90 E and I-94 E run together, **see Illinois Interstate 94, exits 43b thru 59a.**

Exit #	Services
84	I-94 W...Lawrence Ave, **N...gas:** BP
83b a	Foster Ave(from wb), **N...gas:** BP, **food:** Checker's, Dunkin Donuts, **other:** Firestone/auto, Goodyear/auto, Walgreen
82c	Austin Ave, to Foster Ave, no facilities
b	Byrn-Mawr(from wb)
a	Nagle Ave, no facilities
81b	Sayre Ave(from wb)
a	IL 43, Harlem Ave, **S...gas:** BP, Shell
80	Canfield Rd(from wb), **N...other:** Walgreen
79b a	IL 171 S, Cumberland Ave, **N...gas:** Citgo/7-11, Mobil, **food:** Denny's, Hooters, McDonald's, Outback Steaks, Porter's Steaks, **lodging:** AmeriSuites, Holiday Inn, Marriott, **other:** Dominick's Foods, **S...food:** Bennigan's, Clarion, Rennaisance
0mm	River Road Plaza, **N...food:** McDonald's, **lodging:** Marriott, Westin Hotel, **S...**Hyatt(mile markers increase to Rockford)
1mm	I-294, I-190 W, to O'Hare Airport
2mm	IL 72, Lee St(from wb), **N...lodging:** Extended Stay America, Quality Inn, Radisson, **other:** Studio+, **S...food:** McDonald's, **lodging:** Best Western, Holiday Inn Select, Ramada Plaza, Sheraton Gateway, Travelodge
5mm	Des Plaines Oasis both lanes, **gas:** Mobil/diesel/24hr, **food:** McDonald's/24hr
6mm	Elmhurst Rd(from wb), **S...gas:** Marathon, McDonald's, **lodging:** Best Western, Comfort Inn, Day's Inn, Hampton Inn, La Quinta, Microtel
7.5mm	Arlington Hgts Rd, **N on Algonquin...gas:** BP, Shell, **food:** Denny's, Pappadeaux Rest., Yanni's Greek Rest., **lodging:** AmeriSuites, Courtyard, Motel 6, Radisson, Red Roof Inn, **other:** Sam's Club, **S...lodging:** Sheraton
11mm	I-290, IL 53, **N...lodging:** Holiday Inn, **other:** mall, **S...lodging:** AmeriSuites, Extended Stay America, Residence Inn
13mm	Roselle Rd(from wb), **N...**Medieval Times, **S...lodging:** Extended Stay America, **other:** BMW
16mm	Barrington Rd(from wb), **N...lodging:** Hilton Garden, **1 mi S...lodging:** AmeriSuites, Hampton Inn
19mm	IL 59, **N...lodging:** Marriott, **other:** to Poplar Creek Music Theatre
21mm	Beverly Rd(from wb), no facilities
22mm	IL 25, **N...food:** Milk Pail Rest., **lodging:** Day's Inn, **S...gas:** BP, Shell, Speedway/diesel, **food:** Arby's, Baker Hill Pancakes, Subway, **other:** HOSPITAL
24mm	IL 31 N, **N...gas:** BP, Thornton's/diesel, **food:** Alexander's Rest., Bennigan's, Cracker Barrel, **lodging:** Baymont Inn, Crowne Plaza, Courtyard, Hampton Inn, Super 8, TownePlace Suites, **S...lodging:** Best Western
25mm	toll plaza, phone
27mm	Randall Rd, **N...food:** Jimmy's Charhouse, **lodging:** Country Inn Suites, **S...**HOSPITAL
32mm	IL 47(from wb), to Woodstock, **N...other:** Prime Outlets/famous brands, Chevrolet
37mm	US 20, Marengo, **N...gas:** Clark/diesel/24hr/@, Shell/diesel/repair/24hr/@, TA/BP/Burger King/Popeye's/diesel/rest./24hr/@, **food:** McDonald's, Wendy's, **other:** KOA, museums, to Prime Outlets at exit 32(6mi)
41mm	Marengo-Hampshire toll plaza, phone
53mm	Genoa Rd, to Belvidere, **N...**camping
55mm	Belvidere Oasis both lanes, **gas:** Mobil/diesel/24hr, **food:** McDonald's/24hr, phone
56mm	toll plaza
60.5mm	Kishwaukee River

Rockford

Exit #	Services
61mm	I-39 S, US 20, US 51, to Rockford, **S...**funpark
63mm	US 20, State St, **N...gas:** Phillips 66/Subway/diesel, **food:** Cracker Barrel, **lodging:** Baymont Inn, Best Western, Exel Inn, **other:** Time Museum, **S...gas:** BP, Citgo/diesel, Mobil/Blimpie/diesel, **food:** Arby's, Applebee's, BeefARoo, Burger King, Carlos O'Kelly's, Checker's, Cheddar's, ChiChi's, Chili's, Country Kitchen, DQ, Denny's, Don Pablo, Giovanni's Rest., HomeTown Buffet, KFC, Lino's Pizza, LoneStar Steaks, Machine Shed Rest., McDonald's, Old Chicago Grill, Old Country Buffet, Olive Garden, Outback Steaks, Panino's Drive-Thru, Perkins, Red Lobster, Ruby Tuesday, Ryan's, Steak'n Shake, Taco Bell, ThunderBay Grill, Tumbleweed Grill, Wendy's, **lodging:** Candlewood Suites, Comfort Inn, Courtyard, Extended Stay America, Fairfield Inn, Hampton Inn, Holiday Inn Express, Quality Suites, Ramada Inn/rest., Red Roof Inn, Residence Inn, Sleep Inn, Studio+, Super 8, **other:** HOSPITAL, Advance Parts, Aldi Foods, Barnes&Noble, Best Buy, Borders Books, Buick/Pontiac/GMC, Circuit City, CompUSA, Discount Tire, Dodge, $Tree, Home Depot, Iogli Foods, Jo-Ann Fabrics, K-Mart, Kohl's, Lowe's Whse, Marshalls, Michael's, Office Depot, OfficeMax, Old Navy, PepBoys, Sam's Club, Saturn, ShopKO, Target/drugs, Toyota/Lexus, Wal-Mart
66mm	E Riverside Blvd, Loves Park, **1-2 mi S...gas:** BP/24hr, Citgo/diesel/24hr, Mobil/diesel, Phillips 66/diesel, **food:** A&W, Arby's, Basil Café, BeefARoo, Culver's, DQ, India

Interstate 90

House, KFC, Little Caesar's, McDonald's, Sam's Ristorante, Subway, Wendy's, **lodging:** Day's Inn, **other:** Audi/Honda/Jaguar/Mercedes/Porsche/Subaru, Eagle Foods, to Rock Cut SP

75.5mm tollbooth, phone(mile markers decrease from W to E to Chicago)

3 Rockton Rd, no facilities

1.5mm Welcome Ctr/rest area eb, full(handicapped)facilities, info, picnic tables, litter barrels, phone, petwalk, playground, RV dump

1 US 51 N, IL 75 W, S Beloit, **S...gas:** Citgo/Subway/diesel/24hr, Flying J/Country Mkt/diesel/24hr/@, Shell/diesel, **lodging:** Knight's Inn, Ramada Inn, **other:** Ford/Lincoln/Mercury, GMC

0mm Illinois/Wisconsin state line

Interstate 94

Exit # Services

77mm Illinois/Indiana state line

I-94 and I-80 run together 3 mi. See Illinois Interstate 80, exit 161.

74[160]b I-80/I-294 W

a IL 394 S to Danville, no facilities

73 b a US 6,159th St, **N...food:** Fuddrucker's, Outback Steaks, **other:** Chevrolet, Honda, Lincoln/Mercury, Nissan/Hyundai, Target, Tire Barn, Toyota, **S...gas:** Marathon, **food:** Fannie May Candies, Subway, **lodging:** Cherry Lane Motel, **other:** Aldi Foods, Buick/Pontiac, Ford, Stanfa Tire/auto

71b a Sibley Blvd, **N...gas:** Citgo, Mobil/diesel, **food:** McDonald's, Nicky's Gyros, Popeye's, Subway, **lodging:** Baymont Inn, **other:** Dominick's Foods, **S...gas:** BP, Shell, **food:** Dusty's Buffet, Wendy's, White Castle

70b a Dolton, no facilities

69 Beaubien Woods(from eb), Forest Preserve

68b a 130th St, no facilities

66b 115th St, **S...food:** McDonald's

a 111th Ave, **S...gas:** BP, Shell, **other:** Firestone

65 103rd Ave, Stony Island Ave, no facilities

63 I-57 S, no facilities

62 US 12, US 20, 95th St, **N...gas:** Citgo, Shell, **food:** Subway, Taco Bell, **S...gas:** Amoco

61b 87th St, **N...gas:** BP, Shell, **food:** Burger King, McDonald's, **S...other:** Cub Foods, Home Depot, Marshall's

a 83rd St(from eb), **N...gas:** Shell, **other:** st police

60c 79th St, **N...gas:** Mobil, Shell, **S...gas:** Citgo/diesel, **food:** Church's

b 76th St, **N...gas:** BP, Mobil, Shell, **other:** Walgreen/24hr, **S...food:** KFC, Popeye's

a 75th St(from eb), **N...gas:** BP, Mobil, Shell, **S...food:** KFC, Popeye's

59c 71st St, **N...gas:** BP, **S...food:** McDonald's

a I-90 E, to Indiana Toll Rd

58b 63rd St(from eb), **N...gas:** Shell, **S...gas:** BP

a I-94 divides into local and express, 59th St, **S...gas:** BP

57b Garfield Blvd, **N...food:** Checker's, Chinese Kitchen, Popeye's, **other:** Trak Auto, Walgreen, laundry, **S...gas:** Mobil, Shell/24hr, **food:** Famous Burritos, Wendy's, **other:** HOSPITAL

a 51st St, **N...food:** McDonald's

56b 47th St(from eb)

a 43rd St, **S...gas:** Citgo/diesel, Econo

55b Pershing Rd, no facilities

a 35th St, **S...**to New Comiskey Park

54 31st St, **S...**HOSPITAL

53c I-55, Stevenson Pkwy, N to downtown, Lakeshore Dr

b I-55, Stevenson Pkwy, S to St Louis

52c 18th St, **N...gas:** Shell

b Roosevelt Rd, Taylor St(from wb), **N...gas:** Shell

a Taylor St, Roosevelt Rd(from eb), **N...gas:** Shell, **other:** Toyota, **S...gas:** Citgo

51h-i I-290 W, to W Suburbs

g E Jackson Blvd, to downtown

f W Adams St, to downtown

e Monroe St(from eb), downtown, **S...lodging:** Quality Inn, **other:** Walgreen

d Madison St(from eb), downtown, **S... lodging:** Quality Inn, **other:** Walgreen

c E Washington Blvd, downtown

b W Randolph St, downtown

a Lake St(from wb)

50b E Ohio St, downtown, **S...gas:** Marathon

a Ogden Ave, no facilities

49b a Augusta Blvd, Division St, **N...other:** Lexus, **S...gas:** BP, Shell, **food:** Pizza Hut

48b IL 64, North Ave, **N...gas:** BP, **other:** Home Depot, **S...gas:** BP, Shell, **other:** Volvo

a Armitage Ave, **S...gas:** Amoco, **other:** Jaguar, Volvo

47c b Damen Ave, **N...gas:** Citgo, car/vanwash

a Western Ave, Fullerton Ave, **N...gas:** Citgo, **food:** Burger King, Popeye's, **other:** Costco/gas, Home Depot, Target, **S...gas:** Marathon, **food:** KFC

46b a Diversey Ave, California Ave, **S...gas:** Mobil, **food:** IHOP/24hr, Popeye's

45c Belmont Ave, **N...food:** Wendy's

b Kimball Ave, **N...gas:** Marathon/diesel, **S...gas:** Marathon, **food:** Pizza Hut, Subway, Wendy's, **other:** Delray Farms Foods, Dominick's Foods, Radio Shack, Walgreen/24hr

a Addison St(from eb), no facilities

44b Pulaski Ave, Irving Park Rd, **N...gas:** BP, Mobil

ILLINOIS

Interstate 94

E ↕ W

a	IL 19, Keeler Ave, Irving Park Rd, **N...gas:** BP, Shell/24hr, **other:** to Wrigley Field
43c	Montrose Ave, no facilities
b	I-90 W
a	Wilson Ave, no facilities
42	W Foster Ave, **S...gas:** Citgo, Marathon
41mm	Chicago River, N Branch
41c	IL 50 S, to Cicero, to I-90 W
b a	US 14, Peterson Ave, no facilities
39b a	Touhy Ave, **N...gas:** BP/diesel, Shell, **lodging:** Radisson, **other:** Cassidy Tire, **S...gas:** BP, Citgo, Mobil/diesel, Shell, **food:** Burger King, Dunkin Donuts, Jack's Rest./24hr, **other:** Lee's Auto Parts, PepBoys
37b a	IL 58, Dempster St, no facilities
35	Old Orchard Rd, **N...gas:** BP, Shell, **food:** Bloomingdale's, Marshall Fields, **other:** HOSPITAL, Nissan, mall, **S...lodging:** Extended Stay America, Hampton Inn
34c b	E Lake Ave, **N...gas:** BP, **food:** Panda Express, Starbucks, **other:** Borders Books, GNC, Omaha Steaks, **S...gas:** BP, Shell, **food:** DQ
a	US 41 S, Skokie Rd(from eb)
33b a	Willow Rd, **S...gas:** BP, Shell, **food:** Starbucks, **other:** Dominick's Foods, Walgreen
31	E Tower Rd, **S...other:** BMW, Hummer, Jeep, Mercedes, Toyota,
30b a	Dundee Rd(from wb, no EZ return), **S...gas:** Citgo, Marathon, **food:** Bennigan's, Olive Garden, Japanese Steaks, **lodging:** Rennaisance
29	US 41, to Waukegan, to Tri-state tollway
50mm	IL 43, Waukegan Rd, **N...lodging:** Red Roof Inn, Embassy Suites, **other:** Home Depot
53mm	I-294 S
53.5mm	Deerfield Rd toll plaza, phones
54mm	Deerfield Rd, **W...lodging:** Marriott Suites
56mm	IL 22, Half Day Rd, **E...lodging:** Woodfield Suites
59mm	IL 60, Town Line Rd, **E...**HOSPITAL
60mm	Lake Forest Oasis both lanes, **gas:** Mobil/diesel, **food:** Wendy's/24hr, **other:** info
62mm	IL 176, Rockland Rd(no nb re-entry), **E...other:** Harley-Davidson, to Lamb's Farm
64mm	IL 137, Buckley Rd(from wb), **E...other:** to VA HOSPITAL, Chicago Med School
67mm	IL 120 E, Belvidere Rd(no nb re-entry), **E...**HOSPITAL
68mm	IL 21, Milwaukee Ave(from eb), **E...other:** HOSPITAL, Six Flags
70mm	IL 132, Grand Ave, **E...gas:** Speedway/diesel, **food:** Burger King, Cracker Barrel, Culver's, IHOP, Joe's Crabshack, Little Caesar's, McDonald's, Ming's Chinese, Olive Garden, Outback Steaks, Subway, TCBY, **lodging:** Baymont Inn, Comfort Suites, Country Inn Suites, Grand Hotel, Extended Stay America, Hampton Inn, **other:** Six Flags Park, **W...gas:** Mobil, Shell, **food:** Applebee's, Bakers Square, Boston Mkt, Chili's, Denny's, LoneStar Steaks, Max&Erma's, McDonald's, Pizza Hut, Pizzaria Uno, Red Lobster, Schlotsky's, Sizzler, Starbucks, Steak'n Shake, Taco Bell, TGIFriday, Wendy's, White Castle, **lodging:** Comfort Inn, Fairfield Inn, Holiday Inn, **other:** Circuit City, Dominick's Foods, Gurnee Mills Outlet Mall/famous brands, Home Depot, Honda, Hyundai, JC Penney, Jewel-Osco, Kohl's, Lincoln/Mercury, Michaels, OfficeMax, Sam's Club, Sears/auto, Target/drugs, VW, Wal-Mart/drugs
73.5mm	Waukegan toll plaza, phones
76mm	IL 173(from nb, no return), Rosecrans Ave, **E...**to IL Beach SP
1b	US 41 S, to Waukegan, **E...other:** Sky Harbor RV Ctr
a	Russell Rd, **W...gas:** Citgo/diesel/24hr, TA/Mobil/Pizza Hut/diesel/24hr/@, **other:** Peterbilt
0mm	Illinois/Wisconsin state line

Chicago Area

Interstate 255(St Louis)

N ↕ S

E St Louis

Exit #	Services
	I-255 begins/ends on I-270, exit 7.
30	I-270, W to Kansas City, E to Indianapolis
29	IL 162, to Glen Carbon, Granite City, to Pontoon Beach
26	Horseshoe Lake Rd, **E...**st police
25b a	I-55/I-70, W to St Louis, E to Chicago, Indianapolis
24	Collinsville Rd, **E...gas:** BP/24hr, **food:** Jack-in-the-Box, **other:** Shop'n Save, **W...**Fairmount Racetrack
20	I-64, US 50, W to St Louis, E to Louisville, facilities 1 mi E off I-64, exit 9.
19	State St, E St Louis, **E...gas:** Clark, **lodging:** Western Inn, **other:** Holten SP
17b a	IL 15, E St Louis, Centreville, to Belleville, no facilities
15	Mousette Lane, **E...**HOSPITAL, **W...other:** GMC/Volvo Trucks
13	IL 157, to Cahokia, **E...gas:** Casey's, **W...gas:** BP/24hr, QT, **food:** Burger King, Capt D's, China Express, DQ, Domino's, Hardee's, KFC, McDonald's, Pizza Hut, Ponderosa, Popeye's, Rally's, Taco Bell, **lodging:** Holiday Inn Express, **other:** Advance Parts, Aldi Foods, AutoZone, CarQuest, $General, GMC/Pontiac, Goodyear/auto, Schnuck's, Walgreen, Wal-Mart/drugs, Cahokia RV Parque(2mi)
10	IL 3 N, to Cahokia, E St Louis, **W...gas:** Shell
9	to Dupo, no facilities
6	IL 3 S, to Columbia, **E...gas:** Citgo, Shell/24hr, **other:** Chevrolet
4mm	**Missouri/Illinois state line, Mississippi River**
3	Koch Rd, no facilities
2	MO 231, Telegraph Rd, **N...gas:** Shell, **food:** Hardee's, McDonald's, Pizza Hut/Taco Bell, Steak'n Shake, **other:** Dierberg's Foods, $Tree, Wal-Mart SuperCtr/24hr, Jefferson Barracks Nat Cem, **S...gas:** CFM/diesel, **food:** DQ

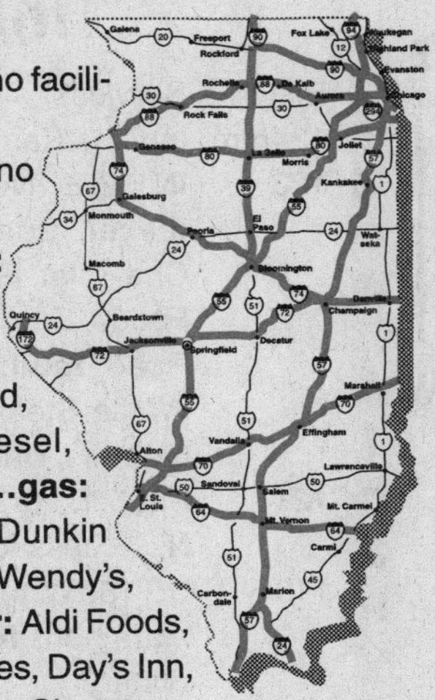

Interstate 255

1d c US 50, US 61, US 67, Lindbergh Blvd, Lemay Ferry Rd, accesses same as I-55 exit 197, **N...food:** Arby's, Hooters, McDonald's, Old Country Buffet, Subway, **other:** Advance Parts, Costco/gas, Dillard's, Discount Tire, Ford, Sears/auto, mall, **S...gas:** Citgo, **food:** Jack-in-the-Box, Papa John's, White Castle, **other:** Firestone, Sam's Club

1b a I-55 S to Memphis, N to St Louis. I-255 begins/ends on I-55, exit 196.

Interstate 294(Chicago)

Exit # Services

I-294 begins/ends on I-94, exit 74. Numbering descends from west to east.

I-294 & I-80 run together 5 mi. See Illinois Interstate 80, exits 155-160.

5mm I-80 W, access to I-57

5.5mm 167th St, toll booth, phones

6mm US 6, 159th St, **E...gas:** BP, Citgo, Mobil, Shell, **other:** Aldi Foods, AutoZone, Walgreen, **W...gas:** Clark, Marathon, **food:** Burger King, Dunkin Donuts/Baskin-Robbins, Hung's Garden Chinese, KFC/Pizza Hut, Popeye's, Taco Bell, USA Rest., White Castle, **lodging:** Holiday Inn Express, **other:** Firestone/auto, Radio Shack, U-Haul, Walgreen

11mm Cal Sag Channel

12mm IL 50, Cicero Ave, **E...gas:** Citgo/7-11, Speedway, **food:** Onion Field Rest., **W...gas:** BP, Gas City/Subway/diesel/24hr, **food:** Boston Mkt, IHOP, Pizza Hut, Pizzaria Uno, Popeye's, Portillo's Dogs, Quizno's, Starbucks, **lodging:** Baymont Inn, Hampton Inn, **other:** Best Buy, Dominick's Foods, NTB, OfficeMax, Pep-Boys, Sears/auto

18mm US 12/20, 95th St, **E...gas:** Clark, **food:** Bennigan's, McDonald's, Papa John's, **other:** HOSPITAL, Buick, Honda, Mazda, Sears/auto, mall, **W...gas:** Citgo/7-11, Shell, Speedway/diesel, **food:** Arby's, Burger King, Denny's, George's Rest., Quizno's, Schoop's Burgers, Wendy's, **lodging:** Exel Inn, **other:** HOSPITAL, Jewel-Osco, Walgreen

20mm toll booth, phones

22mm 75th St, Willow Springs Rd, no facilities

23mm I-55, Wolf Rd, to Hawthorne Park, no facilities

25mm Hinsdale Oasis both lanes, **gas:** Mobil/diesel, **food:** Baskin-Robbins, Wendy's/24hr

28mm US 34, Ogden Ave, **E...**zoo, **W...gas:** BP, Shell/deli, **food:** Dunkin Donuts, McDonald's, Starbucks, **other:** HOSPITAL, Audi/Porsche, Firestone/auto, LandRover, Maserati, Rolls-Royce/Bentley/Ferrari/Lotus, Wild Oats Mkt

28.5mm Cermak Rd(from sb, no return)

29mm I-88 tollway, no facilities

30mm toll booth, phones

31mm IL 38, Roosevelt Rd(no EZ nb return), **E...gas:** Citgo/diesel, **lodging:** Hillside Manor Motel

32mm I-290 W, to Rockford(from nb), no facilities

34mm I-290(from sb), to Rockford, no facilities

38mm O'Hare Oasis both lanes, **gas:** Mobil/diesel, **food:** Burger King, TCBY

39mm IL 19 W(from sb), Irving Park Rd, **E...gas:** Clark, Marathon/diesel, **other:** 7-11, Walgreen, **1 mi E...gas:** BP/repair, Clark, **food:** DQ, Dunkin Donuts, McDonald's, Subway, Wendy's, **lodging:** Comfort Suites, **other:** Aldi Foods, **W...lodging:** Candlewood Suites, Day's Inn, Hampton Inn, Howard Johnson, Sheraton

40mm I-190 W, **E...services from I-90, exit 79...gas:** Mobil, **food:** McDonald's, **lodging:** Courtyard, Doubletree, Embassy Suites, Holiday Inn, Hotel Softel, Hyatt, Marriott, Radisson, Rosemont Suites, Westin

41mm toll booth, phones

42mm Touhy Ave, **W...gas:** Mobil/service, **food:** Tiffany's Rest., **lodging:** Comfort Inn

43mm Des Plaines River

44mm Dempster St(from nb, no return), **E...**HOSPITAL, **W...food:** Dunkin Donuts, Subway

46mm IL 58, Golf Rd, **E...gas:** Citgo/diesel, Shell, **food:** Omega Rest., Senoya Oriental, **other:** Best Buy, CVS Drug, Golf Mill Mall, Target, auto repair

49mm Willow Rd, **W...food:** TGIFriday, **lodging:** Baymont Inn, Doubletree Suites, Courtyard, Fairfield Inn, Motel 6, **1 mi W on Milwaukee...gas:** BP, **food:** Burger King, Denny's, McDonald's, **lodging:** Wingate Inn

53mm Lake Cook Rd(no nb re-entry), **E...**Hyatt, **lodging:** Embassy Suites

I-294 begins/ends on I-94.

Interstate 474(Peoria)

Exit # Services

15 I-74, E to Bloomington, W to Peoria. I-474 begins/ends on I-74, exit 99.

9 IL 29, E Peoria, to Pekin, **N...gas:** Clark, Shell/Arby's, Thornton's, **food:** Creve Coeur Rest., Dan's Pizza, Pizza Hut, Taco John's, **lodging:** Ragon Motel, **other:** Riverboat Casino, **S...gas:** Casey's, Citgo/Subway/diesel, **food:** Denny's, McDonald's, **other:** Buick/Pontiac, Chrysler/Jeep/Dodge, Toyota

8mm Illinois River

6b a US 24, Adams St, Bartonville, **S...gas:** Clark/diesel, Shell/24hr, **food:** Hardee's, KFC, McDonald's, Tyroni's Café

5 Airport Rd, **S...gas:** Phillips 66

3a to IL 116, Farmington, **S...**Wildlife Prairie Park

0b a I-74, W to Moline, E to Peoria. I-474 begins/ends on I-74, exit 87.

INDIANA

Interstate 64

E ↕ W — New Albany

Exit #	Services
124mm	Indiana/Kentucky state line, Ohio River
123	IN 62 E, New Albany, **N...gas:** BP/24hr, Bigfoot/diesel, Speedway, Sunoco, **food:** DQ, **other:** Chevrolet, Firestone/auto, Goodyear/auto, Valu Mkt Foods, **S...gas:** BP, Marathon/diesel/24hr, Tobacco Road, **food:** Minny's Café, Subway/Noble Roman, Waffle Steak, **lodging:** Hampton Inn, Holiday Inn Express, **other:** HOSPITAL
121	I-265 E, to I-65(exits left from eb), no facilities, **N...**access to HOSPITAL
119	US 150 W, to Greenville, **1/2 mi N...gas:** Citgo/diesel, Marathon, **food:** DQ, Sam's Family Rest., Huber Winery
118	IN 62, IN 64W, to Georgetown, **N...gas:** Marathon/diesel/24hr, Shell, **food:** Korner Kitchen, McDonald's, Pizza King, **lodging:** Motel 6, **other:** Thriftway Foods, **S...gas:** Marathon/diesel
115mm	**Welcome Ctr wb, full(handicapped)facilities, vending, phone, picnic tables, litter barrels**
113	to Lanesville, no facilities
105	IN 135, to Corydon, **N...gas:** Citgo/diesel, Shell/24hr, **food:** Big Boy, **lodging:** Quality Inn, **S...gas:** BP, Chevron, **food:** Arby's, Burger King, China Best Buffet, Cracker Barrel, Hardee's, KFC, Lee's Chicken, McDonald's, O'Charley's, Papa John's, Pizza Hut, Ryan's, Subway, Taco Bell, Waffle Steak/24hr, Wendy's, White Castle, **lodging:** Baymont Inn, Hampton Inn, Holiday Inn Express, **other:** MEDICAL CARE, AutoZone, Chevrolet/Pontiac/Buick, $General, $Tree, Ford/Mercury, Radio Shack, Wal-Mart SuperCtr/24hr, RV camping
100mm	Blue River
97mm	parking area both lanes, no facilities
92	IN 66, Carefree, **S...gas:** BP/Kathy's Kitchen/diesel, Citgo/diesel/rest./24hr, Shell/Noble Roman's/diesel/24hr/@, Sunoco/diesel, **food:** Country Style Rest., **lodging:** Day's Inn/rest./diesel, **other:** to Wyandotte Caves, Harrison Crawford SF
88mm	Hoosier Nat Forest eastern boundary
86	IN 37, to Sulphur, **N...**to Patoka Lake, **S...**gas, food, phone, scenic route
81.5mm	**parking area wb, no facilities**
80mm	**parking area eb, no facilities**
79	IN 37, St Croix, **S...**to Hoosier NF, camping, phone, to OH River Toll Br
76mm	Anderson River
72	IN 145, to Birdseye, **N...**to Patoka Lake, **S...**gas, phone, St Meinrad Coll
63	IN 162, to Ferdinand, **N...gas:** Marathon/diesel, **food:** Wendy's, **lodging:** Comfort Inn, **other:** Ferdinand SF, **S...**Holiday World Camping
58mm	**rest areas both lanes, full(handicapped)facilities, info, vending, picnic tables, litter barrels, phone**
57	US 231, to Dale, **N...gas:** 231 Trkstp/diesel/rest./24hr/@, **S...gas:** Marathon/Denny's/24hr, Shell/diesel/24hr, **lodging:** Baymont Inn, Budget Host(2mi), Motel 6, **other:** Lincoln Boyhood Home, Lincoln SP
54	IN 161, to Holland, no facilities
39	IN 61, Lynnville, **N...gas:** Shell/diesel, **lodging:** Old Fox Inn/rest., **other:** Goodyear, **S...**museum(10mi)
32mm	Wabash & Erie Canal
29b a	I-164 S, IN 57 S, to Evansville, **N...gas:** Sunoco/Subway/TCBY/diesel
25b a	US 41, to Evansville, **N...gas:** Flying J/CountryMkt/diesel/24hr/@, Pilot/Wendy's/diesel/24hr/@, Pilot/diesel/24hr/@, **lodging:** Quality Inn, **other:** Blue Beacon, **S...gas:** BP/motel, Busler/diesel/24hr/@, **food:** Arby's, Burger King, Denny's, McDonald's, **lodging:** Best Inn, Comfort Inn, Gateway Inn, Holiday Inn Express, Super 8, **other:** st police, to U S IN
18	IN 65, to Cynthiana, **S...gas:** Motomart/diesel/24hr
12	IN 165, Poseyville, **S...gas:** Citgo/diesel, **other:** Chevrolet, New Harmonie Hist Area/SP
7mm	**Black River Welcome Ctr eb, full(handicapped)facilities, phone, picnic tables, litter barrels, petwalk**
5mm	Black River
4	IN 69 S, New Harmony, Griffin, **1 mi N...**gas/diesel, food, motel, antiques
2mm	Big Bayou River
0mm	Indiana/Illinois state line, Wabash River

Interstate 65

N ↕ S — Merrillville

Exit #	Services
262	I-90, W to Chicago, E to Ohio, I-65 begins/ends on US 12, US 20.
261	15th Ave, to Gary, **E...**Mack Trucks, **W...gas:** Marathon
259b a	I-94/80, US 6W, no facilities
258	US 6, Ridge Rd, **E...gas:** ExpressAmerica Gas, Speedway/diesel, **food:** Diner's Choice Rest., **W...gas:** Citgo, Marathon, Phillips 66
255	61st Ave, Merrillville, **E...gas:** Marathon, Speedway/diesel/24hr, Thornton, **food:** Arby's, Cracker Barrel, McDonald's, Pizza Hut/Taco Bell, Wendy's, **other:** Chevrolet, Chrysler/Jeep, Comfort Inn, $Inn, Lee's Inn, I-65 Repair, **1 mi W...gas:** Shell, **food:** Burger King, LJ Silver, Subway, **other:** HOSPITAL
253b	US 30 W, Merrillville, **W...gas:** Gas City/diesel/24hr, Meijer/diesel/24hr, Shell, Speedway/diesel, **food:** Applebee's, Arby's, Blimpie, Buffalo Wings, Denny's, Dunkin Donuts, Fannie May Candies, Hooters, House of Kobe, KFC, LoneStar Steaks, New Moon Chinese, Pizza Hut, Rio Bravo, Roma Pizza, Schlotsky's, Smokey Bones BBQ, Steak'n Shake, Subway, Texas Corral Steaks, Wendy's, White Castle, **lodging:** Courtyard, $Inn, Fairfield Inn, Hampton Inn, Holiday Inn Express, Radisson, Red Roof Inn, Residence Inn, **other:** Aldi Foods, CarQuest, Celebration Sta, Fire-

Interstate 65

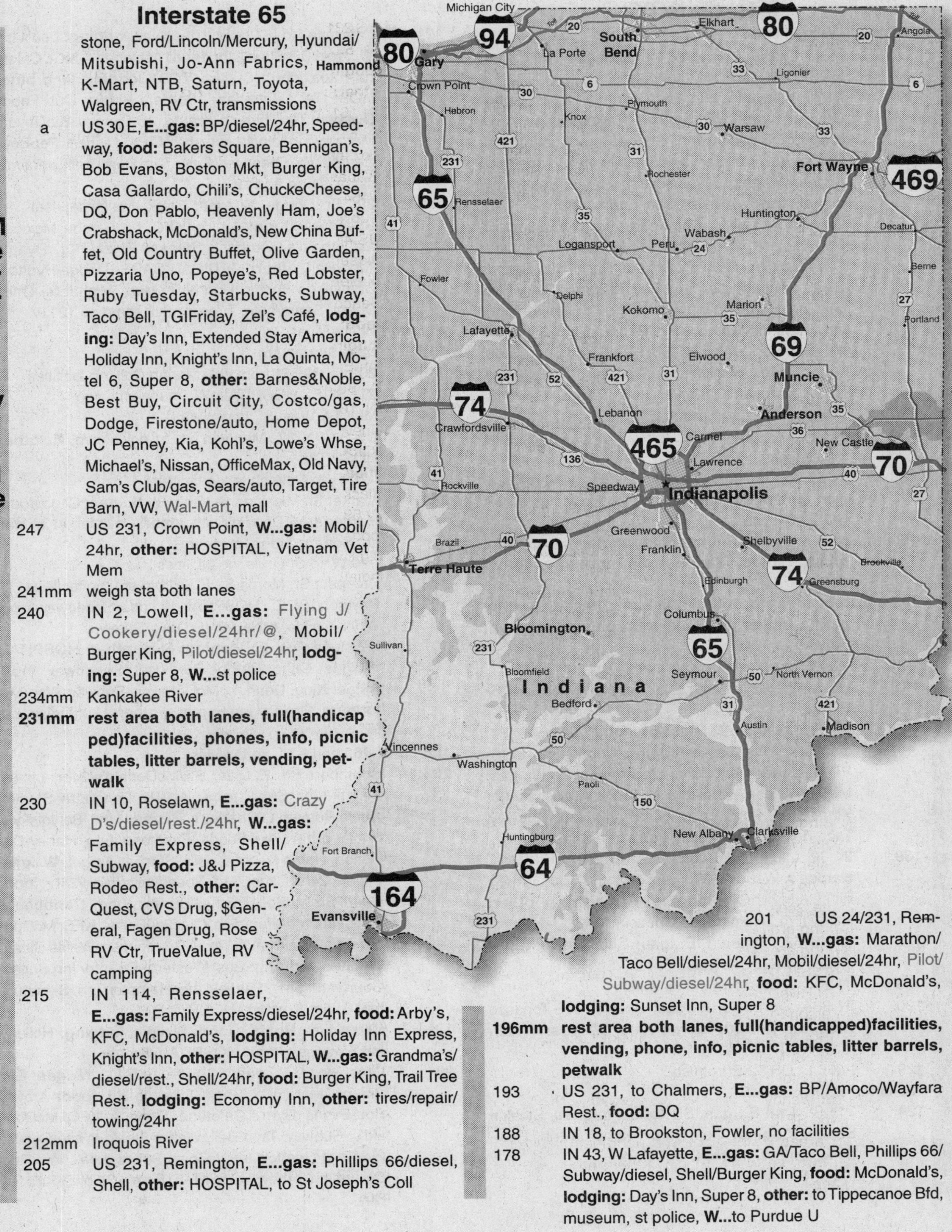

stone, Ford/Lincoln/Mercury, Hyundai/ Mitsubishi, Jo-Ann Fabrics, K-Mart, NTB, Saturn, Toyota, Walgreen, RV Ctr, transmissions

a US 30 E, **E...gas:** BP/diesel/24hr, Speedway, **food:** Bakers Square, Bennigan's, Bob Evans, Boston Mkt, Burger King, Casa Gallardo, Chili's, ChuckeCheese, DQ, Don Pablo, Heavenly Ham, Joe's Crabshack, McDonald's, New China Buffet, Old Country Buffet, Olive Garden, Pizzaria Uno, Popeye's, Red Lobster, Ruby Tuesday, Starbucks, Subway, Taco Bell, TGIFriday, Zel's Café, **lodging:** Day's Inn, Extended Stay America, Holiday Inn, Knight's Inn, La Quinta, Motel 6, Super 8, **other:** Barnes&Noble, Best Buy, Circuit City, Costco/gas, Dodge, Firestone/auto, Home Depot, JC Penney, Kia, Kohl's, Lowe's Whse, Michael's, Nissan, OfficeMax, Old Navy, Sam's Club/gas, Sears/auto, Target, Tire Barn, VW, Wal-Mart, mall

247 US 231, Crown Point, **W...gas:** Mobil/ 24hr, **other:** HOSPITAL, Vietnam Vet Mem

241mm weigh sta both lanes

240 IN 2, Lowell, **E...gas:** Flying J/ Cookery/diesel/24hr/@, Mobil/ Burger King, Pilot/diesel/24hr, **lodging:** Super 8, **W...**st police

234mm Kankakee River

231mm rest area both lanes, full(handicapped)facilities, phones, info, picnic tables, litter barrels, vending, petwalk

230 IN 10, Roselawn, **E...gas:** Crazy D's/diesel/rest./24hr, **W...gas:** Family Express, Shell/ Subway, **food:** J&J Pizza, Rodeo Rest., **other:** CarQuest, CVS Drug, $General, Fagen Drug, Rose RV Ctr, TrueValue, RV camping

215 IN 114, Rensselaer, **E...gas:** Family Express/diesel/24hr, **food:** Arby's, KFC, McDonald's, **lodging:** Holiday Inn Express, Knight's Inn, **other:** HOSPITAL, **W...gas:** Grandma's/ diesel/rest., Shell/24hr, **food:** Burger King, Trail Tree Rest., **lodging:** Economy Inn, **other:** tires/repair/ towing/24hr

212mm Iroquois River

205 US 231, Remington, **E...gas:** Phillips 66/diesel, Shell, **other:** HOSPITAL, to St Joseph's Coll

201 US 24/231, Remington, **W...gas:** Marathon/ Taco Bell/diesel/24hr, Mobil/diesel/24hr, Pilot/ Subway/diesel/24hr, **food:** KFC, McDonald's, **lodging:** Sunset Inn, Super 8

196mm rest area both lanes, full(handicapped)facilities, vending, phone, info, picnic tables, litter barrels, petwalk

193 US 231, to Chalmers, **E...gas:** BP/Amoco/Wayfara Rest., **food:** DQ

188 IN 18, to Brookston, Fowler, no facilities

178 IN 43, W Lafayette, **E...gas:** GA/Taco Bell, Phillips 66/ Subway/diesel, Shell/Burger King, **food:** McDonald's, **lodging:** Day's Inn, Super 8, **other:** to Tippecanoe Bfd, museum, st police, **W...**to Purdue U

INDIANA

Interstate 65

N ↕ S

176mm Wabash River

175 IN 25, Lafayette, **E...gas:** Marathon/24hr, **W...other:** HOSPITAL, **gas:** Marathon(1mi)

172 IN 26, Lafayette, **E...gas:** Meijer/diesel/24hr, **food:** Cracker Barrel, DQ, Steak'n Shake, White Castle, **lodging:** Baymont Inn, Budget Inn, Comfort Inn, Holiday Inn Express, Lee's Inn, Microtel, TownePlace Suites, **W...gas:** BP/diesel/24hr, Shell, Speedway/diesel, **food:** Arby's, Bob Evans, Burger King, Chick-fil-A, Chili's, China Garden, DQ, Damon's, Don Pablo, KFC, Logan's Roadhouse, McDonald's, Olive Garden, Outback Steaks, Pizza Hut, Porky's Rest., Spageddie's, Taco Bell, **lodging:** $Inn, Fairfield Inn, Hampton Inn, Homewood Suites, Knight's Inn, Radisson, Ramada Inn, Red Roof Inn, Signature Inn, Super 8, **other:** HOSPITAL, CVS Drug, $Tree, Marsh Foods, Buick/Nissan/Cadillac, Lowe's Whse, NAPA AutoCare, Sam's Club, Target, Wal-Mart SuperCtr/24hr, to Purdue U

168 IN 38, IN 25, Dayton, **E...gas:** BP/Piccadilly's/24hr, Mobil/diesel

158 IN 28, to Frankfort, **E...gas:** BP/diesel/24hr, Marathon, **2 mi W...lodging:** Lincoln Lodge Motel, **other:** HOSPITAL, camping

150mm rest area sb, full(handicapped)facilities, info, picnic tables, litter barrels, phone, vending, petwalk

148mm rest area nb, full(handicapped)facilities, info, picnic tables, litter barrels, phone, vending, petwalk

146 IN 47, Thorntown, no facilities

141 US 52 W(exits left from sb), Lafayette Ave, **E...**HOSPITAL

Lebanon

140 IN 32, Lebanon, **E...gas:** BP, **food:** Denny's, McDonald's, White Castle, **lodging:** Comfort Inn, HOSPITAL, **other:** AutoZone, Goodyear/auto, **W...gas:** McClure/diesel, Shell/diesel, **food:** Arby's, Burger King, KFC, Ponderosa, Steak'n Shake, Subway, Taco Bell, **lodging:** $Inn, Lee's Inn, Super 8

139 IN 39, Lebanon, **E...gas:** GA, **food:** Arni's Rest., Hardee's, Wendy's, **W...gas:** Flying J/Country Mkt/diesel/LP/24hr/@, **lodging:** Ramada Inn, **other:** HOSPITAL, Homemade Chocolates

138 to US 52, Lebanon, **E...gas:** Citgo/diesel, Shell/diesel, **other:** Chevrolet, Ford

133 IN 267, Whitestown, no facilities

130 IN 334, Zionsville, **E...gas:** Shell/diesel, Tobacco Rd/Subway, **food:** Burger King, **W...gas:** TA/BP/diesel/rest./24hr/@

129 I-865 E, US 52 E(from sb)

126mm Fishback Creek

124 71st St, **1 mi E...gas:** BP, **food:** Hardee's, Steak'n Shake, **lodging:** Courtyard, Hampton Inn, Residence Inn, **W...**Eagle Creek Park

123 I-465, S to airport

121 Lafayette Rd, **E...gas:** Speedway, **lodging:** Lee's Inn, **W...gas:** BP, Shell/24hr, **food:** Applebee's, MCL Cafeteria, Papa John's, Subway, TCBY, **lodging:** $Inn, **other:** HOSPITAL, Batteries+, Borders Books, Cub Foods, Discount Tire, Firestone/auto, JC Penney, Kia/Toyota, Mercury/Lincoln/Mitsubishi, NAPA, Nissan, PepBoys, Sears/auto, Speedway Parts, Tire Barn, mall, transmissions, same as 119

119 38th St, Dodge, **W...gas:** Clark, Meijer's/diesel/24hr, Speedway, **food:** Arby's, KFC, La Bamba Mexican, McDonald's, Outback Steaks, Pizza Hut, Ryan's, Taco Bell, **other:** MEDICAL CARE, Dodge/Hyundai, Dominick's Foods, Honda, K-Mart, Michael's, Office Depot, Sears/auto, Tires+, mall, same as 121

Indianapolis Area

117.5mm White River

117 MLK St(from sb)

116 29th St, 30th St(from nb), Marian Coll, no facilities

115 21st St, **E...**HOSPITAL, **W...**museums, zoo

114 MLK St, West St, downtown

113 US 31, IN 37, Meridian St, to downtown, **E...other:** HOSPITAL

112a I-70 E, to Columbus, no facilities

111 Market St, Michigan St, Ohio St, **E...gas:** Citgo, **food:** Hardee's, McDonald's, **W...other:** City Market, to Market Square Arena, museum

110b I-70 W, to St Louis, no facilities

a Prospect St, Morris St, E St(from sb), no facilities

109 Raymond St, **E...**HOSPITAL, **W...gas:** Speedway, **food:** White Castle, **other:** CVS Drug, Safeway

107 Keystone Ave, **E...lodging:** $Inn, **other:** HOSPITAL, **W...gas:** Citgo, Phillips 66/diesel, Speedway, **food:** Burger King, Denny's, McDonald's, Subway, Wendy's, **lodging:** Holiday Inn Express, **other:** U of Indianapolis

106 I-465 and I-74, no facilities

103 Southport Rd, **E...gas:** BP/McDonald's/24hr, Meijer/diesel/24hr, Shell, **food:** Arby's, Longhorn Steaks, Noble Roman, O'Charley's, Pizzaria Uno, Schlotsky's, Sonic, **other:** Aldi Foods, Firestone/auto, Harley-Davidson, Home Depot, Kohl's, Staples, Target, **W...gas:** Bigfoot/24hr, Citgo/7-11, Speedway/diesel/24hr, **food:** Beef&Brew, Bob Evans, Burger King, Carrabba's, Cheeseburger Paradise, Cracker Barrel, KFC, McDonald's, Steak'n Shake, Texas Roadhouse, Waffle Steak, Wendy's, **lodging:** Best Western, Country Inn Suites, Courtyard, $Inn, Fairfield Inn, Hampton Inn, Signature Inn, Super 8, **other:** HOSPITAL

Greenwood

101 CountyLine Rd, **W...food:** Blimpie, **lodging:** Holiday Inn Express, **other:** HOSPITAL, Kroger

99 Greenwood, **E...gas:** Citgo/diesel/24hr, **W...gas:** BP/Amoco, Marathon, Shell, Tobacco Rd, **food:** Arby's, Bob Evans, Byrd's Cafeteria, Denny's, KFC, McDonald's, Subway, Taco Bell, Waffle Steak, White Castle, **lodging:** Comfort Inn, InTown Suites, Lee's Inn, Red Carpet Inn, **other:** HOSPITAL, Sam's Club, Stout's RV Ctr

Interstate 65

N ↕ S

95 Whiteland, **E...gas:** Flying J/CountryMkt/diesel/24hr@, Marathon/Kathy's Kitchen/diesel, **W...gas:** Pilot/Arby's/diesel/24hr/@, Pilot/McDonald's/diesel/24hr/@

90 IN 44, Franklin, **W...gas:** BP, Shell, **food:** Burger King, Franklin Gardens Rest., McDonald's, Subway, Waffle Steak, **lodging:** Carlton Lodge, Day's Inn/rest., Howard Johnson, Quality Inn, Super 8, **other:** HOSPITAL, golf

85mm Sugar Creek

82mm Big Blue River

80 IN 252, Edinburgh, to Flat Rock, **W...gas:** BP/diesel, Shell/diesel

76b a US 31, Taylorsville, **E...gas:** Shell/diesel, Speedway/diesel, **food:** A&W/KFC, Burger King, Waffle Steak, **lodging:** Comfort Inn, **other:** HOSPITAL, **W...gas:** BP, Citgo/Subway/diesel, Thornton/diesel/café, **food:** Arby's, Cracker Barrel, Hardee's, Max&Erma's, McDonald's, Waffle Steak, **lodging:** Best Western, Hampton Inn, Holiday Inn Express, **other:** Edmundson RV Ctr, Goodyear, Harley-Davidson, Prime Outlets/famous brands, antiques, repair

73mm rest area both lanes, full(handicapped)facilities, phone, vending, info, picnic tables, litter barrels, petwalk

68mm Driftwood River

Columbus

68 IN 46, Columbus, **E...gas:** BP/diesel/24hr, Bigfoot, Shell, Speedway/diesel, **food:** Burger King, McDonald's, Mexico Viejo, Riviera Diner, **lodging:** Courtyard, Holiday Inn/rest., Ramada Inn, Sleep Inn, Super 8, **other:** HOSPITAL, **W...gas:** Marathon, Swifty, **food:** Arby's, Bob Evans, Denny's, KFC/Pizza Hut, Taco Bell, Wendy's, **lodging:** Day's Inn, Knight's Inn, Travelodge, **other:** U-Haul, to Brown Co SP

64 IN 58, Walesboro, **W...gas:** Marathon, **food:** Kathy's Express Diner, **other:** to RV camping

55 IN 11, Seymour, to Jonesville, **E...gas:** BP

54mm White River

51mm weigh sta both lanes

Seymour

50b a US 50, Seymour, **E...gas:** Chevron, Marathon/diesel, Swifty, TA/BP/diesel/24hr/@, **food:** McDonald's, Waffle House, **lodging:** Day's Inn, Econolodge, Motel 6, Super 8, **other:** Tanger Outlet/famous brands, **W...gas:** BP, Shell/diesel, Speedway/diesel, Sunoco/diesel, **food:** Applebee's, Arby's, Bob Evans, Burger King, Cracker Barrel, Denny's, KFC, LJ Silver, McDonald's, Papa John's, Perkins, Pizza Hut, Rally's, Ryan's, Santa Fe Mexican, Steak'n Shake, Subway, Taco Bell, Tumbleweed Grill, Wendy's, **lodging:** Hampton Inn, Holiday Inn/rest., HomeTown Inn, Knight's Inn, Lee's Inn, **other:** HOSPITAL, Aldi Foods, AutoZone, Chevrolet/Buick/Pontiac/GMC, $General, Family$, Foods+, Ford/Lincoln/Mercury, GNC, Home Depot, JC Penney, Radio Shack, Staples, Wal-Mart SuperCtr/24hr

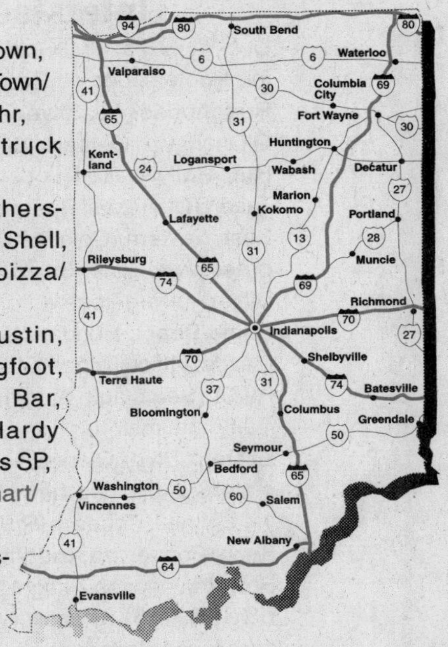

41 IN 250, Uniontown, **W...gas:** UnionTown/diesel/rest./24hr, **other:** auto/truck repair

36 US 31, Crothersville, **E...gas:** Shell, **W...gas:** BP/pizza/subs

34a b IN 256, Austin, **E...gas:** Bigfoot, **food:** Dairy Bar, **other:** to Hardy Lake, Clifty Falls SP, **W...gas:** Fuelmart/A&W/diesel

Scottsburg

29b a IN 56, Scottsburg, to Salem, **E...gas:** BP/diesel, MotoMart, Speedway/diesel, **food:** Burger King, KFC, Ponderosa, Sonic, Subway, Taco Bell, **lodging:** Holiday Inn Express, Mariann Motel/rest., **other:** HOSPITAL, CVS Drug, **W...gas:** Citgo/diesel, Shell, **food:** Arby's, LJ Silver, McDonald's, Pizza Hut, Roadhouse USA, Waffle Steak, Wendy's, **lodging:** Best Western, Hampton Inn, Super 8, **other:** Big O Tire, Jellystone Camping(4mi), Wal-Mart SuperCtr/24hr

22mm rest area both lanes, full(handicapped)facilities, info, phone, picnic tables, litter barrels, vending, petwalk

19 IN 160, Henryville, **E...gas:** Bigfoot, Shell/24hr, Sprint/diesel, **food:** Schuler's Rest.

16 Memphis Rd, Memphis, **E...gas:** BP, Citgo/diesel, **W...gas:** Pilot/Arby's/diesel/24hr/@, **other:** Customers 1st RV Ctr.

9 IN 311, Sellersburg, to New Albany, **E...gas:** BP, Chevron, Shell, Swifty, **food:** Arby's, Cracker Barrel, DQ, Waffle Steak, **lodging:** Ramada Ltd, **other:** Carmerica Tires/service, Ford, O'Reilly Parts, st police, **W...gas:** DM/gas, **food:** Burger King, McDonald's, Taco Bell, **lodging:** Comfort Inn, **other:** city park

7 IN 60, Hamburg, **E...gas:** BP/diesel/24hr, **W...gas:** Citgo, **food:** KFC, **lodging:** Day's Inn

6b a I-265 W, to I-64 W, New Albany, IN 265 E

5 Veterans Parkway, no facilities

4 US 31 N, IN 131 S, Clarksville, New Albany, **E...gas:** Thornton/Subway/diesel, **food:** White Castle, **lodging:** Crest Motel, **W...gas:** Speedway/diesel, **food:** Applebee's, Arby's, Blimpie, Bob Evans, Boston Mkt, Burger King, Capt D's, ChiChi's, Damon's, Denny's,

INDIANA

Interstate 65

N ↕ S — Clarksville

Don Pablo, Fazoli's, Golden Corral, HomeTown Buffet, Hooters, Jerry's Rest., Little Caesar's, Logan's Roadhouse, LJ Silver, McDonald's, Mr Gatti's, O'Charley's, Outback Steaks, Papa John's, Pizza Hut, Rally's, Red Lobster, Steak'n Shake/24hr, Taco Bell, Texas Roadhouse, Wendy's, **lodging:** Best Western, Colonial Motel, $Inn, Hampton Inn, **other:** AutoZone, Buick/Pontiac/GMC, Circuit City, Dillard's, Firestone/auto, Ford, Hancock Fabrics, Home Depot, Honda, JC Penney, Kia, Kroger/deli, Mazda, Office Depot, OfficeMax, PepBoys, Premier RV Ctr, Sears/auto, Target, Toyota, USPO, Walgreen, Wal-Mart, mall

2 Eastern Blvd, Clarksville, **E...lodging:** Day's Inn, Motel 6, Super 8, **other:** U-Haul, **W...gas:** BP, Citgo/7-11, Shell, Tobacco Rd/gas, **food:** KFC, Omelet Shop, Ponderosa, **lodging:** Best Inn, Econolodge, Howard Johnson, Knight's Inn, Quality Inn

1 US 31 S, IN 62, Stansifer Ave, **W...food:** Derby Dinner House, **lodging:** Holiday Inn, Stansifer Hotel, **other:** HOSPITAL, Stinnett RV Ctr

0 Jeffersonville, **E...gas:** BP, Thornton, **food:** DQ, Hardee's, McDonald's, Waffle Steak, **other:** HOSPITAL, Chrysler/Jeep, Hyundai, Nissan, Walgreen, to Falls of OH SP, **W...food:** Hooters, Subway, **lodging:** Fairfield Inn, Ramada Inn, TownePlace Inn

0mm Indiana/Kentucky state line, Ohio River

Interstate 69

N ↕ S

Exit # Services

158mm Indiana/Michigan state line

157 Lake George Rd, to IN 120, Fremont, Lake James, **E...gas:** Petro/Mobil/diesel/24hr/@, **lodging:** Lake George Inn, **other:** Western Star Trucks, **W...gas:** Pilot/Wendy's/diesel/24hr/@, Shell/Subway/diesel/24hr/@, **food:** McDonald's, Red Arrow Rest., **lodging:** Holiday Inn Express(1mi), Redwood Lodge, **other:** Prime Outlets/famous brands(1mi), fireworks

156 I-80/90 Toll Rd, E to Toledo, W to Chicago

154 IN 127, to IN 120, IN 727, Fremont, Orland, **E...food:** Herb Garden Rest., **lodging:** E&L Motel, Hampton Inn, Super 8, **W...gas:** Marathon/diesel, **lodging:** Budgeteer Motel, Holiday Inn Express, **other:** Prime Outlets/famous brands(2mi), to Pokagon SP, Jellystone Camping(4mi)

150 rd 200 W, to Lake James, Crooked Lake, **E...gas:** BP/diesel, **W...gas:** Shell, Pennzoil Gas, **other:** Marine Ctr

148 US 20, to Angola, Lagrange, **E...gas:** BP/Subway, Marathon/diesel, Speedway/diesel, **food:** McDonald's, Wendy's(1mi), **other:** HOSPITAL, **W...lodging:** Best Western

145mm Pigeon Creek

144mm rest area sb, full(handicapped)facilities, info, phone, picnic tables, litter barrels, vending, petwalk

140 IN 4, Ashley, Hudson, to Hamilton, **1 mi W...gas:** Phillips 66

134 US 6, to Waterloo, Kendallville, **W...gas:** Marathon/diesel/24hr

Auburn

129 IN 8, Auburn, to Garrett, **E...gas:** BP/diesel, Clark, GA, Marathon/diesel/24hr, Shell, Speedway/diesel, Ambrosia Rest., **food:** Applebee's, Arby's/24hr, Bob Evans, Burger King, DQ, Fazoli's, KFC, McDonald's, Pizza Hut, Ponderosa, Richard's Rest., Subway, Taco Bell, TCBY, Wendy's, Zesto Drive-In, **lodging:** Auburn Inn, Budget Inn, Comfort Suites, Country Hearth Inn, Holiday Inn Express, Ramada Ltd, Super 8, **other:** HOSPITAL, AutoZone, Chevrolet/Pontiac/Buick/RV Ctr, Chrysler/Jeep, $General, Ford, Kroger, Radio Shack, Staples, Wal-Mart SuperCtr/24hr, museum, **W...**Home Depot

126 IN 11-A, to Garrett, Auburn, **E...**Kruse Auction Park, **W...**KOA

116 IN 1 N, Dupont Rd, **E...gas:** BP/Burger King, **lodging:** Comfort Suites, **W...gas:** BP/Elmo's/diesel, Speedway, **food:** Bob Evans, Ground Level Coffee, McDonald's(1mi), Trolley Grill, **lodging:** AmericInn, Sleep Inn, **other:** HOSPITAL

115 I-469, US 30 E, no facilities

Ft Wayne

112b a Coldwater Rd, **E...gas:** BP/diesel/24hr, Marathon, Sunoco, **food:** Arby's, ChiChi's, Cork'n Cleaver, DeBrand's Chocolate, Hunan Chinese, Joe's CrabShack, Krispy Kreme, LoneStar Steaks, Old Country Buffet, Oriental Seafood Buffet, Papa John's, Red River Steaks/BBQ, Steak'n Shake, Taco Bell, Taco Cabana, Wendy's, Zesto Drive-In, **lodging:** AmeiSuites, Marriott, **other:** $Tree, Hall's Factory Steaks, Walgreen, Wal-Mart SuperCtr/24hr, **W...**DQ

111b a US 27 S, IN 3 N, **E...gas:** Shell, **food:** Cap'n Cork Rest., Golden Corral, Sonic, **lodging:** Residence Inn, **other:** Honda, Infiniti, Kia, Nissan, Pontiac/GMC/Isuzu, Toyota, **W...gas:** BP/diesel, Marathon, Meijer/diesel/24hr, **food:** Applebee's, Cracker Barrel, Golden China, KFC, McDonald's, Sonic, Texas Roadhouse, Tumbleweed Grill, **lodging:** Baymont Inn, Courtyard, County Inn Suites, Day's Inn, **other:** $Inn, Fairfield Inn, Guesthouse Motel, Hampton Inn, Lee's Inn, Signature Inn, Studio+, Home Depot, Lowe's Whse, Sam's Club, VW

109b a US 33, Ft Wayne, **E...gas:** BP, Citgo/Subway/diesel, Sunoco, **food:** Arby's, Liberty Diner, McDonald's, **lodging:** Best Inn, Comfort Inn, $Inn, Econolodge, Holiday Inn, Knight's Inn, Motel 6, Red Roof Inn, ValuLodge, **other:** HOSPITAL, to Children's Zoo

105b a IN 14 W, Ft Wayne, **E...gas:** Meijer/diesel/24hr, Shell/Subway/diesel, Speedway/LP, **food:** Bob Evans, FlatTop Grill, Logan's Roadhouse, O'Charley's, Steak'n Shake, Subway, **lodging:** Klopfenstein Suites, **other:** HOSPITAL, Acura, Barnes&Noble, Best Buy, BMW, Cadillac, Chevrolet, Chrysler/Plymouth/Jeep, Daewoo,

Interstate 69

N

S

Dodge, Harley-Davidson, Hummer, Lexus, Kohl's, Lincoln/Mercury, Lowe's Whse, Mazda, Old Navy, Pontiac/Buick/GMC, Saab, Saturn, Staples, Subaru, Toyota, Volvo, Wal-Mart SuperCtr/24hr, to St Francis U, **W...**Corvette Museum

102 US 24, to Huntington, Ft Wayne, **E...food:** Subway(1mi), Taco Bell(1mi), **lodging:** Extended Stay America, Hampton Inn, **other:** HOSPITAL, to In Wesleyan U, **W...gas:** BP/24hr, Marathon, **food:** Applebee's, Arby's, Bob Evans, Capt D's, Carlos O'Kelly's, Coventry Tavern Rest., McDonald's, Outback Steaks, Pizza Hut, Tumbleweeds Grill, Wendy's, Zesto Drive-In, **lodging:** Best Western, Comfort Suites, Hilton Garden, Holiday Inn Express, **other:** Kroger, Scott's Foods, Walgreen, st police

99 Lower Huntington Rd, no facilities

96b a I-469, US 24 E, US 33 S, **E...**to airport

93mm rest area sb, full(handicapped)facilities, info, phone, vending, picnic tables, litter barrels, pet walk

89mm rest area nb, full(handicapped)facilities, info, phone, vending, picnic tables, litter barrels, pet walk

86 US 224, Markle, to Huntington, **E...gas:** Citgo/diesel(1mi), Marathon/24hr(1mi), Sunoco/Subway, **food:** DQ(1mi), E of Chicago Pizza, **lodging:** Sleep Inn, Super 8, **other:** HOSPITAL, antiques, **W...**to Huntington Reservoir

80mm weigh sta both lanes

78 IN 5, to Warren, Huntington, **E...gas:** Sunoco/diesel, **lodging:** Huggy Bear Motel, **W...gas:** Clark/Subway/diesel/24hr, Crazy D's/diesel/24hr, **food:** Hoosier-Land Rest., McDonald's, **lodging:** Ramada Ltd, Super 8, **other:** HOSPITAL, RV Camping, to Salmonie Reservoir

76mm Salamonie River

73 IN 218, to Warren, no facilities

64 IN 18, to Marion, Montpelier, **W...gas:** BP/Subway/diesel, Marathon/diesel, **food:** Arby's, **lodging:** Country Inn Suites, **other:** HOSPITAL, Harley-Davidson

60mm Walnut Creek

59 US 35 N, IN 22, to Upland, Gas City, **E...gas:** Citgo/Subway, **food:** Burger King, Cracker Barrel, **lodging:** B&B, Best Western, Super 8, **other:** Taylor U, **W...gas:** Marathon/diesel/24hr, McClure Trkstp/diesel/24hr/@, Shell/diesel, **food:** KFC/Taco Bell, **other:** IN Wesleyan

55 IN 26, to Fairmount, **E...gas:** Marathon

50mm rest area both lanes, full(handicapped)facilities, info, phone, picnic tables, litter barrels, vending, pet walk

45 US 35 S, IN 28, to Alexandria, Albany, **E...gas:** Shell/Taco Bell/diesel/24hr, **other:** camping, **W...**camping

Anderson

41 IN 332, to Muncie, Frankton, **E...gas:** Citgo/diesel, **other:** HOSPITAL, to Ball St U

34 IN 67, to IN 32, Chesterfield, Daleville, **E...gas:** Pilot/Subway/diesel/24hr/@, Shell/Burger King, **food:** Arby's, Taco Bell, White Castle, **lodging:** Budget Inn, **other:** HOSPITAL, Factory Shops/famous brands, **W...gas:** GA/diesel, Pilot/diesel/24hr/@, **food:** McDonald's, Subway, Wendy's, **lodging:** Super 8, **other:** flea mkt

26 IN 9, IN 109, to Anderson, **E...gas:** Meijer/diesel/24hr, **food:** KFC/A&W, Ryan's, **lodging:** $Inn, Hampton Inn, Quality Inn, **W...gas:** BP/24hr, Marathon, Shell, Red Barn Mkt/Noble Roman's/diesel, **food:** Applebee's, Arby's, Bob Evans, Burger King, ChiChi's, Cracker Barrel, Great Wall Chinese, Grindstone Charley's, La Charreada Mexican, Little Caesar's, LoneStar Steaks, McDonald's, Perkins, Pizza Hut, Red Lobster, Ruby Tuesday, Steak'n Shake, Taco Bell, TCBY, Texas Roadhouse, Waffle Steak, Wendy's, White Castle, **lodging:** Baymont Inn, Best Inn, Best Western, Comfort Inn, Econolodge, Holiday Inn, Lee's Inn, Super 8, **other:** HOSPITAL, Aldi Foods, Cadillac/GMC, Kohl's, OfficeMax, Old Navy, Payless Foods, Radio Shack, Target, Tire Barn, Toyota, Wal-Mart/auto, to Anderson U, to Mounds SP

22 IN 9, IN 67, to Anderson, **W...gas:** GA, **lodging:** Anderson Country Inn(1mi), **other:** HOSPITAL, st police

19 IN 38, Pendleton, **E...gas:** Marathon, **food:** Burger King, DQ, McDonald's, Subway

14 IN 13, to Lapel, **W...gas:** Pilot/Subway/diesel/24hr/@, **other:** camping

10 IN 238, to Noblesville, Fortville, **E...**outlet mall

5 IN 37 N, 116th St, Fishers, to Noblesville, **W...gas:** Shell/autocare, **food:** Hardee's, McDonald's, O'Charley's, Quizno's, Steak'n Shake, Wendy's, **other:** Target

INDIANA

Interstate 69

E ↕ W

3 96th St, **E...gas:** Meijer/diesel/24hr, Shell, VP/diesel, **food:** Applebee's, Bennigan's, Cracker Barrel, Golden Wok Chinese, Grindstone Charley's, McDonald's, Noble Roman's, Panera Bread, Qdoba Mexican, Red Rock Roadhouse, Ruby Tuesday, Steak'n Shake, Wendy's, **lodging:** Holiday Inn, Holiday Inn Express, Sleep Inn, Studio 6, **other:** Kohl's, Marsh Food/gas, PepBoys, Radio Shack, Sam's Club, Staples, Wal-Mart SuperCtr/24hr, **W...gas:** Marathon, **food:** Arby's, Bob Evans, Burger King, Panda Express, Peterson's Steaks/seafood, Schlotsky's, Taco Bell, **lodging:** Comfort Inn, Residence Inn, Staybridge Suites, **other:** Home Depot, Sam's Club/gas

1 82nd St, Castleton, **E...food:** Golden Corral, **lodging:** Clarion, $Inn, Extended Stay America, Omni Hotel, Super 8, **other:** HOSPITAL, Lowe's Whse, **W...gas:** BP, Speedway, **food:** Arby's, Burger King, Cancun Mexican, Castleton Grill, Charleston Rest., ChiChi's, China Dynasty, Denny's, Fazoli's, Hooters, IHOP, KFC, LJ Silver, McDonald's, Olive Garden, Pizza Hut, Red Lobster, Skyline Chili, Sonic, Starbucks, Steak'n Shake, Tony Roma, Wendy's, **lodging:** Best Western, Candlewood Suites, Day's Inn, Fairfield Inn, Hampton Inn, **other:** Aamco, Best Buy, Discount Tire, Goodyear/auto, Sears/auto, Tire Barn, mall

0mm I-465 around Indianapolis. I-69 begins/ends on I-465,

Interstate 70

E ↕ W

Richmond

Exit # Services

156.5mm Indiana/Ohio state line, weigh sta

156b a US 40 E, Richmond, **N...gas:** Petro/Marathon/diesel/rest./24hr, Swifty, **lodging:** Fairfield Inn, Golden Inn, **other:** Blue Beacon, **S...gas:** Shell/mart, Speedway/mart, Sunoco, **food:** A&W/LJ Silver, Applebee's, Bob Evans, Burger King, Chili's, Cracker Barrel, Fazoli's, Golden Corral, KFC, McDonald's, O'Charley's, Pizza Hut, Ponderosa, Red Lobster, Ruby Tuesday, Ryan's, Steak'n Shake, Super China, Texas Roadhouse, White Castle, **lodging:** Best Western, Day's Inn, $Inn, Hampton Inn, Holiday Inn, Lee's Inn, Motel 6, **other:** Chevrolet/Cadillac, Chrysler/Jeep, $General, Firestone, Ford/Lincoln/Mercury, Goody's, Goodyear/auto, Hastings Books, Honda, JC Penney, Kroger, Lowe's Whse, Nissan, OfficeMax, Sav-A-Lot Foods, Sears/auto, Target, Tires+, U-Haul, Wal-Mart SuperCtr/24hr

153 IN 227, Richmond, to Whitewater, **2 mi N...**Grandpa's Farm RV Park(seasonal)

151b a US 27, Richmond, to Chester, **N...food:** Fricker's Rest., **other:** Best Buy RV Ctr, Dodge, Honda, KOA, **S...gas:** Meijer/diesel/24hr, Speedway, Shell, Sunoco/mart, **food:** Big Boy, Bob Evans, Burger King, Carver's Rest., McDonald's, Pizza Hut, Subway, Taco Bell, Wendy's, **lodging:** Comfort Inn, Super 8, **other:** HOSPITAL, Harley-Davidson

149 US 35, IN 38, Richmond, to Muncie, **N...**Love's/Hardee's/diesel/mart/24hr, **S...**Raper RV Ctr

148mm weigh sta both lanes

145 Centerville, **N...gas:** BP/DQ/Stuckey's, **lodging:** Super 8, **other:** Goodyear/repair

145mm Nolans Fork Creek

144mm rest area both lanes, full(handicapped)facilities, info, vending, phone, picnic tables, litter barrels, petwalk

141mm Greens Fork River

137 IN 1, to Hagerstown, Connersville, **N...**Amish Cheese, **S...gas:** Crazy D's/diesel/rest./24hr, GasAmerica/mart/24hr, Shell/mart/24hr, **food:** Burger King, McDonald's

131 Wilbur Wright Rd, New Lisbon, **S...gas:** Marathon/KFC/Taco Bell/diesel24hr, **other:** RV park

126mm Flatrock River

123 IN 3, Spiceland, to New Castle, **N...gas:** Speedway, **lodging:** Best Western(2mi), Day's Inn, Holiday Inn Express(3mi), **other:** HOSPITAL, Irwin RV Park(1mi), **S...gas:** BP/diesel/mart/@, Flying J/CountyMkt/diesel/mart/24hr/@, **food:** Kathy's Kitchen

117mm Big Blue River

115 IN 109, to Knightstown, Wilkinson, **N...gas:** GA/diesel/rest./24hr, **food:** Burger King

107mm rest area both lanes, full(handicapped)facilities, vending, phone, picnic tables, litter barrels, petwalk, RV dump

104 IN 9, Greenfield, Maxwell, **N...gas:** GA/mart, **S...gas:** GA/diesel, Shell/mart, Sunoco/mart, Swifty/mart, **food:** Applebee's, Arby's, Bamboo Garden, Bob Evans, Burger King, Garfield's Rest., Hardee's, KFC, McDonald's, Pizza Hut, Steak'n Shake, Taco Bell, Waffle House, Wendy's, White Castle, **lodging:** Comfort Inn, $Inn, Holiday Inn Express, Lee's Inn, Super 8, **other:** Advance Parts, Aldi Foods, Big O Tire, CVS Drug, Home Depot, Marsh Foods, Radio Shack, Wal-Mart SuperCtr/gas/24hr

96 Mt Comfort Rd, **N...gas:** GA/mart, Pilot/diesel/mart/24hr, **food:** Burger King, Pizza Hut, Subway, **S...gas:** Shell/mart, **food:** McDonald's, **other:** KOA(seasonal), Mark's RV Ctr

91 Post Rd, to Ft Harrison, **N...gas:** Marathon/7-11, **food:** Big Boy, Cracker Barrel, Denny's, Joe's Crabshack, McDonald's, Outback Steaks, Steak'n Shake, Wendy's, **lodging:** Baymont Inn, InTown Suites, **other:** Lowe's Whse, st police, **S...gas:** BP/mart, Shell/mart, **food:** Hardee's, KFC/Taco Bell, Waffle Steak, **lodging:** Best Western, $Inn, Quality Inn, Super 8, Travelers Inn, **other:** CVS Drug, Home Depot, Marsh Foods

90 I-465(from wb), no facilities

89 Shadeland Ave, I-465(from eb), **N...gas:** Marathon, **food:** Bob Evans, Waffle House, **lodging:** Comfort Inn, Hampton Inn, Hawthorn Suites, Motel 6, **other:** Toyota, U-Haul, **S...gas:** BigFoot, Clark, Marathon, Shell/mart/24hr, Speedway/diesel, **food:** Arby's, Burger King, Cattle Co Steaks, 4Seasons Diner, McDonald's, Omelet Shop, Rally's, Red Lobster, Texas Roadhouse, Wendy's, **lodging:** Budget Inn, Day's Inn, Fairfield Inn,

Interstate 70

E ↕ W

Indianapolis Area

Holiday Inn/Damon's, Knight's Inn, La Quinta, Marriott, Ramada Ltd, **other:** Aamco, Buick, CVS Drug, Chevrolet, Dodge, Ford/Lincoln/Mercury

87 Emerson Ave, **N...gas:** BP/McDonald's, Speedway/mart, **S...gas:** Shell/mart

85b a Rural St, Keystone Ave, **N...**fairgrounds, **S...gas:** Marathon

83b(112) I-65 N, to Chicago

a(111) Michigan St, Market St, downtown, **S...food:** Hardee's

80(110a) I-65 S, to Louisville

79b Illinois St, McCarty St, downtown

a West St, **N...lodging:** Comfort Inn, **other:** HOSPITAL, to Union Sta, Govt Ctr, RCA Dome, zoo

78 Harding St, to downtown

77 Holt Rd, **S...gas:** Clark Gas, Shell/mart, **food:** McDonald's, Mr Dan's Rest., **other:** AllPro Parts

75 Airport Expswy, to Raymond St, **N...gas:** Marathon/mart, Speedway/mart, **food:** Cracker Barrel, Denny's, JoJo's Rest., Schlotsky's, Waffle Steak, **lodging:** Adam's Mark, Baymont Inn, Fairfield Inn, La Quinta, Motel 6, Red Roof Inn, Residence Inn, access to Day's Inn, Hilton, Holiday Inn, Ramada, **other:** to airport

73b a I-465 N/S, I-74 E/W

66 IN 267, to Plainfield, Mooresville, **N...gas:** BP/mart/24hr, Shell/mart, Speedway/diesel/mart, Thornton/diesel/mart, **food:** Arby's, Bob Evans, Burger King, Coachman Rest., Cracker Barrel, Golden Corral, Hog Heaven BBQ, Little Mexico, McDonald's, Perkins, Pizza King, Quizno's, Ritter's Custard, Sonic, Steak'n Shake, Subway, Wendy's, White Castle, **lodging:** AmeriHost, Comfort Inn, Day's Inn, $Inn, Hampton Inn, Holiday Inn Express, Lee's Inn, Super 8, **other:** Chateau Thomas Winery, Harley-Davidson

65mm rest area both lanes, full(handicapped)facilities, info, vending, phone, picnic tables, litter barrels, petwalk

59 IN 39, to Belleville, **N...gas:** Marathon/mart, **S...gas:** TA/Citgo/diesel/rest./24hr/@

51 rd 1100W, **S...other:** Koger's/diesel/mart, repair/towing/24hr

41 US 231, Cloverdale, to Greencastle, **N...food:** Long Branch Steaks, **lodging:** Midway Motel, **other:** HOSPITAL **S...gas:** BP/diesel/mart, Citgo/Subway/diesel/mart/24hr, Shell/mart, **food:** Arby's, Burger King, Chicago's Pizza, KFC, McDonald's, Taco Bell, Wendy's, **lodging:** Best Inn, Day's Inn, $Inn, Holiday Inn Express, Ramada Inn, Super 8, **other:** Clover Tire, Value Mkt Foods, to Lieber SRA

37 IN 243, to Putnamville, **S...gas:** Marathon/diesel/mart, **other:** to Lieber SRA

Terre Haute

23 IN 59, to Brazil, **N...gas:** Pilot/diesel/mart/24hr, **other:** HOSPITAL, **S...gas:** Pilot/Subway/diesel/mart, Shell/Brazil 70/diesel/rest./24hr/@, Sunoco/Rally's/diesel/mart, **food:** Burger King, **lodging:** Howard Johnson Express

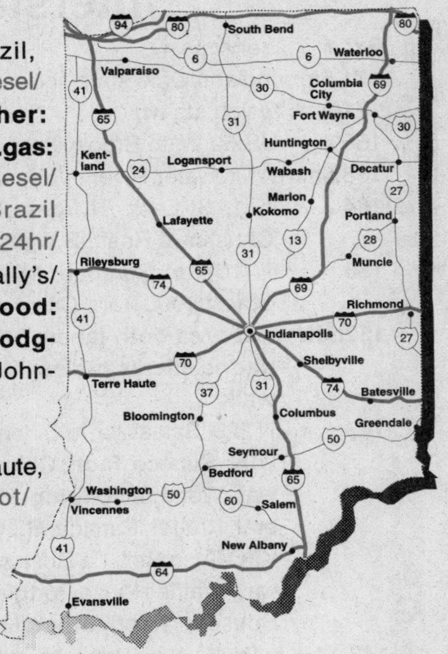

15mm Honey Creek

11 IN 46, Terre Haute, **N...gas:** Pilot/Arby's/diesel/mart/24hr, Thornton/diesel, **food:** Burger King, McDonald's, airport, **S...**KOA

7 US 41, US 150, Terre Haute, **N...gas:** BP/mart, Marathon/diesel/mart, Thornton's/diesel, **food:** Applebee's, Arby's, Bob Evans, Burger King, Cracker Barrel, Fazoli's, Hardee's, IHOP, Little Caesar's, LoneStar Steaks, Pizza Hut, Quizno's, Schlotsky's, Steak'n Shake, Texas Roadhouse, Tumbleweed Mesquite Grill, **lodging:** Comfort Suites, $Inn, Drury Inn, Fairfield Inn, PearTree Inn, Signature Inn, Super 8, **other:** AutoZone, Chrysler/Dodge/Jeep, Daewoo, JiffyLube, S IN Tire, **S...gas:** JiffyMart/24hr, Marathon, Speedway/mart, Sunoco/mart, Thornton's/mart, **food:** Arby's, Burger King, ChiChi's, China Buffet, Garfield's Rest., Denny's, Hardee's, KFC, LJ Silver, McDonald's, Olive Garden, Outback Steaks, Papa John's, Ponderosa, Rally's, Red Lobster, Ritter's Custard, Ryan's, Sonic, Subway, Taco Bell, TGIFriday, Wendy's, **lodging:** Hampton Inn, Holiday Inn, Motel 6, **other:** HOSPITAL, Aldi Foods, BooksAMillion, Buick/Pontiac/Cadillac, Chevrolet/Hyundai/Nissan, Circuit City, Dodge, FashionBug, Ford/Kia, GMC/Mazda, Goodyear/auto, Jo-Ann Crafts, Kroger, Lowe's Whse, OfficeMax, Old Navy, Sam's Club, Saturn, Sears/auto, Staples, Toyota, Wal-Mart SuperCtr/gas/24hr

5.5mm Wabash River

3 Darwin Rd, W Terre Haute, **N...**to St Mary of-the-Woods Coll

1.5mm Welcome Ctr eb, full(handicapped)facilities, info, picnic tables, litter barrels, phone, vending, petwalk

1 US 40 E(from eb, exits left), W Terre Haute, to Terre Haute

0mm Indiana/Illinois state line

Interstate 74

E ↕ W

Exit #	Services
171.5mm	Indiana/Ohio state line
171mm	weigh sta wb
169	US 52 W, to Brookville, no facilities
168.5mm	Whitewater River
164	IN 1, St Leon, **N...gas:** Exxon, Shell/diesel, **food:** Christina's Rest., **S...gas:** BP/Blimpie/diesel
156	IN 101, to Sunman, Milan, **S...gas:** Exxon/diesel, **other:** 1000Trails Camping
152mm	**rest area both lanes, full(handicapped)facilities, phone, picnic tables, litter barrels, vending, petwalk**
149	IN 229, Batesville, to Oldenburg, **N...gas:** Shell/diesel/24hr, Sunoco, **food:** China Buffet, McDonald's, Subway, Wendy's, **lodging:** Hampton Inn, **other:** $General, Kroger, Pamida, **S...gas:** BP, **food:** Arby's, DQ, KFC/Taco Bell, La Rosa's Pizza, Skyline Chili, Subway, Waffle House, **lodging:** Comfort Inn, Sherman House Inn/rest., **other:** HOSPITAL
143	to IN 46, New Point, **N...gas:** Petro/Marathon/diesel/rest./24hr/@, **S...gas:** Marathon
134b a	IN 3, Greensburg, to Rushville, **S...gas:** Bigfoot, BP/diesel, Shell/24hr, Speedway, Tobacco Rd, **food:** Arby's, Big Boy, Burger King, Chili's, El Tapatio Mexican, Great Wall Chinese, KFC, McDonald's, Papa John's, Ponderosa, Subway, Taco Bell, Waffle House, Wendy's, **lodging:** Best Western, Lee's Inn, Holiday Inn Express, **other:** Advance Parts, Aldi Foods, AutoZone, Big O Tire, Chrysler, CVS Drug, Ford/Mercury, Radio Shack, Staples, Wal-Mart SuperCtr/24hr
132	US 421(from eb), to Greensburg, no facilities
129mm	Clifty Creek
123	Saint Paul, **S...**camping
119	IN 244 E, to Milroy, no facilities
116	IN 44, to Shelbyville, Rushville, **N...gas:** Bigfoot/diesel, **S...gas:** BP, Marathon, Shell/24hr, Swifty, **food:** Applebee's, Arby's, Baskin-Robbins/Dunkin Donuts, Bavarian Haus, Bob Evans, Burger King, Denny's, Domino's, Golden Corral(1mi), LJ Silver, McDonald's, New China, Papa John's, Pizza Hut, Subway, Taco Bell, Wendy's, **lodging:** Lee's Inn, Rasner Motel, **other:** HOSPITAL, Aldi Foods, Chevrolet/Nissan, CVS Drug, $General, Ford/Lincoln/Mercury, GNC, Goody's, IGA Foods, Kroger, Marsh Food, NAPA, Osco Drug, Radio Shack, Wal-Mart
115mm	Little Blue River
113mm	Big Blue River
113	IN 9, to Shelbyville, **N...gas:** CF/diesel, **food:** Cracker Barrel, **S...gas:** BP, Shell, **food:** Cow Palace(1mi), McDonald's, Waffle Steak, **lodging:** Comfort Inn, Day's Inn, Hampton Inn, Holiday Inn Express, Super 8, **other:** HOSPITAL, Buick/GMC, Chrysler/Plymouth, Ford/Lincoln/Mercury
109	Fairland Rd, **S...other:** Brownie's Marine, RV camping/funpark
103	London Rd, to Boggstown, no facilities
102mm	Big Sugar Creek
101	Pleasant View Rd, **N...gas:** Marathon, **food:** Chester Fried, **lodging:** Golden Royal Inn
99	Acton Rd, no facilities
96	Post Rd, **N...gas:** Marathon/Subway/diesel/24hr, **food:** McDonald's, **S...gas:** Shell/diesel, **food:** Wendy's, **other:** Chevrolet
94b a	I-465/I-74 W, I-465 N, US 421 N
	I-74 and I-465 run together 21 miles. **See Indiana Interstate 465, exits 2-16, and 52-53.**
73b	I-465 N, access to same facilities as 16a on I-465
a	I-465 S, I-74 E, no facilities
71mm	Eagle Creek
66	IN 267, Brownsburg, **N...gas:** Phillips 66/24hr, Shell, **food:** Applebee's, Happy Wok, Hardee's, Subway, **lodging:** Holiday Inn Express, **other:** Big O Tire, **S...gas:** BP/diesel, Speedway/diesel, **food:** Arby's, Blimpie, Bob Evans, Burger King, China's Best, McDonald's, Papa Murphy's, Taco Bell, Wendy's, White Castle, **lodging:** Comfort Suites, Super 8, **other:** MEDICAL CARE, CVS Drug, $Tree, Ford, Kroger/gas, K-Mart, Radio Shack, Wal-Mart SuperCtr/24hr
61	to Pittsboro, **S...gas:** Blue&White Service/diesel/24hr, **food:** Hap's Place Rest./gas/diesel, tires
58	IN 39, Lizton, to Lebanon, **N...gas:** Phillips 66, **S...**HOSPITAL
57mm	**rest area both lanes, full(handicapped)facilities, phone, picnic tables, litter barrels, vending, petwalk**
52	IN 75, Jamestown, to Advance, **2 mi S...**gas, food, camping
39	IN 32, to Crawfordsville, **S...**antiques(1mi), to Wabash Coll
34	US 231, Crawfordsville, to Linden, **S...gas:** BP, Citgo/diesel/rest./24hr/@, GA, Marathon, Shell, **food:** Burger King, KFC, McDonald's, **lodging:** Comfort Inn, Day's Inn, $Inn, Holiday Inn, Super 8, **other:** HOSPITAL, KOA
25	IN 25, Waynetown, to Wingate, no facilities
23mm	**rest area both lanes, full(handicapped)facilities, phone, picnic tables, litter barrels, vending, petwalk**
19mm	weigh sta both lanes
15	US 41, Veedersburg, to Attica, **1/2 mi S...gas:** Marathon, Phillips 66/Subway/diesel/24hr, **other:** to Turkey Run SP, camping
8	Covington, **N...gas:** Shell, **food:** Maple Corner Rest.(1mi), **other:** fireworks
7mm	Wabash River
4	IN 63, to Newport, **N...gas:** Pilot/Arby's/diesel/24hr/@, **food:** Beefhouse Rest.
1mm	**Welcome Ctr eb, full(handicapped)facilities, info, phone, picnic tables, litter barrels, vending, petwalk**
0mm	Indiana/Illinois state line

Greensburg

Shelbyville

Brownsburg

Interstate 80/90

E ↕ W

Exit # Services

157mm Indiana/Ohio state line

153mm toll plaza, litter barrels

146mm Booth Tarkington Service Area both lanes, Mobil/diesel, DQ, McDonald's, playground

144 I-69, US 27, Angola, Ft Wayne, **N...gas:** Petro/Mobil/diesel/LP/24hr/@, Shell/Subway/diesel/24hr/@, Pilot/Wendy's/diesel/24hr/@, **food:** McDonald's, Red Arrow Rest., **lodging:** Redwood Lodge, Lake George Inn, **S...gas:** Marathon/diesel/24hr, **lodging:** Holiday Inn Express, **other:** Prime Outlets/famous brands, **services on IN 120 E...food:** Herb Garden Rest., **lodging:** E&L Motel, Hampton Inn, Super 8, **other:** Golf/rest., U-Haul/repair(1mi), **W...**to Pokagon SP, Jellystone Camping(7mi)

131.5mm Fawn River

126mm Ernie Pyle Travel Plaza eb, Gene S Porter Travel Plaza wb, Mobil/diesel, Fazoli's, Hardee's, gifts, RV dump

121 IN 9, Howe, to Lagrange, **N...gas:** Golden Buddha, **lodging:** Greenbriar Inn, Hampton Inn, Travel Inn, **other:** HOSPITAL(4mi), **2 mi N...food:** Applebee's, Golden Corral, DQ, Wendy's, **lodging:** Comfort Inn, Knight's Inn, Wood Motel, **S...gas:** Clark, **lodging:** Holiday Inn Express, Super 8, **other:** HOSPITAL(8mi)

120mm Fawn River

108mm trucks only rest area both lanes

107 US 131, IN 13, to Middlebury, Constantine, **N...gas:** Marathon/diesel, **food:** Country Table Rest.(1mi), McDonald's(4mi), **lodging:** PatchWork Quilt Inn(1mi), Plaza Motel, **other:** Tower Motel, **1 mi S...gas:** BP/Blimpie/diesel, **food:** Yup's DairyLand, **other:** KOA(apr-nov), **5 mi S...food:** DQ, Subway, **other:** Coachman RV Factory, Eby's Pines RV Park

101 IN 15, Bristol, to Goshen, **1 mi S...gas:** Citgo/7-11, Speedway/diesel, **food:** River Inn Rest., **other:** MEDICAL CARE, Eby's Pines Camping(3mi), bank

Elkhart

96 rd 17, E Elkhart, **2 mi S...gas:** BP/diesel, Citgo/7-11, Marathon, **food:** DQ, McDonald's, Subway

92 IN 19, to Elkhart, **N...gas:** Citgo/7-11, Phillips 66/Subway/diesel, **food:** Applebee's, Cracker Barrel, Perkins, Steak'n Shake, **lodging:** Best Western, Comfort Suites, Country Inn Suites, Diplomat Motel, Econolodge, Fairway Inn, Hampton Inn, Holiday Inn Express, Knight's Inn, Quality Inn, Sleep Inn, **other:** Aldi Foods, CVS Drug, GNC, K-Mart, Martin's Foods, Radio Shack, Tierra RV Ctr, **S...gas:** Clark, Marathon/diesel, **food:** Arby's, Bennigan's, Blimpie, Bob Evans, Burger King, Callaghan's Rest., Da Vinci's Pizza, King Wha Chinese, Lazy Bones Rest., McDonald's, Olive Garden, Red Lobster, Ryan's, Texas Roadhouse, **lodging:** Budget Inn, Day's Inn, Ramada Inn, Red Roof Inn, Signature Inn, Super 8, Weston Plaza, **other:** HOSPITAL, CarQuest, $Tree, Holiday World RV, Wal-Mart SuperCtr/24hr, truck/RV repair, **1 mi S...gas:** Citgo, Shell, Speedway, Swifty, **food:** DQ, KFC, LJ Silver, Papa John's, Pizza Hut, Matterhorn Rest., Red Dragon Chinese, Taco Bell, Wendy's, **other:** Advance Parts, AutoZone, Family$, Osco Drug, Walgreen

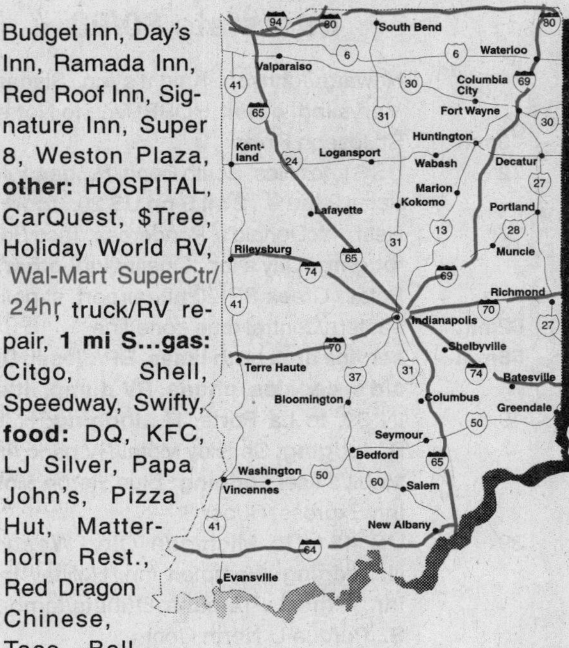

91mm Christiana Creek

90mm Henry Schricker Travel Plaza eb, George Craig Travel Plaza wb, BP/diesel, Arby's, Dunkin Donuts, Pizza Hut, RV dump, travelstore, USPO

83 to Mishawaka, **1-2 mi N on IN 23W...gas:** BP/diesel, Citgo/7-11, Mobil, Phillips 66/Subway/diesel, **food:** Applebee's, Arby's, Famous Dave's, Olive Garden, Pizza Hut, Taco Bell, Wendy's, **lodging:** Carlton Lodge, Fairfield Inn, Hampton Inn, Holiday Inn Express, Super 8, **other:** Best Buy, CVS Drug, Kroger, JC Penney, Marshall Field, Michael's, Office Depot, Sears, Target, Walgreen, KOA(mar-nov), mall, **2 mi S on Grape Rd & Main St(off IN 23W)...gas:** Meijer/diesel/24hr, **food:** Arby's, Burger King, Chili's, LoneStar Steaks, Mancino's Pizza, McDonald's, Old Country Buffet, Outback Steaks, Papa Vino's Italian, Ryan's, Steak'n Shake, Subway, TGIFriday, **lodging:** Best Western, Courtyard, Extended Stay America, SpringHill Suites, **other:** Studio+, Barnes&Noble, Buick/GMC, Chrysler/Plymouth, Circuit City, Discount Tire, Hyundai, Jo-Ann Fabrics, Lowe's Whse, Sam's Club, Wal-Mart SuperCtr/24hr

South Bend

77 US 33, US 31B, IN 933, South Bend, **N...gas:** Admiral, **food:** Arby's, Burger King, Damon's, Family Style Buffet, Fazoli's, Marco's Pizza, McDonald's, Panorama Rest., Papa John's, Pizza Hut, Ponderosa, Steak&Ale, Subway, **lodging:** Comfort Suites, Day's Inn, Hampton Inn, Motel 6, Ramada Inn, Super 8, **other:** AutoZone, Walgreen, **1 mi N on frtge rd...gas:** Meijer/diesel/24hr, Phillips 66, **food:** Burger King, McDonald's, **S...gas:** Marathon, **food:** Bob Evans, Denny's, Great Wall Chinese, King Gyro's, Perkins, Pizza King, Taco Bell, Wendy's, **lodging:** Best Inn,

Interstate 80/90

E ↕ W South Bend

Howard Johnson, Knight's Inn, Signature Inn, St Marys Inn, **other:** HOSPITAL, to Notre Dame

76mm St Joseph River

72 US 31, to Niles, South Bend, **N...gas:** Pilot/Subway/diesel/24hr/@ , **2 mi S on US 20...food:** 4 Seasons Rest., McDonald's, Ponderosa, Taco Bell, Wendy's, **lodging:** Day's Inn, Quality Inn, **other:** RV Ctr, to Potato Creek SP(20mi), airport, st police

62mm eastern/central time zone line

56mm service area both lanes, BP/diesel, DQ, McDonald's, cookies, phone, RV dump, litter barrel

49 IN 39, to La Porte, **N...lodging:** Hampton Inn, **S...lodging:** Cassidy Motel/RV park, **4mi S...gas:** Mobil/diesel, **lodging:** Blue Heron Motel, Holiday Inn Express, Super 8

39 US 421, to Michigan City, Westville, **5 mi N...lodging:** Hampton Inn, Holiday Inn, Knight's Inn, **other:** Premium Outlets/famous brands, **S...**Purdue U North Cent

38mm trucks only rest area both lanes, litter barrels

31 IN 49, to Chesterton, Valparaiso, **N...food:** Hilton Garden, **lodging:** Econolodge(3mi), Super 8(3mi), **other:** Sand Creek RV Park(4mi), to IN Dunes Nat Lakeshore, **S...lodging:** Hampton Inn(8mi), **other:** Yellow Brick Rd Museum/gifts

24mm toll plaza

23 Portage, Port of Indiana, **N...food:** Marko's Rest., **lodging:** Comfort Inn, Holiday Inn Express, **2 mi N...gas:** Marathon, Shell, **lodging:** Day's Inn, $Inn, Ramada Inn, Super 8, **S...gas:** Amoco, Marathon, **food:** Burger King, Dunkin Donuts, First Wok Chinese, KFC, McDonald's, Subway, Wendy's, **other:** Family$, GNC, Town&Country Mkt/24hr, USPO, Walgreen

22mm service area both lanes, info, gas: BP/diesel, food: Fazoli's, Hardee's, other: playground

21mm I-90 and I-80 run together eb, separate wb. **I-80 runs with I-94 wb. For I-80 exits 1 through 15, see Indiana Interstate 94.**

21 I-94 E to Detroit, I-80/94 W, US 6, IN 51, Lake Station, **N...gas:** Dunes Trkstp/diesel/@ , Flying J/diesel/24hr/@ , Pilot/diesel/24hr/@ , TA/Subway/diesel/24hr/@ , **food:** McDonald's, Ponderosa, Wing Wah Chinese, **other:** Aldi Foods, Buick, Parts+, truckwash, **S...gas:** Mobil, Pilot/Subway/diesel/24hr/@ , Shell, **food:** Burger King, DQ, Ruben's Café, **other:** Walgreen

17 I-65 S, US 12, US 20, Dunes Hwy, to Indianapolis, no facilities

15 IN 53, Broadway, to Gary, no facilities

14a Grant St, to Gary, **S...**HOSPITAL

10 IN 912, Cline Ave, to Gary, **N...**casino

5 US 41, Calumet Ave, to Hammond, **S...gas:** Marathon, Speedway, **food:** Arby's, Aurelio's Pizza, Dunkin Donuts, Johnel's Rest., KFC, McDonald's, Taco Bell, White Castle, **lodging:** American Inn, Ramada Inn, Super 8, **other:** Aldi Foods, AutoZone, Murray's Parts, Walgreen

3 IN 912, Cline Ave, to Hammond, to Gary Reg Airport, **S...gas:** Shell

1mm toll plaza

1mm US 12, US 20, 106th St, Indianapolis Blvd, **N...gas:** BP/diesel/24hr, Mobil, Shell/diesel, **other:** casino, **S...food:** Burger King, Giappo's Pizza, KFC, McDonald's, **other:** Jewel-Osco

0mm Indiana/Illinois state line

Interstate 94

E ↕ W

Exit # Services

46mm Indiana/Michigan state line

43mm Welcome Ctr wb, full(handicapped)facilities, info, phone, picnic tables, litter barrels, vending, petwalk

40b a US 20, US 35, to Michigan City, **N...food:** McDonald's, **other:** HOSPITAL, **S...gas:** Speedway/diesel

34b a US 421, to Michigan City, **N...gas:** BP/diesel, Clark, Meijer/diesel/24hr, Mobil/diesel, Shell, Speedway/diesel, **food:** Applebee's, Arby's, Bob Evans, Buffalo Wings, Burger King, Chili's, Damon's, Denny's, El Bracero Mexican, Godfather's, KFC, King Gyro, McDonald's, Micro Brewery, Pizza Hut, Popeye's, Red Lobster, Ryan's, Schoop's Rest., Steak'n Shake, Subway, Taco Bell, Wendy's, **lodging:** Comfort Inn, Hampton Inn, Holiday Inn Express, Knight's Inn, Red Roof Inn, Super 8, Travel Inn, **other:** HOSPITAL, Aldi Foods, AutoZone, $Tree, JC Penney, Jo-Ann Fabrics, Lowe's Whse, OfficeMax, Parts+, Radio Shack, Wal-Mart/auto, **S...gas:** Gas City, **other:** Buick/Pontiac/GMC, Harley-Davidson

29mm weigh sta both lanes

26b a IN 49, Chesterton, **N...**to IN Dunes SP, Sand Cr Camping, **S...gas:** BP/White Castle, Shell/24hr, Speedway, **food:** Arby's, Burger King, Dunkin Donuts, KFC, Little Caesar's, LJ Silver, McDonald's, Pizza Hut, Subway, Taco Bell, Wendy's, **lodging:** Econolodge, Hilton Garden(3mi), Super 8, **other:** MEDICAL CARE, Jewel-Osco, K-Mart, Walgreen, to Valparaiso

22b a US 20, Burns Harbor, **N...gas:** Steel City Express/diesel/@ , TA/Subway/diesel/rest./24hr/@ , **other:** Blue Beacon, **S...gas:** Mobil, Pilot/McDonald's/Subway/diesel/24hr/@ , **other:** Camp-Land RV Ctr, Chevrolet, Chrysler/Dodge/Jeep, Ford/Mercury, Toyota

Interstate 94

19 IN 249, Portage, to Port of IN, **N...gas:** Family Express/diesel, **S...gas:** Marathon/24hr, Shell/24hr, **food:** Denny's, **lodging:** Comfort Inn, Day's Inn, Hampton Inn, Holiday Inn Express, Ramada Inn, Super 8, **2 mi S...food:** Burger King, Subway, Wendy's

16 access to I-80/90 toll road E, I-90 toll road W, IN 51N, Ripley St

I-94/I-80 run together wb

15b US 6W, IN 51, **N...gas:** Flying J/diesel/24hr/@, Pilot/diesel/24hr/@, TA/diesel/24hr/@, **food:** McDonald's, **other:** Blue Beacon, **N on US 20...gas:** Dunes/diesel repair, **food:** Ponderosa, Wing Wah Chinese, **other:** Aldi Foods, Buick, Parts+, Pennzoil

a US 6E, IN 51S, to US 20, **S...gas:** Mobil/diesel, Pilot/Subway/diesel/24hr/@, Shell, **food:** Burger King, DQ, Reuben's Café

13 Central Ave(from eb), no facilities

12b I-65 N, to Gary and toll road

a I-65 S(from wb), to Indianapolis

11 I-65 S(from eb)

10b a IN 53, Broadway, **N...gas:** Citgo, Marathon/24hr, **food:** Broadway BBQ, **S...gas:** BP/24hr, Citgo, **food:** DQ, Rally's

9b a Grant St, **N...gas:** Citgo, **food:** Chicago Hotdogs, **other:** Walgreen, **S...gas:** Citgo, Flying J/Cookery/diesel/24hr/@, Steel City/diesel/rest./24hr, **food:** Burger King, Church's, KFC, McDonald's, Subway, **other:** Aldi Foods, AutoZone, Firestone/auto, Ford, US Factory Outlets

6 Burr St, **N...gas:** BP/24hr, Pilot/Subway/diesel/24hr/@, TA/Pizza Hut/Taco Bell/diesel/24hr/@, **food:** Rico's Pizza, **S...gas:** Shell/diesel/24hr

5b a IN 912, Cline Ave, **S...gas:** BP, Clark, Shell, Speedway/Subway, **food:** Arby's, DQ, Fannie May Candies, Jedi's Garden Rest., KFC, McDonald's, Pizza Hut, Popeye's, White Castle, **lodging:** Hammond Inn, Motel 6, Super 8, K-Mart, Radio Shack

3b a Kennedy Ave, **N...gas:** Clark, Speedway, **food:** Burger King, Domino's, McDonald's, **other:** NAPA AutoCare, Walgreen, **S...gas:** Citgo, Speedway, **food:** Cracker Barrel, DQ, Firehouse Gyros, Squigi's Pizza, Subway, Wendy's, **lodging:** Courtyard, Fairfield Inn, Residence Inn, **other:** IN Welcome Ctr, Radio Shack

2b a US 41S, IN 152N, Indianapolis Blvd, **N...gas:** Luke's, SavAStop, Shell, **food:** Arby's, Dunkin Donuts, Papa John's, Schoop's Burgers, Wheel Rest., Woodmar Rest., **other: S...gas:** Pilot/Subway/diesel/24hr/@, Thornton, **food:** Blue Top Drive-In, Burger King, Steer Rest., Taco Bell, TopNotch Rest., **lodging:** AmeriHost, **other:** Aldi Foods, $General, K-Mart, Mr Transmission, Ultra Foods

1b a US 41N, Calumet Ave, **N...gas:** BP/Subway/diesel, Gas City/diesel, Marathon, **other:** Dodge, Firestone/auto, Walgreen, **S...gas:** BP, Gas City, Marathon, Shell, **food:** Arby's, Boston Mkt, Burger King, Taco Bell, Wendy's, **other:** CVS Drug

0mm Indiana/Illinois state line

Interstate 465(Indianapolis)

Exit # Services

I-465 loops around Indianapolis. Exit numbers begin/end on I-65, exit 108.

53b a I-65 N to Indianapolis, S to Louisville

52 Emerson Ave, **N...gas:** Shell/24hr, Speedway, **food:** Burger King, Domino's, KFC, LJ Silver, Subway, Taco Bell, Wendy's, **lodging:** Motel 6, **other:** HOSPITAL, CVS Drug, **S...gas:** Shell/repair, Speedway/diesel, **food:** Arby's, Blimpie, Dairy Queen, Donato's Pizza, Fazoli's, Hardee's, Hunan House, McDonald's, Papa John's, Pizza Hut, Ponderosa, Steak'n Shake, Subway, Waffle House, White Castle/24hr, **lodging:** Holiday Inn, InnAmerica, Red Roof Inn, Super 8, **other:** AutoZone, Goodyear/auto, K-Mart, Marsh Foods, Radio Shack, Walgreen

I-74 W and I-465 S run together around S Indianapolis 21 miles

49 I-74 E, US 421 S, no facilities

48 Shadeland Ave(from nb)

47 US 52 E, Brookville Rd, **E...gas:** Shell, **food:** Burger King

46 US 40, Washington St, **E...gas:** Marathon, **food:** Arby's, China Buffet, Italian Graden, Old Country Buffet, Perkins, Steak'n Shake, Subway, **other:** Ford, Osco Drug, Target, **W...gas:** Thornton's, **food:** Applebee's, Burger King, Bob Evans, ChiChi's, Don Pablo, Fazoli's, McDonald's, Pizza Hut, Pi's Chinese, Wendy's, **lodging:** Signature Inn, **other:** K-Mart, PepBoys, Pontiac/GM/Mazda, Suzuki

INDIANA

Interstate 465

Indianapolis Area

44b I-70 E, to Columbus
a I-70 W, to Indianapolis
42 US 36, IN 67 N, Pendleton Pike, **E...food:** Bennigan's, Hardee's, Papa's Rest., **lodging:** Days Inn, Sheraton, **W...gas:** Clark, Speedway, Thornton's, **food:** A&W/KFC, Arby's, Denny's, LJ Silver, McDonald's, Pizza Hut/Taco Bell, Subway, **other:** HOSPITAL, K-Mart/gas
40 56th St, Shadeland Ave, **E...gas:** Marathon, to Ft Harrison
37b a I-69, N to Ft Wayne, IN 37, **W...other:** HOSPITAL, facilities on frontage rds
35 Allisonville Rd, **N...food:** Applebee's, Hardee's, LJ Silver, McDonald's, MCL Cafeteria, **lodging:** Courtyard, **other:** Best Buy, CompUSA, Firestone/auto, JC Penney, Jo-Ann Fabrics, Kohl's, Lazarus, Marshall's, Osco Drug, mall, **S...gas:** Shell, Speedway/diesel, **food:** Bob Evans, ChuckeCheese, Hop's Brewery, Papa John's, Perkins/24hr, White Castle, **lodging:** Signature Inn, **other:** Circuit City, Kroger, **S on 82nd...food:** PrimeTime Grill, **other:** Marsh Foods
33 IN 431, Keystone Ave, **N...gas:** BP/McDonald's, Marathon/diesel, Shell, **food:** Arby's, Bob Evans, Burger King, Steak&Ale, Subway, **lodging:** Motel 6, **other:** BMW, Chevrolet/Isuzu, Infiniti, Nissan, Toyota **S...food:** Cooker, Keystone Grill, **lodging:** AmeriSuites, Marriott, Sheraton, Westin Suites, **other:** Champ's, Kohl's, mall, **1 mi S on 82nd...food:** Applebee's, Boston Mkt, Chili's, Don Pablo, O' Charley's, Logan's Roadhouse, LoneStar Steaks, Pizzeria Uno, Prime Time Grill, Schlotsky's, Shell's Seafood, Subway, **other:** Barnes&Noble, OfficeMax
31 US 31, Meridian St, **N...lodging:** Residence Inn, Signature Inn, SpringHill Suites, Wyndham Garden, **other:** HOSPITAL, **S...gas:** Marathon, Shell/diesel, **food:** McDonald's
27 US 421 N, Michigan Rd, **N...food:** Dairy Queen, McDonald's, **lodging:** Red Roof Inn, **other:** Chevrolet, **S...gas:** BP, Marathon, Shell, Sunoco, **food:** Arby's, Bob Evans, Boston Mkt, ChiChi's, China Buffet, Denny's, IHOP, Max&Erma's, O'Charley's, Outback Steaks, Pizza Hut, Qdoba Mexican, Ruby Tuesday, Schlosky's, Steak'n Shake, Subway, Taco Bell, Texas Roadhouse, Wendy's, White Castle, Wildcat Brewing Co/rest., Yen Ching Rest., **lodging:** Best Western, Comfort Inn, $Inn, Drury Inn, Embassy Suites, Extended Stay America, Fairfield Inn, Holiday Inn Select, HomeGate Inn, InTown Suites, Microtel, Quality Inn, Residence Inn, Signature Inn, Wellesley Inn, **other:** Aamco, Costco/gas, Cub Foods, CVS Drug, Discount Tire, $General, Firestone, Lowe's Whse, Office Depot, OfficeMax, PepBoys, Radio Shack, Staples, Wal-Mart SuperCtr/24hr
25 I-465 W, no facilities
23 86th St, **E...gas:** Shell/24hr, Speedway, **food:** Arby's, Burger King, Quizno's, **lodging:** MainStay Suites, Suburban Lodge, **other:** HOSPITAL
21 71st St, **E...gas:** Amoco, **food:** Galahad's Café, Hardee's, McDonald's, Steak'n Shake, Subway, **lodging:** Clarion Inn, Courtyard, Hampton Inn, **other:** DENTIST cleaners
20 I-65, N to Chicago, S to Indianapolis
19 56th St(from nb), **E...gas:** Citgo/7-11, Speedway/diesel
17 38th St, **E...gas:** BP, Marathon, Shell/24hr, **food:** ChiChi's, China Chef, DQ, Olive Garden, Subway, **lodging:** Day's Inn, **other:** Aamco, Circuit City, Home Depot, Kroger, Osco Drug, **W...food:** Arby's, Burger King, Chili's, Cracker Barrel, Don Pablo, McDonald's, Mtn Jack's Rest., Ruby Tuesday, Taco Bell, TGIFriday, **lodging:** Country Hearth Inn, Signature Inn, **other:** Marsh Foods, Target

I-74 E and I-465 run together around S Indianapolis 21 miles

16b I-74 W, to Peoria
a US 136, to Speedway, **N...gas:** Bigfoot, BP, Shell, Thornton's/24hr, **food:** Applebee's, Blimpie, Burger King, Denny's, Dunkin Donuts, Grindstone Charlie's, Hardee's, KFC, LJ Silver, McDonald's, Rally's, Subway, Taco Bell, Wendy's, White Castle, **lodging:** $Inn, Motel 6, Red Roof, Super 8, **other:** Firestone, Goodyear, Kohl's, Kroger, Marsh Foods, MensWhse, Old Navy, Sears, Speedway Museum, **S...lodging:** Clarion
14b a 10th St, **N...gas:** Marathon, Shell, **food:** China Wok, Pizza Hut, Wendy's, **other:** HOSPITAL, Cub Food/24hr, Lowe's Whse, **S...gas:** BP, GA/Subway, Shell, Speedway/24hr, **food:** Arby's, Fazoli's, Hardee's, Little Caesar's, McDonald's, Noble Roman's, Pizza Hut, Rally's, Taco Bell, **other:** CVS Drug, $General

Interstate 465

Indianapolis Area

13b a US 36, Rockville Rd, **N...gas:** Citgo/Burger King, **lodging:** Comfort Inn, Sleep Inn, Wingate Inn, **other:** Sam's Club, **S... gas:** Speedway/24hr, **food:** Bob Evans, **lodging:** Best Western

12b a US 40 E, Washington St, **N...gas:** BP, **food:** Burger King, Church's, Fazoli's, McDonald's, Papa John's, Taco Bell, White Castle, **other:** Advance Parts, AutoZone, $General, Family$, Kroger, Osco Drug, U-Haul, Walgreen, transmissions, **S...gas:** Bigfoot/24hr, Phillips 66/Noble Roman's/TCBY/diesel, Shell, Thornton/24hr, **food:** Arby's, Burger King, Hardee's, KFC, LJ Silver, McDonald's, Omelet Shoppe, Pizza Hut, Steak'n Shake, Wendy's, **lodging:** $Inn, **other:** Aamco, Goodyear, K-Mart, Radio Shack, Target, TireBarn

11b a Airport Expressway, **N...lodging:** Adam's Mark Hotel, Baymont Inn, Day's Inn, Extended Stay America, Motel 6, **S...gas:** BP, **food:** Burger King, **lodging:** Hilton, Holiday Inn, Ramada Inn

9b a I-70, E to Indianapolis, W to Terre Haute

8 IN 67 S, Kentucky Ave, **N...**HOSPITAL, **S... gas:** BP/diesel, Marathon, Speedway, Shell, **food:** Big Boy, Denny's, Hardee's, KFC

7 Mann Rd(from wb), **N...**HOSPITAL

4 IN 37 S, Harding St, **N...gas:** Mr Fuel/diesel, Pilot/Wendy's/DQ/diesel/24hr/@, **food:** Omelet Shoppe, **lodging:** Best Inn, $Inn, Super 8, **other:** Blue Beacon, **S...gas:** Flying J/Conoco/diesel/LP/rest./24hr/@, Marathon, **food:** Hardee's, McDonald's, Taco Bell, Waffle&Steak, White Castle, **lodging:** Knight's Inn, **other:** Freightliner

2b a US 31, IN 37, **N...gas:** BP/24hr, **food:** Arby's, Burger King, Dutch Oven, Golden Wok, Hardee's, KFC, King Ribs, J's Burger, Laughner's Cafeteria, LJ Silver, McDonald's, MCL Cafeteria, Old Country Buffet, Papa John's, Pizza Hut, Ponderosa, Rally's, Steak&Ale, Steak'n Shake, Taco Bell, Wendy's, White Castle, **other:** Aldi Foods, AutoTire, AutoWorks, AutoZone, Chrysler/Jeep, CVS Drug, Dodge, $General, Family$, Firestone, Ford, Goodyear, Hancock Fabrics, Jo-Ann Fabrics, Kroger, Lincoln/Mercury, Marsh Foods, Office Depot, Osco Drug, Radio Shack, Save-A-Lot, Target, U-Haul, **S...gas:** Bigfoot, Shell, Sunoco/Subway, **food:** Applebee's, Bob Evans, Denny's, HH Smorgasbord, McDonald's, Red Lobster, Wendy's, **lodging:** Comfort Inn, Day's Inn, Holiday Inn Express, Quality Inn, Ramada Ltd, Red Roof Inn, Travelodge

53b a I-65 N to Indianapolis, S to Louisville

I-465 loops around Indianapolis. Exit numbers begin/end on I-65, exit 108.

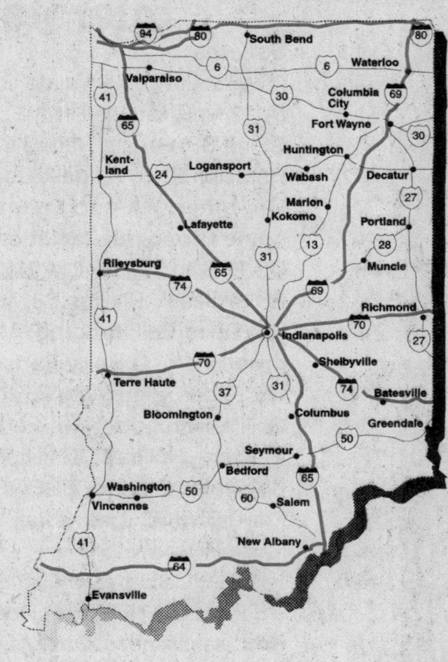

Interstate 469(Ft Wayne)

Ft Wayne

N ↕ S

Exit #	Services
31c b a	I-69, US 27 S. I-469 begins/ends.
29.5mm	St Joseph River
29b a	Maplecrest Rd, **W...gas:** BP/DQ/Subway/diesel
25	IN 37, to Ft Wayne, **W...gas:** Meijer/diesel/24hr, **food:** Applebee's, Kohl's, Wal-Mart SuperCtr/24hr, Steak'n Shake
21	US 24 E, no facilities
19b a	US 30 E, to Ft Wayne, **E...gas:** Sunoco/Taco Bell/diesel, **food:** Wendy's, **W...gas:** Citgo/diesel/mart, **food:** Arby's(2mi), KFC(1mi), Golden Gate Chinese, Richard's Rest., Zesto Drive-In, **lodging:** Holiday Inn Express, **other:** $General, Scott's Foods
17	Minnich Rd, no facilities
15	Tillman Rd, no facilities
13	Marion Center Rd, no facilities
11	US 27, US 33 S, Ft Wayne, to Decatur, no facilities
10.5mm	St Marys River
9	Winchester Rd, no facilities
6	IN 1, Ft Wayne, to Bluffton, **W...**to airport
2	Indianapolis Rd, **W...**to airport
1	Lafayette Ctr Rd, no facilities

IOWA

Interstate 29

N ↕ S

Sioux City

Exit #	Services
152mm	Iowa/South Dakota state line, Big Sioux River
151	IA 12 N, Riverside Blvd, **E...gas:** Casey's, **other:** to Stone SP, Pecaut Nature Ctr
149	Hamilton Blvd, **E...gas:** Conoco, **lodging:** Hamilton Inn, **other:** AAA, to Briar Cliff Coll, **W...Iowa Welcome Ctr sb, full facilities,** Riverboat Museum
148	US 77 S, to S Sioux City, Nebraska, **W...gas:** Conoco/A&W/diesel, Phillips 66, **food:** McDonald's, Pizza Hut, Taco Bell, **lodging:** Marina Inn, Regency Inn, **other:** Ford, O'Reilly Parts
147b	US 20 bus, Sioux City, **E...food:** Arby's, Burger King, Chili's, Hardee's, KFC, Perkins/24hr, **lodging:** Best Western, Holiday Inn, Hilton Inn, **other:** HOSPITAL, Chevrolet, Staples, USPO, Walgreen,
a	Floyd Blvd, **E...gas:** Total, **W...**to Riverboat Casino
146.5mm	Floyd River
144 b	I-129 W, US 20 W, US 75 S, no facilities
a	US 20 E, US 75 N, to Ft Dodge, **1 mi E on Lakeport Rd...gas:** Amoco, Casey's, Shell, **food:** Applebee's, Burger King, Coyote Canyon Steaks, Garfield's Rest., Hardee's, KFC, LJ Silver, Nap's BBQ, Outback Steaks, Piccadilly's, Pizza Hut, Red Lobster, **lodging:** Comfort Inn, Fairfield Inn, Holiday Inn Express, **other:** Buick/Honda/Isuzu, HobbyLobby, Hy-Vee Foods/24hr, Jo-Ann Fabrics/crafts, Michael's, Sears/auto, Target, Younkers, mall
143	US 75 N, Singing Hills Blvd, **E...gas:** Cenex/@, Texaco/diesel/motel/café/24hr/@, **food:** McDonald's, **lodging:** AmericInn, Baymont Inn, Day's Inn, **other:** Sam's Club, Wal-Mart SuperCtr/gas/24hr, Sgt Floyd Mon, **W...gas:** Amoco/diesel/motel/café/24hr/@, **food:** Wendy's, Super 8, **other:** Kenworth/Peterbilt, truckwash
141	D38, Sioux Gateway Airport, **E...gas:** Casey's, Conoco, Phillips 66/diesel, Shell, **food:** China Taste, Godfather's, Steak Block Rest., Subway, **lodging:** Econolodge, **other:** Fairway Foods, mall, **W...lodging:** Motel 6, **other:** museum
139mm	**rest area both lanes, full(handicapped)facilities, phone, info, picnic tables, litter barrels, RV dump**
135	Port Neal Landing, no facilities
134	Salix, **E...gas:** Total, **W...**camping
132mm	weigh sta sb
127	IA 141, Sloan, **E...gas:** Amoco, Shell/diesel, **lodging:** Homestead Inn, WinnaVegas Inn, **3 mi W...**to Winnebago Indian Res/casino
120	to Whiting, **W...**camping
112	IA 175, Onawa, **E...gas:** Conoco/Subway/diesel/@, Phillips 66/diesel, Janz Rest., **food:** McDonald's, Michael's Rest., Oehler Bros Rest., **lodging:** Super 8, **other:** HOSPITAL, Chevrolet/Buick/GMC, Chrysler/Jeep/Dodge, Interchange RV Park, NAPA, Pamida, **2 mi W...other:** KOA, Lewis&Clark SP, Keelboat Exhibit
110mm	**rest area both lanes, full(handicapped)facilities, phone, info, picnic tables, litter barrels, petwalk, RV dump**
105	E60, Blencoe, **1/2 mi E...gas:** TR's Gas
96mm	Little Sioux River
95	IA 301, Little Sioux, **E...gas:** G&N OneStop, **other:** Loess Hills SF(9mi), **W...**Woodland RV Camp
92mm	Soldier River
91.5mm	**rest area both lanes, litter barrels, no facilities**
89	IA 127, Mondamin, **1 mi E...gas:** Jiffy Mart/diesel
82	IA 300, F50, Modale, **1 mi W...gas:** Cenex
80mm	**rest area sb, full(handicapped)facilities, info, phone, picnic tables, litter barrels, RV dump**
78.5mm	**rest area nb, full(handicapped)facilities, info, phone, picnic tables, litter barrels, RV dump**
75	US 30, Missouri Valley, **E...Iowa Welcome Ctr(5mi), gas:** Sinclair, Texaco/diesel/24hr/@, **food:** Arby's, McDonald's, Subway, **lodging:** Hillside Motel(2mi), **other:** HOSPITAL(2mi), Ford/Mercury, to Steamboat Exhibit, **W...gas:** Amoco/diesel, Conoco/Kopper, Kettle, **food:** Burger King, Oehler Bros Café, **lodging:** Day's Inn, Rath Inn, Super 8, **other:** Chevrolet/Pontiac/Buick, Chrysler/Jeep/Dodge
73.5mm	weigh sta both lanes
72.5mm	Boyer River
72	IA 362, Loveland, **E...gas:** Conoco/diesel, **W...**to Wilson Island SP(6mi)
71	I-680 E, to Des Moines, no facilities, **I-29 S & I-680 W run together 10 mi**
66	Honey Creek, **W...gas:** Phillips 66/diesel/LP/Iowa Feed&Grain Co Rest., **other:** camping
61b	I-680 W, to N Omaha, **I-29 N & I-680 E run together 10 mi, W...**Mormon Trail Ctr
a	IA 988, to Crescent, **E...gas:** Phillips 66, **other:** to ski area
56	IA 192 S(sb only, exits left), Council Bluffs, **E...lodging:** Super 7 Inn, **other:** HOSPITAL
55	N 25th, Council Bluffs, **E...gas:** Pump'n Munch, Sinclair/24hr, **lodging:** Travelodge
54b	N 35th St(from nb), Council Bluffs, **E on Broadway... food:** Arby's, Burger King, Wendy's, **lodging:** Best Western, **other:** Honda
a	G Ave(from sb), Council Bluffs, **E...gas:** Shell, **W...**auto repair
53b	I-480 W, US 6, to Omaha, no facilities
a	9th Ave, S 37th Ave, Council Bluffs, **E...gas:** Phillips 66, Shell, Total, **lodging:** Day's Inn, **W...other:** Harrah's Casino/hotel, RiverBoat Casino, camping
52	Nebraska Ave, **E...gas:** Conoco/diesel, **lodging:** Comfort Suites, **W...lodging:** AmeriStar Hotel/casino, Hampton Inn, Holiday Inn, **other:** RiverBoat Casino
51	I-80 W, to Omaha, no facilities

I-29 and I-80 run together 3 miles. See Iowa Interstate 80, exits 1b-3.

Council Bluffs

48	I-80 E(from nb), to Des Moines, **E...**HOSPITAL

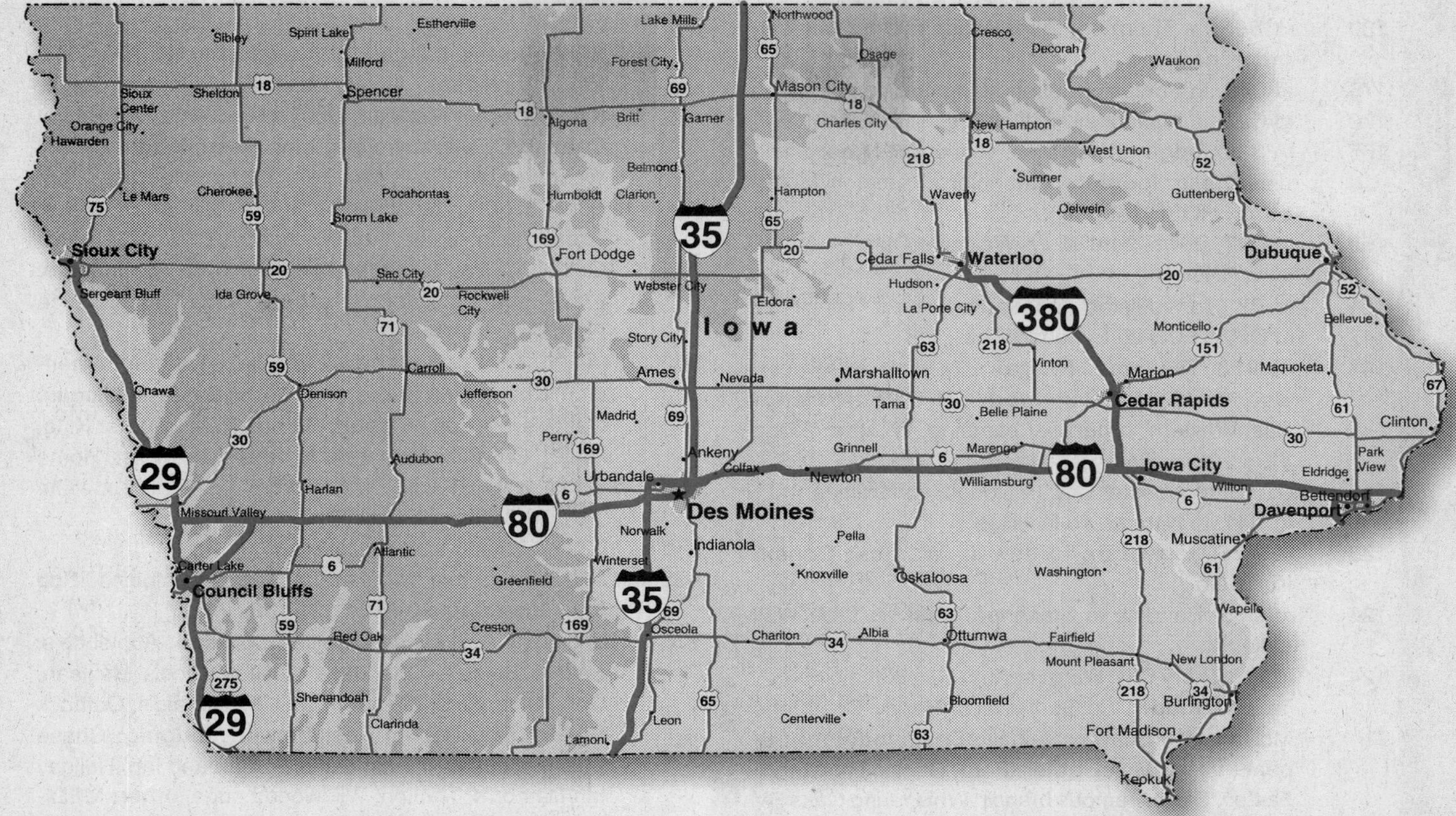

Interstate 29

47	US 275, IA 92, Lake Manawa, **E...gas:** Phillips 66, **other:** Iowa School for the Deaf
42	IA 370, to Bellevue, **W...other:** K&B Saddlery, to Offutt AFB, camping
38mm	**rest area both lanes, full(handicapped)facilities, phone, info, picnic tables, litter barrels, RV dump, petwalk**
35	US 34 E, to Glenwood, **E...lodging:** Western Inn(4mi), **W...gas:** Amoco/diesel, **lodging:** Bluff View Motel, **other:** Ford
32	US 34 W, Pacific Jct, to Plattsmouth, no facilities
24	L31, Bartlett, to Tabor, no facilities
20	IA 145, Thurman, no facilities
15	J26, Percival, **1-2 mi E...**gas/diesel
11.5mm	weigh sta nb
10	IA 2, to Nebraska City, Sidney, **E...**to Waubonsie SP(5mi), **W...gas:** Conoco/diesel/@, Sapp/diesel/rest./24hr/@, Shell/diesel/24hr/@, **lodging:** Super 8, **6 mi W on US 75...food:** A&W/Amigo's, Arby's, Burger King, McDonald's, Pizza Hut, Valentino's, **lodging:** Best Western, Day's Inn, **other:** CountryMart Foods, Pamida, Factory Stores of America/famous brands, to Arbor Lodge SP, camping(4mi)
1	IA 333, Hamburg, **1 mi E...gas:** Casey's/diesel, **food:** Pizza Hut, **lodging:** Hamburg Motel, **other:** HOSPITAL, Soda Fountain
0mm	Iowa/Missouri state line

Interstate 35

Exit #	Services
219mm	Iowa/Minnesota state line
214	rd 105, to Northwood, Lake Mills, **W...Welcome Ctr both lanes, full(handicapped)facilities, picnic tables, litter barrels, vending, petwalk, RV dump,** Cenex/Burger King/diesel/24hr/@
212mm	weigh sta both lanes
208	rd A38, to Joice, Kensett, no facilities
203	IA 9, to Manly, Forest City, **W...gas:** Amoco/diesel, **other:** HOSPITAL, to Pilot Knob SP
202mm	Winnebago River
197	rd B20, **8 mi E...**Lime Creek Nature Ctr
196mm	parking area both lanes, litter barrels, no facilities
194	US 18, Clear Lake, to Mason City, **E...**HOSPITAL(8mi), **W...gas:** Casey's, Conoco/Taco John's/diesel/@, Kum&Go/@, Shell/Wendy's/diesel, **food:** Bennigan's, Burger King, Culver's, Dairy Queen, Denny's, KFC/Taco Bell, McDonald's, Perkins/24hr, Pizza Hut, Subway, **lodging:** AmericInn, Best Western/rest., Budget Inn, Lake Country Inn, Microtel
193	rd B35, Emery, to Mason City, **E...gas:** Amoco/diesel/24hr, **food:** Happy Chef/24hr, **lodging:** Super 8, **W...gas:** Phillips 66, **lodging:** Heartland Inn(3mi), **other:** Chevrolet, Ford, antiques, to Clear Lake SP
190	US 18, rd 27 E, to Mason City, no facilities
188	rd B43, to Burchinal, no facilities
182	rd B60, Swaledale, to Rockwell, no facilities

Clear Lake

IOWA

Interstate 35

N ↕ S

180 rd B65, to Thornton, **2 mi W...gas:** Cenex/diesel, **other:** camping
176 rd C13, to Sheffield, Belmond, no facilities
170 rd C25, to Alexander, no facilities
165 IA 3, to **lodging:** Hampton, Clarion, **E...gas:** Shell/diesel/rest., **lodging:** AmericInn, Hampton Motel, **other:** HOSPITAL(7mi)
159 rd C47, Dows, **2 mi W...**IA Welcome Ctr
155mm Iowa River
151 rd R75, to Woolstock, no facilities
147 rd D20, to US 20 E, no facilities
144 rd 928, Williams, **E...gas:** Phillips 66/diesel/Boondocks Motel/@, **food:** TH Café, **lodging:** Best Western, **other:** RV camping, **W...gas:** Flying J/Conoco/diesel/rest./24hr/@
142b a US 20, to Webster City, Ft Dodge, no facilities
139 rd D41, to Kamrar, no facilities
133 IA 175, Ellsworth, to Jewell, **W...gas:** Cenex, Kum&Go
128 rd D65, Randall, to Stanhope, **5 mi W...**Little Wall Lake Pk
124 rd 115, Story City, **W...gas:** Kum&Go/diesel/24hr/@, Texaco, **food:** DQ, Godfather's, Happy Chef/24hr, McDonald's, Subway, Valhalla Rest., **lodging:** Super 8, Viking Motel, **other:** Ford, Gookin RV Ctr, VF Factory Stores/famous brands, Whispering Oaks RV Park
123 IA 221, rd E18, to Roland, McCallsburg, no facilities
120mm rest area nb, full(handicapped)facilities, info, phone, picnic tables, litter barrels, vending, RV dump/scenic prairie area sb, no facilities
119mm rest area sb, full(handicapped)facilities, phone, picnic tables, litter barrels, vending, RV dump
116 rd E29, to Story, **7 mi W...**Story Co Conservation Ctr
113 13th St, Ames, **W...gas:** BP/Arby's/diesel/@, Kum&Go/Burger King/diesel, **food:** Starlite Village Rest., **lodging:** Best Western/rest., Holiday Inn Express, **other:** HOSPITAL, Harley-Davidson, to USDA Vet Labs, ISU
111b a US 30, Ames, to Nevada, **E...**camping(11mi), **W...gas:** Shell/diesel/rest./@, **food:** Embers Rest., **lodging:** AmericInn, Comfort Inn, Country Inn Suites, Hampton Inn, Heartland Inn, Microtel, Super 8, **other:** to IA St U
109mm S Skunk River
106mm weigh sta both lanes
102 IA 210, to Slater, **3 mi W...food:** DQ
96 to Elkhart, **W...**to Big Creek SP(11mi), Saylorville Lake
94mm rest area both lanes, full(handicapped)facilities, info, phone, picnic tables, litter barrels, vending, petwalk

Ames

92 1st St, Ankeny, **W...gas:** BP/diesel/24hr, Kum&Go, QT, **food:** Applebee's, Arby's, Blue Sky Creamery, Burger King, Cazador Mexican, Duffy's Rest., Fazoli's, Happy Chef, KFC, Subway, Village Inn Rest., **lodging:** Best Western/rest., Day's Inn, Fairfield Inn, Heartland Inn, Super 8, **other:** Goodyear/auto, O'Reilly Parts, Staples, Tires+, auto repair, **1mi W...gas:** BP, Casey's, **food:** Golden Corral, LJ Silver, MaidRite Café, McDonald's, Pizza Hut, Taco John's, **other:** HOSPITAL, Hy-Vee Food/drug, NAPA
90 IA 160, Ankeny, **E...food:** Chip's Diner, **lodging:** AmericInn, Country Inn Suites, Holiday Inn Express, **W...gas:** Casey's, Phillips 66, **food:** B-bops Rest., Burger King, Chili's, Culver's, McDonald's, **other:** Chevrolet, Home Depot, Kohl's, Radio Shack, Target, Wal-Mart SuperCtr/24hr, to Saylorville Lake(5mi)
87b a I-235, I-35 and I-80, no facilities
I-35 and I-80 run together 14 mi around NW Des Moines. **See Iowa Interstate 80 exits 124-136.**
72c University Ave, **E...gas:** Phillips 66, **food:** Applebee's, Bakers Square, Cheddar's, Chili's, Cuco's Mexican, Don Pablo, KFC, Macaroni Grill, McDonald's, Outback Steaks, RockBottom Rest./brewery, **lodging:** Chase Suites, Courtyard, Fairfield Inn, Heartland Inn, Holiday Inn/Damon's, The Inn, Wildwood Lodge, **other:** MEDICAL CARE, Barnes&Noble, Best Buy, CompUSA, K-Mart, Kohl's, Lowe's Whse, Marshall's, SportMart, World Mkt, **W...gas:** Amoco, Kum&Go/Burger King, QT, **food:** Cracker Barrel, **lodging:** Baymont Inn, Best Western, Country Inn Suites, **other:** HOSPITAL
b I-80 W no facilities
a I-235 E, to Des Moines
71 new exit
69b a Grand Ave, W Des Moines, no facilities
68.5mm Racoon River
68 IA 5, **7 mi E...lodging:** Crystal Inn, Hampton Inn, **other:** to airport, to Walnut Woods SP
65 G14, Cumming, to Norwalk, **14 mi W...**John Wayne Birthplace, museum
61mm North River
56 IA 92, to Indianola, Winterset, **W...gas:** Shell/diesel/café/@, Total/diesel, **other:** repair
56mm Middle River
53mm rest area nb, litter barrels, no facilities
52 G50, St Charles, St Marys, **14 mi W...**John Wayne Birthplace, museum
51mm rest area sb, litter barrels, no facilities
47 rd G64, to Truro, no facilities
45.5mm South River
43 rd 207, New Virginia, **E...gas:** Sinclair/diesel, **W...**Total/diesel/@
36 rd 152, to US 69, **3 mi E...**lodging
34 Clay St, Osceola, **W...**Lakeside Casino Resort/camping

Des Moines

Interstate 35

N ↕ S

33 US 34, Osceola, **E...gas:** BP/diesel, Casey's, Cenex/diesel/café/24hr/@, Kum&Go, Shell/diesel/rest./@, **food:** Family Table Rest., Hardee's, McDonald's, Pizza Hut, Subway, 3rd Rail Grill, **lodging:** Best Western, Blue Haven Motel(2mi), Super 8, **other:** HOSPITAL, Ford, Chrysler/Plymouth/Dodge/Jeep, Hy-Vee Foods, O'Reilly Parts, Pamida, st patrol, **W...food:** KFC/Taco Bell, **lodging:** AmericInn

32mm rest area both lanes, full(handicapped)facilities, phone, picnic tables, litter barrels, vending, petwalk, RV dump

30mm weigh sta both lanes

29 rd H45, no facilities

22 rd 258, Van Wert, no facilities

18 rd J20, to Grand River, no facilities

12 rd 2, Decatur City, Leon, **E...gas:** Phillips 66, Shell/diesel/rest./@, **5 mi E...lodging:** Little River Motel, **other:** HOSPITAL

7.5mm Grand River

7mm Welcome Ctr nb/rest area sb, full(handicapped)facilities, info, phone, picnic tables, litter barrels, vending, petwalk, RV dump

4 US 69, Lamoni, to Davis City, **E...**to 9 Eagles SP(10mi), **W...gas:** BP/Kum&Go/diesel, Casey's(2mi), Cenex/diesel(2mi), **food:** Subway(2mi), **lodging:** Chief Lamoni Motel, Super 8, **other:** antiques, IA Welcome Ctr

0mm Iowa/Missouri state line

Interstate 80

E ↕ W

Exit # Services

307mm Iowa/Illinois state line, Mississippi River

306 US 67, to Le Claire, **N...Welcome Ctr wb, full(handicapped)facilities, picnic tables, litter barrels, phone, petwalk, food:** Steventon's Rest., **lodging:** Comfort Inn, Super 8, **other:** Slagle Foods, **1 mi N...gas:** BP, Mobil, **food:** A&W, **other:** Buffalo Bill Museum, **S...gas:** BP/diesel

301 Middle Rd, to Bettendorf, no facilities

300mm rest area both lanes, full(handicapped)facilities, phone, picnic tables, litter barrels, vending, petwalk, RV dump

Davenport

298 I-74 E, to Peoria, **S...other:** to HOSPITAL, st patrol

295b a US 61, Brady St, to Davenport, **N...gas:** BP, to Scott CP, **S...gas:** BP, Shell, **food:** Country Kitchen, Cracker Barrel, McDonald's, ThunderBay Grille, Village Inn Rest., **lodging:** AmericInn, Best Western, Baymont Inn, Casa Loma Suites, Country Inn Suites, Day's Inn, Exel Inn, Heartland Inn, Motel 6, Residence Inn, Super 8, **1-2 mi S...gas:** BP/diesel, Shell, **food:** Burger King, ChiChi's, Country Kitchen, Ground Round, Hardee's, Hooters, LoneStar Steaks, McDonald's, LJ Silver, Rudy's Tacos, Steak'n Shake, **lodging:** Holiday Inn, **other:** AutoZone, Acura, Dodge, Sears/auto, Toyota, mall

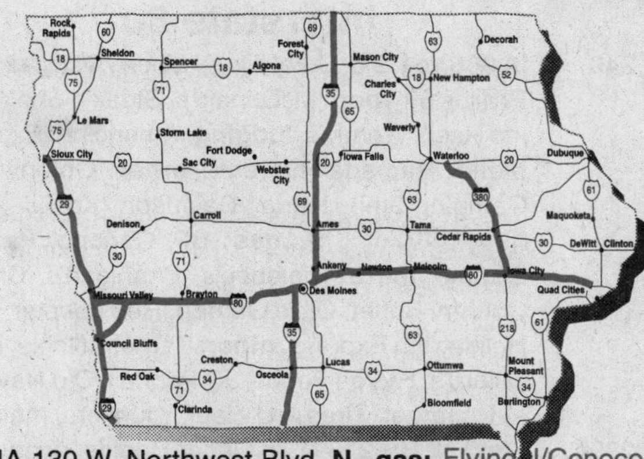

292 IA 130 W, Northwest Blvd, **N...gas:** Flying J/Conoco/diesel/LP/rest./24hr/@, **other:** Interstate RV Park(1mi), Farm&Fleet, waterpark, **S...gas:** BP/McDonald's, Fred's Gas/towing, Sinclair, **food:** Machine Shed Rest., **lodging:** Comfort Inn

290 I-280 E, to Rock Island

284 Y40, to Walcott, **N...gas:** Pilot/Arby's/diesel/24hr/@, TA/IA 80/BP/Blimpie/DQ/Wendy's/diesel/24hr/@, Phillips 66/diesel, **food:** Gramma's Kitchen, **lodging:** Comfort Inn, Super 8, **other:** Blue Beacon, Goodyear, **S...gas:** Pilot/Subway/diesel/24hr/@, **food:** McDonald's, **lodging:** Day's Inn

280 Y30, to Stockton, New Liberty, no facilities

277 Durant, **2 mi S...**food

271 US 6 W, IA 38 S, to Wilton, **S...**lodging

270mm rest area both lanes, full(handicapped)facilities, info, phone, picnic tables, litter barrels, vending, petwalk, RV dump

268mm weigh sta both lanes

267 IA 38 N, to Tipton, **N...other:** Cedar River Camping, **S...food:** The Cove Café

266mm Cedar River

265 to Atalissa, **S...gas:** Phillips 66/diesel/rest./24hr/@

259 Springdale, to West Liberty, **S...gas:** BP/diesel/24hr, **lodging:** Econolodge, **other:** KOA

254 X30, West Branch, **N...gas:** BP/diesel, Casey's, **food:** HeynQtr Steaks, Main St Rest., **other:** Jack&Jill Foods, H Hoover NHS/museum, USPO, **S...gas:** Phillips 66/diesel, **food:** McDonald's, **lodging:** Presidential Motel

249 Herbert Hoover Hwy, **S...**golf

246 IA 1, Dodge St, **N... gas:** BP/A&W/diesel, Phillips 66, **lodging:** Highlander Inn, **S...gas:** Sinclair, **food:** TGIFriday, **lodging:** Kountry Inn

Iowa City

244 Dubuque St, Iowa City, **N...**Coralville Lake, **S...**HOSPITAL, to Old Capitol

242 to Coralville, **N...food:** River City Grille, **lodging:** Hampton Inn, Holiday Inn, **S...gas:** BP, Conoco Kum&Go/diesel/@, **food:** Arby's, Big Mike's Subs, Burger King, Country Kitchen, Hardee's, KFC, LJ Silver, LoneStar Steaks, McDonald's, Old Chicago Pizza, Peking Buffet, Perkins/24hr, Pizza Hut, Subway, Taco Bell, Taco John's, **lodging:** Best Western, Big Ten Inn, Comfort Inn, Day's Inn, Econolodge, Fairfield Inn, Heartland Inn, Iowa Lodge, Motel 6, Red Roof Inn, Super 8, **other:** HOSPITAL, Toyota, Walgreen

IOWA

Interstate 80

E ↕ W

240 IA 965, to US 6, Coralville, N Liberty, **N...gas:** Conoco, Phillips 66, **food:** McDonald's, Steak'n Shake, Village Inn Rest., Wendy's, **lodging:** AmericInn, ExpressWay Motel, Ramada Inn/rest., **other:** Colony Country Camping(3mi), Harley-Davidson, Kohl's, Wal-Mart SuperCtr/24hr, **S...gas:** BP, Conoco, Phillips 66/ Blimpie, **food:** Applebee's, Bennigan's, Chili's, Old Country Buffet, Olive Garden, Red Lobster, **lodging:** Holiday Inn Express, **other:** Barnes&Noble, Best Buy, Dillard's, HyVee Foods, JC Penney, Old Navy, Sears/ auto, Target, Tires+, U-Haul, Younkers, mall

239b I-380 N, US 218 N, to Cedar Rapids, no facilities

a US 218 S, no facilities

237 Tiffin, no facilities

236mm rest area both lanes, full(handicapped)facilities, phone, picnic tables, litter barrels, vending, RV dump, petwalk

230 W38, to Oxford, **N...other:** Sleepy Hollow Camping, Colona Museum

225 US 151 N, W21 S, **N...**to Amana Colonies, **lodging:** Comfort Inn, **S...Welcome Ctr, gas:** BP, Phillips 66, **food:** Colony Village Rest., Little Amana Rest./Winery, Ox Yoke Rest., **lodging:** Day's Inn/rest, Holiday Inn, My Little Inn, Super 8

220 IA 149 S, V77 N, to Williamsburg, **N...gas:** BP, Phillips 66/diesel/@, **food:** Arby's, McDonald's, Pizza Hut, Subway, Taste Of China, **lodging:** Best Western, Crest Motel, Super 8, **other:** GNC, Tanger/famous brands, VF/famous brands, **S...lodging:** Day's Inn, Ramada Ltd

216 to Marengo, **N...gas:** Kum&Go/Texaco/diesel, **lodging:** Sudbury Court Motel(7mi), **other:** HOSPITAL

211 to Ladora, Millersburg, no facilities

208mm rest area both lanes, full(handicapped)facilities, phone, vending, picnic tables, litter barrels, petwalk

205 to Victor, no facilities

201 IA 21, to Deep River, **N...gas:** Sinclair/Nick's Rest., Texaco/diesel/24hr/@, **lodging:** Sleep Inn, **other:** RV camping, **S...gas:** KwikStar/diesel/rest./24hr/@

197 to Brooklyn, **N...gas:** BP/Amoco/diesel/@, **food:** Brooklyn-80 Rest./24hr, **other:** RV camping

191 US 63, to Montezuma, **N...gas:** Sinclair, **S...gas:** Citgo/diesel/rest./@, FuelMart/diesel/rest./24hr/@, to Fun Valley Ski Area(13mi)

182 IA 146, to Grinnell, **N...gas:** Casey's, **food:** Country Kitchen, DQ(3mi), Hardee's(3mi), KFC, Taco Bell, Taco John's, HyVee, **lodging:** Country Inn, Day's Inn, Econolodge, Super 8, **other:** HOSPITAL(4mi), Chrysler/Plymouth/Dodge/Jeep, **S...**Fun Valley Ski Area

180mm rest area both lanes, full(handicapped)facilities, phone, vending, weather info, picnic tables, litter barrels, petwalk, playground

179 IA 124, to Oakland Acres, Lynnville, no facilities

175mm N Skunk River

173 IA 224, Kellogg, **N...gas:** Citgo/diesel/rest./24hr, **other:** Pella Museum, Rock Creek SP(9mi)

168 SE Beltline Dr, to Newton, **1 mi N...gas:** Casey's, **food:** Arby's, Taco John's, **lodging:** Mid-Iowa Motel, **other:** Plymouth/Jeep, Rolling Acres Camping, Wal-Mart SuperCtr/gas/24hr

Newton

164 US 6, IA 14, Newton, **N...gas:** BP/diesel, Casey's, Kum&Go, Phillips 66/Subway/diesel, **food:** Country Kitchen, Culver's, Golden Corral, KFC, Perkins/24hr, **lodging:** Day's Inn, Holiday Inn Express, Radisson, Ramada Ltd, Super 8, **other:** HOSPITAL, museum, **S...lodging:** Best Western/rest., to Lake Red Rock

159 F48, to Jasper, Baxter, **N...**antiques

155 IA 117, Colfax, **N...gas:** BP/McDonald's/diesel/@, **other:** antiques, **S...gas:** Casey's, Kum&Go/Texaco/ Subway/diesel/24hr/@

153mm S Skunk River

151 weigh sta wb

149 Mitchellville, no facilities

148mm rest area both lanes, full(handicapped)facilities, phone, picnic tables, litter barrels, petwalk, vending, RV dump

143 Altoona, Bondurant, **S...gas:** BP(2mi), Casey's, **lodging:** Settle Inn(2mi), **other:** HyVee Foods(2mi)

142b a US 65, Hubble Ave, Des Moines, **S...gas:** Bosselman/ Sinclair/diesel/rest./24hr/@, Git'n Go, **food:** Burger King, Godfather's, Hardee's, McDonald's, Pizza Hut, Subway/TCBY, Taco John's, **lodging:** Country Inn, Heartland Inn, Holiday Inn Express, Howard Johnson Express, Motel 6, Rodeway Inn, Settle Inn, **other:** Blue Beacon, Factory Outlet/famous brands

141 US 6 W, US 65 S(from wb), Pleasant Hill, Des Moines, no facilities

137b a I-35 N, I-235 S, to Des Moines, no facilities

I-80 W and I-35 S run together 14 mi

Des Moines

136 US 69, E 14th St, Camp Sunnyside, **N...gas:** BP/diesel, Phillips 66, **food:** Bonanza, Country Kitchen, Giselle's Rest., Okoboji Grill, **lodging:** Best Western/rest., Motel 6, Red Roof Inn, **other:** Harley-Davidson, Volvo/GMC, **1-2 mi S...gas:** Casey's, Citgo/diesel, **food:** QT/Burger King/diesel/@, Arby's, Fazoli's, KFC, LJ Silver, McDonald's, Pizza Hut, Schlotsky's, Scornovacca's Pizza, Subway, Village Inn Rest., Wendy's, **lodging:** 14th St Inn, Ramada Ltd, **other:** Advance Parts, CarMax, CarX Muffler, Ford Trucks, Goodyear, MidState RV Ctr, Tires+

135 IA 415, 2nd Ave, Polk City, **N...other:** diesel repair, **S...gas:** Git'n Go, QT, **food:** DQ, **other:** HOSPITAL, Earl's Tire, NAPA Autocare, USPO(2mi), st patrol

133mm Des Moines River

131 IA 28 S, NW 58th St, **N... gas:** Casey's, QT, **food:** NorthEnd Diner, Quizno's, Tagliai's Pizza, **lodging:** Best Inn, Ramada Inn, **other:** Acura, Goodyear/auto, HyVee Food, Infiniti, VW/Audi, **S...gas:** BP/diesel/24hr, Phillips 66, QT, Sinclair/diesel, **food:** Arby's, BBQ, Bennigan's, Burger King, Country Kitchen, Denny's, Embers Rest., Famous Dave's BBQ, Ground Round,

Interstate 80

E

W

Des Moines

KFC, McDonald's, Perkins, Pizza Hut, Shangrila Buffet, Tin Alley Grill, Village Inn Rest., Wendy's, **lodging:** Comfort Inn, Day's Inn, Holiday Inn, Quality Inn, Red Roof Inn, Sheraton, Super 8, **other:** HOSPITAL, Best Buy, Chevrolet, Chrysler/Plymouth, Daewoo, Firestone/auto, Ford/Mitsubishi, Goodyear/auto, Isuzu, Lincoln/Mercury, Marshall's, NAPA Autocare, Nissan, Office Depot, Sears/auto, Suzuki, Toyota, Younker's, Walgreen, mall

129 NW 86th St, Camp Dodge, **N...gas:** Kum&Go, **food:** Burger King, McDonald's, Okoboji Grill, Village Inn Rest., **lodging:** Birchwood Creek Inn, **other:** Dahl's Foods, **S...gas:** BP, Phillips 66, **food:** B-Bops Burgers, Culver's, Friedrich's Coffee, Happy Joe's Pizza, **lodging:** Microtel, **other:** Walgreen

127 IA 141 W, Grimes, **N...gas:** BP/Blimpie/diesel/@, Phillips 66/Subway/diesel, to Saylorville Lake, **S...food:** Quizno's, **other:** Radio Shack, Target

126 Douglas Ave, Urbandale, **N...gas:** Pilot/diesel/rest./24hr/@, **S...**Kum&Go/diesel, **food:** Dragon China, **lodging:** Day's Inn, Econolodge, Extended Stay America

125 US 6, Hickman Rd, **N...gas:** Flying J/Conoco/Cookery/diesel/LP/24hr/@, **S... food:** IA Machine Shed Rest., Clarion, **lodging:** Comfort Suites, Sleep Inn, **other:** GMC, Goodyear, Honda, Hyundai, to Living History Farms

124 (72c from I-35 nb), University Ave, **N...gas:** Amoco, Kum&Go/Burger King, QT, **food:** Cracker Barrel, **lodging:** Baymont Inn, Best Western, Country Inn Suites, **other:** HOSPITAL, **S...gas:** Phillips 66, **food:** Applebee's, Bakers Square, Cheddar's, Chili's, Cuco's Mexican, Don Pablo, KFC, Macaroni Grill, McDonald's, Outback Steaks, RockBottom Rest./brewery, **lodging:** Chase Suites, Courtyard, Fairfield Inn, Heartland Inn, Holiday Inn/Damon's, The Inn, Wildwood Lodge, **other:** MEDICAL CARE, Barnes&Noble, Best Buy, CompUSA, K-Mart, Kohl's, Lowe's Whse, Marshall's, World Mkt

I-80 E and I-35 N run together 14 mi

123b a I-80/I-35 N, I-35 S to Kansas City, I-235 to Des Moines

122 (from eb)60th St, W Des Moines, no facilities

121 74th St, W Des Moines, **N...food:** West End Diner, **lodging:** Hampton Inn, Hawthorn Suites, **other:** HyVee Food/gas, **S...gas:** BP, Kum&Go/Blimpie, **food:** Arby's, Burger King, McDonald's, Perkins, Taco John's, **lodging:** Candlewood Suites, Fairfield Inn, Quality Inn, Marriott, Motel 6, Wingate Inn

119mm rest area both lanes, full(handicapped)facilities, info, vending, phone, picnic tables, petwalk, RV dump

117 R22, Booneville, Waukee, **N...food:** Organic Farm Rest., **other:** Timberline Camping(2mi), **S...gas:** Kum&Go/24hr, **food:** Rube's Steaks

115mm weigh sta eb

113 R16, Van Meter, **1 mi S...gas:** Casey's

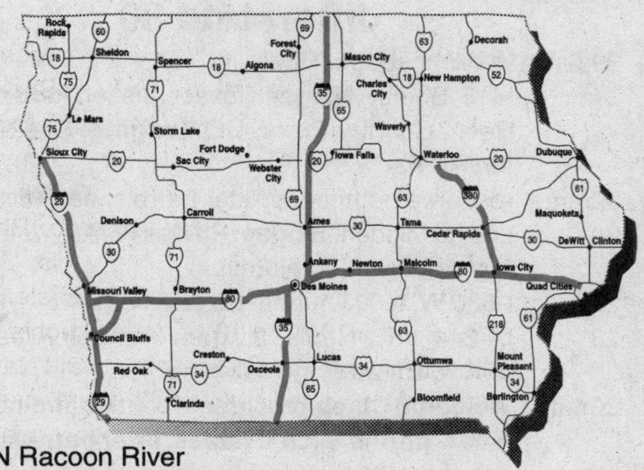

112mm N Racoon River

111mm Middle Racoon River

110 US 169, DeSoto, to Adel, **N...lodging:** Edgetowner Motel, **S...gas:** BP, Casey's, **other:** AirCraft Supermkt

106 F90, P58, **N...**KOA

104 P57, Earlham, **S...gas:** Casey's(2mi)

100 US 6, Dexter, to Redfield, no facilities

97 P48, to Dexter, **N...**camping

93 P28, Stuart, **N...gas:** Amoco/diesel/24hr, Conoco/diesel, **food:** Cyclone Drive-In, Burger King, McDonald's, Subway, AmericInn, Super 8, **other:** Jubilee Foods, NAPA, **S... gas:** Phillips 66/diesel, **food:** Country Kitchen, **lodging:** Stuart Motel

88 P20, Menlo, no facilities

86 IA 25, to Greenfield, Guthrie Ctr, **S...food:** IA Harvest Rest., **other:** HOSPITAL(13mi), to Preston/Spring Brook SP

85mm Middle River

83 N77, Casey, **1 mi N...gas:** Kum&Go, **other:** camping

80.5mm rest area both lanes, full(handicapped)facilities, phone, picnic tables, litter barrels, vending, petwalk, RV dump

76 IA 925, N54, Adair, **N...gas:** Amoco/diesel, Casey's/diesel, Kum&Go/diesel, Happy Chef/24hr, **food:** Mikey's Sandwiches, **lodging:** Adair Budget Inn, Super 8, **other:** camping

75 G30, to Adair, **1 mi N...gas:** Casey's, same as 76

70 IA 148 S, Anita, **S...**to Lake Anita SP(6mi), camping

64 N28, to Wiota, no facilities

61mm E Nishnabotna River

60 US 6, US 71, Lorah, to Atlantic, **S...gas:** Phillips 66/diesel/24hr, **food:** Country Kitchen, **lodging:** Econolodge

57 N16, to Atlantic, **S...**HOSPITAL(7mi)

54 IA 173, to Elk Horn, **7 mi N...Welcome Ctr, lodging:** AmericInn, **other:** Windmill Museum, gas, food

51 M56, to Marne, no facilities

46 M47, Walnut, **N...gas:** Amoco/McDonald's/24hr, **food:** Villager Buffet, **lodging:** Super 8, to Prairie Rose SP(8mi), **S...gas:** Kum&Go/diesel/24hr, **food:** Aunt B's Kitchen, **lodging:** Red Carpet Inn/RV Park, repair

44mm weigh sta both lanes

40 US 59, Avoca, to Harlan, **N...gas:** Conoco/Wings/Taco John/diesel/rest./24hr/@, **other:** HOSPITAL(12mi), **S...gas:** Texaco/diesel, **food:** Embers Rest., **lodging:** Avoca Motel, Capri Motel, **other:** Parkway Camping(2mi), Nishna Museum

IOWA

Interstate 80

39.5mm W Nishnabotna River

34 M16, Shelby, **N...gas:** Texaco/diesel, **food:** Cornstalk Rest., Country Pizza, DQ, **lodging:** Shelby Country Inn/RV Park

32mm rest area both lanes, litter barrels, no facilities

29 L66, to Minden, **S...gas:** Phillips 66/A&W/diesel, **lodging:** Midtown Motel(2mi)

27 I-680 W, to N Omaha, no facilities

23 IA 244, L55, Neola, **S...gas:** Kum&Go/diesel, **other:** to Arrowhead Park, camping

20mm Welcome Ctr eb/rest area wb, full(handicapped)facilities, phone, picnic tables, litter barrels, vending, petwalk, RV dump

17 G30, Underwood, **N...gas:** Phillips 66/Subway/diesel/24hr, **lodging:** Interstate 80 Inn/rest., Underwood Motel, **other:** truck/tire repair

8 US 6, Council Bluffs, **N...gas:** Coastal, Phillips 66/diesel, **lodging:** Chalet Motel(5mi), **other:** HOSPITAL, **S...**st patrol

5 Madison Ave, Council Bluffs, **N...gas:** BP/Amoco, **food:** Burger King, FoodCourt, Great Wall Chinese, KFC, McDonald's, Panera Bread, Pizza Hut, Subway, **lodging:** Heartland Inn, **other:** MEDICAL CARE, Barnes&Noble, Dillard's, DrugTown, HyVee Food/drug, JC Penney, NTB, Old Navy, Sears/auto, Target, Walgreen, mall, **S...gas:** Conoco, Shell, **food:** DQ, Valentino's Rest., Village Inn Rest., **lodging:** Western Inn, **other:** No Frills Foods

4 I-29 S, to Kansas City

3 IA 192 N, Council Bluffs, **N...**to Hist Dodge House, **S...gas:** Phillips 66/diesel/@, Shell/diesel, TA/Pizza Hut/diesel/24hr/@, **food:** Burger King, Applebee's, Beijing Chinese, Cracker Barrel, Dairy Queen, Fazoli's, Golden Corral, Hardee's, LJ Silver, McDonald's, Perkins/24hr, Red Lobster, Subway, Taco Bell, **lodging:** Comfort Inn, Day's Inn, Fairfield Inn, Motel 6, Settle Inn, **other:** Advance Parts, Aldi Foods, Chevrolet/GMC, Buick/Pontiac, Dodge, Ford/Lincoln/Mercury, Home Depot, Kia, Mazda, Nissan/Cadillac, OfficeMax, Plymouth/Jeep/Suzuki, Sam's Club/gas, Subaru, Toyota, TruckOMat, U-Haul, Wal-Mart SuperCtr/24hr, diesel repair

1b S 24th St, Council Bluffs, **N...gas:** Casey's, Conoco, Pilot/Arby's/diesel/24hr/@, Sinclair, Texaco/Burger King/diesel/rest., **lodging:** American Inn, Best Western, Super 8, **other:** Goodyear, RV camping, Peterbilt, SpeedCo, casino

a I-29 N, to Sioux City

0mm Iowa/Nebraska state line, Missouri River

Interstate 235(Des Moines)

Exit # Services

15 I-80, E to Davenport

13 US 6, E Euclid Ave, **E...gas:** Coastal, Phillips 66, **food:** Burger King, Dragon House Chinese, Papa John's, Perkins, **other:** Hancock Fabrics, HyVee Foods, Radio Shack, Walgreen, **W...other:** NAPA

12 Guthrie Ave, **N...gas:** Coastal/diesel/mart, **other:** Jocko's Auto Parts

11 IA 163 W, E University Ave, Easton Dr, no facilities

10 US 65/69, E 14th, E 15th, **N...food:** DQ, **other:** Walgreen, **S...food:** McDonald's, **other:** HOSPITAL, st capitol, zoo

9 E 6th St, Penn Ave(from wb), **N...**HOSPITAL

8.5 3rd St, 5th Ave, **N...lodging:** Holiday Inn, **other:** HOSPITAL, **S...**Conv Ctr, **lodging:** Best Western, Embassy Suites, Park Inn, Marriott

8 Keo Way, **S...gas:** Git'n Go, **other:** HOSPITAL

7.5 Harding Rd(from wb)

7 MLK Blvd, Drake U, **S...**airport

6.5 31st St, Governor's Mansion

6 42nd St, Science & Art Ctr, **N...gas:** Git'n Go, **food:** Papa John's, Taco John's

5 56th St(from wb), **N...**golf

4 IA 28, 63rd St, to Windsor Heights, **S...**Hist Valley Jct, zoo

3 8th St, W Des Moines, **N...gas:** Kum&Go, **food:** B-Bop's Café, Blimpie, Burger King, **other:** NTB, Sam's Club/gas, Sears AutoCtr, Wal-Mart SuperCtr/24hr, **S...gas:** BP, Kum&Go, **food:** Classic Custard, Garcia's Mexican, Jimmy's American Café, **lodging:** Best Western, **other:** Ford

2 22nd St, 24th St, W Des Moines, **N...gas:** BP, Citgo, **food:** ChiChi's, ChuckeCheese, Famous Dave's BBQ, Hardee's, Hooters, LoneStar Steaks, McDonald's, Old Country Buffet, Taco Bell, Village Inn Rest., Zachary's Grill, **lodging:** Studio+, **other:** Firestone/auto, Goodyear/auto, Gordman's, Hancock Fabrics, Michael's, Office Depot, Walgreen

1 35th St, W Des Moines, **N...gas:** BP/diesel, **food:** Red Lobster, **other:** HyVee Foods, JC Penney, SteinMart, Target, Younker's, mall, **S...**MEDICAL CARE

0mm I-235 begins/ends on I-80, exit 123.

Interstate 280(Davenport)

Exit # Services

18b a I-74, US 6, Moline, **S...gas:** Citgo, **food:** Bender's Rest., Denny's, Harold's Rest., McDonald's, Omelet Shoppe, Skyline Rest., **lodging:** Best Western, Comfort Inn, Country Inn Suites, Exel Inn, Hampton Inn, Holiday Inn, Holiday Inn Express, La Quinta, Motel 6, Skyline Inn

15 Airport Rd, Milan, **N...food:** MaidRite Café, **S...gas:** Mobil/diesel

11b a IL 92, Rock Island, to Andalusia, **S...**Camelot Camping(apr-oct)

9.5mm Iowa/Illinois state line, Mississippi River

8 rd 22, Rockingham Rd, to Buffalo

6 US 61, W River Dr, to Muscatine, **W...**food, camping

4 Locust St, rd F65, 160th St, **E...**HOSPITAL, to Palmer Coll, St Ambrose U, **W...gas:** Citgo/Subway/diesel/@

1 US 6 E, IA 927, Kimberly Rd, to Walcott, **E...**lodging, transmissions

0mm I-280 begins/ends on I-80, exit 290.

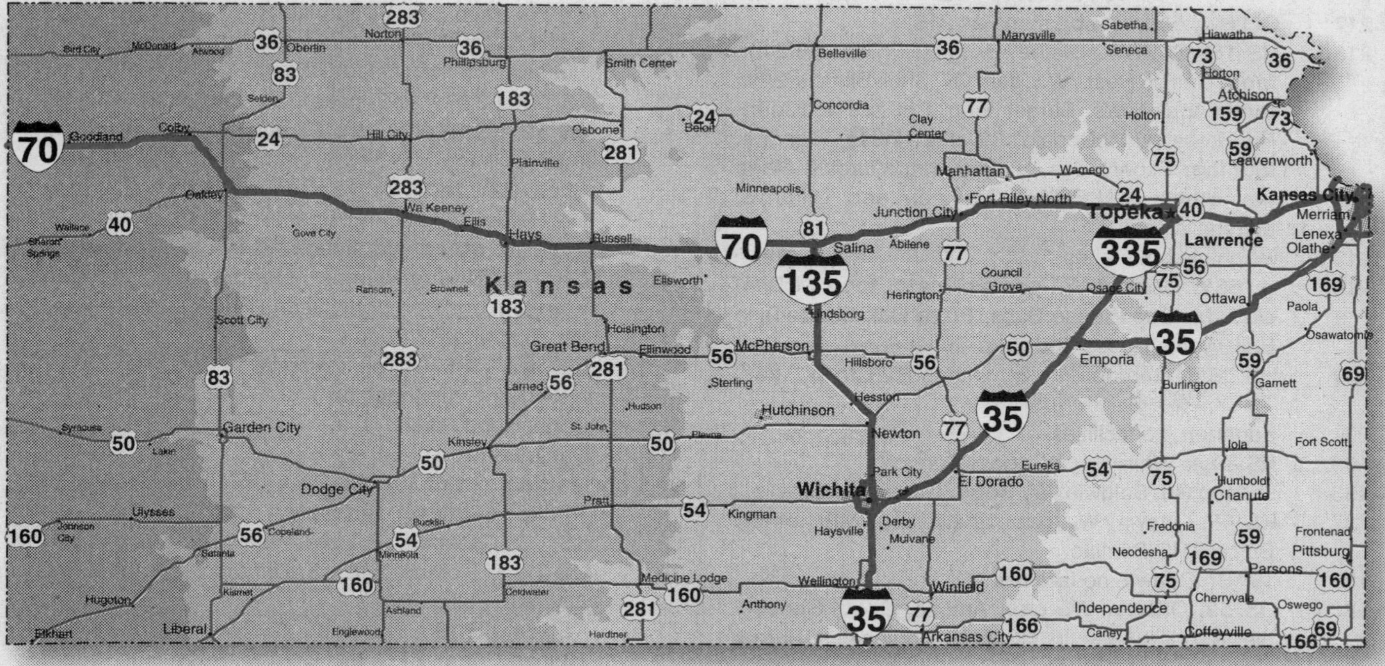

Interstate 35

N ↕ S

Kansas City Area

Exit #	Services
235mm	Kansas/Missouri state line
235	Cambridge Circle, **E...gas:** QT
234b a	US 169, Rainbow Blvd, **E...gas:** Phillips 66, **food:** Applebee's, Arby's, Burger King, McDonald's, Rosedale BBQ, Wendy's, **lodging:** Best Western, Day's Inn, **other:** KU MED CTR
233a	SW Blvd, Mission Rd, no facilities
b	37th Ave(from sb), no facilities
232b	US 69 N, **E...gas:** QT, Phillips 66, **food:** McDonald's, Taco Bell
a	Lamar Ave, **E...gas:** QT
231b a	I-635(exits left from nb), no facilities
230	Antioch Rd(from sb), **E...gas:** QT
229	Johnson Dr, **E...gas:** Shell, **food:** Arby's, Chili's, Papa John's, **other:** GNC, Home Depot, Marshall's, OfficeMax, Old Navy, Walgreen, Walnut Grove RV Park, **W...gas:** Phillips 66/diesel
228b	US 56 E, US 69, Shawnee Mission Pkwy, **W...food:** Burger King, Denny's, LJ Silver, Perkins, Pizza Hut, Steak'n Shake, Taco Bell, Wendy's
a	67th St, **E...gas:** QT, Shell, **food:** Burger King, Chevy's Mexican, Denny's, Winstead's Rest., **lodging:** Comfort Inn, Drury Inn, Fairfield Inn, HomeStead Village, Quality Inn, **other:** BMW, K-Mart, VW, **W...gas:** Phillips 66, **other:** Jaguar, Land Rover, Mercedes
227	75th St, **E...gas:** Circle K, Conoco, QT, **food:** McDonald's, Perkins, **lodging:** Wellesley Inn, **other:** HOSPITAL, Acura, JC Penney, Wal-Mart, **W...gas:** Citgo/7-11, QT/diesel, Shell, **food:** Ryan's, Sonic, Subway, Taco Bell, Wendy's, **lodging:** Hampton Inn
225b	US 69 S(from sb), Overland Pkwy, no facilities
a	87th St, **E...gas:** Amoco, Green Mill Rest., Tippen's Rest., **food:** Wendy's, **lodging:** Holiday Inn, **other:** Gomer's Foods, **W...gas:** Phillips 66, Shell, **food:** Arby's, Kahn Chinese, LongBranch Steaks, Mary's Place Gyros, Taco Bell, **other:** NTB, museum
224	95th St, **E...gas:** Amoco, Phillips 66, Shell, **food:** Applebee's, Burger King, China Buffet, Cielio's Italian, Denny's, Holiday Ham Café, Houlihan's, Italian Oven, KFC, McDonald's, Mimi's Café, Ming Palace, Mongolian BBQ, Old Chicago Pizza, On the Border, Pizza Hut, Ponderosa, Ruby Tuesday, Santa Fe Café, Steak&Ale, Taco Bell, TGIFriday, **lodging:** Comfort Inn, Day's Inn, Holiday Inn, La Quinta, Motel 6, Super 8, **other:** HOSPITAL, Advance Parts, Best Buy, CircuitCity, Dillard's, HyVee Foods, JC Penney, Nordstrom's, OfficeMax, Sam's Club, SteinMart, mall, **W...gas:** Conoco, Costco/gas
222b a	I-435 W & E
220	119th St, **E...gas:** Conoco, Shell, **food:** A&W, Burger King, Chevy's Mexican, China Café, Cracker Barrel, Gambucci's Italian, IHOP, Jersey Boyz Deli, Joe's Crabshack, LJ Silver, Machine Shed Rest., McDonald's, Rio Bravo Cantina, Ruby Tuesday, Schlotsky's, Souper Salad, Steak'n Shake, Subway, Tres Hombres Mexican, Wendy's, Zio's Italian, **lodging:** Comfort Suites, Fairfield Inn, Hampton Inn, Residence Inn, **other:** Aamco, Barnes&Noble, Dodge, GNC, Goodyear/auto, Home Depot, Honda, Hyundai, Mazda, OfficeMax, Old Navy, Radio Shack, Target, U-Haul, transmissions
218	135th, Santa Fe St, Olathe, **E...gas:** Shell, **food:** Backyard Burgers, Burger King, Corona Garden Mexican, Perkins, **other:** Ford, K-Mart, Osco Drug, **W...gas:** Amoco, Phillips 66, QT, **food:** Denny's, McDonald's, Ponderosa, Wendy's, **lodging:** Day's Inn, **other:** Chevrolet, Chrysler/Plymouth/Jeep, Kia, Mazda, Nissan, Pontiac/Buick/GMC, Saturn, Suzuki, Subaru, Toyota

Olathe

KANSAS

Interstate 35

N ↕ S

217 Old Hwy 56(from sb), same as 215

215 US 169 S, KS 7, Olathe, **E...gas:** Phillips 66/24hr, **food:** Catfish Rest., **W...gas:** QT, Shell/Blimpie/24hr, **food:** Applebee's, Burger King, Chili's, FoodCourt, Red Lobster, McDonald's, Waffle House, Wendy's, **lodging:** Econolodge, Holiday Inn, Microtel, Sleep Inn, **other:** HOSPITAL, Chrysler/Jeep, Dillard's, Marshalls, mall

213mm weigh sta both lanes

210 US 56 W, Gardner, **W...gas:** Phillips 66, **food:** McDonald's, Mr GoodSense Subs, Pizza Hut, Sonic, Taco Bell, Waffle House, **lodging:** Super 8

207 US 56 E, Gardner Rd, **E...**Olathe RV Ctr, **W...gas:** Conoco/diesel, Shell/diesel

202 Edgerton, no facilities

198 KS 33, to Wellsville, **W...gas:** Conoco

193 LeLoup Rd, Baldwin, **W...food:** Country Café

187 KS 68, Ottawa, **W...gas:** Shell/diesel/24hr, **other:** Buick/GMC/Pontiac

185 15th St, Ottawa, no facilities

Ottawa

183b a US 59, Ottawa, **W...gas:** Amoco, Citgo, Conoco/diesel, Phillips 66/diesel, **food:** Applebee's, Burger King, Country Kitchen, KFC, LJ Silver, McDonald's, Pizza Hut, Sirloin Stockade, Taco Bell, Wendy's, **lodging:** Econolodge, Hampton Inn, Holiday Inn Express, Super 8, Villager Lodge, **other:** Advance Parts, Chrysler/Plymouth/Dodge/Jeep, CountryMart Foods, $General, $Tree, Wal-Mart SuperCtr/gas/24hr

182b a US 50, Eisenhower Rd, Ottawa, no facilities

176 Homewood, **W...**RV camping

175mm rest area both lanes, full(handicapped)facilities, phone, picnic tables, litter barrels, vending, petwalk

170 KS 273, Williamsburg, **W...gas:** Shell/diesel/café, phone

162 KS 31 S, Waverly, no facilities

160 KS 31 N, Melvern, no facilities

155 US 75, Burlington, Melvern Lake, **E...gas:** BP/Subway/diesel, TA/Wendy's/diesel/24hr/@, Beto Inn

148 KS 131, Lebo, **E...gas:** Coastal/diesel, **food:** Lebo Grill, **lodging:** Universal Inn, **W...**to Melvern Lake

141 KS 130, Neosho Rapids, **E...**NWR(8mi)

138 County Rd U, no facilities

135 County Rd R1, **W...**RV camping/phone

Emporia

133 US 50 W, 6th Ave, Emporia, **1-3 mi E...gas:** Casey's, **food:** Braum's, McDonald's, Pizza Hut, **lodging:** Budget Host

131 KS 57, KS 99, Burlingame Rd, **E...gas:** Conoco/diesel, Phillips 66, **food:** Burger King, DQ, Hardee's, Mr GoodSense Subs

130 KS 99, Merchant St, **E...gas:** Phillips 66/diesel, **food:** Subway, **lodging:** University Inn, **other:** Emporia St U

128 Industrial Rd, **E...gas:** Conoco, **food:** Burger King, Mazzio's, Pizza Hut, Subway, **lodging:** Econolodge, Ramada Inn, Motel 6, **other:** HOSPITAL, CarQuest, Goodyear/auto, JC Penney, **W...gas:** Phillips 66/Wendy's/diesel, Shell, **food:** Applebee's, Cracker Barrel, Golden Corral, McDonald's, MT Mike's Steaks, Taco Bell, Village Inn Rest., **lodging:** Candlewood Suites, Fairfield Inn, Holiday Inn Express, **other:** Staples, Wal-Mart SuperCtr/24hr

127c KS Tpk, I-335 N, to Topeka

b a US 50, KS 57, Newton, **E...gas:** Conoco/diesel, Flying J/Conoco/diesel/rest./24hr/@, Phillips 66/diesel, Shell/A&W, **food:** Arby's, Carlos O'Kelly's, China Buffet, Hardee's, **lodging:** Best Western/rest., Day's Inn, Super 8, **other:** Aldi Foods, Chevrolet/Pontiac/Buick, Chrysler/Dodge/Plymouth/Jeep/Toyota, $General, Ford/Lincoln/Mercury/Nissan, PriceChopper Foods, **W...**Emporia RV Park

127mm I-35 and I-335 KS Tpk, toll plaza

I-35 S and KS Tpk S run together

125mm Cottonwood River

111 Cattle Pens

97.5mm Matfield Green Service Area(both lanes exit left), Phillips 66/diesel, Hardee's

92 KS 177, Cassoday, **E...gas:** Fuel'n Service, phone

76 US 77, El Dorado N, **E...**El Dorado SP, **3 mi E...gas:** Casey's, Phillips 66

71 KS 254, KS 196, El Dorado, **E...gas:** Phillips 66, **food:** Golden Corral, KFC, McDonald's, Pizza Hut, **lodging:** Best Western, Heritage Inn, Sunset Inn, Super 8, HOSPITAL, **other:** $General, Ford/Lincoln/Mercury, Pontiac/Buick/Cadillac, Radio Shack, Wal-Mart/24hr/auto

65mm Towanda Service Area(both lanes exit left), Phillips 66/diesel, McDonald's

62mm Whitewater River

57 21st St, Andover, **W...**golf, phone

53 KS 96, Wichita, **1 mi W...gas:** Conoco, **food:** McDonald's, Taco Bell, Wendy's, **lodging:** Courtyard, **other:** Acura, Lowe's Whse, Mercedes, Wal-Mart SuperCtr/24hr

Wichita

50 US 54, Kellogg Ave, **E...**McConnell AFB, **W...lodging:** Comfort Inn, Clubhouse Inn, Day's Inn, Fairfield Inn, Hampton Inn, Hilton, Marriott, Residence Inn, Scotsman Inn, Studio+, Super 8, **other:** VA HOSPITAL, Wichita Suites, **1 mi E on Kellogg...gas:** Conoco/Wendy's/diesel, **food:** Subway, **other:** Buick/Infiniti, Lowe's Whse, Porsche/Jaguar, Wal-Mart SuperCtr/24hr, **W on Kellogg Ave...gas:** Coastal, **food:** Arby's, Carlos O'Kelly's, Denny's, Green Mill Rest., Hooters, KFC, LJ Silver, McDonald's, Old Chicago Pizza, Pizza Hut, Spangles Rest., Steak&Ale, Taco Bell, **lodging:** LaQuinta, Wichita Inn, Williamsburg Inn, **other:** Advance Parts, Barnes&Noble, Best Buy, Chevrolet/Cadillac, Chrysler/Plymouth, Circuit City, $General, Firestone/auto, Ford, Hancock Fabrics, Honda, JC Penney, Kia/Nissan, K-Mart, Lincoln/Mercury, Michael's, NTB, OfficeMax, PepBoys, Pontiac/GMC/Hyundai, Saturn, Sears/auto, Subaru/Isuzu, Target, Toyota, mall

45 KS 15, Wichita, **E...**Boeing Plant

44.5mm Arkansas River

42 47TH St, I-135, to I-235, Wichita, **services on 47th St, E...gas:** Coastal, **food:** Potbelly's Rest., **lodging:** Best Western, Comfort Inn, Day's Inn, Holiday Inn Express, Red Carpet Inn, **W...gas:** Phillips 66, **food:** Applebee's, Braum's, Burger King, DQ, Godfather's, KFC, LJ Silver, McDonald's, Pizza Hut, Quizno's, Spaghetti Jack's,

KANSAS

Interstate 35

Spangles Rest., Taco Bell, Taco Tico, **other:** Checker's Foods, Dillon's Foods, K-Mart, O'Reilly's Parts, Radio Shack

39 US 81, Haysville, **W...lodging:** Haysville Inn

33 KS 53, Mulvane, **E...**Mulvane Hist Museum, **W...**Wyldewood Winery

26mm Belle Plaine Service Area(both lanes exit left), gas: Phillips 66/diesel, food: McDonald's

19 US 160, Wellington, **3 mi W...food:** Penny's Diner, **lodging:** OakTree Inn, Steakhouse Motel, Sunshine Inn, **other:** RV camping

17mm toll plaza

I-35 N and KS TPK N run together

4 US 166, to US 81, South Haven, **E...gas:** Phillips 66/diesel, **lodging:** Economy Inn/rest., **W...**Oasis RV Park

1.5mm weigh sta nb

0mm Kansas/Oklahoma state line

Interstate 70

Exit # Services

423b 3rd St, James St, no facilties

a 5th St, no facilties

422d c Central Ave, service rd, no facilties

422b a US 69 N, US 169 S

421b I-670, no facilities

a **S...**railroad yard

420b a US 69 S, 18th St Expswy, no facilities

419 38th St, Park Dr, access to 10 motels

418b I-635 N, **N...food:** McDonald's, Taco Bell, Wendy's, Dillard's, **other:** JC Penney, mall

a I-635 S, no facilities

417 57th St, no facilities

415a KS 32 E(from eb), no facilities

b to US 40 W, State Ave, Kansas City, **N...gas:** Conoco, **food:** Alvardo's Café, Arby's, Capt D's, Perkins, McDonald's, Taco Bell

414mm weigh sta wb, parking area both lanes, phone

414 78th St, **N...gas:** QT, **food:** Arby's, Burger King, Cracker Barrel, DQ, Hardee's, Lucky Chinese, Sonic, Wendy's, **lodging:** Microtel, **other:** HOSPITAL, Walgreen, **S...gas:** Conoco, **lodging:** American Motel, Comfort Inn

411b I-435 N, access to Woodlands Racetrack, to KCI Airport

a I-435 S, no facilities

410 110th St, **N...**Cabella's, KS Speedway, last free exit wb before KS TPK

225mm I-70 W and KS TPK run together

224 KS 7, to US 73, Bonner Springs, Leavenworth, **N...gas:** Shell, **food:** KFC/Taco Bell, Mazzio's, Waffle House, Wendy's, **lodging:** Holiday Inn Express, **other:** museum, **S...gas:** Citgo, **food:** McDonald's, **other:** Ford, PriceChopper Foods, Wal-Mart SuperCtr/24hr

217mm toll booth

209mm Lawrence Service Area(both lanes exit left), full facilities, Conoco/diesel, McDonald's

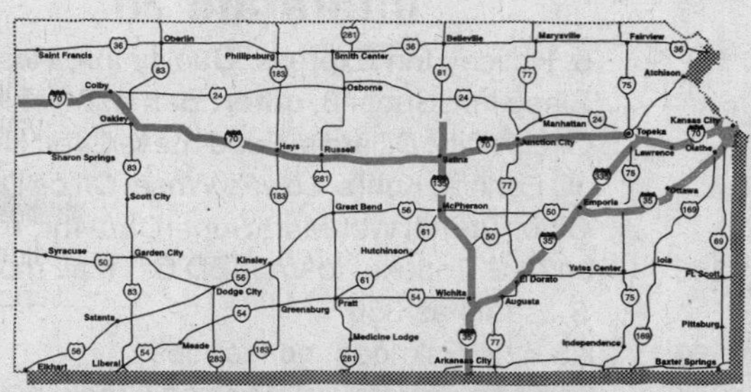

204 US 24, US 59, to E Lawrence, **S...gas:** Citgo, Conoco, **food:** Burger King, Sonic, **lodging:** Bismarck Inn, J-Hawk Motel, SpringHill Suites, **other:** O'Reilly Parts, outlet

203mm Kansas River

202 US 59 S, to W Lawrence, **1 mi S...gas:** Phillips 66, **food:** Capt's Galley, Chili's, MT Mike's Steaks, **lodging:** Best Western, Day's Inn, Hampton Inn, Holiday Inn, Quality Inn, Ramada Inn, Travelodge, Super 8, **other:** HOSPITAL, Firestone/auto, to Clinton Lake SP, to U of KS

197 KS 10, Lecompton, Lawrence, **N...**Perry Lake SP, **S...**Clinton Lake SP,

188mm Topeka Service Area(both lanes exit left), full facilities, Conoco/diesel, Hardee's

182 I-70 W(from wb), to Denver

367mm toll plaza

366 I-470 W, to Wichita, I-70 E and KS TPK E run together

365 21st St, Rice Rd, no facilities

364b US 40 E, Carnahan Ave, to Lake Shawnee

a California Ave, **S...gas:** BP/diesel, Conoco, **food:** Burger King, McDonald's, Pizza Hut, Rosa's Mexican, Sonic, Subway, **other:** AutoZone, Dillon's Food/gas, Family$, Food4Less, Walgreen

363 Adams St, downtown

362c 10th Ave(from wb), **N...lodging:** Ramada Inn, **S...gas:** BP, **other:** st capitol

362b a to 8th Ave, downtown, **N...lodging:** Capital Center Inn, **other:** to St Capitol

361b 3rd St, Monroe St, **N...gas:** BP, **lodging:** Ramada Inn

361a 1st Ave, **S...**Ryder

359 MacVicar Ave, no facilities

358b a Gage Blvd, **S...gas:** gas/diesel, **food:** McDonald's, Wendy's, **other:** HOSPITAL

357b a Fairlawn Rd, 6th Ave, **S...gas:** Conoco, Phillips 66, **food:** A&W, **lodging:** Best Western, Holiday Inn/rest., Motel 6, **other:** NAPA, zoo-rain forest

356b a Wanamaker Rd, **N...lodging:** AmeriSuites, **other:** KS Museum of History, **S...gas:** BP, Phillips 66/diesel, Topeka/diesel/rest./24hr, **food:** Applebee's, Boston Mkt, Burger King, Chili's, ChuckeCheese, Coyote Canyon Café, Cracker Barrel, Denny's, Golden Corral, GoodCents Subs, IHOP, McDonald's, Mesquite Grill, Old Country Buffet, Olive Garden, Panera Bread, Perkins, Pizza Hut, Red Lobster, Ruby Tuesday, Shoney's, Sirloin Stockade, Steak'n Shake, Taco Bell, Timberline Steaks, Wendy's, Winstead's Burgers, **lodging:** Candlewood Suites, Comfort Inn, Country Inn Suites, Courtyard, Day's Inn, Fairfield Inn, Hampton Inn, Motel

KANSAS

Interstate 70

E ↕ W

6, Holiday Inn Express, Quality Inn, Residence Inn, Sleep Inn, Super 8, **other:** Barnes&Noble, Best Buy, Circuit City, Dillard's, Food4Less/24hr, Home Depot, JC Penney, Kohl's, Lowe's Whse, Office Depot, Sam's Club, Target, Wal-Mart SuperCtr/24hr, mall

355 I-470 E, Topeka, to VA MED CTR, air museum, **1 mi S...**same as 356

353 KS 4, to Eskridge, no facilities

351 frontage rd(from eb), Mission Creek, no facilities

350 Valencia Rd, no facilities

347 West Union Rd, no facilities

346 Carlson Rd, Willard, to Rossville, no facilities

343 frontage rd, no facilities

342 Eskridge Rd, Keene Rd, access to Lake Wabaunsee

341 KS 30, Maple Hill, **S...gas:** Amoco/diesel/café

338 Vera Rd, **S...gas:** Texaco/DQ/Stuckey's

336mm rest area(exits left from both lanes), full(handicapped)facilities, phone, picnic tables, litter barrels, RV camping/dump, petwalk

335 Snokomo Rd, Paxico, Skyline Mill Creek Scenic Drive

333 KS 138, Paxico, no facilities

332 Spring Creek Rd, no facilities

330 KS 185, to McFarland, no facilities

329mm weigh sta both lanes

328 KS 99, to Alma, **S...**Wabaunsee Co Museum

324 Wabaunsee Rd, no facilities

322 Tallgrass Rd, no facilities

318 frontage rd, no facilities

316 Deep Creek Rd, no facilities

313 KS 177, to Manhattan, **N...gas:** DeDee's/diesel/café, **8 mi N...food:** Applebee's, Chili's, McDonald's, Schlotsky's, Village Inn Rest., **lodging:** Best Western, Comfort Inn, Fairfield Inn, Hampton Inn, Motel 6, Super 8, **other:** Jeep, Nissan, Sears/auto, to KSU

311 Moritz Rd, no facilities

310mm rest area both lanes, full(handicapped)facilities, phone, picnic tables, litter barrels, petwalk, RV dump

307 McDowell Creek Rd, scenic river rd to Manhattan

304 Humboldt Creek Rd, no facilities

303 KS 18 E, to Ogden, Manhattan, **8 mi N...lodging:** Hampton Inn, Super 8, to KSU

301 Marshall Field, to Ft Riley, **N...other:** Cavalry Museum, Custer's House, KS Terr Capitol

300 US 40, KS 57, Council Grove, **N...lodging:** Dreamland Motel, **S...**hist church

Jct City

299 Flinthills Blvd, to Jct City, Ft Riley, **N...gas:** BP/diesel, **food:** Stacy's Rest., **lodging:** Econolodge, Great Western Inn, Red Carpet Inn, Super 8

298 Chestnut St, to Jct City, Ft Riley, **N...gas:** Shell/Burger King/diesel/24hr, **food:** BBQ, Cracker Barrel, Family Buffet, Taco Bell, **lodging:** Best Western, Holiday Inn Express, Super 8, **other:** $Tree, Wal-Mart SuperCtr/24hr

296 US 40, Washington St, Junction City, **N...gas:** Citgo/diesel, Phillips 66, Shell/diesel/24hr, **food:** Country Kitchen, DQ, Denny's, El Cazador Mexican, KFC, McDonald's, Peking Chinese, Sirloin Stockade, Sonic, Subway, **lodging:** Budget Host/RV Park, Comfort Inn, Day's Inn, Ramada Ltd, **other:** Chevrolet/Pontiac, Food4Less/24hr

295 US 77, KS 18, Marysville, to Milford Lake, **N...gas:** Phillips 66/A&W/diesel/24hr, **lodging:** Motel 6, **other:** HOSPITAL

294mm rest area both lanes, full(handicapped)facilities, phone, picnic tables, litter barrels, RV dump, petwalk

290 Milford Lake Rd, no facilities

286 KS 206, Chapman, **S...gas:** Citgo, **1 mi S...gas:** Casey's

Abilene

281 KS 43, to Enterprise, **N...**4 Seasons RV Ctr/Park

277 Jeep Rd, no facilities

275 KS 15, Abilene, to Clay Ctr, **N...food:** DQ, **lodging:** Brookville Motel, Holiday Inn Express, **S...gas:** Amoco/diesel, Phillips 66/Taco Bell, **food:** Burger King, China Taste, Green Acres Rest., McDonald's, Pizza Hut, Sonic, Subway, **lodging:** Best Western, Day's Inn, Super 8, **other:** HOSPITAL, Alco/gas, AutoZone, Chevrolet/Pontiac/Buick, CountryMart Foods, $General, Ford/Lincoln/Mercury, Chrysler, Plymouth/Jeep/Dodge, to Eisenhower Museum

272 Fair Rd, to Talmage, **S...**Russell Stover Candy

266 KS 221, Solomon, **S...gas:** Total/diesel/rest./24hr/@

265mm rest area both lanes, full(handicapped)facilities, phone, picnic tables, litter barrels, vending, petwalk

264mm Solomon River

260 Niles Rd, New Cambria, no facilities

253mm Saline River

Salina

253 Ohio St, **S...gas:** Flying J/Conoco/Country Mkt/diesel/LP/24hr/@, **other:** HOSPITAL, Harley-Davidson, Kenworth

252 KS 143, Salina, **N...gas:** Amoco/diesel/rest./24hr/@, Petro/Mobil/Phillips 66/Wendy's/Pizza Hut/diesel/@, **food:** Bayard's Café, DQ, McDonald's, Toucan's Mexican, **lodging:** Best Inn, Day's Inn, Holiday Inn Express, Motel 6, Salina Inn, Super 8, **other:** Blue Beacon, KOA, **S...gas:** Bosselman/Sinclair/Blimpie/diesel/24hr/@, **lodging:** Best Western, Travelodge

250b a I-135, US 81, N to Concordia, S to Wichita, no facilities

249 Halstead Rd, to Trenton, no facilities

244 Hedville, **N...**Sundowner West RV Park, **S...gas:** Phillips 66/diesel

238 Glendale, to Brookville, Tescott, no facilities

233 Juniata, to Beverly, no facilities

225 KS 156, to Ellsworth, **S...gas:** Texaco/diesel, **other:** Ft Harker Museum, Ft Larned HS

224mm rest area both lanes, full(handicapped)facilities, phone, picnic tables, litter barrels, petwalk, RV dump

221 KS 14 N, to Lincoln, no facilities

219 KS 14 S, to Ellsworth, **S...gas:** Conoco/diesel, **other:** auto/truck repair

216 to Vesper, **S...gas:** Shell/DQ/Stuckey's

Interstate 70

209 to Sylvan Grove, no facilities

206 KS 232, Wilson, **N...gas:** Conoco/rest., **other:** Wilson Lake(6mi), winery

199 KS 231, Dorrance, **N...**to Wilson Lake, **S...gas:** Agco

193 Bunker Hill Rd, **N...gas:** Shamrock/diesel/Bearhouse Café/24hr, to Wilson Lake

189 US 40 bus, Pioneer Rd, Russell, no facilities

187mm rest area both lanes, full(handicapped)facilities, phone, picnic tables, litter barrels, petwalk

184 US 281, Russell, **N...gas:** Amoco/diesel/24hr, Phillips 66/Mesquite Grill/diesel, **food:** Meridy's Rest., McDonald's, Pizza Hut, Sonic, Subway, **lodging:** AmericInn, Day's Inn, Russell Inn, Super 8, **other:** HOSPITAL, Dumler RV Park, JJJ RV Park, st patrol

180 Balta Rd, to Russell, no facilities

175 KS 257, Gorham, **1 mi N...**gas, food, phone

172 Walker Ave, no facilities

168 KS 255, to Victoria, **S...gas:** Ampride/diesel, to Cathedral of the Plains

163 Toulon Ave, no facilities

161 Commerce Parkway, no facilities

159 US 183, Hays, **N...gas:** Shamrock/diesel/24hr, **food:** Applebee's, Carlos O'Kelly's, Golden Corral, **lodging:** Best Western, Comfort Inn, Fairfield Inn, **other:** Ford/Lincoln/Mercury, Harley-Davidson, Plymouth/Dodge, Radio Shack, Toyota, Wal-Mart SuperCtr/gas/24hr, **S...gas:** Amoco/24hr, Conoco/Golden OX/diesel/24hr, Love's, Phillips 66/diesel, **food:** A&W, Arby's, Burger King, Country Kitchen, KFC, LJ Silver, McDonald's, MT Mike's Steaks, Pheasant Run Café, Pizza Hut, Pizza Inn, Sonic, Subway, Taco Bell, Vagabond Rest., Village Inn Rest., Wendy's, **lodging:** Best Western, Comfort Inn, Day's Inn, Econolodge, Hampton Inn, Holiday Inn, Motel 6, Super 8, **other:** HOSPITAL, Advance Parts, Chevrolet/Mazda, Chrysler, Firestone/auto, Hastings Books, JC Penney, NAPA, SunMart Foods, Walgreen, mall, st patrol

157 US 183 S byp, to Hays, **S...lodging:** Gen Hayes Inn, **other:** museum, to Ft Hays St U

153 Yocemento Ave, no facilities

145 KS 247 S, Ellis, **S...gas:** Casey's, Shell, **food:** Alloway's Rest./TasteeFreez, **lodging:** Ellis House Inn, **other:** to Chrysler Museum, Railroad Museum, antiques

140 Riga Rd, no facilities

135 KS 147, Ogallah, **N...gas:** Schreiner/diesel/café, **other:** Goodyear, **S...**to Cedar Bluff SP(13mi)

132mm rest area both lanes, full(handicapped)facilities, picnic tables, litter barrels, petwalk, RV dump

128 US 283 N, WaKeeney, **N...gas:** Conoco/diesel/24hr, **lodging:** Budget Host, Super 8, **other:** HOSPITAL

127 US 283 S, WaKeeney, **N...gas:** Phillips 66/McDonald's/diesel/24hr, **food:** DQ, Jade Garden Rest., Nobody's Rest., Pizza Hut, **lodging:** KS Kountry Inn, Sundowner Motel, **S...gas:** Amoco/diesel/rest./24hr, Conoco/Subway/diesel, **lodging:** motel, **other:** KOA

120 Voda Rd, no facilities

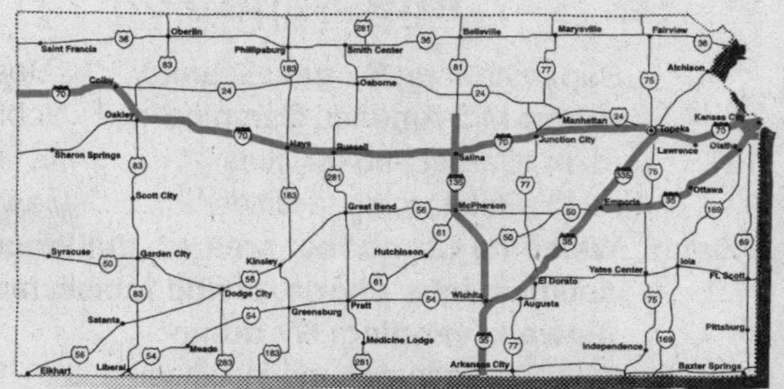

115 KS 198 N, Banner Rd, Collyer, **N...gas:** Sinclair/diesel

107 KS 212, Castle Rock Rd, Quinter, **N...gas:** Phillips 66/diesel, **lodging:** Budget Host/rest., **other:** HOSPITAL, Chevrolet, Sunflower RV Park, **S...gas:** Conoco/diesel/24hr, **food:** DQ

99 KS 211, Park, **1 mi N...gas:** Sinclair/diesel

97mm rest area both lanes, full(handicapped)facilities, picnic tables, litter barrels, vending, petwalk, RV dump

95 KS 23 N, to Hoxie, no facilities

93 KS 23, Grainfield, **N...gas:** Sinclair/diesel

85 KS 216, Grinnell, **S...gas:** Shell/DQ/Stuckey's

79 Campus Rd, no facilities

76 US 40, to Oakley, **S...gas:** Shell/diesel/café/repair/24hr/@, **lodging:** Best Value Inn, 1st Interstate Inn, **other:** HOSPITAL, Blue Beacon

70 US 83, to Oakley, **N...lodging:** Free Breakfast Inn, **S...gas:** Conoco/diesel, Phillips 66/diesel, **food:** Colonial Steaks, **other:** HOSPITAL, Hi-Plains RV Park, Prairie Dog Town, Fick Museum

62 rd 24, Mingo, **S...gas:** Ampride/diesel/24hr, phone

54 Country Club Dr, Colby, **1 mi N...lodging:** Country Club Motel, **other:** HOSPITAL, RV camping

53 KS 25, Colby, **N...gas:** Amoco/diesel, Conoco/DQ/diesel, Phillips 66/Subway, **food:** Arby's, Burger King, KFC/Taco Bell, LJ Silver, McDonald's, MT Mike's Steaks, Pizza Hut, Sonic, Taco John's, **lodging:** Day's Inn, Holiday Inn Express, Quality Inn, Super 8, Welk-Um Inn, **other:** HOSPITAL, AutoZone, Dillon Food, $General, Ford/Lincoln/Mercury, Goodyear, Prairie Art Museum, Radio Shack, Wal-Mart, diesel repair, **S...gas:** Phillips 66/diesel, **food:** Quizno's, Starbucks, Village Inn Rest., **lodging:** Best Western, Comfort Inn, **other:** Chevrolet/Cadillac/Buick/Pontiac, outlets

48.5mm rest area both lanes, full(handicapped)facilities, phone, picnic tables, litter barrels, RV dump, vending, petwalk

45 US 24 E, Levant, no facilities

36 KS 184, Brewster, **N...gas:** Citgo/diesel

35.5mm Mountain/Central time zone

27 KS 253, Edson, no facilities

19 US 24, Goodland, **N...food:** Pizza Hut, **lodging:** Best Western, **other:** KOA, Plains Museum

17 US 24, KS 27, Goodland, **N...gas:** Conoco, Phillips 66/diesel, Sinclair/DQ/diesel, **food:** McDonald's, Subway, Taco John's, Wendy's, **lodging:** Best Western/rest., Comfort Inn, Economy 9 Motel, Howard Johnson, Super 8, **other:** HOSPITAL, Pontiac/GMC, Wal-Mart

KANSAS

Interstate 70

SuperCtr/24hr, **S...gas:** Shamrock/A&W/diesel/24hr, **other:** Mid-America Camping

12 rd 14, Caruso, no facilities

9 rd 11, Ruleton, no facilities

7.5mm Welcome Ctr eb/rest area wb, full(handicapped)facilities, info, phone, picnic tables, litter barrels, petwalk, vending, RV dump

1 KS 267, Kanorado, no facilities

.5mm weigh sta eb

0mm Kansas/Colorado State Line

Interstate 135(Wichita)

Exit # Services

95b a I-70, E to KS City, W to Denver. I-135 begins/ends on I-70, exit 250. US 81 continues nb.

93 KS 140, State St, Salina, no facilities

92 Crawford St, **E...gas:** Amoco/diesel, Citgo, Shell, **food:** Blimpie, Braum's, Spangles, Taco Bell, Western Sizzlin, **lodging:** Best Western, Comfort Inn, Fairfield Inn, Holiday Inn, Super 8, **W...gas:** Phillips 66/diesel, **lodging:** Red Coach Inn

90 Magnolia Rd, **E...gas:** Phillips 66/diesel, Shell, **food:** Carlos O'Kelly's, Chili's, Coyote Canyon Café, Golden Corral, Hong Kong Buffet, IHOP, McDonald's, Mesquite Grill, Schlotsky's, **lodging:** 1st Inn, **other:** Advance Parts, Buick/Subaru, Dillon's Foods, $General, Food4Less, JC Penney, Sears/auto, mall, **W...gas:** Conoco

89 Schilling Rd, **E...gas:** Shell, **food:** Applebee's, Burger King, Fazoli's, Pizza Hut, Red Lobster, Sonic, **lodging:** Candlewood Suites, Country Inn Suites, Hampton Inn, **other:** Aldi Foods, Cadillac/Chevrolet, Honda, OfficeMax, Sam's Club, Target, Wal-Mart SuperCtr/24hr, **W...gas:** Casey's, **lodging:** Baymont Inn

86 Mentor, Smolan, no facilities

82 KS 4, Assaria, no facilities

78 KS 4 W, Lindsborg, **E...gas:** Shell/DQ/Stuckey's

72 US 81, Lindsborg, **4 mi W...**HOSPITAL, gas, food, lodging, phone, camping, museum

68mm rest areas(both lanes exit left), full(handicapped)facilities, phone, picnic tables, litter barrels petwalk, RV dump

65 Pawnee Rd, no facilities

60 US 56, McPherson, Marion, **W...gas:** Conoco/diesel, Phillips 66, **food:** Applebee's, Arby's, Braum's, KFC, McDonald's, Perkins, Pizza Hut, Red Coach Rest., Sirloin Stockade, **lodging:** Best Western, Super 8, **other:** HOSPITAL, Wal-Mart/auto

58 US 81, to Hutchinson, McPherson, no facilities

54 Elyria, no facilities

48 KS 260 E, Moundridge, **2 mi W...**gas, food, phone

46 KS 260 W, Moundridge, **2 mi W...**gas, food, phone

40 Hesston, **W...gas:** Conoco/diesel, **food:** Pizza Hut, Subway, **lodging:** Hesston Heritage Inn

34 KS 15, N Newton, **E...gas:** Phillips 66/diesel/LP, **W... food:** LJ Silver, Subway, **other:** Kaufman Museum

33 US 50 E, to Peabody, no facilities

32 Broadway Ave, **E...food:** Applebee's, **other:** Chevrolet/Cadillac, Chrysler/Plymouth/Dodge/Jeep, Ford/Lincoln/Mercury

31 Newton, **E...gas:** Ampride/diesel, Conoco/diesel, Shell/diesel/motel, **food:** KFC, Red Coach Rest., **lodging:** Day's Inn, 1st Inn, Super 8, **W...gas:** Phillips 66/diesel, **food:** Braum's, Sirloin Stockade, **lodging:** Best Western

30 US 50 W, KS 15(exits left from nb), Newton, to Hutchinson, **W...gas:** Phillips 66, **other:** HOSPITAL, AutoZone, Buick/Pontiac/GMC, Dillon's Foods/24hr, Wal-Mart SuperCtr/24hr

28 SE 36th St, **W...gas:** Texaco/diesel, **food:** Burger King, Subway, Taco Bell, **other:** Newton Outlets/famous brands

25 KS 196, to Whitewater, El Dorado, no facilities

23mm rest areas both lanes, full(handicapped)facilities, phone, picnic tables, litter barrels, vending, petwalk, RV dump

22 125th St, no facilities

19 101st St, phone, camping

17 85th St, **E...**Valley Ctr, KS Coliseum

16 77th St, no facilities

14 61st St, **E...gas:** QT/Blimpie, Total, **food:** Cracker Barrel, Sonic, Taco Bell, Wendy's, **lodging:** Comfort Inn, **W...gas:** Coastal, **food:** KFC, McDonald's, **lodging:** Super 8, **other:** Goodyear/auto

13 53rd St, **W...gas:** Phillips 66, **food:** Red Coach Rest., **lodging:** Best Western, Day's Inn

11b I-235 W, KS 96, to Hutchinson, no facilities

a KS 254, to El Dorado, no facilities

10b 29th St, Hydraulic Ave, no facilities

a KS 96 E, no facilities

9 21st St, **E...gas:** Amoco, **food:** Burger King, Wichita St U

8 13th St, **E...gas:** Total

7b 8th St, 9th St, **E...**School of Medicine

6b 1st St, 2nd St, **E...**AutoZone, **W...**Chevrolet, Chrysler/Jeep

5b US 54, US 400, Kellogg Ave, **1 mi E...gas:** Amoco, Total, **food:** McDonald's, Spangles Rest., Wendy's

a Lincoln St, **W...gas:** QT

4 Harry St, **1 mi E...gas:** QT, **food:** Church's Chicken, Denny's, Dunkin Donuts, McDonald's, Spangles Rest., Wendy's, **W...gas:** Amoco

3 Pawnee Ave, **E...gas:** QT, **W...food:** Burger King, Church's, Papa John's, Spangles, **lodging:** Carpet Inn, Pawnee Inn

2 Hydraulic Ave, **E...gas:** QT, **W...food:** McDonald's, Subway

2mm Arkansas River

1c I-235 N, **2 mi W...**Hilton

b a US 81 S, 47th St, **E...gas:** Coastal, **food:** Potbelly's Rest., **lodging:** Best Western, Comfort Inn, Day's Inn, Holiday Inn Express, **W...gas:** Phillips 66, **food:** Applebee's, Braum's, Burger King, DQ/Super Wok, Godfather's, KFC, LJ Silver, McDonald's, Pizza Hut, Quizno's, Spaghetti Jack's, Spangles Rest., Subway, Taco Bell, Taco Tico, **lodging:** Red Carpet Inn, **other:** Checker's Foods, Dillon's Foods, K-Mart, O'Reilly's Parts, Radio Shack

0mm I-135 begins/ends on I-35, exit 42.

KENTUCKY

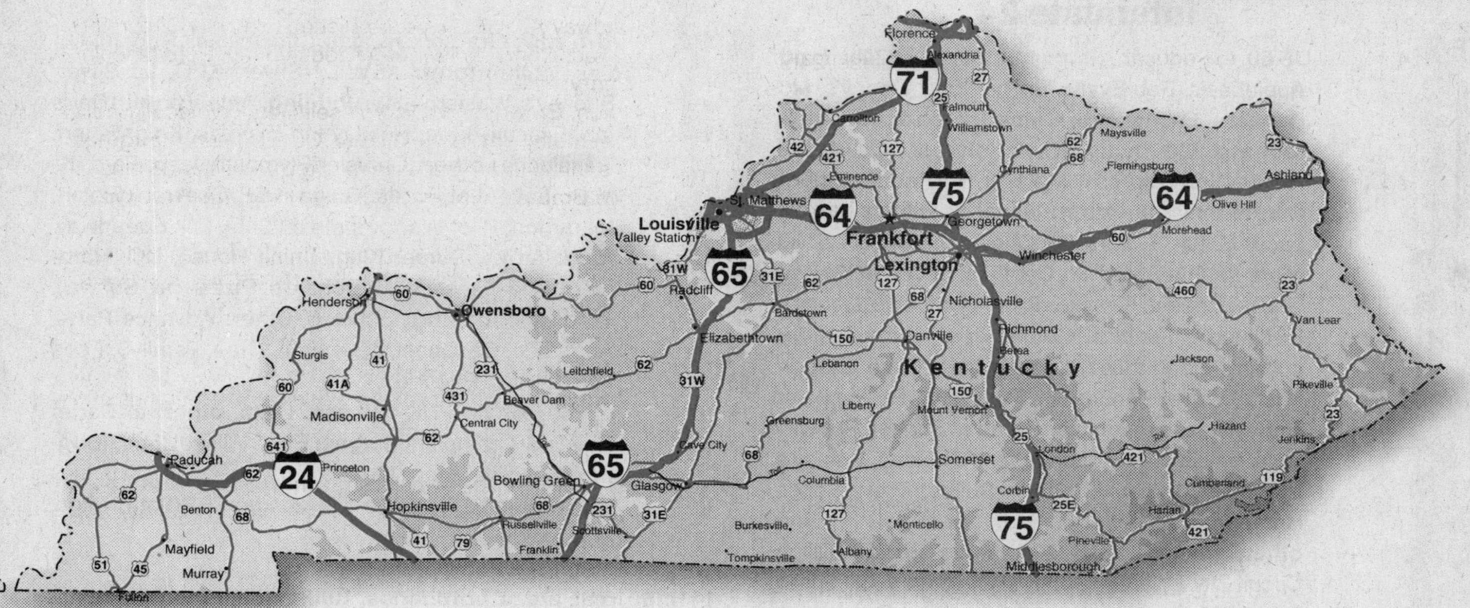

Interstate 24

E ↕ W

Exit #	Services
93.5mm	Kentucky/Tennessee state line
93mm	**Welcome Ctr wb, full(handicapped)facilities, phones, picnic tables, litter barrels, vending, petwalk**
91.5mm	Big West Fork Red River
89	KY 115, to Oak Grove, **N...**to Jeff Davis Mon St HS, **S...gas:** Citgo/diesel, Pilot/Speedway/McDonald's/diesel/24hr/@
86	US 41A, to Ft Campbell, Hopkinsville, Pennyrile Pkwy, **N...gas:** Chevron/Taco Bell/diesel/24hr, **S...gas:** BP/Burger King/diesel/24hr, Flying J/Conoco/Country Mkt/diesel/LP/24hr/@, Pilot/Subway/diesel/24hr/@, Williams/diesel/rest./24hr, **food:** McDonald's, Waffle House, **lodging:** Baymont Inn, Best Western, Comfort Inn, Day's Inn, Econolodge, Fairfield Inn, Holiday Inn Express, Rodeway Inn
79mm	Little River
73	KY 117, Newstead, to Gracey, no facilities
65	US 68, KY 80, to Cadiz, **S...gas:** Amoco, BP/diesel, Phillips 66/diesel/24hr, Shell/diesel/24hr, **food:** Cracker Barrel, KFC, McDonald's, Wendy's, **lodging:** Holiday Inn Express, Knight's Inn, 7 Inn, Super 8, **other:** HOSPITAL, Chevrolet, antiques, golf, to NRA's
56	KY 139, to Cadiz, Princeton, **S...gas:** Chevron/diesel, **other:** Nat Rec Areas
47mm	Lake Barkley
45	KY 293, Saratoga, to Princeton, **N...**to KY St Penitentiary, **S...gas:** Chevron/diesel/pizza, **food:** Old Farmhouse Rest., **lodging:** Regency Inn, **other:** Lake Barkley RV Camping
42	to W KY Pkwy eb
40	US 62, US 641, Kuttawa, Eddyville, **N...lodging:** Relax Inn, **other:** camping, **S...gas:** BP/Wendy's/diesel/24hr, Huck's/diesel/24hr/@, Shell, **food:** Santa Fe Steaks, **lodging:** Day's Inn, Hampton Inn, **other:** W KY Factory Outlet, to Lake Barkley, KY Lake Rec Areas, camping
36mm	weigh sta both lanes, phones
34mm	Cumberland River
31	KY 453, to Grand Rivers, Smithland, **N...gas:** Amoco/diesel, **lodging:** Microtel, **S...gas:** BP/24hr, **food:** Miss Scarlett's, **lodging:** Best Western, Grand Rivers Resort(3mi), **other:** NRA's, camping
29mm	Tennessee River
27	US 62, Calvert City, to KY Dam, **N...gas:** BP, Chevron, Shell, **food:** Cracker Barrel, DQ, KFC, McDonald's, Waffle House, Willow Pond Rest., **lodging:** Cloverleaf Motel, Foxfire Motel, Super 8, **other:** KOA, **S...gas:** Coastal/diesel/rest./24hr, **lodging:** KY Dam Motel, **other:** Cypress Lakes Camp
25b a	to Calvert City, Carroll/Purchase Pkwy, services 1 mi N
16	US 68, to Paducah, **S...gas:** BP/diesel, Roadside, Southern Pride/diesel/24hr/@, **food:** Subway
11	rd 1954, Husband Rd, to Paducah, **N...gas:** Exxon/diesel, **lodging:** Best Western, **other:** Duck Creek RV Park
7	US 45, US 62, to Paducah, **N...gas:** Ashland/Subway/diesel, BP/diesel, Citgo, Pet-tro, Shell/diesel/24hr, **food:** A&W, Burger King, LJ Silver, Taco Bell, **lodging:** Quality Inn, **other:** HOSPITAL, **S... Welcome Ctr both lanes, full(handicapped)facilities, phones, vending, picnic tables, litter barrels, petwalk, gas:** BP/diesel, Shell, Scot Gas, **food:** Arby's, Golden Corral, Hardee's, KFC, Little Caesar's, Mardi Gras Café, McDonald's, Sonic, Taco John's, Waffle House, **lodging:** Denton Motel, Sunset Inn, **other:** FoodTown, K-Mart, Rite Aid, SuperValue Food/24hr

Paducah

KENTUCKY

Interstate 24

E ↕ W — Paducah

4 US 60, to Paducah, **N...gas:** Shell/diesel/24hr, **food:** Applebee's, Bob Evans, Burger King, Denny's, McDonald's, O'Charley's, Outback Steaks, Rafferty's, **lodging:** Courtyard, Day's Inn/rest., Drury Inn, Holiday Inn Express, Motel 6, Ramada Inn, Red Carpet Inn(1mi), **other:** Hancock Fabrics, KY Tobacco Outlet, **S...gas:** BP, Chevron/Domino's, Shell, **food:** Atlanta Bread Co, Capt D's, Chong's Chinese, ChuckeCheese, Cracker Barrel, Damon's, Denny's, El Chico's, Fazoli's, Godfather's, Hardee's/24hr, Logan's Roadhouse, Los Amigos, Olive Garden, Pasta House, Ponderosa, Pizza Hut, Red Lobster, Ruby Tuesday, Ryan's, Steak'n Shake, Subway, Taco Bell, Texas Roadhouse, TGIFriday, Wendy's, **lodging:** Best Inn, Comfort Suites, Drury Suites, Hampton Inn, Motel 6, PearTree Inn, Thrifty Inn, **other:** Advance Parts, Aldi Foods, BooksAMillion, Circuit City, Dillard's, Goody's, Goodyear, JC Penney, Lowe's Whse, Office Depot, OfficeMax, Sam's Club, Sears/auto, Wal-Mart SuperCtr/gas/24hr, Millsprings Funpark, mall

3 KY 305, to Paducah, **N...gas:** Citgo/diesel/24hr, **food:** Casa Mexicana, Huddle House/24hr, **lodging:** Comfort Inn/rest., Ramada Ltd, Super 8, **S...gas:** BP/diesel/24hr, Pilot/Subway/diesel/24hr/2, **food:** Waffle Hut, **lodging:** Baymont Inn, **other:** Fern Lake Camping, antiques

0mm Kentucky/Illinois state line, Ohio River

Interstate 64

E ↕ W — Grayson — Lexington

Exit # Services

192mm Kentucky/West Virginia state line, Big Sandy River

191 US 23, to Ashland, **1-2 mi N...gas:** Exxon, GoMart, Marathon/diesel, **food:** Burger King, Hardee's, McDonald's, Pizza Inn, Subway, **lodging:** Holiday Inn Express(5mi), Ramada Ltd, **other:** HOSPITAL, Rite Aid

185 KY 180, Cannonsburg, **1-3 mi N...gas:** BP/diesel, Chevron, **food:** Arby's, Burger King, Hardee's, Subway, Taco Bell, **lodging:** Ashland Plaza, Day's Inn, Fairfield Inn, Hampton Inn, Knight's Inn, **other:** st police, **S..**Flying J/CountryMkt/diesel/24hr/@, Hidden Valley Camping

181 US 60, to Princess, **N...gas:** Citgo/diesel, **S...gas:** Marathon

179 rd 67, Industrial Parkway, no facilities

173mm rest areas wb, full(handicapped)facilities, phone, vending, picnic tables, litter barrels, petwalk

172 rd 1, rd 7, Grayson, **N...gas:** Citgo/diesel, SuperQuik/diesel/24hr, **food:** A&W/LJ Silver, KFC, LJ Silver, Shoney's, Western Steer, **lodging:** American Inn, Day's Inn, Executive Inn, Holiday Inn Express, Knight's Inn, Travelodge, **other:** Chrysler/Plymouth/Jeep, Ford, K-Mart, SaveALot Foods, **S...gas:** BP, Chevron, Exxon, Marathon, Pilot/Wendy's/diesel/24hr/@, Speedway, **food:** Arby's, Burger King, China House, DQ, Hardee's, Little Caesar's, McDonald's, Pizza Hut, Subway, Taco Bell, **lodging:** Super 8, **other:** Advance Parts, AutoZone, CarQuest, $General, $Tree, Family$, Food Fair, Parts+, Rite Aid

161 US 60, to Olive Hill, **N...gas:** Citgo, **other:** to Carter Caves SP, camping, **S...gas:** Exxon/diesel/24hr, **lodging:** Spanish Manor Motel

156 rd 2, to KY 59, to Olive Hill, **S...gas:** BP(3mi), Citgo, Sunoco/diesel

148mm weigh sta both lanes

141mm rest areas both lanes, full(handicapped)facilities, phone, vending, picnic tables, litter barrels, petwalk

137 KY 32, to Morehead, **N...gas:** BP, **food:** DQ, **other:** Kroger, **S...gas:** BP, Chevron/Burger King/diesel/24hr, Exxon/diesel, **food:** Domino's, Hardee's, KFC, Lee's Chicken, McDonald's, Papa John's, Ponderosa, Shoney's, Subway, **lodging:** Best Western, Day's Inn, Holiday Inn Express, Mtn Lodge Motel, Ramada Ltd, Super 8, **other:** HOSPITAL, Buick/Pontiac, Food Lion, Goodyear, Radio Shack, Wal-Mart, st police

133 rd 801, Farmers, to Sharkey, **N...**Eagle Trace Golf/rest.(4mi), **S...gas:** BP/diesel, **lodging:** Comfort Inn

123 US 60, to Salt Lick, Owingsville, **N...gas:** Chevron/diesel

121 KY 36, to Owingsville, **N...gas:** BP/diesel, Citgo/diesel, Sunoco/diesel, **food:** DQ, McDonald's, Subway, **lodging:** Best Western, **other:** $General

113 US 60, to Mt Sterling, **N...gas:**Chevron/diesel/@

110 US 460, KY 11, Mt Sterling, **N...gas:** Chevron/repair/24hr, Shell/Krystal/diesel, **food:** Cracker Barrel, Fairfield Inn, Ramada Ltd, **other:** golf, **S...gas:** BP/diesel, Exxon/Subway, Marathon, Speedway/diesel, **food:** Applebee's, Arby's, Burger King, Golden Corral, Jerry's Rest., KFC, Lee's Chicken, LJ Silver, McDonald's, Rio Grande Mexican, Wendy's, **lodging:** Budget Inn, Day's Inn/rest., **other:** HOSPITAL, Family$, Ford/Mercury, **S on KY 686...gas:** Ashland, **food:** Hardee's, Little Caesar's, Pizza Hut, Taco Bell, Taco Tico, **other:** Advance Parts, Chevrolet, Chrysler/Plymouth/Dodge/Jeep, Ford, Wal-Mart SuperCtr/24hr

108mm rest area wb, full(handicapped)facilities, phone, vending, picnic tables, litter barrels, petwalk

101 US 60, no facilities

98.5mm rest area eb, full(handicapped)facilities, phone, vending, picnic tables, litter barrels, petwalk

98 KY 402(from eb), no facilities

Interstate 64

E ↕ W

96b a KY 627, to Winchester, Paris, **N...gas:** BP/diesel, Citgo/diesel/rest., **S...gas:** Marathon/diesel, Speedway, **lodging:** Comfort Suites, Day's Inn, Hampton Inn, **other:** Chevrolet

94 KY 1958, Van Meter Rd, Winchester, **N...gas:** Chevron/24hr, Shell/diesel, **lodging:** Best Value Inn, Holiday Inn Express, **other:** flea mkt, **S...gas:** BP/diesel, Citgo, Marathon, Speedway/diesel, **food:** Applebee's, Arby's, Burger King, Cantuckee Diner, Capt D's, Domino's, Fazoli's, Golden Corral, Great Wall Chinese, JB Asian Grill, KFC, Little Caesar's, LJ Silver, McDonald's, Papa John's, Pizza Hut, Popeye's, Rally's, Sonic, Subway, Tacos Too, Waffle House, Wendy's, **lodging:** Best Western, Travelodge, **other:** HOSPITAL, Advance Parts, AutoZone, Chrysler/Plymouth/Dodge/Jeep, Family$, Ford/Mercury, K-Mart, Kroger, Lowe's Whse, Radio Shack, Wal-Mart SuperCtr/24hr, to Ft Boonesborough Camping

87 KY 859, Blue Grass Sta, no facilities

81 I-75 S, to Knoxville

I-64 and I-75 run together 7 mi. See Kentucky Interstate 75, exits 113-115.

75 I-75 N, to Cincinnati, access to KY Horse Park

69 US 62 E, to Georgetown, **N...**antiques(mi), **S...**Equus Run Vineyards(2mi)

65 US 421, Midway, **S...gas:** Citgo/diesel, antiques

60mm rest area both lanes, full(handicapped)facilities, phone, picnic tables, litter barrels, vending, petwalk

Frankfort

58 US 60, to Frankfort, **N...gas:** BP/diesel, Chevron/diesel, Citgo/diesel, Shell, **food:** Arby's, KFC, Mkt Café, McDonald's, Sandy's Steaks, Tumbleweed's, White Castle, **lodging:** Best Western/rest., Blue Grass Inn, Fairfield Inn, University Lodge, **other:** Elkhorn Camping(5mi), Cadillac/Pontiac, Chevrolet/Nissan, Chrysler/Plymouth/Jeep, Ford/Lincoln/Mercury, Toyota, to KY St Capitol, KYSU, to Viet Vets Mem, transmissions

55mm Kentucky River

53b a US 127, Frankfort, **N...gas:** Chevron/24hr, Shell/24hr, Speedway, **food:** A&W/LJ Silver, Applebee's, Big Boy, Burger King, Chili's, ChuckeCheese, Columbia Steaks, DQ, Fazoli's, Hardee's, KFC, McDonald's, O'Charley's, Pizza Hut, Shoney's, Steak'n Shake, Taco Bell, Wendy's, **lodging:** Day's Inn, Hampton Inn, Holiday Inn(4mi), Super 8(1mi), **other:** HOSPITAL, Advance Parts, Goodyear, Goody's, JC Penney, K-Mart, Kroger/24hr, Lowe's Whse, Office Depot, Radio Shack, Rite Aid, Wal-Mart SuperCtr/24hr, Ancient Age Tour, to KY St Capitol, st police, **S...gas:** BP, Marathon/diesel

48 KY 151, to US 127 S, **S...gas:** Chevron/24hr, Shell/Subway/diesel

43 KY 395, Waddy, **N...gas:** Flying J/Conoco/Country Mkt/diesel/LP/24hr/@, **S...gas:** Citgo/Stuckey's/diesel/rest./24hr

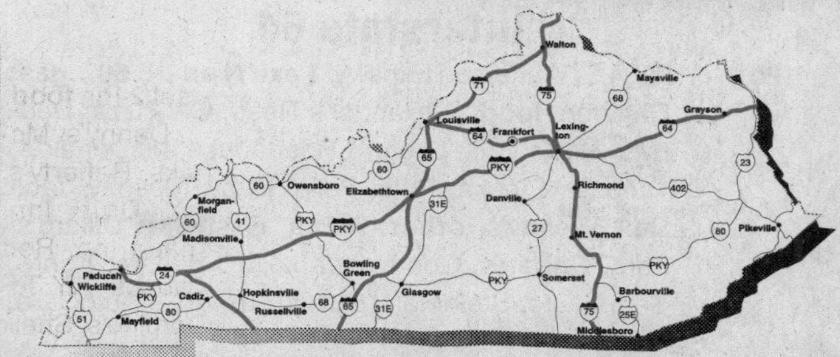

38.5mm weigh sta both lanes

35 KY 53, Shelbyville, **N...gas:** BP/diesel, Chevron/diesel, **food:** Cracker Barrel, KFC, McDonald's(1mi), Subway, **other:** Chevrolet, Ford/Mercury, Kroger/gas/deli, antiques, **S...gas:** Shell/Noble Roman's/diesel, **lodging:** Holiday Inn Express, **other:** golf

32b a KY 55, Shelbyville, **1-3 mi N...gas:** Shell, **food:** Arby's, Burger King, DQ, McDonald's, Pizza Hut, Wendy's, **lodging:** Best Western, Country Hearth Inn, Day's Inn, Shelby Motel, Probus Log Cabin, **other:** HOSPITAL, AutoZone, Buick/Pontiac/GMC, Wal-Mart SuperCtr/gas/24hr, **S...**Taylorsville Lake SP

29mm rest area both lanes, full(handicapped)facilities, info, phone, picnic tables, litter barrels, vending, petwalk

28 Veechdale Rd, Simpsonville, **N...gas:** Citgo, Pilot/Subway/diesel/24hr/@, **food:** Oasis Mkt/diner, **lodging:** Old Stone Inn, **other:** golf, **S...gas:** BP/diesel

19b a I-265, Gene Snyder Fwy, **N...**to Tom Sawyer SP

Louisville

17 S Blankenbaker, **N...gas:** DM/diesel, **lodging:** Staybridge Suites, **S...gas:** BP, Chevron, Shell, Thornton's/Subway/diesel, **food:** Arby's, Big Boy, Burger King, Cracker Barrel, HomeTown Buffet, King Buffet, Kingfish Rest., McDonald's, Ruby Tuesday, Subway, Waffle House, Wendy's, **lodging:** Best Western Signature, Candlewood Suites, Comfort Suites, Country Inn Suites, Hilton Garden, Holiday Inn Express, MainStay Suites, Microtel, Sleep Inn, **other:** Sam's Club/gas, Outlets Ltd

15 Hurstbourne Lane, Louisville, **N...gas:** Amoco, BP/diesel, Chevron/diesel, Shell/diesel, **food:** Arby's, Bob Evans, Burger King, Carrabba's, Chili's, Don Pablo, Harper's Rest., LoneStar Steaks, Macaroni Grill, McDonald's, Olive Garden, Papa John's, Perkins, Sichuan Garden Chinese, Steakout, Subway, TGIFriday, Tumbleweed Mexican, Waffle House, **lodging:** AmeriSuites, Courtyard, Fairfield Inn, Holiday Inn, Red Roof Inn, **other:** Barnes&Noble, CompUSA, Kroger, Lowe's Whse, **S...gas:** BP/diesel, Shell, Meijer/diesel/24hr, Thornton's, **food:** Applebee's, Blimpie, Buc's Rest., China Star, ChuckeCheese, DQ, Damon's, Dillon's Rest., Macaroni Grill, O'Charley's, Piccadilly's, Shoney's, Shogun Japanese, Starbucks, Steak'n Shake, Wendy's, **lodging:** Day's Inn, Hampton Inn, Hurstbourne Hotel, Marriott, Radisson, Red Carpet Inn, **other:** Cadillac, Chevrolet/Subaru, Home Depot, Honda, Infiniti, Michael's, Mitsubishi, Pontiac/GMC, Radio Shack, Staples, Target, Town Fair Foods, Wal-Mart/drugs

KENTUCKY

Interstate 64

E ↔ W — Louisville

12b I-264 E, Watterson Expswy, **1 exit N on US 60...gas:** Chevron, **food:** Alexander's Rest., CA Pizza, Denny's, Hop's Grill, Logan's Roadhouse, McDonald's, Outback Steaks, Rollo Pollo, Ruby Tuesday, Taco Bell, Wendy's, **other:** Acura, Best Buy, Dillard's, Ford, Galyan's, Goodyear/auto, JC Penney, Kohl's, Sears/auto, SteinMart, Suzuki, Towery's AutoCare, mall

a I-264 W, access to HOSPITAL

10 Cannons Lane, no facilities

8 Grinstead Dr, Louisville, **S...gas:** BP, Chevron, **other:** Southern Baptist Seminary, Presbyterian Seminary, Jim Porter's Rest.

7 US 42, US 62, Mellwood Ave, Story Ave, **N...gas:** Petroz

6 I-71 N(from eb), to Cincinnati, no facilities

5a I-65, S to Nashville, N to Indianapolis

b 3rd St, Louisville, **N...food:** Hardee's, **food:** Joe's CrabShack, McDonald's, **lodging:** Ramada Inn, **S...lodging:** Galt House Hotel, **food:** Kingfish Rest., **other:** HOSPITAL

4 9th St, Roy Wilkins Ave, **S...**KY Art Ctr, science museum, downtown

3 US 150 E, to 22nd St, **S...gas:** Chevron, DairyMart, Shell, **food:** DQ, McDonald's, Subway, **other:** MEDICAL CARE

1 I-264 E, to Shively, **S...**airport, zoo

0mm Kentucky/Indiana state line, Ohio River

Interstate 65

N ↔ S — Louisville

Exit # Services

138mm Kentucky/Indiana state line, Ohio River

137 I-64 W, I-71 N, I-64 E, **W...**to Galt House, downtown

136c Jefferson St, Louisville, **E...**HOSPITAL, **W...gas:** Chevron, **food:** McDonald's, Papa John's, **lodging:** Clarion Inn, Doubletree Hotel, Hyatt, Quality Hotel, **other:** Tires+

136b a Broadway St, Chestnut St, **E...other:** Ford/Lincoln/Mercury, Tires+, HOSPITAL, **W...gas:** Speedway, Thornton, **food:** Taco Bell, **lodging:** Cumberland Motel, Day's Inn, Holiday Inn, Hyatt Hotel

135 W St Catherine, **E...gas:** BP/Amoco, Shell, **lodging:** Day's Inn

134b a KY 61, Jackson St, Woodbine St, **W...gas:** BP/Amoco, **lodging:** Day's Inn, Quality Inn, **other:** Harley-Davidson

133b a US 60A, Eastern Pkwy, Taylor Blvd, **E...food:** Denny's, Papa John's, Pizza Mia, Subway, **W...gas:** BP/diesel, Shell, **food:** Cracker Barrel, McDonald's, **lodging:** Country Hearth Inn, **other:** U of Louisville, Churchill Downs, museum

132 Crittenden Dr(from sb), **E...food:** Denny's, same as 133

131b a I-264, Watterson Expswy, **W...**Cardinal Stadium, Expo Center, airport

130 KY 61, Preston Hwy, **E on Ky 61...gas:** BP, DM, Speedway, Thornton, **food:** Blimpie, Bob Evans, Burger King, ChuckeCheese, Fazoli's, KFC, Lindy's Rest., McDonald's, Papa John's, Ponderosa, Rally's, Royal Garden Buffet, Subway, Taco Bell, Waffle House, Wendy's, **lodging:** Econolodge, Red Roof Inn, Super 8, **other:** Big O Tire, Chevrolet/Nissan, Chrysler/Plymouth, $General, Ford, PepBoys, Radio Shack, SavALot Foods, Staples, Tires+, U-Haul, Winn-Dixie

128 KY 1631, Fern Valley Rd, **E...gas:** BP/diesel, Bigfoot/gas, Chevron, Thornton/Subway/diesel, **food:** Arby's, Big Boy, Golden Wall Chinese, Hardee's, McDonald's, Outback Steaks, Shoney's, Waffle House, White Castle, **lodging:** Holiday Inn, InTown Suites, Signature Inn, Thrifty Dutchman, **other:** Cottman Transmissions, Sam's Club, Walgreen, **W...**UPS Depot

127 KY 1065, outer loop, **E...**Texas Roadhouse, **W...food:** McDonald's, to Motor Speedway

125b a I-265 E, KY 841, Gene Snyder Fwy

121 KY 1526, Brooks Rd, **E...gas:** BP/Amoco, Chevron, **food:** Arby's, Burger King, Cracker Barrel, **lodging:** Baymont Inn, Fairfield Inn, **W...gas:** BP/Blimpie/diesel, Pilot/Subway/Taco Bell/diesel/24hr/@, Shell/diesel, **food:** Waffle House, **lodging:** Comfort Inn, Hampton Inn, Holiday Inn Express, Quality Inn

117 KY 44, Shepherdsville, **E...gas:** BP, Shell/diesel, **food:** Denny's, Kitchen Rest., **lodging:** Best Western/rest., Day's Inn, **other:** KOA(2mi), **W...gas:** Amoco/diesel, Chevron/diesel/24hr, Speedway/diesel, **food:** Arby's, Backyard Burger, Burger King, DQ, El Tarasco Mexican, Fazoli's, LJ Silver, KFC, McDonald's, Mr Gatti's, Papa John's, Rio's Steaks, Sonic, Subway, Taco Bell, Waffle House, Wendy's, White Castle, **lodging:** Country Inn Suites, Hampton Inn, Motel 6, Super 8, **other:** $General, Family$, Kroger, NAPA, Rite Aid, Winn-Dixie

116.5mm Salt River

116 KY 480, KY 61, **E...gas:** Love's/Subway/diesel/24hr/@, Shell/diesel, **W...gas:** Marathon/diesel, **other:** Grandma's RV Park, Leisure Life RV Ctr

114mm rest area sb, full(handicapped)facilities, phone, vending, picnic tables, litter barrels, petwalk

112 KY 245, Clermont, **E...gas:** Shell/diesel, **other:** Jim Beam Outpost, Bernheim Forest, to My Old Kentucky Home SP

105 KY 61, Lebanon Jct, **W...gas:** Shell/Subway/Noble Roman/diesel/24hr/@, 105 QuickStop/diesel

102 KY 313, to KY 434, to Radcliff, **E...**to Patton Museum

KENTUCKY

Interstate 65

N ↕ S

Elizabethtown

94 US 62, Elizabethtown, **E...gas:** Exxon/diesel, Marathon, Shell, **food:** Denny's, Golden Corral, KFC/Taco Bell, Waffle House, White Castle, **lodging:** Day's Inn, Quality Inn, Super 8, **other:** KOA(1mi), **W...gas:** BP, Chevron/diesel/24hr, Speedway/diesel, Swifty, **food:** Blimpie, Burger King, BunBakers, Cracker Barrel, McDonald's, Mr Gatti's, Papa John's, Pizza Hut, Ryan's, Shoney's, Stone Hearth, Subway, TX Outlaw Steaks, Texas Roadhouse, Wendy's, **lodging:** Comfort Inn, Hampton Inn, Holiday Inn, Howard Johnson, Motel 6, Ramada Inn, **other:** HOSPITAL, Advance Parts, CVS Drug, $General, $Tree, Kroger/gas, Skagg's RV Ctr, st police

93 to Bardstown, to BG Pky, **E...**to My Old KY Home SP, Maker's Mark Distillery

91 US 31 W, KY 61, Elizabethtown, WK Pkwy, **E...gas:** Big T/Chevron/24hr, Citgo/diesel, Shell, **food:** LJ Silver, Omelet House, **lodging:** Budget Motel, Commonwealth Lodge, Howard Johnson, **other:** Ryder Trucks, to Lincoln B'Place, **W...gas:** Citgo, **food:** Denny's, Jerry's Rest./24hr, Lee's Chicken, **lodging:** Best Western, Rodeside Inn, **other:** HOSPITAL

90mm weigh sta both lanes

86 KY 222, Glendale, **E...gas:** Pilot/McDiner/diesel/24hr/@, **other:** Glendale Camping, **W...gas:** Citgo/diesel/rest./24hr, Petro/diesel/rest./24hr/@, **lodging:** Economy Inn, **other:** Blue Beacon

83mm Nolin River

82mm rest area sb, full(handicapped)facilities, phone, vending, picnic tables, litter barrels, petwalk

81.5mm rest area nb, full(handicapped)facilities, phone, vending, picnic tables, litter barrels, petwalk

81 KY 84, Sonora, **E...gas:** BP, Davis Bros/diesel/rest./24hr/@, Citgo/diesel/rest., **other:** Blue Beacon, to Lincoln B'Place, **W...gas:** Shell

76 KY 224, Upton, **E...gas:** Chevron/diesel, **W...**to Nolin Lake

75mm eastern/central time zone

71 KY 728, Bonnieville, no facilities

65 US 31 W, Munfordville, **E...gas:** BP/Subway/diesel, Citgo/diesel, Marathon, **food:** County Fixen's Rest., DQ, Pizza Hut, McDonald's, Sonic, **lodging:** Super 8, **other:** $General, Family$, **W...gas:** Chevron/diesel/24hr, Shell, **food:** Cave Country Rest., to Nolin Lake

61mm Green River

58 KY 218, Horse Cave, **E...lodging:** Horse Cave Motel, **other:** HOSPITAL, **W...gas:** BP, Chevron/Pizza Hut/diesel/24hr, Marathon/repair, **food:** Bee's Rest./24hr, Subway, **lodging:** Budget Host/rest., Hampton Inn, **other:** Jent Factory Outlet, KOA, to Mammoth Cave NP

55mm rest area sb, full(handicapped)facilities, phone, vending, picnic tables, litter barrels, petwalk

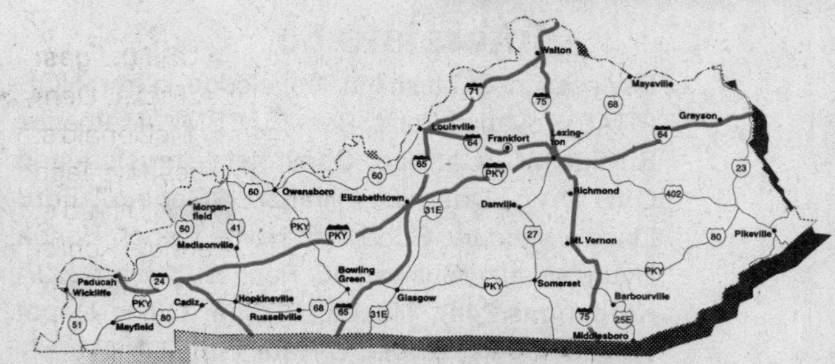

Bowling Green

53 KY 70, KY 90, Cave City, **E...gas:** Amoco/diesel, BP/Burger King, Chevron/diesel/24hr, JR/Subway, Shell, **food:** Country Kitchen, Cracker Barrel, DQ, Jerry's Rest., KFC, LJ Silver/A&W, McDonald's, Pizza Hut, Sahara BBQ/steaks, Taco Bell, Wendy's, **lodging:** Best Western, Comfort Inn, Day's Inn/rest., Howard Johnson, Quality Inn, Ramada Ltd, Super 8, **other:** HOSPITAL, Barren River Lake SP(24mi), **W...gas:** Shell, **other:** Onyx Cave, Mammoth Cave NP, Jellystone Camping

48 KY 255, Park City, **E...gas:** Shell/diesel/24hr, **lodging:** Parkland Motel, **other:** tire repair, **W...**to Mammoth Cave NP, Cedar Hill RV Park

43 Cumberland Pky(toll), to Barren River Lake SP

39.5mm rest area nb, full(handicapped)facilities, phone, vending, picnic tables, litter barrels, petwalk

38 KY 101, Smiths Grove, **W...gas:** BP/diesel, Chevron/diesel, Keystop, Shell, **food:** McDonald's, Bryce Motel, Victorian House B&B, **other:** $General, 7 Springs Park, RV camping

36 US 68, KY 80, Oakland, no facilities

30mm rest area sb, full(handicapped)facilities, phone, vending, picnic tables, litter barrels, petwalk

28 rd 446, to US 31 W, Bowling Green, **W...gas:** BP, Keystop/gas, Shell/Blimpie/24hr, **food:** Hardee's, Jerry's Rest., Wendy's, **lodging:** Best Western, Country Hearth Inn, Value Lodge, **other:** HOSPITAL, Corvette Museum, **3 mi W...**Camping World RV Supply, to WKYU

22 US 231, Bowling Green, **E...gas:** Citgo/diesel, MinitMart/gas, Shell, **food:** Cracker Barrel, Denny's, Domino's, Hardee's, Ryan's, Sonic, Waffle House, **lodging:** Best Western, Comfort Inn, Day's Inn, Econolodge, Fairfield Inn, Microtel, Ramada/rest., Super 8, **other:** USPO, **W...gas:** BP, Chevron/diesel, Exxon/TCBY, RaceWay, Shell/Blimpie/diesel, Speedway, **food:** Applebee's, Arby's, Beijing Chinese, Bob Evans, Buffalo Wings, Burger King, ChiChi's, CiCi's, Fazoli's, HomeTown Buffet, Hop's Grill, KFC, Krystal, Little Caesar's, LoneStar Steaks, Longhorn Steaks, McDonald's, MT Grille, C'Charley's, Olive Garden, Outback Steaks, Pizza Hut, Ponderosa, Quizno's, Rafferty's, Red Lobster, Santa Fe Steaks, Shoney's, Smokey Bones BBQ, Sonic, Steak'n Shake, Subway, Taco Bell, TGIFriday, Tumbleweed Grill, Waffle House, Wendy's, White Castle, **lodging:** Baymont Inn, Courtyard, Drury Inn, Hampton Inn, Motel 6,

KENTUCKY

Interstate 65

Payless Inn, Scottish Inn, Travelodge, **other:** HOSPITAL, Advance Parts, Best Buy, BMW/Mercedes, Buick/GMC, Cadillac, Chevrolet, Chrysler/Jeep, CVS Drug, Daewoo, Dillard's, $General, Ford/Lincoln/Mercury, Goodyear, Home Depot, Honda, Hyundai/Isuzu/Subaru, JC Penney, K-Mart, KOA, Kroger/gas/24hr, Mazda, Nissan, Office Depot, Pontiac, Sears, Toyota, U-Haul, Winn-Dixie, mall

20 WH Natcher Toll Rd, to Bowling Green, access to W KY U, KY st police

6 KY 100, Franklin, **E...gas:** BP/diesel/24hr, Citgo/Blimpie/diesel/24hr/@, **W...gas:** Pilot/Subway/diesel/24hr/@, Pilot/diesel/24hr/@, **lodging:** Day's Inn, Super 8, **other:** HOSPITAL, KOA, PetroLube/tires/repair

4mm weigh sta nb

2 US 31 W, to Franklin, **E...gas:** Flying J/Conoco/diesel/LP/rest./24hr/@, Keystop/Marathon/Burger King/diesel/24hr/@, **W...gas:** BP/Subway/diesel, **food:** Cracker Barrel, McDonald's, Richie's Steaks, Shoney's, Waffle House, **lodging:** Best Western, Comfort Inn, Franklin Inn, Hampton Inn, Holiday Inn Express, Kentucky Motel, **other:** HOSPITAL

1mm Welcome Ctr nb, full(handicapped)facilities, phone, vending, picnic tables, litter barrels, petwalk

0mm Kentucky/Tennessee state line

Interstate 71

Exit # Services

Kentucky/Ohio state line, Ohio River

I-71 and I-75 run together 19 miles. **See Kentucky Interstate 75, exits 175-192.**

77[173] I-75 S, to Lexington, no facilities

75mm weigh sta sb

72 KY 14, to Verona, **E...gas:** BP/diesel, Chevron/diesel, **other:** Oak Creek Camping(5mi)

62 US 127, to Glencoe, **E...gas:** 62 TrkPlaza/diesel/rest./@, **W...gas:** Marathon/diesel/rest., **lodging:** 127 Motel

57 KY 35, to Sparta, **E...gas:** Marathon/diese, **other:** Sparta RV Park(3mi), **W...gas:** BP/diesel, **lodging:** Ramada Inn, **other:** KY Speedway

55 KY 1039, **W...**KY Speedway

44 KY 227, to Indian Hills, **E...gas:** BP/LP, **W...gas:** Chevron/diesel/24hr, Citgo/diesel, Marathon/diesel, Shell, **food:** Arby's, Burger King, Hometown Pizza, KFC, LJ Silver, McDonald's, Subway, Taco Bell, Waffle House, **lodging:** Best Western, Day's Inn, Hampton Inn, Holiday Inn Express, Super 8, **other:** HOSPITAL, Chevrolet, Chrysler/Plymouth/Dodge, Ford/Mercury, $General, Factory Stores/famous brands, Kroger/gas, Rite Aid, Sav-A-Lot Foods, Wal-Mart SuperCtr/24hr, Carroll Butler SP

43.5mm Kentucky River

43 KY 389, to KY 55, English, no facilities

34 US 421, Campbellsburg, **W...gas:** Citgo/Subway/diesel, Marathon

28 KY 153, KY 146, to US 42, Pendleton, **E...gas:** Marathon/diesel, Paul's, Pilot/Subwaydiesel/24hr, **W...gas:** Pilot/McDonald's/diesel/24hr

22 KY 53, La Grange, **E...gas:** BP/24hr, Marathon/diesel, Speedway/Rally's, **food:** Burger King, Lucky Dragon Chinese, Papa John's, Ponderosa, Waffle House, Wendy's, **lodging:** Day's Inn, Holiday Inn Express, Luxbury Inn, **other:** HOSPITAL, Big O Tire, $General, Kroger/gas, Wal-Mart SuperCtr/24hr, **W...gas:** Chevron/diesel/24hr, Shell, Swifty, **food:** Arby's, Cracker Barrel, DQ, Hometown Pizza, KFC, LJ Silver, McDonald's, Subway, Taco Bell, **lodging:** Comfort Suites, Super 8, **other:** Chevrolet/Pontiac/Buick, NAPA, Rite Aid

18 KY 393, Buckner, **W...gas:** Citgo/diesel, **food:** Subway

17 KY 146, Buckner, **E...other:** Ford, **W...gas:** Shell/diesel, Thornton's/diesel/24hr, **other:** USPO, st police

14 KY 329, Crestwood, Pewee Valley, Brownsboro, **E...gas:** Chevron/24hr, Shell, **2 mi E...food:** DQ, Hometown Pizza, Subway

13mm rest area both lanes, full(handicapped)facilities, phone, vending, picnic tables, litter barrels, petwalk

9b a I-265, KY 841, Gene Snyder Fwy, **E...**to Sawyer SP

5 I-264, Watterson Expswy, **E...**to Sawyer SP

2 Zorn Ave, **E...**VA HOSPITAL, **W...gas:** BP, Chevron, **food:** Kingfish Rest., **lodging:** Ramada Inn, **other:** Art Museum

1b I-65, S to Nashville, N to Indianapolis

Interstate 75

Exit # Services

193mm Kentucky/Ohio state line, Ohio River

192 5th St(from nb), Covington, **E...gas:** BP, Chevron, Shell, Speedway, **food:** AllStar Chili, Big Boy, Burger King, GoldStar Chili, McDonald's, Perkins, Subway, Taco Bell, Waffle House, White Castle, **lodging:** Courtyard, Extended Stay America, Holiday Inn, Radisson, **other:** Ford/Lincoln/Mercury, Lexus, Subaru/VW, Riverboat Casino, **W...lodging:** Hampton Inn

191 12th St, Covington, **E...food:** Jillian's Rest., **other:** HOSPITAL, Dodge, museum, same as 192

189 KY 1072(from sb), Kyles Lane, **W...gas:** BP/diesel, Marathon/diesel, Shell/diesel, Speedway, **food:** Big Boy, Hardee's, Pizza Hut, Substation II, **lodging:** Day's Inn, Ramada Inn, **other:** SteinMart, Thriftway Foods, Walgreen, same as 188

188 US 25, US 42, Dixe Hwy, **W...lodging:** Day's Inn, Holiday Inn, Ramada, **other:** DENTIST, Kroger, same as 189

Interstate 75

N ↕ S

Florence

186 KY 371, Buttermilk Pike, Covington, **E...gas:** Ashland, BP/diesel, Citgo/diesel, **food:** DQ, DrawBridge Rest., Oriental Wok, Papa John's, **lodging:** Best Western, Cross Country Inn, **W...gas:** Ashland, BP, Shell, Sunoco/diesel, **food:** Arby's, Bob Evans, Burger King, Domino's, Fazoli's, GoldStar Chili, LJ Silver, McDonald's, Outback Steaks, Pizza Hut, Subway, **other:** CHIROPRACTOR, Drug Emporium, Remke Foods, Walgreen

185 I-275 E and W, **W...**to airport

184 KY 236, Donaldson Rd, to Erlanger, **E...gas:** BP/deli, Marathon, **food:** Double Dragon Chinese, Rally's, **W...gas:** Ashland/Subway, Marathon, Speedway, Sunoco, **food:** Waffle House, **lodging:** Comfort Inn, Day's Inn, Econolodge

182 KY 1017, Turfway Rd, **E...gas:** BP, **food:** Big Boy, Blimpie, Krispy Kreme, Lee's Chicken, Penn Sta Subs, Ryan's, **lodging:** Comfort Inn, Courtyard, Fairfield Inn, Signature Inn, **other:** Big Lots, Office Depot, Winn-Dixie, funpark, **W...gas:** Meijer/diesel/24hr, **food:** Applebee's, Boston Mkt, Burger King, Cracker Barrel, Fuddrucker's, Italianni's Rest., Longhorn Steaks, Ming Garden Chinese, O'Charley's, Rafferty's, Schlotsky's, Shell's Rest., Steak'n Shake, Tumbleweeds Grill, Wendy's, **lodging:** AmeriSuites, Ashley Qtrs Hotel, Extended Stay America, Hampton Inn, Hilton Inn, Studio+ Suites, **other:** HOSPITAL, Best Buy, Biggs Foods, Home Depot, Kohl's, Lowe's Whse, OfficeMax, Sam's Club, Turfway Park Racing, Wal-Mart

181 KY 18, Florence, **E...gas:** Speedway, TA/Citgo/diesel/rest./24hr/@, **food:** Goodfellow's Dining, Waffle House, **lodging:** Best Western, Cross Country Inn, **W...gas:** BP/diesel/Procare, **lodging:** Microtel, Suburban Lodge, **other:** JC Penney, K-Mart, Dodge, Ford, Mazda, Nissan, Toyota

180-A Mall Rd(from sb), **W...food:** ChiChi's, ChuckeCheese, GoldStar Chili, China King, Hardee's, LoneStar Steaks, Old Country Buffet, Olive Garden, Taco Bell, **other:** Barnes&Noble, Home Goods, Jo-Ann Fabrics, Kroger/24hr, Lazarus, Mens Whse, Michael's, Sears/auto, Staples, Walgreen, mall, same as 180

180 US 42, US 127, Florence, Union, **E...gas:** BP/diesel, Speedway, Thornton, **food:** BBQ, Big Boy, Bob Evans, Burger King, Capt D's, Jalapeno's Mexican, LJ Silver, Main Moon Chinese, McDonald's, Pizza Hut, Rally's, Red Lobster, Substation II, Subway, WarmUps Café, Wendy's, **lodging:** Knight's Inn, Motel 6, Ramada Inn/rest., Super 8, **other:** Cadillac, funpark, **W...gas:** BP, Chevron/TCBY/diesel, Shell/diesel/24hr, Speedway, **food:** Arby's, Burger King, DQ, KFC, Little Caesar's, Perkins/24hr, Pizza Hut, Ponderosa, Waffle House, White Castle, Kroger/deli, **lodging:** Budget Host, Holiday Inn, Travelodge, Wildwood Inn, **other:** AutoZone, Circuit City, CVS Drug, Michel Tire, NTB, PepBoys, Walgreen

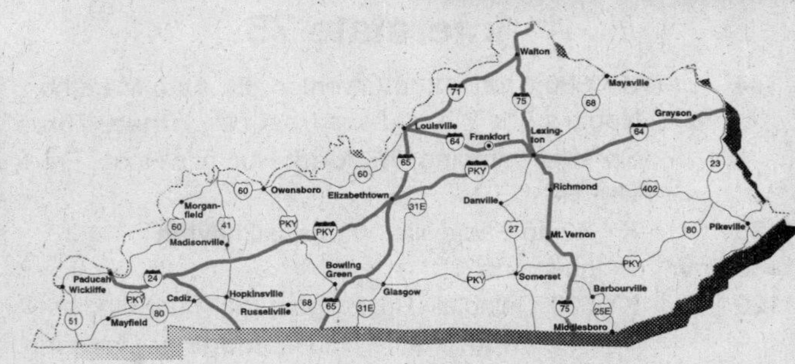

178 KY 536, Mt Zion Rd, **E...gas:** BP/Rally's/diesel, Mobil, Shell/diesel, Sunoco/diesel, **food:** GoldStar Chili, Hometown Pizza, Jersey Mike's Subs, Margarita's Mexican, Steak'n Shake, Subway, **other:** VETERINARIAN, Goodyear/auto, MktPlace Foods, Valvoline

177mm Welcome Ctr sb/rest area nb, full(handicapped)facilities, phone, vending, picnic tables, litter barrels, RV dump

175 KY 338, Richwood, **E...gas:** TA/BP/Taco Bell/diesel/rest./@, Pilot/Subway/diesel/@, **food:** Arby's, Burger King, White Castle/24hr, **lodging:** Holiday Inn Express, **other:** Florence RV Park, **W...gas:** BP/Wendy's, Pilot/Subway/diesel/24hr/@, Shell/diesel, **food:** GoldStar Chili, McDonald's, Snappy Tomato Pizza, Waffle House, **lodging:** Day's Inn/rest., Econolodge, **other:** to Big Bone Lick SP

173 I-71 S, to Louisville

171 KY 14, KY 16, Walton, to Verona, **E...gas:** BP, Citgo/DQ, **food:** Waffle House, **W...gas:** Flying J/Conoco/diesel/LP/rest./24hr/@, **other:** Blue Beacon, Delightful Dave's RV Ctr, to Big Bone Lick SP

168mm weigh sta sb

166 KY 491, Crittenden, **E...gas:** BP, Citgo/diesel, Marathon/A&W/Taco Bell/diesel, **other:** Chrysler/Plymouth/Dodge, KOA(2mi), **W...gas:** Chevron, Shell/Subway/diesel, **food:** Burger King, Country Bumpkins Rest.

159 KY 22, Dry Ridge, to Owenton, **E...gas:** BP, Marathon/DQ, Shell/diesel, **food:** Arby's/24hr, Burger King, KFC/Taco Bell, LJ Silver, McDonald's, Pizza Hut, Subway, Waffle House, Wendy's, **lodging:** Country Inn Suites, Dry Ridge Inn, Microtel, Super 8, **other:** HOSPITAL, $General, Radio Shack, Wal-Mart SuperCtr/24hr, **W...gas:** Speedway/diesel, Sunoco/diesel, **food:** Country Grill, Cracker Barrel, **lodging:** Hampton Inn, Holiday Inn Express, **other:** Toyota, Dry Ridge Outlets/famous brands, Sav-A-Lot, Toyota

154 KY 36, Williamstown, **E...gas:** Citgo/diesel/LP, Shell/diesel, **food:** Chester Fried Chicken, Red Carpet Rest., **lodging:** Knight's Inn, **other:** HOSPITAL, to Kincaid Lake SP, **W...gas:** BP/diesel, Marathon/diesel, **food:** Sterling Rest., **lodging:** Day's Inn, HoJo's

KENTUCKY

Interstate 75

N S Lexington

144 KY 330, Corinth, to Owenton, **E...gas:** Marathon, Noble's Trk Plaza/diesel/rest./@, **other:** Three Springs Camping, **W...food:** Hunter's Rest., Freeway Rest.

136 KY 32, to Sadieville, **W...gas:** Chevron

130.5mm weigh sta nb

129 KY 620, Delaplain Rd, **E...gas:** Pilot/Subway/diesel/24hr/@, **food:** Waffle House, **lodging:** Day's Inn, Motel 6, **W...gas:** Pilot/McDonald's/diesel/24hr/@, Shell/24hr,

127mm rest area both lanes, full(handicapped)facilities, phone, vending, picnic tables, litter barrels, petwalk

126 US 62, to US 460, Georgetown, **E...gas:** BP, Chevron/24hr, Marathon, **food:** Applebee's, Big Boy, McDonald's, O'Charley's, Flag Inn, Lowe's Whse, Wal-Mart SuperCtr/gas/diesel/24hr, **W...gas:** BP, Shell/24hr, Speedway/A&W/diesel, **food:** Cracker Barrel, Fazoli's, KFC, Waffle House, **lodging:** Best Western, Comfort Suites, Country Inn Suites, Hampton Inn, Holiday Inn Express, Microtel, Shoney's Inn, Subway, Wendy's, Super 8, Winner's Circle Motel, **other:** HOSPITAL, Chevrolet/Pontiac/Buick, Ford, Dodge/Jeep, K-Mart/Little Caesar's, Outlets/famous brands, to Georgetown Coll, same as 125

125 US 460(from nb), Georgetown, **E...gas:** BP/diesel, Marathon, Shell, **lodging:** Econolodge, Flag Inn, Super 8, **other:** flea mkt, **W...gas:** DM, Swifty, **food:** Arby's, DQ, LJ Silver, Reno's Roadhouse, Taco Bell, Wendy's, **other:** Outlets/famous brands, Radio Shack, same as 126

120 rd 1973, to Ironworks Pike, KY Horse Park, **E...**KY Horse Park Camping, **W...gas:** Citgo/Stuckey's/diesel/pizza/24hr, **other:** HOSPITAL

118 I-64 W, to Frankfort, Louisville

115 KY 922, Lexington, **E...gas:** Exxon/diesel, Shell/Subway/24hr, **food:** Cracker Barrel, McDonald's, Waffle House, **lodging:** Knight's Inn, La Quinta, Sheraton, **other:** SaddleHorse Museum(4mi), **W...gas:** Chevron/diesel, **food:** Denny's, Post Rest., **lodging:** Embassy Suites, Holiday Inn, Marriott/rest., **other:** museum

113 US 27, US 68, Lexington, to Paris, **E...gas:** BP/diesel(2mi), Speedway, **food:** Waffle House, **lodging:** Ramada Inn, **W...gas:** Chevron/Subway/diesel/24hr, Shell, **food:** Fazoli's, LJ Silver, Siggy's Rest., **lodging:** Catalina Motel, Red Roof Inn, **1 mi W...gas:** Shell, Swifty, **food:** Burger King, Capt D's, Hardee's/24hr, Shoney's, **other:** Chevrolet, Chrysler/Plymouth/Jeep, Hall's RV Ctr, Kroger/deli, Northside RV Ctr, carwash, to UKY, Rupp Arena

111 I-64 E, to Huntington, WV

Lexington

110 US 60, Lexington, **W...gas:** Shell, Speedway/diesel, Thornton/Subway/24hr, **food:** Arby's, Bob Evans, Cracker Barrel, Hardee's, International Buffet, McDonald's, Waffle House, Wendy's, **lodging:** Baymont Inn, Best Western, BlueGrass Suites, Comfort Inn, Country Inn Suites, Hampton Inn, HoJo's, Holiday Inn Express, Knight's Inn, Microtel, Motel 6, Quality Inn, Ramada Ltd, Signature Inn, Super 8, Wilson Inn

108 Man O War Blvd, **W...gas:** Citgo/diesel, Meijer/diesel/24hr, Shell/Wendy's/24hr, Speedway, **food:** Applebee's, Arby's, Backyard Burger, Burger King, Carrabba's, Chick-fil-A, Damon's, Don Pablo, Fazoli's, GoldStar Chili, KFC/Taco Bell, Logan's Roadhouse, Max&Erma's, McDonald's, Outback Steaks, Pizza Hut, Rafferty's, Ruby Tuesday, Steak'n Shake, Taco Bell, TGIFriday, Waffle House, **lodging:** Courtyard, Hilton Garden, Sleep Inn, **other:** HOSPITAL, Barnes&Noble, Goody's, Kohl's, OfficeMax, Old Navy, Radio Shack, Target, Walgreen

104 KY 418, Lexington, **E...gas:** Exxon/Wendy's/diesel/24hr, Shell, **food:** Waffle House, **lodging:** Comfort Suites, Day's Inn, Econolodge, Red Roof Inn, Holiday Inn, **W...gas:** BP/diesel, Chevron, Speedway/Subway, **food:** Jerry's Rest., **other:** HOSPITAL, **4 mi W...food:** Hooters, KFC, Texas Roadhouse

99 US 25 N, US 421 N, no facilities

98mm Kentucky River

97 US 25 S, US 421 S, **E...gas:** Exxon/Huddle House/diesel/24hr, flea mkt, **W...**RV camping(2mi)

95 KY 627, to Boonesboro, Winchester, **E...gas:** BP/Blimpie/diesel, Love's/diesel/24hr/@, **food:** Hall's Diner(6mi), McDonald's, **other:** Ft Boonesborough SP, camping, **W...gas:** Shell/Burger King/diesel/24hr

Richmond

90 US 25, US 421, Richmond, **E...food:** Cracker Barrel, Outback Steaks(4mi), Western Sizzlin, **lodging:** Knight's Inn, La Quinta, Ramada Ltd, Red Roof Inn, **W...gas:** Citgo/24hr, Exxon/Arby's/diesel, Shell, Thorobred Gas, **food:** Big Boy, DQ, Hardee's, Pizza Hut, Subway, Waffle House, Wendy's, **lodging:** Day's Inn, Super 8, **other:** NTB, Pennzoil, antiques

87 KY 876, Richmond, **E...gas:** Amoco/diesel/24hr, BP/diesel, Chevron/24hr, Citgo/diesel, Shell/diesel/24hr, Speedway/diesel, **food:** Arby's, Bojangles, Burger King, DQ, Denny's, Dunkin Donuts, Fazoli's, Hardee's, KFC, Krystal/24hr, Little Caesar's, LJ Silver, McDonald's, Papa John's, Pizza Hut, Rally's, Red Lobster(2mi), Snappy Tomato Pizza, Subway, Taco Bell, Waffle House, Wendy's, **lodging:** Best Western, Econolodge, Holiday Inn, Quality Qtrs Inn, **other:** HOSPITAL, $General, Goodyear/auto, Winn-Dixie, to EKU, **W...gas:** BP/diesel, DM/24hr, **food:** Bob Evans, J Patrick's Grille, Ryan's, Steak'n Shake/24hr, **lodging:** Comfort Suites, Hampton Inn, Holiday Inn Express, Jameson Inn

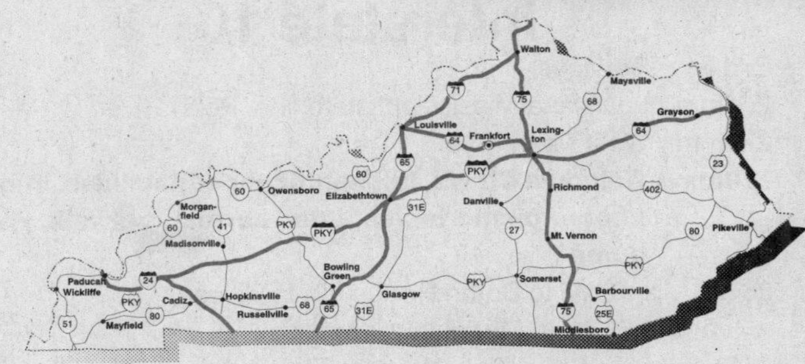

Interstate 75

N ↕ S

Berea

82.5mm rest area both lanes, full(handicapped)facilities, phone, vending, picnic tables, litter barrels, petwalk

77 KY 595, Berea, **E...**HOSPITAL, to Berea Coll, **W...gas:** BP/Subway/24hr, Shell, **food:** Columbia Grill, Denny's, **lodging:** Day's Inn, Holiday Inn Express

76 KY 21, Berea, **E...gas:** BP, Citgo/DQ/Stuckey's, DM/gas, Shell/Burger King, Speedway/diesel, **food:** Arby's, Dinner Bell Rest., KFC, Little Caesar's, LJ Silver, Mario's Pizza, McDonald's, Pizza Hut, Subway, WanTen Chinese/Thai, Wendy's, **lodging:** Holiday Motel, Howard Johnson, Knight's Inn, Super 8, **other:** HOSPITAL, $General, Ford, NAPA, Wal-Mart SuperCtr/24hr, tires, **W...gas:** BP, Chevron/24hr, Marathon/diesel, **food:** Lee's Chicken, Pantry Family Rest., **lodging:** Best Western, Econolodge, Fairfield Inn, Mtn View Motel, **other:** Chrysler/Plymouth/Dodge/Jeep, O Kentucky Camping, Walnut Meadow Camping

62 US 25, to KY 461, Renfro Valley, **E...gas:** Shell/24hr, **food:** Hardee's, Waffle House, **lodging:** Country Hearth Inn, Renfro Valley Inn, **other:** KOA(2mi), **W...gas:** BP/Blimpie/24hr, Citgo/KFC/Wendy's/24hr, Shell/24hr, Marathon/Taco Bell, **food:** DQ, Denny's, Godfather's, McDonald's, Subway, **lodging:** Day's Inn, Econolodge, Mt Villa Motel, **other:** HOSPITAL, to Big South Fork NRA, Lake Cumberland

59 US 25, Mt Vernon, to Livingston, **E...gas:** BP, Marathon/diesel, Shell/diesel, **food:** Jean's Rest., Pizza Hut, **lodging:** Best Western, Kastle Inn/rest., **other:** Nicely Camping, **W...gas:** Citgo, Super 8

51mm Rockcastle River

49 KY 909, to US 25, Livingston, **W...gas:** 49er Fuel Ctr/diesel/rest./@, Shell/diesel/24hr

London

41 KY 80, London, to Somerset, **E...gas:** Chevron, Marathon, Speedway, **food:** Arby's, Burger King, DQ, Ideal Rest., KFC, McDonald's, Pizza Hut, Rax, Sonic, **lodging:** Day's Inn, Economy Inn, Holiday Inn Express, Park Inn, Red Roof Inn, Sleep Inn, Super 8, **other:** HOSPITAL, AutoZone, Chrysler/Jeep, DogPatch Trading, $General, Kroger/deli, Parsley's Tire/repair, Pontiac/GMC, Rite Aid, st police, **W...gas:** Amoco, BP/diesel/24hr/@, Chevron/McDonald's, Citgo/diesel/24hr, Shell/Subway/24hr, **food:** LJ Silver, Jerry's Rest., Patty's Buffet, Shiloh Roadhouse, Taco Bell, Waffle House, Wendy's, **lodging:** Budget Host, **other:** Westgate RV Camping

38 KY 192, London, **E...gas:** BP/diesel, Citgo/diesel, Shell/Arby's/diesel, Speedway/Rally's/diesel, **food:** Big Boy, Burger King, Capt D's, El Dorado Mexican, Fazoli's, Hardee's, Huddle House, Krystal, McDonald's, Pizza Hut, Ponderosa, Rockabilly Café, Ruby Tuesday, Taco Bell, **lodging:** Comfort Suites, Day's Inn, Hampton Inn, Ramada Ltd, **other:** HOSPITAL, Advance Parts, Goody's, Kroger, Office Depot, USPO, Wal-Mart SuperCtr/24hr, airport, camping, toll rd to Manchester/Hazard, Western Star Trucks, to Levi Jackson SP, **W...**to Laurel River Lake RA

34mm weigh sta both lanes, truck haven

30.5mm Laurel River

Corbin

29 US 25, US 25E, Corbin, **E...gas:** BP, Citgo/diesel/24hr, Exxon, Pilot/Subway/diesel/24hr/@, **food:** Arby's(2mi), KFC(2mi), Burger King, Shoney's, Taco Bell, Western Steer, Western Sizzlin, Best Western, **lodging:** Quality Inn/rest., Super 8, **other:** Goodyear, Blue Beacon, to Cumberland Gap NP, **W...gas:** BP/Krystal/diesel, Chevron/diesel, Shell/diesel/24hr, **food:** BBQ, Cracker Barrel, Taco Bell, **lodging:** Baymont Inn, Comfort Inn, Fairfield Inn, Hampton Inn, Knight's Inn, **other:** KOA, to Laurel River Lake RA

25 US 25W, Corbin, **E...gas:** Speedway/diesel, **food:** Burger King, Corbin Burgerhouse, Jerry's Rest., McDonald's, **lodging:** Country Inn Suites, Day's Inn, Holiday Inn Express, Landmark Inn, **other:** HOSPITAL, auto repair/tires, **W...gas:** BP/diesel, Exxon/Buddy's BBQ, Shell/24hr, **food:** Arby's, Reno's Roadhouse, Waffle House, **lodging:** Best Western, Regency Inn, **other:** to Cumberland Falls SP

15 US 25W, Goldbug, to Williamsburg, **W...gas:** Chevron/diesel, Shell, **other:** Cumberland Falls SP

14.5mm Cumberland River

11 KY 92, Williamsburg, **E...gas:** BP/diesel, Exxon/diesel, Shell, **food:** Arby's, DQ, Hardee's, KFC, McDonald's, Pizza Hut, Subway, TCBY, Adkins Motel, Cumberland Inn, Scottish Inn, Super 8, **other:** Chevrolet, Chrysler/Plymouth/Dodge/Jeep, $General, Ford, NAPA, Sav-A-Lot Foods, U-Haul, mufflers/transmissions, **W...gas:** Shell/diesel, Pilot/Wendy's/diesel/@, **food:** BJ's Rest., Burger King, Krystal, LJ Silver, Ribeye Steaks, **lodging:** Day's Inn, Williamsburg Motel/RV Park, **other:** Wal-Mart SuperCtr/24hr, to Big South Fork NRA

1.5mm Welcome Ctr nb, full(handicapped)facilities, phone, vending, picnic tables, litter barrels, petwalk

0mm Kentucky/Tenesee state line

LOUISIANA

Interstate 10

E ↕ W

Exit #	Services
274mm	Louisiana/Mississippi state line, Pearl River
272mm	West Pearl River
270mm	**Welcome Ctr wb, full(handicapped)facilities, info, phone, picnic tables, litter barrels, petwalk, RV dump**
267b	I-12 W, to Baton Rouge, no facilities
a	I-59 N, to Meridian, no facilities
266	US 190, Slidell, **N...gas:** Exxon/diesel, Shell/diesel, TA/Mobil/diesel/rest./24hr/@, Texaco, **food:** Arby's, Burger King, China Wok, CiCi's, Denny's, KFC, LoneStar Steaks, McDonald's, Pizza Hut, Shoney's, Taco Bell, Wendy's, **lodging:** Best Value Inn, Best Western, Day's Inn, Motel 6, Super 8, **other:** HOSPITAL, Harley-Davidson, PepBoys, Radio Shack, U-Haul, **S...gas:** Chevron/diesel/24hr, RaceTrac, **food:** Applebee's, Big Easy Diner, Cracker Barrel, Osaka Grill, Outback Steaks, Sonic, Waffle House, **lodging:** King's Lodge, La Quinta, Ramada Inn, **other:** HOSPITAL, Wal-Mart/auto, auto repair/transmissions, casino
265mm	weigh sta both lanes
263	LA 433, Slidell, **N...gas:** BP, Exxon, Shell, **food:** China Buffet, Ray's Rest., Waffle House, **lodging:** Comfort Inn, Hampton Inn, **other:** Chevrolet, Mitsubishi, **S...gas:** Fleet/Subway/diesel/@, Texaco/Domino's/diesel, **food:** McDonald's, Wendy's, **lodging:** Holiday Inn, **other:** Jeep, Ford/Lincoln/Mercury, Honda, Isuzu, Mazda, Nissan, Pontiac/Buick/GMC, Saturn, Toyota, Slidell Factory Outlet/famous brands, KOA(1mi)
261	Oak Harbor Blvd, Eden Isles, **N...gas:** Exxon/diesel, **food:** Phil's Marina Café, **lodging:** Sleep Inn, **S...gas:** BP/Subway/diesel
255mm	Lake Pontchartrain
254	US 11, to Northshore, Irish Bayou, **S...gas:** BP/diesel
251	Bayou Sauvage NWR, **S...**swamp tours
248	Michoud Blvd, no facilities
246b a	I-510 S, LA 47 N, S to Chalmette, N to Littlewood, **S...**6 Flags of NO
245	Bullard Ave, **N...gas:** Shell, **food:** Jame's Seafood, Kettle, Pizza Hut, Sonic, **lodging:** Comfort Suites, La Quinta, **other:** Daewoo, Honda, Hyundai, Mitsubishi, NAPA, **S...gas:** Exxon, Shell, **food:** Burger King, IHOP, KFC/Taco Bell, McDonald's, Shoney's, Subway, **lodging:** Hampton Inn, Motel 6, **other:** HOSPITAL, Buick/GMC, Circuit City, Ford, Home Depot, Nissan, PepBoys, Toyota
244	Read Blvd, **N...gas:** Shell, **food:** Lama's Seafood, McDonald's, TX BBQ, **other:** Office Depot, Rite Aid, Sam's Club, Walgreen, Wal-Mart, **S...gas:** Spur/diesel, **food:** Popeye's, Wendy's, **lodging:** Best Western, Day's Inn, Holiday Inn Express, **other:** HOSPITAL, Dillard's, Dodge/Jeep, Ford/Lincoln/Mercury, Goodyear/auto, Honda, Kia, Sears/auto, mall
242	Crowder Blvd, **N...gas:** Chevron, **S...gas:** Exxon, **food:** Papa John's, Rally's, Shoney's, Wendy's, **lodging:** La Quinta, **other:** Family$
241	Morrison Rd, **N...gas:** Shell, Spur, **food:** Burger King, **other:** Rite Aid
240b a	US 90 E, Chef Hwy, Downman Rd, **N...gas:** Amoco, Shell, Spur, **lodging:** Family Inn, Super 8, **other:** Chevrolet, Hyundai, U-Haul, **S...gas:** Chevron
239b a	Louisa St, Almonaster Blvd, **N...gas:** Spur, **food:** Burger King, McDonald's, Piccadilly's, Pizza Hut, Red Lobster, Wendy's, **lodging:** Howard Johnson, Knight's Inn, **other:** Firestone, K-Mart, PrecisionTune, Radio Shack, Toyota, Walgreen, Winn-Dixie, mall
238b	I-610 W(from wb)
237	Elysian Fields Ave, **N...gas:** Amoco/diesel
236b	LA 39, N Claiborne Ave, no facilities
a	Esplanade Ave, downtown
235a	Orleans Ave, to Vieux Carre, French Qtr, **S...lodging:** Day's Inn, Holiday Inn, Marriott, Sheraton, **other:** Winn-Dixie
234b	Poydras St, **N...**HOSPITAL, **S...**to Superdome, downtown
a	US 90A, Claiborne Ave, to Westbank, Superdome
232	US 61, Airline Hwy, Tulane Ave, **N...**Pennzoil, **S...gas:** Exxon, **food:** McDonald's, Piccadilly's, **other:** A&P, Chevrolet, Firestone, Radio Shack, Rite Aid, to Xavier U
231b	Florida Blvd, WestEnd
a	Metairie Rd, no facilities
230	I-610 E(from eb), to Slidell
229	Bonnabel Blvd, no facilities
228	Causeway Blvd, **N...gas:** Shell, **food:** Copeland's Rest., **lodging:** Best Western, Hampton Inn, Ramada Ltd, **S...gas:** Amoco, Exxon, Timesaver Gas, **food:** Denny's, Pasta Etc, Steak'n Egg/24hr, **lodging:** Courtyard, Extended Stay America, Holiday Inn, La Quinta, Quality Hotel, Residence Inn, Wyndham, **other:** MEDICAL CARE
226	Clearview Pkwy, Huey Long Br, **N...gas:** Chevron, Exxon, **food:** Ruby Tuesday, **lodging:** Sleep Inn, **other:** Sears, Target, **S...gas:** Chevron, Circle K, **food:** Burger King, Piccadilly's, Subway, **lodging:** Shoney's Inn, Sun Suites, **other:** HOSPITAL, Buick/GMC, Dillard's, mall
225	Veterans Blvd, **N...gas:** Chevron, Shell, Spur/diesel, **food:** Burger King, Denny's, McDonald's, Rouse's Foods, **lodging:** La Quinta, **other:** Aamco, Dodge, Honda, Radio Shack, Rite Aid, **S...gas:** Jubilee, Shell, **food:** Church's, Godfather's, N O Burgers, Piccadilly's, Popeye's, Rally's, Schlotsky's, Tiffin Pancakes, Wendy's, **lodging:** Holiday Inn, Sheraton, **other:** Acura, Best Buy, Chevrolet, CompUSA, GNC, Home Depot, Jo-Ann Fabrics, K-Mart, Michael's, Nissan, Office Depot, PepBoys, VW, Walgreen, Wal-Mart/auto
224	Power Blvd(from wb)

Slidell

New Orleans Area

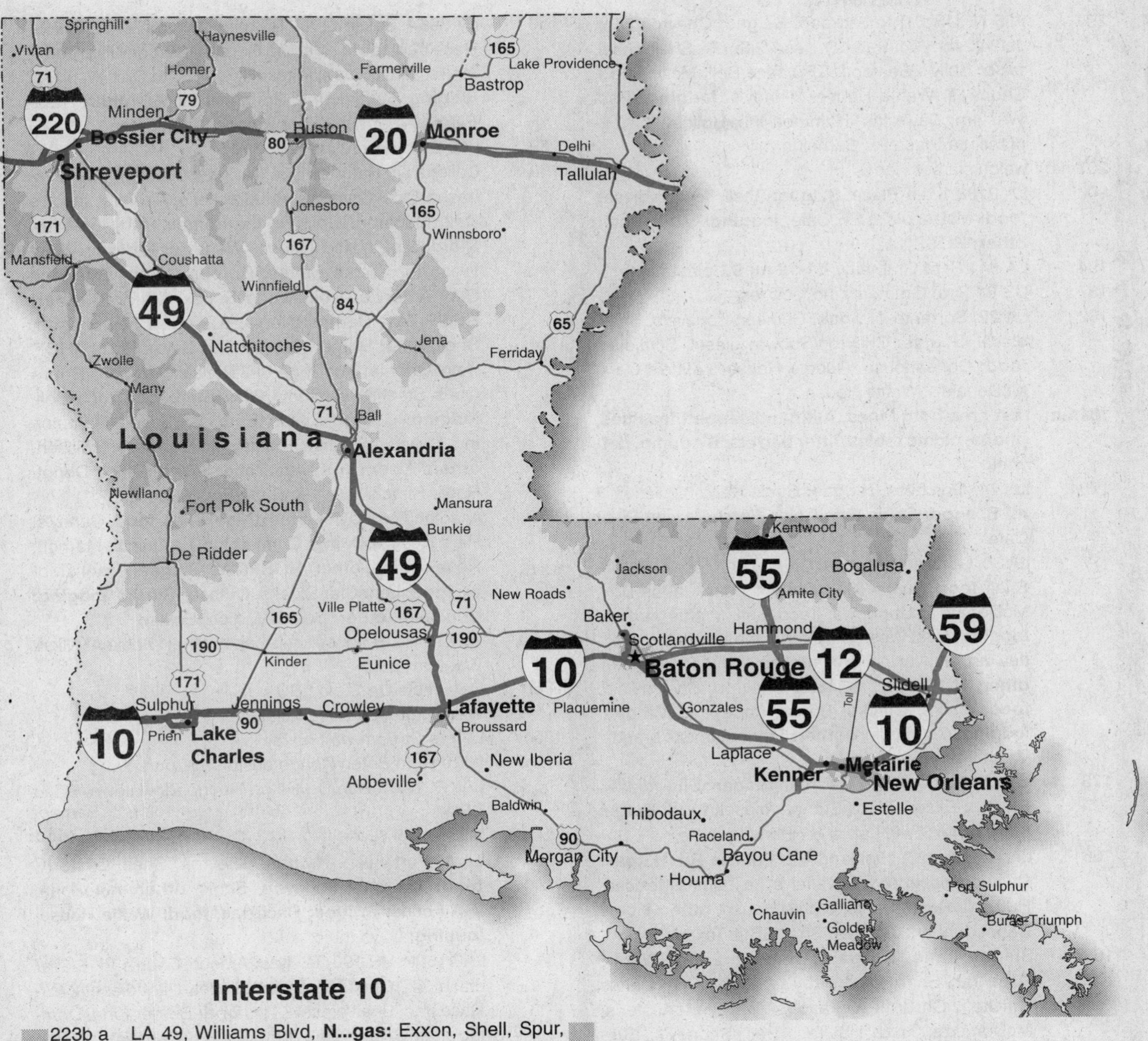

Interstate 10

E ↕ W

223b a LA 49, Williams Blvd, **N...gas:** Exxon, Shell, Spur, **food:** Burger King, Church's, El Patio, Fisherman's Cove, Jade Palace, Pizza Hut, Popeye's, Rally's, Subway, Taco Bell, Tokyo Japanese, Wendy's, **lodging:** Fairfield Inn, **other:** AutoZone, Ford, Office Depot, OfficeMax, Rite Aid, **S...gas:** Exxon/diesel, Shell, **food:** Brick Oven, Burger King, Denny's, Jazz Seafood/steaks, McDonald's, Messina's Rest., Pizza Hut, Sonic, Subway, **lodging:** Best Western, Comfort Inn, Contempra Inn, Day's Inn, Extended Stay America, Holiday Inn, La Quinta, Plaza Inn, Travelodge, Wingate Inn, **other:** Advance Parts, Circuit City, Dillard's, Eckerd, Firestone/auto, Goodyear, Hyundai, NAPA, Radio Shack, U-Haul, mall

221 Loyola Dr, **N...gas:** Circle K, Exxon/diesel, Shell/diesel, Spur, **food:** Church's, McDonald's, Popeye's, Rally's, Subway, Taco Bell, **other:** Advance Parts, Sam's Club/gas, **S...gas:** Amoco, **food:** Rick's Café, Wendy's, **lodging:** Sleep Inn, **other:** airport, info

220 I-310 S, to Houma, no facilities

214mm Lake Pontchartrain

210 I-55N(from wb)

LOUISIANA

Interstate 10

E ↕ W

La Place

209 I-55 N, US 51, to Jackson, **S...gas:** Chevron/24hr, Jet24/24hr, Pilot/Subway/diesel/24hr/@, Shell/diesel, **food:** Bully's Seafood, KFC/Taco Bell, McDonald's, Shoney's, Waffle House, Wendy's, **lodging:** Best Western, Day's Inn, Hampton Inn, Holiday Inn Express, La Place RV Camping

207mm weigh sta both lanes

206 LA 3188 S, La Place, **S...gas:** Shell, Texaco/diesel, **food:** McDonald's, SF Café, **lodging:** Millet Motel, **other:** HOSPITAL

194 LA 641 S, to Gramercy, **11-15 mi S...**plantations

187 US 61 S, to Gramercy, no facilities

182 LA 22, Sorrento, **N...gas:** Chevron/Popeye's, Shell/diesel, **S...gas:** Chevron/Subway/diesel, SJ/diesel, **food:** Coffeehouse, Huddle House, Lafitte's Café, McDonald's, Waffle House

181mm rest area both lanes, full(handicapped)facilities, phone, picnic tables, litter barrels, RV dump, petwalk

179 LA 44, Gonzales, **N...gas:** Circle K, Mobil/diesel, **3 mi S...food:** Cabin Fine Cajun Food, Pelican Point Café

177 LA 30, Gonzales, **N...gas:** Citgo/USA/diesel/24hr/@, Shell, **food:** Burger King, Church's, Jack-in-the-Box, McDonald's, Shoney's, Taco Bell, Waffle House, **lodging:** Best Western, Budget Inn, Day's Inn, Holiday Inn, Quality Inn, Western Inn, White Rose Motel, **other:** HOSPITAL, **S...gas:** Chevron, Shell/diesel, **food:** Chili's, Cracker Barrel, Popeye's, Wendy's, **lodging:** Comfort Inn, **other:** Tanger/famous brands, Vesta RV Park

173 LA 73, Prairieville, to Geismar, **N...gas:** Shell/diesel, **S...gas:** Exxon, Mobil/Subway/diesel, **food:** Burger King, **other:** Twin Lakes RV Park(1mi)

166 LA 42, LA 427, Highland Rd, Perkins Rd, **N...gas:** Chevron/diesel, **food:** Church's, La Palmas Mexican, Ruffino's Rest., Sonic, Waffle House, **other:** Home Depot, funpark, **S...gas:** Shell/BBQ, Texaco

163 Siegen Lane, **N...gas:** Chevron/24hr, Exxon, RaceTrac, Shell, **food:** Arby's, Burger King, Canes Chicken, Chick-fil-A, Fazoli's, IHOP, McAlister's, McDonald's, Pizza Hut/Taco Bell, Shoney's, Subway, Waffle House, Whataburger, **lodging:** Baymont Inn, Holiday Inn, Microtel, Motel 6, **other:** Advance Parts, $Tree, Honda, Office Depot, Radio Shack, Target, **S...food:** Chili's, Joe's Crabshack, Subway, Wendy's, **lodging:** Courtyard, Residence Inn, **other:** BooksAMillion, Lowe's Whse, Sam's Club/gas, Wal-Mart SuperCtr/24hr

162 Bluebonnet Rd, **N...gas:** Chevron/diesel, **lodging:** Quality Suites, **S...gas:** RaceWay, **food:** Bennigan's, Burger King, Copeland's, J Alexander's, Logan's Roadhouse, Ralph&Kacoo's, **lodging:** AmeriSuites, **other:** Best Buy, CompUSA, Dillard's, JC Penney, McRae's, Sears/auto, Mall of LA

Baton Rouge

160 LA 3064, Essen Lane, **S...gas:** Chevron/24hr, Exxon, RaceTrac, **food:** Bamboo Garden, Burger King, Copeland's, McDonald's, Piccadilly's, Tomato Grill, Wendy's, **lodging:** Fairfield Inn, Springhill Suites, **other:** HOSPITAL, Albertson's, Tire Kingdom, Walgreen

159 I-12 E, to Hammond

158 College Dr, Baton Rouge, **N...gas:** Jubilee, **food:** Alabasha Café, Damon's, Fuddrucker's, Hooters, Jason's Deli, Macaroni Grill, On-the-Border, Ruby Tuesday, Starbucks, Waffle House, Wendy's, **lodging:** Best Western, Chase Suites, Corporate Inn, Extended Stay America, Homewood Suites, Marriott, **other:** HOSPITAL, Barnes&Noble, **S...gas:** Chevron/24hr, Shell, **food:** Burger King, Chili's, Gino's Pizza, IHOP, Koto Oriental, McDonald's, Ninfa's Mexican, Ruth's Chris Steaks, Seminola Grill, Starbucks, Taco Bell, **lodging:** Comfort Suites, Embassy Suites, Hampton Inn, Hawthorn Suites, Holiday Inn Express, Radisson, **other:** Albertson's, AutoZone, $Tree, Office Depot, Radio Shack, Rite Aid, SuperFresh Foods

157b Acadian Thruway, **N...gas:** Citgo, Shell, **food:** Denny's, Rib's Rest., **lodging:** Comfort Inn, La Quinta, Marriott, Rodeway Inn, **other:** HOSPITAL, **S...gas:** Exxon, Mobil, **food:** LoneStar Steaks, Outback Steaks, **lodging:** Courtyard, **other:** BooksAMillion, Eckerd

a Perkins Rd, **S...gas:** Shell/diesel, **other:** BooksAMillion, Wal-Mart/auto

156b Dalrymple Dr, **S...**to LSU

a Washington St, no facilities

155c Louise St(from wb), no facilities

b I-110 N, to Baton Rouge bus dist, airport

a LA 30, Nicholson Dr, Baton Rouge, downtown, **S...**to LSU

154mm Mississippi River

153 LA 1, Port Allen, **N...gas:** Chevron, Shell, Circle K, **food:** Church's, Popeye's, Sonic, **other:** AutoZone, IGA Foods, **S...gas:** RaceTrac, **food:** Waffle House, **lodging:** Days Inn

151 LA 415, to US 190, **N...gas:** Amoco, Cash's Trk Plaza/diesel/@, Chevron, Exxon/diesel, Pilot/diesel/24hr, RaceTrac, Shell/diesel/24hr, **food:** Burger King, Domino's, KFC/Taco Bell, McDonald's, Popeye's, Waffle House, Wendy's, **lodging:** Best Western, Chinese Inn/rest., Comfort Inn, Days Inn, Holiday Inn Express, Shoney's Inn, **other:** Cajun Country Camping(2mi), **S...gas:** Love's/Arby's/diesel/24hr, Shell/diesel/24hr, Texaco/diesel/24hr, **lodging:** Motel 6, Ramada Inn, Super 8

139 LA 77, Grosse Tete, **N...gas:** Shell/Subway/diesel, **other:** Chevrolet, **S...gas:** Tiger Trkstp/diesel/rest./@

137.5mm rest area both lanes, full(handicapped)facilities, phone, picnic tables, litter barrels, petwalk, RV dump

135 LA 3000, to Ramah, **N...gas:** Texaco

128mm emergency callboxes begin wb, about 1/2 mi intervals

127 LA 975, to Whiskey Bay, no facilities

Interstate 10

E ↕ W

126.5mm Pilot Channel of Whiskey Bay
122mm Atchafalaya River
121 Butte La Rose, no facilities
117mm emergency callboxes begin eb, about 1/2 mi intervals
115 LA 347, to Cecilia, Henderson, **N...gas:** BP/diesel, Exxon/diesel/24hr, Texaco/diesel, **food:** Boudin's Rest., Landry's Seafood, **lodging:** Holiday Inn Express, **S...gas:** Chevron/DQ/diesel, Citgo, Exxon/Subway/diesel, Pilot/diesel/24hr/@, Shell, **food:** McDonald's, Waffle House
109 LA 328, to Breaux Bridge, **N...gas:** Shell/diesel, Texaco/Blimpie/diesel, **food:** Crawfish Kitchen, **S...gas:** Chevron/Popeye's, Mobil/Burger King/Domino's/diesel, Pilot/Arbys/diesel/24hr/@, Texaco, **food:** Church's, McDonald's, Mulate's Cajun Rest., Waffle House, Wendy's, **lodging:** Best Western, Sonan Motel

Lafayette

108mm weigh sta both lanes
103b I-49 N, to Opelousas
a US 167 S, to Lafayette, **N...gas:** Shell/diesel, **food:** Church's, **lodging:** Motel 6, Ramada Inn, **S...gas:** Chevron/diesel/24hr, RaceTrac, Shell, **food:** Checker's, ChopStix Chinese, Kajun Kitchen, KFC, McDonald's, Pizza Hut, Popeye's, Shoney's, Subway, Taco Bell, Waffle House, Wendy's, Western Sizzlin, **lodging:** Best Western, Comfort Suites, Fairfield Inn, Holiday Inn, Jameson Inn, La Quinta, Quality Inn, Super 8, TravelHost Inn, **other:** HOSPITAL, Albertson's/gas, $General, Firestone/auto, Ford, Home Depot, Rite Aid, Super 1 Foods/gas, VW, Wal-Mart SuperCtr/gas/24hr, transmissions
101 LA 182, to Lafayette, **N...gas:** Chevron/McDonald's, RideUSA, TA/Mobil/diesel/24hr/@, **food:** Arby's, Burger King, Pizza Hut, Waffle House, Whataburger, **lodging:** Red Roof Inn, **other:** Honda Motorcycles, **S...gas:** Circle K, Exxon, RaceTrac, Shell/diesel, **food:** Cracker Barrel, **lodging:** Calloway Inn, Day's Inn, **other:** HOSPITAL, Hyundai, Isuzu/Kia
100 Ambassador Caffery Pkwy, **N...gas:** Exxon/Subway/diesel/24hr, **S...gas:** Chevron/24hr, Citgo/24hr, RaceTrac/24hr, Shell/diesel, **food:** Burger King, McDonald's, Pizza Hut/Taco Bell, Sonic, Waffle House, Wendy's, **lodging:** Hampton Inn, Sleep Inn, Microtel, **other:** HOSPITAL, Goodyear
97 LA 93, to Scott, **N...**Christien Pt RV Park, **S...gas:** Shell/Church's/diesel/24hr, **lodging:** Howard Johnson, **other:** Harley-Davidson, KOA
92 LA 95, to Duson, **N...gas:** Texaco/diesel/casino/24hr, **S...gas:** Chevron/diesel, Exxon/diesel, **lodging:** Super 8

Crowley

87 LA 35, to Rayne, **N...gas:** Chevron/diesel, Exxon/diesel/24hr, **food:** Burger King, Chef Roy's Café, Gabe's Café, McDonald's, **lodging:** Days Inn, **other:** RV camping, **S...gas:** Citgo/diesel, Mobil/diesel/24hr, Shamrock/diesel, Shell/Subway, **food:** DQ, Popeye's, **lodging:** Comfort Inn, **other:** HOSPITAL, Advance Parts, Eckerd, Family$, NAPA, Winn-Dixie
82 LA 1111, to E Crowley, **S...gas:** Chevron/diesel, Murphy USA/gas, Shamrock, **food:** Wendy's, **other:** HOSPITAL, $Tree, GNC, Radio Shack, Wal-Mart SuperCtr/24hr
80 LA 13, to Crowley, **N...gas:** Conoco/diesel/24hr, Shell/diesel, **food:** Rice Palace Rest., Waffle House, **lodging:** Best Western, Crowley Inn, **S...gas:** Circle K/24hr, Exxon/24hr, RaceTrac, Shamrock/diesel, **food:** Burger King, DQ, Domino's, El Dorado Mexican, Fezzo's Seafood/steaks, KFC, Lucky Wok Chinese, McDonald's, Mr Gatti's, Pizza Hut, PJ's Grill, Popeye's, Sonic, Subway, Taco Bell, **other:** AutoZone, Chrysler/Plymouth/Dodge/Jeep, $General, Ford/Mercury/Nissan, Nissan, Radio Shack, Rite Aid, U-Haul, Winn-Dixie
76 LA 91, to Iota, **S...gas:** Conoco/diesel/café/24hr
72 Egan, **S... food:** Cajun Connection Rest.
67.5mm rest areas both lanes full(handicapped)facilities, phone, picnic tables, litter barrels, petwalk, RV dump
65 LA 97, to Jennings, **N...gas:** Spur/diesel, **S...gas:** Phillips 66/diesel, **lodging:** Day's Inn, **other:** to SW LA St School

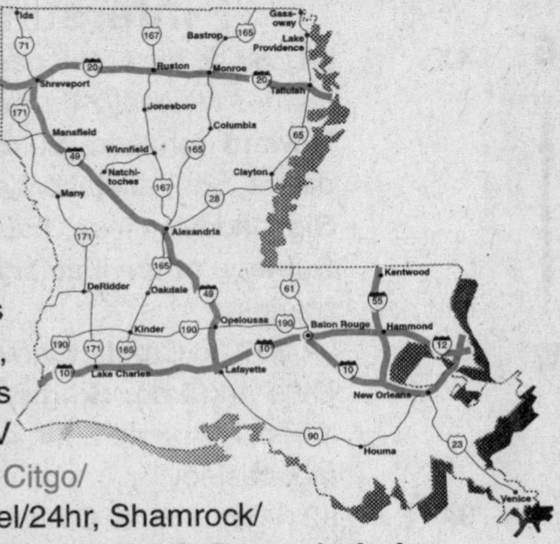

Jennings

64 LA 26, to Jennings, **N...**Budget Inn, **S...gas:** Chevron, Citgo, Exxon, Fina, Jennings Trvl Ctr/diesel, Shamrock/diesel, **food:** Burger King, DQ, Denny's, McDonald's, Mr Gatti's, Pizza Hut, Popeye's, Shoney's, Sonic, Subway, Taco Bell, Waffle House, Wendy's, **lodging:** Comfort Inn, Holiday Inn, **other:** HOSPITAL, AutoZone, Chrysler/Jeep/Dodge, Goodyear/auto, HiLo Parts, Rite Aid, Wal-Mart SuperCtr/gas/24hr, bank
59 LA 395, to Roanoke, no facilities
54 LA 99, Welsh, **S...gas:** Chevron, Conoco/diesel, Exxon/diesel/24hr, **food:** Cajun Tails Rest., DQ, Subway
48 LA 101, Lacassine, **S...gas:** Citgo, Exxon
44 US 165, to Alexandria, **N...other:** Quiet Oaks RV Park(10mi), Grand Casino(22mi), **S...**Wood-n Treasures RV Park

LOUISIANA

Interstate 10

E ↕ W

Lake Charles

Exit	Services
43	LA 383, to Iowa, **N...gas:** Exxon/diesel/24hr, Loves/Hardee's/diesel/24hr, **food:** Burger King, **lodging:** Howard Johnson, **S...gas:** Chevron/24hr, Conoco/diesel, Shell, Texaco/diesel, **food:** Cajun Kwik Deli, Big Daddy's Rest., Fausto's Chicken, McDonald's, Subway, **other:** Factory Stores of America/famous brands
36	LA 397, to Creole, Cameron, **N...**Citgo, Jean Lafitte RV Park(2mi), **S...gas:** Chevron/diesel, Conoco/diesel/RV dump/24hr, **other:** James Mobile Camping, casino
34	I-210 W, to Lake Charles, no facilities
33	US 171 N, **N...gas:** GasWay/diesel, RaceWay, Shamrock, **food:** Burger King, Church's, McDonald's, Subway, Taco Bell, **lodging:** Best Western, Comfort Inn, Day's Inn, La Quinta, **other:** AutoZone, Eckerd, O'Reilly Parts, Walgreen, to Sam Houston Jones SP, **S...lodging:** Holiday Inn Express, Motel 6, Treasure Inn
32	Opelousas St, **N...gas:** Exxon
31b	US 90 E, Shattuck St, to LA 14, **S...gas:** Pakco/diesel, **food:** McDonald's, **lodging:** Econolodge
a	US 90 bus, Enterprise Blvd, **S...gas:** BP/diesel/24hr, **food:** Popeye's
30b a	LA 385, N Lakeshore Dr, Ryan St, **N...gas:** Chevron, **food:** Waffle House, **lodging:** Travel Inn/rest., **S...food:** Montana's Smokehouse, **lodging:** Harrah's Hotel/casino, Holiday Inn, Lakeview Motel
29	LA 385, **N...gas:** Chevron, **food:** Steamboat Bills Rest., Waffle House, **lodging:** Lakeview Motel, Travel Inn/rest., **S...lodging:** Best Suites, **other:** Players Island Casino/hotel
28mm	Calcasieu Bayou, Lake Charles
27	LA 378, to Westlake, **N...gas:** Circle K/24hr, Fina, Shell, **food:** Burger King, DQ, Pizza Hut, **other:** to Sam Houston Jones SP, **S...gas:** Conoco/24hr, **lodging:** Inn at the Isle, **other:** Riverboat Casinos
26	US 90 W, Southern Rd, Columbia, **N...gas:** Circle K/gas
25	I-210 E, to Lake Charles, no facilities
23	LA 108, to Sulphur, **N...gas:** Circle K/gas, Citgo, Exxon, **food:** Burger King, McDonald's, Popeye's, Subway, Taco Bell, **lodging:** Comfort Suites, **other:** AllPro Parts, $General, Radio Shack, Wal-Mart SuperCtr/gas/24hr, **S...gas:** Citgo/diesel, **food:** Cracker Barrel, Waffle House, Winner's Choice Rest./24hr, **lodging:** Best Western, Crossland Suites, Holiday Inn Express, Super 8, **other:** Goodyear, casino
21	LA 3077, Arizona St, **N...gas:** Chevron, Conoco/diesel, Exxon, **food:** A&W/KFC, Boiling Point Deli, DQ, Papa John's, **other:** $General, Ford, Kroger/gas, NAPA, Walgreen, **S...gas:** Chevron/diesel, Citgo/diesel, **other:** HOSPITAL, Hidden Ponds RV Park

Sulphur

Exit	Services
20	LA 27, to Sulphur, **N...gas:** Bayou Gas, Exxon/diesel/24hr, Shell, **food:** Bonanza, Burger King, Cajun Charlie's Rest./gifts, Cajun Cookery, Checker's, Hong Kong Chinese, McDonald's, Mr Gatti's, Popeye's, Subway, Taco Bell, Wendy's, **lodging:** Chateau Motel, Hampton Inn, Holiday Inn, **other:** Brookshire Foods, Family$, Firestone/auto, Goodyear/auto, InstaLube, **S...gas:** Pilot/diesel, Texaco/diesel, **food:** Pit Grill Cajun, Pizza Hut, Sonic, Waffle House, **lodging:** Fairfield Inn, La Quinta, Microtel, Wingate Inn, **other:** HOSPITAL, casino, to Creole Nature Trail
8	LA 108, Vinton, **N...gas:** Citgo/diesel, EZ/diesel, **other:** V RV Park
7	LA 3063, Vinton, **N...gas:** Delta/Exxon/diesel, **food:** Burger King, Lucky Delta Café, Subway
4	US 90, LA 109, Toomey, **N...gas:** Chevron/diesel, Exxon/diesel/24hr, Shell/diesel, **other:** casinos, **S...gas:** Exxon/diesel, **lodging:** Delta Downs Hotel/casino, **other:** Pelican Palace RV Park
2.5mm	weigh sta both lanes
1.5mm	**Welcome Ctr eb, full(handicapped)facilities, phone, picnic tables, litter barrels, petwalk**
1	(from wb), Sabine River Turnaround, no facilities
0mm	Louisiana/Texas state line, Sabine River

Interstate 12

E ↕ W

Exit #	Services
85c	I-10 E, to Biloxi. I-12 begins/ends on I-10, exit 267.
b	I-59 N, to Hattiesburg, no facilities
a	I-10 W, to New Orleans, no facilities
83	US 11, to Slidell, **N...gas:** Chevron/diesel/24hr, Exxon/diesel, **food:** Burger King, McDonald's, Waffle House, **other:** $General, SuperValu Foods, **S...gas:** Mardi Gras Trkstp/diesel, Shell, **lodging:** City Motel(3mi), **other:** HOSPITAL
80	Airport Dr, North Shore Blvd, **N...food:** IHOP, **other:** Target, **S...gas:** Chevron/24hr, Shell/diesel, **food:** Burger King, ChuckeCheese, McDonald's, Pizza Hut/Taco Bell, Subway, Wendy's, **other:** Best Buy, Dillard's, Goodyear/auto, Home Depot, JC Penney, Mervyn's, Sam's Club/gas, Sears/auto, Wal-Mart SuperCtr/24hr, mall
74	LA 434, to Lacombe, **S...gas:** Spur/diesel(3mi)
65	LA 59, to Mandeville, **N...gas:** Chevron/Subway, Danny&Clyde's, Shell, **other:** Abbita Brew Pub, **S...gas:** Conoco/Burger King/diesel, Texaco/Domino's/diesel, **other:** Winn-Dixie, to Fontainebleau SP, camping
63b a	US 190, Covington, Mandeville, **N...gas:** Exxon, RaceTrac, Shell, **food:** Applebee's, Burger King, Copeland's Grill, Ground Pati Rest., IHOP, KFC, Osaka Japanese, Outback Steaks, Piccadilly's, Portofino Italian, Sonic, Subway, TGIFriday, Waffle House, Wendy's, **lodging:**

Interstate 12

E

W

Best Western, Comfort Inn, Courtyard, Hampton Inn, Holiday Inn, Mt Vernon Motel, Super 8, **other:** MEDICAL CARE, Albertson's, BooksAMillion, Circuit City, GNC, Home Depot, Nissan, Office Depot, Toyota, Wal-Mart SuperCtr/24hr, **S...other:** HOSPITAL, Chrysler/Plymouth, st police, to New Orleans via toll causeway

60.5mm rest areas both lanes, full(handicapped)facilities, phone, picnic tables, litter barrels, petwalk

59 LA 21, Madisonville, to Covington, **N...gas:** Chevron/ Church's, Conoco/Burger King/diesel, Shell, **food:** McDonald's, **other:** HOSPITAL, **S...gas:** Shell/ Domino's/diesel, **other:** Fairview Riverside SP

57 LA 1077, to Goodbee, Madisonville, **S...**Family RV Park, to Fairview Riverside SP

47 LA 445, to Robert, **1-3 mi N...other:** Hidden Oaks Camping, Jellystone Camping, Sunset Camping, to Global Wildlife Ctr

42 LA 3158, to Airport, **N...gas:** Amoco, Chevron/ Stuckey's/diesel/24hr, **lodging:** Friendly Inn

Hammond

40 US 51, to Hammond, **N...gas:** Chevron, RaceTrac, Shell/24hr, Texaco/diesel, **food:** Border Café, Burger King, China Garden, Church's, McDonald's, Pizza Hut, Quizno's, Ryan's, Taco Bell, Wendy's, **lodging:** Best Western, Comfort Inn, Supreme Inn, **other:** MEDICAL CARE, Dillard's, Rite Aid, Sears/auto, U-Haul, Walgreen, mall, **S...gas:** Petro/Mobil/diesel/ rest./24hr/@, Pilot/Arby's/diesel/24hr/@, Shell, **food:** Waffle House, **lodging:** Colonial Inn, Ramada Inn, **other:** Blue Beacon, $General, **other:** HOSPITAL, KOA

38b a I-55, N to Jackson, S to New Orleans

37mm weigh sta both lanes

35 Pumpkin Ctr, Baptist, **N...gas:** Exxon, **other:** Punkin RV Park, **S...gas:** Chevron/24hr

32 LA 43, to Albany, **N...**Chevron, **1 mi S...gas:** Citgo/ diesel, **other:** to Tickfaw SP

29 LA 441, to Holden, **N...gas:** Coastal/diesel, **other:** RV RestStop(1mi), st police

28mm rest areas both lanes, full(handicapped)facilities, phone, picnic tables, litter barrels, petwalk

22 LA 63, Livingston, to Frost, **N...gas:** Chevron/diesel, Conoco/diesel, Mobil

19 to Satsuma, no facilities

15 LA 447, to Walker, **N...gas:** Citgo, Shell/24hr, Texaco, **food:** Burger King, Church's, Domino's, Jack-in-the-Box, La Fleur's Seafood, McDonald's, Popeye's, Sonic, Subway, Waffle House, **other:** AutoZone, Rite Aid, Wal-Mart SuperCtr/24hr, Winn-Dixie, **S...gas:** Chevron, Fina/diesel, **other:** Rocky's RV Ctr

10 LA 3002, to Denham Springs, **N...gas:** Chevron, Circle K, Exxon, RaceTrac, Shell/diesel, **food:** Arby's, Burger King, Cactus Café, Crawford's Cajun, KFC, McDonald's, Pizza Hut, Pepper's Rest., Popeye's, Ryan's, Subway, Waffle House, Wendy's, **lodging:** Best Western, Holiday Inn Express, **other:** Advance Parts, Firestone/auto, Home Depot, Radio Shack, Rite Aid, **S...gas:** Pilot/Subway/diesel, Shell, **food:** Piccadilly's, Shoney's, **lodging:** Day's Inn, Highland Inn, **other:** Dodge/Isuzu, Ford, KOA

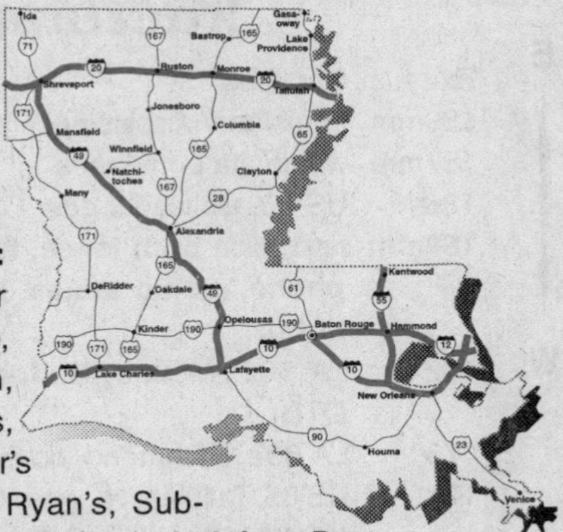

8.5mm Amite River

7 O'Neal Lane, **N...gas:** Mobil, **lodging:** Comfort Suites, **other:** HOSPITAL, Eckerd, HobbyLobby, Knight's RV Park, Office Depot, Toyota, **S...gas:** BP, Chevron/24hr, RaceTrac, Texaco/diesel, **food:** Blimpie, Burger King, China King, Fazoli's, LoneStar Steaks, McDonald's, Pizza Hut/Taco Bell, Popeye's, Sonic, Subway, Waffle House, Wendy's, **other:** $General, Radio Shack, Super Fresh Foods, Walgreen, Wal-Mart SuperCtr/24hr

6 Millerville Rd, **N...gas:** Chevron/24hr

4 Sherwood Forest Blvd, **N...gas:** Exxon, Shell/diesel, **food:** Bamboo House, Burger King, ChuckeCheese, Denny's, Egg Roll King, Jack-in-the-Box, McDonald's, Popeye's, Sonic, Subway, Waffle House, **lodging:** Crossland Suites, Red Roof Inn, Super 8, **other:** Piggly Wiggly, Rite Aid, **S...gas:** Chevron/24hr, Shell/24hr, **food:** Bayou Cajun Seafood, BBQ, Pasta Garden, Pizza Hut, Taco Bell, **lodging:** Calloway Inn, **other:** Harley-Davidson

Baton Rouge

2b US 61 N, **N...gas:** Amoco, Chevron, Exxon/diesel, Mobil/diesel, Shell/24hr, Texaco, **food:** Applebee's, Cracker Barrel, McDonald's, Pizza Hut/Taco Bell, Shoney's, Subway, Taste of China, Wendy's, Wienerschnitzel, **lodging:** Hampton Inn, Holiday Inn, Microtel, Motel 6, Shoney's Inn, Sleep Inn, **other:** Acura/Infiniti, Albertson's, Dodge, $Tree, Ford/Lincoln/Mercury, Marshall's, Michael's, Nissan/Suzuki, PepBoys, SteinMart, Toyota, Walgreen, transmissions

a US 61 S, **S...gas:** Chevron, Circle K/gas, Jubilee/ diesel, **food:** Gustavo's Mexican, McDonald's, Waffle House, **lodging:** Deluxe Inn, Plantation Inn, **other:** Cadillac/Volvo, Chevrolet, Home Depot, Mitsubishi, Winn-Dixie

1b LA 1068, to LA 73, Essen Lane, **N...gas:** Shell/diesel, **food:** Cane's Rest., McDonald's, **other:** HOSPITAL, Eckerd, Family$, Radio Shack

a I-10(from wb). I-12 begins/ends on I-10, exit 159 in Baton Rouge.

LOUISIANA
Interstate 20

E ↕ W

Exit #	Services
189mm	Louisiana/Mississippi state line, Mississippi River
187mm	weigh sta both lanes
186	US 80, Delta, **S...gas:** Chevron/Blimpie/diesel/24hr
184mm	**rest area both lanes, full(handicapped)facilities, phone, picnic tables, litter barrels, petwalk, RV dump**
182	LA 602, Mound, **S...food:** Winner's Circle Rest./OTB
173	LA 602, Richmond, no facilities
171	US 65, Tallulah, **N...gas:** Chevron, Shell/diesel, **food:** KFC, McDonald's, Subway, Wendy's, **lodging:** Day's Inn, Super 8, **other:** HOSPITAL, **S...gas:** Conoco/diesel, Love's/diesel/24hr/@, TA/Mobil/diesel/rest./24hr/@
164mm	Tensas River
157	LA 577, Waverly, **N...gas:** Tiger Trkstp/diesel/rest./24hr/@, **S...**Chevron/Subway/diesel/24hr/@, to Tensas River NWR
155mm	Bayou Macon
153	LA 17, Delhi, **N...gas:** Chevron/Taco Bell, Exxon, **food:** Burger King, DQ, Moby's Rest., Pizza Hut, Sonic, Subway, **other:** HOSPITAL, **S...gas:** Shell, **lodging:** Best Western, Day's Inn
150mm	**rest area both lanes, full(handicapped)facilities, phone, picnic tables, litter barrels, petwalk, RV dump**
148	LA 609, Dunn, no facilities
145	LA 183, rd 202, Holly Ridge, no facilities
141	LA 583, Bee Bayou Rd, **N...gas:** Texaco/diesel
138	LA 137, Rayville, **N...gas:** Pilot/Wendy's/diesel/24hr/@, **food:** Burger King, McDonald's, **lodging:** Day's Inn, **other:** HOSPITAL, Chevrolet/Pontiac/Buick, Family$, Firestone, $General, Wal-Mart, **S...gas:** Citgo/Subway/diesel/24hr, Exxon, **food:** Popeye's, Waffle House, **lodging:** Ramada Ltd, **other:** Goodyear
135mm	Beouf River
132	LA 133, Start, **N...gas:** Exxon
128mm	Lafourche Bayou
124	LA 594, Millhaven, **N...gas:** EZ Mart/diesel, **other:** st police, to Arsage Wildlife Area
120	Garrett Rd, Pecanland Mall Dr, **N...gas:** Citgo/diesel, Shell, **food:** Applebee's, Gator's Rest., McAlister's, Olive Garden, Pizza Hut, Red Lobster, Zipp's Drive-Thru, **lodging:** Comfort Inn, Courtyard, Holiday Inn, Residence Inn, **other:** Dillard's, Firestone/auto, JC Penney, Sears/auto, mall, **S...gas:** Exxon/diesel, Kangaroo/diesel, **lodging:** Best Western, Day's Inn, **other:** Harley-Davidson, Hope's RV Ctr, Lowe's Whse, Pecanland RV Park, Sam's Club, Shilo RV Camp
118b a	US 165, **N...food:** Copeland's Rest., IHOP, O'Charleys, **lodging:** Holiday Inn, La Quinta, **other:** Home Depot, Plymouth/Dodge, Goodyear, Target, to NE LA U, **S...gas:** Chevron, Citgo, Exxon, Shell, **food:** Burger King, McDonald's, **lodging:** Comfort Inn, Hampton Inn, Motel 6, Ramada Ltd
117b	LA 594, Texas Ave, no facilities
a	Hall St, Monroe, **N...**HOSPITAL, Civic Ctr
116b	US 165 bus, LA 15, Jackson St, **N...**HOSPITAL, **S...food:** Popeye's, **lodging:** Guesthouse Inn/rest.
a	5th St, Monroe, **N...gas:** Citgo/Circle K
115	LA 34, Mill St, **N...gas:** Citgo
114	LA 617, Thomas Rd, **N...gas:** RaceTrac, Shell, **food:** BBQ, Bennigan's, Burger King, Capt D's, Chick-fil-A, El Chico, Grandy's, KFC, Las Margaritas Mexican, McAlister's, McDonald's, Pizza Hut, Popeye's, Shoney's, Subway, Taco Bell, Waffle House, Wendy's, **lodging:** Shoney's Inn, Super 8, Wingate Inn, **other:** HOSPITAL, Office Depot, Rite Aid, Walgreen, Wal-Mart SuperCtr/gas/24hr, **S...gas:** Citgo/diesel, Exxon/diesel, Shell, **food:** Chili's, Cracker Barrel, Logan's Roadhouse, LoneStar Steaks, Outback Steaks, Sonic, Waffle House, **lodging:** Fairfield Inn, Holiday Inn Express, Jameson Inn, Red Roof Inn, Super 8
112	Well Rd, **N...gas:** Shell/diesel/24hr, Texaco/24hr, **food:** DQ, Flapjack's, McDonald's, Waffle House, **S...gas:** Pilot/Subway/Wendy's/diesel/24hr/@, **other:** Pavilion RV Park
108	LA 546, to US 80, Cheniere, **N...gas:** Exxon/diesel, Texaco/diesel
107	Camp Rd, rd 25, Cheniere, **N...**Sunset Cove RV Park
103	US 80, Calhoun, **N...gas:** Chevron/diesel/rest., Citgo/diesel, **lodging:** Avant Motel
101	LA 151, to Calhoun, **N...gas:** Texaco
97mm	**rest area wb, full(handicapped)facilities, phone, picnic tables, litter barrels, petwalk, RV dump**
95mm	**rest area eb, full(handicapped)facilities, phone, picnic tables, litter barrels, petwalk, RV dump**
93	LA 145, Choudrant, **S...gas:** Chevron
86	LA 33, Ruston, **N...gas:** Citgo, RaceWay, Shell/diesel, **food:** Cajun Café, Log Cabin Rest., Ryan's, Sonic, **lodging:** Comfort Inn, Day's Inn, Holiday Inn, Lincoln Motel, **other:** Buick/GMC, Chevrolet/Pontiac/Cadillac, Chrysler/Plymouth, Firestone, Ford/Lincoln/Mercury, Toyota, Wal-Mart SuperCtr/gas/24hr, **S...gas:** Texaco/diesel, **lodging:** Holiday Inn Express
85	US 167, Ruston, **N...gas:** Citgo/Subway, Exxon/A&W, Shell, **food:** Burger King, Capt D's, Huddle House, McDonald's, Peking Chinese, Shoney's, Wendy's, **lodging:** Econolodge, Hampton Inn, Ramada Inn, Relax Inn, **other:** Super 1 Foods, JC Penney, Radio Shack, **S...gas:** BP, Shell/diesel, **food:** Pizza Hut, **lodging:** Best Western, **other:** HOSPITAL

Tallulah

Monroe

Ruston

Interstate 20

84 LA 544, Ruston, **N...gas:** Mobil/diesel, **S...gas:** Chevron, Citgo/24hr, Exxon, Shell/diesel, **food:** DQ, Johnny's Pizza, Pizza Inn, Quizno's, Subway, TCBY, Wendy's, **lodging:** Super 8

81 LA 141, Grambling, **S...gas:** Clark/Church's/diesel/24hr, Exxon, **other:** to Grambling St U

78 LA 563, Industry, **S...gas:** Texaco/diesel

77 LA 507, Simsboro, no facilities

69 LA 151, Arcadia, **S...gas:** BP/diesel, Exxon, Texaco, **food:** Country Folks Kitchen, McDonald's, Sonic, Subway, **lodging:** Day's Inn, Nob Hill Inn/rest., **other:** Arcadia Tire, Brookshire Foods, Factory Stores/famous brands, Fred's Drugs, NAPA

67 LA 9, Arcadia, **N...**to Lake Claiborne SP, **S...gas:** Texaco

61 LA 154, Gibsland, **S...gas:** Exxon(1mi)

58mm rest area both lanes, full(handicapped)facilities, phone, picnic tables, litter barrels, petwalk, RV dump

55 US 80, Ada, Taylor, no facilities

52 LA 532, to US 80, Dubberly, **N...**Exxon/Mom's Diner/diesel/24hr, **S...gas:** Citgo/diesel

49 LA 531, Minden, **N...gas:** Trucker's Paradise/diesel/rest./casino/24hr/@, Wal-Mart SuperCtr/gas/24hr(3mi)

47 US 371 S, LA 159 N, Minden, **N...gas:** Chevron/diesel, Mobil/diesel, Texaco/24hr, **food:** Golden Biscuit, **lodging:** Best Western, Exacta Inn/rest., Holiday Inn Express, Southern Inn, **other:** HOSPITAL, Ford/Lincoln/Mercury, **S...**B&B, to Lake Bistineau SP, camping

44 US 371 N, Dixie Inn, Cotton Valley, **N...gas:** Chevron, **food:** Crawfish Hole #2, Nicky's Cantina, **lodging:** Minden Motel(2mi), **other:** Family$

38 Goodwill Rd, Ammo Plant, **S...gas:** BP/Rainbow Diner/diesel/24hr, **other:** Interstate RV Park

36mm rest area both lanes, full(handicapped)facilities, phone, picnic tables, litter barrels, petwalk, RV dump

33 LA 157, Fillmore, **N...gas:** Phillips 66, **other:** Hilltop Camping(2mi), **S...gas:** Citgo, Pilot/Arby's/diesel/24hr/@, **other:** Lake Bistineau SP

26 I-220 W, Shreveport, **1 mi N...**facilities off of I-220

23 Industrial Dr, **N...gas:** Circle K, Exxon/Subway, Texaco/Popeye's/24hr, **food:** Barnhill's Buffet, Burger King, McDonald's, Sue's Kitchen, Taco Bell, **lodging:** Le Bossier Motel, **other:** st police, **S...gas:** Chevron/diesel, Road Mart/diesel, **lodging:** Quality Inn, **other:** RV SuperCtr

22 Airline Dr, **N...gas:** Chevron/McDonald's/diesel, Citgo/Circle K, Exxon/diesel, Mobil, **food:** Applebee's, Arby's, Backyard Burgers, Bennigan's, Burger King, Capt D's, Chili's, ChuckeCheese, DQ, Grandy's, IHOP, Little Caesar's, Luby's, Mr Gatti's, Mr Jim's Chicken, Pizza Hut, Popeye's, Red Lobster, Schlotsky's, Sonic, Taco Bell, Waffle House, **lodging:** Best Western, Crossland Suites, Isle of Capri Hotel, Super 8, **other:** Albertson's/gas, BooksAMillion, Dillard's, Eckerd, Firestone/auto, Goodyear/auto, JC Penney, K-Mart, NAPA, Office Depot, Pep-Boys, Sears/auto, Walgreen, mall, **S...gas:** Texaco/diesel/24hr, Circle K, **food:** Church's, Darryl's Rest., Domino's, Outback Steaks, Popeye's, **lodging:** Baymont Inn, Microtel, Quality Inn, **other:** HOSPITAL, AutoZone, Fabrics+, Super1 Food, to Barksdale AFB

21 LA 72, to US 71 S, Old Minden Rd, **N...gas:** Circle K, Exxon, **food:** Burger King, Cowboy's Rest., El Chico, McDonald's, Morrison's Cafeteria, Ralph&Kacoo's, Subway, Whataburger, **lodging:** Hampton Inn, Holiday Inn, La Quinta, Residence Inn, Shoney's Inn/rest., **other:** Advance Parts, AutoZone, **S...gas:** RaceTrac, **food:** Dragon House Chinese, Waffle House, Wendy's, **lodging:** Day's Inn, Motel 6

20c (from wb), to US 71 S, to Barksdale Blvd

20b LA 3, Benton Rd, same as 21

a Hamilton Rd, Isle of Capri Blvd, **N...gas:** Circle K, Texaco/24hr, **food:** BBQ, **lodging:** Comfort Inn, **S...gas:** Chevron, **lodging:** Ramada/rest., **other:** casino

19b Traffic St, Shreveport, downtown, **N...other:** Chevrolet, casino

a US 71 N, LA 1 N, Spring St, Shreveport, **N...food:** Don's Seafood, **lodging:** Best Western, Holiday Inn

18b-d Fairfield Ave(from wb), downtown Shreveport, **N...other:** radiators, **S...**HOSPITAL

18a Line Ave, Common St(from eb), downtown, **S...gas:** Citgo, **other:** HOSPITAL

17b I-49 S, to Alexandria

a Lakeshore Dr, Linwood Ave, no facilities

16b US 79/80, Greenwood Rd, **N...**HOSPITAL, **S...gas:** Citgo, **food:** Burger King, El Chico, **lodging:** Travelodge

a US 171, Hearne Ave, **N...gas:** Citgo, **food:** Subway, **other:** HOSPITAL, **S...gas:** Exxon, Fina, Texaco/diesel, **food:** KFC, Krystal, **lodging:** Howard Johnson

14 Jewella Ave, Shreveport, **N...gas:** Citgo/diesel, Food-Fast, Texaco/diesel/24hr, **food:** Burger King, Church's, McDonald's, Popeye's, Subway, Taco Bell, Whataburger, **other:** Advance Parts, AutoZone, County Mkt Foods, Eckerd, Family$, Walgreen

13 Monkhouse Dr, Shreveport, **N...food:** Denny's, **lodging:** Best Value Inn, Day's Inn, Holiday Inn Express, Residence Inn, The Lodge, **S...gas:** Chevron, Exxon/Subway/diesel, Texaco/diesel, **food:** Waffle House, **lodging:** Best Western, Hampton Inn, Pelican Inn, Ramada, Super 8, **other:** to airport

LOUISIANA

Interstate 20

E ↕ W

11 I-220 E, LA 3132 E, to I-49 S

10 Pines Rd, **N...gas:** BP/diesel, **food:** DQ, Pizza Hut, Popeye's, Subway, **other:** Brookshire Foods, KOA, **S...gas:** Chevron/McDonald's, Exxon/diesel, Shell, **food:** Burger King, Church's, Cracker Barrel, Domino's, Dragon Chinese, Grandy's, IHOP, KFC, Nicky's Cantina, Subway, Taco Bell, Waffle House, Wendy's, Whataburger, **lodging:** Courtyard, Fairfield Inn, La Quinta, Holiday Inn, Jameson Inn, **other:** Chrysler/Dodge, Kroger, Radio Shack, USPO, Walgreen, Wal-Mart SuperCtr/gas/24hr

8 US 80, LA 526 E, **N...lodging:** Red Roof Inn, **other:** Freightliner, **S...gas:** Chevron/diesel, Petro/Mobil/diesel/rest./@, Pilot/Wendy's/diesel/24hr/@, Speedway, **food:** Crescent Landing Catfish Rest.(3mi), **other:** Blue Beacon

5 US 79 N, US 80, to Greenwood, **N...gas:** Kelly's/diesel/rest./24hr/@, Texaco/diesel, **lodging:** Country Inn, Mid Continent Motel, **other:** Bounder RV Ctr

3 US 79 S, LA 169, Mooringsport, **S...gas:** Flying J/Conoco/diesel/LP/rest./24hr/@, Love's/Arby's/diesel/24hr/@

2mm Welcome Ctr eb, full(handicapped)facilities, phone, picnic tables, litter barrels, petwalk, RV dump

1mm weigh sta both lanes

0mm Louisiana/Texas state line

Interstate 49

N ↕ S

Shreveport

Exit # Services

I-49 begins/ends in Shreveport on I-20, exit 17.

206 I-20, E to Monroe, W to Dallas

205 King's Hwy, **E...food:** McDonald's, Piccadilly's, **other:** Dillard's, Sears/auto, mall, **W...gas:** Shamrock, **food:** Burger King, LJ Silver, Subway, Taco Bell, **other:** HOSPITAL

203 Hollywood Ave, Pierremont Rd, **W...gas:** Fina

202 LA 511, E 70th St, **W...gas:** Chevron, Circle K, **food:** Sonic, SC Chicken

201 LA 3132, to Dallas, Texarkana, no facilities

199 LA 526, Bert Kouns Loop, **E...gas:** Chevron/Arby's/diesel/24hr, Citgo, Exxon, RaceTrac, **food:** Burger King, KFC, Taco Bell, Wendy's, **lodging:** Comfort Inn, **other:** Home Depot, **W...gas:** Texaco/diesel, **food:** McDonald's, **other:** Brookshire Foods

196mm Bayou Pierre

191 LA 16, to Stonewall, no facilities

186 LA 175, to Frierson, Kingston, no facilities

177 LA 509, to Carmel, **E...gas:** Eagles Trkstp/diesel/rest.

172 US 84, to Grand Bayou, Mansfield, no facilities

169 Asseff Rd, no facilities

162 US 371, LA 177, to Evelyn, Pleasant Hill, no facilities

Natchitoches

155 LA 174, to Ajax, Lake End, **W...gas:** Spaulding/diesel/@, **other:** Country Livin' RV

148 LA 485, Powhatan, Allen, no facilities

142 LA 547, Posey Rd, no facilities

138 LA 6, to Natchitoches, **E...gas:** BP/Mkt Express, Exxon/Subway, RaceTrac, **food:** Shoney's, Wendy's, **lodging:** Best Western, Holiday Inn Express, Super 8(5mi), **other:** HOSPITAL, Albertson's(3mi), Wal-Mart SuperCtr/24hr(5mi), **W...gas:** Chevron/diesel, Citgo, Texaco/diesel, **food:** Burger King, Huddle House, McDonald's, Simpatico's Grille, **lodging:** Comfort Inn, Hampton Inn, Microtel, **other:** Nakatosh RV Park, to Kisatchie NF

132 LA 478, rd 620, no facilities

127 LA 120, to Cypress, Flora, **E...gas:** Citgo, **lodging:** Ryder Inn(10mi), **other:** to Cane River Plantations

119 LA 119, to Derry, Cloutierville, **E...**to Cane River Plantations

113 LA 490, to Chopin, **E...gas:** Phillips 66/diesel

107 to Lena, **E...**USPO

103 LA 8 W, to Flatwoods, **E...gas:** Texaco, **other:** to Cotile Lake, RV camping

99 LA 8, LA 1200, to Boyce, Colfax, **6 mi W...**Cotile Lake, RV camping

98 LA 1(from nb), to Boyce, no facilities

94 rd 23, to Rapides Sta Rd, **E...gas:** Rapides/diesel, **W...other:** I-49 RV Ctr

90 LA 498, Air Base Rd, **W...gas:** Chevron/diesel/24hr, Exxon/diesel, Mobil/diesel, Texaco/BBQ/diesel, **food:** Burger King, Cracker Barrel, McDonald's, **lodging:** La Quinta, Super 8, Travel Express Inn

86 US 71, US 165, MacArthur Dr, **1-2 mi W...gas:** Mobil, Texaco, **food:** Burger King, Ryan's, Shoney's, **lodging:** Clarion, Comfort Inn, Hampton Inn, Motel 6, Quality Inn, Travelodge, **other:** Super 1 Foods

85b Monroe St, Medical Ctr Dr(from nb)

a LA 1, 10th St, MLK Dr, downtown

84 US 167 N, LA 28, LA 1, Pineville Expswy(no ez return nb), no facilities

83 Broadway Ave, **E...**Fina, **1 mi W...gas:** Texaco, **food:** Wendy's, **other:** BooksAMillion, Harley-Davidson, Lowe's Whse, Target, Wal-Mart SuperCtr/24hr

Alexandria

81 US 71 N, LA 3250, Sugarhouse Rd, MacArthur Dr(from sb), **W...gas:** Phillips 66/diesel, same as 83

80 US 71 S, US 167, MacArthur Dr, Alexandria, **2-4 mi W...gas:** Chevron/diesel, Exxon, I-49 Trk Plaza/diesel, Mobil, **food:** Burger King, Carino's Italian, Chili's, Cuco's Mexican, KFC, Logan's Roadhouse, McDonald's, Outback Steaks, Pizza Hut, Sonic, Subway, Taco Bell, Western Sizzlin, **lodging:** Best Western, Clarion, Day's Inn, Hampton Inn, Holiday Inn, Ramada Ltd, Super 8, **other:** Albertson's, Dillard's, JC Penney, Sam's Club/gas, U-Haul, mall

73 LA 3265, rd 22, to Woodworth, **W...gas:** Exxon/Blimpie/diesel, **other:** LA Conf Ctr, to Indian Creek RA, RV camping

LOUISIANA

Interstate 49

N ↕ S

66 LA 112, to Lecompte, **E...gas:** Chevron/Burger King/diesel, **food:** Lea's Lunch, **W...**museum

61 US 167, to Meeker, Turkey Creek, **E...**to Loyd Hall Plantation(3mi)

56 LA 181, Cheneyville, no facilities

53 LA 115, to Bunkie, **E...gas:** Chevron/diesel/casino/24hr/@

46 LA 106, to St Landry, **W...**to Chicot SP

40 LA 29, to Ville Platte, **E...gas:** Exxon/diesel

35mm E...rest area/rec area both lanes, full(handicapped)facilities, picnic tables, litter barrels, vending, petwalk, RV dump

27 LA 10, to Lebeau, no facilities

25 LA 103, to Washington, Port Barre, **W...gas:** Exxon, **other:** Family$

Opelousas

23 US 167 N, LA 744, to Ville Platte, **E...gas:** Chevron/Subway/diesel, Texaco/diesel, **W...gas:** 167 Trkstop/diesel/rest./casino/24hr/@, to Chicot SP

19b a US 190, to Opelousas, **W...**HOSPITAL, **1 mi W...gas:** Exxon/diesel, Mobil, **food:** Blimpie, Palace Café, Soileau's Café, **other:** RV camping

18 LA 31, to Cresswell Lane, **E...lodging:** Holiday Inn, **other:** Chrysler/Dodge/Jeep/Isuzu, Wal-Mart SuperCtr/diesel/24hr, **W...gas:** Chevron/diesel/24hr, Shamrock, Shell, **food:** Burger King, Creswell Lane, Domino's, McDonald's, Pizza Hut, Ryan's, Subway, Taco Bell, Wendy's, **lodging:** Best Western, Day's Inn, **other:** Eckerd, Express Lube, Family$, Firestone, Nissan, Pontiac/Buick/Cadillac, Rite Aid, TireWorld

17 Judson Walsh Dr, **E...gas:** Texaco/diesel, **W...food:** Ray's Diner, Ryan's

15 LA 3233, Harry Guilbeau Rd, **W...lodging:** Comfort Inn/rest., **other:** HOSPITAL

11 LA 93, to Grand Coteau, Sunset, **E...gas:** Chevron, Citgo/diesel/24hr, Exxon/Popeye's/diesel, **food:** Beau Chere Rest., **W...lodging:** Sunset Inn

7 LA 182, no facilities

4 LA 726, Carencro, **E...**Evangeline Downs Racetrack, Foreman RV Ctr, **W...gas:** Chevron, Citgo/Domino's, **food:** Burger King, McDonald's, **lodging:** Economy Inn

2 LA 98, Gloria Switch Rd, **E...gas:** Citgo/Blimpie/diesel, **food:** Prejean's Rest., **other:** Stevens RV Ctr, Lowe's Whse, **W...gas:** Shell, **food:** Picante Mexican

1b Pont Des Mouton Rd, **E...gas:** Exxon/diesel, **lodging:** Motel 6, Plantation Motel, Ramada Inn, **other:** Gauthier's RV Ctr, st police, **W...**Ford

a I-10, W to Lake Charles, E to Baton Rouge, **US 167 S...gas:** Chevron/diesel/24hr, RaceTrac, Shell, **food:** Checker's, ChopStix Chinese, Kajun Kitchen, KFC, McDonald's, Pizza Hut, Popeye's, Shoney's, Subway, Taco Bell, Waffle House, Wendy's, Western Sizzlin, **lodging:** Best Western, Comfort Suites, Fairfield Inn, Holiday Inn, Jameson Inn, La Quinta, Quality Inn, Super 8, TravelHost Inn, **other:** HOSPITAL, Albertson's/gas, $General, Firestone/auto, Ford, Home Depot, Rite Aid, Super 1 Foods/gas, VW, Wal-Mart SuperCtr/gas/24hr, transmissions

Lafayette

I-49 begins/ends on I-10, exit 103.

Interstate 55

N ↕ S

Exit # Services

65.5mm Louisiana/Mississippi state line

65mm Welcome Ctr sb, full(handicapped)facilities, tourist info, phone, picnic tables, litter barrels, petwalk

64mm weigh sta nb

61 LA 38, Kentwood, **E...gas:** Chevron/diesel/24hr, Texaco, United/diesel, **food:** Jam Chicken, Sonic, **other:** HOSPITAL, Ford/Mercury, IGA Foods, **W...gas:** Exxon/Subway/diesel, Texaco/diesel/24hr, **other:** Chevrolet, Chrysler/Jeep/Dodge, Great Discovery Camping(3mi)

58.5mm weigh sta sb

57 LA 440, Tangipahoa, **E...**to Camp Moore Confederate Site

54.5mm rest area nb, full(handicapped)facilities, phone, picnic tables, litter barrels, petwalk

53 LA 10, Fluker, to Greensburg, **W...**HOSPITAL

50 LA 1048, Roseland, **E...gas:** Texaco/diesel/24hr

47 LA 16, Amite, **E...gas:** Chevron/Domino's/diesel, Citgo, Conoco, RaceTrac, **food:** Burger King, KFC, Master Chef, McDonald's, Pizza Hut, Popeye's, Sonic, Subway, Wendy's, **lodging:** Comfort Inn, **other:** HOSPITAL, AutoZone, Winn-Dixie, **W...gas:** Amite Trkstp/OysterGrill/diesel(2mi), **food:** Ardillo's, **lodging:** Colonial Motel, **other:** Ford

41 LA 40, Independence, **E...gas:** Conoco, **other:** HOSPITAL, **W...**Indian Cr Camping(2mi)

36 LA 442, Tickfaw, **E...gas:** Chevron/diesel, **other:** camping, to Global Wildlife Ctr(15mi)

32 LA 3234, Wardline Rd, **E...gas:** Spur, Texaco/diesel, **food:** Burger King, Chinese Cuisine, McDonald's, Murphy's Seafood, Wendy's, **lodging:** Best Western, **W...gas:** Chevron

LOUISIANA

Interstate 55

N ↕ S

Hammond

31 US 190, Hammond, **E...gas:** Chevron/diesel, Exxon/Subway/diesel, Pilot/diesel, Saver/diesel, United, **food:** Applebee's, Burger King, Chili's, Country Cookin Seafood, Cracker Barrel, Krystal, McDonald's, Pizza Hut, Shoney's, Sonic, Taco Bell, Waffle House, Wendy's, **lodging:** Executive Inn, Hampton Inn, Super 8, The Inn, **other:** HOSPITAL, Aamco, Advance Parts, AutoZone, BooksAMillion, Chrysler/Plymouth/Buick/Dodge, $General, $Tree, Eckerd, Lowe's Whse, Office Depot, OfficeMax, Radio Shack, Walgreen/24hr, Wal-Mart SuperCtr/gas/24hr, Winn-Dixie, transmissions/repair

29b a I-12, W to Baton Rouge, E to Slidell

28 US 51 N, Hammond, **E...gas:** RaceTrac, **food:** Catfish Charlie's, CiCi's, Don's Seafood Rest., Shoney's(2mi), **lodging:** Econolodge, Holiday Inn/rest., Ramada Inn/rest., Rockwood Inn, **other:** HOSPITAL, KOA, Mitchell RV Ctr

26 LA 22, Ponchatoula, to Springfield, **E...gas:** Amoco, Chevron/diesel, Conoco, Exxon/diesel, Shell, **food:** Burger King, China King, KFC, McDonald's, Popeye's, Sonic, Subway(1mi), Wendy's, **lodging:** Microtel, **other:** AutoZone, $General, Eckerd, Ford, NAPA, O'Reilly Parts, Winn-Dixie, **W...gas:** Texaco/Domino's/diesel

23 US 51, Ponchatoula, no facilities

22 frontage rd(from sb), no facilities

La Place

15 Manchac, **E...food:** Middendorf Café, **other:** phone, swamp tours

7 Ruddock, no facilities

1 US 51, to I-10, Baton Rouge, La Place, **S...gas:** Chevron/24hr, Jet/Citgo/24hr, Shell/diesel, Speedway/Blimpie/Church's/diesel, **food:** Bully's Seafood, Burger King, KFC, McDonald's, Shoney's, Waffle House, Wendy's, **lodging:** Best Western, Holiday Inn Express, **other:** HOSPITAL, La Place RV Camping

I-55 begins/ends on I-10, exit 209.

Interstate 59

See Mississippi Interstate 59

Interstate 220(Shreveport)

E ↕ W

Shreveport

Exit # Services

I-220 begins/ends on I-20, exit 26.

17b I-20, W to Shreveport, E to Monroe

a US 79, US 80, **N...gas:** Exxon, Citgo/Circle K, RaceWay, **food:** Waffle House, **other:** LA Downs Racetrack, Hilltop RV Park(7mi), **S...gas:** Chevron/diesel/mart, **food:** Huddle House

15 Shed Rd, no facilities

13 Swan Lake Rd, no facilities

12 LA 3105, Airline Dr, **N...**HOSPITAL, **S...gas: Citgo,** Exxon/diesel, Shamrock/diesel, Shell/Subway, **food:** Applebee's, Burger King, CiCi's, Grandy's, McDonald's, Quizno's, Sonic, Taco Bell, Wendy's, **lodging:** Best Western, **other:** Home Depot, Wal-Mart SuperCtr/24hr/gas, **1 mi S...gas:** Mobil, Circle K, **food:** Arby's, Chili's, ChuckeCheese, DQ, Mr Gatti's, Popeye's, **other:** HOSPITAL, BooksAMillion, Dillard's, Eckerd, NAPA, Office Depot, mall

11 LA 3, Bossier City, **N...other:** HOSPITAL, Buick/Pontiac/GMC, Ford, Toyota/Lexus, Maplewood RV Park(3mi), **S...gas:** Chevron/McDonald's/diesel/24hr, **other:** Nissan

7b a US 71, LA 1, Shreveport, **N...gas:** Citgo, Exxon/diesel, Fina/diesel, **food:** Domino's, Sonic, Subway, Whataburger/24hr, **other:** Brookshire Foods, NAPA, **S...gas:** Chevron/24hr, RaceTrac, Texaco/diesel/24hr, **food:** BBQ, Burger King, Church's, KFC, McDonald's, Sammy's Rest., Taco Bell, Howard Johnson/rest., **lodging:** Royal Inn, **other:** AutoZone, Eckerd, Family$, Kroger, Radio Shack, Rite Aid, repair/transmissions

5 LA 173, Blanchard Rd, **S...gas:** Citgo

2 Lakeshore Dr, no facilities

1a Jefferson Paige Rd, **S...food:** Denny's, **lodging:** Best Value Inn, Best Western, Day's Inn, Ramada Inn, Super 8

b I-20, E to Shreveport, W to Dallas. I-220 begins/ends on I-20, exit 11.

Interstate 610(New Orleans)

E ↕ W

I-610 begins/ends on I-10

4 Franklin Ave(from eb), no facilities

3 Elysian fields, **N...**HOSPITAL, **S...gas:** Chevron, Shell, **food:** Burger King, McDonald's

2b US 90, N Broad St, New Orleans St, no facilities

2c Paris Ave(from wb, no return), **S...gas:** Shell/24hr, Spur, **food:** Popeye's

2a St Bernard Ave(from eb), to LSU School of Dentistry, auto racetrack

1a Canal Blvd, **S...gas:** Shell

1b I-10, to New Orleans

I-610 begins/ends on I-10

MAINE

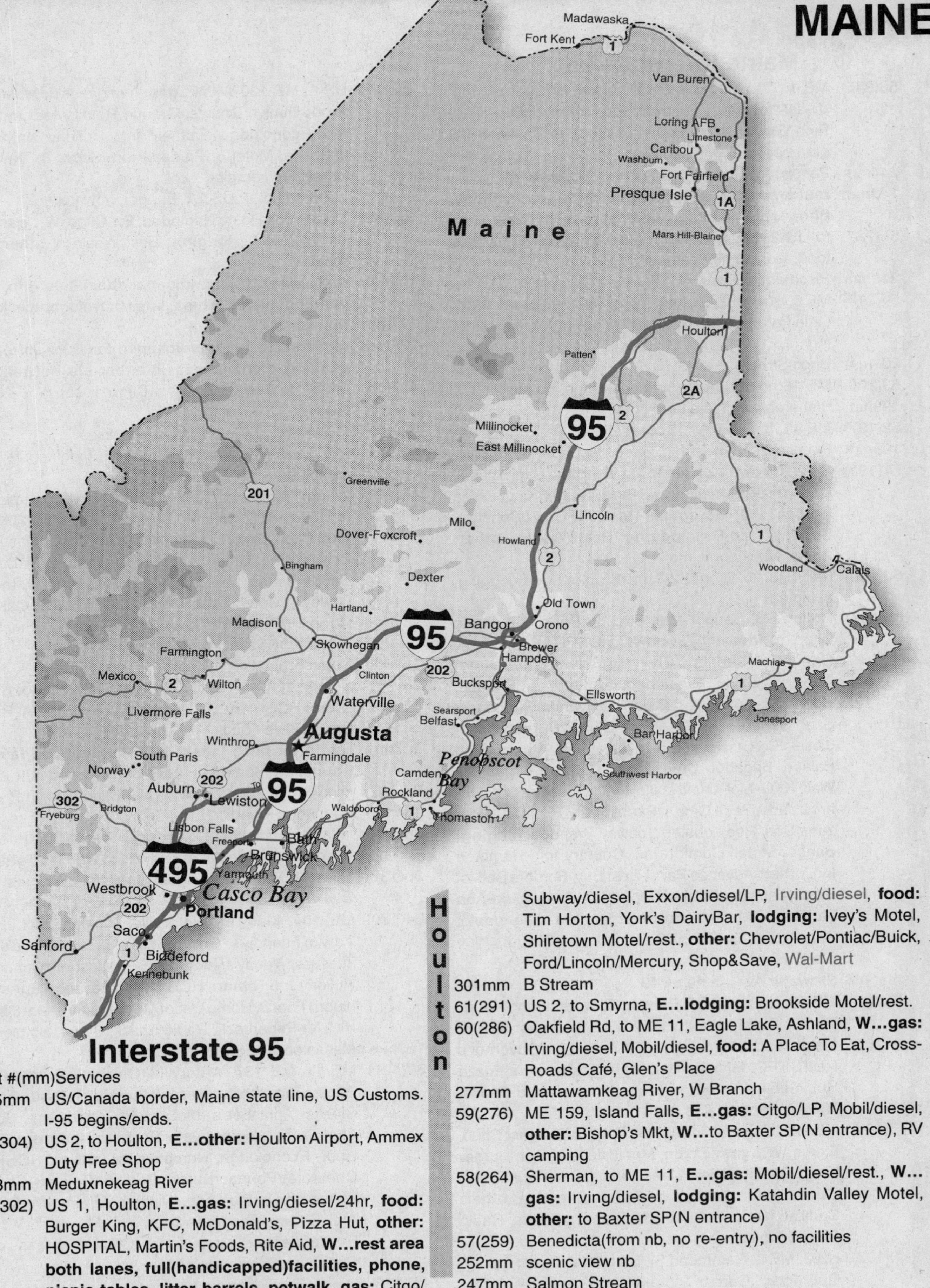

Interstate 95

N ↕ S

Exit #(mm)Services

305mm US/Canada border, Maine state line, US Customs. I-95 begins/ends.

63(304) US 2, to Houlton, **E...other:** Houlton Airport, Ammex Duty Free Shop

303mm Meduxnekeag River

62(302) US 1, Houlton, **E...gas:** Irving/diesel/24hr, **food:** Burger King, KFC, McDonald's, Pizza Hut, **other:** HOSPITAL, Martin's Foods, Rite Aid, **W...rest area both lanes, full(handicapped)facilities, phone, picnic tables, litter barrels, petwalk, gas:** Citgo/ Subway/diesel, Exxon/diesel/LP, Irving/diesel, **food:** Tim Horton, York's DairyBar, **lodging:** Ivey's Motel, Shiretown Motel/rest., **other:** Chevrolet/Pontiac/Buick, Ford/Lincoln/Mercury, Shop&Save, Wal-Mart

Houlton

301mm B Stream

61(291) US 2, to Smyrna, **E...lodging:** Brookside Motel/rest.

60(286) Oakfield Rd, to ME 11, Eagle Lake, Ashland, **W...gas:** Irving/diesel, Mobil/diesel, **food:** A Place To Eat, Cross-Roads Café, Glen's Place

277mm Mattawamkeag River, W Branch

59(276) ME 159, Island Falls, **E...gas:** Citgo/LP, Mobil/diesel, **other:** Bishop's Mkt, **W...**to Baxter SP(N entrance), RV camping

58(264) Sherman, to ME 11, **E...gas:** Mobil/diesel/rest., **W... gas:** Irving/diesel, **lodging:** Katahdin Valley Motel, **other:** to Baxter SP(N entrance)

57(259) Benedicta(from nb, no re-entry), no facilities

252mm scenic view nb

247mm Salmon Stream

MAINE

Maine Interstate 95

N ↕ S

56(245) ME 157, to Medway, E Millinocket, **W...gas:** Irving/diesel, **lodging:** Gateway Inn, **other:** HOSPITAL, Pine Grove Camping(4mi), USPO, to Baxter SP(S entrance)
244mm Penobscot River
243mm rest area both lanes, full(handicapped)facilities, phone, picnic tables, litter barrels, petwalk
55(227) to US 2, ME 6, Lincoln, **4 mi E...**HOSPITAL, gas, food, lodging, RV camping
219mm Piscataquis River
54(216) ME 6, Howland, **E...gas:** Irving/95 Diner/diesel, **food:** Little Peters Rest., **other:** 95er Towing/repair, camping
201mm Birch Stream
53(200) ME 16(no nb re-entry), to LaGrange, no facilities
199mm rest area/weigh sta both lanes
52(197) ME 43, to Old Town, **E...**gas/diesel
196mm Pushaw Stream
51(193) Stillwater Ave, to Old Town, **E...gas:** Citgo/diesel, Irving/diesel, Mobil/diesel, **food:** Burger King, China Garden, DQ, Governor's Rest., KFC, McDonald's, Subway, Taco Bell, **lodging:** Best Western, **other:** Ames, IGA Foods, mall
50(190) Kelly Rd, to Orono, **2-3 mi E...**gas, food, lodging, camping
49(187) Hogan Rd, Bangor Mall Blvd, to Bangor, **E...gas:** Citgo, **food:** Denny's, **other:** HOSPITAL, Audi/VW, Chevrolet/Cadillac, Chrysler/Plymouth/Dodge, Daewoo/Suzuki, Firestone/auto, Ford, GMC/Isuzu, Honda/Nissan/Volvo, Mitsubishi/Hyundai/Mercedes/Saab/Subaru, Saturn, Sam's Club, **W...gas:** Citgo/diesel, Exxon/diesel, **food:** Applebee's, Arby's, Asian Palace, Bugaboo Creek Café, Burger King, China Wall, KFC, McDonald's, 99 Rest., Olive Garden, Oriental Jade, Papa Gino's, Paul's Rest., Pizza Hut, Pizzaria Uno, Red Lobster, Subway, Wendy's, **lodging:** Bangor Motel, Comfort Inn, Country Inn, Hampton Inn, **other:** Advance Parts, Best Buy, Borders Books, Goodyear/auto, Home Depot, JC Penney, Jo-Ann Fabrics, K-Mart, Lincoln/Mercury/Kia, Sears/auto, Shaw's Foods, Shop&Save, Staples, Target, Wal-Mart, mall

Bangor

48a(186) Stillwater Ave, same as 49
48(185) ME 15, to Broadway, Bangor, **E...gas:** Irving, **food:** Tri-City Pizza, **other:** HOSPITAL, **W...gas:** Exxon, Mobil, **food:** China Light, DQ, Friendly's, Governor's Rest., KFC, Mamma Baldacci's, McDonald's, Pizza Hut, Subway, **other:** Firestone, Hannaford Foods, Mazda, Pontiac, Rite Aid
47(184) ME 222, Union St, to Ohio St, Bangor, **E...gas:** Citgo, Exxon, **W...gas:** Exxon, Mobil/diesel, **food:** Burger King, Dunkin Donuts, McDonald's, Nicky's Diner, Papa Gino's, Wendy's, **lodging:** Sheraton, **other:** Cadillac, Chrysler/Jeep, Hannaford's Foods, Radio Shack, Staples
46(183) US 2, ME 2, Hammond St, Bangor, **E...gas:** Exxon, Gulf, **food:** Corner Store, Papa Gambino's Pizza, Subway, **other:** NAPA
45b(182) US 2, ME 100 W, **W...gas:** Irving/diesel, Mobil/diesel, **food:** Dunkin Donuts, Ground Round, **lodging:** Day's Inn, Econolodge, Fairfield Inn, Holiday Inn, Howard Johnson, Motel 6, Ramada Inn, Super 8, Travelodge, **other:** RV camping
a I-395, to US 2, US 1A, Bangor, downtown
44(180) Cold Brook Rd, to Hampden, **E...**Citgo, **W...gas:** Citgo/diesel/24hr/@, **lodging:** Best Western, **other:** diesel repair
178mm rest area sb, full(handicapped)facilities, info, phone, vending, picnic tables, litter barrels, petwalk
177mm Soudabscook Stream
176mm rest area nb, full(handicapped)facilities, info, phone, vending, picnic tables, litter barrels, petwalk
43(174) ME 69, to Carmel, **E...gas:** Citgo/diesel, **W...**RV camping
42(167) ME 69, ME 143, to Etna, no facilities
41(161) ME 7, to E Newport, Plymouth, **E...**lodging, LP, **W...**RV camping
40(159) Ridge Rd(from sb), to Plymouth, Newport, no facilities
39(157) to US 2, ME 7, ME 11, Newport, **E...**HOSPITAL, **W...gas:** Citgo, Exxon, Irving/diesel/24hr, Mobil/diesel, **food:** Burger King, China Way, Dunkin Donuts, McDonald's, Sawyers Dairybar, Scotty's Diner, Subway, **lodging:** Lovley's Motel, **other:** MEDICAL CARE, CarQuest, Chrysler/Plymouth/Jeep, NAPA, Radio Shack, Rite Aid, Shop&Save, Wal-Mart SuperCtr/24hr
151mm Sebasticook River
38(150) Somerset Ave, Pittsfield, **E...gas:** Mobil, **food:** Subway, **other:** HOSPITAL, Chevrolet, Family$, NAPA, Rite Aid, Shop&Save Foods
147mm rest area both lanes, full(handicapped)facilities, phone, picnic tables, litter barrels, petwalk
37(137) Hinckley Rd, Clinton, **W...gas:** Citgo/diesel/LP
134mm Kennebec River
36(133) US 201, Fairfield, **E...gas: food:** Purple Cow Pancakes, **W...other:** Fairfield Creamery, Old NE CandleStore
35(132) ME 139, Fairfield, **E...gas:** Shell/deli, **W...gas:** Citgo/Subway/diesel
34(130) ME 104, Main St, Waterville, **E...gas:** Mobil, **food:** Arby's, Friendly's, Governor's Rest., McDonald's, Ruby Tuesday, Wendy's, **lodging:** Best Western, Comfort Inn, Holiday Inn, **other:** HOSPITAL, Advance Parts, Hannaford Foods, Home Depot, JC Penney, K-Mart, Mazda/VW, Mr Paperback, Radio Shack, Sears, Staples
129mm Messalonskee Stream
33(121) ME 11, ME 137, Waterville, Oakland, **E...gas:** Citgo/Burger King, Irving/diesel/24hr, Mobil, **food:** Angelo's Steaks, Applebee's, McDonald's, Pizza Hut, Subway, Thai Dish, Weathervane Seafood, **lodging:** Budget Host, Econolodge, Hampton Inn, **other:** HOSPITAL, Chevrolet/Pontiac/Buick, Cadillac/Toyota, Chrysler/Plymouth/Dodge/Jeep, Nissan, Mr Paperback, Rite Aid, Shaw's Food/gas/24hr, Wal-Mart/grill, **W...gas:** Exxon/diesel, Valero, **food:** China Express, **other:** CarQuest, Ford/Lincoln/Mercury
32(120) Lyons Rd, Sidney, no facilities

Waterville

Maine Interstate 95

N ↕ S

117mm rest area sb, full(handicapped)facilities, phone, vending, picnic tables, litter barrels, petwalk
113mm rest area nb, full(handicapped)facilities, phone, vending, picnic tables, litter barrels, petwalk
31(106) ME 27, ME 8, ME 11, Augusta, **E...gas:** Citgo, Getty, **food:** Capt's Seafood, Ground Round, Olive Garden, Panera Bread, **lodging:** Holiday Inn, **other:** Barnes&Noble, Home Depot, Old Navy, Sam's Club, Staples, Wal-Mart SuperCtr/24hr, **W...gas:** Irving/diesel/24hr, **food:** 99 Rest., Wendy's, **lodging:** Comfort Inn, **other:** Mitsubishi/Volvo, Vet Cem
105mm Bond Brook
30(103) US 202, ME 11, ME 17, ME 100, Augusta, **E...gas:** Citgo, Irving/diesel, Shell, **food:** Applebee's, Arby's, Burger King, Capitol Buffet, Damon's Subs, Domino's, DQ, Friendly's, KFC, McDonald's, Pizza Hut, Subway, Wendy's, **lodging:** Best Western, **other:** $Tree, K-Mart, Shaw's Foods, USPO, **W...gas:** Exxon, Getty, **food:** Bonanza, Margarita's Mexican, **lodging:** Best Inn, Econolodge, Motel 6, Super 8, **other:** CarQuest, Chrysler/Jeep/Nissan/Subaru, Dodge/Plymouth/Hyundai, Pontiac, Shop&Save/24hr, Sears/auto, Toyota
14 ME TPK/I-495. Maine Turnpike and I-95 run together nb, divide sb.
28(100) ME 9, ME 126, to Gardiner, Litchfield, TOLL PLAZA, **W...**gas, last free nb exit
27(94) US 201, to Gardiner, **E...**gas/diesel, **W...**gas, RV camping
26(88) ME 197, to Richmond, **E...gas:** Citgo/diesel
25(81.5) ME 125, Bowdoinham, no facilities
24(75) ME 196, to Lisbon, Topsham, **E...gas:** Irving, **food:** Arby's, McDonald's, 99 Rest., Subway, Wendy's, **lodging:** Hannaford Foods, NAPA, Radio Shack, Rite Aid, mall
74.5mm Androscoggin River
22(73) US 1, Bath, **1 mi E on US 1...gas:** Gulf, Irving/diesel, Mobil/diesel, **food:** Dunkin Donuts, McDonald's, Thai House, **lodging:** Comfort Inn, Econolodge, MaineLine Motel, Travelers Inn, **other:** HOSPITAL, Chevrolet/Mazda, Ford
71mm parking area southbound
21(68) to Freeport(from nb), facilities 1 mi E on US 1
20(67) ME 125, to Pownal, **E on US 1...gas:** Exxon, **food:** Arby's, Friendly's, McDonald's, Taco Bell, **other:** MEDICAL CARE, LL Bean, USPO, outlet mall/famous brands, **W...**to Bradbury Mtn SP
19(65) Desert Rd, Freeport, **E...gas:** Citgo, **food:** Friendly's, **lodging:** Coastline Inn, Comfort Inn, Hampton Inn, Super 8, **other:** outlet mall/famous brands, RV camping
17(62) US 1, Yarmouth, **E...rest area both lanes, full(handicapped)facilities, info**, **food:** Bill's Pizza, Muddy Rudder Rest., **lodging:** Best Western, **other:** Ford, Delorme Mapping, **W...gas:** Citgo/diesel, Shell, **food:** Bill's Pizza, McDonald's, Pat's Pizza, **lodging:** DownEast Village Motel, **other:** MEDICAL CARE, Shop&Save 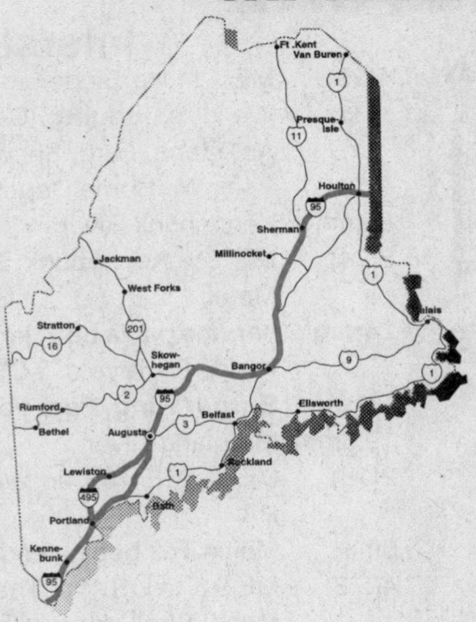
16(59.5) US 1, to Cumberland, Yarmouth, **W...gas:** Exxon, Mobil, **food:** 233 Grill, **lodging:** Brookside Motel, **other:** Rite Aid
15(55) I-295 S, **US 1 S...gas:** Exxon/diesel, Gulf/diesel, Mobil, **food:** Dunkin Donuts, McDonald's, Moose Crossing Rest., **other:** Goodyear, Rite Aid, Shaw's Foods
54mm toll booth
9(49) I-495 N, to Lewiston, no facilities
8(48) ME 25, to Portland, **E...gas:** Citgo, **food:** Applebee's, Burger King, ME Buffet, Subway, **lodging:** Ramada Ltd, **other:** BJ's Whse/gas, Jo-Ann Fabrics, Shaw's Foods, **W...gas:** Exxon, Mobil/diesel, Shell/Subway, **food:** DQ, Denny's, Friendly's, KFC, McDonald's, Pizza Hut, Verrillo's Rest., Wendy's, **lodging:** Howard Johnson, Motel 6, Super 8, Travelodge, **other:** Chrysler/Plymouth/Dodge/Jeep, DD Auto Parts, Ford/Hyundai, Home Depot, NAPA, Shop&Save, Tire Whse, VIP Auto
47mm Stroudwater River
7b to ME 25, Rand Rd, no facilities
7a(46) to ME 22, Congress St, same as 7
7(43) to US 1, Maine Mall Rd, S Portland, **E...gas:** Mobil, Shell/diesel, **food:** Burger King, Bugaboo Creek Steaks, Chili's, Friendly's, Great Wall Chinese, Ground Round, IHOP, LoneStar Steaks, Longhorn Steaks, Macaroni Grill, McDonald's, Old Country Buffet, Olive Garden, On the Border, Panera Bread, Pizza Hut, Pizzaria Uno, Ruby Tuesday, Tim Horton's, Weathervane Seafood, Wendy's, **lodging:** Coastline Inn, Comfort Inn, Day's Inn, Fairfield Inn, Hampton Inn, Residence Inn, Sheraton Tara, **other:** AAA, Best Buy, Borders Books, Circuit City, Filene's, Ground Round, Honda, JC Penney, Lexus/Subaru/Toyota, Macy's, Marshall's, OfficeMax, Sears/auto, Shaw's Foods, Shop'n Save, Staples, mall, **W...food:** Applebee's, **lodging:** AmeriSuites, Marriott, **other:** Target
6a(42) I-295 N(from nb), to S Portland, Scarborough, **E...other:** HOSPITAL, Sam's Club, Wal-Mart(1mi)
41mm Nonesuch River
6(39) to US 1, **E...**Scarborough Downs Racetrack(seasonal)
5(36) I-195 E, to Saco, Old Orchard Beach, no facilities
35mm **E...lodging:** Holiday Inn Express/Saco Hotel Conference Ctr
33mm Saco River

MAINE

Interstate 95

N ↕ S

4(29) ME 111, to Biddeford, **E...gas:** Irving/diesel, **food:** Wendy's, **lodging:** Comfort Inn, **other:** HOSPITAL, AutoZone, Ford, Shaw's Foods, Wal-Mart SuperCtr/24hr, **W...**Home Depot

25mm Kennebunk River

3(24) ME 35, Kennebunk Beach, **E...lodging:** Turnpike Motel

24mm service plaza both lanes, sb...Mobil/diesel, Burger King, Popeye's, TCBY, gifts, nb...Mobil/diesel, Burger King, Popeye's, TCBY, atm, gifts

19.5mm Merriland River

2(18) ME 9, ME 109, to Wells, Sanford, **W...**to Sanford RA

6mm Maine Tpk begins/ends, toll booth

4(5.8) ME 91, to US 1, to The Yorks, **E...gas:** Irving/diesel, Mobil, Shell, **food:** Canellie's Deli, Foodee's Pizza, Norma's Cafe, Ruby's Grill, **other:** HOSPITAL, Family$, Ford, Shop&Save Foods, last exit before toll rd nb

5.5mm weigh sta nb

5mm York River

4mm weigh sta sb

3mm Welcome Ctr nb, full(handicapped)facilities, info, phone, vending, picnic tables, litter barrels, petwalk

Kittery

2(2) (2 & 3 from nb), US 1, to Kittery, **E...gas:** Citgo/Taco Bell/diesel, Getty, Mobil/diesel, **food:** Burger King, Clam Hut Diner, DQ, McDonald's, Quarterdeck Rest., Subway, Weathervane Seafood, **lodging:** Super 8, **other:** FSA/Tanger/famous brands, **W...gas:** Mobil

1 ME 103(from nb, no re-entry), to Kittery, **E...gas:** Citgo, Sunoco, **lodging:** Blue Roof Motel/diner, Day's Inn, NorthEaster Motel, Rex Motel, Super 8, **other:** Navy Yard

0mm Maine/New Hampshire state line, Piscataqua River

Interstate 295

Exit #(mm)Services

I-295 begins/ends on I-95, exit 15.

N ↕ S

10 US 1, to Falmouth, **E...gas:** Exxon/diesel, Gulf/diesel, Mobil, **food:** Dunkin Donuts, McDonald's, Moose Crossing Rest., **other:** Goodyear, Rite Aid, Shaw's Foods

9mm Presumpscot River

9 US 1 S, ME 26, to Baxter Blvd, **W...**The Diner

Portland

8 ME 26 S, Washington Ave, **E...other:** U-Haul

7 US 1A, Franklin St, **E...other:** CarQuest, NAPA

6b a US 1, Forest Ave, **E...gas:** Mobil, **other:** HOSPITAL, AAA, Firestone/auto, Wild Oats Mkt, **W...food:** Arby's, Bleacher's Rest., Burger King, Pizza Hut, **other:** Hannaford Foods

5b a ME 22, Congress St, **E...food:** Denny's, McDonald's, **lodging:** Fairfield Inn, **other:** HOSPITAL, **W...gas:** Citgo, Getty, Mobil/diesel, **food:** Ananias Italian, **lodging:** DoubleTree Hotel

3mm Fore River

4 US 1 S, to Main St, to S Portland, facilities on US 1 away from exit

3 ME 9, to Westbrook St, **W...gas:** Irving/diesel, Mobil/diesel, **food:** Burger King, LoneStar Steaks, Olive Garden, Outback Steaks, TGIFriday, **other:** Chevrolet, Home Depot

2 to US 1 S, to S Portland, services on US 1, **E on US 1...gas:** Citgo/7-11, Exxon, Irving/diesel, Mobil, **food:** Dunkin Donuts, Governor's Rest., Tony Roma's, Yankee Grill, **lodging:** Best Western, Day's Inn, Quality Inn, **other:** Discount Tire

1 to I-95, to US 1, multiple services on US 1, same as 2

I-295 begins/ends on I-95, exit 6a.

Interstate 495

Exit #(mm)Services

Maine Tpk begins/ends at exit 30 on I-95. I-495 portion of Maine Tpk begins/ends at 100mm.

N ↕ S

14b(100) I-95 S, ME 9, ME 126, to Gardiner

a I-95 N

97.5mm toll plaza

95mm service plaza nb, Mobil/diesel, Burger King, TCBY, atm, gifts

82.5mm Sabattus Creek

81mm service plaza sb, Mobil/diesel, Burger King, TCBY, atm, gifts

Lewiston

13(78) to ME 196, Lewiston, **W on ME 196...gas:** Getty, Mobil/diesel, Shell, Sunoco, **food:** Cathay Hut Chinese, Chalet Rest., D'angelo's, Dunkin Donuts, Fanny's Diner, Governor's Rest., KFC/Taco Bell, McDonald's, Wendy's, **lodging:** Motel 6, Ramada Inn, Super 8, **other:** HOSPITAL, Rite Aid, Shaw's Foods

76.5mm Androscoggin River

12(73) US 202, rd 4, rd 100, to Auburn, **E...gas:** Irving/Blimpie/Taco Bell/diesel, **food:** KnuckleHeads Buffet, **lodging:** Auburn Inn, **other:** HOSPITAL, RV camping, **W...**HOSPITAL

69mm Royal River

64.5mm toll plaza

11(61) US 202, rd 115, rd 4, to ME 26, Gray, **E...gas:** Exxon, Gulf, Mobil, Shell, **food:** Dunkin Donuts, Subway, McDonald's, **other:** Rite Aid, Thriftway Foods

57mm service plaza nb, Mobil/diesel, Burger King, TCBY, atm, gifts

56mm service plaza sb, Mobil/diesel, Burger King, TCBY, atm, gifts

53mm Piscataqua River

10(50) to ME 26, ME 100 W, N Portland, **E...food:** Dunkin Donuts, Patty's Rest., **other:** HOSPITAL, Hannaford Foods

49mm Presumpscot River

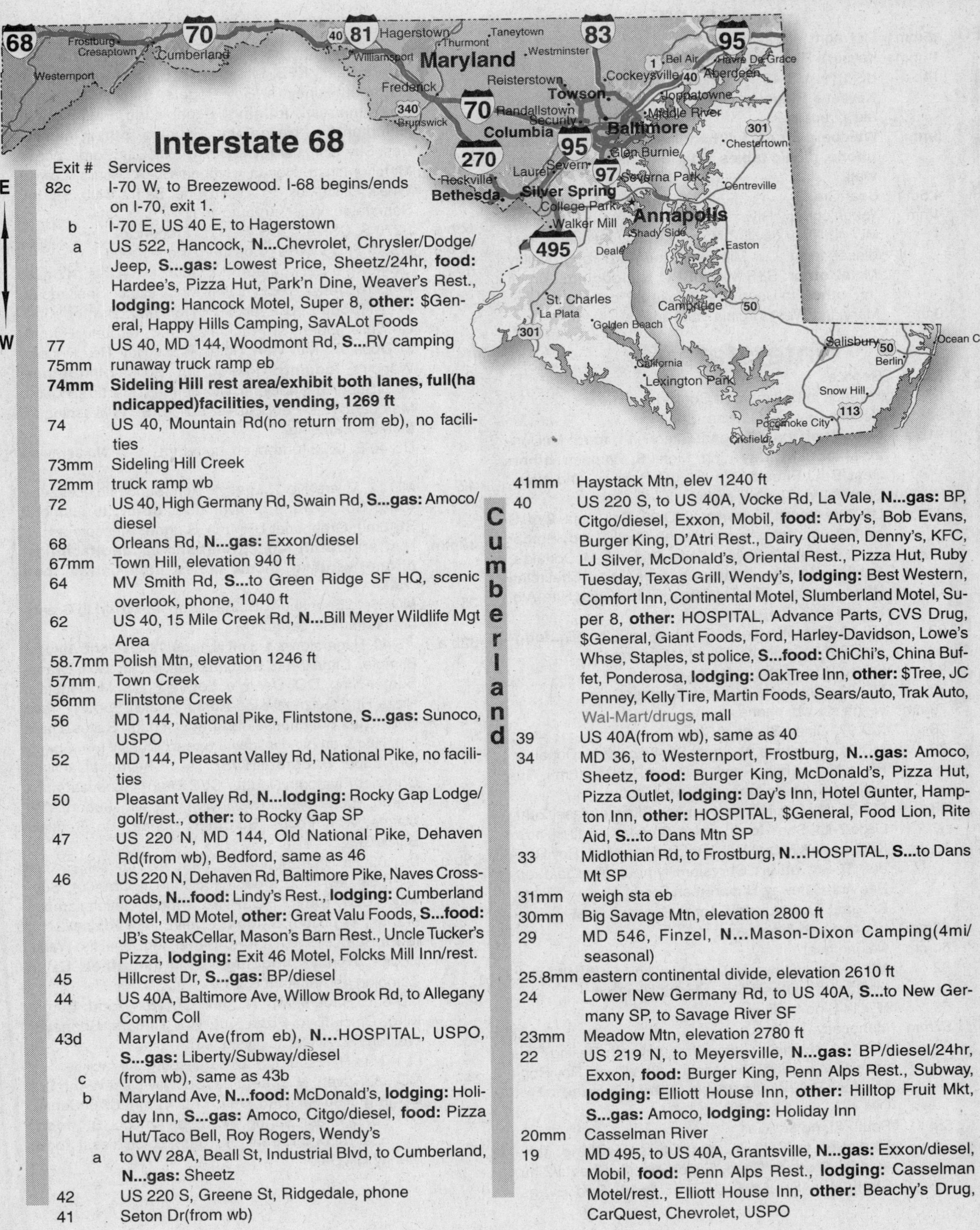

Interstate 68

E ↕ W

Exit #	Services
82c	I-70 W, to Breezewood. I-68 begins/ends on I-70, exit 1.
b	I-70 E, US 40 E, to Hagerstown
a	US 522, Hancock, **N...**Chevrolet, Chrysler/Dodge/Jeep, **S...gas:** Lowest Price, Sheetz/24hr, **food:** Hardee's, Pizza Hut, Park'n Dine, Weaver's Rest., **lodging:** Hancock Motel, Super 8, **other:** $General, Happy Hills Camping, SavALot Foods
77	US 40, MD 144, Woodmont Rd, **S...**RV camping
75mm	runaway truck ramp eb
74mm	**Sideling Hill rest area/exhibit both lanes, full(handicapped)facilities, vending, 1269 ft**
74	US 40, Mountain Rd(no return from eb), no facilities
73mm	Sideling Hill Creek
72mm	truck ramp wb
72	US 40, High Germany Rd, Swain Rd, **S...gas:** Amoco/diesel
68	Orleans Rd, **N...gas:** Exxon/diesel
67mm	Town Hill, elevation 940 ft
64	MV Smith Rd, **S...**to Green Ridge SF HQ, scenic overlook, phone, 1040 ft
62	US 40, 15 Mile Creek Rd, **N...**Bill Meyer Wildlife Mgt Area
58.7mm	Polish Mtn, elevation 1246 ft
57mm	Town Creek
56mm	Flintstone Creek
56	MD 144, National Pike, Flintstone, **S...gas:** Sunoco, USPO
52	MD 144, Pleasant Valley Rd, National Pike, no facilities
50	Pleasant Valley Rd, **N...lodging:** Rocky Gap Lodge/golf/rest., **other:** to Rocky Gap SP
47	US 220 N, MD 144, Old National Pike, Dehaven Rd(from wb), Bedford, same as 46
46	US 220 N, Dehaven Rd, Baltimore Pike, Naves Crossroads, **N...food:** Lindy's Rest., **lodging:** Cumberland Motel, MD Motel, **other:** Great Valu Foods, **S...food:** JB's SteakCellar, Mason's Barn Rest., Uncle Tucker's Pizza, **lodging:** Exit 46 Motel, Folcks Mill Inn/rest.
45	Hillcrest Dr, **S...gas:** BP/diesel
44	US 40A, Baltimore Ave, Willow Brook Rd, to Allegany Comm Coll
43d	Maryland Ave(from eb), **N...**HOSPITAL, USPO, **S...gas:** Liberty/Subway/diesel
c	(from wb), same as 43b
b	Maryland Ave, **N...food:** McDonald's, **lodging:** Holiday Inn, **S...gas:** Amoco, Citgo/diesel, **food:** Pizza Hut/Taco Bell, Roy Rogers, Wendy's
a	to WV 28A, Beall St, Industrial Blvd, to Cumberland, **N...gas:** Sheetz
42	US 220 S, Greene St, Ridgedale, phone
41	Seton Dr(from wb)

Cumberland

Exit #	Services
41mm	Haystack Mtn, elev 1240 ft
40	US 220 S, to US 40A, Vocke Rd, La Vale, **N...gas:** BP, Citgo/diesel, Exxon, Mobil, **food:** Arby's, Bob Evans, Burger King, D'Atri Rest., Dairy Queen, Denny's, KFC, LJ Silver, McDonald's, Oriental Rest., Pizza Hut, Ruby Tuesday, Texas Grill, Wendy's, **lodging:** Best Western, Comfort Inn, Continental Motel, Slumberland Motel, Super 8, **other:** HOSPITAL, Advance Parts, CVS Drug, $General, Giant Foods, Ford, Harley-Davidson, Lowe's Whse, Staples, st police, **S...food:** ChiChi's, China Buffet, Ponderosa, **lodging:** OakTree Inn, **other:** $Tree, JC Penney, Kelly Tire, Martin Foods, Sears/auto, Trak Auto, Wal-Mart/drugs, mall
39	US 40A(from wb), same as 40
34	MD 36, to Westernport, Frostburg, **N...gas:** Amoco, Sheetz, **food:** Burger King, McDonald's, Pizza Hut, Pizza Outlet, **lodging:** Day's Inn, Hotel Gunter, Hampton Inn, **other:** HOSPITAL, $General, Food Lion, Rite Aid, **S...**to Dans Mtn SP
33	Midlothian Rd, to Frostburg, **N...**HOSPITAL, **S...**to Dans Mt SP
31mm	weigh sta eb
30mm	Big Savage Mtn, elevation 2800 ft
29	MD 546, Finzel, **N...**Mason-Dixon Camping(4mi/seasonal)
25.8mm	eastern continental divide, elevation 2610 ft
24	Lower New Germany Rd, to US 40A, **S...**to New Germany SP, to Savage River SF
23mm	Meadow Mtn, elevation 2780 ft
22	US 219 N, to Meyersville, **N...gas:** BP/diesel/24hr, Exxon, **food:** Burger King, Penn Alps Rest., Subway, **lodging:** Elliott House Inn, **other:** Hilltop Fruit Mkt, **S...gas:** Amoco, **lodging:** Holiday Inn
20mm	Casselman River
19	MD 495, to US 40A, Grantsville, **N...gas:** Exxon/diesel, Mobil, **food:** Penn Alps Rest., **lodging:** Casselman Motel/rest., Elliott House Inn, **other:** Beachy's Drug, CarQuest, Chevrolet, USPO

MARYLAND

Interstate 68

E ↕ W

15mm Mt Negro, elevation 2980 ft
14mm Keyser's Ridge, elevation 2880 ft
14b a US 219, US 40 W, Oakland, **N...gas:** Citgo/diesel, Keyser's Ridge/Amoco/diesel/rest., **food:** McDonald's, repair
6mm Welcome Ctr eb, full(handicapped)facilities, info, phone, picnic tables, litter barrels, vending, petwalk
4.5mm Bear Creek
4mm Youghiogheny River
4 MD 42, Friendsville, **N...gas:** Amoco/diesel, Citgo/diesel, **food:** Old Mill Rest., **lodging:** Yough Valley Motel, **other:** S&S Mkt, USPO, **S...lodging:** Sunset Inn, **other:** to Deep Creek Lake SP, camping
0mm Maryland/West Virginia state line

Interstate 70

E ↕ W

Exit # Services
I-70 begins/ends in Baltimore at Cooks Lane.

Baltimore

94 Security Blvd N, **S...gas:** Shell
91b a I-695, **N off exit 17...gas:** Citgo/7-11, **food:** McDonald's, **lodging:** Day's Inn, Motel 6, Ramada, **other:** Best Buy, Firestone/auto, JC Penney, Old Navy, Sears/auto, Staples, mall
87b a US 29(exits left from wb)to MD 99, Columbia, **2 mi S on US 40...gas:** Amoco/diesel, Shell, **food:** Burger King, Giardino's Italian, Lotte Oriental, McDonald's, Subway, Wendy's, **other:** Advance Parts, Chevrolet, Honda, Nissan, Pontiac/Isuzu/GMC/Volvo, Rite Aid, SuperFresh Food, Wal-Mart
83 US 40, Marriottsville(no EZ wb return), **2 mi S...lodging:** Turf Valley Hotel/Country Club/rest.
82 US 40 E(from eb), same as 83
80 MD 32, Sykesville, **N...**golf, **S...gas:** Citgo
79mm weigh sta wb, phone
76 MD 97, Olney, **S...gas:** Citgo
73 MD 94, Woodbine, **N...gas:** Shell, **food:** McDonald's, Pizza Hut, **other:** Ramblin Pines RV Park(6mi), SuperMkt, **S...gas:** Amoco/diesel, Citgo
68 MD 27, Mt Airy, **N...gas:** Amoco/Blimpie/diesel/24hr, Citgo/7-11, Shell, **food:** Arby's, Burger King, Domino's, KFC, Ledo's Pizza, McDonald's, Pizza Hut, Roy Rogers, TCBY, **other:** Chrysler/Plymouth/Dodge/Jeep, Rite Aid, Safeway, SuperFresh Foods, Wal-Mart/auto, **S...gas:** Exxon/diesel/24hr, 4 Seasons Rest.
66mm truckers parking area eb
64mm weigh sta eb
62 MD 75, Libertytown, **N...gas:** Mobil/diesel, Shell, **food:** McDonald's, **other:** New Market Hist Dist
59 MD 144, no facilities
57mm Monocacy River
56 MD 144, **N...gas:** Citgo, Sheetz, **food:** Beijing Chinese, Burger King, McDonald's, JR's Pizza, Roy Rogers, Taco Bell, Waffle House, **other:** $General, to Hist Dist
55 South St, no facilities
54 Market St, to I-270, **N...gas:** Costco, **lodging:** Travelodge, **S...gas:** Citgo, Exxon/diesel, Sheetz/24hr, Shell/24hr, SouStates/diesel, **food:** Bob Evans, Burger King, Checker's, Cracker Barrel, El Paso Cantina, Jerry's Rest., KFC, McDonald's, Pargo's Café, Peking Gourmet, Popeye's, Roy Rogers, Subway, Wendy's, Day's Inn/rest., **lodging:** Econolodge, Fairfield Inn, Hampton Inn, Holiday Inn Express, **other:** Aamco, Best Buy, Chrysler/Plymouth, Circuit City, Ford/Lincoln/Mercury/Isuzu, Honda, Hyundai/Buick, Kohl's, Lowe's Whse, OfficeMax, PrecisionTune, Sam's Club, Saturn, Sears/auto, Wal-Mart/auto, mall

Frederick

53b a I-270 S, US 15 N, US 40 W, to Frederick
52b a US 15 S, US 340 W, Leesburg, no facilities
49 US 40A(no EZ wb return), Braddock Heights, **N...gas:** Amoco, Crown, Exxon/diesel, Mobil/diesel, Shell/repair, 7-11, **food:** Bob Evans, Boston Mkt, Burger King, ChiChi's, Denny's, Fritchie's Rest., Ground Round, McDonald's, Mtn View Diner, Pizza Hut, Roy Rogers, Wendy's, **lodging:** Comfort Inn, Holiday Inn, **other:** Ford/Subaru, Goodyear, JC Penney, Martin's Foods, Merchant Tire, PepBoys, st police, **S...**to Washington Mon SP, camping
48 US 40 E, US 340(from eb, no return), **1 mi N...**same as 49
42 MD 17, Myersville, **N...gas:** Exxon, Sunoco/diesel/24hr, **food:** Burger King, McDonald's, **other:** to Gambrill SP(6mi), Greenbrier SP(4mi), **S...gas:** Amoco/diesel
39mm rest area both lanes, full(handicapped)facilities, phone, vending, picnic tables, litter barrels, petwalk

Hagerstown

35 MD 66, to Boonsboro, **S...gas:** Sheetz, **other:** to Greenbrierington SP, camping
32b a US 40, Hagerstown, **1-3 mi N...gas:** AC&T/24hr, Amoco/Blimpie, Citgo/7-11, Exxon/diesel, **food:** Bob Evans, Burger King, DQ, Denny's, Ledo's Pizza, McDonald's, Pizza Hut, Quizno's, Red Horse Steaks, Subway, Taco Bell, Texas Roadhouse, **lodging:** Comfort Suites, Day's Inn, Hampton Inn, Holiday Inn/rest., Quality Inn, Sheraton, Super 8, **other:** HOSPITAL, Chevrolet/Cadillac, Chrysler/Plymouth/Dodge, CVS Drug, Goodyear/auto, Martin Foods, Mercedes/Toyota, Nissan, Subaru/VW/Mazda, Weis Foods, **S...other:** Honda, Kia, Pontiac/Buick/GMC
29b a MD 65, to Sharpsburg, **N...gas:** ACT/diesel, Exxon/24hr, Sheetz/24hr, **food:** FoodCourt, Pizza Hut, Subway, TCBY, **other:** HOSPITAL, Prime Outlets/famous brands, st police, **S...gas:** Shell/Blimpie/diesel/24hr, **food:** Burger King, Cracker Barrel, McDonald's, Waffle House, Wendy's, **lodging:** Sleep Inn, **other:** Safari Camping, to Antietam Bfd
28 MD 632, Hagerstown, **N...gas:** Chevron, **food:** Burger King, Chick-fil-A, Pizza Hut, Roy Rogers, Shoney's, Western Sizzlin, **S...**Jellystone Camping
26 I-81, N to Harrisburg, S to Martinsburg, no facilities
24 MD 63, Huyett, **N...gas:** Pilot/Subway/diesel/24hr, **S...lodging:** Red Roof Inn, **other:** KOA(2mi), C&O Canal
18 MD 68 E, Clear Spring, **N...gas:** Amoco, BP, **food:** McDonald's, **other:** bank, **S...gas:** Exxon/diesel, **food:** Wendy Hill Café

MARYLAND

Interstate 70

E ↕ W

12 MD 56, Indian Springs, **S...gas:** Exxon/diesel, **other:** Ft Frederick SP

9 US 40 E(from eb), Indian Springs, no facilities

5 MD 615(no immediate wb return), **N...**Log Cabin Rest.(2mi)

3 MD 144, Hancock(exits left from wb), **S...gas:** ACT/diesel, Amoco/diesel/rest./24hr/@, BP/diesel, **food:** Shive's Subs, Hardee's, Park'n Dine, Pizza Hut, Weaver's Rest., **lodging:** Hancock Motel, Super 8, **other:** Ford, NAPA, repair

1b US 522(exits left from eb), Hancock, **N...**Chevrolet, Chrysler/Dodge/Jeep, **S...gas:** Lowest Price/diesel, Sheetz/24hr, **food:** Park'n Dine, Pizza Hut, Weaver's Rest., **lodging:** Hancock Motel, Super 8, **other:** $General, Sav-A-Lot Foods, Happy Hills Camp

a I-68 W, US 40, W to Cumberland

0mm Maryland/Pennsylvania state line, Mason-Dixon Line

Interstate 81

N ↕ S

Exit # Services

12mm Maryland/Pennsylvania state line

10b a Showalter Rd, **E...lodging:** Colonial Motel, Hampton Inn, **W...**Microtel

9 Maugans Ave, **E...gas:** Mobil, Sheetz, Shell/Domino's/diesel, **food:** Antrim House Rest., McDonald's, Pizza Hut, Taco Bell, Waffle House, **lodging:** Colonial Motel, Hampton Inn, **W...food:** Burger King, Family Time Rest., **lodging:** Microtel

Hagerstown

8 Maugansville Rd(from sb, no re-entry), same as 9

7b a MD 58, Hagerstown, same as 6

6b a US 40, Hagerstown, **E...gas:** Exxon/diesel, Liberty, Shell, **food:** Roy Rogers, Wendy's, **lodging:** Clarion, Days Inn, Holiday Motel, Quality Inn, **other:** HOSPITAL, **W...food:** Arby's, IHOP, KFC, McDonald's, #1 Chinese, Pizzaria Uno, Ryan's, Subway, TGIFriday, Wendy's, **other:** Borders Books, Circuit City, $Express, Home Depot, OfficeMax, Trak Parts, Wal-Mart SuperCtr/24hr

5 Halfway Blvd, **E...gas:** AC&T/diesel/rest., Sheetz, Shell, **food:** Boston Mkt, Chick-fil-A, Dynasty Buffet, Fazoli's, Ground Round, Little Caesar's, McDonald's, Olive Garden, Outback Steaks, Pizza Hut, Popeye's, Red Lobster, Roy Rogers, Ruby Tuesday, Shoney's, Taco Bell, Wendy's, **lodging:** Holiday Inn Express, Motel 6, Plaza Hotel, Travelodge, **other:** CVS Drug, $Tree, Firestone/auto, Ford/Lincoln/Mercury, Hyundai, JC Penney, K-Mart, Lowe's Whse, Martin's Foods, Michael's, Sam's Club/gas, Sears/auto, Staples, Target, mall, **W...gas:** AC&T, Exxon

4 I-70, E to Frederick, W to Hancock, to I-68

2 US 11, Williamsport, **E...gas:** AC&T/diesel, **food:** Burger King, **W...gas:** Exxon, Shell/diesel, Sunoco/diesel/24hr, **food:** McDonald's, Waffle House, **lodging:** Red Roof Inn, **other:** KOA(4mi)

1 MD 63, MD 68, Williamsport, **E...gas:** Bowman/diesel, **other:** Jellystone, KOA, to Antietam Bfd, **W...**Citgo

0mm Maryland/West Virginia state line, Potomac River

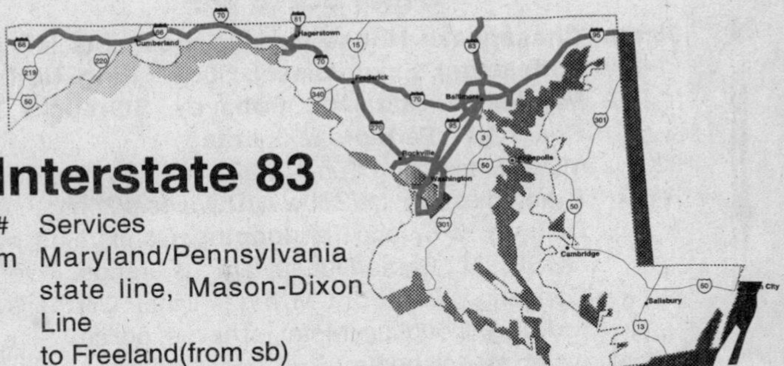

Interstate 83

N ↕ S

Exit # Services

38mm Maryland/Pennsylvania state line, Mason-Dixon Line

37 to Freeland(from sb)

36 MD 439, Bel Air, **5 mi W...**Morris Meadows Camping

35mm weigh/insp sta sb

33 MD 45, Parkton, **E...gas:** Exxon/diesel

31 Middletown Rd, to Parkton, golf

27 MD 137, Mt Carmel, Hereford, **E...gas:** Exxon/diesel, **other:** MEDICAL CARE, Graul's Foods, Hereford Drug, USPO

24 Belfast Rd, to Butler, Sparks, no facilities

20 Shawan Rd, Hunt Valley, **E...gas:** Amoco, Exxon/diesel, 7-11, **food:** Beijing Rest., Burger King, Carrabba's, Cinnamon Tree Rest., McDonald's, Outback Steaks, Valley View Rest, Wendy's, **lodging:** Chase Suites, Courtyard, Econolodge, Embassy Suites, Hampton Inn, Hunt Valley Marriott, **other:** Giant Foods, Goodyear/auto, Sears/auto, Wal-Mart, mall

18 Warren Rd(from nb, no return), Cockeysville, **E...**Exxon, SS/diesel, Residence Inn

17 Padonia Rd, Deereco Rd, **E...**Amoco/diesel, Applebee's, Bob Evans, Chili's, Denny's, Macaroni Grill, Day's Hotel, Extended Stay America, Goodyear/auto, Rite Aid, USPO

16b a Timonium Rd, **E...**Sunoco/diesel, Steak&Ale, Holiday Inn, Red Roof Inn, Infiniti, Saab

Baltimore

14 I-695 N, no facilities

13 I-695 S, Falls Rd, HOSPITAL, st police

12 Ruxton Rd(from nb, no return), no facilities

10b a Northern Parkway, **E...**HOSPITAL, Exxon, Texaco

9b a Cold Spring Lane, no facilities

8 MD 25 N(from nb), Falls Rd

7b a 28th St, **E...**HOSPITAL, **W...**Baltimore Zoo

6 US 1, US 40T, North Ave, downtown

5 MD Ave(from sb), downtown

3 Chase St, Gilford St, downtown

2 Pleasant St(from sb), downtown

1 Fayette St, downtown Baltimore, I-83 begins/ends. **S...**Bennigan's, Mo's Seafood Rest.

Interstate 95

N ↕ S

Exit # Services

110mm Maryland/Delaware state line

109b a MD 279, to Elkton, Newark, **E...gas:** Citgo/diesel, Petro/diesel/rest./24hr/@, **food:** Cracker Barrel, KFC/Taco Bell, McDonald's, Waffle House, **lodging:** Econolodge, Elkton Lodge, Knight's Inn, Motel 6, **other:** HOSPITAL, Blue Beacon, **W...gas:** TA/Mobil/Subway/diesel/24hr/@

100 MD 272, to North East, Rising Sun, **E...gas:** Flying J/diesel/rest./LP/24hr/@, Sunoco, **food:** McDonald's, Roy Rogers, Schroeder's Deli, Wendy's, **lodging:** Crystal Inn, **other:** Eckerd, museum, st police, to Elk Neck SP, **W...gas:** Citgo, Mobil, **other:** zoo

MARYLAND

Interstate 95

N ↕ S

Aberdeen

96mm Chesapeake House service area(exits left from both lanes), Exxon/diesel, Burger King, HotDogs, Mrs Fields, Pizza Hut, Popeye's, Starbucks, Taco Bell, TCBY, Farmers Mkt, gifts

93 MD 275, to Rising Sun, US 222, to Perryville, **E...gas:** Exxon/diesel, Pilot/Subway/DQ/diesel/24hr/@, **food:** Denny's, KFC/Taco Bell, **lodging:** Comfort Inn, **other:** HOSPITAL, Prime Outlets/famous brands, Riverview Camping, **W...food:** CM Tuggs Diner, Crother's Mkt, **lodging:** Douglass Motel, **other:** st police

92mm weigh sta/toll booth

91.5mm Susquehanna River

89 MD 155, to Havre de Grace(last nb exit before toll), **1-3 mi E...food:** KFC, McDonald's, MacGregor's Rest., **lodging:** Best Budget Inn, Super 8, **other:** HOSPITAL, **W...**to Susquehanna SP

85 MD 22, to Aberdeen, **E...gas:** Amoco/24hr, Citgo/7-11, Crown/diesel, Enroy, Sunoco/diesel, Shell/diesel/24hr, **food:** Arby's, Bob Evans, Family Buffet, Golden Corral, Japan House, KFC, King's Chinese, Lee's Hunan, Little Caesar's, McDonald's, Olive Tree Italian, Papa John's, Subway, Taco Bell, Wendy's, **lodging:** Day's Inn, Econolodge/rest., Holiday Inn, Quality Inn/rest., Red Roof, Sheraton, Super 8, Travelodge, **other:** $Express, $General, $Tree, GNC, Klein's Foods, K-Mart, Mars Foods, Pontiac/Cadillac, Radio Shack, Rite Aid, Target, museum

81mm MD House service area(exits left from both lanes), Exxon/diesel, Sunoco/diesel, Big Boy, Cinnamon, Hotdog City, Roy Rogers, Sbarro's, TCBY, gifts

80 MD 543, to Riverside, Churchville, **E...gas:** Amoco/Burger King, Crown/A&W/diesel, Mobil/diesel, **food:** China Moon, Cracker Barrel, McDonald's, Riverside Pizzaria, **lodging:** SpringHill Suites, **other:** Eckerd, Klein's Foods, Bar Harbor RV Park

77b a MD 24, to Edgewood, Bel Air, **E...gas:** Exxon/Blimpie/diesel, Shell, Texaco/diesel, **food:** Burger King, Denny's/24hr, Giovanni's Rest., Taco Bell, Vitali's Rest., **lodging:** Best Western, Comfort Inn, Day's Inn, Edgewood Motel, Hampton Inn, Holiday Inn Express, Sleep Inn, **W...gas:** Exxon/diesel, **food:** KFC/Taco Bell, McDonald's, **other:** HOSPITAL, BJ's Whse, Wal-Mart/drugs, Weis Foods

74 MD 152, Joppatowne, **E...gas:** Amoco, Citgo/High's/diesel, Exxon/diesel, **food:** Friendly's, KFC, IHOP, McDonald's, Mowery's Seafood, Roy Rogers, Venitian Palace, Wendy's, **lodging:** Edgewood Motel, Super 8, **other:** HOSPITAL, RV Ctr, Toyota(1mi)

70mm Big Gunpowder Falls

67b a MD 43, to White Marsh Blvd, US 1, US 40, **E...gas:** Crown/24hr, Enroy, Shell, Sunoco, **food:** Burger King, WhiteMarsh Diner, **lodging:** Williamsburg Inn, **other:** Best Buy, Dodge, Target, to Gunpowder SP, **3 mi E on US 40...other:** CostCo, Home Depot, PepBoys, RV Ctr, **W...gas:** Exxon/diesel, **food:** Bayou Blues Café, Bertucci's, Chili's, Don Pablo, McDonald's, Olive Garden, Red Brick Sta, Red Lobster, Ruby Tuesday, Taco Bell, TGIFriday, Wendy's, **lodging:** Hampton Inn, Hilton Garden, **other:** Barnes&Noble, Giant Foods, GNC, Hecht's, IKEA, JC Penney, Lord&Taylor, Macy's, Old Navy, Sears, USPO, mall, to Gunpowder SP

64b a I-695(exits left), E to Essex, W to Towson

Baltimore

62 to I-895(from sb)

61 US 40, Pulaski Hwy, **E...gas:** Texaco, **food:** McDonald's, **other:** Cooper Tires

60 Moravia Rd, no facilities

59 Eastern Ave, **E...gas:** Shell, Texaco, **food:** Burger King, Denny's, **other:** Chrysler/Plymouth/Dodge/Jeep, Pontiac/GMC, **W...gas:** Amoco/diesel/24hr, Exxon, **food:** Wendy's, **other:** HOSPITAL, Home Depot

58 Dundalk Ave, **E...gas:** Citgo

57 O'Donnell St, Boston St, **E...gas:** TA/Mobil/Sbarro's/Taco Bell/diesel/@, **food:** McDonald's, **lodging:** Best Western, Rodeway Inn

56 Keith Ave, no facilities

56mm McHenry Tunnel, toll plaza(north side of tunnel)

55 Key Hwy, to Ft McHenry NM, last nb exit before toll

54 MD 2 S, to Hanover St, **W...**downtown, HOSPITAL

53 I-395 N, to MLK, **W...**downtown, Oriole Park

52 Russell St N, **W...**HOSPITAL

51 Washington Blvd, no facilities

50 Caton Ave, **E...gas:** Crown Gas, Hess, Shell/24hr, Texaco/diesel, **food:** Caton House Rest., McDonald's, **lodging:** Holiday Inn Express, **W...**HOSPITAL

49b a I-695, E to Key Bridge, Glen Burnie, W to Towson, to I-70, to I-83

47b a I-195 , to BWI Airport, to Baltimore

46 I-895, to Harbor Tunnel Thruway

43 MD 100, to Glen Burnie, **1 mi E...gas:** Citgo, Exxon/Wendy's, **lodging:** Best Western

41b a MD 175, to Columbia, **E...gas:** Citgo, Exxon, Shell, **food:** Burger King, High's Dairy, Jerry's Rest., McDonald's, **lodging:** Fairfield Inn, Super 8, **W...gas:** Exxon, **food:** Applebee's, Bob Evans, McDonald's, Olive Garden, TGIFriday, **lodging:** Studio+, **other:** HOSPITAL, to Johns Hopkins U, Loyola U

38b a MD 32, to Ft Meade, **2 mi E on US 1...gas:** Amoco, Enroy, Exxon, **food:** Burger King, McDonald's, Taco Bell, **lodging:** Comfort Inn, **other:** to BWI Airport, **W...**HOSPITAL

37mm Welcome Ctr both lanes, full(handicapped)facilities, info, phone, vending, picnic tables, litter barrels, petwalk

35b a MD 216, to Laurel, **E...gas:** Crown Gas, Exxon, **food:** McDonald's, **other:** Weis Food/drug, laundry

34mm Patuxent River

33b a MD 198, to Laurel, **E...gas:** Exxon, **food:** High's Dairy, McDonald's, **other:** HOSPITAL, **W...gas:** Exxon, Shell, **food:** Brass Duck Rest., McDonald's, **lodging:** Best Western

29 MD 212, to Beltsville, **E...gas:** 7-11, **W...gas:** Exxon/Blimpie/diesel, **food:** Magic Cue Rest., McDonald's, Wendy's, **lodging:** Fairfield Inn, Sheraton, **other:** CVS Drug, Giant Foods

27 I-495 S around Washington

25b a US 1, Baltimore Ave, to Laurel, College Park, **E...gas:** Amoco, Citgo/7-11, Exxon/diesel, Mobil, Shell/24hr, **food:** Arby's, Burger King, Danny's Rest., El Mexicano, Moose Creek Steaks, Jerry's Subs, Jonesie's Rest., McDonald's, Pizza Hut, Wendy's, **lodging:** Holiday Inn, **other:** Goodyear, Rite Aid, US Agri Library, **W...gas:** Amoco/24hr, Shell, Barnside Diner/24hr, **food:** Baskin-Robbins/Dunkin Donuts, Starbucks, **lodging:** Day's Inn, Econolodge, Hampton Inn, Ramada Ltd, Super 8, **other:** GNC, Home Depot, Honda, Shoppers Foods, VW, to U of MD

MARYLAND

Interstate 95

N
S

23 MD 201, Kenilworth Ave, **E...lodging:** Marriott/rest., **1 mi W on Greenbelt...gas:** Shell, Texaco, **food:** Boston Mkt, Checker's, KFC, McDonald's, Popeye's, TJ's Roadhouse, **lodging:** Courtyard, **other:** Cadillac, CVS Drug, Giant Food/drug, Staples, Target

22 Baltimore-Washington Pkwy, **E...**to NASA

20b a MD 450, Annapolis Rd, Lanham, **E...gas:** Mobil, **food:** Burger King, Jerry's Rest., McDonald's, Pizza Hut, Red Lobster, **lodging:** Best Western, Day's Inn/rest., Red Roof Inn, **other:** Ford/Kia, Harley-Davidson, **W...gas:** Amoco, Chevron, Citgo/7-11/24hr, Shell, Sunoco/24hr, **food:** Chesapeake Bay Seafood, Danny's Diner, KFC, Shoney's, Wendy's, **lodging:** Ramada Inn, **other:** HOSPITAL, Aamco, Chrysler/Plymouth/Jeep, Dodge, Goodyear/auto, JustTires, Lincoln/Mercury, Nissan, Office Depot, Pontiac, Radio Shack, Safeway, Shoppers Foods, Staples

19b a US 50, to Annapolis, Washington, no facilities

17 MD 202, Landover Rd, to Upper Marlboro, **E...food:** Inglewood Rest. Park, **lodging:** DoubleTree Club Hotel, **other:** Capitol Centre, **W...food:** IHOP, **other:** Buick, Circuit City, Goodyear/auto, Hecht's, JustTires, Sam's Club, Sears/auto, mall

16 Arena Dr, **W...**to Arena

15 MD 214, Central Ave, **E...lodging:** Extended Stay America, Hampton Inn/rest., **other:** Capitol Centre, to Six Flags, **W...gas:** Crown, Exxon/diesel, Shell/autocare, Sunoco/24hr, **food:** DQ, KFC, Jerry's Subs, McDonald's, Pizza Hut, Wendy's, **lodging:** Day's Inn/rest., **other:** Goodyear, Home Depot, NTB, Staples, Trak Auto, U-Haul, mall

11 MD 4, Pennsylvania Ave, to Upper Marlboro, **W...gas:** Exxon, Sunoco, **food:** Applebee's, Arby's, IHOP, LD's CrabHouse, LJ Silver, Pizza Hut, Starbucks, Taco Bell, Wendy's, **other:** CVS Drug, Hancock Fabrics, JC Penney, K-Mart, Marshall's, SuperFresh Foods, st police

9 MD 337, to Allentown Rd, **E...gas:** Crown, Shell/autocare, **food:** Checkers, Dunkin Donuts, Popeye's, **lodging:** Holiday Inn Express, Motel 6, Ramada Inn, Super 8, **other:** HOSPITAL, Family$, Trak Auto, U-Haul, to Andrews AFB

7 MD 5, Branch Ave, to Silver Hill, **E...gas:** Exxon, Sunoco, 7-11, **food:** Wendy's, **W...gas:** Shell/diesel, **lodging:** Day's Inn, **other:** HOSPITAL, Ford, **1 mi W...other:** BMW, Buick/Pontiac/GMC, Ford/Mercury/Kia, Nissan

4b a MD 414, St Barnabas Rd, Marlow Hgts, **E...gas:** Citgo, Exxon, **food:** Blackeyed Pea, Bojangles, Burger King, Checkers, KFC, McDonald's, Outback Steaks, Wendy's, **other:** $Tree, Home Depot, K-Mart, Old Navy, Safeway, Staples, **W...gas:** Exxon/dieselDQ, Shell/autocare, **food:** McDonald's

3b a MD 210, Indian Head Hwy, to Forest Hgts, **E...gas:** Mobil, Shell, **food:** Danny's Burgers, Pizza Hut, Ranch House Rest., Taco Bell, **lodging:** Best Western, Susse Chalet, **other:** Radio Shack, Sav-A-Lot Foods, Shoppers Foods, USPO, **W...gas:** Amoco/24hr, Chevron/diesel/24hr, Crown Gas, Exxon, Shell, 7-11, **food:** Arby's, Burger King, KFC, McDonald's, Papa John's, Pizza Hut, Popeye's, Subway, Wendy's, **other:** MEDICAL CARE, CVS Drug, Family$, Giant Foods, Radio Shack, Rite Aid, Safeway

2b a I-295, N to Washingon

0mm Maryland/Virginia state line, Potomac River, Woodrow Wilson Bridge

Washington DC Area

Frederick

Interstate 97

N
S

Exit #	Services
17	I-695. I-97 begins/ends on I-695.
16	MD 648, Ferndale, Glen Burnie, **W...gas:** Mobil
15b	MD 176 W, Dorsey Rd, Aviation Blvd, **W...**to BWI
14b a	MD 100, Ellicott City, Gibson Island, no facilities
13b a	MD 174, Quarterfield Rd, no facilities
12	MD 3, New Cut Rd, Glen Burnie, **E...gas:** Amoco, Enroy, Exxon/24hr, Mobil, **food:** Burger King, Domino's, Pizza Hut, Popeye's, Taco Bell, Wendy's, **other:** Giant Foods, Metro Foods, Target, Wal-Mart
10b a	Benfield Blvd, Severna Park, **E...gas:** Crown, Exxon, Shell/diesel, **food:** McDonald's
7	MD 3, MD 32, Bowie, Odenton, **E...**motel
5	MD 178, Crownsville, no facilities
0mm	I-97 begins/ends on US 50/301.

Interstate 270(Rockville)

E
W

Exit #	Services
32	I-270 begins/ends on I-70, exit 53.
31b a	MD 85, **N...gas:** Exxon, Sheetz, Shell/diesel, **food:** Applebee's, Bob Evans, Burger King, Checker's, Golden Corral, Jerry's Rest., KFC/Taco Bell, LoneStar Steaks, McDonald's, Pargo's, Popeye's, Roy Rogers, Wendy's, **lodging:** Day's Inn, Holiday Inn, Holiday Inn Express, **other:** Best Buy, Borders Books, Chrysler, Circuit City, CVS Drug, Goodyear/auto, Home Depot, Lowe's Whse, OfficeMax, Sam's Club, Wal-Mart/auto, **S...gas:** Amoco/Blimpie, **food:** Cracker Barrel, Macaroni Grill, McDonald's, Panda Express, TGIFriday, **lodging:** Courtyard, Extended Stay America, Fairfield Inn, Hampton Inn, MainStay Suites, **other:** Honda
30mm	Monocacy River
28mm	viewpoint wb
26	MD 80, Urbana, **N...gas:** Exxon
22	MD 109, Hyattstown, to Barnesville, **N...**Food+/gas, **food:** Hyattstown Deli, **S...lodging:** Comus Inn(3mi)
21mm	weigh sta both lanes
18	MD 121, Boyds, to Clarksburg, Little Bennett Pk, Blackhill Pk, **N...**gas, camping(seasonal)
16	MD 27, Father Hurley Blvd, to Damascus, **N...gas:** Chevron/diesel, Exxon, Mobil, **food:** Applebee's, Bob Evans, McDonald's, TCBY, **lodging:** Extended Stay America, **other:** Borders Books, Giant Foods, Home Depot, Kohl's, Michael's, PepBoys, Target, Wal-Mart, **S...gas:** Amoco, 7-11, **food:** McDonald's, Subway, Wendy's

MARYLAND

Interstate 270

Rockville

15b a MA 118, to MD 355, **N...gas:** Chevron/diesel, **food:** Burger King, **lodging:** Hampton Inn, **S...gas:** Amoco, Citgo/7-11, Exxon/24hr, **food:** Pizza Hut, **other:** st police, tire/brake repair
13b a Middlebrook Rd(from wb), no facilities
11b a MD 124, Quince Orchard Rd, **N...gas:** Exxon, **food:** Boston Mkt, ChuckeCheese, McDonald's, Roy Rogers, Starbucks, Subway, **lodging:** Courtyard, Hilton, Holiday Inn, TownePlace Suites, **other:** Borders Books, CompUSA, CVS Drugs, Ford, JC Penney, Sam's Club, mall, **S...gas:** Shell, Texaco/diesel, **food:** Chevy's Mexican, Chili's, Denny's, Friendly's, LoneStar Steaks, Starbucks, **lodging:** Red Roof Inn, **other:** Chevrolet, Circuit City, Giant Foods, McGruder's Foods, Staples, Trak Auto, Seneca Creek SP
10 MD 117, Clopper Rd(from wb), same as 11.
9b a I-370, to Gaithersburg, Sam Eig Hwy, **S...food:** access to Chinese Rest., India Bistro, Pizza Hut, Subway, **other:** Barnes&Noble, Festival Foods, Target, Weis Mkt
8 Shady Grove Rd, **S...lodging:** Marriott, Quality Suites, Residence Inn, Sleep Inn, SpringHill Suites, **other:** HOSPITAL
6b a MD 28, W Montgomery Ave, **N...lodging:** Woodfin Suites, **S...lodging:** Best Western
5b a MD 189, Falls Rd
4b a Montrose Rd, **N...**gas, **S...**st police
2 I-270/I-270 spur diverges eb, converges wb
1 MD 187, Old Georgetown Rd, **S...gas:** Exxon, **food:** Hamburger Hamlet, **other:** HOSPITAL, CVS Drug, Giant Foods
1b a (I-270 spur)Democracy Blvd, **W...gas:** Exxon/Texaco/diesel, **lodging:** Marriott, **other:** Hecht's, JC Penney, Nordstrom's, mall
0mm I-270 begins/ends on I-495, exit 35.

Interstate 495(DC)

See Virginia Interstate 495(DC)

Interstate 695(Baltimore)

Baltimore

Exit # Services
48mm Patapsco River, Francis Scott Key Br
44 MD 695(from nb)
43mm toll plaza
42 MD 151 S, Sparrows Point(last exit before toll sb), **E...**gas/diesel
41 MD 20, Cove Rd, **W...**gas, food
40 MD 150, MD 151, North Point Blvd, **E...**auto repair
39 Merritt Blvd, **W...gas:** Amoco, **other:** Ford, Hyundai
38b a MD 150, Eastern Blvd, to Baltimore, **W...food:** KFC, **other:** JC Penney, Staples
36 MD 702 S(exits left from sb), Essex
35 US 40, **1 mi N...food:** Dunkin Donuts, McDonald's, **other:** Circuit City, NTB, Office Depot, U-Haul, **2 mi N...gas:** Citgo, **other:** Harley-Davidson, Home Depot
34 MD 7, Philadelphia Rd, **N...lodging:** Susse Chalet
33b a I-95, N to Philadelphia, S to Baltimore
32b a US 1, Bel Air, **N...gas:** Exxon, 7-11, **food:** Denny's, Dunkin Donuts, IHOP, Taco Bell, **other:** Giant Foods, K-Mart, Merchant Tire/auto, Salvo Auto Parts, **S...gas:** Crown Gas, Getty, **food:** McDonald's, Mr Crab, Subway, **other:** Valu Food, Goodyear/auto
31c MD 43 E(from eb), no facilities
b a MD 147, Hartford Rd, **N...gas:** Amoco/24hr, Citgo/7-11, Mobil, Shell/diesel, **other:** CVS Drugs, Chrysler/Plymouth, Goodyear
30b a MD 41, Perring Pkwy, **N...food:** Burger King, Denny's, Roy Rogers, **other:** Chevrolet, Ford, Giant Foods, Home Depot, K-Mart, Office Depot, Ross, **S...other:** Dodge, Mazda
29b a MD 542, Loch Raven Blvd, **S...lodging:** Holiday Inn
28 Providence Rd, no facilities
27b a MD 146, Dulaney Valley Rd, **N...**Hampton NHS, **S...gas:** Mobil/diesel, Sheraton, **other:** Hecht's, SuperFresh Food, mall
26b a MD 45, York Rd, Towson, **S...**gas, food
25 MD 139, Charles St, **N...**HOSPITAL, AAA
24 I-83 N, to York
23b a I-83 S, Baltimore, MD 25 N, **N...**gas, food
22 Green Spring Ave, no facilities
21 Stevenson Rd, no facilities
20 MD 140, Reisterstown Rd, Pikesville, **N...**gas, food, lodging, **S...**gas, food, lodging
19 I-795, NW Expswy, no facilities
18b a MD 26, Randallstown, Lochearn, **E...gas:** Crown, HOSPITAL,
17 MD 122, Security Blvd, **E...food:** Red Lobster, **lodging:** Comfort Inn, Day's Inn, Motel 6, **other:** Mitsubishi, **W...gas:** Citgo/7-11, **food:** McDonald's, **lodging:** Holiday Inn, **other:** Best Buy, Firestone, JC Penney, Staples, mall
16b a I-70, E to Baltimore, W to Frederick
15b a US 40, Ellicott City, Baltimore, **E...food:** ChuckeCheese, **lodging:** Day's Inn, **other:** Dodge, Value City Foods, **W...gas:** Amoco, Shell
14 Edmondson Ave, no facilities
13 MD 144, Frederick Rd, Catonsville, **W...**gas, food
12c b MD 372 E, Wilkens, **E...**HOSPITAL
11b a I-95, N to Baltimore, S to Washington
10 US 1, Washington Blvd, **W...**auto repair
9 Hollins Ferry Rd, Lansdowne, **W...**Goodyear
8 MD 168, Nursery Rd, **N...gas:** Exxon, Shell, **food:** KFC, McDonald's, Wendy's, **lodging:** Motel 6
7b a MD 295, **N...**to Baltimore, **S...**BWI Airport
6b a Camp Mead Rd(from nb)
5 MD 648, Ferndale, gas, food, lodging
4b a I-97 S, to Annapolis
3b a MD 2 N, Brooklyn Park, **S...**gas, food, lodging
2 MD 10, Glen Burnie
1 MD 174, Hawkins Point Rd, **S...gas:** Citgo

MASSACHUSETTS

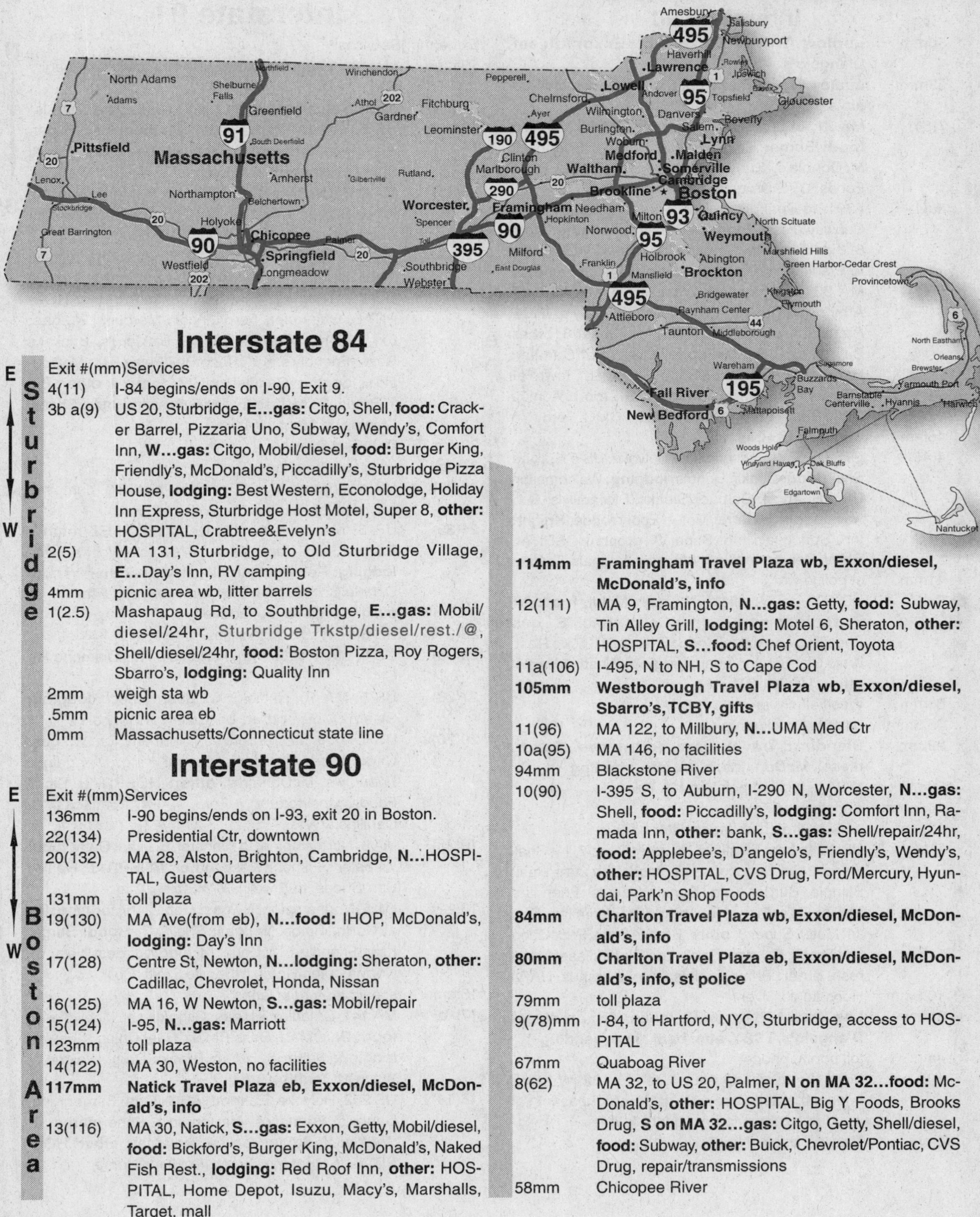

Interstate 84

E ↕ W — Sturbridge

Exit #(mm)	Services
4(11)	I-84 begins/ends on I-90, Exit 9.
3b a(9)	US 20, Sturbridge, **E...gas:** Citgo, Shell, **food:** Cracker Barrel, Pizzaria Uno, Subway, Wendy's, Comfort Inn, **W...gas:** Citgo, Mobil/diesel, **food:** Burger King, Friendly's, McDonald's, Piccadilly's, Sturbridge Pizza House, **lodging:** Best Western, Econolodge, Holiday Inn Express, Sturbridge Host Motel, Super 8, **other:** HOSPITAL, Crabtree&Evelyn's
2(5)	MA 131, Sturbridge, to Old Sturbridge Village, **E...**Day's Inn, RV camping
4mm	picnic area wb, litter barrels
1(2.5)	Mashapaug Rd, to Southbridge, **E...gas:** Mobil/diesel/24hr, Sturbridge Trkstp/diesel/rest./@, Shell/diesel/24hr, **food:** Boston Pizza, Roy Rogers, Sbarro's, **lodging:** Quality Inn
2mm	weigh sta wb
.5mm	picnic area eb
0mm	Massachusetts/Connecticut state line

Interstate 90

E ↕ W — Boston Area

Exit #(mm)	Services
136mm	I-90 begins/ends on I-93, exit 20 in Boston.
22(134)	Presidential Ctr, downtown
20(132)	MA 28, Alston, Brighton, Cambridge, **N...**HOSPITAL, Guest Quarters
131mm	toll plaza
19(130)	MA Ave(from eb), **N...food:** IHOP, McDonald's, **lodging:** Day's Inn
17(128)	Centre St, Newton, **N...lodging:** Sheraton, **other:** Cadillac, Chevrolet, Honda, Nissan
16(125)	MA 16, W Newton, **S...gas:** Mobil/repair
15(124)	I-95, **N...gas:** Marriott
123mm	toll plaza
14(122)	MA 30, Weston, no facilities
117mm	**Natick Travel Plaza eb, Exxon/diesel, McDonald's, info**
13(116)	MA 30, Natick, **S...gas:** Exxon, Getty, Mobil/diesel, **food:** Bickford's, Burger King, McDonald's, Naked Fish Rest., **lodging:** Red Roof Inn, **other:** HOSPITAL, Home Depot, Isuzu, Macy's, Marshalls, Target, mall
114mm	**Framingham Travel Plaza wb, Exxon/diesel, McDonald's, info**
12(111)	MA 9, Framington, **N...gas:** Getty, **food:** Subway, Tin Alley Grill, **lodging:** Motel 6, Sheraton, **other:** HOSPITAL, **S...food:** Chef Orient, Toyota
11a(106)	I-495, N to NH, S to Cape Cod
105mm	**Westborough Travel Plaza wb, Exxon/diesel, Sbarro's, TCBY, gifts**
11(96)	MA 122, to Millbury, **N...**UMA Med Ctr
10a(95)	MA 146, no facilities
94mm	Blackstone River
10(90)	I-395 S, to Auburn, I-290 N, Worcester, **N...gas:** Shell, **food:** Piccadilly's, **lodging:** Comfort Inn, Ramada Inn, **other:** bank, **S...gas:** Shell/repair/24hr, **food:** Applebee's, D'angelo's, Friendly's, Wendy's, **other:** HOSPITAL, CVS Drug, Ford/Mercury, Hyundai, Park'n Shop Foods
84mm	**Charlton Travel Plaza wb, Exxon/diesel, McDonald's, info**
80mm	**Charlton Travel Plaza eb, Exxon/diesel, McDonald's, info, st police**
79mm	toll plaza
9(78)mm	I-84, to Hartford, NYC, Sturbridge, access to HOSPITAL
67mm	Quaboag River
8(62)	MA 32, to US 20, Palmer, **N on MA 32...food:** McDonald's, **other:** HOSPITAL, Big Y Foods, Brooks Drug, **S on MA 32...gas:** Citgo, Getty, Shell/diesel, **food:** Subway, **other:** Buick, Chevrolet/Pontiac, CVS Drug, repair/transmissions
58mm	Chicopee River

MASSACHUSETTS

Interstate 90

E ↕ W

56mm	**Ludlow Travel Plaza wb, Exxon/diesel, D'angelo's**
55mm	**Ludlow Travel Plaza eb, Exxon/diesel, McDonald's**
7(54)	MA 21, to Ludlow, **N...gas:** Gulf, Mobil, Sunoco, **food:** Burger King, Dunkin Donuts, Friendly's, McDonald's, Subway, **other:** HOSPITAL, Big Y Foods, CVS Drug, Jo-Ann Fabrics
6(51)	I-291, to Springfield, Hartford CT, **N...gas:** Pride/Subway/diesel, **food:** McDonald's, **lodging:** Motel 6, Plantation Inn, Ramada Inn, **other:** HOSPITAL, to Bradley Int Airport, Basketball Hall of Fame
5(49)	MA 33, to Chicopee, Westover AFB, **N...food:** Arby's, Burger King, Denny's, Friendly's, IHOP, Pizza Hut, Wendy's, Comfort Inn, Super 8, **other:** BJ's Whse, Big Y Foods, Chevrolet/Cadillac, Honda/Subaru, Stop&Shop Food/gas, TownFair Tire, U-Haul, World Mkt, mall, **S...food:** Admiral DW's Rest., **other:** Buick/Pontiac/GMC, Ford
46mm	Connecticut River
4(46)	I-91, US 5, W Springfield, to Holyoke, **US 5 N...gas:** Shell, **food:** Dunkin Donuts, **lodging:** Welcome Inn, **US 5 S...food:** Outback Steaks, Piccadilly's, Subway, **lodging:** Corral Motel, Econolodge, Knight's Inn, Springfield Inn, Super 8, **other:** HOSPITAL, BMW, Honda, Indian Motorcycles, Lexus, Toyota
41mm	st police wb
3(40)	US 202, to Westfield, **N...gas:** Mobil, **food:** NE Pizza, **lodging:** Country Court Motel, **S...gas:** Shell/Subway/diesel, **food:** Friendly's, Nick's Rest., Whip City Brewery/rest., **lodging:** Westfield Motel, **other:** HOSPITAL
36mm	Westfield River
35.5mm	runaway truck ramp eb
29mm	**Blandford Travel Plaza both lanes...Exxon/diesel, McDonalds, gifts, info, vending**
20mm	1724 ft, highest point on MA Tpk
14.5mm	Appalachian Trail
12mm	parking area both lanes, litter barrels
2(11)	US 20, to Lee, Pittsfield, **N...gas:** Citgo/7-11, Shell/diesel/24hr, Sunoco/repair, **food:** Athena's Rest., Blimpie, Burger King, Dunkin Donuts, Friendly's, McDonald's, Pizza Hut, **lodging:** Pilgrim Inn, Sunset Motel, Super 8, **other:** Brooks Drug, PriceChopper Foods, **S...gas:** Shell, Lee Plaza/diesel/Motel/rest., **other:** Prime Outlets/famous brands, NAPA
10.5mm	Hoosatonic River
8mm	**Lee Travel Plaza both lanes, Exxon/diesel, D'angelo's, TCBY, atm, bank, info, vending**
4mm	toll booth, phone
1(2)	MA 41(from wb, no return), to MA 102, W Stockbridge, the Berkshires, **N...lodging:** Pleasant Valley Motel, **other:** to Bousquet Ski Area
0mm	Massachusetts/New York state line

Springfield

Pittsfield

Interstate 91

N ↕ S

Exit #(mm)	Services
55mm	Massachusetts/Vermont state line, callboxes begin/end
54mm	parking area both lanes, picnic tables, litter barrels
28(51)	US 5, MA 10, Bernardston, **E...food:** Bella Notte Ristorante, **lodging:** Fox Inn, **W...gas:** Citgo/diesel, Sunoco, **other:** RV camping
27(45)	MA 2 E, Greenfield, **E...gas:** Citgo, Mobil, Sunoco, **food:** Burger King, Denny's Pantry, Friendly's, McDonald's, **other:** HOSPITAL, CVS Drug
26(43)	MA 2 W, MA 2A E, Greenfield, **E...gas:** Citgo/diesel, Mobil, Palmer/diesel, **food:** China Gourmet, Dunkin Donuts, **lodging:** Howard Johnson, **other:** HOSPITAL, Chevrolet, Ford/Lincoln/Mercury, **W...gas:** Exxon/24hr, Shell/24hr, **food:** Bickford's, Bricker's Rest., Friendly's, KFC/Taco Bell/Pizza Hut, McDonald's, **lodging:** CandleLight Inn, Super 8, **other:** Big Y Foods, BJ's Whse, Family$, Nissan, Radio Shack, Staples, to Mohawk Tr
39mm	Deerfield River
37mm	weigh sta both lanes
25(36)	MA 116(from sb), S Deerfield, hist dist, camping, same as 24
24(35)	US 5, MA 10, MA 116, Deerfield(no EZ return), **E...gas:** Mobil, **food:** Chandler's Rest., Wolfy's Rest., **lodging:** Red Roof Inn, Whatley Inn, **other:** Yankee Candle Co, **W...gas:** Exxon/diesel/diner/24hr
34.5mm	parking area nb, no facilities
23(34)	US 5(from sb), no facilities
22(30)	US 5, MA 10(from nb), N Hatfield, **W...**Diamond RV Ctr
21(28)	US 5, MA 10, Hatfield, **W...gas:** Sunoco, **lodging:** Stearns Motel, **other:** Long View RV, st police
20(26)	US 5, MA 9, MA 10(from sb), Northampton, **W...gas:** Citgo, **food:** Bickford's, Burger King, D'angelo's, Friendly's, McDonald's, **other:** HOSPITAL, Big Y Foods, Chevrolet/VW, Ford, NAPA, Pontiac/GMC/Cadillac, VW
19(25)	MA 9, Northampton, to Amherst, **E...gas:** Getty, **food:** Webster's Fishook Rest., **other:** HOSPITAL, Hadley BarnShops, to Elwell SP, **W...gas:** Citgo
18(22)	US 5, Northampton, **E...gas:** Mobil/24hr, **lodging:** Inn at Northampton, **W...gas:** Shell/24hr, **food:** Burger King, Friendly's, McDonald's, **lodging:** Best Western, Northampton Hotel, **other:** to Smith Coll
18mm	scenic area both lanes
17b a(16)	MA 141, S Hadley, **E...gas:** Citgo/diesel, Mobil/diesel, **food:** DairyMart, Bess Eaton, Real China, Subway, **lodging:** Super 8, **other:** Brooks Drug, Walgreen, **W...**to Mt Tom Ski Area
16(14)	US 202, Holyoke, **E...food:** ABC Pizza, Burger King, Denny's, Friendly's, McDonald's, Schermerhorn's Seafood, **lodging:** Yankee Pedlar Inn, **other:** HOSPITAL, to Heritage SP, **W...**Soldier's Home

Greenfield

MASSACHUSETTS

Interstate 91

N ↕ S — Springfield

15(12) to US 5, Ingleside, **E...gas:** Shell, **food:** Cracker Barrel, Friendly's, Pizzaria Uno, Ruby Tuesday, **lodging:** Holiday Inn, **other:** HOSPITAL, Barnes&Noble, Best Buy, Circuit City, CompUSA, Filene's, JC Penney, Lord&Taylor, Old Navy, Sears/auto, Target, mall

14(11) to US 5, to I-90(Mass Tpk), E to Boston, W to Albany, **E...**HOSPITAL

13b a(9) US 5 N, W Springfield, **E...gas:** Citgo, **food:** Bickford's, On the Border, Outback Steaks, Piccadilly's, Subway, **lodging:** Comfort Inn, Knight's Inn, Red Roof Inn, Residence Inn, Springfield Inn, Super 8, **other:** BMW, Home Depot, Honda/Lexus/Toyota, mall, **W...gas:** Citgo/diesel, Mobil, Sunoco/diesel, **food:** Arby's, Boston Mkt, Burger King, Calamari's Grill, ChiChi's, Chili's, D'angelo's, Empire Buffet, Friendly's, HomeTown Buffet, Ivanhoe Rest., KFC, McDonald's, Pizza Hut, Wendy's, Wong's Chinese, **lodging:** Best Western, Day's Inn, Econolodge, Hampton Inn, Knoll Motel, Quality Inn, Red Carpet Inn, **other:** Chrysler/Plymouth, Costco, Home Depot, Lincoln/Mercury, Mazda/Mercedes, Michael's, Nissan/Subaru, Stop&Shop Foods, Staples

12(8.5) I-391 N, to Chicopee, no facilities

11(8) Burney Ave(from sb), **E...gas:** Mobil, **other:** HOSPITAL

10(7.5) Main St(from nb), Springfield, **E...gas:** Mobil

9(7) US 20 W, MA 20A E(from nb), **E...food:** McDonald's

8(6.5) I-291, US 20 E, to I-90, **E...**downtown, **lodging:** Holiday Inn, **other:** HOSPITAL,

7(6) Columbus Ave(from sb), **E...lodging:** Marriott, Sheraton, **W...gas:** Pride/diesel/rest., **other:** to Basketball Hall of Fame

6(5.5) Springfield Ctr(from nb), **W...gas:** Pride Autotruck/diesel

5(5) Broad St(from sb), same as 4

4(4.5) MA 83, Broad St, Main St, **E...gas:** Citgo, Mobil/diesel, Shell/diesel, United, **food:** McDonald's, Wendy's, **other:** Buick/GMC, Hyundai, Saturn, **W...gas:** Sunoco/diesel

3(4) US 5 N, to MA 57, Columbus Ave, W Springfield, **E...gas:** Sunoco, **other:** SavMore Foods, **W...**Chevrolet

2(3.5) MA 83 S(from nb), to E Longmeadow, **E...food:** Friendly's

1(3) US 5 S(from sb), no facilities

0mm Massachusetts/Connecticut state line, callboxes begin/end

Interstate 93

N ↕ S — Methuen

Exit #(mm)Services

47mm Massachusetts/New Hampshire state line, callboxes begin/end

48(46) MA 213 E, to Methuen, **E...**HOSPITAL

47(45) Pelham St, Methuen, **E...gas:** Sunoco/24hr, **food:** Dunkin Donuts, McDonald's, Outback Steaks, **W...gas:** Getty, **food:** Fireside Rest., **lodging:** Day's Inn/rest., Guesthouse Inn, **other:** Chrysler/Plymouth/Jeep, Pontiac/Nissan

46(44) MA 110, MA 113, to Lawrence, **E...gas:** Getty, **food:** Burger King, Dunkin Donuts, McDonald's/24hr, PapaGino's, Pizza Hut/D'angelo, MktBasket Foods, **other:** HOSPITAL, **W...gas:** Citgo, Gulf, **food:** Dunkin Donuts, Jimmy's II Rest., Jackson's Rest., Millhouse Rest.

45(43) Andover St, River Rd, to Lawrence, **E...lodging:** Courtyard, Hawthorn Suites, Residence Inn, SpringHill Suites, Wyndham, **W...gas:** Mobil, **food:** Grill 93, **lodging:** Staybridge, Tage Inn

44b a(40) I-495, to Lowell, Lawrence, **E...**HOSPITAL

43(39) MA 133, N Tewksbury, **E...gas:** Mobil/24hr, **lodging:** Ramada Inn/rest.

42(38) Dascomb Rd, East St, Tewksbury, no facilities

41(35) MA 125, Andover, st police

40(34) MA 62, Wilmington, no facilities

39(33) Concord St, **E...**Shriners Auditorium

38(31) MA 129, Reading, **W...gas:** Mobil, **food:** Burger King, Dunkin Donuts, Dynasty Chinese, Lucci's Foods, Michael's Place Rest., 99 Rest.

37c(30) Commerce Way, Atlantic Ave, **W...**Target

37b a(29) I-95, S to Waltham, N to Peabody

36(28) Montvale Ave, **E...gas:** Mobil, **food:** Dunkin Donuts, **W...gas:** Citgo/diesel, Exxon/24hr, Getty, Shell, **food:** Bickford's/24hr, Friendly's, McDonald's, Polcari's Italian, Spud's Rest., **lodging:** Crowne Plaza Hotel, Howard Johnson, **other:** HOSPITAL, BJ's Whse

35(27) Winchester Highlands, Melrose, **E...**HOSPITAL(no EZ return to sb)

34(26) MA 28 N(from nb, no EZ return), Stoneham, **E...gas:** Mobil, **food:** Friendly's, **other:** HOSPITAL

33(25) MA 28, Fellsway West, Winchester, **E...**HOSPITAL

32(23) MA 60, Salem Ave, Medford Square, **W...lodging:** AmeriSuites, **other:** HOSPITAL, to Tufts U

31(22) MA 16 E, to Revere(no EZ return sb), **E...gas:** Shell, **food:** Bertucci's, Subway, **lodging:** Howard Johnson Rest., **other:** Ford/Lincoln/Mercury, mall, st police, **W...gas:** Exxon, **food:** Burger King, Dunkin Donuts, Pizza Hut, **other:** AutoZone, Dodge

30(21) MA 28, MA 38, Mystic Ave, Somerville, **W...gas:** Coastal

MASSACHUSETTS

Interstate 93

N ↕ S

Boston Area

29(20) MA 28(from nb), Somerville, **E...food:** McDonald's, **other:** Circuit City, Home Depot, K-Mart, Tage Inn, mall, **W...gas:** Gulf, **lodging:** Holiday Inn
28(19) Sullivans Square, Charles Town, downtown
27 US 1 N(from nb)
26(18.5) MA 28 N, Storrow Dr, North Sta, downtown
25 Haymarket Sq, Gov't Center
24(18) Callahan Tunnel, **E...**airport
23(17.5) High St, Congress St, **W...lodging:** Marriott
22(17) Atlantic Ave, Northern Ave, South Sta, Boston World Trade Ctr
21(16.5) Kneeland St, ChinaTown
20(16) I-90 W, to Mass Tpk
19(15.5) Albany St(from sb), **W...gas:** Mobil/diesel, **other:** HOSPITAL
18(15) Mass Ave, to Roxbury, **W...**HOSPITAL
17(14.5) E Berkeley(from nb), **E...**New Boston Food Mkt
16(14) S Hampton St, Andrew Square, **W...gas:** Shell/ 24hr, **food:** Bickford's, **lodging:** Holiday Inn Express, **other:** Home Depot, K-Mart/Little Caesar's, Marshall's, OfficeMax, Old Navy
15(13) Columbia Rd, Everett Square, **E...**JFK Library, to UMA, **W...gas:** Shell
14(12.5) Morissey Blvd, **E...**JFK Library, **W...gas:** Shell, **food:** D'angelo's, **lodging:** Howard Johnson, Ramada Inn, **other:** Stop&Shop Foods
13(12) Freeport St, to Dorchester, **W...gas:** Citgo/7-11, **food:** Boston Mkt, **other:** CVS Drug, Dodge, Toyota
12(11.5) MA 3A S(from sb, no EZ return), Quincy, **E...gas:** Shell, **food:** Café Pacific, Domino's, **lodging:** Best Western, **W...gas:** Exxon, Shell, Sunoco, **food:** Arby's, Bickford's, Ground Round, PapaGino's, Wendy's, **other:** AutoZone, CVS Drug, Ford/ Lincoln/Mercury, Pontiac/GMC, Staples, Walgreen
11b a(11) to MA 203, Granite Ave, Ashmont, **W...food:** McDonald's
10(10) Squantum Ave(from sb), Milton, **W...**HOSPITAL
9(9) Adams St, Bryant Ave, to N Quincy, **W...gas:** Shell/repair
8(8) Brook Pkwy, to Quincy, Furnace, **E...gas:** Global, Gulf/diesel, Mobil, **other:** Home Depot, Saturn
7(7) MA 3 S, Braintree, to Cape Cod, **E...lodging:** Marriott
6(6) MA 37, Braintree, to Holbrook, **E...gas:** Mobil/ 24hr, **food:** Boardwalk Café, D'angelo's, Pizzaria Uno, **lodging:** Sheraton/café, **other:** Circuit City, Filene's, Firestone/auto, Lord&Taylor, Macy's, Sears/auto, mall, **W...gas:** Sunoco, **food:** Ascari Café, **lodging:** Candlewood Suites, Day's Inn, Extended Stay America, Hampton Inn, **other:** Barnes&Noble, Ford, Nissan
5b a(4) MA 28 S, to Randolph, Milton, **E...gas:** Citgo, Mutual, Shell/repair/24hr, Sunoco, **food:** D'angelo's, Domino's, Dunkin Donuts/Togo's, Friendly's, IHOP, Legends Café, Lombardo's Rest., Sal's Calzone Rest., Wong's Chinese, **lodging:** Holiday Inn/rest.
4(3) MA 24 S(exits left from sb), to Brockton, no facilities
3(2) MA 138 N, Houghtons Pond, to Ponkapoag Trail, no facilities
2b a(1) MA 138 S, Milton, to Stoughton, **E...**golf, **W...gas:** Gulf, Mobil, Shell/diesel, Sunoco, **food:** Dugout Café
1(0) I-95 N, S to Providence. I-93 begins/ends on I-95, exit 12.

Interstate 95

N ↕ S

Amesbury

Exit #(mm) Services
89.5mm Massachusetts/New Hampshire state line, parking area sb
60(89) MA 286, to Salisbury, beaches, **E...gas:** Mobil/diesel, **food:** Chubby's Diner, Lena's Seafood Rest., **other:** camping(seasonal)
59(88) I-495 S(from sb)
58b a(87) MA 110, to I-495 S, to Amesbury, Salisbury, **E...gas:** Sunoco/diesel, **food:** Crossroads Pizza, Frankie's Café, Sylvan St Grille, Winner's Circle Rest., **other:** Dodge, Plymouth/Jeep, U-Haul, radiators, **W...gas:** Mobil, Sunoco, **food:** Burger King, Dunkin Donuts, Friendly's, McDonald's, Shorty's Diner, **lodging:** Fairfield Inn, **other:** Chevrolet/VW, Stop&Shop Foods
86mm Merrimac River
57(85) MA 113, to W Newbury, **E...gas:** Mobil/24hr, Shell/repair/24hr, Sunoco, **food:** Dunkin Donuts, Friendly's, Jade Chinese, McDonald's, PapaGino's, Wendy's, White Hen Pantry, **other:** HOSPITAL, Brooks Drug, K-Mart, MktBasket Foods, Radio Shack, Shaw's Foods, Walgreen
56(78) Scotland Rd, to Newbury, **E...**st police
55(77) Central St, to Byfield, **E...food:** Gen Store Eatery, Village Diner, **W...gas:** Prime/diesel/repair
54b a(76) MA 133, E to Rowley, W to Groveland, **E...food:** Agawam Diner, McDonald's, **W...**Old Town Tavern
75mm weigh sta both lanes
53b a(74) MA 97, S to Topsfield, N to Georgetown, no facilities
52(73) Topsfield Rd, to Topsfield, Boxford, no facilities
51(72) Endicott Rd, to Topsfield, Middleton, no facilities
50(71) US 1, to MA 62, Topsfield, **E...gas:** Exxon/24hr, Mobil/24hr, **food:** Ristorante Italiano, **W...food:** Supino's Rest., **lodging:** Sheraton , **other:** CVS Drug, Staples, Stop&Shop, st police
49(70) MA 62(from nb), Danvers, Middleton, **W...**same as 50
48(69) Hobart St(from sb), **W...food:** Italian Rest., Jake's Rest., **lodging:** Comfort Inn, Extended Stay America, Motel 6, **other:** Home Depot, Honda

Massachusetts Interstate 95

N ↕ S Peabody

47b a(68) MA 114, Peabody, to Middleton, **E...gas:** Exxon/diesel/24hr, Mobil, Shell, Sunoco, **food:** Dunkin Donuts, Friendly's, PapaGino's, **other:** Chevrolet, Dodge, Infiniti, Lowe's Whse, NTB, Subaru/Toyota, Wal-Mart, **W...food:** Chili's, McDonald's, TGIFriday, **lodging:** Motel 6, Residence Inn, TownePlace Suites, **other:** Circuit City, Costco, Dodge, Home Depot, LandRover, Mazda, NAPA, Pontiac/Hyundai

46(67) to US 1, **W...gas:** Best, Gulf/diesel, Shell, Sunoco, **food:** Bel-Aire Diner, Burger King, **other:** Auto Parts+

45(66) MA 128 N, to Peabody, no facilities

44b a(65) US 1 N, MA 129, **E...gas:** Shell, **W...gas:** Shell, **food:** Bennigan's, Bertucci's, Bickford's, Carrabba's, Wendy's, **lodging:** Hampton Inn, Holiday Inn, Homewood Suites, **other:** HOSPITAL

43(63) Walnut St, Lynnfield, **E...**to Saugus Iron Works NHS(3mi), **W...lodging:** Sheraton, **other:** golf

42(62) Salem St, Montrose, **E...gas:** Mobil, Prime, Sunoco, **food:** Paul's Pizza, **W...lodging:** Sheraton

41(60) Main St, Lynnfield Ctr, **E...gas:** Shell

40(59) MA 129, N Reading, Wakefield Ctr, **E...gas:** Exxon, **W...other:** Chevrolet, diesel repair

39(58) North Ave, Reading, **E...lodging:** Best Western, **other:** Mazda/Isuzu/Volvo/Saab, **W...gas:** Citgo, Exxon/repair, Shell/diesel/24hr, **other:** HOSPITAL, Ford

38b a(57) MA 28, to Reading, **E...gas:** Gulf, Hess, Shell/repair, **food:** Bickford's, Boston Mkt, Burger King, China Moon, Dunkin Donuts, Ground Round, 99 Rest., PapaGino's, Subway, **other:** AutoZone, CVS Drug, Ford, GNC, Marshalls, Radio Shack, Shaw's Foods, **W...gas:** Exxon, Getty, Mobil, Shell, **food:** Harrow's Rest., McDonald's

37b a(56) I-93, N to Manchester, S to Boston

36(55) Washington St, to Winchester, **E...gas:** Getty, **food:** Dunkin Donuts, FarEast Chinese, Italian Express, **lodging:** Crowne Plaza Hotel, **other:** AutoZone, Buick/Pontiac/GMC, CompUSA, Jaguar, Mitsubishi, Nissan, Staples, Toyota, **W...gas:** Shell, **food:** China Pearl, D'angelo's, Joe's Grill, McDonald's, 99 Rest., On the Border, Panera Bread, PapaGino's, Pizza Hut, Pizzaria Uno, TGIFriday, MktBasket Foods, **lodging:** Comfort Inn, Courtyard, Fairfield Inn, Hampton Inn, Red Roof Inn, **other:** CVS Drug, Hogan Tire, NTB, USPO, mall

35(54) MA 38, to Woburn, **E...lodging:** Ramada Inn, **other:** HOSPITAL, **W...gas:** Mobil/diesel, Shell, **food:** Baldwin Park Grill, Dunkin Donuts, Roast Beef Roundup, **lodging:** Sierra Suites, **other:** Stop&Shop Foods

34(53) Winn St, Woburn, no facilities

33b a(52) US 3 S, MA 3A N, to Winchester, **E...food:** Café Escadrille, ChuckeCheese, Outback Steaks, PapaRazzi's, **lodging:** Summerfield Suites, **other:** HOSPITAL, CVS Drug, Honda, Marshalls, Michael's, **W...gas:** Citgo, Hess, **lodging:** Marriott, **other:** HOSPITAL, Porsche

Boston Area

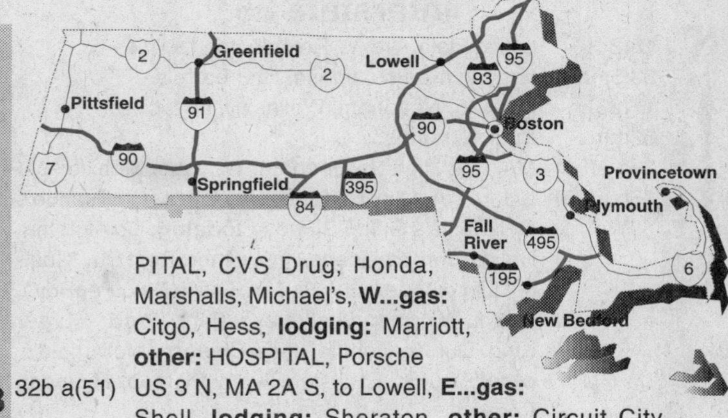

32b a(51) US 3 N, MA 2A S, to Lowell, **E...gas:** Shell, **lodging:** Sheraton, **other:** Circuit City, **W...food:** Boston Mkt, Burger King, Chili's, McDonald's, Pizzaria Regina, Smokey's Café, TCBY, Victoria Sta Rest., **lodging:** Howard Johnson, **other:** Barnes&Noble, Dodge, Filene's, Lord&Taylor, Macy's, Sears/auto, mall

31b a(48) MA 4, MA 225, Lexington, **E...gas:** Mobil/repair, Shell, **food:** Alexander's Pizza, Bertucci's Pizza, **W...gas:** Exxon/24hr, Shell/24hr, **food:** Denny's, Friendly's, McDonald's, **lodging:** Holiday Inn Express, **other:** MEDICAL CARE

30b a(47) MA 2A, Lexington, **E...gas:** Shell, **other:** HOSPITAL, **W...lodging:** Sheraton, **other:** to MinuteMan NP, Hanscom AFB

46.5mm travel plaza nb, Sunoco/diesel/24hr, McDonald's, gifts

29b a(46) MA 2 W, Cambridge, no facilities

28b a(45) Trapelo Rd, Belmont, **E...gas:** Exxon, Mobil, Shell, **food:** Burger King, Dunkin Donuts, Friendly's, McDonald's, PapaGino's, **other:** Osco Drugs, Star Mkt

27b a(44) Totten Pond Rd, Waltham, **E...gas:** Shell, **food:** Naked Fish Rest., **lodging:** Best Western, Courtyard, HolidayInn Express, Home Suites Inn, Sheraton, Westin Hotel, **W...food:** Bertucci's Rest., DoubleTree/rest., **lodging:** Rennaisance Hotel, **other:** Costco, Home Depot

26(43) US 20, to MA 117, to Waltham, **E...gas:**Shell/diesel, **other:** HOSPITAL, **W...gas:** Mobil

25(42) I-90, MA Tpk

24(41) MA 30, Newton, Wayland, **E...gas:** Mobil, **lodging:** Marriott

23(40) Recreation Rd(from nb), to MA Tpk

22b a(39) Grove St, **E...lodging:** Holiday Inn, **other:** golf

38.5mm travel plaza sb, Gulf/diesel, McDonald's, gifts

21b a(38) MA 16, Newton, Wellesley, **E...**HOSPITAL, **W...food:** Pillar House Rest.

20b a(36) MA 9, Brookline, Framingham, no facilities

19b a(35) Highland Ave, Newton, Needham, **E...gas:** Gulf, Hess, **food:** D'angelo's, Dunkin Donuts, Ground Round, McDonald's, Mighty Subs, Sheraton/rest., **other:** Staples, **W...gas:** Shell/24hr, **food:** Bickford's, **other:** Chevrolet, Ford

MASSACHUSETTS

Interstate 95

N ↕ S — Boston Area

18(34) Great Plain Ave, W Roxbury, no facilities
33.5mm parking area sb, phone, litter barrels
17(33) MA 135, Needham, Wellesley, no facilities
32mm truck turnout sb
16b a(31) MA 109, High St, Dedham, **W...gas:** Mobil/diesel
15b a(29) US 1, MA 128, **E...food:** Bickford's, Chili's, Joe's Grill, Testa's Grill, TGIFriday, **lodging:** Comfort Inn, Holiday Inn, Residence Inn, **other:** Best Buy, Costco, Lincoln/Mercury, Nissan, OfficeMax, PepBoys, Volvo, **W...gas:** Shell/diesel/24hr, **food:** Burger King, Dunkin Donuts, Jade Chinese, McDonald's, **other:** Buick, Chrysler/Plymouth/Jeep, Hyundai, Pontiac
14(28) East St, Canton St, **E...lodging:** Hilton
27mm rest area sb, full(handicapped)facilities, phone, picnic tables, litter barrels
13(26.5) University Ave, no facilities
12(26) I-93 N, to Braintree, Boston, motorist callboxes end nb
11b a(23) Neponset St, to Canton, **E...gas:** Citgo/repair, Sunoco/repair, **W...gas:** Gulf/diesel, **lodging:** Ramada Inn, Sheraton, **other:** HOSPITAL
22.5mm Neponset River
10(20) Coney St(from sb, no EZ return), to US 1, Sharon, Walpole, **1 mi W on US 1...gas:** Exxon, Mobil, Shell, US/diesel, **food:** Beacon's Rest., Dunkin Donuts, Friendly's, Ground Round, IHOP, McDonald's, 99 Rest., Old Country Buffet, PapaGino's, Pizza Hut, Taco Bell, **lodging:** Best Western, **other:** Acura, Barnes&Noble, CVS Drug, Home Depot, Isuzu, Jo-Ann Fabrics, OfficeMax, Old Navy, Stop&Shop Foods, Wal-Mart, mall
9(19) US 1, to MA 27, Walpole, **W...food:** Bickford's, **lodging:** Super 8, **lodging:** Sharon Inn, **other:** same as 10
8(16) S Main St, Sharon, **E...food:** Dunkin Donuts, **other:** Osco Drug, Shaw's Foods, Wards Berry Farm, whaling museum
7b a(13) MA 140, to Mansfield, **E...food:** Friendly's, 99 Rest., Piccadilly Rest., **lodging:** Comfort Inn, Courtyard, Holiday Inn, Red Roof Inn, Residence Inn, **other:** Stop&Shop Food, **W...gas:** Mobil, Shell, **food:** PapaGino's, **other:** Radio Shack

Attleboro

6b a(12) I-495, S to Cape Cod, N to NH
10mm Welcome Ctr/rest area both lanes, full(handicapped)facilities, info, phone, picnic tables, litter barrels, petwalk
9mm truck parking area sb
5(7) MA 152, Attleboro, **E...**HOSPITAL, **W...gas:** Gulf/diesel, **food:** Bill's Pizza, Wendy's, **other:** Brooks Drug, Radio Shack, Shaw's Foods
4(6) I-295 S, to Woonsocket
3(4) MA 123, to Attleboro, **E...gas:** Shell/diesel, **other:** HOSPITAL, zoo
2.5mm parking area/weigh sta both lanes, no restrooms, litter barrels, motorist callboxes
2b a(1) US 1A, Newport Ave, Attleboro, **E...gas:** Cumberland, Mobil, Shell, Sunoco, **food:** McDonald's, Olive Garden, **lodging:** Holiday Inn, **other:** Bob's Store, Home Depot, K-Mart, Mazda, OfficeMax, Pontiac, Shaw's Foods
1(.5) US 1(from sb), **E...lodging:** Day's Inn, **other:** Aamco, Brooks Drug, Volvo, **W...gas:** A+, Gulf, **food:** Burger King, McDonald's, Ponderosa, Taco Bell, **other:** Dodge, Mazda, Mitsubishi, Ro Jack's Foods
0mm Massachusetts/Rhode Island state line

Interstate 195

N ↕ S

Exit #(mm)Services
22(41) I-495 N, MA 25 S, to Cape Cod. I-195 begins/ends on I-495, exit 1.
21(39) MA 28, to Wareham, **N...gas:** Maxi/diesel/24hr, **food:** Zeadey's Rest., **S...gas:** Shell/diesel, **other:** HOSPITAL, **other:** NAPA, repair, **1 mi S...gas:** Mobil
37mm rest area eb, info, phone, picnic tables, litter barrels, petwalk, boat ramp
36mm Sippican River
20(35) MA 105, to Marion, **S...**RV camping(seasonal)
19b a(31) to Mattapoisett, **S...gas:** Mobil
18(26) MA 240 S, to Fairhaven, **1 mi S...gas:** Citgo/7-11, Gulf, Mutual, Shell, **food:** Applebee's, Blimpie, Burger King, D'angelo's, Dunkin Donuts, Fairhaven Chowder, Great Wall Chinese, McDonald's, 99 Rest., PapaGino's, Pasta House, Taco Bell, Wendy's, **lodging:** Hampton Inn, **other:** AutoZone, Brooks Drug, $Tree, GMC/Buick/Pontiac, GNC, K-Mart, Marshalls, Mazda, Radio Shack, Shaw's Foods, Stop&Shop Foods, Staples, TownFair Tire, Wal-Mart
25.5mm Acushnet River
17(24) Coggeshall St, New Bedford, **N...gas:** Sunoco, **food:** Dunkin Donuts, EndZone Café, McDonald's, same as 16
16(23) Washburn St(from eb), **N...gas:** Shell, Sunoco, **food:** McDonald's
15(22) MA 18 S, New Bedford, downtown, **S...**Whaling Museum, hist dist
14(21) Penniman St(from eb), New Bedford, downtown
13b a(20) MA 140, **N...**airport, **S...gas:** Buttonwood/diesel, Sunoco, **food:** Dunkin Donuts, **other:** HOSPITAL, Buttonwood Park/zoo, CVS Drug, Honda, Shaw's Foods, VW
12b a(19) N Dartmouth, **N...**Outlet/famous brands, **S...gas:** Hess, Mobil/diesel, **food:** Burger King, D'angelo's, Dunkin Donuts, Friendly's, Jimmy's Pizza, McDonald's, 99 Rest., Old Country Buffet, PapaGino's, Peking Garden, Taco Bell, Wendy's, **lodging:** Comfort Inn, **other:** Best Buy, Chevrolet, Firestone/auto, JC Penney, Saturn, Sears/auto, Stop&Shop Food/gas, TownFair Tire, Toyota, mall, st police
11b a(17) Reed Rd, to Dartmouth, **2 mi S...gas:** Shell/24hr, **lodging:** Dartmouth Motel

MASSACHUSETTS

Interstate 195

10(16) MA 88 S, to US 6, Westport, **S...gas:** Mobil/diesel, Rte 6 Gas, **lodging:** Hampton Inn

9(15.5) MA 24 N(from nb), Stanford Rd, Westport, **S...gas:** Mobil/diesel, Rte 6 Gas, **food:** LePage's Seafood, Priscilla Rest., **lodging:** Hampton Inn

8b a(15) MA 24 S, Fall River, Westport, **S...food:** Dunkin Donuts, Subway

7(14) MA 81 S, Plymouth Ave, Fall River, **N...gas:** Getty, **food:** 99 Rest., **S...gas:** Shell, **food:** Applebee's, McDonald's, **other:** Goodyear/auto, Walgreen

6(13.5) Pleasant St, Fall River, downtown

5(13) MA 79, MA 138, to Taunton, **S...gas:** Citgo/7-11, Hess, **food:** Denny's, **lodging:** Day's Inn

12mm Assonet Bay

4b a(10) MA 103, to Swansea, Somerset, **N...gas:** Getty, **food:** Rogers Rest., **other:** auto repair, **S...gas:** Shell/24hr, **food:** TKO Shea's Rest., **lodging:** Quality Inn

3(8) US 6, to MA 118, Swansea, Rehoboth, **N...gas:** Hess, Shell/diesel, **food:** Bess Eaton, Burger King, D'angelo's, Dunkin Donuts, Friendly's, McDonald's, Ponderosa, **other:** CarQuest, Firestone/auto, Hi-Lo Foods, Sears/auto, mall, **S...gas:** Cumberland/24hr, **food:** Anthony's Seafood, **lodging:** Swansea Motel

6mm rest area eb, full(handicapped)facilities, phone, picnic tables, litter barrels, petwalk

5.5mm parking area wb

2(5) MA 136, to Newport, **S...gas:** Mobil/24hr, Shell/24hr, **food:** Dunkin Donuts, Subway

3mm weigh sta both lanes

1(1) MA 114A, to Seekonk, **N...gas:** Exxon/diesel, Public, Shell/24hr, **food:** Newport Creamery, 99 Rest., **lodging:** Johnson&Wales Inn, Motel 6, **S...gas:** Mobil/24hr, Sunoco/diesel, **food:** Applebee's, Bickford's, Bugaboo Creek Steaks, Burger King, Chili's, China Wok, Cisco's Pizza, D'angelo's, Dunkin Donuts, Friendly's, McDonald's, Old Country Buffet, PapaGino's, Subway, Taco Bell, Testa's Italian, TGIFriday, Wendy's, **lodging:** Gateway Motel, Hampton Inn, Mary's Motel, Park Inn, Ramada Inn/rest., Town'n Country Motel, **other:** Bob's Stores, Circuit City, Daewoo, GNC, Home Depot, Michael's, PepBoys, Sam's Club, Staples, Stop&Shop Foods, Target, TownFair Tire, Volvo, Wal-Mart

0mm Massachusetts/Rhode Island state line. **Exits 8-1 are in RI.**

8(5) US 1A N, Pawtucket, **S...gas:** Mobil/diesel, **food:** Subway, **other:** CVS Drug

7(4) US 6 E, CT 114 S, Seekonk, to Barrington

6(3) Broadway Ave, **N...gas:** Speedy AutoService, **S...gas:** Shell, Sunoco/diesel

5(2.5) RI 103 E, Warren Ave

4(2) US 44 E, RI 103 E, Taunton Ave, Warren Ave, **N...gas:** Exxon

3(1.5) Gano St, **S...lodging:** Radisson

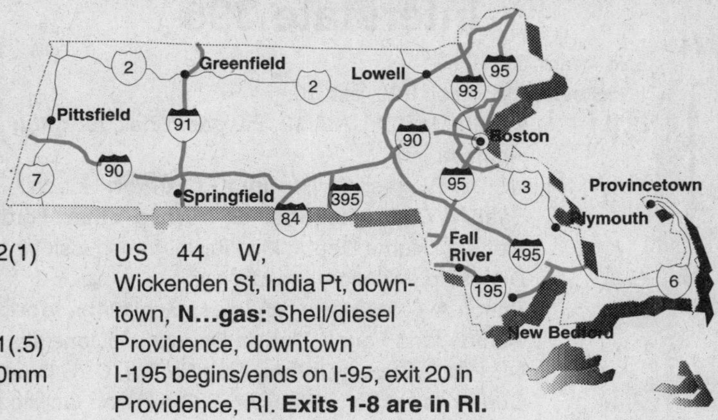

2(1) US 44 W, Wickenden St, India Pt, downtown, **N...gas:** Shell/diesel

1(.5) Providence, downtown

0mm I-195 begins/ends on I-95, exit 20 in Providence, RI. **Exits 1-8 are in RI.**

Interstate 290

Exit #(mm) Services

26b a(20) I-495. I-290 begins/ends on I-495, exit 25.

25b a(17) Solomon Pond Mall Rd, to Berlin, **N...food:** Bertucci's, TGIFriday, **lodging:** Super 8, **other:** Best Buy, Borders Books, JC Penney, Sears/auto, Target, mall, **S...**Solomon Pond Grill

24(15) Church St, Northborough, no facilities

23b a(13) MA 140, Boylston, **N...gas:** Citgo/diesel, Mobil, **food:** Dunkin Donuts, Other Place Rest.

22(11) Main St, Worchester, **N...gas:** Exxon/24hr, **food:** Bickford's, Friendly's, McDonald's, Wendy's, **other:** HOSPITAL

21(10) Plantation St(from eb), **N...lodging:** Best Western, **other:** Lowe's Whse, Staples, Target

20(8) MA 70, Lincoln St, Burncoat St, **N...gas:** Charter/24hr, Exxon/Subway/24hr, Shell, Sunoco, **food:** Bickford's, Denny's, Dunkin Donuts, Friendly's, McDonald's, Papa Gino's, Taco Bell, Wendy's, **lodging:** Day's Inn, Econolodge, Holiday Inn, **other:** Auto Palace, CVS Drug, Radio Shack, Shaw's Food/24hr, Walgreen

19(7) I-190 N, MA 12, no facilities

18 MA 9, Framington, Ware, Worcester Airport, **N...**HOSPITAL

16 Central St, Worcester, **N...lodging:** Crowne Plaza, Hampton Inn, mall

14 MA 122, Barre, Worcester, downtown

13 MA 122A, Vernon St, Worcester, downtown

12 MA 146 S, to Millbury, no facilities

11 Southbridge St, College Square, **N...gas:** Shell/diesel, **food:** Wendy's, **S...gas:** Getty

10 MA 12 N(from wb), Hope Ave, no facilities

9 Auburn St, to Auburn, **E...gas:** Shell, **food:** Arby's, Bickford's, Wendy's, McDonald's, **lodging:** Baymont Inn, Comfort Inn, **other:** Acura, Firestone, Sears/auto, Shaw's Foods, Staples, mall

8 MA 12 S(from sb), Webster, **W...gas:** Shell, **lodging:** Best Western

7 I-90, E to Boston, W to Springfield. I-290 begins/ends on I-90.

MASSACHUSETTS

Interstate 395

N ↕ S

Exit #(mm) Services
I-395 begins/ends on I-90, exit 10.

7(12) to I-90(MA Tpk), MA 12, **E...gas:** Shell, **lodging:** Ramada Inn
6b a(11) US 20, **E...gas:** Gulf, **food:** KFC, **other:** Honda, Saab/VW, **W...gas:** Shell, BJ's Whse, **other:** Ford/Mercury, Home Depot, Mitsubishi, transmissions
5(8) Depot Rd, N Oxford, no facilities
4(6) Sutton Ave, to Oxford, **W...gas:** Mobil/24hr, **food:** Cumberland Farms, Dunkin Donuts, McDonald's, NE Pizza, Subway, **other:** Cahill's Tire, CVS Drug
3(4) Cudworth Rd, to N Webster, S Oxford, no facilities
2(3) MA 16, to Webster, **E...**Subaru, **W...gas:** Exxon/24hr, Getty, Mobil, Shell/24hr, **food:** Burger King, D'angelo's/Papa Gino's, Empire Wok, Friendly's, KFC, McDonald's, **other:** HOSPITAL, Brooks Drug, CVS Drug, Ford, PriceChopper Foods
1(1) MA 193, to Webster, **E...**HOSPITAL
0mm Massachusetts/Connecticut state line

Interstate 495

N ↕ S

Exit #(mm)Services
I-495 begins/ends on I-95, exit 59.

55 MA 110(no return nb), to I-95 S, **E...gas:** Best Choice, Mobil, Sunoco, **food:** Burger King, Friendly's, McDonald's, **lodging:** Fairfield Inn, **other:** Stop&Shop, Chevrolet/VW

Amesbury

54(118) MA 150, to Amesbury, no facilities
53(115) Broad St, Merrimac, **W...gas:** Gulf
114mm parking area sb, phone, restrooms, picnic tables, litter barrels
52(111) MA 110, to Haverhill, **E...**HOSPITAL, **W...gas:** Getty, Mobil
110mm parking area nb, phone, picnic tables, litter barrels
51(109) MA 125, to Haverhill, **E...gas:** Citgo, Mobil, **food:** Bros Pizza, **other:** HOSPITAL
50(107) MA 97, to Haverhill, **E...**HOSPITAL, **W...**Ford
49(106) MA 110, to Haverhill, **E...gas:** Gulf, Sunoco/24hr, **food:** Chunky's Diner, Dunkin Donuts, McDonald's, 99 Rest., PapGino's, **lodging:** Best Western, Comfort Inn, **other:** Buick/Pontiac/GMC, Chrysler/Plymouth, MktBasket Foods
105.8mm Merrimac River
48(105.5) MA 125, to Bradford, no facilities
47(105) MA 213, to Methuen, **1-2 mi W...food:** Bugaboo Steaks, Burger King, ChuckeCheese, McDonald's, TGIFriday, **other:** Borders Books, Home Depot, Marshalls, Old Navy, Wal-Mart, Methuen Mall
46(104) MA 110, **E...gas:** Gulf, Sunoco/24hr, **other:** HOSPITAL, Ford/Lincoln/Mercury
45(103) Marston St, to Lawrence, **W...other:** Chevrolet, Honda, Isuzu, Kia
44(102) Merrimac St, to Lawrence
43(101) Mass Ave, no facilities
42(100) MA 114, **E...gas:** Exxon, Gulf, Mobil, **food:** Denny's, Friendly's, Lee Chin Cninese, Pizza Hut, **lodging:** Hampton Inn, **W...gas:** Shell/diesel, 7-11, **food:** Burger King, Marathon Pizzaria, McDonald's, TCBY, Wendy's, **lodging:** Quality Inn, **other:** HOSPITAL, MktBasket Foods
41(99) MA 28, to Andover, **E...food:** Dunkin Donuts, **other:** Chevrolet
40b a(98) I-93, N to Methuen, S to Boston
39(94) MA 133, to N Tewksbury, **E...gas:** Mobil/diesel/24hr, **food:** McDonald's, **lodging:** Extended Stay America, **W...gas:** Hess, **food:** Cracker Barrel, Wendy's, **lodging:** Fairfield Inn, Holiday Inn/rest., Ramada/rest., Residence Inn
38(93) MA 38, to Lowell, **E...gas:** Shell, **food:** Applebee's, Burger King, Friendly's, IHOP, T-D Waffle, **lodging:** Motel 6, **other:** Home Depot, Honda/VW, Mazda, MktBasket Foods, **W...gas:** Shell/diesel, Sunoco, USA/diesel, **food:** Dunkin Donuts, Milan Pizza, McDonald's, Wendy's, **other:** MEDICAL CARE, Chevrolet/Pontiac/Buick/GMC, CVS Drug, K-Mart, Saturn, Staples
37(91) Woburn St, to S Lowell, **W...gas:** Exxon

Chelmsford

36(90) Lowell ConX, to Lowell SP, **1 mi W...food:** McDonald's, Outback Steaks, **lodging:** Courtyard, **other:** Shop&Save, Walgreen
35b a(89) US 3, S to Burlington, N to Nashua, NH
34(88) MA 4, Chelmsford, **E...gas:** Mobil, Sunoco, **food:** Dunkin Donuts, Skip's Rest., 99 Rest., **lodging:** Radisson, **W...gas:** Shell, **food:** Ground Round, **lodging:** Best Western
33 MA 4, N Chelmsford(from nb)
88mm motorist aid call boxes begin sb
87mm rest area both lanes, full(handicapped)facilities, phone, picnic tables, litter barrels, vending, petwalk
32(83) Boston Rd, to MA 225, **E...gas:** Exxon/24hr, Gulf/service, Mobil/24hr, **food:** Applebee's, B&B Café, Boston Mkt, Burger King, Chili's, D'angelo's, Dunkin Donuts, McDonald's, **other:** CVS Drug, MktBasket Foods, Osco Drug, to Nashoba Valley Ski Area
31(80) MA 119, to Groton, **E...gas:** Mobil/diesel/24hr, **food:** Dunkin Donuts, Ken's Café, Subway
30(78) MA 110, to Littleton, **E...gas:** Shell, **food:** HOSPITAL, **W...gas:** Citgo/diesel, Sunoco/diesel
29b a(77) MA 2, to Leominster, **E...**to Walden Pond St Reserve
28(75) MA 111, to Boxborough, Harvard, **E...gas:** Exxon/repair, **lodging:** Holiday Inn
27(70) MA 117, to Bolton, **E...gas:** Mobil/diesel, **W...gas:** Mobil, **food:** Bolton Pizza, Hebert Ice Cream, **other:** RV camping(seasonal)
26(68) MA 62, to Berlin, **E...**Best Western, **W...gas:** Exxon/24hr, Gulf/24hr, Shell/diesel
66mm Assabet River

MASSACHUSETTS

Interstate 495

N ↕ S

Marlborough

25b(64) I-290, to Worchester, no facilities

a to MA 85, Marlborough, **E...food:** Burger King, Honeydew Donuts, 99 Rest., Piccadilly's

24b a(63) US 20, to Northborough, Marlborough, **E...gas:** Circle M, Mobil, **food:** D'angelo's, Dunkin Donuts, Rocco's Rest., **lodging:** Holiday Inn/rest., **W...gas:** Exxon, Shell, **food:** Boston Mkt, China Taste, Longhorn Steaks, McDonald's, PapaGino's, Starbucks, Subway, Tandoori Grill, Wendy's, **lodging:** Best Western, Embassy Suites, Homestead Suites, Radisson, **other:** GNC, OfficeMax, Victory Foods

23c(60) Crane Meadow Rd, Marlborough

23b a(59) MA 9, to Shrewsbury, Framingham, **E...gas:** Exxon/diesel, **food:** Red Barn Coffee, Wendy's, **lodging:** Red Roof Inn, **other:** Volvo, **W...gas:** Mobil/diesel/24hr, **food:** Burger King, Friendly's, McDonald's, **lodging:** Courtyard, Extended Stay America, Residence Inn, Sierra Suites, Wyndham Hotel, **other:** HOSPITAL

22(58) I-90, MA TPK, E to Boston, W to Albany

21b a(54) MA 135, to Hopkinton, Upton, **E...gas:** Exxon, Gulf, Mobil

20(50) MA 85, to Milford, **W...gas:** Gulf/diesel/LP, Mobil, **food:** Wendy's, **lodging:** Baymont Inn, Courtyard

19(48) MA 109, to Milford, **W...gas:** Mobil/Pizza Hut/diesel/24hr, Shell, **food:** Applebee's, Bugaboo Cr Steaks, Burger King, McDonald's, PapaGino's, Taco Bell, **lodging:** Radisson, Tage Inn, **other:** $Tree, Jo-Ann Fabrics, K-Mart, Radio Shack

18(46) MA 126, to Bellingham, **E...food:** Chili's, McDonald's, **other:** Barnes&Noble, Bread&Circus, MktBasket Foods, Old Navy, Staples, Wal-Mart, **W...gas:** Hess, Mobil/24hr, Sunoco/diesel, **food:** Dunkin Donuts, Outback Steaks, Pizzaria Uno, **other:** Home Depot

17(44) MA 140, to Franklin, Bellingham, **E...gas:** Mobil, Shell, Sunoco, **food:** Applebee's, Burger King, D'angelo's, Dunkin Donuts, Friendly's, KFC, Longhorn Steaks, Panera Bread, PapaGino's, Pipinelle's Rest., Pizza Hut, Subway, Taco Bell, Thai Cuisine, **other:** AutoZone, Buick/GMC, Chrysler/Jeep, CVS Drug, GNC, Marshalls, Stop&Shop, **W...**HOSPITAL, BJ's Whse

16(42) King St, to Franklin, **E...gas:** Sunoco/24hr, **food:** Dunkin Donuts, Gold Fork Rest., Goodfella's Rest., McDonald's, **lodging:** Hampton Inn, **other:** Spruce Pond Creamery, **W...lodging:** Hawthorn Inn

15(39) MA 1A, to Plainville, Wrentham, **E...gas:** Mobil, **other:** HOSPITAL, **W...gas:** Gulf, Mobil/diesel, **food:** Ruby Tuesday, **other:** Premium Outlets/famous brands

14b a(37) US 1, to N Attleboro, **E...gas:** Mobil/D'angelo's/diesel, **food:** Luciano's Rest., **lodging:** Arbor Inn, **W...gas:** Mobil

13(32) I-95, N to Boston, S to Providence, access to HOSPITAL

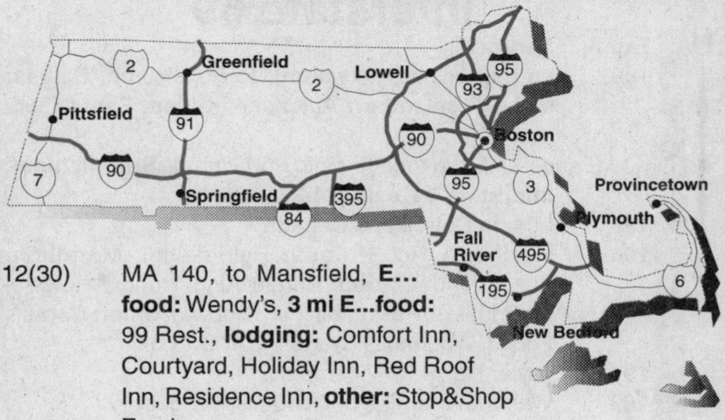

12(30) MA 140, to Mansfield, **E... food:** Wendy's, **3 mi E...food:** 99 Rest., **lodging:** Comfort Inn, Courtyard, Holiday Inn, Red Roof Inn, Residence Inn, **other:** Stop&Shop Food

11(29) MA 140 S(from eb, no return), **1 mi W...gas:** Gulf, **food:** Andrea's Pizza, Boston Pizza, Dunkin Donuts, Mandarin Chinese, McDonald's, **other:** $Tree, GNC, Radio Shack

10(26) MA 123, to Norton, **E...gas:** QuickStop, **other:** McLaughlin RV Park, **W...**HOSPITAL

9(24) Bay St, to Taunton, **W...food:** Dunkin Donuts, HoHo Chinese, Pizza Hut, **lodging:** Holiday Inn, **other:** MEDICAL CARE, Tedeschi Foods

8(22) MA 138, to Raynham, **E...gas:** Mobil/diesel, **food:** Honeydew Donuts, **W...gas:** Central Oil, Exxon/diesel, Mobil/24hr, Shell/diesel/repair, **food:** Bros Pizza, China Garden, La Casa Mia Rest., McDonald's, Pepperoni's Pizza, **other:** HOSPITAL

7b a(19) MA 24, to Fall River, Boston, **1/2 mi E...food:** Burger King

18mm weigh sta both lanes

Middleboro

17.5mm Taunton River

6(15) US 44, to Middleboro, **E...food:** Burger King, Dunkin Donuts, Friendly's, PapaGino's, **W...gas:** 44 Gas, Mobil/diesel, Sunoco/diesel, **lodging:** Fairfield Inn

5(14) MA 18, to Lakeville, **E...gas:** Circle Farm, Citgo, Mobil, **food:** Burger King, Dunkin Donuts, Fireside Grill, Friendly's, Panda Chinese, PapaGino's, USA Pizza, **other:** MEDICAL CARE, CVS Drug, Kelly's Tire, Stop&Shop Food, **W...other:** Massasoit SP, RV camping(seasonal)

4(12) MA 105, to Middleboro, **E...gas:** Exxon/diesel/24hr, Mobil/diesel, Shell/24hr, Sunoco/24hr, **food:** DQ, Dunkin Donuts, McDonald's, Papa Timmy's Pizza, Subway, **lodging:** Day's Inn, **other:** Brooks Drug, Chevrolet, Osco Drug

10.5mm rest area eb, picnic tables

10mm rest area both lanes, picnic tables

3(8) MA 28, to Rock Village, S Middleboro, **E...gas:** Citgo/diesel, **other:** RV camping(seasonal)

2(3) MA 58, W Wareham, **E...other:** Edaville Family Park, auto repair, to Myles Standish SF, **W...food:** Dapper Dan's Hotdogs, **other:** RV camping(seasonal)

2mm Weweantic River

1(0) I-495 begins/ends on I-195, MA 25 S.

MICHIGAN
Interstate 69

N ↕ S — Port Huron

Exit #	Services
199	Lp 69(from eb, no return), to Port Huron, **S...gas:** Mobil/diesel, **other:** AutoZone, K-Mart, Sam's Club/gas
	I-69 E and I-94 E run together into Port Huron. **See Michigan Interstate 94, exit 274-275mm.**
198	I-94, to Detroit and Canada
196	Wadhams Rd, **N...gas:** Bylo/diesel, Marathon, Shell/Wendy's, **food:** Burger King, Hungry Howie's, McDonald's, Peking Kitchen, Subway, **other:** Carter's Foods, Wadham's Drugs, KOA, **S...**golf
194	Taylor Rd, **N...**RV camping
189	Wales Center Rd, to Goodells, **S...**golf
184	MI 19, to Emmett, **N...gas:** Citgo/diesel/rest./24hr, **S...gas:** Marathon/diesel/24hr
180	Riley Center Rd, **N...**RV camping
176	Capac Rd, **N...gas:** BP/McDonald's/diesel, **food:** Subway(2mi)
174mm	**rest area wb, full(handicapped)facilties, phone, picnic tables, litter barrels, vending, petwalk**
168	MI 53, Imlay City, **N...gas:** BP/diesel/24hr, Speedway/diesel, **food:** Big Boy, Burger King, DQ, Hungry Howie's, Jet's Pizza, Jimmy's Coney Island, Little Caesar's, Lucky's Steaks, McDonald's, Taco Bell, Wah Wong Chinese, Wendy's/Tim Horton, **lodging:** Day's Inn, M53 Motel, Super 8, **other:** AutoZone, Chevrolet/Pontiac, Chrysler/Plymouth/Dodge/Jeep, Farmer Jack's, Ford, GNC, IGA Foods, Pamida, **S...**camping
163	Lake Pleasant Rd, to Attica, no facilities
160mm	**rest area eb, full(handicapped)facilities, phone, picnic tables, litter barrels, vending, petwalk**
159	Wilder Rd, no facilities
158mm	Flint River
155	MI 24, Lapeer, **1 mi N...gas:** BP, Marathon/diesel, Meijer/diesel/24hr, **food:** Arby's, Burger King, DQ, Hot'n Now, KFC, Little Caesar's, McDonald's, Michael's Dining, Subway, Taco Bell, Tim Horton, Wendy's, **lodging:** Best Western, Fairfield Inn, **other:** HOSPITAL, K-Mart, Kroger, Radio Shack, SavALot, st police, **S...gas:** Mobil/diesel, Buick/Pontiac
153	Lake Nepessing Rd, **S...**to Thumb Correctional, camping, golf
149	Elba Rd, **S...food:** Woody's Pizza
145	MI 15, Davison, **N...gas:** Shell/diesel, Speedway, **food:** Apollo Rest., Arby's, Big Boy, Big John's Rest., Burger King, Country Boy Rest., Dunkin Donuts, Hungry Howie's, Italia Gardens, KFC, Little Caesar's, Lucky's Steaks, McDonald's, Subway, Taco Bell, **lodging:** Comfort Inn, **other:** AutoValue Parts, GNC, Kessel Foods, Pontiac/Buick/GMC, Radio Shack, Rite Aid/24hr, **S...gas:** Mobil/diesel
143	Irish Rd, **N...gas:** Shell/diesel, **S...gas:** Shell/McDonald's/24hr, 7-11
141	Belsay Rd, Flint, **N...gas:** BP/Wendy's, Shell/diesel/24hr, **food:** Country Kitchen, McDonald's, Taco Bell, **other:** MEDICAL CARE, Harley-Davidson, Kessel Foods, K-Mart, Wal-Mart/auto, **S...gas:** Sunoco/A&W/LJ Silver/diesel

Flint

Exit #	Services
139	Center Rd, Flint, **N...gas:** Marathon, Speedway/diesel, **food:** Applebee's, Boston Mkt, Halo Burger, McDonald's, Moikong Chinese, Old Country Buffet, Ponderosa, Subway, Tim Horton, Wendy's, **lodging:** Budget Host, **other:** Aldi Foods, Buick, Family$, Goodyear/auto, Home Depot, JC Penney, Jo-Ann Fabrics, Lowe's Whse, Mervyn's, OfficeMax, Old Navy, mall, **S...gas:** Meijer/diesel/24hr, **food:** Bob Evans, DQ, McDonald's, Walli's Rest., **lodging:** Super 8, **other:** MEDICAL CARE, FarmerJack's, Staples, Target, to IMA Sports Arena
138	MI 54, Dort Hwy, **N...gas:** BP/24hr, Speedway/diesel, Sunoco, **food:** Anna's Kitchen, Big John's Rest., Little Caesar's, Pumpernik's Rest., Toshi's Café, YaYa's Chicken, **other:** HOSPITAL, Rite Aid, **S...gas:** Speedway, Sunoco, **food:** Angelo's Coney Island, Arby's, Big John's Steaks, Burger King, Chester Fried, China Buffet, KFC, McDonald's, Red Roof Ribs, Subway, Taco Bell, **other:** Aamco, Advance Parts, AutoZone, Cadillac/Pontiac, $General, Goodyear, K-Mart, Radio Shack, Rite Aid, U-Haul, Walgreen
137	I-475, UAW Fwy, to Detroit, Saginaw
136	Saginaw St, Flint, **N...**HOSPITAL, U MI at Flint, **S...other:** ExpertTire, GMC
135	Hammerberg Rd, industrial area, **S...gas:** Sunoco/diesel
133b a	I-75, S to Detroit, N to Saginaw, US 23 S to Ann Arbor
131	MI 121, to Bristol Rd, **1/2 mi N on Miller Rd...gas:** Speedway, **food:** A&W, Big Boy, Burger King, Chili's, ChuckeCheese, Golden Moon Chinese, LJ Silver, Old Country Buffet, Outback Steaks, Ponderosa, Ryan's, Ruby Tuesday, Subway, Taco Bell, Valley Diner, **other:** Best Buy, Borders Books, Circuit City, Discount Tire, Dodge, Firestone/auto, Goodyear/auto, JC Penney, Jo-Ann Fabrics, Marshall Fields, Mervyn's, Michael's, Office Depot, Old Navy, Sears/auto, Target, mall
129	Miller Rd, **S...gas:** Speedway, **food:** Arby's, Burger King, McDonald's, Wendy's, **other:** Kroger/gas
128	Morrish Rd, **S...gas:** BP/24hr, **other:** Sports Creek Horse Racing
126mm	**rest area eb, full(handicapped)facilities, info, phone, picnic tables, litter barrels, petwalk**
123	MI 13, Lennon, to Saginaw, **N...gas:** Speedway/diesel
118	MI 71, Durand, to Corunna, **S...gas:** Marathon, Shell/diesel, **food:** Hardee's, McDonald's, Subway, **lodging:** Sunset Motel, **other:** MEDICAL CARE, Carter's Foods, Chevrolet/Pontiac, Family$, Radio Shack, Rite Aid
115mm	Shiawassee River
113	Bancroft, **S...gas:** BP/diesel, RV camping
105	MI 52, Perry, to Owosso, **S...gas:** Citgo/7-11, Phillips 66/Taco Bell, Sunoco/Subway/diesel, **food:** Burger King, Café Sports, 59er Diner, McDonald's, **lodging:** Heb's Inn, **other:** Family$, Ford, Rite Aid, RV camping, truck repair(1mi)
101mm	**rest area wb, full(handicapped)facilities, phone, picnic tables, litter barrels, petwalk**
98.5mm	Looking Glass River
98	Woodbury Rd, Shaftsburg, to Laingsburg, **S...**RV camping

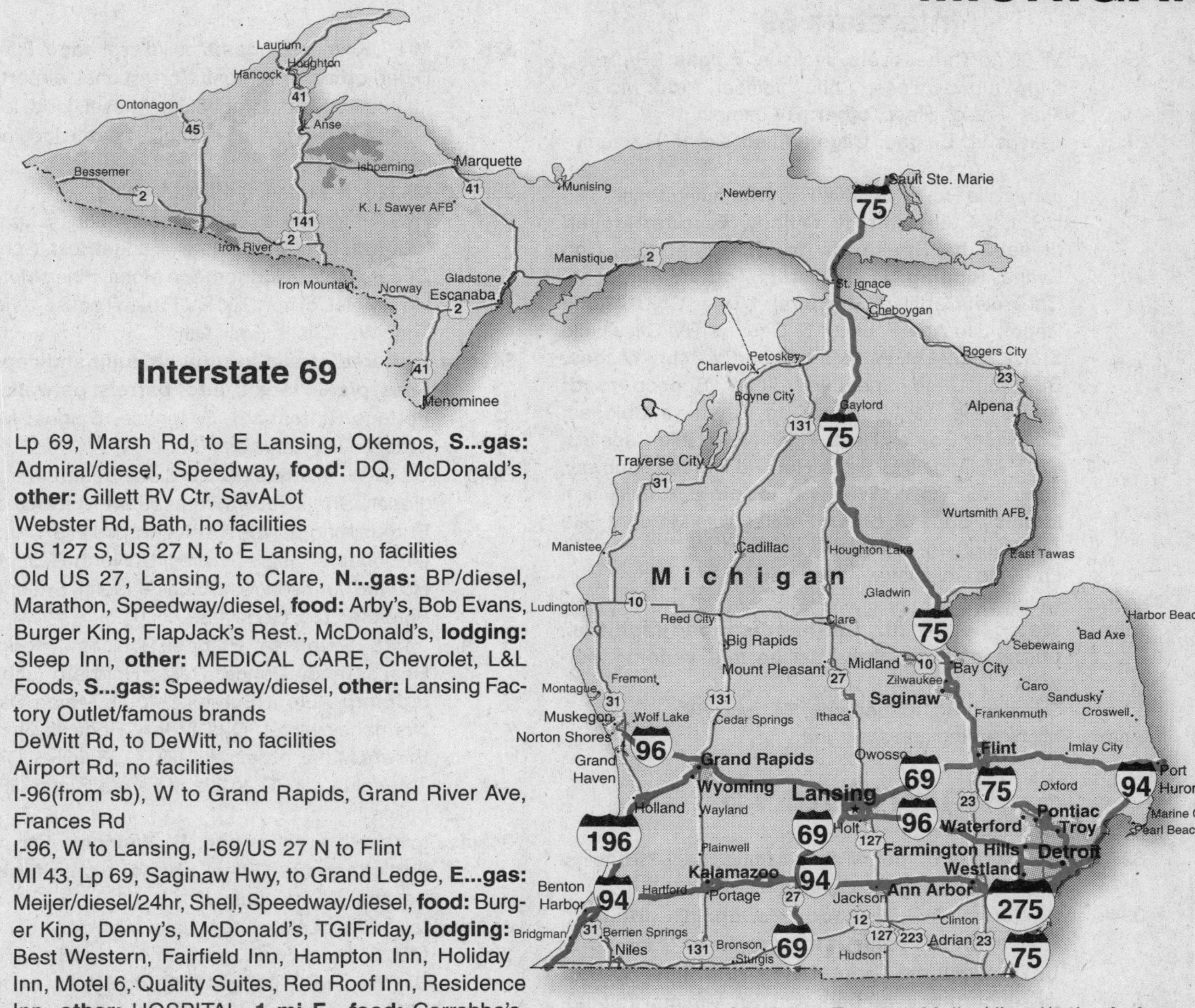

Interstate 69

N ↕ S

Lansing

94 Lp 69, Marsh Rd, to E Lansing, Okemos, **S...gas:** Admiral/diesel, Speedway, **food:** DQ, McDonald's, **other:** Gillett RV Ctr, SavALot

92 Webster Rd, Bath, no facilities

89 US 127 S, US 27 N, to E Lansing, no facilities

87 Old US 27, Lansing, to Clare, **N...gas:** BP/diesel, Marathon, Speedway/diesel, **food:** Arby's, Bob Evans, Burger King, FlapJack's Rest., McDonald's, **lodging:** Sleep Inn, **other:** MEDICAL CARE, Chevrolet, L&L Foods, **S...gas:** Speedway/diesel, **other:** Lansing Factory Outlet/famous brands

85 DeWitt Rd, to DeWitt, no facilities

84 Airport Rd, no facilities

81 I-96(from sb), W to Grand Rapids, Grand River Ave, Frances Rd

91 I-96, W to Lansing, I-69/US 27 N to Flint

93b a MI 43, Lp 69, Saginaw Hwy, to Grand Ledge, **E...gas:** Meijer/diesel/24hr, Shell, Speedway/diesel, **food:** Burger King, Denny's, McDonald's, TGIFriday, **lodging:** Best Western, Fairfield Inn, Hampton Inn, Holiday Inn, Motel 6, Quality Suites, Red Roof Inn, Residence Inn, **other:** HOSPITAL, **1 mi E...food:** Carrabba's, Frank's Grill, Outback Steaks, **other:** Chrysler/Jeep, **W...gas:** BP/24hr, QD, Sunoco/McDonald's, **food:** Arby's, Bob Evans, Cracker Barrel, Subway, **other:** Discount Tire, GMC/Mazda, Lowe's Whse, Michael's, Wal-Mart/auto

95 I-496, to Lansing, no facilities

72 I-96, E to Detroit, W to Grand Rapids

70 Lansing Rd, **1 mi E...gas:** Citgo/diesel/rest./24hr/@, **other:** st police

68mm rest area nb, full(handicapped)facilities, phone, picnic tables, litter barrels, vending, petwalk

66 MI 100, to Grand Ledge, Potterville, **W...gas:** BP, Shell/Subway, **food:** McDonald's, to Fox Co Park

61 Lansing Rd, **E...gas:** Marathon/diesel, Mobil/diesel, **food:** Applebee's, **lodging:** Comfort Inn, **other:** AutoZone, Chevrolet, Chrysler/Jeep/Dodge, Wal-Mart SuperCtr/24hr, **W...gas:** Speedway, QD, **food:** Arby's, Big Boy, Burger King, Hot'n Now, KFC, Little Caesar's, McDonald's, Pizza Hut, Subway, Taco Bell, Top Chinese, Wendy's, **other:** HOSPITAL, Advance Parts, CarQuest, Family$, Ford/Mercury, Geldhof Tire/auto, Jo-Ann Fabrics, Pontiac/Buick/GMC, Radio Shack, SavALot

Marshall

60 MI 50, Charlotte, **E...gas:** Meijer/diesel/24hr, **lodging:** Holiday Inn Express, **W...**HOSPITAL, Super 8, RV camping

57 Lp 69, Cochran Rd, to Charlotte, **E...**RV camping

51 Ainger Rd, **1 mi E...**access to gas, food, RV camping

48 MI 78, Olivet, to Bellevue, **1 mi E...gas:** Citgo/Subway, **food:** Taco Bell, **other:** to Olivet Coll

42 N Drive N, Turkeyville Rd, **W...food:** Cornwell's Rest.(1mi)

41mm rest area sb, full(handicapped)facilities, phone, picnic tables, litter barrels, petwalk

38 I-94, E to Detroit, W to Chicago

36 Michigan Ave, to Marshall, **E...gas:** Mobil/diesel, Shell/Subway, **food:** Arby's, Burger King, McDonald's, Pizza Hut, Taco Bell, Wendy's, **lodging:** AmeriHost, **other:** HOSPITAL, AutoZone, Chevrolet, $Tree, GNC, K-Mart, Parts+, Radio Shack, Rite Aid, **W...lodging:** Arbor Inn, **other:** Chrysler/Dodge/Jeep

32 F Drive S, **3/4 mi E...gas:** Shell, **food:** Moonraker Rest.(3mi)

28mm rest area nb, full(handicapped)facilities, phone, info, picnic tables, litter barrels, petwalk

MICHIGAN

Interstate 69

N ↕ S

25 MI 60, to Three Rivers, Jackson, **E...gas:** BP/diesel, Citgo/Subway/diesel, Sunoco/diesel, **food:** McDonald's, Te-Kon Rest., **other:** RV camping

23 Tekonsha, **E...gas:** Citgo, **W...**access to RV camping

16 Jonesville Rd, **W...**Waffle Farm Camping(2mi)

13 US 12, Coldwater, to Quincy, **E...gas:** Meijer/diesel/24hr, Speedway, **food:** Applebee's, Bob Evans, **lodging:** Red Roof Inn, **other:** AutoZone, Chevrolet/Cadillac, $General, $Tree, GNC, Home Depot, JJo-Ann Fabrics, N Country RV Ctr, Radio Shack, SavALot, Wal-Mart SuperCtr/24hr, **W...gas:** BP/24hr, Citgo, Speedway/diesel, Sunoco, **food:** Arby's, Big Boy, Burger King, Charlie's Chinese, Coldwater Garden Rest., Hot'n Now, Little Caesar's, KFC, McDonald's, Pizza Hut, Ponderosa, Subway, Taco Bell, TCBY, Wendy's, **lodging:** Holiday Inn Express, Super 8, **other:** Ford/Lincoln/Mercury, Rite Aid, Walgreen, st police

10 Lp 69, to Coldwater, no facilities

8mm weigh sta nb

6mm Welcome Ctr nb, full(handicapped)facilities, phone, picnic tables, litter barrels, vending, petwalk

3 Copeland Rd, Kinderhook, **W...gas:** BP

0mm Michigan/Indiana state line

Interstate 75

N ↕ S

Exit # Services

395mm US/Canada Border, Michigan state line, I-75 begins/ends at toll bridge to Canada

394 Easterday Ave, **E...food:** McDonald's, **lodging:** Holiday Inn Express, **other:** to Lake Superior St U, **W...Welcome Ctr/rest area, info, gas:** Holiday/diesel/currency exchange, USA Minimart/diesel, **food:** Freighter's Rest.(2mi), **lodging:** Ramada Inn(2mi)

Sault Ste Marie

392 3 Mile Rd, Sault Ste Marie, **E...gas:** Admiral, Amoco/diesel, Holiday/diesel, Marathon, Mobil/diesel, Shell, USA/diesel/24hr, **food:** Abner's Rest., Arby's, Burger King, Country Kitchen, Great Wall Chinese, Jeff's Café, KFC, La Senorita Mexican, Little Caesar's, Mancino's Pizza, McDonald's, Pizza Hut, Studebaker's Rest., Subway, Taco Bell, Wendy's, **lodging:** Best Western, Budget Host, Comfort Inn, Day's Inn, Hampton Inn, Kewadin Inn, King's Inn, Motel 6, Plaza Motel, Quality Inn, Skyline Motel, Super 8, **other:** HOSPITAL, Buick/Cadillac, Chevrolet/Pontiac, Family$, Glen's Mkt, JC Penney, Jo-Ann Fabrics, K-Mart, NAPA, OfficeMax, Radio Shack, Sav-A-LotWal-Mart, st police, Soo Locks Boat Tours

389mm rest area nb, full(handicapped)facilities, info, phone, picnic tables, litter barrels, petwalk

386 MI 28, **3 mi E...**food, lodging, **W...**to Brimley SP, Clear Creek Camping(5mi)

379 Gaines Hwy, **E...**to Barbeau Area, camping

378 MI 80, Kinross, **E...gas:**Mobil/diesel, **food:** Frank&Jim's Diner, **other:** to Kinross Correctional, airport, golf

373 MI 48, Rudyard, **2 mi W...**gas/diesel, food, lodging

359 MI 134, to Drummond Island, access to lodging, camping

352 MI 123, to Moran, **5 mi W...**lodging

348 H63, St Ignace, to Sault Reservation, **E...gas:** Shell, **lodging:** Birchwood Motel, BudgetHost, Comfort Inn, Cedars Motel, NorthernAire Motel, Pines Motel, Rockview Motel, **other:** Tiki RV Park, st police, to Mackinac Trail, **W...**Castle Rock Gifts

346mm rest area/scenic turnout sb, full(handicapped)facilities, picnic tables, litter barrels, petwalk

345 Portage St(from sb), St Ignace, **E...gas:** Marathon, **other:** other services

344b US 2 W, **W...gas:** Citgo/diesel/rest./24hr, Holiday/diesel, Shell/Subway/diesel/24hr, **food:** Big Boy, Burger King, Clyde's Drive-In, Miller's Camp Rest., McDonald's, Suzi's Pasties, UpNorth Rest., **lodging:** Howard Johnson/rest., Sunset Motel, Super 8, **other:** Ford/Mercury, Goodyear

a Lp 75, St Ignace, **E...gas:** Shell(1mi), **food:** Flame Rest., Gandy Dancer Rest., Northern Lights Rest., **lodging:** Aurora Borealis Motel, Moran Bay Motel, Normandy Motel, Quality Inn, Rodeway Inn, Straits Breeze Motel, **other:** HOSPITAL, Family$, Glen's Mkt, TrueValue, USPO, to Island Ferrys, Straits SP, KOA, st police

343mm toll booth to toll bridge, **E...Welcome Ctr nb, full(handicapped)facilities, phone, picnic tables, litter barrels, W...**museum

341mm toll bridge, Lake Huron, Lake Michigan

339 US 23, Jamet St, **E...gas:** Amoco, **food:** Audie's Rest., Big Boy, KFC, **lodging:** BudgetHost, Econolodge, LaMirage Motel, Motel 6, Parkside Motel, Ramada Inn, Riviera Motel, Super 8, **W...gas:** Shell, **food:** Darrow's Rest., Mackinaw Cookie Co, **lodging:** Chalet Motel, Holiday Inn Express

Mackinaw City

338 US 23(from sb), **E...Welcome Ctr/rest area, gas:** Amoco, Marathon, **food:** Big Boy, Burger King, Cheeping Chinese, DQ, Subway, **lodging:** Baymont Inn, Downing's Motel, Ramada Inn, Rodeway Inn, **other:** IGA Foods/supplies, same as 337, **W...lodging:** Bindel Motel, Chalet Motel, Ft Mackinaw Motel, Trails End Inn

337 MI 108(no EZ return to nb), Nicolet St, Mackinaw City, **E...gas:** Citgo/LP, **food:** Embers Rest., Mancino's Pizza, Mario's Ristorante, **lodging:** Anchor Inn, Beach-Comber Motel, BelAire Motel, Best Western, Budget Inn, Capri Motel, Cherokee Shores Inn, Chippewa Inn, Clarion, Day's Inn, Fairfield Inn, Friendship Inn, Grand Mackinaw Resort, Hamilton Lodge, Hampton Inn, Hawthorn Inn, Howard Johnson, King's Inn, Nicolet Inn, North Pointe Inn, Ottawa Motel, Quality Inn, Ramada Ltd, Starlite Inn, Sundown Motel, Surf Motel, Travelodge, **other:** KOA, Old Mill Creek SP, to Island Ferrys, **W...**Wilderness SP

Interstate 75

N ↕ S

336 US 31 S(from sb), to Petoskey
328mm rest area sb, full(handicapped)facilities, info, phone, picnic tables, litter barrels, petwalk
326 C66, to Cheboygan, **E...gas:** Marathon, **other:** HOSPITAL, Sea Shell City/gifts
322 C64, to Cheboygan, **E...**HOSPITAL, LP, airport, st police
317mm rest area/scenic turnout nb, full(handicapped)facilities, info, phone, picnic tables, litter barrels, petwalk
313 MI 27 N, Topinabee, **E...lodging:** Johnson Motel, gas, food, RV Park
311mm Indian River
310 MI 33, MI 68, **E...lodging:** Holiday Inn Express, **other:** Jellystone Park(3mi), **W...gas:** Amoco/diesel, Shell/McDonald's/24hr, **food:** Burger King, Brown Trout Rest., Don's Burgers, Paula's Café, **lodging:** Coach House Motel, **other:** Ken's Mkt, to Indian River Trading Post/RV Resort, to Burt Lake SP
301 C58, Wolverine, **E...gas:** Marathon/diesel
297mm Sturgeon River
290 Vanderbilt, **E...gas:** BP/diesel/LP/RV dump, **food:** Gateway Diner, **W...gas:** Mobil/diesel
287mm rest area sb, full(handicapped)facilities, info, phone, picnic tables, litter barrels
282 MI 32, Gaylord, **E...gas:** Amoco/diesel, Clark, Holiday/24hr, Speedway/diesel, **food:** Arby's, Burger King, DQ, KFC, La Senorita Mexican, McDonald's, Quizno's, Subway, TCBY, Wendy's, **lodging:** Best Western, Comfort Inn, Quality Inn, Red Roof Inn, Glen's Foods, **other:** HOSPITAL, Harley-Davidson, Rite Aid, st police, **W...gas:** Citgo/diesel, Marathon/diesel, Mobil/diesel, Shell/diesel, **food:** BC Pizza, Big Boy, Bob Evans, China 1, Little Caesar's, Mancino's Pizza, Pizza Hut, Ponderosa, Taco Bell, **lodging:** Day's Inn, Hampton Inn, Super 8, **other:** Chrysler/Plymouth/Dodge, Dayton Tire, Home Depot, K-Mart, Save-A-Lot, Wal-Mart, RV camping

Gaylord

279mm 45th Parallel...halfway between the equator and north pole
279 Old US 27, Gaylord, **E...gas:** Marathon/Subway/diesel, Mobil/diesel, Shell, **food:** Burger King, Gobblers Rest., Mama Leone's, Willabee's Rest., **lodging:** Alpine Motel, Best Western(2mi), Brentwood Motel, Econolodge, Timberly Motel, **other:** Chevrolet, Chrysler/Jeep/Nissan, Ford/Lincoln/Mercury, Pontiac/Buick/GMC, RV Ctr, st police, **W...lodging:** Marsh Ridge Motel(2mi), KOA(3mi)
277mm rest area nb, full(handicapped)facilities, info, phone, picnic tables, litter barrels, petwalk
270 Waters, **E...gas:** Mobil/diesel/rest., **W...food:** McDonald's, lodging, RV repair, to Otsego Lake SP
264 Lewiston, Frederic, **W...**access to food, lodging, camping
262mm rest area sb, full(handicapped)facilities, phone, picnic tables, litter barrels, petwalk

Grayling

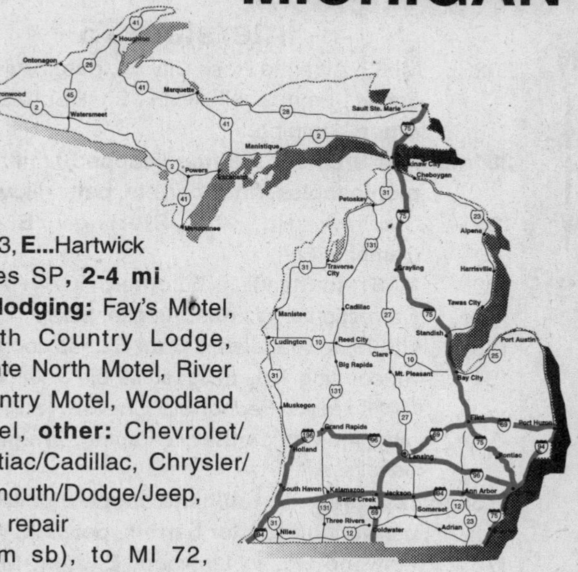

259 MI 93, **E...**Hartwick Pines SP, **2-4 mi W...lodging:** Fay's Motel, North Country Lodge, Pointe North Motel, River Country Motel, Woodland Motel, **other:** Chevrolet/Pontiac/Cadillac, Chrysler/Plymouth/Dodge/Jeep, auto repair
256 (from sb), to MI 72, Grayling, access to same as 254
254 MI 72(exits left from nb, no return), Grayling, **1 mi W... gas:** Amoco, Admiral Gas, BP, Citgo/7-11, Mobil/diesel, Phillips 66, Shell, Speedway, **food:** A&W, Big Boy, Burger King, DQ, KFC, Little Caesar's, McDonald's, Patty's Diner, Pizza Hut, Subway, Taco Bell, Wendy's, **lodging:** Day's Inn, Holiday Inn, Super 7 Inn, **other:** HOSPITAL, Carquest, Family$, Ford/Lincoln/Mercury, Glen's Foods/24hr, K-Mart, NAPA, Rite Aid
251mm rest area nb, full(handicapped)facilities, info, phone, picnic tables, litter barrels, petwalk, vending
251 4 Mile Rd, **E...**Jellystone RV Park, skiing, **W...gas:** Marathon/Arby's/diesel/24hr/@, **food:** Skyline Rest., **lodging:** Super 8
249 US 27 S(from sb), to Clare, no facilities
244 MI 18, Roscommon, **W...gas:** Sunoco/diesel/LP, **other:** N Higgins Lake SP, camping, museum
239 MI 18, Roscommon, S Higgins Lake SP, **E...other:** Ford/Mercury, gas, food, lodging, camping
235mm rest area sb, full(handicapped)facilities, phone, info, picnic tables, litter barrels, petwalk, vending
227 MI 55 W, rd F97, to Houghton Lake, **5 mi W...**food
222 Old 76, to St Helen, **5 mi E...**food, lodging, camping
215 MI 55 E, West Branch, **E...gas:** Kimball/diesel, **food:** Coyle's Rest., **other:** HOSPITAL,
212 MI 55, West Branch, **E...gas:** Marathon/diesel, Shell/Subway, 7-11, **food:** Arby's, Big Boy, Burger King, Lumberjack Rest., McDonald's, Ponderosa, Taco Bell, Wendy's, **lodging:** Quality Inn/rest., Super 8, Tri Terrace Motel, **other:** HOSPITAL, Tanger Outlet/famous brands, st police, **W...gas:** BP/diesel, **other:** Lk George Camping
210mm rest area nb, full(handicapped)facilities, info, phone, picnic tables, litter barrels, petwalk, vending

Interstate 75

N ↕ S

202 MI 33, Alger, to Rose City, **E...gas:** BP/Narski's Mkt/gerky(1/2mi), Mobil/diesel, Shell/Subway/Taco Bell, **other:** camping

201mm rest area sb, full(handicapped)facilities, phone, picnic tables, litter barrels, petwalk, vending

195 Sterling Rd, to Sterling, **E...**Riverview Camping(6mi)

190 MI 61, to Standish, **E...other:** HOSPITAL, Standish Correctional, **W...gas:** Amoco, Mobil

188 US 23, to Standish, **2-3 mi E...**gas, food, camping

181 Pinconning Rd, **E...gas:** Mobil, Shell/McDonald's/diesel, **food:** Pepper Mill Cheese, **lodging:** Pinconning Inn(2mi), **other:** camping, **W...gas:** Sunoco/diesel/rest./24hr

175mm rest area nb, full(handicapped)facilities, phone, picnic tables, litter barrels, petwalk, vending

173 Linwood Rd, to Linwood, **E...gas:** Mobil, **other:** Hoyle's Marina Camping

171mm Kawkawlin River

168 Beaver Rd, to Willard, **E...food:** Turkey Roost Rest.(3mi), **other:** to Bay City SP, **W...gas:** Mobil

166mm Kawkawlin River

164 to MI 13, Wilder Rd, to Kawkawlin, **E...gas:** Meijer Food/diesel/24hr, **food:** McDonald's, **lodging:** AmericInn

162b a US 10, MI 25, to Midland, **E...**HOSPITAL, st police

160 MI 84, Delta, **E...gas:** Mobil/Subway/diesel, Shell/Dunkin Donuts, **W...gas:** Amoco/diesel, Citgo/7-11, Speedway, **food:** Burger King, Howard Johnson Rest., KFC/Taco Bell, McDonald's, **lodging:** Best Value Inn, **other:** Bay Valley RV Park, to Saginaw Valley Coll

158mm rest area sb, full(handicapped)facilities, phone, picnic tables, litter barrels, vending, petwalk

155 I-675 S, to downtown Saginaw, **4 mi W...food:** OutBack Steaks, **lodging:** Hampton Inn, Super 8

154 to Zilwaukee, no facilities

153mm Saginaw River

153 MI 13, E Bay City Rd, Saginaw, **2-3 mi W...**lodging

151 MI 81, to Reese, **E...gas:** Sunoco/diesel, **food:** Burger King

150 I-675 N, to downtown Saginaw, **6 mi W...food:** OutBack Steaks, **lodging:** Hampton Inn, Super 8

Saginaw

149b a MI 46, Holland Ave, to Saginaw, **W...gas:** Admiral, Amoco, BP, Speedway/diesel, Sunoco, **food:** Arby's, Big Boy, Burger King, McDonald's, Taco Bell, Texan Rest., Wendy's, **lodging:** Best Western, Red Roof Inn, Rodeway Inn, **other:** HOSPITAL, Advance Parts, K-Mart, Save-A-Lot Foods

144b a Bridgeport, **E...gas:** Shell/Blimpie, Speedway/diesel/24hr, **lodging:** Heidelburg Inn, **W...gas:** Mobil, TA/diesel/rest./24hr/@, **food:** Arby's, Big Boy, Cracker Barrel, Little Caesar's, McDonald's, Peking City Chinese, Subway, Taco Bell, Wendy's, **lodging:** Baymont Inn, Day's Inn, Villager Lodge, **other:** MEDICAL CARE, Family$, IGA Food, Rite Aid, Radio Shack, st police

143mm Cass River

138mm weigh sta both lanes

136 MI 54, MI 83, Birch Run, **E...gas:** Mobil/diesel/24hr, Shell, **food:** Exit Rest., Halo Burger, KFC, Subway, **lodging:** Best Western, Comfort Inn, Hampton Inn, Holiday Inn Express, Super 8, **other:** CarQuest, Dixie Speedway, RV camping, **W...gas:** Amoco/Burger King, Citgo/7-11, Marathon, Sunoco/diesel, **food:** A&W, Arby's, Applebee's, Big Boy, Bob Evans, Coney Island, DQ, Little Caesar's, McDonald's, Schlotsky's, Taco Bell, Tony's Rest., Uno Pizzaria, Wendy's, **lodging:** Country Inn Suites, **other:** Chevrolet/Buick/Suzuki, Prime Outlet/famous brands

131 MI 57, Clio, to Montrose, **E...gas:** Shell, Sunoco, **food:** Arby's, Burger King, DQ, KFC, McDonald's, Subway, Taco Bell, **other:** AutoZone, Chevrolet, Chrysler/Plymouth, Dodge/Jeep, Farmer Jack's, Ford, K-Mart, Pamida, **W...gas:** Amoco/diesel, Mobil, **food:** Big Boy, Wendy's

129mm rest area both lanes, full(handicapped)facilities, phone, picnic tables, litter barrels, vending, petwalk

126 to Mt Morris, **E...gas:** BP/Burger King/diesel/24hr, **W...gas:** Amoco/diesel, carwash

125 I-475 S, UAW Fwy, to Flint

122 Pierson Rd, to Flint, **E...gas:** Amoco, Clark Gas, Marathon, **food:** Asia Buffet, KFC, McDonald's, Subway, Super 8, **other:** MEDICAL CARE, **W...gas:** Citgo, Meijer/diesel/24hr, Shell, **food:** Arby's, Big John's Steaks, Bob Evans, Burger King, Cracker Barrel, Denny's, Halo Burger, LJ Silver, Pizza Hut, Red Lobster, Taco Bell, Wendy's, YaYa Chicken, **lodging:** Baymont Inn, Great Western Inn, Ramada Inn, **other:** Discount Tire, Home Depot,

118 MI 21, Corunna Rd, **E...gas:** Sunoco, **food:** Badawest Lebanese, Big John's Steaks, Burger King, Coney Island, Hardee's, Little Caesar's, Taco Bell, YaYa Chicken, **other:** HOSPITAL, Advance Parts, $General, Rite Aid, **W...gas:** Amoco, Citgo, Mobil, Shell/Wendy's, Speedway, **food:** Domino's, Schlotsky's, **lodging:** Economy Motel, **other:** AutoZone, Buick, CarQuest, Farmer Jack's Foods, Home Depot, Lincoln/Mercury, Lowe's Whse, Rite Aid, Sam's Club/gas, Wal-Mart, st police

Flint

117b Miller Rd, to Flint, **E...gas:** Speedway/diesel, Sunoco/diesel, **food:** Applebee's, Arby's, Bennigan's, ChiChi's, Don Pablo, Fuddrucker's, KFC, LoneStar Steaks, McDonald's, Papa John's, Subway, **lodging:** Comfort Inn, Motel 6, Sleep Inn, **other:** K-Mart, NTB, Sav-A-Lot Foods, **W...gas:** Amoco/McDonald's, Marathon, **food:** Big Boy, Bob Evans, Burger King, Chili's, ChuckeCheese, Hooters, Mancino's Italian, Old Country Buffet, Olive Garden, Outback Steaks, Pizza Hut, Ryan's, Salvatori's Ristorante, Taco Bell, TCBY, Wendy's, **lodging:** Howard Johnson, Red Roof Inn, Super 8, **other:** MEDICAL CARE, Best Buy, Borders Books, Brake Depot, Circuit City, Dodge, Goodyear, JC Penney, Jo-Ann Fabrics, Marshall Field, Michael's, Office Depot, PepBoys, Radio Shack, Target, U-Haul, mall

Interstate 75

N ↕ S

117a I-69, E to Lansing, W to Port Huron

116 MI 121, Bristol Rd, **E...gas:** Amoco/24hr, Citgo, Speedway/diesel, **food:** Coney Island, KFC, McDonald's, **lodging:** Day's Inn, **other:** AutoZone, GM Plant, **W...gas:** Mobil/diesel, **other:** airport

115 US 23(from sb), **W on Hill Rd...gas:** Citgo, Meijer/diesel/24hr, Mobil, **food:** Maxie's Rest., McDonald's, **lodging:** AmericInn, Courtyard, Holiday Inn, Redwood Lodge, Residence Inn

111 I-475 N, UAW Fwy, to Flint

109 MI 54, Dort Hwy(no EZ return to sb), **1-2 mi E...food:** Big Boy, Damon's, Wendy's

108 Holly Rd, to Grand Blanc, **E...gas:** Sunoco, **food:** Subway, **lodging:** AmeriHost, **other:** BMW/Mercedes/Toyota, **W...gas:** Amoco/McDonald's., **other:** HOSPITAL,

106 Dixie Hwy(no nb return), Saginaw Rd, to Grand Blanc, **E...gas:** Clark

101 Grange Hall Rd, Ortonville, **E...other:** Holly RA, Jellystone Park, st police, **W...other:** to Seven Lakes/Groveland Oaks SP, RV camping

98 E Holly Rd, **E...gas:** Mobil/Subway/diesel/24hr, golf

95.5mm rest area both lanes, full(handicapped)facilities, picnic tables, litter barrels, info, phone, vending, petwalk

93 US 24, Dixie Hwy, Waterford, **E...**Dodge, Saturn, **1-3 mi W...food:** Arby's, Big Boy, McDonald's, Taco Bell, Wendy's, **other:** MEDICAL CARE, Chrysler/Plymouth/Jeep, to Pontiac Lake RA

91 MI 15, Davison, Clarkston, **E...**camping, **W...gas:** Shell, **food:** Dugan's Rest., Mesquite Creek Café, Mrs B's Rest., **lodging:** Millwood B&B

89 Sashabaw Rd, **E...gas:** Shell/diesel, **other:** county park, **W...gas:** Amoco/24hr, **food:** E Ocean Chinese, McDonald's, Subway, **other:** Farmer Jack's Foods, GNC, Pine Knob Music Theatre

86mm weigh sta sb, parking area nb

84b a Baldwin Ave, **E...gas:** Shell/24hr, Sunoco/diesel, **food:** Big Boy, Joe's Crabshack, Wendy's, **other:** Best Buy, CompUSA, Costco/gas, $Castle, Kohl's, Michael's, OfficeMax, Old Navy, **W...gas:** Mobil/24hr, **food:** Chili's, McDonald's, Steak'n Shake/24hr, **other:** Borders Books, Great Lakes Crossing Outlet/famous brands, Marshall's

83b a Joslyn Rd, **E...gas:** Meijer/diesel/24hr, **other:** Jo-Ann Fabrics, Target, **W...food:** McDonald's, FoodTown/24hr, **other:** K-Mart/Little Caesar's, Outlets/famous brands

81 MI 24, Pontiac(no EZ return), **E...**The Palace Arena, **1mi E...gas:** Amoco/24hr

79 University Dr, **E...gas:** Amoco, Domino's, **food:** Dunkin Donuts, Subway, **W...gas:** Speedway, **food:** Big Buck Brewery/steaks, Mtn Jack's Rest., McDonald's, Taco Bell, Wendy's/Tim Horton, **lodging:** AmeriSuites, Courtyard, Extended Stay America, Fairfield Inn, Hampton Inn, Holiday Inn, Motel 6, **other:** HOSPITAL, GM

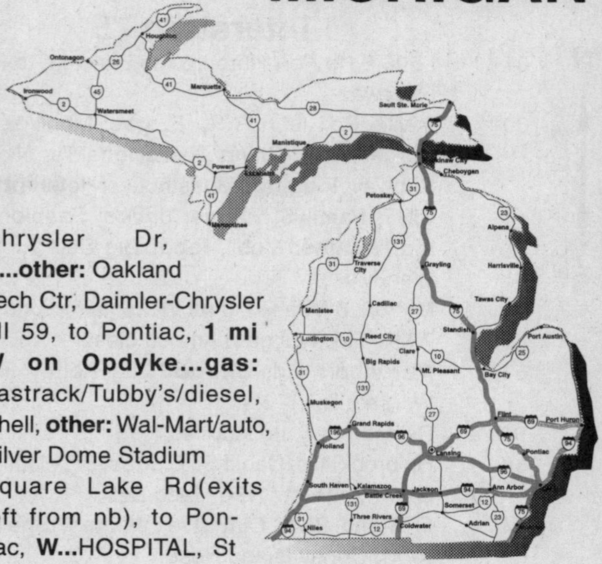

Detroit Area

78 Chrysler Dr, **E...other:** Oakland Tech Ctr, Daimler-Chrysler

77b a MI 59, to Pontiac, **1 mi W on Opdyke...gas:** Fastrack/Tubby's/diesel, Shell, **other:** Wal-Mart/auto, Silver Dome Stadium

75 Square Lake Rd(exits left from nb), to Pontiac, **W...**HOSPITAL, St Mary's Coll

74 Adams Rd, no facilities

72 Crooks Rd, to Troy, **W...food:** Cooker, **lodging:** Embassy Suites, Northfield Hilton Inn

69 Big Beaver Rd, **E...food:** Champp's Grill, O'Grady's Grill, **lodging:** Drury Inn, Marriott, **other:** bank, **W...gas:** Amoco, Shell, 7-11/24hr, **food:** Coney Island, Denny's, Empire Szechuan, Papa Romano's Pizza, Ruth's Chris Steaks, TGIFriday, **other:** MEDICAL CARE

67 Rochester Rd, to Stevenson Hwy, **E...gas:** Clark, Mobil, Shell, **food:** Arby's, Big Boy, Burger King, Coney Island, Dunkin Donuts, KFC, Mr Pita, Pizza Hut/Taco Bell, Ram's Horn Rest., **other:** Discount Tires, Radio Shack, **W...food:** Mtn Jack's Steaks, **lodging:** Holiday Inn, Red Roof Inn, **other:** Belle Tire, repair

65b a 14 Mile Rd, Madison Heights, **E...gas:** Mobil, Shell, **food:** BeefCarver Rest., Bob Evans, Burger King, ChiChi's, Chili's, Country Oven, Denny's, Little Daddy's Grill, Logan's Roadhouse, McDonald's, Panera Bread, Steak&Ale, Taco Bell, Tubby's Subs, **lodging:** Motel 6, Red Roof Inn, **other:** MEDICAL CARE, Belle Tire, Borders Books, Circuit City, CompUSA, Dodge, Fannie May Candy, Ford, Goodyear/auto, JC Penney, Marshall Field, NTB, Office Depot, Sam's Club, Sears/auto, mall, **W...gas:** Mobil/Blimpie, **food:** Applebee's, Bennigan's, Big Fish Seafood, Coney Island, McDonald's, Ponderosa, White Castle, **lodging:** Courtyard, Day's Inn, Econolodge, Extended Stay America, Fairfield Inn, Day's Inn, Hampton Inn, Residence Inn, **other:** CVS Drug, FoodLand

63 12 Mile Rd, **E...gas:** Clark, Marathon, Speedway, **food:** Blimpie, Golden Wheel Chinese, Hacienda Azteca Mexican, Marinelli's Pizza, McDonald's, Red Lobster, TCBY, **other:** Home Depot, K-Mart, Radio Shack, transmissions, **W...gas:** Marathon/Dunkin Donuts, Speedway, **food:** Denny's, Chevrolet, Costco/gas

62 11 Mile Rd, **E...gas:** 7-11, Boodles Rest., **W...gas:** BP, Marathon/diesel, Mobil, **food:** DM, KFC, Pizza Hut, Taco Bell, Tim Horton, Tubby's Subs, **other:** Belle Tire

MICHIGAN

Interstate 75

N
S

Detroit Area

61 I-696 E, to Port Huron, W to Lansing, to Hazel Park Raceway

60 9 Mile Rd, John R St, **E...gas:** Mobil/diesel, **food:** Burger King, China 1, McDonald's, Nick's Pizza, Subway, **lodging:** Guesthouse Hotel, **other:** DENTIST, Family$, Farmer Jack's, FashionBug, Rite Aid, **W...gas:** Mobil, **food:** Big Boy, Tubby's Subs, Wendy's

59 MI 102, 8 Mile Rd, **3 mi W...**st fairgrounds

58 7 Mile Rd, **W...gas:** Amoco/diesel

57 McNichols Rd, **E...food:** La Koney Rest./24hr, **W...gas:** BP

56b a Davison Fwy, no facilities

55 Holbrook Ave, Caniff St, **E...gas:** BP, Mobil, **W...food:** Grandy's Rest., KFC, Taco Bell

54 E Grand Blvd, Clay Ave, **W...gas:** Shell/autocare, **food:** Coney Island Rest.

53 b I-94, Ford Fwy, to Port Huron, Chicago

a Warren Ave, **E...gas:** Mobil, Shell, **W...gas:** Amoco

52 Mack Ave, **E...gas:** Shell, **food:** McDonald's, **W...** HOSPITAL

51c I-375 to civic center, downtown, tunnel to Canada

b MI 3(exits left from nb), Gratiot Ave, downtown

50 Grand River Ave, downtown

49b MI 10, Lodge Fwy, downtown

a Rosa Parks Blvd, **E...**Tiger Stadium, **W...gas:** Mobil, **other:** Firestone

48 I-96 begins/ends, no facilities

47b Porter St, **E...**bridge to Canada, DutyFree/24hr

a MI 3, Clark Ave, **E...gas:** Mobil

46 Livernois Ave, to Hist Ft Wayne, **E...gas:** Marathon, **food:** KFC/Taco Bell

45 Fort St, Springwells Ave, **E...gas:** BP/diesel, **W...gas:** Mobil, **food:** McDonald's

43b a MI 85, Fort St, to Schaefer Hwy, **E...gas:** Amoco, Sunoco, **W...gas:** Marathon, **other:** to River Rouge Ford Plant

42 Outer Dr, **W...gas:** BP/Subway/diesel, Mobil/diesel, **other:** K-Mart

41 MI 39, Southfield Rd, to Lincoln Park, **E...food:** A&W, Bill's Place Rest., **lodging:** Budget Inn, **W...gas:** Mobil/diesel, **food:** Dunkin Donuts, **lodging:** Sleep Inn, **other:** Buick

40 Dix Hwy, **E...gas:** BeeQuik/gas, BP, Citgo, Clark, Speedway, 7-11, **food:** Baffo's Pizza, Coney Island Diner, Ponderosa, **other:** MEDICAL CARE, Farmer Jack's, **W...gas:** Shell, Speedway, **food:** Big Boy, Burger King, Church's, DQ, Dunkin Donuts, LJ Silver, McDonald's, Pizza Hut, Rally's, Taco Bell, **lodging:** Holiday Motel, **other:** Firestone, CVS Drug, Foodland, Sears/auto

37 Allen Rd, North Line Rd, to Wyandotte, **E...gas:** Amoco, Mobil, Speedway, 7-11/24hr, **food:** Anita's Pizza, TCBY, Yum Yum Donuts, **lodging:** Ramada Inn, **other:** HOSPITAL, Sam's Club, transmissions, **W...food:** Arby's, Burger King, McDonald's, **lodging:** Baymont Inn, Cross Country Inn

36 Eureka Rd, **E...gas:** Speedway, **food:** Amigo's Mexican, Bob Evans, Denny's, Orleans Steaks, **lodging:** Ramada Inn, Super 8, **other:** Chevrolet, **W...gas:** Meijer/diesel/24hr, **food:** Bakers Square, Big Boy, Hooters, Mtn Jack's Steaks, Rio Bravo, Ruby Tuesday, Schlotsky's, Wendy's, **lodging:** Red Roof Inn, **other:** MEDICAL CTR, Borders Books, Costco, CVS Drug, Discount Tire, Home Depot, JC Penney, Kohl's, Mervyn's, Staples, mall

35 US 24, Telegraph Rd

34b Sibley Rd, Riverview, **W...gas:** Shell/Dunkin Donuts/Subway

a to US 24(from sb), Telegraph Rd, no facilities

32 West Rd, Woodhaven, to Trenton, **E...gas:** Citgo/diesel/rest., Meijer/diesel/24hr, Mobil/diesel/rest./24hr, Speedway/diesel, **food:** Bob Evans, Burger King, Church's/White Castle, Dunkin Donuts, KFC, LJ Silver, Panera Bread, Pizza Hut, Steak'n Shake, Subway, Taco Bell, **other:** Chevrolet, Chrysler/Plymouth/Dodge, Discount Tire, Firestone/auto, Ford, Home Depot, K-Mart, Kroger, Office Depot, Radio Shack, Target, **W...gas:** Amoco/24hr, Shell, **food:** Marco's Pizza, Millie's Rest., McDonald's, **lodging:** Best Western/rest., Knight's Inn, Holiday Inn Express, **other:** SavOn Drug

29 Gilbralter Rd, to Flat Rock, Lake Erie Metropark, **E...gas:** FasTrack/diesel, **food:** McDonald's, **other:** bank, **W...gas:** Marathon, **lodging:** Sleep Inn, **other:** Ford, st police

28 rd 85(from nb), Fort St, **E...**HOSPITAL

27 N Huron River Dr, to Rockwood, **E...gas:** Marathon, Rich, **food:** Benito's Pizza, Huron River Rest., Marco's Pizza, Ocean Duck Chinese, **other:** Rite Aid, **W...gas:** Speedway/diesel, **food:** Riverfront Rest.

26 S Huron River Dr, to S Rockwood, **E...gas:** Sunoco/diesel, **food:** Dick's Café, **other:** USPO

21 Newport Rd, to Newport, **E...gas:** Amoco/Taco Bell/24hr, **W...gas:** Mobil/Burger King/diesel/24hr

20 I-275 N, to Flint, no facilities

18 Nadeau Rd, **W...gas:** Pilot/Arby's/diesel/24hr/@, **other:** HOSPITAL, RV camping

Monroe

15 MI 50, Dixie Hwy, to Monroe, **E...gas:** Shell, **food:** Bob Evans, Burger King, Dixie Skillet, Red Lobster, **lodging:** Cross Country Inn, Hampton Inn, Hometown Inn, Travel Inn, **other:** to Sterling SP, **W...gas:** Pilot/Subway/diesel/24hr/@, TA/BP/Popeye's/Quizno's/Pizza Hut/diesel/24hr/@, **food:** Beef Jerky Outlet, Big Boy, Cracker Barrel, Denny's, McDonald's, Wendy's, **lodging:** Holiday Inn Express, Knight's Inn, **other:** HOSPITAL, to Viet Vet Mem

14 Elm Ave, to Monroe, no facilities

13 Front St, Monroe, no facilities

11 La Plaisance Rd, to Bolles Harbor, **W...gas:** Amoco, Marathon/Taco Bell/diesel, Speedway, **food:** Burger King, McDonald's, Wendy's, **lodging:** AmeriHost, Comfort Inn, Harbor Town RV Resort, **other:** Outlet Mall/famous brands, st police

Interstate 75

N ↕ S

10mm **Welcome Ctr nb, full(handicapped)facilities, phone, info, picnic tables, litter barrels, vending, petwalk**
9 S Otter Creek Rd, to La Salle, **W...**antiques
7mm weigh sta both lanes
6 Luna Pier, **E...gas:** Sunoco/Blimpie/McDonald's/diesel, **food:** Ganders Rest., Super 8
5 to Erie, Temperance, no facilities
2 Summit St, no facilities
0mm Michigan/Ohio state line

Interstate 94

E ↕ W

Port Huron

Exit #	Services
275mm	I-69/I-94 begin/end on MI 25, **Pinegrove Ave in Port Huron...gas:** BP/24hr, Clark, Marathon, Shell/24hr, Speedway, **food:** Little Caesar's, McDonald's, Tim Horton, Wendy's, White Castle, **lodging:** Best Western, Day's Inn, Holiday Inn Express, **other:** Can-Am DutyFree, Family$, Honda, Rite Aid, tollbridge to Canada
274.5mm	Black River
274	Water St, Port Huron, **N...Welcome Ctr/rest area wb, full facilities, food:** Cracker Barrel, **lodging:** Ramada Inn, **S...gas:** Bylo/diesel, Speedway/Taco Bell/diesel, **food:** Bob Evans, **lodging:** Comfort Inn, Fairfield Inn, Hampton Inn, Knight's Inn, **other:** Lake Port SP, RV camping
271	I-69 E and I-94 E run together eb, **E...**Lp I-69, to Port Huron
269	Dove St, Range Rd, **N...gas:** Speedway/diesel/24hr, **food:** Burger King, **lodging:** AmeriHost
266	Gratiot Rd, Marysville, **S...gas:** BP/diesel/24hr, **food:** Burger King, **1 mi S...gas:** Rich, Shell/24hr, **food:** Big Boy, 4Star Rest., KFC, Little Caesar's, McDonald's, Pelican Café, Pizza Hut, Taco Bell, **lodging:** Days Inn, Microtel, Super 8, **other:** HOSPITAL, AutoZone, Carter's Foods, CVS Drug, Goodyear, Rite Aid
262	Wadhams Rd, **N...**camping, **S...gas:** Marathon/diesel/showers/24hr
257	St Clair, Richmond, **S...gas:** BP/diesel, **other:** st police
255mm	**rest area eb, full(handicapped)facilities, phones, info, picnic tables, litter barrels, petwalk**
251mm	**rest area wb, full(handicapped)facilities, phones, info, picnic tables, litter barrels, petwalk**
248	26 Mile Rd, to Marine City, **N...gas:** BP/Amoco, **food:** McDonald's, **other:** Macomb Correctional, golf, **S...gas:** Citgo/7-11, Mobil, SpeedyQ/diesel
247mm	Salt River
247	MI 19(from eb), New Haven, no facilities
243	MI 29, MI 3, Utica, New Baltimore, **N...gas:** Marathon, Meijer/diesel/24hr, Shell/Subway/diesel, Sunoco/diesel, **food:** Applebee's, Arby's, Burger King, Gus Coney Island, McDonald's, Outback Steaks, Papa Romano's Pizza, Ruby Tuesday, Steak'n Shake, Texas Roadhouse, Town&Country Rest., Wendy's, White Castle/Church's/24hr, **lodging:** Chesterfield Motel, **other:** Belle Tire, GNC, Home Depot, K-Mart, Lowe's Whse, Michael's, NTB, Radio Shack, Staples, Target, Walgreen, **S...gas:** Marathon/diesel/24hr, Pilot/Subway/diesel/24hr/@, **food:** Big Boy, Hot'n Now, Taco Bell, LodgeKeeper, **other:** Chevrolet

Detroit Area

Exit #	Services
241	21 Mile Rd, Selfridge, **N...gas:** Marathon/diesel, **food:** China King, Hungry Howie's, Quizno's, Subway, **other:** Advance Parts, CVS Drug, same as 240
240	to MI 59, **N...gas:** BP/Amoco, Citgo/7-11, Marathon, Speedway, **food:** Arby's, McDonald's, Tim Horton, **lodging:** Best Western, **other:** Ford, Wal-Mart/auto
237	N River Rd, Mt Clemens, **N...gas:** BP/diesel, Mobil/Subway/diesel, **food:** Damon's Grill, McDonald's, **lodging:** Comfort Inn, **other:** General RV Ctr, Gibralter Trade Ctr
236.5mm	Clinton River
236	Metro Parkway, **S...food:** McDonald's
235	Shook Rd(from wb), no facilities
234b a	Harper Rd, 15 Mile Rd, **N...gas:** Amoco/McDonald's, Citgo, Marathon, SpeedyQ, Sunoco/diesel/24hr, **food:** China Moon, Sorrento Pizza, Subway, **S...gas:** Mobil, **food:** China Moon, Little Caesar's, Subway
232	Little Mack Ave, **N...gas:** Sunoco, **food:** Bob Evans, **lodging:** Comfort Inn, Econolodge, Holiday Inn Express, Microtel, Red Roof Inn, Super 8, **S...gas:** BP/24hr, Meijer/diesel/24hr, Speedway/diesel, **food:** Cracker Barrel, IHOP, **lodging:** Baymont Inn, **other:** Circuit City, Home Depot, Jo-Ann Fabrics, K-Mart, same as 231
231	(from eb), MI 3, Gratiot Ave, **N...gas:** Shell, Speedway, Sunoco, **food:** Big Boy, Boston Mkt, Burger King, BBQ, ChuckeCheese, Denny's, McDonald's, Mtn Jack's Rest., Pizza Hut, **lodging:** Day's Inn, Georgian Inn, Knight's Inn, Red Roof Inn, Super 8, **other:** Discount Tire, Firestone/auto, Nissan, Sam's Club, Sears/auto, Target, Toyota, U-Haul, mall

MICHIGAN

Interstate 94

E ↕ W

Detroit Area

230 12 Mile Rd, **N...gas:** Citgo/7-11, Marathon/diesel, **food:** Burger King, Outback Steaks, **other:** CVS Drug, Hyundai, Lincoln/Mercury, Marshall's, Wal-Mart, mall, **S...gas:** Marathon

229 I-696 W, Reuther Fwy, to 11 Mile Rd, **N...gas:** BP, **S... gas:** BP/dieselmart, Speedway

228 10 Mile Rd, **N...gas:** BP/24hr, Shell, **food:** Eastwind Chinese, Jet's Pizza, **other:** CVS Drug

227 9 Mile Rd, **N...gas:** Mobil, Speedway/diesel, Sunoco, **food:** McDonald's, Papa John's, Taco Bell, Wendy's, **other:** CVS Drug, Farmer Jack's, FM Drugs, Office Depot, **S...gas:** Mobil, **other:** Cadillac

225 MI 102, Vernier Rd, 8 Mile Rd, **S...food:** KFC, Wendy's, **other:** Kroger

224b Allard Ave, Eastwood Ave, no facilities

a Moross Rd, **S...gas:** Shell, **other:** Farmer Jack's

223 Cadieux Rd, **S...gas:** BP/Subway, Mobil, Shell, Sunoco, **food:** McDonald's, Taco Bell, Tubby's Subs, Wendy's

222b Harper Ave(from eb), **S...food:** Taco Bell

a Chalmers Ave, Outer Dr, **N...gas:** BP/Subway/diesel, Clark, Marathon, **food:** Coney Island, KFC, White Castle

220b Conner Ave, **N...gas:** BP, KwikFill/gas, **lodging:** Travel Inn

a French Rd, no facilities

219 MI 3, Gratiot Ave, **N...gas:** Citgo, Marathon/Subway, **food:** KFC, McDonald's, **other:** Family$, **S...gas:** BP/diesel

218 MI 53, Van Dyke Ave, **N...gas:** BP

217b Mt Elliott Ave, **S...gas:** Mobil, **food:** BBQ, KFC

a E Grand Blvd, Chene St, no facilities

216b Russell St(from eb), to downtown

a I-75, Chrysler Fwy, to tunnel to Canada

215c MI 1, Woodward Ave, John R St, no facilities

b MI 10 N, Lodge Fwy

a MI 10 S, downtown, tunnel to Canada

214b Trumbull Ave, to Ford Hospital

a (from wb)Grand River Ave, **N...gas:** Citgo

213b I-96 W to Lansing, E to Canada, bridge to Canada, to Tiger Stadium

a W Grand(exits left from eb), no facilities

212b Warren Ave(from eb), no facilities

a Livernois Ave, **S...gas:** Marathon/Subway/diesel

211b Cecil Ave(from wb), Central Ave, no facilities

a Lonyo Rd, **S...**Ford

210 US 12, Michigan Ave, Wyoming Ave, **N...gas:** Mobil/Pizza Hut, **S...gas:** BP/diesel, Citgo/diesel, **food:** YumYum Donuts

209 Rotunda Dr(from wb), no facilities

208 Greenfield Rd, Schaefer Rd, **N...gas:** Mobil, 7-11, **S...**River Rouge Ford Plant

207mm Rouge River

206 Oakwood Blvd, Melvindale, **N...gas:** Marathon, **food:** Oakwood Grill, **other:** Ford Plant, UPS, to Greenfield Village, **S...gas:** BP, Mobil, 7-11, **food:** Burger King, Domino's, Little Caesar's, O Henry's, Pizza Hut, Subway, YumYum Donuts, **lodging:** Best Western, Holiday Inn Express, **other:** Belle Tire, Smirnoff Distillery

205mm Largest Uniroyal Tire in the World

204b a MI 39, Southfield Fwy, Pelham Rd, **N...gas:** Marathon, Mobil, 7-11, **food:** Mancino's Pizza, Ponderosa, **other:** to Greenfield Village, **S...gas:** Mobil, BP, **1/2 mi S on Ecorse Rd...gas:** 7-11, **food:** Burger King, Dunkin Donuts, McDonald's

202b a US 24, Telegraph Rd, **N...gas:** Clark, Shell, **food:** Andoni's Rest., Burger King, KFC, Krispy Kreme, McDonald's, Pizza Hut, Taco Bell, Rally's, Ram's Horn Rest., Subway, Wendy's, **lodging:** Casa Bianca Motel, **other:** Rite Aid, **S...gas:** Marathon/diesel, **lodging:** Nu Haven Motel, **1/2 mi S...gas:** Amoco, Citgo, Mobil, Shell, **food:** Burger King, Hungry Howie's, Marina's Pizza/subs, Old Country Buffet, Pizza Hut, Red Lobster, Super China, YumYum Donuts, **lodging:** Quality Inn, **other:** CVS Drug, Radio Shack, U-Haul, Wal-Mart

200 Ecorse Rd,(no ez eb return), to Taylor, **N...gas:** Marathon/diesel, **food:** Granny's Rest., **S...gas:** BP/diesel, Speedway

199 Middle Belt Rd, **S...gas:** Amoco/diesel/24hr, **food:** Denny's, McDonald's, Wendy's, **lodging:** Day's Inn, Howard Johnson, Super 8

198 Merriman Rd, **N...food:** Bob Evans, **lodging:** Baymont Inn, Best Western, Clarion, Comfort Inn, Courtyard, Crowne Plaza Hotel, Doubletree Inn, Econolodge, Extended Stay America, Fairfield Inn, Hampton Inn, Hilton, Holiday Inn, Howard Johnson, Marriott, Motel 6, PearTree Inn, Sheraton, **S...**Wayne Co Airport

197 Vining Rd, no facilities

196 Wayne Rd, Romulus, **N...gas:** Shell, **food:** McDonald's, **S...gas:** Mobil/diesel, Speedway, **food:** Burger King

194b a I-275, N to Flint, S to Toledo

192 Haggerty Rd, **N...gas:** BP, Mobil/24hr, **food:** Burger King(2mi), Subway, **S...**Lower Huron Metro Park

190 Belleville Rd, to Belleville, **N...gas:** Meijer/diesel/24hr, Amoco/24hr, Marathon, **food:** Applebee's, Arby's, Big Boy, Cracker Barrel, McDonald's, Taco Bell, Wendy's, **lodging:** Hampton Inn, Holiday Inn Express, Red Roof Inn, **other:** Camping World RV Service/supplies, CVS Drug, $Tree, Farmer Jack's, Firestone/auto, Ford, Michal's RV Ctr, U-Haul, Wal-Mart, **S...gas:** Shell, **food:** Burger King, China King, Dimitri's Kitchen, Domino's, Subway, TCBY, **lodging:** Comfort Inn, Super 8, **other:** USPO

MICHIGAN

Interstate 94

E ↕ W

187 Rawsonville Rd, **S...gas:** Mobil/diesel, Speedway/diesel, **food:** Burger King, Denny's, Hardee's, KFC, Little Caesar's, LoneStar Steaks, McDonald's, Pizza Hut, Subway, Tim Horton, Wendy's, **other:** $Tree, GNC, K-Mart, Radio Shack, Rite Aid

185 US 12, Michigan Ave(from eb, exits left, no return), to frontage rds, airport, no facilities

184mm Ford Lake

183 US 12, Huron St, Ypsilanti, **N...gas:** Marathon/diesel, **other:** to E MI U, **S...food:** McDonald's, **lodging:** Marriott, **other:** HOSPITAL, Chevrolet/Pontiac/Buick/GMC, st police

181b a US 12 W, Michigan Ave, Ypsilanti, **N...gas:** Meijer/diesel/24hr, Rich, Speedway, 7-11, **food:** Burger King, Taco Bell, **other:** HOSPITAL, Aamco, Busch's Food/24hr, Firestone, Jo-Ann Fabrics, Wal-Mart, **S...gas:** Shell, **food:** Chessy's Grill, McDonald's, Subway

180b a US 23, to Toledo, Flint, no facilities

Ann Arbor

177 State St, **N...gas:** Amoco/24hr, Mobil, Shell, **food:** Azteca Mexican, Bennigan's, Burger King, Calif Pizza, Graham's Steaks, Macaroni Grill, Max&Erma's, Olive Garden, **lodging:** Best Western, Crowne Plaza Hotel, Comfort Inn, Courtyard, Fairfield Inn, Hampton Inn, Hilton, Holiday Inn Express, Red Roof Inn, Sheraton, Wolverine Inn, **other:** Firestone, JC Penney, Marshall Fields, Mitsubishi, Sears/auto, VW, World Mkt, mall, to UMI, **S...gas:** Clark/diesel, **food:** ChiChi's, Coney Island, McDonald's, Pizza Hut/Taco Bell, **lodging:** Motel 6, **other:** U-Haul

175 Ann Arbor-Saline Rd, **N...gas:** Shell, **food:** Applebee's, Old Country Buffet, Subway, **lodging:** Candlewood Suites, **other:** Mervyn's, Office Depot, mall, to UMI Stadium, **S...gas:** Meijer/diesel/24hr, **food:** Big Boy, Joe's Crabshack, McDonald's, Outback Steaks, TGIFriday, **other:** Best Buy, CompUSA, Jo-Ann Fabrics, Kohl's, OfficeMax, Target

172 Jackson Ave, to Ann Arbor, **N...gas:** Amoco, BP, Marathon, Shell, **food:** KFC, Schlotsky's, **other:** HOSPITAL, K-Mart, Kroger, Rite Aid, mall, **S...gas:** Sunoco/diesel, **food:** Weber's Rest., **lodging:** Best Western, **other:** Chevrolet/Pontiac/Cadillac, Ford

171 MI 14(from eb, exits left), to Ann Arbor, to Flint by US 23, no facilities

169 Zeeb Rd, **N...gas:** BP/24hr, **food:** Baxter's Deli, McDonald's, **S...gas:** Mobil, **food:** Arby's, Burger King, PB's Rest., Pizza Hut, Taco Bell, Wendy's

168mm rest area eb, full(handicapped)facilities, info, phone, picnic tables, litter barrels, vending, petwalk

167 Baker Rd, Dexter, **N...gas:** Pilot/Subway/diesel/24hr/@, **S...gas:** Pilot/Arby's/diesel/24hr/@, TA/BP/diesel/rest./24hr/@, **food:** McDonald's, **other:** Blue Beacon

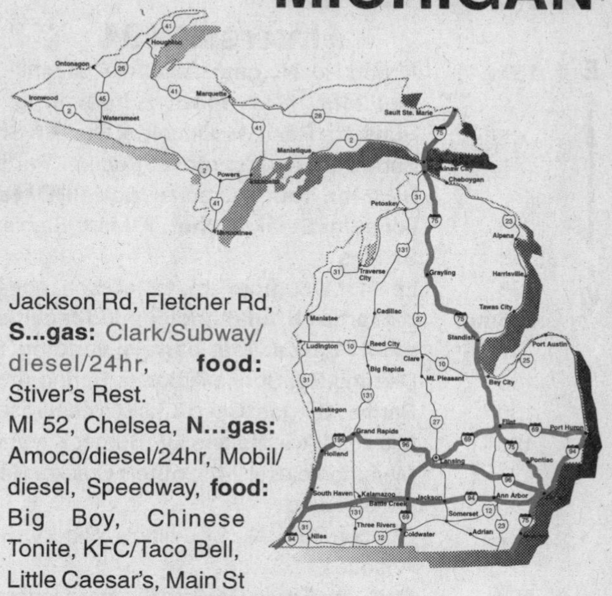

Jackson

162 Jackson Rd, Fletcher Rd, **S...gas:** Clark/Subway/diesel/24hr, **food:** Stiver's Rest.

159 MI 52, Chelsea, **N...gas:** Amoco/diesel/24hr, Mobil/diesel, Speedway, **food:** Big Boy, Chinese Tonite, KFC/Taco Bell, Little Caesar's, Main St Coney Island, McDonald's, Prego's Italian, Subway, Wendy's, **lodging:** Comfort Inn, Holiday Inn Express, **other:** HOSPITAL, Bridges RV Ctr, Chevrolet/Buick, Chrysler/Plymouth/Dodge/Jeep, CVS Drug, Farmer Jack's, Ford, Pamida

157 Jackson Rd, Pierce Rd, **N...**Gerald Eddy Geology Ctr

156 Kalmbach Rd, **N...**to Waterloo RA

153 Clear Lake Rd, **N...gas:** Marathon/diesel

151.5mm weigh sta both lanes

150 to Grass Lake, **S...gas:** Phillips 66/Subway, **other:** RV camping

150mm rest area wb, full(handicapped)facilities, phone, picnic tables, litter barrels, vending, petwalk

147 Race Rd, **N...**to Waterloo RA, camping, **S...**lodging

145 Sargent Rd, **S...gas:** BP/White Castle/diesel, Mobil/diesel/rest./24hr, **food:** McDonald's, Wendy's, Zig's Kettle/brewery, **lodging:** Colonial Inn, **other:** RV camping

144 Lp 94(from wb), to Jackson, same as 145

142 US 127 S, to Hudson, **3 mi S...gas:** Meijer/diesel/24hr, Speedway, **food:** Domino's, McDonald's, Wendy's, **other:** Advance Parts, Kroger, Parts+, Rite Aid

141 Elm Rd, **N...lodging:** Travelodge, **other:** Chevrolet/Dodge/Honda/Hyundai, **S...**HOSPITAL

139 MI 106, Cooper St, to Jackson, **N...**st police/prison, **S...gas:** Citgo/Subway, **other:** HOSPITAL

138 US 127 N, MI 50, Jackson, to Lansing, **N...food:** Gilbert's Steaks, Red Lobster, Yen Kang Chinese, **lodging:** Baymont Inn, Comfort Inn, Fairfield Inn, Hampton Inn, Holiday Inn, Super 8, **S...gas:** Admiral, Marathon, Shell/24hr, **food:** Big Boy, Bob Evans, Fazoli's, Ground Round, LJ Silver, Old Country Buffet, Outback Steaks, Pizza Hut, **lodging:** Country Hearth Inn, Motel 6, **other:** Best Buy, Circuit City, Kohl's, Lowe's Whse, Michael's, OfficeMax, Sears/auto, Target

MICHIGAN

Interstate 94

E ↕ W

137 Airport Rd, **N...gas:** Meijer/diesel/24hr, Shell/Taco Bell/24hr, 7-11, **food:** Burger King, Denny's, Hudson's Rest., McDonald's, Steak'n Shake/24hr, Subway, Wendy's, **other:** Bumper Parts, **S...gas:** BP/24hr, **food:** Cracker Barrel, Olive Garden, LoneStar Steaks, **other:** K-Mart, Sam's Club/gas, Staples

136 Lp 94, MI 60(from eb), to Jackson, no facilities

135mm rest area eb, full(handicapped)facilities, phone, picnic tables, litter barrels, vending, petwalk

133 Dearing Rd, Spring Arbor, to Spring Arbor Coll

130 Parma, **S...gas:** Citgo/Trkstp/diesel/rest./24hr/@

128 Michigan Ave, **N...gas:** BP/Burger King/diesel/24hr, Marathon/diesel/24hr, **other:** Cracker Hill Antiques, RV camping

127 Concord Rd, **N...**St Julian's Winery, **S...**Harley's Antiques

124 MI 99, to Eaton Rapids, **S...**food, lodging

121 28 Mile Rd, to Albion, **N...gas:** Mobil, **food:** Arby's, **lodging:** Day's Inn, **S...gas:** FS/diesel/24hr, Marathon, Speedway/diesel/24hr, **food:** Burger King, Fresh'n Fast Café, KFC, McDonald's, Paradise Oriental, Pizza Hut, **lodging:** Knight's Inn, **other:** HOSPITAL, AutoZone, Chevrolet/Pontiac/Buick, $General, Family$, Felpausch Foods, Ford/Mercury, Radio Shack, Tire City, RV camping

119 26 Mile Rd, no facilities

115 22.5 Mile Rd, **N...gas:** Citgo/diesel/rest./24hr

113mm rest area wb, full(handicapped)facilities, phone, picnic tables, litter barrels, vending, petwalk

Marshall

112 Partello Rd, **S...gas:** Sunoco/diesel/24hr, **food:** Schuler's Rest.

110 Old US 27, Marshall, **N...gas:** Shell/Subway/diesel/24hr, **food:** Country Kitchen/24hr, **S...gas:** Citgo/diesel, **food:** Denny's, KFC, **lodging:** Holiday Inn Express, **other:** HOSPITAL, sheriff

108 I-69, US 27, N to Lansing, S to Ft Wayne, no facilities

104 11 Mile Rd, Michigan Ave, **N...gas:** Pilot/Taco Bell/diesel/24hr/@, Sunoco/Te-Khi Trkstp/rest./24hr/@, **S...gas:** Citgo/Subway/diesel/24hr, **lodging:** Quality Inn/rest.

103 Lp 94(from wb, no return), to Battle Creek, **N...**HOSPITAL, same as 104

102mm Kalamazoo River

100 Beadle Lake Rd, **N...food:** Moonraker Rest., **S...gas:** Citgo/diesel, **other:** Binder Park Zoo

98b I-194 N, to Battle Creek, no facilities

a MI 66, to Sturgis, **S...gas:** Citgo/Blimpie/diesel, Meijer/diesel/24hr, **food:** Chili's, Schlotsky's, Steak'n Shake, **other:** Kohl's, Lowe's Whse, Michael's, Sam's Club, Staples, Wal-Mart/auto, same as 97

Kalamazoo

97 Capital Ave, to Battle Creek, **N...gas:** BP/24hr, Clark, **food:** Arby's, Lakeview Rest., LoneStar Steaks, McDonald's, Red Lobster, **lodging:** Comfort Inn, Knight's Inn, **S...gas:** Citgo, Shell/24hr, Sunoco/Subway/24hr, **food:** Applebee's, Bob Evans, Burger King, Canton Buffet, Cracker Barrel, Denny's, Don Pablo, Fazoli's, NY Burrito, Old Country Buffet, Pizza Hut, Steak'n Shake, Taco Bell, Wendy's, **lodging:** Appletree Inn, Battle Creek Inn, Baymont Inn, Day's Inn, Fairfield Inn, Hampton Inn, Motel 6, Super 8, **other:** Borders Books, Firestone/auto, Goodyear/auto, Harley-Davidson, JC Penney, K-Mart, Marshall Fields, Sears/auto, Target, mall

96mm rest area eb, full(handicapped)facilities, phone, picnic tables, litter barrels, vending, petwalk

95 Helmer Rd, **N...gas:** Citgo/diesel, **other:** st police, **2 mi N...gas:** Meijer/diesel/24hr

92 Lp 94, to Battle Creek, Springfield, **N...gas:** Citgo/Arlene's Trkstp/diesel/rest./24hr/@, Shell/24hr, **other:** RV camping, to Ft Custer RA

88 Climax, **N...**Galesburg Speedway

85 35th St, Galesburg, **N...gas:** Shell/Burger King/diesel/24hr, **food:** McDonald's, **other:** Galesburg Speedway, to Ft Custer RA, **S...other:** Winery Tours, RV camping

85mm rest area wb, full(handicapped)facilities, phone, picnic tables, litter barrels, vending, petwalk

81 Lp 94(from wb), to Kalamazoo, no facilities

80 Cork St, Sprinkle Rd, to Kalamazoo, **N...gas:** Citgo/diesel, Double Xpress, Speedway, **food:** Arby's, Burger King, Chicken Coop, Denny's, Godfather's, Hot'n Now, Perkins, Taco Bell, **lodging:** Best Western, Clarion Hotel, Fairfield Inn, Holiday Inn Express, Red Roof Inn, **S...gas:** BP/diesel/24hr, Speedway/diesel, **food:** Derk's Rest., Holly's Landing Rest., McDonald's, Subway/24hr, **lodging:** Day's Inn, Motel 6, Quality Inn

78 Portage Rd, Kilgore Rd, **N...gas:** Citgo, **food:** Hungry Howie's, Subway, Uncle Ernie's Pancakes, **lodging:** Hampton Inn, **other:** HOSPITAL, **S...gas:** Marathon, Shell/24hr, **food:** Angelo's Italian, Callahan's Rest., Gum Ho Chinese, McDonald's, Taco Bell, Theo&Stacy's Rest., **lodging:** Country Inn Suites, **other:** AutoValue Parts, museum

76b a Westnedge Ave, **N...gas:** Meijer/diesel/24hr, Speedway/diesel, SuperDuper, **food:** Arby's, Bennigan's, Big Boy, Hong Kong Buffet, Hooters, Mancino's Eatery, Outback Steaks, Papa John's, Pappy's Mexican, Peter Piper Pizza, Pizza Hut, Quizno's, Steak'n Shake, Subway, Taco Bell, **lodging:** Quality Inn, **other:** Discount Tire, Goodyear/auto, Lowe's Whse, Office Depot, Rite Aid, **S...gas:** Shell/24hr, **food:** Applebee's, Burger King, Chili's, ChuckeCheese, Empire Chinese, Fazoli's, Finley's Rest., KFC, Little Caesar's, LJ Silver, Mtn Jack's

Interstate 94

E ↕ W

Rest., McDonald's, Old Country Buffet, Olive Garden, Peking Palace, Pizza Hut, Qdoba Mexican, Red Lobster, Schlotsky's, Subway, Taco Bell, Wendy's, **lodging:** Holiday Motel, **other:** Barnes&Noble, Best Buy, Cadillac/Pontiac/Nissan, Circuit City, Fannie Mae Candies, Firestone/auto, Home Depot, JC Penney, Jo-Ann Fabrics, K-Mart, Kohl's, MktPlace Foods, Marshall Fields, Mervyn's, Michael's, OfficeMax, Old Navy, PepBoys, Radio Shack, Sears/auto, Target, Walgreen, WorldMkt, mall

75 Oakland Dr, no facilities

74b a US 131, to Kalamazoo, **N...**to W MI U, Kalamazoo Coll

72 Oshtemo, **N...gas:** Citgo/diesel, Speedway/diesel, **food:** Burger King, Culver's, McDonald's, Taco Bell, Wendy's, **lodging:** Hampton Inn, Saturn, **S...food:** Cracker Barrel, **lodging:** Fairfield Inn

66 Mattawan, **N...gas:** Speedway/Subway/diesel/24hr, **food:** Mancino's Italian, **other:** Rossman Auto/towing, **S...gas:** Shell

60 MI 40, Paw Paw, **N...gas:** BP/24hr, Speedway/diesel/24hr, **food:** Arby's, Big Boy, Burger King, Chicken Coop, McDonald's, Pizza Hut, Subway/TCBY, Taco Bell, Wendy's, **lodging:** Deerfield Inn, Quality Inn, **other:** HOSPITAL, Chrysler/Dodge/Jeep, Felpausch Foods, St Julian Winery, Warner Winery

56 MI 51, to Decatur, **N...**st police, **S...gas:** Citgo/diesel, Marathon/diesel/24hr

52 Lawrence, **N...**gas(1mi), **food:** Waffle House of America

46 Hartford, **N...gas:** Shell/diesel/24hr, **food:** McDonald's, Panel Room Rest.

42mm rest area wb, full(handicapped)facilities, phone, picnic tables, litter barrels, vending, petwalk

41 MI 140, Watervliet, to Niles, **N...gas:** BP/24hr, Citgo, **food:** Burger King, Chicken Coop, Taco Bell, Waffle House, **other:** HOSPITAL

39 Millburg, Coloma, Deer Forest, **N...gas:** Marathon/diesel, Speedway, **food:** McDonald's, **other:** RV Ctr, **1 mi N...gas:** BP/diesel, Westco/diesel, **food:** Pizza Hut, Subway

36mm rest area eb, full(handicapped)facilities, phone, picnic tables, litter barrels, vending, petwalk

34 I-196 N, US 31 N, to Holland, Grand Rapids, no facilities

33 Lp I-94, to Benton Harbor, **2-4 mi N...**airport, sheriff's dept

30 Napier Ave, Benton Harbor, **N...gas:** Flying J/Wendy's/diesel/24hr/@, Shell/24hr, **lodging:** Super 8, **other:** HOSPITAL, Blue Beacon, **S...gas:** Chrysler/Dodge/Honda

Benton Harbor

29 Pipestone Rd, Benton Harbor, **N...gas:** Meijer/diesel/24hr, Speedway/diesel, **food:** Applebee's, Big Boy, Burger King, Denny's, Hacienda Mexican, Hardee's, IHOP, McDonald's, Pizza Hut, Red Lobster, Steak'n Shake, Subway, Texas Corral, **lodging:** Best Western, Courtyard, Motel 6, Red Roof Inn, **other:** MEDICAL CARE, Aldi Foods, Best Buy, $Tree, Ford/Lincoln/Mercury, Goodyear/auto, Home Depot, JC Penney, Jo-Ann Fabrics, Lowe's Whse, OfficeMax, Radio Shack, Sears, Staples, Walgreen, Wal-Mart SuperCtr/24hr, **S...gas:** Citgo/Blimpie/Taco Bell/diesel/24hr, **food:** Bob Evans, **lodging:** Comfort Suites, Holiday Inn Express

28 US 31 S, MI 139 N, to Niles, **N...gas:** Citgo/diesel, Speedway/diesel, **food:** Arby's, Burger King, Capozio's Pizza, Chicken Coop, Country Kitchen, DQ, Henry's Burgers, KFC, Little Caesar's, Pizza Hut, Subway, U-Buffet, Wendy's, **lodging:** Day's Inn/rest., Ramada Inn/rest., **other:** HOSPITAL, AutoZone, Chevrolet, $Tree, Firestone, M&W Tire, OfficeDepot, Old Navy, Rite Aid, Target, st police, **S...gas:** Marathon, **lodging:** Howard Johnson

27mm St Joseph River

27 MI 63, Niles Ave, to St Joseph, **N...gas:** Amoco/24hr, **food:** Nye's Apple Barn, **S...**Goodyear

23 Red Arrow Hwy, Stevensville, **N...gas:** Admiral, Amoco/TacoBell, Marathon/diesel, Mobil, Shell/diesel/24hr, **food:** Big Boy, Burger King, Cracker Barrel, DQ, Fireside Inn Rest., LJ Silver, McDonald's, Papa John's, Popeye's, Subway, **lodging:** Baymont Inn, Park Inn, Ray's Motel, Villager Lodge, **other:** Walgreen, **S...food:** Schuler's Rest., **lodging:** Hampton Inn

22 John Beers Rd, Stevensville, **N...**to Grand Mere SP, **S...gas:** Marathon/diesel

16 Bridgman, **N...gas:** Amoco/A&W/diesel/24hr, **other:** to Warren Dunes SP, **S...gas:** Speedway/diesel/24hr, **food:** McDonald's, Pizza Hut, Subway, **1/2 mi S...food:** Brian's Cove Rest., Chicken Coop Rest., Olympus Rest., Roma Pizza, **other:** Chevrolet/Buick

MICHIGAN

Interstate 94

E ↕ W

12 Sawyer, **N...gas:** Citgo/diesel/rest./24hr, **S...gas:** TA/BurgerKing/Popeye's/Taco Bell/diesel/24hr/@, **lodging:** Super 8, **other:** USPO

6 Lakeside, Union Pier, **N...other:** St Julian's Winery, antiques, **S...**RV camping

4b a US 12, New Buffalo, to Three Oaks, **N...food:** Pizza Hut, st police

2.5mm weigh sta both lanes

1 MI 239, New Buffalo, to Grand Beach, **N...gas:** Shell, **lodging:** Best Western, Edgewood Motel, Holiday Inn Express, **S...gas:** New Buffalo/diesel/24hr, **food:** Arby's, Wendy's, **lodging:** Comfort Inn

.5mm Welcome Ctr eb, full(handicapped)facilities, info, phone, picnic tables, litter barrels, vending, petwalk

0mm Michigan/Indiana state line

Interstate 96

E ↕ W

Exit # Services

I-96 begins/ends on I-75, exit 48 in Detroit.

191 I-75, N to Flint, S to Toledo, US 12, to MLK Blvd, to Michigan Ave, no facilities

190b Warren Ave, **N...gas:** Citgo, **S...gas:** Marathon

a I-94 E to Port Huron

189 W Grand Blvd, Tireman Rd, **N...gas:** BP

188b Joy Rd, **N...food:** Church's

a Livernois, **N...gas:** Mobil, Shell, **food:** Burger King, KFC, McDonald's, **other:** Wendy's

187 Grand River Ave(from eb), no facilities

Detroit Area

186b Davison Ave, I-96 local and I-96 express divide, no exits from express

a (from eb), Wyoming Ave

185 Schaefer Hwy, to Grand River Ave, **N...gas:** BP/24hr, Mobil, **food:** Coney Island, McDonald's, **other:** CVS Drug, **S...gas:** Sunoco

184 Greenfield Rd, no facilities

183 MI 39, Southfield Fwy, exit from expswy and local, no facilities

182 Evergreen Rd, no facilities

180 Outer Dr, **N...gas:** BP/diesel/lube

180mm I-96 local/express unite/divide

179 US 24, Telegraph Rd, **N...food:** Grand Buffet Chinese, Taco Bell, White Castle/Church's, **other:** Chevrolet, Family$, Goodyear, **S...gas:** BP, Marathon/diesel

178 Beech Daly Rd, **N...gas:** Sunoco

177 Inkster Rd, **N...food:** Panda Chinese, Subway, **lodging:** Super 8, **other:** Hancock Fabrics

176 Middlebelt Rd, **N...food:** Bob Evans, ChiChi's, IHOP, Olive Garden, **lodging:** Comfort Inn, Super 8, **other:** MEDICAL CARE, **S...gas:** Meijer/diesel/24hr, **food:** Boss Hog's BBQ, Logan's Roadhouse, **other:** Costco/gas, Home Depot, Marshall's, Wal-Mart

175 Merriman Rd, **N...gas:** Mobil, Speedway/diesel, **other:** CHIROPRACTOR, **S...gas:** Sunoco, **food:** Blimpie

174 Farmington Rd, **N...gas:** Mobil/diesel, Sunoco, **food:** Looney Bakery, **S...gas:** BP/Amoco, **food:** KFC, **other:** bank

173b Levan Rd, **N...**HOSPITAL, to Madonna U

a Newburgh Rd, no facilities

171mm I-275 and I-96 run together 9 miles

170 6 Mile Rd, **N...food:** Andrea's Ristorante, Ground Round, Max&Erma's, **lodging:** Best Western, Courtyard, Holiday Inn, Marriott, **other:** mall, **S...gas:** BP, Mobil, **food:** Applebee's, Buca Italian, Charlie's Grille, Papa Vino's, **lodging:** Fairfield Inn, Residence Inn, TownePlace Suites, **other:** Barnes&Noble, CVS Drug, Office Depot

169b a 7 Mile Rd, **N...food:** Rio Bravo, LoneStar Steaks, **lodging:** Embassy Suites, **S...food:** Alexander's Rest., Bahama Breeze Rest., Bonfire Bistro, Champp's Rest., Cooker Rest., Del Rio Cantina, Macaroni Grill, **lodging:** AmeriSuites, **other:** Home Depot

167 8 Mile Rd, to Northville, **S...gas:** Meijer/diesel/24hr, Speedway, **food:** Benihana, Big Boy, Chili's, McDonald's, Kyoto Steaks, On-the-Border, Taco Bell, **lodging:** Hampton Inn, Hilton, Ramada Ltd, **other:** Best Buy, Costco/gas, Firestone, Home Depot, Kohl's, OfficeMax, Target, to Maybury SP

165 I-696, I-275, MI 5, Grand River Ave, **I-275 and I-96 run together 9 miles**

163 I-696(from eb), no facilities

162 Novi Rd, Novi, to Walled Lake, **N...gas:** BP, **food:** ChuckeCheese, McDonald's, Oaks Grill, Pizza Hut, Red Lobster, Subway, TooChez Rest, **lodging:** DoubleTree Hotel, Sheraton, **other:** HOSPITAL, Circuit City, Galyan's, JC Penney, Jo-Ann Fabrics, Kroger, Marshall's, OfficeMax, Sears/auto, WorldMkt, mall, **S...gas:** Mobil, **food:** Big Boy, Bob Evans, Boston Mkt, Grady's Rest., Kim's Chinese, Olive Garden, Red Robin, TGIFriday, Wendy's, **lodging:** Courtyard, Wyndham Garden, **other:** Borders Books, CompUSA, Mervyn's

161mm rest area eb, full(handicapped)facilities, phone, vending, picnic tables, litter barrels, petwalk

160 Beck Rd, 12 Mile Rd, **N...**HOSPITAL, **S...other:** Home Depot, Kroger, to Maybury SP

159 Wixom Rd, Walled Lake, **N...food:** Wendy's, **lodging:** Baymont Inn, **other:** to Proud Lake RA, **S...gas:** Meijer/diesel/24hr, Mobil, Shell, **food:** Arby's, Burger King, KFC, McDonald's, Taco Bell, Togo's/Baskin-Robbins/Dunkin Donuts, **other:** Lincoln/Mercury, RV Ctr

155 New Hudson, to Milford, **N...**Ford, to RV camping, **S...gas:** Mobil, **food:** Putters Rest.

153 Kent Lake Rd, **N...**Kensington Metropark, **S...gas:** Mobil

151 Kensington Rd, **N...**Kensington Metropark, **S...**Island Lake RA, food, lodging

150 Pleasant Valley Rd, **S...**phone

148b a US 23, N to Flint, S to Ann Arbor, no facilities

147 Spencer Rd, **N...gas:** Mobil, **other:** st police, **S...**to Brighton St RA

145 Grand River Ave, to Brighton, **N...gas:** BP, Shell/diesel, **food:** Arby's, Cracker Barrel, Outback Steaks, Pizza Hut, **lodging:** Courtyard, **other:** Cadillac/GMC, Ford/Mercury, **S...gas:** Clark/Subway/diesel, Meijer/diesel/24hr, **food:** Big Boy, Burger King, Chili's, DQ, KFC, Lil Chef, Little Caesar's, LoneStar Steaks, McDonald's, Red Robin,

Interstate 96

E
W

Taco Bell, Wendy's, **lodging:** Holiday Inn Express, **other:** AAA, Farmer Jack's, Home Depot, Honda, Jo-Ann Fabrics, K-Mart, Mazda, Radio Shack, Staples, Target, USPO, mall, to Brighton Ski Area

141 Lp 96(from wb, no EZ return), to Howell, **N...gas:** Shell, Sunoco/diesel, **food:** Applebee's, Bob Evans, Little Caesar's, McDonald's, Mesquite Jct, TW's Italian, **lodging:** Grandview Inn, **other:** Chevrolet, **S...gas:** Speedway, **food:** Arby's, Big Boy, Taco Bell, Wendy's

141mm rest area wb, full(handicapped)facilities, phone, vending, picnic tables, litter barrels, petwalk

137 D19, Howell, to Pinckney, **N...gas:** Mobil, Shell/diesel, Speedway, **lodging:** Kensington Inn, Ramada Inn, **other:** HOSPITAL, Goodyear, Parts+, **S...food:** Benny's Grill, Country Kitchen, **lodging:** Best Western, **other:** Howell Auto Repair

135mm rest area eb, full(handicapped)facilities, vending, phone, picnic tables, litter barrels, petwalk

133 MI 59, Highland Rd, **N...gas:** Sunoco/McDonald's/diesel/, **food:** Texas Taco, **lodging:** AmeriHost, **other:** Factory Shops/famous brands

129 Fowlerville Rd, Fowlerville, **N...gas:** BP/rest./24hr, Shell/diesel, Sunoco/diesel, **food:** Big Boy, Fowlerville Rest., McDonald's, Subway, Taco Bell, Wendy's, **lodging:** Best Western, **S...gas:** Mobil, **other:** Chysler/Dodge/Jeep, **other:** Ford

126mm weigh sta both lanes

122 MI 43, MI 52, Webberville, **N...gas:** Mobil/diesel/24hr, **food:** Angel's Café, McDonald's, **other:** MI Brewing Co

117 Williamston, to Dansville, **N...gas:** Marathon, **1 mi N...gas:** Admiral, Speedway, **food:** Blimpie, DQ, Red Cedar Grill, Westside Deli, **S...gas:** Sunoco/diesel

111mm rest area wb, full(handicapped)facilities, phone, picnic tables, litter barrels, vending, petwalk

Lansing

110 Okemos, Mason, **N...gas:** BP/24hr, Marathon, Sunoco, 7-11, **food:** Applebee's, Arby's, Big Boy, Burger King, Hook's Grill, Little Caesar's, McDonald's, Stillwater Grill, Subway, **lodging:** Comfort Inn, Fairfield Inn, Hampton Inn, Holiday Inn Express, **other:** to stadium

106b a I-496, US 127, Lansing, to Jackson

104 Lp 96, Cedar St, Lansing, to Holt, **N...gas:** Admiral, Meijer/diesel/24hr, Shell, Speedway, **food:** Arby's, Blimpie, Bob Evans, Church's, Cuby Jack's Rest., Denny's, Hooters, KFC, LJ Silver, Mr Taco, Pizza Hut, Texas Roadhouse, Wendy's, White Castle, **lodging:** Best Western, Day's Inn, Econolodge, Governors Inn, Holiday Inn, Regent Inn, Super 8, **other:** HOSPITAL, Aldi Foods, Belle Tire, Cadillac, Chevrolet, Chrysler/Jeep, Dodge, GMC, Harley-Davidson, Hyundai, Lexus, Lincoln/Mercury, Mitsubishi, NTB, OfficeMax, Saab, Sam's Club, Target, Toyota, **S...gas:** Speedway/24hr, **food:** Buffalo's SW Café, Burger King, China East Buffet, Flapjack's Rest., McDonald's, Ponderosa, Subway, **lodging:** Ramada Ltd, **other:** CarQuest, Family$, Kroger, Lowe's Whse, NAPA

101 MI 99, MLK Blvd, to Eaton Rapids, **1-3 mi N...gas:** Meijer/diesel/24hr, QD, **food:** Arby's, **S...gas:** Speedway/Subway/diesel/24hr, Sunoco/diesel, **food:** McDonald's, Wendy's

98b a Lansing Rd, to Lansing, **S...gas:** Citgo/diesel/rest./24hr, **food:** Windsor Mtn Grill

97 1-69, US 27 S, S to Ft Wayne, N to Lansing, no facilities

95 I-496, to Lansing

93b a MI 43, Lp 69, Saginaw Hwy, to Grand Ledge, **N...gas:** Meijer/diesel/24hr, Shell, Speedway/diesel, **food:** Burger King, Denny's, McDonald's, TGIFriday, **lodging:** Best Western, Fairfield Inn, Hampton Inn, Holiday Inn, Motel 6, Quality Suites, Red Roof Inn, Residence Inn, **other:** HOSPITAL, **1 mi N...food:** Carrabba's, Frank's Grill, Outback Steaks, **other:** Chrysler/Jeep, **S...gas:** BP/24hr, QD, Sunoco/McDonald's, **food:** Arby's, Bob Evans, Cracker Barrel, Subway, **other:** Discount Tire, GMC/Mazda, Lowe's Whse, Michael's, Wal-Mart/auto

92mm Grand River

91 I-69 N, US 27 N(from wb), to Flint

90 Grand River Ave, to airport

89 I-69 N, US 27 N(from eb), to Flint

87mm rest area eb, full(handicapped)facilities, phone, picnic tables, litter barrels, vending, petwalk

86 MI 100, Wright Rd, to Grand Ledge, **S...gas:** Mobil/McDonald's/diesel, Fleet/Subway/diesel/24hr/@

84 to Eagle, Westphalia, no facilities

79mm rest area wb, full(handicapped)facilities, info, phone, picnic tables, litter barrels, vending, petwalk

77 Lp 96, Grand River Ave, Portland, **N...gas:** BP/24hr, Marathon/diesel, Shell, Speedway/diesel, **food:** Arby's, Burger King, Little Caesar's, McDonald's, Oriental Star Chinese, Subway, **lodging:** Best Western, **other:** Family$, Rite Aid, Tom's Foods, **S...food:** Wendy's, **other:** Ford

76 Kent St, Portland, **N...gas:** Marathon/diesel(1mi), food

76mm Grand River

73 to Lyons-Muir, Grand River Ave, no facilities

69mm weigh sta both lanes

67 MI 66, to Ionia, Battle Creek, **N...gas:** Meijer/diesel/24hr(5mi), Pilot/Subway/diesel/24hr/@, **lodging:** AmeriHost, Midway Motel, Super 8, **other:** HOSPITAL, RV camping, st police

MICHIGAN

Interstate 96

E ↕ W

Grand Rapids

64 to Lake Odessa, Saranac, **N...**Ionia St RA, **S...**I-96 Speedway
63mm rest area eb, full(handicapped)facilities, phone, picnic tables, litter barrels, petwalk, vending
59 Clarksville, **N...**auto repair
52 MI 50, to Lowell, **N...**fairgrounds, **S...gas:** Marathon/Taco Bell/diesel(2mi), **other:** RV camping
46 rd 6, to rd 37, no facilities
46mm Thornapple River
45mm rest area wb, full(handicapped)facilities, info, phone, picnic tables, litter barrels, vending
43b a MI 11, 28th St, Cascade, **N...gas:** Marathon/diesel, Meijer/diesel/24hr, **food:** Big Boy, Boston Mkt, Brann's Steaks, Burger King, Panera Bread, Pizza Hut, Shanghai Garden, Subway, Sundance Grill, Wendy's, **lodging:** Baymont Inn, Country Inn Suites, Crowne Plaza Hotel, Days Inn, Lexington Suites, **other:** Wal-Mart, **S...gas:** BP, Citgo, Shell, Speedway, **food:** Applebee's, Arby's, Blimpie, Bob Evans, Burger King, Cheddar's, Chili's, Damon's, Denny's, Dunkin Donuts, Grand Rapids Brewery, Hoffman House Rest., HongKong Garden, Hooters, IHOP, McDonald's, Olive Garden, Outback Steaks, Papa Vino's Italian, Perkins, Pizza Hut, Red Lobster, Rio Bravo, Steak'n Shake, Subway, Wendy's, **lodging:** Comfort Inn, Courtyard, Exel Inn, Extended Stay America, Hampton Inn, Hilton, Knight's Inn, Motel 6, Quality Inn, Red Roof Inn, **other:** Barnes&Noble, CarQuest, Circuit City, CompUSA, Home Depot, Jo-Ann Fabrics, Nissan/Acura/Audi/Subaru, NTB, OfficeMax, Sam's Club, Target, U-Haul
40b a Cascade Rd, **N...gas:** BP, Marathon/diesel, 7-11/24hr, **food:** Subway, **other:** NAPA Autocare, **S...gas:** Shell, Speedway/diesel, **other:** HOSPITAL
39 MI 21(from eb), to Flint, no facilities
38 E Beltline Ave, to MI 21, MI 37, MI 44, **N...**RV camping, **S...food:** Duba's Dining, **other:** HOSPITAL
37mm I-196(from wb, exits left), Gerald Ford Fwy, to Grand Rapids
36 Leonard St, **1-2 mi S...food:** Arby's, Blimpie, McDonald's, **other:** sheriff's dept
33 Plainfield Ave, MI 44 Connector, **N...gas:** BP, Meijer/diesel/24hr, Speedway, 7-11, **food:** Arby's, Big Boy, Blimpie, Burger King, Domino's, Fred's Pizza, Golden Dragon, Hungry Howie's, KFC, Little Caesar's, LJ Silver, McDonald's, Pizza Hut, Russ' Rest., Schlotsky's, Subway, Taco Bell, Wendy's, **lodging:** Grand Inn, Lazy T Motel, **other:** AutoZone, Belle Tire, Chevrolet, Chrysler/Plymouth/Jeep, Discount Tire, Dodge, Ford/Mercury, Goodyear/auto, NAPA, Nissan/VW, NTB, Plymouth/Jeep, Radio Shack, Rite Aid, U-Haul, Walgreen, transmissions, **S...gas:** Amoco/24hr, **food:** Denny's, Traditions Rest.
31mm Grand River
31b a US 131, N to Cadillac, S to Kalamazoo, **1 mi N...food:** McDonald's
30b a Alpine Ave, Grand Rapids, **N...gas:** BP/24hr, Citgo/7-11, Marathon, Shell, **food:** Applebee's, Bennigan's, Blimpie, ChuckeCheese, Clock Rest., Cracker Barrel, Damon's, Fire Mtn Grill, Logan's Roadhouse, McDonald's, Old Country Buffet, Olive Garden, Outback Steaks, Perkins, Russ' Rest., Ryan's, Schlotsky's, Steak'n Shake, Subway, Taco Bell, TGIFriday, **lodging:** Hampton Inn, Holiday Inn Express, Swan Inn, **other:** Aldi Foods, Belle Tire, Best Buy, CarQuest, Circuit City, Discount Tire, Ford/Kia, Kia, Kohl's, Michael's, NAPA, OfficeMax, PepBoys, Radio Shack, Sam's Club, Target, Wal-Mart/auto, **S...gas:** Admiral/diesel, Gas4Less, Meijer/diesel/24hr, Speedway/diesel, **food:** Arby's, Burger King, Fazoli's, KFC, LJ Silver, McDonald's, Papa John's, Pizza Hut, Ponderosa, Wendy's, **lodging:** Motel 6, **other:** Goodyear/auto, Home Depot, Jo-Ann Fabrics, U-Haul
28 Walker Ave, **S...gas:** Meijer/diesel/24hr, **food:** Bob Evans, McDonald's, **lodging:** Amerihost, Baymont Inn
26 Fruit Ridge Ave, **N...gas:** Citgo/diesel, **S...gas:** Amoco/diesel
25mm rest area eb, full(handicapped)facilities, phone, picnic tables, litter barrels, petwalk
25 8th Ave, 4Mile Rd(from wb), **S...gas:** Marathon/diesel, **lodging:** Wayside Motel
24 8th Ave, 4Mile Rd(from eb), **S...gas:** Marathon/diesel, **lodging:** Wayside Motel
23 Marne, **N...other:** tires, fairgrounds/raceway, **S...food:** Depot Café, Rinaldi's Café, **other:** USPO
19 Lamont, Coopersville, **N...**food, **S...food:** Sam's Joint Rest., **other:** LP
16 B-35, Eastmanville, **N...gas:** Amoco/Subway/TCBY/diesel, Fleet/diesel/24hr, Shell/Burger King/diesel, **food:** Arby's, Little Caesar's, McDonald's, Pizza Hut/Taco Bell, **lodging:** AmeriHost, **other:** Family RV Ctr, Prevo's Foods, Rite Aid, **S...gas:** Pacific Pride/diesel, **other:** RV camping
10 B-31, Nunica, **N...food:** Turk's Rest., **S...gas:** Mobil, **other:** RV camping, golf course/rest.
9 MI 104(from wb, exits left), to Grand Haven, Spring Lake, **S...gas:** Mobil, **other:** to Grand Haven SP
8mm rest area wb, full(handicapped)facilities, phone, picnic tables, litter barrels, vending, petwalk
5 Fruitport(from wb, no return), no facilities
4 Airline Rd, **N...gas:** racetrack, **S...gas:** Speedway/diesel, Shell, Wesco/diesel, **food:** Burger Crest Diner, McDonald's, Subway, **other:** Fruitport Foods/24hr, Pleasure Island Water Park(5mi), USPO, to PJ Hoffmaster SP

Muskegon

1c Hile Rd(from eb), **S...gas:** racetrack
b a US 31, to Ludington, Grand Haven, **N...lodging:** Alpine Motel, Bel-aire Motel, Haven Motel, **other:** All Seasons RV, **2 mi N on Sherman Blvd...gas:** Westco/diesel, **food:** Applebee's, Arby's, Fazoli's, McDonald's, Old Country Buffet, Ruby Tuesday, Wendy's, **lodging:** Comfort Inn/rest., Ramada Inn, Super 8, **other:** HOSPITAL, Circuit City, GNC, Lowe's Whse, OfficeMax, Sam's Club, Staples, Target, Wal-Mart SuperCtr/24hr, **S...gas:** Mobil/diesel, **lodging:** AmeriHost, Best Western, Quality Inn, **other:** airport, racetrack

I-96 begins/ends on US 31 at Muskegon.

Interstate 196(Grand Rapids)

E ↕ W

Exit # Services

81mm I-196 begins/ends on I-96, 37mm in E Grand Rapids.

79 Fuller Ave, **N...**sheriff's dept

78 College Ave, **S...gas:** DM/gas, McDonald's, **other:** HOSPITAL, Rite Aid, auto repair, museum

77c Ottawa Ave, downtown, **S...**Gerald R Ford Museum

b a US 131, S to Kalamazoo, N to Cadillac

76 MI 45 E, Lane Ave, **S...gas:** Amoco, **other:** Gerald R Ford Museum, John Ball Park&Zoo

75 MI 45 W, Lake Michigan Dr, **N...**to Grand Valley St U

74mm Grand River

73 Market Ave, **N...**to Vanandel Arena

72 Lp 196, Chicago Dr E(from eb), no facilities

Holland

70 MI 11(exits left from wb), Grandville, Walker, **S...gas:** BP/diesel, Shell/repair, Speedway, **other:** NAPA, USPO

69b a Chicago Dr, **N...gas:** Meijer/diesel/24hr, **food:** KFC, McDonald's, Papa John's, Perkins, Subway, **other:** Aldi Foods, AutoZone, $General, Radio Shack, Target, **S...gas:** Amoco, Clark Gas, Speedway, **food:** Arby's, Burger King, Get'm-n-Go Burger, Little Caesar's, Pizza Hut, Russ' Rest., Wendy's, **lodging:** Best Western, Holiday Inn Express

67 44th St, **N...gas:** Mobil/diesel, **food:** Burger King, Cracker Barrel, Steak'n Shake, **lodging:** Comfort Suites, **other:** AAA, Wal-Mart/auto, **S...other:** Circuit City, Lowe's Whse, Residence Inn(2mi)

65 new exit

62 32nd Ave, to Hudsonville, **N...gas:** BP/diesel/24hr, **food:** Arby's, Burger King, McDonald's, **lodging:** AmeriHost, **other:** Chevrolet, **S...gas:** Mobil/Subway/diesel/24hr, **lodging:** Super 8, **other:** Harley-Davidson

58mm rest area eb, full(handicapped)facilities, phone, picnic tables, litter barrels, vending, petwalk

55 Byron Rd, Zeeland, **N...gas:** 7-11, **food:** McDonald's, **3-5 mi N...**HOSPITAL, to Holland SP

52 16th St, Adams St, **2 mi N...gas:** Meijer/diesel/24hr, Speedway, **food:** Wendy's, **lodging:** Best Inn, Econolodge, **other:** HOSPITAL, **S...gas:** Mobil/Subway/diesel, **food:** Burger King

49 MI 40, to Allegan, **N...gas:** BP/McDonald's/diesel, **S...gas:** Tulip City/diesel/24hr/@, **food:** Rock Island Rest.

44 US 31 N(from eb), to Holland, **3-5 mi N...lodging:** Country Inn, **other:** HOSPITAL, gas, food

43mm rest area wb, full(handicapped)facilities, info, phone, picnic tables, litter barrels, vending, petwalk

41 rd A-2, Douglas, Saugatuck, **N...gas:** Marathon/diesel, Shell/Subway/diesel, **food:** Burger King, **lodging:** AmericInn, Holiday Inn Express, Timberline Motel(3mi), **other:** NAPA, Saugatuck RV Resort, to Saugatuck SP, **S...lodging:** Shangrai-la Motel

38mm Kalamazoo River

36 rd A-2, Ganges, **N...gas:** Shell, **lodging:** AmericInn

Benton Harbor

34 MI 89, to Fennville, **S...gas:** Shell/24hr, **other:** Lyons Fruits, Winery Tours

30 rd A-2, Glenn, Ganges, to Westside Cty Park

25mm rest area eb, full(handicapped)facilities, phone, picnic tables, litter barrels, vending, petwalk

26 109th Ave, to Pullman, no facilities

22 N Shore Dr, **N...food:** Seawolf Café, Tello's Ristorante, **other:** to Kal Haven Trail SP, RV camping

20 rd A-2, Phoenix Rd, **N...gas:** BP/diesel/24hr, Marathon/diesel, **food:** Arby's, Taco Bell, **lodging:** SouthHaven Motel, **other:** HOSPITAL, AutoZone, st police, **S...gas:** BP/diesel, **food:** Big Boy, McDonald's, Sherman's Dairybar, Wendy's, **lodging:** Hampton Inn, Holiday Inn Express, Lighthouse Inn, **other:** Wal-Mart SuperCtr/gas/24hr

18 MI 140, MI 43, to Watervliet, **N...gas:** Shell/diesel/24hr, **food:** Ma's Coffeepot Rest./24hr, **1-2 mi N...gas:** Speedway, **food:** Burger King, CT's Café, McDonald's, Pizza Hut, Platter's Diner, **lodging:** Budget Lodge, LakeBluff Motel, **other:** D&W Foods, Buick/Pontiac/Cadillac/GMC, Chevrolet, Chrysler/Dodge

13 to Covert, **N...**to Van Buren SP, RV camping

7 MI 63, to Benton Harbor, **N...food:** DiMaggio's Pizza, Vitale's Mkt/subs, **other:** RV camping

4 Riverside, to Coloma, **S...gas:** Marathon/diesel, **other:** KOA

2mm Paw Paw River

1 Red Arrow Hwy, **N...**Ross Field Airport

0mm I-94, E to Detroit, W to Chicago

I-196 begins/ends on I-94, exit 34 at Benton Harbor.

Interstate 275(Livonia)

N ↕ S

Exit # Services

I-275 and I-96 run together 9 miles. **See Michigan Interstate 96, exits 165-170.**

29 I-96 E, to Detroit, MI 14 W, to Ann Arbor

28 Ann Arbor Rd, Plymouth, **E...gas:** BP/24hr, Shell, **food:** Atlantis Rest., Denny's, Dunkin Donuts, **lodging:** Day's Inn, Red Roof Inn, **W...food:** Bennigan's, Burger King, Steak&Ale, **lodging:** Quality Inn, **other:** Cadillac, K-Mart, Lincoln/Mercury

MICHIGAN

Interstate 275

N ↕ S — Livonia

25 MI 153, Ford Rd, Garden City, **W...gas:** BP, Shell, Speedway, Sunoco/diesel, **food:** Arby's, Bob Evans, Chili's, ChuckeCheese, Church's, Cooker, Dunkin Donuts, Hunan Empire Chinese, KFC, Little Caesar's, Olive Garden, Outback Steaks, Quizno's, Tim Horton, Wendy's, White Castle, **lodging:** Baymont Inn, Extended Stay America, Fairfield Inn, Motel 6, **other:** Discount Tire, K-Mart, Target

23 rest area nb, full(handicapped facilities), phone, info, picnic tables, litter barrels

22 US 12, Michigan Ave, to Wayne, **E...gas:** BP/24hr, Mobil/diesel, Shell, Speedway/diesel, **food:** Jonathan's Rest., McDonald's, Subway, TCBY, Wendy's, **lodging:** Day's Inn, Fellows Cr Motel, Holiday Inn Express, Super 8, Willo Acres Motel, **W...gas:** Marathon/A&W/diesel, **food:** McDonald's

20 Ecorse Rd, to Romulus, **W...gas:** Mobil/Burger King/diesel/24hr

17 I-94 E to Detroit, W to Ann Arbor, **E...**airport

15 Eureka Rd, **E...gas:** Shell, airport

13 Sibley Rd, New Boston, **W...**gas, food, hardware, to Lower Huron Metro Park

11 S Huron Rd, **1 mi W...gas:** Sunoco/Burger King/diesel, **food:** Jacob's Rest.

8 Will Carleton Rd, to Flat Rock, no facilities

5 Carleton, South Rockwood, **W...**food

4mm rest area sb, full(handicapped)facilties, phone, picnic tables, litter barrels

2 US 24, to Telegraph Rd, **W...gas:** Marathon/diesel, lodging

0mm I-275 begins/ends on I-75, exit 20.

Interstate 475(Flint)

N ↕ S — Flint

Exit # Services

17.5mm I-475 begins/ends on I-75, exit 125.

15 Clio Rd, **W...gas:** BP, **other:** Chevrolet, Northwoods RV Ctr

13 Saginaw St, **E...gas:** BP, **food:** DQ, McDonald's, Papa John's, Ponderosa, Taco Bell, **other:** Family$, Kroger/gas, **W...gas:** Clark, Sunoco, **food:** Burger King, KFC, Little Caesar's

11 Carpenter Rd, no facilities

10 Pierson Rd, no facilities

9 rd 54, Dort Hwy, Stewart Ave, **E...gas:** Citgo, **food:** McDonald's

8mm Flint River

8b Davison Rd, Hamilton Ave, no facilities

a Longway Blvd, **W...food:** China 1 Buffet, **lodging:** Holiday Inn Express, **other:** HOSPITAL

7 rd 21, Court St, downtown Flint

6 I-69, W to Lansing, E to Port Huron

5 Alberton Rd(from sb), **E...gas:** Marathon

4 Hemphill Rd, Bristol Rd, **E...gas:** Speedway, **food:** Subway, **W...gas:** Speedway, **food:** Latina Rest., **other:** Kroger/gas

2 Hill Rd, **E...gas:** Speedway, **food:** Applebee's, Bob Evans, **lodging:** Wingate Inn, **other:** Ford, **W...gas:** Shell, Sunoco, **food:** Arby's, Bob Evans, **lodging:** Courtyard, Holiday Inn, Residence Inn

0mm I-475 begins/ends on I-75, exit 111.

Interstate 696(Detroit)

E ↕ W — Detroit Area

Exit # Services

I-696 begins/ends on I-94.

28 I-94 E to Port Huron, W to Detroit, 11 Mile Rd, **E...gas:** BP/diesel, Speedway, 7-11

27 MI 3, Gratiot Ave, **N...gas:** BP, **food:** National Coney Island, **other:** Costco/gas, **S...gas:** BP, Mobil/McDonald's, **food:** White Castle, **other:** Goodyear/auto

26 MI 97, Groesbeck Ave, Roseville, **N...gas:** Mobil/diesel, **S...gas:** Marathon, **food:** Wendy's

24 Hoover Rd, Schoenherr Rd, **N...gas:** Sunoco, **food:** Burger King, KFC, **S...gas:** BP, Mobil, **food:** ChiChi's, Subway, Taco Bell, Tim Horton, **lodging:** Holiday Inn Express, **other:** CVS Drug, Kroger, Marshall's

23 MI 53, Van Dyke Ave, **N...gas:** BP, **food:** Arby's, Coney Island, Dunkin Donuts, McDonald's, **lodging:** Baymont Inn, **other:** MEDICAL CARE, Cadillac/Pontiac/GMC, Dodge, Jo-Ann Fabrics, radiators, **S...gas:** BP/24hr, **food:** Burger King, **other:** Chevrolet, Ford, Toyota, USPO

22 Mound Rd, no facilities

20 Ryan Rd, Dequindre Rd, **N...gas:** Marathon, **food:** IHOP, **lodging:** Knight's Inn, Red Roof Inn, **S...food:** Bob Evans, McDonald's, **lodging:** Comfort Suites, Ramada Ltd, **other:** Rite Aid, transmissions

19 Couzens St, 10 Mile Rd, **S...**Hazel Park Racetrack

18 I-75 N to Flint, S to Detroit

17 Campbell Ave, Hilton Ave, Bermuda, Mohawk, **S...gas:** Marathon/diesel

16 MI 1, Woodward Ave, Main St, **N...food:** Burger King, **other:** zoo

14 Coolidge Rd, 10 Mile Rd, **S...gas:** Mobil, Speedway, **food:** Dunkin Donuts, **food:** Jade Palace Chinese, Little Caesar's, LJ Silver, Pizza Hut, Subway, Taco Bell, Wendy's, **other:** CVS Drug, Farmer Jack's, Jo-Ann Fabrics

13 Greenfield Rd, **S...gas:** Mobil, Sunoco, **food:** Dunkin Donuts, **other:** Ford

12 MI 39, Southfield Rd, 11 Mile Rd, **S...gas:** Shell

11 Evergreen Rd, **S...lodging:** Residence Inn

10 US 24, Telegraph Rd, **N...gas:** BP, Marathon, **food:** Denny's, Seoul Garden Korean, **lodging:** Hampton Inn, Embassy Suites, **other:** Belle Tire, Best Buy, Chevrolet, Chrysler/Jeep, Circuit City, Dodge/Plymouth, $General, Farmer Jack's, Ford, Honda/Nissan/Isuzu, Hyundai, Jo-Ann Fabrics, K-Mart, Lexus, Lincoln/Mercury, Office Depot, Pontiac/Buick, USPO, mall, **S...gas:** Mobil, **lodging:** Courtyard, Hilton, Holiday Inn, Marriott

8 MI 10, Lodge Fwy, no facilities

5 Orchard Lake Rd, Farmington Hills, **N...gas:** Marathon, Mobil, Shell, **food:** Arby's, Hong Hua Chinese, Roberto's Rest., Ruby Tuesday, Starbucks, Steak&Ale, Steamer's Seafood, Subway, Wendy's, **lodging:** Comfort Inn, **other:** Discount Tire, to St Mary's Coll

1 (from wb), I-96 W, I-275 S, to MI 5, Grand River Ave

Interstate 35

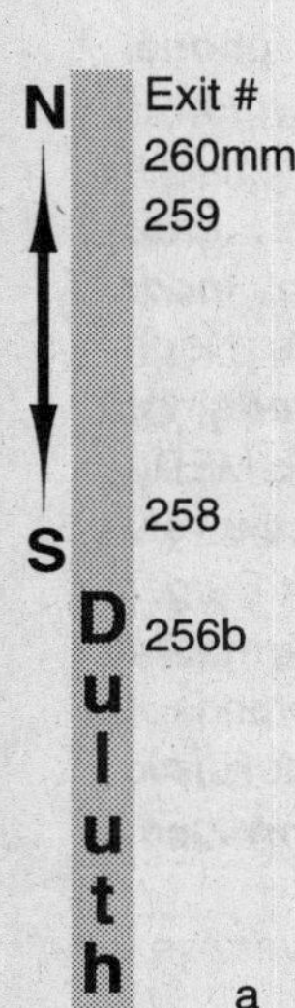

Exit #	Services
260mm	I-35 begins/ends on MN 61 in Duluth.
259	MN 61, London Rd, North Shore, to Two Harbors, **W... gas:** Holiday/diesel, Spur, SA, **food:** Blackwoods Grill, Burger King, KFC, McDonald's, Perkins, Pizza Hut, Subway, Taco John's, Wendy's, **lodging:** Best Western
258	21st Ave E(from nb), to U of MN at Duluth, **W...food:** Perkins, **lodging:** Best Western, same as 259
256b	Mesaba Ave, Superior St, **E...gas:** ICO/DQ, **food:** Burger King, Grandma's Grill, Little Angie's Cantina, Red Lobster, Timberlodge Steaks, Tradewinds Rest., **lodging:** Canal Park Inn, Comfort Suites, Hampton Inn, Hawthorn Suites, Superior Lake Inn, **W...lodging:** Holiday Inn, Radisson
a	Michigan St, **E...**waterfront, **W...**HOSPITAL, downtown
255a	US 53 N, downtown, mall, **W...other:** Kia
b	I-535 spur, to Wisconsin, no facilities
254	27th Ave W, **W...gas:** BP/24hr, Holiday/Burger King/diesel, Spur/diesel, **food:** Embers Rest., Subway, **lodging:** Motel 6
253b	40th Ave W, **W...gas:** BP/diesel/24hr, **food:** Perkins/24hr, **lodging:** Comfort Inn, Super 8
a	US 2 E, US 53, to Wisconsin, no facilities
252	Central Ave, W Duluth, **W...gas:** Conoco/diesel, Holiday/diesel/24hr, **food:** Beaners Coffee, Giant Panda, KFC, McDonald's, Pizza Hut, Sammy's Café, Subway, Taco Bell, White Castle, **other:** K-Mart, Radio Shack, Super 1 Foods, Walgreen
251b	MN 23 S, Grand Ave, no facilities
a	Cody St, zoo, **E...lodging:** Allyndale Motel
250	US 2 W(from sb), to Grand Rapids, **1/2 mi W...gas:** Holiday/diesel, Mobil/diesel/LP, **food:** Blackwoods Grill, Country Kitchen, Wok'n Grill, **lodging:** AmericInn

MINNESOTA

Interstate 35

N ↕ S

249 Boundary Ave, Skyline Pkwy, **E...gas:** Holiday/McDonald's/diesel, **lodging:** Country Inn Suites, Sundowner Motel(1mi), **other:** to ski area, **W...rest area both lanes, full(handicapped) facilities, info, phone, picnic tables, litter barrels, vending, gas:** Phillips 66/diesel/24hr, **food:** Blackwoods Grill, Country Kitchen, **lodging:** Travelodge

246 MN 13, Midway Rd, Nopeming, **W...gas:** Armor/diesel, **food:** Dry Dock Rest.

245 MN 61, **E...food:** Buffalo House Rest./camping

242 rd 1, Esko, Thomson, **E...gas:** BP

239.5mm St Louis River

239 MN 45, Scanlon, to Cloquet, **E...other:** Jay Cooke SP, KOA(May-Oct), **W...gas:** Conoco, **food:** Pantry Rest., Wood City Grille, **lodging:** Golden Gate Motel, **other:** HOSPITAL, Chevrolet, Pontiac/Buick, camping, diesel repair

237 MN 33, Cloquet, **1 mi W...gas:** BP/24hr, Conoco/diesel, Spur, **food:** Country Kitchen, Grandma's Grill, DQ, Hardee's, McDonald's, Perkins/24hr, Pizza Hut, Subway, Taco Bell, Taco John's, **lodging:** AmericInn, Super 8, **other:** HOSPITAL, Chrysler/Plymouth/Jeep, Family$, Ford/Mercury, NAPA, Super 1 Foods, Wal-Mart/24hr, White Drug

236mm weigh sta both lanes

235 MN 210, Carlton, to Cromwell, **E...gas:** BP/diesel/rest., Armor Fuel, Spur/diesel/24hr, **food:** Backyard Grill, Embers Rest., **lodging:** AmericInn, Royal Pines Motel, **other:** to Jay Cooke SP, **W...other:** Black Bear Casino/Hotel/rest.

235mm Big Otter Creek

233mm Little Otter Creek

227 rd 4, Mahtowa, **E...**camping, **W...gas:** Conoco

226mm rest area nb, full(handicapped)facilities, phone, picnic tables, litter barrels, vending, petwalk

220 rd 6, Barnum, **E...**camping, **W...gas:** BP/diesel/café/24hr, **lodging:** Northwoods Motel

219mm Moose Horn River

218mm Moose Horn River

216 MN 27(from sb, no EZ return), Moose Lake, **1-2 mi W...gas:** BP, Holiday/diesel, Phillips 66, **food:** Art's Café, DQ, Wyndtree Rest., **lodging:** AmericInn(4mi), Moose Lake Motel, **other:** HOSPITAL, Chevrolet/Buick/Pontiac, Super Valu Foods, to Munger Trail

214 rd 73(from nb, no EZ return), Moose Lake, **E...other:** Moose Lake SP(2mi), camping, **W...gas:** Conoco/Subway/diesel, **lodging:** AmericInn, **2 mi W...food:** Wyndtree Rest., **lodging:** Moose Lake Motel, **other:** HOSPITAL, Munger Trail, Red Fox Camping

209 rd 46, Sturgeon Lake, **E...gas:** Phillips 66, **W...lodging:** Sturgeon Lake Motel, **other:** Timberline Camping(3mi)

209mm rest area sb, full(handicapped)facilities, phone, picnic tables, litter barrels, vending, petwalk

206.5mm Willow River

205 rd 43, Willow River, **W...gas:** Citgo/diesel, **other:** camping(2mi), laundry

198.5mm Kettle River

198mm rest area nb, full(handicapped)facilities, phone, picnic tables, litter barrels, vending, petwalk

195 rd 18, rd 23 E, to Askov, **E...gas:** BP/diesel/café, **lodging:** Super 8, **other:** to Banning SP, camping, **W...**camping

191 MN 23, rd 61, Sandstone, **E...gas:** BP/diesel/LP, Conoco/diesel, **lodging:** Sandstone 61 Motel(2mi), **other:** MEDICAL CARE, Family Drug

184mm Grindstone Rover

Hinckley

183 MN 48, Hinckley, **E...gas:** Conoco/Tobie's Rest., Holiday/diesel, **food:** Burger King, DQ, Hardee's, Subway, Taco Bell, **lodging:** Day's Inn, Grand Northern Inn, **other:** Chevrolet, flea mkt, to St Croix SP(15mi), **W...gas:** Mobil/24hr, Phillips 66/White Castle/diesel, **food:** Cassidy's Rest., **lodging:** Gold Pine Inn, **other:** Fire Museum

180 MN 23 W, rd 61, to Mora, no facilities

175 rd 14, Beroun, **E...gas:** BP/diesel

171 rd 11, Pine City, **E...gas:** SA/diesel, **food:** McDonald's, **other:** Chrysler/Dodge, **W...**camping

170mm Snake River

169 MN 324, rd 7, Pine City, **E...gas:** BP/diesel, Holiday/diesel, **food:** A&W, DQ, Grizzly's Grill, KFC, Pizza Hut, Red Shed Rest., Subway, **other:** Ford/Mercury, Jubilee Foods, Pamida, Radio Shack, Wal-Mart, camping, **W...**to NW Co Fur Post HS

165 MN 70, Rock Creek, to Grantsburg, **E...gas:** Citgo/diesel, **lodging:** Chalet Motel, camping, **W...gas:** Total/diesel/café/24hr

159 MN 361, rd 1, Rush City, **E...gas:** Holiday/Burger King/diesel, **other:** HOSPITAL, Main St Mkt Foods, **W...**camping(2mi)

154mm rest area nb, full(handicapped)facilities, phone, picnic tables, litter barrels, vending, petwalk

152 rd 10, Harris, **2 mi E...**gas/diesel

147 MN 95, North Branch, to Cambridge, **E...gas:** BP, Casey's, Conoco/diesel, Holiday/diesel, **food:** DQ, Domino's, KFC/Taco Bell, McDonald's, North Branch Café, Perkins, Pizza Hut, Subway, **lodging:** AmericInn, Oak Inn/rest., Super 8, **other:** MEDICAL CARE, CarQuest, Fisk Tire, NAPA, SuperValu Foods, to Wild River SP(14mi), **W...food:** Burger King, Denny's, **other:** Chevrolet, Chrysler/Plymouth/Dodge/Jeep, Ford, Tanger Outlet/famous brands

139 rd 19, Stacy, **E...gas:** BP, Phillips 66, **food:** Rustic Rest., **lodging:** Super 8(8mi), city park, **W...gas:** Conoco/pizza

Interstate 35

N ↕ S

135 US 61 S, rd 22, Wyoming, **E...gas:** BP/diesel, **food:** Cornerstone Café, DQ, Pizza Zone, Subway, **other:** HOSPITAL, CarQuest, IGA Foods, **W...gas:** Citgo/diesel, **food:** McDonald's, Village Inn Rest., **other:** camping(10mi), golf

132 US 8(from nb), to Taylors Falls

131 rd 2, Forest Lake, **E...gas:** Amoco/24hr, Holiday/diesel, SA/diesel, **food:** Applebee's, Arby's, Burger King, Cheung Chinese, Hardee's, McDonald's, Perkins, Quack's Café, Taco Bell, White Castle, **lodging:** AmericInn, **other:** HOSPITAL, Champion Auto, Checker Parts, Kennedy Transmissions, OfficeMax, Rainbow Foods/24hr, Target, Tires+, Wal-Mart, **W...gas:** Holiday/diesel, **food:** Famous Dave's BBQ, Papa Murphy's, Quizno's, Starbucks, Wendy's, **lodging:** Country Inn Suites, **other:** Buick/Pontiac, Chevrolet/Cadillac, Chrysler/Plymouth/Dodge/Jeep, Cub Foods, Ford, GNC

131mm rest area sb, full(handicapped)facilities, phone, picnic tables, litter barrels, vending, petwalk

129 MN 97, rd 23, **E...**camping(6mi), **W...gas:** Conoco/pizza/diesel/24hr, **other:** camping(1mi)

128mm weigh sta both lanes

127 I-35W, S to Minneapolis. **See I-35W.**

123 rd 14, Centerville, **E...**Otter Lake RV Ctr, **W...gas:** Citgo/diesel, Marathon, Shell, **food:** DQ, Embers Rest., Kelly's Rest.

120 rd J(from nb)

117 MN 96, **E...gas:** Mobil, SA/diesel, **food:** Burger King, Casa Lupita Mexican, **lodging:** AmericInn, **other:** Goodyear/auto, NAPA, **W...gas:** BP, PDQ, **food:** Applebee's, Arby's/Sbarro's, Boston Mkt, Culver's, McDonald's, Subway, MEDICAL CARE, **other:** Cub Foods, Tires+, USPO, Walgreen

115 rd E, **E...gas:** BP, Conoco, SA/diesel, **food:** Jimmy's Panera Bread, Perkins, **lodging:** Holiday Inn Express, **W...gas:** KFC/Pizza Hut, **food:** McDonald's, Papa Murphy's, Quizno's, Wendy's, **other:** Festival Foods, GNC, Radio Shack, Target, Wal-Mart/auto

114 I-694 E(exits left from sb), no facilities

113 I-694 W, no facilities

112 Little Canada Rd, **E...gas:** Citgo, **W...gas:** Sinclair, **food:** Porterhouse Steaks

111b MN 36 W, to Minneapolis, no facilities

a MN 36 E, to Stillwater, no facilities

110b Roselawn Ave, no facilities

a Wheelock Pkwy, **E...gas:** BP, Mobil, **food:** Subway, **W...gas:** Sinclair/diesel

109 Maryland Ave, **E...gas:** Citgo, SA/diesel, **W...food:** Wendy's, **other:** K-Mart

108 Pennsylvania Ave, downtown

107c University Ave, downtown, **E...gas:** BP, **W...other:** HOSPITAL, to st capitol

107b a I-94, W to Minneapolis, E to St Paul. I-35 and I-94 run together.

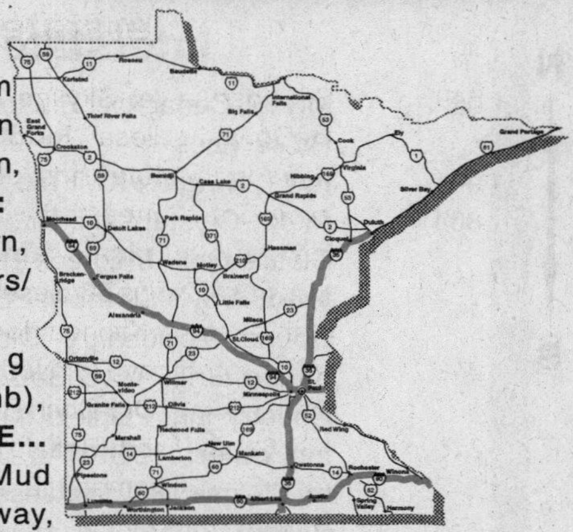

106c 11th St(from nb), Marion St, downtown, **E...lodging:** Best Western, **other:** Sears/auto

106b Kellogg Blvd(from nb), downtown, **E... food:** MS Mud Grill, Subway, **lodging:** Holiday Inn, **other:** HOSPITAL

a Grand Ave, **E...**HOSPITAL

105 St Clair Ave, no facilities

104c Victoria St, Jefferson Ave, no facilities

b Ayd Mill Rd(from nb), no facilities

a Randolph Ave, no facilities

103b MN 5, W 7th St, **E...food:** Burger King, **W...gas:** SA/diesel, **other:** USPO

a Shepard Rd(from nb)

102mm Mississippi River

102 MN 13, Sibley Hwy, **W...gas:** BP, Holiday

101b a MN 110 W, **E...food:** Ziggy's Deli, **W...gas:** SA

99b I-494 W, no facilities

a I-494 E, no facilities

98 Lone Oak Rd, **E...lodging:** Homestead Suites, Microtel, **other:** Sam's Club, USPO, **W...gas:** BP, **food:** Costello's Coffee, Joe Senser's Grill, Magic Thai Café, **lodging:** Hampton Inn

97b Yankee Doodle Rd, **E...gas:** Holiday, **food:** Applebee's, Arby's, Blimpie, Burger King, Cattle Co Rest., Chili's, Culver's, DQ, Don Pablo's, Houlihan's, KFC, McDonald's, New China Buffet, Perkins, Pizza Hut, Red Robin, Taco Bell, **lodging:** Residence Inn, Springhill Suites, TownePlace Suites, **other:** MEDICAL CARE, Barnes&Noble, Byerly's Foods, Checker Parts, GNC, Kohl's, Michael's, Office Depot, OfficeMax, Old Navy, Rainbow Foods, Tires+, **W...gas:** BP, SA/diesel, **lodging:** Al Baker's Rest., Boston Mkt, Dragon Palace Chinese, **lodging:** Best Western, Extended Stay America

a Pilot Knob Rd, same as 97b, **E...gas:** Phillips 66, Hardee's, **lodging:** Best Western, SpringHill Suites, TownePlace Suites, **other:** Firestone, Goodyear, Wal-Mart, mall

94 rd 30, Diffley Rd, to Eagan, **W...gas:** Conoco

93 rd 32, Cliff Rd, **E...gas:** Shell, **food:** Subway, **W...gas:** Holiday/diesel, Mobil/diesel, **food:** Burger King, Bakers Square, Boston Mkt, Burger King, Cherokee Sirloin, DQ, Denny's, Dolittle's Café, Greenmill Rest., KFC, Little Caesar's, McDonald's, Subway, Taco Bell, Wendy's, **lodging:** Hilton, Holiday Inn Express, Sleep Inn, Staybridge Suites, **other:** Checker Parts, Target, USPO, Walgreen

Interstate 35

N ↕ S

92 MN 77, Cedar Ave, **E...**Zoo, **1 m W...**access to Cliff Rd services

90 rd 11, **E...gas:** KwikTrip, **W...gas:** Freedom

88b rd 42, Crystal Lake Rd, **E...food:** Byerly's Rest., Ciatti's Grill, Millcreek Rest., **W...gas:** BP, PDQ, **food:** Arby's/Sbarro's, BBQ, Burger King, Ground Round, McDonald's, Old Country Buffet, Roadhouse Grill, Taco Bell, Vico's Café, **lodging:** Country Inn, Fairfield Inn, Hampton Inn, Holiday Inn, **other:** HOSPITAL, Home Depot, USPO, **1/2 mi W...gas:** Holiday/diesel, SA, **food:** Applebee's, Bakers Square, Champp's Café, ChiChi's, Chili's, ChuckeCheese, Godfather's, KFC, Kings Buffet, Macaroni Grill, Olive Garden, Outback Steaks, Papa John's, Red Lobster, Schlotsky's, Southern China Café, TGIFriday, **lodging:** InTown Suites, **other:** Barnes&Noble, Chevrolet, Circuit City, Cub Foods, Discount Tire, Goodyear/auto, JC Penney, K-Mart, Marshall Field, Mervyn's, Michael's, NTB, OfficeMax, Rainbow Foods, Sears/auto, Target, Tires+, Walgreen, mall

a I-35W(from nb), N to Minneapolis. **See I-35W.**

87 Crystal Lake Rd, **W...gas:** KT, **other:** Buick, Ford/Lincoln/Mercury, Honda/Nissan, Saturn, Toyota, Beaver Mtn Ski Area

86 rd 46, **E...gas:** KT, SA/diesel, **food:** KFC, **other:** Harley-Davidson

85 MN 50, Sinclair, **E...gas:** BP/24hr, F&F/diesel, SA/diesel, **food:** Burger King, DQ, Lakeville Chinese, Pizza Hut, Subway, Taco Bell, **lodging:** Comfort Inn, **other:** MEDICAL CARE, Family Foods, Goodyear, **W...gas:** Holiday/diesel, **food:** ChartHouse Rest., Cracker Barrel, Perkins, **lodging:** AmeriInn

84 185th St W(from sb), Orchard Trail, no facilities

81 rd 70, Lakeville, **E...gas:** Holiday/diesel, **food:** McDonald's, Subway, Tacoville, **lodging:** Motel 6, Super 8/rest., **other:** towing/repai

76 rd 2, Elko, **E...gas:** Phillips 66/diesel/LP, **W...food:** Glenno's Eatery/pizza, HeartThrop Café

76mm rest area sb, full(handicapped)facilities, phone, picnic tables, litter barrels, vending, petwalk

69 MN 19, to Northfield, **E...gas:** Fuel&mart, **food:** Taco Bell(6mi), **8 mi E...lodging:** AmericInn, Country Inn, Super 8, **other:** Carleton Coll, St Olaf Coll, **W... gas:** Conoco/A&W/diesel/24hr, **food:** Embers Rest.

68mm rest area nb, full(handicapped)facilities, phone, picnic tables, litter barrels, vending, petwalk

66 rd 1, to Dundas, **1 mi W...food:** Boonie's Grill

Faribault

59 MN 21, Faribault, **E...gas:** Shell/diesel/rest., **lodging:** AmericInn, Day's Inn, Super 8, **2 mi E...gas:** Mobil, SA, **food:** A&W, Burger King, Hardee's, KFC, Peppermill Grill, Pizza Hut, Taco John's, **lodging:** Galaxie Inn, Lyndale Motel, **other:** Ford/Lincoln/Mercury, **W...other:** Go-Kart rides, camping

56 MN 60, Faribault, **E...gas:** BP, Mobil, **food:** Burger King, Great China Buffet, Hardee's, Perkins, Pizza Hut, Quizno's, Subway, Taco John's, **other:** HOSPITAL, Buick/Pontiac, Chevrolet, Chrysler/Plymouth/Jeep, Dodge, Family$, Goodyear/auto, Hy-Vee Foods, JC Penney, Jo-Ann Fabrics, Tires+, Wal-Mart, mall, **W...gas:** Petro/diesel, **food:** DQ, Happy Chef/24hr, **lodging:** Select Inn, **other:** Sakatah Lake SP, camping

55 (from nb, no return), **1 mi E...gas:** SA, KT, Mobil, **food:** Broaster Rest., Burger King, DQ, El Tequila Mexican, Great China Buffet, Hardee's, KFC, Pizza Hut, Subway, Taco John's, **lodging:** AmericInn, **other:** MEDICAL CARE, Ford/Mercury, Harley-Davidson

48 rd 12, rd 23, Medford, **W...food:** McDonald's, **other:** Outlet Mall/famous brands

45 rd 9, Clinton Falls, **W...gas:** KT/diesel, **food:** Green Mill Rest. Noble Romans, TimberLodge Steaks, Wendy's, **lodging:** Comfort Inn, Holiday Inn, **other:** Cabela's Sporting Goods, museum

Owatonna

43 rd 34, 26th St, Airport Rd, Owatonna, **W...lodging:** Ramada Inn, **other:** MEDICAL CARE

42b a US 14 W, rd 45, Owatonna, to Waseca, **E...gas:** Sinclair/diesel/24hr, **food:** Kernel Rest., **other:** Bumper Parts, CashWise Foods, Chrysler/Dodge/Plymouth/Jeep, Ford/Lincoln/Mercury, **W...gas:** BP/diesel, **food:** Culver's, Happy Chef, McDonald's, Perkins, **lodging:** Best Budget Inn, Ramada Inn, Super 8, **other:** Wal-Mart SuperCtr/gas/diesel/24hr

41 Bridge St, Owatonna, **E...gas:** Mobil/diesel, **food:** Applebee's, Arby's, Burger King, DQ, KFC, Subway, Taco Bell, **lodging:** AmericInn, Country Inn Suites, **other:** HOSPITAL, **W...gas:** Mobil/diesel, **lodging:** Microtel, **other:** Target

40 US 14 E, US 218, Owatonna, **1 mi E on rd 6...gas:** Shell, **food:** El Tequila Mexican, Godfather's, Hardee's, Taco John's, **lodging:** Oakdale Motel, **other:** HOSPITAL, Hy-Vee Foods/24hr, Sterling Drug, WholesaleTire

38mm Turtle Creek

35mm rest area both lanes, full(handicapped)facilities, phone, picnic tables, litter barrels, vending, petwalk

34.5mm Straight River

32 rd 4, Hope, **1/2 mi E...**camping, **1 mi W...**gas, food

MINNESOTA

Interstate 35

N ↕ S

Albert Lea

26	MN 30, Ellendale, to Blooming Prairie, **E...gas:** Cenex/diesel/rest./24hr, **W...gas:** BP/Mel's Diner/diesel/24hr
22	rd 35, Geneva, to Hartland, **1 mi E...**gas, food
18	MN 251, Clarks Grove, to Hollandale, **W...gas:** Phillips 66/diesel/LP, **other:** camping
13b a	I-90, W to Sioux Falls, E to Austin, **W...**HOSPITAL
12	US 65 S(from sb), Lp 35, Albert Lea, same as 11
11	rd 46, Albert Lea, **E...gas:** TA/McDonald's/Pizza Hut/diesel/24hr/@, **food:** Trails Rest., **lodging:** Comfort Inn, **other:** KOA(may-oct/6mi), **W...gas:** Conoco/diesel, Phillips 66, Shell/diesel, **food:** Burger King, China Buffet, Golden Corral, McDonald's, Osa Zamora Mexican, Perkins, Pizza Hut, Tienda Mexico, Trumble's Rest., Wendy's, **lodging:** Budget Host, Country Inn Suites, Day's Inn, Super 8, **other:** HOSPITAL, CarQuest, Buick/Pontiac/Cadillac/Honda, Ford, Home Depot, Mazda, NAPA, Nissan/VW, Toyota, Volvo, diesel repair, to Myre-Big Island SP
9mm	Albert Lea Lake
8	US 65, Lp 35, Albert Lea, to Glenville, **2 mi W...gas:** Cenex/24hr, Citgo, Holiday, **food:** DQ, Hardee's, KFC
5	rd 13, Twin Lakes, to Glenville, **3 mi W...**camping
2	rd 5, no facilities
1mm	**Welcome Ctr nb, full(handicapped)facilities, phone, picnic tables, litter barrels, vending, petwalk**
0mm	Minnesota/Iowa state line

Interstate 35W

N ↕ S

Minneapolis

Exit #	Services
41mm	I-35W begins/ends on I-35, exit 127.
36	rd 23, **E...gas:** BP/diesel, **W...gas:** Phillips 66/diesel, **food:** McDonald's, Subway, **other:** MEDICAL CARE, Kohl's, Target
33	rd 17, Lexington Ave, **E...gas:** BP, **1 mi E...food:** Burger King, McDonald's, **W...food:** Applebee's, Damon's, Green Mill Rest., Quizno's, Wendy's, **other:** Cub Foods, GNC, Home Depot, Michael's, Radio Shack, Wal-Mart
32	95th Ave NE, to Lexington, Circle Pines, **W...**Nat Sports Ctr
31b	Lake Dr, **E...gas:** Shell/diesel
a	rd J, 85th Ave NE(no EZ return to nb), no facilities
30	US 10 W, MN 118, to MN 65, no facilities
29	rd I, no facilities
28c b	rd 10, rd H, **W...gas:** BP, **food:** Best Steaks, Jake's Café, KFC, McDonald's, Mermaid Café, Perkins, Pizza Hut/Taco Bell, RJ Riches Rest., Subway, Saturn, **lodging:** AmericInn, Day's Inn, **other:** carwash
a	MN 96, no facilities
27b a	I-694 E and W
26	rd E2, **W...gas:** Phillips 66/diesel
25b	MN 88, to Roseville(no EZ return to sb), **E...gas:** SA/diesel, **lodging:** Courtyard, Fairfield Inn, Residence Inn, **W...gas:** Mobil, PDQ, **food:** Barley John's, Godfather's, Jake's Café, Main Event Rest., McDonald's, Perkins/24hr, Subway
a	rd D(from nb), same as 25b
24	rd C, **E...food:** Burger King, **lodging:** Holiday Inn, **W...lodging:** Comfort Inn, **other:** Chevrolet/Pontiac/GMC, Chrysler/Plymouth/Dodge/Jeep, Volvo
23b	Cleveland Ave, MN 36, **E...food:** India Palace Rest., Joe Senser's Rest., **lodging:** Day's Inn, Motel 6, Radisson, Super 8
a	MN 280, Industrial Blvd(from sb)
22	MN 280, Industrial Blvd(from nb), **E...lodging:** Sheraton
21b a	rd 88, Broadway St, Stinson Blvd, **E...**Ford Trucks, **W...food:** Burger King, Country Kitchen, Cousins Subs, McDonald's, Pizza Hut/Taco Bell, **other:** Home Depot, OfficeMax, Old Navy, Rainbow Foods/24hr, Target
19	E Hennepin(from nb)
18	US 52, 4th St SE, University Ave, to U of MN, **E...gas:** BP
17c	11th St, Washington Ave, **E...lodging:** Holiday Inn, **W...gas:** Mobil, **other:** HOSPITAL, Goodyear, to Metrodome
b	I-94 W(from sb)
a	MN 55, Hiawatha
16b a	I-94(from nb), E to St Paul, W to St Cloud, to MN 65
15	31st St(from nb), Lake St, **E...food:** McDonald's, Taco Bell, **other: W...**HOSPITAL
14	35th St, 36th St, no facilities
13	46th St, no facilities
13mm	Minnehaha Creek
12b	Diamond Lake Rd, no facilities
a	60th St(from sb), **W...gas:** Mobil, **other:** Cub Foods
11b	MN 62 E, to airport
a	Lyndale Ave(from sb), **E...gas:** Shell
10b	MN 62 W, 58th St, no facilities
a	rd 53, 66th St, no facilities
9c	76th St(from sb), no facilities
b a	I-494, MN 5, to airport

MINNESOTA

Interstate 35W

N ↕ S

8	82nd St, W...**food:** Bennigan's, Red Lobster, **other:** Chevrolet, Infiniti, Kia, Saturn, Suzuki, Toyota
7b	90th St, no facilities
a	94th St, E...**gas:** BP, Goodyear/auto, W...**lodging:** Holiday Inn
6	rd 1, 98th St, E...**gas:** Indian Joe's/gas, **food:** Bakers Square, Byerly's Rest., Caribou Coffee, New China, Starbucks, **other:** Ford, Gander Mtn, Walgreen, W...**gas:** SA/diesel, **food:** Burger King, Denny's, Subway
5	106th St, no facilities
5mm	Minnesota River
4b	113th St, Black Dog Rd, no facilities
a	Cliff Rd, E...Dodge, W...VW
3b a	MN 13, Shakopee, Canterbury Downs, E...**lodging:** Ramada Ltd
2	Burnsville Pkwy, E...**gas:** Citgo, Oasis Mkt/diesel, **food:** Bob's Café, **other:** MEDICAL CARE, AAA, mall, W...**gas:** BP, **food:** Embers Rest., Perkins, TimberLodge Steaks, **lodging:** Day's Inn, Prime Rate Motel, Red Roof Inn, Super 8, **other:** Best Buy
1	rd 42, Crystal Lake Rd, **See Minnesota Interstate 35, exit 88b.**
0mm	I-35W begins/ends on I-35, exit 88a.

Interstate 90

E ↕ W

Exit #	Services
277mm	Minnesota/Wisconsin state line, Mississippi River
275	US 14, US 61, to MN 16, La Crescent, **N...Welcome Ctr wb, full(handicapped)facilities, info, phone, picnic tables, litter barrels, vending, petwalk**
272b a	Dresbach, N...**lodging:** Dresbach Motel, S...Gopher Marine
270	Dakota, N...accesses lodging at 272
269	US 14, US 61, to Winona, N...**other:** to OL Kipp SP, camping, S...camping
266	rd 12, Nodine, N...**other:** Great River Bluff SP, OL Kipp SP, camping, S...**gas:** BP/Subway/diesel/24hr/@, **lodging:** Truckers Inn/rest.
261mm	weigh sta both lanes
257	MN 76, Ridgeway, Witoka, to Houston, N...gas, S...camping
252	MN 43 N, to Winona, **7 mi N...lodging:** AmeircInn, Best Western, Holiday Inn, Quality Inn, Super 8, **other:** HOSPITAL
249	MN 43 S, to Rushford, N...**other:** Peterbilt Trucks/repair, S...Ernie Tuff Museum
244mm	**rest area eb, full(handicapped)facilities, phone, picnic tables, litter barrels, vending, petwalk**
242	rd 29, Lewiston, no facilities
233	MN 74, St Charles, to Chatfield, N...**gas:** KT/LP/24hr, **food:** Pizza Factory, Subway, **other:** Whitewater SP, S...**gas:** Shell/diesel, **food:** Amish Ovens Rest./bakery, **other:** RV dump/LP
229	rd 10, Dover, no facilities
224	rd 7, Eyota, no facilities
222mm	**rest area wb, full(handicapped)facilities, phone, picnic tables, litter barrels, vending, petwalk**
218	US 52, to Rochester, **8 mi N...food:** Old Country Buffet, **lodging:** Hampton Inn, Holiday Inn, Motel 6, Sleep Inn, **other:** Brookside RV Park, S...**gas:** Citgo, **other:** KOA(Mar-Oct)(1mi)
209b a	US 63, MN 30, to Rochester, Stewartville, **8-10 mi N...lodging:** Comfort Inn, Day's Inn, Hampton Inn, Holiday Inn, Super 8, **1 mi S...gas:** KwikTrip, **food:** DQ, **lodging:** AmericInn
205	rd 6, no facilities
202mm	**rest area eb, full(handicapped)facilities, phone, picnic tables, litter barrels, vending, petwalk**
193	MN 16, Dexter, S...**gas:** Phillips 66/Windmill Rest./diesel/24hr, **lodging:** Budget Inn
189	rd 13, to Elkton, no facilities
187	rd 20, no facilities
183	MN 56, to Rose Creek, Brownsdale, S...**gas:** Cenex/diesel/LP
181	28th St NE, no facilities
180b a	US 218, 21st St NE, Oakland Place, to Austin, S...**gas:** Texaco, **lodging:** Austin Motel
179	11th Dr NE, to Austin, N...**gas:** Citgo/diesel/rest./24hr
178b	6th St NE, to Austin, downtown
a	4th St NW, N...**food:** Culver's, Perkins, **lodging:** AmericInn, Day's Inn, Holiday Inn, S...**gas:** BP, Conoco/Subway/diesel, Sinclair/diesel, **food:** A&W, Burger King, **other:** HOSPITAL, Goodyear
177	US 218 N, Austin, Mapleview, to Owatonna, N...**gas:** Holiday, **food:** Applebee's, KFC, King Buffet, Quizno's, **other:** Cashwise Food/gas/24hr, Hy-Vee Foods, JC Penney, K-Mart, Radio Shack, ShopKO, Target, mall, S...**gas:** Sinclair/diesel, **food:** Hardee's, **lodging:** Super 8
175	MN 105, rd 46, to Oakland Rd, N...**gas:** Phillips 66/diesel, **food:** Sportts Rest., **lodging:** Countryside Inn, S...**gas:** BP, Conoco/diesel, **food:** McDonald's(2mi), **lodging:** Downtown Motel(2mi), Sterling Motel(2mi), **other:** Chrysler/Plymouth/Dodge/Jeep, Ford/Mercury, camping
171mm	**rest area wb, full(handicapped)facilities, phone, picnic tables, litter barrels, petwalk**
166	rd 46, Oakland Rd, N...**other:** KOA/LP, golf(par3)
163	rd 26, Hayward, S...**gas:** Cenex, **food:** Pizza Hut(4mi), Trails Rest.(4mi), **other:** Myre-Big Island SP, camping
161.5mm	**rest area eb, full(handicapped)facilities, phone, picnic tables litter barrels, petwalk**
159b a	I-35, N to Twin Cities, S to Des Moines, no facilities

Interstate 90

157 rd 22, Albert Lea, **S...gas:** Conoco/24hr, Mobil/Subway/diesel/24hr, **food:** Applebee's, Café Don'l, DQ, Herberger's, McDonald's, **lodging:** AmericInn, Holiday Inn Express, **other:** HOSPITAL, Chevrolet, Harley-Davidson, Hy-Vee Foods/24hr, Radio Shack, ShopKO, mall

154 MN 13, to US 69, Albert Lea, to Manchester, **N...gas:** SA/diesel, **3 mi S...lodging:** BelAir Motel, **other:** Wal-Mart

146 MN 109, to Wells, Alden, **S...gas:** BP/diesel/rest., Cenex

138 MN 22, to Wells, Keister, **S...**camping

134 MN 253, rd 21, to Bricelyn, MN Lake, no facilities

128 MN 254, rd 17, to Frost, no facilities

119 US 169, Blue Earth, to Winnebago, **S...gas:** KwikTrip/diesel, Phillips 66, Shell/DQ, Sinclair/diesel, **food:** Country Kitchen, McDonald's, Pizza Hut, Subway, AmericInn, Budget Inn, Super 8, **other:** HOSPITAL, Wal-Mart/drugs, Jolly Green Giant

118mm rest area both lanes, full(handicapped)facilities, phone, picnic tables, litter barrels, petwalk, playground

113 rd 1, Guckeen, no facilities

107 MN 262, rd 53, Granada, to East Chain, **S...other:** Flying Goose Camping(May-Oct)(1mi)

102 MN 15, Fairmont, **S...gas:** BP/24hr, Cenex/diesel, Conoco/diesel, Phillips 66/diesel, SA/diesel/24hr, **food:** Burger King, China Rest., Happy Chef/24hr, KFC, McDonald's, Perkins, Pizza Hut, Ranch Family Rest., Subway, **lodging:** Budget Inn, Comfort Inn, Holiday Inn, Super 8, **other:** HOSPITAL, CarQuest, Chrysler/Plymouth/Dodge/Jeep, Goodyear, K-Mart, Pontiac/Buick

99 rd 39, Fairmont, **S...**access to gas, food, lodging

93 MN 263, rd 27, Welcome, **1/2 mi S...gas:** Cenex, camping

87 MN 4, Sherburn, **1 mi S...gas:** Cenex, **food:** Ma Faber's Cookin', **other:** HOSPITAL, camping

80 rd 29, Alpha, no facilities

73 US 71, Jackson, **N...gas:** Conoco/diesel, **food:** Burger King, **lodging:** Best Western/rest., Super 8, **other:** to Kilen Woods SP, **S...gas:** BP, **food:** Embers Rest., Pizza Ranch, Subway, **lodging:** Budget Host, **other:** HOSPITAL, Park-Vu Motel, Chevrolet/Buick/Pontiac, Chrysler/Plymouth/Dodge/Jeep, to Spirit Lake, KOA(May-Sept)

72.5mm W Fork Des Moines River

72mm rest area wb, full(handicapped)facilities, phone, picnic tables, litter barrels, vending, petwalk

69mm rest area eb, full(handicapped)facilities, phone, picnic tables, litter barrels, vending, petwalk

64 MN 86, Lakefield, **N...**HOSPITAL, gas/diesel, food, camping

57 rd 9, Spafford, to Heron Lake, no facilities

50 MN 264, rd 1, to Brewster, Round Lake, **S...**camping

47 rd 53, no facilities

46mm weigh sta eb

45 MN 60, Worthington, **N...gas:** BP/diesel, **S...gas:** Casey's, Shell/diesel/24hr, **food:** McDonald's, **lodging:** Budget Inn, Sunset Inn, camping

43 US 59, Worthington, **N...lodging:** Travelodge, **S...gas:** BP, Casey's, Cenex/diesel, Phillips 66/diesel, Shell, **food:** Burger King, Country Kitchen, DQ, Godfather's, Happy Chef, KFC, McDonald's, Perkins/24hr, Pizza Hut, Subway, Taco John's, **lodging:** AmericInn, Budget Inn, Day's Inn, Holiday Inn Express, **other:** HOSPITAL, County Mkt Foods/24hr, Hy-Vee Foods, Chevrolet/Pontiac/Buick/Cadillac, Family$, Ford, JC Penney, ShopKO, Wal-Mart SuperCtr/gas/24hr

42 MN 266, rd 25, to Reading, **S...lodging:** Super 8, **other:** Wal-Mart SuperCtr/gas/24hr

33 rd 13, Rushmore, to Wilmont, no facilities

26 MN 91, Adrian, **S...gas:** Cenex/diesel, **other:** camping

25mm rest area wb, full(handicapped)facilities, phone, picnic tables, litter barrels, petwalk

24mm rest area eb, full(handicapped)facilities, phone, picnic tables, litter barrels, petwalk

18 rd 3, Kanaranzi, Magnolia, no facilities

12 US 75, Luverne, **N...gas:** BP/Subway/diesel, Casey's, Cenex/diesel, FuelTime/diesel, Phillips 66/diesel, Sinclair, **food:** Country Kitchen, McDonald's, Pizza Hut, Taco John's, Tasty Drive-In, **lodging:** Comfort Inn, Cozy Rest Motel(1mi), Hillcrest Motel(2mi), **other:** HOSPITAL, Chevrolet/Pontiac/Buick/GMC, Chrysler/Dodge/Jeep, Jubilee Foods, NAPA, truckwash, to Blue Mounds SP, Pipestone NM, **S...food:** Magnolia Steaks, **lodging:** Super 8, **other:** Pamida

5 rd 6, Beaver Creek, **N...gas:** Shell/diesel

1 MN 23, rd 17, to Jasper, **N...other:** to Pipestone NM, access to gas/diesel

0mm Minnesota/South Dakota state line, **Welcome Ctr/weigh sta eb, full(handicapped)facilities, info, phone, picnic tables, litter barrels**

MINNESOTA
Interstate 94

Exit #	Services
259mm	Minnesota/Wisconsin state line, St Croix River
258	MN 95 N, to Stillwater, Hastings, Lakeland, no facilities
257mm	weigh sta wb
256mm	**Welcome Ctr wb, full(handicapped)facilities, phone, picnic tables, litter barrels, vending, petwalk**
253	rd 15, Manning Ave, **S...other:** KOA, StoneRidge Golf, to Afton Alps SP, ski area
251	rd 19, Keats Ave, Woodbury Dr, **S...gas:** KT, SA, **food:** Burger King, DQ, FoodCourt, Subway, **lodging:** Extended Stay America, Holiday Inn Express, **other:** Outlets/famous brands, KOA
250	rd 13, Radio Dr, Inwood Ave, **N...**Machine Shed Rest., **S...gas:** Holiday, **food:** Blimpie, Don Pablo, Schlotsky's, Starbucks, Sunset Grill, Taco Bell, TGIFriday, Wendy's, **other:** Borders Books/Café, Champp's, Circuit City, CompUSA, Cub Foods, GNC, Hepner's Auto Ctr, Home Depot, Jo-Ann Crafts, LandsEnd Inlet, Mervyn's Calif, OfficeMax, Old Navy, Tires+
249	I-694 N & I-494 S, no facilities
247	MN 120, Century Ave, **N...food:** Denny's, Toby's Rest., **lodging:** AmericInn, Super 8, **other:** Harley-Davidson, Saturn, **S...gas:** SA, **food:** GreenMill Rest., McDonald's, **lodging:** Country Inn/rest., **other:** Chevrolet
246c b	McKnight Ave, **N...**3M
a	Ruth St(from eb, no return), **N...gas:** BP, Sinclair, **food:** Culver's, HoHo Chinese, Perkins, **other:** Firestone/auto, Michael's
245	White Bear Ave, **N...gas:** SA/Subway, **food:** Hardee's, Embers Rest., N China Buffet, **lodging:** Exel Inn, Ramada Inn, **S...gas:** BP, **food:** Arby's, Bakers Square, Burger King, Davanni's Pizza/subs, Ground Round, KFC/Pizza Hut, Krispy Kreme, McDonald's, Perkins, Taco Bell, **lodging:** Holiday Inn, **other:** Chrysler/Plymouth, Firestone/auto, JC Penney, Target
244	US 10 E, US 61 S, Mounds/Kellogg, no facilities
243	US 61, Mounds Blvd, **S...**River Centre
242d	US 52 S, MN 3, 6th St, **N...gas:** Holiday, **food:** Subway
c	7th St, **S...gas:** SA
b a	I-35E N, US 10 W, I-35E S(from eb)
241c	I-35E S(from wb)
b	10th St, 5th St, to downtown
a	12th St, Marion St, Kellogg Blvd, **N...lodging:** Best Western Kelly Inn, **other:** Sears, **S...gas:** BP, Holiday, SA, **lodging:** Savoy Inn, **other:** HOSPITAL, st capitol
240	Dale Ave, no facilities
239b a	Lexington Pkwy, Hamline Ave, **N...gas:** BP, **food:** Chevy's Mexican, Hardee's/24hr, **lodging:** Sheraton, **other:** HOSPITAL, Cub Foods, K-Mart, Target
238	Snelling Ave, **N...food:** Applebee's, McDonald's, Perkins, **lodging:** Sheraton, **other:** Target, **S...gas:** Citgo, **other:** Tires+, same as 239
237	Cretin Ave, Vandalia Ave, to downtown
236	MN 280, University Ave, to downtown
235b	Huron Blvd, **N...gas:** Citgo, **food:** Arnold's Burger Grill, **other:** HOSPITAL, U of MN
235mm	Mississippi River
235a	Riverside Ave, 25th Ave, **N...gas:** Winner, **food:** Starbucks, **S...food:** Perkins, Taco Bell
234c	Cedar Ave, downtown
234b a	MN 55, Hiawatha Ave, 5th St, **N...lodging:** Holiday Inn, **other:** to downtown
233b	I-35W N, I-35W S(exits left from wb)
a	11th St(from wb), **N...**downtown
231b	Hennepin Ave, Lyndale Ave, to downtown
a	I-394, US 12 W, to downtown
230	US 52, MN 55, 4th St, 7th St, Olson Hwy, **N...**Metrodome, **S...**HOSPITAL, Int Mkt Square
229	W Broadway, Washington Ave, **N...gas:** Holiday, Old Colony/diesel, **food:** Burger King, **S...food:** Taco Bell, Wendy's, **other:** Target
228	Dowling Ave N, no facilities
226	53rd Ave N, 49th Ave N, no facilities
225	I-694 E, MN 252 N, to Minneapolis, no facilities
34	to MN 100, Shingle Creek Pkwy, **N...food:** ChiChi's, Cracker Barrel, Denny's, Olive Garden, TGIFriday, **lodging:** AmericInn, Baymont Inn, Best Western, Comfort Inn, Country Inn Suites, Extended Stay America, Hilton, Motel 6, Super 8, **S...food:** Ground Round, India Passage, New King Buffet, Panera Bread, Perkins, Pizza Hut, Vallarta's Mexican, **lodging:** The Inn on the Farm, **other:** Best Buy, Circuit City, Ford, Kohl's, PepBoys, Target, Tires+
33	rd 152, Brooklyn Blvd, **N...food:** Culver's, **other:** Chevrolet, Dodge, Honda, Mazda, Pontiac, **S...gas:** BP, **food:** Embers Rest., **other:** Family$, Chrysler/Plymouth/Jeep, Rainbow Foods, Walgreen
31	rd 81, Lakeland Ave, **N...gas:** SA/diesel, **food:** DQ, Wagner's Drive-In, Wendy's, **lodging:** Ramada Inn, **S...lodging:** Budget Host, Super 8, **other:** Kennedy Transmissions
30	Boone Ave, **N...lodging:** Northland Inn/rest., Sleep Inn, **S...**Home Depot
29b a	US 169, to Hopkins, Osseo, no facilities
28	rd 61, Hemlock Lane, **N on Elm Creek...gas:** Citgo, **food:** Arby's/Sbarro's, Buca Café, ChuckeCheese, Don Pablo, Famous Dave's, Ground Round, Hop's Grill, Houlihan's, Joe's Crabshack, Krispy Kreme, Mongkok Asian, Olive Garden, Panera Bread, Qdoba Mexican, Red Lobster, Starbucks, TimberLodge Steaks, **lodging:** Hampton Inn, Staybridge Suites, **other:** Best Buy, Borders Books, Cub Foods, Jo-Ann Fabrics, Kohl's, Old Navy, Tires+, same as 215, **S...gas:** BP, **food:** Perkins/24hr, **lodging:** Travelodge

E ↕ W

St Paul

Minneapolis

Interstate 94

E
W

216 I-94 W and I-494, no facilities

215 rd 109, Weaver Lake Rd, **N...gas:** Citgo, SA/diesel, **food:** Burger King, Bakers Square, Cattle Co Steaks, Champp's, DQ, Don Pablo, Hop's Grill, J Cousineau's Rest., Joe's Crabshack, KFC, McDonald's, Old Country Buffet, Papa John's, Pizza Hut, Subway, Taco Bell, Wendy's, **lodging:** Hampton Inn, Staybridge Suties, **other:** MEDICAL CARE, Barnes&Noble, Cub Foods, GNC, Goodyear/auto, Kohl's, K-Mart, Old Navy, Tires+, USPO, Walgreen, mall, same as 28, **S...food:** Applebee's, Fuddrucker's

214mm rest area eb, full(handicapped)facilities, phone, picnic tables, litter barrels

213 rd 30, 95th Ave N, Maple Grove, **N...gas:** SA/diesel, **S...gas:** Holiday/diesel, **food:** Culver's, McDonald's, Orient Buffet, Quizno's, **S...other:** Rainbow Foods, Sam's Club, Target, Wal-Mart/auto, KOA(2mi)

207 MN 101, Rogers, to Elk River, **N...gas:** Holiday/diesel, SA/diesel, TA/Citgo/diesel/24hr/@, **food:** Burger King, Denny's, Domino's, McDonald's, Pizza Hut, Subway, Taco Bell, Wendy's, **lodging:** Super 8, **other:** Camping World(off Rogers Dr), Target, **S...gas:** BP, Sinclair/diesel, **food:** Country Kitchen, DQ, Ember's Rest., Subway, **lodging:** AmercInn, **other:** Chevrolet

205.5mm Crow River

205 MN 241, rd 36, St Michael, **S...gas:** SA/diesel, **3 mi S...gas:** Exxon, **food:** McDonald's

202 rd 37, Albertville, **N...gas:** Conoco/diesel, **food:** Burger King, Subway, **S...gas:** BP, Phillips 66, Shell, **lodging:** Riverwood Hotel/rest.

201 rd 19(rom eb), Albertville, St Michael, **N...other:** Albertville Outlets/famous brands, **S...gas:** BP

195 rd 75(from wb, no EZ return), Monticello, **N...gas:** Conoco/diesel, **food:** Hawk's Grill, Jam'n Go Café, **other:** HOSPITAL

193 MN 25, Monticello, to Buffalo, Big Lake, **N...gas:** Holiday/diesel, **food:** Burger King, Country Grill, DQ, KFC, Perkins, Taco Bell, Wendy's, **lodging:** AmericInn, **other:** AutoValue Parts, BMW, Cub Foods, Honda, K-Mart, Monticello RV Ctr, **S...gas:** BP, Conoco, SA/diesel, **food:** McDonald's, Subway, **lodging:** Best Western, Comfort Inn, Day's Inn, **other:** Checker Parts, Chevrolet, Ford/Mercury, Goodyear/auto, Lake Maria SP

187mm rest area eb, full(handicapped)facilities, phone, picnic tables, litter barrels, vending, petwalk

183 rd 8, Hasty, to Silver Creek, Maple Lake, **N...**Northern RV/boat, **S...gas:** Marathon/diesel/rest./24hr/@, **other:** to Lake Maria SP, camping

St Cloud

178 MN 24, Clearwater, to Annandale, **N...gas:** Citgo/diesel, Holiday/24hr, Marathon/Pizza Hut, **food:** DQ, Burger King, Subway, **lodging:** Best Western, Budget Inn, Day's Inn, **other:** Eagle Trace Golf/grill, KOA(1mi), **S...gas:** Exxon/diesel, **food:** Longhorn Steaks, **other:** A-1 Acres Camping(1mi)

178mm rest area wb, full(handicapped)facilities, phone, picnic tables, litter barrels, petwalk, vending

171 rd 7, rd 75, St Augusta, **N...gas:** Exxon/diesel, Holiday/diesel, **food:** McDonald's, Nathan B's Rest., **lodging:** AmericInn, Holiday Inn Express, Ramada Ltd, Travelodge, **other:** HOSPITAL, Toyota, **S...gas:** Conoco/diesel, **other:** Pleasureland RV Ctr

167b a MN 15, to St Cloud, to Kimball, **4 mi N...gas:** SA/diesel, **food:** Applebee's, Arby's, Bakers Square, Chipotle Mexican, Embers Rest., McDonald's, Old Country Buffet, Outback Steaks, Perkins, Pizza Hut, Taco Bell, TimberLodge Steaks, **lodging:** Baymont Inn, Best Western, Comfort Inn, Country Inn Suites, Fairfield Inn, Holiday Inn, Quality Inn, Ramada Ltd, Radisson, Super 8, **other:** HOSPITAL, CashWise Foods, Kohl's, Sam's Club, ShopKO

164 MN 23, Rockville, to St Cloud, **2-3 mi N...**Taco Bell, **lodging:** Motel 6, Ramada Ltd

162.5mm Sauk River

160 rd 2, St Joseph, to Cold Spring, **N...gas:** BP, SA, **lodging:** Super 8, **other:** Coll of St Benedict

158 rd 75(from eb), to St Cloud, same as 160, 3 mi N

156 rd 159, St Joseph, **N...**St Johns U, no facilities

153 rd 9, Avon, **N...gas:** Citgo, Shell/diesel, **food:** Neighbor's Rest., **lodging:** AmericInn, **S...other:** El Rancho Manana Camping, auto parts

152mm rest area both lanes, full(handicapped)facilities, phone, picnic tables, litter barrels, vending, petwalk

147 MN 238, rd 10, Albany, **N...gas:** Holiday/diesel/24hr, Marathon, Shell/Subway/diesel, **food:** DQ, Hillcrest Rest., **lodging:** Country Inn Suites, **other:** HOSPITAL, IGA Food, **S...food:** KFC, **other:** Chrysler/Plymouth/Dodge/Jeep, NAPA

140 rd 11, Freeport, **N...gas:** Conoco/diesel, **food:** Charlie's Café, **lodging:** Ackie's Pioneer Inn, **other:** USPO, **S...**LP

137 MN 237, rd 65, New Munich, no facilities

MINNESOTA

Interstate 94

E ↕ W

137mm Sauk River

135 rd 13, Melrose, **N...gas:** Mobil/diesel, Phillips 66/Subway/diesel/24hr, **food:** Burger King, **other:** HOSPITAL, Ford, Jublilee Foods, NAPA, **S...gas:** Conoco/diesel, **food:** DQ, El Portal Mexican, **lodging:** Super 8, **other:** Save Foods

132.5mm Sauk River

131 MN 4, Meire Grove, to Paynesville, no facilities

128mm Sauk River

127 US 71, MN 28, Sauk Centre, **N...gas:** Casey's, Holiday/diesel, SA/24hr, **food:** DQ, Hardee's, McDonald's, Pizza Hut, Subway, **lodging:** AmeriInn, BestValue Inn, Super 8, **other:** HOSPITAL, Coborn's Foods, Ford/Mercury, **S...gas:** BP/diesel/café/24hr, **other:** Chevrolet/Pontiac/Buick/Chrysler/Jeep, RV Service

124 Sinclair Lewis Ave(from eb), Sauk Centre, no facilities

119 rd 46, West Union, no facilities

114 MN 127, rd 3, Osakis, to Westport, **3 mi N...**gas/diesel, food, lodging, camping

Alexandria

105mm rest area wb, full(handicapped)facilities, phone, picnic tables, litter barrels, vending, petwalk

103 MN 29, Alexandria, to Glenwood, **N...gas:** Citgo, F&F/diesel, Holiday, **food:** Burger King, Country Kitchen, Culver's, Dolittle's Café, Hardee's, KFC, McDonald's, Pizza Hut, Subway, Taco Bell, **lodging:** AmercInn, Best Inn, Comfort Inn, Day's Inn, SkyLine Motel, Super 8, **other:** HOSPITAL, Chevrolet/Cadillac/Mazda, OfficeMax, Target, Wal-Mart/24hr, **S...gas:** Conoco/diesel, **lodging:** Country Inn Suites, Holiday Inn, **other:** Buick/Pontiac/GMC

100mm Lake Latoka

100 MN 27, no facilities

99mm rest area eb, full(handicapped)facilities, phone, picnic tables, litter barrels, vending, petwalk

97 MN 114, rd 40, Garfield, to Lowery, no facilities

90 rd 7, Brandon, **2-3 N...**gas, food, camping, **S...**camping, ski area

82 MN 79, rd 41, Evansville, to Erdahl, **2 mi N...gas:** BP/diesel, **S...**HOSPITAL, camping

77 MN 78, rd 10, Ashby, to Barrett, **N...**gas/diesel, food, camping, **S...**camping

69mm rest area wb, full(handicapped)facilities, phone, picnic tables, litter barrels, petwalk, vending

67 rd 35, Dalton, **N...**camping, **S...**camping

61 US 59 S, rd 82, to Elbow Lake, **N...gas:** Citgo/diesel/café/LP/24hr, **other:** HOSPITAL, camping(4mi), **S...**camping

60mm rest area eb, full(handicapped)facilities, phone, picnic tables, litter barrels, petwalk, vending

57 MN 210, rd 25, Fergus Falls, **N...**HOSPITAL

55 rd 1, Fergus Falls, to Wendell, no facilities

54 MN 210, Lincoln Ave, Fergus Falls, **N...gas:** Cenex/diesel, F&F/diesel, Holiday, Tesoro, **food:** Applebee's, Burger King, Godfather's, KFC, McDonald's, Pizza Hut, Speedway Grill, Subway, **lodging:** AmericInn, Best Western, Comfort Inn, Day's Inn, Motel 7, Super 8, **other:** HOSPITAL, Chrysler/Jeep/Dodge, Ford/Lincoln/Mercury, Home Depot, JC Penney, K-Mart, Mazda, Parts+, Pontiac/GMC, Radio Shack, SunMart Foods, Target, Tires+, Toyota, mall, **S...food:** Mabel Murphy's Rest., **other:** Wal-Mart/drugs/24hr

Fergus Falls

50 rd 88, rd 52, to US 59, Elizabeth, to Fergus Falls, **N...gas:** AmStar/diesel/rest./24hr

38 rd 88, Rothsay, **S...gas:** Tesoro/diesel/café/24hr, Comfort Zone Inn

32 MN 108, rd 30, Lawndale, to Pelican Rapids, no facilities

24 MN 24, Barnesville, **N...food:** Tastee Freez, **1 mi S...gas:** Tesoro, Cenex/diesel, **food:** DQ

22 MN 9, Barnesville, **1 mi S...gas:** Tesoro, Cenex/diesel, **food:** DQ

15 rd 10, Downer, no facilities

8mm Buffalo River

6 MN 336, rd 11, to US 10, Dilworth, no facilities

5mm Red River weigh sta eb

2 rd 52, Moorhead, **1-2 mi N...gas:** Holiday/diesel, **food:** Bennigan's, Perkins, Speedway Grill, **lodging:** Guesthouse Motel, Travelodge, **other:** HOSPITAL, KOA, Target

Moorhead

2mm Welcome Ctr eb, full(handicapped)facilities, info, phone, picnic tables, litter barrels, vending

1b 20th St, Moorhead(from eb, no return), no facilities

1a US 75, Moorhead, **N...gas:** Phillips 66, **food:** Burger King, Papa Murphy's, Village Inn, **lodging:** Courtyard, **other:** SunMart Foods, **S...gas:** BP/24hr, Casey's, Citgo, **food:** Golden Phoenix Chinese, Hardee's, **lodging:** Day's Inn, Motel 75, Super 8, **other:** Osco Drug, Pontiac/GMC

0mm Minnesota/North Dakota state line, Red River

Interstate 494/694

E ↕ W

Exit # Services

I-494/I-694 loops around Minneapolis/St Paul.

71 rd 31, Pilot Knob Rd, **N...lodging:** Courtyard, Fairfield Inn, **S...lodging:** Holiday Inn Select, **food:** LoneOak Café, Sidney's Café(1mi)

70 I-35E, N to St Paul, S to Albert Lea

69 MN 149, MN 55, Dodd Rd, **N...food:** Ziggy's Deli

St Paul

67 US 52, MN S, Robert Rd, **1 mi N...gas:** BP, Mobil, Holiday, **food:** Acre's Rest., Arby's/Sbarro's, Arnold's Burgers, Bakers Square, Bridgeman's Rest., Burger King, Godfather's, KFC, Old Country Buffet, Pizza Hut, Taco Bell, White Castle, **other:** MEDICAL CARE, Aamco, Best Buy, Buick/Pontiac, Chevrolet, Cub Foods, Dodge, Ford/Lincoln/Mercury, Jo-Ann Fabrics, Kia, K-Mart, Mazda, Nissan, Rainbow Foods/24hr, Sam's Club, Target, Toyota, VW, outlet mall, **S...gas:** PDQ

Interstate 494/694

E

W

66 MN 3 N, MN 103 S, no facilities

65 7th Ave, 5th Ave, no facilities

64b a MN 56, Concord St, **N...gas:** Conoco/diesel, **lodging:** Best Western Drovers, **other:** Ford Trucks, Goodyear, Peterbilt, **S...lodging:** Golden Steer Motel/rest.

63mm Mississippi River

63c Maxwell Ave, no facilities

b a US 10, US 61, to St Paul, Hastings, **S...gas:** BP, SA, **lodging:** Boyd's Motel, Subway

62 Lake Rd, **N...lodging:** Country Inn Suites, **S...gas:** SA

60 Valley Creek Rd, **N...food:** Burger King, Cracker Barrel, McDonald's, Pizza Hut, Subway, **lodging:** Hampton Inn, **other:** Goodyear, **S...gas:** BP, SA/diesel/LP, **food:** Applebee's, Ciatti's Rest., Old Mexico Rest., Oriental Rest., Perkins, Pizza, **lodging:** Red Roof Inn, **other:** Best Buy, Kohl's, Rainbow Foods/24hr, Target, Walgreen

58b a I-94, E to Madison, W to St Paul. **I-494 S begins/ends, I-694 N begins/ends**

57 rd 10, 10th St N, **E...**Wingate Inn, **W...gas:** Tom Thumb Superette, **food:** Burger King, KFC, **other:** K-Mart, Rainbow Foods/24hr, mall

55 MN 5, **W...gas:** BP/diesel, Holiday, **food:** Subway, **other:** st patrol

52b a MN 36, N St Paul, to Stillwater, **W...gas:** F&F/diesel

51 MN 120, **E...gas:** BP, Conoco, SA/diesel, **food:** Best Subs, Taco Bell, Zapata's Café

50 White Bear Ave, **E...gas:** Gas4Less, SA, **other:** K-Mart, **W...gas:** BP, Shell, **food:** Arby's, Applebee's, Bakers Square, Burger King, ChiChi's, Denny's, Dutch Rest., Godfather's, Hardee's/24hr, KFC, Old Country Buffet, Perkins/24hr, Red Lobster, Taco Bell, Wendy's, **lodging:** Best Western, Emerald Inn, **other:** Aamco, Best Buy, Goodyear, Jo-Ann Fabrics, Sears/auto, Tires+, mall

48 US 61, **E...gas:** Citgo, **food:** KFC, **other:** Acura/Honda/Buick, Chrysler/Dodge/Jeep, Ford, Isuzu, Mercury/Lincoln, Saturn, Subaru, Van Sales, **W...food:** Chili's, Gulden's Rest., McDonald's, Olive Garden, **lodging:** Best Western, NorthernAire Motel, **other:** HOSPITAL, Toyota, Audi/Porsche, Venburg Tire

St Paul

47 I-35E, N to Duluth

46 I-35E, US 10, S to St Paul

45 rd 49, Rice St, **N...gas:** Mobil/diesel, Phillips 66, **food:** Taco Bell, **other:** Checker Parts, **S...gas:** Marathon, **food:** A&W, Burger King, Hardee's, Taco John's, **other:** Kath Parts

43b Victoria St, **S...** Bob's Food Mkt

a Lexington Ave, **N...food:** Greenmill Rest., **lodging:** Hampton Inn, Hilton Garden, **S...gas:** BP/diesel, Conoco, Mobil/diesel, Sinclair, **food:** Blue Fox Grill, Burger King, Davanni's Pizza, Perkins, Wendy's, **lodging:** Holiday Inn, Super 8, **other:** Goodyear/auto, Kennedy Transmissions, Target

42b US 10 W(from wb), to Anoka, no facilities

a MN 51, Snelling Ave, **1 mi S...gas:** Shell, **food:** McDonald's, **lodging:** Country Inn Suites, Holiday Inn

41b a I-35W, S to Minneapolis, N to Duluth

40 Long Lake Rd, 10th St NW, no facilities

39 Silver Lake Rd, **N...gas:** BP, Sinclair, **food:** McDonald's, **other:** Ford, Snyder Drug, U-Haul

38b a MN 65, Central Ave, **N...gas:** Holiday/diesel, **food:** Subway, Shorewood Rest., **S...gas:** Ashland, SA, **food:** A&W/KFC, Arby's, Asia Rest., Buffalo Wild Wings, Cousins Subs, Denny's, Embers Rest., Flameburger Rest., Ground Round, La Casita Mexican, McDonald's, Papa John's, Subway/TCBY, Taco Bell, Ududi Indian Cuisine, Wendy's, White Castle, **lodging:** Best Western Kelly, Starlite Motel, **other:** GNC, Radio Shack, Target, Tires+, Welle Parts

37 rd 47, University Ave, **N...gas:** Holiday, Mobil, SA/diesel, Sinclair, **food:** Burger King, Cattle Co Rest., McDonald's, Zantigo's Rest., **other:** CarQuest, Cub Foods, Goodyear, Home Depot, Walgreen, **S...gas:** Bona Bros/repair, Shell

Minneapolis

36 E River Rd, no facilities

35mm I-494 W begins/ends, I-694 E begins/ends

35c MN 252, **N...gas:** Holiday, SA

b a I-94 E to Minneapolis

34 to MN 100, Shingle Creek Pkwy, **N...food:** ChiChi's, Cracker Barrel, Denny's, Olive Garden, **lodging:** AmericInn, Baymont Inn, Best Western, Comfort Inn, Hilton, Super 8, **S...food:** Ground Round, India Passage, New King Buffet, Panera Bread, Perkins, Pizza Hut, Vallarta's Mexican, **lodging:** The Inn on the Farm, **other:** Best Buy, Circuit City, Ford, Kohl's, PepBoys, Target, Tires+

33 rd 152, Brooklyn Blvd, **N...food:** Culver's, **other:** Chevrolet, Dodge, Honda, Mazda, Pontiac, **S...gas:** BP, **food:** Embers Rest., **other:** Family$, Chrysler/Plymouth/Jeep, Rainbow Foods, Walgreen

MINNESOTA

Interstate 494/694

E ↕ W

Exit	Services
31	rd 81, Lakeland Ave, **N...gas:** SA, Shell/diesel, **food:** DQ, Wagner's Drive-In, Wendy's, **lodging:** Ramada Inn, **S...lodging:** Budget Host, Super 8, **other:** Kennedy Transmissions
30	Boone Ave, **N...lodging:** Northland Inn/rest., Sleep Inn, **S...**Home Depot
29b a	US 169, to Hopkins, Osseo, no facilities
28	rd 61, Hemlock Lane, **N on Elm Creek...gas:** Citgo, **food:** Arby's/Sbarro's, Buca Café, Champp's Grill, ChuckeCheese, Don Pablo, Famous Dave's BBQ, Ground Round, Hop's Grill, Houlihan's, Joe's Crabshack, Krispy Kreme, Mongkok Asian, Old Country Buffet, Olive Garden, Panera Bread, Red Lobster, Starbucks, TimberLodge Steaks, **lodging:** Hampton Inn, Staybridge Suites, **other:** Best Buy, Byerly's Rest., Cub Foods, Jo-Ann Fabrics, Kohl's, Old Navy, Tires+, **S...gas:** BP, **food:** Perkins/24hr, **lodging:** Travelodge
27	I-94 W to St Cloud, I-94/694 E to Minneapolis
26	rd 10, Bass Lake Rd, **E...gas:** Conoco, **food:** Culver's, McDonald's, **lodging:** Extended Stay America, **other:** mall, **W...gas:** BP, Sinclair/LP, **lodging:** Hilton Garden
23	rd 9, Rockford Rd, **E...gas:** BP, Holiday, **food:** Chili's, **other:** Checker Parts, Lincoln/Mercury, Old Navy, Radio Shack, Rainbow Foods/24hr, Target, Walgreen, **W...gas:** Conoco, PDQ, **food:** Caribou Coffee, Cousins Subs, DQ, LeAnn Chin Chinese, Starbucks, Subway, TGIFriday
22	MN 55, **E...gas:** Holiday/diesel, **food:** Denny's, Green Mill Rest., McDonald's, **lodging:** Best Western Kelly, Radisson, Red Roof Inn, **W...gas:** Holiday/diesel, **food:** Arby's, Burger King, Davanni's Rest., Grandma's Grill, Mulligan's Grill, New Dynasty Chinese, Perkins, **lodging:** Comfort Inn, Day's Inn, Holiday Inn, **other:** Goodyear/auto, Tires+
21	rd 6, **E...gas:** BP/KwikTrip, **other:** Discount Tire, Home Depot
20	Carlson Pkwy, **E...gas:** Holiday/diesel, **food:** Subway, **W...food:** Italianni's Rest., **lodging:** Country Inn Suites
19b a	I-394 E, US 12 W, to Minneapolis, **1 mi E off of I-394...food:** Applebee's, Byerly's Rest., Godfather's, Uno Pizza, Wendy's, **other:** Best Buy, Borders Books, Circuit City, Ford, JC Penney, Jo-Ann Fabrics, OfficeMax, Marshall Field, Mazda, Mercedes/BMW, Saab, Sears/auto, Target, Tires+, mall, **1/2 mi W...gas:** BP, **food:** Bankok Bowl, BBQ, ChiChi's, Pizza Hut, **other:** MEDICAL CARE,Chevrolet, Lexus, Mitsubishi, Nissan
17b a	Minnetonka Blvd, **W...gas:** Mobil, **food:** Dunn Bros Coffee
16b a	MN 7, **1 mi W...food:** Davanni's Rest., Famous Dave's BBQ, Hopkins House Rest., Lund's Rest., McDonald's, Perkins, Subway, Taco Bell
13	MN 62, rd 62, no facilities
12	Valleyview Rd, rd 39(from sb)
11c	MN 5 W, **N...lodging:** Extended Stay America, **other:** Land Rover, **S...other:** Chevrolet
b a	US 169 S, US 212 W, **N...food:** Don Pablo, **lodging:** AmeriSuites, Courtyard, Fairfield Inn, Hampton Inn, Residence Inn, **S...gas:** Phillips 66, **food:** Hop's Grill, **lodging:** Homestead Suites, SpringHill Suites, TownePlace Suites, **other:** Cub Foods, Office Depot
10	US 169 N, to rd 18, no facilities
8	rd 28(from wb, no return), E Bush Lake Rd, no facilities
7b a	MN 100, rd 34, Normandale Blvd, **N...gas:** Shell/diesel, **food:** Burger King, Chili's, Embers Rest., Subway, TGI-Friday, **lodging:** Radisson, Select Inn, **S...gas:** Citgo, **lodging:** Country Inn Suites, Hilton Garden, Holiday Inn, Hotel Seville, Staybridge Inn
6b	rd 17, France Ave, **N...gas:** Mobil, **food:** Cattle Co Rest., Fuddrucker's, Macaroni Grill, Perkins, **lodging:** Best Western, Park Inn Suites, **other:** HOSPITAL, Circuit City, CompUSA, Office Depot, **S...food:** Denny's, Joe Senser's Grill, Olive Garden, **lodging:** Hampton Inn, **other:** Buick/Pontiac/GMC, Ford, Mercedes, Nissan
a	Penn Ave(no EZ eb return), **N...gas:** Citgo, **other:** Buick, Galyan's, Hyundai, Isuzu, **S...food:** Applebee's, Bennigan's, Edwardo's Café, Starbucks, Steak&Ale, Subway, **lodging:** Embassy Suites, **other:** Chevrolet, Chrysler/Pymouth/Jeep, Dodge, Kohl's, Rainbow Foods, Target
5b a	I-35W, S to Albert Lea, N to Minneapolis
4b	Lyndale Ave, **N...gas:** BP, Conoco, **food:** DQ, **lodging:** Hampton Inn, **other:** Best Buy, Borders, Honda, Mitsubishi, Radio Shack, Tires+, **S...gas:** Phillips 66, **other:** Acura, Lincoln/Mercury, Mazda, Subaru
a	MN 52, Nicollet Ave, **N...gas:** SA/diesel, **food:** Burger King, ChiChi's, **S...gas:** Mobil, Shell, **food:** Kwik Mart, Big Boy, McDonald's, **lodging:** Baymont Inn, Super 8, **other:** Home Depot
3	Portland Ave, 12th Ave, **N...gas:** Phillips 66, Sinclair, PDQ Mart, **food:** Arby's, BBQ, Ground Round, **lodging:** AmericInn, **S...gas:** BP, **food:** Denny's, Outback Steaks, Subway, **lodging:** Comfort Inn/rest., Holiday Inn Express, Microtel, **other:** SuperValu Foods, Walgreen, Wal-Mart
2c b	MN 77, **N...lodging:** Motel 6, **S...gas:** BP, SA, **lodging:** AmeriSuites, Best Western, Courtyard, Embassy Suites, Exel Inn, Marriott, Registry Hotel, Sheraton, Thunderbird Hotel, **other:** Nordstrom's, Sears, Mall of America
a	24th Ave, same as 2c b
1b	34th Ave, Nat Cemetary, **S...lodging:** Embassy Suites, Hilton, Holiday Inn
a	MN 5 E, **N...**airport
0mm	Minnesota River. I-494/I-694 loops around Minneapolis/St Paul.

Minneapolis

Interstate 10

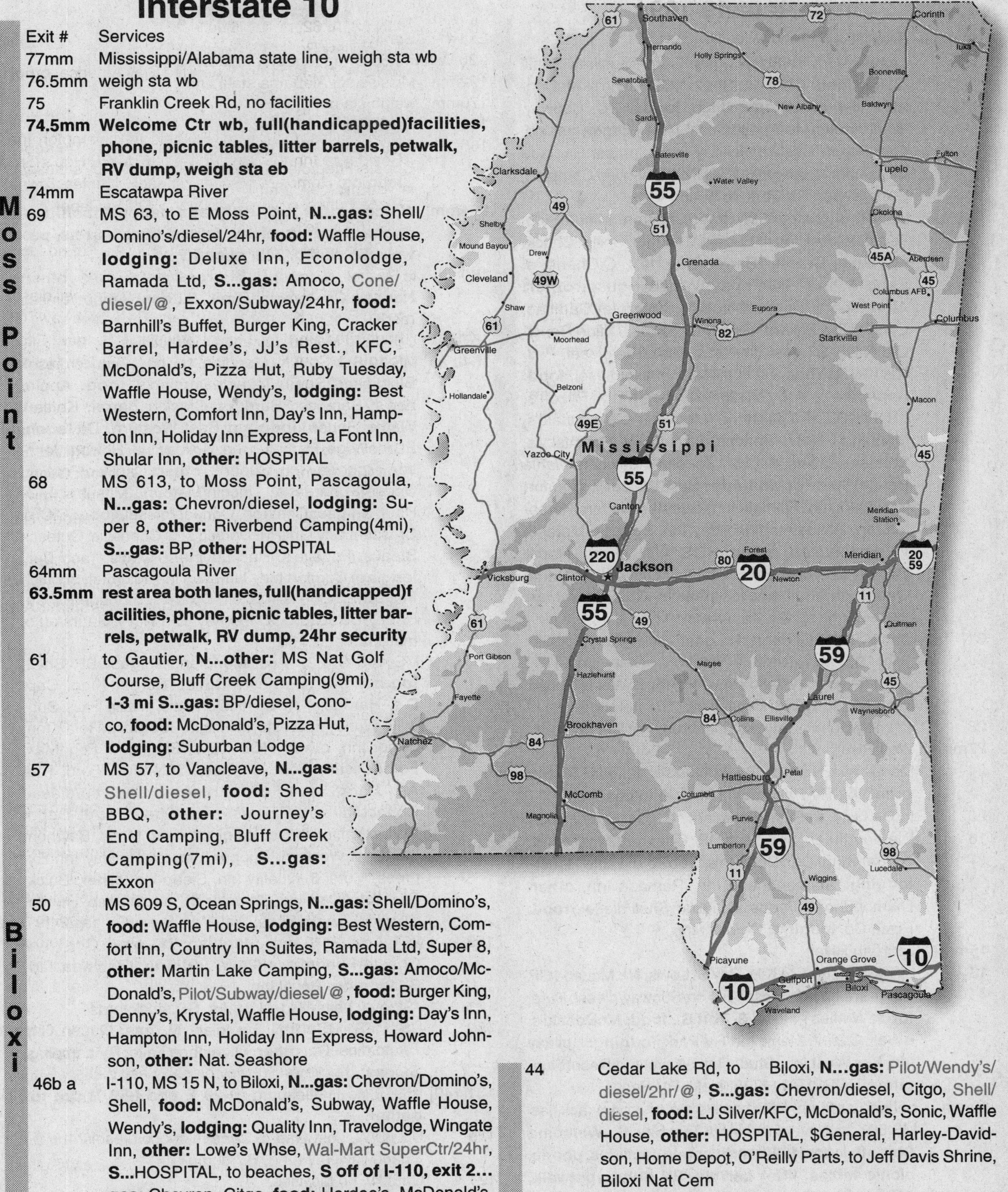

Exit #	Services
77mm	Mississippi/Alabama state line, weigh sta wb
76.5mm	weigh sta wb
75	Franklin Creek Rd, no facilities
74.5mm	**Welcome Ctr wb, full(handicapped)facilities, phone, picnic tables, litter barrels, petwalk, RV dump, weigh sta eb**
74mm	Escatawpa River
69	MS 63, to E Moss Point, **N...gas:** Shell/ Domino's/diesel/24hr, **food:** Waffle House, **lodging:** Deluxe Inn, Econolodge, Ramada Ltd, **S...gas:** Amoco, Cone/ diesel/@, Exxon/Subway/24hr, **food:** Barnhill's Buffet, Burger King, Cracker Barrel, Hardee's, JJ's Rest., KFC, McDonald's, Pizza Hut, Ruby Tuesday, Waffle House, Wendy's, **lodging:** Best Western, Comfort Inn, Day's Inn, Hampton Inn, Holiday Inn Express, La Font Inn, Shular Inn, **other:** HOSPITAL
68	MS 613, to Moss Point, Pascagoula, **N...gas:** Chevron/diesel, **lodging:** Super 8, **other:** Riverbend Camping(4mi), **S...gas:** BP, **other:** HOSPITAL
64mm	Pascagoula River
63.5mm	**rest area both lanes, full(handicapped)facilities, phone, picnic tables, litter barrels, petwalk, RV dump, 24hr security**
61	to Gautier, **N...other:** MS Nat Golf Course, Bluff Creek Camping(9mi), **1-3 mi S...gas:** BP/diesel, Conoco, **food:** McDonald's, Pizza Hut, **lodging:** Suburban Lodge
57	MS 57, to Vancleave, **N...gas:** Shell/diesel, **food:** Shed BBQ, **other:** Journey's End Camping, Bluff Creek Camping(7mi), **S...gas:** Exxon
50	MS 609 S, Ocean Springs, **N...gas:** Shell/Domino's, **food:** Waffle House, **lodging:** Best Western, Comfort Inn, Country Inn Suites, Ramada Ltd, Super 8, **other:** Martin Lake Camping, **S...gas:** Amoco/McDonald's, Pilot/Subway/diesel/@, **food:** Burger King, Denny's, Krystal, Waffle House, **lodging:** Day's Inn, Hampton Inn, Holiday Inn Express, Howard Johnson, **other:** Nat. Seashore
46b a	I-110, MS 15 N, to Biloxi, **N...gas:** Chevron/Domino's, Shell, **food:** McDonald's, Subway, Waffle House, Wendy's, **lodging:** Quality Inn, Travelodge, Wingate Inn, **other:** Lowe's Whse, Wal-Mart SuperCtr/24hr, **S...**HOSPITAL, to beaches, **S off of I-110, exit 2...gas:** Chevron, Citgo, **food:** Hardee's, McDonald's, Pizza Hut, Subway, Taco Bell, Waffle House, **lodging:** Howard Johnson, Suburban Lodge
44	Cedar Lake Rd, to Biloxi, **N...gas:** Pilot/Wendy's/ diesel/2hr/@, **S...gas:** Chevron/diesel, Citgo, Shell/ diesel, **food:** LJ Silver/KFC, McDonald's, Sonic, Waffle House, **other:** HOSPITAL, $General, Harley-Davidson, Home Depot, O'Reilly Parts, to Jeff Davis Shrine, Biloxi Nat Cem
41	MS 67 N, to Woolmarket, **N...gas:** BP, Chevron/ diesel, **other:** Parkers Landing RV Park, golf(6mi), **S...**Mazalea RV Park

MISSISSIPPI

Interstate 10

E ↕ W

Gulfport

39.5mm Biloxi River
38 Lorraine-Cowan Rd, **N...gas:** Exxon/Subway, Shell/diesel, **food:** Capt Al's Seafood, Domino's, McDonald's, **5-7 mi S...gas:** Citgo, **food:** KFC, Subway, Waffle House, **lodging:** Coast Motel, Edgewater Inn, Gulf Beach Resort, Holiday Inn Express, Ramada Ltd, Super 8, **other:** HOSPITAL, Baywood Camping, Sand Beach RV Park, to beaches
34b a US 49, to Gulfport, **N...gas:** Chevron, MinuteStop, Texaco/diesel, **food:** Backyard Burger, Chili's, ChuckeCheese, Cracker Barrel, Hardee's, O'Charley's, Papa John's, TGIFriday, Waffle House, **other:** Albertson's, Barnes&Noble, Chevrolet/Cadillac, Circuit City, Eckerd, Goody's, Honda, Office Depot, Old Navy, **S...gas:** Chevron, FastLane/diesel, Phillips 66, RacTrac, Shell/diesel, Texaco/diesel, **food:** Applebee's, Arby's/24hr, Burger King, Fazoli's, IHOP, KFC, KrispyKreme, McAlister's, McDonald's, Montana's Rest., Perkins, Piccadilly's, Schlotsky's, Shoney's, Sonic, Subway, Toucan's Mexican, Waffle House, Wendy's, **lodging:** Best Western, Comfort Inn, Day's Inn, Fairfield Inn, Guesthouse Inn, Hampton Inn, Holiday Inn, Holiday Inn Express, Motel 6, Villager Suites, **other:** HOSPITAL, Ford, Home Depot, Kia, Michael's, Nissan, OfficeMax, Prime Outlets/famous brands, Sam's Club, Wal-Mart SuperCtr/gas/24hr, transmissions
31 Canal Rd, to Gulfport, **N...gas:** Love's/Arbys/diesel/24hr, **S...gas:** Flying J/Conoco/Cookery/diesel/LP/24hr, Texaco/Krystal/diesel/24hr, **food:** Waffle House, Wendy's, **lodging:** Crystal Inn, Econolodge
28 to Long Beach, **S...gas:** Chevron, Phillips 66
27mm Wolf River
24 Menge Ave, **N...gas:** Chevron/diesel, **S...gas:** Texaco, **other:** A1 RV Park, flea mkt, golf, to beaches
20 to De Lisle, to Pass Christian, **N...gas:** Spur
16 Diamondhead, **N...gas:** BP, Chevron/24hr, **food:** Burger King, DQ, Domino's, Subway, Waffle House, **lodging:** Diamondhead Inn, Ramada Inn, **other:** Diamondhead Foods, **S...gas:** Shell/diesel, **food:** Pizza Co, **lodging:** Comfort Inn
15mm Jourdan River
13 MS 43, MS 603, to Kiln, Bay St Louis, **N...**McLeod SP, **S...gas:** Chevron/diesel, Exxon/Subway/diesel, Pure, **food:** Waffles+ Rest., **3-7 mi S...food:** McDonald's, **other:** Casino Magic Inn/RV Park, **lodging:** Holiday Inn, Key West Inn, Studio Inn, Waveland Resort Inn, **other:** HOSPITAL, KOA, Nella RV Park
10mm parking area eb, litter barrels, no restroom facilities
2 MS 607, to Waveland, NASA Test Site, **S...Welcome Ctr both lanes, full(handicapped)facilities, phone, picnic tables, litter barrels, RV dump, petwalk, 24hr security, no trucks/buses,** to Buccaneer SP, camping, to beaches
1mm weigh sta both lanes
0mm Mississippi/Louisiana state line, Pearl River

Interstate 20

E ↕ W

Meridian

Exit # Services
I-20 W and I-59 S run together to Meridian
172mm Mississippi/Alabama state line
170mm weigh sta both lanes
169 Kewanee, no facilities
165 Toomsuba, **N...gas:** Shell/Subway, Texaco/ChesterFried/diesel, **S...gas:** FuelMart/Arby's/diesel/@, **other:** KOA(2mi)
164mm Welcome Ctr wb, full(handicapped)facilities, phone, vending, picnic tables, litter barrels, petwalk, RV dump, 24hr security
160 to Russell, **N...gas:** TA/BP/diesel/rest./24hr/@, **other:** Nanabe Cr Camping(1mi), **S...gas:** Amoco/diesel/rest.
157b a US 45, to Macon, Quitman, no facilities
154b a MS 19 S, MS 39 N, Meridian, **N...gas:** Amoco/diesel, BP/diesel, Shell, Texaco/Domino's, **food:** Applebee's, Backyard Burgers, Cracker Barrel, Krystal, Waffle House, **lodging:** Best Western, Day's Inn, Econolodge, Hampton Inn, Holiday Inn, Howard Johnson, Rodeway Inn, Super 8, **other:** Cadillac/Pontiac, Dodge/Subaru/Kia, Lincoln/Mercury, Mitsubishi, U-Haul, **S...gas:** Chevron, Conoco/diesel, **food:** CiCi's, Crescent City Grill, McDonald's, O'Charley's, Outback Steaks, Popeye's, Red Lobster, Ryan's, Taco Bell, **lodging:** Comfort Inn, Jameson Inn, Microtel, Scottish Inn, **other:** BooksAMillion, Dillard's, Ethridge RV Ctr, Harley-Davidson, JC Penney, Old Navy, Sears/auto, mall, same as 153
153 MS 145 S, 22nd Ave, Meridian, **N...gas:** BP, Shell, **food:** Arby's, Barnhill's Buffet, Burger King, Capt D's, Hardee's, KFC, McDonald's, Pizza Hut, Subway, Wendy's, Western Sizzlin, **lodging:** Relax Inn, Super Inn, **other:** HOSPITAL, Firestone, FoodMax, Ford/Nissan, Goodyear/auto, $General, Ford, Rite Aid, Sack&Save Foods, **S...gas:** Chevron/diesel, Conoco/diesel, Exxon/diesel, Shell, **food:** Depot Rest., Waffle House, **lodging:** Astro Motel, Baymont Inn, Best Western, Budget 8 Motel, Holiday Inn Express, Motel 6, Quality Inn, Sleep Inn, **other:** Buick, Chevrolet/Cadillac, Chrysler/Plymouth/Jeep, Honda, Suzuki, Lowe's Whse, Wal-Mart SuperCtr/gas/24hr
152 29th Ave, 31st Ave, Meridian, **N...gas:** Chevron/ChesterFried/diesel/24hr, **lodging:** Ramada Ltd, **S...lodging:** Royal Inn
151 49th Ave, Valley Rd, **N...**tires, **S...**stockyards
150 US 11 S, MS 19 N, Meridian, **N...gas:** Queen City Trkstp/diesel@, **other:** Okatibbee Lake, RV camping, **S...gas:** Stuckey's/Subway/diesel, Shell/diesel
131[149] I-59 S, to Hattiesburg. **I-20 E and I-59 N run together.**
129 US 80 W, Lost Gap, **S...gas:** Conoco/diesel/24hr/@, Spaceway/Grill King, RV dump
121 Chunky, no facilities
119mm Chunky River
115 MS 503, Hickory, no facilities
109 MS 15, Newton, **N...gas:** Shell/Wendy's/diesel/24hr, **food:** Bo-Ro Rest., **lodging:** Thrifty Inn, **other:** lube,

Interstate 20

E ↕ W

S...gas: Chevron/diesel/24hr, Conoco/diesel, **food:** Hardee's, KFC/Taco Bell, McDonald's, Pizza Hut, Sonic, Subway, **lodging:** Day's Inn, **other:** HOSPITAL, $General, Piggly Wiggly, Wal-Mart

100 US 80, Lake, Lawrence, **N...gas:** BP/diesel/rest.

96 Lake, no facilities

95mm Bienville Nat Forest, eastern boundary

90mm rest area eb, full(handicapped)facilities, phone, picnic tables, litter barrels, petwalk, RV dump, 24hr security

88 MS 35, Forest, **N...gas:** BP/Subway/diesel, Shell, **food:** KFC, McDonald's, Pizza Hut, Wendy's, **lodging:** AppleTree Inn, Comfort Inn, Day's Inn, Holiday Inn Express, Scott Motel, **other:** HOSPITAL, Chevrolet, Honda, Wal-Mart, **S...gas:** Chevron/diesel/24hr, **food:** Santa Fe Steaks

80 MS 481, Morton, no facilities

77 MS 13, Morton, **N...gas:** Phillips 66/diesel, **other:** HOSPITAL, to Roosevelt SP, RV camping

76mm Bienville NF, western boundary

75mm rest area wb, full(handicapped)facilities, phone, picnic tables, litter barrels, petwalk, RV dump, 24hr security

68 MS 43, Pelahatchie, **N...gas:** Chevron/Subway/diesel/24hr, Conoco/diesel/rest./RV dump/24hr, **food:** Little Red Smokehouse, **other:** RV camping, **S...gas:** BP/diesel

59 US 80, E Brandon, **2 mi S...gas:** Conoco, Shell/diesel

Brandon

56 US 80, Brandon, **N...gas:** Texaco, **food:** BBQ, Burger King, CiCi's, Krystal, McDonald's, Popeye's, Taco Bell, **lodging:** Microtel, **other:** AutoZone, **S...gas:** Exxon, Mac's Gas, Shell/diesel, **food:** DQ, Sonic, Waffle House, **lodging:** Day's Inn, Red Roof Inn, **other:** to Ross Barnett Reservoir

54 Crossgates Blvd, W Brandon, **N...gas:** BP, Exxon, Phillips 66, **food:** Burger King, Domino's, Fernando's Mexican, KFC, Mazzio's, Papa John's, Pizza Hut, Popeye's, Subway, Waffle House, Wendy's, **lodging:** Ridgeland Inn, **other:** HOSPITAL, Buick/GMC, Chevrolet, Eckerd, Firestone/auto, Ford, Goodyear/auto, Kroger, Wal-Mart SuperCtr/gas/24hr, **S...**Shell/Domino's, Home Depot

52 MS 475, **N...gas:** Chevron, Conoco/diesel, **food:** Krystal(3mi), Waffle House, Wendy's(3mi), **lodging:** Quality Inn, Ramada Ltd, Super 8, **other:** Peterbilt, to Jackson Airport

48 MS 468, Pearl, **N...gas:** Conoco, MinuteStop/diesel, Shell/diesel, **food:** Arby's, Bumpers Drive-In, Burger King, Cracker Barrel, Domino's, KFC, McDonald's, O'Charley's, Pizza Hut, Popeye's, Ryan's, Schlotsky's, Shoney's, Sonic, Waffle House, **lodging:** Best Western, Comfort Inn, Econolodge, Fairfield Inn, Hampton Inn, Holiday Inn Express, Jameson Inn, Motel 6, **other:** transmissions, **S...gas:** Chevron/diesel/24hr, Shell/diesel/24hr, **lodging:** Country Inn Suites, Day's Inn, La Quinta

Jackson

47b a US 49 S, Flowood, **N...gas:** Flying J/Conoco/CountryMkt/diesel/LP/24hr/@, **food:** Western Sizzlin, **lodging:** Airport Inn, **2-3 mi S...gas:** Pilot/Krystal/Subway/diesel/24hr/@, **food:** DQ, Waffle House, **lodging:** Day's Inn, Richland Inn, Super 8, **other:** Wal-Mart SuperCtr/gas/24hr, Magnolia RV Camping

46 I-55 N, to Memphis, no facilities

45b US 51, State St, to downtown, **N...gas:** Chevron, **other:** ExpressLube, **S...gas:** Speedway/Hardee's/diesel, **other:** Nissan

a Gallatin St(from wb), to downtown, **N...gas:** Chevron, Petro/diesel/rest/@., **other:** Blue Beacon, **S...gas:** Pilot/McDonald's/diesel/@, **lodging:** Knight's Inn, **other:** Mazda, Toyota

44 I-55 S(exits left from wb), to New Orleans, no facilities

43b a Terry Rd, **N...gas:** Shell, **food:** BBQ, Kim's Seafood, Krystal, **lodging:** Tarrymore Motel

42b a Ellis Ave, Belvidere, **N...gas:** BP, Conoco, Shell, **food:** Burger King, Capt D's, Denny's, McDonald's, Popeye's, Waffle House, Wendy's, **lodging:** Best Western, Comfort Inn, Day's Inn, Econolodge, Ramada, SW Hotel, **other:** AutoZone, Chrysler/Plymouth/Dodge, Family$, Firestone, Radio Shack, U-Haul, transmissions, zoo, **S...gas:** Conoco/diesel, Exxon/diesel, Pump'n Save, **food:** DQ, **other:** Sack&Save Foods

41 I-220 N, US 49 N, to Jackson

40b a MS 18 W, Robinson Rd, **N...gas:** Phillips 66, Shell/diesel, Spur, **food:** Arby's, China Buffet, El Chico, Krystal, Mazzio's, McDonald's, Piccadilly's, Pizza Hut, Popeye's, Wendy's, **lodging:** Day's Inn, Sleep Inn, **other:** CarCare, Home Depot, Office Depot, Sears/auto, **S...gas:** Conoco, **food:** IHOP, Waffle House, **lodging:** Comfort Inn, **other:** HOSPITAL, Wal-Mart SuperCtr/gas/24hr

36 Springridge Rd, Clinton, **N...gas:** Mac's/Burger King, Shell, **food:** Backyard Burger, Bumpers Drive-In, Capt D's, China Garden, DQ, Mazzio's, McDonald's, Papa John's, Smoothie King, Subway, Taco Bell, Waffle House, Wendy's, **lodging:** Clinton Inn, Day's Inn, **other:** Avance Parts, Kroger/gas, Radio Shack, Walgreen, Wal-Mart SuperCtr/gas/24hr(2mi), **S...gas:** Exxon, Shell/diesel, **food:** Applebee's, Fazoli's, Pizza Hut, Popeye's, Shoney's, Xan's Diner, **lodging:** Comfort Inn, Hampton Inn, Holiday Inn Express, Ramada Ltd, Ridgeland Inn

MISSISSIPPI

Interstate 20

E ↕ W

35 US 80 E, Clinton, **N...gas:** Chevron/diesel, Phillips 66/diesel/rest., Shell/diesel, **food:** Backyard Burger, Chick-fil-A, McAlister's Deli, **lodging:** Ridgland Inn, **S...other:** Eagle Ridge RV Park

34 Natchez Trace Pkwy, no facilities

31 Norrell Rd, no facilities

27 Bolton, **N...gas:** Chevron, **S...gas:** BP/diesel

19 MS 22, Edwards, Flora, **N...other:** Askew Landing RV Camping, **S...gas:** BP/diesel, Phillips 66/DQ/Stuckey's, **lodging:** Relax Inn

17mm Big Black River

15 Flowers, no facilities

11 Bovina, **N...gas:** Shell/diesel/24hr, **other:** RV camping

10mm weigh sta wb

8mm weigh sta eb

6.5mm parking area eb

5b a US 61, MS 27 S, **N...gas:** Shell/diesel, Zips/diesel, **food:** Sonic, **S...gas:** Texaco/Domino's/diesel, **food:** Bumpers Rest., Rowdy's Rest., **lodging:** Beechwood Inn, Comfort Inn, Jameson Inn, Scottish Inn, **other:** RV camping, same as 4a

4b a Clay St, **N...gas:** Chevron, **lodging:** Bfd Inn/RV Park, Econolodge, Hampton Inn, Vicksburg Inn, **other:** HOSPITAL, KOA, to Vicksburg NP, **S...gas:** Shell/Domino's/diesel, **food:** China Buffet, Cracker Barrel, Dock Seafood, Pizza Inn, McAlister's, Waffle House, **lodging:** Beechwood Inn/rest., Comfort Inn, Holiday Inn Express, Jameson Inn, Scottish Inn, **other:** Chrysler/Jeep/Toyota, $General, Lincoln/Mercury, Outlet Mall/famous brands/deli, same as 5

3 Indiana Ave, **N...gas:** Texaco/Subway/diesel, **food:** Krystal, McDonald's, Waffle House, **lodging:** Best Western, Deluxe Inn, **other:** Chevrolet, Ford/Lincoln/Mercury, Honda, IGA Foods, Mazda, Rite Aid, **S...gas:** Shell, **food:** KFC, **lodging:** Best Inn, **other:** Buick/GMC/Pontica/Subaru, Family$, Sack&Save Foods

Vicksburg

1c Halls Ferry Rd, **N...gas:** Chevron/24hr, Exxon, **food:** Burger King, Sonic, **lodging:** Travel Inn, **other:** HOSPITAL, **S...gas:** FastLane/diesel, **food:** Capt D's, DQ, Goldie's BBQ, Hardee's, Piccadilly's, Pizza Hut, Popeye's, Ryan's, Shoney's, Subway, Taco Bell, Taco Casa, TCBY, Wendy's, **lodging:** Day's Inn, Fairfield Inn, Super 8, **other:** Dillard's, Home Depot, JC Penney, Kroger, USPO, mall

b US 61 S, **S...gas:** BP, Chevron/Domino's, **other:** Mitsubishi, OfficeMax, Wal-Mart SuperCtr/24hr, same as 1c

a Washington St, Vicksburg, **N...Welcome Ctr both lanes, full(handicapped)facilities, phone, gas:** Kangaroo/diesel, Shell/Subway/diesel, **food:** BBQ, **lodging:** AmeriStar Hotel, **other:** Isle of Capri RV Park, casino, transmissions, **S...food:** Waffle House, **lodging:** La Quinta, Ridgeland Inn

0mm Mississippi/Louisiana state line, Mississippi River

Interstate 55

N ↕ S

Exit # Services

291.5mm Mississippi/Tennessee state line

Southaven

291 State Line Rd, Southaven, **E...gas:** 76/Circle K, **food:** BBQ, Best Pizza, Burger King, Exline's Pizza, McDonald's, Pizza Hut, Subway, Waffle House, **lodging:** Best Western, Comfort Inn, Holiday Inn Express, Quality Inn, **other:** Firestone/auto, Goodyear/auto, K-Mart, Kroger, MegaMkt Foods, Walgreen, **W...gas:** Exxon/diesel, **food:** El Patron Mexican, KFC, Mrs Winner's, Rally's, Wendy's, **other:** Fred's Drug, Rite Aid

289 MS 302, to US 51, Horn Lake, **E...gas:** 76/Circle K, Shell, **food:** Backyard Burger, Burger King, Chick-fil-A, Chili's, Danver's, Fazoli's, IHOP, Krystal, McDonald's, O'Charley's, Outback Steaks, Schlotsky's, Starbucks, Steak'n Shake, TGIFriday, **lodging:** Comfort Suites, Fairfield Inn, Hampton Inn, **other:** HOSPITAL, Aldi Foods, Chevrolet, Chrysler/Plymouth/Jeep, $Tree, Ford, Lowe's Whse, NAPA/repair, Office Depot, Pontiac/GMC Wal-Mart SuperCtr/gas/24hr, **W...gas:** BP, Phillips 66/diesel, Shell/diesel, **food:** Applebee's, Arby's, Bob Evans, ChuckeCheese, Cracker Barrel, Great Wall Chinese, Hooters, KFC/Taco Bell, McDonald's, Mrs Winner's, Papa John's, Pizza Hut, Popeye's, Roadhouse Grill, Ryan's, Waffle House, Wendy's, **lodging:** Day's Inn, Drury Inn, Motel 6, Ramada Ltd, Sleep Inn, Super 8, **other:** Family$, Home Depot, Kroger, OfficeMax, Piggly Wiggly, Target, Walgreen

287 Church Rd, **E...gas:** Texaco/ChesterFried/diesel, **W...gas:** Shell/DQ/diesel, Texaco, **food:** McDonald's, Subway, Waffle House, **lodging:** Magnolia Inn, Super 8

285mm weigh sta both lanes

284 to US 51, Nesbit Rd, **E...gas:** Chevrolet/GMC, **W...gas:** Citgo, Nesbit 1-Stop, **food:** Happy Daze Dairybar, **other:** USPO

280 MS 304, US 51, Hernando, **E...gas:** Exxon, **food:** Huddle House, Sonic, **lodging:** Day's Inn, Hernando Inn, **W...gas:** BP, Chevron/Subway/diesel, Shell/diesel, **food:** BBQ, Church's, McDonald's, Pizza Hut, Sonic, Wendy's, **lodging:** Super 8, **other:** Kroger/gas, NAPA, Piggly Wiggly, Memphis S Camping(2mi), to Arkabutla Lake

279mm Welcome Ctr sb, full(handicapped)facilities, phone, picnic tables, litter barrels, petwalk, RV dump, 24hr security

276mm rest area nb, full(handicapped)facilities, phone, picnic tables, litter barrels, petwalk, RV dump, 24hr security

273mm Coldwater River

271 MS 306, Coldwater, **W...gas:** Amoco, **food:** Subway, **1-2 mi W...gas:** Citgo, Exxon/24hr, **other:** Lake Arkabutla, Memphis S RV Park

265 MS 4, Senatobia, **W...gas:** BP/Huddle House/diesel, Exxon, FuelMart/diesel, Shell/diesel, Texaco/diesel, **food:** KFC, McDonald's, Pizza Hut, Popey's, Sonic, Subway, Taco Bell, Waffle House, Wendy's, Western Sizzlin, **lodging:** Comfort Inn, Motel 6, **other:** HOSPITAL, CarQuest, $General, Fred's Drug, Goodyear/auto, NAPA, Piggly Wiggly, Pontiac/Buick/GMC, USPO

Interstate 55

N ↕ S

257 MS 310, Como, **E...gas:** BP/diesel, **other:** N Sardis Lake

252 MS 315, Sardis, **E...gas:** Amoco/diesel, Chevron/diesel, **food:** BBQ, **lodging:** Lake Inn, Super 8, **other:** NAPA, to Kyle SP, Sardis Dam, RV camping, **W...gas:** BP/diesel, Shell/diesel, **food:** Sonic, **lodging:** Knight's Inn, **other:** HOSPITAL, $General, Fred's Drug

246 MS 35, N Batesville, **E...**to Sardis Lake, **W...gas:** Chevron, Shell/diesel

Batesville

243b a MS 6, to Batesville, **E...gas:** BP/diesel, Texaco/diesel, **food:** Backyard Burger, **other:** Lowe's Whse, Wal-Mart SuperCtr/gas/24hr, to Sardis Lake, U of MS, **W...gas:** Chevron/diesel, Exxon/diesel, FastLane/diesel, Phillips 66/diesel, Shell/diesel, **food:** Burger King, Capt D's, Cracker Barrel, DQ, Domino's, El Charro Mexican, Hardee's, Huddle House, KFC, McDonald's, Pizza Hut, Popeye's, Sonic, Subway, Taco Bell, Wendy's, Western Sizzlin, **lodging:** AmeriHost, Comfort Inn, Day's Inn, Hampton Inn, Ramada Ltd, **other:** HOSPITAL, Advance Parts, AutoZone, $General, Factory Stores/famous brands, Family$, Kroger, Radio Shack

240mm rest area both lanes, full(handicapped)facilities, phone, picnic tables, litter barrels, petwalk, RV dump, 24hr security

237 to US 51, Courtland, **E...gas:** Pure/diesel/rest.

233 to Enid Dam, **E...**to Enid Lake, RV camping, **W...gas:** Benson's/groceries

227 MS 32, Oakland, **E...**to Cossar SP, Sunrise RV Park, **W...gas:** Chevron/diesel

220 MS 330, Tillatoba, **E...gas:** Conoco/diesel/@, **food:** All American Rest.

211 MS 7 N, to Coffeeville, **E...**Frog Hollow RV Park, **W...gas:** BP/diesel, Texaco/diesel

208 Papermill Rd, **E...**Grenada Airport

Grenada

206 MS 8, MS 7 S, to Grenada, **E...gas:** Exxon, RaceTrac, Shell/diesel, Texaco, **food:** BBQ/Steaks, Burger King, Domino's, Hong Kong Chinese, Jake&Rip's Café, La Cabana Mexican, McAlister's Deli, McDonald's, Pizza Hut, Pizza Inn, RagTime Grill, Shoney's, Subway, Taco Bell, Wendy's, Western Sizzlin, **lodging:** Best Western/rest., Comfort Inn, Day's Inn, Hampton Inn, Holiday Inn/rest., Jameson Inn, Super 8, **other:** HOSPITAL, AutoZone, Chrysler/Plymouth/Dodge, $General, Ford/Lincoln/Mercury, Toyota, USPO, Wal-Mart SuperCtr/24hr, to Grenada Lake/RV camping, **W...gas:** Exxon/HuddleHouse, **lodging:** Country Inn Suites, Hilltop Inn

204mm parking area sb, phone, litter barrels

202mm parking area nb, phone, litter barrels

199 S Grenada, to Camp McCain

195 MS 404, Duck Hill, **E...**to Camp McCain, **W...**Conoco/diesel

185 US 82, Winona, **E...gas:** Exxon, Shell/diesel, **food:** KFC, McDonald's, Pizza Hut, **lodging:** Budget Inn, Magnolia Lodge, Relax Inn, Western Inn, **other:** HOSPITAL, **W...gas:** Amoco/diesel/24hr/@, **food:** BBQ

174 MS 35, MS 430, Vaiden, **E...gas:** BP, Chevron/35/55/diesel/motel/24hr/@, Shell/diesel, **other:** NAPA, Vaiden Camping, **W...gas:** Texaco/Stuckey's/24hr, Interstate Grill, **other:** $General

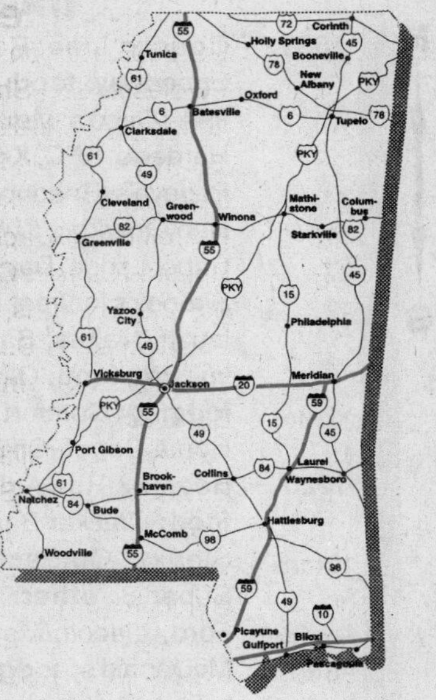

173mm rest area sb, full(handicapped)facilities, phone, picnic tables, litter barrels, petwalk, RV dump, 24hr security

164 to West, **W...gas:** West Trkstp/diesel/@

163mm rest area nb, full(handicapped)facilities, phone, picnic tables, litter barrels, petwalk, RV dump, 24hr security

156 MS 12, Durant, **E...gas:** Shell/diesel, **lodging:** Durant Motel/rest., Super 8, **W...**HOSPITAL

150 **E...**Holmes Co SP, RV camping

146 MS 14, Goodman, **W...**to Little Red Schoolhouse

144 MS 17, to Pickens, **E...gas:** Shell/diesel/24hr/@, **food:** HomePlace Rest., J's Deli, **W...gas:** BP/diesel/rest., **other:** to Little Red Schoolhouse

139 MS 432, to Pickens, no facilities

133 Vaughan, **E...**to Casey Jones Museum

128mm Big Black River

124 MS 16, to N Canton, no facilities

Canton

119 MS 22, to MS 16 E, Canton, **E...gas:** Amoco/Subway/diesel, BP, Chevron/Nancy's, Exxon/diesel, Shell, Texaco/Domino's/diesel, **food:** McDonald's, Pizza Hut, Popeye's, Sombrero Mexican, Wendy's, **lodging:** Best Western, Comfort Inn, Econolodge, Hampton Inn, Holiday Inn Express, **other:** HOSPITAL, Ford, to Ross Barnett Reservoir, **W...gas:** Chevron/KFC/diesel, Citgo/diesel, Love's/Arby's/diesel/24hr/@, **food:** Bumpers Drive-In, 2 Rivers Steaks

118 Nissan Parkway

112 US 51, Gluckstadt, **E...gas:** Exxon/Krystal/diesel, Kangaroo/Subway/diesel, **lodging:** Super 8

108 MS 463, Madison, **E...gas:** Shell/diesel, Texaco/Domino's/diesel, **food:** Backyard Burger, Burger King, Haute Pig Café, **other:** Wal-Mart SuperCtr/24hr

105b Old Agency Rd, **E...gas:** Chevron/diesel, **other:** Pontiac/Buick/GMC

a Natchez Trace Pkwy, no facilities

104 I-220, to W Jackson

MISSISSIPPI

Interstate 55

N ↕ S

Jackson

103 County Line Rd, **E...gas:** BP, Exxon/diesel, Speedway, **food:** Applebee's, Burger King, Chick-fil-A, Cuco's Mexican, Fuddrucker's, Grady's Grill, Hardee's, KFC, Krispy Kreme, Mazzio's, McDonald's, Popeye's, Roadhouse Grill, Ralph&Kacoo's Seafood, Ruby Tuesday, Subway, Taco Bell, Wendy's, **lodging:** Cabot Lodge, Day's Inn, Hilton Garden, Red Roof Inn, Shoney's Inn/rest., **other:** Acura, Dillard's, Goodyear, Isuzu, Mazda, Sam's Club, mall, to Barnett Reservoir, **W...food:** Olive Garden, Red Lobster, Subway, **lodging:** Comfort Suites, Drury Inn, Motel 6, **other:** Home Depot, Office Depot, Target

102b Beasley Rd, Adkins Blvd, **E...gas:** Phillips 66, **food:** Cracker Barrel, El Potrillo Mexican, LoneStar Steaks, OutBack Steaks, **lodging:** La Quinta, Super 8, **other:** BMW, Chrysler/Plymouth/Jeep, Ford, Lincoln/Mercury, Nissan, Toyota, **W...food:** McDonald's, **lodging:** Best Western, Fairfield Inn, InTown Suites, Jameson Inn, **other:** K-Mart, frontage rds access 102a

a Briarwood, **E...food:** Steam Room Grill, **lodging:** Extended Stay America, **W...food:** Capt D's, Chili's, ChuckeCheese, El Chico's, Hops Grill, Jiquilpan Mexican, Perkins, Popeye's, Red Lobster, Steak&Ale, Su Koon Chinese, **lodging:** Best Inn, Best Value Inn, Comfort Inn, Hampton Inn, **other:** Audi/VW, Chevrolet, Dodge, Jaguar/Saab, Mercedes

100 North Side Dr W, **E...gas:** BP, Chevron, Sprint Gas, **food:** Burger King, Dunkin Donuts, McAlister's Deli, McDonald's, Mo's SW Grill, Papa John's, Piccadilly's, Shoney's, SteakOut, Subway, Wendy's, Western Sizzlin, **other:** AutoZone, BooksAMillion, Eckerd, Goodyear/auto, Kroger, Office Depot, **W...gas:** Amoco, Exxon, Shell, **food:** Bennigan's, Broad St Café, Domino's, Hooters, IHOP, Pizza Hut, Waffle House, **lodging:** Holiday Inn, Knight's Inn, Super 8

99 Meadowbrook Rd, Northside Dr E(from nb)

98c b MS 25 N, Lakeland Dr, **E...gas:** Texaco, **lodging:** Parkside Inn, **other:** LaFleur's Bluff SP, **W...**HOSPITAL, museum, airport

a Woodrow Wilson Dr, downtown

96c Fortification St, **E...lodging:** Residence Inn, **W...**HOSPITAL, Bellhaven College

b High St, Jackson, downtown, **E...other:** Chevrolet, Infiniti, Lexus, Saturn, **W...gas:** Shell/diesel, Texaco/diesel, **food:** BBQ, Burger King, DQ, Dennery's, Popeye's, Shoney's, Taco Bell, Waffle House, Wendy's, **lodging:** Clarion, Day's Inn, Hampton Inn, Holiday Inn Express, Quality Inn, Red Roof, **other:** HOSPITAL, Honda, museum, st capitol

a Pearl St(from nb), Jackson, downtown, **W...**access to same as 96b

94 (46 from nb), I-20 E, to Meridian, US 49 S

45b[I-20] US 51, State St, to downtown, **N...gas:** Chevron

a Gallatin St(from sb), downtown, **S...gas:** Pilot/McDonald's/diesel/@, **lodging:** Knight's Inn, **other:** Daewoo, Hyundai/Mazda, Nissan, Toyota

92c (44 from sb), I-20 W, to Vicksburg, US 49 N

b US 51 N, State St, Gallatin St

a McDowell Rd, **E...**Petro/diesel/@, Pilot/McDonald's/diesel/@, **lodging:** Knight's Inn, **W...gas:** Shell, Texaco/diesel, **food:** CiCi's, Waffle House, Wendy's, **lodging:** Super 8

90b Daniel Lake Blvd(from sb), **W...gas:** Shell, **other:** Harley-Davidson

a Savanna St, **E...lodging:** Econolodge, **W...gas:** Amoco, Shell, **food:** BoDon's Catfish, **lodging:** Save Inn

88 Elton Rd, **W...gas:** Chevron, Exxon/Subway/ChesterFried/diesel

85 Byram, **E...gas:** BP/diesel/24hr, Blue Sky, **food:** Double S Grill, **other:** Swinging Bridge RV Park, **W...gas:** Bar, Conoco/diesel, Spur, Texaco/diesel, **food:** McDonald's, Pizza Hut, Popeye's, Sonic, Subway, Taco Bell, Waffle House, Wendy's, **lodging:** Day's Inn, **other:** $General, PawPaw's Camper City, Super D Drug, Winn-Dixie

81 Wynndale Rd, **W...gas:** Conoco/diesel

78 Terry, **E...gas:** Conoco, Shell/Church's/diesel/24hr, **W...gas:** Mac's, **other:** $General, New Deal Food

72 MS 27, Crystal Springs, **E...gas:** Exxon/Subway/diesel, Phillips 66/diesel, **food:** McDonald's, Popeye's, **lodging:** Wisteria B&B, **other:** Ford/Lincoln/Mercury

68 to US 51, S Crystal Springs, no facilities

65 to US 51, Gallman, **E...gas:** Shell/DQ/Stuckey's

61 MS 28, Hazlehurst, **E...gas:** Amoco, Exxon/Subway, Phillips 66, Pump&Save, **food:** Burger King, KFC, McDonald's, Pizza Hut, Stark's Rest., Wendy's, Western Sizzlin, **lodging:** Day's Inn, Ramada Inn, Western Inn, **other:** HOSPITAL, Advance Parts, $General, Family$, Piggly Wiggly, Wal-Mart

59 to S Hazlehurst, no facilities

56 to Martinsville, no facilities

54mm rest area both lanes, full(handicapped)facilities, phone, picnic tables, litter barrels, petwalk, RV dump, vending, 24hr security

Brookhaven

51 to Wesson, **W...gas:** Chevron/Country Jct/diesel/rest./RV camping/@

48 Mt Zion Rd, to Wesson, no facilities

42 to US 51, N Brookhaven, **E...gas:** Exxon/Church's, Phillips 66/diesel/@, Shell, **lodging:** Della's Motel, **other:** HOSPITAL, **W...lodging:** Super 8

40 to MS 550, Brookhaven, **E...gas:** Amoco/Domino's, Exxon/Subway, Shell/diesel/24hr, **food:** BoBo Chinese, Burger King, CiCi's, Cracker Barrel, DQ, El Sombrero Mexican, KFC, Krystal, McDonald's, Pizza Hut, Popeye's, Shoney's, Sonic, Taco Bell, Wendy's, Western Sizzlin, **lodging:** Best Inn, Best Western, Comfort Inn, Day's Inn, Hampton Inn, Spanish Inn, **other:** HOSPITAL, AutoZone, CarQuest, Chevrolet, Chrysler/Plymouth/Dodge/Jeep, Fred's Drug, Ford/Lincoln/Mercury, Honda, Nissan, SaveALot Foods, Wal-Mart SuperCtr/gas/24hr

38 US 84, S Brookhaven, **1 mi E...gas:** Exxon/diesel, **W...gas:** Chevron/diesel/24hr

30 Bogue Chitto, Norfield, **E...gas:** Shell/BogueChitto/diesel/@

24 Johnston Station, **E...**to Lake Dixie Springs

Interstate 55

20b a US 98 W, Summit, to Natchez, **E...gas:** BP/Ward'sBurgers/diesel, RaceWay, Shell/diesel, **W...gas:** Exxon/Subway/Stuckey's/diesel, Phillips 66/diesel

18 MS 570, Smithdale Rd, N McComb, **E...gas:** BP, **food:** Burger King, FoodCourt, McDonald's, Piccadilly's, Ruby Tuesday, **other:** HOSPITAL, JC Penney, Lowe's Whse, Sears/auto, Wal-Mart SuperCtr/24hr, mall, **W...gas:** Chevron/diesel, **food:** Arby's, **lodging:** Deerfield Inn, Hawthorn Inn, **other:** Ford/Lincoln/Mercury

17 Delaware Ave, McComb, **E...gas:** BP/Subway, Chevron/diesel, Exxon/Krystal, Pure, RaceWay, Shell/diesel, **food:** Burger King, China Gourmet, DQ, Golden Corral, Huddle House, McDonald's, Pizza Hut, Pizza Inn, Popeye's, Sonic, Taco Bell, Wendy's, **lodging:** Comfort Inn, Magnolia Inn, Super 8, **other:** HOSPITAL, AutoZone, $General, Eckerd, Family$, O'Reilly Parts, Winn-Dixie, **W...lodging:** Day's Inn, **other:** Chrysler/Plymouth/Dodge/Jeep, Toyota

15b a US 98 E, MS 48 W, McComb, **1 mi E...gas:** Exxon/Subway, Quikmart/gas, Shell, **food:** Church's, Hardee's, KFC, **lodging:** Camellian Motel, Economy Inn, **W...gas:** BP/diesel

13 Fernwood Rd, **W...gas:** Conoco/Fernwood/diesel/rest./24hr/@, **lodging:** Fernwood Motel, **other:** golf, to Percy Quin SP

10 MS 48, Magnolia, **1 mi E...gas:** BP, Exxon, **food:** Subway, **other:** RV camping

8 MS 568, Magnolia, **E...**Pike Co Speedway

4 Chatawa, no facilities

3.5mm Welcome Ctr nb, full(handicapped)facilities, phone, picnic tables, litter barrels, petwalk, RV dump, 24hr security

1 MS 584, Osyka, Gillsburg, **W...**RV camping

0mm Mississippi/Louisiana state line

Interstate 59

Exit # Services

I-59 S and I-20 W run together to Meridian

172mm Mississippi/Alabama state line

For exits 150 to Mississippi/Alabama state line, see Mississippi Interstate 20.

149mm I-59 N and I-20 E run together 22 mi

142 to US 11, Savoy, **W...**to Dunns Falls

137 to N Enterprise, to Stonewall, no facilities

134 MS 513, S Enterprise, no facilities

126 MS 18, Pachuta, to Rose Hill, **E...gas:** Amoco/diesel/24hr, BP/diesel/24hr

118 to Vossburg, Paulding, no facilities

113 MS 528, to Heidelberg, **E...gas:** BP/JR's/diesel/24hr, Exxon/Subway/Pizza Inn/diesel, Stuckey's/pizza/diesel, Shell, **food:** Fly'n Pig BBQ

109mm rest area sb, litter barrels, no restrooms

106mm rest area nb, litter barrels, no restrooms

104 Sandersville, no facilities

99 US 11, **E...gas:** T&B's/diesel, **lodging:** Magnolia Motel, **other:** KOA(1mi)

97 US 84 E, **E...gas:** Exxon/diesel, Kangaroo/Subway/diesel/24hr, **food:** Doc's Rest., Hardee's, **W...gas:** BP/diesel, Texaco/24hr, **food:** KFC, Vic's Biscuits/burgers

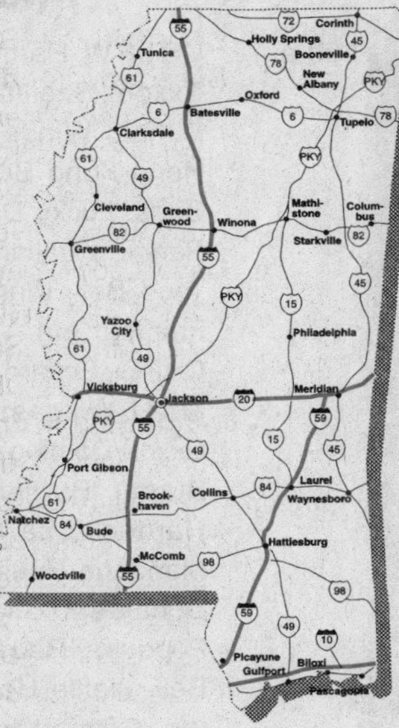

96b MS 15 S, Cook Ave, no facilities

a Masonite Rd, 4th Ave, no facilities

95d (from nb), no facilities

c Beacon St, Laurel, **E...gas:** Texaco, **W...gas:** Chevron, PumpSave Gas, **food:** BBQ, Burger King, Church's, McDonald's, Old Mexico, Popeye's, **lodging:** TownHouse Motel/rest., **other:** Country Mkt Foods, Family$, JC Penney, USPO, XpertTire

b a US 84 W, MS 15 N, 16th Ave, Laurel, **W...gas:** Amoco, Exxon/diesel, **food:** DQ, KFC, McAlister's Deli, McDonald's, Pizza Hut, Shoney's, Subway, Taco Bell, Waffle House, Wendy's, **lodging:** Comfort Suites, Econolodge, Executive Inn, Hampton Inn, Holiday Inn Express, Ramada Inn, Super 8, **other:** HOSPITAL, Advance Parts, $General, Piggly Wiggly

93 US 11, S Laurel, **W...gas:** Citgo/diesel, Exxon/Subway/diesel, Shell/diesel/24hr, **food:** Hardee's

90 US 11, Ellisville Blvd, **W...gas:** Dixie/diesel

88 MS 588, MS 29, Ellisville, **E...gas:** Chevron/diesel, FasTrac, **food:** Domino's, KFC, McDonald's, Pizza Hut, Subway, **other:** Food Tiger, Family$, NAPA, **W...gas:** Exxon/diesel, Shell, **food:** Glenda's Diner, **lodging:** Best Western

85 MS 590, to Ellisville, **W...food:** Red Barn Café

80 to US 11, Moselle, **E...gas:** BP/diesel

78 Sanford Rd, no facilities

76 **W...**Hattiesburg-Laurel Reg Airport

73 Monroe Rd, to Monroe, no facilities

69 to Glendale, Eatonville Rd, no facilities

67b a US 49, Hattiesburg, **E...gas:** Exxon, Shell, Texaco/Krystal, **food:** Arby's, Burger King, Cracker Barrel, DQ, KFC, McDonald's, Pizza Hut, Taco Bell, Waffle House, **lodging:** Comfort Inn, Econolodge, Holiday Inn, Howard Johnson, Inn on the Hill, Motel 6, Ramada Ltd, Regency Inn, Scottish Inn, Super 8, **W...gas:** Amoco/diesel, MapleLeaf/diesel, Pure/diesel, RaceWay, Shell/Subway, Stuckey's/diesel, **food:** Sonic, Waffle House, Ward's Burgers, **lodging:** Best Western, Hawthorn Suites

MISSISSIPPI

Interstate 59

N ↕ S Hattiesburg

65b a US 98 W, Hardy St, Hattiesburg, **E..gas:** Conoco, Exxon, Shell/diesel, Texaco, **food:** Applebee's, Buffalo Wings, Burger King, CiCi's, Domino's, Hong Kong Buffet, IHOP, KFC, Krystal, Lenny's Subs, Lucky Dogs Café, McDonald's, Mr Gatti's, Panino's Italian, Pizza Hut, Steak-Out, Subway, Taco Bell, Ward's Burgers, **lodging:** Day's Inn, Fairfield Inn, Western Motel, **other:** MEDICAL CARE, Eckerd, Goodyear/auto, Home Depot, S MS U, **W...gas:** Amoco/diesel, BP/Subway/diesel, Exxon/Domino's, Kangaroo, Shell, **food:** Backyard Burger, Burger King, Chili's, Copeland's Rest., Hardee's, La Fiesta Brava, LoneStar Steaks, Mandarin House, Mazzio's, McAlister's Deli, McDonald's, O'Charley's, Outback Steaks, Pizza Hut, Popeye's, Red Lobster, Ryan's, Schlotsky's, Taco Bell, Waffle House, Wendy's, **lodging:** Baymont Inn, Comfort Inn, Hampton Inn, Villager Lodge, **other:** HOSPITAL, Advance Parts, BooksAMillion, Dillard's, Firestone/auto, Goodyear/auto, JC Penney, Lowe's Whse, Office Depot, Radio Shack, Rite Aid, SaveRite Foods, Sam's Club/gas, Walgreen, Wal-Mart SuperCtr/24hr, mall

60 US 11, S Hattiesburg, **E...gas:** Shell/diesel, **W...gas:** Amoco/diesel, Kangaroo/Subway/diesel/24hr

59 US 98 E, to US 49, MS Gulf Coast, to Lucedale, Mobile, no facilities

56mm rest area both lanes, litter barrels, no restrooms

51 MS 589, to Purvis, **2 mi W...gas:** Shell/diesel, **food:** Pizza Hut, to Little Black Cr Water Park

48mm Little Black Creek

41 MS 13, to Lumberton, **W...gas:** Pure, **other:** $General, to Little Black Cr Water Park

35 Hillsdale Rd, **E...gas:** Pure/diesel, **lodging:** to Georgetowne Inn, to Lake Hillside Resort

32mm Wolf River

29 MS 26, to Poplarville, **2 mi W...gas:** Kangaroo/diesel, **food:** Burger King

27 MS 53, to Poplarville, **W...gas:** Shell, **other:** Haciendas Camping(2mi)

19 to US 11, Millard, no facilities

15 to McNeill, **W...gas:** McNeill Trkstop/diesel/rest.

13mm rest area sb, litter barrels, no restrooms

10 to US 11, Carriere, **E...gas:** Hilda's/diesel, **food:** Sherryl's Rest., **other:** Clearwater RV Camp(5mi)

8mm rest area nb, litter barrels, no restrooms

6 MS 43 N, N Picayune, **W...gas:** Chevron/diesel, **food:** Paul's Pastries(3mi), **lodging:** Budget Host, Picayune Motel(1mi), **other:** HOSPITAL, Eckerd, Winn-Dixie

Picayune

4 MS 43 S, to Picayune, **E...food:** McDonald's, Ryan's, **other:** Chevrolet/Pontiac/Buick/Cadillac, Wal-Mart SuperCtr/gas/24hr, **W...gas:** BP/diesel, Exxon/diesel, Shell/diesel, Spur, Texaco/diesel, **food:** Burger King, Domino's, Godfather's, Hardee's, KFC, McDonald's, Papa John's, Pizza Hut, Popeye's, Shoney's, Taco Bell, Waffle House, Wendy's, **lodging:** Comfort Inn, Day's Inn, Heritage Inn, **other:** HOSPITAL, Advance Parts, AutoZone, Chrysler/Plymouth/Dodge/Jeep, Firestone/auto, Ford/Lincoln/Mercury, Radio Shack, Rite Aid, Winn-Dixie

3mm Welcome Ctr nb, full(handicapped)facilties, phone, vending, picnic tables, litter barrels, petwalk, RV dump

1.5mm weigh sta both lanes

1 US 11, MS 607, NASA, **W...gas:** Chevron/diesel

0mm Pearl River, Mississippi/Louisiana state line. Exits 11-1 are in Louisiana.

11 Pearl River Turnaround. Callboxes begin sb.

5b Honey Island Swamp, no facilities

a LA 41, Pearl River, **E...gas:** Chevron/gifts

3 US 11 S, LA 1090, Pearl River, **W...gas:** Shell/Subway/diesel, **1 mi W...**Chevron/diesel/24hr, **food:** D&K Rest.

1.5mm Welcome Ctr sb, full(handicapped)facilities, info, phone, picnic tables, litter barrels, petwalk, RV dump

1c b I-10, E to Bay St Louis, W to New Orleans

a I-12 W, to Hammond. I-59 begins/ends on I-10/I-12. **Exits 1-11 are in Louisiana.**

Interstate 220(Jackson)

E ↕ W Jackson

Exit #	Services
11mm	I-220 begins/ends on I-55, exit 104.
9	Hanging Moss Rd, County Line Rd, **E...gas:** BP
8	Watkins Dr, **E...gas:** Shell, Spur
5b a	US 49 N, Evers Blvd, to Yazoo City, **E...lodging:** Star Motel, Family$, Sack&Save Foods, **W...gas:** Amoco, Exxon/Burger King/diesel, Shell/Subway/diesel, **other:** Penske
2b a	Clinton Blvd, Capitol St, **E...**to Jackson Zoo, **W...gas:** RaceWay, Shell, **food:** Burger King, McDonald's, Pizza Hut, Popeye's, Sonic
1b a	US 80, **E...gas:** Jubilee, **food:** BBQ, Capt D's, Denny's, KFC, Taco Bell, Wendy's, Western Sizzlin, **lodging:** Day's Inn, Econolodge, Sleep Inn, **W...gas:** BP, Exxon/Subway/diesel, **food:** Arby's, El Chico, Krystal, McDonald's, Piccadilly's, Pizza Hut, Popeye's, Ruby Tuesday, Wendy's, **other:** Dillard's, Ford, McRae's, Sears/auto, mall
0mm	I-220 begins/ends on I-20, exit 41.

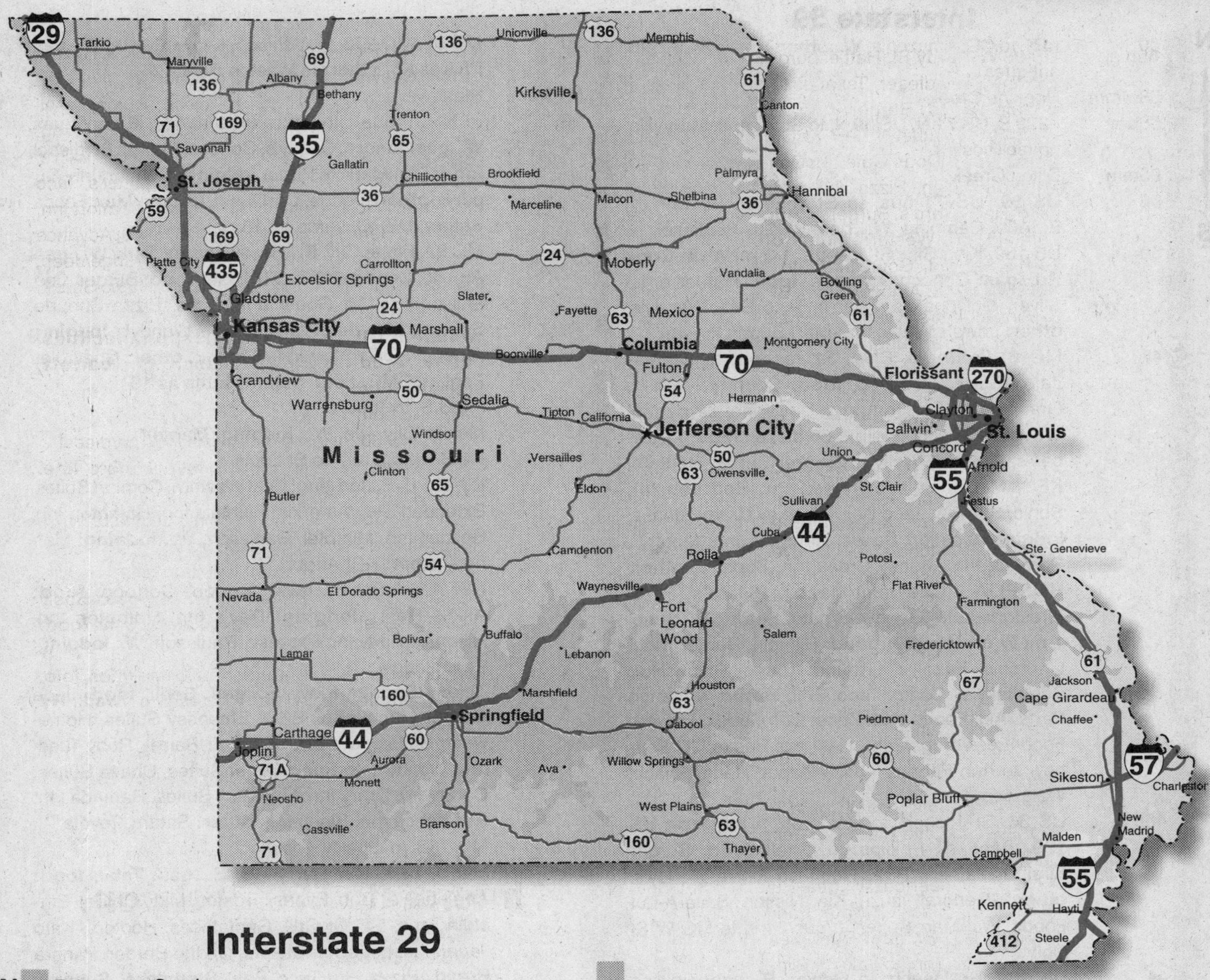

Interstate 29

N

S

Exit #	Services
124mm	Missouri/Iowa state line
123mm	Nishnabotna River
121.5mm	weigh sta both lanes
116	rd A, rd B, to Watson, no facilities
110	US 136, Rock Port, Phelps City, **E...gas:** Conoco/Subway/diesel, Shell/diesel, **lodging:** Rockport Inn, White Rock Motel(2mi), to NW MO St U, **W...gas:** Amoco/diesel/24hr, Phillips 66/diesel/24hr, **food:** McDonald's, Trails End Rest., **lodging:** Super 8, **other:** KOA
109.5mm	**Welcome Ctr sb, full(handicapped)facilities, info, phone, picnic tables, litter barrels, petwalk**
107	MO 111, to Rock Port, **W...lodging:** Elk Inn/RV Park/café
106.5mm	Rock Creek
102mm	Mill Creek
99	rd W, Corning, **E...gas:** Citgo/diesel
97mm	Tarkio River
92	US 59, Craig, to Fairfax, **W...gas:** Shell
90.5mm	Little Tarkio Creek
86.5mm	Squaw Creek
84	MO 118, Mound City, **E...gas:** Phillips 66/diesel, Shamrock/diesel, Sinclair, **food:** Hardee's, Quacker's Steaks, **lodging:** Audrey's Motel, Super 8, **other:** Dodge/Plymouth/Jeep, **W...gas:** King/Shell/Taco Bell/diesel/24hr/@, **other:** Big Lake SP(12mi)
82mm	**rest area both lanes, full(handicapped)facilities, phone, picnic tables, litter barrels, vending, petwalk**
79	US 159, Rulo, **E...gas:** Conoco/diesel/rest./24hr, **other:** RV camping/dump, **W...**to Big Lake SP(12mi), to Squaw Creek NWR(3mi)
78mm	Kimsey Creek
75	US 59, to Oregon, no facilities
67	US 59 N, to Oregon, no facilities
66.5mm	Nodaway River
65	US 59, rd RA, to Fillmore, Savannah, **E...gas:** Conoco/diesel, **other:** antiques

MISSOURI

Interstate 29

N ↕ S

St Joseph

60 rd K, rd CC, Amazonia, **W...other:** Hunt's Fruit Barn, antiques
58.5mm Hopkins Creek
56b a I-229 S, US 71 N, US 59 N, to St Joseph, Maryville, no facilities
55mm Dillon Creek
53 US 59, US 71 bus, to St Joseph, Savannah, **E...**AOK Camping, **W...gas:** Phillips 66/diesel
50 US 169, King City, St Joseph, **1-3 mi W on Cook Rd...gas:** Conoco/Domino's, **food:** Hardee's, LJ Silver, McDonald's, Ryan's, Taco Bell, Wendy's, **other:** Lowe's Whse, Wal-Mart SuperCtr/24hr
47 MO 6, Frederick Blvd, St Joseph, to Clarksdale, **E...gas:** Conoco, **food:** Country Kitchen, Grandma's BBQ, **lodging:** Day's Inn, Drury Inn, **W...gas:** Sinclair, Phillips 66/diesel, **food:** Applebee's, Carlos O'Kelly's, Cracker Barrel, Denny's, KFC, McDonald's, Perkins/24hr, Red Lobster, Sonic, Subway, Taco Bell, Whiskey Creek Steaks, **lodging:** Comfort Suites, Hampton Inn, Motel 6, Ramada Inn, Stoney Creek Inn, Super 8, **other:** HOSPITAL, Chevrolet/Mazda, Dillard's, Ford, Firestone/auto, Goodyear/auto, Sears, RV camp, **1 mi W on US 169...food:** Blimpie, Burger King, Church's, Fazoli's, Ground Round, Pizza Hut, Schlotsky's, Sonic, Taco Bell, **other:** Advance Parts, Aldi Foods, AutoZone, Cub Foods, Eckerd, Food4Less/drugs/24hr, Hastings Books, JC Penney, Jo-Ann Fabrics, Office Depot, Radio Shack, Walgreen
46b a US 36, St Joseph, to Cameron, **1 mi W on US 169...gas:** BP, Phillips 66, Shell, **food:** Burger King, Godfather's, Pizza Hut, Taco John's, Wendy's, **other:** $General, Isuzu, Kia, Nissan, Save-A-Lot Foods, Wal-Mart SuperCtr/gas/24hr, to MO W St Coll
44 US 169, St Joseph, to Gower, **E...gas:** Phillips 66/Subway, **food:** BBQ, LP, **lodging:** Best Western, **other:** tires, **W...gas:** Shell/diesel/24hr/@, **food:** McDonald's, **other:** Chrysler/Jeep/Dodge, Food4Less, Goodyear, Harley-Davidson, Hyundai, Wal-Mart SuperCtr/gas/24hr
43 I-229 N, to St Joseph, no facilities
39.5mm Pigeon Creek
35 rd DD, Faucett, **W...gas:** Farris/Phillips 66/Subway/diesel/motel/24hr/@, **food:** Oliver's Rest.
33.5mm Bee Creek
30 rd Z, rd H, Dearborn, New Market, **E...gas:** Conoco/diesel/24hr
29.5mm Bee Creek
27mm rest area both lanes, full(handicapped)facilities, phone, picnic tables, litter barrels, vending, petwalk
25 rd E, rd U, to Camden Point, **E...gas:** Phillips 66/diesel/rest.
24mm weigh sta both lanes

Platte City

20 MO 92, MO 273, to Atchison, Leavenworth, **W...gas:** Phillips 66, **other:** to Weston Bend SP
19.5mm Platte River
19 rd HH, Platte City(sb returns at 18), **E...**antiques, **W...gas:** Amoco, Casey's, Conoco, Phillips 66/diesel, **food:** DQ, Marko's Pizza, **lodging:** Comfort Inn, Super 8, **other:** Dodge, CarQuest, CountryMart Foods, Saturn, USPO, same as 18
18 MO 92, Platte City, **E...**Basswood RV Park, **W...gas:** Amoco, Conoco/KFC, QT/diesel, **food:** Burger King, McDonald's, Mr GoodCents Subs, Pizza Shoppe, Subway, Taco Bell, Waffle House, Wendy's, **lodging:** AmericInn, Comfort Inn, Super 8, **other:** Chevrolet/Pontiac/GMC, Ford, Saturn, same as 19
17 I-435 S, to Topeka
15 Mexico City Ave, **W...lodging:** Marriott
14 I-435 E(from sb), to St Louis
13 to I-435 E, **E...lodging:** Best Western, Comfort Suites, Extended Stay America, Fairfield Inn, Hampton Inn, Holiday Inn, Microtel, Radisson, **W...lodging:** Marriott, **other:** KCI Airport
12 NW 112th St, **E...gas:** Amoco, Conoco, **food:** Allie's Rest., **lodging:** Day's Inn, Hampton Inn, Hilton, Holiday Inn Express, Radisson, **W...lodging:** Econolodge
10 Tiffany Springs Pkwy, **E...gas:** Shell, **food:** Jade Garden, SmokeBox BBQ, Embassy Suites, Homewood Suites, **W...food:** Cracker Barrel, Ruby Tuesday, Wendy's, **lodging:** AmeriSuites, Chase Suites, Courtyard, Drury Inn, MainStay Suites, Ramada Inn, Residence Inn, Sleep Inn, **other:** Saturn, Toyota
9b a MO 152, to Liberty, Topeka

Kansas City

8 MO 9, rd T, NW Barry Rd, **E...gas:** Total, **food:** Applebee's, Bob Evans, Boston Mkt, Chili's, Einstein Bros, 54th St Grill, Godfather's, Hooters, Kato Japanese, LoneStar Steaks, On the Border, Panera Bread, Pizza Hut/Taco Bell, Starbucks, Subway, Waid's Rest., Wendy's, Winstead's Rest., **other:** HOSPITAL, Barnes&Noble, Eckerd, HyVee Foods, Lowe's Whse, OfficeMax, Old Navy, SteinMart, Wal-Mart SuperCtr/24hr, **W...gas:** Citgo, Phillips 66, QT/diesel, **food:** Hardee's, LJ Silver/A&W, McDonald's, Minsky's Pizza, OutBack Steaks, Rainbow Oriental, Taco John's, **lodging:** Country Hearth Inn, Motel 6, Super 8, **other:** Tires+
6 NW 72nd St, Platte Woods, **E...gas:** Sinclair/diesel, **W...gas:** Phillips 66, Shell, **food:** Jazz Kitchen, Papa John's, Pizza Hut, Pizza Shoppe, Tasty Thai, **other:** IGA Foods, K-Mart/Little Caesar's
5 MO 45 N, NW 64th St, **W...gas:** Shell, **food:** Henhouse Deli, IHOP, McDonald's, O'Quigley's Grill, Silvio's Pizza, Subway, **other:** $General, GNC, Goodyear, Osco Drug, Radio Shack
4 NW 56th St(from nb), **W...gas:** Phillips 66, same as 5

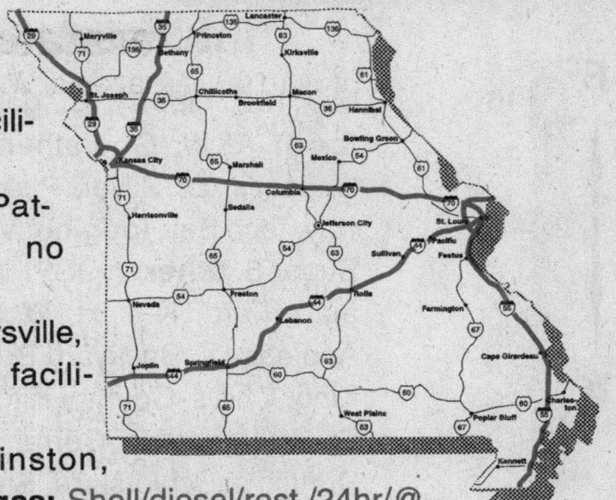

Interstate 29

N ↕ S

3c rd A(from sb), Riverside, **W...gas:** QT, **food:** Argosy Café, Corner Café, Sonic, **lodging:** Skyline Inn, Super 8, **other:** USPO
b I-635 S, no facilities
a Waukomis Dr, rd AA(from nb), no facilities
2b US 169 S(from sb), to KC, no facilities
a US 169 N(from nb), to Smithville, no facilities
1e US 69, Vivion Rd, **E...food:** Steak'n Shake, **other:** Chrysler/Plymouth, Chevrolet/Cadillac, Home Depot, Lincoln/Mercury, Mitsubishi, OfficeMax, PriceChopper Foods/24hr, **W...gas:** QT, **food:** McDonald's
d MO 283 S, Oak Tfwy(from sb)
c Gladstone(from nb), **E...food:** Arby's, Perkins, Pizza St Buffet, Ryan's, Smokehouse BBQ, Tippen's Café
b I-35 N(from sb), to Des Moines
a Davidson Rd, **E...gas:** Shell, **other:** O'Reilly Parts, **W...lodging:** Travelodge
8mm I-35 N. I-29 and I-35 run together 6 mi.

See Missouri Interstate 35, exits 3-8a.

Interstate 35

N ↕ S

Exit #	Services
114mm	Missouri/Iowa state line
114	US 69, to Lamoni, **W...gas:** Conoco/diesel/24hr
113.5mm	Zadie Creek
110	weigh sta both lanes
106	rd N, Blythedale, **E...gas:** Conoco/fireworks, Phillips 66/diesel/café/motel/24hr, **other:** diesel repair, Eagle's Landing Motel, **W...gas:** Shell/diesel/24hr, **other:** camping
99	rd A, to Ridgeway, **5 mi W...**Eagle RV Camping
94mm	E Fork Big Creek
93	US 69, Bethany, **W...food:** Dos Chiquitos Mexican, **other:** RV dump
92	US 136, Bethany, **E...gas:** Conoco/diesel/24hr, Phillips 66/diesel/24hr, **food:** KFC/Taco Bell, McDonald's, **lodging:** Budget Inn, **W...gas:** Amoco/diesel, Casey's, Kum&Go/Wendy's/diesel, MFA Oil/diesel, **food:** Burger King, Country Kitchen, DQ, Pizza Hut, Subway, TootToot Rest., **lodging:** Best Western, Super 8, **other:** HOSPITAL, Chevrolet/Buick, Wal-Mart, **1 mi W...gas:** Ford/Lincoln/Mercury, **other:** Hy-Vee Foods
90mm	Pole Cat Creek
88	MO 13, to Bethany, Gallatin, **3 mi W...lodging:** Bethany Motel
84	rds AA, H, to Gilman City, **E...**Crowder SP(24mi)
81mm	**rest area both lanes, full(handicapped)facilities, phone, picnic tables, litter barrels, vending, petwalk**
80	rds B, N, to Coffey, no facilities
78	rd C, Pattonsburg, **W...gas:** Total/diesel, **other:** antiques
74.5mm	Grand River
72	rd DD, no facilities
68	US 69, to Pattonsburg, no facilities
64	MO 6, to Maysville, Gallatin, no facilities
61	US 69, Winston, Gallatin, **E...gas:** Shell/diesel/rest./24hr/@
54	US 36, Cameron, **E...gas:** Amoco/diesel/24hr, Cenex/diesel, Shell/Wendy's/diesel/24hr, **food:** McDonald's, Subway, **lodging:** Best Western, Comfort Inn, Crossroads Inn/RV Park, **W...gas:** Phillips 66, Shamrock, **food:** Burger King, DQ, Kettle Diner, KFC/Taco Bell, Pizza Hut, Sonic, Subway, **lodging:** Day's Inn, Econolodge, Holiday Inn Express, Super 8, **other:** HOSPITAL, Advance Parts, **other:** Chevrolet, CountryMart Foods, $General, Ford/Mercury, Goodyear, Radio Shack, Wal-Mart SuperCtr/24hr, W MO Corr Ctr
52	rd BB, Lp 35, to Cameron, **E...**MEDICAL CARE, **W...gas:** Casey's, same as 54
49mm	Brushy Creek
48.5mm	Shoal Creek
48	US 69, Cameron, **E...**Down Under RV Park, to Wallace SP(2mi), **W...gas:** Total, fireworks
40	MO 116, Lathrop, **E...gas:** Phillips 66/Country Café/diesel
35mm	**rest area sb, full(handicapped)facilities, phone, picnic tables, litter barrels, vending, petwalk**
34mm	**rest area nb, full(handicapped)facilities, phone, picnic tables, litter barrels, vending, petwalk**
33	rd PP, Holt, **E...food:** Rock Front Steaks, **W...gas:** Conoco/diesel, Phillips 66/diesel, **lodging:** Holt Steel Inn
30mm	Holt Creek
26	MO 92, Kearney, **E...gas:** Casey's/gas, Conoco/diesel, Shell/diesel, **food:** Kookie's Pizza, McDonald's, Sonic, **lodging:** Day's Inn, Super 8, **other:** CountryMart Foods, to Watkins Mill SP, **W...gas:** Conoco/diesel/24hr, **food:** Arby's, Burger King, Hunan Garden Chinese, Subway, **lodging:** Country Hearth Inn, Econolodge, **other:** Chevrolet, Family$, to Smithville Lake
22mm	weigh sta both lanes
20	US 69, MO 33, to Excelsior Springs, **E...**HOSPITAL
17	MO 291, rd A, **1 mi E...food:** Arby's, CiCi's, LJ Silver, Perkins, Ponderosa, **other:** Chevrolet, CountryMart Foods, Eckerd, Hy-Vee Foods, Liberty RV Ctr, Village Lodge, Walgreen, same as 16, **W...gas:** Phillips 66/diesel, **other:** KCI Airport

Cameron

MISSOURI

Interstate 35

E ↕ W

Liberty

16 MO 152, Liberty, **E...gas:** Conoco/diesel, Shell, **food:** A&W, Godfather's, Perkins, KFC, Little Caesar's, LJ Silver, Pizza Hut, Ponderosa, Subway, Taco Bell, **lodging:** Village Inn Rest., Wendy's, Super 8, **other:** HOSPITAL, Chevrolet, Firestone/auto, Ford, K-Mart, **W...gas:** Phillips 66, **food:** Applebee's, Backyard Burger, Bob Evans, Burger King, Chili's, Country Kitchen, Cracker Barrel, 54th St Grill, Golden Corral, LongHorn Steaks, McDonald's, Schlotsky's, SmokeStack BBQ, Steak'n Shake, Waffle House, **lodging:** Comfort Suites, Fairfield Inn, Hampton Inn, Holiday Inn, Express, **other:** Home Depot, Michael's, NAPA AutoCare, Target, Wal-MartSuperCtr/24hr

14 US 69(exits left from sb), Liberty Dr, Pleasant Valley, to Glenaire, **E...gas:** Conoco/diesel, Sinclair, Texaco, **other:** I-35 RV Ctr, **W...gas:** QT/diesel

13 US 69(from nb), to Pleasant Valley, **E...gas:** Phillips 66/diesel, Shell/A&W, Sinclair/24hr, **food:** KFC, McDonald's, **other:** auto repair, **W...gas:** QT/diesel

12b a I-435, to St Louis

11 US 69 N, Vivion Rd, **E...gas:** QT, **food:** Church's, McDonald's, Sonic, Stroud's Rest., same as 10

10 N Brighton Ave(from nb), **E...gas:** QT, **food:** Church's, McDonald's, Sonic, Stroud's Rest.

9 MO 269 S, Chouteau Trfwy, **E...gas:** Phillips 66, **food:** IHOP, Outback Steaks, Papa Murphy's, Popeye's, Subway, **other:** Food Festival, Harrah's Casino/rest., Radio Shack, Target, **W...gas:** Amoco, Wendy's

8c MO 1, Antioch Rd, **E...gas:** Citgo/7-11, Sinclair, **food:** Country Girl Rest., Domino's, **lodging:** Best Western, InnTown Inn, **W...gas:** Phillips 66, **food:** Catfish Rest., Waffle House

b I-29 N, US 71 N, KCI airport

I-35 S and I-29 S run together 6 mi

8a Parvin Rd, **E...gas:** Shell, **other:** O'Reilly Parts, **lodging:** Super 8, **W...lodging:** Travelodge

6b a Armour Rd, **E...gas:** Phillips 66/diesel, **food:** Arby's, Burger King, Capt D's, Denny's, McDonald's, **lodging:** Baymont Inn, Day's Inn, **other:** HOSPITAL, repair, to Riverboat Casino, **W...gas:** QT, Phillips 66, Shell, **food:** DQ, LJ Silver, Juanito's Mexican, Pizza Hut, Taco Bell, Wendy's, **lodging:** American Inn, Country Hearth Suites

Kansas City

5b 16th Ave, industrial district

a Levee Rd, Bedford St, industrial district

4.5mm Missouri River

4b Front St, **E...**Riverboat Casino/rest.

a US 24 E, Independence Ave, no facilities

3 I-70 E, US 71 S, to St Louis, no facilities

2n I-35 N and I-29 N run together 6 mi

2f Oak St, Grand-Walnut St, downtown, **E...lodging:** Super 8, **W...gas:** Conoco

Interstate 35

d Main-Delaware, Wyandotte St, downtown

c Broadway, downtown

a I-70 W, to Topeka

w 12th St, Kemper Arena

u I-70 E, to St Louis

1d 20th St(from sb), no facilities

c b 27th St, SW Blvd, W Pennway(from nb), **E...**HOSPITAL

a SW Trafficway(from sb), no facilities

0mm Missouri/Kansas state line

Interstate 44

E ↕ W

St Louis

Exit # Services

290mm I-44 begins/ends on I-55, exit 207 in St Louis.

290a I-55 S, to Memphis

290c Gravois Ave(from wb), 12th St, **N...gas:** Citgo, **S...food:** McDonald's

290b 18th St(from eb), downtown

289 Jefferson Ave, St Louis, **N...gas:** Citgo, Vickers, **food:** Subway, **lodging:** Holiday Inn Express, **S...food:** McDonald's

288 Grand Blvd, St Louis, **N...**HOSPITAL, **S...food:** Jack-in-the-Box

287b a Kingshighway, Vandeventer Ave, St Louis, **N...gas:** Amoco, **S...gas:** Amoco, **other:** Chevrolet, Chrysler, Walgreen, to MO Botanical Garden

286 Hampton Ave, St Louis, **N...gas:** Mobil, Shell, **food:** Denny's, Jack-in-the-Box, McDonald's, Steak'n Shake, Subway, Taco Bell, **S...gas:** Shell, **food:** Burger King, Church's, Hardee's, Village Inn Rest., **lodging:** Holiday Inn, Red Roof Inn, **other:** museums, zoo

285 SW Ave(from wb, no EZ return), no facilities

284b a Arsenal St, Jamieson St, no facilities

283 Shrewsbury(from wb), some services same as 282

282 Laclede Sta Rd, Murdock Ave(from eb), St Louis, **N...gas:** Amoco, Mobil, **food:** Pantera's Pizza, McDonald's, **other:** Subaru

280 Elm Ave, St Louis, **N...gas:** Amoco/repair, **food:** Steak'n Shake, **other:** Schnuck's Food/24hr, **S...gas:** Shell, **other:** Radiator King

279 (from wb), Berry Rd

278 Big Bend Rd, St Louis, **N...other:** HOSPITAL, Sam's Club, **S...gas:** Mobil/diesel, QT, Sinclair

277b US 67, US 61, US 50, Lindbergh Blvd, **N...gas:** Shell, **food:** Hardee's, **lodging:** Best Western, **other:** HOSPITAL, Hancock Fabrics, Lowe's Whse, Target, Wal-Mart SuperCtr/24hr, **S...gas:** CFM/diesel, Shell, Vickers, **food:** Bob Evans, Burger King, Denny's, Longhorn Steaks, Steak'n Shake, St Louis Bread, Viking Rest., **lodging:** Comfort Inn, Day's Inn, Econolodge, Hampton Inn, Holiday Inn, **other:** CompUSA, Home Depot, Old Navy, WorldMkt

277a MO 366 E, Watson Rd, access to same as 277b S

276b a I-270, S Memphis, N to Chicago, no facilities

275 N Highway Dr(from wb), Soccer Pk Rd, **N...gas:** Texaco/diesel/rest./@

Interstate 44

E ↕ W

274 Bowles Ave, **N...gas:** Shell/diesel, **S...gas:** Amoco, Citgo/diesel/24hr, QT, **food:** Bandana's BBQ, Cracker Barrel, Denny's, Krispy Kreme, McDonald's, Quizno's, Souper Salad, White Castle, **lodging:** Drury Inn, Econolodge, Fairfield Inn, Holiday Inn Express, Motel 6, PearTree Inn, Stratford Inn, **other:** Goodyear

272 MO 141, Fenton, Valley Park, **N...gas:** Motomart, **S...gas:** Citgo/7-11, Phillips 66, QT, Shell, **food:** Burger King, Krispy Kreme, McDonald's, Steak'n Shake, Subway, Taco Bell, **other:** Wet Willie's Waterslide

269 Antire Rd, Beaumont, no facilities

266 Lewis Rd, **N...other:** Rte 66 SP, golf

266mm Meramec River

265 Williams Rd(from eb), no facilities

264 MO 109, rd W, Eureka, **N...gas:** Citgo/7-11, Shell, **food:** Burger King, DQ, KFC, McDonald's, Pizza Hut, Ponderosa, Smokers BBQ, Subway, Taco Bell, Wendy's, White Castle, **lodging:** Day's Inn, **other:** AutoTire, Byerly RV Ctr, Firestone, NAPA, Schnuck's Foods, to Babler SP, **S...gas:** QT/diesel/@, Shell

261 Lp 44, to Allenton, **N...gas:** Motomart/ McDonald'sdiesel, **food:** Applebee's, China King, Country Kitchen, Denny's, KFC, Lion's Choice Rest., Steak'n Shake, **lodging:** Ramada Inn, Red Carpet Inn, Super 8, **other:** MEDICAL CARE, AutoZone, $Tree, GNC, Radio Shack, Wal-Mart SuperCtr/24hr, to Six Flags, same as 264, **S...gas:** Phillips 66/diesel/ rest., Shell/diesel, **other:** Ford, KOA

257 Lp 44, Pacific, **N...lodging:** Comfort Inn, **S...gas:** Mobil/diesel/24hr, Motomart/24hr, Voss/diesel, **food:** Hardee's, KFC, McDonald's, Pizza Hut, Taco Bell, **lodging:** Holiday Inn Express, **other:** Buick/Chevrolet, Chrysler/Jeep/Dodge, IGA Foods, NAPA

253 MO 100 E, to Gray Summit, **S...gas:** Phillips 66, **lodging:** Best Western, Gardenway Motel

251 MO 100 W, to Washington, **N...gas:** Conoco/diesel/ 24hr, FuelMart/Blimpie/diesel/24hr, Mr Fuel/diesel, Phillips 66/Burger King/diesel, **food:** Tri-County Rest.

247mm Bourbeuse River

247 US 50 W, rd AT, rd O, to Union, **N...other:** Harley-Davidson, **other:** Pin Oak Creek Camping, flea mkt, **S...**to Robertsville SP

242 rd AH, to Hist Rte 66

240 MO 47, St Clair, **N...gas:** Phillips 66/Taco Bell/diesel, Sinclair, **food:** Burger King, El Palenque Mexican, **other:** Reed RV Ctr, **S...gas:** Mobil/diesel, **food:** Hardee's, McDonald's, Subway, **lodging:** Budget Lodge, Super 8, **other:** $General, IGA Foods

239 MO 30, rds AB, WW, St Clair, **N...**repair, **S...gas:** Amoco

238mm weigh sta both lanes

235mm rest area both lanes(both lanes exit left), full(handicapped)facilities, phone, picnic tables, litter barrels, vending, petwalk

Sullivan

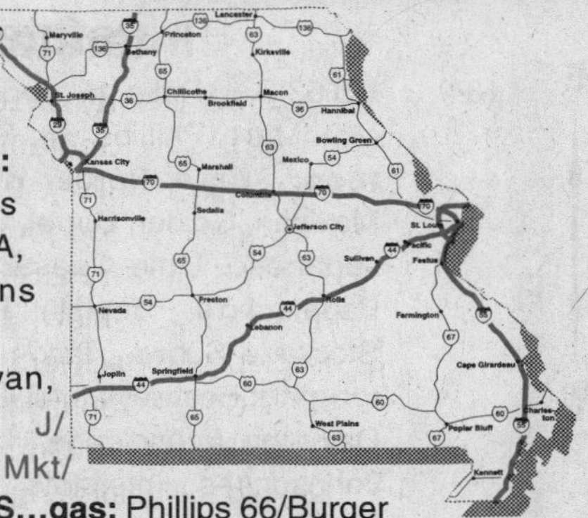

230 rds W, JJ, Stanton, **N...lodging:** Stanton Motel, **S...food:** BS Boogie's Rest., **other:** KOA, Meramec Caverns Camping(3mi)

226 MO 185 S, Sullivan, **S...gas:** Flying J/ Conoco/Country Mkt/ diesel/LP/24hr/@, **S...gas:** Phillips 66/Burger King, **food:** Denny's, Golden Corral, Hardee's, KFC, Steak'n Shake, Taco Bell, **other:** O'Reilly Parts, Wal-Mart SuperCtr/24hr, KOA(1mi), to Meramec SP, same as 225

225 MO 185 N, rd D, Sullivan, **N...gas:** Mobil, Phillips 66/diesel, **food:** Domino's, **lodging:** Baymont Inn, Econolodge, Family Inn, Ramada Inn, Super 8, **other:** Chrysler/Plymouth/ Dodge/Jeep, Ford/Mercury, **S...gas:** Bobber/diesel/café/ @, Citgo, Capt D's, **food:** Jack-in-the-Box, McDonald's, Pizza Hut, Sonic, Subway, **lodging:** Sullivan Motel, **other:** HOSPITAL, Aldi Foods, Chevrolet/Buick, Goodyear, NAPA, same as 226

218 rds N, C, J, Bourbon, **N...gas:** Citgo/diesel, **lodging:** Budget Inn, **S...gas:** Mobil/24hr, **food:** HenHouse Rest., **other:** Suburban RV Ctr, Blue Sprgs Camping(6mi), Riverview Ranch Camping(8mi)

214 rd H, Leasburg, **N...gas:** Mobil/diesel, **S...other:** to Onandaga Cave SP(7mi), camping

210 rd UU, **S...food:** FeedLot Steaks, MO Hick BBQ, Mt Peasant Winery

208 MO 19, Cuba, **N...gas:** Phillips 66, Voss/diesel/rest./24hr/ @, **food:** Country Kitchen, Huddle House, Kum&Get It Buffet, Pizza Hut, **lodging:** Best Western, Super 8, **other:** Blue Beacon, **S...gas:** Casey's, Delano/diesel, Mobil/ Taco Bell/24hr, **food:** Burger King, East Sun Chinese, McDonald's, Pizza Pro, Sonic, Subway, **lodging:** Holiday Inn Express, **other:** Chevrolet/GMC, O'Reilly Parts, Wal-Mart/drugs, to Ozark Nat Scenic Riverways

203 rds F, ZZ, **N...**Blue Moon RV Park, **S...**Rosati Winery(2mi)

195 MO 8, MO 68, St James, Maramec Sprg Park, **N...gas:** Conoco/diesel, Mobil/Taco Bell/diesel, Phillips 66/diesel, **food:** John's Café, McDonald's, Pizza Hut, Subway, **lodging:** Comfort Inn, Economy Inn, **other:** Ford, NAPA, O'Reilly Parts, St James Winery, laundry, **S...gas:** Delano/ diesel, Phillips 66/diesel, S Gas, **food:** Burger King, **lodging:** Finn's Motel, **other:** CountryMart Foods, Pamida

189 rd V, **S...**antiques

Rolla

186 US 63, MO 72, Rolla, **N...gas:** Sinclair, **food:** Steak'n Shake, **lodging:** Drury Inn, Hampton Inn, Sooter Inn, **other:** Lowe's Whse, **S...gas:** Amoco/24hr, Conoco, Mobil, Phillips 66, **food:** Denny's, Domino's, Donut King, Fortune Chinese, Lee's Chicken, St Louis Bread, Waffle House, **other:** HOSPITAL

185 rd E, to Rolla, **S...gas:** Phillips 66, **food:** Arby's, DQ, Hardee's/24hr, Subway, Taco Bell, **other:** HOSPITAL, UMO at Rolla, st patrol

MISSOURI

Interstate 44

E ↕ W — Rolla

184 US 63 S, to Rolla, **N...lodging:** Comfort Inn, **S...gas:** MotoMart, Phillips 66, Shell, StationBreak, Shell, **food:** Arby's, Burger King, Domino's, El Rodeo Mexican, Golden Corral, Ground Round, KFC, Kyoto Japanese, Little Caesar's, LJ Silver, McDonald's, Papa John's, Pizza Hut, Pizza Inn, Shoney's, Sirloin Stockade, Subway, Taco Hut, Wendy's, Zeno's Steaks, **lodging:** Bestway Motel, Best Western, Chalet Motel, Day's Inn, Econolodge, Holiday Inn Express, Howard Johnson/rest., Interstate Motel, Ramada Inn, Super 8, Travelodge, Wayfarer Inn, Western Inn, **other:** HOSPITAL, Chevrolet, Ford/Lincoln/Mercury, Kroger, Wal-Mart, transmissions

179 rds T, C, to Doolittle, Newburg, **S...gas:** BP/24hr, **food:** Cookin' From Scratch Rest.

178mm rest area both lanes, full(handicapped)facilities, phone, picnic tables, litter barrels, vending, petwalk

176 Sugar Tree Rd, **N...lodging:** Vernell's Motel, **S...**camping

172 rd D, Jerome, **N...**camping

169 rd J, no facilities

164mm Big Piney River

166 to Big Piney

163 MO 28, to Dixon, **N...gas:** Voss Truckport/diesel/café/repair/24hr/@, **food:** Ozark Crafts, **S...gas:** Conoco, **food:** Country Café, Sweetwater BBQ, **lodging:** Best Western, Day's Inn, Super 8, Village Lodge

161b a rd Y, to Ft Leonard Wood, **N...gas:** Mobil, **food:** Aussie Jack's Café, Cracker Barrel, Jack's Diner, LJ Silver/A&W, Pizza Hut, Popeye's, Ruby Tuesday, Scottie's Custard, **lodging:** Comfort Inn, Fairfield Inn, Hampton Inn, Red Roof Inn, **other:** $Tree, Toyota, Wal-Mart SuperCtr/24hr, **S...gas:** Cenex, Total, **food:** Arby's, Capt D's, KFC, McDonald's, Papa John's, Pizza Hut, Subway, Taco Bell, Waffle House, Wendy's, **lodging:** Budget Inn, Econolodge, Holiday Inn Express, Motel 6, Ramada Inn, **other:** AutoZone, Dodge/Plymouth, $General, Firestone/auto, Ford/Lincoln/Mercury/Mazda, NAPA, Radio Shack

159 Lp 44, to Waynesville, St Robert, **N...food:** DQ, Sonic, **other:** IGA Foods, O'Reilly Parts, Covered Wagon RV Park(2mi), **S...gas:** Phillips 66/diesel, Shell/repair, **other:** Microtel, Ozark Motel, Cadillac/Chevrolet/GMC, Goodyear/auto, Pontiac, USPO

158mm Roubidoux Creek

156 rd H, Waynesville, **N...gas:** Citgo/diesel, **food:** Imperial Rest., McDonald's, Subway, **lodging:** Star Motel(1mi), **other:** $General, Smitty's Food/gas, Chevrolet/Buick, Covered Wagon RV Park(2mi)

153 MO 17, to Buckhorn, **N...gas:** Cenex/diesel, Citgo/diesel/rest., **food:** Ted Williams Steaks, **lodging:** Ft Wood Inn, **S...gas:** Shell/diesel, **other:** Glen Oaks RV Park

150 MO 7, rd P to Richland, no facilities

145 MO 133, rd AB, to Richland, **N...gas:** Conoco/diesel/rest./24hr, **S...**camping

Lebanon

143mm Gasconade River

140 rd N, to Stoutland, **S...gas:** Conoco, Phillips 66/diesel, **food:** Midway Chinese

139mm Bear Creek

135 rd F, Sleeper, no facilities

130 rd MM, **N...gas:** Phillips 66, **lodging:** Best Budget Inn, Best Western, Red Carpet Inn, **S...gas:** Phillips 66, **other:** HOSPITAL,

129 MO 5, MO 32, MO 64, Lebanon, to Hartville, **N...gas:** Conoco, Phillips 66/diesel, **food:** Applebee's, Bamboo Garden, Burger King, Country Kitchen, DQ, KFC, LJ Silver, McDonald's, Pizza Hut, Shoney's, Sonic, Subway, Taco Bell, Taco Hut, Wendy's, Western Sizzlin, **other:** Advance Parts, Aldi Foods, AutoZone, Chevrolet, Ford, IGA Foods, NAPA, O'Reilly Parts, Walnut Bowl Outlet, to Bennett Sprgs SP, **S...gas:** Amoco, Conoco/diesel, Shell, **food:** Blimpie, Candy's Custard, Capt D's, Hardee's, Pizza Hut, **other:** HOSPITAL, $Tree, Goodyear, Wal-Mart SuperCtr/24hr, to Lake of the Ozarks

127 Lp 44, Lebanon, **N...gas:** Conoco/diesel/rest./24hr, Phillips 66/diesel, **food:** Great Wall Chinese, Waffle House, **lodging:** Best Way Inn, Day's Inn, Econolodge, Hampton Inn, Holiday Inn Express, Scottish Inn, Super 8, **other:** Chicago Cutlery, Chrysler/Plymouth/Dodge/Jeep, Firestone, Ford/Lincoln/Mercury, Walnut Bowl Outlet, **S...other:** Buick/Pontiac/GMC/Cadillac, Harley-Davidson, Russell Stover

123 County Rd, **S...other:** Happy Trails RV Ctr, KOA

118 rds C, A, Phillipsburg, **N...gas:** Conoco/diesel, **S...gas:** Phillips 66

113 rds J, Y, Conway, **N...gas:** Phillips 66, **food:** Rockin Chair Café, **lodging:** Budget Inn, **other:** to Den of Metal Arts, **S...gas:** Conoco

111mm rest area both lanes, full(handicapped)facilities, phone, vending, litter barrels, picnic tables, petwalk

108mm Bowen Creek

107 County Rd, no facilities

106mm Niangua River

100 MO 38, rd W, Marshfield, **N...gas:** Amoco, **food:** Tiny's BBQ, **other:** Chevrolet, Ford, Goodyear/auto, **S...gas:** Cenex, Citgo/diesel, Conoco/diesel, Phillips 66/diesel/24hr, Shell, **food:** Country Kitchen, DQ, KFC, LJ Silver/A&W, McDonald's, Pizza Hut, Sonic, Subway, Taco Bell, **lodging:** Holiday Inn Express, **other:** $General, PriceCutter Foods, Stanley Drug, Wal-Mart/auto

96 rd B, Northview, **N...**Paradise RV Park

89mm weigh sta both lanes

88 MO 125, Strafford, to Fair Grove, **N...gas:** Phillips 66/diesel/rest./24hr/@, TA/Subway/Taco Bell/diesel/24hr/@, **food:** McDonald's, **other:** Goodyear, truckwash, Paradise RV Park(4mi), **S...gas:** Citgo, Conoco/diesel, **lodging:** Super 8, **other:** Harter House Foods, Strafford RV Park

84 MO 744, **S...**Peterbilt

Interstate 44

82b a US 65, to Branson, Fedalia, **S...gas:** Conoco/diesel, Phillips 66, **food:** Waffle House, **lodging:** American Inn, Village Inn, **other:** Truck World, st patrol, to Table Rock Lake, Bull Shoals Lake

80b a Springfield, rd H to Pleasant Hope, **N...gas:** Conoco/diesel/rest./24hr, Phillips 66, Shell, **food:** Waffle House, **lodging:** Day's Inn, Microtel, Motel 6, Super 8, **other:** to SWSU, **S...gas:** Conoco/diesel, Phillips 66, QT, Texaco, Total/diesel/LP, **food:** Andy's Café, Applebee's, Bob Evans, Burger King, Cracker Barrel, DQ, Denny's, Empire Asian, Fazoli's, Hardee's, Jade East Chinese, LJ Silver, KFC, McDonald's, Pizza Hut, Pizza Inn, Ruby Tuesday, Schlotsky's, Shoney's, Sonic, Steak'n Shake, Subway, Taco Bell, Village Inn Rest., Western Sizzlin, **lodging:** Bass Country Inn, Best Western, Comfort Inn, Day's Inn, Drury Inn, Econolodge, Economy Inn, Holiday Inn, Maple Inn, Ozark Inn, PearTree Inn, Plaza Inn, Ramada Inn, RainTree Inn, Red Lion Inn, Red Roof Inn, Sheraton, Solar Inn, **other:** HOSPITAL, AutoZone, Cottman Transmissions, Goodyear/auto, O'Reilly Parts, PriceCutter Foods, Radio Shack, U-Haul, Wal-Mart/auto, mall

77 MO 13, KS Expswy, **N...lodging:** Interstate Inn, **S...gas:** Phillips 66/diesel, QT, **food:** Arby's, Braum's, CiCi's, DQ, McDonald's, Papa John's, Papa Murphys, Pizza Inn, Subway, Taco Bell, Waffle House, Wendy's, **lodging:** Econolodge, **other:** Dillon's Foods, $Tree, GNC, Goodyear/auto, O'Reilly Parts, Radio Shack, Staples, Walgreen, Wal-Mart SuperCtr/24hr

75 US 160 W byp, to Willard, Stockton Lake, **S...**Conoco, The Café, Courtyard

72 MO 266, to Chesnut Expwy, **N...**Travelers RV Park, **1-2 mi S...gas:** Casey's, **food:** Hardee's, McDonald's, Taco Bell, Waffle House, **lodging:** Best Budget Inn, Best Inn

70 rds MM, B, **S...other:** Wilson's Creek Nat Bfd, KOA(1mi)

69 to US 60, Springfield

67 rds N, T, Bois D' Arc, **S...**to Republic, **gas:** Citgo/Ozarks/diesel/@, Conoco

66mm Pond Creek

64.6mm Dry Branch

64.5mm Pickerel Creek

61 rds K, PP, **N...gas:** Amoco, Cenex/diesel/rest./motel

58 MO 96, rds O, Z, Halltown, to Carthage, **S...gas:** Shell/diesel, **lodging:** Cook's Motel/café

57 to rd PP(from wb), no facilities

56.5mm Turnback Creek

56mm Goose Creek

52.5mm rest area both lanes, full(handicapped)facilities, phone, picnic tables, litter barrels, vending, petwalk

49 MO 174E, rd CCW, Chesapeake, no facilities

46 MO 39, MO 265, Mt Vernon, Aurora, **N...gas:** Caseys, Phillips 66/diesel, TA/Conoco/diesel/rest./24hr/@, Sinclair/diesel/24hr/@, **food:** Bamboo Garden Chinese, Country Kitchen, Dalma's Rest., Hardee's, KFC, Mazzio's, McDonald's, Sonic, Taco Bell, **lodging:** American Inn, Budget Host, Super 8, **other:** Family$, O'Reilly Parts, Summer fresh Foods, **S...gas:** Total/diesel/rest., **lodging:** Comfort Inn, **other:** to Table Rock Lake, Stockton Lake

44 rd H, Mt Vernon, to Monett, **N...gas:** Citgo(2mi), **food:** Subway(1mi), **lodging:** Walnuts Motel, **other:** Mid-America Dental/Hearing

43.5mm Spring River

38 MO 97, to Stotts City, Pierce City, **N...**gas/repair, U of MO SW Ctr

33 MO 97 S, to Pierce City, **S...gas:** Sinclair/diesel

29 rd U, Sarcoxie, to La Russell, **N...**WAC RV Park, **S...gas:** Citgo/diesel, **lodging:** Sarcoxie Motel

29mm Center Creek

26 MO 37, Sarcoxie, to Reeds, **N...**truck/tire repair, **S...gas:** Amoco/gifts, **other:** Ford(2mi)

22 rd 100, **N...**RV parts, **S...gas:** Trkstp/diesel/rest./24hr/@

21mm Jones Creek

18b a US 71 N, MO 59 S, to Carthage, Neosho, **N...gas:** Phillips 66, **lodging:** BudgetWay Motel, **other:** Coachlight RV Park, **S...gas:** Total, **other:** George Carver Mon, Ballard's Camping

15 MO 66 W, Lp 44(from wb), Joplin, **N...lodging:** Tara Motel, Timber Motel

15mm Grove Creek

14mm Turkey Creek

11b a US 71 S, MO 249 N, to Neosho, Ft Smith, **S...gas:** Flying J/Conoco/Country Mkt/diesel/LP/24hr/@, **food:** Applebee's(3mi)

8b a US 71, Joplin, to Neosho, **N...gas:** Citgo, Conoco, Sinclair, **food:** Applebee's, Arby's, Benito's Mexican, Bob Evans, Braum's, Burger King, Capt D's, Casa Montez Mexican, CiCi's, Country Kitchen, Denny's, Grandy's, Great Wall Chinese, Gringo's Grill, IHOP, Jim Bob's Steaks, KFC, Kyoto Steaks, LJ Silver, MktPlace Deli, Memphis BBQ, McDonald's, Olive Garden, Outback Steaks, Pizza Hut, Red Lobster, Ruby Tuesday, Shoney's, Sonic, Steak'n Shake, Subway, Taco Bell, Timberline Steaks, Travetti's Italian, Waffle House, Wendy's, **lodging:** Baymont Inn, Best Western, Comfort Inn, Day's Inn, Drury Inn, Fairfield Inn, Hampton Inn, Holiday Inn, Howard Johnson, Motel 6, Ramada Inn, Select Inn, Solar Inn, Super 8, **other:** Chrysler/Plymouth/Dodge, Food4Less/24hr, Ford/Lincoln/Mercury, Hyundai, Jo-Ann Fabrics, Lowe's Whse, NAPA, Nissan/Mercedes, Office Depot, O'Reilly Parts, Pennzoil, Sam's Club/gas, Toyota, VW, Wal-Mart SuperCtr/24hr, **S...gas:** Citgo/diesel, Phillips 66/diesel, **food:** Cracker Barrel, Fazoli's, **other:** Microtel, Wheelen RV Ctr

MISSOURI

Interstate 44

E ↕ W

6	MO 86, MO 43 N, Joplin, to Racine, **1 mi N...gas:** Citgo, **food:** Arby's, McDonald's, Pizza Hut, **lodging:** Capri Motel, West Wood Motel, **other:** HOSPITAL, **S...**Goodyear, Harley-Davidson
5.5mm	Shoal Creek
4	MO 43 to Seneca, **N...gas:** Loves/Hardee's/diesel/24hr/@, **other:** Peterbilt, antiques, **S...gas:** Conoco/Subway/diesel/@, Petro/Blimpie/diesel/@, Pilot/Wendy's/diesel/24hr/@, **food:** McDonald's, **lodging:** Sleep Inn, **other:** KOA
3mm	weigh sta both lanes
2mm	**Welcome Ctr eb, rest area wb, full(handicapped)facilities, picnic tables, litter barrels, phones, vending**
1	US 400, US 166W, to Baxter Springs, KS, no facilities
0mm	Missouri/Oklahoma state line

Interstate 55

N ↕ S

St Louis

Exit #	Services
209mm	Missouri/Illinois state line at St. Louis, Mississippi River
209b	I-70 W to Kansas City
a	to Arch, Busch Stadium
208	7th St, downtown, **W...gas:** BP, **food:** Hardee's, Taco Bell, **lodging:** Adam's Mark Hotel, Drury Plaza, Marriott, Radisson, **other:** Ford Trucks
207c b	**W...**I-44 W, to Tulsa
a	Gravois St(from nb), **E...gas:** Citgo, **W...food:** A-1 Chinese Wok, Jack-in-the-Box
206c	Arsenal St, **E...**Anheuser-Busch Tour Ctr, **W...gas:** Shell
b	Broadway(from nb)
a	Potomac St(from nb)
205	Gasconade, **W...**HOSPITAL
204	Broadway, **E...gas:** Mobil/repair, **W...gas:** Clark, Sinclair, **food:** Crusoe's Rest., Hardee's, McDonald's, Pantera's Pizza, Pizza Hut, Wendy's, **other:** Radio Shack, Walgreen/24hr
203	Bates St, Virginia Ave, **W...gas:** BP, 7-11
202c	Loughborough Ave, **W...**Schnuck's Foods
b	Germania(from sb), no facilities
a	Carondelet(from nb)
201b	Weber Rd, no facilities
a	Bayless Ave, **E...gas:** BP, QT, Shell, **food:** McDonald's, **W...gas:** BP, Citgo/7-11, **food:** DQ, Jack-in-the-Box, Subway, Taco Bell, **other:** Goodyear
200	Union Rd(from sb), no facilities
199	Reavis Barracks Rd, **E...gas:** BP, Shell, **food:** Steak'n Shake/24hr, **other:** Fabric Whse
197	US 50, US 61, US 67, Lindbergh Blvd, **E...gas:** BP, Phillips 66, Shell, **food:** Arby's, KFC, Gingham's Rest., LJ Silver, McDonald's, Steak'n Shake, Subway, **lodging:** Holiday Inn, Super 8, **other:** Advance Parts, Best Buy, Circuit City, Chrysler/Dodge, Dillard's, Goodyear, JC Penney, K-Mart, Marshall's, mall, **W...food:** Bob Evans, Casa Gallardo's, Denny's, Pasta House, Ponderosa, Shoney's, **lodging:** Motel 6, Oak Grove Inn, **other:** Aldi Foods, Ford/Lincoln/Mercury, Honda, Hyundai, Mazda, Saturn
196b	I-270 W, to Kansas City, no facilities
a	I-255 E, to Chicago, no facilities
195	Butler Hill Rd, **E...gas:** Citgo, Phillips 66, **lodging:** Holiday Inn/rest., **W...gas:** Sinclair, **food:** Burger King, Hardee's, Pizza Hut/Taco Bell, Subway, Waffle House, **other:** Schnuck's Foods
193	Meramec Bottom Rd, **E...gas:** Citgo/7-11, Mobil, QT, **food:** Cracker Barrel, **lodging:** Best Western, **other:** Howard RV Ctr
191	MO 141, Arnold, **E...gas:** Citgo, Phillips 66, QT, **food:** Applebee's, BBQ, Burger King, Denny's, Emperor's Wok, Fazoli's, Hardee's, Jack-in-the-Box, LJ Silver, McDonald's, Steak'n Shake, Taco Bell, **lodging:** Drury Inn, Ramada Ltd, **other:** Eckerd, Kohl's, Schnuck's Foods, Shop'n Sav Foods, Wal-Mart/auto, mall, **W...gas:** Mobil, Phillips 66, **food:** Pasta House
190	Richardson Rd, **E...gas:** Citgo, QT, Shell/diesel, **food:** Domino's, DQ, Pizza Hut, Ponderosa, Sonic, Subway, Taco Bell, White Castle, **other:** Firestone, Ford, Mazda, SavALot Foods, **W...gas:** Shell/Blimpie/diesel, **food:** Burger King, McDonald's, Waffle House, **lodging:** Comfort Inn, **other:** Home Depot, Shnuck's Foods/24hr, Target, Walgreen, transmissions
186	Imperial, Kimmswick, **E...gas:** Shell, **food:** Southern Kitchen, Twisters, **W...**to Mastodon SP
185	rd M, Barnhart, Antonia, **W...gas:** Citgo/7-11, Citgo/diesel, **other:** KOA
184.5mm	weigh sta both lanes
180	rd Z, Pevely, to Hillsboro, **E...gas:** Mobil, **food:** BBQ, Burger King, KFC, Subway, **other:** $General, IGA Foods, **W...gas:** Mr Fuel, Phillips 66/McDonald's/diesel, **lodging:** Gateway Inn, Super 8, **other:** KOA(2mi)
178	Herculaneum, **E...gas:** QT/Wendy's/diesel, **W...**Chevrolet, Ford, Pontiac/Cadillac/Buick
175	rd A, Festus, **E...gas:** Phillips 66/diesel, **food:** Arby's, Bob Evans, Burger King, Dohack's, Fazoli's, McDonald's, Papa John's, Sonic, Steak'n Shake, Subway, Taco Bell, Wendy's, White Castle, **lodging:** Drury Inn, Holiday Inn Express, **other:** Advance Parts, Radio Shack, Schnuck's Foods, Toyota, Wal-Mart SuperCtr/gas/24hr, **W...gas:** Citgo/7-11/diesel, Mobil/diesel, **food:** Hardee's, Ruby Tuesday, Waffle House, **lodging:** Baymont Inn, **other:** Dodge, Lowe's Whse
174b a	US 67, Lp 55, Festus, Crystal City, **1 mi E...food:** Arby's, McDonald's, Ryan's, **lodging:** Twin City Motel, **other:** HOSPITAL, Wal-Mart SuperCtr/gas/24hr, same as 175
170	US 61, **W...gas:** Citgo/diesel/LP
162	rds DD, OO, no facilities

Interstate 55

160mm **rest areas both lanes, full(handicapped)facilities, picnic tables, litter barrels, phones, vending, petwalk**

157 rd Y, Bloomsdale, **E...gas:** Phillips 66, **W...gas:** Shamrock/diesel

154 rd O, no facilities

150 MO 32, rds B, A, to St Genevieve, **E...gas:** BP, **food:** DQ, **lodging:** Microtel(4mi), **other:** HOSPITAL, Hist Site(6mi), **W...other:** Pontiac/GMC, Hawn SP(11mi)

143 rds N, M, Ozora, **W...gas:** Shamrock/Subway/diesel/@, Sinclair, **lodging:** Family Inn/rest.

141 rd Z, St Mary, no facilities

135 rd M, Brewer, **E...**propane depot

129 MO 51, to Perryville, **E...gas:** MotoMart, Phillips 66/diesel, **food:** Burger King, KFC, McDonald's, Ponderosa, Taco Bell, **other:** HOSPITAL, Ford, **W...gas:** T-Rex, **food:** DQ, Kelly's Rest., **lodging:** Best Western, Comfort Inn, Super 8, **other:** Chevrolet/Pontiac/Buick, Chrysler/Plymouth/Dodge/Jeep, $Tree, KOA(1mi), Wal-Mart SuperCtr/24hr

123 rd B, Biehle, **W...gas:** Phillips 66, **food:** Country Kettle Rest./gifts

119mm Apple Creek

117 rd KK, to Appleton, **E...food:** Sewing's Rest./repair

111 rd E, Oak Ridge, no facilities

110mm **rest area both lanes, full(handicapped)facilities, picnic tables, litter barrels, phones, vending, petwalk**

105 US 61, Fruitland, **E...gas:** BP/diesel, Casey's, Rhodes/diesel, **other:** CarQuest, Trail of Tears SP(11mi), **W...gas:** D-Mart, **food:** Bavarian Rest., DQ, Pizza Inn, **lodging:** Drury Inn

99 US 61, MO 34, to Jackson, **E...**Holiday Lodge, Super 8, **W...other:** Wal-Mart SuperCtr/gas/24hr(4mi)

96 rd K, to Cape Girardeau, **E...gas:** BP, Citgo/diesel, **food:** Blimpie, Bob Evans, Burger King, ChuckeCheese, Cracker Barrel, DQ, El Acapulco, Great Wall Chinese, Logan's Roadhouse, O'Charley's, Pizza Inn, Red Lobster, Ruby Tuesday, Ryan's, Steak'n Shake, Subway, Taco Bell, **lodging:** Drury Lodge/rest., Holiday Inn Express, PearTree Inn, Victorian Inn, **other:** HOSPITAL, Schnuck's Foods, Barnes&Noble, Best Buy, JC Penney, mall, **other:** AutoZone, Hastings Books, Sears, Walgreen, to SEMSU, **W...gas:** Shell/24hr, **food:** Lion's Choice, McDonald's, Outback Steaks, **lodging:** Drury Inn, Hampton Inn, **other:** Circuit City, Honda, Lowe's Whse, Sam's Club, Saturn, Staples, Target, Wal-Mart SuperCtr/24hr

95 MO 74 E, same as 96

93 MO 74 W, Cape Girardeau, no facilities

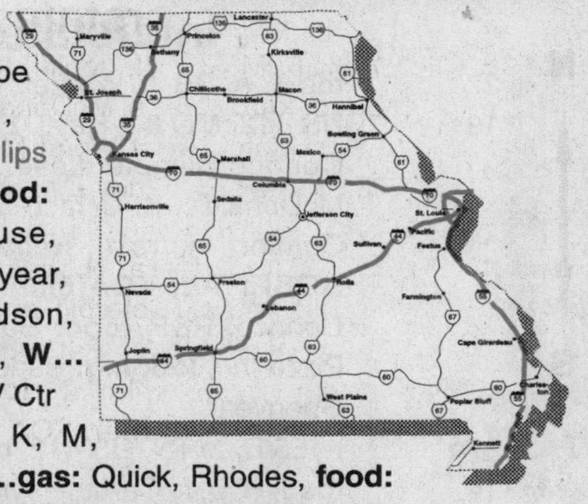

91 rd AB, to Cape Girardeau, **E...gas:** Phillips 66/diesel, **food:** Huddle House, **other:** Goodyear, Harley-Davidson, RV America, **W...** Capetown RV Ctr

89 US 61, rds K, M, Scott City, **E...gas:** Quick, Rhodes, **food:** Burger King, Pizza Pro, Sonic, Waffle Hut

80 MO 77, Benton, **W...gas:** BP, **food:** McDonald's, winery(8mi)

69 rd HH, Miner, to Sikeston, **E...**T&C RV Park(2mi), **W...gas:** Keller Trkstp/diesel/@, golf

67 US 60, US 62, Miner, **E...gas:** Breaktime/diesel, **lodging:** Best Western, Holiday Inn Express, Red Carpet Inn, **other:** T&C RV Park, **1-2 mi W...gas:** Citgo, Hucks, QuickChek, **food:** Bo's BBQ, Burger King, China Pearl, DQ, El Tapatio Mexican, Lambert's Rest., McDonald's, Pizza Hut, Pizza Inn, Sonic, Subway, Taco Bell, Taco John's, Wendy's, **lodging:** Country Hearth Inn, Drury Inn, Holiday Inn Express, PearTree Inn, Ramada Inn, Super 8, **other:** HOSPITAL, Aldi Foods, AutoZone, Chevrolet/Pontiac/Buick, GMC/Cadillac, Family$, Fisher Parts, Goodyear/auto, Pennzoil, Piggly Wiggly, Sikeston Outlets/famous brands

66b US 60 W, to Poplar Bluff, **3 mi W on US 61/62...gas:** Breaktime, **food:** Applebee's, Arby's, DQ, El Bracero Mexican, Hardee's, KFC, McDonald's, Ryan's, Sonic, **lodging:** Day's Inn, **other:** Chrysler/Plymouth/Dodge/Jeep, $Tree, Ford/Lincoln/Mercury, Lowe's Whse, OfficeMax, Radio Shack, Wal-Mart SuperCtr/24hr

a I-57 E, to Chicago, US 60 W

59mm St Johns Bayou

58 MO 80, Matthews, **E...gas:** TA/Taco Bell/diesel/24hr/@, **W...gas:** Flying J/Conoco/diesel/LP/rest./RV dump/24hr/@

52 rd P, Kewanee, **E...gas:** BP/diesel, **W...gas:** Shamrock/diesel

49 US 61, US 62, New Madrid, **3 mi E...lodging:** Relax Inn, **other:** hist site

44 US 61, US 62, Lp 55, New Madrid, **E...**hist site

42mm **Welcome Ctr nb/rest area both lanes, full(handicapped)facilities, picnic tables, litter barrels, phones, vending, petwalk**

40 rd EE, St Jude Rd, Marston, **E...gas:** Pilot/Arby's/diesel/24hr/@, **lodging:** Super 8, **W...gas:** BP/diesel, Breaktime/diesel, **lodging:** Budget Inn

32 US 61, MO 162, Portageville, **W...gas:** BP/diesel, Casey's, **food:** McDonald's, **lodging:** New Orleans Inn, **other:** diesel repair

MISSOURI

Interstate 55

N ↕ S Hayti

27 rds K, A, BB, to Wardell, no facilities

19 US 412, MO 84, Hayti, **E...gas:** Breaktime/diesel, Conoco/Blimpie/diesel, Pilot/diesel/@, **food:** McDonald's, KFC/Taco Bell, Pizza Hut, **lodging:** Comfort Inn/rest., Holiday Inn Express, **other:** HOSPITAL, KOA(6mi), **W...gas:** BP/Subway, Conoco, R&P, **food:** Bavarian Haus Rest., DQ, Pizza Inn, **lodging:** Budget Inn, Drury Inn, **other:** Goodyear

17a I-155 E, to TN, US 412, no facilities

14 rds J, H, U, to Caruthersville, Braggadocio, no facilities

10mm weigh sta both lanes

8 MO 164, Steele, **E...gas:** Duckie's/diesel, **W...lodging:** Deerfield Inn

4 rd E, Cooter, to Holland, no facilities

3mm rest area both lanes, full(handicapped)facilities, picnic tables, litter barrels, phones, vending, petwalk

1 US 61, rd O, Holland, **E...gas:** RaceWay/diesel, **W...gas:** Coastal/diesel

0mm Missouri/Arkansas state line

Interstate 57

N ↕ S Charleston

Exit #	Services
22mm	Missouri/Illinois state line, Mississippi River
18.5mm	weigh sta both lanes
12	US 60, US 62, MO 77, Charleston, **E...gas:** Sunshine Travel Ctr/diesel/@, **lodging:** Economy Motel, **W...gas:** Casey's, Sinclair/diesel, **food:** Apple Valley Buffet, KFC, **lodging:** Econolodge
10	MO 105, Charleston, **E...gas:** BP/Boomland/diesel, Pilot/Subway/diesel/24hr/@, **W...gas:** Casey's, **food:** China Buffet, DQ, McDonald's, Pizza Hut, **lodging:** Comfort Inn, **other:** CountryMart Foods, Plaza Tire
4	rd B, Bertrand, **E...**Jones Jct/diesel
1b a	I-55, N to St Louis, S to Memphis

I-57 begins/ends on I-55, exit 66.

Interstate 64

E ↕ W St Louis

Exit #	Services
41mm	Missouri/Illinois state line, Mississippi River. I-64 and I-70 run together eb.
40b a	Broadway St, to Stadium, to the Arch, **N...lodging:** Sheraton, stadium, **S...other:** Dobb's Tire
c	(from wb), I-44 W, I-55 S
39c	11th St(exits left), downtown
39b	14th St, downtown, **N...lodging:** Sheraton, **S...gas:** BP
a	21st St, Market St(from wb), **N...lodging:** Drury Inn, Hampton Inn
38d	Chestnut at 20th St, **N...lodging:** Drury Inn, Hampton Inn
38c	Jefferson Ave, St Louis Union Sta, **N...**Joplin House
a	Forest Park Blvd(from wb), **N...gas:** Shell
37b a	Market St, Bernard St, Grand Blvd, **N...gas:** Shell, **food:** Del Taco, **lodging:** Courtyard, Hampton Inn, Hyatt, Drury Inn, Adam's Mark Hotel, Marriott
36d	Vandeventer Ave, Chouteau Ave, no facilities
36b a	Kingshighway, **N...lodging:** Best Western, **other:** HOSPITAL, **S...gas:** BP
34d c	Hampton Ave, Forest Park, **N...**museums, zoo, **S...gas:** BP, Mobil, **food:** Courtesy Diner, Hardee's, Imo's Pizza, Jack-in-the-Box, Steak'n Shake, Subway
34a	Oakland Ave, **N...gas:** BP, Del Taco, HOSPITAL
33d	McCausland Ave, **N... gas:** BP, **food:** Del Taco
33c	Bellevue Ave, **N...**HOSPITAL
33b	Big Bend Blvd, no facilities
32b a	Eager Rd, Hanley Rd, **S...gas:** Shell, **other:** Home Depot, Whole Foods Mkt
31b a	I-170 N, **N...gas:** Shell, **food:** Burger King, DQ, IHOP, KFC, Steak'n Shake, TGIFriday, Dillard's, Famous Barr, **other:** mall, **S...gas:** BP, **food:** Macaroni Grill, Subway, **other:** Borders Books, Circuit City, Dierberg's Foods, Goodyear, Target
30	McKnight Rd, no facilities
28c	Clayton Rd(from wb), no facilities
28b a	US 67, US 61, Lindbergh Blvd, **S...lodging:** Hilton, **other:** Shnuck's Foods, mall
27	Spoede Rd, no facilities
26	rd JJ, Ballas Rd, **N...**HOSPITAL, **S...**HOSPITAL
25	I-270, N to Chicago, S to Memphis
23	Mason Rd, **N...lodging:** Courtyard, Marriott, **other:** LDS Temple, hwy patrol
22	MO 141, **N...food:** Regatta Grille, **lodging:** Courtyard, Marriott, **other:** HOSPITAL, **S...food:** Pizza Hut
21	Timberlake Manor Pkwy, no facilities
20	Chesterfield Pkwy(from wb), same as 19b a
19b a	MO 340, Chesterfield Pkwy, **N...gas:** BP, Shell, **food:** Applebee's, Pizzaria Uno, **lodging:** DoubleTree Hotel, Hampton Inn, Residence Inn, **S...gas:** Mobil, **food:** Bahama Breeze Rest., Casa Gallardo's, **other:** Dillard's, mall
17	Boones Crossing, Long Rd, Chesterfield Airport Rd, **1 mi S...gas:** BP, Mobil, Phillips 66, **food:** Annie Gunn's Rest., Gator Flats Rest., Longhorn Steaks, McDonald's, O'Charley's, Old Country Buffet, Olive Garden, Red Lobster, Red Robin, SmokeHouse Rest., Steak'n Shake, Subway, **lodging:** Hampton Inn, Hilton Garden, **other:** Best Buy, $Tree, Ford, Lowe's Whse, Michael's, OfficeMax, Sam's Club, Target, Wal-Mart/auto, WorldMkt
14	Chesterfield Airport Rd(from eb), **S...gas:** Phillips 66, **lodging:** Comfort Inn
13mm	Missouri River, I-64 begins/ends.

Interstate 70

E ↕ W

St Louis

Exit #	Services
252mm	Missouri/Illinois state line, Mississippi River
251a	I-55 S, to Memphis, to I-44, to downtown/no return
250b	Memorial Dr, downtown, Stadium, **S...gas:** Shell, **food:** McDonald's, **lodging:** Day's Inn
a	Conv Center, Arch, Riverfront, **N...lodging:** Econolodge, Embassy Suites, **S...lodging:** Drury Inn, Radisson, TWA Dome
249c	6th St(from eb), no facilities
a	Madison St, 10th St, **N...gas:** Phillips 66/diesel
248b	St Louis Ave, Branch St, no facilities
a	Salisbury St, McKinley Br, **N...**truck repair/24hr, **S...gas:** BP, Mobil/diesel
247	Grand Ave, **N...gas:** Phillips 66/diesel, **lodging:** Western Inn, **S...lodging:** Economy Inn
246b	Adelaide Ave, no facilities
a	N Broadway, O'Fallon Park, **N...gas:** Phillips 66, **other:** Freightliner
245b	W Florissant, no facilities
a	Shreve Ave, **N...**Pillsbury Factory, **S...gas:** BP
244b	Kingshighway, **3/4 mi S...food:** Burger King, McDonald's, Subway
a	Bircher Blvd, Union Blvd, no facilities
243b	(243c from eb)Bircher Blvd, no facilities
243a	Riverview Blvd, no facilities
243	Goodfellow Blvd, **N...gas:** Shell
242b a	Jennings Sta Rd, **N...gas:** Shell, **S...food:** McDonald's, **other:** transmission repair
241b	Lucas-Hunt Rd, **N...gas:** Shell, **3/4 mi S...gas:** Citgo, **food:** McDonald's
a	Bermuda Rd, **S...gas:** Sinclair, **other:** HOSPITAL,
240b a	Florissant Rd, **N...gas:** BP/McDonald's, **food:** DQ, Sonic, Taco Bell, **other:** Schnuck's Foods, Walgreen
239	N Hanley Rd, **N...food:** Jack-in-the-Box, **S...food:** McDonald's
238c b	I-170 N, I-170 S, no return
a	**N...**Lambert-St Louis Airport, **S...lodging:** Renaissance Hotel
237	Natural Bridge Rd(from eb), **S...gas:** Phillips 66, Shell, **food:** Burger King, Denny's, Jack-in-the-Box, KFC, Pizza Hut, Steak'n Shake, Waffle House, Wendy's, DoubleTree, **lodging:** Holiday Inn, Renaissance, Travelodge
236	Lambert-St Louis Airport, **S...gas:** BP, **food:** Big Boy, Coco's, Grone Cafeteria, Hardee's, Lombardo's Café Rafferty's Rest., Tiffany's Rest., **lodging:** Best Western, Day's Inn, Drury Inn/rest., Hampton Inn, Hilton Garden, Holiday Inn, Marriott, Motel 6
235c	Cypress Rd, rd B W, **N...**to airport
b a	US 67, Lindbergh Blvd, **N...gas:** Shell, **lodging:** Executive Intn'l Inn, Holiday Inn/café, Howard Johnson, **S...gas:** Shell, **food:** Lion's Choice Rest., Steak'n Shake, TGIFriday, **lodging:** Congress Inn, Embassy Suites, Homestead Studios, Radisson, **other:** Chevrolet, Dillard's, Firestone, JC Penney, Sears/auto, mall
234	MO 180, St Charles Rock Rd, **N...gas:** Phillips 66, Shell, **food:** Applebee's, Casa Gallardo's, Fazoli's, Hardee's, Hatfield's/McCoy's Rest., LoneStar Steaks, LJ Silver, McDonald's, Old Country Buffet, Ponderosa, Red Lobster, Shoney's, Steak'n Shake, Taco Bell, Tony Bono's Rest., **lodging:** Knight's Inn, **other:** HOSPITAL, Best Buy, Circuit City, GrandPa's Food/drug, Honda, K-Mart, NTB, Office Depot, Sam's Club, Target, Walgreen/24hr, **S...**Isuzu
232	I-270, N to Chicago, S to Memphis, no facilities
231b a	Earth City Expwy, **N...lodging:** Candlewood Suites, Courtyard, Fairfield Inn, Sheraton, Studio+, **S...gas:** Mobil, **food:** Burger King, Dave&Buster's, Stage Left Café, Town Square Café, **lodging:** Holiday Inn, Doubletree Hotel, Wingate Inn, **other:** Harrah's Casino/Hotel, Riverport Ampitheatre
230mm	Missouri River

St Charles

Exit #	Services
229b a	5th St, St Charles, **N...gas:** BP, Mobil/diesel, MotoMart, **food:** Burger King, Denny's, Jack-in-the-Box, KFC, McDonald's, Subway, Waffle House, **lodging:** Baymont Inn, St Charles Inn, **other:** Walgreen/24hr, **S...gas:** Phillips 66, QT/diesel, **food:** Cracker Barrel, **lodging:** Best Western Noah's Ark, Day's Inn, Fairfield Inn, Howard Johnson, Ramada, Suburban Lodge, Townhouse Inn, **other:** JC Penney, malls, RV park
228	MO 94, St Charles, to Weldon Springs, **N...gas:** Citgo, Shell, **food:** Arby's, DQ, Hardee's, Imo's Pizza, LJ Silver, Papa John's, Pizza Hut, Steak'n Shake, Victoria's Creamery, Wendy's, **other:** Advance Parts, AutoValue, AutoZone, Chevrolet, Firestone, Radio Shack, Shop'n Save, Walgreen, Valvoline, **S...gas:** Mobil/diesel, Shell, **food:** ChuckeCheese, Fazoli's, Gingham's Rest., **lodging:** Best Western, **other:** K-Mart, access to 227

MISSOURI

Interstate 70

E ↕ W

227 Zumbehl Rd, **N...gas:** Shell, **food:** Burger King, Culpepper's Grill, **lodging:** Econolodge, **other:** Ford, Lowe's Whse, SavALot Foods, **S...gas:** BP, Citgo, Mobil/FoodCourt, **food:** Applebee's, BBQ, Blackeyed Pea, Bob Evans, Boston Mkt, Capt D's, Chevy's Mexican, Golden Corral, Hardee's, Italian Ristorante, Jack-in-the-Box, Krieger's Grill, LoneStar Steaks, McDonald's, Mr Steak, Old Country Buffet, Popeye's, Subway, Taco Bell, **lodging:** Best Western, Comfort Inn, Red Roof Inn, TownePlace Suites, **other:** Deerborg's Foods/24hr, OfficeMax, Sam's Club, Schnuck's Foods/24hr, Wal-Mart/auto, access to 228

225 Truman Rd, to Cave Springs, **N...gas:** BP, Citgo, Shell, **food:** Taco Bell, Wendy's, **lodging:** Budget Motel, Hampton Inn, Knight's Inn, Motel 6, **other:** Buick/Pontiac, Cadillac, Lincoln/Mercury, Mazda, Saturn, Target, Toyota, U-Haul, **S...gas:** Conoco, Mobil, QT, **food:** Big Boy, Burger King, DQ, Denny's, El Mezcal Mexican, Fazoli's, Ground Round, IHOP, Jack-in-the-Box, Lion's Choice Rest., LJ Silver, McDonald's, Pasta House, Pizza Hut, Ponderosa, Red Lobster, Steak'n Shake, Subway, White Castle, **lodging:** Holiday Inn Select, **other:** HOSPITAL, Chrysler/Jeep, Dodge, Home Depot, Kia, K-Mart, Office Depot, OfficeMax, Shop'n Save, Target

224 MO 370, no facilities

St Peters

222 Mall Dr, St Peters, **N...gas:** QT/diesel/24hr, **food:** Burger King, **other:** Chevrolet, Honda, Mitsubishi, Subaru, **S...gas:** Citgo, Mobil, **food:** Arby's, Bob Evans, Chili's, Domino's, Hardee's, Jack-in-the-Box, Joe's Crabshack, McDonald's, Olive Garden, Pizza Hut, Steak'n Shake, Subway, Taco Bell, Wendy's, **lodging:** Drury Inn, Extended Stay America, **other:** MEDICAL CARE, Aldi Foods, AutoZone, Best Buy, Circuit City, Costco/gas, Deerborg's Foods, Dillard's, Discount Tire, JC Penney, Nissan/Hyundai/VW, Schnuck's Foods, Sears/auto, Walgreen

220 MO 79, to Elsberry, **N...**Cherokee Lakes Camping(7mi), **S...gas:** BP, Citgo/7-11(1mi), **food:** Blimpie(1mi), Hardee's, McDonald's(1mi), Smokehouse Rest., Sonic

217 rds K, M, O'Fallon, **N...gas:** BP, QT, **food:** Blimpie, Burger King, Hardee's, Jack-in-the-Box, Ponderosa, Rally's, Taco Bell, Waffle House, **other:** AutoValue Parts, Firestone, Radio Shack, **S...gas:** Citgo/diesel, DirtCheap, Shell, **food:** Arby's, Bob Evans, Fazoli's, IHOP, KFC, Lion's Choice Rest., Longhorn Steaks, McDonald's, Pizza Hut, Steak'n Shake/24hr, Stefanina's Pizza, **other:** Aldi Foods, AutoZone, K-Mart/drugs, Lowe's Whse, Schnuck's Foods, Shop'n Save Foods, Walgreen, camping

216 Bryan Rd, **N...lodging:** Super 8, **other:** Ford, **S...gas:** Casey's, Mobil, QT

214 Lake St Louis, **N...**Freedom RV Ctr(1mi), **S...gas:** Phillips 66/diesel, Shell, **food:** Cutter's Rest., Denny's, Hardee's, Subway, **lodging:** Day's Inn, **other:** HOSPITAL, IGA Foods

212 rd A, **N...lodging:** Knight's Inn, Ramada Ltd, **S...gas:** Citgo/diesel, **food:** Arby's, Burger King, Imo's Pizza, Texas Willie's Steaks, **lodging:** Holiday Inn, **other:** Chrysler/Plymouth/Dodge/Jeep, Luxury Linens, Wentzville Outlets/famous brands

210b a US 61, US 40, to I-64 E, **S...gas:** Conoco, Phillips 66/diesel, Shell, **other:** HOSPITAL

209 rd Z(from wb), Church St, New Melle, no facilities

208 Pearce Blvd, Wentzville, **N...gas:** Citgo, QT/diesel, **food:** Imo's Pizza, KFC, McDonald's, Palace Buffet, Pizza Hut, Steak'n Shake/24hr, Taco Bell, Waffle House, Wendy's, **other:** HOSPITAL, Chevrolet/Buick, Family$, Home Depot, Sav-A-Lot Foods, Schnuck's Food, Walgreen, **S...gas:** BP, Shell, **food:** Capt D's, Hardee's, KwanYin Chinese, Pantera's Pizza, Ruggeri's Italian, **lodging:** Super 8, **other:** $General, Pinewood RV Park, Plymouth/Dodge, Radio Shack, Thomas RV Ctr, Wal-Mart SuperCtr/24hr

204mm weigh sta both lanes

203 rds W, T, Foristell, **N...gas:** TA/diesel/rest./24hr/@, Mr Fuel/diesel, **lodging:** Best Western, diesel repair, **S...gas:** Phillips 66/diesel/café

200 rds J, H, F, Wright City, **N...gas:** Citgo/diesel, Shell/diesel, **food:** McDonald's, Ruiz Castillo's Mexican(1mi), **S...gas:** Phillips 66, **food:** Big Boy, **lodging:** Super 7 Inn, **other:** Volvo

199 (from wb), same as 200

198mm rest area both lanes, full(handicapped)facilities, phone, picnic tables, litter barrels, petwalk

193 MO 47, Warrenton, **N...gas:** Citgo, Phillips 66/diesel, **food:** Burger King, DQ, Jack-in-the-Box, McDonald's, Pizza Hut, Subway, Waffle House, **lodging:** Day's Inn, Super 8, **other:** Family$, Ford, Moser's Foods, Wal-Mart, **S...gas:** BP, Phillips 66/Blimpie/diesel, Shell/diesel/deli/24hr, **food:** Denny's, Hardee's, Imo's Pizza, KFC, Taco Bell, **lodging:** AmeriHost, BudgetHost, **other:** CarQuest, Chrysler/Plymouth/Dodge/Jeep, Kelly Tire, **1/2 mi on frontage rd...other:** Chevrolet/Pontiac, Outlet Ctr/famous brands

188 rds A, B, to Truxton, **S...gas:** Flying J/Conoco/diesel/LP/24hr/@, **lodging:** Budget Inn

183 rds E, NN, Y, Jonesburg, **1 mi N...**KOA/LP, **S...gas:** BP, Shell/diesel

179 rd F, High Hill, **S...lodging:** Budget Motel, Colonial Inn

175 MO 19, New Florence, **N...gas:** BP/Hardee's/diesel, Phillips 66/diesel/24hr, Shell/diesel/24hr, **food:** Maggie's Café, McDonald's, Pizza Cabin, **lodging:** Best Inn, Day's Inn, Super 8, **other:** Stone Hill Winery/gifts, U-Haul, auto repair, **S...**RV parking

Interstate 70

E

W

Columbia

170 MO 161, rd J, Danville, **N...gas:** Phillips 66, **other:** to Graham Cave SP, Kan-Do RV Park, **S...**Lazy Day RV Park

169.5mm rest area wb, full(handicapped)facilities, phone, vending, picnic tables, litter barrels, petwalk

168mm Loutre River

167mm rest area eb, full(handicapped)facilities, phone, vending, picnic tables, litter barrels, petwalk

161 rds D, YY, Williamsburg, **S...gas:** Conoco/diesel/café/24hr/@

155 rds A, Z, to Calwood, **N...**antiques

148 US 54, Kingdom City, **N...gas:** BP, Phillips 66/Taco Bell/diesel, **lodging:** AmeriHost, **other:** to Mark Twain Lake, **S...gas:** Conoco/Subway/diesel/@, Gasper's/diesel/rest., Petro/Mobil/diesel/rest./24hr/@, Phillips 66/McDonald's/diesel, **food:** Denny's, Comfort Inn, Day's Inn, Red Carpet Inn, Super 8

144 rds M, HH, to Hatton, **S...other:** Crooked Creek Camping, Wilder RV Ctr, fireworks

137 rds DD, J, Stephens, to Millersburg, **S...other:** Walnut Bowls Factory Outlet, to Little Dixie WA

133 rd Z, to Centralia, **N...**Loveall's RV

131 Lake of the Woods Rd, **N...gas:** BP, Phillips 66/Subway/diesel, **S...gas:** Shell/diesel/24hr, **other:** RV Park

128a US 63, Columbia, to Jefferson City, **N...gas:** QT, **food:** Bob Evans, Burger King, Casa Grande Mexican, Cracker Barrel, Golden Corral, KFC, McDonald's, Pizza Hut, Schlotsky's, Steak'n Shake, Taco Bell, Wendy's, **lodging:** Fairfield Inn, Hampton Inn, Super 8, **other:** Aamco, Home Depot, KOA, Cottonwood's RV, **S...gas:** Breaktime/diesel, **food:** Sonic, Subway, **lodging:** Baymont Inn, Best Western, Candlewood Suites, Comfort Inn, Holiday Inn Express, Hawthorn Suites, Howard Johnson, La Quinta, Wingate Inn, **other:** HOSPITAL, Lowe's Whse, MegaMkt Foods, Nowell's Foods, Sam's Club, Staples, Wal-Mart SuperCtr/24hr(1mi)

128 Lp 70(from wb), Columbia, **N...food:** Wendy's, **lodging:** Super 8, **S...gas:** Conoco/diesel, **lodging:** Best Western, Baymont Inn, Comfort Inn, Holiday Inn Express, **other:** HOSPITAL, same as 128a

127 MO 763, Columbia, to Moberly, **N...gas:** Breaktime/diesel, **food:** Honest John's Grill, McDonald's, Waffle House, **lodging:** Budget Host, Ramada, Travelodge, **other:** Acura, Chrysler/Dodge, $General, Harley-Davidson, Pontiac/Cadillac, Saturn, Toyota, **S...gas:** Phillips 66/diesel, **food:** DQ, Everett's Rest., Taco Bell, **lodging:** Econolodge, Super 7 Motel

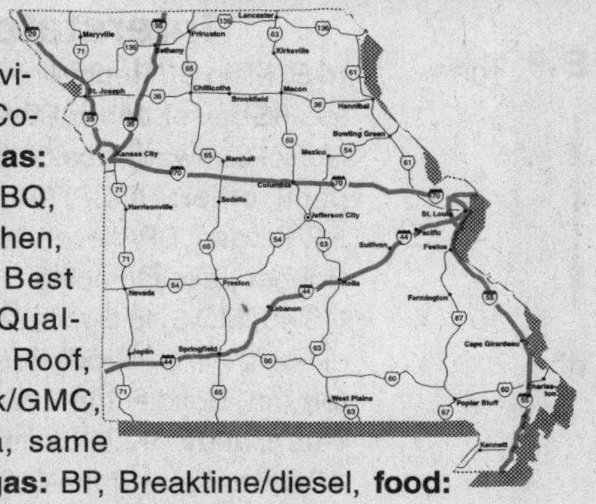

126 MO 163, Providence Rd, Columbia, **N...gas:** BP, **food:** BBQ, Country Kitchen, **lodging:** Best Value Inn, Quality Inn, Red Roof, **other:** Buick/GMC, Ford, Honda, same as 127, **S...gas:** BP, Breaktime/diesel, **food:** Burger King, DQ, McDonald's, Pizza Hut, Sonic, Subway, Taco Bell, **other:** HOSPITAL, Aldi Foods, AutoZone, Chevrolet/Nissan, Chrysler/Jeep, $General, Lincoln/Mercury, O'Reilly Parts

125 Lp 70, West Blvd, Columbia, **S...gas:** Breaktime/diesel, Conoco/diesel, Citgo, Phillips 66/diesel, **food:** Chevy's Mexican, Denny's, Domino's, El Maguey Mexican, Fazoli's, LJ Silver, Olive Garden, Outback Steaks, Perkins, Pizza Hut, Red Lobster, Ryan's, Wendy's, Western Sizzlin, Yen Ching Chinese, **lodging:** Deluxe Inn, Eastwood Inn, Econolodge, Howard Johnson/rest., Scottish Inn, **other:** Advance Parts, Chrysler/Plymouth/Subaru, Firestone/auto, Mitsubishi, Mr Transmissions, PriceChopper Foods, U-Haul, same as 124

124 MO 740, rd E, Stadium Blvd, Columbia, **N...gas:** BreakTime, **lodging:** Extended Stay America, **S...gas:** Phillips 66, **food:** Alexander's Steaks, Applebee's, Burger King, Great Wall Chinese, Hardee's, KFC, Little Caesar's, LJ Silver, McDonald's, Old Chicago Pizza, Pasta House, Pizza Hut, Red Lobster, Ruby Tuesday, Steak'n Shake, Sub Shop, Subway, Taco Bell, Wendy's, **lodging:** Baymont Inn, Day's Inn, Drury Inn, Holiday Inn/rest., Motel 6, Regency Inn, **other:** Circuit City, Dillard's, Ford, Isuzu, JC Penney, K-Mart, Radio Shack, Sears/auto, Toyota, Wal-Mart/auto, mall, to U of MO, same as 125

122mm Perche Creek

121 US 40, rd UU, Midway, **N...gas:** Conoco/diesel/rest./@, **lodging:** Budget Inn, **other:** Goodyear, Flea Mkt/antiques, **S...**golf

117 rds J, O, to Huntsdale, **S...**Furniture World, repair

115 rd BB, Rocheport, **N...**winery, to Katy Tr SP, **S...**antiques

114.5mm Missouri River

111 MO 98, MO 179, to Wooldridge, Overton, **S...gas:** Phillips 66/diesel

106 MO 87, Bingham Rd, to Boonville, **N...gas:** Conoco/diesel/rest., Shell/diesel, **lodging:** Atlasta Motel/rest.

104mm rest area both lanes, full(handicapped)facilities, phone, picnic tables, litter barrels, vending, petwalk

MISSOURI

Interstate 70

E ↕ W

Concordia

103 rd B, Main St, Boonville, **N...gas:** Breaktime, Phillips 66/diesel, **food:** Domino's, KFC, McDonald's, Sonic, Subway, Taco Bell, **lodging:** Day's Inn, Super 8, **other:** HOSPITAL, Wal-Mart/café, to Kay Tr SP, **S...gas:** BP/diesel, Conoco/diesel/24hr, **other:** Bobber Lake Camping

101 US 40, MO 5, to Boonville, **N...gas:** Pilot/Wendy's/diesel/24hr/@, **food:** Burger King, **lodging:** Comfort Inn, Holiday Inn Express, **other:** Russell Stovers Candy, **S...**Chrysler/Plymouth/Dodge/Jeep, **other:** to Lake of the Ozarks

98 MO 41, MO 135, Lamine, **N...**to Arrow Rock HS(13mi), **S...gas:** Conoco/diesel, Shell/diesel/24hr, **food:** Dogwood Rest.

93mm Lamine River

89 rd K, to Arrow Rock, **N...**to Arrow Rock HS

84 rd J, **N...gas:** Citgo/DQ/Stuckey's, truck repair

78b a US 65, to Marshall, **N...gas:** Conoco, **other:** Lazy Days RV Park, **S...gas:** Breaktime/diesel

77mm Blackwater River

74 rds YY, **N...gas:** Shell/diesel/rest./24hr, **lodging:** Betty's Motel, **S...gas:** BP/diesel/rest.

71 rds EE, K, to Houstonia, **N...**flea mkt

66 MO 127, Sweet Springs, **S...gas:** Phillips 66/diesel, Conoco/diesel, **food:** Brownsville Sta Rest., Tastee Freez, **lodging:** People's Choice Motel, Super 8, **other:** HOSPITAL

65.5mm Davis Creek

62 rds VV, Y, Emma, no facilities

58 MO 23, Concordia, **N...gas:** TA/Subway/diesel/24hr/@, **food:** KFC/Taco Bell, McDonald's, **other:** $General, **S...gas:** Breaktime/diesel, Conoco, Shell, **food:** BBQ, Hardee's, Palace Rest., Pizza Hut, Taco John's, **lodging:** Best Western, Day's Inn, **other:** CountryMart Foods, NAPA

57.5mm rest area both lanes, full(handicapped)facilities, phone, picnic tables, litter barrels, vending, petwalk

52 rd T, Aullville, no facilities

49 MO 13, to Higginsville, **N...gas:** BP, Pilot/McDonald's/Subway/diesel/24hr/@, **food:** China Buffet, Pizza Hut, **lodging:** Camelot Inn, Classic Motel(4mi), **other:** to Whiteman AFB, to Confederate Mem, **S...lodging:** Super 8/rest., **other:** GS RV Park

45 rd H, to Mayview, no facilities

43mm weigh sta both lanes

41 rds O, M, to Lexington, Mayview, no facilities

38 MO 131(from wb), Odessa, **S...gas:** BP, Shell, **food:** McDonald's, Sonic, Subway, Taco John's, Wendy's, **other:** camping, same as 37

37 MO 131, Odessa, **N...food:** Countryside Diner, **S...gas:** BP, Shell, **food:** McDonald's, Morgan's Rest., Pizza Hut, Sonic, Subway, Taco John's, Wendy's, **lodging:** Odessa Inn, Parkside Inn, **other:** Chrysler/Plymouth/Dodge/Jeep, Ford, O'Reilly Parts, Prime Outlets/famous brands, Thriftway Foods, RV dump, same as 38

35mm truck parking both lanes

31 rds D, Z, to Bates City, Napoleon, **N...**I-70 Motel/RV Park, **S...gas:** BP/diesel

29.5mm Horse Shoe Creek

28 rd HF, Oak Grove, **N...gas:** TA/Conoco/Popeye's/Pizza Hut/diesel/24hr/@, **lodging:** Day's Inn, **other:** Blue Beacon, KOA, **S...gas:** QT/diesel/24hr, Petro/Blimpie/DQ/Wendy's/diesel/@, **food:** Hardee's, KFC/Taco Bell, McDonald's, Subway, Waffle House, **lodging:** Econolodge, Oak Grove Inn, **other:** Wal-Mart SuperCtr/24hr

Independence

24 US 40, rds AA, BB, to Buckner, **N...gas:** Phillips 66/diesel/rest., **lodging:** Comfort Inn, Travelodge, **other:** Country Campers RV Ctr, **S...gas:** Pilot/Subway/diesel/24hr/@, **food:** Sonic, **other:** GoodSam RV Park/LP, Trailside RV Ctr

21 Adams Dairy Pkwy, **N...**Nationwide RV Ctr(1mi), **S...gas:** Phillips 66/Burger King/diesel, **lodging:** Courtyard, **other:** Home Depot, **2 mi S...food:** Arby's, Fazoli's, Ponderosa

20 MO 7, Blue Springs, **N...gas:** Phillips 66/diesel, Shamrock, Sinclair, **food:** Backyard Burger, Quizno's, Sonic, **lodging:** Motel 6, Ramada Ltd, Sleep Inn, Super 8, **other:** O'Reilly Parts, Osco Drug, PriceChopper Foods, Valvoline, Walgreen, **S...gas:** BP/diesel/24hr, QT, Shell, **food:** Applebee's, BBQ, Burger King, China Buffet, Clancy's, Denny's, Domino's, El Mezcal Mexican, Godfather's, Golden Corral, Jose Pepper's, KFC, LJ Silver, McDonald's, Subway, Thai Place, Texas Tom's Mexican, Village Inn, Wendy's, Winstead's Burgers, **lodging:** Hampton Inn, Holiday Inn Express, Quality Inn, **other:** HOSPITAL, Advance Parts, Chevrolet, Firestone/auto, Hyundai, Office Depot, Radio Shack, Saturn, **1 mi S...food:** Arby's, Fazoli's, **other:** AutoZone, Goodyear/auto, HyVee Foods, NAPA, Wal-Mart/auto

18 Woods Chapel Rd, **N...gas:** BP, **lodging:** American Inn, Day's Inn, Interstate Inn, **other:** Harley-Davidson, **S...gas:** Conoco, Phillips 66/diesel, QT, **food:** Church's, KFC/Taco Bell, McDonald's, Pizza Hut, Taco John's, Waffle House, **other:** All Seasons RV, Ford, Nissan, same as 20

17 Little Blue Pkwy, 39th St, **N...food:** Applebee's, BBQ, Fazoli's, Hereford House, Joe's Crabshack, Macaroni Grill, O'Charley's, On the Border, **lodging:** Hilton Garden, **other:** mall entrance, **S...food:** Carrabba's, Hooters, IHOP, Kobe Steaks, Outback Steaks, Primo Ristorante, Wendy's, **lodging:** Holiday Inn Express, **other:** Costco, Lowe's Whse

16mm Little Blue River

15b MO 291 N, Independence, **1 exit N on 39th St...gas:** Conoco, QT, Phillips 66, **food:** Applebee's, Arby's, BBQ, Bob Evans, Burger King, Chevy's Mexican, Chili's, Denny's, 54th St Grill, Hops Grill, KFC, LJ

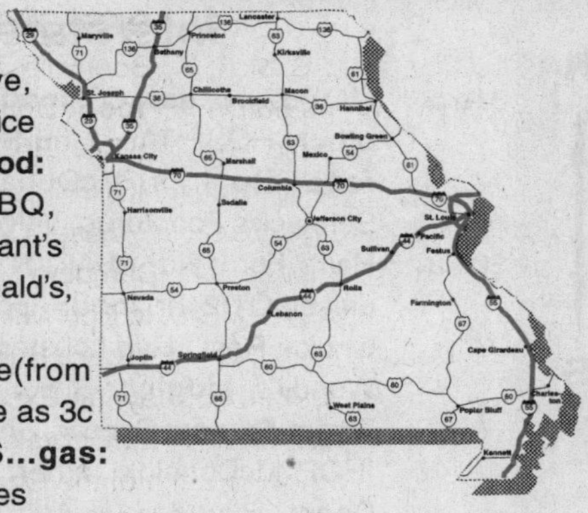

Interstate 70

E ↕ W

Independence

Silver, LoneStar Steaks, Longhorn Steaks, Luby's, McDonald's, Mr GoodCents Subs, Souper Salad, Starbucks, TGIFriday, **lodging:** Fairfield Inn, Residence Inn, **other:** HOSPITAL, Albertson's, Barnes&Noble, Circuit City, Dick's Sports, Dillard's, Jo-Ann Fabrics, Kohl's, Marshall's, NTB, Sam's Club, Sears/auto, Target, Wal-Mart SuperCtr/24hr, mall

a — I-470 S, MO 291 S, to Lee's Summit, no facilities

14 — Lee's Summit Rd, AppleFarm Rest., Boston Mkt, Cracker Barrel, Olive Garden, Steak'n Shake, **lodging:** Budget Host, **other:** Home Depot

12 — Noland Rd, Independence, **N...gas:** QT, Shell/diesel, **lodging:** Best Western, Super 8, **other:** Advance Parts, Firestone, K-Mart, Office Depot, OfficeMax, Osco Drug, Walgreen, U-Haul, transmissions, to Truman Library, **S...gas:** Phillips 66, **food:** Arby's, Burger King, Country Kitchen, Fuddrucker's, KFC/Taco Bell, KrispyKreme, McDonald's, Old Country Buffet, Red Lobster, Ruby Tuesday, Wendy's, **lodging:** American Inn, Comfort Inn, Crossland Inn, Red Roof Inn, **other:** Best Buy, $Tree, Old Navy, HyVee Foods, Tires+

11 — US 40, Blue Ridge Blvd, Independence, **N...gas:** QT, Shell, **food:** A&W/LJ Silver, Burger King, McDonald's, Sonic, Subway, V's Italiano, **lodging:** Budget Host, Deluxe Inn, **other:** Radio Shack, Stadium RV Park, **S...gas:** BP, Citgo/7-11, Sinclair, **food:** Applebee's, Hong Kong Buffet, Old Country Buffet, Papa John's, Steak'n Shake, Taco Bell, **lodging:** Sports Stadium Motel, **other:** Cadillac, JC Penney, mall

10 — Sterling Ave(from eb), same as 11

9 — Blue Ridge Cutoff, **N...gas:** Conoco, **food:** Denny's/24hr, Wendy's, **lodging:** Adam's Mark Hotel/rest., Day's Inn, Drury Inn, Villager Lodge, **other:** HOSPITAL, **S...gas:** BP/24hr, Sinclair, **food:** Taco Bell, **lodging:** Holiday Inn, **other:** Sports Complex

Kansas City

8b a — I-435, N to Des Moines, S to Witchita

7b — Manchester Trafficway, **S...**Ryder Trucks

7mm — Blue River

7a — US 40 E, 31st St, **N...lodging:** Sunset Inn, Villager Lodge, **S...lodging:** Economy Inn, SportsStadium Motel, Travelers Inn

6 — Van Brunt Blvd, **N...gas:** Citgo/7-11, **S...gas:** BP, **food:** KFC, McDonald's, Pizza Hut, Taco Bell, **other:** VA HOSPITAL, Osco Drug

5c — Jackson Ave(from wb), no facilities

b — 31st St(from eb), no facilities

a — 27th St(from eb), no facilities

4c — 23rd Ave, no facilities

b — 18th St, **N...gas:** Phillips 66/Wendy's/diesel

a — Benton Blvd(from eb), Truman Rd, **N...gas:** Phillips 66/Wendy's/diesel, **other:** Advance Parts

Kansas City

3c — Prospect Ave, **N...gas:** Service Oil/diesel, **food:** Kate's BBQ, **S...food:** Bryant's Café, McDonald's, Church's

b — Brooklyn Ave(from eb), **S...**same as 3c

3a — Paseo St, **S...gas:** BP, **other:** tires

2m — US 71 S, downtown

2l — I-670, to I-35 S, no facilities

2j — 11th St, downtown

2g — I-29/35 N, US 71 N, to Des Moines

2h — US 24 E, downtown

2e — MO 9 N, Oak St, **N...gas:** Conoco, **S...gas:** Shamrock, **lodging:** Comfort Inn

2d — Main St, downtown

2c — US 169 N, Broadway, downtown

2b — Beardsley Rd, no facilities

2a — I-35 S, to Wichita

0mm — Missouri/Kansas state line, Kansas River

Interstate 270(St Louis)

N ↕ S

Exit #	Services
15b a	I-55 N to Chicago, S to St Louis. I-270 begins/ends in Illinois on I-55/I-70, exit 20.
12	IL 159, to Collinsville, **N...gas:** Mobil/diesel, **food:** DQ, Hardee's, Ponderosa, **S...**HOSPITAL
9	IL 157, to Collinsville, **N...food:** Comfort Inn, **S...gas:** Phillips 66/24hr
7	I-255, to I-55 S to Memphis
6b a	IL 111, **N...gas:** BP/24hr, Flying J/CountryMkt/diesel/24hr/@, **food:** Hen House Rest., Sawyers Rest., **lodging:** Apple Valley Motel, Best Western, **S...food:** Denny's, McDonald's, **lodging:** Holiday Inn Express, Ramada Ltd, Super 8, to Pontoon Beach
4	IL 203, Old Alton Rd, to Granite City, no facilities
3b a	IL 3, **N...**Riverboat Casino, **S...food:** Hardee's, Waffle House, **lodging:** Chain of Rocks Motel, **other:** KOA
2mm	Chain of Rocks Canal
0mm	Illinois/Missouri state line, Mississippi River, motorist callboxes begin eb
34	Riverview Dr, to St Louis, **N...Welcome Ctr/rest area both lanes, full(handicapped)facilities, info, picnic tables, litter barrels, phones**
33	Lilac Ave, **N...**USPO, **S...gas:** Phillips 66/diesel, QT/diesel/24hr, **food:** Hardee's
32	Bellefontaine Rd, **N...gas:** Mobil, Shell, **food:** Burger King, Denny's, McDonald's, Pizza Hut, Steak'n Shake, **lodging:** Econolodge, Motel 6, **other:** Advance Parts, Firestone, Schnuck's Foods, bank, **S...gas:** BP/24hr, **other:** Aldi Foods

MISSOURI

Interstate 270

N ↕ S

St Louis

31b a MO 367, **N...gas:** QT, **food:** Arby's, Jack-in-the-Box, **other:** HOSPITAL, **1 mi S...gas:** Phillips 66/diesel, **food:** Denny's, McDonald's, Taco Bell, **other:** Schnuck's Food/drug, Valvoline

30b a Hall's Ferry Rd, rd AC, **N...gas:** Mobil, Phillips 66/diesel, QT/24hr, **food:** Applebee's, Hardee's, Lion's Choice Rest., Red Lobster, Taco Bell, White Castle, Wendy's, **lodging:** Super 8, **other:** Discount Tire, Target, **S...gas:** Conoco, Shell, Mobil, **food:** Church's, IHOP, McDonald's, **other:** AutoZone, Buick, Home Depot, Hyundai, Jo-Ann Fabrics, Saturn, Shop'n Save Foods

29 W Florissant Rd, **N...food:** Jack-in-the-Box, **other:** Best Buy, Dierberg's Foods, K-Mart, Office Depot, **S...food:** Blackeyed Pea, Burger King, Krispy Kreme, Malone's Grill, McDonald's, Old Country Buffet, **other:** Circuit City, Saturn, Sam's Club, Wal-Mart

28 Elizabeth Ave, Washington St, **S...gas:** BP/24hr, **N...gas:** Sinclair, **food:** Jack-in-the-Box, Mrs O's Café, Pizza Hut, Subway, Taco Bell, **other:** Chevrolet, JC Penney, OfficeMax, Schnuck's Foods/24hr, Walgreen

27 New Florissant Rd, rd N, **N...gas:** BP, Shell, **food:** Pizza Palace

26b Graham Rd, N Hanley, **N...gas:** Citgo/7-11, **food:** Denny's, Fazoli's, Hardee's, LJ Silver, Rosemari's Rest., **lodging:** Hampton Inn, Red Roof Inn, **other:** HOSPITAL, Mitsubishi, **S...food:** McDonald's, **lodging:** Day's Inn, **other:** $General, Hancock Fabrics

a I-170 S, no facilities

25b a US 67, Lindbergh Blvd, **N...gas:** Shell, Texaco, **food:** Arby's, Burger King, Hardee's, Imo's Pizza, Jack-in-the-Box, McDonald's, Papa John's, Rally's, Ruiz' Mexican, Taco Bell, Village Inn Rest., **lodging:** Baymont Inn, Fairfield Inn, InTown Suites, **other:** AutoZone, Cadillac, Ford, Goodyear, NAPA, Nissan, Schnuck's Foods, Toyota, Walgreen, **S...gas:** Citgo/7-11, Shell, Econolodge, Villa Motel, **other:** VW/Volvo

23 McDonnell Blvd, **E...food:** Bicycle Club Rest., Denny's, **lodging:** La Quinta, **W...gas:** BP, Phillips 66/diesel, QT, **food:** Arby's, Jack-in-the-Box, McDonald's, Steak'n Shake, **other:** Pontiac/GMC

22 MO 370 W, to MO Bottom Rd, no facilities

20c MO 180, St Charles Rock Rd, **E...gas:** BP, Shell, **food:** Casa Gallardo's, Ground Round, Hardee's, McDonald's, Fazoli's, LJ Silver, Old Country Buffet, Ponderosa, Red Lobster, Shoney's, Steak'n Shake, Taco Bell, Tony Bono's Rest., **lodging:** Knight's Inn, **other:** HOSPITAL, Best Buy, Circuit City, K-Mart, Office Depot, Target, Walgreen/24hr, **W...gas:** BP/24hr, Citgo, Mobil, **food:** Bob Evans, Denny's, Olive Garden, Ryan's, Waffle House, **lodging:** Motel 6, Ramada Inn, Red Roof Inn, Super 8, **other:** Ford

20b a I-70, E to St Louis, W to Kansas City

St Louis

17 Dorsett Rd, **E...gas:** BP, QT, **lodging:** Best Western, Drury Inn, Hampton Inn, **W...gas:** Mobil, Phillips 66, Shell, **food:** Arby's, Denny's, Fuddrucker's, McDonald's, Steak'n Shake, Subway, **lodging:** Baymont Inn

16b a Page Ave, rd D, MO 364 W, **E...gas:** BP, CFM, Citgo/7-11, QT, Sinclair, **food:** Blimpie, Copperfield's Rest., Hardee's, Hooters, Malone's Grill, McDonald's, Stazio's Café, **lodging:** Comfort Inn, Courtyard, Holiday Inn, Red Roof Inn, Residence Inn, Sheraton

14 MO 340, Olive Blvd, **E...gas:** BP, Mobil, **food:** Denny's, McDonald's, Lion's Choice Rest., **lodging:** Drury Inn, **other:** HOSPITAL, Chevrolet, **W...food:** Bristol's Café, Culpepper's Café, TGIFriday, **lodging:** Courtyard

13 rd AB, Ladue Rd, no facilities

12b a I-64, US 40, US 61, E to St Louis, W to Wentzville, **E...**HOSPITAL

9 MO 100, Manchester Rd, **E...gas:** BP, **food:** Café America, Houlihan's Rest, IHOP, Lion's Choice Rest., McDonald's, Famous Barr, Galyan's, Lord&Taylor, Nordstrom's, **other:** mall, **W...gas:** Shell, **food:** Applebee's, Casa Gallardo's Mexican, Olive Garden

8 Dougherty Ferry Rd, **S...gas:** Citgo/7-11, Mobil, **food:** McDonald's, **other:** HOSPITAL

7 Big Ben Rd, **N...**HOSPITAL

5b a I-44, US 50, MO 366, E to St Louis, W to Tulsa

3 MO 30, Gravois Rd, **N...gas:** BP, Phillips 66, **food:** Bandana BBQ, Bob Evans, Rich&Charlie's Rest., TGIFriday, **lodging:** Best Western, Comfort Inn, Day's Inn, **S...**Munzert Steaks

2 MO 21, Tesson Ferry Rd, **N...gas:** Phillips 66, **food:** Calico's Rest., Olive Garden, Red Lobster, White Castle, **lodging:** Holiday Inn, **S...gas:** BP, CFM, Shell, **food:** Jack-in-the-Box, Wendy's, Dierberg's Foods

1b a I-55 N to St Louis, S to Memphis

Interstate 435(Kansas City)

Exit # Services

83 I-35, N to KS City, S to Wichita

82 Quivira Rd, Overland Park, **N...food:** Burger King, Old Chicago Pizza, Ponderosa, Taco Bell, **other:** HOSPITAL, **S...food:** McDonald's, Subway, Wendy's, **lodging:** Extended Stay America

81 US 69 S, to Ft Scott, no facilities

79 US 169, Metcalf Rd, **N...gas:** BP, Shell, **food:** Denny's, Dick Clark's Grill, Hooters, Tippin's Café, **lodging:** Clubhouse Inn, Embassy Suites, Hampton Inn, Red Roof Inn, Wyndham Garden, **other:** HOSPITAL, Chrysler/Dodge, **S...food:** McDonald's, **lodging:** Courtyard, Drury Inn, Marriott, PearTree Inn

77b a Nall Ave, Roe Ave, **N...gas:** Amoco, Shell, **food:** DQ, On-the-Border, Panera Bread, Winstead's Grill, **lodging:** Fairfield Inn, **S...gas:** Amoco, **food:** Cactus Grill, McDonald's, Wendy's, **lodging:** AmeriSuites, Courtyard, Hilton Garden, Holiday Inn, Homestead Suites, Sheraton

Interstate 435

Kansas City

75b State Line Rd, **N...gas:** Amoco, Conoco, **food:** Applebee's, McDonald's, Waid's Rest., Wendy's, **other:** Buick/Cadillac, Ford, Goodyear, Infiniti, Lexus, Volvo, **S...**HOSPITAL, city park

a Wornall Rd, **N...gas:** QT, Shell, **other:** Chevrolet, Toyota, VW

74 Holmes Rd, **S...gas:** Amoco, Phillips 66, **food:** Burger King, Guacamole Grill, **lodging:** Courtyard, Extended Stay America

73 103rd St(from sb)

71b a I-470, US 71 S, US 50 E, no facilities

70 Bannister Rd, **E...gas:** Conoco, QT, **food:** Bennigan's, China Buffet, Luby's, McDonald's, Red Lobster, **other:** K-Mart, Sears/auto, mall, **W...food:** KFC/Taco Bell, LJ Silver/A&W, Old Country Buffet, Pizza Hut, **other:** Firestone/auto, Home Depot

69 87th St, Denny's, **E...food:** Darryl's, Denny's, IHOP, Luby's, McDonald's, Tippin's Café, **lodging:** Day's Inn, Motel 6, **other:** Best Buy, NTB, Suzuki, Wal-Mart SuperCtr/24hr, mall, **W...gas:** Amoco/diesel, **lodging:** Baymont Inn

67 Gregory Blvd, **W...**Nature Ctr, IMAX Theatre, zoo

66a 63rd St, **E...gas:** Shell, **food:** Applebee's, Waid's Rest., Wendy's

b MO 350 E, **W...food:** LC's BBQ, **lodging:** Relax Inn

65 Eastwood Tfwy, **W...gas:** Conoco, **food:** KFC, LC's BBQ, McDonald's, Peachtree Buffet, Pizza Hut, **lodging:** Relax Inn

63c Raytown Rd, Stadium Dr, **E...lodging:** Day's Inn, Sports Stadium Motel, Villager Lodge, **other:** Sports Complex

63b a I-70, W to KC, E to St Louis

61 MO 78, no facilities

60 MO 12 E, Truman Rd, 12th St, **E...gas:** Amoco/repair, Shamrock, **W...gas:** QT

59 US 24, Independence Ave, **E...gas:** QT, **food:** Hardee's, **lodging:** Queen City Motel(3mi), **other:** to Truman Library

57 Front St, E...gas: Flying J/Conoco/diesel/rest./24hr/@, food: Burger King, Taco Bell, other: Blue Beacon, W...gas: Phillips 66, QT, food: Denny's, KFC, McDonald's, Pizza Hut, Subway, Waffle House, Wendy's, lodging: Hampton Inn, Park Place Hotel, Smugglers Inn

56mm Missouri River

55b a MO 210, **E...gas:** Phillips 66/diesel, Shell, **lodging:** Red Roof Inn, other: Riverboat Casino, Ford/Volvo/GMC/Mercedes Trucks, **W...food:** Arby's, Denny's, McDonald's, **lodging:** Baymont Inn(2mi), Country Hearth Inn, Day's Inn

54 48th St, Parvin Rd, **E...**funpark, **W...gas:** QT, **food:** Alamo Mexican, Ponderosa, Waffle House, Wendy's, **lodging:** Best Western, Comfort Inn, Country Inn Suites, Crossland Suites, Holiday Inn, Super 8

Kansas City

52a US 69, **E...food:** A&W, KFC, **W...gas:** Amoco/repair, Coastal, Shell, **food:** McDonald's, Pizza Hut, Taco Bell, **other:** $General, Osco Drug, Sav-A-Lot Foods

52b I-35, S to KC

51 Shoal Creek Dr, no facilities

49b a MO 152 E, to I-35 N, Liberty, **E...food:** Applebee's, Bob Evans, Cracker Barrel, Golden Corral, Longhorn Steaks, Steak'n Shake, lodging: Best Western, Comfort Inn, Fairfield Inn, Hampton Inn, Holiday Inn Express, Super 8, Villager Inn

47 NE 96th St, no facilities

46 NE 108th St, no facilities

45 MO 291, NE Cookingham Ave, no facilities

42 N Woodland Ave, no facilities

41b a US 169, Smithville, **N...food:** Burger King, McDonald's, Sonic, lodging: Super 8

40 NW Cookingham, no facilities

37 NW Skyview Ave, rd C, **N...gas:** Total, **S...**golf

36 to I-29 S, to KCI Airport, **N...gas:** Total, **S...gas:** Amoco, lodging: Best Western, Comfort Suites, Fairfield Inn, Hampton Inn, Hilton, Holiday Inn Express, Microtel, Radisson, Wyndham Garden

31mm Prairie Creek

29 rd D, NW 120th St, no facilities

24 MO 152, rd N, NW Berry Rd, no facilities

22 MO 45, Weston, Parkville, no facilities

20mm Missouri/Kansas state line, Missouri River

18 KS 5 N, Wolcott Dr, **E...**to Wyandotte Co Lake Park

15b a Leavenworth Rd, **E...**Woodlands Racetrack

14b a Parallel Pkwy, **E...gas:** QT, **other:** HOSPITAL

13b a US 24, US 40, State Ave, **E...food:** Frontier Steaks, **W...other:** Cabela's Sporting Goods, KS Race Track

12b a I-70, KS Tpk, to Topeka, St Louis

11 Kansas Ave, no facilities

9 KS 32, KS City, Bonner Springs, **W...gas:** Phillips 66/diesel

8b Woodend Rd, **E...**Peterbilt

8.8mm Kansas River

8a Holliday Dr, to Lake Quivira, no facilities

6c Johnson Dr, no facilities

6b a Shawnee Mission Pkwy, **E...gas:** Amoco/diesel, **food:** Sonic, **other:** museum

5 Midland Dr, Shawnee Mission Park, **E...gas:** Conoco, Shell/Blimpie, **food:** Arizona's Grille, Barley's Brewhaus, Jose Pepper's Grill, Paula&Bill's Ristorante, Wendy's, **lodging:** Hampton Inn

3 87th Ave, **E...gas:** Amoco, Phillips 66, Shell, **food:** McDonald's, other: NY Burrito, Panera Bread, Sonic, Zarda BBQ, K-Mart, museum

2 95th St, no facilities

1b KS 10, to Lawrence

a Lackman Rd, **N...gas:** QT, Shell

0mm I-435 begins/ends on I-35.

MONTANA

Interstate 15

Exit #	Services
398mm	Montana/US/Canada Border
397	Sweetgrass, **W...rest area both lanes, full(handicapped)facilities, picnic tables, litter barrels, petwalk, phone, gas:** Sinclair, **lodging:** Glocca Morra Motel/café, **other:** Duty Free
394	ranch access, no facilities
389	MT 552, Sunburst, **W...**gas/diesel, **food:** Kelly's Kitchen, **other:** Sunburst RV Park
385	Swayze Rd, no facilities
379	MT 215, MT 343, Oilmont, to Kevin, **W...food:** Four Corners Café
373	Potter Rd, no facilities
369	Bronken Rd, no facilities
366.5mm	weigh sta sb
364	Shelby, **E...**Lewis&Clark RV Park, **W...**airport
363	US 2, Shelby, to Cut Bank, **E...gas:** Exxon/Subway/diesel/24hr, Sinclair, **food:** Dash Drive-In, Dixie Inn Steaks, Pizza Hut, **lodging:** Comfort Inn, Crossroads Inn, Glacier Motel, O'Haire Motel, **1 mi E...other:** HOSPITAL, Albertson's, CarQuest, Ford/Mercury, GMC, Goodyear/auto, **W...food:** McDonald's, **other:** Pamida/drugs, to Glacier NP
361mm	parking area nb
358	Marias Valley Rd, to Golf Course Rd, **E...**camping
357mm	Marias River
352	Bullhead Rd, no facilities
348	rd 44, to Valier, **W...**Lake Frances RA(15mi)
345	MT 366, Ledger Rd, **E...**to Tiber Dam(42mi)
339	Conrad, **W...gas:** Cenex/diesel, Exxon/diesel, **food:** A&W/KFC, House of Pizza, Keg Rest., Main Drive-In, **lodging:** Conrad Motel, Northgate Motel, Super 8, **other:** HOSPITAL, Dan's Tires, IGA Foods, Olson's Drug, Parts+, Radio Shack, Chevrolet/Pontiac/Buick, Ford/Mercury, Pondera RV Park, RV Ctr/LP
335	Midway Rd, Conrad, **4 mi W...**HOSPITAL, gas, food, phone, lodging, RV camping
328	MT 365, Brady, **1 mi W...gas:** Mtn View Co-op/diesel, **other:** USPO, phone
321	Collins Rd, no facilities
319mm	**Teton River, rest area both lanes, full(handicapped)facilities, phones, picnic tables, litter barrels, petwalk**
313	MT 221, MT 379, Dutton, **W...gas:** Cenex/diesel, **food:** Dutton Café, **other:** USPO
302	MT 431, Power, no facilities
297	Gordon, no facilities
290	US 89 N, rd 200 W, to Choteau, **W...gas:** Exxon, Sinclair/diesel/LP/RV dump, **other:** USPO
288mm	parking area both lanes
286	Manchester, **W...**livestock auction, same as 290(2mi)
282	US 87 N(from sb), weigh sta, **E...gas:** Yellowstone Trkstp/diesel, **1-3 mi E...gas:** Exxon/A&W/Blimpie, **food:** McDonald's, **lodging:** Day's Inn, **other:** Wal-Mart
280	US 87 N, Central Ave W, Great Falls, **E...gas:** Conoco, Flying J/diesel/LP/24hr, **food:** Arby's, Double Barrel Diner, DQ, Ford's Drive-In, KFC, Taco John's, **lodging:** Adelweiss Motel, Alberta Inn, Day's Inn, Starlit Motel, **other:** NAPA, U-Haul/LP, Whalen Tire, to Giant Sprgs SP
280mm	Sun River
278	US 89 S, rd 200 E, 10th Ave, Great Falls, **E...gas:** Exxon/A&W, Sinclair/diesel, **food:** China Town, Classic 50's Diner, DQ, Elmer's Rest., Golden Corral, McDonald's, Quizno's, **lodging:** Airway Motel, Best Western, Budget Inn, Hampton Inn, Holiday Inn Express, Kanga Inn, **other:** Barnes&Noble, Dick's RV Park, Home Depot, OfficeMax, Smith's Food, **1-3 mi E...gas:** Cenex/diesel, Conoco, Holiday/diesel, Sinclair/diesel, **food:** Applebee's, Arby's, Burger King, Cattin's Rest., Country Kitchen, Del Taco, DQ, 4B's Rest., Fuddrucker's, Godfather's, Jaker's Rib/fish, JB's Rest., KFC, Little Caesar's, McDonald's, Ming's Chinese, Papa John's, Papa Murphy's, Pizza Hut, PrimeCut Rest., Sting Rest., Subway, Taco Bell, Taco John's, Wendy's, **lodging:** Comfort Inn, Fairfield Inn, Plaza Inn, Super 8, **other:** HOSPITAL, Albertson's, Checker Parts, Chevrolet/Cadillac/Toyota, County Mkt Food/24hr, Dodge/Hyundai/Suzuki/VW, Firestone/auto, Ford, Hancock Fabrics, Hastings Books, Herberger's, Honda, JC Penney, Jo-Ann Crafts, K-Mart, KOA(6mi), Lincoln/Mercury, McCollum RVs, NAPA, Osco Drug, Nissan, Plymouth/Jeep, Sears/auto, Target, TireRama, USPO, transmissions, to Malmstrom AFB
277	Airport Rd, **E...gas:** Conoco/diesel/café/casino/24hr, **lodging:** Crystal Inn
275mm	weigh sta nb
270	MT 330, Ulm, **E...gas:** Exxon/diesel/LP, **other:** USPO, **W...food:** Griffin's Rest., to Ulm SP
256	rd 68, Cascade, **1/2 mi E...gas:** Sinclair, **food:** Pizza Pro, **lodging:** Badger Motel/café, **other:** NAPA, Tom's Foods, USPO
254	rd 68, Cascade, **1/2 mi E...**same as 256
250	local access, no facilities
247	Hardy Creek, **W...**food, phone, RV camping
246.5mm	Missouri River
245mm	scenic overlook sb
244	Canyon Access, **2 mi W...**camping, food, RV camping, rec area

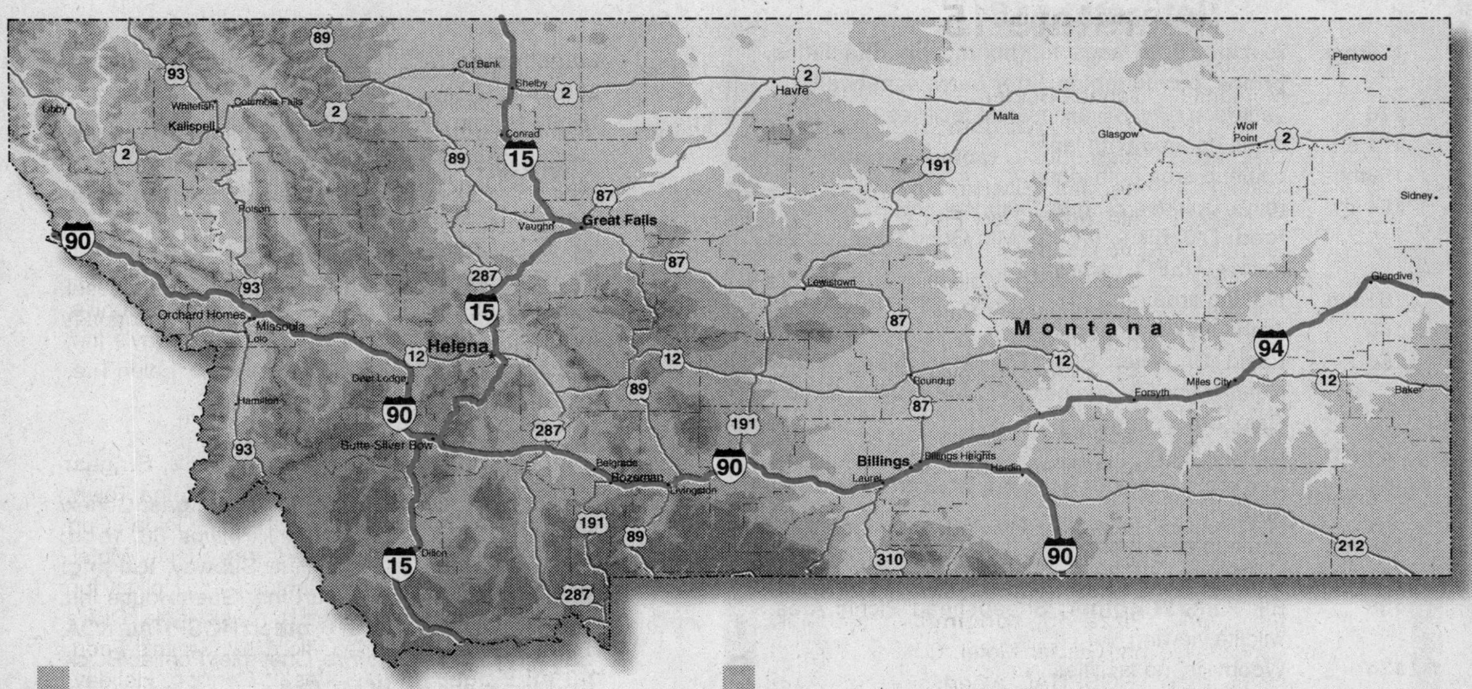

Interstate 15

N ↕ S

240 Dearborn, **E...**RV park, **W...food:** Dearborn Café, **other:** auto repair

239mm **rest area both lanes, full(handicapped)facilities, phone, picnic tables, litter barrels, petwalk**

238mm Stickney Creek

236mm Missouri River

234 Craig, **E...food:** Trout Shop Café/lodge, **other:** rec area, boating, camping

228 US 287 N, to Augusta, no facilities

226 MT 434, Wolf Creek, **E...gas:** Exxon/diesel, **food:** Oasis Café, **other:** Lewis&Clark Canoes, MT Outfitters/flyshop/RV/motel, camping, **W...food:** Frenchman&Me Café, **other:** USPO

222mm parking area both lanes

219 Spring Creek, Recreation Rd(from nb), boating, camping

218mm Little Prickly Pear Creek

216 Sieben, no facilities

209 **E...**to Gates of the Mtns RA, no facilities

205mm turnout sb

202mm weigh sta sb

200 MT 279, MT 453, Lincoln Rd, **W...gas:** Sinclair/Bob's Mkt/diesel, **food:** GrubStake Rest., **other:** Helena Campground(4mi), Lincoln Rd RV Park, to ski area

193 Cedar St, Helena, **E...**Helena RV Park(5mi), Home Depot, **W...gas:** Cenex/diesel, Conoco/diesel, Exxon/diesel, Sinclair/24hr, **food:** Applebee's, Arby's, Dragon Wall Chinese, Godfather's, Jade Garden Chinese, McDonald's, Perkins, Pizza Hut, Subway, Taco Bell, Taco John's, **lodging:** Blackstone Inn/casino, Wingate Inn, **other:** Albertson's/24hr, CarQuest, Checker Parts, Chevrolet, County Mkt Foods, Hastings Books, Kia, K-Mart, NAPA, Shop-KO, Target, TireORama, USPO, radiator/transmissions

Helena

192b a US 12, US 287, Helena, Townsend, **E...gas:** Conoco/diesel/24hr, **food:** Burger King, Golden Corral, Subway, **lodging:** Hampton Inn, **other:** D&D RV Ctr, Schwab Tire, Staples, Wal-Mart SuperCtr/24hr, st patrol, **other:** Buick/Cadillac/GMC, Chrysler/Jeep/Nissan, Ford/Lincoln/Mercury, Honda, Plymouth, Toyota, **W... gas:** Exxon/diesel, Sinclair/24hr, **food:** A&W/KFC, DQ, Frontier Pies, JB's, L&D Chinese, McDonald's, Overland Express Rest., Papa John's, Wendy's, **lodging:** Comfort Inn, Country Inn Suites, Day's Inn, Fairfield Inn, Holiday Inn Express, Jorgenson's Inn, Motel 6, Red Lion Inn, Shilo Inn, Super 8, **other:** HOSPITAL, Albertson's/gas, Country Harvest Foods, Dillard's, Goodyear/auto, Osco Drug, Safeway/gas

187 MT 518, Montana City, **E...other:** Papa Ray's Casino/Pizza, to NF, **W...gas:** Conoco/Mtn City Grill/diesel/casino/24hr, Elkhorn Mtn Inn, Parts+, transmissions

182 Clancy, **E...**RV camping, **W...gas:** Gen Store, **food:** Legal Tender Rest., to NF

MONTANA

Interstate 15

N ↕ S

178mm **rest area both lanes, full(handicapped)facilities, phone, picnic tables, litter barrels, petwalk**
176 Jefferson City, NF access, no facilities
174.5mm chain up area both lanes
168mm chainup area both lanes
164 rd 69, Boulder, **E...gas:** Exxon/diesel/casino/24hr, **food:** DQ, Elkhorn Café, Mtn Good Rest., **other:** Parts+, USPO, camping
161mm parking area nb
160 High Ore Rd, no facilities
156 Basin, **E...other:** Basin Cr Pottery, Merry Widow Health Mine/RV camping, **W...food:** Silver Saddle Café, **other:** camping
154mm Boulder River
151 Bernice, to Boulder River Rd, **W...**camping, picnic area
148mm chainup area both lanes
143.5mm chainup area both lanes
138 Elk Park, **W...other:** Sheepshead Picnic Area, wildlife viewing
134 Woodville, no facilities
133mm continental divide, elev 6368
130.5mm scenic overlook sb
129 I-90 E, to Billings, no facilities
I-15 S and I-90 W run together 8 mi

Butte

127 Harrison Ave, Butte, **N...gas:** Cenex/diesel, Conoco, **food:** Arctic Circle, DQ, Denny's, Derby Steaks, L&D Chinese, Papa John's, Taco John's, **lodging:** Day's Inn, Holiday Inn Express, Red Lion Inn, **other:** Checker Parts, Hastings Books, NAPA, Nissan/Toyota, Safeway, **S...gas:** Conoco/diesel, Exxon/diesel/24hr, Sinclair, **food:** A&W, Arby's, Burger King, 4B's Rest., Godfather's, KFC, McDonald's, Perkins, Pizza Hut, Ray's Rest., Silver Bow Pizza, Subway, Taco Bell, Wendy's, **lodging:** Comfort Inn, Hampton Inn, Ramada Inn, Super 8, **other:** Checker Parts, Chevrolet/Subaru, Chrysler/Plymouth/Dodge/Jeep, Ford/Honda, GMC/Buick/Cadillac/Pontiac, Herberger's, Honda, JC Penney, Jo-Ann Crafts, Lincoln/Mercury, Smith Foods, Staples, Wal-Mart SuperCtr/24hr, Whalen Tire
126 Montana St, Butte, **N...gas:** Cenex/diesel, **lodging:** Eddy's Motel, **other:** HOSPITAL, KOA, Safeway, Schwab Tire, **S...gas:** Conoco, Exxon/diesel
124 I-115(from eb), to Butte, City Ctr
122 Rocker, **N...gas:** Flying J/Arby's/diesel/LP/casino/24hr, **lodging:** Rocker Inn Motel, **other:** weigh sta both lanes, RV camping, **S...gas:** Conoco/4B's Rest./diesel/casino/24hr, **lodging:** Motel 6
I-15 N and I-90 E run together 8 mi
121 I-90 W, to Missoula, no facilities
119 Silver Bow, Port of MT Transportation Hub
116 Buxton, no facilities
112mm Continental Divide, elevation 5879
111 Feely, no facilities
109mm **rest area both lanes, full(handicapped)facilities, phone, picnic tables, litter barrels, petwalk**
102 rd 43, Divide, to Wisdom, **W...gas:** Sinclair, **other:** to Big Hole Nat Bfd
99 Moose Creek Rd, no facilities
93 Melrose, **W...food:** Melrose Café/grill/gas/diesel, Hitchin Post Rest., **other:** Sportsman Motel/RV Park, USPO
85.5mm Big Hole River
85 Glen, no facilities
74 Apex, Birch Creek, no facilities
64mm Beaverhead River

Dillon

63 Lp 15, rd 41, Dillon, Twin Bridges, **E...gas:** Cenex/diesel/LP, Exxon/diesel/24hr, Phillips 66, **food:** KFC, McDonald's, Pizza Hut, Subway, **lodging:** Best Western/rest., Comfort Inn, GuestHouse Inn, Sundowner Motel, Super 8, **other:** HOSPITAL, KOA, Safeway/gas, Schwab Tire, Chevrolet/Pontiac/Buick/Cadillac, museum, W MT Coll
62 Lp 15, Dillon, **E...gas:** Exxon, Sinclair, **food:** Arctic Circle, DQ, Sparky's Rest., **lodging:** Creston Motel, Crosswinds Motel/rest., Flyshop Inn, **other:** HOSPITAL, GS Camping, to WMT
60mm Beaverhead River
59 MT 278, to Jackson, **W...other:** Bannack Ghost Town SP, Countryside RV Park
56 Barretts, **E...**RV camping, **W...gas:** Big Sky Trkstp/diesel/24hr
52 Grasshopper Creek, no facilities
51 Dalys(from sb, no return), no facilities
50mm Beaverhead River
46mm Beaverhead River
45mm Beaverhead River
44 MT 324, **E...other:** Armstead RV Park, Beaverhead Flyshop, **W...other:** Clark Cyn Res, rec area, RV camping
38.5mm Red Rock River
37 Red Rock, no facilities
34mm parking area both lanes, litter barrels
29 Kidd, no facilities
23 Dell, **E...lodging:** Red Rock Inn/rest., **other:** auto repair
16.5mm weigh sta both lanes
15 Lima, **E...gas:** Exxon/diesel, **food:** Jan's Café, **lodging:** Lee's Motel/RV Park, **other:** Big Sky Service/tires, I&J Mkt, USPO, ambulance, auto/tire repair
9 Snowline, no facilities
0 Monida, **E...**phone, to Red Rock Lakes
0mm Monida Pass, elevation 6870, Montana/Idaho state line

Interstate 90

E ↕ W

Exit #	Services
554.5mm	Montana/Wyoming state line
549	Aberdeen, no facilities
544	Wyola, **2 mi S...**gas, food
530	MT 463, Lodge Grass, **1 mi S...gas:** Cenex/diesel/LP, lodging, phone
517.5mm	Little Bighorn River
514	Garryowen, **N...gas:** Conoco, **other:** Custer Bfd Museum
511.5mm	Little Bighorn River
510	US 212 E, **N...gas:** Exxon/diesel/café/gifts, **food:** Crows Nest Café, **other:** HOSPITAL, to Little Bighorn Bfd, **S...other:** Little Bighorn Camping/motel
509.5mm	weigh sta both lanes
509.3mm	Little Bighorn River
509	Crow Agency, **N...gas:** Conoco/24hr, **S...**to Bighorn Canyon NRA
503	Dunmore, no facilities
498mm	Bighorn River
497	MT 384, 3rd St, Hardin, **S...**HOSPITAL, visitors ctr, **2 mi S...lodging:** Lariat Motel, Western Motel, **other:** Casino Rest./lounge
495	MT 47, City Ctr, Hardin, **N...gas:** Shell/diesel, **food:** Purple Cow Rest., **other:** KOA, **S...gas:** Cenex/diesel, Conoco/Subway/diesel/LP/24hr, Exxon/diesel, Sinclair/Blimpie/diesel, **food:** DQ, KFC, McDonald's, Pizza Hut/Taco Bell, Taco John's, **lodging:** American Inn, Lariat Motel, Super 8, Western Motel, **other:** HOSPITAL, RV camping
484	Toluca, no facilities
478	Fly Creek Rd, no facilities
477mm	**rest area both lanes, full(handicapped)facilities, phone, picnic tables, litter barrels, petwalk**
469	Arrow Creek Rd, no facilities
462	Pryor Creek Rd, no facilities
456	I-94 E, to Bismarck, ND, no facilities
455	Johnson Lane, **S...gas:** Exxon/A&W/Blimpie/diesel/24hr, Flying J/Conoco/diesel/LP/rest./24hr/@, **food:** Burger King, Jackpot Diner, Subway, **lodging:** Holiday Inn Express, **other:** RV Ctr(1mi)
452	US 87 N, City Ctr, Billings, **N...gas:** Conoco/Arby's/diesel/LP, Exxon/diesel, **lodging:** Best Western, Chevrolet, transmissions, **2-4 mi N on US 87...gas:** Cenex, Conoco, Holiday/diesel, **food:** Applebee's, Arby's, Burger King, DQ, Elmer's Pancakes, Godfather's, Guadalajara Mexican, Little Caesar's, McDonald's, Papa John's, Papa Murphy's, Peking Express, Pizza Hut, Subway, Taco Bell, Taco John's, Wendy's, **lodging:** Foothills Inn, Metra Inn, **other:** MEDICAL CARE, Albertson's, CarQuest, Champion Parts, Checkers Parts, County Mkt Foods, K-Mart, Radio Shack, Wal-Mart SuperCtr/24hr, **S...gas:** Cenex/diesel
451.5mm	Yellowstone River
450	MT 3, 27th St, Billings, **N...gas:** Conoco/diesel/24hr, Exxon/Subway, Sinclair/repair, **food:** Denny's, Hardee's, Perkins/24hr(1mi), Pizza Hut, **lodging:** Howard Johnson, Rimview Motel(2mi), Sheraton(1mi), War Bonnet Inn/rest., **other:** HOSPITAL, CarQuest, USPO, **S...**KOA, Yellowstone River Camping
447	S Billings Blvd, **N...gas:** Conoco/Subway/diesel/24hr, **food:** Burger King, 4B's Rest., McDonald's, **lodging:** Day's Inn, Extended Stay America, Hampton Inn, Sleep Inn, Super 8
446	King Ave, Billings, **N...gas:** Conoco, Holiday/diesel/LP/RV dump, **food:** Burger King, Country Harvest Buffet, Del Taco, Denny's, Fuddrucker's, Olive Garden, Outback Steaks, Perkins, Pizza Hut, Red Lobster, Taco John's, Texas Roadhouse, **lodging:** C'Mon Inn, Comfort Inn, Day's Inn, Fairfield Inn, Marriott, Quality Inn, Super 8, **other:** Best Buy, Chrysler/Plymouth/Kia, Costco/gas, Dodge, Ford, Kia, NAPA, Nissan, RV Repair, ShopKO, Subaru/Hyundai, USPO, **N on King Ave...gas:** Exxon/Subway, Conoco, Sinclair, **food:** Applebee's, Cactus Creek Steaks, Famous Dave's, IHOP, McDonald's, Quizno's, Subway, Taco Bell, Wendy's, **other:** Albertson's, Barnes&Noble, Hastings Books, Home Depot, Lowe's Whse, Office Depot, OfficeMax, Old Navy, Target, Wal-Mart SuperCtr/24hr, mall, **S...gas:** Conoco/24hr, **food:** Cracker Barrel, Emporium Rest., **lodging:** Best Western, Billings Hotel, Fireside Inn, Holiday Inn, Kelly Inn, Motel 6, Ramada Ltd, Red Roof Inn
443	Zoo Dr, to Shiloh Rd, **N...**Pierce RV Ctr, zoo, **S...**Cenex/diesel
439mm	weigh sta both lanes
437	E Laurel, **S...gas:** Sinclair/diesel/rest./casino/motel/24hr, **other:** EZ Livin' RV Ctr
434	US 212, US 310, Laurel, to Red Lodge, **N...gas:** Cenex/diesel, Conoco/diesel, Exxon/diesel/24hr, **food:** Burger King, Hardee's, Pizza Hut, Subway, Taco John's, **lodging:** Howard Johnson, Super 8, **other:** IGA Foods, Chevrolet, Ford, **S...**to Yellowstone NP
433	Lp 90(from eb), no facilities
426	Park City, **S...gas:** Cenex/diesel/café/24hr, **food:** CJ's Motel, **other:** auto/tire repair
419mm	**rest area both lanes, full(handicapped)facilities, phone, picnic tables, litter barrels, petwalk**

MONTANA

Interstate 90

E ↕ W

Exit	Services
408	rd 78, Columbus, **N...**Mtn Range RV Park, **S...gas:** Conoco/Big Sky Motel, Exxon/diesel/24hr, **food:** Apple Village Café/gifts, McDonald's, **lodging:** Super 8, **other:** HOSPITAL, IGA Foods, casino, museum, to Yellowstone
400	Springtime Rd, no facilities
398mm	Yellowstone River
396	ranch access, no facilities
392	Reed Point, **N...gas:** Sinclair/diesel, **lodging:** Hotel Montana/rest., **other:** RV camping
384	Bridger Creek Rd, no facilities
381mm	**rest area both lanes, full(handicapped)facilities, phone, picnic tables, litter barrels, petwalk**
377	Greycliff, **S...other:** Prairie Dog Town SP, KOA
370	US 191, Big Timber, **1 mi N...gas:** Conoco/diesel, Exxon, Sinclair/diesel, **lodging:** Grand Hotel, Lazy J Motel, **other:** Spring Camp RV Ranch(4mi), USPO
369mm	Boulder River
367	US 191 N, Big Timber, **N...gas:** Exxon/diesel, Conoco/diesel, **food:** Crazy Jane's Eatery/casino, **lodging:** Super 8, **other:** CarQuest, Chevrolet, hist site, visitor ctr
362	De Hart, no facilities
354	MT 563, Springdale, no facilities
352	ranch access, no facilities
350	East End access, no facilities
343	Mission Creek Rd, no facilities
340	US 89 N, to White Sulphur Sprgs, **S...**airport
337	Lp 90, to Livingston, **2 mi N...gas:** Exxon, **lodging:** motels
333mm	Yellowstone River
333	US 89 S, Livingston, **N...food:** Pizza Hut, Taco John's, **lodging:** Best Western, Budget Host, Econolodge, Livingston Inn, Travelodge, **other:** HOSPITAL, Chevrolet, County Mkt Food/24hr, Ford/Lincoln/Mercury, Oasis RV Park, Pamida, Radio Shack, Western Drug, **S...gas:** Cenex/diesel, Conoco/diesel, Exxon/diesel, **food:** Hardee's, McDonald's, Subway, **lodging:** Comfort Inn, Super 8, **other:** Albertson's, KOA(10mi), Osen's RV Park, to Yellowstone
330	Lp 90, Livingston, **1 mi N...gas:** Yellowstone Trkstp/diesel/24hr/rest.
326.5mm	chainup area both lanes
324	ranch access, no facilities
323mm	chainup area wb
322mm	Bridger Mountain Range
321mm	turnouts/hist marker both lanes
319	Jackson Creek Rd, no facilities
319mm	chainup area both lanes
316	Trail Creek Rd, no facilities
313	Bear Canyon Rd, **S...other:** Bear Canyon Camping
309	US 191 S, Main St, Bozeman, **N...other:** Jeep/Subaru, Sunrise RV Park, **S...gas:** Exxon, Sinclair, **food:** Eastside Diner, MT AleWorks, **lodging:** Alpine Lodge, Best Western, Blue Sky Motel, Continental Motel, Ranch House Motel, Western Heritage Inn, **other:** HOSPITAL, Toyota/Mazda, RV service, Goodyear, to Yellowstone
306	US 191, N 7th, Bozeman, **N...gas:** Conoco, Sinclair, **N...food:** McDonald's, Panda Buffet, **lodging:** Best Value Inn, Fairfield Inn, Microtel, Ramada Ltd, Sleep Inn, Super 8, TLC Inn, **other:** RV supplies, ski area, **S...gas:** Conoco/Arby's/diesel, Exxon, Sinclair/diesel, **food:** Applebee's, DQ, Frontier Pies Rest., Hardee's, KFC, McDonald's, Papa John's, Subway, Taco Bell, Taco John's, Village Inn Pizza, Wendy's, **lodging:** Best Western, Bozeman/rest., Comfort Inn, Day's Inn, Hampton Inn, Holiday Inn, **other:** Big O Tire, CarQuest, County Mkt Foods, Firestone/auto, K-Mart, NAPA, Wal-Mart SuperCtr/24hr, Museum of the Rockies
305	MT412, N 19th Ave, **N...gas:** Exxon, **S...food:** A&W/KFC, Carino's Italian, Denny's, McKenzie River Pizza, **other:** Border's Books, Costco, Home Depot, Target, Smith's, UPS, USPO, **2-3 mi S...food:** Arby's, Bennigan's, Burger King, Perkins, Pizza Hut, Spanish Peaks Brewery/Italian Café, **lodging:** Best Western, Wingate Inn, **other:** Ford, museum
298	MT 291, MT 85, Belgrade, **N...gas:** Cenex/diesel, Conoco, Exxon/Subway/diesel, **food:** Burger King, DQ, McDonald's, Pizza Hut, **other:** Albertson's, IGA Foods, NAPA, **S...gas:** Flying J/Conoco/diesel/LP, **food:** Country Kitchen, **lodging:** Holiday Inn Express, La Quinta, Super 8, **other:** Harley-Davidson, InterWest Tire, truckwash, to Yellowstone NP
292.5mm	Gallatin River
288	MT 346, MT 288, Manhattan, **N...gas:** Conoco/diesel, **other:** RV camping
283	Logan, **S...other:** Madison Buffalo Jump SP(7mi)
279mm	Madison River
278	MT 205, rd 2, Three Forks, Trident, **N...**Missouri Headwaters SP, **1 mi S...lodging:** Broken Spur Motel, Sacajawea Inn, **other:** camping, phone
277.5mm	Jefferson River
274	US 287, to Helena, Ennis, **N...gas:** Conoco/diesel, Sinclair/diesel, **food:** Wheat MT Bakery/deli, **other:** to Canyon Ferry SP, Ft 3 Forks, **S...gas:** Exxon/Subway/diesel/24hr, **other:** Lewis&Clark Caverns SP, KOA(1mi), to Yellowstone NP
267	Milligan Canyon Rd, no facilities
261.5mm	chain removal area
257mm	Boulder River
256	MT 359, Cardwell, **S...gas:** Gas-Up/diesel, **other:** to Yellowstone NP, Lewis&Clark Caverns SP, RV camping

Livingston

Bozeman

Belgrade

MONTANA

Interstate 90

E ↕ W

249 rd 55, to rd 69, Whitehall, **S...gas:** Exxon/Subway/diesel/24hr, **food:** A&W/KFC, **lodging:** Chief Motel, Super 8, **other:** camping

241 Pipestone, **S...other:** Pipestone Camping(apr-oct), gas, phone

240.5mm chainup area both lanes

238.5mm runaway ramp eb

237.5mm pulloff eb

235mm parking area both lanes, litter barrels

233 Homestake, Continental Divide, elev 6393, no facilities

230mm chain removal area both lanes

Butte

228 MT 375, Continental Dr, no facilities

227 I-15 N, to Helena, Great Falls, no facilities

I-90 and I-15 run together 8 mi. **See Montana Interstate 15, exits 122-127.**

219 I-15 S, to Dillon, Idaho Falls, no facilities

216 Ramsay, no facilities

211 MT 441, Gregson, **3-5 mi S...**food, lodging, Fairmont RV Park

210.5mm parking area wb, Pintlar Scenic route info

208 MT 1, Opportunity, Anaconda, Pintlar Scenic Loop, Georgetown Lake RA, **3-5 mi S...other:** HOSPITAL, gas, food, lodging, RV camping/dump, ski area

201 Warm Springs, **S...other:** MT ST HOSPITAL, gas/diesel

197 MT 273, Galen, **S...other:** to MT ST HOSPITAL

195 Racetrack, no facilities

Deer Lodge

187 Lp 90, Deer Lodge(no wb return), **2 mi S...gas:** Exxon, MRC/diesel/repair, **food:** A&W, Pizza Hut, R-B Drive-In, **lodging:** Downtowner Motel, Scharf's Motel/rest., **other:** HOSPITAL, IGA Foods, Safeway/deli, Tow Ford Museum, Grant-Kohrs Ranch NHS, KOA(seasonal), Indian Creek RV Park(seasonal)(4mi)

184 Deer Lodge, **S...gas:** Cenex/diesel, Conoco/diesel/casino, **food:** 4B's Rest., McDonald's, **lodging:** Super 8, **other:** Indian Cr Camping, **1 mi S...gas:** Exxon/diesel/casino, **food:** Pizza Hut, **lodging:** Downtowner Motel, Western Big Sky Inn, **other:** Safeway, Schwab Tire

179 Beck Hill Rd, no facilities

175mm Little Blackfoot River

175 US 12 E(from wb), Garrison, **N...**gas/phone, hist site, RiverFront RV Park

174 US 12 E(from eb), same as 175

170 Phosphate, no facilities

168mm rest area both lanes, full(handicapped)facilities, phone, picnic tables, litter barrels, petwalk

166 Gold Creek, **S...other:** Camp Mak-A-Dream

162 Jens, no facilities

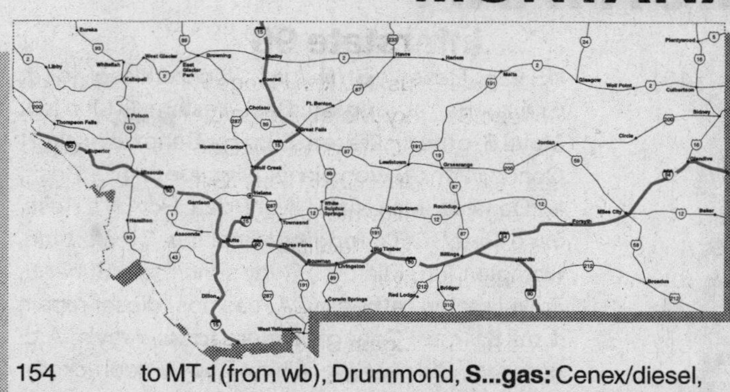

154 to MT 1(from wb), Drummond, **S...gas:** Cenex/diesel, Exxon/diesel, Sinclair/diesel/24hr, **food:** Wagon Wheel Café/Motel, **lodging:** Sky Motel, **other:** Pintlar Scenic Rt, Georgetown Lake RA, Goodtime RV Park(3mi)

153 MT 1(from eb), **N...other:** Garnet GhostTown, **S...food:** D-M Café, **lodging:** Drummond Motel, same as 154

150.5mm weigh sta both lanes

143mm rest area both lanes, full(handicapped)facilities, phone, picnic tables, litter barrels, petwalk

138 Bearmouth Area, **N...other:** Chalet Bearmouth Camp/rest., to gas, food, lodging

130 Beavertail Rd, **S...other:** to Beavertail Hill SP, rec area, camping(seasonal)

128mm parking area both lanes, no facilities

126 Rock Creek Rd, **S...lodging:** Rock Creek Lodge/gas/casino, **other:** Ekstrom Camping/rest., rec area

120 Clinton, **1 mi N...food:** Poor Henry's Café, **S...gas:** Conoco/diesel, **other:** USPO

113 Turah, no facilities

109.5mm Clark Fork

109mm Blackfoot River

109 MT 200 E, Bonner, **N...gas:** Exxon/Arby's/Subway/diesel/casino/LP/24hr/@, **food:** River City Grill, **other:** USPO, hist site, truck/auto repair

108.5mm Clark Fork

107 E Missoula, **N...gas:** Ole's Mkt/Diner/Conoco/diesel/24hr, Sinclair, **food:** Kolb's Café/casino, **lodging:** Aspen Motel, **other:** transmissions, **2 mi S...lodging:** Holiday Inn Express

Missoula

105 US 12 W, Missoula, **S...gas:** Cenex/diesel/24hr, Conoco/diesel/24hr, Pacific Pride/diesel, Sinclair, **food:** Burger King, Finnegan's, Little Caesar's, McDonald's, McKay's Rest./casino, Pasta House, Pizza Hut, PressBox Café, Quizno's, Taco Bell, **lodging:** Best Western, Campus Inn, Creekside Inn, DoubleTree, Family Inn, Holiday Inn, Holiday Inn Express, Ponderosa Motel, Thunderbird Motel, **other:** Albertson's, Champion Parts, Flyshop, Jim's Casino, U of MT, Vietnam Vet's Mem

104 Orange St, Missoula, **S...gas:** Conoco, Sinclair, **food:** KFC, Pagoda Chinese, Subway, **lodging:** Budget Motel, Red Lion Inn, Travelodge, **other:** HOSPITAL, Bakke Tire, to City Ctr

MONTANA

Interstate 90

E ↕ W Missoula

101 US 93 S, Reserve St, **N...gas:** Conoco/diesel, **food:** Cracker Barrel, **lodging:** Best Western, C'Mon Inn, Motel 6, **other:** ski area, **S...gas:** Cenex/diesel/LP, Conoco/24hr, Exxon/diesel/24hr, **food:** 4B's Rest., McDonald's, McKenzie River Pizza, Rowdy's Rest., Taco Time/TCBY, **lodging:** Best Inn, Comfort Inn, Hampton Inn, Microtel, Ruby's Inn/rest., Super 8, Travelers Inn, **other:** KOA, casinos, diesel repair, **1 mi S...gas:** Conoco, Exxon, **food:** Arby's, Arctic Circle, Burger King, China Bowl, Fuddrucker's, Old Country Buffet, Outback Steaks, Subway, Taco Bell, Wendy's, **other:** Albertson's, Barnes&Noble, Best Buy, Chevrolet, Costco/gas, Home Depot, Michael's, Old Navy, Staples, Target, Wal-Mart SuperCtr/24hr, mall

99 Airway Blvd, **S...other:** Chrysler/Plymouth/Dodge, Lincoln/Mercury, airport

96 US 93 N, MT 200W, Kalispell, **N...gas:** Conoco/diesel/rest./24hr, **lodging:** Day's Inn/rest., **other:** Jellystone RV Park, Peterbilt/Ford/Freightliner, to Flathead Lake & Glacier NP, **S...gas:** Sinclair/4B's/diesel/24hr, **lodging:** Redwood Lodge, **other:** RV repair

92.5mm inspection sta both lanes

89 Frenchtown, **S...gas:** Conoco/diesel/café/24hr, Sinclair/rest./laundry, **other:** MEDICAL CARE, USPO, to Frenchtown Pond SP

85 Huson, **S...gas:** Sinclair/café, **other:** phone

82 Nine Mile Rd, **N... other:** Hist Ranger Sta/info, food, phone

81.5mm Clark Fork

80mm Clark Fork

77 MT 507, Alberton, Petty Creek Rd, **S...**access to gas, food, lodging, phone

75 Alberton, **S...lodging:** MT Hotel, River Edge Motel/gas, **other:** MT Book Store, RV camp, casino

73mm parking area wb, litter barrels

72mm parking area eb, litter barrels

70 Cyr, no facilities

70mm Clark Fork

66 Fish Creek Rd, no facilities

66mm Clark Fork

61 Tarkio, no facilities

58.5mm Clark Fork

58mm rest area both lanes, full(handicapped)facilities, phone, picnic tables, litter barrels, petwalk, NF camping(seasonal)

55 Lozeau, Quartz, **N...food:** StageCoach Grill/gas/casino

53.5mm Clark Fork

49mm Clark Fork

47 MT 257, Superior, **N...gas:** Cenex/24hr, Conoco/diesel, Sinclair/Durango's Rest., **lodging:** Bel-vue Motel, Big Sky Motel, Budget Host, **other:** HOSPITAL, IGA Food, Mineral Drug, NAPA, USPO, **S...gas:** Exxon/diesel/casino/mechanic/24hr

45mm Clark Fork

43 Dry Creek Rd, **N...**NP camping(seasonal)

37 Sloway Area, no facilities

34mm Clark Fork

33 MT 135, St Regis, **N...gas:** Conoco/diesel/rest./gifts, Exxon/pizza, Sinclair, **food:** Frosty Drive-In, Jasper's Rest., OK Café/casino, **lodging:** Little River Motel, St Regis Motel/camping, Super 8, **other:** KOA, USPO

30 Two Mile Rd, **S...**fishing access

29mm fishing access, wb

26 Ward Creek Rd(from eb), no facilities

25 Drexel, no facilities

22 Camels Hump Rd, Henderson, **N...other:** camping(seasonal), antiques(1mi)

18 DeBorgia, **N...food:** Pinecrest Rest./casino, **lodging:** Hotel Albert, Riverside Inn/café(1mi), **other:** U-Haul, antiques, auto repair, same as 16

16 Haugan, **N...gas:** Exxon/diesel/24hr, **lodging:** 10,000 Silver $/motel/rest./casino

15mm weigh sta both lanes, exits left from both lanes

10 Saltese, **N...other:** Elk Glen's Store, **food:** MT Café, **lodging:** Mangold's Motel, **other:** USPO, antiques

10mm St Regis River

5 Taft Area, no facilities

4.5mm rest area both lanes, full(handicapped)picnic tables, litter barrels, petwalk, chainup/removal

0 Lookout Pass, **other:** Lookout RV Park/deli/rest., access to ski area, info

0mm Montana/Idaho state line, Mountain/Pacific time zone, Lookout Pass elev 4680

Interstate 94

E ↕ W

Exit # Services

250mm Montana/North Dakota state line

248 Carlyle Rd, no facilities

242 MT 7(from wb), Wibaux, **S...rest area both lanes, full(handicapped)facilities, phone, picnic tables, litter barrels, gas:** Amsler's/diesel, Cenex/diesel, **food:** Tastee Hut, **lodging:** Budget Host, **other:** RV camping

241 MT 261(from eb), to MT 7, Wibaux, **S...gas:** Amsler's, Cenex, **lodging:** Budget Host, same as 242

241mm weigh sta both lanes

236 ranch access, no facilities

231 Hodges Rd, no facilities

224 Griffith Creek, frontage road, no facilities

222.5mm Griffith Creek

215 MT 335, Glendive, City Ctr, **N...gas:** Conoco, **food:** CC's Café, **lodging:** Comfort Inn, Day's Inn, King's Inn, Super 8, **other:** Glendive Camping(apr-oct), museum, **S...gas:** Exxon/diesel, Sinclair/diesel/repair, **food:** DQ, Hardee's, **lodging:** Best Western, Budget Motel, El Centro Motel, **other:** HOSPITAL, to Makoshika SP

Interstate 94

E ↕ W

Glendive

215mm Yellowstone River

213 MT 16, Glendive, to Sidney, **N...gas:** Exxon/diesel, **other:** Green Valley Camping, st patrol, **S...gas:** Conoco/diesel, Sinclair/diesel, **food:** McDonald's, Pizza Hut, Subway, Taco John's, **lodging:** Best Western Downtown, Budget Host, Holiday Lodge, Parkwood Motel, **other:** Albertson's, Ford/Lincoln/Mercury, Radio Shack

211 MT 200S(from wb, no EZ return), to Circle, no facilities

210 Lp 94, to MT 200S, W Glendive, **S...gas:** Cenex, **food:** McDonald's, **other:** Chevrolet/Pontiac/Buick, Chrysler/Plymouth/Dodge/Jeep, Makoshika SP

206 Pleasant View Rd, no facilities

204 Whoopup Creek Rd, no facilities

198 Cracker Box Rd, **1 mi N...**Hess Arabians

192 Bad Route Rd, **S...rest area/weigh sta both lanes, full(handicapped)facilities, weather info, phone, picnic tables, litter barrels, camping, petwalk**

187mm Yellowstone River

185 MT 340, Fallon, **S...food:** access to café, **other:** phone

184mm O'Fallon Creek

176 MT 253, Terry, **N...gas:** Cenex/diesel, **lodging:** Diamond Motel, Kempton Hotel, **other:** HOSPITAL, Terry RV Oasis

170mm Powder River

169 Powder River Rd, no facilities

159 Diamond Ring, no facilities

148 Valley Access, no facilities

141 US 12 E, Miles City, **N...other:** Big Sky RV Camping, casino(4mi), to KOA

Miles City

138 MT 58, Miles City, **N...gas:** Cenex/diesel/24hr, Conoco, Exxon/diesel/24hr, **food:** A&W/KFC, DQ, 4B's Rest., Gallagher's Rest., Hardee's, Jewel's Steaks, Little Caesar's, McDonald's, Pizza Hut/Taco Bell, Subway, Taco John's, Wendy's, **lodging:** Best Western, Budget Inn, Day's Inn, Econolodge, Motel 6, **other:** HOSPITAL, Albertson's, Checker Parts, County Mkt Foods/24hr, Osco Drug, K-Mart, KOA, Wal-Mart/auto, casinos, **S...food:** Hunan Chinese, **lodging:** Comfort Inn, Guesthouse Inn, Holiday Inn Express, Super 8

137mm Tongue River

135 Lp 94, Miles City(no EZ return), no facilities

128 local access, no facilities

126 Moon Creek Rd, no facilities

117 Hathaway, no facilities

114mm rest area eb, full(handicapped)facilities, phone, picnic tables, litter barrels, petwalk

113mm rest area wb, full(handicapped)facilities, phone, picnic tables, litter barrels, petwalk, overlook

106 Butte Creek Rd, to Rosebud, **N...**food, phone

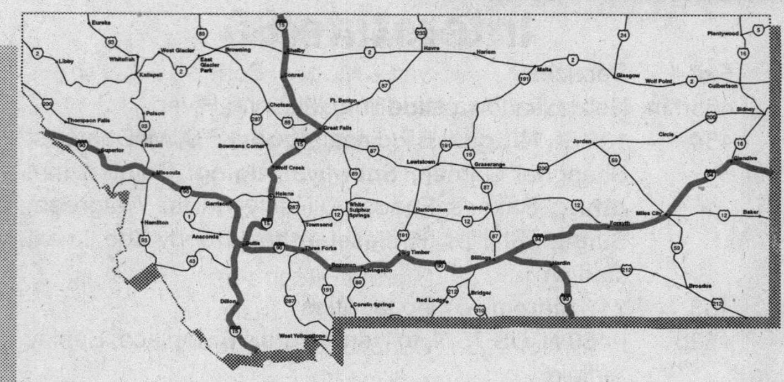

103 MT 446, MT 447, Rosebud Creek Rd, no facilities

98.5mm weigh sta both lanes

95 Forsyth, **N...gas:** Cenex, Exxon/diesel/24hr, **food:** Top That Eatery, **lodging:** Rails Inn Motel(1mi), MT Inn, **other:** Ford/Mercury, Yellowstone Drug, to Rosebud RA, **S...**camping

93 US 12 W, Forsyth, **N...gas:** Cenex, Exxon/diesel/24hr, **food:** Top That Eatery, **lodging:** Crestwell Inn, MT Motel, WestWind Motel, **other:** HOSPITAL, repair/tires

87 MT 39, to Colstrip, no facilities

82 Reservation Creek Rd, no facilities

72 MT 384, Sarpy Creek Rd, no facilities

67 Hysham, **1-2 mi N...**gas, phone, food, lodging

65mm rest area both lanes, full(handicapped)facilities, phone, picnic tables, litter barrels, petwalk

63 ranch access, no facilities

53 Bighorn, access to phone

52mm Bighorn River

49 MT 47, Custer, to Hardin, **S...food:** Ft Custer Café, **other:** to Little Bighorn Bfd, camping

47 Custer, **S...gas:** Conoco/diesel, **food:** Jct City Saloon/café, **lodging:** D&L Motel/café, **other:** Custer Food Mkt

41.5mm rest area wb, full(handicapped)facilities, phone, picnic tables, litter barrels, petwalk

38mm rest area eb, full(handicapped)facilities, phone, picnic tables, litter barrels, petwalk

36 Waco, frontage rd, no facilities

23 Pompeys Pillar, **N...other:** Pompeys Pillar Nat Landmark

14 Ballentine, Worden, **S...food:** Long Branch Café/casino

6 MT 522, Huntley, **N...**gas/phone, **food:** Sam's Café

0mm I-90, E to Sheridan, W to Billings, I-94 begins/ends on I-90, exit 456.

NEBRASKA

Interstate 80

E ↕ W

Exit #	Services
455mm	Nebraska/Iowa state line, Missouri River
454	13th St, **N...gas:** BP/diesel, **food:** KFC, McDonald's, Shanghai Garden, Subway, **lodging:** Comfort Inn, **other:** Baker's Foods, O'Reilly Parts, Walgreen, **S...gas:** Phillips 66/diesel, **other:** Doorly Zoo, Imax, stadium
453	24th St(from eb), no facilities
452b	I-480 N, US 75 N, to Henry Ford's Birthplace, Eppley Airfield
a	US 75 S, no facilities
451	42nd St, **N...gas:** Conoco/diesel, Texaco, **other:** , **S...gas:** Phillips 66, **food:** Burger King, McDonald's, Taco Bell, **other:** HOSPITAL, FastLube, Ford
450	60th St, **N...gas:** Phillips 66, Shell, **other:** NAPA, to U of NE Omaha, **S...gas:** Phillips 66/diesel, **food:** Country Kitchen, **lodging:** Microtel
449	72nd St, to Ralston, **N...gas:** BP/Amoco, **food:** Burger King, Charlie's Seafood Grill, Grover St Rest., Perkins, **lodging:** Clarion, Hampton Inn, Holiday Inn, Homewood Suites, Red Lion Inn, Super 8, Travelodge, **other:** HOSPITAL, **S...gas:** Phillips 66/diesel, **food:** Anthony's Rest.
448	84th St, **N...gas:** BP/Amoco, Shell, **food:** China Garden, Denny's, Farmhouse Café, McDonald's, Subway, Taco Bell, **lodging:** Econolodge, **other:** EYECARE, Baker's Foods, Goodyear/auto, Hancock Fabrics, Mangelson's Crafts, NAPA AutoCare, ShopKO, **S...gas:** Phillips 66/diesel, QT, Sinclair, SuperGas, **food:** Wendy's, **other:** Acura/Isuzu/Kia, Chevrolet, Just Good Meats, U-Haul
446	I-680 N, to Boystown
445	US 275, NE 92, I thru L St, **N...gas:** Cenex, **food:** Austin's Steaks, **lodging:** Clarion, Residence Inn, **other:** Nelsen's RV Ctr, Sam's Club, **S...food:** Village Inn Rest., **lodging:** Baymont Inn, Comfort Inn, Day's Inn, Hampton Inn, Hawthorn Suites, Holiday Inn Express, Howard Johnson, Motel 6, Super 8, **other:** Goodyear, NE Beef Co, **S on 108th...gas:** Conoco/diesel, QT/diesel, **food:** Arby's, Burger King, China 1, Hong Kong Café, LJ Silver, McDonald's, Pizza Hut/Taco Bell, Subway, Valentino's, Wendy's, **other:** Albertson's
444	Q St, **N...gas:** Cenex/diesel
442	126th St, Harrison St, **N...other:** Chrysler/Jeep, Toyota
440	NE 50, to Springfield, **N...gas:** Conoco, Shell/Subway/diesel/24hr/@, **food:** Azteca Mexican, Cracker Barrel, Hardee's, McDonald's, TH Café, **lodging:** Ben Franklin Motel, Budget Inn, Comfort Inn, Day's Inn, Ramada Ltd, **other:** HOSPITAL, Ford, truckwash, **S...gas:** BP/Amoco/diesel, to Platte River SP
439	NE 370, to Gretna, **N...gas:** Phillips 66/diesel, **lodging:** Day's Inn, Suburban Inn, antiques, **S...**HOSPITAL, museum
432	US 6, NE 31, to Gretna, **N...gas:** Bosselman/diesel/rest./24hr, **food:** McDonald's, **lodging:** Super 8, **other:** GNC, Nebraska X-ing/famous brands, **S...gas:** Flying J/Conoco/diesel/LP/rest./24hr/@, **other:** KOA, to Schramm SP
431mm	**rest area wb, full(handicapped)facilities, info, phone, picnic tables, litter barrels, petwalk**
427mm	Platte River
426	to Ashland, **N...**gas, food, RV camping, to Mahoney SP
425.5	**rest area eb, full(handicapped)facilities, phone, picnic tables, litter barrels, petwalk, vending**
420	NE 63, Greenwood, **N...gas:** Conoco/diesel/café, **other:** RV camping, **S...gas:** Phillips 66/diesel, **food:** Cubby's Rest., **lodging:** Big Inn, to Platte River SP
416mm	weigh sta both lanes
409	US 6, Waverly, to E Lincoln, **S...gas:** Phillips 66/Gas'n Shop, **other:** HOSPITAL
405	US 77 N, 56th St, Lincoln, **S...gas:** Phillips 66, **other:** HOSPITAL, **1 mi S...food:** Misty's Rest., **lodging:** Howard Johnson, Motel 6, **other:** antiques
404mm	**rest area wb, full(handicapped)facilities, info, phone, picnic tables, litter barrels, vending, petwalk**
403	27th St, Lincoln, **S...gas:** Conoco/Wendy's/diesel, Phillips 66/Subway/diesel, **food:** Cracker Barrel, Taco Inn, **lodging:** AmericInn, Red Roof Inn, Settle Inn, Staybridge Suites, **other:** Chevrolet/Pontiac/Cadillac/GMC, Ford/Mazda, **1-3 mi S...gas:** Mobil, Phillips 66, Texaco, **food:** Applebee's, Beacon Hill Rest., Burger King, Carlos O'Kelly's, DaVinci's Italian, Godfather's, Golden Corral, HyVee Foods, IHOP, McDonald's, Papa John's, Runza Rest., Schlotsky's, Sonic, Taco John's, Valentino's, **lodging:** Village Inn, Baymont Inn, Comfort Suites, Country Inn Suites, Fairfield Inn, Microtel, Ramada Ltd, Super 8, **other:** $Tree, GNC, Haas Tire, Interstate Battery, Mazda, Michael's, Radio Shack, Sam's Club, ShopKO, Wal-Mart SuperCtr/24hr, to U NE, st fairpark
401b	US 34 W, **N...**RV camping
a	I-180, US 34 E, to 9th St, Lincoln
399	Lincoln, **N...gas:** Amoco/diesel/24hr, Phillips 66, **food:** Baskin-Robbins, McDonald's, NY Pizza, Perkins/24hr, Quizno's, TacoMaker, **lodging:** Airport Inn, Comfort Inn, Day's Inn, Hampton Inn, Holiday Inn Express, Horizon Inn, Motel 6, Ramada Inn, Sleep Inn, Travelodge, to airport, **S...lodging:** Economy Inn, Inn4Less
397	US 77 S, to Beatrice, **S...gas:** Conoco, **lodging:** Congress Inn, Welcome Inn, **other:** Ford/Lincoln/Mercury
396	US 6, West O St(from eb), **S...gas:** Sinclair/diesel/, **lodging:** Cobbler Inn, Senate Inn, Super 8, Travelodge, Welcome Inn
395	US 6, NW 48th St, **N...gas:** Sinclair, **food:** Runza Rest., **other:** Ford/Freightliner Trucks, st patrol, **S...gas:** Shoemaker/Texaco/Popeye's/diesel/@, **lodging:** Cobbler Inn, Senate Inn, Shoney's Inn, Super 8(2mi)
388	NE 103, Pleasant Dale, to Crete, **N...gas:** Sinclair, **other:** RV camping/gas
382	US 6, Milford, no facilities
381mm	**rest area eb, full(handicapped)facilities, phone, picnic tables, litter barrels, petwalk, vending**

Omaha

Lincoln

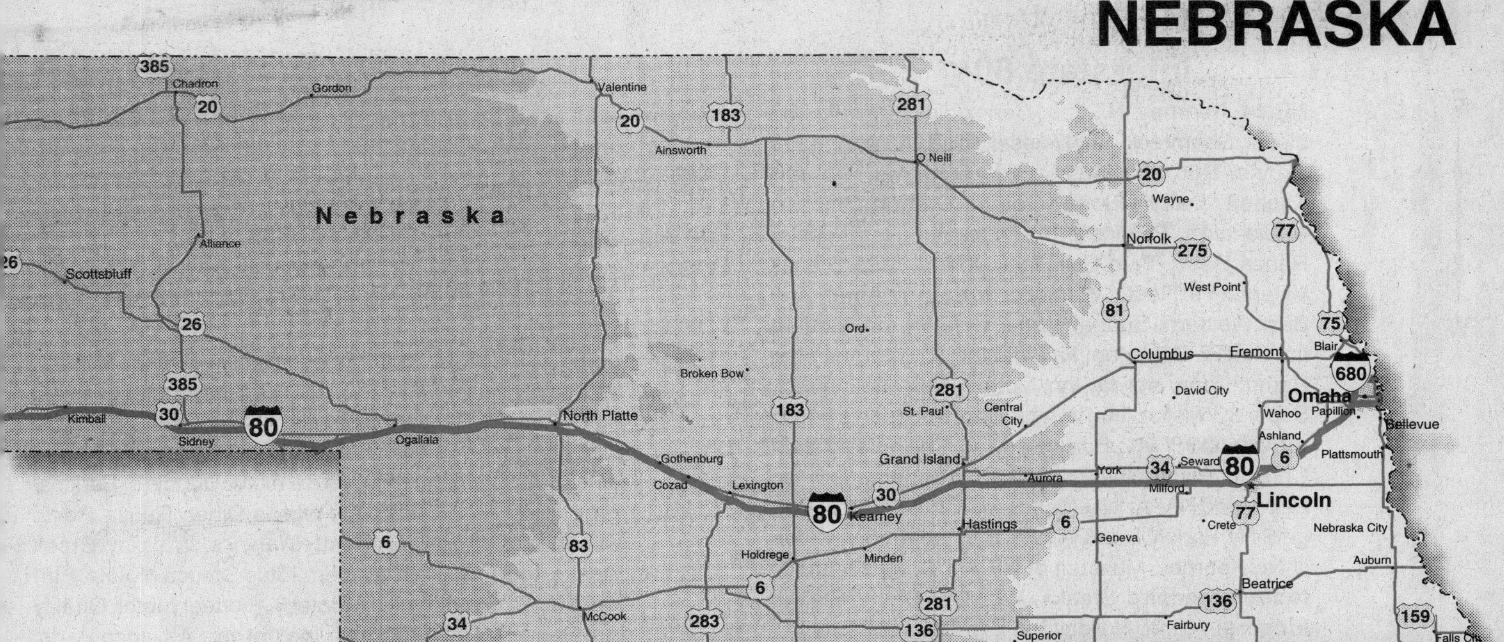

Interstate 80

E ↕ W

York

379 NE 15, to Seward, **2-3 mi N...gas:** Phillips 66, **food:** McDonald's, Valentino's, **lodging:** Dandy Lion Inn, Super 8, **other:** HOSPITAL, antiques, **S...gas:** Phillips 66/diesel

375mm rest area wb, full(handicapped)facilities, info, phone, picnic tables, litter barrels, petwalk, vending

373 80G, Goehner, **N...gas:** Shell

369 80E, Beaver Crossing, **3 mi S...**food, RV camping

366 80F, to Utica, no facilities

360 93B, to Waco, **N...gas:** FuelMart/diesel/rest./@, **S...lodging:** Double Nickel Camping

355mm rest area wb, full(handicapped)facilities, info, phone, picnic tables, litter barrels, vending, petwalk

353 US 81, to York, **N...gas:** Amoco/diesel, SappBros/Sinclair/Subway/diesel/@, Shell, **food:** A&W/Amigo's, Arby's, Burger King, Country Kitchen, Golden Gate Chinese, KFC/Taco Bell, McDonald's, Taco John's, Wendy's, **lodging:** Budget Inn, Comfort Inn, Day's Inn, Quality Inn, Super 8, Yorkshire Motel, **other:** HOSPITAL, Buick/GMC, Chevrolet/Pontiac, Chrysler/Dodge, **S...gas:** Conoco/diesel, Petro/Phillips 66/Pizza Hut/diesel/24hr/@, Shell/diesel/rest./24hr, **food:** Applebee's, **lodging:** 1st Inn, Holiday Inn, Blue Beacon

351mm rest area eb, full(handicapped)facilities, info, phone, picnic tables, litter barrels, petwalk, vending

348 93E, to Bradshaw, no facilities

342 93A, Henderson, **N...other:** Good Sam RV Park, antiques, **S...gas:** FuelMart/diesel, **food:** Eat'n Haus, **lodging:** 1st Inn, **other:** HOSPITAL

338 41D, to Hampton, no facilities

Kearney

332 NE 14, Aurora, **N...gas:** Casey's, Shell/diesel, **food:** McDonald's(3mi), Pizza Hut(3mi), **lodging:** Budget Host(3mi), Hamilton Motel/rest., **other:** HOSPITAL, to Plainsman Museum, **S...gas:** Sinclair/diesel

324 41B, to Giltner, no facilities

318 NE 2, to Grand Island, **S...other:** Grand Island RV Park, KOA

317mm rest area wb, full(handicapped)facilities, info, phone, picnic tables, litter barrels, vending, petwalk

315mm rest area eb, full(handicapped)facilities, info, phone, picnic tables, litter barrels, vending, petwalk

314mm Platte River

314 new exit

312 US 34/281, to Grand Island, **N...gas:** Bosselman/Sinclair/Max's/Subway/Taco Bell/diesel/24hr/@, Phillips 66/Krispy Kreme, **food:** 9 Bridge Rest., **lodging:** USA Inn/rest., **other:** HOSPITAL, Mormon Island RA, to Stuhr Pioneer Museum, **S...gas:** Amoco, **food:** Arby's, **lodging:** Holiday Inn/rest., Holiday Inn Express, **other:** Ford/Peterbilt, Hastings Museum(15mi)

305 40C, to Alda, **N...gas:** Phillips 66/diesel/24hr, TA/Conoco/diesel/rest./24hr/@, **other:** Crane Meadows Nature Ctr/rest area

300 NE 11, Wood River, **S...gas:** Bosselman/Sinclair/Subway/Taco Bell/diesel/24hr/@, **lodging:** Wood River Motel

291 10D, Shelton, **N...other:** War Axe SRA, **S...gas**/diesel

285 10C, Gibbon, **N...gas:** Ampride/diesel, **other:** Windmill RA, RV camping, **rest area both lanes, full facilities, picnic tables, litter barrels, S...lodging:** Country Inn, **other:** Don's Repair

279 NE 10, to Minden, **N...gas:** Shell/diesel, **other:** Cabela's SportsGear, **S...other:** Pioneer Village Camping

275mm The Great Platte River Road Archway Monument

NEBRASKA

Interstate 80

E ↕ W

272 NE 44, Kearney, **N...gas:** Cenex/diesel, Phillips 66/diesel, Shamrock, Shell/diesel, **food:** A&W/Amigo's, Arby's, Burger King, Carlos O'Kelly's, Country Kitchen, Dairy Queen, Golden Dragon Chinese, McDonald's, Perkins/24hr, Pizza Hut, Red Lobster, Runza Rest., Taco Bell, Taco John's, USA Steaks, Valentino's Rest., Wendy's, **lodging:** AmericInn, Best Western, Budget Motel, Comfort Inn, Country Inn Suites, Day's Inn, Fairfield Inn, 1st Interstate Inn, Hampton Inn, Holiday Inn, Motel 6, Ramada Inn/rest., Super 8, Western Inn, Wingate Inn, Boogaart's Foods, **other:** HOSPITAL, Buick/Cadillac, Chevrolet/Mazda, Chrysler/Plymouth/Dodge/Jeep, $General, Pontiac, Goodyear, NAPA, Wal-Mart SuperCtr/24hr(3mi), Budget$ RV Park, Clyde&Vi's RV Park, to Archway Mon, U NE Kearney, Museum of NE Art, **S...gas:** Amoco, **food:** Grandpa's Steaks, Whiskey Creek Steaks, **lodging:** 1st Inn, Holiday Inn Express

271mm rest area wb, full(handicapped)facilities, info, phone, picnic tables, litter barrels, petwalk

269mm rest area eb, full(handicapped)facilities, info, phone, picnic tables, litter barrels, petwalk

263 Odessa, **N...gas:** Sapp/Texaco/diesel/rest./@, **other:** UP Wayside Area, **S...food:** Aunt Lu's Rest.

257 US 183, Elm Creek, **N...gas:** Bosselman/Sinclair/Subway/Little Caesar/diesel/24hr/@, **lodging:** 1st Interstate Inn, **other:** Antique Car Museum, Sunny Meadows Camping

Lexington

248 Overton, **N...gas:** Mian Bros/Amoco/diesel/24hr/@, **food:** MB Rest.

237 US 283, Lexington, **N...gas:** Ampride/diesel/@, Conoco/KFC/Taco Bell/@, Phillips 66/diesel, **food:** A&W/Amigo's, Arby's, Burger King, Dairy Queen, McDonald's, Pizza Hut, Wendy's, **lodging:** Budget Host, Comfort Inn, Day's Inn, 1st Interstate Inn, Gable View Inn, Holiday Inn Express, **other:** HOSPITAL, Advance Parts, Chevrolet/Pontiac/Buick, $General, Goodyear, SavALot Foods, Wal-Mart/café, museum, **S...gas:** Sinclair/diesel/@, **food:** Kirk's Café, **lodging:** Super 8, **other:** Goodyear, to Johnson Lake RA

231 Darr Rd, **S...**truckwash/24hr

227mm rest area both lanes, full(handicapped)facilities, info, phone, picnic tables, litter barrels, vending, petwalk

222 NE 21, Cozad, **N...gas:** Amoco/Burger King, Phillips 66/diesel, Sinclair, **food:** Dairy Queen, McDonald's, Pizza Hut, PJ's Rest., Subway, Taco Time, **lodging:** Best Value Inn, Motel 6, **other:** HOSPITAL, Alco, Ford, museum

211 NE 47, Gothenburg, **N...gas:** Shell/diesel/24hr/@, **food:** Dragon Chinese, McDonald's, Mi Ranchito Mexican, Pizza Hut/Taco Bell, Runza Rest., **lodging:** Super 8, Travel Inn, Western Motel, **other:** HOSPITAL, Pony Express Sta Museum(1mi), Chevrolet/Pontiac/Buick, truck permit sta, **S...**KOA/gas

199 Brady, **N...gas:** Sinclair/DQ/diesel, **other:** RV camping

194mm rest area both lanes, full(handicapped)facilities, phone, picnic tables, litter barrels, vending, petwalk

190 Maxwell, **N...gas:** Sinclair/diesel, **S...other:** to Ft McPherson Nat Cemetary, RV camping

181mm weigh sta both lanes, phones

179 to US 30, N Platte, **N...lodging:** Stanford Motel, **other:** RV camping, **S...gas:** Flying J/Conoco/CountryMkt/diesel/LP/24hr/@

N Platte

177 US 83, N Platte, **N...gas:** Amoco/Subway, Conoco/diesel, Phillips 66/diesel/24hr, Shell/diesel, Sinclair/diesel, **food:** A&W, Amigo's Rest., Applebee's, Arby's, Baskin-Robbins/Blimpie/Dunkin Donuts, BBQ, Burger King, Dairy Queen, Hong King Chinese, KFC, LJ Silver, McDonald's, Perkins/24hr, Pizza Hut, Quizno's, Roger's Diner, Runza Rest., Valentino's, Village Inn Rest., Wendy's, Whiskey Creek Steaks, **lodging:** Best Western, Blue Spruce Motel, 1st Interstate Inn, Hampton Inn, Motel 6, Pioneer Motel, Quality Inn, Sands Motel, Stockman Inn, **other:** Advance Parts, $General, Goodyear/auto, Harley-Davidson, Holiday TravL Park, JC Penney, ShopKO, Staples, SunMart Foods, Wal-Mart SuperCtr/gas/24hr, mall, museum, to Buffalo Bill's Ranch, **S...gas:** Conoco/Taco Bell/diesel/24hr/@, Phillips 66, Texaco/diesel/rest./24hr, **food:** Country Kitchen, Hunan Chinese, **lodging:** Comfort Inn, Day's Inn, Holiday Inn Express, Ramada Ltd, Super 8, **other:** Cadillac, Chevrolet, Chrysler/Jeep, Dodge, Ford/Lincoln/Mercury, Honda, Toyota/Mazda, truck permit sta, to Lake Maloney RA

164 56C, Hershey, **N...gas:** Western/diesel/rest./24hr/@, **other:** Western Wear Outlet

160mm rest area both lanes, full(handicapped)facilities, info, phone, picnic tables, litter barrels, petwalk

158 NE 25, Sutherland, **N...lodging:** Park Motel, Sutherland Lodge, **S...gas:** Conoco/diesel/pizza/subs/24hr

149mm Central/Mountain time zone

145 51C, Paxton, **N...gas:** Shell/24hr, **food:** Ole's Café, **lodging:** Day's Inn

133 51B, Roscoe, no facilities

132mm rest area wb, full(handicapped)facilities, info, phone, picnic tables, litter barrels, petwalk

Ogallala

126 US 26, NE 61, Ogallala, **N...gas:** Amoco, Phillips 66/diesel, Shell/diesel/24hr/@, Texaco/Burger King, **food:** Amigo's Rest., Arby's/RV parking, Country Kitchen, McDonald's, Pizza Hut, Taco Bell, Taco John's, Valentino's, **lodging:** Best Western, Day's Inn, Holiday Inn Express, Ramada Ltd, **other:** HOSPITAL, Ace Hardware, Big A Parts, Chevrolet/Buick, Radio Shack, to Lake McConaughy, **S...gas:** Conoco/Subway, TA/diesel/rest./24hr/@, Phillips 66/diesel, **food:** Dairy Queen, KFC, Panda Chinese, Wendy's, **lodging:** Comfort Inn, Econolodge, 1st Interstate Inn, Super 8, **other:** $General, Open Corral RV Park, Pamida

124mm rest area eb, full(handicapped)facilities, info, phones, picnic tables, litter barrels, petwalk

117 51A, Brule, **N...gas:** Happy Jack's/diesel, **other:** RV camping

Interstate 80

107 25B, Big Springs, **N...gas:** Bosselman/Sinclair/Grandma Max's/diesel/@, Total/diesel, **food:** Blimpie, Little Caesar's, **lodging:** Budget 8 Motel, **other:** McGreer Camping, truckwash
102 I-76 S, to Denver, no facilities
102mm S Platte River
101 US 138, to Julesburg, no facilities
99mm scenic turnout eb
95 NE 27, to Julesburg, no facilities
88mm Lodgepole Creek, rest area wb, full(handicapped)facilities, phone, picnic tables, litter barrels, vending, petwalk
85 25A, Chappell, **N...gas:** Ampride, **other:** Chevrolet/Buick, Creekside Camping, USPO, wayside park, **S... gas:** Texaco/diesel
82.5mm rest area eb, full(handicapped)facilities, phone, picnic tables, litter barrels, vending, petwalk
76 17F, Lodgepole, **1 mi N...**gas/diesel, lodging
69 17E, to Sunol, no facilities
61mm rest area wb, full(handicapped)facilities, phone, picnic tables, litter barrels, vending, petwalk
59 US 385, 17J, Sidney, **N...gas:** Amoco, Conoco/KFC/Taco Bell/TCBY/diesel, Shell/diesel/24hr/@, **food:** Arby's, China 1 Buffet, Little Mexico Rest., McDonald's, Mi Ranchito Mexican, Perkins, Quizno's, Runza Rest., Taco John's, **lodging:** AmericInn, Comfort Inn, Day's Inn, Motel 6, **other:** Cabela's SportsGear, $General, Lovers Leap Vinyards, Naddox RV Ctr, Pamida, Radio Shack, RV camping(2mi), golf, truck permit sta, **3 mi N...food:** KFC, Pizza Hut, **lodging:** Generic Motel, Sidney Motel, Super 8, **other:** HOSPITAL, RV camping, **S...gas:** Phillips 66/diesel, **food:** Country Kitchen, **lodging:** Holiday Inn, **other:** truckwash
55 NE 19, Sidney, to Sterling, CO, **2 mi N...lodging:** Ft Sidney Inn, Super 8
51.5mm rest area/hist marker eb, full(handicapped)facilities, phone, picnic tables, litter barrels, vending, petwalk
48 to Brownson, no facilities
38 Potter, **N...gas:** Cenex/diesel/LP, Shell, **other:** repair
29 53A, Dix, **1/2 mi N...**gas, food
25mm rest area wb, full(handicapped)facilities, phone, picnic tables, litter barrels, vending, petwalk
22 53E, Kimball, **N...lodging:** Day's Inn, **other:** KOA, golf
20 NE 71, Kimball, **N...gas:** Sinclair/diesel/@, **food:** Beef&Brunch Rest., Pizza Hut, Subway, **lodging:** Day's Inn, 1st Interstate Inn, Super 8, **S...food:** Burger King, **other:** HOSPITAL, truck permit sta., Twin Pines RV Park
18mm parking area eb, litter barrel
10mm rest area eb, full(handicapped)facilities, info, phone, picnic tables, litter barrels, petwalk
8 53C, to Bushnell, no facilities
1 53B, Pine Bluffs, **1 mi N...**RV camping
0mm Nebraska/Wyoming state line

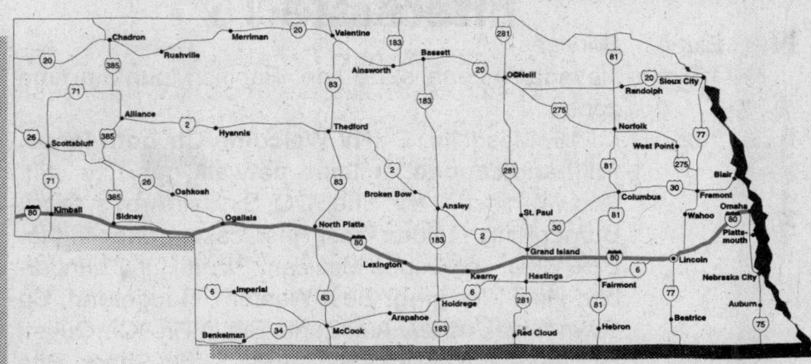

Interstate 680(Omaha)

Exit # Services
29b a I-80, W to Omaha, E to Des Moines. I-680 begins/ends on I-80, exit 27.
28 IA 191, to Neola, Persia, no facilities
21 L34, Beebeetown, no facilities
19mm rest area wb, full(handicapped)facilities, info, phone, picnic tables, litter barrels, petwalk
16mm rest area eb, full(handicapped)facilities, info, phone, picnic tables, litter barrels, petwalk
71 I-29 N, to Sioux City
66 Honey Creek, **W...gas:** Phillips 66/diesel/rest., **food:** Iowa Feed&Grain Co Rest.
3b a I-29, S to Council Bluffs, IA 988, to Crescent, **E...gas:** Phillips 66, **other:** to ski area
1 County Rd, no facilities
14mm Nebraska/Iowa state line, Missouri River, Mormon Bridge
13 US 75 S, Florence, **E...gas:** Shell/diesel, **food:** OJ's Mexican, Zesto Diner, **lodging:** Mormon Trail Motel, **other:** LDS Temple, Mormon Trail Ctr, **W...gas:** Phillips 66
12 US 75 N, 48th St, **E...gas:** Phillips 66, **food:** Burger King
9 72nd St, **3 mi E...food:** Famous Dave's BBQ, IHOP, Sonic, **other:** HOSPITAL, **W...**Cunningham Lake RA
6 NE 133, Irvington, **E...gas:** Conoco/diesel, **food:** Burger King
5 Fort St, **W...gas:** Sinclair, Shell, **other:** Wal-Mart/drugs, USPO
4 NE 64, Maple St, **E...gas:** BP/Amoco, **W...**Kum&Go, **food:** Burger King, KFC, McDonald's, Perkins, Pizza Hut, Runza, Subway, Taco Bell, **lodging:** Comfort Suites, La Quinta, Ramada Ltd, **other:** Albertson's, Champion Parts
3 US 6, Dodge St, **E...food:** Chang's Bistro, Macaroni Grill, Panera Bread, Steak'n Shake, TGIFriday, **lodging:** Hampton Inn, Marriott, **other:** MEDICAL CARE, Dodge, Ford, JC Penney, Mazda, Von Maur, **W...gas:** BP/Amoco, **food:** Blimpie, Boston Mkt, DQ, NY Burrito, **lodging:** Best Western, Crowne Plaza Motel, Super 8, **other:** Cadillac, Chevrolet, Nissan/Hyundai, Toyota
2 Pacific St, **E...gas:** BP/Amoco, Sinclair, **lodging:** Park Inn
1 NE 38, W Center Rd, **E...food:** Don&Millie's Rest., Garden Café, **W...gas:** Phillips, **food:** BBQ, Burger King, Wendy's
0mm I-680 begins/ends on I-80, exit 446.

NEVADA

Interstate 15

Exit #	Services
123mm	Nevada/Arizona state line, Pacific/Mountain time zone
122	Lp 15, Mesquite, **E...NV Welcome Ctr both lanes, full(handicapped)facilities, petwalk, gas:** Chevron/Subway/diesel/24hr, Shell/DQ, Sinclair/Arby's, **food:** Burger King, Golden West Rest./casino, Jack-in-the-Box, KFC, Los Lupes Mexican, Pizza Hut, Thunderbird Rest., **lodging:** Best Western, Budget Inn, Up Town Motel, **other:** AutoZone, Big O Tire, CarQuest, GNC, Great Outdoors RV, NAPA, Radio Shack, Rite Aid, Smith's Foods, USPO, diesel repair, museum, **W...gas:** Virgin River/76/diesel/LP/RV park, **food:** McDonald's, **lodging:** Holiday Inn, Eureka Motel/casino, Mesquite Springs Motel, Virgin River Hotel/casino
120	Lp 15, Mesquite, Bunkerville, **E...gas:** Arco/24hr, Chevron, Terribles, Shell/diesel, **food:** Carollo's Rest., McDonald's, Casablanca Resort/casino/RV Park, Oasis Resort/casino, Peppermill Resort/casino, Players Island Resort/casino, **lodging:** Valley Inn, **other:** USPO, **W...lodging:** Best Western
112	NV 170, Riverside, Bunkerville, no facilities
110mm	truck parking both lanes, litter barrels
100	to Carp, Elgin, no facilities
96mm	truck parking nb, litter barrels
93	NV 169, to Logandale, Overton, **E...lodging:** Best Western(10mi), **other:** Lake Mead NRA, Lost City Museum
91	NV 168, Glendale, **W...gas:** Chevron/diesel/rest.
90.5mm	Muddy River
90	NV 168(from nb), Glendale, Moapa, **W...gas:** Chevron/diesel/rest., **other:** Moapa Indian Reservation
88	Hidden Valley, no facilities
87.5mm	parking area both lanes, litter barrels
84	Byron, no facilities
80	Ute, no facilities
75	NV 169 E, Valley of Fire SP, Lake Mead NRA, **E...other:** casino, fireworks
64	US 93 N, Great Basin Hwy, to Ely, Great Basin NP, no facilities
60mm	livestock check sta sb
58	NV 604, Las Vegas Blvd, to Apex, Nellis AFB, no facilities
54	Speedway Blvd, Hollywood Blvd, **E...gas:** Petro/Mobil/diesel/24hr/@, **other:** Las Vegas Speedway
52	rd 215 W, no facilities
50	Lamb Ave(from sb), no facilities
48	Craig Rd, **E...gas:** Arco/24hr, Chevron/Subway/24hr, Mobil, Pilot/DQ/KFC/Pizza Hut/diesel/24hr, Shell, **food:** Burger King, Jack-in-the-Box, Speedway Grill, **lodging:** Best Western(2mi), Hampton Inn, Super 8, **other:** to Nellis AFB, **W...gas:** Citgo/7-11, **lodging:** Holiday Inn Express
46	Cheyenne Ave, **E...gas:** Arco/24hr, Citgo/7-11, Exxon, **lodging:** Ramada Inn/casino, **other:** NAPA, **W...gas:** Breeze-In/Jack-in-the-Box, Citgo/7-11, Flying J/diesel/LP/rest./24hr/@, **food:** Denny's, McDonald's, **lodging:** Comfort Inn, **other:** Blue Beacon, diesel repair
45	Lake Mead Blvd, **E...gas:** 7-11, McDonald's, **food:** Wendy's
44	Washington Ave(from sb), **E...lodging:** Best Western, casinos
43	D St(from nb), **E...**Best Western, same as 44, **W...**Office Depot
42b a	I-515 to LV, US 95 N to Reno, US 93 S to Phoenix, **E...**76, casinos, **W...gas:** Arco/24hr, Shell
41b a	NV 159, Charleston Blvd, **E...gas:** Arco/diesel, 7-11, **other:** antiques, **W...gas:** 76, Shell, **food:** Carl's Jr, Del Taco, McDonald's, Taco Bell, Wendy's, **other:** HOSPITAL, gifts
40	Sahara Ave, **E...**The Strip, **gas:** 76/diesel/rest./24hr, **lodging:** Las Vegas Inn/casino, Travelodge, **other:** LV Conv Ctr, Goodyear, RV Ctr, **W...gas:** Texaco/diesel/LP, 7-11, **food:** Denny's, **lodging:** Palace Station Hotel/casino, **other:** Lexus, Mazda, Mitsubishi, Mercedes
39	Spring Mtn Rd(from sb), **E...lodging:** Budget Suites, Frontier Hotel, **other:** Mirage, Treasure Island, **W...gas:** Arco/24hr, Circle K, United/diesel, **food:** Schlotsky's, **other:** EconoLube/Tune, Discount Tire, Firestone/auto, Goodyear/auto, Lexus, Mercedes, auto/transmission repair
38b a	Dunes Flamingo Rd, **E...**The Strip, **lodging:** Caesar's Palace, Flamingo Hilton, Monte Carlo, to UNLV, **W...gas:** Arco/24hr, Texaco, **food:** Burger King, Outback Steaks, Subway, Gold **lodging:** Coast Hotel, Palms Hotel, Rio Hotel, **other:** MEDICAL CARE, Terrible Herbst Wash/lube
37	Tropicana Ave, **E...lodging:** Excaliber Hotel, Mandalay Bay, MGM Grand, Motel 6, Tropicana Hotel, **other:** GMC/White/Volvo, airport, casinos, funpark, **W...gas:** Arco/24hr, Chevron/diesel, 76, Shell/Mr Subs, WildWest/diesel/LP, **food:** Burger King, IHOP, In-n-Out, Jack-in-the-Box, KFC, McDonald's, Taco Bell, Taco Cabana, Wendy's, **lodging:** Best Western, Budget Suites, Hampton Inn, Howard Johnson, Motel 6, Orleans Hotel, **other:** CarQuest, Honda Motorcycles, casino
36	Russell Rd, **E...gas:** Shell, McDonald's, **lodging:** Diamond Inn, Klondike Hotel, Pollyanna Motel, **other:** casinos, to airport, **W...gas:** Chevron/Herbst/diesel
34	to I-215 E, Las Vegas Blvd, to The Strip, McCarran Airport
33	NV 160, to Blue Diamond, Death Valley, **E...gas:** Arco/24hr, Chevron/McDonald's, Citgo/7-11/diesel, Mobil/diesel/LP, **other:** factory outlet/famous brands, **W...gas:** Chevron, TA/76/Burger King/diesel/LP/24hr/@, **food:** Jack-in-the-Box, Subway, **lodging:** Firebird Inn, **other:** Oasis RV Resort, Silverton Hotel/RV Resort/casino
27	NV 146, to Henderson, Lake Mead, Hoover Dam, **E...gas:** Arco, **2 mi E...other:** Wheelers RV/LP, factory outlets
25	NV 161, Sloan, **1 mi E...**Wheelers RV/service/LP
24mm	bus/truck check sta nb
12	NV 161, Jean, to Goodsprings, **E... Welcome Ctr nb, full facilities, info, gas:** Mobil/diesel, **other:** Gold Strike Casino/hotel/Burger King, USPO, skydiving, **W...other:** Nevada Landing Casino/Shell/diesel/24hr, NV Correctional
1	Primm, **E...gas:** Chevron, 76/diesel, **food:** Carl's Jr, Denny's, Johnnnie D's Rest., McDonald's, **other:** Buffalo Bill's Resort/casino, Primm Valley Resort/casino, Prima Donna RV Park, factory outlets, **W...gas:** Shell/diesel, **lodging:** Whiskey Pete's Hotel/casino/steaks
0mm	Nevada/California state line

Interstate 80

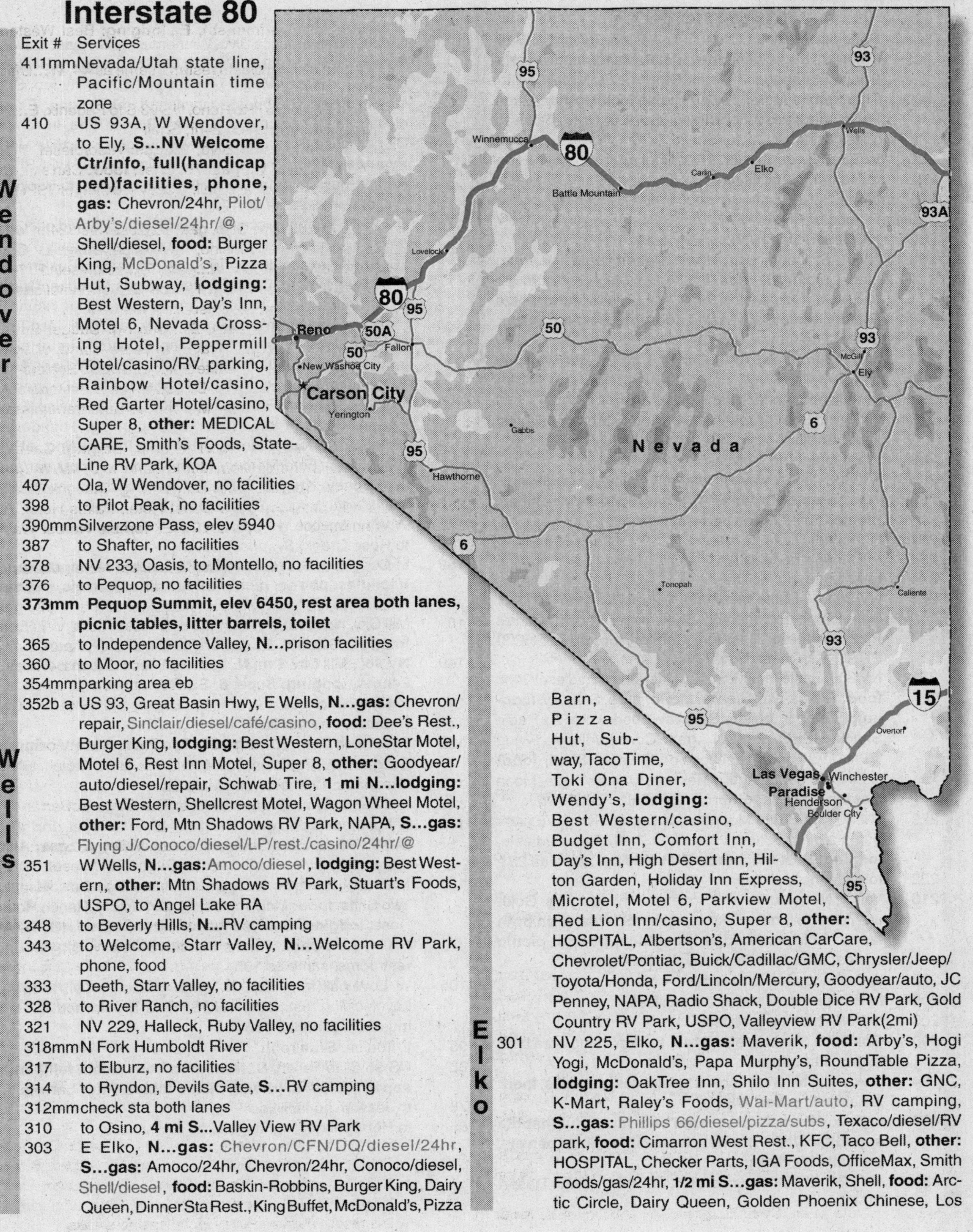

E ↕ W

Exit #	Services
411mm	Nevada/Utah state line, Pacific/Mountain time zone
410	US 93A, W Wendover, to Ely, **S...NV Welcome Ctr/info, full(handicapped)facilities, phone, gas:** Chevron/24hr, Pilot/Arby's/diesel/24hr/@, Shell/diesel, **food:** Burger King, McDonald's, Pizza Hut, Subway, **lodging:** Best Western, Day's Inn, Motel 6, Nevada Crossing Hotel, Peppermill Hotel/casino/RV parking, Rainbow Hotel/casino, Red Garter Hotel/casino, Super 8, **other:** MEDICAL CARE, Smith's Foods, State-Line RV Park, KOA
407	Ola, W Wendover, no facilities
398	to Pilot Peak, no facilities
390mm	Silverzone Pass, elev 5940
387	to Shafter, no facilities
378	NV 233, Oasis, to Montello, no facilities
376	to Pequop, no facilities
373mm	**Pequop Summit, elev 6450, rest area both lanes, picnic tables, litter barrels, toilet**
365	to Independence Valley, **N...**prison facilities
360	to Moor, no facilities
354mm	parking area eb
352b a	US 93, Great Basin Hwy, E Wells, **N...gas:** Chevron/repair, Sinclair/diesel/café/casino, **food:** Dee's Rest., Burger King, **lodging:** Best Western, LoneStar Motel, Motel 6, Rest Inn Motel, Super 8, **other:** Goodyear/auto/diesel/repair, Schwab Tire, **1 mi N...lodging:** Best Western, Shellcrest Motel, Wagon Wheel Motel, **other:** Ford, Mtn Shadows RV Park, NAPA, **S...gas:** Flying J/Conoco/diesel/LP/rest./casino/24hr/@
351	W Wells, **N...gas:** Amoco/diesel, **lodging:** Best Western, **other:** Mtn Shadows RV Park, Stuart's Foods, USPO, to Angel Lake RA
348	to Beverly Hills, **N...**RV camping
343	to Welcome, Starr Valley, **N...**Welcome RV Park, phone, food
333	Deeth, Starr Valley, no facilities
328	to River Ranch, no facilities
321	NV 229, Halleck, Ruby Valley, no facilities
318mm	N Fork Humboldt River
317	to Elburz, no facilities
314	to Ryndon, Devils Gate, **S...**RV camping
312mm	check sta both lanes
310	to Osino, **4 mi S...**Valley View RV Park
303	E Elko, **N...gas:** Chevron/CFN/DQ/diesel/24hr, **S...gas:** Amoco/24hr, Chevron/24hr, Conoco/diesel, Shell/diesel, **food:** Baskin-Robbins, Burger King, Dairy Queen, Dinner Sta Rest., King Buffet, McDonald's, Pizza Barn, Pizza Hut, Subway, Taco Time, Toki Ona Diner, Wendy's, **lodging:** Best Western/casino, Budget Inn, Comfort Inn, Day's Inn, High Desert Inn, Hilton Garden, Holiday Inn Express, Microtel, Motel 6, Parkview Motel, Red Lion Inn/casino, Super 8, **other:** HOSPITAL, Albertson's, American CarCare, Chevrolet/Pontiac, Buick/Cadillac/GMC, Chrysler/Jeep/Toyota/Honda, Ford/Lincoln/Mercury, Goodyear/auto, JC Penney, NAPA, Radio Shack, Double Dice RV Park, Gold Country RV Park, USPO, Valleyview RV Park(2mi)
301	NV 225, Elko, **N...gas:** Maverik, **food:** Arby's, Hogi Yogi, McDonald's, Papa Murphy's, RoundTable Pizza, **lodging:** OakTree Inn, Shilo Inn Suites, **other:** GNC, K-Mart, Raley's Foods, Wal-Mart/auto, RV camping, **S...gas:** Phillips 66/diesel/pizza/subs, Texaco/diesel/RV park, **food:** Cimarron West Rest., KFC, Taco Bell, **other:** HOSPITAL, Checker Parts, IGA Foods, OfficeMax, Smith Foods/gas/24hr, **1/2 mi S...gas:** Maverik, Shell, **food:** Arctic Circle, Dairy Queen, Golden Phoenix Chinese, Los

Wendover — Wells — Elko

NEVADA

Interstate 80

E ↕ W

Sanchez Mexican, New China Café, **lodging:** Best Western, Esquire Inn, Key Motel, Manor Inn, National 9 Inn, Stampede 7 Motel, Stockmen's Motel/casino, Thunderbird Motel, Towne House Motel, **other:** Big A Parts, CarQuest, FoodTown, Sav-On Drug, Schwab Tire, casinos

298 W Elko, **N...**repair, **S...**RV camping

292 to Hunter, no facilities

285mm tunnel

285mm Humboldt River

Carlin

282 NV 221, E Carlin, **N...**prison area

280 NV 766, Carlin, **N...other:** Desert Gold RV Park, diesel repair, **S...gas:** Amoco/diesel, Pilot/Subway/diesel/24hr/@, Texaco/Burger King/diesel, **food:** Pizza Factory, State Café/casino, **lodging:** Best Inn Suites, **other:** FoodTown, USPO

279 NV 278(from eb), to W Carlin, **1 mi S...gas:** Amoco/diesel

271 to Palisade, no facilities

270mm Emigrant Summit, elev 6114, parking area both lanes, litter barrels

268 to Emigrant, no facilities

261 NV 306, to Beowawe, Crescent Valley, no facilities

258mm rest area both lanes, full(handicapped)facilities, picnic tables, litter barrels, petwalk

257mm Humboldt River

254 to Dunphy, no facilities

244 to Argenta, no facilities

Battle Mtn

233 NV 304, to Battle Mountain, **1-2 mi N...gas:** Conoco/diesel/24hr, Exxon/24hr, Shell/diesel, **food:** Mama's Pizza, **lodging:** Best Inn, Comfort Inn, **other:** HOSPITAL, CarQuest, FoodTown

231 NV 305, Battle Mountain, **N...gas:** Chevron/diesel/24hr, **food:** Hide-a-way Steaks, McDonald's, Subway, **lodging:** Super 8, **other:** Bestway Foods, NAPA, Radio Shack, USPO, **1 mi N...gas:** Conoco/diesel, Flying J/Exxon/Blimpie/diesel/casino/24hr/@, Shell, **food:** Donna's Diner, El Aguila Mexican, Mama's Pizza, Moon Garden Chinese, **other:** HOSPITAL, FoodTown

229 NV 304, W Battle Mountain, **N...gas:** Flying J/Exxon/Blimpie/diesel/casino/24hr/@, Shell, Texaco/diesel, **lodging:** Best Inn, **other:** RV camping, same as 231

222 to Mote, no facilities

216 Valmy, **N...gas:** 76/USPO/diesel/24hr, **lodging:** Golden Motel/grill, **other:** RV camping, **S...rest area both lanes, full(handicapped)facilities, phone, picnic tables, litter barrels, petwalk, RV dump**

212 to Stonehouse, no facilities

205 to Pumpernickel Valley, no facilities

203 to Iron Point, no facilities

200 Golconda Summit, elev 5145, truck parking area both lanes, litter barrels

194 Golconda, **N...**Waterhole #1 Hotel/gas/groceries, **food:** Z Bar/Grill, **other:** USPO

187 to Button Point, **N...rest area both lanes, full(handicapped)facilities, phone, picnic tables, litter barrels, petwalk, RV dump**

180 NV 794, E Winnemucca Blvd, **2-4 mi S...**High Desert RV Park

Winnemucca

178 NV 289, Winnemucca Blvd, Winnemucca, **S...gas:** Maverik, Pump'n Save/diesel, **food:** Rte 66 Grill, **lodging:** Best Inn, Budget Inn, Cozy Motel, Frontier Motel, Quality Inn, Scott Motel, **other:** CarQuest, carwash, **1 mi S...gas:** Exxon/diesel, Shell, Texaco/diesel, **food:** Burger King, Imachea's Dinnerhouse, Pizza Hut, Subway, **lodging:** La Villa Motel, Pyrenees Motel, Winners Hotel/casino, **other:** HOSPITAL, Radio Shack, Winnemucca RV Park, casinos, to Buckeroo Hall of Fame, same as 176

176 US 95 N, Winnemucca, **N...gas:** Pacific Pride/diesel, **S...gas:** Chevron/24hr, Flying J/Conoco/diesel/LP/rest./24hr/@, 76, Shell, Texaco/diesel, **food:** A&W, Arby's, Baskin-Robbins, Burger King, Denny's, Dos Amigos Mexican, Griddle Diner, Jerry's Rest., KFC, McDonald's, Pizza Hut, RoundTable Pizza, San Fermin Italian, Subway, Taco Bell, Taco Time, **lodging:** Best Western, Day's Inn, Economy Inn, Holiday Inn Express, La Villa Motel, Model T Motel/RV Park, Motel 6, Nevada Motel, Park Hotel, Ponderosa Motel, Pyrennes Motel, Quality Inn, Ramada Ltd, Red Lion Inn/casino, Santa Fe Inn, Scottish Inn, Super 8/RV parking, Thunderbird Motel, Townhouse Motel, Winner's Hotel/casino, **other:** HOSPITAL, Ford/Mercury, Ford/Mercury, Goodyear/auto, JC Penney, Kragen Parts, Raley's Foods, Schwab Tire, Wal-Mart/auto/gas, RV camping, truck repair

173 W Winnemucca, **1 mi S...**airport, industrial area

168 to Rose Creek, **S...**prison area

158 to Cosgrave, **S...rest area both lanes, full(handicapped)facilities, phone, picnic tables, litter barrels, petwalk, RV dump**

151 Mill City, **N...gas:** TA/Arco/Taco Bell/diesel/casino/24hr/@, **lodging:** Super 8, **S...other:** Trading Post/RV park

149 NV 400, Mill City, **1 mi N...gas:** to TA/Arco/Taco Bell/diesel/24hr/@, **lodging:** Super 8, **S...**RV camping

145 Imlay, no facilities

138 Humboldt, no facilities

129 Rye Patch Dam, **N...other:** to Rye Patch RA, RV camping, **S...gas:** TA/Arco/diesel/café/24hr/@

119 Oreana, to Rochester, no facilities

112 to Coal Canyon, **S...**to correctional ctr

Lovelock

107 E Lovelock(from wb), **N...gas:** Exxon/diesel, **lodging:** Desert Plaza Inn, Ramada Inn, Super 10 Inn, **other:** Lazy K Camping

106 Main St, Lovelock, **N...gas:** Chevron/Taco Bell/diesel/LP, Two Stiffs, **food:** McDonald's, Pizza Factory, Ranch House Rest., **lodging:** Covered Wagon Motel, **other:** HOSPITAL, NAPA AutoCare, Radio Shack, Safeway, playground/restrooms, same as 105

105 W Lovelock(from eb), **N...gas:** Exxon/diesel, **lodging:** Lovelock Inn/rest., **other:** HOSPITAL, Brookwood RV Park, museum, same as 106

93 to Toulon, **S...**airport

83 US 95 S, to Fallon, **S...rest area both lanes, full(handicapped)facilities, phone, picnic tables, litter barrels**

78 to Jessup, no facilities

65 to Hot Springs, Nightingale, no facilities

Interstate 80

E / W

48 US 50A, US 95A, E Fernley, to Fallon, **N...gas:** 76/diesel/rest./casino/@, **lodging:** Truck Inn/KFC/Pizza Hut, **other:** RV camping, tires, **S...gas:** Chevron/diesel/casino, Shell/Taco Bell/diesel/24hr/@, **food:** Domino's, McDonald's, **lodging:** Best Western, Super 8, **other:** American Carcare, Goodyear/auto, Radio Shack, Scolari's Foods, Siverado Rest./casino, to Great Basin NP

46 US 95A, W Fernley, **S...gas:** Pilot/DQ/Wendy's/diesel/24hr/@, **other:** Blue Beacon, Fernley RV Park, **1 mi S...gas:** Chevron, Exxon

45mm Truckee River

43 Wadsworth, to Pyramid Lake, **N...gas:** 76/diesel/camping

42mm rest area wb, full(handicapped)facilities, phone, picnic tables, litter barrels, petwalk, check sta eb

40 Painted Rock, no facilities

38 Orchard, no facilities

36 Derby Dam, no facilities

32 Tracy, Clark Station, no facilities

28 NV 655, Patrick, no facilities

27mm scenic view, eb

25mm check sta wb

23 Mustang, **N...food:** Mustang Sta Café, **other:** RV camping

22 Lockwood, no facilities

21 Vista Blvd, Greg St, Sparks, **N...gas:** Chevron/McDonald's, QwikStop, **food:** Del Taco, **lodging:** Fairfield Inn, **other:** HOSPITAL, **S...gas:** Alamo/diesel/rest./24hr/@, **lodging:** Super 8

20 Sparks Blvd, Sparks, **N...gas:** Shell/diesel/24hr, **food:** Carl's Jr, Outback Steaks, **other:** water funpark, **S...gas:** Alamo/diesel/rest./24hr/@, **lodging:** Super 8

Sparks

19 E McCarran Blvd, Sparks, **N...gas:** Beacon, Chevron/diesel, TA/76/diesel/rest./@, Winners Corner, **food:** Applebee's, Arby's, Black Bear Diner, Burger King, Jack-in-the-Box, KFC, Kraig's Rest., Sierra Sid's, Wendy's, Wienerschnitzel, **lodging:** InnCal, Sunrise Motel, Windsor Inn, **other:** $Tree, Ford/Lincoln/Mercury/Isuzu, GNC, Jo-Ann Fabrics, Mervyn's, Radio Shack, Safeway, Sav-On Drug, Suzuki, Victorian RV Park, books, mall, **1 mi N on Prater Way...food:** El Pollo Loco, IHOP, Jack-in-the-Box, McDonald's, Pizza Hut, Sizzler, Subway, Taco Bell, **lodging:** Lariat Motel, **other:** Albertson's, Goodyear, Kragen Parts, LJ Silver, Longs Drugs, Target, **S...food:** Black Forest Rest., Denny's, **lodging:** McCarran House Hotel, **other:** NAPA AutoCare

18 NV 445, Pyramid Way(from eb), Sparks, **N...gas:** Citgo/7-11, **lodging:** Courtyard, Silver Club Hotel/casino, **S...lodging:** Nugget Hotel/casino

17 Rock Blvd, Nugget Ave, Sparks, **N...gas:** Arco/24hr, Exxon, Winners, **other:** Kragen Parts, casinos, **S...lodging:** Nugget Hotel/casino

16 B St, E 4th St, Victorian Ave, **N...gas:** Arco/24hr, Winners, **lodging:** Motel 6, **other:** Rail City Casino, **S...gas:** Arco/diesel/24hr, Chevron/repair, **lodging:** Gold Coin Motel, Hilton

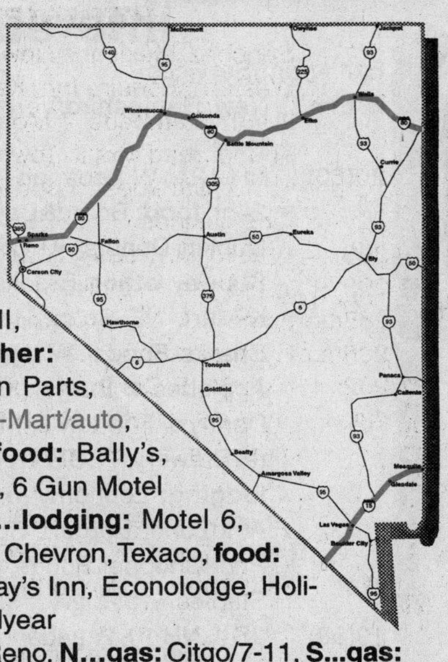

15 US 395, to Carson City, **1 mi N on McCarran Blvd...gas:** Chevron, Shell, Texaco/diesel, **food:** Arby's, Burger King, Del Taco, Szechuan Chinese, Sonic, Subway, Taco Bell, TCBY, Wendy's, **other:** Home Depot, Kragen Parts, OfficeMax, Ross, Wal-Mart/auto, WinCo Foods, **S...food:** Bally's, **lodging:** Holiday Inn, 6 Gun Motel

14 Wells Ave, Reno, **N...lodging:** Motel 6, **other:** bank, **S...gas:** Chevron, Texaco, **food:** Denny's, **lodging:** Day's Inn, Econolodge, Holiday Inn, **other:** Goodyear

13 US 395, Virginia St, Reno, **N...gas:** Citgo/7-11, **S...gas:** Chevron, Shell/diesel, **food:** Dairy Queen, Giant Burger, **lodging:** Ramada Inn, **other:** HOSPITAL, Walgreen, to downtown hotels/casinos, to UNVReno

Reno

12 Keystone Ave, Reno, **N...gas:** Arco/24hr, Citgo/7-11, **food:** Pizza Hut, **lodging:** Gateway Inn, Motel 6, **other:** Raley's Foods, Sav-On Drug, **S...gas:** Chevron, 76/diesel, **food:** Baskin-Robbins, Burger King, Coffee Grinder Rest., Higgy's Pizza, Jack-in-the-Box, McDonald's, Port of Subs, Shakey's Pizza, Taco Bell, Wendy's, **other:** Harrah's, Hilton's, Albertson's, Allied Parts, Olson Tire, Radio Shack, 98 Cents Store, casinos, RV park

10 McCarran Blvd, Reno, **N...gas:** Arco/24hr, Citgo/7-11, Tesoro, **food:** Arby's, Baskin-Robbins, Burger King, Carl's Jr, Chili's, Del Taco, El Pollo Loco, Hacienda Mexican, IHOP, Jack-in-the-Box, KFC, McDonald's, Papa Murphy's, RoundTable Pizza, Schlotsky's, Starbucks, Taco Bell, **other:** MEDICAL CARE, Albertson's, Big O Tire, Kragen Parts, QuikLube/gas, Safeway, Sav-On Drug, ShopKO, Tires+, **S...gas:** Arco/24hr, Citgo/7-11, **lodging:** Summit Ridge Inn, **other:** Home Depot, K-Mart/Little Caesar's

9 Robb Dr, **N...gas:** 76

8 W 4th St(from eb), Robb Dr, Reno, **S...**RV camping

7 Mogul, no facilities

6.5mm truck parking/hist marker/scenic view both lanes

5 to E Verdi(from wb), **N...food:** Backstop Grill, Rattler Ridge Grill(2mi)

4.5mm scenic view eb

4 Garson Rd, Boomtown, **N...gas:** Chevron/diesel/@, **lodging:** Boomtown Hotel/casino, **other:** RV park

3.5mm check sta eb

3 Verdi(from wb), no facilities

2.5mm Truckee River

2 Lp 80, to Verdi, **N...gas:** Arco/diesel/24hr, **food:** Branding Iron Café, Jack-in-the-Box, Taco Bell, **lodging:** Gold Ranch Hotel/casino

1 Gold Ranch Rd(from eb), to Verdi, no facilities

0mm Nevada/California state line

NEW HAMPSHIRE

Interstate 89

N ↕ S Lebanon

Exit #(mm)Services

61mm New Hampshire/Vermont state line, Connecticut River

20(60) NH 12A, W Lebanon, **E...gas:** Mobil/24hr, Sunoco/24hr, **food:** Board&Basket, Brick Oven Pizza, Chili's, Dunkin Donuts, KFC/Taco Bell, Shorty's Mexican, Subway, **other:** Brooks Drug, GNC, Jo-Ann Fabrics, K-Mart, NE Soap&Herb, PowerHouse Mall/shops, Shaw's Foods, **W...gas:** Citgo/diesel/repair, **food:** Applebee's, Burger King, China Light, D'angelo's, Denny's, Friendly's, McDonald's, Pizza Hut, 7 Barrel Brewery, TCBY, Weathervane Seafood, Wendy's, **lodging:** Economy Inn, Fireside Inn, **other:** Ames, AutoZone, Borders Books, CVS Drug, JC Penney, PriceChopper Foods, Radio Shack, Shaw's Foods, Staples, Wal-Mart

19(58) US 4, NH 10, W Lebanon, **E...gas:** Exxon/diesel/24hr, Shell/Blimpie, **food:** China Sta, **other:** Family$, Ford, Harley-Davidson, Honda, NAPA, P&C Foods, Radio Shack, **W...gas:** Sunoco

57mm Welcome Ctr/rest area/weigh sta sb, full(handicapped)facilities, phone, picnic tables, litter barrels, vending, petwalk, weigh sta nb

18(56) NH 120, Lebanon, **E...gas:** Getty/diesel/rest./24hr, **food:** Day's Inn, **other:** Buick/Pontiac/GMC, Chevrolet/Cadillac/VW, Dodge/Mazda, Nissan, to Dartmouth Coll, **W...gas:** Citgo/diesel, Shell, **other:** HOSPITAL, U-Haul

17(54) US 4, to NH 4A, Enfield, **E...food:** Riverside Grill, Shaker Museum, **other:** Tire Kingdom

16(52) Eastman Hill Rd, **E...gas:** Exxon/diesel/24hr, **W...gas:** Mobil/Burger King/diesel/24hr, **other:** Arctic Cat/Kawasaki/Suzuki, Whaleback Ski Area

15(50) Montcalm, no facilities

14(47) NH 10(from sb), no facilities

13(43) NH 10, Grantham, **E...gas:** Gulf/diesel/Gen Store, **food:** Doodle's Diner, **W...gas:** Mobil/repair

40mm rest area nb, full(handicapped)facilities, info, phone, picnic table, litter barrels, vending, petwalk

12A(37) Georges Mills, **W...other:** to Sunapee SP, food, phone, lodging, RV camping

12(34) NH 11 W, New London, **2 mi E...gas:** Exxon/diesel, **lodging:** Maple Hill Country Inn, **other:** HOSPITAL

11(31) NH 11 E, King Hill Rd, New London, **2 mi E...lodging:** Fairway Motel, food

10(27) to NH 114, Sutton, **E...**to Winslow SP, **1 mi W...**lodging, to Wadleigh SB

26mm rest area sb, full(handicapped)facilities, info, phone, picnic tables, litter barrels, vending, petwalk

9(19) NH 103, Warner, **E...gas:** Citgo/Subway/Pizza Hut/TCBY, Exxon, Mobil/diesel/24hr, **food:** Dunkin Donuts, Foothills Rest., McDonald's, MktBasket Foods, **other:** Rollins SP, **W...**to Sunapee SP, ski area

Concord

8(17) NH 103(from nb, no EZ return), Warner, **1 mi E...**gas, food, museum, to Rollins SP

15mm Warner River

7(14) NH 103, Davisville, **E...other:** TrueValue, phone, RV camping(seasonal)

12mm Contoocook River

6(10) NH 127, Contoocook, **1 mi E...gas:** Mobil, Sunoco, **W...other:** Elm Brook Park, Sandy Beach Camping(3mi)

5(8) US 202 W, NH 9(exits left from nb), Hopkinton, **W...**food, RV camping(seasonal)

4(7) NH 103, Hopkinton(from nb, no EZ return), **E...**HorseShoe Tavern, gas

3(4) Stickney Hill Rd(from nb), no facilities

2(2) NH 13, Clinton St, Concord, **E...**HOSPITAL, food, **W...**NH Audubon Ctr

1(1) Logging Mill Rd, Bow, **E...gas:** Mobil/24hr, **lodging:** Hampton Inn

0mm I-93 N to Concord, S to Manchester, I-89 begins/ends on I-93, 36mm.

Interstate 93

Exit#(mm)Services

N ↕ S

2(11) I-91, N to St Johnsbury, S to White River Jct. I-93 begins/ends on I-91, exit 19.

1(8) VT 18, to US 2, to St Johnsbury, **2 mi E...**gas, food, lodging, camping

1mm Welcome Ctr nb, full(handicapped)facilities, info, phone, picnic tables, litter barrels, vending, petwalk

131mm Connecticut River, Vermont/New Hampshire state line. **Exits 1-2 are in VT.**

44(130) NH 18, NH 135, **W...Welcome Ctr(8am-8pm)/scenic vista both lanes, full(handicapped)facilities, info, phone, picnic tables, litter barrels, petwalk**

Littleton

43(125) NH 135(from sb), to NH 18, Littleton, **1-2 mi W...**HOSPITAL, same as 42

42(124) US 302 E, NH 10 N, Littleton, **E...gas:** Citgo, Cumberland, Gulf, Sunoco/24hr, **food:** Burger King, Cantina Di Gerardo, ClamShell Rest., Deluxe Pizza, Dunkin Donuts, Jing Fong Chinese, McDonald's, Oasis Italian, Pizza Hut, Subway, **other:** Brooks Drug, Medicine Shoppe, Parts+, Rite Aid, **W...gas:** Mobil, **lodging:** Travellers Inn, **other:** Butson's Foods, Chevrolet/Buick/Pontiac, Chrysler/Dodge/Jeep, KOA, Radio Shack, Shaw's Foods, Staples, VIP Parts/repair, Wal-Mart

41(122) US 302, NH 18, NH 116, Littleton, **E...gas:** Irving/diesel/24hr, **lodging:** Eastgate Motel/rest.

40(121) US 302, NH 10 E, Bethlehem, **E...gas:** Exxon, **lodging:** Adair Country Inn/rest., **other:** Snowy Mtn Camping, to Mt Washington

39(119) NH 116, NH 18(from sb), N Franconia, Sugar Hill, **W...**lodging

Interstate 93

N ↕ S

Woodstock

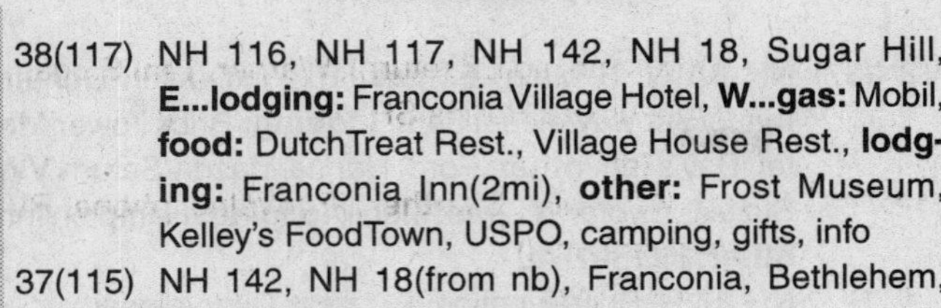

38(117) NH 116, NH 117, NH 142, NH 18, Sugar Hill, **E...lodging:** Franconia Village Hotel, **W...gas:** Mobil, **food:** DutchTreat Rest., Village House Rest., **lodging:** Franconia Inn(2mi), **other:** Frost Museum, Kelley's FoodTown, USPO, camping, gifts, info

37(115) NH 142, NH 18(from nb), Franconia, Bethlehem, **E...lodging:** Inn at Forest Hills

36(114) NH 141, to US 3, S Franconia, **W...**golf, food, lodging

35(113) US 3 N(from nb), to Twin Mtn Lake, no facilities

112mm S Franconia, Franconia Notch SP begins sb

3(111) NH 18, Echo Beach Ski Area, view area, info

2(110) Cannon Mtn Tramway, **W...other:** Boise Rock, Old Man Viewing, Lafayette Place Camping

109mm trailhead parking

108mm Lafayette Place Camping(from sb), trailhead parking

107mm The Basin

1(106) US 3, The Flume Gorge, info, camping(seasonal)

104mm Franconia Notch SP begins nb

33(103) US 3, N Woodstock, **E...food:** Frescolones Pizza, Longhorn Palace Rest., Notchview Country Kitchen, **lodging:** Drummer Boy Motel, Indian Head Resort, Mountaineer Motel/rest., Mt Coolidge Motel, Pemi Motel, Profile Motel, Red Doors Motel, **other:** Indian Head viewing, to Franconia Notch SP, **W...lodging:** Country Bumpkin Cottages/RV Park, Cozy Cabins, Mt Liberty Motel, White Mtn Motel, **other:** Clark's Trading Post, Cold Springs Camping

32(101) NH 112, N Woodstock, Loon Mtn Rd, **E...gas:** Irving, Mobil, Shell/diesel, **food:** Bill&Bob's Roast Beef, Burger King, Dragon Lite Chinese, Earl of Sandwich Rest., GH Pizza, Gypsy Café, House of Pancakes, McDonald's, NE Chowder, 7 Seas Seafood, **lodging:** Comfort Inn, Lincoln Sta Lodge, Loon Mtn Resort, Millhouse Inn/rest., Pollard Brook Resort, River Green Hotel, **other:** MEDICAL CARE, Big A Parts, GNC, Rite Aid, T&C Foods, USPO, to North Country Art Ctr, **W...gas:** Citgo, Mobil, **food:** Café Lafayette, Chalet Rest., Landmark II Rest., Peg's Café, Truant's Rest., **lodging:** Alpine Lodge, Autumn Breeze Motel, Carriage Motel, Woodstock Inn/rest., **other:** NAPA, USPO, candy/fudge/gifts

31(97) to NH 175, Tripoli Rd, **E...**RV camping(seasonal), **W...**KOA(2mi)

30(95) US 3, Woodstock, **E...food:** Frannie's Place Café, **lodging:** Jack-O-Lantern Inn/rest., Pioneer Motel, **other:** golf, **W...**flea mkt, RV camping(seasonal)

29(89) US 3, Thornton, **E...**Pemi River RV Park, **1 mi W...gas:** Citgo/diesel, **lodging:** Gilcrest Motel

28(87) NH 49, Campton, **E...gas:** Citgo, Mobil, **food:** Mad River Rest., **other:** Family Store/deli, USPO, to ski area, RV camping, **W...gas:** Citgo/diesel, **food:** Sunset Grill, **lodging:** Scandinavi-Inn, **other:** Branch Brook Camping

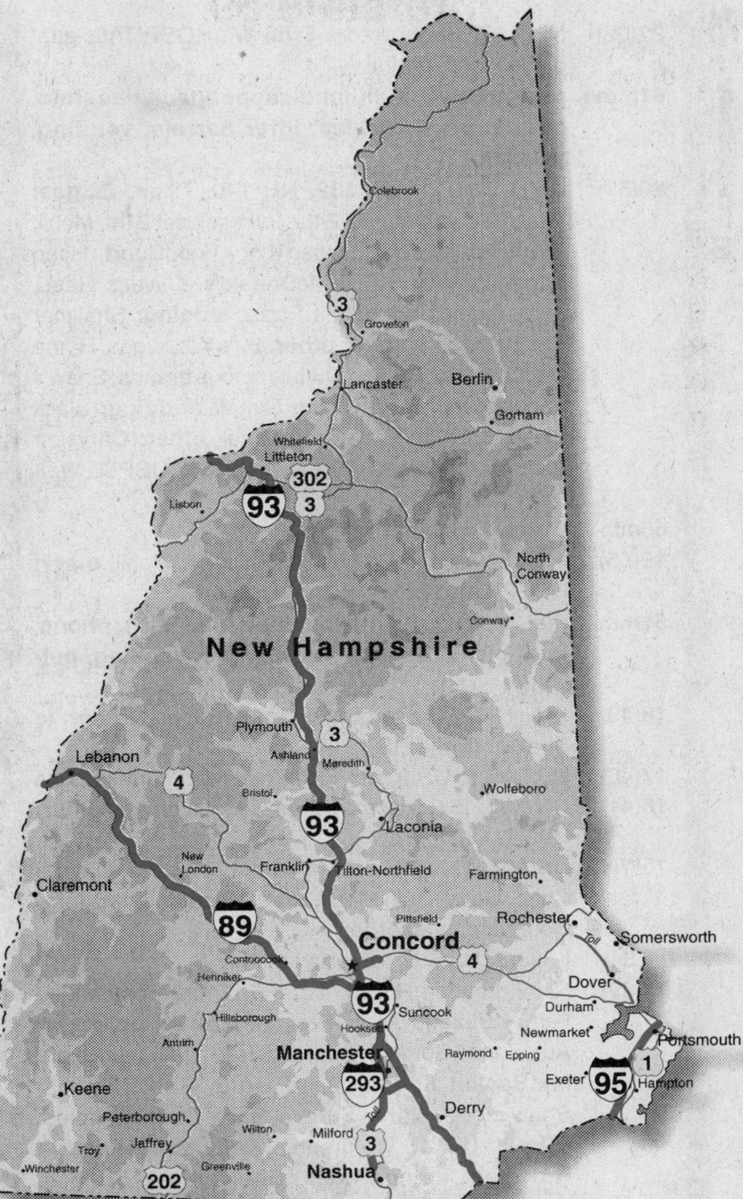

Plymouth

27(84) Blair Rd, Beebe River, **E...food:** Bridge 41 Rest., **lodging:** Red Sleigh Motel/chalets, Super 8

26(83) US 3, NH 25, NH 3A, Tenny Mtn Hwy, **W on US 3...food:** McDonald's, **lodging:** Best Inn, Pilgrim Inn, **other:** HOSPITAL

25(81) NH 175(from nb), Plymouth, **W...gas:** Irving/diesel, Mobil, **food:** Bierhaus Café, Bridgeside Diner, HongKong Garden, Subway, **other:** HOSPITAL, to Holderness School, Plymouth St Coll

24(76) US 3, NH 25, Ashland, **E...gas:** Cumberland, Irving/Subway/diesel, Mobil/diesel, **food:** Burger King, Common Man Diner, **lodging:** Comfort Inn, **other:** Big A Parts, Bob's Foods, USPO, RV camp(4mi)

23(71) NH 104, NH 132, New Hampton, to Mt Washington Valley, **E...gas:** Citgo/diesel, Irving/diesel/24hr, **food:** Dunkin Donuts, Rossi Italian, **other:** USPO, **W...food:** Homestead Rest.(2mi), **other:** Davidson's RV Park(2mi), ski area

NEW HAMPSHIRE

Interstate 93

N ↕ S

22(62) NH 127, Sanbornton, **5 mi W...**HOSPITAL, gas/diesel, food, phone

61mm rest area sb, full(handicapped)facilities, info, phone, picnic tables, litter barrels, vending, petwalk

20(57) US 3, NH 11, NH 132, NH 140, Tilton, **E...gas:** Exxon/Subway/diesel/24hr, Irving/diesel/24hr, Mobil, **food:** Applebee's, Burger King, FoodCourt, Hong Kong Chinese, KFC, McDonald's, Oliver's Rest., Tilt'n Diner, UpperCrust Pizza, **lodging:** Shalimar Resort(3mi), Super 8, **other:** BJ's Whse/gas, Home Depot, Lakes Region Outlet/famous brands, Shaw's Foods, Staples, VIP Auto Ctr, **W...lodging:** Black Swan B&B(2mi), Wayland Motel, **other:** Chrysler/Plymouth/Dodge, Ford/Nissan/Kia, USPO, Wal-Mart/auto

56mm Winnipesaukee River

19(55) NH 132(from nb), Franklin, **W...gas:** Mobil, **other:** HOSPITAL, NH Vet Home, antiques

51mm rest area nb, full(handicapped)facilities, phone, info, picnic tables, litter barrels, vending, petwalk

18(49) to NH 132, Canterbury, **E...gas:** Sunoco, **other:** to Shaker Village HS

17(46) US 4 W, to US 3, NH 132, Boscawen, **4 mi W...**gas

16(41) NH 132, E Concord, **E...gas:** Mobil/diesel, **other:** Quality Cash Mkt

15W(40) US 202 W, to US 3, N Main St, Concord, **W...gas:** Citgo, Getty, Gulf, Mobil, **food:** Friendly's, **lodging:** Courtyard/café, **other:** HOSPITAL

E I-393 E, US 4 E, to Portsmouth

Concord

14(39) NH 9, Loudon Rd, Concord, **E...food:** Boston Mkt, Family Buffet, Panera Bread, Pizzaria Uno, **other:** AutoZone, Borders Books, $Tree, GNC, LLBean, MktBasket Foods, Osco Drug, Radio Shack, Shaw Foods/24hr, Shop'n Save Food, Staples, U-Haul, USPO, Walgreen, **1-2 mi E on Loudon Rd...gas:** Irving, Mobil, Shell/diesel, Sunoco, **food:** Applebee's, Burger King, Chili's, D'angelo's, Dunkin Donuts, Friendly's, KFC, Longhorn Steaks, McDonald's, Olive Garden, PapaGino's, Wendy's, **other:** JC Penney, Sears/auto, Shaw's Foods, Wal-Mart SuperCtr/24hr, **W...gas:** Gulf/diesel, Hess, Exxon/diesel, **food:** Rainbow Buffet, Tea Garden Rest., **lodging:** Holiday Inn, **other:** Ames, Jo-Ann Fabrics, Marshalls, MktBasket Foods, Pill MktPlace, to state offices, hist sites, museum

13(38) to US 3, Manchester St, Concord, **E...gas:** Sunoco/diesel, **food:** Beefside Rest., Cat'n Fiddle Rest., Cityside Grille, Dunkin Donuts, Red Blazer Rest., **other:** Chrysler/Plymouth, Saab, Volvo/Isuzu, **W...gas:** Gulf, Hess, Mobil/diesel/24hr, **food:** Burger King, Common Man Diner, Dunkin Donuts, D'angelo's, Hawaiian Isle Rest., KFC, McDonald's, **lodging:** Best Western, Comfort Inn, Fairfield Inn, **other:** HOSPITAL, BMW, Firestone, GMC, Goodyear/auto, NAPA

12N(37) NH 3A N, S Main, **E...gas:** Exxon/Dunkin Donuts, Irving/Subway/diesel/24hr, **lodging:** Brick Tower Motel, Day's Inn, **other:** Ford, Honda/Mazda/Saturn/VW, Suzuki, Toyota, **W...gas:** Mobil, **lodging:** Hampton Inn, **other:** HOSPITAL

S NH 3A S, Bow Junction, **E...gas:** Citgo/diesel

36mm I-89 N to Lebanon, toll road begins/ends

31mm rest area both lanes, full(handicapped)facilities, info, phone, vending

11(30) NH 3A, to Hooksett, toll plaza, phone, **4 mi E...gas:** Citgo Trkstp/diesel/rest.

28mm I-293(from sb), Everett Tpk

Manchester

10(27) NH 3A, Hooksett, **E...gas:** Irving/diesel, **W...gas:** Exxon, Mobil/diesel, **food:** Big Cheese Pizza

26mm Merrimac River

9N S(24) US 3, NH 28, Manchester, **W...gas:** Exxon/diesel, Mobil, Sunoco/diesel/24hr, **food:** Burger King, D'angelo's, Dunkin Donuts, Happy Garden Chinese, KFC, Little Caesar's, Lusia's Italian, PapaGino's, Shorty's Mexican, **other:** HOSPITAL, Chrysler/Dodge/Jeep, Ford/Lincoln/Mercury, Mercedes, Shop'n Save Foods, U-Haul

8(23) to NH 28a, Wellington Rd, **W...**VA HOSPITAL, Currier Gallery

7(22) NH 101 E, to Portsmouth, Seacoast, no facilities

6(21) Hanover St, Candia Rd, Manchester, **E...food:** Wendy's, **W... gas:** Citgo/diesel, Mobil/diesel, Shell/24hr, **food:** Angelo's Rest., Pizza Boy, McDonald's, **other:** HOSPITAL

19mm I-293 W, to Manchester, to airport

5(15) NH 28, to N Londonderry, **E...gas:** Sunoco/diesel, **food:** Poor Boy's Diner, **3 mi E...gas:** Shell, **food:** Applebee's, Burger King, **other:** Dodge/Jeep, Lincoln/Mercury, NAPA, Sullivan Tire, Victory Foods, Wal-Mart, **W...gas:** Exxon/diesel, **food:** Carboni's Pizza, **lodging:** Sleep Inn, **other:** MEDICAL CARE

Derry

4(12) NH 102, Derry, **E...gas:** Citgo/diesel, Mobil/24hr, Mutual, Shell/24hr, Sunoco/diesel, **food:** Burger King, Cracker Barrel, Derry Rest., **other:** HOSPITAL, **W...gas:** Citgo/7-11, Exxon/diesel, Shell/diesel, **food:** Domino's, Happy Garden Chinese, McDonald's, PapaGino's, Wendy's, **other:** Chrysler/Plymouth, Ford, Home Depot, K-Mart/Little Caesar's, Radio Shack, Shaw's Foods, USPO, VIP Auto, Walgreen

8mm weigh sta both lanes

3(6) NH 111, Windham, **E...gas:** Citgo/diesel, Sunoco/24hr, **food:** Capri Pizza, Dunkin Donuts, House of Pizza, Subway, **W...gas:** Exxon, **other:** Castleton Conference Ctr/rest.

2(3) to NH 38, NH 97, Salem, **E...gas:** Sunoco, **lodging:** Red Roof Inn, **W...gas:** Citgo, **food:** KC Steaks, Lucy's Country Store/subs, **lodging:** Fairfield Inn, Holiday Inn

Interstate 93

N ↕ S

1(2)	NH 28, Salem, **E...gas:** Citgo, Exxon, Getty, **food:** Burger King, Denny's, McDonald's, 99 Rest., **lodging:** Park View Inn, **other:** Barnes&Noble, Best Buy, Dodge/Nissan/Toyota, Filene's, Home Depot, JC Penney, K-Mart, Macy's, MktBasket Foods, Sears/auto, Shaw's Foods, Staples, Target, Walgreen, racetrack, mall
1mm	**Welcome Ctr nb, full(handicapped)facilities, info, phone, picnic tables, litter barrels, vending, petwalk**
0mm	New Hampshire/Massachusetts

Interstate 95

N ↕ S

Portsmouth

Exit #(mm)	Services
17mm	New Hampshire/Maine state line, Piscataqua River
7(16)	Portsmouth, Port Authority, waterfront hist sites, **W...food:** Applebee's, Schoolhouse Rest., Wendy's, **lodging:** Courtyard, **other:** BJ's Whse/gas, K-Mart
6(15)	Woodbury Ave(from nb), Portsmouth, **E...gas:** Gulf, Shell, **lodging:** Anchorage Inn
5(14)	US 1, US 4, NH 16, The Circle, Portsmouth, **E... gas:** Gulf, Shell/diesel, **food:** Bickford's, Momma D's Rest., **lodging:** Anchorage Inn, Best Inn, Best Western, Holiday Inn, **other:** HOSPITAL, Pontiac/Cadillac/GMC, **W...gas:** Exxon, **food:** Dunkin Donuts, McDonald's, Pizza Hut, **lodging:** Hampton Inn, **other:** Ford, Home Depot, Mazda/VW, Nissan, Saturn
4(13.5)	US 4(from nb), to White Mtns, Spaulding TPK, **E...**HOSPITAL, **W...**to Pease Int Trade Port
3a(13)	NH 33, Greenland
3b(12)	NH 101, to Portsmouth, **E...**HOSPITAL, **W...gas:** Mobil/diesel, Sunoco/diesel, TA/diesel/rest./24hr/@, **food:** McDonald's(1mi)
2(6)	NH 51, to Hampton, **1 mi E on US 1...food:** McDonald's, **other:** HOSPITAL
5.5mm	toll plaza
4mm	Taylor River
1(1)	NH 107, to Seabrook, toll rd begins/ends, **E...gas:** Getty, Sunoco, **food:** Applebee's, Burger King, D'Angelo's, KFC, McDonald's, Pizza Hut/Taco Bell, Road Kill Café, Subway, Wendy's, **lodging:** Hampshire Motel, **other:** AutoZone, CVS Drug, GNC, Jo-Ann Crafts, MktBasket Foods, NAPA, Radio Shack, Shaw's Foods, Staples, Wal-Mart, to Seacoast RA, **W...gas:** Citgo, **food:** Capt K's Seafood, McGrath's Dining, **lodging:** Best Western, **other:** Sam's Club, Seabrook Greyhound Pk
.5mm	**Welcome Ctr nb, full(handicapped)facilities, phone, vending, picnic tables, litter barrels, petwalk**
0mm	New Hampshire/Massachusetts state line

Interstate 293(Manchester)

Manchester

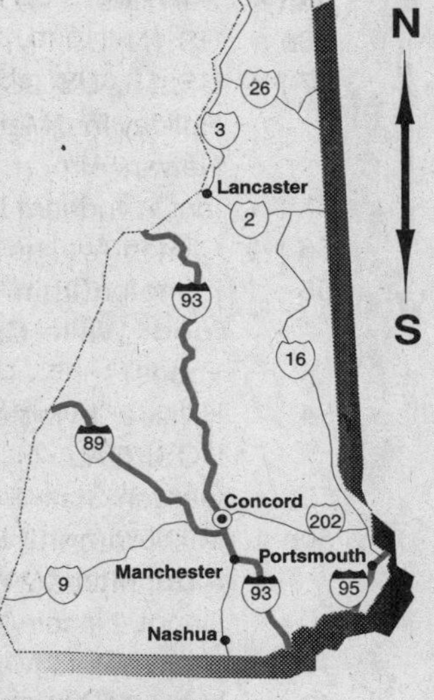

Exit#(mm)	Services
8(9)	I-93, N to Concord, S to Derry. I-293 begins/ends on I-93, 28mm.
7(6.5)	NH 3A N, Dunbarton Rd(from nb), no facilities
6(6)	Singer Park, Manchester, **E...gas:** Sunoco, **food:** Hooters, **lodging:** Ramada Inn, **W...gas:** Mobil, Shell/diesel, **other:** HOSPITAL,
5(5)	Granite St, Manchester(from nb, no EZ return), **E...lodging:** Holiday Inn, **W...gas:** Citgo/7-11, Exxon, M&H, **food:** Dunkin Donuts, **other:** HOSPITAL
4(4)	US 3, NH 3A, NH 114A, Queen City Br, **E...gas:** Citgo/7-11, Sunoco, **lodging:** Queen City Inn, **W on US 3...gas:** Gulf/diesel, Hess/diesel, Mobil, **food:** Applebee's, Bickford's, Burger King, D'angelo's, DQ, KFC, McDonald's, Papa John's, Subway, Wendy's, **lodging:** Comfort Inn, Econolodge, **other:** Goodyear, Osco Drug, Subaru
3(3)	NH 101, **W on US 3...food:** China Buffet, Outback Steaks, T-Bonz Rest., **lodging:** Wayfarer Inn, **other:** Bob's Store, CVS Drug, Macy's, Marshalls, Radio Shack, Shop&Save, Staples, VIP Auto
2.5mm	Merrimac River
2(2)	NH 3A, Brown Ave, **S...gas:** Citgo/Subway/diesel, Citgo/7-11, Shell/repair, **food:** Beijing Chinese, Kwikava, McDonald's, Rick's Café, **lodging:** Super 8
1(1)	NH 28, S Willow Rd, **N...gas:** Mobil/Pizza Hut/diesel, Sunoco/diesel, **food:** Bickford's, Boston Mkt, Burger King, Chili's, Friendly's, McDonald's, PapaGino's, Taco Bell, Wendy's, Yee Dynasty Chinese, **lodging:** Fairfield Inn, Sheraton, **other:** HOSPITAL, AutoZone, Batteries+, Buick/Chevrolet, Circuit City, CVS Drug, $Tree, GMC, Harley-Davidson, Home Depot, Mercedes, Michael's, Nissan/Mitsubishi, OfficeMax, Osco Drug, PepBoys, Pontiac/Cadillac/Mazda, Sam's Club, Tire Whse, Town Fair Tire, U-Haul, VW, **S...gas:** Exxon/diesel, Shell, **food:** Antics Grill, Bertucci's, Bickford's, ChuckeCheese, FoodCourt, Ground Round, Longhorn Steaks, 99 Rest., Olive Garden, Pizzaria Uno, Ruby Tuesday, TGIFriday, **lodging:** Courtyard, TownePlace Suites, **other:** HOSPITAL, Barnes&Noble, Best Buy, Chrysler/Plymouth, Filene's, Ford, Honda, Hyundai, JC Penney, K-Mart, Lexus, NTB, Saturn, Sears/auto, Staples, Toyota, Wal-Mart, mall
0mm	I-93, N to Concord, S to Derry. I-293 begins/ends on I-93.

NEW JERSEY

Interstate 78

E ↔ W — Newark

Exit #	Services
58b a	US 1N, US 9N, NJ Tpk, no facilities
57	US 1S, US 9S, **S...lodging:** Day's Inn, Courtyard, Holiday Inn, Marriott, Ramada Inn, Sheraton, **other:** to Newark Airport, **3 mi S...lodging:** Day's Inn, Hampton Inn, Wyndham Garden
56	Clinton Ave, no facilities
55	Irvington(from wb), **N...gas:** Amoco, Hess/diesel, **food:** White Castle, **other:** HOSPITAL, PathMark Foods
54	Hillside, Irvington(from eb), **N...gas:** Amoco, **other:** HOSPITAL
52	Garden State Pkwy, no facilities
50b a	Millburn(from wb), **N...gas:** Amoco, Exxon, Mobil, **food:** Manny's Weiners, **other:** Firestone/auto, Home Depot, Lincoln/Mercury, USPO
49b	(from eb), to Maplewood, same as 50b a
48	to NJ 24, NJ 124, to I-287 N, Springfield, no facilities
47mm	I-78 eb divides into express & local
45	NJ 527(from eb), Glenside Ave, Summit, no facilities
44	(from eb), to Berkeley Heights, New Providence, no facilities
43	(from wb), to New Providence, no facilities
41	Scotch Plains, to Berkeley Heights, no facilities
40	NJ 531, The Plainfields, **S...gas:** Amoco/24hr(1mi), **other:** HOSPITAL
36	NJ 651, to Warrenville, Basking Ridge, **N...gas:** Exxon/service/24hr, **S...gas:** Amoco(1mi)
33	NJ 525, to Martinsville, Bernardsville, PGA Golf Museum, **N...lodging:** Somerset Hills Inn/rest., **S...gas:** Amoco/24hr
32mm	scenic overlook wb
29	I-287, to US 202, US 206, I-80, to Morristown, Somerville, **S...**HOSPITAL
26	NJ 523 spur, Lamington, to North Branch, no facilities
24	NJ 523, to NJ 517, to Oldwick, Whitehouse, **2 mi S...gas:** Exxon/diesel/24hr
20b a	NJ 639(from wb), Lebanon, to Cokesbury, **S...gas:** Exxon/24hr, Shell/24hr, **food:** Cokesbury Inn Rest., Dunkin Donuts, **other:** to Round Valley RA
18	US 22 E, Annandale, Lebanon, **N...**HOSPITAL, same as 17, **S...**Honda
17	NJ 31 S, Clinton, **N...gas:** Amoco/24hr, Hess, **food:** King Buffet, McDonald's, **1 mi N...food:** TingHo Chinese, **other:** Chrysler/Plymouth/Dodge/Jeep/Ford, ShopRite Foods, to Spruce Run RA, **S...other:** Chevrolet
16	NJ 31 N(from eb), Clinton, **N...food:** King Buffet, McDonald's, A&P, bank, same as 17
15	NJ 173 E, Clinton, to Pittstown, **N...gas:** Citgo, Shell/diesel/24hr, **food:** Clinton House Rest., Subway, **lodging:** Holiday Inn, **other:** museum, **S...food:** Cracker Barrel, Frank's Pizza, Hunan Wok, **lodging:** Hampton Inn, **other:** HOSPITAL, $Tree, Laneco Foods, Wal-Mart/grill
13	NJ 173 W(from wb), **N...food:** Sherwood Crossing Rest., same as 12
12	NJ 173, Norton, to Jutland, **N...gas:** Citgo/Johnny's Rest./diesel, Exxon/diesel, **food:** Coach'n Paddock, **other:** to Spruce Run RA, **S...gas:** Shell/diesel
11	NJ 173, West Portal, Pattenburg, **N...gas:** Coastal/24hr, Shell/diesel, **food:** Chalet Rest., Landslide Rest., **other:** Jugtown RV Park, to st police
8mm	**rest area both lanes, picnic tables, litter barrels, no restrooms**
7	NJ 173, to Bloomsbury, West Portal, **N...**RV camping, **S...gas:** Citgo/diesel/rest./24hr, Pilot/Subway/diesel/24hr/@, TA/Mobil/diesel/rest./24hr/@
6	Warren Glen, Asbury(from eb), no facilities
4	Warren Glen, Stewartsville(from wb), no facilities
3.5mm	weigh sta eb
3	US 22, NJ 173, to Phillipsburg, **N...gas:** PennJersey/diesel/rest./24hr/@, US/diesel/24hr, **other:** HOSPITAL, **1 mi N...gas:** Citgo/diesel, **food:** Almond Tree Rest., Burger King, Domino's, Key City Diner(3mi), McDonald's, Perkins, Ponderosa, Ruby Tuesday, **lodging:** Holiday Inn, Phillipsburg Inn, **other:** Home Depot, Honda, Laneco Foods, ShopRite Foods, Wal-Mart/auto, **S...other:** Chevrolet/Isuzu
0mm	New Jersey/Pennsylvania state line, Delaware River

Clinton

Interstate 80

E ↔ W

Exit #	Services
	I-80 begins/ends at G Washington Bridge in Ft Lee, NJ.
73mm	toll plaza eb
72b	US 1 S, US 9, **N...food:** Red Oak Rest., **other:** Staples
a	US 46, NJ 4, **N...gas:** Amoco, Exxon/Subway, Getty, Gulf, Hess/diesel, Mobil, Sunoco, **food:** Bennigan's, **lodging:** Best Western, Holiday Inn, **S...gas:** Mobil, Shell, **lodging:** Courtesy Inn, Hilton
71	Broad Ave, Leonia, Englewood, **N...gas:** Gulf, **lodging:** Day's Inn, Executive Inn, **S...gas:** Shell
70b a	NJ 93, Leonia, Teaneck, **N...gas:** Marriott, **other:** HOSPITAL
68b a	I-95, N to New York, S to Philadelphia, to US 46
67	to Bogota(from eb), no facilities
66	Hudson St, to Hackensack, **N...gas:** Getty
65	Green St, S Hackensack, **S...gas:** Exxon, **lodging:** Hilton
64b a	NJ 17 S, to US 46 E, Newark, Paramus, **S...gas:** Amoco/24hr, Exxon, **food:** Baskin-Robbins, Crown Plaza, **other:** PathMark Foods
63	NJ 17 N, **N...gas:** Amoco/24hr, Citgo, Gulf, Hess/diesel/24hr; **other:** HOSPITAL, CVS Drug, Harley-Davidson, Home Depot
62b a	GS Pkwy, to Saddle Brook, **N...gas:** Shell, **lodging:** Howard Johnson, Marriott, **S...lodging:** Holiday Inn
61	NJ 507, to Garfield, Elmwood Park, **N...**Marcal Paper Co, **S...gas:** Sunoco

Interstate 80

E ↕ W Paterson

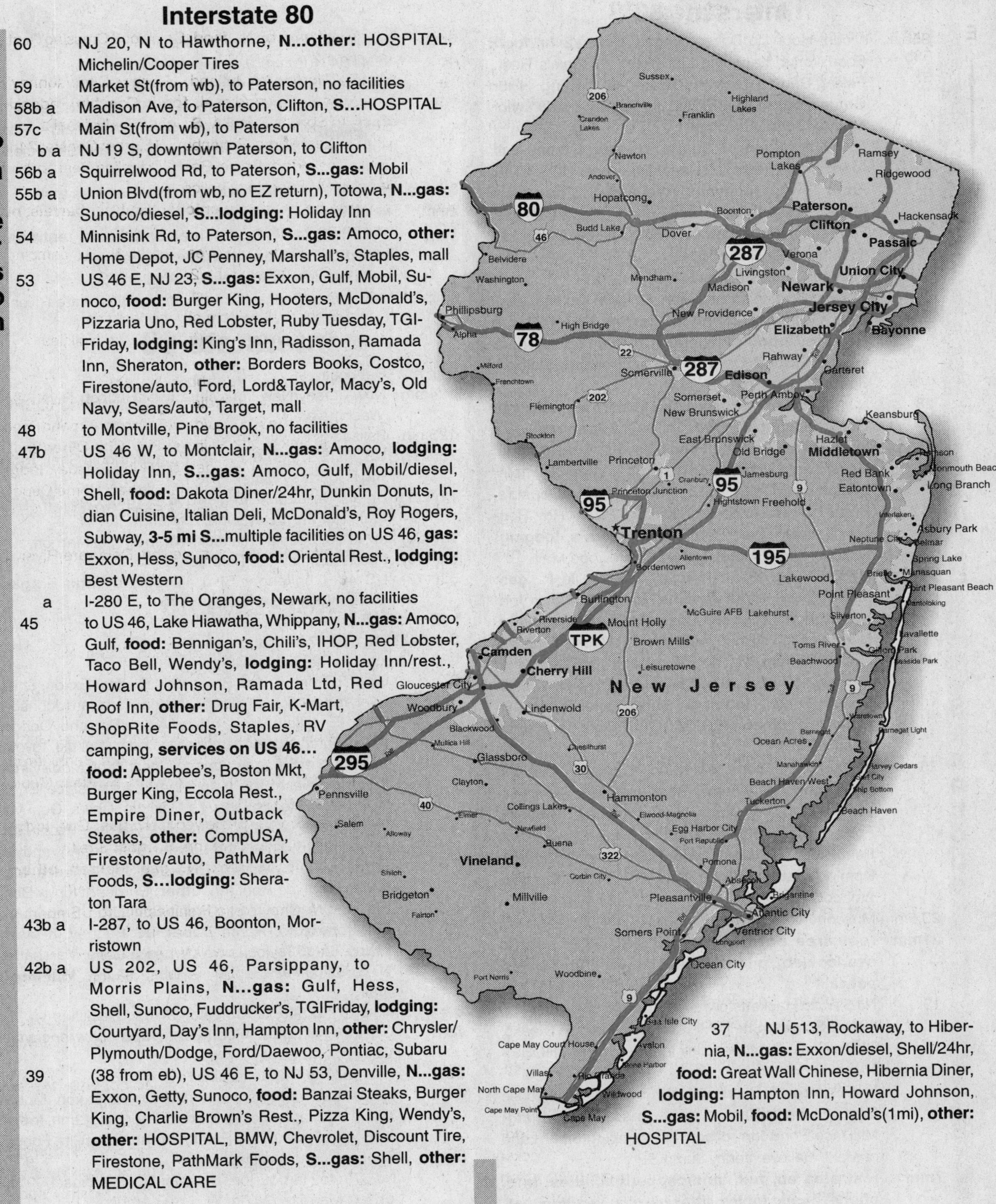

60 NJ 20, N to Hawthorne, **N...other:** HOSPITAL, Michelin/Cooper Tires

59 Market St(from wb), to Paterson, no facilities

58b a Madison Ave, to Paterson, Clifton, **S...**HOSPITAL

57c Main St(from wb), to Paterson

b a NJ 19 S, downtown Paterson, to Clifton

56b a Squirrelwood Rd, to Paterson, **S...gas:** Mobil

55b a Union Blvd(from wb, no EZ return), Totowa, **N...gas:** Sunoco/diesel, **S...lodging:** Holiday Inn

54 Minnisink Rd, to Paterson, **S...gas:** Amoco, **other:** Home Depot, JC Penney, Marshall's, Staples, mall

53 US 46 E, NJ 23, **S...gas:** Exxon, Gulf, Mobil, Sunoco, **food:** Burger King, Hooters, McDonald's, Pizzaria Uno, Red Lobster, Ruby Tuesday, TGI-Friday, **lodging:** King's Inn, Radisson, Ramada Inn, Sheraton, **other:** Borders Books, Costco, Firestone/auto, Ford, Lord&Taylor, Macy's, Old Navy, Sears/auto, Target, mall

48 to Montville, Pine Brook, no facilities

47b US 46 W, to Montclair, **N...gas:** Amoco, **lodging:** Holiday Inn, **S...gas:** Amoco, Gulf, Mobil/diesel, Shell, **food:** Dakota Diner/24hr, Dunkin Donuts, Indian Cuisine, Italian Deli, McDonald's, Roy Rogers, Subway, **3-5 mi S...**multiple facilities on US 46, **gas:** Exxon, Hess, Sunoco, **food:** Oriental Rest., **lodging:** Best Western

a I-280 E, to The Oranges, Newark, no facilities

45 to US 46, Lake Hiawatha, Whippany, **N...gas:** Amoco, Gulf, **food:** Bennigan's, Chili's, IHOP, Red Lobster, Taco Bell, Wendy's, **lodging:** Holiday Inn/rest., Howard Johnson, Ramada Ltd, Red Roof Inn, **other:** Drug Fair, K-Mart, ShopRite Foods, Staples, RV camping, **services on US 46... food:** Applebee's, Boston Mkt, Burger King, Eccola Rest., Empire Diner, Outback Steaks, **other:** CompUSA, Firestone/auto, PathMark Foods, **S...lodging:** Sheraton Tara

43b a I-287, to US 46, Boonton, Morristown

42b a US 202, US 46, Parsippany, to Morris Plains, **N...gas:** Gulf, Hess, Shell, Sunoco, Fuddrucker's, TGIFriday, **lodging:** Courtyard, Day's Inn, Hampton Inn, **other:** Chrysler/Plymouth/Dodge, Ford/Daewoo, Pontiac, Subaru

39 (38 from eb), US 46 E, to NJ 53, Denville, **N...gas:** Exxon, Getty, Sunoco, **food:** Banzai Steaks, Burger King, Charlie Brown's Rest., Pizza King, Wendy's, **other:** HOSPITAL, BMW, Chevrolet, Discount Tire, Firestone, PathMark Foods, **S...gas:** Shell, **other:** MEDICAL CARE

37 NJ 513, Rockaway, to Hibernia, **N...gas:** Exxon/diesel, Shell/24hr, **food:** Great Wall Chinese, Hibernia Diner, **lodging:** Hampton Inn, Howard Johnson, **S...gas:** Mobil, **food:** McDonald's(1mi), **other:** HOSPITAL

NEW JERSEY

Interstate 80

E ↕ W

35b a Mount Hope, to Dover, **S...gas:** Exxon/24hr, **food:** FoodWorks, Laughing Lion Rest., Maggie's Rest., Peking Garden, Sizzler, 13 Eateries, **lodging:** Hilton Garden, **other:** HOSPITAL, JC Penney, Lord&Taylor, Macy's, Sears/auto, mall

34b a NJ 15, Wharton, to Sparta, **N...gas:** Exxon, Gulf, **food:** Donut Town, McDonald's, **other:** HOSPITAL, Food Town, Goodyear, Rite Aid, **S...food:** Ann Marie's Ristorante, Dunkin Donuts, King's Chinese, Townsquare Diner, **other:** Costco, Home Depot, OfficeMax, ShopRite Foods

32mm truck rest area wb, no facilities

30 Howard Blvd, to Mt Arlington, **N...gas:** Exxon/diesel/24hr, Gulf/diesel/24r, **food:** Cracker Barrel, Davy's Hotdogs, **lodging:** Sheraton, **other:** QuickCheck Foods, **S...food:** David's Rest., McDonald's, Outback Steaks

28 NJ 10, to Ledgewood, Lake Hopatcong, **S...gas:** G&N/diesel/repair, **food:** Cliff's Grill, **lodging:** Day's Inn, **other:** ShopRite Foods, Toyota, **1 mi S...gas:** Hess/diesel, Shell, **food:** Burger King, Blimpie, Boston Mkt, ChiChi's, Dunkin Donuts, McDonald's, Pizza Hut, Red Lobster, Roxbury Pizza, Roy Rogers, Subway, Taco Bell, TCBY, Wendy's, **lodging:** Roxbury Circle Motel, **other:** Ledgewood Mall

27 US 206 S, NJ 182, to Netcong, Somerville, **N...gas:** Mobil/diesel, **food:** Perkins, **lodging:** Day's Inn, **other:** Ford, **S...gas:** Coastal, Shell/diesel/24hr, **food:** Joseph's Rest., McDonald's, Rose's Diner

26 US 46 W(from wb, no EZ return), to Budd Lake, **S...gas:** Pennzoil, Shell/diesel, **food:** DQ, Dunkin Donuts, Perkins, **lodging:** Henry's Motel, Budd Lake Motel, A&P, **other:** MEDICAL CARE, Goodyear/auto, Service Tires

25 US 206 N, Stanhope, to Newton, **N...gas:** Exxon/24hr, Shell, **food:** Tasty Family Rest., **lodging:** Black Forest Inn/rest., Wyndham Garden, **other:** ShopRite Foods, to Waterloo Village, Int Trade Ctr, **S...gas:** PetroStop, Shell/24hr, **food:** Budd Lake Diner/rest., Domino's, **other:** URGENT CARE, **1-2 mi S... gas:** Amoco/24hr, 7-11

Stanhope

23.5mm Musconetcong River

21mm rest area both lanes, NO TRUCKS, scenic overlook(eb), phone, picnic tables, litter barrels, petwalk

19 NJ 517, to Hackettstown, Andover, **N...**RV camping, **1-2 mi S...gas:** Shell, 7-11, **food:** Babalou's Steaks, BLD's Rest., Panther Valley Inn/rest., **other:** HOSPITAL

12 NJ 521, Hope, to Blairstown, **N...food:** Maxwell House Rest., Nathan's Rest., **1 mi S...gas:** Shell, **lodging:** MillRace Pond Inn, **other:** RV camping(5mi), Land of Make Believe, Jenny Jump SF

7mm rest area eb, full(handicapped)facilities, info, phone, picnic tables, litter barrels, vending, petwalk

6mm scenic overlook wb, no trailers

4c to NJ 94 N(from eb), to Blairstown

b to US 46 E, to Buttzville

a NJ 94, to US 46 E, Columbia, to Portland, **N...gas:** TA/BP/Taco Bell/diesel/24hr/@, **food:** McDonald's, Pizza Hut, **other:** DayStop, RV camping, **S...gas:** Shell/diesel/24hr

3.5mm Hainesburg Rd(from wb) accesses services at 4

2mm weigh sta eb

1mm Worthington SF, S...rest area both lanes, restrooms, info, picnic tables, litter barrels, petwalk

1 to Millbrook(from wb), **N...**Worthington SF

0mm New Jersey/Pennsylvania state line, Delaware River

Interstate 95

N ↕ S

Exit # Services

124mm New Jersey/New York state line, Hudson River, Geo Washington Br

123mm Palisades Pkwy(from sb)

72(122) US 1, US 9, US 46, Ft Lee, **E...gas:** Mobil, Shell, **lodging:** Courtesy Motel, Hilton

71(121) Broad Ave, Leonia, Englewood, **E...gas:** Shell, **W...gas:** Gulf, **lodging:** Day's Inn, Executive Inn

70(120) to NJ 93, Leonia, Teaneck, **W...lodging:** Marriott

69(119) I-80 W(from sb), to Paterson

68(118) US 46, Challenger Blvd, Ridgefield Park, **E...gas:** Exxon, **lodging:** Hampton Inn

I-95 and NJ Turnpike run together sb

See NJ TPK, exits 7A through 18.

I-95 nb becomes I-295 sb at US 1.

67b a US 1, to Trenton, New Brunswick, **E...gas:** Exxon, Shell/24hr, **food:** Michael's Diner, **lodging:** Howard Johnson, Sleep-E Hollow Motel, **other:** Acura/Porsche, Dodge/Isuzu, Ford/Lincoln/Mercury, Mercedes, Suzuki, Toyota, Volvo, **1-3 mi W...gas:** Amoco/diesel/24hr, Mobil/Circle K/Blimpie/diesel, **food:** Applebee's, Asia Palace, Charlie Brown's Steaks, Chevy's Mexican, Chili's, Denny's, Joe's Crabshack, NY Deli, Olive Garden, Pizza Hut, Princetonian Diner, Red Lobster, TGIFriday, Wendy's, **lodging:** Best Western, Extended Stay America, McIntosh Inn, Red Roof Inn, **other:** Barnes&Noble, Best Buy, BMW, Chevrolet, Circuit City, Drug Emporium, Firestone/auto, Home Depot, JC Penney, K-Mart, Lexus, Lord&Taylor, Lowe's Whse, Macy's, Marshall's, NTB, OfficeMax, PepBoys, Ross, Staples, **Wal-Mart**, mall

Trenton

8 NJ 583, NJ 546, to Princeton Pike, no facilities

7b a US 206, **W...gas:** Mobil/24hr, **food:** Lawrenceville Deli

5b a Federal City Rd, no facilities

4b a NJ 31, to Ewing, Pennington, **W...gas:** Exxon, Mobil/Circle K/Blimpie/diesel, **food:** Burger King(2mi), **lodging:** Wild Flowers Inn Eatery, **other:** ShopRite Foods

3b a Scotch Rd, no facilities

2 NJ 579, to Harbourton, **E...gas:** Coastal/diesel, 7-11, **other:** Marrazzo's Mkt, **W...gas:** Amoco

1 NJ 29, to Trenton, **2 mi W...**museum, st police

0mm New Jersey/Pennsylvania state line, Delaware River

Turnpike

N ↕ S

Exit #(mm)	Services
18(117)	US 46 E, Ft Lee, Hackensack, last exit before toll sb
17(116)	Lincoln Tunnel
115mm	**Vince Lombardi Service Plaza nb...Sunoco/diesel, Big Boy, Nathan's, Roy Rogers, TCBY, gifts**
114mm	toll plaza, phone
16W(113)	NJ 3, Secaucus, Rutherford, **E...gas:** Hess, Shell, **lodging:** Hilton, M Plaza Hotel, **W...lodging:** Sheraton, **other:** Meadowlands
112mm	**Alexander Hamilton Service Area sb...Sunoco, Roy Rogers, gifts**
16E(112)	NJ 3, Secaucus, **E...**Lincoln Tunnel
15W(109)	I-280, Newark, The Oranges
15E(107)	US 1, US 9, Newark, Jersey City, **E...**Lincoln Tunnel
14c	Holland Tunnel
14b	Jersey City
14a	Bayonne
14(105)	I-78 W, US 1, US 9, **2 mi W...lodging:** Holiday Inn, Marriott, Radisson, **other:** airport
102mm	**Halsey Service Area, Sunoco, Roy Rogers, other services in Elizabeth**
13a(102)	Elizabeth, **E...**Ikea Furnishings, **W...lodging:** Hilton, Wyndham Garden
13(100)	I-278, to Verrazano Narrows Bridge
12(96)	Carteret, Rahway, **E...food:** McDonald's, **lodging:** Holiday Inn
93mm	**Cleveland Service Area nb...gas: Sunoco/diesel, food: Roy Rogers, TCBY, T Edison Service Area sb...gas: Sunoco/diesel, food: Big Boy, Dunkin Donuts, Roy Rogers, Starbucks, TCBY**
11(91)	US 9, Garden State Pkwy, to Woodbridge, **E...** Home Depot
10(88)	I-287, NJ 514, to Perth Amboy, **W...gas:** Hess/diesel, **lodging:** Holiday Inn, Ramada/rest.
9(83)	US 1, NJ 18, to New Brunswick, E Brunswick, **E...lodging:** Ramada Inn, **other:** Kinko's, **W...gas:** Exxon, **food:** Bennigan's, Fuddrucker's, **lodging:** Hilton, Howard Johnson Express
79mm	**Kilmer Service Area nb...gas: Sunoco/diesel, food: Big Boy, Roy Rogers, TCBY, other: gifts**
8a(74)	to Jamesburg, Cranbury, **E...lodging:** Holiday Inn/rest., **W...lodging:** Courtyard
72mm	**Pitcher Service Area sb...gas: Sunoco/diesel, food: Big Boy, Cinnabon, Nathan's, Roy Rogers, TCBY**
8(67)	NJ 33, NJ 571, Highstown, **E...gas:** Exxon/diesel, Hess/diesel, Mobil, Shell, **food:** 8 Diner, Prestige Diner, **lodging:** Day's Inn, Ramada Inn, **other:** Thriftway Foods, **W...food:** Coach&4 Rest., **lodging:** TownHouse Motel
7a(60)	I-195 W to Trenton, E to Neptune, no facilities
59mm	Richard Stockton Service Area sb...gas: Sunoco/diesel, food: Big Boy, Roy Rogers, TCBY, Woodrow Wilson Service Area nb...gas: Sunoco, food: Roy Rogers, Big Boy
7(54)	US 206, to Bordentown, Trenton, to Ft Dix, McGuire AFB, to I-295, **Services on US 206...gas:** Mobil/diesel, Petro/diesel/rest./24hr/@, Pilot/Wendy's/diesel/@, Sunoco, WaWa, **food:** Burger King, Denny's, Macedonia Rest., **lodging:** Best Western/rest., Comfort Inn, Day's Inn/rest., Ramada Inn, **other:** RV Ctr, AG Transmissons
6(51)	I-276, to Pa Turnpike, no facilities
5(44)	Willingboro, to Mount Holly, **E...gas:** US/diesel, **food:** Applebee's, Charlie Brown's Steaks, Cracker Barrel, **lodging:** Best Western, Hampton Inn, **W...gas:** Mobil, **food:** Applebee's, TGIFriday, **lodging:** Best Western, Econolodge, Holiday Inn Express, **other:** Home Depot
39mm	**James Fenimore Cooper Service Area nb...gas: Sunoco/diesel, food: Big Boy, Roy Rogers, TCBY, other: gifts**
4(34)	NJ 73, to Philadelphia, Camden, **E...gas:** Exxon, Mobil/diesel, 7-11, **food:** Bennigan's, Chili's, Copperfield's Rest., Denny's, McDonald's, Sage Diner, Wendy's, **lodging:** Candlewood Suites, Extended Stay America, Hampton Inn, Laurel Place Inn, McIntosh Inn, Studio+, Wyndham Hotel, **other:** Cadillac, Ford, Saturn, West Marine, **1-2 mi W...gas:** Exxon, Gulf/diesel, Hess, Mobil/Circle K/diesel, Shell, Texaco, **food:** Bob Evans, Burger King, Dunkin Donuts, KFC, Pizza Hut, **lodging:** Courtyard, Day's Inn, Econolodge, Fairfield Inn, Hampton Inn, Motel 6, Radisson, Ramada Inn/rest., Red Roof Inn, Super 8, Track&Turf Motel, **other:** Lincoln/Mercury, Mazda, transmissions, to st aquarium
30mm	**Walt Whitman Service Area sb...gas: Sunoco, food: Roy Rogers, Nathan's, TCBY, other: gifts**
3(26)	NJ 168, Camden, Woodbury, Atlantic City Expwy, Walt Whitman Br, **E...gas:** WaWa, **lodging:** Comfort Inn, Holiday Inn, **other:** CVS Drug, **W...gas:** BP, Coastal, Gulf, Xtra/diesel, **food:** Dunkin Donuts, Papa John's, Pizza Hut, Wendy's, **lodging:** Econolodge
2(13)	US 322, to Swedesboro, **W...gas:** Shell/diesel
5mm	**Barton Service Area sb...gas: Sunoco, Big Boy, Nathan's, TCBY, gifts, Fenwick Service Area nb...gas: Sunoco, food: Big Boy, Taco Bell, TCBY, gifts**
1(1.2)	Deepwater, **E...gas:** truckstop/diesel, **lodging:** Del Valley Motel, **other:** HOSPITAL, **W...gas:** Mobil/diesel, Pilot/diesel/24hr/Subway/@, Shell/diesel/

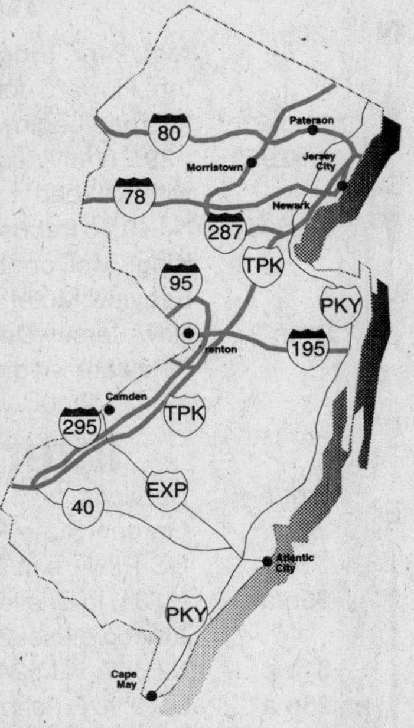

Camden

NEW JERSEY

Turnpike

N ↕ S

	rest./24hr, **lodging:** Friendship Motor Inn, Holiday Inn, Howard Johnson
1mm	toll road begins/ends
2(I-295)	I-295 N divides from toll road, I-295 S converges with toll road
1(I-295)	NJ 49, to Pennsville, **E...gas:** Sunoco, **food:** Burger King, McDonald's, **other:** Cadillac, **W...lodging:** Seaview Motel
0mm	New Jersey/Delaware state line, Delaware River, Delaware Memorial Bridge

Interstate 195

E ↕ W

Freehold

Exit #	Services
36	Garden State Parkway N. I-195 begins/ends on GS Pkwy, exit 99.
35b a	NJ 34, to Brielle, Pt Pleasant, GS Pkwy S. **S...gas:** Amoco/diesel/24hr
31b a	NJ 547, NJ 524, to Farmingdale, **N...**to Allaire SP
28b a	US 9, to Freehold, Lakewood, **N...food:** Ivy League Rest., Lino's Pizza, Stewart's RootBeer, **other:** bank, **S...gas:** Exxon/24hr, Getty, Gulf, Mobil/diesel/24hr, **food:** Arby's, Boston Mkt, Burger King, Jersey Mike's, McDonald's, Taco Bell, **other:** GNC, Grand Union Foods, K-Mart, PathMark Foods, PepBoys, Phar-Mor, Radio Shack, Staples
22	to Jackson Mills, Georgia, **N...**to Turkey Swamp Park
21	NJ 526, NJ 527, to Jackson, Siloam, no facilities
16	NJ 537, to Freehold, **N...gas:** Amoco/24hr, Remington/diesel/LP, Sunoco, **food:** FoodCourt, Java Moon Café, Luigi's Pizza, S&S Deli, **other:** HOSPITAL, 6 Flags Outlet/famous brands, **S...gas:** Wawa/diesel/24hr, **food:** Burger King, KFC, McDonald's, **lodging:** Millstone Inn Rest., Red Cedar Village Pizza
11	NJ 524, Imlaystown, to Horse Park of NJ
8	NJ 539, Allentown, **S...gas:** Amoco/repair, Mobil(1mi), **food:** American Hero Deli, **other:** Crosswicks HP
7	NJ 526(from eb, no return), Robbinsville, Allentown, **1 mi S...food:** La Piazza Ristorante
6	NJ Tpk, N to NY, S to DE Memorial Br
5b a	US 130, **N...gas:** Coastal/diesel, **food:** A Better Pizza, ShrimpKing Rest., **other:** Harley-Davidson, **S...gas:** Gulf/diesel/24hr, **food:** Savoy's Rest., **lodging:** Econolodge(4mi), **other:** Harry's Army Navy, Home Depot, USPO, to state aquarium
3b a	Hamilton Square, Yardville, **N...**HOSPITAL
2	US 206 S, S Broad St, Yardville, **N...gas:** 7-11, **food:** Pizza Star, Taco Bell, **other:** Midas Muffler, **1 mi S...gas:** Amoco, Shell, **food:** Burger King, Ivy Rest., McDonald's, Wendy's
1b a	US 206, **N...food:** Anthony's Pizza, Burger King, McDonald's, **other:** Radio Shack, Rite Aid
0mm	I-295. I-195 begins/ends in Trenton.

Interstate 287

N ↕ S

Exit #	Services
68mm	New Jersey/New York state line
66	NJ 17 S, Mahwah, **E...gas:** Dean Gas, Mahwah Fuel/deli, Mobil/Subway/diesel, **food:** Burger King, Mason Jar Rest., McDonald's, 17 Diner, **lodging:** Comfort Inn, Courtyard, Ramada Inn, Sheraton, Wellesley Inn(3mi), **other:** Saturn
59	NJ 208 S, Franklin Lakes, **W...gas:** Super Stop'n Shop Foods
58	US 202, Oakland, **E...gas:** Mobil, **W...gas:** Exxon/24hr, **food:** Tony's Bros Pizza, **other:** ShopRite Foods
57	Skyline Dr, Ringwood, no facilities
55	NJ 511, Pompton Lakes, **W...food:** Burger King, **other:** A&P, FoodTown
53	NJ 511A, rd 694, Bloomingdale, Pompton Lakes, **E...gas:** Coastal, Sunoco, **food:** Blimpie
52b a	NJ 23, Riverdale, Wayne, Butler, **E...gas:** Amoco, Mobil, Sunoco/diesel, **food:** McDonald's, Rupert's Rest., **other:** A&P, Buick/Pontiac/GMC, **W...gas:** Mobil, Shell/24hr
47	US 202, Montville, Lincoln Park, **E...gas:** Exxon/24hr, **food:** Harrigan's Rest.
45	Myrtle Ave, Boonton, **W...gas:** Citgo, Exxon, **food:** Dunkin Donuts, McDonald's, Subway, **other:** A&P/24hr, Buick/GMC, Drug Fair, GNC
43	Intervale Rd, to Mountain Lakes, **E...gas:** Shell, **W...**Dodge
42	US 46, US 202, **W...gas:** Exxon, Shell, Sunoco, **food:** Applebee's, Fuddrucker's, McDonald's, **lodging:** Courtyard, Day's Inn, Embassy Suites, Garden Suites, Hampton Inn, **other:** Chrysler/Jeep/Pontiac/Subaru, Ford
41b a	I-80, E to New York, W to Allentown
40	NJ 511, Parsippany Rd, to Whippany, **W...gas:** Mobil, Shell, **food:** Fuddrucker's, McDonald's, **lodging:** Day's Inn
39b a	NJ 10, Dover, Whippany, **E...lodging:** Courtyard, Ramada Inn, **W...gas:** Exxon, Mobil, **food:** Hong Kong Buffet, **lodging:** Hilton, Howard Johnson, Marriott, Summerfield Suites, **other:** Buick/GMC/Isuzu
37	NJ 24 E, Springfield, no facilities
36b a	rd 510, Morris Ave, Lafayette, no facilities
35	NJ 124, South St, Madison Ave, Morristown, E...food: Friendly's, W...lodging: Best Western, HQ Plaza Hotel, other: HOSPITAL
33	Harter Rd, no facilities
33mm	rest area nb, full(handicapped)facilities, phone, picnic tables, litter barrels, vending, petwalk
30b a	to US 202, N Maple Ave, Basking Ridge, **E...food:** Ironwood Rest., **W...gas:** Gulf, **food:** Friendly's, Grain-House Rest., **lodging:** Olde Mill Inn/rest.
26b a	rd 525 S, Mt Airy Rd, Liberty Corner, no facilities

Interstate 287

22b a US 202, US 206, Pluckemin, Bedminster, **E...gas:** Amoco, Exxon, Gulf, **food:** Burger King, Golden Chinese, McDonald's, **other:** CVS Drug, King's Foods, **W...gas:** Shell, **food:** Dunkin Donuts

21b a I-78, E to NY, W to PA

17 US 206(from sb), Bridgewater, **W...gas:** Hess, Shell/diesel, **food:** TGIFriday, **other:** Borders Books, Lord&Taylor, Macy's, OfficeMax, mall

14b a US 22, to US 202/206, **E...gas:** Exxon, Hess, **other:** Chevrolet/Lexus, **W...gas:** Amoco, **food:** Felix #9 Diner, Fuddrucker's, Red Lobster, **other:** Acura, Mercedes, Pontiac/Cadillac

13b a NJ 28, Bound Brook, **E...gas:** Amoco/24hr, Mobil/diesel, **food:** Burger King, Costa del Sol Mexican, King Lobster Buffet, Subway, Texas Weiners, **other:** ShopRite Foods, **W...food:** Applebee's, ChuckeCheese, McDonald's, **lodging:** Hilton Garden, **other:** HOSPITAL, Costco, Home Depot, Marshall's, Michael's, Old Navy, PepBoys, Target

12 Weston Canal Rd, Manville, **E...gas:** Shell, **W...food:** SportsTime Rest., **lodging:** Ramada Inn

10 NJ 527, Easton Ave, New Brunswick, **E...gas:** Shell, **other:** Marriott, **W...gas:** Amoco, Coastal, **lodging:** Holiday Inn, Doubletree, Hampton Inn, Summerfield Suites, **other:** HOSPITAL, Garden State Exhibit Ctr

9 NJ 514, River Rd, **W...lodging:** Embassy Suites, Sheraton

8.5mm weigh sta nb

8 Possumtown Rd, Highland Park, no facilities

7 S Randolphville Rd, Piscataway, **E...gas:** Mobil

6 Washington Ave, Piscataway, **W...food:** Applebee's, TGIFriday, **other:** ShopRite Foods, same as 5

5 NJ 529, Stelton Rd, Dunellen, **E...gas:** Amoco/diesel, Gulf, Mobil, Shell, Texaco/diesel, **food:** KFC, Piancone Ristorante, **lodging:** Ramada Ltd, **other:** Home Depot, NAPA, **W...gas:** Exxon, **food:** Burger King, Friendly's, Gianni Pizza, Grand Buffet, McDonald's, Red Lobster, Taco Bell, TGIFriday, Wendy's, **lodging:** Day's Inn, Motel 6, Holiday Inn, **other:** K-Mart, Lowe's Whse, OfficeMax, PathMark Foods, Radio Shack, Staples, Stern's, Wal-Mart/auto

4 Durham Ave, S Plainfield, **E...gas:** Mobil/diesel, **other:** HOSPITAL

3 New Durham Rd(from sb), **W...lodging:** Red Roof Inn

2b a NJ 27, Metuchen, New Brunswick, **W...gas:** Amoco, **other:** Costco

1b a US 1, **1-2 mi N on US 1...gas:** Amoco/24hr, Citgo, Exxon/diesel, Getty, Mobil, Shell, **food:** Bennigan's, Blimpie, Boston Mkt, ChiChi's, Dunkin Donuts, KFC, Macaroni Grill, McDonald's, Menlo Park Diner, Red Lobster, Ruby Tuesday, Sizzler, Steak&Ale, Uno Pizzaria, Wendy's, White Castle, **lodging:** Sheraton, **other:** Best Buy, Drug Fair, Ford, Goodyear/auto, Macy's, Marshall's, Nordstrom's, Sears/auto, ShopRite Foods, Staples, Stern's, mall, **S...gas:** Shell, **food:** Applebee's, Boston Mkt, Burger King, McDonald's, **lodging:** Wellesley Inn, **other:** BJ's Whse, BMW, Home Depot, Infiniti, Mercedes, Office Depot, PepBoys, Stop&Shop Foods

I-287 begins/ends on NJ 440.

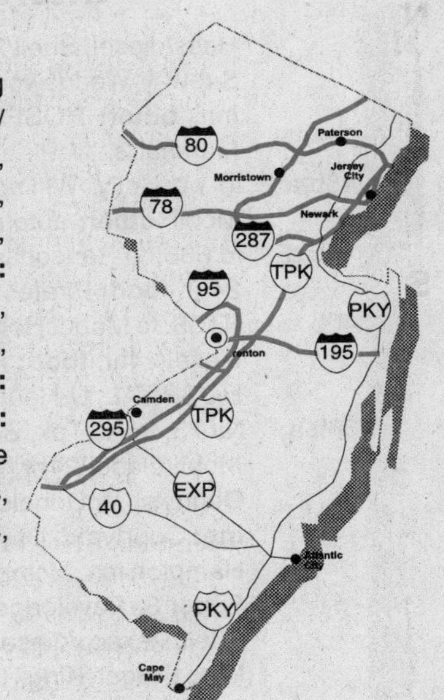

Trenton

Interstate 295

Exit # Services

67b a US 1. I-295 nb becomes I-95 sb at US 1. **See NJ I-95, exit 67b a.**

65b a Sloan Ave, **E...gas:** Exxon, **food:** Burger King, Dunkin Donuts, Taco Bell, **other:** CVS Drug, Goodyear, ShopRite Foods

64 NJ 535 N(from sb), to NJ 33 E, same as 63

63b a NJ 33 W(from nb), rd 535, Mercerville, Trenton, **E...gas:** Citgo, Mobil, **food:** Applebee's, McDonald's, Popeye's, Vincent's Pizza, **other:** Ford/Lincoln/Mercury, **W...gas:** Amoco/diesel, Exxon/24hr, WaWa, **food:** Burger King, Dunkin Donuts, Golden Gate Diner/24hr, Vito's Pizza, **other:** Drug Emporium, ShopRite Foods

62 Olden Ave N(from sb, no return), **W...gas:** Delta

61b a Arena Dr, White Horse Ave, **W...gas:** 7-11

60b a I-195, to I-95, W to Trenton, E to Neptune

58mm scenic overlook both lanes

57b a US 130, US 206, **E...gas:** Mobil, Shell/24hr, **food:** Burger King, Denny's, Ground Round, McDonald's, Rosario's Pizza, **lodging:** Comfort Inn, Econolodge, **other:** Acme Foods, Saturn, **W...**st police

56 US 206 S(from nb, no return), to NJ Tpk, Ft Dix, McGuire AFB, **E...gas:** Sunoco, **lodging:** Day's Inn, Holiday Inn Express, same as 57

52b a rd 656, to Columbus, Florence, **E...gas:** Petro/diesel/rest./24hr/@, Pilot/Wendy's/diesel/24hr/@

50mm rest area both lanes(7am-11pm), full(handicapped)facilities, phone, picnic tables, litter barrels, vending, RV dump

47b a NJ 541, to Mount Holly, Burlington, NJ Tpk, **E...gas:** Exxon/diesel/24hr, Mobil, **food:** Applebee's, Burger King, Cracker Barrel, FoodCourt, McDonald's, Taco Bell, TGIFriday, **lodging:** Best Western, Econolodge, Hampton Inn, Holiday Inn Express, Howard Johnson, **other:** MEDICAL CARE, $Express, Home Depot, Kohl's, OfficeMax, Sears, Target, mall, **W...gas:** Exxon, Gulf/repair,

NEW JERSEY

Interstate 295

N
S

Hess/diesel, Shell/24hr, **food:** Checker's, Friendly's, Subway, Wedgewood Farms Rest., **lodging:** Sunrise Inn, **other:** HOSPITAL, ABC Parts, Acme Foods, Marshall's, Wal-Mart/auto

45b a to Mt Holly, Willingboro, **E...**HOSPITAL, **W...gas:** Mobil, **other:** auto repair

43b a rd 636, to Rancocas Woods, Delran, **W...gas:** Shell/24hr, **food:** Pirates Rest., **other:** HOSPITAL

40b a NJ 38, to Mount Holly, **W...gas:** Mobil, Shell/Subway/diesel/24hr, **food:** FoodCourt, Perkins(3mi), **other:** HOSPITAL, U-Haul

36b a NJ 73, to NJ Tpk, Berlin, Tacony Br, **E...gas:** Exxon, Mobil/diesel/24hr, **food:** Bennigan's, Bob Evans, Denny's, McDonald's, Sage Diner, Wendy's, **lodging:** Courtyard, Day's Inn, Econolodge, Fairfield Inn, Hampton Inn, McIntosh Inn, Radisson, Red Roof Inn, Super 8, Travelodge, Wingate Inn, **W...gas:** Amoco, Shell, Texaco/diesel/24hr, **food:** Bertucci's, Boston Mkt, Burger King, Don Pablo, Dunkin Donuts, Old Town Buffet, Perkins, Pizza Hut, Ponderosa, Togo's, Wendy's, **lodging:** Crossland Suites, Motel 6, Rodeway Inn, Track&Turf Motel, **other:** Barnes&Noble, Best Buy, Chrysler, CompUSA, $Tree, Drug Emporium, Firestone/auto, Filene's, Goodyear/auto, Home Depot, Infiniti, K-Mart, Lexus, Loehmann's, Lord&Taylor, Mitsubishi, OfficeMax, Old Navy, PepBoys, PharMor, Ross, Sears/auto, ShopRite Foods, mall

Cherry Hill

34b a NJ 70, Cherry Hill, to Camden, **E...gas:** Amoco, Exxon/24hr, **food:** Big John's Steaks, Burger King, Dunkin Donuts, Friendly's, Korea Garden Rest., McDonald's, Pizzaria Uno, **lodging:** Extended Stay America, Marriott, Residence Inn, **other:** STS Tire/auto, **W...gas:** Mobil/repair/24hr, Shell/diesel, **food:** Androtti's Café, Denny's, Old Country Buffet, Steak&Ale, **lodging:** Hilton(3mi), Holiday Inn(3mi), Howard Johnson(4mi), Sheraton/rest., **other:** HOSPITAL, Magaziner's Drug

32 NJ 561, to Haddonfield, Voorhees, **3 mi E...gas:** Mobil/diesel/24hr, **food:** Applebee's, FoodCourt, Olive Garden, Vito's Pizza, **lodging:** Hampton Inn, **other:** HOSPITAL, USPO, **W...gas:** Shell, **food:** Burger King

31 Woodcrest Station, no facilities

30 Warwick Rd(from sb), no facilities

29b a US 30, to Berlin, Collingswood, **E...gas:** Amoco, Gulf, Exxon, Shell, **food:** Burger King, Church's, KFC, Oriental Buffet, Wendy's, **lodging:** Barrington Motel, **other:** AutoZone, Drug Emporium, Home Depot, K-Mart, PathMark Foods, transmissions, **W...gas:** Shell

28 NJ 168, to NJ Tpk, Belmawr, Mt Ephraim, **E...gas:** BP, Coastal/diesel, Xtra Fuel, Shell/diesel, **food:** Burger King, Club Diner, Dunkin Donuts, MeiMei Chinese, Papa John's, Wendy's, **lodging:** Comfort Inn, Econolodge, Holiday Inn, Sterling Inn, **other:** Walgreen, **W...gas:** Amoco, Exxon/LP/24hr, Hess, Mobil, **food:** Stewart's RootBeer, McDonald's, Seafood Galley Rest., Taco Bell, **lodging:** Budget Inn, ABC Parts, CVS Drug

26 I-76, NJ 42, to I-676, Walt Whitman Bridge

25b a NJ 47, to Westville, Deptford, no facilities

24b a NJ 45, NJ 551(no EZ sb return), to Westville, **E...gas:** Getty, Gulf, **food:** Colonial Café, **other:** HOSPITAL,**W...**Chevrolet

23 US 130 N, to National Park

22 NJ 644, to Red Bank, Woodbury, **E...gas:** Mobil, **W...gas:** Crown Point Trkstp/diesel/@

21 NJ 44 S, Paulsboro, Woodbury, **W...gas:** WaWa, **lodging:** Westwood Motor Lodge

20 NJ 643, to NJ 660, Thorofare, to National Park, **E...lodging:** Best Western

19 NJ 656, to NJ 44, Mantua, no facilities

18b a NJ 667, to NJ 678, Clarksboro, Mt Royal, **E...gas:** Amoco/diesel, TA/diesel/rest./@, **food:** Dunkin Donuts, KFC/Taco Bell, McDonald's, Wendy's, **W...gas:** Shell/diesel

17 NJ 680, Gibbstown, to Mickleton, **W...gas:** Mobil, **food:** Burger King, Panda House Chinese, **lodging:** Ramada Inn, **other:** Rite Aid, Thriftway Foods

16b NJ 551, to Gibbstown, Mickleton, no facilities

a NJ 653, to Paulsboro, Swedesboro, no facilities

15 NJ 607, to Gibbstown, no facilities

14 NJ 684, to Repaupo, no facilities

13 US 130 S, US 322 W, to Bridgeport, **W...food:** Naples Pizza

11 US 322 E, to Mullica Hill, no facilities

10 Ctr Square Rd, to Swedesboro, **E...gas:** Shell/repair, WaWa/deli, **food:** McDonald's, **lodging:** Hampton Inn, Holiday Inn Select, **W...other:** Camping World RV Supplies/service

7 to Auburn, Pedricktown, **E...gas:** AutoTruck/diesel/rest./motel

4 NJ 48, Woodstown, Penns Grove

3mm weigh sta nb

2mm rest area nb, full(handicapped)facilities, info, phone, picnic table, litter barrels, vending

2c to US 130(from sb), Deepwater, **W...gas:** Flying J/CountryMkt/diesel/LP/24hr/@, TA/Blimpie/Popeye's/diesel/rest./24hr/@, **other:** HOSPITAL

b US 40 E, to NJ Tpk, **E...gas:** Mobil/diesel, Pilot/Subway/diesel/24hr/@, **lodging:** Comfort Inn, Friendship Motel, Holiday Inn Express, Quality Inn, Turnpike Inn, Wellesley Inn

a US 40 W(from nb), to Delaware Bridge

1c NJ 551 S, Hook Rd, to Salem, **E...lodging:** White Oaks Motel, **W...**HOSPITAL

b US 130 N(from nb), Penns Grove

a NJ 49 E, to Pennsville, Salem, **E...gas:** Exxon/diesel/repair, **food:** Burger King, Cracker Barrel, KFC/Taco Bell, McDonald's, **lodging:** Hampton Inn, **W...lodging:** Seaview Motel

0mm New Jersey/Delaware state line, Delaware River, Delaware Memorial Bridge

NEW MEXICO

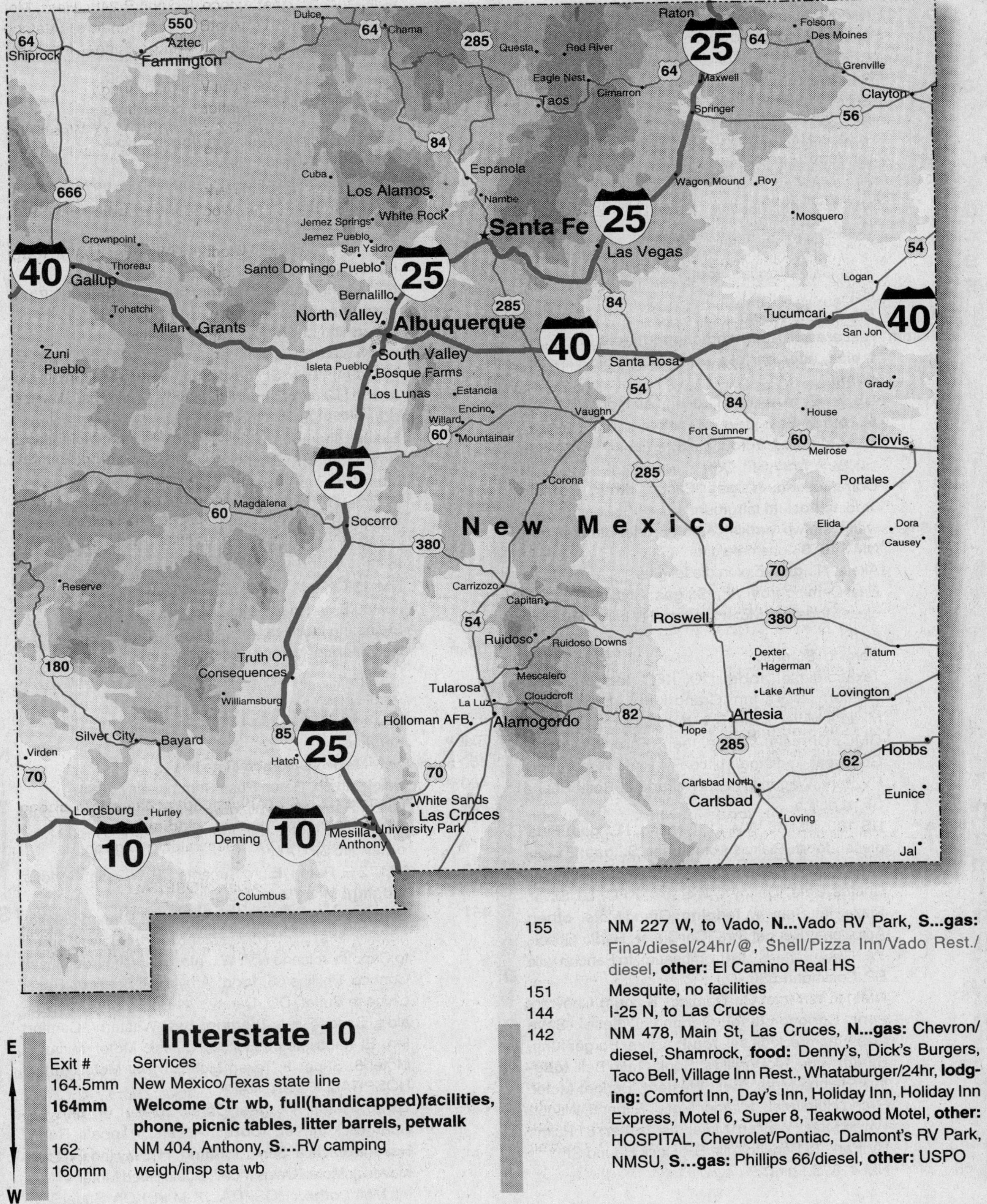

Interstate 10

E ↕ W

Exit #	Services
164.5mm	New Mexico/Texas state line
164mm	**Welcome Ctr wb, full(handicapped)facilities, phone, picnic tables, litter barrels, petwalk**
162	NM 404, Anthony, **S...**RV camping
160mm	weigh/insp sta wb
155	NM 227 W, to Vado, **N...**Vado RV Park, **S...gas:** Fina/diesel/24hr/@, Shell/Pizza Inn/Vado Rest./diesel, **other:** El Camino Real HS
151	Mesquite, no facilities
144	I-25 N, to Las Cruces
142	NM 478, Main St, Las Cruces, **N...gas:** Chevron/diesel, Shamrock, **food:** Denny's, Dick's Burgers, Taco Bell, Village Inn Rest., Whataburger/24hr, **lodging:** Comfort Inn, Day's Inn, Holiday Inn, Holiday Inn Express, Motel 6, Super 8, Teakwood Motel, **other:** HOSPITAL, Chevrolet/Pontiac, Dalmont's RV Park, NMSU, **S...gas:** Phillips 66/diesel, **other:** USPO

NEW MEXICO

Interstate 10

E ↕ W — Las Cruces

140 NM 28, Las Cruces, to Mesilla, **N...gas:** Phillips 66/diesel, **food:** Blake's Lotaburger, BurgerTime, Cracker Barrel, McDonald's, **lodging:** Baymont Inn, Best Western, Hampton Inn, La Quinta, SpringHill Suites, **other:** Wal-Mart SuperCtr/24hr, **N on Valley Dr...gas:** Shell/diesel, **food:** DQ, Domino's, Old Town Rest., **other:** Dodge, Toyota, VW, **S...other:** Harley-Davidson, RV Doc's RV Park, S&H RV Ctr

139 NM 292, Amador Ave, Motel Blvd, Las Cruces, **N...gas:** Pilot/Subway/diesel/24hr/@, TA/Burger King/Taco Bell/diesel/rest./24hr/@, **S...food:** Pit-Stop Café Mexican, **lodging:** Coachlight Inn/RV Park

138mm Rio Grande River

135.5mm rest area eb, full(handicapped)facilities, picnic tables, litter barrels, petwalk, scenic view, RV dump

135 US 70 E, to W Las Cruces, Alamogordo, **1 mi N...other:** Best View RV Park

132 **N**...to airport, fairgrounds, **S...gas:** Love's/Texaco/Subway/diesel/24hr/@

127 Corralitos Rd, **N...gas:** Exxon, **other:** Bowlin's Trading Post, to fairgrounds

120.5mm weigh sta wb, parking area eb, litter barrels

116 NM 549, **S**...gas/café/gifts

102 Akela, **N...gas:** Exxon/diesel/gifts

85 East Deming(from wb), **S...gas:** Chevron, Texaco/diesel, **lodging:** Motel 6, **other:** RV camping, same as 83

83 Deming, **S...gas:** Chevron/diesel, Fina, Save Gas, Texaco/diesel, **food:** DQ, KFC, **lodging:** Best Western, Day's Inn, Grand Motel, Holiday Inn, Mirador Motel, Motel 6, **other:** Chevrolet/Pontiac/GMC, Chrysler/Dodge/Jeep, Ford, Firestone, Goodyear, radiators, Little RV Park, Roadrunner RV Park, Wagon Wheel RV Park, to Rock Hound SP, st police

Deming

82b a US 180, NM 26, NM 11, Deming, **N... gas:** Fina/diesel, **food:** Blake's Lotaburger, **S...gas:** Exxon, Phillips 66, Shell/diesel, **food:** Burger King, Cactus Café, Denny's, K-Bob's, KFC, LJ Silver, Pizza Hut, Subway, **lodging:** Grand Motel, **other:** AutoZone, Budget Tire, CarQuest, Radio Shack, Wal-Mart SuperCtr/24hr, museum, to Pancho Villa SP, Rockhound SP

81 NM 11, W Motel Dr, Deming, **S...gas:** Chevron/24hr, Conoco/diesel, DemingTT/diesel, Save Gas, Shamrock/diesel, **food:** Arby's, Burger King, Burger Time, McDonald's, Sonic, Taco Bell, **lodging:** Balboa Motel, Best Western, Budget Motel, Grand Hotel/rest., Mirador Motel, Super 8, Wagon Wheel Motel, Western Motel/rest., **other:** 81 Palms RV Park, to Pancho Villa SP, Rock Hound SP

68 NM 418, **S...gas:** Savoy/diesel/rest./24hr

62 Gage, **S...gas:** Citgo/DQ/diesel, **other:** Butterfield Station RV Park

61mm rest area wb, full(handicapped)facilities, picnic tables, litter barrels, vending, petwalk

55 Quincy, no facilities

53mm rest area eb, full(handicapped)facilities, picnic tables, litter barrels, vending, petwalk

51.5mm Continental Divide, elev 4585

49 NM 146 S, to Hachita, Antelope Wells, no facilities

42 Separ, **S...gas:** Chevron/diesel, **other:** Bowlin's Continental Divide Gifts

34 NM 113 S, Muir, Playas, no facilities

29 no facilities

24 US 70, E Motel Dr, Lordsburg, **N...gas:** Chevron, Pilot/Arby's/diesel/24hr/@, **lodging:** Budget Motel, **other:** Range RV Park

Lordsburg

23.5mm weigh sta both lanes

22 NM 494, Main St, Lordsburg, **N...gas:** Save Gas, **food:** DQ, McDonald's, **lodging:** Holiday Motel, **other:** CarQuest, Chevrolet, Ford, **S...gas:** Chevron, Exxon, Shamrock, **food:** KFC/Taco Bell, Kranberry's Rest., **lodging:** Best Western, Holiday Inn Express, Motel 10, Super 8, **other:** KOA

20b a W Motel Dr, Lordsburg, **Visitors Ctr/full(handicapped)facilities, info, N...gas:** Love's/Texaco/A&W/Subway/diesel/@, **lodging:** Day's Inn

15 to Gary, no facilities

11 NM 338 S, to Animas, no facilities

5 NM 80 S, to Road Forks, **S...gas:** USA/diesel/rest.

3 Steins, no facilities

0mm New Mexico/Arizona state line

Interstate 25

N ↕ S — Raton

Exit #	Services
460.5mm	New Mexico/Colorado state line
460	weigh sta sb, Raton Pass Summit, elev 7834
454	Lp 25, Raton, **2 mi W...gas:** Texaco, **lodging:** Budget Host, Capri Motel, El Portal Motel, Robin Hood Motel, **other:** HOSPITAL,
452	NM 72 E, Raton, **E**...to Sugarite SP, **W...gas:** Conoco, **lodging:** Mesa Vista Motel
451	US 64 E, US 87 E, Raton, **E...gas:** Chevron/diesel, Texaco/diesel, Total/diesel/24hr, **food:** Subway, **other:** to Capulin Volcano NM, **W**...info, **gas:** Chevron/diesel, Conoco, Phillips 66, **food:** Arby's, All Seasons Rest., Chinese Buffet, DQ, Denny's, K-Bob's, KFC, McDonald's, Sands Rest., **lodging:** Best Western/, Comfort Inn, El Kapp Motel, Holiday Classic Motel, Microtel, Motel 6, Super 8, Texan Motel, Travel Motel, **other:** HOSPITAL, K-Mart, NAPA
450	Lp 25, Raton, **W...gas:** Conoco/diesel, Phillips 66, Shamrock/diesel, **food:** K-Bob's, Pappa's Rest., Rainmaker Café, Sonic, **lodging:** Holiday Inn Express, Maverick Motel, Oasis Motel, Robin Hood Motel, Village Inn Motel, **other:** HOSPITAL, K-Mart, KOA, SuperSave Foods

Interstate 25

N ↕ S

446 US 64 W, to Cimarron, Taos, **4 mi W...**NRA Whittington Ctr, camping
440mm Canadian River
435 Tinaja, no facilities
434.5mm rest area both lanes, full(handicapped)facilities, weather info, picnic tables, litter barrels, petwalk
426 NM 505, Maxwell, **W...**to Maxwell Lakes
419 NM 58, to Cimarron, **E...gas:** Texaco/diesel/24hr, **food:** Heck's Hungry Traveler Rest.
414 US 56, Springer, **E...gas:** Phillips 66/diesel, **food:** Dairy Delite Café, **lodging:** Oasis Motel
412 US 56 E, US 412 E, NM 21, NM 468, Springer, **1 mi E...gas:** Shamrock, **food:** Del Taco, **lodging:** Oasis Motel
404 NM 569, Colmor, Charette Lakes, no facilities
393 Levy, no facilities
387 NM 120, Wagon Mound, to Roy, **E...gas:** Chevron/diesel, Phillips 66, **food:** Santa Clara Café
376mm rest area sb, full(handicapped)facilities, phone, picnic tables, litter barrels, petwalk, RV camping/dump
374mm rest area nb, full(handicapped)facilities, phone, picnic tables, litter barrels, petwalk, RV camping/dump
366 NM 97, NM 161, Watrous, Valmora, **W...**Santa Fe Trail, Ft Union NM, no facilities
364 NM 97, NM 161, Watrous, Valmora, no facilities
361 no facilities
360mm rest area both lanes, litter barrels, no facilities

Las Vegas

356 Onava, no facilities
352 **E...**RV camping, **W...**airport
347 to NM 518, Las Vegas, **E...**CHIROPRACTOR, **1-2 mi W...gas:** Fina/diesel, Phillips 66/Burger King, **food:** Arby's, DQ, Hillcrest Rest., KFC, McDonald's, Pizza Hut, Taco Bell, **lodging:** Comfort Inn, Day's Inn, El Camino Motel, Inn of Las Vegas/rest., Super 8, Townhouse Motel, **other:** KOA, Storrie Lake SP, Las Vegas Civic Ctr
345 NM 65, NM 104, University Ave, Las Vegas, **E...**to Conchas Lake SP, **W...gas:** Fina/diesel, Phillips 66/diesel, **food:** Arby's, Burger King, DQ, Hillcrest Rest., KFC, McDonald's, Mexican Kitchen, Pizza Hut, Subway, Taco Bell, Wendy's, **lodging:** Budget Inn, Comfort Inn, El Camino Motel/rest., Palamino Motel, Plaza Hotel/rest., Sante Fe Trail Inn, Sunshine Motel, Townhouse Motel, **other:** HOSPITAL, Firestone, Hist Old Town Plaza
343 to NM 518 N, Las Vegas, **1 mi W...gas:** Chevron, Citgo, Fina, Phillips 66, **food:** Burger King, McDonald's, Taco Bell, Teresa's Mexican, **lodging:** Comfort Inn,, Day's Inn, El Camino Motel, Plaza Motel, Santa Fe Trail Inn, Thunderbird Motel
339 US 84 S, Romeroville, to Santa Rosa, **E...**KOA, **W...gas:** Texaco/diesel 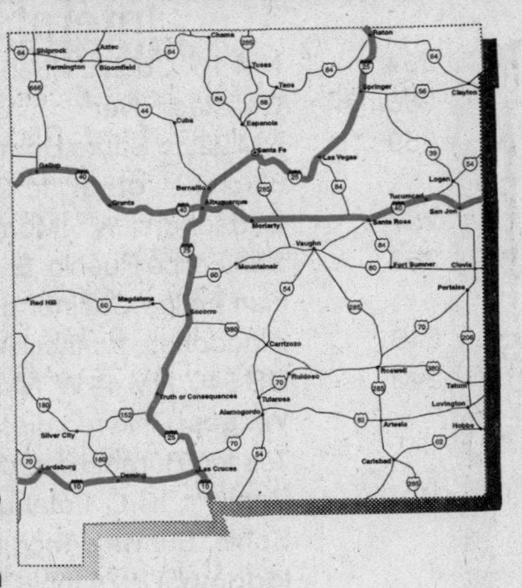
335 Tecolote, no facilities
330 Bernal, no facilities
325mm rest area both lanes, picnic tables, litter barrels, no restroom facilities
323 NM 3 S, Villanueva, **E...**to Villanueva SP, Madison Winery(6mi), RV camping
319 San Juan, San Jose, **3 mi E...**gas/diesel, **W...**Pecos River RV Camp/phone
307 NM 63, Rowe, Pecos, **W...**Pecos NM
299 NM 50, Glorieta, Pecos, **W...gas:** Fina/diesel(4mi), Shell(6mi), **food:** Renate's Rest., **other:** Glorieta Conf Ctr, Pecos NHP
297 Valencia, no facilities
294 Apache Canyon, **W...other:** KOA, Rancheros Camping(Mar-Nov)
290 US 285 S, to Lamy, S to Clines Corners, **W...other:** KOA, Rancheros Camping(Mar-Nov)
284 NM 466, Old Pecos Trail, Santa Fe, **W...gas:** Chevron/diesel, Sunset Gen Store, **lodging:** to Best Western, Desert Inn, Pecos Trail Inn, The Sands, **other:** HOSPITAL, museums

Santa Fe

282 US 84, US 285, St Francis Dr, **W...gas:** Conoco/Wendy's/diesel, Giant, **food:** Church's
278 NM 14, Cerrillos Rd, Santa Fe, **W...lodging:** Sleep Inn, **other:** Santa Fe Outlets/famous brands, **1-4 mi W...gas:** Chevron/diesel/24hr, Conoco, Phillips 66/diesel, Shell, **food:** Applebee's, Arby's, Burger King, China Star, CiCi's, Denny's, Kettle, KFC, LJ Silver, Lotaburger, McDonald's, Olive Garden, Outback Steaks, Panda Express, Pizza Hut, Red Lobster, Schlotsky's, Sonic, Taco Bell, Village Inn Rest., **lodging:** Comfort Inn, Day's Inn, Fairfield Inn, Hampton Inn, Holiday Inn Express, Howard Johnson, La Quinta, Luxury Inn, Motel 6, Quality Inn, Ramada, Red Roof Inn, Santa Fe Lodge, Super 8, **other:** Albertson's, Best Buy, Buick/Pontiac, Chevrolet/GMC, Dillard's, Dodge, Firestone/auto, Ford, Honda/Isuzu, JC Penney, Los Campos RV Resort, PepBoys, Sam's Club, Sears/auto, Subaru, Target, VW, Walgreen, Wal-Mart, mall
276b a NM 599, to NM 14, to Madrid, **E...gas:** Phillips/diesel/24hr, **W...gas:** Conoco, Shell, **other:** Santa Fe Skies RV Park
271 CR 50F, La Cienega, **W...**Pinon RV Park(4mi), racetrack, museum
269mm rest area nb, full(handicapped)facilities, phone, picnic tables, litter barrels, petwalk
267 Waldo Canyon Rd, no facilities

NEW MEXICO

Interstate 25

N ↕ S

Albuquerque

264 NM 16, Cochiti Pueblo, **W...**to Cochiti Lake RA

263mm Galisteo River

259 NM 22, to Santo Domingo Pueblo, **W...gas:** Phillips 66/diesel, **other:** to Cochiti Lake RA

257 Budaghers, **W...**Mormon Battalion Mon

252 San Felipe Pueblo, **E...gas:** Phillips 66/diesel, **food:** San Felipe Casino/rest.

248 Algodones, no facilities

242 US 540, NM 44 W, NM 165 E, to Farmington, Aztec, **W...gas:** Chevron/diesel, Conoco/diesel, Phillips 66, Texaco/Burger King/diesel, **food:** Coronado Rest., Denny's, KFC, Lotaburger, McDonald's, Pizza Hut, Sonic, Subway, Taco Bell, Village Pizza, Wendy's, **lodging:** Day's Inn, Quality Inn, Super 8, **other:** to Coronado SP

240 NM 473, to Bernalillo, **W...gas:** Conoco/diesel, Fina, **food:** Abuelito's Kitchen, Range Café, **other:** KOA, to Coronado SP

234 NM 556, Tramway Rd, **E...gas:** Shamrock, **W...gas:** Phillips 66

233 Alameda Blvd, **E...gas:** Chevron/Burger King, **food:** Comfort Inn, **other:** Toyota, **W...gas:** Phillips 66/diesel, **food:** Carl's Jr, **lodging:** Holiday Inn Express, Ramada Ltd

232 Paseo del Norte, **E...lodging:** Motel 6, **other:** Lowe's Whse, **W...food:** Arby's, **lodging:** Courtyard, Marriott

231 San Antonio Ave, **E...food:** Cracker Barrel, Kettle, **lodging:** Howard Johnson, La Quinta, Quality Suites, Ramada, **other:** HOSPITAL, **W...lodging:** Baymont Inn, Crossland Suites, Hampton Inn, **other:** Mazda, VW

230 San Mateo Blvd, Osuna Rd, Albuquerque, **E...gas:** Chevron, Circle K, Conoco/diesel, **food:** Applebee's, Arby's, Bennigan's, Black-Eyed Pea, Bob's Burgers, Burger King, Carino's Italian, Chili's, Hooters, KFC, LJ Silver, Lotaburger, McDonald's, Olive Garden, Pizza Hut/Taco Bell, Schlotsky's, Sizzler, Sonic, Subway, SweetTomato, Taco Cabana, Teriyaki Chicken, Village Inn Rest., Wendy's, Wienerschnitzel, Wild Oats Mkt, **lodging:** Wyndham, **other:** HOSPITAL, Buick/Pontiac/GMC, Mercedes, Nissan, Subaru/Isuzu, Firestone/auto, NAPA, PepBoys, **W...gas:** Shamrock, **food:** Whataburger, Motel 6

229 Jefferson St, **E...food:** Carrabba's, Landry's Seafood, Olive Garden, OutBack Steaks, **other:** HOSPITAL, same as 230, **W...food:** Chang's, Fuddrucker's, Jersey Jack's, Mimi's Café, Pappadeaux, Red Robin, Rockfish Café, Texas Land&Cattle Steaks, **lodging:** Drury Inn, Residence Inn

228 Montgomery Blvd, **E...gas:** Chevron/diesel, Texaco, **food:** Lotaburger, **lodging:** Best Western, **other:** HOSPITAL, Discount Tire, **W...food:** Arby's, Dickie's Smokehouse, IHOP, McDonald's, Panda Express, Starbucks, Wendy's, **lodging:** InTowne Suites

227b Comanche Rd, Griegos Rd, **E...**UPS Depot

a Candelaria Rd, Albuquerque, **E...gas:** Chevron/rest., Circle K, Fina/Subway/diesel, Shell, TA/diesel/24hr/@, **food:** JB's, IHOP, Village Inn Rest., **lodging:** Comfort Inn, Clubhouse Inn, Fairfield Inn, Hilton, Holiday Inn, Rodeway Inn, Motel 6, Super 8, **W...food:** Waffle House, **lodging:** A-1 Motel, Red Roof Inn, **other:** Volvo

226b a I-40, E to Amarillo, W to Flagstaff

225 Lomas Blvd, **E...gas:** Chevron/7-11, **food:** JB's, Plaza Inn/rest., **other:** HOSPITAL, Chevrolet, Dodge, Ford, Saturn

224b Grand Ave, Central Ave, **W...gas:** Chevron, **lodging:** Econolodge, **other:** HOSPITAL

a Lead Ave, Coal Ave, **E...gas:** Texaco, **food: lodging:** Crossroads Motel, **other:** HOSPITAL

223 Chavez Ave, **E...lodging:** Motel 6, **other:** sports facilities

222b a Gibson Blvd, **E...gas:** Phillips 66, **food:** Applebee's, Burger King, Subway, Waffle House, **lodging:** Country Inn Suites, Courtyard, Hampton Inn, Hawthorn Suites, Quality Suites, Sleep Inn, University Inn, **other:** HOSPITAL, museum, **W...gas:** Fina/7-11, **food:** Church's, LotaBurger

221 Sunport(from nb), **E...lodging:** AmeriSuites, Wyndham, **other:** USPO, airport

220 Rio Bravo Blvd, Mountain View, **E...**golf, **2 mi W...gas:** Shamrock, **food:** Burger King, Church's, McDonald's, Pizza Hut, Subway, Taco Bell, **other:** Albertson's, Family$, Walgreen

215 NM 47, **E...gas:** Conoco/diesel, **other:** to Isleta Lakes RA/RV Camping, casino, st police

214mm Rio Grande

213 NM 314, Isleta Blvd, **W...gas:** Chevron/Subway/diesel/24hr

209 NM 45, to Isleta Pueblo, no facilities

203 NM 6, to Los Lunas, **E...gas:** Chevron/diesel/24hr, Shamrock, Shell/Wendy's/diesel, **food:** Benny's #2, McDonald's, Sonic, Village Inn Rest., **lodging:** Comfort Inn, Day's Inn, **other:** Chevrolet, Ford, Home Depot, **W...gas:** Phillips 66/Subway/diesel, **food:** Carino's Italian, Chili's, KFC, **lodging:** Western Skies Inn, **other:** Wal-Mart SuperCtr/24hr

Belen

195 Lp 25, Los Chavez, **1 mi E...food:** McDonald's, Pizza Hut/Taco Bell, **other:** Wal-Mart SuperCtr/gas/24hr

191 NM 548, Belen, **1 mi E...gas:** Conoco, **food:** KFC, McDonald's, Pizza Hut, Subway, **lodging:** Freeway Inn, Super 8, **other:** to Chavez SP, **W...food:** Casa de Mirada Rest./RV Park, Rio Grande Diner, **lodging:** Best Western, Holiday Inn Express, OakTree Inn

190 Lp 25, Belen, **1-2 mi E...gas:** Akins/diesel, Conoco/diesel, Mustang, **food:** Arby's, Casa de Pizza, Circle T Burger, KFC, McDonald's, Pizza Hut, TJ's Mexican, **lodging:** Freeway Inn, Hub Motel, Super 8, **other:** AutoZone, Big O Tire

Interstate 25

N ↕ S

175 US 60, Bernardo, **E...**Salinas NM, **W...other:** Kiva RV Park
174mm Rio Puerco
169 **E...**La Joya St Game Refuge, Sevilleta NWR
167mm rest area both lanes, full(handicapped)facilities, picnic tables, litter barrels, vending, petwalk
166mm Rio Salado
165mm weigh sta nb/parking area both lanes
163 San Acacia, no facilities
156 Lemitar, **W...**Texaco/diesel/24hr/@
152 Escondida, **W...**to st police

Socorro

150 US 60 W, Socorro, **W...gas:** Chevron, Circle K, Exxon/diesel, Phillips 66/diesel, Shell/diesel, **food:** Burger King, Denny's, Domino's, K-Bob's, KFC, Lotaburger, McDonald's, Pizza Hut, Road-Runner Steaks, Sonic, Subway, Taco Bell, Tina's Rest., **lodging:** Best Inn, Best Western, Economy Inn, Econolodge, El Camino Motel/rest., Holiday Inn Express, Payless Inn, Rio Grande Motel/rest., Sands Motel, San Miguel Inn, Super 8, **other:** Alco, Chevrolet/Pontiac/Buick, Chrysler/Dodge/Jeep, Ford/Mercury, NAPA, Radio Shack, Smith's Foods, to NM Tech
147 US 60 W, Socorro, **W...gas:** Chevron/diesel/RV dump, Conoco/LP, Shell/diesel, Texaco/diesel, **food:** Arby's, Armijo's Mexican, Denny's, KFC, Pizza Hut, **lodging:** Holiday Inn Express, Motel 6, Sands Motel, **other:** HOSPITAL, Parts+, TrueValue, Socorro RV Park, to airport
139 US 380 E, to San Antonio, **E...food:** Manny's Burgers, Owl Café, **other:** Bosque Del Apache NWR
124 to San Marcial, **E...other:** to Bosque del Apache NWR, Ft Craig
115 NM 107, **E...gas:** Truck Plaza/diesel/rest./24hr
114mm rest areas both lanes, full(handicapped)facilities, picnic tables, litter barrels, petwalk, RV parking, vending
107mm Nogal Canyon
100 Red Rock, no facilities
92 Mitchell Point, no facilities
90mm La Canada Alamosa
89 NM 181, to Cuchillo, to Monticello, **4 mi E...gas:** Chevron, Monticello RV Park
83 NM 52, NM 181, to Cuchillo, **3 mi E...lodging:** Elephant Butte Inn/rest., Quality Inn, **other:** Lakeside RV Park, Elephant Butte SP
82mm insp sta nb
79 Lp 25, to Truth or Consequences, **E...gas:** Chevron/diesel, Circle K, Phillips 66/diesel, **food:** China Buffet, DQ, Denny's, Hilltop Café, K-Bob's, KFC/Taco Bell, La Cocina Mexican, Los Arcos Steaks, McDonald's, Pizza Hut, Sonic, Subway, **lodging:** Ace Lodge, Best Western, Holiday Inn, Super 8, **other:** HOSPITAL, AutoZone, NAPA, USPO, to Elephant Butte SP 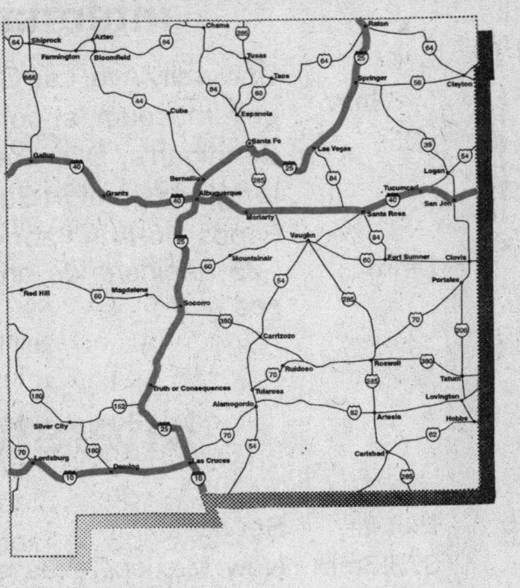
76 (75 from nb)Lp 25, to Williamsburg, **E...gas:** Chevron/24hr, Conoco/diesel, Shell/diesel, **food:** Café Rio, **lodging:** Rio Grande Motel, **other:** Shady Corner RV Park, USPO, city park, **1 mi E...**RJ RV Park
71 Las Palomas, no facilities
63 NM 152, Caballo, to Hillsboro, **E...**Lakeview RV Park/diesel
59 rd 187, Arrey, Derry, **E...**to Caballo-Percha SPs
58mm Rio Grande
51 rd 546, Garfield, to Arrey, Derry, no facilities
41 NM 26 W, Hatch, **1 mi W...gas:** Phillips 66/diesel/24hr, **food:** DQ, **lodging:** Village Plaza Motel, **other:** Chevrolet, Happy Trails RV Park
35 NM 140 W, Rincon, no facilities
32 Upham, no facilities
27mm scenic view nb, picnic tables, litter barrels
26mm insp sta nb
23mm rest area both lanes, full(handicapped)facilities, picnic tables, litter barrels, vending, petwalk
19 Radium Springs, **W...**Leasburg SP, Fort Selden St Mon, RV camping

Las Cruces

9 Dona Ana, **W...gas:** Chevron, Citgo, Conoco, **other:** Family$, RV camping
6b a US 70, Las Cruces, to Alamogordo, **E...gas:** Phillips 66/diesel, Texaco, **food:** IHOP, Outback Steaks, Peter Piper Pizza, Pizzaria Uno, **lodging:** Century 21 Motel, Fairfield Inn, Super 8, **other:** HOSPITAL, K-Mart, Sam's Club, USPO, **W...gas:** Chevron, Shell, **food:** BurgerTime, DQ, Domino's, KFC, Lotaburger, McDonald's, Sonic, Subway, Taco Bell, Whataburger/24hr, **other:** MEDICAL CARE, Albertson's, AutoZone, Checker Parts, IGA Foods, Lowe's Whse, golf
3 Lohman Ave, Las Cruces, **E...gas:** Shamrock, Shell, **food:** Applebee's, Burger King, Cattle Baron Steaks, Carino's Italian, Chili's, Farley's Grill, Garduno's Italian, Golden Corral, Hooters, Jack-in-the-Box, KFC, Luby's, Pizza Hut, Popeye's, Red Lobster, Sonic, Twisters, Village Inn Rest., **lodging:** Hilton, **other:** Albertson's, Barnes&Noble, Dillard's, Discount Tire, Home Depot, JC Penney, OfficeMax, Sears/auto, Target, mall, **W...gas:** Conoco/diesel, **food:** Arby's, China Buffet, McDonald's, Subway, Wendy's, Wienerschnitzel, **other:** Best Buy, Hastings Books, Martin Tires, NAPA, PepBoys, Rainbow Foods, Walgreen, Wal-Mart SuperCtr/24hr

Interstate 25

N ↕ S

1	University Ave, Las Cruces, **E...other:** HOSPITAL, golf, museum, st police, **W...gas:** Conoco, **food:** Bennigan's, DQ, Lorenzo's Italian, McDonald's, **lodging:** Comfort Suites, Sleep Inn, **other:** Furr's Foods, Jo-Ann Fabrics, NMSU
0mm	I-25 begins/ends on I-10, exit 144 at Las Cruces.

Interstate 40

E ↕ W

Exit #	Services
373.5mm	New Mexico/Texas state line, Mountain/Central time zone
373mm	**Welcome Ctr wb, full(handicapped)facilities, phone, picnic tables, litter barrels, petwalk**
369	NM 93 S, NM 392 N, to Endee, no facilities
361	Bard, no facilities
358mm	weigh sta both lanes
356	NM 469, San Jon, **N...gas:** Citgo/KFC/Taco Bell/diesel/24hr, to Ute Lake SP, **S...gas:** Phillips 66/diesel, Shell/diesel
343	ranch access, no facilities
339	NM 278, airport

Tucumcari

335	Lp 40, E Tucumcari Blvd, Tucumcari, **N...gas:** Chevron, Conoco/diesel, Shell, **food:** Denny's, **lodging:** Best Western, Comfort Inn, Econolodge, Hampton Inn, Holiday Inn/rest., Howard Johnson, Motel 6, Super 8, **other:** to Conchas Lake SP, **S...**KOA
333	US 54 E, Tucumcari, **N...gas:** Love's/Godfather's/diesel/@, **other:** Mtn Rd RV Park, **1 mi N...gas:** Shell, Circle K, **food:** Lotaburger, Pizza Hut, Sonic, **lodging:** Best Western, Comfort Inn, Holiday Inn, Palomino Motel, Relax Inn, Travelodge, **other:** K-Mart
332	NM 209, NM 104, 1st St, Tucumcari, **N...gas:** Chevron/Subway/diesel/24hr, Phillips 66, **food:** KFC, K-Bob's, Lotaburger, McDonald's, Sonic, **lodging:** Best Western, Comfort Inn, Day's Inn, Microtel, Travelers Inn, **other:** HOSPITAL, st police, to Conchas Lake SP, **S...gas:** Shell
331	Camino del Coronado, Tucumcari, no facilities
329	US 54, US 66 E, W Tucumcari Ave, **N...gas:** Shell/diesel, **lodging:** Payless Motel, **other:** HOSPITAL, golf
321	Palomas, **S...gas:** Texaco/DQ/Stuckey's/diesel
311	Montoya, no facilities
302mm	**rest area both lanes, full(handicapped)facilities, phone, picnic tables, litter barrels, petwalk, RV dump**
300	NM 129, Newkirk, **N...gas:** Phillips 66/diesel, **other:** to Conchas Lake SP
291	to Rte 66, Cuervo, **N...**Cuervo Gas/repair
284	no facilities
277	US 84 S, to Ft Sumner, **N...gas:** Chevron/diesel, Shell, **food:** DQ, Denny's, Golden Dragon Chinese, Silver Moon Café, **lodging:** Best Western, Budget Inn, Comfort Inn, Holiday Inn Express, Motel 6, **other:** Ford, KOA, **S...gas:** Love's/Carl's Jr/diesel/24hr/@, TA/Shell/Subway/diesel/24hr/@

Santa Rosa

275	US 54 W, Santa Rosa, **N...gas:** Phillips 66, Shell/Burger King, **food:** McDonald's, Rte 66 Rest., Santa Fe Grill, **lodging:** Best Western, Day's Inn, La Quinta, Travelodge, **other:** Santa Rosa Camping, **S...gas:** Shell/diesel/24hr, **food:** Comet Drive-In, Joseph's Grill, Pizza Hut, **lodging:** American Inn, Sun'n Sand Motel, Sunset Motel, Super 8, Tower Motel, Western Motel, **other:** HOSPITAL, CarQuest, st police, USPO
273.5mm	Pecos River
273	US 54 S, Santa Rosa, **N...other:** Santa Rosa Lake SP, **S...gas:** Chevron, **food:** Mateo's Rest.
267	Colonias, **N...gas:** Shell/Stuckey's/rest.
263	San Ignacio, no facilities
256	US 84 N, NM 219, to Las Vegas, no facilities
252	no facilities
251.5mm	**rest area both lanes, full(handicapped)facilities, phone, picnic tables, litter barrels, petwalk, RV dump**
243	Milagro, **N...gas:** Chevron/diesel/café
239	no facilities
234	**N...gas:** Exxon/Flying C/DQ/diesel/gifts, **other:** repair/24hr
230	NM 3, to Encino, **N...other:** to Villanueva SP
226	no facilities
220mm	parking area both lanes, litter barrels
218b a	US 285, Clines Corners, **N...gas:** Phillips 66/diesel/24hr, Shell/diesel/24hr, **food:** Clines Corners Rest., **S...other:** to Carlsbad Caverns NP
208	Wagon Wheel, no facilities
207mm	**rest area both lanes, full(handicapped)facilities, picnic tables, litter barrels, petwalk**
203	**N...**Zia RV Park, **S...lodging:** El Vaquero Motel/rest.
197	to Rte 66, Moriarty, **S...gas:** Lisa's/diesel/rest./@, **1-2 mi S...**same as 194, 196
196	NM 41, Howard Cavasos Blvd, **S...gas:** Circle K/diesel, Shell/Baja Taco, **food:** Lotaburger, Village Grill, **lodging:** Motel 6, Siesta Motel, **other:** Family$, USPO, to Salinas NM(35mi)
194	NM 41, Moriarty, **S...gas:** Chevron/24hr, Phillips 66/diesel, Rip Griffin/Pizza Hut/Subway/Taco Bell/diesel/24hr/@, **food:** Arby's, BBQ, El Comedor Rest., Mama Rosa's Rest., McDonald's, **lodging:** Day's Inn, Econolodge, Holiday Inn Express, Howard Johnson, Motel 6, Super 8, **other:** MEDICAL CARE, Chevrolet/GMC, I-40 RV Park, IGA Foods

Interstate 40

E ↕ W

Albuquerque

187 NM 344, Edgewood, **N...gas:** Conoco/diesel, **food:** DQ, **S...gas:** Exxon, Phillips 66/diesel, **food:** McDonald's, **other:** MEDICAL CARE, Ford, Red Arrow Camping, Smith's Foods, USPO

181 NM 217, Sedillo, no facilities

178 Zuzax, **S...gas:** Chevron/diesel, **other:** Hidden Valley RV Park

175 NM 337, NM 14, Tijeras, **N...food:** Burger Boy(2mi), **other:** to Cibola NF, Turquoise Trail RV Park, **1 mi E...**auto/truck repair/24hr

170 Carnuel, no facilities

167 Central Ave, to Tramway Blvd, **S...gas:** Chevron/24hr, Fina/7-11, Phillips 66, Shell/Burger King, **food:** Einstein Bagels, KFC, Lotaburger, McDonald's, Pizza Hut/Taco Bell, Starbucks, Waffle House, **lodging:** Best Western, Comfort Inn, Day's Inn, Econolodge, Howard Johnson, Motel 6, Travelodge, **other:** GNC, Goodyear/U-Haul/auto, KOA, Meyer's RV, Raley's Foods, Rocky Mtn RV/marine, Smith's/gas, to Kirtland AFB

166 Juan Tabo Blvd, **N...gas:** Chevron, Phillips 66, **food:** Blackeyed Pea, Burger King, Carrow's Rest., LJ Silver, McDonald's, Olive Garden, Oriental Buffet, Paul's Rest., Pizza Hut, Taco Bell, Twisters Diner, Village Inn Rest., Whataburger, Wendy's, **lodging:** Best Inn, Super 8, **other:** Albertson's, Discount Tire, Hastings Books, PepBoys, Radio Shack, Sav-On Drug, transmissions, **S...food:** Wienerschnitzel, **other:** Furr's Foods, Walgreen, KOA

165 Eubank Blvd, **N...gas:** Chevron, Phillips 66, Shell, **food:** JB's, Owl Café, Sonic, **lodging:** Day's Inn, Econolodge, Guesthouse Inn, Holiday Inn Express, Howard Johnson, Ramada Inn, **other:** Best Buy, Target, **S...gas:** Conoco, **food:** Burger King, Bob's Burgers, Boston Mkt, Taco Bell, Wendy's, **other:** Office Depot, Sam's Club/gas, Wal-Mart SuperCtr/24hr

164 Lomas Blvd, Wyoming Blvd, **N...gas:** Phillips 66/Subway, **other:** HOSPITAL, **S...other:** Ford, Dodge, Mazda/Toyota, Subaru, Kirtland AFB

162b a Louisiana Blvd, **N...food:** Bennigan's, Buca Italian, Macaroni Grill, Japanese Kitchen, Steak&Ale, TGIFriday, **lodging:** AmeriSuites, Marriott, Windrock Inn, **other:** Borders Books, Dillard's, JC Penney, Marshall's, Walgreen, **S...**atomic museum

161b a San Mateo Blvd, Albuquerque, **N...gas:** Phillips 66/diesel, Shell/A&W, **food:** Boston Mkt, Burger King, Denny's, McDonald's, Pizza Hut, Quizno's, Starbucks, Taco Bell, Twisters Grill, Wendy's, **lodging:** La Quinta, **other:** Circuit City, CompUSA, Old Navy, **S...gas:** Chevron

Albuquerque

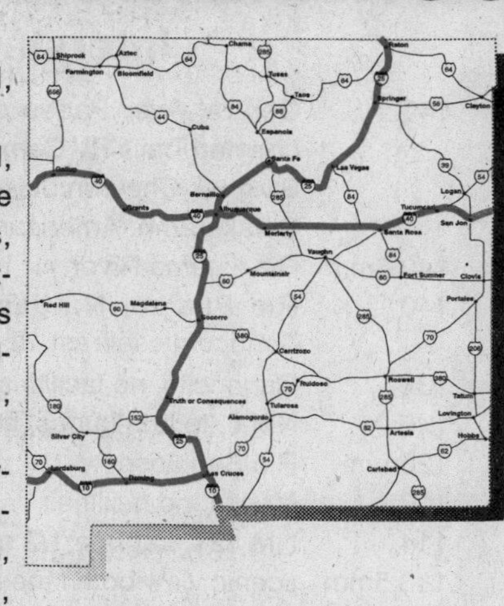

160 Carlisle Blvd, Albuquerque, **N...gas:** Shell, Conoco, Circle K, **food:** JB's, Lotaburger, Pizza Hut, Rudy's BBQ, Sonic, Village Inn Rest., Whataburger, **lodging:** AmeriSuites, Candlewood Suites, Comfort Inn, Courtyard, Econolodge, Equus Hotel, Fairfield Inn, Hampton Inn, Hilton, Holiday Inn, Homestead Village, Motel 6, Quality Inn, Radisson, Residence Inn, Rodeway Inn, Super 8, Travelodge, **other:** BMW, Goodyear/auto, JC Penney, OfficeMax, Smith's Foods, Walgreen, **S...gas:** Shell/Subway/diesel, **food:** Burger King, **other:** HOSPITAL, K-Mart, Wild Oats Mkt

159b c I-25, S to Las Cruces, N to Santa Fe

a 2nd St, 4th St, Albuquerque, **N...gas:** Chevron/24hr, Conoco, Love's/Subway/diesel, **food:** Furr's Café, **other:** U-Haul, **S...food:** Tony's Pizza, **lodging:** Village Inn Rest., Howard Johnson, **other:** Firestone

158 6th St, 8th St, 12th St, Albuquerque, **N...gas:** Love's/Subway/diesel, Phillips 66, **other:** U-Haul, **S...gas:** Chevron, **lodging:** Howard Johnson

157b 12th St(from eb), no facilities

a Rio Grande Blvd, Albuquerque, **S...gas:** Chevron/24hr, Shell, **lodging:** Best Western Rio Grande, Sheraton

156mm Rio Grande River

155 Coors Rd, Albuquerque, **N...gas:** Chevron, Conoco/diesel, Shamrock/diesel/24hr, **food:** Applebee's, Arby's, Burger King, Chili's, Great Wall Chinese, IHOP, McDonald's, Papa Murphy's, Sonic, Subway, Twisters Burritos, Wendy's, **other:** Furr's Foods, Goodyear/auto, Home Depot, Radio Shack, Staples, Walgreen, Wal-Mart SuperCtr/24hr, **S...gas:** Chevron/24hr, Phillips 66/diesel, Shell, **food:** Arby's, Chico's Mexican, Del Taco, Denny's, Furr's Diner, Lotaburger, McDonald's, New China, Pizza Hut/Taco Bell, Subway, Village Inn Rest., **lodging:** Comfort Inn, Day's Inn, Holiday Inn Express, La Quinta, Motel 6, Motel 76, Red Roof Inn, Super 8, **other:** Checker Parts, Discount Tire, U-Haul, carwash

154 Unser Blvd, **N...gas:** Shamrock, **other:** to Petroglyph NM

153 98th St, **S...gas:** Flying J/Conoco/CountryMkt/diesel/LP/24hr/@, **food:** Tumbleweed Steaks(2mi), **lodging:** Microtel

NEW MEXICO

Interstate 40

E ↕ W

149 Central Ave, Paseo del Volcan, **N...other:** Enchanted Trails RV Camping, to Shooting Range SP, **S...gas:** Chevron/diesel/24hr, **food:** Tumbleweed Steaks(2mi), American RV Park

140.5mm Rio Puerco River

140 Rio Puerco, **N...gas:** Exxon/diesel, **S...gas:** Conoco/diesel/rest./@, **other:** Rt 66 Casino

131 Canoncito, no facilities

126 NM 6, to Los Lunas, no facilities

120mm Rio San Jose

117 Mesita, no facilities

114 NM 124, Laguna,**1/2 mi N...**Conoco/diesel

113.5mm scenic view both lanes, litter barrels

108 Casa Blanca, Paraje, **S...gas:** Conoco/Casa Blanca/diesel/24hr, **food:** Taco Bell, **other:** Casa Blanca Mkt, casino

104 Cubero, Budville, no facilities

102 Sky City Rd, Acomita, **N...gas:** Acoma/diesel/24hr, **food:** Huwak'a Rest., **lodging:** Sky City Hotel, **other:** HOSPITAL, RV Park/laundry, casino, **S...rest area both lanes, full(handicapped)facilities, phone, picnic tables, litter barrels, petwalk**

100 San Fidel, no facilities

96 McCartys, no facilities

89 NM 117, to Quemado, **N...gas:** Citgo/Stuckey's, **S...**El Malpais NM

Grants

85 NM 122, NM 547, Grants, **N...gas:** Chevron/diesel/24hr, Conoco/diesel, Pump'n Save/gas, Shell/diesel, **food:** Denny's, Domino's, 4B's Rest./24hr, Lotaburger, Pizza Hut, Subway/TCBY, Taco Bell, **lodging:** Best Western, Comfort Inn, Day's Inn, Econolodge/rest., Holiday Inn Express, Motel 6, Super 8, **other:** HOSPITAL, AutoZone, Checker Parts, Chevrolet/Buick, Chrysler/Jeep/Dodge, Wal-Mart SuperCtr/24hr, **S...**Lavaland RV Park

81b a NM 53 S, Grants, **N...gas:** Chevron, **food:** Burger King, KFC, McDonald's, **lodging:** Sands Motel, SW Motel, **other:** Ford/Lincoln/Mercury, NAPA, USPO, **S...other:** Cibola Sands RV Park, KOA, El Malpais NM

79 NM 122, NM 605, Milan, **N...gas:** Chevron, Love's/Subway/diesel/24hr/@, **food:** DQ, **lodging:** Crossroads Motel, **other:** Bar-S RV Park, **S...gas:** Petro/Mobil/diesel/24hr/@, **other:** st police

72 Bluewater Village, **N...gas:** Exxon/DQ/diesel

63 NM 412, Prewitt, **S...**to Bluewater SP, Grants West RV Camp

53 NM 371, NM 612, Thoreau, **N...gas:** Red Mtn Mkt&Deli, **other:** St Bonaventure RV camp

47 Continental Divide, 7275 ft, **N...gas:** Chevron, **other:** Continental Divide Trdg Post, **S...**USPO

44 Coolidge, no facilities

39 Refinery, **N...gas:** Pilot/diesel/24hr/@

36 Iyanbito, no facilities

33 NM 400, McGaffey, Ft Wingate, **N...other:** to Red Rock SP, RV camping, museum

Gallup

26 E 66th Ave, E Gallup, **N...gas:** Chevron/diesel/24hr, **food:** Denny's/24hr, **lodging:** Sleep Inn, **other:** to Red Rock SP, RV parking/museum, st police, **S...gas:** Conoco/diesel, Fina/diesel, Mustang, **food:** Burger King, KFC, Lotaburger, McDonald's, Sonic, Wendy's, **lodging:** Best Western, Hacienda Motel, Roadrunner Motel, Super 8, **other:** HOSPITAL, Ortega Gifts

22 Montoya Blvd, Gallup, **N...rest area both lanes, full facilities, info, S...gas:** Armco/gas, Chevron, Conoco, Giant Gas, Phillips 66, Shell, Circle K, 7-11, **food:** Burger King, Carl's Jr, Church's, Earl's Rest., LJ Silver, McDonald's, Papa John's, Pedro's Mexican, Pizza Hut, Subway, Taco Bell, **lodging:** Best Western, El Capitan Motel, El Rancho Motel/rest., Redwood Lodge, **other:** Albertson's, Walgreen

20 US 666 N, Gallup, to Shiprock, **N...gas:** Giant/diesel, Phillips 66/diesel, Shell, **food:** Arby's, Burger King, CA Chinese, Church's, Cracker Barrel, DQ, Denny's, Furr's Café, Golden Corral, LotaBurger, McDonald's, Pizza Hut, Sizzler, Sonic, Taco Bell, Wendy's, **lodging:** Holiday Inn Express, Ramada Ltd, **other:** AutoZone, CarQuest, Chrysler/Plymouth/Dodge/Jeep, Family$, Firestone, JC Penney, K-Mart, NAPA, Nissan, Pep-Boys, Safeway, Wal-Mart SuperCtr/24hr, mall, radiators, **S...gas:** Exxon, Shell/diesel, **food:** El Dorado Rest., Lotaburger, Sonic, **lodging:** Best Value Inn, Best Western, Day's Inn, Economy Inn, Royal Holiday Inn, Shalimar Inn, Super 8, Thunderbird Motel, Travelodge, **other:** HOSPITAL, RV camping

16 NM 118, W Gallup, Mentmore, **N...gas:** Armco/diesel/24hr/@, Love's/Subway/diesel/24hr/@, Shell/Pizza Inn/diesel/24hr/@, TA/Blimpie/diesel/24hr/@, **food:** A&W, Howard Johnson, **other:** Blue Beacon, diesel repair, **S...gas:** Chevron/diesel, Conoco, Fina/Allsup's, Shell, **food:** Olympic Kitchen, Ranch Kitchen, Taco Bell, Virgie's Mexican, **lodging:** Best Western, Budget Inn, Comfort Inn, Day's Inn, Econolodge, Holiday Inn, Microtel, Motel 6, Red Roof Inn, Travelers Inn, Travelodge, **other:** USA RV Park

12mm inspection sta eb

8 to Manuelito, no facilities

2mm **Welcome Ctr eb, full(handicapped)facilities, phone, picnic tables, litter barrels, petwalk**

0mm New Mexico/Arizona state line

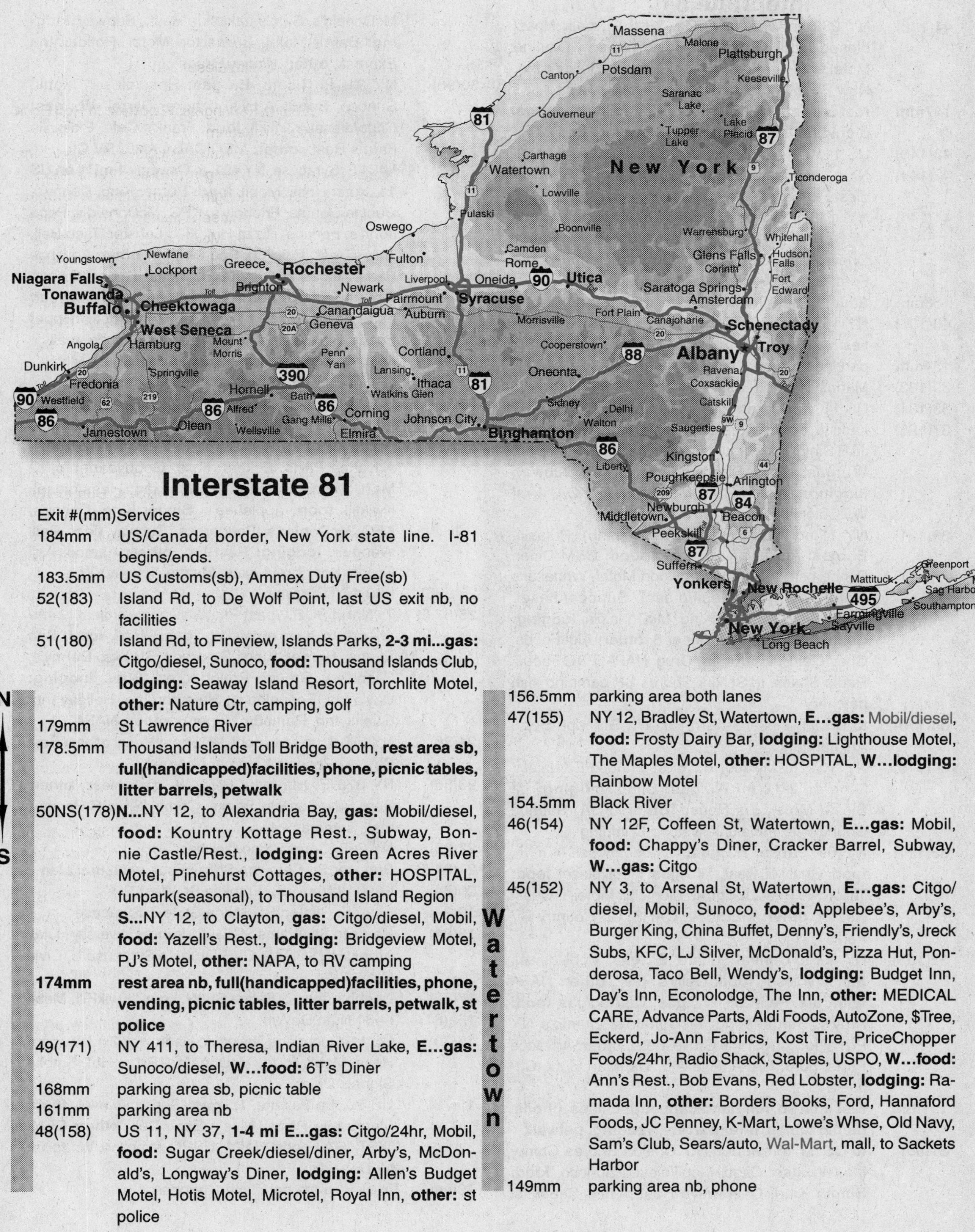

Interstate 81

Exit #(mm)Services

184mm US/Canada border, New York state line. I-81 begins/ends.

183.5mm US Customs(sb), Ammex Duty Free(sb)

52(183) Island Rd, to De Wolf Point, last US exit nb, no facilities

51(180) Island Rd, to Fineview, Islands Parks, **2-3 mi...gas:** Citgo/diesel, Sunoco, **food:** Thousand Islands Club, **lodging:** Seaway Island Resort, Torchlite Motel, **other:** Nature Ctr, camping, golf

179mm St Lawrence River

178.5mm Thousand Islands Toll Bridge Booth, **rest area sb, full(handicapped)facilities, phone, picnic tables, litter barrels, petwalk**

50NS(178) **N...**NY 12, to Alexandria Bay, **gas:** Mobil/diesel, **food:** Kountry Kottage Rest., Subway, Bonnie Castle/Rest., **lodging:** Green Acres River Motel, Pinehurst Cottages, **other:** HOSPITAL, funpark(seasonal), to Thousand Island Region

S...NY 12, to Clayton, **gas:** Citgo/diesel, Mobil, **food:** Yazell's Rest., **lodging:** Bridgeview Motel, PJ's Motel, **other:** NAPA, to RV camping

174mm rest area nb, full(handicapped)facilities, phone, vending, picnic tables, litter barrels, petwalk, st police

49(171) NY 411, to Theresa, Indian River Lake, **E...gas:** Sunoco/diesel, **W...food:** 6T's Diner

168mm parking area sb, picnic table

161mm parking area nb

48(158) US 11, NY 37, **1-4 mi E...gas:** Citgo/24hr, Mobil, **food:** Sugar Creek/diesel/diner, Arby's, McDonald's, Longway's Diner, **lodging:** Allen's Budget Motel, Hotis Motel, Microtel, Royal Inn, **other:** st police

N ↕ S

Watertown

156.5mm parking area both lanes

47(155) NY 12, Bradley St, Watertown, **E...gas:** Mobil/diesel, **food:** Frosty Dairy Bar, **lodging:** Lighthouse Motel, The Maples Motel, **other:** HOSPITAL, **W...lodging:** Rainbow Motel

154.5mm Black River

46(154) NY 12F, Coffeen St, Watertown, **E...gas:** Mobil, **food:** Chappy's Diner, Cracker Barrel, Subway, **W...gas:** Citgo

45(152) NY 3, to Arsenal St, Watertown, **E...gas:** Citgo/diesel, Mobil, Sunoco, **food:** Applebee's, Arby's, Burger King, China Buffet, Denny's, Friendly's, Jreck Subs, KFC, LJ Silver, McDonald's, Pizza Hut, Ponderosa, Taco Bell, Wendy's, **lodging:** Budget Inn, Day's Inn, Econolodge, The Inn, **other:** MEDICAL CARE, Advance Parts, Aldi Foods, AutoZone, $Tree, Eckerd, Jo-Ann Fabrics, Kost Tire, PriceChopper Foods/24hr, Radio Shack, Staples, USPO, **W...food:** Ann's Rest., Bob Evans, Red Lobster, **lodging:** Ramada Inn, **other:** Borders Books, Ford, Hannaford Foods, JC Penney, K-Mart, Lowe's Whse, Old Navy, Sam's Club, Sears/auto, Wal-Mart, mall, to Sackets Harbor

149mm parking area nb, phone

NEW YORK

Interstate 81

N ↕ S

44(148) NY 232, to Watertown Ctr, **3 mi E...gas:** Hess/diesel, Mobil, **lodging:** Best Western, Cityline Motel, Hi-Hat Motel, Hillside Motel, Holiday Inn, New Parrot Motel/rest., **other:** HOSPITAL

147mm rest area sb, full(handicapped)facilities, phone, picnic tables, litter barrels, vending, petwalk

43(146) US 11, to Kellogg Hill, no facilities

42(144) NY 177, Adams Center, **E...gas:** Mobil, Sunoco/diesel, **other:** Harley-Davidson, Polaris

41(140) NY 178, Adams, **E...gas:** Citgo/diesel, **food:** McDonald's, **1 mi E...food:** Tomacy's Rest., Chevrolet/Buick, Pontiac, Chrysler/Jeep/Dodge, Ford, NAPA, **W...**Stony Creek Marina

138mm South Sandy Creek

40(135) NY 193, Pierrepont Manor, to Ellisburg, no facilities

134mm parking area both lanes

39(133) Mannsville, no facilities

38(131) US 11, **E...lodging:** 81-11 Motel

37(128) Lacona, Sandy Creek, **E...gas:** Lacona Gas, **food:** J&R Diner, **lodging:** Harris Lodge, Lake Effect Inn, **W...gas:** Citgo, Sunoco/diesel, **food:** Subway, **lodging:** Salmon River Motel, **other:** KOA, **4 mi W...**Colonial Camping

36(121) NY 13(no immediate return sb or nb), Pulaski, **E...gas:** Agway/diesel, Citgo, **food:** C&M Diner, Ponderosa, **lodging:** Redwood Motel, Whitaker's Motel, **W...gas:** Mobil/diesel, Sunoco/diesel, **food:** Arby's, Burger King, McDonald's, **lodging:** Country Pizza Motel, Super 8, **other:** Aldi Foods, Chevrolet/Buick, Kinney Drug, NAPA, P&C Foods, Radio Shack, to Selkirk Shores SP, camping, fish hatchery

35(118) to US 11, Tinker Tavern Rd, **W...**Grandpa Bob's Animal Park

34(115) NY 104, to Mexico, **E...gas:** Sunoco/EZ/diesel/24hr/@, **2-12 mi W...gas:** Citgo, **lodging:** La Siesta Motel, Eis House, **other:** KOA, Salmon Country/Dowiedale/Jellystone Camping

33(111) NY 69, Parish, **E...gas:** Sunoco/diesel/24hr/@, **food:** Grist Mill Rest., **W...gas:** Mobil/diesel, **food:** Talk Town Rest., **lodging:** Montclair Motel, E Coast Resort, **other:** MEDICAL CARE, Up Country RV Park

32(103) NY 49, to Central Square, **E...gas:** Mobil/diesel, Sunoco/diesel, **food:** Golly's Rest., **other:** NAPA AutoCare, Pennzoil, **W...gas:** FasTrac/gas, **food:** Arby's, Burger King, McDonald's, Quinto's NY Pizza, **lodging:** Pine Grove Motel, **other:** Advance Parts, Ford, NAPA, Rite Aid, Wal-Mart SuperCtr/gas/24hr

101mm rest area sb, full(handicapped)facilities, phone, picnic tables, litter barrels, vending, petwalk

31(99) to US 11, Brewerton, **E...**Oneida Shores Camping, **W...gas:** Citgo, Mobil/diesel, Sunoco, **food:** Burger King, Castaways Rest., Little Caesar's, McDonald's, Sam's Lakeside Rest., Subway, **lodging:** BelAir Motel, Brewerton Motel, Holiday Inn Express, **other:** Kinney Drugs

Syracuse

30(96) NY 31, to Cicero, **E...gas:** Hess/diesel, Mobil, Sunoco, **Food:** Arby's, Cracker Barrel, **W...gas:** Citgo/diesel, Kwikfill, **food:** Frank's Café, Plainville Farms Rest., **other:** MEDICAL CARE, RV Ctr

29(93) I-481 S, Syracuse, NY 481, to Oswego, **1 mi W on US 11...gas:** Hess, Mobil, **food:** Burger King, Denny's, Dunkin Donuts, Friendly's, KFC, McDonald's, Papa John's, Perkins, Pizza Hut, Red Lobster, Taco Bell, Tully's Rest., **lodging:** Rodeway Inn, **other:** Advance Parts, AutoZone, Chrysler/Plymouth, Dodge, Eckerd, Firestone/auto, Ford/Lincoln/Mercury, Goodyear/auto, Home Depot, NAPA, PepBoys, PriceChopper Foods, VW/Porche/Audi, Wegman's Foods, mall

28(91) N Syracuse, Taft Rd, **E...**Eckerd, **W...gas:** Mobil

27(90) N Syracuse, **E...**airport

26(89) US 11, Mattydale, **E...gas:** Mobil, **food:** Doug's Fishfry, Friendly's, Hunan Empire, Paladino's Pizza, **lodging:** Red Carpet Inn, **other:** DENTIST, Advance Parts, Eckerd, Ford, Goodyear/auto, K-Mart, Michael's, Staples, **W...gas:** Hess/diesel, Kwikfill, **food:** Applebee's, Burger King, Denny's, KFC, McDonald's, Ponderosa, Subway, Taco Bell, Wendy's, **lodging:** Rest Inn, **other:** Aamco, Aldi Foods, Kost Tire, Lexus, Mazda, Toyota/VW

25a(88) I-90, NY Thruway

25(87.5) 7th North St, **E...gas:** Pilot/McDonald's/diesel/24hr/@, **other:** auto repair, **W...gas:** Mobil, **food:** Bob Evans, Burger King, Colorado Steaks, Denny's, Friendly's, Ground Round, Jreck Subs, **lodging:** Day's Inn, Econolodge, Hampton Inn, Holiday Inn, Quality Inn, Ramada, Super 8, **other:** NAPA

Syracuse

24(86) NY 370 W, to Liverpool, **W...gas:** Hess, **other:** Best Buy, JC Penney, Kaufmann's, mall

23(86) NY 370 E, Hiawatha Blvd, **W...gas:** Hess, **other:** Best Buy, Borders Books, CompUSA, JC Penney, mall, same as 24

22(85) NY 298, Court St, no facilities

21(84.5) Spencer St, Catawba St(from sb), industrial area

20(84) I-690 W(from sb), Franklin St, West St

19(84) I-690 E, Clinton St, Salina St, to E Syracuse

18(84) Harrison St, Adams St, **E...lodging:** University Hotel, **other:** HOSPITAL, CVS Drug, to Syracuse U, Civic Ctr

17(82) Brighton Ave, S Salina St, **W...gas:** KwikFill, Mobil

16a(81) I-481 N, to DeWitt

16(78) US 11, Onondaga Nation, to Nedrow, **1-2 mi W...gas:** Hess, Mobil, **food:** McDonald's, Pizza Hut, Smoke Signals Diner

15(73) US 20, La Fayette, **E...gas:** Sunoco/diesel, **food:** Mama Mia Pizza, Nice'n Easy Deli, **other:** DENTIST, IGA Foods, NAPA, USPO, st police, **W...food:** McDonald's

70mm truck insp sta both lanes, phones

Interstate 81

14(67) NY 80, Tully, **E...gas:** Sunoco/diesel, **food:** Nice'n Easy Deli, **lodging:** Best Western, **W...food:** Burger King

13(63) NY 281, Preble, **E...**to Song Mtn Ski Resort

60mm rest area nb, full(handicapped)facilities, phone, picnic tables, litter barrels, vending, petwalk

12(53) US 11, NY 281, to Homer, **W...gas:** Mobil/diesel/24hr, KwikFill, **food:** Applebee's, Burger King, Doug's Fishfry, Little Italy Pizzaria, Rusty Nail Rest., **lodging:** Budget Inn, **other:** HOSPITAL, to Fillmore Glen SP

11(52) NY 13, Cortland, **E...food:** Denny's, **lodging:** Comfort Inn, Quality Inn, **W...gas:** Mobil, Arby's, **food:** Bob Evans, China Moon, Friendly's, Little Caesar's, McDonald's, Subway, Taco Bell, Wendy's, **lodging:** Holiday Inn, **other:** Advance Parts, Eckerd, Family$, Jo-Ann Fabrics, Kost Tire, P&C Foods/24hr, Yellow Lantern Camping, museum

10(50) US 11, NY 41, to Cortland, McGraw, **W...gas:** Agway/diesel, Citgo/Burger King/Pizza Hut/diesel/@, Mobil/Subway/diesel/24hr, Sunoco/diesel, **food:** Skyliner Diner, **lodging:** Cortland Motel, Day's Inn

45mm parking area nb, picnic tables

9(38) US 11, NY 221, **W...gas:** Citgo, Sunoco/diesel/24hr, XtraMart, **food:** NY Pizzaria, Taco Express, **lodging:** 3 Bear Inn/rest., Greek Peak Lodge, **other:** NAPA, Country Hills Camping

33mm rest area sb, full(handicapped)facilities, phone, picnic tables, litter barrels, vending, petwalk

8(30) NY 79, to US 11, NY 26, NY 206(no EZ return), Whitney Pt, **E...gas:** Hess, Kwikfill, Mobil/diesel/24hr, **food:** Aiello's Ristorante, Arby's, McDonald's, Subway, **lodging:** Point Motel, **other:** Chevrolet, NAPA, Parts+, Radio Shack, Strawberry Valley Farms(3mi), to Dorchester Park

7(21) US 11, Castle Creek, **W...gas:** Mobil

6(16) US 11, to NY 12, I-88E, Chenango Bridge, **E on US 11...gas:** Citgo/diesel, Exxon, Hess/Blimpie/diesel, KwikFill, Mobil, **food:** Arby's, Burger King, China Buffet, Denny's, Dunkin Donuts, Friendly's, King Grill, McDonald's, Pizza Hut, Ponderosa, Subway, Wendy's, **lodging:** Comfort Inn, Day's Inn, Motel 6, **other:** Advance Parts, CVS Drug, Eckerd, Ford/Mazda, Giant Foods, Harley-Davidson, Kost Tire, Lowe's Whse, Radio Shack

15mm I-88 begins eb

14mm rest area nb, full(handicapped)facilities, phone, picnic tables, litter barrels

5(14) US 11, Front St, **1 mi W...gas:** Mobil/diesel, **food:** Cracker Barrel, Nirchi's Pizza, **lodging:** Day's Inn, Econolodge, Fairfield Inn, Motel 6, Super 8

4(13) NY 17, Binghamton, no facilities

3(12) Broad Ave, Binghamton, **W...gas:** Exxon, **food:** KFC, Papa John's, **other:** CVS Drug, Giant Foods

2(8) US 11, NY 17, **1-2 mi W...gas:** Exxon, Lechner's/diesel, Pilot/Wendy's/diesel/24hr/@, TA/Sunoco/diesel/rest./@, Travelport/diesel, **food:** Arby's, Burger King, Far Out Pizza, McDonald's, Subway, **lodging:** Del Motel, Foothills Motel, Super 8, Thruway Motel

1(4) US 11, NY 7, Kirkwood, **1-2 mi W...gas:** Citgo, Mobil/diesel/24hr, Xtra, **lodging:** Kirkwood Motel, Wright Motel

2mm rest area nb, full(handicapped)facilities, phone, picnic tables, litter barrels, vending, petwalk

1mm weigh sta nb

0mm New York/Pennsylvania state line

Interstate 84

Exit #(mm)Services

71.5mm New York/Connecticut state line

21(68) US 6, US 202, NY 121(from wb), N Salem, same as 20

20(67.5) I-684, US 6, US 202, NY 22, **N...gas:** Mobil/24hr, Shell/diesel, **food:** Bob's Diner, Burger King, McDonald's, **lodging:** BelAire Motel, Heidi's Motel, **other:** Cadillac, Ford, Subaru

19(65) NY 312, Carmel, **S...food:** Applebee's, Friendly's, KFC, McDonald's, Wendy's, **other:** HOSPITAL, Home Depot, Kohl's, st police

18(62) NY 311, Lake Carmel, **S...**Bob's Towing/diesel

17(59) Ludingtonville Rd, **S...gas:** Hess/Blimpie/diesel/24hr, Sunoco, **food:** Lou's Deli, Tina's Rest.

56mm elevation 970 ft

55mm rest area both lanes, full(handicapped)facilities, phone, vending, picnic tables, litter barrels, petwalk

16(53) Taconic Parkway, N to Albany, S to New York, no facilities

15(51) Lime Kiln NY, **3 mi N...gas:** Mobil/24hr, **food:** Dunkin Donuts, Olympic Diner, **lodging:** Royal Inn

13(46) US 9, to Poughkeepsie, **N...gas:** Mobil/diesel, **food:** Boston Mkt, Burger King, Cracker Barrel, Denny's, Ruby Tuesday, Stanley's Eatery, Taco Bell, Wendy's, **lodging:** Courtyard, Hampton Inn, Hilton Garden, Holiday Inn, Homestead Suites, MainStay Suites, Residence Inn, Wellesley Inn, **other:** Sam's Club, Wal-Mart SuperCtr/24hr, **S...gas:** Hess/diesel/24hr, **food:** McDonald's, Pizza Hut, Subway

NEW YORK

Interstate 84

E ↕ W

12(45) NY 52 E, Fishkill, **N...gas:** Coastal/diesel, Gulf, **food:** Friendly's, **S...gas:** Mobil, Sunoco/diesel, **food:** Dunkin Donuts, Hometown Deli, I-84 Diner/24hr, KFC
11(42) NY 9D, to Wappingers Falls, **1 mi N...gas:** Citgo/24hr, Mobil/diesel, Sunoco
41mm toll booth wb
40mm Hudson River
10(39) US 9W, NY 32, to Newburgh, **N...gas:** Citgo/diesel, Mobil, Shell, **food:** Burger King, Alexis Diner, McDonald's, Perkins, **lodging:** Budget Inn, Economy Inn, **S...gas:** Exxon/diesel, Sunoco/diesel, **food:** Subway, **lodging:** Travel Inn, Windsor Inn, **other:** HOSPITAL
8(37) NY 52, to Walden, **N...gas:** Citgo/diesel, Sunoco/24hr
7(36) NY 300, Newburgh, to I-87(NY Thruway), **N...gas:** Exxon/24hr, Mobil/24hr, **food:** McDonald's, Perkins, Taco Bell, Wendy's, **other:** MEDICAL CARE, AutoZone, KOA, Sears, mall, **S...gas:** Sunoco, **food:** Applebee's, Burger King, Cosimos Ristorante, Denny's, Gateway Diner, Neptune Diner, **lodging:** Clarion, Hampton Inn, Holiday Inn, Howard Johnson, Ramada Inn, Super 8, **other:** Auto Mall/dealers, Home Depot, Lowe's Whse, Nissan, Wal-Mart/auto
6(34) NY 17K, to Newburgh, **N...gas:** Mobil/24, Pilot/Arby's/diesel/24hr, **food:** Airport Diner, **lodging:** Comfort Inn, Hampton Inn, **S...gas:** Exxon/diesel, **lodging:** Courtyard
5(29) NY 208, Maybrook, **N...gas:** Exxon/24hr, Mobil, **food:** Burger King, McDonald's, **other:** Eckerd, ShopRite Foods, **S...gas:** Stewarts, TA/diesel/rest./@, **food:** Maybrook Diner, Pizza Hut, Subway, **lodging:** Rodeside Inn, Super 8, **other:** Blue Beacon, Winding Hills Camping
24mm rest area wb, full(handicapped)facilities, phone, vending, picnic tables, litter barrels, petwalk
4(19) NY 17, Middletown, **N...gas:** Getty, Mobil/24hr, Sunoco, **food:** Americana Diner, Applebee's, Boston Mkt, Charlie Brown Steaks, Denny's, Friendly's, Galleria Rest., KFC, McDonald's, Olive Garden, Red Lobster, Ruby Tuesday, Subway, Taco Bell, Wendy's, **lodging:** Howard Johnson, Middletown Motel, Super 8, **other:** HOSPITAL, Best Buy, Circuit City, Firestone/auto, Hannaford Foods, Home Depot, JC Penney, Lowe's Whse, Old Navy, Rite Aid, Sam's Club, Sears/auto, ShopRite Food, U-Haul, Wal-Mart SuperCtr/24hr, mall, **S...gas:** Getty/diesel, Mobil, **food:** El Bandido Mexican, Outback Steaks, TGIFriday, **lodging:** Courtyard, Hampton Inn, Holiday Inn, **other:** st police
17mm rest area eb, full(handicapped)facilities, phone, vending, picnic tables, litter barrels, petwalk

Middletown

3(15) US 6, to Middletown, **N...gas:** Citgo/diesel/24hr, Mobil, **food:** Burger King, Colonial Diner, Ground Round, McDonald's, Perkins, Pizza Hut, Ponderosa, 6-17 Diner, Taco Bell, Wendy's, **other:** HOSPITAL, Acura/Honda, Chevrolet/Isuzu, Mazda, Subaru, **S...gas:** 84 Kwikstop, Sunoco/diesel, **lodging:** Day's Inn, Global Budget Inn, **other:** Chrysler/Jeep, Nissan/BMW/Suzuki, Kia, Toyota, transmissions
2(5) Mountain Rd, **S...**Delaney's Steaks
4mm elevation 1254 ft wb, 1272 ft eb
3mm parking area both lanes
1(1) US 6, NY 23, Port Jervis, **N...gas:** Sunoco/diesel, **food:** Arlene&Tom's Diner, KFC, **lodging:** Deerdale Motel, Painted Aprons Motel, **other:** Ford/Lincoln/Mercury, **S...gas:** Citgo/diesel, Exxon/diesel, Gulf/diesel, **food:** DQ, McDonald's, Ponderosa, **lodging:** Comfort Inn, **other:** HOSPITAL, ShopRite Foods, mall
0mm New York/Pennsylvania state line, Delaware River

Pt Jervis

Middletown

Interstate 86

Exit#(mm)Services
I-86 begins/ends on I-87, exit 16.

E ↕ W

131(386) NY 17, **N...other:** Outlets/famous brands, **S...gas:** Exxon/Subway/diesel, Mobil, Sunoco, **food:** McDonald's, **lodging:** American Budget Inn, Harriman Motel
130a(384)US 6, Bear Mtn, to West Point, **S...other:** Home Depot, Wal-Mart SuperCtr/24hr
130(383) NY 208, Monroe, Washingtonville, **N...gas:** Citgo, Mobil/diesel, **food:** Burger King, Pizza Hut, **lodging:** James Motel, Lake Ann Motel, **other:** Chrysler/Dodge/Jeep, Daewoo, Isuzu, st police
129(380) Museum Village Rd, **S...food:** Plum House Rest
126(378) NY 94, Chester, Florida, **N...gas:** Citgo, Gulf, Mobil, Sunoco/diesel, **food:** Lobster Pier Rest., McDonald's, Sunrise Diner, Wendy's, **other:** Radio Shack, ShopRite Foods, Black Bear Camping, funpark, **S...lodging:** Chester Inn
125(375) NY 17M E, South St, **S...food:** Pizza Deli, White House Rest., **other:** HOSPITAL
124(373) NY 17A, NY 207, **N...gas:** Exxon/diesel, Mobil/diesel, Sunoco/diesel, **food:** Burger King, Country Chicken, Friendly's, Dunkin Donuts, Pizza Hut, Plaza Diner, **other:** Grand Union Foods, **S...other:** Chrysler/Plymouth/Dodge/Jeep, Hyundai
122a(369)Fletcher St, Goshen, no facilities
122(364) rd 67, E Main St, Crystal Run Rd, **N...gas:** Mobil, **food:** El Bandido Rest., FoodCourt, Outback Steaks, Rusty Nail Rest., **lodging:** Hampton Inn, Holiday Inn, **S...gas:** Getty/diesel
121(363) I-84, E to Newburgh, W to Port Jervis
120(362) NY 211, **N...gas:** Sunoco, **food:** American Café, Olive Garden, **lodging:** Howard Johnson, Middletown Motel, Super 8, **other:** Best Buy, Cosimo's, Filene's, Hannaford's Foods, JC Penney, Sam's Club, Wal-Mart, **S...gas:** Getty, Mobil, **food:** Americana Diner, Arby's, Boston Mkt, Burger King, China Buffet, Denny's, Friendly's, Hana Japanese, Pizza Hut,

Interstate 86

Red Lobster, Wendy's, **other:** AutoZone, Circuit City, Eckerd, Ford, Home Depot, Jo-Ann Fabrics, K-Mart, PriceChopper, ShopRite Foods, Staples, Stop&Shop Foods, U-Haul

119(359) NY 309, Pine Bush, **S...gas:** Best Gas/diesel

118a(358) NY 17M, Fair Oaks, no facilities

118(357) Circleville, **N...lodging:** Heritage Motel, **S...gas:** Citgo, Exxon/diesel, Mobil, **food:** Raffael's Italian

116(355) NY 17K, Bloomingburg, **S...gas:** Citgo, Mobil, **food:** Gaudio Diner, Quikway Diner, **other:** Rainbow Valley Camping

113(351) US 209, Wurtsboro, Ellenville, **N...gas:** Citgo/diesel, Mobil/diesel, Stewarts/gas, **food:** Giovanni's Café, **lodging:** Davidman Motel, Gold Mtn Chalet, Day's Inn, Valley Brook Motel, **other:** American Family Campground, Spring Glen Camping

112(350) Masten Lake, Yankee Lake, **S...food:** Potager Diner, **lodging:** ValleyBrook Motel, **other:** WonderWood Camping

111(347) Wolf Lake, **S...gas:** Billy's/diesel

110(345) Lake Louise Marie, **N...lodging:** Dodge Inn Rest.

109(343) Rock Hill, Woodridge, **N...gas:** Exxon/diesel, **food:** Bernie's Diner, LandSea Rest., RockHill Diner, **lodging:** Rosemond Motel, **other:** Hilltop Farms Camping, Lazy G Camping, **S...gas:** Mobil/diesel

108(342) Bridgeville, same as 109

107(340) Thompsonville, **S...food:** Apollo FoodCourt, Hana Rest., Old Homestead Diner, **lodging:** Affordable Inn, Pines Motel, Raleigh Motel, **other:** Chevrolet, Chrysler/Plymouth/Dodge/Jeep, Toyota

105(337) NY 42, Monticello, **N...gas:** Coastal, Exxon/diesel, Mobil, **food:** Bro Bruno Diner, Blue Horizon Diner, Giovanni's Café, KFC, Kutshner's Café, McDonald's, **other:** ShopRite Foods, Wal-Mart SuperCtr/24hr, **S...gas:** Citgo, Stewarts, **food:** Burger King, Monticello Diner, Pizza Hut, Wendy's, **lodging:** Econolodge, Ramada Ltd, **other:** NAPA

104(336) NY 17B, Raceway, Monticello, **S...gas:** Citgo, Exxon, **food:** Bean Bag Eatery, Kelly's Diner, Taco Maker, **lodging:** Best Western, Raceway Motel, Travel Inn, **other:** Swinging Bridge Camp, airport

102(330) Harris, **S...other:** HOSPITAL, Swan Lake Camping

101(328) Ferndale, Swan Lake, **S...gas:** Exxon/diesel

100(327) NY 52 E, Liberty, **N...gas:** Sunoco, **food:** Albert's Rest., Burger King, McDonald's, Taco Bell, Wendy's, **lodging:** Best Inn, Day's Inn, **S...gas:** Citgo, Exxon/diesel, Gulf, Mobil, **food:** Dunkin Donuts, Pizza Hut, **lodging:** Liberty Motel, Lincoln Motel, **other:** Eckerd, Ford/Lincoln/Mercury, Pontiac/Buick, Neversink River Camping, Swan Lake Camping, Yogi Bear Camping

99(325) NY 52 W, to NY 55, Liberty, **S...gas:** Exxon, Sunoco, **food:** Dairy Barn, **lodging:** Catskill Motel

98(321) Cooley, Parksville, **N...gas:** Mobil, **food:** DairyKing, W 17 Diner, **lodging:** Best Western, **S...food:** Tumbleweeds Grill

97(319) Morsston, no facilities

96(316) Livingston Manor, **N...food:** Catskill Rest., **lodging:** Econo Motel, **S...lodging:** OZ B&B, Willowemac Motel

313mm rest area eb, full(handicapped)facilities, picnic tables, litter barrels, phones, vending, petwalk

94(311) NY 206, Roscoe, Lew Beach, **N...gas:** Exxon/diesel, Sunoco, **food:** 1910 Coffeshop, Ramondo's Diner, Roscoe Diner, **lodging:** Reynolds House Motel, Rockland House Motel, Roscoe Motel, Tennanah Lake Motel, **other:** Roscoe Camping, **S...gas:** Mobil/diesel

93(305) to Cooks Falls(from wb), no facilities

92(303) Horton, Cooks Falls, Colchester, **S...gas:** Sunoco/diesel, **food:** Riverside Café/lodge, **other:** Russell Brook Camping

90(297) NY 30, East Branch, Downsville, **N...gas:** Sunoco, **other:** Beaver-Del Camping, Catskill Mtn Camping, Oxbow Camping, Peaceful Valley Camping, **S...lodging:** E Branch Motel

295mm rest area wb, full(handicapped)facilities, picnic tables, litter barrels, phones, vending, petwalk

89(292) Fishs Eddy, no facilities

87a(288) NY 268(from wb), same as 87

87(285) NY 97, to NY 268, to NY 191, Hancock, Cadosia, **S...gas:** Getty, Mobil, **food:** Circle E Diner, Country Bakeshop/rest., Family Rest., Great Wall Chinese, McDonald's, Subway, **lodging:** Colonial Motel, Starlight Lake Inn, **other:** Buick/Chevrolet, NAPA, Parts+

276mm parking area wb, litter barrels

84(274) Deposit, **N...gas:** Citgo/diesel/24hr, Schaeffer's Quickway, Wheeler's, **food:** Wendy's, **lodging:** Deposit Motel, Laurel Bank Motel, **other:** st police

83(273) Deposit, Oquaga Lake

82(270) NY 41, McClure, Sanford, **N...**Kellystone Park, **S...gas:** Sun/diesel, **food:** Alexander's, Marj's Diner/rest., **lodging:** B&B/diner, Chestnut Inn, Scott's Family Resort

265mm parking area eb, picnic tables, litter barrels

81(263) E Bosket Rd, no facilities

80(261) Damascus, **N...gas:** Exxon/diesel, **food:** Damascus Diner, **other:** Forest Hill Lake Park Camping

79(259) NY 79, Windsor, **N...gas:** Citgo, Sunoco, XtraMart, **other:** Lakeside Camping, **S...food:** Marian's Pizza

78(256) Dunbar Rd, Occanum, no facilities

77(254) W Windsor, **N...gas:** Mobil/diesel, ExpressMart/24hr

76(251) Haskins Rd, to Foley Rd, no facilities

75(250) I-81 S, to PA

72(244) I-81 N, US 11, Front St, Clinton St, **S...food:** McDonald's, **other:** Advance Parts, K-Mart

NEW YORK

Interstate 86

E ↕ W

71(242) Airport Rd, Johnson City, **S...gas:** Exxon
70(241) NY 201, Johnson City, **N...gas:** Exxon, **food:** ChiChi's, McDonald's, Pizza Hut, Ponderosa, Taco Bell, **lodging:** Best Inn, Best Western, Hampton Inn, Red Roof Inn, **other:** JC Penney, Kaufmann's, Kost Tire, Wegman's Foods, mall, **S...**Home Depot
69(239) NY 17C, no facilities
238mm Susquehanna River
68(237) NY 17C, Old Vestal Rd, no facilities
67(236) NY 26, NY 434, Vestal, Endicott, **S on NY 434... gas:** Exxon/diesel, **food:** Burger King, China Wok, McDonald's, Old Country Buffet, Olive Garden, Red Lobster, Taco Bell, TGIFriday, Uno Pizzaria, **lodging:** Parkway Motel, SkyLark Motel/rest., **other:** Advance Parts, Barnes&Noble, Chevrolet, Chrysler/Plymouth/Jeep, $Tree, Ford, Grand Union Foods, Jo-AnnFabrics, Kost Tire, Lincoln/Mercury, Lowe's Whse, Nissan, OfficeMax, Subaru, Sam's Club, Target, Wal-Mart SuperCtr/24hr
66(231) NY 434, Apalachin, **S...gas:** KwikFill, Mobil/Subway/diesel, **food:** Blue Dolphin Diner, Donoli's Rest., Dunkin Donuts, McDonald's, **lodging:** Dolphin Inn
65(225) NY 17C, NY 434, Owego, **N...gas:** Mobil/diesel, **food:** Burger King, KFC, McDonald's, Tony's Pizza, Wendy's, **lodging:** Holiday Inn Express, Treadway Motel/rest.
64(223) NY 96, Owego, **N...lodging:** DeepWell Motel, Sunrise Motel, **S...other:** Pennzoil/gas
63(218) Lounsberry, **S...gas:** Exxon/diesel
62(214) NY 282, Nichols, **S...gas:** Citgo/diesel, Sunoco/diesel, **food:** Carmella's Italian
212mm rest area eb, full(handicapped)facilities, picnic tables, litter barrels, phone, vending, petwalk
208mm Susquehanna River
61(206) NY 34, PA 199, Waverly, Sayre, **N...gas:** Sunoco/diesel, **food:** McDonald's, **lodging:** Best Western, **other:** HOSPITAL, Goodyear, **S...**Citgo/24hr
60(204) US 220, Waverly, to Sayre, **S...gas:** Citgo, Mobil, **food:** Wendy's
59a(202) Wilawana, **S...gas:** Sunoco/diesel
59(200) NY 427, Chemung, **N...gas:** Dandy/diesel
199mm rest area wb, full(handicapped)facilities,picnic tables, litter barrels, phone, vending, petwalk
195.5mm parking area
58(195) Lowman, Wellsburg, **N...food:** W Diner, **lodging:** Red Jacket Motel, **S...other:** Gardiner Hill Campsites(4mi), Tillotson Farms Camping(5mi)

Elmira

57(190) Jerusalem Hill, no facilities
56(189) NY 352, Elmira, **S...gas:** Citgo, Sunoco/diesel, **food:** Hoss' Rest., McDonald's, Pizza Hut, **lodging:** Coachman Motel, Holiday Inn, Twain Motel, **other:** HOSPITAL
54(186) NY 13, to Ithaca
185mm I-86 begins ends. **gas:** Mobil, Sunoco, **food:** Dunkin Donuts, LJ Silver, Wendy's, **lodging:** Motel 6, Red Carpet Inn, **other:** Eckerd, K-Mart
52(184) NY 14, to Watkins Glen, **N...food:** Friendly's, **lodging:** Holiday Inn, Knight's Inn, **S...food:** Denny's, Taste of China, **other:** SavALot Foods
52a(183) Commerce Ctr, same as 51
51(182) Chambers Rd, **N...gas:** Mobil/Subway/diesel, Sunoco/diesel, **food:** Lum's, McDonald's, Olive Garden, Outback Steaks, Red Lobster, Rico's Pizza, Ruby Tuesday, **lodging:** Country Inn Suites, Hilton Garden, Knights Inn, **other:** BonTon, JC Penney, Kaufman's, Sears/auto, mall, **S...food:** Applebee's, China Inn, Gino's Pizza, Old Country Buffet, Taco Bell, TGIFriday, Wendy's, **lodging:** Econolodge, Relax Inn, **other:** Barnes&Noble, $Tree, Lowe's Whse, Michael's, Old Navy, Sam's Club, Staples, Top's Foods, Wal-Mart, museum
49(178) Olcott Rd, Canal St, Big Flats, **N...**airport, **S...gas:** Sunoco/diesel, **food:** Picnic Pizza, Shanghai Express

Corning

48(176) NY 352, E Corning, **N...gas:** Citgo, **food:** Tag's Rest., **lodging:** Budget Inn, Gatehouse Motel
47(174) NY 352, Gibson, E Corning, **N...lodging:** Budget Inn
46(171) NY 414, Corning, to Watkins Glen, **S...lodging:** Comfort Inn, **other:** HOSPITAL, Serenbaugh Camping, KOA, museum
45(170) NY 352, Corning, **S...food:** Bob Evans, Burger King, Friendly's, McDonald's, Trixie's Diner, Wendy's, **lodging:** Fairfield Inn, Radisson, **other:** AutoZone, Chrysler/Plymouth/Dodge/Jeep, Eckerd
44(168) US 15 S, NY 417 W, Gang Mills, **N...lodging:** Best Western, Holiday Inn
43(167) NY 415, Painted Post, **N...gas:** Citgo, **food:** Burger King, Friendly's, Magic Wok, McDonald's, Pizza Hut, Ramblers Drive-In, **other:** AutoValue Parts, CarQuest, Eckerd, Firestone/auto, Jo-Ann Fabrics, Radio Shack, **S...gas:** Sunoco, **food:** Denny's, **lodging:** Comfort Inn, Hampton Inn
42(165) Coopers Plains, **N...**st police, **S...lodging:** Lamplighter Motel, Stiles Motel
41(161) rd 333, Campbell, **S...gas:** Shell, **other:** Cardinal Campsites, Camp Bell Camping
160mm rest area eb, full(handicapped)facilities, picnic tables, litter barrels, phone, vending, petwalk
40(156) NY 226, Savona, **N...gas:** Mobil/diesel, **food:** Savona Diner, **other:** Green Acres Camping
39(153) NY415, **N...food:** Chat-a-Whyle Rest., **lodging:** Holland American Country Inn, National Hotel, **S...other:** Babcock Hollow Camping, auto repair

Bath

38(150) NY 54, Bath, to Hammondsport, **N...gas:** Mobil, **food:** Arby's, Burger King, Dunkin Donuts, McDonald's, Pizza Hut, Ponderosa, Subway, **lodging:** Budget Inn, Day's Inn, Super 8, Vinehurst Inn, **other:** HOSPITAL, Advance Parts, AutoValue Parts, Chrysler/Plymouth/Dodge/Jeep, Eckerd, Family$, Ford/Lincoln/Mercury, K-Mart, NAPA, Rite Aid, Top's Foods, museum, st police, winery, to Keuka Lake

Hornell

147mm rest area wb, full(handicapped)facilities, phone, picnic tables, litter barrels, vending, petwalk
37(146) NY 53, Kanona, to Prattsburg, **S...gas:** Sunoco/diesel/rest., **other:** WagonWheel Camping
36(145) I-390 N, NY 15, to Rochester
35(138) Howard, **S...**to Lake Demmon RA, phone
34(130) NY 36, Hornell, Arkport, **N...gas:** Mobil/diesel, **other:** Stony Brook SP, Sun Valley Camping, **S...gas:** Gulf, **food:** Burger King, Country Kitchen, Friendly's,

Interstate 86

McDonald's, Ponderosa, Rupert's Rest., **lodging:** Comfort Inn, Econolodge, Sunshine Motel, Super 8, **other:** Aldi, Chevrolet, Chrysler/Plymouth/ Dodge/Jeep, Ford/Mercury, NAPA, Wal-Mart/auto, Wegman's Foods

125mm scenic overlook eb

33(124) NY 21, Almond, Andover, to Alfred, **S...gas:** Mobil, **food:** Coslo's Rest., Pizza Hut, **lodging:** College Inn, Saxon Inn Hotel, **other:** Lake Lodge Camping, Sage Creek Stores

117mm highest elevation on I-86, elev 2110 ft

32(116) W Almond, no facilities

31(108) Angelica, **N...gas:** Atlantic, Citgo, Sunoco, **lodging:** Angelica Inn B&B

30(104) NY 19, Belmont, Wellsville, **N...**6-S Camping(3mi), **S...gas:** TA/Mobil/diesel/rest./24hr/@, **other:** Park Meadow Camping(6mi)

101mm rest area eb, full(handicapped)facilities, phone, picnic tables, litter barrels, vending, petwalk

29(99) NY 275, Friendship, to Bolivar, **S...gas:** Sunoco, Miller &Brandes Gas

28(92) NY 305, Cuba, **N...lodging:** Coachlight Motel, **other:** Uncle Bo's RV Park, **S...gas:** BP/diesel, Exxon, Sunoco/diesel, **food:** Giant Foodmart, McDonald's, Moonwink's Rest., **other:** HOSPITAL,

27(84) NY 16, NY 446, Hinsdale, **N...**food, **S...**gas, lodging

26(79) NY 16, Olean, **S...gas:** Sunoco, **food:** Burger King, Wendy's, **other:** HOSPITAL

25(77) Olean, **S...gas:** Citgo, **other:** HOSPITAL, **2 mi S on Constitution...gas:** UniMart, **food:** Burger King, Luigi's Pasta, **lodging:** Comfort Inn, **other:** BJ's Whse, K-Mart, Radio Shack, Wal-Mart, St Bonaventure U

24(74) NY 417, Allegany, **S...gas:** Mobil/diesel, **food:** Village Tastee, **other:** Farm&Family, St Bonaventure U

23(68) US 219 S, **N...gas:** M&M/Subway/diesel, lodging, **S...**gas, **lodging:** Howard Johnson(10mi)

66mm Allegheny River

21(61) US 219 N, Salamanca, **S...food:** Red Garter Rest.

20(58) NY 417, NY 353, Salamanca, **N...food:** Nafco Quickstop, Seneca Hawk Petro, **food:** Burger King, McDonald's, **other:** AutoZone, Rail Museum, Seneca-Iroquis Museum

19(54) **S...other:** Allegany SP, Red House Area

18(51) NY 280, **S...other:** Allegany SP, Quaker Run Area

17(48) NY 394, Steamburg, **N...**gas, **food:** Flaherty's Rest., **other:** RV camping, **S...**gas

16(42) W Main St, Randolph, **N...gas:** Mobil/diesel, **food:** R&M Rest., lodging

41mm rest area eb, phone, picnic table, litter barrel

40mm rest area wb, phone picnic table, litter barrel

15(39) School House Rd, no facilities

14(36) US 62, Kennedy, **N...gas:** Keystone Gas, **S...**RV camping

32mm Cassadaga Creek

13(31) NY 394, Falconer, **S...food:** Burger King, McDonald's, Sugar Creek Diner, Wendy's, **lodging:** Budget Inn, Red Roof Inn

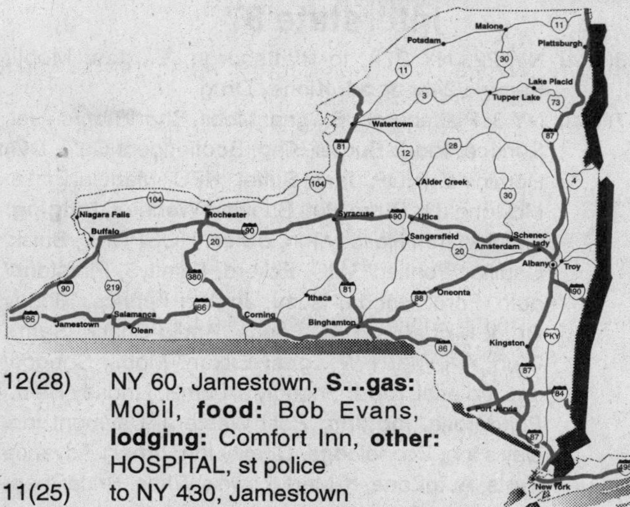

12(28) NY 60, Jamestown, **S...gas:** Mobil, **food:** Bob Evans, **lodging:** Comfort Inn, **other:** HOSPITAL, st police

11(25) to NY 430, Jamestown

10(21) NY 430 W, Bemus Point, **N...**gas, food, lodging, **S...food:** pizzaria, **other:** RV camping

9(20) NY 430 E, no facilities

19mm Chautauqua Lake

8(18) NY 394, Mayville, **N...gas:** Mobil, lodging

7(15) Panama, no facilities

14mm Pendergast Creek

10.5mm French Creek

6(9) NY 76, Sherman, **N...gas:** Mobil, **food:** Village Pizzeria, **other:** Ford, USPO

8mm French Creek

4(1) NY 430, Findley Lake, **N...**motel, **S...**gas, food, lodging, **other:** RV camping, to Peek'n Peak Ski Area

0mm New York/Pennsylvania state line. Exits 3-1 are in PA.

3 PA 89, North East, Wattsburg, **N...**gas, food

1b a I-90, W to Erie, E to Buffalo. I-86 begins/ends on I-90, exit 37.

Interstate 87

Exit #(mm)Services

176mm US/Canada Border, NY state line, I-87 begins/ends.

43(175) US 9, Champlain, **E...**World Duty Free, **W...gas:** Peterbilt Trkstp/diesel/deli/24hr/@, **other:** repair

42(174) US 11 S, Champlain, to Rouse's Point, **E...gas:** Mobil, **food:** Chinese Eatery, Peppercorn Rest., Zachary's Pizza, **lodging:** AmCan Motel, **other:** Chevrolet/ Pontiac(2mi), Kinney Drug, Rite Aid, Tops Foods, USPO, **W...gas:** Irving, Mobil/diesel, Neverett Bros/ Subway/diesel, **food:** Burger King, Dunkin Donuts, McDonald's

41(167) NY 191, Chazy, **E...**st police, **W...**Miner Institute

162mm rest area both lanes, full(handicapped)facilities, info, phone, picnic tables, litter barrels, petwalk

40(160) NY 456, Beekmantown, **E...gas:** Mobil/diesel, **lodging:** Pt Auroche Lodge, Stonehelm Motel/café, **W...**Twin Ells Camping

39(156) NY 314, Moffitt Rd, Plattsburgh Bay, **E...gas:** Stewarts, **food:** Domenic's Rest., Gus' Rest, McDonald's, **lodging:** Pioneer Motel, Rip van Winkle Motel, Super 8, **other:** Plattsburgh RV Park, **W...other:** Shady Oaks Camping, to Adirondacks

NEW YORK

Interstate 87

N Plattsburgh S

38(154) NY 22, NY 374, to Plattsburgh, **E...gas:** Mobil, Sunoco/24hr, **food:** Kinney Drug

37(153) NY 3, Plattsburgh, **E...gas:** Mobil, ShortStop/diesel, Sunoco, **food:** Burger King, Bootleggers Café, DQ, Domino's, IHOP, Jade Buffet, KFC, Mangia Pizza, McDonald's, Pizza Hut, Subway, Wendy's, **lodging:** Comfort Inn, Holiday Inn, **other:** HOSPITAL, Buick, Cadillac/Pontiac/GMC, Eckerd, Family$, Firestone/auto, Ford, Honda, Isuzu, Jo-Ann Fabrics, Kinney Drug, Michael's, P&C Foods, Radio Shack, Sam's Club, Wal-Mart, **W...gas:** Exxon, Mobil, Sunoco/Jreck/diesel, **food:** Friendly's, Lum's, Lindsey Rest., Ponderosa, **lodging:** Best Western, Baymont Inn, Day's Inn, Econolodge, Quality Inn, **other:** Advance Parts, AutoZone, K-Mart, Lowe's Whse, PriceChopper Foods, Sears/auto

151mm Saranac River

36(150) NY 22, Plattsburgh AFB, **E...gas:** Citgo, Mobil/diesel/24hr, **food:** Burger King(3mi), **W...other:** st police

146mm truck insp sta both lanes

35(144) NY 442, Peru, to Port Kent, **2-8 mi E...other:** Iroquois/Ausable Pines Camping, **W...gas:** Citgo/Sugar Creek Diner, Mobil/diesel, Sunoco/Subway/diesel, **food:** Cricket's Rest., McDonald's, **other:** Peru Drug, Tops Foods, USPO

143mm emergency phones at 2 mi intervals begin sb/end nb

34(137) NY 9 N, Ausable Forks, **E...gas:** Sunoco/diesel, **food:** Pleasant Corner Rest., Tastee-Freez, **other:** VETERINARIAN, **W...other:** Prays Mkt, Ausable River RV Camping

136mm Ausable River

33(135) US 9, NY 22, to Willsboro, **E...lodging:** Chesterfield Motel, **other:** RV camping, to Essex Ferry

125mm N Boquet River

32(124) Lewis, **W...gas:** Getty/diesel/24hr, Pierce's Gas/diesel, **food:** Trkstp Diner

123mm rest area both lanes, full(handicapped)facilities, info, phone, picnic tables, petwalk

120mm Boquet River

31(117) NY 9 N, Westport, to Elizabethtown, **E...gas:** Mobil, **lodging:** HillTop Motel, **W...other:** HOSPITAL, st police

30(104) US 9, NY 73, Keene Valley, no facilities

99mm rest area both lanes, full(handicapped)facilities, phone, picnic tables, litter barrels, petwalk

29(94) N Hudson, **E...gas:** Citgo/diesel, **W...**Blue Ridge Falls Camping

28(88) NY 74 E, Schroon Lake, to Ticonderoga, **E...gas:** Sunoco/diesel, **food:** Birches Diner, **lodging:** Schroon Lake B&B, **other:** st police, services on US 9 parallel

83mm rest area both lanes, full(handicapped)facilties, phone, picnic tables, litter barrels, petwalk, vending

27(81) US 9(from nb, no EZ return), Schroon Lake, to gas/diesel, food, lodging

26(78) US 9(no EZ sb return), Pottersville, Schroon Lake, **E...**Ideal Camping, **W...gas:** Mobil/diesel, Black Bear Rest., Big A Parts

25(73) NY 8, Chestertown, **W...gas:** Sunoco/diesel, **other:** RV camping

24(67) Bolton Landing, **E...**RV camping

66mm Schroon River

65mm parking area sb, picnic tables, no facilities

63mm parking area nb, picnic tables, no facilities

23(58) to US 9, Diamond Point, Warrensburg, **W...gas:** Citgo/diesel, Mobil, **food:** McDonald's, **lodging:** Super 8, **other:** Ford/Mercury, RV camping, Central Adirondack Tr, ski area

22(54) US 9, NY 9 N, Lake George, to Diamond Pt, **E...gas:** Citgo, Mobil, **food:** China Wok, Dunkin Donuts, Gino&Tony's Café, Guiseppe's Rest., Jasper's Steaks, JT Kelly's Grill, KFC, Luigi's Italian, Mario's Italian, McDonald's, Pizza Hut, Subway, Taco Bell, Trattoria Siciliano, Trolley Steaks, **lodging:** Admiral Motel, Balmoral Motel, Balsam Motel, Blue Moon Motel, Brookside Motel, Cedarhurst Motel, Econolodge, Ft Henry Resort, Georgian Lodge, Heritage Motel, Knight's Inn, Lakecrest Motel, Lakehaven Motel, Mohawk Cottages, Motel Montreal, Nordick's Motel/rest., Oasis Motel, O'Sullivan's Motel, Park Lane Motel, Quality Inn, 7 Dwarfs Motel, Sundowner Motel, Surfside Motel, Villager Motel, Windsor Lodge, **other:** Rexall Drug, USPO, **W...**parking area both lanes

21(53) NY 9 N, Lake Geo, Ft Wm Henry, **E on US 9...gas:** Mobil, Sunoco, **food:** Adirondack Brewery, A&W, Barnsider Smokehouse, DQ, Mountaineer Rest., Prospect Mt Diner, **lodging:** Best Western, Comfort Inn, Holiday Inn, Holly Tree Inn, Howard Johnson/rest., Nomad Motel, Northland Motel, Ramada Inn, Scottish Inn, Tiki Motel, **W...gas:** Mobil/diesel/LP, **lodging:** Kathy's Motel

51mm Adirondack Park

20(49) NY 149, to Ft Ann, **E...gas:** Mobil/Subway, Sunoco/diesel, **food:** Coach House Diner, Frank's Italian, Logjam Rest., Meeting Place Rest., Montcalm Rest., Trading Post Rest., **lodging:** Day's Inn, French Mtn Motel, Mohican Motel, Rodeway Inn, Samoset Cabins, **other:** Ledgeview RV Park(3mi), Whipporwill/King Phillip/Lake George Camping(2mi), Factory Outlets/famous brands, funpark, st police

Glens Falls

19(47) NY 254, Glens Falls, **E...gas:** Citgo, Hess/Blimpie, Mobil, **food:** Burger King, Dunkin Donuts, FoodCourt, Friendly's, Ground Round, KFC, McDonald's, Mrs B's Café, NY Dogs, Old China Buffet, Olive Garden, Pizza Hut, Ponderosa, Queen Diner, Red Lobster, Silo Rest., Taco Bell, Wendy's, **lodging:** Alpin Haus Motel, Econolodge, Sleep Inn, Welcome Inn, **other:** MEDICAL CARE, Advance Parts, AutoZone, BonTon, CVS Drug, Eckerd, Firestone/auto, Goodyear, JC Penney, Jo-Ann Fabrics, Radio Shack, Rite Aid, Sears, Staples, Wal-Mart, mall, **W...gas:** Mobil, **lodging:** Ramada/rest., st police

Interstate 87

18(45) Glens Falls, **E...gas:** Citgo, Gulf/Subway/24hr, Hess/diesel/24hr, Mobil/24hr, **food:** Carl R's Café, Pizza Hut, Steve's Place Rest., **lodging:** Best Inn, Queensbury Hotel, **other:** HOSPITAL, CVS Drug, Hannaford Foods, U-Haul, **W...gas:** Stewarts, **food:** McDonald's, Super 8

43mm rest area both lanes, full(handicapped)facilities, picnic tables, litter barrels, phone, vending, petwalk

42mm Hudson River

17(40) US 9, S Glen Falls, **E...gas:** Citgo, Getty/Beaver's Diner/diesel, Gulf, Mobil/Waffles+/diesel/24hr, **food:** Moreau Diner, Taco Maker, Wishing Well Rest., **lodging:** Landmark Motel, Sara-Glen Motel, Sunhaven Motel, Swiss American Motel, Town&Country Motel, **other:** American RV Camp, **W...**Moreau Lake SP

16(36) Ballard Rd, Wilton, **E...other:** Coldbrook Campsites, golf, **W...gas:** Mobil, Stewarts, Sunoco/Scotty's Rest./diesel/24hr, **lodging:** Mt View Acres Motel, **other:** Alpin Haus RV Ctr, Ernie's Grocery

15(30) NY 50, NY 29, Saratoga Springs, **E...gas:** Hess/diesel/24hr, Mobil/Blimpie, **food:** Applebee's, Burger King, FoodCourt, Golden Corral, KFC/Taco Bell, McDonald's, Ponderosa, Ruby Tuesday, Uno Pizzaria, **lodging:** Super 8, **other:** Barnes&Noble, BJ's Whse, Dodge, Eckerd, Ford/Mercury, Hannaford Foods, Home Depot, JC Penney, K-Mart, Lowe's Whse, Mazda, Old Navy, PriceChopper Foods, Sears/auto, Staples, Subaru, Target, Toyota, Wal-Mart SuperCtr/24hr, mall, **W...lodging:** Birches Motel, Gateway Motel, Olde Bryan Inn, **other:** HOSPITAL

14(28) NY 9P, Schuylerville, **2 mi E...gas:** Mobil/Lakeside Mkt/deli, **food:** Bayshore Rest./marina, Waterfront Rest., **lodging:** Anchor Inn/rest., Longfellow Inn/rest., Saratoga Lake Inn, Saratoga Springs Motel, **other:** Lee's RV Park, **2 mi W...gas:** Citgo/repair/LP, **lodging:** Holiday Inn, **other:** museum, racetrack

13(25) US 9, Saratoga Springs, **E...food:** Andy's Pizza, Chez Sophie Rest., DeLucia's Deli, **lodging:** Locust Grove Motel, Maggiore's Motel, Post Road Lodge, Unique Posthouse Motel, **other:** Northway RV, Ballston Spa SP, **W...gas:** Mobil, Sunoco/diesel/24hr, **food:** Joe Collins Rest., Packhorse Rest., **lodging:** Design Motel, Hilton Garden, Roosevelt Inn/rest., Thorobred Motel

12(21) NY 67, Malta, **E...gas:** Mobil/diesel, Sunoco, StewartsMart, **food:** Dunkin Donuts, KFC/Taco Bell, Malta Diner, McDonald's, Subway, **lodging:** Cocca's Motel, Riviera Motel, **other:** MEDICAL CARE, CVS Drug, GNC, PriceChopper Foods, st police, **W...**Saratoga NHP

11(18) Round Lake Rd, Round Lake, **W...gas:** StewartsMart, **food:** Adirondack Rest., CiderMill Rest., Good Times Rest.

10(16) Ushers Rd, **E...gas:** Sunoco/diesel, **food:** Ferretti's Rest., **3 mi E...food:** Parkwood Rest., Rusty Nail Rest., **W...gas:** StewartsMart

14mm rest area nb, full(handicapped)facilities, info, phone, picnic tables, litter barrels, vending, petwalk

9(13) NY 146, Clifton Park, **E...gas:** Hess/diesel/24hr, **food:** Burger King, Cracker Barrel, Kabuki Japanese, Pizza Hut, Sam's Pizzaria, Snyder's Rest., **lodging:** Comfort Inn, **other:** Advance Parts, Goodyear/auto, Home Depot, Michael's, OfficeMax, **W...gas:** Mobil, Sunoco/diesel, **food:** Applebee's, Denny's, Dunkin Donuts, Friendly's, KFC, McDonald's, Outback Steaks, Starbucks, Taco Bell, TGIFriday, Wendy's, **lodging:** Best Western, **other:** AutoZone, Chevrolet, CVS Drug, Eckerd, Firestone, Freedom RV Ctr, Hannaford Foods, JC Penney, Jo-Ann Fabrics, K-Mart, Marshall's, PriceChopper Foods, mall, st police

8a(12) Grooms Rd, to Waterford, **2 mi E on US 9...gas:** Getty, Gulf, **food:** 1/2 Moon Diner, Subway

8(10) Crescent, Vischer Ferry, **E...gas:** Hess/24hr, **food:** Krause's Rest.(2mi), McDonald's, **W...gas:** Mobil/Mr Subb/diesel/24hr, Sunoco/24hr, StewartsMart, **other:** CVS Drug

8mm Mohawk River

7(7) NY 7, Troy, **E on US 9 N...lodging:** Hampton Inn, Holiday InnExpress, **other:** Acura, Buick/Pontiac, Eckerd, Ford, Prime Outlets/famous brands, **E on US 9 S...gas:** Mobil, **food:** McDonald's, Subway, **other:** Cottman Transmissions, Infiniti, Marshall's, PriceChopper Foods

6(6) NY 2, to US 9, Schenectady, **E...gas:** Mobil, **food:** Circle Diner, Dakota Steaks, Ground Round, Uno Pizzaria, Vanilla Bean Café, **other:** Caldor, CVS Drug, Goodyear/auto, Sam's Club, Staples, VW, **Wal-Mart**, same as 7, **E on US 9...gas:** Getty, **food:** Burger King, Old Country Buffet, Suns Buffet, Taco Bell, Wendy's, **lodging:** Cocca's Inn, **other:** JC Penney, **W...gas:** Mobil/24hr, **food:** Bennigan's, Friendly's, Kings Buffet, Sebastian's Rest., **lodging:** Clarion, Microtel, Super 8

5(5) NY 155 E, Latham, **E...food:** Vintage Pizza, **lodging:** Latham Inn, **other:** Firestone, USPO, **W...**MEDICAL CARE

NEW YORK

Interstate 87

N ↕ S

Albany

4(4) NY 155 W, Wolf Rd, **E on Wolf Rd...gas:** Hess/diesel, Mobil, Sunoco, **food:** Arby's, Ben&Jerry's, Big House Grill, Burger King, ChiChi's, Denny's, Macaroni Grill, Maxie's Grill, McDonald's, Olive Garden, Outback Steaks, Pizza Hut, Ponderosa, Real Seafood Co, Red Lobster, Subway, Weathervane Seafood, **lodging:** Best Western, Courtyard, Hampton Inn, Holiday Inn, Marriott, Red Roof Inn, **other:** Chevrolet, CVS Drug, Firestone, Ford/Lincoln/Mercury, Hannaford Foods, **W...food:** Gateway Grill, Peony Oriental Rest., **lodging:** Desmond Hotel, Wingate Inn, **other:** Engel's Mkt, to Heritage Park

2(2) NY 5, Central Ave, **E...gas:** Sunoco, **other:** BJ's Whse, Jo-Ann Fabrics, Marshalls, Staples, Target, **E on Wolf Rd...gas:** Mobil, Sunoco, **food:** American Café, Applebee's, Bangkok Thai, Bucca Italian, Dunkin Donuts, Emperor Chinese, Friendly's, Ground Round, Honeybaked Ham, IHOP, LoneStar Steaks, Papa Gino's, Starbucks, **lodging:** Cocca's Inn, Day's Inn, Park Inn, **other:** Barnes&Noble, Borders Books, Firestone/auto, Goodyear/auto, Macy's, OfficeMax, Sears/auto, mall, **W...gas:** Exxon, **food:** BBQ, Delmonico's Steaks, Empress Diner, Garcia's Mexican, Mr Subb, Papa John's, **lodging:** Ambassador Motel, Comfort Inn, Econolodge, Howard Johnson, Northway Inn, Ramada Ltd, Super 8, **other:** AutoZone, Buick, Goodyear

1W(1) NY State Thruway(from sb), I-87 S to NYC, I-90 W to Buffalo

1E(1) I-90 E(from sb), to Albany, Boston

1S(1) to US 20, Western Ave, **on Western Ave...food:** Burger King, Denny's, TGIFriday, **lodging:** Holiday Inn Express, **other:** JC Penney, mall

1N(1) I-87 N(from nb), to Plattsburgh

NY State Thruway goes west to Buffalo(I-90), S to NYC(I-87), I-87 N to Montreal

24(148) I-90 and I-87 N

23(142) I-787, to Albany, US 9 W, **E...gas:** 23 Trkstp/diesel/@, **lodging:** Quality Inn, to Knickerbocker Arena, **W...gas:** Stewarts

139mm parking area sb, phone, picnic tables, litter barrel

22(135) NY 396, to Selkirk, no facilities

21a(134) I-90 E, to MA Tpk, Boston

127mm New Baltimore Travel Plaza sb, Mobil/diesel, Big Boy, Mrs Fields, Roy Rogers, Starbucks, TCBY, atm, gifts, info, UPS

21b(125) US 9 W, NY 81, to Coxsackie, **W...gas:** Citgo/FoxRun/diesel/motel/rest./24hr/@, Sunoco/diesel, **food:** McDonald's(5mi), **lodging:** Best Western, Red Carpet Inn, **other:** Boat/RV Whse

21(114) NY 23, Catskill, **E...gas:** Mobil, Sunoco/diesel/24hr, **lodging:** Catskill Motel/rest., Day's Inn/rest., **other:** to Rip van Winkle Br, **W...food:** Anthony's Italian, LogSider Café, **lodging:** Astoria Motel, Rip van Winkle Motel, **other:** Indian Ridge Camping, to Hunter Mtn/Windham Ski Areas

103mm Malden Service Area nb, Mobil/diesel, Carvel Ice Cream, Hotdogs, McDonald's, atm, gifts, phone, parking area sb

20(102) NY 32, to Saugerties, **E...gas:** Getty, Mobil, Stewarts, **food:** DQ, King Buffet, Main St Rest., McDonald's, Pizza Star, Starway Café, **other:** CarQuest, Chrysler/Plymouth/Dodge/Jeep, CVS Drug, Family$, Grand Union Foods, **W...gas:** Hess/diesel, Sunoco/diesel, **food:** Land&Sea Grill, **lodging:** Catskill Mtn Lodge, Comfort Inn, Howard Johnson/rest., **other:** KOA(2mi), to Catskills

99mm parking area nb, phone, picnic tables, litter barrels

96mm Ulster Travel Plaza sb, Mobil/diesel, Big Apple Bagel, Cinnabon, Nathan's, Roy Rogers, Mrs Fields, TCBY, atm, gifts, phone

19(91) NY 28, Kingston, **E...gas:** Mobil, **food:** Atemus Diner, Friendly's, Gateway Diner, Grand Buffet Rest., Picnic Pizza, **lodging:** Holiday Inn, Super 8, **other:** Advance Parts, Hannaford Foods, Radio Shack, Walgreen, **W...food:** International Diner, **lodging:** Budget 19 Motel, Ramada Inn/rest., Skytop Motel/steaks, SuperLodge, **other:** Buick, Camper's Barn RV, Ford, Nissan, access to I-587, US 209

18(76) NY 299, New Paltz, to Ploughkeepsie, **E...gas:** Citgo/diesel, Mobil, **food:** Cumberland Farms, Austrian Rest., China Buffet, College Diner/24hr, **lodging:** Day's Inn, Econolodge, 87 Motel, Rocking Horse Ranch Resort, to Mid-Hudson Br, **W...gas:** Sunoco/24hr, **food:** Burger King, Dunkin Donuts, Friendly's, McDonald's, New Paltz Grill, Pasquale's Pizza, Plaza Diner, Pizza Hut, TCBY, **lodging:** Mohonk Lodge(6mi), Super 8, **other:** MEDICAL CARE, Advance Parts, Big A Parts, Eckerd, Radio Shack, Rite Aid, ShopRite Foods, Jellystone(9mi), KOA(10mi)

66mm Modena service area sb, gas: Mobil/diesel, food: Arby's, Carvel's Ice Cream/bakery, Mama Ilardo's Pizza, McDonald's, other: atm, fax, gifts, UPS

65mm Plattekill Travel Plaza nb, gas: Mobil/diesel, food: Big Boy, Cinnabon, Nathan's, Roy Rogers, other: atm, gifts, info

Newburgh

17(60) I-84, NY 17K, to Newburgh, **E...gas:** Getty/diesel, Sunoco/diesel/24hr, **food:** Burger King, Neptune Diner, Pizza Hut, Subway, **lodging:** Day's Inn, Holiday Inn, Howard Johnson/rest., **other:** Adams Foods, Caldor, Buick/Pontiac, Chevrolet/Cadillac, Dodge/Plymouth, Ford, Harley-Davidson, Lincoln/Mercury, NAPA, Nissan, Radio Shack, Rite Aid, ShopRite Foods, **W...gas:** Citgo/diesel, **E on NY 300...gas:** Exxon, Mobil, **food:** Applebee's, Cosimo's Rest., Denny's, Dunkin Donuts, King Buffet, McDonald's, Taco Bell, Wendy's, Yobo Oriental, **lodging:** Hampton Inn, Ramada Inn, Super 8, **other:** AutoZone, Discount Tire, Home Depot, Sears/auto, Wal-Mart/auto, Weis Foods, mall

16(45) US 6, NY 17, Harriman, to West Point, **W...gas:** Exxon/Subway/diesel, **lodging:** American Budget Inn, **other:** Chevrolet/Buick, Woodbury Outlet/famous brands, st police

Interstate 87

N ↕ S

34mm Ramapo Service Area sb, gas: Sunoco/diesel/ 24hr, food: Carvel Ice Cream, Lavazza Coffee, McDonald's, other: atm
33mm Sloatsburg Travel Plaza nb, gas: Sunoco/diesel/ 24hr, food: Burger King, Dunkin Donuts, Sbarro's, TCBY, other: atm, gifts, info
15a(31) NY 17 N, NY 59, Sloatsburg
15(30) I-287 S, NY 17 S, to NJ. I-87 S & I-287 E run together.
14b(27) Airmont Rd, Montebello, **E...lodging:** Holiday Inn, **W...gas:** Exxon, **food:** Applebee's, Friendly's, Hong Kong Chinese, Pasta Cucina, Roman Forum Diner, Starbucks, Sutter's Mill Rest., Wellesley Inn, **other:** HOSPITAL, DrugMart, Walgreen, Wal-Mart
14a(23) Garden State Pkwy, Chestnut Ridge, to NJ
14(22) NY 59, Spring Valley, Nanuet, **E...gas:** Amoco, Gulf, Shell, **food:** Burger King, Denny's, McDonald's, Subway, **lodging:** Fairfield Inn, **other:** BMW, CarQuest, Pergament, ShopRite Foods, mall, **W...gas:** Citgo, **food:** Dunkin Donuts, Great China, IHOP, Red Lobster, Taco Bell, White Castle/Church's, **lodging:** Day's Inn, Nanuet Inn, **other:** Barnes&Noble, Daewoo, Home Depot, Macy's, Marshalls, NAPA, OfficeMax, Sears/auto, Staples, Stop'n Shop Foods, mall
13(20) Palisades Pkwy, N to Bear Mtn, S to NJ
12(19) NY 303, Palisades Ctr Dr, W Nyack, **E...**Saturn, **W...gas:** Mobil, Shell/24hr, **food:** Grill 303, **lodging:** Nyack Motel, **other:** Barnes&Noble, Best Buy, BJ's Whse, Circuit City, CompUSA, Dave&Buster's, Filene's, Home Depot, JC Penney, Jo-Ann's Etc, Lord&Taylor, Old Navy, Staples, Target, mall

Nyack

11(18) US 9W, to Nyack, **E...gas:** Mobil, **lodging:** Best Western, **W...gas:** Exxon, Shell, **food:** KFC, McDonald's, **lodging:** Super 8, **other:** HOSPITAL, J&L Repair/tire, Kia, Nissan
10(17) Nyack(from nb), same as 11
14mm Hudson River, Tappan Zee Br
13mm toll plaza
9(12) to US 9, to Tarrytown, **E...gas:** Shell/repair, **food:** Pizza/pasta, **other:** Stop&Shop, **W...gas:** Mobil, **food:** El Dorado West Diner, **other:** Honda/Subaru, Mavis Tire
8(11) I-287 E, to Saw Mill Pkwy, White Plains, **E...lodging:** Marriott
7a(10) Saw Mill River Pkwy S, to Saw Mill River SP, Taconic SP
7(8) NY 9A(from nb), Ardsley, **W...lodging:** Ardsley Acres Motel, **other:** HOSPITAL
6mm Ardsley Travel Plaza nb, Sunoco/diesel, Burger King, Popeye's, TCBY, vending
5.5mm toll plaza, phone
6b a(5) Stew Leonard Dr, to Ridge Hill, **W...other:** Costco, Home Depot, Stew Leonard's Farmfresh Foods
6(4.5) Tuckahoe Dr, Yonkers, **E...gas:** Getty/repair, Gulf, SuperValue, **food:** Buci Italian, Golden Jade Palace, McDonald's, Subway, **lodging:** Tuckahoe Motel, **other:** ShopRite Foods, **W...gas:** Gulf, Mobil, **food:** Chinese Food, Domino's, Dunkin Donuts, **lodging:** Holiday Inn, Regency Hotel
5(4.3) NY 100 N(from nb), Central Park Ave, White Plains, **E...gas:** Getty, Shell, Sunoco, **food:** Ground Round
4(4) Cross Country Pkwy, Mile Sq Rd, **E...gas:** Ford/ Lincoln/Mercury/Subaru, **W...gas:** Shell/diesel/24hr, **food:** Roy Rogers, **other:** to Yonkers Speedway
3(3) Mile Square Rd, **E...gas:** Stop&Shop, Foods, **other:** Circuit City, GNC, Macy's, Thriftway Drug, mall, **W...gas:** Getty, Shell/24hr
2(2) Yonkers Ave(from nb), Westchester Fair, **E...gas:** Mobil, **other:** Yonkers Speedway
1(1) Hall Place, McLean Ave, **E...gas:** Shell, **food:** Dunkin Donuts

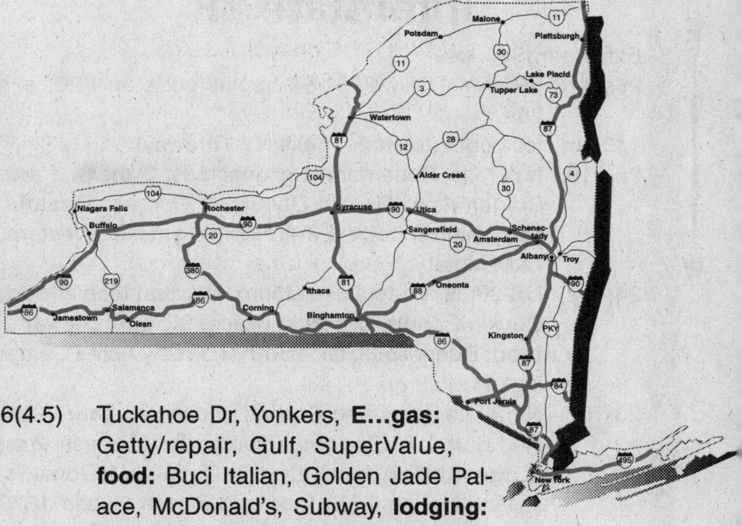

NYC Area

0mm New York St Thruway and I-87 N run together to Albany
14(11) McLean Ave, **E...gas:** Shell, **food:** Dunkin Donuts
13(10) E 233rd, NE Tollway, service plaza both lanes/Mobil
12(9.5) Hudson Pkwy(from nb), Sawmill Pkwy
11(9) Van Cortlandt Pk S, no facilities
10(8.5) W 230th St(from sb), W 240th(from nb), **E...gas:** Getty/ 24hr
9(8) W Fordham Rd, **E...gas:** Gaseteria/diesel, **food:** Jimmy's Bronx Café, **other:** HOSPITAL, Toyota
8(7) W 179th (from nb), **W...**Roberto Clemente SP
7(6) I-95, US 1, S to Trenton, NJ, N to New Haven, CT
6(5) E 153rd t, River Ave, Stadium Rd, **E...**Yankee Stadium
5(5) E 161st, Macombs Dam Br, **E...**Yankee Stadium
3(3) E 138th St, Madison Ave Br, **E...gas:** Gaseteria/ diesel
2(2) Willis Ave, 3rd Ave Br, **E...gas:** Mobil/diesel, **W...food:** McDonald's
1(1) Brook Ave, Hunts Point, no facilities
0mm I-87 begins/ends on I-278.

NEW YORK
Interstate 88

E ↕ W

Exit #(mm)Services

25a(118) I-90/NY Thruway. I-88 begins/ends on I-90, exit 25a.

117mm toll booth (to enter or exit NY Thruway)

25(116) NY 7, to Rotterdam, Schenectady, **3 mi S...food:** Burger King, Dunkin Donuts, 5 Corners Pizzaria, McDonald's, Top's Diner, **lodging:** Best Western, L&M Motel

24(112) US 20, NY 7, to Duanesburg, **N...gas:** Mobil, **food:** Dunkin Donuts, **other:** st police, **S...gas:** Stewarts, **food:** Duanesburg Diner, **other:** Frosty Acres Camping

23(101) NY 30, to Schoharie, Central Bridge, **N...gas:** Mobil, Red Barrel, **S...lodging:** Holiday Inn Express, **2 mi S...gas:** Mobil, **food:** Dunkin Donuts, McDonald's, Hyland House B&B, **lodging:** Parrott House 1870 Inn, Wedgewood B&B, **other:** Hideaway Camping, Locust Park Camping

Cobleskill

22(95) NY 7, NY 145, to Cobleskill, Middleburgh, **2-4 mi N...gas:** Hess/diesel, Kwikfill, Mobil, **food:** Apollo Diner/24hr, Boreali's Diner, Burger King, McDonald's, **lodging:** Best Western, Holiday Motel, Howe Caverns Motel/rest., **other:** HOSPITAL, Twin Oaks Camping, to Howe Caverns, **S...**st police

21(90) NY 7, NY 10, to Cobleskill, Warnerville, **2 mi N...gas:** Hess, Mobil/diesel, **food:** Burger King, Pizza Hut, Sub Express, **other:** HOSPITAL, PriceChopper Foods, **3 mi N...food:** Delaney's Rest., **lodging:** Best Western, Gables B&B, **other:** Wal-Mart SuperCtr/24hr

20(87) NY 7, NY 10, to Richmondville, **S...gas:** Mobil/diesel/24hr, **lodging:** Blue Spruce B&B, Econolodge, **1 mi S...gas:** Sunoco/diesel, **other:** Hi-View Camping

79mm rest area wb, full(handicapped)facilities, phone, vending, picnic tables, litter barrels, petwalk

19(76) to NY 7, Worcester, **N...gas:** Citgo, Stewarts, Sunoco/diesel, **other:** NAPA

73mm rest area eb, full(handicapped)facilities, phones, vending, picnic tables, litter barrels, petwalk

18(71) to Schenevus, **N...gas:** Citgo, **food:** Schenevus Rest.

17(61) NY 7, to NY 28 N, Colliersville, Cooperstown, **2 mi N...gas:** Mobil/diesel, Taylor's, **food:** Homestead Rest., **lodging:** Knott's Motel, Lorenzo's Motel, Redwood Motel, **other:** to Baseball Hall of Fame

16(59) NY 7, to Emmons, **N...food:** Farmhouse Rest., Perrucci's Pizza, **lodging:** Rainbow Inn, **other:** Eckerd, PriceChopper Foods, **1 mi N...food:** Arby's, Burger King, Pizza Hut, **S...food:** Brooks BBQ(4mi)

Oneonta

15(56) NY 28, NY 23, Oneonta, **N...food:** Friendly's, **other:** to Soccer Hall of Fame, **S...gas:** Citgo, Hess, Kwikfill, Mobil, Red Barrel/Taco Bell, **food:** Burger King, Denny's, McDonald's, Neptune Diner/24hr, Sabatini's Italian, Wendy's, **lodging:** Budget Inn, Christopher's Lodge/rest., Holiday Inn, Super 8, Townhouse Motel, **other:** Aldi Foods, BJ's Whse, $Tree, Hannaford's Food, JC Penney, K-Mart/Little Caesar's, Kost Tire, NAPA, OfficeMax, Wal-Mart SuperCtr/24hr

14(55) Main St(from eb), Oneonta, **N...gas:** Citgo, Kwikfill, Stewarts, Sunoco, **food:** Alfresco's Italian, Golden Guernsey Ice Cream, Pepper Joe's Deli, **other:** CVS Drug, cleaners, **S...food:** McDonald's, Taco Bell, Kountry Livin B&B, **other:** Subaru

13(53) NY 205, Citgo, **1-2 mi N...gas:** Citgo, Hess, Mobil, Sunoco/diesel, **food:** Burger King, Duke Diner, Dunkin Donuts, McDonald's, Ponderosa, **lodging:** Cathedral Country Motel/rest., Celtic Motel, Maple Terrace Motel, Oasis Motor Inn, **other:** Chevrolet, Chrysler/Jeep, Honda/Mitsubishi, Nissan, Pontiac/Buick/GMC/Cadillac, Parts+, Rite Aid, to Susquehanna Tr, Gilbert Lake SP(11mi), camping

12(47) NY 7, to Otego, **S...gas:** Mobil/diesel, Sunoco/diesel, **food:** Country Store Kitchen

43mm rest area wb, full(handicapped)facilities, phone, picnic tables, litter barrels, vending, petwalk

11(40) NY 357, to Unadilla, **N...**KOA

39mm rest area eb, full(handicapped)facilities, phone, picnic tables, litter barrels, vending, petwalk

10(38) NY 7, to Unadilla, **2 mi N...gas:** KwikFill, Red Barrel, **lodging:** Country Motel(5mi), **other:** Great American Foods, USPO, st police

9(33) NY 8, to Sidney, **N...gas:** Citgo/diesel, Hess/diesel, Mobil/diesel, **food:** Burger King, China Buffet, McDonald's, Pizza Hut, **lodging:** Algonkin Motel, Country Motel, Super 8, **other:** HOSPITAL, Grand Union, K-Mart/Little Caesar's, Tall Pines Camping, USPO, **S...lodging:** Mason Inn(5mi)

8(29) NY 206, to Bainbridge, **N...gas:** Citgo, Mobil, Sunoco/Taco Bell/diesel/24hr, **food:** Bob's Family Diner, Olde Jericho Tavern, **lodging:** Algonkin Motel, Susquehanna Motel, **other:** Riverside RV Park, Parts+, to Oquage Creek Park

7(22) NY 41, to Afton, **1-2 mi N...gas:** Mobil/24hr, Sunoco/diesel, Xtra, **food:** RiverClub Rest., Tempting Dish Rest., Vincent's Rest., **other:** Afton Golf/rest., Echo Lake Park, Kellystone Park, ValuRite Drug, Smith-Hale HS

6(16) NY 79, to NY 7, Harpursville, Ninevah, **S...gas:** Red Barrel/diesel, **other:** USPO

Binghamton

5(12) Martin Hill Rd, to Belden, **N...gas:** Exxon/diesel, **other:** Belden Manor Camping

4(8) NY 7, to Sanitaria Springs, **S...gas:** Hess/diesel, Lechner's/diesel/repair

3(4) NY 369, Port Crane, **N...**to Chenango Valley SP, **S...gas:** Hess/diesel, KwikFill

2(2) NY 12a W, to Chenango Bridge, **N...gas:** Red Barrel, **food:** Chenango Commons Rest.

1(1) NY 7 W(no wb return), to Binghamton, no facilities

0mm I-81, N to Syracuse, S to Binghamton. I-88 begins/ends on I-81.

NEW YORK

Interstate 90

Exit #(mm)Services

B24.5mm New York/Massachusetts state line

B3(B23) NY 22, to Austerlitz, New Lebanon, W Stockbridge, **N...gas:** Citgo/diesel, **food:** Depot 22 Rest., **S...gas:** Sunoco/diesel, **lodging:** Berkshire Spur Motel, **other:** Woodland Hills Camp

B18mm toll plaza, phone

B2(B15) NY 295, Taconic Pkwy, **1-2 mi S...**gas

B1(B7) US 9, NY Thruway W, to I-87, toll booth, phone

12(20) US 9, to Hudson, **1-3 mi S...gas:** Mobil/diesel/24hr, Sunoco/diesel, Xtra/24hr, **food:** McDonald's, **lodging:** Bel Air Motel, Blue Spruce Motel, **other:** to Van Buren NHS

18.5mm rest area wb, full(handicapped)facilities, phone, picnic tables, litter barrels, vending, petwalk

11(15) US 9, US 20, E Greenbush, Nassau, **N...gas:** Citgo/diesel, Hess/diesel, **food:** Daquiri's Rest., **other:** st police, **S...gas:** Mobil(2mi), **food:** Burger King, My Place Rest., Dewitt Motel, **lodging:** Econolodge, **other:** Grand Union, Rite Aid, USPO

10(10) Miller Rd, to E Greenbush, **1-3 mi S...gas:** Mobil, Stewarts, Sunoco, **food:** Dunkin Donuts, E Greenbush Diner, Pizza Hut, Ponderosa, Weathervane Seafood, **lodging:** Dewitt Motel

9(9) US 4, to Rensselaer, Troy, **N...gas:** Mobil, **food:** Applebee's, Ground Round, McDonald's, OffShore Pier Rest., **lodging:** Holiday Inn Express, **other:** $Tree, Grand Union Foods, Home Depot, Radio Shack, Staples, Wal-Mart, **1-2 mi S...gas:** Citgo/diesel, Mobil, Stewarts, **food:** Cracker Barrel, Denny's, Friendly's, Wendy's, **lodging:** Econolodge, Fairfield Inn, 4 Seasons Motel, Mt Vernon Motel

8(8) NY 43, Defreestville

7(7) Washington Ave(from eb), Rensselaer

6.5mm Hudson River

6mm I-787, to Albany, no facilities

6(4.5) US 9, Northern Blvd, to Loudonville, **N...gas:** Stewarts/gas, **food:** Mr Subb, Ta-Ke Japanese, **lodging:** Red Carpet Inn, **other:** HOSPITAL, David's Fine Foods

5a(4) Corporate Woods Blvd, no facilities

5(3.5) Everett Rd, to NY 5, **S...gas:** Hess, **food:** Bob&Ron's Fishfry, Denny's, Friendly's, Gateway Diner, Ground Round, McDonald's, Subway, Pizza Hut, Popeye's, Taco Bell, **lodging:** Motel 6, Quality Inn, **other:** HOSPITAL, Advance Parts, AutoZone, Chevrolet, Chrysler/Jeep, CVS Drug, $Tree, Eckerd, Ford, Hannaford's Foods/24hr, Honda/Nissan, Mazda, PepBoys, Plymouth/Dodge, Pontiac, PriceChopper Foods, Radio Shack, Suzuki, multiple facilities on NY 5

4(3) NY 85 S, to Slingerlands, no facilities

3(2.5) State Offices, no facilities

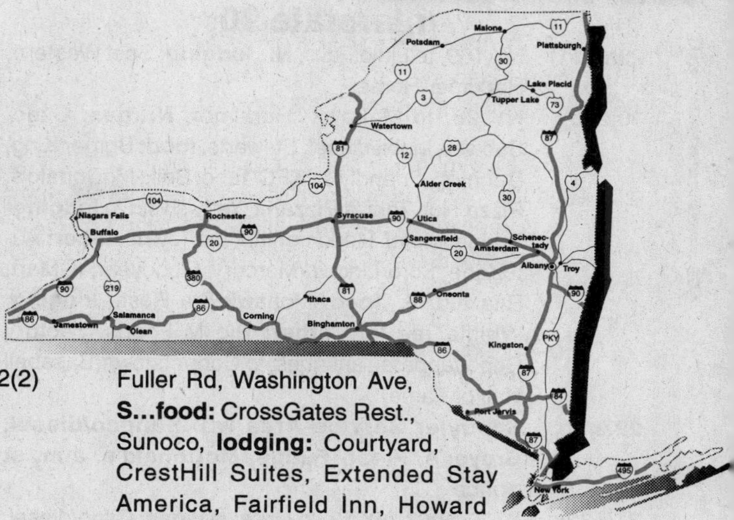

2(2) Fuller Rd, Washington Ave, **S...food:** CrossGates Rest., Sunoco, **lodging:** Courtyard, CrestHill Suites, Extended Stay America, Fairfield Inn, Howard Johnson Express, TownePlace Inn, same as 1S

1N(1) I-87 N, to Montreal, to Albany Airport

1S(1) US 20, Western Ave, **S...**CrossGates Mall Rd, **food:** Bugaboo Creek Steaks, FoodCourt, Hooters, Pizzaria Uno, **other:** Best Buy, Caldor, Filene's, Home Depot, JC Penney, Lord&Taylor, Macy's, Old Navy, Sam's Club, Wal-Mart, mall

24(149) I-87 N, I-90 E

153mm Guilderland Service Area eb, Sunoco/diesel, Ben&Jerry's, McDonald's, Mr Subb

25(154) I-890, NY 7, NY 146, to Schenectady, **1 mi N...**exit 8 off I-890, Mobil

25a(159) I-88 S, NY 7, to Binghamton

26(162) I-890, NY 5 S, Schenectady

168mm Pattersonville Service Area wb, Sunoco/diesel, Big Boy, Cinnabon, Roy Rogers, atm, fax, gifts, info, UPS

172mm Mohawk Service Area eb, Sunoco/diesel, Breyer's, McDonald's, fudge

27(174) NY 30, Amsterdam, **N...gas:** Coastal, Mobil, **lodging:** Super 8/diner/24hr, Valleyview Motel, Windsor Motel, **1 mi N...lodging:** Best Western

28(182) NY 30A, Fonda, **N...gas:** Getty/diesel, Glen Trkstp/Citgo/diesel/rest./24hr, Gulf/repair, Sunoco/diesel/rest./motel, TA/diesel/24hr, **food:** McDonald's, **lodging:** Cloverleaf Inn, Holiday Inn(7mi), Poplars Inn, Super 8, Travelodge, **other:** HOSPITAL

184mm parking area both lanes, phones, litter barrels

29(194) NY 10, Canajoharie, **N...gas:** Gulf, Stewarts, **food:** Chinese Buffet, McDonald's, Pizza Hut, **lodging:** Rodeway Inn, **other:** Grand Union Foods, Radio Shack, Rite Aid, **S...gas:** Mobil, Sunoco, **other:** Chevrolet

210mm Indian Castle Service area eb...gas: Sunoco/diesel, food: Big Boy, Mrs Fields, Roy Rogers, other: atm, gifts, UPS. Iroquois Service Area wb...gas: Sunoco/diesel, Burger King, Dunkin Donuts, TCBY, atm, gifts, UPS

NEW YORK

Interstate 90

E ↕ W

Utica

29a(211) NY 169, to Little Falls, **N...lodging:** Best Western, Herkimer Home

30(220) NY 28, to Mohawk, Herkimer, **N...gas:** Citgo/ Subway, Mobil/diesel, Stewarts, **food:** Burger King, Denny's, Friendly's, KFC/Taco Bell, McDonald's, Pizza Hut, Tony's Pizzaria, Yetty's Pizza, **lodging:** Budget Motel, Herkimer Inn, Inn Towne, **other:** AutoZone, Ford/Lincoln/Mercury, Goodyear, K-Mart, Rite Aid, **S...food:** Mohawk Sta Rest., **lodging:** WhiffleTree Inn, **other:** Big M Foods, Factory Depot/apparel, antiques, to Cooperstown(Baseball Hall of Fame)

227mm **Schuyler Service Area wb, Sunoco/diesel, Breyer's, Fresh Fudge, McDonald's, atm, st police**

31(233) I-790, NY 8, NY 12, to Utica, **N...gas:** Citgo/diesel, Fastrac, **food:** Burger King, Franco's Pizza, Lupino's Pizza, Paesano's Pizza, **other:** BJ's Whse, $Tree, Eckerd, Lowe's Whse, PriceChopper Foods, Rite Aid, Wal-Mart, **S...gas:** Hess/diesel, Sunoco/diesel, **food:** Denny's, Friendly's, Jreck Subs, McDonald's, Pizza Hut, Taco Bell, Wendy's, **lodging:** A-1 Motel, Best Western, Happy Journey Motel, Motel 6, Red Roof Inn, Super 8, **other:** Harley-Davidson

236mm I-790(from eb), to Utica

237.5mm Erie Canal

238mm Mohawk River

32(243) NY 232, Westmoreland, **S...lodging:** Carriage House Motel, Quality Inn, **1 mi S...**gas

244mm **Oneida Service Area eb, Sunoco/diesel, Burger King, Cinnabon, Sbarro's, TCBY, atm, gifts**

250mm parking area eb, phones, picnic tables, litter barrel

33(253) NY 365, Verona, to Vernon Downs, **N...gas:** Citgo, Sunoco, **lodging:** Comfort Suites(6mi), Super 8, Verona Inn, **other:** HOSPITAL, KOA, Wal-Mart, to Griffiss AFB, **S...gas:** SavOn Gas, **lodging:** Super 8, Turning Stone Resort/casino, **other:** repair

256mm parking area wb, phones, picnic tables, litter barrel

34(262) NY 13, to Canastota, **S...gas:** Mobil/diesel, SavOn/ 24hr, **food:** Arby's, Canastota Rest., McDonald's, **lodging:** Days Inn, Graziano Motel/rest., Super 8, **other:** to Sylvan Beach, Boxing Hall of Fame

266mm **Chittenango Service Area wb, Sunoco/diesel, Dunkin Donuts, Sbarro's, TCBY, atm, gifts**

34a(277) I-481, to Syracuse, Chittenango, no facilities

35(279) NY 298, The Circle, Syracuse, **S...gas:** Kwikfill, Mobil/repair, Sunoco/diesel, **food:** Burger King, Denny's, Dunkin Donuts, Jreck Subs, McDonald's, Pepino's Pizza, Seniora Pizza, **lodging:** Candlewood Suites, Carrier Circle Inn, Comfort Inn, Courtyard, Day's Inn, Embassy Suites, Extended Stay America, Fairfield Inn, Hampton Inn, Holiday Inn, Howard Johnson Lodge, John Milton Inn, Marriott, Microtel, Motel 6, Ramada Ltd, Red Roof Inn, Residence Inn, Super 8, Wyndham Garden, **other:** Goodyear/auto, Speedy Transmissions

Syracuse

280mm **Dewitt Service Area eb, Sunoco/diesel, McDonald's, ice cream**

36(283) I-81, N to Watertown, S to Binghamton

37(284) 7th St, Electronics Pkwy, to Liverpool, **N...lodging:** Best Western, **S...gas:** Hess/Godfather's/24hr, KFC/Taco Bell, **lodging:** Holiday Inn, Homewood Suites, Knight's Inn, **1 mi S on 7th St...gas:** Mobil, **food:** Bob Evans, Burger King, Colorado Steaks, Denny's, Friendly's, Ground Round, Jreck Subs, **lodging:** Day's Inn, Econolodge, Hampton Inn, Quality Inn, Ramada Inn, Super 8, **other:** NAPA

38(286) NY 57, Syracuse, to Liverpool, **N...gas:** FasTrac, Hessmart, KwikFill, **food:** Hooligan's Grill, Kirby's Rest., Pier 57 Diner, Pizza Hut, **lodging:** Super 8, **other:** NAPA, **1 mi S...gas:** Mobil, Sunoco/24hr, **food:** Burger King, **other:** Onondaga Lake Park, Salt Museum

39(290) I-690, NY 690, Syracuse, **N...lodging:** Comfort Inn/rest., **other:** Meyers RV Ctr

292mm **Warners Service Area wb, Mobil/diesel/rest., McDonald's, Mama Iraldo's Café, ice cream**

40(304) NY 34, Weedsport, to Owasco Lake, **N...**Riverforest RV Park, **S...gas:** Fastrac, KwikFill, Sunoco/diesel, **food:** Arby's, Arnold's Rest., DB's Drive-In, Old Erie Diner, **lodging:** Best Western, Day's Inn, Microtel, **other:** Big M Foods, NAPA

310mm **Port Byron Service Area eb, Mobil/diesel/rest., Mama Iraldo's Café, McDonald's, ice cream**

318mm parking area wb, picnic tables, phones

41(320) NY 414, Waterloo, to Cayuga Lake, **S...gas:** Mobil/ diesel, Petro/diesel/24hr/@, **food:** MaGee Country Diner, **other:** Waterloo Outlets/famous brands(3mi), NWR

324mm **Junius Ponds Service Area wb, Sunoco/diesel, Dunkin Donuts, Mrs Fields, Roy Rogers, TCBY**

42(327) NY 14, to Geneva, Lyons, **N...**RV camping, **S...gas:** Mobil/diesel, **lodging:** Relax Inn, **other:** Waterloo Outlets/famous brands(3mi)

337mm **Clifton Springs Service Area eb, Sunoco/diesel, Roy Rogers, Sbarro's, TCBY, atm, gifts**

43(340) NY 21, Manchester, to Palmyra, **N...**Hill Cumorah LDS HS(6mi), **S...gas:** Mobil/diesel/24hr, **food:** McDonald's, Steak-Out, **lodging:** Roadside Inn

44(347) NY 332, Victor, **S...gas:** Mobil/diesel, Sunoco/diesel, **food:** Di Pacific's Rest., KFC, McDonald's, Pizza Hut, Subway, **lodging:** Best Value Inn, Budget Inn, Econolodge, **other:** CVS Drug, KOA, st police

350mm **Seneca Service Area wb, gas: Mobil/diesel, food: Burger King, Mrs Fields, Sbarro's, TCBY, other: atm, info, phone**

Interstate 90

45(351) I-490, NY 96, to Rochester, **N...lodging:** Hampton Inn, **S...gas:** KwikFill, **food:** Burger King, Chili's, Dede's Rest., Denny's, **lodging:** Exit 45 Motel, Microtel, **other:** Chevrolet

353mm parking area eb, phone, litter barrels

46(362) I-390, to Rochester, **N on NY 253 W...gas:** Citgo/diesel, Hess, **food:** McDonald's, Peppermints Rest., Tim Horton, Wendy's, **lodging:** Country Inn Suites, Day's Inn, Fairfield Inn, Marriott, Microtel, Red Carpet Inn, Red Roof Inn, Super 8

366mm Scottsville Service Area eb, gas: Mobil/diesel, food: Burger King, Dunkin Donuts, TCBY, other: atm, info

376mm Ontario Service Area wb, gas: Mobil/diesel/deli, food: McDonald's

47(379) I-490, NY 19, to Rochester, no facilities

48(390) NY 98, to Batavia, **N...lodging:** Comfort Inn, **S...gas:** Citgo, **food:** Bob Evans, **lodging:** Best Western, Day's Inn, Holiday Inn, Microtel, Park-Oak Motel, Red Carpet Inn, Sheraton, Super 8, **other:** OfficeMax, Wal-Mart/auto, **1 mi S on NY 63...gas:** Mobil, Sunoco, **food:** Arby's, Burger King, Denny's, McDonald's, Taco Bell, Perkins, Ponderosa, Red Dragon Chinese, Wendy's, **other:** Advance Parts, AutoZone, BJ's Whse, CarQuest, Chevrolet/Cadillac, CVS Drug, $Tree, GNC, Jo-Ann Fabrics, K-Mart, NAPA, Radio Shack, Top's Foods

397mm Pembroke Service Area eb, full(handicapped)facilities, gas: Sunoco/diesel, food: Burger King, Mrs Fields, Popeye's, Starbucks, TCBY, other: atm, gifts, phone, UPS

48a(402) NY 77, Pembroke, **S...gas:** Flying J/diesel/LP/rest./24hr/@, TA/Citgo/diesel/rest./24hr/@, **food:** Subway, **lodging:** Country Cottage Motel, Econolodge, 6 Flags Motel/RV Park

412mm Clarence Service Area wb, full(handicapped)facilities, gas: Sunoco/diesel, food: Burger King, Cinnabon, Nathan's Pizza Hut, TCBY, other: info, phone

49(417) NY 78, Depew, **1-2 mi N...gas:** Mobil, Sunoco, **food:** Applebee's, Arby's, Bennigan's, Boston Mkt, Burger King, ChiChi's, Cracker Barrel, Denny's, Don Pablo, Eatery Rest., Fazoli's, Golden Corral, KFC, McDonald's, Mighty Taco, Old Country Buffet, Perkins, Picasso's Pizza, Pizza Hut, Ponderosa, Protocol Rest., Red Lobster, Roadhouse Grill, Ruby Tuesday, Shogun Japanese, Spilio's Rest., Starbucks, Subway, Ted's Hotdogs, TGIFriday, Wendy's, **lodging:** Clarion, Econolodge, Fairfield Inn, Holiday Inn Express, Microtel, Ramada Ltd, **other:** Acura, Barnes&Noble, Buick, Dodge, Eckerd/24hr, Firestone/auto, Ford, Home Depot, JC Penney, Jo-Ann Fabrics, K-Mart, Mitsubishi, NTB, OfficeMax, Saturn, Sears/auto, Target, Tire-Max, Top's Food/deli, Wal-Mart/auto, Wegman's Foods, mall, **S...gas:** Kwikfill, Mobil, **food:** Bob Evans, John&Mary's Cafe, Salvatore's Italian, **lodging:** Garden Place Hotel, Hospitality Inn, Howard Johnson, Red Roof Inn, Sleep Inn, **other:** Aamco, Top's Foods

419mm toll booth

50(420) I-290 to Niagara Falls, no facilities

50a(421) Cleveland Dr(from eb)

51(422) NY 33 E, Buffalo, **S...**airport, st police

52(423) Walden Ave, to Buffalo, **N...food:** Arby's, Bob Evans, Subway, TGIFriday, Tim Horton, Wendy's, **lodging:** Hampton Inn, Residence Inn, **other:** Aldi, Ford, Goodyear, Target, **S...gas:** Sunoco/diesel/rest./24hr/@, **food:** Alton's Rest., McDonald's, Milton's Rest., Olive Garden, Pizza Hut, **lodging:** Sheraton, **other:** Borders Books, Dodge, JC Penney, K-Mart, Niagara Hobby, Wegman's Foods, mall

52a(424) William St, no facilities

53(425) I-190, to Buffalo, Niagara Falls, **N...food:** McDonald's, **lodging:** Holiday Inn Express

54(428) NY 400, NY 16, to W Seneca, E Aurora, no facilities

55(430) US 219, Ridge Rd, Orchard Park, to Rich Stadium, **S...gas:** KissMart, **food:** Arby's, Denny's, Ponderosa, Subway, Wendy's, **lodging:** Hampton Inn, **other:** Aldi, Home Depot, K-Mart

431mm toll booth

56(432) NY 179, Mile Strip Rd, **N...gas:** Citgo, Sunoco, **food:** Burger King, **lodging:** Econolodge, **other:** CVS Drug, Jubilee Foods, **S...gas:** Citgo, **food:** Applebee's, Boston Mkt, ChiChi's, ChuckeCheese, Garfield's Rest., McDonald's, Olive Garden, Outback Steaks, Pizza Hut, Red Lobster, Roadhouse Grill, Ruby Tuesday, Starbucks, Subway, TGIFriday, Wendy's, **other:** Aldi Foods, BJ's Whse, Firestone/auto, Home Depot, JC Penney, Jo-Ann Etc, OfficeMax, PepBoys, Sears/auto, Wegman's Foods, mall

57(436) NY 75, to Hamburg, **N...gas:** Exit 57/diesel/rest., Mobil/diesel, **food:** Bob Evans, Denny's, McDonald's, Wendy's, **lodging:** Comfort Suites, Day's Inn, Red Roof Inn, Tallyho Motel, **other:** Chevrolet, Chrysler/Plymouth/Jeep/Mitsubishi, Dodge, Ford, GMC/Pontiac, Kia, **S...gas:** Kwikfill/diesel, Mobil, Stop&Gas, **food:** Arby's, Burger King, Camp Rd Diner, Pizza Hut, Subway, **lodging:** Holiday Inn, **other:** Goodyear/auto, USPO

NEW YORK

Interstate 90

E ↕ W

Dunkirk

442mm	parking area both lanes, phone, litter barrels
57a(445)	to Eden, Angola, **2 mi N...gas:** Sunoco/diesel
447mm	**Angola Service Area both lanes, full(handicapped)facilities, Mobil/diesel, Denny's, McDonald's, phone/fax, gifts**
58(456)	US 20, NY 5, Irving, to Silver Creek, **N...gas:** Citgo, Kwikfill, **food:** Burger King, Aunt Millie's Rest., Sunset Grill, Tom's Rest., **other:** HOSPITAL, to Evangola SP
59(468)	NY 60, Fredonia, Dunkirk, **N...lodging:** Dunkirk Motel(4mi), **other:** Lake Erie SP(7mi), **S...gas:** Citgo, Kwikfill/diesel, Mobil/diesel, **food:** Applebee's, Arby's, Bob Evans, Burger King, China King, Cracker Barrel, Denny's, KFC/Taco Bell, Little Caesar's, McDonald's, Perkins, Pizza Hut, Tim Horton, Wendy's, **lodging:** Best Western, Comfort Inn, Day's Inn, **other:** Advance Parts, Aldi, AutoZone, $Tree, Eckerd, Ford/Lincoln/Mercury, GNC, Home Depot, JC Penney, Jo-Ann Fabrics, K-Mart, NAPA, Rite Aid, Top's Foods, Wal-Mart/gas, Woodbury Winery, Arkwright Hills Camping(6mi)
60(485)	NY 394, Westfield, **N...**to Lake Erie SP, camping, **S...gas:** Keystone/diesel, **other:** HOSPITAL
494mm	toll booth
61(495)	Shortman Rd, to Ripley, **N...gas:** Shell/diesel/rest./24hr, **other:** Lakeshore RV Park
496mm	New York/Pennsylvania state line

Interstate 95

N ↕ S

NYC Area

Exit #(mm)	Services
32mm	New York/Connecticut state line
22(30)	Midland Ave(from nb), Port Chester, Rye, **W...gas:** Amoco, Shell, Sunoco, **other:** HOSPITAL, A&P, Home Depot, Staples
21(29)	I-287 W, US 1 N, to White Plains, Port Chester, Tappan Zee
20(28)	US 1 S(from nb), Port Chester
19(27)	Playland Pkwy, Rye, Harrison, no facilities
18b(25)	Mamaroneck Ave, to White Plains, **E...gas:** Shell, **other:** CVS Drug
18a(24)	Fenimore Rd(from nb), Mamaroneck, **E...gas:** Citgo
17(20)	Chatsworth Ave(from nb, no return), Larchmont, no facilities
19.5mm	toll plaza
16(19)	North Ave, Cedar St, New Rochelle, **E...food:** McDonald's, Taco Bell, **lodging:** Ramada Inn, Residence Inn, **other:** Stop&Shop Foods, Toyota, **W...**HOSPITAL
15(16)	US 1, New Rochelle, The Pelhams, **E...gas:** Getty/diesel, PitStop/24hr, **food:** Thru-Way Diner, **other:** Costco, CVS Drug, Home Depot, NAPA, **W...**auto repair
14(15)	Hutchinson Pkwy(from sb), to Whitestone Br, no facilities
13(16)	Conner St, to Mt Vernon, **E...gas:** Gulf/diesel, **lodging:** Econolodge, **W...gas:** Amoco, **food:** McDonald's, **lodging:** Andrea Motel, **other:** HOSPITAL
12(15.5)	Baychester Ave(from nb)
11(15)	Bartow Ave, Co-op City Blvd, **E...gas:** Mobil, **food:** McDonald's, Red Lobster, **other:** Barnes&Noble, JC Penney, K-Mart, Marshalls, Old Navy, PathMark Foods, Staples, **W...gas:** Shell/mart, Sunoco/diesel, **lodging:** Pelham Garden Hotel, **other:** Home Depot
10(14.5)	Gun Hill Rd(from nb), no facilities
9(14)	Hutchinson Pkwy, no facilities
8c(13.5)	Pelham Pkwy W, no facilities
b(13)	Orchard Beach, City Island, no facilities
a(12.5)	Westchester Ave(from sb), no facilities
7c(12)	Pelham Bay Park(from nb), Country Club Rd
b(11.5)	E Tremont(from sb), **E...gas:** Citgo/diesel/24hr, Mobil, **food:** diner
a(11)	I-695(from sb), to I-295 S, Throgs Neck Br, no facilities
6b(10.5)	I-278 W(from sb), I-295 S(from nb), no facilities
a(10)	I-678 S, Whitestone Bridge, no facilities
5b(9)	Castle Hill Ave, **W...gas:** Sunoco, **food:** McDonald's
a(8.5)	Westchester Ave, White Plains Rd, no facilities
4b(8)	Bronx River Pkwy, Rosedale Ave, **W...gas:** Mobil
a(7)	I-895 S, Sheridan Expsy, no facilities
3(6)	3rd Ave, HOSPITAL
2b(5)	Webster Ave, **E...**HOSPITAL
a(4)	Jerome Ave, to I-87, no facilities
1c(3)	I-87, Deegan Expswy, to Upstate, no facilities
b(2)	Harlem River Dr(from sb)
a(1)	US 9, NY 9A, H Hudson Pkwy, 178th St, HOSPITAL
0mm	New York/New Jersey state line, Hudson River, Geo Washington Br

Interstate 190(Buffalo)

E ↕ W

Exit #	Services
25.5mm	US/Canada Border, US Customs
25b a	R Moses Pkwy, NY 104, NY 265, Lewiston, no facilities
24	NY 31, Witmer Rd, **E...**st police
23	NY 182, Porter Rd, Packard Rd, **E...gas:** Sunoco, **food:** Burger King, DQ, **other:** Firestone/auto, K-Mart, NAPA, Prime Outlets/famous brands, U-Haul, **W...food:** Wendy's, **other:** Aldi Foods, Sam's Club, Wal-Mart

Interstate 190

22	US 62, Niagara Falls Blvd, **E...food:** Bob Evans, Taco Bell, Timberlodge Steaks, **lodging:** Budget Host, Howard Johnson, Red Carpet Inn, **other:** Chevrolet/Buick/Pontiac, Ford, Jeep, Target, Top's Foods, Toyota, **W...lodging:** Econolodge, Scottish Inn, **other:** Home Depot
21b	NY 384, Buffalo Ave, R Moses Pkwy, **W...**Getty, NY SP, American Falls
a	La Salle Expsway
20.5mm	Niagara River East, toll booth
20b a	Long Rd, **E...lodging:** Budget Motel, **other:** Country Store
19	Whitehaven Rd, **E...gas:** Getty, **other:** Top's Foods, KOA, **W...other:** Chevrolet
18b a	NY 324 W, Grand Island Blvd, **E...gas:** Mobil, **food:** Burger King, **W...**Beaver Island SP
17.5mm	Niagara River East
17	NY 266, toll booth
16	I-290 E, to I-90, Albany
15	NY 324, Kenmore Ave, **W...**U-Haul
14	Ontario St, **E...gas:** KwikFill, Mobil, **food:** McDonald's, Tim Horton, **other:** Advance Parts, **W...food:** Harry's Grille
11	NY 198, Buffalo, downtown
10mm	toll booth
9	Porter Ave, to Peace Bridge, Ft Erie
8	NY 266, Niagara St, downtown, **E...lodging:** Adam's Mark Hotel
7	NY 5 W, Church St, Buffalo, downtown
6	Elm St, **E...**HOSPITAL, downtown, **W...**HSBC Arena
5	Louisiana St, Buffalo, downtown
4	Smith St, Fillmore Ave, Buffalo, downtown
3	NY 16, Seneca St, **W...other:** Hutchins Auto Parts
2	US 62, NY 354, Bailey Ave, Clinton St, no facilities
1	Ogden St, **E...gas:** Sunoco, **food:** Wendy's, **lodging:** Best Value Inn, Holiday Inn Express, **other:** Volvo/GMC Trucks
.5mm	toll plaza nb
0mm	I-90. I-190 begins/ends on I-90, exit 53.

Interstate 287(NYC)

Exit#	Services
12	I-95, N to New Haven, S to NYC. I-287 begins/ends on I-95, exit 21.
11	US 1, Port Chester, Rye, **N...gas:** Amoco, Mobil, Sunoco, Shell, **food:** Burger King, Maryann 's Mexican, McDonald's, Port Chester Diner, Wendy's, **other:** HOSPITAL, A&P, Goodyear, Kohl's, Medallion Repair, Nissan, Staples
10	Bowman Ave, Webb Ave, no facilities
9N S	Hutchinson Pkwy, Merritt Pkwy, to Whitestone Br
9a	I-684, Brewster, no facilities
8	Westchester Ave, to White Plains, **S...other:** Nordstrom's, Westchester Mall Place
7	Taconic Pkwy(from wb), to N White Plains
6	NY 22, White Plains
5	NY 100, Hillside Ave, **S...gas:** Citgo, Getty, Mobil, **food:** Planet Pizza, **other:** Aamco
4	NY 100A, Hartsdale, **N...**HOSPITAL, **S...gas:** Amoco, **food:** Burger King, **other:** BMW, Dodge/Hyundai, Jaguar, Nissan/Mazda, Staples, Volvo
3	Sprain Pkwy, to Taconic Pkwy, NYC
2	NY 9A, Elmsford, **N...gas:** Amoco, Shell, Sunoco, **food:** Red Fox Diner
1	NY 119, Tarrytown, **N...lodging:** Marriott, **S...gas:** Exxon/diesel, Mobil, **lodging:** Extended Stay America, Hampton Inn

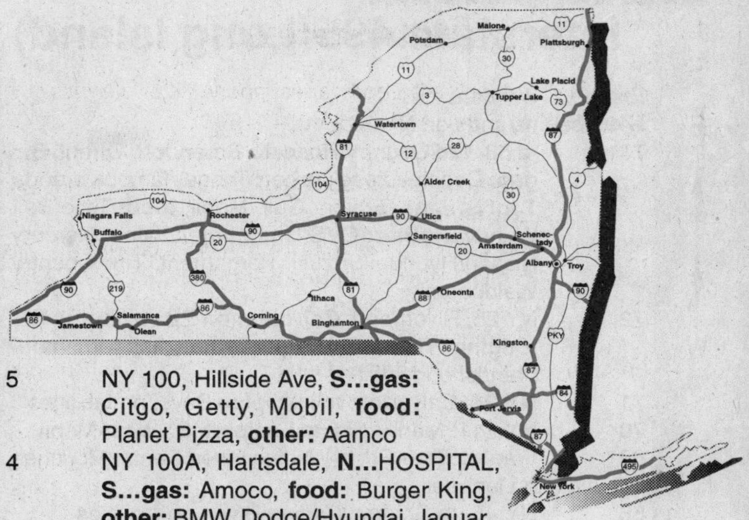

I-287 runs with I-87 N.

Interstate 290(Buffalo)

Exit #	Services
8	I-90, NY Thruway, I-290 begins/ends on I-90, exit 50.
7b a	NY 5, Main St, **N...gas:** Sunoco, **food:** La Nova Wings, Pizza Plant, Tim Horton, **S...gas:** Coastal, **food:** Sonoma Grille, **lodging:** Amherst Motel
6	NY 324, NY 240, **N...gas:** Getty, **lodging:** Courtyard, **other:** Cadillac, **S...other:** MEDICAL CARE, Chrysler/Dodge
5b a	NY 263, to Millersport, **N...gas:** Christino's Bistro, **lodging:** Hampton Inn, Marriott, Red Roof Inn, **S...gas:** Mobil, **lodging:** Homewood Suites, Motel 6, **other:** Nissan, Toyota, VW, Walgreen
4	I-990, to St U, no facilities
3b a	US 62, to Niagara Falls Blvd, **N...gas:** Citgo, Sunoco, **food:** Bob Evans, Max's Grill, Roadhouse Grill, **lodging:** Blvd Inn, Extended Stay America, Holiday Inn, Sleep Inn, Travelodge, **other:** Home Depot, Wal-Mart, **S...gas:** Mobil/mart, **food:** Applebee's, Don Pablo, Montana's Grill, Outback Steaks, Starbucks, Subway, Tim Horton, **other:** Barnes&Noble, Best Buy, Jo-Ann Fabrics, K-Mart, Target
2	NY 425, Colvin Blvd, **N...food:** KFC, McDonald's, Subway, Wendy's, **lodging:** Microtel, **other:** BJ's Whse, Family$, Goodyear/auto, Top's Foods, **S...gas:** Kwikfill, **food:** Old Town Bistro
1b a	Elmwood Ave, NY 384, NY 265, **N...gas:** Kwikfill, **lodging:** Microtel, **other:** Rite Aid, **S...gas:** Mobil/diesel/mart, **food:** Arby's, **other:** HOSPITAL
0mm	I-190. I-290 begins/ends on I-190 in Buffalo.

NEW YORK

Interstate 495(Long Island)

E ↕ W

Long Island

Exit #	Services
I-495 begins/ends on NY 25.	
73	rd 58, Old Country Road, to Greenport, Orient, **S...gas:** Coastal/diesel, **other:** Tanger/famous brands, **1 mi S...gas:** Exxon, Gulf, Mobil, **food:** Taco Bell, Wendy's, **other:** CVS Drug, Ford/Lincoln/Mercury, Nissan/Hyundai/Suzuki, Pergament, Tire Country, Waldbaum's
72	NY 25, Riverhead, Calverton(no EZ eb return), **S...lodging:** Ramada Inn/grill, **other:** Tanger/famous brands/foodcourt
71	NY 24, Calverton, to Hampton Bays, no facilities
70	NY 111, Manorville, to Eastport, **S...gas:** Mobil
69	Wading River Rd, to Wading River, Center Moriches, no facilities
68	NY 46, to Shirley, Wading River, no facilities
66	NY 101, Sills Rd, Yaphank, **N...**gas, food
64	NY 112, Medford, to Coram, **N...other:** Home Depot, King Kullen Foods, Sam's Club, **S...gas:** Amoco, Exxon, Gulf, 7-11, **lodging:** Gateway Inn, **other:** cinema
63	NY 83, **N...gas:** Hess, **S...gas:** Exxon, **food:** Churchill's Rest., **lodging:** Best Western
62	rd 97, to Blue Point, Stony Brook, **N...gas:** Gulf
61	rd 19, Holbrook, to Patchogue, **N...gas:** Mobil, **S...gas:** Exxon/diesel
60	Ronkonkoma Ave, **N...gas:** Exxon, **S...gas:** Shell
59	Ocean Ave, Ronkonkoma, to Oakdale, **S...gas:** Exxon
58	Old Nichols Rd, Nesconset, **N...gas:** Exxon, **food:** Hooters, **lodging:** Marriott, Wyndham Garden, **S...gas:** Amoco
57	NY 454, Vets Hwy, to Hauppauge, **N...gas:** Exxon/diesel, **food:** TGIFriday, **S... gas:** Amoco/24hr, Exxon, Gulf/diesel/24hr, Shell, **food:** Blue Dawn Diner, New Horizon Diner, Subway, **lodging:** Hampton Inn, **other:** Stop&Shop Foods
56	NY 111, Smithtown, Islip, **N...gas:** Exxon/Subway/Domino's/diesel, Mobil, **S...gas:** Mobil, **food:** Café La Strada, **lodging:** Holiday Inn Express
55	Central Islip, **N...gas:** Mobil, **S...gas:** Shell/diesel
54	Wicks Rd, **N...gas:** Amoco, **lodging:** Howard Johnson, Sheraton, **S...gas:** Mobil
53	Sunken Meadow Pkwy, Bayshore, to ocean beaches
52	rd 4, Commack, **N...gas:** Mobil/diesel, Shell/repair, **food:** Conca d'Oro Pizza, Ground Round, **lodging:** Hampton Inn, **other:** Costco
51.5mm	parking area both lanes, phone, litter barrels
51	NY 231, to Northport, Babylon, no facilities
50	Bagatelle Rd, to Wyandanch, no facilities
49N	NY 110 N, to Huntington, **N...lodging:** Marriott
S	NY 110 S, to Amityville
48	Round Swamp Rd, Old Bethpage, **S...gas:** Mobil/diesel, **food:** Old Country Pizza/deli, **lodging:** Rodeway Inn, **other:** USPO
46	Sunnyside Blvd, Plainview, **N...lodging:** Holiday Inn
45	Manetto Hill Rd, Plainview, Woodbury, no facilities
44	NY 135, to Seaford, Syosset, no facilities
43	S Oyster Bay Rd, to Syosset, Bethpage, **N...gas:** Mobil
42	Northern Pkwy, rd N, Hauppauge, no facilities
41	NY 106, NY 107, Hicksville, Oyster Bay, **S...gas:** Amoco, Mobil, Sunoco, **food:** Boston Mkt, Boulder Creek Steaks, Broadway Diner, Burger King, Dunkin Donuts, McDonald's, **lodging:** On the Border, Circuit City, Goodyear/auto, Sears/auto
40	NY 25, Mineola, Syosset, **S...gas:** Amoco, Exxon, Hess/diesel, Shell, 7-11, **food:** Burger King, Friendly's, IHOP, McDonald's, Nathan's Famous, Wendy's, **lodging:** Edgerton Motel, Hostway Motel, Howard Johnson, **other:** Home Depot, Kohl's, OffTrack Betting, Staples
39	Glen Cove Rd, **N...gas:** Mobil
38	Northern Pkwy E, Meadowbrook Pkwy, to Jones Beach
37	Willis Ave, to Roslyn, Mineola, **N...gas:** Exxon, Shell, **other:** repair, **S...gas:** Gulf,
36	Searingtown Rd, to Port Washington, **S...**HOSPITAL
35	Shelter Rock Rd, Manhasset, no facilities
34	New Hyde Park Rd, no facilities
33	Lakeville Rd, to Great Neck, **N...**HOSPITAL
32	Little Neck Pkwy, **N...food:** pizza
31	Douglaston Pkwy, **S...gas:** Amoco, **food:** Stern's, **other:** USPO, Waldbaum's Foods, mall
30	E Hampton Blvd, Cross Island Pkwy
29	Springfield Blvd, **S...gas:** Exxon, Texaco/repair, **food:** Chinese Rest., McDonald's
27	I-295, Clearview Expswy, Throgs Neck, **N...gas:** Gulf, 7-11, **food:** Blue Bay Diner, **other:** Rockbottom Drug
26	Francis Lewis Blvd, S
25	Utopia Pkwy, 188th St, **N...gas:** Citgo, Mobil, Sunoco, **S...gas:** Amoco, Gaseteria, Mobil, Shell/repair, Sunoco, **other:** Filene's Basement, Fresh Meadows, Goodyear, Radio Shack
24	Kissena Blvd, **N...gas:** Exxon/diesel, **food:** Dunkin Donuts, **S...gas:** Mobil
23	Main St, **N...food:** Palace Diner
22	Grand Central Pkwy, to I-678, College Pt Blvd, **N...gas:** Citgo, Mobil, **lodging:** Paris Suites, **S...gas:** Mobil, **lodging:** Best Western
21	108th St, **N...gas:** Gaseteria
19	NY 25, Queens Blvd, Woodhaven Blvd, to Rockaways, **N...other:** JC Penney, Macy's, Stern's, mall, **S...gas:** Amoco, **other:** Circuit City, Marshall's, Old Navy, Sears
18.5	69th Ave, Grand Ave(from wb), no facilities
18	Maurice St, **N...gas:** Amoco, **S...gas:** Gaseteria/Dunkin Donuts, **food:** McDonald's, **other:** diesel repair
17	48th St, to I-278, no facilities
16	I-495 begins/ends in NYC.

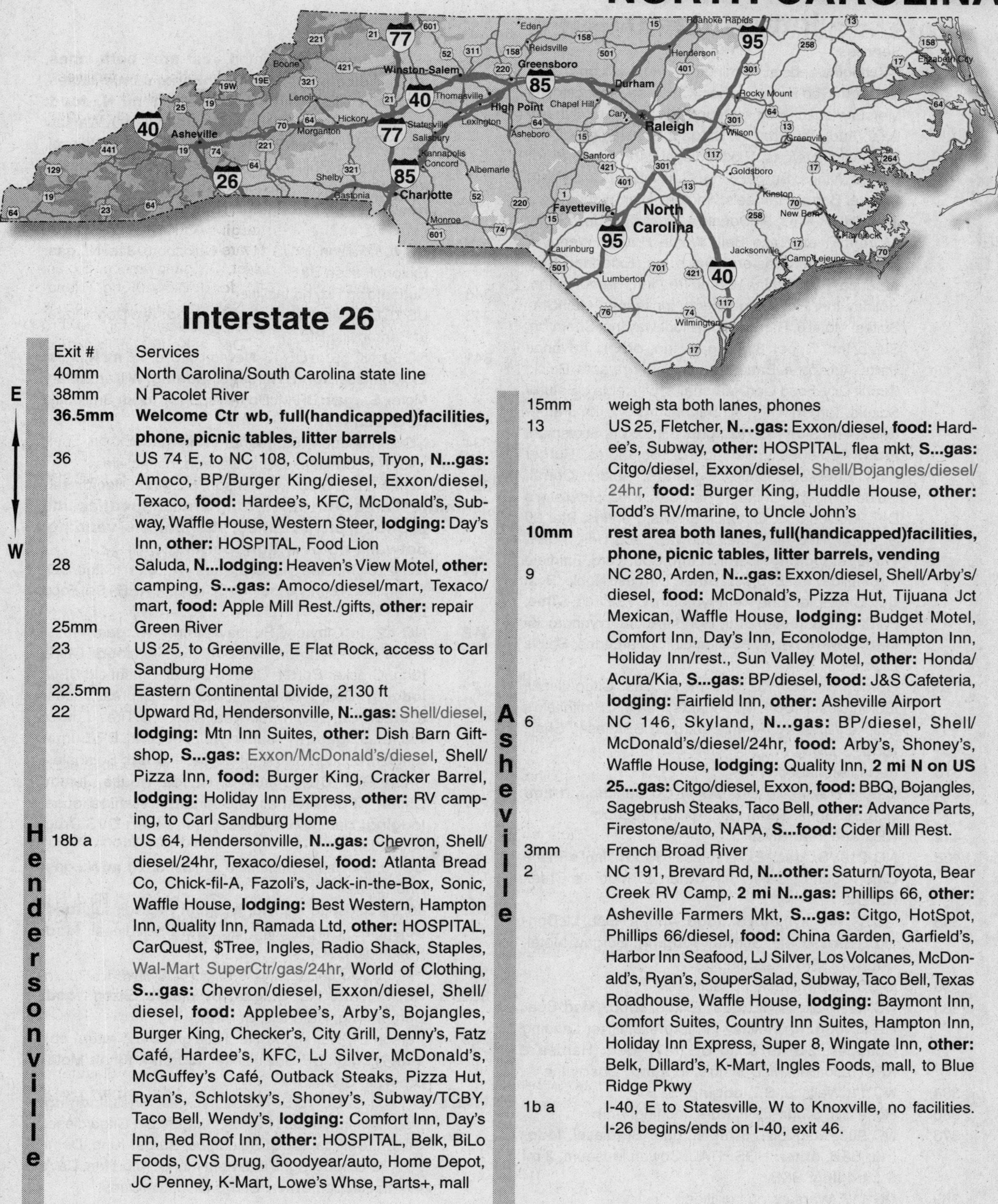

Interstate 26

E ↕ W

Exit #	Services
40mm	North Carolina/South Carolina state line
38mm	N Pacolet River
36.5mm	**Welcome Ctr wb, full(handicapped)facilities, phone, picnic tables, litter barrels**
36	US 74 E, to NC 108, Columbus, Tryon, **N...gas:** Amoco, BP/Burger King/diesel, Exxon/diesel, Texaco, **food:** Hardee's, KFC, McDonald's, Subway, Waffle House, Western Steer, **lodging:** Day's Inn, **other:** HOSPITAL, Food Lion
28	Saluda, **N...lodging:** Heaven's View Motel, **other:** camping, **S...gas:** Amoco/diesel/mart, Texaco/mart, **food:** Apple Mill Rest./gifts, **other:** repair
25mm	Green River
23	US 25, to Greenville, E Flat Rock, access to Carl Sandburg Home
22.5mm	Eastern Continental Divide, 2130 ft
22	Upward Rd, Hendersonville, **N...gas:** Shell/diesel, **lodging:** Mtn Inn Suites, **other:** Dish Barn Giftshop, **S...gas:** Exxon/McDonald's/diesel, Shell/Pizza Inn, **food:** Burger King, Cracker Barrel, **lodging:** Holiday Inn Express, **other:** RV camping, to Carl Sandburg Home
18b a	US 64, Hendersonville, **N...gas:** Chevron, Shell/diesel/24hr, Texaco/diesel, **food:** Atlanta Bread Co, Chick-fil-A, Fazoli's, Jack-in-the-Box, Sonic, Waffle House, **lodging:** Best Western, Hampton Inn, Quality Inn, Ramada Ltd, **other:** HOSPITAL, CarQuest, $Tree, Ingles, Radio Shack, Staples, Wal-Mart SuperCtr/gas/24hr, World of Clothing, **S...gas:** Chevron/diesel, Exxon/diesel, Shell/diesel, **food:** Applebee's, Arby's, Bojangles, Burger King, Checker's, City Grill, Denny's, Fatz Café, Hardee's, KFC, LJ Silver, McDonald's, McGuffey's Café, Outback Steaks, Pizza Hut, Ryan's, Schlotsky's, Shoney's, Subway/TCBY, Taco Bell, Wendy's, **lodging:** Comfort Inn, Day's Inn, Red Roof Inn, **other:** HOSPITAL, Belk, BiLo Foods, CVS Drug, Goodyear/auto, Home Depot, JC Penney, K-Mart, Lowe's Whse, Parts+, mall
15mm	weigh sta both lanes, phones
13	US 25, Fletcher, **N...gas:** Exxon/diesel, **food:** Hardee's, Subway, **other:** HOSPITAL, flea mkt, **S...gas:** Citgo/diesel, Exxon/diesel, Shell/Bojangles/diesel/24hr, **food:** Burger King, Huddle House, **other:** Todd's RV/marine, to Uncle John's
10mm	**rest area both lanes, full(handicapped)facilities, phone, picnic tables, litter barrels, vending**
9	NC 280, Arden, **N...gas:** Exxon/diesel, Shell/Arby's/diesel, **food:** McDonald's, Pizza Hut, Tijuana Jct Mexican, Waffle House, **lodging:** Budget Motel, Comfort Inn, Day's Inn, Econolodge, Hampton Inn, Holiday Inn/rest., Sun Valley Motel, **other:** Honda/Acura/Kia, **S...gas:** BP/diesel, **food:** J&S Cafeteria, **lodging:** Fairfield Inn, **other:** Asheville Airport
6	NC 146, Skyland, **N...gas:** BP/diesel, Shell/McDonald's/diesel/24hr, **food:** Arby's, Shoney's, Waffle House, **lodging:** Quality Inn, **2 mi N on US 25...gas:** Citgo/diesel, Exxon, **food:** BBQ, Bojangles, Sagebrush Steaks, Taco Bell, **other:** Advance Parts, Firestone/auto, NAPA, **S...food:** Cider Mill Rest.
3mm	French Broad River
2	NC 191, Brevard Rd, **N...other:** Saturn/Toyota, Bear Creek RV Camp, **2 mi N...gas:** Phillips 66, **other:** Asheville Farmers Mkt, **S...gas:** Citgo, HotSpot, Phillips 66/diesel, **food:** China Garden, Garfield's, Harbor Inn Seafood, LJ Silver, Los Volcanes, McDonald's, Ryan's, SouperSalad, Subway, Taco Bell, Texas Roadhouse, Waffle House, **lodging:** Baymont Inn, Comfort Suites, Country Inn Suites, Hampton Inn, Holiday Inn Express, Super 8, Wingate Inn, **other:** Belk, Dillard's, K-Mart, Ingles Foods, mall, to Blue Ridge Pkwy
1b a	I-40, E to Statesville, W to Knoxville, no facilities. I-26 begins/ends on I-40, exit 46.

Hendersonville

Asheville

NORTH CAROLINA
Interstate 40

E ↕ W Wilmington

Exit # Services

420mm I-40 begins/ends at Wilmington. **Facilities on US 17, N...food:** Bob Evans, **other:** Chrysler/Jeep, Lincoln/Mercury/Isuzu, Home Depot, Kia, Nissan, Subaru/Saab/Audi, Toyota, VW, **S...gas:** Crown/diesel/24hr, Dodge's Store/gas, Exxon/diesel/24hr, Shell, **food:** Buffalo Wings, Burger King, Carrabba's, Chick-fil-A, Cracker Barrel, Hardee's, Hooters, Hieronymus' Seafood, IHOP, KFC, McDonald's, Ruby Tuesday, Sticky Fingers Rest., Taco Bell, Waffle House, Wendy's, **lodging:** Best Western, Day's Inn, Extended Stay America, Fairfield Inn, GreenTree Inn, Hampton Inn, Holiday Inn, Howard Johnson, Innkeeper, MainStay Suites, Motel 6, Ramada Inn, Rodeway Inn, Sheraton, Sleep Inn, Super 8, Wingate Inn, **other:** Advance Parts, AutoZone, Batteries+, Buffalo Tire/auto, Buick, Circuit City, Food Lion, Marshall's, OfficeMax, Saturn/Suzuki, Target, Wal-Mart SuperCtr/gas/24hr, **Facilities 2-4 mi S on NC 132...gas:** BP, Exxon, Scotsman, **food:** Applebee's, Bennigan's, Bojangles, Burger King, Checker's, Chili's, Domino's, Golden Corral, Golden Phoenix Chinese, Hardee's, KFC, McAlister's Deli, McDonald's, Outback Steaks, Perkins, Pier 20 Seafood, Rockola Café, Subway, Taco Bell, TCBY, Wendy's, **lodging:** Comfort Inn, Courtyard, Fairfield Inn, Holiday Inn Express, **other:** Barnes&Noble, Best Buy, Chevrolet, Chrysler/Plymouth, CVS Drug, $Tree, Ford, Harris-Teeter/24hr, Honda/Acura, Hyundai, K-Mart, Lowe's Whse, Pontiac/GMC/Mercedes, Sam's Club

420b a Gordon Rd, NC 132 N, **2 mi N...gas:** Citgo/diesel, Exxon/diesel, **food:** McDonald's, Perkins, Smithfield's Chicken/BBQ, KOA(4mi), **S...gas:** BP/diesel, Shell, **food:** Subway

416 new interchange

414 Castle Hayne, to Brunswick Co beaches, **1/2mi S...gas:** Shell, Sprint Gas, **food:** Hardee's

412 NE Cape Fear River

408 NC 210, **S...gas:** Exxon/diesel, **food:** Paul's Place Café, Country Café(7mi), **other:** to Moore's Creek Nat Bfd

398 NC 53, Burgaw, **2 mi S...food:** Andy's Rest., McDonald's, Skat's Café, Subway, **lodging:** Burgaw Motel, **other:** HOSPITAL, camping

390 to US 117, Wallace, no facilities

385 NC 41, Wallace, **N...gas:** Exxon, **food:** Mad Boar Rest., **lodging:** Holiday Inn Express, River Landing Cottages, **2-3 mi S...**to US 117, **food:** Hardee's, KFC/Taco Bell, McDonald's, **lodging:** Liberty Inn

384 NC 11, Wallace, **S...lodging:** B&B

380 Rose Hill, **S...gas:** BP, Pure, lodging(1mi)

373 NC 903, Magnolia, **5 mi N...gas:** BP/diesel, **lodging:** B&B, **other:** HOSPITAL, Cowan Museum, **2 mi S...lodging:** B&B

369 US 117, Warsaw, no facilities

364 NC 24, to NC 50, Clinton, **rest area both lanes, full(handicapped)facilities, phone, picnic tables, litter barrels, vending, petwalk, 3 mi N...food:** Hardee's, **lodging:** Country Squire Inn(7mi), Warsaw Inn, **S...gas:** Amoco/Bojangles/diesel, **food:** BP/diesel, Crown/24hr, Phillips 66/diesel/24hr, Texaco/diesel, KFC, McDonald's, Smithfield's BBQ, Subway, Waffle House, Wendy's, **lodging:** Day's Inn, Holiday Inn Express

355 NC 403, Faison, to US 117, to Goldsboro, **3 mi N...gas:** Exxon, Faison B&B

348 Suttontown Rd, no facilities

343 US 701, Newton Grove, **1 mi N...food:** Two Dogs Pizza, to Bentonville Bfd

341 NC 50, NC 55, to US 13, Newton Grove, **1.5 mi N...gas:** Exxon/diesel, **food:** Hardee's, **lodging:** William&Mary Motel, **S...gas:** BP/McDonald's, Shell, **food:** Smithfield BBQ, Subway

334 NC 96, Meadow, **S...gas:** BP(1mi)

328b a I-95, N to Smithfield, S to Benson, no facilities

325 NC 242, to US 301, to Benson, **S...gas:** Citgo/diesel

324mm rest area both lanes, full(handicapped)facilities, phone, picnic tables, litter barrels, vending, petwalk, no overnight parking

319 NC 210, McGee's Crossroads, **N...gas:** Citgo/DQ, Shell/diesel/24hr, **other:** MEDICAL CARE, **S...**Food Lion

312 NC 42, to Clayton, Fuquay-Varina, **N...gas:** Hess/Wendy's/diesel/24hr, Phillips 66/diesel, **food:** China King, Cracker Barrel, Golden Corral, Smithfield BBQ, **lodging:** Best Western, Holiday Inn Express, Super 8, **other:** CarQuest, Goodyear/auto, JustTires, Lowe's Whse, **S...gas:** BP/Subway/diesel/24hr, BP/Burger King/24hr, Citgo/diesel, Shell/diesel, **food:** Bojangles, Brass Grill, DQ, Domino's, Huddle House, Jumbo China, KFC/Taco Bell, McDonald's, Waffle House, **lodging:** Hampton Inn, Sleep Inn, **other:** CVS Drug, Food Lion

306 US 70, Garner, to Smithfield, Goldsboro, **1 mi N...gas:** Shell/diesel

303 Jones Sausage Rd, Rd, **N...gas:** Shell/diesel, **food:** Bojangles, Burger King, **S...gas:** Shell/diesel, **food:** Smithfield BBQ

301 I-440 E, US 64/70 E, to Wilson, no facilities

300b a Rock Quarry Rd, **S...gas:** BP/diesel, Exxon, **food:** Burger King, Hardee's, Subway

299 Person St, Hammond Rd, Raleigh(no EZ return eb), **1 mi N...gas:** BP, Shell/diesel, **lodging:** King's Motel, **other:** to Shaw U

298b a US 401 S, US 70 E, NC 50, **N...gas:** Shell, **lodging:** Red Roof Inn, **other:** Parts+, **S...gas:** BP, Citgo/diesel, Crown, Servco, **food:** Bojangles, Burger King, Domino's, KFC, **lodging:** Claremont Inn, Comfort Inn, Day's Inn, Innkeeper, **other:** Sam's Club, CarQuest

NORTH CAROLINA

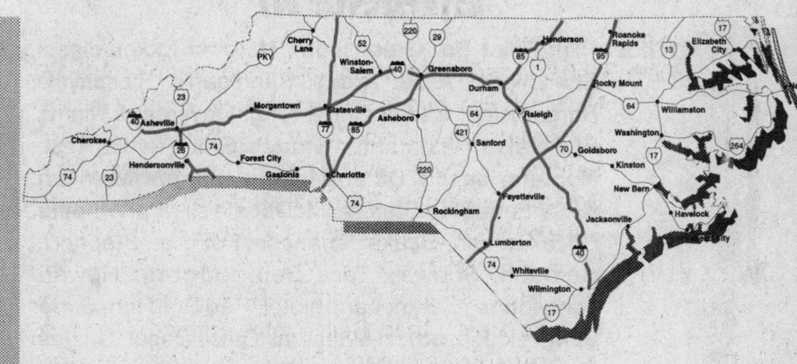

Interstate 40

E ↕ W

Raleigh

297 Lake Wheeler Rd, **N...gas:** Exxon, **food:** Burger King, **other:** HOSPITAL, Farmer's Mkt, **S...gas:** Citgo

295 Gorman St, **1 mi N...gas:** BP, Exxon/diesel, Shell, **food:** Hardee's, Subway, **other:** to NCSU, Reynolds Coliseum

293 US 1, US 64 W, Raleigh, to inner 440 Lp, **S...gas:** Exxon, **lodging:** Motel 6

291 Cary Towne Blvd, Cary, **1 mi S...food:** Burger King, DQ, Hardee's, Jersey Mike's Subs, McDonald's, Olive Garden, Ragazzi's, Taco Bell

290 NC 54, Cary, **1 mi N...gas:** Citgo, **2 mi S...gas:** Citgo, Shell, **lodging:** Hampton Inn

289 to I-440, Wade Ave, to Raleigh, **N...other:** HOSPITAL, museum, **S...**to fairgrounds

287 Harrison Ave, Cary, **N...**to Wm B Umstead SP, **S...gas:** Shell, **food:** Arby's, Burger King, McDonald's, Newton's SW Rest., Subway, Wendy's, **lodging:** Embassy Suites, Studio+

285 Aviation Pkwy, to Morrisville, Raleigh/Durham Airport, **N...lodging:** Hilton Garden

284 Airport Blvd, **N...food:** Chophouse Rest., to RDU Airport, **S...gas:** BP/diesel, Citgo/diesel, Exxon, Shell/diesel, **food:** Cracker Barrel, Jersey Mike's Subs, Quizno's, Schlotsky's, Texas Steaks, Waffle House, Wendy's, **lodging:** Baymont Inn, Courtyard, Day's Inn, Extended Stay America, Fairfield Inn, Hampton Inn, Holiday Inn Express, Microtel, La Quinta, Staybridge Suites, **other:** Prime Outlets/famous brands

283 I-540, to US 70, Aviation Pkwy, no facilities

282 Page Rd, **S...food:** McDonald's, **lodging:** Holiday Inn/rest., Sheraton/rest., Sleep Inn, Wellesley Inn, Wingate Inn, **other:** World Trade Ctr

281 Miami Blvd, **N...food:** Rudino's Grill, Wendy's, **lodging:** Best Western Crown Park, Marriott, Wyndham Garden, **S...gas:** BP, Shell, **lodging:** Clarion, Homewood Suites, Wellesley Inn

280 Davis Dr, **N...**to Research Triangle, **S...lodging:** Radisson Governor's Inn

279b a NC 147, Durham Fwy, to Durham, no facilities

278 NC 55, to NC 54, Apex, Foreign Trade Zone 93, World Trade Ctr, **N...gas:** Citgo, **food:** China 1 Rest., Waffle House, **lodging:** Doubletree Suites, Fairfield Inn, Innkeeper, La Quinta, Red Roof Inn, **S...gas:** Crown, Exxon/diesel, Mobil/diesel, **food:** Arby's, Bojangles, Burger King, Chick-fil-A, Fazoli's, Golden Corral, Hardee's, KFC, McDonald's, Miami Grill, O!Brian's, Papa John's, Pizza Hut, Schlotsky's, Subway, Taco Bell, Wendy's, **lodging:** Candlewood Suites, Courtyard, Crossland Suites, Hawthorn Suites, Homestead Village, Residence Inn, **other:** MEDICAL CARE, $Tree, Eckerd, Food Lion, transmissions/tires

276 Fayetteville Rd, **N...gas:** Exxon/diesel, Phillips 66/diesel, **food:** McDonald's, Quizno's, Ruby Tuesday, Rudino's Pizza, Souper Salad, Subs Etc, TCBY, Waffle House, Wendy's, **other:** Eckerd, GNC, Harris-Teeter, Kroger, to NC Central U

274 NC 751, to Jordan Lake, **1-2 mi N...food:** Burger King, McDonald's, Waffle House, Wendy's, **S...gas:** Citgo

Chapel Hill

273 NC 54, to Durham, UNC-Chapel Hill, **N...gas:** Shell/diesel, **S...gas:** BP/diesel, Shell/diesel, **food:** Hardee's, **lodging:** Best Western(2mi), Hampton Inn, Holiday Inn Express

270 US 15, US 501, Chapel Hill, Durham, **N...food:** Bob Evans, Bojangles, Outback Steaks, Philly Steaks, Tripp's Rest., **lodging:** Comfort Inn, Homewood Suites, **other:** HOSPITALS, Barnes&Noble, Best Buy, $Tree, Home Depot, OfficeMax, Old Navy, Marshall's, Michael's, Saab, Wal-Mart, to Duke U, **S...gas:** BP, Exxon, **food:** Applebee's, Golden Corral, Hardee's, McDonald's, Subway, Wendy's, **lodging:** Hampton Inn, Holiday Inn, Red Roof Inn, Sheraton, Siena Hotel, **other:** BMW, Chevrolet, CVS Drug, Lowe's Whse, Saturn, mall

266 NC 86, to Chapel Hill, **2 mi S...gas:** BP, Citgo, Exxon, Wilco/diesel, **food:** Subway, Zero's Subs, **other:** Harris-Teeter

263 New Hope Church Rd, no facilities

261 Hillsborough, **1.5 mi N...gas:** BP, Citgo/diesel, Shell, **food:** Hardee's, KFC, McDonald's, Pizza Hut, Waffle House, Wendy's

259 I-85 N, to Durham, no facilities

I-40 and I-85 run together 38 mi. See North Carolina Interstate 85, exits 124-161.

219 1-85 S, to Charlotte, US 29, US 70, US 220, no facilities

218b a US 220 S, to I-85 S, Freeman Mill Rd, no facilities

NORTH CAROLINA

Interstate 40

E ↕ W

Greensboro

217b a High Point Rd, Greensboro, **N...gas:** Exxon/diesel, Shell/diesel, **food:** Arby's, Bennigan's, Biscuitville, Burger King, Chili's, China King, Devereaux Dining, El Paraiso Restorante, Grady's Grill, Ham's Rest., Hooters, Jake's Diner/24hr, La Bamba Mexican, KFC, LoneStar Steaks, McDonald's, Mrs Winners, Olive Garden, Osaka Japanese, PoFolks, Stephen's Seafood, Subway, Taco Bell, **lodging:** Howard Johnson/rest., Park Lane Hotel, Red Roof Inn, Super 8, Travelodge, **other:** $General, Office Depot, **S...gas:** Crown, Shell/diesel, **food:** Bojangles, Burger King, Carrabba's, Cookout Café, Darryl's, Hoolihan's, Krispy Kreme, Kyoto Express, Libby Hill Seafood, Mamma Maria Italian, McDonald's, Nascar Café, Oh! Brian's, Pizza Inn, Sonic, Subway, Taco Bell, Tides Seafood, Waffle House, Wendy's, Wok'n Roll, **lodging:** Best Western, Comfort Inn, Day's Inn, Drury Inn, Econolodge, Fairfield Inn, Hampton Inn, Residence Inn, Sheraton, **other:** Aamco, Advance Parts, AutoZone, Belk, Borders Books, Dillard's, Discount Tire, Family$, JC Penney, Lowe's Foods, Merchant Tire/auto, NAPA, NTB, OfficeMax, PepBoys, Radio Shack, Sears/auto, mall

216 NC 6(from eb, exits left), to Greensboro Coliseum

214b a Wendover Ave, **N...gas:** Citgo/diesel, Exxon/diesel, Shell/diesel, **food:** BBQ, Blimpie, Burger King, K&W Cafeteria, Ruby Tuesday, TCBY, Waffle House, **lodging:** Extended Stay America, Holiday Inn Express, Innkeeper, Microtel, **other:** BMW, Chevrolet, Chrysler, Dodge, Ford, Goodyear, Honda/Acura/Nissan, Isuzu/Subaru, Mercedes, Mitsubishi, Saab/Jaguar, Saturn, Staples, Volvo, **S...food:** Applebee's, Arby's, Bojangles, Chick-fil-A, Cracker Barrel, Fuddrucker's, Golden Corral, IHOP/24hr, Imperial Gourmet, Logan's Roadhouse, McDonald's, Red Lobster, Schlotsky's, Steak'n Shake, Subway, TGIFriday, Taco Bell, Tripp's Rest., Wendy's, **lodging:** AmeriSuites, Courtyard, Shoney's Inn/rest., Suburban Lodge, **other:** Best Buy, Circuit City, Ferrari, Goodyear, Harris-Teeter, Home Depot, K-Mart, Lowe's Whse, Porsche, Sam's Club, Wal-Mart SuperCtr/24hr

213 Jamestown, **N...gas:** BP/diesel, **food:** Damon's Ribs, **lodging:** Radisson, to Guilford Coll, **S...other:** Hecht's, Kohl's, Old Navy, Saturn, Target, same as 214

212 Chimney Rock Rd, no facilities

211 new exit

210 NC 68, to High Point, Piedmont Triad, **N...gas:** Phillips 66/diesel, **food:** Arby's, Hardee's, Mr Omelet, Wendy's, **lodging:** Day's Inn, Embassy Suites, Holiday Inn, Homewood Suites, Sleep Inn, **other:** Ford Trucks, Freightliner, to airport, **S...gas:** Exxon/diesel, **food:** Bojangles, McDonald's, Pizza Hut/Taco Bell, Shoney's, Subway, **lodging:** Best Western, Candlewood Suites, Comfort Suites, Hampton Inn, Innkeeper, Motel 6, Ramada Inn, Red Roof Inn, Studio+

208 Sandy Ridge Rd, **N...gas:** Wilco/Hess/diesel/@, **other:** RV Country, **S...gas:** Citgo/diesel, Out Of Doors Mart/Airstream, **other:** Farmer's Mkt

206 Lp 40(from wb), to Kernersville, Winston-Salem, downtown

203 NC 66, to Kernersville, **N...gas:** BP/Amoco, Citgo/McDonald's/diesel, Shell/Subway/diesel, **food:** Capt Tom's Seafood, Clark's BBQ, Suzie's Diner, Waffle House, **lodging:** Sleep Inn, **other:** Ford, Merchant Tire/repair, **S...gas:** Shell/diesel, Holiday Inn Express

201 Union Cross Rd, **N...gas:** Exxon/diesel, QM, **food:** Burger King, China Café, **other:** CVS Drug, Food Lion

196 US 311 S, to High Point, no facilities

195 US 311 N, NC 109, to Thomasville, **S...gas:** Pure, Wilco/Hess/diesel

193c Silas Creek Pkwy(from wb), same as 192

Winston-Salem

193b a US 52, NC 8, to Lexington, **S...gas:** Citgo, Hess/diesel, Shell, **food:** Hardee's

192 NC 150, to Peters Creek Pkwy, Winston-Salem, **N...gas:** Shell, Wilco, **food:** Arby's, Bojangles, Burger King, Checker's, China Buffet, Country Roadhouse, IHOP, KFC, Little Caesar's, Monterrey Mexican, Old Country Buffet, Perkins, Pizza Hut, Red Lobster, Shoney's, Sonic, Taco Bell, Wendy's, **lodging:** Comfort Inn(1mi), Innkeeper, Knight's Inn, **other:** MEDICAL CARE, Acura/Subaru/Isuzu, Audi, AutoZone, Eckerd, Ford, Hyundai, Kroger, Lowe's Foods, Mazda, NAPA, Office Depot, PharMor Drug, Suzuki, VW, **S...gas:** BP, **food:** Libby Hill Seafood, McDonald's, K&W Cafeteria, Wendy's, **lodging:** Holiday Inn Express, **other:** Advance Parts, BiLo, Buick/BMW/Saturn, CVS Drug, Food Lion, Goodyear, Harris Teeter, Honda, K-Mart

190 Hanes Mall Blvd(from wb, no re-entry), **N...food:** McDonald's, O'Charley's, TGIFriday, Tripp's Rest., **lodging:** Day's Inn, **other:** HOSPITAL, Belk, Dillard's, Drug Emporium, Firestone, JC Penney, Marshall's, Sears/auto, mall, same as 189, **S...food:** Baja Fresh Grill, Bojangles, ChuckeCheese, Outback Steaks, Souper Salad, **lodging:** Comfort Suites, Microtel, Sleep Inn

189 US 158, Stratford Rd, Hanes Mall Blvd, **N...gas:** BP, Exxon, **food:** Bojangles, Chili's, Cozumel Mexican, McDonald's, O'Charley's, Olive Garden, Red Lobster, Sagebrush Steaks, Taco Bell, **lodging:** Courtyard, Fairfield Inn, **other:** HOSPITAL, Chevrolet, Hecht's, Jo-Ann Fabrics, OfficeMax, Michael's, NTB, mall, **S...gas:** BP, Shell, **food:** Applebee's, Burger King, Chick-fil-A, Copeland's Grill, Corky's BBQ, Dynasty Buffet, Fuddruckers, Hooters, Jason's Deli, Little Caesar's, LoneStar Steaks, Longhorn Steaks, Macaroni Grill, Schlotsky's, Subway, **lodging:** Extended Stay America, Hampton Inn, Holiday Inn, La Quinta, Sleep Inn, **other:** Barnes&Noble, Best Buy, Circuit City, Costco/gas, CVS Drug, Food Lion, Home Depot, Kohl's, Lowe's Whse, Sam's Club, Target

Interstate 40

E ↕ W

Clemmons

188 US 421, to Yadkinville, Winston-Salem, to WFU(no EZ wb return), **1/2mi N off US 421...gas:** BP/Amoco, Shell, **food:** Boston Mkt, Burger King, McDonald's, Waffle House, Wendy's, **other:** CVS Drug, $Tree, Kroger, Mercedes, Wal-Mart SuperCtr/24hr

184 to US 421, Clemmons, **N...gas:** Shell, Texaco, **food:** Bambini Italian, El Jinet Mexican, KFC, **lodging:** Holiday Inn Express, **S...gas:** BP/diesel, Citgo/diesel, Etna/diesel, Exxon/diesel, Texaco, **food:** Arby's, Brick Oven Pizza, Burger King, Cozumel Mexican, Cracker Barrel, Domino's, JB's Hotdogs, Mandarin Buffet, McDonald's, Mi Pueblo Mexican, Pizza Hut, Quizno's, Sagebrush Steaks, Schlotsky's, Sonic, Subway, Taco Bell, Tokyo Japanese, Waffle House, Wendy's, **lodging:** Holiday Inn, Super 8, Village Inn, **other:** Advance Parts, BiLo Foods, CarQuest, CVS Drug, Food Lion, K-Mart, Lowe's Foods, Merchant Tire, Parts+, Staples, USPO

182 Bermuda Run(from wb, no re-entry), Tanglewood, no facilities

181mm Yadkin River

180 NC 801, Tanglewood, **N...food:** Capt's Galley Seafood, **other:** Eckerd, Lowe's Foods, **S...gas:** BP/diesel, Citgo/Subway/diesel, Exxon, Shell, **food:** Bojangles, DQ, McDonald's, Wendy's, **other:** CVS Drug, Food Lion, Radio Shack

177mm rest areas both lanes, full(handicapped)facilities, phone, vending, picnic tables, litter barrels, petwalk

174 Farmington Rd, **N...gas:** Exxon/diesel, **other:** antiques, **S...other:** Furniture Gallery, vineyards

170 US 601, Mocksville, **N...gas:** Citgo/diesel/LP, Shell/diesel/rest./24hr/@, **S...gas:** BP/diesel, Exxon, Shell/Taco Bell, **food:** Arby's, Bojangles, Burger King, China Grill, Dynasty Chinese, KFC, McDonald's, Pier 601 Seafood, Pizza Hut, Little Caesar's, Subway, Wendy's, Western Steer, **lodging:** Comfort Inn, Day's Inn, High-Way Inn, Scottish Inn, **other:** HOSPITAL, Advance Parts, CVS Drug, $General, Food Lion, Ford/Mercury, Goodyear/auto, Wal-Mart

168 US 64, to Mocksville, **N...gas:** Exxon/diesel, **other:** Lake Myers RV Resort(3mi), **S...gas:** BP

162 US 64, Cool Springs, **N...other:** Lake Myers RV Resort(5mi), **S...gas:** Shell, **other:** TravL Park

161mm S Yadkin River

154 to US 64, Old Mocksville Rd, **N...**HOSPITAL, **S...gas:** Citgo/diesel, **food:** Jaybee's Hotdogs, **lodging:** Hallmark Inn

153 US 64(from eb), **1/2 mi S...gas:** Citgo/diesel, **lodging:** Hallmark Inn, Jaybee's Hotdogs

152b a I-77, S to Charlotte, N to Elkin, no facilities

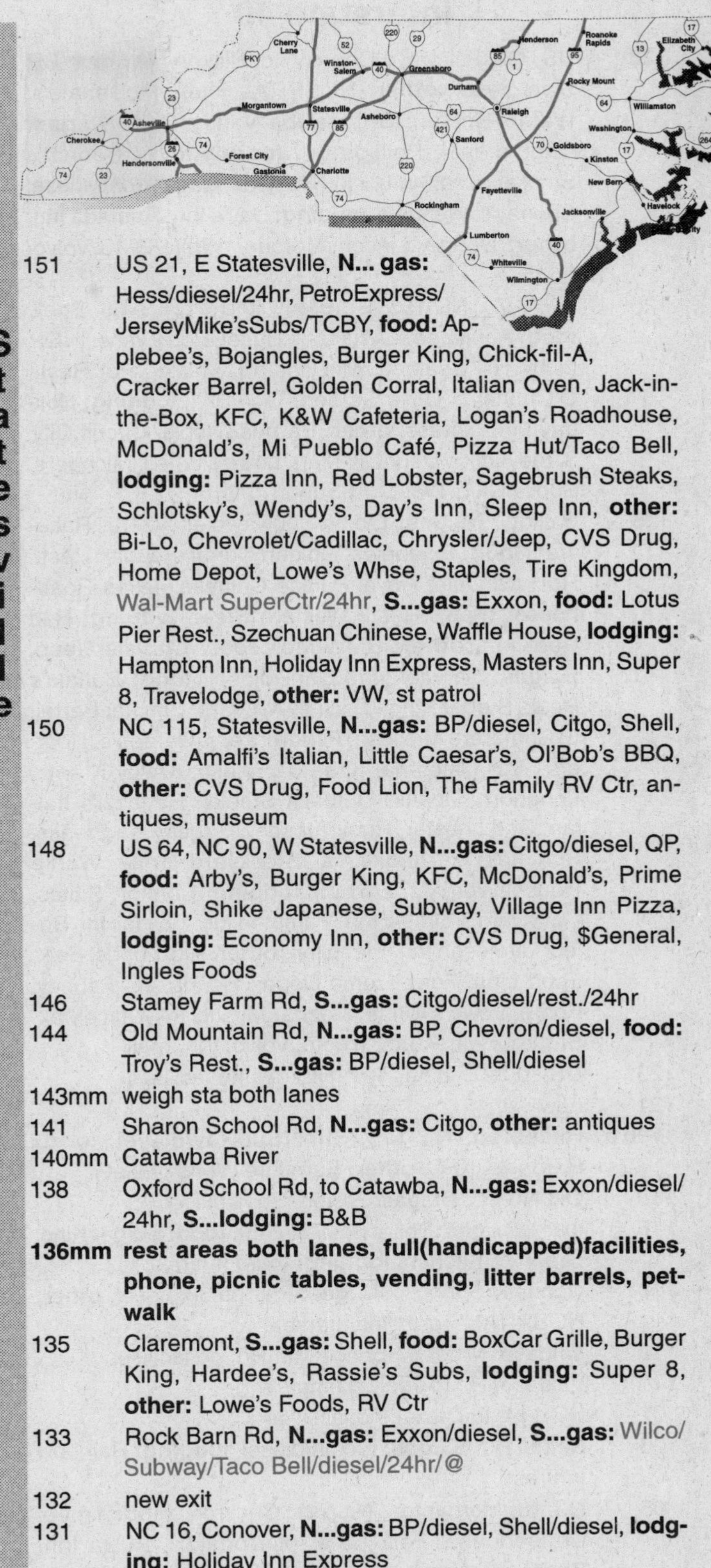

Statesville

151 US 21, E Statesville, **N... gas:** Hess/diesel/24hr, PetroExpress/JerseyMike'sSubs/TCBY, **food:** Applebee's, Bojangles, Burger King, Chick-fil-A, Cracker Barrel, Golden Corral, Italian Oven, Jack-in-the-Box, KFC, K&W Cafeteria, Logan's Roadhouse, McDonald's, Mi Pueblo Café, Pizza Hut/Taco Bell, **lodging:** Pizza Inn, Red Lobster, Sagebrush Steaks, Schlotsky's, Wendy's, Day's Inn, Sleep Inn, **other:** Bi-Lo, Chevrolet/Cadillac, Chrysler/Jeep, CVS Drug, Home Depot, Lowe's Whse, Staples, Tire Kingdom, Wal-Mart SuperCtr/24hr, **S...gas:** Exxon, **food:** Lotus Pier Rest., Szechuan Chinese, Waffle House, **lodging:** Hampton Inn, Holiday Inn Express, Masters Inn, Super 8, Travelodge, **other:** VW, st patrol

150 NC 115, Statesville, **N...gas:** BP/diesel, Citgo, Shell, **food:** Amalfi's Italian, Little Caesar's, Ol'Bob's BBQ, **other:** CVS Drug, Food Lion, The Family RV Ctr, antiques, museum

148 US 64, NC 90, W Statesville, **N...gas:** Citgo/diesel, QP, **food:** Arby's, Burger King, KFC, McDonald's, Prime Sirloin, Shike Japanese, Subway, Village Inn Pizza, **lodging:** Economy Inn, **other:** CVS Drug, $General, Ingles Foods

146 Stamey Farm Rd, **S...gas:** Citgo/diesel/rest./24hr

144 Old Mountain Rd, **N...gas:** BP, Chevron/diesel, **food:** Troy's Rest., **S...gas:** BP/diesel, Shell/diesel

143mm weigh sta both lanes

141 Sharon School Rd, **N...gas:** Citgo, **other:** antiques

140mm Catawba River

138 Oxford School Rd, to Catawba, **N...gas:** Exxon/diesel/24hr, **S...lodging:** B&B

136mm rest areas both lanes, full(handicapped)facilities, phone, picnic tables, vending, litter barrels, petwalk

135 Claremont, **S...gas:** Shell, **food:** BoxCar Grille, Burger King, Hardee's, Rassie's Subs, **lodging:** Super 8, **other:** Lowe's Foods, RV Ctr

133 Rock Barn Rd, **N...gas:** Exxon/diesel, **S...gas:** Wilco/Subway/Taco Bell/diesel/24hr/@

132 new exit

131 NC 16, Conover, **N...gas:** BP/diesel, Shell/diesel, **lodging:** Holiday Inn Express

130 Old US 70, **N...food:** Jack-in-the-Box, Subway, **other:** $General, K-Mart, Lowe's Foods, NAPA AutoCare, **S...gas:** Citgo, Phillips 66, **other:** USPO

Interstate 40

E ↕ W

Hickory

128 US 321, Fairgrove Church Rd, Hickory, **N...gas:** BP, Solo/diesel, **other:** HOSPITAL,Shell, McDonald's, Waffle House, to Catawba Valley Coll, **S...gas:** Citgo/diesel, Phillips 66, **food:** Arby's, Bennitt's Smokehouse, Harbor Inn Seafood, Nagano Japanese, Shoney's, Wendy's, **lodging:** Day's Inn, Ramada Inn, **other:** Dodge, Lincoln/Mercury, White/GMC/Volvo/ Ford

126 to US 70, NC 155, **S...gas:** Citgo, Phillips 66, Shell, **food:** Applebee's, Asia Café Buffet, Bob Evans, IHOP, Libby Hill Seafood, McDonald's, Melting Pot Rest., O'Charley's, Olive Garden, Taco Bell, **lodging:** Holiday Inn Express, **other:** Barnes&Noble, Circuit City, $Tree, Office Depot, K-Mart, Lowe's Whse, Michael's, Sam's Club, Wal-Mart SuperCtr/24hr

125 Hickory, **N...gas:** Exxon/Subway/diesel/24hr, RaceTrac, **food:** Bojangles, Golden Corral, Peddler Rest., Rockola Café, Royal Palace Chinese, Texas Roadhouse, Tripp's Rest., Western Steer, **lodging:** Red Roof Inn, **other:** BMW/Mercedes, Chrysler/Jeep, **S...gas:** Servco/24hr, Shell/diesel, **food:** Buffalo's Rest., Burger King, Chick-fil-A, CiCi's, Cracker Barrel, El Sombrero Mexican, Fuddrucker's, Hardee's, Hooters, J&S Cafeteria, Kobe Japanese, Krispy Kreme, Longhorn Steaks, Outback Steaks, Ragazzi's Italian, Red Lobster, Ruby Tuesday, Sagebrush Steaks, Schlotsky's, Steak&Ale, Stockyard Grille, Waffle House, Wendy's, Zaxby's, **lodging:** Comfort Suites, Courtyard, Fairfield Inn, Hampton Inn, Holiday Inn Select, Jameson Inn, Sleep Inn, **other:** Aldi Foods, Belk, Food Lion, Ford, Home Depot, Honda, JC Penney, Kohl's, Lowe's Whse, Mazda, Mitsubishi, OfficeMax, Saturn, Sears/auto, Toyota, Volvo, VW, mall

123 US 70/321, to NC 127, Hickory, no facilities

121 new exit

119b a Hildebran, **N...gas:** Shell/Subway/diesel, **food:** Hardee's, KFC, **other:** Furniture World Outlet

118 Old NC 10, **N...gas:** Exxon, Shell/diesel

116 Icard, **S...gas:** Phillips/diesel/24hr, **food:** Burger King, Granny's Kitchen, **lodging:** Icard Inn/rest.

113 Connelly Springs, **N...gas:** Phillips 66/diesel, **other:** HOSPITAL, Ford, flea market

112 Valdese, Mineral Springs Mtn Rd, no facilities

111 Valdese, **N...food:** McDonald's

107 NC 114, to Drexel, no facilities

106 Bethel Rd, **S...gas:** Exxon/diesel, **lodging:** Rainbow Inn/rest.

105 NC 18, Morganton, **N...gas:** Chevron, **food:** Arby's, Coffeehouse, Fatz Café, McDonald's, Pizza Inn, Shoney's, Waffle House, Wendy's, Western Sizzlin, **lodging:** Hampton Inn, Red Carpet Inn, **other:** HOSPITAL, Joe's Tire, Pontiac/Cadillac/GMC, **S...**QM/ diesel, Shell, El Paso Mexican, Sagebrush Steaks, Day's Inn, Holiday Inn/rest., Sleep Inn, to South Mtns SP

Morganton

104 Enola Rd, **S...gas:** Citgo, **food:** Chick-fil-A, Jersey Mike's Subs, **other:** Belk, Food Lion, Goody's, Staples, st patrol

103 US 64, Morganton, **N...gas:** Exxon/diesel/24hr, Shell/ diesel, Max' Mexican, Tastee Freez, Super 8, **S...gas:** Citgo, Phillips 66/diesel, RaceTrac, **food:** Butch's BBQ, Checker's, Denny's, Hardee's, KFC, Subway, Taco Bell, Tokyo Diner, **lodging:** Comfort Suites, **other:** Food Lion, Goodyear/auto, Goody's, Honda, Ingles Foods, Lowe's Whse, Radio Shack, Wal-Mart/drugs

100 Jamestown Rd, **N...gas:** BP/diesel/24hr, **other:** Ford/ Mercury, **2 mi N...food:** KFC, Taco Bell, **lodging:** Eagle Motel

98 Causby Rd, to Glen Alpine, **S...**B&B/food

96 Kathy Rd, no facilities

94 Dysartsville Rd, no facilities

90 Nebo, **N...gas:** Exxon/diesel/rest., **other:** to Lake James SP, **S...gas:** BP/diesel, RV Ctr

86 NC 226, Marion, to Spruce Pine, hwy patrol, **N...gas:** Exxon/diesel, **food:** Hardee's, KFC, **lodging:** Comfort Inn(3mi)

85 US 221, Marion, **N...lodging:** Comfort Inn(5mi), Hampton Inn, **other:** to Mt Mitchell SP, **S...gas:** BP/diesel, Shell/diesel/24hr, **food:** Sagebrush Steaks, **lodging:** Day's Inn, Super 8

83 Ashworth Rd, no facilities

82mm rest areas both lanes, full(handicapped)facilities, phone, picnic tables, vending, litter barrels, petwalk

81 Sugar Hill Rd, to Marion, **N...gas:** Amoco/24hr, BP/diesel, Chevron/diesel, Citgo, **other:** HOSPITAL, Chrysler/Plymouth/Dodge/Jeep, **2 mi N...food:** Burger King, McDonald's, **other:** Eckerd, Family$, Ingles Foods, **S...gas:** Shell/diesel/rest./24hr

76mm Catawba River

75 Parker Padgett Rd, **S...gas:** Citgo/DQ/Stuckey's/ diesel

73 Old Fort, Mtn Gateway Museum, **N...gas:** Citgo/diesel, **food:** Hardee's, **S...gas:** Exxon, Super Test/diesel, **food:** McDonald's, **other:** Parts+/repair

72 US 70(from eb), Old Fort, **N...**B&B

71mm Pisgah Nat Forest, eastern boundary

67.5mm truck rest area eb

66 Ridgecrest, no facilities

65 (from wb), to Black Mountain, Black Mtn Ctr, **N...lodging:** Super 8(2mi)

64 NC 9, Black Mountain, **N...gas:** Exxon, Shell/Subway/ 24hr, **food:** #1China, Pizza Hut, **lodging:** Super 8, BiLo/café, **other:** Chevrolet, $General, **S...gas:** Phillips 66, **food:** Arby's, Campfire Steaks, Denny's, Huddle House, KFC, McDonald's, Taco Bell, Wendy's, **lodging:** Comfort Inn, **other:** Eckerd, Ingles Foods, Radio Shack

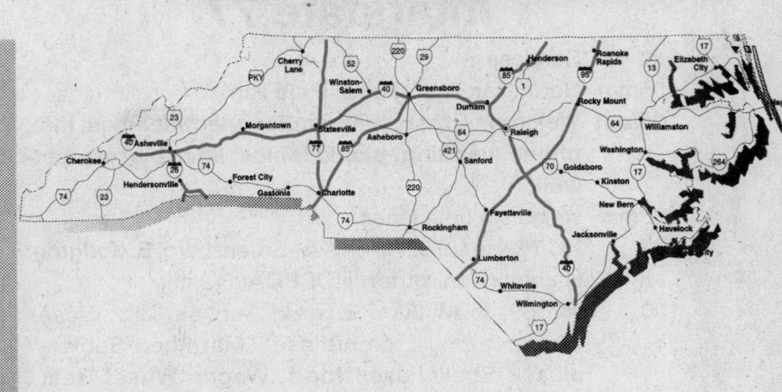

Interstate 40

E ↕ W

Asheville

63mm Swannanoa River

59 Swannanoa, **N...gas:** BP, Citgo/Subway/TCBY, Exxon/diesel, Servco, Shell/diesel, **food:** Athens Pizza, BBQ, Burger King, **other:** Goodyear/auto, Harley-Davidson, Ingles Foods, KOA(2mi), Miles RV Ctr, to Warren Wilson Coll, **S...other:** Gant's Furniture Outlet

55 E Asheville, US 70, **N...gas:** BP, Citgo/Subway, Conoco, **food:** Arby's, Kountry Kitchen, Poseidon Seafood, Waffle House, Zaxby's, **lodging:** Day's Inn, Econolodge, Holiday Inn, Motel 6, Royal Inn, Super 8, **other:** VA HOSPITAL, Go Groceries, Top's RV park, to Mt Mitchell SP, Folk Art Ctr

53b a I-240 W, US 74, to Asheville, Bat Cave, **N...food:** KFC, J&S Cafeteria, McDonald's, **lodging:** Comfort Inn, **other:** Advance Parts, BiLo, CVS Drug, Eckerd, Hamrick's, **1-2 mi N on US 74...gas:** BP, Exxon/diesel, **food:** Applebee's, Burger King, Carrabba's, Chili's, Damon's, IHOP, O'Charley's, Olive Garden, Red Lobster, Subway, Waffle House, **lodging:** Courtyard, Day's Inn, Econolodge, Extended Stay America, Hampton Inn, Ramada Ltd, **other:** Circuit City, Home Depot, Ingles Foods, K-Mart, Office Depot, Sears/auto, mall, **S...gas:** BP/diesel/LP, Phillips 66, **other:** to Blue Ridge Pkwy

51 US 25A, Sweeten Creek Rd, **1/2 mi S...gas:** BP

50 US 25, Asheville, **N...gas:** Exxon/diesel, Shell/diesel, **food:** Arby's, Asaka Japanese, Chapala Mexican, LJ Silver, McDonald's, Pedro's Mexican, Pizza Hut, Popeye's, Subway, Texas Roadhouse, TGIFriday, Wendy's, **lodging:** Baymont Inn, Doubletree Inn, Holiday Inn Express, Howard Johnson, Plaza Motel, Sleep Inn, **other:** HOSPITAL, to Biltmore House, **S...gas:** Phillips 66/diesel, Servco/diesel, **food:** Atl Bread, Huddle House/24hr, **lodging:** Forest Manor Inn

47mm French Broad River

47 NC 191, W Asheville, Farmer's Mkt, **N...other:** Asheville Speedway, **S...gas:** Phillips 66, **food:** Moose Café, Subway, Blackberry's Rest., **2 mi S...lodging:** Comfort Inn, Hampton Inn, Holiday Inn Express, Super 8, Wingate Inn

46b a I-26 & I-240 E, **2 mi N...**multiple facilities from I-240

44 W Asheville, US 74, **N...gas:** BP, Chevron/diesel, Conoco, Exxon, Servco, Shell/Substation II/24hr, **food:** Burger King, Cracker Barrel, El Chapala Mexican, Fatz Café, Pizza Hut, Popeye's, Szechuan Chinese, Waffle House, Wendy's, **lodging:** Best Western, Comfort Inn, Red Roof Inn, Sleep Inn, Super 8, Whispering Pines Motel, **other:** CarQuest, Chevrolet, Chrysler/Plymouth/Jeep, CVS Drug, Family$, Ingles Foods, Lowe's Whse, Mercedes/Mazda, **S...food:** McDonald's, Shoney's, Subway, Budget Motel, Ramada Inn, Home Depot, **1 mi S...gas:** Shell, **food:** BBQ, J&S Cafeteria, Subway, TCBY, **other:** Eckerd, Food Lion

41mm weigh sta both lanes

37 E Canton, **N...gas:** BP, TA/Citgo/diesel/rest./24hr/@, **other:** Goodyear, **S...gas:** Exxon/diesel, Shell, **lodging:** Day's Inn, Plantation Motel, **other:** KOA, Big Cove Camping(2mi)

33 Newfound Rd, to US 74, **S...**gas

31 Canton, **N...food:** Sagebrush Steaks, **lodging:** Econolodge, **S...gas:** BP/diesel, Chevron/Stuckey's, Exxon/McDonald's/24hr, Shell/Arby's/diesel, **food:** Burger King, McDonald's, Pizza Hut(2mi), Subway(1mi), Taco Bell, Waffle House, **lodging:** Comfort Inn, **other:** Ingles Foods, Chevrolet/Pontiac/Buick, Ford, RV/truck repair

27 US 19/23, to Waynesville, Great Smokey Mtn Expswy, **3 mi S...gas:** Shell/Burger King, **food:** Papa's Pizza, Shoney's, Subway, Taco Bell, **other:** HOSPITAL, Food Lion, GNC, Lowe's Whse, Wal-Mart/drugs, to WCU(25mi)

24 NC 209, to Lake Junaluska, **N...gas:** Pilot/diesel/24hr/@, **lodging:** Midway Motel, **S...gas:** Citgo/diesel/24hr/@

20 US 276, to Maggie Valley, Lake Junaluska, **S...gas:** Amoco/diesel, Exxon/diesel/café, Phillips 66/diesel, **lodging:** Quality Inn(5mi), **other:** Creekwood Farm RV Park, Pride RV Resort

16mm Pigeon River

15 Fines Creek, **N...**B&B

12mm Pisgah NF eastern boundary

10mm rest area both lanes, full(handicapped)facilities, phone, vending, picnic tables, litter barrels, petwalk

7 Harmon Den, no facilities

4mm tunnel both lanes

0mm North Carolina/Tennessee state line

NORTH CAROLINA
Interstate 77

N ↕ S

Exit #	Services
105mm	North Carolina/Virginia state line
105mm	**Welcome Ctr sb, full(handicapped)facilities, info, phone, vending, picnic tables, litter barrels, petwalk**
103mm	weigh sta both lanes
101	NC 752, to US 52, to Mt Airy, Greensboro, **E...lodging:** Hampton Inn, **other:** HOSPITAL(12mi),
100	NC 89, to Mt Airy, **E...gas:** Brintle's/Citgo/diesel/rest./24hr/@, Exxon/diesel, Marathon/Subway/diesel, Shell/diesel, **food:** Wagon Wheel Rest., **lodging:** Best Western, Comfort Inn(2mi), **other:** HOSPITAL(12mi), clothing outlet
93	to Dobson, **E...gas:** Citgo/diesel/diner, Shell/DQ/Stuckey's/diesel, **lodging:** Surry Inn
85	NC 1138, CC Camp Rd, to Elkin, **W...gas:** Exxon/diesel, **3 mi W...food:** Burger King, Hardee's, KFC, McDonald's, **lodging:** Elk Inn
83	US 21 byp, to Sparta, no facilities
82.5mm	Yadkin River
	Elkin
82	NC 67, Elkin, **E...gas:** Amoco/diesel/24hr, BP/Case Knife Outlet, Chevron/diesel, Citgo/Subway, **food:** Arby's, Cracker Barrel, Jordan's Rest., **lodging:** Holiday Inn Express, **other:** Holly Ridge Camping(8mi), **W...gas:** Exxon/Baskin-Robbins/TCBY/diesel, **food:** Bojangles, McDonald's, New China, Shoney's, Waffle House, Wendy's, **lodging:** Comfort Inn, Day's Inn, Hampton Inn, Roses Motel, **other:** AutoValue Parts, Buick/Pontiac/GMC, D-Rex Drug, Family$, Food Lion
79	US 21 S, to Arlington, **E...gas:** Shell, **lodging:** Super 8, **W...gas:** Shell/diesel, **food:** Sally Jo's Kitchen, **lodging:** Country Inn, **other:** auto repair
73b a	US 421, to Winston-Salem(20mi), **E...gas:** Amoco/diesel/24hr, Exxon/diesel, **lodging:** Sleep Inn(8mi), Welborn Motel, Yadkin Inn
72mm	**rest area nb, full(handicapped)facilities, phone, vending, picnic tables, litter barrels, petwalk**
65	NC 901, to Union Grove, Harmony, **E...other:** Van Hoy Farms Camping, **W...gas:** Amoco/diesel, BP/diesel, Citgo, Shell/Subway/TCBY/diesel/24hr, **food:** Burger Barn, Honey's Café, **other:** Fiddler's Grove Camping
63mm	**rest area sb, full(handicapped)facilities, phone, vending, picnic tables, litter barrels, petwalk**
59	Tomlin Mill Rd, **W...gas:** Citgo
56.5mm	S Yadkin River
54	US 21, to Turnersburg, **E...gas:** Citgo, **W...gas:** Shell/diesel, **other:** flea mkt
51b a	I-40, E to Winston-Salem, W to Hickory, no facilities
	Statesville
50	E Broad St, Statesville, **E...gas:** Amoco, BP, Crown/diesel, Etna/diesel, **food:** Arby's, Bojangles, Burger King, Domino's, Hardee's, IHOP, McDonald's, Pizza Hut, Shoney's, TCBY, Village Inn Pizza, Wendy's, **lodging:** Fairfield Inn, Red Roof Inn, **other:** MEDICAL CARE, Belk, Eckerd, Harris-Teeter, JC Penney, JR Outlet, K-Mart, Radio Shack, Sears, USPO, Winn-Dixie, mall
49b a	US 70, G Bagnal Blvd, to Statesville, **E...gas:** BP, CircleK, Etna, PDI, Shell/diesel, **food:** KFC, Waffle House, Best Western, **lodging:** Comfort Inn, Holiday Inn, Motel 6, Super 8, **other:** Buick/GMC/Cadillac, Dodge, Ford, Honda, Lincoln/Mercury, Nissan, Subaru, Toyota, **W...gas:** Amoco/diesel, Chevron, Citgo, **lodging:** BestStay Inn, Microtel
45	to Troutman, Barium Springs, **E...**KOA, **W...gas:** Amoco/diesel(2mi), Chevron/BBQ/diesel
42	US 21, NC 115, Oswalt, to Troutman, **E...gas:** Citgo/Subway/Taco Bell/TCBY/diesel/24hr, **W...other:** to Duke Power SP, camping
39mm	**rest area/weigh sta both lanes, full(handicapped)facilities, phone, picnic tables, litter barrels, petwalk, vending**
36	NC 150, Mooresville, **E...gas:** Accel/diesel, Exxon, Shell/24hr, **food:** Bob Evans, Burger King, Denny's, FatBoy's Cafe, McDonald's, Peking Palace, Taco Bell, Texas Steaks, Waffle House, Wendy's, **lodging:** Day's Inn, Ramada Ltd, **other:** Belk, Goody's, Griffin Tire/repair, Harris-Teeter, K-Mart, Staples, Suzuki, Wal-Mart SuperCtr/24hr, **W...gas:** BJ's Whse/gas, BP/diesel, Citgo/KrispyKreme/BBQ, Servco, Shell/diesel/24hr, **food:** Arby's, Chick-fil-A, Cracker Barrel, Golden Corral, Hardee's, Kyoto Japanese, McDonald's, Monterrey Mexican, Subway, **lodging:** Hampton Inn, Super 8, Wingate Inn, **other:** CVS Drug, Food Lion, Lowe's Whse
33	US 21 N, **E...gas:** Phillips 66/diesel, **other:** HOSPITAL, **W...gas:** BP, Citgo/diesel/24hr
30	Davidson, **E...gas:** Exxon/diesel, **other:** to Davidson College
28	US 21 S, NC 73, Cornelius, Lake Norman, **E...gas:** Amoco, Cashion's/diesel, Citgo/24hr, **food:** Bojangles, Denny's, Hardee's, Mom's Country Store/Rest., Prime Buffet Rest., Quincy's, Shoney's, Subway, **lodging:** Hampton Inn, Holiday Inn/rest., **W...food:** Burger King, El Cancun Mexican, Jersey Mike's Subs, KFC, Kobe Japanese, Lake Norman Brewing, Little Caesar's, LoneStar Steaks, Lotus 28 Chinese, McDonald's, Papa John's, Pizza Hut, Taco Bell, Wendy's, **lodging:** Best Western, Comfort Inn, Microtel, Quality Inn, **other:** BiLo/24hr, Chrysler/Jeep, Dodge, Eckerd, Food Lion, Harris-Teeter, Radio Shack, SteinMart
25	NC 73, Concord, Lake Norman, **E...gas:** Shell/diesel, Texaco, **food:** Atlanta Bread Factory, Burger King, Chili's, Fuddrucker's, Hops Rest., Longhorn Steaks, McDonald's, O'Charley's, US Subs, Wendy's, **lodging:** Country Suites, Hawthorn Suites, Ramada Ltd, **other:** MEDICAL CARE, Home Depot, Kohl's, Lowe's Whse, Old Navy, Target, Winn-Dixie, **W...gas:** 76/Circle K/Blimpie, **food:** Arby's, Bob Evans, Bojangles, Carrabba's, DQ, Outback Steaks, Subway, Taipei House, **lodging:** Candlewood Suites, Courtyard, **other:** Food Lion, to Energy Explorium

Interstate 77

N ↕ S

Charlotte

23 NC 73, Huntersville, **E...gas:** Amoco, Shell/24hr, **food:** Hardee's, Mama Mia Mexican, Palace of China, Waffle House, Wendy's, **lodging:** Holiday Inn Express, Red Roof Inn, **other:** MEDICAL CARE, Eckerd, Food Lion, Ford, Hancock Fabrics, Radio Shack, USPO, **W...gas:** Sam's Mart/diesel, **other:** BiLo, CVS Drug, Harris-Teeter

18 Harris Blvd, Reames Rd, **E...gas:** Phillips 66/Arby's/diesel, Shell/diesel, **food:** Bob Evans, Harris Grill, Jack-in-the-Box, Waffle House, **lodging:** Fairfield Inn, Hampton Inn, Hilton Garden, Suburban Lodge, **other:** HOSPITAL, to UNCC, Univ Research Park

16b a US 21, Sunset Rd, **E...gas:** Amoco/Circle K, Jakes Trkstp/diesel/rest./@, Shell/diesel/24hr, **food:** Capt D's, Hardee's, KFC, McDonald's, Subway, Taco Bell, Waffle House, Wendy's, **lodging:** Best Stay Inn, Day's Inn, Super 8, **other:** AllPro Parts, AutoZone, Kerr Drug, Winn-Dixie, **W...gas:** Citgo, Shell/diesel, **food:** BBQ, Bojangles, Burger King, Denny's, Domino's, Waffle House, **lodging:** Sleep Inn, Sunset Motel, **other:** RV Ctr

13b a I-85, S to Spartanburg, N to Greensboro

12 La Salle St, **W...gas:** Citgo/diesel, Shell/diesel

11b a I-277, Brookshire Fwy, NC 16, no facilities

10 Trade St, 5th St(from nb), **E...other:** to Discovery Place, **W...gas:** Citgo, **food:** Bojangles

10a US 21(from sb), Moorhead St, downtown

9 I-277, US 74, to US 29, John Belk Fwy, downtown, **E...lodging:** Quality Inn, Villager Lodge, **other:** HOSPITAL, stadium

8 Remount Rd(from nb, no re-entry), no facilities

7 Clanton Rd, **E...gas:** Citgo/diesel, **food:** Hollywood Grill, Krystal/24hr, McDonald's, Waffle House, Wendy's, **lodging:** Day's Inn, Econolodge, Holiday Inn Express, Motel 6, Ramada, Super 8, **W...gas:** Amoco, Citgo

6b a US 521, Billy Graham Pkwy, **E...gas:** Amoco/diesel, 76/Circle K, Shell/diesel, Speedway/diesel, **food:** Arby's, Azteca Mexican, Bojangles, Buffalo Wings, Burger King, Checker's, China House, Harper's Rest., IHOP, KFC, Krispy Kreme, McDonald's, Shoney's, Steak&Ale, Waffle House, Wendy's, **lodging:** Comfort Inn, Day's Inn, Holiday Inn, Howard Johnson, Sterling Inn, **other:** CVS Drug, to Queens Coll, **W...gas:** Phillips 66, **food:** McDonald's, Wendy's, **lodging:** Clarion, Embassy Suites, Homestead Suites, La Quinta, Sleep Inn

5 Tyvola Rd, **E...gas:** Citgo/diesel, **food:** BBQ, Black-eyed Pea, Chili's, China King, LoneStar Steaks, McDonald's, **lodging:** Comfort Inn, Econolodge, Hampton Inn, Hilton, Marriott, Orchard Inn, Radisson, Residence Inn, Studio+, **other:** BiLo/24hr, Jaguar, Kia, Pontiac/GMC, Target, **1 mi E on US 521...gas:** Texaco, **food:** El Cancun Mexican, Flamingo Rest., Hooters, McDonald's, Ryan's, Taco Bell, Pizza Hut, Wendy's, **other:** Office Depot, OfficeMax, **W...lodging:** Extended Stay America, Wingate Inn, **other:** to Coliseum

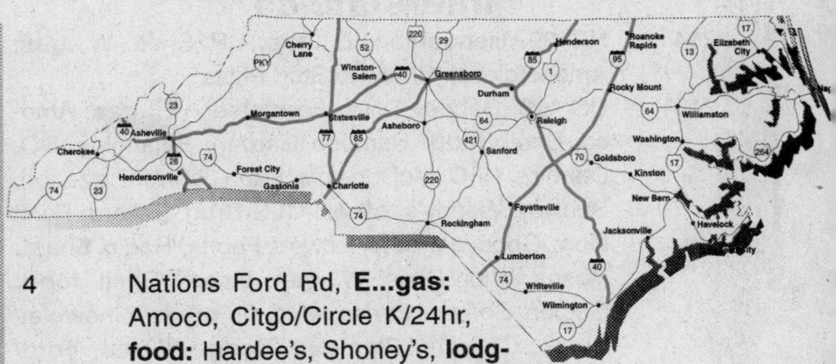

Charlotte

4 Nations Ford Rd, **E...gas:** Amoco, Citgo/Circle K/24hr, **food:** Hardee's, Shoney's, **lodging:** Best Inn, Innkeeper Inn, La Quinta, Red Roof, Villager Lodge, **other:** Sam's Club, **W...gas:** Shell/Burger King

2 Arrowood Rd, to I-485(from sb), **E...gas:** Shell, **food:** Bob Evans, Chick-fil-A, Jack-in-the-Box, LJ Silver, McDonald's, Wendy's, **lodging:** AmeriSuites, Courtyard, Fairfield Inn, Staybridge Suites, TownePlace Suites, **W...food:** Bojangles, **lodging:** Hampton Inn, MainStay Suites, SpringHill Suites

1.5mm Welcome Ctr nb, full(handicapped)facilities, info, phone, vending, picnic tables, litter barrels, petwalk

1 Westinghouse Blvd, to I-485(from nb), **E...gas:** Amoco/diesel, Shell/diesel, **food:** Jack-in-the-Box, Subway, Waffle House, **lodging:** Super 8, **W...gas:** Shell/diesel, **food:** Burger King, McDonald's, **lodging:** Rodeway Inn, **other:** Sears

0mm North Carolina/South Carolina state line

Interstate 85

N ↕ S

Henderson

Exit #	Services
234mm	North Carolina/Virginia state line
233	US 1, to Wise, **E...gas:** Citgo/diesel, Wise Trkstp/Shell/diesel/rest./@, **food:** Budget Inn
231mm	**Welcome Ctr sb, full(handicapped)facilities, phone, picnic tables, litter barrels, petwalk**
229	Oine Rd, to Norlina, no facilities
226	Ridgeway Rd, **W...other:** to Kerr Lake, to St RA, no facilities
223	Manson Rd, **E...gas:** BP/diesel, **other:** camping, **W...**to Kerr Dam
220	US 1, US 158, Fleming Rd, to Middleburg, **E...gas:** Amoco/diesel, **W...gas:** Exxon/diesel, **lodging:** Chex Motel/rest.
218	US 1 S(from sb), to Raleigh
217	Nutbush Bridge, **E...**same as 215 on US 158, **W...gas:** Exxon/diesel, **other:** Kerr Lake RA
215	US 158 BYP E, Henderson(no EZ return from nb), **E...gas:** Citgo/diesel, Shell, Winoco/diesel, **food:** BBQ, Burger King, Mystic Grill, PD Quix Burgers, Tastee Freez, 220 Seafood Rest., Subway, Waffle Pancakes, **lodging:** Budget Host, Comfort Inn, Howard Johnson, Scottish Inn, Travelodge, **other:** Food Lion, Goodyear/auto, Roses, services on US 158

NORTH CAROLINA

Interstate 85

N ↕ S

214 NC 39, Henderson, **E...gas:** BP, Shell, **W...gas:** Amoco/diesel, Shell/HotStuff Pizza

213 US 158, Dabney Dr, to Henderson, **E...gas:** Amoco, Shell, **food:** Bamboo Garden, Bojangles, DQ, Denny's, KFC, McDonald's, Papa John's, Pizza Inn, Subway, Wendy's, **other:** CVS Drug, Eckerd, Food Lion, Goodyear/auto, Lowe's Foods, Radio Shack, Roses, Winn-Dixie, **W...gas:** Exxon, Shell, **food:** Golden Corral, Hurricanes Grill, **other:** Chevrolet/Buick, Chrysler/Plymouth/Dodge, $Tree, Ford/Lincoln/Mercury, K-Mart, Lowe's Whse, Pontiac, Staples, Tires+, same as 212

212 Ruin Creek Rd, **E...gas:** Shell/diesel, **food:** Cracker Barrel, Mazatlan Mexican, SiLo Rest., **lodging:** Day's Inn, **W...gas:** Amoco/Burger King, **food:** Gary's BBQ, Golden Corral, Western Sizzlin, **lodging:** Hampton Inn, Holiday Inn Express, Jameson Inn, Sleep Inn, **other:** HOSPITAL, Belk, Goody's, JC Penney, Wal-Mart SuperCtr/24hr, mall

209 Poplar Creek Rd, **W...**Vance-Granville Comm Coll

206 US 158, Oxford, **E...gas:** Citgo, **W...gas:** Shell/diesel, **food:** Tony's Rest., **other:** airport

Oxford

204 NC 96, Oxford, **E...gas:** Amoco/diesel, **lodging:** Best Western, King's Inn, **other:** Honda, Pontiac/Buick/GMC, **W...gas:** Exxon/DQ/24hr, Shell/24hr, Texaco, Trade/diesel, **food:** Burger King, KFC, Little Caesar's, McDonald's, Pizza Hut, Subway, Taco Bell, Wendy's, Zeko's Italian, **lodging:** Ramada Inn, **other:** HOSPITAL, Byrd's Foods, GNC, Radio Shack, Wal-Mart

202 US 15, Oxford, **2 mi W...lodging:** Crown Motel

199mm rest area both lanes, full(handicapped)facilities, phone, picnic tables, litter barrels, petwalk

198mm Tar River

191 NC 56, Butner, **E...gas:** Amoco/diesel, BP, TradeMart/diesel, **food:** BBQ, Bojangles, Burger King, China Taste Rest., Domino's, KFC/Taco Bell, McDonald's, Pizza Hut, Subway, Wendy's, **lodging:** Comfort Inn, **other:** AutoValue Parts, Eckerd, Food Lion, Herbs4U, M&H Tires, to Falls Lake RA, **W...gas:** Exxon/diesel/24hr, Shell/diesel, **food:** Hardee's, **lodging:** Econolodge, Holiday Inn Express, Ramada Ltd, Sunset Inn, **other:** Goodyear/auto

189 Butner, no facilities

186b a US 15, to Creedmoor, no facilities

185mm Falls Lake

183 Redwood Rd, **E...lodging:** Day's Inn/gas/24hr, **food:** Redwood Café

182 Red Mill Rd, **E...gas:** Exxon/repair, **other:** Kenworth/Volvo Trucks

180 Glenn School Rd, **W...gas:** Heritage

179 E Club Blvd, **E...gas:** Exxon

178 US 70 E, to Raleigh, Research Triangle, RDU Airport, Falls Lake RA

177b c Avondale Dr, NC 55, same as 177a, **E...lodging:** Super 8, **W...food:** Golden Corral

a Durham, downtown, **W...gas:** Amoco, BP, Joy, Shell, **food:** American Hero Subs, Arby's, Dunkin Donuts, Hardee's, KFC, McDonald's, Pizza Hut, Shoney's, Sizzler, **lodging:** Chesterfield Motel, **other:** Advance Parts, Family$, K-Mart

176b a Gregson St, US 501 N, **E...gas:** Crown, Shell, **food:** Biscuitville, Burger King, Subway, Tripp's Rest., **other:** HOSPITAL, Belk, Museum of Life&Science, Sears/auto, mall

175 Guess Rd, **E...gas:** Shell/diesel, **food:** Pizza Hut, **lodging:** Carolina Duke Motor Inn, Holiday Inn Express, Super 8, **W...gas:** Amoco/diesel, BP/diesel, Etna, Exxon, **food:** Bojangles, Honey's Diner/24hr, Tokyo Express, Zero's Subs, **lodging:** Red Roof Inn, **other:** CVS Drug, Home Depot, Kroger

174a Hillandale Rd, **W...gas:** BP/diesel, **food:** PanPan Diner/24hr, **lodging:** Courtyard, Hampton Inn, Howard Johnson, Shoney's Inn, **other:** MEDICAL CARE, Kerr Drug, Winn-Dixie

b US 15 S, US 501 S(from sb), **E...lodging:** Forest Inn

Durham

173 US 15, US 501, US 70, W Durham, **E...gas:** BP, Exxon/diesel, Shell, **food:** Arby's, BBQ, Bojangles, Burger King, Checker's, Cracker Barrel, DogHouse Rest., Domino's, Galley Seafood, Italian Garden Rest., McDonald's, Miami Subs, Subway, Taco Bell, Waffle House, Wendy's, **lodging:** Econolodge, Fairfield Inn, Hilton, Holiday Inn, **other:** HOSPITAL, Byrd's Foods, Dodge/Jeep, Eckerd, Kroger, Rite Aid

172 NC 147 S, to US 15 S, US 501 S(from nb), Durham

170 to NC 751, to Duke U(no EZ return from nb), **E...food:** Harbor Bay Seafood, **lodging:** Scottish Inn, Skyland Inn Best Western/rest., **W...**to Eno River SP

165 NC 86, to Chapel Hill, **E...gas:** Amoco, ExpressAmerica Trkstp/diesel/rest./@, **W...gas:** BP/diesel

164 Hillsborough, **E...gas:** Amoco, Citgo, **food:** McDonald's, **lodging:** Holiday Inn Express, **W...gas:** Exxon/diesel, Shell, **food:** Bojangles, Burger King, Canton House Chinese, Casa Ibarra Mexican, Domino's, Hardee's, KFC, Mayflower Seafood, Occoneechee Steaks, Pizza Hut, Subway, Waffle House, Wendy's, **lodging:** Microtel, Southern Country Inn, **other:** Chevrolet/Buick, Food Lion, Ford, Firestone/auto, GNC, Goodyear/auto, Lowe's Foods, Merchant Tire, Wal-Mart

163 I-40 E, to Raleigh. **I-85 S and I-40 W run together 38 mi.**

161 to US 70 E, NC 86 N, no facilities

160 Efland, **W...gas:** BP/diesel, Exxon/diesel

158mm weigh sta both lanes

157 Buckhorn Rd, **E...gas:** Amoco/diesel, Petro/Mobil/diesel/rest./24hr/@, **W...gas:** Citgo, Exxon

154 Mebane-Oaks Rd, **E...gas:** Shell/Blimpie/diesel/24hr, **W...gas:** Amoco, Citgo, Exxon/diesel, Shell/diesel/24hr, **food:** Biscuitville, Bojangles, Crazy Cow Café, McDonald's, Quizno's, Waffle House, Budget Inn/rest., **other:** Winn-Dixie

Interstate 85

N ↕ S

Burlington

153 NC 119, Mebane, **E...gas:** BP/KFC/Taco Bell/Pizza Hut, **lodging:** Hampton Inn, Holiday Inn Express, **W...gas:** Exxon/Burger King, **food:** Domino's, La Cosina Mexican, Subway, YumYum Chinese, **other:** CVS Drug, Food Lion

152 Trollingwood Rd, **E...gas:** Pilot/McDonald's/diesel/24hr/@, **W...gas:** Fuel City/diesel

150 Haw River, to Roxboro, **W...gas:** Hess/Wilco/DQ/Wendy's/diesel/24hr/@, Flying J/Conoco/diesel/LP/rest./24hr/@, **lodging:** Best Western, **other:** Blue Beacon

148 NC 54, Graham, **E...gas:** Amoco/diesel/24hr, Exxon/diesel/24hr, QP, **food:** Waffle House, **lodging:** ComfortSuites, **W...lodging:** Travel Inn

147 NC 87, Graham, to Pittsboro, **E...gas:** Servco/diesel, **food:** Arby's, Bojangles, Burger King, Domino's, Sagebrush Steaks, Sonic, Subway, Wendy's, **other:** Advance Parts, Chevrolet, Family$, Food Lion, Ford, Goodyear, Plymouth/Jeep, Winn-Dixie, **W...gas:** Citgo/diesel, Exxon, Shell/diesel, **food:** Biscuitville, Hardee's, McDonald's, Taco Bell, **other:** HOSPITAL, CVS Drug, Lowe's Foods

145 NC 49, Burlington, **E...gas:** BP/diesel, Shell/diesel, **food:** Capt D's, **lodging:** Microtel, Motel 6, Red Roof Inn, **W...food:** Biscuitville, Bojangles, Burger King, Hardee's, KFC, Subway, Waffle House, **lodging:** Day's Inn, Holiday Inn, Scottish Inn, **other:** Dodge, $General, Eckerd, Food Lion, Radio Shack

143 NC 62, Burlington, **E...gas:** Citgo/Wendy's, **food:** Bob Evans, Hardee's, Waffle House, to Alamance Bfd, **W...gas:** Exxon, 76/Circle K, **food:** Cutting Board Rest., La Fiesta Mexican, Libby Hill Seafood, Nick's Cuisine, **lodging:** Ramada Inn, **other:** Cadillac, Chevrolet, Food Lion, Ford, Mitsubishi

141 to Burlington, **E...gas:** BP/Amoco, Shell, **food:** IHOP, Mayflower Seafood, Outback Steaks, **lodging:** Hampton Inn, **W...gas:** Crown, Phillips 66/diesel, Shell, **food:** Applebee's, Arby's, Biscuitville, Bojangles, Burger King, Chick-fil-A, Cracker Barrel, Golden Corral, Kabuto Steaks, KFC, McDonald's, Steak'n Shake/24hr, Taco Bell, **lodging:** Best Western, Country Suites, Courtyard, Super 8, **other:** HOSPITAL, Belk, Buick/GMC, Eckerd, Food Lion, Ford/Lincoln/Mercury, Isuzu, K-Mart/gas, Lowe's Foods, Mazda, Nissan, JC Penney, OfficeMax, Sears/auto, Wal-Mart SuperCtr/24hr, Winn-Dixie, mall, to Elon Coll

140 new interchange, no facilities

139mm rest area both lanes, full(handicapped)facilities, phone, picnic tables, litter barrels, vending

138 NC 61, Gibsonville, **W...gas:** Shell/diesel, TA/BP/Burger King/Popeye's/diesel/rest./@, **lodging:** Days Inn

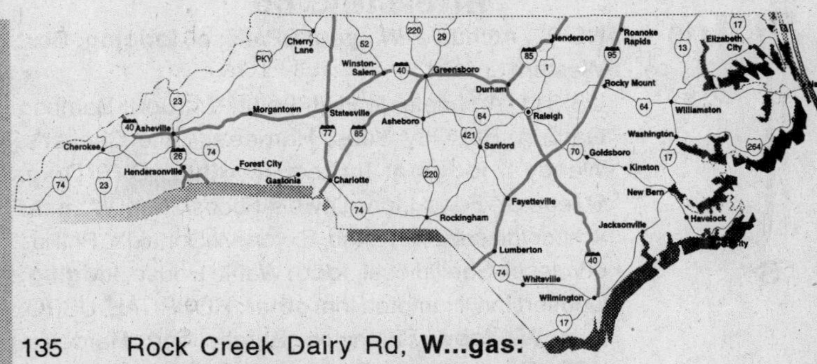

Greensboro

135 Rock Creek Dairy Rd, **W...gas:** Citgo, Exxon, **food:** Jersey Mike's Subs, McDonald's, **other:** Food Lion

132 Mt Hope Church Rd, **W...gas:** Shell/diesel, Texaco, Wilco/Hess/Wendy's/diesel/24hr/@, **lodging:** Hampton Inn

131 to US 70, no facilities

130 McConnell Rd, **E...gas:** Shell/repair, **W...**Replacements LTD Outlet

128 NC 6, E Lee St, **W...gas:** BP/Blimpie/diesel, Phillips 66, **lodging:** Holiday Inn Express, to Coliseum, KOA

127 US 29 N, US 70, US 220 N(from nb), to Reidsville, **W...**KOA

126 US 421 S, to Sanford, **E...gas:** Exxon, **food:** Arby's, Biscuitville, Burger King, Domino's, Golden Pizza, McDonald's, Szechuan Chinese, Subway, Wendy's, **other:** Advance Parts, BiLo, CVS Drug, Food Lion, Goodyear/auto

125 S Elm St, Eugene St, **E...gas:** Amoco, DM, Shell/diesel/24hr, **lodging:** Quality Inn, Super 8, **other:** CarQuest, Home Depot, **W...gas:** Chevron, Citgo/diesel, Crown, **food:** Bojangles, Sonic, **lodging:** Aggie Inn, Ramada Ltd, **other:** AutoZone, Family$, Food Lion

124 Randleman Rd, **E...gas:** Exxon, Shell/24hr, **food:** Cookout Drive-Thru, Mayflower Seafood, Waffle House, Wendy's, **lodging:** Cavalier Inn, **other:** K-Mart, **W...gas:** Amoco, Citgo, Crown, Shell, **food:** Arby's, BBQ, Biscuitville, Burger King, DQ, KFC, McDonald's, Pizza Hut, Substation II, Taco Bell, **lodging:** SouthGate Motel, **other:** Advance Parts, Harley-Davidson

123 I-40 W(from sb), to Winston-Salem. **I-85 N and I-40 E run together 38 mi.**

122c US 220, Rehobeth Church Rd, to Asheboro, **E...lodging:** Motel 6, **W...gas:** Citgo/diesel/rest.

122b a (b only from nb), **N...**to I-40 W, **S...**US 220 S, to Asheboro

121 Holden Rd, **E...gas:** Shell, **food:** Arby's, Burger King, DQ, Denny's, K&W Cafeteria, **other:** GNC, K-Mart, Winn-Dixie, **W...lodging:** Americana Motel, Howard Johnson

120 Groometown Rd, **W...gas:** Phillips 66/diesel/24hr

118 US 29 S, US 70 W, Jamestown, to High Point, **W...lodging:** Grandover Resort, **other:** HOSPITAL

115mm Deep River

NORTH CAROLINA

Interstate 85

N ↕ S

Thomasville

113 NC 62, Archdale, **W...gas:** BP/diesel, **lodging:** Best Western

111 US 311, Archdale, to High Point, **E...food:** Bamboo Garden, Big Guy Subs, Hardee's, Little Caesar's, Wendy's, **lodging:** Innkeeper, **other:** CVS Drug, $General, Food Lion, Lowe's Foods/24hr, **W...gas:** Amoco/diesel/24hr, Citgo, Exxon/McDonald's, Phillips 66/diesel, Shell/diesel, **food:** Waffle House, **lodging:** Comfort Inn, Hampton Inn, **other:** HOSPITAL, USPO, **2 mi W...food:** Bojangles, Burger King, Hardee's, KFC, Papa John's, Pizza Hut, SaltMarsh Annie's Seafood, Taco Bell, **other:** Advance Parts, Eckerd, Firestone, NAPA

108 Hopewell Church Rd, no facilities

106 Finch Farm Rd, **E...gas:** Exxon/diesel

103 NC 109, to Thomasville, **E...gas:** Shell, **food:** Arby's, Taco Bell, **other:** CVS Drug, Ingles Foods, K-Mart, Radio Shack, **W...gas:** Amoco, BP/diesel, Coastal, Crown/24hr, Mobil, Phillips 66, Texaco, Wilco, **food:** Biscuitville, Burger King, Capt Tom's Seafood, China Garden, Flashburger, Golden Corral, Hardee's, KFC, Loflin's Rest., McDonald's, Mr Gatti's, Papa John's, PieZone Pizza, Pizza Hut, Sonic, Sunrise Grille, Waffle House, Wendy's, **lodging:** Howard Johnson, Ramada Ltd, Thomasville Inn, **other:** Advance Parts, AutoZone, Eckerd, Family$, Food Lion, Guy's Drug, Merchant's Tire, Winn-Dixie

102 Lake Rd, **W...gas:** Phillips 66/diesel, Texaco/KrispyKreme/diesel, **lodging:** Day's Inn/rest., **other:** HOSPITAL, Bapt Children Home

100mm rest area both lanes, full(handicapped)facilities, phone, vending, picnic tables, litter barrels, petwalk

96 US 64, Lexington, to Asheboro, **E...gas:** Exxon, **W...gas:** Chevron/diesel, Citgo, Gant/diesel(1mi), **other:** to Davidson Co Coll, NC Zoo

94 Old US 64, **E...gas:** Shell

91 NC 8, to Southmont, **E...gas:** Amoco/diesel, Citgo, Phillips 66, Shell/diesel, **food:** Biscuit King, Capt Stevens Seafood, KFC, McDonald's, Pizza Oven, Sonic, Subway, Wendy's, **lodging:** Comfort Suites, Super 8, **other:** Food Lion, High Rock Lake Camping, **W...gas:** Exxon/diesel, QM, **food:** Arby's, Burger King, Cracker Barrel, Golden Corral, Hardee's, Hunan Chinese, Little Caesar's, Taco Bell, **lodging:** Holiday Inn Express, **other:** HOSPITAL, American Childrens Home, Belks, GNC, Goody's, Hamrick's, Ingles Foods, Wal-Mart

88 Linwood, **W...gas:** BP/diesel, **other:** HOSPITAL,

87 US 29, US 70, US 52(from nb), High Point, **W...lodging:** Best Western, **other:** HOSPITAL, mall

86 Belmont Rd, **W...gas:** Phillips 66/Bill's Trkstp/diesel/rest./24hr/@

Salisbury

85 Clark Rd, to NC 150, **E...food:** Tracks End Rest., **other:** flea mkt

83 NC 150(from nb), to Spencer, no facilities

82 US 29, US 70(from sb), to Spencer, no facilities

81.5mm Yadkin River

81 Spencer, **E...gas:** Amoco/diesel, **W...gas:** Shell

79 Spencer, E Spencer, Spencer Shops St HS, **E...lodging:** Chanticleer Motel, **other:** auto repair

76b a US 52, Salisbury, to Albemarle, **E...gas:** Amoco, Citgo, RaceTrac/24hr, Speedway, **food:** Applebee's, Athena Diner, China Rainbow, Golden Bee Rest., IHOP, Italy Café, Lighthouse Seafood, Little Caesar's, LoneStar Steaks, Schlotsky's, Shoney's, **lodging:** Sleep Inn, **other:** Aldi Foods, Circuit City, CVS Drug, Dodge, Eckerd, Food Lion, GNC, Lowe's Whse, Staples, Super 8, **W...gas:** Exxon/diesel, Servco, 76/diesel, Shell, **food:** Bojangles, Burger King, Capt D's, Chick-fil-A, China Garden, Christo's Rest., Dunkin Donuts, El Cancun Mexican, Ham's Rest., Hardee's, KFC, McDonald's, Outback Steaks, Pizza Hut, Taco Bell, Village Inn Pizza, Waffle House/24hr, Wendy's, **lodging:** Comfort Suites, Howard Johnson, **other:** HOSPITAL, Advance Parts, AutoZone, Family$, Firestone/auto, Goodyear/auto, K-Mart, Office Depot, USPO

75 US 601, Jake Alexander Blvd, **E...food:** Arby's, Farmhouse Rest., **lodging:** Ramada Ltd, **other:** Dan Nicholas Park, **W...gas:** Amoco/24hr, BP, Citgo, Exxon/diesel, Shell/diesel, **food:** Ichiban Japanese, Ryan's, Sagebrush Steaks, Subway, Waffle House, Wendy's, **lodging:** Best Western, Day's Inn, Hampton Inn, Holiday Inn, **other:** Chevrolet/Cadillac, Chrysler/Plymouth/Jeep, Ford/Toyota, Honda/Kia, Nissan/Pontiac/GMC, Wal-Mart

74 Julian Rd, no facilities

72 Peach Orchard Rd, **W...**airport

71 Peeler Rd, **E...gas:** Shell/diesel/rest./24hr, **W...gas:** Citgo/Wilco/Bojangles/Taco Bell/diesel/24hr/@

70 Webb Rd, **E...**flea mkt, **W...**st patrol

68 US 29, US 601, China Grove, to Rockwell, no facilities

63 Kannapolis, **E...gas:** Pilot/Subway/diesel/@, **food:** Waffle House, **lodging:** Best Western, **3 mi W...gas:** Exxon/diesel, **food:** China Buffet, Hardee's, KFC, **other:** repair

60 Earnhardt Rd, **E...gas:** Exxon(1mi), Shell/Burger King, **food:** Cracker Barrel, Kramer&Eugene's Café(1mi), Schlotsky's, Texas Roadhouse, **lodging:** Hampton Inn, Sleep Inn, **other:** HOSPITAL, **W...gas:** BP/diesel, visitor info

59mm rest area both lanes, full(handicapped)facilities, phone, vending, picnic tables, litter barrels, petwalk

Interstate 85

N
S

Concord

58 US 29, US 601, Concord, **E...gas:** Crown/24hr, Exxon, Shell/diesel, Wilco/diesel, **food:** Applebee's, BearRock Café, Burger King, Capt D's, Chick-fil-A, China Orchid, El Cancun Mexican, El Vallarta Mexican, Golden Corral, Italian Oven, KFC, Little Caesar's, Longhorn Steaks, Mayflower Seafood, McDonald's, Mr C's Rest., Pizza Hut, Schlotsky's, Shoney's, Subway, Taco Bell, Texas Steaks, Villa Maria Italian, Waffle House, Wendy's, **lodging:** Colonial Inn, Holiday Inn Express, Mayfair Motel, Rodeway Inn, **other:** HOSPITAL, Belk, Cadillac, Chrysler/Plymouth/Jeep, Eckerd, Food Lion, JC Penney, Sears/auto, U-Haul, mall, st patrol, **W...gas:** Phillips 66, **food:** CiCi's, Bojangles(2mi), Domino's, Hardee's(2mi), IHOP, Ryan's, **lodging:** Cabarrus Inn, Comfort Inn, Fairfield Inn, Microtel, Park Inn, Studio 1 Suites, **other:** $General, Drug Emporium, Eddie's Pizza/funpark, Harris-Teeter, Home Depot, JC Penney, OfficeMax, Target

55 NC 73, Concord, to Davidson, **E...gas:** Exxon/diesel, **food:** Waffle House, **W...gas:** Phillips 66/diesel, 76/diesel, **food:** Huddle House, **lodging:** Day's Inn

54 new exit

52 Poplar Tent Rd, **E...gas:** BP/diesel, Shell/diesel, **other:** to Lowe's Speedway, museum, **W...gas:** Exxon/24hr

49 Speedway Blvd, Concord Mills Blvd, **E...gas:** Shell, Texaco, **food:** BBQ, Bob Evans, Bojangles, Texas Roadhouse, Zaxby's, **lodging:** Hampton Inn, Hawthorn Suites, Holiday Inn Express, Sleep Inn, SpringHill Suites, Wingate Inn, **other:** to Lowes Motor Speedway, **W...gas:** Citgo, **food:** On-the-Border, Roadhouse Grill, Steak'n Shake, **other:** BooksAMillion, Discount Tire, Concord Mills Mall

48 I-485, to US 29, no facilities

46 Mallard Creek Church Rd, **E...gas:** Wilco/Citgo/diesel, **other:** Research Park, **W...gas:** Exxon/24hr, **food:** Subway(1mi)

45 Harris Blvd, **E...gas:** Phillips 66/diesel, **food:** Applebee's, Bojangles, Burger King, Chili's, Chick-fil-A, Hop's Grill, Houlihan's, Max&Erma's, McDonald's, Shoney's, Taco Bell, TGIFriday, Waffle House, **lodging:** Comfort Suites(1mi), Courtyard, Drury Inn, Hampton Inn, Hilton, Holiday Inn, Homewood Suites, Residence Inn, Sleep Inn, **other:** HOSPITAL, Best Buy, Food Lion, GNC, Hannaford's Foods, Kerr Drug, Kohl's, Lowe's Whse, Michael's, Office Depot, Old Navy, Radio Shack, Sam's Club, Walgreen, Wal-Mart/auto, mall, to UNCC, U Research Park, **2 mi W...gas:** Citgo, **food:** Longhorn Steaks, Macaroni Grill, McDonald's, Subway, Wendy's, **other:** Eckerd, Food Lion

43 US 29(from nb), no facilities

Charlotte

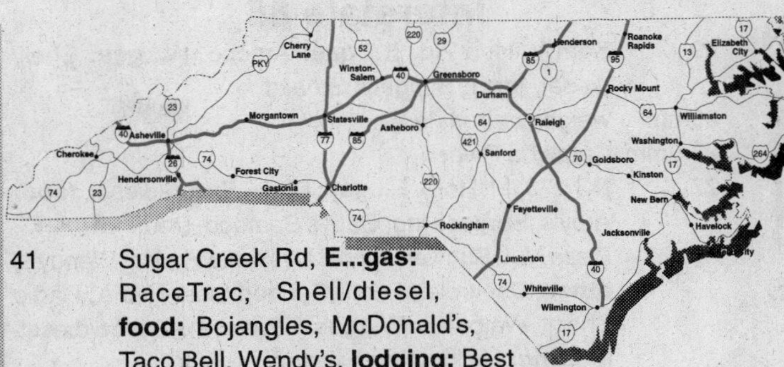

41 Sugar Creek Rd, **E...gas:** RaceTrac, Shell/diesel, **food:** Bojangles, McDonald's, Taco Bell, Wendy's, **lodging:** Best Western, Brookwood Inn, Continental Inn, Econolodge, Microtel, Quality Inn, Red Roof Inn, **W...gas:** BP/diesel, Exxon/diesel, **food:** Shoney's, Texas Ranch Steaks, Waffle House, **lodging:** Comfort Inn, Day's Inn, Fairfield Inn, Holiday Inn Express, Ramada Inn, Rodeway Inn, Super 8

40 Graham St, **E...food:** Hereford Barn Steaks, **lodging:** Travelodge, **other:** Ford Trucks, UPS, **W...gas:** Citgo/diesel, **other:** Goodyear

39 Statesville Ave, **E...gas:** Pilot/Subway/diesel/24hr/@, **food:** CarQuest, **other:** carwash, **W...gas:** Citgo, **food:** Bojangles, **lodging:** Knight's Inn, **other:** auto repair

38 I-77, US 21, N to Statesville, S to Columbia

37 Beatties Ford Rd, **E...gas:** Petro Express, Phillips 66/diesel, Shell/diesel, **food:** Burger King, KFC, McDonald's, Taco Bell, Top China, **other:** CVS Drug, Food Lion, **W...gas:** Amoco, **food:** McDonald's Cafeteria, **lodging:** Travelodge, **other:** funpark, to JC Smith U

36 NC 16, Brookshire Blvd, **E...gas:** Amoco/diesel, **food:** China City, **lodging:** Hornet's Rest Inn, **other:** HOSPITAL, repair, **W...gas:** Exxon, RaceTrac, Speedway, **food:** Bojangles, Burger King, El Toro Mexican

35 Glenwood Dr, **E...gas:** Citgo/Circle K, **lodging:** Innkeeper, **W...food:** Old Europe Rest., **other:** White/GMC

34 NC 27, Freedom Dr, **E...gas:** Amoco/diesel, BP, **food:** Bojangles, Burger King, Capt D's, IHOP, McDonald's, Pizza Hut, Ruby Palace Chinese, Shoney's, Subway, Taco Bell, Tung Hoy Chinese, Wendy's, **other:** MEDICAL CARE, Advance Parts, BiLo, Firestone, Goodyear, NAPA, Pizza Hut, Walgreen, **W...food:** IHOP, **lodging:** GuestHouse Suites, Howard Johnson, Quality Suites, Ramada Ltd, Villager Lodge

33 US 521, Billy Graham Pkwy, **E...gas:** 76/Blimpie/diesel, **food:** Bojangles, Krystal, Wendy's, **lodging:** Day's Inn, Economy Inn, Sheraton, **other:** to Coliseum, airport, **W...gas:** Exxon/diesel, **food:** Cracker Barrel, Prime Buffet, Waffle House/24hr, **lodging:** Fairfield Inn, Hampton Inn, La Quinta, Microtel, Red Roof, Save Inn

32 Little Rock Rd, **E...food:** Waffle House, Courtyard, Econolodge, Holiday Inn, **other:** Toyota, tires, **W...gas:** Citgo/Circle K, Exxon, **food:** Arby's, Hardee's, Shoney's, Subway, **lodging:** Best Western, Comfort Inn, Country Inn Suites, Motel 6, Shoney's Inn/rest., Wingate Inn, **other:** Family$, Food Lion

NORTH CAROLINA

Interstate 85

N ↕ S

29 Sam Wilson Rd, **E...gas:** Amoco, **W...gas:** Shell/diesel, **food:** Stinger's Steaks

28mm weigh sta both lanes

27.5mm Catawba River

27 NC 273, Mt Holly, **E...gas:** Citgo, Exxon/diesel, **food:** Arby's, Burger King, Capt's Seafood, Domino's, KFC, Pizza Hut, Subway, Taco Bell, Waffle House, Wendy's, **other:** Chevrolet, Family$, Food Lion, NAPA, Radio Shack, Walgreen, **W...gas:** BP/diesel, Texaco/diesel, **lodging:** Holiday Inn Express

26 Belmont Abbey Coll, **E...gas:** Amoco, **food:** Bojangles, Hardee's, McDonald's, New China, Papa John's, Western Sizzlin, **other:** Advance Parts, BiLo, Chrysler/Plymouth/Jeep, Ford

24mm South Fork River

23 NC 7, McAdenville, **W...gas:** Chevron/diesel, Shell, **food:** Hardee's, Hillbilly's BBQ/Steaks

22 Cramerton, Lowell, **E...gas:** World Gas, **food:** Applebee's, Burger King, Gator's Rest., Hooters, LJ Silver, Schlotsky's, Zaxby's, **other:** Chevrolet/Cadillac, Honda, Mazda, Kohl's, Lincoln/Mercury, Misubishi, Nissan, Sam's Club, U-Haul

21 Cox Rd, **E...gas:** Citgo/diesel, Exxon, **food:** Arby's, Boston Mkt, Chick-fil-A, Chili's, Don Pablo, Jackson's Cafeteria, Krispy Kreme, Longhorn Steaks, Max' Mexican Eatery, McDonald's, Peking Garden, Pizza Inn, Ryan's, Subway, **other:** Best Buy, BooksAMillion, BiLo/24hr, Dodge, $Tree, Hannaford's Foods, Harris-Teeter/24hr, Home Depot, K-Mart, Lowe's Whse, Michael's, OfficeMax, Old Navy, PepBoys, Tire Kingdom, Upton's, Wal-Mart, mall, **W...gas:** Exxon, Texaco, **food:** IHOP, Super 8, **lodging:** Villager Lodge, **other:** HOSPITAL, Harley-Davidson, Med Ctr Drug, Suzuki

Gastonia

20 NC 279, New Hope Rd, **E...gas:** Amoco, Shell, Texaco, **food:** Arby's, Burger King, Capt D's, Checker's, Hong Kong Buffet, Italian Oven, McDonald's, Morrison's Cafeteria, Pizza Hut, Red Lobster, Sake Japanese, Shoney's, Taco Bell, **lodging:** Holiday Inn Express, **other:** Advance Parts, Belk, Dillard's, Firestone/auto, JC Penney, K-Mart, NAPA, Office Depot, Sears/auto, Target, Winn-Dixie, mall, **W...food:** Bojangles, Cracker Barrel, Hickory Ham Café, KFC, Outback Steaks, Waffle House, **lodging:** Comfort Inn, Fairfield Inn, Hampton Inn, Innkeeper, **other:** HOSPITAL, Circuit City

19 NC 7, E Gastonia, **E...gas:** Shell, **W...gas:** Servco, **food:** Hardee's

17 US 321, Gastonia, **E...gas:** Exxon/diesel/LP, Servco, **lodging:** Day's Inn, **W...gas:** Citgo/diesel, Shell/diesel, **food:** McDonald's, Waffle House, Wendy's, Western Sizzlin, Microtel, Motel 6

14 NC 274, E Bessemer, **E...gas:** Phillips 66, **food:** Burger King, **W...gas:** BP/Subway, Citgo/diesel, **food:** Bojangles, Waffle House, **lodging:** Howard Johnson Express

13 Edgewood Rd, Bessemer City, **E...**to Crowders Mtn SP, **W...gas:** Amoco, Shell/diesel/24hr, **lodging:** Masters Inn

10b a US 74 W, US 29, Kings Mtn, no facilities

8 NC 161, to Kings Mtn, **E...lodging:** Holiday Inn Express, **W...gas:** Amoco, **food:** Burger King, KFC, McDonald's, Taco Bell, Waffle House, Wendy's, **lodging:** Comfort Inn, Ramada Ltd, **other:** HOSPITAL, Chevrolet

6mm rest area sb, full(handicapped)facilities, phone, picnic tables, litter barrels, vending, petwalk

5 Dixon School Rd, **E...gas:** Shell/Subway/diesel, **food:** Classic Diner

4 US 29 S(from sb)

2.5mm Welcome Ctr nb, full(handicapped)facilities, info, phone, vending, picnic tables, litter barrels, petwalk

2 NC 216, Kings Mtn, **E...**to Kings Mtn Nat Military Park, **W...gas:** Chevron

0mm North Carolina/South Carolina state line

Interstate 95

Exit #	Services
181mm	North Carolina/Virginia state line, **Welcome Ctr sb, full(handicapped)facilities, phone, picnic tables, litter barrels, vending, petwalk**
180	NC 48, to Gaston, Pleasant Hill, to Lake Gaston, **W...gas:** Pilot/Subway/diesel/24hr/@
176	NC 46, to Garysburg, **E...gas:** Texaco/Stuckey's, **other:** repair, **W...gas:** Shell, **food:** Aunt Sarah's, Burger King, **lodging:** Best Western
174mm	Roanoke River
173	US 158, Roanoke Rapids, Weldon, **E...gas:** BP/diesel, Shell/Blimpie, Texaco/diesel, **food:** Ralph's BBQ, Trigger's Steaks, Waffle House, **lodging:** Day's Inn, Interstate Inn, Orchard Inn, **other:** HOSPITAL, **W...gas:** BP/diesel, Exxon, RaceTrac, **food:** Arby's, Burger King, Cracker Barrel, Hardee's, KFC, Little Caesar's, McDonald's, Piccolowe's Rest., Pizza Hut, Ruby Tuesday, Ryan's, Shoney's, Subway, Taco Bell, Texas Steaks, Tokyo Sushi, Waffle House, Wendy's, **lodging:** Comfort Inn, Hampton Inn, Jameson Inn, Motel 6, Sleep Inn, **other:** Advance Parts, AutoZone, $General, Eckerd, Firestone/auto, Food Lion, Ford/Lincoln/Mercury/Honda, Piggly Wiggly, Wal-Mart SuperCtr/gas/24hr
171	NC 125, Roanoke Rapids, **W...gas:** Texaco/diesel, **lodging:** Holiday Inn Express, **other:** st patrol

N ↕ S

Roanoke Rapids

Interstate 95

N ↕ S

168 NC 903, to Halifax, **E...gas:** Exxon/diesel, Shell/ Burger King/diesel

160 NC 561, to Brinkleyville, **E...gas:** Exxon/24hr, **W...gas:** Citgo/diesel/rest.

154 NC 481, to Enfield, **E...gas:** Mobil, **W...other:** KOA(1mi)

152mm weigh sta both lanes

150 NC 33, to Whitakers, **E...**golf, **W...gas:** BP/Subway/ DQ/Stuckey's

145 NC 4, to US 301, Battleboro, **E...gas:** Amoco/ diesel, Exxon, Shell/diesel, Texaco, **food:** BBQ, DQ, Denny's, Hardee's, Shoney's, Waffle House, Wendy's, **lodging:** Best Western/rest., Comfort Inn, Day's Inn, Deluxe Inn, Howard Johnson, Masters Inn, Quality Inn, Red Carpet Inn, Scottish Inn, Super 8, Travelodge

142mm rest area both lanes, full(handicapped)facilities, phone, picnic tables, litter barrels, vending, pet-walk

141 NC 43, Red Oak, **E...gas:** Exxon/diesel/LP, Texaco/ diesel, **W...gas:** BP/diesel, **lodging:** Econolodge

138 US 64, Rocky Mount, **5 mi E...lodging:** Comfort Inn, Courtyard, Hampton Inn, Holiday Inn, Residence Inn, **other:** HOSPITAL, to Cape Hatteras Nat Seashore

132 to NC 58, **E...gas:** Citgo/diesel, **1 mi W...gas:** Amoco/diesel

128mm Tar River

127 NC 97, to Stanhope, **E...gas:** BP/diesel, **other:** airport

Wilson

121 US 264, Wilson, **E...gas:** BP, Citgo/Subway, Kangaroo/diesel/LP, Shell, **food:** Aunt Sarah's, Hardee's, KFC/LJ Silver, Waffle House, **lodging:** Comfort Inn, **other:** HOSPITAL, **4 mi E...gas:** Shell/ diesel, **food:** Applebee's, Arby's, Boston Mkt, Burger King, Chick-fil-A, Denny's, Golden Corral, Sonic, Subway, **lodging:** Hampton Inn, **other:** BooksA-Million, Eckerd, Jo-Ann Crafts, K-Mart, Lowe's Whse, Staples, Wal-Mart SuperCtr/24hr, **W...gas:** BP/Blimpie/diesel, **food:** Bojangles, Burger King, Cracker Barrel, McDonald's, **lodging:** Holiday Inn Express, Jameson Inn, Microtel, Sleep Inn, **other:** to Country Doctor Museum

119b a US 264, US 117, no facilities

116 NC 42, to Clayton, Wilson, **E...gas:** Shell/diesel, HOSPITAL, **W...gas:** BP/diesel, **other:** Rock Ridge Camping

107 US 301, Kenly, **E...gas:** BP, Coastal/Subway, Exxon/ McDonald's/diesel, Shell/diesel/24hr, **food:** BBQ, Burger King, Golden China, Nik's Pizza, Patrick's Rest., Waffle House, Willoughby's Seafood, **lodging:** Budget Inn, Deluxe Inn, Econolodge, **other:** Food Lion, Ford, Family$, IGA Food, Tobacco Museum

106 Truck Stop Rd, Kenly, **W...gas:** TA/Wendy's/diesel/ 24hr/@, Wilco/Hess/diesel/24hr/ @, **food:** Kenly Kitchen, Venero's Rest., Waffle House, **lodging:** Day's Inn, Super 8, **other:** Blue Beacon

105.5mm Little River

105 Bagley Rd, Kenly, **E...gas:** Citgo/Stormin Norman/ diesel/rest./24hr/@

102 Micro, **E...gas:** BP/repair, **W...gas:** Phillips 66, USPO

101 Pittman Rd, no facilities

99mm rest areas both lanes, full(handicapped)facilities, vending, phone, picnic tables, litter barrels, pet-walk, hist marker

98 to Selma, **E...**KOA

Selma

97 US 70 A, Selma, to Pine Level, **E...gas:** Citgo/diesel/ 24hr, **food:** Denny's, Subway, **lodging:** Holiday Inn Express, **other:** J&R Outlet, **W...gas:** Amoco/diesel/ 24hr, BP/diesel, Exxon/diesel/24hr, Texaco/diesel, **food:** Bojangles, China Buffet, Golden Corral, Hardee's, KFC, McDonald's, Oliver's Rest., Pizza Hut, Shoney's, Waffle House, **lodging:** Comfort Inn, Day's Inn, Hampton Inn, Luxury Inn, Masters Inn, Regency Inn, Royal Inn, **other:** HOSPITAL

95 US 70, Smithfield, **E...lodging:** Log Cabin Motel/ rest., Howard Johnson Express, Village Motel, **other:** Ava Gardner Museum, **W...gas:** Shell, Speedway/diesel, **food:** Bob Evans, Burger King, Cracker Barrel, Smithfield BBQ(2mi), Texas Roadhouse, **lodging:** Jameson Inn, Super 8, **other:** Harley-Davidson, Factory Outlets/famous brands

93 Brogden Rd, Smithfield, **W...gas:** Amoco/diesel, Shell

91.5mm Neuse River

90 US 301, US 701, to Newton Grove, **E...gas:** Citgo/diesel, **food:** Roz's Rest., **lodging:** Travelers Inn, **other:** Holiday TravLPark, to Bentonville Bfd, **W...gas:** Phillips 66/diesel, **lodging:** Four Oaks Motel

87 NC 96, Four Oaks, no facilities

81b a I-40, E to Wilmington, W to Raleigh

79 NC 50, to NC 27, Benson, Newton Grove, **E...gas:** BP, Citgo, **food:** Waffle House, **lodging:** Dutch Inn, **other:** Food Lion, **W...gas:** Coastal, Exxon, Mobil/McDonald's, **food:** Burger King, Domino's, McDonald's, KFC, Pizza Hut, Subway, **lodging:** Day's Inn, **other:** Family$, Lowe's Foods, Rite Aid

NORTH CAROLINA

Interstate 95

N ↕ S

Dunn

77 Hodges Chapel Rd, **E...gas:** Pilot/Subway/diesel/24hr/@, RV/truckwash

75 Jonesboro Rd, **W...gas:** Sadler/Shell/diesel/rest./24hr/@

73 US 421, NC 55, to Dunn, Clinton, **E...food:** Wendy's, **W...gas:** Exxon/diesel, Chevron/diesel, Texaco, **food:** Bojangles, Burger King, Dairy Freeze, McDonald's(2mi), Sagebrush Steaks, Taco Bell, Triangle Waffle, **lodging:** Comfort Inn, Econolodge, Express Inn, Holiday Inn Express, Jameson Inn, Ramada Inn/rest., **other:** IGA Foods, museum

72 Pope Rd, **E...gas:** BP, **lodging:** Comfort Inn, Royal Inn, **W...gas:** BP, **food:** Brass Lantern Steaks, **lodging:** Budget Inn, Express Inn, **other:** Cadillac/GMC, auto repair

71 Longbranch Rd, **E...gas:** Citgo/Hardee's/Travel World/diesel/24hr, **W...**to Averasboro Bfd

70 SR 1811, **E...lodging:** Relax Inn

65 NC 82, Godwin, **W...other:** Children's Home

61 to Wade, **E...gas:** Citgo/diesel, **other:** KOA, **W...gas:** BP/Subway/diesel/24hr/@

58 US 13, to Newton Grove, **E...lodging:** Day's Inn/rest.

Fayetteville

56 Lp 95, to US 301(from sb), Fayetteville, **W...gas:** Shell, **lodging:** Budget Inn, **other:** HOSPITAL, to Ft Bragg, Pope AFB

55 NC 1832, **W...gas:** Exxon/diesel, Shell, **lodging:** Budget Inn

52 NC 24, Fayetteville, **W...other:** to Ft Bragg, Pope AFB, botanical gardens, museum

49 NC 53, NC 210, Fayetteville, **E...gas:** BP/diesel, Exxon, Texaco/diesel, **food:** Burger King, Denny's, McDonald's, Pizza Hut, Taco Bell, Waffle House, **lodging:** Day's Inn/rest, Deluxe Inn, Motel 6, Quality Inn, **W...gas:** BP/Subway/diesel, Exxon/diesel, Shell/diesel, **food:** Beaver Dam Seafood, Cracker Barrel, Shoney's, **lodging:** Best Western, Comfort Inn, Econolodge, Fairfield Inn, Hampton Inn, Holiday Inn, Innkeeper, Red Roof Inn, Sleep Inn, Sheraton, Super 8

48mm rest areas both lanes, full(handicapped)facilities, phone, picnic tables, litter barrels, vending, petwalk

47mm Cape Fear River

46b a NC 87, to Fayetteville, Elizabethtown, **W...other:** HOSPITAL, Civic Ctr, to Agr Expo Ctr

44 Snow Hill Rd, **W...other:** Lazy Acres Camping, to airport

41 NC 59, to Hope Mills, Parkton, **E...gas:** Kangaroo/24hr, **W...gas:** BP, Spring Valley RV Park

40 Lp 95, to US 301(from nb), to Fayetteville, facilities on US 301(5-7mi)

33 US 301, St Pauls, **E...gas:** Amoco/diesel/repair/24hr

31 NC 20, to St Pauls, Raeford, **E...gas:** Amoco, BP, Mobil, Shell/Huddle House/diesel/24hr, **food:** Burger King, Hardee's, McDonald's, **lodging:** Day's Inn, **W...gas:** Citgo, Exxon/diesel

25 US 301, **E...gas:** BP/diesel

24mm weigh sta both lanes

Lumberton

22 US 301, **E...gas:** Shell/DQ, **food:** Burger King, Denny's, Hardee's, Huddle House, John's Rest., Outback Steaks, Ruby Tuesday, Ryan's, Smithfield BBQ, Texas Steaks, Waffle House, Zaxby's, **lodging:** Best Western, Comfort Suites, Hampton Inn, Holiday Inn, Redwood Lodge, Super 8, **other:** $Tree, Goodyear/auto, Lowe's Foods, Lowe's Whse, Office Depot, OfficeMax, Wal-Mart SuperCtr/24hr, st patrol, **W...gas:** Circle B, Sun-Do/diesel, Texaco/Subway/diesel

20 NC 211, to NC 41, Lumberton, **E...gas:** Amoco, Citgo, Exxon/diesel, **food:** Carolina Steaks, Golden City Chinese, Hardee's, Little Caesar's, McDonald's, New China, Subway, Village Sta Rest., Waffle House, Western Sizzlin, **lodging:** Deluxe Inn, Howard Johnson, Quality Inn, Ramada Ltd, **other:** HOSPITAL, Food Lion/deli, K-Mart, **W...gas:** Texaco/diesel, **food:** BBQ, Cracker Barrel, LungWah Chinese, **lodging:** Comfort Inn, Country Inn Suites, Day's Inn/rest., Econolodge, Fairfield Inn, National 9 Inn

19 Carthage Rd, Lumberton, **E...gas:** BP/diesel, **food:** Mi Casita Mexican, **lodging:** Travelers Inn, **other:** auto repair, **W...gas:** Exxon/diesel, Texaco, **lodging:** Knight's Inn, Motel 6

18mm Lumber River

17 NC 72, **E...gas:** BP/diesel, Citgo, Exxon/Huddle House/diesel, Mobil/diesel, Shell/Wendy's/diesel, **food:** Burger King, Hardee's, McDonald's, Old Foundry Rest., Subway, Waffle House, **lodging:** Budget Inn, Economy Inn, Southern Inn, **other:** AutoZone, Food Lion

14 US 74, Maxton, to Laurinburg, **W...gas:** BP/diesel, **lodging:** Exit Inn, **other:** Sleepy Bear's RV Camp

10 US 301, to Fairmont, no facilities

7 to McDonald, Raynham, no facilities

5mm Welcome Ctr nb, full(handicapped)facilities, phone, picnic tables, litter barrels, vending, petwalk

2 NC 130, to NC 904, Rowland, no facilities

1b a US 301, US 501, Dillon, **E...gas:** Exxon, Shell, **food:** Hot Tamale Rest., Pedro's Diner, Pedro's Ice Cream Fiesta, Sombrero Rest., **lodging:** Golden Triangle Motel, South-of-the-Border Motel, **other:** Pedro's Campground, Ford, **W...gas:** Shell/diesel, Sun-Do, **food:** Tarheel Diner, Waffle House, **lodging:** Budget Motel, Day's Inn, Holiday Inn Express

0mm North Carolina/South Carolina state line

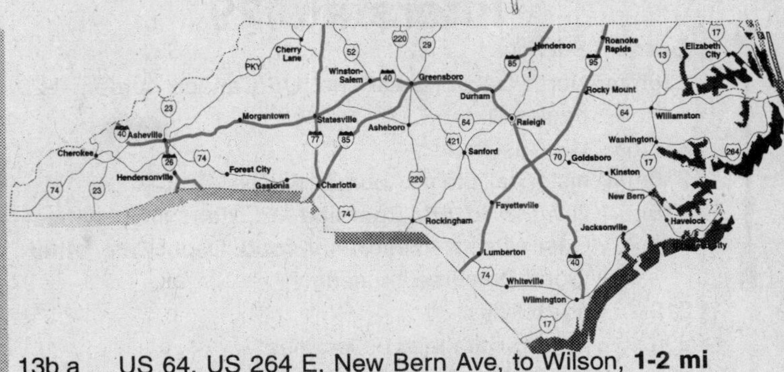

Interstate 240(Asheville)

E ↕ W

Asheville

Exit #	Services
9mm	I-240 begins/ends on I-40, exit 53b a.
8	Fairview Rd, **N...gas:** Shell/Blimpie, **food:** Burger King, J&S Cafeteria, KFC, Little Caesar's, Mandarin Chinese, McDonald's, Subway, **lodging:** Comfort Inn, **other:** Advance Parts, Bilo Foods, CVS Drug, Eckerd, Hamrick's, **S...food:** Pizza Now, **other:** Home Depot, Oakley Foods
7.5mm	Swannanoa River
7	US 70, **N...**U-Haul, **S...gas:** Amoco, Exxon/diesel, **food:** Applebee's, Burger King, Chili's, Cornerstone Rest., Damon's, Greenery Rest., IHOP, Joe's Crabshack, Kell's Grill, McGuffy's Grill, O'Charley's, Olive Garden, Philly Connection, Rio Bravo, Subway, Taco Bell, Waffle House, **lodging:** Courtyard, Day's Inn, Econolodge, Hampton Inn, Holiday Inn, Ramada Ltd, **other:** Belk, Circuit City, Firestone, Food Lion, Goody's, K-Mart, Lowe's Whse, Michael's, Office Depot, OfficeMax, Sears/auto
6	Tunnel Rd(from eb), same as 7
5b	US 70, US 74A, Charlotte St, **N...gas:** Amoco, Exxon, **S...**Civic Ctr
a	**N...gas:** Exxon/diesel, Shell, **food:** Bojangles, 3 Pigs BBQ, **S...lodging:** Interstate Motel
4c	Haywood St, Montford, downtown
b	Patton Ave(from eb), downtown
a	US 19 N, US 23 N, US 70 W, to Weaverville
3b	Westgate, **N...gas:** Servco, **food:** EarthFare Foods, **lodging:** Holiday Inn, **other:** CVS Drug, NTB
a	US 19 S, US 23 S, W Asheville, **N...gas:** Amoco, Exxon, **food:** Arby's, Bojangles, Denny's, KFC, Little Caesar's, LJ Silver, Mandarin Chinese, McDonald's, Pizza Hut, Ryan's, Taco Bell, Wendy's, **other:** Advance Parts, AutoZone, Best Foods, Bilo, Cadillac/Pontiac/GMC, Checker Parts, Goodyear/auto, Ingles, K-Mart, Radio Shack, Sam's Club/gas
2	US 19, US 23, W Asheville, **N...gas:** Shell, **S...gas:** Eblen, **other:** B&B Drug
1c	Amboy Rd(from eb), no facilities
b	NC 191, to I-40 E, Brevard Rd, **S...other:** farmers mkt, camping
a	I-40 W, to Knoxville
0mm	I-240 begins/ends on I-40, exit 46b a.

Interstate 440(Raleigh)

E ↕ W

Raleigh

Exit #	Services
16	I-40
15	Poole Rd, **W...gas:** Amoco/diesel, Citgo/diesel, **food:** Burger King, McDonald's, Subway
13b a	US 64, US 264 E, New Bern Ave, to Wilson, **1-2 mi E...gas:** Amoco, BP, Circle K, Exxon, Phillips 66(1mi), Shell, Speedway, Circle K, **food:** Arby's, Burger King, Checker's, Hardee's, K&S Cafeteria, McDonald's, Miami Subs, O!Brian's, Pizza Hut, Shoney's, Taco Bell, Treacher's Fish, Waffle House, Wendy's, **lodging:** Holiday Inn Express, Microtel, Red Roof Inn, Super 8, **other:** Firestone/auto, Ford, Hamrick's, K-Mart, Kroger, Food Lion, Radio Shack, RV Ctr, Winn-Dixie, **W...**HOSPITAL
12	Yonkers Rd, Brentwood Rd, no facilities
11b a	US 1, US 401, Capital Blvd N, **N...gas:** BP, Citgo, Shell, **food:** Applebee's(1mi), Bojangle's, Don Murray's BBQ, Perkins, Taco Bell, Waffle House, Wendy's, **lodging:** Comfort Inn, Country Inn, Day's Inn, Fairfield Inn, Holiday Inn, MainStay Inn, Sleep Inn, **other:** MEDICAL CARE, **S...gas:** Pontiac/GMC
10	Wake Forest Rd, **N...food:** Denny's, **lodging:** AmeriSuites, Red Roof Inn, **S...lodging:** Courtyard, Extended Stay America, Hampton Inn, Residence Inn, **other:** HOSPITAL
8b a	6 Forks Rd, North Hills, **N...gas:** Exxon, **food:** Bennigan's, **lodging:** Comfort Inn, **other:** Dillard's, Firestone/auto, Winn-Dixie
7b a	US 70, NC 50, Glenwood Ave, Crabtree Valley, **N...gas:** Amoco, BP, Exxon, **food:** McDonald's, Ruby Tuesday, **lodging:** Embassy Suites, Fairfield Inn, Holiday Inn, La Quinta, Marriott, Motel 6, Ramada Inn, Residence Inn, Sheraton, **other:** Barnes&Noble, Belk, Circuit City, Goodyear/auto, Hecht's, Sears/auto, mall
6	Ridge Rd(from nb), same as 7
5	Lake Boone Tr, **W...gas:** Phillips 66, **other:** HOSPITAL
4b a	to I-40 W, Wade Ave, **E...**bank, **W...**to I-40, RDU
3	NC 54, Hillsboro St, **E...gas:** Citgo, **lodging:** Ramada Inn, **other:** to Meredith Coll
2b a	Western Blvd, **E...**to NCSU, Shaw U, **W...**K-Mart
1d	Melbourne Rd(from sb), no facilities
1c	Jones-Franklin Rd, no facilities
1b a	I-40. I-440 begins on I-40. **1-2 mi W on Walnut St...gas:** Amoco, Shell, **food:** Hardee's, McDonald's, Olive Garden, Pizza Hut, Ryan's, Vicky's Seafood, **lodging:** Best Western, Candlewood Suites, Fairfield Inn, Holiday Inn, Motel 6, **other:** Michael's, mall

NORTH DAKOTA
Interstate 29

N ↕ S

Exit #	Services
218mm	North Dakota state line, US/Canada border. I-29 begins/ends.
217mm	US Customs sb
216mm	historical site nb, tourist info sb
215	ND 59, rd 55, Pembina, **E...gas:** Citgo/diesel, Gastrak/pizza/diesel/24hr, **food:** Depot Café, **other:** World DutyFree, museum
212	no facilities
208	rd 1, to Bathgate, no facilities
203	US 81, ND 5, to Hamilton, Cavalier, **W...**weigh sta both lanes
200	no facilities
196	rd 3, Bowesmont, no facilities
193	no facilities
191	ND 11, to St Thomas, no facilities
187	ND 66, to Drayton, **E...gas:** Cenex/diesel, **food:** Rte 66 Café, **lodging:** Motel 66, **other:** CarQuest, USPO
184	to Drayton, **2 mi E...gas:** gas/diesel/hardware, **other:** USPO, camping
180	rd 9, no facilities
179mm	**rest area both lanes(both lanes exit left), full(handicapped)facilities, phone, picnic tables, litter barrels, vending, petwalk**
176	ND 17, to Grafton, **10 mi W...**HOSPITAL, gas, food, lodging
172	no facilities
168	rd 15, Warsaw, to Minto, no facilities
164	no facilities
161	ND 54, rd 19, to Ardoch, Oslo, no facilities
157	no facilities
152	US 81, Manvel, to Gilby, **W...gas:** Co-op/diesel
145	US 81 bus, N Washington St, to Grand Forks, no facilities
141	US 2, Gateway Dr, Grand Forks, **E...gas:** Amoco/diesel/24hr, Conoco/McDonald's/diesel/@, Stamart, **food:** Burger King, Chinese Buffet, **lodging:** Budget Inn, Econolodge, Ramada Inn, Rodeway Inn, Select Inn, Super 8, **other:** AutoValue Parts, Checker Parts, Chrysler/Plymouth/Dodge/Jeep/Toyota, Ford/Lincoln/Mercury, to U of ND, **1 mi E...food:** DQ, Domino's, Hardee's, Taco John's, **other:** HOSPITAL, U-Haul, auto repair, **W...gas:** Simonson/diesel/café/24hr/@, Stamart/diesel/RV dump/@, **food:** Emerald Grill, Perkins, **lodging:** Settle Inn, **other:** Budget RV Ctr, port of entry/weigh sta, airport, to AFB
140	DeMers Ave, **E...gas:** Amoco, Conoco, Hilton Garden, **other:** HOSPITAL, Alerus Ctr, to U of ND
138	32nd Ave S, **E...gas:** Amoco, Holiday/Subway/diesel, Tesoro/diesel, **food:** Applebee's, Brannigan's, Buffalo Wild Wings, Burger King, ChiChi's, China Garden, Domino's, Grizzly's Steaks, Ground Round, McDonald's, Pizza Hut, Quizno's, Red Lobster, Taco Bell, Village Inn Rest., **lodging:** C'mon Inn, Comfort Inn, Country Inn Suites, Day's Inn, Fairfield Inn, Happy Host Inn, Holiday Inn Express, Lakeview Inn, Roadking Inn, **other:** Best Buy, Cadillac, Chevrolet, Chrysler/Toyota, Ford, Gordman's, Honda/Nissan, Hugo's Foods, JC Penney, Jo-Ann Fabrics, K-Mart, Marshall Field, Mazda, Michael's, OfficeMax, Old Navy, Osco Drug, Sam's Club, Sears/auto, Super 1 Foods, Target, Target, Tires+, Wal-Mart, mall, **W...gas:** Conoco/Subway/diesel, **other:** Grand Forks Camping
130	ND 15, rd 81, Thompson, **1 mi W...**gas, food
123	CountyLine Rd, to Reynolds, **E...**to Central Valley School
118	to Buxton, no facilities
111	ND 200 W, to Cummings, Mayville, **W...other:** Big Top Fireworks, to Mayville St U
104	Hillsboro, **E...gas:** Cenex/Burger King/diesel/LP/24hr/@, Tesoro/diesel/24hr, Country **food:** Hearth Rest., **lodging:** Hillsboro Inn, Sunset View Motel, **other:** HOSPITAL, Ford/Mercury, Goodyear, bank, RV park
100	ND 200 E, ND 200A, to Blanchard, Halstad, no facilities
99mm	**rest area both lanes, full(handicapped)facilities, phone, picnic tables, litter barrels, vending, petwalk**
92	rd 11, Grandin, **E...gas:** Co-op/diesel, **W...gas:** Citgo/diesel/hardware
86	Gardner, no facilities
79	Argusville, no facilities
74.5mm	Sheyenne River
74mm	**rest area both lanes, full(handicapped)facilities, phone, picnic tables, litter barrels, vending, petwalk**
73	rd 17, rd 22, Harwood, **E...gas:** Cenex/pizza/diesel/café/24hr
69	rd 20, no facilities
67	US 81 bus, 19th Ave N, **E...**VA HOSPITAL, Hector Int Airport
66	12th Ave N, **E... gas:** Stamart Travel Plaza/diesel/24hr/@, Stop'n Go, **other:** HOSPITAL, to ND St U, **W...gas:** Cenex/diesel, **food:** Arby's, **lodging:** Microtel
65	US 10, Main Ave, W Fargo, **E...gas:** Simonson/diesel, Tesoro/diesel/24hr, **food:** BurgerTime, Kroll's Diner, **other:** Checker Parts, NAPA, OK Tire, U-Haul, transmissions, to Heritage Ctr, **W...gas:** Cenex/Subway/diesel, Simonson Gas, **food:** Embers Rest., Hardee's, Outback Steaks, **lodging:** Best Western, **other:** Aamco, CarQuest, Chevrolet/Buick/Cadillac/Honda, Chrysler/Dodge/Jeep, Cummins Diesel, Hyundai, Isuzu/Volvo/GMC, Kenworth, Mercury/Lincoln, Saturn, Subaru, Toyota
64	13th Ave, Fargo, **E...gas:** Amoco24hr, Cenex, Conoco/diesel, Kum&Go/gas, Phillips 66, Stamart/diesel, **food:** Acapulco Mexican, Applebee's, Arby's, Burger King, ChuckeCheese, DQ, GreenMill Rest., Ground Round, Hardee's, Perkins/24hr, Ponderosa, Quizno's, Subway, Taco John's, TCBY, Wendy's, **lodging:** AmericInn, Best Western, Comfort Inn, Country Suites, Econolodge,

Grand Forks

Grand Forks

Fargo

NORTH DAKOTA

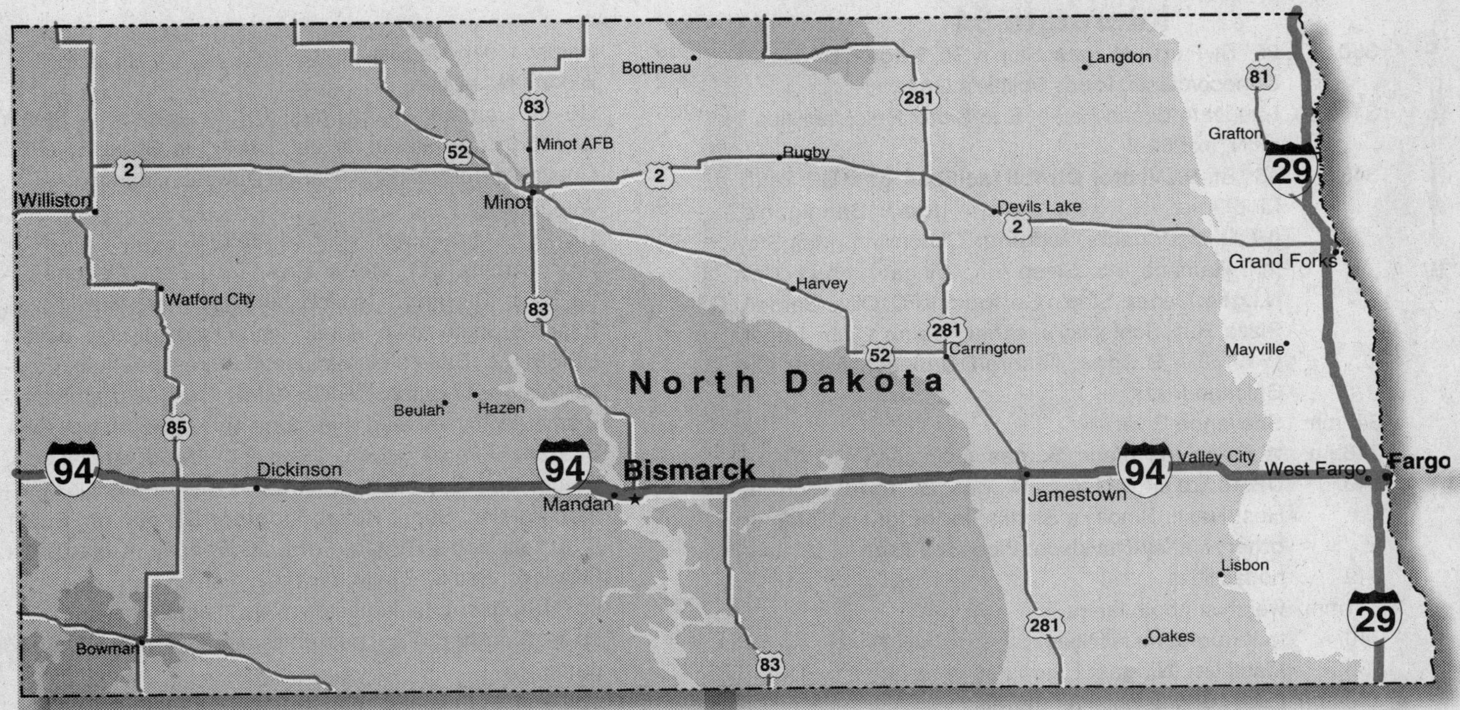

Interstate 29

N ↕ S

Fargo

Hampton Inn, Motel 6, Motel 75, Super 8, **other:** MEDICAL CARE, CashWise Foods/24hr, Goodyear, SunMart Food, Tires+/transmissions, White Drug, **W...gas:** Amoco/24hr, Cenex, Tesoro, **food:** Applebee's, Blimpie, ChiChi's, Chili's, Culver's, Denny's, McDonald's, Fuddrucker's, Grandma's Saloon/deli, Godfather's, Hooters, Krispy Kreme, Kroll's Diner, LoneStar Steaks, Olive Garden, Paradiso Mexican, Pizza Hut, Red Lobster, Royal Fork Buffet, Schlotsky's, Taco Bell, Taco Time, TGIFriday, TimberLodge Steaks, Valentino's Ristorante, **lodging:** Comfort Inn, Day's Inn, Fairfield Inn, Holiday Inn Express, Kelly Inn, Ramada Inn, Red Roof Inn, Select Inn, **other:** Barnes&Noble, Best Buy, Chevrolet, GNC, Herberger's, Hornbacher's Foods, JC Penney, Jo-Ann Crafts, K-Mart, Kohl's, Lowe's Whse, Michael's, Office Depot, OfficeMax, Old Navy, Sam's Club, Sears/auto, SunMart Foods, Target, Wal-Mart, Walgreen, mall

63b a — I-94, W to Bismarck, E to Minneapolis

62 — 32nd Ave S, Fargo, **E...gas:** F&F/diesel, Tesoro, **food:** Country Kitchen, Papa John's, **other:** Ford, **W...gas:** Flying J/Conoco/diesel/LP/motel/24hr/@, **other:** Goodyear/auto, Peterbilt, PleasureLand RV Ctr

60 — 52nd Ave S, to Fargo, **W...other:** Starr Fireworks

56 — to Wild Rice, Horace, no facilities

54 — rd 16, to Oxbow, Davenport, no facilities

50 — rd 18, Hickson, no facilities

48 — ND 46, to Kindred, no facilities

44 — to Christine, **1 mi E...**gas

42 — rd 2, to Walcott, no facilities

40.5mm rest area both lanes, full(handicapped)facilities, phone, picnic tables, litter barrels, vending, petwalk

37 — rd 4, Colfax, to Abercrombie, **E...**to Ft Abercrombie HS, **3 mi W...**gas

Fargo

31 — rd 8, Galchutt, **1 mi E...gas:** Cenex

26 — to Dwight, no facilities

24mm — weigh sta both lanes

23b a — ND 13, Mooreton, to Wahpeton, **10 mi E...**HOSPITAL, ND St Coll of Science

15 — rd 16, Great Bend, to Mantador, no facilities

8 — ND 11, to Hankinson, Fairmount, **E...gas:** Mobil/diesel, **3 mi W...**camping

3mm — Welcome Ctr nb, full(handicapped)facilities, phone, picnic tables, litter barrels, petwalk

2 — rd 22, no facilities

1 — rd 1E, **E...**Dakota Magic Casino/Hotel/rest./gas

0mm — North Dakota/South Dakota state line

Interstate 94

E ↕ W

Exit #	Services
352mm	North Dakota/Minnesota state line, Red River
351	US 81, Fargo, **N...gas:** Conoco, Stop'n Go, Tesoro, **food:** Cousins Subs, Duane's Pizza, Great Harvest, Taco Shop, **other:** HOSPITAL, AutoZone, Hornbacher's Foods, Medicine Shoppe, **S...gas:** Philips 66/diesel, Stop'n Go/diesel, Tesoro, **food:** A&W/LJ Silver, Burger King, El Mariachi Mexican, Embers Rest., Happy Joe's Pizza, KFC, McDonald's, N American Steaks, Papa Murphy's, Pepper's Café, Subway, Taco Bell, **lodging:** Expressway Inn, Rodeway Inn, **other:** Hyundai/Nissan, K-Mart, USPO

NORTH DAKOTA

Interstate 94

E ↕ W

350 25th St, Fargo, **N...gas:** Stop'n Go, **S...gas:** BP/diesel, Conoco/diesel, **food:** Dolittle's Grill

349b a I-29, N to Grand Forks, S to Sioux Falls, facilities 1 mi N, exit 64

348 45th St, **N...Visitor Ctr/full facilities, gas:** BP, Petro/Mobil/diesel/LP/rest./24hr/@, **food:** Bennigan's, IHOP, McDonald's, **lodging:** C'mon Inn, MainStay Inn, Ramada Inn, Sleep Inn, Wingate Inn, **1-2 mi N...gas:** Cenex, Stop'n Go, **food:** KFC, Olive Garden, Pizza Hut, Schlotsky's, **other:** Sam's Club, Target, Wal-Mart, **S...gas:** Tesoro/DQ/diesel, **food:** Old Chicago Pizza

347mm Sheyenne River

346b a W Fargo, to Horace, **S...gas:** Conoco/diesel

343 US 10, Lp 94, W Fargo, **N...gas:** BP, **food:** Highway Host Rest., Smoky's Steaks, **lodging:** Hi-10 Motel, **other:** Harley-Davidson, Pioneer Village

342 no facilities

341mm weigh sta both lanes

340 to Kindred, no facilities

338 Mapleton, **N...gas:** Phillips 66/diesel

337mm truck parking wb, litter barrels

331 ND 18, Casselton, to Leonard, **N...gas:** Phillips 66/diesel/café/motel, **other:** NAPA

328 to Lynchburg, no facilities

327mm truck parking eb, litter barrels

324 Wheatland, to Chaffee, no facilities

322 Absaraka, no facilities

320 to Embden, no facilities

317 to Ayr, no facilities

314 ND 38, Buffalo, to Alice, **3 mi N...**gas, food

310 no facilities

307 to Tower City, **N...gas:** Mobil/diesel/café/repair/24hr, motel

304mm rest area both lanes(both lanes exit left), full(handicapped)facilities, info, phone, picnic tables, litter barrels, vending, petwalk

302 ND 32, Oriska, to Fingal, **1 mi N...**gas, food

298 no facilities

296 no facilities

294 Lp 94, Valley City, to Kathryn, **N...**HOSPITAL, camping

292 Valley City, **N...gas:** Tesoro/diesel/café/24hr, **food:** Sabir's Rest., **lodging:** AmericInn, Super 8, Wagon Wheel Inn/rest., **other:** HOSPITAL, to Bald Hill Dam, camping, **S...other:** Ft Ransom SP(35mi)

291 Sheyenne River

290 Lp 94, Valley City, **N...gas:** Tesoro(1mi), **food:** Kenny's Rest., Pizza Hut, **lodging:** Bel Air Motel, Valley City Motel, **other:** HOSPITAL, Chrysler/Plymouth/Dodge, Pamida, **S...lodging:** Flickertail Inn

288 ND 1 S, to Oakes, no facilities

283 ND 1 N, to Rogers, no facilities

281 Sanborn, to Litchville, **1-2 mi N...**gas, food, lodging

276 Eckelson, **S...other:** Prairie Haven Camping/gas

275mm continental divide, elev 1490

272 to Urbana, no facilities

269 Spiritwood, no facilities

262 Bloom, **N...**airport

260 US 52, Jamestown, **N...gas:** BP/diesel/café/@, Stop'n Go, **lodging:** Starlite Motel, **other:** to St HOSPITAL, Chevrolet/Buick/Dodge, Harley-Davidson, camping

259mm James River

Jamestown

258 US 281, Jamestown, **N...gas:** BP/24hr, Sinclair/diesel, **food:** Arby's, DQ, McDonald's, Taco Bell, Wagonmaster Rest., **lodging:** Comfort Inn, Day's Inn, Holiday Inn Express, Jamestown Motel, Ranch House Motel, **other:** HOSPITAL, Buffalo Herd/museum, Firestone/auto, Frontier Village/RV dump, Cadillac/GMC, CarQuest, Chrysler/Plymouth/Toyota/Jeep, Firestone/auto, Mazda, NW Tire, **S...gas:** Conoco/Subway/diesel/24hr, **food:** Applebee's, Burger King, Embers Rest., Grizzly's Rest., Paradiso Mexican, Perkins, Super Buffet, **lodging:** Dakota Inn, Super 8, **other:** Bob's RV Ctr, Ford, JC Penney, K-Mart/Little Caesar's, Sears, Wal-Mart/drugs, mall

257 Lp 94(from eb), to Jamestown, **N...**diesel repair

256 Lp 94, **S...other:** Wiest truck/trailer repair, **1 mi S...**KOA/RV dump

254mm rest area both lanes, full(handicapped)facilities, phone, picnic tables, litter barrels, petwalk, vending

251 Eldridge, no facilities

248 no facilities

245 no facilities

242 Windsor, **1/4 mi N...**gas

238 Cleveland, to Gackle, **N...gas:** Prairie Oasis/café

233 no facilities

230 Medina, **1 mi N...gas:** Cenex/diesel/LP, **food:** C&R Dairy-Treat, **other:** Medina RV Park, USPO

228 ND 30 S, to Streeter, no facilities

224mm rest area wb, full(handicapped)facilities, phone, picnic tables, litter barrels, vending, petwalk, RV dump

221 Crystal Springs, no facilities

221mm rest area eb, full(handicapped)facilities, phone, picnic tables, litter barrels, vending, petwalk, RV dump

217 Pettibone, no facilities

214 Tappen, **S...**gas/diesel/food

208 ND 3 S, Dawson, **N...**RV camping, **1/2 mi S...**gas, food, to Camp Grassick, RV camping

205 Robinson, no facilities

200 ND 3 N, Steele, to Tuttle, **S...gas:** Cenex, Conoco/diesel/24hr, **food:** Lone Steer Motel/café/24hr/RV dump

195 no facilities

190 Driscoll, no facilities

182 US 83 S, ND 14, Sterling, to Wing, **S...gas:** Cenex/diesel/24hr/RV dump, **food:** Top's Café, **lodging:** Top's Motel(1mi)

176 McKenzie, no facilities

170 Menoken, **S...**to McDowell Dam, no facilities

168mm rest area both lanes, full(handicapped)facilities, phone, picnic tables, litter barrels, vending, petwalk

161 Lp 94, Bismarck Expswy, Bismarck, **N...gas:** Cenex/diesel/24hr, **other:** KOA(1mi), **S...gas:** Tesoro/diesel/rest./24hr, **food:** McDonald's, **lodging:** Ramada Ltd, **other:** Capitol RV Ctr, Dakota Zoo

Interstate 94

E Bismarck W

159 US 83, Bismarck, **N...gas:** BP, Sinclair/diesel, **food:** A&W/LJ Silver, Applebee's, Arby's, Burger King, HongKong Chinese, KFC, Kroll's Diner, McDonald's, Paradiso Mexican, Perkins, Red Lobster, Royal Fork Buffet, Schlotsky's, Space Alien Grill, Taco Bell, **lodging:** AmericInn, Comfort Inn, Country Inn Suites, Fairfield Inn, Motel 6, **other:** Chevrolet, Dan's Foods, K-Mart, Sears, mall, **S...gas:** Conoco/diesel, Tesoro, **food:** DQ, Dominique's Rest., 83 Diner, Hardee's, Intn'l Rest., Pizza Hut, Starbucks, Steak Buffet, Subway, Taco John's, Wendy's, Woodhouse Rest., **lodging:** Best Western, Day's Inn, Kelly Inn, Select Inn, Super 8, **other:** HOSPITAL

157 Divide Ave, Bismarck, **N...gas:** Conoco/diesel/LP/24hr, **food:** Cracker Barrel, McDonald's, **S...gas:** Cenex/A&W, **other:** Econo Foods

156mm Missouri River

156 I-194, Bismarck Expswy, Bismarck City Ctr, **1/2 mi S...lodging:** Colonial Motel, RiverTree Inn

155 to Lp 94(exits left from wb), Mandan, City Ctr, same as 153

Mandan

153 ND 6, Mandan Dr, Mandan, **1/2 mi S...gas:** Cenex/24hr, StaMart/diesel, Tesoro, **food:** Burger King, Bonanza, DQ, Dakota Farms Rest., Domino's, Godfather's, Hardee's, McDonald's, Pizza Hut, Subway, Taco John's, **lodging:** North Country Inn, **other:** CarQuest, Chevrolet, Ford/Mercury, Goodyear/auto, NAPA, Dacotah Centennial Park, Ft Lincoln SP(5mi)

152 Sunset Dr, Mandan, **N...gas:** Conoco, **lodging:** Best Western, Ridge Motel, **S...gas:** Tesoro/diesel/RV dump, **food:** Fried's Rest.

152mm scenic view eb

147 ND 25, to ND 6, Mandan, **S...gas:** Sinclair/diesel/café/24hr

143mm central/mountain time zone

140 to Crown Butte

135mm scenic view wb, litter barrel

134 to Judson, Sweet Briar Lake, no facilities

127 ND 31, to New Salem, **N...**Knife River Indian Village(35mi), **S...gas:** Cenex/diesel, Tesoro/diesel, **lodging:** Sunset Inn/café, **other:** Food Pride, Golden West Shopping Ctr, Biggest Cow in the World

123 to Almont, no facilities

120 no facilities

119mm rest area both lanes, full(handicapped)facilities, phone, picnic tables, litter barrels, petwalk

117 no facilities

113 no facilities

110 ND 49, to Glen Ullin, no facilities

108 to Glen Ullin, Lake Tschida, **3 mi S...**gas, food, lodging, camping

102 Hebron, to Glen Ullin, to Lake Tschida, **3 mi S...**gas, food, lodging, camping

97 Hebron, **2 mi N...**gas, food, lodging

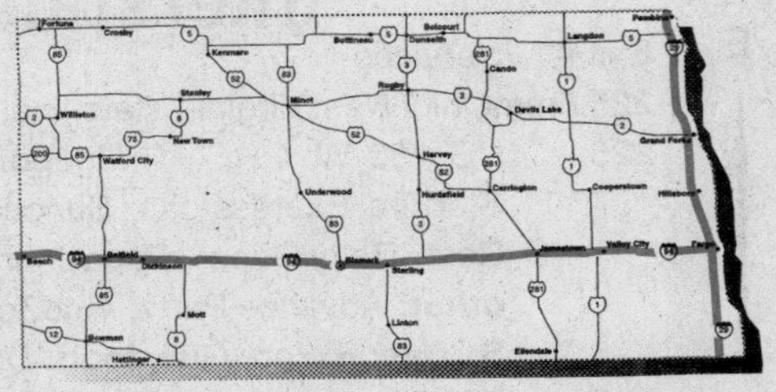

90 no facilities

84 ND 8, Richardton, **N...gas:** Cenex/diesel, **other:** HOSPITAL, to Assumption Abbey, Schnell RA

78 to Taylor, no facilities

72 Gladstone, no facilities

Dickinson

64 Dickinson, **S...gas:** Tesoro/diesel/rest./24hr, **other:** Firestone/auto, Ford/Lincoln/Mercury, Honda/Toyota, diesel repair

61 ND 22, Dickinson, **N...gas:** Cenex/diesel/24hr, Simonson/diesel, **food:** Applebee's, Arby's, Bonanza, Burger King, DQ, Ralphie's Grill, Taco Bell, Taco John's, Wendy's, **lodging:** AmericInn, Comfort Inn, Travelodge, **other:** Albertson's/24hr, Dan's Foods, Goodyear/auto, Herberger's, JC Penney, K-Mart, NAPA, Sears, Wal-Mart/24hr, **S...gas:** BP/Domino's, Cenex/diesel, Conoco/repair, Holiday/diesel/24hr, **food:** A&W/KFC, China Doll, Country Kitchen, Domino's, King Buffet, McDonald's, Perkins, Pizza Hut, Subway, **lodging:** Best Western, Budget Inn, Select Inn, Super 8, **other:** HOSPITAL, info

59 Lp 94, to Dickinson, **S...**to Patterson Lake RA, camping, **3 mi S...**facilities in Dickinson

51 South Heart, no facilities

42 US 85, Belfield, to Grassy Butte, Williston, **N...**T Roosevelt NP(52mi), **S...**info, **gas:** Conoco/diesel, Tesoro/diesel/24hr, **food:** DQ, **lodging:** Trapper's Inn/rest., **other:** NAPA

36 Fryburg, no facilities

32 T Roosevelt NP, Painted Canyon Visitors Ctr, N...rest area both lanes, full(handicapped)facilities, phone, picnic tables, litter barrels, petwalk

27 Lp 94, Historic Medora(from wb), T Roosevelt NP

24.5mm Little Missouri Scenic River

24 Medora, Historic Medora, Chateau de Mores HS, T Roosevelt NP, **S...**visitors ctr

23 West River Rd, no facilities

22mm scenic view eb

18 Buffalo Gap, **N...**Buffalo Gap Camping(seasonal)

12mm rest area eb, full(handicapped)facilities, phone, picnic tables, litter barrels, petwalk

10 Sentinel Butte, Camel Hump Lake, **S...**gas

7 Home on the Range, no facilities

1 ND 16, Beach, **N...lodging:** Outpost Motel, **other:** camping, **S...gas:** Cenex/diesel/LP/24hr, Flying J/diesel/rest./24hr, **lodging:** Buckboard Inn, **other:** HOSPITAL, **Visitor/Welcome Ctr**

1mm weigh sta both lanes, litter barrel

0mm North Dakota/Montana state line

OHIO

Interstate 70

E ↔ W

Exit # Services

225.5mm Ohio/West Virginia state line, Ohio River

225 US 250 W, OH 7, Bridgeport, **N...gas:** Marathon, StarFire Express/gas, Sunoco/24hr, **food:** Abbey's Rest., Dairy Queen, Papa John's, Pizza Hut, Wendy's, **other:** Advance Parts, AutoZone, Family$, Pennzoil, **S...gas:** Exxon, Gulf, **food:** Domino's

220 US 40, rd 214, **N...gas:** Citgo, Exxon/diesel, Sunoco, **lodging:** Hillside Motel(2mi), Holiday Inn Express(2mi), **other:** Aldi Foods, **S...gas:** Marathon/diesel, **food:** Undo's Pizza, Pizza Hut(1mi), **lodging:** Day's Inn

Blaine

218 Mall Rd, to US 40, to Blaine, **N...gas:** BP/diesel, Citgo, Exxon, Marathon, **food:** Applebee's, Arby's, Big Boy, Buffalo Wings, Burger King, Denny's, Eat'n Park, Outback Steaks, Pizza Hut, Red Lobster, Steak'n Shake, Taco Bell, W Texas Steaks, **lodging:** Econolodge, Hampton Inn, Holiday Inn Express, Knight's Inn, Red Roof, Super 8, **other:** AutoZone, Chevrolet/Pontiac/Buick/Cadillac, Circuit City, Kroger, Lowe's Whse, Sam's Club, Staples, Wal-Mart/auto, **S...gas:** USA/diesel, **food:** Bob Evans, Bonanza, Cracker Barrel, Garfield's Rest., LJ Silver, LongHorn Steaks, McDonald's, Rax, **lodging:** Country Inn Suites, **other:** CVS Drug, Jo-Ann Fabrics, JC Penney, NTB, Sears/auto, mall

216 OH 9, St Clairsville, **N...gas:** BP, **S...gas:** Marathon

215 National Rd, **N...gas:** Citgo, **food:** Burger King, Subway, WenWu Chinese, **other:** NAPA, Riesbeck's Foods

213 OH 331, Flushing, **S...gas:** Citgo, Rich, Sunoco/diesel, **lodging:** Twin Pines Motel

211mm rest area both lanes, full(handicapped)facilities, phone, picnic tables, litter barrels, petwalk, vending

208 OH 149, Morristown, **N...gas:** BP/diesel, 208/diesel/rest., **food:** Schlepp's Rest., **lodging:** Arrowhead Motel(1mi), **other:** Ford/Mercury, **S...gas:** Marathon/diesel, **other:** Harley-Davidson, Barkcamp SP

204 US 40 E(from eb), National Rd, no facilities

202 OH 800, to Barnesville, **S...other:** HOSPITAL, gas/diesel, flea mkt

198 rd 114, Fairview, no facilities

193 OH 513, Middlebourne, **N...gas:** BP, FuelMart/diesel, Shell, **other:** fireworks

Cambridge

189mm rest area eb, full(handicapped)facilities, phone, picnic tables, litter barrels, petwalk, vending

186 US 40, OH 285, to Old Washington, **N...gas:** BP, **S...gas:** GoMart/diesel

180b a I-77 N, to Cleveland, to Salt Fork SP, I-77 S, to Charleston

178 OH 209, Cambridge, **N...gas:** BP/diesel, **food:** Bob Evans, Cracker Barrel, Grand Buffet, KFC, McDonald's, Rax, Ruby Tuesday, **lodging:** Best Western, BudgetHost, Comfort Inn, Day's Inn, Holiday Inn, **other:** HOSPITAL, Kroger/deli, **1 mi N...food:** Papa John's, Pizza Hut, Subway, Taco Bell, Wendy's, **other:** AutoZone, Buick/Pontiac/GMC/Cadillac, CVS Drug, Family$, **S...gas:** Pilot/Blimpie/diesel, **food:** Burger King, **lodging:** AmeriHost, **other:** $Tree, K-Mart/gas, Radio Shack, Wal-Mart CuperCtr/gas/24hr, Spring Valley RV Park(1mi)

176 US 22, US 40, to Cambridge, **N...gas:** Sunoco/diesel, **lodging:** Budget Inn, Deluxe Inn, **other:** Western Shop, RV camping, st patrol

173mm weigh sta both lanes

169 OH 83, New Concord, to Cumberland, **N...gas:** BP, **other:** RV camping, to Muskingum Coll

164 US 22, US 40, Norwich, **N...gas:** BP, **lodging:** Baker's Motel, museum

163mm rest area wb, full(handicapped)facilities, phone, picnic tables, litter barrels, petwalk, vending

Zanesville

160 OH 797, Airport, **N...gas:** Love's/Arby's/diesel/24hr/@, **S...gas:** BP, Exxon/Subway/diesel, Starfire, **food:** Denny's, McDonald's, Wendy's, **lodging:** Day's Inn, Holiday Inn, Red Roof Inn, **other:** st patrol

157 OH 93, Zanesville, **N...gas:** BP, **S...gas:** Marathon/Blimpie, Shell/diesel, **other:** KOA(1mi)

155 OH 60, OH 146, Underwood St, Zanesville, **N...**info, **food:** Bob Evans, Olive Garden, Red Lobster, Shoney's, Steak'n Shake, Tumbleweed Grill, **lodging:** Comfort Inn, Fairfield Inn, Hampton Inn, **other:** HOSPITAL, **other:** Pick'n Save Foods, **S...gas:** Exxon/diesel, **food:** Adornetto Café, Cracker Barrel, Subway, Wendy's, **lodging:** AmeriHost, Best Western, **other:** Old Mkt House Inn, Family$, Rite Aid

154 5th St(from eb)

153b Maple Ave(no EZ return from wb), **N...gas:** BP, **food:** Big Boy, Dairy Queen, Wendy's, **other:** HOSPITAL

a State St, **N...gas:** Speedway/diesel, **other:** Harley-Davidson, **S...gas:** BP

153mm Licking River

152 US 40, National Rd, **N...gas:** BP, Exxon/A&W/Blimpie, **food:** McDonald's, **lodging:** Super 8

142 US 40(from wb, no EZ return), Gratiot, **N...**RV camping

141 OH 668, US 40(from eb), to Gratiot, same as 142

132 OH 13, to Thornville, Newark, **N...**Dawes Arboretum(3mi), **S...gas:** BP, Shell, **other:** RV camping

131mm rest area both lanes, full(handicapped)facilitie s, phone, picnic tables, litter barrels, petwalk, vending

129b a OH 79, Hebron, to Buckeye Lake, **N...lodging:** AmeriHost, **S...gas:** BP/Duke/diesel/@, Citgo, Shell, **food:** Burger King, McDonald's, Pizza Hut/Taco Bell, Subway, Wendy's, **lodging:** Super 8, **other:** CarQuest, KOA(2mi), Blue Goose Marina(2mi)

126 OH 37, to Granville, Lancaster, **N...gas:** Citgo/diesel/@, Pilot/DQ/diesel/24hr/@, Starfire Express/diesel, **S...gas:** Sunoco/diesel, TA/BP/Sbarro's/Popeye's/diesel/24hr/@, **lodging:** Deluxe Inn, Red Roof Inn, **other:** truckwash, KOA(4mi),

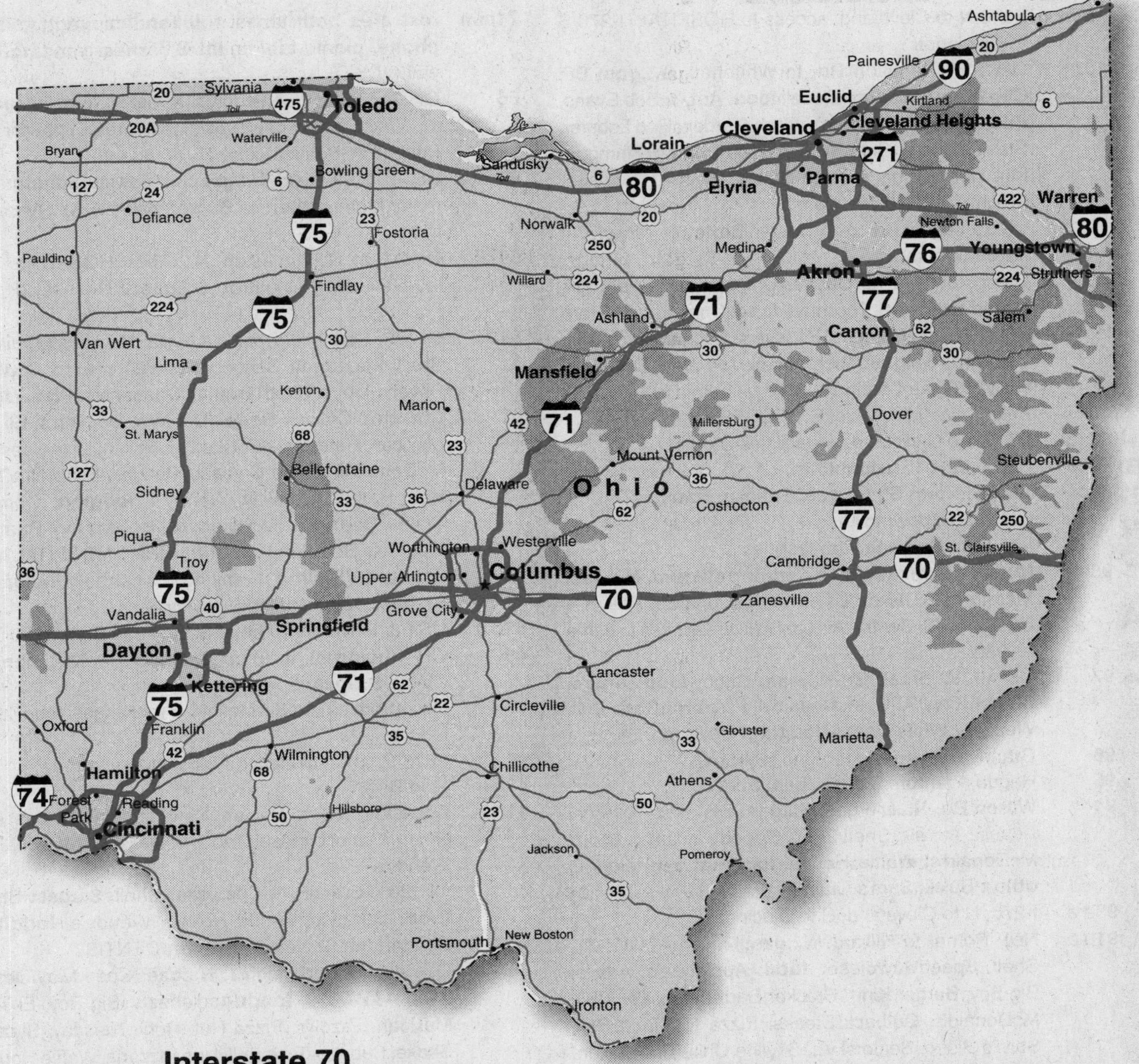

Interstate 70

122 OH 158, Kirkersville, to Baltimore, **N...lodging:** Regal Inn, **S...gas:** Flying J/CountryMkt/diesel/LP/24hr/@

118 OH 310, to Pataskala, **N...gas:** Speedway/diesel, Sunoco/DQ, **S...gas:** Duke's/diesel

112 OH 256, to Pickerington, Reynoldsburg, **N...gas:** BP, Shell, Sunoco/diesel, **food:** KFC, Logan's Roadhouse, McDonald's, O'Charley's, Panera Bread, TGIFriday, **lodging:** Country Inn Suites, Fairfield Inn, **other:** Sam's Club/gas, Tire Kingdom, Wal-Mart SuperCtr/24hr, **S...gas:** Speedway, **food:** Arby's, Boston Mkt, Cracker Barrel, Damon's, KFC, Longhorn Steaks, MT Steaks, Schlotsky's, Steak'n Shake, Wendy's, **lodging:** Best Western, Hampton Inn, Holiday Inn Express, **other:** Barnes&Noble, CVS Drug

110 Brice Rd, to Reynoldsburg, **N...gas:** Shell, Speedway, Sunoco, **food:** Arby's, Burger King, Bob Evans, ChiChi's, Gengi Japanese, Golden China, McDonald's, Max&Erma's, Pizza Hut, Popeye's, Roadhouse Grill, Ryan's, Subway, TeeJaye's Rest., Tim Horton, Waffle House, **lodging:** Best Western, Comfort Inn, Cross Country Inn, Extended Stay America, La Quinta, Ramada Inn, Red Roof, Super 8, **other:** Goodyear/auto, Home Depot, Pennzoil, **S...gas:** BP, Meijer/diesel/24hr, SA/diesel, Sunoco, **food:** Applebee's, Arby's, Asian Star, Boston Mkt, Burger King, China Paradise, KFC/Pizza Hut, McDonald's, Ponderosa, Ruby Tuesday, Skyline Chili, Chipotle Grill, Subway, Steak'n Shake, Taco Bell, Waffle House, Wendy's, White Castle, **lodging:** Comfort Suites, Day's Inn, Econolodge, Motel 6, **other:** Acura, Aldi, Circuit City, CVS Drug, Firestone/auto, GNC, Honda, Hyundai, JC Penney, Jo-Ann Fabrics, Kroger/deli, Lowe's Whse, Michael's, NTB, OfficeMax, Old Navy, Sam's Club, Sears/auto, Target, Toyota, mall

OHIO

Interstate 70

E ↕ W

Columbus Area

108b a I-270 N to Cleveland, access to HOSPITAL, I-270 S to Cincinnati

107 OH 317, Hamilton Rd, to Whitehall, **S...gas:** BP, Citgo/diesel, Sunoco/diesel, **food:** Arby's, Bob Evans, Burger King, McDonald's, Olive Garden, Red Lobster, Steak'n Shake, Subway, Taco Bell, **lodging:** Hampton Inn, Holiday Inn, InTown Suites, Howard Johnson, Knight's Inn, Residence Inn

105b a US 33, James Rd, to Lancaster, Bexley, **N...food:** Tat Italian, Wendy's

103 Livingston Ave, to Capital University, **N...gas:** BP, Speedway/diesel, Thornton, **food:** Domino's, Mr Hero Subs, Peking Chinese, Popeye's, Subway, Taco Bell, Wendy's, **S...gas:** Rich, Shell, **food:** McDonald's, Rally's, White Castle

102 Kelton Ave, Miller Ave, **S...**HOSPITAL

101a I-71 N, to Cleveland, no facilities

100b US 23, to 4th St, downtown

99c Rich St, Town St, **N...gas:** Sunoco, Ford

b OH 315 N, downtown

a I-71 S, to Cincinnati, no facilities

98b Mound St(from wb, no EZ return), stadium, **N...gas:** Marathon, **S...food:** LJ Silver, McDonald's, Rally's

a US 62, OH 3, Central Ave, to Sullivan, access to same as 98b

97 US 40, W Broad St, **N...gas:** Citgo, **food:** Arby's, Burger King, KFC, McDonald's, Pizza Hut/Taco Bell, Wendy's, White Castle, **lodging:** Day's Inn

96 Grandview Ave(from eb), no facilities

95 Hague Ave(from wb), **S...gas:** Sunoco

94 Wilson Rd, **N...**DM/gas, **S...gas:** BP, Pilot/Wendy's/diesel/24hr/@, Shell/24hr, Speedway/24hr, **food:** McDonald's, Waffle House, **lodging:** Econolodge, **other:** Buick, Sam's Club

93b a I-270, N to Cleveland, S to Cincinnati

91b a New Rome, to Hilliard, **N...gas:** Meijer/diesel/24hr, Shell, Speedway/diesel, **food:** Applebee's, Arby's, Big Boy, Burger King, Cracker Barrel, Fazoli's, KFC, McDonald's, Outback Steaks, Pizza Hut/Taco Bell, Salvi's Bistro, Schlotsky's, Skyline Chili, Tim Horton, Texas Roadhouse, White Castle, Wendy's, **lodging:** Comfort Suites, Cross Country Inn, Fairfield Inn, Hampton Inn, Hawthorn Inn, Motel 6, Red Roof Inn, **other:** Giant-Eagle Foods/gas, Ford, Sam's Club, Valvoline, Wal-Mart SuperCtr/24hr, **S...gas:** BP/diesel, Marathon/diesel, **food:** Bob Evans, Steak'n Shake, **lodging:** Best Western, Country Inn Suites, Hilton Garden, Microtel

85 OH 142, W Jefferson, to Plain City, no facilities

80 OH 29, to Mechanicsburg, **S...**hwy patrol

79 US 42, to London, Plain City, **N...gas:** Pilot/Subway/diesel/24hr/@, **food:** Waffle House, **S...gas:** Sunoco/24hr, Speedway/diesel/24hr, TA/BP/Popeye's/Pizza Hut/diesel/24hr/@, **food:** McDonald's, Taco Bell, Wendy's, **lodging:** Holiday Inn Express, Knight's Inn, **other:** HOSPITAL, truckwash

72 OH 56, Summerford, to London, **N...gas:** Shell/24hr, **4 mi S...**HOSPITAL, lodging

71mm rest area both lanes, full(handicapped)facilities, phone, picnic tables, litter barrels, vending, petwalk

Springfield

66 OH 54, South Vienna, to Catawba, **N...gas:** FuelMart/diesel, **S...gas:** Speedway/diesel, **other:** Crawford RV Park(1mi), Beaver Valley RV Park(3mi)

62 US 40, Springfield, **N...gas:** Speedway, **lodging:** Harmony Motel, **other:** to Buck Creek SP, **S...**RV camping

59 OH 41, to S Charleston, **N...other:** HOSPITAL, Harley-Davidson, st patrol, **S...gas:** BP/diesel, Prime Fuel/diesel

54 OH 72, Springfield, to Cedarville, **N...gas:** BP/diesel, Shell, Speedway, Sunoco/diesel/24hr, **food:** A&W/LJ Silver, Arby's, Bob Evans, Cassano's Pizza/subs, Church's, Cracker Barrel, Denny's, Domino's, El Toro Mexican, Hardee's, KFC, Lee's Chicken, Little Caesar's, McDonald's, Panda Chinese, Perkins, Pizza Hut/Taco Bell, Rally's, Subway, Wendy's, **lodging:** Comfort Suites, Day's Inn, Hampton Inn, Holiday Inn, Ramada Ltd, Red Roof Inn, Super 8, **other:** HOSPITAL, Aldi Foods, CVS Drug, Family$, Kroger/deli, Walgreen, **S...gas:** Certified/diesel, Swifty

52b a US 68, to Urbana, Xenia, **S...**to John Bryan SP

48 OH 4(from wb), to Enon, Donnelsville, **N...**Enon RV Camp, **S...gas:** Speedway

47 OH 4(from eb), to Springfield, **5 mi N...**gas, food, lodging

44 I-675 S, to Cincinnati, no facilities

43mm Mad River

41 OH 4, OH 235, to Dayton, New Carlisle, **N...gas:** BP/diesel, Sunoco/diesel, **food:** A&W/KFC, McDonald's, Wendy's

38 OH 201, Brandt Pike, **N...gas:** Shell, **S...gas:** Shell, **food:** Denny's, Waffle House, Wendy's, **lodging:** Comfort Inn, Travelodge, **other:** DENTIST

36 OH 202, Huber Heights, **N...gas:** Speedway/diesel/24hr, A&W/KFC, **food:** Applebee's, Big Boy, El Toro Mexican, Fazoli's, Pizza Hut, Ruby Tuesday, Steak'n Shake, Subway, Taco Bell, Uno Pizzaria, Waffle House, Wendy's, **lodging:** Super 8, **other:** Cub Foods/24hr, GNC, Kohl's, Lowe's Whse, Marshall's, Radio Shack, Saturn, Target, Wal-Mart/auto, **S...gas:** BP/diesel, Sunoco/diesel, **food:** Arby's, Bob Evans, Buffalo Wings, Burger King, Cadillac Jack's Grill, LJ Silver, McDonald's, TGIFriday, White Castle, **lodging:** Days Inn, Hampton Inn, Holiday Inn Express, **other:** CVS Drug, K-Mart, Kroger/gas

33 b a I-75, N to Toledo, S to Dayton

32 Vandalia, **N...**to Dayton Intn'l Airport

29 OH 48, Englewood, to Dayton, **N...gas:** BP, Speedway, Sunoco/24hr, **food:** Arby's, Big Boy, Bob Evans, Perkins, Pizza Hut, Ponderosa, Skyline Chili, Taco Bell, Wendy's, **lodging:** Hampton Inn, Holiday Inn, Motel 6, Super 8, **other:** Advance Parts, Aldi Foods, McNulty RV Ctr, **S...gas:** Meijer/diesel/24hr, **food:** McDonald's, Waffle House, **lodging:** Comfort Inn, Cross Country Inn

Interstate 70

E ↔ W

26 OH 49 S, **S...gas:** Shell

24 OH 49 N, Clayton, to Greenville, **S...gas:** Sunoco/diesel/24hr, **other:** KOA(seasonal)

21 rd 533, Brookville, **N...**gas, **S...gas:** BP/diesel, Speedway/diesel, **food:** Arby's, Dairy Queen, KFC/Taco Bell, McDonald's, Rob's Dining, Waffle House, Wendy's, **lodging:** Day's Inn, Holiday Inn Express, **other:** Chevrolet, $General

14 OH 503, Lewisburg, to West Alexandria, **N...gas:** Sunoco/Subway/diesel, **lodging:** Super Inn, Super-Valu Foods, **S...gas:** Citgo/diesel

10 US 127, to Eaton, Greenville, **N...gas:** Marathon, TA/BP/Burger King/Subway/diesel/24hr/@, st patrol, **S...gas:** Pilot/DQ/diesel/24hr/@, **lodging:** Econolodge

3mm Welcome Ctr eb/rest area both lanes, full(handicapped)facilities, phone, vending, picnic tables, litter barrels, petwalk

1 US 35 E(from eb), to Eaton, New Hope

0mm Ohio/Indiana state line, Welcome Arch, weigh sta eb

Interstate 71

N ↔ S

Cleveland

Exit # Services

247b I-90 W, I-490 E. I-71 begins/ends on I-90, exit 170 in Cleveland.

a W 14th, Clark Ave, no facilities

246 Denison Ave, Jennings Rd(from sb)

245 US 42, Pearl Rd, **E...gas:** BP, Sunoco, **other:** HOSPITAL, zoo

244 W 65th, Denison Ave, no facilities

242b a W 130th, to Bellaire Rd, **W...gas:** Sunoco, **food:** Burger King(1/2mi)

240 W 150th, **E...gas:** Marathon, Speedway/diesel, **lodging:** Marriott, **W...gas:** BP/Subway/diesel, **food:** Burger King, MacKenzie's Grill, Somers Rest., Taco Bell, **lodging:** Baymont Inn, Holiday Inn

239 OH 237 S(from sb), **W...**to airport

238 I-480, Toledo, Youngstown, **W...**airport

237 Snow Rd, Brook Park, **E...gas:** BP, Citgo, Shell, **food:** Bob Evans, McDonald's, **lodging:** Best Western, Fairfield Inn, Holiday Inn Express, **W...**to airport

235 Bagley Rd, **E...food:** Bob Evans, **lodging:** Clarion, **W...gas:** BP/diesel, Shell, Speedway, **food:** Burger King, Damon's, Denny's, Friendly's, McDonald's, Olive Garden, Perkins, Pizza Hut, Taco Bell, **lodging:** Comfort Inn, Courtyard, Cross Country Inn, Motel 6, Radisson, Red Roof Inn, Residence Inn, Studio+, TownePlace Suites, **other:** HOSPITAL, Aldi Foods, GMC, K-Mart

234 US 42, Pearl Rd, **E...gas:** Shell, Speedway, Sunoco/diesel, **food:** Hunan Chinese, Katherine's Rest., Santo's Pizza, Wendy's, **other:** DENTIST, Audi/Porsche, Honda, Hyundai, Saturn, **W...gas:** Marathon/diesel, **food:** Buffalo Wings, Jennifer's Rest., Mad Cactus Café, **lodging:** Colony Motel, Day's Inn, Extended Stay America, La Siesta Motel, Murphy's Motel, Village Motel, **other:** Home Depot, Wal-Mart

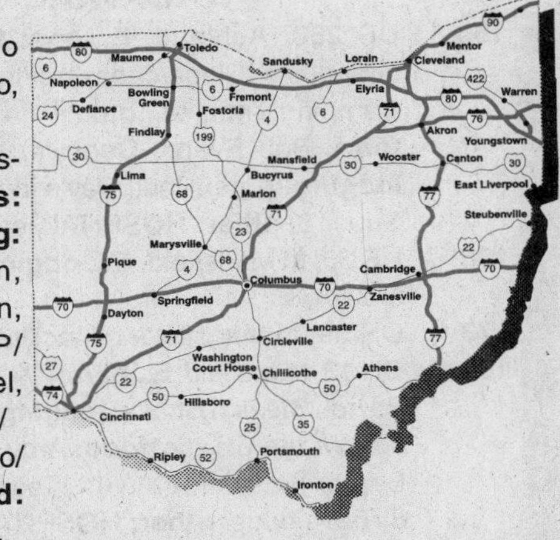

233 I-80 and Ohio Tpk, to Toledo, Youngstown

231 OH 82, Strongsville, **E...gas:** Shell, **lodging:** Holiday Inn, Red Roof Inn, **W...gas:** BP/Subway/diesel, Marathon/diesel, Sunoco/diesel, **food:** Applebee's, Buca Italian, Demetrio's Rest., Longhorn Steaks, Macaroni Grill, Panera Bread, Rio Bravo, TGIFriday, **other:** Borders Books, Dillard's, Giant Eagle Foods, JC Penney, Jo-Ann Fabrics, Kohl's, OfficeMax, Sears/auto, Target, Tire Kingdom, mall

226 OH 303, Brunswick, **E...gas:** Shell/diesel/24hr, **food:** Denny's, Pizza Hut, **other:** Camping World RV Supplies/service, Chrysler/Plymouth/Jeep/Toyota, **W...gas:** BP, Marathon/diesel, Sunoco/diesel, **food:** Arby's, Bob Evans, Burger King, McDonald's, Mi-mi's Rest., Taco Bell, Wendy's, **lodging:** Howard Johnson, Sleep Inn, **other:** Ford, Giant Eagle Food, K-Mart

225mm rest area nb, full(handicapped)facilities, phone, picnic tables, litter barrels, petwalk

224mm rest area sb, full(handicapped)facilities, phone, picnic tables, litter barrels, petwalk

222 OH 3, **W...**st patrol

220 I-271 N, to Erie, Pa

218 OH 18, to Akron, Medina, **E...gas:** BP/diesel/24hr, Citgo/diesel, Shell/diesel, Sunoco/diesel, **food:** Alexandri's Rest., Blimpie, Burger King, Cracker Barrel, Dairy Queen, Hunan Dynasty, Medina Rest., **lodging:** Best Western, Day's Inn, Holiday Inn Express, Suburbanite Motel, Super 8, **other:** $General, GMC, Mitsubishi, **W...**HOSPITAL, Arby's, Bob Evans, Buffalo Wings, Denny's, Pizza Hut, Wendy's, Cross Country Inn, Hampton Inn, Motel 6, Dodge, Harley-Davidson, Honda, Pontiac/Buick/Cadillac, Tire Kingdom

209 I-76 E, to Akron, US 224 **W...gas:** Pilot/Subway/diesel/24hr, TA/BP/Burger King/Popeye's/diesel/24hr/@, **food:** McDonald's, Starbucks, **lodging:** Super 8, **other:** Blue Beacon, Chippewa Valley Camping(1mi)

204 OH 83, Burbank, **E...gas:** BP/diesel, Duke/Taco Bell/diesel, **W...gas:** Pilot/Wendy's/diesel/24hr, **food:** Bob Evans, Burger King, FoodCourt, McDonald's, **other:** HOSPITAL, Buick/Chevrolet/Pontiac, Chrysler/Jeep/Dodge, Prime Outlets/famous brands

198 OH 539, W Salem, **W...other:** Town&Country RV Park(2mi)

196mm rest area both lanes, full(handicapped)facilities, phone, vending, picnic tables, litter barrels, petwalk

196 OH 301(from nb, no re-entry), W Salem, no facilities

191mm weigh sta sb

OHIO

Interstate 71

N ↑ Ashland ↓ S

186 US 250, Ashland, **E...gas:** Citgo, **food:** Perkins, Grandpa's Village/cheese/gifts, **other:** Hickory Lakes Camping(7mi), **W...gas:** TA/BP/diesel/rest./24hr/@, **food:** Bob Evans, Denny's, McDonald's, Wendy's, **lodging:** AmeriHost, Day's Inn, Holiday Inn Express, Super 8, **other:** HOSPITAL, st patrol, to Ashland U

176 US 30, to Mansfield, **E...lodging:** Econolodge, **other:** fireworks

173 OH 39, to Mansfield, no facilities

Mansfield

169 OH 13, Mansfield, **E...gas:** Exxon/diesel, **food:** Cracker Barrel, Steak'n Shake, **lodging:** AmeriHost, Baymont Inn, **W...gas:** Citgo, **food:** Arby's, Big Boy, Bob Evans, Burger King, McDonald's, Taco Bell, **lodging:** Super 8, Travelodge, **other:** HOSPITAL, st patrol

165 OH 97, to Bellville, **E...gas:** BP, Marathon/diesel/24hr, Speedway/diesel, **food:** Burger King, Dutchman Rest., McDonald's, **lodging:** Day's Inn, Comfort Inn, Ramada Ltd, **other:** to Mohican SP, **W...food:** Subway(2mi), Wendy's, **lodging:** Mid Ohio Motel

151 OH 95, to Mt Gilead, **E...gas:** Duke/diesel/rest./24hr, Marathon, **food:** Gathering Inn Rest., McDonald's, Wendy's, **lodging:** Best Western, **other:** st patrol, **W...gas:** BP/diesel, Sunoco/diesel, **lodging:** Knight's Inn, **other:** HOSPITAL, M Camping, Mt Gilead SP(6mi)

149mm truck parking both lanes

140 OH 61, Mt Gilead, **E...gas:** Pilot/Arby's/diesel/24hr/@, **W...gas:** BP/Taco Bell, Sunoco/Subway, **food:** Ole Farmstead Rest.

Columbus Area

131 US 36, OH 37, to Delaware, **E...gas:** Flying J/Conoco/diesel/LP/rest./24hr/@, Pilot/Subway/diesel/24hr/@, **food:** Burger King, **W...gas:** BP/diesel, Shell, **food:** A&W, Arby's, Bob Evans, Cracker Barrel, KFC, McDonald's, Subway, Taco Bell, Waffle House, Wendy's, White Castle, **lodging:** Day's Inn, Hampton Inn, Holiday Inn Express, **other:** HOSPITAL, Alum Cr SP

129mm weigh sta nb

128mm rest area both lanes, full(handicapped)facilities, phone, vending, picnic tables, litter barrels, petwalk

121 Polaris Pkwy, **E...gas:** BP/Blimpie, Shell/24hr, **food:** McDonald's, Polaris Grill, Skyline Chili, Steak'n Shake, **lodging:** Best Western, Wingate Inn, **other:** Polaris Ampitheatre, **W...gas:** Marathon/A&W, Meijer/diesel/24hr, **food:** Applebee's, Arby's, BajaFresh, Bob Evans, Carrabba's, Hoggy's Grille, Hop's Grill, Magic Mtn Grill, Martin's Italian, Max&Erma's, O'Charley's, Olive Garden, Panera Bread, Pizza Hut/Taco Bell, Quaker Steaks, Red Lobster, Starbucks, TGIFriday, Wendy's, **lodging:** Baymont Inn, Hilton Garden, Wellesley Inn, **other:** Barnes&Noble, Best Buy, GNC, JC Penney, Jo-Ann Fabrics, Kroger, Lowe's Whse, OfficeMax, Old Navy, Sears/auto, Target, Wal-Mart SuperCtr/24hr(3mi), mall

119 I-270, to Indianapolis, Wheeling

117 OH 161, to Worthington, **E...gas:** BP/diesel, Shell, Sunoco, **food:** Burger King, KFC, LJ Silver, LoneStar Steaks, Max&Erma's, Outback Steaks, Rally's, Red Lobster, Subway, TeeJaye's Rest., White Castle, **lodging:** Comfort Inn, Day's Inn, Holiday Inn Express, Knight's Inn, Motel 6, **other:** Advance Parts, Big Bear Foods, Firestone, Staples, **W...gas:** Shell, Speedway/diesel, **food:** Bob Evans, McDonald's, Pi's Chinese, Pizza Hut, Skyline Chili, Subway, Waffle House, Wendy's, **lodging:** Best Western, Clarion, Country Inn Suites, Cross Country Inn, Econolodge, Extended Stay America, Hampton Inn, Marriott, Ramada Ltd, Residence Inn, Super 8, **other:** Chevrolet, Giant Eagle/gas

116 Morse Rd, Sinclair Rd, **E...gas:** BP, Shell, Speedway, **food:** China 1st, McDonald's, Fairfield Inn, **other:** MEDICAL CARE, Buick, CVS Drug, **W...gas:** Sunoco, **food:** La Hacienda Real Mexican, TeeJaye's Rest., **lodging:** Cross Country Inn, Motel 6, Ramada Inn, NTB

115 Cooke Rd, no facilities

114 N Broadway, **W...gas:** Sunoco

113 Weber Rd, **W...gas:** Speedway/diesel, **other:** CarQuest, NAPA

112 Hudson St, **E...gas:** BP, Shell, **food:** Wendy's, **lodging:** Holida Inn Express, **W...food:** Big Boy, **other:** Aldi Foods, Lowe's Whse, Tire Kingdom

111 17th Ave, **W...food:** McDonald's, **lodging:** Day's Inn

110b 11th Ave, no facilities

a 5th Ave, **E...gas:** Sunoco, **food:** White Castle, **W...gas:** Citgo, **food:** KFC/Pizza Hut, Wendy's, **other:** AutoZone

109a I-670, no facilities

108b US 40, Broad St, downtown, **W...**Honda

101a[70] I-70 E, US 23 N, to Wheeling

100b a[70] US 23 S, Front St, High St, downtown

106a I-70 W, to Indianapolis

b OH 315 N, Dublin St, Town St

105 Greenlawn, **E...gas:** BP, **food:** White Castle, Wild Bean Café, **other:** HOSPITAL

104 OH 104, Frank Rd, **W...**tires

101b a I-270, Wheeling, Indianapolis

100 Stringtown Rd, **E...gas:** BP, **food:** Bob Evans, Church's/White Castle, **lodging:** Best Western, Cross Country Inn, Hampton Inn, Holiday Inn Express, Hilton Garden, Microtel, Super 8, **W...gas:** Certified/diesel, Speedway/diesel, **food:** Applebee's, Arby's, Burger King, Capt D's, China Bell, Cracker Barrel, Damon's, Fazoli's, Hoggy's Rest., KFC, McDonald's, Perkins/24hr, Pizza Hut, Ponderosa, Rally's, Rancho Alegre Mexican, Roadhouse Grill, Ruby Tuesday, Starbucks, Subway, Taco Bell, TeeJaye's Rest., Tim Horton, Waffle House, Wendy's, **lodging:** Comfort Inn, Day's Inn, Motel 6, Red Roof Inn, Value Inn, **other:** Aldi Foods, All Tune/lube, Big Bear Food/drug, CVS Drug, GNC, Goodyear/auto, K-Mart, Kroger/24hr, NAPA, Radio Shack

97 OH 665, London-Groveport Rd, **E...gas:** Citgo/DM/Taco Bell, Sunoco/Subway, **food:** Arby's, McDonald's, Tim Horton/Wendy's, **other:** to Scioto Downs, **W...other:** Eddie's Repair

94 US 62, OH 3, Orient, **E...gas:** BP, **W...gas:** Sunoco

84 OH 56, Mt Sterling, **E...gas:** BP/Subway, Sunoco, **lodging:** Royal Inn, **other:** to Deer Creek SP(9mi)

75 OH 38, Bloomingburg, **E...**fireworks, **W...gas:** Sunoco

Interstate 71

N

S

69 OH 41, OH 734, Jeffersonville, **E...gas:** Flying J/CountryMkt/diesel/24hr/@, **other:** Walnut Lake Camping, **W...gas:** BP, Shell/Subway/diesel, **food:** Arby's, TCBY, Wendy's, White Castle, **lodging:** AmeriHost, **other:** HOSPITAL, Outlets II/famous brands

68mm rest area both lanes, full(handicapped)facilities, phone, vending, picnic tables, litter barrels, petwalk

65 US 35, Washington CH, **E...gas:** Shell, TA/BP/Pizza Hut/Popeye's/diesel/24hr/@, TrueNorth/diesel, **food:** A&W/KFC, Bob Evans, Burger King, McDonald's, Taco Bell/LJ Silver, Waffle House, Wendy's, **lodging:** AmeriHost, Hampton Inn, **other:** HOSPITAL, Prime Outlets/famous brands, **W...lodging:** Budget Motel

58 OH 72, to Sabina, no facilities

54mm weigh sta sb

50 US 68, to Wilmington, **E...food:** Werner's BBQ, **other:** HOSPITAL, **W...gas:** BP/DQ/diesel, Pilot/Subway/diesel/24hr, Shell/diesel/24hr, **food:** Dairy Queen, Max&Erma's, McDonald's, Wendy's, **lodging:** Budget Inn, Ramada Plaza

49mm weigh sta nb

45 OH 73, to Waynesville, **E...gas:** BP, Marathon/diesel, **other:** HOSPITAL, 1000 Trails RV Park, **W...**Caesar Creek SP(5mi)

36 Wilmington Rd, **E...**to Ft Ancient St Memorial, RV camping

35mm Little Miami River

34mm rest area both lanes, full(handicapped)facilities, scenic view, phone, vending, picnic tables, litter barrels, petwalk

32 OH 123, to Lebanon, Morrow, **E...gas:** BP, Clark, **food:** Country Kitchen, **other:** Morgan's RV Park, **3 mi W...food:** Bob Evans, Skyline Chili, **lodging:** Knight's Inn

28 OH 48, S Lebanon, **E...lodging:** Countryside Inn(1mi), **W...other:** Lebanon Raceway(6mi), hwy patrol

25 OH 741 N, Kings Mills Rd, **E...gas:** Shell/Popeye's, Speedway/diesel, **food:** El Toro Mexican, McDonald's, Ruby Tuesday, Taco Bell, Outback Steaks, **lodging:** Comfort Suites, Kings Island Inn, Quality Inn, **other:** Harley-Davidson, **W...gas:** AmeriStop/Subway, BP, **food:** Arby's, Big Boy, Bob Evans, Burger King, DQ, Perkins, Pizza Hut, Skyline Chili, Waffle House, Wendy's, **lodging:** Best Western, Hampton Inn, Holiday Inn Express, Microtel, **other:** CVS Drug, GNC, Kroger

24 Western Row, King's Island Dr(from nb), **E...gas:** Sunoco, **lodging:** King's Island, **other:** Jellystone Camping

19 US 22, Mason Montgomery Rd, **E...gas:** Meijer/diesel/24hr, Shell, SA/diesel, Sunoco/24hr, **food:** United Dairy Farmers, Arby's, Big Boy, Bennigan's, Bob Evans, Boston Mkt, Cooker, Cracker Barrel, Fazoli's, Golden Corral, KFC, McDonald's, Olive Garden, Pizza Hut, Pizza Tower, Ponderosa, Taco Bell, TGIFriday, Wendy's, White Castle, **lodging:** Comfort Inn, Quality Inn, Signature Inn, SpringHill Suites, TownePlace Suites, **other:** AutoZone, Barnes&Noble, Best Buy, Circuit City, Chevrolet, Firestone/auto, GMC/Buick/Pontiac, Goodyear, Kohl's, Kroger, Lincoln/Mercury, Michael's, Michel's Tires, OfficeMax, Old Navy, Radio Shack, Target, Toyota, Wal-Mart/auto, Walgreen, **W...gas:** BP/diesel, Marathon/diesel/24hr, Shell, **food:** Applebee's, Burger King, Carrabba's, Chipotle Mexican, Copeland's Rest., Fuddrucker's, LoneStar Steaks, O'Charley's, RiverCity Grill, Steak'n Shake, Skyline Chili, Subway, Tumbleweed Grill, Waffle House, Wendy's, **lodging:** AmeriSuites, Baymont Inn, Best Western, Country Hearth Inn, Day's Inn, Marriott, Ramada Ltd, Red Roof Inn, **other:** Bigg's Foods, Home Depot, Lowe's Whse, Staples

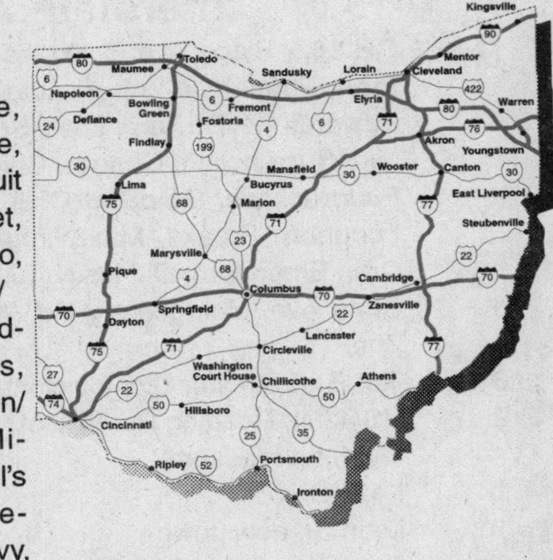

Cincinnati

17b a I-275, to I-75, OH 32, no facilities

15 Pfeiffer Rd, **E...**HOSPITAL, **W...gas:** BP, Shell/diesel, Sunoco/diesel/24hr, **food:** Applebee's, Bennigan's, Bob Evans, Buffalo Wings, Subway, **lodging:** Clarion, Courtyard, Embassy Suites, Hampton Inn, Holiday Inn Express, MainStay Suites, Ramada Inn, Red Roof Inn, Wingate Inn, **other:** Office Depot

14 OH 126, Reagan Hwy, Blue Ash, no facilities

12 US 22, OH 3, Montgomery Rd, **E...gas:** Shell/24hr, Sunoco, **food:** Arby's, Bob Evans, Jalapeno Café, KFC, LoneStar Steaks, LJ Silver, OutBack Steaks, Red Lobster, Ruby Tuesday, Subway, Taco Bell, TGIFriday, Wendy's, **lodging:** Hannaford Suites, Harvey Hotel, Sheraton, **other:** Dodge/Plymouth, Firestone, Goodyear, Hyundai, OfficeMax, PepBoys, Staples, **W...food:** Max&Erma's, McDonald's, Starbucks, **other:** Barnes&Noble, Dillard's, Firestone/auto, Parisian, mall

11 Kenwood Rd, **W...**HOSPITAL, same as 12

10 Stewart Rd(from nb), to Silverton, **W...gas:** Marathon/diesel

9 Redbank Rd, to Fairfax, **E...gas:** Mobil, Speedway, **W...gas:** Marathon

8 Kennedy Ave, Ridge Ave W, **E...gas:** Meijer/diesel, **lodging:** Red Roof Inn, **other:** Sam's Club, Target, **W...gas:** Exxon/Subway, Marathon/diesel, **food:** Denny's, Golden Corral, KFC, LJ Silver, McDonald's, Old Country Buffet, Pizza Hut, Rally's, Taco Bell, White Castle, Wendy's, **other:** Bigg's Foods, Circuit City, Ford, Goodyear, Home Depot, Office Depot, Tire Discounter, Wal-Mart, transmissions

OHIO

Interstate 71

N ↕ S — Cincinnati

7b a OH 562, Ridge Ave E, Norwood, **1/2mi E...gas:** BP, **food:** Ponderosa, **other:** AutoZone
6 Edwards Rd, **E...gas:** Shell, Speedway, **food:** Boston Mkt, Buca Italian, Chang's China Bistro, Don Pablos, Fuddrucker's, GoldStar Chili, J Alexander's Rest., Longhorn Steaks, Max&Erma's, Starbucks, **other:** Drug Emporium, Old Navy, TJ Maxx, **W...gas:** Shell
5 Dana Ave, Montgomery Rd, **W...other:** Xavier Univ, Zoo
3 Taft Rd(from sb), U of Cincinnati
2 US 42 N, Reading Rd, **W...other:** HOSPITAL, downtown, art museum
1k j I-471 S
1d Main St, downtown
1c b Pete Rose Way, Fine St, stadium, downtown
1a I-75 N, US 50, to Dayton, no facilities
I-71 S and I-75 S run together
0mm Ohio/Kentucky state line, Ohio River

Interstate 74

E ↕ W — Cincinnati

Exit # Services
20 I-75(from eb), N to Dayton, S to Cincinnati, I-74 begins/ends on I-75.
19 Gilmore St, Spring Grove Ave, no facilities
18 US 27 N, Colerain Ave, no facilities
17 Montana Ave(from wb), **N...gas:** BP
14 North Bend Rd, Cheviot, **N...gas:** Citgo, Speedway/diesel, **food:** DQ, Happy Chinese, McDonald's, Perkins, Skyline Chili, Wendy's, **other:** Sam's Club/gas, Tires+, Walgreen, **S...gas:** BP, **food:** Bob Evans, **lodging:** Tri-Star Motel
11 Rybolt Rd, Harrison Pike, **S...gas:** BP, Meijer/gas, **food:** Angelo's Pizza, Dante's Rest., **lodging:** Imperial House Motel, **other:** Kohl's
9 I-275 N, to I-75, N to Dayton
8mm Great Miami River
7 OH 128, Cleves, to Hamilton, **N...gas:** BP/diesel, Marathon/diesel, **food:** BierHaus Rest., Wendy's
5 I-275 S, to Kentucky
3 Dry Fork Rd, **N...gas:** Citgo, **S...gas:** Shell/diesel, **food:** Burger King, McDonald's, **other:** Chevrolet
2mm weigh sta eb
1 New Haven Rd, to Harrison, **N...gas:** BP/diesel, **food:** Buffalo Wings, Cracker Barrel, GoldStar Chili, **lodging:** Comfort Inn, **other:** Biggs Foods, Ford, Home Depot, Tires+, **S...gas:** Marathon/diesel, Shell/24hr, Speedway/diesel, Sunoco, A&W/KFC, **food:** Arby's, Big Boy, Burger King, Jersey Mike Subs, McDonald's, Perkins, Pizza Hut, Skyline Chili, Taco Bell, Waffle House, Wendy's, White Castle, **lodging:** Holiday Inn Express, Quality Inn, **other:** AutoZone, CVS Drug, Family$, Firestone, GNC, Goodyear/auto, K-Mart, Kroger, NAPA, Walgreen
0mm Ohio/Indiana state line

Interstate 75

N ↕ S — Toledo

Exit # Services
211mm Ohio/Michigan state line
210 OH 184, Alexis Rd, to Raceway Park, **E...gas:** BP, **other:** FoodTown, **W...gas:** BP/diesel/24hr, Meijer/diesel/24hr, Pilot/Subway/diesel/24hr/@, **food:** Bob Evans, Burger King, Ground Round, McDonald's, Taco Bell, Wendy's, **lodging:** Comfort Inn, Hampton Inn, **other:** Ford Trucks
210mm Ottawa River
209 Ottawa River Rd(from nb), **E...gas:** BP, Citgo, Sunoco, **food:** Little Caesar's, Marco's Pizza, **other:** VETERINARIAN, FoodTown, Rite Aid
208 I-280 S, to I-80/90, to Cleveland
207 Stickney Ave, Lagrange St, **E...gas:** BP, Citgo, Sunoco, **food:** McDonald's, Wendy's, **other:** Kash'nKarry Foods, Family$, K-Mart
206 to US 24, Phillips Ave, **W...**transmissions
205b Burdan St, **E...**HOSPITAL
a to Willys Pkwy, to Jeep Pkwy
204 I-475 W, to US 23, to Maumee, Ann Arbor
203b US 24, to Detroit Ave, **W...gas:** BP/24hr, **food:** KFC, McDonald's, Rally's, **other:** Rite Aid, Sav-A-Lot Foods, U-Haul
a Bancroft St, downtown
202 Washington St, Collingwood Ave(from sb, no EZ return), **E...gas:** BP, **other:** HOSPITAL, Art Museum, **W...food:** McDonald's
201b a OH 25, Collingwood Ave, **W...**Toledo Zoo
200 South Ave, Kuhlman Dr, no facilties
200mm Maumee River
199 OH 65, Miami St, to Rossford, **E...lodging:** Day's Inn
198 Wales Rd, Oregon Rd, to Northwood, **E...gas:** Shell/Subway/diesel/24hr, **food:** Pizza Hut, **lodging:** Comfort Inn, Microtel
197 Buck Rd, to Rossford, **E...gas:** Shell/diesel, **food:** Wendy's/Tim Horton, **W...gas:** BP/24hr, Sunoco/diesel, **food:** Denny's, McDonald's, **lodging:** Knight's Inn, Super 8
195 OH 795, Perrysburg, to I-80/90, OH Tpk(toll), **E...gas:** Barney's/Subway/diesel, BP/diesel, **lodging:** Courtyard
193 US 20, US 23 S, Perrysburg, **E...gas:** BP/diesel/24hr, Sunoco, **food:** Big Boy, Bob Evans, Burger King, Cracker Barrel, McDonald's, Panera Bread, Ralphie's, Shanghai Chinese, Subway, Taco Bell, Wendy's, **lodging:** Best Western, Day's Inn, Holiday Inn Express, **other:** GNC, Kohl's, K-Mart, Kroger/gas/24hr, KOA(7mi), **W...gas:** Marathon/diesel, **lodging:** Baymont Inn, **other:** AutoZone, Harley-Davidson
192 I-475, US 23 N(exits left from nb), to Maumee, Ann Arbor
187 OH 582, to Luckey, Haskins, no facilities
181 OH 64, OH 105, Bowling Green, to Pemberville, **E...gas:** Meijer/diesel/24hr, **W...gas:** BP, Citgo/Subway/diesel, Marathon, Speedway, Sunoco/diesel, **food:** Big Boy, Bob Evans, Burger King, ChiChi's, Domino's, El Zarape Mexican, Fricker's Rest., Hunan Buffet, McDonald's, Waffle House, Wendy's, **lodging:** Best Western, Buckeye Motel, Day's Inn, Quality Inn, Hampton Inn, **other:** HOSPITAL, bank, to Bowling Green U

Interstate 75

179 US 6, to Fremont, Napoleon, **W...**museum

179mm rest area both lanes, full(handicapped)facilities, phone, picnic tables, litter barrels, vending, petwalk

175mm weigh sta nb

171 OH 25, Cygnet, no facilities

168 Eagleville Rd, Quarry Rd, **E...gas:** FuelMart/diesel

167 OH 18, North Baltimore, to Fostoria, **E...gas:** Petro/Mobil/diesel/rest./24hr/@, **food:** McDonald's, Pizza Hut, **other:** Blue Beacon, **other:** truck repair, **W...gas:** Sunoco/diesel, **lodging:** Crown Inn

165mm Rocky Ford River

164 OH 613, to McComb, Fostoria, **E...other:** Shadylake Camping, to Van Buren SP, **W...gas:** Pilot/Subway/Taco Bell/diesel/24hr/@

162mm weigh sta sb, phones

161 OH 99, **E...other:** Ford, camping, hwy patrol

159 US 224, OH 15, Findlay, **E...gas:** BP/diesel, Speedway/diesel, Swifty, **food:** Bob Evans, Burger King, Dakota Grill, KFC, McDonald's, Pizza Hut, Ponderosa, Ralphie's, Spaghetti Shop, Steak'n Shake, Taco Bell, Wendy's, **lodging:** Cross Country Inn, Ramada Inn, Rodeway Inn, Super 8, **other:** HOSPITAL, **W...gas:** Shell/diesel, **food:** China Garden, Cracker Barrel, Denny's, Outback Steaks, Waffle House, **lodging:** Country Hearth Inn, Hampton Inn, Holiday Inn Express

158 Blanchard River

157 OH 12, Findlay, **E...gas:** GA/diesel, Marathon/Blimpie/diesel, **lodging:** Day's Inn, **W...gas:** BP, Hwy Travel Ctr/diesel/24hr/@, **food:** Fricker's Rest., Pilgrim Rest., **lodging:** Econolodge

156 US 68, OH 15, to Carey, **E...**HOSPITAL

153mm rest area both lanes, full(handicapped)facilities, phone, picnic tables, litter barrels, vending, petwalk

145 OH 235, Mount Cory, to Ada, **E...**TwinLakes Camping

142 OH 103, Bluffton, to Arlington, **E...gas:** Sunoco/diesel, **lodging:** Knight's Inn, **W...gas:** Marathon/diesel, Shell/diesel, **food:** Arby's, Burger King, KFC, McDonald's, Subway, Taco Bell, **lodging:** Comfort Inn, **other:** to Bluffton Coll

140 Bentley Rd, to Bluffton, no facilities

135 OH 696, to US 30, Beaverdam, to Delphos, **E...gas:** Pilot/diesel/24hr/@, **W...gas:** Flying J/Cookery/diesel/LP/24hr/@, tires, truck repair

134 Napolean Rd(no nb re-entry), to Beaverdam, no facilities

130 Blue Lick Rd, **E...gas:** Citgo/diesel, **food:** Blue Lick Pizza/subs, **lodging:** Ramada Inn

127b a OH 81, Lima, to Ada, **W...gas:** BP, Marathon/diesel, **food:** Waffle House, **lodging:** Comfort Inn, Day's Inn/rest., Econolodge

126mm Ottawa River

125 OH 309, OH 117, Lima, **E...gas:** BP/diesel, Speedway, **food:** Arby's, Big Boy, Bob Evans, Burger King, Capt D's, China Buffet, Cracker Barrel, Hunan Garden, McDonald's, Olive Garden, Pizza Hut, Ponderosa, Rally's, Ralphie's, Red Lobster, Ryan's, Skyline Chili, Subway, Taco Bell, TCBY, Texas Roadhouse, Wendy's, **lodging:** Hampton Inn, Holiday Inn, Motel 6, **other:** Ford/RV Ctr, Jo-Ann Fabrics, K-Mart, PharmX Drug, Ray's Foods, Sam's Club, Wal-Mart SuperCtr/24hr, **W...gas:** Shell, **food:** Damon's, Papa John's, Pomodoro Pizza, **lodging:** Super 8, **other:** HOSPITAL, $General, Sav-A-Lot Foods

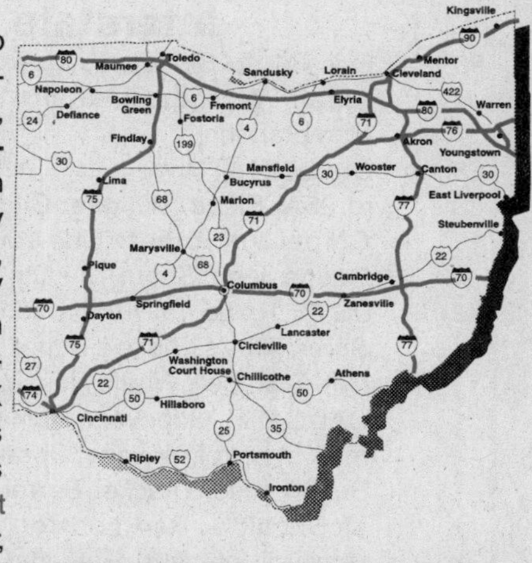

124 4th St, **E...**hwy patrol

122 OH 65, Lima, **E...gas:** Speedway/diesel, **W...gas:** Shell/diesel/24hr, **other:** Freightliner, GMC, Mack , Volvo

120 Breese Rd, Ft Shawnee, **W...other:** Ace Hardware, Harley-Davidson, NAPA/repair

118 to Cridersville, **W...gas:** Fuelmart/Subway/diesel, Speedway/diesel, **food:** Dixie Ley Diner, **other:** $General

114mm rest area both lanes, full(handicapped)facilities, phones, picnic tables, litter barrels, vending, petwalk

113 OH 67, Wapakeneta, to Uniopolis, no facilities

111 Bellefontaine St, Wahpakeneta, **E...gas:** L&G Trkstp/diesel/@, **lodging:** Day's Inn, **other:** KOA, **W...gas:** BP, Citgo, Shell, **food:** Arby's, Bob Evans, Burger King, Capt D's, Dairy Queen, El Azteca Mexican, KFC, Lamplighter Rest., Lucky Steer Rest., McDonald's, Pizza Hut, Ponderosa, Shanghai Grill, Taco Bell, Waffle House, Wendy's, **lodging:** Best Western, Holiday Inn Express, Super 8, Travelodge, **other:** Advance Parts, Family$, Neil Armstrong Museum, Radio Shack, st patrol

110 US 33, to St Marys, Bellefontaine, **E...**hwy patrol, KOA

104 OH 219, Botkins, **W...gas:** Marathon/A&W/diesel/@, Sunoco/diesel, **lodging:** Budget Host

102 OH 274, to Jackson Ctr, New Breman, no facilities

99 OH 119, Anna, to Minster, **E...gas:** Citgo/diesel, 99 Trkstp/diesel/rest./@, **food:** Apple Valley Café, **W...gas:** GA, Sunoco/diesel, **food:** Subway, Wendy's, truckwash

94 rd 25A, Sidney, no facilities

93 OH 29, Sidney, to St Marys, **W...**Lake Loramie SP, RV camping

92 OH 47, Sidney, to Versailles, **E...gas:** Shell, Speedway/diesel, DM, **food:** Arby's, Subway, Wendy's, Winger's, **other:** HOSPITAL, AutoZone, CVS Drug, $General, NAPA, PharmX Drug, Sav-A-Lot Foods, **W...gas:** BP, Citgo/diesel, Sunoco, **food:** Bob Evans, Burger King, Cazador Mexican, El Monterrey Mexican, Highmarks Rest., KFC, McDonald's, Perkins, Pizza Hut, Ponderosa, Rally's, Taco Bell, Waffle House, **lodging:** Comfort Inn, Day's Inn, Econolodge, Holiday Inn/rest., **other:** Aldi Foods, Buick/Pontiac/GMC, Chevrolet, Dodge/Plymouth, $Tree, Ford/Lincoln/Mercury, Kroger, Radio Shack, Staples, Wal-Mart SuperCtr/gas/diesel/24hr

OHIO

Interstate 75

N ↕ S

90 Fair Rd, to Sidney, **E...gas:** Sunoco/diesel, **other:** repair, **W...gas:** Marathon/DQ/diesel, **lodging:** Hampton Inn

88mm Great Miami River

83 rd 25A, Piqua, **W...gas:** Citgo/diesel, **lodging:** Red Carpet Inn, **other:** Chevrolet, Chrysler/Plymouth/Dodge/Jeep, Sherry RV Ctr, to Piqua Hist Area

82 US 36, Piqua, to Urbana, **E...gas:** BP, **food:** A&W/LJ Silver, Arby's, Blake's Buffet, China East, KFC, Pizza Hut, Taco Bell, Waffle House, Wendy's, **other:** MEDICAL CARE, Goodyear, Home Depot, Jo-Ann Fabrics, mall, st patrol, **W...gas:** Speedway, **food:** Bob Evans, Burger King, Cracker Barrel, El Sombrero Mexican, McDonald's, Red Lobster, **lodging:** Comfort Inn, Howard Johnson, Ramada Ltd, **other:** Aldi Foods, JC Penney, Sears/auto, mall

81mm rest area both lanes, full(handicapped)facilities, phones, picnic tables, litter barrels, vending

78 rd 25A, **E...**HOSPITAL

74 OH 41, Troy, to Covington, **E...gas:** BP/diesel, **food:** China Garden, LJ Silver, McDonald's, Perkins, Pizza Hut, Subway, **other:** HOSPITAL, Goodyear/auto, PharmX Drug, Radio Shack, to Hobart Arena, **W...gas:** Meijer/diesel/24hr, Shell, Speedway/diesel, **food:** Applebee's, Big Boy, Bob Evans, Burger King, Crazy H Steaks, Dairy Queen, Fazoli's, Friendly's, KFC, Penn Sta, Skyline Chili, Steak'n Shake, Tego Bay Rest., **lodging:** Fairfield Inn, Hampton Inn, Holiday Inn Express, Knight's Inn, Residence Inn, **other:** AutoZone, County Mkt Foods, CVS Drug, Goodyear, Lowe's Whse, Staples, Tire Discounters, Wal-Mart

Troy

73 OH 55, Troy, to Ludlow Falls, **E...gas:** BP, Shell, **food:** Jersey Mike's Subs, Lincoln Sq Rest., Waffle House, Wendy's, **lodging:** Econolodge, HomeTown Inn, Super 8, **other:** HOSPITAL, Country Folks Gen Store

69 rd 25A, **E...gas:** DM/Taco Bell, Marathon, Starfire/diesel, **other:** Buick/Pontiac/GMC, Chrysler/Plymouth/Dodge, Ford

68 OH 571, Tipp City, to West Milton, **E...gas:** BP/dieselmart, Shell, Speedway, **food:** Burger King, Cassano's Pizza, Chin's Chinese, Domino's, Hong Kong Kitchen, McDonald's, Subway, Taco Bell, **other:** CVS Drug, Family$, Goodyear, Honda, **W...gas:** Citgo, Speedway/diesel, **food:** Arby's, Big Boy, Tipp' O the Town Rest., Wendy's, **lodging:** Heritage Motel, Holiday Inn Express

64 Northwoods Blvd, **E...gas:** Kroger/gas

63 US 40, Vandalia, to Donnelsville, **E...gas:** Speedway/diesel, **food:** Frischer's Rest., **lodging:** Crossroads Motel, **other:** auto repair, **W...gas:** BP/diesel, Shell, Speedway, **food:** Arby's, Burger King, KFC, McDonald's, Pizza Hut, Taco Bell, Waffle House, Wendy's, **lodging:** Cross Country Inn, Travelodge(2mi), **other:** Rexall Drug

61b a I-70, E to Columbus, W to Indianapolis, to Dayton Int Airport

60 Little York Rd, Stop 8 Rd, **E...food:** Damon's, Olive Garden, Red Lobster, Subway, **lodging:** Howard Johnson, Residence Inn, **other:** Discount Tire, Nissan, McNulty RV Ctr, NTB, Volvo/BMW/VW, **W...gas:** Sunoco, **food:** Arby's, Bennigan's, Bob Evans, Cracker Barrel, Don Pablo, El Rancho Grande Mexican, Golden Corral, Joe's Crabshack, LoneStar Steaks, Max&Erma's, O'Charley's, Outback Steaks, Ryan's, Skyline Chili, SmokeyBones BBQ, Wendy's, **lodging:** Comfort Inn, Country Inn Suites, Courtyard, Day's Inn, Extended Stay America, Fairfield Inn, Knight's Inn, Motel 6, Ramada Inn, Red Roof Inn, **other:** Sam's Club/gas

58 Needmore Rd, to Dayton, **E...gas:** BP/diesel, Shell/McDonald's, **food:** Big Boy, Hardee's, **lodging:** Best Western, **other:** Goodyear/auto, Tires UnLtd/repair, to AF Museum, **W...gas:** Marathon/diesel, Speedway/diesel, Sunoco/diesel/24hr, **food:** A&W/LJ Silver, Burger King, Capt D's, Cassano's Rest., Church's, Ma's Chinese, Sam's Pizza, Waffle House, **other:** Advance Parts, Kroger/gas

57b Wagner Ford Rd, Siebenthaler Rd, Dayton, **E...gas:** Sunoco, **lodging:** Holiday Inn, **W...gas:** Speedway, **food:** Marion's Pizza, **lodging:** Day's Inn, Parkway Inn, **other:** Interstate Battery, Kelly Tire, Rite Aid, auto repair

Dayton

a Neva Rd, no facilities

56 Stanley Ave, Dayton, **E...gas:** Shell, **other:** trk repair, **W...gas:** Clark, **food:** Dragon City Chinese, GoldStar Chili, Great Steak Co, McDonald's, Rally's, Taco Bell, Wendy's, **lodging:** Dayton Motel, Plaza Motel, Royal Motel

55b a Keowee St, Dayton, **E...**Arrow Batteries, **W...gas:** BP, **lodging:** Plaza Motel

54c OH 4 N, Webster St, to Springfield, no facilities

54mm Great Miami River

54b OH 48, Main St, Dayton, **E...gas:** Chevrolet/Cadillac, **W...gas:** BP, **other:** HOSPITAL

a Grand Ave(from sb), Dayton, downtown

53b OH 49, 1st St, Salem Ave, Dayton, downtown, no facilities

a OH 49, 3rd St, downtown

52b a US 35, E to Dayton, W to Eaton

51 Edwin C Moses Blvd, Nicholas Rd, **E...**HOSPITAL, to U of Dayton, **W...gas:** BP/diesel, **food:** McDonald's, Wendy's, **lodging:** Econolodge, **other:** SunWatch Indian Village

50b a OH 741, Kettering St, Dryden Rd, **E...gas:** Citgo, **W...gas:** Sunoco/Subway/diesel, **food:** TJ's Rest., **lodging:** Holiday Inn, Super 8

47 Central Ave, W Carrollton, Moraine, **E...gas:** Sunoco, **food:** Big Boy, Quizno's, Waffle House, **other:** Honda, auto repair, transmissions, **W...gas:** Ashland, Speedway, **food:** KFC, McDonald's, Pizza Hut, Taco Bell, Wendy's, **other:** USPO

44 OH 725, to Centerville, Miamisburg, **E...gas:** BP/diesel, Shell, Speedway, **food:** Big Boy, Blimpie, Burger King, ChiChi's, Dunkin Donuts, Fuddrucker's, Golden Corral, Hardee's, KFC, La Pinata Mexican, Max&Erma's, McDonald's, Ponderosa, Red Lobster, Skyline Chili, Wendy's, **lodging:** Comfort Suites, Courtyard, Doubletree Suites, Holiday Inn, Homewood Suites, Motel 6, Residence Inn, **other:** HOSPITAL, Best Buy, Circuit City, CompUSA, Firestone/auto, Goodyear/auto, Home Depot, Honda/Nissan/Mazda, JC Penney, Kia, Lazarus, Lowe's Whse, Michael's, Mitsubishi, OfficeMax, PepBoys, Pontiac, Sears/auto, Tire Discounters, Toyota, Wal-Mart, mall,

Interstate 75

N ↕ S

W...gas: BP, Marathon, Shell, **food:** Bob Evans, Jersey Mike's Subs, LJ Silver, Perkins, **lodging:** Knight's Inn, Ramada Inn, Red Roof Inn, Signature Inn, Yankee Mill Inn, **other:** HOSPITAL, Aamco, $General, Ford

43 I-675 N, to Columbus

38 OH 73, Springboro, Franklin, **E...gas:** BP, Shell, Speedway, Sunoco/diesel, **food:** Arby's, Bob Evans, Chantrell's Rest., China Buffet, KFC/Taco Bell, LJ Silver, McDonald's, Papa John's, Perkins, Pizza Hut, Skyline Chili, Subway, Wendy's, **lodging:** Hampton Inn, Holiday Inn Express, **other:** K-Mart, Kroger, Radio Shack, **W...gas:** Exxon/diesel, Shell, **food:** Big Boy, Domino's, GoldStar Chili, **lodging:** Econolodge, Knight's Inn, **other:** AutoZone, $General, Marsh Foods, NAPA

Middletown

36 OH 123, Franklin, to Lebanon, **E...gas:** Exxon/Wendy's/diesel/24hr/@, Pilot/Subway/Pizza Hut/diesel/@, **food:** McDonald's, Waffle House, **lodging:** Super 8, **W...gas:** BP, Marathon/White Castle

32 OH 122, Middletown, **E...gas:** BP, Duke, **food:** McDonald's, Waffle House, **lodging:** Best Western, Comfort Inn, Ramada Inn, Super 8, **other:** Ford/Mercury/Lincoln, Jeep, **W...gas:** Citgo, Meijer/diesel/24hr, Speedway, **food:** Applebee's, Big Boy, Bob Evans, Cracker Barrel, El Rancho Grande Mexican, KFC, LoneStar Steaks, McDonald's, O'Charley's, Old Country Buffet, Olive Garden, Ponderosa, Schlotsky's, Shell's Rest., Sonic, Steak'n Shake, Wendy's, **lodging:** Fairfield Inn, Hawthorn Inn, Holiday Inn Express, **other:** HOSPITAL, Buick/GMC/Pontiac, Goodyear/auto, Kohl's, Kroger, Lowe's Whse, Sears/auto, Target, Tire Discounters, mall

29 OH 63, Monroe, to Hamilton, **E...gas:** Chevron/WhiteCastle/diesel, Shell/diesel, Stony Ridge Trk Plaza/.diesel/@, **food:** Burger King, GoldStar Chili, Popeye's, Waffle House, Wendy's/Tim Horton, **lodging:** Day's Inn, Stony Ridge Inn, **W...gas:** BP/diesel, Speedway, Sunoco/diesel, **food:** McDonald's, Perkins, Sara Jane's Rest., **lodging:** Hampton Inn, **other:** flea mkt

27.5mm rest area both lanes, full(handicapped)facilities, info, phone, picnic tables, litter barrels, vending, petwalk

24 OH 129 W, to Hamilton, no facilities

22 Tylersville Rd, to Mason, Hamilton, **E...gas:** BP, Marathon, Sunoco, **food:** Arby's, Bob Evans, Burger King, Donato's Pizza, Dudley's Pizza, Fazoli's, GoldStar Chili, KFC, LJ Silver, McDonald's, Perkins, Pizza Hut, Skyline Chili, Taco Bell, Waffle House, Wendy's, **lodging:** Econolodge, **other:** Firestone, GNC, Home Depot, Kroger, Radio Shack, Tires+, bank, **W...gas:** Meijer/diesel/24hr, Shell, Speedway/diesel/24hr, **food:** O'Charley's, Steak'n Shake, **other:** Tire Discounters, Wal-Mart/auto

21 Cin-Day Rd, **E...food:** Big Boy, **lodging:** Holiday Inn Express, **W...gas:** Mobil/Subway/diesel, Shell, **food:** Waffle House, Skyline Chili, **lodging:** Knight's Inn

19 Union Centre Blvd, to Fairfield, **W...gas:** BP/Subway/diesel, DM, Shell, **food:** Applebee's, Bob Evans, Buffalo Wings, Burger King, Great Steak Co, Max&Erma's, River City Grill, Roadhouse Grill, Skyline Chili, Uno Pizzaria, Wendy's, **lodging:** Marriott, Sleep Inn

16 I-275 to I-71, to I-74

15 Sharon Rd, to Sharonville, Glendale, **E...gas:** BP, Chevron, Marathon/diesel, Shell, Sunoco, **food:** BBQ, Big Boy, Bob Evans, Burbank's Rest., Pizza Hut, Skyline Chili, Waffle House, **lodging:** Best Western, Country Inn Suites, Fairfield Inn, Hampton Inn, Hilton Garden, Holiday Inn/rest., Motel 6, Ramada Inn, Red Roof Inn, Woodfield Suites, **other:** UPS, Valvoline, **W...gas:** Speedway, Sunoco, **food:** Capt D's, China Buffet, LJ Silver, McDonald's, Mexican Connection, Shogun Japanese, Subway, Taco Bell, Wendy's, **lodging:** Comfort Inn, Econolodge, Extended Stay America, Radisson, Residence Inn, Signature Inn, Super 8, **other:** Nissan

14 OH 126, to Woodlawn, Evendale, **E...**GE Plant, **W...lodging:** Quality Inn

13 Shepherd Lane, to Lincoln Heights, **E...**GE Plant, **W...food:** Taco Bell, Wendy's, **other:** Advance Parts

12 Wyoming Ave, Cooper Ave, to Lockland, no facilities

10a OH 126, Ronald Reagan Hwy, **E...**Chevrolet

b Galbraith Rd(exits left from nb), Arlington Heights

9 OH 4, OH 561, Paddock Rd, Seymour Ave, to Cincinnati Gardens

8 Towne St, Elmwood Pl(from nb), no facilities

7 OH 562, to I-71, Norwood, Cincinnati Gardens, no facilities

6 Mitchell Ave, St Bernard, **E...gas:** Marathon, Shell, Speedway/diesel, **food:** KFC/Taco Bell, Wendy's, **lodging:** Holiday Inn Express, **other:** Walgreen, to Cincinnati Zoo, to Xavier U, **W...gas:** BP/Subway/diesel, **food:** McDonald's, Rally's, **other:** Family$, Ford, Honda, Kroger, Tires+

Cincinnati

4 I-74 W, US 52, US 27 N, to Indianapolis, no facilities

3 to US 27 S, US 127 S, Hopple St, U of Cincinnati, **E...gas:** Marathon, **food:** White Castle, **lodging:** access to Day's Inn, **W...gas:** Shell, **other:** HOSPITAL

2b Harrison Ave, industrial district, **E...**Ford Trucks, **W...gas:** BP, **food:** McDonald's

a Western Ave, Liberty St(from sb)

1h Ezzard Charles Dr, **W...lodging:** Holiday Inn

g US 50W, Freeman Ave, **W...gas:** Site, **food:** Big Boy, Wendy's, **lodging:** Holiday Inn, **other:** Ford

f 7th St(from sb), downtown, **W...lodging:** Holiday Inn

e 5th St(from sb), downtown, **E...gas:** Crowne Plaza, **lodging:** Sheraton

1a I-71 N, to Cincinnati, downtown, to stadium

0mm Ohio/Kentucky state line, Ohio River

OHIO

Interstate 76

E ↕ W

Exit #	Services
	Ohio/Pennsylvania state line
	For exits 15 through 16A, see Ohio Turnpike.
60mm	I-76 eb joins Ohio TPK(toll)
57	to OH 45, Bailey Rd, to Warren, **S...**access to gas, food, lodging
54	OH 534, Lake Milton, to Newton Falls, **N...**RV camping, **S...gas:** BP, **other:** to Berlin Lake, camping
52mm	Lake Milton
48	OH 225, to Alliance, **N...**to W Branch SP, camping, **S...**to Berlin Lake
45.5mm	**rest area both lanes, full(handicapped)facilities, phone, picnic tables, litter barrels, petwalk**
43	OH 14, to Alliance, Ravenna, **N...**to W Branch SP, **S...gas:** Citgo/diesel, **other:** fireworks
38b a	OH 5, OH 44, to Ravenna, **N...gas:** BP, Speedway/diesel, **food:** Arby's, McDonald's, Wendy's, **other:** HOSPITAL, **S...gas:** DM/Subway, **food:** Burger King, Cracker Barrel, David's Rest., **other:** Giant Eagle Foods, auto repair, RV camping
33	OH 43, to Hartville, Kent, **N...gas:** Amoco, BP/diesel, **food:** Bob Evans(2mi), Burger King(2mi), Country Kitchen, Pizza Hut, **lodging:** Alden Inn, Day's Inn, Hampton Inn, Holiday Inn, Super 8, Tallyho Motel, **other:** to Kent St U, **S...gas:** Marathon, Speedway, **food:** McDonald's, Wendy's
31	rd 18, Tallmadge, **S...food:** Brimfield's Steaks(1mi), Pizza Serena
29	OH 532, Tallmadge, Mogadore, no facilities
27	OH 91, Canton Rd, Gilchrist Rd, **N...food:** Bob Evans, **S...gas:** Marathon/diesel, **food:** Hardee's, Wendy's, **lodging:** Best Western
26	OH 18, E Market St, Mogadore Rd, **N...gas:** Citgo/diesel, Shell, **S...food:** Arby's, McDonald's
25b a	Martha Ave, General St, Brittain, **N...gas:** Citgo, **other:** Goodyear
24	Arlington St, Kelly Ave, **N...**Mercedes, Toyota
23b	OH 8, Buchtell Ave, to Cuyahoga, to U of Akron
a	I-77 S, to Canton
22b	Wolf Ledges, Akron, downtown, **S...gas:** BP, **food:** McDonald's
a	Main St, Broadway, downtown
21c	OH 59 E, Dart Ave, **N...**HOSPITAL
b	Lakeshore St, Bowery St(from eb), no facilities
a	East Ave(from wb), no facilities
20	I-77 N(from eb), to Cleveland
19	Battles Ave, Kenmore Blvd, no facilities
18	I-277, US 224 E, to Canton, Barberton, no facilities
17b a	OH 619, Wooster Rd, State St, to Barberton, **S...gas:** Marathon, **other:** HOSPITAL
16	Barber Rd, **S...gas:** Pilot/diesel/@, **food:** Tomaso's Italian, **lodging:** Shamrock Motel, **other:** Chrysler/Plymouth/Jeep/Nissan/Suzuki
14	Cleve-Mass Rd, to Norton, **S...gas:** BP, Marathon(2mi), **food:** Charlie's Rest., **lodging:** Berlin's Motel(2mi)
13b a	OH 21, N to Cleveland, S to Massillon, **N...gas:** Duke
11	OH 261, Wadsworth, **N...gas:** Speedway
9	OH 94, Wadsworth, to N Royalton, **N...gas:** DM, **food:** Applebee's, Arby's, Bob Evans, Burger King, Galaxy Rest., KFC, McDonald's, Pizza Hut, Ponderosa, Taco Bell, Wendy's, **lodging:** Holiday Inn Express, Ramada Ltd, **other:** Buehler's Foods, DrugMart, Goodyear/auto, K-Mart, Radio Shack, **S...gas:** BP, Marathon, Pennzoil, Shell, Sunoco, **food:** Denny's, Rizzi's Ristorante, **lodging:** Legacy Inn, **other:** Rite Aid
7	OH 57, to Rittman, Medina, **N...gas:** Marathon/diesel, **other:** HOSPITAL, airport
6mm	weigh sta both lanes
2	OH 3, Seville, to Medina, **N...food:** Dairy Queen, Hardee's, Subway, **lodging:** Comfort Inn, **other:** Maple Lakes Camping(seasonal), **S...gas:** Citgo/diesel, Sunoco, **other:** RV camping
1	I-76 E, to Akron, US 224, **W on US 224...gas:** Pilot/Subway/diesel/24hr/@, TA/Burger King/Popeye's/diesel/24hr/@, **food:** McDonald's, **lodging:** Super 8, **other:** Blue Beacon, SpeedCo, Chippewa Valley Camping(1mi)
0mm	I-76 begins/ends on I-71, exit 209.

Akron

Interstate 77

N ↕ S

Exit #	Services
	I-77 begins/ends on I-90 exit 172, in Cleveland.
163c	I-90, E to Erie, W to Toledo
b	E 9th St, Tower City
162b	E 22nd St, E 14th St(from nb)
a	E 30th St, Woodland Ave, Broadway St(from nb), **W...**USPO
161b	I-490 W, E 55th, to I-71, **E...**HOSPITAL
a	OH 14(from nb), Broadway St
160	Pershing Ave(from nb), **W...**HOSPITAL
159b	Fleet Ave, **E...gas:** BP/Subway/diesel
a	Harvard Ave, Newburgh Heights, **W...gas:** BP/Subway/diesel/24hr, Marathon
158	Grant Ave, Cuyahoga Heights
157	OH 21, OH 17(from sb), Brecksville Rd, no facilities
156	I-480, to Youngstown, Toledo
155	Rockside Rd, to Independence, **E...gas:** Sunoco, **food:** Bob Evans, ChiChi's, Denny's, Frank&Pauly's Rest., **lodging:** Baymont Inn, Comfort Inn, Embassy Suites, Holiday Inn, Red Roof Inn, **W...gas:** BP/diesel, **food:** Applebee's, Damon's, Longhorn Steaks, **lodging:** AmeriSuites, Courtyard, Hampton Inn, Residence Inn, Sheraton
153	Pleasant Valley Rd, to Independence, 7 Hills, no facilities
151	Wallings Rd, no facilities
149	OH 82, to Broadview Heights, Brecksville, **W...gas:** BP, **food:** Domino's, Laura's Kitchen, Pazzo's Café, **lodging:** Tallyho Motel
147	to OH 21, Miller Rd(from sb), no facilities
146	I-80/Ohio Tpk, to Youngstown, Toledo

Cleveland

Interstate 77

N ↕ S

145 OH 21(from nb), **E...gas:** BP/repair, Pilot/diesel, **food:** DQ, Wendy's, **lodging:** Brushwood Motel, Hampton Inn, Holiday Inn, Super 8

144 I-271 N, to Erie

143 OH 176, to I-271 S, **E...**to Coliseum, **W...gas:** Sunoco, **food:** Arabica Café, McDonald's, Subway

141mm rest area both lanes, full(handicapped)facilities, phone, picnic tables, litter barrels, vending, petwalk

138 Ghent Rd, **2 mi E...lodging:** Hilton, Sheraton, **W...gas:** Citgo/diesel, **food:** Lanning's Rest., Vaccaro's Italian

137b a OH 18, to Fairlawn, Medina, **E...gas:** BP, Citgo, Marathon, Shell, Speedway, **food:** Applebee's, Backyard Burger, Bob Evans, ChiChi's, Chili's, Cracker Barrel, Friendly's, Golden Corral, KFC, LoneStar Steaks, Macaroni Grill, Max&Erma's, McDonald's, Olive Garden, Ruby Tuesday, Starbucks, Steak'n Shake, Taco Bell, Wendy's, **lodging:** Courtyard, Fairfield Inn, Hampton Inn, Holiday Inn, Red Roof Inn, Super 8, **other:** Acme Foods, Best Buy, Borders Books, Ford, Home Depot, Jo-Ann Fabrics, Lowe's Whse, NTB, Old Navy, Sam's Club, Staples, Wal-Mart, **W...gas:** Citgo, **food:** Amazon Café, Bennigan's, Burger King, Damon's, Don Pablo, Eastside Mario's, Fuddrucker's, Outback Steaks, Thirsty Dog Brewing Co, TGIFriday, **lodging:** Best Western, Comfort Inn, Extended Stay America, Radisson, Residence Inn, Studio+

136 OH 21S, to Massillon, no facilities

135 Cleveland-Massillon Rd(from nb), no facilities

133 Ridgewood Rd, Miller Rd, **E...gas:** Citgo/diesel, **food:** Wendy's

132 White Pond Dr, Mull Ave, **E...**Jasper's Grille, golf

131 OH 162, Copley Rd, **E...gas:** Citgo, **other:** USPO, **W...gas:** BP/diesel/24hr, Marathon/diesel, **food:** McDonald's, Pizza Hut

Akron

130 OH 261, Wooster Ave, **E...gas:** BP, Citgo, **food:** Burger King, Church's, New China, Rally's, Subway, White Castle, **other:** Advance Parts, AutoZone, **W...food:** KFC, **other:** Chevrolet, Top's Foods, Toyota, U-Haul

129 I-76 W, to I-277, to Kenmore Blvd, Barberton

21a East Ave(from nb), no facilities, I-77 S and I-76 E run together

b Lakeshore(from sb), to Bowery St, no facilities

c OH 59 E, Dart Ave, downtown, **E...**HOSPITAL

22a Main St, Broadway St, downtown, **W...**auto parts

b Grant St, Wolf Ledges, **W...gas:** BP, **food:** McDonald's

125b I-76 E, to Youngstown, I-77 and I-76 run together

a OH 8 N, to Cuyahoga Falls, U of Akron

124b Lover's Lane, Cole Ave, no facilities

a Archwood Ave, Firestone Blvd, no facilities

123b OH 764, Wilbeth Rd, **E...**to airport

a Waterloo Rd, **W...gas:** BP, **other:** Acme Foods

122b a I-277, US 224 E, to Barberton, Mogadore

120 Arlington Rd, to Green, **E...gas:** Speedway/diesel, **food:** Applebee's, Church's, Denny's, Friendly's, IHOP, Mike's Ribs, Pizza Hut, Ryan's, Waffle House, White Castle, **lodging:** Comfort Inn, Holiday Inn Express, Red Roof Inn, **other:** Home Depot, Wal-Mart/auto, **W...gas:** BP, **food:** Bob Evans, Burger King, King Buffet, McDonald's, Subway, Taco Bell, TGIFriday, Wendy's, **lodging:** Day's Inn, Econolodge, Fairfield Inn, Hampton Inn, **other:** Buick/Pontiac/GMC, Chevrolet, Honda/Mazda, Sirpilla RV Ctr

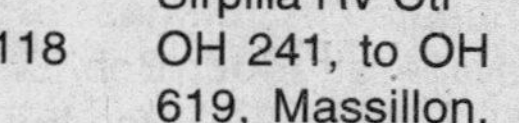

118 OH 241, to OH 619, Massillon, **E...gas:** Speedway/diesel, **food:** Subway, **W...gas:** Citgo/DM, **food:** Arby's, McDonald's, Meneche Rest., Pancho's Mexican, **lodging:** Super 8, **other:** MEDICAL CARE

113 Akron-Canton Airport, **2 mi W...other:** Clay's RV, London Chocolate Factory

111 Portage St, N Canton, **E...gas:** TA/Marathon/diesel/rest./24hr/@, Sunoco/diesel, **food:** BrewHouse Grill, Burger King, Golden Corral, KFC, TrueValue, **other:** Begg's RV Ctr, **W...gas:** BP/diesel, **food:** Carrabba's, ChuckeCheese, Cracker Barrel, Don Pablo, IHOP, Joe's Crabshack, Longhorn Steaks, McDonald's, Pizza Hut, Quizno's, Red Robin, Taco Bell, Wendy's, **lodging:** Best Western, Microtel, Motel 6, **other:** BJ's Whse, Borders Books, DrugMart, Giant Eagle Foods, Goodyear/auto, Harley-Davidson, Home Depot, Lowe's Whse, Marshall's, OfficeMax, Old Navy, Sam's Club/gas, SteinMart, Wal-Mart/auto

109b a Everhard Rd, Whipple Ave, **E...gas:** Citgo/Subway, Speedway/diesel, **food:** Blimpie, Burger King, Denny's, Fazoli's, McDonald's, Taco Bell, **lodging:** Comfort Inn, Fairfield Inn, Hampton Inn, Residence Inn, Super 8, **other:** $General, Ford, Saturn, **W...gas:** Marathon, **food:** Applebee's, Arby's, Bob Evans, Boston Mkt, Chang's Chinese, ChiChi's, Damon's, Donato's Pizza, Eastside Mario's, Eat'n Park, Friendly's, Fuddrucker's, Great Wall Chinese, HomeTown Buffet, Italian Oven, KFC, LoneStar Steaks, Manchu Café, Olive Garden, Outback Steaks, Panera Bread, Pizza Hut, Red Lobster, TGIFriday, Thirsty Dog Grill, Wendy's, **lodging:** Best Suites, Day's Inn, Holiday Inn, Red Roof Inn, Sheraton, Super 8, **other:** B Dalton's, Best Buy, Circuit City, Dillard's, Firestone/auto, Goodyear/auto, Jo-Ann Crafts, Kohl's, Marc's Foods, Michael's, NTB, Radio Shack, Sears/auto, Target, mall

107b a US 62, OH 687, Fulton Rd, to Alliance, **E...**City Park, **W...**Pro Football Hall of Fame

106 13th St NW, **E...**HOSPITAL

105b OH 172, Tuscarawas St, downtown

a 6th St SW(no EZ return from sb), **W...**HOSPITAL

104 US 30, US 62, to E Liverpool, Massillon, no facilities

103 OH 800 S, **E...gas:** Citgo, Speedway, **food:** Arby's, Subway, Taco Bell

101 OH 627, to Faircrest St, **E...gas:** Citgo/Gulliver's 77 Plaza/diesel/rest./@, Marathon/McDonald's, **food:** Wendy's

OHIO

Interstate 77

N ↕ S — Canton — Cambridge

- 99 Fohl Rd, to Navarre, **W...gas:** Shell, KOA(4mi)
- 93 OH 212, Bolivar, to Zoar, **E...gas:** Marathon, **food:** McDonald's, Pizza Hut, Wendy's, Zoar Tavern(3mi), **lodging:** Sleep Inn, **other:** Giant Eagle Foods, NAPA, to Lake Atwood Region, **W...gas:** Citgo/DQ
- 92mm weigh sta both lanes
- 87 US 250W, to Strasburg, **2 mi E...food:** Arby's, Grinders, **W...gas:** Citgo/diesel, **food:** Hardee's, Lugnut Café, Manor Rest., McDonald's, **lodging:** Ramada Ltd, Twins Motel
- **85mm rest areas both lanes, full(handicapped)facilities, info, phone, picnic tables, litter barrels, petwalk**
- 83 OH 39, OH 211, Dover, to Sugarcreek, **E...gas:** BP, Marathon/Subway, Speedway/diesel, **food:** Bob Evans, Denny's, KFC, McDonald's, Shoney's, Wendy's, **lodging:** Hospitality Inn, **other:** HOSPITAL, Ford/Chrysler/Plymouth/Dodge/Jeep, Lincoln/Mercury/Nissan, RV American, **W...gas:** Marathon/DQ, **lodging:** Comfort Inn
- 81 US 250, to Uhrichsville, OH 39, New Philadelphia, **E...gas:** Marathon, **food:** Burger King, Denny's, El San Jose Mexican, Hong Kong Buffet, LJ Silver, McDonald's, Pizza Hut, Taco Bell, Texas Roadhouse, **lodging:** Budget Inn, Hampton Inn, Holiday Inn, Day's Inn, Motel 6, Schoenbrunn Inn, Super 8, Travelodge, **other:** Advance Parts, Aldi Foods, $General, Wal-Mart SuperCtr/24hr, **W...gas:** Eagle/diesel/rest./@
- 73 OH 751, to rd 21, Stone Creek, **W...gas:** Marathon
- 65 US 36, Port Washington, Newcomerstown, **W...gas:** BP, Duke/diesel/rest., Marathon/Wendy's/24hr, **food:** McDonald's, **lodging:** Hampton Inn, Super 8
- 64mm Tuscarawas River
- 54 OH 541, rd 831, Kimbolton, to Plainfield, **W...gas:** BP, **food:** Jackie's Rest.
- 47 US 22, to Cadiz, Cambridge, **E...**to Salt Fork SP(6mi), lodging, RV camping, **W...gas:** BP/repair, **other:** HOSPITAL, to Glass Museum, info
- 46b a US 40, Cambridge, to Old Washington, **W...gas:** BP/24hr, Exxon/Wendy's/diesel, FuelMart/diesel, Speedway/24hr, **food:** Burger King, Hunan Chinese, Lee's Rest., LJ Silver, McDonald's, Wally's Pizza, **lodging:** Long's Motel, **other:** Riesbeck's Food/deli
- 44b a I-70, E to Wheeling, W to Columbus
- 41 OH 209, OH 821, Byesville, **W...gas:** BP/diesel, **food:** McDonald's, **other:** IGA Foods, Family$
- **39mm rest area nb, full(handicapped)facilities, phone, picnic tables, litter barrels, petwalk, vending**
- 37 OH 313, Buffalo, **E...gas:** BP/Subway, Duke/diesel, **food:** Buffalo Grill, **other:** truck repair, to Senecaville Lake
- **36mm rest area sb, full(handicapped)facilities, phone, picnic tables, litter barrels, petwalk, vending**
- 28 OH 821, Belle Valley, **E...gas:** Sunoco/diesel, **food:** Marianne's Rest., **other:** USPO, to Wolf Run SP, RV camping
- 25 OH 78, Caldwell, **E...gas:** BP, Pilot/Arby's/diesel/24hr, Sunoco/Subway/diesel, **food:** Dairy Queen, Lori's Rest., McDonald's, **lodging:** Best Western, **other:** Chevrolet/Pontiac/Buick

Marietta

- 16 OH 821, Macksburg, **E...food:** MiniMart Rest., **other:** antiques
- 6 OH 821, to Devola, **E...gas:** Exxon, **W...**HOSPITAL, BP/diesel/LP, RV camping
- **3mm rest area nb, full(handicapped)facilities, info, phone, vending, picnic tables, litter barrels, petwalk**
- 1 OH 7, to OH 26, Marietta, **E...**GoMart/diesel/24hr, Dairy Queen, Damon's, Ryan's, Comfort Inn, Econolodge, Holiday Inn, Aldi Foods, Chevrolet/Cadillac, Chrysler/Plymouth, Dodge, Ford, IGA Foods, Harley-Davidson, Lowe's Whse, Pontiac/Buick, Toyota, Wal-Mart SuperCtr/24hr, **W...gas:** BP/diesel, Duke/diesel, Exxon, Marathon/diesel, Speedway, **food:** Applebee's, Bob Evans, Burger King, Capt D's, Chicago Pizza, Empire Buffet, LJ Silver, McDonald's, Napoli's Pizza, Papa John's, Pizza Hut, Rax, Shoney's, Subway, Taco Bell, Wendy's, **lodging:** Hampton Inn, Knight's Inn, Super 8, **other:** MEDICAL CARE, AutoZone, CVS Drug, Food4Less, Jo-Ann Crafts, K-Mart, Kroger/24hr, museum, st patrol
- 0mm Ohio/West Virginia state line, Ohio River

Interstate 80

E ↕ W

Exit #	Services
237mm	Ohio/Pennsylvania state line
237mm	**Welcome Ctr wb, full(handicapped)facilities, info, phone, picnic tables, litter barrels, vending, petwalk**
234b a	US 62, OH 7, Hubbard, to Sharon, PA, **N...gas:** Flying J/Country Mkt/diesel/24hr/@, Shell/diesel/rest./motel/24hr, **food:** Arby's, Burger King, McDonald's, **other:** Blue Beacon, RV camping(2mi), tire repair
232mm	weigh sta wb
229	OH 193, Belmont Ave, to Youngstown, **N...gas:** Speedway, **food:** Handel's Ice Cream, Sta Sq Rest., **lodging:** Belmont Inn, Hampton Inn, Holiday Inn, Knight's Inn, Ramada Inn, Super 8, TallyHo-tel, **other:** MEDICAL CARE, **S...gas:** Amoco/24hr, Shell, **food:** Arby's, Armando's Italian, Bob Evans, Burger King, Cancun Mexican, Denny's, Ianazone's Pizza, KFC, LJ Silver, McDonald's, Papa John's, Perkins/24hr, Pizza Hut, Sonic, Subway, Taco Bell, Treacher's Rest., West Fork Roadhouse, Youngstown Crab Rest., **lodging:** Comfort Inn, Econolodge, **other:** Advance Parts, Firestone/auto, Giant Eagle Foods, Goodyear/auto, PharMor Drug
228	OH 11, to Warren, Ashtabula, no facilities
227	US 422, Girard, Youngstown, **N...gas:** Shell/diesel/24hr, **food:** Burger King, HotDog Shoppe, Subway
226	Salt Springs Rd, to I-680(from wb), **N...gas:** BP/diesel, Sheetz/diesel/24hr, **food:** Blimpie, McDonald's, **S...gas:** Mr Fuel/diesel/24hr, Petro/Mobil/diesel/rest./24hr/@, Pilot/Arby's/diesel/24hr/@, **other:** Blue Beacon, SpeedCo, diesel repair
224b	I-680(from eb), to Youngstown
a	OH 11 S, to Canfield
223	OH 46, to Niles, **N...gas:** Citgo/diesel, Pilot/Hardee's/diesel/24hr/@, **food:** Bob Evans, Burger King, Country Kitchen, IceHouse Rest., **lodging:** Day's Inn, Howard Johnson, **S...gas:** BP/diesel, FuelMart/diesel, Sheetz/

Interstate 80

24hr, Sunoco/Subway, TA/diesel/rest./24hr/@, **food:** Arby's, Cracker Barrel, McDonald's, Perkins, Taco Bell, Wendy's, **lodging:** Best Western, Econolodge, Hampton Inn, Motel 6, Sleep Inn, Super 8, **other:** Blue Beacon, Freightliner/24hr

221mm Meander Reservoir

219mm I-80 wb joins Ohio Tpk(toll)

For I-80 exits 1 through 14, see Ohio Turnpike.

Interstate 90

Exit # Services

243mm Ohio/Pennsylvania state line

242mm Welcome Ctr/weigh sta wb, full(handicapped)facilities, info, phone, picnic tables, litter barrels, petwalk

241 OH 7, Conneaut, to Andover, **N...food:** Burger King, McDonald's(2mi), **lodging:** Day's Inn, **other:** HOSPITAL, AutoZone, CVS Drug, Giant Eagle/deli, K-Mart, Evergreen RV Park, **S...food:** Beef&Beer Café

235 OH 84, OH 193, N Kingsville, to Youngstown, **N...gas:** Citgo/diesel, **lodging:** Dav-Ed Motel, **other:** Village Green Camping, **S...gas:** Shell/diesel/24hr, Speedway/Subway/diesel, TA/BP/Burger King/diesel/24hr/@, **food:** Jonathan's Family Dining, **lodging:** Kingsville Motel

228 OH 11, to Ashtabula, Youngstown, N...HOSPITAL(4mi)

223 OH 45, to Ashtabula, **N...gas:** Flying J/diesel/LP/rest./24hr/@, **food:** Mr C's Rest., **lodging:** Comfort Inn, Holiday Inn Express, Travelodge, **other:** Buccaneer Camping, **S...gas:** BP/rest., Pilot/Subway/diesel, **food:** Burger King, McDonald's, **lodging:** Hampton Inn

218 OH 534, Geneva, **N...gas:** BP, Sunoco, **food:** Geneva Rest., KFC, Lighthouse Grill, McDonald's, Season's Grille, Wendy's, **lodging:** Howard Johnson, **other:** HOSPITAL, Goodyear, truck service/diesel, KOA(8mi), Indian Creek Camping, to Geneva SP, **S...gas:** KwikFill/diesel/24hr, **food:** Applewood Rest.

212 OH 528, Madison, to Thompson, **N...food:** JC's Diner, McDonald's, Potbelly's Rest., **S...gas:** Marathon, repair/radiator/towing, **other:** Heritage Hills Camping(4mi)

205 Vrooman Rd, **S...gas:** BP/diesel, **food:** Capp's Eatery(1mi)

200 OH 44, to Painesville, Chardon, **N...**HOSPITAL, **S...gas:** BP/Subway/diesel, **food:** McDonald's, Red Hawk Grille, **lodging:** Quail Hollow Resort, **other:** hwy patrol

198mm rest area both lanes, full(handicapped)facilities, phone, picnic tables, litter barrels, vending, petwalk

193 OH 306, Kirtland, to Mentor, **N...gas:** BP, Shell, Speedway, **food:** Cooker, LJ Silver, McDonald's, Ponderosa, **lodging:** Motel 6, Super 8, **S...gas:** Marathon, **food:** Bob Evans, Burger King, Dino's Rest., Roadhouse Steaks, **lodging:** Day's Inn/café, Red Roof Inn, Travelodge, **other:** HOSPITAL

190.5mm weigh sta eb

190 Express Lane to I-271(from wb)

189 OH 91, to Willoughby, Willoughby Hills, **N...gas:** BP/diesel, Shell/24hr, **food:** Bob Evans, Café Europa, Damon's, Peking Chef, **lodging:** Courtyard, Fairfield Inn, Ramada Inn, Travelodge, **other:** HOSPITAL, CVS Drug, Walgreen, **S...food:** Fazio's Italian

188 I-271 S, to Akron

187 OH 84, Bishop Rd, to Wickliffe, Willoughby, **S...gas:** BP/diesel, Shell, **food:** Dairymart, Bakers Square, Burger King, Friendly's, Manhattan Deli, McDonald's, Quizno's, Sbarro's, Subway, TCBY, **lodging:** Holiday Inn, **other:** HOSPITAL, CVS Drug, Chevrolet, Giant Eagle Foods, Marc's Foods, Mazda/VW, OfficeMax, Sam's Club

186 US 20, Euclid Ave, **N...gas:** Sunoco, **food:** Allegro Rest., Denny's, Joe's Crabshack, McDonald's, **lodging:** Hampton Inn, Sheraton, **other:** DENTIST, Dodge/Saturn/Subaru, Ford, **S...gas:** Shell, **food:** Arby's, KFC, Pizza Hut, Popeye's, R-Ribs, Taco Bell, Wendy's, Zanzibar Rest., **other:** CVS Drug, Firestone/auto, K-Mart

185 OH 2 E(exits left from eb), to Painesville

184b OH 175, E 260th St, **N...gas:** Shell/autocare, **S...other:** Ryder Trucks, tires, transmissions

a Babbitt Rd, same as 183, **S...gas:** BP, **other:** K-Mart

183 222nd St, **N...**Pontiac, **S...gas:** Sunoco/diesel/24hr, **other:** Forest City Parts

182b a E 200th St, E 185th St, **N...gas:** BP/24hr, **other:** Home Depot, Honda, **S...gas:** BP, Citgo/diesel, Marathon, Shell/24hr, Speedway, Sunoco, **food:** Shotz Grill, **other:** HOSPITAL

181b a E 156th St, **N...gas:** Marathon, **S...gas:** BP/24hr

180b a E 140th St, E 152nd St, no facilities

179 OH 283 E, to Lake Shore Blvd, no facilities

178 Eddy Rd, to Bratenahl, no facilities

177 University Circle, MLK Dr, **N...other:** Cleveland Lake SP, **S...other:** HOSPITAL, Rockefeller Park

176 E 72nd St, no facilities

175 E 55th St, Marginal Rds, **S...**AAA

174b OH 2 W, downtown, to Lakewood, Rock&Roll Hall of Fame

a Lakeside Ave

173c Superior Ave, St Clair Ave, downtown, **N...gas:** BP

b Chester Ave, **S...gas:** BP

a Prospect Ave(from wb), downtown

172d Carnegie Ave, downtown, **S...food:** Burger King, **other:** Cadillac

c b E 9th St, **S...other:** HOSPITAL, to Cleveland St U

a I-77 S, to Akron

171b a US 422, OH 14, Broadway St, Ontario St, **N...**downtown, **lodging:** Hilton Garden, **other:** to Stadium

OHIO

Interstate 90

E ↕ W

170c b I-71 S, to I-490
a US 42, W 25th St, **N...gas:** Sunoco, **S...gas:** Citgo
169 W 44th St, W 41st St, **N...**HOSPITAL
167b a OH 10, West Blvd, 98th St, to Lorain Ave, **N...**HOSPITAL, **S...gas:** BP/diesel
166 W 117th St, **N...gas:** BP/diesel, Shell, **other:** Forest City Parts, Home Depot, **S...food:** Chinese Cuisine, Church's/White Castle
165 W 140th St, Bunts Rd, Warren Rd, **N...**HOSPITAL
164 McKinley Ave, to Lakewood, no facilities
162 Hilliard Blvd(from wb), to Westway Blvd, Rocky River, **S...gas:** BP, Shell
161 OH 2, OH 254(from eb, no EZ return), Detroit Rd, Rocky River, no facilities
160 Clague Rd(from wb), **S...other:** HOSPITAL, same as 159
159 OH 252, Columbia Rd, **N...gas:** Speedway, **food:** Carrabba's, Cooker Grill, Outback Steaks, **lodging:** Courtyard, Cross Country Inn, TownePlace Suites, **other:** MEDICAL CARE, DENTIST, **S...gas:** BP, Shell, **food:** Friendly's, Houlihan's, KFC, McDonald's, Taco Bell, **other:** CVS Drug, Mueller Tire, Tops Foods
156 Crocker Rd, Bassett Rd, Westlake, Bay Village, **N...gas:** BP, Shell, **food:** Wallaby's Café, **lodging:** Holiday Inn, Red Roof Inn, Residence Inn, **S...gas:** Marathon/diesel, **food:** Applebee's, Bob Evans, Max&Erma's, McDonald's, Subway, TGIFriday, Wendy's, **lodging:** Hampton Inn, **other:** HOSPITAL, Borders Books, CVS Drug, Giant Eagle, GNC, Jo-Ann Crafts, K-Mart, Marc's Foods, OfficeMax, Radio Shack, mall
153 OH 83, Avon Lake, **N...gas:** Sunoco/diesel, **food:** Perkins, **2 mi N...gas:** Speedway, **food:** Burger King, McDonald's, Wendy's, **S...other:** Kohl's, Marshall's, Michael's, Old Navy, Target
151 OH 611, Avon, **N...gas:** BP/Subway/diesel, Pilot/diesel, **food:** McDonald's, **other:** Avon RV, Goodyear/auto, RV/marine storage, **S...gas:** BJ's Whse/gas
148 OH 254, Sheffield, Avon, **N...gas:** Clark, **other:** Ford, **S...gas:** BP, Speedway, **food:** Arby's, Burger King, Cracker Barrel, Donato's Pizza, KFC, Marco's Pizza, McDonald's, Pizza Hut, Ruby Tuesday, Subway, Taco Bell, **other:** Aldi Foods, CarCare USA, CVS Drug, Giant Eagle, K-Mart
147mm Black River
145 OH 57, to Lorain, Elyria, I-80/Ohio Tpk E, **N...food:** Burger King, Cracker Barrel(2mi), **other:** HOSPITAL, Goodyear, U-Haul, **S...gas:** BP/McDonald's/diesel, Speedway, **food:** Applebee's, Arby's, Blimpie, Bob Evans, Burger King, Country Kitchen, Denny's, Fazoli's, Ground Round, HomeTown Buffet, LoneStar Steaks, Mtn Jack's Rest., Pizza Hut, Red Lobster, Subway, SuperKing Buffet, Wendy's, **lodging:** Best Western, Comfort Inn, Day's Inn, Econolodge, Holiday Inn, Howard Johnson, Knight's Inn, Super 8, **other:** Best Buy, Dillard's, Firestone/auto, Goodyear/auto, JC Penney, Jo-Ann Fabrics, K-Mart, Lowe's Whse, Michael's, NTB, OfficeMax, Sam's Club, Sears/auto, Staples, Wal-Mart/auto, mall
144 OH 2 W(from wb, no return), to Sandusky, **1 mi N...**Broadway Ave, **gas:** Marathon, Shell/24hr, **food:** McDonald's, **other:** HOSPITAL
143 I-90 wb joins Ohio Tpk

For wb exits to Ohio/Indiana state line, see Ohio Turnpike.

Interstate 270(Columbus)

Columbus

Exit # Services
55 I-71, to Columbus, Cincinnati
52b a US 23, High St, Circleville, **N...gas:** Speedway/diesel, Sunoco/Blimpie, Thornton/diesel, **food:** A&W/KFC, Arby's, Bob Evans, LJ Silver, McDonald's, Pizza Hut, Ponderosa, Roadhouse Grill, Skyline Chili, Wendy's, **other:** Kroger, Lowe's, Wal-Mart, **S...gas:** BP/diesel, **lodging:** Budget Inn, **other:** Kioto Downs
49 Alum Creek Dr, **N...gas:** Duke/diesel, Sunoco/diesel, **food:** A&W/KFC, Donato's Pizza, Subway, **S...gas:** BP/diesel, **food:** Arby's, McDonald's, Taco Bell, Wendy's, **lodging:** Comfort Inn, Sleep Inn
46b a US 33, Bexley, Lancaster, no facilities
43b a I-70, E to Cambridge, W to Columbus
41b a US 40, **E...gas:** BP, Shell, **food:** Bob Evans, Boston Mkt, Hooters, McDonald's, Outback Steaks, Rally's, Steak'n Shake, Texas Roadhouse, **other:** Walgreen, **W...gas:** Mobil, Speedway, **food:** Fuddruckers, Golden Corral, Hunan Chinese, LoneStar Steaks
39 OH 16, Broad St, **E...gas:** Meijer/diesel, Speedway/diesel, **food:** Arby's, Chipotle Grill, Church's, Quizno's, Waffle House, White Castle, **lodging:** Country Inn Suites, **other:** HOSPITAL, **W...gas:** Shell, **food:** Applebee's, **lodging:** Ramada Inn
37 OH 317, Hamilton Rd, **E...gas:** BP/diesel, Marathon, Speedway/diesel, Sunoco, **food:** Big Boy, Bob Evans, Burger King, Damon's, Hickory House Rest., KFC, McDonald's, **lodging:** Candlewood Suites, Holiday Inn Express, SpringHill Suites, **other:** Firestone, **W...lodging:** Comfort Inn, Concourse Hotel, Cross Country Inn, Hampton Inn
35b a I-670W, US 62, **E...gas:** Speedway/diesel, **food:** City BBQ, McDonald's, Tim Horton, **other:** CVS Drug, **W...**I-670
33 no facilities
32 Morse Rd, **E...gas:** Citgo/DM, Speedway/diesel, **food:** Donato's Pizza, **other:** Toyota, **W...gas:** BP, Shell, **food:** Applebee's, Cooker, HomeTown Buffet, McDonald's, Pizza Hut/Taco Bell, Wendy's, **lodging:** Extended Stay America, **other:** Best Buy, BMW, Circuit City, Jo-Ann Fabrics, Lowe's Whse, Sam's Club, Target, Wal-Mart SuperCtr/24hr, mall
30b a OH 161 E to New Albany, W to Worthington
29 OH 3, Westerville, **E...gas:** BP/diesel, **food:** Applebee's, Arby's, Chipotle Mexican, McDonald's, Fazoli's, Pizza Hut, Tim Horton, **lodging:** Cross Country Inn, Knight's Inn, **other:** CarQuest, Firestone/auto, Kroger, **W...gas:** Shell, Speedway/diesel, Sunoco/diesel, **other:** Aldi Foods
27 OH 710, Cleveland Ave, **N...gas:** Speedway, **food:** Wendy's, **lodging:** Signature Inn, **S...gas:** Sunoco, **food:** Bob Evans, McDonald's, O'Charley's, Steak'n Shake, TGIFriday, Tim Horton, **lodging:** Embassy Suites, Quality Inn, **other:** Home Depot
26 I-71, S to Columbus, N to Cleveland

Interstate 270

E
W

23 US 23, Worthington, **N...gas:** Speedway, **food:** Alexander's, Bob Evans, Champ's Grill, Chipotle Mexican, El Acapulco, Fuddruckers, Gilbert's Steaks, Panera Bread, Ruth's Chris Steaks, **lodging:** AmeriSuites, Courtyard, Extended Stay America, Microtel, Motel 6, Homewood Suites, Red Roof Inn, Residence Inn, Sheraton, **S...gas:** BP, **food:** McDonald's

22 OH 315, no facitlites

20 Sawmill Rd, **N...gas:** BP, Marathon/diesel, **food:** McDonald's, Olive Garden, Taco Bell, Wendy's, **other:** Buick/Pontiac/GMC, Ford, Lincoln-Mercury, Mazda, NTB, Tire Kingdom, **S...gas:** Shell, Speedway, Sunoco, **food:** Applebee's, BajaFresh, Bob Evans, Boston Mkt, Burger King, Chili's, Don Pablo, Fuddrucker's, Golden Corral, Joe's Crabshack, KFC, Longhorn Steaks, Red Lobster, Ruby Tuesday, **lodging:** Hampton Inn, **other:** Barnes&Noble, Borders Books, Cadillac, Circuit City, Infiniti, Lowe's Whse, SteinMart, Toyota

17b a US 33, Dublin-Granville Rd, **E...gas:** Marathon, Sunoco, **food:** Bob Evans, Cooker, McDonald's, **lodging:** Embassy Suites, Wyndham Garden, **other:** BMW, CVS Drug, Kroger

15 Tuttle Crossing Blvd, **E...gas:** BP, Mobil, **food:** Bob Evans, Boston Mkt, Chang's Chinese, Cozymel's, Longhorn Steaks, Macaroni Grill, McDonald's, Pizza Hut/Taco Bell, Steak'n Shake, Wendy's, **lodging:** AmeriSuites, Baymont Inn, Drury Inn, Homewood Suites, Marriott, Staybridge Suites, Wellesley Inn, **other:** JC Penney, Sears/auto, mall, **W...gas:** Exxon/Subway/diesel, Shell, **food:** Uno Pizzaria, **other:** Best Buy, Wal-Mart/auto

13 Cemetery Rd, Fishinger Rd, **E...gas:** Shell, **food:** Burger King, Chili's, Damon's, Dave&Buster's, HomeTown Buffet, KFC, KrispyKreme, LoneStar Steaks, Skyline Chili, Spaghetti's, TGIFriday, **lodging:** Comfort Suites, Homewood Suites, **other:** Big Bear Foods, Lowe's Whse, NTB, Saturn, **W...gas:** BP, Mobil, Speedway, Sunoco, **food:** Bob Evans, Max&Erma's, McDonald's, Roadhouse Grill, Tim Horton, Wendy's, **lodging:** Hampton Inn, Motel 6, **other:** Nissan

10 Roberts Rd, **E...gas:** Marathon, **food:** Subway, Tim Horton, Wendy's, **W...gas:** Speedway, **food:** Waffle House, **lodging:** Holiday Inn, Royal Inn, Super 8, **other:** Kroger/gas

8 I-70, E to Columbus, W to Indianapolis

7 US 40, Broad St, **E...gas:** BP, Shell, Speedway, **food:** Arby's, Bob Evans, Boston Mkt, ChiChi's, TJ's Grill, Tumbleweed Grill, Wendy's, **other:** Chevrolet, Firestone/auto, NTB, Sears/auto, Staples, **W...gas:** Speedway/diesel, **food:** Arby's, Papa John's, Waffle House, **lodging:** Holiday Inn Express, **other:** Home Depot

5 Georgesville, **E...gas:** Citgo, Sunoco/diesel, **W...gas:** Sunoco, Thornton, **food:** Applebee's, Arby's, Bob Evans, Buffalo Wings, DQ, Fazoli's, LoneStar Steaks, McDonald's, O'Charley's, Pizzaria Uno, Red Lobster, Steak'n Shake, Tim Horton, Wendy's, White Castle, **other:** Hyundai/Isuzu, Kroger, Lowe's Whse, Toyota

2 US 62, OH 3, Grove City, **N...gas:** BP, **S...gas:** Shell, Speedway, Sunoco, **food:** Big Boy, Burger King, McDonald's, Tim Horton/Wendy's, Waffle House, **lodging:** Knight's Inn

0mm I-71.

Interstate 271(Cleveland)

N
S

Exit # Services

38mm I-271 begins/ends on I-90, exit 188.

36 Wilson Mills Rd, Mayfield, Highland Hts, **E...lodging:** Holiday Inn, **W...gas:** BP, Sunoco/diesel, Home Depot

34 US 322, Mayfield Rd, **E...gas:** BP, **other:** Giant Eagle Food, Walgreen, **W...food:** Bob Evans, Longhorn Steaks, McDonald's, Ponderosa, **lodging:** Baymont Inn, **other:** HOSPITAL, Best Buy

32 Brainerd Rd, Cedar Rd, **E...food:** Alexander's Rest., Champ's Grill

29 US 422 W, OH 87, Chagrin Blvd, Harvard Rd, **E...gas:** Gulf, **food:** Uno Café, **lodging:** Holiday Inn, Homestead Suites, Travelodge, **W...gas:** Shell, **lodging:** Embassy Suites, Marriott, Radisson

28 OH 175, Richmond Rd, Emery Rd, **E...gas:** BP, **food:** Country Kitchen, **other:** HOSPITAL, Lowe's Whse, **W...other:** BJ's Whse

27b I-480 W, no facilities

26 Rockside Rd, **E...gas:** Sunoco, **food:** Perkins, **lodging:** Red Roof Inn, **other:** Lowe's Whse

23 OH 14 W, Forbes Rd, Broadway Ave, **E...gas:** Sunoco, **food:** McDonald's, Pizza Hut, Subway, Taco Bell, Wendy's, **lodging:** Holiday Inn Express, **other:** OfficeMax, Sam's Club, **W...gas:** BP, **other:** HOSPITAL

21 I-480 E, OH 14 E(from sb), to Youngstown, no facilities

Macedonia

19 OH 82, Macedonia, **E...gas:** Speedway, **W...gas:** Shell, Sunoco, **food:** Arby's, Burger King, Dairy Queen, Little Caesar's, Outback Steaks, Pizza Hut, Taco Bell, Wendy's, **other:** CVS Drug, Giant Eagle Food, Home Depot, K-Mart/auto, Top's Foods

18 OH 8, Boston Hts, to Akron, **E...gas:** BP/Subway, Shell/diesel, Speedway, **food:** BBQ, Bob Evans, Denny's, **lodging:** Baymont Inn, Country Inn Suites, Knight's Inn, Motel 6, Travelodge, **W...food:** Applebee's, Ground Round, KFC, McDonald's, **other:** Kohl's, Wal-Mart/auto

12 OH 303, Richfield, Peninsula, no facilities

10 I-77, to I-80, OH Tpk(from nb), to Akron, Cleveland

9 I-77 S, OH 176(from nb), to Richfield, **E...gas:** Sunoco

8mm rest area both lanes, full(handicapped)facilities, phone, picnic tables, litter barrels, petwalk

3 OH 94, to I-71 N, Wadsworth, N Royalton, **W...gas:** Marathon

0mm I-271 begins/ends on I-71, exit 220.

OHIO

Interstate 475(Toledo)

N ↕ S

Toledo

Exit # Services
20 I-75. I-475 begins/ends on I-75, exit 204.
19 Jackman Rd, Central Ave, **S...gas:** Shell, **other:** HOSPITAL
18b Douglas Rd(from wb), no facilities
a OH 51 W, Monroe St, no facilities
17 Secor Rd, **N...gas:** BP, Shell/diesel, **food:** Applebee's, Betsy Ross' Rest., Bob Evans, Boston Mkt, Burger King, KFC, **other:** MEDICAL CARE, Best Buy, Kroger, PharmX Drug, Walgreen, radiators, RV/auto repair, transmissions, **S...gas:** BP, **food:** Big Boy, Krispy Kreme, LJ Silver, McDonald's, Pizza Hut, Wendy's, **lodging:** Clarion Hotel, Comfort Inn, **other:** FoodTown, Home Depot, U of Toledo
16 Talmadge Rd(from wb, no return), **N...gas:** BP/diesel, Speedway, **food:** Arby's, ChiChi's, Panera Bread, **other:** JC Penney, Marshall Field, mall
15 Talmadge Rd(from eb, no return), no facilities
14 US 23 N, to Ann Arbor, no facilities
13 US 20, OH 120, Central Ave, **E...gas:** Speedway, **food:** Big Boy, Bob Evans, Burger King, McDonald's, Rally's, BMW, Daewoo, **other:** Ford, Honda, Isuzu, Kia, K-Mart, Lexus, Mitsubishi, Nissan, Saturn, Subaru, Toyota, **W...gas:** BP, Speedway
8b a OH 2, **E...gas:** BP/diesel, **food:** Don Pablo, Texas Roadhouse, **lodging:** Extended Stay America, Knight's Inn, Red Roof Inn, Residence Inn, **other:** HOSPITAL, Home Depot, Kohl's, Old Navy, to OH Med Coll **W...gas:** BP, Shell, Speedway, Sunoco/diesel, **food:** Arby's, Big Boy, Bob Evans, Boston Mkt, Burger King, Chili's, Cooker, Mancino's Pizza, McDonald's, New China, Pizza Hut, Rally's, Subway, Wendy's, **lodging:** Courtyard, Cross Country Inn, Fairfield Inn, **other:** Firestone/auto, Kroger, OfficeMax, Sam's Club/gas, Sears/auto, Target
6 Dussel Dr, Salisbury Rd, to I-80-90/tpk, **E...gas:** Barney's, BP, Speedway, **food:** Applebee's, Arby's, Burger King, Hop's Grill, Marie's Diner, Max&Erma's, McDonald's, Panera Bread, Wendy's, Subway, **lodging:** Country Inn Suites, Cross Country Inn, Fairfield Inn, Hampton Inn, Red Roof Inn, Studio+, Super 8, **W...gas:** BP, **food:** Bob Evans, Briarfield Café, **lodging:** AmeriHost
4 US 24, to Maumee, Napolean, **N...other:** HOSPITAL, Toledo Zoo
3mm Maumee River
2 OH 25, Perrysburg, to Bowling Green, **N...gas:** BP/diesel, Citgo/diesel, Shell, **food:** Café Marie, Charlie's Rest., Gino's Pizza, McDonald's, Papa John's, Subway, Wendy's, **other:** CVS Drug, Farmer Jack's Foods, Goodyear/auto, Young's RV Ctr, **S...gas:** Speedway/diesel, **food:** Bob Evans, Waffle House, **lodging:** Red Carpet Inn
0mm I-475 begins/ends on I-75, exit 192.

Ohio Turnpike

E ↕ W

Youngstown

Exit # Services
241mm Ohio/Pennsylvania state line
239mm toll plaza, phone
237mm Mahoning Valley Travel Plaza eb, Glacier Hills Travel Plaza wb, Sunoco/diesel/24hr, McDonald's, gifts, phone
235 I-680(from wb), to Youngstown
232 OH 7, to Boardman, Youngstown, **N...food:** DQ, Smaldino's Family Rest., **lodging:** Budget Inn, Day's Inn, Econolodge, Microtel, North Lima Inn, Super 8, **S...gas:** Shell/diesel, Speedway/diesel, **food:** Road House Diner, **lodging:** Davis Motel, Rodeway Inn, **other:** truck repair
218 I-80 E, to Youngstown, Niles, OH Tpk runs with I-76 eb, I-80 wb.
216 Lordstown(from wb), **N...**GM Plant
215 Lordstown(from eb), **N...**GM Plant, **S...gas:** BP/diesel
210mm Mahoning River
209 OH 5, to Warren, **N...gas:** ShortStop/diesel/repair(3mi), **lodging:** Budget Lodge, **S...gas:** Marathon/diesel/rest./repair, **lodging:** Rodeway Inn, **other:** RV camping
197mm Portage Service Plaza wb, Bradys Leap Service Plaza eb, Sunoco/diesel/24hr, FoodCourt, McDonald's, gifts, phone
193 OH 44, to Ravenna, no facilities
191mm Cuyahoga River
187 OH 14 S, I-480, to Streetsboro, **S...gas:** Sheetz/24hr, **food:** Ruby Tueday, **lodging:** Comfort Inn, Fairfield Inn, Hampton Inn, Palms Motel, TownePlace Suites, Wingate Inn, **other:** Defer Tire, Firestone/auto, Home Depot, mall **1 mi S...gas:** BP, Clark, DM/24hr, Shell, **food:** Arby's, Big Boy, Bob Evans, Brown Derby Roadhouse, Burger King, Burger Central, DQ, Denny's, Domino's, Golden Flame Steaks, KFC, LJ Silver, McDonald's, Mr Hero, New Peking Chinese, Perkins, Pizza Hut, Rally's, Subway, Taco Bell, **lodging:** Best Western, Holiday Inn Express, Microtel, Starlite Motel, Super 8, Wendy's, **other:** CVS Drug, $General, K-Mart, Save-A-Lot Foods, Staples, Wal-Mart, to Kent St U
180 OH 8, to I-90 E, **N...gas:** Marathon, **food:** MoonBeam's Burgers, **lodging:** Comfort Inn, Holiday Inn, **S...gas:** BP/Subway/diesel, Starfire Express, **other:** to Cuyahoga Valley NRA
177mm Cuyahoga River
173 OH 21, to I-77, **N...gas:** Clark, **food:** My Place Rest., **lodging:** Howard Johnson, Scottish Inn, **other:** tires, **S...gas:** BP/repair, Speedway/diesel, **food:** Dairy Queen, Richfield Family Rest., **lodging:** Brushwood Motel, Holiday Inn, Super 8
170mm Towpath Service Plaza eb, Great Lakes Service Plaza wb, gas: Sunoco/diesel/24hr, food: FoodCourt, Panera Bread, Pizza Hut, Wendy's, other: gifts, phone
161 US 42, to I-71, Strongsville, **N on US 42...gas:** Marathon/diesel, Shell, **food:** DairyMart, Jennifer's Rest., Mad Cactus Mexican, **lodging:** Colony Motel, Day's Inn, Extended Stay America, La Siesta Motel, Metrick's Motel, Murphy's Motel, Village Motel, **other:** Home Depot, Wal-Mart, **S on US 42...food:** Burger King, Dairy Queen, KFC, Nino's Italian, Olympia Treats, **lodging:** Elmhaven Motel, **other:** Dodge, NAPA, Staples

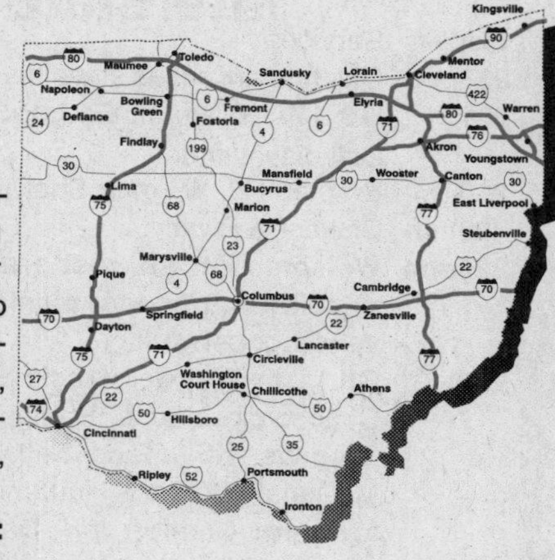

Ohio Turnpike

E ↕ W

Lorain

152 OH 10, to Oberlin, Cleveland, I-480, **N...gas:** BP, Marathon, Shell, Speedway/diesel, Sunoco/diesel, **food:** Kartel's Rest., McDonald's, **lodging:** Super 8, Travelodge, **other:** Giant-Eagle Foods, U-Haul, **S...gas:** BP, **other:** drive-in theatre(seasonal)

151 I-480 E(from eb), to Cleveland, airport

146mm Black River

145 OH 57, to Lorain, Elyria, to I-90, **N...gas:** BP/McDonald's/diesel, Speedway, **food:** Applebee's, Arby's, Blimpie, Bob Evans, Burger King, Country Kitchen, Denny's, Fazoli's, Ground Round, HomeTown Buffet, LoneStar Steaks, Mtn Jack's Rest., Pizza Hut, Red Lobster, Subway, SuperKing Buffet, Wendy's, **lodging:** Best Western, Comfort Inn, Day's Inn, Econolodge, Holiday Inn, Knight's Inn, **other:** Best Buy, Dillard's, Firestone/auto, Goodyear/auto, JC Penney, Jo-Ann Fabrics, Kaufmann's, K-Mart, Lowe's Whse, Michael's, NTB, OfficeMax, Sam's Club, Sears/auto, Staples, Wal-Mart/auto, mall, **S...gas:** Shell/24hr, Speedway/diesel, **lodging:** Howard Johnson, Super 8, **other:** HOSPITAL, laundry, st patrol

142 I-90(from eb), OH 2, to W Cleveland

139mm Middle Ridge Service Plaza wb, Vermilion Service Plaza eb, Sunoco/diesel/24hr, FoodCourt, gifts, phone, RV parking

135 rd 51, Baumhart Rd, to Vermilion, no facilities

132mm Vermilion River

118 US 250, to Norwalk, Sandusky, **N...gas:** DM/diesel, Marathon, Speedway, **food:** 4Monks Italian, McDonald's, Subway, **lodging:** Comfort Inn, Day's Inn, Hampton Inn, Motel 6, Ramada Ltd, Super 8, **other:** Oulet/famous brands, **5 mi N...food:** Perkins, Roadhouse Grill, **lodging:** Econolodge, Fairfield Inn, Red Roof Inn, **S...lodging:** Colonial Inn, Homestead Inn/rest., **food:** Race Café, **other:** Chevrolet, to Edison's Birthplace

110 OH 4, no facilities

100mm Erie Islands Service Plaza wb, Commodore Perry Service Plaza eb, gas: Sunoco/diesel/24hr, food: Burger King, Cinnabon, Max&Erma's, Sbarro's, Starbucks, other: phone

93mm Sandusky River

91 OH 53, to Fremont, Port Clinton, **N...food:** Z's Diner, **lodging:** Best Budget Inn, Day's Inn, **S...gas:** Shell/diesel/24hr, **food:** Applebee's(2mi), **lodging:** Fremont Tpk Motel, Holiday Inn, **other:** HOSPITAL

81 OH 51, Elmore, Woodville, Gibsonburg, no facilities

80.5mm Portage River

77mm Blue Heron Service Plaza wb, Wyandot Service Plaza eb, Sunoco/diesel/24hr, Hardee's/chicken, phone

71 I-280, OH 420, to Stony Ridge, Toledo, **N...gas:** Petro/Mobil/diesel/rest./24hr/@, Flying J/Conoco/diesel/rest./24hr/LP/@, **food:** Charter House Rest., Country Diner, **lodging:** Howard Johnson, Pizza Hut, Knight's Inn, Ramada Ltd, Stony Ridge Inn/truck plaza/diesel/@, **other:** Blue Beacon, **S...gas:** FuelMart/diesel/@, Pilot/diesel/24hr/@, TA/BP/Burger King/Taco Bell/diesel/24hr/@, **food:** McDonald's, Wendy's, **other:** truckwash

Toledo

64 I-75 N, to Toledo, Perrysburg

63mm Maumee River

59 US 20, to I-475, Maumee, Toledo, **N...gas:** Amoco, BP/diesel, Speedway/diesel, **food:** Arby's, Bob Evans, China Gate Rest., Church's, Dominic's Italian, Indian Cuisine, Max's Diner, McDonald's, Pizza Hut, **lodging:** Budget Inn, Econolodge, Holiday Inn, Motel 6, Quality Inn, **other:** Advance Parts, Goodyear/auto, Jo-Ann Fabrics, K-Mart/Little Caesar's, NAPA, Radio Shack, Savers Foods, Sears/auto, to Toledo Stadium, **S...gas:** Meijer/diesel/24hr, Speedway, **food:** Big Boy, ChiChi's, Fazoli's, Fricker's, Friendly's, Ralphie's Burgers, Red Lobster, Schlotsky's, Taco Bell, **lodging:** Best Western, Comfort Inn, Cross Country Inn, Day's Inn, Hampton Inn, Red Roof Inn, Super 8, **other:** Ames, Chevrolet, Ford/Lincoln/Mercury, Honda, Toyota

52 OH 2, to Toledo, **S...lodging:** Super 8, **other:** RV/truck repair

49mm service plaza both lanes, Sunoco/diesel/24hr, gifts/ice cream

39 OH 109, no facilities

34 OH 108, to Wauseon, **S...gas:** Shell/Subway/diesel/24hr/@, **lodging:** Arrowhead Motel, Best Western, Holiday Inn Express, Super 8, **other:** HOSPITAL, Toledo RV Ctr, Woods Trucking/repair(1mi), **2 mi S on US 20A...gas:** DM, Mobil, **food:** Burger King, McDonald's, Pizza Hut, Subway, Wendy's, **lodging:** Wauseon Motel, **other:** Wal-Mart/auto

25 OH 66, Burlington, **3 mi S...other:** Sauder Village Museum

24.5mm Tiffen River

21mm Indian Meadow Service Plaza both lanes, info, Sunoco/diesel/24hr, Hardee's/chicken, travel trailer park

13 OH 15, to Bryan, Montpelier, **S...gas:** Marathon/Subway/diesel, Pennzoil/diesel, **food:** Country Fair Rest., **lodging:** Econolodge, Rainbow Motel, Ramada Inn, **other:** Hutch's Diesel Repair

11.5mm St Joseph River

3mm toll plaza, phone

2 OH 49, to US 20, **N...gas:** Mobil/Subway/diesel, **food:** Burger King, **other:** info

0mm Ohio/Indiana state line

OKLAHOMA

Interstate 35

N ↕ S

Exit #	Services
236mm	Oklahoma/Kansas state line
231	US 177, Braman, **E...gas:** Conoco/Grab'n Dash Deli/diesel/motel
230	Braman Rd, **W...gas:** Shell/diesel/tire repair
229mm	Chikaskia River
225mm	**Welcome Ctr sb, rest area nb, full(handicapped)facilities, phones, picnic tables, litter barrels, vending, petwalk**
222	OK 11, to Blackwell, Medford, Alva, Newkirk, **E...gas:** Conoco/diesel/rest., Phillips 66/diesel, Shell, **food:** Braum's, KFC/Taco Bell, Los Potros Mexican, McDonald's, Pizza Hut(2mi), Sonic(3mi), Subway, **lodging:** Comfort Inn, Day's Inn, Super 8(2mi), **other:** HOSPITAL, **W...gas:** Shell
218	Hubbard Rd, no facilities
216mm	weigh sta both lanes
214	US 60, to Tonkawa, Lamont, Ponka City, N OK Coll, **E...lodging:** Holiday Inn, **W...gas:** Phillips 66/diesel/rest., **lodging:** New Western Inn, **other:** Woodland RV Park
213mm	Salt Fork of Arkansas River
211	Fountain Rd, **E...gas:** Love's/Subway/diesel/24hr/@, **W...gas:** Coulter's Corner/gas
209mm	parking area both lanes, litter barrels
203	OK 15, Billings, to Marland, **E...gas:** Conoco/DQ/diesel/24hr
199mm	Red Rock Creek
195mm	parking area both lanes, no facilities, litter barrels
194b a	US 412, US 64 W, **E...other:** Cimarron Tpk(eb), to Tulsa, **W...**to Enid, Phillips U
193	to US 412, US 64 W(from nb), no facilities
191mm	Black Bear Creek
186	US 64 E, to Fir St, Perry, **E...food:** Subway/diesel, **food:** Braum's, KFC(2mi), McDonald's, Pizza Hut, Taco Mayo, **lodging:** Super 8, **other:** HOSPITAL, museum, **W...gas:** Conoco/diesel/24hr, **lodging:** Day's Inn
185	US 77, Perry, to Covington, **E...gas:** Phillips 66, **lodging:** Best Western/rest., **W...gas:** Shell/diesel/motel/rest./24hr, **other:** RV camping
180	Orlando Rd, no facilities
174	OK 51, to Stillwater, Hennessee, **E...gas:** Shell/diesel, **food:** Charlie's Chicken, **lodging:** Fairfield Inn(12mi), Holiday Inn(13mi), Motel 6(12mi), **other:** Lake Carl Blackwell RV Park
173mm	parking area sb, no facilities, litter barrels
171mm	parking area nb, no facilities, litter barrels
170	Mulhall Rd, no facilities
165mm	Cimarron River
157	OK 33, Guthrie, to Cushing, **E...gas:** Sinclair/diesel/repair, **W...gas:** Conoco, K&L/diesel, Love's/Subway/diesel/24hr, Shell/diesel, Total, **food:** Arby's, Braum's, Burger King, Carl's Jr(3mi), DQ, El Rodeo Mexican, KFC, McDonald's(3mi), **lodging:** Best Western, Interstate Motel, Sleep Inn, **other:** HOSPITAL, OK Terr Museum, Langston U, RV camping
153	US 77 N(exits left from nb), Guthrie, **E...food:** McDonald's, Taco Mayo, **W...other:** Chrysler/Dodge/Jeep, Ford/Mercury, Pontiac/Buick
151	Seward Rd., **E...gas:** Conoco/diesel, Lazy E Arena(4mi), Pioneer RV park
149mm	weigh sta both lanes
146	Waterloo Rd, **E...gas:** Conoco/diesel/24hr, **1/2 mi W...gas:** Citgo/diesel
143	Covell Rd, no facilities
142	Danforth Rd(from nb), no facilities
141	US 77 S, OK 66E, to 2nd St, Edmond, Tulsa, **W...gas:** Conoco, Phillips 66/diesel, **food:** Coyote Café, Denny's, IHOP, KFC/Taco Bell, McDonald's, Western Sizzlin, **lodging:** Best Western, Hampton Inn, Holiday Inn Express, Stafford Inn, **other:** HOSPITAL
140	SE 15th St, Spring Creek, Arcadia Lake, Edmond Park, **W...food:** Braum's
139	SE 33rd St, **W...food:** Applebee's, **lodging:** Sleep Inn
138d	Memorial Rd, **W...other:** Enterprise Square USA
c	Sooner Rd(from sb), no facilities
b	Kilpatrick Tpk, no facilities
a	I-44 Tpk E to Tulsa
	I-35 S and I-44 W run together 8 mi
137	NE 122nd St, to OK City, **E...gas:** Shell/diesel, Total/diesel, **lodging:** Travelodge, **W...gas:** Bosselman/diesel/24hr/@, Flying J/Conoco/CountryMkt/diesel/LP/24hr/@, Love's/Subway/Taco Bell/diesel/24hr/@, **food:** Cracker Barrel, McDonald's, Waffle House, **lodging:** Comfort Inn, Day's Inn, Motel 6, Quality Inn, Super 8, **other:** Abe's RV Park, Frontier City Funpark
136	Hefner Rd, **W...gas:** Conoco/Lil' Italy Rest./diesel, **food:** DQ, same as 137
135	Britton Rd, **E...gas:** Drivers/diesel
134	Wilshire Blvd, **E...gas:** Drivers/diesel, **food:** Braum's, **other:** Gordon Inland Marine, **W...lodging:** Executive Inn, **other:** Blue Beacon
	I-35 N and I-44 E run together 8 mi
133	I-44 W, to Amarillo, **W...**st capitol, Cowboy Hall of Fame
132b	NE 63rd St(from nb), **1/2 mi E...gas:** Conoco/diesel, **food:** Braum's, **lodging:** Remington Inn
a	NE 50th St, Remington Pk, **W...other:** funpark, info, museum, zoo
131	NE 36th St, **W...gas:** Phillips 66/diesel/24hr, **other:** 45th Inf Division Museum
130	US 62 E, NE 23rd St, **E...gas:** Shell/Burger King, **W...**to st capitol
129	NE 10th St, **E...gas:** Conoco/McDonald's/diesel, Total, **W...food:** Tom's BBQ
128	I-40 E, to Ft Smith, no facilities
127	Eastern Ave, OK City, **W...gas:** Petro/diesel/rest./Blue Beacon/24hr/@, Pilot/Wendy's/diesel/24hr/@, Shell/diesel, **food:** BBQ, Waffle House, **lodging:** Best Western, Central Plaza Hotel, **other:** Blue Beacon, Lewis RV Ctr
126a	I-40, W to Amarillo, I-235 N, to st capitol
b	I-35 S to Dallas
125d	SE 15th St, **E...gas:** Conoco/diesel, Total/repair, **lodging:** Green Carpet Inn
b	SE 22nd St(from nb), no facilities
a	SE 25th, **E...food:** Denny's, McDonald's, Sonic, Taco Bell, Waffle House, **lodging:** Day's Inn, Guesthouse Suites, Plaza Inn, Royal Inn, Super 8, **W...gas:** Phillips 66

Blackwell

Guthrie

Okla City

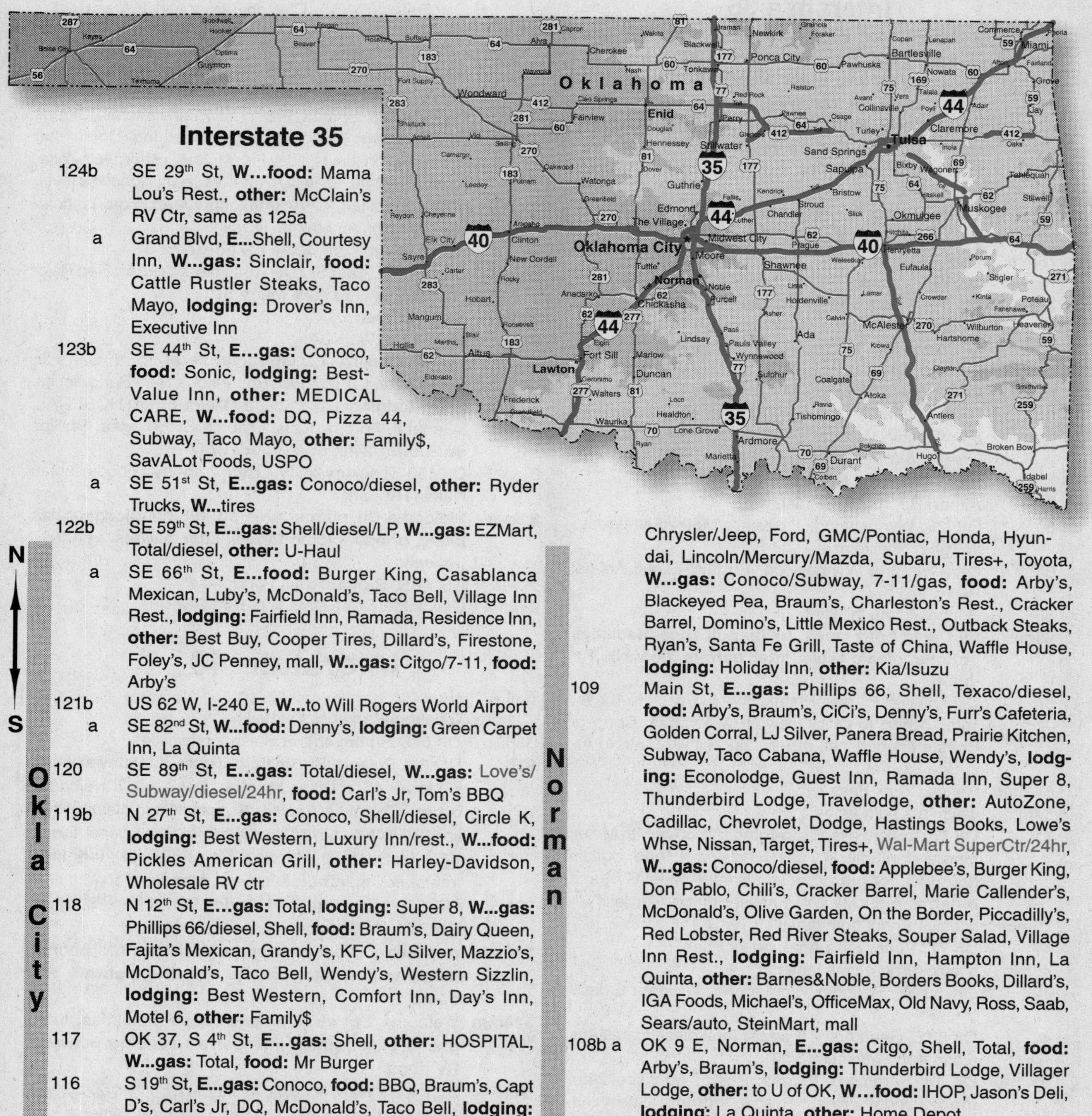

Interstate 35

N ↕ S

Okla City

124b SE 29th St, **W...food:** Mama Lou's Rest., **other:** McClain's RV Ctr, same as 125a

a Grand Blvd, **E...**Shell, Courtesy Inn, **W...gas:** Sinclair, **food:** Cattle Rustler Steaks, Taco Mayo, **lodging:** Drover's Inn, Executive Inn

123b SE 44th St, **E...gas:** Conoco, **food:** Sonic, **lodging:** Best-Value Inn, **other:** MEDICAL CARE, **W...food:** DQ, Pizza 44, Subway, Taco Mayo, **other:** Family$, SavALot Foods, USPO

a SE 51st St, **E...gas:** Conoco/diesel, **other:** Ryder Trucks, **W...**tires

122b SE 59th St, **E...gas:** Shell/diesel/LP, **W...gas:** EZMart, Total/diesel, **other:** U-Haul

a SE 66th St, **E...food:** Burger King, Casablanca Mexican, Luby's, McDonald's, Taco Bell, Village Inn Rest., **lodging:** Fairfield Inn, Ramada, Residence Inn, **other:** Best Buy, Cooper Tires, Dillard's, Firestone, Foley's, JC Penney, mall, **W...gas:** Citgo/7-11, **food:** Arby's

121b US 62 W, I-240 E, **W...**to Will Rogers World Airport

a SE 82nd St, **W...food:** Denny's, **lodging:** Green Carpet Inn, La Quinta

120 SE 89th St, **E...gas:** Total/diesel, **W...gas:** Love's/Subway/diesel/24hr, **food:** Carl's Jr, Tom's BBQ

119b N 27th St, **E...gas:** Conoco, Shell/diesel, Circle K, **lodging:** Best Western, Luxury Inn/rest., **W...food:** Pickles American Grill, **other:** Harley-Davidson, Wholesale RV ctr

118 N 12th St, **E...gas:** Total, **lodging:** Super 8, **W...gas:** Phillips 66/diesel, Shell, **food:** Braum's, Dairy Queen, Fajita's Mexican, Grandy's, KFC, LJ Silver, Mazzio's, McDonald's, Taco Bell, Wendy's, Western Sizzlin, **lodging:** Best Western, Comfort Inn, Day's Inn, Motel 6, **other:** Family$

117 OK 37, S 4th St, **E...gas:** Shell, **other:** HOSPITAL, **W...gas:** Total, **food:** Mr Burger

116 S 19th St, **E...gas:** Conoco, **food:** BBQ, Braum's, Capt D's, Carl's Jr, DQ, McDonald's, Taco Bell, **lodging:** Microtel, **other:** Firestone/auto, Goodyear/auto, Ross, **W...food:** Burger King, **other:** $Tree, Kohl's, Tires+, Wal-Mart SuperCtr/24hr

114 Indian Hill Rd, **E...food:** Barry's Chicken Ranch, **other:** Kerr RV Ctr

113 US 77 S(from sb, exits left), Norman, no facilities

112 Tecumseh Rd, no facilities

110b a Robinson St, **E...gas:** Petrostop, **food:** Hardee's, Krispy Kreme, Sonic, Taco Bell, Western Sizzlin, **lodging:** Day's Inn, Albertson's, **other:** HOSPITAL, Chrysler/Jeep, Ford, GMC/Pontiac, Honda, Hyundai, Lincoln/Mercury/Mazda, Subaru, Tires+, Toyota, **W...gas:** Conoco/Subway, 7-11/gas, **food:** Arby's, Blackeyed Pea, Braum's, Charleston's Rest., Cracker Barrel, Domino's, Little Mexico Rest., Outback Steaks, Ryan's, Santa Fe Grill, Taste of China, Waffle House, **lodging:** Holiday Inn, **other:** Kia/Isuzu

Norman

109 Main St, **E...gas:** Phillips 66, Shell, Texaco/diesel, **food:** Arby's, Braum's, CiCi's, Denny's, Furr's Cafeteria, Golden Corral, LJ Silver, Panera Bread, Prairie Kitchen, Subway, Taco Cabana, Waffle House, Wendy's, **lodging:** Econolodge, Guest Inn, Ramada Inn, Super 8, Thunderbird Lodge, Travelodge, **other:** AutoZone, Cadillac, Chevrolet, Dodge, Hastings Books, Lowe's Whse, Nissan, Target, Tires+, Wal-Mart SuperCtr/24hr, **W...gas:** Conoco/diesel, **food:** Applebee's, Burger King, Don Pablo, Chili's, Cracker Barrel, Marie Callender's, McDonald's, Olive Garden, On the Border, Piccadilly's, Red Lobster, Red River Steaks, Souper Salad, Village Inn Rest., **lodging:** Fairfield Inn, Hampton Inn, La Quinta, **other:** Barnes&Noble, Borders Books, Dillard's, IGA Foods, Michael's, OfficeMax, Old Navy, Ross, Saab, Sears/auto, SteinMart, mall

108b a OK 9 E, Norman, **E...gas:** Citgo, Shell, Total, **food:** Arby's, Braum's, **lodging:** Thunderbird Lodge, Villager Lodge, **other:** to U of OK, **W...food:** IHOP, Jason's Deli, **lodging:** La Quinta, **other:** Home Depot

107mm Canadian River

106 OK 9 W, to Chickasha, **W...gas:** Love's/Subway/diesel/24hr/@, Phillips 66/Burger King/diesel/@, **other:** Chevrolet

104 OK 74 S, Goldsby, **E...other:** Floyd's RV Ctr, **W...gas:** Shell/diesel, Total/diesel

101 Ladd Rd, no facilities

98 Johnson Rd, **E...gas:** Texaco/diesel, **other:** RV camping, **W...other:** muffler repair

OKLAHOMA

Interstate 35

N — S

95 US 77(exits left from sb), Purcell, **1-3 mi E...gas:** Conoco, **food:** Braum's, Carl's Jr, KFC, Mazzio's, Pizza Hut, Subway, **other:** HOSPITAL, Ford

91 OK 74, to OK 39, Maysville, **E...gas:** Conoco, Phillips 66/diesel, **food:** Carl's Jr, Casa Rosa Mexican, McDonald's, Ruby's Inn/rest., Subway, **lodging:** Econolodge, **other:** flea mkt, **W...gas:** Shell/Blimpie/diesel/24hr

86 OK 59, Wayne, Payne, no facilities

79 OK 145 E, Paoli, **E...gas:** Phillips 66

76mm Washita River

74 OK 19, Kimberlin Rd, no facilities

72 OK 19, Paul's Valley, **E...gas:** Citgo, Total/diesel, **food:** Ballard's Drive-In, Braum's, Carl's Jr, Denny's, KFC/Taco Bell, McDonald's, Punkin's Catfish, Sonic, Subway, Taco Mayo, **lodging:** Day's Inn, Garden Inn, Relax Inn, Sands Motel, **other:** Buick/Pontiac/Cadillac/GMC, Chrysler/Dodge/Jeep, $General, Ford/Lincoln/Mercury, Wal-Mart/auto(1mi), **W...gas:** Love's/A&W/diesel/24hr/@, Phillips 66/diesel/24hr, **food:** Chaparral Steaks

70 Airport Rd, **E...**HOSPITAL

66 OK 29, Wynnewood, **E...**Kent's/Motel/diesel/rest., **W...gas:** Shell/diesel

64 OK 17A E, to Wynnewood, **E...**GW Exotic Animal Park

60 Ruppe Rd, no facilities

59mm rest area both lanes, full(handicapped)facilities, phone, picnic table, litter barrels, petwalk, RV dump

55 OK 7, Davis, **E...gas:** Phillips 66/A&W/diesel/24hr/@, Total, **other:** to Chickasaw NRA, **W...gas:** Conoco/ChesterFried/diesel, **other:** Oak Hill RV Park, to Arbuckle Ski Area

54.5mm Honey Creek Pass

54mm weigh sta both lanes

51 US 77, Turner Falls, **E...lodging:** Arbuckle Mtn Motel, Mtnview Inn(3mi), **W...gas:** Sinclair/grill, **food:** Buffalo gap BBQ, **lodging:** Canyon Breeze Motel/RV Park, **other:** to Arbuckle Wilderness, Botanic Gardens

49mm scenic turnout both lanes

47 US 77, Turner Falls Area, no facilities

46mm scenic turnout both lanes

42 OK 53 W, Springer, Comanche, **W...gas:** Exxon/diesel

40 OK 53 E, Gene Autry, **E...gas:** Total/diesel/café/24hr, Gene Autry Museum(8mi)

33 OK 142, Ardmore, **E...gas:** Phillips 66/diesel/24hr, **food:** Ponder's Rest., Ryan's, **lodging:** Guest Inn, La Quinta, Super 8

Ardmore

32 12th St, Ardmore, **1 mi E...gas:** Phillips 66, **food:** Arby's, Braum's, Burger King, Carl's Jr, Fried Pies, Grandy's, KFC, LJ Silver, Pizza Hut, Taco Bell, Taco Bueno, **other:** HOSPITAL, Chevrolet, $General, Hastings Books, O'Reilly Parts, Staples, Toyota, Walgreen, Wal-Mart, **W...gas:** Love's/Godfather's/Subway/diesel/24hr/@, **food:** McDonald's, **lodging:** Microtel

31b a US 70 W, OK 199 E, Ardmore, **E...gas:** Conoco/diesel/24hr, Shamrock/diesel, Shell/diesel, Sinclair/diesel, **food:** Applebee's, Burger King, Cattle Rustler Steaks, Denny's, El Chico's, Golden China, KFC, Little Caesar's, Mazzio's, McDonald's, Pizza Hut, Prairie Kitchen, 2Frogs Grill, **lodging:** Best Western, Comfort Inn, Dorchester Inn, Hampton Inn, Holiday Inn, Motel 6, **other:** AutoZone, Buy4Less/24hr, O'Reilly Parts, **W...gas:** Conoco/diesel, **other:** Cadillac, Chrysler/Dodge/Jeep, Ford/Lincoln/Mercury, Honda, Mazda, Nissan

29 US 70 E, Ardmore, **E...**to Lake Texoma SP

24 OK 77 S, **E...gas:** Sinclair, Total/diesel, **other:** Red River Livestock Mkt, to Lake Murry SP

22.5mm Hickory Creek

21 Oswalt Rd, **W...**KOA

15 OK 32, Marietta, **E...gas:** Total/diesel, **food:** Carl's Jr, Denim's Rest., Pizza Hut, Robertson's Ham Sandwiches, Sonic, **lodging:** Lake Country Motel, **other:** HOSPITAL, $General, Ford, to Lake Texoma SP, **W...gas:** Phillips 66/Subway/24hr, Shell, **food:** BBQ

5 OK 153, Thackerville, **W...other:** Shorty's Foods, Indian Nation RV Park

3.5mm Welcome Ctr nb/rest area sb, full(handicapped)facilities, phone, picnic tables, litter barrels, vending, petwalk

1 US 77 N, **E...gas:** Shamrock/diesel

0mm Oklahoma/Texas state line, Red River

Interstate 40

E — W

Exit # Services

331mm Oklahoma/Arkansas state line

330 OK 64D S(from eb), Ft Smith, no facilities

325 US 64, Roland, Ft Smith, **N...gas:** Total/diesel/24hr/@, **food:** 4Star Diner, **lodging:** Day's Inn, Travelodge, **other:** Cherokee Casino, **S...gas:** Citgo/diesel, Phillips 66, Pilot/Wendy's/diesel/24hr/@, Shell/diesel, **food:** KFC, McDonald's, Mazzio's, Sonic, Subway, **lodging:** Interstate Inn, **other:** $General, Marvin's Foods

321 OK 64b N, Muldrow, **N...food:** Sonic(1mi), **S...gas:** Curt's/diesel/Economy Inn, **other:** repair

316mm rest area eb, full(handicapped)facilities, info, phone, picnic tables, litter barrels, vending, petwalk, RV dump

Sallisaw

314mm Welcome Ctr wb, full(handicapped)facilities, info, phone, picnic tables, litter barrels, vending, petwalk, RV dump

311 US 64, Sallisaw, **N...gas:** Mr Jiff/gas, Phillips 66/diesel, **food:** Hardee's, KFC/Taco Bell, Pizza Hut, Simon's Pizza, Sonic, Subway, Taco Mayo, **lodging:** Econolodge, Motel 6, **other:** HOSPITAL, AutoZone, Pontiac, **1 mi N...food:** Lessley's Café, **other:** to Sallisaw RA, Brushy Lake SP(10mi), Sequoyah's Home(12mi)

Interstate 40

E ↕ W

308 US 59, Sallisaw, **N...gas:** Citgo/diesel, Phillips 66/diesel, Sinclair, **food:** Arby's, Braum's, Dana's Rest., Mazzio's, McDonald's, Western Sizzlin, **lodging:** Best Western, Golden Spur Motel, McKnight Motel, Microtel, Southern Hearth Inn, **other:** HOSPITAL, Wal-Mart SuperCtr/gas/24hr, to Blue Ribbon Downs, **S...gas:** Shell/diesel, **food:** Ole South Rest., **other:** Chevrolet, Chrysler/Plymouth/Dodge/Jeep, Ford, KOA, to Kerr Lake, repair

303 Dwight Mission Rd, **3 mi N...other:** Blue Ribbon Downs

297 OK 82 N, Vian, **N...gas:** Phillips 66, **lodging:** Siesta Motel, **other:** DENTIST, NAPA, to Tenkiller Lake RA

291 OK 10 N, to Gore, **N...other:** Greenleaf SP(10mi), Tenkiller SP(21mi)

290mm Arkansas River

287 OK 100 N, to Webbers Falls, **N...gas:** Love's/Subway/Taco Bell/diesel/24hr/@, **food:** Charlie's Chicken, **lodging:** Knight's Inn, **other:** OK Trading Post, tires/repair

286 Muskogee Tpk, to Muskogee, no facilities

284 Ross Rd, no facilities

283mm parking area both lanes, litter barrels

278 US 266, OK 2, Warner, **N...gas:** Phillips 66diesel, **food:** Big Country Rest., **lodging:** Sleepy Traveler Motel **other:** Auburn RV Park

270 Texanna Rd, to Porum Landing, **S...gas:** Sinclair

265 US 69 bus, Checotah, **N... food:** DQ, Pizza Hut, Sonic, **S...gas:** Citgo/diesel/24hr, **lodging:** Budget Host, **other:** Chevrolet, Chrysler/Plymouth/Dodge/Jeep

264b a US 69, to Eufaula, **1 mi N...gas:** Citgo/diesel/24hr, Flying J/Conoco/Country Mkt/diesel/LP/24hr/@, **food:** Charlie's Chicken, Simon's Pizza, **lodging:** Midway Inn, **other:** $General, Wal-Mart, auto repair

262 to US 266, Lotawatah Rd, **N...gas:** Phillips 66

261mm Lake Eufaula

259 OK 150, to Fountainhead Rd, **S...gas:** Citgo/LP, Shell/café, **lodging:** Lake Eufaula Inn, **other:** to Fountainhead SP

255 Pierce Rd, **N...**KOA

251mm parking area both lanes, no facilities

247 Tiger Mtn Rd, **S...other:** Quilt Barn/antiques

240b a US 62 E, US 75 N, Henryetta, **N...gas:** Conoco, Love's/diesel, Shell, Sinclair, **food:** Arby's, Braum's, DQ, Mazzio's, McDonald's, Sonic, Subway, Taco Mayo, **lodging:** Colonial Motel, Gateway Inn, LeBaron Motel, Relax Inn, **other:** Chrysler/Jeep, Ford, G&W Tire, Wal-Mart, **S...**Indian Nation Tpk

237 US 62, US 75, Henryetta, **N...gas:** Citgo/diesel/24hr, Shell/diesel/24hr, **food:** Pig Out Palace, **lodging:** Green Country Inn, Trail Motel, **other:** HOSPITAL, Henryetta RV Park(2mi), **S...**Hungry Traveler Rest., Super 8

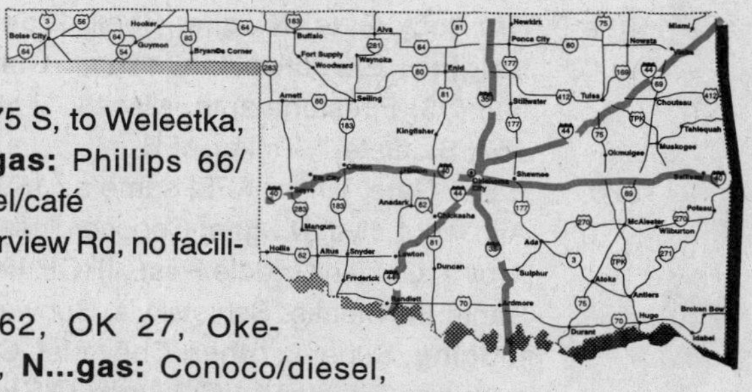

Henryetta

231 US 75 S, to Weleetka, **N...gas:** Phillips 66/diesel/café

227 Clearview Rd, no facilities

221 US 62, OK 27, Okemah, **N...gas:** Conoco/diesel, Total/Subway/diesel/24hr, **food:** Mazzio's, Sonic, **other:** HOSPITAL, **S...gas:** Love's/A&W/Chester/diesel/24hr, **food:** BBQ, Kellogg's Café, **other:** truck repair

217 OK 48, Bearden, to Bristow, **N...**Old West Museum, **S...gas:** Total

216mm N Canadian River

212 OK 56, to Cromwell, Wewoka, **N...gas:** Conoco, **food:** BBQ, **S...gas:** Shell/diesel, to museum

208mm Gar Creek

202mm Turkey Creek

200 US 377, OK 99, to Little, Prague, **S...gas:** Citgo/diesel/24hr, Conoco/diesel/24hr, Love's/Subway/diesel/24hr/@, **food:** Robertson's Ham Sandwiches, **lodging:** Village Inn Motel/rest.

197mm rest area both lanes, full(handicapped)facilities, phone, picnic tables, litter barrels, petwalk

192 OK 9A , Earlsboro, **S...gas:** Shell/diesel, **food:** Biscuit Hill Rest., **lodging:** Rodeside Motel, **other:** CB Shop

189mm N Canadian River

186 OK 18, to Shawnee, **N...gas:** Citgo/diesel, Shell, **food:** Denny's, **lodging:** American Inn, Day's Inn, Motel 6, Ramada Inn, Super 8, **S...lodging:** Colonial Inn, **other:** antique auto museum

185 OK 3E, Shawnee Mall Dr, to Shawnee, **N...food:** Chili's, Garcia's Mexican, Red Lobster, Taco Bueno, **other:** Dillard's, JC Penney, Sears/auto, Wal-Mart/auto mall, **S...gas:** Phillips 66/diesel, **food:** Applebee's, Braum's, Charlie's Chicken, CiCi's, Cracker Barrel, Delta Café, Garfield's Rest., IHOP, Mazzio's, McDonald's, Schlotsky's(2mi), Sonic, **lodging:** Hampton Inn, **other:** Lowe's Whse, Staples

Shawnee

181 US 177, US 270, to Tecumseh, **S...lodging:** Budget Host, **other:** HOSPITAL

180mm N Canadian River

178 OK 102 S, Dale, **N...**trailer sales

176 OK 102 N, McLoud Rd, **S...gas:** Love's/Subway/diesel/24hr, **food:** Curtis Watson Rest.

172 Newalla Rd, to Harrah, **S...gas:** Shell

169 Peebly Rd, no facilities

166 Choctaw Rd, to Woods, **N...gas:** Love's/Subway/diesel/24hr, **other:** KOA, **S...gas:** Phillips 66/diesel, **other:** to Little River SP(11mi)

165 I-240 W(from wb), to Dallas, no facilities

162 Anderson Rd, **N...**LP

159b Douglas Blvd, **N...gas:** Phillips 66, Total, **food:** Denny's, McDonald's, Sonic, Subway, Taco Bell, **other:** RV camping, **S...other:** Tinker AFB, HOSPITAL

OKLAHOMA

Interstate 40

E ↕ W

Okla City

- a Hruskocy Gate, **N...gas:** Shell, **food:** China Grill, **lodging:** Executive Inn, **other:** Chrysler/Dodge, Family$, Firestone/auto, Nissan, U-Haul, same as 157, **S...**Gate 7, Tinker AFB
- 157c Eaker Gate, Tinker AFB, same as 159
- b Air Depot Blvd, **N...gas:** Conoco/diesel, Shell, **food:** Arby's, Golden Griddle Rest., IHOP, KFC, Pizza Inn, Santa Fe Steaks, Schlotsky's, Subway, Taco Mayo, **lodging:** Super 8, **other:** Chevrolet, Cottman Transmissions, Firestone, JC Penney, O'Reilly Parts, Walgreen, **S...**Gate 1, Tinker AFB
- a SE 29th St, Midwest City, **N...gas:** Conoco/diesel, Shell, **lodging:** Planet Inn, **other:** O'Reilly Parts, **S...other:** Ford, Sam's Club
- 156b a Sooner Rd, **N...gas:** Conoco, **food:** BBQ, Cracker Barrel, Ray's Steaks, **lodging:** AmeriSuites, Comfort Inn, Hampton Inn, Holiday Inn Express, La Quinta, **other:** Studio 6, Home Depot, **S...lodging:** Motel 6, **other:** Chevrolet/Pontiac/GMC, Daewoo, Tires+, Toyota
- 155b SE 15th St, Del City, **N...gas:** Shell, **other:** IGA Foods, **S...food:** Ashley's Rest.
- 155a Sunny Lane Rd, Del City, **N...gas:** Conoco/Subway/diesel, **S...gas:** Shell, **food:** Braum's, Pizza Hut, Sonic
- 154 Reno Ave, Scott St, **N...gas:** Sinclair, **S...gas:** Phillips 66/diesel
- 152 I-35 N, to Wichita
- 127 Eastern Ave(from eb), Okla City, **N...gas:** Petro/Mobil/diesel/rest./@, Pilot/Wendy's/diesel/24hr/@, Shell, **food:** G Dale's BBQ, Waffle House, **lodging:** Best Western, Sunshine Inn, **other:** Blue Beacon, Lewis RV Ctr
- 151b c I-35, S to Dallas, I-235 N, to downtown, st capitol
- a Lincoln Blvd, **N...**Bricktown Stadium
- 150c Robinson Ave(from wb), OK City, **N...food:** Spaghetti Whse, **lodging:** Westin Hotel, **other:** U-Haul, Ford
- b Harvey Ave(from eb), downtown, **N...lodging:** Renaissance Hotel, Westin Hotel
- a Walker Ave(from eb), **N...other:** Ford, Goodyear, **S...gas:** Phillips 66, transmissions
- 149b Classen Blvd(from wb), to downtown
- a Western Ave, Reno Ave, **N...gas:** Total/Subway, **food:** McDonald's, Taco Bell, **S...gas:** Conoco/diesel, Shell, **food:** Burger King
- 148c Virginia Ave(from wb), to downtown
- b Penn Ave(from eb), **N...gas:** Shamrock, **S...other:** Isuzu/Ryder Trucks
- a Agnew Ave, Villa Ave, **N...gas:** Phillips 66/diesel, **S...gas:** Conoco/diesel, **food:** BBQ, Braum's, **other:** Freddie's Tires
- 147c May Ave, no facilities
- b a I-44, E to Tulsa, W to Lawton
- 146 Portland Ave(from eb, no return), **N...gas:** Shell/Subway/diesel, **other:** water funpark

Okla City

- 145 Meridian Ave, OK City, **N...gas:** Conoco, Shell, **food:** Boomerang Grill, Denny's, McDonald's, On the Border, Outback Steaks, Shorty Small's Rest., **lodging:** Best Western, Day's Inn, Extended Stay America, Howard Johnson, Motel 6, Red Roof Inn, Residence Inn, Super 8, Travelers Inn, **S...gas:** Phillips 66/diesel, Sinclair, **food:** Arby's, Bennigan's, Burger King, Chili's, Cracker Barrel, Golden Palace Chinese, IHOP, Kona Ranch Steaks, Panera Bread, Quizno's, Rib Crib, Santa Fe Grill, Sonic, Taco Bueno, Tony Roma, Waffle House, Wendy's, Whataburger, **lodging:** AmeriSuites, Candlewood Suites, Clarion Hotel, Comfort Suites, Courtyard, Embassy Suites, Executive Inn, Hampton Inn, Hilton Garden, Holiday Inn Express, La Quinta, Lexington Suites, Motel 6, Ramada Ltd, Regency Inn, Sleep Inn, Wingate Inn
- 144 MacArthur Blvd, **N...gas:** Shell/diesel, **food:** Applebee's, Fire Mtn Steaks, KFC, McDonald's, Sonic, Taco Cabana, **other:** HobbyLobby, Office Depot, Radio Shack, Wal-Mart SuperCtr/24hr, **S...food:** Ruby's Rest., **lodging:** Green Carpet Inn, Microtel, Super 10 Motel, Travelodge, **other:** Kenworth, Sam's Club
- 143 Rockwell Ave, **N...gas:** Shell, **lodging:** Rockwell Inn, **other:** Home Depot, McClain's RV Ctr, Tires+, **S...lodging:** Sands Motel/RV Park/LP, **other:** Rockwell RV Park
- 142 Council Rd, **N...gas:** Shell, Sinclair, **food:** Braum's, McDonald's, Subway, Taco Bell, Waffle House, Wendy's, **lodging:** Best Budget Inn, **S...gas:** TA/Burger King/diesel/24hr/@, **lodging:** Econolodge, **other:** Council Rd RV Park
- 140 Morgan Rd, **N...gas:** Pilot/McDonald's/diesel/24hr/@, TA/Phillips 66/Popeye's/diesel/24hr/@, **other:** Blue Beacon, **S...gas:** Flying J/Conoco/diesel/LP/24hr/@, Love's/Subway/diesel/24hr/@, **food:** Ricky's Mexican, Sonic
- 139 Kilpatrick Tpk, no facilities
- 138 OK 4, to Yukon, Mustang, **N...food:** Denny's, Catcher's Grill, **lodging:** Super 8, **S...gas:** Conoco/diesel, Shell, **food:** Arby's, Burger King, Interurban Grill, Sonic, Subway, Homeland Foods, **lodging:** Best Western
- 137 Cornwell Dr, Czech Hall Rd, **N...**Albertson's
- 136 OK 92, to Yukon, **N...gas:** Shell, **food:** Braum's, Carl's Jr, Harry's Café, KFC, LJ Silver, McDonald's, Taco Mayo, Waffle House, Wendy's, **lodging:** Green Carpet Inn, Hampton Inn, **other:** AutoZone, Chevrolet, Big O Tire, Radio Shack, Rite Aid, Wal-Mart SuperCtr/gas/24hr, **S...food:** Alfredo's, Carino's Italian, Chili's, Jimmy's Egg Café, Quizno's, Rib Crib, Taco Bueno, **other:** HOSPITAL, Ford, Kohl's, Lowe's Whse, Staples

El Reno

- 132 Cimarron Rd, **N...**Statuary World, **S...**airport
- 130 Banner Rd, **N...gas:** Shell/diesel/rest.
- 129mm weigh st both lanes
- 125 US 81, to El Reno, **N...gas:** Conoco, Love's/diesel, **food:** Serapio's Mexican, Taco Mayo, **lodging:** Economy Inn, Super 8, **other:** Chevrolet, Ford/Lincoln/Mercury, Plymouth, Pontiac/GMC/Buick, **S...**truck repair

Interstate 40

E ↕ W

123 Country Club Rd, to El Reno, **N...gas:** Conoco, Shell, **food:** Arby's, Braum's, Carl's Jr, KFC, Mazzio's, McDonald's, Pizza Hut, Subway, Taco Bell, **other:** HOSPITAL, Radio Shack, Wal-Mart SuperCtr/diesel/24hr, **S...gas:** Phillips 66/diesel, **food:** Denny's, Sirloin Stockade, **lodging:** Best Western, Comfort Inn, Day's Inn, Regency Motel, **other:** Family RV Park
119 Lp 40, to El Reno, no facilities
115 US 270, to Calumet, no facilities
111mm picnic area eb, picnic tables, litter barrels
108 US 281, to Geary, **N...gas:** Shell/Subway/diesel, **lodging:** Cherokee Motel/rest., **other:** KOA/Indian Trading Post, to Roman Nose SP, **S...gas:** Love's/diesel/@
105mm S Canadian River
104 Methodist Rd, no facilities
101 US 281, OK 8, to Hinton, **N...**to Roman Nose SP, **S...gas:** Shell/DQ/diesel, **lodging:** Microtel, **other:** picnic area, to Red Rock Canyon SP
95 Bethel Rd, no facilities
94.5mm picnic area wb, picnic tables, litter barrels
88 OK 58, to Hydro, Carnegie, **N...gas:** Shell/diesel/deli
84 Airport Rd, **N...gas:** Shell/diesel, **lodging:** Holiday Inn Express, Travel Inn, **other:** Buick/Pontiac/GMC, Chevrolet/Cadillac, Chrysler/Plymouth/Dodge/Jeep
82 E Main St, Weatherford, **N...gas:** Conoco/diesel, Shell/diesel, **food:** Braum's, Alfredo's Mexican, Arby's, Carl's Jr, Jerry's Rest., KFC/Taco Bell, Mark Rest., Mazzio's, McDonald's, Pizza Hut, Sonic, Subway, Taco Bell, Taco Mayo, **lodging:** Best Western, Day's Inn, Scottish Inn, **other:** HOSPITAL, AutoZone, $General, O'Reilly Parts, Radio Shack, U-Haul, Wal-Mart, to SW OSU
80a W Main St(from eb), **N...gas:** Conoco/diesel, **food:** Casa Sota Mexican, **other:** Ford/Lincoln/Mercury
80 OK 54, Weatherford, **N...gas:** Shell, **food:** Little Mexico Rest./gifts
71 Custer City Rd, **N...gas:** Love's/Subway/diesel/rest./@
69 Lp 40(from wb), to Clinton, **2 mi N...food:** Dairy Queen, **lodging:** Glancey's Motel/rest.
67.5mm Washita River
66 US 183, Clinton, **S...gas:** Shell/diesel, **other:** Ford/Lincoln/Mercury, Chrysler/Dodge/Jeep, Wink's RV Park

Clinton

65a 10th St, Neptune Dr, Clinton, **N...food:** Braum's, KFC, Pizza Hut, Subway, **lodging:** Day's Inn, Relax Inn, Super 8, **S...gas:** Phillips 66/diesel, **lodging:** Clinton Inn
65 Gary Blvd, Clinton, **N...gas:** Conoco, Shell/diesel, **food:** Carl's Jr, DQ, LJ Silver, McDonald's, Pancake House, Rte 66 Rest, Taco Mayo, **lodging:** Best Western, MidTown Inn, Ramada Inn, Travelodge, **other:** HOSPITAL, K-Mart 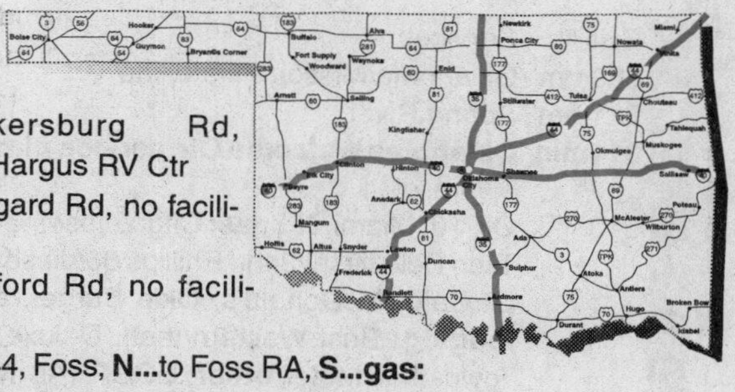
62 Parkersburg Rd, **S...**Hargus RV Ctr
61 Haggard Rd, no facilities
57 Stafford Rd, no facilities
53 OK 44, Foss, **N...**to Foss RA, **S...gas:** Shell/diesel
50 Clinton Lake Rd, **N...other:** KOA/gas/LP/diesel
47 Canute, **S...gas:** Shell

Elk City

41 OK 34(exits left from eb), Elk City, **N...gas:** Love's/Subway/diesel, Shell, **food:** Home Cooking Café, **lodging:** Day's Inn, Holiday Inn, Howard Johnson, Motel 6, Regency Inn, Travelodge, Super 8, **other:** HOSPITAL, Elk Run RV Park
40 E 7th St, Elk City, **N...food:** Portobello Grill, same as 41
38 OK 6, Elk City, **N...gas:** Conoco/diesel, Shell/diesel, **food:** Arby's, Denny's, LJ Silver, McDonald's, Western Sizzlin, **lodging:** Bedford Inn, Day's Inn, **other:** Elk Creek RV Park, **S...gas:** Phillips 66/diesel, **lodging:** Econolodge, Holiday Inn, Ramada Inn, **other:** to Quartz Mtn SP
34 Merritt Rd, no facilities
32 OK 34 S(exits left from eb), Elk City, **3 mi N...gas:** Conoco, **food:** Subway, **lodging:** Best Western, **other:** HOSPITAL
26 Cemetery Rd, **N...food:** Bud's Café, **S...gas:** TA/Subway/diesel/24hr/@
25 Lp 40, Sayre, **N...gas:** Shamrock/diesel, **lodging:** Western Motel, **other:** HOSPITAL, Ford
23 OK 152, Sayre, **S...gas:** Shell/diesel
22.5mm N Fork Red River
20 US 283, Sayre, **N...gas:** Flying J/Conoco/CountryMkt/diesel/24hr/@, **lodging:** AmericInn, **other:** to Washita Bfd Site(25mi)
14 Hext Rd, no facilities
13.5mm check sta both lanes, litter barrels
11 Lp 40, to Erick, Hext, no facilities
10mm Welcome Ctr/rest area both lanes, full(handicapped)facilities, phone, picnic tables, litter barrels, petwalk, RV dump
7 OK 30, Erick, **N...gas:** Shell/diesel/café, **food:** Cal's Café, **lodging:** Comfort Inn, **S...gas:** Love's/A&W/Subway/diesel/@, **food:** Cowboy's Rest./Trading Post, **lodging:** Day's Inn
5 Lp 40, Honeyfarm Rd, no facilities
1 Texola, **S...gas:** gas/diesel/rest., **food:** BBQ, **other:** RV camping
0mm Oklahoma/Texas state line

OKLAHOMA
Interstate 44

E ↔ W

Miami

Exit #	Services
329mm	Oklahoma/Missouri state line
321mm	Spring River
314mm	**Oklahoma Welcome Ctr, service plaza wb,** Phillips 66/diesel
313	OK 10, Miami, **N...gas:** Citgo/diesel, Conoco, Love's/ Taco Bell/diesel/24hr, Phillips 66/diesel, **food:** Arby's, Lil Café, McDonald's, Okie Burger, Stables Rest., **lodging:** Best Western/rest., Deluxe Inn, Super 8, Townsman Motel, **other:** HOSPITAL, Miami RV Park, to NE OK A&M Coll, **S...other:** Chrysler/Plymouth/ Dodge/Jeep
312mm	Neosho River
312mm	picnic area eb, phone, picnic table, litter barrel
310mm	picnic area wb, phone, picnic table, litter barrel
302	US 59, US 69, Afton, **3 mi S...gas, lodging:** Best Western, Grand Lake Country Inn, Shangri-La Inn, **other:** Bears Den Resort Camping
299mm	rest area eb, picnic table, litter barrel
289	US 60, Vinita, **N...gas:** Citgo, Phillips 66/Subway, **food:** Braum's, Carl's Jr, KFC, McDonald's, Pizza Hut, **lodging:** Holiday Inn Express, Vinita Inn, **other:** HOSPITAL, $General, Ford/Mercury, Super H Foods, Wal-Mart, st patrol
288mm	**service plaza both lanes,** Phillips 66/diesel/24hr, **McDonald's, phone**
286mm	toll plaza
283	US 69, Big Cabin, **N...gas:** Shell/diesel/rest./24hr, **lodging:** Super 8, **S...**truck repair
271mm	picnic area eb, picnic table, litter barrel
269	OK 28(from eb, no re-entry), to Adair, Chelsea, **S...gas:** Citgo, golf
269mm	rest area eb, picnic tables, litter barrel
256mm	rest area wb, picnic tables, litter barrel
255	OK 20, Claremore, to Pryor, **N...gas:** Citgo, **food:** Arby's, Carl's Jr, KFC, McDonald's, **lodging:** Best Western, Claremore Motel, Day's Inn, Super 8, **other:** HOSPITAL, to Rogers U, Will Rogers Memorial, museum, **S...gas:** Phillips 66
248	to OK 66, Port of Catoosa, no facilties
244mm	Kerr-McClellan Navigation System
241mm	Will Rogers Tpk begins eb, ends wb, phones
241	OK 66 E, to Catoosa, no facilities
240b	US 412 E, Choteau
240a	OK 167 N, 193rd E Ave, **N...gas:** Phillips 66/diesel/ rest./24hr, SunMart/diesel/24hr, **food:** KFC, McDonald's, Pauline's Buffet, Pizza Hut, Taco Mayo, Waffle House, Wendy's, **lodging:** Super 8, Travelers Inn, **other:** KOA **S...gas:** Citgo, Phillips 66, QT, Shell/A&W/diesel, **food:** Mazzio's, Sonic, Subway, **other:** $General, Family$, Homeland Foods, NAPA, tires/repair
238	161st E Ave, **N...gas:** Shell/diesel/rest./24hr, **S...gas:** QT/diesel/24hr, **food:** Arby's, Burger King, **lodging:** Microtel, **other:** I-44 Auto Auction
236b	I-244 W, to downtown Tulsa, airport
a	129th E Ave, **N...gas:** Flying J/Conoco/diesel/LP/rest./ 24hr/@ , **S...food:** McDonald's
235	E 11th St, Tulsa, **N...gas:** Phillips 66, QT, **food:** Carl's Jr, Fajita Rita's, Lot-a-Burger, Sonic, Waffle House, **lodging:** Executive Inn, Stratford House Inn, Super 8, **other:** $General, May's Drug, O'Reilly Parts, **S...food:** Taco Bueno, **lodging:** National Inn, **other:** Whse Foods
234b	Garnett Rd, **N...food:** Mazzio's, **lodging:** Motel 6, Super 8, **S...gas:** QT/diesel, **food:** Braum's, Denny's, **lodging:** Econolodge, **other:** Whse Foods,
a	US 169, N to Owasso, to airport, S to Broken Arrow, no facilities
233	E 21st St(from wb), **S...gas:** Citgo, **food:** El Chico, **lodging:** Comfort Suites, **other:** MEDICAL CARE, K-Mart, Dean's RV Ctr
231	US 64, OK 51, to Muskogee, E 31st St, Memorial Dr, **N...gas:** Phillips 66, **food:** Whataburger, **lodging:** Day's Inn, Georgetown Plaza Motel, Ramada Inn, Travelodge, **other:** Homeland Foods, **S...gas:** Shell/A&W, **food:** Cracker Barrel, IHOP, McDonald's, Village Inn Rest., **lodging:** Courtyard, Embassy Suites, Extended Stay America, Fairfield Inn, Hampton Inn, Holiday Inn Express, Park Inn, Quality Inn, Super 8, **other:** Chevrolet, Chrysler, Nissan
230	E 41st St, Sheridan Rd, **N...gas:** Shell, **food:** Carl's Jr, On-the-Border, Quizno's, Subway, TGIFriday, Whataburger/ 24hr, **other:** Barnes&Noble, Circuit City, Goodyear/auto, Jo-Ann Fabrics, Michael's, Old Navy, **S...lodging:** Heritage Inn, **other:** Home Depot
229	Yale Ave, Tulsa, **N...gas:** Shell, **food:** McDonald's, **other:** Firestone, Foley's, Mervyn's, Ross, mall, **S...gas:** Phillips 66/diesel, QT/24hr, **food:** Applebee's, Arby's, Braum's, Denny's, Don Pablo, Outback Steaks, Red Lobster, Steak&Ale, Subway, Taco Bell, Taco Cabana, Village Inn Rest., **lodging:** Baymont Inn, Comfort Inn, Holiday Inn, Howard Johnson, Travelodge, **other:** HOSPITAL, Celebration Sta, Kia, Mazda
228	Harvard Ave, Tulsa, **N...gas:** Shell/diesel, **food:** Johnnie's Charcoal Buffet, Subway, **lodging:** Best Western, Towers Hotel, Tradewinds Motel, **S...gas:** Citgo, Phillips 66, **food:** Blimpie, Chili's, Chimi's Mexican, Jamil's Steaks, LoneStar Steaks, LJ Silver/A&W, Marie Callender's, McDonald's, Papa John's, Perry's Rest., Piccadilly's, Pizza Hut, Sol's Grill, Thai Rest., **lodging:** Holiday Inn Express, Ramada Inn, **other:** Albertson's, $Tree, Kelly Tire, K-Mart, SteinMart
227	Lewis Ave, Tulsa, **S...gas:** Shell, Sinclair, **food:** AZ Mexican Rest., El Chico, Goldie's Patio Grill, SteakStuffers USA, Wendy's, **other:** Tires+
226b	Peoria Ave, Tulsa, **N...food:** China Wok, Church's, CiCi's, Pizza Hut, Waffle House, **lodging:** Parkside Hotel, Super 8, **other:** Hancock Fabrics, **S...gas:** QT, Shell, **food:** Braum's, Burger King, **lodging:** Stratford House Inn, **other:** AutoZone, Buy4Less/24hr, $General, Food City
226a	Riverside Dr(from eb), **S...food:** Village Inn
225	Elwood Ave, **N...other:** Chevrolet, Ford
225	Arkansas River
224b a	US 75, to Okmulgee, Bartlesville, **N...gas:** Citgo, QT/ diesel, **food:** KFC, Mazzio's, Subway, **other:** $General, Whse Mkt, **S...lodging:** Royal Inn, **other:** RV park
223c	33rd W Ave, Tulsa, **N...food:** Braum's, Domino's, **S...gas:** Phillips 66, **food:** Rib Crib BBQ, **other:** NAPA Autocare

Tulsa

Interstate 44

E ↕ W

223b 51st St(from wb)
223a I-244 E, to Tulsa, downtown
222c (from wb), **S...lodging:** Value Inn
222b 55th Place, **N...lodging:** Capri Motel, Crystal Motel, **S...lodging:** Day's Inn, Economy Inn
222a 49th W Ave, Tulsa, **N...food:** Carl's Jr, Mama Lou's Rest., Monterey Café, **lodging:** Gateway Motel, Interstate Inn, Motel 6, **other:** $General, May Drug, Radio Shack, **S...gas:** Git'n Go, QT/Wendy's/diesel/24hr, **food:** Arby's, McDonald's, Village Inn Rest., Waffle House, **lodging:** Super 8, Buick/Pontiac/GMC, Volvo Trucks
221mm Turner Tkp begins wb, ends eb
218 Creek Tpk E(from eb)
215 OK 97, Sapulpa, to Sand Sprgs, **N...lodging:** Super 8, **S...gas:** Kum&Go, Phillips 66/diesel, **food:** Arby's, **other:** HOSPITAL, Chrysler/Jeep/Dodge
211 OK 33, to Kellyville, Drumright, Heyburn SP, **S...gas:** Phillip 66/diesel
207mm service plaza wb, **gas:** Phillips 66/diesel
205mm picnic area wb, litter barrels, picnic tables
204mm picnic area eb, litter barrels, picnic tables
197mm service plaza eb, gas: Phillips 66/diesel/24hr, **food:** McDonald's
196 OK 48, Bristow, **S...lodging:** Carolyn Inn, **other:** HOSPITAL
191mm picnic area wb, litter barrels, picnic tables
189mm picnic area eb, litter barrels, picnic tables
182mm toll plaza
179 OK 99, Stroud, to Drumright, **N...gas:** Citgo, **lodging:** Best Western/rest., **S...gas:** Phillips 66/Subway/diesel, **food:** Mazzio's, McDonald's, Sonic, Steak&Eggs Rest., Taco Mayo, **lodging:** Sooner Motel, **other:** HOSPITAL, auto/tire repair
178mm Hoback Plaza both lanes(exits left), gas: Phillips 66/diesel, **food:** McDonald's
171mm picnic area eb, litter barrels, picnic tables
167mm (from eb), **S...gas:** Phillips 66/diesel
166 OK 18, Chandler, to Cushing, **N...other:** Chrysler/Jeep/Dodge, **S...gas:** Phillips 66, **food:** DC Max Pizza, Swirleez Drive-In, **lodging:** Econolodge, Lincoln Motel, **other:** Chandler Tire, Ford
166mm picnic area wb, phones, litter barrels, picnic tables
158 OK 66, to Wellston, no facilities
157 (from wb), **N...gas:** Phillips 66/McDonald's/diesel, **other:** museum info
153mm picnic area both lanes, litter barrels, picnic tables

Okla City

135mm Turner Tpk begins eb, ends wb
138d to Memorial Rd, to Enterprise Square
138a I-35, I-44 E to Tulsa, Turner Tpk, no facilities
I-44 and I-35 run together 8 mi. See Oklahoma Interstate 35, exits 134-137.
130 I-35 S, to Dallas, access to facilities on I-35 S
129 MLK Ave, Remington Park, **N...food:** County Line BBQ, **lodging:** Ramada Ltd, **other:** Cowboy Hall of Fame, **S...food:** McDonald's, **other:** Family$
128b Kelley Ave, OK City, **N...gas:** Conoco, Total/Subway/diesel, **food:** Sonic, **other:** Cowboy Hall of Fame
a Lincoln Blvd, st capitol, **S...lodging:** Comfort Inn, Oxford Inn
127 I-235 S, US 77, City Ctr, Broadway St, **N...gas:** Conoco, Shell, **lodging:** Holiday Inn, Santa Fe Inn, Travel Master Motel
126 Western Ave, **N...food:** Deep Fork Grill, Sonic, TapWorks Grill, **S...lodging:** Guest House Motel
125c NW Expressway(exits left from sb)
b Classen Blvd, OK City, **E...food:** IHOP, McDonald's, **lodging:** Courtyard, Hawthorn Suites, **W...gas:** Shell, **food:** Garcia's Mexican, **other:** Acura, Dillard's, Foley's, JC Penney, Old Navy, Ross, Wal-Mart SuperCtr/24hr, mall
a OK 3A, Penn Ave, to NW Expswy, **E...gas:** Shell, **food:** Braum's, **lodging:** Habana Inn, Homeland Foods, **W...gas:** Conoco/Burger King/diesel24hr
124 N May, **E...other:** Aamco, Ford, **W...gas:** Shell/Subway, **food:** San Marcos Mexican, **lodging:** Day's Inn, Ramada Ltd, Super 8, **other:** Dodge, O'Reilly Parts
123b OK 66 W, NW 39th, to Warr Acres, **W...food:** Burger King, Carl's Jr, Chinese Buffet, McDonald's, Quizno's, Rte 66 Rest., **lodging:** Carlyle Motel, Comfort Inn, Hospitality Inn, Villager Lodge, **other:** Pratt's Foods
a NW 36th St, no facilities
122 NW 23rd St, **E...gas:** Conoco, **food:** Arby's, Sonic, **other:** Big O Tire, Family$, **W...gas:** Conoco, 7-11/gas, **food:** Church's, EggRoll King, LJ Silver, Taco Mayo, **other:** Tires+,
121b a NW 10th St, **E...gas:** 7-11/gas, Shell, **other:** $General, Family$, Whittaker's Foods/24hr, antiques, fairgrounds, **W...gas:** Shell
120b a I-40, W to Amarillo, E to Ft Smith
119 SW 15th St, no facilities
118 OK 152 W, SW 29th St, OK City, **E...gas:** Conoco, 7-11, **food:** Burger King, Capt D's, Grandy's, KFC/Taco Bell, McDonald's, Sonic, Taco Bueno, **other:** AutoZone, $General, Grider's Foods, Walgreen, **W...gas:** Shell, **other:** U-Haul, transmissions
117 SW 44th St, **W...**auto repair
116b Airport Rd, **W...**airport
a SW 59th St, **E...gas:** Conoco, Shell, **W...**Will Rogers Airport
115 I-240 E, US 62 E, to Ft Smith
114 SW 74th St, OK City, **E...gas:** Phillips 66, Sinclair/repair, **food:** Braum's, Burger King, Capt D's, Taco Bell, **lodging:** Ramada Ltd, Villager Lodge, **other:** $General, RV/truckwash
113 SW 89th St, **E...gas:** Love's/Subway/diesel/24hr/@, Total/diesel, 7-11, **food:** McDonald's, Sonic, Taco Mayo
112 SW 104th St, **W...gas:** Shell/rest.
111 SW 119th St, **E...**Walker RV Ctr, **W...**American Dream RV Ctr
110 OK 37 E, to Moore, **E...gas:** Sinclair/diesel
109 SW 149th St, **E...food:** JR's Grill
108mm S Canadian River

OKLAHOMA

Interstate 44

E ↕ W

108 OK 37 W, to Tuttle, **W...gas:** Conoco/Subway/diesel, Phillips 66, **food:** Braum's, Carlito's Mexican, Carl's Jr, Little Caesar's, Mazzio's, **other:** MEDICAL CARE, $General, O'Reilly Parts, Wal-Mart
107 US 62 S(no wb return), to Newcastle, **E...gas:** Shamrock/KFC/diesel/24hr, **lodging:** Newcastle Motel, **other:** Newcastle RV, Walker RV
100mm picnic area eb, picnic tables, litter barrels
99 H E Bailey Spur, rd 4, to Blanchard, Norman
97mm toll booth, phone
95.5mm picnic area wb, picnic tables, litter barrels
85.5mm service plaza, both lanes exit left, Texaco/diesel, McDonald's
83 Chickasha, US 62, **W...gas:** Conoco/diesel, **food:** Subway, **other:** museum

Chickasha

80 US 81, Chickasha, **E...gas:** Conoco, Phillips 66/diesel, Shell/diesel, **food:** Burger King, Eduardo's Café, Western Sizzlin, **lodging:** Day's Inn, Delux Inn, Royal American Inn, **other:** HOSPITAL, Buick/Chevrolet/Pontiac/Cadillac, Chrysler/Plymouth/Dodge/Jeep, $Tree, GNC, Goody's, Wal-Mart/auto, **W...gas:** Conoco, Love's, Shell/diesel, **food:** Arby's, Braum's, Denny's, Domino's, El Rancho Mexican, KFC, LJ Silver, McDonald's, Peking Dragon, Pizza Hut, Sonic, Subway, Taco Bell, Taco Mayo, **lodging:** Best Western, Budget Motel, **other:** AutoZone, Eckerd, Family$, Firestone/auto, Ford/Lincoln/Mercury, Lightner's Foods/24hr, O'Reilly Parts, Radio Shack, Staples
78mm toll plaza, phone
63mm rest area wb, picnic tables, litter barrels
62 to Cyril(from wb)
60.5mm rest area eb, picnic tables, litter barrels
53 US 277, Elgin, Lake Ellsworth, **E...gas:** Conoco/diesel, Total/pizza, **other:** Super H Foods, **W...gas:** Phillips 66/diesel
46 US 62 E, US 277, US 281, to Elgin, Apache, Comanche Tribe, last free exit nb
45 OK 49, to Medicine Park, **W...gas:** Love's/Subway/diesel/24hr/@, **food:** Burger King
41 Key Gate, to Ft Sill, Key Gate, **W...**museum
40c Gate 2, to Ft Sill
40a US 62 W, to Cache, **E...gas:** Fina, **W...lodging:** Super 8
39b US 281(from sb), **W...lodging:** Ramada Inn
a US 281, Cache Rd, Lawton, **1-3 mi W...gas:** Citgo/Circle K, Phillips 66, Total/diesel, **food:** Applebee's, Braum's, Chick-fil-A, Golden Corral, KFC, Ryan's, Subway, Wendy's, **lodging:** Baymont Inn, Day's Inn, Economy Inn, Holiday Inn, Super 8, Super 9 Motel, **other:** U-Haul, transmissions

Lawton

37 Gore Blvd, Lawton, **E...gas:** Phillips 66, Sonic, **food:** Taco Mayo, Woody's Mexican, **lodging:** Howard Johnson, **other:** Comanche Nation Games, **W...food:** Arby's(3mi), Cracker Barrel, Mike's Grille, **lodging:** Ramada Inn(2mi), SpringHill Suites, **other:** Harley-Davidson, Lincoln/Mercury, Nissan
36a OK 7, Lee Blvd, Lawton, **E...gas:** Phillips 66, **W...gas:** Fina/diesel/repair, Welch/diesel, Sun Country Gas/diesel, **food:** Big Chef Rest., KFC/Taco Bell, Leo&Ken's Rest., Salas Mexican, Sonic, **lodging:** Motel 6, **other:** HOSPITAL
33 US 281, 11th St, Lawton, **W...other:** HOSPITAL, gas, food, lodging, airport, to Ft Sill
30 OK 36, Geronimo, no facilities
20.5mm Elmer Graham Plaza, both lanes exit left, Texaco/diesel, McDonald's, info
20 OK 5, to Walters, **E...food:** BBQ
19.5 toll plaza
5 US 277 N, US 281, Randlett, last free exit nb, **E...gas:** Shamrock/diesel
1 OK 36, to Grandfield, no facilities
0mm Oklahoma/Texas state line, Red River

Interstate 240(Okla City)

E ↕ W

Exit # Services
16mm I-240 begins/ends on I-40.
14 Anderson Rd, **S...gas:** Conoco
11b a Douglas Blvd, **N...**Tinker AFB
9 Air Depot Blvd, no facilities
8 OK 77, Sooner Rd, **N...gas:** Love's/Taco Bell/diesel/24hr/@, Phillips 66/Popeye's/diesel, **food:** McDonald's
7 Sunnylane Ave, **S...gas:** Total/A&W/diesel
6 Bryant Ave, no facilities
5 S Eastern Ave, no facilities
4c Pole Rd, **N...food:** Burger King, Luby's, Taco Bell, Texas Roadhouse, **lodging:** Fairfield Inn, Ramada Inn, Residence Inn, **other:** Best Buy, Dillard's, Foley's, JC Penney, Tires+, mall
4b a I-35, N to OK City, S to Dallas, US 77 S, US 62/77 N
3b S Shields, **N...gas:** Total, **other:** Circuit City, Home Depot, **S...other:** Ford, Nissan, Saturn, Wal-Mart SuperCtr/24hr
a S Santa Fe, **S...gas:** Shell, **food:** Chili's, IHOP, **other:** Buick, Chrysler/Jeep, Lowe's Whse, Staples, Wal-Mart SuperCtr/24hr

Okla City

2b S Walker Ave, **N...gas:** 7-11/gas, Shell, **food:** Rib Crib, **S...food:** ChuckeCheese, **other:** PepBoys
2a S Western Ave, **N...gas:** Conoco, **food:** Burger King, House of Szechwan, Nino's Mexican, Taste of China, **other:** Tires+, **S...gas:** Citgo/7-11, **food:** Ashley's Rest./24hr, Grandy's, HomeTown Buffet, KFC, LJ Silver, McDonald's, Red Lobster, Steak&Ale, **lodging:** Holiday Inn Express, Quality Inn, **other:** Big O Tire, Chevrolet, Honda, Office Depot, Radio Shack
1c S Penn Ave, **N...gas:** Conoco, **food:** Carl's Jr, Denny's, Don Pablo, Golden Corral, Harrigan's Rest., Hooters, Olive Garden, Outback Steaks, Pioneer Pies, Santa Fe Grill, Schlotsky's, Michael's, **S...gas:** Shell, **food:** Anna's Gyros, August Moon Chinese, Blackeyed Pea, Hunan Buffet, Mazzio's, McNear's Steaks, Pancho's Mexican, Papa John's, Subway, Taco Bueno, Wendy's, **other:** PharMor Drug, Radio Shack
b S May Ave, **N...gas:** 7-11/gas, **food:** Capt D's, Jimmy's Egg Grill, Waffle House, **other:** Albertson's, **S...gas:** Phillips 66/diesel, Sinclair/diesel, **food:** Braum's, Burger King, Perry's Rest., **lodging:** Ramada Ltd, Villager Lodge
a I-44, US 62, I-240 begins ends on I-44.

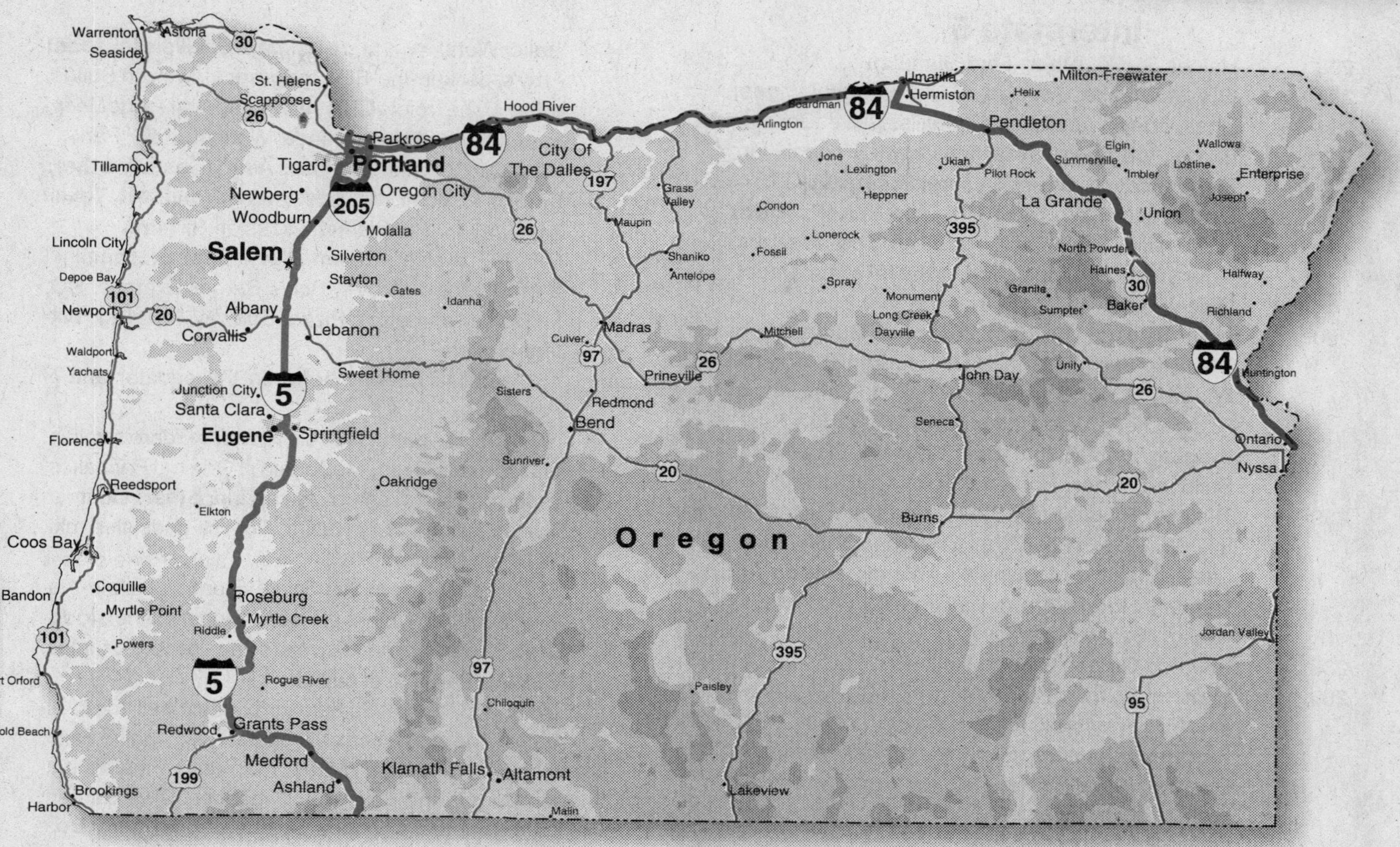

Interstate 5

N ↕ S

Portland

Exit #	Services
308.5mm	Oregonington state line, Columbia River
308	Jansen Beach Dr, **E...gas:** Chevron/24hr, **food:** Burger King, Taco Bell, Waddles Rest., **lodging:** Courtyard, Oxford Suites, DoubleTree Suites, **other:** Safeway, **W...gas:** Arco, 76/diesel, **food:** BJ's Brewery, Damon's, Denny's, McDonald's, Newport Bay Rest., Stanford's Rest., Subway, Tom's Pizza, **lodging:** DoubleTree Hotel, Holiday inn Express, **other:** Barnes&Noble, Circuit City, CompUSA, Firestone, Home Depot, K-Mart, Old Navy, Staples, Target, mall
307	OR 99E S, MLK Blvd, Union Ave, Marine Dr, Expo Ctr, **E...food:** El Burrito, Elmer's Rest., Mo's Deli, Portland Cascade Grill, **lodging:** Best Western
306b	Interstate Ave, Delta Park, **E...gas:** 76, **food:** Burger King, Burrito House, Chinese Cuisine, Elmer's Rest., Shari's, **lodging:** Best Western, Day's Inn, **other:** Baxter Parts, Office Depot, OfficeMax, Portland Meadows
a	Columbia(from nb), **W...gas:** 76, Shell/diesel, 7-11, **food:** Wendy's, Winchell's, **other:** Fred Meyer
305b a	US 30, Lombard St(from nb), same as 306a
304	Portland Blvd, U of Portland, **W...gas:** Arco
303	Alberta St, Swan Island, **E...**HOSPITAL
302b	I-405, US 30 W, **W...**to ocean beaches, zoo
a	Rose Qtr, City Ctr, **E...gas:** Shell, 7-11, **food:** McDonald's, **lodging:** Holiday Inn, Ramada Inn, Travelodge, **other:** HOSPITAL, Ford, **W...food:** Cucina Cucina, **lodging:** Best Western, Red Lion Inn, **other:** coliseum
301	I-84 E, US 30 E, facilities E off I-84 exits
300	US 26 E(from sb), Milwaukie Ave, **W...lodging:** Hilton, Marriott
299b	I-405, no facilities
a	US 26 E, OR 43(from nb), City Ctr, to Lake Oswego
297	Terwilliger Blvd, **W...gas:** Shell, **food:** Burger King, KFC, **other:** HOSPITAL, Fred Meyer
296b	Multnomah Blvd, no facilities
a	Barbur, **W...gas:** Chevron/24hr, Shell, 7-11, **food:** Szechuan Chinese, Subway, Taco Time, Wendy's, **lodging:** Aladdin Motor Inn, Capitol Hill Motel, Portland Rose Motel
295	Capitol Hwy, **E...gas:** Shell, Pacific Pride/diesel, **food:** Dunkin Donuts, McDonald's, RoundTable Pizza, **lodging:** Hospitality Motel, Ranch Inn
294	OR 99W, to Tigard, **W...gas:** Arco/24hr, BP, Shell, **food:** Arby's, Banning's Rest., Burger King, Carrow's Rest., Crab Bowl Rest., Italian Rest., KFC, King's Table, Mexican Rest., Newport Bay Rest., **lodging:** Day's Inn, Tigard Inn, Value Inn, Wayside Inn, **other:** Fred Meyer, U-Haul

Portland

OREGON

Interstate 5

N ↕ S

Wilsonville

293 Haines St, **W...other:** Ford/Diahatsu

292 OR 217, Lake Oswego, **E...**LDS Temple, **gas:** Shell, **food:** Applebee's, Chili's, Olive Garden, Sizzler, **lodging:** Holiday Inn Crown, Phoenix Inn, Residence Inn, **other:** Deseret Books

291 Carman Dr, **W...gas:** Chevron, Shell, **food:** Burgerville, Houlihan's, **lodging:** Best Western, Courtyard, Sherwood Inn, **other:** Home Depot, Office Depot

290 Lake Oswego, **E...gas:** 76, **food:** Burger King, Denny's, Skipper's, Taco Bell, **lodging:** Motel 6, **W...gas:** Arco, Chevron, 76/diesel, Shell, **food:** Fuddrucker's, JB's Roadhouse, Village Inn Rest., **lodging:** Best Suites, Best Western, Quality Inn, Shilo Inn, **other:** Borders Books, CarQuest

289 Tualatin, **E...gas:** BP, Shell, **lodging:** Sweetbrier Inn, **W...gas:** Arco/24hr, Chevron, Shell, **food:** Lee's Kitchen, McDonald's, Wendy's, **lodging:** Century Hotel, **other:** HOSPITAL, Fred Meyer, K-Mart, Safeway, camping

288 I-205, to Oregon City, no facilities

286 Stafford, **E...gas:** Chevron/Burns Bros/diesel/24hr/@, 76/diesel/24hr, **food:** Cheyenne Deli, IHOP, **lodging:** Best Inn, Super 8, **other:** Mercedes, Pleasant Ridge RV Park, **W...lodging:** Holiday Inn/rest., **other:** Camping World RV Service/supplies, Chevrolet, Dodge

283 Wilsonville, **E...gas:** 76/diesel, **food:** Applebee's, Arby's, Bullwinkle's Rest., DQ, Denny's, Domino's, Isleta Bonita Mexican, Izzy's Pizza, Jamba Juice, McDonald's, Papa Murphy's, Quizno's, Red Robin, Shari's/24hr, Subway, Taco Bell, TCBY, Wanker's Café, Wendy's, Wok Chinese, **lodging:** Best Western, Comfort Inn, SnoozInn, **other:** MEDICAL CARE, Fry's Electronics, GNC, Lamb's Foods, NAPA, Rite Aid, Scwab Tire, USPO, **W...gas:** Chevron, Shell/24hr, 7-11, **food:** Burger King/24hr, Chili's, Marvel's Pizza, New Century Chinese, **lodging:** Phoenix Inn, **other:** IGA Food

282.5mm Willamette River

282 Charbonneau District, **E...food:** Charbonneau-on-the-Green Rest., **other:** Langdon Farms Golf

281.5mm rest area both lanes, full(handicapped)facilities, phone, info, picnic tables, litter barrels, petwalk, vending, coffee

278 Donald, **E...gas:** PepStop/diesel/RV Park, **W...gas:** TA/Shell/diesel/rest./24hr/@, Shell/CFN/diesel, **other:** to Champoeg SP

275mm weigh sta sb

274mm weigh sta nb

271 OR 214, Woodburn, **E...gas:** Arco/24hr, Chevron/24hr, Exxon/diesel, 76/repair, Shell, **food:** Burger King, DQ, Denny's, Don Pedro's Express, KFC, McDonald's, Patterson's Rest., Shari's, Taco Bell, Wendy's, **lodging:** Best Western, Fairway Inn/RV Park, Super 8, **other:** Fairway Drug, Lind's Mkt, Trailer World, Wal-Mart, **W...gas:** Shell/diesel, **food:** Arby's, Jack-in-the-Box, **lodging:** Hawthorn Suites, **other:** Chevrolet, Chrysler/Plymouth/Dodge/Jeep, Ford, Outlet/famous brands, Woodburn RV Park

Salem

263 Brooks, Gervais, **E...gas:** Astro Gas/LP, **other:** Brooks Mkt/deli, **W...gas:** Pilot/Subway/Taco Bell/diesel/24hr/@, Willamette Mission SP(4mi)

260b a OR 99E, Keizer, Salem Pkwy, **2 mi E...**camping, **2 mi W...food:** Arby's, Bob's Burger Express, DQ, McDonald's, Pietro's Pizza, Subway, **lodging:** Wittenburg Inn

259mm 45th parallel, halfway between the equator and N Pole

258 N Salem, **E...gas:** 76/Circle K, **food:** Figaro's Italian, Guesthouse Rest., McDonald's, Original Pancakes, **lodging:** Best Western, Sleep Inn, **other:** Cottman Transmissions, Hwy RV Ctr, Roth's Foods, flea mkt, **W...gas:** Chevron, 76/Circle K, Pacific Pride/diesel, Shell/diesel, **food:** Big Shots Steaks, Jack-in-the-Box, LunYuen Chinese, Rock'n Rogers Diner, **lodging:** Rodeway Inn, Travelers Inn, **other:** Staples, Stuart's Parts, to st capitol

256 to OR 213, Market St, Salem, **E...gas:** Shell, **food:** Alberto's Mexican, Carl's Jr, Chalet Rest., China Faith, Denny's, Elmer's, El Mirador Mexican, Figaro's Italian, Jack-in-the-Box, Kyoto Japanese, Olive Garden, Outback Steaks, Skipper's, Taco Bell, **lodging:** Best Western, Cozzzy Inn, Crossland Suites, Tiki Lodge, **other:** Albertson's, American Tire, Best Buy, Bon-Ton, Borders Books, Fred Meyer, Goodyear/auto, NAPA, Pic'n Save Foods, Ross, Safeway, Schwab Tires, Target, Walgreen, mall, **W...gas:** Arco/24hr, Chevron, Pacific Pride/diesel, Shell/diesel/24hr, **food:** Baskin-Robbins, Canton Garden, McDonald's, Newport Bay Seafood, O'Callahan's Rest., Outback Steaks, Pietro's Pizza, Roger's 50's Diner, Subway, Tony Roma's, Village Inn, **lodging:** Holiday Lodge, Motel 6, Phoenix Inn, Quality Inn, Red Lion Hotel, Salem Inn, Shilo Inn, Super 8, **other:** Buick/GMC, Heliotrope Natural Foods, InStock Fabrics, Jack's IGA, Kia/Mazda/Isuzu, Nissan

253 OR 22, Salem, Stayton, **E...gas:** Chevron/repair, Shell/diesel, **food:** Burger King, Carl's Jr, Las Polomas Mexican, McDonald's, Shari's, Subway, **other:** Home Depot, ShopKO, WinCo Foods, Salem Camping, to Detroit RA, **W...gas:** Shell/diesel, **food:** DQ, Denny's, Sybil's Omelet, **lodging:** Best Western, Comfort Suites, Economy Inn, Holiday Inn Express, Motel 6, Travelodge, **other:** HOSPITAL, AAA, Chevrolet/Cadillac/Subaru, Chrysler/Plymouth, Costco, Jeep/Pontiac, K-Mart/auto, Roberson RV Ctr, Schwab Tire, Toyota, st police

252 Kuebler Blvd, **1-3 mi W...gas:** Arco/24hr, 76/24hr, **food:** Burger King, McDonald's, Neufeldt's Rest., Shari's/24hr, **lodging:** Phoenix Inn, **other:** HOSPITAL

Interstate 5

N ↕ S

249 to Salem(from nb), no facilities

248 Sunnyside, **E...gas:** Arco/24hr, **food:** Burger King, Thrillville Funpark, Willamette Valley Vineyards, **other:** RV camping, **W...gas:** Pacific Pride/diesel, **lodging:** Phoenix Inn

244 to Jefferson, no facilities

243 Ankeny Hill, no facilities

242 Talbot Rd, no facilities

241mm rest area both lanes, full(handicapped)facilities, info, phone, picnic tables, litter barrels, RV dump, petwalk

240.5mm Santiam River

240 Hoefer Rd, no facilities

239 Dever-Conner, no facilities

238 Scio, no facilities

237 Viewcrest(from sb), **W...**RV/truck repair

235 Millersburg, no facilities

234 OR 99E, Albany, **E...lodging:** Comfort Suites, **other:** Harley-Davidson, **W...gas:** Arco/24hr, Chevron/24hr, 76, Shell/diesel, **food:** Arby's, Burger King, China Buffet, DQ, Hereford Steer Rest., McDonald's, Pizza Hut, Subway, Taco Bell, TomTom Rest., Wendy's, **lodging:** Bamboo Terrace Motel, Best Western/rest., Budget Inn, Hawthorn Inn, Motel 6, **other:** HOSPITAL, K-Mart, Mervyn's, Chrysler/Jeep, Nissan, Lincoln/Mercury, RV camping, RV repair, to Albany Hist Dist

Albany

233 US 20, Albany, **E...gas:** Chevron/diesel/24hr, 76/diesel, **food:** Burgundy's Rest., LumYuen Chinese, **lodging:** Best Inn Suites, Motel Orleans, Phoenix Inn, **other:** Chevrolet/Toyota, Home Depot, Honda, Lassen RV Ctr, Mazda, RV camping, st police, **W...gas:** Shell, **food:** Abby's Pizza, AppleTree Rest., Baskin-Robbins, Burger King, Burgerville, Cameron's Rest., Carl's Jr, Chalet Rest., Denny's, Elmer's, Los Tequilos Mexican, McDonald's, Sizzler, Skipper's, Taco Time, **lodging:** Valu Inn, **other:** HOSPITAL, Albertson's, Battery Xchange, BiMart, Chrysler/Dodge/Jeep/Subaru/Hyundai, CraftWorld, $Tree, Fred Meyer, Goodyear, Jo-Ann Fabrics, Knecht's Parts, Rite Aid, Schwab Tires, Schuck's Parts, Staples

228 OR 34, to Lebanon, Corvallis, **E...gas:** Shell/diesel/24hr, **food:** Pine Cone Rest., **W...gas:** Arco/24hr, Chevron/A&W/diesel, Shell/CFN/diesel, 76, **other:** to OSU, KOA

222mm Butte Creek

216 OR 228, Halsey, Brownsville, **E...gas:** 76/Blimpie/diesel/24hr, **food:** McDonald's, **lodging:** Best Western/rest., **other:** parts/repair/towing, **W...gas:** Shell/Subway/Taco Bell/diesel

209 Harrisburg, to Jct City, **W...food:** Hungry Farmer Café, **other:** GoodSam RV Park

206mm rest area both lanes, full(handicapped)facilities, info, phone, picnic tables, litter barrels, petwalk

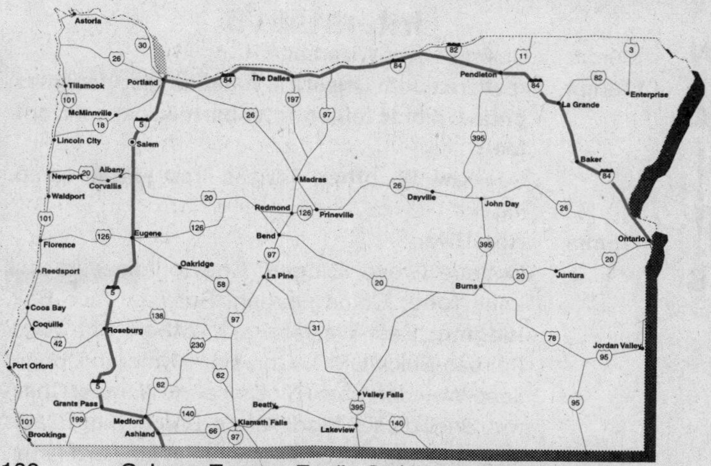

199 Coburg, **E...gas:** Fuel'n Go/diesel, **lodging:** Country Squire Inn, **other:** Coburg Hills RV Park, **W...gas:** Shell/LP, TA/Shell/diesel/rest./24hr/@, **other:** Destinations RV Ctr, Ford/Freightliner/GMC, Guaranty RV Outlet, Marathon RV Ctr, diesel repair, hist dist

197mm McKenzie River

195b a N Springfield, **E...gas:** Arco/24hr, Chevron/24hr, 76/diesel/24hr, **food:** DariMart, A&W, Denny's, Elmer's Rest., FarMan Rest., Gateway Chinese, HomeTown Buffet, IHOP, Jack-in-the-Box, KFC, McDonald's, Outback Steaks, Roadhouse Grill, Schlotsky's, Shari's/24hr, Sizzler, SweetRiver Grill, Taco Bell, **lodging:** Best Western, Comfort Suites, Courtyard, Doubletree Hotel/rest., Gateway Inn, Holiday Inn Express, Motel Orleans, Motel 6, Pacific 9 Motel, Rodeway Inn, Shilo Inn/rest., **other:** Circuit City, Sears/auto, Target, USPO, mall, st police, **W...gas:** Shell, **food:** Taco Bell, **other:** Costco, ShopKO, to airport

194b a **E...**OR 126 E, Springfield, **W...**I-105 W, Eugene, HOSPITAL, **2 mi W...gas:** 76/repair, **food:** Trader Joe's, **lodging:** Red Lion Inn, **other:** Albertson's, Honda, mall

Eugene

193mm Willamette River

192 OR 99(from nb), to Eugene, **W...food:** Burger King, Wendy's, **lodging:** Best Western, Quality Inn

191 Glenwood, **W...gas:** 76/diesel, Shell/diesel/24hr, **food:** Denny's, Lyon's Rest., **lodging:** Motel 6, Phoenix Inn, **other:** RV camping

189 30th Ave S, **E...gas:** Shell/Subway/Taco Bell/diesel/LP, **other:** Harley-Davidson, marine ctr, **W...gas:** Exxon/LP/24hr, **food:** Rainbow Mtn Rest., **other:** RV Ctr, Shamrock RV Park

188b a OR 58, to Oakridge, OR 99S, **W...gas:** Goshen Trkstp/diesel/rest./24hr/@

186 to Goshen(from nb), no facilities

182 Creswell, **E...food:** Emerald Valley Rest.(1mi), **W...gas:** Arco/24hr, 76/Taco Bell/diesel, Shell/diesel, **food:** Country Mouse Deli, DQ, Mr Macho's Pizza, Pizza Sta, TJ's Rest., **lodging:** Creswell Inn, Motel Orleans, **other:** Century Foods, Creswell Drugs, KOA, Kragen Parts, Taylor's Travel Park

OREGON

Interstate 5

N ↕ S

180mm Coast Fork of Willamette River

178mm rest area both lanes, full(handicapped)facilities, phone, picnic tables, litter barrels, petwalk, coffee

176 Saginaw, **W...other:** Taylor's Travel Park, camping

175mm Row River

174 Cottage Grove, **E...gas:** Chevron/diesel/repair/24hr, **food:** China Garden, Subway, Taco Bell, **lodging:** Best Western/rest., **other:** Chevrolet/Pontiac/Buick/GMC, Chrysler/Plymouth/Dodge/Jeep, Wal-Mart/auto, RV Ctr/camp, **W...gas:** Chevron, Shell/diesel, **food:** Arby's, Burger King, Carl's Jr, DQ, KFC, McDonald's, Vintage Inn Rest./24hr, **lodging:** City Ctr Motel, Comfort Inn, Holiday Inn Express, Relax Inn, **other:** HOSPITAL, Safeway, Mazda, Village Green Motel/RV Park

172 6th St, Cottage Grove Lake(from sb), **2 mi W...**RV camping

170 to OR 99, London Rd, Cottage Grove Lake, **6 mi E...**RV camping

163 Curtin, **E...food:** Curtin Café, **lodging:** Stardust Motel, **other:** Pass Creek RV Park, USPO, antiques, **W...food:** Coach House Rest.

162 OR 38, OR 99 to Drain, Elkton, **E...lodging:** Stardust Motel

161 Anlauf(from nb), no facilities

160 Salt Springs Rd, no facilities

159 Elk Creek, Cox Rd, no facilities

154 Yoncalla, Elkhead, no facilities

150 OR 99, to OR 38, Yoncalla, Red Hill, **W...other:** Trees of Oregon RV Park

148 Rice Hill, **E...gas:** Chevron/LP/24hr, Pacific Pride/diesel, Pilot/Subway/diesel/24hr/@, **food:** Homestead Rest./24hr, Peggy's Rest., **lodging:** Best Western, Ranch Motel/rest., **W...food:** K-R Drive-In

146 Rice Valley, no facilities

144mm rest area sb, full(handicapped)facilities, phone, picnic tables, litter barrels, petwalk

143mm rest area nb, full(handicapped)facilities, phone, picnic tables, litter barrels, petwalk

142 Metz Hill, no facilities

140 OR 99(from sb), Oakland, **E...food:** Medley Mkt Deli, Tolly's Rest., **other:** Oakland Hist Dist

138 OR 99(from nb), Oakland, **E...food:** Medley Mkt Deli, Tolly's Rest., **other:** Oakland Hist Dist

136 OR 138W, Sutherlin, **E...gas:** Chevron/A&W/24hr, 76, Shell/Subway/diesel, **food:** Burger King, Dory's Italian, McDonald's, Papa Murphy's, Red Apple Rest., **lodging:** Microtel, Town&Country Motel, Umpqua Regency Inn, **other:** Schwab Tires, **W...gas:** Astro Gas/LP, **food:** DQ, Taco Bell, West Wild Rest./24hr, **lodging:** Best Budget Inn, **other:** Hi-Way Haven RV Camp, diesel repair/towing

135 Wilbur, Sutherlin, **E...**muffler repair

130mm weigh sta sb, phone

129 OR 99, Winchester, **E...**gas, food, camping, diesel repair

128mm N Umpqua River

127 Stewart Pkwy, N Roseburg, **E...gas:** Chevron/diesel/24hr, **lodging:** Motel 6, Super 8, **W...gas:** Shell/Taco Maker/diesel, **food:** Applebee's, Carl's Jr, IHOP, McDonald's, Subway, Taco Bell, **lodging:** Sleep Inn, **other:** Big O Tire, K-Mart, OfficeMax, Parkway Drug, Sears/auto, Sherm's Foods, Staples, Wal-Mart/auto, Mt Nebo RV Park

Roseburg

125 Garden Valley Blvd, Roseburg, **E...gas:** Chevron, 76/diesel, Shell/diesel/24hr, **food:** Jack-in-the-Box, KFC, McDonald's, Sandpiper Rest., Taco Bell, WagonWheel Rest., **lodging:** Best Inn Suites, Comfort Inn, Windmill Inn/rest., **other:** Albertson's, CarQuest, Ford, GMC, NAPA, Rite Aid, transmissions, **W...gas:** Chevron, 76, Shell/LP/repair, **food:** Arby's, Burger King, Carl's Jr, IHOP, Izzy's Pizza, La Hacienda Mexican, RoundTable Pizza, Sizzler, Tequila's Mexican, Wendy's, **lodging:** Best Western, **other:** MEDICAL CARE, BiMart, Fred Meyer, House of Fabrics, JC Penney, Sears/auto, Schuck's Parts, mall

124 OR 138, Roseburg, City Ctr, **E...gas:** 76/diesel/24hr, Tesoro, **food:** Denny's, HiHo Rest., **lodging:** Best Western, Dunes Motel, Holiday Inn Express, Holiday Motel, Travelodge, **other:** MEDICAL CARE, Chevrolet/Pontiac/Buick, Honda, Mazda, Rite Aid, Safeway, **W...gas:** Chevron, Shell/Subway, **food:** Gay 90's Deli, KFC, Pete's Drive-In, Taco Time, **other:** HOSPITAL, Grocery Outlet

123 Roseburg, **E...other:** to Umpqua Park, camping, museum

121 McLain Ave, no facilities

120.5mm S Umpqua River

120 OR 99 N(no EZ nb return), Green District, Roseburg, **E...lodging:** Shady Oaks Motel, **3 mi E...food:** HiHo Rest, **lodging:** Best Western, **W...**RV parts

119 OR 99 S, OR 42 W, Winston, **W...gas:** Chevron/A&W/diesel/24hr, Shell/diesel, **food:** Callahan's Cove Rest., McDonald's, Ocampo's Mexican, Papa Murphy's, Subway, **other:** PriceLess Foods, UPS, RV Park, **3 mi W...lodging:** Greentree Inn/rest., Hillside Court Motel, Wildlife Safari Rest., Sweet Breeze Inn

113 Clarks Branch Rd, Round Prairie, **W...lodging:** QuickStop Motel/mkt, Cubby Hole Mkt, **other:** On the River RV Park, diesel repair

112.5mm S Umpqua River

112 OR 99, OR 42, Dillard, **E...other:** Rivers West RV park, **food:** Southfork Lodge Rest./store, **rest area nb, W...rest area sb, full(handicapped)facilities, phone, picnic tables, litter barrels, petwalk**

111mm weigh sta nb

Interstate 5

N ↕ S

110 Boomer Hill Rd, no facilities

108 Myrtle Creek, **E...food:** DQ, The Hub Rest., **other:** Myrtle Creek RV Park

106 Weaver Rd, **E...**airport

103 Tri City, Myrtle Creek, **E...food:** Broaster House Diner, Kelly's Steaks(1mi), **W...gas:** Chevron/A&W/diesel/24hr, **food:** McDonald's

102 Gazley Rd, **W...other:** Surprise Valley RV Park

101.5mm S Umpqua River

101 Riddle, Stanton Park, **W...**camping

99 Canyonville, **E...food:** Burger King, Cow Creek Café/RV Park/casino, **lodging:** Riverside Motel, 7 Feathers Hotel/RV Park/casino, Valley View Motel, **other:** diesel/RV repair, **W...gas:** Fat Harvey's/diesel/LP/café, Shell/diesel/24hr, **lodging:** Best Western

98 OR 99, Canyonville, Days Creek, **E...gas:** 76/diesel, Shell/diesel/24hr, **food:** Bob's Country Jct Rest., Feedlot Rest., Heaven-on-Earth Café, Natural Foods, **lodging:** Master Host Inn, Leisure Inn, **W...food:** Tastee Burger, **other:** museum, auto repair

95 Canyon Creek, no facilities

90mm Canyon Creek Pass, elev 2020

88 Azalea, **W...other:** Azalea Gen Store/gas

86 Barton Rd, Quine's Creek, **E...gas:** Shell/diesel, **other:** Heaven on Earth Rest./RV camp

83 Barton Rd(from nb), **E...other:** Meadow Wood RV Park(3mi)

82mm rest area both lanes, full(handicapped)facilities, phone, picnic tables, litter barrels, petwalk

80 Glendale, **W...gas:** Sawyer Sta/LP, **food:** Village Inn Rest., **lodging:** Glendale Inn

79.5mm Stage Road Pass, elev 1830

78 Speaker Rd, no facilities

76 Wolf Creek, **E...lodging:** Stage Coach Pass Motel, **W...gas:** Exxon/diesel/24hr, Pacific Pride/diesel, 76, **food:** Bite of Wyo Rest., Wolf Creek Inn Rest., **other:** RV park

74mm Smith Hill Summit, elev 1730

71 Sunny Valley, **E...gas:** 76/diesel, **lodging:** Sunny Valley Motel, **W...food:** Aunt Mary's Tavern, **other:** KOA

69mm Sexton Mtn Pass, elev 1960

66 Hugo, **W...other:** Joe Creek Waterfalls RV Camping

63mm rest area both lanes, full(handicapped)facilities, phone, info, picnic tables, litter barrels, vending, petwalk

61 Merlin, **E...other:** Twin Pines RV Park, **W...gas:** Shell/diesel, **other:** Earl's RV

Grants Pass

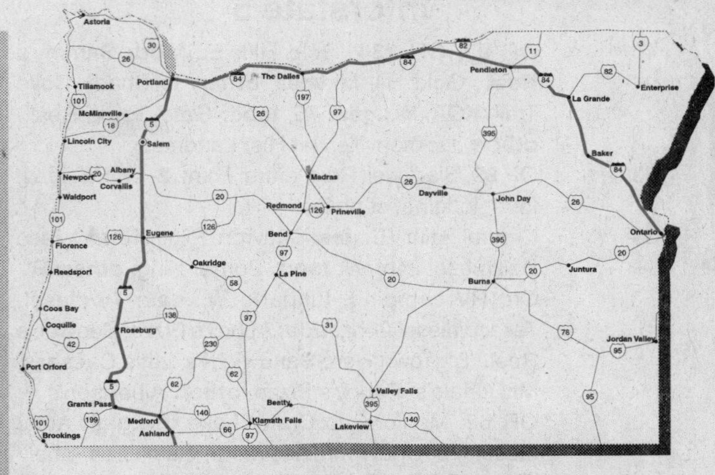

58 OR 99, to US 199, Grants Pass, **W...gas:** Arco, Chevron, Gas4Less/U-Haul, 76/diesel, Shell/repair, Texaco/diesel, TownePump Gas, **food:** Angela's Mexican, Baskin-Robbins, BeeGee's Rest., Burger King, Carl's Jr, DQ, Della's Rest., Denny's, Marco's Pizza, McDonald's, Papa Murphy's, Pizza Hut, Senor Sam's Mexican, Sizzler, Skipper's, Stanbrook's Rest., Subway, Wendy's, **lodging:** Budget Inn, Comfort Inn, Hawk's Inn, Hawthorn Suites, Motel 6, Parkway Lodge, Regal Lodge, Riverside Inn, Royal Vue Motel, Shilo Inn, Super 8, SweetBreeze Inn, TownHouse Motel, Travelodge, **other:** HOSPITAL, AutoZone, Chevrolet/Nissan/Honda, Chrysler/Plymouth/Dodge/Jeep, PriceChopper Foods, Radio Shack, Schwab Tire, ToolBox Repair, st police, towing

55 US 199, Redwood Hwy, E Grants Pass, **W...gas:** Arco/24hr, CFN/diesel, Exxon/diesel/LP/24hr, **food:** Abby's Pizza, Arby's, Carl's Jr, Elmer's, JJ North's Buffet, McDonald's, Shari's/24hr, Si Casa Flores Mexican, Taco Bell, Wild River Brewing Co, **lodging:** Best Western, Discovery Inn, Holiday Inn Express, Knight's Inn, **other:** HOSPITAL, Albertson's, Big O Tire, Fred Meyer, Grocery Outlet, JC Penney, Rite Aid, RiverPark RV Park, Shuck's Parts, Siskiyou RV Ctr, Staples, Wal-Mart

48 Rogue River, Rogue River RA, **E...gas:** Exxon/LP, Fireball Gas, Shell/diesel, **food:** Homestead Rest., **W...food:** Abby's Pizza, Betty's Kitchen, Karen's Kitchen, Tarasco Mexican, **lodging:** Best Western, Rogue River Inn, Rod&Reel Motel, Weasku Inn, **other:** Circle RV Park, MktBasket Foods

45b W...other: Valley of the Rogue SP/rest area both lanes, full(handicapped) facilities, phone, picnic tables, litter barrels, petwalk, camping

45mm Rogue River

45a OR 99, Savage Rapids Dam, **E...other:** Cypress Grove RV Park, **other:** gas, food, lodging

43 OR 99, OR 234, Gold Hill, to Crater Lake, **E...food:** Rock Point Bistro, **lodging:** Lazy Acres Motel/RV Park

OREGON

Interstate 5

N ↕ S

40 OR 99, OR 234, Gold Hill, **E...food:** Sammy's Rest., Gold Hill Mkt/deli, **other:** to Shady Cove Trail, KOA, **W...gas:** 76, **food:** Gato Gordo Rest., **other:** Jacksonville Nat Hist Landmark

35 OR 99, Blackwell Rd, Central Point, **2-4 mi W...**gas, food, lodging, st police

33 Central Point, **E...gas:** Chevron, Pilot/Subway/Taco Bell/diesel/24hr/@, **food:** Burger King, **other:** RV Ctr, RV camping, funpark, **W...gas:** 76/diesel, Texaco/diesel/24hr, **food:** Abbey's Pizza, BeeGee's Rest., BigTown Hero Sandwiches, Little Caesar's, McDonald's, Pappy's Pizza, **other:** Albertson's

Medford

30 OR 62, Medford, to Crater Lake, **E...gas:** Arco/diesel, 76, Chevron/diesel/24hr, Gas4Less, Shell/diesel, **food:** Abby's Pizza, Applebee's, Arby's, Asian Grill, Carl's Jr, Chevy's Mexican, DQ, Denny's, Elmer's, IHOP, India Palace, Marie Callender, McDonald's, Papa John's, Pizza Hut, Quizno's, Red Robin, Schlotsky's, Si Casa Mexican, Sizzler, Starbucks, Subway, Taco Bell, Taco Delite, Thai Bistro, Wendy's, Williams Bakery, **lodging:** Best Western, Cedar Lodge, Comfort Inn, Motel 6, Reston Inn, Rogue Regency Hotel, Shilo Inn, ValleyHai Inn, Windmill Inn, **other:** AAA RV, Albertson's, Aamco, Barnes&Noble, BiMart Foods, Chevrolet, Circuit City, Ford, Fred Meyer, Food4Less, Medford Oaks RV Park, NAPA, OR Tire, Radio Shack, River City RV Ctr, Safeway, Sears, USPO, st police, **W...gas:** Chevron/diesel, Shell/diesel, **food:** Burger King, Domino's, Jack-in-the-Box, KFC, King Wah Chinese, Red Lobster, Skipper's, Wendy's, **other:** HOSPITAL, JC Penney, Krecht's Parts, Mervyn's, Target, U-Haul, mall

27 Barnett Rd, Medford, **E...gas:** Exxon/diesel, Shell/24hr, **food:** Kopper Kitchen, **lodging:** Best Western, Day's Inn/rest., Economy Inn, Motel 6, **W...gas:** Chevron/24hr, Exxon/diesel, Gas4Less, 76, Shell/diesel/24hr, **food:** Abby's Pizza, Apple Annie's, Burger King, Carl's Jr, HomeTown Buffet, Jack-in-the-Box, KFC, Kim's Chinese, McDonald's, McGrath's FishHouse, Pizza Hut, Rooster's Rest., Senor Sam's Mexican, Shari's, Starbucks, Subway, Taco Bell, Wendy's, Zach's Deli, **lodging:** Best Inn, Comfort Inn, Red Lion Inn, Royal Crest Motel, **other:** Ford/Mercury/Lincoln, Food4Less, Fred Meyer, Harry&David's, Hyundai, K-Mart, OfficeMax, Radio Shack, Saturn, Schwab Tires, Staples, Toyota, WinCo Foods

24 Phoenix, **E...gas:** Petro/diesel/rest./RV dump/24hr/@, Shell, **lodging:** PearTree Motel/rest./RV park, **other:** Peterbilt/GMC, **W...gas:** Exxon, **food:** Angelo's Pizza, Courtyard Café, Luigi's Café, McDonald's, Randy's Café, **lodging:** Bavarian Inn, Phoenix Motel, **other:** Ray's Foods, CarQuest, Holiday RV Park, Factory Stores/famous brands

22mm rest area sb, full(handicapped)facilities, phone, picnic tables, litter barrels, vending, petwalk

21 Talent, **W...gas:** Arco/24hr, Gas4Less, Talent's/diesel/rest./repair, **food:** Arbor House Rest., Expresso Café, Figaro's Italian, Senor Sam's Cantina, **lodging:** GoodNight Inn, **other:** OR RV Roundup Camping, Wal-Mart/auto

19 Valley View Rd, Ashland, **W...gas:** Exxon/diesel/LP, Pacific Pride/diesel, Shell/diesel, **food:** Burger King, El Tapatio Mexican, **lodging:** Best Western, Hawthorn Inn, Regency Inn/rest./RV Park, Stratford Inn, **other:** HOSPITAL, U-Haul

Ashland

18mm weigh sta both lanes

14 OR 66, Ashland, to Klamath Falls, **E...gas:** Chevron, 76/diesel/LP, Shell/diesel, **food:** Denny's, OakTree Rest., **lodging:** Ashland Hills Inn/rest., Best Western, Rodeway Inn, Vista Motel, Windmill Inn, **other:** Emigrant Lake Camping(3mi), KOA(3mi), Nat Hist Museum, **W...gas:** Arco/24hr, Astro, 76/LP/24hr, **food:** Azteca Mexican, DQ, McDonald's, Omar's Rest(1mi), Pizza Hut, Taco Bell, Thai Rest., **lodging:** Knight's Inn/rest., Super 8, **other:** Albertson's, BiMart Foods, Rite Aid, Schwab Tire

11.5mm chainup area

11 OR 99, Siskiyou Blvd(no nb return), **2-4 mi W...gas:** Exxon, Shell, **food:** BBQ, DQ, Figaro's Italian, Goodtimes Café, House of Thai, Little Caesar's, Omar's Rest., Senor Sam's Mexican, Subway, Wendy's, **lodging:** Best Western, Cedarwood Inn, Hillside Inn, Rodeway Inn, Stratford Inn, **other:** Radio Shack, Weisinger Brewery

6 to Mt Ashland, **E...lodging:** Callahan's Siskiyou Lodge/rest., **other:** phone, ski area

4mm Siskiyou Summit, elev 4310, brake check both lanes

1 to Siskiyou Summit(from nb)

0mm Oregon/California state line

Interstate 84

E ↕ W

Exit # Services

378mm Oregon/Idaho state line, Snake River

377.5mm Welcome Ctr wb, full(handicapped)facilities, info, phone, picnic tables, litter barrels, vending, petwalk

Ontario

376 US 30, Ontario, to US 20/26, Payette, **N...gas:** Chevron/24hr, **food:** Burger King, Country Kitchen, DQ, Denny's, McDonald's, Taco Time, Wingers, **lodging:** Best Western, Colonial Inn, Holiday Inn, Motel 6, Sleep Inn, Super 8, **other:** Chrysler/Dodge/Plymouth/Jeep, K-Mart, Staples, Wal-Mart SuperCtr/24hr, st police, **S...gas:** Phillips 66, Pilot/Arby's/diesel/24hr/@, Shell, **food:** Domino's, Klondike Pizza, Rusty's Steaks, Sizzler, Subway, Taco Bell, Wendy's, **lodging:** Economy Inn, Holi-

Interstate 84

E ↕ W

day Motel/rest., OR Trail Motel, Stockmen's Motel, **other:** HOSPITAL, Commercial Tire, NAPA, Radio Shack, Schwab Tire, U-Haul, RV repair, 4 Wheeler Museum

374 US 30, OR 201, to Ontario, **N...**to Ontario SP, **S...gas:** Shell/diesel, **food:** North Star Café, **lodging:** Budget Motel, Carlile Motel, **other:** HOSPITAL, parts/repair

373.5mm Malheur River

371 Stanton Blvd, **2 mi S...**to correctional institution

362 Moores Hollow Rd, no facilities

356 OR 201, to Weiser, ID, **3 mi N...**Oasis RV Park

354.5mm weigh sta eb

353 US 30, to Huntington, **N...**weigh sta wb, **gas:** Farewell Bend Travel Plaza/diesel/rest./motel/@, **other:** to Farewell Bend SP, truck repair, RV camping, info

351mm Pacific/Mountain time zone

345 US 30, Lime, Huntington, **1 mi N...**gas, food, lodging, to Snake River Area

342 Lime(from eb), no facilities

340 Rye Valley, no facilities

338 Lookout Mountain, **N...other:** Oregon Tr RV Park

337mm Burnt River

335 to Weatherby, N...rest area both lanes, full(handicapped)facilities, Oregon Trail Info, picnic tables, litter barrels, vending, petwalk

330 Plano Rd, to Cement Plant Rd, **S...**cement plant

329mm pulloff eb

327 Durkee, **N...gas:** Oregon Tr Travel Ctr/Cenex/diesel/café/@

325mm Pritchard Creek

321mm Alder Creek

319 to Pleasant Valley, no facilities

317 to Pleasant Valley(from wb)

315 to Pleasant Valley, no facilities

306 US 30, Baker, **2 mi S...gas:** Chevron/diesel, **food:** DQ, **lodging:** Baker City Motel, Budget Inn, Friendship Inn, Lariat Motel/RV, OR Tr Motel/rest., Royal Motel, **other:** HOSPITAL, to st police, same as 304

Baker

304 OR 7, Baker, **N...gas:** Chevron/Burger King/TCBY/diesel, **lodging:** Super 8, Welcome Inn, **S...gas:** Shell/Blimpie/diesel/24hr, Sinclair/diesel/rest./24hr, **food:** DQ, Joltin Java, Klondike Pizza, McDonald's, Papa Murphy's, Pizza Hut, Subway, Sumpter Jct Rest., Taco Time, **lodging:** Best Western, Eldorado Inn, Quality Inn, Royal Motel, Western Motel, **other:** HOSPITAL, Albertson's, BiMart Foods, Ford/Lincoln/Mercury, Mel's Auto Parts, Mtn View RV Park(3mi), Paul's Transmissions, Rite Aid, Safeway, museum, to hist dist

302 OR 86 E to Richland, **S...other:** HOSPITAL, OR Tr RV Park/gas

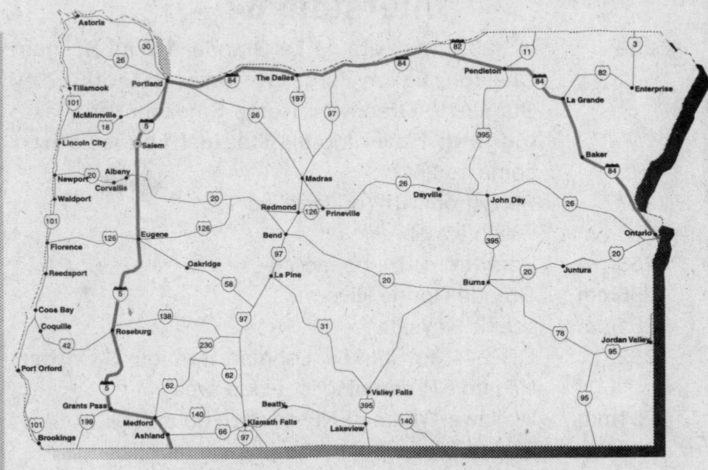

298 OR 203, to Medical Springs, no facilities

297mm Baldock Slough

295mm rest area both lanes, full(handicapped)facilities, info, phone, picnic tables, litter barrels, vending, petwalk

289mm Powder River

287.5mm 45th parallel...halfway between the equator and north pole

286mm N Powder River

285 US 30, OR 237, North Powder, **N...gas:** Cenex/diesel/café, **lodging:** Powder River Motel, **S...other:** to Anthony Lakes, ski area

284mm Wolf Creek

283 Wolf Creek Lane, no facilities

278 Clover Creek, no facilities

273 Ladd Canyon, no facilities

270 Ladd Creek Rd(from eb, no return), no facilities

269mm rest area both lanes, full(handicapped)facilities, info, phone, picnic tables, litter barrels, vending, petwalk

268 Foothill Rd, no facilities

265 OR 203, LaGrande, **N...**airport, **S...gas:** Flying J/Exxon/TCBY/diesel/rest./@, **food:** SmokeHouse Rest., **lodging:** to Broken Arrow Lodge, Quail Run Motel, Travelodge, **other:** Radio Shack, RV camping, to E OR U

LaGrande

261 OR 82, LaGrande, **N...gas:** Chevron/diesel, Shell/diesel, Texaco/diesel, **food:** Denny's, Pizza Hut, Quizno's, Subway, Taco Bell, **lodging:** Howard Johnson, **other:** Chrysler/Plymouth/Dodge/Jeep, Ford/Lincoln/Mercury, Grocery Outlet, Shop'n Kart, Wal-Mart/drugs, LaGrande Rendezvous RV Resort, st police, **S... gas:** Exxon/diesel, 76/Subway/diesel, **food:** DQ, Klondike Pizza, Little Caesar's, McDonald's, Skipper's, Taco Time, Wendy's, Best Western, Sandman Inn, Super 8, **other:** HOSPITAL, Albertson's, Cottman Transmissions, Rite Aid, Safeway, Schuck's Parts, E OR U, Wallowa Lake

260mm Grande Ronde River

OREGON

Interstate 84

E ↕ W

259 US 30 E(from eb), to La Grande, **1-2 mi S...gas:** Chevron, Exxon/Burger King/diesel, **food:** Foley Sta Rest., Greenwell Rest., Smokehouse Rest., **lodging:** Royal Motel, Stardust Lodge, **other:** same as 261

257 Perry(from wb), no facilities

258mm weigh sta eb

256 Perry(from eb), no facilities

255mm Grande Ronde River

254mm scenic wayside

252 OR 244, to Starkey, Lehman Springs, **S...other:** Hilgard SP, camping, chainup area

251mm Wallowa-Whitman NF, eastern boundary

248 Spring Creek Rd, to Kamela, no facilities

246mm Wallowa-Whitman NF, western boundary

243 Summit Rd, Mt Emily Rd, to Kamela, Oregon Trail info, **2 mi N...other:** Emily Summit SP

241mm Summit of the Blue Mtns, elev 4193

238 Meacham, **1 mi N...lodging:** Blue Mountain Lodge, **other:** Oregon Trail info

234 Meacham, **N...other:** Emigrant Sprs SP, RV camping

231.5mm Umatilla Indian Reservation, eastern boundary

228mm Deadman Pass, Oregon Trail info, N...rest area both lanes, full(handicapped)facilities, phone, picnic table, litter barrel, petwalk, vending, RV dump

227mm weigh sta wb, brake check area, phone

224 Poverty Flats Rd, Old Emigrant Hill Rd, to Emigrant Springs SP, no facilities

223mm wb viewpoint, no restrooms

221.5mm eb viewpoint, no restrooms

220mm wb runaway truck ramp

216 Mission, McKay Creek, **N...gas:** Pacific Pride/diesel, Shell/Arrowhead/diesel/@, **food:** Cody's Rest., **other:** Wildhorse Casino/RV Park

213 US 30(from wb), Pendleton, **3-5 mi N...gas:** Chevron/diesel, Exxon/deli, **lodging:** Budget Inn, Economy Inn, Pioneer Motel, Tapadera Budget Motel, Travelers Inn, **other:** HOSPITAL, Pendleton NHD

212mm Umatilla Indian Reservation western boundary

210 OR 11, Pendleton, **N...gas:** Exxon, **other:** HOSPITAL, museum, **S...gas:** Pacific Pride/diesel, 76/diesel, Shell/diesel/LP, **food:** Kopper Kitchen, Shari's/24hr, **lodging:** Best Western, Holiday Inn Express, Motel 6, Red Lion Inn/rest., Super 8, **other:** Mtn View RV Park, st police

Pendleton

209 US 395, Pendleton, **N...gas:** Arco/24hr, **food:** A&W, Dean's Mkt/deli, Jack-in-the-Box, KFC, Taco Bell, **lodging:** Oxford Suites, Travelers Inn, Travelodge, **other:** HOSPITAL, Rite Aid, Safeway/24hr, Schuck's Parts, Wal-Mart SuperCtr/24hr, transmissions, **S...gas:** Exxon/diesel/24hr, Shell/diesel, **food:** Arby's, Burger King, Denny's/24hr, Klondike Pizza, McDonald's, Rooster's Rest., Subway, Wendy's, **lodging:** Econolodge, **other:** MEDICAL CARE, Chevrolet/Pontiac/Buick, Goodyear, Honda, K-Mart, Schwab Tire, Thompson RV Ctr, to Pilot Rock

208mm Umatilla River

207 US 30, W Pendleton, **N...gas:** Chevron/diesel, Shell/diesel/LP, **food:** DQ, Godfather's, Taco Bell, **lodging:** Longhorn Motel, Oxford Suites, Tapadera Budget Motel, Vagabond Inn, **other:** Brooke RV Park, Lookout RV Park

202 Barnhart Rd, to Stage Gulch, **N...**Woodpecker Truck Repair, **S...gas:** Floyd's Truck Ranch/diesel/motel/café/@, **lodging:** 7 Inn, **other:** Oregon Trail info

199 Stage Coach Rd, Yoakum Rd, no facilities

198 Lorenzen Rd, McClintock Rd, **N...other:** trailer/reefer repair

193 Echo Rd, to Echo, Oregon Trail Site

188 US 395 N, Hermiston, **N...gas:** Chevron/diesel(1mi), Pilot/Subway/diesel/24hr/RV park/@, **5 mi N...food:** Denny's/24hr, Jack-in-the-Box, McDonald's, Shari's/24hr, **lodging:** Best Western, Economy Inn, Oxford Suites, **other:** HOSPITAL, **S...other:** Henrietta RV Park, Echo HS

187mm rest area both lanes, full(handicapped)facilities, phone, info, picnic tables, litter barrels, petwalk

182 OR 207, to Hermiston, **N...other:** Buffalo Jct Gas, **5 mi N...gas:** Butter Creek/gas/diesel/RV park, **food:** McDonald's, Shari's

180 Westland Rd, to Hermiston, McNary Dam, **N...**trailer repair, **S...gas:** Shell/diesel

179 I-82 W, to Umatilla, Kennewick, WA

177 Umatilla Army Depot, no facilities

171 Paterson Ferry Rd, to Paterson, no facilities

168 US 730, to Irrigon, **8 mi N...other:** Oregon Trail info, Oasis RV Park

165 Port of Morrow, **S...gas:** Pacific Pride/diesel

164 Boardman, **N...gas:** Chevron/diesel, Shell/diesel, C&D Drive-In, Lynard's Cellar Café, Dodge City Motel, Riverview Motel, USPO, Boardman RV/Marina Park, bank, **S...**76/Taco Bell/diesel/24hr, Nomad Deli/24hr, Econolodge, NAPA Repair/parts, Sentry Foods

161mm rest area both lanes, full(handicapped)facilities, phone, picnic tables, litter barrels, vending, petwalk

159 Tower Rd, no facilities

151 Threemile Canyon, no facilities

Interstate 84

E ↕ W

147 OR 74, to Ione, Heppner, Oregon Trail Site, Blue Mtn Scenic Byway, no facilities

137 OR 19, Arlington, **S...**Chevron, 76/diesel, Happy Canyon Chicken/pizza, Pheasant Grill, Arlington Motel, Village Inn/rest., Thrifty Foods, city park, Columbia River RV Park(1mi)

136.5mm view point wb, picnic tables, litter barrels

131 Woelpern Rd(from eb, no return), no facilities

129 Blalock Canyon, Lewis&Clark Trail, no facilities

123 Philippi Canyon, Lewis&Clark Trail, no facilities

114.5mm John Day River

114 **S...**to John Day River RA

112 **N...**John Day Dam

109 Rufus, **N...**John Day Visitor Ctr, **S...gas:** Pacific Pride/diesel, Shell/diesel, **food:** BBQ, Bob's T-Bone, Frosty's Café, Larry's Rest., **lodging:** Arrowhead Motel, Tyee Motel, Rufus Inn, **other:** RV camping

104 US 97, Biggs, **N...other:** Des Chutes Park Bridge, **S...gas:** Astro/diesel, Chevron, 76/diesel/24hr, Shell/diesel, **lodging:** Biggs Motel/café, Jack's Rest., Linda's Rest., Subway, Dinty's Motel, Riviera Motel, **other:** Maryhill Museum

100mm Deschutes River, Columbia River Gorge Scenic Area

97 OR 206, Celilo, **N...other:** Celilo SP, restrooms, **S...other:** Deschutes SP, Indian Village

88 **N...**to The Dalles Dam

The Dalles

87 US 30, US 197, to Dufur, **N...gas:** 76/Taco Bell/24hr, Shell/diesel, **food:** Big Jim's Drive-In, McDonald's, **lodging:** Comfort Inn, Inn at the Dalles, Shilo Inn/rest., **other:** Columbia Hills RV Park, Lone Pine RV Park, st police, **S...lodging:** Dalles Inn, Schwab Tire

85 The Dalles, **N...Riverfront Park, restrooms, phone, picnic tables, litter barrels, playground, marina, S...gas:** 76, **food:** BurgervilleUSA, Holstein's Coffee, **lodging:** Best Western, Oregon Motel, **other:** HOSPITAL, Fast Auto Repair, NAPA, camping, to Nat Hist Dist

83 (84 from wb)W The Dalles, **N...food:** Orient Café, Windseeker Rest., **other:** NAPA, Tire Factory, **S...gas:** Chevron, Exxon, Shell, **food:** Burger King, Cousins Rest., Denny's, McDonald's, Papa Murphy's, Skipper's, Subway, Taco Bell, Taco Time, **lodging:** Best Western, Day's Inn, Quality Inn, Shilo Inn, Tillicum Inn, Super 8, **other:** HOSPITAL, Albertson's, Chrysler/Plymouth/Dodge, $Store, Emporium, Fred Meyer, Jo-Ann Fabrics, K-Mart, Rite Aid, Safeway, Schuck's Parts, Staples

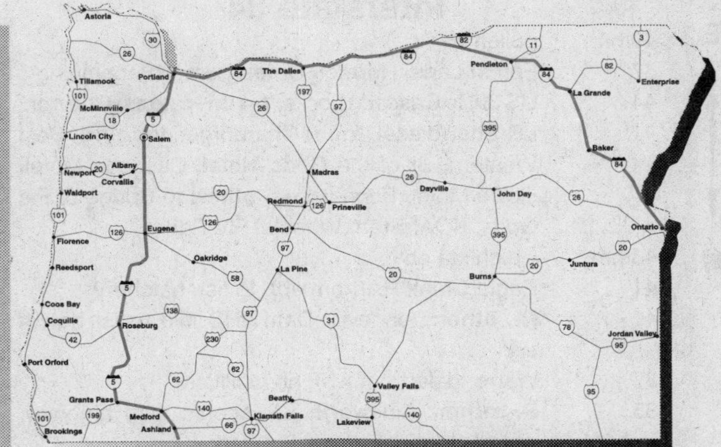

82 Chenowith Area, **S...gas:** Shell/diesel, **1-2 mi S...gas:** Astro/diesel/24hr, Exxon, **food:** Arby's, Burger King, Cousins Rest., KFC, Pietro's Pizza, Stooky's Café, Subway, Wendy's, Day's Inn, BiMart, **other:** Chevrolet/Pontiac/Buick/Jeep/Subaru, Ford/Isuzu/Nissan, Columbia River Discovery Ctr, museum, same as 84

76 Rowena, **N...other:** Mayer SP, Lewis & Clark info, windsurfing

73mm Memaloose SP, rest area both lanes, full(handicapped)facilities, picnic tables, litter barrels, phone, petwalk, RV dump, camping

69 US 30, Mosier, **S...gas:** Rte 30 Store

66mm N...Koberg Beach SP, rest area wb, full facilities, picnic table, litter barrels

Hood River

64 US 30, OR 35, Hood River, to White Salmon, Gov't Camp, **N...gas:** Chevron, Shell/24hr, McDonald's, Riverside Grill, Taco Time, Best Western, marina, museum, st police, **S...gas:** Exxon, **food:** China Gorge Café

63 Hood River, City Ctr, **N...gas:** Shell/diesel, **other:** Visitor Ctr, **S...gas:** Exxon/diesel/24hr, 76, **food:** Burger King, China Gorge, Pasquale's Pizza, Pietro's Pizza, **lodging:** Hood River Hotel, **other:** HOSPITAL, USPO, same as 64

62 US 30, W Hood River, W Cliff Dr, **N...food:** Charburger, **lodging:** Columbia Gorge Hotel, Meredith Motel, Vagabond Lodge, **other:** FruitTree Gifts, **S...gas:** Chevron/diesel/LP, Shell/diesel/LP, **food:** Carolyn's Rest., DQ, McDonald's, Red Carpet Rest., Shari's/24hr, Subway, Taco Bell, **lodging:** Comfort Suites, Econolodge, Prater's Motel, Riverview Lodge, Stonehedge Inn, **other:** HOSPITAL, Chevrolet/Pontiac/Buick, Rite Aid, Safeway, Schwab Tire, Wal-Mart

61mm pulloff wb

60 service rd wb(no return), no facilities

58 Mitchell Point Overlook(from eb)

56 **N...other:** Viento SP, RV camping, phone

55 Starvation Peak Tr Head(from eb), restrooms

54mm weigh sta wb

51 Wyeth, **S...**camping

OREGON

Interstate 84

E ↕ W

49mm pulloff eb
47 Forest Lane, Hermon Creek(from wb), camping
44 US 30, to Cascade Locks, **1-4 mi N...gas:** Chevron/LP, Shell/diesel, **food:** Charburger, **lodging:** Best Western, Br of the Gods Motel, Cascade Motel, Dolce Motel, Econolodge, **other:** to Bridge of the Gods, KOA, Stern Wheeler RV Park
43mm weigh sta eb
41 Eagle Creek RA(from eb), to fish hatchery
40 **N...other:** Bonneville Dam NHS, info, to fish hatchery
37 Warrendale(from wb), no facilities
35 **S...other:** Ainsworth SP, scenic loop highway, waterfall area, Fishery RV Park
31 Multnomah Falls(exits left from both lanes), **S...lodging:** Multnomah Falls Lodge(hist site), camping
30 **S...**Benson SP(from eb)
29 Dalton Point(from wb)
28 to Bridal Veil(7 mi return from eb)
25 **N...**Rooster Rock SP
23mm viewpoint wb, hist marker
22 Corbett, **2 mi S...gas:** Corbett Mkt, **lodging:** Chinook Inn/rest., **other:** Crown Point RV Camping
19mm Columbia River Gorge scenic area
18 Lewis&Clark SP, to Oxbow SP, lodging, food, RV camping
17.5mm Sandy River
17 Marine Dr, Troutdale, **N...food:** Wendy's, **lodging:** Holiday Inn Express, **S...gas:** Chevron/24hr, Flying J/Conoco/Burger King/diesel/LP/24hr/@, TA/Arco/Subway/diesel/24hr/@, **food:** Arby's, McDonald's, Shari's/24hr, Taco Bell, **lodging:** Best Value Inn, Motel 6, Phoenix Inn, **other:** Columbia Outlets/famous brands
16 238th Dr, Fairview, **N...gas:** Arco/diesel/24hr, **food:** Jack-in-the-Box, Yazzi's Rest., **lodging:** Travelodge, **other:** Wal-Mart/auto, **S...gas:** Chevron, **lodging:** Best Western, McMenamin Motel, Shilo Inn, **other:** HOSPITAL, Gresham RV Ctr(3mi)
14 207th Ave, Fairview, **N...gas:** Shell/A&W/Taco Bell/diesel, **food:** GinSun Chinese, **other:** Portland RV Park, Rolling Hills RV Park
13 181st Ave, Gresham, **N...gas:** Chevron, Tesoro, **food:** IHOP, **lodging:** Hampton Inn, **S...gas:** Arco/24hr, 76/Circle K, 7-11, **food:** Blimpie, Burger King, Jung's Chinese, McDonald's, PlumTree Rest., Shari's/24hr, Wendy's, **lodging:** Comfort Suites, Extended Stay America, Hawthorn Suites, Sheraton/rest., Sleep Inn, **other:** Candy Basket Chocolates, Safeway, auto repair
10 122nd Ave(from eb), no facilities
9 I-205, S to Salem, N to Seattle, to airport, (to 102nd Ave from eb)
8 I-205 N(from eb), to airport

Portland

7 Halsey St(from eb), Gateway Dist
6 I-205 S(from eb)
5 OR 213, to 82nd Ave, **N...lodging:** Capri Motel, Day's Inn, **1-3 mi N...gas:** 76, Shell, 7-11, **food:** Arby's, Domino's, Pizza Hut, **lodging:** Quality Inn, Shilo Inn, **S...food:** Elmer's Rest., **lodging:** Microtel
4 68th Ave(from eb), to Halsey Ave
3 58th Ave(from eb), **S...gas:** 76, HOSPITAL
2 43rd Ave, 39th Ave, Halsey St, **N...gas:** 76, Shell, **food:** McDonald's, Winchell's, **lodging:** Banfield Motel, Rodeway Inn, **other:** Rite Aid, **S...other:** HOSPITAL, Buick/Pontiac, Jeep, same as 1
1 33rd Ave, Lloyd Blvd, **N...gas:** 76, Pacific Pride/diesel, Shell, **food:** Burger King, **lodging:** Banfield Motel, Best Western, Holiday Inn, Red Lion Inn, Residence Inn, **other:** JC Penney, Rite Aid, **S...other:** Buick/GMC
0mm I-84 begins/ends on I-5, exit 301.

Interstate 205(Portland)

Portland Area

N ↕ S

Exit # Services
37mm I-405 begins/ends on I-5. **Exits 36-27 are in Washington.**
36 NE 134th St(from nb), **E...gas:** Astro/diesel, **lodging:** University Inn, **other:** Fred Meyer, **W...gas:** Citgo/7-11, 76, TrailMart/diesel, **food:** Billigan's Roadhouse, Burger King, Burgerville, Jack-in-the-Box, McDonald's, Round Table Pizza, Taco Bell, **lodging:** Comfort Inn, Holiday Inn Express, Olympia Motel, Salmon Creek Inn, Shilo Inn, **other:** HOSPITAL, Albertson's, Hi-School Drugs, Zupan's Mkt, 99 RV Park
32 NE 83rd St, Andreson Rd, **W...gas:** Shell/diesel/24hr, **food:** Meadows Kitchen, Wendy's, **other:** Home Depot
30 WA 500, Orchards, Vancouver, **E...gas:** Shell/24hr, **food:** KFC, Burger King, Burgerville, Cisco's Rest., KFC, McDonald's, Subway, **other:** Albertson's, Rite Aid, Toyota, RV park, **W...gas:** Arco, Chevron/24hr, **food:** Chevy's Mexican, Golden Tent Rest., Moshi Japanese, Olive Garden, Red Lobster, Red Robin Rest., RoundTable Pizza, Skipper's, Shari's/24hr, Subway, Taco Bell, TCBY, TGIFriday, Tony Roma, **lodging:** Comfort Suites, Heathman Lodge, Holiday Inn Express, Residence Inn, Sleep Inn, Staybridge Inn, **other:** America's Tire, JC Penney, Meijer&Frank, Mervyn's, Nordstrom's, Pic'n Sav Food, Ross, Sears/auto, Target, mall, RV park
28 Mill Plain Rd, **E...gas:** Chevron/24hr, 76/Circle K, Shell/diesel, Shell/diesel, 7-11, **food:** Applebee's, Burger King, Burgerville, DQ, Elmer's Rest., Ghengis Khan Mongolian, Kings Buffet, McDonald's, Ming Chinese, Muchas Gracias Mexican, Papa's German

Interstate 205

N

S

Rest., Pizza Hut, Shari's, Taco Bell, Trader Joe's, **lodging:** Best Inn, Best Western, Extended Stay America, Guesthouse Inn, Phoenix Inn, **other:** Fred Meyer, Schuck's Parts, Schwab Tire, **W...gas:** Arco/24hr, Shell, **food:** Arby's, Jack-in-the-Box, Old Mill Bread, Subway, **other:** HOSPITAL, Chevrolet, Hyundai, Tire Factory, Wal-Mart/auto

27 WA 14, Vancouver, Camas, Columbia River Gorge, no facilities

25mm Columbia River, Oregoninton state line. **Exits 27-36 are in Washington.**

24 122nd Ave, **E...food:** Burger King, China Wok, CoffeeHouse, McDonald's, Shari's, Subway, **lodging:** Comfort Suites, Courtyard, Fairfield Inn, Hilton Garden, Holiday Inn Express, La Quinta, Shilo Inn/rest., Silver Cloud Inn, Staybridge Suites, Super 8, **other:** Best Buy, Home Depot, **W...lodging:** Hampton Inn, Sheraton/rest.

Portland Area

23b a US 30 byp, Columbia Blvd, **E...gas:** Shell/diesel, **lodging:** Best Western, Econolodge, Red Lion Hotel, Travelodge, **other:** HOSPITAL, **W...gas:** Shell, **food:** Bill's Steaks, Elmer's Rest., **lodging:** Best Inn, Best Western, Clarion, Day's Inn, Holiday Inn, Ramada Inn, **other:** camping

22 I-84 E, US 30 E, to The Dalles

21b I-84 W, US 30 W, to Portland

a Glisan St, **E...gas:** 76, **food:** Applebee's, Carl's Jr, Izzy's Pizza, Quizno's, Szechuan Chinese, **lodging:** Chesnut Tree Inn, **other:** Circuit City, Fred Meyer, Mervyn's, Office Depot, Ross, Tower Books, WinCo Foods, mall, **W...gas:** 76, **food:** Burger King, Elmer's Rest., McDonald's, **lodging:** Best Value Inn, Travelodge, **other:** Nissan

20 Stark St, Washington St, **E...food:** Elmer's Rest., McMenamin's Café, Newport Bay Café, Tony Roma's, **lodging:** Holiday Inn Express, **other:** Cottman Transmissions, mall, **W...gas:** 7-11, **food:** ChuckeCheese, Izzy's Pizza, McDonald's, Stark St Pizza, Taco Bell, Village Inn, **lodging:** Rodeway Inn

19 US 26, Division St, **E...gas:** Exxon, **food:** Burger King, **other:** HOSPITAL, Radio Shack, **W...gas:** Chevron/24hr, Shell/diesel, 7-11, **food:** Izzy's Pizza, McDonald's, Sizzler, Wendy's, **other:** Best Value Inn, Travelodge

17 Foster Rd, **E...gas:** 7-11, **W...gas:** Chevron, Shell, **food:** Arby's, Burger King, IHOP, McDonald's, New Copper Penny Grill, Wendy's, **lodging:** Econolodge, Home Depot

16 Johnson Creek Blvd, **W...gas:** Applebee's, **food:** Burger King, Carl's Jr, Denny's, Fuddrucker's, Old Chicago Pizza, Old Country Buffet, Outback Steaks, Papa Joe's, Ron's Café, Starbucks, Subway, Taco Bell, **other:** Best Buy, Fred Meyer, Home Depot, OfficeMax, RV Ctrs, Shuck's Parts

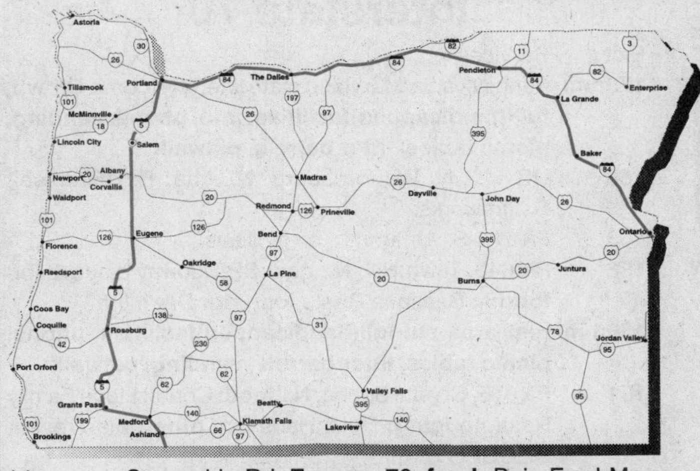

14 Sunnyside Rd, **E...gas:** 76, **food:** Baja FreshMex, Burger King, Domino's, Izzy's Pizza, KFC, McDonald's, McMenamin's Rest., Subway, Taco Time, Thai House, Wendy's, **lodging:** Best Western, Day's Inn, **other:** HOSPITAL, Office Depot, **W...gas:** 76/LP/24hr, **food:** Chevy's Mexican, Gustav's Grill, Olive Garden, Red Robin Rest., **lodging:** Courtyard, Monarch Hotel/rest., Sunnyside Inn/rest., **other:** Barnes&Noble, FabricLand, JC Penney, Mervyn's, Nordstrom's, Old Navy, Sears/auto, Target, World Mkt, mall

13 OR 224, to Milwaukie, **W...**K-Mart

12 OR 213, to Milwaukie, **E...gas:** Chevron/24hr, Shell, 7-11, **food:** Denny's, Elmer's, KFC, McDonald's, Skipper's, Taco Bell/24hr, Wendy's, **lodging:** Clackamas Inn, Cypress Inn, Hampton Inn, **other:** MEDICAL CARE, Fred Meyer, **W...lodging:** Comfort Suites

Portland Area

11 82nd Dr, Gladstone, **W...gas:** Arco/24hr, **food:** High Rock Steakery, Safeway, **lodging:** Oxford Suites

10 OR 213, Park Place, **E...other:** HOSPITAL, to Oregon Trail Ctr

9 OR 99E, Oregon City, **E...gas:** Arco/repair, 76, **food:** KFC, **other:** HOSPITAL, Clackamas Parts, GMC/Pontiac, Mazda, Subaru, Yamaha, **W...gas:** 76, **food:** HongKong Express, La Hacienda Mexican, McDonald's, Shari's, Subway, **lodging:** Budget Inn, Rivershore Hotel, **other:** Firestone/auto, Jo-Ann Fabrics, Michael's, Rite Aid

8.5mm Willamette River

8 OR 43, W Linn, Lake Oswego, **E...gas:** 76, museum, **W...gas:** Shell/diesel

7mm viewpoint nb, hist marker

6 10th St, W Linn St, **E...gas:** Chevron/LP, 76, Ixtapa Mexican, **food:** McDonald's, McMenamin's Café, Shari's/24hr, Thriftway, **other:** Willamette Coffeehouse, **W...food:** Bugatti's Pizza, Jack-in-the-Box, Subway, **other:** Albertson's

4mm Tualatin River

3 Stafford Rd, Lake Oswego, **W...other:** HOSPITAL, Wanker's Country Store/phone

0mm I-205 begins/ends on I-5, exit 288.

PENNSYLVANIA
Interstate 70

E

W

Breezewood

Exit #	Services
173mm	Pennsylvania/Maryland state line. **Welcome Ctr wb, full(handicapped)facilities, info, phone, vending, picnic tables, litter barrels, petwalk**
168	US 522 N, Warfordsburg, **N...gas:** Exxon/diesel, **S...**fireworks
163	PA 731 S, Amaranth, no facilities
156	PA 643, Town Hill, **N...gas:** BP/Subway/diesel/24hr, **food:** 4 Seasons Rest., **lodging:** Day's Inn
156mm	**rest area eb, full(handicapped)facilities, phone, picnic tables, litter barrels, vending, petwalk**
151	PA 915, Crystal Spring, **N...food:** CornerStone Family Rest., **lodging:** DutchHaus Inn, **other:** auto repair, **S...**USPO
149	US 30 W, to Everett, S Breezewood(no immediate wb return), **3 mi S...food:** Denny's, McDonald's, **lodging:** Penn Aire Motel, Redwood Motel, Wildwood Motel
147	US 30, Breezewood, **Services on US 30...gas:** BP/diesel, Citgo, Exxon/diesel, Mobil/diesel/24hr, Sheetz/24hr, Shell, Sunoco/diesel/café, TA/diesel/rest./24hr/@, Texaco/Subway, **food:** Arby's, Big John's Buffet, Bob Evans, Burger King, DQ, Denny's, Domino's, Family House Rest., Hardee's, KFC, McDonald's, Perkins, Pizza Hut, Taco Bell, Wendy's, **lodging:** Best Western, Breezewood Motel, Comfort Inn/rest., Econolodge, Holiday Inn Express, Penn Aire Motel, Quality Inn, Ramada Inn, Wiltshire Motel, **other:** museum
	I-70 W and I-76/PA Turnpike W run together.

For I-70, I-76/PA Turnpike exits 75-146, see PENNSYLVANIA INTERSTATE 76/PA Tpk

Washington

Exit #	Services
58	PA Tpk. I-70 E and I-76/PA Turnpike E run together.
57	I-70 W, US 119, PA 66(toll), New Stanton, **N...food:** Exxon, Sheetz, Bob Evans, Donut Chef, Eat'n Park, KFC, McDonald's, Pagano's Rest., Pizza Hut, Subway, Wendy's, **lodging:** Comfort Inn, Day's Inn, Fairfield Inn, Howard Johnson, Quality Inn, Super 8, **S...gas:** BP/diesel, Sunoco/24hr, **food:** Cracker Barrel, TJ's Rest., **lodging:** New Stanton Motel
54	Madison, **N...**KOA
53	Yukon, no facilities
51b a	PA 31, West Newton, no facilities
49	Smithton, **N...gas:** Citgo/diesel/@, Shell/Perkins/diesel/@, **food:** Old Farmhouse Pizza
46b a	PA 51, Pittsburgh, **N...gas:** BP/diesel, Exxon/24hr, **food:** Burger King, **lodging:** Sleeper Inn, **other:** Chevrolet/Pontiac/Buick/Cadillac/Kia, Harley-Davidson, **S...gas:** Crossroads/diesel/24hr, **lodging:** Holiday Inn, Knotty Pine Motel, Relax Inn
44	Arnold City, no facilities
43b a	(43 from eb)PA 201, Fayette City, **N...**gas/diesel, **S...gas:** Exxon/24hr, Sunoco/24hr, **food:** Burger King, China Wok, Denny's, Eat'n Park, Hoss' Rest., KFC, LJ Silver, McDonald's, Ponderosa, Subway, Wendy's, **lodging:** Best Val-U Motel, **other:** Advance Parts, $General, $Tree, Eckerd, Giant Foods, GNC, K-Mart, Lowe's Whse, Radio Shack, Staples, Wal-Mart SuperCtr/24hr
42a	Monessen, no facilities
42	N Belle Vernon, **S...gas:** BP/McDonald's, Sunoco, **food:** Dairy Queen
41	PA 906, Belle Vernon, no facilities
40mm	Monongahela River
40	PA 88, Charleroi, **N...gas:** Amoco, Crossroads/diesel, **food:** Subway, **other:** HOSPITAL
39	Speers, **N...food:** Loraine's Rest., **S...gas:** Exxon, camping
37b a	PA 43, no facilities
36	Lover(from wb, no re-entry), no facilities
35	PA 481, Centerville, no facilities
32b a	PA 917, Bentleyville, **N...food:** King of the Hill Steaks, **S... gas:** Amoco/diesel, Pilot/DQ/Subway/diesel/24hr, Sheetz/24hr, **food:** Burger King, McDonald's, **lodging:** Best Western, **other:** MEDICAL CARE, Advance Parts, Blue Beacon, $General, Ford, Giant Foods, Rite Aid
31	to PA 136, Kammerer, **N...lodging:** Carlton Motel, **food:** Carlton Kitchen
27	Dunningsville, **S...lodging:** Avalon Motel
25	PA 519, to Eighty Four, **S...gas:** Amoco/24hr, BP/diesel/@, 7-11/diner
21	I-79 S, to Waynesburg. **I-70 W and I-79 N run together 3.5 mi.**
20	PA 136, Beau St, **N...**KOA, **S...**to Washington&Jefferson Coll
19b a	US 19, Murtland Ave, **N...gas:** BP, **food:** Applebee's, Cracker Barrel, McDonald's, Ponderosa, Red Lobster, Texas Roadhouse, TGIFriday, **lodging:** SpringHill Suites, **other:** Aldi Foods, $Tree, Giant Eagle Foods, GNC, Lowe's Whse, Michael's, OfficeMax, Radio Shack, Sam's Club, Target, Toyota/Honda, Wal-Mart SuperCtr/24hr, **S...gas:** Amoco, BP/diesel, Sunoco, **food:** Arby's, Big Boy, Bob Evans, Burger King, Eat'n Park/24hr, Evergreen Chinese, Jade Garden Chinese, KFC, LJ Silver, Old Mexico, Papa John's, Pizza Hut, Shoney's, Taco Bell, **lodging:** Hampton Inn, Motel 6, **other:** HOSPITAL, Buick/Cadillac/GMC, $General, Firestone/auto, Home Depot, JC Penney, Jo-Ann Fabrics, K-Mart, Staples, Subaru, mall, st police
18	I-79 N, to Pittsburgh. **I-70 E and I-79 S run together 3.5 mi.**
17	PA 18, Jefferson Ave, Washington, **N...gas:** Crossroads/diesel, Gulf, **food:** DQ, McDonald's, **other:** CarQuest, Family$, Rite Aid, **S...gas:** Sunoco, **food:** Burger King, 4Star Pizza, **other:** Advance Parts, Foodland
16	Jessop Place, **N...gas:** Citgo, **S...**auto/truck repair
15	US 40, Chesnut St, Washington, **N...food:** StoneCrab Inn Rest., USA Steaks, Foodland, **S...gas:** BP, Crossroads/diesel, Sunoco/24hr, **food:** Bob Evans, China Buffet, Denny's, Eat'n Park/24hr, **other:** Hardee's, LJ Silver, McDonald's, Pizza Hut, Taco Bell, Wendy's, Day's Inn, Econolodge, Ramada Inn, Red Roof Inn, Eckerd, Sears/auto, mall

PENNSYLVANIA

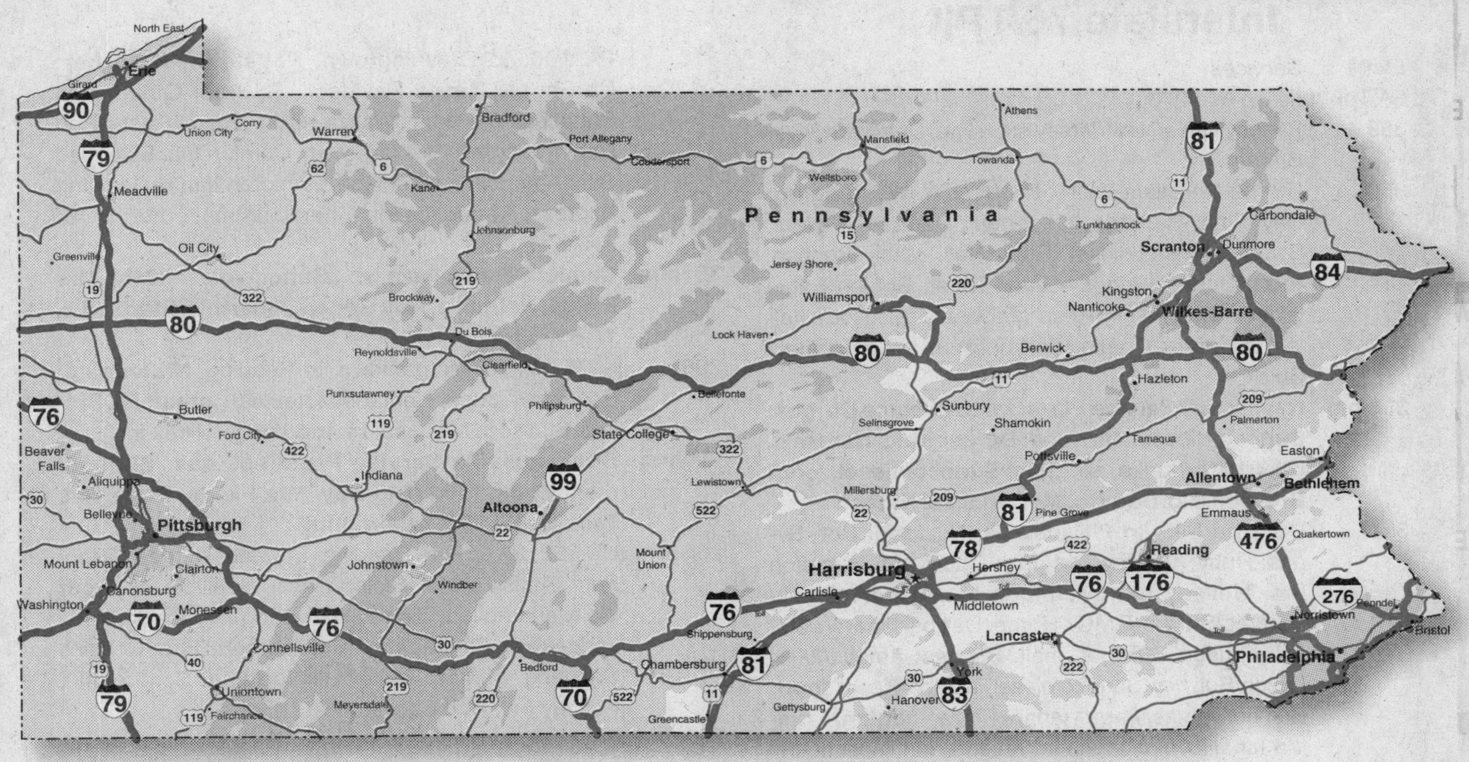

Interstate 70

E ↕ W

11	PA 221, Taylorstown, **N...gas:** Amoco/diesel, **other:** truck repair
6	to US 40, PA 231, Claysville, **N...gas:** Exxon, **other:** NAPA, **S...gas:** Petro/Citgo/Sbarro's/24hr
5mm	**Welcome Ctr eb, full(handicapped)facilities, phone, vending, picnic tables, litter barrels, petwalk**
1	W Alexander, **S...gas:** Shell/diesel
0mm	Pennsylvania/West Virginia state line

Interstate 76

E ↕ W

Philadelphia

Exit #	Service
354mm	Pennsylvania/New Jersey state line, Delaware River, Walt Whitman Bridge
351	Front St, I-95(from wb), N to Trenton, S to Chester
350	Packer Ave, 7th St, to I-95(fromeb), **S...lodging:** Holiday Inn, **other:** to sports complex
349	to I-95, PA 611, Broad St
348	PA 291, W to Chester, **S...lodging:** Ramada Inn
347a	to I-95 S
347b	Passyunk Ave, Oregon Ave, **S...other:** sports complex
346c	28th St, Vare Ave, Mifflin St(from wb)
346b	Grays Ferry Ave, University Ave, civic center, **N...food:** McDonald's, PathMark Foods, **S...gas:** Amoco/24hr, Hess
346a	South St, no facilities
345	30th St, Market St, downtown
344	I-676 E, US 30 E, to Philadelphia(no return from eb)
343	Spring Garden St, Haverford
342	US 13, US 30 W, Girard Ave, Philadelphia Zoo, E Fairmount Park
341	Montgomery Dr, W River Dr, W Fairmount Park
340b	US 1 N, Roosevelt Blvd, to Philadelphia
339	US 1 S, **S...lodging:** Adams Mark Hotel, Holiday Inn
340a	Lincoln Dr, Kelly Dr, to Germantown
338	Belmont Ave, Green Lane, **N...other:** CVS Drug, **S...gas:** Coastal, Sunoco
337	Hollow Rd(from wb), Gladwyne
332	PA 23(from wb), Conshohocken, **N...gas:** Marriott
331b a	I-476, PA 28(from eb), Conshohocken, to Chester
330	PA 320, Gulph Mills, **S...**to Villanova U
328	US 202 N, to King of Prussia, **N...gas:** Exxon/diesel, Mobil, WaWa, **food:** Charlie's Place Rest., Dunkin Donuts, Friendly's, Sizzler, TGIFriday, Uno Pizzaria, **lodging:** Econolodge, Holiday Inn, Howard Johnson, McIntosh Inn, **other:** JC Penney, Macy's, Sears/auto, Thrift Drug, mall, **S...**George Washington Lodge
327	US 202 S, Goddard Blvd, to Valley Forge, Valley Forge Park
326	I-76 wb becomes I-76/PA Tpk to Ohio

For I-76 westbound to Ohio, see I-76/PA Turnpike.

PENNSYLVANIA
Interstate 76/TPK

E

W

Exit # Services

PA Tpk runs wb as I-276

359 Pennsylvania/New Jersey state line, Delaware River Bridge

358 US 13, Delaware Valley, **N...gas:** WaWa, **lodging:** Day's Inn, Ramada Inn, **other:** Cadillac, U-Haul, **S...gas:** Bristol/diesel, Getty Gas, Mobil, Sunoco, **food:** Burger King, DeGrand Diner, Golden Eagle Diner, Italian Family Rest., McDonald's, Russo's Italian, **lodging:** Comfort Inn, Villager Lodge, **other:** Buick

352mm Neshaminy Service Plaza, wb...Welcome Ctr, gas: Sunoco/diesel/24hr, food: Burger King, Nathan's, other: Starbucks, eb...gas: Sunoco/diesel, food: Breyer's, HotDog Co, McDonald's, Nathan's

351 US 1, to I-95, to Philadelphia, **N...food:** Bob Evans, Ruby Tuesday, **lodging:** Courtyard, Hampton Inn, Holiday Inn, McIntosh Inn, **other:** Buick/Pontiac/Saturn/GMC, Home Depot, Sears/auto, Strawbridge's, Target, mall, **S...gas:** Amoco/24hr, Exxon/Subway, Sunoco/diesel, Texaco/diesel, **food:** Dunkin Donuts, Papa Yianni's Pizza, **lodging:** Comfort Inn, Howard Johnson, Knight's Inn, Neshaminy Inn, Radisson, Red Roof Inn, Sunrise Inn, **other:** Cadillac/Toyota

343 PA 611, Willow Grove, **N...gas:** Mobil, **food:** ChiChi's, **lodging:** Candlewood Suites(5mi), Courtyard, **S...gas:** Amoco/24hr, Hess/diesel, Mobil, Shell, Sunoco, 7-11, **food:** Bennigan's, China Garden, Domino's, Dunkin Donuts, Friendly's, McDonald's, Nino's Pizza, Ookaa Japanese, Williamson Rest., **lodging:** Hampton Inn, **other:** Best Buy, Firestone, Infiniti, PepBoys, Staples, transmissions

339 PA 309, Ft Washington, **N...gas:** Exxon, Mobil/Circle K/diesel, **food:** Friendly's, **lodging:** Best Western, Cherry Tree Hotel, Holiday Inn, **other:** BMW, Mercedes, Volvo

25A PA Tpk NE Extension, to I-476

333 Germantown Pike, to Norristown, **N...gas:** Mobil/Circle K, **lodging:** SpringHill Suites, **other:** HOSPITAL, **S...gas:** Mobil/Circle K

328mm King of Prussia Service Plaza wb...Sunoco/diesel/24hr, Breyer's, McDonald's

PA Tpk runs eb as I-276, wb as I-76

326 I-76 E, to US 202, I-476, Valley Forge, **N...gas:** Shell, **food:** Burger King, Cracker Barrel, Hooters, Hoss' Rest., **lodging:** Comfort Inn, Hampton Inn, MainStay Suites, Radisson, Sleep Inn, **S...gas:** Exxon, Mobil, Sunoco, WaWa, **food:** American Grill, CA Pizza, Chili's, Denny's, Houlihan's, McDonald's, **lodging:** Best Western, McIntosh Inn, Motel 6, Sheraton, **other:** Best Buy, Chevrolet, Costco, Crate&Barrel, Home Depot, JC Penney, Sears/auto, mall

325mm Valley Forge Service Plaza eb...gas: Sunoco/diesel/24hr, food: Burger King, Mrs Fields, Nathan's, TCBY, gifts

312 PA 100, to Downingtown, Pottstown, **N...other:** CarSense, Harley-Davidson, **S...gas:** Gulf/diesel, Sunoco/diesel/24hr, WaWa, **food:** Hoss' Rest., Red Robin, **lodging:** Best Western, Comfort Inn, Extended Stay America, Fairfield Inn, Hampton Inn, Holiday Inn Express, Residence Inn, Sheraton(6mi), **other:** HOSPITAL

305mm Camiel Service Paza wb...Sunoco/diesel/24hr, Mrs Fields, Nathan's, Roy Rogers, Sbarro's, Starbucks, TCBY, gifts

298 I-176, PA 10, Morgantown, to Reading, **N...lodging:** Economy Lodge, Heritage Motel/rest., **other:** HOSPITAL **S...food:** McDonald's, **lodging:** Holiday Inn

290mm Bowmansville Service Plaza eb...gas: Sunoco/diesel/24hr, food: Big Boy, Mrs Fields, Pizza Hut, Taco Bell, TCBY, other: gifts

286 US 322, PA 272, to Reading, Ephrata, **N...gas:** Citgo/Penn Amish Motel, Exxon/diesel, Shell/diesel, **food:** Zia Maria Italian, Zinn's Diner, **lodging:** Black Horse Lodge/rest., Penna Dutch Motel, **other:** Dutch Cousins Camping, **S...gas:** Turkey Hill, **lodging:** Comfort Inn, Holiday Inn, Red Carpet Inn

266 PA 72, to Lebanon, Lancaster, **N...gas:** Hess/diesel, Mobil/ChesterFried, **food:** Little Corner of Germany Café, **lodging:** Red Carpet Inn, Rodeway Inn, **S...food:** Hitz Mkt/deli, **lodging:** Hampton Inn, Holiday Inn Express, **other:** HOSPITAL, Mt Hope Winery

259mm Lawn Service Plaza wb...gas: Sunoco/diesel/24hr, food: Burger King, other: TCBY, RV dump

250mm Highspire Service Plaza eb...gas: Sunoco/diesel/24hr, food: Sbarro's

247 I-283, PA 283, Harrisburg East, to Harrisburg, Hershey, **N...gas:** Getty, Sunoco, **food:** Eat'n Park, Taco Bell, Wendy's, **lodging:** Best Western, Day's Inn, Rodeway Inn, **other:** facilities 3-5 mi N

246mm Susquehannah River

242 I-83, Harrisburg West, **N...gas:** BP, Hess, Mobil/diesel, **food:** Bob Evans, Eat'n Park, McDonald's, Pizza Hut, **other:** HOSPITAL, Best Western, Fairfield Inn, Holiday Inn, Knight's Inn, McIntosh Inn, Motel 6, **S...gas:** Keystone Trkstp/diesel/@, **lodging:** Day's Inn

236 US 15, Gettysburg Pike, to Gettysburg, Harrisburg, **N...gas:** Shell, **food:** Subway, **lodging:** Econolodge, Hampton Inn/rest., Holiday Inn Express, Homewood Suites, **other:** HOSPITAL, U-Haul, **S...gas:** Sheetz/24hr, **food:** Hoss' Steaks(1mi), McDonald's(1mi), **lodging:** Best Western, Wingate Inn, **other:** Giant Food/24hr(1mi)

Carlisle

226 US 11, to I-81, Carlisle, to Harrisburg, **N...gas:** Petro/diesel/24hr/@, Citgo/diesel/24hr, Flying J/diesel/LP/rest./24hr/@, Pilot/Wendy's/diesel/24hr, Shell/diesel, Texaco/diesel, **food:** Arby's, BBQ, Big Boy/24hr, Bob Evans, Carelli's Subs, Eat'n Park, McDonald's, Middlesex Diner/24hr, Subway, Waffle House, Western Sizzlin, **lodging:** Appalachian Trail Inn, Best Western, Budget Host, Clarion, Econolodge, Hampton Inn, Holiday Inn,

Interstate 76/TPK

E ↕ W

Quality Inn, Rodeway Inn, Super 8, **other:** HOSPITAL, Blue Beacon, Giant Foods, **S...gas:** Exxon/Taco Bell/24hr, Sheetz/24hr, **food:** Hoss' Rest., **lodging:** Motel 6, **other:** HOSPITAL, Chrysler/Jeep, U-Haul

219mm Plainfield Service Plaza eb...gas: Sunoco/diesel/24hr, food: Roy Rogers, other: TCBY, gifts

203mm Blue Mtn Service Plaza wb...gas: Sunoco/diesel/24hr, food: Mrs Fields, Roy Rogers, TCBY

201 PA 997, Blue Mountain, to Shippensburg, **S...lodging:** Johnnie's Motel/rest., Kenmar Motel

199mm Blue Mountain Tunnel

197mm Kittatinny Tunnel

189 PA 75, Willow Hill, **S...lodging:** Willow Hill Motel/rest.

187mm Tuscarora Tunnel

180 US 522, Ft Littleton, **N...gas:** Amoco, Shell, **food:** The Fort Rest., **lodging:** Downes Motel, HOSPITAL

Breezewood

172mm Sideling Hill Service Plaza both lanes...gas: Sunoco/diesel/24hr, food: Big Boy, Burger King, Mrs Fields, Pretzel Time, TCBY, other: gifts

161 US 30, Breezewood, **Services on US 30...gas:** TA/diesel/rest./24hr/@, BP/diesel, Citgo/Dunkin Donuts, Exxon/diesel, Mobil/diesel/24hr, Sheetz/24hr, Shell, Sunoco/diesel/café, Texaco/Subway, **food:** Arby's, Big John's Buffet, Bob Evans, Bonanza, Burger King, DQ, Denny's, Domino's, Family House Rest., Hardee's, KFC, McDonald's, Perkins, Pizza Hut, Taco Bell, Wendy's, **lodging:** Best Western, Breezewood Motel, Comfort Inn/rest., Econolodge, Holiday Inn Express, Penn Aire Motel, Quality Inn, Ramada Inn, Wiltshire Motel, **other:** camping, museum, truck/tire repair

161mm I-70 W and I-76/PA Turnpike W run together

150mm roadside park wb

148mm Midway Service Plaza both lanes, eb...Sunoco/diesel/24hr, Cinnabon, HotDog City, Mrs Fields, Sbarro's, TCBY, gifts, wb...Sunoco/diesel/24hr, KFC, Mrs Fields, Sbarro's, Starbucks, TCBY, gifts

146 US 220, to I-99, Bedford, **N...gas:** Amoco/McDonald's/diesel/24hr, BP/diesel, Sunoco, **food:** Arena Rest., Baskin-Robbins/Dunkin Donuts, China Inn, Denny's, Ed's Steaks, Hardee's, Hoss' Rest., Pizza Hut, **lodging:** Best Western, Budget Host, Econolodge, Quality Inn, Super 8, Travelodge, **other:** to Shawnee SP(10mi), Blue Knob SP(15mi), **S...lodging:** Golden Eagle Inn(2mi), Hampton Inn, **other:** Suburu

142mm parking area wb

123mm Allegheny Tunnel

112mm Somerset Service Plaza both lanes, eb...gas: Sunoco/diesel/24hr, food: Big Boy, Roy Rogers, TCBY, other: gifts, wb...gas: Sunoco/diesel/24hr, food: Burger King, TCBY, other: gifts

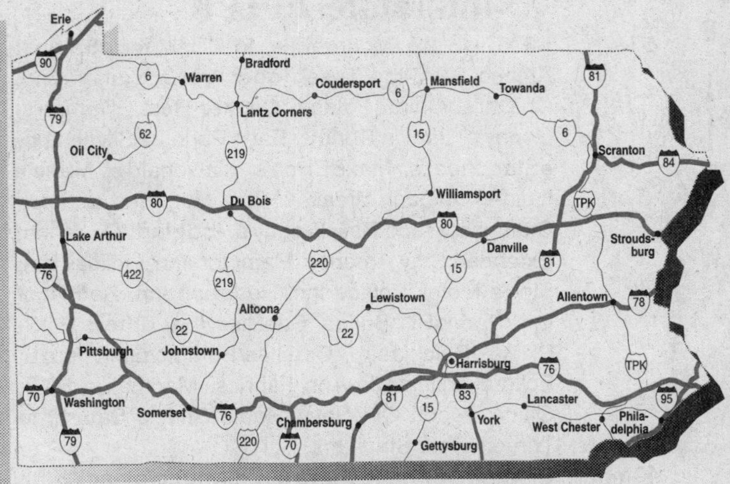

110 PA 601, to US 219, Somerset, **N...gas:** KwikFill, Sheetz/24hr, **food:** Hoss' Rest., King's Rest., Pizza Hut, Taco Bell, **lodging:** $ Inn, Economy Inn, **other:** Advance Parts, Chrysler/Plymouth/Jeep, Ford/Lincoln/Mercury, **S...gas:** Exxon, Shell/diesel, **food:** Arby's, Bruster's Ice Cream, China Garden, Dunkin Donuts, Eat'n Park, Maggie Mae's Café, McDonald's, Pine Grill, Summit Diner, Wendy's, **lodging:** Best Western, Budget Host, Day's Inn, Hampton Inn, Holiday Inn, Knight's Inn, Ramada Inn, Super 8, **other:** Dodge, Eckerd, Harley-Davidson

91 PA 711, Donegal, **N...food:** Tall Cedars Rest./pizza, **S...gas:** BP/Hardee's/Pizza Hut, Exxon/diesel, Sunoco/diesel, **food:** DQ, **lodging:** Day's Inn, Donegal Motel, **other:** golf

78mm service plaza wb...gas: Sunoco/diesel/24hr, food: McDonald's, lodging: Kings Family Rest.

I-70 E runs with I-76/PA Turnpike eb

75 I-70 W, US 119, PA 66(toll), New Stanton, **S... gas:** BP/diesel, Exxon, Sheetz, Sunoco/24hr, **food:** Bob Evans, Cracker Barrel, Donut Chef, Eat'n Park, KFC, McDonald's/24hr, Pizza Hut, Subway, TJ's Rest., Wendy's, **lodging:** Budget Inn, Comfort Inn, Day's Inn, Fairfield Inn, Howard Johnson Express, New Stanton Motel, Ramada Inn, Super 8

74.6mm Hemphill Service Plaza eb...gas: Sunoco/diesel/24hr, food: Breyer's, McDonald's, other: atm

67 US 30, Irwin, to Greensburg, **N...gas:** BP/Blimpie/diesel, Sheetz/24hr, Shell, **lodging:** Motel 3, **other:** HOSPITAL, Ford, **S...gas:** Speedway, Sunoco/24hr, **food:** Angelo's Rest., Arby's, Bob Evans, Burger King, DQ, Denny's, Eat'n Park, KFC, LJ Silver, Los Compasinos Mexican, McDonald's, Pizza Hut, Royal China, Subway, Taco Bell, Teddy's Rest., Wendy's, **lodging:** Conley Inn, Holiday Inn Express, Penn Irwin Motel, **other:** Advance Parts, CarQuest, Giant Eagle Foods/24hr, Kohl's, Shop'n Save

61mm parking area eb

PENNSYLVANIA

Interstate 76/TPK

57 I-376, US 22, Monroeville, to Pittsburgh, **S...gas:** Amoco, BP, Citgo/diesel, **food:** Arby's, Burger King, ChiChi's, China Palace, Cooker Rest., Damon's, Denny's, Dunkin Donuts, Eat'n Park, LJ Silver, LoneStar Steaks, Max&Erma's, McDonald's, Marie's Italian, Outback Steaks, Pizza Hut, Red Lobster, Starbucks, Taco Bell, Wendy's, **lodging:** Day's Inn, Extended Stay America, Hampton Inn, Holiday Inn, King's Motel, Palace Inn, Radisson Inn, Red Roof Inn, SpringHill Suites, SunRise Inn, **other:** HOSPITAL, Buick/Jeep, Cadillac/Pontiac/GMC/Isuzu, Eckerd, Infiniti, Jo-Ann Fabrics, Marshall's, NTB, Office Depot, Old Navy, Radio Shack, Saturn, to Three Rivers Stadium

49mm Oakmont Service Plaza eb...Sunoco/diesel/24hr, Arby's, Hershey's Ice Cream, picnic tables, litter barrels, phone

48.5mm Allegheny River

48 PA 28, Allegheny Valley, to Pittsburgh, New Kensington, **N...gas:** 76/24hr, **food:** Sam Morgan's Rest., **S...gas:** Exxon/diesel, **food:** Bob Evans, Bruster's Yogurt, Burger King, Denny's, Eat'n Park, Fuddrucker's, KFC, King's Rest., McDonald's, Ponderosa, Ripe Tomato, Subway, Taco Bell, Wendy's, **lodging:** Comfort Inn, Day's Inn, Holiday Inn Express, Super 8, Valley Motel, **other:** Advance Parts, Ford, Giant Eagle Food/drug/24hr

41mm parking area/call box eb

39 PA 8, Butler Valley, to Pittsburgh, **N...gas:** BP, Exxon/diesel, Sheetz/24hr, **food:** Bruno's Pizza, Eat'n Park, McDonald's, Venus Diner, **lodging:** Comfort Inn, **other:** Advance Parts, Jo-Ann Fabrics, Shop'n Save Foods, Wal-Mart/auto/drugs, mall, **S...gas:** BP, Sunoco/diesel, **food:** Arby's, Baskin-Robbins, Boston Mkt, Burger King, China Bistro, Denny's, Handel's Ice Cream, Hoss' Rest., KFC, McDonald's, Pizza Hut, Pizza Outlet, Quizno's, Subway, Taco Bell, Wendy's, **lodging:** Day's Inn, Econolodge, **other:** HOSPITAL, AutoZone, CVS Drug, Eckerd, Firestone/auto, Ford, Goodyear/auto, Radio Shack, Thrift Drug

31mm Butler Service Plaza wb...gas: Sunoco/diesel/24hr, food: Burger King, Mrs Fields, Popeye's, TCBY, other: gifts

28 to I-79, to Cranberry, Pittsburgh, **N...gas:** Amoco/24hr, Exxon/diesel, Sheetz, Sunoco/24hr, **food:** Arby's, Bob Evans, Boston Mkt, Burger King, Climo's Pizza/chicken, Denny's, Dunkin Donuts, Hardee's, LJ Silver, LoneStar Steaks, McDonald's, Perkins, Shoney's, Wendy's, **lodging:** AmeriSuites, Comfort Inn, Fairfield Inn, Hampton Inn, Holiday Inn Express, Motel 6, Red Roof Inn, Sheraton, Super 8, **other:** HOSPITAL, Giant Foods, Goodyear/atuo, Jo-Ann Fabrics, K-Mart, Phar-Mor Drug, Shop'n Save/24hr, Wal-Mart, mall, **S...gas:** BP/diesel, **food:** Gulf, Eat'n Park, Hot Dog Shop, **lodging:** Day's Inn, Residence Inn, **other:** Toyota

23.4mm pulloff eb

22mm Zelienople Service Plaza eb...Welcome Ctr, gas: Sunoco/diesel/24hr, food: Roy Rogers, Mrs Fields, TCBY, other: crafts, gifts

17mm parking area eb

13.4mm parking area eb

13mm Beaver River

13 PA 8, Beaver Valley, to Ellwood City, **N...lodging:** Alpine Inn, Beaver Valley Motel, Danny's Motel, HillTop Motel, Holiday Inn, Lark Motel, **other:** HOSPITAL, **S...food:** Giuseppe's Italian, **lodging:** Conley Inn/rest.

10 PA 60(toll), to New Castle, Pittsburgh, **S...**services(6mi), to airport

6mm pulloff eb

2mm pulloff eb

2 (from wb), no facilities

1.5mm toll plaza, phone, call boxes located at 1 mi intervals

0mm Pennsylvania/Ohio state line

Interstate 78

Exit #(mm)Services

77 Pennsylvania/New Jersey state line, Delaware River

76mm Welcome Ctr wb, full(handicapped)facilities, phone, vending, picnic tables, litter barrels, petwalk, toll booth wb

75 to PA 611, Easton, **N...gas:** Citgo/24hr, **food:** McDonald's, Perkins, **lodging:** Best Western, **S...gas:** Shell

71 PA 33, to Stroudsburg

67 PA 412, Hellertown, **N...gas:** Citgo/24hr, **lodging:** Comfort Suites(3mi), **food:** Wendy's, HOSPITAL **S...gas:** Mobil/Subway, **food:** Burger King, McDonald's, Vassi's Drive-In, **other:** Chevrolet

60b a PA 309 S, Quakertown, **S...**The Motor Lodge

59 to PA 145(from eb), Summit Lawn, no facilities

58 Emaus St(from wb), **S...gas:** Shell

57 Lehigh St, **N...gas:** Hess/diesel, **food:** Arby's, IHOP, Queen City Diner, **lodging:** Day's Inn, **other:** Aldi Foods, CVS Drug, Family$, Home Depot, Dodge/Kia/Isuzu, Lincoln/Mercury, Whse Mkt Foods/24hr, **S...gas:** Getty/repair, Gulf, Sunoco, Mobil, Shell/diesel, **food:** Bennigan's, Bob Evans, Brass Rail Rest., Burger King, Domino's, Dunkin Donuts, Dynasty Chinese, Friendly's, McDonald's, Papa John's, Perkins, Pizza Hut/Taco Bell, Subway, Wendy's, **other:** AA Parts, Audi/Mercedes, BonTon, Buick/GMC/Jeep/Saturn, Chevrolet/Pontiac/Saab, Chrysler, Food4Less, Ford/Hyundai/Honda, Lehigh Tire, Mazda/Volvo, Mitsubishi, PharMor, Staples, SteinMart

55 PA 29, Cedar Crest Blvd, **N...gas:** Shell, **S...**HOSPITAL

Interstate 78

E

W

54 US 222, Hamilton Blvd, **N...gas:** Hess, **food:** Ambassador Rest., Boston Mkt, Burger King, Carrabba's, Friendly's, Ice Cream World, McDonald's, Perkins, TGIFriday, Wendy's, **lodging:** Comfort Inn, Holiday Inn Express, **other:** Dorney Funpark, Laneco Foods, Office Depot, **S...gas:** Sunoco, **food:** Charcoal Drive-In, Hunan Chinese, Pizza Hut, Tom Sawyer Diner/24hr, **lodging:** Wingate Inn, **other:** Subaru, U-Haul, Valley Golf

51 to I-476, US 22 E, PA 33 N, Whitehall

49b a PA 100, Fogelsville, **N...gas:** Arby's, **food:** Cracker Barrel, Gyros King, LJ Silver, Orient Express, Pasta Connection, Pizza Hut, **lodging:** Comfort Inn, Hawthorn Inn, **other:** Eckerd, STS Tire/repair, bank, cleaners **S...gas:** Shell, Sunoco/24hr, WaWa, **food:** Burger King, Taco Bell, Yocco's Hotdogs, **lodging:** Cloverleaf Inn, Hampton Inn, Hilton Garden, Holiday Inn, Sleep Inn, **other:** Toyota, Grover Hill Winery, st police

45 PA 863, to Lynnport, **N...gas:** Shell/diesel, **S...lodging:** Super 8

40 PA 737, Krumsville, **N...lodging:** Top Motel, **other:** Pine Hill Campground(N to blinker, rgt onto Old Rte 22, 1.5mi)Robin Hill RV Park(4mi), **S...gas:** Texaco/diesel, **lodging:** Skyview Rest., **other:** to Kutztown U

35 PA 143, Lenhartsville, **3 mi S...**Robin Hill Park

30 Hamburg, **S...gas:** Getty/24hr

29b a PA 61, to Reading, Pottsville, **N...gas:** Mobil, **food:** Burger King, Cracker Barrel, Wendy's, **other:** Harley-Davidson(8mi), st police, **S...other:** Schaeffer's RV(4mi), VF Factory Outlet

23 Shartlesville, **N...gas:** Citgo/Stuckey's/DQ, Shell/diesel, **lodging:** Dutch Motel, **other:** Appalachian Campsites, **S...food:** Blue Mtn Family Rest., **lodging:** Haag's Motel/rest., Fort Motel/rest., **other:** antiques

19 PA 183, Strausstown, **N...gas:** Mobil/Dutch Kitchen Rest., **S...gas:** Shell, **food:** C&C Pizza

17 PA 419, Rehrersburg, **N...gas:** Best/diesel

16 Midway, **N...gas:** Exxon/diesel, Midway/diesel/truckwash, Sunoco/diesel, **food:** Blue Mtn Kitchen, Midway Diner, **lodging:** Comfort Inn, **S...**auto/truck repair

15 Grimes, **S...lodging:** Midway Motel

13 PA 501, Bethel, **N...gas:** Texaco/diesel/24hr, **S...gas:** Amoco/diesel, Exxon/diesel

10 PA 645, Frystown, **S...gas:** Shell/diesel/rest./24hr, Texaco/diesel/24hr, **lodging:** Frystown Motel

6 (8 from wb, US 22)PA 343, Fredricksburg, **1 mi S...food:** Esther's Rest., **other:** Whse Mkt/fuel,

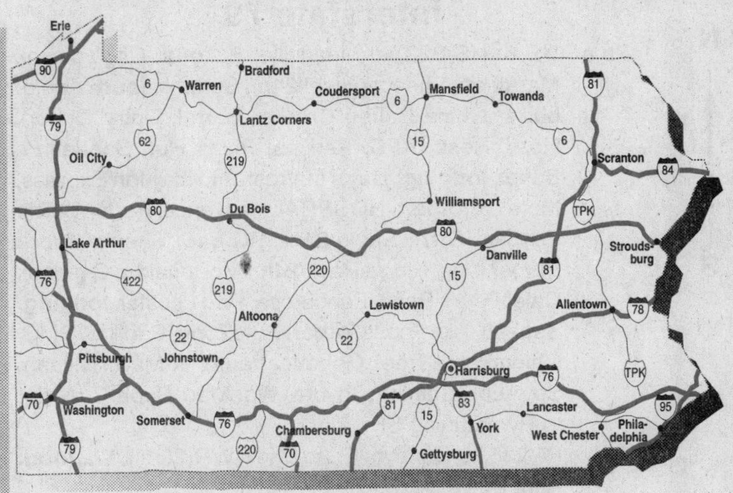

Interstate 79

Erie

Exit # Services

I-79 begins/ends in Erie, exit 183.

N

S

183b a PA 5, 12th St, Erie, **E...**HOSPITAL, **W...gas:** Sunoco, **food:** Bob Evans, Eat'n Park/24hr, Applebee's, KFC, Hooters, McDonald's, Serafini's Italian, Taco Bell, **lodging:** Clarion, Hampton Inn(2mi), **other:** Advance Parts, Aldi Foods, CVS Drug, $General, Eckerd, Giant Eagle Foods, to Presque Isle SP

182 US 20, 26th St, **E...gas:** Citgo, KwikFill, **other:** HOSPITAL, Advance Parts, Family$, Tops Food/24hr, **W...gas:** Citgo, Shell, **food:** Arby's, Burger King, Hoss' Rest., LJ Silver, McDonald's, Pizza Hut, Subway, Super Buffet, Aamco, AutoZone, CVS Drug, Eckerd, Ford, Giant Eagle, K-Mart

180 US 19, to Kearsarge, **E...food:** Arby's, ChiChi's, Don Pablo, Eat'n Park/24hr, KFC, LoneStar Steaks, Max&Erma's, McDonald's, Olive Garden, Outback Steaks, Ponderosa, Red Lobster, Roadhouse Grill, Wendy's, **lodging:** Fairfield Inn, Homewood Suites, **other:** HOSPITAL, Barnes&Noble, Borders Books, Cadillac, Chrysler/Plymouth/Jeep, Isuzu/Audi, JC Penney, Michael's, Sears/auto, SteinMart, mall, **W...gas:** Citgo/diesel, **other:** camping

178b a I-90, E to Buffalo, W to Cleveland, no facilities

174 to McKean, **E...**access to gas/diesel, phone, **W...**camping

166 US 6N, to Edinboro, **E...gas:** Citgo, Sheetz, **food:** Burger King, McDonald's, Perkins, Subway, Taco Bell, Wendy's, **lodging:** Edinboro Inn, Ramada Inn, **other:** $Tree, Radio Shack, Wal-Mart SuperCtr/24hr

163mm rest area both lanes, full(handicapped)facilities, phone, vending, picnic tables, litter barrels, petwalk

154 PA 198, to Saegertown, no facilities

PENNSYLVANIA

Interstate 79

N ↕ S

Meadville

147b a US 6, US 322, to Meadville, **E...gas:** Citgo/diesel, Marathon, Sheetz/diesel/24hr, Sunoco, **food:** Applebee's, China Buffet, Cracker Barrel, Dairy Queen, Hoss' Rest., KFC, Perkins, Pizza Hut, Sandalini's Buffet, **lodging:** Day's Inn/rest., Holiday Inn Express, Motel 6, **other:** HOSPITAL, Advance Parts, Buick/Pontiac, Giant Eagle/24hr, **W...gas:** Sheetz, **food:** Burger King, King's Rest./24hr, McDonald's, Overlook Café, Pete's Rest., Ponderosa, Red Lobster, **lodging:** Super 8, Aldi Foods, **other:** AutoZone, Cadillac/GMC, Chevrolet, $Tree, Goodyear/auto, K-Mart, Nissan, SavALot, Staples, Toyota, Wal-Mart SuperCtr/24hr, to Pymatuning SP

141 PA 285, to Geneva, **E...**to Erie NWR(20mi), **W...food:** Aunt Bee's Rest.

135mm rest area/weigh sta both lanes, full(handicapped)facilities, phone, vending, picnic tables, litter barrels, petwalk

130 PA 358, to Sandy Lake, **E...gas:** Lakeway/diesel/rest./@, **other:** to Goddard SP, camping, **W...other:** HOSPITAL, to Pymatuning SP

121 US 62, to Mercer, **E...gas:** Citgo, **W...gas:** Sunoco/diesel, **other:** st police

116b a I-80, E to Clarion, W to Sharon, no facilities

113 PA 208, PA 258, to Grove City, **E...gas:** BP, Citgo/diesel/24hr, **other:** HOSPITAL, **W...gas:** KwikFill/Subway, Sheetz/24hr, **food:** Eat'n Park/24hr, Elephant&Castle Rest., Hoss' Rest., King's Rest., McDonald's, Wendy's, **lodging:** Amerihost, Comfort Inn, Holiday Inn Express, **other:** KOA(3mi), Prime Outlets/famous brands

110mm rest area sb, full(handicapped)facilities, phone, vending, picnic tables, litter barrels, petwalk

107mm rest area nb, full(handicapped)facilities, phone, vending, picnic tables, litter barrels, petwalk

105 PA 108, to Slippery Rock, **E...gas:** BP(3mi), **lodging:** Apple Butter Inn(3mi), Evening Star Motel/rest., **other:** Slippery Rock Camping, to Slippery Rock U

99 US 422, to New Castle, **E...**to Moraine SP, **W...other:** Coopers Lake Camping, **other:** to Rose Point Camping

96 PA 488, Portersville, **E...**Bear Run Camping, **W...food:** Brown's Country Kitchen

88 (87 from nb), to US 19, PA 68, Zelienople, **1-2 mi W...gas:** Exxon/diesel/24hr, **food:** Burger King, DQ, Pizza Hut, Subway, **lodging:** Zelienople Motel, **other:** Goodyear, Indian Brave RV Camping

85 (83 from nb), PA 528(no quick return), to Evans City, **E...**GoCarts, **W...other:** Pontiac/Buick

81mm picnic area both lanes, phone, picnic table, litter barrel

Pittsburgh

78 (76 from nb, exits left from nb), US 19, PA 228, to Mars, access to I-76, PA TPK, **E...gas:** Citgo, **food:** Applebee's, McDonald's, Quizno's, **lodging:** Marriott, **other:** Kohl's, Lowe's, Staples, Target, Pittsburgh N Camping, **W on US 19...gas:** BP/diesel, Exxon/diesel/24hr, Gulf, 76, Sheetz/24hr, Sunoco/24hr, **food:** Arby's, Bob Evans, Boston Mkt, Burger King, Denny's, Eat'n Park, Hardee's, Hartner's Rest., King's Rest., LoneStar Steaks, LJ Silver, Max&Erma's, Papa John's, Perkins, Shoney's, Subway, TCBY, Wendy's, **lodging:** AmeriSuites, Comfort Inn, Fairfield Inn, Hampton Inn, Holiday Inn Express, Motel 6, Oak Leaf Motel, Red Roof Inn, Residence Inn, Sheraton, **other:** Barnes&Noble, Best Buy, CarQuest, GNC, Giant Eagle, Goodyear/auto, Home Depot, Jo-Ann Fabrics, K-Mart, OfficeMax, PepBoys, Shop'n Save/24hr, Toyota, Wal-Mart/drugs, mall

77 to Cranberry, new exit

75 US 19 S(from nb), to Warrendale, services along US 19

73 PA 910, to Wexford, **E...gas:** BP/24hr, **food:** Eat'n Park, King's Family Rest./24hr, **lodging:** Best Inn, **other:** MEDICAL CARE, **W...gas:** Exxon/diesel/24hr, **food:** Carmody's Rest.

72 I-279 S(from sb), to Pittsburgh

68 Mt Nebo Rd, **W...**HOSPITAL, gas

66 to PA 65, Emsworth, no facilities

65 to PA 51, Coraopolis, Neville Island, **E...gas:** Gulf, **other:** Penske/Hertz Trucks

64.5mm Ohio River

64 PA 51(from nb), to Coraopolis, McKees Rocks

60b a PA 60, Crafton, **E...gas:** Exxon/diesel/24hr, **food:** King's Rest./24hr, **lodging:** Day's Inn, Econolodge, Motel 6, **other:** HOSPITAL, **W...gas:** Sunoco/24hr, **food:** Primanti Rest., **lodging:** Pittsburgh Motel, Red Roof Inn

59b US 22 W, US 30(from nb), **W...**airport

59a I-279 N, to Pittsburgh

57 to Carnegie, **1-3 mi E...gas:** BP, Exxon, **food:** LJ Silver, McDonald's, TCBY, **lodging:** Shop'n Save, Ford, mall

55 to Heidelberg, **1-2 mi E...gas:** Sunoco, **food:** Arby's, ChuckeCheese, DQ, Eat'n Park/24hr, Grand China, KFC, Little Caesar's, Old Country Buffet, Pizza Hut, Ponderosa, Subway, Taco Bell, Wendy's, **other:** HOSPITAL, Eckerd, Firestone/auto, Giant Eagle/24hr, Goodyear/auto, JC Penney, Jo-Ann Fabrics, K-Mart, Radio Shack, mall, **W...food:** LJ Silver, **food:** McDonald's

54 PA 50, to Bridgeville, **E...gas:** BP/diesel, Exxon/diesel, **food:** Burger King, King's Rest./24hr, McDonald's, Wendy's, **lodging:** Comfort Inn, **other:** HOSPITAL, Chevrolet, Dodge, **W...gas:** Sunoco, **lodging:** Knights Inn

Interstate 79

N ↕ S

Washington

50mm **rest area/weigh sta both lanes, full(handicapped)facilities, phone, vending, picnic tables, litter barrels, petwalk**

48 South Pointe, **W...lodging:** Hilton Garden

45 to PA 980, Canonsburg, **E...gas:** Sheetz, **W...gas:** BP/24hr, Citgo, **food:** Hoss' Rest., KFC/Taco Bell, LJ Silver, McDonald's, Pizza Hut, Subway, Wendy's, **lodging:** Super 8, **other:** Advance Parts

43 PA 519, Houston, **E...gas:** Amoco/diesel, **W...gas:** Sunoco/24hr, HOSPITAL,

41 Race Track Rd, **E...food:** McDonald's, Wendy's, **lodging:** Comfort Inn, Holiday Inn, **W...gas:** BP/diesel, **other:** Trolley Museum

40 Meadow Lands(from nb, no re-entry), **W...other:** Trolley Museum(3mi), golf, racetrack

38 I-70 W, to Wheeling

I-79 and I-70 run together 3.5 mi. See Pennsylvania Interstate 70, exits 19-20.

34 I-70 E, to Greensburg

33 US 40, to Laboratory, **W...gas:** Amoco, **other:** KOA

31mm parking area/weigh sta sb

30 US 19, to Amity, **W...gas:** Exxon/Subway

23 to Marianna, Prosperity, no facilities

19 PA 221, to US 19, Ruff Creek, **W...gas:** Amoco/diesel

14 PA 21, to Waynesburg, **E...gas:** Amoco/diesel/24hr, **lodging:** Comfort Inn, **W...gas:** BP/diesel/24hr, Citgo/diesel, Exxon/Taco Bell/diesel, Sheetz, **food:** Burger King, DQ, Golden Corral, Hardee's, KFC, LJ Silver, McDonald's, Wendy's, **lodging:** Econolodge, Super 8, **other:** HOSPITAL, Chevrolet, CVS Drug, More4Less Foods, st police

7 to Kirby, no facilities

6mm **Welcome Ctr/weigh sta nb, full(handicapped)facilities, phone, picnic tables, litter barrels, vending, petwalk**

1 Mount Morris, **E...gas:** Citgo/diesel/rest., **other:** Honda/Mazda, **W...gas:** BP/diesel, Marathon, **other:** Mt Morris Campground

0mm Pennsylvania/West Virginia state line

Interstate 80

E ↕ W

Stroudsburg

Exit # Services

311mm Pennsylvania/New Jersey state line, Delaware River

310.5 toll booth wb, phone

310 PA 611, Delaware Water Gap, **S...Welcome Ctr/rest area, full facilities, info**, Amoco, Gulf/repair, Skillet Rest., Water Gap Diner, Glenwood Hotel/rest., Ramada Inn/rest., Christmas Factory Gifts

309 US 209 N, PA 447, to Marshalls Creek, **N...gas:** Exxon/diesel/24hr, **food:** Gulf, DQ, Landmark Rest., Wendy's, **lodging:** Shannon Motel, **other:** HOSPITAL

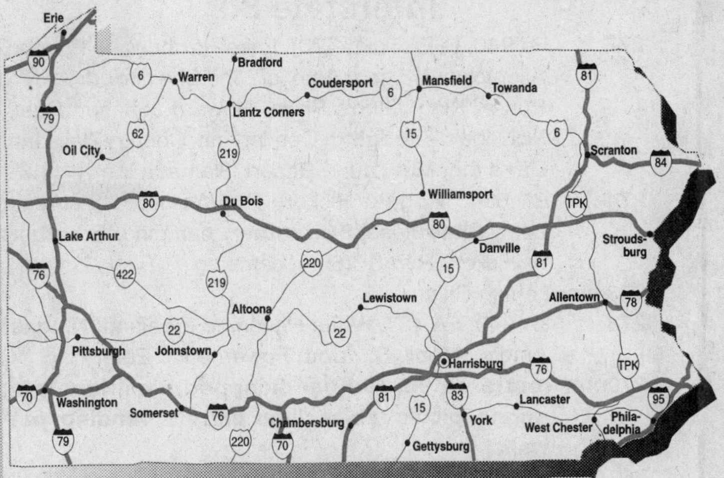

308 East Stroudsburg, **N...gas:** Shell, WaWa, **other:** HOSPITAL, **1 mi N...food:** Arby's, Burger King, China King, Friendly's, McDonald's, **other:** Eckerd, Goodyear/auto, K-Mart, NAPA, Radio Shack, ShopRite Foods, Wal-Mart SuperCtr/24hr, Weis Foods, **S...lodging:** Budget Motel, Super 8

307 PA 191, Broad St, **N...gas:** Gulf, **food:** KFC, McDonald's, **lodging:** Hampton Inn, **other:** HOSPITAL, same as 308

306 Dreher Ave(from wb, no EZ return), **N...gas:** Wawa, **other:** Buick

305 US 209, Main St, **1 mi N...gas:** Gulf, Mobil, **food:** Perkins/24hr, **lodging:** Sheraton, **S...gas:** Exxon/24hr, **lodging:** Colony Motel

304 (303 from eb)US 209, to PA 33, 9th St(no EZ return from wb), no facilities

302 PA 611, to Bartonsville, **N...gas:** Citgo/diesel, Mobil/Subway/Pizza Hut/Taco Bell/diesel/24hr, Shell, **food:** McDonald's, Ponderosa, **lodging:** Holiday Inn, Knight's Inn, Travelodge, **other:** Goodyear

299 PA 715, Tannersville, **N...gas:** BP, Mobil, **food:** Romano's Pizzaria, **lodging:** Pocono Lodge, Ramada Ltd, **other:** The Crossing Factory Outlet/famous brands, **1-3 mi N...food:** Barley Creek Brewing, Friendly's, **lodging:** Brookdale Inn, Chateau Inn, **other:** camping, **S...gas:** Exxon/24hr, **food:** Pocono Diner, Tannersville Diner, **lodging:** Day's Inn, Summit Resort, **other:** to Camelback Ski Area, to Big Pocono SP

298 PA 611(from wb), to Scotrun, **N...gas:** Shell, Sunoco/diesel, **food:** Anthony's Steaks, Plaza Deli, **lodging:** Scotrun Diner/motel, **other:** MEDICAL CARE, to Mt Pocono

295mm **rest area eb, full(handicapped)facilities, phone, picnic tables, litter barrels, vending, petwalk**

293 I-380 W, to Scranton

284 PA 115, Blakeslee, to Wilkes-Barre, **N...gas:** WaWa, **lodging:** Best Western, **other:** Fern Ridge Camping, st police, **S...gas:** Exxon, **other:** to Pocono Raceway

PENNSYLVANIA

Interstate 80

E

W

277 PA 940, to PA Tpk(I-476), Lake Harmony, to Pocono, Allentown, **N...gas:** Amoco/24hr, Shell, **food:** Arby's, Burger King, Gino's Pizza, Howard Johnson Rest., McDonald's, **lodging:** Comfort Inn, CountryPlace Inn, Day's Inn, Mtn Laurel Resort, Ramada Inn

274 PA 534, **N...gas:** Hickory Run/Amoco/diesel/rest./24hr, Shell/diesel/24hr, **other:** camping, **S...other:** to Hickory Run SP(6mi), camping

273mm Lehigh River

273 PA 940, PA 437, White Haven, to Freeland, **N...gas:** Amoco, Mobil, **S...food:** Powerhouse Eatery

270mm rest area eb, full(handicapped)facilities, info, phone, picnic tables, litter barrels, vending, petwalk

262 PA 309, to Hazleton, Mountain Top, **N...gas:** Shell, **food:** Wendy's, **lodging:** Econolodge, MtnView Motel/rest., **other:** Hazleton Camping, **S...gas:** Amoco/24hr, **other:** st police

260b a I-81, N to Wilkes-Barre, S to Harrisburg

256 PA 93, Conyngham, to Nescopeck, **N...gas:** Pilot/Subway/diesel/24hr/@, Sunoco/repair, **S...gas:** Shell/diesel, **food:** Tom's Kitchen(2mi), **lodging:** Best Value Inn, Hampton Inn(4mi), HOSPITAL

251mm Nescopeck River

246mm rest area/weigh sta both lanes, full(handicapped) facilities, weather info, phone, picnic tables, litter barrels, vending, petwalk

242 PA 339, Mifflinville, to Mainville, **N...gas:** Gulf/diesel, Shell/diesel/24hr, **food:** McDonald's, **lodging:** Super 8/rest., **S...gas:** Citgo/diesel

241mm Susquehanna River

Bloomsburg

241b a US 11, Lime Ridge, to Berwick, Bloomsburg, **N... lodging:** Red Maple Inn(2mi), **other:** HOSPITAL, **S...gas:** Shell, **food:** Subway, **lodging:** Budget Host, **2-5 mi S...gas:** Coastal, Sheetz/24hr, Shell, **food:** Applebee's, Arby's, Burger King, Cap'n Jack's Rest., Dairy Queen, Dunkin Donuts, Great Wall Chinese, Little Caesar's, LJ Silver, McDonald's, Pizza Hut, Romeo's Pizza, Taco Bell, Terrapin's Cantina, Wendy's, **lodging:** Tennytown Motel, **other:** Advance Parts, Buick/Pontiac/GMC, Chevrolet/Cadillac, CVS Drug, Eckerd, Ford/Honda, Giant Foods, K-Mart, Kost Tire, Radio Shack, Staples, U-Haul, Wal-Mart, Weis Foods

236 PA 487, Lightstreet, to Bloomsburg, **N...gas:** Citgo, **S...gas:** Coastal, **food:** Denny's/24hr, Ridgeway's Rest., **lodging:** Tennytown Motel(2mi), **other:** HOSPITAL, to Bloomsburg U, camping

232 PA 42, Buckhorn, **N...gas:** Shell/diesel, TA/Amoco/Subway/diesel/rest./24hr/@, **food:** Burger King, Cracker Barrel, KFC, Perkins, Wendy's, Western Sizzlin, **lodging:** Buckhorn Inn, Econolodge, Quality Inn/rest., **other:** JC Penney, Sears, mall, **S...other:** Indian Head camping(3mi)

224 PA 54, to Danville, **N...gas:** Amoco/Subway/diesel/24hr, Mobil, **lodging:** Danville Motel, **S...gas:** Shell/diesel, **food:** Dutch Pantry, Friendly's, McDonald's, Perkins(2mi), **lodging:** Day's Inn, Hampton Inn, Key Motel, Red Roof Inn, **other:** HOSPITAL

219mm rest area both lanes, full(handicapped)facilities, info, phone, picnic tables, litter barrels, vending, petwalk

215 PA 254, Limestoneville, **N...gas:** All American/diesel/rest./24hr, **S...gas:** Petro/Mobil/diesel/rest./24hr/@, Shell/diesel/24hr, **other:** Candlelight Theatre(4mi)

212b a I-180 W, PA 147 S, to Muncy, Williamsport, **N...gas:** Shell/diesel, **S...gas:** Coastal/24hr(1mi), st police

210.5mm Susquehanna River, W Branch

210b a US 15, to Williamsport, Lewisburg, **1 mi N...gas:** Sunoco/repair, **S...gas:** Citgo, **food:** Bonanza, **lodging:** Comfort Inn, Holiday Inn Express, **other:** HOSPITAL

199 Mile Run Rd, no facilities

194mm rest area/weigh sta both lanes, full(handicapped)facilities, phone, picnic tables, litter barrels, vending, petwalk

192 PA 880, to Jersey Shore, **N...gas:** Citgo/diesel/24hr, **food:** Pit-Stop Rest., **S...gas:** Mobil

185 PA 477, Loganton, **N...gas:** Mobil, **other:** Holiday Pines Camping, **S...food:** Watt's Rest.

178 US 220, Lock Haven, **N...food:** Country Barn Rest., **other:** HOSPITAL(7mi), **5 mi N...gas:** Sheetz, **other:** Advance Parts, K-Mart, Wal-Mart SuperCtr/24hr, **S...gas:** Citgo/diesel, Exxon

173 PA 64, Lamar, **N...gas:** Gulf, Speedway/diesel/24hr, **food:** Cottage Family Rest., McDonald's, **lodging:** Comfort Inn/rest., Travelers Delite Motel, **S...gas:** Citgo, TA/Mobil/Subway/diesel/rest./24hr/@, **food:** DQ

161 PA 26, to Bellafonte, **S...gas:** Shell/diesel/repair, **other:** KOA, to PSU

158 US 220 S, PA 150, Milesburg, to Altoona, **N...gas:** Mobil/diesel, Shell/diesel/24hr, TA/Amoco/Subway/diesel/24hr/@, **food:** McDonald's, **lodging:** Bestway Inn(1mi), Holiday Inn, **S...st police**

147 PA 144, to Snow Shoe, **N...gas:** Citgo/diesel/24hr, Exxon/SnowShoe/diesel/repair/2, **food:** Snow Shoe Sandwich Shop, Subway, **other:** IGA Foods, repair

146mm rest area both lanes, full(handicapped)facilities, phone, picnic tables, litter barrels, vending, petwalk

138mm Moshanna River

133 PA 53, Kylertown, to Philipsburg, **N...gas:** KwikFill/motel/rest., Sunoco/LP, **food:** Roadhouse Rest., MktPlace Foods, **other:** USPO, diesel repair, Black Moshannon SP(9mi)

Interstate 80

E ↕ W

123 PA 970, Woodland, to Shawville, **S...gas:** Amoco, Pacific Pride/diesel, **other:** st patrol

120mm Susquehanna River, W Branch

120 PA 879, Clearfield, **N...gas:** Sapp Bros/diesel/24hr/2, **food:** Aunt Lu's Café, Best Western, **S...gas:** Amoco, BP/Subway, Sheetz/24hr, **food:** Arby's, Burger King, Dutch Pantry, McDonald's, **lodging:** Comfort Inn, Day's Inn, Super 8, **other:** HOSPITAL, Buick/Cadillac/GMC, K-Mart, Wal-Mart SuperCtr/24hr

111mm highest point on I-80 east of Mississippi River, 2250 ft

111 PA 153, to Penfield, **N...**to Parker Dam, to SB Elliot SP, **S...**HOSPITAL

Du Bois

101 PA 255, Du Bois, **N...gas:** Amoco/24hr, **other:** camping, **S...lodging:** Ramada Inn, **other:** HOSPITAL, st police, **1-2 mi S...gas:** Citgo, Sheetz/24hr, **food:** Arby's, Bailey's Drive-In, Burger King, Eat'n Park/24hr, Hoss' Rest., Italian Oven, LJ Silver, McDonald's, Perkins/24hr, Ponderosa, Red Lobster, Subway, Taco Bell, Wendy's, **lodging:** Best Western, DuBois Manor Motel, Hampton Inn, **other:** BiLo Foods, Eckerd, Goodyear/auto, JC Penney, K-Mart, Lowe's Whse, Sears, Shop'n Save Foods, Wal-Mart/drugs, mall

97 US 219, Du Bois, to Brockway, **S...gas:** Pilot/Arby's/diesel/24hr/@, Sheetz/diesel/24hr, **food:** Dutch Pantry Rest., Hoss' Rest.(2mi), **lodging:** Pizza Hut, Best Western, Du Bois Manor Motel(2mi), Holiday Inn, **other:** HOSPITAL, Advance Parts

87.5mm rest area both lanes, full(handicapped)facilities, phone, picnic tables, litter barrels, vending, petwalk

86 PA 830, to Reynoldsville, **S...gas:** J's/diesel/rest./motel/24hr, **other:** auto repair

81 PA 28, to Brookville, to Hazen, **S...**to Brookville, hist dist(2mi)

78 PA 36, Brookville, to Sigel, **N...gas:** Flying J/Country Mkt/diesel/24hr/@, TA/BP/Blimpie/Taco Bell/diesel/rest./24hr/@, **food:** DQ, KFC, McDonald's, Pizza Hut, **lodging:** Howard Johnson, Super 8, **other:** Buick/Pontiac/Cadillac, NAPA, to Cook Forest SP, **S...gas:** BP, Citgo/24hr, Exxon, Sunoco/24hr, **food:** Arby's, Burger King, Gilbert's Rest., Subway, **lodging:** Budget Host, Day's Inn, Holiday Inn Express, **other:** MEDICAL CARE

73 PA 949, Corsica, **N...gas:** Corsica/diesel/rest./24hr, **other:** to Clear Creek SP, **S...**USPO

70 US 322, to Strattanville, **N...gas:** Exxon/diesel, Keystone/Shell/diesel/rest./24hr/@

64 PA 66 S, Clarion, to New Bethlehem, **N...**to Clarion U

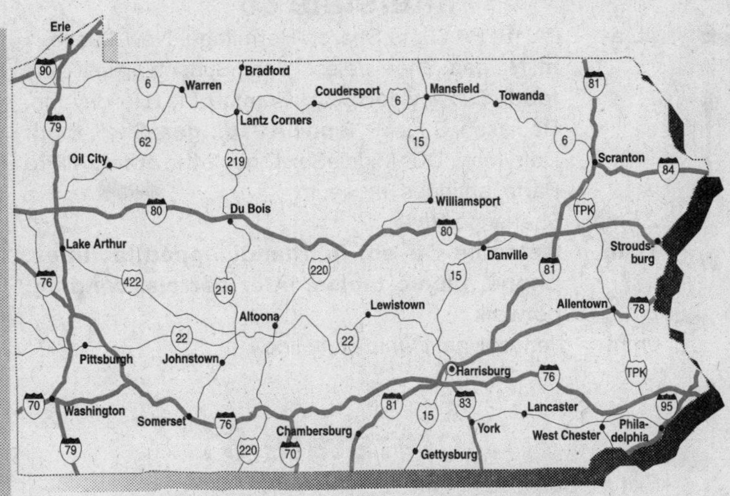

Clarion

62 PA 68, to Clarion, **N...gas:** BP/Subway/24hr, Exxon, KwikFill, **food:** Arby's, Burger King, Eat'n Park, LJ Silver, McDonald's(2mi), Perkins/24hr, Pizza Hut, Sizzler, Taco Bell, **lodging:** Comfort Inn, Day's Inn/rest., Holiday Inn/rest., Microtel, Super 8, **other:** HOSPITAL, Country Mkt/deli/24hr, $Tree, JC Penney, K-Mart, Staples, Wal-Mart SuperCtr/24hr, mall

61mm Clarion River

60 PA 66 N, to Shippenville, **N...gas:** Citgo, **other:** st police, to Cook Forest SP, camping

56mm parking area/weigh sta both lanes

53 to PA 338, to Knox, **N...gas:** Gulf/diesel, **food:** Wolf's Den Rest., Wolf's Camping Resort, **S...other:** Good Tire Service

45 PA 478, Emlenton, to St Petersburg, **N...other:** Chevrolet/Cadillac, **4 mi S...other:** Golf Hall of Fame

44.5mm Allegheny River

42 PA 38, to Emlenton, **N...gas:** Citgo/diesel/rest./24hr, Exxon/Subway/diesel/24hr, **food:** FatChaps Rest., **lodging:** Emlenton Motel, **other:** Gaslight RV Park

35 PA 308, to Clintonville, **N...gas:** Gulf/diesel/LP/24hr

30.5mm rest area both lanes, full(handicapped)facilities, phone, picnic tables, litter barrels, vending, petwalk

29 PA 8, Barkeyville, to Franklin, **N...gas:** Gulf/diesel/24hr, **food:** Arby's, Burger King, King's Rest., **lodging:** Day's Inn, **S...gas:** Citgo/diesel/24hr, KwikFill/diesel/rest./24hr, TA/BP/Subway/diesel/rest./24hr/@, **other:** to Slippery Rock U

24 PA 173, to Grove City, Sandy Lake, **S...other:** HOSPITAL, Wendell August Forge/gifts(3mi)

19b a I-79, N to Erie, S to Pittsburgh

15 US 19, to Mercer, **N...gas:** Marathon/subs, **food:** Burger King, McDonald's, **lodging:** Howard Johnson/rest., **other:** st police, camping, **2 mi S...lodging:** Iron Bridge Inn/rest., **other:** Jct 19&80 Camping, KOA

PENNSYLVANIA

Interstate 80

E

W

4b a PA 18, PA 60, to Sharon-Hermitage, New Castle, **1 mi N...gas:** Sheetz/diesel/24hr, Sunoco/diesel/24hr, **food:** Subway, **lodging:** Comfort Inn, Holiday Inn, Radisson, Super 8, **S on PA 318...gas:** Shell, **food:** DairyMart, DQ, MiddleSex Diner/24hr, **other:** AllPro Parts, antiques, museum

2.5mm Shenango River

1mm Welcome Ctr eb, full(handicapped)facilities, phone, picnic tables, litter barrels, vending, petwalk

0mm Pennsylvania/Ohio state line

Interstate 81

N

S

Exit # Services

233mm Pennsylvania/New York state line

232mm insp sta sb

230 PA 171, Great Bend, **E...gas:** Mobil/24hr, **W...gas:** Exxon/Arby's/diesel/24hr, Sunoco/diesel, **food:** Burger King, Dobb's Country Kitchen, McDonald's, Subway, **lodging:** Colonial Brick Motel/rest., **other:** Ford

223 PA 492, New Milford, **W...gas:** Gulf, Mobil/24hr, **food:** Green Gables Rest.

219 PA 848, to Gibson, **E...**st police, **W... gas:** Exxon/McDonald's/diesel, Flying J/Country Mkt/diesel/24hr/@

217 PA 547, Harford, **E...gas:** Exxon/Subway/diesel/24hr/@, Sunoco/diesel/rest./24hr

211 PA 92, Lenox, **E...**Elk Mtn Ski Area, **W...gas:** Mobil/diesel/24hr, Shell/diesel, **food:** Bingham's Rest., **other:** Lenox Drug

209mm Welcome Ctr sb, full(handicapped)facilities, phone, picnic tables, litter barrel, vending, petwalk

206 PA 374, Lenoxville, to Glenwood, **E...**to Elk Mountain Ski Resort

203mm rest area nb, full(handicapped)facilities, phone, picnic tables, litter barrels, vending, petwalk

202 PA 107, to Fleetville, Tompkinsville, no facilities

201 PA 438, East Benton, **W...gas:** Mobil, **food:** North 40 Rest.

199 PA 524, Scott, **E...gas:** Amoco/diesel, Texaco/diesel/24hr, **W...gas:** Exxon/deli, **food:** Subway, **lodging:** Motel 81, **other:** to Lackawanna SP

197 PA 632, Waverly, **E...other:** Mr Z's Foods, Rite Aid, **W...gas:** Sunoco/24hr, Doc's Deli/24hr

194 US 6, US 11, to I-476/PA Tpk, Clarks Summit, **W...gas:** Shell/diesel, Sunoco/diesel, **food:** Burger King, Friendly's, Krispy Kreme, McDonald's, Pizza Hut, Sabatini's Rest., So-Journer Rest., Subway, Taco Bell, Wendy's, **lodging:** Comfort Inn, Hampton Inn, Nichols Village Inn, Ramada Inn, Summit Inn, **other:** Advance Parts, Eckerd, Kost Tire, Radio Shack, Weis Foods

191b a US 6, US 11, to Carbondale, **E...gas:** Shell, **food:** Applebee's, Arby's, Burger King, China Buffet, ChuckeCheese, Denny's, Don Pablo, Fresno's SW Rest., Hawks Chocolates, LJ Silver, LoneStar Steaks, McDonald's, **other:** MEDICAL CARE, Nathan's Dogs, Old Country Buffet, Olive Garden, Perkins, Pizza Hut, Ruby Tuesday, Texas Steaks, TCBY, Wendy's, Quality Hotel, Aldi Foods, Borders Books, Circuit City, $Express, Firestone/auto, Home Depot, Hyundai, JC Penney, Jo-Ann Crafts, K-Mart, OfficeMax, PepBoys, Radio Shack, Sears/auto, Wal-Mart SuperCtr/24hr, Wegman's Foods, mall, **W...other:** to Anthracite Museum

190 Main Ave, Dickson City, **E...food:** Golden Corral, **lodging:** Fairfield Inn, Residence Inn, **other:** Best Buy, Lowe's Whse, Sam's Club, Staples

188 PA 347, Throop, **E...gas:** Sunoco/diesel, **food:** Big Boy, Boston Mkt, China World Buffet, McDonald's, Wendy's, **lodging:** Day's Inn, Econolodge, **other:** Advance Parts, Kost Tire, PriceChopper Foods, Radio Shack, st police, **W...gas:** Mobil, **food:** Burger King, Friendly's, **other:** Mazda

Scranton

187 to I-84, I-380, US 6(no return from nb)

186 PA 435, Drinker St, **E...gas:** Mobil, **lodging:** Holiday Inn, **W...gas:** Citgo

185 Central Scranton Expwy, **W...**HOSPITAL

184 to PA 307, River St, **W...gas:** Citgo, Exxon, Mobil, **lodging:** Clarion, **other:** HOSPITAL, CVS Drug, $Tree, Gerrity Foods

182 Davis St, Montage Mtn Rd, **E...food:** Mugg's Rest., Rocket's Café, Stadium Club Rest., **lodging:** Comfort Suites, Courtyard, Hampton Inn, **W...gas:** Mobil, Sunoco/diesel, **food:** LJ Silver, McDonald's, Wendy's, **lodging:** Econolodge, Rodeway Inn, **other:** USPO

180 to US 11, PA 502, to Moosic, no facilities

178b a to US 11, Avoca, **E...food:** Damon's, **lodging:** Holiday Inn Express, **W...gas:** Petro/Sunoco/diesel/rest./24hr/@

175b a PA 315 S, to I-476, Dupont, **E...gas:** Mobil/diesel, Sunoco/24hr, **food:** Arby's, McDonald's, Perkins, **lodging:** Knight's Inn, Super 8, **other:** Chevrolet, **W...gas:** Getty, Pilot/Wendy's/diesel/24hr, **lodging:** Victoria Inn, **other:** Wal-Mart

170b a PA 115, PA 309, Wilkes-Barre, **E...gas:** Exxon/diesel, Sunoco/diesel, **lodging:** Best Western, **other:** to Pocono Downs, **W...gas:** Sunoco/24hr, **food:** Friendly's, LJ Silver, McDonald's, Perkins, Pizza Hut, TGIFriday, **lodging:** Candlewood Suites, Day's Inn, Hampton Inn, Holiday Inn, Red Roof Inn, **other:** HOSPITAL, Kia, BMW, Subaru, VW, mall

168 Highland Park Blvd, Wilkes-Barre, **W...gas:** Sheetz, **food:** Applebee's, Bennigan's, Bob Evans, Burger King, Chili's, Cracker Barrel, Ground Round, McDonald's, Olive garden, Outback Steaks, Pizzaria Uno, Red Robin, Wendy's, **lodging:** Best Western, Hilton Garden, Ramada Inn, Travelodge, **other:** Barnes&Noble, Best Buy, Lowe's Whse, Sam's Club/gas, Target, Wal-Mart SuperCtr/24hr, Wegman's Foods

Interstate 81

N ↕ S

Hazleton

165b a PA 309 S, Wilkes-Barre, **W...gas:** BP/diesel, Shell, **food:** Dunkin Donuts, Mark II Rest., McDonald's, Perkins, Taco Bell, **lodging:** Comfort Inn, Econolodge, **other:** Advance Parts, Eckerd, K-Mart

164 PA 29, Ashley, to Nanticoke, no facilities

159 Nuangola, **W...gas:** Amoco/24hr, Godfather's

157mm rest area/weigh sta sb, full(handicapped)facilities, vending, phone, picnic tables, litter barrels, petwalk

156mm rest area/weigh sta nb, full(handicapped)facilities, vending, phone, picnic tables, litter barrels, petwalk

155 to Dorrance, **E...gas:** Sunoco/diesel/24hr, **lodging:** Econolodge(2mi)

151b a I-80, E to Mountaintop, W to Bloomsburg

145 PA 93, W Hazleton, **E...gas:** Shell, Sunoco/diesel/24hr, TurkeyHill, **food:** Bonanza, Damon's, Friendly's, Ground Round, LJ Silver, McDonald's, Perkins, Pizza Hut, Rossi's Rest., Taco Bell, Wendy's, **lodging:** Best Western(2mi), Comfort Inn, Fairfield Inn, Forest Hill Inn, Ramada Inn, **other:** Aldi, Cadillac, Mazda, Plymouth/Jeep, **W...gas:** Shell, **food:** Top of the 80's Rest., **lodging:** Hampton Inn, **other:** st police

143 PA 924, to Hazleton, **E...lodging:** Hazleton Motel, **W...gas:** Exxon

141 PA 424, S Hazleton Beltway, **E...**Mt Laurel Motel

138 PA 309, to McAdoo, **2 mi E...lodging:** Pines Motel

135mm scenic area nb

134 to Delano, no facilities

132mm parking area/weigh sta both lanes

131b a PA 54, Mahanoy City, **E...other:** to Tuscarora/Locust Lake SP, **W...gas:** Exxon

124b a PA 61, to Frackville, **E...food:** Cracker Barrel, McDonald's, **lodging:** Holiday Inn Express, **other:** K-Mart, Sears/auto, mall, **W...gas:** Hess, Mobil/Taco Bell/24hr, **food:** Dutch Kitchen, Rocky's Pizza, Subway, **lodging:** Econolodge, Motel 6, **other:** HOSPITAL, Goodyear/auto, Plymouth/Dodge, Rite Aid, st police

119 High Ridge Park Rd, to Gordon, **E...lodging:** Country Inn Suites, **other:** HOSPITAL

116 PA 901, to Minersville, **E...food:** 901 Rest.

112 PA 25, to Hegins, **W...**camping

107 US 209, to Tremont, no facilities

104 PA 125, Ravine, **E...gas:** Exxon/diesel/24hr, **other:** Echo Valley Camping

100 PA 443, to Pine Grove, **E...gas:** Exxon, **food:** Arby's, McDonald's, **lodging:** Colony Lodge, Comfort Inn, Econolodge, **W...gas:** Shell/diesel/24hr

90 PA 72, to Lebanon, **E...gas:** Exxon, Hess, **food:** Subway, Wendy's, **lodging:** Day's Inn, **other:** KOA, Lickdale Camping, **W...lodging:** Red Carpet Inn

89 I-78 E, to Allentown

85b a PA 934, to Annville, **2 mi W...gas:** Mobil/rest., **other:** to Indian Town Gap Nat Cem

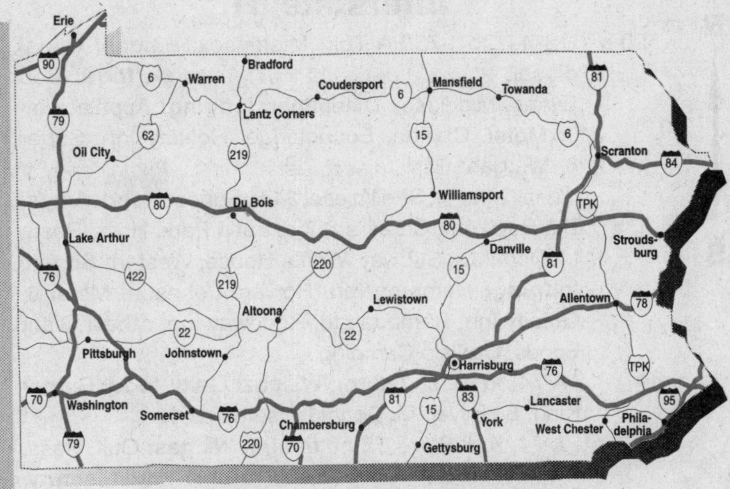

Harrisburg

80 PA 743, Grantville, **E...gas:** Mobil/diesel, **lodging:** Econolodge, Hampton Inn, **W...gas:** Exxon, Shell, **lodging:** Comfort Suites, Holiday Inn, **other:** racetrack

79mm rest area/weigh sta both lanes, full(handicapped)facilities, phone, vending, picnic tables, litter barrels, petwalk

77 PA 39, to Hershey, **E...gas:** Exxon/diesel, Mobil/diesel, Pilot/Pizza Hut/diesel/24hr, **lodging:** Country Inn Suites, Ramada Ltd, Sleep Inn, **other:** to Hershey Attractions, st police, **W...gas:** Shell/Subway/diesel, TA/diesel/24hr/@, Wilco/Perkins/diesel/24hr, **food:** McDonald's, **lodging:** Comfort Inn, Daystop, **other:** Goodyear

72 to US 22, Linglestown, **E...gas:** Citgo/diesel, Hess, Shell/diesel, Sunoco/diesel, **food:** Applebee's, Burger King, El Rodeo Mexican, LJSilver, McDonald's, Malley's Rest., Old Country Buffet, Wendy's, **lodging:** Holiday Inn Express, L&M Motel, Quality Inn, **other:** Advance Parts, C&P Repair, Chrysler/Jeep, CVS Drug, Festival Foods, K-Mart, Toyota, U-Haul, **W...food:** Country Oven Rest., **lodging:** Best Western

70 I-83 S, to York, airport

69 Progress Ave, **E...food:** Cracker Barrel, **other:** st police, **W...food:** Western Sizzlin, **lodging:** Best Western, Red Roof Inn

67b a US 22, US 322 W, PA 230, Cameron St, to Lewistown, no facilities

66 Front St, **E...**HOSPITAL, **W...food:** McDonald's, Ponderosa, Wendy's, **lodging:** Day's Inn

65 US 11/15, to Enola, **1 mi E...gas:** Mobil/24hr, Sunoco/diesel/24hr, **food:** DQ, Eat'n Park, KFC, McDonald's, Subway, Wendy's, **lodging:** Quality Inn, **other:** Advance Parts, K-Mart, Radio Shack, Rite Aid

61 PA 944, to Wertzville, no facilities

59 PA 581, to US 11, to Harrisburg, **3 mi E...food:** Bob Evans, Burger King, Friendly's, McDonald's, Wendy's, **lodging:** Comfort Inn, Hampton Inn, Holiday Inn

57 PA 114, to Mechanicsburg, **1-2 mi E...food:** Arby's, Isaac's Rest., McDonald's, Pizza Hut, Taco Bell, **lodging:** Ramada Ltd

PENNSYLVANIA

Interstate 81

N ↕ S

Carlisle

52b a US 11, to I-76/PA Tpk, Middlesex, **E...gas:** Citgo/diesel, Flying J/diesel/LP/rest./24hr/@, **food:** Bob Evans, Middlesex Diner/24hr, **lodging:** Appalachian Tr Motel, Clarion, Econolodge, Holiday Inn, Super 8, **W...gas:** Petro/diesel/rest./24hr/@, Pilot/Wendy's/diesel/24hr/@, Shell/diesel/24hr, Sunoco, **food:** Arby's, Big Boy/24hr, Carelli's Subs, Eat'n Park, Hoss' Rest., McDonald's, Subway, Waffle House, Western Sizzlin, **lodging:** Hampton Inn, Howard Johnson, Motel 6, Quality Inn, Ramada Ltd, Rodeway Inn, **other:** Giant Foods, Carlisle Camping

49 PA 74(no EZ sb return), **W...gas:** Getty, **food:** Burger King, LJ Silver, McDonald's, same as 48

48 PA 74, York St(no EZ nb return), **W...gas:** Gulf, Hess, KwikFill, **food:** Rillo's Rest., **other:** Ford/Mercury, OfficeMax, **1 mi W...food:** Burger King, LJ Silver, McDonald's, Pizza Hut, Taco Bell, **other:** CVS Drug, JC Penney, K-Mart, Lowe's Whse, Sears/auto

47 PA 34, Hanover St, **E...food:** Cracker Barrel, **lodging:** Sleep Inn, **W...gas:** Mobil

45 College St, **E...gas:** Mobil, Shell, **food:** Bonanza, Carelli's Subs, Friendly's, Great Wall Chinese, McDonald's, **lodging:** Day's Inn, Super 8, **other:** Eckerd, K-Mart, **W...**HOSPITAL

44 PA 465, to Plainfield, **W...gas:** Sheetz/24hr

38mm rest area both lanes, full(handicapped)facilities, phone, picnic tables, litter barrels, petwalk

37 PA 233, to Newville, **E...other:** Pine Grove Furnace SP, **W...**Col Denning SP

Chambersburg

29 PA 174, King St, **E...gas:** Shell/diesel, Sunoco/24hr, **lodging:** Budget Host, **W...food:** Burger King(1mi), DQ, McDonald's(2mi), **lodging:** AmeriHost, **other:** Ford

24 PA 696, Fayette St, **W...gas:** Mobil/diesel

20 PA 997, Scotland, **E...gas:** Exxon/diesel, **food:** McDonald's, **lodging:** Comfort Inn, Super 8, **other:** JC Penney, Sears/auto, mall, **W...gas:** BP/diesel, Sunoco/24hr

16 US 30, to Chambersburg, **E...gas:** Sheetz/24hr, **food:** Boston Mkt, DQ, KFC, Perkins, Popeye's, **lodging:** Day's Inn, **other:** Aldi Foods, $Express, Food Lion, Harley-Davidson, Nissan/Toyota, st police, **W...gas:** Hess/diesel, **food:** Burger King, Golden China, LJ Silver, McDonald's, Pizza Hut, Ponderosa, Taco Bell, **lodging:** Best Western(1mi), Sheraton, Travelodge(1mi), **other:** HOSPITAL, Advance Parts, Family$, Lincoln/Mercury, Sav-A-Lot Food

14 PA 316, Wayne Ave, **E...food:** Bob Evans, Cracker Barrel, **lodging:** Fairfield Inn, Hampton Inn, **W...gas:** Exxon/24hr, KwikFill, Sheetz, Shell/diesel, Sunoco, **food:** Applebee's, Arby's, Denny's, Pizza Hut, Red Lobster, Subway, Wendy's, **lodging:** Econolodge, Holiday Inn Express, Quality Inn, **other:** CVS Drug, Giant Foods, K-Mart, Staples, Weis Foods

12mm weigh sta sb

10 PA 914, Marion, no facilities

7mm weigh sta nb

5 PA 16, Greencastle, **E...gas:** Shell/diesel, TA/BP/diesel/24hr/@, **food:** Arby's, Buckhorn Rest., McDonald's, Subway, **lodging:** Castle Green Motel, Econolodge, Rodeway Inn, **other:** Whitetail Ski Resort, **W...gas:** Exxon/diesel, **food:** Antrim House Rest., Hardee's

3 US 11, **E...food:** Chef Family Rest., **lodging:** Comfort Inn

2mm Welcome Ctr nb, full(handicapped)facilities, phone, picnic tables, litter barrels, vending, petwalk

1 PA 163, Mason-Dixon Rd, **W...food:** Black Steer Rest., Mason-Dixon Rest., **lodging:** Econolodge, State Line Motel, **other:** Keystone RV

0mm Pennsylvania/Maryland state line, Mason-Dixon Line

Interstate 83

N ↕ S

Exit # Services

51b a I-83 begins/ends on I-81, exit 70.

Harrisburg

50b a US 22, Jonestown Rd, Harrisburg, **E...gas:** Shell, Sunoco, **food:** Applebee's, Arby's, Colonial Diner, LJ Silver, McDonald's, Pizza Hut, Red Lobster, Subway, Taco Bell, **other:** Aamco, Borders Books, CVS Drug, Goodyear/auto, Home Depot, Kohl's, Michael's, NTB, PepBoys, Sears/auto, Target, Tires+, Weis Foods, mall, **W...gas:** Citgo/7-11, Exxon, **food:** Friendly's, KFC, Outback Steaks

48 Union Deposit Rd, **E...gas:** Sunoco, **food:** Arby's, Burger King, Denny's, Evergreen Chinese, LoneStar Steaks, Panera Bread, Wendy's, **lodging:** Hampton Inn, Sheraton, **other:** HOSPITAL, Giant Foods, Staples, mall, **W...gas:** Shell, **food:** ChiChi's, Hardee's, McDonald's, OutBack Steaks, Rita's Drive-Thru, Subway, TGIFriday, Waffle House, Your Place Rest., **lodging:** Comfort Inn, Fairfield Inn, **other:** Lowe's Whse, Phar-Mor Drugs, Radio Shack, Weis Foods

47 (46b from nb), US 322 E, to Hershey, Derry St, **E...gas:** Hess Gas, **food:** Papa John's, **other:** Home Depot

46a I-283 S, to I-76/PA Tpk, **facilities E off I-283 S...gas:** Amoco, Exxon/diesel, Sunoco, **food:** Bob Evans, Capitol Diner, Doc Holliday's Steaks, Eat'n Park, Leed's Grill, McDonald's, **lodging:** Baymont Inn, Econolodge, Holiday Inn, Howard Johnson, Marriott, Red Roof Inn, Super 8, Travelodge, Wyndham, **other:** Buick, LandRover, VW/Audi

45 Paxton St, **E...gas:** Texaco, **food:** Burger King, Dunkin Donuts, Pizza Hut, Ponderosa, Santo's Pizza, S Philly Hoagies, Wendy's, **other:** Chrysler/Plymouth, JC Penney, Mazda/Subaru/Toyota, mall

44b 17th St, 19th St, **E...gas:** Pacific Pride/diesel, Sunoco, A+ Minimart, **food:** Benihana Japanese, Hardee's, Massimo's Pizza/subs, Royal Thai Rest., **other:** Big A Parts, Cadillac/GMC, Dodge, Firestone, Honda, Hyundai/Suzuki/Isuzu, Nissan, Pontiac

Interstate 83

44a PA 230, 13th St, Harrisburg, downtown, **W...gas:** Chevrolet, **other:** Saturn

43 2nd St, Harrisburg, downtown, st capitol, **W...gas:** Crowne Plaza, **other:** HOSPITAL

42.5mm Susquehanna River

42 Lemoyne, **E...gas:** Hess, Mobil, Turkey Hill Gas/food, **food:** Burger King, KFC

41b Highland Park, **W...gas:** Mobil, **food:** KFC, Rascal's Pizza, Royal Subs, Weis Foods

41a US 15, PA 581 W, to Gettysburg, no facilities

40b New Cumberland, **W...gas:** Shell, **food:** JoJo's Pizza, McDonald's, Subway, **other:** $General

40a Limekiln Rd, to Lewisberry, **E...gas:** BP, Mobil, **food:** Bob Evans, Eat'n Park, McDonald's, Pizza Hut, **lodging:** Comfort Inn, Fairfield Inn, Holiday Inn, Rodeway Inn, Travelodge, **W...gas:** Hess/diesel, **lodging:** Motel 6, Travel Inn

39b I-76/PA Tpk

39a PA 114, Lewisberry Rd, **E...lodging:** Day's Inn

38 Reesers Summit, no facilities

36 PA 262, Fishing Creek, **E...gas:** Hess, **food:** Culhanes Steaks, **W...gas:** Shell

35 PA 177, Lewisberry, **E...food:** Hillside Café, **W...gas:** Mobil, **food:** Family Rest.

35mm parking area/weigh sta sb

34 Valley Green(from nb), same as 33

33 PA 392, Yocumtown, **E...gas:** Hess/Blimpie/diesel, Henry's Trkstop/diesel, Rutter's Gas, **food:** Alice's Rest., Burger King, Maple Donuts, McDonald's, Newberry Diner, **lodging:** Super 8, **other:** MEDICAL CARE, Eckerd, Family$, Radio Shack, SuperFresh Food, Thrift Drugs

33mm parking area/weigh sta nb

32 PA 382, Newberrytown, **E...gas:** Sunoco/diesel, Rutter's/diesel, **food:** Pizza Hut, **W...gas:** Exxon/diesel

28 PA 295, Strinestown, **W...gas:** Exxon/Rutter's/24hr, **food:** Wendy's

24 PA 238, Emigsville, **W...gas:** Mobil, **food:** Sibol's Steaks

22 PA 181, N George St, **E...gas:** Exxon/24hr, Getty, **lodging:** Comfort Inn, **W...gas:** Sunoco/24hr, **food:** LJ Silver, McDonald's, Wendy's, **lodging:** Day's Inn, Motel 6, Super 8, same as 21b

21b a US 30, Arsenal Rd, to York, **E...food:** Bob Evans, San Carlo's Rest., **lodging:** Day's Inn, Hampton Inn(2mi), Holiday Inn, Ramada Inn, Red Roof Inn, Sheraton, **other:** Pontiac, **W...gas:** Crown Gas, Exxon, Mobil, Texaco/diesel, **food:** Burger King, China Kitchen, Domino's, Dunkin Donuts, El Rodeo Mexican, Friendly's, Hardee's, Hooters, KFC, LoneStar Steaks, LJ Silver, McDonald's, Old Country Buffet, Pizza Hut, Popeye's, Subway, Taco Bell, Wendy's, **lodging:** Holiday Inn, Motel 6, Super 8, **other:** Chevrolet/Subaru, Chrysler/Mitsubishi, CVS Drug, Harley-Davidson, NTB, PepBoys, Radio Shack, Staples, Weis Foods

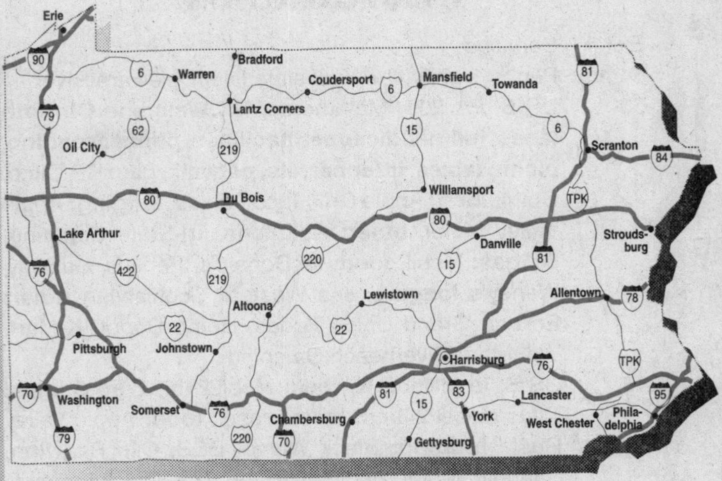

York

19 PA 462, Market St, **E...gas:** Sunoco, **food:** Applebee's, Eat'n Park, Perkins, **lodging:** Quality Inn Suites, **other:** HOSPITAL, Nissan, Saturn, **W...gas:** Sunoco

18 PA 124, Mt Rose Ave, Prospect St, **E...gas:** Exxon, Mobil, Rutters, **food:** Sunoco/Pizza Hut, Burger King, Denny's, Little Caesar's, **lodging:** Budget Host, Spirit of 76 Motel, **other:** CVS Drug, K-Mart, Nello Tire, Weis Foods, **W...gas:** Mobil(1mi)

16b a PA 74, Queen St, **E...gas:** Mobil/24hr, **food:** Cracker Barrel, Pizza Hut, Ruby Tuesday, **lodging:** Country Inn Suites, **other:** Ford/Lincoln/Mercury, Giant Foods, **W...gas:** Exxon, **food:** Chap's Rest., McDonald's, Subway, Taco Bell, **other:** CVS Drug, Cadillac/BMW/Hyundai, CVS Drug, $General, Honda, Jo-Ann Fabrics, Weis Foods

15 (from nb)S George St, I-83 spur into York, **W...**HOSPITAL

14 PA 182, Leader Heights, **E...**Subway, **W...gas:** Exxon/Pizza Hut, Sunoco/diesel/24hr, **food:** McDonald's, **lodging:** Comfort Inn

10 PA 214, Loganville, **W...food:** Lee's Rest., Mamma's Pizza, **lodging:** Midway Motel, **other:** st police

8 PA 216, Glen Rock, **E...lodging:** Rocky Ridge Motel, **other:** Amish Farmers Mkt(2mi)

4 PA 851, Shrewsbury, **E...gas:** Crown/diesel/@, Mobil/diesel/24hr, **lodging:** Hampton Inn, **W...gas:** Exxon/diesel/24hr, **food:** Arby's, Coachlight Rest., KFC/Taco Bell, McDonald's, Subway, Wendy's, **other:** Advance Parts, CVS Drug, $Tree, Giant Foods/24hr, GNC, Radio Shack, Wal-Mart SuperCtr/24hr

2mm Welcome Ctr nb, full(handicapped)facilities, phone, vending, picnic tables, litter barrels, petwalk

0mm Pennsylvania/Maryland state line

PENNSYLVANIA

Interstate 84

E ↕ W

Exit #	Services
54mm	Pennsylvania/New York state line, Delaware River
53	US 6, PA 209, Matamoras, **N...Welcome Ctr/both lanes, full(handicapped)facilities, phone, vending, picnic tables, litter barrels, petwalk, gas:** BP, Citgo, Go24, **food:** Apple Grill, Taco Palace, **lodging:** Apple Valley Motel, **other:** AutoZone, Tri-State Camping, **S...gas:** Mobil, **food:** McDonald's, Perkins, Subway, Wendy's, **lodging:** Best Western, Scottish Inn, **other:** Eckerd, Grand Union Foods, Home Depot, K-Mart, Wal-Mart, Riverbeach Camping
46	US 6, to Milford, **N...gas:** Mobil/24hr, **2 mi S...gas:** Citgo/diesel/24hr, Sunoco/diesel, **food:** Apple Valley Rest., **lodging:** Black Walnut B&B, Cliff Park Inn, Sherelyn Motel, Red Carpet Inn, Tom Quick Inn/rest.
34	PA 739, to Lords Valley, Dingmans Ferry, **S...gas:** Mobil, Sunoco/Taco Bell/diesel, **food:** China Dynasty, McDonald's, Pizza/pasta, **other:** Rite Aid, USPO
30	PA 402, to Blooming Grove, **N...**st police, to Lake Wallenpaupack
26	PA 390, to Tafton, **N...**Exxon/diesel, to Lake Wallenpaupack, **S...other:** to Promised Land SP
26mm	**rest area/weigh sta both lanes, full(handicapped)facilities, phone, vending, picnic tables, litter barrels, petwalk**
20	PA 507, Greentown, **N...gas:** Exxon/diesel, Mobil, **food:** John's Italian, **other:** Animal Park
17	PA 191, to Newfoundland, Hamlin, **N...gas:** Exxon/24hr, Howe's 84/diesel/24hr, **food:** Twin Rocks Rest., **lodging:** Comfort Inn/rest.
8	PA 247, PA 348, Mt Cobb, **N...gas:** Gulf, **other:** golf, **S...gas:** Mobil/diesel/24hr
4	I-380 S, to Mount Pocono, no facilities
2	PA 435 S, to Elmhurst, no facilities
1	Tigue St, **N...lodging:** Holiday Inn, **S...gas:** Mobil
0mm	I-84 begins/ends on I-81, exit 54.

Interstate 90

E ↕ W

Exit #	Services
46mm	Pennsylvania/New York state line, **Welcome Ctr/weigh sta wb, full(handicapped)facilities, phone, vending, picnic tables, litter barrels, petwalk**
45	US 20, to State Line, **N...gas:** KwikFill/diesel/@, TA/Taco Bell/diesel/rest./@, **food:** McDonald's, Pizza Hut, **other:** Heritage Wine Cellars, **S...gas:** BP/Subway/diesel, **lodging:** Red Carpet Inn, **other:** Niagara Falls Info
41	PA 89, North East, **N...gas:** Shell, **lodging:** Super 8, Vineyard B&B, **S...**winery
37	I-86 E, to Jamestown, no facilities
35	PA 531, to Harborcreek, **N...gas:** TA/BP/diesel/rest./24hr/@, **food:** Pizza Hut, **lodging:** Rodeway Inn, **other:** Blue Beacon
32	PA 430, to Wesleyville, **N...gas:** Citgo, **S...other:** camping, st police
29	PA 8, to Hammett, **N...gas:** Citgo, **food:** Wendy's, **other:** HOSPITAL, **S...lodging:** Ramada/rest., **other:** Ford/Peterbilt, Cummins Repair
27	PA 97, State St, Waterford, **N...gas:** Citgo/diesel/24hr, Kwikfill, Petro, **food:** Arby's, Barbato's Italian, Big Boy, McDonald's, **lodging:** Best Western, Day's Inn, Red Roof Inn, TalleyHo Inn, **other:** HOSPITAL, **S...gas:** Pilot/Subway/diesel/24hr, Shell/diesel, **lodging:** Quality Inn, Super 8
24	US 19, Peach St, to Waterford, **N...gas:** Citgo/diesel, KwikFill, **food:** Applebee's, Burger King, China Garden, ChuckeCheese, Cracker Barrel, Damon's, Eat'n Park, Fazoli's, Longhorn Steaks, McDonald's, Old Country Buffet, Panera Bread, Ponderosa, QuakerSteak/lube, Taco Bell, TGIFriday, Wendy's, **lodging:** Courtyard, Motel 6, **other:** HOSPITAL, Advance Parts, Best Buy, Circuit City, Country Fair/deli, $Tree, Giant Eagle, Home Depot, Jo-Ann Fabrics, K-Mart, Kohl's, Lowe's Whse, Pontiac, Sam's Club, Staples, Target, VW, Wal-Mart/auto, Wegman's Foods, **S...gas:** Citgo, Sunoco, **food:** Bob Evans, **lodging:** Comfort Inn, Country Inn Suites, Econolodge, Hampton Inn, Holiday Inn Express, Microtel, Residence Inn
22b a	I-79, N to Erie, S to Pittsburgh, **3-5 mi N...**facilities in Erie
18	PA 832, Sterrettania, **N...gas:** Citgo/diesel/24hr, Shell/diesel/24hr, **food:** Burger King, **other:** Hill's Family Camping, to Presque Isle SP, **S...gas:** Gulf/diesel/rest./repair/24hr, Shell/diesel/24hr, **lodging:** Best Western, **other:** tires/service
16	PA 98, Fairview, to Franklin Center, **S...other:** Follys Inn Camping(2mi), Mar-Jo-Di Camping(5mi)
9	PA 18, Platea, to Girard, **N...other:** diesel repair, st police
6	PA 215, East Springfield, to Albion, **S...gas:** Sunoco, **lodging:** Miracle Motel
3	US 6N, West Springfield, to Cherry Hill, **N...**lodging on US 20, **S...gas:** BP/diesel/rest./repair/24hr
2.5mm	**Welcome Ctr/weigh sta eb, full(handicapped)facilities, info, phone, picnic tables, litter barrels, vending, petwalk**
0mm	Pennsylvania/Ohio state line

Erie

PENNSYLVANIA

Interstate 95

N ↕ S

Exit # Services

51mm Pennsylvania/New Jersey state line, Delaware River

51 PA 32, to New Hope, **W...**Washington Crossing Hist Park

49mm Welcome Ctr sb, full(handicapped)facilities, vending, phone, picnic tables, litter barrels, petwalk

49 PA 332, to Yardley, Newtown, **W...lodging:** Hampton Inn, **other:** HOSPITAL, to Tyler SP

46 US 1, to I-276, Langhorne, Oxford Valley, no facilities

Levittown

44 US 1, PA 413, to Penndel, Levittown, **E...gas:** Mobil/diesel/24hr, Shell/diesel/24hr, **food:** ChuckeCheese, Dunkin Donuts, Friendly's, Great American Diner, HongKong Pearl, Wendy's, **other:** HOSPITAL, Acura, Chevrolet/Buick, Chrysler/Dodge, $Express, Drug Emporium, Ford, Goodyear/auto, Honda, Jeep/Hyundai, K-Mart, Lincoln/Mercury, Marshalls, NTB, Radio Shack, Sam's Club, Subaru, VW/Volvo, Whse Mkt, **W...gas:** Mobil/diesel/24hr, **food:** Denny's, McDonald's, **other:** Toyota, U-Haul

40 PA 413, I-276(from nb), to Bristol Bridge, Burlington, **E...food:** Golden Eagle Diner/24hr, McDonald's, Taco Bell, **other:** HOSPITAL

37 PA 132, to Street Rd, **W...gas:** Amoco/24hr, Coastal, Gulf/diesel, Sunoco/diesel, **food:** Burger King, Denny's, IHOP, KFC, McDonald's, Wendy's, **other:** Cottman Transmissions, Firestone, GNC, K-Mart, PepBoys, Radio Shack

35 PA 63, to US 13, Woodhaven Rd, Bristol Park, **W...gas:** Coastal, Mobil, Shell, WaWa, **food:** Old Haven Pizza, **lodging:** Hampton Inn, **other:** HOSPITAL, Acme Foods, Hancock Fabrics, Home Depot, **1 mi W...gas:** Exxon, Mobil, **food:** Boston Mkt, China Buffet, Don Pablo, Dynasty Rest., Farm Buffet, KFC, McDonald's, Pizza Hut, Taco Bell, Wendy's, **other:** CompUSA, JC Penney, Marshall's, Nordstrom's, NTB, OfficeMax, SuperFresh Foods, Wal-Mart, mall

32 Academy Rd, **W...other:** HOSPITAL, K-Mart,

30 PA 73, Cottman Ave, **W...gas:** Sunoco

27 Bridge St, **W...gas:** Getty Gas, Eckerd, **other:** HOSPITAL

26 to NJ 90, Betsy Ross Brdg, Pennsauken, NJ, **W...gas:** Sunoco, **food:** Burger King, McDonald's, **lodging:** Hampton Inn

25 Allegheny Ave, **W...gas:** Sunoco, Wawa, **other:** HOSPITAL

23 Lehigh Ave, Girard Ave, **W...gas:** Exxon, Shell, **food:** Dunkin Donuts, Pizza Hut, Ruby Tuesday, **other:** HOSPITAL, Radio Shack

22 I-676, US 30, to Central Philadelphia, Independence Hall, **W...lodging:** Comfort Inn

20 Columbus Blvd, Penns Landing, **E...gas:** Amoco, Mobil, WaWa, **food:** Burger King, Boston Mkt, Dave&Buster's, ChartHouse Rest., ChuckeCheese, Hooters, McDonald's, **other:** Hyatt, Home Depot, OfficeMax, PepBoys, SavALot Foods, ShopRite Foods, Staples, Wal-Mart

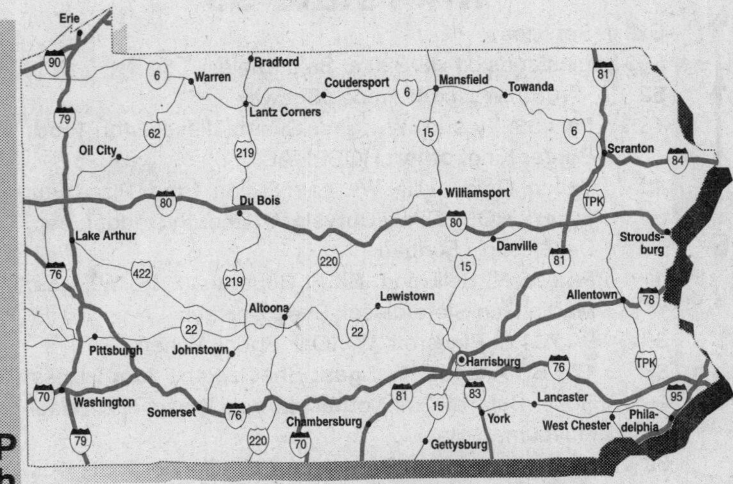

Philadelphia Area

19 I-76 E, to Walt Whitman Bridge, **W on Oregon Ave...gas:** Amoco, Shell, Sunoco/diesel/24hr, **food:** Burger King, Church's Chicken, McDonald's, Subway, Wendy's, **lodging:** Holiday Inn, **other:** Aldi, K-Mart, to stadium

17 PA 611, to Broad St, Pattison Ave, **W...other:** HOSPITAL, to Naval Shipyard, to stadium

15mm Schuykill River

15 Enterprise Ave, Island Ave(from sb), no facilities

14 Bartram Ave, Essington Ave(from sb), no facilities

13 PA 291, to I-76 W(from nb), to Central Philadelphia, **E...gas:** Exxon/diesel, **lodging:** Day's Inn, Guest Quarters, Hilton, Residence Inn, Sheraton Suites, Westin Suites

12 **E...**Philadelphia Intl Airport

10 PA 291 E, **E...lodging:** Marriott, Rennaisance Hotel, **W...lodging:** Courtyard, Hampton Inn, Embassy Suites, Extended Stay America, Fairfield Inn, Microtel, Studio+

9b a PA 420, to Essington, Prospect Park, **E...gas:** Coastal/diesel, **food:** Denny's, Shoney's, **lodging:** Comfort Inn, Econolodge, Holiday Inn, Motel 6, Radisson, Ramada Inn, Red Roof Inn

8 Ridley Park, to Chester Waterfront, **W on US 13...gas:** Sunoco, WaWa, **food:** McDonald's, **other:** Wal-Mart

7 I-476 N, to Plymouth, Meeting, no facilities

6 PA 352, PA 320, to Edgmont Ave, **1 mi E on US 13...food:** McDonald's, **other:** Wal-Mart, **W...food:** Edgmont Diner, **other:** HOSPITAL, to Widener U

5 Kerlin St(from nb), **E...gas:** Amoco

4 US 322 E, to NJ, **W...lodging:** Highland Motel

3 (3 from nb, no EZ return)US 322 W, Highland Ave, **E...gas:** Sunoco/diesel/24hr, Ford/Lincoln/Mercury, Goodyear

2 PA 452, to US 322, Market St, **E...gas:** Getty, **W...gas:** Citgo, Exxon, **food:** McDonald's

1 Chichester Ave, **E...gas:** Sunoco, **W...gas:** Amoco

0mm Pennsylvania/Delaware state line, **Welcome Ctr/weigh sta nb, full(handicapped)facilities, phone, picnic tables, litter barrels, petwalk**

PENNSYLVANIA

Interstate 99

N ↕ S

Exit # Services

I-99 begins/ends on US 220 at Bald Eagle.

52 PA 350, **W...gas:** Amoco/Subway

48 PA 453, Tyrone, **W...gas:** Sheetz/diesel/24hr, **food:** Burger King, **other:** HOSPITAL

45 Tipton, Grazierville, **W...gas:** Exxon, **food:** Pizza Hut, **other:** HOSPITAL, Chrysler/Plymouth/Dodge/Jeep, DelGrosso's Funpark

41 PA 865 N, Bellwood, **E...**Ft Roberdeau HS, **W...gas:** Martin Gen Store/diesel, Sheetz/diesel

39 PA 764 S, Pinecroft, **W...**Oak Spring Winery

33 17th St, Altoona, **W...gas:** Sheetz/24hr, **food:** Hoss' Rest., Subway(2mi), **other:** Lowe's Whse, Railroader Museum, U-Haul

32 PA 36, Frankstown Rd, Altoona, **E...**Canoe Cr SP, **W... gas:** Sheetz, **food:** Dunkin Donuts, HongKong Buffet, McDonald's, Olive Garden, Papa John's, Perkins, Pizza Hut, Red Lobster, Subway, Wendy's, **lodging:** Day's Inn, Econolodge, Holiday Inn, Super 8, **other:** HOSPITAL, AutoZone, Big A Parts, Cadillac, CVS Drug, Daewoo, Dodge, Eckerd, Lincoln/Mercury, NAPA, Nissan, Radio Shack, Subaru

Altoona

31 Plank Rd, Altoona, **E...food:** Fazoli's, Friendly's, Jethro's Rest., King's Rest., Outback Steaks, Ruby Tuesday, TGIFriday, **lodging:** Comfort Inn, Ramada Inn, **other:** Circuit City, Firestone/auto, Sam's Club, Target, Wal-Mart, **W...gas:** BP/Subway, **food:** Applebee's, Arby's, Burger King, Denny's, Don Pablo, Eat'n Park, KFC, LJ Silver, Ponderosa, Taco Bell, **lodging:** Hampton Inn, Motel 6, **other:** Advance Parts, BiLo Foods, $General, Giant Eagle Foods, JC Penney, Kaufmann's, K-Mart, PharMor, Sears/auto, Staples, Trak Auto, Weis Foods

28 US 22, Holidaysburg, to Ebensburg, **1 mi E...food:** McDonald's

23 PA 36, PA 164, Roaring Spring, Portage, **E...gas:** Exxon/LittleCaesar's/24hr, Mobil/Blimpie/diesel, Sheetz/24hr, **food:** Lynn's Rest., **lodging:** Rax, Haven Rest Motel, **other:** HOSPITAL, Chrysler/Plymouth/Dodge/Jeep, truck repair

15 Claysburg, King, **W...**gas, food

10 to Imler, **W...**gas, food, Blue Knob SP(8mi)

7 PA 869, Osterburg, St Clairsville, **W...**gas, food

3 PA 56, Johnstown, Cessna, **E...gas:** Amoco/diesel

1 I-70/76. I-99 begins/ends on US 220.

Interstate 476

E ↕ W

Exit # Services

131 US 11, US 6. I-476 begins/ends on I-81.

122 Keyser Ave, Old Forge, Taylor, no facilities

121mm toll plaza

115 I-81, PA 315, Wyoming Valley, Pittston, **W...gas:** Mobil, Pilot/Wendy's/diesel/24hr, Sunoco, **food:** Arby's, McDonald's, Perkins, **lodging:** Knight's Inn, Super 8, **other:** Chevrolet

112mm toll plaza

105 PA 115, Wilkes-Barre, Bear Creek, **E...gas:** Amoco, Mobil/diesel, Texaco

103mm parking area sb

100mm parking areas both lanes

97mm parking areas both lanes

95 I-80, PA 940, Pocono, Hazleton, **E...food:** Burger King, **W...gas**: Amoco/24hr, Texaco, WaWa, **food:** A&W/LJ Silver, Arby's, Gino's Pizza, Howard Johnson Rest., McDonald's, **lodging:** Comfort Inn, CountryPlace Inn, Day's Inn, Mtn Laurel Resort, Ramada Inn

90mm parking area sb

86mm Hickory Run Service Plaza both lanes, **gas:** Sunoco/diesel, **food:** Breyer's, McDonald's

74 US 209, Mahoning Valley, Lehighton, Stroudsburg, **W...gas:** Exxon/diesel, **food:** Subway

71mm Lehigh Tunnel

56 I-78, US 22, PA 309, Lehigh Valley, **E...lodging:** Comfort Inn, Day's Inn, McIntosh Inn, Super 8

56mm Allentown Service Plaza both lanes, **gas:** Sunoco/diesel, **food:** Big Boy, Nathan's, Pizza Hut, Roy Rogers, TCBY

44 PA 663, Quakertown, Pottstown, **E...lodging:** Best Western, Econolodge, Hampton Inn, Holiday Inn Express, Rodeway Inn, **other:** HOSPITAL

37mm parking area sb

31 PA 63, Lansdale, **E...gas:** Amoco, Mobil, **lodging:** Best Western, Lansdale Motel

20 Germantown Pike W, to I-276 W, PA Tpk W

19 Germantown Pike E

Philadelphia

18b a (18 from sb), Conshoshocken, Norristown, **E...gas:** Mobil, **food:** Burger King, LoneStar Steaks, McDonald's, Outback Steaks, **lodging:** Hampton Inn, **W...food:** Papa John's, Uno Pizzaria, Wendy's, **other:** BJ's Whse, Home Depot, Honda, Nissan, OfficeMax

16b a (16 from sb), I-76, PA 23, to Philadelpia, Valley Forge, no facilities

13 US 30, St Davids, Villanova, **E...gas:** Coastal, **food:** Campus Pizza, Villanova Diner, **other:** HOAPITAL, Radnor Drugs, USPO, Villanova Hardware

9 PA 3, Broomall, Upper Darby, **E...food:** PathMark Foods, **other:** HOSPITAL, carwash

5 US 1, Lima, Springfield, **N...**mall

3 Media, Swarthmore, Baltimore Pike, **E...**HOSPITAL

1 McDade Blvd, **E...gas:** Exxon, **food:** Dunkin Donuts, KFC, McDonald's

0mm I-476 begins/ends on I-95, exit 7.

Interstate 95

N ↕ S

Providence

Exit #(mm)Services
43mm Rhode Island/Massachusetts state line
30(42) East St, to Central Falls, **E...food:** Dunkin Donuts
29(41) US 1, Cottage St, **W...food:** D'angelo's, **other:** Firestone
28(40) RI 114, School St, **E...gas:** Sunoco, **other:** HOSPITAL, Hyundai, to hist dist
27(39) US 1, RI 15, Pawtucket, **E...gas:** Sunoco, **W...gas:** Shell/repair, Sunoco/diesel/24hr, **food:** Burger King, Dunkin Donuts, Ground Round, **lodging:** Comfort Inn, **other:** HOSPITAL
26(38) RI 122, Lonsdale Ave(from nb), **E...other:** U-Haul
25(37) US 1, RI 126, N Main St, Providence, **E...gas:** Hess Gas, **food:** Chili's, **other:** HOSPITAL, Brooks Drug/24hr, Shaw's Foods, **W...gas:** DB, Gulf/diesel, **food:** Burger King, Chelo's Italian, **other:** Aamco
24(36.5) Branch Ave, Providence, downtown, **W...other:** Sears Repair, Stop&Shop Foods
23(36) RI 146, RI 7, Providence, **E...gas:** Shell, **lodging:** Marriott, **other:** HOSPITAL, **W...**USPO
22(35.5) US 6, RI 10, Providence, downtown
21(35) Broadway St, Providence, **W...other:** Engle Tire, Goodyear/auto
20(34.5) I-195, to E Providence, Cape Cod
19(34) Eddy St, Allens Ave, to US 1(from sb), **W...food:** Wendy's, HOSPITAL
18(33.5) US 1A, Thurbers Ave, **W...gas:** Shell, **food:** Burger King, **other:** HOSPITAL
17(33) US 1(from sb), Elmwood Ave, **W...other:** Cadillac/Mazda, Tires Whse
16(32.5) RI 10, Cranston, **W...**zoo
15(32) Jefferson Blvd, **E...gas:** Getty/diesel, Global/diesel, **food:** Bickford's, Dunkin Donuts, **lodging:** Motel 6, **W...other:** Ford Trucks, Ryder
14(31) RI 37, Post Rd, to US 1, **W...gas:** Exxon, HOSPITAL
13(30) **1 mi E...**TF Green Airport, **lodging:** Hampton Inn, Holiday Inn Express, MainStay Suites, Masterhost Inn, Quality Suites, Residence Inn
12b(29) RI 2, I-295 N(from sb)
a RI 113 E, to Warwick, **E...gas:** Shell/Dunkin Donuts/diesel, **lodging:** Crowne Plaza Hotel, **W...**mall
11(29) I-295 N(exits left from nb), to Woonsocket
10b a(28) RI 117, to Warwick, **W...**HOSPITAL

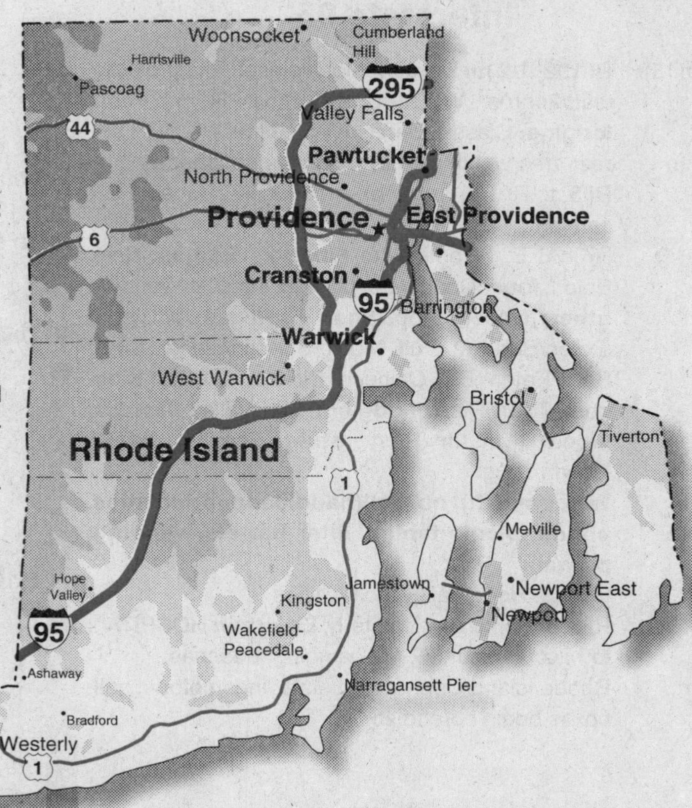

9(25) RI 4 S, E Greenwich, no facilities
8b a(24) RI 2, E Greenwich, **E...gas:** Shell/diesel, **food:** China Buffet, Dunkin Donuts, McDonald's, Outback Steaks, Ruby Tuesday, **other:** MEDICAL CARE, Ro Jack's Foods, Walgreen, **W...gas:** Sunoco/diesel, **food:** Applebee's, Denny's, Hops Rest., PapaGino's, Weathervane Seafood, Wendy's, **lodging:** Fairfield Inn, SpringHill Suites, **other:** Arlington RV, GNC, Goodyear/auto, Honda/Volvo, Jennings CarCare, Lowe's Whse, Mazda/Hyundai, Mitsubishi, Nissan, PepBoys, Pontiac/GMC/VW, Stop&Shop Foods, mall
7(21) to Coventry, **E...gas:** Mobil/diesel, **W...food:** Applebee's, Cracker Barrel, Denny's, Wendy's/rv parking, **other:** BJ's Whse/gas, auto repair
6a(20) Hopkins Hill Rd, **W...**park&ride
6(18) RI 3, to Coventry, **W...gas:** Shell/diesel, Sunoco/diesel/repair, **food:** Bess Eaton, Dunkin Donuts, Mark's Grill, **lodging:** Best Western, Super 8

RHODE ISLAND

Interstate 95

5b a(15) RI 102, **1-2 mi E...gas:** Mobil/diesel, Trkstp/diesel/rest./24hr/@ , **W...food:** Deli Store, Family Rest., **lodging:** Classic Motel

10mm rest area/weigh sta nb, weigh sta sb, phones

4(9) RI 3, to RI 165(from,nb), Arcadia, **W...**Arcadia SP, camping

3b a(7) RI 138 E, Wyoming, to Kingston, **E...gas:** Bess Eaton, **food:** Dunkin Donuts, McDonald's, Wendy's, **other:** NAPA, Stop&Shop Food/gas, **W...gas:** Exxon/Subway, Gulf, Mobil, Sunoco/diesel, **food:** Bess Eaton, Bali Chinese, Bickford's, Pizza Kingdom, Town Pizza, **lodging:** Sun Valley Inn/rest., Wood River Inn Rest., **other:** Family$, NAPA, Ocean Drug

6mm Welcome Ctr nb, full(handicapped)facilities, phone, picnic tables, litter barrels, vending, petwalk

2(4) to RI 3, Hope Valley, no facilities

1(1) RI 3, to Hopkinton, Westerly, **E...other:** HOSPITAL, to Misquamicut SP, RV camping, beaches

0mm Rhode Island/Connecticut state line, motorist callboxes begin nb/end sb

Interstate 295 (Providence)

Exit # Services

2b a(4) I-95, N to Boston, S to Providence. I-295 begins/ends on I-95, exit 4 in MA. **Exits 2-1 are in MA.**

1b a(2) US 1, **E...food:** Charlie's Rest., Friendly's, Hearth'n Kettle, Longhorn Steaks, 99 Rest., Panera Bread, TGIFriday, **other:** Best Buy, Borders, Circuit City, CompUSA, Filene's, JC Penney, Lord&Taylor, Lowe's Whse, Marshalls, Michael's, Old Navy, Sears/auto, Target, Wal-Mart, mall, **W...gas:** Exxon, Mutual/diesel, Shell/Subway, **food:** Applebee's, **lodging:** Holiday Inn Express, Super 8, **other:** Ford, Dodge/Kia, Nissan, Toyota

0mm Rhode Island/Massachusetts state line. **Exits 1-2 are in MA.**

11(24) RI 114, to Cumberland, **E...gas:** Shell/diesel, **food:** Honeydew Donuts, **other:** CVS Drug, Dave's Foods, **W...food:** Sakis Pizza/subs, **other:** Tedeschi Foods, Diamond Hill SP

10(21) RI 122, **E...gas:** Mutual Gas, P&A Conv/gas, **food:** Burger King, Dunkin Donuts, Jim's Deli, McDonald's, **W...food:** Chicken Power, Pamfilio's Italian, Pastry Gourmet, **other:** Brooks Drug, CVS Drug, $Depot, Newport Creamery, Ro Jack's Foods

20mm Blackstone River

19.5mm weigh sta both lanes, phone

9b a(19) RI 146, Woonsocket, Lincoln, **E...**mall, **2 mi W...gas:** Mobil, **other:** Chrysler/Plymouth, Honda, Isuzu

8b a(16) RI 7, N Smithfield, **W...gas:** Citgo/diesel/7-11, **food:** Cactus Grille, House of Pizza, Smith-Appleby House

7b a(13) US 44, Centerdale, **E...gas:** Shell, **food:** Isabella's Deli, Nicole's Bistro, **other:** HOSPITAL, Parts+, **W...gas:** Exxon/Subway/diesel, Mobil, Shell, **food:** A&W, Applebee's, Burger King, D'angelo's, Dunkin Donuts, KFC, McDonald's, PapaGino's, Pizza Hut, Subway, TinTsin Chinese, Wendy's, **other:** MEDICAL CARE, Brooks Drug, CVS Drug, Home Depot, Radio Shack, Stop&Shop Foods, to Powder Mill Ledges WR

6(10) US 6, to Providence, **E...gas:** Mobil, Shell/Dunkin Donuts, **food:** Burger King, China Jade, Del's Deli, KFC, Luigi's Italian, McDonald's, Quikava, Wendy's, **lodging:** Hi-Way Motel, **other:** AutoZone, BJ's Whse, Chevrolet/Buick, CVS Drug, Honda, Pontiac/GMC, Shaw's Foods, USPO, **W...lodging:** Bel-Air Motel

5(9) US 6 E Expswy

4(7) RI 14, Plainfield Pk, **W...gas:** Mobil/diesel/24hr

3b a(4) rd 37, Phenix Ave, **E...**TF Green Airport

2(2) RI 2 S, to Warwick, **E...gas:** Exxon, **food:** Longhorn Steaks, Macaroni Grill, Pizzaria Uno, **other:** Filene's, JC Penney, Macy's, Marshalls, Radio Shack, mall, **W...gas:** Mobil, Shell, Sunoco, **food:** Bickford's, Chili's, ChuckeCheese, Dunkin Donuts, HomeTown Buffet, Kwikava, LoneStar Steaks, McDonald's, PapaGino's, Subway, Taco Bell, Wendy's, **other:** Brooks Drug, CompUSA, Dodge/Subaru, Home Depot, NAPA, OfficeMax, Sam's Club, Saturn, Sears/auto, Staples, TownFair Tire, Wal-Mart, mall

1(1) RI 113 W, to W Warwick, same as 2

0mm I-295 begins/ends on I-95, exit 11.

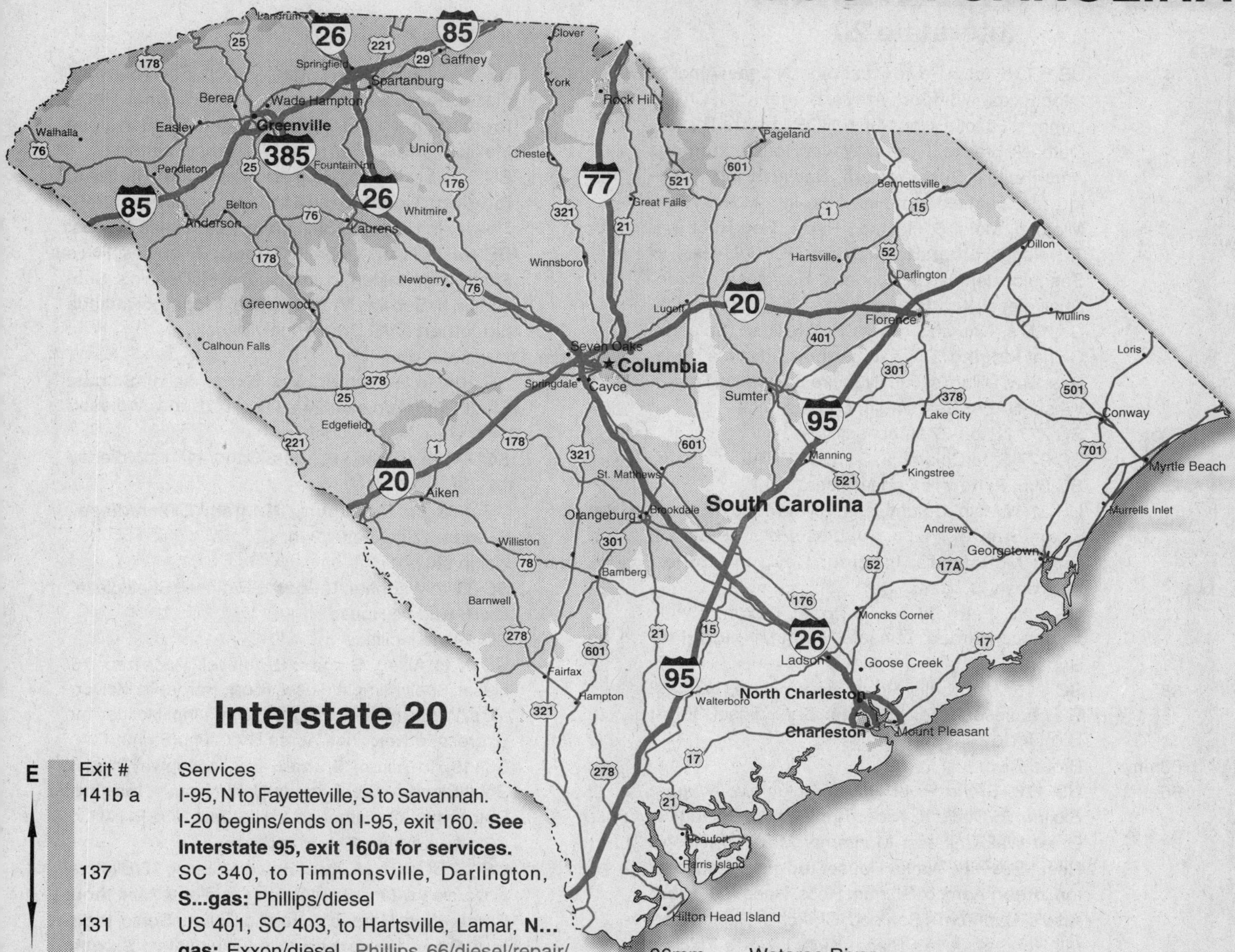

Interstate 20

E ↕ W

Exit #	Services
141b a	I-95, N to Fayetteville, S to Savannah. I-20 begins/ends on I-95, exit 160. **See Interstate 95, exit 160a for services.**
137	SC 340, to Timmonsville, Darlington, **S...gas:** Phillips/diesel
131	US 401, SC 403, to Hartsville, Lamar, **N... gas:** Exxon/diesel, Phillips 66/diesel/repair/rest./24hr/@, **other:** to Darlington Int Raceway
123	SC 22, Lamar, **N...gas:** BP, Lee SP
121mm	Lynches River
120	SC 341, Bishopville, Elliot, **N...lodging:** Bishopville Motel(3mi), **S...gas:** Exxon/diesel, **food:** Taste of Country Rest., **lodging:** Howard Johnson Express, **other:** HOSPITAL
116	US 15, Bishopville, to Sumter, Shaw AFB, **N...gas:** Shell/KFC/diesel/24hr, **food:** McDonald's, Pizza Hut, Subway(1mi), Waffle House, **lodging:** Econolodge, **S...gas:** Wilco/Hess/DQ/Wendy's/diesel/24hr/@
108	SC 34, to SC 31, Manville, **N...gas:** Shell/diesel, **S...gas:** Citgo/diesel
101	rd 329, no facilities
98	US 521, to Camden, **N...gas:** Citgo/diesel, Exxon/McDonald's, Shell, **lodging:** Fairfield Inn, **other:** HOSPITAL, **3-5 mi N...food:** Golden Corral, **lodging:** Colony Inn, Greenleaf Inn, Knight's Inn, **other:** Revolutionary War Pk

Columbia

Exit #	Services
96mm	Wateree River
93mm	**rest area both lanes, full(handicapped)facilities, phones, vending, picnic tables, litter barrels, petwalk**
92	US 601, to Lugoff, **N...gas:** Pilot/DQ/Subway/diesel/24hr/@, Shell/diesel, **food:** Hardee's, Waffle House, **lodging:** Day's Inn, Ramada Ltd, Travelodge, **other:** Camden RV Park(1mi), **2-3 mi N... lodging:** Best Western, KFC, McDonald's, Shoney's, Holiday Inn, **other:** Ford/Lincoln/Mercury
87	SC 47, to Elgin, **N...gas:** BP/diesel, Shell/diesel
82	SC 53, to Pontiac, **N...gas:** Shell, **S...other:** Clothing World Outlet
80	Clemson Rd, **N...gas:** Exxon/diesel, 76/Circle K, Shell/Bojangles, **food:** McDonald's, Waffle House, Zaxby's, **lodging:** Holiday Inn Express, **other:** CVS Drug, **S...other:** Chevrolet
76b a	Alpine Rd, to Ft Jackson, **N...**Sesquicentennial SP (76 from eb), I-77, N to Charlotte, S to Charleston

SOUTH CAROLINA

Interstate 20

E ↕ W

74 US 1, Two Notch Rd, to Ft Jackson, **N...gas:** Amoco/24hr, Exxon, 76, **food:** Arby's, Burger King, Chili's, Denny's, Fazoli's, Hops Grill, IHOP, Lizard's Thicket, Outback Steaks, Ryan's, Waffle House, **lodging:** AmeriSuites, Best Western, Baymont Inn, Comfort Inn, Fairfield Inn, Hampton Inn, Holiday Inn, Microtel, Motel 6, Ramada Plaza, Red Roof Inn, Travelodge, **other:** Home Depot, USPO, U-Haul, to Sesquicentennial SP, **S...gas:** Hess/diesel, Exxon, Shell/diesel, **food:** Applebee's, BBQ, Bojangles, Capt D's, Church's, Santa Fe Mexican, Splendid China, **lodging:** Day's Inn, **other:** Advance Parts, Best Buy, Dillard's, Family$, Firestone/auto, Lowe's Whse, NAPA, Sears/auto, Staples, mall

73b SC 277 N, to I-77 N, no facilities

a SC 277 S, to Columbia, **S...**HOSPITAL

72 SC 555, Farrow Rd, no facilities

71 US 21, N Main, Columbia, to Blythewood, **N...gas:** Exxon/Subway/Pizza Hut/diesel/@ , BP/diesel, **food:** McDonald's, **lodging:** Day's Inn, **other:** truckwash, **S...gas:** Shell

70 US 321, Fairfield Rd, **S...gas:** Exxon, Flying J/Conoco/Hardee's/diesel/LP/24hr/@ , **lodging:** Super 8

68 SC 215, Monticello Rd, to Jenkinsville, **N...gas:** Exxon/diesel, Shell, **S...gas:** Shell/diesel, **food:** Big Daddy's Café

66mm Broad River

65 US 176, Broad River Rd, to Columbia, **N...gas:** Exxon, 76/Circle K, **food:** Applebee's, Bojangles, Great Wall Chinese, Monterrey Mexican, Rush's Rest., Subway, Waffle House, **lodging:** Economy Inn, **other:** Aamco, **S...gas:** Hess, RaceWay, **food:** Arby's, Capt Tom's Seafood, Church's, Golden Corral, Hooters, Julie's Place, KFC, Lizard's Thicket, McDonald's, Pizza Hut, Sandy's HotDogs, Taco Bell, Taco Cid, Wendy's, **lodging:** American Inn, Best Inn, InTowne Suites, Ramada Ltd, Royal Inn, **other:** Advance Parts, Belk, CVS Drug, Eckerd, Family$, Food Lion, Mr Transmission, PepBoys, mall

64b a I-26, US 76, E to Columbia, airport, W to Greenville, Spartanburg

63 Bush River Rd, **N...gas:** 76/Circle K/diesel, **food:** Cracker Barrel, Steak-Out, Subway, **lodging:** Travelodge, **other:** CVS Drug, Hamrick's, **S...gas:** Citgo, **food:** El Chico, Fuddrucker's, Key West Grill, Villa Rest., Waffle House, **lodging:** Best Western, Courtyard, Knight's Inn, Sheraton, Sleep Inn

61 US 378, W Cola, **5 mi N...food:** Ryan's, Wendy's, **lodging:** Holiday Inn Express, **S...gas:** Amoco/diesel/24hr, 76(2mi), **food:** Waffle House, **other:** HOSPITAL, antiques

58 US 1, W Columbia, **N...gas:** Exxon, Shell/Subway/diesel, **food:** Waffle House, **2 mi S...gas:** Hess, **food:** Burger King, KFC, McDonald's, San Jose Mexican, **other:** Barnyard RV Park, to airport

55 SC 6, to Lexington, **N...gas:** Shell, **food:** Hardee's, **lodging:** Comfort Inn(2mi), Hampton Inn(2mi), Holiday Inn Express(3mi), **other:** CarQuest, **S...gas:** BP/diesel, Citgo, Depot/DQ, **food:** Bojangles, Fox's Pizza Den, Golden Town Chinese, McDonald's, Substation II, Subway, Waffle House, **lodging:** Ramada Ltd, **other:** CVS Drug, Piggly Wiggly

52.5mm weigh sta wb

51 SC 204, to Gilbert, **N...gas:** Exxon/diesel, **S...gas:** Shell/Gertie's/diesel/24hr, Texaco/Subway/diesel/24hr/@

44 SC 34, to Gilbert, **N...gas:** Citgo/44Trkstp/diesel/rest./@

39 US 178, to Batesburg, **N...gas:** Exxon/diesel, **S...gas:** Citgo/diesel/24hr

35.5mm weigh sta eb

33 SC 39, to Wagener, **N...gas:** BP/diesel, Shell/diesel, **food:** Huddle House

29 SC 49, no facilities

22 US 1, to Aiken, **S...gas:** BP/diesel, RaceTrac, 76/diesel, Shell/Blimpie/diesel, **food:** Hardee's, McDonald's, Waffle House, **lodging:** Day's Inn, Holiday Inn Express, **other:** Pine Acres RV Camp(5mi)

18 SC 19, to Aiken, **S...gas:** Exxon/Subway/diesel, Shell/Blimpie/diesel, **food:** Waffle House, **lodging:** Deluxe Inn, Guesthouse Inn, **other:** HOSPITAL

11 SC 144, Graniteville, no facilities

5 US 25, SC 121, **N...gas:** Bryants/diesel, 76/Blimpie/pizza/diesel/24hr, Shell/Bojangles/diesel/24hr, **food:** Burger King, Hardee's, Huddle House, Sonic, **lodging:** Sleep Inn, **other:** Winn-Dixie/24hr, **S...gas:** Citgo/Taco Bell/diesel, Speedway/diesel/24hr, **food:** Waffle House

1 SC 230, Martintown Rd, N Augusta, **S...gas:** 76/Blimpie/diesel/24hr, **food:** Tastee Freez, Waffle House, **other:** to Garn's Place

.5mm **Welcome Ctr eb, full(handicapped)facilities, phone, picnic tables, litter barrels, vending, petwalk**

0mm South Carolina/Georgia state line, Savannah River

Interstate 26

Exit # Services

E ↕ W

I-26 begins/ends on US 17 in Charleston, SC.

221 Meeting St, Charleston, **2 mi E...food:** Church's, KFC, **lodging:** Hampton Inn, **other:** Visitors Ctr, Family$, Piggly Wiggly

221b US 17 N, to Georgetown

a US 17 S, to Kings St, to Savannah, **N...**HOSPITAL

Interstate 26

E / W

Charleston

220 Romney St(from wb), no facilities

219b Morrison Dr, East Bay St(from eb), **N...gas:** Shell, Sam's Gas, **food:** Huddle House

a Rutledge Ave(from eb, no EZ return), to The Citadel, College of Charleston

218 Spruill Ave(from wb), N Charleston, no facilities

217 N Meeting St(from eb), no facilities

216b a SC 7, Cosgrove Ave, **S...food:** Arby's, McDonald's, SunFire Grill, Wendy's, **other:** to Charles Towne Landing

215 SC 642, Dorchester Rd, N Charleston, **N...gas:** Hess/diesel, **lodging:** Howard Johnson, **S...gas:** Amoco/diesel, **food:** Alex's Rest./24hr

213b a Montague Ave, Mall Dr, **N...food:** Piccadilly's, Red Lobster, **lodging:** Courtyard, Sheraton, **other:** Charles Towne Square, Firestone, **S...gas:** Amoco/diesel, Hess/Bojangles/diesel, **food:** Waffle House, **lodging:** Comfort Inn, Day's Inn, Embassy Suites, Extended Stay America, Hampton Inn, Hilton Garden, HomePlace Suites, Homestead Suites, Quality Inn, Ramada Inn, Suite 1, Super 8, Wingate Inn

N Charleston

212c b I-526, E to Mt Pleasant, W to Savannah, airport

a Remount Rd(from wb, no EZ return), Hanahan, **N on US 52/78...gas:** Exxon, Hess/diesel, **food:** Burger King, KFC, McDonald's, Pizza Hut/Taco Bell, **other:** Dodge, Ford, Office Depot

211b a Aviation Pkwy, **N on US 52/78...gas:** Amoco, Exxon, **food:** Arby's, Burger King, Capt D's, China Town, Church's, Grandy's, Huddle House, McDonald's, Old Country Buffet, Pizza Hut, Pizza Inn, Schlotsky's, Shoney's, Sonic, Subway, Tokyo Japanese, Wendy's, **lodging:** Masters Inn, Radisson, **other:** Aamco, Batteries+, $General, $Tree, Goodyear, PepBoys, Radio Shack, Sam's Club, **S...gas:** Citgo/diesel, El Cheapo/diesel, **food:** Waffle House, **lodging:** Best Western, Seagrass Inn, Travelodge

209 Ashley Phosphate Rd, to US 52, **N...gas:** Exxon, Kangaroo, **food:** Applebee's, Chick-fil-A, China Buffet, ChuckeCheese, Denny's, Don Pablo, Fazoli's, Hardee's, Hooters, Hops Grill, K&W Cafeteria, Krispy Kreme, Noisy Oyster Grill, Olive Garden, Outback Steaks, Perkins, Pizza Hut, Ryan's, Sticky Fingers Rest., Subway, Taco Bell, Waffle House, Wendy's, **lodging:** Clarion, Holiday Inn Express, Red Roof Inn, Residence Inn, Studio+ Hotel, Super 8, **other:** MEDICAL CARE, Barnes&Noble, Belk, Best Buy, BooksAMillion, Cicuit City, Dillard's, Firestone/auto, Home Depot, JC Penney, Lexus, Lowe's Whse, Mitsubishi, Nissan, OfficeMax, Sears/auto, Target, Toyota, Wal-Mart SuperCtr/24hr, mall, **S...gas:** Amoco, Hess, RaceWay, **food:** Bojangles, Cracker Barrel, Domino's, IHOP, Kobe Japanese, McDonald's, Waffle House, **lodging:** Fairfield Inn, Hampton Inn, Howard Johnson, InTowne Suites, La Quinta, Motel 6, Relax Inn, Sleep Inn

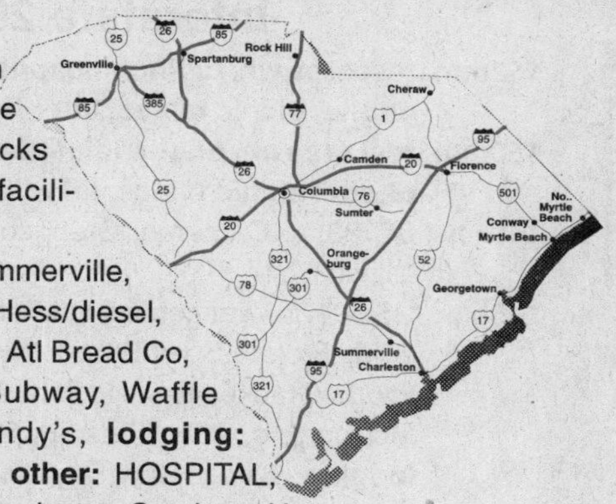

208 to US 52(from wb), to Goose Creek, Moncks Corner, no facilities

205b a US 78, to Summerville, **N...gas:** BP, Hess/diesel, **food:** Arby's, Atl Bread Co, Bruster's, Subway, Waffle House, Wendy's, **lodging:** Fairfield Inn, **other:** HOSPITAL, DENTIST, Charleston Southern U, **S...gas:** Speedway/diesel, **other:** KOA

204mm rest area eb, full(handicapped)facilities, vending, phone, picnic tables, litter barrels, petwalk

203 College Park Rd, Ladson, **N...gas:** 76, Speedway/diesel, **food:** McDonald's, Waffle House, Wendy's, **lodging:** Best Western, Day's Inn, **S...other:** KOA(2mi)

202mm rest area wb, full(handicapped)facilities, vending, phone, picnic tables, litter barrels, petwalk

199b a US 17 A, to Moncks Corner, Summerville, **N...gas:** BP, Citgo/diesel, Hess/diesel, Pilot/McDonald's/diesel/24hr, **food:** KFC, Pizza Hut, Subway, **other:** Advance Parts, AutoZone, BiLo, Buick/Pontiac/GMC, CVS Drug, $General, Family$, Food Lion, Ford/Mercury, **S...gas:** 76/Circle K, Enmark/diesel, **food:** Applebee's, Bojangles, Burger King, China Town, Fazoli's, Hardee's, Huddle House, IHOP, Papa John's, Perkins/24hr, Ryan's, Shoney's, Waffle House, **lodging:** Comfort Inn, Econolodge, Hampton Inn, Holiday Inn Express, Sleep Inn, **other:** Belk, Chevrolet, Chrysler/Plymouth/Jeep, GNC, Home Depot, Lowe's Whse, Radio Shack, Staples, Target, Wal-Mart SuperCtr/24hr, Winn-Dixie

194 SC 16, to Jedburg, access to Foreign Trade Zone 21, no facilities

187 SC 27, to Ridgeville, St George, **N...gas:** Phillips 66, **S...gas:** BP/diesel, **10 mi S...other:** Francis Beidler Forest

177 SC 453, Harleyville, to Holly Hill, **S...gas:** Shell/diesel/LP, **food:** Derrick's Kitchen, **lodging:** Ashley Lodge

174mm weigh sta both lanes

172b a US 15, to Santee, St George, **S...gas:** Horizon/Subway/diesel/24hr

169b a I-95, N to Florence, S to Savannah

165 SC 210, to Bowman, **N...gas:** Exxon/diesel, **S...gas:** BP/diesel/rest., Texaco/Blimpie/diesel/repair

159 SC 36, to Bowman, **N...gas:** Pilot/McDonald's/diesel/24hr/repair/@

154b a US 301, to Santee, Orangeburg, **N...lodging:** Days Inn, **S...gas:** Exxon/Blimpie/diesel, Shell/diesel/24hr, **lodging:** Best Western(7mi), Holiday Inn(8mi), **other:** auto repair

SOUTH CAROLINA

Interstate 26

E ↕ W

Columbia

152mm rest area wb, full(handicapped)facilities, vending, phone, picnic tables, litter barrels, petwalk

150mm rest area eb, full(handicapped)facilities, vending, phone, picnic tables, litter barrels, petwalk

149 SC 33, to Cameron, Orangeburg, to SC State Coll, Claflin Coll

145b a US 601, to Orangeburg, St Matthews, **S...gas:** Amoco/24hr, Exxon, Shell/Burger King, Speedway/diesel, **food:** Cracker Barrel, Fatz Café, Hardee's, KFC, McDonald's, Ruby Tuesday, Subway, Waffle House, **lodging:** Comfort Inn, Day's Inn, Fairfield Inn, Hampton Inn, Holiday Inn Express, Sleep Inn, Southern Lodge, **other:** HOSPITAL, **other:** Cadillac/Nissan, Chevrolet, Chrysler/Plymouth/Dodge, Nissan

139 SC 22, to St Matthews, **S...gas:** Phillips 66, Shell, Wilco/Hess/Arby's/diesel/24hr/@, **other:** Sweetwater Lake Camping(2.5mi)

136 SC 6, to North, Swansea, **N...gas:** BP, Exxon/diesel/LP/rest./24hr, **other:** auto/tire repair

129 US 21, **N...gas:** Shell/diesel

125 SC 31, to Gaston, **N...other:** Wolfe's Truck/trailer repair

123mm rest area both lanes, full(handicapped)facilities, vending, phone, picnic tables, litter barrels, petwalk

119 US 176, US 21, to Dixiana, **N...gas:** 76/Circle K/diesel, **S...gas:** Exxon, Shell/Subway/TCBY/diesel/@

116 I-77 N, to Charlotte, US 76, US 378, to Ft Jackson

115 US 176, US 21, US 321, to Cayce, **N...gas:** Amoco, Coastal, RaceTrac/24hr, Texaco, **food:** Waffle House, **other:** Harley-Davidson, **S...gas:** Pilot/DQ/Wendy's/diesel/24hr/@, United/diesel/24hr, **food:** Bojangles, Great China, Hardee's, McDonald's, Subway, Wendy's, **lodging:** Ramada Ltd, **other:** Firestone, Piggly Wiggly

113 SC 302, Cayce, **N...gas:** Exxon, Texaco/diesel, **food:** Waffle House, **lodging:** Airport Inn, Knight's Inn, Masters Inn, **other:** Peak's Tire, **S...gas:** Exxon, RaceTrac, 76/Circle K, **food:** Denny's, Lizard's Thicket, Ryan's, Shoney's, Subway, Waffle House/24hr, **lodging:** Comfort Inn, Day's Inn, Sleep Inn, Travelodge, **other:** NAPA, airport

111b a US 1, to W Columbia, **N...gas:** RaceTrac/diesel, 76/Circle K, **food:** BBQ, Domino's, Dragon City Chinese, Hardee's, Maurice's BBQ, Ruby Tuesday, Sonic, Subway, TCBY, Waffle House, **lodging:** Holiday Inn, Super 8, **other:** CHIROPRACTOR, BiLo Foods, $Tree, Harlan Tire, JiffyLube, Kroger, Wal-Mart SuperCtr/gas/24hr, to USC, **S...gas:** Hess, **food:** Applebee's, Wendy's, **other:** CVS Drug, Lowe's Whse, U-Haul

110 US 378, to W Columbia, Lexington, **N...food:** BBQ, Lizard's Thicket, McDonald's, Rush's Rest., Subway, Waffle House, Western Sizzlin, **lodging:** Day's Inn, Hampton Inn, Ramada/rest., **other:** MEDICAL CARE, CVS Drug, Eckerd, Food Lion, U-Haul, **S...gas:** 76/Circle K, **food:** Bojangles, Hardee's, Pizza Hut, **lodging:** Executive Inn, **other:** HOSPITAL

108 I-126 to Columbia, Bush River Rd, **N...gas:** Shell/diesel, **food:** Blimpie, Capt D's, Chick-fil-A, Hardee's, KFC, Royal China Buffet, Schlotsky's, Shoney's, Wendy's, **lodging:** Baymont Inn, Villager Lodge, **other:** Advance Parts, Firestone/auto, K-Mart, Office Depot, OfficeMax, mall, **S...gas:** RaceWay, Speedway/diesel, **food:** Cracker Barrel, **lodging:** Courtyard, Day's Inn, Howard Johnson, **multiple facilities 1-3 mi N off I-126, Greystone Blvd, N...gas:** Amoco, Shell, **food:** Waffle House, **lodging:** Embassy Suites, Extended Stay America, Residence Inn, Studio+, **other:** Chrysler/Jeep, Dodge, Ford, GMC, Lincoln/Mercury, Honda, Kia, Mitsubishi, **S...**Riverbanks Zoo

107b a I-20, E to Florence, W to Augusta

106b a St Andrews Rd, **N...gas:** Exxon/Blimpie, **food:** Chuck-eCheese, IHOP, Papa John's, **lodging:** Motel 6, **other:** DENTIST, BiLo Foods, Buick/Pontiac, CVS Drug, Eckerd, Infiniti, Jaguar, Kroger/deli, Nissan, **S...gas:** Hess/diesel, 76/Circle K, Shell, **food:** Bojangles, Domino's, Hilltop Rest., Maurice's BBQ, McDonald's, Old Country Buffet, Pizza Hut, Ryan's, Steak&Ale, TCBY, Thai Lotus, Waffle House, Wendy's, **lodging:** Red Roof Inn, Super 8, **other:** $General, Eckerd, Food Lion, NTB

104 Piney Grove Rd, **N...gas:** Speedway/diesel, **food:** Hardee's, San Jose Mexican, Waffle House, **lodging:** Comfort Inn, Knight's Inn, **other:** $General, to Subaru, RV/Marine Ctr, **S...gas:** Exxon/diesel, Shell, **lodging:** Comfort Suites, Microtel, **other:** Land Rover, auto repair

103 Harbison Blvd, **N...food:** Applebee's, Hops Grill, **lodging:** Hampton Inn, Wingate Inn, **other:** Chevrolet, Home Depot, Lowe's Whse, funpark, **S...gas:** Amoco/24hr, Exxon/Taco Bell, Hess/diesel, Shell, **food:** Bojangles, Blimpie, Carrabba's, Chili's, Chick-fil-A, Denny's, Fazoli's, LongHorn Steaks, Macaroni Grill, McAlister's Grill, McDonald's, Olive Garden, Outback Steaks, Roadhouse Grill, Ruby Tuesday, Rush's Rest., Shoney's, Sonic, Steak'n Shake, Sticky Fingers, Subway, Texas Roadhouse, Yamato Japanese, **lodging:** Comfort Suites, Country Inn Suites, Fairfield Inn, Suite 1, Holiday Inn Express, TownePlace Suites, **other:** MEDICAL CARE, Belk, Best Buy, BooksAMillion, Circuit City, Dillard's, Goodyear, Goody's, Marshall's, Michael's, OfficeMax, Old Navy, Publix, Rite Aid, Sam's Club, Saturn, Sears/auto, Staples, Target, Wal-Mart SuperCtr/24hr, mall

102 SC 60, Ballentine, Irmo, **N...lodging:** AmeriSuites, Wellesley Inn, **S...gas:** 76/Circle K, Exxon, Shell, **food:** Bellacino's Pizza, Maurice's BBQ, Papa John's, TCBY, Zaxby's, **other:** CVS Drug, Piggly Wiggly, same as 103

101b a US 76, US 176, to N Columbia, **1/2 mi N...gas:** Exxon/Subway/diesel, **food:** Blimpie, Fatz Café, Food Lion, **other:** Eckerd, Publix, **S...gas:** Amoco, 76, **food:** Waffle House

Interstate 26

E ↕ W

97 US 176, to Ballentine, **N...**Woodsmoke Camping, **S...gas:** Exxon/diesel
94mm weigh sta wb, phones
91 SC 48, to Chapin, **S...gas:** Amoco/diesel, Exxon/diesel, Shell/diesel, **food:** Capital City Subs, Hardee's(3mi), McDonald's, Subway(2mi), Taco Bell, Waffle House, **other:** to Dreher Island SP
85 SC 202, Little Mountain, Pomaria, **S...**to Dreher Island SP
82 SC 773, to Prosperity, Pomaria, **N...gas:** Amoco/Subway/diesel/@, **other:** Farmer's/Flea Mkt
81mm weigh sta eb
76 SC 219, to Pomaria, Newberry, **2 mi S...gas:** BP, **food:** Burger King, Wendy's, **lodging:** Hampton Inn, Holiday Inn Express, **other:** Wal-Mart SuperCtr/gas/24hr, to Newberry Opera House
74 SC 34, to Newberry, **N...gas:** BP, Shell/diesel/24hr, **lodging:** Best Western/rest., **S...gas:** Texaco/diesel, **food:** Bill&Fran's Café, Capt D's, Hardee's(2mi), McDonald's(2mi), Waffle House, **lodging:** Comfort Inn, Day's Inn, Economy Inn(2mi), Holiday Inn Express(2mi), **other:** HOSPITAL, to NinetySix HS
72 SC 121, to Newberry, **S...gas:** Citgo/Blimpie/diesel, **other:** HOSPITAL, to Newberry Coll
66 SC 32, to Jalapa, no facilities
63.5mm rest area both lanes, full(handicapped)facilities, phone, vending, picnic tables, litter barrels, petwalk
60 SC 66, to Joanna, **S...gas:** Exxon/diesel, Chevron, **other:** Magnolia Camping
54 SC 72, to Clinton, **N...gas:** Citgo/diesel/24hr, **S...gas:** Exxon/Blimpie/diesel, **other:** HOSPITAL, to Presbyterian Coll, Thornwell Home
52 SC 56, to Clinton, **N...gas:** Pilot/Subway/diesel/24hr/@, **food:** Blue Ocean Rest., McDonald's, Waffle House, **lodging:** Comfort Inn, **S...gas:** Phillips 66/diesel, Shell/diesel, **food:** Hardee's, Waffle House, Wendy's, **lodging:** Day's Inn, Ramada Inn, Travelers Inn(2mi), **other:** HOSPITAL
51 I-385, to Greenville(from wb), no facilities
45.5mm Enoree River
44 SC 49, to Cross Anchor, Union, no facilities
41 SC 92, to Enoree, **S...gas:** Phillips 66
38 SC 146, to Woodruff, **N...gas:** Hot Spot/Shell/Hardee's/diesel/24hr, **food:** Big Country Rest./lounge
35 SC 50, to Woodruff, **S...gas:** Citgo/diesel/rest./24hr, **other:** HOSPITAL
33mm S Tyger River
32mm N Tyger River
28 US 221, to Spartanburg, **N...gas:** Citgo/AuntM's/diesel/24hr, Crown(2mi), Shell/Subway/diesel/24hr, **food:** Burger King, Walnut Grove Seafood Rest., **other:** HOSPITAL, Pine Ridge Camping(3mi), to Walnut Grove Plantation

Spartanburg

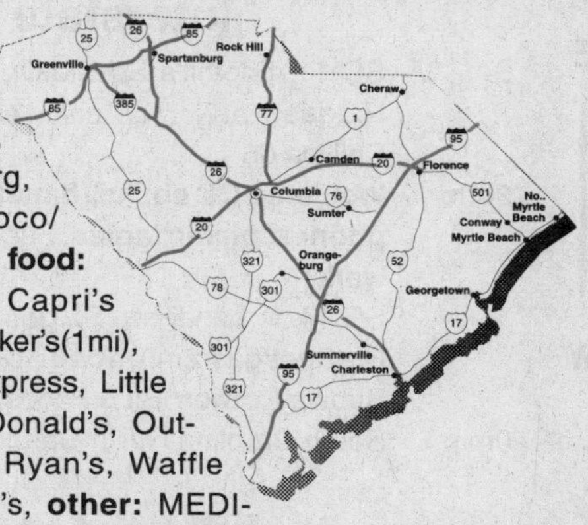

22 SC 296, Reidville Rd, to Spartanburg, **N...gas:** Amoco/diesel, Exxon, **food:** Arby's, BBQ, Capri's Italian, Fuddrucker's(1mi), Hong Kong Express, Little Caesar's, McDonald's, Outback Steaks, Ryan's, Waffle House, Zaxby's, **other:** MEDICAL CARE, Advance Parts, Rite Aid, to Croft SP, **S...gas:** BP, **food:** Burger King, Denny's, Domino's, Hardee's, Subway, TCBY, Waffle House/24hr, **lodging:** Sleep Inn, Southern Suites, Super 8, **other:** Abbot Farms/fruit, BiLo, BMW, CVS Drug, Eckerd, Harris-Teeter, Saturn, Toyota
21b a US 29, to Spartanburg, **N...gas:** BP, Crown/24hr, Exxon/Subway, Phillips 66, **food:** Burger King, Calzone's Rest., Checker's, Chick-fil-A, CiCi's, Dunkin Donuts, Hardee's, Hop's Grill, Japanese Rest., KFC, LoneStar Steaks, LJ Silver, Mr Gatti's, O'Charley's, Old Country Buffet, Papa John's, Pizza Hut, Pizza Inn, Quincy's, Red Lobster, Substation II, Wendy's, **other:** Barnes&Noble, Belk, Circuit City, Dillard's, Firestone/auto, Home Depot, JC Penney, K-Mart/gas, Office Depot, OfficeMax, Sears/auto, mall, **S...gas:** Citgo/diesel, Texaco/diesel, **food:** Applebee's, Aunt M's Café, IHOP, McDonald's, Piccadilly's, Prime Sirloin, Taco Bell, **other:** Advance Parts, Best Buy, Ingles, Lowe's Whse, Rite Aid, Sam's Club, Wal-Mart
19b a Lp I-85, Spartanburg, **N...gas:** Amoco, Phillips 66/diesel, **food:** Cracker Barrel, Econolodge, Radisson, Ramada Inn, Residence Inn, Quality Hotel, **S...lodging:** Hampton Inn, Tower Motel
18b a I-85, N to Charlotte, S to Greenville
17 New Cut Rd, **S...gas:** Chevron/diesel, Speedway/diesel, **food:** Burger King, Fatz Café, McDonald's, Waffle House, **lodging:** Comfort Inn, Day's Inn, Howard Johnson Express, Relax Inn
16 John Dodd Rd, to Wellford, **N...gas:** Citgo/diesel, Phillips 66, **food:** Arby's, Aunt M's, **other:** Camping World RV Supply Ctr, Cunningham RV Park
15 US 176, to Inman, **N...gas:** FuelStop, 76/Circle K/diesel, Phillips 66, **food:** Waffle House, **other:** HOSPITAL **S...gas:** Exxon/Blimpie/diesel, **food:** Taco Bell(2mi)
10 SC 292, to Inman, **N...gas:** HotSpot/Shell/Subway/diesel/24hr
9.5mm parking area both lanes, litter barrels
7.5mm Lake William C. Bowman

SOUTH CAROLINA

Interstate 26

E ↕ W

5 SC 11, Foothills Scenic Dr, Chesnee, Campobello, **N...gas:** Kangaroo/Aunt M's Café/diesel/@, **S...gas:** Phillips 66

3mm Welcome Ctr eb, full(handicapped)facilities, info, phones, picnic tables, litter barrels, vending, petwalk

1 SC 14, to Landrum, **S...gas:** BP/Burger King/diesel, HotSpot/gas(2mi), **food:** Denny's, Pizza Hut(1mi), Subway, **other:** BiLo Foods, Ingles/café/gas/24hr

0mm South Carolina/North Carolina state line

Interstate 77

N ↕ S

Exit # Services

91mm South Carolina/North Carolina state line

90 US 21, Carowinds Blvd, **E...gas:** Shell, World Gas, **food:** Bojangles, Denny's, **lodging:** Day's Inn, **other:** HOSPITAL, RV Ctr, RV camping(4mi), **W...gas:** Citgo, Exxon/café, 76/Circle K/Wendy's/diesel, **food:** El Cancun Mexican, KFC, Mom's Rest., Shoney's, **lodging:** Comfort Inn, Holiday Inn Express, Motel 6, Ramada Inn, Sleep Inn, **other:** Carowinds Funpark, Carolina Pottery/outlet mall/famous brands

89.5mm Welcome Ctr sb, full(handicapped)facilities, info, phone, vending, picnic tables, litter barrels, petwalk/weigh sta nb

88 Gold Hill Rd, to Pineville, **E...gas:** Shell/diesel, **W...gas:** Exxon/diesel, **food:** McDonald's(2mi), **other:** Dodge/Jeep, Ford, KOA

85 SC 160, Ft Mill, Tega Cay, **E...gas:** Exxon, **food:** Subway, Winn-Dixie/café, **other:** New Peach Stand, **W...gas:** BP/diesel, Crown, **food:** Burger King

84.5mm weigh sta sb

83 SC 49, Sutton Rd, no facilities

82.5mm Catawba River

82b a US 21, SC 161, Rock Hill, Ft Mill, **E...gas:** Exxon, Phillips 66, **food:** BBQ, IHOP, **lodging:** Holiday Inn/rest., **other:** Home Depot, museum, **W...gas:** Amoco, Citgo, Exxon, Phillips 66, RaceTrac/diesel, Speedway, Texaco, **food:** Arby's, BBQ, Bojangles, Burger King, Capt's Galley Seafood, Chick-fil-A, CiCi's, Denny's, El Cancun Mexican, Godfather's, Little Caesar's, LJ Silver, McDonald's, Outback Steaks, Pizza Hut, Pizza Inn, Sagebrush Steaks, Sakura Chinese, Shoney's, Subway, Taco Bell, TCBY, Waffle House, Wendy's, **lodging:** Bestway Inn, Best Western, Comfort Inn, Country Inn Suites, Courtyard, Day's Inn, Econolodge, Howard Johnson, Microtel, Quality Inn, Ramada/rest., Super 8, **other:** HOSPITAL, Advance Parts, Aldi, AutoZone, BiLo, Chevrolet, Chrysler/Jeep, Eckerd, Family$, Firestone/auto, Ford, Honda, K-Mart, Nissan, Office Depot, PepBoys, Toyota, U-Haul, Winn-Dixie, XpertTire

Rock Hill

79 SC 122, Dave Lyle Blvd, to Rock Hill, **E...gas:** BP, **food:** Applebee's, Chick-fil-A, Cracker Barrel, Dairy Queen, Hardee's, J&K Cafeteria, Longhorn Steaks, O'Charley's, Ryan's, Ruby Tuesday, **lodging:** Hampton Inn, Wingate Inn, **other:** Belk, Food Lion, Goody's, Honda, JC Penney, Lowe's Whse, Sears/auto, Staples, Wal-Mart/drugs/24hr, mall, **W...gas:** Citgo, **food:** Bob Evans, Chili's, RoadHouse Grill, Wendy's, **lodging:** Hilton Garden, **other:** isitor ctr

77 US 21, SC 5, to Rock Hill, **E...gas:** BP/Subway/diesel, Citgo/diesel/24hr, **other:** to Andrew Jackson SP(12mi), **W...gas:** Cone/diesel, Exxon/diesel, Phillips 66/diesel, **food:** Bojangles, KFC, McDonald's, Waffle House, **other:** to Winthrop Coll

75 Porter Rd, **E...gas:** Shell

73 SC 901, to Rock Hill, York, **E...gas:** Exxon/diesel, **W...gas:** Exxon(1mi), HOSPITAL

66mm rest area both lanes, full(handicapped)facilities, phone, picnic tables, litter barrels, vending, petwalk

65 SC 9, to Chester, Lancaster, **E...gas:** Amoco/Subway/24hr, BP, Shell/diesel, **food:** Waffle House, **lodging:** Day's Inn, Econolodge, **lodging:** Relax Inn, **W...gas:** Exxon/diesel, **food:** Burger King, Country Omelet/24hr, KFC, McDonald's, **lodging:** Comfort Inn, Microtel, Super 8, **other:** HOSPITAL

62 SC 56, Richburg, to Fort Lawn, no facilities

55 SC 97, Great Falls, to Chester, **E...gas:** BP/diesel, **food:** Home Place Rest., **W...**HOSPITAL

48 SC 200, to Great Falls, **E...gas:** Shell/diesel, **food:** Grand Central Rest.

46 SC 20, to White Oak, no facilities

41 SC 41, to Winnsboro, **E...**to Lake Wateree SP

34 SC 34, Ridgeway, to Winnsboro, **E...gas:** BP/diesel/24hr, **lodging:** Ridgeway Motel, **other:** camping(1mi), **W...gas:** Citgo/diesel/store, Exxon/Blimpie/diesel, **food:** Waffle House, **lodging:** Ramada Ltd

27 Blythewood Rd, **E...gas:** Citgo/diesel, Exxon/Bojangles/diesel/24hr, **food:** Blythewood Pizza/subs, KFC, McDonald's, Oaks Farm/rest., Waffle House, Wendy's, WG's Wings, **lodging:** Comfort Inn, Day's Inn, Holiday Inn Express, **other:** IGA Foods

24 US 21, to Blythewood, **E...gas:** BP, Shell/Subway/diesel, **food:** Taco Bell

22 Killian Rd, no facilities

19 SC 555, Farrow Rd, **E...gas:** Shell, **food:** Cracker Barrel, **lodging:** Courtyard, Longs Drug, **W...food:** Waffle House, **other:** Carolina Research Pk, SC Archives

18 to SC 277, to I-20 W(from sb), Columbia, **W...gas:** 76/Circle K/diesel

SOUTH CAROLINA

Interstate 77

17	US 1, Two Notch Rd, **E...gas:** Amoco/24hr, Kangaroo, 76/Circle K/diesel, **food:** Arby's, Burger King, Denny's, Texas Roadhouse, Waffle House, **lodging:** Fairfield Inn, InTown Suites, Ramada Plaza, Wingate Inn, **other:** U-Haul, USPO, to Sesquicentennial SP, **W...food:** Chili's, Fazoli's, Hop's Grill, IHOP, Lizard's Thicket, Outback Steaks, Waffle House, **lodging:** AmeriSuites, Comfort Inn, Econolodge, Hampton Inn, Holiday Inn, Microtel, Quality Inn, Red Roof Inn, **other:** MEDICAL CARE, Home Depot
16b a	I-20, W to Augusta, E to Florence, Alpine Rd
15b a	SC 12, to Percival Rd, **W...gas:** Shell, **1/2 mi W...gas:** Exxon
13	Decker Blvd(from nb), **W...gas:** El Cheapo
12	Forest Blvd, Thurmond Blvd, **E...**to Ft Jackson, **W...gas:** BP/diesel, 76/diesel, Shell/diesel/24hr, **food:** Bojangles, Chick-fil-A, Fatz Café, Golden Corral, Hardee's, McDonald's, RedBone Rest., Steak&Ale, Subway, Wendy's, **lodging:** Extended Stay America, Super 8, **other:** HOSPITAL, $Tree, Sam's Club/gas, Wal-Mart SuperCtr/24hr, museum
10	SC 760, Jackson Blvd, **E...**to Ft Jackson, **2 mi W...food:** Applebee's, Bojangles, Maurices BBQ, Ruby Tuesday, Subway, **lodging:** Econolodge, Liberty Inn
9b a	US 76, US 378, Columbia, to Sumter, **E...gas:** Amoco, Citgo, Hess/diesel, Speedway/diesel, **food:** Capt D's, Chick-fil-A, China Chef, Domino's, KFC, McDonald's, Pizza Hut, Rush's Rest., Shoney's, Subway, Waffle House, **lodging:** Best Western, Comfort Inn, Country Inn Suites, Day's Inn, Hampton Inn, Holiday Inn Express, Sleep Inn, **other:** MEDICAL CARE, Advance Parts, Family$, Firestone/auto, Food Lion, Goodyear/auto, Interstate Batteries, Lowe's Whse, NAPA, Piggly Wiggly, Pontiac/GMC, Radio Shack, U-Haul, USPO, Wal-Mart/auto, **W...gas:** Corner Pantry/gas, 76/Circle K(1mi), **food:** CiCi's, Hardee's, Mark&Sue's, Sonic, Substation II, Wendy's, **lodging:** Economy Inn, **other:** HOSPITAL, $General, Eckerd, Food Lion, Target
6b a	Shop Rd, **W...**to USC Coliseum, fairgrounds
5	SC 48, Bluff Rd, **1 mi E...gas:** 76, **W...gas:** Shell/Burger King/diesel, **food:** Bojangles(2mi)
3mm	Congaree River
2	Saxe Gotha Rd, no facilities
1	US 21, US 176, US 321(from sb), Cayce, **W...**accesses same as SC I-26, exit 115.
0mm	I-77 begins/ends on I-26, exit 116.

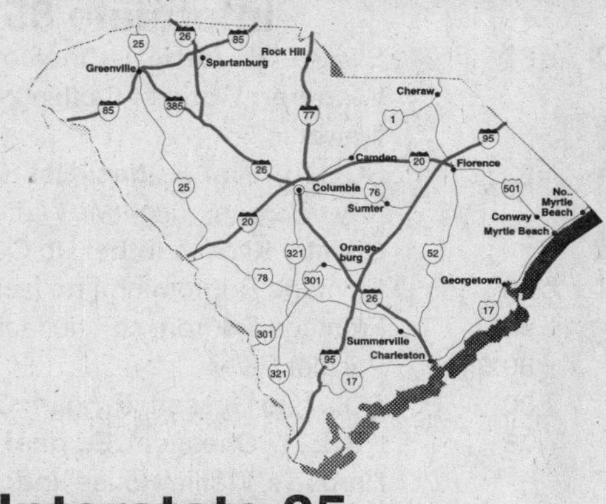

Interstate 85

Exit #	Services
106.5mm	South Carolina/North Carolina state line
106	US 29, to Grover, **W...gas:** Crown, Exxon/diesel, Wilco/Hess/DQ/Wendy's/diesel
104	SC 99, **E...gas:** Citgo/diesel/rest./24hr
103mm	**Welcome Ctr sb, full(handicapped)facilities, info, phone, picnic tables, litter barrels, vending, petwalk**
102	SC 198, to Earl, **E...gas:** Citgo/diesel, Exxon/diesel, **food:** Hardee's, **W...**Flying J/Conoco/diesel/LP/rest./24hr/@, Shell/diesel, **food:** McDonald's, Waffle House
100mm	Buffalo Creek
100	SC 5, to Blacksburg, Shelby, **W...gas:** Speedway/Subway/diesel/24hr, Shell/diesel
98	Frontage Rd(from nb), **E...food:** Broad River Café
97mm	Broad River
96	SC 18(from sb), **W...gas:** Exxon/diesel
95	SC 18, to Gaffney, **E...gas:** Citgo/24hr, Exxon/diesel, **food:** Mr Petro/Mr Waffle, Aunt M's Rest., Fatz Café, **other:** HOSPITAL, Daewoo, to Limestone Coll
92	SC 11, to Gaffney, **E...food:** Applebee's, Blue Bay Seafood, Bojangles, Burger King, Chinese Buffet, Domino's, McDonald's, Pizza Hut, Ruby Tuesday, Ryan's, Sagebrush Steaks, Sonic, Subway, Taco Bell, Wendy's, Western Sizzlin, **lodging:** Holiday Inn Express, Jameson Inn, **other:** MEDICAL CARE, Advance Parts, Belk, BiLo, $Tree, Eckerd, Ford/Mercury, Ingles Foods, Radio Shack, Wal-Mart SuperCtr/24hr, to Limestone Coll, **W...gas:** Chevron, Texaco/diesel, **food:** Waffle House, **lodging:** Comfort Inn, Day's Inn, to The Peach, Foothills Scenic Hwy
90	SC 105, SC 42, to Gaffney, **E...gas:** BP/DQ/diesel, Pilot/diesel/24hr/@, **food:** Waffle House, **lodging:** Red Roof Inn, Sleep Inn, **W...gas:** Citgo/Burger King, Phillips 66/diesel, **food:** Cracker Barrel, FoodCourt, Mel's Diner, **lodging:** Hampton Inn, **other:** Hamrick's, Prime Outlets/famous brands
89mm	**rest area both lanes, full(handicapped)facilities, phone, picnic tables, litter barrels, vending, petwalk**

SOUTH CAROLINA

Interstate 85

N / S

87 SC 39, **E...other:** PineCone Camping(1mi), **W...other:** World of Clothing, fruit stand/peaches/ fireworks

83 SC 110, **1 mi E...gas:** Hot Spot/gas, **food:** Subway, **W...gas:** Citgo/Mr Waffle/diesel/24hr, **food:** Country Kitchen, **other:** to Cowpens Bfd

82 Frontage Rd(from nb), no facilities

81 Frontage Rd(from sb), no facilities

80.5mm Pacolet River

80 SC 57, to Gossett, **E...gas:** Citgo/Bullets/diesel

78 US 221, Chesnee, **E...gas:** Shell/diesel, **food:** Hardee's, Waffle House, **lodging:** Motel 6, **other:** fruit stand, **W...gas:** BP, Exxon/Burger King/diesel, RaceTrac/diesel, **food:** BBQ, McDonald's, Subway, Wendy's, **lodging:** Holiday Inn Express, **other:** Advance Parts, **other:** $General, Ingles Foods

Spartanburg

77 Lp 85, Spartanburg, facilities along Lp 85 exits E

75 SC 9, Spartanburg, **E...food:** Denny's, **lodging:** Fairfield Inn, **1 mi E...gas:** Exxon, **lodging:** Best Western, Comfort Inn, Day's Inn, **W...gas:** BP/ Burger King/LJSilver/diesel, Phillips 66, RaceTrac, **food:** Capri's Italian, Fatz Café, McDonald's, Pizza Hut, Waffle House, Zaxby's, **lodging:** Hawthorn Inn, Jameson Inn, **other:** Advance Parts, CVS Drug, Ingles, USPO, Valvoline

72 US 176, to I-585, **E...other:** to USC-S, Wofford/ Converse Coll, **W...gas:** Amoco, RaceTrac, **other:** Masters RV Ctr

70b a I-26, E to Columbia, W to Asheville

69 Lp 85, SC 41(from nb), to Fairforest, **E...lodging:** Hampton Inn, Tower Motel, **other:** camping

68 SC 129(from sb), to Greer, no facilities

67mm N Tyger River

66 US 29, to Lyman, Wellford, no facilities

63 SC 290, to Duncan, **E...gas:** Citgo/diesel, Exxon/ Arby's, **food:** A&W/KFC, Atlanta Bread Co, Burger King, Denny's, Pizza Inn, Taco Bell, Waffle House, **lodging:** Hampton Inn, Jameson Inn, Microtel, **W...gas:** Pilot/Wendy's/diesel/24hr/@, TA/BP/ DQ/diesel/rest./@, Shell, **food:** Arby's, BBQ, Bojangles, Hardee's, McDonald's, Waffle House, **lodging:** Comfort Inn, Day's Inn, Travelodge, **other:** Sonny's RV Ctr

62.5mm S Tyger River

60 SC 101, to Greer, **E...gas:** Amoco, Citgo/diesel, **W...gas:** Exxon/Burger King, Phillips 66, **food:** Waffle House, **lodging:** Super 8

57 **W...other:** Greenville-Spartanburg Airport

56 SC 14, to Greer, **E...gas:** Citgo/DQ, Texaco/diesel, **W...gas:** Amoco/diesel, **other:** HOSPITAL

55mm Enoree River

54 Pelham Rd, **E...gas:** Amoco, BP/diesel, Citgo/ diesel/24hr, **food:** Burger King, Corona Mexican, Waffle House, **lodging:** Holiday Inn Express, **W...gas:** Amoco/diesel, Exxon, **food:** Applebee's, Atlanta Bread Co, California Dreaming Rest., Hardee's, Joe's Crabshack, J&S Cafeteria, Logan's Roadhouse, Macaroni Grill, Max&Erma's, Mayflower Seafood, McDonald's, Miami Grill, On the Border, Ruby Tuesday, Schlotsky's, Tony Roma, Wendy's, **lodging:** Comfort Inn, Courtyard, Extended Stay America, Fairfield Inn, Hampton Inn, MainStay Suites, Marriott, Microtel, Residence Inn, Wingate Inn, **other:** BiLo/24hr, CVS Drug, Goodyear/auto, Ingles, Radio Shack

52mm weigh sta nb

51 I-385, SC 146, Woodruff Rd, **E...gas:** Exxon, **food:** Fatz Café, Fuddrucker's, IHOP, Midori's Café, **other:** Goodyear/auto, Wal-Mart SuperCtr/24hr(1mi), **other:** VETERINARIAN, **W...gas:** Amoco, BP, RaceTrac/ 24hr, Shell, **food:** Atl Bread Co, Burger King, Capri's Italian, Cracker Barrel, McDonald's, Prime Sirloin, Remington's Rest., TGIFriday, Waffle House, **lodging:** Day's Inn, Embassy Suites, Fairfield Inn, Holiday Inn Express, La Quinta, Marriott(3mi), Microtel, **other:** BJ's Whse, Dillard's, Firestone/auto, Goody's, Home Depot, Lowe's Whse, Old Navy, Target, mall

Greenville

48b a US 276, Greenville, **E...food:** Waffle House, Red Roof Inn, **lodging:** Super 8, **other:** CarMax, Nissan, **W...gas:** BP, Exxon/diesel, **food:** Arby's, Bojangles, Burger King, Hooters, Jack-in-the-Box, Olive Garden, Ryan's, Taco Bell, **lodging:** Day's Inn, Embassy Suites, Valu Lodge, **other:** Acura/Honda, Best Buy, BMW, BooksAMillion, Buick, Cadillac, Chrysler/Plymouth/Jeep, Daewoo/Suzuki, Dodge, Ford, Goody's, Kia, Lexus, Lincoln/Mercury, Marshall's, Mazda, Mercedes, Michael's, Office Depot, OfficeMax, PepBoys, Pontiac/GMC, Sam's Club/gas, SteinMart, Toyota, Volvo, VW/Audi

46c rd 291, Pleasantburg Rd, Mauldin Rd, **W...gas:** Shell/diesel, **food:** Spinx/Arby's, Steak-Out, Subway, **lodging:** Comfort Inn, InTowne Suites, Quality Inn, **other:** Aamco, BiLo/gas, CVS Drug

46b a US 25 bus, Augusta Rd, **E...gas:** Amoco, Chevron, Exxon, Phillips 66, **food:** Bojangles, Burger King, Waffle House, **lodging:** Camelot Inn, Holiday Inn, Motel 6, Southern Suites, **W...food:** Dixie Rest., Jack-in-the-Box, **lodging:** Economy Inn, Travelodge, **other:** Home Depot

44 US 25, White Horse Rd, **E...gas:** Spinx/Subway/ diesel, **W...gas:** RaceTrac, **food:** McDonald's, BBQ, Quincy's, Waffle House, **other:** HOSPITAL

44a SC 20(from sb), to Piedmont, no facilities

42 I-185 toll, US 29, to Greenville, **W...**HOSPITAL

40 SC 153, to Easley, **E...gas:** Exxon/diesel, **food:** Waffle House, **W...gas:** RaceTrac, Shell/diesel/24hr, **food:** Arby's, Burger King, Hardee's, KFC, Pizza Hut/Taco Bell, Subway, Zaxby's, **lodging:** Executive Inn, Super 8, **1 mi W...gas:** Shell, **food:** Little Caesar's, McDonald's, Sonic, **other:** BiLo Foods, Eckerd, GNC, Ingles Foods

SOUTH CAROLINA

Interstate 85

N S

39 SC 143, to Piedmont, **E...gas:** BP/diesel, **W...gas:** Shell/diesel

35 SC 86, to Easley, Piedmont, **E...gas:** Pilot/diesel/24hr/@, **W...gas:** Amoco/Bullets/diesel

34 US 29(from sb), to Williamston, no facilities

32 SC 8, to Pelzer, Easley, **E...gas:** Shell/diesel

27 SC 81, to Anderson, **E...gas:** Amoco/diesel, Citgo, Exxon, Phillips 66/diesel, **food:** Arby's, Carolina Country Café, KFC/Pizza Hut, McDonald's, Waffle House, **lodging:** Holiday Inn Express, **other:** HOSPITAL **W...gas:** Shell/KrispyKreme/diesel/24hr, **food:** Charlie's Wings

23mm rest area sb, full(handicapped)facilities, phone, vending, picnic tables, litter barrels, petwalk

Anderson

21 US 178, to Anderson, **E...gas:** Shell/diesel, **2 mi E...food:** Applebee's, Fazoli's, **lodging:** La Quinta, Quality Inn, Studio 1, Super 8

19b a US 76, SC 28, to Anderson, **E...gas:** Amoco/diesel, Exxon/diesel, **food:** BBQ, Chick-fil-A, Chili's, DockMasters Seafood, Grand China, Hardee's, Texas Roadhouse, **lodging:** Day's Inn, La Quinta, Royal American Inn, **other:** Buick/GMC, Chrysler/Plymouth, **W...gas:** RaceTrac/diesel/24hr, **food:** Buffalo's Café, Cracker Barrel, Hooters, Outback Steaks, Paparazzi's Italian, Shrimp Shack, Waffle House, Wendy's, **lodging:** Comfort Suites, Country Inn Suites, Fairfield Inn, Hampton Inn, Jameson Inn, **other:** to Clemson U

18mm rest area nb, full(handicapped)facilities, phone, vending, picnic tables, litter barrels, petwalk

15mm Lake Hartwell

14 SC 187, to Clemson, Anderson, **E...gas:** FuelMart/diesel/24hr, **food:** Huddle House/24hr, **other:** KOA(1mi), **W...gas:** Amoco/diesel, **lodging:** Budget Inn, **other:** to Clem Research Pk

12mm Seneca River, Lake Hartwell

11 SC 24, SC 243, to Townville, **E...gas:** Exxon/diesel, Speedway/diesel/24hr, **other:** Savannah River Scenic Hwy, **W...gas:** Shell/TCBY/diesel, **food:** Townville Café, **other:** Hartwell RV Park(3mi)

9mm weigh sta nb

4 SC 243, to SC 24, Fair Play, **E...gas:** Exxon/diesel/LP/rest./24hr, **other:** Thousand Trails Camping

2 SC 59, to Fair Play, **E...lodging:** LivingStone Motel, **other:** fireworks, **W...**fireworks

1 SC 11, to Walhalla, **W...food:** Gazebo Rest., **other:** fireworks, to Lake Hartwell SP

.5mm Welcome Ctr nb, full(handicapped)facilities, info, phone, picnic tables, litter barrels, vending, petwalk

0mm South Carolina/Georgia state line, Lake Hartwell, Tugaloo River

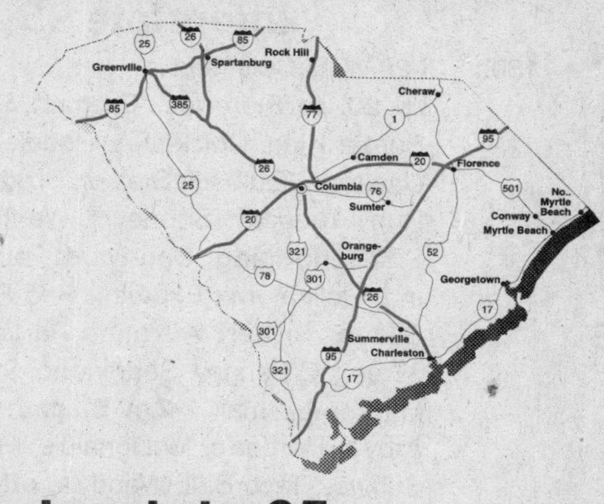

Interstate 95

N S

Exit # Services

198mm South Carolina/North Carolina state line

196mm Welcome Ctr sb, full(handicapped)facilities, info, phone, vending, picnic tables, litter barrels, petwalk

Dillon

195mm Little Pee Dee River

193 SC 9, SC 57, Dillon, to N Myrtle Beach, **E...gas:** Amoco/24hr, Exxon, Speedway/diesel, **food:** Bojangles, Burger King, Golden Corral, Shoney's, Waffle House, Wendy's, **lodging:** Best Value Inn, Comfort Inn, Day's Inn/rest., Hampton Inn, Holiday Inn Express, Howard Johnson, Ramada Ltd, **other:** HOSPITAL **W...gas:** BP/diesel, **food:** Hubbard House, Waffle House, **lodging:** Econolodge, Super 8

190 SC 34, to Dillon, **E...gas:** BP/Stuckey's/Dairy Queen, **other:** repair, **W...gas:** Dillon Gas/diesel

181 SC 38, Oak Grove, **E...gas:** BP, Flying J/Conoco/diesel/LP/rest./24hr/@, Shell/Subway, **W...gas:** Wilco/Hess/DQ/Wendy's/diesel/@, **other:** auto/truck repair

175mm Pee Dee River

172mm rest area both lanes, full(handicapped)facilities, phone, picnic tables, vending, litter barrels, petwalk

170 SC 327, **E...gas:** BP, Pilot/Wendy's/diesel/24hr/@, **food:** McDonald's, **lodging:** Holiday Inn Express, **other:** to Myrtle Beach, Missile Museum, **W...gas:** Citgo/diesel

169 TV Rd, to Florence, **E...other:** KOA(1mi), Peterbilt, diesel repair, **W...gas:** Amoco, Petro/Exxon/diesel/rest./24hr/@, Texaco/diesel, **lodging:** Rodeway Inn, **other:** Blue Beacon

Florence

164 US 52, Florence, to Darlington, **E...gas:** Citgo, Exxon/Pizza Hut/diesel, RaceWay/24hr, Shell, **food:** Cracker Barrel, Denny's, Hardee's, Kobe Japanese, McDonald's, Ruby Tuesday, Waffle House, Wendy's, **lodging:** Best Western, Comfort Inn, Econolodge, Hampton Inn, Holiday Inn, Knight's Inn, Motel 6, Suburban Lodge, Super 8, **other:** HOSPITAL, Chrysler/Jeep, Pontiac/Buick, **W...gas:** Hess/diesel, Patlo/diesel/24hr, Pilot/Subway/Taco Bell/diesel/@, **food:** Arby's, Bojangles, Burger King, Fatz Café, KFC, Shoney's, **lodging:** Country Inn Suites, Day's Inn, Guesthouse Inn, Microtel, Ramada Inn, Sleep Inn, Thunderbird Inn, Wingate Inn, **other:** to Darlington Raceway

SOUTH CAROLINA

Interstate 95

N ↕ S

160b I-20 W, to Columbia

a Lp 20, to Florence, **E...gas:** Shell/diesel, **food:** Burger King, Chick-fil-A, Huddle House, Morrison's Cafeteria, Outback Steaks, Pizza Hut, Red Lobster, Ruby Tuesday, Shoney's, Waffle House, Western Sizzlin, **lodging:** Courtyard, Fairfield Inn, Hampton Inn, Holiday Inn Express, Red Roof Inn, SpringHill Suites, **other:** Advance Parts, Belk, Chevrolet, $Tree, JC Penney, Sears/auto, Staples, Target, Wal-Mart/drugs, mall, **1-2 mi E...gas:** Exxon, Shell, **food:** Arby's, Hardee's, McDonald's, Percy&Willie's Rest., Subway, Taco Bell, Wendy's, **other:** BooksAMillion, Chevrolet/BMW/Isuzu, Circuit City, Lowe's Whse, Piggly Wiggly, CVS Drug, K-Mart, Firestone/auto, Nissan, NAPA, Nissan, Sam's Club, mall

157 US 76, Timmonsville, Florence, **E...gas:** BP/diesel, Exxon/McDonald's/diesel, Phillips 66, **food:** Swamp Fox Diner, Waffle House, **lodging:** Day's Inn, Howard Johnson Express, Villager Lodge, **W...gas:** Sunoco, **lodging:** Tree Room Inn/rest., Young's Plantation Inn/Magnolia Dining Room, Swamp Fox Camping(1mi)

153 Honda Way, **W...**Honda Plant

150 SC 403, to Sardis, **E...gas:** BP/diesel, **lodging:** Budget Inn, **W...gas:** Exxon/diesel, **other:** Honeydew RV Camp

147mm Lynches River

146 SC 341, to Lynchburg, Olanta, **E...lodging:** Relax Inn

141 SC 53, SC 58, to Shiloh, **E...gas:** Exxon/diesel, **other:** DonMar RV Ctr, to Woods Bay SP, **W...gas:** Shell

139mm rest area both lanes, full(handicapped)facilities, phone, vending, picnic tables, litter barrels, petwalk

135 US 378, to Sumter, Turbeville, **E...gas:** BP, Citgo, **food:** Compass Rest., **lodging:** Day's Inn, Knight's Inn, **W...gas:** Exxon/diesel, **other:** Pineland Golf Course

132 SC 527, to Sardinia, Kingstree, no facilities

130mm Black River

122 US 521, to Alcolu, Manning, **E...food:** MD Fried Chicken(2mi), **lodging:** Manning Motel(3mi), **W...gas:** Exxon/diesel, **food:** Shrimper Rest.

119 SC 261, Manning, to Paxville, **E...gas:** Shell/24hr, TA/Amoco/Blimpie/LJS/Pizza Hut/Sbarro's/diesel/24hr/@, **food:** Huddle House, Mariachi's, Shoney's, Waffle House, Wendy's, **lodging:** Best Western, Comfort Inn, Holiday Inn Express, Ramada Ltd, **other:** HOSPITAL, Chrysler/Jeep/Dodge, Ford, **1 mi E...gas:** Exxon, **food:** Burger King, KFC, Sonic, Subway, **other:** CVS Drug, $General, Food Lion, Goodyear/auto, Radio Shack, Wal-Mart/drugs, to McDonald's(2mi), Campers Paradise RV Park, **W...gas:** Exxon/24hr, Horizon/diesel, **lodging:** Super 8, **other:** auto repair

115 US 301, to Summerton, Manning, **E... gas:** Exxon/diesel, **lodging:** Carolina Inn, **W...gas:** Texaco/diesel/24hr, **food:** Georgio's Greek, **lodging:** Day's Inn, Econolodge, Sunset Inn

108 SC 102, Summerton, **E...gas:** BP/DQ/Stuckey's, **other:** TawCaw RV Parl(6m), **W...lodging:** Day's Inn, Deluxe Inn, Knight's Inn, Travelodge

102 US 15, US 301 N, to Santee, **E...lodging:** motel, **other:** RV camping, **W...gas:** Shell/diesel, **other:** to Santee NWR

100mm Lake Marion

99mm rest area both lanes, full(handicapped)facilities, phone, info, vending, picnic tables, litter barrels, petwalk

98 SC 6, Santee, to Eutawville, **E...gas:** BP, Chevron/LP, Citgo, **food:** Huddle House, KFC, Pizza Hut, Shoney's, **lodging:** Best Western, Day's Inn, Hampton Inn, Howard Johnson, Super 8, **other:** $General, Piggly Wiggly, Russell Stover Candy, Santee Outlets/famous brands, **W...gas:** BP/diesel, Citgo, Exxon, Hess/diesel, Horizon/Pizza Hut/diesel/24hr, Shell/diesel, **food:** BBQ, Burger King, Cracker Barrel, Hardee's, Denny's, McDonald's, Waffle House, Wendy's, **lodging:** Budget Motel, Clark Inn/rest., Comfort Inn, Country Inn Suites, Economy Inn, Holiday Inn, Lake Marion Inn, **other:** BiLo, CarQuest, CVS Drug, Family$, Food Lion, NAPA, Radio Shack, USPO, to Santee SP(3mi)

97 US 301 S(from sb, no return), to Orangeburg, no facilities

93 US 15, to Santee, Holly Hill, no facilities

90 US 176, to Cameron, Holly Hill, **W...gas:** Exxon/diesel

86b a I-26, W to Columbia, E to Charleston, no facilities

82 US 178, to Bowman, Harleyville, **E...gas:** Amoco, Wilco/Hess/Wendy's/DQ/diesel/24hr/@, **lodging:** Peachtree Inn, **W...gas:** Texaco/diesel

77 US 78, St George, to Bamberg, **E...gas:** Exxon/KFC, Shell/Subway/TCBY, **food:** Empire Asian, Georgio's Rest., Hardee's, McDonald's, Pizza Hut, Waffle House, Western Sizzlin, **lodging:** American Inn, Comfort Inn/RV park, Quality Inn, **other:** Chevrolet/Pontiac/GMC, CVS Drug, Family$, Food Lion, Ford, USPO, **W...gas:** BP, Texaco/diesel, **food:** Huddle House, Taco Bell, **lodging:** Best Western, Day's Inn, Southern Inn, Super 8

68 SC 61, Canadys, **E...gas:** Amoco, Citgo, Texaco/Subway/diesel, **other:** to Colleton SP(3mi)

62 SC 34, **W...other:** Lakeside RV camping

57 SC 64, Walterboro, **E...gas:** BP/Subway/Pizza Hut/TCBY/diesel/24hr, Exxon/diesel, Shell/DQ, Speedway, Texaco/Blimpie/diesel, **food:** Burger King, Capt D's, Huddle House, Little Caesar's, Longhorn Steaks, McDonald's, Olde House Café, Taco Bell, Waffle House, Wendy's, **lodging:** Sleep Inn, Southern Inn, **other:** HOSPITAL, Advance Parts, AutoZone, BiLo, CVS Drug, Food Lion, GNC, K-Mart, Piggly Wiggly, Wal-Mart, **W...gas:** Amoco/diesel, **lodging:** Super 8

Interstate 95

N ↕ S

53 SC 63, Walterboro, to Varnville, Hampton, **E...gas:** Amoco/McDonald's, Citgo/diesel, El Cheapo, Shell, Texaco, **food:** Burger King, Dairy Queen, KFC, Longhorn Steaks, McDonald's, Ruby Tuesday, Shoney's, Waffle House, **lodging:** Best Western, Comfort Inn/rest., Econolodge, Quality Inn, Ramada Inn, Rice Planter's Inn, Thunderbird Inn, **W...gas:** BP, **food:** Cracker Barrel, **lodging:** Day's Inn, Deluxe Inn, Hampton Inn, **other:** Green Acres Camping

47mm rest area both lanes, full(handicapped)facilities, phone, vending, picnic tables, litter barrels, petwalk

42 US 21, to Yemassee, Beaufort, no facilities

40mm Combahee River

38 SC 68, to Hampton, Yemassee, **E...gas:** Chevron, **W...gas:** BP/Subway/TCBY, Exxon, Shell/diesel, **food:** J's Rest., **lodging:** Palmetto Lodge/rest., Super 8

33 US 17 N, to Beaufort, **E...gas:** BP/diesel, Citgo, Exxon, Shell, Texaco/Subway/24hr, **food:** Denny's, McDonald's, TCBY, Waffle House, Wendy's, **lodging:** Best Western, Day's Inn/rest., Holiday Inn Express, Knight's Inn, **other:** KOA

30.5mm Tullifinny River

29mm Coosawhatchie River

28 SC 462, to Coosawhatchie, Hilton Head, Bluffton, **W...gas:** Amoco, Chevron/diesel, Citgo/Stuckey's/DQ, Exxon/diesel/rest.

22 US 17, Ridgeland, **E...food:** El Ranchito Mexican, **W...gas:** Shell, Plantation Inn, HOSPITAL

21 SC 336, to Hilton Head, Ridgeland, **W...gas:** Chevron/Blimpie/diesel/24hr, Citgo, Exxon, Texaco/diesel, **food:** Burger King, Hong Kong Chinese, Huddle House, Jasper's Porch Rest., KFC, Main St Pizza, Subway, Waffle House, **lodging:** Carolina Lodge, Comfort Inn/rest., Econolodge, Ramada Ltd, **other:** HOSPITAL, $General, Eckerd, Food Lion

18 SC 13, to US 17, US 278, to Switzerland, Granville, Ridgeland, no facilities

17mm parking area both lanes, litter barrels

8 US 278, Hardeeville, to Bluffton, **E...gas:** BP/Joker Joe's/diesel/24hr/@, Exxon, Shell/McDonald's, **food:** Huddle House, Wendy's, **W...gas:** Chevron/Subway, Kangaroo/24hr, **food:** KrispyKreme, Pizza Hut, TCBY, **lodging:** Ramada Ltd

5 US 17, US 321, Hardeeville, to Savannah, **E...gas:** El Cheapo, Exxon/Blimpie, Shell/24hr, **food:** KFC, Waffle House, **lodging:** Day's Inn, Economy, Sleep Inn, **other:** to Savannah NWR, **W...gas:** BP/diesel, Speedway/diesel, **food:** Burger King, McDonald's, New China Rest., Shoney's, Subway, Wendy's, **lodging:** Comfort Inn, Deluxe Inn, Holiday Inn Express, Howard Johnson Express, Knight's Inn, Scottish Inn, Super 8, **other:** NAPA, antiques

Hardeeville

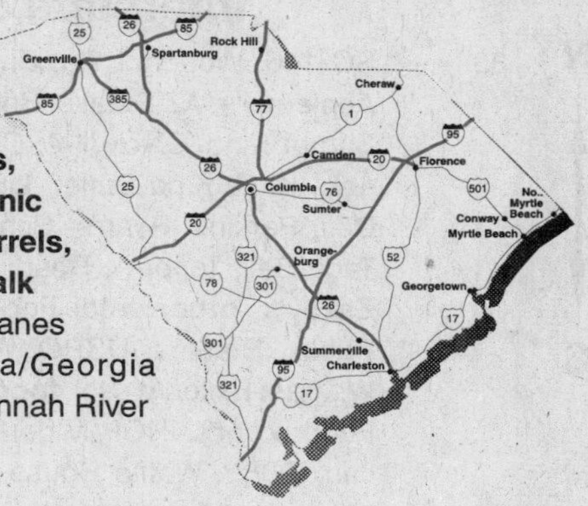

4.5mm Welcome Ctr nb, full(handicapped)facilities, info, phone, picnic tables, litter barrels, vending, petwalk

3.5mm weigh sta both lanes

0mm South Carolina/Georgia state line, Savannah River

Interstate 385(Greenville)

N ↕ S

Exit #	Services
42	US 276, Stone Ave, to Travelers Rest., to Greenville Zoo, **E...other:** CarQuest, **W...gas:** Amoco, **1-2 mi W...**multiple facilities on US 276, I-385 begins/ends on US 276.
40b a	SC 291, Pleasantburg Dr, **E...gas:** Conoco, Speedway, **food:** Jack-in-the-Box, Jalisco Mexican, Little Caesar's, Lizard's Thicket, Pizza Hut, S&S Cafeteria, Sonic, Steak&Ale, Subway, Taco Casa, Wendy's, **other:** CVS Drug, to BJU, Furman U, **W...gas:** Shell, **food:** Domino's, Dragon Den Chinese, Krispy Kreme, **lodging:** Comfort Inn, Sleep Inn, **other:** Advance Parts, transmissions
39	Haywood Rd, **E...gas:** BP, Exxon/diesel, **food:** Domino's, LongHorn Steaks, Outback Steaks, Shoney's, **lodging:** AmeriSuites, Courtyard, GuestHouse Suites, Hilton, La Quinta, Quality Inn, Residence Inn, **other:** Firestone, **W...gas:** Crown, Shell, Texaco, **food:** Arby's, Applebee's, Bennigan's, Blackeyed Pea, Buffalo's Café, Burger King, Chili's, ChuckeCheese, CityRange Steaks, Don Pablo, Hardee's, Italian Mkt/grill, Jack-in-the-Box, Jason's Deli, Kanpai Tokyo, O'Charley's, Senor Wrap's, Steak'n Shake, Waffle House, Wendy's, **lodging:** Hampton Inn, Studio+, **other:** Barnes&Noble, Belk, Circuit City, Dillard's, Discount Tire, Goodyear, Harley-Davidson, JC Penney, NTB, Sears/auto, mall
37	Roper Mtn Rd, **E...other:** BiLo Foods, **W...gas:** Amoco, BP/diesel, Exxon/Pantry, RaceTrac, **food:** Atl Bread Co, Backyard Burger, Burger King, Capri's Italian, Cracker Barrel, Fazoli's, LoneStar Steaks, McDonald's, Miyabi Japanese, Rafferty's, Remington's Rest., Waffle House, **lodging:** Day's Inn, Crowne Plaza, Embassy Suites, Fairfield Inn, Holiday Inn Select, La Quinta, Travelodge, **other:** BJ's Whse, CompUSA, Goody's, Home Depot, Lowe's Whse, Old Navy, Target, mall
36b a	I-85, N to Charlotte, S to Atlanta

Greenville

SOUTH CAROLINA

Interstate 385

N ↕ S

Simpsonville

35 SC 146, Woodruff Rd, **E...gas:** Amoco, BP, **food:** Applebee's, AZ Steaks, Bojangles, Boston Pizzaria, Burger King, Chick-fil-A, Chili's, DQ, Fazoli's, Hardee's, KFC, King Buffet, Little Caesar's, McAlister's Deli, Perkins, Ryan's, Schlotsky's, Sonic, Subway, Taco Bell, Topper's Rest., Waffle House, Wendy's, Zaxby's, **other:** Aldi Foods, BiLo Foods, $Tree, Publix, Staples, USPO, Wal-Mart SuperCtr/24hr, **W...gas:** Exxon/diesel, **food:** Burger King, Fatz Café, Fuddrucker's, IHOP, Midori's Rest., Monterrey Mexican, TCBY, Waffle House, **lodging:** Hampton Inn, **other:** Goodyear/auto, Hamrick's Outlet, funpark

34 Butler Rd, Mauldin, **E...gas:** Exxon, **food:** Arby's, **other:** CVS Drug, **W...gas:** Phillips 66, **lodging:** Super 8(3mi)

33 Bridges Rd, Mauldin, no facilities

31 I-185 toll(from sb), SC 417, to Laurens Rd, **E...gas:** Amoco, **food:** Hardee's, **other:** HOSPITAL, **W...gas:** BP, **food:** LJSilver, **lodging:** Masters Inn

30 I-185 toll(from nb), US 276, Standing Springs Rd, no facilities

29 Georgia Rd, to Simpsonville, **W...other:** MountainTop RV/Marine Ctr

27 Fairview Rd, to Simpsonville, **E...gas:** Amoco, Shell, **food:** Hardee's, McDonald's, **lodging:** Palmetto Inn, **other:** HOSPITAL, Advance Parts, BiLo Food, Chevrolet, $General, Rite Aid, **W...gas:** Amoco/Arby's, BP, **food:** Applebee's, AZ Steaks, Burger King, Cracker Barrel, Dragon Den Chinese, KFC, Ryan's, Pizza Hut, Taco Bell, Waffle House, Wendy's, **lodging:** Comfort Inn, Day's Inn, Hampton Inn, Holiday Inn Express, Microtel, **other:** $Tree, GNC, Ingles, Lowe's Whse, Radio Shack, Wal-Mart SuperCtr/gas/24hr

26 Harrison Bridge Rd(from sb), no facilities

24 Fairview St, Fountain Inn, **E...gas:** Phillips 66, **food:** Hardee's, Waffle House, **other:** carwash

23 SC 418, to Fountain Inn, Fork Shoals, **E...gas:** Exxon/Subway/diesel/24hr

22 SC 14 W, Old Laurens Rd, to Fountain Inn, no facilities

19 SC 14 E, to Gray Court, Owings, no facilities

16 SC 101, to Woodruff, Gray Court, no facilities

10 SC 23, to Ora, no facilities

9 US 221, to Laurens, Enoree, **E...gas:** Exxon/Subway/diesel/24hr, **food:** Waffle House, **lodging:** Budget Lodge, **W...**Wal-Mart Dist Ctr, **lodging:** Travel Inn

6mm rest area both lanes(both lanes exit left), full(handicapped)facilities, phone, vending, picnic tables, litter barrels, petwalk

5 SC 49, to Laurens, Union, no facilities

2 SC 308, to Clinton, Ora, **W...other:** HOSPITAL, to Presbyterian Coll in Clinton

0mm I-26 S to Columbia, I-385 begins/ends on I-26 at 52mm.

Interstate 526(Charleston)

E ↕ W

Charleston

Exit # Services

33mm I-526 begins/ends.

32 US 17, **N...gas:** Exxon, Hess, **food:** Subway, **lodging:** Day's Inn, Red Roof Inn, **other:** Advance Parts, CVS Drug, **1 mi N...gas:** Shell, **food:** Burger King, Chili's, IHOP, LongHorn Steaks, On The Border, TGIFriday, **other:** Barnes&Noble, Belk, Eckerd, Lowe's Whse, Old Navy, **S...gas:** Amoco, Speedway, **food:** Applebee's, Arby's, Chick-fil-A, China Buffet, Domino's, KFC, La Hacienda Mexicana, McDonald's, Papa John's, **other:** MEDICAL CARE, $General, Office Depot, Publix, USPO, VW, Wal-Mart, **1 mi S...gas:** Hess, 76, Shell, **food:** Hardee's, Huddle House, Outback Steaks, Shoney's, Wendy's, **lodging:** Comfort Inn, Day's Inn, Extended Stay America, Holiday Inn, Masters Inn, **other:** Cadillac/Chevrolet, Ford, Firestone/auto, Radio Shack, Staples

30 Long Point Rd, **N...gas:** Exxon, **food:** Bamboo Garden, Mo's Café, Sonic, Starbucks, Subway, Waffle House, **other:** Food Lion, Harris Teeter Foods, Charles Pinckney NHS

26mm Wando River

24 Daniel Island, **S...**Queen Anne's Steaks/seafood, Hampton Inn

23b a Clements Ferry Rd, no facilities

21mm Cooper River

20 Virginia Ave(from eb), **S...gas:** Hess Depot, **other:** Marathon Refinery

19 N Rhett Ave, **N...gas:** Hess, **food:** Hardee's, **other:** Eckerd, Food Lion, **S...gas:** Amoco

18b a US 52, US 78, Rivers Ave, **N...gas:** Amoco/diesel, Shell, **food:** McDonald's, **other:** Family$, Merchant Auto, NAPA, Piggly Wiggly, **S...lodging:** Catalina Inn

17b a I-26, E to Charleston, W to Columbia

16 Montague Ave, Airport Rd, **S...food:** Wendy's, **lodging:** Embassy Suites, Hilton Garden

15 SC 642, Dorchester Rd, Paramount Dr, **N...gas:** BP, 76, **food:** Wendy's, **S...gas:** Amoco, Exxon, **food:** Burger King, Checker's, Huddle House, **lodging:** Super 8, **other:** Buick/Pontiac/GMC

14 Leeds Ave, **S...other:** HOSPITAL, boat marina

13mm Ashley River

12 SC 61, Ashley River Rd, **N...food:** Chick-fil-A, McDonald's, O'Charley's, Quizno's, Sonic, **other:** HOSPITAL, Home Depot

11 Sam Rittenburg Blvd, **S...other:** Belk, Dillard's, JC Penney, Sears/auto, mall

10 US 17, SC 7, **services from US 17, E...gas:** BP, Shell, Speedway, **food:** Capt D's, Checker's, China Gourmet, CiCi's, McDonald's, Red Lobster, Ruby Tuesday, Taco Bell, **lodging:** Holiday Inn Express, Motel 6, **other:** Mazda, Mitsubishi, Piggly Wiggly, **W...gas:** Exxon, Hess, 76/Circle K, **food:** Waffle House, **lodging:** Econolodge, Hampton Inn, InTown Suites, **other:** Acura, Advance Parts, Chrysler/Plymouth/Jeep, Costco/gas, CVS Drug, Food Lion, Toyota

I-526 begins/ends on US 17.

SOUTH DAKOTA

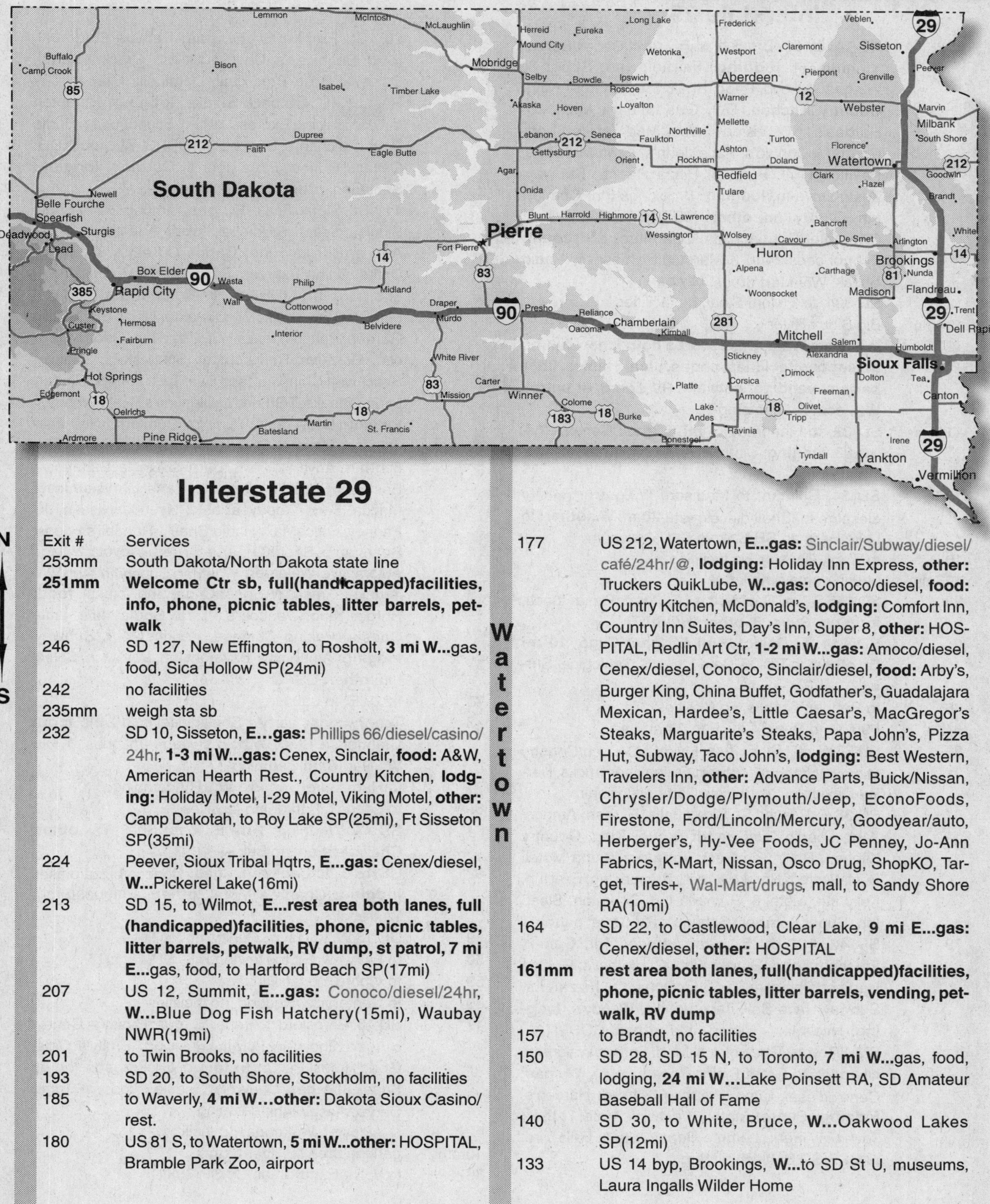

Interstate 29

N ↕ S

Exit #	Services
253mm	South Dakota/North Dakota state line
251mm	**Welcome Ctr sb, full(handicapped)facilities, info, phone, picnic tables, litter barrels, petwalk**
246	SD 127, New Effington, to Rosholt, **3 mi W...**gas, food, Sica Hollow SP(24mi)
242	no facilities
235mm	weigh sta sb
232	SD 10, Sisseton, **E...gas:** Phillips 66/diesel/casino/24hr, **1-3 mi W...gas:** Cenex, Sinclair, **food:** A&W, American Hearth Rest., Country Kitchen, **lodging:** Holiday Motel, I-29 Motel, Viking Motel, **other:** Camp Dakotah, to Roy Lake SP(25mi), Ft Sisseton SP(35mi)
224	Peever, Sioux Tribal Hqtrs, **E...gas:** Cenex/diesel, **W...**Pickerel Lake(16mi)
213	SD 15, to Wilmot, **E...rest area both lanes, full (handicapped)facilities, phone, picnic tables, litter barrels, petwalk, RV dump, st patrol, 7 mi E...**gas, food, to Hartford Beach SP(17mi)
207	US 12, Summit, **E...gas:** Conoco/diesel/24hr, **W...**Blue Dog Fish Hatchery(15mi), Waubay NWR(19mi)
201	to Twin Brooks, no facilities
193	SD 20, to South Shore, Stockholm, no facilities
185	to Waverly, **4 mi W...other:** Dakota Sioux Casino/rest.
180	US 81 S, to Watertown, **5 mi W...other:** HOSPITAL, Bramble Park Zoo, airport

Watertown

Exit #	Services
177	US 212, Watertown, **E...gas:** Sinclair/Subway/diesel/café/24hr/@, **lodging:** Holiday Inn Express, **other:** Truckers QuikLube, **W...gas:** Conoco/diesel, **food:** Country Kitchen, McDonald's, **lodging:** Comfort Inn, Country Inn Suites, Day's Inn, Super 8, **other:** HOSPITAL, Redlin Art Ctr, **1-2 mi W...gas:** Amoco/diesel, Cenex/diesel, Conoco, Sinclair/diesel, **food:** Arby's, Burger King, China Buffet, Godfather's, Guadalajara Mexican, Hardee's, Little Caesar's, MacGregor's Steaks, Marguarite's Steaks, Papa John's, Pizza Hut, Subway, Taco John's, **lodging:** Best Western, Travelers Inn, **other:** Advance Parts, Buick/Nissan, Chrysler/Dodge/Plymouth/Jeep, EconoFoods, Firestone, Ford/Lincoln/Mercury, Goodyear/auto, Herberger's, Hy-Vee Foods, JC Penney, Jo-Ann Fabrics, K-Mart, Nissan, Osco Drug, ShopKO, Target, Tires+, Wal-Mart/drugs, mall, to Sandy Shore RA(10mi)
164	SD 22, to Castlewood, Clear Lake, **9 mi E...gas:** Cenex/diesel, **other:** HOSPITAL
161mm	**rest area both lanes, full(handicapped)facilities, phone, picnic tables, litter barrels, vending, petwalk, RV dump**
157	to Brandt, no facilities
150	SD 28, SD 15 N, to Toronto, **7 mi W...**gas, food, lodging, **24 mi W...**Lake Poinsett RA, SD Amateur Baseball Hall of Fame
140	SD 30, to White, Bruce, **W...**Oakwood Lakes SP(12mi)
133	US 14 byp, Brookings, **W...**to SD St U, museums, Laura Ingalls Wilder Home

SOUTH DAKOTA

Interstate 29

N ↕ S

Brookings

132 US 14, Lp 29, Brookings, **E...gas:** Cenex/Burger King/diesel, **lodging:** Fairfield Inn, Super 8, **W...gas:** Amoco, Citgo, Shell, **food:** Burger King, Country Kitchen, DQ, Guadalajara Mexican, Hardee's, KFC, King's Wok, Mad Jack's Food-Court, McDonald's, Papa John's, Papa Murphy's, Pavilion Grill, Perkins, Pizza Ranch, Subway, Zesto Drive-In, **lodging:** Brookings Inn, Comfort Inn, Quality Inn, **other:** HOSPITAL, Big O Tire, Chevrolet/Pontiac/Buick/Cadillac, $Discount, EconoFoods/24hr, K-Mart/Little Caesar's, Radio Shack, Wal-Mart/drugs, city park

127 SD 324, to Elkton, Sinai, no facilities

124mm Big Sioux River

121 to Nunda, Ward, **E...rest area both lanes, full(handicapped)facilities, phone, picnic tables, litter barrels, vending, petwalk, RV dump, st patrol, W...**food, RV camping

114 SD 32, to Flandreau, **7 mi E...gas:** Cenex, Phillips 66, **lodging:** Sioux River Motel, **other:** Santee Tribal Hqtrs

109 SD 34, Colman, to Madison, **W...gas:** Conoco/diesel/rest., Shell/diesel/rest., **20 mi W...other:** to Lake Herman SP, Dakota St U, museum

104 to Trent, Chester, no facilities

103mm parking area both lanes

98 SD 115 S, Dell Rapids, **3 mi E...food:** Pizza Ranch, **lodging:** Super 8, **other:** HOSPITAL

94 SD 114, to Baltic, **2 mi E...gas:** Citgo, **10 mi E...other:** to EROS Data Ctr, US Geological Survey

86 to Renner, Crooks, no facilities

84b a I-90, W to Rapid City, E to Albert Lea

83 SD 38 W, 60th St, **E...gas:** Flying J/Conoco/Country Mkt/diesel/24hr/@, **other:** Freightliner Trucks, Harley-Davidson, Northview Campers, repair

Sioux Falls

81 SD 38 E, Russell St, Sioux Falls, **E...gas:** Amoco/24hr, Food'n Fuel, **food:** Burger King, Country Kitchen, Roll'n Pin Rest., **lodging:** Arena Motel, Best Western Ramkota/rest., Brimark Inn, Exel Inn, Kelly Inn, Motel 6, Ramada Inn, Sheraton, Sleep Inn, Super 8, **other:** Schaap's RV Ctr, st patrol

79 SD 42, 12th St, **E...gas:** Amoco/24hr, Cenex, Freedom, **food:** Burger King, Godfather's, Golden Harvest Chinese, KFC, McDonald's, Pizza Hut, Subway, Taco Bell, Taco John's, Wendy's, **lodging:** Nite's Inn, Ramada Ltd, **other:** HOSPITAL, BMW/Toyota, Chevrolet, K-Mart, Saturn, Walgreen, city park, to Great Plains Zoo/museum, **W...gas:** Cenex/diesel, Citgo, Phillips 66, **food:** Hardee's, **lodging:** Sunset Motel, Westwick Motel, **other:** Tower RV Park, Lemme Repair, Sioux Falls Tire, to USS SD Battleship Mem

78 26th St, Empire St, **E...gas:** Phillips 66/diesel, **food:** Bennigan's, ChuckeCheese, Cracker Barrel, Culver's, Dixie Bros Grill, Domino's, Granite City Rest., KFC, Outback Steaks, **lodging:** Hampton Inn, Holiday Inn Express, **other:** EconoFoods, Home Depot, Michael's, Sam's Club, USPO, **W...food:** DQ, Oscar's Coffee, Papa John's, Quizno's, **lodging:** Settle Inn, **other:** Hy-Vee Foods

77 41st St, Sioux Falls, **E...gas:** Amoco/24hr, Shell, Sinclair/diesel, SA/diesel, **food:** Andolini's Italian, Arby's, Burger King, Carlos O'Kelly's, ChiChi's, Chili's, China Express, Fry'n Pan Rest., Fuddrucker's, Green Mill Rest., KFC, LoneStar Steaks, MacGregor's Steaks, McDonald's, Nap's BBQ, Olive Garden, Perkins, Pizza Hut, Pizza Inn, Qdoba Mexican, Quizno's, Red Lobster, Schlotsky's, Subway, Szechwan Chinese, Taco Bell, Taco John's, Timber-Lodge Steaks, TGIFriday, Valentino's Rest., Wendy's, **lodging:** Best Western Empire, Comfort Suites, Fairfield Inn, Microtel, Radisson, Residence Inn, Super 8, **other:** Advance Parts, Barnes&Noble, Batteries+, Best Buy, Big O Tire, Checker Parts, Chrysler/Jeep/Mazda, Ford, Goodyear/auto, Hyundai/Nissan, JC Penney, OfficeMax, Radio Shack, Randall's Foods, Sears/auto, ShopKO, Target, Tires+, Toyota, Village Automotive, Walgreen, Wal-Mart SuperCtr/24hr, VW, Younkers, mall, **W...gas:** Citgo, Shell/diesel, **food:** Burger King, Denucci's Pizza, Godfather's, Little Caesar, Peking Chinese, Perkins/24hr, Subway, **lodging:** AmericInn, Baymont Inn, Day's Inn, Select Inn, **other:** USPO

75 I-229 E, to I-90 E

73 Tea, **E...gas:** Larry's Shell/diesel/café/24hr, **food:** Crabhouse Rest., **other:** U-Haul, antiques, **1.5mi W...**Red Barn Camping

71 to Harrisburg, Lennox, **W...**RV camping

68 to Lennox, Parker, no facilities

64 SD 44, Worthing, **1 mi E...gas:** Shell, **W...other:** Chevrolet/Pontiac/Buick

62 US 18 E, to Canton, **E...gas:** Conoco/pizza/diesel, **lodging:** Charlie's Motel, **other:** antiques(9mi), **W...**repair

59 US 18 W, to Davis, Hurley, no facilities

56 to Fairview, **E...**to Newton Hills SP(12mi)

53 to Viborg, no facilities

50 to Centerville, Hudson, no facilities

47 SD 46, Beresford, to Irene, **E...gas:** Casey's, Cenex/Burger King, Sinclair/diesel, **food:** Emily's Café, GoodTimes Pizza, **lodging:** Crossroads Motel, Super 8, **other:** Chevrolet, Fiesta Foods, **W...gas:** Cenex/diesel/24hr, camping

42 to Alcester, Wakonda, no facilities

40mm parking area sb, litter barrel

38 to Volin, **E...**to Union Co SP(7mi)

N
S

31 SD 48, Spink, to Akron, no facilities
26 SD 50, to Vermillion, **E...Welcome Ctr/rest area both lanes, full(handicapped)facilities, info, phone, picnic tables, litter barrels, petwalk, RV dump, W...gas:** Conoco/diesel/24hr, **6-7 mi W...gas:** Casey's/gas, Phillips 66, **food:** Amigo's Mexican, Burger King, Pizza Hut, Subway, Taco John's, **lodging:** Comfort Inn, Super 8, Travelodge, **other:** Hy-Vee Foods, to UofSD
18 Lp 29, Elk Point, to Burbank, **E...gas:** Amoco/diesel, Phillips 66/pizza/subs, **food:** Cody's Rest., Dairy Queen, **lodging:** HomeTowne Inn
15 to Elk Point, **1 mi E...**gas, food, lodging
9 SD 105, Jefferson, **E...gas:** Amoco/Choice Cut Rest.
4 McCook, **1 mi W...other:** KOA(seasonal), Adams Homestead/nature preserve
3mm weigh sta nb
2 N Sioux City, **E...gas:** Ampride/diesel/rest./24hr, Cenex, **food:** Glass Palace Rest.(1mi), McDonald's, Taco John's, **other:** Dakota Valley Foods, Gateway Computers, USPO, **W...gas:** Casey's/gas, Citgo/Taco Bell, **lodging:** Comfort Inn, Econolodge, Hampton Inn, Super 8, **other:** to Sodrac Dogtrack
1 **E...other:** Dakota Dunes Golf Resort, **W...gas:** Citgo/diesel, **food:** Graham's Grill, **lodging:** Country Inn Suites
0mm South Dakota/Iowa state line, Big Sioux River

Interstate 90

E
W

Exit # Services
412.5mm South Dakota/Minnesota state line
412mm **Welcome Ctr wb/rest area eb, full(handicapped)facilities, info, phone, picnic tables, litter barrels, petwalk, RV dump(wb), weigh sta both lanes**
410 Valley Springs, **N...**Palisades SP(7mi), **S...**Beaver Creek Nature Area, gas, food
406 SD 11, Brandon, Corson, **S...gas:** Amoco, **lodging:** Holiday Inn Express, **S...gas:** Amoco, Ampride, Shell, **food:** DQ, Pizza Ranch, Taco John's, **other:** to Big Sioux RA
402 EROS Data Ctr, **N...other:** Jellystone RV Park
400 I-229 S, no facilities
399 SD 115, Cliff Ave, Sioux Falls, **N...gas:** Phillips 66/diesel, Sinclair/diesel, **food:** Cody's Grill, Frontier Village, **other:** Spader RV Ctr, KOA, **S...gas:** Cenex/diesel, Holiday/diesel, Pilot/Subway/diesel/24hr/@, **food:** Arby's, Burger King, **lodging:** Grain Bin Rest., Great American Rest., McDonald's, Perkins, Taco John's, Cloud Nine Motel, Comfort Inn, Country Inn Suites, Day's Inn, Econolodge, Super 8, **other:** HOSPITAL, Blue Beacon, Goodyear, Kenworth, Peterbilt, Volvo

Sioux Falls

396b a I-29, N to Brookings, S to Sioux City, no facilities
390 SD 38, Hartford, **N...other:** Camp Dakota RV Park, Goos RV Ctr, **S...gas:** Phillips 66/diesel, Buffalo Ridge/gas, **food:** Pizza Ranch
387 rd 17, Hartford, **N...gas:** Phillips 66/diesel
379 SD 19, Humboldt, **1 mi N...gas:** Shell/diesel, **food:** Home Café/Grill, **other:** Town&Country Store
375mm E Vermillion River
374 to SD 38, Montrose, **2 mi N...**gas, food, **5 mi S...other:** Lake Vermillion RA, RV camping
368 Canistota, **4 mi S...lodging:** Best Western
364 US 81, Salem, to Yankton, **4 mi N...gas:** Cenex, Conoco, **lodging:** Home Motel, **other:** RV camp
363.5mm W Vermillion River
363mm **rest area both lanes, full(handicapped)facilities, phone, picnic tables, litter barrels, vending, petwalk, RV dump, st patrol**
357 to Bridgewater, Canova, no facilities
353 Spencer, Emery, **S...gas:** TA/Amoco/Subway/diesel/24hr/@
352mm Wolf Creek
350 SD 25, Emery, Farmer, **N...other:** to DeSmet, Home of Laura Ingalls Wilder
344 SD 262, Alexandria, to Fulton, **N...**KOA, **S...gas:** Shell/diesel
337mm parking area both lanes
335 Riverside Rd, **N...**RV camping
334.5mm James River
332 SD 37 S, Mitchell, to Parkston, **N...gas:** Amoco/Burger King/24hr, Cenex/diesel/@, Phillips 66/Blimpie, Shell/Subway/diesel/24hr, **food:** Arby's, Bonanza, Country Kitchen, Dairy Queen, Embers Rest., Hardee's, KFC, McDonald's, Perkins, Pizza Hut, Pizza Ranch, Twin Dragon Chinese, **lodging:** AmericInn, Best Western, Chief Motel, Comfort Inn, Corn Palace Motel, Day's Inn, Super 8, Thunderbird Motel, **other:** HOSPITAL, Advance Parts, Chrysler/Plymouth/Dodge, K-Mart, transmissions, **1-2 mi N...other:** to Corn Palace, Museum of Pioneer Life, RV camping, **S...gas:** Shell/Taco Bell/diesel/24hr, **food:** Culver's, **lodging:** Hampton Inn, Kelly Inn, **other:** Cabela's, Wal-Mart SuperCtr/gas/24hr

Mitchell

SOUTH DAKOTA

Interstate 90

E ↕ W

330 SD 37 N, Mitchell, weigh sta, **N...gas:** Cenex/24hr, Shell, **food:** Country Kitchen, **lodging:** Anthony Motel, Econolodge, Holiday Inn/rest., Motel 6, Siesta Motel, **other:** HOSPITAL, County Fair Foods, to Corn Palace, museum, **S...other:** Dakota RV Park

325 Betts Rd, **S...**RV camping

319 Mt Vernon, **1 mi N...gas:** Cenex

310 US 281, to Stickney, **S...gas:** Conoco/A&W/diesel/24hr, **other:** to Ft Randall Dam

308 Lp 90, to Plankinton, **N...gas:** Phillips 66/Al's Café/diesel, **lodging:** Cabin Fever Motel, Super 8, **other:** RV camping

301.5mm rest area both lanes, full(handicapped)facilities, phones, picnic tables, litter barrels, RV dump

296 White Lake, **1 mi N...gas:** Cenex/diesel, Shell, **lodging:** White Lake Motel

294mm Platte Creek

293mm parking area both lanes

289 SD 45 S, to Platte, **S...other:** to Snake Cr/Platte Cr RA(25mi)

284 SD 45 N, Kimball, **N...gas:** Amoco/tires, Phillips 66/diesel/24hr, **food:** Ditty's Diner, Frosty King Drive-In, Ponderosa Café, **lodging:** Super 8, Travlers Motel, **other:** RV Park, **S...lodging:** Kimball Motel

272 SD 50, Pukwana, **2 mi N...**gas, food, lodging, **S...other:** Snake/Platte Creek Rec Areas(25mi)

265 SD 50, Chamberlain, **N...gas:** Amoco, **food:** DQ, **lodging:** AmericInn, **3 mi N...food:** McDonald's, Subway, **lodging:** Bel Aire Motel, Hillside Motel, Lakeshore Motel, **other:** HOSPITAL, Honda, Lakota Museum, **S...gas:** Conoco/diesel, **other:** Happy Camper Park

264mm rest area both lanes, full(handicapped)facilities, scenic view, info, phones, picnic tables, litter barrels, RV dump

Chamberlain

263 Chamberlain, Crow Creek Sioux Tribal Hqtrs, **N...gas:** Sinclair/diesel, **food:** A&W, Casey's Café, McDonald's, Pizza Hut, Rainbow Café, Subway, Taco John's, **lodging:** The Plaza Motel/groceries/gas, Best Western(1mi), Bel Aire Motel, Hillside Motel, Lakeshore Motel, Riverview Inn, Super 8, **other:** Buche's IGA/deli

262mm Missouri River

260 SD 50, Oacoma, **N...gas:** Amoco/Burger King/diesel, Conoco/diesel, **food:** Taco John's, **lodging:** Al's Oasis Motel, Cedar Shore Motel, Comfort Inn, Day's Inn, Holiday Inn Express, **other:** Chevrolet/Buick/Pontiac, Familyland Camping, Cedar Shore Resort, Hi Dri Camping, Old West Museum

251 SD 47, to Winner, Gregory, no facilities

248 SD 47, Reliance, **N...other:** Sioux Tribal Hqtrs, to Big Bend RA

241 to Lyman, no facilities

235 SD 273, Kennebec, **N...gas:** Conoco/diesel, **food:** Pony Express Café, **lodging:** Budget Host, Kings Inn, **other:** KOA

226 US 183 S, Presho, **N...gas:** Conoco/diesel, **food:** Norma's Drive-In Café, **lodging:** Coachlight Inn, Hutch's Motel/café, **other:** museum

225 Presho, same as 226

221mm rest area wb, full(handicapped)facilities, info, phone, picnic tables, litter barrels, RV dump, petwalk

220 no facilities

218mm rest area eb, full(handicapped)facilities, info, phone, picnic tables, litter barrels, RV dump, petwalk

214 Vivian, no facilities

212 US 83 N, SD 53, to Pierre, **N...gas:** Phillips 66/diesel, **food:** Vivian Jct Rest., **other:** HOSPITAL(34mi)

208 no facilities

201 Draper, **N...**gas/diesel, **food:** Hilltop Café

194mm parking area both lanes

Murdo

192 US 83 S, Murdo, **N...gas:** Amoco/diesel, HHH/diesel/@, Phillips 66, Sinclair/diesel, **food:** Buffalo Rest., Food Court, KFC, Murdo Drive-In, Star Rest., **lodging:** Anchor Inn, Best Western, Chuck's Motel, Day's Inn, Hospitality Inn, Lee Motel, Super 8, TeePee Motel/RV Camp, **other:** Super Value Foods, camping, **S...lodging:** Landmark Country Inn, **other:** to Rosebud

191 Murdo, **N...**access to same as 192

190mm Central/Mountain time zone

188mm parking area both lanes, litter barrels

183 Okaton, **S...**gas, Ghost Town

177 no facilities

172 to Cedar Butte, no facilities

170 SD 63 N, to Midland, **N...gas:** Shell, **other:** 1880's Town, KOA

167mm rest area wb, full(handicapped)facilities, phones, picnic tables, litter barrels, RV dump, petwalk

165mm rest area eb, full(handicapped)facilities, phones, picnic tables, litter barrels, RV dump, petwalk

163 SD 63, Belvidere, **S...gas:** Amoco/diesel/café, Sinclair/diesel, **lodging:** motel

152 Lp 90, Kadoka, **N...gas:** Phillips 66/diesel/rest./24hr, **S...lodging:** Best Western, Budget Host, Leewood Motel, **other:** Badlands Petrified Gardens, camping

150 SD 73 S, Kadoka, **N...lodging:** Dakota Inn/rest., **S...gas:** Amoco, Conoco/diesel, Shell/café, **food:** Happy Chef, Sidekicks Rest., **lodging:** Best Western, Budget Host, Downtowner Motor Inn, Ponderosa Motel, Super 8, **other:** Kadoka Camping, to Buffalo Nat Grasslands

Interstate 90

E ↕ W

143 SD 73 N, to Philip, **15 mi N...**HOSPITAL

138mm scenic overlook wb

131 SD 240, **S...**to Badlands NP, **gas:** Amoco(seasonal), Conoco(11mi), **lodging:** Badlands Inn(9mi), Cedar Pass Lodge/rest.(9mi), **other:** Circle 10 Camping, Prairie Home NHS, KOA(15mi), Good Sam Camping

129.5mm scenic overlook eb

127 no facilities

121 no facilities

116 no facilities

112 US 14 E, to Philip, no facilities

Wall

110 SD 240, Wall, **N...gas:** Amoco/diesel, Exxon, Phillips 66/Subway, **food:** Cactus Café, DQ, Elkton House Rest., **lodging:** Best Value Inn, Best Western, Day's Inn, Econolodge, Elk Motel, Fountain Hotel, Hitching Post Motel, Homestead Motel, Kings Inn, Knight's Inn, Sunshine Inn, Super 8, The Wall Motel, Welsh Motel, **other:** NAPA, Wall Drug/gifts/rest., museum, **S...**to Badlands NP, RV camping

109 Wall, **1-2 mi N...**access to same as 110

107 Cedar Butte Rd, no facilities

101 rd T-504, Jensen Rd, to Schell Ranch, no facilities

100mm rest area both lanes, full(handicapped)facilities, info, phone, picnic tables, litter barrels, RV dump, vending, petwalk

99.5mm Cheyenne River

99 Wasta, **N...gas:** Amoco/diesel, **lodging:** Redwood Motel, **other:** Bryce's RV Camping

90 to Owanka, no facilities

88 rd 473(from eb, no re-entry), no facilities

84 rd 497, **N...**Olde Glory Fireworks

78 New Underwood, **1/2 mi S...**gas, **lodging:** Jake's Motel, **other:** Steve's General Store

69mm parking area both lanes

67 new exit

66 Box Elder, **N...gas:** Flying J/Conoco/diesel/@, Shell(1mi), **food:** McDonald's, Pizza Hut, **other:** Ellsworth AFB, SD Space & Air Museum, Box Elder Trading Post, fireworks

Rapid City

61 Elk Vale Rd, **N...gas:** Flying J/Conoco/CountryMkt/diesel/LP/RV dump/24hr/@, **other:** Langland RV Ctr, **S...other:** KOA(seasonal)(3mi), transmissions

60 Lp 90(exits left from wb), Rapid City, to Mt Rushmore, **1-3 mi S...food:** KFC, LJ Silver, **lodging:** Holiday Inn Express, Stardust Motel, **other:** HOSPITAL, K-Mart, Nat Coll of Mines/Geology

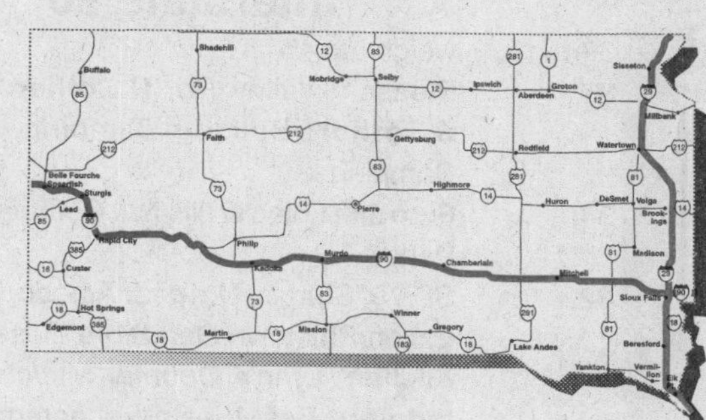

59 La Crosse St, Rapid City, **N...gas:** Amoco/24hr, Phillips 66/A&W, Shell, **food:** Boston Pizza, Burger King, Denny's, Minerva's Rest., Outback Steaks, TGIFriday, **lodging:** Best Western, Country Inn Suites, Holiday Inn Express, Super 8, **other:** Sears/auto, mall, st patrol, **S...gas:** Cenex/diesel, Exxon/24hr, **food:** Golden Corral, McDonald's, MillStone Rest., Perkins/24hr, Schlotsky's, Sirloin Buffet, **lodging:** AmericInn, Comfort Inn, Day's Inn, Fair Value Inn, Foothills Inn, Microtel, Motel 6, Quality Inn, Ramada Inn, Rushmore Motel, Thrifty Motel, **other:** Sam's Club, Wal-Mart SuperCtr/gas/24hr

58 Haines Ave, Rapid City, **N...gas:** Conoco, Shell, **food:** Applebee's, Chili's, Fuddrucker's, Hardee's, Red Lobster, Su Casa Mexican, **lodging:** Travelodge, **other:** Borders, Hancock Fabrics, Herbergers, JC Penney, Lowe's Whse, Target, Tires+, to Rushmore Mall, **S...gas:** Conoco, **food:** Taco John's, **other:** HOSPITAL, OfficeMax, ShopKO, same as 59

57 I-190, US 16, to Rapid City, to Mt Rushmore, **1 mi S on North St...gas:** Conoco, **lodging:** Best Western, Holiday Inn, Howard Johnson, Radisson, **other:** Albertson's

55 Deadwood Ave, **N...other:** Lazy JD Camp(6mi), **S...gas:** Sinclair/Subway/diesel, **food:** A&W, Culver's, **lodging:** Best Western Sun Inn(3mi), **other:** Black Hills Dogtrack, diesel repair

51 Black Hawk Rd, **N...other:** Fort Welikit Camping(1mi), **S...other:** MidStates RV Ctr

48 Stagebarn Canyon Rd, **N...food:** Cattleman's Steaks, **other:** RV camping, **S...gas:** Sinclair/Stagebarn Plaza/food, **food:** Classick's Rest., Mike's Pizza, **lodging:** Super 8, **other:** MEDICAL CARE

46 Piedmont Rd, Elk Creek Rd, **N...food:** Elk Creek Steaks, **lodging:** Covered Wagon Resort, **other:** to Petrified Forest, camping, **S...gas:** Conoco/Subway/diesel/@, **other:** camping

44 Bethlehem Rd, **S...lodging:** Bethlehem Lodge(6mi), **other:** Bethlehem RV Park(2mi)

42mm rest area both lanes, full(handicapped)facilities, info, phones, picnic tables, litter barrels, RV dump, petwalk, vending

40 Tilford, **N...**antiques

SOUTH DAKOTA

Interstate 90

E ↔ W

39mm	weigh sta eb
37	Pleasant Valley Rd, **N...other:** Elkview Camp, **S...other:** Bulldog Camping, Rush-No-More Camping
34	**S...other:** Black Hills Nat Cemetary, No Name RV Park
32	SD 79, Sturgis, **N...gas:** Amoco, Conoco/Subway, Exxon/Phil-town Gen Store/diesel, **food:** Country Kitchen, Lynn's Country Mkt/café, Taco John's, **lodging:** Best Western, Lantern Motel, National 9 Inn, StarLite Motel, **other:** HOSPITAL, Ford/Lincoln/Mercury, Motorcycle SuperStore, Southside RV Park, to Bear Butte SP
30	US 14A W, SD 34E, Sturgis, to Deadwood, **N...gas:** Cenex/diesel, Conoco, Sinclair, **food:** Pizza Hut, McDonald's, Pizza Hut, Subway, Taco John's, **other:** CarQuest, Mr Tire, Pamida, Radio Shack, Day's End Camping, **S...gas:** RanchMart, Shell/diesel, **food:** Burger King, **lodging:** Day's Inn, Super 8/rest., **other:** Chevrolet
23	SD 34 W, Whitewood, to Belle Fourche, **N...other:** Northern Hills RV Ctr, **S...gas:** Amoco, Phillips 66, **food:** Pronto Diner, **lodging:** Tony's Motel
17	US 85 S, to Deadwood, **9-12 mi S in Deadwood...food:** Cadillac Jack's Diner, 4Aces Buffet, Silverado Café, **lodging:** AmericInn, Best Western, Day's Inn, Holiday Inn Express, Palace Hotel, Super 8, White House Inn, Deadwood Gulch Resort, **other:** KOA, Winner's Casino
14	US 14A, Spearfish Canyon, **N...food:** Applebee's, **lodging:** Comfort Inn, Fairfield Inn, Holiday Inn/rest., **S...gas:** Amoco, Conoco, **food:** Dairy Queen, KFC, Perkins, Pizza Ranch, All **lodging:** American Inn, Howard Johnson, Super 8, **other:** Ford/Lincoln/Mercury, K-Mart, auto museum, cinema, Mt View Camping, Chris' Camping
12	Spearfish, **S...gas:** Amoco, Conoco/diesel, Sinclair/diesel, **food:** Arby's, Burger King, DQ, McDonald's, Millstone Rest., Papa Murphy's, Pizza Ranch, Subway, Wendy's, **lodging:** Day's Inn, Kelly Inn, **other:** HOSPITAL, Chevrolet/Buick/Pontiac, Black Hills St U, fish hatchery, same as 10
10	US 85 N, to Belle Fourche, **S...food:** Burger King, Cedar House Rest., DQ, Domino's, Golden Dragon Chinese, McDonald's, Subway, Taco Bell, Wendy's, **lodging:** Best Western, Day's Inn, **other:** Cadillac/GMC, Chevrolet/Buick/Cadillac, Jeep, Jo's Camping, KOA, Safeway, Thrift Foods, USPO, Wal-Mart, same as 12
9	W Spearfish, no facilities
2	**1 mi N...**McNenny St Fish Hatchery, no facilities
1mm	**Welcome Ctr eb, full(handicapped)facilities, info, phone, picnic tables, litter barrels, RV dump, petwalk**
0mm	South Dakota/Wyoming state line

Sturgis — Spearfish

Interstate 229(Sioux Falls)

N ↔ S

Exit #	Services
10b a	I-90 E and W. I-229 begins/ends on I-90, exit 400.
9	Benson Rd, **W...**Amoco/burgers/pizza
7.5mm	Big Sioux River
7	Rice St, **E...**winter sports, **W...**to stockyards
6	SD 38, 10th St, **E...**Citgo, Phillips 66, Applebee's, Arby's, Baxter Café, DQ, Domino's, Fry'n Pan Rest., Golden star Buffet, KFC, Pizza Hut, Quizno's, Taco Bell, Tomacelli's Italian, Budget Host, Suburban Motel, Super 8, Big O Tire, Checker Parts, Family$, Hy-Vee Foods, K-Mart, Pronto Parts, ShopKO, Sunshine Foods, **W...**Amoco, Phillips 66/diesel/mart, Shell, Burger King, BurgerTime, Godfather's, Hardee's, LaBamba Mexican, Little Caesar's, Pizza Inn, Puerto Vallarta, Steak-Out, Subway, Taco John's, Wendy's, Rushmore Motel, Jim's Repair, Lewis Drug, Radio Shack, USPO
5.5mm	Big Sioux River
5	26th St, **E...**HOSPITAL, Shell/diesel, Cherry Creek Grill, Keg Chicken Café, McDonald's, city park
4	Cliff Ave, **E...**Phillips 66/TCBY/diesel, Sinclair/diesel, Runza Rest., Walgreen
3	SD 115, Lp 229, Minnesota Ave, **E...**city park, **1 mi W...**Sinclair, Burger King, Culver's, Famous Dave's BBQ, Hardee's, Little Caesar's, McDonald's, Subway, Holiday Inn, Dodge, GMC, Hy-Vee Foods, K-Mart, Lewis Drug, Mitsubishi/Toyota, Sunshine Foods, USPO
2	Western Ave, **E...**Shell, **W...**MEDICAL CARE, Cenex/diesel, Shell, Burger King, Champ's Café, China Buffet, Nap's BBQ, Pizza Hut, Valentino's Italian, Advance Parts, Goodyear/auto, Radio Shack
1.5mm	Big Sioux River
1c	Louise Ave, **E...**Homewood Suites, **W...**Amoco, Phillips 66/diesel, A&W, Burger King, McDonald's, Royal Fork Buffet, Wendy's, Honda/Mercedes, mall
1b a	I-29 N and S. I-229 begins/ends on I-29, exit 75.

Sioux Falls

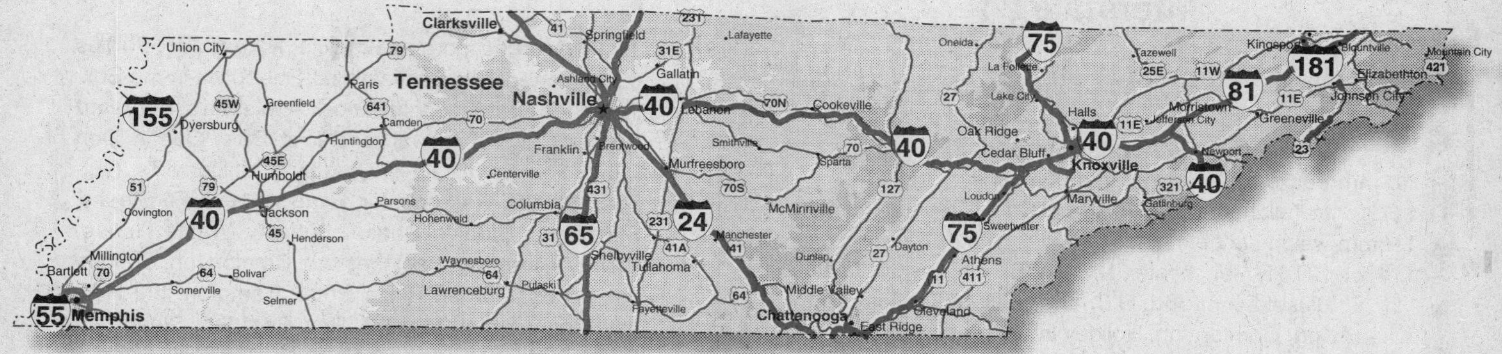

Interstate 24

E ↕ W

Exit #	Services
185b a	I-75, N to Knoxville, S to Atlanta. I-24 begins/ends on I-75, exit 2 in Chattanooga.
184	Moore Rd, **S...food:** Chef Lin Buffet, Trovino's Italian, **other:** $Tree, K-Mart
183	(183a from wb), Belvoir Ave, Germantown Rd, no facilities
181a	US 41 S, to East Ridge(from eb), **S...food:** Westside Grill, King's Lodge, **other:** Ford Trucks
181	Fourth Ave, Chattanooga, to TN Temple U, **N...gas:** Citgo/diesel, Conoco, Exxon/Blimpie/diesel, **food:** Bojangles, Burger King, Capt D's, Central Park, Hardee's, Krystal/24hr, Subway, Waffle House, **lodging:** Rodeway Inn, **other:** BiLo, $General, Goodyear, Mr Transmission, repair, **S...gas:** Citgo
180b a	US 27 S, TN 8, Rossville Blvd, **N...other:** U-Haul, to Chickamauga, UT Chatt, **S...gas:** Fast TravelCtr/diesel, RaceTrac/diesel/24hr, **food:** KFC, **lodging:** Hamilton Inn, **other:** NTB
178	US 27 N, Market St, Chattanooga, to Lookout Mtn, **N...gas:** Amoco/diesel, **lodging:** Day's Inn, Knight's Inn, Ramada Inn, **other:** Ford, Nissan, U-Haul, to Chattanooga ChooChoo, **S...food:** KFC, **lodging:** Comfort Suites, Hampton Inn, Motel 6
175	Browns Ferry Rd, to Lookout Mtn, **N...gas:** Citgo, Exxon/diesel, **food:** Mike's Pizza, **lodging:** Best Value Inn, **other:** CVS Drug, $General, Food Lion, **S...gas:** Conoco/diesel, Shell/diesel, **food:** Hardee's, McDonald's, Subway, **lodging:** Comfort Inn, Econolodge, Sleep Inn
174	US 11, US 41, US 64, Lookout Valley, **N...food:** Waffle House, **lodging:** Day's Inn, Racoon Mtn Camping(2mi), **S...gas:** BP/diesel/24hr, Exxon, Pure, **food:** BBQ, Cracker Barrel, Taco Bell, Waffle House, **lodging:** Baymont Inn, Best Western, Comfort Inn, Country Inn Suites, Hampton Inn, Holiday Inn Express, Knight's Inn, Ramada Ltd, Super 8, **other:** Lookout Valley Camping, st patrol
172mm	**rest area eb, full(handicapped)facilities, phone, picnic tables, litter barrels, vending, petwalk**
171mm	Tennessee/Georgia state line
169	GA 299, to US 11, **N...gas:** SavATon/diesel/24hr, **S...gas:** Fast/Subway/TCBY/diesel/24hr/@, Cone/diesel/24hr/@, RaceTrac/24hr
167	I-59 S, to Birmingham
167mm	Tennessee/Georgia state line, Central/Eastern time zone
161	TN 156, to Haletown, New Hope, **N...gas:** Amoco, **other:** On The Lake Camping, **S...gas:** Chevron/fireworks
160mm	Tennessee River/Nickajack Lake
159mm	**Welcome Ctr wb/rest area eb, full(handicapped)facilities, phone, vending, picnic tables, litter barrels, petwalk**
158	US 41, TN 27, Nickajack Dam, **N...gas:** Texaco, **S...gas:** Phillips 66/diesel/fireworks
155	TN 28, Jasper, **N...gas:** Amoco/diesel, Citgo/diesel(1mi), **food:** Dairy Queen(1mi), Hardee's, Western Sizzlin, **lodging:** Acuff Country Inn, **S...**HOSPITAL
152	US 41, US 64, US 72, Kimball, S Pittsburg, **N...gas:** Amoco/fireworks, Cone/diesel, Phillips 66/fireworks, RaceTrac, **food:** A&W/LJ Silver, Arby's, Domino's, Hardee's, KFC, Krystal, McDonald's, Pizza Hut, Shoney's, Subway, Taco Bell, Waffle House, Wendy's, **lodging:** Budget Host, Comfort Inn, Day's Inn, Holiday Inn Express, **other:** HOSPITAL, BiLo, Chevrolet/Pontiac/Buick, $Tree, Goody's, Radio Shack, Wal-Mart SuperCtr/24hr, to Russell Cave NM, **3 mi S...other:** Lodge Cast Iron
143	Martin Springs Rd, **N...gas:** Chevron/diesel/fireworks
135	US 41 N, Monteagle, **N...gas:** Phillips 66/diesel/rest./24hr, Pure/diesel, **food:** HappyLand Rest., **other:** AutoSure Parts, S Cumberland RV Park, **S...**Day's Inn
134	US 64, US 41A, Monteagle, to Sewanee, **N...gas:** Amoco/McDonald's, **other:** CVS Drug, to S Cumberland SP, **S...gas:** Chevron/diesel, Citgo, **food:** Bluewater Lodge Rest., Pizza Hut, Smokehouse BBQ, Best Western, **lodging:** Budget Host, **other:** $General, Firestone/U-Haul/auto, Monteagle Winery, Piggly Wiggly, to U of The South
133mm	**rest area both lanes, full(handicapped)facilities, phone, picnic tables, litter barrels, vending, petwalk**
128mm	Elk River

Chattanooga

Monteagle

TENNESSEE

Interstate 24

E ↕ W — Manchester

127 US 64, TN 50, Pelham, to Winchester, **N...gas:** Amoco, Phillips 66, Texaco/Stuckey's, **S...gas:** Exxon/diesel, **other:** to Tims Ford SP

119mm trucks only parking area both lanes

117 to Tullahoma, USAF Arnold Ctr, UT Space Institute

116mm weigh sta both lanes

114 US 41, Manchester, **N...gas:** BP, Phillips 66, Texaco/diesel/24hr, **food:** O'Charley's, Ruby Tuesday, **lodging:** Comfort Inn, Holiday Inn Express, Ramada Inn, Scottish Inn, Super 8, **other:** Chrysler/Dodge/Toyota, KOA, Nissan, Toyota, Wal-Mart SuperCtr/gas/24hr, museum, **S...gas:** Exxon/24hr, RaceWay, **food:** Arby's, Burger King, Capt D's, KFC, Krystal, McDonald's, Pizza Hut, Taco Bell, Waffle House, Wendy's, **lodging:** Country Inn Suites, Day's Inn, Knight's Inn, Red Roof Inn, **other:** Advance Parts, AutoZone, BiLo Foods, Chevrolet, Family$, Ford/Lincoln/Mercury, Goodyear, Russell Stover, carwash

111 TN 55, Manchester, **N...gas:** Amoco, Chevron, Citgo/diesel/24hr, **other:** to Rock Island SP, **S...gas:** BP, **food:** Hardee's, Sonic, **other:** HOSPITAL, to Jack Daniels Dist HS, Old Stone Fort

Murfreesboro

110 TN 53, Manchester, **N...gas:** BP, Exxon/TCBY/24hr, Shell, **food:** Cracker Barrel, D Crockett's Roadhouse, Oak Rest., **lodging:** Ambassador Inn, Day's Inn, Hampton Inn, **S...gas:** Texaco/diesel/24hr, **food:** Waffle House, **lodging:** Econolodge, **other:** HOSPITAL

109mm Duck River

105 US 41, **N...gas:** Busy Corner/BP/diesel/24hr, Shell, **food:** RanchHouse Rest., **S...gas:** Amoco, to Normandy Dam

97 TN 64, Beechgrove, to Shelbyville, **N...other:** auto parts/repair, **S...gas:** Phillips 66/diesel

89 Buchanan Rd, **N...gas:** Texaco/diesel, **S...gas:** Citgo/diesel/rest./24hr, **food:** Huddle House

81 US 231, Murfreesboro, **N...gas:** BP/diesel/24hr, Exxon, RaceWay/24hr, Shell, **food:** Arby's, Burger King, Cracker Barrel, King's Table Rest., Krystal, Parthenon Steaks, Ponderosa, Shoney's, Waffle House/24hr, Wendy's, **lodging:** Best Inn, Guesthouse Inn, Knight's Inn, Ramada Ltd, Regal Inn, Scottish Inn, **other:** HOSPITAL, Dodge, Honda, Mazda, **S...**Citgo/24hr, Express/diesel/24hr, Golden Gallon, Phillips 66/diesel/24hr, Texaco/24hr, BBQ, La Siesta Mexican, McDonald's, Pizza Hut/Taco Bell, Sonic, Subway, Waffle House, Howard Johnson, Quality Inn, Safari Inn, Gateway Tire, Toyota

78 TN 96, Murfreesboro, to Franklin, **N...gas:** BP, Phillips 66/Church's/White Castle/diesel, Shell/Jack-in-the-Box, Texaco/Burger King/24hr, **food:** Applebee's, Backyard Burger, Chick-fil-A, Cracker Barrel, Dairy Queen, Don Pablo, Fazoli's, IHOP, KFC, Luby's, McDonald's, OutBack Steaks, Red Lobster, Ryan's, Santa Fe Steaks, Starbucks, Steak'n Shake, Subway, Waffle House, Wendy's, **lodging:** Best Western, Comfort Inn, Country Inn Suites, Garden Plaza Hotel, Hampton Inn, Holiday Inn, Microtel, Motel 6, Red Roof Inn, Sleep Inn, Super 8, Wingate Inn, **other:** BooksAMillion, Dillard's, HobbyLobby, Home Depot, JC Penney, Lowe's Whse, OfficeMax, Sears, Staples, Target, Wal-Mart SuperCtr/gas/24hr, mall, to Stones River Bfd, **S...gas:** Amoco/diesel/24hr, Chevron/24hr, Citgo/diesel/24hr, Express, Exxon/24hr, Texaco, **food:** Hardee's, Sonic, Taco Bell, Waffle House, **other:** $General, Kohl's, Kroger, River Rock Outlet/famous brands, Sam's Club, Walgreen

74b a TN 840, to Lebanon, Franklin, no facilities

Nashville

70 TN 102, Lee Victory Pkwy, Almaville Rd, to Smyrna, **S...gas:** Amoco, Citgo/diesel/24hr, Express, Exxon, **food:** Dad's Rest., McDonald's, **lodging:** Deerfield Inn

66 TN 266, Sam Ridley Pkwy, to Smyrna, **N...gas:** Cone/diesel/24hr, Shell/diesel, **food:** Logan's Roadhouse, Sonic, **lodging:** Day's Inn, **other:** MEDICAL CARE, Kroger/gas, Nashville I-24 Camping(3mi), **S...food:** Cracker Barrel, O'Charley's, **lodging:** Fairfield Inn, Sleep Inn, **other:** I-24 Expo

64 Waldron Rd, to La Vergne, **N...gas:** Exxon/24hr, Marathon, Pilot/Subway/diesel/24hr/@, **food:** Arby's, Hardee's, Krystal/24hr, McDonald's, Waffle House, **lodging:** Comfort Inn, Holiday Inn Express, Super 8, **other:** Music City Camping(3mi), **S...gas:** Express/diesel/24hr, **lodging:** Driftwood Inn

62 TN 171, Old Hickory Blvd, **N...gas:** Chevron, Citgo, Shell/diesel/24hr, TA/BP/Burger King/Popeye's/diesel/24hr/@, **food:** Waffle House, **lodging:** Best Western

60 Hickory Hollow Pkwy, **N...gas:** BP, Citgo/24hr, Express, Shell, **food:** Applebee's, Arby's, Bailey's Grill, Burger King, ChuckeCheese, Courtyard Café, Cracker Barrel, KFC, Logan's Roadhouse, McDonald's, O'Charley's, Outback Steaks, Pizza Hut, Red Lobster, Subway, TGIFriday, Wendy's, **lodging:** Day's Inn, Fairfield Inn, Hampton Inn, Holiday Inn, Ramada Inn, **other:** MEDICAL CARE, Best Buy, Chevrolet, Circuit City, Dillard's, Dodge, Eckerd, Firestone/auto, Kroger, Mazda, NTB, Office Depot, mall, transmissions, **S...gas:** BP/diesel, Shell, **food:** IHOP, Olive Garden, Shoney's, Steak'n Shake, Waffle House/24hr, **lodging:** Knight's Inn, Quality Inn, Quarters Inn, Super 8, **other:** Acura, Goodyear, Home Depot, Target

Interstate 24

E ↕ W

59 TN 254, Bell Rd, same as 60

57 Haywood Lane, **N...gas:** Marathon, **food:** Hardee's, Pizza Hut, **other:** $General, Food Lion, Walgreen, **S...gas:** Phillips 66/diesel/24hr

56 TN 255, Harding Place, **N...gas:** Chevron/diesel, Exxon, Shell/diesel/24hr, **food:** Applebee's, Arby's, KFC, McDonald's, Pizza Hut/Taco Bell, Subway, Waffle House, Wendy's, White Castle/Church's, **lodging:** Drury Inn, Executive Inn, Motel 6, PearTree Inn, Suburban Lodge, Super 8, **other:** Sam's Club/gas, **S...gas:** Express, Shell, **food:** Burger King, Hooters, Jack-in-the-Box, Waffle House, **lodging:** Economy Inn, Motel 6, **other:** HOSPITAL

Nashville

54b a TN 155, Briley Pkwy, **N...other:** to Opryland, Camping World RV Supplies, KOA

53 I-440 W, to Memphis

52 US 41, Murfreesboro Rd, **N...gas:** BP, Texaco, **food:** Bennigan's, Dunkin Donuts, Golden Corral, Krystal, Piccadilly's, Pizza Hut, Red Lobster, Taco Bell, Waffle House, **lodging:** Day's Inn, Econolodge, Holiday Inn Express, Howard Johnson, Quality Inn, Ramada Inn, Scottish Inn, **other:** CarQuest, Office Depot, bank, **S...food:** Jack-in-the-Box, **other:** Chevrolet, Dodge

52b a I-40, E to Knoxville, W to Memphis

I-24 and I-40 run together 2 mi. See Tennessee Interstate 40, exits 212-213.

50b I-40 W

48 James Robertson Pkwy, **N...gas:** Shell, **S...gas:** Exxon, TA/Subway/diesel/24hr/@, **food:** Shoney's, **lodging:** Ramada Ltd, Stadium Inn, **other:** st capitol

47a US 31E

47 N 1st St, Jefferson St, **N...gas:** Express/diesel, **S...lodging:** Day's Inn, Knight's Inn, **other:** U-Haul

I-24 and I-65 run together. See Tennessee Interstate 65, exit 87b a.

44b a I-65, N to Louisville, S to Nashville, no facilities

43 TN 155, Briley Pkwy, Brick Church Pike, **N...gas:** Citgo

40 TN 45, Old Hickory Blvd, **N...gas:** Citgo/Subway/diesel, Cone/diesel, Phillips 66/diesel/24hr, **lodging:** Super 8

35 US 431, to Joelton, Springfield, **S...gas:** Amoco/diesel/24hr, BP/diesel/24hr, **food:** McDonald's, Subway, **lodging:** Day's Inn, **other:** Family$, OK Camping

31 TN 249, New Hope Rd, **N...gas:** Shell, **S...gas:** Citgo/diesel/24hr, **food:** Buddy's ChopHouse, **other:** to Nashville Zoo

24 TN 49, to Springfield, Ashland City, **N...gas:** Amoco, Texaco, Williams/diesel/24hr, **other:** HOSPITAL, **S...gas:** Shell, **food:** Subway

19 TN 256, Maxey Rd, to Adams, **N...gas:** BP/diesel, Phillips 66/diesel/rest./24hr, **S...gas:** Shell/diesel/24hr

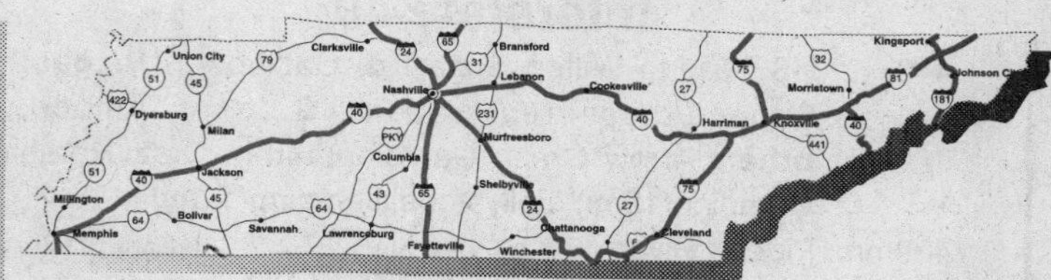

Clarksville

11 TN 76, to Adams, Clarksville, **N...gas:** Texaco/diesel/24hr, **S...gas:** Amoco/diesel/24hr, Citgo/Subway/24hr, **food:** Home Place Rest., McDonald's, Waffle House, **lodging:** Comfort Inn, Day's Inn, Holiday Inn Express, Super 8, **other:** HOSPITAL

9mm Red River

8 TN 237, Rossview Rd, no facilities

4 US 79, to Clarksville, Ft Campbell, **N...gas:** BP/diesel/24hr, **food:** Cracker Barrel, **other:** Spring Creek Camping(2mi), RV Ctr, **S...gas:** Amoco/diesel/24hr, Citgo/diesel, Exxon/Blimpie/diesel/24hr, Texaco/diesel, **food:** Applebee's, Arby's, Burger King, ChiChi's, Church's/White Castle, Cracker Barrel, KFC, Krystal, Logan's Roadhouse, LJ Silver, McDonald's, O'Charley's, Olive Garden, Outback Steaks, Ponderosa, Rafferty's, Red Lobster, Ruby Tuesday, Ryan's, Santa Fe Steaks, Steak'n Shake, Sub's Grill, Suzie's Drive-Thru, Taco Bell, Uncle Bud's Catfish, Waffle House, Wendy's, **lodging:** Best Western, Comfort Inn, Country Inn Suites, Day's Inn, Econolodge, Fairfield Inn, Hampton Inn, Holiday Inn, Microtel, Ramada Ltd, Red Roof Inn, Royal Inn, Shoney's Inn/rest., Super 8, Travelodge, Wingate Inn, **other:** Advance Parts, Goodyear/auto, K-Mart, Lowe's Whse, OfficeMax, Target, Wal-Mart SuperCtr/gas/24hr, mall, winery, to Austin Peay St U, to Land Between the Lakes

1 TN 48, to Clarksville, Trenton, **N...gas:** Shell/diesel, **other:** Clarksville Camping, antiques, **S...gas:** Amoco, Exxon

.5mm Welcome Ctr eb, full(handicapped)facilities, phones, vending, picnic tables, litter barrels, petwalk

0mm Tennessee/Kentucky state line

Interstate 40

E ↕ W

Exit # Services

451mm Tennessee/North Carolina state line

451 Waterville Rd, no facilities

447 Hartford Rd, **N...gas:** Citgo/diesel, **S...gas:** Exxon/towing, **food:** River Co Deli, **other:** Fox Fire Camping, whitewater rafting

446mm Welcome Ctr wb, full(handicapped)facilities, phones, vending, picnic tables, litter barrels, petwalk, NO TRUCKS

443 Foothills Pkwy, to Gatlinburg, Great Smokey Mtns NP, **S...camping**

443mm Pigeon River

TENNESSEE

Interstate 40

E ↕ W — Newport

440 US 321, to Wilton Spgs Rd, Gatlinburg, **N...gas:** Sunoco/diesel/rest./repair, **S...gas:** Amoco, **other:** Arrow Creek Camping(14mi), CrazyHorse Camping(12mi), Jellystone Camping(12mi)

439mm Pigeon River

435 US 321, Newport, to Gatlinburg, **N...gas:** Exxon/diesel/24hr, Marathon/24hr, Shell, **food:** Arby's, Burger King, Capt D's, Hardee's, KFC, La Carreta Mexican, McDonald's, Pizza Hut, Pizza+, SageBrush Steaks, Shoney's, Subway, Taco Bell, **lodging:** Bryant Town Motel, Motel 6/RV park, **other:** HOSPITAL, Goodyear/auto, **S...gas:** Amoco, BP/TCBY, **food:** Cracker Barrel, Ryan's, Shiner's BBQ, Waffle House/24hr, Wendy's, **lodging:** Best Western, Family Inn, Holiday Inn, **other:** CVS Drug, Sav-A-Lot, Wal-Mart SuperCtr/gas/24hr

432b a US 70, US 411, US 25W, to Newport, **N...gas:** BP/diesel, Exxon/diesel/24hr, TimeOut Travel Ctr/diesel, Krystal, **food:** Lois' Country Kitchen, Rodeo Rest., Sonic, **lodging:** Budget Motel, Comfort Inn, Relax Inn, **other:** Chevrolet/Pontiac/Buick, Chrysler/Jeep/Dodge, Ford/Mercury, KOA, TMC Camping, **S...gas:** BP, Citgo/24hr, Shell/diesel, **lodging:** Family Inn/rest.

426mm rest area wb, full(handicapped)facilities, phone, vending, picnic tables, litter barrels, petwalk

425mm French Broad River

424 TN 113, Dandridge, **N...gas:** Marathon/diesel

421 I-81 N, to Bristol, no facilities

420mm rest area eb, full(handicapped)facilities, phone, vending, picnic tables, litter barrels, petwalk

417 TN 92, Dandridge, **N...gas:** Marathon, Pilot/Subway/diesel/@, **food:** Hardee's, McDonald's, Perkins, **lodging:** Tennessee Mtn Inn, **S...gas:** Shell/Wendy's/diesel, Texaco/KFC/diesel, **food:** Shoney's, Waffle House, **lodging:** Comfort Inn, Holiday Inn Express, Super 8

415 US 25W, US 70, to Dandridge, **S...gas:** Shell/diesel

412 Deep Sprgs Rd, to Douglas Dam, **N...gas:** Sunshine/diesel/@, **food:** Apple Valley Café, **S...gas:** Chevron/diesel

407 TN 66, to Sevierville, Pigeon Forge, Gatlinburg, **N...gas:** Citgo/Huddle House/diesel, **food:** McDonald's, **lodging:** Motel 6, KOA, **S...gas:** Amoco, **food:** BP/DQ/Pizza Inn, Exxon/diesel, Shell/Krystal/diesel, Shell/Subway/diesel, Ole Southern Rest., Wendy's, **lodging:** Best Western, Comfort Inn, Day's Inn, Holiday Inn Express, Quality Inn, Ramada Ltd, **other:** Chrysler/Jeep/Dodge, Foretravel RV Ctr, Honda, RV camping, flea mkt, **3-10 mi S...gas:** Citgo, **lodging:** Clarion Inn, Ramada Ltd, Wingate Inn, **other:** Lee Greenwood Theatre, USPO, multiple services/outlets

Knoxville

402 Midway Rd, no facilities

398 Strawberry Plains Pk, **N...gas:** Amoco/diesel, BP/diesel, Exxon/Pizza Hut/diesel, **food:** McDonald's, Ruby Tuesday, Waffle House, Wendy's, **lodging:** Comfort Inn, Country Inn Suites, Hampton Inn, Holiday Inn Express, Ramada Ltd, Super 8, **S...gas:** Pilot/DQ/Subway/diesel/24hr/@, Pilot/diesel/24hr/@, **food:** Weigel's, Arby's, Burger King, Cracker Barrel, KFC, Krystal, Puleo's Grill, Taco Bell, **lodging:** Baymont Inn, Fairfield Inn

395mm Holston River

394 US 70, US 11E, US 25W, Asheville Hwy, **N...gas:** BP, Mobil/diesel, **lodging:** Sunbeam Motel(2mi), **other:** $General, city park, **1 mi N...gas:** RaceTrac, **food:** Subway, Wendy's, **lodging:** Gateway Inn, **other:** Advance Parts, Food Lion, flea mkt, **S...gas:** Exxon, Shell/diesel, **food:** Waffle House/24hr, **lodging:** Day's Inn, **1 mi S...food:** China City, **lodging:** Family Inn/rest., **other:** CVS Drug, Kroger/gas, **other:** Walgreen

393 I-640 W, to I-75 N, no facilities

392 US 11 W, Rutledge Pike, **N...gas:** Shell/diesel, **food:** CookHouse Rest., **other:** $General, U-Haul, repair, **S...gas:** BP, **food:** BBQ, Hardee's, Shoney's, **lodging:** Family Inn, **other:** AutoValue Parts, transmissions, to Knoxville Zoo

390 Cherry St, Knoxville, **N...gas:** Pilot/diesel, Shell/diesel, **food:** Weigel's, Country Table Rest., Hardee's, **lodging:** Red Carpet Inn, **other:** Goodyear, **1 mi S...gas:** Amoco, Exxon, **food:** Arby's, KFC, Krystal, LJ Silver, Mrs Winner's, Subway, Wendy's, **lodging:** Budget Motel, Regency Inn, **other:** Advance Parts, AutoZone, Walgreen

389 US 441 N, Broadway, 5th Ave, **1/2 mi N...gas:** BP, Conoco, Star, **food:** Burger King, Capt D's, KFC, Krystal, Steak-Out, Subway, Taco Bell, Wendy's, **other:** CVS Drug, $General, Family$, Firestone, Kroger/deli/24hr, Radio Shack, Tires+, USPO, Walgreen/24hr, transmissions

388 US 441 S(exits left from wb), downtown, **S...gas:** BP, **lodging:** Radisson, **other:** to Smokey Mtns, to U of TN

387b TN 62, 17th St, **N...gas:** Pilot, **lodging:** Best Inn, **1/2 mi S...lodging:** Hilton, Holiday Inn, **other:** Goodyear

a I-275 N, to Lexington

386b a US 129, University Ave, to UT, airport

385 I-75 N, I-640 E, no facilities

I-40 W and I-75 S run together 17 mi

383 Papermill Rd, **N...lodging:** Holiday Inn/rest., **S...gas:** Amoco, BP, Citgo, Pilot/diesel, Spur Gas, **food:** Applebee's(1mi), Burger King, China Buffet, Darryl's, Dunkin Donuts, IHOP, Longhorn Steaks, McDonald's, Morrison's Cafeteria, Pizza Hut, Red Lobster, Regas Café, Ruby Tuesday, Showbiz Pizza, Taco Bell, Taco Rancho Mexican, Waffle House, Wendy's, Western Sizzlin, **lodging:** Econolodge, Howard Johnson, Super 8, **other:** Buick/GMC, Firestone, same as 380

Interstate 40

E ↕ W

Knoxville

380 US 11, US 70, West Hills, **S...gas:** BP, Citgo, Conoco, Pilot, Texaco/diesel, **food:** Arby's, Applebee's, Backyard Burger, Blackeyed Pea, Cancun Mexican, Checker's, Chick-fil-A, Chili's, Cozymel's Grill, Honeybaked Ham, KFC, Macaroni Grill, Michael's Prime Rib, Mr Gatti's, O'Charley's, Olive Garden, Papa John's, PlumTree Chinese, Schlotsky's, Subway, Taco Bell, Texas Roadhouse, **lodging:** Comfort Hotel, Howard Johnson, Quality Inn, **other:** BiLo Foods, Borders Books, Dillard's, $General, Food Lion, Goody's, JC Penney, K-Mart, Kohl's, Office Depot, Old Navy, Staples, U-Haul, Walgreen, mall, st patrol, **1 mi S on Kingston Pike...gas:** Citgo/7-11, **food:** Morrison's Cafeteria, Central Park, Little Caesar's, **lodging:** Family Inn, **other:** Office Depot, Radio Shack

379 Bridgewater Rd, **N...gas:** Exxon/Subway, Pilot/diesel, **food:** McDonald's, Pizza Hut/Taco Bell, **lodging:** Red Carpet Inn, **other:** Sam's Club, Wal-Mart SuperCtr/24hr, **S...gas:** BP/diesel, Pilot/diesel, Texaco/diesel, **food:** Burger King, ChuckeCheese, Don Pablo, Logan's Roadhouse, Mrs Winners, Old Country Buffet, Omelet House, Ryan's, Shoney's, Tony Roma, Wendy's, **lodging:** Family Inn, Holiday Inn, Scottish Inn, **other:** AutoZone, BooksAMillion, Buy4Less Foods, Cadillac, Firestone/auto, Ford, Dodge, GMC, Goodyear, Isuzu, Mitsubishi, Nissan, SuperX Drug

378 Cedar Bluff Rd, **N...gas:** Amoco/24hr, Pilot/Taco Bell, Texaco, **food:** Arby's, Burger King, Cracker Barrel, KFC, LJ Silver, McDonald's, Papa John's, Pizza Hut, Subway, Waffle House, Wendy's, **lodging:** Budget Inn, Hampton Inn, Holiday Inn, Ramada Inn, Sleep Inn, **other:** HOSPITAL, Food Lion, Walgreen, **S...food:** Applebee's, Bob Evans, Carrabba's, Corky's Ribs/BBQ, Denny's, Fazoli's, Friendly's, Grady's Grill, Hops Grill, IHOP, Outback Steaks, **lodging:** Clubhouse Inn, Courtyard, Extended Stay America, Guesthouse Suites, La Quinta, Luxbury Best Western, Microtel, Red Roof Inn, Residence Inn, Signature Inn, **other:** Best Buy, Celebration Sta, Chevrolet, Chrysler, Circuit City, Ford, Jo-Ann Fabrics, Kia, Lowe's Whse, Michael's, Staples, Walgreen

376 I-140 E, TN 162 N, to Maryville, **N...**to Oak Ridge Museum

374 TN 131, Lovell Rd, **N...gas:** Amoco, BP, Texaco/diesel, TA/diesel/rest./24hr/@, **food:** McDonald's, Taco Bell, Waffle House, **lodging:** Best Western, Knight's Inn, La Quinta, Travelodge, **other:** Passport RV Ctr, **S...gas:** Citgo, Pilot/Wendy's/diesel/24hr/@, Speedway, **food:** Arby's, Chili's, Krystal, McDonald's, Shoney's, **lodging:** Candlewood Suites, Day's Inn/rest., Motel 6, **other:** CarMax, Goody's, Honda, Land Rover, Lexus, Mercedes, OfficeMax, Target, Toyota, Wal-Mart SuperCtr/24hr

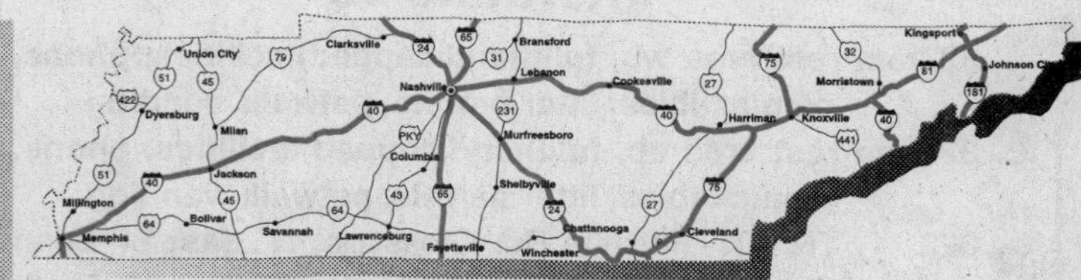

373 Campbell Sta Rd, **N...gas:** Amoco, Shell/diesel, **lodging:** Comfort Suites, Ramada Ltd, Super 8, **other:** Buddy Gregg RV Ctr, **S...gas:** BP, Conoco/diesel, Pilot/diesel, **food:** Cracker Barrel, Wendy's, **lodging:** Baymont Inn, Holiday Inn Express

372mm weigh sta both lanes

369 Watt Rd, **N...gas:** Flying J/Conoco/diesel/LP/24hr/@, Speedco, **S...gas:** Exxon, Petro/Mobil/diesel/24hr/@, TA/BP/Burger King/Perkins/Pizza Hut/diesel/24hr/@, **other:** Blue Beacon

I-40 E and I-75 N run together 17 mi

368 I-75 and I-40, no facilities

364 US 321, TN 95, Lenoir City, Oak Ridge, **N...gas:** Shell, **other:** Crosseyed Cricket Camping(2mi), **S...food:** Ruby Tuesday(4mi)

363mm parking area wb, phone, litter barrel

362mm parking area eb, phone, litter barrel

360 Buttermilk Rd, **N...**Soaring Eagle RV Park

356 TN 58 N, Gallaher Rd, to Oak Ridge, **N...gas:** BP/diesel, **food:** Huddle House, Simply Subs, **lodging:** Day's Inn, Family Inn/rest., Kings Inn, **other:** 4 Seasons Camping, **S...gas:** Citgo/diesel

355 Lawnville Rd, **N...gas:** Pilot/diesel

352 TN 58 S, Kingston, **N...lodging:** Knight's Inn, **other:** NAPA, **S...gas:** Exxon/diesel, RaceWay, Shell, **food:** DQ, Hardee's, McDonald's, Pizza Hut, Sonic, Subway, Taco Bell, **lodging:** Comfort Inn, **other:** Marina RV Park, to Watts Bar Lake

351mm Clinch River

350 US 70, Midtown, **S...other:** Lowe's Whse, Patterson RV Supplies

Harriman

347 US 27, Harriman, **N...gas:** Phillips 66/Subway/diesel, **food:** Cancun Mexican, Hardee's, KFC, LJ Silver, McDonald's, Pizza Hut, Ruby Tuesday, Taco Bell, Wendy's, **lodging:** Best Western, to Frozen Head SP, Big S Fork NRA, **S...gas:** BP, Exxon, Shell/Krystal/diesel/24hr, **food:** Cracker Barrel, Reno's Grill, Shoney's, **lodging:** Holiday Inn Express, Super 8, **2-3 mi S...food:** Capt D's, Domino's, Subway, **other:** HOSPITAL, Advance Parts, Goody's, Kroger, Radio Shack, Wal-Mart SuperCtr/gas/24hr

340 TN 299 N, Airport Rd, no facilities

339.5mm eastern/central time zone line

338 TN 299 S, Westel Rd, **N...gas:** BP/diesel, **S...gas:** Shell/diesel, E-WTrkstp/diesel/rest./24hr/@, **other:** Top Mtn Camping

336mm parking area/weigh sta eb, litter barrel

329 US 70, Crab Orchard, **N...gas:** BP/diesel, Exxon/mechanic, **other:** Lakes Camping

TENNESSEE

Interstate 40

E ↕ W

Crossville

327mm rest area wb, full(handicapped)facilities, phone, picnic tables, litter barrels, petwalk, vending

324mm rest area eb, full(handicapped)facilities, phone, picnic tables, litter barrels, petwalk, vending

322 TN 101, Peavine Rd, Crossville, **N...gas:** BP/Bean Pot Rest., Exxon/Taco Bell/diesel, Phillips 66, **food:** Hardee's, McDonald's, **lodging:** Holiday Inn Express, **other:** Roam+Roost RV Campground, to Fairfield Glade Resort, **S...lodging:** Comfort Inn, Super 8, **other:** HOSPITAL, Chesnut Hill Winery/rest., Cumberland Mtn SP

320 TN 298, Crossville, **N...**antiques, golf, winery, **S...gas:** BP/DQ/Pizza Hut/diesel, Shell/24hr, **food:** Catfish Cove Rest., Krystal(2mi), Wendy's(2mi), **other:** HOSPITAL, Factory Outlet/famous brands, antiques, auto repair

318mm Obed River

317 US 127, Crossville, **N...gas:** BP/diesel, Citgo/diesel, Exxon/Subway/diesel/24hr, Shell/Blimpie/diesel, **lodging:** Best Western, La Quinta, Ramada Inn, **1-2 mi S...gas:** Citgo, Phillips 66/diesel, Sunoco, **food:** Cracker Barrel, Ponderosa, Ruby Tuesday, Ryan's, Schlotsky's, Shoney's, Taco Bell, Waffle House, Wendy's, **lodging:** Days Inn, Heritage Inn, Scottish Inn, Villager Lodge, **other:** HOSPITAL, Chevrolet/Cadillac, Chrysler/Plymouth/Dodge/Jeep, $Tree, GNC, Goodyear, Lowe's Whse, Staples, Wal-Mart SuperCtr/gas/24hr, to Cumberland SP

311 Plateau Rd, **N...gas:** Citgo/diesel, **S...gas:** BP/diesel, Exxon

306mm parking area/weigh sta wb, litter barrels

301 US 70 N, TN 84, Monterey, **N...gas:** Phillips 66, Shell, **food:** Burger King, DQ, Subway

300 US 70, Monterey, **N...gas:** Citgo/diesel, **food:** Hardee's

291mm Falling Water River

Cookeville

290 US 70, Cookeville, **N...gas:** BP, **S...gas:** Citgo, **lodging:** Alpine Inn

288 TN 111, Cookeville, to Livingston, Sparta, **S...gas:** Citgo, Mid Tenn Trkstp/diesel/@, Phillips 66/Subway/diesel, **food:** Huddle House, **lodging:** Knight's Inn

287 TN 136, Cookeville, **N...gas:** BP/TCBY, Chevron/diesel, Citgo, Shell/diesel, **food:** Applebee's, Arby's, Burger King, Capt D's, Chili's, China Star, Cracker Barrel, DQ, Fazoli's, Golden Corral, Huddle House, IHOP, Jack-in-the-Box, King Buffet, Krystal, Logan's Roadhouse, LJ Silver, McDonald's, Mr Gatti's, O'Charley's, Outback Steaks, Pizza Hut, Ponderosa, Quizno's, Rafferty's, Red Lobster, Ryan's, Schlotsky's, Shoney's, Sonic, Steak'n Shake, Subway, Taco Bell, Waffle House, Wendy's, **lodging:** Best Western, Comfort Suites, Day's Inn, Executive Inn, Hampton Inn, Holiday Inn/rest., Ramada Ltd, Super 8, **other:** Auto Value Parts, Cadillac/Honda, CVS Drug, $Tree, Firestone, Goody's, Harley-Davidson, JC Penney, K-Mart, Kroger, Lowe's Whse, OfficeMax, Radio Shack, Tires+, Toyota, Wal-Mart SuperCtr/24hr, mall, st patrol, transmissions, **S...gas:** Exxon/diesel, Pilot/Blimpie/diesel, **food:** Gondola Pizza, KFC, Waffle House, **lodging:** Baymont Inn, Country Inn Suites, Econolodge, **other:** Dodge

286 TN 135, Burgess Falls Rd, **N...gas:** BP, Exxon, RaceWay/diesel, Shell/diesel, **food:** Applebee's, Arby's, Hardee's, Steak'n Shake, Thai Cuisine, Waffle House, **lodging:** KeyWest Inn, **other:** HOSPITAL, Chrysler/Plymouth/Jeep, Goodyear, Kia/Mitsubishi, Mazda, Nissan, Toyota, U-Haul, to TTU, **S...gas:** Amoco/diesel, Citgo/diesel, **lodging:** Star Motor Inn/rest.

280 TN 56 N, Baxter, **N...gas:** Shell/diesel, **other:** Camp Discovery

276 Old Baxter Rd, **S...gas:** Citgo/diesel, **other:** fireworks

273 TN 56 S, to Smithville, **S...gas:** BP/diesel, Phillips 66, **food:** Rose Garden Rest., **lodging:** Timber Ridge Inn

268 TN 96, Buffalo Valley Rd, **S...**to Edgar Evins SP

267mm Caney Fork River

267mm rest area both lanes, full(handicapped)facilities, info, phone, picnic tables, litter barrels, petwalk, vending

266mm Caney Fork River

263mm Caney Fork River

258 TN 53, Gordonsville, **N...gas:** BP, Exxon/KFC/Taco Bell, Shell, **food:** Connie's BBQ, McDonald's, Timberloft Café, Waffle House, **lodging:** Comfort Inn, **other:** to Cordell Hull Dam, **S...gas:** Citgo/diesel, KeyStop/diesel, **lodging:** Courtyard Country Buffet

254 TN 141, to Alexandria, no facilities

252mm parking area/weigh sta both lanes, picnic tables, litter barrels

Lebanon

245 Linwood Rd, **N...gas:** BP/diesel

239 US 70, Lebanon, **N...gas:** BP, RaceWay, **S...gas:** Phillips 66/diesel/rest/@

238 US 231, Lebanon, **N...gas:** BP, Express, Exxon, Shell, **food:** Applebee's, Arby's, BBQ, Cracker Barrel, Demo's Steaks, Gondola Rest., Hardee's, Jack-in-the-Box, McDonald's, Mrs Winner's, Pizza Hut, Ponderosa, Ryan's, Shoney's, Subway, Taco Bell, Waffle House, Wendy's, **lodging:** Best Western, Comfort Inn, Economy Inn, Guesthouse Inn, Hampton Inn, Holiday Inn Express, **other:** HOSPITAL, OfficeMax, Wal-Mart SuperCtr/24hr, **S...gas:** Cone/diesel, Pilot/Subway/diesel/24hr/@, **food:** O'Charley's, Santa Fe Steaks, Sonic, **lodging:** Comfort Suites, Country Inn Suites, Day's Inn, Knight's Inn, Super 8, **other:** Prime Outlets/famous brands, flea mkt, to Cedars of Lebanon SP, RV camping

236 S Hartmann Dr, **N...food:** Jack-in-the-Box(2mi)

235 TN 840 W, to Murfreesboro, no facilities

Interstate 40

E ↕ W

Nashville

232 TN 109, to Gallatin, **N...gas:** Citgo, Express, Shell/diesel/24hr, **food:** Brewster's Grille, McDonald's, Sonic, Subway, Waffle House, Wendy's, **lodging:** Sleep Inn, **2 mi S...other:** Countryside Resort Camping

226 TN 171, Mt Juliet Rd, **N...gas:** BP/McDonald's/diesel, Express/diesel, Exxon/diesel, Shell/diesel/24hr, **food:** Arby's, Capt D's, **S...gas:** Express/diesel, **food:** Cracker Barrel, Ruby Tuesday, Waffle House, **lodging:** Microtel, **other:** to Long Hunter SP

221 TN 45 N, Old Hickory Blvd, to The Hermitage, **N...gas:** BP, Exxon, Express/diesel, RaceWay, Shell/24hr, **food:** Applebee's, DQ, Hardee's, IHOP, Jack-in-the-Box, Music City Café, O'Charley's, Waffle House, **lodging:** Best Inn, Comfort Inn, Holiday Inn Express, Suburban Lodge, **other:** HOSPITAL, CVS Drug, Kroger, Walgreen, **S...gas:** Phillips 66/White Castle, Shell/McDonald's

219 Stewart's Ferry Pike, **N...gas:** Express, **S...gas:** Express/Subway, Shell/diesel, **food:** Cracker Barrel, Uncle Bud's Catfish, Sal's Pizza, Waffle House, **lodging:** Best Value Inn, Best Western, Country Inn Suites, Day's Inn, Family Inn, Sleep Inn, **other:** $General

216 (216 c from eb)TN 255, Donaldson Pk, **N...gas:** BP/diesel, Citgo, Express, RaceWay, Shell/Subway/diesel/24hr, **food:** Arby's, Backyard Burger, BBQ, Burger King, Domino's, Jalisco's Cantina, KFC, Little Caesar's, McDonald's, New China, Papa John's, Pizza Hut/Taco Bell, Ruby Tuesday, Shoney's, Subway, Waffle House, Wendy's, **lodging:** Baymont Inn, Country Inn Suites, Drury Inn, Hampton Inn, Holiday Inn Express, Howard Johnson, Red Roof, Springhill Suites, Super 8, Wingate Inn, Wyndham Hotel, **other:** Advance Parts, K-Mart, Walgreen

b a (from eb), **S...**Nashville Intn'l Airport

215b a TN 155, Briley Pkwy, to Opryland, **N...gas:** Shell, **food:** Denny's, Day's Inn, **lodging:** Econolodge, Embassy Suites, Holiday Inn, La Quinta, Marriott, Park Suite Hotel, Quality Inn, Rodeway Inn, Sheraton, **other:** bank, **2 mi N on Lebanon Pike...other:** to Camping World RV Service, KOA, Capt D's, Waffle House, Hampton Inn, **S...gas:** Shell, **lodging:** Clarion, Radisson, Royal Inn, Villager Lodge

213b I-24 W

a I-24 E/I-440, E to Chattanooga

213 US 41(from wb), to Spence Lane, **N...gas:** Shell/diesel, **S...food:** Denny's, McDonald's, Red Lobster, Shoney's, Waffle House, Western Sizzlin, **lodging:** Day's Inn, Econolodge, Holiday Inn Express, Ramada Inn, Scottish Inn, Tudor Inn, same as 212

212 Fessler's Lane(from eb, no return), **N...**Harley-Davidson, **S...gas:** Shell/diesel, **food:** Burger King, Krystal, McDonald's, Mrs Winners, Sonic, Wendy's, same as 213

211mm Cumberland River

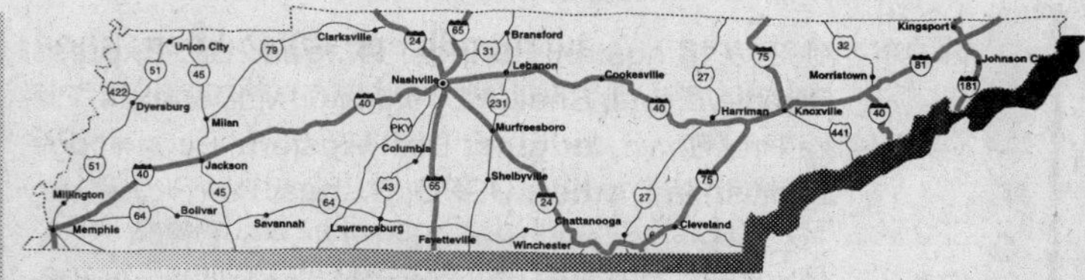

Nashville

211b I-24 W, no facilities

a I-24E, I-40 W

210c US 31 S, US 41A, 2nd Ave, 4th Ave, **N...lodging:** Stouffer Hotel, **S...**museum

210b a I-65 S, to Birmingham

209b a US 70, Charlotte Ave, Nashville, **N...lodging:** Holiday Inn, **other:** Chevrolet, Lincoln/Mercury, Nissan, Pontiac/GMC, Suzuki, Toyota, Country Music Hall of Fame, Conv Ctr, transmissions, **S...gas:** BP/diesel, Exxon, **food:** Burger King, Subway, White Castle, **lodging:** Guesthouse Inn, Chrysler/Plymouth

208b a I-65, N to Louisville, S to Birmingham

207 28th Ave, Jefferson St, Nashville, TN St U, **N...gas:** Citgo, Phillips 66, **food:** Subway, Wendy's, **S...**HOSPITAL

206 I-440 E, to Knoxville, no facilities

205 46th Ave, W Nashville, **N...**Harley-Davidson, **S...gas:** Express, Shell, **food:** McDonald's, Mrs Winner's

204 TN 155, Briley Pkwy, **N...gas:** Exxon, Shell/diesel, **S...food:** Burger King, Church's/White Castle, Domino's, Jack-in-the-Box, KFC, Krystal, New China, Uncle Bud's Catfish, Waffle House, Wendy's, **lodging:** Baymont Inn, Best Western, Comfort Inn, **other:** AutoZone, CVS Drug, Ford, Goodyear/auto, Kroger, NTB, PepBoys, Walgreen

201b a US 70, Charlotte Pike, **N...gas:** Exxon, Shell/diesel/24hr, **food:** Cracker Barrel, Subway, Super China, Waffle House, **lodging:** Super 8, **other:** $Tree, GNC, Lowe's Whse, Radio Shack, Wal-Mart SuperCtr/24hr, **S...lodging:** Howard Johnson/rest.

199 rd 251, Old Hickory Blvd, **S...gas:** BP, Express/Subway, **food:** Waffle House, **other:** Sam's Club

196 US 70, Newsom Sta, to Bellevue, **N...gas:** Express, **food:** Shoney's, **S...gas:** BP, Express/diesel, Shell/diesel/24hr, **food:** Applebee's, Jack-in-the-Box, O'Charley's, Pizza Hut, Princeton's Grille, Ruby Tuesday, Sam's Grill, Sir Pizza, Sonic, Subway, Taco Bell, Waffle House, Wendy's, **lodging:** Hampton Inn, Microtel, **other:** MEDICAL CARE, Circuit City, Dillard's, $Tree, Firestone/auto, Home Depot, Michael's, Old Navy, Piggly Wiggly, Staples, USPO, Walgreen/24hr, mall

195mm Harpeth River

192 McCrory Lane, to Pegram, **S...**Natchez Trace Pkwy

190mm Harpeth River

188mm Harpeth River

TENNESSEE

Interstate 40

E ↕ W

Dickson

188 rd 249, Kingston Springs, **N...gas:** BP, Express/Blimpie/diesel, Shell/Arby's, **food:** McDonald's, Pizza Pro, Sonic, **lodging:** Best Western, Econolodge, Scottish Inn, **other:** USPO, **S...gas:** Petro/Chevron/Pizza Hut/diesel/showers/24hr/@

182 TN 96, to Dickson, Fairview, **N...gas:** Citgo/diesel, **lodging:** Deerfield Inn, Fairview Inn, **other:** M Bell SP(16mi), **S...gas:** BP/diesel, Flying J/Conoco/Country Mkt/diesel/LP/24hr/@

175 TN 840, no facilities

172 TN 46, to Dickson, **N...gas:** BP/diesel/24hr, Pilot/Wendy's/diesel/24hr/@, Shell, **food:** Arby's, Burger King, Cracker Barrel, McDonald's, Ruby Tuesday, Subway, Waffle House/24hr, Wang's China, **lodging:** Baymont Inn, Comfort Inn, Econolodge, Hampton Inn, Knight's Inn, Motel 6, Ramada Ltd, Super 8, **other:** HOSPITAL, Chevrolet, KOA, to M Bell SP, **S...gas:** Phillips 66, Shell, O'Charley's, **lodging:** Day's Inn, Holiday Inn

170mm rest area both lanes, full(handicapped)facilities, phone, picnic tables, litter barrels, vending, petwalk

166mm Piney River

163 rd 48, to Dickson, **N...gas:** Phillips 66/Reed's/diesel, **S...gas:** Shell, **other:** Tanbark Camping

152 rd 230, Bucksnort, **N...gas:** BP, **food:** Rudy's Rest., **lodging:** Bucksnort Motel, Travel Inn

149mm Duck River

148 rd 50, Barren Hollow Rd, to Turney Center, **S...gas:** Shell

143 TN 13, to Linden, Waverly, **N...gas:** Phillips 66/diesel, Pilot/Arby's/diesel/24hr/@, Pilot/Subway/diesel/24hr/@, Shell, **food:** Las Fuentes Mexican, Loretta's Kitchen, McDonald's, **lodging:** Best Western, Day's Inn, Holiday Inn Express, Super 8, **other:** KOA, **S...gas:** Exxon/diesel, Shell, **lodging:** Southside Motel/rest.

141mm Buffalo River

137 Cuba Landing, **S...**gas

133mm Tennessee River

133 rd 191, Birdsong Rd, **N...lodging:** Birdsong RV Resort/marina(9mi)

131mm rest area both lanes, full(handicapped)facilities, phone, vending, picnic tables, litter barrels, petwalk

126 US 641, TN 69, to Camden, **N...gas:** Exxon/Subway/TCBY/diesel, Phillips 66/North 40/diesel/rest./@, SugarTree Trkstp/diesel/@, Shell, **other:** tire/truck repair, to NB Forrest SP, **S...gas:** BP/diesel, Citgo/DQ/Stuckey's, Shell/diesel, **lodging:** Day's Inn/rest., **other:** HOSPITAL

116 rd 114, **S...other:** to Natchez Trace SP, RV camping

110mm Big Sandy River

Jackson

108 TN 22, Parkers Crossroads, to Lexington, **N...gas:** BP/McDonald's/24hr, Citgo/diesel/24hr, Phillips 66/diesel, **food:** Bailey's Rest., Dairy Queen, Subwat/TCBY, **lodging:** Knight's Inn, **other:** USPO, city park, **S...gas:** Coastal, Exxon, **food:** Cotton Patch Rest., **lodging:** Best Western, **other:** HOSPITAL, RV camping, to Shiloh Nat Bfd(51mi)

103mm parking area/weigh sta eb, litter barrels, phone

102mm parking area/weigh sta wb, litter barrels

101 rd 104, **N...gas:** Exxon, **other:** golf(3mi)

93 rd 152, Law Rd, **N...gas:** Phillips 66/diesel/deli/24hr, **S...gas:** Shell/diesel

87 US 70, US 412, Jackson, **N...gas:** Coastal/diesel, **S...gas:** Love's/Hardee's/diesel/24hr/@, Shell/diesel

85 Christmasville Rd, to Jackson, **N...gas:** Amoco/Subway/diesel, Exxon/diesel/24hr, **lodging:** Howard Johnson Express, **other:** $General, **S...gas:** Shell(1mi)

83 new exit

82b a US 45, Jackson, **N...gas:** Shell, **food:** Cracker Barrel, **lodging:** Knight's Inn, Microtel, **other:** Batteries+, **S...gas:** BP, Citgo, RaceWay, **food:** Backyard Burger, Barley's Brewhouse, Burger King, Capt D's, China Palace, DQ, Folks Rest., KFC, Krystal, LJ Silver, McDonald's, Pizza Hut, Pizza Inn, Popeye's, Shoney's, Sonic, Subway, Suede's Rest., Taco Bell, Waffle House, Wendy's, **lodging:** Baymont Inn, Executive Inn, Ramada Ltd, Sheraton/rest., Super 8, **other:** Advance Parts, AutoZone, Belk, CarQuest, Firestone/auto, Goodyear/auto, JC Penney, Kroger/24hr, Office Depot, Radio Shack, Sears/auto, WaldenBooks, mall

80b a US 45 Byp, Jackson, **N...gas:** BP/diesel, Exxon, **food:** Backyard Burger, Buffalo Wings, Chili's, Chick-fil-A, Corky's BBQ, Domino's, Fazoli's, 5&Diner, IHOP, Jason's Deli, KFC, Lenny's Subs, LoneStar Steaks, Longhorn Steaks, Peking Chinese, Perkins, Schlotsky's, Starbucks, Steak'n Shake, Wendy's, **lodging:** AmeriHost, Comfort Inn, Country Inn Suites, Jameson Inn, Red Roof Inn, **other:** Circuit City, Home Depot, Lowe's Whse, Nissan, Sam's Club/gas, Saturn, Wal-Mart SuperCtr/24hr, **S...gas:** BP, Citgo, Coastal/diesel, Phillips 66/diesel, 76, **food:** Applebee's, Arby's, Barnhill's Buffet, Burger King, Dunkin Donuts, El Chico's, Logan's Roadhouse, Madison's Rest., McDonald's, Mrs Winner's, O'Charley's, Pizza Hut, Sakura Japanese, Shakey's Custard, Sonic, Subway, Village Pizza, Waffle House, **lodging:** Best Western, Comfort Inn, Day's Inn, Econolodge, Fairfield Inn, Hampton Inn, Holiday Inn, Old Hickory Inn, **other:** HOSPITAL, Cadillac/Pontiac/Buick/Toyota, $General, Hancock Fabrics, Harley-Davidson, King Tires, K-Mart, to Pinson Mounds SP, Chickasaw SP

79 US 412, Jackson, **S...gas:** BP/repair, Citgo/diesel, Exxon, **lodging:** Day's Inn, **other:** Jackson RV Park

78mm Forked Deer River

76 rd 223 S, **S...other:** McKellar-Sites Airport, Whispering Pines RV Park

Interstate 40

74 Lower Brownsville Rd, no facilities

73mm rest area both lanes, full(handicapped)facilities, info, phone, picnic tables, litter barrels, vending, petwalk

68 rd 138, Providence Rd, **N...gas:** Amoco/diesel, **lodging:** Scottish Inn, **S...gas:** Pure, TA/Citgo/diesel/rest./24hr/@, **other:** Joy-O RV Park, truck repair

66 US 70, to Brownsville, **S...gas:** FuelMart/Blimpie/diesel/24hr, **lodging:** Motel 6

60 rd 19, Mercer Rd, no facilities

56 TN 76, to Brownsville, **N...gas:** Amoco, Citgo/Subway/diesel/24hr, **food:** Dairy Queen, KFC, McDonald's, Pizza Hut/Taco Bell, **lodging:** Best Western, Comfort Inn, Day's Inn, Holiday Inn Express, **S...gas:** BP/diesel, Exxon/Huddle House/diesel/24hr

55mm Hatchie River

52 TN 76, rd 179, Koko Rd, to Whiteville, no facilities

50mm weigh sta both lanes, phone

47 TN 179, to Stanton, Dancyville, **S...gas:** Exit 47 Trkstp/diesel/rest./24hr/@

42 TN 222, to Stanton, **N...lodging:** Countryside Inn, **S...gas:** Exxon/diesel, Shell/Baker's Diiner/diesel/@, **lodging:** Deerfield Inn

35 TN 59, to Somerville, **S...gas:** BP/diesel, **food:** Longtown Rest.

29.5mm Loosahatchie River

25 TN 205, Airline Rd, to Arlington, **N...gas:** Chevron/diesel, Exxon/Subway/diesel, **other:** vistor ctr

24 TN 385, rd 204, to Arlington, Millington, Collierville

Memphis

20 Canada Rd, Lakeland, **N...gas:** 76/diesel/24hr, Shell/McDonald's, **food:** Waffle House, **lodging:** Day's Inn/rest., Relax Inn, Super 8, **S...gas:** Exxon/Subway/TCBY/diesel, **other:** Factory Outlet/famous brands, **other:** KOA

18 US 64, to Bartlett, **N...gas:** Shell, **food:** Bob Evans, Buffalo Wings, Don Pablo, Hooters, Luby's, Memphis Pizza, Olive Garden, Schlotsky's, Steak'n Shake, Waffle House, **lodging:** Country Inn Suites, Holiday Inn Express, SpringHill Suites, **other:** Firestone, Goodyear/auto, Lowe's Whse, Pontiac/GMC, Sam's Club/gas, Wal-Mart SuperCtr/24hr, same as 16, **S...gas:** BP, Citgo/diesel, 76/Circle K, **food:** Backyard Burger, KFC, **other:** Kroger, Walgreen

16b a TN 177, to Germantown, **N...gas:** 76, Shell, **food:** Alexander's Rest., Bahama Breeze, Burger King, Chili's, Chick-fil-A, IHOP, Joe's Crabshack, Logan's Roadhouse, Macaroni Grill, McDonald's, On-the-Border, Red Lobster, Sessel's Café, Taco Bell, Wendy's, **lodging:** AmeriSuites, Hampton Suites, Wellesley Inn, **other:** Barnes&Noble, Best Buy, Chevrolet, Chrysler/Plymouth/Dodge, Circuit City, Dillard's, Ford, Home Depot, Honda, JC Penney, Michael's, Office Depot, OfficeMax, Old Navy, Sears/auto, Target, Walgreen, mall, **S...**Shell, Shogun Japanese, Waffle House, Best Inn, Comfort Suites, Microtel, Wingate Inn, Costco/gas

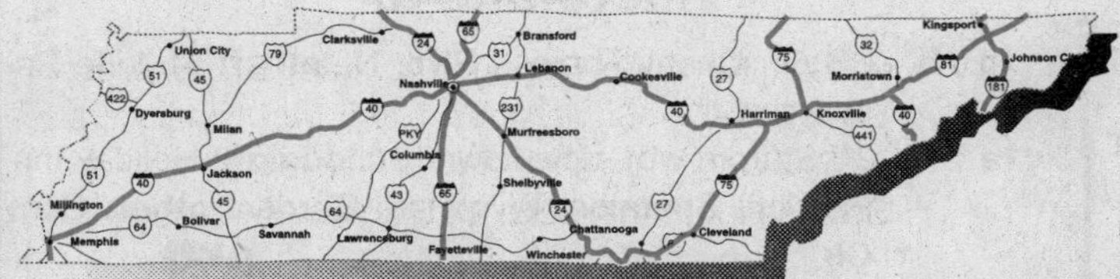

15b a Appling Rd, **N...**BP, **1 mi N...gas:** Shell, **food:** Coletta's Italian, Suburban Lodge, **S...gas:** Chevron/diesel

14 Whitten Rd, **N...gas:** Express/Blimpie, 76/diesel, Shell/Burger King, **food:** Sidecar Café, **other:** Harley-Davidson, **S...gas:** BP, Chevron, **food:** Backyard Burger, **lodging:** Travelers Inn

12 Sycamore View Rd, **N...gas:** Citgo/diesel, Phillips 66, **food:** Capt D's, Church's, Cracker Barrel, IHOP, KFC, Krystal, McDonald's, Mrs Winner's, Perkins, Ruby Tuesday, Shoney's, Sonic, Subway, Taco Bell, Waffle House, **lodging:** Baymont Inn, Drury Inn, Hampton Inn, Holiday Inn Express, Red Roof Inn, **other:** Walgreen, **S...gas:** Exxon, 76/diesel, **food:** Burger King, India Cuisine, Jimmy C's Café, Top's BBQ, Wendy's, **lodging:** Best Western, Comfort Inn, Day's Inn, Fairfield Inn, Hawthorn Inn, La Quinta, Memphis Inn, Motel 6, Super 8

10.5mm Wolf River

10b a (from wb)I-240 W around Memphis, I-40 E to Nashville

12c (from eb)I-240 W, to Jackson, I-40 E to Nashville

12b Sam Cooper Blvd(from eb)

12a US 64/70/79, Summer Ave, **N...gas:** Express/diesel, Texaco/diesel, **food:** Luby's, Pappy&Jimmie's Rest., Waffle House, **lodging:** Ramada Inn, **other:** Ford, OfficeMax, U-Haul, mall, **S...gas:** Amoco, Exxon, **food:** Arby's, Great China, McDonald's, NamKing Chinese, Pizza Hut, Wendy's, Western Sizzlin, **other:** Firestone/auto, Fred's Drug, Goodyear/auto, Hancock Fabrics, K-Mart

10 TN 204, Covington Pike, **N...gas:** Amoco, **food:** McDonald's, Wendy's, **other:** Audi/VW, Buick, Cadillac, Chevrolet, Dodge, Honda, Hyundai, Isuzu/Mazda, Kia/Toyota, Mitsubishi, Nissan, Pontiac/GMC, Sam's Club, SuperLo Food/gas, Volvo

8b a TN 14, Jackson Ave, **N...gas:** Citgo/diesel, 76, Sonic, **lodging:** Day's Inn, Sleep Inn, **other:** Raleigh Tire, **S...gas:** Citgo/diesel, **food:** Central Park, **other:** AutoZone, Family$, Kelly Tire, O'Reilly Parts, transmissions

6 Warford Rd, no facilities

5 Hollywood St, **N...gas:** Amoco, Express, **food:** Burger King, **other:** Walgreen

3 Watkins St, **N...gas:** Amoco, Express/diesel, Oil City USA, **other:** U-Haul

2a rd 300, to US 51 N, Millington, **N...other:** Meeman-Shelby SP

2 Smith Ave, Chelsea Ave, no facilities

1g f TN 14, Jackson Ave, **S...gas:** Exxon, Express, **other:** Don's Transmissions

1e I-240 E, no facilities

TENNESSEE

Interstate 40

E ↕ W

1d c b	US 51, Danny Thomas Blvd, **N...other:** St Jude Research Ctr
1a	2nd St(from wb), downtown, **S...lodging:** Holiday Inn, Marriott, Sheraton, Wyndham Garden, **other:** Conv Ctr
1	Riverside Dr, Front St(from eb), Memphis, **S...lodging:** Comfort Inn, **other:** Conv Ctr, Riverfront
0mm	Tennessee/Arkansas state line, Mississippi River

Interstate 55

N ↕ S

Memphis

Exit #	Services
13mm	Tennessee/Arkansas state line, Mississippi River
12c	Delaware St, Memphis, **W...lodging:** Super 8
b	Riverside Dr, downtown Memphis, **E...**TN Welcome Ctr
a	E Crump Blvd(from nb), **E...**museum
11	McLemore Ave, Presidents Island, industrial area
10	S Parkway, **1/2mi E...gas:** Conoco/diesel
9	Mallory Ave, industrial area
8	Horn Lake Rd(from sb), no facilities
7	US 61, 3rd St, **E...gas:** Amoco, Exxon/mart, **food:** BBQ, LotABurger, McDonald's, Taco Bell, **W...gas:** Citgo/Subway, Express/diesel, **food:** KFC, McDonald's, **lodging:** Rest Inn, Starliet Inn, **other:** CarQuest, Fuller SP, Indian Museum
6b a	I-240, no facilities
5b	US 51 S, Elvis Presley Blvd, to Graceland, **W...gas:** Citgo/diesel, Exxon, Phillips 66/diesel, **food:** Capt D's, Exline's Pizza, Kettle, KFC, Peking Chinese, Rally's, Taco Bellfs, **lodging:** American Inn, Day's Inn, Graceland Inn, Heartbreak Hotel, Motel 6, **other:** HOSPITAL, Advance Parts, Davis RV Ctr, Dodge, KOA, Walgreen, transmissions, to Graceland
a	Brooks Rd, **E...gas:** Express/diesel, Exxon, **food:** Popeye's, **lodging:** Airport Inn, Clarion, Travelodge, **other:** Toyota
3mm	**Welcome Ctr nb, full(handicapped)facilities, phone, vending, picnic tables, litter barrels, petwalk**
2b a	TN 175, Shelby Dr, Whitehaven, **E...gas:** Citgo/Subway, Conoco, Exxon, **lodging:** Shelby Inn, Super 8, **W...gas:** 76/mart, Shell, **food:** Burger King, CK's Coffee, Crumpy's Wings, Hook's Fish/chicken, **other:** Family$, Goodyear/auto, SaveALot Food, Seessel's Food/gas, U-Haul
0mm	Tennessee/Mississippi state line

Interstate 65

N ↕ S

Nashville

Exit #	Services
121.5mm	Tennessee/Kentucky state line
121mm	**Welcome Ctr sb, full(handicapped)facilities, phone, picnic tables, litter barrels, vending, petwalk**
119mm	weigh sta both lanes
117	TN 52, Portland, **E...gas:** Shell/diesel/fireworks, **other:** HOSPITAL, **W...gas:** Amoco, **other:** Jiffy Oil Trkstp/diesel/@, **lodging:** Budget Host, **other:** fireworks
116mm	Red River
113mm	Red River
112	TN 25, Cross Plains, **E...gas:** Amoco/diesel, **food:** Sad Sam's Pizza, **W...gas:** Express/diesel, Exxon/diesel/24hr
108	TN 76, White House, **E...gas:** Keystop, Nervous Charlie's/diesel, **food:** Dairy Queen, Hardee's, KFC/A&W, McDonald's, Sonic(1mi), Taco Bell, Waffle House, Wendy's, **lodging:** Comfort Inn, Holiday Inn Express, **other:** MEDICAL CARE, USPO, park/playground, **W...gas:** Amoco/diesel/24hr, **food:** BBQ, **lodging:** Day's Inn
104	TN 257, Bethel Rd, **E...gas:** Phillip 66/diesel/rest./24hr, **W...gas:** Shell, **other:** Owl's Roost Camping
98	US 31 W, Millersville, **E...gas:** Citgo/diesel, RaceWay, Shell/diesel, **food:** Waffle House, **lodging:** Holiday Rest Motel/RV park(2mi), **W...gas:** Amoco/diesel, **lodging:** Economy Inn, **other:** Nashville N Camping
97	TN 174, Long Hollow Pike, **E...gas:** BP, Exxon, Mapco, **food:** Arby's, Capt D's, Cracker Barrel, Domino's, KFC, McDonald's, Subway, Waffle House, Wendy's, **lodging:** Comfort Inn, Guesthouse Inn, Hampton Inn, Holiday Inn Express, Knight's Inn, Red Roof Inn, **other:** MEDICAL CARE, K-Mart, Kroger, Music City Outlets, **W...gas:** Shell/diesel, **food:** BBQ, Bob Evans, Dairy Queen, Hardee's, Jack-in-the-Box, Krystal/24hr, Poncho Villa Grill, Sonic, **lodging:** Baymont Inn, Motel 6, **other:** Eckerd
96	Two Mile Pky, **E...gas:** BP/diesel, Shell, **food:** Coach's Grill, Cooker, Copeland's Rest., Cracker Barrel, El Chico, Hooters, Krystal, Las Cebolla's Mexican, Las Palmas Mexican, McDonald's, Mr Gatti's, Mrs Winner's, O'Charley's, Papa John's, Pargo's Café, Pizza Hut, Rio Bravo, Schlotsky's, Subway, Uncle Bud's Catfish, Waffle House, Wendy's, **lodging:** Comfort Suites, Day's Inn, Quality Inn, Super 8, **other:** HOSPITAL, BooksAMillion, Cadillac, CVS, Dillard's, Firestone, Goodyear, Home Depot, JC Penney, Nissan, NTB, Sears/auto, Universal Tire, mall, **E on Gallatin...food:** Arby's, Burger King, Calhoun's Cafe, Checker's, Chick-fil-A, Chili's, ChuckeCheese, Fazoli's, IHOP, Krispy Kreme, LJ Silver/A&W, Logan's Roadhouse, Longhorn Steaks, Old Country

Interstate 65

N ↕ S

Nashville

Buffet, Olive Garden, Outback Steaks, Rafferty's, Red Lobster, Santa Fe Steaks, Starbucks, Steak'n Shake, Taco Bell, **other:** Best Buy, Chevrolet, Chrysler/Jeep, Circuit City, Goody's, Harley-Davidson, Honda, Isuzu, Lincoln/Mercury, Marshall's, Michael's, OfficeMax, Old Navy, Sam's Club/gas, Target, Walgreen, Wal-Mart/drugs, **W...gas:** Chevron, Phillips 66

95 TN 386, Vietnam Veterans Blvd(from nb)

92 TN 45, Old Hickory Blvd, **E...other:** HOSPITAL, to Old Hickory Dam

90 TN 155 E, Briley Pkwy, **E...**to Opreyland

90b a US 31W, US 41, Dickerson Pike, **E...gas:** BP, Citgo/diesel, Express/diesel, Phillips 66, **food:** Arby's, Burger King, Capt D's, Domino's, KFC, Lee's Chicken, McDonald's, Mrs Winner's, Pizza Hut, Pizza Inn, Subway, Taco Bell, Waffle House, Wendy's, **lodging:** Colony Motel, Congress Inn, Day's Inn, Econolodge, Sleep Inn, Super 8, **other:** Advance Parts, AutoZone, Camping World RV Supply, CVS Drug, Family$, KOA, Kroger, Sam's Club, Walgreen

88b a I-24, W to Clarksville, E to Nashville, no facilities

87b a US 431, Trinity Lane, **E...gas:** Phillips 66/Blimpie, Pilot/Arby's/diesel, **food:** Krystal, White Castle/Church's, **lodging:** Cumberland Inn, Delux Inn, **W...gas:** BP/diesel, Chevron, Exxon, Shell/24hr, Texaco, **food:** Burger King, Capt D's, Denny's, Jack-in-the-Box, Jack's BBQ, McDonald's, Ponderosa, Taco Bell, Waffle House, **lodging:** Baymont Inn, Day's Inn, Drury Inn, Econolodge, Hampton Inn, Holiday Inn Express, Knight's Inn, Liberty Inn, Motel 6, Quality Inn, Ramada Inn, Regency Inn, Super 8, **other:** Family$, to American Bapt Coll

86 I-24 E, to I-40 E, to Memphis

86mm Cumberland River

85 US 41A, 8th Ave, **E...**to st capitol, **W...gas:** Exxon, Arby's, **food:** Krystal, McDonald's, Pizza Hut, Subway, Taco Bell, **other:** Cadillac/Honda

84b a I-40, E to Knoxville, W to Memphis

209[I-40] US 70, Charlotte Ave, Church St, **E...food:** McDonald's, **other:** Nissan, **W...gas:** Exxon, **food:** Burger King, White Castle, **lodging:** Best Western, Shoney's Inn

82b a I-40, W to Memphis, E to Nashville

81 Wedgewood Ave, **W...gas:** BP, Exxon, **other:** U-Haul, **services on 8th Ave...gas:** Citgo, Cone/diesel/, **food:** Burger King, Krystal, McDonald's, Mrs Winner's, **other:** $General, $Tree, Kroger, Walgreen

80 I-440, to Memphis, Knoxville

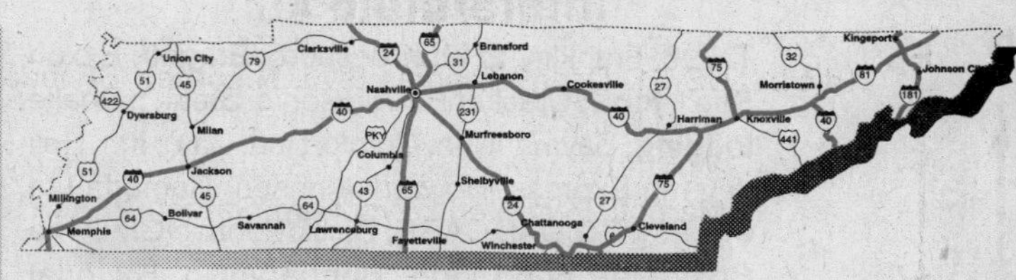

79 Armory Dr, **E on Powell...gas:** BP, Citgo, **food:** Applebee's, Rafferty's, Subway, Wendy's, **other:** CHIROPRACTOR, BMW, CarMax, CompUSA, Firestone/auto, Home Depot, Michael's, mall

78b a TN 255, Harding Place, **E...gas:** Amoco, Express, Texaco, **food:** Cracker Barrel, Mama Mia's Italian, Santa Fe Grill, Waffle House, **lodging:** La Quinta, Red Roof Inn, Traveler's Rest Hist Home

74 TN 254, Old Hickory Blvd, to Brentwood, **E...food:** Capt D's, Shoney's, Waffle House, **lodging:** AmeriSuites, Hilton Suites, Holiday Inn, Steeplechase Inn, **W...gas:** BP, Exxon, Shell, Texaco/diesel, **food:** BBQ, Mazatlan Mexican, Mrs Winner's, O'Charley's, Papa John's, Pargo's Rest., Ruby Tuesday, Vittles Rest., Wendy's, **lodging:** Brentwood Suites, Courtyard, Extended Stay America, Hampton Inn, Studio+, **other:** USPO, Walgreen, **facilities on US 31...food:** Burger King, Little Caesar's, **other:** Eckerd, Harris-Teeter, OfficeMax

71 TN 253, Concord Rd, to Brentwood, no facilities

69 Moore's Lane, Galleria Blvd, **E...gas:** Express/diesel, **food:** Applebee's, Backyard Burgers, Cooker, Cozymel's, Houlihan's, Joe's Crabshack, Outback Steaks, Sonic, **lodging:** AmeriSuites, Homestead Suites, Red Roof Inn, Wingate Inn, **other:** Acura/Lexus, Bruno's Foods, Circuit City, Home Depot, Mercedes, Michael's, Walgreen, **W...gas:** BP, Marathon, Shell/diesel, **food:** J Alexander's Rest., Buca Italian, Macaroni Grill, McDonald's, Pizza Hut/Taco Bell, Red Lobster, Rio Bravo, Schlotsky's, Stony River Steaks, Subway, **lodging:** Sleep Inn, **other:** Barnes&Noble, Best Buy, CompUSA, Dillard's, Infiniti, JC Penney, Sears/auto, Target, mall

68b a Cool Springs Blvd, **E...lodging:** Embassy Suites, Marriott, **W...gas:** Exxon, Shell, **food:** Atl Bread, Carrabba's, Chili's, Jack-in-the-Box, Luby's, McDonald's, Ming Chinese, Off the Grill, Ruby Tuesday, Starbucks, TGIFriday, Wendy's, **lodging:** Country Inn Suites, Hampton Inn, **other:** MEDICAL CARE, Borders Books, Harley-Davidson, Harris-Teeter, Home Depot, Jo-Ann Fabrics, Kohl's, Kroger, Lowe's Whse, Marshall's, Sam's Club, Saturn, Staples, Walgreen, Wal-Mart SuperCtr/24hr, to Galleria Mall

TENNESSEE

Interstate 65

N ↕ S — Franklin

65 TN 96, Franklin, to Murfreesboro, **E...gas:** Exxon, Shell, **food:** Cracker Barrel, Sonic, Steak'n Shake, **lodging:** Baymont Inn, Comfort Inn, Day's Inn, Holiday Inn Express, Howard Johnson, Ramada Ltd, **other:** MEDICAL CARE, Buick/Pontiac/GMC/Kia, Chevrolet, Food Lion, Honda/Volvo, Hyundai, Walgreen, **W...gas:** BP/diesel, Express/diesel, Shell/diesel, **food:** Arby's, Backyard Burger, BBQ, Camino Real Mexican, ChopHouse Chinese, CiCi's, Hardee's, KFC, McDonald's, O'Charley's, Papa John's, Pizza Hut, Shoney's, Starbucks, Subway, Taco Bell, Waffle House, Wendy's, **lodging:** Best Western, Super 8, **other:** BiLo, Chrysler/Plymouth/Dodge, CVS Drug, $General, Eckerd, Ford/Mercury, Goody's, HobbyLobby, Home Depot, Kroger, Mazda, Nissan, SteinMart, Toyota, USPO, to Confederate Cem at Franklin

64mm Harpeth River

61 TN 248, Peytonsville Rd, to Spring Hill, **E...gas:** TA/BP/diesel/rest./24hr/@, **W...gas:** Cone, Express/24hr, Shell, **other:** Goose Creek Inn/rest.

59b a TN 840, no facilities

58mm W Harpeth River

53 TN 396, Saturn Pkwy, to Spring Hill, Columbia, TN Scenic Pkwy

48mm parking area/weigh sta nb, litter barrels

46 US 412, TN 99, to Columbia, Chapel Hill, **E...gas:** Chevron, **other:** Campers RV Park, **W...gas:** BP, Exxon/Burger King, Shell/diesel/rest., **food:** Waffle House, **lodging:** Best Value Inn, Comfort Inn, Hampton Inn, Holiday Inn Express, Relax Inn, **other:** HOSPITAL

40.5mm Duck River

37 TN 50, to Columbia, Lewisburg, **E...other:** HOSPITAL, TN Walking Horse HQ, **W...gas:** Shell/diesel, **lodging:** Richland Inn, **other:** to Polk Home

32 rd 373, Mooresville, to Lewisburg, **E...gas:** Exxon/diesel

27 rd 129, Cornersville, to Lynnville, **E...other:** Texas T Camping

25mm parking area sb, litter barrels

24mm parking area nb, litter barrels

22 US 31A, to Pulaski, **E...gas:** BP/diesel/rest./@, **food:** McDonald's, Subway, **lodging:** Econolodge, **W...gas:** Pilot/diesel, Shell/diesel/24hr, **other:** flea mkt

14 US 64, to Pulaski, **E...gas:** BP/diesel, Shell/diesel, **food:** Sands Rest., Sarge's Shack Rest., **lodging:** Super 8, **other:** KOA, to Jack Daniels Distillery, **W...**to David Crockett SP

6 rd 273, Bryson, **E...gas:** Phillips 66/diesel/rest./@, **lodging:** Best Value Inn

4mm Elk River

3mm **Welcome Ctr nb, full(handicapped)facilities, info, phone, picnic tables, litter barrels, petwalk**

1 US 31, rd 7, Ardmore, **E...gas:** Chevron/diesel/24hr, Exxon/Church's/diesel, **other:** antiques, **1-2 mi E... gas:** Shell/repair, **food:** DQ, Hardee's, McDonald's, Subway

0mm Tennessee/Alabama state line

Interstate 75

N ↕ S

Exit # Services

161.5mm Tennessee/Kentucky state line

161mm **Welcome Ctr sb, full(handicapped)facilities, phone, vending, picnic tables, litter barrels, petwalk**

160 US 25W, Jellico, **E...gas:** Citgo, Exxon/Subway/diesel, Texaco/Stuckey's, **food:** KFC, **lodging:** Jellico Motel/rest., **other:** auto parts, **W...gas:** Shell/Arby's/diesel, **food:** Hardee's, Wendy's, **lodging:** Best Western, Day's Inn/rest., **other:** HOSPITAL, Flowers Bakery, camping, fireworks, to Indian Mtn SP

144 Stinking Creek Rd, no facilities

141 TN 63, to Royal Blue, **E...gas:** BP/diesel, **food:** Perkins/24hr, **W...gas:** Exxon/Stuckey's, Pilot/Subway/diesel/24hr/@, **food:** Dairy Queen, **lodging:** Comfort Inn, **other:** fireworks, to Big South Fork NRA

134 US 25W, TN 63, Caryville, **E...gas:** Exxon/diesel, Shell/24hr, **food:** Pizza Hut, Waffle House/24hr, Western Sizzlin, **lodging:** Hampton Inn, Lakeview Inn/rest., Super 8, Thacker Christmas Inn, **other:** HOSPITAL, to Cove Lake SP, **W...gas:** Amoco, **food:** Shoney's, Scotty's Hamburgers, **lodging:** Budget Host

130mm weigh sta both lanes, phones

129 US 25W S, Lake City, **E...**antiques, LP, **W...gas:** BP, Citgo, Exxon/Subway/diesel/24hr, Shell, Texaco/Blimpie/diesel, **food:** Burger King, Cottage Rest., Cracker Barrel, KFC, McDonald's, **lodging:** Day's Inn, Blue Haven Motel, Lake City Motel, Lamb's Inn/rest., **other:** $General, same as 128

128 US 441, to Lake City, **E...gas:** BP, **other:** Coastal, Mountain Lake Marina(4mi), **W...gas:** Exxon/diesel/24hr, Shell, **food:** Cottage Rest., Subway, **lodging:** Blue Haven Motel, Lake City Motel, Lamb's Inn, **other:** $General, Hillbilly Mkt/deli, antique cars, to Norris Dam SP, same as 129

126mm Clinch River

122 TN 61, Bethel, Norris, **E...gas:** Shell, **other:** Fox Inn Camping, antiques, museum, **W...gas:** Citgo/diesel, Exxon/Subway/diesel/24hr, Marathon/diesel/24hr, Texaco, **food:** Burger King, Hardee's, Krystal/24hr, McDonald's, Waffle House, Wendy's, **lodging:** Best Western, Comfort Inn, Holiday Inn Express, Super 8, **other:** Big Pine Ridge SP

Interstate 75

N ↕ S

Knoxville

117 TN 170, Racoon Valley Rd, **E...gas:** BP, Pilot/Burger King/Subway/diesel/24hr/@ , **W...lodging:** Valley Inn, **other:** Vaughn Camping(2mi)

112 TN 131, Emory Rd, to Powell, **E...gas:** BP/diesel, Chevron, Pilot/DQ/Taco Bell/diesel/24hr/@ , **food:** Aubrey's Rest., Buddy's BBQ, McDonald's, KFC, Krystal, Steak'n Shake, Wendy's, **lodging:** Country Inn Suites, Holiday Inn Express, **other:** CVS Drug, $General, Family$, Ingles, Toyota, **W...gas:** Exxon/24hr, Shell/diesel/24hr, **food:** Hardee's, Shoney's, Waffle House/24hr, **lodging:** Comfort Inn

110 Callahan Dr, **E...gas:** Coastal, Weigel's/gas, **lodging:** Knight's Inn, Quality Inn/rest., **W...gas:** Amoco, **food:** Burger King, Chick-fil-A, Chili's, Golden Corral, McDonald's, Wendy's, **lodging:** Scottish Inn, **other:** GMC/Volvo

108 Merchant Dr, **E...gas:** BP/diesel, Citgo/diesel, Pilot/diesel, Texaco/diesel, **food:** Applebee's, Cracker Barrel, Denny's, El Chico's, Logan's Roadhouse, O'Charley's, Pizza Hut, Sonic, Rafferty's, Ryan's, Waffle House, **lodging:** Comfort Inn, Day's Inn, Hampton Inn, Howard Johnson, Ramada Ltd, Sleep Inn, **other:** CVS Drug, Ingles, Valvoline, **W...gas:** Citgo, Exxon/Godfather's, Pilot/Conoco, Shell, **food:** Arby's, Burger King, Cancun Mexican, Capt D's, Darryl's Rest, Great American Steaks, IHOP, Mandarin House, McDonald's, Outback Steaks, Pizza Inn, Red Lobster, Subway, Waffle House/24hr, **lodging:** Clarion Inn, Econolodge, Family Inn, Motel 6, Super 8, **other:** Food Lion, Walgreen, **1 mi W on US 25W...food:** Arby's, Krystal, LJ Silver, Shoney's, Taco Bell, **other:** Advance Parts, CVS Drug, Firestone, K-Mart, Kroger

107 I-640 & I-75

3b[I-640] US 25W, **N...gas:** Amoco, BP, Texaco/diesel, **food:** Hardee's, KFC, Krystal, LJ Silver, Mr Gatti's, Pizza Hut, Quincy's, Taco Bell, Wendy's, **other:** Chevrolet, CVS Drug, Firestone, Ford, K-Mart, Kroger, transmissions, same as 108

1[I-640] TN 62, Western Ave, **N...gas:** Cargo/diesel, RaceTrac, Shell/diesel, **food:** Central Park, Golden Corral, KFC, LJ Silver, McDonald's, Mixon's Deli, Ruby Tuesday, Shoney's, Subway, Taco Bell, Wendy's, **other:** CVS Drug, Kroger, Walgreen, **S...gas:** BP, **food:** Dad's Donuts, Domino's, Hardee's, Krystal, **other:** Advance Parts, USPO

I-75 and I-40 run together 17 mi. See Tennessee Interstate 40, exits 369 through 385.

84[368] I-40, W to Nashville

81 US 321, TN 95, to Lenoir City, **E...gas:** BP/diesel, Exxon/Subway/diesel, Phillips 66, Shell/diesel, **food:** BelAir Grill, Burger King(1mi), Dinner Bell Rest., El Arriero Mexican, KFC, McDonald's, Shoney's, Waffle House, Wendy's, **lodging:** Crossroads Inn, King's Inn/rest., **other:** to Great Smokies NP,

Athens

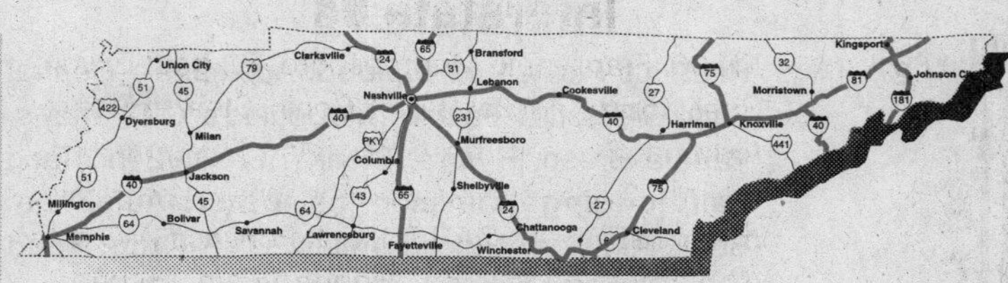

Ft Loudon Dam, **W...gas:** Citgo/diesel, Shell/diesel, Krystal, **food:** Ruby Tuesday, **lodging:** Comfort Inn, Econolodge, Ramada Ltd, **other:** Chevrolet, Pontiac/Buick/GMC

76 rd 324, Sugar Limb Rd, **W...**to TN Valley Winery

74mm Tennessee River

72 TN 72, to Loudon, **E...gas:** BP/McDonald's, Shell/Wendy's/diesel, **food:** BBQ, China King, **lodging:** Holiday Inn Express, Super 8, **other:** to Ft Loudon SP, **W...**Citgo, Marie's Kitchen, Knight's Inn, Express Camping

68 TN 323, to Philadelphia, **E...gas:** BP/diesel

62 TN 322, Oakland Rd, to Sweetwater, **E...food:** Dinner Bell Rest., **W...other:** KOA

60 TN 68, Sweetwater, **E...gas:** Marathon, RaceWay, Shell/diesel, **food:** Burger King, KFC, McDonald's, Wendy's, **lodging:** Best Value Inn, Budget Host, Comfort Inn, Day's Inn, Super 8(2mi), **other:** HOSPITAL, to Lost Sea Underground Lake, **W...gas:** BP/diesel, Exxon/diesel, Phillips 66, **food:** BBQ, Cracker Barrel, **lodging:** Best Western, Quality Inn, **other:** flea mkt, to Watts Bar Dam

56 TN 309, Niota, **E...gas:** BP/Trkstop/diesel/rest./@ , **other:** Country Music Camping, **W...**tires

52 TN 305, Mt Verd Rd, to Athens, **E...gas:** BP(1mi), Phillips 66, **other:** Overniter RV Park, **W...gas:** Exxon, **lodging:** Ramada Inn

49 TN 30, to Athens, **E...gas:** BP, Exxon, RaceWay, Shell/DQ/diesel/24hr, **food:** Applebee's, Burger King, Hardee's, KFC, Krystal, McDonald's, Mexi-Wing, Monterrey Mexican, Shoney's, Subway, Waffle House, Wendy's, **lodging:** Day's Inn, Hampton Inn, Holiday Inn Express, Homestead Inn, Knight's Inn, Motel 6, Super 8, **other:** HOSPITAL, KOA, Russell Stover, to TN Wesleyan Coll, **W...gas:** Shell/diesel, **lodging:** Homestead Inn, **other:** Jeep, Pontiac/Buick/Cadillac/GMC

45.5mm rest area both lanes, full(handicapped)facilities, phone, vending, picnic tables, litter barrels, petwalk

42 TN 39, to Riceville, **E...gas:** Express/diesel, **food:** Callie's Kitchen, **lodging:** Relax Inn, Rice Inn(2mi)

36 TN 163, to Calhoun, no facilities

35mm Hiwassee River

33 TN 308, to Charleston, **E...gas:** Citgo, **other:** 33 Camping, **W...gas:** Shell/diesel/rest./24hr/@

TENNESSEE

Interstate 75

N ↕ S

Cleveland

27 Paul Huff Pkwy, **1 mi E...food:** Applebee's, Central Park, CiCi's, DQ, Fazoli's, McDonald's, O'Charley's, Panera Bread, Ryan's, Steak'n Shake/24hr, Taco Bell, **lodging:** Jameson Inn, **other:** AutoZone, BooksAMillion, Buick/Pontiac, CVS Drug, Food Lion, Goodyear/auto, HobbyLobby, JC Penney, K-Mart, Lowe's Whse, OfficeMax, Sears, Staples, Wal-Mart SuperCtr/gas/24hr, mall, **W...gas:** BP/diesel, Conoco, Exxon, Shell, **food:** Denny's/24hr, Hardee's, Waffle House, Wendy's, **lodging:** Comfort Inn, EQ Motel, Hampton Inn, Ramada Ltd, Royal Inn, Super 8

25 TN 60, Cleveland, **E...gas:** BP, Chevron/diesel, RaceTrac, Shell/diesel, **food:** Burger King, Cancun Mexican, Cracker Barrel, Hardee's, McDonald's, Roblyn's Steaks, Schlotsky's, Shoney's, Waffle House, Wendy's, Zaxby's, **lodging:** Colonial Inn, Day's Inn, Douglas Inn, Econolodge, Economy Inn, Knight's Inn, Quality Inn, **other:** HOSPITAL, to Lee Coll, **W...gas:** Shell, **food:** TN Jack's Rest., **lodging:** Baymont Inn, Holiday Inn, Wingate Inn

23mm parking area/weigh sta nb

20 US 64 byp, to Cleveland, **1-3 mi E...gas:** Exxon, Shell, **food:** Golden Corral, Hardee's, McDonald's, Subway, Taco Bell, **other:** Chrysler/Jeep/Plymouth, Food Lion, Honda, Toyota, **W...gas:** Exxon/diesel/24hr, KOA(1mi)

16mm scenic view sb

13mm parking area/weigh sta sb, phone

11 US 11 N, US 64 E, Ooltewah, **E...gas:** Chevron, Citgo, RaceTrac, Shell, **food:** Arby's, Bohangles, Burger King, Hardee's, McDonald's, Subway, Taco Bell, Wendy's, **other:** MEDICAL CARE, BiLo, **W...gas:** Exxon/diesel, **food:** Krystal, Waffle House, **lodging:** Super 8, **other:** to Harrison Bay SP

7b a US 11, US 64, Lee Hwy, **W...gas:** Chevron, Shell, **food:** Waffle House, **lodging:** Best Inn, Best Western/rest., Day's Inn, Econolodge, Motel 6, Park Inn, Wellesley Inn, **other:** Harley-Davidson, Land Rover

Chattanooga

5 Shallowford Rd, **E...food:** Alexander's, Arby's, Backyard Burgers, BBQ, Blimpie, Capt D's, Central Park, CiCi's, Country Place Rest., Famous Dave's, Hop's Grill, Krystal, Logan's Roadhouse, Macaroni Grill, McDonald's, Old Country Buffet, Pizza Hut, Schlotsky's, Steak'n Shake/24hr, Taco Bell, TGIFriday, **lodging:** Comfort Suites, Wingate Inn, **other:** MEDICAL CARE, Best Buy, BooksAMillion, Firestone/auto, FoodMaxx/24hr, Ford, FreshMkt Foods, Home Depot, Lowe's Whse, OfficeMax, Walgreen, Wal-Mart SuperCtr/24hr, **W...gas:** Exxon, Shell, **food:** Applebee's, Blimpie, Burger King, Cancun Mexican, Cracker Barrel, Domino's, El Chico's, Fazoli's, GlenGene Deli, Godfather's, KFC, McDonald's, Ocean Ave Seafood, O'Charley's, Papa John's, Pizza Hut, Rio Bravo, Sonic, SteakOut Rest., Shoney's, Subway, Texas Roadhouse, Waffle House, Wendy's, **lodging:** Country Inn Suites, Day's Inn, Fairfield Inn, Guesthouse Inn, Hampton Inn, Holiday Inn, Holiday Inn Express, Homewood Suites, MainStay Suites, Ramada Ltd, Red Roof Inn, Sleep Inn, **other:** HOSPITAL, BiLo, CVS Drug, Goodyear, U of TN/Chatt

4a (from nb)Hamilton Place Blvd, **E...food:** DQ, El Meson Mexican, Grady's Grill, Olive Garden, Outback Steaks, Piccadilly's, Red Lobster, Ruby Tuesday, Sticky Fingers, **lodging:** Courtyard, **other:** Barnes&Noble, Circuit City, Dillard's, Goody's, JC Penney, Michael's, Old Navy, Sears/auto, Staples, mall

4 TN 153, Chickamauga Dam Rd, no facilities

3b a TN 320, Brainerd Rd, **E...gas:** Exxon, **food:** Subway

2 I-24 W, to I-59, to Chattanooga, Lookout Mtn, no facilities

1.5mm **Welcome Ctr nb, full(handicapped)facilities, phone, vending, picnic tables, litter barrels, petwalk**

1b a US 41, Ringgold Rd, to Chattanooga, **E...gas:** BP, Exxon, **lodging:** Airport Inn, Comfort Inn, Econolodge, Howard Johnson, Ramada Inn, **other:** BiLo Foods, Family$, Shipp's RV Ctr/park, **W...gas:** Conoco/diesel, Pure, Shell/diesel, **food:** Arby's, Burger King, Central Park Burger, Cracker Barrel, Hardee's, Krystal, LJ Silver/A&W, McDonald's, Pizza Hut, PortoFino Italian, Shoney's, Subway, Taco Bell, Teriyaki House, Uncle Bud's Catfish, Waffle House, **lodging:** Best Inn, Day's Inn, Holiday Inn Express, Super 8, Travelodge, Waverly Motel, **other:** U-Haul

0mm Tennessee/Georgia state line

Interstate 81

N ↕ S

Bristol

Exit #	Services
75mm	**Tennessee/Virginia state line, Welcome Ctr sb, full(handicapped)facilities, info, phone, vending, picnic tables, litter barrels, petwalk**
74b a	US 11 W, to Bristol, Kingsport, **E...lodging:** Day's Inn, Hampton Inn, **other:** HOSPITAL, **1-2 mi E...gas:** Shell, **food:** Burger King, KFC, LJ Silver, McDonald's, Pizza Hut, Shoney's, Taco Bell, Wendy's, **W...gas:** Exxon, **food:** Truby's Diner, **lodging:** Best Western
69	TN 394, to Blountville, **E...gas:** BP/Subway/diesel, **food:** Arby's, Burger King(1mi), **other:** Bristol Int Raceway

Interstate 81

N ↕ S

Johnson City

66 TN 126, to Kingsport, Blountville, **E...gas:** Exxon/diesel, **W...gas:** Chevron/24hr, **food:** McDonald's, **other:** FSA/famous brands

63 rd 357, Tri-City Airport, **E...gas:** Exxon/Taco Bell/Krystal/diesel, Shell/Subway/diesel/24hr, **food:** Cracker Barrel, Wendy's, **lodging:** La Quinta, Sleep Inn, **other:** Hamrick's Clothing Outlet, **W...gas:** Phillips 66/diesel, **lodging:** Red Carpet Inn, **other:** $General, KOA, Sam's Club, Rocky Top Camping

60mm Holston River

59 TN 36, to Johnson City, Kingsport, **E...gas:** Citgo/diesel, **lodging:** Super 8, **W...gas:** Amoco/LP, Exxon, Shell/diesel, Sunoco, **food:** Arby's, Burger King, Domino's, Fazoli's, Hardee's, HotDog Hut, Huddle House, Jersey Mike's Subs, La Carreta Mexican, Little Caesar's, McDonald's, Pal's HotDogs, Perkins/24hr, Piccadilly's, Pizza Hut, Sonic, Subway, Wendy's, **lodging:** Comfort Inn, Holiday Inn Express, **other:** Advance Parts, CVS Drug, $Store, Firestone/auto, Ingles, USPO, to Warrior's Path SP

57b a I-181, to Kingsport, I-26 S, to Johnson City, to ETSU, no facilities

56 Tri Cities Crossing, no facilities

50 TN 93, Fall Branch, **W...other:** auto auction, st patrol

44 Jearoldstown Rd, **E...gas:** Amoco, **W...other:** Exit 44 Mkt/gas

41mm rest area sb, full(handicapped)facilities, phone, vending, picnic tables, litter barrels, petwalk

38mm rest area nb, full(handicapped)facilities, phone, vending, picnic tables, litter barrels, petwalk

36 TN 172, to Baileyton, **E...gas:** Pilot/Subway/diesel/@, **other:** repair, **W...gas:** BP/diesel/24hr, Marathon/diesel/24hr/@, Shell/Subway/diesel/24hr, **lodging:** 36 Motel, **other:** Baileyton Camp(2mi)

30 TN 70, to Greeneville, **E...gas:** Exxon/DQ/Stuckey's/diesel

23 US 11E, to Greeneville, **E...gas:** Amoco/Wendy's, BP, **other:** to Andrew Johnson HS, **W...gas:** Exxon/Taco Bell/diesel, Phillips 66/diesel/rest., **food:** McDonald's, NY Pizza/Italian, Tony's Rest., **lodging:** Comfort Inn, Super 8

21mm weigh sta sb

15 TN 340, Fish Hatchery Rd, **E...gas:** BP/diesel/24hr, **W...other:** truck/trailer repair

12 TN 160, to Morristown, **E...gas:** Phillips 66, **W...gas:** Shell/diesel, **other:** to Crockett Tavern HS

8 US 25E, to Morristown, **E...gas:** Shell/repair, **food:** Sonic(2mi), **lodging:** Twin Pines Motel(3mi), **W...gas:** BP/diesel, Exxon, **food:** Cracker Barrel, Hardee's, **lodging:** Holiday Inn, Parkway Inn, Super 8, **other:** to Cumberland Gap NHP

4 rd 341, White Pine, **E...gas:** Exxon/diesel, Pilot/diesel/24hr, **food:** McDonald's, **lodging:** Crown Inn, **W...gas:** Citgo, Kwikshop, Shell/diesel, **food:** Huddle House/24hr, **lodging:** Day's Inn, Hillcrest Inn, **other:** to Panther Cr SP

2.5mm rest area sb, full(handicapped)facilities, phone, picnic tables, litter barrels, vending, petwalk

1b a I-40 E to Asheville, W to Knoxville. I-81 begins/ends on I-40, exit 421.

Interstate 640(Knoxville)

Knoxville

E ↕ W

Exit # Services

9mm I-640 begins/ends on I-40, exit 393.

8 Millertown Pike, Mall Rd N, **N...gas:** Conoco/Backyard Burgers, Exxon/DQ/24hr, **food:** Applebee's, Burger King, Don Pablos, KFC, McDonald's, Piccadilly's, Pizza Inn, Ruby Tuesday, Taco Bell, Texas Roadhouse, Wendy's, **other:** Circuit City, Dillard's, JC Penney, Kohl's, OfficeMax, Sam's Club, Sears/auto, Wal-Mart/auto, farmer mkt, mall, **S...gas:** Conoco, **food:** Subway, **other:** Food Lion, Home Depot, Lowe's Whse, Pep-Boys

6 US 441, to Broadway, **N...gas:** BP, Chevron, Conoco, Phillips 66, Pilot/diesel, **food:** Arby's, Austin's Steaks, Cancun Mexican, CiCi's, Fazoli's, Krispy Kreme, Larry's Subs, LJ Silver, McDonald's, Papa John's, Ruby Tuesday, Sonic, Subway, Taco Bell, **lodging:** Best Western, **other:** Advance Parts, AutoZone, Batteries+, CVS Drug, $General, Firestone, Goodyear, Kroger/24hr, NAPA, Target, Walgreen, **S...food:** Buddy's BBQ, Sam's Rest., Shoney's, YumYum Buffet, **other:** BiLo Foods, CVS Drug, Food City, K-Mart, NAPA, Office Depot, Walgreen

3a I-75 N to Lexington, I-275 S to Knoxville

b US 25W, Clinton Hwy, **N...gas:** Phillips 66, **other:** Chevrolet, Dodge, Ford, Nissan, facilities on frontage rds

1 TN 62, Western Ave, **N...gas:** Cargo/diesel, RaceTrac, Shell/diesel, **food:** Central Park, KFC, LJ Silver, McDonald's, Nixon's Deli, Ruby Tuesday, Shoney's, Sonic, Subway, Taco Bell, Wendy's, **other:** CVS Drug, Kroger, Walgreen, **S...gas:** BP, **food:** Hardee's, Krystal, **other:** Advance Parts, USPO

0mm I-640 begins/ends on I-40, exit 385.

TEXAS

Interstate 10

E ↕ W

Orange

Exit #	Services
880.5mm	Texas/Louisiana state line, Sabine River
880	Sabine River Turnaround, RV camping
879mm	**Welcome Ctr wb, full(handicapped)facilities, phone, picnic tables, litter barrels, vending, pet-walk**
878	US 90, Orange, **N...gas:** Mobil/diesel, **other:** air-boat rides, **S...other:** Western Store
877	TX 87, 16th St, Orange, **N...gas:** Chevron, Shamrock/diesel, **food:** Cajun Cookery, Gary's Café, Little Caesar's, Pizza Hut, Subway, Waffle House, **lodging:** Best Western, Day's Inn, Holiday Inn Express, Motel 6, Super 8, **other:** Buick/Pontiac/Toyota, $General, Eckerd, MktBasket/deli, Radio Shack, **S...gas:** Shell/diesel, **food:** Burger King, Church's, Cody's Rest., DQ, Jack-in-the-Box, McDonald's, Popeye's, Taco Bell, **other:** Buick/Pontiac, Cadillac/GMC, HEB Foods, Kroger, Modica Tires, O'Reilly Parts, Toyota
876	Adams Bayou, frontage rd, **N...gas:** Exxon, **food:** Cajun Cookery, Gary's Café, Waffle House, **lodging:** Best Western, Best Value Inn, Motel 6, Ramada Inn, Super 8, **S...gas:** Chevron/diesel, same as 877
875	FM 3247, MLK Dr, **N...food:** Luby's, **S...other:** HOSPITAL, Chrysler/Dodge/Plymouth/Jeep, RV Ctr
874	US 90, Womack Rd, to Orange, **S...**HOSPITAL, Oakleaf Park RV Park
873	TX 62, TX 73, to Bridge City, **N...gas:** Exxon/diesel/24hr, Flying J/Conoco/diesel/LP/24hr/@, tires, **S...gas:** Pilot/Wendy's/diesel/24hr/@, Shamrock, Texaco/diesel, **food:** Jack-in-the-Box, Burger King, McDonald's, Waffle House
870	FM 1136, no facilities
869	FM 1442(from wb), to Bridge City, **S...**Lloyd RV Ctr
867	frontage rd(from eb), no facilities
866.5mm	**rest areas both lanes, full(handicapped)facilities, vending, picnic tables, litter barrels**
865	Doty Rd(from wb), frontage rd, no facilities
864	FM 1132, FM 1135, **N... food:** Burr's BBQ, **lodging:** Budget Inn
862c	Timberlane Dr(from eb), no facilities
b	Old Hwy(from wb), no facilities
a	Railroad Ave, no facilities
861d	TX 12, Deweyville, no facilities
c	Denver St, **N...gas:** Conoco/diesel
b	Lamar St(from wb), **N...gas:** Conoco/diesel
a	FM 105, Vidor, **N...gas:** Chevron/diesel, Shamrock, Shell, **food:** DQ, Domino's, McDonald's, Popeye's, Waffle House, **other:** Family$, Mktbasket Foods, Radio Shack, **S...gas:** Conoco, Exxon/diesel, **food:** Burger King, Church's, Great Wall Chinese, KFC, Pizza Hut, Sonic, Subway, Taco Bell, Whataburger, **other:** MEDICAL CARE, tires

Beaumont

Exit #	Services
860b a	Dewitt Rd, W Vidor, frontage rd, no facilities
859	Bonner Turnaround, no facilities
858b	Asher Turnaround, **N...other:** Boomtown RV Park, **S...food:** Denny's
a	Rose City East, **S...gas:** Chevron, Gateway/diesel, **food:** Denny's
857	Rose City, no facilities
856	Old Hwy, no facilities
855a	US 90 bus, to downtown, Port of Beaumont, no facilities
854	ML King Pkwy, Beaumont, **N...gas:** Conoco, **S...gas:** Exxon, Texaco, **food:** McDonald's, **other:** Chrysler/Jeep
853c	7th St, **N...gas:** Fina, **food:** Burger King, McDonald's, Ninfa's Mexican, Red Lobster, Waffle House, **lodging:** Holiday Inn, Scottish Inn, Super 8, Travel Inn, **other:** bank, same as 853b
b	11th St, **S...gas:** Conoco, Fina, **food:** Jack-in-the-Box, Luby's, **lodging:** Best Western, Interstate Inn, Motel 6, Quality Inn, Ramada Inn, **other:** HOSPITAL, Chevrolet/Cadillac/GMC
a	US 69 N, to Lufkin
852	Harrison Ave, Calder Ave, Beaumont, **N...gas:** Chevron/diesel/24hr, Texaco/diesel, **food:** BBQ, Bennigan's, Cajun Cookery, Casa Ole Mexican, Chili's, Olive Garden, Steak&Ale, **S...gas:** Chevron, **food:** Church's, McDonald's, **lodging:** Day's Inn, Econolodge, La Quinta, **other:** Chevrolet, transmissions
851	US 90, College St, **N...gas:** Exxon/diesel, RaceTrac, **food:** Acapulco Mexican, Carrabba's, China Border, Fujiyama Japanese, Golden Corral, Outback Steaks, Waffle House, **lodging:** Best Western, Comfort Inn, **other:** AutoZone, O'Reilly Parts, Pennzoil, Subaru/Suzuki, **S...gas:** Chevron/Burger King/24hr, Mobil, Shell, Texaco, **food:** DQ, IHOP, Jason's Deli, KFC, Pizza Hut, Taco Bell, Wendy's, Whataburger, **lodging:** Courtyard, Econolodge, Fairfield Inn, Hilton/rest., Motel 6, **other:** HOSPITAL, Discount Tire, Dodge, Eckerd, Firestone/auto, Ford/Lincoln/Mercury, GMC/Cadillac, Honda, Jeep, MktBasket Foods, Mazda, Mercedes, Mitsubishi, Nissan, NTB, Office Depot, Sam's Club/gas, U-Haul, Volvo, Walgreen
850	Washington Blvd(from wb), same as 851
849	US 69 S, Washington Blvd, to Port Arthur, airport, no facilities
848	Walden Rd, **N...gas:** Texaco, **food:** Pappadeaux Seafood, **lodging:** Holiday Inn/rest., La Quinta, **S...gas:** Chevron/Subway/diesel/24hr, Petro/Mobil/diesel/24hr/@, **food:** Carino's Italian, Cheddar's, Cracker Barrel, Jack-in-the-Box, Joe's Crabshack, Waffle House, **lodging:** Hampton Inn, Ramada Ltd, **other:** Blue Beacon
846	Brooks Rd(from eb), **S...other:** Gulf Coast RV Resort

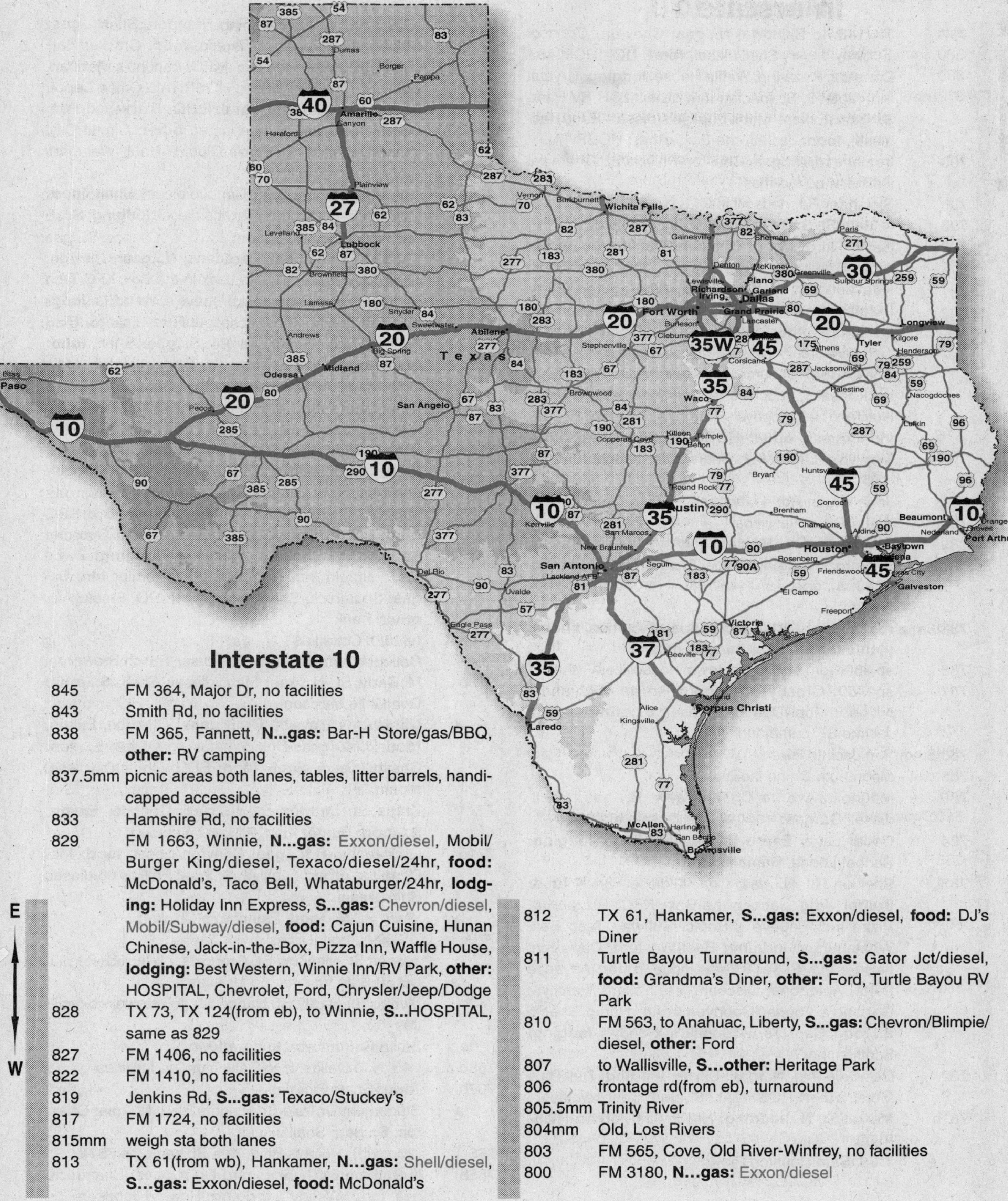

Interstate 10

E ↕ W

845 FM 364, Major Dr, no facilities
843 Smith Rd, no facilities
838 FM 365, Fannett, **N...gas:** Bar-H Store/gas/BBQ, **other:** RV camping
837.5mm picnic areas both lanes, tables, litter barrels, handicapped accessible
833 Hamshire Rd, no facilities
829 FM 1663, Winnie, **N...gas:** Exxon/diesel, Mobil/Burger King/diesel, Texaco/diesel/24hr, **food:** McDonald's, Taco Bell, Whataburger/24hr, **lodging:** Holiday Inn Express, **S...gas:** Chevron/diesel, Mobil/Subway/diesel, **food:** Cajun Cuisine, Hunan Chinese, Jack-in-the-Box, Pizza Inn, Waffle House, **lodging:** Best Western, Winnie Inn/RV Park, **other:** HOSPITAL, Chevrolet, Ford, Chrysler/Jeep/Dodge
828 TX 73, TX 124(from eb), to Winnie, **S...**HOSPITAL, same as 829
827 FM 1406, no facilities
822 FM 1410, no facilities
819 Jenkins Rd, **S...gas:** Texaco/Stuckey's
817 FM 1724, no facilities
815mm weigh sta both lanes
813 TX 61(from wb), Hankamer, **N...gas:** Shell/diesel, **S...gas:** Exxon/diesel, **food:** McDonald's
812 TX 61, Hankamer, **S...gas:** Exxon/diesel, **food:** DJ's Diner
811 Turtle Bayou Turnaround, **S...gas:** Gator Jct/diesel, **food:** Grandma's Diner, **other:** Ford, Turtle Bayou RV Park
810 FM 563, to Anahuac, Liberty, **S...gas:** Chevron/Blimpie/diesel, **other:** Ford
807 to Wallisville, **S...other:** Heritage Park
806 frontage rd(from eb), turnaround
805.5mm Trinity River
804mm Old, Lost Rivers
803 FM 565, Cove, Old River-Winfrey, no facilities
800 FM 3180, **N...gas:** Exxon/diesel

Interstate 10

E ↕ W

Baytown

797 TX 146, to Baytown, **N...gas:** Chevron, Conoco/Subway/diesel, Shell/diesel, **food:** DQ, IHOP, McDonald's, Pizza Inn, Waffle House, **lodging:** Crystal Inn, Motel 6, Scanadian Inn, **other:** L&R RV Park, **S...gas:** Exxon, Mobil/Popeye's/diesel, RaceTrac/diesel, **food:** Jack-in-the-Box, **other:** HOSPITAL

796 frontage rd, **N...gas:** Chevron/Phillips/BP Chemical Refinery, no facilities

795 Sjolander Rd, no facilities

793 N Main St, **S...gas:** Citgo/KFC/diesel/24hr

792 Garth Rd, **N...gas:** Chevron/24hr, **food:** Burger King, Cracker Barrel, Denny's, Jack-in-the-Box, Red Lobster, Waffle House, Whataburger/24hr, **lodging:** Best Western, Baymont Inn, Hampton Inn, La Quinta, **other:** Chrysler/Jeep, Honda, Hyundai, Lincoln/Mercury, Nissan, Toyota, **S...gas:** RaceTrac, Shell, **food:** Cozumel Mexican, McDonald's, Outback Steaks, Pancho's Mexican, Piccadilly's, Pizza Hut/Taco Bell, Popeye's, Wendy's, **lodging:** Holiday Inn Express, **other:** HOSPITAL, Ford, Marshall's, Mervyn's, OfficeMax, Sears/auto, Vaughn RV Ctr, mall

791 John Martin Rd, no facilities

790 Wade Rd, no facilities

789 Thompson Rd, **N...gas:** Pilot/McDonald's/diesel, Shamrock, **lodging:** Super 8, **other:** Buick/Pontiac/GMC, **S...gas:** TA/diesel/rest./24hr/@, **other:** truck repair

788.5mm rest area eb, full(handicapped)facilities, phone, picnic tables, litter barrels, petwalk

788 sp 330(from eb), to Baytown, no facilities

787 sp 330, Crosby-Lynchburg Rd, to Highlands, **N...gas:** Mobil/Domino's/diesel, **S...other:** to San Jacinto SP, camping

786.5mm San Jacinto River

786 Monmouth Dr, no facilities

785 Magnolia Ave, to Channelview, **N...gas:** Shell/diesel, **S...gas:** Phillips/diesel, same as 784

Houston

784 Cedar Lane, Bayou Dr, **N...gas:** Citgo, **lodging:** Budget Lodge, Ramada Ltd

783 Sheldon Rd, **N...gas:** Coastal/diesel, Shell, **food:** Burger King, Jack-in-the-Box, KFC, Pizza Hut, Pizza Inn, Popeye's, Sonic, Subway, Taco Bell, Whataburger, **lodging:** Best Western, Day's Inn, Leisure Inn, Super 8, Travelodge, **other:** Advance Parts, AutoZone, DiscountTire, Eckerd, Family$, Garland's Foods, Goodyear/auto, Radio Shack, **S...food:** Capt D's, McDonald's, Wendy's, **lodging:** Scottish Inn

782 Dell-Dale Ave, **N...gas:** Exxon, **lodging:** Dell Dale Motel, **other:** HOSPITAL, **S...gas:** Conoco/diesel

781b Market St, **N...lodging:** Holiday Inn, **other:** HOSPITAL

a TX 8, Sam Houston Pkwy

780 (779 from wb)Uvalde Rd, Freeport St, **N...gas:** Chevron/diesel, Mobil, Texaco, **food:** Cracker Barrel, IHOP, Jack-in-the-Box, KFC, Pancho's Mexican, Subway, Taco Bell, **other:** HOSPITAL, Office Depot, **S...gas:** Mobil/diesel, **food:** BBQ, Blackeyed Pea, Marco's Mexican, Whataburger, **other:** Circuit City, Home Depot, NTB, Sam's Club, U-Haul, Wal-Mart/auto/24hr

778b Normandy St, **N...gas:** Conoco/diesel, Shell, **food:** Golden Corral, **S...gas:** Texaco/diesel, **lodging:** Scottish Inn

a FM 526, Federal Rd, Pasadena, **N...gas:** Chevron, Shell, **food:** BBQ, Blimpie, Jack-in-the-Box, KFC/Taco Bell, LJ Silver, Pizza Hut, Popeye's, Wendy's, **lodging:** La Quinta, **other:** DiscountTire, Eckerd, HEB Foods, Radio Shack, Target, **S...gas:** Shell, **food:** Bennigan's, Chili's, Church's, Coney Island, Joe's Crabshack, McDonald's, Ninfa's Mexican, Pappa's Seafood, Peking Chinese, **other:** MEDICAL CARE, AutoZone, Family$, O'Reilly's Parts

Houston

776b John Ralston Rd, Holland Ave, **N...gas:** Citgo, Mobil, **food:** Luby's, **lodging:** Best Western, **other:** Kroger/deli/24hr, NTB, Walgreen, **S...**same as 778

a Mercury Dr, **N...gas:** Conoco, Shamrock/diesel, **food:** Burger King, E China Rest., Island Gourmet Seafood, McDonald's, Pizza Inn, **lodging:** Day's Inn, Fairfield Inn, Hampton Inn, Premier Inn, **S...gas:** Shamrock, Shell/diesel, **food:** DQ, Steak&Ale, **other:** bank

775b a I-610, no facilities

774 Gellhorn(from eb) Blvd, Anheuser-Busch Brewery

773b McCarty St, **N...gas:** Mobil/diesel, Shell, **S...food:** Don Chile Mexican

a US 90A, N Wayside Dr, **N...gas:** Chevron, Exxon, **food:** Jack-in-the-Box, Whataburger/24hr, **S...gas:** Coastal/diesel, Shell, **food:** BBQ, Church's, diesel repair

772 Kress St, Lathrop St, **N...gas:** Conoco, Exxon, **S...food:** Burger King, 7 Mares Seafood

771b Lockwood Dr, **N...gas:** Chevron/diesel, **food:** McDonald's, **other:** Family$, **S...gas:** Phillips 66/diesel, Shell/diesel

a Waco St, **N...food:** Frenchey's Chicken

770c US 59 N, no facilities

b Jenson St, Meadow St, Gregg St, no facilities

a US 59 S, to Victoria, no facilities

769c McKee St, Hardy St, Nance St, downtown, no facilities

a Smith St(from wb), to downtown

768b a I-45, N to Dallas, S to Galveston, no facilities

767b Taylor St, no facilities

a Studemont Dr, Yale St, Heights Blvd, **N...gas:** Chevron, **S...gas:** Shell/diesel

766 (from wb), Heights Blvd, Yale St, same as 767a

765b N Durham Dr, N Shepherd Dr, **N...gas:** Shamrock/gas, **food:** Wendy's, **lodging:** Howard Johnson

Interstate 10

E ↕ W

Houston

a TC Jester Blvd, **S...gas:** Exxon/diesel, Texaco/diesel

764 Westcott St, Washington Ave, Katy Rd, **N...food:** Denny's, **lodging:** Comfort Inn, **S...gas:** Chevron, **food:** IHOP

763 I-610, no facilities

762 Silber Rd, Post Oak Rd, **N...food:** Aubrey's Ribs, Red Robin, **other:** Dodge, **S...gas:** Shell, **food:** Jack-in-the-Box, **lodging:** Holiday Inn, Ramada Inn, **other:** Chevrolet, carwash

761b Antoine Rd, **N...food:** Country Harvest Buffet, Hunan Chinese, **S...gas:** Shell, **food:** Blue Oyster Grill, Denny's, Papa John's, Whataburger/24hr, **lodging:** La Quinta, Wellesley Inn, **other:** NTB

a Wirt Rd, Chimney Rock Rd, **N...food:** Capt Penny's Seafood, **S...gas:** Chevron, Exxon/TCBY, Shell, **food:** El Tiempo Cantina, 59 Diner, McDonald's, Planter's Seafood, Steak&Ale

760 Bingle Rd, Voss Rd, **S...gas:** Exxon/diesel, Texaco/diesel, **food:** Goode Co Café, Marie Callender, Mason Jar Rest., Pappy's Café, Redwood Grill, SaltGrass Steaks, Southwell's Burgers, Sweet Tomatos, TX BBQ, Ugo's Italian, **other:** HOSPITAL, DENTIST

759 Campbell Rd(from wb), same as 758b

758b Blalock Rd, Campbell Rd, **N...food:** Ciro's Italian, Fiesta Foods, Sonic, **other:** Adam's Automotive, LubeStop, Mail It, cleaners, **S...gas:** Chevron/McDonald's/diesel, Exxon, Texaco, **other:** HOSPITAL, Kroger, Walgreen

a Bunker Hill Rd, **N...gas:** Exxon, **food:** CiCi's, **other:** Best Buy, Costco, Lowe's Whse, Michael's, PepBoys, Radio Shack, **S...gas:** Texaco/diesel, Circle K, **food:** Charlie's Burgers, Guadalajara Mexican, Quizno's, Subway, **lodging:** Day's Inn, Howard Johnson, Super 8, **other:** Ford, Goodyear/auto, Marshall's, Nissan, Ross, Target

757 Gessner Rd, **N...gas:** Exxon, **food:** BBQ, Bennigan's, Chili's, DQ, McDonald's, Schlotsky's, Wendy's, Whataburger/24hr, **other:** MEDICAL CARE, BrakeCheck, Eckerd, Home Depot, Honda, Kroger, NAPA, OfficeMax, Sam's Club/gas, U-Haul, Wal-Mart, **S...gas:** Shell, Texaco/diesel, **food:** Fuddrucker's, Jack-in-the-Box, Jason's Deli, Macaroni Grill, Olive Garden, Pappasito's, Papadeaux Seafood, Taste of TX Rest., **lodging:** Radisson, Sheraton, **other:** HOSPITAL, Circuit City, Cost+, Foley's, Ford, Goodyear, Mervyn's, Office Depot, Sears/auto, mall

756 TX 8, Sam Houston Tollway, no facilities

755 Willcrest Rd, **N...other:** Discount Tire, Kia, Mazda, NTB, **S...gas:** Citgo/diesel, Exxon/McDonald's/24hr, Texaco, **food:** China Buffet, Denny's, IHOP, Steak&Ale, **lodging:** La Quinta

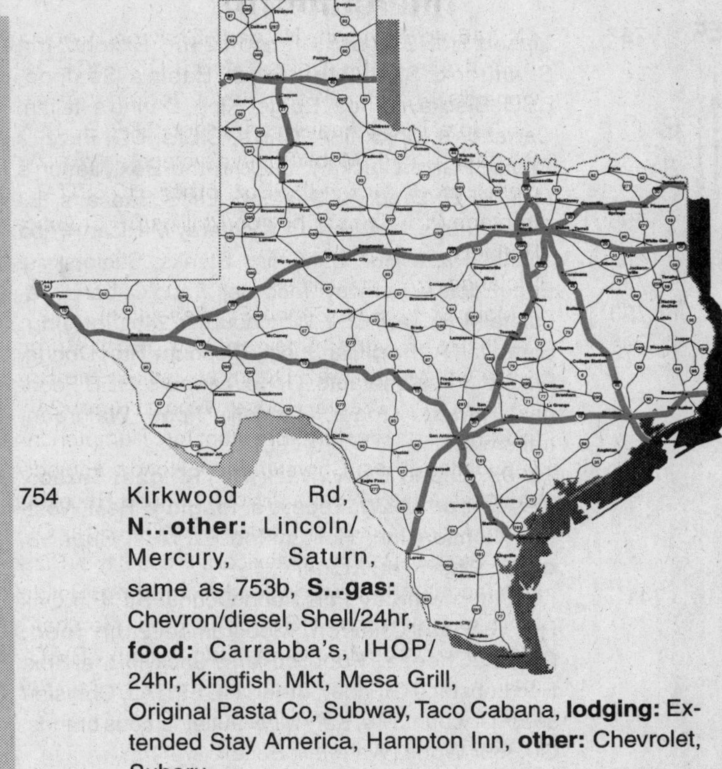

754 Kirkwood Rd, **N...other:** Lincoln/Mercury, Saturn, same as 753b, **S...gas:** Chevron/diesel, Shell/24hr, **food:** Carrabba's, IHOP/24hr, Kingfish Mkt, Mesa Grill, Original Pasta Co, Subway, Taco Cabana, **lodging:** Extended Stay America, Hampton Inn, **other:** Chevrolet, Subaru

753b Dairy-Ashford Rd, **N...other:** Buick, Chrysler/Dodge, Infiniti, K-Mart, Lexus, Nissan, Toyota, Volvo, **S...gas:** Exxon/TCBY/diesel, Shamrock, **food:** Beck's Prime Rest., Subway, TX Cattle Steaks, Whataburger, **lodging:** Courtyard, Guesthouse Inn, **other:** Audi/Porsche, Cadillac, Mitsubishi, Pontiac/GMC/Suzuki

a Eldridge Rd, **N...gas:** Conoco/diesel, **lodging:** Omni Hotel, **S...gas:** Shamrock/24hr, **other:** Pennzoil

751 TX 6, to Addicks, **N...gas:** Texaco, **food:** Cattlegard Rest., Waffle House, **lodging:** Drury Inn, Holiday Inn, Red Roof Inn, **other:** Sam's Club/gas, **S...gas:** Exxon, Chevron, Conoco/diesel, Texaco/diesel, **food:** Blimpie, DQ, Denny's/24hr, El Yucatan Mexican, Jack-in-the-Box, Wendy's, **lodging:** Bradford HomeSuites, Hearthside Extended Stay, La Quinta, Motel 6, Super 8, **other:** JiffyLube, **other:** USPO, carwash

748 Barker-Cypress Rd, **S...food:** Cracker Barrel, Lulu's Buffet, **lodging:** Fairfield Inn, **lodging:** TownePlace Inn, **other:** Chrysler/Plymouth/Jeep, Dodge, Hoover RV Ctr, Hyundai, VW

747 Fry Rd, **N...gas:** Chevron, Phillips 66, Shamrock/diesel, Shell/24hr, **food:** Bennigans, Burger King, Church's, DQ, Denny's, Godfather's, McDonald's, Pizza Hut, Sonic, Souper Salad, Subway, Taco Bell, Victor's Mexican, Whataburger, **other:** MEDICAL CARE, Goodyear, HEB Food/gas, Home Depot, Sam's Club/gas, Walgreen, Wal-Mart/auto, **S...gas:** Chevron, Citgo, Shell, **food:** Baskin-Robbins, Boston Mkt, Capt Tom's Seafood, El Chico, Fazoli's, IHOP, Jack-in-the-Box, Ninfa's Café, Omar's Mexican, Orient Express, Outback Steaks, Quizno's, Wendy's, **other:** Albertson's, Ford, Lowe's Whse, Radio Shack, Target

Interstate 10

E ↕ W

745 Mason Rd, **S...gas:** Chevron/24hr, Exxon/24hr, Shamrock, Shell/24hr, **food:** Babin's Seafood, BBQ, Blackeyed Pea, Burger King, Carino's Italian, Carrabba's, Chick-fil-A, Chili's, CiCi's, DQ, Fuzzy's Pizza, Hartz Chicken, Jack-in-the-Box, Jason's Deli, KFC, Landry's Seafood, Little Caesar's, LJ Silver, Luby's, McDonald's, Monterey Mexican, Papa John's, Pizza Hut, SaltGrass Steaks, Schlotsky's, SpagEddie's, Subway, Taco Bell, Taco Cabana, Taquiera Mexican, TCBY, Whataburger/24hr, **lodging:** Sleep Inn, **other:** CarQuest, Discount Tire, Dodge, Eckerd, Firestone/auto, Goodyear/auto, HEB Food/gas, K-Mart, Kroger, Randall's Food, Walgreen, transmissions

743 TX 99, Grand Pkwy, Peek Rd, **S...gas:** Texaco/diesel, **food:** A&W, Popeye's, **lodging:** Best Western, Comfort Inn, Holiday Inn Express, Super 8, **other:** Chevrolet, Kroger

741 (742 from wb)Katy-Fort Bend County Rd, Pin Oak Rd, **S...gas:** Chevron, Mobil/diesel/24hr, **food:** ChuckeCheese, Fuddruckers, Jack-in-the-Box, Red Lobster, TGIFriday, **other:** HOSPITAL, Chrysler/Jeep, Discount Tire, Katy Mills Outlet/famous brands, Outdoor World, Wal-Mart SuperCtr/24hr

740 FM 1463, **N...food:** McDonald's, Sonic, **other:** Yamaha, **S...gas:** Chevron, **food:** RainForest Café, **other:** Books-A-Million, Pyle RV Ctr

737 Pederson Rd, **S...other:** Holiday World RV Ctr

732 FM 359, to Brookshire, **N...gas:** Exxon/diesel, Phillips 66/diesel/rest./24hr, Shell, **lodging:** Executive Inn, **other:** KOA, **S...gas:** Chevron/diesel, Citgo/diesel, Exxon/Burger King/diesel/24hr, **food:** Jack-in-the-Box, **other:** Ford Trucks, truckwash

731 FM 1489, to Koomey Rd, **N...gas:** Exxon/diesel, Shell, **food:** Villa Fuentes Mexican, **lodging:** Brookshire Motel, Travelers Inn, **other:** KOA

730mm picnic areas(both lanes exit left), tables, litter barrels

729 Peach Ridge Rd, Donigan Rd, no facilities

726 Chew Rd(from eb), **S...**golf

725 Mlcak Rd(from wb), no facilities

724mm weigh sta wb

723 FM 1458, to San Felipe, **N...gas:** Knox/Subway/diesel/24hr, **other:** to Stephen F Austin SP, **S...other:** Outlet Ctr/famous brands, Food Court

721 (from wb), **S...**to Outlet Ctr

720a Outlet Ctr Dr, **S...**Outlet Ctr/famous brands

Sealy

720 TX 36, to Sealy, **N...gas:** Shell/diesel, **food:** DQ, Hartz Chicken, McDonald's, Sonic, Tony's Rest., **other:** Chevrolet/Pontiac/Buick/GMC, Jones RV Ctr, **S...gas:** Chevron/diesel/24hr, Mobil/diesel, Shell/diesel/24hr, **food:** Hinze's BBQ, Hunan Chinese, KFC/Taco Bell, Omar's Mexican, Pizza Hut, Subway, Whataburger/24hr, **lodging:** Best Western, Holiday Inn Express, Rodeway Inn, **other:** Bill's Foods, Chrysler/Plymouth/Dodge/Jeep, Radio Shack, Wal-Mart

718 US 90(from eb), to Sealy, no facilities

716 Pyka Rd, **N...gas:** Sealy Trk Plaza/diesel/rest./showers/24hr/@

713 Beckendorff Rd, no facilities

709 FM 2761, Bernardo Rd, no facilities

704 FM 949, no facilities

701mm picnic area wb, tables, litter barrels

699 FM 102, to Eagle Lake, **N...other:** Happy Oaks RV Park, antiques, **S...other:** Eagle Lake SP(14mi)

698 Alleyton Rd, **N...food:** BBQ, **S...gas:** Shell/Taco Bell/diesel, **other:** Chrysler/Jeep/Dodge, Ford

697mm Little Colorado River

Columbus

696 TX 71, Columbus, **N...gas:** Chevron/diesel/24hr, Shell/diesel, **food:** Burger King, DQ, Denny's, Guadalajara Mexican, Jack-in-the-Box, Pizza Hut, Schobel's Rest., Whataburger, **lodging:** Columbus Inn, Holiday Inn Express, **other:** HOSPITAL, Buick/Chevrolet, HEB Foods, Radio Shack, Wal-Mart/drugs, **S...gas:** Mobil/Church's/Subway/diesel, Shamrock/diesel, **food:** McDonald's, Sonic, **lodging:** Country Hearth Inn, **other:** Columbus RV Park

695 TX 71(from wb), to La Grange

693 FM 2434, to Glidden, no facilities

692mm rest areas both lanes, full(handicapped)facilities, vending, phone, picnic tables, litter barrels, RV dump, petwalk

689 US 90, to Hattermann Lane, **N...**Motorcoach RV Park

682 FM 155, to Wiemar, **N...gas:** Chevron, Exxon/diesel, Shell/diesel, **food:** BBQ, DQ, Quizno's, **lodging:** Super 8, **other:** HOSPITAL, $General, **S...other:** Buick/Chevrolet

678mm E Navidad River

677 US 90, **N...food:** Nannie's Café, **other:** Fostoria Glass, OutPost Art Gallery

674 US 77, Schulenburg, **N...gas:** Chevron/diesel, Exxon/diesel, **food:** BBQ, McDonald's, **lodging:** Executive Inn, Oak Ridge Motel/rest., **other:** Ford, **S...gas:** Exxon, Phillips 66/diesel, Shamrock/Subway, Shell/diesel, **food:** Burger King, DQ, Frank's Rest., Guadalajara Mexican, Whataburger, **other:** Schulenberg RV Park

672mm W Navidad River

668 FM 2238, to Engle, no facilities

661 TX 95, FM 609, to Flatonia, **N...gas:** Mobil, **food:** BBQ, **S...gas:** Exxon/24hr, Shamrock, Shell/Grumpy's Rest./motel, **food:** DQ, McDonald's, **lodging:** Sav-Inn

657.5mm picnic areas both lanes

653 US 90, **N...gas:** Shell/diesel

649 TX 97, to Waelder, no facilities

642 TX 304, to Gonzales, **N...other:** Kactus Korral RV Park(2mi)

637 FM 794, to Harwood, no facilities

632 US 90/183, to Gonzales, **N...gas:** Love's/Subway/diesel/24hr, **lodging:** Coachway Inn(2mi), **S...other:** to Palmetto SP, camping

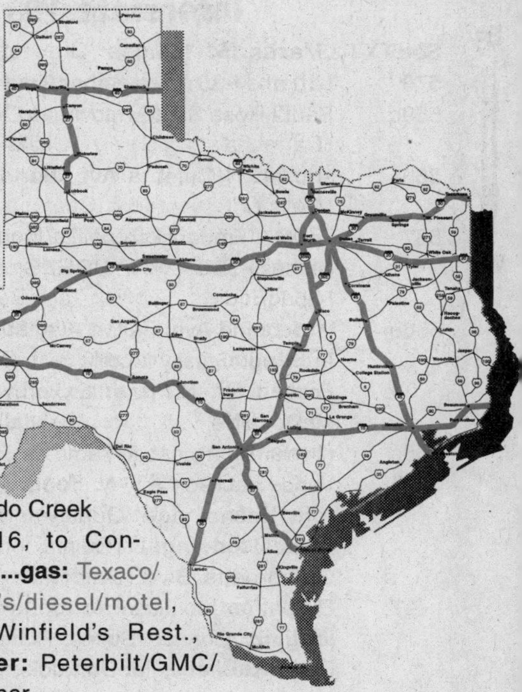

Interstate 10

E

W

630mm San Marcos River
628 TX 80, to Luling, **N...gas:** Shamrock/24hr, **food:** DQ, **other:** HOSPITAL, Riverbend RV Park, **S...gas:** Shell
625 Darst Field Rd, no facilities
624.5mm Smith Creek
623mm Allen Creek
621mm rest areas both lanes, full(handicapped)facilities, phone, picnic tables, litter barrels, vending, petwalk
620 FM 1104, no facilities
617 FM 2438, to Kingsbury, no facilities
616mm truck weigh sta both lanes
614.5mm Mill Creek
612 US 90, no facilities
611mm Geronimo Creek
610 TX 123, to San Marcos, **N...gas:** Exxon/diesel, Chevron/Subway/diesel, **food:** K&G Steaks, Los Cucos Mexican, Luby's, Subway, **lodging:** Comfort Inn, Holiday Inn, **other:** Tire Whse, **S...gas:** Shamrock/diesel, **food:** Taco Cabana, **other:** HOSPITAL, River Shade RV
609 TX 123, Austin St, **S...gas:** Mobil/diesel, **other:** Chevrolet
607 TX 46, FM 78, to New Braunfels, **N...gas:** Texaco/Jack-in-the-Box/diesel, **food:** Huddle House, **lodging:** Alamo Inn, **S...gas:** Exxon/DQ/diesel, **food:** BBQ, Hong Kong Chinese, Kettle, McDonald's, Soilitas Mexican, **lodging:** Best Western, Super 8, **other:** Chrysler/Plymouth/Dodge
605 FM 464, **N...other:** Twin Pines RV Park, **S...gas:** EZ Gas/24hr
605mm Guadalupe River
604 FM 725, to Lake McQueeney, **N...**RV park
603 US 90 E, US 90A, to Seguin, **N...other:** Explorer USA RV Sales, **S...other:** S Texas RV SuperStore
601 FM 775, to New Berlin, **N...gas:** Mobil/Subway/diesel/24hr
600 Schwab Rd, no facilities
599 FM 465, to Marion, no facilities
599mm Santa Clara Creek
597 Santa Clara Rd, no facilities
595 Zuehl Rd, no facilities
594mm Cibolo Creek
593 FM 2538, Trainer Hale Rd, **N...gas:** Citgo/DQ/diesel/24hr, **S...gas:** Exxon/diesel/rest./24hr
593mm Woman Hollering Creek
591 FM 1518, to Schertz, **N...gas:** Exxon/diesel/rest./motel/repair/24hr, **other:** camping
590.5mm rest areas both lanes, full(handicapped)facilities, phone, picnic tables, litter barrels, petwalk, RV dump
589mm Salitrillo Creek
589 Pfeil Rd, Graytown Rd, no facilities
587 LP 1604, Randolph AFB, to Universal City, no facilities
585.5mm Escondido Creek
585 FM 1516, to Converse, **N...gas:** Texaco/Church's/diesel/motel, **food:** Winfield's Rest., **S...other:** Peterbilt/GMC/Freightliner
585mm Martinez Creek
583 Foster Rd, **N...gas:** Flying J/Conoco/diesel/LP/rest./24hr/@, Shamrock/24hr, **food:** Jack-in-the-Box/24hr, **lodging:** Holiday Inn Express, Hillcrown Inn, **other:** truckwash, **S...gas:** TA/Chevron/Burger King/Pizza Hut/Popeye's/diesel/24hr/@
582.5mm Rosillo Creek
582 Ackerman Rd, Kirby, **N...gas:** Pilot/Arby's/diesel/24hr, **S...gas:** Petro/Mobil/diesel/24hr/@, KFC/Pizza Hut/Taco Bell, **food:** Wendy's, **lodging:** Relay Station Motel, **other:** Blue Beacon, Petrolube
581 I-410, no facilities

San Antonio

580 LP 13, WW White Rd, **N...gas:** Chevron, Fina, **food:** Hailey's Rest./24hr, Wendy's, **lodging:** Comfort Inn/rest., Motel 6, Scotsman Inn, **other:** RV camping, **S...gas:** Exxon/diesel, **food:** BBQ, McDonald's, Mexican Rest., Pizza Hut, **lodging:** Econolodge, Quality Inn, Super 8, **other:** Ford/Freightliner, Volvo, tires
579 Houston St, **N...gas:** Shamrock, **lodging:** Ramada Ltd, **S...gas:** Chevron, **lodging:** Day's Inn, Passport Inn
578 Pecan Valley Dr, ML King Dr, **N...gas:** Phillips 66, **S...gas:** Shell/diesel
577 US 87 S, to Roland Ave, **S...food:** Whataburger/24hr, **other:** transmissions
576 New Braunfels Ave, Gevers St, **S...gas:** Shamrock, **food:** McDonald's, Taco Snack
575 Pine St, Hackberry St, **S...food:** Little Red Barn Steaks
574 I-37, US 281, no facilities
573 Probandt St, **N...food:** Miller's BBQ, **S...gas:** Conoco, Shamrock, **other:** to SA Missions HS
572 I-10 and I-35 run together 3 miles

Interstate 10

E ↕ W

See TX I-35, exits 153-155a b.

570 I-10 and I-35 run together 3 miles

569c Santa Rosa St, downtown, to Our Lady of the Lake U

568 spur 421, Culebra Ave, Bandera Ave, **S...**to St Marys U

567 Lp 345, Fredericksburg Rd(from eb upper level accesses I-35 S, I-10 E, US 87 S, lower level accesses I-35 N)

566b Hildebrand Ave, Fulton Ave, **S...gas:** Exxon, 7-11, **lodging:** Galaxy Motel

a Fresno Dr, **N...gas:** Exxon, Shamrock, **food:** McDonald's

565c (from wb), access to same as 565 a b

b Vance Jackson Rd, **N...food:** Miller's BBQ, **lodging:** Econolodge, Quality Inn, **S...gas:** Exxon, Texaco, **lodging:** La Quinta

a Crossroads Blvd, Balcone's Heights, **N...gas:** Exxon, Texaco/diesel, **food:** Denny's, Whataburger, **lodging:** Comfort Suites, Rodeway Inn, **S...food:** Dave&Buster's, McDonald's, **lodging:** Sumner Suites, Super 8, **other:** Firestone/auto, Mazda, RV Ctr, Target, Toyota, mall, transmissions

564b a I-410, facilities off of I-410 W, Fredericksburg Rd

563 Callaghan Rd, **N...gas:** Mobil, **food:** Las Palapas Mexican, Subway, TGIFriday, **lodging:** Embassy Suites, Marriott, **other:** CHIROPRACTOR, Ford, Lexus, Malibu Grand Prix, Mazda, Sun Harvest Foods, Toyota, **S...gas:** Exxon, **food:** Mama's Rest., **other:** Lowe's Whse

561 Wurzbach Rd, **N...gas:** Mobil/diesel, Phillips 66, **food:** Bennigan's, Fuddrucker's, Golden Corral, Jason's Deli, Pappasito's Cantina, Popeye's, Sea Island Shrimphouse, TX Land&Cattle, **lodging:** AmeriSuites, Homewood Suites, Ramada Ltd, Wyndham, **other:** MEDICAL CARE, Albertson's, HEB Food/gas, Eckerd/24hr, **S...gas:** Texaco/diesel, **food:** Alamo Café, Arby's, Benihana, Church's, Denny's, IHOP, Jack-in-the-Box, Luby's, McDonald's, Pizza Hut, Sombrero Rosa Café, Taco Bell, Taco Cabana, Tony Roma, Wendy's, **lodging:** Candlewood Suites, Drury Inn, Hawthorn Suites, Holiday Inn Express, La Quinta, Motel 6, Residence Inn, Sleep Inn, Thrifty Inn

560b frontage rd(from eb), **N...food:** Water St Seafood, **other:** Chrysler/Plymouth, Kia, Nissan

a Huebner Rd, **N...food:** BBQ, Champ's, Macaroni Grill, On the Border, SaltGrass Steaks, **other:** Borders, Land Rover, Old Navy, Ross, cinema, **S...gas:** Exxon, Shell/Jack-in-the-Box, **food:** Burger King, Cracker Barrel, Jim's Rest., **lodging:** AmeriSuites, Day's Inn, Hampton Inn, Homestead Village, **other:** Cadillac/Hummer

559 Lp 335, US 87, Fredericksburg Rd, **N...food:** Carrabba's, Chili's, Outback Steaks, Joe's Crabshack, Logan's Roadhouse, **other:** Buick/GMC, **S...gas:** Texaco, **food:** Krispy Kreme, Acura

558 De Zavala Rd, **N...gas:** Chevron, Exxon/diesel, **food:** BBQ, McDonald's, Sonic, Subway, Taco Cabana, **lodging:** Best Western, Howard Johnson, Radford Inn, Super 8, **other:** Barnes&Noble, Chevrolet, HEB Food/gas, Home Depot, Marshall's, OfficeMax, Target, **S...food:** IHOP, Schlotsky's, TGIFriday, Whataburger, Zio's Italian, **other:** Discount Tire, Wal-Mart SuperCtr/24hr

557 Spur 53, Univ of TX at San Antonio, **N...other:** Jaguar/Mazerati/Ferrari, **S...other:** Costco/gas

556b frontage rd, **S...lodging:** Motel 6

a to Anderson Lp, **S...lodging:** Comfort Inn, **other:** to Seaworld

555 La Quintera Pkwy, no facilities

554 Camp Bullis Rd, **N...gas:** Citgo, **other:** Russell Park, **S...gas:** Shell, **lodging:** Rodeway Inn, Motel 6(2mi)

551 Boerne Stage Rd(from wb), to Leon Springs, same as 550

550 FM 3351, Ralph Fair Rd, **N...gas:** Shamrock/Pico's/diesel, **S...gas:** Texaco/Domino's/diesel, **food:** Las Palapas Mexican, Macaroni Grill, Starbucks, **other:** GNC, HEB Foods

546 Fair Oaks Pkwy, Tarpon Dr, **S...gas:** Chevron/diesel/café, Exxon/diesel/café, **other:** Hoover RV Ctr

543 Boerne Stage Rd, to Scenic LP Rd, **N...gas:** Citgo/diesel/24hr, **food:** Alamo Café, Copeland's Seafood/steaks, lCaverns Inn/rest., **other:** Chevrolet, Chrysler/Dodge/Jeep, Ford, Pontiac/Buick/GMC, Alamo Fiesta RV Park, Ancira RV Ctr, Wal-Mart SuperCtr/24hr, to Cascade Caverns

540 TX 46, to New Braunfels, **N...gas:** Exxon/Taco Bell/diesel, Texaco/diesel/24hr, **food:** Burger King, Church's, DQ, Denny's, Little Caesar's, Margarita's Café, Pizza Hut, Quizno's, Shanghai Chinese, Sonic, Taco Cabana, Wendy's, **lodging:** Best Western, Holiday Inn Express, Key to the Hills Motel, **other:** HEB Food/gas, Walgreen, **S...**Chili's, Home Depot

539 Johns Rd, **S...gas:** Shamrock/diesel/LP, **food:** Pico's Chicken, **lodging:** Tapatio Springs Motel(4mi)

538mm Cibolo Creek

537 US 87, to Boerne, **2 mi N...gas:** Chevron, Shamrock, **food:** La Hacienda Rest., Maque's Mexican, Pete's Place, Pico's Chicken, Subway, **lodging:** Key to the Hills Motel

533 FM 289, Welfare, **N...food:** Po-Po Family Rest., **other:** Top of the Hill RV Park(1mi)

532mm Little Joshua Creek

531mm picnic area wb, tables, litter barrels

530mm Big Joshua Creek

529.5mm picnic area eb, tables, litter barrels

527 FM 1621(from wb), to Waring

526.5mm Holiday Creek

Interstate 10

E ↕ W

Kerrville Ozona

524 TX 27, FM 1621, to Waring, **N...**VETERINARIAN, **S...gas:** Chevron/diesel, Texaco/24hr, **food:** DD Family Rest.

523.5mm Guadalupe River

523 US 87 N, to Comfort, **N...gas:** Chevron/McDonald's/diesel, **S...gas:** Exxon/diesel/24hr, Texaco/diesel, **food:** DQ, **lodging:** Inn at Comfort, **other:** USA RV Park

521.5mm Comfort Creek

520 FM 1341, to Cypress Creek Rd, no facilities

515mm Cypress Creek

514mm rest areas both lanes, full(handicapped)facilities, vending, phone, picnic tables, litter barrels, petwalk, playground

508 TX 16, Kerrville, **N...gas:** Exxon/diesel, **other:** Chevrolet/Pontiac/Buick/Cadillac, RV camping, **S...**Chamber of Commerce, **gas:** Chevron/Subway/diesel, Shamrock/diesel, TC/diesel, Shell/McDonald's/diesel/24hr, **food:** Acapulco Mexican, BBQ, Cracker Barrel, DQ, Denny's, Luby's, Schlotsky's, **lodging:** Best Western, Budget Inn, Comfort Inn, Day's Inn, Econolodge, Hampton Inn, Holiday Inn Express, Motel 6, Super 8, YoYo Ranch Hotel, **other:** HOSPITAL, Home Depot, Kerrville RV Ctr, Lowe's Whse, **1-2 mi S...food:** Burger King, Jack-in-the-Box, KFC, Pizza Hut/Taco Bell, **other:** AutoZone, $General, Firestone, Hastings Books, HEB Foods, Pennzoil, Walgreen, to Kerrville-Schreiner SP

505 FM 783, to Kerrville, **S...gas:** Exxon/diesel, **3 mi S on TX 27...lodging:** Inn of the Hills, **food:** Chili's, DQ, Pizza Hut, Sonic, Taco Casa, Wal-Mart SuperCtr/24hr, **other:** Classic Car Museum

503.5mm scenic views both lanes, litter barrels

501 FM 1338, **N...other:** Buckhorn RV Resort, **S...other:** KOA(2mi)

497mm picnic area both lanes, tables, litter barrels

492 FM 479, **S...**Lone Oak Store

490 TX 41, no facilities

488 TX 27, Mountain Home, to Ingram, no facilities

484 Midway Rd, no facilities

477 US 290, to Fredericksburg, no facilities

476.5mm service rd eb

472 Old Segovia Rd, no facilities

465 FM 2169, to Segovia, **S...gas:** Phillips 66/diesel, **food:** Safari Rest., **lodging:** Best Western, **other:** RV camping

464.5mm Johnson Fork Creek

462 US 83 S, to Uvalde, no facilities

461mm picnic area eb, tables, litter barrels

460 (from wb), to Junction, no facilities

459mm picnic area wb, tables, litter barrels

457 FM 2169, to Junction, **N...gas:** Texaco/diesel, **S...lodging:** Day's Inn/rest., **other:** RV camping

456.5mm Llano River

Junction

456 US 83/377, Junction, **N...gas:** Chevron/diesel, Conoco, Shamrock/McDonald's/diesel/24hr, **food:** BBQ, JR's Rest., **lodging:** Comfort Inn, **S...gas:** Exxon, Shell, **food:** DQ, Git-It Rest., **lodging:** Hills Motel, Slumber Inn/rest., Sun Valley Motel, **other:** HOSPITAL, KOA, Lakeview RV Park(3mi), Lazy Daze RV Park, to S Llano River SP

452.5mm Bear Creek

451 RM 2291, to Cleo Rd, **S...**camping

448mm North Creek

445 RM 1674, **S...**camping

444.5mm Stark Creek

442.5mm Copperas Creek

442 RM 1674, to Ft McKavett, no facilities

439mm N Llano River

438 Lp 291(from wb), to Roosevelt, same as 437

437 Lp 291(from eb, no EZ return), to Roosevelt, **1 mi N...gas:** Simon Bros Mercantile/diesel, **other:** USPO

429 RM 3130, to Harrell, no facilities

423mm parking area both lanes, litter barrels

420 RM 3130, to Baker Rd, no facilities

412 Allison Rd, RM 3130, no facilities

404 RM 3130, RM 864, **N...**to Ft McKavett St HS, **S...lodging:** Best Value Inn, **other:** HOSPITAL

Sonora

400 US 277, Sonora, **N...gas:** Texaco/diesel, **food:** Sutton Co Steaks, **lodging:** Day's Inn, **other:** Chevrolet/Buick/Pontiac, **S...gas:** Chevron/diesel, Conoco/diesel, Exxon/diesel/24hr, Fina/diesel, Phillips 66, Shell/diesel, **food:** Country Cookin Café, DQ, La Mexicana Rest., Pizza Hut, Sonic, Taco Grill, **lodging:** Best Value Inn, Best Western, **other:** Alco, Buster's RV Park, Family$, Parts+, museum

399 (from eb)LP 467, Sonora, **S...gas:** Chevron/diesel, Fina/24hr, Phillips 66, Exxon/diesel/24hr, **food:** DQ, Subway, **lodging:** Day's Inn, **other:** HOSPITAL, RV camping

TEXAS

Interstate 10

E ↕ W

394mm **rest area both lanes, full(handicapped)facilities, phone, picnic tables, litter barrel, petwalk, RV dump**
392 RM 1989, Caverns of Sonora Rd, **8 mi S...other:** Caverns of Sonora Camping, phone
388 RM 1312(from eb), no facilities
381 RM 1312, no facilities
372 Taylor Box Rd, **N...gas:** Chevron/diesel/rest./24hr, **lodging:** Super 8/RV Park, **other:** auto museum
368 LP 466, **N...**same as 365 & 363
365 TX 163, Ozona, **N...gas:** Chevron/diesel, Texaco/diesel/café, T&C/Taco Bell/diesel, **food:** Burger King, Café NextDoor, DQ, Subway, **lodging:** Best Western, Economy Inn/RV Park, **other:** HOSPITAL, NAPA, to David Crockett Mon, **S...gas:** Chevron, Frank's Fuels, Shell
363 Lp 466, to Ozona, no facilities
361 RM 2083, Pandale Rd, no facilities
357mm Eureka Draw
351mm Howard Draw
350 FM 2398, to Howard Draw, no facilities
349mm parking area wb, litter barrels
346mm parking area eb, litter barrels
343 US 290 W, no facilities
337 Live Oak Rd, no facilities
336.5mm Live Oak Creek
328 River Rd, Sheffield, **S...gas:** Phillips 66/diesel
327.5mm Pecos River
325 US 290, TX 349, to Iraan, Sheffield, **N...**HOSPITAL
320 frontage rd, no facilities
314 frontage rd, no facilities
308mm rest area both lanes, full(handicapped)facilities, phone, picnic tables, litter barrels, petwalk
307 US 190, FM 305, to Iraan, **N...**HOSPITAL
298 RM 2886, no facilities
294 FM 11, Bakersfield, **N...gas:** Exxon, **S...gas:** Chevron/diesel/café, **other:** phone
288 Ligon Rd, no facilities
285 McKenzie Rd, **S...other:** Domaine Cordier Ste Genevieve Winery
279mm picnic area eb, tables, litter barrels
277 FM 2023, no facilities
273 US 67/385, to McCamey, **N...other:** picnic area wb, tables, litter barrels
272 University Rd, no facilities
264 Warnock Rd, **N...other:** KOA/gas/BBQ
261 US 290 W, US 385 S, **N...gas:** Exxon/TCBY/diesel, **other:** RV camping, **S...**HOSPITAL
259b a (259 from eb)TX 18, FM 1053, Ft Stockton, **N...gas:** Fina/diesel, Shell/Burger King/diesel, Texaco/diesel, **other:** I-10 RV Park
257 US 285, Ft Stockton, to Pecos, **N...other:** Comanche Land RV Park, golf, **S...gas:** Chevron/diesel, Exxon/diesel/rest., Shamrock/diesel, **food:** BBQ, KFC/Taco Bell, McDonald's, Pizza Hut, Sonic, Subway, **lodging:** Atrium West Motel, Best Western, Comfort Inn, Day's Inn, Holiday Inn Express, La Quinta, Motel 6, Sands Motel, **other:** Chevrolet/Pontiac/Buick, Ford/Lincoln/Mercury, Goodyear/auto, Mktbasket Foods, Wal-Mart

Ft Stockton

256 to US 385 S, Ft Stockton, **1 mi S...gas:** Shamrock/diesel, Shell/diesel, Texaco/diesel, **food:** China Inn, DQ, K-Bob's Steaks, KFC, Pizza Express, Sonic, Subway, **lodging:** Alpine Lodge/rest., Best Western, Comfort Inn, Econolodge, Motel 6, Sands Motor Inn, Super 8, **other:** HOSPITAL, to Ft Stockton Hist Dist, Big Bend NP
253 FM 2037, to Belding, no facilities
248 US 67, FM 1776, to Alpine, **S...**to Big Bend NP, no facilities
246 Firestone, no facilities
241 Kennedy Rd, no facilities
235 Mendel Rd, no facilities
233mm rest area both lanes, full(handicapped)facilities, phone, picnic tables, litter barrels, petwalk
229 Hovey Rd, no facilities
222 Hoefs Rd, no facilities
214 (from wb), FM 2448, no facilities
212 TX 17, FM 2448, to Pecos, **S...gas:** Fina/diesel/café
209 TX 17, **S...other:** to Davis Mtn SP, Ft Davis NHS
206 FM 2903, to Balmorhea, **S...other:** to Balmorhea SP
192 FM 3078, to Toyahvale, **S...other:** to Balmorhea SP
188 Giffin Rd, no facilities
186 I-20, to Ft Worth, Dallas
185mm picnic area both lanes, tables, litter barrels
184 Springhills, no facilities
181 Cherry Creek Rd, **S...gas:** Chevron/24hr
176 TX 118, FM 2424, to Kent, **N...gas:** Chevron/diesel, **S...other:** to McDonald Observatory, Davis Mtn SP, Ft Davis
173 Hurd's Draw Rd, no facilities
166 Boracho Sta, no facilities
159 Plateau, **N...gas:** Fina/diesel/24hr
153 Michigan Flat, no facilities
146 Wild Horse Rd, no facilities
146mm weigh sta wb
144.5mm rest area both lanes, full(handicapped)facilities, picnic tables, litter barrels, petwalk

Van Horn

140b Ross Dr, Van Horn, **N...gas:** Chevron, Exxon/diesel, Love's/Subway/diesel/24hr, **lodging:** Bell's Motel, Comfort Inn, Day's Inn/rest., Motel 6, Sands Motel/rest., **other:** El Campo RV Park, Van Horn Drug, **S...other:** Mountain RV Park/dump
a US 90, TX 54, Van Horn Dr, **N...gas:** Shamrock, Texaco/diesel, **lodging:** Comfort Inn, Village Inn, **other:** HOSPITAL, NAPA, USPO, **S...gas:** Exxon, Pilot/Wendy's/diesel/24hr, **food:** Papa's Café

Interstate 10

138 Lp 10, to Van Horn, **N...food:** Chuey's Rest., DQ, Pizza Hut, **lodging:** Best Western, Budget Inn, Comfort Inn, Economy Inn, Motel 6, Ramada Ltd, **other:** Eagles Nest RV Park, Ford/Mercury, Goodyear, IGA Foods, **S...gas:** Chevron/diesel/24hr, **food:** McDonald's, **lodging:** Holiday Inn Express, Super 8

137mm truck weigh sta eb

136mm scenic overlook wb, picnic tables, litter barrels

135mm Mountain/Central time zone line

133 (from wb)frontage rd, no facilities

129 Allamore, to Hot Wells, no facilities

108 to Sierra Blanca(from wb), same as 107

107 RM 1111, Sierra Blanca Ave, **N...gas:** Exxon/diesel/24hr, Texaco/diesel, **lodging:** Sierra Motel, **other:** Good Sam RV Park, truck/tire repair, to Hueco Tanks SP, **S...gas:** Chevron, **food:** Cactus Grill

105 (106 from wb)Lp 10, Sierra Blanca, same as 107

102.5mm inspection sta eb

99 Lasca Rd, **N...other:** picnic area both lanes, picnic tables, litter barrels, no restrooms

98mm picnic area eb, tables, litter barrels, no restrooms

95 frontage rd(from eb), **S...**gas/motel/café

87 FM 34, **S...gas:** Trkstp/diesel/rest./24hr/@

85 Esperanza Rd, no facilities

81 FM 2217, no facilities

78 TX 20 W, to McNary, no facilities

77mm truck parking area wb

72 spur 148, to Ft Hancock, **S...gas:** Shell/diesel, Texaco, **food:** Angie's Rest., **other:** RV park, motel

68 Acala Rd, no facilities

55 Tornillo, no facilities

51mm rest area both lanes, full(handicapped)facilities, picnic tables, litter tables, petwalk

49 FM 793, Fabens, **S...gas:** Phillips 66/diesel, RnR/diesel, **food:** Church's, McDonald's, **lodging:** Fabens Inn, **other:** Barton Parts, Big 8 Foods, Family$

42 FM 1110, to Clint, **S...gas:** Exxon/diesel, **lodging:** Cotton Valley Motel/RV Park/rest./dump

37 FM 1281, Horizon Blvd, **N...gas:** Exxon, Love's/Subway/diesel/24hr, **lodging:** Americana Inn, **S...gas:** Petro/Mobil/Blimpie/diesel/24hr/@, **food:** McDonald's, **lodging:** Deluxe Inn, **other:** Blue Beacon

34 TX 375, Americas Ave, **N...gas:** Chevron/diesel/24hr, Shamrock/diesel, Texaco/diesel/24hr, **S...other:** RV camping, El Paso Mus of Hist

32 FM 659, Zaragosa Rd, **N...gas:** Chevron/diesel, Phillips 66, **food:** Arby's, Cheddar's, Furr's Buffet, IHOP, Logan's Roadhouse, Macaroni Grill, McDonald's, Outback Steaks, Starbucks, Village Inn Rest., Whataburger/24hr, **lodging:** Microtel, **other:** Chevrolet, Circuit City, Lowe's Whse, Office Depot, **S...gas:** Chevron, Shamrock/diesel, **food:** Howah Chinese

30 Lee Trevino Dr, **N...gas:** TGIFriday, **lodging:** Red Roof Inn, **other:** Discount Tire, Firestone, Ford, Isuzu, Home Depot, Lexus, NTB, Sears/auto, mall, **S...gas:** Shamrock/24hr, **other:** Nissan

29 Lomaland Dr, **N...gas:** Exxon, **food:** Denny's, Edelweiss Rest., KwikWok, Whataburger, **lodging:** AmeriSuites, La Quinta, Motel 6, **other:** Lexus, Toyota, **S...gas:** Fina/7-11, **food:** Dot's BBQ, Julio's Café, Tony Roma, **lodging:** HomeGate Studios, Westar Suites, **other:** Harley-Davidson

28b Yarbrough Dr, El Paso, **N...gas:** Chevron/24hr, **food:** Beijing Chinese, Bennigan's, Burger King, Grandy's, LJ Silver, McDonald's, Sonic, Subway, Wendy's, Whataburger, Wienerschnitzel, Wyatt's Cafeteria, **lodging:** Day's Inn, **other:** Marshall's, Mervyn's, PepBoys, Radio Shack, Ross, Wal-Mart SuperCtr/gas/24hr, **S...gas:** Shamrock/24hr, **food:** Applebee's, LaMalenche Café, Pizza Hut, **lodging:** Baymont Inn, Comfort Inn, InTown Suites, Suburban Lodge

a FM 2316, McRae Blvd, **N...gas:** Chevron/24hr, **food:** Chico's Taco, ChuckeCheese, Jack-in-the-Box, KFC, Marie Callender, Pancho's Mexican, Pepe's Tomales, Pizza Hut, **other:** HOSPITAL, Best Buy, Firestone/auto, Goodyear/auto, K-Mart, Michael's, OfficeMax, Walgreen, **S...gas:** Chevron, Fina/7-11, Phillips 66/diesel, **food:** Gabriel's Mexican, Hyundai/Saturn

27 Hunter Dr, Viscount Blvd, **N...gas:** Shamrock, Fina/7-11, **food:** Carrow's Rest., K-Bob's, Red Lobster, Taco Bell, **lodging:** La Quinta, **other:** Barnes&Noble, CompUSA, Firestone, **S...gas:** Exxon/Subway/diesel, Shell, Whataburger/24hr, **other:** Family$, Food City

Interstate 10

E ↕ W

26 Hawkins Blvd, El Paso, **N...gas:** Chevron, Shamrock, Texaco, **food:** Arby's, Burger King, Country Kitchen, DQ, Golden Corral, IHOP, Landry's Seafood, Luby's, Olive Garden, Taco Cabana, Wyatt's Cafeteria, **lodging:** Howard Johnson, **other:** Circuit City, Dillard's, JC Penney, Office Depot, Pennzoil, Sam's Club, Sears/auto, Wal-Mart SuperCtr/gas/24hr, **S...gas:** Shamrock/diesel, **food:** China King, McDonald's, Village Inn Rest., **lodging:** Best Western

25 Airway Blvd, El Paso Airport, **N...gas:** Shell/diesel/24hr, **food:** Courtyard, **lodging:** Hampton Inn, Holiday Inn, Radisson, **other:** VW/Volvo/Mercedes, **S...gas:** Chevron/diesel/rest./24hr, **other:** Goodyear, Subaru

24b Geronimo Dr, **N...gas:** Chevron/24hr, **food:** Seafood Galley, Steak&Ale, **other:** MEDICAL CARE, Dillard's, Mervyn's, Office Depot, Target, Walgreen, mall, **S...gas:** Fina/7-11, Phillips 66, **food:** Bombay Bicycle Club, Denny's, **lodging:** AmeriSuites, Embassy Suites, La Quinta

a Trowbridge Dr, **N...gas:** Fina, Thunderbird Gas, **food:** Alexandrio's Mexican, Luby's, McDonald's, Steak&Ale, Whataburger, **lodging:** Budget Inn, **other:** CHIROPRACTOR, Ford, Nissan, Toyota

23b US 62/180, to Paisano Dr, **N...food:** Jack-in-the-Box, McDonald's, **other:** Ford, U-Haul, to Carlsbad

a Raynolds St, **S...food:** Arby's, **lodging:** Motel 6, Super 8, **other:** HOSPITAL

22b US 54, Patriot Fwy, no facilities

a Copia St, El Paso, **N...gas:** Fina/7-11, Shamrock, **food:** KFC

21 Piedras St, El Paso, **N...gas:** Exxon, **food:** Burger King, McDonald's, **other:** Family$

20 Dallas St, Cotton St, **N...gas:** Exxon, Church's

19 TX 20, El Paso, downtown, **N...gas:** Chevron, **S...gas:** Texaco, **lodging:** Holiday Inn, Travelodge

18b Franklin Ave, Porfirio Diaz St, no facilities

a Schuster Ave, **N...**Sun Bowl, **S...**to UTEP

16 Executive Ctr Blvd, **N...gas:** Shamrock/24hr, **food:** Burger King, **lodging:** Executive Inn, **other:** Ford

13b a US 85, Paisano Dr, to Sunland Park Dr, **N...gas:** Shamrock/24hr, **food:** Barriga's Café, Carino's Italian, ChuckeCheese, Grand China, Great American Steaks, Olive Garden, Red Lobster, Sonic, Whataburger/24hr, **other:** Barnes&Noble, Best Buy, Circuit City, Dillard's, JC Penney, Office Depot, OfficeMax, PetsMart, Sears/auto, Target, mall, **S...gas:** Shamrock/diesel/24hr, Shell, **food:** La Malinche Mexican, McDonald's, Sonic, Subway, **lodging:** Best Western, Comfort Suites, Holiday Inn, Sleep Inn, Studio+, **other:** GMC/Pontiac/Buick, Sunland Park RaceTrack

12 Resler Dr(from wb), no facilities

11 TX 20, to Mesa St, Sunland Park, **N...gas:** Chevron/diesel/24hr, Circle K/gas, Shamrock/diesel/24hr, **food:** Carrow's/24hr, Chili's, CiCi's, Cracker Barrel, Denny's, Golden Corral, Jaxon's Rest/brewery, K-Bob's, LJ Silver, Papa John's, Popeye's, Rancher's Grill, Red Lobster, Souper Salad, Subway, Taco Bell, Tony Roma, Wienerschnitzel, Wendy's, Whataburger, **lodging:** Baymont Inn, Comfort Inn, La Quinta, Red Roof Inn, **other:** Albertson's, Checker Parts, Fabric Whse, Firestone/auto, Goodyear/auto, Home Depot, PepBoys, Wal-Mart SuperCtr/24hr, **S...gas:** Chevron/diesel/24hr, Shamrock/diesel/24hr, **food:** Burger King, Church's, Golden China, Hudson's Grill, KFC, Leo's Mexican, Luby's, McDonald's, Subway, Taco Cabana, Village Inn Rest., **lodging:** Best Value Inn, Day's Inn, Extended Stay America, Motel 6, Travelodge, **other:** AutoZone, Big 8 Foods, Furr's Foods, Martin Tires, Radio Shack, Sam's Club/gas, Walgreen

9 Redd Rd, **N...**Ford, **S...gas:** Phillips 66/diesel, **food:** Burger King, Pizza Hut, **other:** Albertson's/gas, Chevrolet, Honda, Lowe's Whse

8 Artcraft Rd, no facilities

6 Lp 375, to Canutillo, **N...gas:** Texaco/Taco Bell/diesel, **other:** to Trans Mountain Rd, Franklin Mtns SP, **S...gas:** Shell/Subway/diesel, **other:** RV camping

5mm truck check sta eb

2 Westway, Vinton, **N...gas:** Petro/Mobil/Blimpie/diesel/rest./Petrolube/tires/24hr/@, **S...gas:** gas/24hr, **food:** Great American Steaks

1mm **Welcome Ctr eb, full(handicapped)facilities, info, phone, picnic tables, litter barrels, petwalk,** weigh sta wb

0 FM 1905, Anthony, **N...gas:** Flying J/Conoco/diesel/LP/24hr/@, **lodging:** Super 8, **rest area wb, full(handicapped) facilties, picnic tables, litter barrels, S...gas:** Chevron/deli/diesel, Exxon/Burger King/diesel/24hr, Pilot/Wendy's/diesel/24hr/@, **lodging:** Holiday Inn Express, **other:** Big 8 Foods, American RV/Marine(1mi), truckwash

0mm Texas/New Mexico state line

Interstate 20

E ↕ W

Exit # Services

636mm Texas/Louisiana state line

635.5mm **Welcome Ctr wb/parking area eb, full(handicapped)facilities, phone, picnic tables, litter barrels, petwalk**

635 TX 9, TX 156, to Waskom, **N...gas:** Chevron/Burger King/diesel, Exxon/diesel, **food:** Burger King, DQ, Jim's BBQ, **other:** Family$

633 US 80, FM 9, FM 134, to Waskom, **N...gas:** Texaco, **food:** Catfish Village Rest.

628 to US 80(from wb), to frontage rd(from eb), no facilities

Interstate 20

E ↕ W

Marshall

624 FM 2199, to Scottsville, no facilities

620 FM 31, to Elysian Fields, no facilities

617 US 59, Marshall, **N...gas:** Exxon/24hr, Texaco/24hr, **food:** Applebee's, Domino's, Golden Corral, Gucci's Pizza, IHOP, Marshall City Steaks, McDonald's, Subway, Waffle House, Wendy's, **lodging:** Best Western, Express Inn, Hampton Inn, Holiday Inn Express, La Quinta, **other:** Chevrolet/Cadillac, Chrysler/Plymouth/Dodge/Jeep, Ford/Lincoln/Mercury, Toyota, Country Pines RV Park(8mi), **S...gas:** Chevron/diesel, Conoco/diesel/@, Shamrock/diesel, Total, **food:** Hungri Maverick Rest., **lodging:** Day's Inn, Econolodge, Motel 6, Super 8

614 TX 43, to Marshall, **S...**to Martin Creek Lake SP

610 FM 3251, no facilities

608mm rest area both lanes, full(handicapped)facilities, phone, vending, picnic tables, litter barrels

604 FM 450, Hallsville, **N...**gas/diesel, **other:** 450 Hitchin' Post RV Park, to Lake O' the Pines

600mm Mason Creek

599 FM 968, Longview, **N...lodging:** Wingate Inn(8mi), **other:** Kenworth Trucks, **S...gas:** Exxon/diesel, Fina/diesel/rest./@, Phillips 66, **other:** Goodyear, truck repair

596 US 259 N, TX 149, to Lake O' Pines, **N...gas:** Exxon/Grandy's/diesel, Texaco/diesel, **food:** Burger King, Whataburger, **lodging:** Microtel, Super 8, **other:** HOSPITAL, **S...gas:** Total/diesel, **lodging:** Holiday Inn Express, **other:** to Martin Lake SP

595b a TX 322, Estes Pkwy, **N...gas:** Arco, Chevron/Subway/diesel, Shamrock, Texaco/diesel/24hr, **food:** DQ, Jack-in-the-Box, Lupe's Mexican, McDonald's, Pizza Hut, Stratford Inn, Waffle House, **lodging:** Best Western, Day's Inn, Econolodge, Guest Inn, **S...gas:** Chevron/diesel, Fina/diesel, **food:** KFC/Taco Bell, Shone's rest., **lodging:** Hampton Inn, La Quinta, Motel 6

593mm Sabine River

591 FM 2087, FM 2011, no facilities

589b a US 259, TX 31, Kilgore(exits left from wb), **N...other:** E TX Oil Museum, **1-3 mi S...food:** Kilgore Café, **lodging:** Budget Inn, Comfort Inn, Day's Inn, Holiday Inn Express, Homewood Suites, Ramada Inn

587 TX 42, Kilgore, **N...gas:** Shamrock, **food:** BBQ, **other:** E TX Oil Museum, **S...gas:** Exxon

583 TX 135, to Kilgore, Overton, **N...gas:** EZMart/gas, **other:** Shallow Creek RV Resort, **S...gas:** Exxon/diesel

582 FM 3053, Liberty City, **N...gas:** Exxon/Subway/diesel, Fina, Texaco, **food:** BBQ, DQ

579 Joy-Wright Mtn Rd, no facilities

575 Barber Rd, no facilities

574mm picnic area both lanes, picnic tables, litter barrels, handicapped accessible

571b FM 757, Omen Rd, to Starrville, no facilities

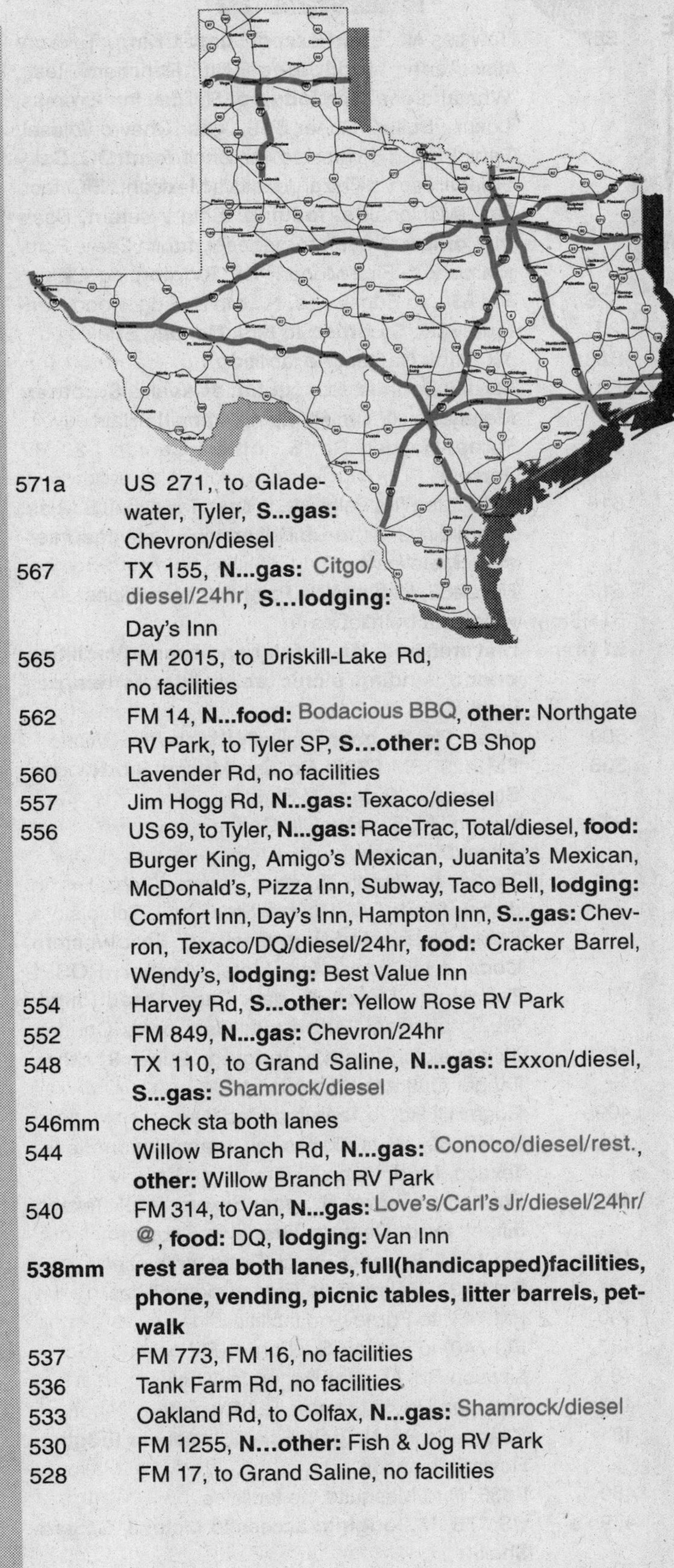

571a US 271, to Gladewater, Tyler, **S...gas:** Chevron/diesel

567 TX 155, **N...gas:** Citgo/diesel/24hr, **S...lodging:** Day's Inn

565 FM 2015, to Driskill-Lake Rd, no facilities

562 FM 14, **N...food:** Bodacious BBQ, **other:** Northgate RV Park, to Tyler SP, **S...other:** CB Shop

560 Lavender Rd, no facilities

557 Jim Hogg Rd, **N...gas:** Texaco/diesel

556 US 69, to Tyler, **N...gas:** RaceTrac, Total/diesel, **food:** Burger King, Amigo's Mexican, Juanita's Mexican, McDonald's, Pizza Inn, Subway, Taco Bell, **lodging:** Comfort Inn, Day's Inn, Hampton Inn, **S...gas:** Chevron, Texaco/DQ/diesel/24hr, **food:** Cracker Barrel, Wendy's, **lodging:** Best Value Inn

554 Harvey Rd, **S...other:** Yellow Rose RV Park

552 FM 849, **N...gas:** Chevron/24hr

548 TX 110, to Grand Saline, **N...gas:** Exxon/diesel, **S...gas:** Shamrock/diesel

546mm check sta both lanes

544 Willow Branch Rd, **N...gas:** Conoco/diesel/rest., **other:** Willow Branch RV Park

540 FM 314, to Van, **N...gas:** Love's/Carl's Jr/diesel/24hr/@, **food:** DQ, **lodging:** Van Inn

538mm rest area both lanes, full(handicapped)facilities, phone, vending, picnic tables, litter barrels, petwalk

537 FM 773, FM 16, no facilities

536 Tank Farm Rd, no facilities

533 Oakland Rd, to Colfax, **N...gas:** Shamrock/diesel

530 FM 1255, **N...other:** Fish & Jog RV Park

528 FM 17, to Grand Saline, no facilities

TEXAS

Interstate 20

E ↕ W — Canton

527 TX 19, **N...gas:** Exxon/Burger King, Texaco/diesel/24hr, **food:** Jewl's Rest., Ranchero Rest., Whataburger/24hr, **lodging:** Holiday Inn Express, Luxury Suites, Super 8, **S...gas:** Chevron/diesel/24hr, Phillips 66/diesel/24hr, Shell, **food:** DQ, Dairy Palace, Jerry's Pizza, Juanita's Mexican, KFC/Taco Bell, McDonald's, **lodging:** Best Western, Day's Inn, **other:** Chrysler/Dodge/Plymouth/Jeep, Ford/Mercury, to First Monday SP, RV camping, LP

526 FM 859, to Edgewood, **N...other:** Edgewood Heritage Park, **S...other:** to First Monday SP

523 TX 64, to Canton, no facilities

521 Myrtle Springs Rd, **N...**trailer sales, **S...other:** Marshall's RV Ctr, RV camp/dump, U-Haul

519 Turner-Hayden Rd, **S...other:** Canton I-20 RV Park

516 FM 47, to Wills Point, **N...**to Lake Tawakoni, **S...gas:** Shamrock/24hr, **food:** Robertson's Café/gas, Interstate Motel/café

512 FM 2965, Hiram-Wills Point Rd, no facilities

511.5mm weigh sta both lanes

511mm rest area both lanes, full(handicapped)facilities, phone, vending, picnic tables, litter barrels, petwalk

509 Hiram Rd, **S...gas:** Phillips 66/diesel/BBQ Café

506 FM 429, FM 2728, College Mound Rd, **N...gas:** Bluebonnet Ridge RV Park

503 Wilson Rd, **S...gas:** Rip Griffin/Subway/Pizza Hut/diesel/LP/24hr/@

Terrell

501 TX 34, to Terrell, **N...gas:** Chevron/24hr, Exxon/diesel, **food:** DQ, Double Steak/grill, Schlotsky's, Waffle House, **lodging:** Best Inn, Best Western, Comfort Inn, Day's Inn, Motel 6, **other:** HOSPITAL, Home Depot, **S...gas:** Citgo/diesel, Phillips 66, Total/diesel/24hr, **food:** Carmona's Cantina, McDonald's, Wendy's, **lodging:** Super 8, **other:** Tanger Outlet/famous brands

499b Rose Hill Rd, to Terrell, no facilities

a to US 80, W to Dallas, **N...gas:** Exxon/diesel, Texaco, **food:** Dennys, Grandy's, Subway

498 FM 148, to Terrell, **N...gas:** Exxon/diesel, Texaco/diesel, **food:** Denny's, Grandy's, Subway

493 FM 1641, **S...gas:** Exxon/Pizza Inn/diesel

491 FM 2932, Helms Tr, to Forney, no facilities

490 FM 741, to Forney, no facilities

487 FM 740, to Forney, **S...**Forney RV park

483 Lawson Rd, Lasater Rd, no facilities

482 Belt Line Rd, to Lasater, **S...**RV park

481 Seagoville Rd, **N...gas:** Fina, Total/diesel, **lodging:** Howard Johnson

480 I-635, N to Mesquite, no facilities

479b a US 175, **N...lodging:** access to Motel 6, **S...gas:** Shell

477 St Augustine Rd, no facilities

476 Dowdy Ferry Rd, no facilities

Dallas

474 TX 310 N, Central Expsy, no facilities

473b a I-45, N to Dallas, S to Houston, no facilities

472 Bonnie View Rd, **N...gas:** Flying J/Conoco/diesel/LP/rest./24hr/@, Shell, **food:** Jack-in-the-Box, **lodging:** Ramada Ltd, **S...gas:** TA/Exxon/Burger King/diesel/24hr/@

470 TX 342, Lancaster Rd, **N...gas:** Chevron/24hr, Pilot/DQ/Wendy's/diesel/24hr/@, **S...gas:** Pilot/diesel/24hr/2, **food:** McDonald's, Whataburger, **lodging:** Day's Inn, Quest Inn

468 Houston School Rd, **S...gas:** Exxon/diesel, **food:** Whataburger

467b a I-35E, N to Dallas, S to Waco, **1 mi N...**off of I-35E, **gas:** Shell, **food:** McDonald's

466 S Polk St, **N...gas:** Citgo, Conoco/diesel, **food:** DQ, **S...gas:** Love's/Carl's Jr/diesel/24hr/2

465 Wheatland/S Hampton Rds, **N...gas:** Shell/diesel, **S...gas:** Chevron/McDonald's, RaceWay, **food:** Arby's, BBQ, Cheddar's, Jack-in-the-Box, Popeye's, Sonic, Taco Bell, Wendy's, **lodging:** Comfort Inn, **other:** HOSPITAL, Home Depot, Buick/GMC/Hyundai, Home Depot, Kia, Lincoln/Mercury, Lowe's Whse, Mazda, OfficeMax, Sam's Club/gas, Saturn

464b a US 67, Love Fwy, no facilities

463 Camp Wisdom Rd, **N...gas:** Chevron/McDonald's, Exxon, **food:** Catfish King Rest., Denny's, Taco Cabana, **lodging:** Best Value Inn, Hampton Inn, Holiday Inn, Ramada Inn, Royal Inn, **other:** Chief Parts, Chrysler/Jeep, Ford, Nissan, **S...gas:** Fina, Texaco/diesel, **food:** Bennigan's, Blimpie, Burger King, Jack-in-the-Box, McDonald's, Olive Garden, Owens Rest., Red Lobster, Subway, Wendy's, **other:** Advance Parts, Best Buy, Circuit City, K-Mart, NTB, PepBoys, Pontiac, Target, Toyota

462b a Duncanville Rd(no EZ wb return), **S...gas:** Exxon, Shell/diesel, **food:** Arby's, KFC, Mr Gatti's, Whataburger, **lodging:** Motel 6, **other:** Goodyear, Kroger, Radio Shack

461 Cedar Ridge Rd, **S...gas:** RaceTrac

460 TX 408, no facilities

458 Mt Creek Pkwy, no facilities

457 FM 1382, to Grand Prairie, **N...gas:** Shamrock/diesel/café, Shell/diesel, **food:** Waffle House, **S...gas:** RaceTrac, **food:** Jack-in-the-Box, **other:** to Joe Pool Lake

456 Carrier Pkwy, to Corn Valley Rd, **N...food:** Chick-fil-A, Don Pablo, Taco Cabana, Whataburger, **other:** Home Depot, Kohl's, Target, **S...gas:** Fina, **food:** BBQ, Boston Mkt, Cheddar's, Chili's, Denny's, IHOP, Little Caesar's, McDonald's, Subway, TCBY, **other:** Albertson's, Eckerd, Walgreen

Interstate 20

E ↕ W

454 Great Southwest Pkwy, **N...gas:** Chevron/24hr, Conoco/diesel, **food:** Carino's Italian, Chuck-eCheese, KFC, McDonald's, Taco Bell, Taco Bueno, Texas Roadhouse, Waffle House, Wendy's, Wiener-schnitzel, **lodging:** Day's Inn, Quality Inn, **other:** HOSPITAL, Harley-Davidson, **S...gas:** Exxon, Shamrock/Burger King, Shell/Subway/diesel, **food:** Applebee's, Arby's, Schlotsky's, **lodging:** Comfort Inn, **other:** Discount Tire, Dodge, Sam's Club, Wal-Mart SuperCtr/24hr, to Joe Pool Lake

453b a TX 360, **1-2 mi N...**Mayfield Rd, **gas:** Chevron/24hr, Fina, RaceTrac, Shell, **food:** Pizza Hut, Waffle House, Whataburger, mall, to airport, **S...**Watson Rd, **gas:** Shell

452 Frontage Rd, no facilities

451 Collins St, New York Ave, **N...gas:** Mobil, RaceTrac, **food:** Jack-in-the-Box, Pizza Hut, **other:** Acura, Mazda/VW/Kia, Saturn, **S...gas:** Shamrock, Shell, **food:** McDonald's, **other:** Nissan

450 Matlock Rd, **N...gas:** Citgo/7-11, Fina/diesel, **food:** Abuelo's Mexican, BBQ, IHOP, Mercado Juarez Café, SaltGrass Steaks, Spaghetti Whse, Tony Roma's, Wendy's, **lodging:** Comfort Inn, Hampton Inn, La Quinta, **other:** HOSPITAL, CompUSA, Lowe's Whse, Michael's, Old Navy, **S...gas:** Citgo/7-11, Shamrock, Shell, **food:** Joe's Pizza, **other:** Fry's Electronics, NTB

449 FM 157, Cooper St, **N...gas:** Fina, Mobil, Shell, 7-11, **food:** BBQ, Bennigan's, Blackeyed Pea, Chili's, China Café, CiCi's, Don Pablo, Golden Corral, Grandy's, Jack-in-the-Box, Jason's Deli, KFC, McDonald's, On the Border, Outback Steaks, Owens Rest., Razzoo's Cajun Café, Red Lobster, Schlotsky's, Souper Salad, Spaghetti Whse, Starbucks, Thai Cuisine, Wendy's, Whataburger, **lodging:** Days Inn, Holiday Inn Express, Homestead Village, Studio 6, **other:** Barnes&Noble, Best Buy, Dillard's, Discount Tire, Hancock Fabrics, Hyundai, JC Penney, Mervyn's, Office Depot, Sears/auto, Subaru, Target, mall, **S...gas:** Chevron, Citgo/7-11, Conoco, Mobil, **food:** Applebee's, Arby's, Boston Mkt, Burger King, Burger St, Chick-fil-A, Denny's, Dos Gringo's Mexican, El Fenix Mexican, HomeTown Buffet, LJ Silver, Luby's, Macaroni Grill, McDonald's, Old Country Buffet, Olive Garden, Popeye's, Shoney's, Sonic, Taco Bueno, TGIFriday, **other:** Circuit City, Ford, GMC, Home Depot, Isuzu, K-Mart, Kroger, OfficeMax, Pontiac, Wal-Mart SuperCtr/24hr

448 Bowen Rd, **N...gas:** Shell/24hr, **food:** Cracker Barrel, **S...gas:** Shell

447 Kelly-Elliot Rd, Park Springs Blvd, **N...gas:** Citgo, **S...gas:** Exxon, Fina/Blimpie, **other:** camping

445 Green Oaks Blvd, **N...gas:** Conoco, Minyard, Shell, **food:** Arby's, BBQ, Boston Mkt, Burger King, Grandy's, Jack-in-the-Box, KFC, Mac's Grill, Pizza Hut, Pizza Inn, Taco Bell, Taipan Chinese, Whataburger, **other:** Albertson's, Eckerd/24hr, **S...gas:** Chevron/24hr, Citgo/7-11, Shamrock, **food:** Cheddar's, IHOP, Fazoli's, McDonald's, Pancho's Mexican, Schlotsky's, Sonic, Steak&Ale, Taco Bueno, Waffle House, **other:** AutoZone, Discount Tire, $General, Winn-Dixie

444 US 287 S, to Waxahatchie, no facilities

443 Bowman Springs Rd(from wb), no facilities

442b a I-820 to Ft Worth, US 287 bus, **N...gas:** Fina, **lodging:** Great Western Inn, **S...gas:** Phillips 66, Shell, **food:** DQ

Ft Worth

441 Anglin Dr, Hartman Lane, **N...gas:** Conoco/diesel, **lodging:** Super 8, **S...gas:** Conoco/diesel

440b Forest Hill Dr, **S...gas:** Chevron/24hr, Conoco, Shell/diesel, **food:** Braum's, Capt D's, CiCi's, DQ, Denny's, Domino's, Jack-in-the-Box, Luby's, McDonald's, Sonic, Starbucks, Subway, **lodging:** Comfort Inn, **other:** Brookshire Foods, Discount Tire, Eckerd, Walgreen

a Wichita St, **N...gas:** Chevron, **food:** Taco Bell, Taco Casa, Wendy's, **S...gas:** Conoco, Fina, **food:** Chicken Express, McDonald's, Schlotsky's, Taco Bueno, Whataburger

439 Campus Dr, **N...other:** Ford, Chrysler/Plymouth/Jeep, **S...other:** Sam's Club/gas

438 Oak Grove Rd, **1 mi N...gas:** Shell, **food:** Burger King, Denny's, Jack-in-the Box, McDonald's, Whataburger, **lodging:** Day's Inn, **S...gas:** Conoco

437 I-35W, N to Ft Worth, S to Waco

436b Hemphill St, **N...gas:** Shell/diesel, **S...other:** Chevrolet

a FM 731(from eb), to Crowley Ave, **N...other:** $General, SavALot Food, **S...gas:** Chevron, Conoco/diesel, DQ, Pizza Hut/Taco Bell

435 McCart St, **N...gas:** Conoco/diesel, Fina, **S...gas:** Shell/24hr

Interstate 20

E

W

434 Trail Lake Dr, **N...gas:** Phillips 66, **S...gas:** Citgo, Shell, **food:** Pancho's Mexican

433 Hulen St, **N...gas:** Shell/diesel, **food:** ChuckeCheese, Grady's Grill, Hooters, Olive Garden, Red Lobster, Souper Salad, TGIFriday, **lodging:** TownePlace Suites, **other:** MEDICAL CARE, Albertson's, Circuit City, Home Depot, Office Depot, **S...**BBQ, Bennigan's, Denny's, Jack-in-the-Box, McDonald's, Hampton Inn, mall

431 (432 from wb), TX 183, Bryant-Irvin Rd, **N...food:** Mimi's Café, **other:** Best Buy, CompUSA, Lowe's Whse, Sam's Club, **S...gas:** Chevron/24hr, Exxon, Shell, **food:** Blackeyed Pea, IHOP, Outback Steaks, Rio Mambo, SaltGrass Steaks, Sam's Rest., Subway, **lodging:** AmeriSuites, Holiday Inn Express, La Quinta, **other:** HOSPITAL, Buick, Ford, Goodyear/auto, Mazda, Saturn, Suzuki, Target

430mm Clear Fork Trinity River

429b Winscott Rd, no facilities

a US 377, to Granbury, **N...gas:** Phillips 66/diesel, **food:** Cracker Barrel, **lodging:** Best Western, **S...gas:** Chevron, Exxon, RaceTrac/24hr, Shell, **food:** DQ, McDonald's, Waffle House, Whataburger/24hr, **other:** Albertson's

428 I-820, N around Ft Worth, no facilities

426 RM 2871, Chapin School Rd, no facilities

425 Markum Ranch Rd, no facilities

421 I-30 E(from eb), to Ft Worth, no facilities

420 FM 1187, Aledo, Farmer, parking, **S...other:** Cowtown RV Camping

419mm weigh sta eb

418 Ranch House Rd, Willow Park, **N...gas:** Exxon, Shell/diesel, **food:** BBQ, Pizza Hut, Subway, Taco Casa, **S...gas:** Shell/ChickenExpress/diesel, **food:** McDonald's, **lodging:** Ramada Ltd, Brookshire Foods, Cowtown RV Park(1mi)

417mm weigh sta wb

415 FM 5, Mikus Rd, Annetta, **S...gas:** Citgo/diesel/rest., Shell

413 (414 from wb), US 180 W, Lake Shore Dr, **N...gas:** RaceTrac, Shamrock, Texaco/diesel, **food:** DQ, Sonic, **other:** Chevrolet/Buick, Ford, Jeep, Lincoln/Mercury, Nissan, Pontiac/GMC, Toyota, **S...gas:** Chevron/diesel

Weatherford

410 Bankhead Hwy, **S...gas:** Love's/Subway/diesel/24hr/@

409 FM 2552 N, Clear Lake Rd, **N...gas:** Petro/Mobil/diesel/rest./24hr/@, **food:** Catfish O'Charlie's, Jack-in-the-Box, **lodging:** Best Western, **other:** HOSPITAL, Blue Beacon, **S...gas:** Chevron/diesel

408 TX 171, FM 1884, FM 51, Tin Top Rd, Weatherford, **N...gas:** Exxon/Popeye's/24hr, Mobil, **food:** Applebee's, BBQ, Braum's, China Garden, Golden Corral, IHOP, McDonald's, Montana Rest., Schlotsky's, Subway, Taco Bell, Taco Bueno, Whataburger/24hr, **lodging:** La Quinta, Super 8, **other:** AutoZone, Home Depot, OfficeMax, Wal-Mart SuperCtr/gas/24hr, **S...gas:** Exxon/diesel, Shell/Burger King/diesel/24hr, **food:** Waffle House, **lodging:** Best Value Inn, Comfort Inn, Hampton Inn, Holiday Inn Express, Motel 6

407 Tin Top Rd(from eb), same as 408

406 Old Dennis Rd, **N...gas:** Conoco/diesel/24hr/@, **lodging:** Day's Inn, **S...gas:** Pilot/Wendy's/diesel/24hr/@

402 (403 from wb), TX 312, to Weatherford, **S...other:** RV camping

397 FM 1189, to Brock, **N...gas:** Shamrock/diesel, **S...**tires

394 FM 113, to Millsap, **N...gas:** gas/diesel/RV camping

393mm Brazos River

391 Gilbert Pit Rd, no facilities

390mm rest area both lanes, full(handicapped)facilities, phone, vending, picnic tables, litter barrels, petwalk

386 US 281, to Mineral Wells, **N...gas:** Fina

380 FM 4, Santo, **S...other:** Windmill Acres RV Park/Roadrunner Rest./gas

376 Blue Flat Rd, Panama Rd, no facilities

373 TX 193, Gordon, no facilities

370 TX 108 S, FM 919, Gordon, **N...gas:** Citgo/Bar-B/diesel/rest., **S...other:** Longhorn Inn/RV Park

367 TX 108 N, Mingus, **N...gas:** Thurber Sta/gas, **food:** Smoke Stack Café, **S...food:** NY Hill Rest.

364mm Palo Pinto Creek

363 Tudor Rd, picnic area, tables, litter barrels

362mm Bear Creek, picnic area both lanes, tables, litter barrels

361 TX 16, to Strawn, no facilities

358 (from wb), frontage rd, no facilities

356mm Russell Creek

354 Lp 254, Ranger, **2 mi N...food:** Lillie's Café, **lodging:** Relax Inn

351 (352 from wb), College Blvd, no facilities

349 FM 2461, Ranger, **N...gas:** Conoco(2mi), Love's/Subway/Godfather's/diesel/24hr/@, **food:** DQ, **lodging:** Best Value Inn, Relax Inn(2mi), **S...gas:** Chevron/diesel

347 FM 3363(from wb), Olden, **S...food:** TX Cattle Exchange Steaks

345 FM 3363(from eb), Olden, no facilities

343 TX 112, FM 570, Eastland, Lake Leon, **N...gas:** Conoco/diesel, Fina/Subway, Shell, **food:** BBQ, DQ, McDonald's, Sonic, Taco Bell, **lodging:** Super 8/RV park, **other:** AutoZone, Buick/Chevrolet/Cadillac, GMC/Pontiac $General, Ford/Mercury, Wal-Mart/drugs, **S...gas:** Exxon/Burger King/diesel/24hr, **food:** Pulido's Mexican, **lodging:** Budget Host, Ramada Inn, **other:** Chrysler/Plymouth/Dodge/Jeep

340 TX 6, Eastland, **N...gas:** Chevron/diesel, **other:** HOSPITAL, **S...gas:** Texaco/diesel

337 spur 490, no facilities

Interstate 20

E ↕ W

332 US 183, Cisco, **N...gas:** Chevron, Citgo/diesel, **food:** BBQ, Cisco Café, DQ, Pizza Heaven, Sonic, Subway, **lodging:** Oak Motel, **S...gas:** Fina/diesel, **other:** Ford

330 TX 206, Cisco, **N...gas:** Chevron/diesel/White Elephant Rest./24hr, **lodging:** Best Western, **other:** HOSPITAL

329mm picnic area wb, tables, litter barrels, handicapped accessible

327mm picnic area eb, tables, litter barrels, handicapped accessible

324 Scranton Rd, no facilities

322 Cooper Creek Rd, no facilities

320 FM 880 N, FM 2945 N, to Moran, no facilities

319 FM 880 S, Putnam, **N...gas:** gas/diesel/café, **other:** USPO

316 Brushy Creek Rd, no facilities

313 FM 2228, no facilities

310 Finley Rd, no facilities

308 Lp 20, Baird, **1 mi S...**antiques

307 US 283, Clyde, **N...food:** DQ, **S...gas:** Conoco/diesel, **food:** Allsup's, Robertson's Café, **lodging:** Baird Motel/RV park

306 FM 2047, Baird, **N...other:** Chevrolet/Pontiac/GMC, Chrysler/Plymouth/Dodge/Jeep

303 Union Hill Rd, no facilities

301 FM 604, Cherry Lane, **N...gas:** Chevron/diesel/24hr, **food:** Subway, Whataburger/24hr, **S...gas:** Fina/diesel/café, Shell/diesel/24hr, **food:** DQ/24hr, **other:** Franklin RV Ctr, IGA Foods

300 FM 604 N, Clyde, **N...other:** Dodge, **S...gas:** Conoco, **other:** White's RV Park

299 FM 1707, Hays Rd, no facilities

297 FM 603, Eula Rd, no facilities

296.5mm rest area both lanes, full(handicapped)facilities, phone, picnic tables, litter barrels, petwalk

294 Buck Creek Rd, no facilities

292b Elmdale Rd, no facilities

a Lp 20(exits left from wb), **S...lodging:** Travelodge

290 TX 36, Lp 322, **S...**airport, zoo

288 TX 351, **N...gas:** Allsup's/diesel, Chevron, Fina/Subway/diesel, **food:** DQ, Skillet's Café, **lodging:** Comfort Inn, Day's Inn, Executive Inn, Holiday Inn Express, Whitten Inn, **S...lodging:** Super 8, **other:** HOSPITAL

Abilene

286c FM 600, Abilene, **N...gas:** Exxon/diesel, Fina/diesel, **food:** Denny's/24hr, **lodging:** Best Western, La Quinta, **S...gas:** Chevron/diesel, **other:** Stover's Candies

286 US 83, Pine St, Abilene, **N...**Firestone, **S...gas:** Fina, Shamrock, **lodging:** Budget Host, **other:** HOSPITAL

285 Old Anson Rd, **N...gas:** Texaco, **lodging:** Travel Inn, **S...gas:** Texaco/diesel, **lodging:** Econolodge, Quality Inn(2mi)

283 US 277 S, US 83(exits left from wb), no facilities

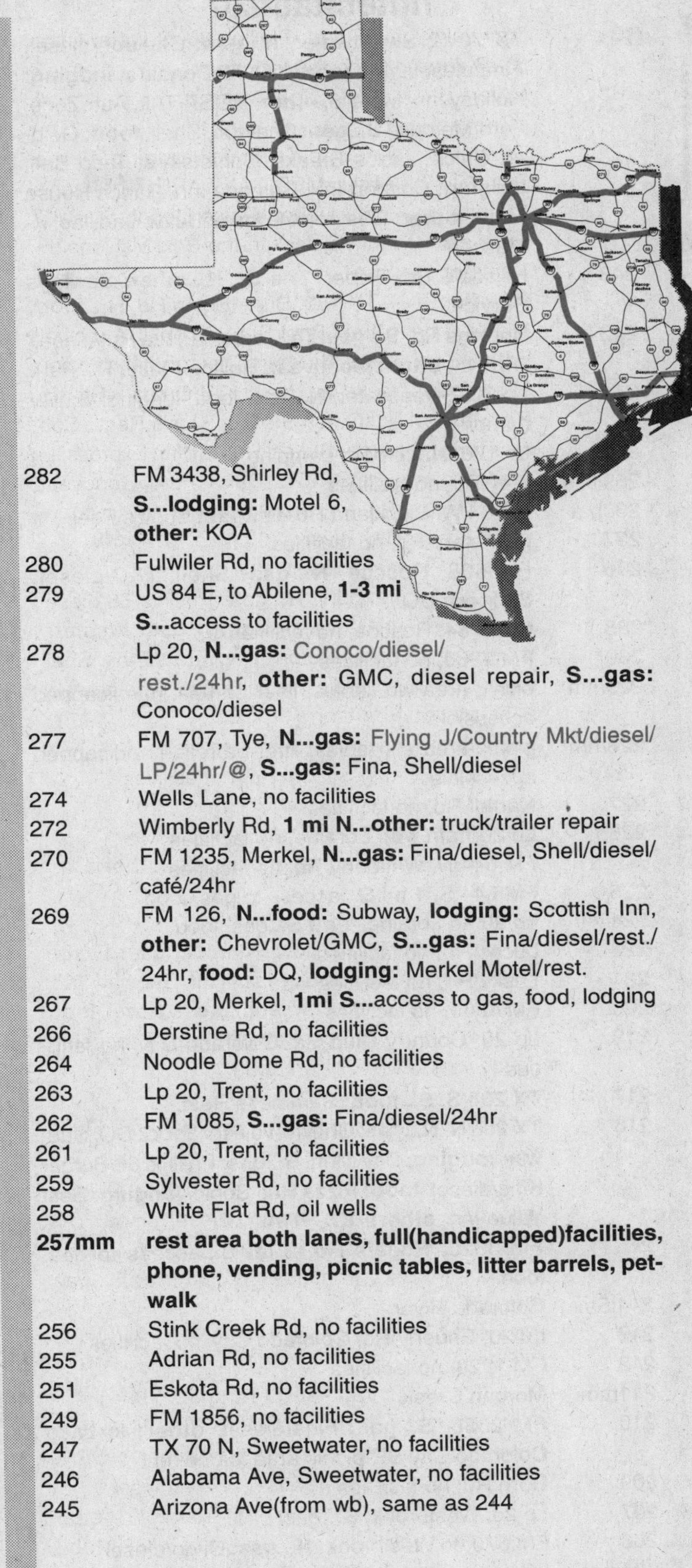

282 FM 3438, Shirley Rd, **S...lodging:** Motel 6, **other:** KOA

280 Fulwiler Rd, no facilities

279 US 84 E, to Abilene, **1-3 mi S...**access to facilities

278 Lp 20, **N...gas:** Conoco/diesel/rest./24hr, **other:** GMC, diesel repair, **S...gas:** Conoco/diesel

277 FM 707, Tye, **N...gas:** Flying J/Country Mkt/diesel/LP/24hr/@, **S...gas:** Fina, Shell/diesel

274 Wells Lane, no facilities

272 Wimberly Rd, **1 mi N...other:** truck/trailer repair

270 FM 1235, Merkel, **N...gas:** Fina/diesel, Shell/diesel/café/24hr

269 FM 126, **N...food:** Subway, **lodging:** Scottish Inn, **other:** Chevrolet/GMC, **S...gas:** Fina/diesel/rest./24hr, **food:** DQ, **lodging:** Merkel Motel/rest.

267 Lp 20, Merkel, **1mi S...**access to gas, food, lodging

266 Derstine Rd, no facilities

264 Noodle Dome Rd, no facilities

263 Lp 20, Trent, no facilities

262 FM 1085, **S...gas:** Fina/diesel/24hr

261 Lp 20, Trent, no facilities

259 Sylvester Rd, no facilities

258 White Flat Rd, oil wells

257mm rest area both lanes, full(handicapped)facilities, phone, vending, picnic tables, litter barrels, petwalk

256 Stink Creek Rd, no facilities

255 Adrian Rd, no facilities

251 Eskota Rd, no facilities

249 FM 1856, no facilities

247 TX 70 N, Sweetwater, no facilities

246 Alabama Ave, Sweetwater, no facilities

245 Arizona Ave(from wb), same as 244

Interstate 20

E ↕ W

244 TX 70 S, Sweetwater, **N...gas:** Chevron/diesel, Fina/diesel/24hr, **food:** DQ, McDonald's, **lodging:** Holiday Inn, Motel 6, **other:** HOSPITAL, AutoZone, Ford/Mercury, **S...gas:** Chevron, Shell, **food:** Golden Chick, Jack's Steaks, Schlotsky's, Taco Bell, **lodging:** Comfort Inn, Ramada Inn, Ranch House Motel, **other:** Chevrolet/Pontiac/Buick/Cadillac, K-Mart

243 Hillsdale Rd, Robert Lee St, **N...other:** Bewley's Service

242 Hopkins Rd, **S...gas:** TA/Conoco/Pizza Hut/diesel/24hr/@, **other:** Goodyear, Rolling Plains RV Park

241 Lp 20, Sweetwater, **N...**gas, food, lodging, **S...**RV camping

240 Lp 170, **N...**airport, camping

239 May Rd, no facilities

238b a US 84 W, Blackland Rd, **N...gas:** Scott's Fuel

237 Cemetery Rd, no facilities

236 FM 608, Roscoe, **N...gas:** Shell, T&C/diesel, **S...food:** DQ

235 to US 84, Roscoe, no facilities

230 FM 1230, no facilities

229mm picnic area wb, tables, litter barrels, handicapped accessible

228mm picnic area eb, tables, litter barrels, handicapped accessible

227 Narrell Rd, no facilities

226b Lp 20(from wb), Loraine, no facilities

a FM 644 N, Wimberly Rd, no facilities

225 FM 644 S, **1 mi S...**access to gas, food

224 Lp 20, to Loraine, **1 mi S...**gas, food

223 Lucas Rd, no facilities

221 Lasky Rd, no facilities

220 FM 1899, no facilities

219 Lp 20, Country Club Rd, Colorado City, no facilities

217 TX 208 S, **S...food:** Summer's Rest.

216 TX 208 N, **N...gas:** Chevron/diesel, **food:** DQ, Subway, **lodging:** Day's Inn, **S...gas:** Phillips 66/Burger King/diesel, **food:** Pizza Hut, Sonic, **lodging:** Best Value Inn, **other:** HOSPITAL

215 FM 3525, Rogers Rd, **2 mi S...**access to gas, food

214.5mm Colorado River

213 Lp 20, Enderly Rd, Colorado City, no facilities

212 FM 1229, no facilities

211mm Morgan Creek

210 FM 2836, **S...gas:** Fina/diesel, **other:** to Lake Colorado City SP, picnic area, camping

209 Dorn Rd, no facilities

207 Lp 20, Westbrook, **S...**gas

206 FM 670, to Westbrook, **N...gas:** Citgo/diesel

204mm rest area wb, full(handicapped)facilities, phone, picnic tables, litter barrels, petwalk

200 Conaway Rd, no facilities

199 Iatan Rd, no facilities

195 frontage rd(from eb), no facilities

194 E Howard Field Rd(from wb), no facilities

192 FM 821, many oil wells

191mm rest area eb, full(handicapped)facilities, phone, picnic tables, litter barrels, petwalk

190 Snyder Field Rd, no facilities

189 McGregor Rd, no facilities

188 FM 820, Coahoma, **N...gas:** T&C/diesel, **food:** DQ, **lodging:** motel, **other:** USPO

186 Salem Rd, Sand Springs, no facilities

184 Moss Lake Rd, Sand Springs, **N...gas:** Phillips 66/diesel, **S...**RV camping

182 Midway Rd, no facilities

Big Spring

181b Refinery Rd, **N...gas:** Fina Refinery

a FM 700, **N...**airport, RV camping, **2 mi S...**HOSPITAL

179 US 80, Big Spring, **S...gas:** Fina/7-11, Texaco, **food:** DQ, Denny's, **lodging:** Comfort Inn, Great Western Inn, **other:** IGA Foods, Eckerd, Chevrolet/Pontiac/Buick

178 TX 350, Big Spring, **N...gas:** Texaco/diesel

177 US 87, Big Spring, **N...gas:** Exxon/diesel, Rip Griffin/Subway/diesel/24hr/@, **lodging:** Econolodge, Motel 6, Super 8, **S...gas:** Chevron/diesel, Fina/diesel, **food:** DQ, **lodging:** Holiday Inn Express

176 TX 176, Andrews, no facilities

174 Lp 20 E, Big Springs, **S...gas:** Texaco/diesel, **other:** airport

172 Cauble Rd, no facilities

171 Moore Field Rd, no facilities

169 FM 2599, no facilities

168mm picnic area both lanes, tables, littter barrels

165 FM 818, no facilities

158 Lp 20 W, to Stanton, **N...**RV camping

156 TX 137, Lamesa, **S...gas:** Shamrock/Subway/diesel/24hr, **food:** DQ, Sonic

154 US 80, Stanton, **2 mi S...**access to gas, food, lodging

151 FM 829(from wb), no facilities

144 US 80, **2-3 mi N...**facilities in Midland

143mm frontage rd(from eb), no facilities

142mm picnic area both lanes, tables, litter barrels, hist marker

Midland

138 TX 158, FM 715, Greenwood, **N...gas:** Texaco/diesel, **food:** BBQ, Whataburger, **S...gas:** T&C/Subway/diesel

137 Old Lamesa Rd, no facilities

136 TX 349, Midland, **N...gas:** Phillips 66/diesel, **food:** McDonald's, Sonic, **lodging:** Howard Johnson, Super 8, **other:** IGA/gas, Family$, Petroleum Museum, **S...gas:** Exxon/Burger King/diesel, T&C, Texaco/diesel

Interstate 20

E ↕ W

134 Midkiff Rd, **N...gas:** T&C/Subway/diesel, **1 mi N on Wall St...**Fina/7-11, Exxon, **food:** Denny's, **lodging:** Best Western, Day's Inn, Executive Inn, La Quinta, Sleep Inn, **other:** HOSPITAL, Chevrolet, Chrysler/Plymouth/Jeep, Honda, Kia, Lincoln/Mercury, Mercedes/Volvo, Nissan

131 TX 158, Midland, **N...lodging:** Travelodge, **other:** RV camping

Odessa

126 FM 1788, **N...gas:** Chevron/diesel, Warfield/Mobil/Subway/diesel/@, **other:** museum, airport

121 Lp 338, Odessa, **N...food:** Denny's, McDonald's, **lodging:** Day's Inn, Holiday Inn Express, La Quinta, Motel 6, **other:** U of TX Permian Basin, **1 mi N...gas:** Fina/7-11, **lodging:** Elegante Hotel, **3 mi N on TX 191 W...food:** Chili's, Fazoli's, Logan's Roadhouse, McDonald's, On-the-Border, Quizno's, Whataburger, **lodging:** Fairfield Inn, Hampton Inn, **other:** Albertson's, Circuit City, Home Depot, Sears/auto, Sam's Club/gas, Wal-Mart SuperCtr/24hr

118 FM 3503, Grandview Ave, **N...gas:** Fina/diesel, **other:** Freightliner/Peterbilt, HOSPITAL

116 US 385, Odessa, **N...gas:** T&C, **food:** DQ, **lodging:** Best Western, Delux Inn, Villa West Inn, **other:** HOSPITAL, **S...gas:** Phillips 66/diesel, Texaco/diesel, **lodging:** Motel 6, **other:** city park

115 FM 1882, **N...gas:** Fina/Country Cookin

113 TX 302, Odessa, no facilities

112 FM 1936, Odessa, **N...gas:** Citgo/diesel

108 Moss Ave, Meteor Crater, no facilities

104 FM 866, Meteor Crater Rd, no facilities

103.5mm weigh sta wb/parking area eb, litter barrels

101 FM 1601, Penwell, no facilities

92 (93 from wb), FM 1053, no facilities

86 TX 41, **N...**Monahans Sandhills SP, camping

83 US 80, Monahans, **2 mi N...gas:** Citgo, **other:** HOSPITAL, RV camping

Monahans

80 TX 18, Monahans, **N...gas:** Chevron/diesel/24hr, Exxon, **food:** Bar H Steaks, Big Burger, DQ, McDonald's, Sonic, **other:** HOSPITAL, Alco Discount, CarQuest, Chrysler/Plymouth/Dodge/Jeep, Furr's Foods, Lowe's Foods, Country Club RV Park(2mi), **S...gas:** Fina/diesel/24hr, Kent Gas, Phillips 66/diesel, **lodging:** Texan Inn, **other:** Chevrolet/Pontiac/Buick/GMC

79 Lp 464, Monahans, no facilities

76 US 80, Monahans, **2 mi N...other:** to Million Barrel Museum, RV camping

73 FM 1219, Wickett, **N...gas:** Texaco/Allsup's, **S...gas:** Mobil/Subway/diesel/24hr

70 TX 65, no facilities

69.5mm rest area both lanes, full(handicapped)facilities, phone, picnic tables, litter barrels, petwalk

66 FM 1927, to Pyote, no facilities

58 frontage rd, multiple oil wells

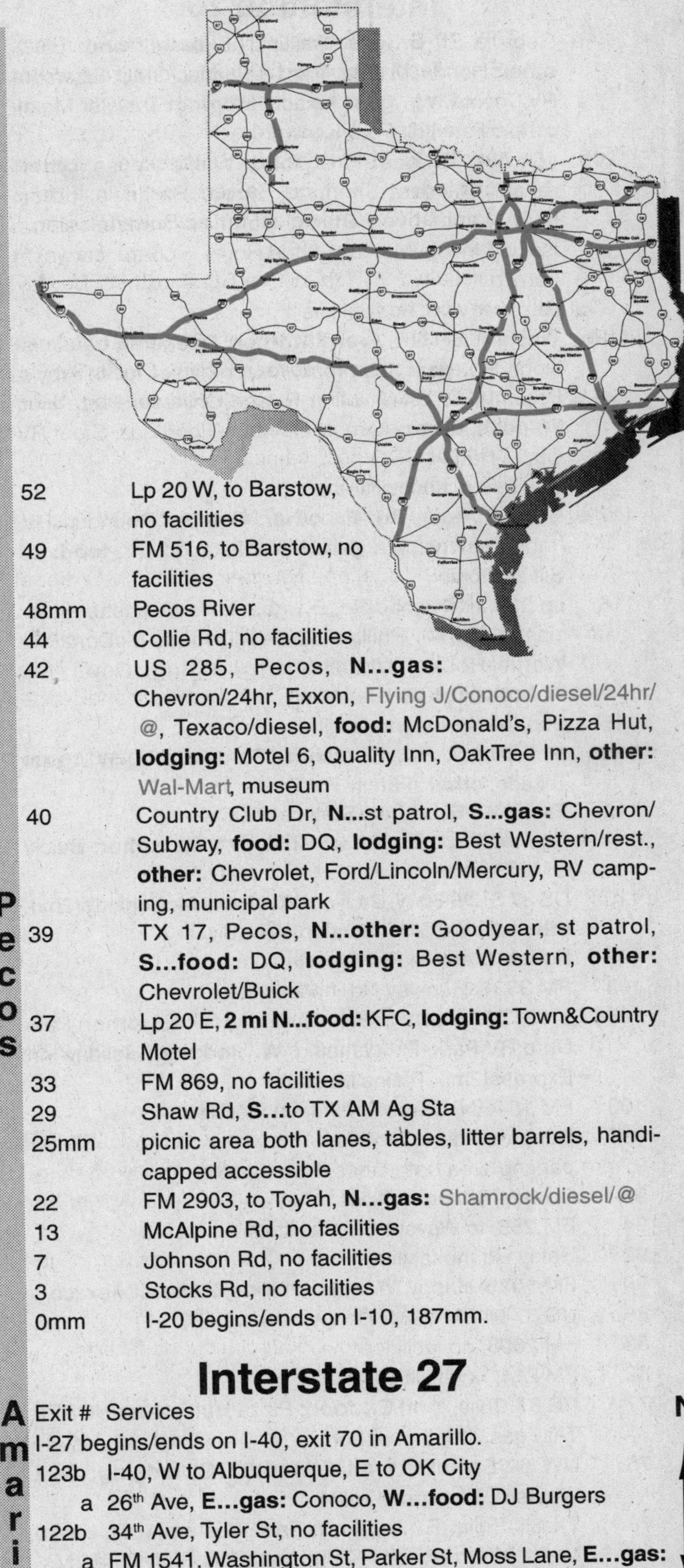

52 Lp 20 W, to Barstow, no facilities

49 FM 516, to Barstow, no facilities

48mm Pecos River

44 Collie Rd, no facilities

Pecos

42 US 285, Pecos, **N...gas:** Chevron/24hr, Exxon, Flying J/Conoco/diesel/24hr/@, Texaco/diesel, **food:** McDonald's, Pizza Hut, **lodging:** Motel 6, Quality Inn, OakTree Inn, **other:** Wal-Mart, museum

40 Country Club Dr, **N...**st patrol, **S...gas:** Chevron/Subway, **food:** DQ, **lodging:** Best Western/rest., **other:** Chevrolet, Ford/Lincoln/Mercury, RV camping, municipal park

39 TX 17, Pecos, **N...other:** Goodyear, st patrol, **S...food:** DQ, **lodging:** Best Western, **other:** Chevrolet/Buick

37 Lp 20 E, **2 mi N...food:** KFC, **lodging:** Town&Country Motel

33 FM 869, no facilities

29 Shaw Rd, **S...**to TX AM Ag Sta

25mm picnic area both lanes, tables, litter barrels, handicapped accessible

22 FM 2903, to Toyah, **N...gas:** Shamrock/diesel/@

13 McAlpine Rd, no facilities

7 Johnson Rd, no facilities

3 Stocks Rd, no facilities

0mm I-20 begins/ends on I-10, 187mm.

Interstate 27

N ↕ S

Amarillo

Exit # Services

I-27 begins/ends on I-40, exit 70 in Amarillo.

123b I-40, W to Albuquerque, E to OK City

a 26th Ave, **E...gas:** Conoco, **W...food:** DJ Burgers

122b 34th Ave, Tyler St, no facilities

a FM 1541, Washington St, Parker St, Moss Lane, **E...gas:** Texaco, **food:** Sonic **W...gas:** Texaco, **food:** Taco Bell

121b Hawthorne Dr, Austin St, **E...lodging:** Amarillo Motel, **other:** Honda Motorcycles, **W...gas:** Texaco/diesel, **other:** Scottie's Transmissions

Interstate 27

N ↕ S

a Georgia St, **E...gas:** Phillips 66/diesel, **food:** BBQ, **other:** Honda, Mazda, Nissan, Pontiac/GMC, Sizemore RV, Toyota, **W...gas:** Texaco, **lodging:** Traveler Motel, **other:** Family$, Ford/Kenworth

120b 45th Ave, **E...gas:** Fina, **food:** Waffle House, **other:** repair, **W...gas:** Shamrock, **food:** Hardee's, **other:** BMW/LandRover, Buick, Cottman Transmissions, Isuzu, Lincoln/Mercury, Land Rover, Subaru, carwash, donuts

a Republic Ave, no facilities

119b Western St, 58th Ave, **E...other:** $General, transmissions, **W...gas:** Shamrock, Texaco/diesel, **food:** Arby's, Braum's, LJ Silver, Ming Palace Chinese, Pizza Hut, Wendy's, **other:** Aamco, Rainbow Food/gas, Stout RV Ctr, U-Haul, USPO

a W Hillside, no facilities

117 Bell St, Arden Rd, **E...other:** Camper Roundup RV, transmissions, **W...gas:** Fina, Texaco/24hr, **food:** LJ Silver, Sonic

116 Lp 335, Hollywood Rd, **E...gas:** Love's/Chester Fried/diesel/24hr/@, Phillips 66/diesel, **food:** McDonald's, Waffle House, Whataburger, **lodging:** Day's Inn, **W...other:** HOSPITAL(8mi)

115 Sundown Lane, no facilities

113 McCormick Rd, **E...other:** Ford/Suzuki, **W...gas:** Texaco, **other:** Family RV Ctr

112 FM 2219, **E...other:** Stater's RV Ctr

111 Rockwell Rd, **E...other:** Chevrolet, **W...other:** Buick/GMC/Pontiac

110 US 87 S, US 60 W, Canyon, **W...food:** McDonald's(2mi), **other:** Buick/GMC/Pontiac, WTSU

109 Buffalo Stadium Rd, **W...**stadium

108 FM 3331, Hunsley Rd, no facilities

106 TX 217, Canyon, to Palo Duro Cyn SP, **E...other:** Palo Duro RV Park, RV camping, **W...lodging:** Holiday Inn Express(2mi), Plains Museum

103 FM 1541 N, Cemetery Rd, no facilities

99 Hungate Rd, no facilities

97mm parking area both lanes, litter barrels

96 Dowlen Rd, no facilities

94 FM 285, to Wayside, no facilities

92 Haley Rd, no facilities

90 FM 1075, Happy, **W...gas:** Phillips 66/diesel, Texaco

88b a US 87 N, FM 1881, Happy, same as 90

83 FM 2698, no facilities

82 FM 214, no facilities

77 US 87, Tulia, **1 mi E...food:** Pizza Hut, **other:** HOSPITAL, gas, lodging, airport

75 NW 6th St, Tulia, **1 mi E...food:** DQ, **lodging:** Best Western, **W...**same as 74

74 TX 86, Tulia, **E...lodging:** Best Western(1mi), Lasso Motel, **other:** HOSPITAL, **W...gas:** Rip Griffin/Grandy's/Subway/diesel/24hr/@, **lodging:** Select Inn

70mm parking area both lanes, litter barrels

68 FM 928, no facilities

63 FM 145, Kress, **1 mi E...**gas/diesel, food, phone

61 US 87, County Rd, no facilities

56 FM 788, no facilities

54 FM 3183, to Plainview, **W...**truck service

53 Lp 27, Plainview, **E...other:** HOSPITAL, access to gas, food, lodging

Plainview

51 Quincy St, no facilities

50 TX 194, Plainview, **E...gas:** Phillips 66, **other:** HOSPITAL, Wal-Mart Dist, to Wayland Bapt U

49 US 70, Plainview, **E...gas:** Fina, Phillips 66, Shamrock/diesel, Texaco/Subway/diesel, **food:** Carlito's Mexican, Cotton Patch Café, Domino's, FarEast Chinese, Furr's Café, Kettle, LJ Silver/A&W, Pizza Hut, Sonic, Taco Bell, Tokyo Steaks, **lodging:** Best Western, Comfort Suites, Day's Inn, **other:** Buick/Pontiac/Cadillac/GMC, Chrysler/Jeep, Ford/Lincoln/Mercury/Toyota, GNC, Hastings Books, NAPA, O'Reilly Parts, Radio Shack, United Foods, **W...gas:** Chevron, Phillips 66/diesel, **food:** Burger King, Chicken Express, Little Mexico, McDonald's, Mr Gatti's, Subway, **lodging:** Holiday Inn Express, Ramada Ltd, **other:** JC Penney, Wal-Mart

45 Lp 27, to Plainview, no facilities

43 FM 2337, no facilities

41 County Rd, no facilities

38 Main St, no facilities

37 FM 1914, Cleveland St, **E...gas:** Co-op, **food:** DQ, **W...**HOSPITAL

36 FM 1424, Hale Center, no facilities

32 FM 37 W, no facilities

31 FM 37 E, no facilities

29mm rest area both lanes, full(handicapped)facilities, phone, picnic tables, litter barrels, petwalk

27 County Rd, no facilities

24 FM 54, **W...**RV park/dump

22 Lp 369, Abernathy, **E...gas:** Phillips 66, **W...gas:** Phillips 66/diesel, **food:** DQ

21 FM 597, Main St, Abernathy, **W...gas:** Conoco/diesel, Co-op/diesel, **food:** Cyclone Rest., DQ

20 Abernathy(from nb), no facilities

17 County Rd 53, no facilities

15 Lp 461, to New Deal, **1/2mi E...gas:** Texaco/Subway/diesel/24hr, **other:** phone

14 FM 1729, same as 15

13 Lp 461, to New Deal, no facilities

12 access rd(from nb), no facilities

11 FM 1294, Shallowater, no facilities

10 Keuka St, **E...other:** Airborne Express, Fed Ex

Lubbock

9 Airport Rd, **E...**airport, **W...other:** Lubbock RV Park/dump

8 FM 2641, Regis St, no facilities

7 Yucca Lane, **W...lodging:** Country Creek Motel, Texas Star Inn/rest.

6b a Lp 289, Ave Q, Lubbock, **E...other:** Pharr RV, **W...lodging:** Texas Motel/rest.

5 Ave H, Municipal Dr, **E...other:** Mackenzie Park

4 US 82, US 87, 4th St, to Crosbyton, **E...**fairgrounds, **W...**to TTU

Interstate 27

E ↕ W

3 US 62, TX 114, 19th St, no facilities
2 34th St, **E...gas:** Phillips 66, **lodging:** Budget Motel, **W...**MEDICAL CARE
1c 50th St, **E...gas:** Fina, **food:** El Jalapeno Café, JoJo's Burgers, **W...gas:** Fina/7-11, Shamrock/diesel, **food:** Bryan's Steaks, Burger King, ChinaStar Buffet, Church's, DQ, Domino's, KFC, LJ Silver/A&W, McDonald's, Pizza Hut/Taco Bell, Subway, Taco Villa, Whataburger/24hr, Wienerschnitzel, **other:** MEDICAL CARE, Chrysler/Plymouth, $General, O'Reilly Parts, United Food/drug/gas, USPO, Walgreen, Woody Tires
b US 84, **E...lodging:** Circus Inn, Day's Inn, Super 8, **W...gas:** Skillet's Burgers, **lodging:** Best Western, Comfort Inn, Holiday Inn Express, Motel 6, Ramada Ltd
a Lp 289, **W...other:** Sims RV Ctr
1 82nd St, **W...gas:** Phillips 66
I-27 begins/ends on US 87 at 82nd St in S Lubbock.

Interstate 30

E ↕ W

Texarkana

Exit #	Services
223mm	Texas/Arkansas state line
223b a	US 59, US 71, State Line Ave, Texarkana, **N...gas:** Citgo/diesel, EZ Mart, Shell, **food:** Denny's, IHOP, Pizza Inn, Red Lobster, Waffle House, **lodging:** Baymont Inn, Best Western, Comfort Suites, Holiday Inn, Hampton Inn, Holiday Inn Express, Quality Inn, Sheraton, Super 8, **other:** tires, **S...gas:** Conoco/diesel, Exxon, RaceTrac, Texaco, Total, **food:** Arby's, Backyard Burger, Baskin-Robbins, Bennigan's, Burger King, Cattlemen's Steaks, CiCi's, El Chico, KFC, La Carreta Mexican, Lee's China, LJ Silver, Mandarin House, McDonald's, Papa John's, Pizza Hut, Pizza Inn, Schlotsky's, Subway, Taco Bell, Taco Tico, Wendy's, Whataburger/24hr, **lodging:** Best Western, Comfort Inn, Day's Inn, Econolodge, Economy Inn, Express Inn, Knight's Inn, La Quinta, Motel 6, **other:** Albertson's, AutoZone, Chevrolet/Buick, Chrysler/Jeep, Radio Shack, Wal-Mart SuperCtr/24hr, Walgreen
223mm	**Welcome Ctr wb, full(handicapped)facilities, info, phone, picnic tables, litter barrels, vending, petwalk**
222	TX 93, FM 1397, Summerhill Rd, **N...gas:** Shell, Total/Subway, **food:** Applebee's, McDonald's, Waffle House, **lodging:** Motel 6, **other:** MEDICAL CARE, Ford/Freightliner, Goodyear/auto, Honda, **S...gas:** Chevron, Exxon, Texaco/24hr, **food:** Bryce's Rest., **lodging:** Ramada Inn, **other:** Mazda/Isuzu/GMC
220b	FM 559, Richmond Rd, **N...gas:** Exxon, EZ Mart, **food:** Burger King, Carino's Italian, Cracker Barrel, DQ, Domino's, McAlister's Deli, Pizza Hut, Poncho's Mexican, Popeye's, Sonic, Taco Bell, TaMolly's Mexican, Texas Roadhouse, **lodging:** Comfort Suites, **other:** Sam's Club, Super 1 Food/gas, **S...gas:** Total/diesel, **food:** Arby's, Chili's, El Chico's, Golden Corral, Grandy's, Lee's Chinese, Luby's McDonald's, Outback Steaks, Subway/Baskin-Robbins, **other:** AutoZone, Albertson's, BooksAMillion, Dillard's, JC Penney, Michael's, Office Depot, Sears/auto, Target, Walgreen, mall

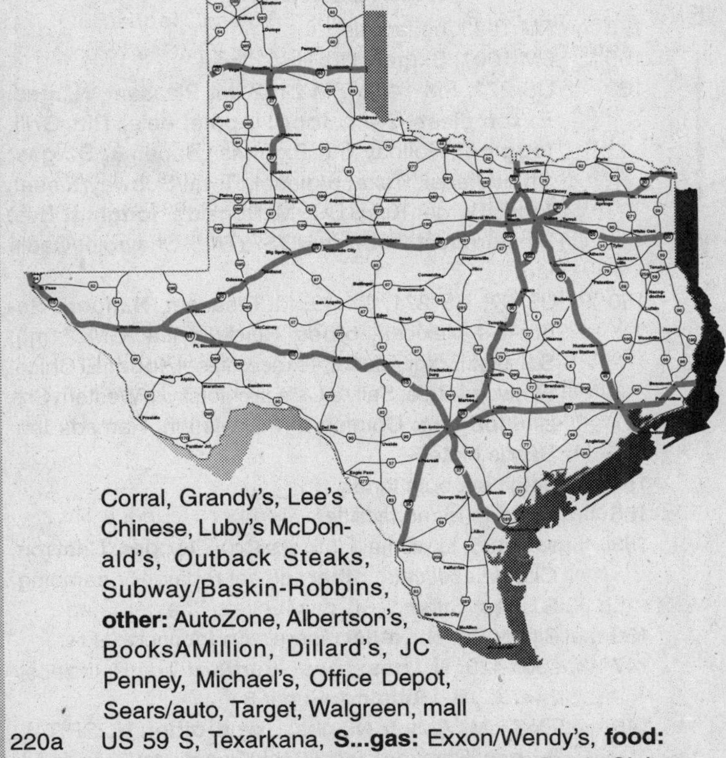

New Boston

Exit #	Services
220a	US 59 S, Texarkana, **S...gas:** Exxon/Wendy's, **food:** DQ, **other:** Lowe's Whse, Radio Shack, Sam's Club, Wal-Mart SuperCtr/gas/24hr, mall
218	FM 989, Nash, **N...gas:** Citgo/diesel/24hr, **other:** cinema, **S...gas:** Exxon/Burger King/diesel, **other:** White/GMC/Volvo, to Lake Patman
213	FM 2253, Leary, **N...other:** Palma RV Ctr
212	spur 74, Lone Star Army Ammo Plant, **S...gas:** Texaco
208	FM 560, Hooks, **N...gas:** Citgo/diesel/24hr, Texaco/diesel/24hr, **food:** Farm Mkt BBQ, **lodging:** Hooks Motel, **S...gas:** Total/diesel/24hr, **food:** DQ, **other:** Family$
206	TX 86, **S...other:** Red River Army Depot
201	TX 8, New Boston, **N...gas:** Texaco/diesel, Total/diesel, **lodging:** Tex Inn, **other:** Chevrolet, Chrysler/Dodge, **S...gas:** Chevron/Subway/diesel, Exxon/Burger King, EZ/24hr, Phillips 66/diesel, **food:** Catfish King, Church's, DQ, KFC/Taco Bell, McDonald's, Pizza Hut, TCBY, **lodging:** Best Western, Bostonian Inn, **other:** HOSPITAL, Brookshire's Foods, Eckerd, Ford/Mercury, Wal-Mart/drugs
199	US 82, New Boston, **N...gas:** Texaco
198	TX 98, **N...gas:** Texaco
193mm	Anderson Creek
192	FM 990, **N...gas:** FuelStop/diesel/café
191mm	**rest area both lanes, full(handicapped)facilities, phone, picnic tables, litter barrels, vending, petwalk**
186	FM 561, no facilities
181mm	Sulphur River
178	US 259, to DeKalb, Omaha, no facilities
174mm	White Oak Creek

TEXAS

Interstate 30

E ↕ W

170 FM 1993, no facilities

165 FM 1001, **S...gas:** Chevron/diesel

162 US 271, FM 1402, FM 2152, Mt Pleasant, **N...gas:** Exxon/diesel/24hr, **food:** Applebee's, Pitt Grill, **lodging:** Holiday Inn Express, Super 8, **S...gas:** Shell/diesel, Texaco/diesel, Total/Subway/diesel, **food:** Burger King, DQ, McDonald's, **lodging:** Best Western/rest., **other:** HOSPITAL, Chevrolet/Cadillac

160 US 67, US 271, TX 49, Mt Pleasant, **N...food:** Senorita's Mexican, **other:** Buick/Pontiac/GMC(1mi), **S...gas:** Exxon/diesel, Texaco/diesel, **food:** El Chico, Elmwood Café, Sally's Café, Schlotsky's, Western Sizzlin, **lodging:** Comfort Inn, Day's Inn, Ramada Inn, Sands Motel

157mm weigh sta both lanes

156 frontage rd, no facilities

153 spur 185, to Winfield, Miller's Cove, **N...gas:** Chevron, Citgo/diesel/café, **other:** diesel repair, RV camping, **S...gas:** Citgo

150 Ripley Rd, **N...other:** Lowe's Distribution

147 spur 423, **N...gas:** Love's/Subway/Taco Bell/diesel/24hr/@, **S...lodging:** Super 8

146 TX 37, Mt Vernon, **N...gas:** Exxon, **other:** HOSPITAL, **S...gas:** Chevron/diesel/24hr, Fina/diesel/24hr, **food:** BarnStormer's Café, Burger King, DQ, Hubbard's Café, La Cabana Mexican, Sonic, TX BBQ, **lodging:** Super 8, **other:** to Lake Bob Sandlin SP

143 rest area both lanes, full(handicapped)facilities, phone, picnic tables, litter barrels, vending, petwalk

142 County Line Rd, no facilities

141 FM 900, Saltillo Rd, no facilities

136 FM 269, Weaver Rd, **N...gas:** Phillips 66

135 US 67 N, no facilities

Greenville

131 FM 69, no facilities

127 US 67, Lp 301, **N...lodging:** Budget Inn, Comfort Inn, Holiday Inn, **S...gas:** Chevron, Texaco, Burton's Rest./24hr, Best Western

126 FM 1870, College St, **S...gas:** Chevron/diesel/rest., Exxon, Texaco/24hr, **food:** Burton's Rest./24hr, **lodging:** Best Western, **other:** Firestone/auto

125 Frontage Rd, same as 124

124 TX 11, TX 154, Sulphur Springs, **N...gas:** Chevron/diesel, Exxon, **food:** BBQ, Catfish King Rest., Domino's, Hal's Diner, Happy Moon Chinese, KFC, Peddlar's Pizza, Pitt Grill, Pizza Hut, San Rimo Italian, Sonic, Subway, TaMolly's Mexican, **lodging:** Royal Inn, **other:** HOSPITAL, AutoZone, Cadillac, Chevrolet/Buick/GMC, Chrysler/Jeep, $General, Family$, Ford, GNC, Kroger/24hr, Nissan, USPO, VF Outlet/famous brands, **S...gas:** Exxon/diesel, Shell, Texco/diesel, **food:** Braum's, Burger King, Chili's, China House, Furr's Rest., Grandy's, Jack-in-the-Box, K-Bob's Steaks, McDonald's, Pizza Inn, San Remo's Italian, Taco Bell, Whataburger, Wendy's, **lodging:** Holiday King Motel, **other:** Eckerd, Wal-Mart SuperCtr/gas/24hr(1mi), factory outlet

123 FM 2297, League St, **N...gas:** Texaco

122 TX 19, to Emory, **N...**HOSPITAL, **S...gas:** Phillips 66/diesel/rest./24hr, Pilot/Arby's/diesel/24hr/@, **other:** Shady Lakes RV Park, to Cooper Lake

120 US 67 bus, no facilities

116 US 67, FM 2653, Brashear Rd, no facilities

110 FM 275, Cumby, **N...gas:** Phillips 66, **S...gas:** Texaco/24hr

104 FM 513, FM 2649, Campbell, **S...**to Lake Tawakoni

101 TX 24, TX 50, FM 1737, to Commerce, **N...gas:** Phillips 66/diesel, **other:** to E TX St U

97 Lamar St, **N...gas:** Exxon/diesel, **lodging:** Dream Lodge Motel

96 US 67, Lp 302, **S...gas:** Fina

95 Division St, **S...other:** HOSPITAL, Puddin Hill Fruit Cakes

94b a US 69, US 380, Greenville, **N...gas:** Texaco, Total/diesel, **food:** Ninfa's Mexican, **lodging:** American Inn, Best Western, Royal Inn, **S...gas:** Chevron/24hr, Exxon, Fina, **food:** Arby's, Burger King, Catfish King Rest., McDonald's, **lodging:** Comfort Inn, Economy Inn, Motel 6, Ramada Inn, Super 8, **other:** Chrysler/Dodge/Jeep

93b a US 67, TX 34 N, Greenville, **N...gas:** Exxon, Mobil, Phillips 66, Texaco, **food:** Applebee's, CiCi's, Grandy's, IHOP, Jack-in-the-Box, KFC, LJ Silver/A&W, Royal Drive-In, Ryan's, Schlotsky's, Sonic, Subway, Taco Bell, Taco Bueno, TaMolly's Mexican, TCBY, Tony's Italian, Wendy's, Whataburger/24hr, **other:** HOSPITAL, Belk, Brookshire's Foods, Buick/Pontiac, Cadillac, Goody's, JC Penney, Staples, USPO, mall, **S...gas:** Chevron/diesel, Exxon/diesel/24hr, **food:** Chili's, Cracker Barrel, Dickie's BBQ, Luby's, Red Lobster, **lodging:** Holiday Inn Express, **other:** Ford/Lincoln/Mercury, Home Depot, Radio Shack, RV Ctr, Wal-Mart SuperCtr/24hr

90mm Farber Creek

89 FM 1570, **S...lodging:** Luxury Inn, **other:** Lake Country RV Ctr

89mm E Caddo Creek

87 FM 1903, **N...gas:** Chevron/Pizza Inn/diesel, **S...gas:** Exxon/Pancake House/diesel, Texaco/diesel/24hr

87mm Elm Creek

85 FM 36, Caddo Mills, **N...**RV camping, **S...**auto repair

85mm W Caddo Creek

83 FM 1565 N, **N...gas:** Exxon/diesel

79 FM 2642, no facilities

77b FM 35, Royse City, **N...gas:** Exxon/diesel, Knox/Subway/diesel/24hr/@, **food:** BBQ

a TX 548, **N...gas:** Texaco/diesel, **food:** Jack-in-the-Box, McDonald's, **lodging:** Sun Royse Inn, **S...gas:** Conoco

73 FM 551, Fate, no facilities

70 FM 549, **S...gas:** Love's/diesel/24hr/@

69 (from wb), frontage rd

68 TX 205, to Rock Wall, **N...gas:** RaceTrac, Shell, Texaco, **food:** Braum's, DQ, KFC, Luigi's Italian, Pizza Hut, Pizza Inn, Whataburger, **lodging:** Holiday Inn Express, Super 8, **other:** Chevrolet, Dodge, Ford/Mercury, **S...gas:** TA/diesel/rest./24hr/@

Interstate 30

E ↕ W

67b FM 740, Ridge Rd, **N...gas:** Chevron, Mobil, **food:** Arby's, Burger King, Cajun Catfish, Grandy's, IHOP, McDonald's, Schlotsky's, Waffle House, **other:** Goodyear/auto, Kwik Kar Lube, MailBoxes Etc, Wal-Mart SuperCtr/24hr, cleaners, **S...gas:** Chevron, Exxon/Pizza Inn, Texaco, Total, **food:** Applebee's, Blackeyed Pea, Carino's Italian, Chick-fil-A, Chili's, ChuckeCheese, El Chico, Jack-in-the-Box, McDonald's, On-the-Border, Starbucks, Subway, Taco Bell, TCBY, **lodging:** Country Inn Suites, **other:** Albertson's, Discount Tire, Eckerd, GNC, Home Depot, Kohl's, Kroger, Lowe's Whse, Michael's, OfficeMax, Old Navy, Radio Shack, Ross, SteinMart, Target, to Lake Tawakoni

a Horizon Rd, Village Dr, **N...gas:** Total, **food:** Café Express, RanchHouse Rest., Saltgrass Steaks, Culpeper Cattle Steaks

66mm Ray Hubbard Reservoir

64 Dalrock Rd, Rowlett, **N...gas:** Exxon, Shamrock/diesel, **food:** Dickie's BBQ, **lodging:** Comfort Suites, **other:** HOSPITAL, Express Drug

63mm Ray Hubbard Reservoir

62 Chaha Rd, **N...food:** Martinez Mexican, **lodging:** Best Western, **other:** cleaners, to Hubbard RA, **S...gas:** Shamrock, Texaco, **other:** $General

61 Zion Rd, **N...gas:** Conoco/diesel, **lodging:** motel

60b Bobtown Rd, **N...gas:** Mobil, **food:** Jack-in-the-Box, **S...gas:** Texaco, **food:** Catfish King Rest.

a Rose Hill Dr, no facilities

59 Beltline Rd, Garland, **N...gas:** Citgo/7-11, Total, **food:** Church's, Denny's, LJ Silver, McDonald's, Whataburger, Wendy's, Taco Bell, **lodging:** MEDICAL CARE, **other:** Albertson's, Chief Parts, Eckerd, Goodyear, Wal-Mart SuperCtr/24hr, **S...gas:** Exxon/diesel, Shell, **food:** Burger King, DQ, Grandy's, Waffle House, Williams Chicken, lodging: Day's Inn, I-30 Inn, Motel 6, **other:** Kroger

58 Northwest Dr, **N...gas:** Shamrock, Texaco, **other:** Nissan, **S...gas:** Fina, **food:** Jack-in-the-Box, **other:** Lowe's Whse

56c b I-635 S, I 635 N

a Galloway Ave, Gus Thomasson Dr, **N...gas:** Shamrock, **food:** KFC, **S...gas:** Citgo/7-11, **food:** Checker's, Grandy's, Luby's, On-the-Border, Subway, Wendy's, Kroger, **lodging:** Courtyard, Crossland Studios, Delux Inn, Fairfield Inn, **other:** MEDICAL CARE, Nichols RV Ctr, other multiple facilities, Bigtown Mall...Hooters, Olive Garden, Outback Steaks, Red Lobster, Steak&Ale, Celebration Sta, Circuit City, NTB, Sears

55 Motley Dr, **N...gas:** Texaco/diesel, **food:** Castillo Mexican, **lodging:** Astro Inn, Ramada Ltd, **S...gas:** Chevron, Fina, **food:** Golden Ox Café, **lodging:** Mesquite Inn, Microtel, **other:** HOSPITAL, Dodge, to Eastfield Coll

Dallas

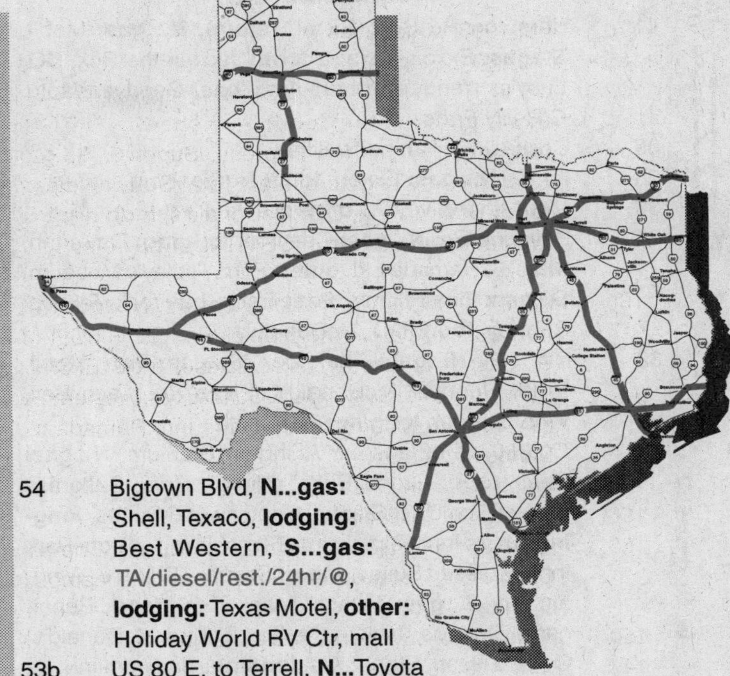

54 Bigtown Blvd, **N...gas:** Shell, Texaco, **lodging:** Best Western, **S...gas:** TA/diesel/rest./24hr/@, **lodging:** Texas Motel, **other:** Holiday World RV Ctr, mall

53b US 80 E, to Terrell, **N...**Toyota

a Lp 12, **N...lodging:** Luxury Inn, **other:** Chevrolet, **S...food:** CiCi's, Whataburger, **lodging:** Holiday Inn Express, **other:** Ford, K-Mart, Sam's Club, Staples, Wal-Mart SuperCtr/gas/24hr

51 Highland Rd, **N...gas:** Exxon, **food:** Country China, Denny's, Kettle, Luby's, McDonald's, Owen's Rest., **lodging:** La Quinta, **S...gas:** RaceWay, Texaco/diesel, **food:** Burger King, Capt D's, Furr's Dining, Grandy's, KFC, Pizza Hut, Wendy's, **lodging:** Exel Inn, Howard Johnson, Red Roof, **other:** AutoZone, Eckerd

50b a Ferguson Rd, **N...gas:** Shamrock, Phillips 66, Texaco, **lodging:** FairPark Inn, **S...other:** U-Haul

49b Dolphin Rd, Lawnview Ave, Samuell Ave, **N...lodging:** Welcome Inn

a Winslow St, **N...gas:** Fina, Phillips 66, Texaco/diesel/repair, **other:** Texas FoodLand, **S...gas:** Phillips 66, Shell/24hr

48b TX 78, E Grand, **S...**fairpark, arboreteum

a Carroll Ave, Central Ave, Peak St, Haskell Ave, **N...gas:** Shamrock, **other:** HOSPITAL, **S...gas:** Exxon, **food:** Joe's Burgers

47 2nd Ave, **S...food:** McDonald's, **other:** Cotton Bowl, fairpark

46b I-45, US 75, to Houston

a Central Expswy, downtown

45 I-35E, N to Denton, to Commerce St, Lamar St, Griffin St, **S...gas:** Fina, **food:** McDonald's, **lodging:** Ramada Inn

44b I-35E S, Industrial Blvd, no facilities

a I-35E N, Beckley Ave(from eb)

43b a Sylvan Ave(from wb), **N...gas:** Texaco/Quizno's/diesel, **other:** HOSPITAL, Family$, USPO/24hr

42 Hampton Rd N, **1 mi N...food:** Burger King, KFC/Taco Bell

TEXAS

Interstate 30

E ↕ W

41 Hampton Rd S(no EZ eb return), **N...gas:** Mobil, **S...gas:** Exxon, Texaco, **food:** Jack-in-the-Box, DQ, Luby's, Wendy's, **other:** AutoZone, Goodyear/auto, O'Reilly Parts

39 Cockrell Hill Rd, no facilities

38 Lp 12, **N...gas:** Exxon, **food:** Burger King

36 MacArthur Blvd, **S...other:** U-Haul

34 Belt Line Rd, **N...gas:** Chevron, **lodging:** Day's Inn, Motel 6, Ramada Ltd, **other:** Ford, Ripley's Museum, **S...gas:** Fina/Blimpie, RaceTrac, Shamrock, Texaco/Subway, **food:** DQ, McDonald's

32 NW 19th, **N...gas:** Shamrock, **S...gas:** Fina, Mobil, **food:** Denny's, McDonald's, Pizza Hut, Taco Bell, Whataburger, **lodging:** La Quinta

Dallas

30 TX 360, Six Flags Dr, Arlington Stadium, **N...gas:** Shell, **food:** Grand Buffet, Ninfa's Café, Saltgrass Steaks, TrailDust Steaks, Candlewood Suites, **lodging:** Day's Inn, Fairfield Inn, Flagship Inn, Hilton, Park Inn, Radisson Suites, **other:** Studio+, Super 8, Wingate Inn, **S...gas:** Texaco/diesel, Total, **food:** Bennigan's, Denny's, Jack-in-the-Box, Luby's, McDonald's, Owen's Rest., Steak&Ale, **lodging:** Baymont Inn, La Quinta, **other:** Dillard's, JC Penney, K-Mart, Plymouth, Sears/auto, Six Flags Funpark, mall

29 Ball Park Way, **N...gas:** Chevron, Citgo, **food:** Frijoles Café, Grady's Grill, Macaroni Grill, TrailDust Steaks, **lodging:** Fairfield Inn, **other:** Toyota, **S...gas:** Fina/diesel, **food:** On-the-Border, Texas Steaks, **lodging:** Howard Johnson, Marriott, Stadium Inn, Wyndham Hotel, **other:** Six Flags Funpark

28b TX 157, Nolan Ryan Expswy, **N...gas:** Mobil, **food:** Waffle House, **lodging:** Country Inn Suites, **S...food:** Chili's, Cozymel's, Harrigan's Grill, Joe's Crabshack, Landry's Seafood, Olive Garden, Pappadeaux Seafood, **lodging:** Courtyard, Day's Inn, **other:** Wyndham Garden, **other:** Barnes&Noble, SteinMart, TX Stadium

a FM 157, Collins St, **N...food:** Whataburger, **other:** HOSPITAL, Plymouth/Dodge, **S...food:** Pappasito's Cantina, **other:** Home Depot

27 Lamar Blvd, Cooper St, **N...gas:** Mobil, **food:** Jack-in-the-Box, **other:** Eckerd, Kroger, **S...gas:** Citgo/7-11, Texaco, **food:** Burger King, Denny's, **other:** MEDICAL CARE

26 Fielder Rd, **S...other:** to Six Flags(from eb)

25mm Village Creek

24 Eastchase Pkwy, **N...food:** Jack-in-the-Box, **other:** CarMax, Sam's Club/gas, Wal-Mart SuperCtr/24hr, **S...gas:** Chevron, Texaco/diesel, **food:** IHOP, McDonald's, Whataburger, **other:** Office Depot, Old Navy, Ross, Target

23 Cooks Lane, **S...gas:** Mobil

21c Bridgewood Dr, **N...gas:** Mobil, Texaco, **food:** Bennigan's, Luby's, Wendy's, **other:** Discount Tire, Home Depot, Kroger, U-Haul, **S...gas:** Fina, Shamrock, Texaco/diesel/24hr, **food:** Burger King, McDonald's, Pizza Hut, Taco Bueno, Whataburger/24hr, **other:** MEDICAL CARE

b a I-820, no facilities

19 Brentwood Stair Rd(from eb), **N...gas:** Chevron, Texaco/diesel, **food:** Chuy's Mexican, Steak&Ale, **other:** Kroger, **S...gas:** Citgo/diesel, Texaco

18 Oakland Blvd, **N...gas:** Phillips 66, Texaco/diesel, **food:** Burger King, Taco Bell, Waffle House, **lodging:** Motel 6

Ft Worth

16c Beach St, **S...gas:** Citgo/7-11, **lodging:** Best Western, Comfort Inn

16b a Riverside Dr(from wb), **S...lodging:** Great Western Inn

15b a I-35W N to Denton, S to Waco

14b Jones St, Commerce St, Ft Worth, downtown

14a TX 199, Henderson St, Ft Worth, downtown

13b Summit Ave, downtown, no facilities

13a 8th Ave, downtown

12d Forest Park Blvd, **N...food:** Pappadeaux Café, Pappasito's, Tony Roma, **other:** HOSPITAL

12b Rosedale St, no facilities

a University Dr, City Parks, **S...lodging:** Fairfield Inn, Ramada Inn

11 Montgomery St, **S...gas:** Texaco/diesel, **food:** Whataburger, **other:** visitor info

10 Hulen St, Ft Worth, **S...other:** Borders Books, World-Mkt

9b US 377, Camp Bowie Blvd, Horne St, **N...food:** Uncle Julio's Mexican, **S...gas:** Citgo/7-11, Fina, Texaco, **food:** Burger King, Dunkin Donuts, Jack-in-the-Box, Pizza Hut/Taco Bell, Purple Cow Diner, Qdoba Mexican, Szechuan Chinese, Subway, Taco Bueno, Tejano Café, Wendy's, Whataburger

a Bryant-Irvin Rd, **S...gas:** Texaco, same as 9b

8b Ridgmar, Ridglea, **N...gas:** Citgo

a TX 183, Green Oaks Rd, **N...food:** Applebee's, Blimpie, Jack-in-the-Box, Olive Garden, Taco Bueno, TGIFriday, **other:** MEDICAL CARE, Albertson's, Best Buy, Dillard's, Firestone, Foley's, JC Penney, Mervyn's, NTB, Office Depot, Ross, Sears/auto, U-Haul, **S...food:** Tommy's Burgers, **lodging:** Hawthorn Suites

7b a Cherry Lane, TX 183, spur 341, to Green Oaks Rd, **N...gas:** Texaco, **food:** ChuckeCheese, CiCi's, IHOP/24hr, Luby's, Papa John's, Popeye's, Ryan's, Subway, Taco Bell, Wendy's, **lodging:** La Quinta, Super 8, **other:** Ford, Home Depot, O'Reilly Parts, Sam's Club/gas, Wal-Mart/auto, **S...lodging:** Best Western, Hampton Inn, Holiday Inn Express, **other:** MEDICAL CARE, Dodge, Mitsubishi, Nissan, Target

6 Las Vegas Trail, **N...gas:** Chevron/24hr, **food:** McDonald's, Waffle House, **lodging:** Day's Inn, **other:** Acura, Lincoln/Mercury, **S...gas:** Citgo, Texaco/diesel, **food:** Pancake House, **lodging:** Best Budget Suites, Comfort Inn, Motel 6, **other:** AutoZone, Kia, Subaru

5b c I-820 S and N

Interstate 30

E ↕ W

5a Alemeda St(from eb, no EZ return), no facilities
3 RM 2871, Chapel Creek Blvd, no facilities
2 spur 580 E, no facilities
1b Linkcrest Dr, **S...gas:** Chevron, Fina/diesel, Mobil/diesel, Shamrock
0mm I-20 W. I-30 begins/ends on I-20, exit 421.

Interstate 35

N ↕ S

Exit # Services
504mm Texas/Oklahoma state line, Red River
504 frontage rd, no facilities
503mm parking area both lanes, no facilities
502 Welcome Ctr sb, full(handicapped)facilities, TX Tourist Bureau/info, phone, picnic tables, litter barrels
501 FM 1202, **E...other:** Chrysler/Plymouth/Dodge/Jeep, Ford/Mercury, **W...gas:** Hilltop/Conoco/diesel/café/@, **food:** Applebee's, Harper's Steaks/seafood, **other:** Prime Outlets/famous brands, Western Outfitter, Harper's Steaks, RV camping
500 FM 372, Gainesville, **E...gas:** Hitchin' Post/Texaco/diesel/rest./24hr/@
498b a US 82, Gainesville, to Wichita Falls, Sherman, **E...gas:** Citgo/diesel, Exxon, Phillips 66/diesel, Shamrock, Texaco, **food:** Catfish Louie's, Denny's, Whatburger/24hr, **lodging:** Bed&Bath Inn, Budget Host, Comfort Inn, Delux Inn, 12 Oaks Inn, **other:** HOSPITAL, **W...gas:** Exxon/diesel, **lodging:** Best Western, Day's Inn

Gainesville

497 frontage rd, no facilities
496b TX 51, FM 51, California St, Gainesville, **E...gas:** Chevron, Conoco, **food:** Bonanza, Braum's, Burger King, Grandy's, McDonald's, Taco Bell, Taco Mayo, Wendy's, **lodging:** Holiday Inn Express, Ramada Inn, **other:** Cadillac, Dodge/Plymouth, Goodyear/auto, N Central TX Coll, **W...gas:** Texaco, **food:** Chili's
496a to Weaver St, no facilities
496mm Elm Fork of the Trinity River
495 frontage rd, no facilities
494 FM 1306, no facilities
492mm picnic area sb, tables, litter barrels
491 Spring Creek Rd, no facilities
490mm picnic area nb, picnic tables, litter barrels
489 FM 1307, to Hockley Creek Rd, no facilities
487 rd 922, Valley View, **W...gas:** Chevron/diesel/24hr, **food:** DQ, **other:** USPO
486 frontage rd, no facilities
485 frontage rd(from sb), no facilities
483 FM 3002, Lone Oak Rd, **E...other:** Lone Oak RV Park, RV Ranch Ctr
482 Chisam Rd, no facilities
481 View Rd, **W...other:** Sundown Ranch RV Park
480 Lois Rd, **E...other:** Wal-Mart Dist Ctr
479 Belz Rd, Sanger, same as 478
478 FM 455, to Pilot Pt, Bolivar, **E...gas:** Phillips 66, Texaco, **food:** DQ, Sonic, **lodging:** Sanger Inn, **other:** USPO, cleaners/laundry, **W...gas:** Chevron/Subway/24hr, **food:** Jack-in-the-Box, McDonald's, **other:** Chevrolet, IGA Foods, RV Park, Ray Roberts Lake and SP
477 Keaton Rd, **E...gas:** Phillips 66, **food:** No Frills Grill, **W...gas:** Shamrock/diesel, **other:** RV Ctr
475b Rector Rd, no facilities
a FM 156, to Krum, no facilities
474 Cowling(from nb), no facilities
473 FM 3163, Milam Rd, **E...gas:** Love's/Subway/diesel/24hr/@

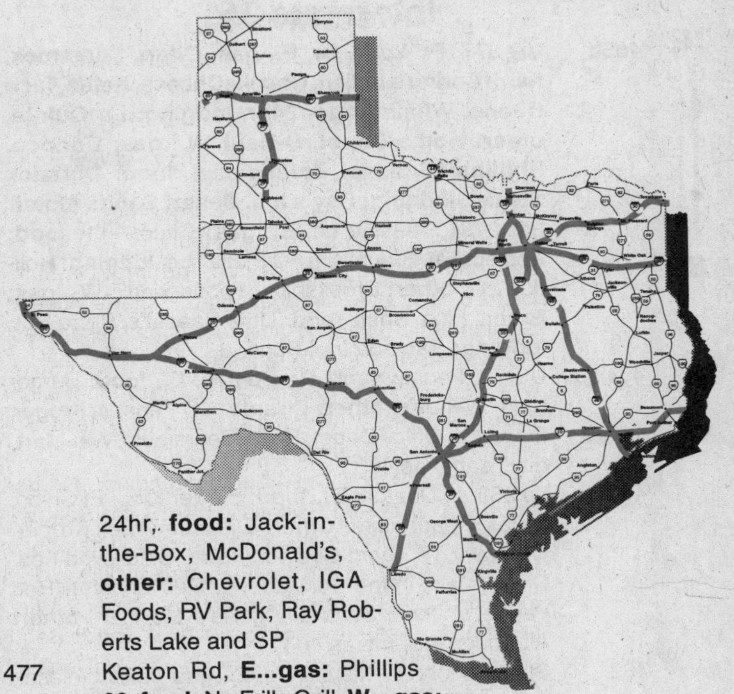

Denton

472 Ganzer Rd, **W...other:** Texas RV Resort
471 US 77, FM 1173, Lp 282, to Denton, Krum, **E...gas:** TA/Conoco/diesel/rest./24hr/@, **food:** Good Eats Café, **other:** HOSPITAL, Denton Stores/famous brands, **W...gas:** Citgo/diesel/café/24hr, Fina, **other:** Foster's Western Shop, to Camping World RV Supply
470 Lp 288, same services as 469 from sb
469 US 380, University Dr, to Decatur, McKinney, **E...gas:** Phillips 66/diesel, RaceTrac, **food:** Braum's, ChinaTown Café, Cracker Barrel, Luigi's Pizza, McDonald's, **lodging:** Best Western, **other:** Albertson's/drugs, Dodge, K-Mart, Toyota, **W...gas:** Conoco/diesel, Shamrock/service, Texaco/diesel, **food:** DQ, Denny's, Waffle House, **lodging:** Exel Inn, Howard Johnson, Motel 6, **other:** HOSPITAL, Ancira RV Ctr, Camping World RV Supply, to TX Woman's U
468 FM 1515, Airport Rd, W Oak St, no facilities
467 I-35W, S to Ft Worth, no facilities

I-35 divides into E and W sb, converges into I-35 nb. **See Texas I-35 W.**

466b Ave D, **E...gas:** Citgo, Exxon/diesel, **food:** Burger King, IHOP/24hr, McDonald's, Pancho's Mexican, Taco Cabana, **lodging:** Comfort Suites, **other:** $General, Sack'n Save Foods, to NTSU, **W...lodging:** Radisson
a McCormick St, **E...gas:** Phillips 66, Texaco/diesel, **lodging:** Comfort Suites, **W...gas:** Citgo, Fina/diesel/U-Haul

Interstate 35

N ↕ S

465b **US 377, Ft Worth Dr, E...gas: Citgo, Shamrock, food: Carino's Italian, ChuckeCheese, Kettle, Taco Bueno, Whataburger/24hr, lodging: La Quinta, other: Home Depot, U-Haul, W...gas: Conoco, Phillips 66/diesel, Total/diesel, food: Outback Steaks, lodging: Day's Inn, Desert Sands Motel**

a FM 2181, Teasley Ln, **E...gas:** Citgo/7-11, **food:** Applebee's, Braum's, KFC/Pizza Hut, **lodging:** Holiday Inn, **other:** Brookshires Foods, bank, **W...gas:** Exxon, Fina, Shell, **food:** Little Caesar's, Pizza Hut, **lodging:** Ramada Inn, Super 8

464 US 77, Pennsylvania Dr, Denton, **E...food:** Burger King, Wendy's, **other:** Dillard's, JC Penney, Kroger, Mervyn's, Office Depot, Ross, Sears/auto, Wal-Mart, mall, same as 463

463 Lp 288, to Denton, **E...food:** Burger King, El Chico, Texas Roadhouse, **other:** Discount Tire, Kroger, Old Navy, **W...gas:** Chevron, **food:** Blackeyed Pea, Chili's, Jack-in-the-Box, Luby's, Red Lobster, Red Pepper's Rest., Schlotsky's, Tia's Mexican, **other:** Albertson's, same as 464

462 State School Rd, Mayhill Rd, **E...gas:** Texaco/diesel, **other:** HOSPITAL, Hyundai, **W...gas:** Exxon/café, **other:** Cadillac, Chevrolet, Dodge/Toyota, Lincoln/Mercury/Mazda/Isuzu, Pontiac/Buick/GMC

461 Sandy Shores Rd, Post Oak Dr, **E...other:** Ford, McClain RV Ctr, **W...other:** Chrysler/Plymouth/Jeep/Kia, Nissan

460 Corinth Pkwy, **E...gas:** Chevron/diesel/repair, **other:** McClain RV Ctr, camping, **W...other:** Harley-Davidson

459 frontage rd, **W...other:** Destiny RV Resort

458 FM 2181, Swisher Rd, **E...gas:** Phillips 66, Texaco/Subway, **W...gas:** Chevron/McDonald's, Exxon/Wendy's, **food:** Burger King, Chick-fil-A, Jack-in-the-Box, KFC/Pizza Hut/Taco Bell, Mr Gatti, Starbucks, Whataburger, **other:** Albertson's, Discount Tire, GNC, Radio Shack, Wal-Mart SuperCtr/gas/24hr

457b Denton Rd, Hundley Dr, Lake Dallas, **E...gas:** Chevron

a Lake Dallas, Hundley Dr(from nb)

456 Highland Village, no facilities

456mm Lewisville Lake

455 McGee Lane, no facilities

454b Garden Ridge Blvd, **W...gas:** Citgo, **other:** city park

a FM 407, Justin, **E...gas:** Shamrock, **W...gas:** Fina/diesel, Texaco, **food:** McDonald's

453 Valley Ridge Blvd, **E...other:** Ford, May RV Ctr

452 FM 1171, to Flower Mound, **E...gas:** Mobil, **food:** IHOP, Taco Bueno, **lodging:** Howard Johnson, HOSPITAL, **W...gas:** Chevron, Exxon/diesel, **food:** Burger King, Golden Corral, Grandy's, Whataburger/24hr, **other:** Home Depot, Kohl's, Lowe's Whse, Staples, U-Haul, same as 451

451 Fox Ave, **E...gas:** Texaco/diesel, **food:** Braum's, **W...gas:** Chevron/24hr, Conoco/Quizno's/diesel, Shamrock, **food:** Blackeyed Pea, Cracker Barrel, El Chico, **lodging:** Hampton Inn, Microtel, **other:** Atlas Transmissions, VW

Grapevine

450 TX 121, Grapevine, **E...gas:** Citgo/7-11, RaceTrac, **food:** BBQ, Owens Rest., Pancho's Mexican, **lodging:** Pines Motel, Ramada Ltd, **other:** Chevrolet/Subaru, Dodge, **W...gas:** Chevron, Citgo/7-11, Conoco, Fina, Shamrock, Texaco/diesel, **food:** Alfredo's Pizza, Burger King, Chili's, Church's, Don Pedro's, Furr's Dining, IHOP, Ming Garden Chinese, KFC, LJ Silver, McDonald's, Rodarte's Cantina, Subway, Taco Bell, Tia's Mexican, Waffle House, Whataburger/24hr, **lodging:** Budget Inn, Day's Inn, J&J Motel, Spanish Trails Inn, Super 8, **other:** Chief Parts, Eckerd, Firestone/auto, Food Lion, Kroger, Nissan/Saturn, transmissions

449 Corporate Drive, **E...food:** China Dragon, Fox&Hound Grill, Hartford Grill, Hooters, On the Border, **lodging:** Extended Stay America, Hearthside Inn, Motel 6, **other:** Cavender's Boots, **W...gas:** Exxon/Quizno's/Pizza Inn/TCBY, Fina/diesel, **food:** Chili's, El Fenix Mexican, Jack-in-the-Box, Kettle, **lodging:** Best Western, La Quinta, Sun Suites, Honda, NTB

448b a FM 3040, Round Grove Rd, **E...food:** Abuelo's Mexican, Bennigan's, ChuckeCheese, Jack-in-the-Box, Olive Garden, SaltGrass Steaks, Subway, **lodging:** Homewood Suites, **other:** Best Buy, Ross, Target, **W...gas:** Chevron, Exxon, RaceTrac, Texaco, **food:** Applebee's, Carino's Italian, Chick-fil-A, Christina's Mexican, Cotton Patch Café, Don Pablo, Famous Dave's BBQ, Good Eats Grill, IHOP, Logan's Roadhouse, Luby's, Macaroni Grill, McDonald's, OutBack Steaks, Red Lobster, Schlotsky's, Sonic, SpagEddie's Italian, Taco Cabana, TGIFriday, Tony Roma, Water Garden Chinese, Wendy's, **lodging:** Comfort Inn, Country Inn Suites, **other:** Barnes&Noble, Borders Books, Circuit City, CompUSA, Dillard's, Discount Tire, Foley's, JC Penney, Marshall's, Michael's, Office Depot, OfficeMax, Old Navy, Sears/auto, Target, mall

446 Frankford Rd, **E...food:** La Hacienda Ranch Grill, **other:** Volvo

445b Pres Geo Bush Tpk

445 Trinity Mills Rd, **E...other:** HOSPITAL, Buick/GMC/Pontiac, Home Depot, PepBoys, RV Ctr

444 Whitlock Lane, Sandy Lake Rd, **E...gas:** Texaco, **other:** RV camping, **W...gas:** Chevron, **food:** McDonald's, **lodging:** Delux Inn

443 Belt Line Rd, Crosby Rd, **E...gas:** Conoco, Shell, **other:** NTB

442 Valwood Pkwy, **E...gas:** Texaco, **food:** DQ, Denny's, El Chico, Grandy's, Jack-in-the-Box, Rosita's Mexican, Taco Bueno, Waffle House, **lodging:** Comfort Inn, Guest Inn, Red Roof, Royal Inn, **other:** Ford, **W...gas:** Fina/diesel, **lodging:** Day's Inn, **other:** Chevrolet, U-Haul, transmissions

Dallas

441 Valley View Lane, **W...gas:** Exxon, Mobil, **lodging:** Best Western, Day's Inn, Econolodge, La Quinta

440b I-635 E, no facilities

c I-635 W, to DFW Airport, no facilities

439 Royal Lane, **E...gas:** Texaco, **food:** McDonald's, Whataburger/24hr, **other:** Daewoo, **W...gas:** Chevron, **food:** Jack-in-the-Box, Wendy's

Interstate 35

N ↕ S

Dallas

438 Walnut Hill Lane, **E...gas:** Fina/Quizno's/diesel, Mobil, Shell, **food:** Bennigan's, Burger King, Chili's, Denny's, Old San Francisco Steaks, Red Lobster, Steak&Ale, Taco Bell, TGIFriday, Tony Roma's, Trail Dust Steaks, Wild Turkey Grill, **lodging:** Country Inn Suites, Drury Inn, Hampton Inn, **W...gas:** Chevron, Texaco/diesel, **other:** RV Ctr

437 Manana Rd(from nb), same as 438

436 TX 348, Irving, to DFW, **E...gas:** Exxon/diesel, **food:** IHOP, Luby's, Schlotsky's, Waffle House, **lodging:** Clarion Suites, Comfort Suites, Courtyard, Homestead Suites, Radisson, Studio 6, **W...gas:** Exxon, **food:** Blackeyed Pea, Chili's, Don Pablo, Humperdinck's Grill, Jack-in-the-Box, Joe's Crabshack, McDonald's, Olive Garden, Outback Steaks, Papadeaux Seafood, Pappas Bros Steaks, Red Lobster, Taco Bell/Pizza Hut, Tony Roma's, Wendy's, **lodging:** Red Roof Inn

435 Harry Hines Blvd(from nb), **E...gas:** RaceTrack, **food:** Arby's, **other:** U-Haul, same as 436

434b Regal Row, **E...gas:** Fina/Grandy's, **food:** Denny's, Whataburger/24hr, **lodging:** La Quinta, Red Roof Inn, **W...lodging:** Fairfield Inn

a Empire, Central, **E...gas:** Chevron, **food:** Monald's, Sonic, Wendy's, **lodging:** Budget Suites, Candlewood Suites, InTown Suites, Wingate Inn, **other:** Office Depot, **W...gas:** Exxon, **food:** Burger King, Schlotsky's, Taco Bell/Pizza Hut

433b Mockingbird Lane, Love Field Airport, **E...gas:** Mobil, **food:** Jack-in-the-Box, **lodging:** Clarion Hotel, Crowne Plaza, Harvey Hotel, Residence Inn, **other:** Sheraton, **W...gas:** Chevron, **food:** McDonald's, **other:** Goodyear

a (432b from sb)TX 356, Commonwealth Dr, **E...gas:** Texaco/diesel, **lodging:** Marriott, **other:** OfficeMax, **W...lodging:** Delux Inn

432a Inwood Rd, **E... other:** HOSPITAL, Chevrolet, **W...gas:** Fina, Texaco, **food:** Whataburger/24hr, **lodging:** Homewood Suites

431 Motor St, **E...gas:** Mobil, **food:** Denny's, **lodging:** Stouffer Hotel, **W...gas:** Shell, **food:** Ninfa's Grill, Wok Chinese, **lodging:** Embassy Suites, Marriott Suites

430c Wycliff Ave, **E...food:** JoJo's Rest., **lodging:** Renaissance Hotel, **other:** Intn'l Apparel Mart

b Mkt Ctr Blvd, **E...other:** World Trade Ctr, **W...food:** Denny's, **lodging:** Courtyard, Fairfield Inn, Ramada Inn, Sheraton, Wilson World Hotel, Wyndham Garden

a Oak Lawn Ave, **W...gas:** Texaco/diesel, **food:** Denny's, Medieval Times Rest., **lodging:** Holiday Inn, **other:** to Merchandise Mart

429c HiLine Ave(from nb)

b Continental Ave, Commerce St W, downtown, **E... food:** Hooters, **W...gas:** Exxon, **food:** McDonald's

a to I-45, US 75, to Houston, no facilities

428e Commerce St E, Reunion Blvd, Dallas, downtown

d I-30 W, to Ft Worth

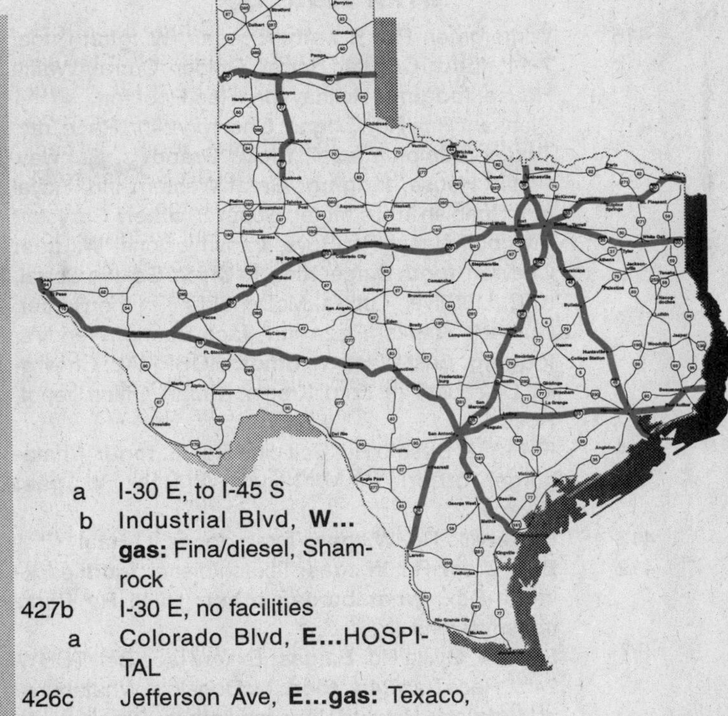

a I-30 E, to I-45 S

b Industrial Blvd, **W... gas:** Fina/diesel, Shamrock

427b I-30 E, no facilities

a Colorado Blvd, **E...HOSPITAL**

426c Jefferson Ave, **E...gas:** Texaco, **W...gas:** Shell

b TX 180 W, 8th St, **E...gas:** Texaco, **W...gas:** Shell, **lodging:** Mustang Inn

a Ewing Ave, **E...food:** McDonald's, **W...other:** Chrysler/Jeep, Pontiac/GMC, Honda, Hyundai

425c Marsalis Ave, **E...lodging:** Dallas Inn, **W...gas:** Mobil, Shamrock

b Beckley Ave, 12th St, **W...gas:** Exxon, **food:** Wendy's

a Zang Blvd, **W...gas:** Shamrock, Texaco/diesel

424 Illinois Ave, **E...gas:** Chevron, **food:** BBQ, Dunkin Donuts, **other:** HOSPITAL, **W...gas:** Exxon, **food:** Church's, IHOP, Jack-in-the-Box, Little Caesar's, Sonic, Taco Bell, OakTree Inn, **other:** Brake Ctr, Eckerd

423b Zaner Ave, **W...food:** Big Boy, Spin's Rest., **lodging:** Westerner Motel

a (422b from nb)US 67 S, Kiest Blvd, **W...gas:** Shell/repair, Texaco/diesel, **food:** McDonald's, Wendy's, **lodging:** Quality Inn, **other:** Subaru/VW

421b Lp 12W, Ann Arbor St, **W...food:** Luby's, Red Lobster, **lodging:** Big Couple Motel, Sunbelt Motel, **other:** Sam's Club

a Lp 12E, **E...gas:** RaceWay, Texaco/diesel, **lodging:** Budget Inn, Howard Johnson, Motel 6, **other:** K-Mart

420 Laureland, **E...lodging:** Master Suite Motel, **other:** **W...gas:** Conoco, Mobil, **lodging:** Embassy Motel, Linfield Inn

419 Camp Wisdom Rd, **E...gas:** Exxon, **W...gas:** Shell/24hr, **food:** McDonald's, **lodging:** Oak Cliff Inn, Suncrest Inn, **other:** U-Haul

418c Danieldale Rd(from sb)

418b I-635/I-20 E, to Shreveport, no facilities

a I-20 W, to Ft Worth, no facilities

417 Wheatland Rd(from nb), no facilities

TEXAS

Interstate 35

N ↕ S

416 Wintergreen Rd, **E...other:** repair, **W...gas:** Citgo/7-11, **food:** Cracker Barrel, Golden Corral, Waffle House, **lodging:** Holiday Inn, Red Roof Inn
415 Pleasant Run Rd, **E...gas:** Chevron/24hr, RaceTrac, Texaco/Blimpie/diesel, **food:** Grandy's, Subway, Waffle House, **lodging:** Great Western Inn, Royal Inn, Spanish Trails Motel, Super 8, **other:** Chrysler/Plymouth/Jeep, PepBoys, transmissions, **W...gas:** Chevron, **food:** Burger King, El Chico, Golden Corral, KFC, LJ Silver, Luby's, McDonald's, On the Border, Outback Steaks, Pizza Inn, Taco Bueno, Wendy's, **lodging:** Best Western, **other:** HOSPITAL, Chevrolet, Discount Tire, Ford, Kroger, K-Mart, Office Depot, Ross
414 FM 1382, Desoto Rd, Belt Line Rd, **E...food:** Whataburger, **other:** Wal-Mart SuperCtr/24hr, **W...gas:** Texaco
413 Parkerville Rd, **W...gas:** Total, Honda, U-Haul
412 Bear Creek Rd, **W...gas:** Texaco/diesel, **food:** Jack-in-the-Box, Whataburger, **other:** HiHo RV Park, transmissions
411 FM 664, Ovilla Rd, **E...gas:** Exxon/Taco Bell/TCBY/24hr, RaceTrac/24hr, **food:** McDonald's, Whataburger, **lodging:** Howard Johnson, **other:** Brookshire's Foods, Eckerd, **W...gas:** Exxon, Texaco
410 Red Oak Rd, **E...gas:** Fina/Subway/diesel/24hr, Texaco/diesel, **food:** Denny's, **lodging:** Day's Inn, **W...other:** Hilltop Travel Trailers
408 US 77, **E...**golf
406 Sterrett Rd, **E...**fireworks
405 FM 387, **E...gas:** Chevron
404 Lofland Rd, industrial area, no facilities
403 US 287, to Ft Worth, **E...gas:** Texaco, **food:** McDonald's, **other:** Chevrolet/Cadillac, Jeep, **W...other:** Buick/Pontiac/GMC, Chrysler/Dodge, Ford/Mercury
401b US 287 bus, Waxahatchie, **E...lodging:** Best Western, Super 8
a Brookside Rd, **E...lodging:** Brookside Inn, Ramada Ltd
399b FM 1446, no facilities
a FM 66, FM 876, Maypearl, **E...lodging:** Texas Inn, **W...gas:** Chevron/diesel, Texaco/diesel/24hr
397 to US 77, no facilities
393mm rest area both lanes, full(handicapped)facilities, phone, picnic tables, litter barrels, vending, petwalk
391 FM 329, Forreston Rd, no facilities
386 TX 34, Italy, **E...gas:** Texaco/diesel/24hr, **food:** DQ, **W...gas:**Exxon/diesel, **lodging:** Italy Inn
384 Derrs Chapel Rd, no facilities
381 FM 566, Milford Rd, no facilities
377 FM 934, no facilities
374 FM 2959, Carl's Corner, **W...gas:** Carl's/diesel/rest.
I-35E**********
371 I-35 W. I-35 divides into E and W nb, converges sb. **See Texas I-35 W.**
370 US 77 N, FM 579, Hillsboro, no facilities

Hillsboro

368b FM 286, **E...food:** LoneStar Café, Taco Bell, Wendy's, **other:** Prime Outlets/famous brands, **W...gas:** Exxon/Domino's, Shamrock/diesel, Texaco/diesel, **food:** Braum's, DQ, El Conquistador Mexican, McDonald's, Pizza Hut, **lodging:** Best Western, Comfort Inn, **other:** HOSPITAL
a TX 22, TX 171, to Whitney, **E...gas:** Citgo/7-11, Love's/Subway/Pizza Hut/diesel/24hr/@ , **food:** Arby's, Black-eyed Pea, Burger King, Golden Corral, Grandy's, IHOP, McDonald's, **lodging:** Holiday Inn Express, Motel 6, Wyndham Mill Inn, **W...gas:** Chevron, Exxon, Mobil, Shell/diesel, **food:** Jack-in-the-Box, KFC, Schlotsky's, Whataburger/24hr, **lodging:** Thunderbird Motel/rest., **other:** Buick/Pontiac/GMC, Chevrolet/Cadillac, Chrysler/Plymouth/Dodge/Jeep, Ford/Mercury, Wal-Mart SuperCtr/gas/24hr
367 Old Bynum Rd(from nb), no facilities
364b TX 81 N, to Hillsboro, no facilities
a FM 310, **E...gas:** Conoco/diesel/24hr, **W...gas:** Fina/KrispyKreme/diesel/24hr, **food:** BBQ
362 Chatt Rd, no facilities
359 FM 1304, **W...gas:** Mobil/Subway/diesel/24hr, **other:** antiques
358 FM 1242 E, Abbott, **E...gas:** Exxon, **food:** Turkey Shop Café
356 Co Rd 3102, no facilities
355 County Line Rd, **E...other:** KOA
354 Marable St, **E...other:** KOA
353 FM 2114, West, **E...gas:** Citgo/Subway, Fina, Shell, **food:** DQ, Little Czech Bakery, **other:** Ford, **W...gas:** Citgo/diesel/repair, Exxon, **other:** Chevrolet, Goodyear
351 FM 1858, **W...other:** West Auction
349 Wiggins Rd, no facilities
347 FM 3149, Tours Rd, no facilities
346 Ross Rd, **E...gas:** Shell/diesel/24hr, **W...gas:** Exxon/diesel/24hr, **other:** I-35 RV Park
345mm picnic area/litter barrels both lanes
345 Old Dallas Rd, **E...**antiques, **W...other:** I-35 RV Park
343 FM 308, Elm Mott, **E...gas:** Exxon/DQ, Fina/diesel, Texaco/diesel/24hr, **W...gas:** Chevron/diesel/24hr, **food:** BBQ, Heitmiller Steaks
342b US 77 bus, **W...**RV Park
a FM 2417, Crest Dr, **W...gas:**Shamrock/diesel, **food:** DQ, **lodging:** Everyday Inn, **other:** Family$, auto repair
341 Craven Ave, Lacy Lakeview, **E...gas:** Chevron, **W...gas:** BP/diesel, Shell//pizza, **lodging:** Interstate North Motel, **other:** Chief Parts
340 Myers Lane(from nb), no facilities
339 to TX 6 S, FM 3051, Lake Waco, **E...gas:** Shamrock/diesel, **food:** Casa Ole, ChiChi's, Domino's, El Conquistador, Jack-in-the-Box, Luby's, Pizza Hut, Popeye's, Sonic, Subway, Wendy's, Whataburger/24hr, **lodging:** Country Inn Suites, **other:** MEDICAL CARE, $General, Radio Shack,Wal-Mart SuperCtr/24hr, **W...gas:** Chevron, Citgo, Texaco, **food:** Burger King, Cracker Barrel, KFC, McDonald's, Papa John's, Starbucks, **lodging:** Hampton Inn, Hawthorn Inn, Knight's Inn, **other:** to airport

Interstate 35

N ↕ S Waco

338b Behrens Circle(from nb), **E...gas:** Texaco, same as 339, **W...gas:** Texaco/diesel/LP, **lodging:** Day's Inn, Delta Inn, Knight's Inn, Motel 6, **other:** Eckerd

337 (338a from nb)US 84, to TX 31, Waco Dr, **E...other:** AutoZone, Family$, HEB Food/gas, Sam's Club/gas, **W...gas:** Texaco, **other:** HOSPITAL

335c Lake Brazos Dr, MLK Blvd, **E...food:** Summer Palace Chinese, **lodging:** Holiday Inn, RiverPlace Inn/café, **W...lodging:** Travel Inn, Victorian Inn, **other:** HOSPITAL

335mm Brazos River

335b FM 434, University Parks Dr, **E...food:** China Grill, IHOP, Jim's Rest., Quizno's, Thai Cuisine, **lodging:** Best Western, **other:** Baylor U, **W...food:** Arby's, Jack-in-the-Box, **lodging:** Clarion, Lexington Inn, Residence Inn

a 4th St, 5th St, **E...gas:** Exxon/Subway/TCBY/diesel, Texaco/diesel, **food:** Denny's, IHOP, Lupito's Mexican, Pizza Hut, **lodging:** Best Western, La Quinta, **other:** Baylor U, **W...gas:** BP, Shamrock, **food:** Fazoli's, LJ Silver, McDonald's, Taco Bell, Taco Cabana, Wendy's, Whataburger/24hr, **lodging:** Clarion, **other:** to Baylor U

334b US 77 S, 17th St, 18th St, **E...gas:** BP, Chevron, Texaco/diesel, **food:** Burger King, Popeye's, Schlotsky's, Vitek's BBQ, **lodging:** Budget Inn, Comfort Inn, Super 8, **other:** Harley-Davidson, **W...gas:** Phillips 66/diesel, Texaco, **food:** Mexico Lindo, **other:** HOSPITAL

333a Lp 396, Valley Mills Dr, **E...gas:** Chevron, **food:** El Chico, Elite Café, Texas Roadhouse, Trujillo's Mexican, **lodging:** Astro Motel, Motel 6, **other:** Isuzu/Mazda, **W...gas:** RaceWay, Shamrock, **food:** Bush's Chicken, Church's Chicken, DQ, Jack-in-the-Box, Papa John's, Sonic, **lodging:** Comfort Inn, **other:** Eckerd, Jeep, Lincoln/Mercury, Volvo/Freightliner

331 New Rd, **E...gas:** Chevron, **lodging:** New Road Inn, Relax Inn, Rodeway Inn, **W...gas:** Flying J/CountryMkt/diesel/24hr/@, **lodging:** Quality Inn

330 Lp 340, TX 6, **E...gas:** Chevron, **lodging:** New Road Inn, Rodeway Inn, **2 mi W...gas:** Citgo/diesel, **food:** Chick-fil-A, Luby's, McDonald's, Outback Steaks, TGIFriday, Wienerschnitzel, **lodging:** Extended Stay America, Fairfield Inn, **other:** CompUSA, Ford, Honda, Lowe's Whse, Toyota, Wal-Mart SuperCtr/24hr

328 FM 2063, FM 2113, Moody, **E...gas:** Pilot/DQ/diesel/24hr/@, **food:** McDonald's, **W...gas:** Shamrock, Texaco/24hr

325 FM 3148, Moonlight Dr, **W...gas:** Shell/Subway/TCBY/diesel/24hr, **food:** Laredo's Rest.

323 FM 2837, Lorena, **W...gas:** Brookshire Bros/Conoco, **food:** Pizza House, **other:** $General

322 Lorena, **E...gas:** Phillips 66/diesel, **W...gas:** Chevron/diesel

319 Woodlawn Rd, no facilities

318mm picnic area both lanes, litter barrels, picnic tables

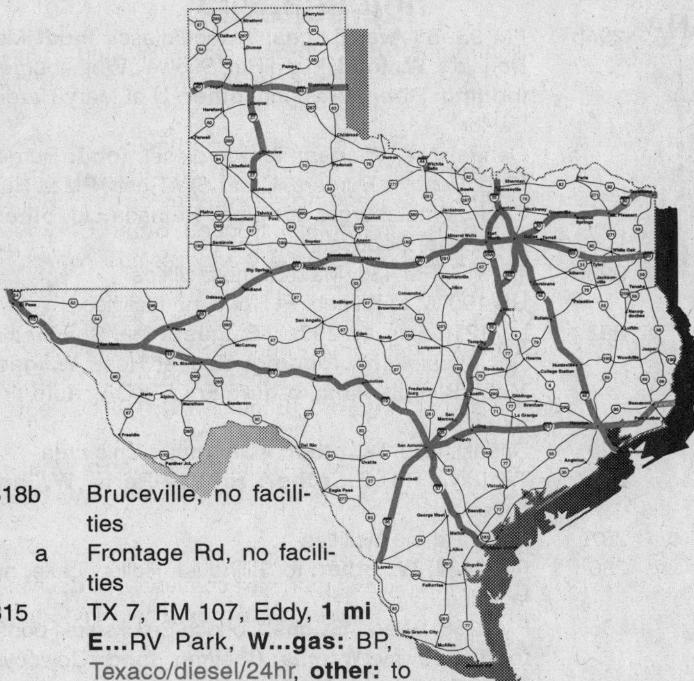

318b Bruceville, no facilities

a Frontage Rd, no facilities

315 TX 7, FM 107, Eddy, **1 mi E...**RV Park, **W...gas:** BP, Texaco/diesel/24hr, **other:** to Mother Neff SP

314 Old Blevins Rd, no facilities

311 Big Elm Rd, no facilities

308 FM 935, Troy, **E...gas:** Texaco, **other:** Troy Foods, **W...gas:** Exxon, **other:** Nick's Campers, Troy Lube

306 FM 1237, Pendleton, **W...gas:** Love's/Citgo/Subway/A&W/diesel/24hr, **other:** Temple RV Park

305 Berger Rd, **W...other:** Temple RV Park, repair

304 Lp 363, Dodgen Loop, **W...gas:** Shamrock/diesel/24hr, Shell/Wendy's/diesel

Temple

303 spur 290, N 3rd St, Temple, **E...lodging:** TX Inn, **W...lodging:** Continental Inn

302 Nugent Ave, **E...gas:** Exxon/diesel, Texaco/diesel, **lodging:** Comfort Suites, Econolodge, Holiday Inn Express, **W...gas:** Chevron, **food:** Denny's, **lodging:** Day's Inn, Motel 6, Stratford House Inn, Travelodge

301 TX 53, FM 2305, Adams Ave, **E...gas:** Shamrock, **food:** Jim's Rest., KFC, LJ Silver, McDonald's, Pizza Hut, Starbucks, Taco Bell, Wendy's, Whataburger, **lodging:** La Quinta, **other:** Ford, **W...food:** Catfish Shack, **lodging:** Best Western, **other:** Albertson's/drugs, Chrysler/Jeep, $General, Lincoln/Mercury, Harley-Davidson, Jeep

300 Ave H, 49th –57th Sts, **E...gas:** Shell, Texaco, **food:** Las Casas Mexican, **lodging:** Oasis Motel, **other:** Dodge, **W...gas:** Texaco

299 US 190 E, TX 36, **E...gas:** Shell, Texaco/diesel, **food:** El Conquistador Mexican, Golden Corral, Jack-in-the-Box, Luby's, **lodging:** Budget Inn, Regency Inn, **other:** HOSPITAL, Ancira RV Ctr, Chevrolet/Toyota, Dodge, K-Mart, Saturn, Subaru, **W...gas:** Exxon/diesel/24hr, Texaco, **food:** Burger King, Chili's, IHOP

297 FM 817, Midway Dr, **E...gas:** Citgo, **lodging:** Day's Inn, Super 8/rest., **other:** BMW, Nissan, Saab, Volvo, **W...gas:** Shamrock, **other:** Buick/Pontiac/GMC, Fed Ex, VW

294b FM 93, 6th Ave, **E...gas:** Texaco/diesel, **food:** McDonald's, **W...food:** Pizza Hut, Subway, Whataburger, **lodging:** River Forest Inn, **other:** U of Mary Hardin Baylor

a Central Ave, **W...gas:** Texaco/diesel, **food:** Burger King, Bobby's Burgers, Great SW Rest., Pizza Hut, Sonic, Whataburger, **lodging:** Ramada Ltd, **other:** AutoZone, Goodyear

293b TX 317, FM 436, Main St, no facilities

a US 190 W, to Killeen, Ft Hood, no facilities

292 Lp 121(same as 293a), **E...gas:** Fina, Shamrock/diesel/rest./24hr, **lodging:** Budget Host, **W...gas:** Mobil/Blimpie/24hr, **other:** Ford, KOA, auto/tire repair

290 Shanklin Rd, **W...other:** KOA(1mi), picnic area

289 Tahuaya Rd, **E...other:** Hi-Way Parts, **W...**antiques

287 Amity Rd, no facilities

286 FM 2484, **W...other:** to Stillhouse Hollow Lake, no facilities

285 FM 2268, Salado, **E...gas:** Conoco/Brookshire Foods, **food:** Subway, **W...gas:** Chevron, **food:** Cowboys BBQ, Robertson's Rest.

284 Robertson Rd, **E...gas:** Exxon/Burger King, **lodging:** Stagecoach Inn, **W...gas:** Texaco/diesel, **food:** DQ, **lodging:** Super 8

283 FM 2268, FM 2843, Salado, to Holland, no facilities

282 FM 2115, **E...gas:** Texaco/diesel/lube/repairs, **food:** Salado Creek Grill, **other:** RV camping

281.5mm rest area both lanes, full(handicapped)facilities, phone, picnic tables, litter barrels, vending, petwalk

280 Prairie Dell, no facilities

279 Hill Rd, **W...other:** Emerald Lake RV Park

277 Yankee Rd, no facilities

275 FM 487, Jarrell, to Florence, **E...gas:** Exxon, Shamrock/diesel, **W...gas:** Texaco, **other:** Jarrell Country Mkt, USPO

271 Theon Rd, **W...gas:** Texaco/Subway/diesel/24hr

268 FM 972, Walburg, no facilities

266 TX 195, **E...gas:** Mobil/Arby's/diesel/24hr, **W...gas:** Exxon/diesel

264 Lp 35, Georgetown, **E...lodging:** San Gabriel Motel, **other:** All Seasons RV Ctr, Live Oaks RV Park

262 RM 2338, Lake Georgetown, **E...gas:** Shamrock, **food:** KFC, Luby's, McDonald's, Quizno's, Sonic, Subway, **lodging:** Holiday Inn Express, **other:** Albertson's, Eckerd, Parts+, Radio Shack, **W...gas:** Phillips 66, Texaco, **food:** Chuck Wagon Café, DQ, Popeye's, Taco Bueno, Wendy's, Whataburger/24hr, **lodging:** Day's Inn, La Quinta

261 TX 69, Georgetown, **E...gas:** Texaco/diesel, **food:** Applebee's, Burger King, Chili's, KFC/Taco Bell, Schlotsky's, **other:** HEB Foods, same as 262, **W...other:** Home Depot, Wal-Mart SuperCtr/24hr, antiques

260 RM 2243, Leander, **E...other:** HOSPITAL, USPO, **W...gas:** Chevron, Conoco, Mobil, **food:** Jack-in-the-Box, **lodging:** Comfort Inn

259 Lp 35, **E...other:** Candle Factory, **W...other:** RV Outlet Mall, to Interspace Caverns

257 Westinghouse Rd, **E...other:** Chevrolet/Buick, Chrysler/Plymouth/Dodge/Jeep, Ford, Mazda, Mitsubishi, VW

256 RM 1431, Chandler Rd, **rest area sb, full(handicapped)facilities, phone, picnic tables, litter barrels, vending, petwalk**

255mm rest area nb, full(handicapped)facilities, vending, phone, picnic tables, litter barrels, vending, petwalk

254 FM 3406, Round Rock, **E...gas:** Chevron, Citgo/7-11, Texaco, **food:** Arby's, Castaways Seafood, Giovanni's Italian, McDonald's, Schlotsky's, Sonic, **other:** Firestone, GMC/Pontiac, Honda, Pennzoil, Toyota, **W...gas:** Phillips 66/24hr, **food:** Carino's Italian, China One, Chuy's Mexican, Cracker Barrel, Denny's, Golden Corral, SaltGrass Steaks, **lodging:** AmeriSuites, Courtyard, Hilton Garden, La Quinta, SpringHill Suites, Super 8, **other:** Nissan

253b US 79, to Taylor, **E...gas:** Phillips 66, Shamrock/diesel, **food:** Baskin-Robbins, DQ, Famous Sam's Café, KFC, LoneStar Café, LJ Silver, **other:** HOSPITALAutoZone, HEB/deli, **W...gas:** Exxon/diesel, Texaco/diesel/24hr, **food:** BBQ, IHOP, K-Bob's Rest., Taco Bell, Thundercloud Subs, **lodging:** La Quinta, Red Roof Inn, Sleep Inn, **other:** Eckerd, USPO

a Frontage Rd, **E...gas:** Shell, **food:** Arby's, Castaway's Seafood/steaks, DQ, Damon's, KFC, Sirloin Stockade, Taco Bell, **lodging:** Best Western, Wingate Inn, **W...food:** La Marguarita, Mr Gatti, Popeye's, Ramada Ltd, **other:** Eckerd

252b a RM 620, **E...gas:** Texaco/diesel/24hr, **lodging:** Candlewood Suites, Crossland Suites, **other:** bank, **W...gas:** Fina, Phillips 66, **food:** Grandy's, Little Caesar's, McDonald's, **lodging:** Comfort Suites, Staybridge Suites, **other:** Albertson's, mall

251 Lp 35, Round Rock, **E...food:** Outback Steaks, Whataburger, **lodging:** Residence Inn, **other:** Aamco, Diahatsu, transmissions, **W...gas:** Exxon, Texaco, **food:** Burger King, Jack-in-the-Box, Luby's, Peter Piper Pizza, Taco Cabana, **lodging:** Day's Inn, **other:** Albertson's, Hastings Books, NTB, Walgreen

250 FM 1325, **E...gas:** Chevron, Mobil/diesel, **food:** Applebee's, Chick-fil-A, Chili's, El Chico, Jason's Deli, Joe's Crabshack, Macaroni Grill, McDonald's, Subway, **lodging:** Hampton Inn, **other:** Discount Tire, Goodyear/auto, Home Depot, OfficeMax, Ross, Target, Wal-Mart SuperCtr/24hr, **W...gas:** Texaco, **food:** Antonio's Cantina, Hooters, Krispy Kreme, Olive Garden, Starbucks, **lodging:** Baymont Inn, **other:** Barnes&Noble, Circuit City, Kohl's, Lowe's Whse, Marshall's, Office Depot, Old Navy, Sam's Club

Interstate 35

Austin

248 Grand Ave Pkwy, no facilities

247 FM 1825, Pflugerville, **E...gas:** RaceTrac, **food:** Jack-in-the-Box, Sonic, Taco Cabana, Wendy's, **other:** Firestone/auto, HEB Foods, cinema, **W...gas:** Exxon, Shell/Church's, **food:** BBQ, KFC, **lodging:** Quality Suites, **other:** Goodyear/auto

246 Dessau Rd, Howard Lane, **E...gas:** Shell/diesel, Texaco, **food:** Baby Acapulco, **other:** Home Depot, Kohl's, NTB, **W...gas:** Shamrock, **food:** IHOP, Whataburger

245 FM 734, Parmer Lane, to Yeager Lane, **E...food:** Subway, **other:** HEB Food/gas, Radio Shack, **W...gas:** Citgo/7-11, Exxon, **lodging:** Residence Inn, SpringHill Suites

243 Braker Lane, **E...gas:** Shamrock, **food:** Jack-in-the-Box, Whataburger/24hr, **other:** Harley-Davidson, **W...gas:** Texaco/diesel, **lodging:** Austin Motel

241 Rundberg Lane, **E...gas:** Exxon, **food:** Golden Corral, Mr Gatti's, **lodging:** Ramada Inn, **other:** Albertson's, U-Haul, **W...gas:** Chevron, Texaco, **lodging:** Budget Inn, Home-Style Inn, Motel 6

240a US 183, Lockhart, **E...gas:** Exxon, **food:** DQ, Jack-in-the-Box, Old San Francisco Steaks, **lodging:** Day's Inn, Ramada Inn, Wellesley Inn, **other:** Chevrolet, **W...gas:** Chevron/diesel/24hr, Texaco/diesel, **lodging:** Motel 6, Red Roof Inn, Super 8, Travelodge Suites, Wingate Inn

239 St John's Ave, **E...gas:** Texaco, **food:** Chili's, Jim's Rest., Steak&Egg, **lodging:** Budget Host, Day's Inn, Hampton Inn, **other:** Dodge, Home Depot, Volvo, Wal-Mart SuperCtr/24hr, **W...gas:** Conoco/diesel, Exxon, **food:** Antonio's TexMex, Applebee's, Bennigan's, Denny's, **lodging:** AmeriSuites, Comfort Inn, Country Inn Suites, Holiday Inn Express, La Quinta, Sheraton, Sumner Suites

238b US 290 E, RM 222, same as 238a, frontage rds connect several exits

a 51st St, **E...gas:** Exxon, Chevron, Phillips 66, Shell, **food:** Burger King, Dixie's Roadhouse, El Torito, Fuddrucker's, Grandy's, Jim's Rest., LJ Silver, McDonald's, Owens Rest., Pappasito's, Sonic, Texas Steaks, Whataburger, **lodging:** Doubletree Hotel, Drury Inn, Econolodge, Embassy Suites, Holiday Inn, Homestead Village, Red Lion Hotel, Studio 6 Suites, **other:** Advance Parts, Firestone, FoodLand, Jo-Ann Crafts, OfficeMax, Volvo, **W...gas:** Texaco, **food:** Baby Acapulco, Bombay Bicycle Club, Capt's Seafood, Carrabba's, IHOP, India Cuisine, Outback Steaks, Quizno's, **lodging:** Courtyard, Drury Inn, Fairfield Inn, Hilton, Motel 6, Quality Inn, Ramada Ltd, Rodeway Inn, Super 8, **other:** Dillard's, Ford, Office Depot

237b 51st St, same as 238a

a Airport Blvd, **E...food:** BBQ, U-Haul, **W...food:** Jack-in-the-Box, Wendy's, GNC, Goodyear, **other:** HEB Foods, Old Navy, PetCo, Sears/auto

upper level is I-35 thru, lower level accesses downtown

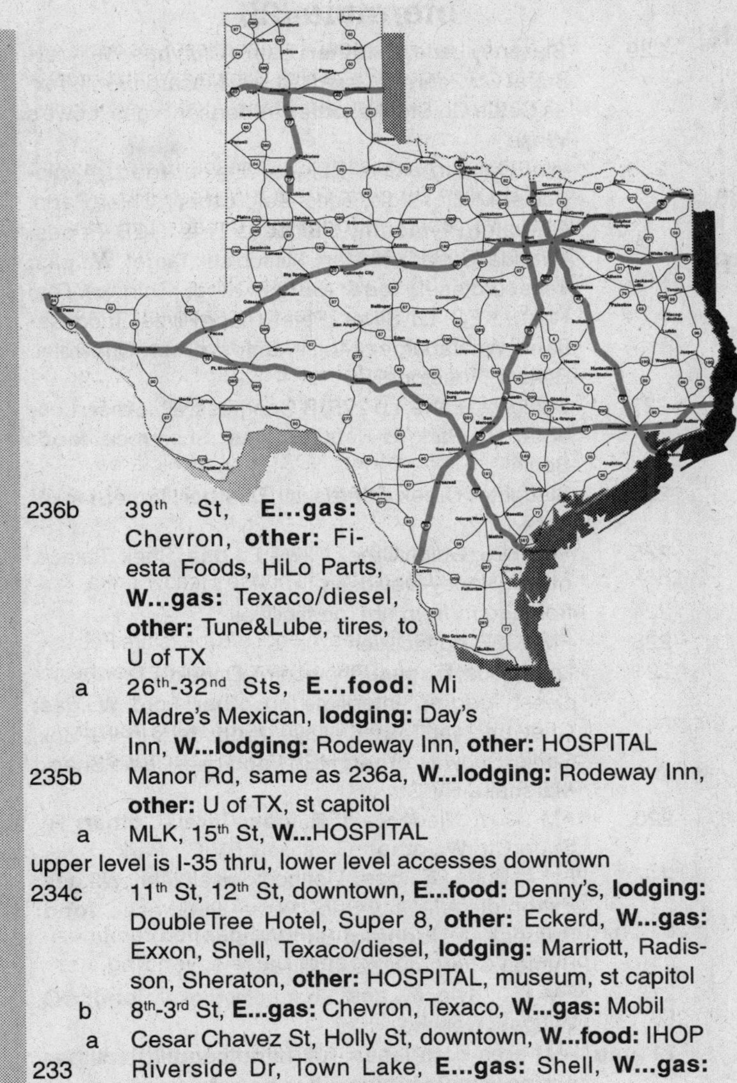

236b 39th St, **E...gas:** Chevron, **other:** Fiesta Foods, HiLo Parts, **W...gas:** Texaco/diesel, **other:** Tune&Lube, tires, to U of TX

a 26th-32nd Sts, **E...food:** Mi Madre's Mexican, **lodging:** Day's Inn, **W...lodging:** Rodeway Inn, **other:** HOSPITAL

235b Manor Rd, same as 236a, **W...lodging:** Rodeway Inn, **other:** U of TX, st capitol

a MLK, 15th St, **W...**HOSPITAL

upper level is I-35 thru, lower level accesses downtown

234c 11th St, 12th St, downtown, **E...food:** Denny's, **lodging:** DoubleTree Hotel, Super 8, **other:** Eckerd, **W...gas:** Exxon, Shell, Texaco/diesel, **lodging:** Marriott, Radisson, Sheraton, **other:** HOSPITAL, museum, st capitol

b 8th-3rd St, **E...gas:** Chevron, Texaco, **W...gas:** Mobil

a Cesar Chavez St, Holly St, downtown, **W...food:** IHOP

233 Riverside Dr, Town Lake, **E...gas:** Shell, **W...gas:** Chevron/diesel, **lodging:** Holiday Inn

232mm Little Colorado River

232b Woodland Ave, **E...lodging:** Wellesley Inn

a Oltorf St, Live Oak, **E...gas:** Texaco/diesel, **food:** Carrow's, Luby's, **lodging:** La Quinta, Suburban Lodge, **W...gas:** Chevron, Exxon, Shell, Texaco/repair, **food:** Denny's, Marco Polo Rest., **lodging:** Clarion, Quality Inn

231 Woodward St, **E...gas:** Shell/diesel, **food:** Country Kitchen, **lodging:** Exel Inn, Holiday Inn, Motel 6, Park West Inn, Ramada Ltd, Super 8, same as 232, **W...other:** MEDICAL CARE, Home Depot

230b a US 290 W, TX 71, Ben White Blvd, St Elmo Rd, **E...gas:** Texaco, **food:** Domino's, Jim's Rest., McDonald's, Subway, Western Choice Steaks, **lodging:** Best Western, Comfort Suites, Courtyard, Fairfield Inn, Hampton Inn, Marriott, Omni Hotel, Red Roof Inn, Residence Inn, SpringHill Suites, **other:** bank, **W...food:** Burger King, Furr's Cafeteria, IHOP, Pizza Hut, Taco Cabana, **lodging:** Candlewood Suites, Day's Inn, Hawthorn Suites, La Quinta, **other:** HOSPITAL, BMW, Dodge/Jeep, Ford, GMC, Honda, Hyundai, Lincoln/Mercury, NTB, Nissan, Pontiac/Cadillac/Mazda, Suzuki/Kia, Toyota

TEXAS

Interstate 35

N ↑↓ S

229 Stassney Lane, **E...other:** Sam's Club/gas, Wal-Mart Super Ctr/24hr, **W...food:** Chili's, Macaroni Grill, Texas Cattle Co Steaks, **other:** Albertson's/gas, Lowe's Whse

228 Wm Cannon Drive, **E...gas:** Exxon, **food:** Applebee's, McDonald's, Taco Bell, **other:** Chief Parts, Chrysler/Plymouth, Discount Tire, HEB Foods, Hyundai/Subaru, K-Mart, Mitsubishi, Target, **W...gas:** Texaco/diesel, **food:** Burger King, Chinese/Thai Rest., KFC, LJ Silver, Peter Piper Pizza, Taco Cabana, Whataburger/24hr, Wendy's, **other:** Chevrolet, Eckerd, Firestone

227 Slaughter Lane, Lp 275, S Congress, **E...other:** LoneStar RV Park, U-Haul, **W...gas:** Shamrock, **food:** Sonic

226 Slaughter Creek Overpass, **E...other:** LoneStar RV Park

225 FM 1626, Onion Creek Pkwy, **E...gas:** Shell, Texaco, **other:** Harley-Davidson

224 frontage rd(from nb), no facilities

223 FM 1327, no facilities

221 Lp 4, Buda, **E...gas:** Chevron/McDonald's, Phillips 66/diesel, **lodging:** Interstate Inn, **other:** Ford, **W...gas:** Chevron/24hr, Texaco/diesel, **food:** Jack-in-the-Box, Sonic, Subway, **other:** HEB Food/gas, Radio Shack, Marshall's RV Ctr

220 FM 2001, Niederwald, **E...gas:** Texaco, **other:** RV SuperCtr, **W...other:** Crestview RV Ctr/Park

217 Lp 4, Buda, **E...gas:** Conoco/diesel/24hr, **W...gas:** Exxon/diesel, Shamrock/Pizza Hut/diesel, **food:** Burger King, **lodging:** Best Western

215 Bunton Overpass, no facilities

213 FM 150, Kyle, **E...gas:** Shamrock/diesel, **food:** DQ, **W...gas:** Conoco

211mm rest area both lanes, full(handicapped)facilities, phone, picnic tables, litter barrels, vending, petwalk

211mm truck check sta nb

210 Yarrington Rd, **W...other:** Plum Creek RV Resort

209mm truck check sta sb

208mm Blanco River

208 Frontage Rd, Blanco River Rd, no facilities

206 Lp 82, Aquarena Springs Rd, **E...gas:** Conoco, Shamrock, **W...gas:** Exxon/diesel, Mobil/diesel, Phillips 66/diesel, Shell, Texaco, **food:** Jim's Rest., Popeye's, Sonic, Tortuga's Rest., **lodging:** Comfort Inn, La Quinta, Motel 6, Quality Inn, Ramada Ltd, Stratford Inn, Super 8, University Inn, **other:** to SW TX U, RV camping

San Marcos

205 TX 80, TX 142, Bastrop, **E...gas:** Chevron, Conoco, Mobil, Shamrock, Shell/diesel, **food:** Arby's, BBQ, DQ, Jason's Deli, Pantera's Pizza, Schlotsky's, Subway, Taste of China, **other:** Eckerd, Hastings Books, Wal-Mart SuperCtr/24hr, **W...gas:** Chevron, Shamrock, Circle K/gas/24hr, **food:** Applebee's, Burger King, Church's, CiCi's, Furr's Cafeteria, IHOP, KFC, LJ Silver, Logan's Roadhouse, McDonald's, MT Mike's Steaks, Pizza Hut, Sirloin Stockade, Taco Cabana, Wendy's, **lodging:** Best Western, Budget Inn, Day's Inn, Microtel, Red Roof Inn, Rodeway Inn, **other:** HEB Foods, JC Penney, Office Depot, OfficeMax, Target, Walgreen

204mm San Marcos River

204b CM Allen Pkwy, **W...gas:** Chevron, Conoco/diesel, Texaco/diesel, **food:** Chinese Buffet, DQ, Sonic, **lodging:** Best Western, Econolodge, Mustang Motel

a Lp 82, TX 123, to Seguin, **E...gas:** Conoco, Phillips 66, Shamrock, Texaco/diesel, **food:** Burger King, Chili's, FasTaco, Golden Corral, Hardee's, Luby's, McDonald's, Red Lobster, Whataburger/24hr, **lodging:** Holiday Inn Express, **other:** HOSPITAL, Chevrolet/Buick, Ford/Mercury, Jeep/Chrysler, transmissions

202 FM 3407, Wonder World Dr, **E...gas:** Shell, **food:** Jack-in-the-Box, Wienerschnitzel, **other:** HOSPITAL, **other:** Discount Tire, Lowe's Whse, **W...gas:** Shamrock/diesel, **food:** BBQ, **other:** Plymouth/Dodge, transmissions

201 McCarty Lane, **E...other:** Pontiac/GMC, Subaru, **W...other:** Chrysler/Plymouth/Dodge, Nissan

200 Center Point Rd, **E...food:** Bennigan's, Cracker Barrel, Food Court, LoneStar Café, Outback Steaks, Subway, Taco Bell, Wendy's, **other:** Old Navy, Prime Outlets/famous brands, Tanger Outlet/famous brands, **W...gas:** Shamrock/diesel, **food:** Schlotsky's, Whataburger/24hr, AmeriHost, Honda

New Braunfels

199 Posey Rd, **E...other:** Tanger Outlets/famous brands, Toyota

196 FM 1106, York Creek Rd, no facilities

195 Watson Lane, Old Bastrop Rd, **E...**antiques

193 Conrads Rd, Kohlenberg Rd, **W...gas:** Rip Griffin/Shell/Subway/diesel/24hr/@, **food:** Country Fair Rest., **other:** Camping World RV Supply

191 FM 306, FM 483, Canyon Lake, **E...gas:** Conoco/Quizno's/diesel, Texaco, **other:** RV camping, Wal-Mart Dist Ctr, **W...gas:** Chevron, Exxon/diesel **food:** Burger King, GristMill Rest., **other:** Camping World RV Supply, transmissions

190c Post Rd, no facilities

b Lp 35 S, New Braunfels, **W...**gas/diesel, **food:** Capparelli's Italian, **lodging:** Hawthorn Inn

a frontage rd, **E...gas:** Shell, **other:** Discount Tire, Home Depot, **W...gas:** McDonald's, **food:** Wendy's, **lodging:** Best Western, Comfort Suites, Motel 6

189 TX 46, Seguin, **E...gas:** Conoco/diesel, Exxon, Texaco/diesel, **food:** Luby's, Oma's Haus Rest., **lodging:** Oakwood Inn, Stratford House, Super 8, **other:** Discount Tire, K-Mart, Office Depot, **W...gas:** Chevron/24hr, Shamrock, **food:** Applebee's, IHOP, McDonald's, New Braunfels Smokehouse, Pizza Hut, Skillet's Rest., Taco Bell, Taco Cabana, Wendy's, **lodging:** Adelweiss Inn, Day's Inn, Hampton Inn, Holiday Inn, Motel 6, Rodeway Inn, **other:** HOSPITAL

188 Frontage Rd, **W...food:** Mamacita's, Ryan's, **other:** Hastings Books

188mm Guadalupe River

Interstate 35

N ↕ S

187 FM 725, Lake McQueeny Rd, **E...gas:** Chevron/ 24hr, **food:** Arby's, CiCi's, Guadalajara Mexican, LJ Silver, Subway, Whataburger/24hr, **other:** Jeep, Radio Shack, **W...gas:** Exxon/diesel, **food:** Adobe Café, DQ, Jack-in-the-Box, Rally's, Steaks to Go, **lodging:** Budget Host, **other:** HOSPITAL, NAPA AutoCare, transmissions

186 Walnut Ave, **E...gas:** Exxon/Subway, Shamrock, **food:** Chick-fil-A, Marina's Mexican, McDonald's, Popeye's, Schlotsky's, Taco Bell, **lodging:** Executive Lodge, **other:** Chevrolet, Wal-Mart/auto, **W...gas:** Conoco, Shamrock, Texaco/diesel, **food:** KFC, Mr Gatti's, Papa John's, Shanghai Chinese, **other:** AutoZone, HEB/deli/gas, Ross, Target, U-Haul, Walgreen

185 FM 1044, no facilities

184 FM 482, Lp 337, Ruekle Rd, **E...gas:** Texaco/Blimpie/ diesel, **other:** Buick/Pontiac/GMC, Hill Country RV Park

183 Solms Rd, **W...gas:** Exxon, **other:** Mazda/Kia

182 Engel Rd, **E...food:** Pam's Country Kitchen, 1st RV Ctr, **W...other:** Mazda/Kia

180 Schwab Rd, no facilities

179mm rest area both lanes, full(handicapped)facilities, phone, picnic tables, litter barrels, vending, pet-walk, RV dump

178 FM 1103, Cibolo Rd, Hubertus Rd, **E...gas:** Shell/ diesel

177 FM 482, FM 2252, **W...other:** Stone Creek RV Park

176 Weiderstein Rd, no facilities

175 FM 3009, Natural Bridge, **E...gas:** Shamrock, **food:** BBQ, McDonald's, Schlotsky's, Sonic, Taco Cabana, **other:** HEB Food/gas, Radio Shack, **W...gas:** Shamrock/Subway, Texaco/diesel, **food:** Arby's, Denny's, Jack-in-the-Box, KFC/Taco Bell/Pizza Hut, Wendy's, **lodging:** Atrium Inn, Country Inn, **other:** Factory Shoestore

174b Schertz Pkwy, no facilities

a FM 1518, Selma, **E...other:** Diahatsu, Honda/ Mitsubishi, Saturn, **W...other:** Tex-All RV Ctr

173 Old Austin Rd, Olympia Pkwy, **E...food:** Chick-fil-A, Chili's, IHOP, Macaroni Grill, Outback Steaks, Subway, **other:** Best Buy, Borders Books, Home Depot, OfficeMax, Old Navy, Ross, Target, WorldMkt, **W...other:** Retama Park RaceTrack

172 TX 218, Anderson Lp, P Booker Rd, **E...lodging:** Comfort Inn, **other:** to Randolph AFB, **W...other:** to SeaWorld

171 Topperwein Rd, same as 170

170 Judson Rd, to Converse, **E...gas:** Texaco/diesel, **food:** India Cuisine, Kettle, Subway, Whataburger/ 24hr, **lodging:** La Quinta, **other:** HOSPITAL, Chevrolet, Chrysler/Plymouth, Ford, Gunn Auto Parts, Hyundai, Nissan, Pontiac/GMC, Toyota, **W...gas:** Exxon, Holiday Inn Express, **other:** Mazda, Sam's Club, Subaru

San Antonio

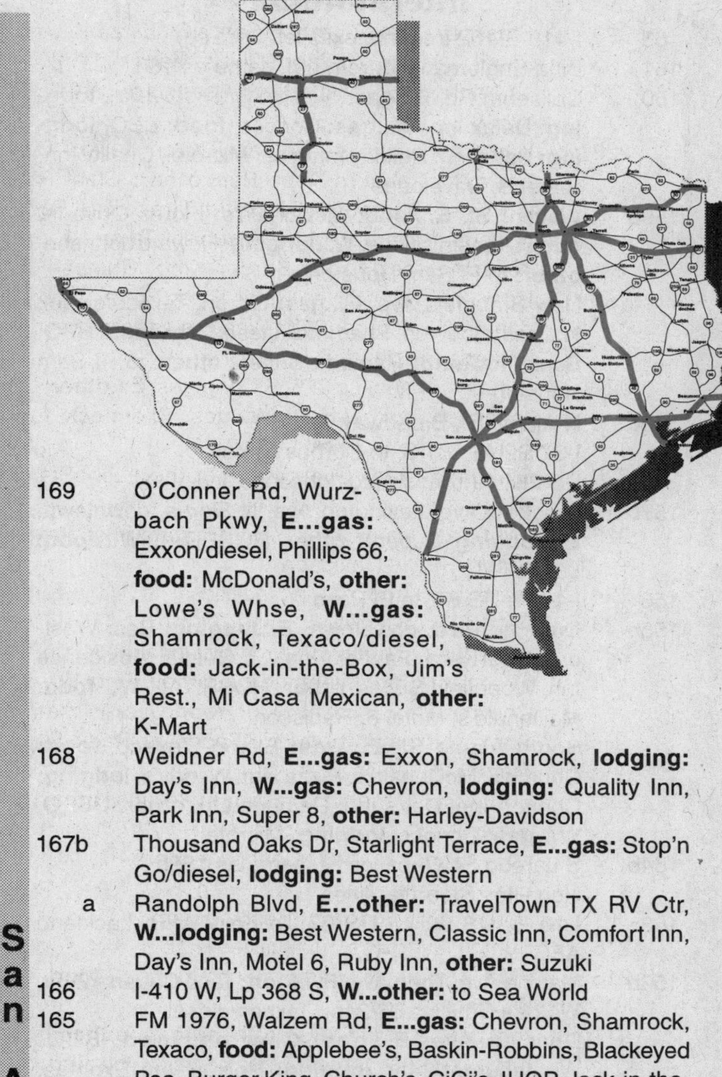

169 O'Conner Rd, Wurzbach Pkwy, **E...gas:** Exxon/diesel, Phillips 66, **food:** McDonald's, **other:** Lowe's Whse, **W...gas:** Shamrock, Texaco/diesel, **food:** Jack-in-the-Box, Jim's Rest., Mi Casa Mexican, **other:** K-Mart

168 Weidner Rd, **E...gas:** Exxon, Shamrock, **lodging:** Day's Inn, **W...gas:** Chevron, **lodging:** Quality Inn, Park Inn, Super 8, **other:** Harley-Davidson

167b Thousand Oaks Dr, Starlight Terrace, **E...gas:** Stop'n Go/diesel, **lodging:** Best Western

a Randolph Blvd, **E...other:** TravelTown TX RV Ctr, **W...lodging:** Best Western, Classic Inn, Comfort Inn, Day's Inn, Motel 6, Ruby Inn, **other:** Suzuki

166 I-410 W, Lp 368 S, **W...other:** to Sea World

165 FM 1976, Walzem Rd, **E...gas:** Chevron, Shamrock, Texaco, **food:** Applebee's, Baskin-Robbins, Blackeyed Pea, Burger King, Church's, CiCi's, IHOP, Jack-in-the-Box, Jim's Rest., KFC, Las Palapas Mexican, LJ Silver, Luby's, Marie Callender's, McDonald's, Olive Garden, Pizza Hut, Red Lobster, Schlotsky's, Subway, Taco Bell, Taco Cabana, Taco Kitchen, Wendy's, Whataburger, **lodging:** Drury Inn, Hampton Inn, **other:** Albertson's, AutoZone, CarQuest, Cavender's Boots, Circuit City, Dillard's, Discount Tire, Eckerd, Firestone/ auto, HEB Foods, Home Depot, JC Penney, Mervyn's, Michael's, Office Depot, OfficeMax, PepBoys, Radio Shack, Target, Wal-Mart SuperCtr/24hr, mall, **W...gas:** Mobil, **food:** Sonic, **other:** NTB

164b Eisenhauer Rd, **E...gas:** Exxon/diesel, **other:** $General, Hancock Fabrics

a Rittiman Rd, **E...gas:** Conoco/diesel, Exxon/ TacoMaker, RaceTrac, Shamrock, Texaco/diesel, Circle K/24hr, **food:** Burger King, Church's Chicken, Cracker Barrel, Denny's, McDonald's, Rally's, Taco Cabana, Whataburger/24hr, **lodging:** Comfort Suites, Knight's Inn, La Quinta, Motel 6, Ramada Inn, Scotsman Inn, Stratford House, Super 8, **other:** HEB Foods, **W...gas:** Chevron/diesel, Shamrock, **food:** BBQ, Popeye's, Sonic, Wendy's

Interstate 35

N ↕ S

163 I-410 S(162 from nb, exits left from sb)
161 Binz-Engleman Rd(from nb), same as 160
160 Coliseum Rd, **E...gas:** Shamrock/diesel/24hr, **lodging:** Delux Inn, **W...gas:** Conoco, **food:** BBQ, **lodging:** Day's Inn, Holiday Inn/rest., Microtel, Quality Inn, Super 8, Travelodge
159b Walters St, **E...food:** McDonald's, Flores Drive-In, **other:** transmissions, **W...lodging:** Howard Johnson, **other:** to Ft Sam Houston
a New Braunfels Ave, **E...gas:** Exxon, Texaco/diesel, **W...gas:** Chevron, Shamrock/diesel/24hr, **food:** BBQ, Sonic, **lodging:** Ramada Suites, **other:** to Ft Sam Houston
158c N Alamo St, Broadway
b I-37 S, US 281 S, to Corpus Christi
a US 281 N(from sb), to Johnson City
157b a Brooklyn Ave, Lexington Ave, N Flores, downtown, **E...lodging:** Super 8, **other:** HOSPITAL, **W...food:** Luby's
156 I-10 W, US 87, to El Paso
155b Durango Blvd, downtown, **E...lodging:** Best Western, Courtyard, Fairfield Inn, La Quinta, Residence Inn, Woodfield Suites, **other:** HOSPITAL, **W...food:** McDonald's, Motel 6, Radisson
a South Alamo St, **E...gas:** Exxon, Texaco, **food:** Church's, McDonald's, Pizza Hut, Wendy's, **lodging:** Comfort Inn, Day's Inn, Ramada Ltd, **other:** USPO, **W...gas:** Conoco, **lodging:** Microtel
154b S Laredo St, Ceballos St, same as 155b
a Nogalitos St, no facilities
153 I-10 E, US 90 W, US 87, to Kelly AFB, Lackland AFB
152b Malone Ave, Theo Ave, **E...food:** Taco Cabana/24hr, **W...gas:** Phillips 66/24hr, Texaco/diesel
a Division Ave, **E...gas:** Chevron, **food:** BBQ, Whataburger/24hr, **lodging:** Holiday Inn Express, **W...gas:** Exxon, Phillips 66, **other:** transmissions
151 Southcross Blvd, **E...gas:** Exxon, Shell, **food:** Shop'n Save, **W...gas:** Circle K, Texaco/diesel
150b Lp 13, Military Dr, **E...gas:** Chevron, Conoco, Texaco, **food:** Denny's, KFC, Pizza Hut, Taco Cabana, **lodging:** La Quinta, **other:** AutoZone, Discount Tire, U-Haul, **W...gas:** Exxon, Mobil, Shamrock, **food:** Golden Corral, Hungry Farmer Steaks, Jack-in-the-Box, KFC, LJ Silver, Luby's, McDonald's, Mr Gatti, Pizza Hut, Wendy's, Whataburger, **other:** Albertson's, Eckerd, Goodyear, HEB Foods, JC Penney, Mervyn's, Office Depot, Old Navy, Sears/auto, Target, mall,
a Zarzamora St(149 fom sb), same as 150b
149 Hutchins Blvd(from sb), **E...gas:** Shamrock, **lodging:** Motel 6, **other:** HOSPITAL, **W...other:** Chevrolet, Ford, Kia
148b Palo Alto Rd, **W...gas:** Shamrock
a TX 16 S, spur 422(exits left from sb), Poteet, **E...gas:** Chevron, **W...gas:** Phillips 66, **other:** $General
147 Somerset Rd, **E...gas:** Texaco/diesel, **W...other:** Dodge
146 Cassin Rd(from nb), no facilities
145b Lp 353 N, no facilities
a I-410, TX 16, no facilities
144 Fischer Rd, **E...gas:** Shamrock/Subway/diesel/24hr, **lodging:** D&D Motel, **other:** RV camping, **W...gas:** Love's/Carl's Jr/diesel/24hr/@
142 Medina River Turnaround(from nb), no facilities
141 Benton City Rd, Von Ormy, **W...gas:** Texaco/diesel/café
140 Anderson Lp, 1604, **E...gas:** Exxon/Burger King/diesel/24hr, **W...gas:** Texaco/Church's/Pizza Hut/diesel/24hr, **other:** to Sea World
139 Kinney Rd, **E...**RV camping
137 Shepherd Rd, no facilities
135 Luckey Rd, no facilities
133 TX 132 S, Lytle, access to same as 131
131 FM 3175, FM 2790, Benton City Rd, **W...gas:** Conoco/diesel/24hr, **food:** BBQ, DQ, McDonald's, PigStand Rest., Sonic, Topis Mexican, **lodging:** Day's Inn, **other:** $General, HEB Food/gas
129mm rest area both lanes, full(handicapped)facilities, phone, picnic tables, litter barrels, vending, petwalk
127 FM 471, Natalia, no facilities
124 FM 463, Bigfoot Rd, **E...**Ford
122 TX 173, Divine, **E...gas:** Exxon/Church's/diesel, **other:** Chevrolet, Plymouth/Jeep/Dodge, **W...gas:** Chevron/Subway/diesel, **food:** CCC Steaks, **lodging:** Country Corner Inn
121 TX 132 N, Devine, **E...other:** Gusville RV Park
118.5mm weigh sta both lanes
114 FM 462, Bigfoot, **E...gas:** Shamrock/diesel
111 US 57, to Eagle Pass, no facilities
104 Lp 35, **3 mi E...gas:** Shamrock, **food:** Sonic, **lodging:** Executive Inn, **other:** HOSPITAL
101 FM 140, Pearsall, **E...**Chevron, BBQ, Royal Inn, **W...gas:** Exxon/Blimpie/diesel/24hr, **food:** Cowpokes BBQ, **lodging:** Budget Inn, **other:** HOSPITAL
99 FM 1581, Pearsall, to Divot, **W...**LP
93mm parking/picnic area both lanes, litter barrels, handicapped accessible
91 FM 1583, Derby, no facilities
90mm Frio River
86 Lp 35, Dilley, no facilities
85 FM 117, **E...food:** Garcia's Café/motel, **W...gas:** Exxon/DQ/diesel, **lodging:** Safari Motel/café
84 TX 85, Dilley, **E...other:** Super S Foods, **other:** HOSPITAL, Chevrolet/Pontiac, NAPA, **W...gas:** Shamrock/diesel/24hr, Texaco/Church's/diesel/24hr, **lodging:** Executive Inn
82 County Line Rd, Dilley, no facilities
77 FM 469, Millett, no facilities
74 Gardendale, no facilities
68 Lp 35(69 from sb), Cotulla, **1 mi E...gas:** Mobil, **food:** Chuck Wagon Steaks, **lodging:** Cotulla Motel, **other:** Family$
67 FM 468, to Big Wells, **E...gas:** Exxon/Wendy's/diesel/24hr, **other:** Conoco/Country Store/rest., Shamrock/Church's/Pizza Hut/diesel/24hr, **food:** DQ, **lodging:** Executive Inn, Village Inn, tire repair, **W...gas:** Chevron/McDonald's/diesel

Pearsall

Interstate 35

65 Lp 35, Cotulla, **1-2 mi E...gas:** Mobil, **food:** Chuck Wagon Steaks, **lodging:** Cotulla Motel
63 Elm Creek Interchange, no facilities
59mm parking/picnic area both lanes, litter barrels, handicapped accessible
56 FM 133, Artesia Wells, **E...**gas
48 Caiman Creek Interchange, no facilities
39 TX 44, Encinal, **E...gas:** Love's/Subway/Chester Fried/diesel/24hr/@
38 TX 44(from nb), Encinal, no facilities
32 San Roman Interchange, no facilities
27 Callaghan Interchange, no facilities
24 Camino Colombia toll rd, to Monterrey
22 Webb Interchange, no facilities
18 US 83 N, to Carrizo Springs, **E...Tx Travel Info Ctr(8am-5pm)**
15mm parking/picnic area both lanes, insp area nb
13 Uniroyal Interchange, **E...gas:** Pilot/Subway/diesel/24hr/@, **other:** Blue Beacon
10 Port Laredo Carriers Dr(from nb), no facilities
9 Lp 20 W, to World Trade Bridge
8 FM 1472, Milo
7 Shilo Dr, Las Cruces Dr, **E...lodging:** Motel 9
6mm Texas Tourist Bureau, info
4 FM 1472, Del Mar Blvd, **E...gas:** Chevron/repair, Exxon/diesel, **food:** Applebee's, Bennigan's, Burger King, Carino's Italian, DQ, IHOP, Jack-in-the-Box, Las Asadas Mexican, McDonald's, Whataburger, **lodging:** Extended Stay America, Hampton Inn, **other:** Albertson's, Best Buy, HEB Foods, Lowe's Whse, Marshall's, Old Navy, Radio Shack, Target, **W...gas:** Texaco/diesel, **food:** Golden Corral, **lodging:** Executive House Motel, Motel 6

Laredo

3b Mann Rd, **E...food:** Logan's Roadhouse, Luby's, Sirloin Stockade, Tony Roma, **other:** Buick, Dillard's, Foley's, Ford/Lincoln/Mercury, Honda, Mazda, Mervyn's, Pontiac/Cadillac/GMC, Sears/auto, Toyota, mall, **W...food:** Chili's, Outback Steaks, Pancake House, Subway, Taco Palenque, **lodging:** Family Garden Inn, Fiesta Inn, La Hacienda Motel, Motel 6, **other:** $General, Home Depot, Michael's, Office Depot, OfficeMax, Ross, Wal-Mart/auto/24hr
a San Bernardo Ave, **E...gas:** Texaco/diesel, **food:** Chick-fil-A, Fuddrucker's, LJ Silver, Peter Piper Pizza, **other:** HEB Foods, K-Mart, NAPA, PepBoys, SteinMart, mall, **W...gas:** Citgo/Circle K, Chevron, Phillips 66/diesel, **food:** Burger King, Coyote Creek Rest., DQ, Dunkin Donuts, El Pollo Loco, Hunan Chinese, Julep's Rest., King Dynasty Chinese, McDonald's, Pizza Hut, Popeye's, Taco Bell, Taco Palenque, Wendy's, Whataburger, **lodging:** Best Western, Gateway Inn, Monterey Inn, Red Roof Inn, **other:** Gonzales Auto Parts, Goodyear/auto, Radio Shack, Sam's Club
2 US 59, Saunders Rd, **E...gas:** Conoco, Shamrock, Texaco, **food:** Jack-in-the-Box, **other:** HOSPITAL, **W...gas:** Chevron/diesel/24hr, Exxon/diesel, Phillips 66/diesel, **food:** Church's Denny's, **lodging:** Civic Ctr Inn, Courtyard, El Cortez Motel, Holiday Inn, La Quinta, Mayan Inn, **other:** AutoZone, Mexico Insurance, Ramirez Tire

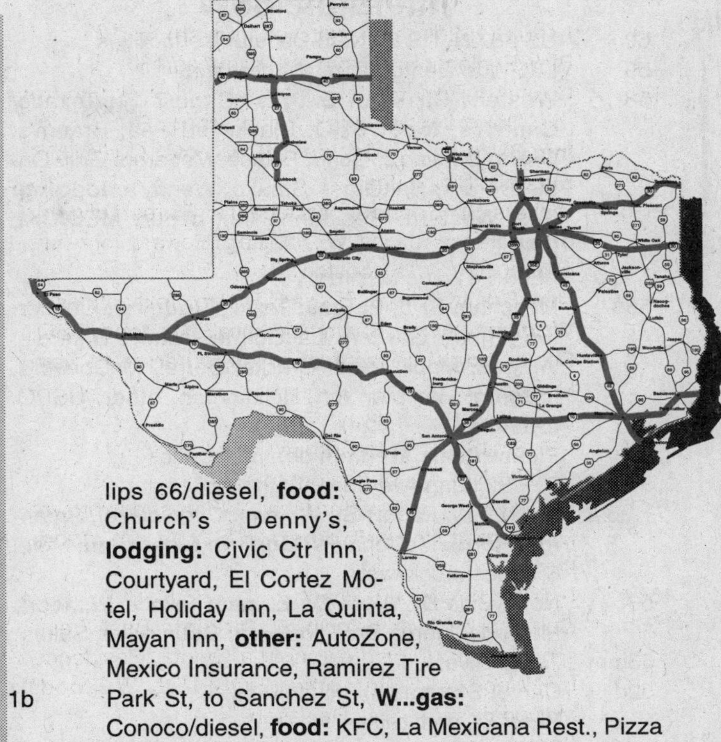

1b Park St, to Sanchez St, **W...gas:** Conoco/diesel, **food:** KFC, La Mexicana Rest., Pizza Hut, Popeye's
1a Victoria St, Scott St, Washington St, **E...gas:** Exxon, Citgo/Circle K, Texaco, **W...gas:** Exxon/24hr, Texaco, Circle K, **food:** KFC, Mariachi Express, McDonald's, Wendy's, **other:** Firestone/auto, Goodyear/auto, transmissions
I-35 begins/ends in Laredo at Victoria St...access to multiple facilities

Interstate 35W

Exit # Services
I-35W begins/ends on I-35, exit 467.
85a I-35E S, no facilities
84 FM 1515, Bonnie Brae St, **E...**HOSPITAL
82 FM 2449, to Ponder, no facilities
79 Crawford Rd, no facilities
76 FM 407, Argyle, to Justin, no facilities
76mm picnic area both lanes, litter barrels, picnic tables
74 FM 1171, to Lewisville, no facilities
70 TX 114, to Dallas, Bridgeport, **E...gas:** Texaco/Church's/diesel, **other:** to DFW Airport, **W...other:** TX Motor Speedway
68 Eagle Pkwy, **W...**airport
67 Alliance Blvd, **W...other:** to Alliance Airport, FedEx
66 to Westport Pkwy, Keller-Haslet Rd, **E...lodging:** Hampton Inn, Hawthorn Suites, **W...gas:** Mobil/Wendy's/diesel, **food:** BBQ, Bryan's Smokehouse, Cactus Flower Café, Oriental Garden, Schlotsky's, Subway, Taco Bueno, **other:** USPO
65 TX 170 E, **E...gas:** Pilot/diesel/24hr/@
64 Golden Triangle Blvd, to Keller-Hicks Blvd, no facilities
63 Park Glen, no facilities

TEXAS

Interstate 35W

N ↕ S

60 US 287 N, US 81 N, to Decatur, no facilities
59 I-35 W to Denton(from sb), turnaround
58 Western Ctr Blvd, **E...gas:** Citgo/7-11, Texaco/Church's, **food:** BBQ, Blackeyed Pea, Braum's, Chili's, Domino's, Donut Palace, Macaroni Grill, On-the-Border, SaltGrass Steaks, Wendy's, **lodging:** Best Western, Residence Inn, **other:** MEDICAL CARE
57b a I-820 E&W, no facilities
56 Meacham Blvd, **E...gas:** Texaco, **lodging:** Comfort Inn, Hilton Garden, La Quinta, **other:** Dillard's, **W...gas:** Mobil, **food:** Cracker Barrel, McDonald's, **lodging:** Hampton Inn, Holiday Inn, **other:** USPO, cleaners
55 Pleasantdale Ave(from nb), no facilities
54c 33rd St, Long Ave(from nb), no facilities
b a TX 183 W, Papurt St, **W...gas:** Citgo/diesel, Shamrock, **food:** McDonald's, **lodging:** Classic Inn, Motel 6, **other:** truckwash
53 North Side Dr, Yucca Dr, **E...gas:** Texaco, **W...food:** Mercado Juarez Café, **lodging:** Country Inn Suites
53mm Trinity River
52d Carver St(from nb), no facilities
c Pharr St, no facilities
b Belknap(from sb), no facilities
a US 377 N, TX 121, to DFW, no facilities
51 spur 280, downtown Ft Worth
50c a I-30 W, E to Dallas
b TX 180 E(from nb), no facilities
49b Rosedale St, **W...**HOSPITAL
a Allen Ave, **E...gas:** Chevron, **W...**HOSPITAL
48b Morningside Ave(from sb), same as 48a
a Berry St, **E...gas:** Chevron/McDonald's, Citgo, **W...gas:** RaceTrac, **other:** Sack'n Save Foods, U-Haul
47 Ripy St, **E...other:** transmissions
46b Seminary Dr, **E...food:** Grandy's, Golden Corral, Jack-in-the-Box, Taco Cabana, Wyatt's Cafeteria, **lodging:** Day's Inn, Delux Inn, Regency Inn, Super 7 Inn, **W...gas:** Exxon, Texaco, **food:** Denny's, El Chico, Peony Chinese, **other:** Dillard's, Firestone/auto, JC Penney, Sears
a Felix St(from nb), **E...gas:** Mobil, **food:** Pulido's Mexican, **lodging:** S Oaks Inn, **W...food:** Burger King, McDonald's, **other:** Dodge
45b a I-20, E to Dallas, W to Abilene
44 Altamesa, **E...lodging:** Holiday Inn, **W...gas:** Citgo, **food:** Rig Steaks, Waffle House, **lodging:** Best Western, Comfort Suites, Motel 6, South Lp Inn, **other:** RV Ctr
43 Sycamore School Rd, **W...gas:** Exxon, **food:** Beefer's Rest./24hr, Jack-in-the-Box, Subway, Taco Bell, Whataburger/24hr, **other:** Aaron's Foods, $General, Home Depot, Radio Shack
42 Everman Pkwy, **E...gas:** Exxon, **W...other:** RV Ctr
41 Risinger Rd, **W...**auto repair
40 Garden Acres Dr, **E...gas:** Love's/diesel/24hr, **lodging:** Microtel, **other:** HOSPITAL, **W...other:** RV Lite Ctr
39 FM 1187, McAlister Rd, **E...**HOSPITAL, **W...gas:** Citgo/diesel, Shamrock/diesel/24hr, **food:** Taco Bell, Waffle House, **lodging:** Howard Johnson
38 Alsbury Blvd, **E...gas:** Chevron, Mobil/diesel, **food:** Chili's, Country Steaks, Cracker Barrel, McDonald's, Taipan Chinese, **lodging:** Super 8, **other:** Ford, Lowe's Whse, **W...gas:** Citgo, Texaco/24hr, **food:** Arby's, Burger King, Denny's, Grandy's, Pancho's Mexican, **other:** Albertson's, Chevrolet, K-Mart
37 TX 174, Wilshire Blvd, to Cleburne, **W...gas:** Exxon, Shell, **other:** Eckerd
36 FM 3391, Burleson, **E...gas:** Citgo, Mobil, **food:** Luby's, Steak Exchange, Waffle House, **lodging:** Comfort Suites, Day's Inn, **W...gas:** Chevron, Fina/diesel, Shamrock
34 Briaroaks Rd(from sb), **W...**RV camping
33mm rest area sb, full(handicapped)facilities, phone, picnic tables, litter barrels
32 Bethesda Rd, **E...gas:** Citgo, **lodging:** 5 Star Inn/rest., Bill&Martin's Seafood Rest., **W...other:** RV Ranch Park
31mm rest area nb, full(handicapped)facilities, phone, picnic tables, litter barrels
30 FM 917, Mansfield, **W...gas:** Fina, Texaco/Snappy Jack's/diesel
27 County Rds 604 & 707, **E...other:** Travel Villa RV Ctr
26b a US 67, Cleburne, **E...gas:** Citgo/Pop'sChicken/diesel, Exxon/Subway/24hr, Texaco
24 FM 3136, FM 1706, Alvarado, **E...gas:** Chevron, Texaco/diesel/24hr, **food:** Alvarado House Rest., **W...other:** McClain's RV Ctr
21 Barnesville Rd, to Greenfield, no facilities
17 FM 2258, no facilities
16 TX 81 S, County Rd 201, Grandview, **E...**RV camping, **W...**RV camping
15 FM 916, Maypearl, **W...gas:** Phillips 66(1mi), Shamrock/diesel, **food:** BBQ
12 FM 67, no facilities
8 FM 66, Itasca, **E...gas:** Chevron/diesel/café/24hr, **W...gas:** Citgo/diesel, **food:** DQ, **other:** Ford, picnic tables, litter barrels
7 FM 934, **E...**picnic tables, litter barrels
3 FM 2959, **E...**to Hillsboro Airport

I-35W begins/ends on I-35, 371mm.

Interstate 37

San Antonio

N ↕ S

Exit # Services
142b a I-35 S to Laredo, N to Austin. I-37 begins/ends on I-35 in San Antonio.
141c Brooklyn Ave, Nolan St(from sb), downtown
b Houston St, downtown, **E...lodging:** Red Roof Inn, **W...food:** Denny's, **lodging:** Crockett Hotel, Day's Inn, Hampton Inn, Holiday Inn, Hyatt Hotel, Marriott, Residence Inn, **other:** to The Alamo
a Commerce St, downtown, **W...lodging:** La Quinta, Marriott
140b Durango Blvd, downtown, **E...food:** Bill Miller BBQ, **other:** to Aladome
a Carolina St, Florida St, no facilities
139 I-10 W, US 87, US 90, to Houston, **W...other:** to Sea World

Interstate 37

N ↕ S

138c Fair Ave, Hackberry St, **E...gas:** Chevron, **food:** DQ, Jack-in-the-Box, KFC, Peter Piper Pizza, Popeye's, Taco Bell, **other:** Family$, Home Depot, **W...gas:** Exxon, Texaco
b E New Braunfels Ave(from sb), **E...food:** Chick-fil-A, Hong Kong Buffet, Jim's Rest., Luby's, McDonald's, Taco Cabana, Pizza Hut, Wendy's, **other:** mall
a Southcross Blvd, W New Braunfels Ave, **W...gas:** Exxon, **food:** Sonic
137 Hot Wells Blvd, **E...**bank, **W...food:** IHOP, **lodging:** Motel 6
136 Pecan Valley Dr, **E...gas:** Citgo/diesel, **food:** KFC/ Taco Bell, Pizza Hut, **other:** O'Reilly Parts, **W...**HOSPITAL
135 Military Dr, Lp 13, **E...gas:** Shamrock, Texaco, **food:** Jack-in-the-Box, **lodging:** Best Western, Mission Trail RV Resort, **W...gas:** Shamrock, **food:** Burger King, Lotus Chinese, **other:** HEB Food/gas, K-Mart, to Brooks AFB
133 I-410, US 281 S, no facilities
132 US 181 S, no facilities
130 Donop Rd, Southton Rd, **E...gas:** Shamrock/diesel/ RV dump, **food:** Braunig Lake Café, **lodging:** San Antonio Inn, **other:** I-37 RV Ctr/flea mkt, **W...gas:** Texaco/diesel, **other:** car/truckwash
127 San Antonio River Turnaround(from nb), Braunig Lake
127mm San Antonio River
125 FM 1604, Anderson Lp, **E...gas:** Conoco/Burger King/diesel/24hr, **food:** Mi Reina Mexican, **W...gas:** Exxon/diesel, Fina/diesel/burgers, **food:** BBQ
122 Priest Rd, Mathis Rd, no facilities
120 Hardy Rd, no facilities
117 FM 536, no facilities
113 FM 3006, no facilities
112mm picnic area both lanes, handicapped accessible
109 TX 97, to Floresville, **E...gas:** Chevron/diesel, **food:** DownHome Burgers/BBQ, Harpers Landing Rest., **other:** Chrysler/Plymouth/Dodge/Jeep, Yamaha
106 Coughran Rd, no facilities
104 spur 199, Leal Rd, to Pleasanton(no immediate sb return), same as 103
103 US 281 N, Leal Rd, to Pleasanton, **E...gas:** Citgo, Shamrock/diesel, **food:** DQ, K&K Steak&Egg, **lodging:** Kuntry Inn
98 TX 541, McCoy, no facilities
92 US 281A, Campbellton, no facilities
88 FM 1099, to FM 791, Campbellton, no facilities
83 FM 99, Whitsett, Peggy, **E...gas:** Texaco/diesel, **W...gas:** Chevron, Exxon/diesel/deli/RV Park/dump
82mm rest area sb, full(handicapped)facilities, phone, picnic tables, litter barrels
78mm rest area nb, full(handicapped)facilities, phone, picnic tables, litter barrels
76 US 281Alt, FM 2049, Whitsett, no facilities
75mm truck weigh sta sb
74mm truck weigh sta nb
72 US 281 S, Three Rivers, **4 mi W...lodging:** Best Western, **other:** to Rio Grande Valley

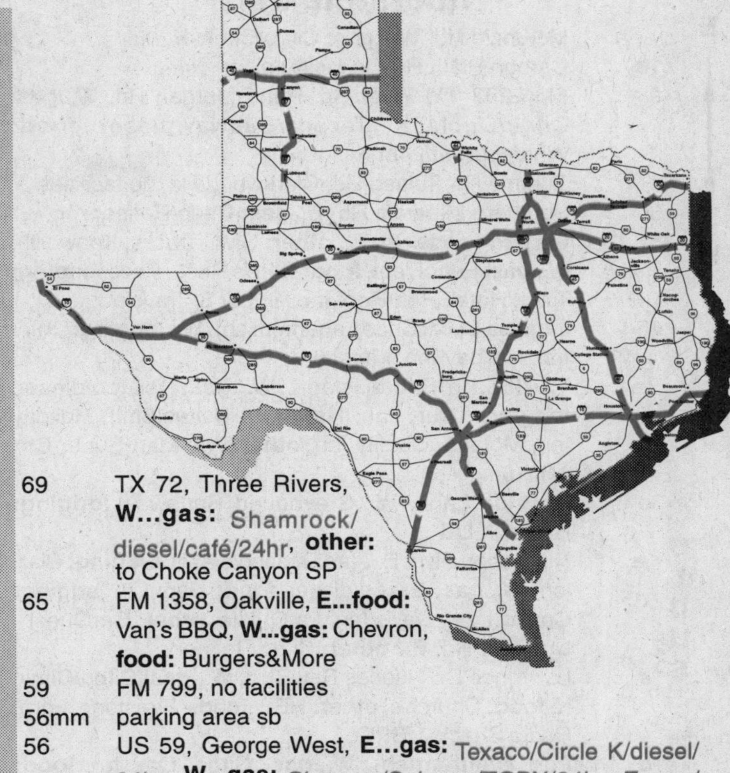

69 TX 72, Three Rivers, **W...gas:** Shamrock/ diesel/café/24hr, **other:** to Choke Canyon SP
65 FM 1358, Oakville, **E...food:** Van's BBQ, **W...gas:** Chevron, **food:** Burgers&More
59 FM 799, no facilities
56mm parking area sb
56 US 59, George West, **E...gas:** Texaco/Circle K/diesel/ 24hr, **W...gas:** Chevron/Subway/TCBY/24hr, Exxon/ Burger King/diesel/24hr, **other:** Rockin'N RV Park
51 Hailey Ranch Rd, no facilities
47 FM 3024, FM 534, Swinney Switch Rd, **W...other:** to KOA
44mm parking area sb
42mm parking area nb
40 FM 888, no facilities
36 TX 359, Mathis, to Skidmore, **W...gas:** Texaco/diesel, **food:** Pizza Hut
34 TX 359 W, **W...gas:** Shamrock/diesel, Texaco, **food:** Taqueria Vallarta Mexican, **other:** Ford, to Lake Corpus Christi SP
31 TX 188, Rockport, to Sinton
22 TX 234, FM 796, Edroy, to Odem, no facilities
20b Cooper Rd, no facilities
19.5mm rest area both lanes, full(handicapped)facilities, phone, picnic tables, litter barrels, vending, petwalk
17 US 77 N, to Victoria, no facilities
16 LaBonte Park, **W...**info, picnic tables
15 Sharpsburg Rd(from sb), Redbird Ln, no facilities
14 US 77 S, Rebird Ln, Robstown, to Kingsville, **1 mi W on UpRiver Rd...gas:** Chevron/Burger King, Citgo/Circle K, RaceTrac, Taxaco, **food:** BBQ, CiCi's, Denny's, Good'n Crisp Chicken, K-Bob's, Pizza Hut, Popeye's, Sonic, Subway, Whataburger/24hr, Wienerschnitzel, **lodging:** Comfort Inn, **other:** HOSPITAL, Beall's, Eckerd, Firestone, Home Depot, Radio Shack, Wal-Mart SuperCtr/24hr
13b Sharpsburg Rd(from nb)
a FM 1694, Callicoatte Rd, Leopard St, no facilities
11b FM 24, Violet Rd, Hart Rd, **E...gas:** NewWay/diesel/24hr, **W...gas:** Citgo, Exxon/Circle K, **food:** DQ, Domino's, KFC, McDonald's, Schlotsky's, Sonic, Subway, Taco Bell, Whataburger/24hr, **lodging:** Best Western, **other:** AutoZone, Family$, HEB Food/gas, O'Reilly Parts

TEXAS

Interstate 37

E–W

a McKinzie Rd, **W...gas:** Citgo/Circle K

10 Carbon Plant Rd, no facilities

9 FM 2292, Up River Rd, Rand Morgan Rd, **W...gas:** Citgo/Circle K, Texaco/Subway/diesel, **food:** Whataburger/24hr

7 Suntide Rd, Tuloso Rd, Clarkwood Rd, no facilities

6 Southern Minerals Rd, **E...gas:** Citgo Refinery

5 Corn Products Rd, **E...other:** GMC Trucks, Kenworth, **W...gas:** PetroFleet, **food:** Gem's Rest., Race **lodging:** Track Hotel, Red Roof Inn, Super 8, Travelodge

4b Lantana St, McBride Lane(from sb), **W...lodging:** Drury Inn, Holiday Inn, Motel 6

a TX 358, to Padre Island, **W...gas:** Texaco/diesel, **lodging:** Drury Inn, Hawthorn Suites(6mi), Holiday Inn, Motel 6, Quality Inn, **other:** Wal-Mart Super Ctr/24hr(6mi)

Corpus Christi

3b McBride Lane, **W...**Greyhound Raceway, **lodging:** Ramada Ltd

a Navigation Blvd, **E...gas:** Texaco/diesel, **lodging:** Clarion, **W...gas:** Exxon/diesel, **food:** Denny's, **lodging:** Comfort Inn, Day's Inn, La Quinta, **other:** CarQuest

2 Up River Rd, **E...other:** Citgo Refinery

1e Lawrence Dr, Nueces Bay Blvd, **W...gas:** Citgo/Circle K, **food:** Church's, **other:** HEB Foods, Firestone, Ford, Radio Shack, USPO

1d Port Ave(from sb), **W...gas:** Citgo, Coastal, **food:** Vick's Burgers, **lodging:** Howard Johnson, **other:** Port of Corpus Christi

1c US 181, TX 286, Shoreline Blvd, Corpus Christi, **W...**HOSPITAL

1b Brownlee St(from nb), no facilities

1a Buffalo St(from sb). **S on Shoreline...gas:** Citgo/Circle K, **food:** Joes Crabshack, Landry's Seafood, **lodging:** Omni Hotel, Ramada Inn. I-37 begins/ends on US 181 in Corpus Christi.

Interstate 40

E–W

Exit # Services

177mm Texas/Oklahoma state line

176 spur 30(from eb), to Texola, no facilities

175mm picnic area wb, picnic tables, litter barrels

173mm picnic area eb, picnic tables, litter barrels

169 FM 1802, Carbon Black Rd, no facilities

Shamrock

167 FM 2168, Daberry Rd, **N...gas:** Shell/diesel/Butch's BBQ/24hr

164 Lp 40(from wb), to Shamrock, **1 mi S...lodging:** Budget Inn, Econolodge, **other:** HOSPITAL, museum

163 US 83, Shamrock, to Wheeler, **N...gas:** Chevron/diesel, Conoco, Shell/diesel/24hr, **food:** Hasty's Burgers, Pizza Hut, **lodging:** Best Western Irish/rest., Western Motel, **other:** mall, **S...gas:** Phillips 66/Subway/24hr, Shell, **food:** DQ, McDonald's, **lodging:** Budget Host

161 Lp 40, Rte 66(from eb), to Shamrock, **S...gas:** Chevron

157 FM 1547, Lela, **2 mi S...other:** W 40 RV Park

152 FM 453, Pakan Rd, **S...**gas

150mm picnic area wb, tables, litter barrels

149mm picnic area eb, tables, litter barrels

148 FM 1443, Kellerville Rd, no facilities

146 County Line Rd, **S...**camping

143 Lp 40(from wb), to McLean, to gas, phone, food, lodging, museum

142 TX 273, FM 3143, to McLean, **N...gas:** Shell/diesel, **lodging:** Texas Motel, **other:** CarQuest, Country Corner RV Park

141 Rte 66(from eb), McLean, **N...food:** Red River Steaks, **lodging:** Cactus Inn, same as 142

135 FM 291, Rte 66, Alanreed, **S...gas:** Conoco/motel/café/RV park, **other:** USPO

132 Johnson Ranch Rd, ranch access, no facilities

131mm rest area wb, full(handicapped)facilities, phone, picnic tables, litter barrels, petwaik

129mm rest area eb, full(handicapped)facilities, phone, picnic tables, litter barrels, petwalk

128 FM 2477, to Lake McClellan, **S...other:** camping, RV dump

124 TX 70 S, to Clarendon, **N...**gas/diesel, café, RV camping

121 TX 70 N, to Pampa, no facilities

114 Lp 40, Groom, **N...**auto/diesel/service, **S...**to gas/diesel, food, lodging

113 FM 2300, Groom, **S...gas:** Shell/diesel, **food:** DQ, **lodging:** Chalet Inn

112 FM 295, Groom, **S...other:** Biggest Cross, **1 mi S...**gas

110 Lp 40, Rte 66, no facilities

109 FM 294, no facilities

108mm parking area wb, litter barrels

106mm parking area eb, picnic tables, litter barrels

105 FM 2880, grain silo, no facilities

98 TX 207 S(from wb), to Claude, no facilities

96 TX 207 N, to Panhandle, **N...gas:** Love's/Subway/diesel/24hr/@, **S...gas:** Shell/repair, **food:** A&W, **lodging:** Budget Host, Conway Inn

89 FM 2161, to Rte 66, no facilities

87 FM 2373, no facilities

87mm picnic areas both lanes, litter barrels

85 Amarillo Blvd, Durrett Rd, access to camping

81 FM 1912, **S...gas:** TA/Subway/diesel/rest./24hr/@

80 FM 228, **N...other:** AOK RV Park, to Texas Tech Institute

78 US 287 S(from eb), FM 1258, Pullman Rd, same as 77

77 FM 1258, Pullman Rd, **N...gas:** Pilot/Arby's/diesel/24hr/@, **S...gas:** Shell/diesel/24hr/@, **other:** Custom RV Ctr

76 spur 468, **N...gas:** Flying J/Conoco/diesel/LP/rest./24hr/@, Shell/diesel, **other:** tourist info

75 Lp 335, Lakeside Rd, **N...gas:** Pilot/Subway/diesel/rest./24hr/@, **food:** Country Barn Rest., McDonald's, Waffle House, **lodging:** Quality Inn, Super 8, Trailer Inn, **other:** UPS, Peterbilt Trucks, KOA(2mi), **S...gas:** Petro/Mobil/diesel/rest./@, **other:** Blue Beacon

74 Whitaker Rd, **N...lodging:** Big Texan Inn/café, **other:** RV camping, **S...gas:** Love's/Subway/diesel/@, TA/FoodCourt/diesel/24hr/@, **lodging:** Budget Inn, **other:** Blue Beacon

Interstate 40

E ↕ W

Amarillo

73 Eastern St, Bolton Ave, Amarillo, **N...gas:** Shamrock/diesel, **food:** Polly's Rest., **lodging:** Fiesta Motel, Motel 6, Red Roof Inn, **S...gas:** Chevron/diesel, Citgo/diesel, Pacific Pride/diesel, **food:** Cally's Corner Rest., **lodging:** Best Western, **other:** Ford Trucks

72b Grand St, Amarillo, **N...gas:** Fina, Texaco, **food:** KFC, **lodging:** Motel 6, **other:** Nissan, U-Haul, **S...gas:** Phillips 66, **food:** Braum's, McDonald's, Pizza Hut, Sonic, Subway, Taco Cabana, Taco Villa, **lodging:** Motel 6, **other:** AutoZone, $General, Wal-Mart SuperCtr/gas/24hr, same as 73

a Nelson St, **N...food:** Cracker Barrel, KFC, **lodging:** Ashmore Inn, Budget Host, Econolodge, Kiva Hotel, Ramada Inn, Sleep Inn, Super 8, Travelodge, **other:** Qtrhorse Museum, **S...gas:** Chevron, Shamrock/diesel, **lodging:** Camelot Inn

71 Ross St, Osage St, Amarillo, **N...gas:** Conoco/diesel, Shamrock, Shell/diesel, **food:** Burger King, El Tapatio Mexican, Grandy's, Longhorn Diner, LJ Silver, McDonald's, Popeye's, Schlotsky's, Subway, **lodging:** Coachlight Inn, Comfort Inn, Day's Inn, Holiday Inn, Microtel, **S...gas:** Shamrock, **food:** Arby's, Denny's, Fiesta Grande Mexican, Sonic, Taco Bell, Wendy's, **lodging:** Hampton Inn, La Quinta, Ramada Ltd, **other:** Chevrolet, Ford, Hyundai, Sam's Club/gas, USPO

70 I-27 S, US 60 W, US 87, US 287, to Canyon, Lubbock, **N...other:** Goodyear/auto, bank

69b Washington St, Amarillo, **N...other:** Albertson's, **S...gas:** Phillips 66, Shell, **food:** DQ, Subway, **other:** Eckerd

a Crockett St, access to same as 68b

68b Georgia St, **N...gas:** Shell/Subway, Texaco, **food:** TGIFriday, **lodging:** Ambassador Hotel, **S...gas:** Phillips 66, **food:** Burger King, BBQ, Church's, Denny's, Furr's Café, Taco Villa, Whataburger, **lodging:** Econolodge, Quality Inn, **other:** HOSPITAL, Chrysler/Dodge, Hastings Books, K-Mart, Mitsubishi, Office Depot, Saturn

a Julian Blvd, Paramount Blvd, **N...gas:** Chevron, Shell, **food:** Arby's, Nick's Rest., Pancho's Mexican, Pizza Hut, Schlotzsky's, Wendy's, **lodging:** Harley Hotel, same as 67, **S...gas:** Shamrock, **food:** Bennigan's, Caboose Diner, Cactus Grill, Cajun Magic, Calico Country Café, El Chico, Godfather's, Kabuki's Japanese Steaks, LJ Silver, Orient Express, Peking Rest., Pizza Planet, Popeye's, Red Lobster, Ruby Tequila's Mexican, Steak&Ale, Texas Roadhouse, **lodging:** Comfort Suites, Holiday Inn Express, Motel 6, Travelodge, **other:** Cadillac, Discount Tire, Pennzoil

67 Western St, Amarillo, **N...gas:** Citgo, Phillips 66/diesel, Shell, **food:** Beef Rigger Rest., Blackeyed Pea, Braum's, Burger King, Chili's, Cty Line BBQ, Legends Grill, Marie Callender's, McDonald's, Pancho's Mexican, Subway, Taco Bell, **S...gas:** Phillips 66, Shamrock, **food:** Catfish Shack, Dairy Queen, Furr's Café, Gary's BBQ, IHOP, Olive Garden, Taco Cabana, Vince's Pizza, Waffle House, Wienerschnitzel, **lodging:** Holiday Inn Express, **other:** Firestone/auto, NAPA, Radio Shack, same 68

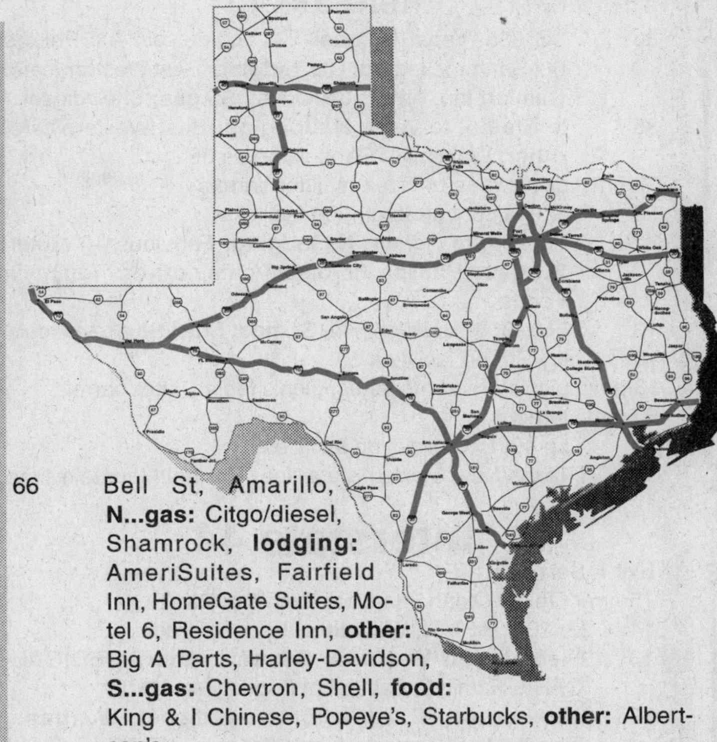

66 Bell St, Amarillo, **N...gas:** Citgo/diesel, Shamrock, **lodging:** AmeriSuites, Fairfield Inn, HomeGate Suites, Motel 6, Residence Inn, **other:** Big A Parts, Harley-Davidson, **S...gas:** Chevron, Shell, **food:** King & I Chinese, Popeye's, Starbucks, **other:** Albertson's

65 Coulter Dr, Amarillo, **N...gas:** Phillips 66/diesel, **food:** Arby's, Golden Corral, Luby's, My Thai Café, Taco Bell, Waffle House, **lodging:** Best Western, Comfort Inn, Courtyard, Day's Inn, Executive Inn, La Quinta, **other:** HOSPITAL, Chevrolet, Firestone/auto, Nissan, **S...gas:** Chevron/KFC, Citgo, Shell, **food:** BBQ, Braum's, ChinaStar, ChuckeCheese, CiCi's, Hoffbrau Steaks, Jason's Deli, McDonald's, Outback Steaks, Pizza Hut, Santa Fe Rest., Sonic, Subway, Taco Villa, TCBY, Wendy's, Whataburger, Wienerschnitzel, **lodging:** Hampton Inn, 5th Season Inn, **other:** Best Buy, Goodyear/auto, IGA Foods, Lowe's Whse, Sears/auto

64 Soncy Rd, to Pal Duro Cyn, **N...food:** Carino's Italian, Joe's Crabshack, Logan's Roadhouse, **lodging:** Comfort Inn, Homewood Suites, Extended Stay America, **other:** Discount Tire, **S...gas:** Shamrock/diesel/24hr, **food:** Applebee's, DQ, Fazoli's, Hooters, Legends Steaks, McDonald's, On-the-Border, Ruby Tuesday, **other:** MEDICAL CARE, Barnes&Noble, Circuit City, Dillard's, Ford, Home Depot, K-Mart, Mervyn's, OfficeMax, Old Navy, Target, mall

62b Lp 40, Amarillo Blvd, RV camping

a Hope Rd, Helium Rd(from eb), **S...other:** RV camping, antiques

60 Arnot Rd, **S...gas:** Love's/A&W/Subway/diesel/@, Texas Trading Co/gifts, **other:** camping

57 RM 2381, to Bushland, **N...**grain silo, **S...gas:** Shell/diesel, **other:** USPO, RV camping/dump(1mi)

55mm parking area wb, litter barrels

54 Adkisson Rd, **S...**RV park

53.5mm parking area eb, litter barrels

49 FM 809, to Wildorado, **S...gas:** Phillips 66/diesel, **food:** Cookie's Café, **lodging:** Royal Inn, **other:** repair

42 Everett Rd, no facilities

37 Lp 40, to Vega, **1 mi N...other:** Walnut RV Park, same as 36, **S...**airport

TEXAS

Interstate 40

E ↔ W

Exit #	Services
36	US 385, Vega, **N...gas:** Conoco/diesel/24hr, Phillips 66, Shamrock, **food:** DQ, **lodging:** Best Western/café, Comfort Inn, **other:** CarQuest, **S...gas:** Shell/diesel
35	to Rte 66, to Vega, **N...lodging:** Best Western/café, **other:** Walnut RV Park, same as 36
32mm	picnic area both lanes, litter barrels
28	to Rte 66, Landergin, no facilities
22	TX 214, to Adrian, **N...lodging:** Fabulous 40 Motel, **S...gas:** Phillips 66/diesel/café, **other:** Tommy's Foods
18	FM 2858, Gruhlkey Rd, **S...gas:** Shell/Stuckey's/rest.
15	Ivy Rd, no facilities
13mm	picnic area both lanes, picnic tables, litter barrels
5.5mm	turnout
0	Lp 40, to Glenrio, no facilities
0mm	Texas/New Mexico state line, Central/Mountain time

Interstate 44

E ↔ W

Wichita Falls

Exit #	Services
15mm	Texas/Oklahoma state line, Red River
14	Lp 267, E 3rd St, **W...other:** Burk RV Park
13	Glendale St, **W...food:** Subway, **other:** MEDICAL CARE, Family$, Sav-A-Lot Foods, Wal-Mart
12	Burkburnett, **E...gas:** Chevron/diesel, **W...gas:** Fina/7-11, Shamrock, **food:** Braum's, KFC/Taco Bell, Mazzio's, McDonald's, Subway, Whataburger/24hr, **other:** Chevrolet/Pontiac, Ford
11	FM 3429, Daniels Rd, **W...gas:** Fina
9mm	picnic area both lanes, picnic table, litter barrels, petwalk
7	East Rd, no facilities
6	Bacon Switch Rd, no facilities
5a	FM 3492, Missile Rd, **E...other:** st patrol, **W...gas:** Exxon/diesel
5	Access Rd, no facilities
4	City Loop St, no facilities
3c	FM 890, **W...gas:** Shamrock, **other:** $Tree, Wal-Mart SuperCtr/gas/24hr
3b	sp 325, Sheppard AFB, no facilities
a	US 287 N, to Amarillo
2	Maureen St, **E...gas:** Fina/7-11/diesel, Texaco/diesel, **lodging:** Comfort Inn, King's Inn, Motel 6, Travelodge, **other:** Chevrolet, Mazda, Nissan/Volvo/VW, **W...gas:** Fina/7-11, **food:** China Star, DQ, Denny's, El Chico, LJ Silver, Waffle Time, Whataburger/24hr, **lodging:** Hampton Inn, La Quinta, Super 8, Travelers Inn
1d	US 287 bus, Lp 370, **W...gas:** Conoco/diesel, **lodging:** Day's Inn, River Oaks Inn
1c	Texas Tourist Bureau, **E...gas:** Citgo, **W...lodging:** Radisson
1b	Scotland Park(from nb), **E...lodging:** Scotland Park Motel, **W...**RV park
1a	US 277 S, to Abilene
0mm	I-44 begins/ends in Witchita Falls. **1-2 mi S in Wichita Falls...gas:** Citgo/Circle K/diesel, Conoco, Fina/7-11/diesel, **food:** Arby's, Burger King, Carl's Jr, IHOP, McDonald's, Papa John's, Popeye's, Subway, Whataburger/24hr, Wendy's, **lodging:** Econolodge, Holiday Inn, **other:** HOSPITAL

Interstate 45

N ↔ S

Dallas

Exit #	Services
286	to I-35 E, to Denton. I-45 begins/ends in Dallas.
285	Bryan St E, US 75 N, no facilities
284b a	I-30, W to Ft Worth, E to Texarkana, access to HOSPITAL
283b	Pennsylvania Ave, to MLK Blvd, **E...gas:** to Shamrock, Shell, **food:** BBQ, **W...food:** KFC/Taco Bell
a	Lamar St, no facilities
281	Oberton St(from sb), **W...gas:** Chevron
280	Illinois Ave, Linfield St, **E...lodging:** Linfield Motel, Star Motel, **W...gas:** Texaco
279b a	Lp 12, no facilities
277	Simpson Stuart Rd, **W...other:** to Paul Quinn Coll
276b a	I-20, W to Ft Worth, E to Shreveport
275	TX 310 N(from nb, no re-entry), no facilities
274	Dowdy Ferry Rd, Hutchins, **E...gas:** Texaco/diesel, **lodging:** Gold Inn, **W...food:** DQ, Jack-in-the-Box, Smith's Rest.
273	Wintergreen Rd, no facilities
272	Fulghum Rd, no facilities
271	Pleasant Run Rd, no facilities
270	Belt Line Rd, to Wilmer, **E...gas:** Texaco/diesel, Total/diesel, **W...gas:** Citgo/diesel, Exxon/Subway, **food:** DQ
269	Mars Rd, no facilities
268	Malloy Bridge Rd, no facilities
267	Frontage Rd, no facilities
266	FM 660, **E...gas:** Fina/diesel, **W...gas:** Shamrock/diesel, **food:** DQ
265	Lp 45, Ferris, no facilities
263	Lp 561, no facilities
262	Newton Rd, to Trumbull, no facilities
261	County Rd(from nb), no facilities
260	Hampel Rd, **W...other:** Goodyear
259	FM 813, FM 878, no facilities
258	Lp 45, Palmer, **E...gas:** Knox/Subway/diesel/24hr/@, **other:** golf, **W...gas:** Mobil/diesel/24hr, **lodging:** Palmer Motel
255	FM 879, Garrett, **E...gas:** Exxon/diesel, **W...gas:** Chevron/diesel
253	Lp 45, **W...gas:** Texaco/diesel, **food:** Papa Tino's Mexican

Ennis

Exit #	Services
251b a	TX 34, Ennis, **E...gas:** Fina, Texaco/diesel, **food:** Bubba's BBQ, McDonald's, **lodging:** Best Western, Travelers Inn, **W...gas:** Chevron/diesel, Exxon/diesel/24hr, **food:** Arby's, Braum's, Burger King, Chili's, DQ, Domino's, Golden Corral, Jack-in-the-Box, KFC, Sonic, Subway, Taco Bell/Pizza Hut, Waffle House, Wall Chinese Café, Whataburger/24hr, **lodging:** Ennis Inn, Quality Inn, **other:** HOSPITAL, AutoZone, Chevrolet/Pontiac, Chrysler/Plymouth/Dodge, Ford/Mercury, Pennzoil, Pontiac/Buick, Wal-Mart SuperCtr/24hr, RV camping
249	FM 85, Ennis, **E...lodging:** Budget Inn, **W...gas:** Total/diesel, **other:** Blue Beacon
247	US 287 N, to Waxahatchie, no facilities
246	FM 1183, Alma, **W...gas:** Chevron, Phillips 66
244	FM 1182, no facilities
243	Frontage Rd, no facilities
242	Rice, **W...**bank
239	FM 1126, **W...gas:** Phillips 66

Interstate 45

N
S

238 FM 1603, **E...gas:** Fina/diesel, **other:** Casita RV Trailers, tires
237 Frontage Rd, no facilities
235b Lp I-45(from sb), to Corsicana
a Frontage Rd, no facilities
232 Roane Rd, no facilities
231 TX 31, Corsicana, **E...gas:** Texaco/diesel, **food:** Jack-in-the-Box, **lodging:** Colonial Inn, **other:** Chevrolet, **W...gas:** Chevron, Exxon/Subway/diesel, Shell/diesel, **food:** Bill's Cafeteria, DQ, McDonald's, **lodging:** Comfort Inn, **other:** HOSPITAL, Chrysler/Plymouth/Dodge/Jeep, Ford, to Navarro Coll
229 US 287, **E...gas:** Exxon/Wendy's/diesel, Shell/diesel/24hr, **food:** Sonic, Russell Stover Candies, **other:** VF Outlet/famous brands, **W...gas:** Chevron, **food:** Catfish King Rest., Waffle House, **lodging:** Corsicana Inn, Day's Inn, Royal Inn, Travelers Inn
228b Lp 45(exits left from nb), Corsicana, **2 mi W...**facilities in Corsicana
a 15th St, Corsicana, **E...gas:** Phillips 66/diesel
225 FM 739, Angus, **E...gas:** Chevron/diesel, Exxon/diesel, **other:** to Chambers Reservoir, **W...gas:** Citgo/diesel, Shell, **other:** Camper Depot
221 Frontage Rd, no facilities
220 Frontage Rd, no facilities
219b Frontage Rd, no facilities
a TX 14(from sb), Richland, to Mexia
218 FM 1394, Richland, **W...gas:** Shell
217mm rest area both lanes, full(handicapped)facilities, phone, picnic tables, litter barrels, vending, petwalk, RV dump
213 FM 246, to Wortham, **W...gas:** Chevron, Texaco/diesel
211 FM 80, to Streetman, no facilities
206 FM 833, no facilities
198 FM 27, to Wortham, **E...gas:** Shell/BBQ, **food:** Gilberto's Mexican, **other:** HOSPITAL, **W...gas:** Exxon, Love's/Burger King/diesel/24hr/@, **lodging:** Budget Inn, **other:** I-45 RV Park
197 US 84, Fairfield, **E...gas:** Exxon/Jack-in-the-Box, Fina/Sam's, Texaco, **food:** DQ, McDonald's, Ponte's Diner, Sonic, Subway/Texas Burger, **lodging:** Holiday Inn Express, Super 8, **other:** Chevrolet, Chrysler/Plymouth/Dodge, **W...gas:** Shell/diesel, Texaco/diesel, **food:** Dalia's Mexican, I-45 Rest., KFC/Taco Bell, Pizza Hut, Sammy's Rest., **lodging:** Regency Inn, Sam's Motel, **other:** Ford/Mercury
189 TX 179, to Teague, **E...gas:** Exxon/Chester Fried/Dinner Bell/diesel, StarUSA Gas/café
187mm picnic area both lanes, tables, litter barrels
180 TX 164, to Groesbeck, no facilities
178 US 79, Buffalo, **E...gas:** Shell/diesel, Texaco/diesel, **food:** Subway/Texas Burger, Westhervane Rest., **other:** Brookshire Food/gas, Parts+, **W...gas:** Exxon/Church's/diesel, Mobil/diesel, Shamrock/diesel/24hr, **food:** DQ, Pitt Grill/24hr, Rainbow Rest., Sonic, **lodging:** Best Western, Economy Inn, Super 8
175mm Bliss Creek
166mm weigh sta sb
164 TX 7, Centerville, **E...gas:** Chevron, Texaco/diesel, **food:** Country Cousins Café, Subway, Texas Burger, **lodging:** Day's Inn, **W...gas:** Exxon/24hr, Shell/diesel, **food:** DQ, Jack-in-the-Box, Mama Mike's BBQ
160mm picnic area sb, tables, litter barrels, hist marker, handicapped accessible
159mm Boggy Creek
156 FM 977, to Leona, **W...gas:** Exxon/diesel
155mm picnic area nb, handicapped accessible
152 TX OSR, to Normangee, **W...gas:** Chevron/diesel, **other:** Yellow Rose RV Park/café
146 TX 75, no facilities
142 US 190, TX 21, Madisonville, **E...gas:** Exxon/diesel, Texaco/diesel/24hr, **food:** Church's, Corral Café, **lodging:** Madisonville Inn, **W...gas:** Shamrock/Popeye's/diesel, Shell/Subway/24hr, **food:** China Café, Jack-in-the-Box, Lakeside Rest., McDonald's, Pizza Hut, Sonic, Texas Burger, **lodging:** Budget Motel, Western Lodge, **other:** HOSPITAL, Ford, Parts+
136 spur 67, no facilities
132 FM 2989, no facilities
126mm rest area sb, full(handicapped)facilities, phone, picnic tables, litter barrels, vending, petwalk, RV dump
124mm rest area nb, full(handicapped)facilities, phone, picnic tables, litter barrels, vending, petwalk, RV dump
123 FM 1696, no facilities
121mm parking area nb
118 TX 75, **E...gas:** Texaco/diesel/24hr, **other:** truckwash, **W...gas:** Pilot/Wendy's/diesel/24hr/@
116 US 190, TX 30, **E...gas:** Citgo, Shamrock/diesel, **food:** Church's, El Chico, Golden Corral, Imperial Garden Chinese, McDonald's, TCBY, Tejas Café, Texas Burger, Whataburger/24hr, **lodging:** Comfort Inn, Econolodge, La Quinta, Motel 6, **other:** HOSPITAL, Nissan, Plymouth/Jeep/Dodge, Pontiac/GMC, **W...gas:** Exxon, Chevron/24hr, Shell/24hr, Texaco/diesel, **food:** Burger King, Chili's, CiCi's, Denny's, IHOP, KFC, Luby's, Pizza

Huntsville

TEXAS

Interstate 45

N ↕ S

Hut, Subway, Taco Bell, **lodging:** Holiday Inn Express, **other:** Discount Tire, Hastings Books, Kroger, Office Depot, Radio Shack, Walgreen, Wal-Mart SuperCtr/gas/24hr

114 FM 1374, **E...gas:** Exxon/diesel, Texaco, **food:** Casa Tomas Mexican, DQ, **lodging:** Gateway Inn, Super 8, **other:** Ford/Lincoln/Mercury, **W...gas:** Chevron, Shamrock/diesel, **food:** Country Inn Steaks, **lodging:** Sam Houston Inn, **other:** HOSPITAL

113 TX 19(from nb), Huntsville, **E...food:** Catfish Palace Rest.(2mi)

112 TX 75, **E...gas:** Citgo, **lodging:** Baker Motel, **other:** Houston Statue, to Sam Houston St U, museum

109 Park 40, **W...other:** to Huntsville SP

105mm picnic area both lanes, tables, litter barrels

103 FM 1374/1375(from sb), to New Waverly, **W...gas:** Citgo/diesel

102 FM 1374/1375, TX 150(from nb), to New Waverly, **E...gas:** Shell, **1 mi W...gas:** Citgo/diesel

101mm weigh sta nb

98 TX 75, Danville Rd, Shepard Hill Rd, **E...other:** Fishpond RV Park/dump, **2 mi W...lodging:** B&B

95 Longstreet Rd, no facilities

94 FM 1097, to Willis, **E...food:** Jack-in-the-Box, Mr Gatti, Sonic, **other:** $General, Kroger/gas, **W...gas:** Chevron/Popeye's, Exxon/Burger King, Texaco/Taco Bell/diesel/24hr, **food:** McDonald's, Subway, **lodging:** Best Western

92 FM 830, Seven Coves Dr, **W...other:** RV Park on the Lake(3mi)

91 League Line Rd, **E...gas:** Chevron/McDonald's, **food:** LoneStar Café, Subway, Wendy's, **lodging:** Comfort Inn, La Quinta, **other:** Prime Outlets/famous brands, **W...gas:** Texaco, **food:** Cracker Barrel

90 FM 3083, Teas Nursery Rd, Montgomery Co Park

88 Lp 336, to Cleveland, Navasota, **E...gas:** Mobil/diesel, Shamrock/diesel, Shell/24hr, **food:** Arby's, Blackeyed Pea, Domino's, Grandy's, Hofbrau Steaks, Hunan Chinese, KFC, Little Caesar's, LJ Silver, Margarita's Mexican, McDonald's, Papa John's, Sonic, Subway, TX Roadhouse, Whataburger, **other:** MEDICAL CARE, Buick/Pontiac, Discount Tire, Goodyear/auto, Hastings Books, Kroger, Michael's, Pennzoil, Walgreen, **W...gas:** Chevron/24hr, **food:** Ryan's, **other:** Eckerd, Goody's, GNC, Hancock Fabrics, JC Penney, Lowe's Whse, Randall's Foods, Radio Shack, Sam's Club, Wal-Mart SuperCtr/24hr

Conroe

87 TX 105, Conroe, **E...gas:** Shamrock, **food:** Burger King, CiCi's, Imperial Garden Chinese, Jack-in-the-Box, Luther's BBQ, McDonald's, Outback Steaks, Steak&Ale, Taco Bell, **other:** HOSPITAL, Eckerd/24hr, Firestone/auto, Kia, Kroger, NTB, Suzuki, **W...gas:** Exxon/TCBY, Texaco/diesel, **food:** Golden Corral, Luby's, **other:** Buick/GMC/Isuzu, Home Depot, Hyundai, Office Depot, Randall's Food/gas, Target

85 FM 2854, Gladstell St, **E...gas:** Citgo, **other:** HOSPITAL, Ford/Mercury, Honda, Mitsubishi, Nissan, **W...gas:** Shamrock, Texaco/diesel, **food:** IHOP, **lodging:** Baymont Inn, Day's Inn, Motel 6, **other:** Cadillac, Chrysler/Plymouth/Jeep, Daewoo, Dodge, Mazda, Toyota

84 TX 75 N, Frazier St, **E...gas:** Conoco/diesel, Exxon/diesel, Texaco/diesel, **lodging:** Corporate Inn, Holiday Inn, Ramada Ltd, **other:** U-Haul, **W...gas:** Shell, **food:** Pizza Hut, Porky's Rest., Taco Cabana, **other:** Albertson's, Discount Tire, K-Mart, Kroger

83 Crighton Rd, Camp Strake Rd, no facilities

82 River Plantation Dr

82mm San Jacinto River

81 FM 1488, to Hempstead, Magnolia, **E...gas:** Citgo/diesel, **W...gas:** Shamrock, **other:** CamperLand RV Ctr

80 Needham Rd(from sb), no facilities

79 TX 242, Needham, **E...gas:** Texaco/McDonald's, **other:** Woodland Lakes RV Resort(1mi), **W...food:** Chuck-eCheese, Willie's Grill, **lodging:** Country Inn Suites, **other:** Firestone, Kohl's, Wal-Mart SuperCtr/24hr

78 Needham Rd(from sb), Tamina Rd, access to same as 77

77 Woodlands Pkwy, Robinson, Chateau Woods, **E...gas:** Conoco/diesel, Texaco, **food:** Babin's Steaks, Buca italian, Luther's BBQ, Pancho's Mexican, Pappadeaux Rest., Pizza Hut, Red Lobster, Saltgrass Steaks, **lodging:** Budget Inn, **other:** Discount Tire, Home Depot, JoAnn Fabrics, Michael's, NTB, Office Depot, Old Navy, Sam's Club, SteinMart, Walgreen, **W...gas:** Shamrock, Texaco, **food:** Guadalajara Mexican, Landry's Seafood, Luby's, Macaroni Grill, Outback Steaks, Pancho's Mexican, **lodging:** Comfort Inn, Day's Inn, Drury Inn, Hampton Inn, Homewood Suites, La Quinta, **other:** HOSPITAL, Best Buy, Dillard's, Marshall's, Mervyn's, OfficeMax, Target, World Mkt, mall

76 Research Forest Dr, Tamina Rd, **E...gas:** Chevron/diesel, Coastal/lube, Shamrock, Stop'n Go, Texaco, **food:** Casa Elena Mexican, LJ Silver, **other:** MEDICAL CARE, Food Basket, Firestone, **W...food:** Carrabba's, El Chico, IHOP, Kyoto Japanese, Olive Garden, Tortuga Mexican, **lodging:** Crossland Suites, **other:** Goodyear/auto

Houston

73 Rayford Rd, Sawdust Rd(to Hardy Toll Rd from sb), **E...gas:** Conoco, Shell, **food:** Hartz Chicken, Jack-in-the-Box, LJ Silver, McDonald's, Popeye's, Sonic, Thomas BBQ, **lodging:** Hawthorn Suites, Holiday Inn Express, **other:** AutoZone, O'Reilly Parts, **W...gas:** Mobil, Shell, Texaco, **food:** Grandy's, Sam's Rest., Woodland Chinese, **lodging:** Red Roof Inn, **other:** Discount Tire, Eckerd, HEB Foods, Kroger

72 Frontage Rd(from nb), no facilities

70b Spring-Stuebner Rd, no facilities

a FM 2920, to Tomball, **E...gas:** Exxon, **food:** El Palenque Mexican, McDonald's, Pizza Hut, Wendy's, **other:** Radio Shack, Vaughn's RV Ctr, Walgreen, transmissions, **W...gas:** Chevron, Shell, **food:** Burger King, Taco Bell, Whataburger/24hr, **lodging:** Travelodge, **other:** Ford, U-Haul

Interstate 45

N
S

68 Holzwarth Rd, Cypress Wood Dr, **E...gas:** Texaco/diesel, **food:** Burger King, Chick-fil-A, Hartz Chicken, Pizza Hut/Taco Bell, Sonic, Wendy's, Whataburger, **other:** Albertson's, $Tree, GNC, Kohl's, Kroger, Lincoln/Mercury, Ross, Toyota, Wal-Mart SuperCtr/24hr, **W...gas:** Chevron/24hr, **food:** Denny's, Jack-in-the-Box, Pizza Hut, Popeye's, **lodging:** Day's Inn, Motel 6, **other:** Ford, Home Depot, Lowe's Whse, Office Depot, Target, Walgreen

66 FM 1960, to Addicks, **E...gas:** Chevron, RaceTrac, Shell, **food:** Jack-in-the-Box, Sonic, **lodging:** Day's Inn, **other:** BMW, Chevrolet, Honda, Mercedes, Radio Shack, **W...gas:** Exxon, Shell/diesel/24hr, Texaco/diesel, **food:** Bennigan's, Grandy's, Jack-in-the-Box, Jojo's Rest., Luby's, McDonald's, Outback Steaks, Pizza Hut, Popeye's, Red Lobster, Steak&Ale, Subway, Taco Bell, **lodging:** Comfort Suites, Fairfield Inn, Hampton Inn, La Quinta, **other:** GolfSmith, Infiniti, Jaguar, LandRover, Lexus, NTB, Saturn, mall

64 Richey Rd, **E...gas:** Texaco/Church's, **food:** Atchafalaya River Café, Pappasito's Cantina, **lodging:** Holiday Inn, Lexington Suites, **other:** Cadillac, Discount Tire, Nissan, Sam's Club, **W...gas:** Flying J/Conoco/diesel/24hr/@, **food:** Cracker Barrel, House of Creole, Jack-in-the-Box, Joe's Crabshack, Lupe Tortillo, SaltGrass Steaks, Whataburger, Zio's Italian, **lodging:** La Quinta, Shoney's Inn, **other:** U-Haul

Houston

63 Airtex Dr, **E...other:** Acura, Cadillac, LoneStar RV Ctr, Nissan, **lodging:** Howard Johnson, Scottish Inn, **W...gas:** Chevron, RaceTrac, **food:** McDonald's, **lodging:** Best Western, Studio+, **other:** Celebration Sta

62 Rankin Rd, Kuykendahl, **W...gas:** Shell, **food:** Luby's, **lodging:** Baymont Inn, Rodeway Inn, Sun Suites, **other:** BMW, Buick/Subaru, Hyundai, Kia, Mercedes, Mitsubishi, Saab, Suzuki, Volvo, VW

61 Greens Rd, **E...food:** Whataburger, **lodging:** Day's Inn, Marriott, Wyndham Hotel, **other:** Circuit City, Dillard's, Foley's, JC Penney, Mervyn's, mall, **W...**Burger King, Luby's, Kroger, Office Depot, OfficeMax, Target

60c Beltway E, no facilities

b TX 8, **E...lodging:** La Quinta, Marriott, **other:** Dillard's, Sears/auto, mall, **W...food:** Marco's Mexican

a TX 525, **E...gas:** Exxon, Shamrock, Shell, Texaco, **food:** Burger King, Champ's Rest., China Border, Denny's/24hr, Furr's Cafeteria, LJ Silver, Mucho Mexico, Pizza Hut, Steak&Ale, **other:** Firestone/auto, Honda, Randall's Foods, Walgreen, **W...food:** Gordito's Mexican, Pappa's Rest., Quizno's, Wendy's, **other:** Best Buy, Dodge, GNC, Home Depot, Pontiac/GMC, Wal-Mart SuperCtr/24hr

59 FM 525, West Rd, **E...gas:** Exxon, Shell, **food:** McDonald's, Pizza Hut, Wendy's, **other:** Fiesta Foods, **W...gas:** Exxon, **food:** Taco Bell, Taco Cabana, **lodging:** Best Western, GreenChase Inn, Holiday Inn Express, **other:** Fry's Electronics, K-Mart, Lincoln/Mercury, PepBoys

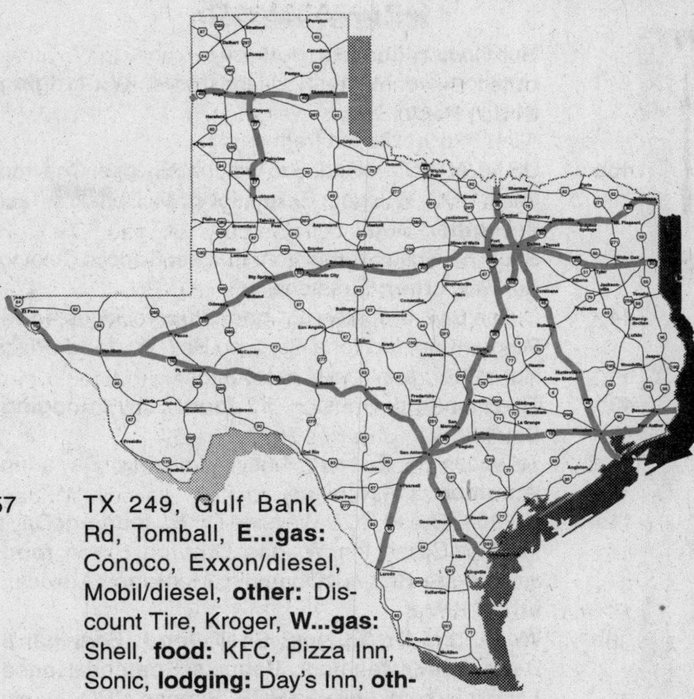

57 TX 249, Gulf Bank Rd, Tomball, **E...gas:** Conoco, Exxon/diesel, Mobil/diesel, **other:** Discount Tire, Kroger, **W...gas:** Shell, **food:** KFC, Pizza Inn, Sonic, **lodging:** Day's Inn, **other:** Chevrolet, Chrysler/Plymouth/Jeep, Daewoo, Eckerd, Family$, Ford, Mazda, Saturn

56 Canino Rd, **E...lodging:** Taj Inn, **W...gas:** Shell, **food:** Luby's, **other:** Nissan, Toyota

55b a Little York Rd, Parker Rd, **E...gas:** Chevron, Exxon, Mobil/diesel, Shamrock, Shell, **food:** Schlotsky's, Whataburger, **lodging:** Olympic Motel, **other:** HOSPITAL, FoodTown, Goodyear, **W...gas:** Chevron/24hr, Shell, **food:** Capt D's, Denny's, Hartz Chicken, Jack-in-the-Box, KFC, LJ Silver, McDonald's, Popeye's, **lodging:** Best Value Inn, Econolodge, Town Inn, **other:** Walgreen

54 Tidwell Rd, **E...gas:** Exxon, **food:** Pancho's Mexican, Pizza Inn, Subway, Taco Cabana, Thomas BBQ, **other:** Eckerd, Jo-Ann Fabrics, Radio Shack

53 Airline Dr, **E...gas:** Chevron, Citgo, Conoco, same as 52

52 Crosstimbers Rd, **E...gas:** Shell, Texaco/diesel, **food:** Burger King, CiCi's, IHOP, James Coney Island, McDonald's, Pancho's Mexican, Pappas BBQ, Taco Bell, Taco Cabana, Wendy's, **other:** Discount Tire, Fiesta Foods, Firestone, mall, **W...gas:** Chevron/diesel, Citgo, **food:** Little Mexico Rest., Whataburger/24hr, **lodging:** Howard Johnson, Luxury Inn, Palace Inn, Super 8, **other:** Coach USA RV Ctr, U-Haul

Houston

51 I-610, no facilities

50b Calvacade St, Link Rd, **E...gas:** Exxon/Taco Bell, Texaco, **W...lodging:** Astro Inn

a Patton St, **E...gas:** Chevron/24hr, Pilot/Wendy's/diesel/24hr/@, **lodging:** Classic Inn, Luxury Inn, **W...gas:** Texaco/diesel/24hr

49b N Main St, Houston Ave, **E...food:** Casa Grande Mexican, **W...gas:** Exxon/diesel, **food:** KFC, McDonald's, Whataburger/24hr, **other:** Auto Supply

48b a I-10, E to Beaumont, W to San Antonio

47d Dallas St, Pierce St(from sb), **E...other:** HOSPITAL

Interstate 45

N ↕ S

c McKinney St(from sb, exits left)
b Houston Ave, Memorial Dr, downtown, **W...lodging:** Best Western
a Allen Pkwy(exits left from sb)
46b a US 59, N to Cleveland, S to Victoria, **E...gas:** Chevron, **food:** BBQ, **W...gas:** Exxon, **food:** McDonald's, Taco Bell, **other:** BMW
45b a South St, Scott St, Houston, **E...gas:** Conoco, Texaco/ Subway, **other:** Firestone
44 Cullen Blvd, Houston, **E...gas:** Shamrock/gas, **food:** Burger King, McDonald's, Taco Bell, **W...food:** Pizza Hut, **other:** bank, to U of Houston
43b Telephone Rd, Houston, **E...food:** Luby's, **lodging:** Day's Inn
a Tellepsen St, **E...food:** Luby's, **lodging:** Day's Inn, **W...other:** U of Houston
41b US 90A, Broad St, S Wayside Dr, **E...lodging:** Day's Inn, Red Carpet Inn, **W...gas:** Chevron, Exxon, **food:** Jack-in-the-Box, McDonald's, Monterrey Mexican, **other:** K-Mart
a Woodridge Dr, **E...gas:** Shell, **food:** Bennigan's, Denny's, McDonald's, Pappa's Seafood House, Schlotsky's, **W...food:** IHOP, Pappas BBQ, Sonic, Subway, Whataburger, Wendy's, **other:** Chevrolet/ Buick, Dillard's, HEB Food/gas, Home Depot, Lowe's Whse, Marshall's, Office Depot, Old Navy, Radio Shack, mall
40c I-610 W
b I-610 E, to Pasadena
a Frontage Rd(from nb), no facilities
39 Park Place Blvd, Broadway Blvd, **E...gas:** Texaco, **food:** Dante Italian, **W...gas:** Shell, Phillips 66, Texaco/Blimpie, **food:** Kelly's Rest., May Moon Café, **other:** Chevrolet, Dodge
38b Howard Dr, Bellfort Dr(from sb), **E...gas:** Texaco, **food:** Blue Oyster Seafood, Dante Italian, **W...gas:** Citgo, **food:** Chilo's Seafood, **lodging:** Palace Inn, Passport Inn, **other:** HEB Food/gas, PepBoys
38 TX 3, Monroe Rd, **E...gas:** Chevron, Exxon, Shell, **food:** DQ, Fat Maria's Mexican, Jack-in-the-Box, Lonesome Steer Steaks, Wendy's, **other:** NTB, U-Haul, **W...gas:** Chevron/diesel, Texaco/diesel, **food:** Luby's, Luther's BBQ, **lodging:** Best Western, Quality Inn, Smile Inn, **other:** Firestone, Radio Shack, Suzuki, U-Haul
36 College Ave, Airport Blvd, **E...gas:** Shamrock, Shell, **food:** DQ, Waffle House, **lodging:** Fairfield Inn, Rodeway Inn, **other:** RV Ctr, **W...gas:** Exxon, Texaco, **food:** Church's Chicken, Denny's, Lucky Dragon Chinese, Taco Cabana, **lodging:** AmeriSuites, Courtyard, Drury Inn, La Quinta, Marriott/Damon's, Red Roof Inn, Super 8, Travel Inn, **other:** Discount Tire
35 Edgebrook Dr, **E...gas:** Chevron, Exxon, RaceTrac, **food:** Burger King, Aranda's Bakery, Grandy's, Jack-in-the-Box, Popeye's, Subway, Taco Bell, Waffle House, **lodging:** Airport Inn, **other:** Eckerd, Fiesta Foods, Firestone, Office Depot, Thompson RV Ctr, Walgreen, **W...gas:** Exxon, Shell, Circle K, **food:** James Coney Island, KFC, LJ Silver, McDonald's, Pizza Hut, Whataburger

League City

34 S Shaver Rd, **E...gas:** Conoco, **food:** McDonald's, **other:** Acura, Honda, Kia, Pontiac/GMC, Saturn, Toyota, Vaughn's RV Ctr, **W...gas:** Chevron/24hr, Exxon, Mobil, **food:** Arby's, Burger King, Pancho's Mexican, Wendy's, **other:** Best Buy, Circuit City, $Tree, Foley's, Holiday World RV Ctr, Jo-Ann Fabrics, K-Mart, Marshall's, Nissan, NTB, OfficeMax, Target
33 Fuqua St, **E...gas:** Shamrock, **food:** Chili's, Fuddrucker's, Luby's, Mexico Lindo, Olive Garden, TGIFriday, **lodging:** Sun Suites, **other:** Chrysler/Plymouth/Jeep, Dodge, Ford, Honda, Hyundai, Isuzu, Lincoln/Mercury, **W...food:** Barco's Mexican, Bennigan's, Blackeyed Pea, CiCi's, Golden Corral, Gringo's Mexican, IHOP, Joe's Crabshack, Steak&Ale, Subway, Taco Cabana, Taco Bell, TX Cattle Steaks, Whataburger, **other:** Firestone, Home Depot, JC Penney, Kroger, Old Navy, Radio Shack, Ross, Sam's Club, Subaru, Tire Station, Wal-Mart, mall
32 Sam Houston Tollway
31 FM 2553, Scarsdale Blvd, **W...gas:** Exxon, Shell, **food:** DQ, McDonald's, **other:** Chevrolet, Mitsubishi
30 FM 1959, Ellington Field, Dixie Farm Rd, **E...gas:** Conoco/diesel, Shell/diesel, **other:** HOSPITAL, Dodge, **W...gas:** Texaco/diesel, **food:** McDonald's, Popeye's, **other:** VW
29 FM 2351, Clear Lake City Blvd, Friendswood, to Clear Lake RA
27 El Dorado Blvd, **E...food:** DQ, **other:** mall, **W...food:** Texas Roadhouse, Whataburger, **other:** Circuit City, Kohl's, Lexus, Mervyn's, Radio Shack, Sam's Club/gas, Wal-Mart SuperCtr/24hr
26 Bay Area Blvd, **E...food:** Red Lobster, **other:** HOSPITAL, Barnes&Noble, CompUSA, Lowe's Whse, Michael's, Old Navy, to Houston Space Ctr, **W...gas:** Shell, **food:** Baskin-Robbins, Bennigan's, Denny's/24hr, McDonald's, Olive Garden, On-the-Border, Steak&Ale, **lodging:** Best Western, Suburban Inn, **other:** Dillard's, Macy's, Sears/auto, Target, Outlet Mall/famous brands, mall, U of Houston
25 FM 528, NASA rd 1, **E...gas:** Conoco, Shamrock, Texaco, **food:** Chili's, CiCi's, IHOP, Macaroni Grill, Mason Jar Grill, Pappasito's Cantina, Saltgrass Steaks, Tony Roma's, Waffle House, **lodging:** Motel 6, **other:** HOSPITAL, Audi, Best Buy, Home Depot, Honda, K-Mart, Mazda, Office Depot, SteinMart, Volvo, **W...food:** Cinco de Mayo Mexican, China Square, DQ, Hooters, Hot Wok Chinese, Luther's BBQ, Subway, **other:** Radio Shack, Wal-Mart/auto
23 FM 518, League City, **E...gas:** RaceTrac, Texaco/diesel, **food:** Applebee's, Burger King, Grand Buffet, Jack-in-the-Box, KFC, Little Caesar's, Pancho's Mexican, Sonic, Subway, **other:** Academy Sports, BMW, Eckerd, JiffyLube, Kroger, Walgreen, **W...gas:** Chevron, Exxon/ 24hr, **food:** Cracker Barrel, Hartz Chicken, McDonald's, Taco Bell, Waffle House, Wendy's, **lodging:** Super 8, **other:** Discount Tire, U-Haul
22 Calder Dr, Brittany Bay Blvd, **E...other:** Toyota, camping
20 FM 646, Santa Fe, Bacliff, **W...gas:** Shamrock/diesel
19 FM 517, Dickinson Rd, Hughes Rd, **E...gas:** Shell, Shamrock, **food:** Jack-in-the-Box, Monterey Mexican,

Interstate 45

N

S

Pizza Inn, **other:** Buick/Pontiac/GMC/Subaru, Due's Camping Ctr, Eckerd, Family$, Food King, Radio Shack, **W...gas:** Exxon, Texaco/diesel, Circle K, **food:** Burger King, KFC, McDonald's, Pizza Hut, Subway, Taco Bell, Wendy's, Whataburger/24hr, **other:** Ford, Kroger, Walgreen

17 Holland Rd, **W...**to Gulf Greyhound Park

16 FM 1764 E(from sb), Texas City, **E...other:** HOSPITAL, Demontrond RV Ctr, mall, same as 15

15 FM 2004, FM 1764, Hitchcock, **E...gas:** Shell, **food:** Carino's Italian, Jack-in-the-Box, **lodging:** Fairfield Inn, Hampton Inn, **other:** HOSPITAL, Chevrolet/Toyota/RV Ctr, Dillard's, Foley's, JC Penney, Lowe's Whse, mall, **W...gas:** Mobil/Subway, Shell, Texaco, **food:** Waffle House, Wendy's, Whataburger, **other:** Gulf Greyhound Park, Wal-Mart SuperCtr/24hr

13 Century Blvd, Delany Rd, **E...gas:** Shamrock, **W...lodging:** Ramada Inn, Super 8, **other:** Outlet Mall/famous brands

12 FM 1765, La Marque, **E...gas:** Chevron/24hr, **food:** Domino's, Jack-in-the-Box, Kelley's Rest., Sonic, **lodging:** HiWay Motel, **W...gas:** Mobil/diesel

11 Vauthier Rd, no facilities

10 FM 519, Main St, **E...gas:** Shamrock, **food:** McDonald's, **W...gas:** Texaco/diesel

9 Frontage Rd(from sb), no facilities

8 Frontage Rd(from nb), no facilities

7c Frontage Rd, no facilities

b TX 146, TX 6(exits left from nb), Texas City, **W...gas:** Texaco

a TX 146, TX 3, no facilities

6 Frontage Rd(from sb), no facilities

5 Frontage Rd, no facilities

4 Village of Tiki Island, Frontage Rd, **W...gas:** Conoco/diesel, **other:** public boat ramp

4mm West Galveston Bay

1c TX 275, FM 188(from nb), Port of Galveston, Port Ind Blvd, Teichman Rd, **E...gas:** Chevron, Citgo, Texaco/diesel, **lodging:** Howard Johnson, Motel 6, **other:** Chevrolet, Chrysler/Dodge/Plymouth/Jeep, Ford, Mazda, Mitsubishi, Nissan, Toyota

1b 71st St(from sb), **E...gas:** EZ Mart/gas, same as 1c

Galveston

1a TX 342, 61st St, to W Beach, **E...gas:** EZMart/gas, **food:** Denny's, **other:** Target, **W...gas:** RaceTrac, Texaco, **food:** Burger King, Church's, McDonald's, Taco Bell, **lodging:** Day's Inn, **other:** Big Lots, Chevrolet/Pontiac/Buick/Cadillac, Chrysler/Jeep, Family$, Honda, U-Haul, USPO, **1-2 mi W...gas:** Chevron, Exxon/diesel, Shamrock, Shell, Texaco, **food:** Arby's, Burger King, China Border, Domino's, Golden Wok, Jack-in-the-Box, KFC, LJ Silver, Luby's, Marco's Mexican, Mario's Italian, McDonald's, Papa John's, Pizza Hut, Popeye's, Subway, Taco Cabana, TCBY, Whataburger, **lodging:** Beachcomber Inn, Best Western, Super 8, **other:** Eckerd, Firestone/auto, Hastings Books, K-Mart, Office Depot, O'Reilly Parts, Randall's Food/gas, Walgreen,

I-45 begins/ends on TX 87 in Galveston.

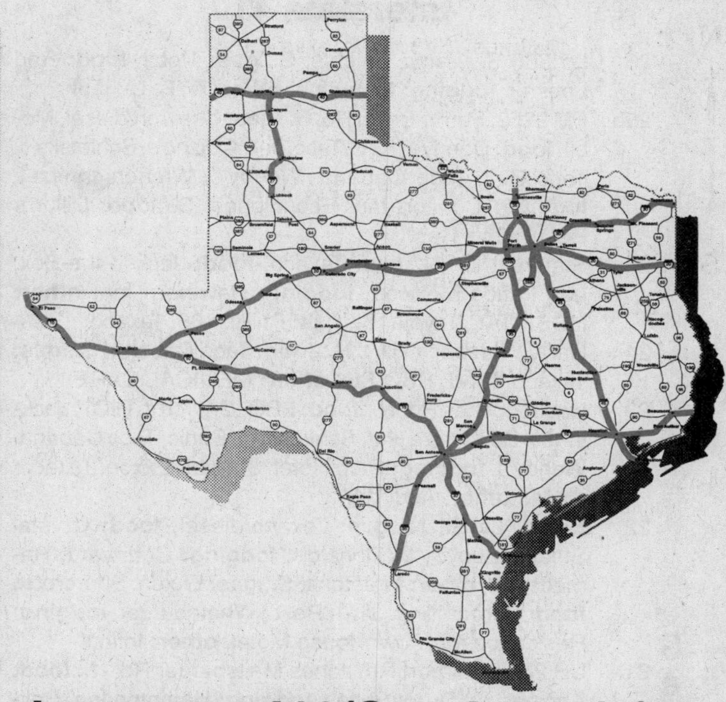

Interstate 410(San Antonio)

Exit # Services

53 I-35, S to Laredo, N to San Antonio

51 FM 2790, Somerset Rd, no facilities

49 TX 16 S, spur 422, **N...gas:** Chevron, **food:** Church's Chicken, **other:** HOSPITAL, to Palo Alto Coll

48 Zarzamora St, no facilities

46 Moursund Blvd, no facilities

44 US 281 S, spur 536, Roosevelt Ave, **N...gas:** Texaco/diesel, **other:** RV camping

43 Espada Rd(from eb), no facilities

42 spur 122, S Presa Rd, to San Antonio Missions Hist Park, **S...gas:** Whiteside/diesel

41 I-37, US 281 N, no facilities

39 spur 117, WW White Rd, no facilities

37 Southcross Blvd, Sinclair Rd, Sulphur Sprs Rd, **N...**HOSPITAL

35 US 87, Rigsby Ave, **E...gas:** Exxon/TacoMaker, Shamrock/diesel, **food:** Denny's, Jack-in-the-Box, McDonald's, Taco Bell, **other:** Radio Shack, Wal-Mart SuperCtr/gas/24hr, **W...gas:** Chevron, **food:** Barnacle Bill's Seafood, BBQ, Luby's, Pizza Hut, Sonic, Subway, Taco Cabana, Whataburger, **lodging:** Day's Inn, **other:** Aamco, Advance Parts

34 FM 1346, E Houston St, **W...gas:** Chevron, Shamrock, **food:** McDonald's, Wendy's, **lodging:** Comfort Inn, Motel 6

33 I-10 E, US 90 E, to Houston, I-10 W, US 90 W, to San Antonio

32 Dietrich Rd(from sb), FM 78(from nb), to Kirby, no facilities

31b Lp 13, WW White Rd, no facilities

a FM 78, Kirby, no facilities

30 Space Center Dr(from nb), **E...gas:** Coastal, Shamrock

I-410 and I-35 S run together 7 mi, **See Texas I-35, exits 162 thru 165.**

27 I-35, N to Austin, S to San Antonio

Interstate 410

San Antonio

26 Lp 368 S, Alamo Heights, **S...gas:** Mobil, **food:** Red Lobster, **lodging:** Drury Inn, **other:** NTB, U-Haul

25b FM 2252, Perrin-Beitel Rd, **N...gas:** Chevron/diesel, Mobil, **food:** Denny's, KFC/Taco Bell, Quizno's, Schlotsky's, Taco Bell, Taco Cabana, Wendy's, Wienerschnitzel, **lodging:** Comfort Inn, Econolodge, **S...food:** Dillon's Rest., Jim's Rest.

25a Starcrest Dr, **N...gas:** Texaco, **food:** Jack-in-the-Box, Los Patios Mexican, **lodging:** Hawthorn Inn, **other:** HOSPITAL, Toyota, **S...gas:** Phillips 66, Texaco

24 Harry Wurzbach Hwy, **N...food:** Taco Cabana, **S...gas:** Texaco, **food:** BBQ Sta, **other:** MEDICAL CARE

23 Nacogdoches Rd, **N...food:** BBQ, Church's, IHOP, Jack-in-the-Box, Pizza Hut, Schlotsky's, Sonic, Taco Cabana, Wendy's, **lodging:** Club Hotel, **S...gas:** Exxon, Texaco/diesel, **other:** Audi/VW

22 Broadway St, **N...gas:** Texaco/diesel, **food:** Crystal Steaks, Luby's, McDonald's, **lodging:** Courtyard, Ramada Inn, **other:** Firestone, **S...gas:** Exxon, Shamrock, **food:** Burger King, Jim's Rest., Whataburger, **lodging:** Residence Inn, TownHouse Motel, **other:** Infiniti

21 US 281 S, Airport Rd, Jones Maltsberger Rd, **N...food:** Applebee's, Drury Suites, **lodging:** Hampton Inn, Holiday Inn Select, PearTree Inn, **S...gas:** Texaco/diesel, **food:** Pappadeaux, Red Lobster, Texas Land&Cattle, **lodging:** Courtyard, Day's Inn, Fairfield Inn, La Quinta, Renaissance Hotel, Staybridge Suites, **other:** Hyundai/Kia, Mitsubishi, Subaru, Wal-Mart/24hr

20 TX 537, **N...food:** Jason's Deli, TGIFriday, **lodging:** DoubleTree Hotel, Hilton, **other:** Barnes&Noble, Best Buy, Chevrolet, Circuit City, Honda, Lincoln/Mercury, Marshall's, Mazda, Ross, **S...food:** Arby's, Bennigan's, El Pollo Loco, Luby's, McDonald's, Taco Cabana, **other:** Dillard's, Dodge, Foley's, Macy's, Mervyn's, Saks 5th, Sears/auto, mall

19b FM 1535, FM 2696, Military Hwy, **N...food:** Gyro/Sub Shop, Souper Salad, **S...gas:** Exxon, **food:** Denny's, Jim's Rest.

19a Honeysuckle Lane, Castle Hills

17b (from wb), **S...food:** DQ, Dunkin Donuts, **other:** Firestone, HEB Foods

17 Vance Jackson Rd, **N...gas:** Mobil, Phillips 66, Shamrock, **food:** Burger King, Jack-in-the-Box, KFC, McDonald's, Steak&Ale, Sonic, Taco Cabana, Whataburger, **lodging:** Marriott, **other:** Aamco, CarQuest, Discount Tire, Target, Tire Sta, transmissions, **S...gas:** Exxon, **food:** Subway, **other:** U-Haul

16b a I-10 E, US 87 S, to San Antonio, I-10 W, to El Paso, US 87 N

15 Lp 345, Fredericksburg Rd, **E...gas:** Texaco, **food:** Church's, Dave&Buster's, Jack-in-the-Box, Jim's Rest., Kettle, Luby's, N China Rest., **lodging:** AmeriSuites, Best Value Inn, **other:** BMW, Target, **W...gas:** Mobil, **lodging:** Holiday Inn, **other:** K-Mart

14 Callaghan Rd, Babcock Ln, **E...gas:** Chevron, Exxon, Shamrock, **food:** Marie Callender's, **lodging:** Comfort Inn, Hampton Inn, Travelodge Suites, **other:** GMC/Pontiac, **W...gas:** Conoco, **food:** Burger King, Chili's, ChopSticks Chinese, DingHow Chinese, El Chico, Golden Corral, HomeTown Buffet, Joe's Crabshack, Landry's Seafood, Pizza Hut, Quizno's, Red Lobster, Wendy's, Whataburger, **other:** HOSPITAL, Home Depot, Sam's Club, Wal-Mart SuperCtr/24hr

13b Rolling Ridge Dr, **W...food:** Jack-in-the Box, KFC, Las Palapas Mexican, same as 14

13a TX 16 N, Bandera Rd, Evers Rd, Leon Valley, **E...food:** Outback Steaks, **other:** Albertson's, Audi, Office Depot, OfficeMax, Old Navy, Saturn, Target, Toyota, U-Haul, **W...gas:** Exxon, Shamrock, Texaco, **food:** Applebee's, BBQ, IHOP, Jack-in-the-Box, Jim's Rest., KFC, Luby's, McDonald's, Olive Garden, Schlotsky's, Taco Cabana, **lodging:** Super 8, **other:** Aamco, Best Buy, Chevrolet, Circuit City, Dillard's, Eckerd, Honda, Marshall's, NTB

11 Ingram Rd, **E...gas:** Texaco/diesel, **food:** Bennigan's, Calloway's Rest., Fazoli's, Texas Roadhouse, **lodging:** Day's Inn, Econolodge, **other:** Aamco, BrakeCheck, **W...food:** Applebee's, Burger King, Denny's, Jack-in-the-Box, Jason's Deli, Olive Garden, Subway, Whataburger, **lodging:** Super 8, **other:** Barnes&Noble, Best Buy, Dillard's, $Tree, Foley's, JC Penney, Mervyn's, Michael's, Ross, Sears/auto, mall

10 FM 3487, Culebra Rd, **E...food:** Barnacle Bill's Seafood, BBQ, Denny's, McDonald's, Wendy's, **lodging:** Holiday Inn Express, La Quinta, Red Roof Inn, **other:** Chrysler/Plymouth/Dodge/Jeep, Mazda/Nissan/Daewoo, to St Mary's U, **W...gas:** Exxon, Phillips 66, RaceTrac, **food:** Blimpie, ChuckeCheese, Fuddrucker's, **lodging:** Best Western, InTown Inn, **other:** Firestone/auto, Ford, Mitsubishi

9b a TX 151, **W...gas:** Chili's, **lodging:** Quality Inn, **other:** Home Depot, Lowe's Whse, Wal-Mart SuperCtr/gas/24hr, to Sea World

7 (8 from sb)Marbach Dr, **E...gas:** Exxon, **food:** McDonald's, **other:** PepBoys, **W...gas:** Chevron/diesel, Texaco/dieel, **food:** Acadiena Café, Burger King, Golden Wok, Jack-in-the-Box, Jim's Rest., KFC, LJ Silver, Luby's, McDonald's, Mr Gatti's, Pancho's Mexican, Peter Piper Pizza, Pizza Hut, Red Lobster, Sonic, Subway, Taco Bell, Taco Cabana, Whataburger/24hr, **lodging:** Motel 6, Super 8, **other:** Advance Parts, Discount Tire, $General, $Tree, Eckerd, Firestone/auto, HEB Food, K-Mart, Target

6 US 90, to Lackland AFB, **E...lodging:** Country Inn Motel, **other:** Explore USA RV Ctr, **W...gas:** Shamrock, Texaco/diesel, **food:** Andrea's Mexican

4 Valley Hi Dr, San Antonio, to Del Rio, **E...gas:** Mobil, Phillips 66/diesel, Shamrock, **food:** Church's Chicken, McDonald's, Pizza Hut, Sonic, **other:** AutoZone, HEB Food/gas, Radio Shack, **W...gas:** Texaco/diesel, **other:** to Lackland AFB

3b a Ray Ellison Dr, Medina Base, **W...gas:** Shamrock

2 FM 2536, Old Pearsall Rd, **E...gas:** Texaco/diesel, **food:** BBQ, McDonald's, Sonic

1 Frontage Rd, no facilities

Interstate 610(Houston)

Houston

Exit #	Services
38c a	TX 288 N, downtown, access to zoo
37	Scott St, **N...gas:** Texaco
36	FM 865, Cullen Blvd, **S...gas:** Chevron/McDonald's, Mobil, Shamrock, **lodging:** Crown Inn, Cullen Inn
35	Calais Rd, Crestmont St, MLK Blvd, **N...gas:** Exxon, **food:** Burger King
34	S Wayside Dr, Long Dr, **N...gas:** Exxon, Texaco, **food:** Wendy's, **other:** Fiesta Foods, **S...gas:** Coastal/diesel, Conoco
33	Woodridge Dr, Telephone Rd, **N...gas:** Texaco/diesel, **food:** IHOP, McDonald's, Papa John's, Wendy's, **S...gas:** Shell, **food:** Burger King, KFC, Piccadilly's Cafeteria, Spanky's Pizza, Whataburger, **other:** Dodge, Ford, mall
32b a	I-45, S to Galveston, N to Houston, to airport
31	Broadway Blvd, **N...gas:** Conoco, **S...gas:** Texaco
30c b	TX 225, to Pasadena, San Jacinto Mon, no facilities
29	Port of Houston Main Entrance
28	Clinton Dr, no facilities
27	Turning Basin Dr, industrial area
26b	Market St, no facilities
a	I-10 E, to Beaumont, I-10 W, to downtown
24b	Wallisville Rd, **E...gas:** Mobil/diesel, Texaco/diesel, **food:** McDonald's
24	US 90 E, **E...gas:** Chevron, Phillips 66, **food:** Luby's, Wendy's, **W...gas:** Texaco
23b	N Wayside, **E...gas:** Exxon
23a	Kirkpatrick Blvd, no facilities
22	Homestead Rd, Kelley St, **N...gas:** Texaco/diesel, **food:** Whataburger
21	**Lockwood Dr, N...gas: Chevron/McDonald's, Texaco, food: Burger King, other: Popeye's, Family$, S...gas: Conoco, food: CJ's Rest., other: HOSPITAL**
20	US 59, to downtown
19	Hardy Toll Rd, no facilities
18	Irvington Blvd, Fulton St, **N...gas:** Chevron, **S...gas:** Texaco/diesel, **food:** Jack-in-the-Box
17	I-45, N to Dallas, S to Houston
16	Yale St, N Main St, Shamrock, **N...gas:** Exxon, **S...gas:** Mobil, Shell, **food:** Burger King, Church's Chicken, **lodging:** Western Inn
15	TX 261, N Shepherd Dr, **N...food:** Sonic, Taco Cabana, **S...gas:** Chevron, Shell, Texaco/diesel, **food:** Wendy's, Whataburger, **other:** Home Depot, PepBoys
14	Ella Blvd, **N...gas:** Exxon, Shell/24hr, Texaco, **food:** Blimpie, Burger King, Jack-in-the-Box, KFC, LJ Silver, McDonald's, Popeye's, Taco Bell, **S...gas:** Shell, **food:** BBQ, **other:** HOSPITAL, Lowe's Whse
13c	TC Jester Blvd, **N...gas:** Chevron, Texaco, **food:** Atchafalaya Kitchen, Denny's, Golden Gate Chinese, **lodging:** Courtyard, SpringHill Suites, **S...gas:** Phillips 66
13b a	US 290, no facilities
12	W 18th St, **N...food:** CiCi's, **lodging:** Sheraton, **other:** Foley's, JC Penney, OfficeMax, mall, **S...food:** Whataburger
11	I-10, W to San Antonio, E to downtown Houston

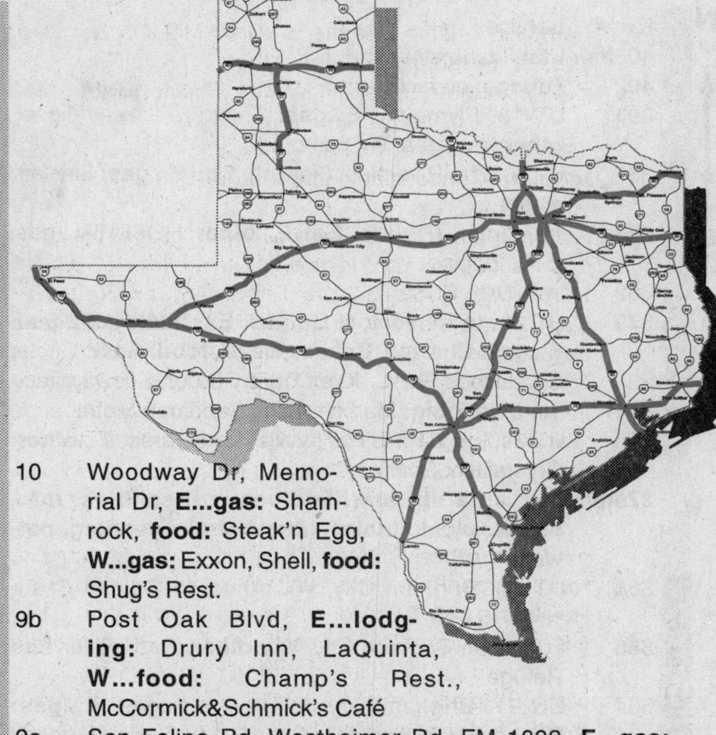

Houston

Exit #	Services
10	Woodway Dr, Memorial Dr, **E...gas:** Shamrock, **food:** Steak'n Egg, **W...gas:** Exxon, Shell, **food:** Shug's Rest.
9b	Post Oak Blvd, **E...lodging:** Drury Inn, LaQuinta, **W...food:** Champ's Rest., McCormick&Schmick's Café
9a	San Felipe Rd, Westheimer Rd, FM 1093, **E...gas:** Exxon/diesel, Texaco, **lodging:** Courtyard, Hampton Inn, **other:** Circuit City, NTB, Target, **W...gas:** Shell, **food:** Luke's Burgers, **lodging:** Crowne Plaza Hotel, HomeStead Village Studios, Marriott, Sheraton, **other:** Best Buy, Dillard's, Nieman-Marcus
8	US 59, Richmond Ave, no facilities
7	Bissonet St, Fournace Place, **E...other:** Home Depot, **W...gas:** Texaco/diesel/repair
6	Bellaire Blvd, no facilities
5b	Evergreen St, no facilities
5a	Beechnut St, **E...gas:** Chevron, **food:** Boston Mkt, IHOP, McDonald's, Outback Steaks, **other:** bank, **W...gas:** Shell, **food:** Escalante Mexican Grill, James Coney Island, Saltgrass Steaks, Smoothie King, **other:** Borders Books, Marshall's, mall
4a	Brasswood, S Post Oak Rd, **E...gas:** Exxon, **lodging:** Day's Inn
3	Stella Link Rd, **N...gas:** Chevron, **food:** Jack-in-the-Box, **other:** DiscountTire, Food City, Radio Shack, **S...gas:** Exxon, Phillips 66, Texaco
2	US 90A, **N...gas:** Chevron, Conoco, Shamrock, **food:** Arby's, Bennigan's, Burger King, Church's, Denny's/24hr, KFC, McDonald's, Taco Bell, Wendy's, **lodging:** Howard Johnson, Villa Motel, **other:** Ford, Honda, **S...gas:** Chevron, **food:** Whataburger/24hr, **lodging:** La Quinta, Motel 6, Super 8, **other:** Firestone, Nissan, Toyota, to Buffalo Speedway
1c	Kirby Dr(from eb), **N...lodging:** Radisson, Shoney's Inn/rest., **S...food:** Joe's Crabshack, Papadeaux Seafood, Pappasito's Cantina, **other:** Cavender's Boots, Chevrolet, NTB, Pontiac/GMC, Toyota
1b a	FM 521, Almeda St, Fannin St, **N...gas:** Chevron, Conoco, **other:** Astro Arena, **S...gas:** Texaco, **food:** McDonald's, **other:** Aamco, Sam's Club, to Six Flags

UTAH

Interstate 15

N ↕ S

Exit #	Services
403mm	Utah/Idaho state line
402	Portage, no facilities
394	UT 13, Plymouth, **E...gas:** Chevron/Subway/diesel, **other:** rec area, RV camping
387	UT 30 E, to Riverside, Fielding, **1 mi E...gas:** Sinclair/diesel
383	Tremonton, Garland, **2 mi E...other:** HOSPITAL, gas, food, lodging
382	I-84 W, to Boise
379	UT 13, to Tremonton, **E...gas:** Exxon/Arby's, **2-3 mi E...gas:** Chevron, Conoco/diesel, **food:** Arctic Circle, Crossroads Rest., JC's Country Diner, Subway, Taco Time, **lodging:** Marble Motel, Sandman Motel
375	UT 240, to UT 13, Honeyville, to rec area, **E...other:** Crystal Hot Springs Camping
370mm	**rest area sb, full(handicapped)facilities, info, phone, picnic tables, litter barrels, vending, petwalk**

Brigham City

Exit #	Services
368	UT 13, Brigham City, **W...other:** to Golden Spike NHS
366	Forest St, Brigham City, **W...other:** Bear River Bird Refuge
364	US 91, Brigham City, to US 89, Logan, **E...gas:** Chevron/Blimpie/24hr, Citgo/7-11, Flying J/diesel/rest./24hr, Sinclair, **food:** Arby's, Aspen Grill, Beto's Mexican, Burger King, Hunan Chinese, J&D's Rest., KFC/Taco Bell, Little Caesar's, McDonald's, Pizza Hut, Pizza Press, Sonic, Subway, Taco Time, Wendy's, **lodging:** Bushnell Motel, Crystal Inn, Galaxie Motel, Howard Johnson Express, **other:** HOSPITAL, AutoZone, Checker Parts, Chevrolet/Pontiac/Buick/Cadillac, Chrysler/Dodge/Jeep, Radio Shack, ShopKO, Wal-Mart SuperCtr/gas/24hr, RV camping, to Yellowstone NP via US 89
363mm	**rest area nb, full(handicapped)facilities, phone, picnic tables, litter barrels, vending, petwalk**
361	Port of Entry both lanes
360	UT 315, to Willard, Perry, **E...gas:** Flying J/Country Mkt/diesel/LP, **other:** KOA(2mi)
354	UT 126, to US 89, Willard Bay, to Utah's Fruit Way, no facilities
352	UT 134, Farr West, N Ogden, **E...gas:** Citgo/7-11, Maverik, Phillips 66/Wendy's/diesel, **food:** Arby's, Domino's, McDonald's, Melino's Mexican, Subway, **W...gas:** Conoco/diesel
349	to Harrisville, Defense Depot, **W...gas:** Shell/diesel, diesel repair

Ogden

Exit #	Services
347	UT 39, 12th St, Ogden, **E...gas:** Phillips 66, Shell/diesel, **lodging:** Best Western/rest., **1-2 mi E...gas:** Chevron, **food:** Denny's, KFC, McDonald's, Sizzler, Village Inn Rest., **lodging:** Motel 6, **other:** to Ogden Canyon RA, **W...gas:** Pilot/DQ/Subway/Taco Bell/diesel/24hr/@, **lodging:** Western Inn
346	UT 104, 21st St, Ogden, **E...gas:** Chevron/Arby's/diesel, Flying J/Conoco/diesel/LP/24hr, Phillips 66/diesel, **food:** Cactus Red's Rest., Outlaw Rest., **lodging:** Big Z Motel/rest., Comfort Suites, Holiday Inn Express, Marriott, **other:** RV Repair, **W...gas:** Shell/diesel/café, **lodging:** Super 8/café/diesel, **other:** Century RV Park (from nb), UT 53, Ogden, 24th St, **E...gas:** Sinclair/diesel
345	
344b a	UT 79 W, 31st St, Ogden, **1-2 mi E on Wall St...gas:** Citgo/7-11, **food:** Arby's, Golden Corral, JJ North's Buffet, Sizzler, **lodging:** Day's Inn, Radisson, **other:** HOSPITAL, Dillard's, Chevrolet, Ford/Lincoln/Mercury, RV Ctr, mall, to Weber St U, **W...**airport
343	I-84 E(from sb), to Cheyenne, Wyo, no facilities
342	UT 26(from nb), to I-84 E, Riverdale Rd, **E...gas:** Conoco/diesel, Sinclair, **food:** Applebee's, Boston Mkt, Carl's Jr, Chili's, La Salsa Mexican, McDonald's, **lodging:** Red Roof Inn, **other:** Chrysler/Plymouth/Jeep, Circuit City, Harley-Davidson, Home Depot, Honda/Nissan, Isuzu, Lincoln/Mercury/Toyota/Kia, Mazda, Mitsubishi, Office-Max, Pontiac/Buick/GMC, Saturn, Target, Toyota, Wal-Mart SuperCtr/24hr, Wilderness RV

Roy

Exit #	Services
341	UT 97, Roy, Sunset, **E...other:** Air Force Museum, **W...gas:** Citgo/7-11, Exxon/diesel, Phillips 66, Sinclair, Texaco, **food:** Arby's, Arctic Circle, Blimpie, Burger King, Central Park, DQ, Denny's, KFC, McDonald's, Pizza Hut, Ponderosa, Sonic, Subway, Taco Bell, Village Inn Rest., Wendy's, **lodging:** Quality Inn, Motel 6, **other:** Albertson's, AutoZone, BrakeWorks, Checker Parts, Citte RV Ctr, Early Tires, Goodyear, Discount Tire, Radio Shack, RiteAid, Smith's/gas, transmissions, same as 342
338	UT 103, Clearfield, **E...**Hill AFB, **W...gas:** Chevron, Conoco, Citgo/7-11, PetroMart, Texaco, Circle K, **food:** Arby's, Carl's Jr, Central Park, KFC, McDonald's, Skipper's, Subway, Taco Bell, Winger's, **lodging:** Alana Motel, Crystal Cottage Inn, Super 8, **other:** Big O Tire, Sierra RV, same as 341
336	UT 193, Clearfield, to Hill AFB, **E...gas:** Maverik, Tesoro/diesel, **W...gas:** Chevron
335	UT 108, Syracuse, **E...gas:** Chevron, Phillips 66/diesel, Circle K, **food:** Applebee's, Cracker Barrel, Famous Dave's, Golden Corral, JB's, Marie Callender's, Outback Steaks, Quizno's, Red Robin, SF Pizza, TimberLodge Steaks, **lodging:** Courtyard, Fairfield Inn, Hampton Inn, Holiday Inn Express, La Quinta, TownePlace Suites, **other:** Barnes&Noble, Lowe's Whse, Office Depot, Old Navy, Target, **W...gas:** Citgo/7-11, Conoco, **other:** HOSPITAL, Arby's, McDonald's, RV Ctr

Layton

Exit #	Services
334	UT 232, UT 126, Layton, **E...gas:** Phillips 66, Texaco, **food:** Denny's, Garcia's, McDonald's, Olive Garden, Red Lobster, Sizzler, Tony Roma, Training Table Rest., Wendy's, **lodging:** Comfort Inn, **other:** JC Penney, Mervyn's, mall, to Hill AFB S Gate, **W...gas:** Flying J, **food:** Blimpie, Burger King, China Buffet, Fuddrucker's, IHOP, KFC, LoneStar Steaks, McGrath's FishHouse, Taco Bell, **other:** Batteries+, Chevrolet, Dodge, NTB, OfficeMax, Plymouth/Jeep, Pontiac/Cadillac/GMC, Ream's Foods, Sam's Club, ShopKO, Staples, Wal-Mart SuperCtr/24hr
332	to UT 126(from nb), Layton, **E...food:** Little Orient Chinese, **other:** repair, **W...gas:** Texaco, **other:** Jensen's RV
331	UT 273, Kaysville, **E...gas:** Chevron/McDonald's, Citgo/7-11, Phillips 66/diesel, Sinclair, **food:** Cutler's Sandwiches,

Interstate 15

N ↕ S

DQ, Joanie's Rest., KFC, Subway, Taco Time, Wendy's, Far **lodging:** West Motel, **other:** Albertson's, Checker Parts, **W...other:** 1st Choice Cars, Kia, Jensen's RV

329mm parking area both lanes

327 UT 225, Lagoon Dr, Farmington, **E...food:** Subway, **other:** amusement park, camping

326 US 89 N, UT 225(from nb), **1 mi E...gas:** Maverik/gas, **food:** Arby's, Aunt Pam's, Burger King, Little Caesar's, **other:** Smith's Foods, Goodyear/auto, RV Park, to I-84

325 UT 227(from nb), Lagoon Dr, to Farmington, **E...food:** Subway, **other:** Lagoon Funpark/RV Park

322 Centerville, **E...gas:** Chevron, Phillips 66/diesel, **food:** Arby's, Arctic Circle, Burger King, Carl's Jr, Dairy Queen, Del Taco, IHOP, Jake's Shakes, LoneStar Steaks, McDonald's, Subway, Taco Bell, TacoMaker, Wendy's, **other:** Albertson's, Home Depot, LandRover, Radio Shack, Schwab Tire, Target/foods, **W...other:** RV Ctr

321 US 89 S(exits left from sb), UT 131, 500W, S Bountiful, **E...gas:** Chevron/24hr, Exxon/diesel, Phillips 66/diesel, Tesoro, **food:** Alicia's Rest., **lodging:** Country Inn Suites, **other:** Goodyear

320 UT 68, 500 S, W Bountiful, Woods Cross, **E...gas:** Exxon, Tesoro/diesel, **food:** Blimpie, Burger King, Carl's Jr, China Gourmet, Christopher's Steaks, ChuckaRama, Dee's Rest., HogiYogi, KFC, McDonald's, Papa Murphy's, Pizza Hut, SF Pizza, Sizzler, Subway, SuCasa Mexican, Taco Bell, Winger's, **lodging:** Country Inn Suites, **other:** HOSPITAL, Aamco, Albertson's, AllA$, AutoZone, Barnes&Noble, Checker Parts, Early's Tire, Firestone/auto, GNC, OfficeMax, Radio Shack, Rite Aid, ShopKO, Walgreen, **W...gas:** Chevron/diesel, Phillips 66/A&W/diesel, **lodging:** InTown Suites

318 26th S, N Salt Lake, **E...gas:** Chevron, Sinclair, Texaco, **food:** Apollo Burger, Arby's, Burger King, La Frontera Mexican, KFC, McDonald's, Peter Piper Pizza, Pizza Hut, Skipper's, Subway, Village Inn, Wendy's, **lodging:** Best Western, Comfort Inn, **other:** Chevrolet/Pontiac/Buick/Kia, Diahatsu, Ford/Lincoln/Mercury, Honda, Mazda, Nissan, Smith's Foods, Toyota, **W...gas:** Conoco, Denny's, Lorena's Mexican, Hampton Inn, Motel 6, Goodyear

317 Center St, Cudahy Lane(from sb), N Salt Lake, **E...**gas

316 I-215 W(from sb), to airport, no facilities

315 US 89 S, to Beck St, N Salt Lake, no facilities

314 Redwood Rd, Warm Springs Rd, no facilities

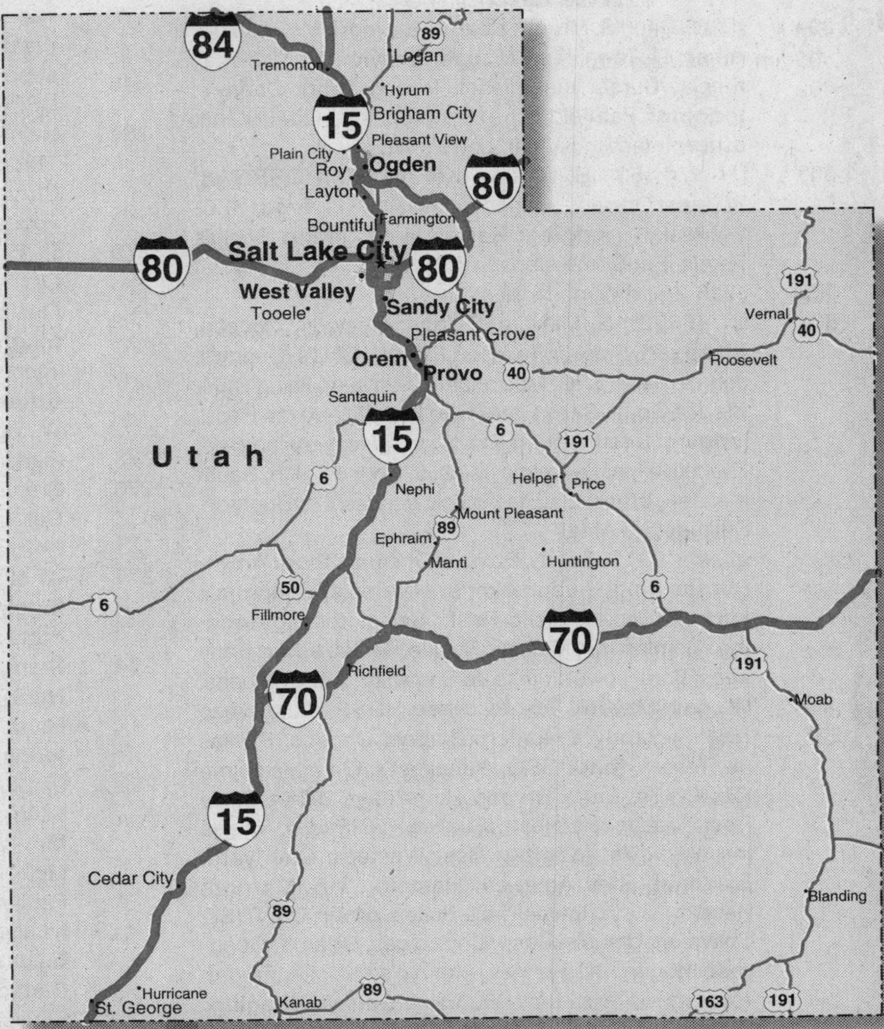

Salt Lake

313 9th St W, 7-11, Self's conv/rest., Tia Maria's Mexican, Regal Inn

312 6th St N, **E...other:** HOSPITAL, LDS Temple, downtown, to UT State FairPark

311 I-80 W, to Reno, airport, no facilities

310 6th S, SLC City Ctr, info, **1 mi E...gas:** Chevron, Phillips 66/diesel, Circle K, **food:** Burger King, Dairy Queen, Denny's, McDonald's, Wendy's, **lodging:** Embassy Suites, Hampton Inn, Little America, Motel 6, Quality Inn, Ramada Inn, Residence Inn, Super 8, **other:** Ford, Toyota, to Temple Square, LDS Church Offices

309b a 9th S, 13th S, SLC, downtown, **E...gas:** Texaco, **W...gas:** to Flying J/Conoco/diesel/LP/rest./24hr, **food:** Wendy's, **other:** Blue Beacon, Chevrolet, Goodyear, Mitsubishi

308 UT 201, 21st St S, 13th St S, 9th St S(from nb), **E...gas:** Chevron, Phillips 66, **food:** Atlantis Burgers, Carl's Jr, McDonald's, **other:** CompUSA, Costco/gas, Home Depot, Office Depot, U-Haul, same as 309

307 I-80 E, to Denver, Cheyenne, no facilities

306 UT 171, 33rd S, S Salt Lake, **E...gas:** Citgo/7-11, Phillips 66, **food:** Apollo Diner, Burger King, McDonald's, Taco Bell, **lodging:** Bonneville Inn, Day's Inn, Roadrunner Motel, **W...gas:** Maverik/gas, **other:** Sam's Club, GMC

UTAH

Interstate 15

N ↕ S

304 UT 266, 45th S, Murray, Kearns, **E...food:** McDonald's, **other:** UpTown Tire, **W...gas:** Chevron, Shell/diesel, Sinclair/Burger King/diesel, Texaco, **food:** Denny's, **lodging:** Fairfield Inn, Hampton Inn, Quality Inn, **other:** InterMtn RV Ctr, Lowe's Whse

303 UT 173, 53rd S, Murray, Kearns, **E...**HOSPITAL, **W...gas:** Chevron, Conoco, Sinclair, 7-11, **food:** KFC, Schlotsky's, **lodging:** Reston Hotel, **other:** Smith's Foods, FunDome, Jenson's RV Ctr

302b a I-215 E and W, no facilities

301 UT 48, 72nd S, Midvale, **E...gas:** Chevron, Conoco, Phillips 66, Sinclair, Texaco/LP, **food:** Chili's, Denny's, John's Place, KFC, McDonald's, Midvale Mining Café, Sizzler, South Seas Café, Taco Bell, Village Inn Rest., **lodging:** Best Western, Day's Inn, Discovery Inn/café, Executive Inn, La Quinta, Motel 6, Rodeway Inn, Sandman Inn, **other:** Cadillac/Buick, carwash, to Brighton, Solitude Ski Areas

Sandy

298 UT 209, 90th S, Sandy, **E...gas:** Chevron, **food:** Arby's, Burger King, Fuddrucker's, Hardee's, Johanna's Kitchen, Sconecutter's Rest., Sweet Tomato, **lodging:** Comfort Inn, Majestic Rockies Motel, **other:** Early Tires, Ford, Lowe's Whse, to Snowbird, Alta Ski Areas, **W...gas:** Maverik, Tesoro, **other:** HOSPITAL, Aamco

297 106th S, Sandy, S Jordan, **E...gas:** Conoco, Phillips 66, Tesoro, **food:** BBQ, Bennigan's, Carver's Prime Rib, Chili's, Eat a Burger, HomeTown Buffet, Jim's Rest., Johanna's Rest., Subway, TGIFriday, Village Inn, Wendy's, **lodging:** Best Western, Courtyard, Extended Stay America, Hampton Inn, Marriott, Residence Inn, TownePlace Suites, **other:** DENTIST, Chevrolet, Chrysler/Jeep, Costco/gas, Dillard's, Goodyear, Honda, JC Penney, Mervyn's, Nissan, Target, Toyota, Wal-Mart, mall, **W...food:** Denny's, **lodging:** Country Inn Suites, Sleep Inn, Super 8, **other:** Buick/GMC/Pontiac

Draper

294 UT 71, Draper, Riverton, **E...gas:** Flying J/diesel, Holiday/diesel, **food:** Arctic Circle, Café Rio Mexican, Carl's Jr, Fazoli's, Guadalahonky's Mexican, Jamba Juice, KFC, McDonald's, Panda Express, Pizza Hut, Quizno's, Ruby Tuesday, Sonic, Teriyaki Express, Wendy's, Wienerschnitzel, Wingers Diner, **lodging:** Fairfield Inn, Holiday Inn Express, Ramada Ltd, **other:** Camping World RV Supplies(1mi), Early Tire, Goodyear/auto, Greenbax, Mountain Shadows Camping, Smith's Foods, FSA Outlets/famous brands

291 UT 140, Bluffdale, **E...other:** Hyundai, Isuzu, Camping World RV Supplies(2mi), **W...gas:** Citgo/7-11, Common Sense/gas, **other:** st prison

287 UT 92, to Alpine, Highland, **E...**to Timpanogas Cave, **W...gas:** Phillips 66/diesel, **food:** Iceberg Café, **other:** Lone Peak RV Ctr, Thanksgiving Point/café

285 US 89 S, 12th W, to UT 73, Lehi, **W...gas:** Chevron/diesel

282 UT 73, to Lehi, **E...gas:** Conoco/diesel, **food:** 1 Man Band Diner, **lodging:** Motel 6, **W...gas:** Chevron/diesel/24hr, Phillips 66/Wendy's/24hr, **food:** Arctic Circle, Dutch Oven Rest., KFC/Pizza Hut, McDonald's, Papa Murphy's, Subway, Wingers Diner, **lodging:** Best Western, Comfort Inn, Day's Inn, Super 8, **other:** Albertson's, Big O Tire, Checker Parts, GNC, Uncle Dave's, USPO, museum

281 Main St, American Fork, **E...gas:** Phillips 66/diesel/24hr, Texaco, **food:** Wendy's, **other:** HOSPITAL, Chevrolet, Chrysler/Plymouth/Dodge/Jeep, Home Depot, Smith's Foods, Target, Wal-Mart SuperCtr/24hr

279 5th E, Pleasant Grove, **E...gas:** Conoco/Blimpie, **food:** Carl's Jr, Denny's, McDonald's, Taco Bell, **lodging:** Quality Inn, **other:** OfficeMax, Stewart's RV Ctr, **1-2 mi E...gas:** Circle K, Phillips 66, Texaco, **food:** Arby's, Del Taco, Golden Corral, Hardee's, KFC, Subway, Wendy's, **other:** HOSPITAL, American Camping, Chevrolet, **W...other:** Buick/GMC/Pontiac, Ford, Land Rover

278 Pleasant Grove, **E...food:** Sonic

Orem

276 Orem, Lindon, **E...gas:** Exxon/diesel, Phillips 66, **food:** Del Taco, **other:** Home Depot, Schwab Tire, **W...gas:** Chevron/diesel

275 UT 52, to US 189, 8th N, Orem, **E...gas:** Phillips 66/diesel, **lodging:** La Quinta, **1 mi E...food:** Arby's, Dairy Queen, **other:** to Sundance RA

274 Orem, Center St, **E...gas:** Citgo/7-11, Conoco, **other:** HOSPITAL, funpark, **1-2 mi E...food:** Burger King, Hardee's, KFC, Taco Bell, Wendy's, **W...gas:** Tesoro, **lodging:** Econolodge, **other:** LP

Provo

272 UT 265, 12th St S, University Pkwy, **E...gas:** Phillips 66/Wendy's/diesel/24hr, Sinclair, Tesoro, **food:** Chevy's Mexican, IHOP, Krispy Kreme, Lucky Buns Creamery, McDonald's, McGrath's FishHouse, Subway, **lodging:** Fairfield Inn, Hampton Inn, La Quinta, **other:** Ford, JiffyLube, Mazda, Saturn, Wal-Mart SuperCtr/24hr, **1-3 mi E...gas:** Chevron, **food:** Applebee's, Arby's, Black Angus, Carrabba's, Chili's, Fuddrucker's, Golden Corral, Outback Steaks, Ponderosa, Pizza Hut, Red Lobster, Sizzler, Village Inn, **lodging:** Best Western, Courtyard, **other:** Barnes&Noble, Circuit City, Honda, JC Penney, Jo-Ann Fabrics, Lowe's Whse, Mervyn's, Mitsubishi, Nissan, Office Depot, OfficeMax, Old Navy, Subaru, mall, to BYU, many services on US 89

268b a UT 114, Center St, Provo, **E...gas:** Conoco, Phillips 66, Shell, Sinclair, 7-11, **other:** HOSPITAL, **1 mi E...lodging:** Marriott, Travelers Inn, Travelodge, **other:** Albertson's, Checker Parts, **W...gas:** Chevron, Conoco, **lodging:** Econolodge, **other:** KOA, Lakeside RV, Utah Lake SP

266 US 189 N, University Ave, Provo, **E...gas:** Chevron/24hr, Conoco/diesel, Maverik, Phillips 66, Tesoro/diesel, **food:** Arby's, Blimpie, Burger King, ChuckaRama, Hogi Yogi, KFC, McDonald's, Papa Murphy's, Ruby River Steaks, Sizzler, Taco Bell, Taco Time, Village Inn Rest., Wendy's, **lodging:** Best Western, Colony Inn, Fairfield Inn, Hampton Inn, Holiday Inn, Howard Johnson, Motel 6, National 9 Inn, Sleep Inn, Super 8, **other:** Dillard's, GoodEarth Foods, Home Depot, JC Penney, K-Mart, NAPA, OfficeMax, Sam's Club, Sears/auto, Staples, Silver Fox RV Camping, mall, to BYU, **1 mi E...food:** Los Three Amigos Mexican, **lodging:** Best Western, Hotel Roberts, Safari Motel, Western Inn, **other:** CarQuest, VW/Audi, auto repair

Interstate 15

N ↕ S

265 UT 75, Springville, **E...gas:** Flying J/diesel/rest./24hr/@, Maverik, **food:** McDonald's(1mi), **lodging:** Best Western, **other:** E Bay RV Park
263 UT 77, Springville, Mapleton, **E...gas:** Phillips 66/diesel, **food:** DQ, IHOP, Quizno's, Wendy's, **other:** Big O Tire, JiffyLube, Wal-Mart SuperCtr/gas/24hr, **W...gas:** Conoco/Arby's/diesel, **food:** Cracker Barrel, **lodging:** Day's Inn, **other:** Quality RV Ctr
261 US 89 S, US 6 E(from sb), to Price, **E...gas:** Chevron, Phillips 66, Texaco, **food:** Arby's, Burger King, Carl's Jr, JB's, KFC, McDonald's, Papa Murphy's, Taco Bell, Taco Time, Wendy's, Winger's, **lodging:** Holiday Inn Express, Western Inn, **other:** Albertson's/gas, Checker Parts, Fakler's Tire, Food4Less, K-Mart, Radio Shack, RV Ctr
260 US 6 E, UT 156, Spanish Fork, **E...gas:** Chevron, Conoco/diesel, Phillips 66, Texaco/diesel/LP, **food:** Arby's, Burger King, Hogi Yogi, JB's, KFC, Little Caesar's, McDonald's, North's Buffet, Subway, Taco Bell, Taco Time, Wendy's, **lodging:** Escalante B&B, **other:** Macey's Foods, ShopKO, **W...gas:** Conoco/diesel, **other:** Chevrolet, Chrysler/Plymouth/Jeep, Ford, RV Ctr
256 UT 164, to Spanish Fork, no facilities
254 UT 115, Payson, **E...gas:** Chevron/diesel, Flying J/diesel/LP/rest./24hr/@, Sinclair, **food:** McDonald's, Subway/Fruizle, **lodging:** Comfort Inn, **other:** HOSPITAL, Checker Parts, Payson Foods, RiteAid, diesel repair, Mt Nebo Loop
252 Payson, Salem, **E...gas:** Chevron, Sinclair/Arby's/diesel, **food:** Hogi Yogi, **other:** Wal-Mart SuperCtr/24hr, **W...gas:** Phillips 66/Wendy's/diesel
248 US 6 W, Santaquin, **E...other:** TrueValue, **W...gas:** Chevron, Conoco/diesel, Phillip 66/diesel, **food:** Main St Pizza, Main St Mkt, SantaQueen Burgers, Subway, Sorenson's Apple Farm, **other:** Nat Hist Area, Tintic Mining Dist, auto/tire care
245 to S Santaquin, no facilities
236 UT 54, Mona, no facilities
228 UT 28, to Nephi, **2-4 mi W...gas:** CashSaver/diesel, Citgo/7-11, Conoco, **food:** Reed's Drive-In, **lodging:** Safari Motel, **other:** HOSPITAL, Chevrolet/Pontiac/Buick, Goodyear, Thriftway Foods, to Great Basin NP

Nephi

225 UT 132, Nephi, **E...gas:** Tesoro/diesel/LP, **food:** Taco Time, **other:** KOA(5mi), **W...gas:** Chevron/Arby's/diesel, Phillips 66/Wendy's/diesel, Sinclair, **lodging:** Economy lodge, **other:** HOSPITAL, Big O Tire, Hi-Country RV Park
222 UT 28, Nephi, to I-70, **E...gas:** Chevron/diesel, Sinclair/diesel/24hr, Tesoro/diesel/24hr, **food:** Burger King, Mickelson's Rest., Subway/Fruizle, **lodging:** Motel 6, Roberta's Cove Motel, Super 8, **W...gas:** Flying J/Pepperoni's/diesel/LP/24hr/@, **food:** Tiara Café, Wayne's Rest., **lodging:** Best Western, Safari Motel, **other:** HOSPITAL, Ford/Mercury, Big A Parts, diesel repair
207 to US 89, Mills, no facilities

202 Yuba Lake, phone, access to boating, camping, rec facilities
188 US 50 E, Scipio, to I-70, **E...gas:** Chevron/diesel, Phillips 66/diesel, **lodging:** Super 8
184 ranch exit, no facilities
178 US 50, Delta, Holden, **W...**gas, phone, to Great Basin NP
174 to US 50, Holden, **W...**gas, phone, to Great Basin NP
167 Lp 15, Fillmore, **1-3 mi E...gas:** Chevron/diesel, Shell/diesel/LP, Sinclair/diesel, **lodging:** Best Western/rest., Fillmore Motel, **other:** HOSPITAL, WagonsWest RV Park, **W...gas:** Phillips 66/Subway/diesel/24hr, Tesoro/diesel
163 Lp 15, to UT 100, Fillmore, **E...gas:** Chevron/Arby's/diesel/24hr, Maverik, **lodging:** AppleCreek Inn, Best Western, Fillmore Motel, **other:** HOSPITAL, KOA, **W...gas:** Phillips 66/Burger King/24hr
158 UT 133, Meadow, **E...gas:** Chevron, Texaco/diesel
153mm view area sb
151mm view area nb
146 Kanosh, **2 mi E...**gas, chainup area
138 ranch exit, no facilities
137mm rest area sb, full(handicapped)facilities, picnic tables, litter barrels, vending, petwalk
135 Cove Fort, Hist Site, **E...gas:** Chevron
132 I-70 E, to Denver, Capitol Reef NP, Fremont Indian SP
129 Sulphurdale, chainup area, no facilities
126mm rest area nb, full(handicapped)facilities, picnic tables, litter barrels, vending, petwalk
125 ranch exit, no facilities
120 Manderfield, chainup area nb, no facilities
112 to UT 21, Beaver, Manderfield, **E...gas:** Chevron/diesel, Conoco/diesel, Sinclair/diesel, **food:** Arby's, El Bambi Café, Hunan Chinese, McDonald's, Subway, **lodging:** Best Western/rest., Country Inn, Day's Inn, Motel 6, Stag Motel, **other:** HOSPITAL, KOA(1mi), **W...gas:** Texaco/diesel, **food:** Wendy's, **lodging:** Super 8, **other:** to Great Basin NP

Beaver

109 to UT 21, Beaver, **E...gas:** Phillips 66, Sinclair, Texaco/Burger King/diesel/24hr, **food:** Arshel's Café, **lodging:** Aspen Lodge, Best Western, Comfort Inn, Day's Inn, Delano Motel/RV Park, Granada Inn, Sleepy Lagoon Motel, **other:** HOSPITAL, Mike's Foodtown, Cache Valley Cheese, NAPA, RV Parts/repair/dump, **W...gas:** Chevron/DQ/diesel/24hr, **food:** KanKun Mexican, Timberline Rest., **lodging:** Quality Inn, RV park, **other:** truckwash, to Great Basin NP
100 ranch exit, no facilities
95 UT 20, to US 89, to Panguitch, Bryce Canyon NP, no facilities

UTAH

Interstate 15

N ↕ S

88mm **rest area both lanes, full(handicapped)facilities, phone, picnic table, litter barrel, petwalk, hist site**

82 UT 271, Paragonah, no facilities

78 UT 141, Parowan, **E...lodging:** Crimson Hills Motel, Day's Inn, Swiss Village Inn, **other:** ski areas, **W...gas:** TA/Subway/Taco Bell/diesel/24hr

75 UT 143, Parowan, **2 mi E...lodging:** Jedadiah's Inn/rest., Day's Inn, **other:** to Brian Head/Cedar Breaks Ski Resorts

71 Summit, **W...gas:** Sunshine Travel Plaza/diesel/rest./@

62 UT 130, Cedar City, **E...gas:** Phillips 66/diesel, **lodging:** Best Western(3mi), Holiday Inn(1mi), **other:** KOA(2mi), st patrol, **W...gas:** Sinclair, Texaco/diesel/24hr, **food:** Steak&Stuff Rest., **lodging:** Travelodge

Cedar City

59 UT 56, Cedar City, **E...gas:** Maverik, Phillips 66/diesel/LP, Tesoro, Texaco/diesel, **food:** Arby's, Burger King, Denny's, KFC, McDonald's, Shoney's, Sonic, Taco Bell, Wendy's, **lodging:** Abbey Inn, Comfort Inn, Econolodge, **other:** MEDICAL CARE, Chevrolet/Buick, L&S Tire, NAPA, **1 mi E...gas:** Texaco/service, **food:** China Garden, Godfather's, Papa Murphy's, Pizza Factory, Sizzler, Sullivan's Café, **lodging:** Best Western, Rodeway Inn, Valu Inn, Zion Motel, **other:** Dodge/Chrysler/Jeep, Goodyear, GMC, Lin's Mkt, USPO, **W...gas:** Sinclair/diesel, **food:** Gondola Italian, Subway, **lodging:** Crystal Inn, Motel 6, Super 8

57 Lp 15, to UT 14, Cedar City, **1 mi E...gas:** Chevron/repair/24hr, Phillips 66/diesel, Sinclair/diesel, **food:** Dairy Queen, Domino's, Hogi Hogi, Hunan Chinese, JB's, Pizza Hut, Subway, Taco Time, **lodging:** Cedar-Rest Motel, Days Inn, Rodeway Inn, Super 7 Motel, Zion Motel, **other:** HOSPITAL, Albertson's, Allied Tire, AutoZone, Checker Parts, Radio Shack, Smith's Food/gas/24hr, to Cedar Breaks, Navajo Lake, Bryce Cyn, Duck Crk, **W...gas:** Chevron/diesel, **food:** Applebee's, Baker House B&B, **other:** Wal-Mart SuperCtr/gas/24hr

51 Kanarraville, Hamilton Ft, no facilities

44mm **rest area both lanes, full(handicapped)facilities, phone, picnic tables, litter barrels, petwalk, hist site**

42 New Harmony, Kanarraville, **W...gas:** Texaco/diesel

40 to Kolob Canyon, Zion's NP, **E...other:** tourist info/phone, scenic drive

36 ranch exit, no facilities

33 ranch exit, no facilities

31 Pintura, no facilities

30 Browse, no facilities

27 UT 17, Toquerville, **9 mi E...food:** Subway, **lodging:** Super 8, **other:** to Zion NP, Grand Cyn, Lake Powell

23 Leeds, Silver Reef(from sb), **3 mi E...other:** Harrisburg RV Resort/gas, hist site, museum

22 Leeds, Silver Reef(from nb), same as 23

16 UT 9, to Hurricane, **E...**Wal-Mart Dist Ctr, **10 mi E...gas:** Chevron, Shell, **lodging:** Comfort Inn, Motel 6, Travelodge, **other:** to Zion NP, Grand Canyon, Lake Powell, RV Camping

10 Middleton Dr, Washington, **E...gas:** Phillips 66/diesel, Sinclair, Tesoro/diesel, **food:** Alberto's Mexican, Arby's, Arctic Circle, Burger King, IHOP, Jack-in-the-Box, Ruby Tuesday, Toro Moro Mexican, Wendy's, **other:** Albertson's, AutoZone, Costco/gas, Home Depot, JC Penney, QwikLube, Redlands RV Park, Sears/auto, Wal-Mart SuperCtr/24hr/gas, mall, **W...gas:** Chevron/diesel/LP, Shell/24hr, **other:** Dixie Radiator, auto repair

8 St George Blvd, St George, **E...gas:** Shell, Texaco/Subway/diesel, **food:** Applebee's, Blimpie, Carl's Jr, Chili's, ChuckaRama, Don Jose Mexican, Fazoli's, Outback Steaks, Red Lobster, Village Inn Rest., Winger's, **lodging:** Hampton Inn, Ramada Inn, Shoney's Inn/rest., **other:** HOSPITAL, Harmon's Foods, Lowe's Whse, Michael's, Old Navy, Settler's RV Park, Staples, Sunrise Tire, Target, Zion Factory Stores/famous brands, same as 10, **W...gas:** Chevron, Maverik/gas, Sinclair/Domino's/LP/diesel, Texaco/diesel, **food:** Burger King, China King, Denny's, KFC/A&W, McDonald's, Pizza Hut, Taco Bell, Taco Time, Wendy's, Wienerschnitzel, **lodging:** Best Western, Comfort Inn, Day's Inn, Desert Edge Inn, Econolodge, Howard Johnson, Motel 6, Sands Motel, Singletree Inn, SunTime Inn, Travelodge, **other:** Big O Tire, Checker Parts, Honda Motorcycles, NAPA, Old Home Bakery, Rite Aid, St Geo RV, to LDS Temple

St George

6 UT 18, Bluff St, St George, **E...gas:** Chevron/diesel/24hr, Shell/24hr, Tesoro/A&W/diesel/24hr, **food:** Jack-in-the-Box, **lodging:** Ambassador Inn, Fairfield Inn, **other:** Buick/Pontiac/GMC, Firestone/auto, Hyundai, Saturn, U-Haul, funpark, **W...gas:** Chevron/diesel, Texaco, **food:** Arby's, Burger King, Carl's Jr, Claimjumper Steaks, DQ, Denny's, JB's, McDonald's, Palms Rest., Pancho&Lefty's Mexican, Pizza Hut, Tony Roma, **lodging:** Best Western, Bluffs Inn, Budget 8 Inn, Claridge Inn, Comfort Suites, Crystal Inn, Holiday Inn, Quality Inn, Super 8, **other:** HOSPITAL, Albertson's, AutoZone, Big O Tire, Chevrolet/Cadillac, Daewoo, Ford/Lincoln/Mercury, DixieLube, Goodyear, Honda, Jo-Ann Fabrics, Mazda, NAPA, Nissan, Plymouth/Chrysler/Dodge/Jeep, Radio Shack, TempleView RV Park, Toyota, Vacation World RV Ctr

4 Bloomington, **E...gas:** Flying J/Burger King/diesel/24hr, **W...gas:** Chevron/Taco Bell, **other:** Foodcourt, Wal-Mart SuperCtr/24hr

2 **Welcome Ctr nb, full(handicapped)facilities, picnic tables, litter barrels, phone, petwalk**

1mm Port of Entry/weigh sta both lanes

0mm Utah/Arizona state line

Interstate 70

Exit #	Services
230mm	Utah/Colorado state line
226mm	**view area wb, restrooms(handicapped), litter barrels**
225	Westwater, no facilities
220	ranch exit, no facilities
212	to Cisco, no facilities
202	UT 128, to Cisco, no facilities
190	Yellowcat Ranch Exit, no facilities
188mm	**Welcome Ctr wb, full(handicapped)facilities, info, picnic tables, litter barrels**
185	Thompson, **N...gas:** Shell/diesel, **other:** café, camping, lodging
180	US 191 S, Crescent Jct, to Moab, **N...**gas/diesel/café, **S...**lodging
178mm	**rest area eb, full(handicapped)facilities, scenic view, picnic tables, litter barrels**
173	ranch exit, no facilities
	Green River
162	UT 19, Green River, info, **1-2 mi N...gas:** Sinclair/diesel, Phillips 66/Burger King/diesel/24hr, Tesoro/diesel, **food:** Ben's Café, Chow Hound Drive-In, Lemieux Café, McDonald's, Westwinds Rest., **lodging:** Best Western/rest., Book Cliff Lodge/rest., Budget Host, Comfort Inn, Deluxe Inn, Holiday Inn Express, Motel 6, Rodeway Inn, Super 8, **other:** OK Anderson City Park, museum, same as 158
158	UT 19, Green River, **N...gas:** Chevron/diesel, Conoco/Arby's/diesel/24hr/@, Phillips 66/diesel/24hr, Tesoro/diesel, Sinclair/diesel, **food:** Ben's Café, Cathy's Rest., ChowHound Drive-In, **lodging:** Budget Inn, Mancose Rose Hotel, Oasis Motel/café, **other:** MEDICAL CARE, Big A Parts, Goodyear/auto, NAPA Repair, USPO, KOA, Shady Acres RV Park, Green River SP, same as 162, NO SERVICES WB FOR 100 MILES
156	US 6 W, US 191 N, to Price, Salt Lake, no facilities
147	UT 24 W, to Hanksville, to Capitol Reef, Lake Powell, no facilities
144mm	**rest area wb, restrooms(handicapped), litter barrels**
141.5mm	runaway truck ramp eb
140mm	**rest area both lanes, view area, restrooms (handicapped), litter barrels**
139mm	runaway truck ramp eb
136mm	brake test area eb
129	ranch exit, no facilities
120mm	**rest area both lanes, restrooms(handicapped), litter barrels**
114	to Moore, **N...rest area both lanes, restrooms(handicapped), litter barrels**
105	ranch exit, no facilities
102mm	**rest area both lanes, restrooms(handicapped), litter barrels**
91	ranch exit, no facilities
89	UT 10 N, UT 72, to Emery, Price, **12 mi N...**gas, **S...**to Capitol Reef NP
84mm	**S...rest area both lanes, full(handicapped)facilities, litter barrels, petwalk**
72	ranch exit, no facilities
61	Gooseberry Rd, no facilities
	Salina
54	US 89 N, to Salina, US 50 W, to Delta, **N...gas:** Chevron/Burger King/diesel, Phillips 66/diesel, Sinclair/diesel, **food:** China Gate, Denny's, Subway, **lodging:** Best Western, Luxury Inn, Super 8, **other:** Butch Cassidy RV Camp, **1 mi N...gas:** Conoco/diesel, **other:** NAPA, NEXT SERVICES 108 MI EB
48	UT 24, to US 50, Sigurd, Aurora, **1-2 mi S...**gas, food, to Fishlake NF, Capitol Reef NP
	Richfield
40	Lp 70, Richfield, **S...gas:** Chevron, Flying J/diesel/LP/rest./24hr/@, **food:** Arby's, Chuckwagon Steaks, Subway, **lodging:** Luxury Inn, Super 8, **other:** HOSPITAL, RV/truck repair, **1-2 mi S...food:** McDonald's, Taco Time, **lodging:** Best Western, Budget Host, Day's Inn/rest., Quality Inn, **other:** Albertson's, **other:** Buick/Pontiac/Cadillac/GMC, KOA, Lin's Mkt
37	Lp 70, Richfield, **S...gas:** Phillips 66/Wendy's/diesel, KFC/Taco Bell, **lodging:** Comfort Inn, Hampton Inn, **1-2 mi S...gas:** Conoco/diesel/Munchie's RV Park, Tesoro/Burger King/diesel, **food:** McDonald's, Papa Murphy's, **lodging:** Best Western, Day's Inn, Quality Inn, **other:** Albertson's, Checker Parts, Chevrolet, Ford/Mercury, KOA, Wal-Mart SuperCtr/24hr, to Fish Lake/Capitol Reef Parks, st patrol
32	Elsinore, Monroe, **1/2 mi S...gas:** Chevron, Silver Eagle/gas
26	UT 118, Joseph, Monroe, **S...gas:** Diamond D/diesel, Shell/RV Park
23	US 89 S, to Panguitch, Bryce Canyon, no facilities
17	**N...other:** Fremont Indian Museum, info, phone, camping
13mm	brake test area eb
8	Ranch Exit, no facilities
3mm	Western Boundary Fishlake NF
1	Historic Cove Fort, **N...gas:** Chevron(2mi)
0mm	I-15, N to SLC, S to St George. I-70 begins/ends on I-15, exit 132.

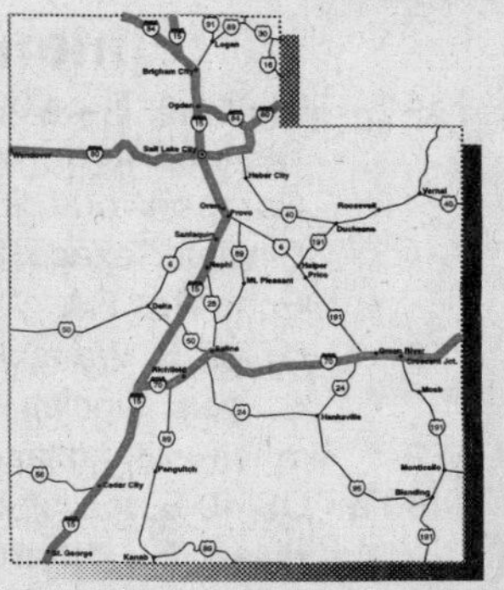

Interstate 80

Exit #	Services
197mm	Utah/Wyoming state line, no facilities
193	Wahsatch, no facilities
189	ranch exit, no facilities
185	Castle Rock, no facilities
182mm	Port of Entry/weigh sta wb
180	Emery(from wb), no facilities
170	**Welcome Ctr wb/rest area eb, full(handicapped)facilities, phone, vending, picnic tables, litter barrels, petwalk, RV dump**
169	Echo, **1 mi N...**gas/diesel, **food:** Kozy Rest./lodging
168	I-84 W, to Ogden, I-80 E, to Cheyenne, no facilities
166	view area both lanes, litter barrels

UTAH

Interstate 80

E ↕ W

Kimball Jct

164 Coalville, **N...gas:** Phillips 66/diesel/mart, **lodging:** Best Western, **other:** Holiday Hills RV Camp/LP, CamperWorld RV Park, **S...gas:** Chevron/diesel, Sinclair, Texaco, **food:** Holiday Hills Rest., **other:** to Echo Res RA

156 UT 32 S, Wanship, **N...food:** Spring Chicken Café, **S...gas:** Sinclair/diesel, **other:** to Rockport SP

152 ranch exit, no facilities

148b a US 40 E, to Heber, Provo, **N...gas:** Sinclair/Blimpie/diesel, **S...other:** Home Depot

147mm rest area wb, full(handicapped)facilities, phone, vending, picnic tables, litter barrels, petwalk

145 UT 224, Kimball Jct, to Park City, **N...other:** Ford/Mercury, RV camping, **S...gas:** Chevron, Shell/diesel, **food:** Arby's, Denny's, Loco Lizard Cantina, McDonald's, Subway, Ruby Tuesday, Taco Bell, Wendy's, **lodging:** Best Western, Hampton Inn, Holiday Inn Express, **other:** Smith's Foods, USPO, Wal-Mart, Outlet Mall/famous brands, RV camping, **4 mi S...gas:** Citgo/7-11, **lodging:** Olympia Park Hotel, Radisson, **other:** ski areas

144mm view area eb

143 ranch exit, **N...gas:** Phillips 66/Blimpie, **food:** Pizza Hut, **other:** to Jeremy Ranch, **S...**camping, ski area

140 Parley's Summit, **S...gas:** Sinclair/diesel, **food:** No Worries Café

137 Lamb's Canyon, no facilities

134 UT 65, Emigration Canyon, East Canyon, Mountaindale RA

133 utility exit(from eb), no facilities

132 ranch exit, no facilities

131 (from eb) Quarry, no facilities

130 I-215 S(from wb), no facilities

129 UT 186 W, Foothill Dr, Parley's Way, **N...**HOSPITAL

128 I-215 S(from eb), no facilities

127 UT 195, 23rd E St, to Holladay, no facilities

126 UT 181, 13th E St, to Sugar House, **N...gas:** Chevron, Texaco, **food:** Olive Garden, Red Lobster, Sizzler, Training Table Rest., Wendy's, **other:** ShopKO

125 UT 71, 7th E St, **gas:** Texaco, **other:** Firestone, **N...food:** McDonald's

124 US 89, S State St, **N...gas:** Citgo/7-11, Chevron, Texaco/diesel, **food:** Burger King, Skipper's, Taco Bell, Uncle Sid's Rest., Wendy's, Woody's Drive-In, **other:** Buick, Chrysler/Jeep, Discount Tire, Dodge, Honda, Jeep, Suzuki, transmissions, **S...food:** KFC, Pizza Hut, **lodging:** Ramada Inn

Salt Lake

123mm I-15, N to Ogden, S to Provo, no facilities

I-80 and I-15 run together approx 4 mi. See Utah Interstate 15, exits 308-310.

121 600 S, to City Ctr

120 I-15 N, to Ogden

118 UT 68, Redwood Rd, to N Temple, **2-3 mi N on N Temple...gas:** Amoco, Chevron/Subway/diesel, Circle K, **food:** Burger King, Denny's, KFC, Taco Bell, **lodging:** Airport Inn, Candlewood Suites, Comfort Suites, Day's Inn, Holiday Inn Express, Motel 6, Radisson, Utah St Fairpark, **S...**HOSPITAL

117 I-215, N to Ogden, S to Provo, no facilities

115b a 40th W, W Valley Fwy, **N...**to Salt Lake Airport

114 Wright Bros Dr(from wb), **N...lodging:** La Quinta, Microtel, Residence Inn, same as 113

113 5600 W(from eb), **N...gas:** Phillips 66/mart, **food:** Perkins, Pizza Hut, **lodging:** Best Western, Comfort Inn, Courtyard, Fairfield Inn, Hilton, Holiday Inn, La Quinta, Microtel, Quality Inn, Residence Inn, Sheraton, Super 8

111 7200 W, **N...**visitor ctr

104 UT 202, Saltair Dr, to Magna, **N...other:** Great Salt Lake SP, beaches

102 UT 201(from eb), to Magna, no facilities

101mm view area wb

99 UT 36, to Tooele, **S...gas:** Chevron/Subway, Flying J/Conoco/Country Mkt/diesel/LP/24hr/@, TA/Amoco/Burger King/Taco Bell/diesel/rest./24hr/@, Texaco/diesel, KFC(10mi), **food:** McDonald's, **lodging:** Oquirrh Motel/RV Park, **other:** HOSPITAL

88 to Grantsville, no facilities

84 UT 138, to Grantsville, Tooele, no facilities

77 UT 196, to Rowley, Dugway, no facilities

70 to Delle, **S...gas:** Delle/Sinclair/diesel/café/motel/24hr/@, phone

62 to Lakeside, Eagle Range, military area, no facilities

56 to Aragonite, no facilities

54mm rest area both lanes, full(handicapped)facilities, phone, picnic tables, litter barrels, petwalk, vending

49 to Clive, no facilities

41 Knolls, no facilities

26mm architectural point of interest

10mm rest area both lanes, full(handicapped)facilities, phone, picnic tables, litter barrels, vending, petwalk, observation area

Wendover

4 Bonneville Speedway, **N...gas:** Phillips 66/diesel/café/24hr/@

3mm Port of Entry, weigh sta both lanes

2 UT 58(no EZ wb return), Wendover, **S...gas:** Amoco/diesel, Sinclair/diesel, Shell/diesel, Texaco/diesel, **food:** McDonald's, Subway, Taco Burger, **lodging:** Best Western, Bonneville Motel,Day's Inn, Econolodge, Heritage Motel, Motel 6, Super 8, Western Ridge Motel, **other:** Fred's Foods, Bonneville Speedway Museum, Silversmith Casino, Stateline Inn/casino, RV park, USPO, auto repair

0mm Utah/Nevada state line, Mountain/Pacific time zone

Interstate 84

E ↕ W

Exit #	Services
120	I-84 begins/ends on I-80, exit 168 near Echo, Utah.
115	to Henefer, Echo, **1/2 mi S...other:** USPO, to E Canyon RA
112	Henefer, **S...**gas, food, lodging
111	Croydon, no facilities

Interstate 84

E ↕ W

111mm Devil's Slide Scenic View
108 Taggart, **N...**gas, food, phone
106 ranch exit, no facilities
103 UT 66, Morgan, E Canyon RA, **N...**Ford, **S...gas:** Chevron, Phillips 66, Shell, **food:** Chicken Hut, Spring Chicken Café, Steph's Drive-In, **other:** MEDICAL CARE, Jubilee Foods, USPO, city park
96 Peterson, **N...gas:** Sinclair(3mi), **other:** to Snow Basin, Powder Mtn, Nordic Valley Ski Areas, **S...gas:** Phillips 66/diesel
94mm rest area wb, full(handicapped)facilities, picnic tables, litter barrels, petwalk
92 UT 167(from eb), to Huntsville, **N...gas:** Sinclair/diesel(2mi), **other:** trout farm(1mi), to ski areas
91mm rest area eb, full(handicapped)facilities, picnic tables, litter barrels, petwalk
87b a US 89, Ogden, to Layton, Hill AFB, **N...food:** McDonald's(2mi), **1/2 mi S...gas:** Shell
85 S Weber, Uintah, no facilities
81 to I-15 S, UT 26, Riverdale Rd, **N...gas:** Conoco/diesel, Sinclair, **food:** Applebee's, Boston Mkt, Carl's Jr, Chili's, La Salsa Mexican, McDonald's, **other:** Chrysler/Plymouth/Jeep, Circuit City, Harley-Davidson, Home Depot, Honda/Nissan, Isuzu, Lincoln/Mercury/Toyota/Kia, Lowe's Whse, Mazda, Mitsubishi, OfficeMax, PepBoys, Pontiac/Buick/GMC, Sam's Club/gas, Target, Wal-Mart SuperCtr/24hr, Wilderness RV, **S...food:** McDonald's, **lodging:** Motel 6

Roy

I-84 and I-15 run together. See Utah Interstate 15, exits 344 through 379.

41 I-15 N to Pocatello
40 UT 102, Tremonton, Bothwell, **N...gas:** Chevron/Burger King/diesel/24hr, Shell/Quizno's/diesel/wash/24hr, **food:** Denny's/24hr, McDonald's, **lodging:** Western Inn, **other:** HOSPITAL(4mi), Jack's RV, **1 mi N...gas:** Amoco/diesel, Sinclair, **lodging:** to Marble Motel, Sandman Motel, **other:** Alco, **S...other:** to Golden Spike NM
39 to Garland, Bothwell, **N...**HOSPITAL
32 ranch exit, no services
26 UT 83 S, to Howell, no services
24 to Valley, no services
20 to Blue Creek, no facilities
17 ranch exit, no facilities
16 to Hansel Valley, no facilities
12 ranch exit, no facilities
7 Snowville, **N...gas:** Chevron/diesel, Flying J/Pepperoni's/diesel/LP/24hr/@, **food:** Mollie's Café, Ranch House Diner, **lodging:** Outsiders Inn, **other:** RV camping
5 UT 30, to Park Valley, no facilities
0mm Utah/Idaho state line

Snowville

Interstate 215 (Salt Lake)

N ↕ S

Exit # Services
29 I-215 begins/ends on I-15.
28 UT 68, Redwood Rd, **W...gas:** Flying J/diesel/rest./mart/24hr/@, Maverik/24hr, **other:** BMW(motorcycles)
25 22nd N, no facilities
23 7th N, **E...gas:** Amoco, **food:** KFC, McDonald's, Taco Bell, **lodging:** Day's Inn, Holiday Inn, Motel 6, **W...lodging:** Holiday Inn Express, Radisson
22b a I-80, W to Wendover, E to Cheyenne
21 California Ave, **E...gas:** Phillips 66, Sapp Bros/Sinclair/Burger King/diesel/@, Shell/Subway/diesel, **food:** Great American Diner, **other:** Goodyear
20b a UT 201, W to Magna, 21st S, **W... other:** Goodyear
18 UT 171, 3500 S, W Valley, **E...food:** Applebee's, Chili's, Cracker Barrel, Country Kitchen, **lodging:** Baymont Inn, Country Inn Suites, Crystal Inn, Extended Stay America, La Quinta, Sleep Inn, **other:** HOSPITAL, PepBoys, **W...other:** Early Tire, JCPenney, Mervyn's, Michael's, mall
15 UT 266, 47th S, **E...gas:** Conoco, **food:** KFC, Taco Bell, Village Inn, Wendy's, **lodging:** Fairfield Inn, Hampton Inn, **W...gas:** Chevron, **food:** Arby's
13 UT 68, Redwood Rd, **E...gas:** Chevron, Tesoro, **food:** Applebee's, Arby's, Carl's Jr, Frontier Pies, Fuddrucker's, Hometown Buffet, Taco Bell, **lodging:** Homestead Suites, **other:** Circuit City, ShopKO, Wal-Mart/auto
12 I-15, N to SLC, S to Provo
11 same as 10(from eb)
10 UT 280 E, **E...other:** Sam's Club, **W...food:** Applebee's, Arby's, Hooters, La Salsa Mexican, Macaroni Grill, Olive Garden, Red Lobster, Taco Bell, Wendy's, Village Inn, **other:** HOSPITAL
9 Union Park Ave, **E...food:** Black Angus, Carl's Jr, Chili's, Famous Dave's BBQ, LaSalsa Mexican, Marie Callender's, Outback Steaks, Sweet Tomato, Tony Roma, **lodging:** Best Western, Crystal Inn, Extended Stay America, Homewood Suites, **other:** Albertson's, Barnes&Noble, Circuit City, Home Depot, OfficeMax, Old Navy, Ross, Smith's Foods, Target, Wal-Mart/auto, **W...gas:** Tesoro, **lodging:** Crystal Inn, Motel 6, Super 8
8 UT 152, 2000 E, **E...gas:** Chevron, **food:** KFC, Taco Bell, **W...food:** Wendy's
6 6200 S, **E...food:** Loco Lizards Café, Mikado Café, Quizno's, **other:** Alta, Brighton, Snowbird, Solitude/ski areas
5 UT 266, 45th S, Holladay, **W...gas:** Tesoro
4 39th S, **E...gas:** Chevron, Sinclair, **food:** Rocky Mtn Pizza, **other:** Dan's Foods, **W...**HOSPITAL
3 33rd S, Wasatch, **W...gas:** Tesoro, **food:** Burger King, KFC, McDonald's, Taco Bell, Wendy's
2 I-80 W, no facilities

I-215 begins/ends on I-80, exit 130.

Salt Lake

VERMONT

Interstate 89

N ↕ S

St Albans

Exit #(mm)Services

130mm US/Canada Border, Vermont state line, I-89 begins/ends.

129.5mm rest area sb, full facilities, phone, picnic tables, litter barrels, petwalk

22(129) US 7 S, Highgate Springs, **E...other:** Ammex DutyFree, **3 mi E...gas:** Mobil/diesel

129mm Latitude 45 N, midway between N Pole and Equator

128mm Rock River

21(123) US 7, VT 78, Swanton, **E...gas:** Exxon/diesel/24hr, **W...gas:** Mobil/diesel, Shell, Sunoco/diesel, **food:** Big Wok Chinese, Dunkin Donuts, McDonald's, **other:** Grand Union Foods

20(118) US 7, VT 207, St Albans, **W...gas:** Mobil, Shell/diesel, **food:** Burger King, Dunkin Donuts, KFC/Taco Bell, McDonald's, Panda China, Pizza Hut, **other:** Chevrolet, Ford, Hannaford Foods, Indian Motorcycles, Jo-Ann Fabrics, Kinney Drug, Radio Shack, Sears, Staples

19(114) US 7, VT 36, VT 104, St Albans, **W...gas:** Exxon, Gulf/diesel, Mobil, Shell/diesel, **lodging:** Comfort Inn, **other:** HOSPITAL, Lincoln/Mercury, USPO, st police

111mm rest area both lanes, full(handicapped)facilities, info, phone, picnic tables, litter barrels, vending, petwalk

18(107) US 7, VT 104A, Georgia Ctr, **E...gas:** Citgo, Mobil/diesel, Shell, **food:** Potbelly Café, **other:** GA Auto Parts, Homestead Camping, Interstate Auto Service

17(98) US 2, US 7, Lake Champlain Islands, **E...gas:** Mobil, Shell/diesel, **other:** camping(4mi), **W...other:** to NY Ferry, camping(6mi)

96mm weigh sta both lanes

16(92) US 7, US 2, Winooski, **E...gas:** Mobil, **food:** Friendly's, Lighthouse Rest., **lodging:** Hampton Inn, **other:** Shaw's Foods, **W...gas:** Citgo, GoGo Gas, Shell/diesel, **food:** Burger King, Libby's Diner, McDonald's, Rathskellar Rest., **lodging:** Fairfield Inn, Motel 6

15(91) VT 15(no EZ nb return), Winooski, **E...lodging:** Day's Inn, Handys Extended Stay Suites, **W...gas:** Citgo, Exxon, Mobil, **food:** Westside Deli, **other:** USPO

90mm Winooski River

Burlington

14(89) US 2, Burlington, **E...gas:** Citgo/rerpair, Coastal, Mobil, Shell/diesel, Sunoco, **food:** Al's Fry's, Applebee's, Burger King, CheeseTraders, Dunkin Donuts, Friendly's, KFC, McDonald's, Outback Steaks, Zachary's Pizza, **lodging:** Anchorage Inn, Best Western, Clarion, Comfort Inn, Holiday Inn, SwissHost Motel, University Inn, **other:** Barnes&Noble, BonTon, Brooks Drug, Grand Union Foods, Hannaford's Foods, JC Penney, Jo-Ann Fabrics, Natural Foods Mkt, Sears/auto, mall, **W...gas:** Exxon, Mobil, **lodging:** Sheraton, **other:** HOSPITAL, Advance Parts, Michael's, Staples

13(87) I-189, to US 7, Burlington, **2 mi W on US 7 N...gas:** Citgo, Shell, **food:** China Express, KFC, TGIFriday, **lodging:** Colonial Motel, Town&Country Motel, **other:** Hyundai/Subaru, Nadeau Drug, PriceChopper, Radio Shack, **2 mi W on US 7 S...gas:** Exxon, Gulf, Sunoco, Texaco, **food:** Burger King, Cactus Pete's Rest., Denny's, Friendly's, Koto Japanese, McDonald's, Olive Garden, Perry's Rest., Pizza Hut, **lodging:** Super 8, **other:** Audi/VW, Chrysler/Plymouth/Saturn, Hannaford's Foods, K-Mart, Pontiac/Cadillac, Tire Whse

12(84) VT 2A, to US 2, Williston, to Essex Jct, **E...gas:** Citgo, Mobil/24hr, Sunoco/diesel/subs/24hr, **food:** Friendly's, Susse Chalet, **other:** Best Buy, Circuit City, City Drug, Hannaford's Foods, Home Depot, Staples, Wal-Mart, st police, **W...lodging:** Courtyard, Residence Inn

82mm rest area both lanes(7am-11pm), full(handicapped)facilities, phone, picnic tables, litter barrels, vending, petwalk

11(79) US 2, to VT 117, Richmond, **E...lodging:** Chequered House Motel, **W...gas:** Mobil/diesel/24hr

67mm rest area sb, no facilities

66mm rest area nb, no facilities

Montpelier

10(64) VT 100, to US 2, Waterbury, **E...gas:** Exxon/diesel/24hr, Mobil/diesel/24hr, **food:** Mist Hill Café, **lodging:** Blush Hill Inn, Holiday Inn, Thatcher Brook Inn/rest., **W...gas:** Citgo, **food:** Zachary's Pizza, **other:** USPO

9(59) US 2, to VT 100B, Middlesex, **W...gas:** Getty, **lodging:** Camp Meade Motel/rest., **other:** museum, st police

8(53) US 2, Montpelier, **1 mi E...gas:** Citgo, Exxon/diesel, Gulf/diesel, Mobil, Sunoco/repair, **food:** La Pizzaria, Sarducci's Rest., **lodging:** Capitol Plaza Hotel, Montpelier Inn, **other:** Bond Parts, Shaw's Foods, camping(6mi), to VT Coll

Interstate 89

7(50) VT 62, to US 302, Barre, **E...gas:** Mobil/diesel/24hr **food:** Maplewood Rest., **lodging:** Comfort Suites **other:** Shaw's Foods, Staples, **1 mi E...lodging** LaGue Inn, **other:** HOSPITAL, Cadillac/GMC/Toyota, JC Penney, Jo-Ann Fabrics, camping(7mi)

6(47) VT 63, to VT 14, S Barre, **4 mi E...**gas, food, lodging, camping, info

5(43) VT 64, to VT 12, VT 14, Williamstown, **6 mi E...**gas diesel, food, lodging, camping, **W...**to Norwich U

41mm highest elevation on I-89, 1752 ft

34.5mm rest area/weigh sta both lanes(7am-11pm) full(handicapped)facilities, info, phone, litter barrels, petwalk

4(31) VT 66, Randolph, **E...other:** RV camping(1mi) **W...gas:** Mobil, **food:** McDonald's, lodging(3mi) **other:** HOSPITAL, RV camping(5mi)

3(22) VT 107, Bethel, **E...gas:** Shell/diesel, **food:** Village Pizza, **lodging:** Fox Stand Inn, **other:** to Jos Smith Mon(8mi), **1 mi W...gas:** Citgo/diesel/LP, **other** MEDICAL CARE, NAPA, USPO

14mm White River

2(13) VT 14, VT 132, Sharon, **E...lodging:** 1/2 Acre Motel, **W...gas:** Citgo/diesel, Gulf/diesel, Mobil, **food** Dixie's Kitchen, **lodging:** Columns Motel, **other** Sharon Trading Post, USPO, Jos Smith Mon(6mi)

9mm rest area/weigh sta both lanes(7am-11pm), full facilities, phone, info, picnic tables, litter barrels, vending, NO HANDICAPPED FACILITIES

7mm White River

1(4) US 4, to Woodstock, Quechee, **3 mi E...gas:** Shell diesel/24hr, **lodging:** Hampton Inn, Super 8

1mm I-91, N to St Johnsbury, S to Brattleboro

0mm Vermont/New Hampshire state line, Connecticut River

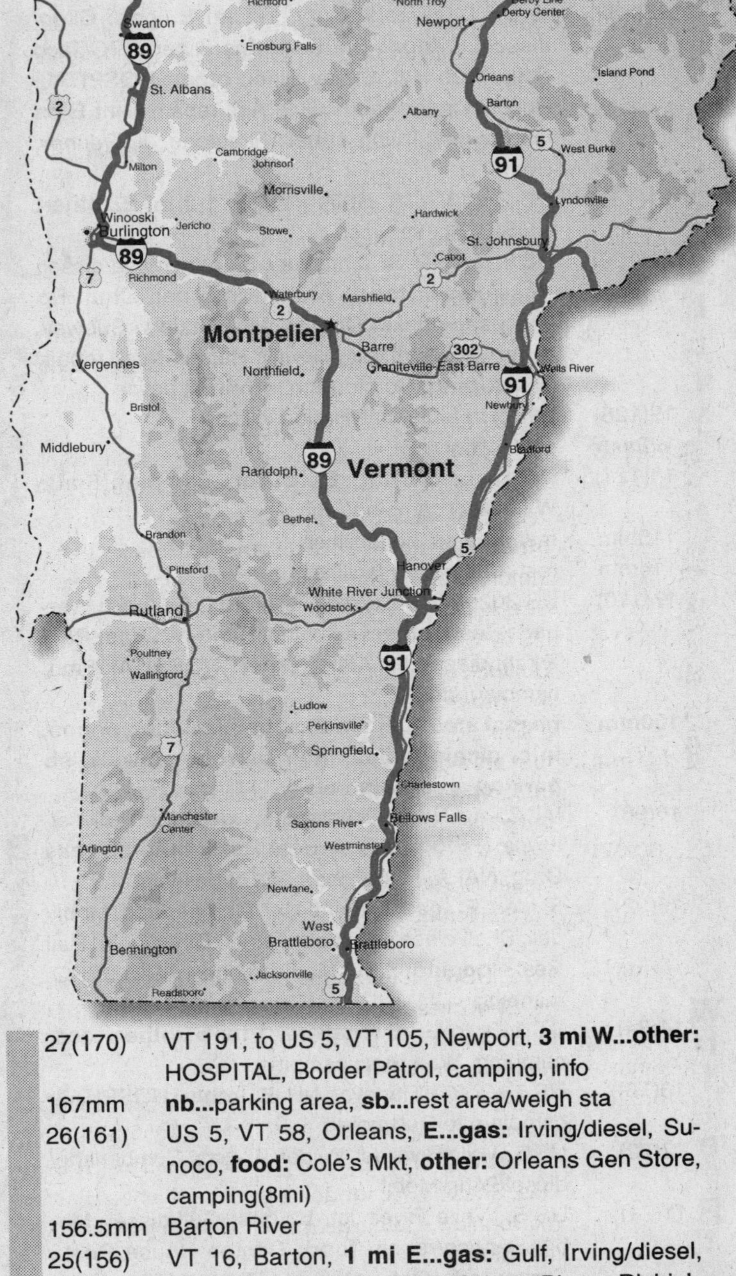

Interstate 91

Exit #(mm)Services

178mm US/Canada Border, Vermont state line, US Customs, I-91 begins/ends.

29(177) US 5, Derby Line, **E...**Ammex Dutyfree, **1 mi W...gas:** Irving/diesel

176.5mm Welcome Ctr sb, full(handicapped)facilities, info, picnic tables, litter barrels, phone, petwalk, Midpoint between the Equator and N Pole

28(172) US 5, VT 105, Derby Ctr, **E...gas:** Exxon/diesel/24hr, Petrol King/diesel, **other:** Fireside Camping, st police, **W...gas:** Gulf/Dunkin Donuts/diesel, Shell/diesel/24hr, **food:** McDonald's, Village Pizza, **lodging:** Inn at The Hill, Pepin's Motel, Super 8, **other:** HOSPITAL, Chevrolet/GMC/Pontiac/Cadillac, Chrysler/Jeep, Kinney Drug, Parts+, Plymouth/Dodge, Rite Aid, Shop&Save Foods, RV camping

27(170) VT 191, to US 5, VT 105, Newport, **3 mi W...other:** HOSPITAL, Border Patrol, camping, info

167mm **nb...**parking area, **sb...**rest area/weigh sta

26(161) US 5, VT 58, Orleans, **E...gas:** Irving/diesel, Sunoco, **food:** Cole's Mkt, **other:** Orleans Gen Store, camping(8mi)

156.5mm Barton River

25(156) VT 16, Barton, **1 mi E...gas:** Gulf, Irving/diesel, Mobil/diesel/repair, **food:** Orlean Pizza, Richie's Rest., Village Coffeehouse, **lodging:** PineCrest Motel, **other:** C&C Foods, Cole's Mkt, Ford, Orlean Gen Store, USPO, camping(2mi)

154mm parking area nb

150.5mm highest elevation on I-91, 1856 ft

143mm scenic overlook nb

141mm rest area sb, full(handicapped)facilities, info, picnic tables, litter barrels, phone

24(140) VT 122, Wheelock, **2 mi E...**gas, food, lodging

23(137) US 5, to VT 114, Lyndonville, **E...gas:** Gulf/diesel, Mobil/Dunkin Donuts, **food:** McDonald's, **lodging:** Colonade Inn, **other:** NAPA, Rite Aid, White Mkt Foods, **W...lodging:** Lyndon Motel

VERMONT

Interstate 91

N ↕ S

St Johnsbury

22(132) to US 5, St Johnsbury, **1-2 mi E...gas:** Citgo/diesel/LP, **food:** Brit-Da-Brans Diner, KFC/Taco Bell, Pizza Hut, St Jay Diner, **other:** HOSPITAL, PriceChopper Foods, Rite Aid, repair, **4 mi E on US 5...gas:** Irving, **other:** Firestone, JC Penney, Sears

21(131) US 2, to VT 15, St Johnsbury, **1-2 mi E...other:** HOSPITAL, services

20(129) US 5, to US 2, St Johnsbury, **E...gas:** Irving/diesel, Shell/diesel, **food:** Anthony's Diner, Chun Bo Chinese, Dunkin Donuts, McDonald's, Subway, **other:** Brooks Drug, Kevin's Repair, truck repair, **W...lodging:** Comfort Inn, **other:** st police

19(128) I-93 S to Littleton NH, no facilities

122mm scenic view nb

18(121) to US 5, Barnet, **E...other:** camping(5mi), **W...other:** camping(5mi)

115mm rest area sb, no facilities

114mm rest area nb, no facilities

17(110) US 302, to US 5, Wells River, NH, **E...food:** Warner's Rest., **other:** camping(10mi), **W...gas:** P&H Trkstp/diesel/rest./24hr, **other:** HOSPITAL(5mi), camping(9mi)

100mm nb rest area, full(handicapped)facilities, phone, info, picnic tables, litter barrels, petwalk, sb parking area/weigh sta

16(98) VT 25, to US 5, Bradford, **E...gas:** Mobil/diesel/LP/café, **food:** Hungry Bear Rest., **other:** Kinney Drug, NAPA, P&C Foods, **W...**st police

15(92) Fairlee, **E...gas:** Citgo/diesel, Cumberland, Mobil/deli, Shell/diesel/LP, **food:** Fairlee Diner, Third Rail Rest., **lodging:** Silver Maple Lodge, **other:** USPO, camping

White River Jct

14(84) VT 113, to US 5, Thetford, **1 mi E...other:** food, camping, **W...other:** camping

13(75) US 5, VT 10a, Hanover, NH, **E...other:** HOSPITAL, camping, to Dartmouth

12(72) US 5, White River Jct, Wilder, **E...gas:** Cumberland/diesel/24hr, Mobil

11(71) US 5, White River Jct, **E...gas:** Gulf/diesel, Mobil, Sunoco/repair, **food:** Canton House Rest., Crossroads Café, Gillam's Rest., McDonald's, **lodging:** Coach an' Four Motel, Comfort Inn, Pines Motel, Ramada Inn, **other:** Ford/Lincoln/Mercury/Hyundai, Jct Mktplace, Toyota, USPO, **W...gas:** Citgo, Shell, Texaco/diesel, **lodging:** Best Western, Hampton Inn, Super 8, **other:** HOSPITAL

10N(70) I-89 N, to Montpelier

S I-89 S, to NH, airport

68mm rest area/weigh sta both lanes(7am-11pm), full(handicapped)facilities, picnic tables, litter barrels, phone, vending, petwalk

9(60) US 5, VT 12, Hartland, **W...**info, **gas:** Mobil(1mi), **other:** HOSPITAL

8(51) US 5, VT 12, VT 131, Ascutney, **E...gas:** Citgo/diesel, Gulf/diesel, Mobil, Sunoco/diesel, **food:** Ascutney House Rest., Mr G's Rest., **lodging:** Yankee Village Motel, **other:** HOSPITAL, Max' Country Store

7(42) US 5, VT 106, VT 11, Springfield, **W...gas:** Mobil/diesel/24hr, Shell/diesel/LP, **lodging:** Howard Johnson Rest., Holiday Inn Express, **other:** HOSPITAL, camping

39mm rest area both lanes, no facilities

6(34) US 5, VT 103, Rockingham, to Bellows Falls, **E...gas:** Shell, **food:** Leslie's Rest., **lodging:** Rockingham Motel/rest., **W...gas:** Sunoco/diesel/24hr, **other:** st police(6mi)

5(29) VT 121, to US 5, Westminster, to Bellows Falls, **3 mi E...**gas, food, phone, lodging

24mm rest area both lanes, no facilities

22mm weigh sta sb

20mm parking area nb

4(18) US 5, Putney, **E...lodging:** Putney Inn/rest., **W...gas:** Sunoco/diesel/LP/24hr, **other:** camping(3mi)

Brattleboro

3(11) US 5, VT 9 E, Brattleboro, **E...gas:** Agway, Citgo/diesel/24hr, Mobil, Sunoco, **food:** Bickford's, Dunkin Donuts, Friendly's, KFC, McDonald's, Michele's Ristorante, Pizza Hut, Village Pizza, **lodging:** Colonial Motel, Day's Inn, Holiday Inn Express, Motel 6, Quality Inn, Super 8, **other:** Ford/Mercury, GNC, Hannaford Foods, NAPA, Pontiac/Buick/GMC, Radio Shack, Rite Aid, Subaru, U-Haul, USPO

2(9) VT 9 W, to rd 30, Brattleboro, **E...gas:** Sunoco, **W...gas:** Mobil, Shell, **food:** Country Deli, **other:** to Marlboro Coll, st police

1(7) US 5, Brattleboro, **E...gas:** Coastal/diesel, Getty, Mobil/Dunkin Donuts, Shell/Subway/diesel, Sunoco, **food:** Burger King, Millenium Pizzaria, VT Inn Pizza, **lodging:** Econolodge, **other:** HOSPITAL, Brooks Drug, CarQuest, Chevrolet/Cadillac, Chrysler/Jeep, PriceChopper Foods, to Ft Dummer SP

6mm Welcome Ctr nb, full(handicapped)facilities, info, phone, picnic tables, litter barrels, vending, petwalk, playground

0mm Vermont/Massachusetts state line

Interstate 93

See New Hampshire Interstate 93

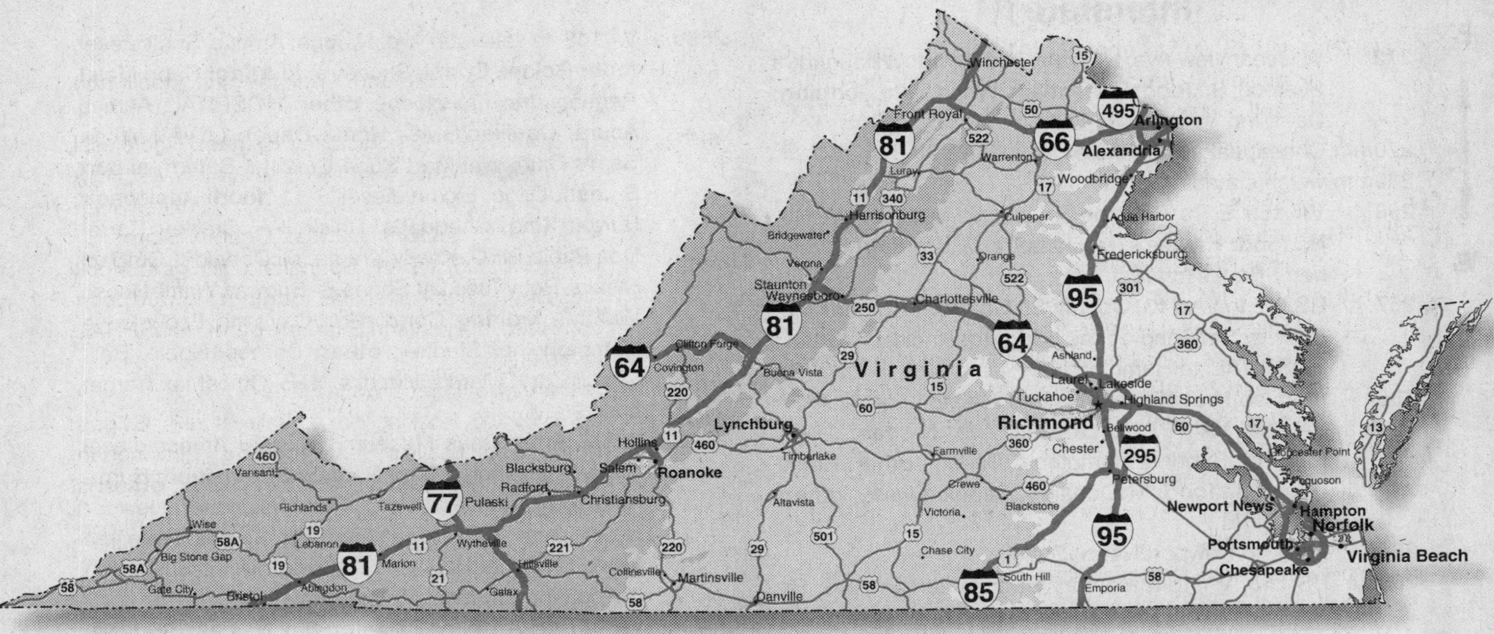

Interstate 64

E ↕ W — Norfolk

Exit #	Services
299b a	I-264 E, to Portsmouth. I-64 begins/ends on I-264.
297	US 13, US 460, Military Hwy, **N...gas:** Exxon
296b a	US 17, to Portsmouth, **N...other:** VETERINARIAN, **4 mi S...**camping
294mm	S Br Elizabeth River
292	VA 190, to VA 104(from eb, no EZ return), Dominion Blvd, **S...gas:** BP, Shell, **food:** Burger King, Hardee's, **other:** MEDICAL CARE, Family$, Food Lion, Rite Aid
291b a	I-464 N, VA 104 S, to Elizabeth City, Outer Banks, same services as 292
290b a	VA 168, Battlefield Blvd, to Nag's Head, Manteo, **N...other:** Merchant's Auto Ctr, **S...gas:** Amoco/ diesel/24hr, Shell/Blimpie, **food:** Applebee's, Chik-fil-A, ChuckeCheese, Dunkin Donuts, Golden Corral, Grand China Buffet, Hardee's, Ryan's, Taco Bell, Waffle House, Wendy's, **lodging:** Day's Inn, Super 8, **other:** $Tree, Lowe's Whse, Sam's Club, USPO, Wal-Mart SuperCtr/24hr
289b a	Greenbrier Pkwy, **N...gas:** Citgo, **food:** Burger King, Nathan's Deli, Subway, Taco Bell, Wendy's, **lodging:** Hampton Inn, Holiday Inn, Motel 6, Red Roof Inn, Wellesley Inn, **other:** Acura, BMW, Chevrolet, Cloth World, Dodge, Food Lion, Ford, Honda, Hyundai, Isuzu, Mitsubishi, Pontiac, Subaru, Volvo, U-Haul, transmissions, **S...food:** Blimpie, Boston Mkt, Cheers Grill, Cooker, Don Pablo, Fazoli's, LoneStar Café, McDonald's, Old Country Buffet, Olive Garden, Pargo's, Ruby Tuesday, Starbucks, TCBY, Winston's Café, Food Lion, Harris-Teeter/24hr, **lodging:** Comfort Suites, Courtyard, Extended Stay America, Fairfield Inn, Sun Suites, **other:** Barnes&Noble, **other:** Circuit City, Dillard's, $General, Drug Emporium, Hecht's, Marshall's, Michael's, Office Depot, OfficeMax, Old Navy, Sears/auto, Target, mall
286b a	Indian River Rd, **N...gas:** Amoco/24hr, Citgo/Wilco/ diesel, Crown, Exxon, Shell, 7-11, **food:** Hardee's, **S...gas:** Exxon/diesel, 7-11, **food:** Capt D's, Golden Corral, Shoney's, Waffle House, **lodging:** Founder's Inn
285	E Branch Elizabeth River
284b a	I-264, to Norfolk, VA 44, to VA Beach(exits left from eb), **1/2 mi E off 1 exit N, Newtown Rd...gas:** Amoco, Chevron, Exxon, Shell, 7-11, **food:** Adam's Rest., Denny's/24hr, Golden Corral, Texas Steaks, Wendy's, **lodging:** Hampton Inn, Holiday Inn, La Quinta, Ramada Inn
282	US 13, Northampton Blvd, **N...lodging:** Quality Inn, **other:** to Chesapeake Bay Br Tunnel
281	VA 165, Military Hwy(no EZ eb return), **N...gas:** Amoco/diesel, Robo, Shell/diesel/24hr, **food:** Andy's Pizza, Pizza Hut, Wendy's, **other:** Chevrolet/Kia, Chrysler/Nissan, Mazda/Suzuki, Econolodge, Aamco, Food Lion, **S...gas:** Exxon, **food:** BBQ, DQ, **lodging:** Hampton Inn, Hilton, **other:** Firestone, Target
279	Norview Ave, **N...gas:** 7-11, **food:** Golden Corral, **other:** K-Mart, to airport, botanical garden
278	VA 194 S, Chesapeake Blvd(no EZ wb return), **N...gas:** Crown, **other:** Eckerd, NAPA, **S...food:** Burger King
277b a	VA 168, to Tidewater Dr, **N...gas:** Citgo/7-11, **food:** Hardee's, **S...**HOSPITAL
276c	to US 460 W, VA 165, Little Creek Rd, **N...gas:** Shell, **S...gas:** Amoco, Exxon, **food:** McDonald's, Mr Jim's Submarines, Taco Bell, Wendy's, **other:** AutoZone, Eckerd, Farm Fresh, Hannaford Foods
276b a	I-564 to Naval Base
274	Bay Ave(from wb), to Naval Air Sta
273	US 60, 4th View St, Oceanview, **N...gas:** Exxon/diesel/ 24hr, **lodging:** Chesabay Motel, Econolodge, **other:** Harrison Boathouse/Pier, **S...other:** to Norfolk Visitors Ctr, info

VIRGINIA

Interstate 64

E ↕ W

Hampton

272 W Oceanview Ave, **N...gas:** 7-11, **food:** Willoughby's Seafood, **S...food:** Fisherman's Wharf Rest., **lodging:** Day's Inn

270mm Chesapeake Bay Tunnel

269mm weigh sta eb

268 VA 169 E, to Buckroe Beach, Ft Monroe, VA Ctr, **N...food:** Hardee's, McDonald's, **S...lodging:** Strawberry Banks Inn/rest.

267 US 60, to VA 143, County St, **S...food:** Burger King, Subway Sta Sandwiches, **lodging:** Radisson, **other:** HOSPITAL, to Hampton U

265c (from eb)**N...other:** Armistead Ave, to Langley AFB

265b a VA 134, VA 167, to La Salle Ave, **N...gas:** Citgo, **lodging:** Super 8, Hampton Coliseum, **other:** Home Depot, **S...food:** McDonald's, Seafood Rest., **other:** HOSPITAL,

264 I-664, to Newport News, Suffolk

263b a US 258, VA 134, Mercury Blvd, to James River Br, **N...gas:** Exxon, Shell, **food:** Applebee's, Bennigan's, Blimpie, Boston Mkt, Burger King, Chi Chi's, Chili's, Darryl's Rest., Das Wiener Works, Denny's, Golden Corral, Grandy's, Grate Steak, Hooters, KFC, McDonald's, Olive Garden, Pizza Hut, Rally's, Red Lobster, Rockola Café, Steak&Ale, Taco Bell, Waffle House, Wendy's, **lodging:** Courtyard, Day's Inn, Fairfield Inn, Hampton Inn, Holiday Inn, Quality Inn, Red Roof Inn, Sheraton, **other:** Chevrolet/Mazda, Ford/Diahatsu, Chrysler/Jeep, Hecht's, JC Penney, Office Depot, Target, Wal-Mart SuperCtr/24hr, **S...gas:** Amoco, Citgo/7-11, **food:** Old Country Buffet, Pizza Hut, Waffle House, **lodging:** Econolodge, Interstate Inn, La Quinta, **other:** Advance Parts, Auto Express, CarQuest, Circuit City, Nissan, OfficeMax, PepBoys, Radio Shack, Toyota, Volvo

262 VA 134, Magruder Blvd(no EZ wb return), **N...gas:** Citgo/7-11, Exxon, **other:** Dodge/Acura

261b a Center Pkwy, to Hampton Roads, **S...gas:** Citgo, **food:** McDonald's, Peking Chinese, Ruby Tuesday, Subway, Taco Bell, Topeka's Steaks, Zero's Pizza, **other:** BooksAMillion, $Tree, Eckerd, FarmFresh Foods, Winn-Dixie

258 US 17, J Clyde Morris Blvd, **N...gas:** Amoco, Crown, Exxon, 7-11/24hr, **food:** Domino's, Hardee's, New China, Waffle House, Wendy's, **lodging:** BudgetLodge, Host Inn, Ramada Inn/rest., Super 8, **other:** Advance Parts, Food Lion, Rite Aid, **S...gas:** Citgo/diesel/24hr, Exxon, 7-11/24hr, **food:** BBQ, Burger King, Hong Kong Chinese, Papa John's, Pizza Hut, Sammy&Angelo's Steaks, Subway, Taco Bell, **lodging:** Motel 6, Omni Hotel/rest., **other:** HOSPITAL, BMW/Honda, $Tree, Eckerd, Radio Shack, museum

256b a Victory Blvd, Oyster Point Rd, **N...gas:** Amoco, Citgo/diesel, Texaco, **food:** BBQ, Bagel Bakery, Burger King, Fuddrucker's, Hardee's, Starbucks, **S...other:** Coll of Wm&Mary

255b a VA 143, to Jefferson Ave, **N...gas:** Amoco, Shell/diesel, **food:** Golden Corral, Shoney's, **lodging:** Capri Motel, Regency Inn, Travelodge, **other:** HOSPITAL, Aamco, Acura, Cadillac/GMC, Home Depot, Lowe's Whse, Sam's Club, Wal-Mart SuperCtr/24hr, Saturn, airport, **S...gas:** Citgo, Exxon/diesel, 7-11, **food:** Applebee's, Burger King, Cheddar's, Chick-fil-A, Cracker Barrel, Don Pablo, KFC, Krispy Kreme, McDonald's, OutBack Steaks, Ruby Tuesday, Shoney's, Subway, Waffle House, Wendy's, **lodging:** Comfort Inn, Day's Inn, Econolodge, Hampton Inn, Studio+, **other:** Barnes&Noble, Belk, Circuit City, Dillard's, Hecht's, NTB, OfficeMax, Target, mall

250b a to US Army Trans Museum, **N...gas:** Amoco/diesel, Citgo/7-11, Shell, **2-4 mi N...gas:** Exxon, **food:** Burger King, **lodging:** Capri Motel, Tudor Inn, **other:** Newport News Camp, to Yorktown Victory Ctr, **S...gas:** RaceTrac, **food:** McDonald's, Wendy's, **lodging:** Ft Eustis Inn, Holiday Inn Express, Mulberry Inn, TDY Inn

Williamsburg

247 VA 143, to VA 238(no EZ return wb), **N...gas:** BP/diesel, Citgo/7-11, **other:** to Yorktown, **S...other:** to Jamestown Settlement

243 VA 143, to Williamsburg, **S...**same as 242a

242b a VA 199, to US 60, to Williamsburg, **N...gas:** BP(2mi), **lodging:** Day's Inn/rest., **other:** water funpark, to Yorktown NHS, **1 mi S...gas:** Frank's Trkstp/diesel/rest./@, Citgo/7-11, Crown Gas, Shell, **food:** Burger King, LJ Silver, McDonald's, Wendy's, **lodging:** Best Western, Courtyard, Howard Johnson, Marriott, Quality Inn, Rodeway Inn, **other:** 1st Settlers Camping, to William&Mary Coll, Busch Gardens, to Jamestown NHS

238 VA 143, to Colonial Williamsburg, Camp Peary, **2-3 mi S...gas:** Citgo, EC/diesel, Shell, **food:** Cracker Barrel, Golden Corral, Hardee's, Ledo's Pizza, McDonald's, Williamsburg Woodlands Grill, **lodging:** Best Western/rest., Comfort Inn, Day's Inn, Econolodge, Holiday Inn/rest., Homewood Suites, Howard Johnson/rest., King William Inn, Quality Inn/rest., **other:** HOSPITAL, Anvil Camping

234 VA 646, to Lightfoot, **1-2 mi N...other:** KOA, Colonial Camping, Pottery Camping, **2-3 mi S...gas:** Exxon/diesel, Mobil/diesel, Shell/diesel, **food:** BBQ, Burger King, Hardee's, KFC, Lightfoot Rest., McDonald's, Subway, **lodging:** Colonial Hotel, Day's Inn, Quality Inn, Super 8, **other:** Kincaid Camping

231b a VA 607, to Norge, Croaker, **N...gas:** Citgo/7-11, **other:** to York River SP, **1-2 mi S...gas:** Shell, **food:** KFC, Candle Factory Rest., Wendy's, **lodging:** Econolodge, Williamsburg Camping(5mi)

227 VA 30, to US 60, Toano, to West Point, **S...gas:** Shell/Stuckey's/diesel, **food:** McDonald's, Welcome South Rest., **lodging:** Anderson's Corner Motel(2mi), **other:** Ed Allen's Camping(10mi)

220 VA 33 E, to West Point, **N...gas:** Exxon/diesel

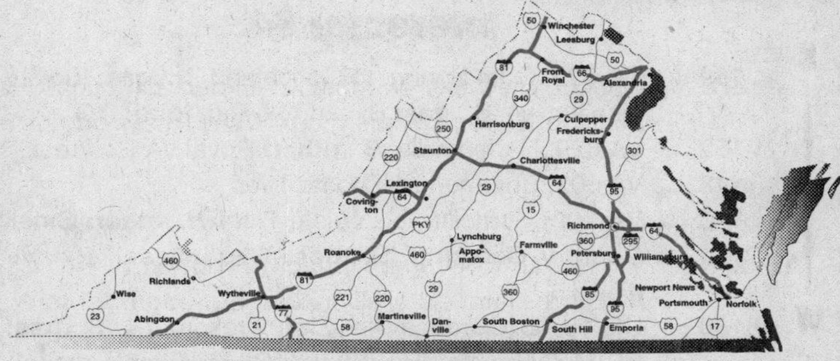

Interstate 64

214 VA 155, to New Kent, Providence Forge, **S...gas:** Exxon/diesel, **food:** DQ, Allen's **other:** Camping(10mi), Colonial Downs Racetrack

213mm rest area both lanes, full(handicapped)facilities, phone, vending, picnic tables, litter barrels, petwalk

211 VA 106, to Talleysville, to James River Plantations, no facilities

205 VA 33, VA 249, to US 60, Bottoms Bridge, Quinton, **N...gas:** BP/diesel, Exxon/diesel, **food:** New Peking Chinese, Subway, **other:** Eckerd, Food Lion, USPO, **S...gas:** Shell/diesel, **food:** McDonald's, MarketPlace Foods

204mm Chickahominy River

203mm weigh sta both lanes

200 I-295, N to Washington, S to Rocky Mount, to US 60

197b a VA 156, Airport Dr, to Highland Springs, **N...gas:** BP/diesel, Citgo/7-11, Shell/diesel, **food:** Bojangles, Domino's, Hardee's, Pizza Hut, Subway, **other:** Advance Parts, CVS Drug, Winn-Dixie, **S...gas:** BP, EC/diesel, Shell/diesel, **food:** Arby's, Aunt Sarah's, Burger King, Waffle House, **lodging:** Comfort Inn, Courtyard, Day's Inn, DoubleTree, Econolodge, Hampton Inn, Hilton/rest., Microtel, Motel 6, Super 8, Wingate Inn, **other:** to airport

195 Laburnum Ave, **N...gas:** Chevron/repair, Shell, **S...gas:** Applebee's, **food:** Subway, Taco Bell, **other:** Ukrop's Foods, **3/4 mi S...gas:** BP/24hr, Exxon, 7-11, **food:** Aunt Sarah's, Bojangles, Burger King, Capt D's, China King, DQ, Hardee's, KFC, McDonald's, Papa John's, Wendy's, Western Sizzlin, **lodging:** Airport Inn, Hampton Inn, Holiday Inn, Sheraton/rest., Super 8, Wyndham Garden, **other:** CVS Drug, $General, $Tree, Firestone/auto, Ford, Hannaford Foods, Radio Shack, Rite Aid, Trak Auto

193b a VA 33, Nine Mile Rd, **N...gas:** BP, Exxon/Subway, **food:** Burger King, McDonald's, **S...**HOSPITAL

192 US 360, to Mechanicsville, **N...gas:** Citgo, **food:** McDonald's, **S...gas:** BP, Citgo, **food:** Church's

190 I-95 S, to Petersburg, 5th St, **N...other:** Richmond Nat Bfd Park, **S...lodging:** Marriott, **other:** st capitol, coliseum. **I-64 W and I-95 N run together. See Virginia Interstate 95, exits 76-78.**

187 I-95 N(exits left from eb), to Washington. **I-64 E and I-95 S run together.**

186 I-195, Richmond, to Powhite Pkwy

185b a US 33, Staples Mill Rd, Dickens Rd, no facilities

183 US 250, Broad St, Glenside Dr, **N...gas:** Chevron/DQ, **food:** Bob Evans, **lodging:** Best Western, Comfort Inn, Embassy Suites, **other:** K-Mart, same as 181, **S...other:** HOSPITAL, to U of Richmond

181 Parham Rd, **N on Broad...gas:** BP/24hr, Citgo, Crown/diesel, Exxon, Shell, **food:** Aunt Sarah's, Bennigan's, Blue Marlin Seafood, Bojangles, Burger King, Casa Grande Mexican, Famous Dave's BBQ, Friendly's, Fuddruckers, Hardee's, Hooters, KFC, LoneStar Steaks, LJ Silver, Olive Garden, OutBack Steaks, Piccadilly's, Red Lobster, Shoney's, Steak&Ale, Taco Bell, TGIFriday, Waffle House, Wendy's, **lodging:** Fairfield Inn, Quality Inn, Suburban Lodge, Super 8, **other:** HOSPITAL, BooksAMillion, CVS Drug, Ford/Lincoln/Mercury, Honda/Mitsubishi, Hyundai/Subaru, Infiniti, Mazda/BMW, Mercedes, Nissan, PepBoys, Staples, Toyota, Ukrop's Foods, transmissions, **1 mi S...gas:** BP, Exxon, **food:** McDonald's, Topeka Steaks, **lodging:** Ramada Inn

180 Gaskins Rd, **N...gas:** BP/24hr, Shell/diesel, **food:** O'Charley's, **lodging:** Courtyard, Holiday Inn Express, Residence Inn, Studio+, **N on Broad...food:** Applebee's, Arby's, Blackeyed Pea, Boston Mkt, Burger King, Golden Corral, IHOP, KFC, McDonald's, Peking Chinese, Rockola Café, Ruby Tuesday's, Ryan's, Subway, Taco Bell, Tripp's Rest., Wendy's, Zorba's Greek/Italian, **other:** Borders Books, Cadillac, Chrysler/Jeep, Circuit City, Costco, Drug Emporium, Evans Foods, Food Lion, Fresh Fields Foods, Goodyear/auto, Hannaford Foods, Lowe's Whse, Sam's Club, VW, mall

178b a US 250, Short Pump, **N...gas:** BP/diesel, Citgo, Exxon/diesel, Shell/diesel, **food:** Leonardo's Pizza, Starbucks, Thai Garden Rest., **lodging:** AmeriSuites, Comfort Suites, Hampton Inn, Hilton Garden, Homestead Village, Homewood Suites, **other:** CompUSA, Firestone/auto, OfficeMax, **1 mi S...gas:** BP, Citgo/7-11, Crown, **food:** Burger King, Capt D's, Domino's, McDonald's, Taco Bell, TGIFriday, Wendy's, **lodging:** Candlewood Suites, **other:** Barnes&Noble, Best Buy, CarQuest, Goodyear/auto, Home Depot, Kohl's, Lowe's Whse, Target, Ukrop's Foods, Wal-Mart SuperCtr/24hr

177 I-295, to I-95 N to Washington, to Norfolk, VA Beach, Williamsburg

175 VA 288, no facilities

173 VA 623, to Rockville, Manakin, **N...gas:** Citgo(2mi), **S...gas:** BP/DQ/diesel, Exxon/diesel(1mi), Shell/diesel, **food:** BBQ, **lodging:** Alley's Motel(1mi), **other:** $General, Food Lion

169mm rest area both lanes, full(handicapped)facilities, vending, phone, picnic tables, litter barrels, petwalk

167 VA 617, Oilville, to Goochland, **N...gas:** Exxon, **S...gas:** BP/Bullets/diesel/24hr

VIRGINIA

Interstate 64

E ↕ W

159 US 522, Gum Spring, to Goochland, **N...gas:** Exxon/diesel/mart, **S...gas:** BP(2mi), Citgo, **food:** DQ
152 VA 629, Hadensville, **S...other:** Royal VA Golf/rest.
148 VA 605, Shannon Hill, no facilities
143 VA 208, Ferncliff, to Louisa, **7 mi N...other:** Small Country Camping, **S...gas:** Citgo/diesel, Exxon/diesel
136 US 15, to Gordonsville, Zion Crossroads, **S...gas:** BP/McDonald's/diesel/24hr, Citgo/Blimpie/diesel, Exxon/Burger King/diesel, Shell/diesel, **lodging:** Crescent Inn/rest., Zion Roads Motel
129 VA 616, Keswick, Boyd Tavern, **N...lodging:** Keswick Hotel, **S...gas:** BP(1mi)
124 US 250, to Shadwell, **2 mi N...gas:** Amoco, Liberty, Shell, **food:** Aunt Sarah's, Burger King, McDonald's, Ponderosa, Taco Bell, Wendy's, **lodging:** Town&Country Motel, White House Motel, **other:** HOSPITAL, **S...lodging:** Ramada Inn
123mm Rivanna River
121 VA 20, to Charlottesville, Scottsville, **N...gas:** Amoco/diesel, **food:** Blimpie, **S...gas:** Exxon, **other:** KOA(9mi), to Monticello
120 VA 631, 5th St, to Charlottesville, **N...gas:** Exxon/diesel, Shell, **food:** Burger King, Domino's, Hardee's, Jade Garden, McDonald's, Pizza Hut/Taco Bell, Waffle House, Wendy's, **lodging:** Holiday Inn, Omni Hotel(2mi), Sleep Inn, **other:** CVS Drug, Family$, Food Lion, laundry
118b a US 29, Charlottesville, to Lynchburg, **1-4 mi N...gas:** Amoco, Citgo/diesel, Exxon, Shell, **food:** Blimpie, Hardee's, Shoney's, Subway, **lodging:** Best Western, Boar's Head Inn, Budget Inn, English Inn, Econolodge, **other:** HOSPITAL, UVA, **S...gas:** Exxon/diesel
114 VA 637, to Ivy, no facilities
113mm rest area wb, full(handicapped)facilities, phone, vending, picnic tables, litter barrels, petwalk
111mm Mechum River
108mm Stockton Creek
107 US 250, Crozet, **1 mi N...gas:** Exxon, **1 mi S...other:** Misty Mtn Camping
105mm rest area eb, full(handicapped)facilities, phone, vending, picnic tables, litter barrels, petwalk
104mm scenic area eb, litter barrels, no truck or buses
100mm scenic area eb, litter barrels, hist marker, no trucks or buses
99 US 250, Afton, to Waynesboro, **N...lodging:** Colony Motel, **other:** to Shenandoah NP, Skyline Drive, ski area, to Blue Ridge Pkwy, **S...lodging:** Afton Inn
96 VA 622, Waynesboro, to Lyndhurst, **3 mi N...gas:** Shell, Quality Inn
95mm South River
94 US 340, Waynesboro, to Stuarts Draft, **N...gas:** Citgo/7-11/diesel, Exxon/diesel, **food:** Arby's, Burger King, KFC, Shoney's, S River Grill, Taco Bell(1mi), Wendy's, Western Sizzlin, **lodging:** Best Western, Day's Inn, Deluxe Motel(2mi), Holiday Inn Express, Skyline Motel(2mi), Super 8, **other:** HOSPITAL, Waynesboro N 340 Camping(9mi), **S...gas:** Shell/diesel, **other:** Waynesboro Outlet Village, museum
91 Va 608, Fishersville, to Stuarts Draft, **N...gas:** Shell/diesel, **lodging:** Hampton Inn, **other:** HOSPITAL, **S...gas:** Exxon/McDonald's, **other:** Shenadoah Acres Camping(8mi), **other:** Walnut Hills Camping(9mi)
89mm Christians Creek
87 I-81, N to Harrisonburg, S to Roanoke
I-64 and I-81 run together 20 miles. See Virginia Interstate 81, exits 195-220.
56 I-81, S to Roanoke, N to Harrisonburg
55 US 11, to VA 39, Lexington, info, **N...gas:** Exxon/diesel, **food:** Burger King, Ruby Tuesday, Waffle House, **lodging:** Best Western, Country Inn Suites, Super 8, Wingate Inn, **other:** HOSPITAL(3mi), $Tree, Radio Shack, Wal-Mart SuperCtr/24hr, Lee-Hi Camping(3mi), VA Horse Ctr, **S...gas:** Citgo/Subway/diesel, **food:** Redwood Rest., **lodging:** Comfort Inn, Econolodge, Holiday Inn Express, **other:** to Wash&Lee U, VMI
50 US 60, VA 623, to Lexington, **3 mi S...lodging:** Day's Inn
43 VA 780, to Goshen, no facilities
35 VA 269, VA 850, Longdale Furnace, **S...lodging:** Longdale Inn, **2 mi S...lodging:** North Mtn Motel
33mm truck rest area eb
29 VA 269, VA 850, **S...gas:** Exxon/diesel/rest.
27 US 60 W, US 220 S, VA 629, Clifton Forge, **N...other:** to Douthat SP, Alleghany Highlands Arts/crafts, Buckhorne Camping(2mi), **S...gas:** Citgo/diesel, Exxon, **lodging:** The Park Motel
24 US 60, US 220, Clifton Forge, **1 mi S...gas:** Shell/diesel, **food:** DQ, Hardee's, Taco Bell
21 to VA 696, Low Moor, **S...**HOSPITAL
16 US 60 W, US 220 N, Covington, to Hot Springs, **N...gas:** Amoco, Etna, Exxon/Burger King/24hr, Shell, **food:** Western Sizzlin, **lodging:** Best Value Inn, Best Western, Holiday Inn Express, **other:** Buick/Pontiac/GMC, to ski area, **S...food:** McDonald's, **lodging:** Comfort Inn, **other:** $General, K-Mart, Radio Shack
14 VA 154, Covington, to Hot Springs, **N...gas:** Exxon/Arby's, Sunoco, **food:** Great Wall Chinese, Hardee's, KFC, Little Caesar's, Subway, Wendy's, **lodging:** Budget Motel, Highland Motel, Townhouse Motel, **other:** Advance Parts, AutoZone, CVS Drug, Family$, Food Lion, Kroger, **S...food:** China House, Mama Pizza, **other:** $Tree, GNC, Wal-Mart SuperCtr/24hr
10 US 60 E, VA 159 S, Callaghan, **S...gas:** Marathon/diesel/LP
7 VA 661, no facilities
2.5mm Welcome Ctr eb, full(handicapped)facilities, phone, picnic tables, litter barrels, petwalk
1 Jerry's Run Trail, **N...**to Allegheny Trail

Charlottesville

Lexington

Covington

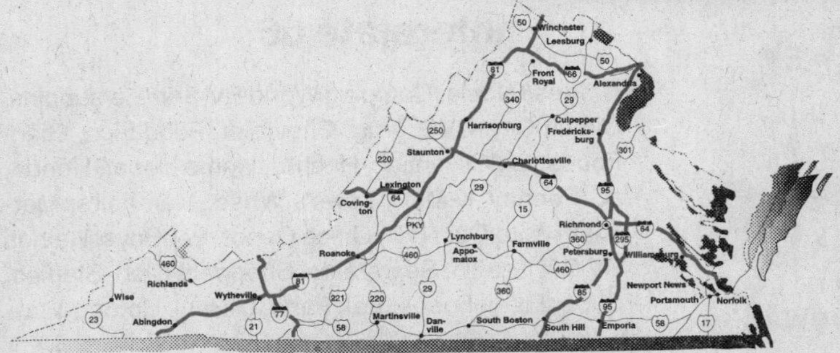

Interstate 66

E ↕ W

DC Area

Exit #	Services
77mm	Independence Ave, to Lincoln Mem. I-66 begins/ends in Washington, DC.
76mm	Potomac River, T Roosevelt Memorial Bridge
75	US 50 W(from eb), to Arlington Blvd, G Wash Pkwy, I-395, US 1, **S...**Iwo Jima Mon
73	US 29, Lee Hwy, Key Bridge, to Rosslyn, **N...lodging:** Marriott, **S...lodging:** Best Western
72	to US 29, Lee Hwy, Spout Run Pkwy(from eb), **N...gas:** Shell, **lodging:** Econolodge, **S...other:** CVS Drug, Eckerd/24hr, Starbucks, Giant Foods
71	VA 120, Glebe Rd(no EZ return from wb), **N...**HOSPITAL, **S...gas:** Mobil, **food:** Blackeyed Pea, **lodging:** Comfort Inn, Holiday Inn
69	US 29, Sycamore St, Falls Church, **N...gas:** Exxon, **S...gas:** 7-11, **lodging:** Econolodge
68	Westmoreland St(from eb), same as 69
67	to I-495 N(from wb), to Baltimore, Dulles Airport
66	VA 7, Leesburg Pike, to Tysons Corner, Falls Church, **N...gas:** Exxon, Mobil, **food:** Chinese Cuisine, Jerry's Subs/Pizza, Ledo's Pizza, Starbucks, TCBY, **other:** FreshFields Foods, SuperCrown Books
64b a	I-495 S, to Richmond
62	VA 243, Nutley St, to Vienna, **S...gas:** Exxon, **1 mi S on Lee Hwy...gas:** Citgo/7-11, Exxon, Shell, Sunoco/diesel, Texaco, **food:** Applebee's, Dunkin Donuts, Estella's Italian, IHOP/24hr, LoneStar Steaks, McDonald's, NY Pizzaria, Subway, TCBY, **lodging:** Anchorage Motel, Econolodge, **other:** Harley-Davidson, Jeep, Radio Shack, Safeway, Saturn, Trak Parts
60	VA 123, to Fairfax, **S...gas:** Exxon, Shell/24hr, Sunoco, **food:** Denny's, Fuddrucker's, Hooters, Indian Cuisine, KFC, Outback Steaks, Red Lobster, 29 Diner, **lodging:** Wellesley Inn, **other:** MEDICAL CARE, Buick/Isuzu, Chevrolet, Chrysler/Dodge, Ford/Lincoln/Mercury, Honda, Hyundai, Mazda, Rite Aid, Toyota, to George Mason U
57	US 50, to Dulles Airport, **N...food:** Bennigans, Ruby Tuesday, Subway, **lodging:** Extended Stay America, Holiday Inn, **other:** MEDICAL CARE, Hecht's, JC Penney, Lord&Taylor, Macy's, Sears/auto, mall, **1 mi N...food:** Grady's Grill, Silver Diner, **S...gas:** Amoco, Shell, 7-11, **food:** Burger King, Italian Rest., Wendy's, **lodging:** Candlewood Suites, Comfort Inn/rest., Courtyard, Hampton Inn, **other:** Borders Books, Circuit City, Ford, Giant Foods
56mm	weigh sta both lanes

Manassas

Exit #	Services
55	Fairfax Co Pkwy, to US 29, **N...**4 Lakes Mall, **gas:** Exxon, Mobil, **food:** Applebee's, Blue Iguana Café, Burger King, Cooker Rest., Don Pablo, Eatery Rest., Food-Court, Fresh Fare Rest., Olive Garden, Pizza Hut, Red Robin, TCBY, TGIFriday, Tony's Pizza, Wendy's, **lodging:** Hyatt Hotel, **other:** HOSPITAL, Barnes&Noble, Best Buy, BJ's Whse, CompUSA, Food Lion, Galyan's, Kohl's, Radio Shack, Wal-Mart
53b a	VA 28, to Centreville, Dulles Airport, Manassas Museum, **S...gas:** Exxon, Mobil/diesel, 7-11, **food:** Chesapeake Bay Seafood, Jake's Rest., LoneStar Steaks, McDonald's, **lodging:** SpringHill Suites, **other:** Drug Emporium, Giant Foods, Jo-Ann Fabrics, Peoples Drug, same as 52
52	US 29, to Bull Run Park, **N...gas:** Shell, **other:** Goodyear/auto, camping, **S...gas:** Exxon, Mobil/diesel, 7-11, **food:** BBQ, Copeland's Café, Domino's, Hunter Mill Deli, LoneStar Steaks, McDonald's, Ruby Tuesday, Wendy's, **other:** CVS Drug, Jo-Ann Fabrics, Radio Shack, Shoppers Foods, Tire Express, same as 53
49mm	**Welcome Ctr both lanes, full(facilities)facilities, phone, picnic tables, litter barrels, petwalk**
47b a	VA 234, to Manassas, **N...gas:** Shell/diesel, **food:** Blimpie, Cracker Barrel, Hershey's IceCream, Uno Pizzaria, Wendy's, **lodging:** Country Inn Suites, Courtyard, Fairfield Inn, Holiday Inn, **other:** Borders, Kohl's, Old Navy, Manassas Nat Bfd, cinema, **S...gas:** Amoco, Citgo/7-11, Costco/gas, Exxon, RaceTrac/diesel/24hr, Shell/repair, Sunoco/24hr, **food:** American Steak/buffet, Anita's Mexican, Bertucci's Pizza, Bob Evans, Boston Mkt, Burger King, Checker's, Chelsea's Rest., Chili's, Damon's, Denny's, Domino's, Don Pablo's, Hooters, KFC, Little Caesar's, Logan's Roadhouse, McDonald's, Old Country Buffet, Olive Garden, Pizza Hut, Red Lobster, Ruby Tuesday, Schlotsky's, Shoney's, Starbucks, Subway, Taco Bell, TGIFriday, Wendy's, Wok'n Roll, Zipani Bread Café, **lodging:** Best Western, Day's Inn, Hampton Inn, Red Roof Inn, Super 8, **other:** MEDICAL CARE, Aamco,

VIRGINIA

Interstate 66

Exit #	Services
	Barnes&Noble, Camping World RV Service/supples, Circuit City, CVS Drug, Chevrolet, Food Lion, Giant Foods, GMC/Pontiac, Hecht's, Home Depot, Honda, JC Penney, K-Mart, Lowe's Whse, Marshall's, Merchant Auto Ctr, NTB, Office Depot, PepBoys, Reines RV Ctr, Saturn, Sears/auto, Shoppers Club, Staples, Super Fresh Foods, Trak Parts, U-Haul, Upton's, Wal-Mart
44	VA 234(from wb), Manassas, airport
43b a	US 29, Gainesville, to Warrenton, **S...gas:** Citgo/7-11, Exxon/diesel, Mobil, RaceTrac, Shell/diesel/24hr, **food:** Burger King, Joe's Italian/pizza, McDonald's, Subway, Wendy's, **other:** Giant Foods, Hillwood Camping
40	US 15, Haymarket, **N...other:** Yogi Bear's Camping(5mi), **S...gas:** Mobil/diesel/24hr, Sheetz/diesel/24hr, **lodging:** Lee-Hi Motel(5mi)
31	VA 245, to Old Tavern, **1 mi N...gas:** BP/diesel
28	US 17 S, Marshall, **N...gas:** Amoco/diesel, Citgo, **food:** McDonald's, **other:** HOSPITAL
27	VA 55 E, VA 647, Marshall, **1-2 mi N...gas:** Chevron/diesel, Citgo, Exxon/diesel, **food:** Old Salem Rest.
23	US 17 N, VA 55, Delaplane(no re-entry from eb), no facilities
20mm	Goose Creek
18	VA 688, Markham, no facilities
13	VA 79, to VA 55, Linden, Front Royal, **S...**Chevron/diesel/24hr, Mobil/24hr, Applehouse Rest., BBQ, **5-6 mi S...food:** Burger King, Donut Express, KFC, **lodging:** Central City Motel, Quality Inn, Pioneer Motel, Super 8, **other:** KOA(seasonal), to Shenandoah NP, Skyline Drive, ski area
11mm	Manassas Run
7mm	Shenandoah River
6	US 340, US 522, Front Royal, to Winchester, **S...gas:** Exxon/Baskin-Robbins, Mobil/24hr, **food:** McDonald's, **other:** HOSPITAL, **1-2 mi S...gas:** East Coast, **food:** Arby's, Hardee's, Pizza Hut, Tastee Freez Rest., Wendy's, **lodging:** Bluemont Motel, Blue Ridge Motel, Front Royal Motel, Relax Inn, Shenandoah Motel, Twin Rivers Motel, **other:** Gooney Creek Camping(7mi), KOA(6mi), Poe's Southfork Camping(2mi)
1b a	I-81, N to Winchester, S to Roanoke
0mm	I-66 begins/ends on I-81, exit 300.

Wytheville

Interstate 77

Exit #	Services
67mm	Virginia/West Virginia state line, East River Mtn
66	VA 598, to East River Mtn, no facilities
64	US 52, VA 61, to Rocky Gap, no facilities
62	VA 606, to South Gap, no facilities
61.5mm	**Welcome Ctr sb, full(handicapped)facilities, info, phone, vending, picnic tables, litter barrels, petwalk**
60mm	**rest area nb, full(handicapped)facilities, phone, vending, picnic tables, litter barrels, petwalk**
58	US 52, to Bastian, **E...gas:** BP/diesel, **W...gas:** Citgo/diesel, Exxon/diesel
56mm	runaway ramp nb
52	US 52, VA 42, Bland, **E...gas:** Citgo, **food:** Bland Square Rest., **W...gas:** Shell/DQ/diesel, **food:** Log Cabin Rest., **lodging:** Big Walker Motel
51.5mm	weigh sta both lanes
48mm	Big Walker Mtn
47	VA 717, **6 mi W...other:** to Deer Trail Park/NF Camping
41	VA 610, Peppers Ferry, Wytheville, **E...food:** Sagebrush Steaks, **lodging:** Best Western, Sleep Inn, Super 8, **W...gas:** Shell/diesel/24hr, TA/BP/Subway/Taco Bell/diesel/24hr/@, **food:** Country Kitchen, Wendy's, **lodging:** Hampton Inn, Ramada/rest.
40	I-81 S, to Bristol, US 52 N
I-77 and I-81 run together 9 mi. See Virginia Interstate 81, exits 73-80.	
32	I-81 N, to Roanoke
26mm	New River
24	VA 69, to Poplar Camp, **E...other:** to Shot Tower SP, New River Trail Info Ctr, **W...gas:** Citgo/diesel
19	VA 620, airport
14	US 58, US 221, to Hillsville, Galax, **E...gas:** Citgo/Subway, **food:** Burger King(2mi), Peking Palace, Pizza Hut(2mi), **lodging:** Nob Hill Motel, Red Carpet Inn, **other:** HOSPITAL, **W...gas:** BP/24hr, Chevron/Pizza Inn/diesel/24hr, Exxon/DQ/diesel, **food:** McDonald's, Shoney's, **lodging:** Best Western, Comfort Inn, Hampton Inn, Holiday Inn Express, **other:** Carrollwood Camping, Ford/Mercury
8	VA 148, VA 775, to Fancy Gap, **E...gas:** Chevron(2mi), Citgo/diesel, **lodging:** Lakeview Motel/rest., Mountaintop Motel/rest., **other:** Fox Trail Camping, Utt's Camping, to Blue Ridge Pkwy, **W...gas:** BP, Exxon/diesel, **food:** On the Way Rest., **lodging:** Countryview Inn, Day's Inn
6.5mm	runaway truck ramp sb
4.5mm	runaway truck ramp sb
3mm	runaway truck ramp sb
1	VA 620, no facilities
.5mm	**Welcome Ctr nb, full(handicapped)facilities, info, phone, picnic tables, litter barrels, petwalk**
0mm	Virginia/North Carolina state line

Interstate 81

N ↕ S

Exit #	Services
324mm	Virginia/West Virginia state line
323	VA 669, to US 11, Whitehall, **E...gas:** Exxon, **W...gas:** Flying J/Country Mkt/diesel/LP/24hr/@
321	VA 672, Clearbrook, **E...gas:** Mobil/diesel, **food:** Olde Stone Rest.
320mm	**Welcome Ctr sb, full(handicapped)facilities, phone, vending, picnic tables, litter barrels, petwalk**
317	US 11, Stephenson, **W...gas:** Exxon/diesel, Liberty/diesel, Sheez/diesel, **food:** Burger King, Denny's, McDonald's, Pizza Hut/Taco Bell, Tastee Freez, Venice Italian, **lodging:** Comfort Inn, Econolodge, **other:** HOSPITAL, Candy Hill Camping(4mi)
315	VA 7, Winchester, **E...gas:** Exxon, Sheetz/24hr, **other:** Dodge/Volvo, mall, **W...gas:** Chevron/diesel, Liberty/diesel, Shell/diesel, **food:** Arby's, Capt D's, Hardee's, KFC, Little Caesar's, LJ Silver, McDonald's, Pizza Hut, Subway, Wendy's, **lodging:** Hampton Inn, Shoney's Inn/rest., **other:** Pharmor Drug
314mm	Abrams Creek
313	US 17/50/522, Winchester, **E...gas:** BP/diesel, Exxon, Mobil/diesel, Shell/diesel, **food:** Asia Garden, Chason's Buffet, Cracker Barrel, Golden Corral, Hoss' Steaks, IHOP, Texas Roadhouse, Waffle House, **lodging:** Comfort Inn, Holiday Inn, Red Roof Inn, Super 8, Travelodge, **other:** Costco, Food Lion, Ford/Lincoln/Mercury/Nissan, Harley-Davidson, JoAnn Fabrics, Target, **W...gas:** Sheetz/24hr, **food:** Bob Evans, Chick-fil-A, Chili's, China Jade, CiCi's, El Ranchero, KFC, McDonald's, Pargo's, Perkins, Pizza Hut/Taco Bell, Ruby Tuesday, Sam's Hotdogs, Subway, Wendy's, **lodging:** Baymont Inn, Best Western, Hampton Inn, Wingate Inn, **other:** BooksAMillion, Circuit City, $Tree, Home Depot, JC Penney, K-Mart, Kohl's, Kroger, Lowe's Whse, Martin Foods, OfficeMax, PepBoys, Sears/auto, Staples, Trak Parts, Target, Wal-Mart SuperCtr/24hr, mall, to Shenandoah U
310	VA 37, to US 11, **1 mi W...lodging:** Best Value Inn, Day's Inn, Echo Village Motel, Relax Inn, Royal Inn, **other:** HOSPITAL, Candy Hill Camping(6mi)
307	VA 277, Stephens City, **E...gas:** Citgo/7-11, Shell/diesel, **food:** Burger King, KFC/Taco Bell, McDonald's, Roma Italian, Subway, Waffle House, Wendy's, Western Steer, **lodging:** Comfort Inn, Holiday Inn Express, **other:** MEDICAL CARE, White Oak Camping, **W...**Exxon, Sheetz/24hr, Redwood Budget Inn
304mm	weigh sta both lanes
302	VA 627, Middletown, **E...gas:** Exxon/diesel, **W...gas:** Citgo/7-11, Liberty/diesel, **food:** Godfather's, **lodging:** Super 8, Wayside Inn/rest., **other:** to Wayside Theatre
300	I-66 E, to Washington, to Shenandoah NP, Skyline Dr

Winchester

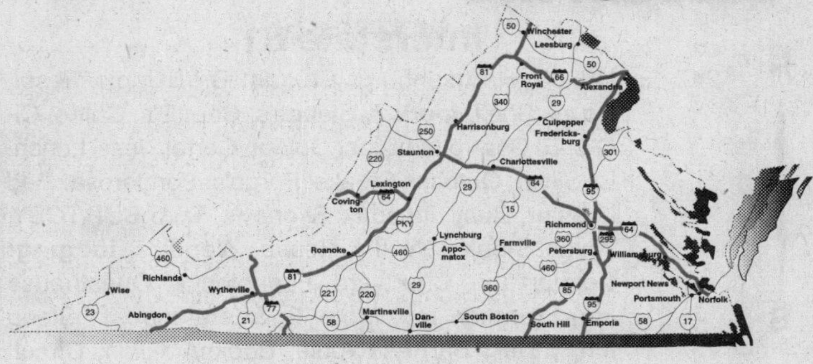

Exit #	Services
298	US 11, Strausburg, **E...gas:** BP/diesel, Exxon/diesel/LP, **food:** Burger King, McDonald's, **lodging:** Hotel Strausburg/rest., **other:** Battle of Cedar Creek Camping, **W...other:** to Belle Grove Plantation
296	VA 55, Strausburg, **E...other:** to Hupp's Hill Bfd Museum
291	VA 651, Toms Brook, **E...lodging:** Budget Inn, **W...gas:** Love's/Arby's/diesel/24hr/@, Wilco/Hess/DQ/diesel/24hr/@, **other:** truckwash
283	VA 42, Woodstock, **E...gas:** Chevron/7-11, Sheetz, Shell, **food:** Arby's, Hardee's, KFC, McDonald's, Pizza Hut, Ponderosa, Taco Bell, Wendy's, **lodging:** Budget Host, Comfort Inn, Ramada/rest., **other:** HOSPITAL, to Massanutten Military Academy, **W...gas:** Exxon/diesel/24hr, Sunoco, **food:** China Wok, Subway, **other:** $Tree, Wal-Mart SuperCtr/24hr
279	VA 185, VA 675, Edinburg, **E...gas:** BP/diesel, Exxon/diesel, Shell/diesel/24hr, **food:** Edinburg Mill Rest., Subway, **other:** Creek Side Camping(2mi)
277	VA 614, Bowmans Crossing, no facilities
273	VA 292, VA 703, Mt Jackson, **E...gas:** Citgo/7-11, Exxon/diesel, Liberty/Blimpie/diesel, Sheetz/Wendy's/diesel/24hr, **food:** Burger King, Denny's, Godfather's, **lodging:** Best Western/rest., **other:** $General, Food Lion/24hr, Radio Shack, USPO
269	VA 730, to Shenandoah Caverns, **E...gas:** Chevron/diesel
269mm	N Fork Shenandoah River
264	US 211, New Market, **E...gas:** BP/Blimpie/diesel, Chevron/diesel, Exxon/diesel, Shell/diesel, **food:** Burger King, McDonald's, Pizza Hut, Southern Kitchen, Taco Bell, **lodging:** Budget Inn, Quality Inn, Shenvalee Motel/rest., **other:** Rancho Camping, to Shenandoah NP, Skyline Dr, **W...gas:** Citgo/7-11, **lodging:** Day's Inn, **other:** to New Market Bfd
262mm	**rest area both lanes, full(handicapped)facilities, phone, vending, picnic tables, litter barrels, petwalk**
257	US 11, VA 259, to Broadway, **3-5 mi E...other:** KOA, Endless Caverns Camping
251	US 11, Harrisonburg, **W...gas:** Exxon/diesel, **lodging:** Economy Inn

VIRGINIA

Interstate 81

N ↕ S Harrisonburg

247 US 33, Harrisonburg, **E...gas:** BP/Blimpie/diesel, Royal, Shell, **food:** Applebee's, Capt D's, Chili's, Ci-Ci's, El Charro Mexican, Golden Corral, Jess' Lunch, LJ Silver, Outback Steaks, Pargo's, Ponderosa, Red Lobster, Ruby Tuesday, Shoney's, Taco Bell, TCBY, Texas Steaks, Waffle House, Wendy's, **lodging:** Comfort Inn, Courtyard, Econolodge, Guesthouse Inn, Hampton Inn, Motel 6, Sheraton/rest., Sleep Inn, **other:** Barnes&Noble, BooksAMillion, Circuit City, Food Lion, Home Depot, Kroger, K-Mart, Lowe's Whse, Nissan, OfficeMax, PepBoys, Staples, Wal-Mart SuperCtr/24hr, to Shenandoah NP, Skyline Dr, mall, **W...gas:** Chevron/diesel, Exxon/diesel, Sheetz, **food:** Arby's, Golden China, Hardee's, KFC, Kyoto, McDonald's, Mr Gatti's, Pizza Hut, Sam's Hotdogs, Subway, **lodging:** Marvilla Motel, **other:** HOSPITAL, Advance Parts, CVS Drug, Radio Shack

245 VA 659, Port Republic Rd, **E...gas:** Exxon/Subway/diesel, Liberty/Blimpie/diesel, Shell, **food:** DQ, **lodging:** J Day's Inn, Howard Johnson, **W...other:** HOSPITAL, to James Madison U

243 US 11, to Harrisonburg, **W...gas:** BP/diesel, Citgo/7-11, Exxon/diesel, Harrisonburg Trkstp/diesel, Liberty/diesel, **food:** Burger King, Cracker Barrel, McDonald's, Taco Bell, Waffle House, **lodging:** Holiday Inn Express, Ramada Inn, Red Carpet Inn, Rockingham Motel, Super 8, **other:** Advance Parts, BMW, Chrysler, Ford/Lincoln/Mercury, Hyundai, Kia, Subaru, Toyota

240 VA 257, VA 682, Mount Crawford, **1-3 mi W...gas:** Exxon/diesel, Liberty/gas, **food:** Burger King, **lodging:** Village Inn, **other:** Natural Chimneys Camping

235 VA 256, Weyers Cave, **E...gas:** Mobil/diesel, **W...gas:** BP/Subway/diesel, Exxon/diesel, **lodging:** Augusta Motel, **other:** to Grand Caverns

232mm rest area both lanes, full(handicapped)facilities, phone, vending, picnic tables, litter barrels, petwalk

227 VA 612, Verona, **E...gas:** BP/Subway/diesel, **lodging:** Waffle Inn, **other:** North 340 Camping(11mi), **W...gas:** Citgo/diesel, Exxon, Plaza/diesel, **food:** Arby's, Burger King, Hardee's, KFC, McDonald's, Wendy's, **lodging:** Ramada Ltd, **other:** CVS Drug, Food Lion, KOA(3mi)

225 VA 275, Woodrow Wilson Pkwy, **E...lodging:** Quality Inn/rest., **W...lodging:** Day's Inn, Holiday Inn/rest.

222 US 250, Staunton, **E...gas:** Citgo, Exxon/McDonald's/24hr, Shell/diesel, **food:** Cracker Barrel, Rowe's Rest., Shoney's, Texas Steaks, Wendy's, **lodging:** Best Western, Guesthouse Inn, Sleep Inn, **W...gas:** Sheetz, **food:** Burger King, Ryan's, Shorty's Diner, Waffle House, **lodging:** Comfort Inn, Econolodge, Microtel, Super 8, **other:** AutoZone, Lowe's Whse, TireMart, Toyota, Wal-Mart SuperCtr/24hr, American Frontier Culture Museum

221 I-64 E, to Charlottesville, to Skyline Dr, Shenandoah NP

220 VA 262, to US 11, Staunton, **1 mi W...gas:** Citgo, Etna, Exxon, Shell, **food:** Applebee's, Arby's, Burger King, Country Cookin', Hardee's, KFC, McDonald's, Red Lobster, Taco Bell, **lodging:** Budget Inn, Hampton Inn, **other:** Advance Parts, Harley-Davidson, Honda, JC Penney, Pontiac/Buick, Rule RV Ctr

217 VA 654, to Mint Spring, Stuarts Draft, **E...gas:** BP/Subway/diesel, Exxon/diesel, **lodging:** Day's Inn, Shenandoah Acres Resort(8mi), **W...gas:** Citgo/diesel/24hr, Crown, Liberty/gas, **lodging:** Red Carpet Inn, Walnut Hill Camping(4mi)

213b a US 11, US 340, Greenville, **E...gas:** BP/Subway, Pilot/Arby's/diesel/24hr/@, Shell, **lodging:** Budget Host

205 VA 606, Raphine, **E...gas:** Exxon/Burger King, Fuel City/diesel, Sunoco, Whites/diesel/24hr/motel/@, **W...gas:** Wilco/Wendy's/diesel/24hr/@, **lodging:** Day's Inn/rest.

200 VA 710, Fairfield, **E...gas:** Amoco/diesel/24hr, **food:** McDonald's, **W...gas:** Citgo/Sunshine/diesel/rest./@, Exxon/Subway/diesel, Shell/diesel

199mm rest area sb, full(handicapped)facilities, phone, vending, picnic tables, litter barrels, petwalk

195 US 11, Lee Highway, **E...lodging:** Maple Hall Lodging/dining, **W...gas:** Citgo/diesel/24hr, Shell/diesel, **food:** Aunt Sarah's, **lodging:** Howard Johnson/rest., Ramada Inn, Red Oak Inn, **other:** Lee-Hi Camping

191 I-64 W(exits left from nb), US 60, to Charleston

Lexington

188 US 60, to Lexington, Buena Vista, **3-5 mi E...gas:** Exxon, **food:** Country Cookin', Hardee's, KFC, LJ Silver, McDonald's, Pizza Hut, Taco Bell, Wendy's, **lodging:** Budget Inn, Buena Vista Inn, Comfort Inn, Day's Inn, **other:** HOSPITAL, to Glen Maury Park, to Stonewall Jackson Home, Marshall Museum, to Blue Ridge Pkwy, **W...gas:** Exxon/diesel/24hr, **lodging:** Day's Inn, Hampton Inn, **other:** to Washington&Lee U, VMI

180 US 11, Natural Bridge, **E...gas:** Pure/diesel, Shell, **food:** Fancy Hill Diner, **lodging:** Econo Inn, **W...gas:** Shell/diesel, **food:** Pink Cadillac Diner, **lodging:** Budget Inn, **other:** KOA

175 US 11 N, to Glasgow, Natural Bridge, **E...gas:** Exxon, **lodging:** Natural Bridge Hotel/rest., **other:** to James River RA, Jellystone Camping

168 VA 614, US 11, Arcadia, **E...gas:** Shell, **food:** MtnView Rest., **lodging:** Wattstull Inn, **other:** Wonderful Life Camping(6mi), **W...food:** Burger King

167 US 11(from sb), Buchanan

162 US 11, Buchanan, **E...gas:** Exxon/diesel, **other:** to BR Pkwy, **W...gas:** Shell/Subway/24hr

158mm rest area sb, full(handicapped)facilities, phone, vending, picnic tables, litter barrels, petwalk

156 VA 640, to US 11, **E...gas:** Exxon/diesel, Shell, **food:** Greenwood Rest.

150 US 11/220, to Fincastle, **E...gas:** Citgo/diesel/24hr, Dodge's/diesel, Exxon, Pilot/Subway/diesel/24hr, TA/BP/diesel/@, **food:** Country Cookin', Cracker Barrel, Hardee's, McDonald's, Shoney's, Taco Bell, Waffle

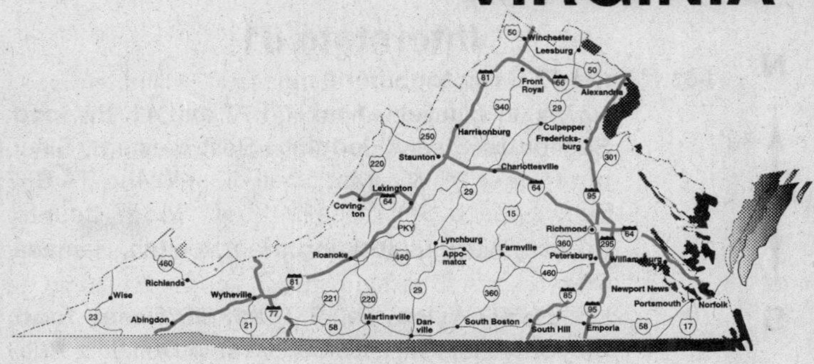

Interstate 81

N ↕ S

House, Wendy's, **lodging:** Comfort Inn, Day's Inn, Holiday Inn Express, Red Roof Inn, Travelodge, **other:** Berglun RV Ctr, CVS Drug, Winn-Dixie, **W...gas:** BP/diesel, Exxon/diesel/24hr, **food:** Bojangles, Pizza Hut, Teng Fi Chinese, **lodging:** Best Western, Econolodge

149mm weigh sta both lanes

146 VA 115, Cloverdale, **E...gas:** Exxon, Shell/diesel, **food:** Burger King, Chico&Billy's, Hardee's, McDonald's, Subway, Wildflour Café, **lodging:** Budget Motel, Country Inn Suites, Day's Inn/rest., Hampton Inn, Knight's Inn, Roanoker Motel

Roanoke

143 I-581, US 220, to Roanoke, Blue Ridge Pkwy(exits left from sb), **1 mi E...food:** Waffle House, **lodging:** Hampton Inn, Holiday Inn, Ramada Ltd, Super 8, **2-3 mi E on Herschberger...food:** Applebee's, Hardee's, IHOP, Logan's Roadhouse, O'Charley's, Ruby Tuesday, Texas Steaks, TGIFriday, **lodging:** AmeriSuites, Best Western, Clarion, Comfort Inn, Courtyard, Extended Stay America, Howard Johnson, Wyndham, **other:** Sears/auto, Target, Wal-Mart SuperCtr/gas/24hr, mall

141 VA 419, Salem, **1-2 mi E...gas:** BP, Exxon, Shell, **food:** Burger King, Hardee's, Country Cookin' Rest., McDonald's, **lodging:** Baymont Inn, Econolodge, Embassy Inn, Holiday Inn Express, Park Inn, Quality Inn, **other:** HOSPITAL, Chevrolet, **W...gas:** BP/diesel, Citgo

140 VA 311, Salem, **1 mi W...food:** Hanging Rock Grill/golf

137 VA 112, VA 619, Salem, **E...gas:** BP, Crown, Exxon, Sheetz, Shell/diesel, **food:** Applebee's, Arby's, Bojangles, Denny's, Dynasty Buffet, El Rodeo Mexican, Fazoli's, Hardee's, KFC, Mamma Maria Italian, McDonald's, Omelet Shoppe, Shoney's, Taco Bell, **lodging:** Comfort Inn, Econolodge, Super 8, **other:** AutoZone, Food Lion, Snyder's RV, Walgreen, Wal-Mart SuperCtr/24hr, **W...lodging:** Ramada Inn

132 VA 647, to Dixie Caverns, **E...gas:** Citgo, Shell, **lodging:** Budget Host, **other:** Dixie Caverns Camping, st police

129mm rest area nb, full(handicapped)facilities, phone, vending, picnic tables, litter barrels, petwalk

128 US 11, VA 603, Ironto, **E...gas:** Citgo/24hr, **W...gas:** Citgo/Subway/diesel/24hr

118c b a US 11/460, Christiansburg, **E...gas:** Shell/diesel, **food:** Denny's, Cracker Barrel, **lodging:** Day's Inn, Fairfield Inn, Hampton Inn, Holiday Inn Express, Super 8, **other:** Interstate RV Camping, **W...gas:** BP, Crown, Exxon/Subway, RaceWay, Shell/Bojangles, **food:** Country Cookin Rest., McDonald's, Pizza Hut, Shoney's, Waffle House, Wendy's, Western Sizzlin, **lodging:** Econolodge, Howard Johnson, **other:** HOSPITAL, Advance Parts, Chevrolet, Chrysler/Dodge, Ford/Toyota, Honda, to VA Tech

114 VA 8, Christiansburg, **W...gas:** Citgo, **food:** Burger King, Hardee's, Macado's Rest., Pizza Inn, **lodging:** Budget Inn

109 VA 177, VA 600, **W...gas:** BP/diesel, Marathon, **lodging:** Comfort Inn, **other:** HOSPITAL

107mm rest area both lanes, full(handicapped)facilities, phone, vending, picnic tables, litter barrels, petwalk

105 VA 232, VA 605, to Radford, **W...lodging:** Executive Inn

101 VA 660, to Claytor Lake SP, **E...lodging:** Claytor Lake Inn, Sleep Inn, **W...gas:** Chevron/diesel/@, Citgo/diesel, **food:** DQ, Omelet Shoppe, Taco Bell

98 VA 100 N, to Dublin, **E...gas:** BP, Exxon/Subway/diesel, **food:** Shoney's, **lodging:** Comfort Inn/rest., Hampton Inn, Holiday Inn Express, **W...gas:** Marathon, Shell/diesel, **food:** Blimpie, Burger King, McDonald's, Waffle House, Wendy's, **lodging:** Super 8, Travel Inn, **other:** HOSPITAL, to Wilderness Rd Museum

94b a VA 99 N, to Pulaski, **E...lodging:** Day's Inn, **W...gas:** Exxon, HOSPITAL

92 VA 658, to Draper, **E...gas:** BP, **other:** to New River Trail SP

89b a US 11 N, VA 100, to Pulaski, no facilities

86 VA 618, Service Rd, **W...gas:** I-81/Citgo/diesel/rest, **lodging:** Gateway Motel

84 VA 619, to Grahams Forge, **W...gas:** Love's/Subway/diesel/24hr/@, Shell/DQ/diesel/24hr, **lodging:** Fox Mtn Inn/rest., Trail Motel

81 I-77 S, to Charlotte, Galax, to Blue Ridge Pkwy. **I-81 S and I-77 N run together 9 mi.**

80 US 52 S, VA 121 N, to Ft Chiswell, **E...gas:** BP/Burger King/diesel, Flying J/diesel/rest/24hr/@, **food:** Wendy's, **lodging:** Hampton Inn, Super 8, **other:** Blue Beacon, FSA/famous brands, GS Camping, **W...gas:** Amoco, Citgo/diesel, **food:** McDonald's, **lodging:** Comfort Inn, **other:** Little Valley RV Ctr

Wytheville

77 Service Rd, **E...gas:** Citgo/Subway/diesel/24hr, Flying J/diesel/LP/rest./24hr/@; Hess/diesel, **food:** Burger King, **other:** KOA, **W...gas:** Exxon/diesel, Wilco/Hess/Arby's/diesel/24hr, **other:** st police

73 US 11 S, Wytheville, **E...gas:** Citgo, Mobil, Shell/diesel, **food:** Applebee's, Bob Evans, Burger King, Cracker Barrel, Great Wall Buffet, Hardee's, KFC, Pizza Hut, Shenanigan's Steaks, Shoney's, Waffle House, **lodging:** Budget Host, Day's Inn, Holiday Inn, Motel 6, Quality Inn, Red Carpet Inn, Travelodge, **other:** HOSPITAL, Buick

VIRGINIA

Interstate 81

N ↕ S

I-81 N and I-77 S run together 9 mi

72 I-77 N, to Bluefield, **1 mi N, I-77 exit 41, E...food:** Sagebrush Steaks, **lodging:** Best Western, Sleep Inn, Super 8, **W...gas:** Shell/diesel/24hr, TA/BP/Subway/Taco Bell/diesel/24hr/@, **food:** Country Kitchen, Wendy's, **lodging:** Hampton Inn, Ramada/rest.

70 US 21/52, Wytheville, **E...gas:** BP/diesel, **food:** Arby's, China Wok, Little Caesar's, McDonald's, Ruby Tuesday, Subway, Wendy's, **other:** HOSPITAL, CVS Drug, $Tree, Food Lion, Lowe's Whse, Wal-Mart SuperCtr/24hr, **W...gas:** Citgo, Etna, Exxon, **food:** DQ, LJ Silver, Pizza Hut, Scrooge's Rest., **lodging:** Comfort Inn, Econolodge, Koala Motel, Travelite Motel

67 US 11(from nb, no re-entry), to Wytheville, no facilities

61mm rest area nb, full(handicapped)facilities, phone, vending, picnic tables, litter barrels, petwalk, NO TRUCKS

60 VA 90, Rural Retreat, **E...gas:** Chevron/diesel, Citgo/Yesterdaze Diner/diesel, **food:** McDonald's, **other:** to Rural Retreat Lake, camping

54 rd 683, to Groseclose, **E...gas:** Exxon/DQ/diesel, Shell/diesel, **lodging:** Relax Inn

53.5mm rest area sb, full(handicapped)facilities, phone, vending, picnic tables, litter barrels, petwalk

50 US 11, Atkins, **W...gas:** Citgo/diesel/24hr, **food:** Subs on the Way, **lodging:** Comfort Inn

47 US 11, to Marion, **W...gas:** Amoco, Chevron/diesel/24hr, Exxon/diesel, **food:** Arby's, Burger King, McDonald's, Pizza Hut, **lodging:** Best Western/rest., Econolodge, VA House Inn, **other:** HOSPITAL, K-Mart, Radio Shack, SuperX Drug, to Hungry Mother SP(4mi)

Marion

45 VA 16, Marion, **E...food:** AppleTree Rest., **other:** to Grayson Highlands SP, Mt Rogers NRA, **W...gas:** Chevron, **food:** Hardee's, KFC, LJ Silver, Wendy's, **lodging:** Royal Inn

44 US 11, Marion, no facilities

39 US 11, VA 645, Seven Mile Ford, **E...lodging:** Budget Inn/rest., **W...other:** Interstate Camping/groceries

35 VA 107, Chilhowie, **E...gas:** Shell, **lodging:** Knight's Inn, **W...gas:** Chevron, Exxon, Rouse Fuel, **food:** McDonald's, Subway, TasteeFreez, **lodging:** Budget Inn(1mi), Rainbow Autel/rest., **other:** $General, Food City/gas

32 US 11, to Chilhowie, no facilities

29 VA 91, Glade Spring, to Damascus, **E...gas:** Petro/diesel/rest./24hr/@, **food:** Giardino's Italian, Pizza+, Wendy's, **lodging:** Swiss Inn/rest., Travelodge, **W...gas:** Chevron/diesel/24hr, Coastal, Exxon, **other:** CarQuest

26 VA 737, Emory, **W...other:** to Emory&Henry Coll

24 VA 80, Meadowview Rd, **W...**auto repair

22 VA 704, Enterprise Rd, no facilities

Abingdon

19 US 11/58, to Abingdon, **E...gas:** Shell/Subway/diesel, **other:** to Mt Rogers NRA, **W...gas:** Chevron/diesel/24hr, Citgo, Exxon/diesel, **food:** Burger King, Cracker Barrel, Harbor House Seafood, Huddle House, Omelet Shoppe, Wendy's, **lodging:** Alpine Motel, Day's Inn, Holiday Inn Express, Quality Inn

17 US 58A, VA 75, Abingdon, **E...gas:** Valero, **food:** Domino's, LJ Silver, **lodging:** Hampton Inn, **other:** Mr Transmission, **W...gas:** Chevron, Citgo/diesel, Exxon, **food:** Arby's, China Wok, Hardee's, KFC, McDonald's, Papa John's, Pizza Hut, Shoney's, Taco Bell, Wendy's, **lodging:** Martha Washington Inn, Super 8, **other:** HOSPITAL, Advance Parts, CVS Drug, $General, Food City, Kroger, K-Mart, Radio Shack

14 US 19, VA 140, Abingdon, **W...gas:** Chevron/diesel/24hr, Exxon, Shell/diesel, **food:** DQ, McDonald's, **lodging:** Budget Inn(3mi), Comfort Inn, **other:** Ford, Riverside Camping(10mi)

13.5mm TRUCKERS ONLY rest area nb, full(handicapped) facilities, phone, vending, picnic tables, litter barrels

13 VA 611, to Lee Hwy, **E...other:** Harley-Davidson, **W...gas:** Shell/diesel

10 US 11/19, Lee Hwy, **W...gas:** BP/diesel, Chevron, **lodging:** Beacon Inn, Deluxe Inn, Evergreen Inn, Skyland Inn

7 Old Airport Rd, **E...gas:** Citgo, Shell/diesel, **food:** Bob Evans, Bojangles, Sonic, **lodging:** La Quinta, **W...gas:** BP/diesel, Citgo/Wendy's, Conoco/diesel, **food:** Chop's Rest., Damon's, Fazoli's, Golden Corral, IHOP, Jumbo Buffet, Kobe Japanese, Logan's Roadhouse, O'Charley's, Outback Steaks, Pizza Hut, Ruby Tuesday, Subway, Taco Bell, **lodging:** Holiday Inn, Microtel, Motel 6, **other:** MEDICAL CARE, Advance Parts, Lowe's Whse, Office Depot, Wal-Mart SuperCtr/24hr, Sugar Hollow Camping

5 US 11/19, Lee Hwy, **E...gas:** Citgo, Shell, **food:** Arby's, Burger King, Hardee's, KFC, LJ Silver, McDonald's, Shoney's, Wendy's, **lodging:** Budget Inn, Crest Motel, Siesta Motel, Super 8, **other:** CVS Drug, Family$, Parts+, USPO, **W...gas:** Exxon, **lodging:** Comfort Inn, **other:** Blevins Tire, Buick/Pontiac, Lee Hwy Camping

Bristol

3 I-381 S, to Bristol, **1 mi E...gas:** Chevron, Citgo/diesel, Conoco, **food:** Applebee's, Pizza Hut, **lodging:** Econolodge

1 US 58/421, Bristol, **1 mi E...gas:** Chevron, Phillips 66, **food:** Burger King, Chick-fil-A, KFC, Krispy Kreme, LJ Silver, McDonald's, Taco Bell, Wendy's, **lodging:** Budget Host, Ramada Inn, **other:** HOSPITAL, CarQuest, CVS Drug, Dodge, Family$, Food Lion, Kroger, Lincoln/Mercury, Sears/auto, Walgreen, Wal-Mart/grill, mall, **W...gas:** Shell(1mi)

0mm Virginia/Tennessee state line, Welcome Ctr nb, full(handicapped)facilities, info, phone, vending, picnic tables, litter barrels, petwalk, NO TRUCKS

Interstate 85

N ↕ S

Petersburg

Exit #	Services
69mm	I-85 begins/ends on I-95.
69	US 301, Petersburg, Wythe St, Washington St, **W...lodging:** Regency Inn
68	I-95 S, US 460 E, to Norfolk, Crater Rd, **E...**HOSPITAL, **3/4 mi E...gas:** Exxon/diesel, RaceTrac/diesel, Shell, **food:** Hardee's, **lodging:** California Inn, **other:** to Petersburg Nat Bfd
65	Squirrel Level Rd, **E...other:** to Richard Bland Coll, **W...gas:** BP/diesel
63b a	US 1, to Petersburg, **E...gas:** Chevron/diesel, Exxon/diesel/24hr, Shell, Texaco/diesel/24hr, Thriftmart Plaza/diesel, **food:** Burger King, Hardee's, Waffle House, **W...gas:** Amoco, **food:** McDonald's
61	US 460, to Blackstone, **E...gas:** Amoco, EastCoast/Subway/TCBY/diesel/LP, **lodging:** Day's Inn(3mi), **W...gas:** Shell/diesel, **other:** Picture Lake Camping(2mi), airport
55mm	**rest area both lanes, full(handicapped)facilities, phone, picnic tables, litter barrels, vending, petwalk**
53	VA 703, Dinwiddie, **W...gas:** Exxon/diesel, **food:** HomePlace Rest., ThatsaBurger, **other:** to 5 Forks Nat Bfd
52mm	Stony Creek
48	VA 650, DeWitt, no facilities
42	VA 40, McKenney, **W...gas:** Citgo, Exxon, **other:** auto repair, **1.5 mi W...lodging:** Economy Inn
40mm	Nottoway River
39	VA 712, to Rawlings, **E...other:** VA Battlerama, **W...gas:** Chevron/diesel/24hr, Circle Dmart/diesel, Citgo/diesel, **lodging:** Nottoway Motel/rest.
34	VA 630, Warfield, **W...gas:** Exxon/diesel
32mm	**rest area both lanes, full(handicapped)facilities, phone, picnic tables, litter barrels, vending, petwalk**
28	US 1, Alberta, **W...gas:** Exxon
27	VA 46, to Lawrenceville, **E...other:** to St Paul's Coll
24	VA 644, to Meredithville, no facilities
22mm	weigh sta both lanes
20mm	Meherrin River
15	US 1, to South Hill, **E...gas:** Citgo/deli, **W...gas:** Shell, **food:** Kahill's Diner
12	US 58, VA 47, to South Hill, **E...gas:** RaceTrac, Shell/SlipIn, **food:** Arnold's Diner, Bojangles, Domino's, **lodging:** Hampton Inn, Holiday Inn Express, Super 8, **other:** $Tree, Wal-Mart, **W...gas:** Amoco/diesel, Chevron/diesel/repair, Exxon/diesel, Petrol, Shell/diesel, **food:** Brian's Steaks, Burger King, Denny's, Golden Corral, Hardee's, KFC, McDonald's, New China, Pizza Hut, Subway, Taco Bell, Wendy's, **lodging:** Best Western, Comfort Inn, Econolodge, **other:** HOSPITAL, CVS Drug, $General, Farmers Foods, Goodyear/auto, Roses, Winn-Dixie
4	VA 903, to Bracey, Lake Gaston, **E...gas:** Amoco/DQ/Subway/diesel, Exxon/diesel/rest./24hr, **other:** Americamps Camping(5mi), **W...gas:** Shell/Pizza Hut, **lodging:** Day's Inn/rest.
3mm	Lake Gaston
1mm	**Welcome Ctr nb, full(handicapped)facilities, phone, picnic tables, phones, litter barrels, vending, petwalk**
0mm	Virginia/North Carolina state line

South Hill

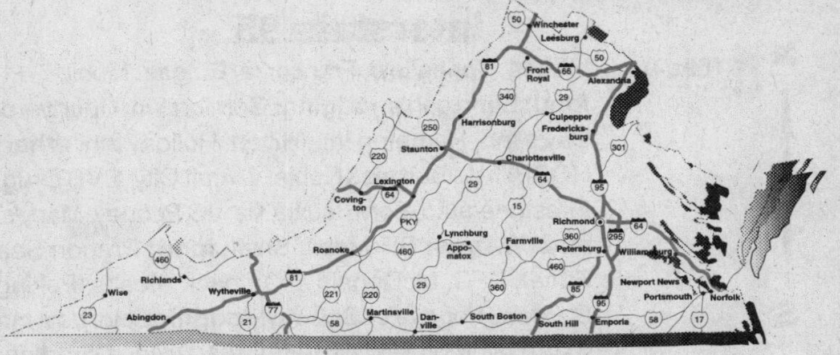

Interstate 95

N ↕ S

DC Area

Exit #	Services
178mm	Virginia/Maryland state line, Potomac River, W Wilson Mem Br
177c b a	US 1, to Alexandria, Ft Belvoir, **E...gas:** Amoco, Mobil, Shell/diesel, Sunoco, **food:** Alexandria Diner, Domino's, Great American Steak Buffet, **lodging:** Day's Inn, Hampton Inn, Red Roof Inn, Travelers Motel, **other:** Chevrolet, Chrysler/Plymouth/Jeep, Dodge, **W...gas:** Exxon/24hr, Hess
176b a	VA 241, Telegraph Rd, **E...gas:** Amoco, Exxon, Hess/diesel, **food:** Honolulu Rest., **other:** U-Haul, repair, **W...lodging:** Courtyard, Holiday Inn, **W on Duke St...gas:** Mobil, Shell/Subway/24hr, 7-11, **food:** Dunkin Donuts, Generous George's Pizza, McDonald's, Wendy's, **lodging:** Homestead Suites, **other:** CVS Drug, LandRover
174	Eisenhower Ave Connector, to Alexandria
172	rd 613, Van Dorn St, to Franconia, **E...lodging:** Comfort Inn, **1 mi W...gas:** Exxon, Shell, **food:** Dunkin Donuts, Jerry's Rest., McDonald's, Papa John's, Red Lobster, **other:** Aamco, Giant Foods, NTB, Radio Shack
170a	I-495 N, to Rockville. I-495 & I-95 N run together to MD.
b	I-395 N, to Washington

VIRGINIA

Interstate 95

N ↕ S

169b a VA 644, Springfield, Franconia, **E...gas:** Mobil, 7-11, **food:** Bennigan's, **lodging:** Comfort Inn, Courtyard, Day's Inn, Hampton Inn, Hilton, Holiday Inn, **other:** HOSPITAL, Barnes&Noble, Circuit City, CVS Drug, Firestone/auto, Ford, Isuzu/Kia, JC Penney, Macy's, mall, **W...gas:** BP, Mobil, Shell, **food:** Dragon Sea Buffet, KFC, McDonald's, Outback Steaks, Peking Garden, Popeye's, Subway, **lodging:** Holiday Inn Express, Motel 6, **other:** CVS Drug, Diahatsu, Dodge, Giant Foods, Goodyear/auto, K-Mart, Radio Shack, Subaru/VW, Toyota

167 VA 617, Back Lick Rd(from sb), no facilities

166b a VA 7100, to Ft Belvoir, Newington, **E...gas:** Exxon/diesel, **lodging:** Hunter Motel/rest., **W...gas:** Exxon, InterFuel/diesel, **food:** McDonald's, **other:** Chevrolet, Nissan

163 VA 642, Lorton, **E...gas:** Citgo, Shell/24hr, **W...gas:** Shell, **food:** Burger King, Café Platters, Gunston Wok, **lodging:** Comfort Inn

161 US 1 S(no nb re-entry, exits left from sb), to Ft Belvoir, Mt Vernon, Woodlawn Plantation, Gunston Hall, **1 mi E**...access to same as 160, along US 1

160.5mm Occoquan River

160b a VA 123 N, Woodbridge, Occoquan, **E...gas:** BP/diesel, Exxon, Mobil, Shell, **food:** Lum's, Subway, Taco Bell, TexMex, **lodging:** Comfort Inn, Econolodge, Friendship Inn, Hampton Inn, **other:** Aldi Foods, Ford, Food Lion, GNC, K-Mart, Radio Shack, Trak Auto, **W...gas:** BP, Exxon/diesel, Mobil, Shell, 7-11, **food:** KFC, McDonald's, **other:** VA Grill, Wendy's

158b a VA 3000, Prince William Pkwy, Woodbridge, **W...gas:** Exxon, Mobil, Shell, **food:** Boston Mkt, Taco Bell, Wendy's, **lodging:** Fairfield Inn

156 VA 784, Potomac Mills, **E...gas:** Exxon, Wawa/gas, **food:** Checkers, McDonald's, Taco Bell, **other:** HOSPITAL, Hyundai, Kia, Lincoln/Mercury, Mazda, Mitsubishi, Nissan, Radio Shack, Safeway, Trak Auto, to Leesylvania SP, **W...gas:** Exxon, Mobil, Shell, **food:** Blackeyed Pea, Bob Evans, Burger King, Chesapeake Bay Seafood, Chili's, Domino's, El Charro Mexican, Jazz St Grill, Jerry's Subs, McDonald's, Olive Garden, Outback Steaks, Pizza Hut, Popeye's, Silver Diner, Wendy's, **lodging:** Day's Inn, Wytestone Suites, **other:** Circuit City, CompUSA, Firestone/auto, K-Mart, Marshall's, Michael's, NTB, Staples, U-Haul

155mm **rest area both lanes, full(handicapped)facilities, phone, vending, picnic tables, litter barrels, petwalk, no trucks**

154mm truck rest area/weigh sta both lanes

152 VA 234, Dumfries, to Manassas, **E...gas:** BP/diesel/24hr, Chevron/service, Shell/diesel, **food:** Golden Corral, KFC, McDonald's, Taco Bell, **lodging:** Sleep Inn, Super 8, **other:** NAPA Autocare, Weems-Botts Museum, **W...gas:** Citgo/7-11, Exxon/Blimpie, Shell, **food:** Cracker Barrel, MontClair Rest., Tizieno Italian, Waffle House, **lodging:** Econolodge, Hampton Inn, Holiday Inn Express

150 VA 619, to Triangle, Quantico, **E...gas:** BP/diesel, Citgo/7-11, Exxon, Shell/diesel, **food:** Burger King, Dunkin Donuts, Jim's Subs/pizza, McDonald's, Wendy's, **lodging:** Ramada Inn, US Inn, **other:** auto repair, to Marine Corps Base, **W...**Prince William Forest Park

148 to Quantico, **2 mi E...gas:** Mobil/diesel, Spring Lake Motel, to Marine Corps Base

143b a to US 1, VA 610, Aquia, **E...gas:** Exxon, Shell/diesel/24hr, **food:** Carlos O'Kelly's, DQ, DaVanzo's Italian, Imperial Garden, KFC, Little Caesar's, McDonald's, Pizza Hut, Ruby Tuesday, Shoney's, Subway, Wendy's, **lodging:** Day's Inn, Hampton Inn, **other:** GNC, Radio Shack, Rite Aid, Shoppers Foods, Tires+, **W...gas:** BP/diesel, Citgo/7-11/diesel, Exxon, Shell/diesel, **food:** Burger King, Chick-fil-A, China Buffet, China Wok, Dunkin Donuts, Golden Corral, McDonald's, Perkins, Popeye's, Taco Bell, Wendy's, **lodging:** Comfort Inn, Country Inn, Holiday Inn Express, Super 8, **other:** CVS Drug, $General, Giant Foods, Home Depot, Merchants Tire, Wal-Mart/auto, Aquia Pines Camping

140 VA 630, Stafford, **E...gas:** BP, Mobil, Shell/diesel, **food:** McDonald's, Plaza Subs, **lodging:** Bradshaw Motel(3mi), **W...gas:** BP/diesel, Shell/diesel

137mm Potomac Creek

133b a US 17 N, to Warrenton, **E...gas:** Exxon/diesel, Mobil/diesel, RaceTrac, 7-11, **food:** Arby's, Illiano Pizzaria, Paradise Diner, **lodging:** Howard Johnson Express, Motel 6, **W...gas:** BP/diesel, Chevron, Citgo/7-11, EastCoast/Subway/diesel, Shell/diesel, **food:** Burger King, Johnny Appleseed Rest., McDonald's, Pizza Hut, Ponderosa, Taco Bell, Waffle House, Wendy's, ServiceTown Rest., **lodging:** Best Inn, Comfort Inn, Day's Inn, Holiday Inn, Quality Inn, Ramada Ltd, Sleep Inn, Super 8, Travelodge, Wingate Inn, **other:** Blue Beacon, CVS Drug, Food Lion

132.5mm Rappahannock River

132mm **rest area sb, full(handicapped)facilities, phone, picnic tables, litter barrels, petwalk, vending**

130b a VA 3, to Fredericksburg, **E...gas:** BP/diesel/24hr, Mobil/diesel, RaceTrac, Shell, 7-11, Wawa/24hr, **food:** Arby's, Bob Evans, Café daVanzo, Carlos O'Kelly's, Chesapeake Bay Seafood, CiCi's, Dunkin Donuts, Friendly's, KFC, LoneStar Steaks, LJSilver, McDonald's, Mkt St Buffet, Popeye's, Shoney's, Subway, TCBY, Top's Chinese, Wendy's, **lodging:** Best Western, Hampton Inn, **other:** HOSPITAL, Batteries+, $King, Hancock Fabrics, Home Depot, Pep-Boys, Radio Shack, Staples, **W...gas:** BP, Citgo/7-11, Crown Gas, Exxon/diesel/24hr, Shell, Wawa/24hr,

Fredericksburg

Interstate 95

N ↑↓ S

Fredericksburg

food: Applebee's, Aunt Sarah's, BBQ, Boston Mkt, Burger King, Denny's, Fuddrucker's, Great Steak, IHOP, Ledo Pizza, Little Caesar's, McDonald's, NY Diner, Old Country Buffet, Olive Garden, Outback Steaks, Piccadilly, Pizza Hut, Popeye's, Prime Rib, Red Lobster, Ruby Tuesday, Santa Fe Grill, Starbucks, Taco Bell, TGIFriday, Tia's TexMex, Waffle House, **lodging:** Econolodge, Holiday Inn, Ramada Inn, Sheraton, Super 8, **other:** Belk, Best Buy, BJ's Whse, Borders Books, Circuit City, Giant Foods, GNC, Hecht's, JC Penney, Kohl's, K-Mart, Lowe's Whse, Merchants Tire, Michaels, NTB, Office Depot, Old Navy, Sears/auto, Shoppers Foods, Target, Wal-Mart SuperCtr/24hr, mall

126 US 1, US 17 S, to Fredericksburg, **E...gas:** Amoco, BP, Citgo/7-11, Exxon/Subway, Mobil, Shell/diesel, **food:** Arby's, Denny's, El Charro Mexican, McDonald's, Pizza Hut, Ruby Tuesday, Shoney's, Taco Bell, Waffle House, Wendy's, Western Sizzlin, **lodging:** Day's Inn/rest., Econolodge, Fairfield Inn, Holiday Inn, Howard Johnson, Ramada Inn, Super 8, **other:** Buick/Pontiac/GMC, Cadillac, CarQuest, CVS Drug, Goodyear/auto, Honda/Nissan/Mazda/VW, Merchants Tire, Rite Aid, **W...gas:** Exxon/Blimpie, RaceTrac/diesel/24hr, **food:** Aunt Sarah's, Burger King, Cracker Barrel, Damon's, Durango's Steaks, Golden China, KFC, McDonald's, **lodging:** Comfort Inn, WyteStone Suites, **other:** Massaponax Outlet Ctr/famous brands, KOA(6mi)

118 VA 606, to Thornburg, **E...gas:** Shell/diesel, **other:** to Stonewall Jackson Shrine, **W...gas:** BP, Citgo/diesel, Exxon, Mobil/diesel/24hr, **food:** Burger King, McDonald's, **lodging:** Holiday Inn Express, Lamplighter Motel, **other:** KOA(7mi), to Lake Anna SP

110 VA 639, to Ladysmith, **E...gas:** Shell/diesel, **W...gas:** Citgo/diesel, Exxon/diesel

108mm rest area both lanes, full(handicapped)facilities, vending, phone, picnic tables, litter barrels, petwalk

104 VA 207, to US 301, Bowling Green, **E...gas:** BP/diesel, Chevron, Exxon/diesel, Mr Fuel/diesel, Petro/diesel/rest./24hr/@, Pilot/Subway/DQ/diesel/24hr/@, Shell/diesel, **food:** McDonald's, Wendy's, **lodging:** Holiday Inn Express, Howard Johnson, **other:** Blue Beacon, Russell Stover Candies, to Ft AP Hill, **W...gas:** Exxon/diesel, Flying J/Country Mkt/diesel/24hr/@, **food:** Aunt Sarah's, Kristina's Pizza, Waffle House, **lodging:** Comfort Inn, Day's Inn/rest., Ramada Inn, Travelodge, **other:** CarQuest

98 VA 30, Doswell, **E...**to King's Dominion Funpark, **gas:** Citgo/7-11, Shell/diesel, **food:** Burger King, Denny's, **lodging:** Best Western, Econolodge, **other:** All American Camping, King's Dominion Camping, truckwash

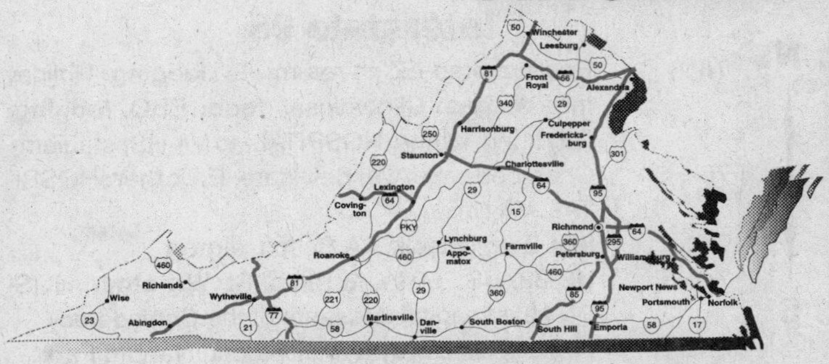

92 VA 54, Ashland, **E...gas:** Mobil, **W...gas:** BP, TA/diesel/rest./@, Chevron, Citgo/diesel, EastCoast/Blimpie/diesel, Exxon/Subway, Shell/diesel, **food:** Arby's, Burger King, Capt D's, Cracker Barrel, DQ, Hardee's, Jersey Mike's Subs, KFC, Los Amigos Mexican, McDonald's, PapaLou Pizza, Pizza Hut, Ponderosa, Popeye's, Shoney's, Taco Bell, Waffle House, Wendy's, **lodging:** Budget Inn, Comfort Inn, Day's Inn, Econolodge, Hampton Inn, Microtel, Quality Inn, Ramada Inn, Super 8, **other:** Travelodge, Buick/Pontiac, CarQuest, Family$, Food Lion, Radio Shack, Rite Aid, Trak Auto, U-Haul, Ukrop's Foods

89 VA 802, to Lewistown Rd, **E...gas:** Shell, TA/Mobil/Pizza Hut/diesel/café/24hr/@, **other:** Americamps RV Camp, **W...lodging:** Cadillac Motel, **other:** Kosmo Village Camping

86 VA 656, to Atlee, Elmont, **E...gas:** Sheetz(1mi), **food:** McDonald's(1mi), **W...gas:** Citgo, Mobil, Shell/Subway/diesel, **food:** Applebee's, Burger King, Chili's, FoodCourt, Gino's Ristorante, McDonald's, Ruby Tuesday, Sbarro's, Shoney's, Wendy's, **lodging:** Best Western/rest., SpringHill Suites, **other:** Circuit City, Dillard's, Firestone/auto, Goodyear/auto, Hecht's, JCPenney, Michael's, OfficeMax, Sears/auto, Target, Ukrop's Foods, mall

84b a I-295 W, to I-64, E to Norfolk

83b a VA 73, Parham Rd, **W...gas:** Citgo/7-11, EC/diesel, Exxon/DQ, Shell/diesel, **food:** Aunt Sarah's, Burger King, Denny's, El Paso Mexican, Hardee's, KFC, Little Caesar's, McDonald's, Papa Lou's Pizza, Subway, Waffle House, Wendy's, **lodging:** Broadway Motel, Econolodge, Holiday Inn, Knight's Inn, Northbrook Inn, Quality Inn, Shoney's Inn, Sleep Inn, **other:** CVS Drug, Food Lion, Hannaford Foods, Kroger, Lowe's Whse, Wal-Mart SuperCtr/24hr

82 US 301, Chamberlayne Ave, **E...gas:** BP, Chevron, Citgo, Exxon/diesel, Mobil/diesel, Shell, **food:** Blimpie, Bojangles, Dunkin Donuts, Friendly's, McDonald's, Subway, Wendy's, **lodging:** Quality Inn, Ramada Ltd, Super 8, Town Motel

81 US 1, Chamberlayne Ave(from nb), same as 82

80 Hermitage Rd, Lakeside Ave(from nb, no return), **W...gas:** BP, EC/Subway, **other:** Goodyear/auto, Ginter Botanical Gardens

79 I-64 W, to Charlottesville, I-195 S, to U of Richmond

VIRGINIA

Interstate 95

N ↕ S

Richmond

78 Boulevard(no EZ nb return), **E...lodging:** Holiday Inn, **W...gas:** Citgo/diesel, **food:** BBQ, **lodging:** Day's Inn, **other:** HOSPITAL, to VA HS, stadium

76 Chamberlayne Ave, Belvidere, **E...other:** HOSPITAL, VA Union U

75 I-64 E, to Norfolk, VA Beach, airport

74c US 33, US 250 W, to Broad St, **W...other:** HOSPITAL, st capitol, Museum of the Confederacy

b Franklin St, **E...other:** Richmond Nat Bfd Park

a I-195 N, to Powhite Expswy, downtown

73.5mm James River

73 Maury St, to US 60, US 360, industrial area

69 VA 161, Bells Rd, **E...**Port of Richmond, **W...gas:** Exxon/diesel/24hr, Shell/diesel, **food:** Hardee's, McDonald's, **lodging:** Candlewood Suites, Holiday Inn, Red Roof Inn

67b a VA 895 toll E, VA 150, to Chippenham Pkwy, Falling Creek, **W...gas:** BP, Chevron/diesel, RaceTrac, Shell/diesel, **food:** Blimpie, Burger King, Hardee's, Wendy's

64 VA 613, to Willis Rd, **E...gas:** Exxon, Shell, **food:** Arby's, Aunt Sarah's, Waffle House, Econolodge, Ramada, Drewy's Bluff Bfd, **W...gas:** Chevron, Citgo/7-11, Mobil/diesel, Shell/diesel, **food:** Bridgette's Rest., Burger King, DQ, McDonald's, **lodging:** Country Inn Suites, Sleep Inn, Super 8, VIP Inn, **other:** flea mkt

62 VA 288 N, to Chesterfield, Powhite Pkwy, to airport

Chester

61b a VA 10, Chester, **E...gas:** RaceTrac/24hr, **food:** Hardee's, Imperial Seafood, **lodging:** Comfort Inn, Courtyard, Hampton Inn, Holiday Inn Express, Homewood Suites, Quality Inn, **other:** HOSPITAL, to James River Plantations, City Point NHS, **W...gas:** BP, Citgo/7-11/diesel, Crown/diesel, EC/diesel, Exxon/diesel, Shell, **food:** Applebee's, Burger King, Capt D's, Cracker Barrel, Denny's, Friendly's, Hardee's, KFC, McDonald's, Pizza Hut, Shoney's, Subway, Taco Bell, Waffle House, Wendy's, Western Sizzlin, **lodging:** Day's Inn, Fairfield Inn, Howard Johnson, Super 8, **other:** Aamco, Chevrolet, CVS Drug, K-Mart, Lowe's Whse, Rite Aid, Target, Trak Auto, Ukrops Foods, Winn-Dixie, Roadrunner Camping(2mi), to Pocahontas SP

58 VA 746, **E...gas:** Texaco/diesel, **lodging:** Chester Inn, **W...gas:** Amoco, Chevron/diesel, Exxon/diesel, **food:** Subway, **lodging:** Day's Inn, Interstate Inn/rest.

54 VA 144, Temple Ave, to Ft Lee, Hopewell, **E...gas:** BP/24hr, Chevron/diesel, Citgo, Crown, Exxon/Subway, **food:** Applebee's, Arby's, Burger King, Golden Corral, La Carreta Mexican, LoneStar Steaks, McDonald's, Old Country Buffet, Outback Steaks, Red Lobster, Ruby Tuesday, Sagebrush Steaks, Taco Bell, Wendy's, **lodging:** Comfort Inn, Hampton Inn, Holiday Inn Express(5mi), Innkeeper, **other:** MEDICAL CARE, Belk, BooksAMillion, Chevrolet/Cadillac/Buick/Nissan, Circuit City, Dillard's, Hecht's, Home Depot, JC Penney, Jo-Ann Fabrics, K-Mart, Marshall's, Michael's, Sam's Club, Sears/auto, Staples, Target, Wal-Mart SuperCtr/24hr, mall, **W...gas:** Shell, **food:** Hardee's, **other:** Colony Tire, U-Haul, to VSU

Petersburg

53 S Park Blvd(from nb), **E...**same as 54

52.5mm Appomattox River

52 Washington St, Wythe St, **E...gas:** Amoco, BP, Crown, Shell/diesel, **food:** DQ, Steak&Ale, **lodging:** Econolodge, Holiday Inn, Howard Johnson, King Motel, Ramada, Royal Inn, Star Motel, Super 8, **other:** Petersburg Nat Bfd, **W...gas:** Shell, **food:** Aunt Sarah's, **lodging:** Best Inn, Radisson, HOSPITAL

51 I-85 S, to South Hill, US 460 W

50a b c d US 301, US 460 E, to Crater Rd, County Dr, **E...gas:** BP, Citgo/7-11, Exxon, RaceTrac, **food:** Hardee's, McDonald's, Wendy's, **lodging:** American Inn, Best Inn, California Inn, Flagship Inn, Knight's Inn, Super 8, **other:** HOSPITAL

48b a Wagner Rd, **E...gas:** Exxon, **food:** McDonald's, **W...gas:** BP, Chevron/diesel, Citgo, Exxon, Shell, **food:** Arby's, BBQ, Burger King, DQ, Hardee's, Honey B's Rest., KFC, McDonald's, Pizza Hut, Ponderosa, Shoney's, Subway, Taco Bell, **lodging:** Crater Inn, **other:** Dodge, Food Lion, Ford/Lincoln/Mercury, PepBoys

47 VA 629, to Rives Rd, **1-2 mi E...food:** McDonald's, **W...gas:** BP, Citgo, Shell, **lodging:** Heritage Motel, **1-2 mi W...lodging:** Crater Inn, LaSalle Motel, **other:** Softball Hall of Fame Museum, same as 48 on US 301

46 I-295 N(exits left from sb), to Washington

45 US 301, **E...gas:** Shell/diesel, **W...gas:** Exxon, **food:** Pumpkins Rest., Stephen-Kent Rest., **lodging:** Best Western, Comfort Inn, Day's Inn/rest., Hampton Inn, Holiday Inn Express, Quality Inn

41 US 301, VA 35, VA 156, **E...gas:** Chevron/diesel, **lodging:** Econolodge, **other:** KOA(1mi), **W...lodging:** Knight's Inn, Travelodge

40mm weigh sta both lanes

37 US 301, Carson, **W...gas:** BP/diesel, Shell/RV park

36mm rest area nb, full(handicapped)facilities, phone, vending, picnic tables, litter barrel, petwalk

33 VA 602, **W...gas:** Chevron/diesel, Davis TrkStp/diesel/@, Exxon/diesel, **food:** Burger King, Denny's/24hr, **lodging:** Sleep Inn, Stony Creek Motel

31 VA 40, Stony Creek, to Waverly, **W...gas:** Petrol/diesel, Shell/diesel/24hr, **food:** Carter's Rest.

24 VA 645, no facilities

20 VA 631, Jarratt, **W...gas:** Exxon/diesel/24hr, Shell/Blimpie/diesel, **food:** Jarratt Rest.

Interstate 95

N S

17 US 301, **1 mi E...food:** China Star Rest., **lodging:** Knight's Inn, Reste Motel, **other:** Jellystone Park Camping

13 VA 614, to Emporia, **E...gas:** Shell/diesel, **food:** Slip-In Rest., **lodging:** Dixie Motel

12 US 301(from nb), **E...lodging:** Dixie Motel

Emporia

11b a US 58, Emporia, to South Hill, **E...gas:** BP/Subway/Taco Bell/diesel, Exxon, Shell, **food:** Arby's, Burger King, DQ, Hardee's, KFC, LJ Silver, McDonald's, Pizza Hut, Wendy's, Western Sizzlin, **lodging:** Fairfield Inn, Holiday Inn, **other:** HOSPITAL, Advance Parts, CVS Drug, Eckerd, Food Lion, Radio Shack, Wal-Mart SuperCtr/24hr, Winn-Dixie, **W...gas:** Citgo, Exxon, Shell/Sadler/diesel/rest., **food:** Bojangles, Shoney's, TJ's Family Rest., **lodging:** Best Western, Day's Inn, Hampton Inn

8 US 301, **E...gas:** Amoco, Citgo, Exxon/Simmon's/diesel/rest./@, **food:** Denny's, **lodging:** Comfort Inn, Red Carpet Inn/rest.

4 VA 629, to Skippers, **W...gas:** Citgo/diesel, **lodging:** Econolodge, **other:** Cattail Creek Camping(2mi)

3.5mm Fountain's Creek

.5mm **Welcome Ctr nb, full(handicapped)facilities, phone, vending, picnic tables, litter barrels, petwalk**

0mm Virginia/North Carolina state line

Interstate 264(Norfolk)

E W

Exit # Services

14b a I-64. I-264 begins/ends on I-64.

13 US 13, Military Hwy, **N...food:** Wendy's, **lodging:** Best Western, Day's Inn

12 Ballentine Blvd, **N...other:** HOSPITAL, Norfolk SU

11b a US 460, VA 166/168, Brambleton Ave, Campostello Rd, **N...gas:** 7-11, Spur

10 Tidewater Dr, City Hall Ave, **N...lodging:** Omni Hotel

9 St Paul's Blvd, Waterside Dr, **S...other:** Harbor Park Waterslide

8 I-464 S, to Chesapeake, no facilities

7.5mm tunnel

7b a VA 141, Effingham St, Crawford St, **N...other:** Naval HOSPITAL, **S...other:** Shipyard

6.5mm weigh sta eb

6 Des Moines Ave(from eb), no facilities

5 US 17, Frederick Blvd, Midtown Tunnel, **S...gas:** Amoco

4 VA 337, Portsmouth Blvd, no facilities

3 Victory Blvd, **N...other:** Advance Parts, **S...gas:** Amoco

2b a Greenwood Dr, no facilities

0mm I-264 begins/ends on I-64, exit 299.

14 I-664 begins/ends on I-64, exit 299.

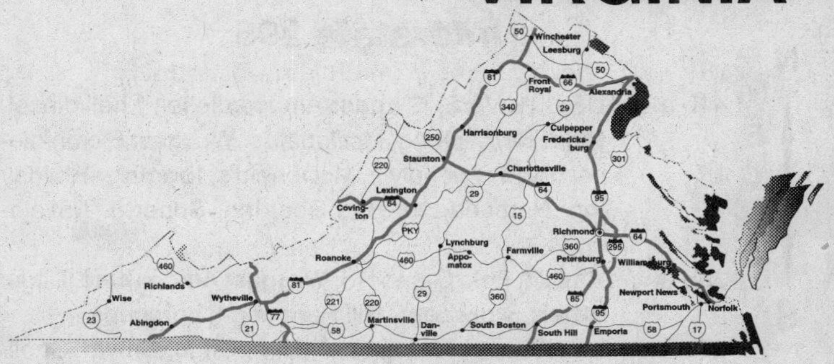

Portsmouth

13b a US 13, US 58, US 460, Military Hwy, **E...**gas, food lodging

12 VA 663, Dock Landing Rd, no facilities

11b a VA 337, Portsmouth Blvd, **E...**gas, food

10 VA 659, Pughsville Rd, no facilites

9b a US 17, US 164, **E...**gas, food, lodging, **W...other:** to James River Br, museum

8b a VA 135, College Dr, no facilities

11.5mm insp sta wb

9mm James River

8mm tunnel

7 Terminal Ave, **W...**museum

6 25th St, 26th St, **E...gas:** Citgo/7-11, **food:** McDonald's

5 US 60 W, 35th St, Jefferson Ave, **E...gas:** Shell, **food:** Burger King, Church's, KFC

4 Chesnut Ave, Roanoke Ave, **E...**food mkt

3 Aberdeen Rd, **E...gas:** Citgo/diesel, **W...food:** Hardee's, McDonald's, Wendy's, **other:** museum

2 Powhatan Pkwy, no facilities

1b a I-64, W to Richmond, E to Norfolk. I-664 begins/ends on I-64.

Interstate 295(Richmond)

N S

Exit # Services

53b a I-64, W to Charlottesville, E to Richmond, to US 250, I-295 begins/ends.

51b a Nuckols Rd, **1 mi N...gas:** Amoco, **S...food:** McDonald's, Wendy's

49b a US 33, Richmond, **N...gas:** Shell, **S...food:** Debbie's Kitchen, Hardee's, Shoney's

45b a Woodman Rd, **S...food:** Hardee's, **other:** Meadow Farm Museum

43 I-95, US 1, N to Washington, S to Richmond(exits left from nb), **services on US 1, N...gas:** Amoco/diesel, Mobil, Shell, **food:** Burger King, Chili's, FoodCourt, **lodging:** Best Western, SpringHill Suites, **other:** AmeriCamps, Kosmo Village, mall, **1-2 mi S...gas:** Exxon, EastCoast/diesel, Shell, **food:** Aunt Sarah's, El Paso Mexican, Hardee's, McDonald's, Subway, Taco Bell, Waffle House, Wendy's, **lodging:** Broadway Motel, Cavalier Motel, Econolodge, Quality Inn, Shoney's Inn, **other:** Food Lion, Eckerd, Firestone, Lowe's Whse, Wal-Mart SuperCtr/24hr

Interstate 295

N ↕ S — Mechanicsville

Exit #	Services
41b a	US 301, VA 2, **E...gas:** Amoco/diesel, Shell/diesel, **food:** Burger King, McDonald's, **W...gas:** Exxon/diesel, **food:** Friendly's, McDonald's, **lodging:** Holiday Inn, Ramada Ltd, Red Roof Inn, Super 8, Travelodge
38b a	VA 627, Pole Green Rd, **W...gas:** Amoco/café, Citgo, **other:** Strawberry Hill Funpark, fairgrounds
37b a	US 360, **1 mi E...gas:** Amoco, Citgo, Crown, Shell/diesel, **food:** Arby's, Cracker Barrel, Gus' Italian, IHOP, McDonald's, Mexico Rest., Ruby Tuesday, Shoney's, Taco Bell, Tumbleweeds Steaks, Wendy's, **lodging:** Hampton Inn, Holiday Inn Express, **other:** Home Depot, Kohl's, OfficeMax, Ukrops Foods, Wal-Mart SuperCtr/24hr, **W...gas:** Citgo/7-11, Mobil/diesel, NAPA, to Mechanicsville
34b a	VA 615, Creighton Rd, **E...gas:** Amoco/diesel, Citgo/7-11, **5 mi W...gas:** Citgo, **food:** McDonald's
31b a	VA 156, **E...gas:** Citgo/diesel, **other:** to Cold Harbor, **4 mi W...gas:** Amoco/diesel, Citgo, Shell, **food:** Bojangles, Hardee's, **lodging:** Courtyard, Day's Inn, Econolodge, Hampton Inn, Hilton, Holiday Inn, Microtel, Motel 6, Wingate Inn
28	US 60, to I-64, **E...gas:** Amoco, Shell/FoodCourt/diesel, **W...gas:** Citgo, **other:** museum
22b a	VA 5, Charles City, **E...other:** Shirley Plantation, **W...gas:** Amoco, **other:** Richmond Nat Bfd
18mm	James River
15b a	VA 10, Hopewell, **E...gas:** Amoco, Citgo, **lodging:** Evergreen Motel, **other:** HOSPITAL, James River Plantations, **W...gas:** Chevron/diesel, Citgo/diesel, EastCoast, **food:** Burger King, Denny's, Friendly's, McDonald's, Subway, Waffle House, Wendy's, **lodging:** Comfort Inn, Hampton Inn, Holiday Inn Express, Howard Johnson
13mm	Appomattox River
9b a	VA 36, Hopewell, **E...gas:** Chevron, **food:** Honey B's Rest., Mexico Rest., **lodging:** Econolodge, Innkeeper, **other:** Advance Parts, AutoZone, $General, **W...gas:** Amoco/diesel/24hr, Exxon/Bullets, Pilot/diesel/24hr, Shell, **food:** Burger King, Denny's, Japanese Steaks, McDonald's, Papa John's, Pizza Hut, Shoney's, Subway, Taco Bell, Waffle House, Wendy's, Western Sizzlin, Willie's Diner, **lodging:** Comfort Inn, Hampton Inn, Holiday Inn Express, **other:** Chevrolet, Food Lion, Rite Aid, U-Haul, US Army Museum, Winn-Dixie
5.5mm	Blackwater Swamp
3b a	US 460, Petersburg, to Norfolk, **E...gas:** EastCoast/diesel, **food:** KrispyKreme, Subway, **W...gas:** Exxon, **food:** Hardee's, McDonald's
1	I-95, N to Petersburg, S to Emporium, I-295 begins/ends.

Hopewell

Interstate 495(DC)

N ↕ S — DC Area

Exit #	Services
27	I-95, N to Baltimore, S to Richmond. I-495 & I-95 S run together.
28b a	MD 650, New Hampshire Ave, **N...gas:** Amoco/24hr, Exxon/diesel, Shell/autocare/24hr, 7-11, **food:** KFC, Shoney's, **other:** CVS Drug, Radio Shack, Safeway
29b a	MD 193, University Blvd, no facilities
30b a	US 29, Colesville, **N...gas:** Amoco, Shell, 7-11/Jerry's Subs, **food:** McDonald's, **other:** Safeway
31b a	MD 97, Georgia Ave, Silver Springs, **S...gas:** Amoco/diesel, Exxon/diesel, Shell, Texaco/diesel, **food:** Hunan Chinese, **other:** CVS Drug, Merchants Tire, Snider's Foods, Staples
33	MD 185, Connecticut Ave, **N...other:** LDS Temple, **S...gas:** Amoco, Citgo, Sunoco, **food:** Chevy Chase Foods
34	MD 355, Wisconsin Ave, Bethesda, no facilities
35	(from wb), I-270
36	MD 187, Old Georgetown Rd, **S...other:** HOSPITAL
38	I-270, to Frederick
39	MD 190, River Rd, Washington, Potomac, no facilities
40	Cabin John Pkwy, Glen Echo(from sb), no trucks, no facilities
41	Clara Barton Pkwy, Carderock, Great Falls, no trucks
42mm	**Potomac River, Virginia/Maryland state line. Exits 41-27 are in Maryland.**
43	G Washington Mem Pkwy, no trucks, no facilities
44	VA 193, Langley, no facilities
45b a	VA 267 W, to I-66 E, no facilities
46b a	VA 123, Chain Bridge Rd, **W...lodging:** Hilton
47b a	VA 7, Leesburg Pike, Falls Church, Tysons Corner, **E...**Doubletree, **W...gas:** Amoco/diesel, Crown Gas, Exxon, Mobil, Shell, Shell, 7-11, **food:** Bertucci's, Boston Mkt, Chili's, McDonald's, NY Deli, Olive Garden, On-the-Border, Pizza Hut, **lodging:** Marriott, **other:** Ford, Nordstrom's, mall
49c b a	I-66(exits left from both lanes), to Manassas, Front Royal, no facilities
50b a	US 50, Arlington Blvd, Fairfax, Arlington, **N...lodging:** Marriott, **S...lodging:** Residence Inn
51	VA 657, Gallows Rd, **S... gas:** Exxon, 7-11, **other:** HOSPITAL
52b a	VA 236, Little River Tpk, Fairfax, **N...gas:** Citgo, Mobil/repair, 7-11, **food:** McDonald's, **other:** GNC, Rite Aid, Safeway
54b a	VA 620, Braddock Rd, Ctr for the Arts, Geo Mason U, **S...gas:** Mobil/diesel, **other:** Safeway
56c b a	I-95 S, I-395 N, I-95 N. I-495 & I-95 N run together.

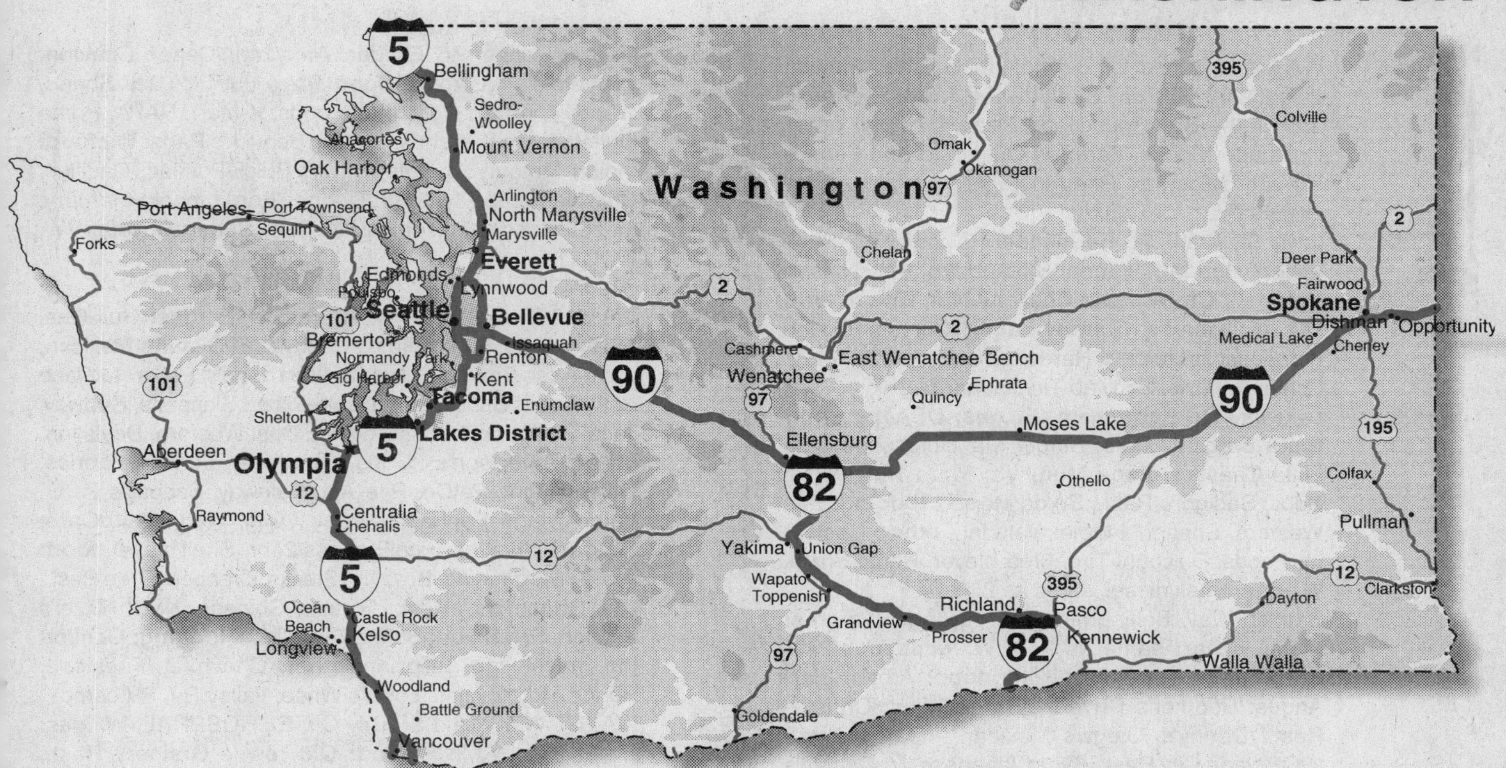

Interstate 5

N ↕ S

Blaine

Exit #	Services
277mm	USA/Canada Border, Washington state line, customs
276	WA 548 S, Blaine, **E...gas:** Arco, Exxon/diesel, USA/diesel/24hr, **food:** Denny's, Pasa del Norte Mexican, **lodging:** Northwoods Motel, **other:** Ammex Duty Free, to Peace Arch SP, **W...gas:** Chevron/repair, Exxon, **food:** Golden Chopstix Rest., Harbor Café, Pizza Factory, Portal Café, Subway, WheelHouse Grill, **lodging:** Anchor Inn, Bayside Motel, International Motel, **other:** Coast Hardware, NAPA
275	WA 543 N(from nb, no return), truck customs, **E...gas:** Exxon, **W...gas:** Chevron/diesel
274	Peace Portal Drive(from nb, no return), Blaine, **W...gas:** Chevron, **lodging:** Martin Inn, **other:** Duty Free, Semi-ah-moo Resort, camping
270	Lynden, Birch Bay, **W...gas:** Shell/Subway/Taco Bell/diesel, **lodging:** Semi-ah-moo Resort, **other:** Peace Arch Outlet/famous brands, SeaBreeze RV Park(5mi)
269mm	**Welcome Ctr sb, full(handicapped)facilities, info, phone, picnic tables, litter barrels, petwalk, vending**
267mm	**rest area nb, full(handicapped)facilities, info, phone, picnic tables, litter barrels, petwalk, vending**
266	WA 548 N, Custer, Grandview Rd, **W...gas:** Arco/24hr, Birch Bay SP
263	Portal Way, **E...gas:** Texaco/diesel, **other:** Cedars RV Park
263mm	Nooksack River
262	Main St, Ferndale, **E...gas:** 76/diesel, Tesoro/diesel, **food:** Denny's, McDonald's, **lodging:** Super 8, **other:** RV Park, U-Haul, **W...gas:** Exxon/diesel/LP, Shell/diesel, **food:** Bob's Burgers, DQ, Grant's Drive-In, Monnt's Café, Murdock's Steaks, Papa Murphy's, **lodging:** Scottish Lodge, **other:** Costcutter Foods, Haggen's Foods, NAPA, Scwab Tire
260	Slater Rd, Lummi Island, **E...gas:** Arco/24hr, **other:** El Monte RV, antiques, **5 mi W...gas:** 76, Shell/diesel, **other:** Eagle Haven RV Park, Lummi Casino/café(10mi), Lummi Ind Res
258	Bakerview Rd, **W...gas:** Arco/24hr, Exxon/diesel/24hr, 76, **food:** Mykono's Greek Rest., **lodging:** Hampton Inn, Shamrock Motel, **other:** airport, RV Park, st patrol
257	Northwest Ave, **E...other:** Chevrolet/Cadillac, **W...gas:** Shell
256b	Bellis Fair Mall Pkwy, **E...other:** Sears, Target, mall
a	WA 539 N, Meridian St, **E...gas:** Chevron, Exxon/diesel, Shell/diesel, Texaco/diesel, **food:** Arby's, Burger King, China Buffet, DQ, Denny's, Godfather's, Izzy's Pizza, Kowloon Garden, McDonald's, McHale's Rest., Old Country Buffet, Olive Garden, Pizza Hut, Quizno's, Red Robin, Shari's/24hr, Starbucks, Taco Time, Teriyaki House, Thai House, Wendy's, **lodging:** Best Western, Comfort Inn, Day's Inn, Holiday Inn Express, Quality Inn, **other:** Barnes&Noble, Best Buy, Bon-Marche, Circuit City, Costco, Costcutter Foods, Home Depot, JC Penney, Mervyn's, Nordstrom's, Office Depot, Rite Aid, Ross, Safeway, Schuck's Parts, Schwab Tire, Sears, Target, Walgreen, Wal-Mart/auto, mall, st patrol, to Nooksack Ind Res, **W...food:** Eleni's Rest., **lodging:** Rodeway Inn, Travelers Inn

WASHINGTON

Interstate 5

N ↕ S

Bellingham

255 WA 542 E, Sunset Dr, Bellingham, **E...gas:** Chevron/diesel/24hr, Exxon, Shell/diesel, **food:** Expresso, Jack-in-the-Box, RoundTable Pizza, Taco Bell, **other:** Costcutter Foods, Farmers Outlet, Jo-Ann Fabrics, K-Mart, OfficeMax, Rite Aid, to Mt Baker, **W...other:** HOSPITAL

254 Iowa St, State St, Bellingham, **E...gas:** 76, Shell, **other:** Honda, Hyundai, Mitsubishi, Kia, Nissan, Volvo, RV Ctr, **W...gas:** Chevron/24hr, Exxon, **food:** DQ, McDonald's, Subway, **other:** Chrysler/Dodge, Ford/Lincoln/Mercury, Hardware Sales, Isuzu, NAPA, Schuck's Parts, Schwab Tire, Subaru

253 Lakeway Dr, Bellingham, **E...gas:** USA/gas, 7-11, **food:** Bergsma Café, Burger Me, Horseshoe Café, Little Caesar's, Papa Murphy's, Pizza Hut, Port of Subs, Sadighi's Rest., So de Mexico, **lodging:** Best Western, Shangrila Motel, Valu Inn, **other:** Costcutter Foods, Discount Tire, Fred Meyer, Radio Shack, **W...gas:** Shell/diesel, same as 252

252 Samish Way, Bellingham, **E...lodging:** Evergreen Motel, **other:** same as 253, **W...gas:** Arco/24hr, Chevron, 76, Shell/diesel/24hr, **food:** Arby's, Black Angus, Boomer's Drive-In, Burger King, Christo's Rest., Denny's, Diego's Mexican, Figaro's Pizza, IHOP, Jade City Rest., Kyoto Japanese, McDonald's, New Peking, NW Viet Rest., Rib'n Reef, RoundTable Pizza, Starbucks, Subway, **lodging:** Aloha Motel, Bay City Motel, Cascade Inn, Coachman Motel, Key Motel, Motel 6, Ramada Inn, Travelodge, Villa Inn, **other:** Audi, Chrysler/Jeep, Haggen Foods, Rite Aid, VW

250 WA 11 S, Chuckanut Dr, Bellingham, Fairhaven Hist Dist, **W...gas:** Arco/24hr, Chevron/repair, **food:** Dos Padres Mexican, SkyLark Café, Tony's Café, Win's Drive-In, **other:** Larrabee SP, to Alaska Ferry

246 N Lake Samish, **W...gas:** Shell/diesel, **other:** Lake Padden RA, RV camping

242 Nulle Rd, S Lake Samish, no facilities

240 Alger, **E...gas:** Texaco/diesel/LP/RV dump, **W...food:** Alger Grille, **lodging:** Sudden Valley Motel/RV Park

238mm rest area both lanes, full(handicapped)facilities, phone, picnic tables, litter barrels, vending, petwalk

236 Bow Hill Rd, **E...other:** Harrah's Casino/rest., **W...**fish mkt

235mm weigh sta sb

234mm Samish River

232 Cook Rd, Sedro-Woolley, **E...gas:** Shell/diesel, Tesoro/24hr, **food:** Burger King(4mi), DQ, Iron Skillet Rest.(4mi), **lodging:** 3 Rivers Inn(5mi), **other:** KOA

231 WA 11 N, Chuckanut Dr, **E...other:** Skagit RV/marine, st patrol, to Larrabee SP

230 WA 20, Burlington, **E...gas:** Chevron, Exxon, Shell/diesel, **food:** Beary Patch Rest., Jack-in-the-Box, Outback Steaks, Pizza Factory, Red Robin, Subway, **lodging:** Cocusa Motel, **other:** HOSPITAL, Bon-Marche, Fred Meyer, Haggen Foods, JC Penney, Schwab Tire, Sears/auto, OfficeMax, Target, mall, to N Cascades NP, **W...gas:** Arco/diesel/24hr, Chevron/diesel, **food:** McDonald's, **lodging:** Holiday Inn Express, Mark II Motel, **other:** Harley-Davidson, to San Juan Ferry

Mt Vernon

229 George Hopper Rd, **E...gas:** Arco/24hr, Cenex, Chevron, USA/diesel, Costco/gas, **food:** Pizza Hut/Taco Bell, Shari's, Wendy's, **other:** Costcutter Foods, K-Mart, NAPA, Prime Outlets/famous brands, Saturn, Schuck's Parts, **W...food:** Indian Motorcycle Café, **other:** Buick/Pontiac, Cadillac, Chrysler/Jeep/Plymouth/Dodge, Ford/Lincoln/Mercury, Mazda/Honda, Mitsubishi, Nissan, Subaru/Toyota, VW, RV Ctr

228mm Skagit River

227 WA 538 E, College Way, Mt Vernon, **E...gas:** Gull Gas, 76, **food:** Big Scoop Rest., Denny's, El Gitano's Mexican, Jack-in-the Box, McDonald's, Papa John's, Pizza Hut/Taco Bell, Port of Subs, RoundTable Pizza, Skipper's, Subway, Taco Time, Winchell's, **lodging:** Best Western, Day's Inn, **other:** Albertson's, $Plus, Goodyear, Jo-Ann Fabrics, Office Depot, PetCo, Rite Aid, Safeway, Schuck's Parts, ValueVillage Foods, Wal-Mart/auto, Walt's AutoCare, **W...gas:** Chevron, FuelExpress/24hr, Shell/diesel, **food:** Arby's, Burger King, Buzz Inn Steaks, Cranberry Tree Rest., DQ, Drummond'sRest., Fortune Chinese, KFC, Mitzel's Kitchen, Royal Fork Buffet, Taco Time, **lodging:** Comfort Inn, Travelodge, Tulip Inn, **other:** Chevrolet, Firestone, Honda Motorcycles, Lowe's Whse, Valley RV, RV camp

226 WA 536 W, Kincaid St, City Ctr, **E...**HOSPITAL, **W...gas:** Pacific Pride/diesel, **food:** Old Towne Grainery Rest., Skagit River Brewing Co, **other:** NAPA, Valley RV Ctr, RV camping

225 Anderson Rd, **E...gas:** CFN/diesel, 76, **W...gas:** Chevron

224 WA 99 S(from nb, no return), S Mt Vernon, **E...**gas/diesel, food

221 WA 534 E, Conway, Lake McMurray, **E...gas:** Shell/diesel/24hr, **W...gas:** 76, Shell, **food:** Channel Lodge Rest., **lodging:** Ridgeway B&B, Valentine House B&B, Wild Iris B&B, **other:** Blake's RV Park/marina

218 Starbird Rd, **W...lodging:** Hillside Motel

215 300th NW, no facilities

214mm weigh sta nb

212 WA 532 W, Stanwood, Bryant, **W...gas:** Shell/24hr, Texaco/diesel, **4 mi W...food:** Burger King, DQ, Mkt St Café, McDonald's, **other:** Haggen Foods/24hr, Camano Island SP(19mi)

210 236th NE, no facilities

209mm Stillaguamish River

208 WA 530, Silvana, Arlington, **E...gas:** Chevron/24hr, 76/Circle K, Shell, Texaco/diesel/24hr, **food:** Denny's, O'Brien Manor Rest., **lodging:** Arlington Motel, Weller's Rest., **other:** HOSPITAL, to N Cascades Hwy, **W...gas:** Exxon/diesel/LP/24hr

207mm rest area both lanes, full(handicapped)facilities, phone, picnic tables, litter barrels, coffee, vending, RV dump, petwalk

206 WA 531, Lakewood, **E...gas:** Arco/24hr, 76/diesel/LP/RV dump, Shell/24hr, 7-11/Citgo, **food:** Alfy's Pizza, Buzz Inn Steaks, Jack-in-the-Box, McDonald's, Taco Time, **lodging:** Crossroads Inn, Hawthorn Suites, **other:** Chrysler/Jeep, Food Pavilion, Lowe's Whse, Pontiac/Buick/GMC, Rite Aid, Safeway/24hr, **W...gas:** Chevron/24hr, **food:** Petosa's Rest., **lodging:** Smokey Point Motel, **other:** Cedar Grove Shores RV(6mi), to Wenburg SP

Interstate 5

N ↕ S

202 116th NE, **E...gas:** Shell/diesel, Texaco/diesel/24hr, **W...gas:** Chevron/diesel/24hr, **other:** st patrol

200 88th St NE, Quil Ceda Way, **E...gas:** Chevron, Citgo/7-11, Shell/Blimpie/diesel, **other:** Haggen's Foods/24hr, **W...other:** Home Depot, Wal-Mart/auto

199 WA 528 E, Marysville, Tulalip, **E...gas:** Arco/24hr, Chevron/24hr, 76, Shell/Subway/diesel, **food:** Burger King, DQ, Jack-in-the-Box, Las Margaritas Mexican, Royal Fork Buffet, Village Inn Rest., **other:** Albertson's, Big O Tire, JC Penney, Lamont's, Rite Aid, Schwab Tire, Staples, **W...gas:** 76, **food:** Arby's, Golden Corral, McDonald's, Taco Time, Wendy's, **lodging:** Best Western/rest., Fairfield Inn, Holiday Inn Express, **other:** Chevrolet/Subaru, RV SuperMall, to Tulalip Indian Res

198 Port of Everett(from sb), Steamboat Slough, st patrol

195mm Snohomish River

195 Port of Everett(from nb), Marine View Dr, no facilities

194 US 2 E, Everett Ave, City Ctr, **W...gas:** Shell/diesel, Schwab Tire

193 WA 529, Pacific Ave, **W...gas:** Chevron, 76, **food:** Denny's, Roaster Rest., **lodging:** Best Western, Gardner Bay Inn, Howard Johnson, Marina Village Inn(3mi), **other:** HOSPITAL

Everett

192 Broadway(exits left from nb), Evergreen Way, City Ctr, **W...gas:** Arco/24hr, Chevron, Exxon, 76, Shell, **food:** Alfy's Pizza, Iver's Seafood, Jack-in-the-Box, King's Table, McDonald's, O'Donnell's Café, Petosa's On Broadway, Taco Bell, **lodging:** Day's Inn, Royal Motor Inn, Travelodge, **other:** Ford

189 WA 526 W, WA 527, Everett Mall Way, Everett, **E...gas:** Arco/24hr, Shell/diesel, **food:** Alfy's Pizza, Burger King, Buzz Inn Steaks, McDonald's, Wendy's, **lodging:** Studio+, Travelodge, **other:** Costco, **1 mi W on Evergreen Way...gas:** Chevron, Shell, Texaco/diesel, 7-11, **food:** Denny's, Godfather's, Taco Bell, Taco Time, Village Inn Rest., **lodging:** Cherry Motel, Comfort Inn, Extended Stay America, Motel 6, Rodeway Inn, Sunrise Inn, **other:** Bon-Marche, Buick/Pontiac, Discount Tire, Dodge/Jeep, Firestone/auto, Fred Meyer, K-Mart, mall

188mm rest area/weigh sta sb, full(handicapped)facilities, info, phone, picnic tables, litter barrels, coffee, RV dump, weigh sta nb

186 WA 96, 128th SW, **E...gas:** 76, Shell/diesel/24hr, **lodging:** Holiday Inn, **other:** Lakeside RV Park, Silver Lake RV Park, **W...gas:** Arco/24hr, Chevron/24hr, Citgo/7-11, Shell, Texaco, **food:** Alfy's Pizza, Burger King, DQ, Denny's, Great River Rest., KFC, McDonald's, Mitzel's Kitchen, Mongolian Grill, Pizza Hut, Skipper's, Subway, Taco Bell/24hr, Teriyaki Rest., **lodging:** Cypress Inn, Everett Inn, Motel 6, **other:** Albertson's, Goodyear/auto, Tony's Autocare, transmissions

183 164th SW, **E...gas:** Arco, Shell/diesel/24hr, **food:** Jack-in-the-Box/24hr, Shari's, Subway, Taco Time, **other:** Wal-Mart, **W...gas:** Exxon, Shell, Texaco/Quizno's/diesel, **other:** Twin Cedars RV Park, Alderwood Mall Blvd

182 **E...**I-405 S, to Bellevue, **W...**WA 525, Alderwood Mall Blvd, to Alderwood Mall, **gas:** Arco/24hr, **food:** Japanese Rest., Keg Steaks/seafood, TCBY, **lodging:** Residence Inn, **other:** Marshall's, Michael's, Nordstrom's, Sears/auto, Target, Evans Tire

Seattle

181 44th Ave W, to WA 524, Lynnwood, **E...gas:** Arco, 76, Shell, Texaco, **food:** McDonald's, **lodging:** Embassy Suites, Extended Stay America, Hampton Inn, **other:** Albertson's, Barnes&Noble, Best Buy, Circuit City, Lowe's Whse, Old Navy, Staples, **W...gas:** Chevron/24hr, 76/diesel, 7-11, Shell/repair, **food:** Applebee's, Black Angus, Buca Italian, Burger King, Chevy's Mexican, Country Harvest Rest., Denny's, El Torito, Evergreen Donuts, IHOP, Jack-in-the-Box, Japanese Rest., KFC, McDonald's, Old Country Buffet, Olive Garden, Red Lobster, Starbucks, Subway, Tony Roma, Wendy's, **lodging:** Courtyard, Holiday Inn Express, Lynnwood Inn, **other:** MEDICAL CARE, Firestone/auto, Fred Meyer, Goodyear/auto, Radio Shack, mall

179 220th SW, Mountlake Terrace, **W...gas:** Shell, Texaco/diesel, 7-11, **food:** Azteca Mexican, China Passage, Countryside Donuts, Starbucks, Subway, Thai Terrace Rest., **other:** HOSPITAL, Honda, Schuck's Parts, **1 mi W on WA 99...gas:** Shell, **food:** Jack-in-the-Box, McDonald's, **other:** Acura, Big O Tire, Nissan, Toyota

178 236th St SW(from nb), Mountlake Terrace, no facilities

177 WA 104, Edmonds, **E...gas:** Chevron/24hr, Shell/diesel, **food:** Buzz Inn Steaks, Canyons Rest., McDonald's, Starbucks, Subway, **lodging:** Homestead Village Suites, **other:** CompUSA, RiteAid, Schuck's Parts, Thriftway Foods, **1-2 mi W on WA 99...gas:** 76, Shell, Texaco, **food:** China Clipper Rest., Coco's, Denny's, Godfather's, Todo Mexico, **lodging:** Day's Inn, Harbor Inn, K&E Motel, Travelodge, **other:** Costco, GNC, Home Depot, OfficeMax, QFC Foods, Radio Shack, Schwab Tire, VW

176 NE 175th St, Aurora Ave N, to Shoreline

175 WA 523, NE 145th, 5th Ave NE, **1 mi W on WA 99...food:** Las Margaritas Mexican, Shari's, Taco Time, Wendy's, **other:** $Store, Schuck's Parts

174 NE 130th, Roosevelt Way, **1 mi W on WA 99...food:** Burger King, KFC, **lodging:** Best Western, **other:** Albertson's, Buick/GMC, Firestone, K-Mart, Office Depot, Rite Aid, Sam's Club

173 1st Ave NE, Northgate Way, **E...gas:** Arco/24hr, 76, **food:** Azteca Mexican, Baskin-Robbins, Marie Callender's, Pancake Haus, Red Robin, Seattle Crab Co, Subway, Taco Time, Tony Roma, **other:** B&B Parts, Best Buy, Discount Tire, JC Penney, Longs Drug, Nordstrom's, Pacific Fabrics, QFC Foods, Target, mall, **W...gas:** Chevron, 76, Shell/diesel, 7-11, **food:** Arby's, Barnaby's Café, Denny's, McDonald's, **lodging:** Birkshire Inn, Ramada Inn

172 N 85th, Aurora Ave, **1 mi W on Aurora...gas:** Arco, 76/diesel, **food:** Jack-in-the-Box

WASHINGTON

Interstate 5

N ↕ S

171 WA 522, Lake City Way, Bothell, no facilities
170 Ravenna Blvd, **E...gas:** Arco, Texaco/diesel, **other:** MEDICAL CARE, QFC Foods,
169 NE 45th, NE 50th, **E...gas:** 76, **lodging:** University Inn, **other:** HOSPITAL, U of WA, **W...lodging:** University Plaza Inn, **other:** to Seattle Pacific U, zoo
168b WA 520, to Bellevue, no facilities
a Lakeview Blvd, downtown
167 Mercer St(exits left from nb), Fairview Ave, Seattle Ctr, **W...gas:** Shell
166 Olive Way, Stewart St, **E...other:** HOSPITAL, **W...lodging:** SpringHill Suites, **other:** Honda
165a Seneca St(exits left from nb), James St, **E...other:** HOSPITAL, **W...lodging:** Renaissance Hotel
b Union St, downtown
164b 4th Ave S, to Kingdome, **1 mi W...**same as 163
a I-90 E, to Spokane, no facilities
163 6th Ave, S Spokane St, W Seattle Br, Columbian Way, **1 mi W on 4th Ave S...gas:** Arco, **food:** Arby's, Burger King/24hr, Denny's, McDonald's, Subway, Taco Bell, **other:** OfficeMax, Sears, auto repair, transmissions

Seattle

162 Corson Ave, Michigan St(exits left from nb), same as 161
161 Swift Ave, Albro Place, **W...gas:** Shell, **food:** Thai Rest., **lodging:** Georgetown Inn
158 Pacific Hwy S, E Marginal Way, **W...gas:** Chevron, **food:** Randy's Rest., **lodging:** Econolodge, Holiday Inn, Travelodge, **other:** HOSPITAL
157 ML King Way, no facilities
156 WA 539 N, Interurban Ave, Tukwila, **E...gas:** Pacific Pride/diesel, 7-11, **W...gas:** 76, Shell/diesel, **food:** Denny's, Jack-in-the-Box, **lodging:** Quality Inn, Towne&Country Suites, **other:** Harley-Davidson
154b WA 518, Burien, S Center Blvd, **E...gas:** Arco, **food:** Denny's, Domino's, **other:** JC Penney, Nordstrom's, Sears/auto, Target, mall, **see WA I-405, exit 1.** **W...lodging:** Extended Stay America
a I-405, N to Bellevue
152 S 188th, Orillia Rd, **W...gas:** 76, **food:** Denny's, Jack-in-the-Box, Omni Rest., Schaumski's Rest., **lodging:** Airport Plaza Hotel, Clarion, Comfort Inn, Day's Inn, DoubleTree Hotel, Motel 6, Super 8, **other:** KOA
151 S 200th, Military Rd, **E...gas:** Shell/diesel, **lodging:** Motel 6, **W...gas:** Chevron, Citgo/7-11, 76, **food:** Bob's Burgers, Burgers Teriyaki, Godfather's, **lodging:** Best Western, Econolodge, Hampton Inn, Howard Johnson, MiniRate Motel, Skyway Inn, Sleep Inn, **other:** U-Haul
149 WA 516, to Kent, Des Moines, **E...lodging:** Best Western, Day's Inn, **other:** Poulsbo RV Ctr, **W...gas:** Arco/24hr, Shell/diesel/24hr, 7-11, **food:** Burger King, Dunkin Donuts, McDonald's, Pizza Hut, Starbucks, Subway, Taco Bell/24hr, Wendy's, **lodging:** Century Motel, Kings Arms Motel, New Best Inn, **other:** QFC Foods, Radio Shack, to Saltwater SP
147 S 272nd, **W on Pacific Hwy...gas:** Arco/24hr, Citgo/7-11, Shell/diesel, **food:** DQ, Jack-in-the-Box, KFC, Little Caesar's, Papa Murphy's, Subway, Taco Bell, Taco Time, Viva Mexican, Wendy's, **lodging:** Travel Inn, **other:** Albertson's, Bartell Drug, CarQuest, Firestone/auto, Rite Aid, Safeway/24hr, Schuck's Parts
143 Federal Way, S 320th, **W...gas:** Arco/24hr, 76/Circle K, Shell/diesel/24hr, **food:** Applebee's, Arby's, Azteca Mexican, Black Angus, Blimpie, Burger King, Coco's, CucinaCucina, Denny's, Dunkin Donuts, Godfather's, Ivar's Seafood, KFC, Marie Callender, McDonald's, McHale's Rest., Mongolian Grill, Old Country Buffet, Outback Steaks, Pizza Hut, Red Lobster, Red Robin, Subway, Taco Bell, Taco Time, TCBY, Tony Roma, Torero's Mexican, Wendy's, **lodging:** Best Western, Comfort Inn, Courtyard, Extended Stay America, La Quinta, **other:** MEDICAL CARE, Best Buy, Borders Books, Firestone/auto, Goodyear/auto, Jo-Ann Fabrics, K-Mart, Mervyn's, OfficeMax, Old Navy, Rite Aid, Ross, Safeway/24hr, Sears/auto, Target, Top Foods, Wal-Mart/auto, mall, to Dash Point SP
142b a WA 18 E, S 348th, Enchanted Pkwy, **E...other:** funpark, **W...gas:** Chevron/24hr, Ernie's/diesel, Flying J/diesel/LP/rest./24hr/@, Shell/diesel, **food:** Burger King, DQ, Denny's, Jack-in-the-Box, McDonald's, Olive Garden, Shari's, Subway, Teriyaki Rest., **lodging:** Eastwind Motel, Holiday Inn Express, Roadrunner Motel, Super 8, **other:** HOSPITAL, Chevrolet, Circuit City, Costco, Ford, Home Depot, Lowe's Whse, NAPA
141mm weigh sta sb
137 WA 99, Fife, Milton, **E...gas:** Arco/24hr, Chevron/diesel/24hr, 76/diesel/RV dump, Shell/24hr, **food:** DQ, Johnnie's Rest., **lodging:** Best Western, Motel 6, Acura, Baybo's RV Ctr, Tacoma RV Ctr, Volvo, **W...gas:** Arco, 76/Circle K, **food:** Arby's, Baskin-Robbins, Burger King, Christy's Rest., Denny's, KFC, McDonald's, Mitzel's Kitchen, Pizza Experience, Pizza Hut/Taco Bell, Wendy's, **lodging:** Comfort Inn, Kings Motel, **other:** Camping World/RV Service/supplies, Fife Drug, Great American RV Ctr, NAPA, Schwab Tire

Tacoma

136b a Port of Tacoma, **E...other:** BMW, Honda, Mercedes, Sam's Club, RV Sales, **W...gas:** Chevron, Flying J/diesel/LP/rest./24hr/@, Shell/diesel, **food:** Fife City Grill, Jack-in-the-Box, **lodging:** Best Inn, Day's Inn, Econolodge, Extended Stay America, Hometel Inn, Ramada Ltd, Travelers Inn, **other:** Goodyear/auto, Harley-Davidson, Nissan, World Trade Ctr
135 Bay St, Puyallup, **E...gas:** Exxon, Shell, **W...gas:** Arco/24hr, **lodging:** La Quinta, **other:** to Tacoma Dome
133 WA 7, I-705, City Ctr, **W...other:** Tacoma Dome, **lodging:** Ramada Inn, Sheraton, Travel Inn, **other:** museum
132 WA 16 W, S 38th, to Bremerton, Gig Harbor, **W...food:** Azteca Mexican, Cucina Cucina, TGIFriday, **lodging:** Extended Stay America, **other:** Circuit City, Diahatsu, Ford, Hyundai, JC Penney, Tire Sta, Toyota, mall, to Pt Defiance Pk/Zoo
130 S 56th, Tacoma Mall Blvd, **W...gas:** Shell, **food:** ChuckeCheese, El Torito, Subway, Tony Roma, **other:** Firestone, House of Fabrics, JC Penney, Sears/auto

Interstate 5

N ↕ S

129 S 72nd, S 84th, **E...gas:** Arco/24hr, Chevron/24hr, Exxon, 76, **food:** Applebee's, Burger King, DQ, Elmer's Rest., Great Wall Buffet, IHOP, Jack-in-the-Box, Mitzel's Kitchen, Olive Garden, Red Lobster, Shari's, Starbucks, Taco Bell, Zoopa Café, **lodging:** Best Western, Howard Johnson, Motel 6, Shilo Inn, Travelodge, Longs Drug, MegaFoods, **W...gas:** Arco/24hr, **food:** Calzone's Italian, Jack-in-the-Box, Yankee Diner, **lodging:** Day's Inn, **other:** Gart Sports, Home Depot, Nevada Bob, to Steilacoom Lake

128 (from nb)same as 129, **E...gas:** 76, Shell/diesel, **food:** Copperfield's Rest., Denny's, Subway, **lodging:** Best Western, Comfort Inn, Crossland Suites, Holiday Inn Express, King Oscar Motel, Rothem Inn, Sherwood Motel, Tacoma Inn, **W...gas:** Tesoro, **food:** Ruby Tuesday, **other:** Discount Tire, cinema

127 WA 512, S Tacoma Way, Puyallup, Mt Ranier, **W...gas:** Arco/24hr, Chevron, 76, Shell/diesel, **food:** Burger King, DQ, Denny's, IHOP, Ivar's Seafood, Mazatlan Mexican, McDonald's, McHale's Rest., Sizzler, Subway, Taco Time, Wendy's, **lodging:** Best Western, Budget Inn, Quality Inn, **other:** Baybo's RV Ctr, Schuck's Parts, transmissions

125 Lakewood, to McChord AFB, **W...gas:** 76/diesel, Shell/diesel, Tesoro, **food:** Black Angus, Denny's, El Toro Mexican, KFC, Pizza Hut, Wendy's, **lodging:** Best Western, **other:** Ft Lewis Motel, Lakewood Lodge, Madigan Motel, Rose Garden Motel, HOSPITAL, Aamco, BMW, CarQuest, Goodyear/auto, U-Haul, mall

124 Gravelly Lake Dr, **W...gas:** Arco/repair, 76/24hr, **other:** same as 125

123 Thorne Lane, Tillicum Lane, no facilities

122 Camp Murray, **E...other:** HOSPITAL, **W...gas:** Arco, Chevron/repair, 7-11, **food:** Baskin-Robbins, BBQ Inn, Burrito Mexican, Domino's, Gertie's Grill, KFC, McDonald's, Papa John's, Pizza Hut, Subway, Taco Bell, Taco Time, Teriyaki House, **other:** SpeedZone Parts

120 Ft Lewis, **E...other:** Ft Lewis Military Museum

Nisqually

119 Du Pont Rd, Steilacoom, **W...gas:** 76, **food:** Happy Teriyaki, Starbucks, Steilacoom Deli

118 Center Dr, **W...lodging:** GuestHouse Inn

117mm weigh sta nb

116 Mounts Rd, Old Nisqually, **W...other:** Riverbend Camping(seasonal)

115mm Nisqually River

114 Nisqually, **E...gas:** Chevron/repair, Exxon/diesel, Shell/LP, **food:** Nisqually Grill, Shipwreck Café, Tiny's Burgers/gifts

111 WA 510 E, Marvin Rd, to Yelm, **E...gas:** Chevron/24hr, 76/Circle K, Shell/diesel, Tesoro/Taco Bell, **food:** Blimpie, Burger King, DQ, Godfather's, Hawk's Prairie Rest., McDonald's, Papa Murphy's, Ruby Tuesday, Subway, Taco Time, **lodging:** King Oscar Motel, **other:** MegaFoods/24hr, Radio Shack, Rite Aid, Safeway/24hr, Schuck's Parts, Schwab Tire, **W...gas:** Pacific Pride/diesel, **food:** Country Jct Rest., **other:** Tolmie SP(5mi), RV camping

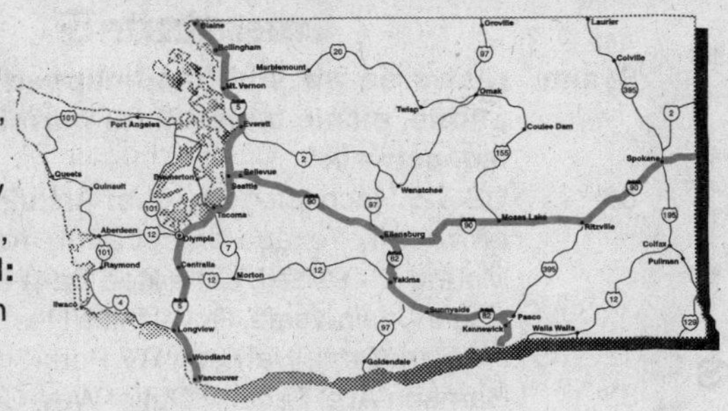

109 Martin Way, Sleator-Kenny Rd, **E...food:** Main Chinese Buffet, Pizza Hut/Taco Bell, **other:** Discount Tire, ShopKO, Top Food/24hr, **W...gas:** Arco/24hr, Exxon/diesel, 76/Circle K, Shell/diesel/24hr, **food:** Bailey's Rest., Burger King, Casa Mia Rest., Denny's, El Serape Mexican, IHOP, Jack-in-the-Box, Mandarin House, Red Lobster, Shari's Rest./24hr, Subway, **lodging:** AmeriTel, Bailey Motel, Comfort Inn, Day's Inn, Holiday Inn Express, Holly Motel, Super 8, **other:** HOSPITAL, Firestone/auto, K-Mart, NAPA

108 Sleator-Kenny Rd, **E...gas:** Shell/diesel, **food:** Applebee's, Arby's, Baskin-Robbins, Godfather's, McDonald's, Red Coral Rest., Starbucks, Wendy's, Winchell's/24hr, **other:** Firestone/auto, Fred Meyer, Jo-Ann Fabrics, Mervyn's, Michael's, Office Depot, Radio Shack, Rite Aid, Target, **W...other:** HOSPITAL, same as 109

107 Pacific Ave, **E...gas:** Shell/diesel, **food:** Izzy's Café, Schlotsky's, Shari's, Sizzler, Taco Time, **other:** Albertson's, Home Depot, Ross, mall, **W...**Ford

Olympia

105 St Capitol, City Ctr, **E...food:** Figaro's Pizza, Izzy's Pizza, Pacific Terrace Rest., Rainier Rest., Ribeye Rest., Sizzler, Taco Time, **other:** Food Pavilion, Foreign Auto Works, RV Ctr, mall, **W...gas:** Chevron/24hr, Shell/diesel/24hr, **food:** Casa Mia Rest., Chinese Buffet, DQ, Jack-in-the-Box, McDonald's, Plum St Deli, Saigon Rest., **lodging:** Best Western, Carriage Inn, Golden Gavel Motel, Phoenix Inn, Ramada Inn, **other:** Pontiac/Cadillac/Saturn

104 US 101 N, W Olympia, to Aberdeen, **W...gas:** Arco, Chevron, Citgo/7-11, Shell/diesel, **food:** Jack-in-the-Box, **lodging:** Extended Stay America, West Coast Motel, **other:** HOSPITAL, to Capitol Mall

103 2nd Ave, no facilities

102 Trosper Rd, Black Lake, **E...gas:** Arco/24hr, Citgo/7-11, Shell/diesel/24hr, **food:** Arby's, Burger King, Cattin's Rest./24hr, El Sarape Mexican, Jack-in-the-Box, KFC, McDonald's, Pizza Hut, Subway, Taco Bell, Teriyaki Rest., **lodging:** Best Western, Motel 6, **other:** Goodyear, Schuck's Parts, **W...gas:** Chevron/24hr, 76/Circle K, Shell/24hr, **food:** Nickelby's Rest., **lodging:** Tyee Hotel/rest., **other:** Albertson's, Costco, Fred Meyer, MegaFoods/24hr

101 Airdustrial Way, **E...gas:** Chevron, Shell, **food:** Quizno's, **lodging:** Comfort Inn, GuestHouse Inn, Olympia Camping

99 WA 121 S, 93rd Ave, Scott Lake, **E...other:** American Heritage Camping, **W...gas:** Exxon/diesel, Shell/diesel/LP, **food:** Hannah's Pantry Rest., **lodging:** Restover Motel

95 WA 121, Littlerock, **3 mi E...other:** Millersylvania SP, RV camping, **W...food:** Farmboy Drive-In

93.5mm rest area sb, full(handicapped)facilities, info, phone, picnic tables, litter barrels, vending, coffee, petwalk

WASHINGTON

Interstate 5

N ↕ S

Centralia

91mm **rest area nb, full(handicapped)facilities, info, phone, picnic tables, litter barrels, vending, coffee, petwalk**

88 US 12, Rochester, **W...gas:** Arco/24hr, Shell/diesel/LP/repair, Texaco/diesel/24hr, **food:** DQ, Grand Mound Pizza/deli, Little Red Barn Rest./24hr, Lucky Eagle Casino/café, Royal India Rest., **other:** Outback RV Park(2mi), Harrison RV Park(3mi)

82 Harrison Ave, Factory Outlet Way, Centralia, **E...gas:** Arco/24hr, Shell/diesel, **food:** Alberto's Mexican, Burger King, Burgerville, Casa Ramos Mexican, DQ, Godfather's, Panda Inn, Pizza Hut, Shari's/24hr, TCBY, Wendy's, **lodging:** Centralia Inn, Ferryman's Inn, King Oscar Motel, Riverside Motel, **other:** HOSPITAL, VF/famous brands, **W...gas:** Chevron, 76/Circle K, Shell, **food:** Arby's, Country Cousin Rest., Denny's, Jack-in-the-Box, McDonald's, Papa Murphy's, Starbucks, Subway, Taco Bell, **lodging:** Day's Inn, Motel 6, **other:** Fuller's Foods, GNC, Outlet Mall/famous brands, Rite Aid, Safeway, Schuck's Parts, Scwab Tire

82mm Skookumchuck River

81 WA 507, Mellen St, **E...gas:** Shell, Texaco/diesel, **food:** Buchanan's Rest., King Solomon Rest., **lodging:** Holiday Inn Express, Pepper Tree Motel/RV Park, Travelodge, **W...**HOSPITAL

79 Chamber Way, **E...gas:** Shell/diesel/24hr, **food:** Burger King, McDonald's, Plaza Jalisco Mexican, Subway, **other:** Ford/Lincoln/Mercury/Toyota, Goodyear/auto, RV Ctr, museum, **W...gas:** 76/Burger King/diesel/LP, **other:** K-Mart/Little Caesar's, Wal-Mart/auto, st patrol

77 WA 6 W, Chehalis, **E...gas:** Arco/24hr, Cenex, **food:** Dairy Bar, **lodging:** St Helens Inn/rest., **other:** Healthy Harvest Foods, Hustons Parts, **W...gas:** Exxon(2mi), **food:** Desi's Kitchen, **other:** Rainbow Falls SP(16mi), RV camping

76 13th St, **E...gas:** Arco/24hr, Chevron, 76, **food:** Denny's, Jack-in-the Box, Jade Garden Chinese, Kit Carson Rest., **lodging:** Best Western, Howard Johnson, Relax Inn, **other:** Safeway, **W...**RV Park/dump

72 Rush Rd, Napavine, **E...gas:** Shell/Taco Bell/diesel, **food:** McDonald's, RibEye Rest./24hr, Subway, **other:** Dave's RV Ctr, RV park, **W...gas:** Chevron/diesel/24hr, Pacific Pride/diesel, Shell/diesel, **food:** FoodCourt

72mm Newaukum River

71 WA 508 E, Onalaska, Napavine, **E...gas:** 76/diesel

68 US 12 E, **E...gas:** Arco/24hr, Chevron/diesel/RV Park, 76/diesel/LP, Spiffy's Rest./24hr, **other:** KOA, to Lewis&Clark SP, Mt Ranier NP, **W...gas:** Shell/diesel, **food:** The Mustard Seed Rest.

63 WA 505, Winlock, **E...other:** RV park(3mi), **W...gas:** Shell/diesel/LP, Texaco/LP

60 Toledo, no facilities

59 WA 506 W, Vader, **E...gas:** 76/diesel, **food:** Mrs Beesley's Burgers, **W...gas:** Shell/diesel/24hr, **food:** Country House Rest., Grandma's Café, **other:** River Oaks RV Park

59mm Cowlitz River

57 Barnes Dr, Jackson Hwy, **W...gas:** GeeCee's/diesel/café/24hr/@, **other:** repair, RV camping

55mm **rest area both lanes, full(handicapped)facilities, phone, picnic tables, litter barrels, vending, petwalk**

52 Toutle Park Rd, **E...other:** Paradise Cove RV Park/gas

50mm Toutle River

49 WA 504 E, Castle Rock, **E...gas:** Arco/24hr, Chevron, Shell, Texaco/diesel/24hr, **food:** Burger King, C&L Burgers, El Compadre Mexican, 49er Diner, Papa Pete's Pizza, RoseTree Rest., Subway, **lodging:** Mt St Helens Motel, 7 West Motel, Silver Lake Motel/resort, Timberland Inn, **other:** Seaquest SP(5mi), **W...gas:** Gasco

48 Huntington Ave, no facilities

46 Pleasant Hill Rd, **E...other:** Cedars RV Park

44mm weigh sta sb, phone

42 Ostrander Rd, no facilities

Kelso

40 to WA 4, Kelso-Longview, **1 mi W...gas:** 76, **lodging:** Best Value Inn, Best Western, Budget Inn, Townhouse Motel, **other:** HOSPITAL, Parts+, transmissions

39 WA 4, Kelso, to Longview, **E...gas:** Arco/24hr, Shell, **food:** Denny's, Hilander Rest., Jitter's Drive-Thru, Little Caesar's, McDonald's, Shari's/24hr, Subway, **lodging:** Motel 6, Red Lion Motel, Super 8, **other:** Rite Aid, Safeway, **W...gas:** Chevron/repair, Texaco/diesel, **food:** Azteca Mexican, Burger King, DQ, Izzy's Pizza, North's Buffet, Red Lobster, Taco Bell, **lodging:** Comfort Inn, GuestHouse Inn, **other:** Emporium, JC Penney, Sears/auto, Target, Top Foods, mall, museum

36 WA 432 W, to WA 433, US 30, Kelso, **E...other:** U-Neek RV Ctr, **1-3 mi W...gas:** 76, Shell/24hr, **lodging:** Patrician Inn, **other:** HOSPITAL, Longview RV ctr, Toyota, Oaks RV Park, st patrol

32 Kalama River Rd, **E...food:** Fireside Café, **other:** Camp Kalama RV Park/gifts

31mm Kalama River

30 Kalama, **E...gas:** Chevron, **food:** Burger Bar, Key Grill, Subway, **lodging:** Columbia Inn/rest., Kalama River Inn, **other:** Big A Parts, USPO, **W...gas:** Shell/diesel, **other:** RV camping

27 Todd Rd, Port of Kalama, **E...gas:** Shell/diesel/café/24hr

22 Dike Access Rd, **W...gas:** CFN/diesel/24hr, **other:** Columbia Riverfront/Lewis River/Woodland Shores RV Parks

Woodland

21 WA 503 E, Woodland, **E...gas:** Arco/24hr, Chevron, Shell/diesel, Texaco/diesel/LP, **food:** Burgerville, Casa Maria's, DQ, Figaro's Italian, Grandma's House(8mi), OakTree Rest., Riverside Rest., Rosie's Rest., South China Rest., Subway, **lodging:** Best Inn, Best Western, Lewis River Inn, Woodlander Inn, **other:** Hi-School Drug, Letterbox, Sav-On Foods, Woodland Shores RV Park, **W...gas:** Exxon/24hr, **food:** McDonald's, ParkPlace Pizza, Whimpy's Rest., **lodging:** Hansen's Motel, Lakeside Motel, Scandia Motel, **other:** Chevrolet, NAPA, Safeway/gas

WASHINGTON

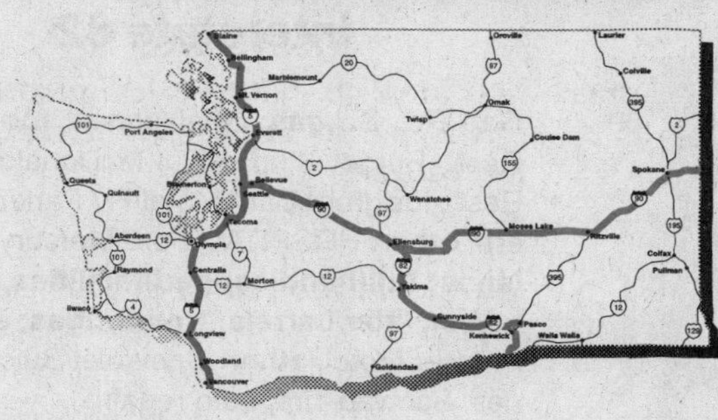

Interstate 5

N ↕ S

Exit #	Services
20mm	N Fork Lewis River
18mm	E Fork Lewis River
16	NW 319th St, La Center, **E...gas:** Texaco/diesel/24hr, **food:** Lucky Dragon Rest., **other:** Paradise Point SP
15mm	weigh sta nb
14	WA 501 W, NW 269th St, **E...gas:** Arco/24hr, 76/Circle K, **food:** Country Café, to **other:** Battleground Lake SP(14mi), Big Fir RV Park(4mi), **W...gas:** Chevron/diesel
13mm	**rest area sb, full(handicapped)facilities, info, phone, picnic tables, litter barrels, vending, petwalk, RV dump**
11mm	**rest area nb, full(handicapped)facilities, info, phone, picnic tables, litter barrels, vending, petwalk, RV dump**
9	NE 179th St, **E...food:** Jollie's Rest./24hr, **other:** Poulsbo RV, **W... gas:** Chevron/diesel
7	I-205 S(from sb), to I-84, WA 14, NE 134th St, Portland Airport, **E...gas:** Citgo/7-11, 76, TrailMart/diesel, **food:** Billigan's Roadhouse, Burger King, Burgerville, Jack-in-the-Box, McDonald's, Round Table Pizza, Taco Bell, **lodging:** Comfort Inn, Holiday Inn Express, Olympia Motel, Salmon Creek Inn, Shilo Inn, **other:** HOSPITAL, Albertson's, Hi-School Drugs, Zupan's Mkt, 99 RV Park, **W...gas:** Astro/diesel, **lodging:** University Inn, **other:** Fred Meyer
5	NE 99th St, **E...gas:** Arco/24hr, Citgo/7-11, Shell, **food:** Burgerville, Carl's Jr, Domino's, Fat Dave's Rest., Quizno's, **other:** Nissan/Kia, Walgreen, Winco Foods/24hr, **W...gas:** Arco/24hr, Chevron/24hr, **food:** Applebee's, Bortolami's Pizza, McDonald's, **other:** Albertson's, Hi-School Drug, Wal-Mart
4	NE 78th St, Hazel Dell, **E...gas:** Exxon, 76, Shell, **food:** BBQ, Burger King, Burgerville, Buster's BBQ, Dragon King Chinese, Izzy's Rest., KFC, Mar-Bo Chinese, McDonald's, Pizza Hut, Skipper's, Smokey's Pizza, Starbucks, Steakburger, Subway, Taco Bell, Taco Time, **lodging:** Edelweiss Inn, Quality Inn, Value Motel, **other:** America's Tire, CarQuest, Firestone, Fred Meyer, Dodge, Ford, Goodyear, Mazda, Nissan, Radio Shack, Schuck's Parts, U-Haul, transmissions, **W...gas:** Shell/diesel/LP, Texaco/diesel, **food:** Blimpie, Denny's, Figaro's Pizza, RoundTable Pizza, Wendy's, **other:** Rite Aid, Safeway
3	NE Hwy 99, Hazel Dell, Main St, **E...other:** HOSPITAL, **W...gas:** Arco, **other:** Safeway, transmissions
2	WA 500 E, 39th St, to Orchards, no facilities
1d	E 4th, Plain Blvd W, to WA 501, Port of Vancouver, no facilities
1c	Mill Plain Blvd, City Ctr, **W...gas:** Chevron, Texaco, **food:** Cattle Co Rest., Burgerville, Denny's, **lodging:** DoubleTree Hotel, Fort Motel, Shilo Inn, Vancouver Inn, **other:** Ford, Lincoln/Mercury, Pontiac/Cadillac/GMC, Jeep/Eagle, Mitsubishi, Suzuki, Clark Coll, st patrol
1b a	WA 14 E, to Camus, **E...food:** ChartHouse Rest.
0mm	Washington/Oregon state line, Columbia River

Vancouver

Interstate 82

E ↕ W

Exit #	Services
11mm	I-82 Oregon begins/ends on I-84, exit 179.
10	Westland Rd, **E...other:** to Umatilla Army Depot, **lodging:** to Best Western, **other:** HOSPITAL
5	Power Line Rd, no facilities
1.5mm	Umatilla River
1	US 395/730, Umatilla, **E...lodging:** Best Western, Desert Inn, **other:** Hatrock Camping(8mi), to McNary Dam, **W...gas:** Amoco/diesel/LP, Arco/diesel/24hr, Shell/diesel/rest., **food:** Dojack's Rest., G&J Burgers, **lodging:** Heather Inn, McNary Hotel, Rest-a-Bit Motel, Tillicum Motel, **other:** NAPA, Red Apple Mkt, USPO, st police, Welcome Ctr, weight sta
132mm	Columbia River, Washington/Oregon state line
131	WA 14 W, Plymouth, **N...other:** RV camping, to McNary Dam
130mm	weigh sta wb
122	Coffin Rd, no facilities
114	Locust Grove Rd, no facilities
113	US 395 N, to I-182, Kennewick, Pasco, st patrol, **2-5 mi N...gas:** Arco/24hr, Exxon, **food:** Billigan's Roadhouse, Bruchi's Café, Carl's Jr, China Café, Denny's, Godfather's, Jack-in-the-Box, KFC, McDonald's, Starbucks, Subway, Taco Bell/24hr, **lodging:** Best Western, Hawthorn Suites, Holiday Inn Express, Nendel's Inn, Tapadera Budget Motel, Travelodge, **other:** GNC, Harley-Davidson, Hastings Books, Radio Shack, Rite Aid, Safeway
109	Badger Rd, W Kennewick, **N...gas:** Shell/BYOBurger/diesel/24hr, **3 mi N...food:** Chico's Tacos, McDonald's, Subway, **lodging:** Clearwater Inn, Silver Cloud Inn, Super 8, West Coast Inn
104	Dallas Rd, **3 mi N...gas:** Conoco/diesel/24hr, **food:** Hotstuff Pizza/subs
102	I-182, US 12 E, to US 395, Spokane, HOSPITAL, facilities in Richland, Pasco
96	WA 224, Benton City, **N...gas:** Conoco/diesel/24hr, **food:** BearHut Rest., **other:** Beach RV Park
93	Yakitat Rd, no facilities
88	Gibbon Rd, no acilities
82	WA 22, WA 221, Mabton, **2 mi S...food:** Blue Goose Rest., **lodging:** Prosser Motel, **other:** HOSPITAL, to WA St U Research, to Wine Tasting Facilities, museum
82mm	Yakima River

Kennewick

WASHINGTON

Interstate 82

E ↕ W

80 Gap Rd, **S...gas:** Shell/diesel, **food:** Blue Goose Rest., Burger King, KFC, McDonald's, NorthWoods Rest., **lodging:** Barn Motel/RV Park/rest., Best Western, **other:** HOSPITAL, Ford/Mercury, **rest area both lanes, full(handicapped)facilities, phone, picnic tables, litter barrels, 1 mi S...gas:** Exxon, **lodging:** Prosser Motel, **other:** Chevrolet/Buick, Chukar Cherries, Schwab Tire, auto repair

75 County Line Rd, Grandview, **1 mi S...gas:** Cenex/diesel, Conoco/diesel/24hr, **lodging:** Apple Valley Motel, Grandview Motel, **other:** same as 73

73 Stover Rd, Wine Country Rd, Grandview, **S...gas:** Conoco/diesel/24hr, Shell/Quizno's/TCBY/diesel, **food:** Eli&Kathy's Breakfast, Morrie's Pizza, New Hong Kong, 10-4 Café, **lodging:** Apple Valley Motel, Grandview Motel, **other:** Plymouth/Jeep/Dodge, Red Apple Foods, RV Ctr, RV Park/dump, auto repair

69 WA 241, to Sunnyside, **N...gas:** Arco/diesel/24hr, Shell/TacoMaker/diesel/24hr, **food:** Arby's, Burger King, DQ, McDonald's, Pizza Hut, Skipper's, Subway, Taco Bell, **lodging:** Rodeway Inn, Travelodge, **other:** BiMart Foods, Buick/Chevrolet/Nissan, GNC, JC Penney, K-Mart/Little Caesars, Schuck's Parts, Staples, Wal-Mart/auto

67 Sunnyside, Port of Sunnyside, **N...gas:** Chevron/diesl, **other:** HOSPITAL, BiMart Foods, **S...other:** DariGold Cheese

63 Outlook, Sunnyside, **3 mi N...lodging:** Sunnyside B&B, Townhouse Motel, Travelodge, **other:** RV camping

58 WA 223 S, to Granger, **S...gas:** Conoco/diesel, **other:** OK Tire, RV camping

54 Division Rd, Yakima Valley Hwy, to Zillah, **N...food:** El Ranchito Rest., **S...other:** Teapot Dome NHS, diesel/LP, RV dump

52 Zillah, Toppenish, **N...gas:** Arco/24hr, Chevron, 76/diesel, **food:** Mario's Cantina, McDonald's, Subway, **lodging:** Comfort Inn, **other:** RV dump, Wine Tasting

50 WA 22 E, to US 97 S, Toppenish, **N...lodging:** Best Western, **food:** Gold Nugget Café/casino, **3 mi S... food:** Legends Buffet/casino, McDonald's, **lodging:** Toppenish Inn, **other:** HOSPITAL, Murals Museum, RV Park, to Yakima Nation Cultural Ctr

44 Wapato, **N...gas:** Texaco/diesel, **2 mi S...food:** DQ

40 Thorp Rd, Parker Rd, Yakima Valley Hwy, **N...other:** Sagelands Winery

39mm Yakima River

38 Union Gap(from wb), **1 mi S...food:** Peppermint Stick Drive-In, **other:** gas, lodging, museum

37 US 97(from eb), **1 mi S...gas:** Exxon, Texaco, **other:** Alpenlite RV, NAPA

Yakima

36 Valley Mall Blvd, Yakima, **N...other:** st patrol, **S...gas:** Arco/diesel/24hr, Cenex/diesel, Texaco/Gearjammer/diesel/rest./24hr, **food:** Burger King, Denny's/24hr, Godfather's, Hill's Café, IHOP, Jack-in-the-Box, KFC, Miner's Drive-In, Outback Steaks, SeaGalley Rest., Shangrila Chinese, Shari's, Taco Bell, **lodging:** Best Western, Cobblestone Inn, Quality Inn, Super 8, **other:** MEDICAL CARE, Big A Parts, Goodyear, Lowe's Whse, Office Depot, Rite Aid, Sears/auto, ShopKO, diesel/repair, mall

34 WA 24 E, Nob Hill Blvd, Yakima, **N...gas:** CFN/diesel, **other:** K-Mart, Sportsman SP, KOA, diesel/repair, **S... gas:** Arco/24hr, Chevron/Subway/TCBY/diesel/24hr, Citgo/7-11, Shell/diesel, **food:** Arby's, McDonald's, **other:** HOSPITAL, Al's Parts, Circle H Ranch RV Park, Family Foods, museum

33 Yakima Ave, Yakima, **N...gas:** Chevron/Quizno's/TCBY/24hr, Shell/Chester's/diesel, **food:** Burger King, Marti's Café, McDonald's, **lodging:** Oxford Suites, **other:** Chevrolet/GMC/Isuzu, Honda, Mazda, Wal-Mart SuperCtr/24hr, **S...gas:** Arco/24hr, Citgo/7-11, **food:** DQ, FoodCourt, Taco Bell, **lodging:** Budget Suites, Holiday Inn Express, West Coast Inn, **other:** JC Penney, Mervyn's, OfficeMax, Red Apple Mkt, Schwab Tire, Target, mall

31b a US 12 W, N 1st St, to Naches, **S...gas:** Arco/diesel/24hr, Shell/repair, **food:** Arctic Circle, Black Angus, China Buffet, Denny's, Jack-in-the-Box, Mel's Diner/24hr, Peking Palace, Pizza Hut, Red Apple Rest., Red Lobster, Sizzler, Subway, Waffles'n More, Wendy's, **lodging:** Best Western, Big Valley Motel, DoubleTree Hotel, Economy Inn, Motel 6, **other:** Nendel's, Red Lion Inn, Sun Country Inn, Tourist Motel, Twin Bridges Inn, Vagabond Inn, Yakima Inn, RV Park, **2 mi W on N 40th Ave...gas:** Arco, Conoco/diesel/café, **food:** Jack-in-the-Box, McDonald's, Shari's, Subway, Taco Bell, **lodging:** Comfort Suites, **other:** Fred Meyer

30 WA 823 N, Rest Haven Rd, to Selah, no facilities

29 E Selah Rd, **N...other:** fruits/antiques

26 WA 821 N, to WA 823, Canyon Rd, **N...gas:** Shell/Noble Roman/Quizno's/TCBY/diesel/24hr

24mm rest area eb, full(handicapped)facilities, phone, picnic tables, litter barrels

23mm Selah Creek

22mm rest area wb, full(handicapped)facilities, phone, picnic tables, litter barrels

21mm S Umptanum Ridge, 2265 elev

19mm Burbank Creek

17mm N Umptanum Ridge, 2315 elev

15mm Lmuma Creek

11 Military Area, no facilities

8mm view point both lanes, Manastash Ridge, 2672 elev

3 WA 821 S, Thrall Rd, no facilities

0mm I-90, E to Spokane, W to Seattle. I-82 begins/ends on I-90, exit 110.

Interstate 90

E ↕ W

Spokane

Exit #	Services
300mm	Washington/Idaho state line, Spokane River
299	State Line, Port of Entry, **N...Welcome Ctr/rest area both lanes, weigh sta, full(handicapped)facilities, phone, picnic tables, litter barrels, petwalk,** Exxon
296	Otis Orchards, Liberty Lakes, **N...gas:** Shell/Subway/diesel, **food:** HomePlate Grill, **lodging:** Best Western, **other:** GMC/Pontiac, **S...gas:** Chevron/LP, 76, **food:** Burger King, Carl's Jr, Domino's, McDonald's, Papa Murphy's, Quizno's, Taco Bell, **other:** Albertson's, Alton Tire, GNC, ForeTravel RV Ctr, Land Rover, Safeway/gas
294	Sprague Ave(from wb, no EZ return), **S...other:** North Country RV/marine, Nut Factory, auto repair
293	Barker Rd, Greenacres, **N...gas:** Conoco/Wendy's/diesel, GTX Trkstp/diesel/café, **food:** Slapshot Café, Wendy's, **other:** Alpine Motel/RV Park, KOA, **S...gas:** Conoco/24hr, Exxon/Subway/24hr, **other:** NW RV Ctr
291	Sullivan Rd, Veradale, **N...gas:** Chevron/Blimpie/TCBY, **food:** Arby's, McDonald's, Outback Steaks, Tony Roma, **lodging:** Hawthorn Inn, Oxford Suites, Residence Inn, **other:** Barnes&Noble, Best Buy, Circuit City, JC Penney, Sears/auto, Staples, mall, **S...gas:** Chevron, Conoco, 76, Shell/diesel, **food:** A&W, Bruchi's Rest., DQ, Godfather's, Jack-in-the Box, KFC, McDonald's, Mongolian BBQ, Noodle Express, Pizza Hut, Schlotsky's, Shari's/24hr, Starbucks, Subway, Taco Bell, **lodging:** Comfort Inn, DoubleTree Hotel, **other:** Fred Meyer, Goodyear/auto, Hastings Books, K-Mart, Michael's, Rite Aid, Ross, Wal-Mart/auto
291a	Evergreen Rd, **N...food:** Black Angus, Boston Pizza, IHOP, **other:** BonMarche, Greenbax, Old Navy, Sears/auto, mall, **S...gas:** Shell
289	WA 27 S, Pines Rd, Opportunity, **N...gas:** Citgo/7-11, **food:** Old Matthews Rest., **S...gas:** Holiday, Shell/diesel, 76, **food:** Applebee's, DQ, Jack-in-the-Box, **lodging:** Best Western, **other:** HOSPITAL, Standard Battery
287	Argonne Rd, Millwood, **N...gas:** Holiday/diesel, **food:** Burger King, Denny's, Godfather's, Hungry Farmer Rest., Jack-in-the-Box, Longhorn BBQ, Marie Callender's, McDonald's, Papa Murphy's, Subway, Taco Bell, Wendy's, Wolffy's Burgers, **lodging:** Motel 6, RedTop Motel, Super 8, **other:** Albertson's, Schuck's Parts, Tidyman's Foods, Walgreen, **S...gas:** 76/Circle K, Chevron, Exxon, **food:** Casa de Oro Mexican, Godfather's, GoodTymes Grill, Perkins, **lodging:** Holiday Inn Express, Quality Inn, **other:** Rite Aid/24hr, Safeway
286	Broadway Ave, **N...gas:** Flying J/Conoco/Sak's Rest./diesel/LP/24hr/@, Shell, **food:** Zip's Burgers, Best Inn, Comfort Inn, Goodyear, Schwab Tire, White/Volvo/GMC, **S...**CFN/diesel, 7-11
285	Sprague Ave, **N...gas:** Shell, **food:** Denny's, IHOP, Jack-in-the-Box, McDonald's, **lodging:** ParkLane Motel, **other:** Costco/gas, Grocery Outlet, Home Depot, K-Mart, Lowe's Whse, Radio Shack, Shuck's Parts, Tidyman's Foods, **S...gas:** Exxon, **food:** Mandarin House, Puerta Vallarta Mexican, Subway, Taco Time, Zip's Burger, **other:** Alton's Tire, Chevrolet, Chrysler/Plymouth, Dodge, Ford, Hyundai, L&L RV Ctr, Nissan/Saab, RV camping, transmissions
284	Havana St(from eb, no EZ return), **N...food:** Jack-in-the-Box, McDonald's
283b	Freya St, Thor St, **N...gas:** Chevron, Conoco/diesel, **food:** Peking Garden, Subway, Wolf Lodge Steaks, **other:** Park Lane Motel/RV Park, Fred Meyer, **S...gas:** Citgo/7-11, Texaco/Taco Bell
a	Altamont St, **S...gas:** 76
282b	2nd Ave, **N...lodging:** Shilo Inn, **other:** Office Depot
a	WA 290 E, Trent Ave, Hamilton St, **N...gas:** Shell/diesel, **lodging:** Shilo Inn, **other:** Shogun Japanese, Office Depot
281	US 2, US 395, to Colville, **N...gas:** Citgo/7-11, Conoco, Shell/repair, Texaco/diesel, **food:** Arby's, Just Like Home Buffet, McDonald's, Perkins, Pizza Hut, Rancho Chico's Rest., Subway, Taco Time, Waffles'n More, **lodging:** Best Western/rest., Howard Johnson, **other:** Firestone, Ford, Schwab Tire, U-Haul, **S...lodging:** WestCoast Hotel, **other:** HOSPITAL
280b	Lincoln St, **N...gas:** Chevron, Conoco/diesel, Shell, **food:** Burger King, Carl's Jr, Godfather's, IHOP, Jack-in-the-Box, McDonald's, Taco Bell, Wendy's, Zip's Burgers, **lodging:** Best Western, Ramada Inn, **other:** Cadillac, Lincoln/Mercury, Honda, Lexus, Mazda, Mercedes, Saturn, Toyota, **S...**HOSPITAL
a	downtown, **N...gas:** Chevron/McDonald's, Conoco/diesel, Shell, Texaco, **food:** Arctic Circle, Perkins, Subway, **lodging:** Select Inn, **other:** AAA, Chevrolet, NAPA, Safeway
279	US 195 S, to Colfax, Pullman, **N...lodging:** West Wynn Hotel, Shangri-la Motel
277b a	US 2 W, Fairchild AFB, to Grand Coulee Dam, **N...lodging:** Day's Inn, Hampton Inn, Motel 6, Ramada, Rodeway Inn, Shangri-la Motel, Spokane House Hotel
276	Geiger Blvd, **N...gas:** Flying J/Exxon/diesel/LP/rest./24hr/@, **food:** Denny's, Subway, Airway **lodging:** Express Inn, Best Western, **other:** USPO, st patrol, **S...gas:** Shell/diesel/LP, Sunset RV Park/dump
272	WA 902, Medical Lake, **N...gas:** Shell/diesel, **other:** Overland Sta/RV Park, **S...lodging:** Super 8, **other:** Yogi Bear Camping
270	WA 904, Cheney, Four Lakes, **S...gas:** Exxon, **lodging:** Rosebrook Inn(6mi), Willow Springs Motel(6mi), **other:** Peaceful Pines RV Park, Ford, E WA U
264	WA 902, Salnave Rd, to Cheney, Medical Lake, **2 mi N...**camping
257	WA 904, Tyler, to Cheney, no facilities
254	Fishtrap, **S...other:** Fishtrap RV camping/tents

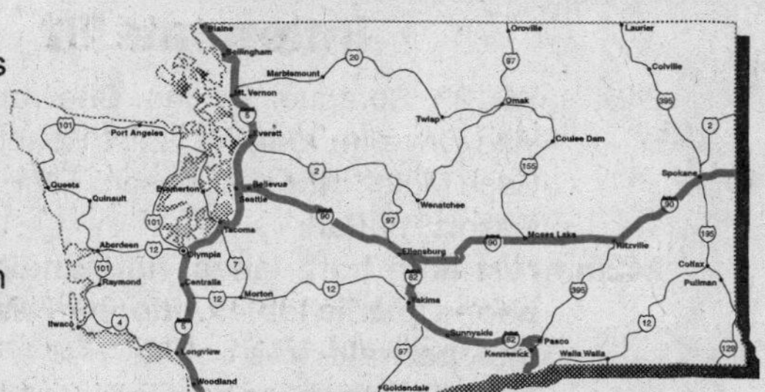

WASHINGTON

Interstate 90

E ↕ W

245 WA 23, Sprague, **S...gas:** Chevron/diesel, **food:** Viking Drive-In, **lodging:** Last Roundup Motel, Purple Sage Motel, **other:** 4 Seasons RV Park, Sprague Lake Resort/RV Park

242mm rest area both lanes, full(handicapped)facilities, phone, picnic tables, litter barrels, tourist/weather info, petwalk, free coffee

231 Tokio, **S...**weigh sta both lanes, **gas:** Exxon/Templin's Café/diesel, **other:** RV Park

226 Coker Rd, **S...other:** Cottage RV Park

221 WA 261 S, Ritzville, City Ctr, **N...gas:** Astro, Cenex, Chevron/McDonald's, Exxon, Shell/Taco Bell/diesel, Texaco/diesel/pizza, **food:** Perkins, Zip's Burgers, **lodging:** Best Inn/RV Park, Colwell Motel, Empire Motel, Top Hat Motel, **other:** HOSPITAL, hist dist

220 to US 395 S, Ritzville, **N...gas:** Cenex, Chevron, Exxon/diesel/café, **food:** Jake's Café, Texas John's Café, **lodging:** Caldwell Inn, Westside Motel, **other:** st patrol

215 Paha, Packard, no facilities

206 WA 21, to Lind, Odessa, no facilities

199mm rest area both lanes, full(handicapped)facilities, phone, picnic tables, litter barrels, vending, RV dump, petwalk

196 Deal Rd, to Schrag, no facilities

188 U Rd, to Warden, Ruff, **10 mi S...**food

184 Q Rd, no facilities

182 O Rd, to Wheeler, no facilities

Moses Lake

179 WA 17, Moses Lake, **N...gas:** Chevron/diesel/café/24hr, Conoco/diesel, Exxon, 76/diesel, Shell, **food:** Arby's, Burger King, DQ, Denny's, McDonald's, Shari's Rest./24hr, **lodging:** Holiday Inn Express, Moses Lake Inn, Shilo Inn/rest./24hr, Travelodge, **other:** HOSPITAL, **1 mi N...food:** Subway, **lodging:** El Rancho Motel, Sage'n Sand Motel, **other:** MEDICAL CARE, Honda, Nissan, USPO, **2 mi N...food:** Godfather's, KFC, Pizza Hut, **other:** Buick/Chevrolet/Pontiac, CarQuest, Chrysler/Plymouth, Ford/Lincoln/Mercury, Radio Shack, Rite Aid, Safeway, Scwab Tire, **S...other:** I-90 RV, Sun Country RV, Willows RV Park(2mi), Potholes SP(15mi)

177mm Moses Lake

176 WA 171, Moses Lake, **1 mi N...gas:** Cenex/24hr, Exxon/diesel, Shell, Texaco/diesel, **food:** El Rodeo Mexican, Godfather's, Kiyoji's Rest., Perkins/24hr, **lodging:** Best Western/rest., Interstate Inn, Maples Motel, Motel 6, Oasis Budget Inn, Super 8, Motel 6, **other:** HOSPITAL, OK Tires, Big Sun Resort/RV Hookups, **S...lodging:** Lakeshore Motel

175 Westshore Dr(from wb), **N...other:** Moses Lake SP, to Mae Valley, **S...other:** st patrol

174 Mae Valley, **N...other:** Suncrest Resort/RV, **S...gas:** Conoco/diesel, **other:** st patrol

169 Hiawatha Rd, no facilities

164 Dodson Rd, no facilities

162mm rest area wb, full(handicapped)facilities, phone, picnic tables, litter barrels, petwalk, RV dump

161mm rest area eb, full(handicapped)facilities, phone, picnic tables, litter barrels, petwalk, RV dump

154 Adams Rd, no facilities

151 WA 281 N, to Quincy, **N...gas:** Shell/diesel/pizza/subs, **other:** HOSPITAL(12mi), Shady Tree/RV camp

149 WA 281 S, George, **N...**HOSPITAL(12mi), **S...gas:** 76/Subway/diesel, Exxon/diesel/24hr, **food:** Martha Inn Café, **other:** RV camp

143 Silica Rd, to The Gorge Ampitheatre

139mm Wild Horses Mon, scenic view both lanes

137 WA 26 E, to WA 243, Othello, Richland, no facilities

137mm Columbia River

136 Huntzinger Rd, Vantage, **N...gas:** Shell, Texaco/diesel/repair, **food:** Golden Harvest Café, Wanapum Rest., **lodging:** Motel Vantage, **other:** KOA, to Ginkgo/Wanapum SP, auto repair, **4 mi S...other:** Gettys Cove RV Park

126mm Ryegrass, elev 2535, rest area both lanes, full(handicapped)facilities, phone, picnic tables, litter barrels, petwalk

115 Kittitas, **N...gas:** 76/24hr, Shell/diesel/24hr, **food:** RJ's Café, **other:** Olmstead Place SP

110 I-82 E, US 97 S, to Yakima, no facilities

Ellensburg

109 Canyon Rd, Ellensburg, **N...gas:** Astro, Chevron/24hr, Eagle Trkstp/diesel/@, Shell/24hr, Texaco, **food:** Arby's, Baskin-Robbins, Burger King, Casa de Blanca Mexican, Fiesta Mexican, Golden Dragon Chinese, KFC, McDonald's, Palace Café, Pizza Hut, RanchHouse Rest., Skipper's, Subway, Taco Bell, Tanum Rest., **lodging:** Comfort Inn, Ellensburg Inn, Goose Creek Inn, Nites Inn, Super 8, **other:** HOSPITAL, Al's Parts, BiMart Foods, CarQuest, Chevrolet, NAPA, Radio Shack, Rite Aid, Scwab Tire, Super 1 Food/24hr, **S...gas:** Flying J/Sak's/diesel/LP/24hr/@, **food:** Leaton's Rest., **lodging:** Best Inn/RV park

106 US 97 N, to Wenatchie, **N...gas:** Chevron, Conoco/diesel/RV dump, Pilot/Subway/diesel/24hr/@, **food:** Blue Grouse Rest., 76, Copper Kettle(2mi), DQ, Jack-in-the-Box, Perkins, **lodging:** Harold's Motel, I-90 Inn, Regal Lodge(2mi), **other:** Ford, **S...other:** KOA, st patrol

101 Thorp Hwy, **N...other:** antiques/fruits/vegetables

93 Elk Heights Rd, Taneum Creek, no facilities

92.5mm Elk Heights, elev 2359

89mm Indian John Hill, elev 2141, rest area both lanes, full(handicapped)facilities, phone, picnic tables, litter barrels, RV dump, petwalk, vending

Cle Elum

85 WA 970, WA 903, to Wenatchie, **N...gas:** Conoco/repair, 76/diesel, Shell/diesel/24hr, **food:** Cottage Café/24hr, DQ, Homestead Rest., McKean's Drive-In, **lodging:** Aster Inn, Cascade Mtn Inn, Cedars Motel, Chalet Motel, Wind Blew Inn, **other:** CarQuest, PriceChopper Foods, Trailer Corral RV Park

84 Cle Elum(from eb, return at 85), **N...gas:** Chevron/diesel, Conoco, Shell/Subway/diesel, **food:** Burger King, DQ, El Caporal Mexican, Sunset Café, YumYang Chinese, **lodging:** Cle Elum Motel, Timber Lodge Motel, Stewarts Lodge, **other:** HOSPITAL, Safeway/gas, museum

81mm Cle Elum River

80 Roslyn, Salmon la Sac, no facilities

80mm weigh sta both lanes, phone

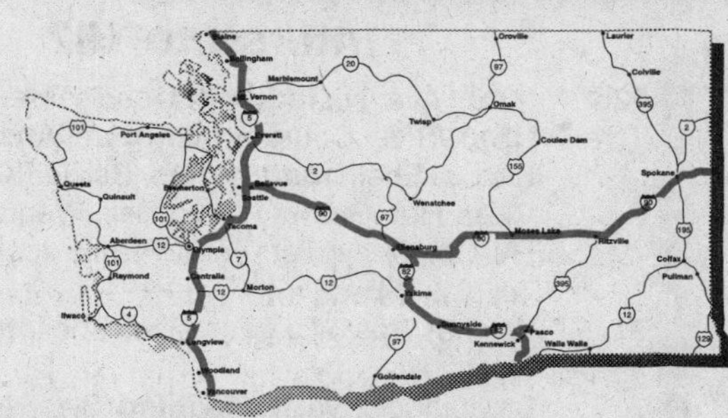

Interstate 90

E ↕ W

78 Golf Course Rd, **S...other:** Sun Country Golf/RV Park

74 W Nelson Siding Rd, no facilities

71 Easton, **S...gas:** CB's Store, **lodging:** Silver Ridge Ranch B&B, **other:** USPO, John Wayne Tr, Iron Horse SP

71mm Yakima River

70 Lake Easton SP, **N...gas:** Texaco/café, **food:** Mtn High Burger, Parkside Café, **S...other:** Silver Ridge Ranch RV Park

63 Cabin Creek Rd, no facilities

62 Stampede Pass, elev 3750, to Lake Kachess, **N...lodging:** Kachess Lodge

54 Hyak, Gold Creek, no facilities

53 Snoqualmie Pass, elev 3022, info, **S...gas:** Chevron, **food:** Family Pancake House, **lodging:** Best Western/Summit Inn, **other:** to rec areas

52 W Summit(from eb), same as 53

47 Denny Creek, Asahel Curtis, Tinkham Rd, **N...other:** chain area, **S...other:** RV camping/dump

45 USFS Rd 9030, **N...other:** to Lookout Point Rd, no facilities

42 Tinkham Rd, no facilities

38 **N...other:** fire training ctr

35mm S Fork Snoqualmie River

34 468th Ave SE, Edgewick Rd, **N...gas:** Pacific Pride/diesel, 76/Pizza Hut/Taco Bell/diesel, Seattle E/diesel/Ken's Rest./24hr, Shell/Subway/diesel/24hr, **lodging:** Edgewick Inn, NW Motel/RV Park

32 436th Ave SE, North Bend Ranger Sta, **1 mi N...**gas, food, lodging

31 WA 202 W, North Bend, Snoqualmie, **N...gas:** Chevron/diesel, Shell/diesel, Texaco/diesel, **food:** Arby's, Blimpie, Carribean Burger, DQ, Denny's, McDonald's, Taco Time, **lodging:** North Bend Motel, Old Honey Farm Inn, Sallish Lodge, Sunset Motel, **other:** HOSPITAL, NorthBend Stores/famous brands, Safeway/24hr, museum, st patrol

27 North Bend, Snoqualmie(from eb), no facilities

25 WA 18 W, Snoqualmie Pkwy, to Auburn, Tacoma, **N...**weigh sta

22 Preston, **N...gas:** Chevron/diesel/24hr, **food:** Expresso Café, Savannah's Burgers, Green Bank Cheese, **other:** USPO, Snoqualmie River RV Park(4mi), **S...other:** Blue Sky RV Park

20 High Point Way, **1 mi N...**Country Store

Issaquah

18 E Sunset Way, Issaquah, **S...gas:** Shell, **food:** Domino's, Flying Pie Pizza, Issaquah Brewhouse, Jak's Grill, Shagrila Garden Chinese, Front St Mkt, **other:** Radio Shack

17 E Sammamish Rd, Front St, Issaquah, **N...gas:** 76, **food:** Cojo Café, McDonald's, Starbucks, **other:** Albertson's, Fred Meyer, Home Depot, **S...gas:** Arco/repair, Chevron/24hr, Shell, Texaco/diesel/24hr, **food:** Domino's, Front St Deli, Skipper's, **other:** U-Haul

15 WA 900, Issaquah, Renton, **N...gas:** Arco/24hr, **food:** Georgio's Subs, IHOP, Red Robin, Tully's Coffee, **lodging:** Holiday Inn, Motel 6, **other:** Barnes&Noble, Costco, Lowe's Whse, Office Depot, Trader Joe's, Unique Foods, to Lk Sammamish SP, **S...gas:** Shell, **food:** Acapulco Mexican, Baskin-Robbins, Boston Mkt, Burger King, Denny's, Georgio's Subs, Godfather's, Honey B Ham, Jack-in-the-Box, JayBerry's Rest., KFC/Taco Bell, La Costa Mexican, Lombardi's Rest., McDonald's, O'Char Bistro, RoundTable Pizza, Schlotsky's, Subway, Taco Del Mar, Taco Time, Tokyo Garden, 12th Ave Café, **other:** Big O Tire, Firestone/auto, Ford, GNC, Harley-Davidson, QFC Foods, Rite Aid, Ross, Safeway Foods, Schuck's Parts, Target, USPO

Bellevue

13 SE Newport Way, W Lake Sammamish, no facilities

11 SE 150th, 156th, 161st, Bellevue, **N...**LDS Temple, **gas:** Shell, 7-11, **food:** DQ, Lil' Jon's Rest., Mandarin Chinese, McDonald's, Samurai Sam's Rest., **lodging:** Day's Inn, Eastgate Motel, Embassy Suites, Kane's Motel, **other:** Ford, Jo-Ann Fabrics/crafts, Subaru/VW, Safeway, **S...gas:** 76, Standard/24hr, Shell/diesel/24hr, **food:** Baskin-Robbins, Domino's, Outback Steaks, Pizza Hut, **lodging:** Candlewood Suites, **other:** Albertson's, Rite Aid, Schuck's Parts

10 I-405, N to Bellevue, S to Renton, facilities located off I-405 S, exit 10

9 Bellevue Way, no facilities

8 E Mercer Way, Mercer Island, no facilities

7c 80th Ave SE(exits left from wb)

7b a SE 76th Ave, 77th Ave, Island Crest Way, Mercer Island, **S...gas:** Chevron, 76/repair, Shell/diesel/repair, **food:** McDonald's, Mi Pueblo Mexican, 7Star Chinese, Starbucks, Subway, Tully's Coffee, **lodging:** Travelodge, **other:** Island Foods, Walgreen

6 W Mercer Way(from eb), same as 7

5mm Lake Washington

3b a Ranier Ave, Seattle, downtown, **N...gas:** Texaco

2c b I-5, N to Vancouver, S to Tacoma

a 4th Ave S, to King Dome

I-90 begins/ends on I-5 at exit 164.

Interstate 182(Richland)

E ↕ W

Exit # Services

14b a US 395 N, WA 397 S, OR Ave, **N...gas:** Flying J/diesel/mart/24hr, Shell, **food:** Burger King, Subway, **other:** Goodyear, **S...lodging:** Budget Inn. **I-182 begins/ends on US 395 N.**

13 N 4th Ave, Cty Ctr, **N...gas:** CFN/diesel, **lodging:** Airport Motel, Starlite Motel, **S...other:** HOSPITAL, RV park, museum

WASHINGTON

Interstate 182

12b N 20th Ave, **N...lodging:** DoubleTree Hotel

a US 395 S, Court St, **S...gas:** Arco/24hr, Conoco, Exxon, Shell, **food:** Arby's, Burger King, McDonald's, Pizza Hut, Subway, Taco Bell, Wendy's, **other:** Chief RV Ctr, Chevrolet, Food Pavilion/café, Ford, K-Mart, Toyota, U-Haul

9 WA 68, Trac, **N...gas:** Arco, Shell, **food:** Heidi Haus Rest.

7 Broadmoor Blvd, **N...lodging:** Sleep Inn, **other:** Broadmoor Outlet Mall/famous brands, **S...other:** Broadmoor RV Ctr, Sandy Heights RV Park

6.5mm Columbia River

5b a WA 240 E, Geo Washington Way, to Kennewick, no facilities

4 WA 240 W, **N...gas:** CFN/diesel, Conoco/diesel, 7-11, **food:** McDonald's, **other:** Fred Meyer

3.5mm Yakima River

3 Queensgate, **N...gas:** Arco/mart, Shell, **other:** Wal-Mart/auto, **S...gas:** Shell/diesel, **other:** RV Park(3mi)

0mm I-182 begins/ends on I-82, exit 102.

Interstate 405(Seattle)

Exit # Services

30 I-5, N to Canada, S to Seattle, I-405 begins/ends on I-5, exit 182.

26 WA 527, Bothell, Mill Creek, **E...food:** Canyon's Rest., Denny's, McDonald's, QFC Foods, **lodging:** Sierra Suites, **other:** MEDICAL CARE, Lake Pleasant RV Park, **W...gas:** Arco, Shell/diesel, 7-11, **food:** Arby's, Burger King, DQ, Denny's, Godfather's, Jack-in-the-Box, Mongolian Grill, Outback Steaks, Papa Murphy's, Quizno's, Starbucks, Taco Time, Tully's Coffee, **lodging:** Comfort Inn, Extended Stay America, **other:** Albertson's, Bartell Drug, QFC Foods, Rite Aid

24 NE 195th St, Beardslee Blvd, **E...gas:** Shell/Quizno's/diesel, **lodging:** Residence Inn, Wyndham Garden

23b WA 522 W, Bothell

a WA 522 E, to WA 202, Woodinville, Monroe, no facilities

22 NE 160th St, **E...gas:** Chevron, Shell/diesel/24hr

20 NE 124th St, **E...gas:** Arco/24hr, 76, Chevron/24hr, Shell/diesel/24hr, 7-11, **food:** Denny's, Evergreen China, Old Country Buffet, Pizza Hut, Shari's, **lodging:** Best Western, Clarion Inn, Motel 6, Silver Cloud Inn, **other:** HOSPITAL, CompUSA, Discount Tire, Infiniti, Larry's Mkt, OfficeMax, Rite Aid, Ross, mall, **W...gas:** Arco/24hr, 76, **food:** Burger King, Domino's, McDonald's, Milestone Grill, Olive Garden, Starbucks, Subway, Taco Time, Wendy's, **other:** Buick/Pontiac/GMC, Fred Meyer, GNC, QFC Food/24hr, Schuck's Parts

18 WA 908, Kirkland, Redmond, **E...gas:** Arco/24hr, Chevron/24hr, 76/Circle K, Shell, Texaco/diesel, **food:** Burger King, Domino's, Gandhi Cuisine, McDonald's, Outback Steaks, Pegasus Rest., Teriyaki, Tres Hermanos Mexican, **other:** Chevrolet, Honda, Mazda, Nissan, Safeway, Schuck's Parts, U-Haul, Walgreen, **W...food:** Subway, TGIFriday

17 NE 70th Pl, no facilities

14b a WA 520, Seattle, Redmond, no facilities

13b NE 8th St, **E...gas:** Arco/24hr, Chevron/diesel, Shell/diesel, **food:** Burger King, Denny's, Hunan Garden, Pumphouse Rest., **lodging:** Extended Stay America, **other:** HOSPITAL, Buick/Pontiac, Ford, Home Depot, Larry's Mkt, Saab, **W...food:** DQ, **lodging:** DoubleTree

a NE 4th St, **E...other:** Ford, **W...food:** Azteca Mexican, Jonah's Rest., **lodging:** Bellevue Inn, Best Western, Doubletree Hotel, Hilton, Hyatt

12 SE 8th St, no facilities

11 I-90, E to Spokane, W to Seattle

10 Cold Creek Pkwy, Factoria, **E on Factoria Blvd...gas:** 76/Circle K, 7-11, **food:** Applebee's, KFC, Keg Steaks, McDonald's, McHale's Rest., Old Country Buffet, Peking Wok, Presto Pizza, Red Robin, Starbucks, Subway, Taco Bell, Taco Time, Thai Rest., Tully's Coffee, Winchell's, **lodging:** Homestead Suites, **other:** Honda, Mervyn's, Nordstrom's, Old Navy, Oriental Foods, QFC Foods, Rite Aid, Safeway, Schuck's Parts, Target, mall

9 112th Ave SE, Newcastle, phone

7 NE 44th St, **E...food:** Denny's/24hr, McDonald's, **lodging:** Travelers Inn

6 NE 30th St, **E...gas:** Arco/24hr, **W...gas:** Chevron/24hr, Shell, 7-11

5 WA 900 E, Park Ave N, Sunset Blvd NE, no facilities

4 WA 169 S, Wa 900 W, Renton, **E...food:** Shari's, **lodging:** Silver Cloud Inn, **other:** Aqua Barn Ranch Camping, **W...gas:** Shell/diesel, **food:** Burger King, 7-11, Golden Palace Chinese, **lodging:** Renton Inn, **other:** IGA Foods

2 WA 167, Rainier Ave, to Auburn, **E...**HOSPITAL, **W...gas:** Arco/24hr, Chevron, 76, Shell, USA Minimart, **food:** Arby's, Burger King, China Garden, Denny's, IHOP, Jack-in-the-Box, KFC, Lucky Thai, Mazatlan Mexican, McDonald's, Pizza Hut, Quizno's, Taco Bell, Torero's Mexican, Tully's Coffee, Wendy's, Yankee Grill, **lodging:** Holiday Inn, **other:** Cadillac, Chevrolet, Chrysler/Plymouth/Jeep, Dodge/Toyota, Ford, Fred Meyer, Firestone, Honda/Mazda/Hyundai/Suzuki/Kia, Isuzu, K-Mart/Little Caesar's, Lincoln/Mercury, Mitsubishi, Pontiac/Buick/GMC, Radio Shack, Safeway/gas, Schuck's Parts, Schwab Tire, Subaru/Peugeot, Walgreen, Wal-Mart/auto

1 WA 181 S, Tukwila, **E...gas:** Chevron/diesel, 76/diesel, Shell/diesel, **food:** 7-11, Barnaby's Rest., Burger King, Chili's, Jack-in-the-Box, McDonald's, Quizno's, Sizzler, Starbucks, Taco Bell, Teriyaki Wok, Wendy's, Zoopa Café, **lodging:** Best Western, Courtyard, DoubleTree Suites, Embassy Suites, Hampton Inn, Homestead Village, Red Lion Hotel, Residence Inn, **other:** Acura, Barnes&Noble, Bon-Marche, Circuit City, Firestone, Goodyear, JC Penney, Lowe's Whse, Mervyn's, Nordstrom's, Office Depot, Sears/auto, Target, **W...gas:** 76, Shell, **lodging:** Homewood Suites, Studio+

0mm I-5, N to Seattle, S to Tacoma, WA 518 W. I-405 begins/ends on I-5, exit 154.

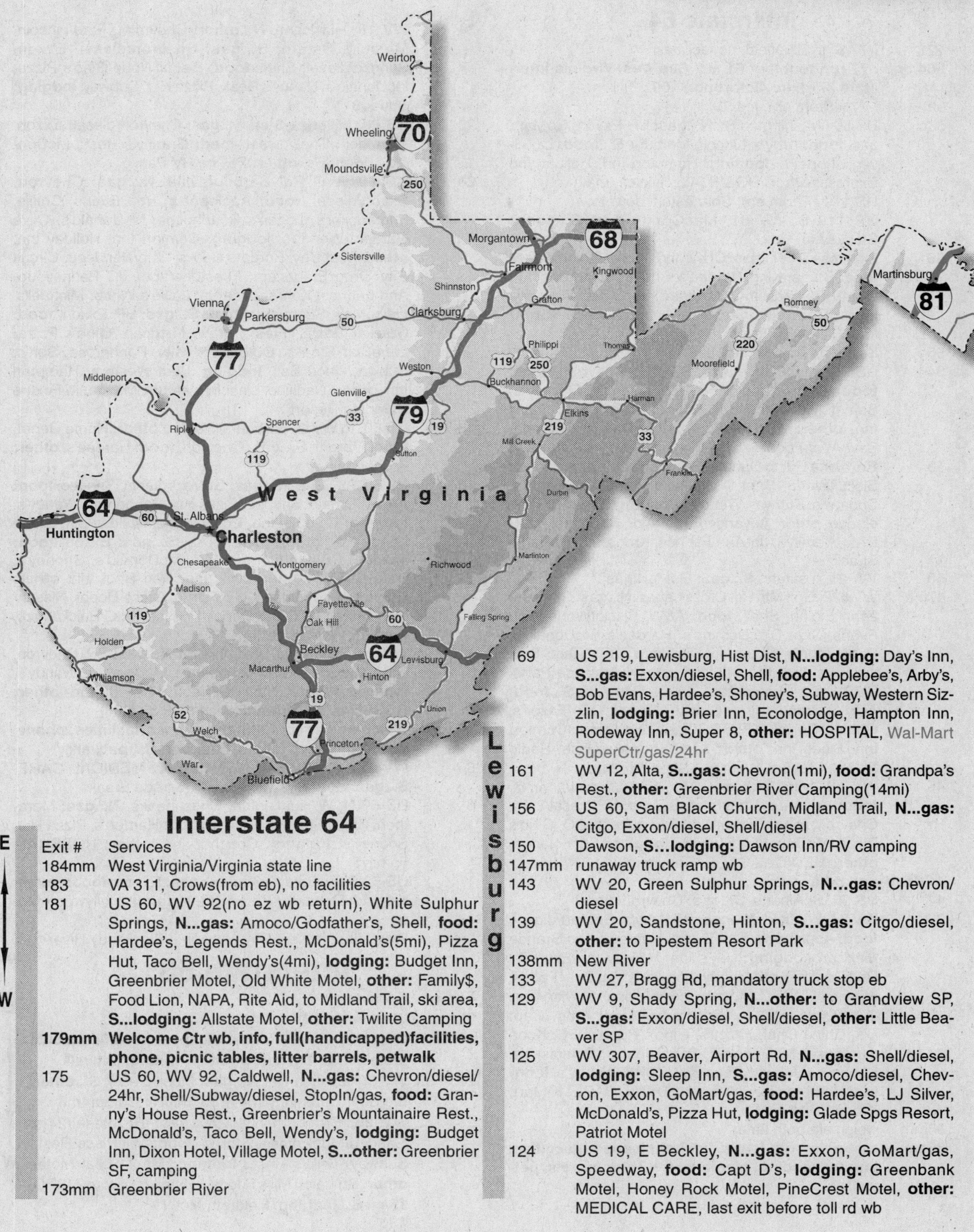

Interstate 64

E ↕ W

Exit #	Services
184mm	West Virginia/Virginia state line
183	VA 311, Crows(from eb), no facilities
181	US 60, WV 92(no ez wb return), White Sulphur Springs, **N...gas:** Amoco/Godfather's, Shell, **food:** Hardee's, Legends Rest., McDonald's(5mi), Pizza Hut, Taco Bell, Wendy's(4mi), **lodging:** Budget Inn, Greenbrier Motel, Old White Motel, **other:** Family$, Food Lion, NAPA, Rite Aid, to Midland Trail, ski area, **S...lodging:** Allstate Motel, **other:** Twilite Camping
179mm	**Welcome Ctr wb, info, full(handicapped)facilities, phone, picnic tables, litter barrels, petwalk**
175	US 60, WV 92, Caldwell, **N...gas:** Chevron/diesel/24hr, Shell/Subway/diesel, StopIn/gas, **food:** Granny's House Rest., Greenbrier's Mountainaire Rest., McDonald's, Taco Bell, Wendy's, **lodging:** Budget Inn, Dixon Hotel, Village Motel, **S...other:** Greenbrier SF, camping
173mm	Greenbrier River

Lewisburg

169	US 219, Lewisburg, Hist Dist, **N...lodging:** Day's Inn, **S...gas:** Exxon/diesel, Shell, **food:** Applebee's, Arby's, Bob Evans, Hardee's, Shoney's, Subway, Western Sizzlin, **lodging:** Brier Inn, Econolodge, Hampton Inn, Rodeway Inn, Super 8, **other:** HOSPITAL, Wal-Mart SuperCtr/gas/24hr
161	WV 12, Alta, **S...gas:** Chevron(1mi), **food:** Grandpa's Rest., **other:** Greenbrier River Camping(14mi)
156	US 60, Sam Black Church, Midland Trail, **N...gas:** Citgo, Exxon/diesel, Shell/diesel
150	Dawson, **S...lodging:** Dawson Inn/RV camping
147mm	runaway truck ramp wb
143	WV 20, Green Sulphur Springs, **N...gas:** Chevron/diesel
139	WV 20, Sandstone, Hinton, **S...gas:** Citgo/diesel, **other:** to Pipestem Resort Park
138mm	New River
133	WV 27, Bragg Rd, mandatory truck stop eb
129	WV 9, Shady Spring, **N...other:** to Grandview SP, **S...gas:** Exxon/diesel, Shell/diesel, **other:** Little Beaver SP
125	WV 307, Beaver, Airport Rd, **N...gas:** Shell/diesel, **lodging:** Sleep Inn, **S...gas:** Amoco/diesel, Chevron, Exxon, GoMart/gas, **food:** Hardee's, LJ Silver, McDonald's, Pizza Hut, **lodging:** Glade Spgs Resort, Patriot Motel
124	US 19, E Beckley, **N...gas:** Exxon, GoMart/gas, Speedway, **food:** Capt D's, **lodging:** Greenbank Motel, Honey Rock Motel, PineCrest Motel, **other:** MEDICAL CARE, last exit before toll rd wb

WEST VIRGINIA

Interstate 64

E ↕ W

Charleston

121 I-77 S, to Bluefield, no facilities

I-64 and I-77 run together 61 mi. See West Virginia Interstate 77, exits 42 through 100.

59 I-77 N(from eb), to I-79

58c US 60, Washington St, **N...gas:** BP, Exxon, GoMart/gas, **food:** Arby's, Lincoln/Mercury, **S...food:** LJ Silver, Shoney's, **lodging:** Hampton Inn, Holiday Inn Express, **other:** HOSPITAL, civic ctr, mall

b US 119 N(from eb), Charleston, downtown

a US 119 S, WV 61, MacCorkle Ave, **S...food:** Steak&Ale

56 Montrose Dr, **N...gas:** Chevron/Blimpie, Exxon/diesel, **food:** Burger King, Hardee's, Shoney's, **lodging:** Microtel, Ramada Inn, Wingate Inn, **other:** Advance Parts, Chevrolet, Chrysler/Plymouth/Jeep, Kia, K-Mart, Rite Aid, Toyota, VW

55 Kanawha Tpk, no facilities

54 US 60, MacCorkle Ave, **S...gas:** Chevron, Citgo, **food:** Bob Evans, KFC, LJ Silver, McDonald's, Schlotsky's, Taco Bell, Wendy's, **lodging:** Day's Inn, **other:** HOSPITAL, Aamco, Daewoo, Honda, SaveALot Foods

53 Roxalana Rd, to Dunbar, **S...gas:** GoMart/gas, **food:** BiscuitWorld, Capt D's, Gino's Pizza, McDonald's, Shoney's, Subway, Wendy's, **lodging:** Super 8, Travelodge, **other:** Advance Parts, Aldi, CarQuest, CVS Drug, Family$, Jo-Ann Fabrics, Kroger, NTB, Radio Shack

50 VW 25, Institute, **S...gas:** GoMart/gas

47b a WV 622, Goff Mtn Rd, Cross Lanes, **N...gas:** Chevron/24hr, Exxon, Shell, **food:** A&W, BiscuitWorld, Bob Evans, Capt D's, Domino's, Hardee's, McDonald's, Papa John's, Pizza Hut, Subway/TCBY, Taco Bell, Wendy's, **lodging:** Motel 6, **other:** Advance Parts, CVS Drug, Kroger/gas, NAPA, Rite Aid, **S...food:** Arby's, Burger King, Cracker Barrel, DQ, Fazoli's, Golden Corral, KFC, TGIFriday, **lodging:** Comfort Inn, Sleep Inn, **other:** $Tree, Lowe's Whse, Radio Shack, Staples, Wal-Mart SuperCtr/24hr

45 WV 25, Nitro, **N...gas:** Pilot/Arby's/diesel/24hr/@, **food:** Hardee's, Chevrolet, **S...gas:** BP/diesel/24hr, Chevron, **food:** BiscuitWorld, Checker's, DQ, Gino's Pizza, McDonald's, Subway, **lodging:** Econolodge, **other:** MEDICAL CARE, Chevrolet

44.3mm Kanawha River

44 US 35, St Albans, **S...gas:** Chevron/diesel

39 WV 34, Winfield, **N...gas:** BP/Arby's, GoMart/diesel, **food:** Applebee's, Bob Evans, Hardee's, Rio Grande Mexican, **lodging:** Day's Inn, Holiday Inn Express, Red Roof Inn, **other:** Advance Parts, Big Bear Foods, $General, USPO, **S...gas:** Exxon/diesel, GoMart/gas, TA/diesel/rest./24hr/@, **food:** Burger King, Capt D's, China Chef, Fazoli's, Gino's Pizza, KFC, Kobe Japanese, McDonald's, Papa John's, Schlotsky's, Shoney's, Subway, Taco Bell, TCBY, Wendy's, **lodging:** Hampton Inn, **other:** MEDICAL CARE, K-Mart, Kroger, Rite Aid

38mm weigh sta both lanes

35mm rest area both lanes, full(handicapped)facilities, phone, vending, picnic tables, litter barrels, petwalk

Huntington

34 WV 19, Hurricane, **N...other:** Chevrolet, Ford/Lincoln/Mercury, Saturn, **S...gas:** Chevron/diesel, Exxon, Sunoco/diesel, Shell, **food:** BiscuitWorld/Gino's Pizza, McDonald's, Nancy's Rest., Pizza Hut, Subway, **lodging:** Super 8

28 US 60, Milton, **1-3 mi S...gas:** Chevron/diesel, Exxon, Marathon, Shell/diesel, **food:** Granny's Rest., McDonald's, Wendy's, **other:** Foxfire RV Park

20 US 60, Mall Rd, Barboursville, **N...gas:** Chevron, Exxon/diesel, **food:** Applebee's, Bob Evans, Chili's, Fuddrucker's, Logan's Roadhouse, McDonald's, Olive Garden, Wendy's, **lodging:** Comfort Inn, Holiday Inn, **other:** Best Buy, Borders Books, Chrysler/Jeep, Circuit City, Drug Emporium, Firestone/auto, JC Penney, Jo-Ann Fabrics, Kohl's, Lazarus, Lowe's Whse, Michael's, OfficeMax, Sears/auto, mall, **S...gas:** BP, Exxon, **food:** Cracker Barrel, Fiesta Bravo Mexican, Gino's Pizza, LoneStar Steaks, Outback Steaks, Ponderosa, Sonic, Subway, Taco Bell, **lodging:** Best Western, Hampton Inn, **other:** Cadillac, Lincoln/Mercury, Mazda, to Foxfire Camping Resort

18 US 60, to WV 2, Barboursville, **N...other:** Home Depot, **other:** Target, **S...gas:** Chevron, **food:** Hardee's, **other:** Kroger/gas

15 US 60, 29th St E, **N...gas:** GoMart/diesel, Sunoco, **food:** Arby's, Omelet Shoppe, Pizza Hut, Ponderosa, Wendy's, **lodging:** Colonial Inn, Econolodge, Holiday Inn, Stone Lodge Inn, **other:** HOSPITAL, **S...gas:** Exxon, **food:** Fazoli's, Golden Corral, KFC, McDonald's, Shoney's, Taco Bell, **lodging:** Day's Inn, Red Roof Inn, **other:** Chrysler/Dodge/Jeep, CVS Drug, Office Depot, Nissan/Mitsubishi/VW, Office Depot, Pontiac/GMC/Buick/Isuzu, Subaru, Wal-Mart/auto

11 WV 10, Hal Greer Blvd, **1-3 mi N...gas:** BP, Chevron, Shell, **food:** Arby's, Marshall Café, McDonald's, Wendy's, **lodging:** Holiday Inn, Radisson, Ramada Ltd, **other:** HOSPITAL, **S...other:** Beech Fork SP(8mi)

10mm Welcome Ctr eb, full(handicapped)facilities, phone, vending, picnic tables, litter barrels, petwalk

8 WV 152 S, WV 527 N, **N...other:** MEDICAL CARE, **S...gas:** Speedway, **food:** DQ, Laredo Steaks

6 US 52 N, W Huntington, Chesapeake, **N...gas:** Marathon, Shell, Speedway/24hr, **food:** Hardee's, Pizza Hut, Shoney's, **lodging:** Coaches Inn, **other:** HOSPITAL, Family$

1 US 52 S, Kenova, **1-3 mi N...gas:** Exxon, **food:** Burger King, McDonald's, Pizza Hut, **lodging:** Hollywood Motel

0mm West Virginia/Kentucky state line, Big Sandy River

Interstate 68

E ↕ W

Exit # Services

32mm West Virginia/Maryland state line

31mm Welcome Ctr wb, full(handicapped)facilities, picnic tables, litter barrels, phone, vending, petwalk

29 WV 5, Hazelton Rd, **N...gas:** Mobil/diesel, **S...other:** Big Bear Camping(3mi), Pine Hill RV Camp(4mi)

23 WV 26, Bruceton Mills, **N...gas:** BP/diesel/24hr, Sandy's/Mobil/diesel/24hr/@, **food:** Mill Place Rest., Subway, Twila's Rest., **lodging:** Maple Leaf Motel, **other:** Bruceton Mills Foods, Hostetler's Store, USPO, **15 mi S...lodging:** Heldreth Motel

Interstate 68

18mm Laurel Run

17mm runaway truck ramp eb

16mm weigh sta wb

15 WV 73, WV 12, Coopers Rock, **N...other:** Chestnut Ridge SF, GS Camping(2mi)

12mm runaway truck ramp wb

10 WV 857, Fairchance Rd, Cheat Lake, **N...gas:** BP/diesel/24hr, Exxon/diesel, **food:** La Casita Mexican, Pizza'n Pasta, Ruby&Ketchy's Rest., Subway, **S...food:** Burger King, Dimitri's Steaks, **lodging:** Lakeview Resort, Stone Crab Inn

9mm Cheat Lake

7 WV 857, Pierpont Rd, **N...gas:** BP/Subway, Exxon/diesel, **Food:** Bob Evans, Outback Steaks, Ruby Tuesday, Taco Bell, Wendy's, **lodging:** Holiday Inn Express, Super 8, **other:** HOSPITAL, BooksAMillion, Lowe's Whse, Michael's, Shop'n Save Food, to WVU Stadium, **S...food:** Tiberio's Rest.

4 WV 7, to Sabraton, **N...gas:** BP, Exxon/Blimpie/24hr, **food:** Burger King, Hardee's, Hero's Hut, KFC, LJ Silver, McDonald's, Pizza Hut, Ponderosa, Subway, Wendy's, **other:** Chrysler/Dodge, CVS Drug, $General, Food Lion, Ford, Kroger/diesel, NAPA, USPO

3mm Decker's Creek

1 US 119, Morgantown, **N...gas:** Exxon/diesel, **food:** Subway, **lodging:** Comfort Inn, Morgantown Motel(2mi), Ramada Inn/rest., **S...gas:** Chevron/diesel, **other:** to Tygart L SP

0mm I-79, N to Pittsburgh, S to Clarksburg. I-68 begins/ends on I-79, exit 148.

Interstate 70

Exit # Services

14mm West Virginia/Pennsylvania state line

13.5mm Welcome Ctr wb, full(handicapped)facilities, phone, vending, picnic tables, litter barrels, petwalk

11 WV 41, Dallas Pike, **N...gas:** TA/diesel/rest./@, **lodging:** Day's Inn, **S...gas:** BP/DQ/diesel, Citgo/A&W/Taco Bell/diesel, Exxon, **lodging:** Holiday Inn Express, **other:** RV camping

5 US 40, WV 88 S, Tridelphia, **N...gas:** Marathon, **food:** Christopher's Café, Hoss' Rest., Pizza Hut, Subway, Wendy's, **lodging:** Super 8, **other:** Riesbeck's Foods, **S...gas:** Amoco, Exxon/diesel, **food:** DQ, Ernie's Rest.(2mi), McDonald's, **other:** Advance Parts, NAPA, Rite Aid, museum

5a I-470 W, to Columbus, no facilities

4 WV 88 N(from eb), Elm Grove, **S...gas:** Amoco, Exxon/diesel, same as 5

3.5mm weigh sta wb

2b Washington Ave, **N...gas:** Exxon, **food:** Greco's Rest., **S...food:** Figaretti's Italian, **other:** HOSPITAL

a WV 88 N, to Oglebay Park, **N...gas:** Exxon, **food:** Big Boy, Bob Evans, DQ, Hardee's, LJ Silver, Papa John's, Rax, Subway, Texas Roadhouse, **lodging:** Hampton Inn, **other:** Advance Parts, CVS Drug, Kroger/gas, NTB, Radio Shack

1b US 250 S, WV 2 S, S Wheeling, no facilities

a US 40 E, WV 2 N, Main St, downtown, **S...lodging:** Best Western

1mm tunnel

0 US 40 W, Zane St, Wheeling Island, **N...gas:** Exxon/diesel, **food:** Conv Mart, DQ , FoodCourt, KFC

0mm West Virginia/Ohio state line, Ohio River

Interstate 77

Exit # Services

186mm West Virginia/Ohio state line, Ohio River

185 WV 14, WV 31, Williamstown, **W...gas:** Exxon, Shell, **food:** Dutch Pantry, Subway, **lodging:** Day's Inn, **other:** Glass Factory Tours

179 WV 2 N, WV 68 S, to Waverly, **E...gas:** Exxon, **other:** airport, **W...gas:** BP, **food:** Pepper's Mexican, **lodging:** Expressway Motel, **other:** HOSPITAL

176 US 50, 7th St, Parkersburg, **E...lodging:** Best Western, **other:** to North Bend SP, **W...gas:** Shell/24hr, Speedway/diesel, **food:** Bob Evans, Burger King, Little Caesar's, LJ Silver, McDonald's, Mountaineer Rest./24hr, Omelet Shoppe, Shoney's, Wendy's, **lodging:** Econolodge, Holiday Inn, Knight's Inn, Motel 6, Red Roof Inn, **other:** Advance Parts, Buick/Mercedes/Isuzu, Kroger/diesel, Toyota, Family$, to Blennerhassett Hist Park

174 WV 47, Staunton Ave, **1 mi E...gas:** BP, Exxon/diesel, **food:** Subway, **W...gas:** Citgo/diesel

173mm Little Kanawha River

173 WV 95, Camden Ave, **E...gas:** Marathon/diesel, **1-4 mi W...gas:** BP, **food:** Hardee's, **lodging:** Blennerhassett Hotel, **other:** HOSPITAL

170 WV 14, Mineral Wells, **E...gas:** BP/diesel/repair/24hr, Chevron, Citgo/diesel, Liberty Trkstp/diesel/24hr, **food:** BBQ, McDonald's, Subway, Taco Bell, Wendy's, **lodging:** Comfort Suites, Hampton Inn, **other:** USPO, **W...food:** Cracker Barrel, Napoli's Pizza, **lodging:** AmeriHost, Microtel

169mm weigh sta both lanes, phone

166mm rest area both lanes, full(handicapped)facilities, phone, picnic tables, litter barrels, vending, petwalk

161 WV 21, Rockport, **W...gas:** Marathon

154 WV 1, Medina Rd, no facilities

WEST VIRGINIA

Interstate 77

N ↕ S

Charleston

146 WV 2 S, Silverton, Ravenswood, **W...gas:** BP/diesel, Exxon/24hr, Marathon/diesel/24hr, **food:** DQ, **lodging:** Scottish Inn

138 US 33, Ripley, **E...gas:** BP/diesel/24hr, Exxon/24hr, Marathon/diesel, **food:** KFC, LJ Silver, McDonald's, Pizza Hut, Taco Bell, Wendy's, **lodging:** Best Western/rest., Super 8, **other:** Kroger, NAPA, Rite Aid, Sav-A-Lot, Wal-Mart, **W...gas:** Exxon/diesel/24hr, Ponderosa, Shoney's, **food:** Subway, **lodging:** Holiday Inn Express, **other:** HOSPITAL

132 WV 21, Fairplain, **E...gas:** BP/Burger King/diesel, Shell/diesel, **other:** Ford, **W...lodging:** 77 Motel

124 WV 34, Kenna, **E...gas:** Exxon, **food:** Your Family Rest.

119 WV 21, Goldtown, no facilities

116 WV 21, Haines Branch Rd, Sissonville, **4 mi E...other:** Rippling Waters Campground

114 WV 622, Pocatalico Rd, **E...gas:** MtnMart/gas, **other:** Fascheck Foods

111 WV 29, Tuppers Creek Rd, **W...gas:** BP/Subway/diesel, **food:** Tudor's Biscuit World

106 WV 27, Edens Fork Rd, **W...gas:** Chevron/diesel/country store, **lodging:** Sunset Motel(3mi)

104 I-79 N, to Clarksburg

102 US 119 N, Westmoreland Rd, **E...gas:** Chevron/7-11/24hr, GoMart/24hr, **food:** Hardee's/24hr, **lodging:** Parsley Motel, **other:** Foodland, Pennzoil/24hr,

101 I-64, E to Beckley, W to Huntington

100 Broad St, Capitol St, **W...food:** Charleston House Rest., **lodging:** Fairfield Inn, Holiday Inn, Marriott, Super 8, **other:** HOSPITAL, CVS Drug, Family$, GMC, Honda Motorcycles, JC Penney, Kroger

99 WV 114, Capitol St, **E...**airport, **W...gas:** Exxon, Domino's, **food:** KFC/Taco Bell, McDonald's, Wendy's, **other:** to museum, st capitol

98 35th St Bridge(from sb), **W...gas:** Sunoco, **food:** KFC/Taco Bell, McDonald's, Steak Escape, Shoney's, Subway, Wendy's, **other:** HOSPITAL, to U of Charleston

97 US 60 W(from nb), Kanawha Blvd, no facilities

96 US 60 E, Midland Trail, Belle, **W...lodging:** Budget Host

96mm W Va Turnpike begins/ends

95.5mm Kanawha River

95 WV 61, to MacCorkle Ave, **E...gas:** BP/diesel, GoMart/diesel/24hr, **food:** Bob Evans, IHOP, LoneStar Steaks, McDonald's, Subway, Wendy's, **lodging:** Comfort Suites, Country Inn Suites, Day's Inn, Knight's Inn, Motel 6, **other:** Red Roof, Advance Parts, K-Mart, **W...gas:** Ashland/Blimpie/24hr, Chevron/7-11, Exxon/diesel/24hr, Marathon, GoMart/24hr, **food:** Applebee's, Azteca Mexican, Burger King, Capt D's, ChiChi's, China Buffet, Hooters, Pizza Hut/Taco Bell, Ponderosa, Shoney's, Southern Kitchen/24hr, Shoney's, **other:** MEDICAL CARE, Foodland, Kroger, Lowe's Whse, NAPA, Subaru, Suzuki, mall

Beckley

89 WV 61, WV 94, to Marmet, **E...gas:** Exxon/Subway/diesel/24hr, Shell, Sunoco, **food:** Biscuit World, Gino's Pizza, Hardee's, KFC, LJ Silver, Wendy's, **other:** Family$, Kroger/deli, Rite Aid, **W...other:** Ford(1mi)

85 US 60, WV 61, East Bank, **E...gas:** GoMart/diesel/24hr, **food:** Gino's Pizza, McDonald's, Shoney's, **other:** Chevrolet, Gilmer Foods, Kroger, tire repair

82.5mm toll booth

79 Cabin Creek Rd, Sharon, no facilities

74 WV 83, Paint Creek Rd, no facilities

72mm Morton Service Area nb, gas: Exxon/diesel, food: Burger King, Starbucks, TCBY, atm

69mm rest area sb, full(handicapped)facilities, phone, picnic tables, litter barrels

66 WV 15, to Mahan, **1/2 mi W...gas:** Sunoco/diesel/24hr

60 WV 612, to Mossy, Oak Hill, **1/2 mi E...gas:** Exxon/diesel/repair/24hr, **other:** RV camping

56.5mm toll plaza, phone

54 rd 2, rd 23, Pax, **E...gas:** BP/rest.

48 US 19, N Beckley, **1 mi E...gas:** Amoco/Subway/diesel, **food:** Garfield's Rest., **lodging:** Ramada Inn, **other:** JC Penney, Sears/auto, **4 mi E on US 19/WV 16 S...gas:** Exxon, **food:** Bob Evans, Burger King, Checker's, Fazoli's, Hardee's, LoneStar Steaks, LJ Silver, McDonald's, Rio Grande Mexican, Ryan's, Wendy's, **other:** Acura, AutoZone, Buick, Chevrolet/Cadillac, Chrysler/Plymouth, CVS Drug, Dodge, Honda, Hyundai, Staples, Subaru/Kia, U-Haul, Wal-Mart SuperCtr/24hr

45mm Tamarack Service Area both lanes, W...gas: Exxon/diesel, food: BiscuitWorld, Sbarro's, Starbucks, TCBY, other: gifts

44 WV 3, Beckley, **E...gas:** Chevron/diesel, Exxon, Marathon, Shell/Hardee's/24hr, **food:** Applebee's, BBQ, Burger King, DQ, Hibachi Japanese, McDonald's, Outback Steaks, Pancake House, Pizza Hut, **lodging:** Best Western, Comfort Inn, Courtyard, Fairfield Inn, Holiday Inn, Howard Johnson, Super 8, **other:** MEDICAL CARE, CVS Drug, Kroger/gas, **W...gas:** BP/Subway, GoMart/diesel, **food:** Bob Evans, Cracker Barrel, Texas Steaks, Wendy's, **lodging:** Country Inn Suites, Day's Inn, Hampton Inn, Microtel, Park Inn

42 WV 16, WV 97, to Mabscott, **2 mi E...food:** Tudor's Biscuits, **lodging:** Budget Inn, **other:** HOSPITAL, **W...gas:** Amoco/diesel, **food:** Godfather's, Subway

40 I-64 E, to Lewisburg, no facilities

30mm toll booth, phone

28 WV 48, to Ghent, **E...gas:** BP, Exxon/diesel, Marathon/diesel, **lodging:** Glade Springs Resort(1mi), Appalachian Resort Inn(12mi), **other:** to ski area, **W...lodging:** Econolodge

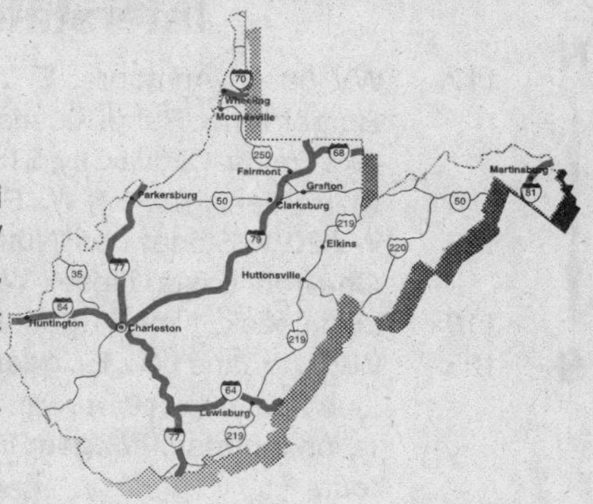

Interstate 77

26.5mm Flat Top Mtn, elevation 3252
20 US 19, to Camp Creek, **E...gas:** Exxon/diesel, Tolliver's T-stop, **W...other:** Camp Creek SP
18.5mm scenic overlook/parking area/weigh sta sb, no facilities
18mm Bluestone River
17mm Bluestone Service Area/weigh sta nb, full(handicapped)facilities, scenic view, picnic area, Exxon/diesel, Starbucks, TCBY, atm/fax
14 WV 20, Athens Rd, **E...gas:** Citgo, **other:** Green Acres RV Park, Pipestem Resort SP
9mm WV Turnpike begins/ends
9 US 460, Princeton, **E...Welcome Ctr,** I-77 Trkstp/diesel/@, Wal-Mart SuperCtr/24hr, **W...gas:** Amoco/diesel, Chevron/diesel/24hr, Exxon/diesel/24hr, Marathon/diesel, **food:** Applebee's, Bob Evans, Burger King, Capt D's, Cracker Barrel, DQ, Hardee's, McDonald's, Omelet Shoppe, RomaX Italian, Shoney's, Subway, Taco Bell, Texas Steaks, Wendy's, **lodging:** Budget Inn, Comfort Inn, Day's Inn, Hampton Inn, Johnston's Inn/rest., Ramada Ltd, Sleep Inn, Super 8, **other:** HOSPITAL, Town&Country Motel, Turnpike Motel, K-Mart
7 WV 27, Ingleside Rd(from nb, no re-entry), no facilities
5 WV 112(from sb, no re-entry), to Ingleside, no facilities
3mm East River
1 US 52 N, to Bluefield, **4 mi W...food:** LJ Silver, Wendy's, **lodging:** Brier Motel, Econolodge, Highlander Motel, Holiday Inn/rest., Knight's Inn, Ramada Inn, **other:** HOSPITAL
.5mm East River Mtn
0mm West Virginia/Virginia state line

Princeton

Interstate 79

Exit # Services
160mm West Virginia/Pennsylvania state line
159 Welcome Ctr sb, full(handicapped)facilities, info, picnic tables, litter barrels, phone, vending, petwalk
155 US 19, WV 7, **E...gas:** Sheetz, **3 mi E...gas:** Shell, **food:** Burger King, Eat'n Park, LJ Silver, McDonald's, Shoney's, Wendy's, **lodging:** Day's Inn, Econolodge, Euro Suites, Friends Inn, Hampton Inn, Holiday Inn, **other:** HOSPITAL, to WVU, **W...gas:** Exxon/diesel
152 US 19, to Morgantown, **E...gas:** BP/diesel, Exxon, Getty, **food:** Arby's, McDonald's, Pizza Hut, Subway, Taco Bell, Western Sizzlin, **lodging:** Clarion, Econolodge, Advance Parts, **W...food:** Bob Evans, Burger King, Garfield's Rest., **other:** JC Penney, K-Mart, Lowe's Whse, Sears/auto, mall

Morgantown

150mm Monongahela River
148 I-68 E, to Cumberland, MD, **1 mi E...gas:** Exxon/diesel/24hr, **lodging:** Comfort Inn, Morgantown Motel, Ramada Inn/rest.
146 WV 77, to Goshen Rd, no facilities
141mm weigh sta both lanes
139 WV 33, E Fairmont, **E...gas:** Chevron, **W...gas:** Exxon/24hr, K&T/BP/diesel/@, **other:** RV camping
137 WV 310, to Fairmont, **E...gas:** BP, Exxon/diesel/24hr, **food:** Simmering Pot Rest., Subway, **lodging:** Holiday Inn, **other:** to Valley Falls SP, **W...gas:** Chevron, **food:** KFC, McDonald's, Wendy's, **other:** HOSPITAL
135 WV 64, Pleasant Valley Rd, no facilities
133 Kingmont Rd, **E...gas:** BP/Subway/diesel, Exxon/diesel, **food:** Cracker Barrel, **lodging:** Super 8, **W...gas:** Chevron/diesel/24hr, King/diesel, **food:** DJ's Diner, **lodging:** Comfort Inn, Country Club Motel, Day's Inn, Red Roof Inn
132 US 250, S Fairmont, **E...food:** Arby's, Bob Evans, Dragon Buffet, Hardee's, McDonald's, Subway, Taco Bell, TJ's Rest., **lodging:** Day's Inn, Red Roof Inn, **other:** Advance Parts, Chrysler/Dodge, $General, FoodLand, Harley-Davidson, JC Penney, Jo-Ann Fabrics, Sam's Club, Shop'n Save, Wal-Mart/drugs, mall, to Tygart Lake SP, **W...gas:** Exxon/diesel/24hr, GoMart/diesel/24hr, Sunoco, **lodging:** Colonial Inn(4mi), Country Club Motel(4mi), **other:** HOSPITAL, Buick/Pontiac/GMC, Ford/Lincoln/Mercury, Toyota
125 WV 131, Saltwell Rd, to Shinnston, **E...food:** Oliverio's Rest., **W...gas:** Exxon/Subway/diesel/24hr
124 rd 279, Jerry Dove Dr, no facilities
123mm rest area both lanes, full(handicapped)facilities, info, phone, picnic tables, litter barrels, vending, petwalk
121 WV 24, Meadowbrook Rd, **E...gas:** GoMart/Blimpie/24hr, Sheetz, **food:** Bob Evans, **lodging:** Hampton Inn, **other:** MEDICAL CARE, **W...gas:** Exxon/diesel, **food:** Arby's, Burger King, Garfield's Rest., **other:** Jo-Ann Fabrics, **food:** Outback Steaks, Ponderosa, **lodging:** Super 8, Honda, **other:** JC Penney, OfficeMax, Phar-Mor, Target, mall
119 US 50, to Clarksburg, **E...gas:** Chevron/diesel/24hr, Exxon/diesel, GoMart/gas, Speedway, **food:** China Buffet, Damon's, Denny's, Eat'n Park, Hardee's, KFC, Little Caesar's, LJ Silver, McDonald's, Panera Bread, Taco Bell, Texas Roadhouse, Uno Pizzaria, USA Steaks, Wendy's, **lodging:** Comfort Inn, Day's Inn, Holiday Inn, Knight's Inn, Ramada Ltd, Sleep Inn, **other:** HOSPITAL, Chevrolet, K-Mart, Kroger/gas/24hr, Lowe's Whse, Nissan, Radio Shack

Clarksburg

WEST VIRGINIA

Interstate 79

N

S

Charleston

117 WV 58, to Anmoore, **E...food:** Applebee's, Arby's, Burger King, Ruby Tuesday, Ryan's, Subway, **other:** Aldi Foods, Circuit City, $Tree, Goody's, Staples, Wal-Mart SuperCtr/24hr, **W...**BP/diesel

115 WV 20, to Stonewood, Nutter Fort, **E...gas:** BP/diesel, Chevron, Exxon/diesel, **W...**HOSPITAL

110 Lost Creek, **1 mi E...gas:** BP/diesel

105 WV 7, to Jane Lew, **E...gas:** Chevron/diesel/rest., Jane Lew Trkstp/diesel/rest./@, **lodging:** Wilderness Plantation Inn/rest., **W...gas:** Exxon, **other:** glass factory tours

99 US 33, US 119, to Weston, **E...gas:** BP, Exxon/diesel, Sheetz/24hr, **food:** Gino's Pizza, McDonald's, Subway, Western Sizzlin, **lodging:** Bicentennial Motel, Budget Host, Comfort Inn/rest., Super 8, **other:** Advance Parts, Family$, GNC, Kroger, Radio Shack, Wal-Mart, **W...gas:** BP, Rich, **food:** Hardee's, KFC, LJ Silver, Pizza Hut, Wendy's, **other:** HOSPITAL, $General, Ford, NAPA, SavALot, Twin Lakes Camper Sales, to Canaan Valley Resort, Blackwater Falls

96 WV 30, to S Weston, **E...other:** to S Jackson Lake SP, Broken Wheel Camping, **W...lodging:** Weston Motel

91 US 19, to Roanoke, **E...other:** Whisper Mtn Camping, to S Jackson Lake SP

85mm rest area both lanes, full(handicapped)facilities, info, picnic tables, litter barrels, phone, vending, petwalk, RV dump

79.5mm Little Kanawha River

79 WV 5, Burnsville, **E...gas:** Exxon/24hr, **lodging:** 79 Motel/rest., **other:** NAPA, **W...gas:** Shell, Cedar Cr SP

78mm Saltlick Creek

67 WV 4, to Flatwoods, **E...gas:** Ashland/diesel, Chevron/diesel, Exxon/diesel, Shell/diesel, **food:** DQ, KFC/Taco Bell, Larry's Steaks, McDonald's, Subway, **lodging:** Day's Inn, Sutton Lake Motel, **other:** Ace Hardware, Chevrolet/Buick, to Sutton Lake RA, camping, **W...gas:** Ashland/diesel, Citgo, **food:** Shoney's, Wendy's, **other:** Flatwood Stores/famous brands

62 WV 4, to Sutton, Gassaway, **E...food:** Simplicity Café, **lodging:** Elk Motel, **W...gas:** GoMart, **food:** LJ Silver, Pizza Hut, **other:** HOSPITAL, CVS Drug, Ford/Mercury, Jeep/Dodge, Kroger/deli, Super$

57 US 19 S, to Beckley, no facilities

52mm Elk River

51 WV 4, to Frametown, **E...**antiques

49mm rest area both lanes, full(handicapped)facilities, picnic tables, phone, litter barrels, vending, petwalk, RV dump

46 WV 11, Servia Rd, no facilities

40 WV 16, to Big Otter, **E...gas:** Shell/diesel, **W...gas:** Exxon/diesel

34 WV 36, to Wallback, **E...food:** Gino's Diner, BiscuitWorld

25 WV 29, to Amma, **E...gas:** Exxon/diesel

19 US 119, VW 53, to Clendenin, **E...gas:** BP/diesel/24hr, **food:** BiscuitWorld, Gino's Diner, **other:** Shafer's Superstop

9 WV 43, to Elkview, **W...gas:** Exxon/Arby's/diesel, Speedway/diesel/24hr, **food:** Bob Evans, McDonald's, Pizza Hut, Ponderosa, Subway, **lodging:** Holiday Inn Express, **other:** Advance Parts, CVS Drug, GNC, K-Mart, Kroger, Radio Shack

5 WV 114, to Big Chimney, **1 mi E...gas:** Exxon, **food:** Hardee's/24hr, **other:** Rite Aid, Smith's Foods

1 US 119, Mink Shoals, **E...food:** Harding's Family Rest., **lodging:** Sleep Inn

0 I-77, S to Charleston, N to Parkersburg. I-79 begins/ends on I-77, exit 104.

Interstate 81

N

S

Martinsburg

Exit # Services

26mm West Virginia/Maryland state line, Potomac River

25mm Welcome Ctr sb, full(handicapped)facilities, info, phone, picnic tables, litter barrels, petwalk

23 US 11, Marlowe, Falling Waters, **1 mi E...other:** Falling Waters Camping, **W...gas:** BP/diesel, **other:** Outdoor Express RV Ctr

20 WV 901, Spring Mills Rd, **E...gas:** TA/diesel/rest./24hr/@, **lodging:** Econolodge, **other:** I-81 Flea Mkt, **W...gas:** Shell/diesel, **food:** Domino's, **lodging:** Holiday Inn Express

16 WV 9, N Queen St, Berkeley Springs, **E...gas:** Citgo, Exxon/Subway/diesel, Sheetz, Denny's, Golden China, Hoss's, KFC, LJ Silver, McDonald's, Ollie's Rest., Pasta House, Waffle House, **lodging:** Bavarian Inn, Comfort Inn, Knight's Inn, Stone Crab Inn, Super 8, Travelodge, **W...gas:** Citgo, Shell/diesel

14 rd 13, Dry Run Rd, **E...**HOSPITAL

13 WV 15, Kings St, Martinsburg, **E...gas:** BP/diesel, Sheetz/24hr, **food:** Applebee's, Asia Garden, Burger King, Cracker Barrel, El Ranchero Mexican, Fazoli's, Outback Steaks, Pizza Hut, Shoney's, Wendy's, **lodging:** Day's Inn, Holiday Inn/rest., **other:** HOSPITAL, OfficeMax, Tanger/famous brands, Wal-Mart SuperCtr/24hr, same as 12

12 WV 45, Winchester Ave, **E...gas:** Citgo/diesel, Martins/gas, Sheetz/24hr, Shell/diesel, **food:** Arby's, Bob Evans, McDonald's, Papa John's, Ryan's, Ruby Tuesday, Taco Bell, Wendy's, **lodging:** Economy Inn, Hampton Inn, Heritage Motel, Kristalite Inn, Relax Inn, Scottish Inn, **other:** AutoZone, JC Penney, Lowe's Whse, Sears/auto, mall, Nahkeeta RV Camping(3mi), same as 13

8 WV 32, Tablers Station Rd, **2 mi E...lodging:** Pikeside Motel

5 WV 51, Inwood, to Charles Town, **E...gas:** Exxon, Sheetz, Shell/diesel, **food:** Luwegee's Rest., McDonald's, Pizza Hut, Pizza Oven, Subway, Viva Mexican, Waffle House, **other:** Food Lion, **W...other:** Lazy-A Camping(9mi)

2mm Welcome Ctr nb, full(handicapped)facilities, info, phone, vending, picnic tables, litter barrels, petwalk

0mm West Virginia/Virginia state line

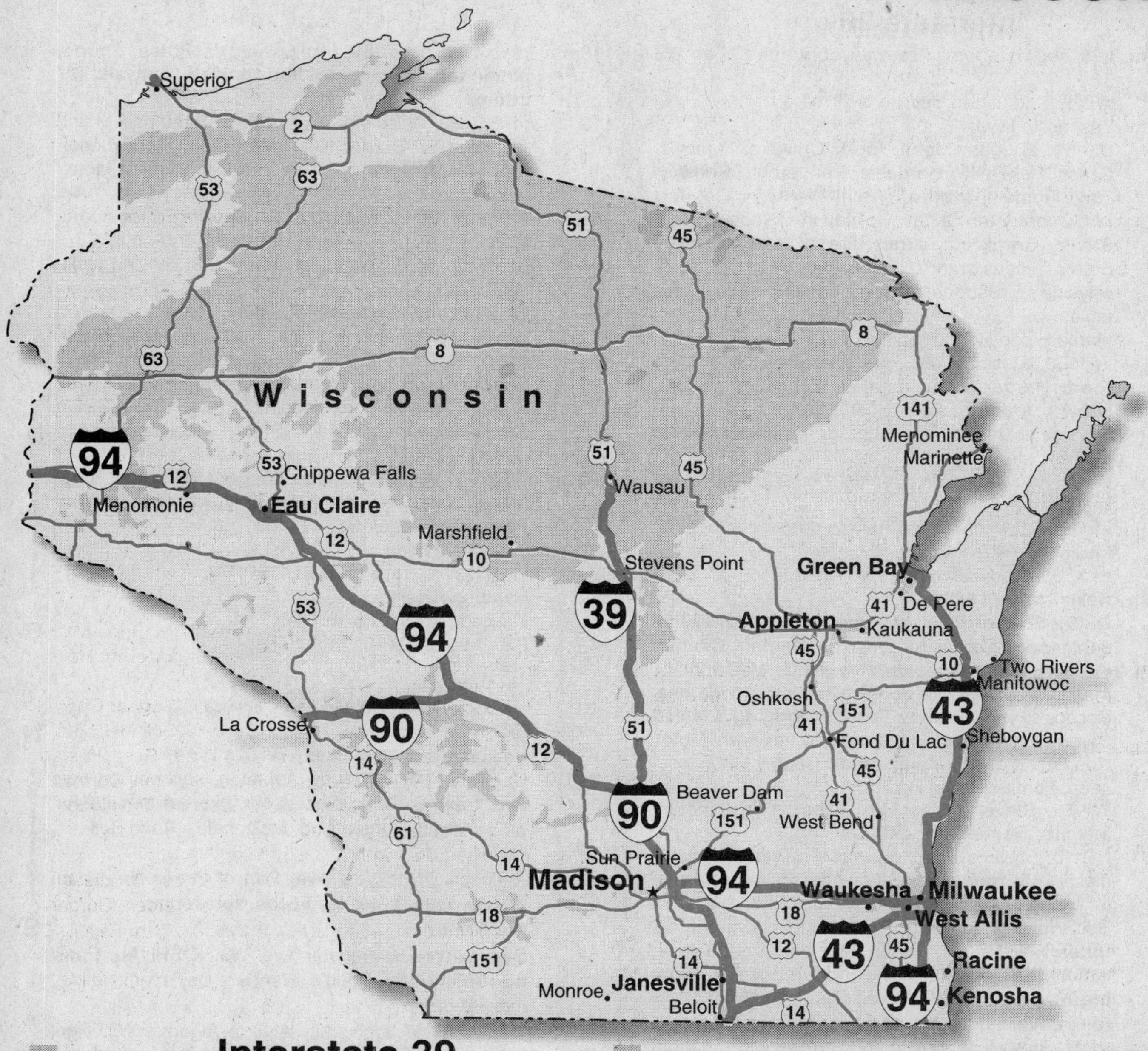

Interstate 39

N ↕ S

Wausau

Exit #	Services
211	US 51, rd K, Merrill, **E...**antiques
210mm	Prairie River
208	WI 64, WI 70, Merrill, **W...gas:** BP/diesel/24hr, KwikTrip/diesel, Mobil/diesel, **food:** Burger King, Diamond Dave's Tacos, Hardee's, McDonald's, Pine Ridge Rest., Taco Bell, Three's Company Dining, **lodging:** Best Western, Super 8, **other:** Piggly Wiggly, Radio Shack, Wal-Mart, to Council Grounds SP
206mm	Wisconsin River
205	US 51, rd Q, Merrill, **E...gas:** Citgo/diesel/rest./24hr, **other:** antiques
197	rd WW, to Brokaw, **W...gas:** Citgo/diesel
194	US 51, rd U, rd K, Wausau, **E...gas:** F&F/gas, KwikTrip/gas, Mobil, **food:** A&W, McDonald's, Taco Bell, **other:** Chrysler/Jeep, Toyota/Isuzu/Mercedes
193	Bridge St, **W...**HOSPITAL
192	WI 29 W, WI 52 E, Wausau, to Chippewa Falls, **E...food:** Annie's Rest., King Buffet, Little Caesar's, **lodging:** Baymont Inn, Exel Inn, Ramada, Subway, Country Inn Suites, **other:** County Mkt Foods, same as 191
191	Sherman St, **E...gas:** BP, **food:** Applebee's, Cousins Subs, Hudson's Grill, McDonald's, **lodging:** Courtyard, Hampton Inn, Super 8, **other:** HOSPITAL, **W...food:** Burger King, Hardee's, Schlotsky's, 2510 Deli, **other:** Audi/Nissan/VW, Home Depot
190mm	Rib River
190	rd NN, **E...food:** Krumbee's Bakery, **lodging:** Park Inn, **W...gas:** Citgo/diesel/24hr, Mobil/diesel, **food:** Hoffman House Rest., Shakey's Pizza, Subway, **lodging:** Best Western, **other:** MEDICAL CARE, Rib Mtn Ski Area, st patrol
188	rd N, **E...gas:** BP/24hr, Phillips 66, **food:** Country Kitchen/24hr, Fazoli's, HongKong Buffet, McDonald's, Wendy's, **lodging:** Country Inn Suites(1mi), Day's Inn, **other:** Aldi, Best Buy, Chevrolet, King's RV Ctr, Mazda, OfficeMax, Sam's Club, Saturn, Wal-Mart

WISCONSIN

Interstate 39

N ↕ S

187mm **I-39 begins/ends. Freeway continues N as US 51.**
187 WI 29 E, to Green Bay, no facilities
186mm Wisconsin River
185 US 51, **E...gas:** Mobil, **food:** Culver's, Denny's, Green Mill Rest., Hardee's, Ponderosa, Subway, Tony Roma's, **lodging:** Best Western, Comfort Inn, Country Inn Suites, Holiday Inn, Rodeway Inn, Stoney Creek Inn, **other:** Cedar Creek Factory Stores/famous brands, mall
183mm wayside sb, restroom facilities, drinking water, picnic tables
181 Maple Ridge Rd, no facilities
179 WI 153, Mosinee, **W...gas:** BP, Shell/diesel/24hr, **food:** Hardee's, McDonald's, StageStop Rest., Subway, **lodging:** AmeriHost, **other:** Ford
178mm wayside nb, restroom facilities, drinking water, picnic tables
175 WI 34, Knowlton, to WI Rapids, **1 mi W...other:** Mullins Cheese Factory
171 rd DB, Knowlton, **W...other:** to gas, food, lodging, Mullins Cheese Factory
165 rd X, **E...**food, camping
164mm weigh sta both lanes
161 US 51, Stevens Point, **W...gas:** BP, Citgo, KwikTrip/24hr, **food:** Burger King, China Garden, Country Kitchen, Domino's, Hardee's, KFC, McDonald's, Mesquite Grill, Papa John's, Perkins, Ponderosa, Rococo's Pizza, Subway, Taco Bell, **lodging:** Comfort Suites, Country Inn Suites, Holiday Inn, Point Motel, Roadstar Motel, Super 8, **other:** County Mkt Foods, Jeep, Pontiac/Buick, Radio Shack
159 WI 66, Stevens Point, **W...other:** Ford/Lincoln/Mercury, Honda, Plymouth
158 US 10, Stevens Point, **E...gas:** F&F/diesel, Mobil/diesel/24hr, **food:** Applebee's, Arby's, Culver's, Fazoli's, Hong Kong Buffet, McDonald's, Shoney's, Taco Bell, Wendy's, **lodging:** Fairfield Inn, Hawthorn Inn, **other:** Aldi, Mazda, Nissan, Staples, Target, Tires+, Wal-Mart, **W...gas:** BP/24hr, **food:** Hilltop Grill, **lodging:** Baymont Inn, Best Western, Point Motel
156 rd HH, Whiting, no facilities
153 rd B, Plover, **W...gas:** BP/Burger King, Mobil/diesel, **food:** Cousins Subs, El Tapatio Mexican, McDonald's, Subway, **lodging:** AmericInn, **other:** IGA Foods, ShopKO
151 WI 54, to Waupaca, **E...gas:** Shell/Arby's/diesel/24hr, **food:** 4Star Family Rest., Shooter's Rest., **lodging:** Day's Inn, Elizabeth Inn/Conv Ctr
143 rd W, Bancroft, to WI Rapids, **E...gas:** Citgo/diesel, Cedarwood Rest.
139 rd D, Almond, no facilities
136 WI 73, Plainfield, to WI Rapids, **E...gas:** BP, Mobil/diesel, **other:** NAPA, **W...gas:** Phillips 66/Subway/diesel
131 rd V, Hancock, **E...gas:** Citgo, **other:** camping
127mm weigh sta both lanes(exits left)
124 WI 21, Coloma, **E...gas:** Mobil/A&W/diesel, **other:** camping
120mm **rest area sb, full(handicapped)facilities, phone, picnic tables, vending, litter barrels, petwalk, RV dump**
118mm **rest area nb, full(handicapped)facilities, phone, picnic tables, vending, litter barrels, petwalk, RV dump**
113 rd E, rd J, Westfield, **E...lodging:** Sandman Motel, **W...gas:** BP/Burger King, Marathon, Mobil/diesel, **food:** McDonald's, Subway, **lodging:** Pioneer Motel/rest.
106 WI 82 W, WI 23 E, Oxford, **E...lodging:** Crossroads Motel
104 (from nb, no EZ return)rd D, Packwaukee, no facilities
100 WI 23 W, rd P, Endeavor, **E...gas:** Cenex

Portage

92 US 51 S, Portage, **E...gas:** KwikTrip/diesel, Mobil, **food:** Culver's, Dino's Rest., KFC, McDonald's, Subway, Taco Bell, Wendy's, **lodging:** Ridge Motel, Super 8, **other:** Ford/Lincoln/Mercury, $Tree, Pick'n Save, Piggly Wiggly, Radio Shack, Staples, Wal-Mart SuperCtr/24hr
89b a WI 16, to WI 127, Portage, **E...gas:** BP/Burger King/diesel, **food:** Sharpshooter Grill, **other:** Chrysler/Plymouth/Dodge/Jeep
88.5mm Wisconsin River
87 WI 33, Portage, **5 mi E...**HOSPITAL
86mm Baraboo River
85 Cascade Mt Rd, no facilities
84 I-39, I-90 & I-94 run together sb.

Interstate 43

N ↕ S

Exit # Services
192mm I-43 begins/ends at Green Bay on US 41.
192b US 41 S, US 141 S, to Appleton, services on Velp Ave, **1 exit S...**Citgo/diesel/24hr, Express/diesel/24hr, Mobil/Arby's, Burger King, McDonald's, Taco Bell
a US 41 N, US 141 N
189 Atkinson Dr, to Velp Ave, Port of Green Bay, **1 mi W...**Glen's Gas, Jubilee Foods, auto repair
188 Fox River
187 East Shore Dr, Webster Ave, **W...**HOSPITAL, Shell/diesel/24hr, McDonald's, Wendy's, Day's Inn, Holiday Inn, RV dump

Green Bay

185 WI 54, WI 57, University Ave, to Algoma, **W...**Citgo, Marathon, Mobil, Shell/A&W, Cousins Subs, GB Pizza, Lee's Cantonese Chinese, Pizza Hut, Ponderosa, Subway, Taco Bell, Tower Motel, SuperValu Foods, Walgreen, U of WI GB
183 Mason St, rd V, **E...**HOSPITAL, AmeriHost, **1 mi W...**BP, Citgo, Mobil/diesel, Applebee's, Burger King, China Kitchen, Country Kitchen, Fazoli's, Godfather's, Julie's Café, McDonald's, Papa John's, Papa Murphy's, Perkins, Pizza Hut, Schlotsky's, Taco Bell, Candlewood Suites, Cadillac, Champion Parts, Chevrolet, Cub Foods, Dodge, Goodyear/auto, Hyundai, K-Mart, Kohl's, Mazda, Nissan, OfficeMax, Osco Drug, ShopKO, Tires+, Wal-Mart/24hr, mall
181 Eaton Rd, rd JJ, **E...**Citgo/Blimpie/diesel, Hardee's, Harley-Davidson, Ford, Home Depot, **W...**Express/Subway/diesel, Festival Foods
180 WI 172 W, to US 41, **1 exit W...**HOSPITAL, BP/Taco Bell/24hr, Citgo/diesel/24hr, Burger King, Country

Interstate 43

N ↕ S

Express Rest./24hr, McDonald's, Best Western, Hampton Inn, Radisson Inn, Ramada, to stadium

178 US 141, to WI 29, rd MM, Bellevue, **E...**Shell/Arby's/diesel, **W...**BP/diesel/repair/24hr

171 WI 96, rd KB, Denmark, **E...**Citgo/diesel, Chubby's Subs, Lorrie's Café, McDonald's, Steve's Cheese, Shady Acres Camping

168mm rest area both lanes, full(handicapped)facilities, phone, vending, picnic tables, litter barrels, RV dump, petwalk

166mm Devils River

164 WI 147, rd Z, Maribel, **W...**Citgo/diesel, Cedar Ridge Rest., Devils River Camp

160 rd K, Kellnersville, **2-3 mi W...**food

157 rd V, Hillcrest Rd, Francis Creek, **E...**Citgo/diner/diesel

154 US 10 W, WI 310, Two Rivers, to Appleton, **E...**HOSPITAL, Mobil, **W...**Cenex

153mm Manitowoc River

152 US 10 E, WI 42 N, rd JJ, Manitowoc, **E...**HOSPITAL, Inn on Maritime Bay(3mi), maritime museum

149 US 151, WI 42 S, Manitowoc, **E...**HOSPITAL, Mobil/diesel/24hr, Shell/diesel/24hr, Applebee's, Burger King, Country Kitchen, Culver's, Fazoli's, 4Seasons Rest., Perkins, Ponderosa, Wendy's, Comfort Inn, Heritage Inn, Holiday Inn, Super 8, Buick/Pontiac/GMC/Cadillac, Chrysler/Plymouth/Dodge/Jeep, OfficeMax, Tires+, Wal-Mart, museum, **W...**BP/24hr, McDonald's, AmericInn

144 rd C, Newton, **E...**Mobil/diesel, antiques

142mm weigh sta sb, phone

137 rd XX, Cleveland, **E...**Citgo/Burger King/diesel, Cleveland Family Rest.

128 WI 42, Howards Grove, **E...**HOSPITAL, BP/diesel/24hr, Mobil/diesel, Hardee's, Comfort Inn, Jo-Ann Fabrics, **W...**Citgo/Cousins Subs/diesel

126 WI 23, Sheboygan, **E...**HOSPITAL, Applebee's, Culver's, Flame Rest., Hardee's, IHOP, McDonald's, New China, Nino's Café, Pitstop Pizza, Pizza Hut/Taco Bell, Ponderosa, Baymont Inn, BrownStone Inn, Ramada Inn, Super 8, Aldi Foods, Chrysler/Jeep/Subaru, Firestone/auto, Ford/Lincoln/Mercury, Honda/Mazda/Toyota, Hyundai, JC Penney, Kohl's, OfficeMax, Piggly Wiggly, Sears/auto, ShopKO, Walgreen, Wal-Mart/24hr, mall, **W...**Pinehurst Inn

123 WI 28, rd A, Sheboygan, **E...**Citgo/diesel/24hr, Mobil/McDonald's/diesel, Cruisers Burgers, Perkins, Taco Bell, Wendy's, AmericInn, Holiday Inn Express, Harley-Davidson, **W...**Chili's, $Tree, Elder Beerman, Home Depot, Michael's

120 rds OK, V, Sheboygan, **E...**Phillips 66/diesel, Judie's Rest., Best Value Inn, Sleep Inn, Glove Outlet, to Kohler-Andrae SP, camping, **1 mi W...**Horn's RV Ctr

116 rd AA, Foster Rd, Oostburg, **W...**Sandpiper Diner

113 WI 32 N, rd LL, Cedar Grove, **W...**Citgo/diesel/repair, Dr Zwann Rest., Lakeshore Motel

107 rd D, Belgium, **E...**Harrington Beach SP, **W...**BP/DQ/diesel/24hr, Mobil/McDonald's/diesel/24hr, Hobo's Korner Kitchen, AmericInn

100 WI 32 S, WI 84 W, Port Washington, **E...**Citgo/diesel, Arby's, Burger King, McDonald's, Subway, Best Western, Country Inn Suites, Allen-Edmonds Shoes, Goodyear/auto, Sentry Foods, **W...**Nisleit's Country Inn

97 (from nb), WI 57, Fredonia, no facilities

96 WI 33, to Saukville, **E...**Mobil/diesel/24hr, Best Western, Buick/Pontiac/Cadillac, Dodge, Ford, Piggly Wiggly, Wal-Mart, **W...**BP/24hr, Bublitz' Rest., DQ, Ducati Café, Subway, Super 8, Kelly Tire

93 WI 32 N, WI 57 S, Grafton, **1-2 mi E...**Dairy House Rest., Pied Piper Rest., Smith Bros Fish, Best Western

92 WI 60, rd Q, Grafton, **E...**GhostTown Rest., **W...**Citgo/DQ/diesel, Baymont Inn, Home Depot, OfficeMax, Target

89 rd C, Cedarburg, **W...**HOSPITAL, Mobil/diesel, Cedar Crk Settlement Café(6mi), StageCoach Inn, Washington House Inn

Milwaukee

85 WI 57 S, WI 167 W, Mequon Rd, **W...**Citgo/diesel, Mobil/24hr, Café 1505, Chancery Rest., Cousins Subs, DQ, Damon's, Hong Palace Chinese, McDonald's, Panera Bread, Subway, Wendy's, Best Western, Chalet Motel, Jewel-Osco, Kohl's, Walgreen

82b a WI 32 S, WI 100, Brown Deer Rd, **E...**MEDICAL CARE, BP/24hr, PDQ/diesel, Cousins Subs, Heineman's Rest., McDonald's, Pizza Hut, Qdoba Mexican, SpeakEasy Grill, Courtyard, Borders Books, Kohl's Foods, Osco Drug, Walgreen, **W...**Sheraton/rest.

80 Good Hope Rd, **E...**BP, Peking Palace, Manchester East Hotel, Residence Inn, to Cardinal Stritch U

78 Silver Spring Dr, **E...**BP, Mobil, Applebee's, Burger King, Denny's, Ground Round, Little Caesar's, LK Chinese, McDonald's, Papa John's, Pizza Hut, Subway, Taco Bell, Tumbleweed Grill, Wendy's, Zappa's Rest., Baymont Inn, Exel Inn, NorthShore Motel, Woodfield Suites, Barnes&Noble, Cadillac, Firestone/auto, Goodyear/auto, Kohl's, Radio Shack, Sears/auto, Walgreen, mall, **W...**HOSPITAL

77b a (from nb), **E...**Anchorage Rest., Home Depot

76b a WI 57, WI 190, Green Bay Ave, **E...**Anchorage Rest., Home Depot, **W...**Citgo, Burger King, Buick, Jaguar/Volvo

75 Atkinson Ave, Keefe Ave, **E...**Mobil, **W...**BP, Citgo

74 Locust St, no facilities

73c North Ave(rom sb), **E...**Wendy's, **W...**McDonald's

a WI 145 E, 4th St(exits left from sb), Broadway, downtown

72c Wells St, **E...**HOSPITAL, Civic Ctr, museum

b (from sb), I-94 W, to Madison

WISCONSIN

Interstate 43

N ↕ S

Milwaukee

a (310c from nb, exits left from sb), I-794 E, to Lakefront, downtown, I-94 W to Madison

311 WI 59, National Ave, 6th St, downtown

312a Lapham Blvd, Mitchell St, Old Towne Serbian Gourmet House

b (from nb), Becher St, Lincoln Ave

314a Holt Ave, **E...**Citgo/diesel, Pick'n Save Food, **W...**HOSPITAL, to Alverno Coll

b Howard Ave, no facilities

10b (316 from sb), I-94 S to Chicago, airport, no facilities

9b a US 41, 27th St, **E...**MEDICAL CARE, BP, Citgo, Mobil, Arby's, Burger King, Chancery Rest., Cousins Subs, Pizza Hut, Rusty Skillet Rest., Togo's/Baskin-Robbins/Dunkin Donuts, Suburban Motel, AutoZone, CarQuest, Dodge, K-Mart, Rainbow Foods, Target, Walgreen, **W...**HOSPITAL, Denny's, Los Burritos Tapatios, McDonald's, Taco Bell, Hospitality Suites, AAA, Advance Parts, Chevrolet, Chrysler/Jeep, Goodyear, GMC/Hyundai, Kohl's

8a WI 36, Loomis Rd, **E...**BP, Citgo, Los Mariachis Mexican, Walgreen, **W...**Citgo, to Alverno Coll

7 60th St, **E...**Speedway/diesel, Mineo's Rest., Harley-Davison, **W...**Speedway

5b 76th St(from sb, no EZ return), **E...**Applebee's, Boston Mkt, Burger King, Ground Round, Hooters, KFC, Kopp's Burgers, McDonald's, Olive Garden, Outback Steaks, Pizza Hut, Red Lobster, TGIFriday, Wendy's, Barnes&Noble, Best Buy, Borders Books, BreadSmith, Circuit City, Cub Foods, Firestone/auto, Goodyear/auto, Isuzu, Office Depot, SteinMart, Valvoline, **W...**Trak Auto

a WI 24 W, Forest Home Ave, **E...**Citgo, Boerner Botanical Gardens

61 (4 from sb), I-894/US 45 N, I-43/US 45 S

60 US 45 S, WI 100, 108th St(exits left from sb), **E...**BP, Citgo, Clark Gas, Phillips 66, A&W, Amore Italian, Charcoal Grill, MegaOne Rest., **W...**Phillips 66, Forum Rest., McDonald's, Omega Custard, Aldi Foods, Badger Transmisions, Goodyear, Mr P Tire, Saturn, Walgreen, Wal-Mart/drugs

59 WI 100, Layton Ave(from nb), Hales Corner, same as 60

57 Moorland Rd, **E...**cinema, **1-3 mi W...**Mobil/24hr, Speedway/diesel/24hr, Applebee's, Atlanta Bread, Fazoli's, McDonald's, Quizno's, Rococo's Pizza, Taco Bell, Tumbleweed Grill, Baymont Inn, Best Western, Country Inn Suites, Embassy Suites/rest., Holiday Inn Express, Michael's, Target

54 rd Y, Racine Ave, **1-2 mi E...**Citgo/diesel, KwikTrip, Culver's, Cousins Subs, McDonald's

50 WI 164, Big Bend, **W...**Citgo/diesel, McDonald's, Pizza Stop

44mm Fox River

43 WI 83, Mukwonago, **E...**BP/diesel, **W...**Citgo, Shell, Burger King, Culver's, DQ, McDonald's, Subway, Taco Bell, Sleep Inn, Wal-Mart

38 WI 20, East Troy, **W...**BP, Clark/Subway/diesel/24hr/@, Shell/McDonald's, Burger King, Roma Ristorante, CarQuest, Chrysler/Plymouth/Dodge, NAPA

36 WI 120, East Troy, **W...**Country Inn Suites, gas/diesel

33 Bowers Rd, **E...**to Alpine Valley Music Theatre

32mm rest area both lanes, full(handicapped)facilities, phone, picnic tables, litter barrels, vending, petwalk

29 WI 11, Elkhorn, fairgrounds, no facilities

27b a US 12, to Lake Geneva, no facilities

25 WI 67, Elkhorn, **E...**MEDICAL CARE, Mobil/diesel, AmericInn, Chevrolet, Chrysler/Dodge/Jeep, **W...**Speedway/diesel/24hr, Burger King, Dehaan Auto/RV Ctr

Delavan

21 WI 50, Delavan, **E...**Shell/diesel/24hr, Greyhound DogTrack, Kohl's, Wal-Mart SuperCtr/24hr, **W...**MEDICAL CARE, Mobil, Speedway/diesel/24hr, Burger King, Cousins Subs, KFC, McDonald's, Perkins, Pizza Hut, Subway, Taco Bell, Wendy's, Delavan Inn, Super 8, Ace Hardware, Chevrolet/Cadillac, Ford/Lincoln/Mercury, K-Mart, Pick'n Save, Piggly Wiggly, ShopKO, Walgreen

17 rd X, Delavan, Darien, **W...**BP

15 US 14, Darien, **E...**Citgo/diesel, West Wind Diner

6 WI 140, Clinton, **E...**BP, Citgo, Subway, Ford

2 rd X, Hart Rd, **E...**Butterfly Fine Dining

1b a I-90, E to Chicago, W to Madison, **W...**BP/24hr, BP/Subway/diesel, Citgo/diesel, Phillips 66, Pilot/DQ/Taco Bell/diesel/24hr/@, Speedway/diesel, Applebee's, Arby's, Asia Buffet, Burger King, Cousins Subs, Country Kitchen, Culver's, Fazoli's, Hong Kong Buffet, McDonald's, Papa Murphy's, Perkins, Wendy's, Comfort Inn, Econolodge, Fairfield Inn, Holiday Inn Express, Super 8, Aldi Foods, Buick/Pontiac, Chevrolet/Cadillac/Nissan, $Tree, Radio Shack, Staples, Tires+, Wal-Mart SuperCtr/24hr

I-43 begins/ends on I-90, exit 185 in Beloit.

Interstate 90

E ↕ W

Exit # Services

187mm Wisconsin/Illinois state line. I-90 & I-39 run together nb.

187mm Welcome Ctr wb, full(handicapped)facilities, info, phones, picnic tables, litter barrels, vending, petwalk

Beloit

185b I-43 N, to Milwaukee

a WI 81, Beloit, **S...gas:** BP, BP/Subway/diesel, Citgo/diesel/24hr, Phillips 66, Pilot/DQ/Taco Bell/diesel/24hr/@, Speedway/diesel, **food:** Applebee's, Arby's, Asia Buffet, Burger King, Cousins Subs, Country Kitchen, Culver's, DQ, Fazoli's, Hong Kong Buffet, McDonald's, Perkins, Wendy's, **lodging:** Comfort Inn, Econolodge, Fairfield Inn, Holiday Inn Express, Super 8, **other:** Buick/Pontiac, Chevrolet/Cadillac/Nissan, Staples, Tires +, Wal-Mart SuperCtr/24hr

183 Shopiere Rd, rd S, to Shopiere, **S...gas:** Citgo/diesel/24hr, **other:** HOSPITAL, camping

177 WI 351, Janesville, **S...other:** to Blackhawk Tec Coll, Rock Co Airport

Interstate 90

E / W

Janesville

175b a WI 11, Janesville, to Delavan, **N...gas:** BP/Subway/diesel/24hr, **food:** Denny's, **lodging:** Baymont Inn, **S...gas:** BP, **food:** DQ, Hardee's, **lodging:** Lannon Stone Motel

171c b US 14, WI 26, Janesville, **N...gas:** TA/Mobil/Wendy's/diesel/@, Damon's, Old Country Buffet, Steak'n Shake, Subway, Holiday Inn Express, Microtel, Home Depot, Kamp Dakota, Michael's, Old Navy, Staples, Tires+, **S...gas:** BP, Citgo/diesel/24hr, KwikTrip/diesel/24hr, Phillips 66/diesel, **food:** Applebee's, Arby's, BBQ, Big Boy, Burger King, ChiChi's, Country Kitchen, Cousins Subs, Fazoli's, Ground Round, Gyro's Greek, Hardee's, Hooters, KFC, McDonald's, McRaven's Rest., Olive Garden, Papa Murphy's, Perkins, Pizza Hut, Shakey's Pizza, Taco Bell, **lodging:** Ramada Inn/rest., Select Inn, Super 8, **other:** HOSPITAL, Aldi Foods, Firestone/auto, Ford/Lincoln/Mercury, Harley-Davidson, JC Penney, Jo-Ann Fabrics, Mazda, Mercedes, K-Mart, ShopKO, Target, VW, Wal-Mart/drugs, mall

171a **S...**same as 171c b, **N...gas:** Phillips 66, **food:** Cracker Barrel, Best Western/rest., Motel 6, Hampton Inn

168mm rest area eb, full(handicapped)facilities, phone, picnic tables, litter barrels, vending, petwalk

163.5mm Rock River

163 WI 59, Edgerton, to Milton, **N...gas:** Mobil, Shell/Burger King, **food:** Cousins Subs, McDonald's, Red Apple Rest., **lodging:** Newville Drive-In, Comfort Inn, **other:** Hickory Hill/Lakeland Camping, marina, **S...gas:** BP

160 US 51S, WI 73, WI 106, to Deerfield, Oaklawn Academy, **N...other:** Hickory Hill Camping, **S...gas:** Shell/diesel/24hr/@, **food:** Ray's Rest., Subway, **lodging:** Towne Edge Motel, HOSPITAL

156 US 51N, to Stoughton, **S...lodging:** Coachman's Inn, HOSPITAL

147mm weigh sta wb

147 rd N, to Stoughton, Cottage Grove, **N...**Corner Store, **S...gas:** BP/Burger King/24hr, Citgo/Cousins Subs/diesel, **other:** Lake Kegonsa SP

146mm weigh sta eb

142b a (142a exits left from wb)US 12, US 18, Madison, to Cambridge, **N...gas:** Mobil/diesel, **food:** McDonald's, Subway, **lodging:** Knight's Inn, Motel 6, Ramada Inn, Wingate Inn, **other:** Harley-Davidson, **S...gas:** Cenex, Phillips 66/diesel, Shell/diesel, **food:** Arby's, Denny's, Noodles Rest., Wendy's, **lodging:** AmericInn, Day's Inn, Edgewood Inn, Holiday Inn Express, Quality Inn, **other:** HOSPITAL, UWI

138a I-94, E to Milwaukee, W to La Crosse, **I-90 W and I-94 W run together for 93 miles**

Madison

b **S...other:** WI 30, to Madison, airport

135c b US 151, Madison, **N...food:** Cheesehaus, **lodging:** Courtyard, Woodfield Suites, **other:** Buick, Chevrolet, Chrysler/Plymouth/Dodge, Ford, Isuzu, Nissan, Toyota

a **S...gas:** BP/24hr, Shell, Sinclair, **food:** Applebee's, Carlos O'Kelly's, Chili's, Country Kitchen, Cracker Barrel, Denny's, Dunkin Donuts, Hardee's, Heritage House Smorgasbord, IHOP, KFC, McDonald's, Mtn Jack's Rest., Old Country Buffet, Olive Garden, Perkins, Pizza Hut, Ponderosa, Pizza Hut, Red Lobster, Rococo's Pizza, Steak'n Shake, Tumbleweed Grill, Wendy's, **lodging:** Best Western, Comfort Inn, Crowne Plaza Hotel, Econolodge, Exel Inn, Fairfield Inn, Hampton Inn, Holiday Inn/rest., Microtel, Motel 6, Red Roof Inn, Residence Inn, Roadstar Inn, Select Inn, **other:** MEDICAL CARE, Best Buy, Circuit City, Firestone/auto, Home Depot, JC Penney, Jo-Ann Fabrics, K-Mart, Kohl's, Office Depot, OfficeMax, Old Navy, Sears, ShopKO, mall, st patrol

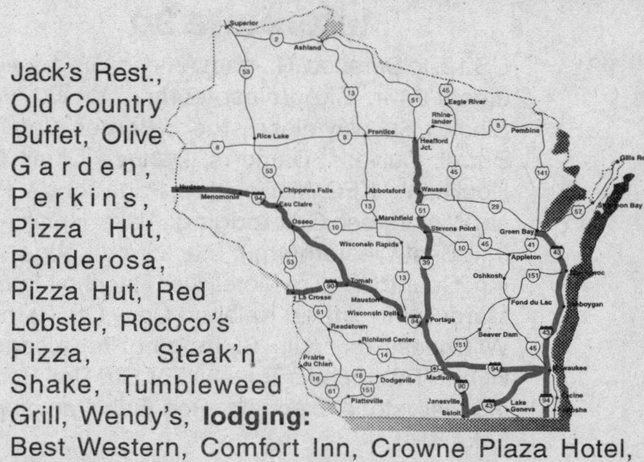

132 US 51, Madison, De Forest, **N...gas:** Citgo/diesel/rest., Shell/diesel, **food:** Pine Cone Rest., **S...gas:** TA/Mobil/Subway/diesel/rest./24hr/@, **other:** Goodyear, Peterbilt, Volvo/White/GMC/Freightliner, WI RV World, camping

131 WI 19, Waunakee, **N...gas:** Citgo, KwikTrip, Mobil, Speedway/Taco Bell/diesel/@, **food:** A&W, McDonald's, Roadside Grill, **lodging:** Day's Inn, Super 8, **other:** Mousehouse Cheesehaus, Kenworth Trucks, **5 mi S...lodging:** Country Inn Suites

126 rd V, De Forest, to Dane, **N...gas:** BP, Phillips 66/Arby's/diesel, **food:** Burger King, Culver's, McDonald's, 7E Rest., Subway, **lodging:** Holiday Inn Express, **other:** KOA, **S...gas:** Citgo, Exxon/diesel

119 WI 60, to Lodi, Arlington, **S...gas:** Mobil/Cousins/diesel, **food:** A&W, Rococo's Pizza, **lodging:** Best Western, **other:** Interstate RV Ctr

115 rd CS, to Lake Wisconsin, Poynette, **N...gas:** Citgo/Subway/diesel, Gas4Less, **food:** McDonald's, **other:** Smokey Hollow Camping, diesel truck/trailer repair, trout fishing

113mm rest area both lanes, full(handicapped)facilities, phone, picnic tables, litter barrels, vending, petwalk, RV dump

111mm Wisconsin River

108b a I-39 N, WI 78, to US 51 N, Portage, **N...other:** HOSPITAL, to WI Dells, **S...gas:** BP, Petro/diesel/rest./24hr/@, **food:** DQ, Little Caesar's, Subway, **lodging:** Comfort Suites, Day's Inn, Devil's Head Resort/Conv Ctr, **other:** Blue Beacon

106mm Baraboo River

106 WI 33, Portage, **N...gas:** Mobil/diesel/rest., **other:** HOSPITAL, **S...gas:** BP, **other:** Kamp Dakota, SkyHigh Camping, to Cascade Mtn Ski Area, Devil's Lake SP, Circus World Museum

WISCONSIN

Interstate 90

92 US 12, to Baraboo, **N...gas:** Amoco, BP/diesel, Cenex/diesel/24hr, Citgo/diesel/24hr, Mobil/diesel/24hr, Sinclair/Subway/diesel, **food:** Burger King, Cracker Barrel, Culver's, Damon's, Danny's Diner, Denny's, Houlihan's, KFC, McDonald's, Papa John's, Ponderosa, Wintergreen Grill, **lodging:** Alakai Hotel, American Inn, Best Western(4mi), Black Wolf Lodge, Camelot Inn, Country Squire Motel, Dell Rancho Motel, Grand Marquis Inn, **other:** Kalahari Conv Ctr, Ramada Ltd, WI Cheese, museum, **S...lodging:** Travelodge, **other:** HOSPITAL, Scenic Traveler RV Ctr, Dell Boo Camping, Jellystone Camping, Red Oak Camping, Mirror Lake SP

89 WI 23, Lake Delton, **N...gas:** Marathon, Mobil/diesel, **food:** Houlihan's, Howie's Rest., Internet Café, KFC, **lodging:** Copacabana Motel, Olympia Motel, RainTree Motel, Rodeway Inn, Travelodge, Wilderness Motel, **other:** Crystal Grand Music Theatre, Springbrook Camping, Jellystone Camping, **S...other:** Home Depot, Wal-Mart SuperCtr/gas/24hr, Country Roads RV Park

87 WI 13, Wisconsin Dells, **N...gas:** BP/diesel, Citgo/diesel, Mobil/diesel, Shell, **food:** Burger King, Country Kitchen, Denny's, Pedro's Mexican, Perkins, Rococo's Pizza, Taco Bell, Wendy's, Best Western, Christmas Mtn Village, **lodging:** Comfort Inn, Day's Inn, Holiday Inn/rest., Howard Johnson, Polynesian Hotel, Super 8, **other:** KOA, Sherwood Forest Camping, Tepee Park Camping, golf, info

85 US 12, WI 16, Wisconsin Dells, **N...other:** to Rocky Arbor SP, Good Sam Camping, Sherwood Forest Camping, **S...lodging:** Summer Breeze Resort

79 rd HH, Lyndon Sta, **N...other:** Dreamfield RV Ctr, **S...**Shell/diesel/rest.

76mm rest area wb, full(handicapped)facilities, phone, picnic tables, litter barrels, vending, petwalk

74mm rest area eb, full(handicapped)facilities, phone, picnic tables, litter barrels, vending, petwalk

69 WI 82, Mauston, **N...gas:** Cenex/Taco Bell/diesel/24hr/@, Pilot/Wendy's/diesel/24hr/@, Shell/24hr, **food:** Country Kitchen, **lodging:** Best Western Oasis, Country Inn, Super 8, **other:** to Buckhorn SP, **S...gas:** Citgo/diesel, KwikTrip/diesel, **food:** Culver's, McDonald's, Pizza Hut, Roman Castle Rest., Subway, **lodging:** Alaskan Motel/rest., **other:** HOSPITAL, Family$, K-Mart, Pick'n Save, Walgreen

61 WI 80, New Lisbon, to Necedah, **N...gas:** Citgo/Bunkhouse Rest./diesel/24hr/@, Mobil/A&W/Subway/diesel/@, **lodging:** Edge O' the Wood Motel, Travelodge, **other:** Buckhorn SP, **S...gas:** KwikTrip/24hr

55 rd C, Camp Douglas, **N...other:** wayside, to Camp Williams, Volk Field, **S...gas:** BP/diesel, Mobil/Subway/diesel, **food:** Target Bluff Rest., **lodging:** K&K Motel, **other:** to Mill Bluff SP

51mm weigh sta eb

48 rd PP, Oakdale, **N...gas:** Citgo/Old Rig Diner/diesel/24hr/@, **other:** Kamp Dakota/showers, KOA, antiques, **S...lodging:** Oakdale Motel, **other:** repair

47.5mm weigh sta wb

45 I-94 W, to St Paul, **I-90 E and I-94 E run together for 93 miles**

43 US 12, WI 16, Tomah, **N...gas:** Citgo, KwikTrip/diesel/24hr, **food:** A&W, Burnstadt's Café, DQ, Embers Rest., European Café, Hearty Platter Rest., **lodging:** Villager Lodge, **other:** HOSPITAL

41 WI 131, Tomah, to Wilton, **N...gas:** Mobil, KwikTrip/diesel, **food:** A&W, European Café, **lodging:** Brentwood Inn, **other:** VA MED CTR, **S...**st patrol

28 WI 16, Sparta, Ft McCoy, **N...gas:** BP, Kwiktrip/diesel, **lodging:** Holiday Inn Express, **other:** HOSPITAL

25 WI 27, Sparta, to Melvina, **N...gas:** Cenex/diesel, Citgo/diesel, Conoco/Taco Bell, KwikTrip/diesel/24hr, **food:** Burger King, Country Kitchen, DQ, Happy Chef, Hardee's, KFC, McDonald's, Pizza Hut, Subway, **lodging:** Country Inn, Super 8, **other:** Chevrolet/Buick/Pontiac, Chrysler/Dodge, Family$, Ford/Mercury, Jubilee Foods, Radio Shack, Wal-Mart, **S...**camping

22mm rest area wb, full(handicapped)facilities, phone, picnic tables, litter barrels, vending, petwalk

20mm rest area eb, full(handicapped)facilities, phone, picnic tables, litter barrels, vending, petwalk

15 WI 162, Bangor, to Coon Valley, **N...**gas, **S...other:** Chevrolet

12 rd C, W Salem, **N...gas:** Cenex/diesel/24hr, **other:** Coulee Region RV Ctr, NAPA, Neshonoc Camping, **S...lodging:** AmericInn

10mm weigh sta eb

5 WI 16, La Crosse, **N...food:** Outback Steaks, **lodging:** Baymont Inn, Hampton Inn, Microtel, **other:** Woodman's Food/gas/lube, Aldi Foods, Home Depot, Pennzoil, Valvoline, bank, **S...gas:** Holiday/A&W/diesel, KwikTrip/diesel/24hr, **food:** Applebee's, ChiChi's, ChuckeCheese, Culver's, Fazoli's, McDonald's, Old Country Buffet, Olive Garden, Perkins, TGIFriday, Wendy's, **lodging:** Holiday Inn Express, **other:** HOSPITAL, Barnes&Noble, Best Buy, Goodyear/auto, Kohl's, Mashall Field, Michael's, OfficeMax, Sears/auto, ShopKO, Target, mall

4 US 53 N, WI 16, to WI 157, La Crosse, **N...other:** Harley-Davidson, **S...gas:** Citgo, Kwiktrip/gas, **food:** Applebee's, Bakers Square, Burger King, ChiChi's, Ciatti's Italian, El Patio Mexican, Famous Dave's BBQ, Grizzly's Café, Little Caesar's, McDonald's, Red Lobster, Rococo's Pizza, Subway, Taco Bell, Wendy's, **lodging:** Comfort Inn, Day's Inn, **other:** HOSPITAL, Cub Foods/24hr, Food Festival/24hr, GNC, Goodyear/auto, JC Penney, K-Mart, NW Fabrics/crafts, Office Depot, Sam's Club, ShopKO, Tires+, Wal-Mart SuperCtr/24hr, Bluebird Springs Camping, La Crosse River St Trail, mall

3 US 53 S, WI 35, to La Crosse, **S...gas:** Kwiktrip, Speedway/diesel, **food:** Burger King, Coney Island, Country Kitchen, Edwardo's Pizza, Embers Rest./24hr, KFC, McDonald's, North Country Steaks, Old Country Cheese, Pizza Hut, Rococo's Pizza, Subway, **lodging:** Best Western, Brookstone Inn, Exel Inn, Hampton Inn, Nightsaver Inn, Roadstar Inn, Super 8, **other:** ShopKO, U-Haul, to Great River St Trail, Viterbo Coll

2.5mm Black River

2 rd B, French Island, **N...gas:** Mobil/diesel, **other:** airport, **S...gas:** Citgo/diesel/IGA Food, **lodging:** Day's Inn/rest.

1mm Welcome Ctr eb, full(handicapped)facilities, info, phone, picnic tables, litter barrels, vending, petwalk

0mm Wisconsin/Minnesota state line, Mississippi River

Interstate 94

E ↕ W

Exit # Services

349mm Wisconsin/Illinois state line, rd ML(from nb), weight sta nb

347 WI 165, rd Q, Lakeview Pkwy, **E...gas:** BP/diesel, **food:** Culver's, McDonald's, Radisson/rest., **other:** Prime Outlets/famous brands, **Welcome Ctr, full facilities, W...other:** GolfShack Whse

345 rd C, **E...gas:** Phillips 66/diesel, **food:** Chester Fried, **4 mi W...gas:** BP

Kenosha

345mm Des Plaines River

344 WI 50, to Kenosha, Lake Geneva, **E...food:** Citgo/diesel, Shell, Woodman's/gas, **food:** Quizno's, Starbucks, Texas Roadhouse, White Castle, **lodging:** Baymont Inn, Country Inn Suites, Super 8, **other:** HOSPITAL, **W...gas:** BP, Speedway/Subway/diesel, **food:** Arby's, Burger King, Cracker Barrel, Denny's, KFC, LJ Silver, McDonald's, Perkins, Taco Bell, Wendy's, **lodging:** Best Western, Country Inn Suites, Day's Inn, Quality Suites, Value Inn, **other:** BMW, Cadillac, Chevrolet, Ford, GM, Jeep, Mitsubishi, Subaru, Toyota, Outlet Mall/famous brands

342 WI 158, to Kenosha, **E...food:** Culver's, **lodging:** Holiday Inn Express(7mi), **other:** Harley-Davidson, dog track

340 WI 142, rd S, to Kenosha, **E...gas:** Citgo/diesel, Mobil/diesel, **other:** HOSPITAL, **W...food:** Mars Cheese Castle Rest., StarBar Rest., **lodging:** Easterday Motel, **other:** to Bong RA

339 rd E, **E...gas:** Marathon/diesel/24hr

337 County Line Rd, rd KR, **E...other:** to Great Lakes Dragway, **W...food:** Apple Holler Rest.

335 WI 11, to Racine, Burlington, **E...gas:** KwikTrip/diesel/24hr

333 US 20, to Racine, Waterford, **E...gas:** KwikTrip/diesel/24hr, Shell/Cousins Subs/diesel, **food:** Burger King, McDonald's, **lodging:** Holiday Inn Express, Paul's Motel, Ramada Ltd, **other:** Hyundai, HOSPITAL, **7 mi E...lodging:** Comfort Inn, Fairfield Inn, Marriott, Quality Inn, Super 8, **W...gas:** Citgo/5th Wheel Grill/diesel/24hr/@, Petro/Mobil/Wendy's/diesel/24hr/@, **food:** Culver's, Subway, **lodging:** Best Western

Milwaukee

329 rd K, Thompsonville, to Racine, **E...gas:** Pilot/Arby's/diesel/24hr/@, **W...gas:** Mobil/A&W

328mm weigh sta eb

327 rd G, **W...other:** Trader Jack's Fireworks

326 7 Mile Rd, **E...gas:** BP/24hr, **other:** Jellystone Park, RV repair, **W...gas:** Mobil/24hr, antiques

325 US 41 N(from wb), to 27th St, **W...food:** Acropolis Rest., Charcoal Grill, SandTrap Rest.

322 WI 100, to Ryan Rd, **E...food:** McDonald's, Wendy's, **other:** Goodyear/Cummins Diesel, **W...gas:** Citgo, Mobil, Pilot/Subway/diesel/24hr/@, Shell/Burger King/diesel, **food:** Arby's, Cousins Subs, Perkins, **lodging:** Value Inn, **other:** Blue Beacon, Freightliner/repair

320 rd BB, Rawson Ave, **E...gas:** BP/24hr, Mobil, **food:** Applebee's, Burger King, **lodging:** Baymont Inn, **other:** Honda

319 rd ZZ, College Ave, **E...gas:** Shell/Subway, Speedway/diesel, **food:** McDonald's, Perkins, **lodging:** Comfort Suites, Country Inn Suites, Exel Inn, Hampton Inn, **other:** MainStay Suites, Radisson, Ramada/rest., Red Roof, **W...gas:** BP/24hr, Citgo/diesel, **other:** VIP Foodmart, Boy Blue DairyMart

318 WI 119, no facilities

317 Layton Ave, **E...gas:** Andy's Gas, Clark Gas, **food:** Martino's Rest., Porterhouse Rest., Prime Qtr Steaks, **other:** Checkers Parts, Radio Shack, **W...food:** Spring Garden Rest., **lodging:** Howard Johnson

316 I-43 S, I-894 W(exits left from wb), to Beloit

314b Howard Ave, to Milwaukee, **W...other:** HOSPITAL, to Alverno Coll

a Holt Ave, **E...gas:** Andy's/diesel, **food:** Arby's, Chucke-Cheese, DQ, Subway, Wendy's, **other:** Jewel-Osco/gas, K-Mart, Pik'n Sav Foods, **W...**HOSPITAL

312b a Becher St, Mitchell St, Lapham Blvd, **W...gas:** BP, Citgo

311 WI 59, National Ave, 6th St, downtown

Milwaukee

310a 13th St(from eb), **E...**HOSPITAL

b I-43 N, to Green Bay

c I-794 E, **E...lodging:** Holiday Inn, Ramada Inn, **other:** to downtown and Lake Michigan Port of Entry

309b 26th St, 22nd St, Clybourn St, St Paul Ave, **N...other:** HOSPITAL, to Marquette U

a 35th St, **N...gas:** Speedway

308c b US 41, no facilities

a VA Ctr, **N...other:** Miller Brewing, **S...other:** County Stadium

307b 68th-70th St, Hawley Rd, **S...other:** to County Stadium

a **N...**68th St, **N...other:** Pennzoil

306 WI 181, to 84th St, **N...**HOSPITAL, **S...other:** Olympic Training Facility

305b US 45 N, to Fond du Lac, **N...**HOSPITAL

a I-894 S, to Chicago, to airport

304b a WI 100, **N...gas:** Citgo, Shell/diesel, **food:** Cousins Subs, Edwardo's Pizza, Ground Round, Giuseppi's Pizza, McDonald's, Pizza Hut, Schlotsky's, Steak Escape, Taco Bell, **lodging:** Best Western/rest., Exel Inn, **other:** zoo, **S...gas:** Phillips 66, Speedway/diesel, **other:** U-Haul, Walgreen

WISCONSIN

Interstate 94

E ↕ W

301b a Moorland Rd, **N...gas:** BP/diesel/24hr, Mobil, **food:** Bakers Square, Fuddrucker's, Houlihan's, Maxwell's Rest., McDonald's, Pizzaria Uno, **lodging:** Courtyard, Marriott, Sheraton, Wyndham Garden, **other:** Audi, Barnes&Noble, BMW, Firestone/auto, Goodyear/auto, JC Penney, Office Depot, Saab, Sears/auto, Walgreen, **S...gas:** Mobil, **food:** Champp's Rest., **lodging:** Best Western, Country Inn Suites, Embassy Suites/rest., Residence Inn, **other:** Walgreen, golf

297 US 18, rd JJ, Blue Mound Rd, Barker Rd, **1-2 mi N...gas:** BP/24hr, Mobil, **food:** Applebee's, Boston Mkt, Burger King, ChiChi's, ChuckeCheese, Gondola Grille, KFC, Kopp's Custard, McDonald's, Olive Garden, Pano's Charhouse, Perkins, Starbucks, Subway, Tony Roma's, Wendy's, Zorba's Grill, **lodging:** Baymont Inn, Comfort Inn, Courtyard, Fairfield Inn, Hampton Inn, Motel 6, Wyndham Garden, **other:** MEDICAL CARE, Acura, Advance Parts, Best Buy, Circuit City, CompUSA, Drug Emporium, K-Mart, Mazda/Lexus, NTB, Pick'n Save, VW, **S...gas:** PDQ Gas, **food:** Arby's, Dunkin Donuts, McDonald's, Schlotsky's, Taco Bell, **lodging:** Extended Stay America, Holiday Inn, Select Inn, Super 8, **other:** Chrysler, Home Depot, Target, Tires+, Walgreen, st patrol

295 WI 164, Waukesha, **N...gas:** Citgo/diesel, KwikTrip/gas, **lodging:** Marriott, **other:** HOSPITAL, **S...other:** HOSPITAL, to Carroll Coll

294 rd J, to Waukesha, **N...gas:** Mobil, **food:** Machine Shed Rest., Thunder Bay Grill, **lodging:** Comfort Suites, Radisson, **S...other:** Expo Ctr

293c WI 16 W, Pewaukee(from wb), **N...other:** GE Plant

b a rd T, Wausheka, Pewaukee, **S...gas:** Mobil, **food:** Brisco Co Grill, Cousins Subs, Denny's, Fazoli's, Peking House, Rococo's Pizza, Subway, Taco Amigo, Weissgerber's Gasthaus Rest., Wendy's, **lodging:** Best Western, **other:** Firestone/auto, Jo-Ann Fabrics, Osco Drug, Pick'n Save Foods, Radio Shack, Walgreen

291 rd G, Pewaukee, **N...food:** Culver's, McDonald's, **lodging:** Country Inn

290 rd SS, no facilities

287 WI 83, to Wales, Hartland, **N...food:** Hardee's, McDonald's, Perkins, Water St Brewery/rest., **lodging:** Country Pride Inn, Holiday Inn Express, **other:** Amish Barn Gifts, GNC, Kohl's, Sentry Foods, Walgreen, **S...gas:** BP/diesel/24hr, PDQ/diesel/24hr, **food:** Breadworks Café, Burger King, DQ, Marty's Pizza, Rococo's Pizza, Subway, **lodging:** Baymont Inn, **other:** MEDICAL CARE, Home Depot, OfficeMax, Target, Tires+, Wal-Mart/drugs

285 rd C, Delafield, **N...gas:** Mobil, **other:** to St John's Military Academy, **S...other:** to Kettle Moraine SF

283 rd P, to Sawyer Rd(from wb), no facilities

282 WI 67, to Oconomowoc, Dousman, **N...gas:** Mobil, **food:** Culver's, Pizza Hut, Schlotsky's, Subway, K-Mart, **lodging:** Olympia Resort, **other:** HOSPITAL, Pick'n Save, Sentry Foods, **S...other:** to Kettle Moraine SF(8mi), Old World WI Hist Sites(13mi)

Madison

277 Willow Glen Rd(from eb, no return), no facilities

275 rd F, to Sullivan, Ixonia, **N...gas:** BP/diesel, **other:** Concord Gen Store, **S...**camping

267 WI 26, Johnson Creek, to Watertown, **N...gas:** BP/McDonald's/diesel, Shell/diesel/rest./24hr/@, **food:** Arby's, **lodging:** Day's Inn, **other:** Goodyear/auto, Johnson Creek Outlet Ctr/famous brands, **S...gas:** Citgo/Hardee's/diesel/24hr, **food:** Culver's, **other:** HOSPITAL, Kohl's, to Aztalan SP

265mm Rock River

264mm rest area wb, full(handicapped)facilities, phone, picnic tables, litter barrels, vending, petwalk

263mm Crawfish River

261mm rest area eb, full(handicapped)facilities, phone, picnic tables, litter barrels, vending, petwalk

259 WI 89, Lake Mills, to Waterloo, **N...gas:** Citgo/diesel/24hr, **lodging:** Lake Country Inn, **S...gas:** BP/diesel/24hr, KwikTrip/diesel/24hr, **food:** McDonald's, Pizza Pit, Subway, **lodging:** Pyramid Motel/RV park, **other:** Buick/Chevrolet/Cadillac, Country Campers RV Ctr, to Aztalan SP

250 WI 73, to Marshall, Deerfield, no facilities

246mm weigh sta eb

244 rd n, Sun Prairie, Cottage Grove, **N...gas:** BP/diesel, Citgo/diesel, **S...food:** McDonald's

240 I-90 E. I-94 and I-90 run together 93 miles. **See Wisconsin I- 90, exits 48-138.**

Tomah

147 I-90 W, to La Crosse

143 US 12, WI 21, Tomah, **N...gas:** Mobil/diesel, **food:** Country Kitchen, Perkins, **lodging:** AmericInn, Holiday Inn, Super 8, **other:** Humbird Cheese/gifts, **S...gas:** BP/diesel/rest./24hr, Citgo, Shell/diesel/cheese, **food:** Burnstad's Amish Café, Culver's, KFC, McDonald's, Subway, Taco Bell, **lodging:** Comfort Inn, Cranberry Suites, Econolodge, **other:** HOSPITAL, County Mkt Foods, $Tree, Ford/Lincoln/Mercury, U-Haul, Wal-Mart SuperCtr/gas/diesel/24hr, to Ft McCoy(9mi), **S on US 12...food:** Burger King, Pizza Hut, **other:** Chevrolet/Buick, Chrysler/Plymouth/Dodge/Jeep, Firestone/auto, NAPA, Radio Shack

135 rd EW, Warrens, **N...other:** Jellystone Camping

128 rd O, Millston, **N...other:** Black River SF, camping, **S...gas:** Hartland/diesel, **lodging:** Millston Motel

122mm rest area/scenic view both lanes, full(handicapped)facilities, phone, picnic tables, litter barrels, vending, petwalk

116 WI 54, **N...gas:** BP/Subway/diesel/LP/@, **food:** Perkins, **lodging:** Best Western Arrowhead/rest., Holiday Inn Express, Super 8, **other:** Black River RA, Parkland Camp, **S...gas:** Flying J/Cookery/diesel/24hr/@, KwikTrip/diesel, **food:** Burger King, DQ, Hardee's, McDonald's, Oriental Kitchen, Pizza Hut, **lodging:** Day's Inn, **other:** $Tree, Wal-Mart

115mm Black River

115 US 12, Black River Falls, to Merrillan, **N...lodging:** Pines Motel, **S...gas:** Holiday, Mobil/diesel, **food:** Hardee's, KFC, Pizza Hut, Subway, Sunrise Rest., **other:** HOSPITAL, Harley-Davidson, NAPA, Pontiac/Buick/GMC

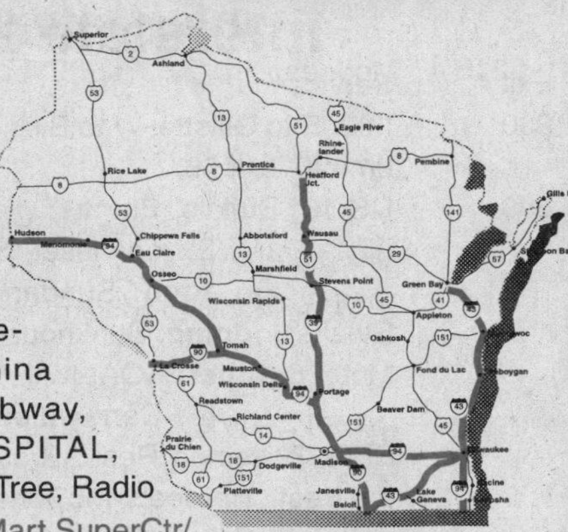

Interstate 94

E ↕ W

Eau Claire

105 to WI 95, Hixton, to Alma Center, **N...lodging:** Motel 95, **other:** KOA(3mi), **S...gas:** Cenex/diesel, Hixton Trvl/diesel/rest./24hr

98 WI 121, Northfield, to Alma Center, Pigeon Falls, **S...gas:** Cenex/diesel, **lodging:** Jackie's Café/Inn

88 US 10, Osseo, to Fairchild, **N...gas:** BP/DQ, Mobil, Shell/Elderberry's/diesel, **food:** Hardee's, Heckel's Rest., **lodging:** 10-7 Inn, Super 8, **other:** Chevrolet, Ford, Stony Cr RV Park, **S...gas:** Citgo, Speedway/diesel, **food:** McDonald's, Subway, **lodging:** Red Carpet Inn, **other:** HOSPITAL

81 rd HH, rd KK, Foster, **S...gas:** Cenex/diesel/LP, **food:** Foster Cheesehaus

70 US 53, Eau Claire, **N off Golf Rd...gas:** Conoco/diesel, **food:** A&W, Applebee's, Bakers Square, Oakwood Café Court, Fazoli's, Jade Garden, McDonald's, Northwoods Grill, Olive Garden, TGIFriday, **lodging:** Country Inn Suites, Heartland Inn, **other:** Aldi Foods, Best Buy, Borders Books, Dayton's, Kohl's, Michael's, Office Depot, Sam's Club, Target, Wal-Mart SuperCtr/24hr, mall, **S...other:** st police

68 WI 93, to Eleva, **N...gas:** BP, KwikTrip, Speedway/24hr, **food:** Burger King, DQ, Hardee's, **lodging:** Econolodge, **other:** Chrysler, Firestone/auto, Goodyear/auto, Jeep, Lincoln/Mercury, Nissan, Saturn, Subaru, VW, same as 70, **S...gas:** Citgo, **other:** Buick/Pontiac/Cadillac/GMC/Hyundai, Ford

65 WI 37, WI 85, Eau Claire, to Mondovi, **N...gas:** BP, Citgo/diesel, **food:** Arby's, ChiChi's, China Buffet, Godfather's, GreenMill Rest., Hardee's, Heckel's Rest., McDonald's, Randy's Rest., Red Lobster, Subway, Taco Bell, TCBY, Wendy's, YenKing Chinese, **lodging:** Best Western, Comfort Inn, Day's Inn/rest., Exel Inn, Hampton Inn, Holiday Inn/rest., Park Inn, Plaza Hotel, Quality Inn, Roadstar Inn, **other:** HOSPITAL, Castle Foods, Mazda/Toyota, Radio Shack, ShopKO

64mm Chippewa River

59 to US 12, rd EE, to Eau Claire, **N...gas:** Citgo/Burger King/diesel/24hr, Holiday/Subway/diesel/24hr, **food:** Anderson's Grill, Embers Rest., McDonald's, **lodging:** AmericInn, Day's Inn, Super 8, **other:** HOSPITAL, Fox RV Ctr(10mi), auto repair/towing, **S...**US RV Ctr, trailer repair

52 US 12, WI 29, WI 40, Elk Mound, to Chippewa Falls, **S...gas:** U-Fuel, **food:** Elk Mound Café

49mm weigh sta wb

Menomonie

45 rd B, Menomonie, **N...gas:** Cenex/diesel/rest., **S...gas:** KwikTrip/Subway/diesel/24hr, **food:** Culver's, Heckel's Rest., **lodging:** AmeriHost, **other:** HOSPITAL, Wal-Mart Dist Ctr

44mm Red Cedar River

43mm rest areas both lanes, full(handicapped)facilities, phone, picnic tables, litter barrels, vending, petwalk, weather info

41 WI 25, Menomonie, **N...gas:** Cenex/Burger King, **food:** Applebee's, China Buffet, Subway, **other:** HOSPITAL, Aldi Foods, $Tree, Radio Shack, Wal-Mart SuperCtr/24hr, Edgewater Camping, GS Camping, **S...gas:** Citgo, F&F/diesel, Holiday, Speedway/diesel/24hr, **food:** Arby's/Sbarro's, Country Kitchen, DQ, Hardee's, Kernel Rest., KFC, Little Caesar's, McDonald's, Perkins, Pizza Hut, Taco Bell, Taco John's, Wendy's, **lodging:** AmericInn, Best Western, Country Inn Suites, Motel 6, Super 8, **other:** Chevrolet, Chrysler, K-Mart, to Red Cedar St Tr

32 rd Q, to Knapp, no facilities

28 WI 128, Wilson, to Glenwood City, Elmwood, **N...gas:** KwikTrip/diesel/24hr, **food:** Hearty Platter Rest., **S...other:** Eau Galle RA, camping

24 rd B, Woodville, to Baldwin, **N...gas:** Mobil, **lodging:** Woodville Motel, **S...other:** Eau Galle RA, camping

19 US 63, Baldwin, to Ellsworth, **N...gas:** Freedom/diesel, KwikTrip/Subway/diesel, **food:** A&W, DQ, Hardee's, McDonald's, **lodging:** AmericInn, **other:** HOSPITAL, **S...gas:** Citgo/diesel/LP/24hr, **lodging:** Super 8

Hudson

16 rd T, Hammond, **N...other:** Sheepskin Outlet

10 WI 65, Roberts, to New Richmond, no facilities

8mm weigh sta eb

4 US 12, rd U, Somerset, **N...gas:** Citgo/diesel/24hr, TA/Mobil/diesel/rest./24hr/@, **other:** JR Ranch Motel/steaks, to Willow River SP

3 WI 35, to River Falls, U of WI River Falls, no facilities

2 rd F, Carmichael Rd, Hudson, **N...gas:** BP, Holiday, **food:** Applebee's, Cousins Subs, Culver's, KFC, Papa Murphy's, Taco John's, **lodging:** Royal Inn, **other:** Econo Foods, Pontiac/GMC, Target, **S...Welcome Ctr both lanes, full(handicapped)facilities, phone, picnic table, litter barrel, info, petwalk, gas:** Holiday, KwikTrip/diesel, **food:** Arby's, Burger King, Country Kitchen, Denny's, McDonald's, Perkins/24hr, Pizza Hut, Subway, Taco Bell, Wendy's, **lodging:** Best Western, Comfort Inn, Fairfield Inn, Holiday Inn Express, Super 8, **other:** Checker Parts, Chevrolet/RV Ctr, County Mkt Foods, Ford/Mercury, Home Depot, Tires+, Wal-Mart, Yamaha, to Kinnickinnic SP

1 WI 35 N, Hudson, **1 mi N...gas:** Freedom, Holiday, **food:** DQ, Subway, **other:** City Mkt Foods

0mm Wisconsin/Minnesota state line, St Croix River

WYOMING

Interstate 25

Exit #	Services
300	I-90, E to Gillette, W to Billings. I-25 begins/ends on I-90, exit 56.
299	US 16, Buffalo, **E...gas:** Cenex/diesel, Conoco/diesel/24hr, Exxon/diesel, Sinclair/diesel, Shell/diesel/24hr, **food:** Sundance Grill, Winchester Steaks, **lodging:** Bunkhouse Motel, Comfort Inn, Motel 6, **other:** KOA, NAPA, **W... gas:** Bighorn/diesel/24hr/@, Cenex/diesel/rest./24hr, **food:** BBQ, Bozeman Rest., Breadboard Rest., Dash Inn Rest., Hardee's, McDonald's, Pizza Hut, Subway, Taco John's, **lodging:** Crossroads Inn/rest., Econolodge, Horsemen's Inn, Motel Wyo, Super 8, **other:** HOSPITAL, Indian RV Camp
298	US 87, Buffalo, **W...gas:** Sinclair/diesel/pizza, **other:** Nat Hist Dist Info
291	Trabing Rd, no facilities
280	Middle Fork Rd, no facilities
274mm	parking area both lanes, litter barrels
265	Reno Rd, no facilities
254	Kaycee, **E...gas:** Exxon/diesel, Shell/diesel, **food:** Country Inn Diner, **lodging:** Cassidy Inn, Siesta Motel, **other:** Kaycee Foods, NAPA Repair, Powder River RV Park, USPO, **W...rest area both lanes, full(handicapped)facilities, phone, picnic tables, litter barrels, petwalk, gas:** Sinclair/diesel/LP/motel, **other:** KC RV Park
249	TTT Rd, no facilities
246	Powder River Rd, no facilities
235	Tisdale Mtn Rd, no facilities
227	WY 387 N, Midwest, Edgerton, no facilities
223	no facilities
219mm	parking area both lanes, litter barrels
216	Ranch Rd, no facilities
210	Horse Ranch Creek Rd, Midwest, Edgerton, no facilities
197	Ormsby Rd, no facilities
191	Wardwell Rd, to Bar Nunn, **W...gas:** Conoco/diesel, **other:** TM camping
189	US 20, US 26 W, to Shoshone, Port of Entry, airport
188b	WY 220, Poplar St, **E...gas:** Sinclair, **food:** El Jarro Mexican, JB's, La Costa Mexican, **lodging:** Econolodge, Hampton Inn, Holiday Inn, Motel 6, Radisson, Super 8, **other:** Westridge Inn, Ryder Trucks, **W...gas:** Exxon, Shell/Burger King/diesel, **food:** Casper's Rest., DQ, **other:** Harley-Davidson, to Ft Casper HS
188a	Center St, Casper, **E...gas:** Conoco/diesel, Shell/diesel, JB's, Taco John's, **lodging:** Holiday Inn, National 9 Inn, Showboat Motel, **W...gas:** Cenex, **food:** Denny's, **lodging:** Day's Inn, Parkway Plaza Motel
187	McKinley St, Casper, **E...gas:** Minimart/diesel, **lodging:** Ranch House Motel, **other:** repair/transmissons
186	US 20, US 26, US 87, Yellowstone St, Casper, **E...other:** VW/Audi, **W...lodging:** Best Western, **other:** HOSPITAL, Chevrolet/Subaru, Pontiac, VW, diesel repair
185	WY 258, Wyoming Blvd, E Casper, **E...gas:** Conoco/diesel, Kum&Go, **food:** Applebee's, Outback Steaks, **lodging:** Comfort Inn, Shilo Inn, **other:** KOA(1mi), **W...gas:** Cenex, Exxon/diesel, Flying J/Conoco/diesel/LP/24hr/@, **food:** Arby's, Burger King, DQ, Hardee's, HomeTown Buffet, KFC, LJ Silver, McDonald's, Perkins, Pizza Hut, Red Lobster, Taco Bell, Taco John's, Village Inn Rest., Wendy's, **lodging:** Holiday Inn Express, 1st Interstate Inn, **other:** AutoZone, Buick/Cadillac/Pontiac/GMC, Ford/Mercury, Home Depot, Hyundai, JC Penney, K-Mart, Nissan, OfficeMax, Old Navy, Safeway, Sam's Club, Sears/auto, Target, Volvo, Wal-Mart SuperCtr/24hr, to Oregon Tr, mall
182	WY 253, Brooks Rd, Hat Six Rd, **E...gas:** Sinclair/diesel/@, **food:** Lou's Rest., **other:** to Wilkins SP
175mm	parking area sb, litter barrels
171mm	parking area nb, litter barrels
165	Glenrock, **2 mi E...gas:** Phillips 66, **other:** Deer Creek Village RV Camping(apr-nov)
160	US 87, US 20, US 26, E Glenrock, **E...gas:** Exxon, Phillips 66, **food:** Subway, **lodging:** All American Motel, Glenrock Motel, Hotel Higgins B&B, **other:** Deer Creek RV Camping, to Johnston Power Plant
156	Bixby Rd, no facilities
154	Barber Rd, no facilities
153mm	parking area both lanes, litter barrels
151	Natural Bridge, no facilities
150	Inez Rd, no facilities
146	La Prele Rd, no facilities
140	WY 59, Douglas, **E...gas:** Conoco/Subway/diesel, Maverik, **food:** Arby's, McDonald's, **lodging:** Best Western, Plains Motel, Super 8, **other:** HOSPITAL, Buick/Chevrolet/GMC/Pontiac, CarQuest, Chevrolet, Jackalope Camping, WY St Fair, Pioneer Museum, **W...other:** KOA
135	US 20, US 26, US 87, Douglas, **E...gas:** Broken Wheel/Sinclair/diesel/rest./@, **lodging:** Country Inn Rest., Alpine Inn, 1st Interstate Inn, **other:** HOSPITAL, auto repair, **1-2 mi E...food:** Clementine's Pizza, KFC/Taco Bell, Pizza Hut, Taco John's, Village Inn Rest., **lodging:** Chieftain Motel, **other:** Dodge/Plymouth, Ford/Mercury, Pamida, Safeway
129mm	parking area both lanes
126	US 18, US 20 E, Orin, **E...Orin Jct Rest Area both lanes, full(handicapped)facilities, phones, picnic tables, litter barrels, petwalk, RV dump, gas:** Orin Jct Trkstp/diesel/café
125mm	N Platte River
111	Glendo, **E...gas:** Sinclair/diesel, **food:** Glendo Marina Café, **lodging:** Howard's Motel, **other:** to Glendo SP, RV camping

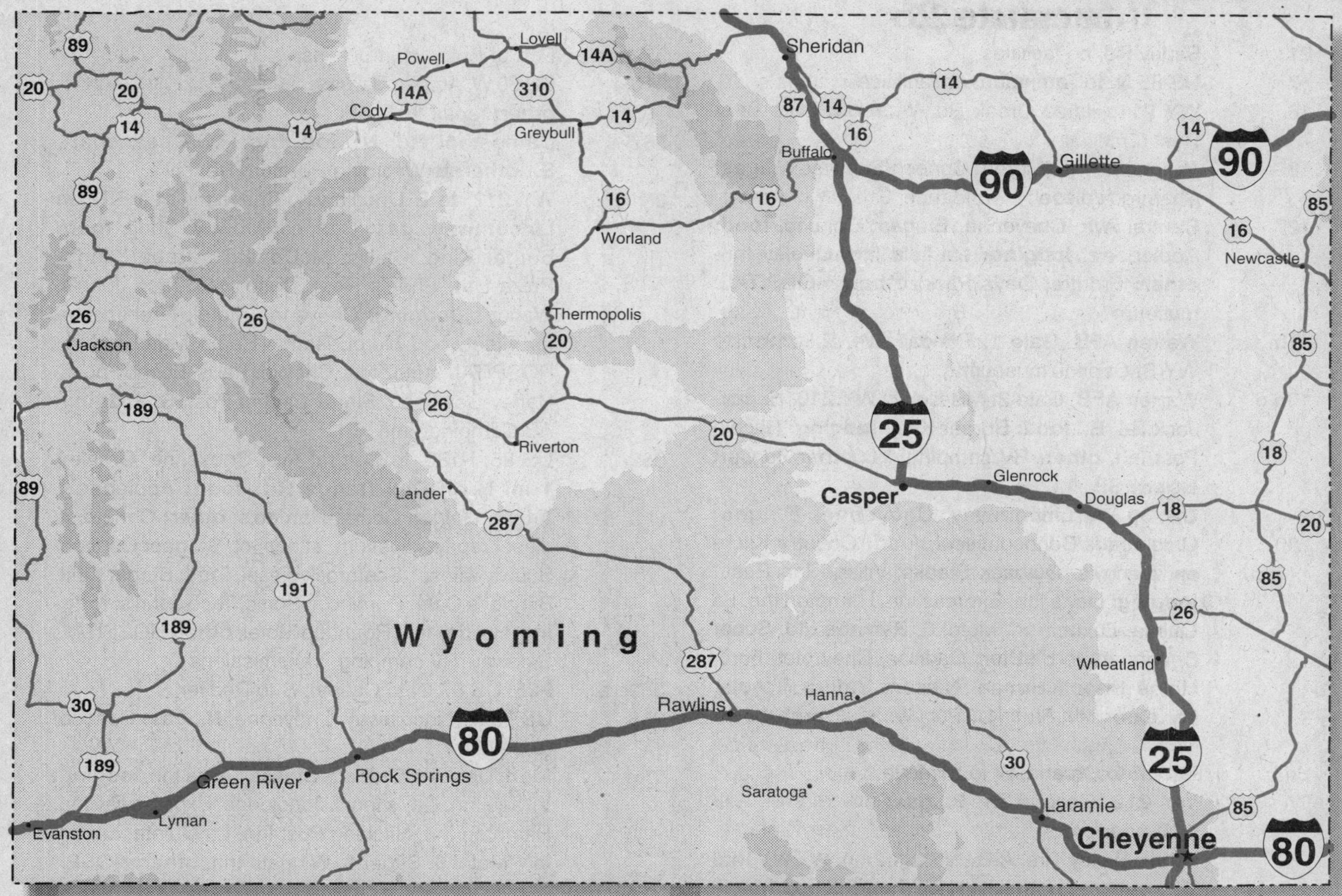

Interstate 25

N ↕ S

Wheatland

104 to Middle Bear, no facilties

100 Cassa Rd, no facilities

94 El Rancho Rd, no facilities

92 US 26 E, Dwyer, **E...other:** to Guernsey SP, Ft Laramie NHS

91.5mm rest area both lanes, full(handicapped)facilities, picnic tables, litter barrel, petwalk, RV dump

87 Johnson Rd, no facilities

84 Laramie River Rd, no facilities

83.5mm Laramie River

80 US 87, Wheatland, Laramie Power Sta, **E...gas:** Sinclair/A&W/diesel/24hr, **food:** Pizza Hut, Timberland Rest., **lodging:** Best Western, **other:** Chevrolet/Pontiac/Buick/Cadillac, Chrysler/Dodge/Plymouth/Jeep, Pamida, Safeway, same as 78

78 US 87, Wheatland, **E...gas:** Cenex/diesel, Conoco/diesel, **food:** Arby's, Burger King, Subway, Taco John's, **lodging:** Best Western, Motel 6, Plains Motel, Vimbo's Motel/rest., Westwinds Motel, Wyo Motel, **other:** HOSPITAL, Safeway, **W...gas:** Exxon/diesel, Conoco/diesel, **other:** Ford/Mercury, Radio Shack, RV park

73 WY 34 W, to Laramie, Sybille Wildlife Ctr(seasonal)

70 Bordeaux Rd, no facilities

68 Antelope Rd, no facilities

67.5mm parking area nb, litter barrels

66 Hunton Rd, no facilities

65.5mm parking area both lanes, litter barrels

65 Slater Rd, no facilities

64mm Richeau Creek

57 TY Basin Rd, Chugwater, no facilities

54 Lp 25, Chugwater, **E...gas:** Sinclair/diesel, **food:** Buffalo Grill, **lodging:** Super 8, **other:** GS RV Park, **rest area both lanes, full(handicapped)facilities, phone, picnic tables, litter barrels, petwalk, RV dump**

47 Bear Creek Rd, no facilities

39 Little Bear Community, no facilities

36mm Little Bear Creek

34 Nimmo Rd, no facilities

33mm Horse Creek

29 Whitaker Rd, no facilities

25 ranch exit, no facilities

WYOMING

Interstate 25

N ↕ S

Cheyenne

21 Ridley Rd, no facilities
17 US 85 N, to Torrington, no facilities
16 WY 211, Horse Creek Rd, **W...food:** Little Bear Rest.(2mi)
13 Vandehei Ave, **E...gas:** Conoco/Subway, **W...gas:** Shamrock/diesel
12 Central Ave, Cheyenne, **E...gas:** Conoco, **food:** Applebee's, **lodging:** Fairfield Inn, Quality Inn, **other:** Frontier Days Park, **other:** HOSPITAL, museum
11b Warren AFB, Gate 1, Randall Ave, **E...other:** to WY St Capitol, museum
10b d Warren AFB, Gate 2, Missile Dr, WY 210, Happy-Jack Rd, **E...food:** Burger King, **lodging:** Hitchin Post Inn, **other:** RV camping, **W...other:** to Curt Gowdy SP
9 US 30, W Lincolnway, Cheyenne, **E...gas:** Crossroads/Conoco/diesel, **food:** Country Kitchen, Denny's, Outback Steaks, Village Inn Rest., **lodging:** Day's Inn, Express Inn, Hampton Inn, La Quinta, Luxury Inn, Motel 6, Ramada Ltd, Super 8, Wingate Inn, **other:** Cadillac, Chevrolet, Ford, Home Depot, Honda, Nissan, Saturn, Toyota, **W...gas:** Little America/Sinclair/diesel/rest./motel/@
8d b I-80, E to Omaha, W to Laramie
7 WY 212, College Dr, **E...gas:** Love's/Wendy's/diesel/24hr/@, Shamrock/Subway/diesel/24hr/@, **other:** Bailey Tire, A-B RV Park(2mi), **W...WY Info Ctr/rest area both lanes, full(handicapped)facilities, phone, picnic tables, litter barrels, petwalk, gas:** Flying J/Conoco/diesel/LP/rest./24hr/@, **food:** McDonald's, **lodging:** Comfort Inn
6.5mm Port of Entry, nb
2 Terry Ranch Rd, **2 mi E...**Terry Bison Ranch/rest./hotel, **other:** RV camping
0mm Wyoming/Colorado state line

Interstate 80

E ↕ W

Exit # Services
402mm Wyoming/Nebraska State line
401 WY 215, Pine Bluffs, **N...gas:** Cenex/A&W/diesel/24hr/@, Conoco/Subway/diesel, Shamrock/diesel/@, Sinclair/repair, **food:** Uncle Fred's Rest., **lodging:** Gator's Motel, Sunset Motel, Travel Inn, **other:** USPO, Pine Bluff RV Park, **S...Welcome Ctr/rest area both lanes, full(handicapped)facilities, info, phone, playground, nature trail, picnic tables, litter barrels, petwalk**
391 Egbert, no facilities
386 WY 213, WY 214, Burns, no facilities
377 WY 217, Hillsdale, **N...gas:** TA/Amoco/Burger King/Taco Bell/diesel/motel/24hr/@, **other:** Wyo RV Camping
372mm Port of Entry wb, truck insp
370 US 30 W, Archer, **N...gas:** Sapp/diesel/rest./24hr/@, **other:** repair, RV park
367 Campstool Rd, **N...lodging:** KOA(seasonal), **S...other:** to Wyoming Hereford Ranch
364 WY 212, to E Lincolnway, Cheyenne, **1 mi N on Lincolnway...gas:** Conoco/Subway, Shell, **food:** Burger King, Chili's, McDonald's, Papa John's, Pizza Hut, Shari's Rest., Taco Bell, Taco John's, Wendy's, **lodging:** Cheyenne Motel, Firebird Motel, Fleetwood Motel, Ranch Home Motel, **other:** HOSPITAL, AutoZone, Checker Parts, Econo Foods, Harley-Davidson, Sierra Trading Post, **S...lodging:** AB Camping(4mi)
362 US 85, I-180, to Central Ave, Cheyenne, Greeley, **1 mi N on Dell Range Rd...food:** Applebee's, Arby's, Golden Corral, Hardee's, **other:** CarQuest, diesel repair, museum, st capitol, **S...gas:** Conoco/Subway/diesel, Shamrock/diesel, **food:** Burger King, Byrider's Café, Domino's, Sonic, Taco John's, **lodging:** Holiday Inn, Roundup Motel, **other:** HOSPITAL, Safeway, RV camping, transmissions
359c a I-25, US 87, N to Casper, S to Denver
358 US 30, W Lincolnway, Cheyenne, **N...gas:** Conoco/diesel/24hr, Little America/Sinclair/diesel/motel/@, **food:** Denny's, Outback Steaks, Pizza Inn, **lodging:** Village Inn, Day's Inn, Econolodge, Expressway Inn, Hampton Inn, Hitching Post Inn, La Quinta, Luxury Inn, Motel 6, Super 8, Wingate Inn, **other:** HOSPITAL, Chevrolet, Home Depot, Honda
348 Otto Rd, no facilities
345 Warren Rd, no facilities
344mm parking area wb
343.5mm parking area eb
342 Harriman Rd, no facilities
341mm parking area both lanes
339 Remount Rd, no facilities
335 Buford, **S...gas:** Sinclair/Lone Tree Jct/diesel/24hr
333mm point of interest, parking area both lanes
329 Vedeauwoo Rd, **S...**to Ames Monument, Nat Forest RA
323 WY 210, Happy Jack Rd, **N...rest area both lanes, full(handicapped)facilities, phone, picnic tables, litter barrels, petwalk, Lincoln Monument, elev. 8640,** to Curt Gowdy SP

Laramie

322mm chain up area both lanes
316 US 30 W, Grand Ave, Laramie, **1-2 mi N...gas:** Conoco, **food:** Applebee's, Arby's, Bailey's Rest., Burger King, Godfather's, Hong Kong Buffet, JB's, McDonald's, Sonic, Taco Bell, Taco John's, Teriyaki Bowl, Vitale Italian, Wendy's, Winger's, **lodging:** Comfort Inn, Sleep Inn, University Inn, Wyo Motel, **other:** HOSPITAL, Albertson's/gas, Toyota, Wal-Mart SuperCtr/24hr

Interstate 80

E ↕ W

313 US 287, to 3rd St, Laramie, Port of Entry, **N...gas:** Conoco, Exxon, Phillips 66, Sinclair, Shell/diesel, **food:** Chuck Wagon Rest., Corona Village Mexican, Great Wall Chinese, **lodging:** 1st Inn Gold, Laramie Inn/rest., Motel 8, Sunset Inn, **other:** HOSPITAL, Honda/Nissan/Isuzu, Laramie Plains Museum, **S...lodging:** Best Western, Motel 6

312mm Laramie River

311 WY 130, WY 230, Snowy Range Rd, Laramie, **S...gas:** Conoco/diesel, Phillips 66/diesel, Sinclair/diesel, **food:** McDonald's, **lodging:** Best Value Inn, Howard Johnson, Travel Inn, **other:** to Snowy Range Ski Area, WY Terr Park

310 Curtis St, Laramie, **N...gas:** Pilot/Wendy's/diesel/24hr/@, Shamrock/café/diesel, **lodging:** Day's Inn, Econolodge, Super 8, **other:** HOSPITAL, Goodyear/service/towing, KOA, **1 mi N on 3rd...food:** Pizza Hut, Shari's Rest., **other:** Checker Parts, Jeep/Subaru, K-Mart, Safeway Foods, **S...gas:** Petro/Mobil/diesel/24hr/@

307mm parking area both lanes, litter barrels

297 WY 12, Herrick Lane, no facilities

290 Quealy Dome Rd, **S...gas:** Cenex/diesel/24hr

279 Cooper Cove Rd, no facilities

272mm Rock Creek

272 WY 13, to Arlington, **N...gas:** Exxon, **other:** RV camping

267 Wagonhound Rd, S...rest area both lanes, full(handicapped)facilities, phone, picnic tables, litter barrels, petwalk

262mm parking area both lanes

260 WY 402, **S...**towing

259mm Medicine Bow River, E Fork

257mm Medicine Bow River

255 WY 72, Elk Mtn, to Hanna, **N...gas:** Conoco/diesel/@

238 Peterson Rd, no facilities

235 US 30/87, WY 130, Walcott, **N...gas:** Shell/diesel/café

229mm N Platte River

228 Ft Steele HS, N...rest area both lanes, full(handicapped)facilities, phone, picnic tables, litter barrels, petwalk

221 E Sinclair, **N...gas:** Phillips 66/diesel/rest./24hr, **other:** to Seminoe SP, camping

219 W Sinclair, **N...other:** to Seminoe SP, camping

Rawlins

215 Cedar St, Rawlins, **N...gas:** Conoco/diesel, Kum&Go, Phillips 66, Shell/KFC/Taco Bell/diesel, **food:** McDonald's, Pizza Hut, Rustler's Rest., Subway, Taco John's, Wendy's, **lodging:** Bridger Inn, Day's Inn, 1st Choice Inn, Key Motel, Weston Inn, **other:** Alco, Buick/Chevrolet/Pontiac/GMC, CarQuest, Checker Parts, Chrysler/Plymouth/Dodge/Jeep, City Mkt Food, Pamida, TDS Tire, museum, Frontier Prison NHS, to Yellowstone/Teton NP

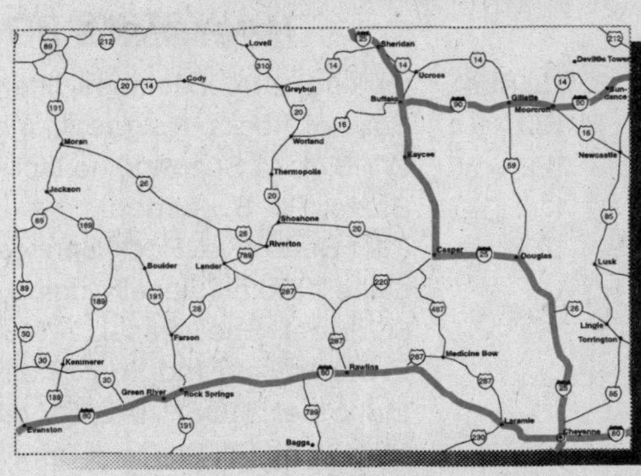

214 Higley Blvd, Rawlins, **N...**KOA, **S...gas:** Rip Griffin/Subway/diesel/24hr/@, **lodging:** Sleep Inn

211 WY 789, to US 287 N, Spruce St, Rawlins, **N...gas:** Conoco/diesel, Exxon/diesel, Phillips 66, Sinclair/diesel, **food:** Cappy's Rest., JB's, **lodging:** Best Western/rest., Bucking Horse Lodge, Cliff Motel, Ideal Motel, National 9 Inn, Sunset Motel, Super 8, **other:** HOSPITAL, RV World Camping, **1 mi N...lodging:** Economy Inn, Rawlins Motel, **other:** Ford/Lincoln/Mercury

209 Johnson Rd, **N...gas:** Flying J/diesel/LP/rest./24hr/@

206 Hadsell Rd(no eb return), no facilities

205.5mm continental divide, elev 7000

204 Knobs Rd, no facilities

201 Daley Rd, no facilities

196 Riner Rd, **13 mi N...**Strong Ranch

190mm parking area wb, litter barrels

189mm parking area eb, picnic tables, litter barrels

187 WY 789, Creston, Baggs Rd, **S...**fireworks, **50 mi S...gas:** Baggs Jct Gas/diesel

184 Continental Divide Rd, no facilities

173 Wamsutter, **N...gas:** Loves/Subway/diesel/24hr/@, Sinclair/diesel/LP/@, **S...gas:** Conoco/diesel/repair/café/24hr, Phillips 66/diesel/@, **food:** Broadway Café, **lodging:** Wamsutter Motel

170 Rasmussen Rd, no facilities

168 Frewen Rd, no facilities

166 Booster Rd, no facilities

165 Red Desert, **S...gas:** SaveWay, lodging, **other:** 24hr towing

158 Tipton Rd, continental divide, elev 6930

156 GL Rd, no facilities

154 BLM Rd, no facilities

152 Bar X Rd, no facilities

150 Table Rock Rd, **S...gas:** Sinclair/Major Gas/diesel, **other:** camping

146 Patrick Draw Rd, no facilities

144mm rest area both lanes, full(handicapped)facilities, phone, picnic tables, litter barrels, petwalk

143mm parking area both lanes, litter barrels

142 Bitter Creek Rd, no facilities

139 Red Hill Rd, no facilities

136 Black Butte Rd, no facilities

WYOMING

Interstate 80

E ↕ W

135mm parking area both lanes, litter barrels
130 Point of Rocks, **N...gas:** Conoco/diesel/motel
122 WY 371, to Superior, no facilities
111 Baxter Rd, **S...**airport
107 Pilot Butte Ave, Rock Springs, **S...gas:** Conoco/diesel, Exxon/diesel/lodging, Kum&Go, Phillips 66/diesel, Shell/diesel, 7-11, **food:** Lew's Rest., El Sands Café, **lodging:** Knotty Pine Motel, Sands Inn, **other:** HOSPITAL, RV camping, repair
104 US 191 N, Elk St, Rock Springs, **N...gas:** Exxon, Flying J/Conoco/diesel/LP/rest./24hr/@, Kum&Go/gas, Phillips 66/diesel/24hr, Sinclair/Burger King/diesel, **food:** McDonald's, Renegade Rest., Taco Time, **lodging:** Best Western, Outlaw Inn/rest., Econolodge/rest., **other:** Buick/Pontiac/GMC, Chrysler/Jeep, to Teton, Yellowstone Nat Parks via US 191, **S...gas:** Exxon/diesel, **lodging:** Day's Inn

Rock Springs

103 Rock Springs, College Dr, **S...gas:** Conoco/diesel/24hr, **other:** HOSPITAL, W WY Coll
102 WY 430, Dewar Dr, Rock Springs, **N...gas:** Exxon, Sinclair/diesel, China Buffet, **food:** Taco Time, **lodging:** Motel 6, Ramada Ltd, The Inn, **other:** Chevrolet/Cadillac, Chrysler/Dodge/Subaru, Don's RV Ctr, Harley-Davidson, JC Penney, NAPA, Smith's Food, **S...gas:** Kum&Go, Phillips 66, **food:** Arby's, Burger King, Golden Corral, JB's, KFC, McDonald's, Pizza Hut, Sizzler, Subway, Taco Bell, Village Inn Rest., Wendy's, Wonderful House Chinese, **lodging:** Comfort Inn, Holiday Inn Express, Super 8, **other:** HOSPITAL, Albertson's, AutoZone, Big O Tire, Checker Parts, Hastings Books, NAPA, Wal-Mart SuperCtr/gas/24hr
99 US 191 S, E Flaming Gorge Rd, **N...other:** KOA(1mi), **S...gas:** Conoco/diesel/café/24hr/@, **food:** Big Wheeler Rest., Log Inn Steaks, **other:** fireworks, transmissions

Green River

94mm Kissing Rock
91 US 30, to WY 530, Green River, **S...gas:** Conoco, **food:** Arctic Circle, China Garden, McDonald's, Pizza Hut, Subway, Taco John's, Taco Time, **lodging:** Coachman Inn, Mustang Motel, Super 8, **other:** Expedition NHS, to Flaming Gorge NRA, same as 89
89 US 30, Green River, **S...gas:** Exxon, Sinclair/diesel, **food:** Green River Rest., McDonald's, Penny's Diner, Taco Time, **lodging:** Desmond Inn, OakTree Inn, Super 8, Western Inn, Adams RV Service, **other:** Tex's RV Camp, NAPA, to Flaming Gorge NRA
87.5mm Green River
85 Covered Wagon Rd, **S...other:** Tex's Travel Camp, Adam's RV parts/service
83 WY 372, La Barge Rd, **N...**to Fontenelle Dam
78 (from wb), no facilities
77mm Blacks Fork River
72 Westvaco Rd, no facilities
71mm parking area both lanes
68 Little America, **N...gas:** Sinclair/diesel/Little America Hotel/rest./24hr@, **other:** RV camping
66 US 30 W, Kemmerer, to Teton, Yellowstone, Fossil Butte NM, no facilities
61 Cedar Mt Rd, to Granger, no facilities
60mm parking area both lanes, litter barrels
54mm parking area eb, litter barrels
53 Church Butte Rd, no facilities
49mm parking area wb, litter barrels
48 Lp 80, Lyman, Ft Bridger, Hist Ft Bridger, **S...lodging:** Valley West Motel
45mm Blacks Fork River
41 WY 413, Lyman, **N...gas:** Gas'n Go/diesel/café/@, **other:** Terry's Diesel Repair/café, **S...rest area both lanes, full(handicapped)facilities, phone, picnic tables, litter barrels, petwalk,** Valley West Motel(2mi), KOA(1mi)
39 WY 412, WY 414, to Carter, Mountain View, no facilities
34 Lp 80, to Ft Bridger, **S...gas:** Phillips 66/diesel/LP, **lodging:** Wagon Wheel Motel, **other:** Ft Bridger NHS, to Flaming Gorge NRA
33.5mm parking area eb, litter barrels
33 Union Rd, no facilities
30 Bigelow Rd, **N...gas:** TA/Tesoro/Burger King/Taco Bell/diesel/@, **S...**fireworks
28 French Rd, no facilities
27.5mm parking area both lanes
24 Leroy Rd, no facilities
23 Bar Hat Rd, no facilities
21 Coal Rd, no facilities
18 US 189 N, to Kemmerer, to Nat Parks
15 Guild Rd(from eb), no facilities
14mm parking area both lanes
13 Divide Rd, no facilities
10 Painter Rd, to Eagle Rock Ski Area

Evanston

6 US 189, Bear River Dr, Evanston, **N...gas:** Sinclair, Pilot/Subway/diesel/24hr/@, **food:** Don Pedro Mexican, **lodging:** Motel 6, Prairie Inn, Super 8, Vagabond Motel, **other:** CarQuest, Ford/Mercury, Goodyear, Bear River RV Park, Phillips RV Park, Wyo Downs Racetrack, **S...Welcome Ctr both lanes, full(handicapped)facilities, phone, picnic tables, litter barrels, petwalk, RV dump(seasonal), playground,** Bear River SP
5 WY 89, Evanston, **N...gas:** Chevron/Domino's/diesel, Maverik, Sinclair, **food:** Arby's, DragonWall Chinese, McDonald's, Papa Murphy's, Shakey's Pizza, Subway, Taco John's, Wendy's, **lodging:** Super 8, **other:** HOSPITAL, AutoZone, Chevrolet/Buick, Jubilee Foods, NAPA, Radio Shack, Wal-Mart SuperCtr/24hr, **S...**WY St Hospital

Interstate 80

E ↕ W

3	US 189, Harrison Dr, Evanston, **N...gas:** Chevron/diesel, Flying J/diesel/rest./24hr/@, Phillips 66, Sinclair, Tesoro, Shell/diesel, **food:** Burger King, JB's, Lottie's Rest., Taco Time, **lodging:** Best Western/rest., Comfort Inn, DX Motel, Economy Inn, HighCountry Inn, The Lodge, Weston Inn, **other:** HOSPITAL, Automotive+, Chrysler/Plymouth/Jeep, GMC/Pontiac/Cadillac, Goodyear/auto, **S...gas:** Phillips 66/A&W/diesel, **food:** KFC, **other:** HOSPITAL, fireworks
.5mm	Port of Entry eb, weigh sta wb
0mm	Wyoming/Utah state line

Interstate 90

E ↕ W

Sundance

Exit #	Services
207mm	Wyoming/South Dakota state line
205	Beulah, **N...gas:** Conoco/Golden Buffalo Café/diesel/LP/@, **other:** Camp-Fish Camping
204.5mm	Sand Creek
199	WY 111, to Aladdin, no facilities
191	Moskee Rd, no facilities
189	US 14 W, Sundance, **N...gas:** Amoco/diesel/24hr, **food:** Aro Rest., Subway(2mi), Log Cabin Café, **lodging:** Best Value Inn, Best Western, Budget Host Arrowhead, **other:** HOSPITAL, Mountain View Camping, to Devil's Tower NM, museum, **S...rest area both lanes, full(handicapped)facilities, info, phone, picnic tables, litter barrels, playground, petwalk,** RV dump, port of entry/weigh sta
187	WY 585, Sundance, **N...gas:** Amoco/diesel, Conoco/24hr, **food:** Flo's Place Café, Subway, **lodging:** Best Western, Decker's Motel, Sundance Mtn Inn
185	to WY 116, to Sundance, **S...gas:** Shell/diesel/service
178	Coal Divide Rd, no facilities
177mm	parking area both lanes, litter barrels
172	Inyan Kara Rd, no facilities
171mm	parking area both lanes, litter barrels
165	Pine Ridge Rd, to Pine Haven, **N...**to Keyhole SP
163mm	parking area both lanes, litter barrels
160	Wind Creek Rd, no facilities
154	US 14, US 16, Moorcroft, **S...gas:** Conoco/diesel, Donna's Diner, Subway, Cozy Motel, Moorcourt Motel
153	US 16 E, US 14, W Moorcroft, **N...rest area both lanes, full(handicapped)facilities, phone, picnic tables, litter barrels, petwalk**
152mm	Belle Fourche River
141	Rozet, **2 mi S...**gas, food, phone
138mm	parking area both lanes
132	Wyodak Rd, no facilities
129	Garner Lake Rd, **S...other:** Harley-Davidson, High Plains Camping, WY Marine/RV Ctr

Gillette

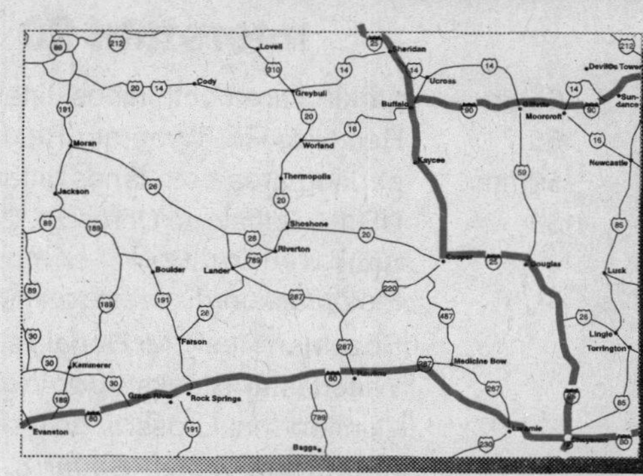

128	US 14, US 16, Gillette, Port of Entry, **N...gas:** Conoco, Kum&Go, Phillips 66/LP, Shell, **food:** Burger King, KFC, Mona's Café American/Mexican, Taco John's, Village Inn Rest., **lodging:** Econolodge, Motel 6, National 9 Inn, Rolling Hills Motel, Thrifty Inn Motel, **other:** Advance Parts, Crazy Woman Camping(2mi)
126	WY 59, Gillette, **N...gas:** Cenex/diesel, Conoco, **food:** Hardee's, McDonald's, Pizza Etc, Prime Rib Rest., Subway, **lodging:** Ramada Ltd, Rolling Hills Motel, **other:** Plains Tire, Radio Shack, Smith's Foods, **S...gas:** Conoco/diesel, Exxon, Phillips 66/Flying J/diesel/rest./24hr/@, Shell, **food:** Applebee's, Arby's, Blimpie, Burger King, China Buffet, DQ, Golden Corral, KFC, Las Margaritas Mexican, Papa Murphy's, Perkins/24hr, Pizza Hut, Taco Bell, Wendy's, **lodging:** Clarion, Comfort Inn, Day's Inn, Holiday Inn Express, Wingate Inn, **other:** Advance Parts, Albertson's, Big O Tire, Checker Parts, Chrysler/Plymouth/Dodge/Jeep, Dan's Foods, Drug Fair, GNC, Goodyear/auto, K-Mart, Wal-Mart/drugs, city park
124	WY 50, Gillette, **N...gas:** Conoco/24hr, Shell/Burger King/diesel, **food:** Fireside Café, LJ Silver, Pizza Hut, Tully's Café, **lodging:** Best Western/rest., Budget Inn, Hampton Inn, Motel 6, Super 8, **other:** HOSPITAL, Dan's Mkt, **S...gas:** Kum&Go/diesel
116	Force Rd, no facilities
113	Wild Horse Creek Rd, no facilities
110mm	parking area both lanes
106	Kingsbury Rd, no facilities
102	Barber Creek Rd, no facilities
91	Dead Horse Creek Rd, no facilities
89mm	Powder River
88	**Powder River Rd, N...rest area both lanes, full(handicapped)facilities, phone, picnic tables, litter barrels, petwalk**
82	Indian Creek Rd, no facilities
77	Schoonover Rd, no facilities
73.5mm	Crazy Woman Creek
73	Crazy Woman Creek Rd, no facilities
69	Dry Creek Rd, no facilities

WYOMING

Interstate 90

E ↔ W

68.5mm	parking area both lanes, litter barrels
65	Red Hills Rd, Tipperary Rd, no facilities
59mm	parking area both lanes, litter barrels
58	US 16, Buffalo, to Ucross, **1-2 mi S...**Nat Hist Dist, **gas:** Cenex/diesel/@, Conoco/diesel/24hr/@, Exxon/diesel, Shell/diesel, Sinclair/diesel, **food:** Bozeman Rest., McDonald's, Pizza Hut, Subway, Winchester Steaks, **lodging:** Bunkhouse Motel, Comfort Inn, Crossroads Inn, Econolodge, Motel 6, Mtnview Motel, Super 8, Wyo Motel, **other:** HOSPITAL, Deer Park Camping, Indian Camping, NAPA, KOA
56b	I-25 S, US 87 S, to Buffalo
a	25 Bus, 90 Bus, to Buffalo
53	Rock Creek Rd, no facilities
51	Lake DeSmet, **2 mi N...**gas, food, lodging
47	Shell Creek Rd, no facilities
44	US 87 N, Piney Creek Rd, to Story, Banner, **N...other:** Ft Phil Kearney, museum, **5 mi S...lodging:** Tunnel Inn
39mm	scenic turnout wb, litter barrel
37	Prairie Dog Creek Rd, to Story, no facilities
33	Meade Creek Rd, to Big Horn, no facilities
31mm	parking area eb, litter barrel
25	US 14 E, Sheridan, **N...lodging:** Comfort Inn, **S...gas:** Amoco, Conoco/diesel, Exxon, Sinclair, **food:** Arby's, Burger King, JB's, LBM Pizza, Perkins/24hr, Subway, Taco Bell, Wendy's, **lodging:** Appletree Inn, Day's Inn, Holiday Inn, Lariat Motel, Mill Inn, Parkway Motel, **other:** Carl's SuperFoods, Firestone, NAPA, Pamida, Pontiac/Cadillac, Toyota, Wal-Mart, mall, to Hist Dist, Sheridan Coll
23	WY 336, 5th St, Sheridan, **N...rest area both lanes, full(handicapped)facilities, info, phone, picnic tables, litter barrels, petwalk, 1-2 mi S...gas:** Shell, **food:** Arctic Circle, DQ, **lodging:** Energy Inn, Trails End Motel, **other:** HOSPITAL, museum
20	Main St, Sheridan, **S...**Port of Entry, **gas:** Cenex, Conoco, Exxon/diesel/24hr, Gas4Less, MiniMart/gas, Shell, **food:** Cattleman's Cut Rest., Country Kitchen, McDonald's, Pizza Hut, Subway, Taco John's, **lodging:** Holiday Lodge, Trails End Motel, Triangle Motel, Super 8, **other:** K-Mart, KOA, Safeway
16	to Decker, Montana, no facilities
15mm	parking area wb, litter barrels
14.5mm	Tongue River
14	Acme Rd, no facilities
9	US 14 W, Ranchester, **S...**to Yellowstone, Teton NPs, Conner Bfd NHS, Ski Area
1	Parkman, no facilities
0mm	Wyoming/Montana state line

Buffalo

Sheridan

Help a friend with

Updated and published annually, ***the Next EXIT®*** provides the best USA Interstate Highway information available. Use this form to order ***the Next EXIT®*** as a present for someone special. Thank you!

Please send________copies of ***the Next EXIT***® to the address below. I enclose my check or money order for $12.95 + $4.00 s&h per copy.

(Please add $2.00 per copy for priority delivery.)

name...

street...

city...

state.................. zip...

4 ways to order:

**1) mail to: the Next EXIT, inc.
PO Box 888
Garden City, UT 84028**

2) order on the web at *www.thenextexit.com*

3) call: 1-800-NEX-EXIT(639-3948), and use your visa/mastercard.

4) fax: 1-435-946-8808, and use your visa/mastercard.

Electronically, ***the Next EXIT***® is provided for Palm handheld devices through the highly acclaimed software application, **I-WayInfo**. Please visit www.iWayInfo.com for order information.

email us at nextexit@cut.net *visit our website at www.thenextexit.com*